Smith, Hogan, and Ormerod's
CRIMINAL LAW

Sixteenth edition

David Ormerod CBE, QC (Hon)

*Professor of Criminal Justice, University College London,
Barrister, Bencher of Middle Temple,
Door Tenant at Red Lion Chambers*

Karl Laird

*Stipendiary Lecturer and Tutor in Law, St Edmund Hall, Oxford,
Barrister, 6KBW College Hill*

OXFORD

UNIVERSITY PRESS

OXFORD

UNIVERSITY PRESS

Great Clarendon Street, Oxford, OX2 6DP,
United Kingdom

Oxford University Press is a department of the University of Oxford.
It furthers the University's objective of excellence in research, scholarship,
and education by publishing worldwide. Oxford is a registered trade mark of
Oxford University Press in the UK and in certain other countries

Published in the United States of America by Oxford University Press
198 Madison Avenue, New York, NY 10016, United States of America

British Library Cataloguing in Publication Data

Data available

Library of Congress Control Number: 2017964393

ISBN 978-0-19-884970-4

Printed in Great Britain by
Bell & Bain Ltd., Glasgow

For Olivia and Scarlet

David Ormerod

For Philip

Karl Laird

New to this edition

Key developments in the 16th edition include:

- *Wallace, Broughton*, and *A* on causation.
- *Lane and Letts* on strict liability.
- *SFO v Barclays* and *Alstom* on corporate liability.
- *Tas* on complicity.
- *Thompson* on conspiracy.
- *Taj* on intoxication and self-defence.
- *Cheeseman* on self-defence.
- *Goodwin, Islam*, and *Dawson* on loss of control.
- *Foy* on diminished responsibility.
- *Kuddus* and *Broughton* on gross negligence manslaughter.
- *Veysey, Melin*, and *BM* on offences against the person.
- *Pringle* on child abduction.
- *Lawrance* and *Attorney General's Reference (No 1 of 2020)* on sexual offences.
- *Barton* on dishonesty.
- *Varley, D* and *Smith* on fraud.
- *Bush* on false accounting.
- *Chablosz* on Communications Act offences.

Preface

This edition of *Smith, Hogan, and Ormerod's Criminal Law*, like its predecessors, is intended to provide an accessible and authoritative analysis of the doctrinal criminal law that appeals to a broad readership. It is a source of immense pride that the book continues to be cited with such frequency both by the courts in England and Wales and in other common law jurisdictions. It was particularly gratifying to see the book's influence in so many decisions including, in particular, the analysis of innocent agency and fraud being cited with approval by the Court of Appeal in *Varley*. However, our aim in this edition, as with every other, has been to produce a book that can primarily be used by undergraduate law students. We have made a number of presentational changes in this edition to ensure the book continues to be an accessible resource for students. To make the book easier to navigate, we have provided tables of contents at the beginning of each chapter. We have also made changes to the footnotes, to ensure they do not interrupt the flow of the text. As with the previous edition, a number of chapters have been made available free of charge on OUP's **online resources**.

The text has been fully updated to incorporate the developments in the criminal law which have taken place since the publication of the previous edition. Most notably, the Court of Appeal has now decided, in *Barton*, that the Supreme Court's *obiter* analysis of dishonesty in *Ivey v Genting Casinos* should be treated as binding. We analyse that judgment—and its implications for the criminal law—in Chapter 18. There are two other noteworthy cases which have required substantial parts of several chapters to be rewritten. First, in *Taj* the Court of Appeal stated, in an analysis which was *obiter*, that the principles articulated by the House of Lords in *Majewski* might apply not only when the defendant is intoxicated, but also where he is suffering from the proximate effects of earlier intoxication. Secondly, the Court of Appeal has provided guidance on how principles of causation ought to apply in the context of gross negligence manslaughter where the defendant fails to summon medical help for someone who is suffering an adverse reaction to the drugs he supplied. These judgments, and many others, demonstrate that the criminal law continues to be an area that is ripe for doctrinal analysis and scholarly debate.

The manuscript for this edition was delivered to OUP in October 2020, but we have been able to incorporate a number of important developments that have taken place since then, most notably *Attorney General's Reference (No 1 of 2020)*.

David Ormerod
Karl Laird

Acknowledgements

We would like to thank the friends and colleagues from both academia and practice with whom we have discussed the issues analysed in the book. In particular we have benefited from discussions with David Perry QC, Annabel Darlow QC, Anthony Shaw QC and Rudi Fortson QC. David Ormerod would also like to thank Chloe Reddock for her assistance. Karl Laird would like to thank the students at St Edmund Hall and Merton College who have provided valuable feedback on their experience of using the previous edition.

At OUP we were fortunate to work once again with such a dedicated team with Jessica Lehmani, Lucia Perez, Joy Ruskin-Tompkins, and Karen Moore. Despite the many additional hardships generated by the pandemic, they managed the entire publication process with skill and patience.

Contents

Part I General Principles

Part II Particular Crimes

Table of statutes

Table of cases

Abbreviations

The following are the abbreviations used for the principal textbooks and legal journals cited in this book. References are to the latest editions, as shown below, unless it is specifically stated otherwise. The particulars of other works referred to in the text are set out in full in the relevant footnotes. A full bibliography of all references is **available free** via the **online resources** at www.oup.com/he/SHO-textbook16e.

Throughout the book the neutral citation system (UKSC, UKHL, UKPC, EWCA Crim, EWHC (Admin), etc) is commonly adopted in relation to cases in England and Wales since 2001.

Archbold	*Criminal Pleading, Evidence and Practice* by JF Archbold (2021) by M Lucraft QC and others
Arlidge and Parry on Fraud	*Arlidge and Parry on Fraud* (2nd edn, 1996; 6th edn, 2020) by J Fisher QC, J Bewsey, A Herd and A Milne QC
Blackstone, *Commentaries*, i–iv	*Commentaries on the Laws of England* by Sir William Blackstone, vol i–iv (4 vols) (17th edn, 1830) by E Christian
Blackstone's Criminal Practice	*Blackstone's Criminal Practice* (2021) by D Ormerod and D Perry (eds)
CLJ	Cambridge Law Journal
CLP	Current Legal Problems
Co 3 Inst	*Institutes of the Laws of England*, vol 3 (4 vols) (1797) by Sir Edward Coke
Cr App R	Criminal Appeal Reports
Crim LR	Criminal Law Review
Crime, Proof and Punishment	*Crime, Proof and Punishment: Essays in Memory of Sir Rupert Cross* edited by CFH Tapper (1981)
Criminal Law Essays	*Criminal Law: Essays in Honour of JC Smith* edited by PF Smith (1987)
Draft Code	*A Criminal Code for England and Wales*, Law Com No 177 (1989)
Duff, *Answering for Crime*	*Answering for Crime: Responsibility and Liability in the Criminal Law* (2007) by RA Duff
Duff and Green, *Defining Crimes*	*Defining Crimes: Essays on the Special Part of the Criminal Law* (2005) by RA Duff and SP Green (eds)
East, I/II PC	*A Treatise of the Pleas of the Crown* by EH East, vol I/II (2 vols) (1803)
Edwards, *Mens Rea*	*Mens Rea in Statutory Offences* (1955) by J Ll J Edwards
Eighth Report	Criminal Law Revision Committee, Eighth Report, *Theft and Related Offences* (1966) Cmnd 2977
Emmerson, Ashworth and Macdonald, HR&CJ	*Human Rights and Criminal Justice* (3rd edn, 2012) by B Emmerson, A Ashworth and A Macdonald
Fourteenth Report	Criminal Law Revision Committee, Fourteenth Report, *Offences Against the Person* (1980) Cmnd 7844
Glazebrook, *Reshaping the Criminal Law*	*Reshaping the Criminal Law: Essays in Honour of Glanville Williams* edited by PR Glazebrook (1978)
Green, *Lying, Cheating and Stealing*	*Lying, Cheating and Stealing: A Moral Theory of White Collar Crime* (2006) by SP Green

Green, *13 Ways*	*13 Ways to Steal a Bicycle: Theft Law in the Information Age* (2012) by SP Green
Griew, *Theft*	*The Theft Acts 1968 and 1978* (7th edn, 1995) by EJ Griew
Hale, I/II PC	*The History of the Pleas of the Crown* by Sir Matthew Hale, vol I/II (2 vols) (1736)
Hall, *General Principles*	*General Principles of Criminal Law* (2nd edn, 1960) by J Hall
Hart and Honoré, *Causation in the Law*	*Causation in the Law* (2nd edn, 1985) by HLA Hart and T Honoré
Harv LR	Harvard Law Review
Hawkins, I/II PC	*A Treatise of the Pleas of the Crown* by W Hawkins, vol I/ II (2 vols) (8th edn, 1795) by J Curwood
Horder, APOCL	*Ashworth's Principles of Criminal Law* (9th edn, 2019) by J Horder
Howard, SR	*Strict Responsibility* (1963) by C Howard
J Crim L	Journal of Criminal Law (English)
Kenny, *Outlines*	*Outlines of Criminal Law* by CS Kenny (19th edn, 1966) by JWC Turner
LCCP	Law Commission Consultation Paper
LQR	Law Quarterly Review
LS	Legal Studies, the Journal of the Society of Public Teachers of Law
MACL	*The Modern Approach to Criminal Law* edited by L Radzinowicz and JWC Turner (1948)
MLR	Modern Law Review
OJLS	Oxford Journal of Legal Studies
Ormerod and Williams, *Smith's Law of Theft*	*The Law of Theft* (9th edn, 2007) by D Ormerod and DH Williams
Russell	*Crime* by Sir WO Russell (12th edn, 1964) by JWC Turner (2 vols)
Shute and Simester, *Criminal Law Theory*	Criminal Law Theory: Doctrines of the General Part (2002) edited by S Shute and A Simester
Simester, *Appraising Strict Liability*	*Appraising Strict Liability* (2005) edited by A Simester
Simester, Spencer, Stark, Sullivan and Virgo, CLT&D	*Simester and Sullivan's Criminal Law: Theory and Doctrine* (7th edn, 2019) by AP Simester, JR Spencer, F Stark, GR Sullivan, and G Virgo
Smith, *Justification and Excuse*	*Justification and Excuse in the Criminal Law* by JC Smith (The Hamlyn Lectures, 1989)
Smith, *Property Offences*	*Property Offences* (1994) by ATH Smith
Stephen, *Digest*	*A Digest of the Criminal Law* by Sir James Fitzjames Stephen (9th edn, 1950) by LF Sturge
Stephen, I–III HCL	*A History of the Criminal Law of England* by Sir James Fitzjames Stephen, vols I–III (3 vols) (1883)
Tadros, *Criminal Responsibility*	*Criminal Responsibility* (2005) by V Tadros
Williams, CLGP	*Criminal Law: The General Part* (2nd edn, 1961) by GL Williams
Williams, TBCL	*Textbook of Criminal Law* (2nd edn, 1983) by GL Williams
Wilson, *Central Issues*	*Central Issues in Criminal Theory* (2002) by W Wilson

Part I
General Principles

1

An introduction to the criminal law

1.1 A universal definition of 'a crime'?

It is now rather unfashionable to begin law books with definitions.[1] One reason for this is that it is notoriously difficult to define the subject matter of a particular branch of the law; and this is particularly true of the criminal law. But this is a book about crimes, and if it did not at least attempt to tell the reader what a crime is, it would be deficient. It would allow the reader to proceed with preconceived notions about what constitutes a crime. In particular, there would be a danger that the reader might assume the popular meaning of crime which is different from, less precise and narrower than the legal meaning. A criminal law book must be concerned with the legal meaning of crime; and the reader is entitled to know what it is, or at least why it is so difficult to describe.

Common definitions from non-legal dictionaries do not provide much help as a starting point, as they offer only bland definitions such as 'an act or omission prohibited and

---

[1] For classical accounts of the problem of definition, see Kenny, *Outlines* (15th edn, 1935) Ch 1; G Williams, 'The Definition of Crime' (1955) 8 CLP 107; G Hughes, 'The Concept of Crime: An American View' [1959] Crim LR 239 and 331. For more contemporary philosophical accounts, see in particular the collections of essays edited by Duff and Green, *Defining Crimes*; Duff, *Answering for Crime*; A Halpin, *Definition in the Criminal Law* (2004); and essays in J Gardner, *Offences and Defences: Selected Essays in the Philosophy of Criminal Law* (2007).

punished by law'. Although they may inform us that the meaning of the word 'crime' can be traced to the Latin 'crimen' (accusation), that takes us no further forward to an understanding of the subject. A simple definition of a crime as a wrong, which is prosecuted and carries a penalty might satisfy the layman without providing any sufficient answer for the lawyer.

Some might think that an exercise in further definition is futile since every lawyer knows a crime when they see it, but a ready response to this claim is that not all crimes are readily identifiable even to the lawyer. This is inevitable when there are well in excess of 10,000 crimes in England and Wales[2] covering such diverse activities as murder, rape, being in possession of certain breeds of dangerous dog[3] and obstructing a clergyman in the discharge of his duties in a place of worship or on his way thither.[4] But given the importance of the criminal law in terms of what is at stake for the individual and society and how often the criminal law is used, surely a definition could and should be produced.

An attempt to define *a crime* at once encounters a difficulty. If the definition is a good one, it should enable us to recognize any behaviour—whether involving an act or omission—as a crime, or not a crime, by seeing whether it contains all the ingredients of the definition. When this proposition is given serious consideration it is impossible. When Parliament enacts that particular conduct (doing X) shall become a crime or that conduct (doing X) which is now criminal shall cease to be so, the conduct (doing X) does not change in nature in any respect other than that of legal classification. All its observable characteristics are precisely the same before as after the statute comes into force. Making the conduct criminal does not change the conduct itself; it changes the legal classification of that conduct. By way of example, suicide was a crime until 3 August 1961, when, by the Suicide Act 1961,[5] it became perfectly lawful to kill oneself. The nature of the act in question, its morality or immorality and the consequence did not change overnight; but its legal nature did.

1.2 A universal purpose in criminal law?

Our quest for a definition of criminal law is not assisted greatly by looking for a declared purpose which underpins every criminal law in England and Wales.[6] The criminal law of this country has developed over many centuries, and with many and varied purposes of those who have framed it and those who have enforced it. Consequently, it is not easy to state confidently what the aims of the criminal law are.

The position would be different if we were starting from scratch—if we were drawing up a new criminal code. The authors of a completely new code of criminal law are in a position to state their objectives at the outset. 'The general purposes of the provisions governing the definition of offenses' in the American Law Institute's Model Penal Code[7] might be taken as a statement of the proper objectives of the substantive law of crime in a modern legal system. The purposes are:

(a) to forbid and prevent conduct that unjustifiably and inexcusably inflicts or threatens substantial harm to individual or public interests;

(b) to subject to public control persons whose conduct indicates that they are disposed to commit crimes;

---

[2] Not including the thousands of by-laws created at a local level.
[3] See the Dangerous Dogs Act 1991.
[4] Offences Against the Person Act 1861, s 36.   [5] See Ch 15.
[6] For analyses of various theories of criminalization, see Chs 1–5 of RA Duff and SP Green (eds), *Philosophical Foundations of Criminal Law* (2011) and the essays in RA Duff, L Farmer, SE Marshall, M Renzo, and V Tadros (eds), *Criminalization: The Political Morality of the Criminal Law* (2014).
[7] Proposed Official Draft, §1.02(1). Cf N Walker, *The Aims of the Penal System* (1966).

(c) to safeguard conduct that is without fault from condemnation as criminal;

(d) to give fair warning of the nature of the conduct declared to be an offense;

(e) to differentiate on reasonable grounds between serious and minor offenses.[8]

Whether English criminal law fulfils these purposes is a matter to think about while studying the general principles and particular offences discussed throughout the rest of this book. For example, whether our law is confined to forbidding conduct that is 'inexcusable', or whether it adequately safeguards conduct that is without fault from condemnation as criminal, are matters which are particularly considered in Ch 3 but which frequently arise elsewhere.

1.3 Universal characteristics of a crime?

Struggling to define crimes and even to identify a clear declared purpose in criminalizing forms of conduct, the student might turn instead to search for characteristics that are universal to every crime so that at least all crimes can be identified even if not readily defined. Those hoping for a straightforward checklist of criteria guaranteed to allow someone to identify any and every crime are destined for disappointment. It is nigh on impossible to agree any determinate criteria. There is considerable force in Professor Duff's concession that we should resist the:

desire to find some single concept or value that will capture the essence of crime or the essential characteristic in virtue of which crimes are properly punished . . . in favour of a pluralism that recognises a diversity of reasons for criminalisation, matching the diversity of kinds of wrong which can legitimately be the criminal law's business.[9]

Despite the lack of a universally accepted definition of criminal law, it is possible to point to certain characteristics which are *generally* found in conduct which is criminal; in particular, it usually involves a public wrong and a moral wrong.[10]

1.3.1 A 'public' wrong

Crimes generally involve behaviour which has a particularly harmful effect on the public and goes beyond interfering with merely private rights. This has been recognized for decades. Writing 90 years ago, Sir Carleton Allen noted that:

Crime is crime because it consists in wrongdoing which directly and in serious degree threatens the security or well-being of society, and because it is not safe to leave it redressable only by compensation of the party injured.[11]

This statement explains why certain behaviours may have originally been made crimes either by judicial decision or by legislation, but it does not necessarily accurately represent

---

[8] For criticism, see PH Robinson, 'The Modern General Part—Three Illusions' in Shute and Simester, *Criminal Law Theory*, 79.

[9] Duff, *Answering for Crime*, 139.

[10] Recent years have seen a huge outpouring of theoretical writing on the criminal law. For an interesting reflection on some of this, see RA Duff, 'Theorising About Criminal Law' (2005) 25 OJLS 353.

[11] CK Allen, 'The Nature of a Crime' (1931) *Journal of Society of Comparative Legislation*, Feb, reprinted in *Legal Duties* 221, 233–4.

the present state of the entire catalogue of criminal offences. A crime may remain a crime long after it has ceased to be a threat to the security or well-being of society.[12] Allen's proposition tells us what—as he thinks—*ought to be* criminal rather than what is criminal.

There is a further dimension to the concept of public wrong.[13] This emphasizes not that the wrong is one done against the public, but rather that a 'public wrong' is significant for defining crimes because it reflects the important role that the public has in punishing crimes. As Duff explains:

we should be held criminally responsible for wrongdoings which are public in the sense that they properly concern all members of the polity, and merit a formal public response of censure and condemnation.[14]

As Duff acknowledges, that does not assist in determining what wrongdoing should count as 'public'.[15]

This 'public' nature of crimes is evidenced by the contrast between the rules of civil and criminal procedure. Any member of the public can, as a general rule and in the absence of some provision to the contrary, bring a criminal prosecution. That is true whether or not he[16] has suffered any special harm over and above other members of the public. As a member of the public he has an interest in the enforcement of the criminal law. D steals V's watch. V may prosecute him—so may X, Y, Z or any other citizen.[17] As the then Lord Chief Justice made clear in *Smith*,[18] for example, the law of theft protects the Queen's peace and is not a means of enforcing personal property rights.

In practice, of course, the vast majority of prosecutions are performed by the Crown Prosecution Service (CPS) or Director of the Serious Fraud Office or other public officers who have no personal interest in the outcome. The victim of an offence cannot prevent the prosecution of the offender.[19] The consent of the Director of Public Prosecutions (DPP) to a prosecution is subject to judicial review in very limited circumstances. Proceedings may be stopped by the Crown through the entry of a *nolle prosequi* by the Attorney General who may stay the proceedings at any time[20] without the consent of the prosecutor.

If the prosecution succeeds and a sentence is imposed by the court, the instigator of the prosecution has no power to pardon the offender. This power belongs exclusively to the Crown, representing the public interest in the matter. It is important not to confuse the position of the Crown with that of the victim. The recognition of the significance of the victim in the criminal process has been marked over the last two decades or so,[21] but in terms of substantive law, the formal position is that the prosecution is usually brought by the Crown, and the Crown is not seen as a surrogate victim.[22]

---

[12] G Williams (1955) 8 CLP at 126–7.   [13] G Lamond, 'What is a Crime' (2007) 27 OJLS 609.

[14] Duff, *Answering for Crime*, 123. See generally Ch 6 of that work.

[15] Lamond, n 13, argues that it is because they represent blameworthy conduct, in terms of mens rea.

[16] Throughout the book, for the sake of convenience, we use the male pronoun.

[17] The right of private prosecution is unaffected by the Prosecution of Offences Act 1985; but s 24 empowers the High Court, on the application of the Attorney General (AG), to restrain a vexatious prosecutor: *Ewing v DPP* [2010] EWCA Civ 70. The DPP may take over a private prosecution at any stage (s 6(2)) and may discontinue a prosecution during its 'preliminary stage': s 23. See generally *Blackstone's Criminal Practice* (2021) D2.

[18] [2011] EWCA Crim 66.

[19] See on victim waiver and settlement, G Dingwall and C Harding, *Diversion in the Criminal Law* (1998) Ch 3.

[20] The DPP may intervene and offer no evidence: *Turner v DPP* (1978) 68 Cr App R 70 (Mars Jones J), (1978) Crim LR 754; *Raymond v AG* [1982] QB 839.

[21] For discussion, see SL Walklate, *Victimology: The Victim and the Criminal Justice Process* (1989); A Bottoms and J Roberts, *Hearing the Victim: Adversarial Justice, Crime Victims and the State* (2012). It has been suggested that the criminal justice system's increased awareness of the rights of victims is attributable to the ECHR. See K Starmer, 'Human Rights, Victims and the Prosecution of Crime in the 21st Century' [2014] Crim LR 777.

[22] See *Weir* [2001] 1 WLR 421.

All this public control over the proceedings in criminal law stands in sharp contrast with the position regarding civil wrongs—torts and breaches of contract. There, only the person injured may sue. He (and only he) may freely discontinue the proceedings at any time and, if he succeeds and an award of damages is made in his favour, it is entirely at his discretion whether to forgive the defendant and terminate his liability.

Crimes, then, are wrongs which the judges have held, or Parliament has enacted, to be sufficiently injurious to the public to warrant the application of criminal procedure to deal with them. Of course, this does not enable us to recognize conduct as criminal when we see it. Some forms of conduct are so obviously public wrongs that *anyone* would say they should be criminal—murder or rape, for example.[23] These are often referred to by the Latin expression *mala in se*—which means simply intrinsically wrong. All such types of obviously harmful conduct almost certainly are criminal. But there are many other types of conduct—sometimes labelled by the Latin expression *mala prohibita*—about which opinions may differ widely: what, for example, of substance abuse, or prostitution?

It is important not to overstate the significance of public condemnation of a form of conduct. Parliament and the courts alone declare the range and scope of the criminal law. When a citizen is heard urging that, 'There ought to be a law against X . . .', he is expressing his personal conviction that some variety of behaviour is so harmful to society that it ought to be discouraged by being made the subject of criminal proceedings. There will almost invariably be a body of opinion which disagrees. But even if *everyone* in England and Wales agreed with him, X would not thereby become a crime. Public condemnation is ineffective without the endorsement of an Act of Parliament or a decision of a court.[24]

In recent years politicians have been too willing to accede to public condemnation of particular forms of conduct and the clamour to make new crimes.[25] The Law Commission reports that:

Since 1997, more than 3000 criminal offences have come on to the statute book. That figure should be put in context, taking a longer perspective. Halsbury's Statutes of England and Wales has four volumes devoted to criminal laws that (however old they may be) are still currently in force. Volume 1 covers the offences created in the 637 years between 1351 and 1988. Volume 1 is 1382 pages long.

Volumes 2 to 4 cover the offences created in the 19 years between 1989 and 2008. Volumes 2 to 4 are no less than 3746 pages long. So, more than 2 and a half times as many pages were needed in Halsbury's Statutes to cover offences created in the 19 years between 1989 and 2008 than were needed to cover the offences created in the 637 years prior to that. Moreover, it is unlikely that the Halsbury volumes devoted to 'criminal law' capture all offences created in recent times.[26]

---

[23] See the comments in the appeals against rape convictions on Pitcairn: *Christian* [2006] UKPC 47.

[24] Witness the Radio 4 poll to find the listeners' law, which prompted a Bill to redefine the defence of self-defence as applicable to householders injuring burglars, discussed in Ch 10 and on the interpretation of the Court of Appeal having made little difference to the law in terms of whether the householder is prosecuted: *Ray* [2017] EWCA Crim 1391.

[25] For a quantitative analysis, see J Chalmers and F Leverick, 'Tracking the Creation of Criminal Offences' [2013] Crim LR 543.

[26] See LCCP 195, *Criminal Liability in Regulatory Contexts* (2010) para 1.17. The claim of recent growth has been challenged by F Leverick, J Chalmers et al, 'Is Formal Criminalisation Really on the Rise? Evidence from the 1950s' [2015] Crim LR 177.

There are, it is argued, just too many criminal offences.[27] In particular, there has been a disproportionate number of offences created to deal with regulatory misconduct. The Law Commission has proposed that:

the criminal law should only be employed to deal with wrongdoers who deserve the stigma associated with criminal conviction because they have engaged in seriously reprehensible conduct. It should not be used as the primary means of promoting regulatory objectives.[28]

It is important at this point to emphasize one of the unique features of the criminal law of which it seems that Parliament may recently have lost sight. The criminal sanction is the most coercive method of regulating an individual's behaviour which the State can deploy. The whole criminal justice system involves State infringements of personal autonomy from the possibility of investigation and surveillance, arrest, search, seizure, detention, questioning, public court hearings, to a trial process which may include pre-trial detention, and lead to punishment, including the ultimate infringement—imprisonment. Thereafter the consequences of a criminal record will have an impact on the defendant for many years after release—and in serious cases for life. Even if no term of imprisonment is imposed, the range of other punishments available to the criminal courts all have one thing in common: a degree of stigma.[29] Even if individuals are not taken through the entire process of the criminal trial, but are diverted[30] before trial and dealt with by way of cautioning, conditional cautions, etc they suffer the stigma. There is a marked public condemnation which is publicly communicated.[31]

This degree of coercion is qualitatively different from the outcome in a dispute in civil law. For the liberal minded at least, criminalization should be a matter of last resort because of this stigmatization and the most intrusive forms of State intervention it entails. As Husak has stated, 'a criminal statute cannot be necessary to accomplish a purpose if other means could do so more easily'.[32] Readers will be able to judge for themselves whether English law really respects this principle of what Ashworth calls 'minimal criminalisation'.[33] The point is not so much to reduce criminal law to its absolute minimum, as to ensure that resort is only had to criminalization in order to protect individual autonomy, or to protect those social arrangements necessary to ensure that individuals have the capacity and facilities to exercise their autonomy.[34]

It is important also to note that in English law there is no category of 'violations' or 'administrative wrongs' that sits between criminal and civil wrongs as exists in some jurisdictions.[35]

---

[27] See DN Husak, *Overcriminalization: The Limits of the Criminal Law* (2008) Ch 1.

[28] LC 195, para 1.29.

[29] See N Walker and C Marsh, 'Do Sentences Affect Public Disapproval?' (1984) *British Journal of Criminology* 27; N Walker, *Punishment, Danger and Stigma* (1980).

[30] See G Dingwall and C Harding, *Diversion in the Criminal Process* (1998) and more recently RA Duff, L Farmer, S Marshall and V Tadros, *The Trial on Trial*, vol 3 (2007) 180 et seq.

[31] See Tadros, *Criminal Responsibility*, 2.

[32] DN Husak, 'The Criminal Law as a Last Resort' (2004) 24 OJLS 207, 212.

[33] For an excellent and accessible account of the principles of criminalization, see Horder, APOCL, Chs 1–4. See also the suggestion by Jeremy Horder that the focus is too narrow and fails to acknowledge the need for criminalization of conduct giving rise to remoter harms: J Horder, 'Bribery as a Form of Criminal Wrongdoing' (2011) 127 LQR 37.

[34] N Lacey, *Unspeakable Subjects* (1998); *State Punishment* (1988).

[35] See LCCP 195, para 3.32 and the excellent discussion in R White, 'Civil Penalties: Oxymoron, Chimera and Stealth Sanction' (2010) 126 LQR 593 and K Reid, 'Strict Liability: Some Principles for Parliament' (2008) 29 Stat LR 173.

1.3.2 A 'moral' wrong

The second characteristic of crimes which is usually emphasized is that they involve conduct which is morally wrong.[36] As with 'public wrong', the characteristic is hopelessly vague.

1.3.2.1 Morality

As seen from the previous discussion, the traditional attitude of the common law has been that crimes are essentially immoral acts deserving of punishment. Centuries ago, when the number of crimes was relatively few and only the most outrageous acts were prohibited—murder, robbery, rape, etc—this was, no doubt, true. But the criminal law is no longer coextensive with morality. A review of the current vast range of criminal offences in England demonstrates that proposition. Many acts are now prohibited on the grounds of social expediency and not because of their immoral nature. This is especially so in the field of summary offences (those that can be tried only in the magistrates' court)—and summary offences are crimes.[37] Moreover, many acts which are generally regarded as immoral—for example, adultery—are not crimes in England.[38] The test of immorality is not a very helpful one in seeking to identify *universal* characteristics of a crime.[39]

There is a further difficulty which arises in classifying action as criminal on the basis of its purported immorality—whose morality should form the benchmark for criminalization? This problem is illustrated well by the problem of drawing appropriate legal limits on the level of physical harm which an adult, who is not lacking in mental capacity, might consent to being inflicted on him. Very different answers would be provided depending on whether the respondent is, for example, a liberal,[40] a paternalist[41] or a legal moralist.[42] The issue also arises in other contexts. For example, the Fraud Act 2006 creates offences which come close to criminalizing lying: it is sufficient that the defendant dishonestly makes a misleading statement with intent to gain.[43]

Whether conduct ought to be a crime *simply* on the ground of its immoral nature has been the subject of vigorous debate on different issues through the decades. One of the most well known was the debate in the 1960s about whether consensual homosexual conduct between men in private ought to be decriminalized. The Wolfenden Committee on Homosexual Offences and Prostitution reviewed the position. Its conclusion was that enforcement of morality is not a proper object of the criminal law. The function of the criminal law, as they saw it, is:

to preserve public order and decency, to protect the citizen from what is offensive or injurious, and to provide sufficient safeguards against exploitation and corruption of others, particularly those

[36] For an accessible account of this complex area, see Wilson, *Central Issues*, Ch 1, and Duff, *Answering for Crime*, Chs 4 and 6.

[37] G Williams (1955) 8 CLP at 110. It is true that courts have frequently treated regulatory offences differently on the grounds that they are 'not truly criminal' or are 'quasi-criminal': *Harrow London Borough Council v Shah* [1999] 3 All ER 302, [2000] Crim LR 692; p 163. But this is a dubious argument. By any recognized test, the offence is criminal: it carries criminal consequences.

[38] Adultery is criminal in some countries. See Duff, *Answering for Crime*, 144.

[39] See LCCP 195, para 4.39 on the usefulness of the harm principle in general.

[40] With focus on whether harm is caused to another's interests.

[41] For whom it will be sufficient that harm is caused to another or the accused.

[42] For whom it is sufficient that the conduct is immoral. See the decision of the House of Lords in *Brown* [1994] 1 AC 212, discussed in Ch 16 in full and LCCP 139, *Consent in the Criminal Law* (1995) Appendix C. Cf P Roberts, 'The Philosophical Foundations of Consent in the Criminal Law' (1997) 17 OJLS 389 and S Shute, 'The Law Commission's Second Consultation Paper on Consent' [1996] Crim LR 684.

[43] See D Ormerod, 'Criminalising Lying?' [2007] Crim LR 193 and see Ch 22. Professor Horder categorizes this as a harm-centred, minimalist conception of the criminal law: Horder (2011) 127 LQR 37.

who are specially vulnerable . . . It is not . . . the function of the law to intervene in the private lives of citizens, or to seek to enforce any particular pattern of behaviour, further than is necessary to carry out the purposes we have outlined.[44]

This view was challenged by Lord Devlin,[45] who argued that there is a public morality which is an essential part of the bond which keeps society together; and that society may use the criminal law to preserve morality in the same way that it uses it to preserve anything else that is essential to its existence. The standard of morality is that of 'the man in the jury box', based on the 'mass of continuous experience half-consciously or unconsciously accumulated and embodied in the morality of common sense'. To this it was answered[46] that it is not proper for the State to enforce the general morality without asking whether it is based on ignorance, superstition or misunderstanding; that it is not a sufficient ground for prohibiting an act that 'the thought of it makes the man on the Clapham omnibus sick'.

In the midst of this debate, the House of Lords delivered its controversial decision in *Shaw v DPP*,[47] in which Lord Simonds asserted that:

there remains in the courts of law a residual power to enforce the supreme and fundamental purpose of the law, to conserve not only the safety and order *but also the moral welfare of the state*;

and that the appellate courts were the custodian of the morality of the people and had the superintendency of offences that are contrary to good morals (sometimes given the Latin tag *contra bonos mores*). 'Lord Devlin, regarded *Shaw's* case', as settling 'for the purpose of the law that morality in England means what twelve men and women think it means—in other words it is to be ascertained as a question of fact' by a jury.[48] Subsequently, however, the particular legal rule (that homosexual conduct between consenting male adults is an offence) that caused the Wolfenden Committee to formulate its general principle[49] was repealed by the Sexual Offences Act 1967. The House of Lords has since also accepted that it does not have power to extend the criminal law to enforce good morals.[50]

This same moral debate is echoed in more recent times with the question of what levels of harm or injury an adult not lacking in mental capacity might consent to in the course of consensual sexual sadomasochism. The issue divided the House of Lords in the case of *Brown*,[51] prompted two Law Commission Consultation Papers and provoked a torrent of legal academic writing.[52] Many other instances of the debate about morality and criminal law can be seen in recent years and will be replayed in the future.[53] For example, Parliament recently introduced an offence for an adult to possess extreme pornography depicting images of consenting adult conduct.[54] At the time of writing, Parliament is in the process of removing the possibility for someone to consent to rough sex if the activity carries a risk of death (see the Domestic Abuse Bill 2021).

---

[44] Cmnd 247 (1957), para 13.   [45] *The Enforcement of Morals* (1965) 1.

[46] HLA Hart, *The Morality of the Criminal Law* (1964). Hart challenges the view that society is as morally homogenous as Devlin's approach would require.

[47] [1962] AC 220, 267; p 491.

[48] 110 U Pa L Rev at 648. See also HLA Hart, *Law, Liberty, and Morality* (1963); G Hughes, 'Morals and the Criminal Law' (1962) 71 Yale LJ 662. For an excellent discussion of the whole controversy, see B Mitchell, *Law, Morality and Religion in a Secular Society* (1967).

[49] See n 44.

[50] *Knuller (Publishing, Printing and Promotions) Ltd v DPP* [1973] AC 435, p 491. Such judicial offence-creation would contravene Art 7 of the ECHR which protects against retrospective criminalization. See the recognition of the appropriate limits of judicial law-making in *Rimmington* [2005] UKHL 63.

[51] [1994] 1 AC 212.   [52] See the materials in Ch 16, p 712.

[53] See the special issue of the *British Journal of Criminology* 'Moral Panics—36 Years On' (2009) 49(1).

[54] See Ch 30.

1.3.2.2 Harms or wrongs to others

Implicit in a requirement that every crime involves a moral wrong is the acceptance that a 'wrong' is done or harm to another or others is involved.[55] Conduct can be treated as a 'wrong' if it violates some moral duty or rule, and harmful if it infringes the autonomy of another or causes serious offence to another. Conduct can be wrongful without being harmful (an insignificant lie to V's benefit); and harmful without being wrong (D undercutting his competitor's prices and causing him to go out of business).

Again, this poses a problem since it is only if there is agreement as to the moral bases for criminalizing that there is likely to be agreement as to whether the conduct in question involves a harm.[56] What will be 'wrong' or 'harmful' for the paternalist will not necessarily be so for the liberal.

In the last few decades, academic writing has focused heavily on the issue of the harm principle. By far the most refined examination of this has been that of Professor Feinberg,[57] but he is not alone in recognizing the utility of the harm principle in defining what is characteristic about crimes.[58] In the late 1970s, Gross dealt with the issue as had Packer a decade earlier.[59]

The harm to others formula seems to me to have two uses that justify its inclusion in a list of limiting criteria for invocation of the criminal sanction. First, it is a way to make sure that a given form of conduct is not being subjected to the criminal sanction purely or even primarily because it is thought to be immoral. It forces an inquiry into precisely what bad effects are feared if the conduct in question is not suppressed by the criminal law. Second, it immediately brings into play a host of secular inquiries about the effects of subjecting the conduct in question to the criminal sanction. One cannot meaningfully deal with the question of harm to others without weighing benefits against detriments. In that sense, it is a kind of threshold question, important not so much in itself, as in focusing attention on the further considerations relevant to the ultimate decision. It is for these two instrumental reasons rather than for either its intrinsic rightness or ease of application that it deserves inclusion.[60]

It is easy to think of the harm principle in a narrow, constrained way as meaning only direct harms to others. For some this fails to provide necessary protection against more remote harms.[61] A valuable refined statement of the harm principle is that by Professors Gardner and Shute:

It is no objection to the harm principle that a harmless action was criminalised nor even that an action with no tendency to cause harm was criminalised. It is enough to meet the demands of the harm principle that, if the actions were not criminalised that would be harmful. . . . Noninstrumental

---

[55] The philosophical literature on this topic is vast. See, inter alia, Wilson, *Central Issues*, Ch 1, and references therein.

[56] Harm can be defined to include endangerment to V's interests where D foresees that he might damage those interests although he is not acting intentionally to damage them. See further Duff, 'Criminalising Endangerment' in Duff and Green, *Defining Crimes*; cf C Clarkson, 'Aggravated Endangerment' (2007) 60 CLP 279.

[57] See the review of 25 years to 2005 by Duff (2005) 25 OJLS 353.

[58] For arguments that the harm principle is over- and under-inclusive, see Duff, *Answering for Crime*, Ch 6.

[59] J Feinberg, *Harm to Others* (1984); H Packer, *The Limits of the Criminal Sanction* (1968) 266; H Gross, *A Theory of Criminal Justice* (1979) 119.

[60] Packer, ibid, 262.

[61] Professor Horder advances a 'true' understanding of Mill's harm principle, based upon harm prevention and the risk of the harm that might result if the conduct were not criminalized. Horder (2011) 127 LQR 37. However, he does not propose any *de minimis* threshold nor does he establish how remote the risk of harm must be before it may be legitimately the subject of the criminal law.

wrongs, even when they are perfectly harmless in themselves, can pass this test if their criminalisa-tion diminishes the occurrence of them, and would detract from people's prospects—for example diminishing some public good.[62]

Whether an activity can be classified as involving a 'setback to interests' or a 'diminution of a public good' will often be a controversial question.[63] As noted, Parliament has in recent years too readily accepted that a form of behaviour is sufficiently harmful or wrong to war-rant criminalization rather than some alternative less coercive form of regulation.[64] This has been particularly striking in the context of so-called regulatory offences.[65]

In identifying the interests to be protected by the criminal law, it is increasingly impor-tant to recognize the State's obligation to protect the rights of citizens as protected by the European Convention on Human Rights (ECHR). Where Art 3 guarantees a right to be free from inhuman and degrading treatment, it is incumbent on the State through the process of the criminal law to provide adequate protection against the infliction of such harm as corporal punishment. Similarly, where Art 2 of the ECHR guarantees a right to life, it is incumbent on the State to provide adequate protection of that right for each citizen.

1.3.2.3 Agreed basis of criminalization?

Numerous scholarly analyses have devoted thousands of pages to an attempt to identify the basis on which conduct *ought* to be criminalized. These philosophical inquiries lie beyond the scope of this work which is focused on providing a doctrinal analysis of the criminal law.[66] A compelling examination of the criminalization problem is offered by Husak in his work *Overcriminalization*.[67] He advances a number of factors which should guide whether conduct ought to be criminal. These are in brief: that the criminal law ought not to be used to prohibit 'non trivial harm or evil';[68] that a criminal offence must target some wrongful conduct by the defendant;[69] that punishment for an offence is justified only when and to the extent it is deserved;[70] the burden on justifying the creation of a criminal offence is on those who seek to introduce it;[71] that the crime to be created must identify a substantial and legiti-mate State interest to be protected;[72] that the criminal law introduced will directly advance that interest;[73] and that criminalization will ensure that criminal law ought not to be more extensive in scope than is necessary to achieve its purpose.[74]

1.3.3 Definition by process?

As the brief discussion above has demonstrated, it is impossible in relation to any particular form of conduct to define the intrinsic qualities which render it criminal. It is also impos-sible to identify any universal purpose, and difficult to agree readily on any universal moral foundation for a crime. Because of this, most writers—and the courts—have been driven to 'define' whether conduct is criminal by turning to the nature of the legal proceedings which may follow from its commission.[75] The criminal quality of conduct cannot be discerned by intuition; nor can it be discovered by reference to any standard but one: is the conduct prohibited with penal consequences?[76]

---

[62] J Gardner and S Shute, 'The Wrongness of Rape' in J Horder (ed), *Oxford Essays in Jurisprudence* (2000) 216.

[63] Elaborate systems for differentiating levels of harm and relative offence seriousness have been devised, see A von Hirsch and N Jareborg, 'Gauging Criminal Harm: A Living Standard Analysis' (1991) 11 OJLS 1.

[64] See A Ashworth, 'Interpreting Criminal Statutes: A Crisis of Legality' (1991) 117 LQR 419.

[65] See LCCP 195.

[66] See n 36 and references therein.   [67] (2008).   [68] ibid, 66.   [69] ibid, 72.

[70] ibid, 82.   [71] ibid, 100.   [72] ibid, 120.   [73] ibid, 145.   [74] ibid, 153.

[75] See LCCP 195, para 3.39.

[76] *Proprietary Articles Trade Association v A-G for Canada* [1931] AC 310 at 324 per Lord Atkin.

The problem then becomes one of distinguishing criminal proceedings from civil proceedings. Any attempt to distinguish between crimes and torts comes up against the same kind of difficulty encountered in defining crimes generally: that most torts are crimes as well, though some torts are not crimes and some crimes are not torts. It is not in the nature of the conduct but in the nature of the proceedings that the distinction consists; and both types of proceeding may follow where conduct is both a crime and a tort.[77]

Professor Kenny,[78] in his famous book in which he attempted to define a crime, directed his attention to identifying the essential distinction between civil and criminal procedure. He rejected any distinction based on: (a) the extent to which the State was involved in the two types of proceeding, because that was incapable of being applied with precision; (b) the tribunals involved, because both civil and criminal cases may be heard in the magistrates' courts and the Supreme Court; (c) the object of the proceedings, because, while 'the object of criminal procedure is always *Punishment*', the award of exemplary damages in civil actions is also punitive; (d) the nature of the sanctions, because, while criminal sanctions never enrich any individual, it was not true to say that all civil actions do, since some civil actions for penalties could be brought only by the Crown. The action in civil law is subject to a limitation period which does not apply in criminal law—prosecutions for conduct as long as 63 years earlier have been successful.[79]

Kenny finally seized upon the degree of control exercised over the two types of proceedings by the Crown as the criterion, and defined 'crimes' as:

wrongs whose sanction is punitive and is in no way remissible by any private person, but is remissible by the Crown alone, *if remissible at all*.[80]

Kenny's definition has been much criticized. Professor Winfield[81] thought it led to a vicious circle:

What is a crime? Something that the Crown alone can pardon. What is it that the Crown alone can pardon? A crime.[82]

Winfield thought it advisable not to accept this part of Kenny's definition; and he concentrated on the question, what is punishment? The answer he arrived at is that: 'The essence of punishment is its inevitability . . . no option is left to the offender as to whether he shall endure it or not'; whereas, in a civil case, 'he can always compromise or get rid of his liability with the assent of the injured party'.[83] Thus we seem to arrive back at the test we have just rejected: who can remit the sanction.

More substantial is the point made by Professor Williams.[84] If we are going to define crime by reference to procedure, we ought to make use of the whole law of procedure, not just one item of it—the power to remit the sanction. If a court has to decide whether a particular act which has been prohibited by Parliament is a crime, it may be guided by a reference in the statute to any element which exists only in civil, or only in criminal, procedure as the case may be. A crime is:

an act that is capable of being followed by criminal proceedings, having one of the types of outcome (punishment, etc) known to follow these proceedings.[85]

---

[77] A civil action for assault or battery is barred by the Offences Against the Person Act 1861, ss 44 and 45 if criminal proceedings brought in the magistrates' court by or on behalf of the victim (a) have been dismissed and a certificate of dismissal has been issued; or (b) have resulted in conviction and the defendant has paid anything he was ordered to pay or has served any imprisonment imposed. See *Stevens and Whitehouse* (1991) 155 JP 697.

[78] Kenny, *Outlines*, Ch 1.

[79] See *D* [2013] EWCA Crim 2398. Note that there are some offences to which time limits apply, notably summary only ones.

[80] Kenny, *Outlines*, 1.   [81] *Province of the Law of Tort* (1931) Ch VIII.

[82] ibid, 197.   [83] ibid, 200.   [84] (1955) 8 CLP at 128.   [85] ibid, 123.

This definition is by no means so unhelpful as at first sight it may appear; for there are many points of distinction between civil and criminal procedure, and if the statute prescribes one procedural step peculiar to the criminal law that will point to the provision creating a criminal offence. In some instances, this may mean that the determination of whether a provision creates a crime or a civil wrong turns on whether a rule of criminal or a rule of civil procedure should be followed.[86] Of course, using procedural clues to classify a provision as one creating a crime tells us nothing about what acts *ought* to be crimes, but that is not its purpose.[87]

There is a further problem with reliance on the procedural differences between crime and civil law to identify a crime. In recent years, Parliament has introduced a series of measures which although formally civil orders have a quasi-criminal nature: for example, Football Banning Orders, Sexual Harm Prevention Orders, Serious Crime Prevention Orders.[88] Although civil procedures and civil rules of evidence may apply, the consequences of breaching such an order are criminal.[89] In addition, the stigma attached to such orders is greater than that which would usually be associated with a civil order.[90] The Anti-social Behaviour, Crime and Policing Act 2014 created new Anti-Social Behaviour Injunctions and Criminal Behaviour Orders (for convicted offenders).[91] Whether these new orders are in fact less punitive than the original Anti-Social Behaviour Orders has been doubted by many commentators including, for example, the campaign group Liberty.

1.3.4 The practical test: is it a crime?

From time to time, the courts have found it necessary to determine whether particular proceedings are criminal or not. Before the Criminal Evidence Act 1898, the defendant could not give evidence on oath on his own behalf in a criminal case whereas (since the Evidence Act 1851) he had been able to do so in a civil action. If he wished to give evidence, the nature of the proceeding had to be ascertained.[92] The same problem could arise today if it were sought to *compel* the defendant to give evidence.[93]

This problem arose frequently under legislation[94] that provided that no appeal should lie to the Court of Appeal 'in any criminal cause or matter'. The question whether a

---

[86] cf PJ Fitzgerald, 'A Concept of Crime' [1960] Crim LR 257, 259–60.

[87] Writers who set out to define a crime by reference to the nature of the conduct, on the other hand, inevitably end by telling us not what a crime is but what the writer thinks it ought to be; and that is not a definition of a crime.

[88] Serious Crime Act 2007, Part 1, on which see R Fortson, *Blackstone's Guide to the Serious Crime Act 2007* (2008). See generally E Freer, *A Practitioner's Guide to Ancillary Orders in Criminal Courts* (2018).

[89] There is a danger that these orders can create 'personal' criminal laws—eg, while it is not an offence for a person to enter a particular shopping centre, if D is made subject to an order not to do so, his entering the shopping centre becomes a crime personal to him. Admittedly, he is criminally liable for the breach of the court order and not the entry per se, but the effect is the same and the dangers for misuse are obvious. See for discussion S Hoffman and S Macdonald, 'Should ASBOs be Civilized?' [2010] Crim LR 457; P Ramsay, 'Substantively Uncivilized ASBOs' [2010] Crim LR 761; S Hoffman and S Macdonald, 'Substantively Uncivilized ASBOs: A Response' [2010] Crim LR 764.

[90] See on these, A Ashworth, 'Social Control and "Anti-Social Behaviour": The Subversion of Human Rights' (2004) 120 LQR 263. See also White (2010) 126 LQR 593.

[91] For discussion, see KJ Brown, 'Replacing the ASBO with the Injunction to Prevent Nuisance and Annoyance: A Plea for Legislative Scrutiny and Amendment' [2013] Crim LR 623; P Jarvis, 'The New Criminal Behaviour Order' [2015] Crim LR 275.

[92] *Cattell v Ireson* (1858) EB & E 91; *Parker v Green* (1862) 2 B & S 299.

[93] He is compellable in a civil but not in a criminal case.

[94] The Judicature Act 1873, s 47, and its successor, the Judicature Act 1925, s 31(1)(a) in force until 1968. Appeal now lies to the Court of Appeal (Crim Div) as provided by the Criminal Appeal Act 1968. See LCCP 184, *The High Court's Jurisdiction in Relation to Criminal Proceedings* (2007), and Report of that name LC 324 (2010). The government has yet to respond to the Law Commission's report. See also on this *Belhaj v DPP* [2018] UKSC 33.

particular proceeding was a criminal cause or matter frequently came before the Court of Appeal and the House of Lords. The test which was regularly applied was whether the proceedings may result in the punishment of the offender. If they may, then it was a criminal proceeding.[95] As a practical test, this seems to work well enough. However, it must always be remembered that it is a rule with exceptions, because some actions for penalties are undoubtedly civil actions, and yet they have the punishment of the offender as their objective; for this reason the test of punishment is jurisprudentially unsatisfactory.[96]

The meaning of punishment itself is not easy to ascertain; for the defendant in a civil case, who is ordered to pay damages by way of compensation, may well feel that he has been punished. It has been suggested[97] that:

What distinguishes a criminal from a civil sanction and all that distinguishes it . . . is the judgment of community condemnation which accompanies and justifies its imposition.

According to this view it is the condemnation, plus the consequences of the sentence—fine or imprisonment, etc—which together constitute the punishment; but the condemnation is the essential feature. From this, it is argued that we can say readily enough what a 'crime' is:

It is not simply anything which the legislature chooses to call a 'crime'. It is not simply anti-social conduct which public officers are given a responsibility to suppress. It is not simply any conduct to which a legislature chooses to attach a 'criminal' penalty. It is conduct which, if duly shown to have taken place, will incur a formal and solemn pronouncement of the moral condemnation of the community.[98]

But if 'the formal and solemn pronouncement' means the judgment of a criminal court (and what else can it mean?) we are driven back to ascertaining whether the proceeding is criminal or not. How is the judge to know whether to make 'solemn and formal pronouncement of condemnation' or to give judgment as in a civil action? Surely, only by ascertaining whether the legislature (or the courts in the case of a common law crime) have prescribed that the proceedings shall be criminal; and this must depend, primarily, upon whether it is intended to be punitive.

1.3.5 Conclusion

Readers will by now have realized that the task of defining 'crime' by reference to a universal purpose for criminalization or by identifying some universally accepted ingredients such as public wrongs and harms would be extremely difficult. There is no sufficient agreement as to what these purposes or ingredients are. The best that can be offered in practical terms is to consider the trial process and likely outcomes if liability is established.

---

[95] eg *Mellor v Denham* (1880) 5 QBD 467; *Seaman v Burley* [1896] 2 QB 344; *Robson v Biggar* [1908] 1 KB 672; *Re Clifford and O'Sullivan* [1921] 2 AC 570; *Amand v Home Secretary and Minister of Defence of the Royal Netherlands Government* [1943] AC 147; *Re Osman (No 4)* [1991] Crim LR 533. In a different context, see recently *Belhaj v DPP* [2018] UKSC 33.

[96] It is thought not to be a substantial objection that exemplary damages may be awarded in some civil cases; for this is merely ancillary to the main object and the occasions for their award are now much restricted: *Rookes v Barnard* [1964] AC 1129, 1221; *Cassell & Co Ltd v Broome* [1972] AC 1027; *AB v South West Water Services Ltd* [1993] QB 507.

[97] By HM Hart, 'The Aims of the Criminal Law' (1958) 23 *Law and Contemporary Problems* 401, 404.

[98] ibid, 405.

1.4 The sources of the criminal law

Having considered whether there is a universal definition of a crime, it is useful to consider the sources of the criminal law. As this section will demonstrate, there is no criminal code in England and Wales. The criminal law is therefore dispersed throughout not only the common law, but also a multitude of legislative provisions.

1.4.1 Common law

A particular difficulty in English criminal law is that many important and serious offences, including for example, murder, manslaughter, misconduct in public office and conspiracy to defraud, derive from the common law rather than statute. It may seem surprising that the courts in the twenty-first century are still relying on definitions of offences from judicial pronouncements of centuries ago, or even from the ancient common law writers and reporters—East,[99] Hale,[100] Coke,[101] Hawkins,[102] etc. This poses problems in terms of the principle of legality and of potentially retrospective application. Challenges to some of the best established common law offences—for example, the gross negligence manslaughter offence,[103] public nuisance[104] and conspiracy to defraud—have been mounted in recent years on the grounds of uncertainty and retrospectivity.

There has been a growing concern that these old common law offences are being used inappropriately. For example, in *Norris v USA*[105] and *GG Plc*[106] the House of Lords rejected attempts to use the ancient common law crime of conspiracy to defraud to deal with an alleged price-fixing cartel. For centuries, the common law offence had been available but at no time had anyone, whether an individual or a company, been successfully prosecuted for being a party or giving effect to a price-fixing agreement per se.[107] It was a novel, yet inappropriate, use of this common law offence.

It has been accepted repeatedly by the courts in recent decades that they will not create new offences. This stance is to be welcomed since it is well recognized that judicial law-making is an undemocratic process with a tendency to create uncertainty. In *Jones* et al,[108] the House of Lords made clear that statute law was the sole source of new criminal offences and it was for those elected representatives of the country in Parliament, not the executive and not the judges, to decide what conduct should be treated as criminal. This echoed their lordships' statements in *Goldstein and Rimmington*,[109] where it was observed that just as the courts had no power to create new offences so they had no power to abolish offences (public nuisance in that case).

A further problem with common law offences arises in relation to their overlap with statute. The House of Lords has since accepted that where Parliament has defined the ingredients of an offence, that statutory offence should ordinarily be charged rather than a common law offence which might not include the same defences and for which the potential penalty is unlimited.[110] This issue has arisen with increasing frequency in relation to the

---

[99] East, I/II PC.   [100] Hale, I/II PC.   [101] Co 1 Inst.
[102] J Curwood (ed), *A Treatise of the Pleas of the Crown* (8th edn, 1795).
[103] *Misra* [2004] EWCA Crim 2375, see Ch 15.
[104] *Rimmington* [2005] UKHL 63, see Ch 31. See also LCCP 193, *Simplification of Criminal Law: Public Nuisance and Outraging Public Decency* (2010) and report LC 358 (2015).
[105] [2008] UKHL 16.   [106] [2008] UKHL 17.
[107] Parliament criminalized price-fixing cartels under the Enterprise Act 2002.
[108] [2006] UKHL 16.   [109] [2005] UKHL 63.
[110] ibid, [30]. There is no strict prohibition on a prosecution for the common law offence in such circumstances. But note *Stockli* [2017] EWCA Crim 1410 in which the court stated that a calculated decision to deny a defendant the benefit of a statutory defence might constitute an abuse of process.

common law offences of conspiracy to defraud and cheating the Revenue, which overlap with a number of statutory offences.[111]

There have been repeated calls to abolish common law offences.[112] The problems posed by common law offences are examined further in the relevant chapters in which the offences are discussed.

It should not be forgotten that the common law also provides most of the 'defences' in English law, including insanity, automatism, intoxication, mistake,[113] duress, duress of circumstances and necessity;[114] even self-defence, which in 2008 Parliament claimed to clarify by statute, rests on common law principles.[115]

The Law Commission has been prolific in recent years in producing Consultation Papers and Reports affecting many areas of the substantive criminal law including in the last few years: murder, manslaughter, infanticide, provocation, diminished responsibility, incitement, conspiracy, attempt, secondary liability, bribery and corruption, intoxication, insanity and automatism, hate crime, unfitness to plead, offences against the person, and kidnapping. The papers produced are high quality with analysis of the present law and its defects, often providing empirical and comparative materials and stimulating discussion of the law. Much of the Law Commission's work consists of analysing common law offences and recommending that they be placed on a statutory footing. Reference to the Law Commission's valuable work is made throughout the book at the relevant points.

1.4.2 Statute

Notwithstanding the common law—with all its ambiguities and flexibility—most of English criminal law is now contained in thousands of independent statutory offences.[116] These are not collected together as a catalogue of 'criminal legislation', and many offences appear in an otherwise unrelated statute as, for example, with offences in the Companies Act 2006 or the Insolvency Act 1986. In addition, there are thousands of statutory instruments to consider as ministers and bodies such as local authorities are commonly provided with powers to create criminal offences by subordinate legislation. A striking example of the use of secondary legislation is the many, frequently changing, offences during the Covid-19 period introduced under the Health Protection (Coronavirus, Restrictions) (England) Regulations 2020.

Even within the exclusively criminal statutes it is often difficult to discern the present law since the statutes are too readily and heavily amended without being republished in consolidated form. As Toulson LJ noted in *Chambers*,[117] in a case dealing with tobacco importation:

To a worryingly large extent, statutory law is not practically accessible today, even to the courts whose constitutional duty it is to interpret and enforce it. There are four principal reasons. . . . First, the

---

[111] In *R (Redcar Cleveland BC) v Dady* [2013] EWHC 475 (QB), [17], Coulson J stated: 'It seems to me, therefore, that the court must look, first, at whether there is a relevant statutory offence and, if so, how and why the Crown has chosen not to prefer conspiracy charges by reference to that offence, and whether it is proper in all the circumstances to allow the common law allegation of conspiracy to defraud to be maintained.' In the subsequent case of *Dosanjh* [2013] EWCA Crim 2366 D was charged with cheating the public revenue and sought to argue that it offended the principle of legality for him not to have been charged with a statutory offence when one was available. The Court of Appeal rejected this contention, finding that there was a good reason for the Crown to have preferred the common law offence.

[112] See G McBain, 'Abolishing Some Obsolete Common Law Crimes' (2009) 20 KLJ 89.

[113] All dealt with in Ch 9.   [114] See Ch 10.

[115] See Ch 10 and the Criminal Justice and Immigration Act 2008, s 76 as repeatedly amended.

[116] This makes it extremely difficult to ascertain how many criminal offences actually exist. For discussion, see J Chalmers and F Leverick, 'Tracking the Creation of Criminal Offences' [2013] Crim LR 543.

[117] [2008] EWCA Crim 2467, [24]–[27]. On the unfairness this creates, see A Ashworth (2011) 74 MLR 1, 21, and Ch 9.

majority of legislation is secondary legislation. . . . Secondly, the volume of legislation has increased very greatly over the last 40 years.[118] Thirdly, on many subjects the legislation cannot be found in a single place, but in a patchwork of primary and secondary legislation. Fourthly, there is no comprehensive statute law database . . . This means that the courts are in many cases unable to discover what the law is, or was at the date with which the court is concerned, and are entirely dependent on the parties for being able to inform them what were the relevant statutory provisions which the court has to apply.

So extensive is the problem of criminalizing by secondary legislation that the Law Commission proposed that no new criminal offence-making provision should be created otherwise than in primary legislation.[119]

Even once the relevant provision has been identified and it has been ascertained that it is in force, as any student of the English legal system will know, the fact that an offence is laid down in a statute is no guarantee that its meaning is clear and undisputed. Many of the decisions discussed in this book involve the appellate criminal courts wrestling with matters of statutory construction. This has the potential to generate vast numbers of appellate decisions (all of which are now accessible via the internet and legal research databases) and there is a real danger that the principle under consideration in a given case is lost in the voluminous citation of authority.[120]

This is not the place to rehearse general principles of statutory construction. However, it is worth emphasizing one particular principle of statutory construction in criminal law: that if a provision is ambiguous it ought to be interpreted in the manner favourable to the accused.[121] The courts have acknowledged a new dimension to that principle where the ambiguity might be resolved by reference to ministerial statements. In *Thet v DPP*,[122] it was suggested that it is not permissible to use the doctrine in *Pepper v Hart*[123] and refer to the parliamentary debates to enlarge the scope of liability. However, in *Tabnak*,[124] Lord Philips CJ, again giving the judgment of the court, qualified, *obiter*, what had been said in *Thet v DPP*.[125] Defence reliance on *Pepper v Hart*, to admit parliamentary material as an aid to statutory construction, may be more readily received by the court than where the prosecution rely on *Pepper v Hart*. The criminal courts' use of *Pepper v Hart* continues to be rather unorthodox.[126]

1.4.3 EU

The law of the European Union is an often overlooked source of English criminal law.[127] There is little doubt that the domestic criminal lawyer in England experienced the influence of EU law in criminal process (with extradition and European Arrest Warrants, and

---

[118] His lordship referred to 'The Law Commission's Report on Post-Legislative Scrutiny' (2006) Law Com 302, which gave some figures in Appendix C. In 2005, there were 2,868 pages of new Public General Acts and approximately 13,000 pages of new Statutory Instruments, making a total well in excess of 15,000 pages (which is equivalent to over 300 pages a week) excluding European Directives and European Regulations, which were responsible for over 5,000 additional pages of legislation. See also LCCP 195, *Criminal Liability in Regulatory Contexts* (2010). Cf F Leverick, J Chalmers et al, 'Is Formal Criminalisation Really on the Rise? Evidence from the 1950s' [2015] Crim LR 177.

[119] See LCCP 195, para 3.144.

[120] See *Erskine* [2009] EWCA Crim 1425, [2010] Crim LR 48 and commentary.

[121] *Tuck v Priester* (1887) 19 QBD 627.   [122] [2006] EWHC 2701 (Admin), [15].

[123] [1993] AC 593.   [124] [2007] EWCA Crim 380.   [125] [2006] EWHC 2701 (Admin).

[126] See eg the decision in *JTB* [2009] UKHL 20 on *doli incapax*, discussed in Ch 9 in full and see F Bennion [2009] Crim LR 757.

[127] See for an accessible account, E Baker, 'The European Union's "Area of Freedom, Security and (Criminal) Justice" 10 Years On' [2010] Crim LR 833. For more detailed analysis, see V Mitsilegas, *EU Criminal Law* (2009). See also E Baker, 'Taking European Criminal Law Seriously' [1998] Crim LR 361; H Jung, 'Criminal Justice—A European Perspective' [1993] Crim LR 237; J Dine, 'European Community Criminal Law' [1993] Crim LR 246; N Bridge, 'The European Communities and the Criminal Law' [1976] Crim LR 88.

European Investigation Orders, etc).[128] In terms of substantive criminal law rather than process, although it might seem as if there is little English case law dealing explicitly with EU criminal law, in fact EU law had an important influence on a number of areas of mainstream criminal law in this country. One way EU law influenced domestic criminal law was by introducing criminal law measures at EU level. Another way was to influence the interpretation of domestic law by EU principles. Obvious examples include: cartels in competition law that are now criminalized by the Enterprise Act 2002,[129] consumer protection offences, areas of VAT evasion and carousel frauds and environmental crimes.[130] EU law was clearly an important source of statutory criminal law in England and will remain so even after the UK leaves the EU. This is because s 2(1) of the European Union (Withdrawal Agreement) Act 2020 inserts s 1B into the European Union (Withdrawal) Act 2018 so that s 1B(2) provides that, 'EU-derived domestic legislation, as it has effect in domestic law immediately before exit day, continues to have effect in domestic law on and after exit day'.

1.4.4 International law

As supranational legal regimes have begun to exert more of an influence on English criminal law, the range of sources extends ever wider. There are several aspects to acknowledge. First, there are of course some crimes created by English law which can be committed abroad but these are not international at all, simply extraterritorial.[131]

In addition, there are numerous crimes of a transnational form, in particular money laundering offences.

There is also the potential for international law[132] to influence domestic law directly as was illustrated in *Jones*[133] where the appellants sought to argue that the definition of crime in s 3 of the Criminal Law Act 1967 should be interpreted to include the crime of aggression recognized in international law. This would have permitted them to argue that they were acting in prevention of a 'crime' (the international crime of aggression) when they damaged property at military establishments in England as a protest against the Iraq war. The House of Lords rejected that interpretation, recognizing that it was for Parliament to incorporate such international crimes into English law, and not for the courts.[134]

International law also influences domestic criminal law because the *origin* of domestic criminal law may be found in the UK's obligations to give effect to international law, specifically those obligations contained in treaties. For example, the offences contained in the International Criminal Court Act 2001 (genocide, war crimes and crimes against humanity) are defined by reference to the Rome Statute.[135]

---

[128] For detailed analysis, see D Atkinson (ed), *EU Law in Criminal Practice* (2013).

[129] C Graham, 'The Enterprise Act 2002 and Competition Law' (2004) 67 MLR 273; C Harding and J Joshua, 'Breaking Up the Hardcore: The Prospects for the Proposed Cartel Offence' [2002] Crim LR 933. See also *Norris v USA* [2008] UKHL 16.

[130] As an illustration of the way that EU law might impact on domestic criminal law, see the relatively recent realization that the Video Recordings Act 1984 was invalid since it was never referred to the EU Commission. The Video Recordings Act 2010 was then enacted in identical terms. See *Buidimir* [2010] EWCA Crim 1486.

[131] See P Alldridge, *Relocating Criminal Law* (2000) Ch 7.

[132] See generally the essays contained in V Mitsilegas, P Alldridge and L Cheliotis (eds), *Globalisation, Criminal Law and Criminal Justice* (2014).

[133] [2006] UKHL 16; see also the commentary at [2007] Crim LR 66.

[134] See Lord Bingham [2006] UKHL 16, [12], [23], [28].

[135] See the excellent review by K Grady, 'International Crimes in the Courts of England and Wales' [2014] Crim LR 693.

1.5 The ECHR and Human Rights Act 1998

The enactment of the Human Rights Act 1998 (HRA 1998) was one of the most significant developments in English law in the last century. Its impact has been felt on the criminal law as elsewhere. Detailed consideration of the Act and the ECHR can be found in specialist texts, and the following pages offer simply an introductory overview of the most important aspects of the ECHR and its impact on substantive criminal law.[136] The Convention rights are dealt with at relevant points throughout the book.

As with other areas of law, every criminal court is, by virtue of s 2 of the HRA 1998, obliged to 'take account' of the jurisprudence of the European Court of Human Rights (ECtHR) in construing English law. This is problematic since much of the Strasbourg jurisprudence is vague and general in nature and not in the familiar form of common law case precedents. In addition, there is the problem that all too often in criminal matters the ECtHR accepts that the actions of the relevant State are within the margin of appreciation. This accommodates the Member States' distinctive criminal law traditions and cultures, but renders the protection in substantive law relatively weak.[137]

Under s 3 of the HRA 1998 the courts must ensure that statutes 'so far as it is possible to do so, be read and given effect in a way which is compatible with the Convention rights'. Examples of the criminal courts' approach to that duty can be seen in numerous cases. Lord Bingham summarized the position:

> First, the interpretative obligation under s 3 is a very strong and far reaching one, and may require the court to depart from the legislative intention of Parliament. Secondly, a Convention-compliant interpretation under s 3 is the primary remedial measure and a declaration of incompatibility under s 4 an exceptional course. Thirdly, it is to be noted that during the passage of the Bill through Parliament the promoters of the Bill told both Houses that it was envisaged that the need for a declaration of incompatibility would rarely arise. Fourthly, there is a limit beyond which a Convention-compliant interpretation is not possible. . . . In explaining why a Convention-compliant interpretation may not be possible, members of the committee used differing expressions: such an interpretation would be incompatible with the underlying thrust of the legislation, or would not go with the grain of it, or would call for legislative deliberation, or would change the substance of a provision completely, or would remove its pith and substance, or would violate a cardinal principle of the legislation. . . . All of these expressions, as I respectfully think, yield valuable insights, but none of them should be allowed to supplant the simple test enacted in the Act: 'So far as it is possible to do so . . .'. While the House declined to try to formulate precise rules . . . it was thought that cases in which s 3 could not be used would in practice be fairly easy to identify.[138]

Where necessary the High Court, Court of Appeal or Supreme Court may declare a statute to be incompatible (HRA 1998, s 4) but cannot 'strike down' legislation. The courts have held some criminal statutes incompatible in controversial circumstances.[139] A court may 'read down' a statute to avoid a declaration of incompatibility. This has proved necessary in some criminal cases.[140]

---

[136] See generally Emmerson, Ashworth and Macdonald, HR&CJ; J Cooper and M Colvin, *Human Rights in the Investigation and Prosecution of Crime* (2009). For a review of developments in the past decade and a half, see A Ashworth, 'A Decade of Human Rights in Criminal Justice' [2014] Crim LR 325.

[137] See K Cavanagh, 'Policing the Margins: Rights Protection and the European Court of Human Rights' [2006] EHRLR 422.

[138] *A-G's Reference (No 4 of 2002)* [2004] UKHL 43, [28]. See *R (Hicks) v Commissioner of Police for the Metropolis* [2014] EWCA Civ 3.

[139] See eg *A v Secretary of State for the Home Department* [2004] UKHL 56 on the Anti-terrorism, Crime and Security Act 2001.

[140] See eg *Lambert* [2002] 2 AC 545.

The ECHR imposes positive and negative obligations. Thus, the State cannot infringe a person's rights by, for example, denying his right to life (negative obligation). Equally, the State is obliged to provide protection for an individual's rights by ensuring that the criminal law punishes and deters those who infringe rights (positive obligation).[141]

Some Articles of the Convention expressly impose such positive obligations,[142] as for example with Art 2 providing that the right to life 'shall be protected by law'. Many other guarantees under the Convention have been interpreted by the ECtHR to impose an obligation on the State to create laws which will protect the Convention rights of one individual from being infringed by another.[143]

1.5.1 Convention rights and substantive criminal law

Although the ECHR's impact is most significant in the context of evidence and procedure, the ECHR also has a direct impact on the operation of the substantive criminal law in many ways.[144]

1.5.1.1 Definition and interpretation

In terms of definition of crimes, the greatest impact might be under Art 7, which proscribes retrospective criminalization. Article 7 has been interpreted so as to prohibit vague criminal offences, as well as those that are truly retrospective. Article 7 provides:

1. No one shall be held guilty of any criminal offence on account of any act or omission which did not constitute a criminal offence under national or international law at the time when it was committed. Nor shall a heavier penalty be imposed than the one that was applicable at the time the criminal offence was committed.

2. This Article shall not prejudice the trial and punishment of any person for any act or omission which, at the time it was committed, was criminal according to the general principles of law recognized by civilized nations.

The European Court held in *Kokkinakis v Greece*,[145] and has reiterated many times since, that:

Article 7 . . . is not confined to prohibiting the retrospective application of the criminal law to an accused's disadvantage. It also embodies, more generally, the principle that only the law can define a crime and prescribe a penalty (*nullum crimen, nulla poena sine lege*) and the principle that the criminal law must not be extensively construed to an accused's detriment, for instance by analogy; it follows that an offence must be clearly defined in law.

The Strasbourg Court looks to whether the individual can know from the wording of the relevant provision and, if need be, with the assistance of the courts' interpretation of it,

---

[141] See further L Lazarus, 'Positive Obligations and Criminal Justice: Duties to Protect or Coerce?' in L Zedner and JV Roberts (eds), *Principles and Values in Criminal Law and Criminal Justice* (2013); J Rogers, 'Applying the Doctrine of Positive Obligations in the European Convention of Human Rights to Domestic Substantive Criminal Law in Domestic Proceedings' [2003] Crim LR 690. See also on the State's duty to protect life: *Van Colle v CC of Hertfordshire* [2008] UKHL 50. The principle was affirmed in *Van Colle v UK* (2013) 56 EHRR 23. For the impact this has on failures properly to investigate crime, see *Commissioner of Police for the Metropolis v DSD* [2018] UKSC 11.

[142] See generally S Fredman, *Human Rights Transformed* (2008).

[143] See Emmerson, Ashworth and Macdonald, HR&CJ, para 2.53.

[144] There was a substantial debate as to how significant an impact the HRA would have: for a minimalist view, see Buxton LJ, 'The Human Rights Act and the Substantive Criminal Law' [2000] Crim LR 331; and for a more radical expectation, see A Ashworth, 'HRA 1998 and Substantive Law' [2000] Crim LR 564.

[145] (1994) 17 EHRR 397 (App no 14307/88), Judgment of 25 May 1993, para 52.

which acts and omissions will make him criminally liable. This is not a prohibition on the development of the common law. As the Court noted in *SW*:[146]

However clearly drafted a legal provision may be, in any system of law, including criminal law, there is an inevitable element of judicial interpretation. There will always be a need for elucidation of doubtful points and for adaptation to changing circumstances. Indeed, in the United Kingdom, as in the other Convention States, the progressive development of the criminal law through judicial law-making is a well entrenched and necessary part of legal tradition. Article 7 of the Convention cannot be read as outlawing the gradual clarification of the rules of criminal liability through judicial interpretation from case to case, provided that the resultant development is consistent with the essence of the offence and could reasonably be foreseen.

In general, the English courts have taken a very narrow view of the protection afforded by Art 7[147] and have failed to accept that common law crimes such as manslaughter by gross negligence,[148] and public nuisance,[149] are incompatible with Art 7 on the grounds of their vagueness. One striking example of the English courts' narrow approach is *Haw v Secretary of State*,[150] where the court held that there was no infringement when the Serious Organised Crime and Police Act 2005 imposing restrictions on demonstrations in Parliament Square was applied to someone whose protest there had started before the Act was even drafted.

The House of Lords[151] did rely on Art 7 in rejecting the Crown's use of conspiracy to defraud when that offence had never previously been used to prosecute the alleged wrong-doing—price fixing. The House acknowledged the 'consistent message . . . through cases decided from 1875 through to 1984, was that price-fixing was not of itself capable of constituting a crime. . . . There was no reported case, indeed, it would appear, no unreported case, no textbook, no article which suggested otherwise.'[152] As such, it would infringe the principle of legality to impose the offence without warning. The House of Lords distinguished *SW* since in that case there was a gradual change in the law incrementally criminalizing marital rape and hence the availability of the charge had become reasonably foreseeable.

We anticipate that challenge on Art 7 grounds will continue to be mounted to the recent redefinition of dishonesty in the criminal trial.[153]

Many of the other Articles of the Convention will also affect the application of existing and future[154] crimes.

1.5.2 The Convention rights

Many of the ECHR rights as specified in Sch 1 to the HRA 1998, are of importance in determining the appropriate scope and application of offences. There are numerous examples provided throughout the book, but a few simple examples show how widely the impact of the Convention can be felt in substantive criminal law:

- Art 2 impacts on the scope of the protection offered by the law of homicide and the qualifications on the scope of self-defence, on abortion and euthanasia.[155] In *R (Pretty)*

---

[146] See *SW v UK* (1995) 21 EHRR 363, para 35.

[147] See C Murphy, 'The Principle of Legality in Criminal Law under the ECHR' [2010] EHRLR 194.

[148] *Misra* [2004] EWCA Crim 2375.   [149] *Rimmington* [2006] UKHL 63.

[150] [2005] EWCA Civ 532.   [151] *Norris v USA* [2008] UKHL 16; *GG* [2008] UKHL 17.

[152] At [55].   [153] Despite *Bermingham* [2020] EWCA Crim 1662. See below and *Barton* [2020] EWCA Crim 575.

[154] As the minister must give an assurance to Parliament that any Bill is compatible with the ECHR: HRA 1998, s 19. Note, however, this assurance is provided when the Bill is in its original form when presented to Parliament. See generally ATH Smith, 'The Human Rights Act and the Criminal Lawyer: The Constitutional Context' (1999) 197 CLR 251. The Law Commission's proposals are very keenly influenced by ECHR concerns; see eg LC 282, *Children: Their Non-Accidental Deaths or Serious Injury* (2003); LC 348, *Hate Crime: Should the Current Offences be Extended* (2014).

[155] See Chs 12 and 15.

v DPP,[156] as confirmed in *Pretty v UK*,[157] Art 2 does not enshrine the right to self-determination so as to require the State to permit the terminally ill to determine for themselves when they die;[158]

- Art 3 impacts on the regulation of the parental administration of corporal punishment;[159]
- Art 4 led to the introduction of a slavery offence in 2009 and its amendment in 2015;
- Art 5 affects the manner in which defendants found unfit to plead or not guilty by reason of insanity will be treated[160] and also, for example, the definition of the offence of false imprisonment;[161]
- Art 6 impacts on the use of reverse burden of proof defences;[162]
- Art 8 is relevant in protecting the rights of consenting adults to engage in sexual behaviour;[163]
- Art 9 could impact on the public order offences and the right of a religious group to conduct a service in public;
- Art 10 could offer a defence to those charged with offences in which they are expressing themselves in the form of protest—criminal damage or public order or obscenity;[164]
- Art 11 could affect the way the public order restrictions on a meeting are enforced;[165] and
- Art 14 could impact on the way that the criminal law discriminates against spouses or non-married couples.[166]

1.5.3 Article 6(2) of the ECHR and the burden of proof

The famous case of *Woolmington v DPP*[167] makes clear that the requirement for the prosecution to prove the guilt of the defendant beyond a reasonable doubt is a fundamental principle of English law.[168] Article 6(2) of the ECHR reinforces this, providing that a person 'charged with a criminal offence shall be presumed innocent until proved guilty according to the law'. The effect of the presumption is that in any criminal trial the prosecution bear the burden of proving (beyond a reasonable doubt) that the defendant performed the relevant actus reus with the requisite mens rea in the crime alleged. The defendant will bear the burden of raising sufficient evidence to get any defences off the ground. For example, where it is alleged that D murdered V, the prosecution must establish all the elements of murder, and D will have an obligation to adduce sufficient evidence to raise his defence, for example self-defence. The defendant bears what is called an evidential burden. The prosecution will then be obliged to rebut that defence to the criminal standard of proof; that is, making the jury satisfied so that they are sure that D was not acting in self-defence. The prosecution bear the legal burden of disproving it.

In exceptional circumstances, D bears the legal burden of proof. This is a more onerous duty: to prove a fact on the balance of probabilities, rather than merely to adduce evidence of it. The first exception is where D pleads insanity. His obligation is to prove that it is

---

[156] [2001] UKHL 61.   [157] (2002) 35 EHRR 1.

[158] See also *R (on the application of Nicklinson and another) v Ministry of Justice* [2014] UKSC 38.

[159] See Ch 16.   [160] See Ch 9.   [161] See Ch 16.   [162] See Ch 10.   [163] See Ch 17.

[164] Chs 27, 30, 31.   [165] Ch 31.   [166] Ch 11.   [167] [1935] AC 462.

[168] See generally HL Ho, 'The Presumption of Innocence as a Human Right' in P Roberts and J Hunter (eds), *Criminal Evidence and Human Rights: Reimagining Common Law Procedural Traditions* (2012); D Hamer, 'A Dynamic Reconstruction of the Presumption of Innocence' (2011) 31 OJLS 417; A Stumer, *The Presumption of Innocence, Evidential and Human Rights Perspectives* (2010).

more probable than not that he was 'insane' in law.[169] A second exception is where D pleads diminished responsibility under s 2 of the Homicide Act 1957. Again, it is for D to prove that it is more probable than not that he suffered from an abnormality of mental functioning arising from a recognized medical condition that substantially affected his relevant capacity and caused him to kill (see further the discussion in Ch 13). Further exceptional categories are created by Parliament, but these must be treated with caution, since all must comply with Art 6(2).[170] Finally, there are implied statutory exceptions where the offence provides any 'exception, exemption, proviso, excuse or qualification whether or not it accompanies the description of the offence in the enactment creating the offence'.[171] It is rather unsatis-factory that such an important matter as who bears the burden of proof turns on the matter of form in the statutory drafting, and is not obvious in every offence-creating provision.

Where an offence imposes a *legal burden* on the accused to *prove* a matter, rather than imposing merely an *evidential burden* to *raise* evidence of a matter, the question of compat-ibility with Art 6(2) arises. The leading ECtHR authority on the application of Art 6(2) is *Salabiaku v France*.[172] The Court recognized that Art 6(2) does not regard presumptions of fact or of law provided for in the criminal law with indifference. It requires States to confine them within reasonable limits which take into account the importance of what is at stake and maintain the rights of the defence.[173]

The English courts rapidly, though not consistently, developed a domestic jurisprudence on the imposition of a burden on the accused.[174] No fewer than four visits to the House of Lords failed to produce definitive guidance on the matter.[175] In the most important deci-sion, the House held that the court's responsibility in construing statutory provisions which appear to place a burden on a defendant is not to decide whether a reverse burden should be imposed on a defendant, but rather to evaluate whether Parliament's enactment unjustifi-ably infringes the presumption of innocence. Consider the case of a legal burden of proof placed on the accused on a charge of membership of a proscribed organization under s 11 of the Terrorism Act 2000,[176] where Lord Bingham identified five reasons[177] for his conclusion that the presumption was unjustifiably infringed:

(a) the reverse burden created a real risk that innocent individuals might be convicted, since the section is capable of applying to people who have no culpability;

(b) it could be difficult for any individual to prove that he has not participated in activi-ties, since terrorist organizations do not often keep records;

(c) if the legal burden rested on defendants, courts would in some cases convict those who could not establish their innocence;

---

[169] See T Jones, 'Insanity, Automatism and the Burden of Proof on the Accused' (1995) 111 LQR 475. For a full discussion see, Ch 9, p 318.

[170] Arguably these are not so exceptional—see A Ashworth and M Blake, 'The Presumption of Innocence in English Criminal Law' [1996] Crim LR 306, who found around 40 per cent of crimes imposing a burden on the accused.

[171] See the Magistrates' Courts Act 1980, s 101, in relation to summary offences. The House of Lords applied the same essential criteria in finding implied burdens in indictable offences: *Hunt* [1987] AC 352.

[172] (1988) 13 EHRR 379.   [173] Para 28.

[174] See IH Dennis, 'Reverse Onuses and the Presumption of Innocence' [2005] Crim LR 901.

[175] See *R v DPP, ex p Kebeline* [2000] 2 AC 326; *Lambert* [2002] 2 AC 545; *Johnstone* [2003] 1 WLR 1736; *A-G's Reference (No 4 of 2002)* [2004] UKHL 43. See also *Chargot Ltd* [2008] UKHL 73.

[176] Section 11(2) provides: It is a defence for a person charged with an offence under subsection (1) to prove that the organisation was not proscribed on the last (or only) occasion on which he became a member or began to profess to be a member, and that he has not taken part in the activities of the organisation at any time while it was proscribed.

[177] At [51].

(d) the potential punishment for the relevant offence is up to ten years' imprisonment;

(e) the security considerations, although important, do not absolve Member States from their duty to ensure that basic standards of fairness are observed.

This can be contrasted with their lordships' conclusion in the conjoined appeal in *Sheldrake*, dealing with s 5(2) of the Road Traffic Act 1988 which provides a defence to the offence of drink-driving.[178] The House of Lords held unanimously that Parliament had not acted unjustifiably in placing the legal burden on the accused in relation to that defence.[179]

The defendant has a full opportunity to show that there was no likelihood of his driving, a matter so closely conditioned by his own knowledge and state of mind at the material time as to make it much more appropriate for him to prove on the balance of probabilities that he would not be likely to drive than for the prosecutor to prove, beyond reasonable doubt, that he would . . . If a driver tries and fails to establish a defence under section 5(2), I would not regard the resulting conviction as unfair.

The guiding principles in determining the compatibility of a reverse onus provision appear to be the severity of sentence, the ease of proof for the defence and the risk of convicting the innocent.[180] These principles do not form a sufficiently solid or clear basis to guide the lower courts in future decision-making, and it is likely that the matter will require further appellate attention.[181]

Further reading

RA Duff and SP Green (eds), *Philosophical Foundations of Criminal Law*

RA Duff, L Farmer, SE Marshall, M Renzo, and V Tadros (eds), *Criminalization: The Political Morality of the Criminal Law*

HLA Hart, *Law, Liberty, and Morality*

DN Husak, *Overcriminalization: The Limits of the Criminal Law*

H Packer, *The Limits of the Criminal Sanction*

---

[178] Which provides that it is a defence for the defendant to prove that although he was in charge of the vehicle and was intoxicated beyond the legal limit 'the circumstances were such that there was no likelihood of his driving the vehicle whilst the proportion of alcohol' in his body exceeded the limit.

[179] At [41]. See also *Chargot Ltd* [2008] UKHL 73.

[180] For cogent criticism, see A Ashworth, commenting in [2005] Crim LR 215.

[181] See especially Dennis [2005] Crim LR 901.

2

The elements of a crime: actus reus

2.1 Introduction

It is a fundamental principle of criminal law that a person may not be convicted of a crime unless he has manifested his wrongdoing in some behaviour. There is no thought crime. Different crimes identify different forms of proscribed behaviour. Some are conduct crimes, where the acts or omissions of the accused are (with any required mental element) sufficient to constitute the offence. Examples include perjury and fraud. In these conduct offences there is no need to prove that any result was caused by D's conduct. Some crimes are result crimes and in those it must be proved that D's conduct caused a proscribed result. Murder, criminal damage and causing death by dangerous driving are examples.

The prosecution must prove beyond reasonable doubt (a) in a conduct crime that responsibility is to be attributed to D for certain behaviour or the existence of a certain state of affairs, in circumstances forbidden by criminal law; and (b) in a result crime, that responsibility is to be attributed to D for conduct in specified circumstances that has caused a proscribed event. That is the actus reus or external elements of the offence. To convict D, the prosecution must also prove that he had a defined state of mind in relation to the behaviour, existence of the state of affairs or causing of the event. The state of mind is the mens rea, or mental element, of the crime. The principle that a person is not criminally liable for his conduct unless the prescribed state of mind (mens rea) coincides with the prohibited actus reus also being present is frequently stated in the form of a Latin maxim: *actus non facit reum nisi mens sit rea*.[1]

2.1.1 Proof and the elements of the offence

As an example of these fundamental principles in operation, consider a charge of murder. The actus reus of murder is that D unlawfully caused the death of a human being under the Queen's peace; the mens rea is that D intended to kill or cause GBH. If it is absolutely clear that D killed V—that is, he has caused an actus reus—he must be acquitted of murder if there is a reasonable possibility that the killing was accidental. If that is the case, it has not been proved beyond reasonable doubt that he had the requisite mens rea. That was laid down by the House of Lords in *Woolmington v DPP*[2] where it was held, overruling earlier authorities, that it is a misdirection to tell a jury that D must *satisfy* them that the killing was an accident. The true rule is that the jury must acquit even though they are not satisfied that D's story is true, if they think it might reasonably be true. They should convict only if satisfied beyond reasonable doubt that D's account is *not* true.

At common law, this rule is of general application[3] and there is only one exception to it at common law—the defence of insanity.[4] If D pleads a defence of insanity, he must prove that defence, on the balance of probabilities.[5] For other common law defences, for example duress, the only burden on D is to raise enough evidence of the existence of the constituents of the defence;[6] whereupon it is for the prosecution to satisfy the jury that at least one of those constituents did not exist.[7] If there is evidence of a defence, though it has not been specifically raised by D, the judge must direct the jury to acquit unless they are satisfied that the defence has been disproved.[8]

By statute, however, a legal burden may expressly or impliedly be placed on the defendant to prove his defence.[9] Since the HRA 1998 such provisions may not always

[1] 'Properly translated, this means "An act does not make a man guilty of a crime, unless his mind be also guilty." It is thus not the *actus* which is "*reus*" but the man and his mind respectively' per Lord Hailsham in *Haughton v Smith* [1975] AC 476 at 491–2. It is, however, convenient to follow the established usage of 'actus reus'. Cf Lord Simon in *DPP for Northern Ireland v Lynch* [1975] AC 653 at 690, and Lord Diplock in *Miller* [1983] 2 AC 161.
[2] [1935] AC 462. See Lord Cooke, 'One Golden Thread' in *Turning Points in the Common Law* (The Hamlyn Lectures, 1997) 28.
[3] *Mancini v DPP* [1942] AC 1; *Chan Kau v R* [1955] AC 206; *Lobell* [1957] 1 QB 547 (self-defence) and see now s 76 of the Criminal Justice and Immigration Act 2008, p 400; *Bratty v A-G for Northern Ireland* [1963] AC 386 (automatism); *Gill* [1963] 1 WLR 841 (duress). But the onus of proving procedural bars to trial such as *autrefois convict* or *acquit*, may be on D: *Coughlan* (1976) 63 Cr App R 33 at 36.
[4] See Ch 9. [5] He has a legal burden of proof.
[6] This is known as an evidential burden. [7] The Crown has the legal burden of proof.
[8] *Palmer v R* [1971] AC 814; *Wheeler* (1967) 52 Cr App R 28 at 30–1; *Hamand* (1985) 82 Cr App R 65. See *Batchelor* [2013] EWCA Crim 2638 and *Brandford* [2016] EWCA Crim 1794.
[9] *Hunt* [1987] AC 352.

be fully effective,[10] and the court will be required to examine their compatibility with Art 6(2) of the ECHR. Whenever a legal burden of proof is put upon D, he satisfies it if he proves the issue on a balance of probabilities—the same standard as that on the claimant in a civil action—and he need not prove it beyond reasonable doubt.[11] There are numerous statutory offences and defences which impose legal burdens of proof on the defendant. The Law Commission has in recent reports also recommended creating defences for which D bears a legal burden of proof,[12] and this may become a more common feature in statutes.

2.1.2 Identifying elements of actus reus and mens rea

It is impossible to catalogue every type of conduct, circumstance or result that might constitute the actus reus of a crime. There are many thousands of offences, and in each case it is necessary to look to the specific terms of the offence, as defined by statute or common law, to determine what the elements of actus reus will be. As ever, care must be taken to be precise about the form of the actus reus of the particular offence. For example, the actus reus of murder is not simply the result—'a killing'—but includes elements of conduct and circumstances: the unlawful causing of the death of a human being under the Queen's peace. Similarly, the actus reus of rape is not simply non-consensual sex but, more specifically, consists of elements of conduct (penile penetration of the vagina, anus or mouth of a person) and proscribed circumstances (without the person's consent). A key skill that the criminal lawyer must develop is the ability to identify which elements of an offence are those of actus reus and which relate to the mens rea. It is usually easier to identify the elements of a crime that comprise the mens rea since these are represented by common expressions— intentionally, knowingly, wilfully, recklessly, etc—all of which are examined fully in the next chapter.

It should be noted that the separation of elements into actus reus and mens rea in this manner is principally to allow for the most convenient exposition and discussion of any given crime.[13] In practical terms, there is no need for the prosecution to approach its case by breaking down the crime into constituent parts of actus reus and mens rea to prove each element in turn to the jury's satisfaction; it will, sensibly, approach the task as one of proving all the elements of the crime as a whole. Moreover, it is not always possible to separate precisely actus reus from mens rea.[14] Sometimes a word that describes the actus reus, or part of it, implies a mental element. Without that mental element the actus reus simply cannot exist. For example, there are many offences of possession of specified objects (drugs, knives, etc) and it has always been recognized that 'possession', which might appear to be an element of actus reus, consists also in a mental element.[15] The same is true of words like

---

[10] See p 23. On the HRA 1998 and the burden of proof, see, *inter alia*, Emmerson, Ashworth and Macdonald, HR&CJ, Ch 29.

[11] *Carr-Briant* [1943] KB 607.

[12] See eg the defence of reasonableness in s 50 of the Serious Crime Act 2007 (LC 300, *Inchoate Liability for Assisting and Encouraging Crime* (2006); a similar defence was recommended for conspiracy in LC 318, *Conspiracy and Attempts* (2009) (see Ch 11); and that recommended for duress to murder in LC 304 (discussed in Ch 12)).

[13] See ATH Smith, 'On Actus Reus and Mens Rea' in P Glazebrook, *Reshaping the Criminal Law*; see also the more recent analysis of the significance of the differentiation: Duff, *Answering for Crime*, 202–8.

[14] See ACE Lynch, 'The Mental Element in the Actus Reus' (1982) 98 LQR 109.

[15] See Ch 5. For an interesting analysis of possession offences, see MD Dubber, 'The Possession Paradigm' in Duff and Green, *Defining Crimes*.

'permits',[16] 'appropriates',[17] 'cultivates',[18] 'abandons'[19] and many more that appear across the range of offences. Having an offensive weapon in a public place is the actus reus of an offence; but whether an article is an offensive weapon depends, in some circumstances, on the intention with which it is carried. In the absence of that intention, the thing is not an offensive weapon and there is no actus reus.[20] Making a false representation is the actus reus of fraud, but the element of falsity requires D to know the representation was untrue or misleading.[21] Similarly, transferring criminal property is a money laundering offence, but the definition of criminal property depends in part on whether D knows or suspects it is criminal property.[22]

The significance of this is that where the crime has an actus reus which incorporates a mental element, that necessarily becomes an element of the offence. It is the combination of the two which becomes the complete definition of the prohibited conduct.

2.1.3 The nature of an actus reus

Since the actus reus includes all the elements in the definition of the crime except D's mental element or fault,[23] it follows that the actus reus is not merely an 'act'. It may comprise conduct and any relevant circumstances and/or results.

Usually the actus reus requires proof of an act or an omission by D (which might be better described as 'conduct'). In fraud, D's conduct (making a false representation) is the full actus reus. For some conduct crimes the actus reus comprises conduct *and* circumstances: perjury is committed as soon as D makes a statement (conduct) on oath (circumstance) that he does not believe to be true. It is irrelevant whether there is a result in terms of whether his testimony is believed or not. In result crimes,[24] in addition to conduct and circumstances it must also be proved that the proscribed conduct caused a particular result. In murder, for example, it must be shown that D's conduct unlawfully caused the death. The actus reus of murder consists of elements of conduct (stabbing, shooting etc), circumstance (that the victim was a human being under the Queen's peace who had been born alive—a foetus is not yet a person to the law) and result (that the victim died).

In some rare instances, the actus reus may consist in a set of circumstances or 'state of affairs', not including any conduct or action by D at all.[25] An example might be where D is charged with 'being found' drunk in a public place.

2.1.3.1 Result crimes

There are many examples of result crimes, some of the most obvious being murder, manslaughter, wounding, etc. It has been said[26] that in 'result crimes' the law is interested only in

[16] See Ch 5.

[17] See Ch 18. In *Gomez* [1993] AC 442 at 495, [1993] Crim LR 304. Lord Browne-Wilkinson regarded 'appropriation' in the offence of theft as not involving any mental state; but this is hard to believe. See the discussion, p 865.

[18] *Champ* (1981) 73 Cr App R 367, [1982] Crim LR 108 and commentary.

[19] *Hunt v Duckering* [1993] Crim LR 678 (abandoning a dog in circumstances likely to cause unnecessary suffering).

[20] See online Chapter on offensive weapons.   [21] See Ch 22, s 2 of the Fraud Act 2006.   [22] See Ch 26.

[23] It should be said that this is not the only possible definition of an actus reus, and that a more limited view is taken of it by some writers. It is thought, however, that it is the most useful conception of the actus reus and is adopted throughout this book. Cf Williams, CLGP, 16, who suggests that the elements of actus reus ought also to incorporate the absence of some defences. See also the discussion in Duff, *Answering for Crime*, 202.

[24] Some crimes can be both—bribery can be committed by causing B to receive (result) or by offering to B (conduct): Green, *Lying, Cheating and Stealing*, 35. See the Bribery Act 2010, s 1 dealing with D who bribes and s 2 with R who receives.

[25] See p 43.   [26] GH Gordon, *Criminal Law of Scotland* (2nd edn, 1978) 61.

the result and not in the conduct bringing about the result. Similarly, a well-known definition of actus reus is 'such result of human conduct as the law seeks to prevent'.[27] But a dead
person with a knife in his back is not the actus reus of a murder. It is putting the knife in
the back thereby causing the death that is the actus reus. The law is just as interested in the
conduct that brings about the result in a 'result crime' as it is with a 'conduct crime'.[28]

2.1.3.2 Conduct crimes

True conduct crimes, such as perjury, are rare. The term 'conduct crime' has been interpreted more widely by Glanville Williams to include wounding and abduction—in these
crimes, 'you do not have to wait to see if anything happens as a result of what the defendant
does'.[29] This method of classification is controversial. If the test is whether you 'have to wait
to see', wounding is a conduct crime if committed with a knife but a result crime if committed with a gun, crossbow or catapult. If the distinction between conduct and result crimes is
to be made,[30] these offences of wounding and abduction are better regarded as result crimes.
A result has to flow from D's physical movements, whether you have to wait for it or not.

Since the Criminal Attempts Act 1981,[31] it is possible to charge someone with an offence
of attempt if they have done an act more than merely preparatory to the commission of an
indictable offence (with intent thereby[32] to commit that offence). So all indictable offences are
now, in a sense, potentially conduct crimes. D who aims a rifle at V and is about to shoot is, by
that conduct, attempting to murder him. The actus reus of the substantive offence attempted
need never happen and may, indeed, be impossible (eg if the gun is unloaded). The definition
of the elements of the substantive offence serves only to define the mens rea of the attempt.

An argument can be made that the law should always have regard only to the conduct and
not to the result. Whether the conduct results in harm is generally a matter of chance
and does not alter the blameworthiness and dangerousness of the actor.[33] But English law
has not gone so far.[34] If D hurls a stone, being reckless whether he injures anyone but not
intending to harm anyone, he is guilty of an offence if the stone strikes V but of no offence—
not even an attempt—if no one is injured. From a retributive point of view, it might be argued
that D should be equally liable in either event. This could be achieved by the creation of
general offences of reckless endangerment.[35] On utilitarian grounds, however, it is probably
undesirable to turn the whole criminal law into 'conduct crimes'. The needs of deterrence are
probably adequately served in most cases by 'result crimes'; and the criminal law should be
extended only where a clear need is established.

---

[27] Kenny, *Outlines*, 17.   [28] See Lord Diplock in *Treacy v DPP* [1971] AC 537 at 560.

[29] 'The Problem of Reckless Attempts' [1983] Crim LR 365 at 366, 368.

[30] It is not clear that it has, or should have, any practical consequences except perhaps as to jurisdiction.

[31] As interpreted in *Shivpuri*, p 516.

[32] ie D intends to cause the result by that act; it is the last act D intends, and needs to do not a merely preparatory act. An earlier act is sufficient, if 'more than merely preparatory': Ch 11.

[33] A Ashworth, 'Belief Intent and Criminal Liability' in J Eekelaar and J Bell (eds), *Oxford Essays in
Jurisprudence* (1987); 'Taking the Consequences' in S Shute, J Gardner and J Horder (eds), *Action and Value in
Criminal Law* (1993) and 'Defining Offences Without Harm' in *Criminal Law Essays*.

[34] As noted in the 12th edn, the Court of Appeal rejected this type of argument in a sentencing appeal where
D who had stabbed V was guilty of her murder, even though unknown to anyone V had a very short life expec-
tancy owing to a deep vein thrombosis. D claimed that his sentence ought to reflect this fact. He also sought to
argue that his sentence should be reduced because V's pre-existing medical condition meant that she would die
young and V's family had not been deprived of her 'long life': *Master* [2007] EWCA Crim 142.

[35] See, *inter alia*, the discussion in Duff, 'Criminalising Endangerment' in Duff and Green, *Defining Crimes*;
Duff, *Answering for Crime*, Ch 7; KJM Smith, 'Liability for Endangerment: English Ad Hoc Pragmatism and
American Innovation' [1983] Crim LR 127; D Lanham, 'Danger Down Under' [1999] Crim LR 960; C Clarkson,
'Aggravated Endangerment Offences' (2007) 60 CLP 278; A Ashworth and L Zedner, *Preventive Justice* (2014) Ch 5.

It has been argued that in some offences it may be that the actus reus can take different forms (result or conduct) depending on the circumstances.[36] Thus, theft can be committed where D assumes only one of the rights of the owner over his property (conduct crime)[37] or where he assumes them all (result crime). This ambiguity is all the less satisfactory because the different categorization of a crime as a conduct or result crime may have implications for procedure, in terms of the form of the indictment, and for jurisdictional issues.

The fact that an offence is a 'conduct offence' does not mean that it should automatically be classified as a 'continuing' offence. The term 'conduct' is being used to distinguish the type of crime from a 'result' crime. The conduct crime of perjury is completed once the testimony leaves the lips of the witness. It is not a continuing crime in any real sense. Identifying the starting and finishing points of the actus reus will be important in ensuring that the element of mens rea coincides in time, and may as noted be significant for procedural purposes of charging, in terms of the specific dates and actions alleged in the indictment and the territorial jurisdiction of the courts.

2.1.3.3 Actus reus includes circumstances

Circumstances, like consequences, are relevant if they are included in the definition of the crime. The definition of theft, for example, requires proof that D dishonestly appropriated property *belonging to another* with intention permanently to deprive the other of it. If the property belonged to no one (because it had been abandoned), D's appropriation in those circumstances could not constitute the actus reus of theft. However dishonest he might be, he could not be convicted of theft because an essential constituent of the crime is missing.[38] In child sex offences, the prohibited conduct (eg of sexual touching, etc) must be committed in the prescribed circumstance of the child being under a specified age (13 or 16 depending on the charge). In burglary, D's conduct of entering a building must be in prescribed circumstances: as a trespasser; and so on.

2.1.3.4 Victim's conduct/state as part of the actus reus

Sometimes a particular state of mind on the part of the *victim* is an essential element of the actus reus of a crime and, if the prosecution are unable to prove its existence, they must fail. If D is prosecuted for rape, it must be proved that V did not consent to the act of penile penetration. The absence of consent by V is an essential constituent of the actus reus. But in many crimes the consent or other state of mind of the victim is entirely irrelevant. If D is charged with the murder of V, it is no defence for him to show that V asked to be killed.

2.1.3.5 Summary

It is apparent from these examples that we can only see what elements comprise the actus reus of any particular crime by looking at the definition of that crime. We find this definition, in the case of common law crimes, in the decisions of the courts and, in the case of statutory crimes, in the words of the statute as construed by the courts. The actus reus elements of crimes are as diverse as the criminal offences themselves; for example, in bigamy, the fact that D is validly married; in wounding that D caused a break in the skin; in handling stolen goods, that the goods have, in fact, been stolen; and so on.

---

[36] See M Hirst, *Jurisdiction and the Ambit of the Criminal Law* (2003) 128.
[37] See *Morris* [1984] AC 320, p 864.
[38] He might, however, be convicted of an attempt to steal.

2.1.4 The effect of penalty provisions in determining the elements of the actus reus

Sometimes Parliament provides that an offence shall be more severely punishable when a particular fact, say 'X', is present. For example, causing a person to engage in sexual activity is part of the actus reus of a narrow group of offences. In all of those, if the sexual activity the person is caused to engage in involves penile penetration, the maximum sentence is higher.[39] When this happens, it is 'plain beyond argument that Parliament has created two offences', according to Lord Diplock (on behalf of a unanimous House of Lords) in *Courtie*.[40] The offence when condition X is present is a different and graver offence than when X is not present. X is an element in the actus reus, or the mens rea, or both, of the greater offence. The courts apply this principle where it can be presumed that Parliament intended to create two offences by giving one form of the offence a higher penalty. The courts will disapply the principle if it would lead to such inconvenient and absurd results that, in the opinion of the courts, Parliament could not have intended it to apply: *DPP v Butterworth*.[41]

When *Courtie* applies, the effect is (a) that D can be convicted of the greater offence only if the charge alleges that additional element X, and (b) it is for the jury to decide whether X is proved and to give their verdict accordingly, not a matter for the judge to decide after verdict.

Where Parliament provides an elaborate structure of maximum penalties, as in the case of drug offences, the criminal offences are correspondingly complex.[42] But the *Courtie* principle is sound. Where proof of fact X will result in D being liable to a higher penalty, the requirement to prove X should be no less stringent than in the case of the other facts of the offence.

2.1.5 Actus reus and the relationship with justifications or excuses

There is a long-standing debate not only as to the value of the use of terms such as actus reus and mens rea,[43] but precisely how the terminology ought to be applied. In the terminology used by Glanville Williams:[44]

Actus reus includes . . . the absence of any ground of justification or excuse, whether such justification or excuse be stated in any statute creating the crime or implied by the courts in accordance with general principle . . .

An alternative view is that of David Lanham:[45]

As a matter of analysis we can think of a crime as being made up of three ingredients, *actus reus, mens rea* and (a negative element) absence of a valid defence.

---

39 See Ch 17.   40 [1984] AC 463 at 471; *Grout* [2011] EWCA Crim 299.

41 [1995] 1 AC 381. Section 7(6) of the Road Traffic Act 1988 on its face creates only one offence of failing to provide a specimen of breath; but there is a higher penalty where the offender was driving or attempting to drive than when he was merely in charge. Nevertheless, there is only one offence. By contrast, s 5(1)(a) of the Act (driving/attempting to/being in charge of a motor vehicle on a road after consuming so much alcohol that the proportion of it in the breath/blood/urine exceeds the prescribed limit) creates nine offences, all punishable with the same penalty: *Bolton Justices, ex p Khan* [1999] Crim LR 912.

42 *Shivpuri* [1987] AC 1, [1986] Crim LR 536 and commentary; *Ellis, Street and Smith* (1986) 84 Cr App R 235, [1987] Crim LR 44, and commentary; *Bett* [1999] Crim LR 218. *Courtie* seems to have been completely overlooked in *Leeson* [2000] 1 Cr App R 233, [2000] Crim LR 195. See commentary at 196.

43 See PH Robinson, 'Should the Criminal Law Abandon the Actus Reus–Mens Rea Distinction?' in Shute, Gardner and Horder (eds), *Action and Value in Criminal Law*, arguing for the abandonment of the oversimplistic categorization which obscures the doctrines lying beneath the overarching labels. See also Duff, *Answering for Crime*, Ch 5.

44 CLGP, 19. See also TBCL, Ch 2.   45 [1976] Crim LR 276.

Other variations on these two basic views can be advanced including, for example, the suggestion that the actus reus includes the absence of any elements of justification, but not those of excuse.[46]

A simple example illustrates these different approaches. D punches V hard in the stomach, but does so in self-defence. No offence would be committed—according to Williams, because there is no actus reus (or, indeed, mens rea) and, according to Lanham, because, although there is both actus reus and mens rea (the intentional assault) there is a valid defence. Williams' opinion is attractive both because it seems strange to describe an act which is required or permitted by the law as an actus reus[47] and because there are practical difficulties in distinguishing (as Lanham's analysis requires) between the definitional elements of an offence and defence elements.[48] On the other hand, the cataloguing of every element of an offence becomes impossibly cumbersome if it has to include all conceivable defences to each element—as the authors of the Draft Criminal Code put it, 'the inapplicability of every exception admitted by the definition of an offence must be treated as an element of it'.[49] Moreover, defences may also require mental as well as external elements. Duress is a defence but only, of course, if D is aware of the threatening facts.[50] If the purpose of using the terms actus reus and mens rea is convenience of explaining and examining the law, there is much to be said for the Lanham approach and it is generally (but not invariably) followed in this book.[51]

2.1.6 No conviction without actus reus

There must be proof of actus reus. There are no 'thought crimes'.[52] In some instances, the actus reus of a crime might be relatively minimal in physical terms, and may even otherwise seem innocuous—as in conspiracy where the actus reus comprises 'an agreement'. This underlines the importance of keeping in mind the crime as a whole, and not allowing the fragmentation into elements of actus reus and mens rea to distort one's understanding of the offence.

It is important however that every element of the actus reus is proved. For example, taking the actus reus of assault—causing a person to apprehend immediate unlawful personal violence[53]—that might be broken down into elements of conduct towards 'a person', 'causing apprehension', of 'immediate', 'unlawful', 'personal violence'. Unless the prosecution can make the jury sure D's conduct fulfilled *all* of these requirements there would be no actus reus. Thus, if D caused V to apprehend personal violence, but not immediately, as where D telephoned V in Leeds and said 'I'm in London, but when I get back tomorrow I will hit you', there would be no assault. Similarly, if D caused V to apprehend immediate personal violence, but D was acting with V's consent such as at the outset of a professional boxing match, there would be no unlawfulness and hence no assault.

---

[46] See MS Moore, *Act and Crime: The Philosophy of Action and its Implications for Criminal Law* (1993) 177–83. See further Ch 9.

[47] But, as noted earlier, actus reus implies no moral judgement, the only point of the analysis being convenience in exposition.

[48] Although arguably the same is true of Williams' analysis since it requires us to exclude any ground of justification or excuse.

[49] Draft Code, vol 2, 7.2, 7.3.   [50] See p 369.

[51] The Latin terms are frequently used by the courts but no detailed analysis has been made of them and it cannot be said that there is a standard judicial usage. The judicial trend has long been to avoid Latin in the criminal trial. '"Throw Latin out of court" says Woolf': The Times, 20 July 2000.

[52] For a theoretical analysis of why this is so, see Duff, *Answering for Crime*, 95 et seq. Cf DN Husak, 'Does Criminal Liability Require an Act?' in RA Duff, *Philosophy and the Criminal Law* (1998).

[53] See p 691.

Offences can exist without any requirement for proof of mens rea in whole or in part—offences of strict or absolute liability—but, except in the anomalous case of an intoxicated offender,[54] the courts will not dispense with the actus reus element.

If the crime does require mens rea and that has been proved, unless the actus reus is proved that crime is not committed. Although D with a dishonest state of mind believes that he is appropriating V's property he cannot in any circumstances be guilty of theft if the property belongs to no one. D has the mens rea but the actus reus, the other fundamental element of the crime, is lacking. D may penetrate V with his penis with intent to have intercourse with her without her consent but, if in fact she consents, his act cannot amount to rape. D may act with intent to marry during the lifetime of his wife but if, unknown to him, she is dead, he cannot commit bigamy. If D makes a statement, which he believes to be false, with intent to gain, he cannot be convicted of fraud if the statement is, in fact, true. In each case, D may now be convicted of attempting to commit the crime in question.[55]

In *Deller*,[56] D induced V to purchase his car by representing (*inter alia*) that D had ownership and was entitled to sell it. In fact, D had previously executed a document that purported to mortgage the car to a finance company and, no doubt, D thought he was telling a lie. He was charged with obtaining by false pretences.[57] It then appeared that the document dealing with the purported mortgage of the car was probably void in law for the technical reason that it was as an unregistered bill of sale. If the document was void the car *was* owned by D and he was entitled to sell it: 'quite accidentally and, strange as it may sound, dishonestly, the appellant had told the truth'.[58] D's conviction was, therefore, quashed by the Court of Criminal Appeal, for, though he had mens rea, no actus reus had been established. Under the present law, D could be convicted of an attempted fraud.[59]

2.1.6.1 The problematic case of *Dadson*

A case which is sometimes said to be inconsistent with this fundamental principle, but which is worth discussing because it illustrates the difficulties that may arise in connection with its application, is *Dadson*.[60] A full discussion of the case occurs in the context of defences in Ch 10.

D was a constable, employed to watch a copse from which wood had been stolen. He carried a loaded gun. V emerged from the copse carrying wood that he had stolen, and, ignoring D's calls to stop, ran away. D, having no other means of bringing him to justice, fired and wounded him in the leg. He was convicted of shooting at V with intent to cause him grievous bodily harm. V had been repeatedly convicted of stealing wood, but D did not know this. Under s 39 of the Larceny Act 1827, stealing wood was a felony if the thief already had two previous convictions for the same offence. V had two previous convictions and so was a felon. D did not know that V was a felon when he shot him. It was lawful to wound an escaping felon[61] if this was the only way of arresting him.[62] Could D rely on what would be a compelling justifying circumstance when D was unaware of its existence? Erle J told the jury that the alleged felony, *being unknown to D*, constituted no justification. On a

---

54 See *Lipman* [1970] 1 QB 152. See also the discussion of *Heard* [2007] EWCA Crim 125, p 337.

55 See Ch 11.

56 (1952) 36 Cr App R 184. Cf *Brien* (1903) 3 SRNSW 410; *Dyson* [1908] 2 KB 454.

57 Under the Larceny Act 1916, s 32, now replaced by the Fraud Act 2006, s 2, see p 974.

58 (1952) 36 Cr App R 184 at 191.

59 See p 980. This was confirmed in *Cornelius* [2012] EWCA Crim 500, although the Court of Appeal declined to substitute D's conviction for fraud for one of attempted fraud and quashed his conviction.

60 (1850) 2 Den 35. Cf *Tooley* (1709) 11 Mod Rep 242 at 251 per Holt CJ; and see Williams, CLGP, 23 et seq.

61 A term used before the Criminal Law Act 1967 to denote those committing serious offences.

62 This was assumed in the case.

case reserved, the judges thought the conviction was correct: D was not justified in firing at V because the fact that V was committing a felony was not known to D at the time.

Many have argued that this case is wrong because, if we ignore D's state of mind and look at the actual facts, what he did was lawful; there was no actus reus.[63] It is submitted that this approach is incorrect. It is important to distinguish between two types of 'defence' that may be raised. In the first type, D merely denies the existence of an element (other than the mens rea) in the definition of the crime. If D successfully raises that plea he certainly cannot be convicted of that crime, whatever his state of mind. This is what happened in *Deller*—there was no false representation.[64] In the second type, D admits that all the elements in the definition of the crime have been established and goes on to assert other facts that afford him a defence in law. The establishment of this type of defence may require D to assert the existence of a mental element as well as external facts.

In *Dadson*,[65] D did not deny that he shot at V or that he intended to cause him grievous bodily harm. He admitted the necessary constituents of the crime (other than 'unlawfulness') but went on to assert other facts that, he alleged, made his act lawful. He was pleading a defence. Whether his act was lawful depended on what were the constituents of the *defence* that he raised; and all that the case decided was that that defence, like duress and self-defence, required the assertion not merely of external facts but also of a state of mind.[66] *Dadson*, then, is perfectly reconcilable with *Deller*. It does *not* decide that a person can be convicted where there is no actus reus. There was an actus reus for D did unlawfully wound V. All that the case decided was that the defence to wounding, 'I was arresting an escaping felon', was a defence which required a mental as well as a physical element and, because the mental element was lacking (D was not aware that V was a felon), the wounding was unlawful.[67]

2.1.7 Coincidence of actus reus and mens rea

Not only must the prosecution establish every element of the actus reus of the crime in question and the relevant mens rea, they must, as a general rule, establish that they occurred at the same time—that there was a coincidence of actus reus and mens rea. This principle is examined in greater detail in the following chapter.

The actus reus amounts to a crime only when it is accompanied by the appropriate mens rea. To cause an actus reus without the requisite mens rea is not a crime and may be an ordinary, innocent act. For example, the offence of perjury[68] consists in D's conduct of making a statement, whether true or not, in the prescribed circumstances of D being on oath in a judicial proceeding, with the mens rea of knowing the statement to be false or not believing it to be true.[69] Thus, every statement on oath in a judicial proceeding might be seen as the actus reus of perjury. The offence turns on D's mens rea. When we say that certain conduct

---

[63] See Williams, CLGP, 22; Lady HM Trevelyan (ed), *The Works of Lord Macaulay*, vol 7 (1866) 552; PH Robinson, 'Competing Theories of Justification' in A Simester and ATH Smith (eds), *Harm and Culpability* (1996) 45. Cf J Gardner, 'Justifications and Reasons' in A Simester and ATH Smith (eds), *Harm and Culpability*, 103.

[64] See the previous section.   [65] See n 60.

[66] A doctrine of actus reus which says that such a course *must* be wrong, as contravening a fundamental principle, is much too constricting. Whether the defence should consist simply in the external facts, or in the facts plus the state of mind, is a matter of policy; and it was a not unreasonable decision of policy to say that a person who deliberately shot another should be guilty of an offence unless he knew of circumstances justifying or excusing his conduct.

[67] See p 724. For a defence of *Dadson*, see Hall, *General Principles*, 228 and R Perkins, *Criminal Law* (2nd edn, 1969) 39. And cf the crime of perjury where D may be convicted if he makes a statement on oath which he believes to be false though it is in fact true.

[68] Perjury Act 1911, s 1(1), Stephen, *Digest*, 95–6.

[69] Cf the apparent misinterpretation of the mens rea of the offence in *Purvis v DPP* [2020] EWHC 3573 (Admin).

comprises the actus reus of a crime, what we mean is that the conduct or result would be a crime if it were perpetrated by a person with mens rea. The description of the conduct as an actus reus does not necessarily imply any judgement whatever as to its moral or legal quality. The analysis into actus reus and mens rea is for convenience of exposition only. The only concept known to the law is the crime; and the crime exists only when actus reus and mens rea coincide.

2.2 Analysis of an actus reus

We have seen that the actus reus of the offence comprises all those elements that are not identifiable as mens rea or fault. Central to the element of the actus reus is the voluntary conduct of the defendant. That usually involves some act on his part, but we must take care not to oversimplify things by describing the actus reus as simply D's 'act'. Some writers have suggested that 'an act' is nothing more than a willed muscular movement—for example, the deliberate crooking of a finger. But, if D crooked his finger around the trigger of a loaded pistol which was pointing at V, with the result that V was killed, to say 'D crooked his finger' would be a most misleading way of describing D's 'act'. 'Again, suppose a person orally demands money backed by threats of injury. Can the action of his vocal chords be separated from the resulting sound issuing from his mouth and its intended meaning to the hearer?'[70] We naturally say, 'D shot V' or 'D demanded money from V'. This way of describing the act takes account of the circumstances surrounding the actual movement of the body (insofar as they are relevant) and its consequences (again, insofar as they are relevant), and, for ordinary purposes, it is obviously the sensible way of describing it.[71] But for the purposes of the criminal law as we have seen it is sometimes necessary to break down an 'act', so comprehensively described, into the constituents of: (a) the conduct which is the central feature of the crime; (b) the surrounding material circumstances; and (c) the consequences. One reason for so doing is that the law may require different mental elements for the various constituents.

2.2.1 D's conduct must be voluntary

If the actus reus of the crime includes an act, it must, of course, be proved that D performed that act voluntarily. Although generally expressed as a requirement of 'voluntariness' there is a degree of confusion as to whether the law is truly concerned that D was 'conscious' of his actions, whether he 'willed' them or whether they were 'voluntary'.[72] These terms are not synonymous, and their precise definition involves complex

---

70 *Timbu Kolian v R* (1968) 119 CLR 47 at 69 per Windeyer J. D's act was demanding with menaces.

71 See eg the discussion of crimes involving hate speech in J Jaconelli, 'Context-Dependent Crime' [1995] Crim LR 771. For a more theoretical analysis of the significance of considering the actus reus as more than a bodily willed movement, see Duff, *Answering for Crime*, 98 et seq discussing how 'action' in this context cannot be seen as simply a natural or mechanical phenomenon.

72 See generally RD Mackay, *Mental Condition Defences in the Criminal Law* (1995) Ch 1, and HLA Hart, *Punishment and Responsibility* (1968) Ch 4. There is considerable philosophical literature on the subject, including MS Moore, *Act and Crime: The Philosophy of Action and its Implications for Criminal Law* (1993). See also Wilson, *Central Issues*, Ch 4; A Norrie, *Crime, Reason and History* (3rd edn, 2014) 140–51. In addition, there is a growing body of literature evaluating the insights that neuroscience can provide in this area. Eg see NA Vincent (ed), *Neuroscience and Legal Responsibility* (2013). For a sceptical account of the relevance of neuroscience to criminal law doctrine, see MS Pardo and D Patterson, *Minds, Brains and Law* (2013).

questions of philosophy and neurology,[73] presenting distractions which for pragmatic reasons the criminal courts are keen to avoid. The requirement that the act was voluntary is fundamental to the imposition of criminal liability since it reflects the underlying respect for the individual's autonomy and the principle that 'unless a man has the capacity and fair opportunity to adjust his behaviour to the law its penalties ought not to be applied to him'.[74]

The clearest cases of involuntariness might be thought to be those where D is unconscious. If D is unconscious or, for example, asleep, he *cannot* exercise his will, he cannot control his movement so any movements of his body that are made are involuntary.[75] This is subject to an important exception where the reason for the lack of consciousness is D's own voluntary intoxication or other prior fault.

Even where D is conscious, there are many well-established circumstances in which the act will be found to be involuntary for the purposes of the criminal law. Suppose the offence is 'wounding' and the evidence shows that, while D was holding a knife in his hand, E seized D's hand and, against D's will, plunged the knife still held by D's hand into V. Plainly D is not guilty of wounding because it was not 'his' act. Similarly, D would not be guilty of a battery if he was afflicted by St Vitus' dance and his fist shot out in an uncontrolled spasm and struck V; or if D who was carefully carrying a heavy weight was startled by an unexpected explosion and dropped it onto V's foot; or if D tripped onto V. If D, while driving, is attacked by a swarm of bees and, in his panic at having been suddenly engulfed by the swarm, is temporarily disabled from controlling the vehicle, which crashes into V, he may be held to be no longer 'driving'.[76] In each of these cases the movement of D's limbs was involuntary in that it did not flow from an exercise by D of his will.[77] The event happened either against, or at least without, his will. In these examples, note that D was conscious but exercised no control over his movements.

If D is conscious and the physical movement is voluntary, D may be liable for its consequences if the crime is one of strict liability or negligence, even though it is unintentionally misdirected, as where D put his foot on the accelerator of a bus instead of, as he intended, the brake.[78]

In Ch 9 we discuss the rules governing pleas of automatism—where D claims to have lacked voluntariness. For present purposes it is important to be aware that these rules will not exclude liability if the reason for involuntariness was D's voluntary intoxication.

---

[73] See eg DW Denno, 'How Psychological Research on Consciousness can Enlighten the Criminal Law' [2002] Amicus Curiae 28; R Schopp, *Automatism, Insanity and the Psychology of Criminal Responsibility: A Philosophical Inquiry* (1991); B McSherry, 'Voluntariness, Intention and the Defence of Mental Disorder: Towards a Rational Approach' (2003) 21 Behavioural Sciences and the Law 581; K Saunders, 'Voluntary Acts and the Criminal Law: Justifying Culpability Based on the Existence of Volition' (1988) 49 U Pitt LR 443. See also I Ebrahim et al, 'Violence Sleepwalking and the Criminal Law: (1) The Medical Aspects' [2005] Crim LR 601; W Wilson et al, 'Violence, Sleepwalking and the Criminal Law: (2) The Legal Aspects' [2005] Crim LR 614, criticizing the current law and exposing the dissonance with medical knowledge.

[74] HLA Hart, *Punishment and Responsibility*, 181.

[75] Viscount Kilmuir LC in *Bratty* suggested that automatism is a term connoting the state of a person who, though capable of action, is not 'conscious of what he is doing . . . it means unconscious voluntary action', *Bratty v A-G for Northern Ireland* [1963] AC 386, 401.

[76] *Hill v Baxter* [1958] 1 QB 277 at 286. See the discussion in the Law Commission Discussion Paper, *Criminal Liability: Insanity and Automatism* (2013) Ch 5.

[77] Duff provides an interesting account of how, rather than focusing on action in terms of willed movement, this aspect of actus reus might be better described as turning on whether D had control: *Answering for Crime*, 99–106.

[78] *A-G's Reference (No 4 of 2000)* [2001] Crim LR 578 and commentary (causing death by dangerous driving).

2.2.1.1 Self-induced involuntarism

As noted, there is an exception to the rule that there is no liability for an involuntary act: where the 'act' was done while in a state of self-induced intoxication.[79] The rule is a complex one to be examined in full in Ch 9. In short, if D has voluntarily intoxicated himself so that D was unconscious or otherwise 'acting' involuntarily, that will provide no excuse for any crimes he commits while in that state if they are crimes of 'basic intent' (ie those crimes that do not require proof of mens rea of intention—on an orthodox interpretation at least[80]). D who is not at fault in inducing his involuntariness will be able to rely on that involuntariness as an excuse for any crimes he committed while in that state.

So, for example, consider D who, owing to his voluntary ingestion of LSD, kills his girlfriend V, mistakenly believing that he is slaying a serpent at the centre of the earth.[81] At the time of the killing D is acting involuntarily. However, D's prior fault by voluntarily reducing himself to that drug-induced state provides a sufficient basis of fault in law to regard his subsequent involuntary conduct as blameworthy. He is guilty of manslaughter. It has been argued[82] that this is part of a wider rule that any automatism induced by D's 'fault' whether involving drugs or not is no defence. 'Fault' here means doing or omitting to do something that could reasonably be foreseen to be likely to bring about such a state. The decided cases, however, all appear to involve the use or misuse of drink or drugs (including prescribed medicines)[83] and it may be that the anomalous rule whereby the courts hold a defendant liable despite his automaton state at the time of the offence is properly confined to cases of voluntary intoxication. The basis for the courts adopting that exceptional course is the grave social danger presented by intoxicated individuals.[84] One can imagine (perhaps fanciful) scenarios in which D causes some harm while in a state of automatism but he has carelessly or knowingly set up the circumstances for his involuntariness without the involvement of intoxicants. An example might be where D visits a hypnotist to receive the suggestion that he should kill V and goes on to carry out that homicide when in the trance, but such circumstances have not been addressed by the courts.[85]

Of course, if the 'fault' exhibited by D's 'prior' conduct is itself sufficient to found liability for the offence charged, then D is properly convicted of it under ordinary principles.[86] An elementary example is where a driver, feeling sleepy, continues to drive until he falls asleep and has an accident. His failure to take a break from driving may itself constitute the fault element of the offence of careless driving or even dangerous driving.[87] The subsequent conduct of falling asleep is not blameless: D's culpability lies precisely in the failure to safeguard against its occurrence.

---

[79] *Hardie* [1985] 1 WLR 64. See the discussion in Ch 10 and LC 314, *Intoxication and Criminal Liability* (2009).

[80] cf *Heard* [2007] EWCA Crim 125, see p 337.

[81] *Lipman* [1970] 1 QB 152; approved in *DPP v Majewski* [1977] AC 443. See p 336.

[82] RD Mackay, 'Intoxication as a Factor in Automatism' [1982] Crim LR 146, 147.

[83] See *Poole* [2003] All ER (D) 448 (Mar) where D's failure to take his epilepsy medicine led to his loss of consciousness.

[84] These issues are discussed in full in Ch 9.

[85] C Finkelstein, 'Involuntary Crimes, Voluntarily Committed' in Shute and Simester, *Criminal Law Theory*, 143; PH Robinson, 'Causing the Condition of One's Own Defense: A Study in the Limits of the Criminal Law Doctrine' (1985) 71 Virg LR 1. See also *Finnegan v Heywood* (2000), 10 May, High Ct of Justiciary, where D's transitory state of sleepwalking (and driving) was induced by his voluntary intoxication and he was aware of the likelihood of that outcome. The decision does not make it clear whether D would have had a defence of automatism if he was unaware of the likelihood. See also the valuable discussion by Wilson et al, n 72, proposing a defence of 'not guilty by reason of sleep disorder'.

[86] The *dictum* of Martin JA in *Rabey* (1977) 79 DLR (3d) 414, 425 quoted by Mackay as a 'typical example of a *dictum* in support of "fault liability"', n 71, seems to be saying no more than this.

[87] *Kay v Butterworth* (1945) 173 LT 191, see n 109.

2.2.1.2 Voluntariness as actus reus or mens rea?

Writers dispute whether the voluntariness of D's conduct should be regarded as part of the actus reus or as part of the mens rea.[88] On the one hand, it is a mental element; on the other, it is said that it is an essential constituent of the act, which is part of the actus reus. Some have argued that the classification is important. The argument runs: some offences, known as offences of strict liability, do not require mens rea. If voluntariness is part of the mens rea of an offence because it relates to D's state of mind, a person charged with an offence of strict liability might be convicted for a mere involuntary act because, since the court is not inquiring into D's state of mind, it will not be considering voluntariness. The fallacy in this argument lies in the proposition that offences of strict liability require 'no mens rea'.[89] This is not so.

If the actus reus of the offence requires regard to be had to D's state of mind (as in, eg, possession) then there is certainly no way of dispensing with it;[90] but it does not follow that it must be dispensed with where an offence is held to be one of strict liability. An actus reus must be proved, even for an offence of strict liability; therefore if voluntariness is part of the actus reus, no one can be convicted of any crime if his act was involuntary. Voluntariness is best regarded as an element of the actus reus. That reflects the true basis of the defence as a denial of voluntary 'conduct'.

For 125 years, *Prince*[91] was regarded as the leading case on strict liability. Although now superseded by statute,[92] it remains a good illustration of the principle that even strict liability crimes require proof of voluntary conduct. *Prince* decided that D may be convicted of the offence (now repealed) of taking a girl under the age of 16 out of the possession and against the will of her father, even though D believed in good faith and on reasonable grounds that the girl he was taking was over 16. Even if this was an offence 'requiring no mens rea' as to the age of the girl (ie strict liability as to that part of the actus reus), it is quite clear that it involved a substantial mental element. It would be essential to have proved that D intended to take a girl out of the possession of her parents. If he thought the girl was in no one's possession, he was not guilty. If he thought the girl was a boy, he was probably not guilty. No one suggests, however, that we should say that his knowledge that the girl was in the possession of her parents is part of the actus reus. The fact is that, even in offences of strict liability, some degree of mens rea must be proved. Therefore, even though the elements of an offence may suggest that D can be guilty without having regard to his state of mind, this will not necessarily be the case.

What is missing in cases where D's act is involuntary appears to most people as a vital link between mind and body; and both the ordinary person and the lawyer might well insist on this by saying that in these cases there is not 'really' a human *action* at all and certainly nothing for which anyone should be made criminally responsible however 'strict' legal responsibility might be.[93]

---

[88] Turner (MACL, 195 and 199 and Kenny, *Outlines*, 23) thought 'voluntariness' an element of mens rea. Williams, CLGP, s 8 and I Patient, 'Some Remarks about the Element of Voluntariness in Offences of Absolute Liability' [1968] Crim LR 23 think it part of the actus reus. See generally PH Robinson, 'Should the Criminal Law Abandon the Actus Reus–Mens Rea Distinction?' in S Shute, J Gardner and J Horder (eds), *Action and Value in Criminal Law* (1993) 187, 196–7.

[89] cf *Blackburn v Bowering* [1994] 1 WLR 1324, p 738; Howard, SR 1; RS Clark (ed), *Essays on Criminal Law in New Zealand* (1971) 49; HL Packer, *The Limits of the Criminal Sanction* (1968) 126.

[90] See p 166.   [91] (1875) LR 2 CCR 154.   [92] See p 766.

[93] See the classic account by HLA Hart, 'Acts of Wills and Responsibility', Jubilee Lectures of the Faculty of Law, University of Sheffield (1960) 115 at 137. Note that Turner, while regarding voluntariness as mens rea, thought it a different and more fundamental element than foresight of consequences; MACL, 195–205.

2.2.1.3 Automatism

The defendant's claim of a lack of voluntariness is described in criminal law as a plea of automatism; that is, that D was acting as an automaton. Automatism has narrow limits as a 'defence'. According to Lord Denning,[94] it is restricted to acts done while unconscious and to spasms, reflex actions and convulsions.[95] The courts approach the defence with great scepticism.[96] It commonly arises in driving cases, particularly where diabetic defendants claim that they were suffering from hyperglycaemic or hypoglycaemic states.[97] The Law Commission has acknowledged the difficulty in defining automatism, but suggested that:

the correct definition of the defence is focused not on whether the accused was conscious or unconscious,[98] but on whether he or she was conscious of what he or she was doing, in other words, whether he or she was acting with or without control at the time of the alleged offence.[99]

Automatism is not a defence to a driving charge unless there is 'a total destruction of voluntary control'.[100] In *Broome v Perkins*,[101] D, though in a hypoglycaemic state, was held guilty of driving without due care and attention because from time to time he apparently exercised conscious control over his car, veering away from other vehicles so as to avoid a collision, braking violently, and so on. A condition described by an expert witness as 'driving without awareness' was not sufficient where it in fact amounted to merely reduced or imperfect awareness. Clearly, policy plays a part in the courts' adoption of such a strict approach to the degree of involuntariness constituting automatism, particularly in road traffic offences. Passages in some judgments suggest that the plea applies only if there is a complete lack of consciousness rather than a lack of voluntariness. That seems unduly narrow and to risk losing sight of the focus on whether D had the capacity to control his actions. In relation to other crimes, the courts have not consistently adopted such a strict approach. In the case of *Charlson*,[102] for example, where the evidence was that D was 'acting as an automaton without any *real knowledge* of what he was doing' (emphasis added) as a result of a cerebral tumour, Barry J directed the jury to acquit if the defence might reasonably be true.

More recently, in *Coley*,[103] the Court of Appeal affirmed that D cannot successfully plead automatism unless he suffers from a 'complete destruction of voluntary control'. Hughes LJ

---

[94] In *Bratty* [1961] 3 All ER 523 at 532. It is confined to 'involuntary movement of the body or limbs of a person': *Watmore v Jenkins* [1962] 2 All ER 868 at 878 per Winn J. This case was cited with approval by the Court of Appeal in *Coley* [2013] EWCA Crim 223. In a Canadian case, *Racimore* (1976) 25 CCC (2d) 143, a 'failure to remain' after an accident was held to be involuntary because D did not know there had been an accident. This seems to be an unsatisfactory device for introducing a requirement of mens rea into an offence of strict liability. Cf *Davey v Towle* [1973] RTR 328.

[95] See the discussion in the Scottish case of *Ross v HM Advocate* 1991 SCCR 823 where the court identified four criteria: an external factor; which was not self-induced; which D was not bound to foresee; and which caused a total alienation of reason rendering him incapable of controlling or appreciating what he was doing. See on this P Ferguson, 'The Limits of the Automatism Defence' (1991) 36 JLSS 446. In *Foye* [2013] EWCA Crim 475, Lord Hughes observed that *Ross* is entirely in accordance with the English law of automatism.

[96] See H Phoenix, 'Automatism: A Fading Defence' (2010) 56 *Criminal Law Quarterly* 328, 332.

[97] For discussion, see J Rumbold and M Wasik, 'Diabetic Drivers, Hypoglycaemic Unawareness, and Automatism' [2011] Crim LR 863.

[98] As the Court of Appeal held in *Coley* [2013] EWCA Crim 223, [23]: 'automatism does not require that'.

[99] Discussion Paper, *Criminal Liability: Insanity and Automatism* (2013), para 5.2. See also the comment of Bastarache J of the Canadian Supreme Court in *Stone* [1999] 2 SCR 290, [156] that the term 'unconscious' is in fact inaccurate in this context, preferring 'impaired consciousness in which an individual, though capable of action, has no voluntary control over that action'.

[100] This has been criticized on the basis that it could be considered 'unduly harsh' to restrict automatism to cases such as these. See Horder, APOCL, 103.

[101] (1987) 85 Cr App R 321.

[102] [1955] 1 All ER 859.   [103] [2013] EWCA Crim 223.

emphasized that while automatism does not require D to be unconscious, it does require his actions to be involuntary. His lordship stated that disinhibition is similarly insufficient. D was convicted of attempted murder, demonstrating that the principle that was originally developed in the context of road traffic offences applies more generally throughout the criminal law.

2.2.1.4 Automatism as physical involuntariness

Although the courts have sometimes confused the issue of consciousness and voluntariness in seeking to determine the scope of the 'defence' of automatism, they have been clear and consistent in holding that automatism is about physical, not moral, involuntariness. Pleas of 'irresistible impulse' have been consistently rejected as a defence even where arising from insanity. The fact that, as a result of hysterical amnesia, or hysterical fugue, D was unaware of 'legal restrictions or moral concern', is no defence if he knew the facts which constitute the offence charged.[104] An irresistible craving for drink is not a defence to a charge of stealing alcohol.[105] Similarly, if D has punched V it is no defence (though it may mitigate the sentence) to say that this was an immediate and irresistible reaction to provocation by V. But the borderline between this and a 'reflex action' must be a fine one. The legal nature and legal effect of a reflex action is, itself, uncertain. In *Ryan v R*,[106] D with one hand pointed a loaded shotgun at V whom he had robbed, while with the other hand he attempted to tie V up. V moved. D was startled and, he said, 'involuntarily' pressed the trigger because of a 'reflex action'. Barwick CJ thought that, if this story had been true, D would not have been responsible in law for the 'act' of pressing the trigger; but Windeyer J held that, while that act may have been 'involuntary' in a dictionary sense, it was one for which he was responsible in law and not properly analogous to an act done in convulsions or an epileptic seizure. With respect, however, it seems closer to these than to 'the sudden movement of a tennis player retrieving a difficult shot; not accompanied by conscious planning but certainly not involuntary'.[107]

It is, of course, very important to identify the precise conduct which it is alleged is voluntary and for which D is therefore to be held responsible. In *Ryan v R*, the pointing of the loaded gun and the placing of the finger on the trigger were clearly voluntary acts and, provided that it could be said that these acts caused death, the accused would be liable for homicide, whether the pressing of the trigger was an act for which he was responsible or not. Similarly, in the English civil case of *Gray v Barr*[108] D approached V with a loaded gun and fired a shot to frighten V. D and V grappled together and V fell on the gun and was shot and killed. The trial judge and Salmon LJ thought that the real cause of V's death was the accident of his falling on the gun; whereas Lord Denning MR and Phillimore LJ thought that the cause was D's deliberate act in approaching V with the gun. All the judges agreed, however, that D could properly have been convicted of manslaughter on these facts. The act for which D would be held responsible was not the firing of the fatal shot—that was not his act—but deliberately approaching V in that threatening way. Similarly, a person who is in an unconscious state through an epileptic seizure is not liable for an offence involving 'driving', though he is sitting at the controls of a moving vehicle, unless, having regard to the degree and

---

104 *Isitt* [1978] Crim LR 159.

105 *Dodd* (1974) 7 SASR 151 at 157. See generally LS Tao, 'Legal Problems of Alcoholism' (1969) 37 Fordham LR 405; J Tolmie, 'Alcoholism and Criminal Liability' (2001) 64 MLR 688.

106 (1967) 40 ALJR 488, discussed by ID Elliott, 'Responsibility for Involuntary Acts: *Ryan v The Queen*' (1968) 41 ALJ 497.

107 Elliott, n 105.

108 [1971] 2 QB 554. Cf *Jarmain* [1946] KB 74; *Blayney v Knight* (1975) 60 Cr App R 269. Cf *A-G's Reference (No 3 of 2004)* [2005] EWCA Crim 1882.

frequency of epilepsy and the probability that he might have an attack, he is liable because of his conscious act of starting or continuing to drive.[109]

An interesting scenario arose in *Brady*[110] where, having voluntarily consumed alcohol and drugs, D had fallen from a balcony in a nightclub onto the dance floor below and had landed on the victim, thereby causing her serious injuries. The prosecution's evidence was to the effect that D had climbed onto the balcony railings and had jumped from them deliberately; D's account was that he perched his bottom against the railings and lost his balance and fell. The single issue in the trial was whether D had acted with the requisite mens rea. The Court of Appeal noted, *obiter*, that there was arguably evidence of 'deliberate non-accidental conduct on the part of the accused that inflicted grievous bodily harm', in that D had deliberately perched precariously on a low railing above a crowded dance floor and having consumed considerable quantities of alcohol and drugs. This deliberate act, on any view, led almost immediately and directly to the fall over the railing and to the infliction of grievous bodily harm. It is submitted that there was an actus reus. A contrasting factual scenario would have been if a person was perched on the railings and fell because he lurched backwards involuntarily to avoid that unforeseen swarm of bees which academics often pray in aid.[111]

2.2.1.5 Involuntariness not arising from automatism

A person may have full control over his body but no control over events in which it is involved. A driver's brakes fail without his fault and, consequently, he inevitably fails to accord precedence to a pedestrian on a pedestrian crossing.[112] Although it has been said that this offence is absolute,[113] in the sense of requiring no evidence of negligence, it was held in *Burns v Bidder*[114] that such a driver has a 'defence'. The court equated the driver's situation with that of one stunned by a swarm of bees, or propelled by a vehicle hitting his car from behind. The offence is therefore not truly an absolute one, as 'voluntariness' is essential. On the other hand, it seems to have been held that it is no defence that the failure to accord precedence on the zebra crossing arises inevitably from the unforeseeable behaviour of the pedestrian.[115] That seems inconsistent because the driver in such a case has no more power to avert the failure than where his brakes fail. It is submitted that D should never be held criminally liable for an 'act' or result of an 'act' over which he has no control.[116]

2.2.1.6 Reform

In 2013 the Law Commission published a Discussion Paper, setting out its provisional proposals for reform of the defences of insanity and automatism.[117] This was derived from an earlier Scoping Paper[118] and is discussed in Ch 9.

---

[109] *Hill v Baxter* [1958] 1 QB 277 at 286 per Pearson LJ; *McBride* [1962] 2 QB 167. Similarly where D goes to sleep: *Kay v Butterworth* (1945) 173 LT 191.

[110] [2006] EWCA Crim 2413, [2007] Crim LR 564 and commentary.

[111] See further the commentary at [2007] Crim LR 564.

[112] Contrary to the Zebra, Pelican and Puffin Pedestrian Crossings Regulations and General Directions 1997, SI 1997/2400, reg 25.

[113] *Hughes v Hall* [1960] 1 WLR 733.   [114] [1967] 2 QB 227.

[115] *Neal v Reynolds* [1966] Crim LR 393. The case is only briefly reported and may be explained on another ground.

[116] See also KJM Smith and W Wilson, 'Impaired Voluntariness and Criminal Responsibility' (1993) 13 OJLS 69, considering the question of voluntariness in terms of a person's capacity to conform to the law's requirements. See also DN Husak, *Philosophy of Criminal Law* (1987) 102 and Duff, *Answering for Crime* on the significance of the issue of control. Duff suggests that use of the concept of control avoids many of the difficulties experienced in trying to distinguish acts and omissions.

[117] Ashworth [2013] Crim LR 787.

[118] For discussion of which, see J Peay, 'Insanity and Automatism: Questions From and About the Law Commission's Scoping Paper' [2012] Crim LR 927.

2.3 A 'state of affairs' as an actus reus

A crime may be so defined that it can be committed although there is no 'act' in the sense considered previously.[119] There may be no necessity for any 'willed muscular movement'. Instead, it may be enough if a specified 'state of affairs' is proved to exist. These offences are sometimes called 'status'[120] or 'situation'[121] offences. Under s 4(2) of the Road Traffic Act 1988, for example, any person who, when in charge of a mechanically propelled vehicle on a road or other public place,[122] is unfit to drive through drink or drugs, commits an offence. One cannot take charge without consciously doing so, but it is not *taking* charge of the vehicle, or *becoming* unfit, which is the offence, but simply *being* in charge and *being* unfit. So long as this state of affairs continues, the actus reus of the crime is committed. The actus reus may even be in the process of being committed while D is sleeping,[123] for he may still be 'in charge'. A further example is provided by the offence under s 25 of the Theft Act 1968: a person commits an offence if, when not at his place of abode, he *has with him* any article for use in the course of, or in connection with, burglary, etc.[124] So long as he has the article with him, he is committing the offence. Of course, in all these examples D will, almost invariably, have done the acts of taking charge, getting drunk or taking up the article, but these acts are not part of the crime. Although attempts have been made to defend these offences on the basis of D's prior fault, these are not wholly convincing.[125]

Offences of this type must be treated with great caution. They are commonly associated with tyrannical regimes in which offences of 'status' are enacted, for example offences of being a member of a particular political organization[126] or being of a particular race or religion (criminalization of which is arguably yet worse because the person may have made no conscious choice to become such a member). It has been suggested that criminalizing such conduct may contravene the ECHR.[127]

Even in modern-day England and Wales this type of offence has led to extraordinary results in offences of 'being found' in a particular situation. In *Larsonneur*,[128] D was convicted under the Aliens Order 1920 in that she, 'being an alien to whom leave to land in the United Kingdom has been refused' was found in the UK. She had been brought from Ireland into the UK against her will in the custody of the police. Notwithstanding the wide condemnation of that decision,[129] similar results were reached in respect of the offence under s 12 of the Licensing Act 1872 of being found drunk in a highway. In *Winzar v Chief Constable of Kent*,[130] D was taken to hospital on a stretcher but was found to be drunk and told to leave.

---

[119] See P Glazebrook, 'Situational Liability' in *Reshaping the Criminal Law*, 108.

[120] Howard, SR, Ch 3.

[121] MD Cohen, 'The Actus Reus and Offences of Situation' (1972) 7 Israel L Rev 186.

[122] See the unusual case of *DPP v Richardson* [2019] EWHC 428 (Admin).

[123] *Duck v Peacock* [1949] 1 All ER 318; but see the defence provided by Road Traffic Act 1956, s 9(1) proviso, now re-enacted in the Road Traffic Act 1988, s 4(3), on which see K McCormac (ed), *Wilkinson's Road Traffic Offences* (29th edn, 2019) Ch 4.

[124] Theft Act 1968, s 25, p 1066.   [125] See *Crime, Reason and History*, 148.

[126] See *Scales v US*, 327 US 203 (1961) re Communist Party membership.

[127] See GR Sullivan, 'Strict Liability and the ECHR' in Simester, *Appraising Strict Liability*, 207.

[128] (1933) 24 Cr App R 74. Cf *Walters* [1969] 1 QB 255 (being an incorrigible rogue). See the criticism of *Larsonneur* by Howard, SR, 47. For a spirited but unconvincing defence of the case, see DJ Lanham, '*Larsonneur* Revisited' [1976] Crim LR 276 and RC Doegar, 'Strict Liability in Criminal Law and *Larsonneur* Revisited' [1998] Crim LR 791 with response by JC Smith [1999] Crim LR 100, and DJ Lanham, Letter [1999] Crim LR 683.

[129] 'The acme of strict injustice', Hall, *General Principles*, 329 fn 14; Williams, CLGP, 11; Howard, SR, 47; Gordon, n 26, 287. J Horder, *Excusing Crime* (2004) explains such cases as 'far from being exceptional', rather they were 'all too characteristic of the period', at 251.

[130] (1983) The Times, 28 Mar, DC. Cf *Palmer-Brown v Police* [1985] 1 NZLR 365, CA (D not 'found' behaving in a particular way when behaviour occurred some time after encounter with constable).

When he was seen slumped on a seat in the corridor, the police were called and they took him to a police car parked in the highway outside the hospital. He was convicted of being 'found drunk' in the highway. The words 'found drunk' were held to mean 'perceived to be drunk'. The decision is a controversial one: 'perceive' means 'to become aware of' and it seems that the police became aware of D's condition in the hospital and not in the highway.

Larsonneur and Winzar were convicted of offences the commission of which was in fact procured by the police;[131] and this seems peculiarly offensive. These offences of 'being found' are unusual[132] in that they require an act on the part of the finder but no act or mens rea on the part of D. As a matter of principle, even 'state of affairs' offences ought to require proof that D either caused the state of affairs or failed to terminate it or act in order to do so when it was within his control and possible to do so.[133]

The Court of Appeal cited the previous paragraph with approval in *Robinson-Pierre*,[134] in which Pitchford LJ stated:

we have no doubt that the supremacy of Parliament embraces the power to create 'state of affairs' offences in which no causative link between the prohibited state of affairs and the defendant need be established. The legal issue is not, in our view, whether in principle such offences can be created, but whether in any particular enactment Parliament intended to create one.

This decision is a welcome affirmation that while the principle of parliamentary sovereignty dictates that Parliament can create situational offences of absolute liability, this is not something that will be lightly inferred. If Parliament considers it appropriate for a defendant to be guilty in the absence of any causative link between his conduct and the prohibited state of affairs, then unequivocal language must be used.

Physical impossibility of compliance with the law should be a defence, at least where it is not proved that the impossibility arose through D's own fault.[135] So, situational offences are rightly condemned when they do not allow D to adjust his behaviour to remain within the law.[136]

It has been held by the Privy Council that the offence of 'remaining' in Singapore, having been prohibited from entering that country, could not be committed by one who was ignorant of the prohibition.[137] Implicit in the decision is that if D 'remained' in the country because he was being detained he would not commit the offence. It is true that 'remaining'

---

[131] It might be argued that the police action breaks the chain of causation between any prior wrongdoing of D and the ultimate forbidden status.

[132] But not unique. Being the parent of a child of compulsory school age who was a registered pupil at a school was an offence under the Education Act 1944, s 39(1) if the child failed to attend that school regularly. It was unnecessary to prove any knowledge or neglect on the part of the parent: *Crump v Gilmore* [1970] Crim LR 28. Glazebrook, 'Situational Liability' in *Reshaping the Criminal Law*, 108, contends that *Larsonneur*-type liability is by no means unusual, pointing, *inter alia*, to the similarity, from the defendant's point of view, of vicarious liability (on which see Ch 8).

[133] *Patient* [1968] Crim LR 23. Cf *Burns v Nowell* (1880) 5 QBD 444. Other jurisdictions have avoided the result in *Larsonneur*: *Achterdam* 1911 EDL 336 (EM Burchell and PMA Hunt, *South African Criminal Law and Procedure* (1970) 105); *O'Sullivan v Fisher* [1954] SASR 33. In the United States, similar offences have been held unconstitutional: *Robinson v California*, 370 US 660, 8 L Ed 2d 758 (1962) (being addicted to the use of narcotics).

[134] [2013] EWCA Crim 2396.

[135] See A Smart, 'Criminal Responsibility for Failing to do the Impossible' (1987) 103 LQR 532.

[136] Wilson, *Central Issues*, 83.

[137] *Lim Chin Aik v R* [1963] AC 160. See also *Finau v Department of Labour* [1984] 2 NZLR 396 (failure to leave New Zealand after revocation of permit not an offence where impossible to leave because of pregnancy). But cf *Grant v Borg* [1982] 1 WLR 638, where an immigrant was held guilty of knowingly remaining beyond the time limit although, because of a mistake of law, he may have believed the time had been extended.

may be said to be D's act while 'being found' is the act of another; but the substance of the two offences is the same.

Historically, it was held[138] at common law that 'being in possession' was an insufficient act to constitute the actus reus of a crime, but there are now many cases where, by statute, mere possession is enough. Thus, possession of dangerous drugs, explosive substances, firearms, articles for fraud and forged banknotes all constitute the actus reus of various crimes. 'Being in possession' does not involve an act in the sense of a muscular movement at all, for a person may possess goods merely by knowingly[139] keeping them in his house. Possession which is initially lawful may become criminal because of a change of circumstances without any act by D,[140] but only after he has failed to divest himself of possession within a reasonable time.[141] 'Being in possession' is simply a state of affairs which in certain circumstances involves criminal liability.

2.4 Omissions

cant do sth   vs must do sth

Considerable controversy persists over whether, and to what extent, the law ought to regard inactivity as a sufficient basis for criminal liability.[142] There are powerful arguments of principle and practicality against the imposition of general criminal liability for failing to act in circumstances which give rise to a prohibited harm.[143] The strongest argument against imposing any such general criminal liability is that to do so would infringe the autonomy of the citizen in a qualitatively different manner to circumstances where liability is imposed for positive action. It is argued that it is legitimate for the law to criminalize holding V under water so that he drowns, but not to seek to compel a person to act by criminalizing, for example, his refusal to save a drowning stranger.[144] However, in some circumstances the law can, consistent with this principle of autonomy, impose liability for omission—as where the drowning V is not a stranger but is D's child. These categories of exceptional liability for omission are examined in the following sections. Irrespective of the existence of these exceptions, the arguments of individual autonomy have been challenged for their failure generally to respect obligations of social responsibility, particularly where the potential harm that can be averted (eg death) is disproportionate to the infringement of the person's liberty (eg the simple act of plucking a child from a shallow pool of water).[145]

---

138 *Heath* (1810) Russ & Ry 184; *Dugdale v R* (1853) 1 E & B 435.

139 A person may possess a thing in the civil law although he does not know of its existence; but knowledge will usually be required in criminal law: cf *Warner v Metropolitan Police Comr*, see p 166; *Cugullere* [1961] 1 WLR 858.

140 cf *Buswell* [1972] 1 WLR 64.

141 *Burns v Nowell*, n 132; *Levine* [1927] 1 DLR 740 is contrary.

142 There is a wealth of academic literature on the topic, see in particular: A Ashworth, 'Positive Duties, Regulation and the Criminal Sanction' (2017) 133 LQR 606; A Ashworth, *Positive Obligations in Criminal Law* (2013); G Fletcher, *Rethinking Criminal Law* (1978) Ch 8; G Hughes, 'Criminal Omissions' (1958) 67 Yale LJ 590; Duff, *Answering for Crime*, Ch 5; P Glazebrook, 'Criminal Omissions: The Duty Requirements in Offences Against the Person' (1960) 76 LQR 386; A Ashworth, 'The Scope of Criminal Liability for Omissions' (1989) 105 LQR 424; JC Smith, 'Liability for Omissions in Criminal Law' (1984) 4 LS 88. See on Scots law: R Shiels, 'Scots Law and Liability for Omissions' (2006) 70 J Crim L 413.

143 cf Tadros, *Criminal Responsibility*, 184.

144 See G Williams, 'Criminal Omissions—The Conventional View' (1991) 107 LQR 86. For criticism, see Tadros, *Criminal Responsibility*, 189 arguing that such cases are better dealt with by providing defences of justification.

145 See especially A Ashworth (1989) 105 LQR 424. On qualitative moral differences between act and omission, see A Simester 'Why Omissions are Special' (1995) 1 *Legal Theory* 311.

A further argument against imposing general liability for omissions is that to do so would infringe principles of legality. It is questioned whether the law can impose liability with sufficient clarity, specificity and certainty to respect adequately the principles of fair warning, fair labelling, maximum certainty, coherence with civil law, etc.[146] An additional argument is that failing to act cannot be regarded as a cause of harm, so there should be no general liability for omission in result crimes. But these denials of causation often take an unduly simplistic approach. Further arguments against the imposition of general criminal liability for omissions include the practical difficulty in defining the standard of duty which the law would impose on the person required to act, and of the potential unfairness in singling out for punishment a particular individual from the population as a whole, or a group of individuals, none of whom acted. In the discussion that follows, we can examine the extent to which the law has satisfactorily overcome these objections in those exceptional categories of case in which liability for failure to act has been recognized.[147]

2.4.1 Offences of mere omission

Statutes frequently make it an offence to omit to do something. There are many legislative provisions requiring companies and others to submit returns of various kinds (tax, licences, etc) and making it an offence to fail to do so.[148] This type of offence is not restricted to corporate regulation: the driver of a vehicle which is involved in an accident must give his details to anyone who has reasonable grounds for requesting them, or must report the accident.[149] A motorist who fails to provide a police officer with a specimen of breath when properly required to do so commits an offence.[150] So does a person legally liable to maintain a child if he fails to provide him with adequate food, clothing, medical aid or lodging.[151] These offences, although they provide that D is liable for a criminal offence by omission, are uncontroversial provided that they respect the general principles of criminal law. Most of them are of a regulatory nature, but there are controversial examples relating to more serious crimes. Modern legislation has created a number of offences for failure to report criminal activities, such as ss 19 and 38B of the Terrorism Act 2000,[152] which respectively criminalize failure to report suspicions of certain terrorist offences having been committed, when the information is acquired in a professional capacity, and failure to disclose information which would be of material assistance in the prevention of an act of terrorism.[153] There are also numerous examples of offences of failing to control others, including even adult strangers, such as the offence in s 111A(1B) of the Social Security Administration Act 1992 (allowing false benefit claim).[154]

[146] For an accessible account of the academic concerns, see Wilson, *Central Issues*, 82–102. and A Ashworth, 'Ignorance of the Criminal Law and Duties to Avoid It' (2011) 74 MLR 1.
[147] For an interesting comparison with some continental European systems, see J Keiler, *Actus Reus and Participation in European Criminal Law* (2012) 68–110.
[148] See eg: Companies Act 1985, s 444 (as amended by the Companies Act 2006, Sch 3, para 1), (Secretary of State's power to require a company or individual to produce documents); Insolvency Act 1986, s 235 (duty on officers and employees of a company to cooperate with the 'office-holder' or official receiver of a company).
[149] Road Traffic Act 1988, s 170(4).   [150] ibid, s 6.
[151] Children and Young Persons Act 1933, s 1(2)(a). Non-reporting of the harm caused by others to children could amount to 'neglect' under the Children and Young Persons Act 1933, s 1(1) (see W [2006] EWCA Crim 2723) or in the case of wilfully neglecting a mental patient contrary to the Mental Health Act 1983, s 127(1) (*Morrell* [2002] EWCA Crim 2547). See also the offences in ss 20 and 21 of the Criminal Justice and Courts Act 2015. Note also failure to safeguard a girl from risks of FGM: Serious Crime Act 2015, s 72.
[152] See C Walker, *Blackstone's Guide to the Anti-Terrorism Legislation* (3rd edn, 2014) para 3.89.
[153] Section 330 of the Proceeds of Crime Act 2002 also creates an offence for failing to disclose suspicions of money laundering.
[154] See *Tilley* [2009] EWCA Crim 1426 and [2009] Crim LR 162 and commentary.

Parliament has demonstrated an increased willingness to impose positive duties upon citizens. As Ashworth explains,[155] there are an increasing number of duties to report, duties to prevent[156] and duties to protect. Ashworth argues that there is now a trend towards the 'responsibilization' of professionals, other individuals and commercial organizations. Some of these positive duties are enforced by way of criminal offences. In a recent discussion of this issue, Ashworth analyses the development of these offences, which he argues represent a new generation of omissions-based liability.[157] As he points out, these offences are not of general application, but only apply selectively. Ashworth suggests that the enactment of offences of this nature reflects the particular concerns of government and the legislature at given points in history and do not proceed from a holistic examination of whether there are good arguments for general offences such as these. Ashworth convincingly concludes that it is necessary to consider whether it is right to have omissions offences in relation to money laundering but not murder, female genital mutilation but not other forms of child abuse, and bribery and tax offences rather than wounding.

At common law, offences of pure omission are also to be found, though rarely. A police officer was held to be guilty of a common law crime when, without justification or excuse, he failed to perform his duty to preserve the Queen's peace by protecting a citizen who was being kicked to death.[158] A citizen is guilty of an offence if he fails to respond to a constable's call for assistance in keeping the peace.[159] The courts appear reluctant to extend common law offences to include liability for omission.[160] There has been some debate about the desirability of a general offence of failing to report a crime.[161]

2.4.2 Offences of omission causing a result

Where, as in the examples in the previous section, the offence is defined in terms of the failure to act itself, there are no special difficulties. Problems with omissions arise when the offence requires proof of a result as, for example, in homicide and other offences against the person. Stephen stated the rule for these offences as follows: 'It is not a crime to cause death or bodily injury, even intentionally, by any omission . . .'[162]

He gave the following famous illustration:

A sees B drowning and is able to save him by holding out his hand. A abstains from doing so in order that B may be drowned, and B is drowned. A has committed no offence.

---

[155] A Ashworth, 'Positive Duties, Regulation and the Criminal Sanction' (2017) 133 LQR 606.

[156] These offences are discussed in Ch 8.

[157] A Ashworth, 'A New Generation of Omissions Offences?' [2018] Crim LR 351.

[158] *Dytham* [1979] QB 722, [1979] Crim LR 666. For a definitive modern definition of misconduct in public office see *A-G's Reference (No 3 of 2003)* [2004] EWCA Crim 868, holding that D must be subjectively aware of the duty and subjectively reckless in its fulfilment (at [30]). See also *Belton* [2010] EWCA Crim 2857 where it is not even clear D knew of her public office status and *Cosford* [2013] EWCA Crim 466. The Criminal Justice and Courts Act 2015, s 26 creates an offence of corrupt or improper exercise of police powers and privileges, triable only on indictment and punishable by up to 14 years' imprisonment. See for discussion, LCCP 229, *Misconduct in Public Office* (2016) Ch 3 and the subsequent Report No 397 (2020).

[159] *Brown* (1841) Car & M 314, p 199. See D Nicholson, 'The Citizen's Duty to Assist the Police' [1992] Crim LR 611. PACE Code C, para 1K provides 'all citizens have a duty to help police officers to prevent crime and discover offenders'. This is a civic rather than a legal duty. Cf J Wanik, 'Forcing the Bystander to Get Involved' (1985) 94 Yale LJ 1787.

[160] eg rejection of perverting the course of justice by omission: *Clark* [2003] EWCA Crim 991; cf the extension in relation to cheating the public revenue: *Mavji* (1987) 84 Cr App R 34 which may be explained on the basis of the Court of Appeal's exceptional preparedness to read dishonesty offences broadly, see p 870.

[161] See Ashworth, *Positive Obligations*, 62, and see Ch 7.

[162] Stephen, *Digest* (4th edn, 1887) art 212.

Stephen went on to state exceptional cases where the law imposes a duty to act. If A in the example were B's parent, A would have a duty to act and would be guilty of murder if he did not act and the child drowned. There are a number of problems which need to be considered.

(1) Is the offence in question one under which conviction can arise for omission?

(2) If so, is A under a duty to act?

(3) If so, can we truly say that A has 'caused' the prohibited result?

(4) Is the conduct in question properly regarded as an omission? In many cases the courts may strain the concept of an act so as to avoid difficulties, particularly in cases involving medical care terminating life.

2.4.2.1 Is the offence one capable of being committed by omission?

Assuming that the defendant's conduct can properly be described as an omission, for example standing by and watching a person drowning or failing to feed a person, the question to determine is whether the offence with which he is charged can be fairly interpreted to apply to omissions.

Statutes generally

In statutory offences this question becomes one of construction. Is the verb, in its context, properly construed to include an omission? Glanville Williams has written:

In my opinion the courts should not create liability for omissions without statutory authority. Verbs used in defining offences and *prima facie* implying active conduct should not be stretched by interpretation to include omissions. In general the courts follow this principle. They do not say, for instance, that a person 'wounds' another by failing to save him from being wounded, or 'damages' a building by failing to stop a fire. At least, this has never been decided.[163]

But Professor Williams himself pointed out that the courts have often held offences to be capable of being committed by omission although the statute did not expressly provide for it. As a matter of principle, it might be argued that the interpretation of a statute that is ambiguous in this regard ought to be resolved in the defendant's favour. However, in many cases the words of the statute can be read to include omissions without straining their meaning.

There are numerous examples of the courts' construction of words to include liability for omission. In *Shama*,[164] a conviction was upheld for falsifying a document required for an accounting purpose contrary to s 17(1)(a) of the Theft Act 1968 where D omitted entirely to fill in a form which it was his duty to complete. In *Firth*,[165] a doctor was held to have deceived a hospital contrary to s 2(1) of the Theft Act 1978 (now repealed), by failing to inform the hospital that certain patients were private patients. 'Obstruct', 'falsify' and 'deceive' are all verbs which the courts have held to be capable of satisfaction by omission. So why not any other verb? The difficulty is to find any principle to limit such construction.

In *Ahmad*,[166] it was held that the words 'does acts' in a modern statute, the Protection from Eviction Act 1977, were to be strictly construed and were not satisfied by proof of an omission. A person commits an offence if he 'does acts' likely to interfere with the peace

163 Letter to the Editor [1982] Crim LR 773.   164 [1990] 2 All ER 602.
165 (1990) 91 Cr App R 217.
166 (1986) 84 Cr App R 64. It will be noted that the court did not regard the act plus omission as an act. Cf 'Creating a dangerous situation/supervening fault' at p 54.

or comfort of a residential occupier with intent to cause him to give up occupation of the premises. D, having done such acts without any such intent, omitted, with the required intention, to rectify the situation he had created. He was not guilty. But in some instances even the word 'act' has been held to be satisfied by an omission.[167] It was held that a man 'commits an act of gross indecency' with a child by totally passive submission to an act done by the child.[168] As noted, the courts often sidestep the issue by treating the whole of the circumstances as forming the basis for liability, as in B[169] where the issue was regarded as whether D 'acted with or towards a child' by remaining motionless as the boy pressed his erect penis against D.

Homicide

The courts have long accepted without debate that murder and manslaughter are capable of commission by omission.[170] Most cases of homicide by omission have resulted in convictions for manslaughter but there is at least one reported case of murder. In *Gibbins and Proctor*,[171] a man and the woman with whom he was living were convicted of murder of the man's child by withholding food. By living with the man and receiving money from him for food, the woman had assumed a duty towards the child (see later on why that is a sufficient duty). The judge was held to have rightly directed that they were guilty of murder if they withheld food with intent to cause the child grievous bodily harm, as a result of which she died. If the child had sustained grievous bodily harm but not died, the court would no doubt have held the defendants guilty of an offence under s 18 of the Offences Against the Person Act 1861.[172] The commission of this offence seems to have been an essential constituent of the Ds' liability, in the way the case was left to the jury. It would be strange indeed if causing death should be capable of commission by omission and causing grievous bodily harm not. If that were the case it would mean that D was not in breach of a duty to act until death occurred, at which point the duty was retrospectively imposed, and one of the aims of the criminal law, to deter wrongdoing or prevent wrongdoing from continuing, would be impossible to fulfil. Those are surely unacceptable consequences.

Parliament has intervened to create specific statutory offences of causing or allowing the death or serious injury of a child in the same household as the offender. These are discussed in detail in Ch 15.

Non-fatal offences against the person

Although the courts have accepted that homicide can be perpetrated by omission, they have assumed that assault or battery requires an act.[173] The words 'kill' and 'slay' in an indictment have been held to be satisfied by proof of an omission, so why not 'assault' or 'battery'? It is said that if D digs a pit for V to fall into, he commits an assault.[174] Why should it be different if he digs the pit without any such intention but then, forming the intention, leaves it unfilled, intending for V to fall in? Glanville Williams argues in respect of a similar case that 'in such circumstances of act-omission the total conduct should be regarded as

---

[167] This has particular significance because the entire law of attempts is based on the requirement of an 'act': Criminal Attempts Act 1981.

[168] *Speck* [1977] 2 All ER 859.   [169] [1999] Crim LR 594.

[170] For discussion of whether the state of the law is so uncertain as to undermine the rule of law, see A Ashworth, 'Manslaughter by Omission and the Rule of Law' [2015] Crim LR 563.

[171] (1918) 13 Cr App R 134.   [172] See p 729.

[173] Leaving aside for now the case where D creates a dangerous situation and fails to take steps within his power to avert that: *Santana-Bermudez* [2003] EWHC 2908 (Admin).

[174] The 'indirect violence' cases are doubted by M Hirst, 'Assault, Battery and Indirect Violence' [1999] Crim LR 577. Cf Smith (1984) 4 LS 88.

an act . . .'.[175] But 'should be regarded as' suggests a fiction and criminal liability should not turn on fictions. And his proposal would not meet the case where the hole has been dug by D's gardener and D, hearing that V is coming, decides to leave it unfilled.

Why should not the court legitimately interpret this situation as one where D causes V immediate unlawful violence? This view may derive some support from the decision in *Ireland*[176] that D's silent telephone call can constitute an assault. Again, however, it is likely that the courts would regard the assault as deriving from D's whole course of conduct by making the call coupled with his remaining silent. It is submitted that it would be realistic for the courts to recognize that one can 'assault', no less than 'kill', by omission.[177]

As for committing battery by omission, whereas assault only requires proof that D caused V to apprehend unlawful violence, battery requires the application of unlawful violence. Can it be said that D can apply force by omission? Such an interpretation of 'apply' might be a more difficult extension than with assault where the word 'cause' is the operative one.[178]

The discussion in the previous two paragraphs has dealt with the issue of whether there can be liability for assault and battery by omission, assuming that the elements of duty and causation can be established.

As a separate matter, there can be liability for supervening fault in assault or battery—where D's course of conduct creates a dangerous situation towards any person and D omits to negate or remove the risk. In *Fagan v Metropolitan Police Commissioner*,[179] where D accidentally drove his car onto a policeman's foot and then intentionally left it there, the majority of the court held that there was an assault (technically a battery) on the ground that, because D remained sitting in the car, there was a continuing act, not a mere omission. This again suggests, if not a fiction, a straining of words. Why should it be different if D had got out immediately, leaving the car on the officer's foot? The case would nowadays be decided under the exceptional category of duty recognized in *Miller*,[180] namely that D had created a dangerous situation by his act of driving onto V's foot and he then came under a duty to take reasonable steps to alleviate that danger. In *Santana-Bermudez*,[181] this reasoning was applied to uphold D's conviction for assault occasioning actual bodily harm where D told a police officer who was about to search him that there were no needles on his person. The officer was pricked by a needle in D's pocket.

On the basis of *Gibbins* (the child neglect case discussed in the previous section), it would seem that causing grievous bodily harm contrary to s 18 of the 1861 Act may be committed by omission. Although under s 20 of the 1861 Act the offence of wounding or inflicting grievous bodily harm would require proof of an 'infliction' of a 'wound' or grievous bodily harm, it is not clear that the words would be construed more narrowly than 'cause' in this context.[182] Since the offence under s 47 of the 1861 Act requires proof of an assault or battery and the 'occasioning', that is, 'causing' of actual bodily harm, subject to what was said earlier regarding assault, there is no reason to assume that this offence cannot also be committed by omission.

The Criminal Law Revision Committee (CLRC) recommended that liability for omissions in offences against the person should be confined to murder, manslaughter and their proposed offences of causing serious injury with intent, unlawful detention, kidnapping, abduction and aggravated abduction.[183] The Home Office in its reform proposals[184] redrafted the

---

175 G Williams, 'What Should the Code do about Omissions?' (1987) 7 LS 92.
176 [1998] AC 147.   177 cf Wilson, *Central Issues*, 101.
178 See Lord Hope in *Ireland* [1998] AC 147, 165.   179 [1969] 1 QB 439.   180 [1983] 2 AC 161.
181 [2003] EWHC 2908 (Admin).   182 *Mandair* [1995] 1 AC 208, [1994] Crim LR 666.
183 Fourteenth Report, *Offences Against the Person* (1980) Cmnd 7844, paras 252–5.
184 *Violence: Reforming the Law of Offences Against the Person* (1998). See now the Law Commission's Scoping Consultation Paper No 217 (2014) and Report No 361 (2015), Ch 5 discussed in Ch 16.

offences against the person in terms of causing injury and serious injury. This approach would present few problems in relation to liability for commission by omission. The law would be greatly simplified.[185]

2.4.2.2 Who owes a duty?

Assuming that the offence itself is one capable of being committed by omission, the next question is whether the individual defendant is one who may be under a duty to act.[186] Since most cases of omission have concerned homicide, the duties so far recognized[187] have been examined in the context of the duty to preserve life. This context is important because when a fatality occurs there is an enhanced danger that the courts will find a duty in previously unrecognized circumstances where the inquiry involves an entirely *ex post facto* rationalization of the relationships involved. Ashworth has convincingly argued that the duty-situations developed by the courts in the current law of manslaughter by omission are unprincipled, unpredictable and capable of producing injustice.[188]

Family and other relations

It is difficult to describe with precision the categories of relationship that might trigger criminal liability based on an omission. Ashworth, in an illuminating analysis of the cases, has suggested that liability for omission may arise if there is a settled relationship of dependence.[189]

Parents owe a duty to their children to act to save them from harm.[190] Presumably children above the age of responsibility owe a corresponding duty to their parents.[191] Other close relationships, whether of a family,[192] domestic, business or other nature, possibly impose similar duties. The criminal law is increasingly willing to protect wide categories of individuals on the basis of their existence within an extended family,[193] but it is unclear how far it would be willing to extend liability. The courts have managed to avoid identifying with precision those relationships which can be sufficient to ground liability. Indeed, they have failed to identify what is significant about those relationships in which a duty has been imposed. As a matter of principle, it can be argued that the important issue is not one of blood or formal legal relationship, but of interdependence.[194]

A further unresolved issue is what the relationship duty obliges D to do if it does arise. This would seem to be resolved on a case-by-case basis. One important issue will be whether the offence can be committed where D performed an act which he believed to be sufficient

---

[185] See also the Law Commission recommendations on Offences Against the Person LC 361 (2015) para 4.107.

[186] See generally L Alexander, 'Criminal Liability for Omissions: An Inventory of Issues' in Shute and Simester, *Criminal Law Theory*.

[187] Other than in cases of 'supervening fault', p 54.

[188] A Ashworth, 'Manslaughter by Omission and the Rule of Law' [2015] Crim LR 563.

[189] Ashworth, *Positive Obligations*, 44–6.

[190] In some instances there are specific statutory offences such as that of child neglect under the Children and Young Persons Act 1933 or the Domestic Violence, Crime and Victims Acts 2004 and 2012.

[191] eg if a muscular 14-year-old leaves his fainting mother to drown in the notorious shallow pool. In *Evans* [2009] EWCA Crim 650, [2009] Crim LR 661 and commentary a teenager did not owe a duty on the basis of family relationships to her half-sister to whom she had supplied drugs.

[192] eg marriage—in *Hood* [2003] EWCA Crim 2772, [2004] 1 Cr App R (S) 73: D was convicted of gross negligence manslaughter for failing to call medical assistance for his wife for three weeks after she fell and broke bones. See also *Broadhurst* [2019] EWCA Crim 2026: sadomasochistic beating while intoxicated, D left V severely injured. See also the discussion of the imposition of liability in such cases in J Horder and L McGowan, 'Manslaughter by Causing Another's Suicide' [2006] Crim LR 1035.

[193] See eg the extensive definition of family in the Sexual Offences Act 2003, s 27.

[194] Fletcher, *Rethinking Criminal Law*, 613.

to fulfil his duty, or if he had a reasonable belief that what he was doing was sufficient. These issues will become intertwined with the mens rea of the offence.

It is equally unclear when, if ever, the relationship duty ends. In the case of a parent and child, for example, a parent of a child of normal capacity may well be absolved on the attainment of the child turning 18, but this could hardly be so in the case of a disabled dependent child.

Voluntarily incurred obligations

The need to define precisely the categories of relationship which trigger a duty has often been avoided by the courts because the particular case calling for adjudication has involved a number of overlapping bases of liability including, significantly, the fact that D has voluntarily undertaken a position of responsibility towards V. For example, a person who has undertaken to care for a helpless and infirm relative[195] who has become dependent on him may be held to owe a duty, particularly where he is to receive some reward for caring for the other.[196] The holder of a public office requiring him to care for others may also incur criminal liability by failing to do so.

There may be wide-ranging circumstances in which a person might be treated as owing a legal duty because he voluntarily engaged in a certain activity and can therefore be treated as also voluntarily assuming a positive obligation to V. D's voluntary engagement in a business, or in a specific activity,[197] or in a relationship with V may all suffice.[198]

It is submitted that people who jointly engage in a hazardous activity whether lawful (like mountaineering), or unlawful (eg involving misuse of drugs offences[199]) may also owe duties to one another. The courts have exhibited reluctance to impose obligations on this basis alone. In *Sinclair Johnson and Smith*,[200] the court considered the manslaughter liability for those who failed to seek medical care for a comatose fellow drug-taker, but any duty was based on the previous friendship and bond between the individuals, rather than the joint act of drug administration. The convictions were overturned, but on a different point relating to causation.[201] The duty of care point was only relevant (though in effect *obiter*) as far as Sinclair and Johnson were concerned. Johnson *would not* have had a duty of care—he was a medically unqualified stranger. Sinclair would have had a duty of care in part because of their close bond, but also because he paid for and supplied V with the methadone and because he remained with V throughout his unconsciousness. In *Ruffell*,[202] a manslaughter conviction was upheld where D had been jointly involved in drug taking with the deceased. D, who had placed V outside in temperatures of six degrees, had also been a friend and host to V, and it is unclear on precisely which basis his duty arose. The matter is discussed further later in relation to the case of *Evans*.

This category of duty could surely extend to unrelated persons who voluntarily undertake responsibility. It is arguable, therefore, that D who sees a stranger, V, drowning, but who voluntarily begins to go to V's assistance could be liable should he then abandon the rescue.

---

[195] *Marriott* (1838) 8 C & P 425; *Nicholls* (1874) 13 Cox CC 75 (D was V's grandmother).

[196] *Instan* [1893] 1 QB 450 (D was V's niece, living in V's house, consuming food provided at V's expense but not supplying any to V); *Stone and Dobinson* [1977] QB 354.

[197] Such as storing hazardous materials, see *Winter and Winter* [2010] EWCA Crim 1474 in Ch 14.

[198] See Ashworth, *Positive Obligations*, 49–52.

[199] The point was not decided in *Dalby* [1982] 1 All ER 916, [1982] Crim LR 439. Cf *People v Beardsley* (1967) 113 NW 1128.

[200] *Sinclair Johnson and Smith* (1998) 148 NLJ 1353, (1998) 21 Aug, CA.

[201] See also most recently *Broughton* [2020] EWCA Crim 1093: D supplied his girlfriend with Class A drug and 'bumped it up'. He remained present as she experienced medical difficulties in the secluded woodland to which they had gone.

[202] [2003] EWCA Crim 122.

Underlying bases for imposing a duty in such circumstances include the argument that in such cases D may be the best placed to act and that V may have relied to his detriment on D's actions—in the case of the drowning swimmer, V may be worse off by relying on D since he may, for example, have stopped calling for assistance from other potential rescuers.[203]

The extent to which a 'voluntary assumption of responsibility' is a free-standing basis for the imposition of a duty, and the scope of circumstances in which it might apply, remain unresolved. One of the most controversial cases may well turn on the existence of this duty. In *Stone and Dobinson*,[204] although the defendants' liability for manslaughter arose in part from their family relationship, and their cohabitation with the victim, their voluntary undertaking of responsibility for the victim seems to have been significant in the court's conclusion that a duty was owed, although it seems that the voluntary undertaking was implied.

As in other categories of duty, the courts have failed to define the content of the duty arising from voluntary assumption. The conviction of the defendants in *Stone and Dobinson*, both of whom had limited mental capacity, suggests that the courts might adopt a strict line when faced with claims that the accused had done what he believed to be sufficient to fulfil his duty. In terms of the termination of such a duty, one who has undertaken the duty can probably divest himself of it only by passing it on to some responsible authority or other person.

Contractual duties

A well-established basis for imposing criminal liability for omissions is where D has contractually accepted the obligation. This could be seen as a subset of the previous category—the voluntary assumption of responsibility.[205]

A contract may give rise to a duty in criminal law to persons, including those not party to the contract but likely to be injured by failure to perform it. The most obvious examples in this category are those who are employed as carers or health-care professionals. In *Pittwood*,[206] a railway crossing gate-keeper opened the gate to let a cart pass and went off to his lunch, forgetting to shut it again. Ten minutes later a haycart was struck by a train while crossing the line and V was killed. D was convicted of manslaughter. It was argued on his behalf that he owed a duty of care only to his employers, the railway company, with whom he contracted. Wright J held, however, that:

there was gross and criminal negligence, as the man was paid to keep the gate shut and protect the public . . . A man might incur criminal liability from a duty arising out of contract.[207]

Again, the courts have not addressed the issue of whether the duty owed under a contract exists strictly within the bounds of the terms of that contract. If D is a lifeguard whose terms of employment stipulate that he finishes at 5 pm daily, is he under a duty to save V who is drowning at 5.05 pm? It seems clear at least that the duty will terminate when the relationship ends, as when an employee leaves the service of his employer.

---

[203] See for analysis of the problems, G Mead, 'Contracting into Crime: A Theory of Criminal Omissions' (1991) 11 OJLS 147.

[204] [1977] QB 354.   [205] See Ashworth, *Positive Obligations*, 51.   [206] (1902) 19 TLR 37.

[207] Wright J said that this was not a mere case of non-feasance, but of misfeasance. However, D's breach of duty was not in opening the gate, but in omitting to close it again. Cf, however, *Smith* (1869) 11 Cox CC 210, where Lush J ruled that there was no duty because D's employer had no duty to provide a watchman. (If D makes a practice of seeing old ladies across the road, he is not responsible if one day he fails to be present and an old lady is killed.) H Beynon, 'Doctors as Murderers' [1982] Crim LR 17 at 22 suggests that opening and not shutting might be regarded as one 'act'; but would it really have been different if the gate had been opened by D's colleague who had just gone off duty? One hopes not.

Creating a dangerous situation/supervening fault

Where D's conduct puts in peril V's person, his property, his liberty or any other interest protected by the criminal law, and D is aware that he has created the peril, he has a duty to take reasonable steps to prevent the harm in question resulting.[208] The initial conduct may be done without any kind of fault but, if D fails to intervene, it is undoubtedly his conduct which is the cause of the harm. For this reason the principle may apply to a wider range of offences than can be committed by simple omission. This category of liability might therefore be treated as entirely separate from the four bases for imposing liability previously discussed. This category of liability differs from the voluntary assumption of responsibility category discussed earlier because this category can give rise to liability where D's original conduct creating the danger was accidental.[209]

The principle derives from *Miller*,[210] where D, a squatter in V's house, went to sleep holding a lighted cigarette. He awoke to find the mattress smouldering. He did nothing to put it out but moved into an adjoining room and went to sleep there. The house caught fire. D was convicted of arson contrary to s 1(1) and (3) of the Criminal Damage Act 1971. The House of Lords held that the judge had rightly directed the jury that, when D woke up, he was under a duty to take some action to put the fire out. Lord Diplock said:[211]

> I see no rational ground for excluding from conduct capable of giving rise to criminal liability conduct which consists of failing to take measures that lie within one's power to counteract a danger that one has oneself created, if at the time of such conduct one's state of mind is such as constitutes a necessary ingredient of the offence.

The Court of Appeal had upheld the conviction on a different basis:

> We would only say that an unintentional act followed by an intentional omission to rectify it or its consequences, or a reckless omission to do so when recklessness is a sufficient *mens rea* for the particular case, should only be regarded *in toto* as an intentional or reckless act when reality and common sense so require; this may well be a matter to be left to the jury. Further, in the relevant analysis we think that whether or not there is on the facts an element of adoption on the part of the alleged offender of what he has done earlier by what he deliberately or recklessly fails to do later is an important consideration.

In some cases the application of this 'continuous act' theory would apparently produce different results from the duty theory. For example, in *Ahmad*[212] if D could be deemed to have acted intentionally (ie with intent to cause the residential occupier to give up occupation) when he rendered the flat uninhabitable, the difficulty of convicting him would have disappeared. This theory, again, involves an undesirable legal fiction. Fictions should have no place in the criminal law. Lord Diplock preferred the 'duty to avert danger' to the 'continuous act' theory but only on the ground that the former is easier to explain to a jury. It is submitted, however, that they are different in substance, as the example based on *Ahmad* shows.[213] Under *Miller*, D must, at the time of the omission to avert the danger he has created, have the mens rea required for the crime with which he is charged at the time of the omission to avert the danger he has created.

---

[208] See M Bohlander, *Principles of German Law* (2009) 44.

[209] See Ashworth, *Positive Obligations*, 53–4.

[210] [1983] 2 AC 161. See [1982] Crim LR 466 and commentary. See [1982] QB 532, [1982] Crim LR 526 and 773–4. The principle is replicated in the Home Office Draft Bill, cl 16 in *Violence: Reforming the Law of Offences Against the Person* (1998). Cf LC 361.

[211] [1983] 2 AC 161. See on the Scots law application of the principle, J Chalmers, 'Fireraising by Omission' 2004 SLT 59.

[212] See p 48.   [213] See commentary [1982] Crim LR 526 and 773–4 and (1984) 4 LS 88 at 91.

Again, one issue to be resolved is the extent of any such duty. Although expressed in terms of 'reasonable' steps, it is unclear how objective this test is to be in application, and in particular whether it is sufficient that D believes on the facts as he sees them that the remedial measures he took were sufficient. Moreover, it is unclear how the law would deal with an individual who claimed impossibility of performance of such a duty.[214]

The scope of the *Miller* doctrine remains unclear. The Court of Appeal has been prepared to adopt an extended interpretation of the *Miller* principle in the case of *Evans*.[215] In that case D gave her half sister, V, heroin to take, knowing that she was a recovering addict. V slipped into a coma. D became aware of that and chose not to call the emergency services but to sit with V. V died. The Court of Appeal upheld D's conviction for gross negligence manslaughter. The court faced two difficulties in doing so: (a) identifying a duty; and (b) establishing that D's act caused V's death. For present purposes we are interested in the duty question. The court did not resolve the case on the basis of a sibling duty nor on the basis solely that D had supplied the drugs, nor on the basis that they were engaged in a dangerous activity together. The court focused on whether D owed a duty when her sister lapsed into a coma. In applying *Miller*, albeit in extended form, the court held that there was a duty.

The extension of *Miller* was significant. Although Miller was charged with criminal damage which at that time was satisfied by proof of objective recklessness, the House of Lords held that his duty only arose on his *subjective* realization of the danger. Gross negligence manslaughter is also a crime based on objective fault, but in *Evans* the court held that the duty arises when D realizes or *ought* to have realized the danger.[216] The court did not provide further detailed examination of whether the duty arises from the creation or the realization of the danger.[217] It is certainly the case that the full scope of the *Miller* doctrine has not been satisfactorily explained. Nevertheless, it is submitted that the courts will be likely to continue applying a *Miller*-type analysis in these cases on various possible bases.

In these exceptional cases where D supplies drugs and remains present but fails to make reasonable efforts to seek medical attention when V experiences serious illness, Lord Diplock's statements in *Miller* are likely to be construed broadly to establish that a duty arises when D became aware (or ought to have become aware) of the events resulting from his act. Liability might also be imposed for V's death caused or contributed to by D's failure to act[218] where a sufficient duty is imposed when D realized/ought to have realized V's post-injection predicament and: (a) D is in a pre-existing relationship of interdependence (parent, carer, etc) which persists irrespective of V's self-administration (eg the husband of a woman who has self-injected and who realizes or ought to have realized that she is having breathing difficulty); or (b) because D has voluntarily assumed responsibility being engaged with V in a dangerous joint enterprise; or (c) where D has voluntarily assumed a duty to care for V who is in such a state. An example might be where V becomes dependent on D's assistance (eg where D starts to care for V, who has overdosed at a party, by moving him from one room to a more secluded space, but then abandons him, leaving V worse off as he is less likely to be seen and rescued by others).[219]

One aspect of the scope of *Miller* is at least clear: it is necessary to invoke the *Miller* principle only in the case of a result crime requiring fault where the act causing the result is done without the relevant fault at that time. Where the offence requires no

---

[214] See Smart (1987) 103 LQR 532.   [215] [2009] EWCA Crim 650.   [216] Per Judge LCJ at [31].

[217] Norrie argues that 'there is a whiff of ad hoc, and misdirected, legal moralism about *Evans*', A Norrie, *Crime, Reason and History* (3rd edn, 2014) 162. See also Glenys Williams, 'Gross Negligence Manslaughter and Duty of Care in "Drugs" Cases: *R v Evans*' [2009] Crim LR 631. For interesting comparison with some continental European systems, see J Keiler, *Actus Reus and Participation in European Criminal Law* (2012) 145.

[218] See *Broughton* [2020] EWCA Crim 1093.

[219] Ashworth argues that the significance of acts of assistance remains unclear. See Ashworth, n 169.

proof of fault, there is no need to rely on it. In *Wings Ltd v Ellis*,[220] D Ltd, a tour operator, published a brochure which, unknown to D, contained misrepresentations. On discovering the truth, D did all they could to correct the errors but, subsequently, V read
an uncorrected brochure and booked a holiday in reliance on it. D was convicted under
s 14(1)(a) of the Trade Descriptions Act 1968 of making a statement which they knew to
be false and, s 14(1)(b), recklessly making a false statement. The statement was 'made'
when it was read by V and, by then, D knew it was false. The Divisional Court, applying
Miller, quashed both convictions. D had done all that could reasonably be expected to
correct the false trade descriptions. The prosecutor appealed in respect of the offence
under s 14(1)(a) only. The appeal was allowed. Subject to a statutory defence which was
not pleaded, the House held that s 14(1)(a) created an 'absolute' offence.[221] D knew the
statement was false and no other fault was required. There was no room for the application of *Miller*.

Where the offence is one requiring fault, whether mens rea strictly so called or negligence,
it is submitted that the *Miller* principle is of general application.[222] If D, sitting alone in the
passenger seat of a car, were accidentally to knock off the handbrake, so that the car rolled
away, it is submitted that he could be convicted of murder if he wilfully omitted to put the
brake on again, intending the car to run over and kill or cause grievous bodily harm to V.
Similarly, D who locks the door of a room not knowing that V is inside and, having learned
that V is within, omits to unlock the door should be liable for false imprisonment.[223] Since
the principle requires the appropriate element of fault at the time of the subsequent omission, it is submitted that liability should arise in such a case.[224]

Further clarification from the courts would be welcome on how it is to be determined
when the duty imposed under *Miller* comes to an end. In the case of *Lewin v CPS*,[225]
a decision not to prosecute was upheld where D left his heavily intoxicated friend,
V, asleep in a car in the summer heat in Spain where he died. The Divisional Court
observed that D's responsibility for the welfare of his passenger 'persisted for so long as
the vehicle was in motion, but . . . would normally have come to an end as soon as the
vehicle was properly parked in a safe place at the end of its journey . . . [it] could only
persist in a way which would be relevant to the offence of manslaughter if a reasonable
person would have foreseen [the risk of death]'. The court went on, 'the young man
who was left in the unlocked car was an adult, not a small child or dog'.[226] Had not
D created a dangerous situation by leaving V, heavily intoxicated, in the car? Was he
not at fault for not summoning help when he realized the temperature had risen so high?
Is the case distinguishable from *Evans*? Ashworth argues that the court's conclusion
emphasizes that an assumption of responsibility alone is not enough for manslaughter,
without knowledge (or reasonable grounds for realizing) that the other person is in a
life-threatening situation.[227]

---

220 [1984] 1 WLR 731; revsd [1985] AC 272.   221 See p 149.

222 As eg in *Green v Cross* (1910) 103 LT 279—D innocently caught a dog in a trap. Instead of releasing it he
left it until it was freed two hours later by the police. Held, Channell J dissenting, that there was evidence on
which he could be convicted of 'cruelly ill-treating' the dog.

223 See the unusual case of *Bowell* [2003] EWCA Crim 3896 in which D falsely imprisoned V in his car,
V jumped from the car and escaped, but D put V back in the car and falsely imprisoned her again before tak-
ing her to hospital several hours later: she was rendered paraplegic by these actions. The court suggested that
D 'could have left her in the road without committing an offence' when she had jumped out.

224 What of the case in which D hosts a party and X drinks alcohol to excess? If D allows X to drive home
and X kills V, should D be liable?

225 [2002] EWHC 1049 (Admin).   226 At [24].   227 Ashworth, n 169 at 572.

2.4.2.3 Causation and omissions

Once it has been determined that there is an offence that can be committed by omission and a defendant who can be held liable owing to the existence of a relevant duty, there remains the question of whether his failure to act has caused the prohibited harm.[228]

Considering again the example of the child, B, left to drown by his parent, A, Stephen saw no difficulty in saying that the death (or bodily injury) was caused by A's omission. Others have taken a different view.[229] It has been argued that B's death would have occurred in precisely the same way if his parent, A, had not come on the scene for any reason, so how can A be said to have caused it? He simply allowed it to happen. The cause of B's death could be said to be simply his falling into the water. Nothing else had to happen. He just drowned. If A and strangers C, D and E had walked by the pool together ignoring B's plight it is impossible to say that, as a matter of fact, A has caused the death but C, D and E have not.

There is a danger of oversimplifying things and seeking to resolve the entire issue of liability on the basis of causation without regard to the prior question of duty.[230] In the case of A, C, D and E, it is possible to describe their failure as *a* factual cause of B's death, and if A is under a duty towards B, it is therefore possible to say that A's failure to act may be *a* legal cause of B's death.[231] As the Draft Code puts it (cl 17(b)):

a person causes a result which is an element of an offence when . . . (b) he omits to do an act which might prevent its occurrence and which he is under a duty to do according to the law relating to the offence.

This provision goes beyond the present law (and beyond what is desirable) in one respect: it extends liability to results which the act D omitted to do *might have* prevented. The present law limits liability to results which D's unperformed act *would have* prevented.[232] In the drowning child example, if A is B's parent and fails to act, under the present law the prosecution would have to establish that the failure on A's part *would* have, not might have, prevented B's death.

In *Broughton*,[233] the Court of Appeal recently confirmed this interpretation in the context of gross negligence manslaughter. D, V's boyfriend, supplied her with Class A drugs at a music festival. He had 'bumped up' the dose he gave her, either by giving her an increased dose or mixing it with ecstasy or ketamine. D and V then left the main festival ground and went to nearby woodland. V experienced a bad reaction to the drugs and D videoed her on numerous occasions, on his phone, at her request over the next few hours. D made ineffectual attempts to get medical assistance—giving someone the wrong location. V died seven hours after taking the drugs. The prosecution's case was that, having supplied the drugs and remaining with the victim, D owed her a duty of care to secure timely medical assistance as her condition deteriorated to the point where her life was obviously in danger. His failure to do so was said by the prosecution to be a substantial cause of her death. The prosecution's resuscitation expert described the deceased as being 'seriously unwell and in need of urgent medical care' four hours after taking the drugs. He concluded that she would have stood a 90 per cent chance of survival with medical intervention had it been available after 4½ hours. The prosecution's expert was unable to rule out that death would have occurred even

---

[228] See AP Simester, 'Causation in (Criminal) Law' (2017) 133 LQR 416; Wilson, *Central Issues*, 186–92; H Beynon, 'Causation, Omissions and Complicity' [1987] Crim LR 539; Tadros, *Criminal Responsibility*, 171.

[229] See B Hogan, 'Omissions and the Duty Myth' in *Criminal Law Essays*.

[230] See A Leavens, 'A Causation Approach to Criminal Omissions' (1988) 76 Cal LR 547.

[231] As considered, p 64, it is sufficient that D's conduct is a substantial and operative cause of V's death for homicide; there is no need to prove that D's conduct is the sole cause of death.

[232] Williams (1987) 7 LS 92 at 106–7, citing *Morby* (1882) 15 Cox CC 35.

[233] [2020] EWCA Crim 1093.

had V received medical assistance. The judge rejected D's submission of no case to answer and declined a request to give a further direction to the jury that, even taken at its highest, the prosecution's evidence was that there was a 10 per cent possibility that medical intervention could never have saved the deceased's life so that he was entitled to be acquitted unless there was evidence to fill the gap between that and the jury being sure that any breach of duty of his had caused or significantly contributed to her death.

The Court of Appeal quashed D's conviction. The judge's direction to the jury did not make it clear that in a case concerning a negligent lack of medical attention, in order to establish that a breach of duty was a substantial cause of death, the prosecution had to prove to the criminal standard that the person concerned would have lived. The court rejected the prosecution argument that the test should be whether the jury was sure that the negligence deprived the victim of a significant or substantial chance of survival that was otherwise available at the time of the negligence. The court emphasized that, as in any homicide, it was sufficient for the prosecution to prove that D's act or omission was a significant contributory cause of death, rather than the sole or principal cause. The opinion of the prosecution expert of a 90 per cent chance of survival had V had medical help 4½ hours after taking the drugs left a realistic possibility that she would have lived.

The decision has been subjected to criticism on the basis that this approach creates an incentive for defendants to challenge causation. The prosecution must be able to exclude plausible possibilities that the victim would have died anyway. Failure to do so means that the case should be withdrawn from the jury. Experts may be reluctant to state emphatically that the victim would have survived had the defendant summoned medical treatment.

2.4.2.4 Act or omission?

It is not always easy to distinguish between an act and an omission. Some of the most difficult examples of the distinction arise in the context of a cessation of medical treatment. If a doctor is keeping a patient alive by cranking the handle of a machine and he stops, this looks like a clear case of omission. So, too, if the machine is electrically operated but switches itself off every 24 hours and the doctor deliberately does not restart it. Switching off a functioning machine looks like an act; but is it any different in substance from the first two cases?[234] On the other hand, is it any different from cutting the high-wire on which a tightrope walker is balancing[235] (which is an act, if ever there was one)? Is the ending of a programme of dialysis an omission, while switching off a ventilator an act? Is the discontinuance of a drip feed, which is keeping a patient alive, by withdrawing the tube from his body an act[236] and failure to replace an emptied bag an omission? In theory, it might be possible to distinguish between these cases. It seems offensive if liability for homicide is so heavily dependent on such very fine distinctions of this kind; but it appears that that is the case.[237]

A doctor is, no doubt, under a duty to make reasonable efforts, in the light of customary medical practice and all other relevant factors, to keep a patient alive.[238] Unfortunately, this does not solve the problem because the content of any duty there may be to 'keep alive' is different from that of the duty 'not to kill'. The issue has become further complicated

---

[234] Examples put by I Kennedy, 'Switching Off Life Support Machines: The Legal Implications' [1977] Crim LR 443.

[235] See Kennedy, ibid at 452. See the discussion by Beynon [1982] Crim LR 17.   [236] Beynon, ibid.

[237] See also S Ost, *An Analytical Study of the Legal, Moral and Ethical Aspects of the Living Phenomenon of Euthanasia* (2003), discussing public perceptions of whether these types of act are equivalent. In *R (on the application of Nicklinson) v Ministry of Justice* [2014] UKSC 38 Lord Neuberger stated that characterizing these cases as involving omissions was 'somewhat uncomfortable'.

[238] Williams, TBCL (1st edn, 1978) 236. See the discussion in *R (Burke) v GMC* [2004] EWHC 1879 (Admin), overruled and regarded as going too far in the discussion of some of these issues: *R (Burke) v GMC* [2006] QB 273.

with recognition that public authorities must respect not only the right to life under Art 2 of the ECHR, but also the right to be free, in the course of treatment, from inhuman and degrading treatment under Art 3. The doctor must also respect the Art 8 privacy rights of the patient which might involve a declared wish to die, or for treatment to be withheld in specific circumstances. The Mental Capacity Act 2005 (ss 24–6) provides statutory recognition of the ability of a competent person to give a binding refusal of treatment (eg 'do not resuscitate'). The individual can provide a binding advance refusal where he is presently competent but anticipates that he may lose that competence as his condition deteriorates.

The difficulties are brought into sharp focus where parents refuse their consent to operations on young children suffering from disabilities knowing that without the operation the child will die. It has been held that such parents are not necessarily guilty of a homicide offence if death ensues.[239] In *Re B (A Minor)*,[240] on these facts, the child was made a ward of court, and the court gave consent as being in the interests of the child. Dunn LJ said that the decision of the parents to allow the child to die was one which everyone accepted as 'entirely responsible'. It was a decision, it seems, that the parents could lawfully take, so that the death of the child, if it had followed, would not have been an actus reus. Templeman LJ thought there might possibly be cases 'where the future is so certain and where the life of the child is bound to be full of pain and suffering that the court might be driven to a different conclusion'—that is, to allow the child to die.[241] Yet there is no doubt that if the parents—or anyone—did any positive act to kill the child, they would be guilty of murder, subject to a relevant defence of necessity.[242] The undoubted duty of parents to preserve the life of their child is different from, and more restricted than, their duty not to kill it.

In *Arthur*,[243] a doctor, having noted that the parents of a Down's Syndrome child did not wish the child to survive, ordered 'nursing care only' and the administration of a drug, allegedly to stop the child seeking sustenance. At the trial of the doctor for attempted murder of the child, Farquharson J directed the jury that it was for them to decide whether 'there was an act properly so-called on the part of Dr Arthur, as distinct from simply allowing the child to die'. Simply allowing the child to die would apparently have been lawful,[244] and withholding food was, according to the medical evidence put by the judge to the jury, 'a negative act'—a mere omission. It is submitted that a better view is that an omission to provide such a child with food and the ordinary necessities of life ought to be equated with an act causing death rather than with an omission to perform an operation or to take some other extraordinary action. The position seems to be the same with a helpless, elderly person, incapable of taking decisions. It may be lawful for his family and the doctor to decide that an operation which would prolong a useless and painful life should not be performed; but it surely cannot be lawful to starve him to death, whether with the assistance of drugs or not.

---

[239] If it were an offence, it would (in the absence of diminished responsibility) be murder, because the parents intend the death of the child.

[240] [1981] 1 WLR 1421.   [241] cf the views in *R (Burke) v GMC* [2004] EWHC 1879 (Admin).

[242] See the discussion of *Re A* [2001] Fam 147 in the following section, and *Inglis* [2010] EWCA Crim 2637. For a discussion of whether necessity can operate successfully as a defence in these cases, see P Lewis, 'The Failure of the Defence of Necessity as a Mechanism of Legal Change on Assisted Dying in the Common Law World' in DJ Baker and J Horder (eds), *The Sanctity of Life and the Criminal Law* (2013). There are some who argue that there ought to be a specific partial defence of 'compassionate killing'. See H Keating and J Bridgeman, 'Compassionate Killings: The Case for a Partial Defence' (2012) 75 MLR 697. The authors conceptualize *Inglis* as a case concerning pity rather than compassion.

[243] (1981) 12 BMLR 1, discussed by M Gunn and JC Smith, '*Arthur's Case* and the Right to Life of a Down's Syndrome Child' [1985] Crim LR 705 and I Kennedy, *Treat Me Right* (1991) Ch 8.

[244] It is submitted that nothing turned on the fact that the charge had been reduced from murder to attempted murder—see [1986] Crim LR 760–2 and D Poole, '*Arthur's Case*: A Comment' [1986] Crim LR 383; D Brahams, 'Putting *Arthur's Case* in Perspective' [1986] Crim LR 387.

Terminating life

The distinction between act and omission was the basis of the important decision in *Airedale National Health Service Trust v Bland*.[245] B, a victim of the Hillsborough stadium disaster, had been in a persistent vegetative state for three and a half years and medical opinion was that there was no hope of improvement or recovery. The Trust, with the support of B's parents, applied for a declaration that they might lawfully discontinue ventilation, nutrition and hydration by artificial means and end medical treatment except to allow B to die peacefully. The application was resisted by the Official Solicitor, who argued that the withdrawal of artificial feeding would constitute murder. The judge granted the declaration and the House of Lords, affirming the Court of Appeal, upheld it. There was no doubt about the intention to kill. The object of the exercise was to terminate B's life. It was accepted that to kill by administering a lethal injection or any similar act would be murder; but what was proposed was held to be not an act, but an omission. Lord Goff said:

> The question is not whether the doctor should take a course which will kill his patient, or even take a course which has the effect of accelerating his death. The question is whether the doctor should or should not continue to provide his patient with medical care which, if continued, will prolong his patient's life.

Lord Goff added that it might be difficult to say that it was in the patient's best interests that the treatment should be ended but that it could sensibly be said that it was not in his best interests that it should be continued. 'Ending' and 'not continuing' look uncommonly like the same thing; but the former expresses the conduct as an act, which could not be justified, and the latter as an omission, which could.[246] In *Re A (Conjoined Twins: Surgical Separation)*, the Court of Appeal held, rightly, it is submitted, that surgery to separate twins was an act.[247] In *R (Burke) v GMC*,[248] Lord Phillips stated that *Bland* should not be read as requiring a persistent vegetative state (PVS) patient to be kept alive simply because he has made an advance directive to that effect. Section 26 of the Mental Capacity Act requires compliance with a valid advance directive to refuse treatment, but the crucial issue is what is in the best interests of a patient.[249]

---

[245] [1993] 1 All ER 821, [1993] Crim LR 877. See J Keown, 'Restoring Moral and Intellectual Shape to the Law After *Bland*' (1997) 113 LQR 481. For an analysis of the *Bland* case and its implications for euthanasia, see D Price, 'What Shape to Euthanasia after *Bland*? Historical, Contemporary and Futuristic Paradigms' (2009) 125 LQR 142. The Scottish courts have reached the same result by a different route: *Law Hospital NHS Trust v Lord Advocate* [1996] 2 FLR 407. *Bland*'s case was distinguished in *Re A (Children; Conjoined Twins: Surgical Separation)*, p 394. *Bland* was relied upon in a number of the speeches in *R (on the application of Nicklinson) v Ministry of Justice* [2014] UKSC 38. The approach has been held to be compatible with the obligations of the State to secure the right to life under Art 2 of the ECHR: *NHS Trusts, A v M* [2001] 1 All ER 801; *A Hospital v W* [2007] EWHC 425 (Fam). There is no mandatory requirement for a court order to be obtained before clinically assisted nutrition and hydration be withdrawn provided the provisions of the Mental Capacity Act 2005 are followed: *NHS v Y* [2018] UKSC 46.

[246] It has been argued that the importance of the judgment is its discussion of the content of the duty of care in respect of an insensate patient. See A du Bois-Pedain, 'The Duty to Preserve Life and its Limits in English Criminal Law' in DJ Baker and J Horder (eds), *The Sanctity of Life and the Criminal Law* (2013).

[247] For criticism of the approach in *Bland* and the consequences for the conjoined twin case, see also J McEwan, 'Murder by Design: The Feel-Good Factor and the Criminal Law' (2001) 9 Med L Rev 246. See also M Wilks, 'Medical Treatment at the End of Life' in C Erin and S Ost, *Criminal Justice System and Health Care* (2007).

[248] [2006] QB 273. See, for discussion, C Dupré, 'Human Dignity and the Withdrawal of Medical Treatment: A Missed Opportunity' [2006] EHRLR 678, lamenting the Court of Appeal's refusal to engage with the human dignity and ECHR arguments.

[249] At [57].

ECHR concerns

In *Glass v UK*,[250] the ECtHR gave detailed consideration to the position under English law, acknowledging first that: 'the regulatory framework . . . is firmly predicated on the duty to preserve the life of a patient, save in exceptional circumstances. Secondly, that same frame-work prioritises the requirement of parental consent [in the case of a child] and, save in emergency situations, requires doctors to seek the intervention of the courts in the event of parental objection.'

In *R (Burke) v GMC*,[251] the High Court recognized that a withdrawal of artificial feed-ing and hydration which a competent patient wishes to continue or which an incompetent person has previously, when competent, directed to continue would infringe Art 8 of the ECHR.[252] It was also held that withdrawal of treatment would breach Art 3 if it exposed the patient to acute mental and physical suffering, irrespective of the awareness of the patient to that suffering. The court in *Burke* also suggested that it would be difficult to envisage circumstances in which the withdrawal of artificial feeding from a sentient patient would be compatible with the Convention. The Court of Appeal subsequently reversed the High Court's decision, upholding the legitimacy of the GMC Guidelines on the withdrawal of nutrition and hydration. The Lord Chief Justice emphasized the duty on doctors to take rea-sonable steps to keep the patient alive. The Court of Appeal concluded that the guarantees in Arts 2, 3 and 8 did not alter the common law position. The court endorsed the comments of Munby J in the High Court,[253] that Art 2 does not entitle anyone to continue with life-prolonging treatment where to do so would expose the patient to 'inhuman or degrading treatment' breaching Art 3, but that at the same time, withdrawal of life-prolonging treat-ment within the common law parameters will not breach Art 2. Lord Phillips stated that this conclusion:

does not, however, lead to the further conclusion that if a National Health doctor were deliberately to bring about the death of a competent patient by withdrawing life-prolonging treatment contrary to that patient's wishes, Article 2 would not be infringed. It seems to us that such conduct would plainly violate Article 2. Furthermore, if English law permitted such conduct, this would also vio-late this country's positive obligation to enforce Article 2. As we have already indicated, we do not consider that English criminal law would countenance such conduct. However, the fact that Articles 2, 3 and 8 of the Convention may be engaged does not, in our judgment, advance the argu-ment or alter the common law.[254]

In *NHS Trust A v M, NHS Trust B v H*,[255] it was confirmed that the withdrawal of nutrition and hydration by artificial means from a patient in a persistent vegetative state would not infringe Art 2.

It will be appreciated from the discussion of these difficult medical cases that the courts struggle to distinguish between acts and omissions. The difficulty all too often leads to dis-tinctions without any apparent difference, or in some cases to a sidestepping of the issue by a convenient treatment of the actus reus as the defendant's conduct viewed *in toto*.

[250] [2004] 1 FLR 1019, [75]. The case concerned the treatment of a child whom doctors thought was dying and to whom they administered diamorphine by way of palliative care despite the objections of the mother.
[251] [2004] EWHC 1879 (Admin). See also *Re OT* [2009] EWHC 633 (Fam): withdrawal of life-sustaining treatment which was no longer in the patient's best interests was not a breach of Art 2 or 8.
[252] On the GMC Guidelines, see J Keown, 'Beyond *Bland*: A Critique of the BMA Guidance on Withholding and Withdrawing Medical Treatment' (2000) 20 LS 66; cf D Price, 'Fairly Bland: An Alternative View of a Supposed New "Death Ethic" and the BMA Guidelines' (2001) 21 LS 618. See also the discussion of the *Schiavo* case in the United States—RA Destro, 'Lessons in Legal and Judicial Ethics from *Schiavo*' in C Erin and S Ost, *The Criminal Justice System and Health Care* (2007).
[253] [2005] QB 424, [162].   [254] At [39].   [255] [2001] Fam 348.

2.4.2.5 'Easy rescue' statutes

As noted, there are hotly contested philosophical arguments about the desirability of creating liability for omissions in general, and much of the academic discussion has centred on the liability for failing to rescue.[256] Many jurisdictions have dealt with Stephen's 'shallow pool' case by creating a specific offence for anyone failing to take steps which he could take without any personal risk, to save another from death or injury. It is important to note that these statutes do not equate omissions with acts. The offender is liable for a specific statutory offence of failing to rescue (with its own penalty) and not the harmful result which D may have prevented and has allowed to happen. Thus, D is not necessarily guilty of homicide if the victim dies.[257]

Some commentators have called for the enactment of an 'easy rescue' or 'Bad Samaritan' offence such as that adopted by our European neighbours,[258] certain US states[259] and elsewhere. A clear example of the type of offence is provided in the Northern Territory in Australia in the Criminal Code Act, s 155. This makes it an offence for any person who, being able to provide rescue, resuscitation, medical treatment, first aid or succour of any kind to a person urgently in need of it and whose life may be endangered if it is not provided, to 'callously'[260] fail to do so. Powerful arguments have been made that such an offence would promote social cooperation, which is itself worthy of promotion by criminal regulation and that such laws are ultimately necessary for individual autonomy to be realized.[261]

The objections to Bad Samaritan laws are well rehearsed.[262] They have been criticized as being so vague that they are either unenforceable and/or contravene the principle of legality. Some of the examples from around the world, including those such as the Northern Territory's offence, may support the criticisms. They are alleged to impose too great a burden on investigators and leave too much to prosecutorial discretion since there may be hundreds of potential defendants who failed to rescue (as opposed to the usual scenario with one individual who acted). In addition, it is questionable how well they operate in practice

---

[256] See, especially, J Feinberg, *Harm to Others* (1984) Ch 4. Compare H Gross, *A Theory of Criminal Justice* (1979) 61–5; M Menlowe, 'The Philosophical Foundations of a Duty to Rescue' and A McCall Smith, 'The Duty to Rescue and the Common Law' in M Menlowe and A McCall Smith (eds), *The Duty to Rescue: The Jurisprudence of Aid* (1993). See also T Elliott and D Ormerod, 'Acts and Omissions: A Distinction Without a Defence' (2009) 39 Cambrian L Rev 40.

[257] J Andanaes, *The General Part of the Criminal Law of Norway* (1965) 132.

[258] eg France: Code pénal, art 223–6 (which replaces art 63 of the previous criminal code). See A Ashworth and E Steiner, 'Criminal Omissions and Public Duties: The French Experience' (1990) 10 LS 153. For more recent analysis, see M Vranken, 'Duty to Rescue in Civil Law and Common Law: Les Extrêmes se Touchent?' (1998) 47 ICLQ 934 at 937–8, and A Cadoppi, 'Failure to Rescue and the Continental Criminal Law' in MA Menlowe and A McCall Smith (eds), *The Duty to Rescue: The Jurisprudence of Aid* (1993) 93, which discusses the imposition of legal duties to rescue in European countries.

[259] Other examples of 'rescue' legislation can be seen in Rhode Island (Gen Laws RI, ss 11-37-3.1, 11-37-3.3 and 11-56-1), Massachusetts (Gen Laws Ann Ch 268, s 40), Minnesota (Stat Ann, ss 604.01(a), 609.02), Hawaii (Haw Rev Stat Ann, s 663–1.6) and Wisconsin (Wis Stat Ann, s 940.34 [1], [2]).

[260] 'Callous' here means with more than normal intent, which requires that 'it be proved that a person deliberately and consciously chose not to provide help or assistance': *Salmon v Chute* (1994) 115 FLR 176, Kearney J at 199. For a brief discussion of this case, see JT Pardun, 'Good Samaritan Laws: A Global Perspective' (1998) 20 Loyola LA Int'l & Comp LJ 591 at 595–6. Murphy suggests that there is a greater need for imposing upon individuals a positive requirement to assist in the Northern Territory because its terrain and climate are particularly harsh and it is sparsely populated: L Murphy, 'Beneficence, Law and Liberty: The Case of Required Rescue' (2001) 89 Georgetown LJ 605 at 659.

[261] A Ashworth, 'The Scope of Criminal Liability for Omissions' (1989) 105 LQR 424 at 432. Cf A Norrie, *Crime, Reason and History* (3rd edn, 2014) 162–8. See also EJ Weinrib, 'The Case for a Duty to Rescue' (1980) 90 Yale LJ 247 and compare J Dressler, 'Some Brief Thoughts (Mostly Negative) about Bad Samaritan Laws' (2000) 40 Santa Clara LR 971.

[262] See JT Pardun, 'Good Samaritan Laws a Global Perspective' (1997–8) 20 Loyola LA Int'l & Comp LJ 591.

since there seem to be very few prosecutions, at least in common law jurisdictions, which is not to say that they do not operate at a symbolic level in encouraging greater communitarianism.[263] More fundamentally, they are claimed to represent a more significant infringement on autonomy (being told you must do X) and impose ambiguous burdens (what to do if someone else has started to rescue?) of uncertain duration (when does the duty end?).

Despite this, the Bad Samaritan laws are numerous[264] and have an ancient pedigree.[265] It is possible to draft legislation narrowly enough to meet or outweigh the objections. In particular, it is possible to include elements of mens rea such as that in the Northern Territory's offence which requires 'callousness'.[266]

2.4.2.6 Act, omission or control?

The numerous complications which flow from the law's attempts to distinguish between acts and involuntary movement, states of affairs and omissions has prompted some academics[267] to argue that the problems can be avoided if the focus shifts to whether D had 'control' of the potential consequences of his behaviour at the relevant time.[268] Duff suggests:

A control requirement does not distinguish action from omission: whether X is an outcome of my action or an event that I could do but do not prevent, I have the same degree of control over whether X ensues, and thus can be criminally responsible on just the same basis in both cases.[269]

Adopting a focus on whether the defendant had control will, Duff claims, make 'criminal responsibility for omissions unproblematic'.[270] There are many theoretical benefits to be gained from a control approach, but the criminal law's practical response to omissions would nevertheless remain problematical in several ways.[271]

2.5 Causation

In every result crime causation is, by definition, an issue.[272] Although the issue often arises in the context of homicide, causation is important in all result crimes.[273] In many cases it is not a contentious issue because it is not disputed.[274] When it is disputed, the prosecution must prove that D, by his own act or unlawful omission, caused the relevant result.[275] Theoretical disputes abound as to whether the element of causation can be properly seen as being exclusively an element of actus reus or whether it ought also to be seen as including consideration of D's fault. Tadros argues that the causal inquiry is sensitive to both moral

---

[263] See ibid, 597.   [264] See ibid, Appendix.
[265] See ibid, 593 and references therein to similar laws in Ancient Egypt.
[269] See eg Duff, *Answering for Crime*. Cf DN Husak, *Philosophy of Criminal Law: Selected Essays* (2010) 38.
[267] *Answering for Crime*, 105.   [268] ibid, 107.   [269] ibid, 107.   [270] ibid, 107.
[271] See Elliott and Ormerod, n 255.
[272] See generally H Hart and T Honoré, *Causation in the Law* (2nd edn, 1985); A Norrie, *Crime, Reason and History* (3rd edn, 2014) Ch 7; Wilson, *Central Issues*, Ch 6.
[273] Especially in cases of strict liability where, in the absence of mens rea elements, disputes over causation become the most critical, eg in environmental offences: N Padfield, 'Clean Water and Muddy Causation' [1995] Crim LR 683.
[274] In *Kimel* [2016] EWCA Crim 1456, the Court of Appeal observed that the fact that a pathologist may be unable to identify a clear cause of death does not mean that the issue of causation could or should not be left to the jury. It was also held that if there is any suggestion that death may have been caused by the actions of some person other than D, this may need to be addressed with care in the trial judge's directions and in any route to verdict provided to the jury. See also *Broughton* [2020] EWCA Crim 1093.
[275] On the issue of causing an event through the use of an innocent agent, see p 188.

factors and to the states of mind of the defendant.[276] There is no doubt that the cases are heavily policy-laden, and it is clear that the courts are keen to avoid an unduly theoretical approach to the issue.

2.5.1 Law or fact?

A common approach of the courts has been[277] to assert that causation is a question of fact to be answered by the application of common sense. The view that it is so simple is belied by the existence of a book on causation in law of over 500 pages with a 24-page table of cases.[278] What D did and what happened are certainly questions of fact. Whether D's act caused what happened is more complicated. If that is a question of fact, it is one which is closely circumscribed by cases deciding what is incapable in law of being a cause, and what cannot reasonably be held to be a cause. Questions of fact *and law* are involved.

Whether D's act caused the result is a question that must be left to the jury but, in answering the question, they must apply legal principles, which it is the judge's duty to explain to them.[279] In one case[280] Lawton LJ said that where 'there is no conflict of evidence and all the jury has to do is to apply the law to the admitted facts, the judge is entitled to tell the jury what the result of that application will be'. Other cases,[281] however, show that the jury may have a substantial role in evaluating the primary facts, and that carries the attendant problems involved in their exercising moral judgement.

In some cases, particularly homicides, expert witnesses will play an important role. Where the question is whether the act caused a prohibited result such as certain injuries or death, the expert's function is to give the court an opinion on the medical issues. It is then for the jury to find the facts and apply the legal principles under the direction of the judge. Thus, cases such as *Jordan* (discussed in the following section) have been criticized[282] because medical experts were permitted to say that the cause of V's death was certain medical treatment, and not wounds inflicted by D.[283] Whether the wound was capable of being 'a cause', for the purpose of the decision, was a question of law, not of medicine. Certainly it was relevant and proper for the court to know if the medical treatment was effective to cause death, either in conjunction with, or independently of, the wound; and perhaps all that the witnesses intended to say was that the treatment alone was the medical cause of death.[284] This concern was again recognized by the Court of Appeal in *Broughton*.[285]

---

[276] *Criminal Responsibility*, 159. Tadros poses an example (p 179) of D stabbing V in the leg. In the first scenario D is unaware that there is a bomb nearby. It explodes killing V. D would not be liable for murder even though he stabbed with intent to kill. In the second scenario, D stabs V and leaves him, being aware that a bomb is nearby. He concludes that in this second example the bomb would not break the chain of causation because D was aware of it. The law already asks whether the explosion of the bomb was reasonably foreseeable, however.

[277] But see now the *Empress Car* case, p 73.   [278] Hart and Honoré, *Causation in the Law.*

[279] *Pagett* (1983) 76 Cr App R 279. See *The Crown Court Compendium* (2020) which provides illustrative directions.

[280] *Blaue* [1975] 3 All ER 446 at 450, p 81. In *Malcherek* [1981] 1 WLR 690, p 78, it was held that the jury were bound to conclude that D caused V's death.

[281] eg *Cheshire* [1991] 1 WLR 844, p 77.

[282] (1956) 40 Cr App R 152, p 77. See G Williams, 'Causation in Homicide' [1957] Crim LR 431 and F Camps and J Havard, 'Causation in Homicide—A Medical View' [1957] Crim LR 576.

[283] cf *Cato* [1976] 1 All ER 260 at 264, [1976] Crim LR 59, p 593 where the medical experts said it was not for them to state the cause of death; they spoke to facts, and deductions therefrom were for the jury.

[284] The medical evidence may take on an additional significance in the case of an omission. See *Sinclair* (1998) 148 NLJ 1353, and *Gowans* [2003] EWCA Crim 3935.

[285] [2020] EWCA Crim 1093.

Of course, it is not necessary in every case for the trial judge to give detailed directions on every aspect of causation set out in the following sections.[286]

2.5.2 The 'but for' principle

The first legal principle to apply is that D's act cannot be regarded as the cause of an event if the event would have occurred in the same way had D's conduct never been performed. For D to be liable, it must be proved that, *but for* D's conduct, the event would not have occurred.[287] Thus, if D poisons V's drink but V dies of natural causes before the poison has had any effect on V, D's conduct is not a 'but for' cause of V's death.[288] When deciding whether D's act was a 'but for' cause, a simple approach is to eliminate D's behaviour from the narrative and ask whether the result would have occurred anyway. If so, D is not liable. In the traditional Latin terminology, D's act must be a *sine qua non* of the prohibited consequence (eg death in murder). But this is only a starting point. There are many acts that are *sine qua non* of an event but are not, either in law or common sense, the cause of it. It is necessary to keep the test in perspective; otherwise blame could be attributed to D's ancestors!

If D invites V to dinner and V is run over and killed on the way, V would not have died but for the invitation; but as a matter of common sense, no one would say 'D killed V', and in law D has not caused his death. In *Jordan*,[289] D stabbed V inflicting a wound that was certainly a *sine qua non* of the death of V because it led directly to the badly performed medical treatment that, according to the medical experts, caused death. It did not necessarily follow that the treatment was, in law, the only cause of the death. That depended on the application of the further principles considered in the following sections. The 'but for' principle is a starting point in the causation inquiry, but nothing more.[290]

2.5.3 Contributory causes

It is clear that D's conduct need not be the sole or the main cause of the result. It is wrong to direct a jury that D is not liable if he is, for example, less than one-fifth to blame.[291] So, where D struck V who was suffering from meningitis and V died, it was enough that the death would not have been caused by the meningitis at the time when it occurred *but for* the blows (and it was immaterial that the blows would not have caused death but for the meningitis).[292] In *L*, a case concerning death by driving, the Court of Appeal, after referring to *Hennigan*, *Skelton* and *Barnes*, stated:

Those authorities establish or recognise these principles: first, the defendant's driving must have played a part not simply in creating the occasion for the fatal accident, i.e. causation in the 'but for' sense, but in bringing it about; secondly, no particular degree of contribution is required beyond a negligible one; thirdly, there may be cases in which the judge should rule that the driving is too

---

[286] See *Ogunbowale* [2007] EWCA Crim 2739. The *Crown Court Compendium* (2020) contains further guidance at Ch 7, section 9.

[287] Even this basic rule may have exceptions, but only in very unlikely circumstances, eg D and E, independently and simultaneously, shoot at V. D's bullet goes through V's heart and E's bullet blows his brains out. It seems safe to assume that both will be held to have caused V's death. Cf Hall, *General Principles*, 267.

[288] See *White* [1910] 2 KB 124; D may be liable for the attempted murder of V.

[289] Discussed in detail, p 77.

[290] This point was emphasized in unequivocal terms by the Supreme Court in *Hughes* [2013] UKSC 56 and reaffirmed in *Taylor* [2016] UKSC 5.

[291] *Hennigan* [1971] 3 All ER 133. And see *Williams* [2010] EWCA Crim 2552, [2011] Crim LR 471 and commentary.

[292] *Dyson* [1908] 2 KB 454.

remote from the later event to have been the cause of it, and should accordingly withdraw the case from the jury.[293]

The principles are equally applicable beyond the context of road traffic offences.

Contributory causes may be the acts or omissions of others, including the conduct of the deceased himself. The contributory negligence of the claimant in civil actions of negligence was an absolute defence at common law, but no such principle applied in the criminal law. In *Swindall and Osborne*,[294] where one or other of the two accused ran over and killed an old man, Pollock CB directed the jury that it was immaterial that the victim was deaf or drunk or negligent and contributed to his own death. One or other of the two accused was a cause of death and, on the evidence, the other was an accessory.

An example of a case in which third parties contributed to V's death is *Benge*.[295] D, a foreman, was employed to take up a certain section of railway line. He misread the timetable and as a result the repairs to the line meant there was no track in place and a train crashed causing deaths. D had placed a man with a flag to warn oncoming trains but had ordered the flagman to go to a distance of only 540 yards, instead of 1,000 yards as required by the company's regulations. D also entirely omitted to place fog signals, although the regulations specified that these should be put at 250-yard intervals for a distance of 1,000 yards. At D's trial for manslaughter it was urged that, in spite of his mistakes, the accident could not have happened if the other servants of the company had done their duty—if the flagman had gone the proper distance or if the engine driver had been keeping a proper look-out, which he was not. Pigott B ruled that this was no defence; if D's negligence mainly or substantially caused the accident, it was irrelevant that it might have been avoided if other persons had not been negligent.

In *Warburton and Hubbersty*,[296] the Court of Appeal rejected a submission that 'where a person has died from a number of injuries caused by different people and the defendant has caused (or been a party to causing) only injuries "A", then the defendant would not have caused the death unless the jury were sure that the deceased would have died from injuries "A" on their own'. Hooper LJ, delivering the judgment of the court, emphasized that 'the test for the jury is a simple one: did the acts for which the defendant is responsible *significantly contribute* to the victim's death'.

2.5.4 Connection between fault and result

The proscribed result is not attributable to D if the *culpable element* in his conduct in no way made a relevant contribution to the result. This is a difficult principle that is often misunderstood. A good illustration of its operation is in *Dalloway*.[297] D was driving a cart on a highway with reins not in his hands but loose on the horse's back. A three-year-old child ran into the road a few yards in front of the horse and was killed. Erle J directed the jury that, if D had reins and by using the reins could have saved the child, he was guilty of manslaughter; but that, if they thought D could not have saved the child by the use of the reins, then they should acquit him. If D had not been driving the cart at all the incident could not have occurred, and in that sense, he 'caused' it; but it was necessary to go further and show that the death was due to the culpable element in his conduct—his negligence in not using the reins.[298]

---

[293] [2010] EWCA Crim 1249, [9]. See also *Jenkins* [2012] EWCA Crim 2909.

[294] (1846) 2 Car & Kir 230. *Ledger* (1862) 2 F & F 857 is contrary but was regarded by Stephen J as 'a very peculiar case': *Digest*, 161 fn 4.

[295] (1865) 4 F & F 504. See also *Walker* (1824) 1 C & P 320 (Garrow B).

[296] [2006] EWCA Crim 627.

[297] (1847) 2 Cox CC 273, cf *Marsh* [1997] 1 Cr App R 67, [1997] Crim LR 205.

[298] cf the discussion of *Clarke* (1990) 91 Cr App R 69.

In *Williams*,[299] W was convicted of the draconian offence of causing death by driving without insurance and without a licence contrary to s 3ZB of the Road Traffic Act 1988. W drove his car without a driving licence or insurance. V crossed a dual-carriageway and stepped out in front of W's car. W argued that he could not avoid the accident. The Court of Appeal held that W's driving was 'a cause' if it was 'more than negligible or de minimis'. The court rejected the value of applying *Dalloway*. It is respectfully submitted that the case does assist. *Dalloway* serves as a reminder that the causation analysis must focus on the relevant act—which act is it alleged is the cause of the death? In *Dalloway* it was the negligent driving by misuse of the reins. In *Williams* it is submitted that the statute makes clear that it is the act of 'driving', not the existence of the car on the road. There has to be a causal link between the *driving* and not just the fact that the car was on the road at the time of the death. The Court of Appeal's interpretation focused only on the link between the fact of the vehicle being on the road and the death. The statutory wording is not limited to that fact, but requires that the act of 'driving' causes the death. Consider a truly extreme case of a suicidal person jumping from a high motorway bridge and landing on D's uninsured car. Has D's *driving* caused V's death? V's death would have arisen if he had hit V's stationary car or the road. D's *driving* is not a cause of death.

In *Hughes*,[300] the Supreme Court overruled *Williams*. Lords Hughes and Toulson emphasized that s 3ZB is not only a penal provision, but is one that creates a homicide offence. For that reason, it had to be construed in a way favourable to the defendant. It was held, therefore, that to be guilty of the offence in s 3ZB it was not enough for D simply to put his car on the road for it to be struck. It was necessary for the Crown to prove that there was something that D did or omitted to do *by way of driving* it that contributed in a more than minimal way to the death. Their lordships emphasized that the Crown does not need to prove that D's driving is careless or inconsiderate, but there must be 'something open to proper criticism in the driving of the defendant, beyond the mere presence of the vehicle on the road, and which contributed in some more than minimal way to the death'. In *Taylor*, the Supreme Court upheld in emphatic terms the approach adopted in *Hughes*.[301] Delivering the judgment of a unanimous seven-member Supreme Court, Lord Sumption held that, for the purposes of aggravated vehicle-taking, there must have been some act or omission in the control of the car, which involved some element of fault, and which contributed in some more than minimal way to the death of V. The approach adopted in *Hughes* has been criticized on the basis that it demonstrates an under-appreciation of the core, physical, dimension of causation.[302]

2.5.5 Negligible causes

It is sometimes said[303] that D's conduct must be a 'substantial' cause, but the use of the word is misleading and seems to mean only that D's contribution must be more than negligible or not be so minute that it will be ignored under the '*de minimis*' principle.[304]

It may, therefore, be misleading to direct a jury that D is not liable unless his conduct was a 'substantial' cause, but that is not the same as saying that D is always liable, no matter how

---

[299] [2010] EWCA Crim 2552, [2011] Crim LR 471 and commentary. For criticism, see GR Sullivan and AP Simester, 'Causation Without Limits: Causing Death While Driving Without a Licence, While Disqualified, or Without Insurance' [2012] Crim LR 753. See also *Carey* [2006] EWCA Crim 17 discussed in Ch 14.

[300] [2013] UKSC 56.

[301] [2016] UKSC 5. For discussion, see K Laird, 'The Decline of Criminal Law Causation Without Limits' (2016) 132 LQR 566.

[302] AP Simester, 'Causation in (Criminal) Law' (2017) 133 LQR 416.

[303] See eg *Benge*, discussed earlier; *Smith* [1959] 2 QB 35 at 42–3 (p 78); Hall, *General Principles*, 283; Perkins (1946) 36 J Crim Law & Crimin at 393, and *Criminal Law*, 606–7.

[304] *Cato* [1976] 1 All ER 260 at 265–6; 'it need hardly be added that [that cause] need not be substantial to render the accused guilty': *Malcherek* [1981] 2 All ER 422 at 428. But note that there is no defence of *de minimis* per se in English criminal law: *Scott* [2007] EWCA Crim 2757 (D 30 minutes late in answering bail).

trivial his contribution to the outcome.[305] For example, D and V are roped mountaineers. V has fallen over a 1,000-foot precipice and is dragging D slowly after him. D cuts the rope and V falls to his death five seconds before both V and D would have fallen. Any acceleration of death is killing but factors that produce a very trivial acceleration may be ignored. D's act is not a cause of V's death because it is merely *de minimis*. Similarly, where two persons independently inflict wounds on V:

suppose one wound severed the jugular vein whereas the other barely broke the skin of the hand, and as the life blood gushed from the victim's neck, one drop oozed from the bruise on his finger ... metaphysicians will conclude that the extra drop of lost blood hastened the end by the infinitesimal fraction of a second. But the law will apply the *substantial factor* test and for juridical purposes the death will be imputed only to the severe injury in such an extreme case as this.[306]

These are, perhaps, rather unlikely examples but the principle would apply, for example, to a person visiting a dying man and contributing to his exhaustion by talking with him; and probably to the administration of pain-killing drugs which accelerate death.[307] In the context of homicide, the problems raise controversial questions of science, law and morality as to the degree of acceleration of death that needs to be established to constitute a cause of death.[308] The Court of Appeal has made clear in *Broughton* that, in the words of Lord Burnett CJ:

The prosecution must prove to the criminal standard that the [defendant's culpable conduct] was at least a substantial contributory cause of death. That means that the prosecution must prove that the deceased would have lived in the sense that life would have been significantly prolonged. It is well established that being 'sure' is not the same as scientific certainty.[309]

The problem of an intervening cause, which is discussed in the following section,[310] is sometimes put on the basis of substantial cause. Thus, Hall writes:

For example, a slight wound may have necessitated going to a doctor or drugstore, and *en route* the slightly injured person was struck by an automobile or shot by his mortal enemy. The slight wound, though a necessary condition of the death, did not contribute substantially to it.[311]

In *Williams*,[312] the court emphasized that the judge must explain to the jury what is meant by 'cause'. A simple reference to 'significant' or 'substantial' might be insufficient, as the terms could easily be misunderstood.

2.5.6 Intervening acts or events

Although D's culpable conduct is a factual (but for) and more than *de minimis* cause of the prohibited result, he is not necessarily legally responsible for it on that basis alone. If there is an intervening event (act or omission) either as a naturally occurring phenomenon or

---

[305] *Hennigan*, n 290. Something more than a 'slight or trifling link' is required: *Kimsey* [1996] Crim LR 35. See also eg *Fitzgerald* [2006] EWCA Crim 1655.

[306] R Perkins and R Boyce, *Criminal Law* (3rd edn, 1982) 779. But cf *Garforth* [1954] Crim LR 936.

[307] See n 308.

[308] Numerous high-profile cases involved doctors who have 'eased the passing' of a terminally ill patient. Examples include: *Cox* (1992) 12 BMLR 38 (see Editorial, 'Hard Cases Make Bad Law: Mercy Killing and Dr Cox' (1992) 142 NLJ 1293) and *Adams*, H Palmer, 'Dr Adams' Trial for Murder' [1957] Crim LR 365. There was considerable comment following the case of David Moor: see A Arlidge, 'The Trial of Dr David Moor' [2000] Crim LR 31; JC Smith, 'A Comment on *Moor's Case*' [2000] Crim LR 41 and also J Goss, 'A Postscript to the Trial of Dr David Moor' [2000] Crim LR 568. The trial judge, Hooper J, was prepared to leave the question of unlawfulness to the jury—if the act was proper treatment for the illness and pain management, it would be lawful even if the effect was fatal.

[309] At [23].   [310] See later.   [311] Hall, *General Principles*, 283, 393.

[312] See n 403; see also *Barnes* [2008] EWCA Crim 2726.

by some human conduct, it may operate to 'break the chain of causation', precluding D's liability for the ultimate result although D may remain liable for an attempt in many cases. The Supreme Court of Canada has framed the issue in the following terms: 'Any assessment of legal causation should maintain focus on whether the accused should be held legally responsible for the consequences of his actions, or whether holding the accused responsible for the death would amount to punishing a moral innocent.'[313]

If, despite the intervening events, D's conduct remains a 'substantial and operative cause' of the result, D will remain responsible (and if the intervention is by another person, that actor may also become liable in such circumstances but that is a matter for a separate criminal investigation distinct from the question whether D is liable). Subject to this, and some exceptional cases, the principles appear to be as follows.

(1) D will remain liable if *his* subsequent act is part of the same transaction perpetrated by D. For example, D stabs V and then shoots him. D remains liable.

(2) D will not be liable if a natural event which is extraordinary, not foreseen by D or not *reasonably foreseeable*, supervenes and renders D's contribution merely part of the background.

(3) In relation to third party interventions, D will not be liable if a third party's intervening act is either:

 (a) one of a *free, deliberate and informed nature* (whether reasonably foreseeable or not);[314]

 (b) if not a free, deliberate informed act, one which was not reasonably foreseeable.

(4) D will not be liable if a medical professional intervenes to treat injuries inflicted by D and the treatment is so *independent* of D's conduct[315] and *so potent* as to render D's contribution part of the history and not a substantial and operating cause of death. The jury must remain focused on whether D remains liable, not whether the medical professional's conduct ought to render him criminally liable for his part. Even where incorrect treatment leads to death or more serious injury, it will only break the chain of causation if it is (a) unforeseeably bad, and (b) the sole significant cause of the death (or more serious injury) with which D is charged.

(5) In relation to victims:

 (a) D *will* be liable if the victim has a pre-existing condition rendering him unusually vulnerable to physical injury (which includes, after *Blaue*, a religious belief); D must accept liability for any unusually serious consequences which result: *Hayward*;[316] *Blaue*.[317]

 (b) D *will not* be liable if the victim's subsequent conduct in response to D's act is not within a range of responses that could be regarded as reasonable and foreseeable in the circumstances. Was V's act so daft as to be wholly disproportionate to D's act? If so, it will break the chain.

313 *Maybin* [2012] 2 SCC 24, [29].
314 This includes acts instinctively done for self-preservation and acts of an involuntary nature by the third party. Cf *Empress Car* [1999] 2 AC 22, in the case of a strict liability environmental offence only if the intervening act was extraordinary would it break causation.
315 Although usually an act, it can be an omission to act. In *McKechnie* (1992) 94 Cr App R 51, [1992] Crim LR 194 where doctors discovered that V had an ulcer but decided that it would be too dangerous to operate because V was still unconscious from D's beating. V died as a result of the ulcer bursting: 'The Recorder's statement of the question of the intervening events—the doctor's decision not to operate on the duodenal ulcer because [V's] head injuries made such an operation dangerous—properly directed the jury, not to the correctness of the medical decision, but to its reasonableness', at 58 per Auld J.
316 (1908) 21 Cox CC 692.   317 [1975] 1 WLR 1411.

In summary, in a homicide case D, who did what would have been a fatal act but for some independent intervention, is not responsible where the intervening independent act or unforeseen event is the immediate and sufficient cause of death. For example, D administers poison to V but, before it takes any effect on V's body, V is struck by lightning, shot dead by a burglar or dies of a heart attack not induced by the poison. In such cases, D may be guilty of attempted murder, but he cannot be convicted of murder.

The courts have struggled to produce a clear approach in this complex area. This problem is exacerbated by the diversity of factual circumstances in which such interventions arise, thereby encouraging the courts to distinguish cases too readily. Decisions have also been heavily influenced by policy considerations and this is illustrated by the willingness to conclude, for example, that interventions do not break the chain of causation where the intervention is by a health-care professional. The courts have also adopted rather loose language in determining whether intervening events 'break the chain of causation', often resorting simply to the use of that metaphor. The best that can be offered by way of guidance is an examination of this series of principles, some of which are openly in conflict.

2.5.6.1 D's subsequent conduct

Where D has performed the conduct element of the offence a subsequent act by him will not break the chain of causation so as to excuse him where that subsequent act is part of the same transaction.[318] The earlier example is a clear one: D stabs V and then shoots him before V has died from the wound. The position is different if the act which causes the proscribed result for the crime (eg death) is part of a completely different transaction from D's original act. For example D, having wounded V, visits him in hospital and accidentally infects him with smallpox of which he dies.[319] D is not liable for V's death.

2.5.6.2 Naturally occurring interventions

The accepted principle in relation to naturally occurring events is illustrated by the examples given by the academic Perkins:[320]

if one man knocks down another and goes away leaving his victim not seriously hurt[321] but unconscious, on the floor of a building in which the assault occurred, and before the victim recovers consciousness he is killed in the fall of the building which is shaken down by a sudden earthquake, this is not homicide. The law attributes such a death to the 'Act of God' and not to the assault, even if it may be certain that the deceased would not have been in the building at the time of the earthquake, had he not been rendered unconscious. The blow was the occasion of the man's being there, but the blow was not the cause of the earthquake, nor was the deceased left in a position of obvious danger. On the other hand if the blow had been struck on the seashore, and the assailant had left his victim in imminent peril of an incoming tide which drowned him before consciousness returned, it would be homicide.[322]

In the second example, V's being drowned was a 'natural' consequence of D's action—that is, a consequence which might be expected to occur in the normal course of events. It was foreseeable as likely to occur in the normal course of events.[323] There is no break in the chain of causation by this naturally occurring intervening act and D remains liable for the result if the prosecution

---

318 See p 69; Russell, 53–60, where the cases are set out; Williams, CLGP, 65; Hart and Honoré, *Causation in the Law*, 333.

319 This paragraph was cited by the court in *Le Brun* (1991) 94 Cr App R 101.

320 (1946) 36 J Crim Law & Crimin at 393.

321 The result would appear to be the same if he were seriously hurt.

322 cf *Hallett* [1969] SASR 141, where the court followed this passage in relation to similar facts.

323 The courts use these terms interchangeably, but there is a difference. Not all naturally occurring events are foreseeable. In *Empress Car*, Lord Hoffmann used the term 'extraordinary' events rather than unforeseeable events in this context.

have established factual and legal causation as discussed earlier. In contrast, in the first example, V's being killed by the falling building was an abnormal and unforeseeable consequence. The act or event was not the natural consequence of D's act. This is sufficient to break the chain of causation. D may be liable for an attempted murder or some relevant offence against the person. D may also be liable if he has personally seen the risk of the high tide (because of specialist knowledge) even though it is not reasonably forseeeable.

2.5.6.3 Third party interventions

Several categories of actor need to be considered.

Innocent agent

Where D knowingly employs an innocent agent[324]—for example, a person who is under the age of criminal responsibility, or insane or merely someone without mens rea—to commit an offence, D, in law, causes the result, though the immediate cause is the innocent agent.

Involuntariness

A truly involuntary act clearly does not break the chain: D so startles E that E involuntarily drops a weight he is carrying which causes damage to V's property. There is no true intervening 'act' and D has caused the damage.

Justified and excused responses to D's act

The principles applicable to involuntary actors have been extended beyond innocent agency, and beyond what might naturally be regarded as 'involuntariness'. It is clear that human intervention, where it consists in a foreseeable act instinctively done for the purposes of self-preservation, or in the execution of a legal duty, does not break the chain of causation. In the case of *Pagett*,[325] D, to resist lawful arrest, held a girl in front of him as a shield and shot at armed police officers. The police 'instinctively'[326] fired back and killed the girl. D was held to have caused her death and to be guilty of manslaughter.[327] Though the court regarded the officer's instinctive act as 'involuntary', they also held that neither a reasonable act of self-defence nor an act done in the execution of a duty to prevent crime or arrest an offender, using such force as is reasonable in the circumstances, will break the chain of causation. It is not clear that such acts of self-defence or in the prevention of crime are necessarily in the same class as a truly 'involuntary' act. Moreover, it cannot be 'reasonable' for anyone intentionally to kill V, an *innocent* person, in order to save his own life[328] or to arrest X; and whether it is reasonable for him to take a risk of killing V must be doubtful. *Pagett* does not deal with the case where the officer's intervening act is unlawful. If it is, it does not necessarily follow that D's act is not a cause of death. There may be two unlawful causes.

The same principles should apply in determining whether in a *Pagett*-like case the killing of an innocent bystander, or another policeman, by police bullets should be taken to be caused by D. It is obvious that in such a case the police firearms officer causes death[329] but, if the officer's shot was a reasonable act of self-defence then he has no liability; as far as the officer is concerned he has not unlawfully caused a death.[330]

---

[324] See p 188.   [325] (1983) 76 Cr App R 279.

[326] Is not the purpose of firearms training to avoid acts of an 'instinctive' nature such as this?

[327] Since the jury acquitted of murder, it must be taken that they were not satisfied D had the necessary mens rea as was then defined in *Hyam* [1975] AC 55—that he knew it was highly probable that the girl would suffer death or grievous bodily harm.

[328] *Dudley and Stephens* (1884) 14 QBD 273, p 392; *Howe* [1987] AC 417. Cf commentary on *Pagett* [1983] Crim LR 394.

[329] cf *Malcherek* [1981] 1 WLR 690, [1981] Crim LR 401, p 78.

[330] The court said that its comments were confined to homicide: but the same principles must surely apply to non-fatal offences.

Third party act which is not free, deliberate, informed, but is reasonably foreseeable

If the third party human intervention is not a free, deliberate and informed one, but is reasonably foreseeable, the third party will not break the chain and D will have caused the result.[331] The challenge in such cases is in identifying what it is that must be foreseeable and with what precision. In *Maybin*,[332] the Supreme Court of Canada considered what exactly needs to have been reasonably foreseeable and held that:

it is the general nature of the intervening acts and the accompanying risk of harm that needs to be reasonably foreseeable. Legal causation does not require that the accused must objectively foresee the precise future consequences of their conduct. Nor does it assist in addressing moral culpability to require merely that the risk of some non-trivial bodily harm is reasonably foreseeable. Rather, the intervening acts and the ensuing non-trivial harm must be reasonably foreseeable in the sense that the acts and the harm that actually transpired flowed reasonably from the conduct of the appellants. If so, then the accused's actions may remain a significant contributing cause of death.

In *Girdler*,[333] D had driven dangerously. D shunted the car driven by V into the path of oncoming traffic. V's car was avoided by most oncoming traffic but not by C. She drove into V killing him and herself. D was charged with causing both their deaths by dangerous driving. The Court of Appeal quashed the convictions after concluding that the trial judge's direction did not give sufficient assistance to the jury. The court concluded that if the immediate cause of the death of V was the 'free, deliberate, and informed' intervention of C then the chain of causation would be broken, but that there were problems in applying that test in this case. C's driving which led to the collision with V could not readily be described as falling within that category even if her driving was careless or dangerous. The court went on to recognize that a test based on reasonable foreseeability was applicable, but doubted whether directing a jury with those words would be apt. The court preferred a simpler expression of the concept:

a jury could be told, in circumstances like the present where the immediate cause of death is a second collision, that if they were sure that the defendant drove dangerously and were sure that his dangerous driving was more than a slight or trifling link to the death(s) then: *the defendant will have caused the death(s) only if you are sure that it could sensibly have been anticipated that a fatal collision might occur in the circumstances in which the second collision did occur.*

Doubt was cast on that aspect of the decision in *Girdler* in the recent case of *A*.[334] The defendant was charged with causing death by dangerous driving and causing serious injury by dangerous driving. She had been out one evening with some friends and was the designated driver. She stopped the car on the hard shoulder of the motorway at 4.30 am because her drunken passengers were irritating her. D opened the car door and did not activate the hazard lights and nor were any other lights visible on the car. One driver in the inside lane of the motorway had to swerve to avoid the door. He sounded the horn and the car door was then closed. Subsequently, X, who was driving a truck in the outside lane of the motorway, was seen to swerve across the other lanes and onto the hard shoulder. The truck struck the defendant's car. It was assumed X had fallen asleep. One of the defendant's passengers died as a result of the collision. The defendant and another passenger suffered serious injury. The trial judge

---

331 At [38]. D's conviction for manslaughter was upheld on the basis that when he got into a fight with V, physical intervention by the bar staff, with its risk of non-trivial harm, was objectively foreseeable. That sufficed to ground D's liability, as the specific details of that intervention did not need to be foreseen. That a member of the bar staff struck V on the back of the head with significant force was therefore insufficient to break the chain of causation.

332 [2012] 2 SCR 30.   333 [2009] EWCA Crim 2666.

334 [2020] EWCA Crim 407, citing the 15th edition of this book on this point.

acceded to a submission of no case and stopped the trial. The test the judge applied was to ask whether a properly directed jury could conclude that it was <u>reasonably foreseeable</u> that a third party (X)—at 4.30 am on a Saturday morning when the traffic was very light—would be so distracted by tiredness <u>or some other prevailing condition that he would</u> suddenly at high speed <u>career across all three lanes of the motorway and onto the hard shoul</u>der, coming to his senses too late to avoid colliding with defendant's car. The prosecution appealed.

The Court of Appeal upheld that appeal and ordered a retrial. The court held that the trial judge had adopted too narrow and specific a test. The Court of Appeal held that it would not be necessary for the jury to be sure that the particular circumstances of the collision or 'the exact form' of the subsequent act was reasonably foreseeable.

Third party voluntary actors

If the intervening event between D's conduct and V's death comprises the conduct of a third party acting in a 'fully voluntary' manner, the position should be straightforward. As Glanville Williams put it:

What a person does (if he has reached adult years, is of sound mind and is not acting under mistake, intimidation or similar pressure) is his own responsibility and is not regarded as having been caused by other people. An intervening act of this kind, therefore, breaks the causal connection that would otherwise have been perceived between previous acts and the forbidden consequence.[335]

So, in a homicide case, the 'free, deliberate and informed' intervention by a third party has been held to have the effect of relieving D of criminal responsibility.[336] As a matter of principle, this seems right since the voluntary actor has chosen his course of action which leads to a prohibited result, and on orthodox principles of criminal liability he is liable for his voluntary actions which are now the immediate cause.

In *Latif*,[337] British customs officers in Pakistan intercepted heroin which D intended to import into England. The officers brought it to England where D took delivery. It was held that D was not guilty of being concerned in the fraudulent evasion of the prohibition on importation because this had been effected by the 'free, deliberate and informed act' of the officers, exploiting the situation created by, but not acting in concert with, D. This broke the chain of causation. This can be contrasted with non-intentional intervening acts, for example a failure by an employer to establish a safe system of work may remain a legal cause of death although the fatal accident would not have occurred but for the inadvertent, probably negligent, act of an employee operating the system.[338]

This is a fundamental principle, but one that has given rise to difficulty in two categories of case that can be examined in more detail.

Empress Car

In the *Empress Car* case,[339] D Ltd was held by the House of Lords to have caused the pollution of a river by bringing oil on to a site and failing to take precautions against the ever-present and foreseeable possibility that someone would release the oil into the river. The escape may have been caused by the fully voluntary act of a stranger, but it was also, in the opinion of the House, caused by the company. In reaching this conclusion, Lord Hoffmann appears to confuse culpability with causation.[340] A householder may be blameworthy for

---

[335] TBCL, 391. See, to the same effect, Hart and Honoré, *Causation in the Law*, 364–5.

[336] *Pagett* (1983) 76 Cr App R 279, 339.

[337] [1996] 2 Cr App R 92.   [338] *R v DPP, ex p Jones* [2000] Crim LR 858.

[339] *Environmental Agency (formerly National Rivers Authority) v Empress Car Co (Abertillery) Ltd* [1998] 1 All ER 481.

[340] See his example of the irate wife at [1998] 1 All ER 487a–c.

forgetting to lock his door and set the burglar alarm at night but he could hardly be said to have 'caused' an ensuing burglary, though it would not have occurred if he had taken the proper precautions.[341] He may have been a factual cause, but as noted earlier with the example of the dinner invitation, that can never be enough to found liability in law. Lord Hoffmann put the case of a factory owner who carelessly leaves a drum containing highly inflammable vapour in a place where it could easily be accidentally ignited. He thought the owner would have caused an explosion if it occurred when a workman threw in a cigarette butt, believing the drum to be empty, but he would not have done so if a person knowing exactly what the drum contained, had thrown in a lighted match. In the former case, the workman's act is not fully voluntary because he is making a fundamental mistake of fact; he is not acting with all the relevant information. In the latter case, the act is fully voluntary—and it appears to be indistinguishable from the actual facts of the *Empress Car* case. Lord Hoffmann concludes, it is submitted rightly, that, in the latter case, the carelessness of the owner had merely provided the person with an opportunity to do what he did—which appears to be equally true of the Empress Car Co Ltd. In suggesting that the chain of causation would be broken by the trespasser's act if it were an extraordinary one, but not merely by its being a free, voluntary and informed act, his lordship seems to confuse the principles dealing with natural interventions and those with third party human interventions.

The principal authority relied on was that from the law of tort—Lord Hoffmann cited *Stansbie v Troman*.[342] In that case a decorator, left in charge of a house, went out to buy wallpaper, leaving the door open. He was held liable in negligence for an ensuing theft. Hart and Honoré[343] cite, along with *Stansbie v Troman*, an American case in which it was held that a railway company would be liable if a girl they put down at nightfall in a dangerous area were raped. That may be true for the law of tort, but clearly, the railway or its officials could not be *criminally* liable for rape.

Empress ought to be regarded as an aberrant authority. On a charitable view, it might be explained on its own facts by the House of Lords being too heavily influenced by the policy of protecting the environment. In such cases, the original actor has control of the potentially hazardous product and is under a duty to protect against environmental harm. Fortunately, the House of Lords confirmed in *Kennedy (No 2)*[344] that the extreme interpretation of the principles as set down in *Empress* is applicable in relation to offences of pollution and is not of general application throughout the criminal law. The Court of Appeal decisions which had sought to apply *Empress* to, for example, manslaughter, were overruled.[345]

Lord Hoffmann further recognized in *Empress* that common sense is not a sufficient guide to resolving causation issues, and that legal principles are involved. This is valuable, but the guidance offered may be baffling to the courts. Causation, it appears, is a variable concept. According to Lord Hoffmann, the answer to the causation question requires the court to ascertain the purpose and scope of the rule alleged to have been broken; and 'Not only may there be different answers to questions about causation when attributing responsibility to different people under different rules . . . but there may be different answers when attributing responsibility to different people under the same rule.' This suggests that the principles of causation have, in this narrow category of pollution and environmental offences, become merely a matter of fact to be determined on a case-by-case basis.[346]

---

[341] As we saw earlier, it may be accurate to describe the householder as *a* cause where he has a duty to lock up, p 65.

[342] [1948] 2 KB 48.   [343] See n 335.   [344] [2007] UKHL 38.

[345] *Finlay* [2003] EWCA Crim 3868 was the most striking example.

[346] This might reflect Lord Hoffmann's preference for issues to be left for jury determination in the criminal trial.

In *Natural England v Day*,[347] the Court of Appeal declined the opportunity to address the continued validity of the approach in *Empress*. The court noted that there were strong arguments for following the *Empress Car* approach if the issue ever arose on the facts of any properly developed appeal.

Drug administration cases

The principle that a fully voluntary act breaks the chain of causation was overlooked, ignored and circumvented in a series of cases dealing with drug administration. The problem in these cases is simple to state. V self-injects what turns out to be a fatal overdose of drugs. D has either: supplied the drugs, made up the syringe, assisted by holding the tourniquet for V to find an injection site or otherwise encouraged V's self-injection. In what circumstances is D liable for manslaughter of V? On a charge of unlawful act manslaughter, requiring proof of an unlawful, intentional and dangerous act causing death (see Ch 14), the sticking point is in establishing causation. On orthodox principles of causation, V's free, voluntary, deliberate informed act by self-injecting should break the chain of causation. As Glanville Williams explained:

The new intervening act (*novus actus interveniens*) of a responsible actor, who had full knowledge of what he is doing, and is not subject to mistake or pressure, will normally operate to relieve the defendant of liability for a further consequence, because it makes the consequence too remote . . . What a person does (if he has reached adult years, is of sound mind and is not acting under mistake, intimidation or other similar pressure) is his own responsibility, and is not regarded as having been caused by other people.[348]

The Court of Appeal adopted a confused approach to these cases in *Kennedy*, *Dias*, *Richards*,[349] *Rogers*[350] and *Finlay*.[351] In *Kennedy (No 2)*,[352] the conclusion was that 'if [D] either caused [V] to administer the drug or was acting jointly with the deceased in administering the drug, [D] would be acting in concert with [V] and there would be no breach in the chain of causation'. The jury is entitled to convict if it finds that the actions of D and V are a 'combined operation'. The conclusion was heavily criticized.[353] The Court of Appeal certified the following question of general public importance:

When is it appropriate to find someone guilty of manslaughter where that person has been involved in the supply of a class A controlled drug, which is then freely and voluntarily self-administered by the person to whom it was supplied, and the administration of the drug then causes his death?

The House of Lords, in a clear and concise unanimous judgment delivered by Lord Bingham, provided an unequivocal and welcome answer to the certified question. D who supplies drugs for V to self-inject can *never* be guilty of unlawful act manslaughter if V is a fully informed adult making a voluntary decision to self-inject. The House emphasized that the criminal law generally assumed the existence of free will; a defendant was not to be treated as causing an adult of sound mind to act in a certain way if the latter made a voluntary and informed

---

[347] [2014] EWCA Crim 2683.
[348] TBCL, 391.   [348] [2002] EWCA Crim 3175.   [350] [2003] EWCA Crim 945.
[351] [2003] EWCA Crim 3868.   [352] [2005] EWCA Crim 685.
[353] See D Ormerod and R Fortson, 'Drug Suppliers as Manslaughterers (Again)' [2005] Crim LR 819. For a defence of manslaughter charges in this scenario and proposals for a specific offence to achieve that, see T Jones, 'Causation, Homicide and the Supply of Drugs' (2006) 26 LS 139, and see L Cherkassky (2008) 72 J Crim L 387.

decision to act in that way.[354] The heroin was 'freely and voluntarily self-administered' by V who chose to inject himself knowing what he was doing. The House of Lords went further and overruled *Rogers*,[355] where D had provided the drugs for V and had held the tourniquet for V as V freely and voluntarily injected himself with what turned out to be a lethal dose of heroin.[356] The House also overruled *Finlay*,[357] where the Court of Appeal held that the question of whether V's act broke the chain of causation was one of fact for the jury and, following *Empress*, involved the assessment of whether V's act was extraordinary.

Norrie argues that while it may be right from a moral, political and policy point of view to restrict the scope of causation based on the principle enunciated in *Kennedy (No 2)*, he questions whether the principle is as compelling as Lord Bingham suggests.[358] When presented with a loaded syringe, Norrie suggests that it is reasonable to expect a drug addict to inject and questions whether the idea of joint, concerted action is really so implausible. He suggests that there are defensible moral grounds for culpability in drug supply cases. He states that these conflict with the idea that V's final act of pushing the plunger represents an instance of irreducible human agency. Depending upon how one contextualizes or decontextualizes this final act, Norrie argues that the outcome of *Kennedy (No 2)* could have gone either way. Norrie's ultimate point is that the principle Lord Bingham placed such reliance upon is malleable and he suggests that it may have been deployed to achieve moral and policy outcomes of which the House of Lords approved. It is submitted that while there is merit in much of what Norrie claims, the decision in *Kennedy (No 2)* is nevertheless a welcome one for its reaffirmation of the orthodox approach to causation.

In *Burgess*,[359] the Court of Appeal subsequently suggested that had the matter fallen for consideration (on the facts D had pleaded on a basis that could not stand in the light of *Kennedy*), D raising the vein for V to self-inject would suffice for a manslaughter conviction. It was held that 'if a defendant may be convicted on the basis that the fatal dose was jointly administered then it follows that he is not automatically entitled to be acquitted if the deceased rather than the defendant physically operated the plunger'.[360] There is obviously a difficult borderline between contributory acts which might properly be regarded as administering a noxious thing and acts which might not. The evidence is likely to be disputed—one participant is dead and the other, the defendant, commonly heavily intoxicated. *Burgess* might therefore serve as an example falling just the other side of the line from *Rogers*. Whether the necessary proximity existed between the actions of D and V is for the

---

[354] The Supreme Court endorsed the principle enunciated in *Kennedy (No 2)* in *Hughes* [2013] UKSC 56. In that case, however, it was held that the principle stated by the House of Lords was not applicable. The Supreme Court held that the fact that V drove whilst under the influence of drugs did not break the chain of causation connecting D's driving to V's death. The Supreme Court distinguished *Kennedy (No 2)* in *Hughes* on the basis that V did not deliberately set out to kill himself. At first glance this may seem confusing, as the victim in *Kennedy (No 2)* did not set out to kill himself either. As a number of commentators have explained, however, the basis for distinguishing the two cases lies in the fact that *Kennedy (No 2)* concerned liability for unlawful act manslaughter. The issue in that case was whether D caused V to inject heroin, whereas the issue in *Hughes* was whether D's driving caused V's death. See Ormerod [2014] Crim LR 234; AP Simester and GR Sullivan (2014) 73 CLJ 14. Norrie suggests that a dangerous and thoughtless act can break the chain of causation and questions whether the Supreme Court ought to have distinguished *Kennedy (No 2)*. See A Norrie, *Crime, Reason and History* (3rd edn, 2014) Ch 7 fn 13.

[355] [2003] EWCA Crim 945.

[356] It is submitted that there will be few of the imaginable 'factual scenarios', aside from where D injects V, in which D can be said to be administering.

[357] [2003] EWCA Crim 3868. D was found to have 'caused to be administered'.

[358] A Norrie, *Crime, Reason and History* (3rd edn, 2014) 183–5.

[359] [2008] EWCA Crim 516. See Hughes (2008) 72 J Crim L 516. See also *Keen* [2008] EWCA Crim 1000.

[360] At [12].

jury to determine. Liability for manslaughter will exist where D has provided the drugs to V whose act of self-administration was not free and voluntary and probably also where V is a child.

The House of Lords in *Kennedy (No 2)* emphasized that nothing it had said cast doubt on liability for gross negligence manslaughter in such cases and the Court of Appeal in *Evans*[361] has confirmed that convictions for that offence can be secured although not for supply alone.[362]

2.5.6.4 Medical interventions

Largely for reasons of policy, the courts have adopted a particularly strict approach in cases where the alleged break in the chain of causation involves the conduct[363] of medical professionals. These are third parties who are intervening in a fully informed manner (although not fully voluntarily since they are under a duty to act[364]), but whose conduct is generally insufficient to break the chain of causation in this context.

Before the advent of a rigorous science of forensic pathology, it was less easy to establish causes of death. The nineteenth-century cases held that, where the immediate cause of death was the medical treatment received by V consequent upon his injury by D, D was guilty of homicide, whether the treatment was proper or improper, negligent or not. If the treatment was given bona fide by competent medical officers, evidence was not admissible to show that it was improper or unskilful. In the earlier cases, this rule was applied only where the wound was dangerous to life. Later, and logically, it was extended to less serious injuries. Those cases must now be regarded in the light of the modern decisions in *Jordan*,[365] *Smith*[366] and *Cheshire*.[367]

In *Jordan*, D stabbed V who was admitted to hospital and died eight days later. At the trial 'it did not occur to the prosecution, the defence, the judge or the jury that there could be any doubt but that the stab caused death'.[368] In the Court of Criminal Appeal, the fresh evidence of two doctors was allowed to the effect that, in their opinion, death had not been caused by the stab wound, which was mainly healed at the time of the death. Rather, their view was that it was caused by the reaction to large quantities of liquid and to a drug called terramycin which had been administered with a view to preventing infection despite the deceased man having already shown he was intolerant to that drug. This treatment, according to the evidence, was 'palpably wrong'. The court quashed the conviction, holding that if the jury had heard this evidence they would have felt precluded from saying that they were satisfied that the death was caused by the stab wound.

The case has been interpreted by Glanville Williams[369] as one where the medical treatment was grossly negligent, but he argues[370] that any degree of negligence which would be recognized by the civil courts should be enough. The court did not say in express terms that there was evidence of negligence, gross or otherwise, though it may reasonably be inferred that 'palpably wrong' treatment is negligent. While anxiously disclaiming any intention of setting a precedent[371] they stated the basis of their decision in even broader terms. They

361 [2009] EWCA Crim 650, [2009] Crim LR 661 and commentary.
362 See p 610 for discussion and Ch 14.
363 Although usually an act, it can be an omission to act, *McKechnie* (1992) 94 Cr App R 51.
364 As Wilson points out, 'doctors who have emergency surgery thrust upon them cannot be expected to get it right all the time', *Central Issues*, 181.
365 (1956) 40 Cr App R 152. For an historical account, see D Ibbetson, '*R v Jordan*' in P Handler, H Mares and I Williams (eds), *Landmark Cases in Criminal Law* (2017).
366 [1959] 2 QB 35. Followed in *Gowans* [2003] EWCA Crim 3935.   367 [1991] 3 All ER 670.
368 See (1956) 40 Cr App R 152 at 155.   369 [1957] Crim LR at 430.   370 ibid, 513.
371 But no court has the right to preclude future courts from considering the effects of its decisions.

were 'disposed to accept it as law that death resulting from any normal treatment employed to deal with a [criminal] injury may be regarded as caused by the [criminal] injury'; but it was 'sufficient to point out here that this was not normal treatment'. Surely, treatment that is 'not normal' is not necessarily negligent, even in the civil law?[372] The case gave rise to some concern in the medical profession and it was predicted[373] that the result of it would be that if, in future, the victim of a homicidal assault died as a result of the medical treatment instituted to save his life, it would be considered homicide by the assailant only if the treatment was 'normal'.

Jordan was distinguished by the court in Smith[374] and by the Court of Appeal in Blaue[375] as 'a very particular case depending upon its exact facts'.

In Smith,[376] in the course of a fight between soldiers of different regiments, D stabbed V twice with a bayonet. One of V's comrades, trying to carry V to the medical reception station, twice tripped and dropped him. At the reception station the medical officer, who was trying to cope with a number of other cases, did not realize that one of the wounds had pierced a lung and caused haemorrhage. He gave V treatment which, in the light of the information regarding V's condition available at the time of the trial, was 'thoroughly bad and might well have affected his chances of recovery'. D's conviction for murder was upheld and counsel's argument that the court must be satisfied that the treatment was normal, and that this was abnormal, was brushed aside:

if at the time of death the original wound is still an operating cause and a substantial cause, then the death can properly be said to be the result of the wound, albeit that some other cause of death is also operating. Only if it can be said that the original wounding is merely the setting in which another cause operates can it be said that the death does not result from the wound. Putting it in another way, only if the second cause is so overwhelming as to make the original wound merely part of the history can it be said that death does not flow from the wound.[377]

In Malcherek,[378] the court thought that if a choice had to be made between Jordan and Smith, Smith was to be preferred; but they did not believe it was necessary to choose. In Blaue, Jordan was thought to be 'probably rightly decided on its facts'. It is submitted that this is so. Smith is distinguishable. Jordan was a case where a jury might have found, in the light of the new evidence, that the wound was, or may have been, merely the setting in which medical treatment caused death—as if a nurse had, with gross negligence, administered a deadly poison in mistake for a sleeping pill or, as in a Kentucky case, Bush v Commonwealth,[379] the medical officer attending V inadvertently infected him with scarlet fever and he died of that. None of these is an act which might be expected to occur in the ordinary course of events and they free D from liability. But, if the injured V is receiving proper and skilful medical attention and he dies from the treatment or the operation, D will be liable.

In Cheshire,[380] the bullet wounds which D inflicted upon V had ceased to be a threat to life and there was evidence that V's death was caused by the tracheotomy performed and negligently treated by the doctors so that it narrowed his windpipe and caused asphyxiation. The Court of Appeal held that the judge had misdirected the jury by telling them that only

---

[372] See Bolam v Friern Hospital Management Committee [1957] 1 WLR 582 and Bolitho v City and Hackney HA [1998] AC 232 and the discussion in J Goudkamp and D Nolan, Winfield and Jolowicz on Tort (20th edn, 2020) Ch 5.

[373] By Camps and Havard [1957] Crim LR 576 at 582–3.   [374] [1959] 2 QB 35 at 43.

[375] [1975] 3 All ER 446. Likewise in Evans and Gardiner (No 2) [1976] VR 523 at 531.

[376] [1959] 2 QB 35 at 43.

[377] Per Lord Parker CJ [1959] 2 QB 35 at 42–3. The passage was applied in Gowans, n 365.

[378] [1981] 2 All ER 422.

[379] 78 Ky 268 (1880) (Kentucky Court of Appeals).   [380] [1991] 3 All ER 670.

recklessness on the part of the doctors would break the chain of causation but upheld the conviction, asserting that 'the rare complication . . . was a direct consequence of the appellant's acts, which remained a significant cause of his death'. The test proposed by the court is not easy to apply:

Even though negligence in the treatment of the victim was the immediate cause of his death, the jury should not regard it as excluding the responsibility of the accused unless the negligent treatment was so independent of his acts, and in itself so potent in causing death, that they regard the contribution made by his acts as insignificant.

It is difficult to know what 'so independent' and 'so potent' mean. In all these cases, D's act caused V to undergo the treatment and if that renders it 'dependent', D would be taken to have caused death, however outlandish the treatment; but it is clear that this is not intended. There is a similar problem with 'potent'. Suppose that the tracheotomy would have caused death even if the wound had been completely healed which on the facts is not entirely clear.[381] No greater potency can then be imagined; but it is unlikely that the court would regard D as not having caused death. The wound would not have been an operating and substantial cause but the ultimate question is whether D's act was a cause and it is clear that it might be, even if the wound was not. The problem could well surface if a victim who has been hospitalized due to a wound inflicted by D contracts MRSA in an unclean hospital.

It is submitted that the following propositions[382] at present represent the law.

(1) Medical evidence is admissible to show that the medical treatment of an injury was the cause of death and that the injury itself was not.[383] This is so whether or not the injury is life-threatening. The conflict of medical evidence may present the jury with a difficult decision as to the potency of the medical intervention.[384] Juries will need careful guidance on such issues.[385]

(2) If an injury inflicted by D was an operating and substantial cause of death, D is guilty of homicide, however badly the injury was treated.[386]

(3) If an injury inflicted by D was not an operating and substantial cause of death (eg it was effectively healed) but V was killed by, for example, the inadvertent administration of deadly poison by a nurse, the wrongful administration of a drug or the ill-treatment of a tracheotomy, D may or may not be guilty of homicide. The test we must now apply is the *Cheshire* independence/potency test. A better test, it is submitted, would be whether the treatment, or the manner of administering it, was so extraordinary as to be unforeseeable—which may be much the same thing as asking whether it was grossly negligent.

Jordan and *Cheshire* were cases where the medical treatment, not the wound, may have been the cause of death. The same principle applies where the injury prevents medical treatment

---

[381] Indeed, according to the Court of Appeal (at 678) the judge directed the jury that the prosecution must prove that 'the bullets were one operative and substantial cause of death'; but the bullets (unless they were still in V's body) could not be an *operating* cause, if that is what is meant, in the sense that a wound might be.

[382] Approved in *Dear* [1996] Crim LR 595.

[383] *Jordan* must be authority for this at least. Moreover, at the trial in *Smith*, Dr Camps gave evidence that, with proper treatment, V's chances of recovery were as high as 75 per cent. See the previous discussion of *Broughton* [2020] EWCA Crim 1093.

[384] See eg *Gowans* [2003] EWCA Crim 3935 where V contracted fatal septicaemia in hospital.

[385] *Suratan* [2004] EWCA Crim 1246.

[386] But cf Hart and Honoré, *Causation in the Law*, 361, discussing *Blaue*, suppose that V had called for a blood transfusion and the doctor had refused because he wanted to play golf, whereupon V bled to death. They argue that death would have been 'caused by the doctor's callousness, not the original wound'. Surely, it would have been caused by both. The wound would certainly have been an operating and substantial cause.

for an independent condition which would have saved V's life: *McKechnie*,[387] where the injuries inflicted by D precluded medical treatment for the duodenal ulcer which killed V. Only an 'extraordinary and unusual' medical decision that the life-saving treatment was not possible would have broken the chain of causation.

It is important to keep in mind that where the question at D's trial is whether the medical professional has broken the chain of causation, the medical professional is *not* on trial. In *Malcherek*,[388] D inflicted upon V injuries which resulted in brain damage. She was put on a life-support machine. Some days later, after carrying out five of the six tests[389] for brainstem death prescribed by the Royal Colleges, doctors disconnected the machine and half an hour later she was pronounced dead. The judge withdrew the question of causation from the jury, ruling that there was no evidence on which they could decide that D did not cause V's death.

On appeal, it was argued that there was evidence on which the jury could have found that the doctors caused death by switching off the machine. The appeal was dismissed. There was no doubt that the injury inflicted by D was an operating and substantial cause of death. Whether or not the doctors were also *a* cause of death was immaterial. They were not on trial;[390] D was. It was enough that a continuing and substantial cause of V's death was the injury inflicted by D.

In the controversial decision in *Wallace*,[391] discussed in the following section, the doctors in Belgium, acting in accordance with Belgian law, euthanized the victim of D's attack at V's request. Their actions were held to not necessarily have broken the chain of causation. It was for the jury to determine whether V's request to the doctors and the act of euthanasia carried out in accordance with his wishes were not discrete acts or events independent of D's conduct in causing him catastrophic disabling burns by soaking him in sulphuric acid. It was open to the jury to conclude that these acts were not voluntary, as they were not the product of free and unfettered volition by V.

2.5.6.5 Victim's conduct breaking the chain of causation

General principle (1): D takes his victim as found

It is a well-established principle in civil law that the defendant takes the victim of his wrong-doing as he finds him—with all V's subsisting weaknesses that might exacerbate the injury resulting from D's act, as where D pricks a haemophiliac with a pin, or slaps the head of a person with an 'egg-shell' skull. According to *Blaue*,[392] in the criminal law as in the civil, the defendant must 'take his victim as he finds him'.

If the principle is restricted to taking V as found in physical terms, little difficulty arises. It seems unnatural to describe V's body's 'response' to D's act as an intervening 'act' between D's infliction of injury and V's death. It is correct, therefore, that D takes V as he finds him with all V's subsisting physical conditions being taken into account.[393] However, controversially, the court in *Blaue* held that the principle applies so that D takes the victim as found in a more holistic sense—taking the victim's *mind* as well as his body as found.

---

[387] (1992) 94 Cr App R 51.

[388] [1981] 1 WLR 690. The appeal of *Steel*, heard at the same time, was materially the same.

[389] There were reasons for not applying the sixth test.

[390] The court remarked, *obiter*, that they thought the suggestion that the doctors had caused the death 'bizarre'—they had done their skilful best to save life, but failed and so discontinued treatment. The policy dimension to causation in homicide where medical negligence is alleged is obvious.

[391] [2018] EWCA Crim 690.

[392] [1975] 3 All ER 446, [1975] Crim LR 648 and commentary. *Smithers* (1976) 34 CCC (2d) 427 (Sup Ct of Canada) is to the same effect. It was immaterial that death was caused in part by malfunctioning epiglottis, where a kick was a contributing cause, outside the *de minimis* range.

[393] See eg *Masters* [2007] EWCA Crim 142, D liable for murder where V had deep vein thrombosis which hastened death and would have killed her soon anyway.

In *Blaue*, D stabbed V, a young girl, and pierced her lung. She was told that she would die if she did not have a blood transfusion. Being a Jehovah's Witness, she refused on religious grounds. She died from the bleeding caused by the wound. D was convicted of manslaughter and argued that V's refusal to have a blood transfusion, being unreasonable, had broken the chain of causation. It was held that the judge had rightly instructed the jury that the wound was a cause of death. Lawton LJ said:[394]

It has long been the policy of the law that those who use violence on other people must take their victims as they find them. This in our judgment means the whole man, not just the physical man. It does not lie in the mouth of the assailant to say that his victim's religious beliefs which inhibited him from accepting certain kinds of treatment were unreasonable. The question for decision is what caused the death. The answer is a stab wound.

In this case, the wound was 'an operating cause and a substantial cause', so the *dictum* was unnecessary to the decision. It is unclear whether the court would take the same approach if V had not previously held the religious belief, but had adopted it to spite D (an unlikely scenario).[395]

The *Blaue* principle, if valid, would impose liability upon D for unforeseeable intervening events causing death and is probably confined to acts or omissions by the victim in person. If the parents of a rape victim were to kill their daughter on the ground that their religion required them to do so, it is thought that D would not be liable for the death. If, however, in *Blaue*, V had been too young to make a decision about a blood transfusion and her parents had succeeded on religious grounds in preventing a transfusion being given, it is thought that the wound would have remained an operating and substantial cause, so D would still have been liable. The parents might also have been guilty of some homicide offence.

Blaue followed *Holland*[396] in which D waylaid and assaulted V, cutting him severely across one of his fingers with an iron instrument. V refused to follow the surgeon's advice to have the finger amputated, although he was told that if he did not his life would be in great danger. The wound caused lockjaw, the finger was then amputated, but it was too late and V died of lockjaw. The surgeon's evidence was that if the finger had been amputated at first, V's life could probably have been saved. Maule J told the jury that it made no difference whether the wound was in its own nature instantly mortal, or whether it became the cause of death by reason of the deceased not having adopted the best mode of treatment. The question was whether, in the end, the wound inflicted by the prisoner was the real cause of death. The argument[397] that medical science has advanced greatly since 1841 and that a refusal to undergo medical treatment, reasonable then, would be unreasonable now, did not impress the court in *Blaue*. Whether V's conduct was reasonable or not was irrelevant.

The principle stated by the court in *Blaue*, if valid, is capable of wider application. Given that D would be liable for wounding or attempted murder, it is arguable that the principle can operate unduly harshly, but the same harshness would apply where the victim has an egg-shell skull, and that rule is not commonly criticized. The true force of the criticisms levelled against the decision is perhaps against the emphasis the law places on the result (death) rather than the blameworthiness of the life-threatening conduct (unlawful wounding).[398]

---

[394] [1975] 3 All ER 446, 450.

[395] On advance decisions to refuse life-sustaining treatment, see now Mental Capacity Act 2005, s 25.

[396] (1841) 2 Mood & R 351. Cf *Mubila* 1956 (1) SA 31.

[397] By Hart and Honoré, *Causation in the Law*, at 360.

[398] See the discussion, p 30 and A Ashworth, 'Belief Intent and Criminal Liability' in J Eekelaar and J Bell (eds), *Oxford Essays in Jurisprudence*; 'Taking the Consequences' in Shute, Gardner and Horder (eds), *Action and Value in Criminal Law* and 'Defining Offences Without Harm' in *Criminal Law Essays*.

General principle (2): self-neglect by the victim

The common law rule is that neglect or maltreatment by the injured person of himself does not exempt D from liability for his ultimate death. In *Wall's* case,[399] where the former Governor of Goree was convicted[400] of the murder of a man by ordering the illegal infliction on him of a flogging of 800 lashes, there was evidence that V had aggravated his condition by drinking spirits. MacDonald LCB told the jury:[401]

there is no apology for a man if he puts another in so dangerous and hazardous a situation by his treatment of him, that some degree of unskilfullness and mistaken treatment of himself may possibly accelerate the fatal catastrophe. One man is not at liberty to put another into such perilous circumstances as these, and to make it depend upon his own prudence, knowledge, skill or experience what may hurry on or complete that catastrophe, or on the other hand may render him service.

In any event, the drink might have been regarded as a merely *de minimis* cause.

General principle (3): subsequent conduct of the victim

A long line of cases has established that D will be held to have caused death or injury by so frightening V that V has jumped from a window or a car or behaved in some other manner dangerous to himself.[402] If D's unlawful conduct has prompted the response from V, D will remain liable if V's reaction was within the range of responses which might be expected from a victim in his situation.[403] If the reaction was 'so daft as to make it [V's] own voluntary act' the chain of causation is broken. Where V's act is daft it will not be reasonably foreseeable so it seems right that D may be absolved of criminal liability. The range of responses to be expected will, of course, vary according to the age and perhaps the sex of the victim.[404] This approach was followed in *Lewis*.[405] L chased V into the road following an argument and V was knocked down by an oncoming car. The Court of Appeal held, dismissing the appeal, that in cases of death during flight from an unlawful act it had to be shown that there was cause and effect; that is, but for the unlawful act, flight and therefore death would not have taken place. In the flight cases V is seeking to avoid further harm.

What of the position where V inflicts greater harm in response to that inflicted by D already and which remains a substantial and operative cause? It is submitted that if D's act is a continuing and operative cause, D remains liable even if the victim is a contributory cause of the final result (eg death in a murder case).

In *People v Lewis*,[406] V, having received a mortal gunshot wound from which he would have died within the hour, cut his throat and died within five minutes. D was held liable for manslaughter on the ground that the original wound was an operating cause. 'Here, when the throat was cut, [V] was not merely languishing from a mortal wound; he was actually dying; and after the throat was cut he continued to languish from both wounds. Drop by drop the life current went out from both wounds, and at the very instant of death the gunshot wound was contributing to the event.'[407] The application of this principle would have

---

[399] (1802) 28 State Tr 51.   [400] Twenty years after the event.   [401] At 145.

[402] *Pitts* (1842) Car & M 284; *Halliday* (1889) 61 LT 701; *Curley* (1909) 2 Cr App R 96 at 109; *Lewis* [1970] Crim LR 647; *Mackie* [1973] Crim LR 54 (Cusack J); *Boswell* [1973] Crim LR 307 (Judge Gower); *Daley* (1979) 69 Cr App R 39.

[403] *Williams and Davies* (1991) 95 Cr App R 1; *Corbett* [1996] Crim LR 594. Cf *Roberts* (1971) 56 Cr App R 95 at 102.

[404] Presumably, following *Blaue*, religions, no matter how esoteric, cannot be regarded as 'daft'. What of an irrational but entrenched fear of hospitals?

[405] [2010] EWCA Crim 151.   [405] 124 Cal 551 (1899) (Sup Ct of California).

[407] But was the contribution of the gunshot wound substantial or *de minimis* (slight or trifling)? Cf the example given by R Perkins, *Criminal Law* (2nd edn, 1969) 69 and Hart and Honoré, *Causation in the Law*, 243.

provided a different answer if V had blown his brains out and died instantly, for then the bleeding from the original wound would not have been an operating cause. The conviction could then have been upheld only by applying a different principle—that the first act provided a reason for the second[408]—and the court would indeed have decided the case on that ground if they had been satisfied that the first act *was* the cause of the second; but they thought that V's suicide might have been out of remorse or a desire to shield D.

If the victim of a rape were to be so traumatized as to commit suicide by shooting herself it might be argued that it was the bullet that caused the death and not the rape. Certainly the rape is not 'an operating and substantial cause' in the same sense as the wound in *Blaue*; depending upon the circumstances, the response may be found by the jury not to be daft and unforeseeable and D may therefore be guilty. This may be the effect of *Dear*[409] where D's conviction for murder was upheld, even though V may have intentionally caused his own death by aggravating the wounds inflicted on him by D. If V would not have killed himself but for those injuries, D caused his death. It would have been different if V had so acted only for some reason unconnected with D's attack on him—for example, shame at his own disgraceful conduct (paedophilia) which had led D to attack him. The decision is, perhaps, not quite conclusive of the rape victim/suicide case: the wounds as well as V's acts may have been the physical cause of death, whereas in the rape case the bullet is the sole physical cause of death. In *Dear*, it was apparently regarded as immaterial that V's conduct was unforeseeable. In this respect, the decision is not easily reconcilable with the line of authority establishing that V's 'daft' conduct will break the chain of causation.

In *Dhaliwal*,[410] the accused had struck his partner a minor blow on the forehead and she had then committed suicide. This was against a lengthy background of domestic abuse amounting to psychological, but not psychiatric, injury by D. The charge of manslaughter was dismissed since the Crown relied on the history of abuse as founding an unlawful and dangerous act. The trial judge held that this was incapable of amounting to actual bodily harm absent psychiatric injury and the Court of Appeal agreed.[411] In an *obiter dictum*, the Court of Appeal left open the possibility that a manslaughter conviction might be available: 'where a decision to commit suicide has been triggered by a physical assault which represents the culmination of a course of abusive conduct, it would be possible . . . to argue that the final assault played a significant part in causing the victim's death'. In terms of causation, even if D's conduct was treated as a sufficient unlawful and dangerous act, could it ever be a sufficient *cause* in law? There may be little doubt that in fact it operated as a cause of the suicide, but does V's action in choosing to commit suicide break the chain of causation?

Can D ever be liable for homicide where V has committed suicide and D's act is not at that moment a continuing and operative cause of death? It has been argued that in such cases a jury might be willing to conclude that suicide was not outside the range of reasonable responses to be expected of someone in V's position, particularly where the jury were made aware of the history of abuse.[412] It should be noted that in none of the reported 'flight' cases does it appear that the victims have chosen to commit suicide; rather, they have behaved in a dangerous fashion, being aware that their choice of escape may expose them to danger of injury or death.

In *Wallace*,[413] the Court of Appeal considered this issue directly. D was alleged to have inflicted catastrophic injuries upon V which left him severely disfigured, permanently paralysed and in a state of unbearable physical and psychological suffering. V travelled to Belgium, where euthanasia is lawful, to be with his family. V was euthanized by doctors in accordance

---

408 Hart and Honoré, *Causation in the Law*, 244.   409 [1996] Crim LR 595.
410 [2006] EWCA Crim 1139.   411 See p 101.
412 See further Horder and McGowan [2006] Crim LR 1035.   413 [2018] EWCA Crim 690.

with Belgian law. The issue for the Court of Appeal was whether the conduct of the defendant was a legally sufficient cause of V's death, or whether V's actions in asking to be euthanized combined with the actions of the Belgian doctors in complying with his request broke the chain of causation between D's conduct and his death. After a comprehensive review of the applicable authorities, the Court of Appeal held that it was open to the jury to conclude that V's request to his doctors and the act of euthanasia carried out in accordance with his wishes were not discrete acts or events independent of the defendant's conduct. It was open to the jury to conclude that these acts were not voluntary, as they were not the product of the sort of free and unfettered volition to which Lord Bingham referred in *Kennedy (No 2)*. It was held that a jury could find that the acts which led to V's death were the direct response to the injuries inflicted by D and to the circumstances created by them for which she was responsible. One of the difficulties with the court's approach is that nowhere in *Kennedy (No 2)* did Lord Bingham state that V's decision must be the result of 'free and unfettered' volition. It could be argued that the decision of a heroin addict to self-inject heroin when it is presented to them is not the product of free and unfettered volition. The requirement that the intervention be 'unfettered' by the consequences of D's unlawful act appears to be a novel qualification. Furthermore, as Simester and Sullivan argue, *Kennedy (No 2)* can also be distinguished on the basis that the mere supply of the drug lacked causal potency and played no ongoing role in explaining V's death, as it merely created the opportunity for the victim to inject himself.[414]

2.5.6.6 Intended consequences

It is sometimes said that intended consequences cannot be too remote; that is, that D must always be liable for them. This, however, is an oversimplification,[415] and is not always accurate because the *sine qua non* rule remains applicable. Thus, in *White*,[416] the consequence intended by D—the death of his mother—occurred; but its occurrence—a fatal heart attack—had nothing to do with D's act in administering the poison and would have happened just the same if D had done nothing. Even where the but for—*sine qua non*—rule is satisfied, the consequence, though intended, may be too remote where it occurs as a result of the intervention of some new cause. So in the cases of *Bush*[417] and *Jordan*[418] it may be that D intended V's death, and V's death occurred; moreover, in neither case would death have occurred without D's act; but in the one case it was caused by scarlet fever and not by D's bullet, and in the other it was caused by medical treatment and not by D's knife.

Where the death occurs in the manner intended by D, he will be guilty even if the course of events was not what he expected; for example, he shoots at V's head, but the bullet misses, ricochets and kills V by striking him in the back. The case of *Michael*[419] is perhaps a rather extreme example of this. D's child, V, was in the care of a nurse, X. D, intending to murder the child, delivered to X a large quantity of laudanum, telling her it was a medicine to be administered to V. X did not think the child needed any medicine and left it untouched in her room. In X's absence, one of her children, Y, aged five, took the laudanum and administered a large dose to V who died. All the judges held that the jury were rightly directed that this administration by 'an unconscious agent' was murder. Hart and Honoré[420] criticize the case on the ground that the child was:

not in any sense an agent, conscious or unconscious, of the mother, who intended [X] alone to give the poison to the child; but the decision may be justified on the ground that, in our

414 AP Simester and GR Sullivan, 'Causing Euthanasia' (2019) 135 LQR 21.
415 But note the rather stronger rejection by some—'slogans like intended consequences are never too remote simply cannot be accepted': C Finkelstein, 'Involuntary Crimes, Voluntarily Committed' in Shute and Simester (eds), *Criminal Law Theory*, 150.
416 [1910] 2 KB 124.   417 78 Ky 268 (1880); p 78.   418 (1956) 40 Cr App R 152.
419 (1840) 9 C & P 356.   420 *Causation in the Law*, 337.

terminology, the act of the child of five did not negative causal connexion between the prisoner's act and the death.

According to this view, the result would have been different if Y had been, not five, but 15. It does not appear that Y knew, from the labelling of the bottle or otherwise, that this was 'medicine' for V. If she did know this, and acted on that knowledge, then there seems no difficulty in imputing the death to D, whatever Y's age. No such fact being reported, however, the case must be treated as one where Y's intervention was in no way prompted by D's instructions. Thus, if Y had taken the poison herself, her death would have been just as much caused by D's act as was V's in the actual case; but it would require an extension of the decision to hold D guilty in such a case, for Y's death was not an intended consequence.[421] If such an extension is not made, the result is quite arbitrary, because it was pure chance whether Y administered the poison to V, or to herself or another child.

2.5.7 Special instances of causation

There are a few instances of causation which require special mention, by reason of the unsatisfactory state of the authorities.

2.5.7.1 Killing by mental suffering or shock

The view of earlier writers was that the law could take no cognizance of a killing caused merely by mental suffering or shock, because 'no external act of violence was offered, whereof the common law can take notice and secret things belong to God'.[422] Stephen thought that the fear of encouraging prosecutions for witchcraft was the reason for the rule and that it was 'a bad rule founded on ignorance now dispelled'.[423]

Suppose a man were intentionally killed by being kept awake till the nervous irritation of sleeplessness killed him, might not this be murder? Suppose a man kills a sick person intentionally by making a loud noise when sleep gives him a chance of life; or suppose knowing that a man has aneurysm of the heart, his heir rushes into his room and roars in his ear, 'Your wife is dead!' intending to kill and killing him, why are not these acts murder? They are no more 'secret things belonging to God' than the operation of arsenic.

This view now represents the law. Hale's proposition was first modified in *Towers*[424] where D violently assaulted a young girl who was holding a four-and-a-half-month-old child in her arms. The girl screamed loudly, so frightening the baby that it cried till it was black in the face. From that day it had convulsions and died a month later. Denman J held that there was evidence to go to the jury of manslaughter. In the case of an adult person, he said that murder could not be committed by using language so strong or violent as to cause that person to die:

mere intimidation, causing a person to die from fright by working upon his fancy, was not murder, but that rule did not apply to a child of such tender years as this:

if the man's act brought on the convulsions or brought them to a more dangerous extent, so that death would not have resulted otherwise, then it would be manslaughter.[425]

This was extended to the case of an adult person by Ridley J in *Hayward*.[426] D, who was in a condition of violent excitement and had expressed his determination to 'give his wife

---

[421] But the doctrine of transferred malice (p 125) would support such an extension.
[422] Hale, I PC, 429; and see East, I PC, 225.   [423] Stephen, *Digest*, 217 fn 9.
[424] (1874) 12 Cox CC 530.   [425] ibid, 533.   [426] (1908) 21 Cox CC 692.

something', chased her from the house into the road using violent threats against her. She fell dead. She was suffering from an abnormal heart condition, such that any combination of physical exertion and fright or strong emotion might cause death. Ridley J directed the jury that no proof of actual physical violence was necessary, but that death from fright alone, caused by an illegal act, such as a threat of violence, was enough. D was unaware of V's condition, and following the general principle outlined earlier, he must take his victim as found. It is irrelevant to the issue of causation whether the fright is one that would have an effect on a reasonable person or only one of exceptional timidity. D's awareness of the likely effect of his conduct will be a relevant issue in determining his mens rea.

2.5.7.2 Killing by perjury

With the abolition of the death penalty, discussion of D 'causing' V's death by giving false testimony leading to V's conviction for a capital crime seems now to be redundant. The principles are discussed in the 10th edition of this book, at p 57.

2.5.7.3 Reform

The Criminal Law Team of the Law Commission produced a Working Paper on causation in 2002. The proposal was to codify the law as follows:

(1) Subject to subsections (2) to (5), a defendant causes a result which is an element of an offence when—

    (a) he does an act which makes a substantial and operative contribution to its occurrence; or

    (b) he omits to do an act, which he is under a duty to do accord ing to the law relating to the offence, and the failure to do the act makes a substantial and operative contribution to its occurrence.

(2)

    (a) The finders of fact may conclude that a defendant's act or omission did not make a substantial and operative contribution to the occurrence of a result if compared with the voluntary intervention of another person, unless:

        (i)   the defendant is subject to a legal duty to guard against the very harm that the intervention or event causes; and

        (ii) the intervention was not so extraordinary as to be unforeseeable to a reasonable person in the defendant's position; and

        (iii) it would have been practicable for the defendant to have taken steps to prevent the intervention.

    (b) The intervention of another person is not voluntary unless it is:

        (i)   free, deliberate and informed; and

        (ii) performed or undertaken without any physical participation from the defendant.

(3)

    (a) The finders of fact may conclude that a defendant's act or omission did not make a substantial and operative contribution to the occurrence of a result if compared with an unforeseeable natural event;

    (b) A natural event is not unforeseeable unless:

        (i)   the defendant did not foresee it; and

        (ii) it could not have been foreseen by any reasonable person in the defendant's position.

(4) A person who procures, assists, or encourages another to cause a result that is an element of an offence does not himself cause that result so as to be guilty of the offence as a principal except when—

    (a) section 26(1)(c) applies; or

    (b) the offence itself consists in the procuring, assisting or encouraging another to cause the result.[427]

These were not formal recommendations of the Law Commission and have not been acted upon since.

Further reading

A Ashworth, *Positive Obligations in Criminal Law*

P Glazebrook, *Reshaping the Criminal Law: Essays in Honour of Glanville Williams*

H Hart and T Honoré, *Causation in the Law*

A Norrie, *Crime, Reason and History: A Critical Introduction to Criminal Law*

S Shute, J Gardner and J Horder (eds), *Action and Value in Criminal Law*

---

[427] This was referred to in *Williams* [2010] EWCA Crim 2552.

3

The elements of a crime: mens rea

3.1 Introduction

In the preceding chapter the actus reus or external elements of the offence were examined. This chapter deals with the mens rea or mental fault of the accused.[1] An actus reus is, in the eyes of the law, a 'bad' thing. The particular conduct that constitutes the actus reus of a given crime is not necessarily a bad thing in everyone's eyes or even in the eyes of the

---

[1] Theoretical analyses of this vast topic include RA Duff, *Intention, Agency and Criminal Liability* (1990); Tadros, *Criminal Responsibility*, esp Chs 8 and 9; A Brudner, *Punishment and Freedom: A Liberal Theory of Penal Justice* (2009) Ch 2; W Chan and AP Simester, 'Four Functions of Mens Rea' (2011) 70 CLJ 381; F Stark, 'It's Only Words: On Meaning and Mens Rea' (2013) 72 CLJ 155. For more classical writings (which although largely historical are still pertinent) on the topic, see: JWC Turner, 'The Mental Element in Crimes at Common Law', MACL, 195; G Williams, *The Mental Element in Crime* (1965) and CLGP, in Ch 2; HLA Hart, 'Negligence, Mens Rea and Criminal Responsibility' in *Oxford Essays in Jurisprudence* (1961) 29; JC Smith, 'The Guilty Mind in the Criminal Law' (1960) 76 LQR 78; A Ashworth, 'Reason, Logic and Criminal Liability' (1975) 91 LQR 102; G Williams, 'Oblique Intention' (1987) 46 CLJ 417.

majority of people. But the law requires us to accept the actus reus as legally 'bad'. Many people think that, in certain circumstances, mercy killing is morally right. In law it is the actus reus of murder, legally very bad indeed.[2] It follows from the fact that an actus reus is treated in law as a bad thing that an intention to cause it is, in law, a bad intention, a guilty mind. Similarly, consciously taking an unjustified risk of causing an actus reus—that is, being reckless whether the actus reus be caused—is also a bad state of mind, though less so than intentionally causing the actus reus. Inadvertently causing an actus reus by failing to take reasonable care—negligence—may also be regarded as legally blameworthy, though still less than intention or recklessness. Intention, recklessness and negligence imply different degrees of 'fault' in the criminal law.

Most serious crimes and many minor offences require proof that D had the specified blameworthy state of mind; that is, fault element with respect to all the elements of the actus reus. For example, in the offence of criminal damage, for the actus reus D must be shown to have (a) destroyed or damaged (b) property (c) belonging to another. The mens rea requires that D (a) intended or was reckless as to whether his conduct would destroy or damage; (b) intended or was reckless as to the article constituting property; and (c) intended or was reckless that it belonged to another. If D intended V to damage his own property he would be acquitted. The fault element for that part of the actus reus would not have been established.

In some offences—which we call 'offences of strict liability'—some elements of the actus reus do not require proof of fault. For example, where D is charged with rape of a child under 13. The prosecution must establish that D penetrated V's vagina, anus or mouth with his penis, and that at the time V was under 13. However, in terms of mens rea the prosecution are only required to prove that D intended to penetrate V with his penis. There is no requirement to prove that D knew or was reckless as to V being under 13—liability as to that element of the actus reus relating to age is 'strict'.[3]

The traditional term for the state of mind which must be proved, 'mens rea', is unfortunately sometimes used by courts to include all degrees of fault, including failure to comply with a standard of conduct—negligence. Frequently the terminology is of no consequence, but it can lead to confusion.[4] In this book we use 'mens rea' to mean the state of mind (intention, recklessness, knowledge, belief, suspicion, wilfulness, malice, etc), required by the particular crime and we use the term 'negligence' to describe failures by the defendant to comply with a prescribed standard of conduct irrespective of his personal state of mind. We consider negligence in the next chapter and strict liability in Ch 5.

3.1.1 Subjective and objective fault

There is an ongoing debate between subjectivist and objectivist approaches to crime. In simple terms, 'subjectivists' assert that, for serious crimes at least, the mental element should require proof that D has personal awareness of his actions and of the relevant circumstances and consequences comprising the actus reus of the offence. Objectivists, in contrast, assert that it is sufficient to prove that the reasonable person would have been aware of the relevant circumstances/consequences comprising the actus reus, irrespective of whether D himself was aware of them. This is, of course, a grossly oversimplistic summary of the competing positions. A more realistic view is that there are shades of subjectivism and objectivism along a spectrum.

[2] See *Inglis* [2010] EWCA Crim 2637 and see Ch 12.   [3] G [2008] UKHL 37.
[4] Commentary on *Seaboard Offshore Ltd v Secretary of State for Transport* [1993] 1 WLR 1025; affd [1994] 2 All ER 99; *Peterssen v RSPCA* [1993] Crim LR 852.

There are competing claims as to the merits of the approaches, both in terms of their princi-pled foundations and their practical application.[5] Some subjectivists argue that the requirement of personal awareness on the part of D is crucial since it secures respect for the autonomy of the individual: D is punished where he has chosen to act in a way contrary to law. Objectivists point out that D might also be regarded as sufficiently culpable to deserve criminal punishment where his inadvertence related to a substantial and obvious risk of the proscribed harm, of which D *had the capacity* to be aware even if he was not actually aware on the occasion in question.

Despite weighty academic opinion that 'the torch of orthodox subjectivism carried by Glanville Williams and *Smith and Hogan* and then by the Law Commission should be doused',[6] the subjective approach continues to be that favoured by the courts, at least in serious crimes, and this was emphasized in the clearest terms by the highest tribunal. In the landmark case of *G*[7] Lord Bingham stated that:

it is a salutary principle that conviction of serious crime should depend on proof not simply that the defendant caused (by act or omission) an injurious result to another but that his state of mind when so acting was culpable. This, after all, is the meaning of the familiar rule *actus non facit reum nisi mens sit rea*. The most obviously culpable state of mind is no doubt an intention to cause the injurious result, but knowing disregard of an appreciated and unacceptable risk of causing an injurious result or a deliberate closing of the mind to such risk would be readily accepted as culpable also. It is clearly blameworthy to take an obvious and significant risk of causing injury to another. But it is not clearly blameworthy to do something involving a risk of injury to another if (for reasons other than self-induced intoxication: *Majewski* [1977] AC 443) one genuinely does not perceive the risk. Such a person may fairly be accused of stupidity or lack of imagination, but nei-ther of those failings should expose him to conviction of serious crime or the risk of punishment.[8]

However, despite this strong endorsement of the subjectivist position from the House of Lords, Parliament has demonstrated a willingness to create serious offences in which the fault element is explicitly objective. Examples include many sexual offences in the Sexual Offences Act 2003, the Terrorism Acts; some of the money laundering offences in the Proceeds of Crime Act 2002 (POCA 2002); and offences involving organized crime in the Serious Crime Act 2015.

3.1.2 Mens rea concerns legal not moral guilt

The literal meaning of 'mens rea' is 'a guilty mind.' This is misleading unless we remember that we are concerned with legal not moral guilt. In some exceptional circumstances the law will treat D as having mens rea though neither D, nor any reasonable person, would regard D's state of mind as blameworthy.[9] Mens rea is simply the label used to describe the mental element required by the definition of the particular crime. Typically this will be an intention to fulfil the elements of the actus reus of that crime, or recklessness whether they be fulfilled. The term refers to the criminality of the act, not its moral quality. At trial the

---

[5] The major proponents of the subjectivist view have been Glanville Williams and Sir John Smith. The subjectivist view has been challenged by prominent academic writers including Horder, APOCL; RA Duff, *Intention Agency and Criminal Liability* (1990); and A Norrie, *Crime, Reason and History* (3rd edn, 2014): see the articles cited later in this chapter. For an excellent account of the positions in the context of manslaughter, see LC 237, *Involuntary Manslaughter* (1996) Part IV.

[6] A Ashworth, *Principles of Criminal Law* (5th edn, 2006) 253. See also A Norrie, 'Between Orthodox Subjectivism and Moral Contextualism' [2006] Crim LR 486, 487.

[7] [2003] UKHL 50.   [8] At [32] per Lord Bingham.

[9] *Dodman* [1998] 2 Cr App R 338, C-MAC, holding that 'Mens rea does not . . . involve blameworthiness', citing the 8th edn of this book and disapproving the *Manual of Air Force Law* (6th edn, 1983) s 69 fn 2.

focus is on proof of the relevant element of mens rea not whether D was acting in a morally culpable manner.[10]

In *Yip Chiu-Cheung*,[11] D was charged with conspiring with E to export drugs from Hong Kong to Australia. E was an undercover drug-enforcement officer who was called as a prosecution witness and testified that he made the agreement with D and intended, with the authority of his superiors, to carry it out. He was going to take the drugs to Australia to entrap other drug dealers. It takes two conspirators to make a conspiracy and D's unsuccessful defence was that E was not a conspirator because he lacked mens rea. It was held that E *did* have the mens rea of conspiracy—that is, an intention to commit the agreed crime. Neither E's good motives nor the superior orders under which he was acting would have been a defence if he had been charged. *Yip* was followed in *Kingston*.[12]

In *Kingston*,[13] D, a paedophile, was charged with indecent assault on a 15-year-old boy, V. D and V had both been drugged surreptitiously by P. P knew of D's tendencies, and he drugged D and V in the hope that D would indecently assault V and that he, P, would be able to video-record the events so as to blackmail D. D did indeed indecently assault V and P video-recorded the events. The House of Lords held that D had been rightly convicted; simply because D lacked blame or moral fault did not mean that he lacked the necessary mens rea. Lord Mustill stated that:

Each offence consists of a prohibited act or omission coupled with whatever state of mind is called for by the statute or rule of the common law which creates the offence. In those offences which are not absolute the state of mind which the prosecution must prove to have underlain the act or omission—the 'mental element'—will in the majority of cases be such as to attract disapproval. The mental element will then be the mark of what may properly be called a 'guilty mind'. The professional burglar is guilty in a moral as well as a legal sense; he intends to break into the house to steal, and most would confidently assert that this is wrong. But this will not always be so. In respect of some offences the mind of the defendant, and still less his moral judgment, may not be engaged at all. In others, although a mental activity must be the motive power for the prohibited act or omission the activity may be of such a kind or degree that society at large would not criticize the defendant's conduct severely or even criticize it at all. Such cases are not uncommon. Yet to assume that contemporary moral judgments affect the criminality of the act, as distinct from the punishment appropriate to the crime once proved, is to be misled by the expression '*mens rea*', the ambiguity of which has been the subject of complaint for more than a century.[14]

The circumstances of these two cases are exceptional. An actus reus generally is, or includes, some very undesirable results—killing, wounding, theft or damage to property, etc. An intention to cause the actus reus is nearly always a state of mind which ordinary people would regard as blameworthy. Nevertheless, moral blameworthiness is not the legal test.

3.2 Forms of mens rea

It is generally accepted that the different types of mens rea form a hierarchy, with intention and knowledge being the most culpable, followed by recklessness, belief and then suspicion. There are other specific forms of mens rea arising in the context of individual offences,

---

[10] For a criticism of equating mens rea with culpability, see W Chan and AP Simester, 'Four Functions of *Mens Rea*' (2011) 70 CLJ 381. The authors argue that denoting culpability is merely one of the functions of mens rea.

[11] [1995] 1 AC 111.

[12] [1994] 3 WLR 519. See also *Hales* [2005] EWCA Crim 1118, on the difference between intention and motive.

[13] ibid.   [14] At 526.

which it is difficult to fit within this hierarchy. We can now turn to examine each form of mens rea commonly found in English criminal law.

3.2.1 Intention

Numerous offences are defined so as to require proof of 'intention' to cause speci-fied results.[15] These commonly include the more serious crimes. It might therefore be expected that the meaning of such a fundamental term would have been settled long ago, but this is not so. The cases are inconsistent, judicial opinion has changed and there is still some measure of uncertainty.[16] We may begin, however, with one well-settled proposition. Everyone agrees that a person intends to cause a result if he acts with the purpose of doing so.[17] If D has resolved to kill V and he fires a loaded gun at him with the object of killing V, he intends to kill. It is immaterial that he is aware that he is a poor shot, that V is nearly out of range and that his chances of success are small. It is sufficient that killing is D's object or purpose: that D acts in order to kill.[18] Note that the focus is on D's purpose,[19] not his desire[20] or wish as to the consequences. D can intend a result by having that as his purpose without desiring it, as where D kills V with a lethal injection to put him out of his pain, but wishes he did not have to. Note also that the definition of intention is wider than 'premeditation' where that term is used to denote planning or calculated acts. 'Intention' in English law extends beyond such cases to include sponta-neous conduct.[21]

One view is that in law 'intention' should be limited to the narrow definition of purposive or direct intention. On this view, a result should never be regarded as intended unless it was the actor's purpose; that is, unless he acted in order to bring about that result. This is often considered to be the ordinary meaning given to the word.[22] However, the courts have fre-quently given the word a wider meaning, sometimes described as 'oblique' (as distinct from

---

[15] The literature on this topic is voluminous. Many of the publications are of a philosophical nature. See, inter alia, JC Smith, 'Intention in Criminal Law' (1974) 27 CLP 93; Lord Goff, 'The Mental Element in the Crime of Murder' (1988) 104 LQR 30; G Williams, 'The Mens Rea for Murder—Leave it Alone' (1989) 105 LQR 387; J Buzzard, 'Intent' [1978] Crim LR 5 and JC Smith, 'A Reply' [1978] Crim LR 14; AR White, *Misleading Cases* (1991) 47; J Finnis, '*Bland*: Crossing the Rubicon' (1993) 109 LQR 329; N Lacey, 'A Clear Concept of Intention' (1993) 56 MLR 621; J Horder, 'Intention in the Criminal Law—A Rejoinder' (1995) 58 MLR 678; N Lacey, 'In(de) terminable Intentions' (1995) 58 MLR 692; MC Kaveny, 'Inferring Intention from Foresight' (2004) 120 LQR 81; I Kugler, *Direct and Oblique Intention in the Criminal Law* (2002); Tadros, *Criminal Responsibility*, Ch 8; MS Moore, 'Intention as a Marker of Moral Culpability and Legal Punishability' in RA Duff and SP Green (eds), *Philosophical Foundations of Criminal Law* (2011); RA Duff, 'Intention Revisited' in DJ Baker and J Horder (eds), *The Sanctity of Life and the Criminal Law* (2013). See also the discussion in LCCP 177, *A New Homicide Act for England and Wales* (2006) Chs 3 and 4; LC 304, *Murder, Manslaughter and Infanticide* (2007); G Coffey, 'Codifying the Meaning of "Intention" in the Criminal Law' (2009) 73 J Crim L 394.

[16] The fact that the main cases defining intention are all murder cases, with the difficult policy issues that offence entails, exacerbates inconsistency and uncertainty. See also the discussion in Tadros, *Criminal Responsibility*, 232.

[17] A majority of the Supreme Court in *Hayes v Willoughby* [2013] UKSC 17 held, in the context of s 1(3)(a) of the Protection from Harassment Act 1997, that 'purpose' denotes a wholly subjective state of mind.

[18] Duff suggests that this can be ascertained by asking: would D treat his action as a failure if he did not achieve the result? If so, D intended the result. Duff, *Intention, Agency and Criminal Liability*, 61.

[19] See the recognition of this by the Supreme Court in *Jogee* [2016] UKSC 8, [90].

[20] The danger of using this term was acknowledged in *Hales* [2005] EWCA Crim 1118, [28].

[21] See M Kremnitzer, 'On Premeditation' (1998) Buffalo Crim LR 627. LCCP 177 rejects it as an option owing to difficulties of proof.

[22] On the problems of using the ordinary language approach in this context, see Lacey (1993) 56 MLR 621.

'direct') intention.[23] Under this alternative approach, it may be sufficient that D has foreseen the prohibited result as one which is highly probable, or virtually certain to occur, even if achieving that result is not his purpose.[24]

3.2.1.1 Current legal position

The cases in which this issue arises almost always involve murder. The mens rea for murder is that D intends to kill or do GBH. The question that recurs is whether D has a sufficient mens rea where he does not have as his purpose that V will be killed or caused GBH by his conduct, but he foresees V's death or GBH as probable, or highly probable or virtually certain to result.

Until relatively recently, the predominant judicial view was that D intended a result if he knew that it was a highly probable (or perhaps merely probable) result of his conduct, although it was not his purpose or object to cause that result. In 1975, Lord Diplock in *Hyam v DPP*[25] endorsed this view. A majority of the House in *Hyam* were certainly of the opinion that this was the law. The actual decision was that foresight of a high probability of GBH was a *sufficient* mens rea for murder, not that such a state of mind *necessarily* amounted to an intention to cause GBH. In *Moloney*,[26] however, the House held that the mens rea of murder is intention to cause death or GBH so it was essential to determine the meaning of 'intention'. *Moloney* must be read in the light of the explanation of it by the House in *Hancock and Shankland*,[27] the Court of Appeal in *Nedrick*[28] and by the House in *Woollin*.[29] The effect of these numerous pronouncements from the appellate courts is that the current state of the law (at least in murder) has remain settled for over 20 years. It is:

(1) a result is intended when it is the actor's purpose to cause it;

(2) a court or jury *may also find* that a result is intended, though it is not the actor's purpose to cause it, when—

(a) the result is a virtually certain consequence of his act, and

(b) the actor knows that it is a virtually certain consequence.

It seems clear that (1) and (2) are distinct forms of intention. In *MD*,[30] the Court of Appeal described the second form of intention—oblique intention—as:

designed to help the prosecution fill a gap in the rare circumstances in which a defendant does an act which caused death without the purpose of killing or causing serious injury, but in circumstances where death or serious bodily harm had been a virtual certainty (barring some unforeseen intervention) as a result of the defendant's action and the defendant had appreciated that such was the case. *Woollin* is not designed to make the prosecution's task more difficult. Many murderers whose purpose was to kill or cause serious injury would escape conviction if the jury was only [directed under (2)(a) and (b)]. The man who kills another with a gun would be able to escape liability for murder if he could show[31] that he was such a bad shot that death or serious bodily harm was

---

[23] cf J Bentham, *Principles of Morals and Legislation* (Harrison edn, 2007).

[24] Williams (1987) 46 CLJ 417. See also A Norrie, 'Oblique Intention and Legal Politics' [1989] Crim LR 793; A Norrie, 'Intention—More Loose Talk' [1990] Crim LR 642; RA Duff, 'The Politics of Intention: A Response to Norrie' [1990] Crim LR 637; Tadros, *Criminal Responsibility*, 215–18 and 228–9; Kugler, *Direct and Oblique Intention*, Ch 1.

[25] [1975] AC 55.   [26] [1985] AC 905.   [27] [1986] AC 455.   [28] [1986] 1 WLR 1025.

[29] [1999] 1 AC 82, [1998] Crim LR 890 and commentary. See LCCP 177, para 4.38.

[30] [2004] EWCA Crim 1391.

[31] Surely this is a slip and the burden is on the prosecution to rebut such a defence?

not a virtual certainty or that the defendant had thought that death or serious bodily harm was not a virtual certainty.[32]

3.2.1.2 Difficulties with the present law

The blurring of evidence and substantive law

Within the definition of oblique intention, why is it a requirement that the result was a virtually certain consequence of D's act? That should not be part of D's mens rea. The fact is very good evidence that D knew that the result was a virtually certain consequence; but it is difficult to see why it should be regarded as a necessary condition as a matter of substantive criminal law.[33] If D thinks that the result is virtually inevitable, but is making a mistake, surely he intends the result even though it was not, in fact, inevitable? If D fires a gun pointed at V's heart, his intention can hardly be affected by the fact, unknown to D, that V is wearing a bullet-proof vest. D's state of mind is as culpable whether V is wearing the vest or not. The difference is in the external circumstances. This point may not be of great practical importance because the best evidence that D knew that the consequence was virtually certain will be the fact that it *was* virtually certain; but this is not invariably so.

Equally, the fact that a result is virtually certain is not proof of intention—the inquiry into intention is one involving an assessment of D's state of mind. Did he have the result as his purpose or did he foresee the result as virtually certain? It is easy to lose sight of this. In *Stringer* M, aged 14, was alleged to have started a fire in his family home early one morning and walked off, knowing that five occupants were asleep upstairs. The Court of Appeal upheld the conviction for murder and arson with intent to endanger life:

if the jury were satisfied (as they must have been) that M started the fire after putting accelerant at the foot of the stairs, that he watched it take hold and then walked away, there *could be only one answer* to the question whether in fact it was a virtual certainty that somebody in the house would suffer really serious harm or death from M's actions. It would be wholly unrealistic to imagine all the occupants escaping from the house by jumping from the upstairs windows without any of them suffering any serious harm. This must have been obvious to any ordinary person at the time. Even taking account of M's age and the fact that his IQ was low/average, the inference that he must have appreciated it on that morning was also overwhelming. On the facts as the jury must have found them, the conclusion that M had the necessary intent was bound to follow.[34]

In practice that may be true, but strictly there is a difference between finding that the result was virtually certain and finding that D foresaw it as such.

---

[32] The extended intention direction is only rarely needed. It is needed where D denies his purpose, not where, eg, D denies any part in the crime: *Phillips* [2004] EWCA Crim 112. The trial judge is best placed to make the decision on the appropriate direction. In *Allen* [2005] EWCA Crim 1344 the Court of Appeal emphasized that it 'is only in an exceptional case that the extended direction by reference to foresight becomes necessary', [63]. See also *Hales* [2005] EWCA Crim 1118, [27]; *Ogunbowale* [2007] EWCA Crim 2739; *Royle* [2013] EWCA Crim 1461. More recently, in *R (on the application of Charles) v Criminal Cases Review Commission* [2017] EWHC 1219 (Admin), Gross LJ stated at [57] that 'save very exceptionally, a judge directing a jury in a case of murder ought not to elaborate on what is meant by intent, leaving it to the jury's good sense to decide whether the Crown has made them sure that the defendant killed the victim with the necessary intent for murder'.

[33] This criticism as stated in the 10th edn of this book was acknowledged by the Court of Appeal in *MD* [2004] EWCA Crim 1391.

[34] [2008] EWCA Crim 1222 (emphasis added).

'Finding' intention

The second major criticism with the present description of the law offered in *Woollin*, and summarized earlier, concerns the use of the phrase, italicized in point (2), 'may also find'. There has been a long-standing debate about whether the descriptions of intention offered in the House of Lords cases in recent decades define intention exhaustively, or whether they merely describe states of mind which a jury may choose to categorize as intention if they wish. In other words, is D's foresight of a virtually certain result conclusive proof that he intended that result? Or is D's foresight of a virtually certain result merely evidence from which the jury may go on to find that he intended that result, if they wish so to categorize his state of mind?

In *Nedrick*, the Court of Appeal had stated that foresight of virtual certainty is merely evidence *from which intention may be inferred*. On that approach a jury may conclude that D foresaw V's death as virtually certain and yet the jury may choose not to treat that as intention. At one point in his speech in *Woollin* Lord Steyn said that, 'The effect of the critical direction is that a result foreseen as virtually certain *is* an intended result' (emphasis added). That was welcomed by many commentators since it seemed to be an unequivocal statement from the House of Lords that there was no room for any 'finding' of intention by the jury. On a literal reading, it seemed to follow from Lord Steyn's statement that once a court or jury was satisfied that D had such foresight, it *must* (not 'may') find that the result was intended by D. Such an approach, equating foresight of virtual certainty with intention, would be advantageous, in terms of optimizing the certainty and consistency in application of this important mens rea element.

An alternative view was that *Woollin* did leave a degree of flexibility for the jury; the decision of the House of Lords was that the jury 'may' find intention. This suggests there is something further for the jury to decide once they have concluded that D foresaw[35] the result as virtually certain. It has been suggested by, amongst others, Professor Norrie, that a test in which foresight of virtual certainty *was* intention, rather than something from which intention *may* be found, would be over-inclusive and would not reflect the degree of 'moral malevolence' in D's act. The argument is that the jury, having decided that D did foresee some prohibited consequence as virtually certain, should go on to consider whether, in all the circumstances, he was so 'wicked' that an intention to cause the evil should be attributed to him.[36] Although this might enhance the prospects of achieving justice in the individual case, it does little to secure certainty and consistency in general application.

The Court of Appeal remains unwilling to interpret *Woollin* as laying down a clear rule that foresight of virtually certain consequences *is* intention. In *Matthews and Alleyne*,[37] M and A were convicted of robbery, kidnapping and murder. V was attacked on leaving a club in the early hours of the morning, and was ultimately thrown off a bridge 25 feet high into a river 64 feet wide. V, being unable to swim, drowned. A co-accused gave evidence that V had said he could not swim. One ground of appeal against convictions for murder was that the judge had directed the jury that foresight of virtual certainty of consequences *was* intention. The Court of Appeal held that *Woollin* did not reach or lay down such a rule of

---

[35] There is a further criticism that the word foresight adds to the confusion. It suggests that D must have a mental picture of the result in his mind, but that is not required. For this reason some prefer the use of the terms 'knowledge or belief', ie that the jury may find intention from D's knowledge or belief that the result will occur. See Tadros, *Criminal Responsibility*, 218–19.

[36] A Norrie, 'After *Woollin*' [1999] Crim LR 532; Norrie, *Crime, Reason and History*, 67–71. See also Kugler, *Direct and Oblique Intention*, 17.

[37] [2003] EWCA Crim 192, [2003] Crim LR 553 and commentary.

substantive law; *Woollin* was concerned with the law of evidence. The judge had gone further than permitted.

[T]he law has not yet reached a *definition* of intent in murder in terms of appreciation of a virtual certainty . . . On the contrary, it is clear from the discussion in *Woollin* as a whole that *Nedrick* was derived from the existing law, at that time ending in *Moloney* and *Hancock*, and that the critical direction in *Nedrick* was approved, subject to the change of one word.

The proper direction should have been in the terms from *Woollin* quoted earlier. However, the court acknowledged that once it was accepted that what was required was appreciation of virtual certainty, and not a lesser foresight of probable consequences, there was very little to choose between evidence and substantive law.

It seems, then, that following *Woollin* the jury retain their 'moral elbow room'.[38] A defendant who is found to have (or admits to having) seen the result as virtually certain will not necessarily be found to have intended the result; the jury will have the discretion to find that he did. This is, it is submitted, an unsatisfactory position, leaving undefined a key term of fault applicable in the most serious crimes. The potential for inconsistent decisions on identical facts is stark. Professor Mitchell's empirical work for the Law Commission[39] confirms that the discretionary element in the definition has the potential to impact on the way crimes are investigated and prosecuted. It renders it more difficult to predict accurately the outcome of cases. This approach does not merely pose problems of a practical nature. If this 'moral threshold' test is to be applied to oblique intention so as to save hard cases from conviction, why should it not also apply to direct intention—that is, purpose? The typical mercy-killer acts with the purpose of killing—and his may be the hardest case of all.[40]

Lord Lane CJ recognized the force of the criticism of this aspect of his judgment in *Nedrick* in the debate on the Report of the House of Lords Select Committee on Murder when he stated:

in *Nedrick* the court was obliged to phrase matters as it did because of earlier decisions in your Lordships' House by which it was bound. We had to tread very gingerly indeed in order not to tread on your Lordships' toes. As a result, *Nedrick* was not as clear as it should have been. However, I agree with the conclusions of the committee that 'intention' should be defined in the terms set out [in the Draft Code]. That seems to express clearly what in *Nedrick* we failed properly to explain.[41]

The definition referred to is that stated in cl 18(b) of the Draft Code:

A person acts 'intentionally' with respect to . . . a result when he acts either in order to bring it about or being aware that it will occur in the ordinary course of events.

In *Woollin*, Lord Steyn, stressing '*will* occur', noted the similarity between the Code and the virtual certainty test. In *Moloney*, Lord Bridge gave a notable example of a man who boards a plane which he knows to be bound for Manchester—the last place he wants to be—in order to escape pursuit: by boarding the Manchester plane, the man '*conclusively* demonstrates his intention to go there, because it is a moral certainty that that is where he will arrive'.[42]

---

[38] Horder (1995) 58 MLR 678, 688. V Tadros, 'The Homicide Ladder' (2006) 69 MLR 601, 604, argues that the moral elbow room allows for the jury to convict in cases where D believes that the result will occur where he does not desire it. See also the discussion in LCCP 177, paras 4.43–4.49 and 4.66, and LC 304, para 3.32.

[39] See LCCP 177, Appendix A; B Mitchell, 'Distinguishing between Murder and Manslaughter in Practice' (2007) 71 J Crim L 318.

[40] See *Inglis* [2010] EWCA Crim 2637.   [41] HL Paper 78-I, 1989; HL vol 512, col 480, 6 Nov 1989.

[42] [1985] AC 905 at 926 (emphasis in original).

There is nothing here about this being merely evidence upon which the jury may find intention—intention is *conclusively* demonstrated.[43] Nevertheless, the Court of Appeal in *Matthews and Alleyne*, having been referred to the above passage in the 10th edition of this book, remained unconvinced that the law had yet reached that position.

In summary, aside from the complexity and lack of definition, the present law may be seen by some as too wide in treating as intention those cases in which D has foreseen as a very high probability that a particular consequence will arise, but where D asserts that that result was not his purpose. The Law Commission recommends a codification of the present law (see later), having provisionally considered and rejected various forms of exhaustive definition.[44]

3.2.1.3 Intention and results known to be a condition of achievement of purpose

It may be said that no one can ever know that a result is certain to follow from an act. This is why courts and writers are driven to speak of 'virtually' or 'almost' certain results. But a person may know that he cannot achieve his purpose, A, without bringing about some other result, B. If he is to bring about A, he knows he must also, at the same time or earlier, bring about B. It may be that, in any other circumstances, he would much rather B did not happen, indeed its occurrence may be abhorrent to him. But, the choice being between (i) going without A and (ii) having A and B, he decides to have A and B. It seems fair to say that he intends to cause B as well as A.

Suppose that V has made a will, leaving the whole of his large estate to D. D loves V but he has an overwhelming desire to enjoy his inheritance immediately. If he gives V what he knows to be a fatal dose of poison, he intends to kill V, though he says truthfully that it causes him anguish. Similarly, consider D who wishes to injure his enemy, V, who is standing inside the window of the house of D's friend. If, knowing the window to be closed, D throws the stone through it at V, can it be doubted that he intends to break his friend's window? Since result 'A' is the actor's purpose, it is immaterial that he is not certain that it will happen. He does not have a good throwing arm and he knows the stone may miss—but he intends to strike V. And, since he knows that if he strikes V it will be because he has broken his friend's window, he intends to break the window. It seems from these examples that we might safely say that where D knows or believes a result to be a condition of the achievement of his purpose, D intends it.

Yet even this modest conclusion is not beyond doubt; there are a number of cases in which the generally accepted principles of intention seem to have been qualified in their application by the appellate courts. In *Moloney*,[45] Lord Bridge referred with approval to *Steane*[46] where D, who, during the Second World War in order to save himself and his family from the horrors of the concentration camp, gave broadcasts which would assist the enemy. He was held not to have had an 'intent to assist the enemy' in performing those broadcasts. Steane may have been a loyal citizen who, in other circumstances, would have wished to do nothing to assist the enemy; but, being faced with the choice, 'Assist us—or go back to the concentration camp', he chose to do as the enemy required. Of course, his purpose was to keep his wife and children out of the camp; but it seems plain that he knew

---

[43] This was the view taken by Ward and Brooke LJJ in Re A *(Conjoined Twins)* [2000] 4 All ER 961, [2001] Crim LR 400 and commentary.

[44] See LCCP 177; Norrie [2006] Crim LR 486, 495. See p 102.

[45] [1985] AC 905 at 929.

[46] [1947] KB 997. See also Duff, *Intention, Agency and Criminal Liability*, 95. For a historical account see GR Rubin, 'New Light on *Steane's Case*' (2003) 24 *Legal History* 143.

that that purpose could only be achieved by doing required acts that might assist the enemy. Reading the broadcast script and making the propaganda films were the acts likely to assist the enemy.[47] There are numerous similar cases. In *Ahlers*,[48] a German consul who assisted German nationals to return home after the declaration of war in 1914 was held to have intended only to do his duty as consul. In *Gillick's* case,[49] some of the judges seem to have been of the opinion that a doctor, who knew or believed that his provision of contraceptive advice to a girl under 16 would encourage a man to have sexual intercourse with her, would not be guilty of abetting the man's commission of the sexual offence, because the doctor's intention was to protect the girl, not to encourage sexual intercourse with her.

In some of these cases, it seems that the concept of intention is strained to do a job for which it is not fitted. The courts appear, in some of these admittedly hard cases, to examine the motives or justifications of the defendant while purporting to be determining his intention. Steane's acquittal would more properly have been based on duress and the case envisaged in *Gillick* seems to have been, in substance, one of necessity—some degree of encouragement of sexual intercourse was a lesser evil than an unwanted pregnancy in the young girl.[50] In each of these cases, D had an 'honourable' purpose. Where D's purpose is disreputable, the court is most unlikely to interpret intention so narrowly. If Steane, being a chain-smoker deprived of cigarettes, had performed the broadcast in order to get a packet, it is probable that Lord Goddard CJ would have had no hesitation in holding that, of course, he intended to assist the enemy. Yet, from the point of view of intention, there seems to be no difference between the cases.[51] If this is so, it produces an undesirable distortion of the concept of intention and it would be better if the true reason for the decision were admitted by the courts.[52] *Moloney*, and *Woollin*, however, encourage such decisions—the jury appears to be left a measure of discretion to say whether they think the state of mind should be categorized as intention or not.

It is arguable that intention, in law, should extend to results known or believed by the actor to be conditions of the achievement of his purpose but should go no further. This would give effect to the constantly reiterated opinion of the courts that intention is different from desire. If D acts in order to cause 'A' and knows 'B' will follow, 'B' is not desired, at least it is not desired for its own sake; but it is intended. The court can avoid treating this as a case of recklessness as to B. D is not merely taking a risk of causing B; he *knows* or thinks he knows that, if he achieves his aim of causing 'A', 'B' will happen or will have already happened.

---

[47] It might be argued that, even in these circumstances, B is not necessarily a condition of A. Someone might open the window while the stone is in flight towards it. The microphone into which Steane spoke might have been disconnected or the transmitter broken down. Lord Bridge's man who boards the plane for Manchester (the last place he wishes to go) to escape arrest intends (as Lord Bridge says [1985] AC at 986) to go to Manchester although it is possible that the plane will be diverted to Luton. Even in the case of D who gives V the fatal dose of poison to accelerate his inheritance, it is possible that V will die of natural causes before the poison takes effect: cf *White* [1910] 2 KB 124. See the discussion in Tadros, *Criminal Responsibility*, 219.

[48] [1915] 1 KB 616.

[49] *Gillick v West Norfolk and Wisbech Area Health Authority* [1986] AC 112, [1986] Crim LR 113 and commentary. See also *Salford Health Authority, ex p Janaway* [1989] AC 537.

[50] See now the Sexual Offences Act 2003, s 73, p 835.   [51] Williams, *The Mental Element in Crime*, 21.

[52] For consideration of the importance of the role of motive in defining intention, see Norrie, *Crime, Reason and History*, 43 et seq; DN Husak, *The Philosophy of Criminal Law: Selected Essays* (2010) Ch 2; Tadros, *Criminal Responsibility*, 202. After a lengthy philosophical account, Tadros concludes that D's intention must be motive-related. He suggests that where D does X believing that in doing X, D will also do Y, if Y is a reason that motivated D to do X, D intends Y. If D believes that Y was a reason against him doing X despite which he still did X, D intentionally did Y, although he did not intend to do Y (at 225). The courts are best avoiding such sophistications.

3.2.1.4 Results known or believed to be virtually certain to accompany achievement of purpose

The definition of intention extends yet further. Result B may be intended, according to *Moloney*, where B is not a condition of A. D can be said to have intended result B where it is possible for result A (D's purpose) to occur without result B also happening, but as D knows, causing A is virtually certain to cause B as well.[53]

To take an example, D, wishing to collect the insurance on a cargo (result A), puts a time bomb in a plane to blow up in the mid-Atlantic. He has no wish to kill the crew. It is *possible* for the plane and cargo to be destroyed and the crew to escape—people do occasionally fall from aircraft at great heights and survive—but the possibility is so remote as to be negligible; and D knows that.[54] There is certainly a strong argument for saying that he intends to kill (result B). This is so even if, as D knows, this type of bomb has a 50 per cent failure rate. There is an even chance that nothing will happen. But he wants the explosion (result A) to happen and, if it does, killing (result B) is, as he knows, a virtual certainty. So a jury may (not must) find that there is an intention to kill.[55]

The difficulty is that once we depart from absolute certainty, there is a question of degree and an uncertain boundary between intention and recklessness. In *Hyam*,[56] D, in order to frighten Mrs Booth, her rival for the affections of X, put blazing newspaper through the letter box of Booth's house and caused the death of two of her children. Ackner J directed the jury that D was guilty of murder if she knew that it was highly probable that her act would cause at least serious bodily harm. The jury convicted so they clearly found that she did know that. In the light of *subsequent cases*, that direction was wrong (foresight of virtual certainty is required before a jury can find intention) but in *Moloney* Lord Bridge[57] thought that, on a proper direction, no reasonable jury could have failed to convict Hyam. Is that really so? Might not a jury have been satisfied that D knew that serious injury to the occupants was a highly probable result without being satisfied that D knew it was virtually certain?

In *Moloney*,[58] Lord Hailsham and Lord Bridge gave the example of the case of a terrorist who plants a time bomb in a public building and gives a warning to enable the public to be evacuated. He knows that it is virtually certain that a bomb disposal squad will attempt to defuse the bomb. The squad does so, the bomb explodes and a member of the squad is killed. It is assumed by their lordships that this is murder.[59] The bomber intends to endanger the squad's lives (because he knows that it is virtually certain they will attempt to defuse the bomb) but he does not, surely, know that it is virtually certain that one of them will be killed or even seriously injured. It is doubtful if this would be murder even under the 'highly probable' formula of *Hyam*. It looks like recklessness, which is not enough for murder.

---

[53] For comparisons of English, Dutch and German approaches to intention and recklessness, see J Blomsma, *Mens Rea and Defences in European Criminal Law* (2012). See in particular the discussion of the mens rea of 'dolus eventualis': the conscious acceptance of a risk. It is enough that D has, with the purpose of achieving result A, foreseen B as a probability and accepted that B can occur or takes that for granted, at 99–134.

[54] This and the example in n 59, have prompted a voluminous literature, see A Pedain, 'Intention and the Terrorist Example' [2003] Crim LR 579 and references therein. Kaveny (2004) 120 LQR 81 argues that in the virtual certainty cases D's gross disregard for human life justifies D's conviction as a murderer.

[55] cf the view of I Kugler, 'Conditional Oblique Intention' [2004] Crim LR 284, seemingly suggesting that the question will depend on whether D has a guilty motive or Parliament's motive in creating an offence of that form or the degree of harm actually caused. It is difficult to see how these issues affect D's intention in substantive law.

[56] [1975] AC 55.   [57] [1985] AC 905 at 926.   [58] ibid at 913, 927.

[59] cf A Pedain [2003] Crim LR 579, suggesting that this is a form of intent because of D's 'motive'. Pedain argues that the terrorist in these cases is sufficiently morally culpable because of his willingness to risk another's death such that he can properly be regarded as having a direct intent for murder.

The example might be justified if it could be proved that the terrorist wants the bomb to go off *at a time* when he knows it is virtually certain that the squad will be attempting to defuse it. That would be indistinguishable from the 'bomb-in-the-plane' case, earlier in this section, where the bomber wants the bomb to go off in the mid-Atlantic.

In *Moloney*, D shot his stepfather, whom he loved, when, in the course of a drunken game to establish who was quicker 'on the draw' with loaded shotguns, he pulled the trigger in response to a challenge, 'if you have [the guts] pull the trigger'. He may not have realized that the gun was aimed, at point-blank range, at V's head. His conviction was quashed because the judge misdirected the jury that D intended serious bodily harm if he foresaw that it would 'probably' happen. In the House of Lords, Lord Bridge insisted on the need for 'a moral certainty', a probability which is 'little short of overwhelming' and an act that 'will lead to a certain event unless something unexpected supervenes to prevent it'.[60] Unfortunately, in summing up his opinion in the form of guidelines for trial judges, he used the term, 'natural consequence' to mean a consequence that is virtually certain to ensue.

In *Hancock and Shankland*,[61] two miners taking industrial action pushed from the parapet of a bridge heavy concrete blocks which struck a taxi carrying a working miner to work and killed the taxi-driver. They said they intended to push the blocks on to the middle lane of the road, not the lane in which the taxi was travelling, and that they intended to frighten the working miner and prevent him going to work, but not to hurt anyone. At their trial for murder, the judge closely followed the *Moloney* 'guidelines'. The Court of Appeal held that the conviction must be quashed. The guidelines were defective. The jury might well have understood 'natural consequence' to mean 'direct consequence' and not to convey the notion of moral certainty or overwhelming probability of which Lord Bridge spoke. The House of Lords agreed. Both courts stressed that even if D has awareness that the consequence is virtually certain that is not intention, but only evidence from which a jury may infer intention, if they are satisfied beyond reasonable doubt that this is the right inference. The difficulties with this approach are considered earlier.

3.2.1.5 Intention in crimes other than murder

Nearly all the leading cases relate to murder and Lord Steyn prefaced his decision in *Woollin* by remarking that 'intent' does not necessarily have precisely the same meaning in every context of the criminal law.[62]

Earlier the House in *Moloney* said that they were laying down the law not only for murder but for offences requiring 'specific intent' generally (which, here, seems to mean merely offences requiring intent). The approval in *Moloney* of cases like *Steane* and the difficulty of reconciling the example of the bomber with intention as defined in that case suggests that the word may well be held to bear different shades of meaning in different contexts. Sometimes the context may indicate a narrower meaning—that nothing less than purpose will do. This may be the explanation of *Steane*, though that decision has been regularly cited in murder cases. A strong case can be made that the very nature of an attempt involves purpose, and that 'intent' in the Criminal Attempts Act[63] should be construed accordingly. The Draft Criminal Code recognizes that the context may require some modification of its proposed definition.

---

60 [1985] AC 905 at 925, 926, 929. See also *R (Tait)* v *CICAP* [2009] EWHC 767 (Admin), [2010] RTR 6.

61 [1986] AC 455.

62 For criticism, see F Stark, 'It's Only Words: On Meaning and Mens Rea' (2013) 72 CLJ 155. Stark objects to the idea that mens rea terms ought to be defined differently depending upon context. He argues that such an approach undermines the criminal law's goal of guiding effectively the conduct of citizens who wish to avoid punishment and that it leaves too much discretion to the criminal law's institutions.

63 See p 434. See LCCP 183, *Conspiracy and Attempts* (2007) para 14.27; LC 318, *Conspiracy and Attempts* (2009).

But, while the context may require a narrower meaning, it is submitted that a court should be slow to give the term a wider one. *Woollin* draws a clear line between intention and recklessness and it is desirable to preserve that clarity throughout the criminal law.

3.2.1.6 Intention as to conduct and circumstances

Most of the cases arise in the context of murder where the issue is whether D has intent as to the consequences of his conduct—death or GBH. In some offences, the issue will be about D's intent as to circumstances which must exist for the offence to be committed. In such cases, intention means either hope that the circumstance exists—which corresponds to purpose in relation to consequences—or knowledge (or belief that it is virtually certain) that the circumstance exists—which corresponds to foresight of certainty in relation to consequences. D charged with murder must intend GBH or death, but also the relevant circumstances— that V is a human being under the Queen's peace.[64] D charged with criminal damage must intend (or be reckless) whether the property belongs to another. If D knows or believes that it is virtually certain it belongs to another, he intends that circumstance.

Where an offence requires proof of an intent as to circumstances, a lesser mens rea will not suffice. So, if D receives a car which he knows to be stolen, that is an intentional handling of stolen goods even though D would, perhaps, much prefer that the car was not stolen. If, however, D believed merely that it was probable, or highly probable, that the car was stolen, this would not be an intentional handling. He neither hoped it was stolen, nor knew it was.

3.2.1.7 Reform

The definition[65] in cl 18(b) of the Draft Code provides:

A person acts 'intentionally' with respect to . . . a result when he acts either in order to bring it about or being aware that it will occur in the ordinary course of events.

There were two possible defects in the definition proposed in the Draft Code:

(a) it did not provide for the case where D knows that the relevant result will occur if, but only if, he succeeds in achieving some other purpose[66] and he is not certain that he will achieve that other purpose—this is exemplified by the case of the bomb with the 50 per cent failure rate;[67]

(b) in certain, admittedly rather unlikely, circumstances, the definition might mean that a person intended a result which it was his purpose to avoid—which does not seem to be very good sense. The starkest example is that of D who throws his child from the upper window of a burning house when he believes that death from the flames is inevitable.[68]

To avoid these difficulties, the Law Commission[69] proposed a definition of intention for the purposes of non-fatal offences against the person which, slightly modified, was included in the draft Bill, cl 14(1) in the Home Office Consultation Paper of February 1998:[70]

---

[64] See p 528.   [65] See the discussion in LCCP 177, para 4.22.   [66] See p 99.   [67] See n 59.

[68] As to whether this is properly seen as a case of intention where a defence of necessity should apply, see the discussion at p 98. See also LCCP 177, para 4.26; Norrie [2006] Crim LR 486, 495.

[69] LC 218, paras 7.1–7.14 and cl 1 of draft Bill, following LCCP 122, *Legislating the Criminal Code: Offences Against the Person and General Principles* (1992) paras 5.4–5.11 and JC Smith, 'A Note on Intention' [1990] Crim LR 85.

[70] JC Smith, 'Offences Against the Person: The Home Office Consultation Paper' [1998] Crim LR 317. See also A Khan, 'Intention in the Criminal Law: Time to Change' (2002) 23 Stat LR 235. See also Law Commission Scoping Consultation Paper No 217, *Reform of Offences Against the Person* (2014) Ch 4 and LC 361 (2015).

... a person acts intentionally with respect to a result if—

(a) it is his purpose to cause it; or

(b) although it is not his purpose to cause it, he knows that it would occur in the ordinary course of events if he were to succeed in his purpose of causing some other result.

Woollin, however, shows that this may be too narrow. D lost his temper and threw down his three-month-old son on to a hard surface, killing him. The prosecution did not contend that his purpose was to kill or cause serious injury. He was convicted of murder on a direction that it was enough that he knew there was a 'substantial risk' that he would cause serious injury. His conviction was upheld by the Court of Appeal but quashed by the House of Lords. If the law was as stated in cl 14, even if Woollin knew that serious bodily injury was certain, he would not have an intention to cause it—it was not his purpose and he had no other purpose, except to vent his anger, which is not a purpose to cause a result. To meet this point it was suggested that the clause should be amended to read '... he knows that it *will occur in the ordinary course of events, or* that it would do so if he were to succeed in his purpose of causing some other result'. The Law Commission more recently rejected that suggestion on the ground that it presents problems where the result is the very thing that D is seeking to avoid (as in the case of the burning house and the father who throws his child to her virtually certain death).[71]

Parliament has accepted in one context at least that a person has intention in relation to a consequence where he means to cause the consequences or is aware that it will occur in the ordinary course of events.[72]

The Law Commission's homicide review led it to consider a number of proposals in relation to intention, finally settling on one retaining the flexibility inherent in the present law (and the moral elbow room it provides):[73]

(1) A person should be taken to intend a result if he or she acts in order to bring it about.

(2) In cases where the judge believes that justice may not be done unless an expanded understanding of intention is given, the jury should be directed as follows: an intention to bring about a result may be found if it is shown that the defendant thought that the result was a virtually certain consequence of his or her action.

This definition removes the unnecessary requirement that the result was a virtual certainty.

3.2.1.8 The distinction between motive and intention

If D's conduct amounts to the causes an actus reus with mens rea, he is guilty of the crime and on the orthodox view it is entirely irrelevant to his guilt that he had a good motive.[74] The mother who kills her severely disabled and suffering child out of motives of compassion is just as guilty of murder as is the person who kills for gain or hatred. On the other hand, if either the actus reus or the mens rea of any crime is lacking, no motive, however evil, will make a person guilty of a crime. The orthodox view that motive should not be confused with mens rea has come under challenge.[75] Consider, for example, that

---

[71] LCCP 177, paras 4.26 and 4.42–4.44.   [72] See the International Criminal Courts Act 2001, s 66(3)(a).

[73] Academics tended to favour a full definition and practitioners and judges favoured the codification proposal adopting the present law (LC 304, para 3.17).

[74] See *A-G's Reference (No 1 of 2002)* [2002] EWCA Crim 2392, where D, a police officer, was prepared to fabricate evidence to convict a person who was factually guilty. Her 'good' motive was not an excuse for perverting the course of justice. It may affect sentence: *Inglis* [2010] EWCA Crim 2637.

[75] See Wilson, Central Issues, Ch 5; Norrie, *Crime, Reason and History*, 43–53; Norrie, *Punishment, Responsibility and Justice* (2002) 170–81; J Horder, 'On the Irrelevance of Motive in Criminal Law' in J Horder (ed), *Oxford Essays in Jurisprudence*; Tadros, *Criminal Responsibility*, Ch 8.

V is about to commit a serious terrorist attack and D takes the justified step of killing V thereby preventing the serious crime. Some argue that if D was motivated to do so by the desire to promote social well-being, he should not be guilty; if D was simply motivated by hatred of V, a long-standing enemy, D should be liable. The intent is the same in either case—to kill the person; the difference between innocence and guilt lies in the motive which prompted this intent.

It is submitted, however, that, assuming that D knew of the facts which justified the killing, this view is contrary to principle. If it were correct, it would seem to follow that D, the public executioner, would be guilty of murder in hanging X, who had been condemned to death by a competent court, if it were shown that D had postponed his retirement to carry out this particular execution because he had a grudge against X and derived particular pleasure from hanging him. This can hardly be the law. If a surgical operation, though dangerous to life, is clearly justifiable on medical grounds, a surgeon who performs it with all proper skill cannot be said to be guilty of attempted murder, or, if the patient dies, murder, because he hopes the patient will die so that he can marry his wife, or inherit his property, or so that the patient will avoid the thoroughly miserable life he will face if he survives.[76]

One of the difficulties in determining the relevance of motive in criminal law lies in the ambiguity of language. Sometimes, when we speak of motive, we mean an emotion such as jealousy or greed, and sometimes we mean a species of intention. For example, D intends: (a) to put poison in his uncle's tea; (b) to cause his uncle's death; and (c) to inherit his money. We would normally say that (c) is his motive. Applying our previous test of intention (p 93), (c) is certainly also intended, but the reason why it is considered merely a motive is that it is a consequence ulterior to the mens rea and the actus reus; it is no part of the crime. The courts are not always consistent in their terminology. For example, if D an employer dismisses E an employee, who has given evidence against him, in accordance with the terms of E's contract, D will be guilty of contempt of court, if his 'motive' was to punish E for his evidence but not if it was for any other reason—for example, incompetence or redundancy.[77] A desire for consistency in terminology would suggest that in such a case we should speak of intent or purpose rather than motive. For example, if this variety of contempt were to be defined, the definition might say, 'with intent to punish the witness'.

In some exceptional cases motive does form an element of an offence. A conspicuous example is the series of 'aggravated offences' first created by the Crime and Disorder Act 1998.[78] Any of the existing offences specified in the Act[79] become racially or religiously aggravated offences with an enhanced penalty if, inter alia, the offence is motivated (wholly or partly) by hostility towards members of a racial group, based on their membership or presumed membership of that group. In blackmail, contrary to s 21 of the Theft Act 1968,[80] the accused's motive may be relevant in ascertaining whether his demand was unwarranted.[81] There are other circumstances in which motive may be relevant to the offence (eg dishonesty) or defence (eg revenge denies a defence of loss of self-control).[82]

As *evidence*, motive is always relevant.[83] This means simply that if the prosecution can prove that D had a motive for committing the crime, they may do so since the existence of a motive makes it more likely that D in fact did commit it. People do not usually act without a motive.

---

[76] See ATH Smith in *Reshaping the Criminal Law*, 95.

[77] *A-G v Butterworth* [1963] 1 QB 696. Cf *Rooney v Snaresbrook Crown Court* (1978) 68 Cr App R 78.

[78] See Ch 16.   [79] See p 734.   [80] See Ch 25.   [81] p 1039; *Chandler v DPP* [1964] AC 763.

[82] This restriction is made explicit in the new defences discussed in Ch 13.

[83] *Williams* (1986) 84 Cr App R 299, not following *Berry* (1986) 83 Cr App R 7.

In *sentencing*, motive is again important. When the law allows the judge a discretion in sentencing, he will obviously be influenced by the culpability of the offender's motive.

3.2.2 Recklessness

The definitions of many crimes specify that either intention to cause the proscribed result or recklessness as to whether that result is caused is sufficient mens rea for liability. A person who did not intend to cause a harmful result may nonetheless have taken an unjustifiable risk of causing it. If so, he may be held to be reckless. Unjustifiably taking risks in conduct which might harm others is culpable behaviour. In some scenarios, if we factor in the justifications for the conduct we might even say that some cases of intended action are less culpable than those involving recklessness.[84]

The test for recklessness involves assessing two issues: (a) whether D foresaw a risk of the proscribed result or circumstance specified in the actus reus of the crime in question; and (b) whether it was reasonable for D to take the risk in the circumstances known to him. These two elements are closely interrelated.

3.2.2.1 The current law

In the landmark case of G Lord Bingham based his definition of recklessness in the context of the Criminal Damage Act 1971 on the Draft Criminal Code, cl 18(c):

A person acts recklessly within the meaning of section 1 of the Criminal Damage Act 1971 with respect to—

(i) a circumstance when he is aware of a risk that it exists or will exist;

(ii) a result when he is aware of a risk that it will occur;

and it is, in the circumstances known to him, unreasonable to take the risk.

It is submitted that this subjective definition of recklessness ought to be applied in all statutory offences of recklessness unless Parliament has explicitly provided otherwise.[85] In *A-G's Reference (No 3 of 2003)*,[86] the Court of Appeal emphasized that although the House of Lords in G had stated that their decision was one specifically on recklessness under the Criminal Damage Act, 'general principles were laid down'. It was established that a defendant could not be culpable under the criminal law of doing something involving a risk of injury to another or damage to property if he genuinely did not perceive the risk.[87] The court refused to restrict the application of G to cases of positive action rather than those where liability arose by D's omission, and applied the subjective test to D's foresight of circumstances as well as consequences.[88]

---

[84] See eg the discussion in Kugler, *Direct and Oblique Intention in the Criminal Law*, 27. Considering D1 who intentionally terminates V's life to spare him pain, compared to D2 who recklessly shoots at an apple on V's head and misses, killing V.

[85] cf the offences relating to the Uranium Enrichment Technology (Prohibition on Disclosure) Regulations 2004, SI 2004/1818, made under the Anti-terrorism Crime and Security Act 2001, s 80(2) where an objective form of recklessness is expressly adopted. For an argument that the *Caldwell* test applies in some consumer offences, see Professor Cartwright in Appendix B to LCCP 195, *Criminal Liability in Regulatory Contexts* (2010) para B17.

[86] [2004] EWCA Crim 868.   [87] At [12].

[88] See also *Mbagwu* [2007] EWCA Crim 1068, where Hughes LJ noted at [20], 'the element of recklessness necessarily meant that the Defendant in question would have to be shown to be reckless in the sense understood in *Cunningham* (1957) 41 Cr App Rep 155. As is well known, recklessness in that sense requires *(and indeed these days in every sense requires)* that it be shown that the Defendant in question actually foresaw some harm to such a person' (emphasis added).

3.2.2.2 Subjective awareness of 'a' risk

The standard test of recklessness set out in the previous paragraph is traditionally called *'Cunningham'* recklessness after the case of that name. It requires proof that D was aware of the existence of *a* risk of the proscribed result or circumstance. It is a subjective form of mens rea, focused on D's own cognition of the existence of a risk.[89]

In *Cunningham*,[90] D tore a gas meter from the wall of the cellar of an unoccupied house to steal the money in it. He left the gas gushing out. It seeped into a neighbouring house and was inhaled by V whose life was endangered. D was convicted under s 23 of the Offences Against the Person Act (OAPA) 1861[91] of maliciously[92] administering a noxious thing so as to endanger life. Because the judge directed the jury that 'malicious' meant simply 'wicked', D's conviction was quashed. The Court of Criminal Appeal quoted with approval the principle first propounded by Professor Kenny in 1902:[93]

in any statutory definition of a crime 'malice' must be taken not in the old vague sense of 'wickedness' in general, but as requiring either (i) an actual intention to do the particular *kind* of harm that in fact was done, or (ii) recklessness as to whether such harm should occur or not (ie the accused has foreseen that the particular kind of harm might be done, and yet has gone on to take the risk of it). It is neither limited to, nor does it indeed require, any ill-will towards the person injured.

Cunningham was not guilty unless *he* was aware, when he broke off the gas meter, or left the broken pipe with the gas gushing out,[94] that it might be inhaled by someone. It is not sufficient that, if D had stopped to think, it would have been obvious to him that there was a risk. He must actually recognize the existence of such a risk and deliberately take it. In *Cunningham*, the court was considering the requirement of 'malice', a form of recklessness, but the definition in *Cunningham* applies generally to crimes of recklessness.[95]

It is well established that where D closes his mind to the risk he can be found reckless within the subjective definition, as where he claims that his extreme anger blocked out of his mind the risk involved in his action.[96] As Lane LJ put it, 'knowledge or appreciation of a risk of [the proscribed harm] must have entered the defendant's mind even though he may have suppressed it or driven it out'.[97]

---

[89] It is important to point out that if D merely asserts that he did not foresee the risk, this will not prevent him from being found guilty. Juries remain free to come to conclusions about D's subjective state of mind and may simply disbelieve his claim. This may be especially likely to occur if the risk was an obvious one and D has no cognitive dysfunction that would have rendered him unable to perceive it. The Administrative Court emphasized that this does not turn a subjective test into an objective one in *Seray-Wurie v DPP* [2012] EWHC 208 (Admin). See also *R (on the application of Pinkney) v DPP* [2017] EWHC 854 (Admin).

[90] [1957] 2 QB 396.   [91] See p 748.

[92] Subject to what is said later, we can treat malice as equivalent to recklessness for the purposes of this discussion.

[93] *Outlines* (16th edn, 1952) 186.   [94] See on omissions, p 54.

[95] In one sense the definition pronounced by the court in *Cunningham* is defective since it fails to make explicit that not only must D foresee the risk of the proscribed harm, but he must take it *unjustifiably* as discussed, p 106.

[96] *Parker* [1977] 1 All ER 475 (D slammed phone down in anger and broke it). Ashworth describes this case as 'troublesome'. He states that cases such as these, involving sudden reaction or rage, leave little room for the kind of reasoning presupposed by the subjectivist paradigm. A Ashworth, 'A Change of Normative Position: Determining the Contours of Culpability in Criminal Law' (2008) 11 New Crim LR 232.

[97] *Stephenson* [1979] QB 695, 704. See also the comments of Lord Bingham in *G* [2004] 1 AC 1034 at [39] and Lord Steyn at [58]. As a more striking example, see *Booth* [2006] EWHC 192 (Admin), where D damaged V's car when he was knocked down by V. D was convicted of criminal damage since he was reckless as to the damage having seen the risk of being knocked down and closed his mind to that risk.

It is only necessary for D to foresee *a* risk of the proscribed harm. In *Brady*,[98] D was drunk when he climbed on railings at a nightclub and fell onto the dance floor below causing serious injuries to V who was dancing there. The issue at trial was whether D had the mens rea: recklessness (strictly speaking for the offence in question it was malice but for present purposes they are not distinguishable). D argued that the effect of the decision in *G*[99] was to require the jury to be directed that the Crown had to establish that D had foreseen 'an obvious and significant risk' of injury to another by his actions, or else that he would have done so had he been sober. The Court of Appeal rejected that argument. The definition of recklessness provided in *G* does not require proof that D had foreseen 'an obvious and significant risk' of the relevant consequence. It followed that there was no need for a trial judge directing a jury as to malice or recklessness to qualify the word 'risk' by the words obvious and significant. The court was surely right to reject this argument: to introduce a requirement that the risk was 'obvious and significant' would create uncertainty and complexity in an area of mens rea which desperately does not need it. The question would certainly arise whether the requirement was to prove that the degree of risk was 'obvious and significant', or whether that qualifying expression related to the consequences should the risk materialize.[100]

3.2.2.3 An unjustified risk

Not all risk-taking constitutes recklessness. Sometimes the accused will have identified a risk and rejected it as being so negligible as to be a reasonable one to take.[101] In other circumstances, the risk may have been rightly recognized to be much greater, but the social utility of the action justifies taking it.[102] It can be justifiable to take a risk of causing harm to another's property or his person or even of causing his death. The pilot of an aircraft, the surgeon performing an operation and the promoter of a tightrope act in a circus must all know that their conduct might cause death but none of them would properly be described as reckless unless the risk taken was an unreasonable one. The law allows the use of reasonable force in the lawful arrest of an offender or in private defence. If D, in the course of an act of reasonable self-defence, damages V's window, he is not guilty of reckless criminal damage.[103]

Whether it is justifiable to take a risk depends on the social value of the activity involved relative to the probability and the gravity of the harm which might be caused. The question is whether the risk was one which a reasonable and prudent person might have taken. It might be reasonable for D to shoot V's ferocious dog which is attacking his sheep, but it does not follow that it would be reasonable to take a risk of causing injury or death to V—still less a bystander. This element of the test is objective—that is to say, the court or jury lays down the required standard of care.

---

[98] [2006] EWCA Crim 2413.

[99] *G* [2004] 1 AC 1034.

[100] Difficulties with a similar qualification were experienced when the House of Lords in *Lawrence* [1982] AC 626 held that in reckless driving the risk must be an obvious and 'serious' one. On the difficulties of that aspect of that test see: G Williams, 'Recklessness Redefined' (1981) 40 CLJ 252, 276; J Brabyn, 'A Sequel to Seymour, Made in Hong Kong' [1987] Crim LR 84 at 90–1.

[101] In LC 304 the definition of recklessness for the purposes of the Law Commission's proposed second degree murder requires awareness of a serious risk, where seriousness does not denote the degree of risk, but that the risk is one that should not be ignored. See LC 304, para 3.39.

[102] For discussion of the relative moral culpability of these two scenarios, see W Wilson, 'The Structure of Criminal Homicide' [2006] Crim LR 471; J Rogers, 'The Law Commission's Proposed Restructuring of the Law of Homicide' (2006) 70 J Crim L 223.

[103] *Sears v Broome* [1986] Crim LR 461.

What degree of risk? It is impossible to say in general terms that recklessness requires any particular degree of probability of the occurrence of the harm in question.[104] If the conduct has no social utility—for example, a game of 'Russian roulette' or an armed robbery—the slightest possibility of any harm should be enough. If the act has a high degree of social utility—for example, the performance of a surgical operation—then only a very high degree of probability of grave harm that outweighs the social utility will suffice to condemn it as reckless.[105]

3.2.2.4 Malice

In *Cunningham*, it will be recalled, the mens rea of the offence was that of 'malice'. That form of mens rea is found in many old offences, including some commonly used offences under the OAPA 1861.

It is clear that the test for malice requires proof that D foresaw a risk of the relevant result. In *Cunningham* the court stated: 'In our opinion, the word "maliciously" in a statutory crime postulates foresight of consequence.' Cunningham was not guilty unless *he* was aware, when he broke off the gas meter, or left the broken pipe with the gas gushing out,[106] that it might be inhaled by someone. In a series of cases, of which the most important is the House of Lords decision in *Parmenter*,[107] convictions for malicious wounding were quashed because trial judges wrongly directed the jury that it was enough that D 'should have foreseen' the risk.[108] This led the jury to think that it is enough that D ought to have foreseen the risk of harm; it is not. To be 'malicious', D must actually foresee some harm and the fact that he ought to have foreseen is, at best, some evidence that he did foresee.

The test of recklessness requires, as we have seen, that D not only foresaw a risk, but unjustifiably went on to take it. The question arises whether that further element is also a requirement for the mens rea of malice.

On the one hand, in the case of *Cunningham*, the court did not include within its definition of malice any requirement that D's taking of the risk was unjustifiable. Subsequent cases, including the House of Lords in *Parmenter and Savage* have approved the *Cunningham* formulation when interpreting the word malice.[109] The *Cunningham* formulation was based, as noted, on Professor Kenny's definition. That definition made no reference to the requirement that D has to act unjustifiably or unreasonably in taking the risk he has foreseen. *Mowatt*[110] also followed *Cunningham*, but did not expressly require that D was unjustified in taking the risk.[111]

On the other hand, the Court of Appeal in *Brady*[112] accepted the decision in G defining recklessness as applicable in s 20 for malice without acknowledging the point under discussion. The G definition is also followed in the *Crown Court Compendium*.[113] While the House of Lords in G expressed itself to be dealing with s 1 of the Criminal Damage Act 1971, the Court of Appeal Criminal Division has accepted the wider application of the decision.[114]

---

[104] See *Vehicle Inspectorate v Nuttall* [1999] 1 WLR 629.

[105] See A Norrie, 'Subjectivism, Objectivism and the Limits of Criminal Recklessness' (1992) 12 OJLS 45; PH Robinson, 'The Modern General Part: Three Illusions' in Shute and Simester, *Criminal Law Theory*, 88–91.

[106] See on omissions, p 45.   [107] [1992] 1 AC 699.

[108] The trial judges fell into error by taking the words of Diplock LJ out of their context in *Mowatt* [1968] 1 QB 421 at 426.

[109] Reference is made in *Savage* to the dissenting views in *Caldwell* [1982] AC 341, [1981] Crim LR 392 and commentary in which reference is made to justification, but the final conclusion in *Savage* was based on *Cunningham*: [1992] 1 AC 699, 750, [1992] Crim LR 288 and commentary.

[110] [1968] 1 QB 421.   [111] See n 109.   [112] [2006] EWCA Crim 2413.

[113] See *Crown Court Compendium* (2020) Part 1, para 8–2.

[114] *AG's Reference (No 3 of 2003)* [2004] EWCA Crim 868 (misconduct in public office); *Brady* [2006] EWCA Crim 2413 (s 20 OAPA 1861).

The mens rea of offences requiring malice, such as s 20 of the OAPA 1861, remains intention or subjective recklessness and is therefore in line with *G* (ie the defendant was aware of a risk of some harm which he then, unreasonably, went on to take).[115]

Despite the absence of express reference to this element in the malice test, it is submitted that the definition of malice ought to be construed as requiring proof that D was aware of a risk and that it was an unjustifiable risk to take in the circumstances known to him. As the Law Commission noted, a 'surgeon may justifiably carry out a surgical procedure despite knowing that there is a risk of serious harm, and should not be guilty of an offence if the operation miscarries'.[116]

3.2.2.5 The rise and fall of objective recklessness

The *Cunningham*, subjective, approach to recklessness or 'advertent recklessness' as it is also called, was the accepted definition until a controversial and, it is now accepted, erroneous turn by the House of Lords in the 1980s. Although the House of Lords in *G* restored orthodoxy by affirming that the definition of recklessness is as stated in *Cunningham*, set out earlier, it is valuable to examine, briefly,[117] the temporary shift of English law towards objective recklessness in some offences.

Caldwell v MPC

It was accepted that the *Cunningham* definition of recklessness applied, inter alia, to the offences of damaging property under the Malicious Damage Act 1861. The Law Commission in its *Report on Criminal Damage*[118] made many proposals for the reform of that law but considered that the mental element, as interpreted in *Cunningham*, was satisfactory. In relation to the mens rea, it proposed only that it be 'expressed with greater simplicity and clarity' and that this should be achieved by using 'intentionally or recklessly' in place of the archaic and misleading term 'maliciously'. Parliament adopted the proposals in the Criminal Damage Act 1971. Unfortunately, the Commission proposed no definition of recklessness and the Act contains none. It was assumed that the definition under *Cunningham* would apply. The Court of Appeal held, though after some hesitation, that 'reckless' in the 1971 Act bore the *Cunningham* meaning. But in 1981, the House of Lords decided in *Caldwell*[119] (Lords Wilberforce and Edmund-Davies dissenting) and in *Lawrence*[120] that where the statute uses the word 'reckless' a different test applied. In *Caldwell*, Lord Diplock said that a person is reckless as to whether any property would be destroyed or damaged:

if (1) he does an act which in fact creates an obvious risk that property would be destroyed or damaged and (2) when he does the act he (i) either has not given any thought to the possibility of there being any such risk or (ii) has recognised that there was some risk involved and has nonetheless gone on to do it.

[115] *Brady*, ibid.

[116] Scoping Paper, para 2.96, citing the CLRC, Fourteenth Report, *Offences against the Person* (1980) Cmnd 7844, para 8.

[117] For a full examination and compelling critique of the *Caldwell* definition and its implications, see the 10th edn of this book, and the references cited therein.

[118] LC 29 (1970), confirming proposals in Working Paper No 23 (1969).

[119] [1982] AC 341, [1981] Crim LR 392 and commentary. See, especially, EJ Griew, 'Reckless Damage and Reckless Driving—Living with *Caldwell* and *Lawrence*' [1981] Crim LR 743; J McEwan and J Robilliard, 'Recklessness: The House of Lords and the Criminal Law' (1981) 1 LS 267; G Syrota, 'A Radical Change in the Law of Recklessness?' [1982] Crim LR 97; Williams (1981) 40 CLJ 252; G Williams, 'The Unresolved Problem of Recklessness' (1988) 8 LS 74.

[120] [1982] AC 510. For discussion of these decisions see also the commentaries at [1981] Crim LR 393 and 410.

Under both limbs (i) and (ii) of the direction, as formulated, it had to be proved that the risk taken was an 'obvious [and serious[121]] risk'. The further element of culpability was either:

(1) D's failure to give thought to whether there was 'such a risk' (which might be designated 'inadvertent recklessness'); or

(2) D's knowledge that there was 'some risk' ('advertent recklessness').

This represented a very different test to that in *Cunningham*.[122] It was sufficient to convict D for an offence to which the *Caldwell* recklessness test applied where the reasonable person would have seen the risk even if D did not, nor even where D could not see the risk because of some limitation in his capacity.[123]

The 'model direction' contained inconsistencies and lacked precision,[124] in particular it left the knotty question whether there was a loophole or lacuna: D would not be reckless if he had considered the matter and decided that there was no risk. It was questionable whether such an individual was any less culpable than one who had given no thought (and who was therefore guilty).[125] There were also more principled objections to the test. First, it resulted in an indefensible distinction in law between the tests applicable to various offences. To take an example based on *W (A Minor) v Dolbey*,[126] if D took an air rifle and, not even considering the possibility that it might be loaded (as was the fact), aimed and fired it at V, breaking V's spectacles and destroying his eye, D would, under *Caldwell*, have been liable for recklessly causing criminal damage to the spectacles but would not have been criminally liable at all for the destruction of the eye because that offence (s 20 OAPA 1861) imposes a subjective test of malice. The law appeared to give greater protection to spectacles than to eyes.

Secondly, it failed to respect the principle that for serious crimes at least, the defendant should be proved to have a culpable *state of mind*. *Caldwell* allowed for conviction on the basis of D having no state of mind as to the risk of the proscribed harm. The most significant principled failing of the *Caldwell* approach was its potential to create injustice, and this led, ultimately, to its downfall. The test worked harshly in cases of young people and those whose capacity to see risk was diminished for reasons which involved no fault on their part. Recklessness was proved if the reasonable person would have foreseen the risk even if D did not or could not because of his lack of experience or understanding or intelligence.[127] For example, in *Stephenson*,[128] a homeless person sheltered in a hollow in a

---

[121] According to the definition in *Lawrence*, decided in the House on the same day.

[122] The difference can be seen by considering post-*G* cases applying *Cunningham* to overturn convictions where the direction had, erroneously, been based on *Caldwell*: eg *Castle* [2004] EWCA Crim 2758; *Cooper* [2004] EWCA Crim 1382.

[123] See S Field and M Lynn, 'The Capacity for Recklessness' (1992) 12 LS 74; S Field and M Lynn, 'Capacity Recklessness and the House of Lords' [1993] Crim LR 127.

[124] To whom must the risk be obvious? Was it always necessary for the risk to be obvious to a reasonable person? What if D was an expert who would have foreseen the risk but the reasonable person would not have done? (See further the commentary on the decision of the Court of Appeal in *Reid* (1989) 91 Cr App R 263 at [1991] Crim LR 269, 271.) Was the degree of risk that ought to have been foreseen restricted to serious risks?

[125] D Birch, 'The Foresight Saga: The Biggest Mistake of All' [1988] Crim LR 4. The relative culpability of one who gives no thought to the risk as compared to one who wrongly believes that there is no risk is difficult to assess. We need to know why the person had the state of mind. If it was because although he had the capacity to see the risk he was too careless or lazy to investigate the risks properly we would properly describe him as culpable: Tadros, *Criminal Responsibility*, 255.

[126] (1983) 88 Cr App R 1.

[127] 'The criminal law ought not to be used to criminalise the merely stupid or irrational': Tadros, *Criminal Responsibility*, 239.

[128] [1979] QB 695, [1979] Crim LR 590 and commentary.

haystack. Feeling cold, he lit a fire in the hollow. The haystack was destroyed. Any reasonable person would have been aware of the risk but Stephenson was suffering from schizophrenia and may not have been aware of it. Because this was not clearly left to the jury, the court—pre-*Caldwell*—quashed his conviction. Even if he had stopped to think whether a risk existed, it is possible that, because of his condition, he might not have realized that there was a risk of damage. Stephenson would have been convicted under *Caldwell*. The objective test therefore had the potential to criminalize the blind person who damaged property being unaware of a risk which would have been obvious to a sighted person. And those with temporary disabilities—the person who strikes a match, being unaware because of his heavy cold that the premises reek of petrol fumes, could be convicted. Sir John Smith wrote of *Caldwell*: 'The decision sets back the law concerning the mental element in criminal damage in theory to before 1861.'[129]

R v G

In *G*,[130] Ds aged 11 and 12 went camping. During the night they set fire to newspapers in the yard at the back of a shop and threw the lit newspapers under a bin. They left without putting out the fire. The fire spread to the wheelie bin and to the shop causing £1m worth of damage. Ds' case was that they expected the newspapers to burn themselves out on the concrete floor. Neither appreciated the risk of the fire spreading as it did. They were charged with arson contrary to s 1(1) and (3) of the 1971 Act. The judge directed the jury in accordance with *Caldwell*, expressing reservations about that being a harsh test in this context. The Court of Appeal upheld the convictions stating that *Caldwell* had been rightly applied and certified the issue of recklessness as one of general public importance. The House of Lords reviewed the history of the term 'recklessness'[131] and unanimously overruled *Caldwell*. It was recognized that having regard to the Law Commission Report No 29 on which the Criminal Damage Act 1971 was based, and the parliamentary intent, the majority in *Caldwell* erred in redefining 'reckless' in s 1 of the Act. The subjective test of recklessness required proof that the accused had foreseen the risk and yet had gone on unjustifiably to take it.[132] That was a much broader conclusion than was necessary to dispose of the certified question. The decision in *Caldwell* was acknowledged to be based on 'fragile foundations' because the House of Lords was not referred to the Law Commission Report. Moreover, Lord Bingham in *G* noted the fact that the majority decision in *Caldwell* had been in the face of a powerful dissent from Lord Edmund-Davies, and had been subjected to sustained and cogent academic[133] and judicial criticism.[134]

---

[129] [1981] Crim LR 393. Note that inadvertent recklessness is established in other jurisdictions: see eg the discussion of German law in JR Spencer and A Pedain, 'Approaches to Strict and Constructive Liability in Continental Criminal Law' in Simester, *Appraising Strict Liability*, 241.

[130] For criticism, see A Halpin, *Definition in the Criminal Law* (2004) Ch 3, especially 102–21; M Davies, 'Lawmakers, Law Lords and Legal Fault' (2004) 68 J Crim L 130, noting the 'delicious irony' that G was decided at a time when Parliament was introducing objective fault elements for serious sex offences in the Sexual Offences Act 2003. See also D Kimel, 'Inadvertent Recklessness in Criminal Law' (2004) 120 LQR 548 suggesting that the problem lay with the application of *Caldwell* in subsequent cases such as *Elliott*; and K Amirthalingham, '*Caldwell* Recklessness is Dead: Long Live Mens Rea's Fecklessness' (2004) 63 MLR 491.

[131] Norrie suggests that a historical analysis reveals yet another approach to recklessness of which their lordships in *G* were seemingly unaware. In some of the earlier authorities, Norrie argues, the issue of cognitive foresight is stated separately from the question of recklessness. Norrie's point is that the definition of recklessness that was favoured in the late nineteenth century juxtaposed a morally substantive element with the cognitive psychological test. Norrie relies on this to suggest that the opposition between subjective and objective recklessness is simplistic. See Norrie, *Crime, Reason and History*, 80–2.

[132] *Cunningham* [1957] 2 QB 396, and commentary [1957] Crim LR 326.   [133] See n 119.

[134] Notably, Ackner LJ in *Stephen Malcolm R* (1984) 79 Cr App R 334, and Goff LJ in *Elliott v C (A Minor)* (1983) 77 Cr App R 103.

Acknowledging the force of the principled criticisms outlined above, the House of Lords in *G* concluded that it should depart from *Caldwell* because it was 'just' to do so. *Caldwell* was castigated as being 'unfair', Lord Bingham referred to it as 'neither just nor moral' and Lord Steyn as a 'cynical strategy'. Lord Steyn also cited UK treaty obligations and the general shift in recent years towards greater subjectivity in mens rea as supporting the outright overruling of *Caldwell*. In short, as Lord Bingham observed, whilst it is clearly blameworthy to take a risk obvious to the individual, it is not 'clearly blameworthy' to do something involving a risk of harm when D has not perceived that risk.[135] Professor Keating's empirical work,[136] based on hypothetical scenarios similar to those in *G*, reveals that a large majority (69 per cent) of members of the public *do* regard behaviour such as that of the boys as criminally blameworthy. Most of those believed that the boys of that age (11 and 12) were old enough to have realized the risks involved. Of those who would not support convicting such boys, the majority were against doing so because of what they considered to be the inappropriateness of the application of the criminal process in such a case.

In *G*, their lordships rejected the narrower solution of a capacity-based exception to the *Caldwell* test. This approach had been suggested as a compromise between the subjectivism of *Cunningham* and the objectivism of *Caldwell*. It would have restricted *Caldwell* recklessness to cases in which D himself, having regard to *his* capacity to see risk, ought to have foreseen the risk of the proscribed harm. The House of Lords held that such an exception would be likely to create further difficulties in defining the relevant exceptional category, and would still impose liability generally on those who caused damage inadvertently.[137] Lord Bingham noted that:

this refinement also has attractions, although it does not meet the objection of principle and does not represent a correct interpretation of the section. It is, in my opinion, open to the further objection of over-complicating the task of the jury (or bench of justices). It is one thing to decide whether a defendant can be believed when he says that the thought of a given risk never crossed his mind. It is another, and much more speculative, task to decide whether the risk would have been obvious to him if the thought had crossed his mind. The simpler the jury's task, the more likely is its verdict to be reliable.[138]

In practical terms, the House of Lords expressed concern at the complexity of *Caldwell* directions. Their lordships were confident that juries could be trusted to apply the *Cunningham* test without blindly accepting a defendant's assertion that he never thought of a certain risk when all the circumstances and probabilities and evidence of what he did and said at the time showed that he did or must have done. It was noted that there is nothing to suggest that this was seen as a problem before *Caldwell*.[139]

The decision in *G* is also welcome for its explicit adoption of the key provision from the Draft Criminal Code defining recklessness. Lord Bingham based his conclusion on the Draft Criminal Code, cl 18(c) as quoted earlier.

Does *Caldwell* still have a role to play?

At one stage in the mid-1980s it looked as if the *Caldwell* test was destined to be the principal form of recklessness in English criminal law. Lord Roskill, when holding the *Caldwell/*

---

[135] cf Lord Rodger of Earlsferry at [69], 'there is much to be said for treating as reckless D who does not trouble his mind to a risk that would have been obvious to him', and see the important article by J Horder, 'Two Histories and Four Hidden Principles of *Mens Rea*' (1997) 113 LQR 95. See also Kimel, n 130, commenting that this conclusion of Lord Bingham is 'clearly unsatisfactory'. See also the review of the two approaches by S Cunningham, 'Recklessness: Being Reckless and Acting Recklessly' (2010) 21 KLJ 445–7.

[136] 'Reckless Children' [2006] Crim LR 546.   [137] See also A Norrie, *Crime, Reason and History*, 80–1.

[138] At [38].   [139] At [39].

Lawrence test to be applicable to manslaughter, said that 'reckless' should be given the *Caldwell* meaning in all offences, 'unless Parliament has otherwise ordained'.[140] Even before *G* it was clear that its application was much more limited. Lord Bingham explicitly limited his judgment in that case to overruling *Caldwell* in its application to criminal damage,[141] so the question remains: post-*G*, are there any offences to which the *Caldwell* formula applies? Other offences to which *Caldwell* had been applied included s 5 of the Data Protection Act 1984[142] but that was repealed by the Data Protection Act 1998 and is now superseded by the 2018 Act. *Blackstone's Criminal Practice* (2003), immediately prior to *G*, suggested *Caldwell* applied to recklessly making a declaration, etc which is false in a material particular;[143] recklessly giving false information in purported compliance with any obligation under the Misuse of Drugs Act 1971,[144] and recklessly making a misleading or deceptive statement or forecast.[145] Although some authority supported these propositions, it is submitted that there is now no basis for applying anything other than the test set out in the Draft Criminal Code, cl 18 as applied in *G*, to each of these offences.[146]

The courts are vigilant in stopping any slide back into the *Caldwell* test. For example, in *Foster v CPS*[147] the Administrative Court quashed D's conviction for interfering with a badger sett by destroying it with intent or being reckless as to whether his actions would have that consequence, contrary to s 3 of the Protection of Badgers Act 1992. The case stated indicated that D had been convicted on the basis of his having been reckless in destroying the sett, rather than his destroying it intentionally. D claimed that he did not realize that badgers were still occupying the sett. In rejecting D's claim, the magistrates found that he was reckless on the basis that he would have been able to recognize the continued presence of badgers had he made rudimentary checks. King J held that the justices had applied the 'now discredited' test of inadvertent recklessness, which necessitated the quashing of D's conviction. This case demonstrates the importance of not conflating recklessness, which is a subjective test, with inadvertence, which has objective connotations.

3.2.2.6 The relative merits of subjective and objective recklessness

The decision in *G* is important in reasserting the primacy of subjectivism, echoing other significant decisions in the House of Lords.[148] Lord Rodger[149] acknowledged that there are academic arguments of substantial pedigree in favour of an objective approach to recklessness.[150] The choice is not simply between strict subjective and objective approaches.[151] Norrie suggests that *G* merely gives the law of recklessness the appearance of a fixed and stable nature. He argues that underneath the surface, recklessness still consists of two incompatible approaches, neither of which seems right on its own, but that no synthesis seems possible either.[152] Many commentators have put forward versions of a compromise position in which

---

140 *Seymour* [1983] 2 All ER 1058 at 1064.   141 At [28].

142 *Data Protection Registrar v Amnesty International* [1995] Crim LR 633.

143 Customs and Excise Management Act 1979, s 167(1).   144 Misuse of Drugs Act 1971, s 18(3).

145 Financial Services and Markets Act 2000, s 397(1)(c). This offence has since been replaced by the Financial Services Act 2012, s 89.

146 For a theoretical discussion of why there ought to be uniform definitions of mens rea that are not context dependent, see F Stark, 'It's Only Words: On Meaning and *Mens Rea*' (2013) 72 CLJ 155.

147 [2013] EWHC 3885 (Admin). See also *Westlake v DPP* [2016] EWHC 825 (Admin).

148 *DPP v B* [2000] 2 AC 428; *K* [2002] 1 AC 462, (strict liability); *(Morgan) Smith* [2001] 1 AC 146 (provocation).

149 At [69].

150 See J Horder (1997) 113 LQR 95. For a comparative perspective of English, Dutch and German approaches to recklessness, see J Blomsma, *Mens Rea and Defences in European Criminal Law* (2012) 134 et seq.

151 For extensive analysis, see Norrie, *Crime, Reason and History*, 82–8.   152 ibid, 88.

the unacceptable harshness of a purely objective test is avoided. These approaches seek to reflect D's culpability in failing to advert to a risk that would have been obvious *to him*, that is, one that was within his capacity to recognize.[153] Alternative suggestions have included tests of 'practical indifference'.[154]

3.2.2.7 Indifference as to results

It is submitted that D's indifference to the risk of a relevant result, where it is proved to exist, is an aggravating factor, but not an element in the definition of the required fault.[155] A person who knowingly takes an unreasonable risk of causing a forbidden result may hope, sincerely and fervently, that it will never happen; but he is, surely, reckless. In *Reid*, Lord Goff suggested that a person may be indifferent to a risk without being aware of its existence.[156] Surely, however, the most we can say is that D would have been indifferent to the risk if he had been aware of it. Such a conclusion could usually be drawn only from evidence as to his general character and habits which the law of evidence does not allow.[157]

The Law Commission did provisionally propose a form of reckless indifference in its offence of second degree murder. This concept was treated as a more culpable form of mens rea than 'simple' recklessness.[158] The Commission proposed that indifference to causing the proscribed result (in that case death) would be defined as follows:

D is indifferent, manifesting a 'couldn't care less' attitude to the result, when he or she realises that there is an unjustified risk of the result being caused by his or her conduct, but goes ahead with that conduct, causing the result. D's own assessment of the justifiability of taking the risk, in the circumstances, is to be considered, along with all the other evidence, in deciding whether D was recklessly indifferent and 'couldn't care less' about causing the result.[159]

This would have created confusion by introducing a further test of recklessness into the law when it had only recently settled to a universally accepted test in *G*. The Law Commission resiled from this proposal in its final report, preferring a test based on one of subjective recklessness.[160]

3.2.2.8 Recklessness and indifference to circumstances

There is a particular difficulty in requiring proof of subjective recklessness as to an actus reus element which is of a morally neutral character. Many offences include in their definition that D does some act in specified circumstances, where the circumstances may appear to be completely arbitrary. For example, it is an offence to possess a shotgun with a barrel length of less than 24 inches unless you have a firearm certificate (as distinct

---

[153] See HLA Hart, 'Negligence, *Mens Rea* and Criminal Responsibility' in *Punishment and Responsibility* (1968). See also Tadros, *Criminal Responsibility*, Ch 9; Duff, *Answering for Crime*, 70.

[154] Duff, *Intention, Agency and Criminal Liability*, arguing that a test of practical indifference could be applied where D's conduct, 'including any conscious risk taking, any failure to notice an obvious risk created by her action and any unreasonable beliefs on which she acted, display a seriously culpable practical indifference to the interests which the agent's actions in fact threatened', p 172. For a critique see Norrie, *Crime, Reason and History*, 90–6. Norrie argues that Duff's approach is incompatible with the prevailing social and legal order.

[155] cf *Gardiner* [1994] Crim LR 455 and commentary.

[156] (1992) 95 Cr App R 391. L Leigh, 'Recklessness after *Reid*' (1993) 56 MLR 208.

[157] cf the proposals by V Tadros, 'Recklessness and the Duty to Take Care' in Shute and Simester, *Criminal Law Theory* arguing that D should be liable if he did not fulfil his duty of investigating the risks which his 'background beliefs' led him to realize were present. See further Tadros, *Criminal Responsibility*, Ch 9.

[158] LCCP 177, para 3.21.

[159] ibid, para 3.150. For criticism, see A Norrie, 'Between Orthodox Subjectivism and Moral Contextualism: Intention and the Consultation Paper' [2006] Crim LR 489, 491; Wilson, n 102.

[160] LC 304, para 2.56.

from a shotgun certificate).[161] The circumstance element of the offence is that the barrel is less than 24 inches. Should there be a requirement to prove mens rea as to that particular circumstance?

The answer will lie in the statutory definition of the offence. Definitions of various crimes involve such circumstance elements based on seemingly arbitrary lines as to a person's age, or as to time, weight, size and other matters of degree. There is no reason why a person who is unaware of the law should direct his mind to the question whether the arbitrary line has been crossed in the particular case, and ignorance of the law is no defence.[162] The possessor of the shotgun has no reason to consider whether the barrel is less than 24 inches in length unless he knows that, if it is, possession without a firearm certificate is an offence.[163] The case is different in a material respect from that of the person who has a positive but mistaken belief that the shotgun is under that length.

Glanville Williams[164] sought to resolve the difficulty by distinguishing between cases of 'mistaken belief' (where there is a positive belief) which would mean that D was not reckless and 'simple ignorance' (where there is no advertence to the question) which would not necessarily preclude a finding of recklessness. This distinction gained some support from *Caldwell*.[165] D can truly be said to be indifferent as to the circumstance—he does not care whether the barrel of the gun is more or less than 24 inches, because he is unaware that it matters. This principle, however, could only be properly applicable in respect of age, time, weight, size and other circumstances which everyone knows to exist in some degree. D knows that the barrel has length and, *ex hypothesi*, he does not care what it is. Where the circumstance is not simply a matter of degree but of kind, it is no longer possible to say that D was indifferent.[166] D may buy and deliver to V a book with an attractive cover without looking at the contents and without considering whether it might contain obscene material, but to infer that he was indifferent about the content would be quite unwarranted. It might be that, when he learned the facts, he might be quite horrified.[167] An objective form of mens rea may be appropriate in such a case.[168]

3.2.2.9 Wilfulness and recklessness

The mens rea term 'wilful' appears in hundreds of statutory offences including some which are commonly prosecuted (eg wilfully obstructing a police officer: Police Act 1996, s 89). It also features in important common law offences including misconduct in public office.[169] It is surprising that the definition of the mens rea element 'wilful' or 'wilfully' is not as clear as it might be. Clarity of definition would certainly seem to be important. Historically, the term generated a great deal of inconsistent case law, particularly in the nineteenth century.[170]

The primary meaning of 'wilful' is 'deliberate' but it may also include recklessness, as accepted by the majority of the House of Lords in *Sheppard*.[171] To be guilty of the offence

---

161 Firearms Act 1968, ss 1 and 4(4).   162 cf Horder [2001] Crim LR 15.   163 Firearms Act 1968, s 1.

164 Williams, CLGP (1st edn) 122, (2nd edn) 151. Cf *A-G's Reference (No 1 of 1995)* [1996] 2 Cr App R 320.

165 See p 108; cf *Pigg* (1982) 74 Cr App R 352.

166 There is an argument that in relation to sex offences the fact that V is under 16 renders D's acts towards her qualitatively different. See Horder [2001] Crim LR 15.

167 The possessor of the shotgun might be equally horrified when they learned the law, but that is not the same thing. We are considering recklessness as to facts, not law. Cf *Mousir* [1987] Crim LR 561 and commentary.

168 See Ch 30.   169 *Attorney-General's Reference (No 3 of 2003)* [2005] QB 73.

170 See Edwards, *Mens Rea*, Ch II; J Andrews, 'Wilfulness: A Lesson in Ambiguity' (1981) 1 LS 303. Andrews suggests (p 305) that one of the reasons that the meaning remained ambiguous in criminal law for so long was the 'relative sloppiness' in the 'construction and practice' of criminal law compared with the greater degree of intellectual discipline which is commonly observed by those who make and practice in 'commercial, chancery and revenue' law!

171 [1981] AC 394 at 408.

under s 1 of the Children and Young Persons Act 1933, the parent must neglect the child 'intending, or at least foreseeing, that the probable consequence of neglect is that the child will suffer injury to his health'.[172] *Sheppard* left a number of ambiguities, but in the light of subsequent case law, including *D*,[173] these appear to have been resolved. First, few if any problems arise in satisfying the wilfulness test when it is alleged that D's conduct was 'deliberate' or 'intentional': that suffices for wilfulness. Secondly, when the allegation is that the alleged 'wilfulness' is demonstrated by D being reckless, it is now settled that the question is whether D was reckless in the subjective (*G*)[174] sense rather than the objective (*Caldwell*) sense of the word.[175] In other words, if D has seen the risk of the proscribed circumstances or consequences and has nevertheless gone on unreasonably to take that risk, his conduct can be described as wilful. Thirdly, the definition of wilful applies whether the allegation is that D performed acts or omissions within the definition of the relevant offence.[176] It would be illogical and create great practical difficulties if the definition of wilfulness for the offence differed depending on the form of harm alleged.

3.2.2.10 Reform of recklessness

The Law Commission's draft Criminal Law Bill (cl 1) reproducing, with a slight modification, the definition in the Draft Code (cl 18(b)) provides that:

a person acts—

  (a) 'recklessly' with respect to—

   (i) a circumstance, when he is aware of a risk that it exists or will exist, and

   (ii) a result when he is aware of a risk that it will occur,

   and it is unreasonable, having regard to the circumstances known to him, to take that risk . . .

The draft Criminal Law Bill would apply this definition to non-fatal offences against the person, and the draft Code Bill would apply it to criminal offences generally. That would result in a substantial simplification of the law. It is submitted that it would also be a great improvement.

3.2.3 Negligence

After *G* and the eradication of *Caldwell* and *Lawrence*, it is possible once again confidently to draw a clear distinction between recklessness and negligence.[177] Recklessness is the conscious taking of an unjustifiable risk, while negligence is the inadvertent taking

---

[172] At 408 per Lord Diplock. Note that the Serious Crime Act 2015, s 66 extends the offence so that ill-treatment may be 'physical or otherwise' and may in particular include a likelihood of injury 'of a physical or psychological nature'.

[173] [2008] EWCA Crim 2360. See also *Patel* [2013] EWCA Crim 965 and *Turbill* [2013] EWCA Crim 1422, both of which concern the interpretation of 'wilful' in s 44 of the Mental Capacity Act 2005.

[174] [2003] UKHL 50.

[175] It was reiterated in *Turbill* [2013] EWCA Crim 1422, that wilfulness connotes a subjective state of mind and that *Sheppard* is the decisive precedent. It was also held, however, that 'recklessness per se was not enough' to be guilty of the offence of wilful neglect, contrary to s 44 of the Mental Capacity Act 2005. This is at odds with the definition of wilfulness that has now become reasonably settled, thus demonstrating how this term continues to be misinterpreted. See the commentary at [2014] Crim LR 388.

[176] See also *Emma W* [2006] EWCA Crim 2723. Lord Diplock in *Sheppard* had equivocated on this. His lordship sought expressly to confine his definition to omissions, but rejected as not a 'natural meaning' a narrower interpretation for positive acts which would limit wilful to mean only that the accused had mens rea as to the doing of the act and not its consequences: *Sheppard* at 404.

[177] See Ch 4, and J Brady, 'Recklessness, Negligence, Indifference and Awareness' (1980) 43 MLR 381.

of an unjustifiable risk. If D is aware of the risk and decides to take it, he is reckless if that was unjustifiable; if he is unaware of the risk, but ought to have been aware of it, he is negligent.[178] Where D did consider whether or not there was a risk and concluded, wrongly and unreasonably, either that there was no risk, or the risk was so small that it would have been justifiable to take it, he is negligent.

3.2.4 Intention, recklessness and negligence as to circumstances

It is worth emphasizing again that intention, recklessness and negligence may be relevant not only to result elements of the actus reus but with respect to the circumstance elements too. Moreover, in some crimes intention as to one or more elements of the actus reus is needed, but mere recklessness or negligence will suffice as to another or other elements. For example, in the offence of sexual touching of a child under 16, D must intend to touch, but he need not intend that the child is under 16; it is sufficient to found liability that D does not have a reasonable belief that the child is 16 or older.

It would seem that, in determining whether D's fault amounted to intention, recklessness or negligence, the same criteria should be applied to circumstances as to consequences. So an act is intentional as to a circumstance[179] when D wants the circumstance to exist or knows that it exists; or, if the broader view of intention[180] is accepted, he is virtually certain that it exists. D is reckless whether a circumstance exists or will exist if he is aware of a risk that it exists or will exist and unjustifiably takes the risk. D is negligent with respect to a circumstance when a reasonable person would know that it exists or will exist and he fails to appreciate that it exists, whether he has given thought to the question or not.

3.2.5 Knowledge

By comparison with mens rea elements such as intention and recklessness, knowledge has attracted comparatively little scholarship. Academic attention has focused on how knowledge plays a part in the general scheme of mens rea and to what extent it factors into negative fault elements (ie mistaken beliefs) that displace mens rea. It is, however, a term deserving attention as it features in many statutes. It is usually considered to sit alongside intention in the mens rea hierarchy, but whereas intention is usually descriptive of states of mind as to consequences (eg I intend to kill), knowledge is usually used in relation to circumstances (eg importing an article or substance knowing it is prohibited).

Knowledge is not the only legislative term to describe prohibited states of mind as to circumstances. Parliament has deployed a range of terms: 'knowledge', 'belief', 'suspicion', 'having reasonable grounds to suspect' and even 'recklessness'. These different terms do not share the same meaning in law.[181] The terms are used in many offences as alternative mens rea requirements.[182] The difficult issue lies in identifying the respective boundaries of each concept. More light has been shed on the matter by academic scholarship, with Professors

---

[178] Orthodoxy suggests that negligence is an objective state of mind; however, there are those who argue that negligence can be reconciled with subjectivism by adding the element that D had the personal capacity to reach the required standard. See Horder, APOCL, 205–8.

[179] This is not the same as saying that the circumstance is intended, because that implies a belief by D that he may be able to influence the existence of the circumstance.

[180] See p 93.

[181] See *Godir* [2018] EWCA Crim 2294 expressly recognizing the difference between recklessness and knowledge.

[182] See the comprehensive catalogue provided by S Shute, 'Knowledge and Belief in the Criminal Law' in Shute and Simester, *Criminal Law Theory*, Ch 8, and see GR Sullivan, 'Knowledge, Belief and Culpability', ibid, Ch 9.

Shute and Sullivan[183] in particular seeking to identify essential conditions which must exist before a state of mind might legitimately be described as 'knowledge'.

The current definition of knowledge in English criminal law is that it is satisfied by proof of a true belief. For example, D knows goods are stolen when he correctly believes that they are. The judicial view is clear: knowledge is true belief and one cannot know something or some circumstance that has yet to occur. As the Canadian Supreme Court explained in *USA v Dynar*:[184]

In the Western legal tradition, knowledge is defined as *true* belief: 'The word "know" refers exclusively to true knowledge; we are not said to "know" something that is not so'.

This view has been endorsed in the House of Lords in two modern cases. In *Montila*,[185] the House accepted that:

A person cannot know that something is A when in fact it is B. The proposition that a person knows that something is A is based on the premise that it is true that it is A. The fact that the property is A provides the starting point. Then there is the question whether the person knows that the property is A.[186]

Subsequently, in *Saik* the House of Lords concluded:

the word 'know' should be interpreted strictly and not watered down. In this context knowledge means true belief.[187]

In conspiracy, for example, if D1 and D2 agree that they will, in the future, exchange money that comes into their bureau de change, they cannot be said to be agreeing to launder money which they *know* to be from a criminal source if they merely see the risk that it might be from a criminal source.[188]

3.2.5.1 Distinguishing knowledge from belief and suspicion

The orthodox view is that 'one cannot know a thing unless it is so',[189] and 'one cannot know a thing will be so unless it will be so'.[190] The critical feature distinguishing knowledge and belief is that the fact or circumstance 'is'.[191] As Shute acknowledges 'there are good reasons why the law should decline to extend its definition of knowledge generally to include knowledge that [the disputed proposition] is possible, likely, etc'.[192] Mere suspicion is therefore not knowledge.[193] The more difficult question lies in distinguishing knowledge from mere belief.[194]

---

[183] See n 182.   [184] [1997] 2 SCR 462 (emphasis added).   [185] [2004] 1 WLR 3141.   [186] At [27].

[187] At [26]. See also Hooper LJ in *Liaquat Ali and others* [2005] EWCA Crim 87 (at [98]).

[188] They might be said to intend that circumstance. See *Saik* [2006] UKHL 18, [2006] Crim LR 998 and commentary. Relied upon in *Sentamu* [2013] EWCA Crim 248.

[189] JC Smith, 'Conspiracy under the Criminal Law Act 1977 (1)' [1977] Crim LR 598, 603.

[190] ibid. See also Williams, CLGP (1953) 133, and more generally writings on knowledge in philosophy—eg AJ Ayer, *The Problem of Knowledge*, 'I conclude that the necessary and sufficient conditions for knowing that something is the case are first that what one is said to know be true, secondly that one be sure of it and thirdly that one should have the right to be sure' at 35, cited by R Buxton, 'Complicity in the Criminal Code' (1969) 85 LQR 252.

[191] As is made clear in *Hall* (1985) 81 Cr App R 260 knowing a fact might be is not the same as knowing it is.

[192] Shute, 'Knowledge and Belief in the Criminal Law' in Shute and Simester, *Criminal Law Theory*, 195.

[193] 'Suspicion in its ordinary meaning is a state of conjecture or surmise where proof is lacking: "I suspect but I cannot prove"': *Hussein v Chong Fook Kam* [1970] AC 942, 948. See also Griffiths (1974) 60 Cr App R 14. These authorities have been cited with approval in numerous cases. For a more recent example, see *R (on the application of 'A') v Chief Constable of 'C' Constabulary* [2014] EWHC 216 (Admin). For further discussion, see LCCP 236, *Anti-Money Laundering: The SARs Regime* (2018) Ch 7.

[194] *Hall* (1985) 81 Cr App R 260, 264, see p 1088.

3.2.6 Belief

The relationship between knowledge and belief has been examined in close detail in the context of handling stolen goods. According to the Court of Appeal in *Hall*:[195]

Belief, of course, is something short of knowledge. It may be said to be the state of mind of a person who says to himself: 'I cannot say I know for certain that [the circumstance exists] but there can be no other reasonable conclusion in the light of all the circumstances, in the light of all that I have heard and seen'.

In *Forsyth*,[196] the court said that the judgment in *Hall* is 'potentially confusing'. In *Moys*,[197] the court suggested simply that the question whether D knew or believed that the proscribed circumstance existed is a subjective one and that suspicion, even coupled with the fact that D shut his eyes to the circumstances, is not enough.

3.2.7 Wilful blindness

For centuries the courts have[198] willingly interpreted knowledge as including 'shutting one's eyes to an obvious means of knowledge' or 'deliberately refraining from making inquiries the results of which the person does not care to have'.[199] Even the House of Lords controversially adopted this proposition:

It is always open to the tribunal of fact, when knowledge on the part of a defendant is required to be proved, to base a finding of knowledge on evidence that the defendant had deliberately shut his eyes to the obvious or refrained from inquiry because he suspected the truth but did not want to have his suspicion confirmed.[200]

A precise definition of wilful blindness or connivance[201] remains elusive.[202] Perhaps the best known exposition of the concept is that of Devlin J in *Roper v Taylor's Central Garages (Exeter)*. His lordship distinguished: (a) actual knowledge; (b) wilful blindness (knowledge in the second degree); and (c) constructive knowledge (knowledge in the third degree).[203] Actual knowledge has been considered: it means true belief. As for wilful blindness, Devlin J emphasized:

a vast distinction between a state of mind which consists of deliberately refraining from making inquiries, the result of which a person does not care to have [wilful blindness], and a state of mind

---

[195] ibid at 264, [1985] Crim LR 377.

[196] A *Hall* direction is not necessary in every case—*Toor* (1987) 85 Cr App R 116.

[197] (1984) 79 Cr App R 72.

[198] See the discussion of the early case law in Edwards, *Mens Rea* (1955) Ch IX, 'The Criminal Degrees of Knowledge in Statutory Offences', 194.

[199] *Roper v Taylor's Central Garages (Exeter)* [1951] 2 TLR 284 (Devlin J). See also eg *Warner v Metropolitan Police Comr* [1969] 2 AC 256, 279 (Lord Reid); *Atwal v Massey* (1972) 56 Cr App R 6.

[200] *Westminster City Council v Croyalgrange Ltd* (1986) 83 Cr App R 155, 164 (Lord Bridge).

[201] See *Winson* [1969] 1 QB 371, 383 (Parker LCJ). Old statutes often used the word 'connivance' but none currently seem to use wilful blindness.

[202] It seems this was owing to the confusion historically over its relationship with vicarious liability: Edwards, *Mens Rea*, 196–8.

[203] More sophisticated subdivisions have been attempted including Peter Gibson J's five categories in the *Baden* case [1993] 1 WLR 509, para 250. Although these were rejected as unhelpful by the House of Lords in the particular context of dishonesty in *Royal Brunei Airlines v Tan* [1995] 2 AC 378, they are worth noting: '(i) actual knowledge; (ii) wilfully shutting one's eyes to the obvious; (iii) wilfully and recklessly failing to make such inquiries as an honest and reasonable man would make; (iv) knowledge of circumstances which would indicate the facts to an honest and reasonable man; (v) knowledge of circumstances which would put an honest and reasonable man on inquiry.'

which is merely neglecting to make such inquiries as a reasonable and prudent person would make [constructive knowledge].[204]

Other judicial definitions[205] have variously incorporated elements of:

(1) a deliberate or intentional refusal to investigate the circumstances suspected;

(2) an opportunity to investigate them;

(3) an absence of doubt as to outcome or at least an awareness by D of the likely outcome of investigation and that the outcome would not be one D desired if he investigated his suspicions;

(4) a causal link between the refusal to investigate and the assumed likely outcome.[206]

The core elements appear to be a degree of awareness of the likely existence of the prohibited circumstances coupled with a blameworthy conscious refusal to enlighten oneself. Academic opinion seems united in requiring proof of more than mere suspicion.[207] Glanville Williams described it in terms of suspicion *'plus'* a deliberate omission to inquire.[208] More recently Sullivan described it in terms of 'suspicion coupled with *deliberate* failure to use *readily available* and effective means to resolve the suspicion'.[209] However it is described, the second limb of the test requires that D must have possessed more than a state of awareness of the risk—he must demonstrate a blameworthiness[210] in his lack of inquiry that justifies treating his state of mind as akin to actual knowledge.[211]

The boundaries of 'wilful blindness' are imprecise. None of the core elements are defined with adequate precision. It is unclear what degree of awareness of risk D must hold. Is suspicion sufficient or must D hold a belief?[212] It is unclear how readily available the bases of enlightenment must be to D. Is he only wilfully blind if he can reasonably or immediately discover the truth, or is the matter one of proportionality depending on the degree of risk and the severity of the harm posed if the risk materializes? It is unclear how convinced of the outcome of investigation D must be—must it be proved, as Horder suggests, that D refrained from making inquiries because he was virtually certain that suspicion would be *confirmed*?[213] Further, to constitute wilful blindness it is unclear what motivation or purpose D must have in seeking to avoid the enlightenment for his refusal. In principle, there

---

[204] *Roper v Taylor's Central Garages (Exeter)* [1951] 2 TLR 284, 288. See also Davis LJ in *Wheeler* [2014] EWCA Crim 2706: 'wilfully shutting eyes to the obvious may constitute evidence connoting knowledge or belief; and it need not necessarily be assumed in all cases that suspicion is all that can safely be inferred from the relevant facts' (at [10]).

[205] See those discussed by Edwards, *Mens Rea*, 199. The Draft Criminal Code also suggests that knowledge includes wilful blindness in cl 18(1)(a); a person acts knowingly 'with respect to a circumstance not only when he is aware that it exists or will exist but also when he avoids taking steps that might confirm his belief that it exists or will exist'.

[206] See eg *Roper*; *Agip (Africa) Ltd v Jackson* [1990] Ch 265, 293 'deliberately shutting eyes to facts he would prefer not to know'; 'it is a commonplace that, if the accused had a suspicion but deliberately shut his eyes, the court or jury is well entitled to hold him guilty'; *Warner v MPC* [1969] AC 256, 279 (Lord Reid). See also *Evan v Dell* [1937] 1 All ER 349, 353: 'deliberately refraining from making inquiries, the results of which [D] might not care to have'.

[207] Although not judicially accepted in the nineteenth century: see Edwards, *Mens Rea*, 207.

[208] CLGP (1953) 127, para 41. In his article on mens rea in secondary liability, 'Complicity, Purpose and the Draft Criminal Code' [1990] Crim LR 98, he described the element as 'an attempted fraud on the law', fn 4.

[209] See Sullivan, 'Knowledge, Belief and Culpability' in Shute and Simester, *Criminal Law Theory*, 214.

[210] See generally M Wasik and MP Thompson, 'Turning a Blind Eye as Constituting *Mens Rea*' (1981) 32 NILQ 324, 337–41.

[211] Described as 'purposeful avoidance' by W Wilson, *Criminal Law: Doctrine and Theory* (2001) 167.

[212] G Williams argued that it should be 'realisation that the fact in question is probable, or at least possible above average', CLGP, 127, para 41. The Law Commission proposed a formula based on D having 'no substantial doubt'. See Wasik and Thompson (1981) 32 NILQ 324, 333.

[213] Horder, APOCL, 204–5.

are strong arguments against the courts applying a mens rea element of wilful blindness unless its elements can be defined with much greater precision.

Some commentators[214] suggest that recklessness is akin to wilful blindness, but academic consensus seems to be that wilful blindness is a narrower category of mens rea.[215] It is narrower for several reasons including: (a) it assumes that D has the opportunity to avail himself of the facts or circumstances that he is aware may exist; (b) that D's assessment of the likelihood of the fact is higher than foresight of *a* risk (as required for recklessness);[216] and (c) he intentionally chooses not to enlighten himself. The distinction has been acknowledged in other jurisdictions, for example the Canadian Supreme Court has observed:

Wilful blindness is distinct from recklessness because, while recklessness involves knowledge of a danger *or risk* and persistence in a course of conduct which creates *a risk* that the prohibited result will occur, wilful blindness arises where a person who has become aware of the need for some inquiry declines to make the inquiry because he does not wish to know the truth. He would prefer to remain ignorant.[217]

3.2.8 Suspicion and reasonable grounds to suspect

Parliament has demonstrated a greater willingness in recent years to create offences with low-level mens rea requirements such as 'suspicion' and 'having reasonable grounds to suspect'. The money laundering offences in POCA 2002 are some of the most obvious examples.[218] The Terrorism Acts also include offences based on suspicion. By s 18(1) of the Terrorism Act 2000, a person commits an offence if he enters into an arrangement which facilitates another person's retention or control of terrorist property, but it is a defence for D to prove that he 'did not know and had no reasonable cause to suspect' that the arrangement related to such property.[219] Requiring only that D 'suspects' relevant facts is a remarkably low threshold for a criminal offence; 'suspicion' and 'reasonable suspicion' have been criticized as too low even as a threshold for the exercise of certain police powers (in which area of law they are commonly found in statutes).

3.2.8.1 The meaning of 'suspicion'

In *Da Silva*,[220] 'suspicion' was held to impose a subjective test: D's suspicion need not be based on 'reasonable grounds'.[221] D must think that there is a possibility, which is more than fanciful, that the relevant facts exist. The court held that:

A vague feeling of unease would not suffice. But the statute does not require the suspicion to be 'clear' or 'firmly grounded and targeted on specific facts' or based on 'reasonable grounds'.[222]

---

214 IH Dennis, 'The Mental Element for Accessories' in *Criminal Law Essays*. Edwards treated them as similar in his *Mens Rea in Criminal Statutes*, citing only very few instances where they were treated as synonymous, 203.

215 See the characteristically forthright statements of EJ Griew, 'Consistency, Communication and Codification Reflection on Two Mens Rea Words' in *Reshaping the Criminal Law*, 73.

216 Especially when recklessness is construed in its subjective sense following G [2004] 1 AC 1034.

217 *Williams* [2004] 2 LRC 499, [27], quoting from *Sansregret v R* [1985] 1 SCR 570 at 584 (McIntyre J).

218 The offences are much broader in respect of mens rea than the international treaties demand as noted by their lordships in *Montila* [2004] UKHL 50 at [28], [2005] Crim LR 479 and commentary.

219 See the Terrorism Act 2000, s 18(2).

220 [2006] EWCA Crim 1654. See generally LCCP 236, *Anti-Money Laundering: The SARs Regime* (2018) Ch 7 and the subsequent report LC 384 (2019), Ch 5.

221 For further discussion as to what is meant by 'knowledge', 'belief' and 'suspicion': see G Williams, 'Handling, Theft and the Purchaser Who Takes a Chance' [1985] Crim LR 432 and see *Hall* [1985] Crim LR 377; *Toor* (1987) 85 Cr App R 116.

222 At [16]. Applied in *Afolabi* [2009] EWCA Crim 2879.

The court stated that using words such as 'inkling' or 'fleeting thought' is liable to mislead.

The Civil Division of the Court of Appeal has endorsed this subjective test of suspicion. In *Shah v HSBC*,[223] the court held that a bank had suspicion that property was criminal if it thought there was a possibility, which was more than fanciful, that it was criminal. There was no requirement to show that that suspicion had been clear or firmly grounded and targeted on specific facts or based on reasonable grounds.

The courts have adopted the dictionary definitions, which are consistent with the previous judicial interpretations of the concept of suspicion in the related field of criminal procedure. One of the most famous statements is that of Lord Devlin in *Hussien v Chang Fook Kam*:[224]

> Suspicion in its ordinary meaning is a state of conjecture or surmise where proof is lacking: 'I suspect but I cannot prove'. Suspicion arises at or near the starting point of an investigation of which the obtaining of prima facie proof is the end.

Further (albeit limited) guidance might be derived from the numerous decisions of the Court of Appeal on the mens rea of handling stolen goods, in which the distinction between belief and 'mere' suspicion has been problematic.[225] The court in *Da Silva* was right, it is submitted, not to impose a gloss on the definition by requiring that the suspicion be 'clear' or 'firmly grounded and targeted on specific facts', even though that approach has been adopted by the House of Lords in various civil law contexts.

The court in *Da Silva* expressed concern about the need for a more detailed direction in cases in which D has suspected but then 'honestly dismissed' his suspicion. This should not be made complicated. This is not a situation in which there is 'a lacuna' where D has failed to form the suspicion despite addressing his mind to it. The appropriate question is, it is submitted, whether D has formed the suspicion and whether he holds that state of mind at the time at which he performs the acts alleged to constitute the actus reus. If D had been suspicious, but by the time of the act those suspicions had been allayed by the receipt of other information, this will mean that he lacked the necessary mens rea.

As the Privy Council confirmed in *Holt v Attorney-General*,[226] the test is a subjective one: actual suspicion is essential, it is not enough to show that D 'ought to have realised'.[227]

3.2.8.2 'Reasonable grounds for knowing or suspecting'

In *Saik*,[228] the House of Lords held that the mens rea element 'reasonable grounds to suspect' in the context of s 93C(2) of the Criminal Justice Act 1988, and now found, for example, in many of the money laundering provisions[229] includes a requirement that D had actual suspicion.[230] Lord Hope concluded that 'the first requirement contains both a subjective part—that the person suspects—and an objective part—that there are reasonable grounds for the suspicion'.[231]

---

[223] [2010] EWCA Civ 31. The court's interpretation of suspicion was held to apply in the civil law relating to money laundering, *K Ltd v National Westminster Bank Plc* [2006] EWCA Civ 1039.

[224] [1970] AC 942 at 948.   [225] See *Hall* (1985) 81 Cr App R 260; *Forsyth* [1997] 2 Cr App R 299.

[226] [2014] UKPC 4.

[227] In that case involving money laundering, D had to shown to have applied mind to the circumstances in which the money had been produced and to have knowledge or suspicion that it would be irregular to receive trust money.

[228] [2006] UKHL 18.

[229] The expression 'reasonable grounds for knowing or suspecting' appears in POCA, s 330 (failure to disclose: regulated sector), s 331 (failure to disclose: nominated officers in the regulated sector), and s 337 (protected disclosure). The shorter phrase 'reasonable grounds for suspecting' appears in many other sections of POCA.

[230] See principally Lord Hope's speech at [52]–[55]. See further the commentary at [2006] Crim LR 998.

[231] At [53].

It had previously been widely assumed that this fault element was a purely objective one,[232] requiring proof only that the reasonable person would have formed the suspicion on the facts available, irrespective of whether the individual defendant formed such suspicion himself. The test is now confirmed, in the POCA context, as a mixed one comprising elements that are subjective (D suspects) and objective (there are reasonable grounds for D doing so). This echoes the approach in police powers contexts, although arguably those are distinguishable because the dual requirement there serves as a check on the abuse of authority. It is easy to envisage circumstances in which the Crown will fail to prove this element because D lacked suspicion (through naivety or stupidity) even though reasonable grounds existed for forming suspicion. But in what circumstances is a prosecution ever likely to falter because D had suspicion, but his suspicion was one not based on reasonable grounds? There is a strong case for saying that, as a matter of policy, a person ought not to be criminally culpable for his failure to suspect even if, objectively viewed, there were grounds for suspecting.

In *Lane and Letts*,[233] the Supreme Court considered the construction of s 17 of the Terrorism Act 2000. This provision makes it an offence to enter into or become concerned in an arrangement as a result of which money or other property is made available or is to be made available to another and D knows or has reasonable cause to suspect that it will or may be used for the purposes of terrorism. Lord Hughes, delivering the judgment of the court, held that its task was to determine how Parliament intended for 'reasonable grounds to suspect' to be interpreted. The court observed that s 17 is not silent as to the state of mind required for the commission of the offences of funding terrorism. The legislative history of the terrorism funding offences indicated that, in adopting the words 'knows or has reasonable cause to suspect', instead of the words 'knows or suspects' which had been used in earlier statutes, Parliament had clearly intended not to require proof of actual suspicion. The scope of the offences extends to include those who had, objectively assessed, reasonable cause to suspect that the money might be put to terrorist use. It was not open to the court to ignore that clear parliamentary intention. The court rejected the argument that such an interpretation rendered s 17 an offence of strict liability. Although the state of mind of such a person was less culpable than that of a person who knew that the money might be used for terrorism, the court stated that it could not be described as being in no way blameworthy. Unlike in the money laundering offences which apply *Saik*, to commit the terrorism offence, it suffices for the jury to be sure that there existed reasonable grounds for suspecting that the property would or might be used for a prohibited purpose.[234]

3.3 Further principles of mens rea

Mens rea is a term which has no single meaning. Every crime has its own mens rea which can be ascertained only by reference to its statutory definition or the case law. The most we can do is to state a general principle, or presumption, which governs its definition.

---

[232] The assumption that the term 'reasonable grounds to suspect' was in this context a purely objective one is supported by the use of that term as a form of fault in some POCA offences (cf Lord Brown at [110]). Eg in s 330 of the 2002 Act it is a sufficient mens rea either that the defendant suspected, or that he had reasonable grounds to suspect, the relevant facts.

[233] [2018] UKSC 36.

[234] One issue that was not considered is the position of an individual whose mental disorder means that he is unable to appreciate that there exist reasonable grounds for suspecting that the money will be used to fund terrorism.

Having understood the meaning attaching to each mens rea element as discussed earlier, it is necessary to apply them in the context of the particular offence charged. It is necessary to examine the structure of the offence with care, seeking to identify each of the elements of the actus reus and then to identify what mens rea element, if any, attaches to each actus reus element.

For example, in criminal damage, the actus reus elements are D's conduct, towards property belonging to another (circumstances), which results in its damage or destruction (result). The mens rea elements are that D's conduct is voluntary, that he intends or is reckless whether the property belongs to another and he intends or is reckless whether it is damaged. There is complete 'correspondence' in that offence because every element of actus reus has an element of mens rea attaching to it.

3.3.1 The correspondence principle

The general principle,[235] which is a desirable one though not always respected by Parliament, is expressed in the Draft Criminal Code as follows:

24—(1) Unless a contrary intention appears, a person does not commit a Code offence unless he acts intentionally, knowingly or recklessly in respect of each of its elements . . .

The justification for requiring some mens rea as to *every* element of the actus reus is that it must be presumed that every element contributes to the criminality of it. If it does not, it should not be there.[236] The requirement is therefore described as one of correspondence between the elements of actus reus and mens rea. This is an important aspect of the subjective approach to mens rea.

However, under the present law very many offences fall far short of precise correspondence; there are elements of the actus reus to which no corresponding mens rea attaches.[237] For example, in assault occasioning actual bodily harm contrary to s 47 of the OAPA 1861,[238] the actus reus elements are that D's conduct causes V to (1) either (a) apprehend immediate unlawful personal violence or (b) have direct physical force applied to his body and (2) suffer some minor injury as a result. The mens rea elements are that D's conduct is voluntary and that he intentionally or recklessly causes (1)(a) or (b). There is no mens rea attaching to (2).

3.3.1.1 Constructive crime

Sometimes the mens rea for a crime 'X' requires no more than proof that D had the mens rea of a lesser offence 'Y'—this is sometimes called 'constructive' crime. Liability for X is constructed from D performing the actus reus for X with the mens rea for Y. For example, an intention to cause GBH is the mens rea of murder. There is no need to prove that D intended to cause, or was reckless whether he caused, death—although death is the crucial element in the definition.[239] Lords Mustill and Steyn have criticized the application of this rule in

---

[235] For comparisons of English, Dutch and German approaches correspondence, see J Blomsma, *Mens Rea and Defences in European Criminal Law* (2012) 206–34.

[236] A view criticized by J Horder in writing on the requirement of mens rea as to age in sex crimes, 'How Culpability Can, and Cannot, be Denied in Under-Age Sex Crimes' [2001] Crim LR 15. See also the more general debate about the application of the correspondence principle and its merits: J Horder, 'A Critique of the Correspondence Principle' [1995] Crim LR 759; B Mitchell, 'In Defence of a Principle of Correspondence' [1999] Crim LR 195; Tadros, *Criminal Responsibility*, Ch 3 and 256–8; see also LCCP 177, Ch 2.

[237] For the relationship between strict liability and constructive liability, see SP Green, 'Six Senses of Strict Liability' in Simester, *Appraising Strict Liability*.

[238] The offence is examined in full in Ch 16, this is a simplified summary.

[239] For criticism see LCCP 177, paras 3.17 et seq, A Ashworth (2008) 11 New Crim LR 232.

murder as a 'conspicuous anomaly' and an example of 'constructive crime'.[240] Similarly, manslaughter may be committed by doing an unlawful and dangerous act which happens to cause death, although D has no mens rea as to the death.

Those are common law offences, but statutes are sometimes similarly interpreted. For example, constructive crime (ie where the mens rea of a lesser offence suffices for a greater) is the general rule in offences against the person. D may be convicted of inflicting grievous bodily harm (s 20 OAPA 1861), if he foresaw some harm, not necessarily 'grievous'.[241] Section 47 of the OAPA 1861 (as set out in the previous section) is another example: D is liable for the s 47 offence even though he foresaw no harm to V but had only the mens rea for the lesser offence of assault or battery.

Some offences are defined in such a way that it is sufficient to prove intention with respect to only one or more elements in the definition of the actus reus. Sometimes it is enough to prove only negligence; sometimes even this is not necessary and D may be convicted although he was blamelessly inadvertent as to a circumstance of the actus reus. In the latter case, we shall say that the crime imposes 'strict liability' as to that circumstance.[242] Strict liability is discussed in Ch 5.

3.3.1.2 Ulterior intent

There is another way in which some offences fail to respect precise correspondence between actus reus and mens rea. Unlike constructive crimes where there are elements of actus reus without mens rea, with some crimes there are elements of mens rea that do not attach to an element of actus reus. These are called crimes of ulterior intent. Crimes are quire commonly defined so that the mens rea includes an intention to produce some further consequence beyond the actus reus of the crime in question. Burglary is an example. It is not enough that D intended to enter a building as a trespasser; that is, to achieve the actus reus of burglary. It is necessary to go further and to show that D had the intention of committing one of a number of specified offences in the building. To be guilty of burglary it is not necessary that D went on to commit any one of those offences—that is not part of the actus reus of burglary which is complete as soon as D enters. Other examples include causing grievous bodily harm with intent to resist the lawful apprehension of any person,[243] and placing gunpowder near a building with intent to do bodily injury to any person.[244] Where such an ulterior intent must be proved, it is sometimes referred to as a 'specific intent'.[245] This term, however, is one which should be regarded with caution.[246] Courts and commentators do not always adopt a consistent interpretation. It can be variously understood to mean: (a) whatever intention has to be proved to establish guilt of the particular crime before the court;[247]

---

[240] In *A-G's Reference (No 3 of 1994)* [1998] 1 Cr App R 91, p 127 and *Powell and Daniels* [1999] 1 AC 1, p 219. Simester suggests that constructive crimes are not unfair if the element of actus reus to which lesser mens rea attaches is not unrelated to the actus reus for which D is required to have mens rea. So in an offence of causing death by dangerous driving, the fact that no mens rea as to death is required does not render the crime unfair since there is an element of mens rea as to the driving and the element of death is an 'intrinsic' risk to the element of driving. Seemingly, on this test, unlawful act manslaughter is not fair since although there is a requirement of mens rea as to some harm being caused to V, death (as to which no mens rea attaches) is not an intrinsic risk to that harm: see *Appraising Strict Liability*, 46.

[241] cf the proposals of the Law Commission in its Report No 218, on offences against the person where the correspondence principle is respected in full. See Ch 16. Note also LCCP 217, *Reform of Offences Against the Person* (2014) and the report LC 361 (2015).

[242] See Ch 5.   [243] OAPA 1861, s 18.   [244] ibid, s 30.

[245] See R Perkins, 'A Rationale of *Mens Rea*' (1939) 52 Harv LR 905, 924.

[246] See R Cross, 'Specific Intent' [1961] Crim LR 510.

[247] *DPP v Beard* [1920] AC 479 at 501–2; p 328.

(b) a 'direct' as distinct from an 'oblique' intention;[248] or (c) an intention ulterior to the actus reus; or (d) a category of crime where D may successfully plead lack of the prescribed mens rea notwithstanding the fact that he relies on evidence that he was intoxicated at the time.[249] The phrase 'ulterior intent' is therefore preferred.

The nature of the ulterior intent which does not relate to an element of actus reus varies widely from crime to crime—in burglary it is an intention to commit one of a number of specified offences; in forgery it is an intention to cause V to act to his prejudice, in theft it is an intention permanently to deprive the owner, and so on.[250]

Where an ulterior *intent* is required, it is obvious that recklessness is not enough. On a charge of wounding with intent to cause grievous bodily harm, proof that D was reckless whether he caused grievous bodily harm will not suffice.[251]

It should again be emphasized that most crimes do not require ulterior intent. In rape, for example, it is enough that D intentionally perpetrated the actus reus—penile penetration of a person's vagina, anus or mouth without their consent—and no ulterior intention need be proved.

Bearing in mind the existence of constructive crimes and crimes of ulterior intent, it is obvious that careful analysis of the offence is always required. It cannot be assumed that there will be perfect correspondence between actus reus and mens rea.

3.3.2 Transferred malice or transferred mens rea

If D, with the mens rea of a particular crime, causes the actus reus of the same crime,[252] he is guilty, even though the result, in some respects, is an unintended one. D intends to murder X and, in the dusk, shoots at a person whom he believes to be X. He hits and kills the person at whom he aims, who is in fact V.[253] In one sense this is obviously an unintended result; but D did intend to cause the actus reus which he has caused and he is guilty of murder. Similarly, where D intends to enter a house, No 6 King Street, and steal property. In the dark he mistakenly enters No 8. He is guilty of burglary.[254]

The law, however, carries this principle still further. Suppose that D, intending to murder X, shoots at a man who is in fact X, but *misses* and kills V who unknown to D was standing close by. This is an unintended result in a different—and more fundamental—respect than the example considered above. Yet, once again, D, with the mens rea of a particular crime, has caused the actus reus of the same crime; and, once again, he is guilty of murder. So, where D struck X, who fell against V, who also fell and sustained a fatal injury, D was guilty of manslaughter: 'The criminality of the doer of the act is precisely the same whether it is [X] or [V] who dies.'[255] The application of the principle to cases of this second type is known as the doctrine of 'transferred malice'.[256]

---

[248] See p 93. *Steane* [1947] KB 997 at 1004.

[249] See p 333. See the discussion of *Heard* [2007] EWCA Crim 125, [2007] Crim LR 654 and commentary, p 337.

[250] See J Horder, 'Crimes of Ulterior Intent' in A Simester and ATH Smith (eds), *Harm and Culpability* (1996) 153, arguing for more crimes of this nature to reflect more accurately the moral differences in wrongdoing.

[251] *Belfon* [1976] 3 All ER 46, where this passage was cited at 49, [1976] 1 WLR 741, 744.

[252] See *Hussain* [1969] 2 QB 567, [1969] Crim LR 433 and commentary; *Ellis, Street and Smith* (1987) 84 Cr App R 235, [1987] Crim LR 44 and commentary; cf *Kundeus* (1976) 24 CCC (2d) 276 at 282–3.

[253] Horder calls this an 'impersonality doctrine' [2006] Crim LR 383 at 384.

[254] See *Wrigley* [1957] Crim LR 57.

[255] *Mitchell* [1983] QB 741. Cf *Haystead v Chief Constable of Derbyshire* [2000] 3 All ER 890.

[256] See Ashworth, *Reshaping the Criminal Law*, 77–94 and *Crime, Proof and Punishment*, 45–70; G Williams, 'Convictions and Fair Labelling' (1983) 42 CLJ 85; J Chalmers and F Leverick, 'Fair Labelling in Criminal Law' (2008) 71 MLR 217; J Horder, 'Transferred Malice and the Remoteness of Unexpected Outcomes from Intentions' [2006] Crim LR 383, and comparing the German system, M Bohlander, 'Problems of Transferred Malice in Multiple-Actor Scenarios' (2010) 74 J Crim L 145; P Westen, 'The Significance of Transferred Intent' (2013) 7 Crim L & Phil 321.

In *Latimer*,[257] D had a quarrel in a public house with X. He took off his belt and aimed a blow at X which struck him lightly, but the belt bounced off and struck V who was standing close by and wounded her severely. The jury found that the blow was unlawfully aimed at X, but that the striking of V 'was purely accidental and not such a consequence of the blow as the prisoner ought to have expected'—that is, he was not even negligent with respect to this result. It was held that D was properly convicted of unlawfully and maliciously wounding V.

It is important to notice the limitations of this doctrine. It operates only when the actus reus and the mens rea of the *same* crime coincide.[258] Consider a case where D shoots at V's dog with intent to kill it but misses and kills V who, unknown to D, was standing close by. Obviously, he cannot be liable for criminal damage in respect of killing the dog, for he has not done so; nor can he be convicted of murder,[259] because D does not have the mens rea for that crime. A similar result follows in the scenario where D shoots at V with intent to kill him and, quite accidentally, kills V's dog—which in law is property: D is guilty of neither crime.[260] As Horder puts it, such 'alchemy', translating fault elements and external elements between crimes is not permitted and would undermine the moral distinctiveness of each individual crime.[261] In such a case, D would be liable for attempting to murder V and the availability of the attempt charge in most cases prompts Ashworth to question whether the transferred malice doctrine is needed.[262]

In *Pembliton*,[263] D was involved in a fight outside a public house and, as a result, was charged with maliciously breaking a window. The jury found:

that the prisoner threw the stone which broke the window, but that he threw it at the people he had been fighting with, intending to strike one or more of them with it, but not intending to break the window.[264]

His conviction was quashed by the Court for Crown Cases Reserved, because there was no finding that he had the mens rea of the crime, the actus reus of which he had caused. Lord Coleridge pointed out that it would have been different if there had been a finding that he was reckless as to the consequence which had occurred—but there was no such finding.[265] The intent which is transferred must be a mens rea, whether intention or recklessness. If D shoots X with intent to kill, because X is making a murderous attack on him and this is the only way in which he can preserve his own life, D does not intend an actus reus (in the broader sense, described earlier), for to kill in these circumstances is justified. If, however, D misses X and inadvertently kills V, an innocent bystander, he does cause an actus reus but he is not guilty of murder for there is no mens rea (in the broader sense) to transfer; the result which he intended was a perfectly lawful one.[266]

The case of *Grant*[267] is significant in this regard, as it is one of the few cases in which the Court of Appeal has had the opportunity to examine the application of the doctrine of transferred malice. DD were chasing V1, who ran into a shop to escape them. DD then fired a number of shots into the shop, with the purpose of killing V1. Their intention was therefore to kill. None of the bullets hit V1, but they did hit V2 and V3, who suffered serious injuries. DD were convicted of one count of attempted murder of V1. That is uncontroversial—their intent was to kill. DD were also convicted of two counts of causing GBH with intent in respect of

257 (1886) 17 QBD 359.   258 This is subject to what is said later about *Grant* [2014] EWCA Crim 143.
259 As to whether it could be manslaughter, see p 599.
260 For a contrary view, see S Eldar, 'The Limits of Transferred Malice' (2012) 32 OJLS 633.
261 [2006] Crim LR 383, 393.   262 ibid.   263 (1874) LR 2 CCR 119.   264 ibid, 120.
265 Under *Caldwell*, recklessness was easy to establish in such a case and there was less need to rely on the doctrine of transferred malice.
266 cf *Gross* (1913) 23 Cox CC 455.   267 [2014] EWCA Crim 143. See also T Storey (2014) 78 J Crim L 214.

V2 and V3. DD appealed arguing that the Crown ought to have been required to choose between prosecuting attempted murder of V1 or the GBH offences. This was founded on the argument that it was not possible to seek a conviction for two different offences of specific intent that had an identical actus reus and mens rea. The court upheld the conviction. DD had mens rea for intent to kill V1 and that was transferred to the actus reus of GBH that they actually caused to V2 and V3. In dismissing their argument, Rafferty LJ held that:

Proof of the mens rea for attempted murder by definition involves proof of the mens rea for causing grievous bodily harm with intent. Once that is clear the fallacy in the submissions is exposed. A useful test of whether submissions to us were well founded lies in considering the obverse. If the point were well made it would follow that an intent to kill must exclude an intent to cause grievous bodily harm.[268]

Although *Grant* might at first seem to represent a departure from orthodoxy, it is merely the application of the principles discussed earlier. DD had the intent to kill, and that mens rea was more than adequate for the actus reus they actually caused—GBH (for which intent to do GBH would suffice). The more controversial issue, and the one not addressed by the Court of Appeal, is whether DD could have been guilty of the attempted murder of V2 and V3. This, it is submitted, would be to extend the doctrine too far.

   In *A-G's Reference (No 3 of 1994)*,[269] D stabbed a pregnant woman. Her child was born prematurely because of the stabbing and died in consequence of the premature birth. The fact that death resulted from premature birth, not directly from the stab wound, 'an unexpected difference of mode', was immaterial. Whether D was negligent in relation to the child was also irrelevant. In fact, D knew that the woman was pregnant but it seems that it would have made no difference if he had not known, and had had no reason to know that. His 'malice' against the mother was transferred to the child whose death he had in fact caused. The Court of Appeal gave full effect to the doctrine as described earlier, declining to impose two limitations advocated by Glanville Williams:[270] (a) that 'an unexpected difference of mode will be regarded as severing the chain of causation if it is sufficiently removed from the intended mode'; and (b) that the doctrine 'should be limited to cases where the consequence was brought about by negligence in relation to the actual victim'.

   The House of Lords, unenthusiastically, confirmed the existence of this ancient principle of transferred malice but declined to extend it to what they regarded as a double transfer of intent—from the mother to the foetus, and from the foetus to the child. D was not guilty of murder. Remarkably, however, they held that D might be convicted of manslaughter by an unlawful and dangerous act—the assault on the mother. This looks like the application of the very doctrine of transferred malice they had just rejected. But D did not intend a merely unlawful and dangerous act. He intended to cause grievous bodily harm; and the act, done with that intention, admittedly caused death—which looks like murder.[271] Horder argues that the correct question should have been whether murder was a representative label for D given that there was (a) an unintended victim and (b) the death arose in a way that was not intended.[272] This is an attractive though complex theoretical model, but leaving the issue of the remoteness of the manner of infliction of the harm and the representativeness of the label of conviction to the jury is an impractical solution.

---

[268] At [36].   [269] [1996] 1 Cr App R 351.

[270] CLGP, 48. Williams would abolish the doctrine for criminal damage. It results in 'unfair labelling' where the property damaged is more valuable than the property D intended to damage. He would retain it for offences against the person: (1983) 42 CLJ 85. Injury to one person is (presumably) as bad as the same injury to any other person.

[271] For criticism see S Gough (1999) 62 MLR 128.   [272] [2006] Crim LR 383, 386–7.

3.3.3 Coincidence in time of actus reus and mens rea

The mens rea must coincide in point of time, even if fleetingly,[273] with the act which causes the actus reus.[274] 'If I happen to kill my neighbour accidentally, I do not become a murderer by thereafter expressing joy over his death. My happiness over the result is not the same as a willingness to commit the illegal act.'[275] Mens rea implies an intention to do a present act, not a future act.[276]

Suppose that D is driving to V's house, set on killing V. A person steps under the wheels of D's car, giving D no chance to avoid him, and is killed. It is V. Clearly, D is not guilty of murder. Similarly, D who walks out of prison while in a state of automatism does not commit the offence of escape by deliberately remaining at large.[277] Suppose that D, having resolved to kill his wife, V, prepares and conceals a poisoned apple with the intention of giving it to her tomorrow. She finds the apple today, eats it and dies. D is not guilty of murder. He might be guilty of manslaughter on the ground that the act of leaving the apple where it might be found was reckless or grossly negligent and caused death.[278] However, if D does an act with intent thereby to cause the actus reus, and does so, it is immaterial that he has repented before the actus reus occurs. Where D dispatched suitcases from Ghana to London which she knew to contain cannabis, her repentance before the importation took place was no defence.[279]

Where D has, with mens rea, gone beyond mere preparation and is in the course of committing an offence, it should be no answer that the final step was involuntary or accidental—as where D is on the point of pulling the trigger with intent to murder and, being startled by an explosion, does so involuntarily.[280]

Where the actus reus of the crime charged is a continuing act, it is sufficient that D has mens rea at some point during the continuance of the actus reus.[281] Where the actus reus is part of a larger transaction, it may be sufficient that D has mens rea during the transaction, though not at the moment the actus reus is accomplished. D inflicts a wound upon V with intent to kill him. Then, believing that he has killed V, he disposes, as he thinks, of the 'corpse'. In fact V was not killed by the wound but dies as a result of the act of disposal. D has undoubtedly caused the actus reus of murder by the act of disposal but he did not, at that time, have mens rea. In cases in India and what was then Rhodesia,[282] it was held,

---

273 See *Styles* [2015] EWCA Crim 1619.

274 *Jakeman* (1982) 76 Cr App R 223, [1983] Crim LR 104 and commentary thereon. See also G Marston, 'Contemporaneity of Act and Intention' (1970) 86 LQR 208; AR White, 'The Identity and Time of the *Actus Reus*' [1977] Crim LR 148. For comparisons of English, Dutch and German approaches to contemporaneity, see J Blomsma, *Mens Rea and Defences in European Criminal Law* (2012) 250–68.

275 J Andanaes, *The General Part of the Criminal Law of Norway* (1965) 194.

276 'There is no law against a man's intending to commit a murder the day after tomorrow. The law only deals with conduct': OW Holmes, *The Criminal Law* (John Harvard edn, 2009) 54.

277 See *Scott* [1967] VR 276; discussed by C Howard, 'Escaping from Gaol' [1967] Crim LR at 406.

278 cf *Burke* [1987] AC 417, [1987] Crim LR 480 and commentary at 484.

279 *Jakeman*, n 274. Cf *Wings Ltd v Ellis*, p 56.

280 See commentary on *Burke* [1987] Crim LR 480. Note the possibility of applying the *Miller* principle (p 53) where D has created the dangerous situation and comes under a duty to avert risk.

281 *Fagan v Metropolitan Police Comr* [1969] 1 QB 439, p 50. Cf *Miller* [1983] 2 AC 161; *Singh (Gurdev) v R* [1973] 1 WLR 1444. See also *Styles* [2015] EWCA Crim 1619.

282 *Khandu* (1890) ILR 15 Bom 194; *Shorty* [1950] SR 280.

accordingly, that D must be acquitted of murder and convicted only of attempted murder. But in *Thabo Meli*,[283] the Privy Council opined that it was:

impossible to divide up what was really one series of acts in this way. There is no doubt that the accused set out to do all these acts in order to achieve their plan, and as parts of their plan: and it is much too refined a ground of judgment to say that, because they were at a misapprehension at one stage and thought that their guilty purpose was achieved before it was achieved, therefore they are to escape the penalties of the law.

This suggests that the answer might be different where there was no antecedent plan to dispose of the body. *Thabo Meli* was distinguished on this ground in New Zealand[284] and, at first, in South Africa.[285] But in England, in *Church*[286] the Court of Criminal Appeal applied *Thabo Meli* where D, in a sudden fight, knocked V unconscious and, wrongly believing her to be dead, threw her into the river where she drowned. He was charged with murder and his conviction for manslaughter was upheld. Here there was no antecedent plan. The point was not considered by the court, but it was apparently thought to be enough that D's conduct constituted 'a series of acts which culminated in [V's] death'. This is an extremely flexible approach to the principle of concurrence or contemporaneity as it is sometimes called, and it facilitates convictions in awkward fact scenarios.

In *Le Brun*,[287] the court followed *Church*, holding that it was immaterial that there was no preconceived plan and that the same principles apply to manslaughter as to murder.[288] D, in a quarrel, knocked his wife unconscious and while attempting to drag her body away dropped and killed her. The jury were rightly told that they could convict D if either he accidentally dropped V while (a) attempting to return her to her home against her wishes and/or (b) attempting to dispose of her body or otherwise cover up the assault. It would be murder if D struck her the original blow with intent to do GBH or kill, and manslaughter if he intended to assault her or cause her injury. The court appears to uphold the manslaughter conviction on both of two alternative principles, as follows.

3.3.3.1 The transaction principle

This appears to operate so that D is guilty of homicide if he kills during the continuance of the transaction, the sequence of events initiated by the unlawful blow, and that transaction continues at least during the conduct described under (a) and (b) in the previous paragraph. This suggests that it certainly continues while D is engaged in some kind of wrongdoing arising out of, and immediately following, the unlawful blow. Though *Le Brun* does not decide this, the result might have been different if D had dropped V in the same manner and at the same time and place while attempting to get her to hospital, or to her home if he had thought that was where she would wish to be taken; or, if he believed her to be dead, while he was attempting to deliver the corpse to the police. Under this principle it is immaterial that the second act is the sole cause of death.

---

[283] [1954] 1 All ER 373. Followed in *Moore and Dorn* [1975] Crim LR 229. For forceful criticism of this decision, see KJ Arenson, '*Thabo Meli* Revisited: The Pernicious Effects of Result-Driven Decisions' (2013) 77 J Crim L 41. Arenson argues that the effect of this decision has been to, 'emasculat[e] the doctrine of temporal coincidence beyond recognition.'

[284] *Ramsay* [1967] NZLR 1005.   [285] *Chiswibo* 1960 (2) SA 714.

[286] [1966] 1 QB 59.   [287] [1992] QB 61.

[288] In *A-G's Reference (No 4 of 1980)* [1981] 2 All ER 617 at 620, the court left open the question whether the principle applies to manslaughter and whether it was part of the *ratio decidendi* of *Church* that it does so. Commentary at [1981] Crim LR 493.

3.3.3.2 The causation principle

This approach holds that the initial blow is a cause of death. As that blow was struck with mens rea, there is no further problem—Le Brun is guilty of murder or manslaughter as the case may be. The second event was also a cause of death but it is clear that there may be more than one cause (see p 65). This may suggest that Le Brun would have been guilty if V had been similarly dropped by a passer-by who was trying to get her to hospital. But it may be that an intervening act by a third party is regarded as breaking the chain of causation, particularly where it is unforeseeable, whereas the same thing done by the original actor is not.[289]

The causation principle represents the *ratio decidendi* of the South African case of *S v Masilela*.[290] D, intending to kill V, knocked him unconscious and, believing him to be dead, set fire to the house. V died from the fumes. If he had not been unconscious he would have been able to walk out, so knocking him unconscious was a cause of death. But it is probable that the chain of causation would be regarded as broken if the house had been set on fire by a stranger who happened to come along after D's departure.

In all these cases the second act was a cause of the death. Where it is impossible to say which act caused death, it has been held that D may be convicted only if it can be proved that he acted with mens rea (or other appropriate degree of fault) on both occasions. Where D knocked V downstairs and then, believing that he had killed her, cut her throat in order to dispose of the body, and it was impossible to say which act caused death, it was held that the jury should have been directed that they should convict of manslaughter if they were satisfied *both* (a) that knocking V downstairs was an intentional act which was unlawful and dangerous[291] *and* (b) that the act of cutting the throat was one of gross criminal negligence.[292] If manslaughter was committed, it was immaterial that it was impossible to prove on which of these two closely related occasions it occurred.[293] If the jury were not satisfied on both points, there was a 50 per cent chance that this was a case of accidental death, in which case acquittal must follow. But if *Thabo Meli* applies to manslaughter,[294] the direction is too favourable. Assuming it was all one 'transaction', it should have been enough to prove that D had the required mens rea on the first occasion.

3.3.4 Ignorance of the law is no defence

In our discussion of the general principles of mens rea nothing has been said about whether D knows his act is against the law, for, in the great majority of cases, it is irrelevant whether he knows it or not:[295] 'the principle that ignorance of the law is no defence in crime' said Lord Bridge, 'is so fundamental that to construe the word "knowingly" in a criminal statute as requiring not merely knowledge of facts material to the offender's guilt, but also knowledge of the relevant law, would be revolutionary and, to my mind, wholly unacceptable'.[296] This view has been powerfully criticized by Ashworth[297] who describes the proposition that ignorance of the criminal law is no defence as preposterous. He suggests that the doctrine is

---

[289] See the passage earlier, cited by the court in *Le Brun*.   [290] 1968 (2) SA 558 (AD).

[291] This is manslaughter. See p 590.

[292] This may be considered to be manslaughter and, indeed, was held to be so in this case. See p 68.

[293] *A-G's Reference (No 4 of 1980)* [1981] 1 WLR 705, [1981] Crim LR 493 and commentary.

[294] This question was left open. *Church* suggests that it does; and that seems right in principle.

[295] See Ch 9, and A Ashworth, 'Excusable Mistake of Law' [1974] Crim LR 652; M Matthews, 'Ignorance of the Law is No Excuse' (1983) 3 LS 174.

[296] *Grant v Borg* [1982] 2 All ER 257 at 263, but cf *Curr* [1968] 2 QB 944. Acts done by D to V in the reasonable belief that V was committing a by-law offence may be justified even if it turns out that the by-law was void for uncertainty: *Percy v Hall* [1997] QB 924 (Civ Div).

[297] 'Ignorance of the Criminal Law, and Duties to Avoid it' (2011) 74 MLR 1.

unfair and that it fails to recognize the State's duty to render the criminal law accessible to citizens to 'respect the right of individuals not to be convicted of offences for which it is not reasonable to expect them to have knowledge'.[298]

As the law presently stands, it must usually be proved that D intended to cause, or was reckless whether he caused, the event or state of affairs which, as a matter of fact, is forbidden by law; but it is quite immaterial to his conviction (though it may affect his sentence) whether he *knew* that the event or state of affairs was forbidden by law. This is so even though it also appears that D's ignorance of the law was quite reasonable and even, apparently, if it was quite impossible[299] for him to know of the prohibition in question. It was no defence for a man visiting from Baghdad, charged with a sexual offence on board a ship lying in an English port, to show that the act he performed was lawful in his own country and that he did not know English law.[300] It was held that a Frenchman might be guilty of murder in the course of duelling in England, even if he did not know that duelling was against English law.[301] In *Bailey*,[302] D was convicted of an offence created by a statute which was passed while he was on the high seas although he committed the act before the end of the voyage when he could not possibly have known of the statute.[303]

In some of these cases it might be argued that D at least intended something immoral; but that makes no difference. A motorist's mistaken belief that a constable has no right in the particular circumstances to require a specimen of breath is not a reasonable excuse for not providing the specimen.[304]

A mistaken belief that a firearm certificate was current was held to be incapable of being a reasonable excuse under the Firearms Act 1968, on the ground that it was a mistake of law.[305] Ignorance that certain banking transactions require the consent of the Bank of England is no defence to a charge of unauthorized deposit-taking.[306]

Since the courts are keen on saying that the meaning of an ordinary word in a statute is not a question of law,[307] it is easy to see how many cases might involve an argument by D that he did not interpret the statutory words to apply to his conduct and therefore did not realize his act was criminal. If D studies the Public Order Act 1986 and concludes that the conduct in which he proposes to indulge is not 'abusive', but the court takes a different view, it is most unlikely that a court would entertain D relying on his mistake 'of fact'. It is thought that such a defence would be regarded as subversive of the criminal law;[308] but, if it is accepted that *Brutus v Cozens* applies (so that statutory words be interpreted as ordinary English words), it is in theory a principled approach.[309]

In the case of the most serious crimes the problem does not arise; everyone knows it is against the law to murder, rob or rape.[310] In the case of many less serious crimes, however, a

---

[298] ibid, 5. This is particularly true of offences based on omissions.
[299] *Bailey*, see later in this paragraph.   [300] *Esop* (1836) 7 C & P 456.
[301] *Barronet and Allain* (1852) Dears CC 51.   [302] (1800) Russ & Ry 1.
[303] But the judges recommended a pardon. Where a continuing act was made unlawful it was held that a reasonable time must be allowed for its discontinuance and that ignorance of the law was relevant to determine this question: *Burns v Nowell* (1880) 5 QBD 444.
[304] *Reid* [1973] 1 WLR 1283: 'if you choose at the street side to act out the part of Hampden, you have got to be right': at 1289 per Scarman LJ.
[305] *Jones* [1995] 1 Cr App R 262. But was not this really a mistake of fact—though probably an unreasonable one?
[306] *A-G's Reference (No 1 of 1995) (B and F)* [1996] 2 Cr App R 320. The more difficult question was whether the ignorant directors 'consented' to the commission of the offence. It was held that they did.
[307] *Brutus v Cozens* [1973] AC 854.
[308] cf *Sancoff v Halford* [1973] Qd R 25. (Belief that books were not obscene is a mistake of law.)
[309] See Ashworth, n 295.
[310] But see *Christian* [2006] UKPC 47 in which Pitcairn islanders charged with sexual offences claimed to have no access to the English law making that conduct criminal. See the fascinating article by H Power [2007] Crim LR 609.

person may very easily, and without negligence, be ignorant that a particular act is a crime. In such cases there will usually be nothing immoral about the act; and the conviction of a morally innocent person requires justification. Various justifications have been advanced for the rule that ignorance is not a defence. Blackstone[311] thought that all sane people know the law—a proposition which is manifestly untrue today. Austin[312] based the rule upon the difficulty of disproving ignorance of the law, while Holmes,[313] who considered this no more difficult a question than many which are investigated in the courts, thought that to admit the plea of ignorance would be to encourage ignorance of the law. A more modern writer, Jerome Hall,[314] argued that to allow the defence would be to contradict one of the fundamental tenets of a legal order: that rules of law enforce objective meanings, to be ascertained by the courts:

If that plea [ie ignorance of the law] were valid, the consequence would be: whenever a defendant in a criminal case thought that the law was thus and so, he is to be treated as though the law were thus and so, that is, *the law actually is thus and so.*[315]

As Hall points out, the criminal law represents an objective code of ethics which must prevail over individual convictions and he therefore argues:[316]

Thus, while a person who acts in accordance with his honest convictions is certainly not as culpable as one who commits a harm knowing it is wrong, it is also true that conscience sometimes leads one astray. *Mens rea* underlines the essential difference. Penal liability based on it implies the objective wrongness of the harm proscribed—regardless of motive or conviction. This may fall short of perfect justice but the ethics of a legal order must be objective.

Much modern legislation is devoid of moral content, apart from the moral obligation to obey the law. Ashworth regards the rule as one based on shaky foundations.[317]

The common law rule is not universally followed and the arguments by which it is supported have been found 'not very convincing to those used to another system'.[318] In Scandinavian criminal law, ignorance of the law is, in varying degrees, a defence. Thus, in Norway, a person will not be excused for ignorance of 'the general rules of society which apply to everybody' or 'the special rules governing the business or activity in which the individual is engaged'. But 'a fisherman need not study the legislation on industry'; an employee may be excused for bona fide and reasonable obedience to illegal orders of his employer; or a stranger for breaking a rule which he could not be expected to know about; or liability may be negatived because the legislation is very new, or its interpretation doubtful. Such rules seem to have much to commend them, compared with the rigid and uncompromising attitude of English law. They seek to relate guilt to moral responsibility in a way in which our rule does not.[319]

---

[311] *Commentaries*, iv, 27.   [312] *Lectures on Jurisprudence* (1885) 497.
[313] *The Common Law* (1881) 48.
[314] 'Ignorance and Mistake in Criminal Law' (1957) 33 Ind LJ 1. Cf *General Principles*, 382–3.
[315] (1957) 33 Ind LJ at 19. In *Cooper v Simmons* (1862) 7 H & N 707 at 717, Martin B thought that to allow the defence would be 'to substitute the opinion of a person charged with a breach of the law for the law itself'.
[316] 33 Ind LJ at 22.   [317] See n 297.
[318] J Andenaes, '*Ignorantia Juris* in Scandinavian Law' in GOW Mueller (ed), *Essays in Criminal Science* (1961) 217 at 222. For South African law, see *S v De Blom* 1977 (3) SA 513 (AD) discussed by C Turpin (1978) 37 CLJ 8.
[319] An exception to the general rule is created by the Statutory Instruments Act 1946, s 3. See D Lanham, 'Delegated Legislation and Publication' (1974) 37 MLR 510. On a charge brought under a statutory instrument it is a defence for D to prove that the instrument had not been issued at the time of the alleged offence; unless the Crown then proves that reasonable steps had been taken to bring it to the notice of the public, or persons likely to be affected by it, or D. See *Defiant Cycle Co Ltd v Newell* [1953] 2 All ER 38. The Privy Council has opined that, in a jurisdiction where there is no similar provision, a person who is unaware that a ministerial order applying a prohibition to him has been made may set up his ignorance as a lack of mens rea: *Lim Chin Aik v R* [1963] AC 160, p 44.

3.3.5 Mistake of law may negative mens rea

If D, has been proved to have the specified mens rea of an offence and has caused the proscribed actus reus, he is guilty and it will not help him to say that he did not know the actus
reus was forbidden by the criminal law. But the actus reus may be so defined that if D makes
a mistake of law it may mean that he was not acting intentionally or recklessly with respect
to some element in the actus reus and so he would lack mens rea. In such a case, his mistake,
whether reasonable or not, is a defence.[320] '[A]n honest belief in a certain state of things does
afford a defence, including an honest though mistaken belief about legal rights.'[321] Unless
the prosecution can prove that the mistake was not made, they have not established the
requisite mens rea. For example, if D is charged with intentionally or recklessly damaging
property belonging to another, even if he admits intentional damage to the property, his
honest belief, arising from a mistake of law, that the property is his own, is a 'defence'. He
will not have an intention or recklessness as to the element of actus reus—that the property
belongs to another. The court so held, in *Smith*,[322] not because of any special provision in
the Criminal Damage Act but by 'applying the ordinary principles of *mens rea*'. The plea of
mistake is considered in full in Ch 9.

3.3.6 Absence of a 'claim of right' as an element in mens rea

Sometimes the mens rea of an offence is so defined as to require the absence of a claim of
right. In other words, if D believed he had a right to do the act in question, he had no mens
rea and therefore was not guilty of the crime. This 'defence' will prevail even if D's belief is
mistaken and is based upon an entirely wrong view of the law. It is available in a number of
important crimes, including theft,[323] criminal damage to property[324] and a number of other
offences requiring wilfulness or fraud. This is in accordance with the ordinary principle that
a mistake of law may, indirectly, operate as a defence by preventing D from having mens rea
in acting as he did. It is important to notice the limits within which this excuse operates. The
mistake must be one which leads D to believe he has a right to act as he does; it is not enough
that he simply believes his act is not a crime. Here, too, the distinction between mistake as to
the criminal and as to the civil law seems to be important. Thus, if D, having read in an out-
of-date book on criminal law that it is not stealing to take another's title deeds to land,[325] were
to take V's deeds, thinking that this was a way in which he could injure V without any risk of
being punished, he could, no doubt, be convicted of theft under s 1 of the Theft Act 1968. He
had no claim of right. It would be otherwise if D, owing to a misunderstanding of the law of
property, thought that the title deeds were his, and that V was wrongfully withholding them
from him. Here, clearly, he had a claim of right. Therefore, while a mistake as to the criminal
law only will not give rise to a claim of right, an error as to the civil law may do so.

It certainly cannot be asserted with confidence that the absence of a claim of right is a
general requirement of mens rea, as it is in the case of theft and the other crimes referred to
previously. The question will therefore be considered in relation to specific crimes discussed
throughout this book.

---

[320] See Ch 9, p 358. Kenneth Simons argues that a distinction ought to be made within the category of mistake of law. The distinction he is in favour of is between mistakes about the criminal law itself and mistakes
about non-criminal law norms that the criminal law makes relevant, such as about the civil law of property in
the context of theft. See KW Simons, 'Ignorance and Mistake of Criminal Law, Noncriminal Law, and Fact'
(2012) 9 Ohio St J Crim L 487.

[321] *Barrett and Barrett* (1980) 72 Cr App R 212 at 216.

[322] [1974] QB 354; p 1104.

[323] See p 908.   [324] See p 1107.   [325] This was the rule at common law.

3.3.7 Proof of intention and foresight

There was formerly House of Lords authority[326] for the view that there is an irrebuttable presumption of law that a person foresees and intends the natural consequences of his acts. Proof that D did an act, the natural consequence of which was death, was conclusive proof that D intended to kill, in the absence of evidence of insanity or incapacity to form an intent. To what extent, if at all, this actually represented the law was disputed: but it is now clear beyond all doubt that it is not the law. The question in every case is as to the actual intention of the person charged at the time when he did the act. Section 8 of the Criminal Justice Act 1967 provides:

A court or jury in determining whether a person has committed an offence,

  (a) shall not be bound to infer that he intended or foresaw a result of his actions by reason only of its being a natural and probable consequence of those actions; but

  (b) shall decide whether he did intend or foresee that result by reference to all the evidence drawing such inferences from the evidence as appear proper in the circumstances.

To what extent intention or foresight need be proved in any particular case depends on the law relating to the crime which is in issue. Section 8 is concerned with *how* intention or foresight must be proved, not *when* it must be proved.[327] On a charge of unlawful act manslaughter, for example, it remains unnecessary to prove that D intended or foresaw that death was likely to result from his act.[328] Section 8 was once construed so as to affect the substantive definition of the law of murder[329] but it is now clear that it applies only to proof and never affects the substantive law.

Although s 8 requires the court to have regard to *all* the evidence, that is, all the evidence relevant to the question whether D did intend or foresee, there is one exception. The courts have consistently held that evidence that D did not intend or foresee because he had taken drink or drugs is no defence, except in the case of crimes requiring 'specific intent'. This practice has been reconciled with the words of s 8 by holding that where D relies on evidence that he had taken drink or drugs for the purpose of showing that he lacked any mens rea, there is a rule of substantive law that the prosecution need prove no mens rea unless the offence is one of 'specific intent'.[330] This is discussed further in Ch 9.

It might be thought, at first sight, that proof of intention, foresight and knowledge presents almost insuperable difficulties. Direct evidence of a person's state of mind, except through his own confession, is not available. But the difficulties, in practice, are not so great. If D points a loaded gun at V's head, pulls the trigger and shoots him dead, it is reasonable to infer that D intended and foresaw V's death. A jury might well be convinced by such evidence that D intended to kill. If D offered an explanation of any kind—he thought the gun was unloaded, or he intended to fire above V's head—and the jury thought that it might reasonably be true, then they should acquit him of an intention to kill. If he offered no explanation, as s 8 makes clear, the jury would not be bound to convict him of having such an intention; they would have to ask themselves whether, in the light of all the evidence, they were satisfied beyond reasonable doubt. Sometimes D's acts may afford apparently overwhelming evidence of his intention to produce a particular result but evidence to

---

[326] *DPP v Smith* [1961] AC 290. The decision cannot be technically overruled by the Privy Council but five judges, all members of the House of Lords, declared that it was wrongly decided in *Frankland* [1987] AC 576. Cf the facts in *Hales* [2005] EWCA Crim 1118.

[327] *DPP v Majewski* [1977] AC 443.   [328] *DPP v Newbury* [1977] AC 500. See Ch 14.

[329] *Hyam v DPP* [1975] AC 55, p 99.   [330] *DPP v Majewski* [1977] AC 443.

the contrary is always admissible and the question must be left to the jury.[331] Similarly, the fact that any reasonable person would, in the circumstances, have known of a fact is cogent evidence that D knew of it.

The difficulty of distinguishing between 'he foresaw' and 'he ought to have foreseen', 'he knew' and 'he ought to have known', is not a good reason for not drawing the line at this point. It is an inescapable difficulty when we have a law which requires us to look into individuals' minds; and such a requirement is essential to a civilized system of criminal law.

[A] lack of confidence in the ability of a tribunal correctly to estimate evidence of states of mind and the like can never be sufficient ground for excluding from enquiry the most fundamental element in a rational and humane criminal code.[332]

Further reading

RA Duff, *Intention, Agency and Criminal Liability: Philosophy of Action and the Criminal Law*

A Norrie, *Crime, Reason and History: A Critical Introduction to Criminal Law*

V Tadros, *Criminal Responsibility*

G Williams, *The Mental Element in Crime*

---

[331] *Riley* [1967] Crim LR 656, is a striking instance of the rebuttal of apparently conclusive evidence of an intent.
[332] *Thomas v R* (1937) 59 CLR 279 at 309 per Dixon J.

4
Crimes of negligence

4.1 Negligence as failure to comply with an objective standard

Negligence[1] describes conduct that falls below the standard to be expected of a reasonable person in the relevant circumstances.[2] Offences can be drafted with requirements to prove D's negligence as to consequences or circumstances.[3] The question in either case is whether D's conduct falls below the reasonable standard.[4] That might be because he has seen the risk of the proscribed consequence or circumstance but reacted unreasonably to it (more usually seen as recklessness), or because he has not seen the risk when he ought to. If the reasonable person would have seen the risk of the proscribed consequence or circumstance, D can be liable for crimes of negligence even if he personally failed to see the risk.

---

[1] See generally HLA Hart, *Punishment and Responsibility* (1968) Ch VI, 'Negligence, *Mens Rea* and Criminal Responsibility'; liability for negligence in manslaughter and road traffic offences is considered in detail in Ch 14 and Ch 32. For a review of approaches in European jurisdictions, see J Blomsma, *Mens Rea and Defences in European Criminal Law* (2012) 166 et seq.

[2] Some commentators argue that there is no principled and rational way to construct the 'reasonable person' against whom D is judged and who it is assumed would have adverted to the risk D failed to advert. See L Alexander and K Ferzan, 'Beyond the Special Part' in RA Duff and SP Green, *Philosophical Foundations of Criminal Law* (2011).

[3] There are occasions when it is unclear whether Parliament has intended to create a crime of negligence. In such instances the court must have regard to the statutory language and the purpose underlying the creation of the offence to ascertain whether it can be committed negligently. For an example of this exercise in the context of s 4(1) of the Animal Welfare Act 2006, see *R (on the application of Gray) v Crown Court at Aylesbury* [2013] EWHC 500 (Admin).

[4] It has been argued that asking whether a defendant's conduct fell short of a reasonable person's conduct is insufficient to ground personal blame, as there is an insufficient linkage between the defendant and wrongdoing that ought to be required for conviction. Objective accounts do have a role to play, however. See F Stark, *Culpable Carelessness* (2016).

Negligence involves a failure by D to comply with an objective standard of behaviour set by the law. Intention, recklessness and negligence all involve a failure to comply with an objective standard of conduct; that is, they are all forms of fault.[5] It is important to appreciate the difference between (a) negligence and (b) intention or *Cunningham/G* recklessness.[6] Intention requires proof of D's personal state of mind—acting with the purpose of causing the harm or foresight of a virtual certainty. Subjective recklessness requires personal foresight of a risk of the proscribed harm and an unjustified taking of the risk. In contrast to both, negligence may be conclusively proved by simply showing that D's conduct failed to measure up to an objective standard irrespective of D's personal state of mind.[7]

The now discredited form of *Caldwell* recklessness was also said by the House of Lords to involve proof of a state of mind; but this is misleading. *Caldwell* recklessness was only a state of mind in the sense that *not* giving thought might be described as a state of mind.[8] An important distinction between *Caldwell* recklessness and negligence was the subject of much of the debate. Under *Caldwell* recklessness, D would not have been liable if he had given thought to the matter of the risk of harm his conduct posed, and wrongly concluded that there was no risk.[9] In contrast, in a crime of negligence D would be liable on such facts. In a crime based on negligence, evidence of D's personal state of mind is no excuse. Negligence is proved by D's *conduct* failing to measure up to an objective standard. It is no answer for him to say, 'I considered whether there was a risk and decided there was none.' Where the risk is one that he *ought to have* foreseen, that is an admission of negligence.[10]

Furthermore, it could never be a 'defence' to a charge of negligence to show that the careless act was done recklessly or intentionally. If D were charged with manslaughter and the prosecution's case was that he killed V by gross negligence it is inconceivable that it could be a defence for him to say convincingly, 'I wasn't negligent; I *intended* to kill him'; or 'I was aware of a risk of killing him and I took it'. The more blameworthy state of mind must include the less; so, if D failed to comply with the objective standard, he is liable whatever his state of mind.[11]

4.1.1 Negligence as mens rea

Writers differ as to whether negligence can properly be described as mens rea. If the term mens rea is used simply as a compendious expression for the varieties of fault that may give rise to criminal liability, then it does, of course, include negligence. If it is taken in its more literal sense of 'guilty mind', the usage is inappropriate.

It is sometimes argued that the absence of foresight or knowledge is just as much a state of mind as its presence;[12] but, since negligence may be proved without establishing anything as to what was going on in D's mind or not, it seems more appropriate and convenient to restrict the label mens rea to intention, recklessness, knowledge, belief, etc, and that is the

---

[5] cf the argument that since negligence involves no culpable choice by the accused it is not properly a fault element: RA Duff, 'Criminalising Endangerment' in Duff and Green, *Defining Crimes*, 48.

[6] See p 104.

[7] It is important not to conflate different states of mind. The Court of Appeal in *Turbill* [2013] EWCA Crim 1422 confirmed that wilful neglect is not the same as negligence, as the former embodies a subjective test.

[8] See p 108. See G Williams, 'Recklessness Redefined' (1981) 40 CLJ 252 at 256–8. On the justification for culpability when D has not troubled to investigate risks that would be obvious to the reasonable person, see Tadros, *Criminal Responsibility*, Ch 3.

[9] See p 109.

[10] See generally J Brady, 'Recklessness, Negligence, Indifference and Awareness' (1980) 43 MLR 381. Note also the conclusion in *A-G's Reference (No 2 of 1999)* [2000] QB 796, that it is not necessary to produce evidence of the 'state of mind' of the accused on a charge of gross negligence manslaughter.

[11] A cold-blooded murderer does not behave reasonably, but we would not describe him as negligent.

[12] G Williams, *Salmond on Jurisprudence* (11th edn, 1957) 329. See also P Brett, *An Inquiry into Criminal Guilt* (1963) 99.

sense in which it is used in this book. Crimes requiring mens rea are contrasted with crimes of negligence discussed in this chapter and strict liability crimes (discussed in the next).[13]

The courts have not engaged with the niceties of these distinctions, but have at least made abundantly clear that negligence is not a form of 'knowledge'. Devlin J emphasized that there is 'a vast distinction between a state of mind which consists of deliberately refraining from making inquiries, the result of which a person does not care to have [wilful blindness], and a state of mind which is merely neglecting to make such inquiries as a reasonable and prudent person would make [constructive knowledge]'.[14] In *Flintshire County Council v Reynolds*,[15] it was reiterated that a person who has 'constructive notice' of a fact may be negligent, but this is not the same as 'knowing' that fact.[16]

4.1.2 Purely objective standards?

Although negligence is conduct that departs from the standard to be expected of a reasonable person that is not to say that a person's state of mind is always completely irrelevant when negligence is in issue. Two factors need to be considered: (a) is it permissible to take into account D's state of mind where that involves special knowledge that a reasonable person would not possess; and (b) is it possible to take into account D's state of mind where he has less knowledge or capacity to see a relevant risk?

4.1.2.1 Where D possesses special knowledge

If D has special knowledge that an ordinary person would not possess, the appropriate question becomes whether a reasonable person, *with that knowledge*, would have acted as he did. For example, behaviour with a revolver that is possibly not negligent in the case of an ordinary person with no special knowledge might be grossly negligent if committed by a firearms expert.[17] D has *more* knowledge or capacity for foresight, and a higher standard will legitimately be expected of him.

Section 2A(3) of the Road Traffic Act 1988, defining dangerous driving,[18] also recognizes that in deciding whether a driver drove dangerously, the standard is 'what would be expected of a competent and careful driver'; but, in determining that standard:

regard shall be had not only to the circumstances of which he could be expected to be aware, but also to any circumstances shown to be within the knowledge of the accused.

So, if D is aware of facts which would not be obvious to a reasonable driver, D may nevertheless be guilty since the Act provides that regard must be had to any circumstances shown to be within his knowledge. If D is unaware on reasonable grounds, for example, of the tendency of a car to swerve to the right when braked hard, D cannot be held to have driven dangerously or even carelessly, but once D becomes aware of this tendency he may properly be held to have driven dangerously if it would then be obvious to a competent and careful driver that to drive the car with this tendency would be dangerous.[19] Similarly, D's actual knowledge of an uneven road surface may count against him though other drivers would be unaware of the hazard.

Several cases have highlighted the difficulty in applying the objective test in situations where a driver has superior driving ability. The Court of Appeal has confirmed that the test is objective: *Bannister*.[20] The current state of the law is that the superior driving *ability* of the

---

[13] cf Duff, *Answering for Crime* who summarizes Hart's position that if D was negligently responsible for bringing about the creation of the risk of the harm he is at 'fault', at 70–1.

[14] *Taylor's Central Garages (Exeter) Ltd v Roper* [1951] 2 TLR 284, 288.

[15] [2006] EWHC 195 (Admin) obtaining benefit contrary to Social Security Administration Act 1992, s 112.

[16] At [17].   [17] cf *Lamb* [1967] 2 QB 981; see p 592.   [18] See Ch 32.

[19] cf *Haynes v Swain* [1975] RTR 40, see Ch 32.

[20] [2009] EWCA Crim 1571. Discussed in full in Ch 32. See also J Goudkamp (2010) 69 CLJ 8.

driver is irrelevant when a driver is charged with dangerous driving. To have regard to those *abilities* is inconsistent with the objective test of the competent and careful driver set out in the Act. These are not relevant to the dangerousness test because they go to the *standard* of the competent and careful driver and not the knowledge or *circumstances*. That distinction is a fine one.

4.1.2.2 Where D is unable to appreciate the relevant risk

More controversial is the question of whether the negligence test should take account of the individual defendant's personal *inability* to appreciate the risk of the proscribed harm. The orthodox answer is that if D has *less* knowledge or capacity for foresight than the reasonable person this will not generally provide him with an excuse. For example, on a charge of careless driving a learner driver, who was exercising all the skill and attention to be expected from a person with his short experience but who has failed to attain the required standard of the competent and careful driver, would be held guilty.

A further example arises in the offence of harassment under the Protection from Harassment Act 1997, s 1(1)(b) read with s 1(2), which imposes a requirement that the course of conduct (which is alleged to amount to harassment) must be one which D knew *or ought to have known* amounts to harassment. That is a statutory crime of negligence. The test of whether D knew or ought to have known is, under s 1, whether a reasonable person *in possession of the same information* as D would think the course of conduct did amount to harassment. In C,[21] the defendant, who suffered from paranoid schizophrenia, had performed the conduct for the offence by sending offensive letters to his MP on at least two occasions. He was convicted and appealed on the basis that the judge should have directed the jury to consider his mental disorder as a relevant condition of the hypothetical reasonable person in s 1(2). The Court of Appeal held that s 1(2) involved a purely objective test relating to the reasonable person and reasonable conduct. D's illness was not relevant to that question. Section 1(2) seeks to endow the reasonable person with knowledge of circumstances that would render otherwise seemingly innocuous conduct harassing (eg when D knows that previous advances towards V have been rejected and continues to send gifts). In such cases, D's inculpatory state of mind is taken into account. Why, then, should the reasonable person not also be possessed with knowledge about D's *exculpatory* states of mind (eg his Asperger's preventing him picking up the cues that his attention is not wanted) in order to assess whether the conduct is harassment? This is not the same as asking whether a reasonable person with the characteristics of the accused would regard it as harassment, particularly where the characteristic inhibits cognition of the wrongdoing.[22]

However, the courts have accepted that the strictness of the objective test ought, in some circumstances, to be modified where the defendant is a child. In *R (RSPCA) v C*,[23] it was held that the question whether a young person (15) was negligent in not taking an injured cat to the vet should be judged by the standards of a reasonable girl of *her* age. It is submitted that this was a sensible qualification of the negligence standard, but it poses two problems.

First, it must be treated with caution. Should account of the defendant's age only be taken when that will affect his ability to appreciate the risk of the relevant harm? Some risks are obvious even to very young children. Equally importantly the question arises whether taking into account the defendant's age (and capacity to appreciate risk) will undermine the

---

[21] [2001] EWCA Crim 1251, [2001] Crim LR 845 and commentary.

[22] Arguably the strong policy grounds of protection on which the Act is founded justify the court's rejection of any attempt to diminish the objective stance under this offence. See the discussion of *Loake v CPS* [2017] EWHC 2855 (Admin) at p 320.

[23] [2006] EWHC 1069 (Admin).

policy underpinning negligence-based crimes. What of the 14-year-old tearaway who is driving a car illegally and causes injury? Should the evaluation of his carelessness in driving take account of his age? Surely not.[24]

Secondly, if the courts accept this qualification of the purely objective standard for young defendants, that begs the question whether modification of the objective test on grounds of recognized disabilities ought also to be unacceptable. Some commentators have suggested that the objective standard ought to be qualified to the extent necessary to take account of the defendant's shortcomings that affect his ability to behave reasonably and which are not a result of his fault.[25] This would include characteristics such as age, hearing, sight, cognitive capacity, etc. It is doubtful that the courts would entertain such a radical qualification of the objective standard. The only English case following this approach seems to be *Hudson*.[26] In deciding whether a man who had sexual intercourse with a 'defective woman', contrary to s 7 of the Sexual Offences Act 1956 (now repealed), had 'no reason to suspect her to be a defective', the court was bound:

to take into account the accused himself. There may be cases of which this is not one, where there is evidence before the jury that the accused himself is a person of limited intelligence, or possibly suffering from some handicap which would prevent him from appreciating the state of affairs which an ordinary man might realize.

The decisions in *Caldwell* and *Lawrence* in 1981 were open to the interpretation that an 'obvious' risk meant obvious to the particular defendant but the courts rejected that notion. 'Obvious' under that test meant obvious to the reasonable person, even if the defendant was a 14-year-old schoolgirl with a learning disability.[27] Some academics rely on the cases decided under *Caldwell* to support the argument that the courts are (and ought to be) amenable to an interpretation of the concept of the reasonable person that is not entirely objective. Some further support for this might derive from the decision of the House of Lords in *G*.[28] However, a response to this claim might be that these cases[29] are merely examples of the courts' desperate attempts to mitigate the harshness of the *Caldwell* formulation of recklessness which applied to serious offences, and that the cases do not provide support for any broader judicial willingness to subjectivize the test of negligence. In other contexts, the court has rejected an opportunity to endow the reasonable person with the personal characteristics of the accused.[30]

The Court of Appeal had the opportunity to consider this issue in *Price*,[31] in which D was convicted of negligently performing a duty, contrary to s 15(2) of the Armed Forces Act 2006. The issue was whether the test should be based on a reasonable person with the same limited skills, professional training, knowledge and experience as D. The Court of Appeal approved the Judge Advocate's direction to the board (the equivalent of the

---

[24] For an argument that in crimes of gross negligence at least the age of the actor ought to be considered, see A Ashworth, *Positive Obligations in Criminal Law* (2013) 193–4.

[25] See Simester, Spencer, Stark, Sullivan and Virgo, CLT&D, 170–1; Horder, APOCL, 205–8; Norrie, *Crime, Reason and History*, 82–3. See further T Hörnle, 'Social Expectation in the Criminal Law: The Reasonable Person in a Comparative Perspective' (2008) 11 New Crim LR 1 at 19.

[26] [1966] 1 QB 448. But see now the many offences under the Sexual Offences Act 2003 where the issue turns on the reasonableness of D's belief. In *B* [2013] EWCA Crim 3, the court rejected D's reliance on his paranoid schizophrenia as a factor to be taken into account in assessing the reasonableness of his belief in consent. See Ch 18.

[27] *Elliott v C (A Minor)* (1983) 77 Cr App R 103; *Stephen Malcolm R* (1984) 79 Cr App R 334.

[28] [2003] UKHL 50.   [29] And those relating to driving such as *Reid* (1992) 95 Cr App R 391.

[30] See eg *C* [2001] Crim LR 845 discussed earlier. See more generally on negligence as an element of harassment under the Protection from Harassment Act 1997, E Finch, 'Stalking the Perfect Stalking Law: An Evaluation of the Efficacy of the Protection from Harassment Act 1997' [2002] Crim LR 703, 714.

[31] [2014] EWCA Crim 229.

jury in a military trial) that D's conduct was to be measured against the standard to be expected of the reasonable serviceman having similar lack of training, knowledge and experience as him. Pitchford LJ went on to state, however, that the direction had been overly generous to D. There was the possibility that, by referring to D's 'skills', the Judge Advocate had inadvertently diluted the objective nature of the test. The Court of Appeal emphasized that the word 'skills' was intended to add nothing to the endowment of the reasonable man with D's training, knowledge and experience. It was observed that if the court accepted D's contention that the reasonable person ought to be endowed with all of D's shortcomings, then no one could ever be found to be negligent. The court stated emphatically that a subjective consideration of D's 'skills' or 'weaknesses' has no place in an objective judgement about whether he reached the appropriate standard of care. Attempts in other contexts to dilute the concept of the reasonable person resulted in an unsatisfactory state of affairs.[32]

4.2 Negligence as the basis of liability

There are few serious crimes in English law in which negligence is the gist of the offence. Manslaughter, causing or allowing a child to die or suffer serious injury by an unlawful act under the Domestic Violence, Crime and Victims Acts 2004 and 2012, and public nuisance[33] are the most conspicuous examples, although arguably manslaughter is a separate form of offence because it requires 'gross negligence'. Other examples where negligence *is* the central feature of the crime include s 3 of the Road Traffic Act 1988 under which it is an offence to drive a mechanically propelled vehicle on a road without due care and attention or without reasonable consideration for other persons using the road. The offence may be committed by making an error of judgement of a kind that a reasonably prudent and skilful driver would not make. It will be noted that it is not necessary to prove that any harmful consequence ensued; it is enough to show that D drove in a manner in which a reasonable person would not have driven because the reasonable person would have realized that it involved an unjustifiable risk. The same considerations apply to the more serious offence of dangerous driving (see Ch 32).

In a number of other serious crimes negligence is not the gist of the offence because intention or recklessness is required as to the central features of the offence, but negligence with respect to some subsidiary element in the actus reus is sometimes enough. So, under s 9 of the Sexual Offences Act 2003, it is an offence intentionally to touch a person, B, aged under 16 where that touching is sexual and either B is under 16 and D *does not reasonably believe* that B is 16 or over, or B is under 13. The conduct element of the offence in the form of 'touching' has to be shown to be intentional, but as to the circumstance of B's age (where between 13 and 16), it is expressly provided that D is guilty if he does not reasonably believe B to be 16 or over. An honest but unreasonable belief that B is 16 is no excuse. Negligence with respect to that circumstantial element of the actus reus will suffice. Such a provision, as well as catching the negligent person, disposes of another difficult case. It deals satisfactorily with the case of D who does not stop to think about B's age at all (simple ignorance),[34] for he cannot say that he reasonably believed B to be 16 or over.

[32] See the discussion in relation to the old law of provocation in Ch 13.
[33] The Law Commission proposes making this a crime of recklessness. See Ch 31.
[34] For philosophical arguments about whether D who does not think about the risk in such circumstances can be described as reckless or culpable at all, see Tadros, *Criminal Responsibility*, Ch 3 and 255–8.

It should be noted that the Sexual Offences Act, although changing the law from what had been a purely subjective approach to recklessness as to consent, has not produced an offence of rape (nor other offences) in which the fault element is *exclusively* objective. The question for the jury in rape is whether the prosecution has made them sure that the particular defendant did not have a reasonable belief in consent in all the circumstances including whether any steps *he* took to ascertain consent were reasonable, and whether he intentionally penetrated the victim's vagina, anus or mouth.

In *B*,[35] rape charges related to occasions when D had sex with V despite her objections. Expert medical evidence was adduced that D suffered from a mental disorder, probably paranoid schizophrenia, at the time of the offences but D was not insane. D claimed that he had a reasonable belief in V's consent and that what was 'reasonable' must take account of his personal mental state. The judge directed the jury that they should ignore D's mental illness when asking whether any belief that he might have had in V's consent had been reasonable. The Court of Appeal upheld the conviction. D must genuinely believe that V is consenting, and must have some objective foundation for that belief, but the belief that D holds must be assessed by the jury on purely objective bases. 'Unless the state of mind amounted to insanity in law, beliefs in consent arising from conditions such as delusional psychotic illness or personality disorders had to be judged by objective standards of reasonableness and not by taking into account a mental disorder that induced a belief which could not reasonably arise without it.'[36] However, the court recognized that there may be cases in which D's personality or abilities might be relevant to whether his positive belief in consent was reasonable, but that was for determination on specific facts. So, for example, a defendant with Asperger's might not understand subtle and non-verbal cues to desist. Such beliefs would not be so irrational as to be ignored under the Act. This leaves scope for some fine distinctions to be drawn in future cases.

4.2.1 Negligent mistakes

Historically it was thought that a mistake was never a defence unless it was reasonable, and that such a rule was capable of turning almost any crime into a crime of negligence. It is now clear since *Morgan*,[37] *B (A Minor)*[38] and *K*[39] that there is no such general rule. For example, before those cases it was held that if D went through a ceremony of marriage to V, believing wrongly but without reasonable grounds that he was no longer married to X because he believed X was dead, or his marriage had been dissolved or annulled, he was guilty of bigamy.[40] This, in effect, was to turn bigamy into a crime of negligence so far as this element of the offence is concerned. D was to be held liable because he did not take sufficient care to ascertain that his first marriage was at an end, before going through the second ceremony. It appears that these cases would be decided differently today. D would be guilty only if he knew that his wife was or might be alive, or that his first marriage was or might be subsisting, as the case may be.

4.3 Degrees of negligence

It has been said that there can be no 'degrees of inadvertence when that word is used to denote a state of mind, since it means that in the man's mind there has been a complete absence of a particular thought, a nullity; and of nullity there can be no degrees'.[41]

---

[35] [2013] EWCA Crim 3. See further P Rook and R Ward, *Rook and Ward on Sexual Offences: Law and Practice* (6th edn, 2021) paras 1.392–1.395.

[36] At [40] per Hughes LJ.   [37] See p 350.   [38] See p 155.   [39] See p 156.

[40] *Tolson* (1889) 23 QBD 168, CCR; *Gould* [1968] 2 QB 65.

[41] Kenny, *Outlines*, 39, criticized by Hart, *Punishment and Responsibility*, n 1, who writes: 'Negligence is gross if the precautions to be taken against harm are very simple, such as persons who are but poorly endowed with physical and mental capacities can easily take.'

It is true that there can be no degrees of inadvertence but there can be degrees of fault in failing to appreciate a risk. The more obvious the risk, and the greater D's capacity to advert to it, the greater his fault in failing to be aware of it. If negligence is regarded as non-attainment of a required standard of conduct then it is clear that there are degrees of it. One person may fall just short of the required standard, another may fall far short. The existence of degrees of negligence is recognized by s 2A of the Road Traffic Act 1988 (as substituted by the Road Traffic Act 1991)[42] when it provides that a person drives dangerously if:

(a) the way he drives falls far below what would be expected of a competent and careful driver, and

(b) it would be obvious to a competent and careful driver that driving in that way would be dangerous.

A driver whose driving falls below, but not *far* below, what would be expected of a competent and careful driver is negligent and probably guilty of careless driving contrary to s 3 of the 1988 Act; but he is not sufficiently negligent to be guilty of the more serious offence of dangerous driving.

The fault required for the present offence of causing death by dangerous driving probably falls short of that required by the law of manslaughter as restated in *Adomako*:[43] that is, 'whether, having regard to the *risk of death* involved, the conduct of the defendant was so bad as in all the circumstances as to amount in [the jury's] judgement to a criminal act or omission'. There are two possible distinctions. First, driving may fall far below what would be expected of a competent and careful driver without involving any apparent risk *to life*. The only apparent risk may be to property but, if the driving unforeseeably causes death, that will amount to a Road Traffic Act offence. Secondly, the Road Traffic Act offence is not subject to the jury's assessment of its 'grossness'. True, the jury find, or, more accurately, have to accept the judge's direction, that even careless driving is a 'criminal act'; but the principle in *Adomako* has to be read against the background that the crime charged is manslaughter; and clearly the jury will be looking to see whether the conduct is bad enough to amount to that very serious crime, not careless driving. Conceivably, a jury of motorists might think that the particular driving, though falling far below the standard expected of a competent and careful driver, ought *not* to amount to a crime. It would be their duty to convict of causing death by dangerous driving, but not of manslaughter.[44] The more likely charge in such a case is now one of causing death by careless driving. Section 20(1) of the Road Safety Act 2006 created an offence (inserting s 2B into the 1988 Act) of causing death by careless or inconsiderate driving.[45]

4.4 Should negligence be a ground of liability?

4.4.1 Negligence as a form of culpable fault

Distinguished academic writers have strongly contended that negligence should have no place in criminal liability.[46] Their arguments for the most part assume a clear-cut distinction between conscious and inadvertent risk-taking that clearly distinguishes *Cunningham/G*

---

[42] See Ch 32. [43] [1995] 1 AC 171, see p 607.

[44] There has to be a serious and obvious risk of death for gross negligence manslaughter: *Misra* [2004] EWCA Crim 2375; *Kuddus* [2019] EWCA Crim 837. See Ch 14, p 613.

[45] The maximum penalty on conviction on indictment is five years' imprisonment or a fine, or both.

[46] See eg J Hall, 'Negligent Behaviour Should be Excluded from Criminal Liability' (1963) 63 Col LR 632; L Alexander and K Kessler Ferzan with S Morse, *Crime and Culpability: A Theory of Criminal Law* (2009), but note Leipold's response, see A Leipold, 'A Case for Criminal Negligence' (2010) 29 Law & Phil 455.

recklessness from negligence.[47] *Caldwell* brought much inadvertent risk-taking within the criminal law, but it no longer has any application (although there are numerous serious offences with an objective element including, eg: manslaughter, dangerous driving, various terrorism offences,[48] money laundering offences[49] and many sexual offences under the Sexual Offences Act 2003).

Turner acknowledged that negligence implies that D was 'in some measure blameworthy, and that we should expect an ordinary reasonable man to foresee the possibility of the consequences and to regulate his conduct so as to avoid them';[50] however, he also contended that the moral test on which criminal liability should be (and, indeed, is) based is the proof of subjective fault of foresight of the consequences of one's conduct. Hall goes further and finds it difficult to accept that negligently caused harm reflects a moral fault.[51] He rejects the thesis that negligent persons may be ethically blameworthy insofar as they are insensitive to the rights of others. He also rejects the view that punishment encourages people to be more careful, arguing that the deterrent theory postulates a person who weighs the possibility of punishment in the balance before acting; but the inadvertent harm-doer, by definition, does not do this. Hall appears to suggest that the courts themselves do not really believe that punishment deters negligence, suggesting that sentences, even for negligent homicides, are relatively light. In the case of negligently caused car accidents, for example, he argues that it seems much more probable that a dull mind, slow reactions, awkwardness and other ethically irrelevant factors were the underlying cause. Other commentators take a different view. Brett, for example, suggests that it is:

common knowledge that as soon as traffic police appear on the roads, drivers begin to pay greater attention to what they are doing and the standard of driving rises sharply.[52]

The negligent performance or certain functions or handling of certain articles—notably driving vehicles—can have such drastic consequences that society is almost bound to adopt any measures that seem to have a reasonable prospect of inducing greater care; and it seems reasonable to suppose that the threat of punishment does have an effect on the care used in their handling.

Glanville Williams acknowledges that 'it is possible for punishment to bring about greater foresight, by causing the subject to stop and think before committing himself to a course of conduct'; but thinks that this justification does not go very far and that the law is wise in penalizing negligence only exceptionally.[53]

Lord Nicholls, in rejecting the former rule that only a reasonable mistake will excuse, invoked a presumption against liability for mere negligence:

When [a person is held liable because his mistake, though negating *mens rea*, was made without reasonable grounds] the defendant's 'fault' lies exclusively in falling short of an objective standard. His crime lies in his negligence. A statute may so provide expressly or by necessary implication. But this can have no place in a common law principle, of general application, which is concerned with the need for a mental element as an essential ingredient of a criminal offence.[54]

---

[47] There are, however, those who argue that the distinction between the two is in fact an uncertain one. See KW Simons, 'The Distinction between Negligence and Recklessness is Unstable' in PH Robinson, SP Garvey and K Ferzan (eds), *Criminal Law Conversations* (2009). See also DN Husak, 'Negligence, Belief and Criminal Liability: The Special Case of Forgetting' (2011) 5 Crim L & Phil 199. Husak states that it is 'scandalous' that there is not a greater body of literature analysing the distinction between recklessness and negligence.

[48] Terrorism Act 2000, ss 15–18.   [49] POCA 2002, ss 330–3.   [50] MACL, 207.

[51] *General Principles*, 136.   [52] Brett, *An Inquiry into Criminal Guilt*, 173.

[53] Chan and Simester proffer a different reason for why negligence should be used rarely, which is based on the proposition that mens rea performs functions other than denoting culpability. See W Chan and AP Simester, 'Four Functions of *Mens Rea*' (2011) 70 CLJ 381.

[54] *B (A Child) v DPP* [2000] 2 AC 428 at 462.

In an impressive account of recklessness and negligence in the criminal law, Stark argues that negligence ought to be recognized as culpable only when certain conditions are met. The conditions he specifies are that the defendant was possessed of background beliefs and perceptions that could have led to the belief that a risk was present, but he failed to form that belief—in circumstances demonstrating insufficient concern for others—because of an accepted facet of his character.[55]

4.4.2 Negligence and capacity

Hart famously challenged the commonly accepted criterion of foresight. The reason why in most cases it is thought proper to punish the person who foresees the forbidden harm is that he can choose to cause it or not; but in some cases of negligence, at least, it may be said:

'he could have thought about what he was doing' with just as much rational confidence as one can say of an intentional wrong-doing, 'he could have done otherwise'.[56]

Hart's approach to negligence, however, differs from that so far generally adopted by the courts. He would not enforce an objective, external and impersonal standard which took no account of the individual's lack of capacity. He would recognize that punishment might be proper only if two questions are answered in the affirmative.[57]

(1) Did the accused fail to take those precautions which any reasonable man with normal capacities would in the circumstances have taken?

(2) Could the accused, given his mental and physical capacities, have taken those precautions?

As noted earlier, the courts have not yet demonstrated a willingness to subjectivize the negligence standard in this way.

4.4.3 Due diligence defences

There have been many suggestions to include more negligence-based liability in the criminal law by replacing strict liability offences—usually by accepting as a defence to strict liability offences that D acted with all due diligence. The 'no negligence' defence is examined further in the context of strict liability in the next chapter.

Further reading

HLA Hart, *Punishment and Responsibility: Essays in the Philosophy of Law*
F Stark, *Culpable Carelessness: Recklessness and Negligence in the Criminal Law*

---

[55] F Stark, *Culpable Carelessness* (2016).
[56] *Oxford Essays in Jurisprudence*, 29.
[57] ibid, 46. Hart was not advocating the punishment of negligence, only seeking to dispel the belief that negligence is a form of strict liability.

5

Crimes of strict liability

5.1 The nature of strict liability

Crimes which do not require mens rea or even negligence as to one or more elements in the actus reus are known as offences of strict liability or, sometimes, 'of absolute prohibition'.[1] An example is s 58(2) of the Medicines Act 1968 which prohibited the sale by retail of specified medicinal products except in accordance with a prescription given by an appropriate medical practitioner.[2] In *Pharmaceutical Society of Great Britain v Storkwain Ltd*,[3] D, a pharmacist,

---

[1] For more detailed discussion of this topic, see especially A Norrie, *Crime, Reason and History* (2014), 102–17; A Ashworth, 'Should Strict Criminal Liability be Removed from all Imprisonable Offences?' in A Ashworth, *Positive Obligations in Criminal Law* (2013); J Horder, 'Strict Liability, Statutory Construction and the Spirit of Liberty' (2002) 118 LQR 458; the collection of essays edited by Simester, *Appraising Strict Liability* and see K Reid, 'Strict Liability: Some Principles for Parliament' (2008) 29 St LR 173.

[2] Section 58(2) has been repealed, but is replaced by very similar provisions in the Human Medicines Regulations 2012, SI 2012/1916, regs 214 and 255.

[3] [1986] 2 All ER 635 discussed by BS Jackson in '*Storkwain*: A Case Study in Strict Liability and Self Regulation' [1991] Crim LR 892, who shows that the Society's policy was to prosecute only where the pharmacist had not acted with due diligence; but the Society does not have a monopoly of the right to prosecute; and if, in practice, fault is required, should not the decision whether it exists be made in court? See also R Cooke, *Turning Points* (Hamlyn Lectures, 1997) 40.

supplied to X specified drugs on prescriptions purporting to be signed by a Dr Irani. The prescriptions were forged. There was, therefore, no prescription given by an appropriate medical practitioner. There was no finding that D acted dishonestly, improperly or even negligently as a pharmacist in acting on that prescription and providing X with the medicines. It appeared that the forgery was good enough to deceive the pharmacists without any negligence on their part. Yet the House of Lords held that the Divisional Court was right to direct the magistrates to convict. The case highlights the difficulties with imposing strict liability, particularly in offences of a serious nature: there is a real sense of unfairness in convicting someone for conduct which on his part was 'faultless'.[4]

It should not be imagined that strict liability applies only in 'regulatory' offences, assuming indeed that such a category of crimes can be defined.[5] For example, s 5 of the Sexual Offences Act 2003 creates an offence where D intentionally penetrates with his penis the vagina, anus or mouth of a child under 13. The conduct element of the offence—penile penetration—must be intentional; that much is clear. But as to the circumstance element that V is under 13, the House of Lords[6] held that Parliament intended this element of the offence to be strict. So, even if V told D she was 16, and even if it was reasonable for D to believe her in the circumstances, D will be guilty of the offence if he intentionally penetrates her. The offence carries a maximum sentence of life imprisonment and, obviously, serious stigma. Numerous other serious criminal offences are strict as to at least one element of the actus reus, including possession of firearms,[7] terrorism offences, possession of indecent images of children[8] and many sexual offences.[9] The imposition of criminal liability and punishment (including imprisonment) for such conduct where D had no mens rea and was not negligent as to one or more elements of the actus reus seems 'unjust'.[10] In one case in which D was convicted of possessing a firearm which he claimed had been slipped into his bag without his knowledge, the court, following a strong line of binding authority stated:

The effect of the authorities is that ignorance of the contents of a bag of which a person is in possession can afford no defence where the contents include a firearm. It makes no difference whether there is something in the bag that the carrier is unaware of, or is mistaken to its nature, or does not know that the bag has any contents, far less that it contains a gun. In each case the question for the jury for consideration relates to possession, which in turn depends on control. This may or may not be harsh, but it is not for this court to re-write the statute, far less when it has already been interpreted by different constitutions of this court on separate occasions.[11]

---

[4] Duff provides an interesting account of the relationship between strict liability and strict responsibility, classifying crimes into categories where liability is 'formally' strict (no intention, recklessness or negligence) and/or those where it is 'substantially' strict (ie no moral fault). See *Answering for Crime*, Ch 10.

[5] See later where LCCP 195, *Criminal Liability in Regulatory Contexts* (2010) is examined. This point is emphasized by Ashworth. See A Ashworth, 'Should Strict Criminal Liability be Removed from all Imprisonable Offences?' in A Ashworth, *Positive Obligations in Criminal Law* (2013).

[6] *G* [2008] UKHL 37. D's application to the ECtHR on the basis that his conviction violated Arts 6 and 8 was found inadmissible. See *G v UK* (2011) 53 EHRR SE25, [2012] Crim LR 47 and commentary.

[7] See *Deyemi* [2007] EWCA Crim 2060, [2008] Crim LR 327 and commentary; *Zahid* [2010] EWCA Crim 2158; *Gregory* [2011] EWCA Crim 1712.

[8] See eg *Price* [2006] EWCA Crim 3363—Protection of Children Act 1978, s 1. For a comprehensive and accessible review of the issues, see A Gillespie, 'Child Pornography: Balancing Substantive and Evidential Law to Safeguard Children' (2005) 9 E & P 29.

[9] Some have argued that rape ought to be a strict liability offence: see, for discussion, K Huigens, 'Is Strict Liability Rape Defensible' in Duff and Green, *Defining Crimes*, 196.

[10] See Duff, *Answering for Crime*, 231–2.

[11] *Tinarwo* [2014] EWCA Crim 1409 at [12]–[13] per HHJ Goldstone QC.

The offence carries a mandatory minimum sentence of five years' imprisonment unless there are exceptional circumstances.

It is worth examining, briefly, the historical background to the use of strict liability. The first case to impose strict liability is said[12] to be that of *Woodrow*.[13] D was found guilty of having in his possession adulterated tobacco, although he did not know it was adulterated. The prosecution emphasized the absence of the word 'knowingly' or any similar word in the definition of the offence and the purpose of the relevant statute—it was for the protection of the Revenue. The court, in interpreting the offence, relied on a section of the Act which gave the Commissioners of Excise a power not to prosecute where there was no 'intention of fraud or of offending against this Act', the implication being that the crime was still committed even when there was no fraud or intention of offending against the Act. Practical problems were also weighed in the balance. Parke B thought that the prosecution would very rarely be able to prove knowledge in such cases if that were an element; and that the public inconvenience which would follow if they were required to do so would be greater than the injustice to the individual if they were not. Even the exercise of reasonable care would not have saved D; according to Parke B, he was liable even if the adulteration was discoverable only by a 'nice chemical analysis'. Liability was strict.

Notwithstanding the subsequent mass of case law, the considerations taken into account in this early case are very much the same as those which influence the courts today when interpreting a statutory offence to determine whether it is one of strict liability:[14] the public welfare purpose of the legislation, the precise statutory form of words in creating the offence, the penalty and whether the offence would otherwise be impossible or almost impossible to prove. These issues will be considered later in this chapter.

It is important to appreciate that where an offence is interpreted to be one of strict liability, the fact that D could not have avoided the prescribed harm even if he had tried to will not absolve him of liability. For example, in *Hobbs v Winchester Corpn*,[15] the case turned on whether a butcher had sold contaminated meat. The butcher was unaware, and the evidence was clear that *he could not have discovered* by any examination which he could reasonably be expected to make, that the meat was contaminated. He was guilty of the crime of selling such meat. Kennedy LJ, having regard to the policy of the statute in protecting consumers said:[16]

> I think that the policy of the Act is this: that if a man chooses for profit to engage in a business which involves the offering for sale of that which may be deadly or injurious to health he must take that risk, and that it is not a sufficient defence for anyone who chooses to embark on such a business to say 'I could not have discovered the disease unless I had an analyst on the premises'.

Similarly, in the famous case of *Cundy v Le Cocq*,[17] D was convicted of selling intoxicating liquor to a drunken person contrary to what was then s 13 of the Licensing Act 1872. It was proved that D did not know the person was drunk and nothing had occurred to show that he was drunk. While some sections of the 1872 Act contained the word 'knowingly', s 13 did not do so. The Divisional Court held that it was not necessary to consider whether D knew, or had means of knowing, *or could with ordinary care have detected*, that the person served was drunk. If D served a drink to a person who was in fact drunk, he was guilty.

---

12 By Sayre (1933) 33 Col LR 55.   13 (1846) 15 M & W 404.
14 See eg recently *Highbury Poultry Farm Produce Ltd v CPS* [2020] UKSC 39 on whether offences relating to the human slaughter of chickens were strict liability under the Welfare of Animals at the Time of Killing (England) Regulations 2015, reg 30(1)(g).
15 [1910] 2 KB 471.   16 ibid, 483. Note the modern statutory defence, p 175.
17 (1884) 13 QBD 207.

In each of these cases D was not even negligent. He intended the conduct element of the offence—to sell medicine or meat or liquor or to possess tobacco—but he was blamelessly unaware of the crucial circumstance element in the actus reus—that the tobacco was adulterated, that the meat was contaminated, that the person was drunk, etc. In each case he was criminally liable despite not having been at fault in relation to this material element of the actus reus of the offence.

5.1.1 Irrelevance of mens rea

Where an offence is held to be one of strict liability, not only is it unnecessary for the prosecution to tender evidence of any mens rea as to the matter of strict liability (eg that D, a pharmacist, had knowledge of or was negligent as to the prescription being duly signed by a practitioner, or D, a retailer, that the tobacco is adulterated, etc), they *must* not adduce evidence of D's mens rea as to that aspect of the offence. Such evidence is irrelevant and, as it shows the defendant to be at fault, it is prejudicial. In *Sandhu*,[18] D was charged with the strict liability offence of causing a listed building to be altered without authority. Although D objected, the prosecution were allowed to prove that he knew the work went beyond what was permitted. This was an error and D's conviction was quashed.[19] This seems an unnecessarily narrow view on the facts.

5.1.2 Distinction from 'absolute' liability

Until relatively recently, only limited academic attention had been paid to defining what was meant by strict liability. One consequence of that is that there is no universally accepted definition of the terms 'strict liability' and 'absolute liability' and how they relate.

It is commonly said that 'no mens rea' need be proved in strict liability offences: 'D can be convicted on proof by the prosecution of *actus reus* only'.[20] In fact it is only in an extreme case[21] that this is true.[22] The label 'absolute offence' is best reserved for those rare situations where the offence criminalizes D whose conduct has caused[23] an actus reus with no mens rea and who is precluded from relying on defences.[24] Absolute liability denotes those crimes

---

[18] [1997] Crim LR 288 and commentary. See *Hill* [1997] 2 Cr App R (S) 243, and commentary at [1997] Crim LR 459 on the sentencing implications.

[19] For proof of strict liability offence by D's previous similar misconduct, see eg *Vehicle and Operator Services Agency v Ace Crane and Transport Ltd* [2010] EWHC 288 (Admin).

[20] Howard, SR, 1.   [21] *Larsonneur*, p 43.

[22] Confusingly, some offences are referred to as being 'double strict liability' offences. These are offences where the underlying or qualifying condition is an offence (eg uninsured driving) which can be committed without mens rea, *and* the aggravating element can be constituted by an event for which D has no fault. The Supreme Court in *Hughes* [2013] UKSC 56 held that the offence in s 3ZB of the Road Traffic Act 1988, causing death by driving while uninsured or without a licence was an offence of strict liability in the sense that it did not require the prosecution to prove mens rea, but it did require proof of some fault in the manner of D's driving which contributed to V's death in a more than minimal way. See also *Taylor* [2016] UKSC 5. For further discussion, see Ch 32.

[23] In *Kilbride v Lake* [1962] NZLR 590, discussed by M Budd and A Lynch, 'Voluntariness, Causation and Strict Liability' [1978] Crim LR 74, D was acquitted of permitting a vehicle not displaying a current warrant of fitness to be on the highway, when the warrant was detached during his absence. The court took the view that there was an actus reus (*sed quaere?*) but that D had not caused it and he was not liable even if the offence was one of strict liability. Cf *Strowger v John* [1974] RTR 124. See the discussion at Ch 2, p 37.

[24] In *Gregory* [2011] EWCA Crim 1712, Lord Judge CJ stated that the judge had been wrong to characterize the offence in s 1(1) of the Firearms Act 1968 as being one of absolute liability. It is an offence of strict liability, as there is nothing that precludes D from pleading a defence.

in which there is no mens rea attaching to any element of the actus reus and no due diligence defence available.[25]

Strict liability is different. The label 'strict liability' should be used to denote crimes in which one element or more (but not all) of the actus reus requires no proof of mens rea. Even this definition of strict liability is problematical since it encompasses constructive crimes. Lord Edmund-Davies said that 'an offence is regarded—and properly regarded—as one of strict liability if no *mens rea* need be proved as to a single element in the *actus reus*'.[26] By this test, even murder is an offence of strict liability because no mens rea is required as to the crucial element of death.[27] Murder, however, does require an intention to cause grievous bodily harm, the mens rea of a lesser offence but nevertheless a substantial mens rea.[28]

Care should also be taken with loose definitions related to whether the offence can be committed without proof of moral fault: the focus is on whether there needs to be mens rea, and as the House of Lords has reminded us, mens rea is not necessarily synonymous with moral fault.[29] Unfortunately, the courts and practitioners do not always adopt consistent and clear terminology.[30]

In this book, we define an offence as one of strict liability where one or more elements of actus reus requires no proof of any mens rea. The element(s) as to which liability is strict will usually be of great significance. In many cases the courts have held that Parliament intended to impose strict liability and have convicted defendants who lacked mens rea, not merely as to some subsidiary matter, but as to the central feature of the actus reus. For example, in a case of sexual touching of a child under 13, liability to the age of the child is strict. D is guilty whether he thought the child was older, whether he had good reason to think so or not. If the child is under 13 that element of the offence is satisfied.

The fact that liability as to the central element of the offence is strict does not necessarily mean that mens rea will be required as to the remaining actus reus elements of the offence. In one of the leading cases, *Gammon (Hong Kong) Ltd v A-G of Hong Kong*, construing the Hong Kong Building Ordinance, Lord Scarman said: 'Each provision clearly requires a degree of mens rea, but each is silent whether it is required in respect of all the facts which together constitute the offence created.' The Privy Council held that D was liable for deviating in a

---

[25] See on this SP Green, 'Six Senses of Strict Liability: A Plea for Formalism' in Simester, *Appraising Strict Liability*. Green identifies six possible uses of 'strict liability' and concludes that the correct one is where the offence lacks mens rea as to at least one element. See also DN Husak, 'Varieties of Strict Liability' (1995) 8 Canadian J L & Jurisprudence 189. Similarly, Ashworth adopts the following definition: 'an offence should be treated as a crime of strict liability if it provides for conviction without requiring fault as to at least one material element'. See A Ashworth, 'Should Strict Criminal Liability be Removed from all Imprisonable Offences?' in A Ashworth, *Positive Obligations in Criminal Law* (2013) 112.

[26] *Whitehouse v Gay News Ltd* [1979] AC 617 at 656, quoting the 4th edn of this book, at p 79 where 'single' was clearly meaning 'one' and not 'any'. See on the constructive crime and strict liability relationship, Green, n 25, 2.

[27] It is for this reason that some regard murder as an anomaly and an instance of 'constructive crime'. See p 532.

[28] See p 535.

[29] See Lord Mustill in *Kingston* [1995] 2 AC 355. For theoretical discussion of the moral issues, see RA Duff, 'Strict Liability, Legal Presumption and the Presumption of Innocence' in Simester, *Appraising Strict Liability*. A similar point is also made by Chan and Simester, who argue that it is a mistake to view mens rea as constituting the fault element of an offence. They argue that it is a necessary but not a sufficient component for a finding of culpability. See W Chan and AP Simester, 'Four Functions of *Mens Rea*' (2011) 70 CLJ 381.

[30] cf *Nicholson* [2006] EWCA Crim 1518 where the Court of Appeal declined to adopt the term strict liability to describe an absence of a reasonable excuse. See also *Charles* [2009] EWCA Crim 1570 in the context of ASBOs.

material way from the approved building plan, even though there was no evidence that he knew that his act constituted a material deviation from the plan—liability as to *that* element was strict.[31]

5.1.3 Common law and statute

The crimes which the courts interpret to be ones of strict liability are almost invariably statutory. There are many thousands of these offences, mostly involving offences triable in the magistrates' court,[32] but with many triable on indictment.[33] There has been an increase in such offences being introduced by Parliament on matters of regulation.[34] This was the subject of close scrutiny in the Macrory Report[35] which led to the Regulatory Enforcement and Sanctions Act 2008. That Act encourages the use of civil administrative sanctions rather than criminal offences in regulatory contexts. In 2010, the Law Commission addressed the problem in Consultation Paper No 195[36] in which more radical proposals were made to avoid the use of criminal offences in regulatory sectors.[37]

As for the common law, it used to be said that there were only two exceptions to the rule requiring mens rea. These were public nuisance and criminal libel. Public nuisance, however, is an anomalous crime and is treated in several respects rather as if it were a civil action than an indictable offence. Criminal libel has now been abolished, although Parliament has now expressly recognized the existence of strict liability in this context by the Contempt of Court Act 1981.[38] Other contempts of court at common law require mens rea.[39]

Apart from these instances, the common law generally required mens rea, though sometimes the mens rea of a lesser offence—as in the case of murder where intention to cause grievous bodily harm is sufficient.

5.1.4 Strict liability and the presumption of innocence

The HRA 1998 prompted challenges to strict liability offences on the basis that they might infringe rights guaranteed under the European Convention. Since the HRA 1998 does not empower courts to 'strike down' statutes, the challenge is not of the same magnitude as that in, for example, the United States where it is possible for some strict liability offences to be held to be unconstitutional.[40] It has been argued that the imposition of strict

---

[31] *Gammon (Hong Kong) Ltd v A-G of Hong Kong* [1985] AC 1 PC.

[32] See Justice, *Breaking the Rules* (1980).

[33] A Ashworth and M Blake, 'The Presumption of Innocence in English Criminal Law' [1996] Crim LR 306 found almost half of the offences in *Archbold* were strict in one sense.

[34] See R Baldwin, 'The New Punitive Regulation' (2004) 67 MLR 351. Cf Leverick et al [2015] Crim LR 177.

[35] *Macrory Review of Regulatory Penalties* (2006). See J Norris and J Phillips, *The Law of Regulatory Enforcement and Sanctions* (2011).

[36] *Criminal Liability in Regulatory Contexts* (2010).

[37] The most radical suggestion in LCCP 195 is for all criminal offences with strict liability to be read subject to a defence for the accused to show that he had acted with all due diligence. See para 1.68.

[38] See: *B* [2006] EWCA Crim 2692; *Attorney General v Associated Newspapers Ltd* [2011] EWHC 418 (Admin).

[39] *Akthar* [2006] EWCA Crim 469.

[40] See A Michaels, 'Imposing Constitutional Limits on Strict Liability: Lessons from the American Experience' in Simester, *Appraising Strict Liability*. See also the Irish Supreme Court decision in *CC v Ireland* [2006] IESC 33 noted by L McGowan, 'Irish Supreme Court: Sexual Offence: Constitutionality' (2006) 70 J Crim L 406. The English courts may of course read down statutes incompatible with the HRA—see eg the reverse burden case of *Keogh* [2007] EWCA Crim 528 (Official Secrets Act 1989), and *Webster* [2010] EWCA Crim 2819 (corruption).

liability might engage, for example, Art 3 (freedom from inhuman or degrading treatment),[41] Art 8 (respect for privacy),[42] Art 10 (freedom of expression)[43] and possibly Art 7 (guarantees against retrospectivity) owing to the ambiguity over whether the courts will hold liability to be strict.

The controversy has been over whether strict liability offences infringe the presumption of innocence guaranteed under Art 6(2) of the ECHR.[44] Some commentators argued that strict liability offences may offend against Art 6(2) because once the prohibited act is proved, D is 'presumed' to be liable.[45] It was argued that the effect of the presumption and the imposition of strict liability is the same.[46] That alleged functional equivalence was keenly disputed by others,[47] who regard the rules of procedure and substantive law as fundamentally distinct. Professor Ashworth has summarized the objection to strict liability as:

that it is wrong to convict people of serious offences without proof of culpability, and that is a separate argument from the presumption of innocence. It is not an argument about evidence and procedure at all but an argument about the proper preconditions of criminal liability.[48]

Although there is some faint support in the ECtHR case law for the application of Art 6(2) to strict liability offences,[49] the European Court has held that strict liability offences are compatible with the Article: 'in principle the contracting States may, under certain conditions, penalize a simple or objective fact as such irrespective of whether it results from criminal intent or from negligence'.[50]

The English courts have taken account of that conclusion in holding that Art 6(2) is restricted to providing procedural protection and does not render the imposition of strict liability incompatible with Art 6(2).[51] As Lord Bingham stated in *Sheldrake*:[52]

The overriding concern is that a trial should be fair, and the presumption of innocence is a fundamental right directed to that end. The Convention does not outlaw presumptions of fact or law but requires that these should be kept within reasonable limits and should not be arbitrary. *It is open*

41 See GR Sullivan, 'Strict Liability for Criminal Offences in England and Wales Following Incorporation into English Law of the ECHR' in Simester, *Appraising Strict Liability*, 206; Michaels, n 40, 229–31. See also S Salako, 'Strict Criminal Liability: A Violation of the Convention' (2006) 70 J Crim L 531, arguing that 'it is degrading and inhuman to put a person who is not culpable through the process of a criminal trial'. The issue is most acute where D is sentenced to a lengthy term of imprisonment for a strict liability offence.

42 As in the *Barnfather* case discussed later. See also on this Michaels, n 40, 233.

43 eg in contempt of court cases: Michaels, n 40. This might also be significant in offences involving communication: *DPP v Collins* [2006] UKHL 40, Ch 30, on the communication of racist views and the element of mens rea.

44 A full examination of the issues of Art 6 belongs more properly in an evidence textbook.

45 See V Tadros and S Tierney, 'The Presumption of Innocence and the Human Rights Act' (2004) 67 MLR 402.

46 See RA Duff, 'Strict Liability, Legal Presumptions and the Presumption of Innocence' in Simester, *Appraising Strict Liability*, 125.

47 See P Roberts, 'Strict Liability and the Presumption of Innocence' in Simester, *Appraising Strict Liability*, 151.

48 A Ashworth, 'Four Threats to the Presumption of Innocence' (2006) 10 E & P 241, 252–3. Cf the views of eg S Salako (2006) 70 J Crim L 53, who suggests such a distinction is 'artificial'.

49 See *Hansen v Denmark* (App no 28971/95).

50 *Salibaku v France* (1998) 13 EHRR 379; Emmerson, Ashworth and Macdonald, HR&CJ, paras 9.74–9.77. For analysis, see *Williams* [2012] EWCA Crim 2162 and Ashworth's criticisms at [2013] Crim LR 447.

51 *G* [2008] UKHL 37. D's application to the ECtHR on the basis that his conviction violated Arts 6 and 8 was judged inadmissible. See *G v UK* (2011) 53 EHRR SE25. See also *Barnfather v Islington LBC* [2003] EWHC 418 (Admin). On which see Tadros and Tierney (2004) 67 MLR 402, and J Horder, 'Whose Values Should Determine Whether Liability is Strict' in Simester, *Appraising Strict Liability*, 105 and see the valuable comment by B Fitzpatrick, 'Divisional Court—Strict Liability and Article 6(2) of the European Convention on Human Rights: School Non-Attendance Offence' (2004) 68 J Crim L 16.

52 [2005] 1 AC 264, [21] (emphasis added).

to states to define the constituent elements of a criminal offence, excluding the requirement of mens rea. But the substance and effect of any presumption adverse to a defendant must be examined, and must be reasonable. Relevant to any judgment on reasonableness or proportionality will be the opportunity given to the defendant to rebut the presumption, maintenance of the rights of the defence, flexibility in application of the presumption, retention by the court of a power to assess the evidence, the importance of what is at stake and the difficulty which a prosecutor may face in the absence of a presumption.[53]

Examples of the domestic courts' approach include the rejection of the argument that strict liability offences restricting press publication of trial proceedings are incompatible with Arts 6 and 10,[54] that strict liability offences are incompatible with Art 7 on the basis of their ambiguity[55] and that the imposition of strict liability in sexual offences with children is incompatible with Art 6.

In *G*,[56] G, who was aged 15, pleaded guilty to rape of a child under 13 (Sexual Offences Act 2003, s 5). G's basis of plea was that V consented and that he reasonably believed her to be older than 13, because she had told him so. The House of Lords confirmed that s 5 creates an offence of strict liability to which belief in consent or the age of the victim has no application. The actus reus of the offence is penile penetration of the vagina, anus or mouth of a victim under 13, whether the victim consented or not and irrespective of how old the defendant thought she was. Section 5 criminalizes this conduct even where the defendant reasonably believed that the child he was penetrating was 16 or older. The House of Lords reached that conclusion having regard to a number of factors including, in particular, the fact that in other sections of the 2003 Act[57] it is expressly stated that the offence is not committed if D believes that V is at least 16; but in s 5 there is no reference to D having a reasonable belief as to age. In relation to the offences dealing with children under 13, liability as to age is strict. This may seem harsh, particularly where D is of similar age and had every reason to believe that V was over 13 (including because she told him so), but the court construed Parliament's intention to impose strict liability in order to protect such young children, and D would have been convicted of an offence on his admitted belief in any event.

5.2 The presumption of mens rea

Since, as noted, strict liability offences are almost always found in statutes, the courts, in enforcing them, profess merely to be implementing the intention of Parliament, express or implied, as they find it in the statute.

It is only rarely that the statute makes explicit that the offence is one of strict liability. An example is s 53A of the Sexual Offences Act 2003,[58] criminalizing use of exploited sex workers. It is made clear that it is 'irrelevant ... whether [D] is, or ought to be, aware that [a third party linked to V] has engaged in exploitative conduct'.[59] It is unfortunate that Parliament

---

[53] See also the comments of leading commentators such as Emmerson, Ashworth and Macdonald, HR&CJ, para 9.74, concluding that even the landmark decisions in *DPP v B* and *K* (discussed later) have no bearing on the relationship between the presumption of innocence and the imposition of strict liability.

[54] *O'Riordan v DPP* [2005] EWHC 1240 (Admin).

[55] *Muhamed* [2002] EWCA Crim 1856, and *Kearns* [2002] EWCA Crim 748.

[56] [2008] UKHL 37, see Lord Hope at [28]–[29].

[57] cf the approach in *Ireland* in a very similar case: *CC v Ireland* [2006] IESC 33.

[58] Inserted by s 14 of the Policing and Crime Act 2009.

[59] The drafting of the offence is very poor in other respects.

does not as a matter of routine make clear that offences are strict liability. The truth is, as Devlin J wrote in 1958:

The fact is that Parliament has no intention whatever of troubling itself about *mens rea*. If it had, the thing would have been settled long ago. All that Parliament would have to do would be to use express words that left no room for implication. One is driven to the conclusion that the reason why Parliament has never done that is that it prefers to leave the point to the judges and does not want to legislate about it.[60]

Where Parliament has not made explicit whether the offence is one of strict liability, that question will be for the courts to determine as a matter of interpreting the statute. If there is an existing precedent on the same offence deciding whether the offence is strict liability, the court should follow that.[61]

In all other cases the courts retain a fairly free-hand in this matter effectively exercising a legislative function. In recent years, the courts have engaged in a more rigorous analysis of the question whether to interpret an offence as one of strict liability. As Lady Arden explained recently in the Privy Council:

The correct approach to the interpretation of legislation of any kind when an issue arises as to the mental element for an offence is very well established. The courts presume that Parliament intended that the prosecution should have to show that the defendant knew the ingredients of the offence, and that presumption is not displaced with respect to any such ingredient unless there is clear wording to that effect or it is necessarily implicit in the language of the statute that it is displaced.[62]

There are two issues to be addressed.[63]

(a) Whether the court should assume that an offence is to be interpreted as one of mens rea.

(b) What factors will influence the court in deciding whether to impose strict liability?

5.3 A strong presumption of mens rea

It is clear that under the current law the highest courts now repeatedly acknowledge that there is a strong presumption against strict liability and that the threshold for interpreting an offence in that way is a high one.[64]

Historically, judges were willing to state that there is a presumption in favour of mens rea, but did not regard the threshold as particularly high. They commonly recited the well-known statement by Wright J in *Sherras v De Rutzen*:[65]

There is a presumption that *mens rea*, or evil intention, or knowledge of the wrongfulness of the act, is an essential ingredient in every offence; but that presumption is liable to be displaced either by the words of the statute creating the offence or by the subject-matter with which it deals, and both must be considered.

---

[60] *Samples of Lawmaking* (1962) 71. Cf GC Thornton, *Legislative Drafting* (2006) 264. Lord Reid in *Sweet v Parsley* [1969] 1 All ER 347 at 351.

[61] See the discussion later as to whether even if there is a binding precedent, if it predates *B* [2000] 2 AC 428 the courts should now reconsider the matter of interpretation from first principles as declared in *B*.

[62] *Nurse v Republic of Trinidad and Tobago* [2019] UKPC 43, [2].

[63] In *Pwr* [2020] EWHC 798 (Admin), the court noted that there has been a divergence in the cases as to the order in which these two questions should be addressed. The case is on appeal to the Supreme Court.

[64] *B* [2000] 2 AC 428; *K* [2002] 1 AC 46.   [65] [1895] 1 QB 918 at 921.

Adopting that approach, the judges readily found the presumption rebutted.[66] The courts' interpretative approach to strict liability is said[67] to have reached its nadir when even bigamy was held to be a crime of strict liability in *Wheat*,[68] now happily overruled. The trend in the years before *Warner v Metropolitan Police Comr*[69] (the first case on the point to reach the House of Lords) seems to have been in favour of strict liability; but Lord Reid in that case (where he dissented) and in *Sweet v Parsley*[70] powerfully reaffirmed the presumption: 'whenever a section is silent as to mens rea there is a presumption that, in order to give effect to the will of Parliament, we must read in words appropriate to require *mens rea*'; and 'it is a universal principle that if a penal provision is reasonably capable of two interpretations, that interpretation which is most favourable to the accused must be adopted'.[71] In 1980, in *Sheppard*,[72] Lord Diplock noted that, 'The climate of both parliamentary and judicial opinion has been growing less favourable to the recognition of absolute [*sic*] offences over the last few decades . . .'[73]

The current law on this point is founded on the decisions of the House of Lords in *B (A Minor) v DPP*[74] and *K*[75] which signalled an emphatic reassertion of the presumption that all serious offences ought to be offences of mens rea.

The House of Lords in those cases declared that there is a constitutional presumption of mens rea in offences. In interpreting a statute, the courts will ask whether that presumption[76] is rebutted, with the consequence that the offence is one of strict liability: 'the test is not whether it is a reasonable implication that the statute rules out *mens rea* as a constituent part of the crime—the test is whether it is a *necessary* implication': *B*.[77] In *K*, the House followed this emphatically.[78] Section 14 of the Sexual Offences Act 1956 (indecent assault—now repealed)[79] provided that neither a girl under 16 (s 14(2)) nor a 'defective' (as the Act labelled someone with a learning disability or mental disorder) (s 14(4)) could give consent

---

[66] In *Brown* [2013] UKSC 43, Lord Kerr, at [29], cited the 13th edn of this work and noted how the authors 'deprecated the tendency of some judges to declaim that the presumption was well-embedded only to willingly find that it was easily rebutted'. It is arguable that the judgment in that case exhibits the same flaw.

[67] Williams, CLGP, 178.

[68] [1921] 2 KB 119, overruled by *Gould* [1968] 2 QB 65.

[69] [1969] 2 AC 256. The case is more fully considered at p 166.

[70] [1970] AC 132, p 162 but the House again imposed strict liability in *Alphacell Ltd v Woodward* [1972] AC 824 p 169.

[71] At 349–50 per Lord Reid. See more recently *Nurse v Republic of Trinidad and Tobago* [2020] UKPC 43.

[72] [1981] AC 394.   [73] At 407.   [74] [2000] 2 AC 428, [2000] Crim LR 403 and commentary.

[75] [2002] 1 AC 462, [2001] Crim LR 993 and commentary.

[76] In the Divisional Court in *Highbury Poultry Farm Produce Ltd v CPS* [2018] EWHC 3122 (Admin), at [75], doubt is cast on whether the word presumption is appropriate in this context. 'In my view, strict liability should not be conceptualised in these terms. The correct analysis is that strict liability only arises if the general or ordinary presumption is displaced, and the noun "presumption" in the context of strict liability is something of a misnomer. Further, as Lord Reid has explained the threshold for rebutting the presumption of mens rea is a high one and regard must be had to all the relevant circumstances in divining the intention of Parliament. This mandates consideration being given to the purposes, policies and objects of the legislation in point, whether the offences in question are truly or only quasi-criminal (see further below), and an analysis of the statutory language directly and indirectly in play' (per Jay J). The Supreme Court agreed with the Crown that the true issue was the proper interpretation of the EU Regulation, not the provision of domestic law: [2020] UKSC 39.

[77] [2000] 2 AC 428, [2000] 1 All ER at 855d–e per Lord Hutton.

[78] For strong criticism, see J Horder, 'How Culpability Can, and Cannot, Be Denied in Under-Age Sex Crimes' [2001] Crim LR 15, commenting that the decision in *B v DPP* 'flies in the face of legislation and case law across much of the rest of the common law world'; PR Glazebrook, 'How Old Did You Think She Was?' (2001) 60 CLJ 26. For criticism of the decision for failing to take a more radical look at the use of due diligence defences, see LCCP 195, para 6.15.

[79] See Ch 17, p 829.

which would prevent an act being an assault for the purposes of the section. It was, however, a defence for the person who had acted indecently towards a consenting 'defective' to prove that he did not know and had no reason to suspect her to be a 'defective'. It necessarily followed that a person who failed to prove this was guilty, although he honestly believed the woman was not a defective; that is, subject to the statutory defence, the section imposed strict liability on that person. Section 14(3) provided that where D had gone through a ceremony of marriage with V which was invalid because she was under 16, it was a defence for him to prove that he believed, and had reasonable cause to believe, her to be his wife. Again, it necessarily followed that a person who was unable to prove that fact was guilty, although he honestly believed the girl to be his wife. Subject to the statutory defence, the section therefore imposed strict liability. But, in contrast, there was no comparable statutory defence for the person who 'assaulted' the consenting girl under 16. Previous decisions over many years had held that, in this scenario, the section imposed unmitigated strict liability.

In *K*, the House overruled those cases and decided that it was for the prosecution to prove that D did not honestly believe that V was 16 or over. The section creating the offence did not, expressly or by necessary implication, exclude full mens rea with respect to age; mens rea as to age was therefore required to be proved in every case. The decision was a controversial one. While Lord Bingham thought this result was not absurd, Lord Millett thought that, 'To afford a defendant who has not married the girl a more generous defence than one who believes he has is grotesque.'[80] Nevertheless, to do justice in the case before him, he concurred in the decision. He, at least, seemed ready to abandon all pretence that he was implementing the intention of Parliament. Parliament had failed to discharge its responsibility. Although the Sexual Offences Act 2003 has reversed the effect of the decision by creating offences in which liability as to age is strict,[81] the decisions in *B* and *K* afford a pre-eminence to the presumption of mens rea which, if applied generally, should result in a substantial diminution of strict liability in English law.

It is important to note that the principle of these decisions is not confined to offences of this type. The judges thought that: 'In principle, an age-related ingredient of a statutory offence stands on no different footing from any other ingredient.'[82] The strength of the presumption of mens rea and of a requirement of mens rea in the subjective sense was endorsed in the strongest terms in the case of *G*[83] on recklessness.[84]

Arguably, all offences of strict liability are vulnerable to challenge by the revitalized presumption declared by the House.[85] In *Cambridgeshire CC v Assoc Lead Mills Ltd*,[86] Walker J, having regard to the discussion in this book of the 'revitalised presumption', questioned whether even an offence based on 'use', on which there is plenty of binding authority, is to be construed as one of strict liability. In other cases, the courts have read *B* and *K* restrictively to mean that where

[80] [2002] 1 AC 462 [43].

[81] *G* [2008] UKHL 37. D's application to the ECtHR on the basis that his conviction violated Arts 6 and 8 was found inadmissible. See *G v UK* (2011) 53 EHRR SE25.

[82] Lord Nicholls in *B* [2000] 2 AC 428. Lord Hobhouse in *K* [2002] 1 AC 462.

[83] [2003] UKHL 50, [2004] 1 AC 1034.

[84] At [32]. Lord Steyn observed that the 'general tendency in modern times is towards adopting a subjective approach' (at [55]).

[85] A key contender could be the strictness as to age in offences of possession of indecent images of children, following *Land* [1999] QB 65, cf the commentary on *Smith and Jayson* [2002] EWCA Crim 683, [2002] Crim LR 659. Other likely challenges have been rejected, eg to the offences of possession of a weapon: see *Deyemi* [2007] EWCA Crim 2060—liability for possession even where D was unaware it (stun gun) was a firearm, believing it to be a torch. For critique of the prevalence of strict liability in the context of firearms offences, see A Ashworth [2013] Crim LR 447.

[86] [2005] EWHC 1627 (Admin).

there is an existing interpretation of an offence which holds it to be one of strict liability and that is a binding precedent, *B* and *K* are not sufficient in themselves to cause a reassessment.[87]

Some of their lordships in *K*[88] refused, *obiter*, to apply the presumption to what was the offence of sexual intercourse with a girl under 13. That was an offence punishable with a maximum of life imprisonment and there was nothing in the words of that section itself which could possibly import mens rea. In *Kumar*,[89] the Court of Appeal applied *B* and *K* to hold that the offence of buggery (under the 1956 Act, now repealed by the Sexual Offences Act 2003) did *not* impose strict liability as to the age of the participants. A degree of caution must, however, be exercised as the impact of *B* and *K* is felt in the lower courts. It would be misleading to think that since *B* and *K* the courts have consistently rejected strict liability; far from it. There are numerous instances of provisions being interpreted as imposing strict liability as, for example, in *Muhamed*[90] (materially contributing to insolvency by gambling carrying two years' imprisonment); *Matudi*[91] (importing prohibited animal products); *Hart v Anglian Water Services Ltd*[92] (causing sewage effluent to be discharged); *Jackson*[93] (low-flying aircraft); *K*[94] (possession of a ball-bearing gun constituting an imitation firearm); *Deyemi*[95] (possession of an electronic stun gun constitutes possession of firearm where D unaware it was a weapon); *Zahid*[96] (possession of ammunition for a firearm); *Thames Water Utilities*[97] (depositing controlled waste on land without a waste management licence); *Ezeemo and others*[98] (EU waste trans-frontier shipment regulations prohibiting export of hazardous waste to a non-OECD country for recovery requiring no proof of knowledge that the product transported was waste nor intention to transport waste to such a country); *Johnson*[99] (conveying prohibited articles into prison); *Highbury Farms*[100] (EU requirement to ensure chickens' throats cut before being immersed in boiling water in food processing); *Pwr*[101] (Terrorism Act 2000, s 13).

The Supreme Court had the opportunity to examine what impact, if any, the revitalized presumption of mens rea had on the offence of 'having unlawful carnal knowledge of a girl under the age of 14', contrary to s 4 of the Criminal Law (Amendment) Acts (Northern Ireland) 1885–1923. Lord Kerr, delivering the judgment of the court in *Brown*,[102] observed that:

The constitutional principle that *mens rea* is presumed to be required in order to establish criminal liability is a strong one. It is not to be displaced in the absence of clear statutory language or unmistakably necessary implication. And true it is, as the appellant has argued, that the legislative history of an enactment may not always provide the framework for deciding whether the clearly identifiable conditions in which an implication must be made are present. It is also undeniable that where the statutory offence is grave or 'truly criminal' and carries a heavy penalty or a substantial social stigma, the case is enhanced against implying that *mens rea* of any ingredient of the offence is not needed.

---

[87] See *Deyemi* [2007] EWCA Crim 2060, [25]. See also the comments of Lord Phillips, President of the Supreme Court, in *R (Child Poverty Action Group) v Secretary of State for Work and Pensions* [2011] 2 WLR 1 describing the House in *B* as 'doing no more than applying a well-established common law presumption or requirement' (at [30]).

[88] [2000] 1 All ER 833 at 843g–h per Lord Steyn and 854h–j per Lord Hutton, [2001] UKHL 41 at [33] per Lord Bingham.

[89] [2004] EWCA Crim 3207.   [90] [2002] EWCA Crim 1856.   [91] [2003] EWCA Crim 697.

[92] [2003] EWCA Crim 2243.

[93] [2006] EWCA Crim 2380. The Court of Appeal's decision provides a very clear example of the discussion of the relevant factors to consider.

[94] [2006] EWHC 2183 (Admin).

[95] [2007] EWCA Crim 2060. See also *Rehman and Wood* [2006] 1 Cr App R (S) 404.

[96] [2010] EWCA Crim 2158. See also *Tinarwo* [2014] EWCA Crim 1409.

[97] [2013] EWHC 472 (Admin). See also *Southern Water Services Ltd* [2014] EWCA Crim 120. For discussion of offences relating to the environment, see J Adshead, 'Doing Justice to the Environment' (2013) 77 J Crim L 215.

[98] [2012] EWCA Crim 2064.   [99] [2017] EWCA Crim 189.

[100] *Highbury Poultry Farm Produce Ltd v CPS* [2020] UKSC 39.

[101] [2020] EWHC 798 (Admin). The Divisional Court's judgment is being appealed to the Supreme Court.

[102] [2013] UKSC 43.

Although Lord Kerr's recognition of the robust nature of the constitutional presumption in favour of mens rea is welcome, his lordship ultimately concluded that there could be no doubt that s 4 was intended to impose strict liability as to the age of V and that none of the subsequent amendments made to it suggested a parliamentary intention for it to be interpreted any differently. Citing *G*, it was held that there were policy considerations that militated against reading s 4 as being subject to a defence that D had a reasonable belief that V was over the prescribed age. In *Lane and Letts*[103] the Supreme Court held that, despite its constitutional significance, the presumption of mens rea is no more than a principle of statutory construction. As such, it must yield to unambiguous statutory language. Lord Hughes explained:[104]

But it is not a power in the court to substitute for the plain words used by Parliament a different provision, on the grounds that it would, if itself drafting the definition of the offence, have done so differently by providing for an element, or a greater element, of mens rea. The principle of Parliamentary sovereignty demands no less.

His lordship rejected the submission that the court should begin with the presumption of mens rea and then consider whether it was displaced by the statutory language. The court's 'first port of call' must be the words of the offence creating provision. In the more recent case of *Attorney General's Reference (No 1 of 2020)*, the Court of Appeal, citing *Lane and Letts*, stated:[105]

There is a presumption that mens rea is an essential ingredient of every offence unless some reason can be found for holding that that is not necessary. This is of great importance in relation to the approach to the construction of criminal statutes, but it remains a principle of construction. Mens rea should not be inadvertently, silently or ambiguously removed from the ingredients of a statutory offence, but it is not a power in the court to substitute for the plain words of Parliament a different provision, on the grounds that it would, if itself drafting the offence, have done so. The first duty of the court is therefore to consider the words of the statute. Finally, the presumption is a principle of construction which must give way to either the plain meaning of the words of the statute, or to other relevant pointers to meaning which clearly demonstrate what Parliament intended.

5.3.1 What mens rea is to be presumed?

Although the highest court has stated that there is a presumption of mens rea in statutory offences, the courts do not usually tell us what they mean by mens rea—what type: recklessness? Negligence? A commonly cited statement is that of Cave J in *Tolson*:[106]

At common law an honest . . .[107] belief in the existence of circumstances, which, if true, would make the act for which a prisoner is indicted an innocent act has always been held to be a good defence.

This is ambiguous. Does 'an innocent act' mean:

(1) not the crime charged; or

(2) neither the crime charged nor some lesser offence; or

(3) not a civil wrong; or

(4) not a moral wrong?

The Draft Criminal Code, cl 20, 'General requirement of fault', would provide a clear rule based on (1):

Every offence requires a fault element of recklessness with respect to each of its elements other than fault elements, unless otherwise provided.

---

[103] [2018] UKSC 36.   [104] At [9].   [105] [2020] EWCA Crim 1665, at [42].
[106] (1889) 23 QBD 168 at 181.
[107] The words 'and reasonable' are omitted as being no longer applicable in the light of *B v DPP*.

If that were enacted, we would know exactly where we stood with respect to offences to which the Code applied. In the meantime there remains a degree of uncertainty.

5.4 Recognizing offences of strict liability

As noted, in some rare instances Parliament makes it explicit that it is imposing an offence of strict liability. Surely there is an argument for imposing an obligation on Parliament always to use one of a specified list of mens rea words when drafting offence-creating legislation and to make explicit if an offence is to be one of strict liability? The level of scrutiny of criminal legislation in Parliament is so appalling that such matters do not always seem to be understood. An obligation of this nature on Parliamentary Counsel would at least assist those in Parliament and clarify matters for the courts.[108]

As noted above, in all cases where Parliament has not made the matter of mens rea explicit, the courts are obliged to interpret the will of Parliament relating to the elements of mens rea.[109] The court must start from the presumption of mens rea as just discussed. Thereafter, by reference to a number of interpretative techniques, the court must decide whether Parliament displaced that presumption by necessary implication.[110] The courts have not adopted a clear and consistent approach. Indeed, Glazebrook has suggested that there is an 'all too familiar litany of vague overlapping criteria which from time out of mind has signally failed to compel from judges predictable consensus'.[111]

An oft-quoted summary of the approach is taken from the opinion of Lord Scarman in *Gammon (Hong Kong) Ltd v A-G Hong Kong*:[112]

(1) There is a presumption of law that *mens rea* is required before a person can be held guilty of a criminal offence. (2) The presumption is particularly strong where the offence is 'truly criminal' in character. (3) The presumption applies to statutory offences, and can be displaced only if this is clearly or by necessary implication the effect of the statute. (4) The only situation in which the presumption can be displaced is where the statute is concerned with an issue of social concern . . . (5) Even where a statute is concerned with such an issue, the presumption of *mens rea* stands unless it can also be shown that the creation of strict liability will be effective to promote the objects of the statute by encouraging greater vigilance to prevent the commission of the prohibited act.

5.4.1 The offence in its statutory context

One of the principal methods of determining if the presumption of mens rea is displaced in an offence is by reference to the statutory terminology. The decisions in *B* and *K* in the House of Lords illustrate the supreme importance attached to the words of the statute. The presumption, we are told, 'can only be displaced by specific language, that is an express provision or a necessary implication'.[113] If that is taken literally, many, if not most, cases of strict liability were wrongly decided; but subsequent case law has demonstrated that that is not the effect of *B* and *K*. In some instances the courts have taken greater notice of *B* and *K*. In *M*,[114] in which the court upheld the judge's ruling that the offence of bringing a prohibited article into a prison[115] was not an offence of strict liability, Rix LJ said:

The default position is that, despite the absence of any express language, there is a presumption, founded in constitutional principle, that *mens rea* is an essential ingredient of the offence. Only a compelling

---

[108] See Reid (2008) 29 St LR 173.   [109] See generally LCCP 195, Part 6.
[110] This was emphasized by the Supreme Court in *Brown* [2013] UKSC 43.
[111] 'How Old Did You Think She Was?' (2001) 60 CLJ 26.   [112] [1985] AC 1.
[113] *K* [2001] UKHL 41 at [32] per Lord Steyn.   [114] [2009] EWCA Crim 2615.
[115] Contrary to the Prison Act 1952, s 40C(1). See now Serious Crime Act 2015, s 79. See also *Johnson* [2017] EWCA Crim 189.

case for implying the exclusion of such an ingredient as a matter of necessity will suffice. Therefore the absence of express language, even in the presence of express language elsewhere in the statute, is not enough to rebut the presumption unless the circumstances as a whole compel such a conclusion.

5.4.1.1 Verbs importing a mental element

We have already noticed that a particular verb may imply a mental element.[116] The obvious examples are to intend, to be malicious or reckless, to know, to suspect, to have reasonable grounds to suspect, etc.[117] With other verbs the courts take a less clear position. The use of one verb in the definition of an offence may import a requirement of fault when the use of a different verb with no such implication would result in an offence of strict liability.

A good example is *M*[118] in which the court upheld the judge's ruling that the offence of bringing, throwing or conveying a prohibited article into a prison[119] was not an offence of strict liability. Rix LJ had regard to the statutory language:

It is hard to think that the verb 'throws' does not involve an intentional act of some kind. It is difficult to conceive (but I do not say impossible) of a person throwing some [proscribed] article into or out of prison without knowing what he is doing. The verb 'brings' is perhaps more neutral, but it takes its colour from the verb 'throws'. The expression 'otherwise conveys', being of a catch-all nature, must plainly take its colour from what has gone before. These are therefore unpromising words with which to begin to find an offence of [strict] liability.[120]

A further illustration is provided by the offence for a person to 'use or cause or permit to be used' a motor vehicle in contravention of certain regulations. 'Using', 'causing' and 'permitting' are three separate offences. In *James & Son Ltd v Smee*,[121] the court held that *using* a vehicle in contravention of a regulation (in that it had a defective braking system) was an offence of strict liability; but D was charged with *permitting* the use which, said the court, 'in our opinion, at once imports a state of mind'; that is, mens rea. A person might 'use' a vehicle with defective brakes although he had no idea that the brakes were defective; but he would not properly be said to 'permit' use with defective brakes unless he knew that the brakes were defective or, at least, was turning a blind eye to that fact. Knowledge is not necessarily the only mental element required. Does a person who knows that his premises are being used for producing or supplying drugs 'permit' if he does nothing about it? Is mere acquiescence enough?[122]

Unfortunately, the courts are inconsistent in their interpretation of this and similar words in other statutes. An example is the offence of 'permitting' a vehicle to be used without insurance. Take the common case where D lends his car to X on condition that it is only driven by an insured driver. If it is in fact driven by a person who is uninsured, the courts have held that D commits the offence. The court ignores the ordinary meaning of the word 'permit'. D who says: 'Here is my car, but you must not drive it until you have insurance' is taken in law 'to permit' what he actually forbids: driving without insurance.[123]

---

116 See Ch 3.

117 In *Riley v DPP* [2016] EWHC 2531 (Admin) it was held that the offence in s 4(2) of the Animal Welfare Act 2006 is not a strict liability offence. The Divisional Court reached this conclusion on the basis that one element of the offence is that D failed to take such steps as were reasonable in all the circumstances to prevent an animal suffering unnecessarily. Gross LJ stated that it is the circumstances which determine what steps were reasonable and knowledge of the circumstances is an essential ingredient of the charge.

118 [2009] EWCA Crim 2615.

119 Contrary to the Prison Act 1952, s 40C(1), as inserted by the Offender Management Act 2007.

120 At [25].   121 [1955] 1 QB 78. Cf *Lomas v Peek* [1947] 2 All ER 574.

122 *Bradbury* [1996] Crim LR 808. Perhaps this is a case where the alternative verb, 'suffer', more appropriately describes the conduct. There are lots of other examples in drugs offences.

123 *DPP v Fisher* [1991] Crim LR 787, distinguishing *Newbury v Davis* [1974] RTR 367.

In what appears to be the first case to reach the House of Lords on this, *Vehicle Inspectorate v Nuttall*,[124] it was said that the meaning depends on the context but it remains difficult to discern how and when the context operates. In *Nuttall*, two judges held that D had a duty to take reasonable steps to detect and prevent breaches and that, if he failed to do so, he 'permitted'. Two judges thought that a mental element of recklessness, in the sense of not caring whether a breach took place, was required. What is reasonable is an objective question and D's opinion is irrelevant.[125] Similar inconsistency is to be found in the interpretation of the verbs, 'suffer', 'allow' and 'cause'.[126]

It seems that the courts will generally give verbs their natural meaning, including any mental element they imply, unless they consider that social policy requires them to decide otherwise. In relation to the offences of uninsured driving, the courts take a strict approach, presumably because of the danger to the public. In that context, the courts refuse to give effect to what they recognize in other social contexts to be the natural meaning of the words used by Parliament.[127]

5.4.1.2 The use of adverbs

'Knowingly'

The use of an adverb in a statute is a more explicit way in which Parliament can make clear that mens rea is required. The clearest example is the word 'knowingly'.[128] Devlin J said that 'knowingly' only says expressly what is normally implied[129]—it does expressly what the presumption in favour of mens rea would do by implication. The use of the word suggests that Parliament wanted to make sure that the courts would not displace the presumption and hold the offence to be one of strict liability. Similarly, where Parliament provides that it is an offence to 'knowingly permit' something to be done, Parliament intends the presumption of mens rea to apply—perhaps the word 'permit' would have been sufficient to import mens rea, but Parliamentary Counsel uses the word knowingly for the avoidance of doubt. When 'knowingly' is used, it should be difficult for any court to hold that mens rea is not required as to *all* the elements of the offence, though it might not extend to an exception clause in the definition of the crime.[130]

As a matter of evidence, the substantive law requirement that D acted 'knowingly' may be proved by what is sometimes called 'wilful blindness':[131] 'it is always open to the tribunal of fact, when knowledge on the part of a defendant is required to be proved, to base a finding of knowledge on evidence that the defendant had deliberately shut his eyes to the obvious or refrained from enquiry because he suspected the truth but did not want to have his suspicion confirmed'.[132] Sometimes, however, the courts take a stricter view, as in handling stolen goods, on which see Ch 26. In *Kwan Ping Bang*,[133] it was accepted that proof of knowledge by inference is possible provided the inference was compelling—'one (and the only one) that no reasonable man could fail to draw from the direct facts proved'.

---

[124] [1999] 1 WLR 629 HL (employer (D) permitting driver to contravene rules regarding rest periods). Cf *Yorkshire Traction Co v Vehicle Inspectorate* [2001] RTR 518.

[125] *Brock and Wyner* [2001] 2 Cr App R (S) 48 (permitting premises to be used for supplying drugs).

[126] A modern example is the approach in *Tilley* [2009] EWCA Crim 1426 interpreting the offence of dishonestly 'allowing' a person to fail to give prompt notification of a change in her social benefit circumstances under s 111A(1B) of the Social Security Administration Act 1992.

[127] But is uninsured driving a greater social evil than driving with defective brakes?

[128] See C Manchester, 'Knowledge Due Diligence and Strict Liability in Regulatory Offences' [2006] Crim LR 213.

[129] *Roper v Taylor's Central Garage (Exeter) Ltd* [1951] 2 TLR 284 at 288. See also S Shute, 'Knowledge and Belief in the Criminal Law' in Shute and Simester, *Criminal Law Theory*.

[130] cf *Brooks v Mason* [1902] 2 KB 743, and *Wings Ltd v Ellis*, p 56.

[131] This is discussed in Ch 3.

[132] *Westminster City Council v Croyalgrange Ltd* [1986] 2 All ER 353 at 359 HL; *Manifest Shipping Co Ltd v Uni-Polaris Shipping Co Ltd* [2001] 1 All ER 743.

[133] [1979] AC 609, 615.

'Wilfully'

The word 'wilfully' looks like a 'mens rea word' and it is sometimes treated as such. It was considered in Ch 3. D does not 'wilfully' obstruct a police officer simply because he does a deliberate act which in fact obstructs the officer; an intention to obstruct must be proved.[134] There are, however, cases in which the courts have imposed strict liability notwithstanding the use of this word. 'Wilful' in these cases is held to apply only to the conduct element of the offence but not to some circumstance or consequence which is an element of the crime. In these cases, liability as to the consequences or circumstances elements of the offence has been held to be strict. So, for example, D was held guilty of wilfully fishing in private water, although he believed there was a public right to fish there;[135] of wilfully killing a house pigeon when he shot a bird, believing it was a wild pigeon;[136] and of wilfully destroying an oak tree in contravention of a tree preservation order when he was unaware of the order and believed that permission had been given for the tree to be felled.[137] In these cases, the *conduct* of fishing, killing a bird and cutting down a tree were all 'wilful'; but in none of them was the commission of the crime 'wilful'.

Following the most important authority, *Sheppard*,[138] discussed in Ch 3, it is arguable that 'wilfully' should be construed to mean wilfully committing *the crime*; but in practice it may be that the courts are still willing to interpret elements of an offence as imposing strict liability despite that word appearing in the statute.

5.4.1.3 Effect of mens rea words appearing in some sections but not others

Where a mens rea word is used in one section of a statute but not in another that may suggest that the second creates an offence of strict liability; but Lord Reid has said:

It is also firmly established that the fact that other sections of the Act expressly require *mens rea*, for example because they contain the word 'knowingly', is not itself sufficient to justify a decision that a section which is silent as to *mens rea* creates an absolute offence.[139]

In the famous example of *Sherras v De Rutzen*,[140] D was charged with supplying liquor to a constable on duty.[141] The policeman was not wearing the armband which would signal that he was a police officer, and it was admitted that the failure to wear it was an indication that he was off duty. D, who was in the habit—quite lawfully—of serving constables in uniform but without their armlets, made no inquiry and took it for granted that this policeman was off duty. The Act provided an offence (in s 16(1)) for a licensee *knowingly* to harbour or suffer to remain on his premises any constable on duty. In contrast, the offence with which D was charged (s 16(2)) did not include the word 'knowingly', but D's conviction was quashed. Day J said that the only inference to be drawn was that under s 16(1) the prosecution had to prove knowledge, while under s 16(2) the defendant had to prove he had no knowledge.[142]

---

134 *Willmott v Atack* [1977] QB 498.
135 *Hudson v MacRae* (1863) 4 B & S 585.   136 *Cotterill v Penn* [1936] 1 KB 53.
137 *Maidstone Borough Council v Mortimer* [1980] 3 All ER 552.
138 [1981] AC 394. Cf *Turner* [2008] EWCA Crim 272.
139 *Sweet v Parsley* [1970] AC 132 at 149.   140 [1895] 1 QB 918.
141 Contrary to the Licensing Act 1872, s 16(2).
142 This view was doubted by Devlin J in *Roper v Taylor's Central Garage (Exeter) Ltd* [1951] 2 TLR 284. If Day J intended to refer to the *evidential* burden only, the *dictum* is unobjectionable. See Edwards, *Mens Rea*, 90–7.

Wright J made no attempt to reconcile the two subsections, contenting himself with pointing out that:[143]

if guilty knowledge is not necessary, no care on the part of the publican could save him from conviction . . . since it would be as easy for the constable to deny that he was on duty when asked, or to produce a forged permission from his superior officer as to remove his armlet before entering the public house.[144]

This factor was influential in many cases including the modern-day cases of *G* in the House of Lords (dealing with sexual offences against under 13s where the statute is explicit about mens rea as to under 16s and silent as to under 13s); *Muhamad*[145] (Insolvency Act offences); and *Matudi*[146] (importation of endangered species).

5.4.2 The offence in its social context

In addition to the statutory context of the offence, the court must have regard to the broader social context of the legislation and the purpose it was designed to serve, and this has historically been highly influential. Cases where strict liability was imposed primarily on social grounds may be even more vulnerable to attack after *B* and *K*. If mens rea is not ruled out expressly or by necessary implication from the text, it cannot, according to *dicta* in *K*, be excluded. As noted, this has not prevented the Court of Appeal subsequently imposing strict liability in cases such as *Muhamed*,[147] *Matudi*,[148] *Ezeemo and others*[149] and *Highbury Poultry*.[150]

5.4.2.1 'Real' or 'quasi' crime?

An important matter is whether the court considers the offence to be a 'true' or 'real' crime or a 'quasi-crime'.[151] Parliament makes no such distinction. A form of behaviour either is, or it is not, declared by Parliament to be a crime.[152] Unlike many European jurisdictions, England does not create a separate category of administrative offences called 'violations' in which strict liability is imposed.[153] The Law Commission rejected the idea of adopting such a system.

Determining what is meant by 'real' crime is not easy. Mitchell J said that he did not regard the offence of selling a lottery ticket to a child under 16 as 'truly criminal in character' although it was punishable on indictment with two years' imprisonment.[154] This is a peculiar understanding of the word 'truth'. The truth is that it is a crime. It is the courts that take it upon themselves to decide whether it is a 'real' or 'quasi' crime. They do so on the basis that an offence which, in the public eye, carries little or no stigma and does not involve 'the disgrace of criminality',[155] is only a quasi-crime. Then, strict liability may be imposed because 'it does not offend the ordinary man's sense of justice that moral guilt is not of the essence of the offence'.[156]

---

[143] [1895] 1 QB 918 at 923.

[144] An example of this criterion as a determinant of strict liability is the case of *Matudi* [2003] EWCA Crim 697 dealing with the importation of endangered species.

[145] [2002] EWCA Crim 1856.   [146] [2003] EWCA Crim 697.

[147] [2002] EWCA Crim 1856.   [148] [2003] EWCA Crim 697.   [149] [2012] EWCA Crim 2064.

[150] [2018] EWHC 3122 (Admin).

[151] See J Horder (2002) 118 LQR 458, noting that regulatory offences are also stigmatizing for the accused. See also G Lamond, 'What is a Crime' (2007) 27 OJLS 609.

[152] See Ch 1.

[153] See the interesting discussion by Reid (2008) 29 St LR 173, and JR Spencer and A Pedain, 'Approaches to Strict and Constructive Liability in Continental Criminal Law' in Simester, *Appraising Strict Liability*.

[154] *London Borough of Harrow v Shah* [2000] Crim LR 692. See further LCCP 195, Part 3.

[155] *Warner v Metropolitan Police Comr* [1969] 2 AC 256 at 272 per Lord Reid.

[156] ibid. Cf *Wings Ltd v Ellis*, p 56. See also *Matudi* [2003] EWCA Crim 697.

The attempt to distinguish an offence on the basis of whether it is a regulatory or real crime is not particularly helpful.[157] In academic terms, the question is often posed as being whether the offence is *malum in se* (intrinsically morally wrong, eg murder or rape) or merely *malum-pro-hibitum* (wrong being prescribed by law) but this too provokes as many disputes as it solves.[158]

Judicial utterances are no more helpful in giving the meaning of 'real' or quasi-crime. In *Sherras v De Rutzen*, Wright J distinguished 'a class of acts ... which are not criminal in any real sense, but are acts which in the public interest are prohibited under a penalty'.[159] More recently, in *Taylor*, Lord Sumption held that 'quasi-crimes' tend to have two characteristic features.[160] First, the requirements of such legislation are founded on collective convenience rather than moral imperatives. Secondly, his lordship held that although fault in the actual commission of the offence may be unnecessary, there are nevertheless positive steps that the prospect of criminal liability may cause people to take, with the aim of preventing the offence from occurring.

In determining whether the offence involves a 'stigma', it is necessary to consider the case where the offence is committed intentionally. If Parliament prohibits the causing of results because it deems them in some measure harmful, the intentional causing of the harm in question probably deserves some measure of moral condemnation. Stigma attaches to, or should attach to, the person who deliberately sells lottery tickets to children or even the motorist who *deliberately* leaves his car in a parking space for longer than is permitted by law—it is an anti-social act, likely to cause inconvenience to others. But few people, even 'right-thinking' people, would consider such an act so iniquitous, even when done intentionally, that the actor ought to be locked up or even shunned and avoided. Since offences of strict liability do not distinguish between degrees of fault and no fault at all, a conviction fixes the offender with whatever stigma might attach to the offence and that is the same stigma as would attach to an intentional offender convicted of that offence.[161] Despite the difficulty in distinguishing between 'real' and quasi-crimes, the judgment in *Taylor* demonstrates that the distinction remains influential amongst judges in determining whether the presumption of mens rea is displaced.[162]

5.4.2.2 A crime of general or special prohibition?

A second factor which may be of great significance when considering social context is whether the provision is of general application or relates only to those following a particular trade, profession or special activity (especially where D has voluntarily engaged in that activity). In the latter type of case, the court may be much more ready to hold such a 'regulatory offence' to impose strict liability.[163] Lord Diplock put it as follows:[164]

Where penal provisions are of general application to the conduct of ordinary citizens in the course of their everyday life, the presumption is that the standard of care required of them in informing themselves of facts which would make their conduct unlawful is that of the familiar common law duty of care. But where the subject-matter of a statute is the regulation of a particular activity involving potential danger to public health, safety or morals, in which citizens have a choice whether they participate or not, the court may feel driven to infer an intention of Parliament to impose, by penal sanctions, a higher duty of care on those who choose to participate and to place on them an obligation to take whatever measures may be necessary to prevent the prohibited act, without regard to those

---

[157] cf A Norrie, *Crime, Reason and History*, 116; A Simester, 'Is Strict Liability Always Wrong?' in Simester, *Appraising Strict Liability*, 37–41.

[158] See DN Husak, '*Malum Prohibitum* and Retributivism' in Duff and Green, *Defining Crimes* and SP Green, 'Why It's a Crime to Tear the Tag off a Mattress' (1997) 46 Emory LJ 1533.

[159] [1895] 1 QB 918 at 922.   [160] [2016] UKSC 5, [26].

[161] See JC Smith in *Barbara Wootton, Essays in Her Honour*, 141 and in commentary on *B* at [2000] Crim LR 408. And see *Harrow v Shah*, n 151.

[162] For further discussion, see K Laird, 'The Decline of Criminal Law Causation Without Limits' (2016) 132 LQR 566.

[163] See further A Brudner, 'Imprisonment and Strict Liability' (1990) 40 U Toronto LJ 738.

[164] In *Sweet v Parsley* [1970] AC 132 at 163.

considerations of cost or business practicability which play a part in the determination of what would be required of them in order to fulfil the ordinary common law duty of care.

So we find most instances of strict liability in statutes regulating the sale of food, and drugs, the management of industrial activities, the management of waste,[165] the conduct of licensed premises, the humane killing of animals for food consumption[166] and the like.[167] That said, the 'particular activity' may be one in which citizens generally engage, like driving a car, but this is something which people choose to do and, as it involves potential danger to others, it is not inconsistent with this statement of principle that some offences regulating the conduct of motorists should be strict.

Some commentators have argued that this factor, and in particular whether the activity involved is one for which a licence is required, is the most important in the courts' decision as to whether a statute should be interpreted as imposing strict liability.[168] Lord Clyde recognized this in *Lambert*:[169]

A strict responsibility may be acceptable in the case of statutory offences which are concerned to regulate the conduct of some particular activity in the public interest. The requirement to have a licence in order to carry on certain kinds of activity is an obvious example. The promotion of health and safety and the avoidance of pollution are among the purposes to be served by such controls. These kinds of cases may properly be seen as not truly criminal. Many may be relatively trivial and only involve a monetary penalty. Many may carry with them no real social disgrace or infamy.

5.4.2.3 Possibility of compliance

According to Devlin J, it is:

a safe general principle to follow . . . that where the punishment of an individual will not promote the observance of the law either by that individual or by others whose conduct he may reasonably be expected to influence, then, in the absence of clear and express words, such punishment is not intended.[170]

This principle has been restated many times, for example by the Privy Council in both *Lim Chin Aik*[171] and *Gammon (Hong Kong) Ltd v A-G of Hong Kong*,[172] by the Divisional Court in *Pharmaceutical Society of Great Britain v Storkwain Ltd*[173] and more recently by the Supreme Court in *Taylor*.[174] But, if implemented more widely, it would seem to require negligence, though not perhaps of a high degree, rather than impose strict liability. D, it appears, must be shown to have fallen short in some respect of the standard to be expected of him. But was the principle applied in *Storkwain*? Was the pharmacist expected to keep a handwriting expert on the premises to scrutinize the prescriptions? Or to telephone the doctor each time he received a prescription for confirmation that he wrote it?[175] In *Harrow v Shah*, it was acknowledged

---

[165] *Ezeemo* [2012] EWCA Crim 2064.

[166] *Highbury Poultry* [2018] EWHC 3122 (Admin) and [2020] UKSC 39.

[167] See generally LCCP 195.

[168] See R Glover, 'Regulatory Offences and Reverse Burdens: The Licensing Approach' (2007) 71 J Crim L 259, arguing that the licence holders have accepted an obligation to prove defences to avoid liability, and therefore reverse burdens are not problematical in this context. See also Green (1997) 46 Emory LJ 1586; Husak in Duff and Green, *Defining Crimes*, 82–4.

[169] [2002] 2 AC 545, [154].

[170] *Reynolds v GH Austin & Sons Ltd* [1951] 2 KB 135.   [171] [1963] AC 160 at 174.

[172] [1985] AC 1 at 14–15.

[173] [1985] 3 All ER 4, approved by the House of Lords [1986] 2 All ER 635 at 640.

[174] [2016] UKSC 5, [26].

[175] It appears that in *Storkwain* the pharmacist, not knowing Dr Irani, *did* telephone the number on the prescription but it was false and he was deceived by the forger or his accomplice who answered: Jackson [1991] Crim LR at 895.

that D had done all he could to ensure compliance with the law. What else could he do, except stop selling lottery tickets? Obviously, the courts do not expect such wholly unreasonable steps to be taken—but how, then, can the principle be satisfied in such cases?

It is worth noting that the evidence from empirical studies is that use of strict liability crimes is not necessarily successful in securing compliance with regulations.[176]

5.4.2.4 Social danger

Fourthly, in construing social context, the courts are influenced by the degree of social danger which, in their opinion, will follow from breach of the particular prohibition.[177] They take judicial notice of the problems with which the country is confronted. The greater the degree of social danger, the more likely it is that the offence will be interpreted as one of strict liability. Drug misuse, road accidents and pollution are constantly brought to our attention as pressing evils; and in each case the judges have at times invoked strict liability as a protection for society.

Dangerous drugs

Legislation concerning dangerous drugs has had a chequered recent history.[178] Lord Parker declared in 1966[179] that he took judicial notice of the fact that drugs are a great danger and the Divisional Court imposed strict liability of a most draconian character in a number of cases at about that time. In one case, D was held to be guilty of being 'concerned in the management of premises used for the purpose of smoking cannabis' though he did not know and had no means of knowing that such smoking was taking place.[180] In other cases, it was held that D was guilty of being in unauthorized possession of a drug[181] if he knew he had control of a thing which was in fact a dangerous drug, even though he did not know, and had no reason to know, that it was either dangerous or a drug.[182] He might have reasonably believed that he had a bottle of sweets, but that would have been no defence.

Problems of possession

The first case on strict liability considered by the House of Lords, *Warner v Metropolitan Police Comr*,[183] concerned possession of prohibited drugs.[184] D, who as a part-time job sold perfume, collected two boxes which had been left for him at a cafe. One box contained perfume, the other controlled drugs. D said he assumed both boxes contained perfume. The jury were told that such a belief went only to mitigation. The Court of Appeal agreed. If D was in possession of the box and he knew the box contained something, he was in possession of the contents, whatever they were; and, as it was an 'absolute' offence, that was all the prosecution had to prove.

The House of Lords, Lord Reid dissenting, agreed with the courts below that the section created an 'absolute' offence, not requiring any mens rea as such. But it was, of course, necessary to prove the actus reus, that is, possession, and that involved proving a mental element. Lord Guest agreed with the Court of Appeal—D's knowledge that he had a box containing *something* under his control was enough—but the other judges held that more was required.

---

[176] G Richardson, 'Effective Means of Regulating Industry Strict Liability for Regulating Crime: The Empirical Evidence' [1987] Crim LR 295. See Appendix A to LCCP 195 by Professor Black.

[177] In *R (on the application of Thames Water Utilities) v Bromley Magistrates' Court* [2013] EWHC 472 (Admin), Gross LJ stated that this criterion concerned him, on the ground that most statutes are, at least in the view of the legislators who enact them, to do with some social danger or concern.

[178] See generally R Fortson, *The Misuse of Drugs and Drug Trafficking Offences* (6th edn, 2012).

[179] In *Yeandel v Fisher* [1966] 1 QB 440 at 446.   [180] ibid.

[181] Contrary to s 1(1) of the Drugs (Prevention of Misuse) Act 1964.

[182] eg *Lockyer v Gibb* [1967] 2 QB 243.   [183] [1969] 2 AC 256.

[184] See for a theoretical consideration of the issues raised by possession offences, MD Dubber, 'The Possession Paradigm' in Duff and Green, *Defining Crimes*, 115; A Ashworth, 'The Unfairness of Risk-Based Possession Offences' (2011) 5 Crim L & Phil 237. See also A Ashworth and L Zedner, *Preventive Justice* (2014) Ch 5.

Though D's possession of the box gave rise to a strong inference that he was in possession of the contents, that inference might be rebutted. Their lordships' opinions are obscure and various but it seems that the inference certainly would be rebutted if: (a) D believed the box contained perfume; (b) perfume was something of 'a wholly different nature' from the drugs; (c) D had no opportunity to ascertain its true nature; and (d) he did not suspect there was 'anything wrong' with the contents. These issues (or at least some of them, for the majority of the House were far from being in complete accord) ought to have been left to the jury and, as they had not, three judges held that there had been a misdirection (but upheld the conviction under the proviso which was then available to the appellate courts).

Possession is a neutral concept, not implying any kind of blame or fault but experience has shown that, when it becomes the determinant of guilt, it tends to acquire a refined and artificial meaning of great complexity. It seems the most obvious common sense to say that a person firmly grasping a parcel is in possession of it and a distinction between the parcel and its contents is too absurd to contemplate. However, if it is a grave offence merely to possess a particular article and that is what is contained in the parcel, courts may strive to find means to say that an 'innocent' person is not in possession, by refining the meaning of that concept. Of course, this problem would not arise if it were held that the offence required some element of fault—possession, as observed, is neutral and in itself incapable of being 'fault'—but, sadly, of all the judges involved, only Lord Reid was willing to take this sensible course. The result was a calamitous decision by the House.

The five speeches delivered in *Warner* differ so greatly and it is so difficult to make sense of parts of them that courts in later cases have found it impossible to extract a *ratio decidendi*. The law has been modified by the Misuse of Drugs Act 1971 but the onus remains on the Crown to prove possession and the Act has nothing to say about that concept. It has, however, influenced the approach of the courts. In *McNamara*,[185] the Court of Appeal, while paying lip-service to the House of Lords, has gone back to the view of the Court of Appeal and the dissenting opinion (on this issue) of Lord Guest. D was in possession of a cardboard box containing cannabis resin. He said he thought it contained pornographic material. Because he knew he was in control of the box and that the box contained something, he was in possession of cannabis. The court was able to reach this conclusion without misgiving because it no longer followed automatically from that finding that D was guilty of the offence: under s 28 of the Misuse of Drugs Act 1971 it is a defence to prove[186] that he neither believed nor suspected nor had reason to suspect that the thing of which he was in possession was a controlled drug.

McNamara provides a welcome simplification of the law where D knows he has the thing or a container with something in it but claims he thought it was something else. It does not solve the problem when D claims he was unaware of the existence of an article in the container. In *Warner*,[187] there was unanimous agreement about a hypothetical case posed earlier by Lord Parker CJ[188]—if something is slipped into a woman's bag and she has no idea that it is there, she is not in possession of it. It is easy to find authority in the vast case law on possession to contradict that proposition but Parker LCJ, the Court of Appeal and the House were entirely confident about it: the woman is in possession of the bag and the known contents but not the thing secretly inserted. The judges refused to say that the hypothetical woman was in possession of the thing because they were thinking of a packet of controlled

---

[185] (1988) 87 Cr App R 246, [1988] Crim LR 440 and commentary.

[186] Interpreted, *obiter*, by the House of Lords in *Lambert* [2002] 2 AC 545 to mean not 'prove' but 'introduce evidence of' so as to comply with the HRA 1998. For a case in which it was held that there was a clear intention to impose a legal burden upon D, see *Williams* [2012] EWCA Crim 2162 and Ashworth's criticisms at [2013] Crim LR 447.

[187] [1969] 2 AC 256 at 282, 286, 300, 303 and 311.   [188] *Lockyer v Gibb* [1967] 2 QB 243 at 248.

drugs and, if she was in possession, she would have been guilty of a grave offence. If the thing were a box of chocolates dropped in by a friend as a birthday present it is unlikely that they would have hesitated to hold that she was in possession of it. Suppose that, before she discovered it, the box had been removed by a pickpocket; would they have hesitated to hold that it was stolen from her (it was not stolen from anyone else) and that the pickpocket was a thief? Of course not. So far as possession is concerned, there is no rational distinction between the drugs and the chocolates.

In *Lewis*,[189] it was held that the judge had not misdirected the jury by telling them that the tenant of a house might be found to be in possession of drugs found on the premises although he did not know they were there, provided he had had an opportunity to find out that they were. But there is no material difference between planting drugs in a person's house and planting them in her basket.[190] The decision seems to contradict the one thing on which their lordships in *Warner* were unanimous. In introducing the idea of opportunity, the court relied on a statement of Lord Morris. But Lord Morris was dealing with a quite different question: possession, he said, was 'being *knowingly in control of a thing* in circumstances which have involved an opportunity (whether availed of or not) to learn or discover, at least in a general way, *what the thing is*'.[191] In *Lewis*, D was not knowingly in control of the thing.

Warner does not affect the law where the drug was not in a container. D must know he has the thing, but it is not necessary that he should know or comprehend its nature.[192] In *Marriott*,[193] D was convicted of being in possession of 0.03 grains of cannabis adhering to a penknife. It was held that the jury had been wrongly directed that he was guilty if he knew he was in possession of the penknife. It was necessary to prove at least that he knew that there was some 'thing' adhering to the knife. The court thought that no further mens rea was necessary—so that the accused would be guilty if he thought the matter was tobacco or toffee—but now, under the Misuse of Drugs Act 1971, it would be a defence for him to prove[194] that he neither believed, nor suspected, nor had reason to suspect, that the 'thing' attached to the knife was a controlled drug.

Being concerned in the management of premises

The second case concerning strict liability to reach the House of Lords was *Sweet v Parsley*.[195] On this occasion, the House overruled the cases which decided that being 'concerned in the management of premises used for the purpose of smoking cannabis' is an offence of strict liability. D, a schoolmistress, let the rooms of a country farmhouse, retaining one room for her own use and visiting the farm occasionally to collect rent and see that all was well. Cannabis was smoked in the farmhouse but it was found as a fact that she had no knowledge whatsoever of this. The Divisional Court nevertheless upheld her conviction.[196] She was

---

[189] (1987) 87 Cr App R 270, [1988] Crim LR 517 and commentary.

[190] 'First of all man does not have possession of something which has been put into his pocket or into his house without his knowledge': *McNamara* (1988) 87 Cr App R 246 at 248.

[191] [1969] 2 AC 256 at 289 (emphasis in original).

[192] *Boyesen* [1982] AC 768. (It is immaterial how minute the quantity is provided only that it amounts to something and D knows he has it.)

[193] [1971] 1 WLR 187.

[194] Interpreted, *obiter*, by the House of Lords in *Lambert* [2001] 3 All ER 577 to mean not 'prove' but 'introduce evidence of' so as to comply with the HRA 1998. For a case in which it was held that there was a clear intention to impose a legal burden upon D, see *Williams* [2012] EWCA Crim 2162.

[195] [1970] AC 132.

[196] It has been suggested that strict liability in such a case might infringe Art 3 of the ECHR by subjecting D to degrading treatment. See Sullivan, 'Strict Liability for Criminal Offences' in Simester, *Appraising Strict Liability*, 206.

'concerned in the management' and that was enough. The House of Lords quashed her conviction. The 'purpose' referred to in the section must be that of the person concerned in the management; and D had no such purpose. Only Lord Wilberforce was content to stop with this 'prosaic interpretation'. The remainder relied, in varying degrees, on a presumption in favour of mens rea. The actual decision in *Warner* was not affected,[197] but the attitude of the House, with the exception of Lord Reid who saw no reason to alter what he had said in the earlier case, is very different. The judges are no less sensitive to the public's view of injustice than to their need for protection; and, for once, a case of strict liability had excited public interest. The public outcry and sense of injustice may not have been without influence.[198]

The corresponding provisions of the Misuse of Drugs Act now require mens rea and leave the onus of proof more appropriately on the prosecution. It is an offence if an occupier[199] or person concerned in the management of premises 'knowingly permits or suffers' the smoking of cannabis and other specified activities in connection with drugs. The word 'knowingly' was introduced for the first time in the Act; but it does not alter the decisions under the Dangerous Drugs Act 1965 that knowledge or wilful blindness is enough, but reasonable grounds for suspicion are not.[200]

Pollution

In view of the ever greater concern about the environment,[201] it is scarcely surprising that modern examples of strict liability crimes should arise in this context. In *Alphacell Ltd v Woodward*,[202] the House of Lords held that D Ltd was guilty of causing polluted matter to enter a river, contrary to s 2(1)(a) of the Rivers (Prevention of Pollution) Act 1951.[203] They had built and operated settling tanks with an overflow channel into the river and provided pumps designed to prevent any overflow taking place. Because the pumps became obstructed with vegetation, an overflow of polluted water occurred. There was no evidence that D knew that pollution was taking place or that they had been in any way negligent. Lord Salmon stressed the public importance of preventing pollution and the risk of pollution from the vast and increasing number of riparian industries and said:[204]

If . . . it were held to be the law that no conviction could be obtained under the 1951 Act unless the prosecution could discharge the often impossible onus of proving that the pollution was caused intentionally or negligently, a great deal of pollution would go unpunished and undeterred to the relief of many riparian factory owners. As a result, many rivers which are now filthy would become filthier still and many rivers which are now clean would lose their cleanliness.

Another example is *Atkinson v Sir Alfred McAlpine& Son Ltd*,[205] where it was held that the company was guilty of failing to give written notice, as required by the Asbestos Regulations 1969, that they were going to undertake work involving crocidolite though they neither

---

[197] *Fernandez* [1970] Crim LR 277 where it was held to be enough that D knew a package might contain some prohibited article and was prepared to take it, whatever the contents were.

[198] 'fortunately the press in this country are vigilant to expose injustice . . .', *Sweet v Parsley* at 150 per Lord Reid.

[199] The occupier is a person whose degree of control is sufficient to enable him to exclude anyone likely to commit an offence under the Act. It is not limited to persons in legal possession and includes a student with rooms in college: *Tao* [1977] QB 141.

[200] *Thomas* (1976) 63 Cr App R 65.

[201] For detailed discussion, see J Adshead, 'Doing Justice to the Environment' (2013) 77 J Crim L 215.

[202] [1972] AC 824. Cf *Empress Car Co (Abertillery) Ltd v National Rivers Authority* [1998] 1 All ER 481, p 73; *Maidstone Borough Council v Mortimer* [1980] 3 All ER 552; *Kirkland v Robinson* [1987] Crim LR 643 (possession of live wild birds an offence of strict liability under the Wildlife and Countryside Act 1981, s 1(1)(a), taking into account the outstanding social importance of an Act designed to protect the environment).

[203] Now repealed.   [204] [1972] AC 824 at 848.   [205] (1974) 16 KIR 220.

knew nor had reason to know that the work involved crocidolite. The court distinguished *Harding v Price*,[206] where Lord Goddard CJ, holding that D was not guilty of failing to report an accident, the happening of which he was unaware, said:

If a statute contains an absolute prohibition against the doing of some act, as a general rule *mens rea* is not a constituent of the offence, but there is all the difference between prohibiting an act and imposing a duty to do something on the happening of a certain event. Unless a man knows that the event has happened, how can he carry out the duty imposed? . . . Any other view would lead to calling on a man to do the impossible.

In *McAlpine*, the court said that, unlike the accident, it was 'probably possible' to ascertain whether crocidolite was involved; but since they held that the mischief would not be met if 'knows or ought to know' were read into the regulation, it is clear that impossibility would not be regarded as a defence.

5.4.2.5 The severity of the punishment

It is often argued that the provision for a severe maximum punishment shows that strict liability could not have been intended by Parliament. To some extent, this is in conflict with the principle previously discussed, since the provision for only a slight punishment would suggest that Parliament thought the social danger involved to be slight. In *Muhamed*,[207] accepting that materially contributing to the extent of insolvency by gambling was an offence of strict liability, the seriousness of the offence was described as the 'starting point' for the court in its determination. The court explained that the more serious the offence, the greater the weight to be attached to the mens rea presumption and vice versa.

However, the courts do not seem to have been deterred in recent years from imposing strict liability in the case of offences carrying heavy maximum sentences—the offence under the Dangerous Drugs Act 1965 of which Ms Sweet was convicted was punishable on indictment with ten years' imprisonment. Causing death by dangerous driving was (originally) punishable with five. The fact that an offence under s 58(2) of the Firearms Act 1968 was punishable with three years' imprisonment did not deter the court from holding that an honest and reasonable belief that the firearm was an antique was no defence.[208] The maximum sentence of life imprisonment in *G* did not prevent the House of Lords interpreting s 5 of the Sexual Offences Act 2003 as strict.[209] In *Gammon (Hong Kong) Ltd v A-G of Hong Kong*,[210] the Privy Council admitted that the fact that the offence was punishable with a fine of HK\$250,000 and imprisonment for three years was 'a formidable point'; but found 'there is nothing inconsistent with the purpose of the ordinance in imposing severe penalties for offences of strict liability'. Of relevance in *Taylor* to whether aggravated vehicle-taking could be characterized as a 'quasi-crime' was the fact that s 12A of the Theft Act 1968 imposes a maximum sentence of 14 years' imprisonment if death is caused.[211] It was held that such a lengthy maximum sentence suggested the offence was in no way a 'quasi-crime'.

---

[206] [1948] 1 KB 695.

[207] [2002] EWCA Crim 1856.

[208] *Howells* [1977] QB 614. Section 19 of the Act (carrying a firearm in a public place) also imposes strict liability, although the maximum penalty (in the case of non-imitation firearms) is seven years: *Vann and Davis* [1996] Crim LR 52.

[209] This is a striking example because G's argument was not that he should be acquitted because he was not at fault but that he should only be liable for the lesser offences (sex with under 16-year-old which on his version he had admitted) carrying a lesser sentence.

[210] [1985] AC 1 at 17.   [211] [2016] UKSC 5.

5.4.3 Other factors

It is impossible to catalogue all factors that may assist the court in interpretation but, in addition to those discussed previously, factors influencing the court's decision as to whether the presumption of mens rea is necessarily rebutted include: the presence of due diligence defences; the stigma of the offence;[212] the need for such offences as a method of prosecuting corporate entities; and the ease of proof for the prosecution unless strict liability is imposed.[213] This final factor must be treated with caution since, logically, it would allow for strict liability in, for example, murder because the prosecution face a difficult task in proving D's mens rea of intention.[214]

5.4.3.1 Liability is strict, not 'absolute'

It was observed at the beginning of this chapter that the fact that an offence is one of strict liability does not rule out the need for any mental element whatsoever. It may be necessary to prove that D had mens rea as to the conduct or circumstances of the offence save the one element in respect of which strict liability was imposed. In addition, a strict liability offence does not preclude reliance on defences.[215] When the court holds that it is an offence of strict liability to sell meat which is unfit for human consumption, it decides that a reasonable mistake as to that particular fact is not a defence. It does not decide that no other defence is available to D; and, as we have seen, a mistake as to other circumstances of the actus reus may afford a defence depending on the statutory form of words.[216] There is no reason why all other defences should not be available as they are in the case of offences requiring full mens rea. Even when the former offence of dangerous driving was thought to impose strict liability,[217] it was held to be a 'defence' if D was in a state of automatism when he 'drove' the vehicle.[218] Similarly, it is perfectly clear that a child under the age of ten could in no circumstances be convicted of an offence of strict liability.[219] It is submitted that other general defences—insanity,[220] necessity,[221] duress[222] and coercion—should be available equally on a charge of an offence of strict liability as in the case of any other offence.[223]

[212] See *Barnfather v Islington Education Authority* [2003] EWHC 418 (Admin). In terms of the potential use of strict liability offences as evidence of D's bad character, see *Goss* [2003] EWCA Crim 3208.

[213] See *Ezeemo* [2012] EWCA Crim 2064 recognizing that if the offence was not one of strict liability then proof of knowledge would be required and that would render the offence very difficult to prove, frustrating Parliament's intention.

[214] See the comparative study by J Spencer and A Pedain, 'Approaches to Strict and Constructive Liability in Continental Criminal Law' in Simester, *Appraising Strict Liability* noting that a reason for continental systems avoiding strict liability is that their procedures allow for proof more easily than the strict adversarial system in England.

[215] For judicial acceptance of this proposition, see *Gregory* [2011] EWCA Crim 1712.

[216] See p 358.   [217] cf *Gosney* [1971] 3 All ER 220.

[218] *Hill v Baxter* [1958] 1 QB 277; *Budd* [1962] Crim LR 49; *Watmore v Jenkins* [1962] 2 QB 572.

[219] See p 360.

[220] See *H v DPP* [1997] 1 WLR 1406, discussed later, in which insanity was wrongly regarded as a defence displacing mens rea. See now the welcome rejection of that approach in *Loake v CPS* [2017] EWHC 2855 (Admin).

[221] This proposition was accepted in *Santos v CPS* [2013] EWHC 550 (Admin). But see *Cichon v DPP* [1994] Crim LR 918 (defence of necessity not open under Dangerous Dogs Act 1991, s 1(2)(d), because an 'absolute' offence).

[222] See *Eden DC v Baird* [1998] CODS 209. *Hampshire CC v E* [2007] EWHC 2584 (Admin), p 392 seems too narrow, and unfair. See J Donoghue (2011) 74 MLR 216 at 235 et seq.

[223] For discussion of this question, see F Sayre, 'Public Welfare Offences' (1933) 33 Col LR 55 at 75–8; Howard, SR, Ch 9.

Larsonneur[224] and *Winzar v Chief Constable of Kent*[225] establish that *lawful* compulsion is not a defence to offences of 'being found'. It does not follow that unlawful duress would not be a defence. If D, being drunk, were forced at gunpoint into the highway he should not be guilty of being found drunk there. Nor does it follow that even lawful compulsion may not found a defence to other, less extreme, cases of strict liability than those of 'being found'.

5.4.3.2 ECHR

The arguments based on Art 6(2) were considered earlier.

5.5 Arguments for and against strict liability

The proliferation of offences of strict liability, while generally deplored by legal writers, was welcomed by some commentators. They argue that strict liability is necessary to promote the punitive and deterrent effects of the criminal law. The argument is made that strict liability could be more readily applied with the factors which the court currently considers when deciding whether to impose strict liability being relevant to the court's sentencing decision.

The difficulty with this approach is that it assumes that the function of the courts is to interpret the statute so as to prevent forbidden acts. But surely that is overly simplistic. Suppose that a butcher, who has taken all reasonable precautions, has the misfortune to sell some meat which is unfit for human consumption. That it was so unfit is undiscoverable by any precaution which a butcher can be expected to take. Ought the butcher to have acted as he did? Unless we want butchers to stop selling meat, or to take precautions so extreme as to be unreasonable (like employing an analyst),[226] it would seem that the answer should be 'yes'; we want butchers, who have taken all reasonable precautions, to sell meat—the act of this butcher was not one which the law should seek to prevent. The imposition of strict liability rather than liability for negligence seems wholly inappropriate.[227]

The most prominent opponent of strict liability offences in recent times is Andrew Ashworth.[228] In his analysis of this issue, Ashworth limits his focus to serious offences. He argues that there are two arguments explaining why the principle of mens rea is so influential in the common law world. The first he calls the 'rule of law' argument and it is founded upon the proposition that it would be wrong to convict and punish anyone who has not been given a 'fair opportunity' to exercise the capacity for 'doing what the law requires and abstaining from what it forbids'.[229] Ashworth therefore identifies the principle of mens rea as being central to fairness in the criminal law. Strict liability is so objectionable because it leads to the conviction of people who it has not been proved were sufficiently at fault in respect of a material element of the offence. Ashworth terms the second argument the 'censure-based' argument and it is a corollary of the seriousness with which a criminal

---

[224] (1933) 24 Cr App R 74; p 43.

[225] (1983) The Times, 28 Mar, p 70. Cf *O'Sullivan v Fisher* [1954] SASR 33, discussed by Howard, SR at 193; *Achterdam* 1911 EDL 336 (EM Burchell and PMA Hunt, *South African Criminal Law and Procedure* (1970) 114).

[226] See Kennedy LJ cited p 148 and see p 149.

[227] This point is also made by Ashworth, who criticizes Lady Hale's speech in *G* on the basis that she did not consider the case for having a negligence standard as an alternative to imposing strict liability. See A Ashworth, 'Should Strict Criminal Liability be Removed from All Imprisonable Offences?' in A Ashworth, *Positive Obligations in Criminal Law* (2013) 121.

[228] ibid.

[229] Here Ashworth is citing HLA Hart, *Punishment and Responsibility: Essays in the Philosophy of Law* (2008) 152.

conviction should be treated. This, it is argued, provides a strong reason for requiring fault. Failure to do so, he argues, imposes public condemnation without properly laying the foundations for it. Ashworth argues that, either separately or in combination, these arguments provide convincing reasons for regarding strict liability as wrong in principle. He states:

The rule-of-law rationale links with the criminal law's function of guiding behaviour and the censure-based rationale links with the criminal conviction's function of expressing official censure. Thus, both rationales connect the criminal law with wider issues of political obligation, in the sense that they emphasise the importance of respect for individuals as rational and autonomous persons.[230]

Some commentators take a different view, arguing that strict liability offences perform a valuable role[231] in 'setting out schemes of conduct that have the effect of co-ordinating risk reduction or the promotion of certain goods'. In the famous, but now overruled, case of *Prince* where D was convicted of taking a girl under 16 out of the possession of her parents, even though he had no mens rea as to her age, some of the judges reached their conclusion on the ground that men should be deterred from taking girls out of the possession of their parents, whatever the girl's age. This reasoning can hardly be applied to many modern offences in which strict liability is adopted. We do not wish to deter people from driving cars, being concerned in the management of premises or canning peas.[232] These acts, if done with all proper care, are not such acts as the law should seek to prevent. The fallacy in the argument lies in looking at the harm done in isolation from the circumstances in which it was brought about. Many acts, which have in fact caused harm, *ought* to have been done. The surgeon performing a justified operation with all proper skill may cause death, yet we would still want him to perform the operation.

Another argument that is frequently advanced in favour of strict liability is that, without it, many guilty people would escape—'that there is neither time nor personnel available to litigate the culpability of each particular infraction'.[233] This argument assumes that it is possible to deal with these cases without deciding whether D had mens rea or not, whether he was negligent or not. Certainly, D may be convicted without deciding these questions, but how can he be fairly sentenced? Clearly, the court ought to deal differently with: (a) the butcher who knew that the meat was contaminated; (b) the butcher who did not know, but ought to have known; and (c) the butcher who did not know and had no means of finding out. Sentence cannot properly be imposed without deciding into which category the convicted person falls. Treating the offence as one of strict liability, in the case of jury trial, merely removes the decision of these vital questions of fact from the jury and puts them in the hands of the judge; in the case of summary trial, it removes the questions from the sphere of strict proof according to law and leaves them to be decided in the much more informal way in which questions of fact relating purely to sentence are decided.[234]

---

[230] See n 227, 118.   [231] Lamond (2007) 27 OJLS 609.

[232] See *Smedleys Ltd v Breed* [1974] AC 839. 'Obviously any consequence is avoidable by the simple expedient of not engaging in the process at all. But that clearly is not what is meant unless the process itself is open to serious criticism as unnecessary or inefficient', [1974] 2 All ER 21 at 28 per Lord Hailsham.

[233] H Wechsler, 'The Model Penal Code' in JL Edwards (ed), *Modern Advances in Criminology* (1965) 73. The argument was met by the authors of the code by 'the creation of a grade of offence which may be prosecuted in a criminal court but which is not denominated criminal and which entails upon conviction no severer sentence than a fine or civil penalty or forfeiture'.

[234] Disputed facts affecting sentence may be decided by the judge in a 'Newton hearing' after conviction—see *Newton* (1982) 77 Cr App R 13. In some cases judges have preferred the use of additional counts to obtain the jury's decision on important issues of culpability which would not appear from a verdict of guilty on a single count. See *Hoof* (intentional or reckless arson?), Ch 27. This course is not open where the offence is one of strict liability. In *Warner* (p 166) the recorder asked the jury after verdict whether D knew the box contained drugs but they said, reasonably, that they had not decided that question.

There is a further problem with strict liability and sentencing.[235] If the offence is one of strict liability, then strictly speaking evidence is not admissible at the trial either to show that D was blameworthy—*Sandhu*[236]—or that he was not—*Gosney*.[237] On the assumption (held, on appeal, to be wrong) that the former offence of dangerous driving was one of strict liability, the judge, no doubt rightly, excluded evidence alleged to show that D was blameless. If the rules relating to proof at the trial have any value at all, it is extraordinary that they should not be applied to the most important facts in the case. That the sentence should be imposed by the judge on a basis of fact different from that on which the jury convicted is deplorable; but it is always possible in the case of strict liability unless the judge questions the jury as to the grounds of their decision—and there are difficulties about this.[238]

An illustration of how mens rea may be relevant to sentence even where strict liability is imposed is in cases of under-age sex. As a child under 13 cannot, in law, give consent to any sexual activity, an offender's belief in the age of the child, even if reasonably held, is irrelevant. However, when considering culpability, actual consent has been recognized as being capable of being a mitigating factor.[239]

The argument which is probably most frequently advanced by the courts for imposing strict liability is that it is necessary to do so in the 'interests of the public'.[240] Of course, it may be conceded that in many of the instances where strict liability has been imposed, the public does need protection against negligence and, assuming that the threat of punishment can make the potential harm-doer more careful, there may be a valid ground for imposing liability for negligence as well as where there is mens rea. But that is an argument for negligence offences, and it is only valid as an argument for strict liability if the courts are not prepared to hold that where the presumption of mens rea is rebutted, it is replaced with a requirement to prove negligence. The judges have generally proceeded on the basis that there is no such 'middle way': where the presumption of mens rea is rebutted liability is strict.[241]

The case against strict liability crimes being created then is, first, that it is unnecessary. It results in the conviction of persons who have behaved impeccably and who should not be required to alter their conduct in any way. Secondly, that it is unjust.[242] Even if an absolute discharge can be given (as in *Ball*),[243] D may feel rightly aggrieved at having been formally convicted of an offence for which he bore no responsibility. It is significant that Ball thought it worthwhile to appeal. Moreover, a conviction may have far-reaching consequences outside the courts,[244] so that it is no answer to say that only a nominal penalty is imposed.[245]

[235] These problems are discussed in A Ashworth, 'Should Strict Criminal Liability be Removed from All Imprisonable Offences?' in A Ashworth, *Positive Obligations in Criminal Law* (2013) 127.

[236] [1997] Crim LR 288.	[237] [1971] 2 QB 674.

[238] cf comment on *Lockyer v Gibb* [1966] Crim LR 504 and on *Sheppard* [1981] AC 394, [1981] Crim LR 171 at 172; *Dalas* [1966] Crim LR 692; *Warner* [1967] 3 All ER 93; *Lester* (1976) 63 Cr App R 144; *Foo* [1976] Crim LR 456 and commentaries on these cases.

[239] *F* [2007] EWCA Crim 2550. See also the *obiter* comments in *Jackson* [2006] EWCA Crim 2380, p 157.

[240] This rationale is derided by Ashworth as being 'vacuous'. See A Ashworth, 'Should Strict Criminal Liability be Removed from All Imprisonable Offences?' in A Ashworth, *Positive Obligations in Criminal Law* (2013) 117.

[241] See the rejection of that approach in *Nurse v Trinidad* [2019] UKPC 43.

[242] See for a philosophical account, A Simester, 'Is Strict Liability Always Wrong?' and DN Husak, 'Strict Liability, Justice and Proportionality' in Simester, *Appraising Strict Liability*.

[243] (1966) 50 Cr App R 266 (blameless driver guilty of causing death by dangerous driving).

[244] With employment, travel restrictions, etc. See the case of *Sweet v Parsley* [1970] AC 132.

[245] This was accepted by the Privy Council in *Lim Chin Aik* [1963] AC 160 at 175 and by Lord Reid in *Warner* [1968] 2 All ER 356 at 366.

5.6 Negligence/lack of due diligence as a preferred approach

The imposition of liability for negligence would meet the arguments of most of those who favour strict liability. Roscoe Pound, in a passage which has been frequently and uncritically accepted as a justification for such offences, wrote:[246]

The good sense of the courts has introduced a doctrine of acting at one's peril with respect to statutory crimes which expresses the needs of society. Such statutes are not meant to punish the vicious but to put pressure upon the thoughtless and inefficient to do their whole duty in the interest of public health or safety or morals.

The 'thoughtless and inefficient' are, of course, the negligent. The objection to offences of strict liability is not that these negligent persons are penalized, but that others who are completely innocent are also liable to conviction. There is therefore a strong argument for saying that where the presumption of mens rea is rebutted on the grounds discussed earlier, then liability should not be strict but should turn on whether D was negligent. One way of achieving this is by including 'due diligence' defences.

These might be made available by statute (usually the statute creating the offence) or at common law.

5.6.1 Statutory due diligence defences

It is common for the drastic effect of a statute imposing strict liability to be mitigated by the provision of a statutory defence allowing the defendant to prove that he acted with all due diligence. The Law Commission has reviewed the use of due diligence defences and the various forms they take—the most general ones based on whether D has taken all reasonable precautions and exercised all due diligence to avoid the commission of the offence.[247]

As an example, the Trade Descriptions Act 1968 created a number of offences, some of which replaced earlier offences of strict liability, and s 24 provided that it is a defence to prove (a) that the commission of the offence was due (inter alia) to a mistake or accident and (b) that D 'took all reasonable precautions and exercised all due diligence to avoid the commission of such an offence by himself or any person under his control'.[248] Thus, though the prosecution do not have to prove negligence, it is a defence for D to show that he was not negligent. Similar provisions have been included in some offences in the Misuse of Drugs Act 1971.

A further more recent example is in s 7 of the Bribery Act 2010 which creates a strict liability offence for a commercial organization where a person associated with it bribes another person intending to obtain or retain a business advantage. This is a very widely defined offence.[249] Section 7 provides:

(1) A relevant commercial organisation ('C') is guilty of an offence under this section if a person ('A') associated with C bribes another person intending—

(a) to obtain or retain business for C, or

(b) to obtain or retain an advantage in the conduct of business for C.

---

[246] *The Spirit of the Common Law* (1921) 52.   [247] LCCP 195, para 6.28.

[248] See generally DL Parry, 'Judicial Approaches to Due Diligence' [1995] Crim LR 695. See P Cartwright, *Consumer Protection and the Criminal Law* (2001).

[249] Section 7 is triable only on indictment (s 11(3)). The maximum sentence is an unlimited fine. See the valuable analysis by S Gentle [2011] Crim LR 101.

There is, crucially, a due diligence defence in s 7(2) for C to prove that it had in place adequate procedures designed to prevent persons associated with C from undertaking such conduct.[250]

Sometimes due diligence defences are extremely complex with various specific elements that D must prove. Examples include those relating to the treatment and sale of food. Several of the offences enacted by ss 7 to 20 of the Food Safety Act 1990 are strict liability offences. Section 21(1), however, provides that it shall be a defence for the person charged with any of the offences to prove that he took all reasonable precautions and exercised all due diligence to avoid the commission of the offence by himself or by a person under his control.[251] But, where this defence involves an allegation that the offence was in consequence of the act or default of another person, the defendant may not, without the leave of the court, rely on it unless within a prescribed period he has served on the prosecutor a notice in writing giving such information identifying or assisting in the identification of the other person as was then in his possession (s 21(5)).

The statutory due diligence defences usually impose on D a burden of proving both that he had no mens rea and that he took all reasonable precautions and exercised all due diligence to avoid the commission of an offence.[252] The effect of such provisions is that the prosecution need do no more than prove that the accused did the prohibited act and it is then for D to establish, if he can, that he did it innocently. Such provisions are a distinct advance on unmitigated strict liability; but they are still a deviation from the fundamental principle that the prosecution must prove the whole of the allegation.

Arguments over what the particular statutory due diligence defence requires D to prove can also arise. In *Croydon LBC v Pinch a Pound (UK) Ltd*,[253] P Co sold knives. An employee at P Co sold a utility knife to two 15-year-olds. P was convicted in the magistrates' court under s 141A of the Criminal Justice Act 1988 ('selling' a knife to anyone under 18). P argued successfully in the Crown Court that the company had exercised all due diligence and taken all reasonable precautions to prevent the commission of the offence, and therefore had the statutory defence in s 141A(4). The Divisional Court held that the Crown Court had misconstrued the due diligence test.[254] The defence in s 141A(4) comprised two elements: (a) taking reasonable precautions (eg a no sales policy, signage and staff training) and (b) the exercise of due diligence in the management and operation of sales of the items (ensuring that the policy was adhered to, recording refused sales correctly, etc). The Crown Court appeared to have focused on whether D had shown an absence of negligence *and an absence of a reprehensible state of mind*. That was too generous to the defendant as it imported mens rea into the offence. The case was remitted with an order to convict.

---

[250] The offences of failing to prevent the facilitation of tax evasion in ss 45 and 46 of the Criminal Finances Act 2017 contain similar defences. There is a crucial difference, however. In the Criminal Finances Act, it is open to the corporate to prove that it was not reasonable in all the circumstances to expect it to have in place prevention procedures. For discussion, see K Laird, 'The Criminal Finances Act 2017—An Introduction' [2017] Crim LR 915.

[251] It has been held that there is no liability for D where he has taken all reasonable steps to delegate his duty to another who then fails to perform to the relevant standard. See eg *R (Keam) v DEFRA* [2005] EWHC 1582 (Admin).

[252] See *X Ltd* [2013] EWCA Crim 818.   [253] [2010] EWHC 3283 (Admin).

[254] Misapplying words from Lord Diplock's speech in *Tesco Supermarkets Ltd v Nattrass* [1972] AC 153; see Ch 8, p 265.

5.6.1.1 Due diligence and reasonable excuse as a cloak for mens rea

In 2011, in *Unah*,[255] the Court of Appeal considered the relationship between strict liability and the defence of reasonable excuse in the context of the Identity Card Act 2006.[256] D was a Nigerian citizen with indefinite leave to remain in the UK. In D's possession was found a false passport, which had expired, in addition to a valid current passport. D's contention was that the passport was genuine. D was charged with an offence under s 21(5) of the Identity Cards Act 2006 and sought to argue that her belief that the passport was genuine ought to constitute a 'reasonable excuse' within the meaning of that section. The judge ruled that the offence was one of strict liability and therefore 'reasonable excuse' could not include D's state of mind as to the genuineness of the passport. The Court of Appeal noted that the offence in s 21(5), unlike s 21(1), did not refer to D having intention or knowledge that the passport was false. To that extent, the judge was right to infer that Parliament had intended to create an offence of strict liability. Elias LJ, however, also stated that it did not follow that lack of knowledge or belief would not be relevant at all to a defence of reasonable excuse. The jury ought to have been directed to consider objectively whether D had a reasonable excuse for possessing the passport and her conviction was quashed.[257] A similar approach was taken in the case of *JB* where the allegation was of a breach of an ASBO.[258] The court noted that the statute:

does not require the Crown to prove a specific mental element on the part of a defendant at the time he committed the acts which constitute the breach of an ASBO. However, if the issue of reasonable excuse arises in any given case a Defendant can raise his state of mind at the time of the alleged breach since the state of mind will usually be relevant to the issue of reasonable excuse. As the effect of s 1(10) is to criminalise conduct that would otherwise not be criminal (cf paras 10 and 11 of the judgment in *Charles* [[2009] EWCA Crim 1570]), it would not be right, on principle, to exclude matters that go to a Defendant's state of mind (such as forgetfulness or a misapprehension about the meaning of the order or an accidental breach).[259]

5.6.2 Due diligence defences imposed at common law?

In some common law jurisdictions it has become commonplace for the courts to adopt a 'halfway house' between strict liability and full mens rea. Once the actus reus has been proved, an onus is imposed on D, sometimes to introduce evidence and sometimes to prove, that he had reasonable grounds for his failure to be aware of, or to foresee, relevant facts, as the case may be. The lead first came from Australia.[260] In Canada also, the Supreme Court, in a notable judgment delivered by Dickson J, held that public welfare offences prima facie fall into an intermediate class between offences requiring mens rea and offences 'of absolute liability'. The prosecution need prove only that D caused the actus reus but he may escape liability by proving that he took all reasonable care to avoid the commission of the offence.[261]

---

255 [2011] EWCA Crim 1837.

256 This has since been repealed and been replaced by similar offences in the Identity Documents Act 2010. The provisions are similar and the decision in this case ought to be applicable to the new offences.

257 It has been argued that this case demonstrates how the reasonable excuse defence acts as a bulwark against the imposition of strict liability. See A Reed, 'Strict Liability and the Reasonable Excuse Defence' (2012) 76 J Crim L 293.

258 *JB v DPP* [2012] EWHC 72 (Admin).   259 At [17].

260 *Maher v Musson* (1934) 52 CLR 100; *Proudman v Dayman* (1941) 67 CLR 536.

261 *City of Sault Ste Marie* (1978) 40 CCC (2d) 353.

Where there is no such express due diligence provision in a statute, it is unlikely that the courts will hold it to be implied. It is true that the House of Lords in *Sweet v Parsley*[262] looked favourably on such a doctrine:[263]

When a statutory prohibition is cast in terms which at first sight appear to impose strict responsibility, they should be understood merely as imposing responsibility for negligence but emphasising that the burden of rebutting negligence by affirmative proof of reasonable mistake rests upon the defendant.[264]

However, the English courts have subsequently showed no inclination to put such a principle into practice. In *Gammon (Hong Kong) Ltd v A-G of Hong Kong*,[265] the Privy Council, while stressing the need for very high standards of care, regarded the choice as a straight one between mens rea and strict liability. Just as the judges invented the presumption in favour of mens rea, they could have invented a presumption of a negligence requirement in particular types of case. They chose not to do so. Lord Devlin has explained this:

It is not easy to find a way of construing a statute apparently expressed in terms of absolute liability so as to produce the requirement of negligence. Take, for example, an offence like driving a car while it has defective brakes. It is easy enough to read into a statute a word like 'wilfully' but you cannot just read in 'carelessly'. You cannot show that no one should carelessly drive a car with defective brakes; you are not trying to get at careless driving. What you want to say is that no one may drive a car without taking care to see that the brakes are not defective. That is not so easy to frame as a matter of construction and it has never been done.[266]

The judicial reluctance to read due diligence defences into strict liability is in part born of a reluctance to impose a burden of proof on the defence. But as the former Law Lord, Lord Cooke of Thorndon observed:

It does seem odd that in the home of *Woolmington* absolute (or strict) liability is so extensively accepted by the courts, and with some equanimity. It is as if the great case has created a judicial mindset which recoils at a shifting of the onus, yet tolerates a harsher solution.[267]

There is nothing wrong, it is submitted, with the 'judicial mindset' which recoils at a shifting of the onus onto the defendant—that reflects a healthy commitment to the presumption of innocence—but when combined with a refusal to imply a requirement of either mens rea or negligence, it does indeed lead to an unduly harsh solution. The opportunity to adopt the halfway house was presented to the House of Lords in *B (A Minor) v DPP*[268] but was declined in favour of a requirement of full mens rea. It seems the halfway house has no future in England and Wales, except where it is embodied in a statute. It could be argued that the judgments in *Unah* and *JB* indicate a different attitude, at least amongst certain members of the Court of Appeal, and Lady Arden did not close the door completely when rejecting the application of the halfway house in *Nurse*.[269] The extent to which these cases

---

[262] [1969] 1 All ER 347 at 351 per Lord Reid, at 357 per Lord Pearce and at 362 per Lord Diplock.

[263] As it had developed in Australia, see n 260.

[264] G Orchard, 'The Defence of Absence of Fault in Australia and Canada' in *Criminal Law Essays*.

[265] [1985] AC 1, [1984] 2 All ER 503 at 509.   [266] *Samples of Lawmaking* (1962) 76.

[267] 'One Golden Thread' in *Turning Points of the Common Law* (Hamlyn Lectures, 1997) 28 at 47. See also *City of Sault Ste Marie* (1978) 85 DLR 3d 161 (Can). On defences of due diligence, see G Orchard, 'The Defence of Absence of Fault in Australia and Canada' in *Criminal Law Essays*.

[268] [2000] 2 AC 428.

[269] '[I]t is not appropriate for the Board to consider the halfway house on this appeal. The matter would in any event have to be fully argued and it would be necessary to overcome the point made by the Court of Appeal, on which the Board expresses no view, that only Parliament could make a decision of this magnitude' (at [60]).

represent a more general willingness to accept the halfway house remains to be seen but the situation does not look promising.

5.6.3 Reform

The Law Commission made the welcome recommendation that:

In an ideal world, criminal offences created by statute would always indicate when fault need not be proved, or if it needs to be proved what kind of fault (or defence) is involved. Since there are so many criminal offences under statute that fall short of the ideal, we believe that, subject to some possible exceptions, the courts should be given the power to apply a defence of due diligence in all the circumstances to statutory offences that would otherwise involve strict liability with no adequate defence. This approach has the advantage of leaving the strict basis of liability in the relevant provision intact. That means the courts will no longer need to search for what may be non-existent Parliamentary intention respecting fault requirements and will no longer need to decide whether a presumption that fault must be proved applies, and if so, whether the presumption has been displaced.[270]

Further reading

A Ashworth and L Zedner, *Preventive Justice*

HLA Hart, *Punishment and Responsibility: Essays in the Philosophy of Law*

A Norrie, *Crime, Reason and History: A Critical Introduction to Criminal Law*

A Simester, *Appraising Strict Liability*

---

[270] LCCP 195, para 6.92, recognizing that in some contexts, eg road traffic, due diligence would not be an appropriate innovation.

6

Parties to crime

6.1 Introduction

A person may be liable for an offence as a 'principal' or 'joint principal' where he has fulfilled the actus reus of the offence.[1] To be a principal offender the person must directly and immediately perform the actus reus of an offence (in this chapter we will refer to the principal as 'P').

Plainly, the principal is not necessarily the only one who can be criminally liable for an offence. A person (in this chapter, D), might also be liable as an 'accessory', or as it is also called, a 'secondary party'. Specific common law and statutory rules govern whether a person is liable as an accessory; these rules apply to all offences, unless expressly[2] or impliedly excluded.[3] Where D is liable as an accessory, he is liable because he aided, abetted, counselled or procured (for convenience we can say 'assisted or encouraged') P who committed the principal offence.

A person, D, other than the principal, P, might also be liable for an inchoate offence—assisting or encouraging P under the Serious Crime Act 2007 (SCA 2007) or for conspiring with P that the offence would be committed. There is a crucial difference from secondary liability: D's liability for inchoate offences arises irrespective of whether P has committed the offence. We deal with inchoate liability in Ch 11.

In secondary liability we can describe D's liability as 'derivative' on the commission of the principal offence.[4] It arises if and only if the principal offence is committed. Logically, therefore, the easiest way of ascertaining D's potential liability is to assess whether the principal offence has been committed, then to consider whether D has fulfilled the requirements of aiding and abetting it. This does *not* involve asking whether D fulfilled the actus reus and mens rea of the principal offence. Instead, we ask whether D performed the relevant conduct sufficient to constitute assisting or encouraging and did so with the mens rea required for liability as an accessory (which is not the same as asking whether D had the mens rea for the principal offence).

Occasionally, statutory offences are drafted in such a way that assisting or encouraging someone to commit an offence is itself a statutory offence[5] (the statute provides: it is an offence to 'do x' and it is an offence to assist any person 'to do x'). In those cases D can be liable for the statutory offence of assisting even if the offence D has assisted is not committed. There are also numerous offences of 'being knowingly concerned in' a type of behaviour such as drug importation or supply of drugs, and the person 'knowingly concerned in' the conduct commits an offence of his own accord not merely as an accessory to someone else's.[6]

Within the scope of secondary liability there also existed at common law a controversial and much misunderstood form of liability known as joint enterprise liability. We will consider that in detail later in this chapter, but following the seminal[7] decision of the Supreme Court in *Jogee*[8] that doctrine no longer exists as a separate basis of liability.

---

[1] See generally KJM Smith, *A Modern Treatise on Complicity* (1991). For an excellent discussion of the current law, see Law Commission Report No 305, *Participating in Crime* (2007) Part 2 and Appendix B.

[2] eg under the Corporate Manslaughter and Corporate Homicide Act 2007 there is no secondary liability for individuals.

[3] Arguably this occurs where a statute creates offences of 'using or causing or permitting to be used'. See *Carmichael & Sons (Worcester) Ltd v Cottle* [1971] RTR 11. Cf *Farr* [1982] Crim LR 745 and commentary.

[4] Russell, 128; *Surujpaul v R* [1958] 3 All ER 300 at 301. This is now subject to the rule in *Millward* [1994] Crim LR 527, p 235.

[5] See eg Female Genital Mutilation Act 2003. Note the Serious Crime Act 2015, ss 70–5, extending the extra-territorial effect of the offence, adding protective orders and adding an offence of failing to protect a girl from the risk of genital mutilation.

[6] See eg the Misuse of Drugs Act 1971, s 4(3)(b).

[7] The term used by Sir Brian Leveson P in *Anwar* [2016] EWCA Crim 551, [20].   [8] [2016] UKSC 8.

6.1.1 Summary

Before discussing in detail the different bases of liability,[9] it is worth summarizing them to provide an overview. D may be liable in the following ways:

(1) As a principal or joint principal where he has played a part in the commission of the actus reus of the offence; or where he acts through an innocent agent.[10]

(2) As an accessory under s 8 of the Accessories and Abettors Act 1861 where D has aided, abetted, counselled or procured P in his conduct where P committed the principal crime.

(3) For the commission of a full statutory offence itself if it is one defined in terms of assisting or encouraging.

(4) Prior to the Supreme Court's judgment in *Jogee*,[11] there was an additional basis upon which D could be liable. Under the common law, D could be liable on the basis of what was known as 'joint enterprise' or 'parasitic accessory'[12] liability. This was a controversial doctrine that was held by the Supreme Court in *Jogee* to have been the result of a 'legal wrong turn' that the court concluded it was necessary to correct. The rise and fall of this doctrine is discussed later in this chapter.[13]

Despite the Supreme Court's efforts to clarify the law in *Jogee*, the current law of secondary liability remains unsatisfactorily complex, and displays many of the characteristic weaknesses of a common law doctrine that has been allowed to develop in a pragmatic and unprincipled way. Statutory reform would be welcome, although there is considerable doubt whether that should be in the form the Law Commission proposed in 2007 (Report No 305 discussed later).[14]

6.2 Bases of liability

By s 8 of the Accessories and Abettors Act 1861, as amended by the Criminal Law Act 1977:

Whosoever shall aid, abet, counsel or procure the commission of any indictable offence whether the same be an offence at common law or by virtue of any act passed or to be passed, shall be liable to be tried, indicted and punished as a principal offender.[15]

The section does not create an offence. It specifies the procedure and punishment for the aiders, abettors, counsellors and procurers, conveniently called 'accessories'.

---

[9] We do not include in this summary any possible inchoate liability. See Ch 11.

[10] See p 188. See recently *Lewis and others* [2017] EWCA Crim 1734.

[11] [2016] UKSC 8. For extensive discussion, see p 223.

[12] This expression was coined by Professor Sir John Smith. See JC Smith, 'Criminal Liability of Accessories: Law and Law Reform' (1997) 113 LQR 453.

[13] At the risk of oversimplifying, D could be liable for P's crime B where D and P had set out with a common purpose to commit crime A and P had gone on to commit crime B and D foresaw as a real possibility that P might commit crime B.

[14] See R Buxton [2009] Crim LR 230; cf W Wilson, 'A Rational Scheme of Liability for Participation in Crime' [2008] Crim LR 3, suggesting the proposals generally 'succeed admirably'; cf GR Sullivan, 'Participating in Crime' [2008] Crim LR 19, suggesting the proposals on joint ventures show a 'disregard for the minimum standards of clarity and comprehensibility' and RD Taylor 'Procuring, Causation, Innocent Agency and the Law Commission' [2008] Crim LR 32, who is also critical of the complexity and incoherence of the proposals.

[15] Similar provisions relating to summary trial are to be found in the Magistrates' Courts Act 1980, s 44.

6.2.1 Distinguishing accessories and principals

English law treats principals and the individuals who are accessories in identical terms for the purposes of procedure and punishment. It has always been sufficient to prove that the defendant was either the principal[16] or accessory.[17] A person who is charged with an offence, say theft, may be convicted whether the evidence proves that he committed the theft (ie was a principal), or aided, abetted, counselled or procured it (ie was an accessory). But the charge should, wherever possible, specify whether the accused is alleged to have been the principal offender or an accessory.[18] The prosecution can nevertheless secure a conviction without specifying precisely what role they allege D played. So, in *Giannetto*, it was acceptable for the prosecution to allege that D killed his wife or that he was an accessory to her killing (by contracting a killer to do so).[19] The jury could convict on that basis. The prosecution could not be sure whether D was the principal offender or an accessory, but could establish beyond doubt that he was involved in plotting her killing.[20] The Supreme Court confirmed in *Jogee* that, 'in some cases the prosecution may not be able to prove whether a defendant was principal or accessory, but it is sufficient to be able to prove that he participated in the crime in one way or another'.[21]

Difficulties of this type are commonplace as, for example, where V is attacked by a group of individuals and killed but the medical evidence points to death resulting from a single stab wound.[22] Unless the evidence can establish that a particular member of the group must have been responsible for inflicting the fatal wound, the prosecution may have no alternative but to allege that each member was either the principal offender or an accessory. Considerable difficulty would arise in such cases if the prosecution had to choose. If there is only one fatal stab wound, the Crown cannot simply allege that each defendant was the principal. As a matter of fact, that is most unlikely to be true; only one person will have plunged the knife in. Equally, the Crown would face difficulty if they alleged that each defendant was an accessory; unless the jury could be sure when considering the case against a particular defendant that he was not the principal, he would have to be acquitted. In view of these forensic difficulties, the pragmatic solution of being able to charge D with being either an accessory or principal is understandable. The lack of precision in such an indictment has been held not to render it incompatible with Art 6 of the ECHR on the basis of the requirement that a defendant must know 'in detail' the nature of the case against him.[23]

Although the law treats the accessory and principal in identical terms for the purposes of procedure and punishment, it is important to distinguish them for several reasons.

---

[16] The common law of felonies designated the actual perpetrator 'the principal in the first degree' and distinguished secondary parties into principals in the second degree—those who participated at the time when the felony was actually perpetrated—and accessories before the fact—those who participated at an earlier time. It was traditional to state that the distinction was that the principal in the second degree was *present* at the commission of the offence; but in fact he might be a considerable distance away—in a US case (*State v Hamilton and Lawrie*, 13 Nev 386 (1878)—signals from mountain top, 30–40 miles away), so long as he was assisting or available to assist, at the time. Hawkins, II PC, c 29, ss 7 and 8; Sir Michael Foster, *A Report on Crown Cases and Discourses on the Crown Law* (ed M Dodson, 3rd edn, 1792) 350. The abolition of felonies in the Criminal Law Act 1967 renders the distinction redundant.

[17] *Mackalley's Case* (1611) 9 Co Rep 61b; *Fitzgerald* [1992] Crim LR 660.

[18] *DPP for Northern Ireland v Maxwell* [1978] 3 All ER 1140; *Taylor* [1998] Crim LR 582.

[19] [1997] 1 Cr App R 1 and commentary [1996] Crim LR 722 for criticism. See also *Morton* [2004] Crim LR 73.

[20] See also *Montague* [2013] EWCA Crim 1781, [2014] Crim LR 615 and commentary.

[21] *Jogee* [2016] UKSC 8, [88].

[22] cf the observations made by Davis LJ in *Lewis* [2017] EWCA Crim 1734, [46].

[23] *Mercer* [2001] All ER (D) 187. Cf A Ashworth, 'A Decade of Human Rights in Criminal Justice' [2014] Crim LR 325, 327.

First, the accessory is only liable once the principal offence has been committed.[24] Secondary liability derives from the commission of the principal offence.[25] This derivative approach to secondary liability means that, with a murder for example, D may supply the weapon to P, who kills V, but it is not until that killing takes place that D can be liable as an accessory. This contrasts with inchoate liability where D who supplies the weapon is liable (depending on his mens rea) as soon as he performs his act of supply, irrespective of whether P goes on to kill V or, indeed, whether P does any further act.

Secondly, in some cases, it is only an offence to do something *to another* and not to assist someone to do it to themselves (eg injecting drugs). It is essential to establish if it is alleged that D helped P to perform the conduct on himself (no liability), or whether D performed it on P (potential liability).[26]

A third reason for distinguishing principals and accessories is that, even in offences of strict liability, accessories must always be proved to have mens rea.[27]

Fourthly, in some instances offences are defined in such a way that they can be committed, as a principal offender, only by someone who is a member of a particular group or who has a particular qualification (eg the 'driver' of a vehicle or the licensee of a pub).[28]

Fifthly, in some offences vicarious liability may be imposed for the act of another who is a principal offender or does the act of a principal offender; but there is no vicarious liability for the act of an accessory.[29]

Finally, in some exceptional cases the available sentencing differs significantly between principal and accessory.[30]

6.2.2 Secondary as distinct from inchoate liability

As noted, with inchoate offences D's liability crystallizes as soon as he has assisted or encouraged P or agreed with him to commit an offence irrespective of whether that leads to P committing or even attempting to commit the substantive offence.[31] Under ss 44 to 46 of the SCA 2007 there is an overlap with secondary liability. Where D does an act which is capable of encouraging or assisting, for example supplying a gun to P for him to murder V, D will be liable under ss 44 to 46 (see Ch 11), subject to mens rea, irrespective of whether the anticipated offence is committed or attempted by P. The offences in ss 44 to 46 are extremely wide-reaching. If P commits the murder, D can be charged as an accessory *or* under ss 44 to 46. There will

---

24 Committing the offence includes 'attempting' to commit the offence. If P, with D's aid, has attempted to murder V, D, as well as P, can be convicted of the offence of attempted murder.

25 See GP Fletcher, *Rethinking Criminal Law* (1978) Ch 8; KJM Smith, *A Modern Treatise on Complicity* (1991) Ch 4; D Lanham, 'Primary and Derivative Criminal Liability: An Australian Perspective' [2000] Crim LR 707; LC 300, paras 2.7 et seq. The law in application fails to remain true to this theory: Wilson describes English law as 'fudging' the theoretical basis: *Central Issues*, Ch 7. An alternative analysis sees the secondary as causally responsible for the principal's crime (see Smith, above, Ch 3; MS Moore, *Causation and Responsibility An Essay in Law, Morals and Metaphysics* (2009); J Gardner, *Offences and Defences: Selected Essays in the Philosophy of Criminal Law* (2007), Ch 4).

26 *Kennedy (No 2)* [2008] 1 AC 269; cf *Empress Car* [1999] 2 AC 22.   27 See p 212.   28 See p 198.

29 See p 283. There is no vicarious liability at common law, as confirmed in *R (Chief Constable of Northumbria) v Newcastle Magistrates' Court* [2010] EWHC 935 (Admin).

30 In road traffic offences, where disqualification of the principal is obligatory, disqualification of accessories is discretionary: Road Traffic Offenders Act 1988, s 34(5).

31 At common law D had no inchoate liability for assisting P to commit an offence which P did not subsequently commit or attempt to commit. The SCA 2007, ss 44–6, introduced such offences following the recommendation of the Law Commission in LC 300, *Inchoate Liability for Assisting and Encouraging Crime* (2006). See the discussion in Buxton, n 14.

often be little advantage in charging D as an accessory.[32] The procedure and sentence will be the same for the offence under the SCA 2007 as for the anticipated substantive offence.

There is an even more complex relationship between conspiracy and secondary liability. A conspiracy is complete as soon as A and B agree to commit an offence (say, murder) with the intention[33] that the offence should be committed. In contrast, there is no secondary liability for anyone unless and until the murder is committed. If B commits murder, A is liable as an accessory to murder by having agreed with B and thereby provided B with encouragement.[34] Liability as an accessory might also arise in this scenario if A assists or encourages B even without an agreement.[35] If B commits the offence, A and B can also still be charged with conspiracy to do so (see Ch 11). Finally, there is the issue of being an accessory to a conspiracy—for example, A intentionally assists D1 and D2 (eg providing D1 and D2 with facilities to meet) when they are making an agreement to murder V; A does not assist in the murder itself, but merely in setting up the agreement. If D1 commits murder as part of his conspiracy with D2, D2 is liable as an accessory (as well as for the conspiracy) because D2 has encouraged D1. Arguably, A has assisted D1 and D2 to commit the conduct element of conspiracy, but it cannot reasonably be said that A has done any act that has assisted or encouraged[36] D1 to *perpetrate the conduct element* of murder. It is submitted that A's act is not enough to render him an accessory to murder.

6.3 The principal offender

It is important to identify the principal offender.[37] Where there are several participants in a crime, the principal offender is the one whose act is the most immediate cause of the actus reus. In murder, for example, he is the person who, with mens rea, fires the gun or administers the poison which causes death; in theft, the person who, with mens rea, appropriates the property belonging to another which is stolen; in bigamy, the person who, knowing himself to be already married, goes through a second ceremony of marriage; and so on. With offences in which there is no result or consequence to be proved, the principal offender is perhaps more accurately the person who engages in the conduct element of the actus reus. In the case of statutory offences, whether a person is a principal offender will turn on whether he satisfies the precise form of words used to describe the conduct element of the offence.[38] One of the reasons why it is important to identify the principal is because he can be guilty if liability is strict as to one of the elements of the substantive offence, but this will not be the case with the secondary party. The Supreme

---

[32] Section 45 requires that D should believe that P *will* commit the conduct element of the actus reus of the principal offence.

[33] cf *Anderson* [1986] AC 27 which is surely wrong on this.

[34] Even in the unusual case where it is not A's intention that the murder be committed. See p 233.

[35] *Rook* [1993] 2 All ER 955, [1993] Crim LR 698 and commentary. Cf Stephen, *Digest* (9th edn) art 28; Williams, CLGP, 363; *Pinkerton v United States*, 328 US 640 (1946). See, however, D Lanham, 'Complicity, Concert and Conspiracy' (1980) 4 Crim LJ 276.

[36] Arguably there is no encouragement by A in this conduct. Some light may be shed on the meaning of that concept when the courts grapple more fully with the SCA 2007 provisions.

[37] Sometimes this is overlooked, as is evident from the judge's direction in *Bristow* [2013] EWCA Crim 1540. Even if P cannot be identified, it is crucial that the jury are directed to consider first whether there was a principal offender before going on to evaluate the other possible bases of liability.

[38] See eg *Corporation of London v Eurostar* [2004] EWHC 187 (Admin), where Eurostar were guilty as principals for 'landing' an Alsatian dog as prohibited under anti-rabies legislation.

Court confirmed in *Jogee* that to be guilty the secondary party must have knowledge of any facts or circumstances necessary for the principal's conduct to be criminal.[39] To take an example, the principal can be guilty of making an indecent image of a child even though he may not have known that the victim was under the age of 18. This is because liability as to the age of V is strict. To be guilty of being an accomplice to this offence, however, the secondary party must have known that the victim was under the age of 18. Failure to identify accurately who is the principal and who is the secondary party risks the latter being convicted even though he may not have possessed the requisite mens rea.

It is a fundamental principle that criminal liability arises from wrongdoing for which a person is himself responsible and not for the wrongdoing of others. If, by performing acts of assistance, an accessory were taken to have brought about the commission of the offence he would for all purposes become a principal offender. If D, having persuaded P to murder V, were taken to have caused V's death, that is, killed V, he would satisfy the definition of murder as a principal. Anyone whose assistance or encouragement in fact caused another to commit a crime would then be a principal. That is not the law. Accessorial liability is based on the assumption that the accessory does not cause the actus reus.[40] The distinction between principal and accessory is fundamental and the two should not be confused.[41] As Lord Kerr pointed out in *Gnango*: 'To speak of joint principal offenders being involved in a joint enterprise is, at least potentially, misleading. The essential ingredient for joint principal offending is a contribution to the cause of the *actus reus*.'[42]

The House of Lords in *Kennedy (No 2)*[43] reaffirmed these fundamental principles.[44] As Lord Bingham made clear, referring to Glanville Williams' article '*Finis* for *Novus Actus*', the doctrine of secondary liability was developed precisely because an informed voluntary choice was ordinarily regarded as a *novus actus interveniens* breaking the chain of causation:

Principals cause, accomplices encourage (or otherwise influence) or help. If the instigator were regarded as causing the result he would be a principal, and the conceptual division between principals (or, as I prefer to call them, perpetrators) and accessories would vanish. Indeed, it was because the instigator was not regarded as causing the crime that the notion of accessories had to be developed. This is the irrefragable argument for recognising the *novus actus* principle as one of the bases of our criminal law. The final act is done by the perpetrator, and his guilt pushes the accessories, conceptually speaking, into the background. Accessorial liability is, in the traditional theory, 'derivative' from that of the perpetrator.[45]

Despite these clear statements, the courts still occasionally refer to D as a 'cause' of P's act. In *Mendez and Thompson*,[46] Toulson LJ, after a scholarly analysis of the historical position, concluded that 'at its most basic level secondary liability is founded on a principle of causation, that a defendant (D) is liable for an offence committed by a principal actor (P) if by his conduct he has caused or materially contributed to the commission of the offence (with the requisite mental element); and a person who knowingly assists or encourages another to commit an offence is taken to have contributed to its commission'.[47] If 'cause' is read strictly,

---

[39] *Jogee* [2016] UKSC 8, [99].
[40] HLA Hart and T Honoré, *Causation in the Law* (2nd edn, 1985) 380; SH Kadish, *Blame and Punishment: Essays in the Criminal Law* (1987) 143–4.
[41] This passage in the 14th edn of this work was cited with approval by Spencer J in *R v Maughan and others* (CCC, 29 July 2016).
[42] [2011] UKSC 59, [129]. It is submitted that the reference to 'contributing to the cause of the actus reus' should be treated with caution.
[43] [2007] UKHL 38.   [44] See p 75.   [45] [2007] UKHL 38, [17].
[46] [2010] EWCA Crim 516, criticized by G Virgo [2010] 5 Arch Rev 4 and D Ormerod [2011] Crim LR 151.
[47] At [18], referring to *Foster's Crown Law* (republished 3rd edn, 1809) 369. Toulson LJ does add 'contributing to'.

this approach seems to run contrary to the fundamental principle reiterated in *Kennedy (No 2)* and does not reflect the practical reality that D might be liable for providing assistance to someone who had already made up his mind to commit the offence. There would be no causal contribution to the offence in such a case.[48] In *Stringer*,[49] Toulson LJ acknowledged that the accessory need not 'cause' the principal to commit the offence in the sense that 'but for' the defendant's conduct, the principal would not have committed the offence. His Lordship suggests instead that the accessory's conduct has to have some relevance to the commission of the principal offence; there had to be a 'connecting link'.[50] This is far less controversial:[51]

The way that the court put it in *Mendez and Thompson* was that D's conduct must (objectively) have constituted assistance or encouragement, even if P (subjectively) did not need assistance or encouragement. Whereas the provision of assistance need not involve communication between D and P, encouragement by its nature involves some form of transmission of the encouragement by words or conduct, whether directly or via an intermediary. An un-posted letter of encouragement would not be encouragement unless P chanced to discover it and read it. Similarly, it would be unreal to regard P as acting with the assistance or encouragement of D if the only encouragement took the form of words spoken by D out of P's earshot.[52]

Writing extrajudicially, Sir Roger Toulson elaborated as follows:

It is plainly right and just that there should have to be some 'connecting link'. It would be morally repugnant to find a person guilty of murder for behaving in a way which on a fair view was unconnected with the crime . . . This analysis involves a concept of causation which is appropriate to the context. I do not see an alternative foundation on which secondary liability can satisfactorily be said to rest.[53]

Whilst this may seem relatively uncontroversial, the spectre of further case law on causation and secondary liabilities arose because of the disagreement between Lords Clarke and Dyson and Lord Kerr in the case of *Gnango*.[54] In that infamous case[55] D was convicted of murder. He had voluntarily engaged in an exchange of gunfire with an opponent (P) in a public place. One of P's shots, aimed at D, killed a passer-by. P was not prosecuted, but would have been guilty of murder by the law of transferred malice. D was convicted of possessing a firearm with intent to endanger life, attempted murder and, by way of joint enterprise, the murder of the passer-by. Lord Dyson felt that it was not possible to uphold D's liability on the basis that D's act of shooting was a cause of the death. If P's act of shooting at D was a free, deliberate and informed act, it broke the chain of causation between D's shooting at P and P's shooting and killing V.[56] His lordship agreed with Lord Clarke that the court could not uphold the conviction on the basis that D caused P to fire the fatal shot. But Lord Clarke took the view that the mere fact that the immediate cause of the death was

[48] See, however, the argument advanced by Gardner, *Offences and Defences*, n 25.
[49] [2011] EWCA Crim 1396, [2011] Crim LR 886 and commentary.   [50] At [48].
[51] Virgo contends, however, that in order to conform with existing doctrine, the connection justification would need to be extended in an artificial fashion. See G Virgo, 'Joint Enterprise Liability is Dead: Long Live Accessorial Liability' [2012] Crim LR 850.
[52] See also *Jogee* [2016] UKSC 8, [12].
[53] R Toulson, 'Complicity in Murder' in DJ Baker and J Horder (eds), *The Sanctity of Life and the Criminal Law: The Legacy of Glanville Williams* (2012) 239.
[54] [2011] UKSC 59. For criticism, see GR Sullivan, 'Accessories and Principals after *Gnango*' in A Reed and M Bohlander (eds), *Participation in Crime: Domestic and Comparative Perspectives* (2013) and R Buxton, 'Being an Accessory to One's Own Murder' [2012] Crim LR 275.
[55] [2010] EWCA Crim 1691.   [56] [2011] UKSC 59, [106].

a criminal and deliberate act on the part of P does not as a matter of law break the chain of causation.[57] It might have been possible to hold D liable for murder on the basis of his shot at P, but that was not left to the jury.[58] Resurrecting the debate about secondary liability and causation would be undesirable after the House of Lords had so definitively and succinctly clarified the law in *Kennedy (No 2)*.[59] It is submitted that the statement from Lord Bingham quoted earlier should be faithfully followed.[60]

6.3.1 Innocent agency

The actus reus of a crime may be directly brought about by the conduct of someone who has no mens rea, or who has some defence,[61] for example infancy or insanity. Such a person is usually described as an 'innocent agent'.[62] The principal offender in such a case is the participant whose act is the most immediate[63] cause of the innocent agent's act. Examples are plentiful. If D sends to V through the post a letter-bomb which injures V when it explodes, the postman who delivers the letter being unaware of its contents is an innocent agent. If D, intending to kill V, provides to V's daughter a poison which he says will cure V's cold, and the daughter innocently (ie without knowing the true nature of the drug) administers the poison, causing V's death, then D is guilty of murder as the principal offender and the daughter is an innocent agent.[64] If in these examples the daughter or the postman had mens rea then he or she would, of course, be a principal offender. Where D, an employee, makes a false statement to his employer's accountant, knowing that the statement will be entered in the accounts, and the innocent accountant does enter it, D is guilty, as a principal offender, of falsifying his employer's accounts.[65] Where D induces a child, aged nine, to take money from a till and give it to D, D is a principal offender as the child is exempt from criminal liability. If the child is over ten and liable to conviction, then he is the principal offender if he has mens rea and D is an accessory.[66]

There are some crimes to which the doctrine of innocent agency is inapplicable because it is impossible to say that D has *personally* performed the conduct required by the definition of the actus reus.[67] Bigamy is a good example (except in the case of a marriage by proxy). Compare it with murder. If D causes an innocent person, say the postman E, to kill V by delivering a letter which E does not know contains a bomb, it is right for the law to take the view that *D has killed V*—the

[57] The only case his lordship relied upon was *Pagett* (1983) 76 Cr App R 279. In that case, however, PP were police officers acting in the execution of a duty and/or in self-defence, which is why it could be said that their acts were no longer voluntary and were caused by D in the strict sense of the term.

[58] [2011] UKSC 59, [91].   [59] [2007] UKHL 37.

[60] Lord Kerr in dissent in *Gnango* placed significant reliance upon Lord Bingham's *dicta* in *Kennedy (No 2)*. His lordship observed that even if it could be said that D's firing at P made it more likely that P would fire again, that is simply insufficient to demonstrate that D *caused* P to shoot.

[61] Other than duress: *Bourne* (1952) 36 Cr App R 125.

[62] See P Alldridge, 'The Doctrine of Innocent Agency' (1990) 2 Crim Law Forum 45; G Williams, 'Innocent Agency and Causation' (1992) 3 Crim Law Forum 289; RD Taylor, 'Complicity and Excuses' [1983] Crim LR 656.

[63] This description of relative proximity can be problematical. D1 passes poison to D2, who passes it to D3 who, unaware that it is poison, passes it to V who dies. D3 is the innocent agent. Is D2 the principal offender and D1 a secondary party? Are both D1 and D2 principal offenders? See Smith, *A Modern Treatise on Complicity*, 98. We are grateful to David Hughes for this example.

[64] *Anon* (1634) Kel 53; *Michael* (1840) 9 C & P 356.   [65] *Butt* (1884) 15 Cox CC 564.

[66] *Manley* (1844) 1 Cox CC 104 In *DPP v K & B* [1997] 1 Cr App R 36, it was said, *obiter*, that if D procured a child under ten to have sexual intercourse without consent, D could not be guilty of rape because there would be no actus reus. That seems wrong: see [1997] Crim LR 121, 122. See also *Mazeau* (1840) 9 C & P 676.

[67] cf *Woby v AJB and LCO* [1986] Crim LR 183 (boys under 18 not guilty of buying intoxicating liquor in licensed premises when they sent in an adult to buy it).

actus reus of murder. In contrast take the case of bigamy, if D knows that F is married, but induces E, an innocent person who has no knowledge of F's marital status, to marry F it is impossible to say that *D has married during the lifetime of his wife*—the actus reus of bigamy. He has not done so. The innocent agency doctrine seems equally inapplicable, it is submitted, in rape and other crimes involving sexual intercourse.[68] In *Varley* the Court of Appeal accepted that there is no 'closed list' of offences where innocent agency cannot be invoked. The court held that for innocent agency to be relied upon, the charge must not entail contradicting the statute defining the offence and the defendant must not lack some characteristic essential for liability as a principal.[69]

6.3.2 Joint principal offenders

There may be more than one person engaged in perpetrating the conduct element of the actus reus of the principal offence. So there may be two or more principal offenders in the same crime. If D1 and D2 make an attack on V intending to kill or cause him serious injury and the combined effect of their blows is to kill him, both are guilty of murder[70] as joint principal offenders. A different type of joint responsibility is where each of two or more parties does an act which is an element of, or part of, the actus reus of the principal offence.[71]

There is, however, no joint principalship if D induces another person, P (not an innocent agent), by persuasion or otherwise, to commit the offence: that does not amount to D causing the actus reus. P's voluntary intervening act 'breaks the chain of causation'[72] so that D is not a principal offender. P is the principal offender; D may be an accessory.[73]

What if the principal offender himself is not present at the moment of the completion of the crime? This can arise in the context of innocent agency. If D1 and D2 agree to employ an innocent agent, E, both D1 and D2 are liable as principal offenders for E's acts when they are committed and it is immaterial that E was instructed by the one in the absence of the other.[74] The innocent agent's acts are considered the acts of both D1 and D2.[75] Where there is no innocent agent, the same considerations cannot apply. D encourages or assists P, who leaves poison to be taken by V, or sets a trap into which V falls. D is liable as a secondary party; P as the principal offender.

6.3.3 Joint principals or principal and accessory?

The distinction between a joint principal offender and a secondary party is sometimes a fine one. There is a view that all who act together with a common purpose are principal offenders.[76] That would mean that if D provided assistance to P by providing a gun for him to murder V

68 There are *dicta* in *Cogan and Leak* [1976] QB 217, p 234, that rape may be committed through an innocent agent but these are contrary to principle. The Law Commission propose replacing the innocent agency doctrine with a specific offence; see p 244.
69 [2019] EWCA Crim 1074, [99].
70 *Macklin and Murphy's Case* (1838) 2 Lew CC 225.
71 *Bingley* (1821) Russ & Ry 446 (A and B each forged part of a banknote).
72 See *Kennedy (No 2)* [2007] UKHL 38.
73 Or liable under ss 44–6 of the SCA 2007 depending on his mens rea.
74 This qualifies the idea that generally the principal is the person who is the immediate cause of the conduct element of the actus reus.
75 *Bull and Schmidt* (1845) 1 Cox CC 281. Arguably D1 is liable as an accessory to D2 who causes E to act. This passage was cited with approval by the Court of Appeal in *Varley* [2019] EWCA Crim 1074, [88].
76 Such a rule has found favour at some times in some jurisdictions: see in Australia *Osland v R* (1998) 73 ALJR 173, HC of A. See further JC Smith, 'Joint Enterprise and Secondary Liability' (1999) 50 NILQ 153; cf A Simester, 'The Mental Element in Complicity' (2006) 122 LQR 578.

and P alone fired the shot, D might be liable as a principal for murder if he shared P's purpose to kill V, even though D did not perform the actus reus of murder. This is not the law in England.[77] As noted, under s 8 of the 1861 Act generally it is immaterial whether D is alleged to have participated in the crime as principal or accessory. Either way, he is equally responsible and liable to conviction. When it is necessary to distinguish, the test would seem to be: did D by his own act (as distinct from anything done by P with D's advice or assistance) contribute to the actus reus? If he did, he is a principal or joint principal offender. The distinction may be important where the jury acquit P and convict D. If D caused the actus reus by his own act, he is a principal offender and there is no problem. But, if he did not, there is a difficulty. If P is innocent, there is no crime which D can have aided or abetted. The difficulty can be overcome (a) if P can be regarded as an innocent agent, or (b) under a somewhat uncertain principle[78] that it is an offence for D to procure the commission of P's actus reus;[79] but it is surely wrong to overcome it by a fiction, a pretence that D 'did it', if he did not.

Where the actus reus is a 'state of affairs'[80]—for example, being in the UK illegally—the test for determining who is a principal offender is: ignoring D, does the statutory description of the state of affairs fit P?

6.4 The liability of secondary parties who assist or encourage crime

To be liable as a secondary party, a person who is not the principal offender must be proved to have aided, abetted, counselled[81] or procured, though it is quite sufficient to show that he did one of these things.[82]

An accessory is liable when and where the principal offence he has aided, abetted, counselled or procured is committed. So an employer, D, who sends P to drive a lorry, which D and P know to be in a dangerous condition, from Scotland to England may be held liable in England for a death caused by P in England because of the lorry's condition.[83]

6.4.1 Actus reus of the accessory

The actus reus and mens rea of the principal offender will be prescribed by the relevant statute or common law, so with murder it would be killing a human being with malice aforethought, etc; with assault it will be intentionally or recklessly causing a person to apprehend immediate unlawful personal violence, etc. If D is alleged to be an accessory to any crime, his liability as an accessory comprises the actus reus of aiding, abetting, counselling or procuring, with the relevant mens rea of an accessory (intention to assist, intention for P to have mens rea, knowledge of the relevant circumstances rendering P's act criminal). The conduct sufficient to satisfy the elements of being an accessory will often contrast starkly

---

[77] See, historically, Stephen's *Digest*, arts 37 and 38. In *Gnango* [2011] UKSC 59 the approach adopted by Lords Brown and Clarke comes close to suggesting that D can be the principal even though he has not caused the actus reus of the substantive offence. With respect, this is incorrect for the reasons given above. Cf GR Sullivan, 'Accessories and Principals after *Gnango*' in A Reed and M Bohlander (eds), *Participation in Crime: Domestic and Comparative Perspectives* (2013); R Buxton, 'Being an Accessory to One's Own Murder' [2012] Crim LR 275 and G Virgo, 'Joint Enterprise Liability is Dead: Long Live Accessorial Liability' [2012] Crim LR 850.

[78] See p 235.   [79] *Millward*, p 235.   [80] See p 43.

[81] 'Counselling' must not be taken literally. Mere incitement to commit an offence, not followed by its actual commission, is not 'counselling'—*Assistant Recorder of Kingston-upon-Hull, ex p Morgan* [1969] 2 QB 58.

[82] *Ferguson v Weaving* [1951] KB 814.

[83] *Robert Millar (Contractors) Ltd* [1970] 2 QB 54. See Law Commission proposals on jurisdiction: LC 305, Ch 6.

with the requirements of the principal offence. In a case of murder, D can be convicted as an accessory as a result of *conduct* that consists of no more than acting as a lookout whereas P must be shown to have killed V, but under s 8 of the 1861 Act both D and P will be convicted as murderers, labelled as such and punished as such.

It is important to remember that there is no secondary liability for a person whose participation in the relevant events does not involve him advising or encouraging P to commit the crime, and who does not assist P in the commission of it in any way. Accepting a lift on a motorbike known to have been taken without consent does not amount to aiding and abetting the use of the vehicle without insurance.[84] It would be different if D had participated in or assisted/encouraged the taking.[85] Liability as an accessory does not extend to cases where D has not assisted or encouraged in fact, but has merely attempted or conspired to do so.[86]

Once encouragement or assistance is proved to have been given by D, the Supreme Court in *Jogee*[87] stated that the prosecution does not have to prove that it had a positive effect on either P's conduct or the outcome. The court expressed concern that such a positive effect would, in many cases, be impossible to prove. The example given by the court is where there were many supporters encouraging P. The court stated that it would be difficult to prove that the encouragement of a single one made a difference. According to the court, that does not mean that D will be guilty if he counselled P to commit the offence many years before. The Supreme Court held that it is ultimately a question of fact and degree whether D's act of assistance or encouragement was so distanced in time, place or circumstances from the conduct of P that it would be unrealistic to regard P's offence as having been encouraged or assisted by it.

It is submitted that there is a risk that these comments will be taken out of context. If it is truly the case that there is no requirement for D's act of assistance or encouragement to have had a positive effect on P, then why does it matter whether D's conduct was committed a long time ago, or has faded to the point of mere background? It is respectfully submitted that the Supreme Court in *Jogee* may have overstated its position. As was discussed earlier, secondary liability is not based upon causation, so the Supreme Court was correct not to resurrect the misleading proposition that D's act of assistance or encouragement must have caused P to commit the offence in question. As Toulson LJ confirmed in *Stringer*, however, there must be some connecting link between D's act of assistance or encouragement and P's offence. In most cases, the presence of this connecting link will be self-evident. In more marginal cases, the sufficiency of the connecting link between D's act of assistance or encouragement and P's conduct will be a question of fact and degree, taking into consideration all the surrounding circumstances. It is disappointing that the Supreme Court in *Jogee* chose to 'fudge'[88] this issue and rely so much upon the jury to decide whether D made a sufficient contribution to be liable as an accessory to P's offence. The decision not to engage with this issue directly perhaps reveals a lack of clarity on the theoretical foundations underpinning secondary liability.

It is also necessary to bear in mind that in *Jogee* the Supreme Court abolished what had become known as the 'fundamental difference rule', which enabled D to avoid liability if the

---

84 *D (Infant) v Parsons* [1960] 1 WLR 797.

85 *Ross v Rivenall* [1959] 1 WLR 713. Cf the Theft Act 1968, s 12(1) and *Boldizsar v Knight* [1980] Crim LR 653, p 951.

86 *Kenning* [2008] EWCA Crim 1534. Liability might arise under the SCA 2007, ss 44–6 or for conspiracy.

87 [2016] UKSC 8, [12].   88 M Dyson, 'Letter to the Editor' [2016] Crim LR 638.

weapon P used to kill V was more dangerous than any weapon D contemplated he might use.[89] The Supreme Court did state, however, that 'it is possible for death to be caused by some overwhelming supervening act by the perpetrator which nobody in the defendant's shoes could have contemplated might happen and is of such a character as to relegate his acts to history'.[90] In such a case, the court stated that D will bear no responsibility for the death. The court's use of the concept of an 'overwhelming supervening act' has replaced the fundamental difference rule.[91] The trial judge is not required, however, to direct the jury in such terms in every case.[92] In *Ibrar*, for example, Hallett LJ concluded that on the facts of the case, P's use of a knife was not an 'overwhelming supervening act' that D could not have contemplated so as to require the judge to direct the jury more fully on the issue of fundamental departure.[93] The Supreme Court's reliance upon the concept suggests a degree of incoherence. The court holds that D's conduct need not have a causative impact on P's crime (causation not necessary to inculpate D) (see [12]), but when considering the exculpation, the court's use of the language of supervening event is that associated with a break in the chain of causation (causation is relevant to exculpation). The language of 'overwhelming supervening acts' echoes precisely that of causation and *novus actus interveniens*. We return to this discussion later.

6.4.1.1 Aid, abet, counsel, procure

In *A-G's Reference (No 1 of 1975)* Lord Widgery CJ said:

We approach s 8 of the 1861 Act on the basis that the words should be given their ordinary meaning, if possible. We approach the section on the basis also that if four words are employed here, 'aid, abet, counsel or procure', the probability is that there is a difference between each of those four words and the other three, because, if there were no such difference, then Parliament would be wasting time in using four words where two or three would do.[94]

The four words had previously been regarded as technical terms and it is clear that they cannot be given their ordinary meaning in all respects.[95]

In the modern law, secondary participation almost invariably consists of 'assisting' or 'encouraging' the commission of the crime. In *Jogee*, the Supreme Court held that the requisite conduct element is that D has encouraged or assisted the commission of the offence by P.[96] As this section will discuss, the terms used in s 8 have historically been interpreted to mean subtly different things.

The only possible exception to the use of the terms 'assisting' or 'encouraging' may be the procurer who succeeds in causing the principal to commit the crime (as in the *A-G's Reference*) without doing anything which could be fairly described as encouragement or

---

[89] *Powell and Daniels, English* [1999] 1 AC 1, 30. Historically, the doctrine also applied if the principal committed the murder in a manner not contemplated by the secondary party. The secondary party's knowledge that the principal was in possession of a weapon is now relevant to the jury's assessment of whether he possessed the requisite intent. See p 220.

[90] *Jogee* [2016] UKSC 8, [97]. The Supreme Court cited *Anderson and Morris* [1966] 2 QB 110; *Wesley* [1963] 1 WLR 1200.

[91] cf M Dyson, 'Shorn-Off Complicity' (2016) 75 CLJ 196.   [92] *Tas* [2018] EWCA Crim 2603.

[93] [2017] EWCA Crim 1841.   [94] [1975] 2 All ER 684 at 686.

[95] Under the old law of felonies, 'aiding and abetting' was used to describe the activity of the principal 'in the second degree' and 'counselling and procuring' that of the accessory before the fact: *Ferguson v Weaving*, n 82, at 818–19; Stephen, *Digest* (4th edn) arts 37–9; *Bowker v Premier Drug Co Ltd* [1928] 1 KB 217 ('aid and abet' implies presence). Aid and abet was, however, sometimes used in relation to acts committed before the actual perpetration of the crime.

[96] [2016] UKSC 8, [8].

assistance. Assisting or encouraging can be by practically any means—supply of weapons, tools, information, support, keeping watch, filming an attack on a mobile phone, etc. It is generally irrelevant whether the accessory is present or absent or whether his assistance or encouragement was given before or at the time of the commission of the offence.

All four words—aid, abet, counsel, procure—may be used together to charge a person, D, who is alleged to have participated in an offence otherwise than as a principal offender.[97] As long as the evidence establishes that D's conduct satisfied one of the words, that is enough to prove his actus reus as an accessory. However, where the indictment uses only one term—for example, 'procures'—it is necessary to prove that D's conduct fits that term.

Each element of the actus reus of the accessory deserves further brief examination to consider three particular issues: (a) what forms of conduct constitute aiding, abetting, counselling or procuring; (b) whether there need be a causal link between the aiding, etc and the principal offence; and (c) whether there need be a meeting of minds or consensus between the aider, etc and the principal offender.

In short, the law is almost certainly that:

(1) 'aiding' requires actual assistance but neither consensus nor causation;[98]

(2) 'abetting' and 'counselling' imply consensus but not causation;

(3) 'procuring' implies causation but not consensus.

Aiding

It has sometimes been said[99] that 'aid and abet' is a single concept, 'aid' denoting the actus reus and 'abet', the mens rea. The natural meaning of s 8 is, however, that stated in the *A-G's Reference*. Moreover, the words aid and abet do connote different kinds of activity. The natural meaning of to 'aid' is to 'give help, support or assistance to'.[100] The courts have taken a broad view of what suffices for 'aid'. Although historically the term was commonly used to describe someone present assisting the principal at the time of the offence, there is now no such restriction.

Aiding can be satisfied by any act of assistance before or at the time of the offence.[101] Supplying a weapon or transporting P to the scene of the crime[102] are obvious examples.

Aiding does not imply any causal connection between D's act and P's. D may assist P and enable him to commit the offence more easily, earlier or with greater safety and, if so, D is surely guilty even if P would have committed the same offence if D had not intervened.[103] In *Bryce*,[104] however, the court seemed to imply a causal requirement. D was convicted of murder as an accessory. In the course of a drug dealers' dispute D assisted P, who was acting on the orders of the gang leader B. D transported P and a gun to a caravan near V's home. More than 12 hours later, P, acting alone, shot V. D's ground of appeal was that the delay meant that what

---

[97] *Re Smith* (1858) 3 H & N 227; *Ferguson v Weaving* [1951] KB 814.

[98] cf Stephen, *Digest* (4th edn) who argued that D who abets or counsels or commands (as well as procures) is liable and, by implication liable only, for an offence 'which is committed *in consequence* of such counselling, procuring, or commandment'.

[99] *Lynch v DPP for Northern Ireland* [1975] 1 All ER 913 at 941 per Lord Simon quoting the 3rd edn of this book and Devlin J in *National Coal Board v Gamble* [1959] 1 QB 11 at 20.

[100] *Oxford English Dictionary*.   [101] *Coney* (1882) 8 QBD 534.

[102] See eg *Nedrick-Smith* [2006] EWHC 3015 (Admin) where D3 was a party to D2 and D1 attacking V in her home. D3 drove them and stood watching as they attacked. The magistrates were entitled to find her guilty as an accessory.

[103] See WR Le Fave and AW Scott, *Criminal Law* (1986) 504. See also *Luffman* [2008] EWCA Crim 1739, n 117. Cf *Mendez*, n 46.

[104] [2004] EWCA Crim 1231. D would be liable for an offence under s 45 or 46 of the SCA 2007.

D did (transporting P) was too remote in time and place to the killing to constitute assistance, particularly since at that stage P had not formed the intention to kill. The Court of Appeal, after a comprehensive survey of the case law, upheld D's conviction concluding that no intervening event occurred hindering the plan, this despite the fact that in the 12-hour delay P's gun barrel was shortened and B visited P to encourage him. The court concluded that there was no 'overwhelming supervening event' sufficient to break the chain of causation, nor had D effected a withdrawal in that time. That implies a causal requirement. More explicit statements to this effect were made in *Mendez*[105] discussed earlier. In the light of the explanation given in *Stringer*,[106] and the powerful statement of Lord Bingham for a unanimous House of Lords in *Kennedy (No 2)*, it is submitted that despite these *dicta*, it remains the case that there is no need for D's acts to have caused the commission of the actus reus of the principal offence. This is supported by the statements of the Supreme Court in *Jogee*.[107] Although there must be some link between D and P in the sense that D must have provided assistance or encouragement in fact, that is a far cry from establishing causation.[108]

Nor does aiding imply any consensus between D and P. If D sees P committing a crime and comes to his assistance by, for example, restraining the policeman who would have prevented P from committing the crime, D is surely guilty even though his assistance is unforeseen and unwanted by P and unknown to him. The same might apply to aid given beforehand. D, knowing that P is going to meet a blackmailer, V, slips a gun into P's pocket in the hope that he will kill V—which P does.[109]

Abetting

The natural meaning of 'abet' is 'to incite, instigate or encourage'.[110] Abetting is usually defined in terms of encouragement. There is little to distinguish abetting from counselling;[111] perhaps there is no difference except that historically 'abet' was used to refer to encouragement at the time of the offence and 'counsel' to encouragement at an earlier time.[112] It is clear that either type of activity is sufficient to found liability as an accessory.

The natural meaning of 'abet' does not imply any causal element, because the word (like counselling[113]) does not even imply that the offence has been committed.[114] As a matter of law, however, the principal offence must have been committed before anyone can be convicted as an abettor or counsellor of it.[115] But, even when the principal offence has been committed, it is true to say that D 'abetted' or 'counselled' it, in the ordinary meaning of the words, even if his encouragement or counsel was ignored by P. Abetting and counselling may be treated alike on causation and, although historically there was scholarly opinion to the contrary,[116] the courts have unequivocally confirmed that there need not be any causal link

---

[105] [2010] EWCA Crim 516.   [106] See p 186.   [107] At [12].

[108] Virgo suggests that 'association' might provide the link. See G Virgo, 'Joint Enterprise Liability is Dead: Long Live Accessorial Liability' [2012] Crim LR 850.

[109] D would on those facts be liable under s 44 of the SCA 2007. The passage in the text was quoted with approval by the Court of Appeal in *Fury* [2006] EWCA Crim 1258.

[110] *Oxford English Dictionary*.

[111] Lord Widgery's analysis of the four terms leaves considerable confusion. His lordship suggests that 'abet' and 'counsel' do imply different forms of activity.

[112] *DPP v Maxwell* [1978] 3 All ER 1140 at 1158 per Lord Lowry CJ.

[113] See eg *Wilcox v Jeffery* [1951] 1 All ER 464; p 201; *Du Cros v Lambourne* [1907] KB 40.

[114] As a matter of ordinary language one would say that D had instigated, incited, encouraged, counselled, P even though P did not then commit the principal offence.

[115] Liability under the SCA 2007, Part 2 will arise if the anticipated offence does not occur. See p 493.

[116] Stephen argued that if D is charged with abetting or counselling, his acts must have caused P to commit the offence. Stephen, *Digest* (4th edn) art 39. On his view, D who abets or counsels or commands (as well as procures) P is liable only for an offence by P 'which is committed *in consequence* of such counselling, procuring, or commandment'.

between D's encouragement and P's commission of the offence in a case alleging counselling: *Luffman*.[117] The Supreme Court adopted the same approach in *Jogee*.[118]

Where the prosecution relies on counselling as the basis for D's secondary liability it must, however, establish that the commission of the offence was within the scope of the principal's authority.[119] Requiring proof of causation in abetting or counselling cases would present problems. To require that before D could be liable as an accessory his abetting/counselling must have caused P to commit the principal offence could, if causation is interpreted strictly, be to insist that, but for D's abetting/counselling, P's offence would not have been committed.[120] This would confine abetting and counselling much too narrowly. Moreover, D would then not be liable if, when he encouraged P, he knew that P had already made up his mind to commit the offence.[121] That is not to deny that D must have counselled in fact:[122] proffered advice or encouragement which has no effect on the mind of P is not counselling.[123]

As for consensus, there must be some connection between D's abetting (or counselling) and the commission of the principal offence. It is probably not necessary to prove that P was influenced in any way by D, but P must at least be aware that he has the authority, or the encouragement or the approval, of D to do the relevant acts.

For example, if the principal offender happened to be involved in a football riot in the course of which he laid about him with a weapon of some sort and killed someone who, unknown to him, was the person whom he had been counselled to kill, he would not, in our view, have been acting within the scope of his authority; he would have been acting outside it, albeit what he had done was what he had been counselled to do.[124]

It was suggested in *A-G's Reference (No 1 of 1975)* that in the case of abetting and counselling the concepts might require a meeting of minds of secondary party and principal. If counselling and abetting must be, in some degree, operative, as suggested previously, this is clearly right.[125]

Counselling

To 'counsel' means to advise or solicit or encourage. The relevance of causation and consensus has been examined in the discussion of abetting in the previous section.

Procuring

'To procure means to produce by endeavour.'[126] 'You cannot procure an offence unless there is a causal link between what you do and the commission of the offence.'[127] In *A-G's*

---

[117] [2008] EWCA Crim 1752. See also the explanation by Toulson LJ in *Stringer* [2011] EWCA Crim 1396 (p 186).

[118] At [12].

[119] *Calhaem* [1985] QB 808.

[120] '... it does not make any difference that the person [*sc*, the person counselled] would have tried to commit suicide anyway': *A-G v Able* [1984] 1 All ER 277 at 288 per Woolf J.

[121] *Giannetto* [1997] 1 Cr App R 1. Trial judge's example: 'I am going to kill your wife'; husband: 'Oh goody.'

[122] But, it is clearly the law that an attempt to counsel does not amount to counselling. Liability for D's acts capable of encouraging P arises under ss 44–6 of the SCA 2007, and this includes attempts by D to encourage P which fail to do so.

[123] *Clarkson* [1971] 1 WLR 1402, C-MAC.

[124] *Calhaem* [1985] QB 808 per Parker LJ; *Schriek* [1997] 2 NZLR 139, 149. Cf the view taken in W Wilson, *Criminal Law: Doctrine and Theory* (3rd edn, 2008).

[125] Consider the case of D, a persistent troublemaker, who comes across P and V in the middle of an argument. D urges P to punch V. Just before doing so, P tells D to 'mind your own business'. See LC 305, Appendix B, para B.63.

[126] *A-G's Reference (No 1 of 1975)* [1975] 2 All ER 684 at 686; *Reed* [1982] Crim LR 819. See KJM Smith, 'Complicity and Causation' [1986] Crim LR 663; H Beynon, 'Causation, Omissions and Complicity' [1987] Crim LR 539.

[127] *A-G's Reference*, ibid, 687.

Reference, D added alcohol to P's drink without P's knowledge or consent. P drove home and thereby committed a strict liability offence of driving with a blood/alcohol concentration above the prescribed limit.[128] D was held to have procured that offence by P if it was proved that D knew that P was going to drive and that the ordinary and natural result of the added alcohol would be to bring P's blood/alcohol concentration above the prescribed limit. D had caused the actus reus (circumstance element) of the offence by putting P over the limit. This is in accordance with the natural meaning of 'procure'.[129] It is different if the driver is aware of the 'lacing'. In that situation P has, by his free, informed act of choosing to imbibe the laced drink, caused the actus reus (circumstance element) of the offence.[130] D might then be convicted as an accessory to P's offence of drink-driving on the basis that, although D has not procured its commission, he has certainly assisted its commission.[131]

What must be proved by way of a causal link in procuring? Glanville Williams cast doubt on the language of the court in *A-G's Reference*.[132] Williams relied on the facts of the famous case of *Beatty v Gillbanks*[133] to suggest that causation and procuring are not synonymous. In *Beatty*, Salvation Army members held a lawful meeting in Weston-super-Mare even though the members knew from experience that this would cause a hostile organization, 'the Skeleton Army', to attack them. The Salvation Army members clearly anticipated that the Skeleton Army would attack them and that the attack would result in damage to others, for example broken shop windows. Williams regarded it as absurd to say that the Salvationists were liable as accessories for the attack on themselves.

There are three responses to Williams' criticism: (a) Lord Widgery did not say that 'procure' means merely 'cause'. He said 'To procure means to produce by endeavour.' The Salvationists may have caused the Skeletons to make the attack (and to break the supposed windows) but these were certainly not results that they were 'endeavouring' to produce. Against this, it might be said that in *A-G's Reference*, D's awareness that he was causing the commission of the offence also fell short of proof of an endeavour to cause it; and, in *Blakely*,[134] the court thought *obiter* that D 'procured' a result if he contemplated it as a possible result of his act—which is far removed from endeavouring to produce it. (b) The Skeletons knew exactly what they were doing and in *A-G's Reference* Lord Widgery made it clear that the decision would not necessarily be the same where a driver knew that his drink was laced. The unaware driver 'in most instances . . . would have no means of preventing the offence from being committed', whereas the aware driver would. Lord Widgery thus contemplated that the act of the aware driver might break the chain of causation even for the purposes of secondary liability, but it is unclear whether his lordship meant that there would be no secondary liability. (c) The Supreme Court in *Gnango*[135] accepted that D could be liable as an accessory to a crime on himself where he encouraged P in the commission of that crime. That extension, making D liable as a secondary party to crimes on himself, would seem to apply at least if the Salvationists and the Skeletons 'formed a mutual plan or agreement to have a fight'. If this approach were held to apply generally, it would mean that in the context of a street brawl, P would be liable for inflicting GBH on D and D would be liable as an accessory to his own GBH provided he were taken to have encouraged P to hit him, which would be possible even if P threw the first punch. The Supreme Court

---

[128] Road Traffic Act 1972, s 6(1), now replaced by Road Traffic Act 1988, s 5.

[129] cf P Glazebrook, 'Attempting to Procure' [1959] Crim LR 774.

[130] See *Kennedy (No 2)* [2007] UKHL 38.

[131] LC 300, para 5.25.

[132] 'in so far as [it] purports to decide that merely causing an offence can be said to be a procuring of it, it should be regarded as too incautious a generalisation'.

[133] (1882) 9 QBD 308; TBCL, 339.   [134] See p 213.   [135] [2011] UKSC 59.

recognized that this could lead to incongruous results and advised restraint on the part of prosecuting authorities.[136] Liability is, of course, subject to D having the requisite mens rea.

If D procures X, an innocent agent, to commit an offence D is taken to have caused the actus reus for all purposes.[137] If D procures P, a guilty agent, to commit the offence, to be liable as an accessory D must be proved to have in fact 'produced by endeavour' the act of P; but, in law, D is not regarded as having caused the actus reus.

In *A-G's Reference (No 1 of 1975)*, D's act of procuring was done without the knowledge or consent, and perhaps against the will, of P. The impact of *Jogee* on procuring is unclear. As discussed later, D must intend P to have the mens rea for the offence. In cases such as this, D did not have that intent. Whether procuring will be treated as an exception to *Jogee* remains to be seen.

6.4.1.2 The timing of the accessory's assistance/encouragement

Assistance given by D before P even starts to commit the principal offence may be sufficient to found D's liability as an accessory if P then completes the offence. What is more important is to ascertain whether D has assisted or encouraged P before P has *concluded* the offence. Assistance given when P is no longer in the course of the commission of the offence—for example, help to enable P to escape or to reap the benefits of the commission of the offence—does not make D an accessory. Where P broke into a warehouse, stole butter and deposited it in the street 30 yards from the warehouse door, D who then came to assist in carrying it off was held not guilty of abetting P's theft.[138] Assistance given by D to a murderer, after his victim is dead or to a rapist after the act of penetration has concluded, does not render D an accessory.[139] D who, without any pre-arranged plan, joins P in an attack on V after V has received a fatal injury, is not guilty as a principal or accessory of homicide (though he may be guilty of an attempt) if his action in no way contributes to V's subsequent death.[140] If D1 and D2 carry out an armed robbery, and D3 drives past the bank as D1 and D2 flee from the scene of the crime with the proceeds, is D3 a party to the robbery if he allows D1 and D2 to get in the car to make good their escape?[141]

6.4.1.3 Omission as a sufficient actus reus of secondary liability?

As discussed in Ch 2, the law does not generally impose criminal liability for a failure to act. In the context of secondary liability, the question that arises is whether D's omission to prevent P committing the crime is sufficient to make D an accessory. Two categories of case need to be distinguished.

First, there are the established categories in which the law imposes a *duty* on an individual to act. Thus, a husband who stands by and watches his wife drown their children is guilty as an accessory to the homicide, subject to his having the requisite mens rea.[142]

---

[136] For criticism, see R Buxton, 'Being an Accessory to One's Own Murder' [2012] Crim LR 275, 280. For similar criticism, see GR Sullivan, 'Accessories and Principals after *Gnango*' in A Reed and M Bohlander (eds), *Participation in Crime: Domestic and Comparative Perspectives* (2013).

[137] The driver whose drink, unknown to him, is 'laced' is not an innocent agent because the offence he is guilty of is a strict liability offence.

[138] *King* (1817) Russ & Ry 332; see also *Kelly* (1820) Russ & Ry 421.

[139] The act is a continuing one: Sexual Offences Act 2003, s 79.

[140] *S v Thomo* 1969 (1) SA 385 (AD); EM Burchell and PMA Hunt, *South African Criminal Law and Procedure* (1970) 352. Some fine distinctions have begun to be drawn. In *Grundy* (1989) 89 Cr App R 333, it was held that if D struck a blow to V after P had caused grievous bodily harm, D might still be liable for assisting grievous bodily harm. In *Percival* [2003] EWCA Crim 1561, D who punched V after P had wounded V could not be liable as an aider and abettor to wounding.

[141] See also *Self* [1992] Crim LR 574 and commentary.   [142] *Russell* [1933] VLR 59.

Secondly, the law extends liability even wider: where D has a *power or right to control* the actions of P and he deliberately refrains from exercising that control, his inactivity *may* be a positive encouragement to P to perform an illegal act and, therefore, an aiding and abetting by D subject to D's mens rea. So, for example, if a licensee of a pub stands by and watches his customers drinking after hours, he is guilty of aiding and abetting them in doing so.[143] In *Du Cros v Lambourne*,[144] it was proved that D's car had been driven at a dangerous speed but it was not proved whether D or E was driving. It was held, nevertheless, that D could be convicted. If E was driving she was doing so in D's presence, with his consent and approval; for he was in control and could and ought to have prevented her from driving in a dangerous manner. D was equally liable whether he was a principal or an accessory.[145] The result would presumably have been different if it had been E's own car, for D would then have had no right of control, and could only have been convicted if proved to have actively encouraged E to drive at such speed.

In *Webster*,[146] the Court of Appeal approved *Du Cros v Lambourne*, holding that 'a defendant might be convicted of aiding and abetting dangerous driving if the driver drives dangerously in the owner's presence *and with the owner's consent and approval*'.[147] *Webster* emphasizes that it must be proved that D knew of those features of P's driving which rendered it dangerous and failed to take action within a reasonable time.[148] The court in *Webster* recognized the:

need to establish not only knowledge of the dangerous driving but knowledge at a time when there was an opportunity to intervene. . . . We conclude that the prosecution had to prove that [D] knew that [P] was, by virtue of the speed the vehicle was travelling, driving dangerously at a time when there was an opportunity to intervene. It was [D's] failure to take that opportunity and, exercise his right as owner of the vehicle, which would lead to the inference that he was associating himself with the dangerous driving.

In *Baldessare*,[149] P and D unlawfully took X's car and P drove it recklessly and caused V's death. It was held that D was guilty of manslaughter as an accessory. In this case (as prosecuting counsel put it):

The common purpose to drive recklessly was . . . shown by the fact that both men were driving in a car which did not belong to them and the jury were entitled to infer that the driver was the agent of the passenger. It matters not whose hand was actually controlling the car at the time.

In *Martin*,[150] D was convicted as an accessory to P's offence of causing death by dangerous driving. P was a learner driver and D was supervising him. P lost control of the vehicle on a bend and crashed, killing himself and a passenger.[151] Unlike *Baldessare*, there was no evidence that D had shared a common purpose with P to drive in this manner. The Court of Appeal, having considered *Webster*, tentatively proffered a direction that ought to have

---

143 *Tuck v Robson* [1970] 1 WLR 741. The principal offence is committed by the drinkers, not the licensee.

144 [1907] 1 KB 40; cf also *Rubie v Faulkner* [1940] 1 KB 571; *Harris* [1964] Crim LR 54. See D Lanham, 'Drivers, Control and Accomplices' [1982] Crim LR 419; M Wasik, 'A Learner's Careless Driving' [1982] Crim LR 411.

145 cf *Swindall and Osborne* (1846) 2 Car & Kir 230: *Salmon* (1880) 6 QBD 79; *Iremonger v Wynne* [1957] Crim LR 624; Williams, CLGP, 137 fn 23.

146 [2006] EWCA Crim 415.

147 The court quashed the conviction in that case on the ground that the trial judge had not directed the jury that they had to consider whether there was an opportunity for Webster to intervene.

148 *Dennis v Pight* (1968) 11 FLR 458 at 463.   149 (1930) 22 Cr App R 70.

150 [2010] EWCA Crim 1450.

151 The conviction for being an accessory to P causing his own death by dangerous driving was quashed as there is no such offence: it is an offence to cause the death of another by driving.

been given. D would be liable if: (a) P committed the offence; (b) D knew that P was driving in a manner which D knew fell far below the standard of a competent and careful driver [whether it is necessary for D to have knowledge is debatable]; (c) knowing that he had an opportunity to stop P from driving in that manner, D deliberately did not take that opportunity; and (d) by not taking that opportunity D intended to assist or encourage P to drive in this manner and D did in fact by his presence and failure to intervene encourage P to drive dangerously.[152]

Whichever category of exception (duty or control) is relied on to prove the actus reus by omission, it is not necessary that the inactive accessory be present at the commission of the offence. For example, a company and its directors may be convicted as accessories to the false making of tachograph records by the company's drivers if they knew that their inactivity was encouraging the practice on the roads miles away.[153]

6.4.1.4 Mere presence at the crime as a sufficient basis for secondary liability?

Can D's mere voluntary presence at P's commission of the principal offence, without anything more, satisfy the actus reus of secondary liability? If there is some conduct on the part of D which goes beyond 'mere' presence, then the principles already discussed will apply. The question will be whether D assisted or encouraged P by his actions or by his failure to act when under a duty/power to control. Where the case involves D's *mere* presence, several issues will commonly call for consideration including: whether D attended the location knowing an offence is being or is about to be committed; the effect that D's presence has on P; and D's state of mind when present.

Mere presence at the scene of a crime is *capable* of constituting encouragement or assistance, but D is not necessarily guilty as an accessory merely because he is present and does nothing to prevent P's crime.[154] In some cases, D's presence will constitute encouragement or assistance because he is present in pursuance of an agreement that the crime be committed. In other cases, D's presence may be sufficient even though there was no prior agreement,[155] and no positive act,[156] provided that by his presence D intentionally provides assistance or encouragement to the principal.[157] In *Jogee*, the Supreme Court observed that both association and presence are likely to be very relevant evidence on the question of whether assistance or encouragement was provided. The Supreme Court did confirm, however, that neither association nor presence is necessarily proof of assistance or encouragement; it depends on the facts.[158]

There are numerous examples of these principles in operation. D who stands outside a building while his friends commit a burglary inside cannot be convicted of burglary without

---

[152] At [32] per Hooper LJ. A further possible element advanced by the court is not necessary (relating to D's foresight of death). See n 165 for discussion of the question whether liability might arise for D by reason of his participation in dangerous driving by P earlier in the journey, coupled with D's foresight that P might commit the offence of causing death by dangerous driving.

[153] *JF Alford Transport Ltd* [1997] 2 Cr App R 326, citing the 8th edn of this book, at p 334. See also *Gaunt* [2003] EWCA Crim 3925, where D, the manager, failed to control P (employees) in racial harassment of V (employee).

[154] *Atkinson* (1869) 11 Cox CC 330; but it is an offence to refuse to assist a constable to suppress a breach of the peace when called upon to do so: *Brown* (1841) Car & M 314. See Ch 7.

[155] *Rannath Mohan v R* [1967] 2 AC 187.

[156] *Wilcox v Jeffery* [1951] 1 All ER 464.

[157] It is insufficient to prove that D arrived even only 30 seconds after P has finished attacking V if there is no evidence of D encouraging P: *Rose* [2004] EWCA Crim 764.

[158] *Jogee* [2016] UKSC 8, [11].

proof that he was assisting or encouraging by, for example, acting as lookout.[159] Similarly, for D to continue to sit beside the driver of a car, P, until the end of a journey after learning that P is uninsured does not amount to abetting P's uninsured driving.[160] If D continues to share a room with a person known to be in unlawful possession of drugs, D is not an accessory unless encouragement or control is proved.[161] If prohibited drugs, found in a van belonging to a party of tourists, are the property of and under the exclusive control of one of them, the others are not guilty as accessories simply because they are present and know of the existence of the drugs.[162]

Both assistance or encouragement in fact *and* an intention to assist or encourage must be proved.[163] When these are proved, it is immaterial that D joined in the offence without any prior agreement.[164] The same principle applies in the case of omissions as in that of positive acts, and it has been held that where two drivers, without any previous arrangement between them, enter into competitive driving on the highway so as knowingly to encourage each other to drive at a dangerous speed or in a dangerous manner, the one is liable as a secondary party for a death or other criminal result caused by the other.[165]

Intention alone without encouragement or assistance in fact is insufficient. In *Allan*,[166] it was held that D who remains present at an affray, nursing a secret intention to help P if the need arises but doing nothing to evince that intention, does not thereby become an accessory. This was reiterated by the Privy Council in *Robinson*:[167]

The commission of most criminal offences, and certainly most offences of violence, could be assisted by the forbidding presence of another as back-up and support. If D's presence could properly be held to amount to communicating to P (whether expressly or by implication) that he was there to help in any way he could if the opportunity or need arose, that was perfectly capable of amounting to aiding. . . . It is important to make clear to juries that mere approval of (ie 'assent' to, or 'concurrence' in) the offence by a bystander who gives no assistance, does not without more amount to aiding.[168]

If some positive act of assistance or encouragement is voluntarily performed by D, with knowledge of the circumstances constituting the offence, it is irrelevant that it is not done with the motive or purpose of encouraging the crime.[169] Nevertheless, the onus on the Crown to prove D's intent can be a heavy one where liability is based solely on D's presence at the scene.[170]

---

159 *S v DPP* [2003] EWHC 2717 (Admin); *L v CPS* [2013] EWHC 4127 (Admin). See also *Rose* [2004] EWCA Crim 764 where D's only actions at the scene were to discourage P from his attack on V. Cf *Ellis* [2008] EWCA Crim 886.

160 *Smith v Baker* [1971] RTR 350.

161 *Bland* [1988] Crim LR 41; see also *Kousar* [2009] EWCA Crim 139.

162 *Searle* [1971] Crim LR 592 and commentary; see also *Montague* [2013] EWCA Crim 1781, [2014] Crim LR 615 and commentary.

163 *Clarkson* [1971] 1 WLR 1402; *Jones and Mirrless* (1977) 65 Cr App R 250.

164 *Rannath Mohan v R* [1967] 2 AC 187.

165 *Turner* [1991] Crim LR 57 and commentary. (Williams, TBCL, 360, thinks otherwise, citing *Mastin* (1834) 6 C & P 396.) If one of two racing drivers is killed, the other may be convicted of causing death by dangerous driving; and it is immaterial whether his act or that of the deceased was the immediate cause of death: *Kimsey* [1996] Crim LR 35; *Lee* [2006] EWCA Crim 240. See also *Martin* [2010] EWCA Crim 1450, n 150.

166 [1965] 1 QB 130; see also *Tansley v Painter* (1968) 112 Sol Jo 1005; *Danquah* [2004] EWCA Crim 1248 (presence alone insufficient to show that Ds formed part of the gang that robbed V when no evidence of contribution to the intimidation or threats).

167 [2011] UKPC 3.

168 At [14] per Sir Anthony Hughes. This passage was cited with approval by the Court of Appeal in *Robinson* [2014] EWCA Crim 2385, [15].

169 *National Coal Board v Gamble* [1959] 1 QB 11; see p 204.   170 eg *Miah* [2004] EWCA Crim 63.

That was reiterated more recently in N[171] where it was unclear whether D was one of the individuals who got out of a car and repeatedly stabbed V or one of those who remained in the car. If he was not the attacker but merely one of those present in the car, knowledge that there was going to be an attack was not sufficient to render him liable. He would have to intend to encourage by his presence in the car. The Court of Appeal described this in terms of an intent 'by his presence to help or encourage the others to commit the crime by either giving moral support to another or by contributing simply to the force of numbers involved'. The concept of 'contributing by force of numbers' was founded on passages in *Jogee*[172] where the Supreme Court made clear that the act of assisting or encouraging 'may take many forms' and 'may include providing support by contributing to the force of numbers in a hostile confrontation'. What the Court of Appeal was at pains to point out is that although the contribution by force of numbers may satisfy the actus reus necessary to make D an accessory, D must also have the intention to encourage or assist P by that presence.

This issue has troubled the courts since at least the case of *Coney*.[173] There it was held that proof of D's mere voluntary presence at a prize-fight (illegal boxing match), without more, was, at the most, only prima facie and not conclusive evidence of abetting the offence of which the contestants were guilty. Presence at such an event is certainly capable of amounting to an actual encouragement. As has already been explained, this point was made by the Supreme Court in *Jogee*. If there were no spectators there would be no fight and, therefore, each spectator, by his presence, contributes to the incentive to the contestants. In the words of the Supreme Court, 'most people are bolder when supported or fortified by others than they are when they are alone'.[174] Voluntary presence at such an event is some evidence on which a jury might find that D was there with the intention of encouraging P's fight. Coney's conviction was quashed because the majority of the court thought that the judge's direction was capable of being understood to mean that voluntary presence was *conclusive* evidence of an intention to encourage. If the direction had made it clear that presence was only prima facie evidence, no doubt the conviction would have been sustained.

In *Wilcox v Jeffrey*,[175] D was found to be an accessory by his presence at a public jazz performance by P. P was the celebrated American saxophonist Coleman Hawkins, who had been given permission to enter the UK only on condition that he would take no employment. D's presence at P's performance was a sufficient aiding and abetting of P in his contravention of the relevant immigration provisions. D's behaviour before and after P's performance supplied further evidence of D's intention to encourage P; he had met P at the airport and D afterwards reported the performance in laudatory terms in his jazz periodical. There was no finding that D applauded the performance. Had there been such a finding then the normal principles described earlier would apply—it would not have been a case of 'mere' voluntary presence but one of active encouragement by D.

Public order offences often raise particular problems in this context since the principal offence will often turn on proof of acts by a specific number of individuals, and in cases of spontaneous violence between groups, it is difficult to identify who is a principal involved in the fight, who is present actively encouraging and who is merely present without more.[176]

Note that there is no requirement that D is present when P commits the offence. As Toulson LJ observed in *Stringer*: 'for centuries secondary liability has attached to a person

---

171 [2019] EWCA Crim 2280.

172 [2016] UKSC 8, [89].   173 (1882) 8 QBD 534.   174 *Jogee* [2016] UKSC 8, [11].

175 [1951] 1 All ER 464. It is arguable that Art 11 of the ECHR may be engaged where the effect is to restrict D's right to assemble with others, see Horder, APOCL, 461.

176 See *Blackwood and others* [2002] EWCA Crim 3102 and *Ellis* [2008] EWCA Crim 886.

who aided or abetted another to commit an offence but was absent at the time of the offence.
. . . To require D to be present assisting at the time of the offence is unsupported by authority and would be wrong in principle.' It is one thing to say that D cannot be liable as an
aider or abettor unless P acted with D's assistance or encouragement when he committed
the offence; it is quite another to suggest that the act or words providing the assistance
or encouragement must be performed or spoken at the moment of the commission of the
offence. Such a limitation would exclude, for example, a person who supplied a murder
weapon in advance of the crime knowing the purpose for which P wanted it. The law would
be defective if an aider and abettor could escape liability by saying that there was a gap in
time between his conduct and the conduct of P. This makes the Supreme Court's statement
in *Jogee* about an 'overwhelming supervening event' (discussed later) all the more obscure.

6.4.1.5 Problems of proving the accessory's actus reus

If all that can be proved is that the principal offence was committed either by P1 or by P2,
both must be acquitted.[177] Only if it can be proved that the one who did not commit the
crime as principal must have aided, abetted, counselled or procured the other to commit
it can both be convicted.[178] Take the case of two nurses, P1 and P2, whose patient V is
injured while in their care. The injuries might have been inflicted by P1 alone, P2 alone,
by P1 with P2's as accessory or vice versa. It is for the prosecution to prove to the criminal standard that the nurse who did not inflict the injuries must have aided or abetted
the infliction either by positive acts or by failure to fulfil the duty owed as a health-care
worker.[179] This problem often arises in a domestic situation. It differs from most other
cases only because parents owe a duty to intervene to prevent the ill-treatment of their
child when a stranger would have no such duty. The case of the parent or carer of the child
or vulnerable adult who dies or suffers serious injury in their household is now governed
by an exceptional procedure under the Domestic Violence, Crime and Victims Acts 2004
and 2012,[180] but the general principle remains: if all that can be proved is that the offence
was committed *either* the first or second defendant, both must be acquitted. A recent
affirmation of that principle is provided in *Banfield*.[181] S and L were convicted of the
murder of V. S was his wife and L his daughter. V had disappeared but no body had ever
been found. There were five postulations as to what might have explained the death: (a) S
killed V and L encouraged her; (b) L killed him and S encouraged her; (c) S killed him in
the absence of L; (d) L killed him in the absence of S; and (e) S and L acted together to kill
him.[182] Rafferty LJ concluded:

> The first four show how obvious were the tenable alternatives which could have led to [V]'s death.
> Once the Crown was unable to identify of which of the four options the jury could be sure, the fifth
> could not on the evidence provide a backstop.[183]

[177] *Richardson* (1785) 1 Leach 387; *Abbott* [1955] 2 QB 497.
[178] *Russell and Russell* [1987] Crim LR 494; *Lane and Lane* (1985) 82 Cr App R 5. For a valuable direction where one of two interrogating police officers has caused injury, see *Forman* [1988] Crim LR 677 (Judge
Woods). See generally G Williams, 'Which of You Did It?' (1989) 52 MLR 179; EJ Griew, 'It Must Have Been One
of Them' [1989] Crim LR 129. *Gibson and Gibson* (1984) 80 Cr App R 24 is misleading and should be used with
care; see commentary at [1984] Crim LR 615.
[179] See for an extreme case *Pinto* [2006] EWCA Crim 749 (D aided and abetted torture of V by P believing
V to be possessed).
[180] Considered at p 666. For comment see P Glazebrook, 'Insufficient Child Protection' [2003] Crim LR 541.
[181] [2013] EWCA Crim 1394.   [182] At [61].
[183] At [62]. The court cited the 13th edn of this work with approval.

6.4.2 Mens rea of the accessory

The mens rea requirements of the accessory were restated in *Jogee*. They can be summarized as follows:

(1) the accessory must intend to assist or encourage the principal's conduct, or in the case of procuring, to bring the offence about;

(2) if the crime requires a particular mens rea, the accessory must intend to assist or encourage the principal to act with that mens rea.[184] Innocent agency and procuring an actus reus would appear to be exceptions to this rule;

(3) the accessory must have knowledge of any existing facts or circumstances necessary for the principal's conduct to be criminal.

We discuss each in detail here noting that this is where the decision of the Supreme Court in *Jogee* has had the greatest impact.

6.4.2.1 Mens rea (1): an intention to aid, etc

It must be proved that D intended to do the acts which he knew to be capable of assisting or encouraging the commission of the crime. There are two elements: an intention to perform the act capable of encouraging or assisting, and an intention, or a belief, that that act will be of assistance. So, where D supplies a weapon to P, which P uses in a murder, proof of D's intention will turn on whether he meant to hand it over (as opposed to accidentally leaving it and P discovering it) and whether D intended that his supply would assist P; there is no further element that D must intend the consequences of P's conduct—that the murder be committed. As Devlin J said:[185]

If one man deliberately sells to another a gun to be used for murdering a third, he may be indifferent whether the third man lives or dies and interested only in the cash profit to be made out of the sale, but he can still be an aider and abettor.

The Supreme Court confirmed in *Jogee* that D's intention to assist or encourage P to commit the offence, and to act with whatever mental element is required of P, will often be coextensive on the facts with an intention by D that the offence be committed. So, in many cases it will be enough to prove that D himself intended the circumstances and/or consequences as required by the relevant offence. In murder, for example, it may be sufficient to direct the jury that if D intended that V would suffer GBH or be killed, that is a sufficient mens rea, rather than directing them to consider, the rather more abstract question, whether D intended that P would intend that V suffer GBH or be killed. (As discussed in (2) below.)

The court did confirm, however, that there will be cases where D gives intentional assistance or encouragement to P, but without D having a positive intent that the particular offence be committed. The example given by the court is where, at the time that the encouragement is given, it remains uncertain what P might do.[186] It is disappointing that the court did not make matters clearer. Some have suggested that the court should have held that D must intend P to, or believe that P will, commit the crime.[187]

---

184 *Jogee* [2016] UKSC 8, [9]–[10].

185 [1959] 1 QB 11 at 23, applied in *JF Alford Transport Ltd* [1997] 2 Cr App R 326, 334–5.

186 *Jogee* [2016] UKSC 8, [11].

187 M Dyson, 'Letter to the Editor' [2016] Crim LR 638. See the formulation proposed by W Wilson and D Ormerod, n 300, when challenging the Supreme Court to remove the parasitic accessorial liability approach to joint enterprise.

Intention to perform the act of assistance

This element of the mens rea is unlikely to give rise to difficulty. D must intend to perform the act that does in fact provide assistance. There is only likely to be a problem in circumstances of potential involuntariness and other rare situations.

Intention thereby to assist

There is no judicial agreement on what the requirement of an intention to assist actually means and unfortunately there was no explicit consideration of this issue in *Jogee*. It is clearly a requirement of intention,[188] but must it be proved that D acted in order to assist P (direct intent); or is it sufficient to prove only that D knew his acts would be virtually certain to assist P (oblique intent)?[189] It seems to be generally accepted that D's knowledge that his act will assist is sufficient.[190] The weight of authority certainly supports the view that it is not necessary to prove that D had as his purpose or desire to assist and if D had the (oblique) intention, it is no excuse that D's motives in performing the act of assistance were unimpeachable.[191]

Oblique intention to assist sufficient

In *National Coal Board v Gamble*,[192] P, a lorry driver, had his employer's lorry filled with coal at a colliery belonging to the defendant Board [D1]. When the lorry was driven on to the weighbridge operated by the defendants' employee, D2, it appeared that its load greatly exceeded that permitted by the relevant regulation.[193] D2 informed P of this but P said he would take the risk, D2 gave him a weighbridge ticket and P committed the offence as principal by driving the overloaded lorry on the highway. As a matter of contract law, the property in the coal did not pass until the ticket was handed over and, therefore, P could not properly have left the colliery without the ticket from D2. It was held that the Board, D1, through its employee D2,[194] was guilty of the offence as an accessory. The decision was based on the assumption that D2 knew that he had the right to prevent the lorry leaving the colliery with the coal. Had D2 not known this, he should have been acquitted. Presumably D2 was indifferent whether P drove his overloaded lorry on the road or not—he probably thought that it was none of his business—but D2's motive was irrelevant and it was enough that his positive act of assistance had been voluntarily done (ie intentional performance of the act of assistance) with knowledge that by doing so he would be assisting P and knowledge of the circumstances constituting the offence.[195]

Despite the fact that it did not say so explicitly, the Supreme Court's judgment in *Jogee* confirms that oblique intention will suffice. The court stated that there is a difference between intention and desire and that the jury may have to be reminded of this fact. This echoes what was earlier held in *Lynch v DPP for Northern Ireland*, where D drove P to the place where he knew that P intended to murder a policeman.

---

[188] The offence is therefore one of specific intent for the purposes of rules on voluntary intoxication: see Ch 9: *McNamara* [2009] EWCA Crim 2530.

[189] See RA Duff, 'Can I Help You? Accessorial Liability and the Intention to Assist' (1990) LS 165. See generally KJM Smith, *A Modern Treatise on Complicity* (1991) Ch 5.

[190] cf IH Dennis, 'The Mental Element for Accessories' in *Essays in Honour of JC Smith* (1987); *contra* GR Sullivan, 'Intent, Purpose and Complicity' [1988] Crim LR 641; and IH Dennis, 'Intention and Complicity: A Reply' [1988] Crim LR 649; Williams [1990] Crim LR 4, 12.

[191] Woolf J in *Gillick v West Norfolk and Wisbech Area Health Authority* [1984] QB 581 at 589. Woolf J's discussion of the criminal aspects of this case was adopted by Lords Scarman and Bridge in the House of Lords [1986] AC 112.

[192] [1959] 1 QB 11, Slade J dissenting.   [193] Motor Vehicles (Construction and Use) Regulations 1955.

[194] See, however, p 205.   [195] D2 would commit an offence under s 45 of the SCA 2007.

It was held that the fact that D does not 'want' or 'aim' to assist does not prevent him being liable as an accessory if he has an oblique intent to assist, so D's intentional driving of the car was aiding and abetting, 'even though he regretted the plan or indeed was horrified by it'.[196]

Must D intend that his conduct 'will' or 'might' assist?

There is a potential difficulty where D believes his act is capable of assisting P but does not believe that in fact it *will* assist P. An example is offered by the Law Commission[197] where D, believing that P is going to murder V, sells P rat poison. If D believes that there is only a 50 per cent chance that P will use it to murder V but D foresees the risk that P *might* murder V by some other means, it cannot be said that D believes that his act *will* assist P. The Law Commission suggest that the case law is inconclusive as to whether D is liable.[198] The judgment of the Supreme Court in *Jogee* has not clarified matters very much. The court confirmed that D must intend to assist or encourage P. The court also confirmed, however, that D need not intend for P to commit the offence in question.[199] The example of such a scenario given by the court is where, at the time that the encouragement is given, it remains uncertain what P might do. D supplying arms to P was the example the court gave of such a scenario. This seems to suggest that it is sufficient for D to intend that his conduct *might* assist, even though he cannot be sure that it necessarily *will* assist.

'Intention' even if D is legally obliged to supply to P?

If P has loaned a weapon to D, and P demands it back, when D hands it over, it is arguable that D aids in the commission of P's subsequent crime committed with that weapon as much as if D had sold or lent the article to P in the first place, but this has never been held to be aiding in law.[200] *National Coal Board v Gamble* suggests a distinction between the cases:

(1) where the seller (D) is aware before ownership has passed to the buyer (P) of P's illegal purpose the delivery amounts to abetting, but

(2) where the seller (D) learns of the illegal purpose for the first time after ownership has passed but before delivery to P the supply does not amount to abetting. The seller is merely complying with his legal duty to give P what is by then P's own property.

This seems to be an unsatisfactory distinction. If D delivers weedkiller to P, knowing that P intends to use it to murder his wife, it would be remarkable if D's guilt as an accessory to murder turned on whether the ownership passed before or after D learned of P's intention.[201] The important thing is that D knows of P's intention when he makes delivery. It should not be an answer that P has a right to possession of the thing in the civil law because the civil law should not afford a right in such a case.[202] In *Garrett v Arthur Churchill (Glass)*

---

[196] [1975] AC 653 at 678 per Lord Morris, approving the judgment of Lowry LCJ on this point. *Fretwell* (1862) Le & Ca 161 appears to be a merciful decision and unsound in principle.

[197] Taken from LC 305, Appendix B, para B.75.

[198] See the speech of Lord Simon in *Lynch* [1975] AC 653, 698h.

[199] *Jogee* [2016] UKSC 8, [10].

[200] [1959] 1 QB 11 at 20 per Devlin J.

[201] D would be liable under ss 44–6 of the SCA 2007.

[202] See Williams, CLGP, s 124 and JC Smith, 'Civil Law Concepts in the Criminal Law' (1972) 31 CLJ 197 at 208. In *K v National Westminster Bank Plc* [2006] EWCA Civ 1039, the court noted that if the criminal law (under POCA 2002) makes it an offence for a bank to honour a customer's instructions to transfer money which it is suspected is criminal property, there can be no breach of contract for the bank to refuse to do so.

Ltd,[203] D, who had bought a goblet as agent of P, was held guilty of being knowingly concerned in the exportation of goods without a licence, when, on P's instructions, he delivered P's own goblet to P's agent who was to take it to the United States:

. . . albeit there was a legal duty in ordinary circumstances to hand over the goblet to the owners once the agency was determined, I do not think that an action would lie for breach of that duty if the handing over would constitute the offence of being knowingly concerned in its exportation.[204]

It is probably the law that the seller is liable whether or not the ownership has passed before delivery. Williams' view, however, is that the seller ought to be liable in neither case. He argues:[205]

The seller of an ordinary marketable commodity is not his buyer's keeper in criminal law unless he is specifically made so by statute. Any other rule would be too wide an extension of criminal responsibility.

A rule based on the nature of the thing as 'an ordinary marketable commodity' is not workable. Weedkiller is an ordinary marketable commodity but it may be acquired and used to commit murder. A more feasible distinction is one based on the seriousness of the offence contemplated:

The gravity of the social harm resulting from the unlawful conduct is used to determine whether mere knowledge of the intended use will be sufficient to carry the taint of illegality.[206]

This could operate on the basis of some balance of the respective harms, but would have the disadvantage of being uncertain. No such distinction has been made in English law. Alternatively, a distinction could be drawn between summary and indictable offences. This would create some arbitrary results.[207] A third approach would be to restrict the scope of the liability of the seller, D, to cases in which his purpose was to assist P. There would be difficulties in establishing that mens rea in some cases.

At present, English authorities suggest a general rule of liability for sellers subject to mens rea, which after *Jogee* requires an intention to assist or encourage. This applies, *a fortiori*, in the case of lenders or those who rent out premises intended for unlawful purposes. In such cases, the owner has a continuing interest in and right to control the property.[208]

6.4.2.2 Mens rea (2): intention that P commit the crime with the requisite mens rea

In *Jogee*, the Supreme Court restated the principle that D must intend to assist P to act with the requisite mens rea for the offence. The court clarified that D must intend, at the time D is performing acts of assistance or encouragement, that P will have the mental element when P is performing the conduct element of the offence. As the court explained:

The second issue is likely to be whether the accessory intended to encourage or assist [P] to commit the crime, *acting with whatever mental element the offence requires of [P]*. If the crime requires a

---

[203] [1970] 1 QB 92. How far does this go? If X lends a picture to a museum, does the museum really commit an offence if, on demand, it returns the picture to X, knowing that he intends to export it without the licence required by law?

[204] [1969] 2 All ER 1141 at 1145 per Parker LCJ.   [205] CLGP, s 124 at 373. TBCL (1st edn) 293–4.

[206] R Perkins and R Boyce, *Criminal Law* (3rd edn, 1982) 746. See also G Williams, 'Obedience to Law as a Crime' (1990) 53 MLR 445.

[207] GR Sullivan [1994] Crim LR 272.

[208] eg the hotelier who lets a room to a man accompanied by a 15-year-old girl, knowing that he intends to have sex with her.

particular intent, [D] must intend (it may be conditionally) to assist [P] to act with such intent. To take a homely example, if [D] encourages [P] to take another's bicycle without permission of the owner and return it after use, but [P] takes it and keeps it, [P] will be guilty of theft but [D] of the lesser offence of unauthorised taking, since he will not have encouraged [P] to act with intent permanently to deprive. In cases of concerted physical attack there may often be no practical distinction to draw between an intention by [D] to assist [P] to act with the intention of causing grievous bodily harm at least and [D] having the intention himself that such harm be caused. In such cases it may be simpler, and will generally be perfectly safe, to direct the jury . . . that the Crown must prove that [D] intended that the victim should suffer grievous bodily harm at least. However, as a matter of law, it is enough that [D] intended to assist [P] to act with the requisite intent. That may well be the situation if the assistance or encouragement is rendered some time before the crime is committed and at a time when it is not clear what [P] may or may not decide to do. Another example might be where [D] supplies a weapon to [P], who has no lawful purpose in having it, intending to help [P] by giving him the means to commit a crime (or one of a range of crimes), but having no further interest in what he does, or indeed whether he uses it at all.[209]

The significant shift from the *Chan Wing-Siu* doctrine, which is discussed in full later, is that D *must intend* that P will intentionally commit the offence (say murder) whereas under the *Chan Wing-Siu* doctrine it was enough that D foresaw as a possibility that P might intentionally commit the offence.

This begs the question of what 'intention' means in this context. It is clear that it is not limited to purpose, as the court confirmed that:

It will therefore in some cases be important when directing juries to remind them of the difference between intention and desire.[210]

The question then remains whether intention can be inferred from foresight. In *Jogee*, the Supreme Court recognized that in the common law, foresight of what might happen is evidence from which a jury can infer the presence of the requisite intention.[211] The court observed that, 'foresight may be good evidence of intention but it is not synonymous with it'.[212] Inferring intention from foresight is the hallmark of oblique or indirect intention. Therefore, although foresight cannot be equated with intention as a matter of law, it is evidence the jury can take into account when they are considering whether D intended to assist or encourage P to act with whatever mens rea is necessary for him to commit the full offence. In the subsequent case of *Anwar*, Sir Brian Leveson P confirmed that, 'the jury will, of course, continue to look at the full picture or factual matrix in order to determine whether the relevant necessary intent can be inferred'.[213]

That the jury may infer intent from foresight begs the following questions: (a) in what circumstances, (b) foresight of what and (c) foresight to what degree?

One of the factors identified by the Supreme Court that may be relevant to the assessment of whether D possessed the requisite intent is whether there was a common purpose between D and P to commit the offence in question.[214] The Supreme Court confirmed, however, that liability as a secondary party does not depend on there being some form of agreement between the parties.[215] The Supreme Court also clarified that knowledge or ignorance that weapons generally, or a particular weapon, is being carried by P will be evidence going to what the intention of D was, and indeed may be irresistible evidence one way or the other, but it is evidence and no more.[216] This was confirmed by the Court of Appeal in

---

[209] *Jogee* [2016] UKSC 8, [90] (emphasis added).   [210] ibid, [91].   [211] ibid, [83].
[212] ibid, [73].   [213] [2016] EWCA Crim 551, [20].   [214] *Jogee* [2016] UKSC 8, [87].
[215] ibid, [95].   [216] ibid, [98].

the subsequent case of *Brown*, in which Hallett LJ stated that, 'Post-*Jogee*, knowledge of a weapon used by a principal to inflict harm is not determinative of secondary party liability. It is evidence that may inform a jury's decision as to whether a defendant who did not himself wield a weapon intended to cause harm to the victim; and if he did, the level of harm.'[217] Her ladyship therefore rejected the submission that the judge ought to have directed the jury that they could only convict D if they were sure that he knew P had a knife. That was echoed in *Tas*.[218]

What the Supreme Court did not address, however, is whether oblique intention in the context of secondary liability has the same strict meaning it has, for example, in the law of murder. As a result of the judgment of the House of Lords in *Woollin*,[219] in a murder trial the jury are only entitled to find that D had the necessary intention if death or GBH was a *virtually certain* consequence and D appreciated that this was the case. If death or GBH was not virtually certain, then the jury are not entitled to find that D had the requisite intention. In the context of secondary liability, the Supreme Court confirmed that the jury can infer intention from foresight, but did not address the question of whether D's foresight of even the slightest possibility of P intentionally acting in the proscribed way is sufficient for the jury to be entitled to infer that he possessed the requisite intention.

To take an example of why this is not merely a theoretical problem, consider *Matthews and Alleyne*.[220] The defendants were convicted of murder after throwing the victim from a bridge and into a river, where he drowned. In the light of *Woollin*, the judge directed the jury that in relation to each defendant they could only convict him of murder as a principal if, when he threw the victim from the bridge and into the river, he appreciated that death or really serious harm was a virtually certain consequence, barring some unforeseen intervention. To amend the facts, rather than being joint principals, if P was the principal and D was the accessory, how should the judge direct the jury in relation to D's liability? What is clear is that the judge should direct the jury that they can only convict D of murder as a secondary party if they are sure that he intended to assist or encourage the principal intentionally to kill or do GBH. If D admits being present when V was murdered by P, but denies having the requisite intent, should the judge direct the jury that they can only infer the requisite intent if D foresaw that the principal might intentionally kill or do GBH, so long as D's foresight of that was more than *de minimis*? Alternatively, should the jury be directed that they are only entitled to infer the requisite intent if D foresaw intentional GBH or killing by P as a *virtually certain* consequence of D's act of assistance or encouragement?

The issue becomes particularly striking if the Crown cannot establish the identity of the principal. As discussed earlier, this is not an uncommon scenario. Can the jury be directed that: (a) they can infer the requisite intent if the defendant they are considering foresaw that the other might intentionally kill or cause GBH so long as this foresight was more than *de minimis*; but (b) to be sure D is guilty as a principal he must have foreseen that death or GBH was a virtually certain consequence barring some unforeseen intervention. The jury would then have to be told that there are two different routes to 'finding' intention, depending upon whether the defendant whose guilt they are considering is the principal or the accessory. Given that the jury would have to be sure that a murder was committed by one of the defendants, there is potentially no avoiding directing the jury as to the applicability of two different routes. This is surely an undesirable state of affairs in directing a jury on the same word in the gravest of crimes.[221]

---

[217] [2017] EWCA Crim 1870, [28]. See also *Ibrar* [2017] EWCA Crim 1841.
[218] [2018] EWCA Crim 2603, [20]–[41].   [219] [1999] 1 AC 82. For discussion, see p 95.
[220] [2003] EWCA Crim 192. For discussion, see p 95.
[221] Courts and Tribunals Judiciary, *Crown Court Compendium* (2020).

It is submitted that there are three significant practical issues arising as a result of this uncertainty around foresight and intention. First, it is unclear how judges are to direct juries on the law. Different judges may direct juries in different ways, which makes resolution of this issue a priority. Secondly, as a matter of principle, there is lack of clarity on whether there ought to be parity as to the level of foresight required of the principal and the accessory.[222] Resolution of this issue is made more complicated by the fact that two different questions are being asked. In relation to the principal, the issue relates to a consequence, whereas for the accessory, the issue is partly about their perception of someone else's likely future state of mind. Thirdly, without resolution by the Court of Appeal there is the danger that the debate the House of Lords sought to put an end to in *Woollin* will be replayed, which would be undesirable as the law would be thrown into a state of confusion.[223] One solution is for the jury to be directed in the following terms:

You (the jury) are entitled to conclude that the greater the likelihood or chance of [X] happening that you are sure that the defendant foresaw, the more weight you can place on this conclusion when you come to decide, as a matter of fact, whether the defendant intended [X]. So if you conclude that the defendant either did not foresee [X] or thought it a remote possibility only, you may conclude that he did not intend [X] to happen; if he foresaw that it was virtually certain to happen but carried on assisting, it may not be difficult to conclude that he intended [X]. How you weigh up that evidence to decide what the defendant intended is a matter for you.

It is important to bear in mind that even if D did not intend to assist or encourage P to kill or cause really serious harm, but the violence escalates and results in death, although D will not be guilty of murder he will be guilty of manslaughter. D will also be guilty of manslaughter if he participates by encouragement or assistance in any other unlawful act which all sober and reasonable people would realize carried the risk of some harm (not necessarily serious) to another and death in fact results.[224] (Subject to the potential application of the 'overwhelming supervening act' exception discussed later, p 219.) When applied in the context of secondary liability, the law of manslaughter may seem particularly harsh, especially since the test of harm is an objective one.

Conditional intent

The Supreme Court confirmed in *Jogee* that D must intend to assist or encourage P to commit the offence, and to act with whatever mental element is required of P. Importantly, the Supreme Court stated that in some cases arising out of a prior joint criminal venture, it will also often be necessary to draw the jury's attention to the fact that the intention to assist, and perhaps also the intention that the crime should be committed, may be conditional.[225] The Supreme Court's discussion of conditional intent was confined to those cases in which D and P are engaged in a joint prior criminal venture, such as a burglary, during the course of which a further offence is committed. Whilst conditional intent may be particularly apposite in scenarios such as these, it can apply with equal force to cases in which there was no prior joint criminal venture.[226]

---

222 This issue is considered further at p 227.

223 For further discussion, see D Ormerod and K Laird, '*Jogee*: Not the End of a Legal Saga But the Start of One?' [2016] Crim LR 539.

224 *Jogee* [2016] UKSC 8, [96].

225 ibid, [92]. Conditional intention is a concept that is also discussed in Ch 11, in the context of statutory conspiracies. This section deals exclusively with the concept as it relates to accessorial liability.

226 For discussion, see Horder, APOCL, 469–75. C Cowley, '*Jogee*, Parasitic Accessory Liability and Conditional Intention' in B Krebs (ed), *Accessorial Liability after Jogee* (2020) Ch 3.

This aspect of the Supreme Court's judgment could prove controversial in three respects. First, there is the practical question of how the concept of conditional intent ought to be explained to the jury. The court gave the following example of a scenario where it might be necessary to draw to the jury's attention the fact that D's intent can be conditional:

The bank robbers who attack the bank when one or more of them is armed no doubt hope that it will not be necessary to use the guns, but it may be a perfectly proper inference that all were intending that if they met resistance the weapons should be used with the intent to do grievous bodily harm at least.

In this example, the Supreme Court seems to be suggesting that the jury will only be entitled to infer that D had the requisite intent if he foresaw that it might be *necessary* for the guns to be used in the course of the robbery. If necessity were the test, then it would impose a high threshold. In the next paragraph of the judgment, however, the Supreme Court gives an example which seems to suggest that the test is not as stringent as this:

If the jury is satisfied that there was an agreed common purpose to commit crime A, and if it is satisfied also that [D] must have foreseen that, in the course of committing crime A, [P] might well commit crime B, it may in appropriate cases be justified in drawing the conclusion that [D] had the necessary conditional intent that crime B should be committed, if the occasion arose; or in other words that it was within the scope of the plan to which [D] gave his assent and intentional support.

This paragraph could be interpreted as entitling the jury to find that D had the requisite intent if he foresaw that the further offence might be committed, not out of necessity, but merely if the opportunity arose. In the subsequent case of *Anwar* Sir Brian Leveson P offered the following formulation: 'What is now required is that [D] intended that [P] cause grievous bodily harm or kill *if the circumstances arise*.'[227] There is the danger that the misapplication of conditional intention could lead to the reintroduction of the problems the Supreme Court sought to address in *Jogee*. For example, the prosecution could invite the jury to infer that merely because D foresaw as a possibility that P might, in the course of their joint venture to burgle V's house, commit murder, that D must have conditionally intended to assist P to commit that crime. Such a formulation bears a striking resemblance to parasitic accessory liability and cannot be what the Supreme Court intended to achieve in *Jogee*.

What must not be lost sight of is the fact that the requisite mens rea is intention. As Krebs explains, 'intent contingent upon the existence of certain facts still requires proof of full-blown intent'.[228] This point ought to be emphasized to the jury, to ensure that they do not labour under the misapprehension that by referring to conditional intention the judge is somehow sanctioning the application of a less demanding form of mens rea. In *Chan Kam Shing*, Ribeiro PJ stated that the Court of Appeal's analysis of conditional intent in *Anwar* and *Johnson* suggests that English law is 'drifting back' to a position resembling parasitic accessory liability.[229] It is submitted that to avoid this the jury ought to be directed that D will be liable if he intended to assist or encourage P to commit the offence if a particular condition was met. For example, where D and P engage in a joint criminal venture to commit robbery, during the course of which P murders the bank clerk, D will be guilty of murder if he intended to assist or encourage P to murder the bank clerk should the bank clerk attempt to raise the alarm during the course of the robbery.

---

[227] *Anwar* [2016] EWCA Crim 551, [22]. Emphasis added.
[228] B Krebs, 'Accessory Liability: Persisting in Error' (2017) 76 CLJ 7, 10.
[229] [2016] HKCFA 87, [92]–[93].

Many factors will be relevant to the jury's assessment of whether D possessed the requisite intention. Of particular relevance will be the jury's assessment of the range of responses D foresaw from P in the event that the bank clerk attempted to raise the alarm during the robbery. Evidence that D, when he embarked on the robbery with P, foresaw that P might murder the bank clerk should he attempt to raise the alarm, but nevertheless continued in the joint venture,[230] would be strong evidence from which the jury could infer that D intended to assist or encourage P to commit murder should that eventuality arise. Foresight is only evidence from which the jury will be entitled to infer the requisite intention, however. Even if D foresaw that P's response to the bank clerk's attempt to raise the alarm might be to commit murder, the jury could conclude that D lacked the requisite intent because, for example, he explicitly told P that he did not want violence to be used. Again, it is crucial to ensure that the jury understands that the requisite mens rea is nothing less than intention.

Secondly, the Supreme Court's discussion of conditional intent was subject to sustained criticism by the Hong Kong Court of Final Appeal in *Chan Kam Shing*.[231] Ribeiro PJ stated that the Supreme Court relied upon the idea of conditional intent in order to deal with what his lordship characterized as 'situational uncertainties'.[232] The HK Court of Final Appeal took the view, however, that conditional intent is unsuited to this purpose and criticized the Supreme Court for explaining the concept solely 'in the context of joint criminal enterprise'. The court also stated that, 'The proposition that a finding of foresight is only evidence of conditional intent [was] . . . difficult to follow.'[233] Krebs agrees that the Supreme Court's analysis of conditional intent was 'somewhat opaque' but concludes that the language of joint enterprise is consistent with using the concept to determine the scope of the undertaking that was to be assisted or encouraged.[234] In *Miller v The Queen*, the High Court of Australia was also critical of the Supreme Court's reliance upon conditional intention.[235]

The final reason why the Supreme Court's discussion of conditional intention could prove controversial is of a more theoretical nature.[236] The Supreme Court's discussion of conditional intent has been found wanting by a number of commentators. For example, it has been argued that particularly problematic is the fact the Supreme Court referred to D's conditional intention to assist or encourage by his *present* conduct. Simester argues that any reference to conditional intention in a scenario where D's act of assistance or encouragement is rendered some time before the crime is committed is a 'red herring'.[237] He argues that once D renders his act of assistance or encouragement, there can be no question of D having any conditional intention. This is because D's part in the commission of the crime has been fulfilled and that any conditional intention to do something requires that the thing to be done lies in the future. At the time of D's act of assistance or encouragement, he must therefore hold the crystallized, unconditional intention to assist or encourage the very crime that P ultimately commits. Simester makes the point that what lies in the future are P's actions and that as D cannot intend P's actions, nor P's mens rea, he cannot conditionally intend them either.[238] Child argues that conditional intention can never apply in these circumstances on

---

[230] The Court of Appeal in *Johnson* [2016] EWCA Crim 1613 made reference to the fact that the court could safely draw the conclusion that DD had the necessary conditional intent that the knife would be used with intent to kill or cause GBH should the occasion arise, on the basis that use of the knife with intent to kill or cause GBH was *within the scope of the plan* to which they gave their assent and conditional support. At [82].

[231] [2016] HKCFA 87.   [232] ibid, [72].   [233] ibid, [78].

[234] B Krebs, 'Hong Kong Court of Final Appeal: Divided by a Common Purpose' (2017) 81 J Crim L 271.

[235] [2016] HCA 30, [21] and [38].

[236] For further discussion, see DJ Baker, *Reinterpreting Criminal Complicity and Inchoate Participation Offences* (2016) Ch 2.

[237] AP Simester, 'Accessory Liability and Common Unlawful Purposes' (2017) 133 LQR 73.

[238] For an alternative view, see DJ Baker, 'Unlawfulness's Doctrinal and Normative Irrelevance to Complicity Liability: A Reply to Simester' (2017) 81 J Crim L 393.

the basis that it is irrational to apply conditional intention to present conduct and results. It is argued that, 'D's intention to aid or abet murder at t1 [time 1] cannot be conditioned by an event that happens later at t2 [time 2]. D's intention may be specific to a certain future view of the world (i.e. to encourage killing on specific terms), but once it has motivated conduct which provides that encouraging effect, it can no longer be conditional.'[239]

Despite the compelling nature of these criticisms, the Supreme Court confirmed in unequivocal terms that D's intent can be conditional. For the reasons that have already been given, it is imperative to convey to juries that conditional intent is not a less stringent form of intention and that foresight is merely evidence from which the requisite intention can be inferred.

6.4.2.3 Mens rea (3): knowledge of facts or circumstances

In addition to proof of intention to do the acts and to assist or encourage, there is a further element of the accessory's mens rea: D must 'know' of the facts or circumstances necessary for P's conduct to be criminal.[240] He need not actually know that an offence has been committed, because he may not know that the facts constitute an offence and because ignorance of the criminal law is not a defence.[241] In *Jogee*, the Supreme Court expressed this element in the following terms: 'knowledge of any existing facts necessary for [P's conduct] to be criminal'.[242]

Two questions arise:

(1) What does 'knowledge' mean in this context?

(2) As to what must D have knowledge—what are the 'facts or circumstances necessary for P's conduct to be criminal'?

Knowledge/foresight/wilful blindness

The Supreme Court in *Jogee* was explicit in stipulating that the mental element in assisting or encouraging includes an intention to assist or encourage the commission of the crime, which requires knowledge of any existing facts necessary for it to be criminal.[243]

This requirement to prove D's knowledge is especially difficult to apply in the context of secondary liability. D's knowledge must relate to P's conduct and the prescribed circumstances. The conduct may or may not be happening contemporaneously with D's act(s) of assistance or encouragement. Frequently, D's acts of assistance or encouragement will have occurred before the commission of the offence by P, and D cannot have 'knowledge' of something that has yet to occur.[244] Where the circumstances have yet to arise or materialize, D cannot know them because they are not yet in existence. The problem of proving

---

[239] J Child, 'Understanding Ulterior *Mens Rea*: Future Conduct Intention is Conditional Intention' (2017) 76 CLJ 311.

[240] See generally KJM Smith, *A Modern Treatise on Complicity*, Ch 6 and LC 305, Appendix B.

[241] *Johnson v Youden* [1950] 1 KB 544 at 546 per Lord Goddard CJ. See also *Ackroyds Air Travel Ltd v DPP* [1950] 1 All ER 933 at 936; *Thomas v Lindop* [1950] 1 All ER 966 at 968; *Ferguson v Weaving* [1951] 1 KB 814; *Bateman v Evans* [1964] Crim LR 601; *Smith v Jenner* [1968] Crim LR 99; *Dial Contracts Ltd v Vickers* [1971] RTR 386; *D Stanton & Sons Ltd v Webber* [1973] RTR 87, [1972] Crim LR 544 and commentary.

[242] *Jogee* [2016] UKSC 8, [9] and [99].

[243] [2016] UKSC 8, [9] and [16].

[244] For discussion of the philosophical nature of knowledge and its relevance to the criminal law, see S Shute, 'Knowledge and Belief in the Criminal Law' at 171 and GR Sullivan, 'Knowledge, Belief and Culpability' at 207 both in Shute and Simester, *Criminal Law Theory*. See also the essay by R Bagshaw, 'Legal Proof of Knowledge' in P Mirfield and R Smith (eds), *Essays in Honour of Colin Tapper* (2003) on evidential influences of substantive law definitions of knowledge.

knowledge may even arise if the principal offence *has* materialized contemporaneously with D's assistance.

In the face of practical difficulties in applying a strict test of knowledge, the concept was diluted by the courts to such an extent that this element of mens rea required of D could more accurately be expressed as a realization of a possibility of the essential elements of P's offence.[245] Knowledge in this context was the equivalent to D foreseeing (or in some cases turning a blind eye to) the likelihood of the essential matters. As a matter of substance this was more like a test of subjective recklessness. For example, the court adopted a relaxed interpretation of 'knowledge' in *Carter v Richardson*[246] where D, the supervisor of a learner driver, P, was convicted of abetting P's driving with excess alcohol. The court said, *obiter*, that it was sufficient that D knew that it was 'probable' that P was 'over the limit'—that D was, in effect, 'reckless' in the *Cunningham* sense[247] to the circumstance element of the crime that P was over the limit. In *Carter v Richardson*, P's offence comprised two main elements: a conduct element—driving—and a circumstances element—with excess alcohol. D intentionally encouraged the act of driving and was reckless as to the circumstance of the excess alcohol. That was sufficient to render him liable. There were a number of cases in which a similar formulation was adopted. For example, in *Bryce* it was held that D's foresight of the 'real or substantial risk' of P's crime was sufficient.[248]

The correctness of this approach must now be doubted in the light of *Jogee*. Unfortunately, the Supreme Court did not discuss the body of case law that had developed in the years since *Johnson v Youden* that sanctioned the application of a less stringent test than knowledge. As noted, the court did, however, explicitly endorse the approach in *Johnson v Youden*: the mental element for accessories includes a requirement for knowledge of any existing facts necessary for it to be criminal.[249] Although the Supreme Court did not do so explicitly, those cases in which knowledge seemed to have been equated with recklessness have been implicitly overturned and should no longer be applied. Knowledge in the context of secondary liability therefore now bears a stricter meaning than the one that had previously been sanctioned. As we discuss later, however, D does not have to intend to assist or encourage a specific offence. It will suffice for D to have intended to assist or encourage P to commit one of a range of offences which might take various forms, such as a terrorism offence or a sexual offence.

D must know any 'existing' facts necessary for P's conduct to be criminal

As has already been explained, D must have 'knowledge of any existing facts necessary for [P's conduct] to be criminal'.[250] As Horder points out, given that P's conduct will take place in the future, there are as of yet no 'existing facts' necessary to make P's act criminal. Therefore, what the Supreme Court must have meant is that what matters is whether D knows that, when P acts on D's assistance or encouragement, the facts making P's act criminal will exist at that later time.[251]

---

[245] See LC 305, para 2.65. For a defence of the dilution of mens rea, see A Simester (2006) 122 LQR 578 at 588–92.

[246] [1974] RTR 314, discussed by G Williams (1975) 34 CLJ 182 and TBCL, 309. But in *Giogianni* (1984) 156 CLR 473 the High Court of Australia held that recklessness is not sufficient on a charge of aiding and abetting.

[247] It is quite clear that inadvertent *Caldwell/Lawrence* recklessness was never enough: *Blakely and Sutton v DPP* [1991] Crim LR 763.

[248] [2004] EWCA Crim 1231, [71].   [249] [2016] UKSC 8, [9] and [16].

[250] ibid, [9] and [99]. See also LC 305, paras 2.51 et seq.   [251] Horder, APOCL, 480.

Knowledge in abetting an offence of strict liability

Where P's offence is one of strict liability, D must have mens rea, namely 'knowledge' of the essential elements of P's wrongdoing. The principal may, but an accessory may not, be convicted without mens rea. The reason is that secondary participation is a common law notion.[252] Application of the normal common law principles of liability requiring mens rea highlights the peculiar nature of offences of strict liability. In a strict liability offence, an accessory who has no mens rea as to the relevant actus reus element must be acquitted even if he was negligent,[253] whereas the principal who has caused the actus reus must be convicted even if he took all proper care and was not even negligent. In *Jogee*, the Supreme Court, citing *National Coal Board v Gamble*, held that where the offence charged does not require mens rea, the only mens rea required of the secondary party is that he intended to assist or encourage P to do the prohibited act, with knowledge of any facts or circumstances necessary for it to be a prohibited act.[254]

The Supreme Court was simply recognizing the application of a longstanding principle. For example, in *Callow v Tillstone*,[255] D, a veterinary surgeon, was charged with abetting the exposure for sale of unsound meat. At the request of a butcher, P, he examined the carcass and gave P a certificate that the meat was sound. The examination had been negligently conducted and the meat was tainted. P, relying on the certificate, exposed the meat for sale and was convicted. The magistrates, holding that D's negligence had caused the exposure, convicted him of abetting. It was held that his conviction must be quashed.[256]

The principle would apply also in a case where, for example, P is charged with taking indecent images of a child under 18. If P had been assisted in his taking of the images by D, who had supplied the camera, it would have been a 'defence' for D (even though not for P) to show that he believed the child to be over 18 or even (at least if he was unaware of the relevance of the age of 18) that he did not know what age she was.

The same principle must apply, *a fortiori*, to offences where negligence as to circumstances will found liability for the principal. Take the offence of bigamy as an example. If D encourages P to marry, both believing honestly but mistakenly and on unreasonable grounds that P's husband is dead, P may be convicted of bigamy but D cannot be convicted as an accessory. This principle applies only to D's negligence as to circumstances forming part of P's crime. Whether a secondary party may be liable for unforeseen consequences of P's crime is considered later.[257]

Knowledge of what type of crime?

Liability for crimes of same type

If D aids, abets, counsels or procures, that is, performs acts of assistance or encouragement to P and D intends that P will commit an offence of a certain 'type' (X), neither party specifying any particular victim, time or place, D may be convicted as a secondary party to any crime *of that type* which P commits. For example, D intentionally provides P with a knife, knowing that P intends to threaten someone: if P does, D is liable.

The principle applies where, as is common, D and P have a shared common purpose to commit an offence, say burglary, but the act of P alone is the immediate cause of the

---

[252] It was never necessary for a statute creating an offence to specify that it should also be an offence to aid, etc, its commission. Cf *McCarthy* [1964] Crim LR 225.

[253] *Carter v Mace* [1949] 2 All ER 714 is to the contrary, but in *Davies, Turner & Co Ltd v Brodie* [1954] 1 WLR 1364 that case was said to lay down no principle of law and to be decided on its own particular facts. See J Montgomerie in 'Aiding and Abetting Statutory Offences' (1950) 66 LQR 222.

[254] *Jogee* [2016] UKSC 8, [99]. See *W(P)* [2016] EWCA Crim 745.   [255] (1900) 83 LT 411.

[256] See also *Bowker v Premier Drug Co Ltd* [1928] 1 KB 217 at 227.   [257] See p 21.

commission of that offence. D is liable as an accessory for that crime provided he intentionally performed acts of assistance or encouragement (driving P to the scene) intending thereby to assist/encourage.

The principle also applies where D does not have a common purpose with P, but assists/ encourages being indifferent whether P commits the crime. A leading case is *Bainbridge*.[258] D purchased some oxygen-cutting equipment which was used six weeks later for breaking into a bank at Stoke Newington. D's story was that he had bought the equipment for P, that he suspected P wanted it for something illegal—perhaps melting down stolen goods—but that he did not know that it was going to be used for any such purpose as it was in fact used. It was held that it was essential to prove that D knew the *type of crime* that was going to be committed: it was not enough that he knew that some kind of illegality was contemplated; but that, if D knew breaking and entering and stealing were intended, it was not necessary to prove that D knew the precise details, for example that the Midland Bank, Stoke Newington, was going to be broken into.[259] That would be too great a degree of specificity for the prosecution to establish and would narrow the scope of secondary liability unduly.

The principle applies equally whether D has assisted by supplying equipment or assisted or encouraged P in some other way. For example, D is liable as an accessory where he provides P with information on how to commit a crime of a particular type, although neither D nor P has any particular crime in view when the advice is given.[260] Where D opened a bank account for P, giving P a false name, D was convicted of aiding and abetting P in the fraudulent use of the particular forged cheque which P subsequently drew upon the account. D had demonstrated an intention that the account be used as a vehicle for presenting forged cheques like the one in fact presented.[261] D knew the type of crime. D is liable even though he does not share P's intent that the offence be committed as, for example, with the supplier of the gun in Devlin's example in *Gamble*. This principle might be regarded as unduly broad. Can it really be said that where D does not even know the precise crime that P will commit he 'knows the essential elements'?

In *DPP for Northern Ireland v Maxwell*,[262] the House of Lords, relying upon the principle enunciated in *Bainbridge*, held that there was no strict requirement that D knows the precise offence P will commit. D assisted P by intentionally driving him to a pub, realizing that P intended to commit one or more of a number of offences, including: planting a bomb at the pub, shooting people at the pub or committing a robbery at the pub. In fact, P intended to plant, and did plant, a bomb there. D was liable as an accessory to that offence. Lord Scarman held that, 'an accessory who leaves it to his principal to choose is liable, provided always the choice is made from the range of offences from which the accessory contemplates the choice will be made'.[263] The principle derived from *Maxwell* was that if D gives assistance to P, knowing that P intends to commit a crime, *foreseeing* that it is one or more of crime X, or crime Y, or crime Z, but being uncertain as to which, D was liable as a secondary party to whichever of those crimes P in fact committed. He would not be liable for crime W, even if it was the same (type) as XYZ, unless it was one D contemplated that P might commit

---

[258] [1960] 1 QB 129. The result would be different under the LC 305 proposals because D can only be liable for those offences by P as to which D intended P commit the conduct element. If D has not intended P to commit the conduct element of burglary (as opposed to handling) he is not liable. He would be liable under the SCA 2007, s 46.

[259] cf the narrower interpretation that the Law Commission placed on it in para B85 of Appendix B of LC 305.

[260] *Baker* (1909) 28 NZLR 536. G Williams thinks the case is wrongly decided: CLGP, s 125. But is it distinguishable in principle from *Bainbridge*? Cf *McLeod and Georgia Straight Publishing Co Ltd* (1970) 75 WWR 161 (newspaper liable for incitement through article on how to cultivate marijuana).

[261] *Thambiah v R* [1966] AC 37.   [262] [1978] 1 WLR 1350.   [263] ibid, 1363.

with mens rea.[264] It is not difficult to understand why the court reached the decision it did. A narrow approach to the mental element might lead to the acquittal of those who are sufficiently culpable.

The approach adopted by the House of Lords did not permit blanket liability, however. On the facts of *Maxwell*, D would have been liable for murder if P had shot and killed: murder was an offence D had foreseen that P might commit in that manner with mens rea and P carried out that crime. D would not be liable if P had committed a 'type' of offence not in D's contemplation when D performed his acts of assistance.[265] So, D would not have been liable if, on arrival at the pub, P had raped V. Nor would it be enough if D had a 'general criminal intention'. So an intention to assist another in the possession of a bag, whatever its contents may be, is insufficient to found an indictment for assisting the possession of cannabis.[266] If D had guessed that the bag contained either cannabis or some other article, proscribed or not, that should have been enough.

The Supreme Court in *Jogee* endorsed the approach in *Maxwell*, but in doing so narrowed it. The court held that the intention to assist or encourage will often be specific to a particular offence. The court recognized, however, that in other cases it may not be. In endorsing *Maxwell* the court recognized that D may intentionally assist or encourage P to commit one of a range of offences, such as an act of terrorism which might take various forms. In such cases the court held that:

> [D] does not have to 'know' (or intend) in advance the specific form which the crime will take. It is enough that the offence committed by [P] is within the range of possible offences which [D] intentionally assisted or encouraged him to commit.[267]

The court held that the decision in *Maxwell* did not derogate from the principle that an intention to assist or encourage the commission of an offence requires *knowledge* by D of any facts necessary to give P's conduct or intended conduct its criminal character. As has already been explained, the principle in *Maxwell* had been interpreted to mean that it was sufficient that P committed one of a range of offences that D had in mind as possibilities. In holding that D will be guilty only if he intentionally assists or encourages P to commit one of a range of offences which D *intends* P will commit, so long as P commits an offence within that range, of which D knows the essential elements the Supreme Court has narrowed the approach in *Maxwell*.

Where are the limits to such liability? If D has supplied P with the means of committing, or information on how to commit, a crime of a particular type, is D to be held liable for *all* the crimes of that type which P may thereafter commit? What if the Midland Bank at Stoke Newington was the second, third or fourth bank which P had burgled with Bainbridge's apparatus? Glanville Williams questioned whether D should be subject to such unforeseeable and perhaps far-reaching liability.[268] If D can be liable for any one crime of *the type* contemplated even if he need not know the details of any specific crime, should D not also be liable for *others* of that type?[269] In endorsing *Maxwell*, the Supreme Court in *Jogee* must be taken to have confirmed the correctness of this approach subject to the narrowing that has already been discussed.

---

264 The prosecution may well now prefer to lay charges under s 46 of the SCA 2007. See p 508.

265 cf Lord Scarman who, unlike Lord Hailsham who refers to the type of offence, relies on the judgment of Lowry LCJ in the Northern Ireland Court of Appeal, upholding the conviction on the basis that D 'knew' that P was going to commit one or more offences and although D did not 'know' which offence he knew that at least one would be committed and the offence P committed was one of those.

266 *Patel* [1970] Crim LR 274 and commentary thereon. Cf *Fernandez* [1970] Crim LR 277.

267 *Jogee* [2016] UKSC 8, [14]–[15].   268 CLGP, s 124.

269 On the question of the withdrawal of an accessory, see p 236.

There are further unresolved problems in relation to this principle. None of these were considered by the Supreme Court in *Jogee*. Whether a crime is of the 'same type' as another may not always be easy to discover. If D lends a jemmy to P, contemplating that P intends to enter a house in order to steal (burglary), is D guilty of any offence if P enters a house intending to commit grievous bodily harm (which is also burglary)? Clearly, D cannot be convicted of grievous bodily harm, because that is an offence of a different type; but he is probably guilty of burglary, because burglary was the crime he had in view—though this particular variety of burglary may be abhorrent to him. If D contemplates theft and P commits robbery, D is not guilty of robbery but might be convicted of the theft which is an essential element of robbery and included in it. Is theft an offence of the same type as removing an article from a place open to the public[270] or taking a motor vehicle without authority?[271] Is robbery an offence of the same type as blackmail? What of D who provides a stolen credit card to P assuming it will be used in fraud, but P uses it to slip the latch on V's door and commit theft. Is it sufficient that these are both dishonesty offences? This is an aspect of the law desperately in need of clarification, at least from a theoretical perspective; in practice, the principle does not seem to have given rise to problems.

D not liable if P intentionally changes victim/target of crime X

If D aids, abets, counsels or procures, that is, assists or encourages, P to commit a crime of a certain 'type' (X), against a particular person, or in respect of a particular thing, D is *not* liable if P *intentionally* commits an offence of the same type against some other person, or in respect of some other thing.

As an example of the principle in operation, consider D who intentionally provides P with a knife, knowing that P intends to use the knife to threaten his ex-wife V and rape her. P deliberately rapes W, a complete stranger, instead. D had not known or intended that. D is not liable for P's act of rape.[272] In *Reardon*,[273] it was accepted[274] that if D intentionally gives assistance to P to kill an identified person, V, D is not liable if P *deliberately* kills a different person, W.

This principle is described well by Hawkins:[275]

But if a man command another to commit a felony on a particular person or thing and he do it on another; as to kill A and he kill B or to burn the house of A and he burn the house of B or to steal an ox and he steal an horse; or to steal such an horse and he steal another; or to commit a felony of one kind and he commit another of a quite different nature; as to rob J S of his plate as he is going to market, and he break open his house in the night and there steal the plate; it is said that the commander is not an accessory because the act done varies in substance from that which was commanded.

As the second part of that quotation makes clear, the principle applies where there is an intentional substantial variation from the proposed course of conduct, even if the victim and property are the same. Hawkins also stated:[276]

if the felony committed be the same in substance with that which was intended, and variant only in some circumstance, as in respect of the time or place, at which, or the means whereby it was effected, the abettor of the intent is altogether as much an accessory as if there had been no variance

---

[270] Theft Act 1968, s 11. See p 941.   [271] ibid, s 12. See p 944.
[272] This is different from the case where D gives P a gun to shoot V. P shoots at V and misses killing X. P is liable for murder because his intent is transferred. D is liable as an accessory to the murder of X. See p 125.
[273] [1999] Crim LR 392.
[274] Referring to the 8th edn of this book, at p 142.
[275] II PC, c 29, s 21. See also Foster, *Crown Law*, n 16, 369. Stephen, *Digest* (4th edn) art 43.
[276] II PC, c 29, s 20.

at all between it and the execution of it; as where a man advises another to kill such a one in the night, and he kills him in the day, or to kill him in the fields, and he kills him in the town, or to poison him, and he stabs or shoots him.[277]

The distinction depends on whether the variation is one 'of substance' and any such distinction must produce difficult borderline cases.

In *Dunning and Graham*, an unreported case at Preston Crown Court,[278] D had a grievance against V. P offered to set fire to V's house. D accepted the offer and gave P V's address. P went to V's house, changed his mind, and set fire to V's Mercedes instead. D did not know that V owned such a car. Nevertheless, Macpherson J held that it was open to the jury to convict D on the ground that she must have authorized or envisaged the possibility of property such as a car in the driveway being damaged by fire. If the car had been so damaged as a consequence of P's setting fire to the house, D would have been liable for arson of the car on the basis of transferred malice discussed in the following section. The case, however, on is facts seems to involve a deliberate variation from the plan. The result might be justified on this basis that D had authorized P to take revenge on V by damaging his property and that it did not really matter to her what the property was. Whether the variation is, or is not, one of substance, depends on the purpose of D as expressed to P.

The South African case of *S v Robinson*[279] provides a controversial illustration of the difficulties of applying this principle. It is an especially difficult case because there is no change of victim as such, but arguably a fundamental change of substance relating to the proposed offence. D1, D2 and P agreed with V that P should kill V to procure the money for which V's life was insured and to avoid V's prosecution for fraud. At the last moment, V withdrew his consent to die but P nevertheless killed him. It was not proved that D1 and D2 foresaw the possibility that P might kill V even if he withdrew his consent or that they had been reckless whether he did so kill him. It was held that the common purpose was murder with the consent of the victim and that P had acted outside that common purpose. D1 and D2, accordingly, were not guilty of murder—though they were guilty of attempted murder, since P had reached the stage of an attempt before V withdrew his consent. Holmes JA, dissenting, thought 'looking squarely at the whole train of events, the conspiracy was fulfilled in death, and there is no room for exquisite niceties of logic about the exact limits of the mandate in the conspiratorial common purpose'.

The division of judicial opinion in this case highlights the problem. What constitutes a change of 'substance' could be interpreted narrowly, being limited to changes which would alter the nature of the criminal charge that could be prosecuted. A broader view of change of 'substance' seems more desirable, but the problem then arises of how to delimit 'changes of substance'. If P knows that a condition precedent of the agreement has not been performed (whether or not forming part of the definition of the crime), he might naturally be said to be no longer engaged on the joint enterprise. If D agrees with P that P shall murder V if he finds out that V is committing adultery with D's wife and P, having discovered that V is *not* committing adultery, nevertheless kills him, D should not be liable for murder, though, if this conditional intention is enough, he may be liable for conspiracy to murder.

D liable if P commits crime X by doctrine of transferred malice

If D intentionally aids, abets, counsels or procures P to commit a crime against a particular person V and P, endeavouring to commit that crime against V, mistakenly commits the crime against another (W), P is liable under the doctrine of transferred

---

[277] This is related to the principle in *Bainbridge* that D need not know all the details of P's offence.
[278] December 1985, unreported.   [279] 1968 (1) SA 666.

THE LIABILITY OF SECONDARY PARTIES 219

malice;[280] and so, therefore, is D. To take an example, if D assists P by intentionally supplying a knife intending to assist P, and P kills W mistaking W for V, D is guilty as a secondary party, and P as a principal offender, of murder. It is important to note that in this scenario P has not *deliberately* departed from the course that D assisted him with; P was attempting to commit the crime which D has assisted him with and D is as responsible for the unintended results of the acts he has assisted.

The old and famous case of *Saunders and Archer*,[281] in its result at least, is reconcilable with this principle. P intended to murder his wife. Following the advice of D, P gave her a poisoned apple to eat. She ate a little of it and gave the rest to their child. P loved the child, yet he stood by and watched it eat the poison, of which it soon died. It was held that P was guilty of murder of the child, but the judges agreed that D who, of course, was not present when the child ate the apple, was not an accessory to this murder. If P had been absent when the child ate the apple it is thought that this would have been a case of transferred malice and D would have been liable; but P's presence and failure to act made the killing of the child, in effect, a deliberate, and not an accidental, departure from the agreed plan. It was—as Kenny explained—'as if Saunders had changed his mind and on a later occasion had used such poison as Archer had named in order to murder some quite different person of whom Archer had never heard'.[282]

6.4.2.4 P's overwhelming supervening act

Under the law prior to *Jogee*, D would not be liable for murder where P's conduct in killing V was of a fundamentally different nature from that which D had foreseen. Recall that D's liability was satisfied on the basis of proof of foresight that P might kill with intent to kill or do GBH. That was such a broad and harsh doctrine that it was appropriate to temper it where P's conduct was so different from what D foresaw—even though D had foreseen at least GBH. Typically, the law draws no distinctions: if D has the mens rea as to a particular harm it does not lie in his mouth to claim that the manner of that harm being caused was not what he anticipated. If D encourages P to damage V's new car, it cannot be for D to say he had no liability because P used the hammer to wreck the vehicle when D merely thought he might scratch it slightly.

Prior to *Jogee*, the question was phrased in terms of whether the actions of P were 'fundamentally different' from what D foresaw that P's offence might be: *English*[283] and *Rahman*.[284] In *English*, both D and P armed themselves with wooden stakes to attack a police officer (crime A). D knew that P might intentionally cause grievous bodily harm with a stake (crime B) and, if he had done and V had died, D would have been guilty of murder. But P killed V with a knife (crime C), which D did not know he had. The House of Lords quashed D's conviction for murder because it was not left to the jury to decide whether the killing with a knife was an act of a fundamentally different kind from any foreseen by D. That test was ambiguous and in the House of Lords in *Rahman*[285] Lord Brown restated the law as follows:

If D realises (without agreeing to such conduct being used) that P may kill or intentionally inflict serious injury, but nevertheless continues to participate with P in the venture, that will amount to

---

[280] Hawkins, I PC, c 29, s 22; Foster, *Crown Law*, n 16, 370; Stephen, *Digest* (4th edn) art 41, illustration (1). See also D Lanham, 'Accomplices and Transferred Malice' (1980) 96 LQR 110.

[281] (1573) 2 Plowd 473.

[282] *Outlines* at 112. See the perceptive jury questions and clear directions in *Gordon-Butt* [2004] EWCA Crim 961 on changes of victim.

[283] An appeal heard together with *Powell and Daniels*, n 89.

[284] [2008] UKHL 45. Horder has argued that the House of Lords, rather than clarifying the law, exacerbated the existing problems with it. See J Horder, *Homicide and the Politics of Law Reform* (2012) 160.

[285] cf the Court of Appeal decision at [2007] EWCA Crim 342. For critical comment on the decision of the House of Lords, see Ormerod [2008] Crim LR 979. See *English* [1997] UKHL 57.

a sufficient mental element for D to be guilty of murder if P, with the requisite intent, kills in the course of the venture unless (i) P suddenly produces and uses a weapon of which D knows nothing and which is more lethal than any weapon which D contemplates that P or any other participant may be carrying and (ii) for that reason P's act is to be regarded as fundamentally different from anything foreseen by D.[286]

Arguably, the definition was too harsh on D: the fundamentally different plea was available only if there was a change of weapon (or the use of a weapon when none at all was contemplated). Arguably also, this position was too generous to D. If D had committed himself to a venture seeing that P might kill with intent, should it matter what method of killing D foresaw? After *Rahman*, the Court of Appeal preferred to focus on whether the conduct of P was 'altogether more life threatening' (in a 'different league'). That test may have been preferable. In *Mendez and Thompson*,[287] Toulson LJ, as he then was, stated: 'In cases where the common purpose is not to kill but to cause serious harm, D is not liable for the murder of V if the direct cause of V's death was a deliberate act by P which was of a kind (a) unforeseen by D and (b) likely to be altogether more life-threatening than acts of the kind intended or foreseen by D' (at [45]). 'What matters is not simply the difference in weapon but the way in which it is likely to be used and the degree of injury which it is likely to cause' (at [42]).

The Supreme Court in *Jogee* rejected the idea that D's foresight that P might intentionally kill or do GBH was a sufficient mens rea for murder. It also rejected the significance that had previously been placed on D's knowledge of P's weapon. There is therefore no scope or need for a fundamental difference test to operate in the way that it did. However, at [97]–[98] of the judgment, the Supreme Court recognized that if P's acts constitute an 'overwhelming supervening act' they preclude D's liability.

The Supreme Court began the discussion of this concept by reaffirming that D will be liable for manslaughter where he participates by encouragement or assistance in any unlawful act by P which all sober and reasonable people would realize carried the risk of some harm (not necessarily serious) to another, and death in fact results.[288] It then went on to state the 'qualification'—seemingly, therefore, a qualification that would reduce D's liability even from unlawful act manslaughter:

97. The qualification to this (recognised in *Wesley Smith*, *Anderson and Morris* and *Reid*) is that it is possible for death to be caused by some overwhelming supervening act by the perpetrator which nobody in the defendant's shoes could have contemplated might happen and is of such a character as to relegate his acts to history; in that case the defendant will bear no criminal responsibility for the death.

98. This type of case apart, there will normally be no occasion to consider the concept of 'fundamental departure' as derived from *English*. What matters is whether D2 encouraged or assisted the crime, whether it be murder or some other offence. He need not encourage or assist a particular way of committing it, although he may sometimes do so. In particular, his intention to assist in a crime of violence is not determined only by whether he knows what kind of weapon D1 has in his possession. The tendency which has developed in the application of the rule in *Chan Wing-Siu* to focus on what D2 knew of what weapon D1 was carrying can and should give way to an examination of whether D2 intended to assist in the crime charged. If that crime is murder, then the question is whether he intended to assist the intentional infliction of grievous bodily harm at least, which question will often, as set out above, be answered by asking simply whether he himself intended

---

[286] At [68]. It is unclear whether his lordship thought himself merely to be describing the law as previously declared. His lordship uses the expression 'restatement'. The Ministry of Justice Consultation Paper No 19/08, *Murder, Manslaughter and Infanticide: Proposals for Reform of the Law* (2008) regards this as a 'step in the right direction' at para 101. See also Buxton [2009] Crim LR 330.

[287] [2010] EWCA Crim 516.

[288] *Church* [1965] 1 QB 59, approved in *Director of Public Prosecutions v Newbury* [1977] AC 500.

grievous bodily harm at least. Very often he may intend to assist in violence using whatever weapon may come to hand. In other cases he may think that D1 has an iron bar whereas he turns out to have a knife, but the difference may not at all affect his intention to assist, if necessary, in the causing of grievous bodily harm at least. *Knowledge or ignorance that weapons generally, or a particular weapon, is carried by D1 will be evidence going to what the intention of D2* was, and may be irresistible evidence one way or the other, but it is evidence and no more. [Emphasis added]

Following *Jogee*, whether P committed the crime in a fundamentally different manner is usually irrelevant, but if P's conduct amounts to 'some overwhelming supervening act by the perpetrator which nobody in the defendant's shoes could have contemplated might happen and is of such a character as to relegate his acts to history' D will not be liable for homicide.

This is one of the most enigmatic and unsatisfactory elements of the decision in *Jogee*. The first question to ask is why there should be such a qualification at all. One reason is that it was recognized historically (as noted in the cases cited). That is not, of itself, a sufficient justification given that: the definition of manslaughter had changed since those cases with the introduction of the *Church* test; the definition of joint enterprise liability had changed; and the Supreme Court was seeking to set the law on a clearer unhindered foundation as demonstrated by its willingness to overrule over 30 years of appellate case law.

There are theoretical problems with the overwhelming supervening act test as pronounced as a qualification to secondary liability to manslaughter. It uses the language of causation, but that begs the question why D should be exculpated on causal grounds (a break in the chain by a supervening event) when his secondary liability is not based on causation in the first place as the Supreme Court itself notes.[289] It is clear that D can be liable as a secondary party without having caused P to commit the offence. Even if we ignore the language of causation and say that the overwhelming supervening act test is designed to recognize the need to excuse D where there is insufficient connection between D's assistance and P's act, it is problematic in at least three important ways.

First it is unclear if it applies only where D faces a manslaughter charge and has the effect of excusing D of all homicide liability, or whether in a case where D is charged with murder it can excuse all homicide liability. It is clear that the test is not designed to reduce murder to manslaughter. As stated in *Jogee*, it does not reduce murder to manslaughter but rather manslaughter to nothing.[290]

Dealing with manslaughter first, as expressed at [97] of the Supreme Court's judgment, it seems clear that the court regards it as a qualification that can definitely apply when D is at risk of a manslaughter verdict. The plea can operate in narrow circumstances. Unlawful act manslaughter requires only that D intentionally performs an unlawful act that a sober and reasonable person would realize *would cause some physical harm* to some person and in fact caused death. The overwhelming supervening act test asks about whether someone in D's shoes could have seen the *risk of the act* of P. In a case where a reasonable person would see a risk of some harm (and perhaps D even admits seeing that risk himself) he can be excused if the manner of P's causing the harm was not foreseeable by someone in D's shoes. An overwhelming supervening act operates to excuse D's liability for manslaughter.

In relation to murder, the position is less clear. There is scope for overwhelming supervening act to be applicable in extreme cases to excuse even murder, and the Supreme Court has not categorically ruled that application out. On one hand it could be argued that there is no scope for such a plea where D has intentionally assisted or encouraged P, and has intended

---

[289] At [12].

[290] A sensible prosecutor would have alternatives on the indictment—conspiracy to do GBH, conspiracy to commit violent disorder etc.

that P cause GBH with intent.[291] In such a case D has satisfied the elements of the offence and the manner of P killing V should not matter. A GBH is a GBH and a killing is a killing; the different manner of P carrying the act out is, on this view, irrelevant. Nor, on this view is P's change of mens rea sufficient for an overwhelming supervening act in murder. It was clear from *Rahman* that if D had the relevant mens rea to be guilty as an accessory to murder, the fact that P killed with an intention to kill when D had only intended P intentionally cause GBH would not preclude D being liable for murder. So, a change of mens rea by P is not an overwhelming supervening act. On this view overwhelming supervening act is unavailable to murder and applies only to manslaughter.

On the other hand, it might be argued that in an extreme case D should not be liable for murder (or manslaughter) if P's act was so different in nature as to relegate D's acts to history. The Northern Ireland Court of Appeal case of *Gamble* is perhaps such a case: D intentionally assists in knee capping (GBH); P intentionally kills by slashing V's throat. There is a change of act, intent and weapon, and the manner of the attack was not one anyone in D's shoes could have contemplated. The House of Lords in *Rahman* were divided on whether Gamble would be guilty of murder. It is unclear still whether he would be guilty or could plead overwhelming supervening act in such a case post-*Jogee*. What is clear is that further explanation from the courts of its scope is required.

Secondly, it is worth noting that irrespective of whether it applies to manslaughter only or murder as well, the test is a very narrow one, (which perhaps supports its application to murder). In *Jogee*, the court held that if P's conduct amounts to 'some overwhelming supervening act by the perpetrator which nobody in the defendant's shoes could have contemplated might happen and is of such a character as to relegate his acts to history' will D not be liable for it.[292] The requirement is that 'nobody' in the defendant's shoes *could have* contemplated the acts. The Court of Appeal has been at pains to point this out in the cases in which an overwhelming supervening act has been considered to date. The most important decision on the point is *Tas*.[293] The Court of Appeal in *Tas* firmly underlines that the test is a narrow one and is not analogous to fundamental difference. The President of the Queen's Bench Division stated:

It is important not to abbreviate the test articulated above which postulates an act that 'nobody in the defendant's shoes could have contemplated might happen and is of such a character as to relegate his acts to history'. In the context of this case, the question can be asked whether the judge was entitled to conclude that there was insufficient evidence to leave to the jury that if they concluded (as they must have) that, in the course of a confrontation sought by Tas and his friends leading to an ongoing and moving street fight (which had Tas driving his car following the chase to ensure that his friends could be taken from the scene), the production of a knife is a wholly supervening event rather than a simple escalation.[294]

Thirdly, there is the question of what evidence will suffice to mean that the plea of OSA should be left to the jury. It is clear from the language of the Supreme Court that it is not enough that violence has 'escalated' beyond what D has anticipated or intended. Nor is it sufficient that there has been a change of weapon (unlike the old law). In *Tas*, the Court of Appeal also emphasized as in earlier cases,[295] that care must be taken to avoid the issue of knowledge of a weapon, which following *Jogee* is no longer necessarily a central issue, being reintroduced as a matter of an overwhelming supervening event. Sir Brian Leveson stated:

one of the effects of *Jogee* is to reduce the significance of knowledge of the weapon so that it impacts as evidence (albeit very important if not potentially irresistible) going to proof of intention, rather than being a pre-requisite of liability for murder. We do not accept that if there is no necessary requirement that the secondary party knows of the weapon in order to bring home a charge of

---

[291] We doubt that it should apply where D has intended that P kill with intent.
[292] At [97]–[98].   [293] [2018] EWCA Crim 2603.   [294] At [40].
[295] *Brown* [2017] EWCA Crim 1870, [28]–[30].

murder (as is the effect of *Jogee*), the requirement of knowledge of the weapon is reintroduced through the concept of supervening overwhelming event for manslaughter.[296]

The presence of a weapon does not constitute an overwhelming supervening act. There have now been a number of cases in which this submission has been made and rejected; for example, in *Harper*.[297] Sir Brian Leveson P went so far as to say that were such a submission to succeed, it would reverse the development of the law identified in *Jogee*. The Court of Appeal in *Tas* also distinguished *Rafferty*[298] where the secondary party had taken part in beating the victim but then left the principals (in order to obtain money using the victim's debit card) whereupon the principals drowned the victim. Quashing that conviction, the court held that no jury could properly have concluded that the drowning of the deceased was other than a new and intervening act in the chain of events: the court did not suggest that this should not generally be a question for the jury.

The court in *Tas* also recognized the distinction between the overwhelming supervening act plea and cases of withdrawal. In that case, with the concept of joint enterprise explained in a way that does not attract any criticism, the critical first question left to the jury was (in effect) whether D participated in a joint enterprise in which V was stabbed. In the light of the way in which the law is now expressed, that, in the court's judgment, was the correct way to put it.

6.4.2.5 Summary of mens rea

For liability as a secondary party:

- a criminal offence must have been committed by P (whether P is identified or not);
- D must have intentionally aided, abetted, counselled or procured P, or in other words assisted or encouraged him, to commit an offence of the type that P in fact committed;
- D must have intended to assist or encourage P's conduct, or in the case of procuring, to bring the offence about, it being sufficient that D has oblique intent;
- D must have knowledge of any existing facts or circumstances necessary for P's conduct to be criminal; and
- if the offence is one of mens rea, D must intend to assist or encourage P to act with that mens rea. Procuring and innocent agency appear to be exceptions to this rule although this has yet to be determined.

6.5 The rise and fall of 'parasitic accessory' or 'joint enterprise' liability

6.5.1 Introduction

Prior to the Supreme Court deciding that it was the consequence of a legal 'wrong turn', the problem in identifying the scope of D's liability for P's offences arose most keenly in the context of so-called 'joint enterprise' or 'parasitic accessory' liability. That doctrine gave rise to a vast number of appeals and to much academic debate.[299] To understand why the Supreme Court characterized the doctrine as a legal wrong turn, it is necessary to set out

---

[296] At [37].   [297] [2019] EWCA Crim 343.   [298] [2007] EWCA Crim 1846.

[299] See JC Smith, 'Criminal Liability of Accessories: Law and Law Reform' (1997) 113 LQR 453; J Burchell, 'Joint Enterprise and Common Purpose' (1997) 10 SACJ 125; cf A Simester, 'The Mental Element in Complicity' (2006) 122 LQR 578, for a review see LC 305. See B Krebs, 'Joint Criminal Enterprise' (2010) 73 MLR 578; G Virgo, 'Joint Enterprise Liability is Dead: Long Live Accessorial Liability' [2012] Crim LR 850; W Wilson and D Ormerod, 'Simply Harsh to Fairly Simple: Joint Enterprise Reform' [2015] Crim LR 3.

the basis upon which it enabled D to be liable for a crime committed by P. D was liable as a parasitic accessory where:

(1) D intentionally participated in the commission of crime 'A' with P or Ps (D's role could be either as a principal or accessory); and

(2) D shared a common purpose with P to commit crime 'A'; and

(3) P or Ps (whether identified or not) committed crime 'B' with the relevant mens rea for that crime; and

(4) P's commission of crime B was in the course or furtherance of crime 'A';

(5) D foresaw as a possibility that P or Ps might commit crime 'B' with the relevant mens rea; and

(6) P or Ps did commit it in a not fundamentally different manner from that which D foresaw; and

(7) D was at the time of the commission of crime 'B' still an active participant with P or Ps in crime 'A'.

It was said by the Supreme Court that this form of liability was developed by the Privy Council in *Chan Wing-Siu v R*,[300] as interpreted in *Hyde* and *Hui Chi-ming* and approved by the House of Lords in *Powell and Daniels, English*[301] and *Rahman*.[302] It was also endorsed in numerous Court of Appeal decisions[303] and by the seven-member constitution of the Supreme Court in *Gnango*.[304]

The House of Lords in *Powell and Daniels, English*[305] confirmed that it was sufficient to found a conviction for murder for D to have realized that P *might* kill with intent to do so or with intent to cause GBH. It was not necessary that D himself held an intention to kill. The particular difficulties in application in murder stemmed from the breadth of the mens rea of that offence and the fact that it is a constructive crime—it is sufficient that P has intended GBH.

The consequences of the joint enterprise principle were especially significant in cases of murder. Once it had been proved that a murder was committed, even if the principal could not be identified, the fact that the jury could not be sure which of the members of a group delivered the fatal blow did not prevent murder convictions for all or any members of the joint enterprise who foresaw that intentional GBH might occur: *Rahman*.[306]

Parasitic accessory liability meant that D could be liable for an offence requiring proof of an intention on the part of the principal offender, P, although D was only reckless about P's likely intentional conduct.[307] Recklessness whether death be caused is a sufficient mens rea for manslaughter but not for murder; yet in a joint enterprise case D could be convicted of murder if D was reckless as to whether P might intentionally perpetrate the conduct element of the actus reus of murder. In *Powell and Daniels, English*, Lord Steyn rejected the

---

[300] (1985) 80 Cr App R 117. See the 7th edn of this book, at pp 143–5, for an account of the cases ending in *Chan Wing-Siu* in *Hyde* (1991) 92 Cr App R 131 and the decision in *Hui Chi-ming* (1992) 94 Cr App R 236.

[301] [1999] AC 1, [1997] 4 All ER 545. See also the comment by G Virgo (1998) 33 CLJ 3. See also *Neary* [2002] EWCA Crim 1736.

[302] [2008] UKHL 45.

[303] See eg *Smith* [2008] EWCA Crim 1342; *ABCD* [2010] EWCA Crim 1622; *Mendez* [2010] EWCA Crim 516; *Lewis* [2010] EWCA Crim 496; *Badza* [2010] EWCA Crim 1363; *Montague* [2013] EWCA Crim 1781; *Bristow* [2013] EWCA Crim 1540; *Ali* [2014] EWCA Crim 2169.

[304] [2011] UKSC 59.　　　[305] [1999] 1 AC 1.　　　[306] [2008] UKHL 45.

[307] For extensive analysis of why parasitic accessory liability was controversial, see W Wilson and D Ormerod, 'Simply Harsh to Fairly Simple: Joint Enterprise Reform' [2015] Crim LR 3; B Crewe, A Liebling, N Padfield and G Virgo, 'Joint Enterprise: The Implications of an Unfair and Unclear Law' [2015] Crim LR 252; M Dyson, 'Might Alone Does Not Make Right: Justifying Secondary Liability' [2015] Crim LR 967.

argument that joint enterprise imposed a form of constructive liability for murder. His lord-ship held that if this were the case it would be contrary to principle and would be a defect of the criminal law. It was accepted that the liability of the secondary party is 'undoubtedly' predicated upon a lesser form of mens rea, but his lordship went on to state that it was unre-alistic to say that joint enterprise *as such* imposed constructive criminal liability. What D must have foreseen was P's *intentional* act: recklessness *whether the conduct element of the offence of murder be committed* is a different and more culpable state of mind than reckless-ness *whether death be caused*—a point which was regarded as persuasive by Lord Steyn.[308]

An example will illustrate how this form of secondary liability applied. Consider D who intentionally performed acts of assistance or encouragement to P, intending for P to have the mens rea for the offence in question: he gave P a gun to assist in his robbery, for exam-ple. D is liable as an accessory to the robbery even though P was the one who completed the offence. That is orthodox accessorial liability as we have discussed it so far in this chap-ter. But, if in the course of the robbery P shot and murdered V, D was *also* liable as an accessory for murder which he did *not* intend or assist or encourage P to commit, pro-vided: (a) D intentionally encouraged or assisted P to commit robbery; (b) D foresaw that in the course of[309] committing robbery, P might perform the conduct element of murder in the prescribed circumstances making that an offence; (c) D foresaw that P might do so with the mens rea of murder; and (d) the manner of P committing the murder was not fundamen-tally different from what D foresaw might occur.

Consider a second example. D, the accessory, intentionally assisted or encouraged P to commit theft by shoplifting from a major electrical retailer, contemplating that in the course of committing that offence P 'might well' do an act with intent to cause grievous bodily harm if challenged by the security staff. If P did an act of the kind D foresaw/contemplated and punched V in order to make off with the goods he was stealing, P was guilty of robbery. D was guilty as accessory to both the theft and to the robbery.

These principles applied: whether D was present with P or not;[310] irrespective of whether D caused any conduct by P; irrespective of whether D agreed with P that P might do so; and irrespective of whether D shared a common intent with P to commit crime B (eg murder).[311]

6.5.1.1 The judgment in *Jogee*

Extensive reference has already been made to the joint judgment of the Supreme Court and Privy Council in *Jogee; Ruddock*. This section will consider why the Supreme Court con-cluded that the doctrine of 'parasitic accessory' or 'joint enterprise' liability constituted a legal wrong turn. As has already been explained, the Supreme Court attributed the develop-ment of parasitic accessory liability to the opinion of the Board in *Chan Wing-Siu*, in which Sir Robin Cooke stated:

In the typical case [of aiding and abetting] the same or the same type of offence is actually intended by all the parties acting in concert. In view of the terms of the directions to the jury here, the Crown does not seek to support the present convictions on that ground. The case must depend rather on the wider principle whereby a secondary party is criminally liable for acts by the primary offender of a type which the former foresees but does not necessarily intend. That there is such a principle is not in doubt. It turns on contemplation or, putting the same idea in other words, authorisation, which may be express but is more usually implied. It meets the case of a crime foreseen as a possible

---

[308] [1999] 1 AC 1, 13–16.

[309] Irrespective of whether it is completed. Simester argued that it was a fiction to say that D aids and abets crime B: see n 76. But the actus reus of aiding is D's participation in crime A despite D foreseeing that B might occur.

[310] *Rook* [1993] Crim LR 698.   [311] cf *Gnango* [2011] UKSC 59.

incident of the common unlawful enterprise. The criminal liability lies in participating in the venture with that foresight.

After an extensive review of the relevant authorities, the Supreme Court in *Jogee* concluded that the Privy Council in *Chan Wing-Siu* and the House of Lords in *Powell and Daniels, English* had in fact laid down a new principle. The authorities relied upon by the Privy Council and accepted by the House of Lords in *Powell* and subsequent cases did not support the proposition that if two people set out to commit an offence (crime A), and in the course of it one of them commits another offence (crime B), the second person is guilty as an accessory to crime B if he foresaw it as a possibility, but did not necessarily intend it. The Supreme Court also stated that the Privy Council had made the error of eliding foresight with intention.

Although it confirmed that it was open to the courts to alter the common law in a way that made it more severe, the Supreme Court stated that judges must be cautious before doing so. The Supreme Court recognised that the policy arguments relied upon in subsequent cases to justify the imposition of liability, specifically the problems of escalation associated with group violence, were important, but the court ultimately concluded that they were insufficient to justify making D guilty of murder as opposed to manslaughter. Of particular relevance to this issue was the fact there was no consideration in *Chan Wing-Siu* or in *Powell and Daniels, English* of the fundamental policy question of whether and why it was necessary and appropriate to reclassify such conduct as murder rather than manslaughter. It was held that such a discussion would necessarily have to entail the consideration of questions about fair labelling and fair discrimination in sentencing. The Supreme Court concluded that the principle enunciated in *Chan Wing-Siu* was based upon an incomplete, and in some respects, erroneous, reading of previous case law, coupled with generalized and questionable policy arguments. The court gave the following reasons for why it was right to correct the error and reverse a statement of principle despite it having been made and followed by the Privy Council and the House of Lords on a number of occasions:

- the court had the benefit of a much fuller analysis than on previous occasions when the topic had been considered;

- it could not be said that the law was now well established and working satisfactorily. Rather, it was highly controversial and a continuing source of difficulty for trial judges, leading to a large number of appeals;

- secondary liability is an important part of the common law, and if a wrong turn has been taken, it should be corrected;

- in the common law, foresight of what might happen is ordinarily no more than evidence from which a jury can infer the presence of the requisite intention. The court recognized that it may be strong evidence, but its adoption as a test for the mental element for murder in the case of a secondary party was a serious and anomalous departure from the basic rule, which resulted in over-extension of the law of murder and reduction of the law of manslaughter. The court noted that murder already has a broad mens rea threshold, because it is sufficient that D has an intention to cause serious injury, without intent to kill or to cause risk to life. The *Chan Wing-Siu* principle extended liability for murder to a secondary party on the basis of a still lesser degree of culpability, namely foresight only of the possibility that the principal may commit murder but without there being any need for there to exist an intention to assist him to do so;

- the rule brings what was characterized as 'the striking anomaly' of requiring a lower mental threshold for guilt in the case of the accessory than in the case of the principal.

The Supreme Court restated the principles that govern secondary liability and emphasized that nothing less than an intention to assist or encourage will suffice for D to be guilty as a secondary party. The mens rea for secondary liability was considered earlier in this chapter.

6.5.1.2 Evaluating *Jogee*

In correcting the 'wrong turn' that led to the development of parasitic accessory liability, the Supreme Court's judgment in *Jogee* simplifies the law.[312] The court has also clarified that, in agreement with the previous editions of this work, 'there is no reason why ordinary principles of secondary liability should not be of general application'.[313] In concluding that nothing less than intention will suffice for D to be guilty as an accessory, the judgment also ensures that the threshold for imposing liability upon the accessory is no longer significantly lower than that of the principal. Moreover, the judgment reduces the injustices in cases where it cannot be proved to the criminal standard which of a number of defendants was the principal. Under the old law, if, say, four defendants were charged with murder and the jury could be sure in relation to each of them only that he participated in the attack and foresaw that the V might be killed by one of the others acting with intent, they were all guilty of murder. Applying *Jogee* on those facts, unless the jury is prepared to infer from the foresight that the particular defendant intended that another in the group would kill with intent, they are all likely to be guilty of manslaughter. Under the old law, there were three injustices by overcriminalizing, as three who should[314] have been convicted of manslaughter were guilty of murder. Under the new law, there is an injustice in that one person who deserves to be labelled and punished as a murderer is instead dealt with as a manslaughterer. There are fewer injustices, and arguably more palatable ones. For all those reasons, the judgment is to be welcomed.[315]

The judgment has, however, proved to be controversial for a number of reasons. First, it has been cogently argued that the Supreme Court's conclusion that *Chan Wing-Siu* introduced a 'new principle' that changed the common law in a way which made it more severe is highly suspect.[316] Stark argues that the Supreme Court cited selectively from the relevant case law, giving the most sympathetic view of history that it could. On his analysis of the case law relied upon by the Supreme Court, Stark argues that *Chan Wing-Siu* confirmed was what already beginning to become clear, namely that there was a 'wider principle' beyond standard aiding and abetting, 'whereby a secondary party is criminally liable for acts by the primary offender of a type which the former foresees but does not necessarily intend'.[317] Stark's analysis leads him to conclude, convincingly it is submitted, that the Supreme Court in *Jogee* engaged in substantive law reform. As he notes, there are clear constitutional issues that arise from the court undertaking such a significant change to the common law.

Secondly, the practical impact of *Jogee* is contestable. Whilst the Supreme Court held in emphatic terms that nothing less than intention will suffice for D to be guilty as an accessory, it confirmed that foresight is evidence of intention and that conditional intention will suffice for D to be guilty. Sir Brian Leveson P confirmed subsequently in *Anwar* that the

---

[312] cf R Buxton, '*Jogee*: Upheaval in Secondary Liability for Murder' [2016] Crim LR 324; M Dyson, 'Shorn-Off Complicity' (2016) 75 CLJ 196.

[313] *Jogee* [2016] UKSC 8, [76].   [314] Adopting the standards prescribed in *Jogee*.

[315] For academic reviews, see GR Sullivan, 'Law Reform in the Supreme Court: The Abolition of Joint Enterprise Liability' in B Krebs (ed), *Accessorial Liability after Jogee* (2020) Ch 1; E van Sliedregt, 'Joint Criminal Confusion: Exploring the Merits and Demerits of Joint Enterprise Liability' and M Weinberg, 'Extended Joint Criminal Enterprise—"Top-Down" or "Bottom-up" Legal Reasoning?', Chs 9 and 10 in the same volume.

[316] F Stark, 'The Demise of "Parasitic Accessorial Liability": Substantive Judicial Law Reform, not Common Law Housekeeping' (2016) 75 CLJ 550.

[317] *Chan Wing-Siu* [1985] AC 168, 175.

same facts which would previously have been used to support the inference of mens rea before the decision in *Jogee* will equally be used post the judgment. His lordship stated that the evidential requirements justifying a decision that there is a case to answer are likely to be the same even if, applying the facts to the different directions in law, the jury might reach a different conclusion.[318] It could transpire, however, that juries are just as likely to convict after *Jogee* as they were before. Indeed, in *Chan Kam Shing* the Hong Kong Court of Final Appeal stated that the concept of conditional intent was interpreted in *Johnson* and *Anwar* in much the same way as the foresight requirement in *Chan Wing-Siu*. This 'drift back to joint criminal enterprise' led Ribeiro PJ to question the true extent of the changes effected by the Supreme Court's decision.[319]

Finally, the judgment has been subject to sustained criticism by courts in other common law jurisdictions. In *Chan Kam Shing*, the Hong Kong Court of Final Appeal declined to follow *Jogee* and held that parasitic accessory liability should continue to be applied in Hong Kong. Ribeiro PJ gave three reasons for this conclusion. First, that secondary parties to a joint criminal enterprise deserve 'to be regarded as gravely culpable'. Secondly, that the abolition of joint enterprise would 'deprive the law of a valuable principle for dealing with dynamic situations involving evidential and situational uncertainties which traditional accessorial liability rules are ill-adapted to addressing'. Finally, the court expressed concern about the introduction of the concept of conditional intent, on the basis that it 'gives rise to significant conceptual and practical problems'. Key to the court's decision to retain parasitic accessory liability was its conclusion that there are two distinct doctrines: basic joint enterprise or 'common purpose' liability, and parasitic accessory liability or 'extended joint criminal enterprise'. In reaching this conclusion, the court disagreed with *Jogee* in which the Supreme Court, citing with approval the previous edition of this work,[320] held that there is no reason why ordinary principles of secondary liability should not be of general application. Krebs argues that this difference in taxonomy means that the two judgments are at cross-purposes.[321]

The judgment in *Jogee* was also criticized by the High Court of Australia in *Miller v The Queen*. A majority of the High Court were not persuaded by the arguments of policy and principle that led the Supreme Court in *Jogee* to declare that *Chan Wing-Siu* constituted a 'legal wrong turn'. The High Court identified six broad reasons for retaining the doctrine of parasitic accessory liability. First, it rejected claims of overcriminalization as being unfounded. Secondly, it held that parasitic accessory liability is an independent type of secondary liability rather than a sub-species of accessory liability, so the differences between the two are not unprincipled. Thirdly, the court expressed concern about the practical difficulties in proving individual contributions in multi-handed situations. Fourthly, it expressed disagreement with the proposition that parasitic accessory liability makes trials unduly complex. Fifthly, it was considered 'undesirable' to alter parasitic accessory liability without reviewing the law of homicide and secondary liability generally. Finally, the court regarded judicial reform as being inappropriate against a background of legislative reform efforts in various Australian states. Krebs argues that the majority judgment in *Miller* does little more than reassert the well-rehearsed arguments in favour of parasitic accessory liability without engaging with the relevant counter-arguments.[322] Gageler J dissented and agreed with the view expressed by the Supreme Court in *Jogee* that escalating group violence does

318 *Anwar* [2016] EWCA Crim 551, [22].   319 [2016] HKCFA 87, [92]–[93].
320 *Jogee* [2016] UKSC 8, [76].
321 B Krebs, 'Hong Kong Court of Final Appeal: Divided by a Common Purpose' (2017) 81 J Crim L 271.
322 B Krebs, 'Accessory Liability: Persisting in Error' (2017) 76 CLJ 7.

not, without more, provide support for parasitic accessory liability. In *Miller*, the majority were concerned that requiring intent on the part of the secondary party set the threshold of liability too high. Whilst foresight sets the threshold of liability too low, Krebs suggests that the decision in *Miller* could indicate that requiring full-blown intention is 'beginning to look a step too far in the opposite direction'.[323] She states that it may be necessary to find a middle ground between foresight and full-blown intention to deal with the phenomenon of incidental crimes.

The judgment in *Jogee* is clearly not a panacea. As this section has demonstrated, the juridical foundation of the Supreme Court's decision is controversial[324] and there are a number of matters that the courts still need to resolve.

One of the most pressing issues for the courts was what to do about those defendants who were convicted on the basis of parasitic accessory liability. In *Jogee*, the Supreme Court stated that, 'the effect of putting the law right is not to render invalid all convictions which were arrived at over many years by faithfully applying the law as laid down in the *Chan Wing-Siu* case and in *R v Powell; R v English*'.[325] Where a conviction has been arrived at by faithfully applying the law as it stood at the time, the court held that it can be set aside only by seeking exceptional leave to appeal to the Court of Appeal out of time. In the subsequent case of *Johnson* the Court of Appeal confirmed that it will be for the applicant for exceptional leave to appeal out of time to demonstrate that a substantial injustice would be done.[326] In determining whether that high threshold has been met, the court stated that it will primarily and ordinarily have regard to the strength of the case advanced that the change in the law would, in fact, have made a difference.[327] If the particular crime is a crime of violence which the jury concluded must have involved the use of a weapon, so that the inference of participation with an intention to cause really serious harm is strong, the court concluded that is likely to be very difficult. If, however, the crime did not involve intended violence or use of force, the court stated that it may well be easier to demonstrate substantial injustice. It is submitted that the approach adopted by the Court of Appeal will preclude most of those whose convictions are based upon the 'wrong turn' taken in *Chan Wing-Siu* from appealing their convictions. The impact of *Jogee* may therefore only be felt prospectively.[328] Many will feel disappointed by this state of affairs. This sense of disappointment is likely to be compounded by the fact that the Court of Appeal's application of *Johnson*,[329] confirmed in the subsequent case of *Garwood*, that it has no jurisdiction to certify a point of law of general public importance in cases where leave to appeal has been refused. This means that an individual in such a case will be unable to challenge before the Supreme Court the Court of Appeal's conclusion that there was no substantial injustice.[330]

---

[323] ibid, 10.

[324] R Williams, 'What is the Theoretical Basis for Accomplice Liability?' in B Krebs (ed), *Accessorial Liability after Jogee* (2020) Ch 2.

[325] [2016] UKSC 8, [100].   [326] [2016] EWCA Crim 1613.

[327] The same approach was adopted by the Northern Ireland Court of Appeal in *Skinner* [2016] NICA 40.

[328] For further discussion, see K Laird [2017] Crim LR 216. At the time of writing, the Court of Appeal has quashed a conviction and ordered a retrial in only one murder case; see *Crilly* [2018] EWCA Crim 168.

[329] eg *Jackson* [2019] EWCA Crim 1461; *Johnson-Haynes* [2019] EWCA Crim 1217.

[330] There are numerous cases on which the Court of Appeal has rejected the submission of substantial injustice. See *Grant-Murray* [2017] EWCA Crim 1228; *Agera* [2017] EWCA Crim 740; *Varley* [2017] EWCA Crim 268. In all these cases, the court concluded that even if the jury had been directed in accordance with *Jogee*, it would have 'made no difference'. See generally K Laird, 'Commentary on *Towers*' [2019] Crim LR 791.

6.6 Accomplice must be participating in 'an offence'

6.6.1 Can there be secondary liability in an inchoate offence?

It is an offence to do acts capable of assisting or encouraging,[331] or to conspire, or to attempt, to commit an offence.[332] It is *not* an offence to attempt[333] or, it is submitted, to conspire[334] to do an act which would involve no more than secondary liability for the offence if it were committed.

Secondary liability is triggered by the commission of the substantive principal offence. To demonstrate the operation of the rules, consider the following example. Knowing that P intends to drive his car, D2 urges D1 to 'lace' P's drink with so much alcohol that if P drives after consuming the drink he will inevitably commit an offence under s 5(1) of the Road Traffic Act 1988.[335] D1 agrees to do so and attempts to, or does, lace the drink. If P consumes the drink, drives his car and thus commits the offence under the Road Traffic Act 1988, D2 and D1 will be guilty as secondary parties.[336] However, if P declines the drink, or does not drive the car, D2 is not guilty of conspiracy and D1 is guilty neither of conspiracy nor of attempt to commit the offence. The act encouraged, agreed upon, attempted and indeed done, lacing the drink, is not the offence.[337] D may be liable under s 44 of the SCA 2007.[338]

Assuming that P consumes the laced drink and drives, P could be guilty as the principal offender, notwithstanding his lack of mens rea, on the ground that the offence is one of strict liability. Where the offence is one requiring mens rea, which the actual perpetrator of the actus reus lacks, then those who procured him to act will be liable because they, or one of them, will be principal offenders acting through an innocent agent.

In the case of conspiracy, one who abets or counsels the commission of the crime appears to be a principal offender in the conspiracy. It is also possible to abet or counsel an attempt.[339] For the scope of D's liability for assisting or encouraging P to assist or encourage P2, see Ch 11.

---

[331] The SCA 2007 replaced common law incitement with three statutory inchoate offences of assisting or encouraging in ss 44–6.

[332] See Ch 11.

[333] Criminal Attempts Act 1981, s 1(4)(b); *Dunnington* [1984] QB 472. Cf *Chief Constable of Hampshire v Mace* (1986) 84 Cr App R 40. See the debate between M Bohlander and J Child in [2009] Crim LR, discussed in Ch 11, p 453.

[334] *Kenning* [2008] EWCA Crim 1534; *Hollinshead* [1985] 1 All ER 850 at 857–8. The House of Lords left the question open: [1985] AC 975. See JC Smith, 'Secondary Participation and Inchoate Offences' in *Crime, Proof and Punishment*, 21.

[335] Driving or being in charge of a motor vehicle with an alcohol concentration above a prescribed limit.

[336] *A-G's Reference (No 1 of 1975)*, p 196.

[337] The adulteration of the drink might possibly amount to the administration of a noxious thing, contrary to the OAPA 1861, s 24, see Ch 16.

[338] Virgo argues that the inchoate offences could in future be deployed to avoid the Supreme Court's restrictive interpretation of accessorial liability in *Jogee*. See G Virgo, 'The Relationship Between Inchoate and Accessorial Liability after *Jogee*' [2016] 9 Arch Rev 6. Given the complexity of the offences in the SCA 2007, this seems unlikely.

[339] *Hapgood and Wyatt* (1870) LR 1 CCR 221; *S v Robinson* 1968 (1) SA 666.

6.7 The relationship between the liability of the principal and secondary party

6.7.1 Procedural issues

Even if the alleged principal offender has been acquitted, a conviction of another person as an accessory may be logical. This is so even if it is assumed[340] that an accessory may be convicted only when the principal offender himself is guilty. The acquittal of the alleged principal offender, far from being conclusive that no crime was committed, is not generally admissible in evidence at a subsequent trial of the secondary parties.[341] A second jury may be satisfied beyond reasonable doubt that the crime was committed upon evidence which the first jury found unconvincing; evidence may be admissible against D which was not admissible against P, or fresh evidence may have come to light or P may have been acquitted because the prosecution offered no evidence against him.

The position would seem to be the same where D is tried first and convicted and P is subsequently acquitted[342] and when the parties are jointly indicted.[343] In *Hughes*,[344] after the prosecution had offered no evidence against P, he was acquitted and called as a witness for the Crown, with the result that D was convicted by the same jury as an accessory to P's alleged crime. Where principal and secondary parties are tried separately, this result is supported by the analogous rule laid down in *DPP v Shannon*[345] that the acquittal of one party to a conspiracy does not invalidate the conviction of the only other party on an earlier or later occasion. *Shannon* left open the question whether one party may be convicted of conspiracy when the other is acquitted at the same trial;[346] and in *Anthony*[347] it was said, *obiter*, that a jury cannot acquit P and at the same time find D guilty of counselling him to commit the crime.

If P and D are tried together and the evidence tending to show that P committed the crime is the same against both, then it would be inconsistent to acquit P and convict D.[348] Where, however, there is evidence admissible against D but not against P that P committed the crime (eg a confession by D that he counselled P to commit the crime and saw him commit it), it would be perfectly logical to acquit P and convict D of counselling him (and of conspiring with him). In *Humphreys and Turner*,[349] which was just such a case, Chapman J held that D might be convicted as an accessory, distinguishing the *dicta* in *Anthony* as applicable only to felonies. It is submitted that, ever since the Criminal Law Act 1967 came into force, the rule stated in *Humphreys and Turner* is applicable to all offences.

It is one thing for a court which is trying D alone to reject or ignore the holding of another court that P was not a principal offender and to hold that he was; and that, therefore, D might be convicted as an accessory to P's crime. It is quite another thing for a court to

---

340 Contrary to the view expressed, see p 233.

341 *Hui Chi-ming v R* [1991] 3 All ER 897. Under the Police and Criminal Evidence Act 1984, s 74, a conviction is now admissible to prove the commission of the offence by the principal: *Turner* [1991] Crim LR 57.

342 In *Rowley* [1948] 1 All ER 570, D's conviction was quashed when, after he had pleaded guilty as an accessory, the alleged principals were acquitted by the jury. But the decision is criticized in *Shannon* [1974] 2 All ER 1009 at 1020 and 1049. Cf *Zaman* [2010] EWCA Crim, on which see Ch 7, p 250.

343 See also *Petch* [2005] 2 Cr App R 657.   344 (1860) Bell CC 242.   345 [1975] AC 717; Ch 12.

346 The point is now settled by the Criminal Law Act 1977, and *Longman and Cribben* (1981) 72 Cr App R 121, p 479; but *Shannon* is relevant to the common law governing secondary participation.

347 [1965] 2 QB 189. Cf *Surujpaul v R* [1958] 1 WLR 1050.   348 *Surujpaul v R* [1958] 1 WLR 1050.

349 [1965] 3 All ER 689 (Liverpool Crown Court).Followed in *Sweetman v Industries and Commerce Department* [1970] NZLR 139. Cf *Davis* [1977] Crim LR 542, and commentary and *Fuller* [1998] Crim LR 61.

hold at one and the same time: (a) that P was, in law, not guilty[350] and (b) that D was guilty, as a secondary party, of P's crime. These propositions seem, at first sight, to be inconsistent with the derivative nature of secondary liability.[351]

6.7.2 Secondary party guilty of a greater offence than the principal

Since secondary liability is said to derive from that of the principal, it may seem hard to see how the liability of the secondary party can properly be held to be greater than that of the principal offender. Historically,[352] distinctions were drawn based on the presence at the crime and it was thought that the liability of the accessory who was absent could never 'rise higher' than that of the principal offender. The distinctions depending on whether the accessory is present at, or absent from, the commission of the crime are no longer applicable.[353]

There are some cases where it seems obvious that a person who, at least, appears to be an accessory ought to be convicted of a greater offence than the immediate perpetrator of the actus reus. We have already noticed that offences may be committed through innocent agents and that if D, with intent to kill, sends a letter-bomb through the post to V who is killed by the explosion, D is guilty of murder as a principal offender and E, the postman, is an innocent agent. Suppose, however, that E notices some wires sticking out of the parcel and that he is aware that a number of letter-bombs have been sent by terrorists lately with fatal results. He thinks, 'This could be a letter-bomb—but it's not likely and I'm in a hurry, I'll risk it' and pushes the letter through V's letter box where it explodes and kills V. If these facts are proved, E behaved recklessly and is guilty of manslaughter. He is no longer an innocent agent. But it would be absurd if D who sent the letter with intent to kill should escape liability for murder.

Alternative approaches to this issue have been advanced by academics. Glanville Williams suggests that a person like our postman should be regarded as a semi-innocent agent.[354] Professor Kadish[355] prefers to say that D can properly be said to have caused V's death. Because P's actions are not 'fully voluntary' they do not break the chain of causation.[356] His approach explains the following difficult example:

[D] hands a gun to [P] informing him that it is loaded with blank ammunition only and telling him to go and scare [V] by discharging it. The ammunition is in fact live (as [D] knows) and [V] is killed. [P] is convicted only of manslaughter. . . . It would seem absurd that [D] should thereby escape conviction for murder.[357]

P's act would be regarded by Kadish as not 'fully voluntary' because, through his ignorance of material facts, he was not fully aware of what he was doing or its consequences; so D has caused the death, intending to kill and is a principal murderer.[358]

---

[350] Not merely that there was not enough evidence to convict him, but that there was evidence which established his innocence.

[351] See p 181.   [352] Hawkins, II PC, c 29, s 15.

[353] It depended on the distinction in the law of felonies between a principal in the second degree and an accessory which has been abolished.

[354] TBCL, 373.   [355] *Blame and Punishment* (1987) 183.

[356] eg P shoots at V, intending to kill but only wounds. D treats the wound recklessly and V dies of the maltreated wound. P and D have both caused V's death. P is guilty of murder and D of manslaughter. Both are principals.

[357] *Burke and Howe* [1986] QB 626 at 641–2. Lord Mackay agreed with the Court of Appeal who found this example convincing: [1987] AC 417.

[358] It is not so clear that the causation theory is a satisfactory explanation of the case where D intends the result and E is reckless whether he causes it—eg the postman case discussed earlier. It seems to be straining rather to say that the postman's act is not 'fully voluntary'.

For many years English law seemed to accept that D could not be liable for a more serious offence than P. This flowed from *Richards*,[359] which the Court of Appeal and Lord Mackay (in *Howe*) considered to be wrongly decided. D, a woman, hired P1 and P2 to beat up her husband 'bad enough to put him in hospital for a month'. She signalled to P1 and P2 when V left the house. They inflicted a wound upon V, not amounting to a serious injury. D was convicted of wounding with intent to cause grievous bodily harm but P1 and P2 were acquitted of that offence and convicted of the lesser offence of unlawful wounding. D's conviction was quashed and a conviction for unlawful wounding substituted.[360]

Richards was heavily criticized and, in view of the disapproval expressed in *Burke* (conjoined with *Howe* on appeal), though only *obiter*, may not be followed in future. It has some academic supporters.[361]

The anomaly of holding D liable for the greater offence is emphasized if we consider a case like *Richards* in which V, by some unforeseeable mischance, had died of the slight injury inflicted by P1 and P2. This would have been manslaughter by P1 and P2. If D was guilty of the s 18 offence, it would follow logically that she was guilty of murder. It may be argued that this would be wrong (though she had the necessary mens rea), because no act was ever done with *intent thereby* to kill or cause serious bodily harm—there was no 'murderous act'. If, however, P1 and P2 had acted with intent to do serious bodily harm but succeeded in inflicting only a slight injury it would have been murder by all three if V had died of that. But then the act would have been done in pursuance of a joint enterprise to cause serious bodily harm. In fact, there was no GBH committed and no charges of such. For that reason, though not for the reasons given, it may be that the decision in *Richards* was right after all.

The position is more straightforward where D and P both have the mens rea for the greater offence but P's liability is reduced for some reason to that of a lesser offence. If P causes the actus reus in carrying out the agreed plan but his liability is reduced 'for some reason special to himself',[362] such as loss of self-control or diminished responsibility,[363] it seems clearly right that D should not be able to shelter behind P's personal exemption from liability for the greater offence.

In the case considered in *Burke* (conjoined with *Howe* on appeal), however, the reduction in P's liability did not depend on a personal consideration of this kind. P's defence was that he had agreed to shoot V out of fear of D, but that, when it came to the event, the gun went off accidentally. The killing was therefore unintentional and amounted to no more than manslaughter. The judge, following *Richards*, directed that if the jury found P guilty only of manslaughter, then D could at most be guilty of manslaughter. The implication of the decision of the House is that this was wrong. It is submitted that the true position is that if P has gone beyond a merely preparatory act and is attempting to commit the crime when he 'accidentally' kills, both D and P are guilty of murder; but, if P is doing only a preparatory act when he happens to kill—he is driving to V's house with intent to blow it up when the bomb in his car goes off and kills V who has unexpectedly gone out for a walk—P is liable only for manslaughter and so is D. The killing which occurs is not the killing he intended, though the victim happens to be the same.[364]

---

[359] [1974] QB 776.

[360] This followed Hawkins's view, n 352. It was assumed that under the old law of felonies, D would have been an accessory and not a principal in the second degree.

[361] Kadish ('Complicity and Causation' (1985) 73 Cal L Rev 323 at 329) supports the *Richards* view arguing (a) that D did not cause the actions of P1 and P2 because they were not her unwitting instruments but chose to act freely as they did and (b) she could not be held liable 'for an aggravated assault [ie an assault with intent to cause grievous bodily harm] that did not take place'.

[362] The phrase used by Lord Mackay in *Burke*, n 357.

[363] This case is covered by s 2(4) of the Homicide Act 1957. D's liability for murder is not affected by E's diminished responsibility. The Coroners and Justice Act 2009, s 54(8) applies the same rule to loss of self-control.

[364] See commentary [1987] Crim LR 481 at 484.

6.7.3 Where the 'principal' is not guilty

Here we are concerned with cases where the immediate perpetrator of the actus reus is not guilty of the offence alleged and the offence is one which is incapable of being committed by a person as a principal offender acting through an innocent agent. Examples include rape and other offences involving sexual intercourse, driving offences and bigamy (except where the bigamous marriage is by proxy). There are three possible situations:

(1) P has committed the actus reus of the offence with mens rea but has a defence;

(2) P has committed the actus reus but has no mens rea;

(3) P has not committed the actus reus.

The approach to these is best examined by analysis of a series of cases in which the issues have arisen.

6.7.3.1 P performs actus reus and mens rea but has a defence

In *Bourne*,[365] D by duress compelled his wife (P) to have sex with a dog. His conviction of abetting her to commit buggery was upheld although it was assumed that the wife, if she had been charged, would have been acquitted on the ground of coercion.[366] Sir Rupert Cross[367] argued that this was in accordance with principle because 'The wife committed the "*actus reus*" with the "*mens rea*" required by the definition of the crime in question and the husband participated in that "*mens rea*".' The wife had mens rea in the sense that she knew exactly what she was doing, though she was to be excused for doing it. According to some theorists, where the defence relied upon by the principal is excusatory, that does not preclude the accessory from being convicted.

6.7.3.2 P performs the actus reus but lacks mens rea

In *Cogan and Leak*,[368] D terrorized his wife, V, into submitting to sexual intercourse with P. P was convicted of rape and D of abetting him but, on appeal, P's conviction had to be quashed because the jury had not been directed correctly, and it may have been that P lacked the mens rea as to V's consent. D's conviction was upheld but primarily on the ground that D was the principal offender acting through an innocent agent. The agency theory is misconceived. If it were right, a woman could be convicted of rape as the principal offender and it is plain that she cannot commit that offence; she does not have a penis. To suggest that D raped his wife V using P's penis is nonsense. The court's second reason was that D was rightly convicted as a procurer because V had been raped ('no one outside a court of law would say she had not been') and 'therefore the particulars of offence accurately stated what [D] had done, namely that he procured [P] to commit the offence'. But if P believed V was consenting, V had not, as a matter of law, been raped. If X's bike is taken from the place he left it by Y who owns an exactly similar model and thinks this is his, X, who has lost his bike forever, reasonably believes it has been stolen, but he is wrong. Y has not committed theft. The court's distinguishing of *Walters v Lunt*[369] (trike not stolen goods because taken by a seven-year-old) was erroneous. If the hypothetical bike and trike were not stolen,

---

[365] (1952) 36 Cr App R 125. See JL Edwards, 'Duress and Aiding and Abetting' (1953) 69 LQR 297; R Cross, 'Duress and Aiding and Abetting (A Reply)' (1953) 69 LQR 354.

[366] See p 399.

[367] (1953) 68 LQR 354.

[368] [1976] QB 217, [1975] Crim LR 584 and commentary. Discussed in *Watkins* [2010] EWCA Crim 2349.

[369] [1951] 2 All ER 645, p 360.

and plainly they were not, V was not raped by P in *Cogan*. The court's opinion that D had procured not merely the actus reus but the offence of rape is wrong.

If a conviction is to be upheld in such a case, and policy and justice seem to require it,[370] this could be on the ground that it is an offence to procure the commission of an actus reus; and the courts took this step in *Millward*.[371] D instructed his employee, P, to drive on a road a vehicle which D knew, but P did not know, was in a dangerous condition. It was assumed that the actus reus of reckless driving was committed simply by the driving of the vehicle on the road. The condition of the vehicle resulted in a collision causing death. P was charged with causing death by reckless driving and D of abetting him. P was acquitted, D was convicted and his conviction upheld on the ground that he had procured the actus reus. This approach was advocated in the first seven editions of this book and it seems the best available to the courts; but there is force in the opinion of Kadish[372] that it 'at least technically . . . amounts to creating a new crime'. As there is no principal offender, there is no question of participation in the guilt of another or of 'secondary liability' and it becomes, in effect, a substantive offence to procure the commission of the actus reus of any crime.

Bourne, Cogan and Leak and *Millward* were all cases of alleged procuring and it is not certain whether the principle of *Millward* extends to other modes of secondary participation. Procuring is narrower than the other modes in that (a) it must be the cause of the conduct or circumstance element of the actus reus and, perhaps, (b) it must be the procurer's purpose to bring about the result—'To procure means to produce by endeavour'[373]—but that may be too restrictive. Bourne and Leak were endeavouring to bring about the whole actus reus; but Millward, while he was 'endeavouring' to have the dangerous vehicle driven on the road, which was assumed to amount to reckless driving, was certainly not endeavouring to have anyone killed. If the driver had been guilty of reckless driving, then both he and Millward would have been guilty of causing death by reckless driving; but it does not necessarily follow that Millward should be guilty of that offence when the driver is not guilty. If 'procure' does imply purpose and if the principle is limited to procuring, then he ought to have been convicted only of reckless driving and not of causing death. The cases may also be approached in terms of justification and excuse, although it is doubtful that this assists greatly—the principal offender in each case was acquitted on the basis of an excusing factor (duress or lack of mens rea), and according to the theory this does not preclude secondary liability.[374] It is unclear what impact *Jogee* will have on these cases. Are they an exception to the rule that D must intend P to act with mens rea, or does *Jogee* implicitly overturn them? It is submitted that the former is the preferable approach.

6.7.3.3 No actus reus by P

In *Morris v Tolman*,[375] D was charged with abetting the owner of a vehicle in using that vehicle for a purpose for which the vehicle had not been licensed. The statute (the Roads Act 1920) was drafted in such a way that the offence could be committed only by the

---

[370] The conduct may well be caught by the offences in the SCA 2007, ss 44–6.
[371] [1994] Crim LR 527. See RD Taylor, 'Complicity, Legal Scholarship and the Law of Unintended Consequences' (2009) 29 LS 1. In *DPP v K and B* [1997] 1 Cr App R 36, some teenage girls procured a boy to 'rape' V. He may have been *doli incapax* (ie at that time incapable of committing the crime). They were held guilty of rape. It was said that it would have been different if the unidentified boy had been, or may have been, under ten because then there would have been no actus reus of rape. It is submitted that that is wrong. The actus reus was the voluntary penetration of the vagina by the penis, whatever the age of the boy.
[372] *Essays in Criminal Law*, 180.   [373] See p 232.
[374] See JC Smith, *Justification and Excuse*; G Williams, 'Theory of Excuses' [1982] Crim LR 722, especially 735–8; Taylor [1983] Crim LR 656.
[375] [1923] 1 KB 166.

licence-holder. It was held that, there being no evidence that the licence-holder, P, had used the vehicle for a purpose other than that for which it was licensed, D must be acquitted. Though he, in fact, had so used the vehicle, that was not an actus reus. Again, in *Thornton v Mitchell*,[376] D, a bus conductor, negligently signalled to the driver of his bus, P, to reverse. Two pedestrians, whom it was not possible for the driver to see, were knocked down and one of them killed. The driver having been acquitted of careless driving, it was held that the conductor must be acquitted of abetting. Again, there was no actus reus. The driver's acquittal shows that he committed no actus reus, for careless driving is a crime which requires no mens rea beyond an intention to drive and D could not be said to have driven the bus. There would have been no such obstacle in the way of convicting D for manslaughter. That would, at that time, simply have raised the question whether D's negligence was sufficiently gross.[377]

Thornton and Mitchell was distinguished in *Millward* on the ground that there was no actus reus of careless driving in the former case. And in *Loukes*[378] where the facts were similar to those in *Millward*, D's conviction for procuring the offence of causing death by *dangerous* driving was quashed. The actus reus of dangerous driving[379] is more precisely defined and a condition of the liability of the driver, P, in this situation is that 'it would be obvious to a competent and careful driver that driving the vehicle in its current state would be dangerous'. The judge directed an acquittal of the driver on the ground that there was no evidence that the dangerous condition of the vehicle would have been obvious to a competent and careful driver. The conviction of Loukes, who was responsible for the maintenance of the vehicle, for procuring the commission of the offence, was quashed. There being no actus reus, he could not be held to have procured one.[380]

6.8 Withdrawal by a secondary party

Where D has counselled P to commit a crime, or is present, aiding P in the commission of it, it may still be possible for him to escape liability by withdrawal before P goes on to commit the crime.[381] An effective withdrawal will not, however, affect any liability he may have already incurred for conspiracy, or, if the withdrawal took place after P had done a more than merely preparatory act,[382] attempting to commit the crime.[383] It is important also to note that the Serious Crime Act offences in ss 44 to 46 allow for D to be prosecuted where he has done acts *capable of* assisting or encouraging P, irrespective of whether P commits any offence. Liability arises once D performs the acts capable of assisting or encouraging,

---

[376] [1940] 1 All ER 339. See Taylor [1983] Crim LR 656, and (2009) 29 LS 1.   [377] See Ch 14.

[378] [1996] Crim LR 341. See commentary doubting whether there was an actus reus in *Millward*. And cf *Roberts and George* [1997] Crim LR 209.

[379] See Ch 32. It seems that there is no room for procuring the actus reus as distinct from the offence because there is no actus reus unless the fault element is present—ie the full offence is committed: *Roberts and George* [1997] Crim LR 209 and commentary.

[380] In *Pickford* [1995] 1 Cr App R 420, 429–30 it was held that it was not an offence to aid and abet a boy under the age of 14 (at that time presumed to be incapable of sexual intercourse) to commit incest with his mother. The act would not be an actus reus.

[381] See A Reed, 'Repentance and Forgiveness: Withdrawal from Participation and the Proportionality Test' in A Reed and M Bohlander (eds), *Participation in Crime: Domestic and Comparative Perspectives* (2013); KJM Smith, 'Withdrawal in Complicity' [2001] Crim LR 769; D Lanham, 'Accomplices and Withdrawal' (1981) 97 LQR 575; Williams, TBCL, 310–11.

[382] See p 445.   [383] Withdrawal does not affect liability for an attempt; see p 456.

irrespective of whether the acts do in fact assist or encourage. There is no withdrawal defence unless what D has done is 'reasonable' within s 50.

Although the principle that 'a person who unequivocally withdraws before the moment of the actual commission of the crime by the principal offender should not be liable for that crime',[384] is clear, it is less easy to identify not only what is meant by 'unequivocal withdrawal' but also on what basis the defence operates. It is unclear whether it is designed primarily to serve as an incentive to D to withdraw or to reflect his diminished degree of blameworthiness.[385]

There are at least three bases on which a withdrawal defence might be constructed.

(1) The defence operates only where D brings to an end the actus reus of assisting or encouraging P. On this interpretation the defence would be relatively narrowly constructed.

(2) The defence may operate because D's withdrawal negates his mens rea of intention to assist or encourage. Such an approach would create an extremely broad defence, potentially D's unannounced unilateral decision to take no part would suffice. That would seem unworkable. It also seems to be unprincipled. If D does acts assisting or encouraging with the requisite mens rea, his subsequent withdrawal cannot negate his mens rea in relation to his completed actus reus.

(3) It is possible to construe the defence as a 'true' defence operating despite the presence of D's continuing actus reus and mens rea as a secondary party.[386]

English law has yet to address these issues in detail and they were not considered by the Supreme Court in *Jogee*. The Law Commission identifies the basis of the defence as 'negating the effect of the assistance, encouragement or agreement'[387] with the ultimate decision whether D has so managed being one for the jury.[388]

6.8.1 An effective withdrawal?

For any withdrawal to be effective, it must be voluntary, real and effective and communicated in some form in good time.[389] If D is arrested, he can hardly be said to have 'withdrawn'. His arrest does not necessarily demonstrate any repentance on his part, nor undo any aid, advice or encouragement he may have already given.[390] Of course, D's arrest precludes any future secondary participation by him;[391] but in this section we are concerned with absolution from the potential liability arising from D's past acts. Withdrawal has no part to play if D denies that he was involved in the offence in any way.[392]

---

[384] *O'Flaherty* [2004] EWCA Crim 526; applied in *Mitchell* [2008] EWCA Crim 2552; *Campbell* [2009] EWCA Crim 50; and *Rajakumar* [2013] EWCA Crim 1512.

[385] For a comprehensive discussion of these approaches, see KJM Smith [2001] Crim LR 769.

[386] This is the approach favoured by Reed, see n 357. He argues that withdrawal is not predicated upon the neutralization of actus reus or mens rea, but rather is a true defence that represents D's reduced level of culpable dangerousness. Unlike other defences, Reed suggests that withdrawal does not fit into the excuse/justification dichotomy, but is more analogous to consent.

[387] LC 305, para 3.60.   [388] ibid, para 3.65.   [389] *Otway* [2011] EWCA Crim 3.

[390] *Johnson and Jones* (1841) Car & M 218. *Jackson* (1673) 1 Hale PC 464 at 465 appears *contra* but is an obscure and unsatisfactory case. See Lanham (1981) 97 LQR 575 at 577.

[391] For an infamous example where it did not, see *Craig and Bentley* (1952) The Times, 10–13 Dec.

[392] *Gallant* [2008] EWCA Crim 1111. Mr Gallant was subsequently pardoned following his acts of bravery in the London Bridge terror attack in 2019.

In addition to a general voluntary awareness on D's part, a clear precondition for the defence to operate is an unequivocal communication of withdrawal.[393] This can be communication to the principal offender, and if more than one to all principal offenders, or by communication with the law enforcement agency.[394]

Mere repentance, without any action, is not a sufficient or necessary condition for the defence.[395] D's 'innocent' state of mind at the time of the commission of the crime is no answer if he had mens rea when he did the act of counselling or aiding. English courts are generally reluctant to inquire into questions of motive. D may have seen the error of his ways, or he may be acting out of malice against his accomplices or because of fear of detection or because he has decided that the risks outweigh the possible rewards. It is submitted that it should make no difference. It has been recognized, for example, that if D neutralizes the effect of any assistance or encouragement he has given, he is not liable, even if he did not intend to neutralize its effect.[396]

6.8.1.1 Preventing or attempting to prevent the crime

To be effective must D's withdrawal involve his taking all reasonable steps to prevent the crime? It is submitted that this is not a necessary, although clearly it should be a *sufficient*, basis for the defence. Where D gives timely warning to the police, the effect ought in most cases to be that the crime will be prevented; but this may not always be so and, even where it is, there remains D's potential liability for abetting P's attempt, if P has gone beyond mere preparation. Surely, however, efforts to prevent the commission of the crime by informing the police ought to be an effective withdrawal, whether D has or has not attempted to persuade P to desist. Apart from being the best evidence of repentance, it is conduct which the law should and does encourage.[397]

6.8.1.2 Withdrawal by cancelling assistance provided

The question of withdrawal is usually approached by ascertaining whether D has 'neutralized' any input his assistance or encouragement might have had irrespective of whether that will in fact prevent the crime being committed. However, this is a difficult test to apply.[398] For example, where D has supplied information it may be impossible in any meaningful sense to cancel the effect of that assistance by merely communicating withdrawal to P and suggesting that D will have no further part to play. In such cases, D's communicated countermand must go further if it is to be effective in neutralizing *the effect* of the assistance. It may be that D in such cases would be obliged to inform the police or do some act to prevent the crime, but the courts have not insisted on this.

---

[393] *O' Flaherty* [2004] EWCA Crim 526.

[394] cf the Law Commission's view that D ought not to be automatically denied the defence if he has not informed all parties: LC 305, para 3.65.

[395] Hale, I PC, 618; Stephen, *Digest* (4th edn) art 42; Williams, CLGP, s 127; *Croft* [1944] 1 KB 295; *Becerra*, n 403.

[396] *Rook* [1993] 2 All ER at 963. See the discussion in LC 305, para 3.126.

[397] cf the large 'discounts' on sentence which may be earned for information given after D has become liable for and been convicted of the offence.

[398] The Supreme Court of Canada, by a majority, held in *Gauthier* [2013] SCC 32 that an effective withdrawal requires D, in a manner proportional to his participation in the commission of the planned offence, to take reasonable steps in the circumstances either to neutralize or otherwise cancel out the effects of his participation or to prevent the commission of the offence. Dissenting, Fish J held that Canadian law had never required D to have taken steps to neutralize his participation and that such steps would strengthen the defence, but that they were not necessary.

Although no clear test has evolved, what seems to be involved in these cases is an unarticulated proportionality test, assessing the exculpatory conduct (what was done or said, to whom, at what stage of the criminal conduct), and the mode of D's participation in the contemplated offence (supply of weapons or advice, mere encouragement, presence at the crime, having been the instigator[399]). In *O'Flaherty*, the court suggested that in evaluating the effectiveness of the withdrawal, account will be taken of 'the nature of the assistance and encouragement already given and how imminent the [principal offence] is, as well as the nature of the action said to constitute the withdrawal'.[400] The court emphasized that it is not necessary for D to have taken reasonable steps to prevent the crime in order to have successfully withdrawn.

If D's assistance consisted only in advising or encouraging P to commit the crime, it may be enough for him to tell P to desist.[401] If P then commits the crime he does so against D's advice and without his encouragement. It may be that P would never have committed the crime if D had not put it into his head in the first place; but then D may be properly and adequately dealt with by conviction under ss 44 to 46 of the SCA 2007. If D has counselled more than one person, then it seems that he must communicate his countermand to all of those who perpetrate the offence, for otherwise his counselling remains operative.[402] To be effective, the communication must be such as 'will serve unequivocal notice upon the other party to the common unlawful cause that if he proceeds upon it he does so without the further aid and assistance of those who withdraw'.[403] The position might be different where D has supplied P with the means of committing the crime. Aid may be no less easily neutralized than advice.

In *Grundy*,[404] D had supplied P, a burglar, with information which was presumably valuable to P in committing the crime; but, for two weeks before P did so, D had been trying to stop him breaking in. It was held that there was evidence of an effective withdrawal which should have been left to the jury. In *Whitefield*,[405] there was evidence that D had served unequivocal notice on P that if he proceeded with the burglary they had planned together, he would do so without D's aid or assistance. The jury should have been told that if they accepted the evidence, that was a defence. D would now be liable for an offence under ss 44 to 46 of the SCA 2007.

If there can be an effective withdrawal even on the basis of a rejected countermand, as in *Grundy*, it is arguable that an attempt to countermand should be the same. D has done all in his power to communicate his countermand to P but failed. In all these cases, the countermand has, *ex hypothesi*, failed; and, if the question is whether D has done his best to neutralize his input, the answer does not depend on the reasons for the failure.[406] It could be argued that where D has failed to communicate, he can escape only by going to the police; but this was not insisted on in *Grundy* when persuasion failed. This suggests that the basis for the defence lies not in neutralizing the actus reus of assisting so far performed by D, but on some broader principle operating to exculpate D despite his continuing actus reus.

An effective withdrawal may often be made more easily at the preparatory stage than where the crime is in the course of commission. Thus, in *Beccara* where D handed P a knife

---

[399] *Mitchell* [2008] EWCA Crim 2552 (D started fight, paused for short period while some others fetched weapons including a mace, and violence recommenced with D present. V killed. D guilty of murder).

[400] [2004] EWCA Crim 526, [60].

[401] *Saunders and Archer* (1573) 2 Plowd 473.

[402] *State v Kinchen* (1910) 52 So 185, quoted by Lanham, n 381.

[403] *Whitehouse* [1941] 1 WWR 112, per Sloan JA (Court of Appeal of British Columbia) approved in *Becerra* (1975) 62 Cr App R 212. Cf *Fletcher* [1962] Crim LR 551; *Grundy* [1977] Crim LR 543.

[404] [1977] Crim LR 543.   [405] (1984) 79 Cr App R 36.   [406] Lanham, n 381.

so that he could use it on anyone interfering in a burglary, D did not make a sufficient communication of withdrawal when, on the appearance of V, he said 'Come on, let's go', and got out through a window. Something 'vastly different and vastly more effective' was required and, possibly, nothing less than physical intervention to stop P committing the crime would be required.[407] In that case, the 'withdrawal' occurred at a very late stage. When the knife is about to descend, the only effective withdrawal may be physical intervention to prevent it reaching its target. This reasoning has been echoed in numerous cases.[408]

6.8.1.3 Spontaneous violence

In all the cases discussed above the offence was pre-planned. It was held in *Mitchell and King* that cases of spontaneous violence are different.[409] On this view, if A and B spontaneously attack V, they are aiding and abetting one another, so long as each is aware that he is being assisted and encouraged by the other; but, if B simply withdraws, his participation in the offence apparently ceases without the need for any express communication to A, so that he will not be liable for acts done by A thereafter. This was reiterated in *Rajakumar*[410] in which Davis LJ stated that:

Classically, as the authorities make clear, issues of withdrawal are a matter of fact and degree (and the authorities also make clear there can be some quite tight requirements if withdrawal is to be satisfied—albeit the burden of proving continuation of participation, and lack of withdrawal, remains on the Crown). Moreover, what may suffice to constitute withdrawal in spontaneous and unplanned group violence may not necessarily so suffice in pre-planned group violence.

The appropriateness of this test depends on which basis the defence rests. If it is regarded as a defence which operates by D neutralizing his actus reus, it can be seriously doubted: if P was encouraged by D's participation and was unaware that D had withdrawn, P continues to be encouraged. There is still an effective actus reus. As noted earlier, there are cases in which the defence has been successful where D has failed to neutralize the effect of his acts of assistance.

In the case of *Robinson*,[411] the Court of Appeal explained *Mitchell and King* as an exceptional case. Referring to the criticisms outlined earlier, the court stated that:

it can only be in exceptional circumstances that a person can withdraw from a crime he has initiated. Similarly in those rare circumstances communication of withdrawal must be given in order to give the principal offenders the opportunity to desist rather than complete the crime. This must be so even in situations of spontaneous violence unless it is not practicable or reasonable so to communicate as in the exceptional circumstances pertaining in *Mitchell* where the accused threw down his weapon and moved away before the final and fatal blows were inflicted.

More recently, however, in *O'Flaherty*, the court again followed the distinction between 'planned' and 'spontaneous' violence drawn in *Mitchell and King*. The Court of Appeal concluded that 'in a case of spontaneous violence such as this where there has been no prior agreement, the jury will usually have to make inferences as to the scope of the joint enterprise from the knowledge and actions of individual participants'.[412] The courts seem to avoid a more precise definition, favouring regarding the matter as one of fact and degree to be left to the jury.

[407] *Becerra*, n 403. Cf *Baker* [1994] Crim LR 444.
[408] See *Campbell* [2009] EWCA Crim 50; *Mitchell* [2008] EWCA Crim 2552.
[409] *Mitchell and King* (1998) 163 JP 75, [1999] Crim LR 496. Reed is extremely critical of this distinction, characterizing it as 'nebulous'. See n 381.   [410] [2013] EWCA Crim 1512, [42].
[411] [2000] 5 Arch News 2. See also *Mitchell* [2008] EWCA Crim 2552.
[412] [2004] EWCA Crim 526, [65].

The ambiguity surrounding the availability of the defence and its elements renders it all too easy for the courts to apply it in a confusing fashion. A good illustration of the confusion is the case of *Rafferty*.[413] D and his co-defendants, P1 and P2, attacked V. D punched V twice. He then left the scene with V's cash card heading for an ATM. Meanwhile, P1 and P2 continued the attack on V escalating the violence by kicking him in the head and, finally, drowning him in the sea. D returned to find V dead. The trial judge left to the jury the question whether D had withdrawn from the enterprise (and, if so, whether he was then liable for causing the death as a principal). The Court of Appeal concluded, rightly it is submitted, that D could not be guilty as a principal—he was not a cause of death. Nor, applying the joint enterprise doctrine then in place, was D necessarily a secondary party: the acts of P1 and P2 could have constituted what was then a 'fundamentally different act' and could now, post-*Jogee*, be seen as an overwhelming supervening event; see earlier p 219. It is submitted that there was no issue of withdrawal.

6.9 Victims as parties to crime

It has been noted[414] that when a statute creates a crime it does not generally provide that it shall be an offence to aid, abet, counsel or procure it. Such a provision is unnecessary, for it follows by implication of law. There is, however, one exception to this rule. Where the statute is designed for the protection of a certain class of persons it may be construed as excluding by implication the liability of any member of that class who is the victim of the offence, even though that member does in fact aid, abet, counsel or procure the offence.[415]

In *Tyrrell*,[416] D, a girl between the ages of 13 and 16, abetted P to have unlawful sexual intercourse with her. This was an offence by P under s 5 of the Criminal Law Amendment Act 1885.[417] It was held, however, that D could not be convicted of abetting because the Act 'was passed for the purpose of protecting women and girls against themselves'.[418] In *Pickford*,[419] the court held (though it was probably not necessary for the court to reach its decision) that *Tyrrell* was applicable to the case of a woman committing incest with her 13-year-old son, but it is not obvious that s 11 of the Sexual Offences Act 1956 (which made it an offence for the woman to permit 'her grandfather, father, brother or son' to have intercourse with her) was intended for the protection of anyone. Under the Sexual Offences Act 2003, there is nothing to prevent the boy being treated as a principal offender.

It has been held that a woman who is not pregnant can be convicted of abetting the use upon herself by another of an instrument with intent to procure her miscarriage, although the clear implication of the statute[420] is that such a woman cannot be convicted of *using* an

---

[413] [2007] EWCA Crim 1846.   [414] See p 181.

[415] See LC 305, para 5.24. See also: B Hogan, 'Victims as Parties to Crime' [1962] Crim LR 683; G Williams, 'Victims as Parties to Crimes—A Further Comment' [1964] Crim LR 686; G Williams, 'Victims and Other Exempt Parties in Crime' (1990) 10 LS 245; Criminal Law Revision Committee, Fifteenth Report, *Sexual Offences* (1984) Cmnd 9213, Appendix B.

[416] [1894] 1 QB 710.   [417] See now Sexual Offences Act 2003, s 9; see p 838.

[418] At 712 per Lord Coleridge. Both the Chief Justice and Mathew J pointed out that there was nothing in the Act to say that the girl should be guilty of aiding and abetting; but, it is submitted, no importance could be attached to that, for statutes hardly ever do.

[419] [1995] 1 Cr App R 420, 428.   [420] OAPA 1861, s 58; see Ch 15.

instrument on herself with that intent.[421] However, a pregnant woman can be convicted (under the same section) of using an instrument on herself so it cannot be argued that this section was passed for the protection of *women* and it would be curious that Parliament should have intended to protect non-pregnant women from themselves, but not pregnant women. How far the rule in *Tyrrell* extends has not been settled. The court referred to 'women' as well as girls and it may well be that it extends to the offences of procuration of women to be prostitutes and of brothel-keeping which were in the 1885 Act and then in the Sexual Offences Act 1956.[422] It was held that it applied to the prostitute who abets a man who is living off her earnings.[423]

In all the reported cases, it seems clear that the protection of the law extended only to a person of the class who is a *victim*. Thus, a child under 16 could be convicted of abetting P in having intercourse with another child under 16; a boy under 14 could be convicted, even before the Sexual Offences Act 1993, of abetting P in intercourse with another boy under 14; a prostitute could abet P in keeping a brothel in which she was not a participant, or of living on the earnings of another prostitute. There are many instances other than sexual offences where laws are passed for the protection of a particular class of persons.

The Supreme Court stated in *Gnango*[424] that the principle should only apply if the offence is one that is intended to protect a specified class. This means, for example, that it does not apply to murder or offences against the person. By way of example, Lord Phillips suggested that the sadomasochists in *Brown*[425] would not only be guilty of GBH for inflicting that harm on each other, but could also be guilty of aiding and abetting the infliction of those injuries upon themselves.[426]

The Law Commission propose to preserve the *Tyrell* principle. There will be no liability where the principal offence is for the protection of a particular category of persons and both (a) D falls within that category and (b) he is the victim.[427]

6.10 Instigation for the purpose of entrapment

Police or other law enforcement officers or their agents sometimes do acts for the purpose of entrapping, or getting evidence against offenders, which would certainly amount to counselling or abetting an offence if they were not done for that purpose.[428] The difficult question is how far an officer may go without himself incurring liability for the offence. Law enforcement officers have no general licence to aid and abet crime.

---

[421] *Sockett* (1908) 72 JP 428; see p 679.

[422] Sections 22–4, 28 and 29. Repealed, see now Sexual Offences Act 2003, ss 52–55.

[423] *Congdon* [1990] NLJR 1221 (Judge Addison); Hogan [1962] Crim LR 683 at 692–3; Williams (1990) 10 LS 245 at 248–9. The offence is repealed by the Sexual Offences Act 2003, under which children are a protected class, but liable to conviction for participating in the sexual activity. *Tyrell* seems to be largely ignored in the 2003 Act. See the article developing this point and cataloguing the instances in which the Act deviates from the principle: M Bohlander, 'The Sexual Offences Act 2003—The *Tyrrell* Principle—Criminalising the Victims' [2005] Crim LR 701.

[424] [2011] UKSC 59, [44]–[53].   [425] [1994] 1 AC 212. See Ch 16.

[426] For criticism, see J Herring, 'Victims as Defendants: When Victims Participate in Crimes Against Themselves' in A Reed and M Bohlander (eds), *Participation in Crime: Domestic and Comparative Perspectives* (2013).

[427] LC 305, cl 16 of the Draft Bill.   [428] Williams, CLGP, s 256.

Two separate questions are involved: (a) in what circumstances will the law enforcement agency official have committed a crime by his encouragement and (b) in what circumstances will the person encouraged by the officer be entitled to rely on such entrapment to excuse his conduct? We are concerned here only with the first of those questions, the second being a matter only of a procedural defence in terms of a stay of proceedings.[429]

It should be noted that where charges are brought in these circumstances for offences under ss 44 to 46 of the SCA 2007, a defence is available under s 50 where D proves (a) that he knew[430] certain circumstances existed; and (b) that it was reasonable for him to act as he did in those circumstances.

6.10.1 Secondary liability for the agent provocateur

As long ago as 1929, the Royal Commission on Police Powers stated:[431]

As a general rule, the police should observe only, without participating in an offence, except in cases where an offence is habitually committed in circumstances in which observation by a third party is *ex hypothesi* impossible. Where participation is essential it should only be resorted to on the express and written authority of the Chief Constable.

In *Sang*,[432] Lord Salmon said:

I would now refer to what is, I believe and hope, the unusual case, in which a dishonest policeman, anxious to improve his detection record, tries very hard with the help of an agent provocateur to induce a young man with no criminal record to commit a serious crime; and ultimately the young man reluctantly succumbs to the inducement . . . The policeman and the informer who had acted together in inciting him to commit the crime should . . . both be prosecuted and suitably punished.

It is not clear that the word 'dishonest' adds anything to the postulated facts and it should make no difference that the policeman's motive is hatred of crime. It can hardly be necessary that the person induced to act should be 'young'; and it might be even more serious to induce a person with a bad record who was 'going straight', for the consequences for him would be worse. These matters go to sentence, not liability.

The essence of the *dictum* seems to be that a person who would not otherwise have committed a particular crime is induced to do so,[433] and the House of Lords in *Looseley* confirmed that this is the essential basis of the concept of entrapment in English law:

Whether the police conduct preceding the commission of the offence was no more than might be expected from others in the circumstances?[434]

An officer who agrees, and intends, to participate in such an offence is guilty of conspiracy.[435] Merely to provide the opportunity for and temptation to commit an offence will be

---

[429] See, generally, the decision of the House of Lords in *Looseley* [2001] UKHL 53, [2002] 1 Cr App R 360 and *Moore* [2013] EWCA Crim 85. A Ashworth, 'Redrawing the Boundaries of Entrapment' [2002] Crim LR 161; D Ormerod and A Roberts, 'The Trouble with *Teixeira*: Developing a Principled Approach to Entrapment' (2002) Int J E & P 38; A Ashworth, 'Testing Fidelity to Legal Values: Official Involvement in Criminal Justice' (2000) 63 MLR 633, 642–52.

[430] Note that it is not enough that D believed they existed.   [431] (1929) Cmd 3297, 116.
[432] (1979) 69 Cr App R 282 at 296.   [433] cf *Birtles* [1969] 1 WLR 1047.
[434] Lord Nicholls, [23].
[435] *Yip Chiu-Cheung v R*, see p 91. See the Law Commission proposals on Conspiracy discussed at p 473.

lawful,[436] as is participation in an offence which has already been 'laid on' and is going to be committed in any event, in order to trap the offenders.[437] In such a case it makes no difference that the police intervention may have affected the time or other circumstances of the commission of the offence.[438]

Where there is a continuing general conspiracy—for example, to supply drugs to anyone asking for them—it seems that a law enforcement officer commits no offence by inducing the general conspirators to enter into a particular conspiracy within the ambit of the general conspiracy, for example to supply him with specified drugs.

It cannot be the law that the police may properly participate in a crime to the point at which irreparable damage is done. A policeman who assists P to commit murder in order to entrap him must be guilty of murder. It is submitted that the same must be true of any injury to the person, unless it is trivial and V consents to it; and probably to any damage to property, unless the owner consents.

The Law Commission propose a new defence where D shows (on the balance of probabilities) that he was acting in order to prevent the commission of an offence or occurrence of harm and it was reasonable to act as he did.[439]

6.11 Reform of secondary liability

The recommendations in Law Commission Report No 305 would, if implemented, transform the scope of accessorial liability. Taken together with Part 2 of the SCA 2007, there will, in effect, be eight types of liability for conduct that assists or encourages crime or is capable of doing so. Only a very short overview can be offered here. The likelihood of them being enacted is very low particularly since the decision in *Jogee* has sought to deal with one of the most troubling issues—that of joint enterprise.

(1) First, D may be liable for an inchoate offence where he intentionally does acts capable of assisting or encouraging the commission of a crime by P. D must believe or be reckless as to whether P will act with the mens rea of the offence and D must intend or believe that any relevant consequences or circumstances of P's offence will be satisfied (SCA 2007, s 44). This offence can be charged whether or not P commits the full offence.

(2) Second, D may be liable for an inchoate offence where he does acts capable of assisting or encouraging the commission of a crime by P, and believes that the conduct element of the actus reus of the crime will be committed by P, believing or being reckless as to whether P will have the mens rea for the offence, and believing or being reckless as to whether any relevant consequences or circumstances of P's offence will be satisfied (SCA 2007, s 45). The offence can be charged whether or not P commits the full offence.

(3) Third, D may be liable for an inchoate offence where he does acts capable of assisting or encouraging the commission of one of a number of specified crimes by P, and believes that one of those crimes will be committed by P, believing or being reckless as

---

[436] *Williams v DPP* (1993) 98 Cr App R 209, where the 'bait' was cartons of cigarettes left in a vulnerable position. The court said that the police had not aided, abetted, etc: but had they not procured the commission of the offence? They would have regarded the operation as a failure if no one had stolen the cartons.

[437] *McCann* (1971) 56 Cr App R 359.   [438] *McEvilly* (1973) 60 Cr App R 150.

[439] cf s 50 of the SCA 2007, discussed at p 502 in which Parliament corrupted the Law Commission's similar proposals in relation to incitement.

to whether P will possess any mens rea required for one of the offences, and believing or being reckless as to whether any relevant consequences or circumstances of one of those offences will be satisfied (SCA 2007, s 46). This offence can be charged whether or not P commits the full offence.

In each of these offences under the SCA 2007, liability is inchoate. It is arguable that the scope of criminal liability has extended too far by allowing for conviction and sentence for serious offences where D's conduct is so remote from the harm of the full offence—P need not even have attempted the principal crime.

(4) Fourth,[440] D may be liable as an accessory[441] if D's conduct assists or encourages P in fact, whether directly or not, and whether the assistance or encouragement is substantial or not. The assistance or encouragement may be by acts (words or conduct), or omission if D is under a relevant duty (eg by contract or relationship), but not by failure to control P where D has a specific entitlement to do so. D must have a direct or oblique intent[442] that P commit the conduct element of the offence. This mens rea element is central to the Commission's proposals reflecting the need for parity of culpability between D and P[443] if D is to be prosecuted, labelled and sentenced in the same manner as P. It is not necessary that D intends P to commit the full offence. D must believe that the circumstances and consequences of P's offence will be satisfied, *or* D must himself have the mens rea for the full offence of which P commits the conduct element.[444]

(5) Fifth, D will be liable for a joint venture[445] where he agrees with P to commit an offence or shares a common intention with P and D intended (directly or obliquely) that P or another party to the venture should commit the conduct element of the principal offence or believed that P or another would or might commit the conduct element of the offence. D would not be liable if P's act is outside the scope[446] of the joint venture.[447] This would take the law back to the approach before *Jogee* in most respects.

It is significant that these fourth and fifth forms of liability replace aiding and abetting, counselling and procuring. They are considerably narrower than the present secondary liability presumably because there is no need to extend liability in view of the offences under ss 44 to 46 of the SCA 2007.

(6) Sixth, in the case of homicide,[448] a joint venture will be caught by the fifth category— D will be liable for murder[449] if D intended to assist or encourage P to commit the relevant offence or D engaged in a joint criminal venture with P and realized that P or

---

[440] LC 305, Part III, especially at paras 3.15 et seq.   [441] Neither term is defined.
[442] LC 305, para 3.88. Cf Wilson arguing that it should be purposive intent—[2008] Crim LR 16.
[443] LC 305, para 3.80.   [444] ibid, para 3.109.   [445] Which is undefined.
[446] Not defined.
[447] For criticism, see Sullivan [2008] Crim LR 19, commenting on the absence of definition, heavy reliance on the existing law and the undue complexity resulting, and Buxton [2009] Crim LR 230, n 14, who regards them as 'unreasonably and unnecessarily' extending the scope of criminal liability and being 'very burdensome' to apply, at 243.
[448] Special proposals for joint venture were made in LC 304, *Murder, Manslaughter and Infanticide* (2006) Part 4.
[449] As defined in the LC Report, see Ch 12.

another party to the venture might commit the relevant offence. D would be liable for manslaughter if D and P were parties to a joint venture, P committed murder in relation to the fulfilment of that venture and D intended or foresaw that non-serious harm or the fear of harm might be caused by a party to the venture and a reasonable person in D's position and with D's knowledge of the relevant facts would have foreseen an obvious risk of death or serious injury being caused by a party to the venture.[450] Again this would take the law back to the position before *Jogee*.

(7) Seventh, D may be liable under a new statutory form of innocent agency.[451] D will be liable if he intentionally caused P to commit the conduct element of the offence, but, although P does commit the conduct element, P is not guilty of the full offence because he is under ten, insane or lacks mens rea.[452] D must also be proved to have the mens rea element of the offence he intended to cause. In the case of strict liability offences, D must know or believe that P would commit the offence (which he would commit even if he lacked mens rea) in the circumstances and with the consequences it requires.[453] The new offence will extend to cases where the offence committed by P is only capable of being committed by a person of a particular description (eg a licensee), even if D is not such a person. There is no requirement that D needs to believe that the full offence will be committed or that it will be committed by P himself.[454]

(8) Eighth, D may be liable where he intentionally causes a 'no fault' offence[455] to be committed by P and D knew or believed that his conduct would cause the offence to be committed.[456] It will be sufficient that D causes the circumstances of the no fault offence to be committed, for example with drink-driving, it is enough that D laces P's drinks causing the circumstance element (that P is over the limit) without causing the conduct element (the driving of a motor vehicle).

The Law Commission also propose to preserve the *Tyrell* principle, and create a defence for those acting in order to prevent the commission of an offence or occurrence of harm where it was reasonable to act in that way.

The Law Commission's proposals for secondary liability as set out in its Report No 305[457] were designed to represent a coherent scheme complementing the inchoate offences recommended by the Commission in Report No 300. However, the coherence has been lost. First, Parliament enacted the inchoate liability provisions in the SCA 2007, but in doing so made fundamental changes to the scope of those provisions. Secondly, although the SCA 2007 is in force, the proposals in relation to secondary liability are not likely to be enacted. Finally, and more worryingly, the government's amendment of the scheme for

---

[450] The proposal was supported by the government in its paper *Murder, Manslaughter and Infanticide* (2008), 19/08 at paras 89–90. The proposals were not taken forward into the Coroners and Justice Act 2009.

[451] See LC 305, Part IV.

[452] It is not enough that P was under duress, etc.

[453] D aged ten tells P aged nine to have sex with V aged nine. D must know or believe that V will be under 13 (circumstances as to age being strict under s 5 of the Sexual Offences Act 2003).

[454] For critical comment, see RD Taylor [2008] Crim LR 19.

[455] ie a strict liability offence—where no proof of mens rea is required as to one or more elements of the actus reus.

[456] LC 305, para 4.31.

[457] (2007) on which see Wilson [2008] Crim LR 3; Taylor [2008] Crim LR 32; Sullivan [2008] Crim LR 19; J Horder, 'Joint Criminal Ventures and Murder' in J Horder, *Homicide and the Politics of Law Reform* (2012).

incitement proposed in Report No 300 and enacted in the SCA 2007 led to wider offences and a change to the scope of the defences available. To maintain coherence, it seems that the Law Commission proposals on secondary parties will have to be similarly expanded. The logical conclusion is that in its future proposals in this area the Commission is now forced to offer wider offences to maintain consistency and coherence with the SCA 2007 provisions.[458]

Further reading

GP Fletcher, *Rethinking Criminal Law*

B Krebs, *Accessorial Liability after Jogee*

A Reed and M Bohlander (eds), *Participation in Crime: Domestic and Comparative Perspectives*

KJM Smith, *A Modern Treatise on the Law of Criminal Complicity*

---

[458] See the proposals on conspiracy and attempts discussed in Ch 11.

7

Assistance after the offence

7.1 Impeding the apprehension or prosecution of offenders

Someone who assists or encourages another to commit a crime may be liable as a secondary party under the common law and s 8 of the Accessories and Abettors Act 1861 as discussed in the previous chapter. Someone who does acts capable of assisting or encouraging a crime by another may be liable under Part 2 of the Serious Crime Act 2007 (as discussed in Ch 11). There are also specific statutory offences for assisting and encouraging in various contexts, including notably terrorism.[1] In this chapter, we focus on the specific offences for those who offer assistance to an offender *after* the commission of his offence.[2]

The general offence is found in s 4 of the Criminal Law Act 1967:

(1) Where a person has committed a relevant offence,[3] any other person who, knowing or believing him to be guilty of the offence or of some other relevant offence, does without lawful authority or reasonable excuse any act with intent to impede his apprehension or prosecution shall be guilty of an offence.

---

[1] Similar offences are provided for in specific contexts, including the wide offences of failing to disclose information related to terrorism: s 38B(1)(B) and s 38B(2) of the Terrorism Act 2000. See C Walker, 'Conscripting the Public in Terrorism Policing: Towards Safer Communities or a Police State?' [2010] Crim LR 441, and on the relationship with s 4 see *Girma* [2009] EWCA Crim 912; *Sherif* [2008] EWCA Crim 2653. A defendant can be charged with both offences, see *Abdurahman* [2019] EWCA Crim 2239.

[2] G Williams, 'Evading Justice' [1975] Crim LR 430; KJM Smith, *A Modern Treatise on Complicity* (1991) Ch 1.

[3] The Serious Organised Crime and Police Act 2005 abolished the concept of 'arrestable offence'; and in this context replaced it with the term 'relevant offence'.

(1A) In this section and section 5 below, 'relevant offence' means—

    (a) an offence for which the sentence is fixed by law,

    (b) an offence for which a person of 18 years or over (not previously convicted) may be sentenced to imprisonment for a term of five years (or might be so sentenced but for the restrictions imposed by section 33 of the Magistrates' Courts Act 1980).

(2) If on the trial of an indictment for a relevant offence the jury are satisfied that the offence charged (or some other offence of which the accused might on that charge be found guilty) was committed, but find the accused not guilty of it, they may find him guilty of any offence under subsection (1) above of which they are satisfied that he is guilty in relation to the offence charged (or that other offence).

(3) A person committing an offence under subsection (1) above with intent to impede another person's apprehension or prosecution shall on conviction on indictment be liable to imprisonment according to the gravity of the other person's offence, as follows:—

    (a) if that offence is one for which the sentence is fixed by law, he shall be liable to imprisonment for not more than ten years;

    (b) if it is one for which a person (not previously convicted) may be sentenced to imprisonment for a term of fourteen years, he shall be liable to imprisonment for not more than seven years;

    (c) if it is not one included above but is one for which a person (not previously convicted) may be sentenced to imprisonment for a term of ten years, he shall be liable to imprisonment for not more than five years;

    (d) in any other case, he shall be liable to imprisonment for not more than three years.

(4) No proceedings shall be instituted for an offence under subsection (1) above except by or with the consent of the Director of Public Prosecutions.[4]

The effect of the decision in *Courtie*[5] is that the section creates four offences, punishable with ten, seven, five and three years' imprisonment respectively.

The CPS suggests that examples of the type of conduct appropriate for a charge of assisting an offender (the 'principal offender', 'O' in this chapter) include: hiding a principal offender; otherwise assisting a principal offender to avoid arrest; assisting a principal offender to abscond from bail; lying to the police to protect principal offenders from investigation and prosecution; hiding the weapon used in an assault/robbery; and washing clothes worn by a principal offender to obstruct any potential scientific examination.[6] In some instances, those who have assisted offenders are charged with perverting the course of justice rather than s 4.[7] Indeed, in *Begum* the Court of Appeal observed that assisting an offender to flee

---

[4] Consent may be granted after charge but must be before proceedings commence. Consent must be obtained before proceedings are started by way of summons. In *Walker* [2016] EWCA Crim 751, Treacy LJ concluded that as matter of statutory construction, if the DPP institutes the proceedings the requirements of the subsection are satisfied and there is no need for a separate consent to be given. Consent is only required if some person other than the DPP, such as the police, institutes the criminal proceedings.

[5] See p 32. That is, if the maximum sentence differs depending on how the crime is committed, each form of offence with a different maximum is a separate offence.

[6] Charging Standard for Public Justice Offences: www.cps.gov.uk/legal-guidance/public-justice-offences-incorporating-charging-standard/.

[7] On which see SM Edwards, 'Perjury and Perverting the Course of Justice Considered' [2003] Crim LR 525. The CPS suggests that perverting the course of justice should be considered when: the assisting is aimed at preventing or hindering the trial process (as opposed to the arrest or apprehension of an accused); the facts are so serious that the court's sentencing powers for the statutory offence are considered inadequate; admissible evidence of the principal offence is lacking: Charging Standard for Public Justice Offences. Cf *T* [2011] EWCA Crim 729.

the country shares characteristics with perverting the course of justice as both strike at the heart of the justice system.[8]

7.1.1 Actus reus

There are two elements in the actus reus where D is charged with impeding the apprehension or prosecution of an offender, O: (a) a relevant offence must have been committed by the offender; and (b) D must have done 'any act' with the appropriate intent. No one may be convicted of an attempt to commit this offence.[9]

7.1.1.1 Proof of a relevant offence

The relevant offence alleged to have been committed by O must be specified in the indictment.[10] If, however, it turns out that O was not guilty of the specified offence, D may still be convicted if O was guilty of another relevant offence for which O might have been convicted on an indictment for the original specified offence.[11] So, for example, if it is alleged that O committed murder and it transpires at D's trial for an offence under s 4 that O was not guilty of murder but was guilty of manslaughter, because O *could*, at his trial for murder, have been convicted of that offence, D may be convicted of assisting under s 4. It is not necessary to direct the jury to find what offence D thought O had committed, though this may be a material factor in the imposition of sentence.[12]

It is only necessary to prove that the offence was committed, not that O was guilty.[13] If O is tried first, it is immaterial that O is acquitted if it can be proved at D's later trial that O was guilty. Even where O and D are tried together, O's acquittal should not, in principle, be conclusive if it can be proved, as against D, that O committed the offence.[14] However, O's conviction is presumptive evidence that he did commit the offence: PACE 1984, s 74. If D is tried first, it is not necessary to prove O's guilt, merely that the offence was committed. In *Zaman*,[15] D pleaded guilty before O was even tried. O was subsequently acquitted. D appealed claiming that there could be no offence under s 4. The Court of Appeal rightly rejected that argument. The court held that it was immaterial whether D 'knew' or merely 'believed' O had committed the offence. With respect, it is submitted that a distinction may need to be drawn in practice between cases of belief and knowledge. In a case where D merely *believes* O has committed the offence, D's plea does not establish that O has committed the offence. Whereas, in a case where D *knows*[16] that O has committed the offence, the plea can fulfil the prosecution's obligation to establish that the offence was committed. Perhaps D ought not to have pleaded at all unless he knew (and not merely believed) that O had committed the offence.

---

[8] [2019] EWCA Crim 323, [27].   [9] Criminal Attempts Act 1981, s 1(4)(c).

[10] Presumably this can include O's liability for secondary or inchoate offences.

[11] Criminal Law Act 1967, s 6(3); *Morgan* [1972] 1 QB 436. It is unclear whether the same principle is applicable to other provisions allowing conviction of offences other than that charged. NB: n 5.

[12] ibid.

[13] In *Saunders* [2011] EWCA Crim 1571, D's conviction was quashed because the judge had failed to direct the jury as to the elements of the relevant offences.

[14] cf *Shannon* [1975] AC 717; *Donald* (1986) 83 Cr App R 49; G Williams [1975] Crim LR 430 at 432. On the use of an offender's incriminating statements at a joint trial, see *Hayter* [2005] UKHL 6 and for their use by the Crown in a subsequent trial, see *Y* [2008] EWCA Crim 10; cf *Girma*, n 1.

[15] [2010] EWCA Crim 209, citing with approval this paragraph in the 12th edn. See further commentary at [2010] Crim LR 574; see also *Saunders* [2011] EWCA Crim 1571.

[16] ie had belief of a true fact: *Saik* [2006] UKHL 18.

7.1.1.2 An act of assistance

Once O's relevant offence has been proved, the remaining element in D's actus reus—'any act'—is almost unlimited.[17] There must be an *act*—an omission will not suffice[18]—but it need not be an act having a natural tendency to impede the apprehension or prosecution of an offender. Where the act does not have such a tendency, however, it will be difficult to prove the intent, in the absence of an admission. Common examples of sufficient 'acts' will be concealing the offender, providing him with transport, food or money to enable him to escape, or destroying evidence against him. The mere making of an oral offer of accommodation may be a sufficient act for these purposes.[19] It does not matter that D regrets his acts and persuades O to turn himself in; the offence is committed.[20]

When drafting this offence, the Criminal Law Revision Committee (CLRC),[21] observed that, 'The requirement that there should be an attempt to "impede" a prosecution will exclude mere persuasion not to prosecute.' However, there is no doubt that words can be a sufficient act; so that the offence would be committed by intentionally misdirecting police who were pursuing an offender, or by making a false statement to the police.[22]

An act done through an agent would be sufficient. Indeed, when done with intent to impede, the mere authorization of the agent would be a sufficient act to constitute the offence, though the agent never acted on it.

7.1.1.3 Relationship to the offence of escape

It is clearly not an offence under s 4 to enable a convicted offender (as opposed to one awaiting trial) to escape from gaol; but this is not important as such acts will amount to other offences.[23] Whether it is an offence to assist an offender who has escaped to remain at large depends on the interpretation of 'apprehension' in s 4. Does it extend beyond its obvious meaning of apprehension with a view to prosecution and include the re-arrest of the escaped convicted prisoner? There seems to be no reason why it should not be so interpreted.

7.1.2 Mens rea

There are two elements in the mens rea: (a) D must know or believe the offender to be guilty of the relevant offence which he had actually committed, or some other relevant offence; and (b) D must intend to impede the apprehension or prosecution of the offender.

---

[17] For discussion of the broader question of when citizens should have a duty to report offences, see A Ashworth, *Positive Obligations in Criminal Law* (2013) 60–5 and A Ashworth and L Zedner, *Preventative Justice* (2014) 100–1. For discussion of a citizen's general duty to disclose, see S Wallerstein, 'On the Legitimacy of Imposing Direct and Indirect Obligations to Disclose Information on Non-Suspects' in GR Sullivan and IH Dennis (eds), *Seeking Security, Pre-Empting the Commission of Criminal Harms* (2012) 37.

[18] cf the offence under s 38B of the Terrorism Act 2000 whereby a person may commit the offence through total inactivity, eg by not answering police questions or by not volunteering information.

[19] *Sherif* [2008] EWCA Crim 2693.

[20] That is a matter of mitigation in sentence: *Roberts* [2008] EWCA Crim 59; *Robinson* [2007] EWCA Crim 3120, [2008] 2 Cr App R (S) 201.

[21] Cmnd 2659, para 28.

[22] This would amount to other offences as well. See Law Commission, *Offences Relating to Interference with the Course of Justice* (1979), Law Com No 96, HC Paper No 213 (Session 1979/80) Pt III.

[23] Prison breaking, escape and rescue are offences at common law. See the 6th edn of this book, at Ch 19.3.

7.1.2.1 Know or believe

'Know' presumably means hold a true belief.[24] Belief is, presumably, to be construed as elsewhere, for example as in handling stolen goods; if so it adds little to 'knowing'.[25] If the mens rea was limited to knowledge alone, it would be difficult to prove. Is wilful blindness sufficient? If D has a mere suspicion that O is an offender and, shutting his eyes to an obvious means of knowledge, assists O, he can hardly be said to 'believe' in O's guilt. Arguably, the subsection is unduly narrow in this respect.[26] In *Sherif*,[27] dealing with the offence under the Terrorism Act 2000, S was held, under s 38B, to have known or believed that the London bombings of 21 July 2005 were to take place and failed to give information. The judge was entitled in his direction to make it plain 'that it was not sufficient for the prosecution to establish that a defendant had closed his eyes, but that the jury was entitled to conclude, if satisfied that he had deliberately closed his eyes to the obvious because he did not wish to be told the truth, that that fact was capable of being evidence to support a conclusion that that defendant either knew or believed the fact in question'.

Where the allegation is that D knew *or* believed of '. . . *the* offence'—the relevant offence which has actually been committed—the mens rea is probably governed both by 'knowing' and 'believing'. Where the allegation is that the knowledge or belief relates to some 'other relevant offence', the issue must be governed only by 'believing' since, *ex hypothesi*, the offence has not been committed and, therefore, D cannot 'know' it has.

7.1.2.2 Knowledge or belief as to what?

In order to know or believe that a relevant offence has been committed, D need not know the law. It will be enough that he believes in the existence of facts which, whether D knows it or not, amount in law to a relevant offence.[28] His ignorance of the law cannot afford a defence.

It is immaterial that D is unaware of O's identity.[29] What if he makes a mistake of identity? If D thinks he sees R committing a relevant offence and acts, intending to impede his apprehension or prosecution, is D guilty under s 4 if he was in fact witnessing O commit the crime?

Perhaps the question should be answered by making a distinction. If D does an act which he intends to assist the person whom he in fact observed, his mistake of identity should be immaterial. For example, D sends a police officer, who is pursuing the offender, in the wrong direction. Here D knows that the *person he is assisting* has committed a relevant offence, and that person has in fact done so. Suppose, on the other hand, that D fabricates evidence the following day so as to provide an alibi for R and this evidence could not, and was of course not, intended to assist O, of whom D has never heard. Here he does not intend to assist the person whom he in fact observed. An indictment in these circumstances charging D with doing an act, knowing O to be guilty of a relevant offence and with intent to impede his prosecution, is plainly bad. If R has never committed a relevant offence, it would seem that D is not guilty under the section;[30] if R once did commit a relevant offence, then D is guilty unless the limitation tentatively suggested in the previous paragraph be imposed.

---

[24] *Saik* [2006] UKHL 18.

[25] *Ismail* [1977] Crim LR 557; *Grainge* [1974] 1 All ER 928; *Griffiths* (1974) 60 Cr App R 14; see p 1089.

[26] See p 253.   [27] [2008] EWCA Crim 2653, [27].

[28] cf *Sykes v DPP* [1962] AC 528 at 563.   [29] *Brindley* [1971] 2 QB 300.

[30] Nor could D be convicted of an attempt to commit the offence. See Criminal Attempts Act 1981, s 1(4)(c), n 9; for discussion of the offence as a specific form of preparatory offence, see Duff, *Answering for Crime*, 160.

7.1.2.3 Some other relevant offence

'Some other relevant offence' must refer to an offence which O has not committed, for otherwise the words are redundant.[31] If D sees O running from a bank brandishing a gun and thinks O committed a robbery and D acts with intent to conceal this, D will be guilty, though O had in fact committed a murder and not a robbery. This is obviously correct, where, as in this example, D's belief relates to the transaction which constituted the actual offence. Suppose, however, that unknown to D, O committed murder last week. D believes, wrongly, that O committed bigamy two years ago. If D does an act with intent to impede O's prosecution for bigamy—such as burning O's letters—it would seem very odd indeed that D should be liable only because O committed murder last week—the murder has nothing to do with the case. This suggests that the offence D supposes O to have committed must arise from the same transaction as the actual offence (and, undoubtedly, this will normally be the case) but to so hold would require the imposition of some limitation on the express words of the section.[32]

7.1.2.4 With intent

D's act must be done with intent to impede the offender's apprehension or prosecution. It does not matter that D's act done with intent proves to be of no assistance to O whatsoever. It must be proved that D's *purpose* was to impede; it is not enough that D knew his act would certainly impede if that was not his object or one of his objects; that is, a 'direct' and not merely an 'oblique' intention is required.[33] This, at least, seems to be the CLRC's view of the clause which became s 4. Discussing the case of harbouring, the CLRC wrote:

> If the harbouring is done with the object of impeding apprehension or prosecution . . . it will be within the offence; if it is done merely by way of providing or continuing to provide the criminal with accommodation in the ordinary way, it will not; and juries will be able to tell the difference.[34]

If this is the correct interpretation of the section, then a handler of stolen goods will not be guilty of an offence under s 4, even where he knows that his conduct has the effect of impeding the apprehension or prosecution of the thief, if that is not his object or purpose.[35] Nor is D guilty under s 4 if, by acts done with the object of avoiding his own arrest or prosecution, he knowingly impedes the arrest or prosecution of another.[36] Where there is prima facie evidence of the necessary intent, it is for D to lay a foundation for a defence by introducing evidence that his sole purpose was of a different character. In the absence of such evidence, there is no duty to direct a jury to consider whether D might have had a different intent.[37] If D has the dual object of saving himself and the other from arrest or prosecution then, no doubt, he is guilty.

7.1.2.5 Lawful authority

Even though the act is done with intent to impede, it is not an offence if there is 'lawful authority or reasonable excuse' for it. According to the CLRC:[38]

> The exception for 'lawful authority' will cover an executive decision against a prosecution, and that for 'reasonable excuse' will avoid extending the offence to acts such as destroying the evidence of an offence (for example a worthless cheque) in pursuance of a legitimate agreement to refrain from prosecuting in consideration of the making good of loss caused by that offence.

---

[31] NB: p 252.   [32] cf the discussion of s 5, p 254.

[33] See pp 93–100.   [34] Cmnd 2659, para 30.   [35] *Andrews and Craig* [1962] 3 All ER 961n.

[36] *Jones* [1949] 1 KB 194.   [37] *Brindley* [1971] 2 QB 300 at 304.   [38] Cmnd 2659, para 28.

It is possible that the exception may have some application outside this situation.[39] As with the Prevention of Crime Act 1953,[40] it enables the courts to afford a defence in circumstances in which they think it reasonable to do so.

7.1.3 The sentence

Section 4(3)[41] provides for a sliding scale of sentences which is related to the relevant offence which has actually been committed. Where D believes that some other relevant offence has been committed, the punishment to which he is liable is fixed according to the actus reus, not according to the mens rea. If D acts with intent to impede the apprehension of O whom he believes to have committed malicious wounding[42] (maximum, five years), he is liable to three years' imprisonment if his belief is correct; but if O has in fact committed murder, he is liable to ten years.

   It is clear that the relevant offence by O which fixes the maximum sentence for D under s 4 must have been committed when the act of impeding by D takes place. So, for example, if D rightly believes O to be guilty of malicious wounding, and D acts to impede his arrest, D is liable to only three years. If, subsequently, O's victim, V, dies, and O becomes guilty of murder, D remains liable to three not ten years' imprisonment.

7.2 Compounding an offence

Section 5(1) of the Criminal Law Act 1967 enacts an offence, triable either way, as follows:

Where a person has committed a relevant offence,[43] any other person who, knowing or believing that the offence or some other relevant offence has been committed, and that he has information which might be of material assistance in securing the prosecution or conviction of an offender for it, accepts or agrees to accept for not disclosing that information any consideration other than the making good of loss or injury caused by the offence, or the making of reasonable compensation for that loss or injury, shall be liable on conviction on indictment to imprisonment for not more than two years.

Proceedings may not be instituted without the consent of the DPP.[44]

   Historically, there were two much wider common law misdemeanours: 'compounding a felony'[45] and 'misprision of felony'.[46] The former consisted in an agreement for consideration not to prosecute, or to impede a prosecution for, a felony. The latter consisted simply in an omission to report a felony to the police. Section 5 replaces both. Section 5 is narrower than misprision in that the offence is committed only if D accepts or agrees to accept consideration for not disclosing the information relating to the relevant offence. It is narrower than compounding in that it is not now criminal to accept or agree to accept consideration for not disclosing information relating to the relevant offence, if the consideration is no more than the making good of the loss or injury caused by the offence or the making of reasonable compensation for that loss or injury. No one may be convicted of attempting to commit an offence under s 5(1).[47]

---

[39] Would a spouse have a reasonable excuse for assisting their spouse? See PJ Pace, '"Impeding Arrest": A Wife's Right as a Spouse?' [1978] Crim LR 82. According to *Lee Shek Ching v R* [1986] LRC (Crim) 718 (Hong Kong, CA), 1985, No 53, being O's wife is not, as such, a reasonable excuse. See *T* [2011] EWCA Crim 729.
[40] See Ch 34.   [41] See p 249.   [42] See p 724.
[43] The Serious Organised Crime and Police Act 2005, Sch 7, replaced 'arrestable offence' with 'relevant offence'.
[44] Section 5(3).   [45] G Williams [1975] Crim LR 430.
[46] See the 1st edn of this book, at pp 539–44.   [47] Criminal Attempts Act 1981, s 1(4)(c), n 9.

7.2.1 Actus reus

There are two elements in the actus reus: (a) a relevant offence must actually have been committed; and (b) D must accept or agree to accept consideration for not disclosing information which he knows or believes to be material.

The offence extends to all relevant offences. The limit on the scope of s 5 is provided by s 5(5): 'The compounding of an offence other than treason shall not be an offence otherwise than under this section.' D commits no offence by agreeing to accept any consideration for not prosecuting a non-relevant offence, though whether as a matter of public policy the resulting contract is enforceable is another matter.

The offence is committed only where D 'accepts or agrees to accept' the consideration. The section envisages an offer being made to D; if the offer comes *from* D, then he might also be guilty of the more serious offence of blackmail.[48] Consideration presumably bears much the same meaning as in the law of contract and extends to money, goods, services or any act or forbearance.

7.2.2 Mens rea

There are two elements in the mens rea. It must be proved that: (a) D knew or believed that a relevant offence had been committed; and (b) D intended to accept or to agree to accept consideration other than the making good of loss or the making of reasonable compensation.

7.2.2.1 Knowledge or belief

These terms should be construed in the same manner as in s 4.

7.2.2.2 Knowledge or belief as to what?

Where D's knowledge or belief relates to the relevant offence (A) which has actually been committed, the application of the section seems quite straightforward. But D's belief may relate to some other relevant offence (B) which, *ex hypothesi*, has not been committed. Here D's acceptance, or agreement to accept consideration, must relate to the offence B which D believes to have been committed and thus not to the offence which has actually been committed since they are different. Under this section, D's belief need not be—as, under s 4, it probably must[49]—that a relevant offence has been committed by the same person who has in fact committed such an offence. If D wrongly supposes that he has seen a relevant offence committed by R and accepts consideration for not disclosing what he saw, he will be guilty if, in fact, he saw O committing a relevant offence.

The argument advanced in connection with s 4, that D's belief must relate to the transaction which resulted in the actual offence, is much stronger in relation to s 5. If D wrongly supposes that R has committed a relevant offence and accepts consideration for not disclosing that fact, his guilt can hardly be established by proving that some time, somewhere, someone committed a relevant offence—for example, that Harold Shipman committed murder. The offence which D supposes to have been committed must have something to do with the offence which has actually been committed. The most obvious point of connection is that the real and the supposed offence must both arise out of the same transaction. An alternative view might be that it is sufficient if either (a) the two offences arise out of the same transaction or (b) they both relate to the same person. Unknown to D, O committed murder last week. D believes, wrongly, that O committed bigamy two years ago. O offers money to D 'to keep his mouth shut'. D, believing that O is talking about the bigamy,

---

[48] See Ch 24.   [49] See p 252.

accepts. According to the first view put above, D is not guilty; according to the alternative view, he is. It is submitted that the first view is better; according to the second, D's liability depends entirely on chance.

If D's acceptance of consideration relates to the transaction in question, then it seems that it will be immaterial that he is mistaken as to both (a) the nature of the relevant offence and (b) the identity of the perpetrator. He supposes he saw R perpetrating a robbery. Actually, he saw O committing murder. If he accepts consideration for not disclosing what he saw he should be guilty.

The CLRC stated:[50]

the offence will not apply to a person who refrains from giving information because he does not think it right that the offender should be prosecuted or because of a promise of reparation by the offender. It would be difficult to justify making the offence apply to those cases.

It is difficult to see, however, how it can be a defence for D simply to say that he did not 'think it right that the offender should be prosecuted', if he has accepted consideration for not disclosing information. Even if the court believes D's views as to the impropriety of the contemplated prosecution, he still falls within the express words of the section. He could be acquitted only if the section were interpreted so as to require that D's object or motive be the acquisition of the consideration. As we have seen,[51] on a charge under s 4 it is probable that a *purpose* of impeding must be proved, but this may be justified by giving a narrow meaning to the ulterior intent specified in that section. No ulterior intent is specified in s 5 and, consequently, it is difficult to see how the section can be limited in the same way.

7.2.2.3 Relationship with advertising for return of stolen goods

It may seem a little surprising that a specific offence of advertising rewards for the return of goods stolen or lost has been retained.[52] Section 23 of the Theft Act provides:

Where any public advertisement of a reward for the return of any goods which have been stolen or lost uses any words to the effect that no questions will be asked, or that the person producing the goods will be safe from apprehension or inquiry, or that any money paid for the purchase of the goods or advanced by way of loan on them will be repaid, the person advertising the reward and any person who prints or publishes the advertisement shall on summary conviction be liable to a fine not exceeding level 3 on the standard scale.

Insofar as an advertisement states that 'no questions will be asked' this is only proposing what is perfectly lawful under s 5(1) of the Criminal Law Act.[53] It is not clear why this should be an offence because it is done through a public advertisement. Nor is it clear why it should be an offence to offer a reward for the return of stolen goods, even their return by the thief. The promise to pay the reward might be unenforceable for lack of consideration but, if it were actually paid, there would be nothing unlawful about that. Possibly the theory is that, if such advertisements were common, theft might be encouraged in that thieves would have an easy and safe way of disposing of the stolen goods for reward. This cannot apply to an advertisement addressed to the bona fide purchaser offering to recompense him if he will return the stolen goods; this seems quite a reasonable thing to do, especially since the bona fide purchaser commits no offence by retaining the goods for himself.[54]

---

[50] Cmnd 2659, para 41.   [51] See p 253.

[52] The section replaced the Larceny Act 1861, s 102 which provided for a penalty of £50 recoverable by a common informer. The fine was increased to £100 by the Common Informers Act 1951. The CLRC hesitantly recommended retention 'as advertisements of this kind may encourage dishonesty': Eighth Report, para 144.

[53] See p 254.   [54] See p 1087.

The section creates what the courts sometimes call a 'quasi-criminal' offence, not requiring mens rea. So, the advertising manager of a company was liable for the publication of an advertisement which he had not read.[55]

'Stolen' bears the wide meaning given to that word by s 24(4) of the Theft Act so the bona fide purchaser may indeed have become the absolute owner of the goods where, for example, they have been obtained by fraud and the property in the goods passed.

7.3 Refusal to aid a constable

It is a common law offence for D to refuse to go to the aid of a constable who, on seeing a breach of the peace, calls on D to assist him in restoring the peace.[56] A ticket collector was held to be guilty of the offence when he failed to come to the assistance of a police officer struggling with a thief. His defence that he had obeyed instructions not to leave his post was not accepted.[57] There must be a reasonable necessity for the constable to request assistance. It is no defence that D's aid would have been ineffective. So where a constable requested D to assist him in suppressing a breach of the peace among four or five hundred people at a prize-fight, Alderson B directed that D's refusal was an offence.[58] It seems that it was no answer that he had his horses to take care of. Alderson B[59] recognized that physical impossibility or a lawful excuse would be an answer; but it is not clear what would constitute 'lawful excuse'. Is the citizen required to act where there would be a grave risk of death or serious injury? Surely the State cannot criminalize D for a failure to put his life on the line?

By s 65(3) of the Serious Crime Act 2007 a person does not perform an act capable of assisting or encouraging crime by the offender merely because he fails to respond to a constable's request for assistance in preventing a breach of the peace.

7.4 Reform

In the wake of scandals involving the failure by schools and other public bodies to report systemic child abuse, there were calls from a number of quarters to introduce into English law a duty to report child abuse and criminal offences for failing to do so.[60] Sir Keir Starmer QC, the former DPP, stated: 'If you're in a position of authority or responsibility in relation to children, and you have cause to believe that a child has been abused, or is about to be abused, you really ought to do something about it.'[61] Such an offence exists in all the jurisdictions in the United States and applies to those who may come into professional contact with children.[62] In his analysis of such offences,[63] Andrew Ashworth states that their justification is to improve the protection afforded to victims. As Ashworth also points out, however, the problem with offences such as these is that, at least in the familial context, it

---

[55] *Denham v Scott* (1983) 77 Cr App R 210.

[56] See the valuable article by D Nicholson, 'The Citizen's Duty to Assist the Police' [1992] Crim LR 611.

[57] *Waugh* (1976) The Times, 1 Oct (Knightsbridge Crown Court).

[58] *Brown* (1841) Car & M 314. Cf *Sherlock* (1866) LR 1 CCR 20.   [59] In *Brown*, ibid.

[60] See the editorial at [2014] Crim LR 1. As Ashworth points out, if such an offence were to be created, it would need to be widely publicized so that citizens were aware they were under such a duty.

[61] www.bbc.co.uk/news/uk-24772777.

[62] SG Thompson, 'The White-Collar Police Force: "Duty to Report" Statutes in Criminal Law Theory' (2002) 11 *William and Mary Bill of Rights Journal* 3.

[63] A Ashworth, *Positive Obligations in Criminal Law* (2nd edn, 2015) 62–6.

may be the case that the individual who has failed to discharge the duty is herself a victim of abuse. Ashworth states that this does not necessarily militate against enacting offences such as these, but does serve to emphasize the importance of sensitivity in the familial context, especially given the possibility for potential gendered unfairness.

The most intractable problem with offences of failure to report generally, according to Ashworth, is definition. How far should the duty extend? This difficulty would, however, be overcome if the duty to report was limited to sexual abuse against children and, perhaps, only extended to those who occupy a duty of care. It remains to be seen whether such offences will be enacted more widely in England and Wales. Note that s 5B of the Female Genital Mutilation Act 2003 imposes duties on health-care professionals and teachers (and social workers in Wales) to notify the police of acts of female genital mutilation that they discover to have been carried out.[64] Failure to make the required notification is not, however, an offence.

Further reading

A Ashworth, *Positive Obligations in Criminal Law*

KJM Smith, *A Modern Treatise on the Law of Criminal Complicity*

---

[64] For further discussion, see K Cook, 'Female Genital Mutilation in the UK Population: A Serious Crime' (2016) 80 J Crim L 88.

8

Corporate and vicarious liability

8.1 Liability of corporations

8.1.1 Introduction

This chapter deals with the potential criminal liability of organizations, focusing predominantly on corporations.[1] It is common to speak of the criminal liability of companies, but of course a company is only one type of incorporated business. Corporations include public limited companies (plc) and private limited companies (Ltd) as well as limited liability partnerships (LLP) and other organizations such as local authorities. The formality of incorporation and its extensive legal ramifications need not detain us.[2] What is important

---

[1] For detailed study, see C Wells, *Corporations and Criminal Responsibility* (2nd edn, 2001); D Bergman, *The Case for Corporate Responsibility* (2000); J Gobert and M Punch, *Rethinking Corporate Crime* (2003); A Pinto QC and M Evans, *Corporate Criminal Liability* (2003); C Harding, *Criminal Enterprise: Individuals Organisation and Criminal Responsibility* (2007); J Gobert, 'Corporate Criminality: New Crimes for the Times' [1994] Crim LR 722; GR Sullivan, 'Expressing Corporate Guilt' (1995) 15 OJLS 281. For reviews of more recent developments, see C Wells, 'Corporate Criminal Liability: A Ten Year Review' [2014] Crim LR 847 and 'Corporate Failure to Prevent Economic Crime—A Proposal' [2017] Crim LR 426. The meaning of the corporation for the purposes of the criminal law was also reviewed in a valuable appendix to LCCP 195, *Criminal Liability in Regulatory Contexts* (2010) by Professor Wells. See also Wells, 'Corporate Crime: Opening the Eyes of the Sentry' (2010) 30 LS 370 at 380–2.

[2] See the Companies Act 2006, ss 1 et seq.

for present purposes is that corporations have a separate legal identity. They are treated in law as having a legal personality distinct from the natural persons—members, directors, employees, etc—who make up the corporation. That presents the opportunity, in theory, of imposing criminal liability on the corporation separately from any liability which might be imposed on the individual members for any criminal wrongdoing.

The number of corporations and the involvement they have in diverse aspects of daily life has expanded dramatically over the last century. In more recent years, it appears that the public perception of corporations has moved towards the true legal position: that the corporation is a free-standing entity, distinct from the people who manage and control it.[3] With this perception has come an expectation that a corporation might properly be regarded as culpable in criminal law separately from, although in addition to, its directors for deaths, breaches of health and safety, etc.[4]

Historically, the pressure for the imposition of criminal liability focused specifically on the issue of punishing companies for manslaughter. The various disasters, each with large loss of life—in particular the *Herald of Free Enterprise* ferry disaster and various rail crashes (Southall, Ladbroke Grove, Paddington, Hatfield)—all prompted calls for new legislation fixing the corporation with liability. The Corporate Manslaughter and Corporate Homicide Act 2007 (hereafter in this chapter 'the 2007 Act') seeks to meet these demands, and is examined in detail in Ch 14 along with other manslaughter offences. The 2007 Act imposes liability for manslaughter on 'organizations'. This concept is much wider than corporations.[5] The special policy considerations that flow from the unique harm of causing a death make it desirable for the corporate manslaughter provisions to apply to a wide range of organizations. This chapter deals with the potential criminal liability of associations—including corporations—other than for manslaughter. In recent years, there has been greater pressure to hold companies liable for various financial and economic crimes, such as fraud, money laundering and tax evasion.

As the expectation that corporations will be held criminally liable has grown, so too has the concern that English law's approach to corporate criminal liability is unsatisfactory at a fundamental level. At the time of writing, there is renewed political interest in reforming corporate criminal liability.[6] This chapter considers the different methods by which corporations may be held liable in English law and examines the problems each poses.

Historically, it was thought that a corporation could not be indicted for a crime at all.[7] As a matter of procedure, personal appearance was necessary at court in the assizes and quarter-sessions. Since the corporation has no physical person, it could not appear. In the

---

[3] See Wells, n 1 and N Lacey, 'Philosophical Foundations of the Common Law' in J Horder (ed), *Oxford Essays in Jurisprudence* (2000) 33. See also P Alldridge, *Relocating Criminal Law* (2000) considering how corporate liability challenges our perceptions of personhood, at 76–82.

[4] As this perception develops, there is a stronger argument that the appropriate basis for imposing criminal liability should be on a corporation's cultures and attitudes towards risk and harm. See p 278. See also Wells, n 1. There is now growing pressure for corporations to be accountable for their contribution to offences in international law (eg by supplying arms to dictators): see W Kalick, 'Corporate Accountability for Human Rights Violations Amounting to International Crimes' (2010) 30 LS 370.

[5] By s 25, 'corporation' does not include a corporation sole but includes any body corporate wherever incorporated. This includes companies incorporated under companies legislation, as well as bodies incorporated under statute (as is the case with many non-Departmental Public Bodies and other bodies in the public sector) or by Royal Charter.

[6] In 2017 the Ministry of Justice conducted a call for evidence surveying the options for reform of the law. See Ministry of Justice, *Corporate Liability for Economic Crime: Call for Evidence* (2017) Cm 9370. In November 2020, the Law Commission announced that the government had asked it to investigate the laws around corporate criminal liability and provide options to reform them.

[7] *Anon* (1701) 12 Mod Rep 560, per Holt CJ.

Court of King's Bench, however, appearance by attorney was allowed and the difficulty was circumvented by removing the indictment into that court by writ of *certiorari*;[8] but now this is unnecessary and, by statute,[9] a corporation may appear and plead through a representative. Further objections which have been raised to imposing criminal liability are that, since a corporation is a creature of the law, it can only do such acts as it is legally empowered to do, so that any crime is necessarily *ultra vires* (outside its powers); and that the corporation, having neither body nor mind, cannot perform the acts or form the intents which are a prerequisite of criminal liability. The *ultra vires* doctrine, however, seems to have been ignored in both the law of tort and crime and appears to apply only in the law of contract and property.[10]

Although a corporation is in law a separate legal entity, in relation to most serious offences English law still relies on the culpability of the individual directors in fixing liability on the corporation. To take an example, if a company is alleged to have committed fraud by making false representations in order to secure lucrative contracts, the criminal culpability of the company will depend on the actions and fault of the directors and managers of the company. The traditional concepts of actus reus and mens rea can be applied to the company via its human controllers. A controller of the company must be proved to have had the relevant mens rea of the offence (acting dishonestly) and to have fulfilled the conduct element of the offence—making a false representation, etc. At one level this seems logical, since although the company is in law a separate legal entity, it can only operate through the medium of its human actors. There are, however, difficulties. At a practical level, as we will see, there are problems in fixing blame on the company through relevant controllers. Moreover, at a principled level some argue that the criminal law ought to be capable of attributing blame to a corporation on account of wrongs done and harms caused by its corporate culture or policies. With larger corporations an ethos or culture can develop quite independently of the controlling officers. That culture might itself form the basis for proof of the criminal wrongdoing. These arguments are keenly contested socio-legal and economic issues which lie beyond the scope of this work.[11] Some of the language of the courts in modern times has also emphasized systemic failings—in the Hatfield rail prosecution, the failings of Balfour Beatty were described in such terms,[12] and the judge castigated the 'total vacuum of management' in the relevant area.[13] Such comments do suggest a failure of the corporation rather than any individual.

Many recent reform proposals urge the use of innovative enforcement and civil law methods of dealing with corporate wrongdoing where the conduct involves breaches of regulations as opposed to commission of 'real' crimes such as those leading to injury or loss of property.[14] These civil law proposals lie beyond the scope of this work. The focus here is on the use of the criminal law.[15]

---

[8] *Birmingham and Gloucester Rly Co* (1842) 3 QB 223.   [9] Criminal Justice Act 1925, s 33.

[10] cf J Goudkamp and D Nolan, *Winfield and Jolowicz on Tort* (20th edn, 2020) Ch 21.

[11] See GR Sullivan, 'The Attribution of Culpability to a Limited Company' (1996) 55 CLJ 515, and Lacey, n 3.

[12] Note also the oft-quoted description in the P&O prosecution of corporate 'sloppiness' (1990) 93 Cr App R 72. See on the *Balfour* decision and others, C Wells (2010) 30 LS 370.

[13] At [14].

[14] In LCCP 195 the Commission seeks to apply the principles espoused in the Macrory Report, *Regulatory Justice: Making Sanctions Effective* (2006) in trying to reduce the volume of criminal offences that exist in relation to regulatory behaviour.

[15] See the valuable discussion in Appendix A to LCCP 195 by Julia Black, examining the merits of these alternatives such as public civil sanctions, administrative sanctions, private civil law, warning notices, restorative justice initiatives, etc.

8.1.2 Bases of criminal liability

There are currently six ways in which a prosecution may be brought against a corporation or its directors.

8.1.2.1 Personal liability of corporate directors, etc

First, individuals within a corporation can be prosecuted for their personal wrongdoing just as any other human being can. For example, a managing director of a company who bribes an agent of a company with whom he is making a contract will be at risk of personal prosecution. So too will a manager who commits offences of driving carelessly or committing frauds while on company business, etc. No more need be said about such criminal liability since it is discussed throughout the rest of the book. If a corporation has been found to be criminally liable, the individual employee or director, etc can also be liable as a secondary party to the corporation's wrongdoing under s 8 of the Accessories and Abettors Act 1861 (see Ch 6). A director can also in some cases be liable for conspiring with the company. A company can conspire with its directors as long as there are at least two directors involved in the conspiracy (neither of whom need to be on trial)[16] (see Ch 11). Occasionally, Parliament excludes personal liability when creating corporate offences as, for example, with the corporate manslaughter offence discussed in Ch 14.[17]

8.1.2.2 For offences of strict liability

Secondly, in some instances offences of strict or absolute liability can be committed by a corporation. If no mens rea needs to be proved there is no difficulty in establishing any fault on the part of the corporation. Depending on which element of the actus reus attracts strict liability, establishing liability for a corporation will be no different from a human actor. It is, of course, important in the application of strict liability to corporations to consider the availability of due diligence defences, allowing the corporation an opportunity to prove that it took all reasonable steps to avoid the commission of the offence. No more need be said about this form of liability and the due diligence defence.[18] They are considered in full in Ch 5.

8.1.2.3 Statutory offences imposing duties on corporations

Thirdly, the corporation, as distinct from its employees or managers, can be criminally liable for any offences laid down by Parliament as applying specifically to corporations performing the relevant activity. A corporation is a legal person but it has no physical existence. As a legal entity, a corporation may be placed under a duty by Parliament to conduct itself in a particular way on pain of criminal sanction for non-compliance. For example, Parliament may create an offence for a corporation to fail to keep records, or to label itself in a particular way.

The type of case where it is most obviously proper that a corporation should be held liable arises where a statute imposes a duty upon a corporation to act and the corporation breaches that duty by failing to act.

It was in such cases that the earliest developments in corporate liability took place. In 1842, in *Birmingham and Gloucester Rly Co*,[19] a corporation was convicted for failing to

---

[16] See *Alstom Network UK Ltd* [2019] EWCA Crim 1318.   [17] 2007 Act, s 18(1).

[18] For a discussion of the difference types of due diligence defences and their merits, see LCCP 195, Part 6. See also the valuable appendix by Professor Cartwright examining the use of due diligence defences in consumer regulation in particular.

[19] (1842) 3 QB 223. Cf *British Steel plc* [1995] 1 WLR 1356.

fulfil a statutory duty. Four years later, in *Great North of England Rly Co*,[20] it was argued that the effect of that decision was limited to cases of non-feasance where there was no agent who could be indicted. It was argued that, in the case of misfeasance, only the agents who had done the wrongful acts were liable. The court held that the distinction was unfounded. Even if it were possible to discover which had occurred, it was incongruous that the corporation should be liable for the one type of wrong and not the other.

A more recent example of an offence specifically created for corporations is that in s 7 of the Bribery Act 2010, creating an offence for a commercial organization to fail to prevent bribery by a person associated with it, intending to obtain or retain a business advantage. This is a very widely defined offence. The due diligence defence in s 7(2) will be crucial as will be the guidance published by the Justice Secretary under s 9.[21] Similar offences are contained in Part 3 of the Criminal Finances Act 2017. These offences criminalize commercial organizations which fail to prevent the facilitation of domestic and foreign tax evasion. There are some suggestions that this is the model, or more accurately range of models, of criminal liability that might be imposed more widely on corporations in future reform.

8.1.2.4 Vicarious liability

It was not a great step forward from holding that a corporation could be liable for breach of statutory duty, as in *Birmingham and Gloucester Railway*, to the courts imposing liability vicariously in these circumstances.[22] Fourthly, then, a corporation can be vicariously liable for the acts of its employees and agents where a natural person would similarly be liable for such acts; for example, when a statute imposes vicarious responsibility.[23] See below.[24]

8.1.2.5 The identification doctrine

Aside from these four categories, prosecuting the corporation within the orthodox model of criminal law creates difficulties. The fact that the corporation has a legal identity does not alter the fact that the corporation has no body and mind. The criminal law's solution to the lack of a corporate body to perform the actus reus and a corporate mind capable of forming mens rea has been to treat the minds and bodies of the officers and servants of the corporation as supplying its mental and physical faculties. The fifth way that the corporation can be liable for offences is therefore on the basis that the controlling officers of the corporation performed the proscribed conduct with the relevant fault element. This is the so-called 'identification' doctrine.[25] The questions are: (1) who is a controlling officer?; (2) is the offence one to which a special statutory rule applies?; (3) is the act within the scope of the corporate duty?

Within every corporation there are certain persons (conveniently labelled in the Draft Criminal Code as 'controlling officers')[26] who are the 'directing mind and will'[27] of the

---

[20] (1846) 9 QB 315.

[21] See S Gentle, 'The Bribery Act 2010: (2) The Corporate Offence' [2011] Crim LR 101.

[22] *Mousell Bros Ltd v London and North-Western Rly Co* [1917] 2 KB 836; *Griffiths v Studebakers Ltd* [1924] 1 KB 102.

[23] *Griffiths v Studebakers Ltd*, ibid; *Mousell Bros Ltd v London and North-Western Rly Co* [1917] 2 KB 836.

[24] See p 281.

[25] See LCCP 195, Part 5 and Appendix C by Professor Wells. For criticism, see N Cavanagh, 'Corporate Criminal Liability: An Assessment of the Models of Fault' (2011) 75 J Crim L 414. For a review from a European perspective, see J Keiler, *Actus Reus and Participation in European Criminal Law* (2012) 459 (comparing Germany) and 463 (comparing the EU).

[26] LC 143, para 11.6, and cl 34. Ministry of Justice, *Corporate Liability for Economic Crime: Call for Evidence* (2017) Cm 9370.

[27] *Lennard's Carrying Co Ltd v Asiatic Petroleum Co Ltd* [1915] AC 705 at 713 per Viscount Haldane LC. Applied in *JF Alford Transport Ltd* [1997] 2 Cr App R 326 at 331, [1997] Crim LR 745 and commentary.

corporation and who, when acting in the company's business, are considered to be the 'embodiment of the company'.[28] Their acts and states of mind are the company's acts and states of mind and the company is held liable, not for the acts of others, but for what are deemed to be its own acts. In a corporate prosecution, the court looks to which person within the organization performed the proscribed conduct and then whether that person is sufficiently senior to be treated as a person who is a directing mind and will of the company.

The courts' willingness to attribute the blameworthy acts and mens rea of the controlling officers to the company developed rapidly in criminal law in the mid-1940s.[29] In *DPP v Kent and Sussex Contractors Ltd*,[30] the fraud alleged required an intention to deceive and it was held that the transport manager's intent was the intent of the company. *Kent* was approved in *ICR Haulage Ltd*[31] and applied to common law offences. The company was convicted of a conspiracy to defraud, with the act and intent of the managing director being the act and intent of the company. The doctrine was memorably described by Denning LJ:[32]

> A company may in many ways be likened to a human body. It has a brain and a nerve centre which controls what it does. It also has hands which hold the tools and act in accordance with directions from the centre. Some of the people in the company are mere servants and agents who are nothing more than hands to do the work and cannot be said to represent the mind or will. Others are directors and managers who represent the directing mind and will of the company and control what it does. The state of mind of these managers is the state of mind of the company and is treated by the law as such.[33]

A person is not a 'controlling officer' simply because his work is 'brain' work (as opposed to physical work) and he exercises some managerial discretion, since not all such persons 'represent the directing mind and will of the company and control what it does'.[34] Nor is someone occupying a position entitled 'manager' necessarily a controlling mind. The manager of a supermarket belonging to a company owning hundreds of supermarkets is not the company's 'brains' and does not act as the company.[35] Companies have been held not to be criminally liable for the acts of a depot engineer[36] or a weighbridge operator[37] or the European Sales Manager of the company.[38] Only the very senior managers or those explicitly authorized by the Board to act on the company's behalf in relation to specific matters[39] will be likely to fit the description as the directing mind and will of the company. This illustrates one of the major shortcomings of the identification doctrine—that it fails to reflect the reality of the internal structure of modern-day large multinational

---

[28] *Essendon Engineering Co Ltd v Maile* [1982] RTR 260.

[29] See for discussion of the development of the doctrine, LCCP 195, paras 5.14–5.80.

[30] [1944] KB 146.   [31] [1944] KB 551, cf *McDonnell* [1966] 1 QB 233, p 461.

[32] *HL Bolton (Engineering) Co Ltd v TJ Graham & Sons Ltd* [1957] 1 QB 159 at 172. Though this *dictum* has been frequently followed, the Privy Council has said in the *Meridian* case, see p 266, that the anthropomorphism distracts attention from what the Board regarded as the true principle determining whether acts should be attributed to the corporation—ie the interpretation of the particular statute.

[33] Thus, it is thought that a company could be guilty of abetting an offence through its managing director—though there is no *vicarious* liability in abetting, p 190. See *Robert Millar (Contractors) Ltd* [1970] 2 QB 54.

[34] *Tesco Supermarkets Ltd v Nattrass* [1972] AC 153 at 171 per Lord Reid, at 187 per Lord Dilhorne and at 200 per Lord Diplock. See Gobert and Punch, *Rethinking Corporate Crime* (2003) 59–70.

[35] ibid.   [36] *Magna Plant Ltd v Mitchell* [1966] Crim LR 394.

[37] *John Henshall (Quarries) Ltd v Harvey* [1965] 2 QB 233.

[38] *Redfern and Dunlop Ltd (Aircraft Division)* (1992) 13 Cr App R (S) 709.

[39] cf *VOSA v FM Conway Ltd* [2012] EWHC 2930 (Admin) where the court held that even though the plant manager had been given a written authorization to that effect he was not the 'brains' of the company.

corporations.[40] Although there are instances of a wide application, in general it produces what many regard as an unsatisfactorily narrow scope for criminal liability. It also renders it disproportionately easy to prosecute smaller companies in which the controllers are more readily identifiable and allows larger corporations to avoid liability by disguising their true organizational structure.[41] There are further difficulties because the test remains so ambiguous—it is unclear which individuals will qualify, and whether the same approach is applicable in all contexts. It is difficult to apply the test to companies of all sizes and structures working in different sectors.

How are the courts to determine which individuals are controllers? In the leading case of *Tesco Supermarkets Ltd v Nattrass*,[42] it was said that the company may be criminally liable only for the acts of:

the board of directors, the managing director and perhaps other superior officers of a company [who] carry out the functions of management and speak and act as the company . . . [43]

or of a person:

who is in actual control of the operations of a company or of part of them and who is not responsible to another person in the company for the manner in which he discharges his duties in the sense of being under his orders . . . [44]

Lord Diplock[45] thought that the question is to be answered by:

identifying those natural persons who by the memorandum and articles of association [of the company] or as a result of action taken by the directors or by the company in general meeting pursuant to the articles are entrusted with the exercise of the powers of the company.

Lord Pearson too thought that the constitution of the company concerned must be taken into account; and Lords Dilhorne, Pearson and Diplock thought that the terms used frequently by Parliament[46]—'any director, manager, secretary or other similar officer of the body corporate'—afford a useful indication. If the persons who are responsible for the general management of the company delegate their duties to another, then the acts of that other will be the acts of the company.[47]

Once the facts have been ascertained, it is a question of law whether a person, in doing particular things, is to be regarded as the company or merely as the company's employee or agent.[48] Accordingly, the judge should direct the jury that if they find certain facts proved then they must find that the act and intention of the agent is the act and the intention of the company. It is not sufficient to direct that the company is liable for its 'responsible agents' or 'high executives', for such persons are not necessarily the company.[49] The test is the same whether the offence be serious or trivial.

The decision in *Tesco* failed to provide the clarity of definition that is needed in fixing the scope of criminal liability, and was heavily criticized.[50]

---

[40] For criticism see LCCP 195, Part 5 and Appendices B and C; Wells, *Corporations and Criminal Responsibility*.

[41] According to the Law Commission in 2010, 96 per cent of UK businesses have between 0–9 employees. See LCCP 195, para 7.6.

[42] See n 34.   [43] At 171 per Lord Reid.   [44] At 187 per Viscount Dilhorne.

[45] At 200, followed in *Seaboard Offshore Ltd v Secretary of State for Transport* [1994] 2 All ER 99, 104.

[46] This is a form of words used in many criminal statutes as discussed later: see p 271.

[47] [1972] AC 153 at 193.   [48] ibid at 170, 173 per Lord Reid.   [49] *Sporle* [1971] Crim LR 706.

[50] See LCCP 195 and references in Part 5; RJ Wickins, 'Confusion Worse Confounded: The End of the Directing Mind Theory' [1997] J Bus Law 524.

Meridian: all a matter of statutory construction?

In the more recent *Meridian* case,[51] the Privy Council, in a valuable review of the nature of corporate liability, held that where the criminal liability alleged is under a statutory offence, whether conduct is to be attributed to a corporation is a question of the construction of the particular statute under which proceedings are brought. Thus, the statute may impose corporate liability in respect of an agent who could not be said to be the 'directing mind and will' of the corporation under the primary rules of attribution.[52] This is a controversial extension of the potential scope of corporate liability. For many it represents a welcome relaxation of the identification doctrine, with the potential to impose corporate liability more flexibly in a broader range of circumstances, but in doing so it reduces the degree of certainty in the law. Indeed, Buxton LJ, in a powerful dissent in a subsequent case in the Court of Appeal (Civil Division), commented that *Meridian* represents an 'imperfect guide to the approach to the rule for attribution of a crime'.[53]

The Privy Council in *Meridian* contrasted the *Tesco* case with the case of *Re Supply of Ready Mixed Concrete (No 2)*.[54] In *Tesco*, a narrow approach to liability was adopted. In the *Concrete* case, the House of Lords held a company liable for contempt of court for the act of a regional employee who made an arrangement in breach of an undertaking given by the company to the Restrictive Practices Court. The board of directors knew nothing of the arrangement and had given instructions that no such arrangements were to be made. But the arrangement made by the regional employee was an agreement binding on the company.[55] The company had given an undertaking that no such arrangement would be made and it had made such an arrangement. Should it not have been exactly the same if the undertaking had been given by an individual employer and the arrangement made by an employee with ostensible authority?[56] *Ready Mixed Concrete (No 2)* was a case of civil contempt of court and the result would not necessarily have been the same if it had been a criminal offence requiring mens rea. In *Meridian* itself, it was held that the acts of the company's investment manager were properly attributed to the company for the purposes of the New Zealand Securities Act 1988. Perhaps all that these cases demonstrate is that a statute imposes liability if that appears to be the intention of the legislature. The Court of Appeal has subsequently emphasized that the *Meridian* approach is only applicable to offences of statutory origin.[57] The *Meridian* approach was endorsed by the Law Commission in LCCP 195, which recommended that courts should look at the underlying purposes of the statutory scheme for guidance on the bases for holding a company liable.[58]

It is increasingly doubtful how far in practice the *Meridian* approach displaces *Tesco* by allowing corporate liability when the acts are those of individuals who would not be seen as a controller applying *Tesco*. In some cases it may have made a difference. For example, *Moore v I Bresler Ltd*,[59] which has been criticized for going too far down the scale of seniority in

---

[51] *Meridian Global Funds Management Asia Ltd v Securities Commission* [1995] 2 AC 500. See E Ferran (2011) 127 LQR 239; E Lim, 'A Critique of Corporate Attribution: "Directing Mind and Will" and Corporate Objectives' [2013] JBL 333.

[52] This passage in the 12th edn was cited with approval by the Court of Appeal in *St Regis Paper Co Ltd* [2011] EWCA Crim 2527, [20].

[53] *Re Odyssey (London) Ltd v OIC Run Off Ltd* (2000) The Times, 17 Mar, Court of Appeal (Civ Div).

[54] [1995] 1 AC 456. See C Wells, 'A Quiet Revolution in Corporate Liability for Crime' (1995) 145 NLJ 1326.

[55] Lord Nolan [1995] 1 All ER 135 at 150–1.

[56] 'In my opinion . . . the act [in breach of an injunction] need not be done by the person himself': Warrington J in *Stancomb v Trowbridge UDC* [1910] 2 Ch 190 at 193–4, a decision which Lord Nolan said should have been followed in *Ready-Mixed Concrete (No 2)*.

[57] *A-G's Reference (No 2 of 1999)* [2000] QB 796, [2000] Crim LR 475 and commentary.

[58] See in particular Part 5 and recommendation at para 5.110.   [59] [1944] 2 All ER 515.

identifying a controlling officer,[60] was approved in *Meridian* by the Privy Council as an example of its 'construction' principle. The company was convicted of making false returns with intent to deceive, contrary to the Finance (No 2) Act 1940, when the returns were made by the company secretary and a *branch* sales manager.[61]

More recent cases suggest that *Meridian* may not have made such a radical change after all.

In *St Regis Paper Co Ltd*[62] the company was held not to be liable as the individual involved was not a directing mind and will of the company. S was the technical manager of one of the company's five plants and falsified environmental records, committing an offence under the relevant pollution regulations.[63] The offence required proof of mens rea. In a preliminary ruling, it was held that the regulation created criminal liability for the acts of an employee although he could not be said to be the directing mind and will of the company. It was held to be sufficient that the employee in question carried out management functions and was therefore in control of the operations of the company in the relevant area. The company appealed. The Court of Appeal acknowledged that several cases had rejected the idea that *Meridian* expressed a new approach which departed from *Tesco*[64] and that Rose LJ in *A-G's Reference (No 2 of 1999)* stated that *Meridian* represented a restatement of the law rather than a departure from existing principles. Moses LJ cited with approval a passage from the 12th edition of this book (p 262) recognizing that the significance of *Meridian* is that it emphasizes the importance of construing the statute which creates the offence in order to determine the applicable rules of attribution.

The Court of Appeal held that having regard to the terms of the regulations, it was not possible to impose criminal liability on the company as S, a technical manager, was not the directing mind and will of the company. The court noted the numerous strict liability offences in the regulations, but that the offence charged against the company required proof of mens rea. The scheme was described as being devised in a 'carefully graduated way', creating some offences requiring proof of mens rea and some that do not. The court concluded that it was respecting the structure of the regulations in holding that the mens rea offences were ones that could only be attributed to the company if committed by someone who was the directing mind and will.[65]

In *R v A Ltd*,[66] Sir Brian Leveson P stated that 'save in those cases where consideration of the legislation creating the offence in question leads to a different and perhaps broader approach, as discussed in *Meridian Global Funds Management Asia Ltd v Securities Commission*, the test for determining those individuals whose actions and state of mind are to be attributed to a corporate body remains that established in *Tesco Supermarkets Ltd v Nattrass*'.[67] In this case it was accepted that BK, a director of the company, was properly regarded as the directing mind and will of A Ltd and that the prosecution could use his diary entries to prove both his guilty mind and that of the company.

---

[60] By R Welsh, 'The Criminal Liability of Corporations' (1946) 62 LQR 345 at 358, Williams, TBCL, 973.

[61] But the company secretary might perhaps be regarded, when acting within the scope of his authority, as the company's 'directing mind and will' for this purpose. *Kent and Sussex Contractors Co* [1944] KB 146 seems more doubtful in this respect, as only the transport manager was involved.

[62] [2011] EWCA Crim 2527.

[63] The Pollution Prevention and Control (England and Wales) Regulations 2000, SI 2000/1973, reg 32(1)(g).

[64] Buxton LJ in his dissent in *Re Odyssey (London) Ltd v OIC Run-Off Ltd* regarded the principle expressed in *Tesco Supermarkets* as the authoritative statement of the law.

[65] The Court of Appeal's reasoning has been heavily criticized. The Court of Appeal refused to certify a point of law: *St Regis Paper Co Ltd* [2012] EWCA Crim 1847.

[66] [2016] EWCA Crim 1469.   [67] At [27].

In *Serious Fraud Office v Barclays Bank Plc*, Davis LJ heard an application by the SFO to reinstate proceedings against Barclays Bank Plc.[68] His lordship relied on *Nattrass* to hold that the criminal courts do not adopt the more extensive approach to corporate attribution which the civil courts may possibly be prepared to adopt. In this case, the relevant corporate officers (one of whom was the CEO) did not have full discretion to act independently in relation to the relevant transactions and they were responsible to others (the board) for the manner in which they discharged their duties. Davis LJ held that despite the executives' seniority it followed that they could not be regarded as the directing mind and will of the bank for the purpose of performing the functions in question. His lordship accepted that the relevant individuals had some degree of autonomy, however this was insufficient; it had to be shown that they had complete autonomy to 'do the deal' in question. Furthermore, there was nothing in the policy or scheme of the statutory offence with which they were charged—under the Fraud Act 2006—to justify fashioning a special rule of attribution in the circumstances of the case. There was therefore no justification for departing from *Tesco v Nattrass*.

The judgment of Davis LJ demonstrates how narrow the approach in *Tesco v Nattrass* is in application. It serves to highlight how difficult it will be to impose criminal liability upon large complex corporates, such as the bank in this case. Not even the CEO had complete autonomy to 'do the deal', as his decisions had to be ratified by the board. His lordship recognized that some may prefer a wider approach than that articulated by the House of Lords in *Tesco*, but it still represents the law.

Davis LJ's judgment may lend weight to the arguments which have been made by successive Directors of the SFO that the identification doctrine needs to be replaced. The judgment also highlights that *Meridian* will only apply if there is some particular policy behind the statute which would justify departing from *Tesco v Nattrass*. Davis LJ could discern no such policy from the background to the Fraud Act 2006 or from its text. His lordship stated that it was difficult to discern any particular policy behind the statute aside from that applicable to analogous common law offences; namely, that it is in the public interest that persons dishonestly conducting themselves in such a way should be liable to criminal sanctions. These observations probably apply with equal force to most criminal offences. This serves to highlight that *Meridian* may only be capable of applying to a small number of criminal offences which have an identifiable purpose (other than that which justifies the enactment of criminal offences generally).

Acting 'as' and yet 'against' the corporation

The *Moore v I Bresler Ltd*[69] decision is subject to criticism because the two officers had as their objective to conceal their fraudulent sale of the company's property. In *Serious Fraud Office v Barclays*,[70] Davis LJ accepted that whilst the courts will be slow to attribute criminal culpability to a company where the acts of the individual(s) in question have operated to defraud the company or otherwise make it a victim, criminal culpability may still, depending on the circumstances and context and on the wording of the statutory offence in question, be capable of attaching to the company by virtue of that conduct of individual(s) representing its directing mind and will. As authority for this proposition, his lordship cited *Belmont Finance Corpn Ltd v Williams Furniture Ltd*.[71]

Acting within the scope of corporate duty

The controlling officer must be acting within the scope of his authority as a corporate officer at the time that he performs the necessary elements of the offence in terms of actus reus and

---

68 [2018] EWHC 3055 (QB).   69 [1944] 2 All ER 515.   70 [2018] EWHC 3055 (QB), [86].
71 [1979] Ch 250. Williams, TBCL, 973, refers to *Belmont Finance Corpn Ltd v Williams Furniture Ltd* as 'a much more sensible decision of a civil court' than the decision in *Moore v I Bresler Ltd*.

mens rea before these can be treated as the criminal acts of the corporation itself under the identification doctrine.

A corporation's 'state of mind'

Having located the relevant controlling individual with whom the corporation may be identified, it is necessary to prove that he performed the relevant actus reus with the accompanying mens rea. Where the offence is one of strict liability, the corporation may be held liable for the acts of any of its employees or agents where those acts are, in law, the company's acts, under the attribution principle discussed later (p 287).[72] Wherever the offence requires mens rea, it must be proved that a controlling officer had the mens rea.[73] Similarly, where a defence requires evidence of a belief or other state of mind, this must usually be the belief or state of mind of a controlling officer;[74] but the belief of one officer, A, will not suffice if another, B (especially if he is superior to A) knows that A's belief is ill-founded.[75] Probably, each controlling officer who is concerned in the offence must have the required state of mind. If, however, no controlling officer is involved and all the employees or agents who are involved do have the required state of mind, the defence ought clearly to be available. For example, if a branch manager, not being a controlling officer, finds a controlled drug in supplies delivered to his branch and takes control of it, intending to hand it to the police, the company may surely rely on this intention to establish the defence provided by s 5(4) of the Misuse of Drugs Act 1971, if it is charged with unlawful possession of the drug.[76]

Many of the offences for which corporate liability can arise turn on proof of knowledge, but other familiar forms of mens rea can be relevant. For example, in *R v X Ltd*[77] the Court of Appeal dealt with proof of recklessness against a company through the state of mind of its sales force. X Ltd was charged with four counts involving engaging in an unfair commercial practice in contravention of different provisions of the Consumer Protection from Unfair Trading Regulations 2008.[78] The Crown had to establish knowledge or recklessness on the part of the company as to the way in which its commercial practices failed (in fact) to meet its obligations to consumers. The Court of Appeal, in construing the offence, held that at least one of the controlling minds had to be proved to be at least reckless, confirming the view in *Airtours v Shipley*.[79] With offences of this technicality, care will be needed to identify precisely what result or circumstance that recklessness must relate to.

No aggregation of several controlling individuals' culpability

A question that was raised by many critics of the identification doctrine was whether it must be proved that an individual controlling officer (whether identifiable or not) was guilty of the crime alleged against the company or whether it is permissible to 'aggregate' the conduct of a number of officers, none of whom would individually be guilty, so as to constitute in sum the elements of the offence.[80] It is submitted that it is not possible artificially to construct the mens rea in this way.[81] Two (semi) innocent states of mind cannot be added

---

[72] Agent's acts are the principal's act in law.
[73] *Tesco Supermarkets Ltd v Nattrass* [1972] AC 153. Draft Criminal Code, cl 34(2).
[74] *GJ Coles & Co Ltd v Goldsworthy* [1985] WAR 183. See G Orchard in *Criminal Law Essays*, 114, 117, 118–19.
[75] *Brambles Holdings Ltd v Carey* (1976) 15 SASR 270 at 280.
[76] See LC 177, Draft Criminal Code, Appendix B, Example 30(vi).
[77] [2013] EWCA Crim 818, [2014] Crim LR 73 and commentary.
[78] SI 2008/1277.   [79] (1994) 58 JP 835. See also *MFI Warehouses v Nattrass* [1973] 1 WLR 307.
[80] See especially C Wells, 'Culture, Risk and Criminal Liability' [1993] Crim LR 551, 563.
[81] cf *Armstrong v Strain* [1952] 1 KB 232, Devlin J: 'You cannot add an innocent state of mind to an innocent state of mind and get as a result a dishonest state of mind.'

together to produce a guilty state of mind.[82] Any such doctrine could certainly have no application in offences requiring knowledge, intention or recklessness.

It is in relation to offences of negligence (particularly gross negligence) that the aggregation principle has been most forcefully advocated. The argument proceeds as follows: a company owes a duty of care and if its operation falls far below the standard required it is guilty of gross negligence. A series of minor failures by officers of the company might add up to a gross breach by the company of its duty of care. There is authority for such a doctrine in the law of tort[83] and the concept of negligence is the same in the criminal law, the difference being one of degree—criminal negligence must be 'gross'. It is immaterial that the doctrine of vicarious liability in tort does not apply in criminal law, because this is a case not of vicarious, but of personal, liability and that is a proper concern of the criminal law. It was argued that a corporation ought to be open to prosecution for manslaughter by gross negligence on the aggregation principle.[84] This argument was rejected by the Court of Appeal in *A-G's Reference (No 2 of 1999)*.[85] The prosecution arose from the Southall train crash in which seven passengers died. The trial judge ruled that the gross negligence manslaughter offence required negligence to be proved under the identification doctrine. The Court of Appeal approved that ruling, holding that unless an identified individual's conduct, characterized as gross criminal negligence, could be attributed to the company, the company was not, in the state of the common law, liable for manslaughter.[86] The specific statutory offence under the Corporate Manslaughter and Corporate Homicide Act 2007 will now apply, but the general principle in corporate liability that the identification doctrine cannot be satisfied by an aggregation of several officers' states of mind remains good law for all other offences.

Several interesting issues remain in relation to the aggregation argument, including to what extent it is necessary for a conviction that an individual controlling mind be identifiable. Can a company waive the need to establish that fact by pleading guilty on the basis that, although no controller was identifiable, the corporation is prepared to accept liability? There would seem no reason in principle why not. The bar on aggregation is to protect the company and if it chooses it may waive that protection. It would not be akin to a company pleading guilty to an offence that was not known to law. Consider the case where the company accepts that it must have been director A or B who performed the criminal acts, but it cannot be established beyond reasonable doubt which of them did. Surely the company should be capable of accepting guilt? Indeed, it is arguable that in such a case the law ought to allow the Crown to establish corporate liability in a contested trial.

Impact of the Corporate Manslaughter and Corporate Homicide Act 2007

The 2007 Act is discussed in full in Ch 14. It imposes liability for manslaughter on the basis of a breach of a relevant duty by the organization *as a result of the way the activities are managed or organized*. The italicized words are designed to ensure that the focus is on a 'management failure'; at least for manslaughter, the limitations of the identification doctrine

---

[82] Wells argues to the contrary that 'aggregation needs to be seen as a recognition that individuals within a company contribute to the whole machine; it is the whole that is judged not the parts': *Corporations and Criminal Responsibility*, 155. See also LCCP 195, Appendix C.

[83] *WB Anderson & Sons Ltd v Rhodes (Liverpool) Ltd* [1967] 2 All ER 850, Cairns J, discussed by M Dean, '*Hedley Byrne* and the Eager Business Man' (1968) 31 MLR 322; JW Salmond, RVF Heuston and RA Buckley, *Salmond on Torts* (21st edn, 1996) 406–9; *Fleming on Torts* (8th edn, 1992) 376–85.

[84] In the *P&O* case, Turner J seems to have proceeded on the basis that recklessness must be proved.

[85] [2000] QB 796; considering *Great Western Trains Co* (1999) 3 June, CCC. It was also rejected in Scotland in *Transco PLC v HM Advocate (No 1)* 2004 SLT 41.

[86] The court's conclusion that there can *in general* be no corporate liability in the absence of an identified human offender ignores the principle discussed earlier of corporate liability where a duty is specifically imposed on the corporation as a legal person: *Birmingham & Gloucester Railway* (1842) 3 QB 223.

are removed.[87] Some commentators suggest that this would be a better approach to adopt in determining corporate liability for all offences.[88]

The Act does, however, place a restriction on the test. Under s 1(3), the offence is committed by an organization only if 'the way in which its activities are managed and organised *by its senior management* is a substantial element in the breach referred to in subsection 1'. Who are the senior managers? By s 1(4)(c):

'senior management', in relation to an organisation, means the persons who play significant roles in—

    (i) the making of decisions about how the whole or a substantial part of its activities are to be managed or organised, or

    (ii) the actual managing or organising of the whole or a substantial part of those activities.

This extends beyond the narrow category of senior individuals who would be caught at common law as the directing mind and will under the identification doctrine. The merits of this test in the context of the offence are considered in Ch 14. The test is linked to a senior level of management but also considers how an activity was managed within the organization as a whole. It will now be possible in manslaughter to aggregate the shortcomings of a wide variety of individuals within the organization to prove a failure of management *by the organization*. The language is designed to reflect the concentration of things done consistently within the organization's culture and policies more generally.[89]

The courts or law reformers could draw upon this definition of 'senior managers' from the 2007 Act in consideration of the scope of the 'relevant controlling minds' in application of the identification doctrine more generally.[90]

8.1.2.6 Statutory liability of corporate officers

The sixth form of liability which, for the sake of completeness, deserves to be mentioned is the statutory liability of a corporate officer as a secondary party to the company's principal offending. The following provision commonly appears in statutes creating offences likely to be committed by corporations:[91]

Where an offence committed by a body corporate is proved to have been committed with the consent or connivance of, or to be attributable to neglect on the part of, a director, secretary or other similar officer of the body corporate, or a person purporting to act in any such capacity, he as well as the body corporate is guilty of the offence and liable to be proceeded against and punished accordingly.

---

[87] Norrie argues that the Act represents a return to an identification approach, given that it focuses upon senior managers. See A Norrie, *Crime, Reason and History* (3rd edn, 2014) 124–7. This is discussed further in Ch 14.

[88] See the discussion in LCCP 195, Part 5 and Appendices B and C.

[89] For discussion of the advantages of basing liability on corporate organizational models, see LCCP 195 and Appendix C in particular, considering the Australian experience.

[90] See the discussion by Cartwright in LCCP 195, Appendix B.

[91] eg Outer Space Act 1986, s 12(3). Other versions of this provision refer also to the 'manager' of a body corporate. The provision in the Fraud Act 2006, s 12 is even wider: '(1) Subsection (2) applies if an offence under this Act is committed by a body corporate. (2) If the offence is proved to have been committed with the consent or connivance of—(a) a director, manager, secretary or other similar officer of the body corporate, or (b) a person who was purporting to act in any such capacity, he (as well as the body corporate) is guilty of the offence and liable to be proceeded against and punished accordingly. (3) If the affairs of a body corporate are managed by its members, subsection (2) applies in relation to the acts and defaults of a member in connection with his functions of management as if he were a director of the body corporate.'

Whether a director or other officer is under a duty is a question which can be answered only by looking at the facts of each case; and the onus of proving that there was a duty which has been neglected is on the prosecution.[92]

As far as 'consent' and 'connivance' are concerned, these provisions probably effect only a slight extension of the law; because the officer who expressly consents or connives in the commission of the offence will be liable as a secondary party under the principles considered in Ch 6. There may, however, be a case of consent which does not amount to counselling or abetting; and the words 'attributable to any neglect on the part of'[93] clearly impose a wider liability in making the officer liable for his negligence in failing to prevent the offence. As the Court of Appeal noted:

the nature of these regulatory statutes with their provisions for secondary liability by directors and managers in accordance with their consent, connivance or neglect is to ensure that they are held to proper standards of supervision and that the size of the company and the distance of directors and managers from the coal face of individual acts should not, where there is consent, connivance or neglect, afford directors or managers with the necessary knowledge a defence.[94]

Note that this common form of provision[95] does not create an offence. It creates an extended form of secondary liability for an offence committed by a body corporate under some other provision of the relevant Act.[96] It is submitted that, like the general law of secondary liability, it applies automatically and does not have to be, and indeed is incapable of being, charged as an offence.[97]

In a House of Lords case dealing with such sections, *Chargot Ltd*,[98] a case under s 37 of the Health and Safety Act 1974, Lord Hope (with whom the other Lords agreed) said:

No fixed rule can be laid down as to what the prosecution must identify and prove in order to establish that the officer's state of mind was such as to amount to consent, connivance or neglect. In some cases, as where the officer's place of activity was remote from the work place or what was done there was not under his immediate direction and control, this may require the leading of quite detailed evidence of which fair notice may have to be given. In others, where the officer was in day to day contact with what was done there, very little more may be needed . . . the question, in the end of the day, will always be whether the officer in question should have been put on inquiry so as to have taken steps to determine whether or not the appropriate safety procedures were in place.

The Law Commission examined the use of this type of provision,[99] and concluded that in principle there cannot be consent and connivance without at least a subjective awareness that wrongdoing is or will be taking place, and that a requirement for proof of at least that level of fault is desirable. On this proposal it would not be possible to establish individual

---

[92] *Huckerby v Elliott* [1970] 1 All ER 189. 'Manager' means someone managing the affairs of the company and not, eg, the manager of a store: *Tesco Supermarkets Ltd v Nattrass* [1972] AC 153 at 178.

[93] These words are omitted from the Theft Act 1968, s 18.

[94] *Hutchins* [2011] EWCA Crim 1056, [25].

[95] Commonly used examples are discussed in LCCP 195, Part 7 including the Trade Descriptions Act 1968, s 20 and the Food Safety Act 1990, s 14.

[96] See *Wilson* [2013] EWCA Crim 1780.

[97] *Contra, Wilson* [1997] 1 All ER 119, [1997] Crim LR 53 and commentary.

[98] [2008] UKHL 73. See also *Knowles v Department for Business, Enterprise and Regulatory Reform* [2009] EWHC 3899 (Admin) and *Tangerine Confectionery Ltd and Veolia ES (UK) Ltd* (2011) 176 JP 349.

[99] LCCP 195, Part 7.

directors' liability for an offence committed by the company, unless there was true, subjective consent or connivance at the offence by the director in question. This would be:

> in keeping with an understanding of the doctrine of consent and connivance as an extension of the complicity doctrine, to fit the reality of corporate decision-making. Moreover, where crimes requiring proof of fault or involving stigma are in issue, a requirement of at least subjective awareness on a director's part would appear to be essential, in point of justice, given that a finding of consent and connivance makes a director (or equivalent person) guilty of the offence itself.[100]

The Commission's provisional proposal is that rather than these connivance provisions being extended to include instances where the company's offence is attributable to mere neglect, instead, where appropriate, new offences should be created based on liability for the conduct of an individual whom the company has negligently failed to prevent from committing the offence.[101]

8.1.3 Limits of corporate liability

When any statute makes it an offence for 'a person' to do or omit to do something, that offence is capable of commission by a corporation, unless the contrary appears: the Interpretation Act 1889 (and now the Interpretation Act 1978) defined 'person' to include 'a body of persons corporate or unincorporate' and provided that the definition, so far as it includes bodies corporate, applies to any provision of an Act whenever passed, relating to an offence punishable on indictment or summary conviction.[102] The fact that the offence requires mens rea does not preclude corporate liability since, as discussed earlier, the state of mind of the corporation's controlling officers, as well as their acts, may be attributed to the corporation using the identification doctrine. However, the nature of the offence may be such that a corporation is physically incapable of committing it even through its controlling officers.

There are numerous other limitations on the liability of a corporation.

8.1.3.1 Categories of offence

There are offences which it is extremely unlikely that an official of a corporation could commit within the scope of his employment; for example, bigamy,[103] rape, some other sexual offences and, possibly, perjury.[104]

8.1.3.2 Penalty and punishment

A corporation cannot be sentenced to a physical punishment such as imprisonment. A corporation cannot therefore be guilty of murder. The lack of imagination in the law's response to sentencing corporations when they are found liable has been cogently criticized.[105] One of the most welcome aspects of the Corporate Manslaughter and Corporate Homicide Act 2007 lies in the innovative sentencing and disposal powers available to the courts. The court may, if the prosecution apply, impose a remedial order. A remedial order under s 9 is one

---

[100] ibid, para 7.34.   [101] ibid.   [102] See the Interpretation Act 1978, s 5 and Sch 1.

[103] Even in some of these cases it is not inconceivable that a corporation might be held liable as a secondary party. Eg the managing director of an incorporated marriage advisory bureau negotiates a marriage which he knows to be bigamous. Or a pornographic film company liable as an accessory to rape.

[104] In *Re Odyssey (London) Ltd v OIC Run Off Ltd* (2000) The Times, 17 Mar, CA (Civ Div), the majority considered, *obiter*, that a company could be liable for perjury through acts of director and managing director, if he had the 'status' of the company when testifying.

[105] See generally on the sentencing of corporations: Gobert and Punch, *Rethinking Corporate Crime*, Ch 7; and for a review of the punishments that might be available, see M Jefferson, 'Corporate Criminal Liability: The Problems of Sanctions' (2001) 65 J Crim L 235.

'requiring the organisation to take specified steps' to remedy the breach or anything result-ing from it which caused death, or any deficiency as to health and safety matters of which the breach appears to be an indication.[106] Under s 10 a publicity order may be made 'requir-ing the organisation to publicise in a specified manner' its conviction, specified particulars, the amount of any fine and the terms of any remedial order. This provision, added during the Bill's passage in the Lords, is clearly intended to deter by impact of adverse publicity.[107]

8.1.4 Unincorporated bodies

An unincorporated association, such as a partnership or trade union, is not a legal person at common law and therefore could not incur criminal liability, though its members could. This is still the position for common law offences. Statutory offences are different.

8.1.4.1 Liability for what offences?

In short, an unincorporated association can be liable for a statutory offences enacted after 1889 subject to the terms of the Act evidencing a contrary intention of Parliament.

The effect of the Interpretation Act 1889 was that in all enactments relating to offences, whenever passed, the word 'person' includes bodies corporate (s 2) and, in enactments passed after 1889, both bodies corporate *and unincorporate* (s 19). The Interpretation Act 1978 preserves this position.[108] Since 1889 unincorporated bodies have been able to commit any offence under an enactment passed after 1889 which makes it an offence for a 'person' to do or omit to do anything which an unincorporated body is capable of doing. The potential liability of unincorporated bodies seems to have been little noticed. In *A-G v Able*, Woolf J, dealing with an alleged offence under the Suicide Act 1961 said, 'It must be remembered that the [Voluntary Euthanasia Society] is an unincorporated body and there can be no question of the society committing an offence';[109] but since that offence may be committed by 'a person' it seems that it may be committed by an unincorporated body. An unincorpo-rated body, being the registered keeper of a vehicle, was held capable of liability as a 'person' to fixed penalties for illegal parking under the Transport Act 1982.[110]

Schedule 1 to the Interpretation Act 1978 provides that '"person" includes a body of per-sons corporate or unincorporate', and by s 5 of the Act 'in any Act, unless the contrary intention appears, words and expressions listed in Schedule 1 to this Act are to be construed according to that Schedule'. Statutes across English law do not adopt a set form of words to help to determine whether 'a contrary intention appears'. The Court of Appeal in *L*[111] accepted that although several statutes do make specific provision for the criminal liability of unincorporated associations, the provisions are so varied that no settled policy can be discerned from them. The court found it impossible to derive any general proposition that:

there is a form of enactment which is to be expected if an unincorporated association is to be crimi-nally liable, and of which the absence signals a contrary intention for the purposes of section 5 of the Interpretation Act.[112]

---

[106] Failure to comply is an offence punishable with a fine.

[107] See the Sentencing Council definitive guidance on these powers: www.sentencingcouncil.org.uk/wp-content/uploads/HS-offences-definitive-guideline-FINAL-web.pdf.

[108] Sch 2, para 4(5) maintains the existing application of 'person' to corporate bodies (and, implicitly, its non-application to unincorporated bodies) in pre-1889 statutes creating offences. The definition of 'person' in Sch 1 applies to all statutes passed after the commencement of the 1889 Act, so that they continue to be capable of commission by unincorporated bodies.

[109] [1984] QB 795.   [110] *Clerk to Croydon Justices, ex p Chief Constable of Kent* [1989] Crim LR 910.

[111] [2008] EWCA Crim 1970.   [112] At [22].

The court accepted that the absence of procedural provisions to govern such prosecutions is not determinative of whether they were intended to apply to unincorporated associations. Different considerations may apply in mens rea offences and those at common law than from strict liability statutory offences.

According to the Court of Appeal in *W Stevenson & Sons (A Partnership)*,[113] in relation to partnerships one consideration may be whether there is some restriction upon the assets that will properly be available to meet any penalty imposed. It is submitted that this is a doubtful interpretation. The court does not address in detail the impact of s 10 of the Partnership Act 1890.[114] It is arguable that once a partnership (or indeed a partner) has been convicted, if s 10 applies all the partners are liable to pay the fine as a matter of partnership law.[115]

It is disappointing that the law offers no clearer definition on these matters.

8.1.4.2 Which members of the unincorporated association can be liable?

It was thought that when an unincorporated association is prosecuted the courts would normally proceed by analogy to the law relating to corporations and that only officials corresponding to the controlling officers of corporations would bear some liability. The Court of Appeal has rejected that narrow approach, adopting an interpretation with the potential to impose liability on many thousands of individuals. In *L*,[116] the chairman and treasurer of a golf club with 900 members were prosecuted for the strict liability offence of polluting a watercourse by an escape of heating oil from the premises caused directly by an independent contractor. The question arose as to whether it was correct to prosecute the individuals rather than the association. The trial judge ruled that the individuals could not be prosecuted. The Court of Appeal disagreed. Irrespective of the lack of personal fault, liability arose as a result of membership. Criminal liability of unincorporated associations was said to involve quite separate principles from those relating to corporations:

A corporation has, for all legal purposes, independent legal personality. It is also regulated, often heavily. It must have a registered address and registered directors and secretary. An unincorporated association may indeed look very like a corporation in some cases, and it may have standing and de facto independence, but equally it may not. A prosecution which could only be brought against an informal grouping of building workers, or sportsmen, or campaigners would be likely to be wholly ineffective. It is a necessary consequence of the different nature of an unincorporated association that all its members remain jointly and severally liable for its actions done within their authority.[117]

The court's conclusion is that liability can be imposed on the individual members irrespective of the lack of personal fault of any individual member. It appears to be heavily influenced by the potential ineffectiveness of a prosecution against a body which might be

---

[113] [2008] EWCA Crim 273. W was convicted under an offence for failing 'to submit a sales note which accurately indicated the quantities and price at first sale of each fish species'. The question for the Court of Appeal was whether it was possible for legislation to render a partnership criminally liable as a separate entity from the individual partners.

[114] 'Where, by any wrongful act or omission of any partner acting in the ordinary course of the business of the firm, or with the authority of his co-partners, loss or injury is caused to any person not being a partner in the firm, or any penalty is incurred, the firm is liable therefor to the same extent as the partner so acting or omitting to act.'

[115] Even if only the partnership is liable to pay, as the Court of Appeal thought, then if the partnership assets are insufficient to pay the fine, s 10 would require an additional contribution from the partners' own assets in any event since it is by definition a partnership liability. If that is right, the court's careful attempts to avoid unjust imposition of penalties on individuals are thwarted.

[116] [2008] EWCA Crim 1970.   [117] At [33] per Hughes LJ.

as informal as some unincorporated ones no doubt are.[118] This has very serious potential ramifications for the presumably tens of thousands of members of unincorporated bodies that exist in England and Wales. Personal criminal liability might result simply by virtue of a person's voluntary membership of a lawful association. Liability is not dependent on any personal fault. Where individual members of an unincorporated association are prosecuted, it is not on the basis of some form of vicarious liability. Nor, unlike corporations, does liability turn on the person holding a position of responsibility or office so that he might be regarded as a controlling officer. Given the enormous number of strict liability offences that such organizations might commit in the course of performing their usual businesses, the prospect of personal liability of all members seems astounding. Of course, there is the potential for prosecution agencies to select individuals within a club since it is for the CPS to determine the defendants in any given case and the courts will interfere only if there is an abuse of process. As Hughes LJ commented in *L*, relevant considerations will no doubt include 'the extent of the association's stability and assets and the nature of the act or omission said to constitute an offence'. Exceptionally, the Crown might choose to prosecute both the association and its members.

If the decision is correct, it is submitted that the potential criminal liability of members of unincorporated associations deserves parliamentary consideration. Provisions akin to those dealing with the criminal liability of company officers discussed earlier at p 271 would produce fairer results.

In *Riley v CPS*,[119] the prosecution, relying on the Partnership Act 1890, argued that even where the terms of the statutory offence do not render all of the partners liable as joint principal offenders, all the partners are so liable simply by virtue of their status as co-partners. The Divisional Court rejected that analysis on the basis that the Act is concerned with satisfying debts and liabilities for which a partnership has become liable and not with criminal liability.

8.1.5 Rationale and reform of corporate criminal liability

The English courts have created the identification principle through which corporate liability might be imposed without addressing the broader social purposes of imposing such liability,[120] or (leaving aside the 2007 Act) the effectiveness of the punishments administered. The fines imposed are ultimately borne by the shareholders who, in most cases, are not responsible in any sense for the offence. If they really had control over the directors and so over the management of the company, this might afford some justification; but it is generally recognized that they have little control over large public companies.[121] Moreover, fines may be inflicted on the boards of nationalized industries, where there are no shareholders and the consumers of the product, who ultimately pay the fine, have no rights whatever to appoint or dismiss the officials concerned. Since the persons actually responsible for the offence may, in the great majority of cases, be convicted, it has been questioned whether there is any need to impose this additional penalty.

Arguments in favour of wider corporate liability include that there may be difficulty in fixing individuals with liability where someone among the 'brains' of the corporation has undoubtedly authorized the offence. Since, moreover, the names of the officers will mean

---

[118] It should be noted that this has not prevented the imposition of injunctions against such bodies albeit with necessary elaboration, eg *Huntingdon Life Sciences v Stop Huntingdon Animal Cruelty* [2003] EWHC 1967 (QB).

[119] [2016] EWHC 2531 (Admin).

[120] cf other jurisdictions, and, eg, J Gobert and E Mugnai, 'Coping with Corporate Criminality—Some Lessons from Italy' [2002] Crim LR 617; S Adam, N Cosette-Basecqz and M Nihoul (eds), *Corporate Criminal Liability in Europe* (2008).

[121] R Pennington, *Company Law* (8th edn, 2001) Part III.

nothing to the public, only the conviction of the corporation itself will serve to warn the public of the wrongful acts—operating buses with faulty brakes, trains on defective tracks or selling mouldy pies—which are committed in its name. Corporate liability, of course, also ensures that the offence will not go unpunished and that a fine proportionate to the gravity of the offence may be imposed, when it might be out of proportion to the means of the individuals concerned. Further, the imposition of liability on the organization gives all of those directing it an interest in the prevention of illegalities—and they are in a position to prevent them, though the shareholders are not. In the case of *Balfour Beatty Rail Infrastructure Ltd*,[122] the company appealed against a sentence of £10m imposed on the company for a conviction under s 3 of the Health and Safety at Work etc Act 1974 arising from the Hatfield train crash where several people died and many were injured. The Lord Chief Justice noted that the knowledge that a breach can result in a fine of sufficient size to impact on the shareholders 'will provide a powerful incentive for management to comply with the duty' while accepting that the fine need not always be so high as to affect dividends or share prices.[123]

In *R v Sellafield; R v Network Rail Infrastructure Ltd*,[124] the Lord Chief Justice examined in detail the principles applicable in imposing fines for breaches of safety and environmental protection legislation on very large companies—Sellafield Ltd with a turnover of £1.6bn and Network Rail with a turnover of £6.2bn. The court upheld the fines (Sellafield Ltd was fined £700,000 for offences arising out of the disposal of radioactive waste and Network Rail was fined £500,000 for an offence arising out of a collision at an unmanned level crossing, causing very serious injuries to a child).[125] The Sentencing Council has since issued a definitive sentencing guideline.[126]

As noted earlier, the courts have taken a relatively simplistic approach to imposing criminal liability on corporations by shoehorning them into the orthodox model of criminal liability via the identification doctrine.[127] This has pre-empted discussion of the more fundamental question, namely whether an entirely separate model of criminal responsibility ought to be created to reflect corporate structures and activities.[128] For some, the company is no more than the collection of individuals which make it up, while for others the company has a distinct personality which should be reflected in the law's treatment. Whether a company as a non-human entity can properly be found to be morally culpable in its own right raises issues extending well beyond the scope of this work, but four options for distinctly corporate criminal liability deserve mention.[129]

8.1.5.1 Aggregation

This approach has been noted previously and involves aggregating the mens rea of various individuals within the corporation to combine as a sufficient blameworthy 'state of mind' of the company. This approach has been considered and rejected by the Court of Appeal.[130]

---

122 [2006] EWCA Crim 1586.   123 At [42].   124 [2014] EWCA Crim 49.

125 Relying upon *Southern Water Services Ltd* [2014] EWCA Crim 120 in which a fine of £200,000 was upheld.

126 *Environmental Offences: Definitive Guideline* (2014). It has effect from 1 July 2014. It is available in full at www.sentencingcouncil.org.uk/wp-content/uploads/ Environmental-offences-definitive-guideline-web.pdf.

127 See A Norrie, *Crime, Reason and History* (3rd edn, 2014) Ch 5.

128 See further the discussion in LCCP 195, particularly the appendices.

129 J Gobert, 'Corporate Criminality: Four Models of Fault' (1994) 14 LS 393; J Gobert, 'Corporate Criminality: New Crimes for the Times' [1994] Crim LR 722; R Grantham, 'Corporate Knowledge: Identification or Attribution?' (1996) 59 MLR 732; R Lööf, 'Corporate Agency and White Collar Crime—An Experience-Led Case for Causation-Based Corporate Liability for Criminal Harms' [2020] Crim LR 275. For a review of approaches in Europe, particularly in the Netherlands and Germany, see J Keiler, *Actus Reus and Participation in European Criminal Law* (2012) Ch 5. Different models of liability are considered at p 262 et seq.

130 *A-G's Reference (No 2 of 1999)* [2000] QB 796, [2000] Crim LR 475. See also Bingham LJ in *R v HM Coroner for East Kent, ex p Spooner* (1989) 88 Cr App R 10.

This approach would, however, be practically attainable and would not require radical deviation from the orthodox model of criminal responsibility. But for this reason some commentators would regard it as an inadequate solution. It would serve only to maintain the fiction of attributing liability through the acts of the company controllers rather than looking deeper for a culpable corporate culture or ethos. As Fisse and Braithwaite argue 'organisations are systems . . . not just aggregations of individuals'.[131]

8.1.5.2 Culpable corporate culture

Professor Wells has also criticized the narrow understanding of the aggregation approach, arguing that it is not simply the sum of the parts—addition of director A's mens rea and director B's knowledge—to comprise the relevant mens rea for the offence. Wells rejects the identification doctrine as too narrow and advocates an extension of the availability of direct corporate liability.[132] Having regard to the organizational structures of corporations and their corporate policies and practices, she argues that the law should recognize that 'responsibility can . . . be found in the corporation's structures themselves'.[133] Wells concludes that there should be a form of corporate mens rea. Under this proposal a corporation can be responsible for the corporation's conduct. The difficulty with such a proposal lies in determining how errant the policy and/or practice of the company must be to be treated in law as being equally deserving of blame as the mens rea of an individual offender.

Some jurisdictions have introduced a corporate culture-based approach to liability.[134] In the Australian Capital Territory, for example, the statutory equivalent to the corporate manslaughter offence[135] turns on proof of a culpable corporate culture, with corporate culture defined as an: 'attitude, policy, rule, course of conduct or practice existing within the corporation generally or in that part of the corporation where the relevant conduct happens'.

English law has not adopted anything quite so radical, even in the 2007 Act. Under the corporate manslaughter offence, the jury's duty in relation to determining the breach of duty is provided in s 8 and includes an obligation to consider whether the evidence shows that the organization failed to comply with any health and safety legislation[136] that relates to the alleged breach and, if so, how serious that failure was and how much of a risk of death it posed. The jury *may* also:

consider the extent to which the evidence shows that there were attitudes, policies, systems or accepted practices within the organisation that were likely to have encouraged any such [health and safety] failure . . . or to have produced tolerance of it; [and] have regard to any health and safety guidance that relates to the alleged breach.

This section does not prevent the jury from having regard to any other matters they consider relevant. Section 8(3) emphasizes that the jury may have reference to general organizational and systems failures. One difficulty with this provision, as with establishing something as

---

[131] B Fisse and J Braithwaite, 'The Allocation of Responsibility for Corporate Crime: Individualism, Collectivism and Accountability' (1988) 11 Sydney LR 468, 479.

[132] See also the summary in LCCP 195, Appendix C.

[133] Wells, *Corporations and Criminal Responsibility*, 157.

[134] For criticism, see N Cavanagh, 'Corporate Criminal Liability: An Assessment of the Models of Fault' (2011) 75 J Crim L 414. Although Cavanagh argues that this model is preferable to the other options, he suggests that it nevertheless poses issues of evidential uncertainty and that it might not act as an effective deterrent.

[135] Crimes (Industrial Manslaughter) Amendment Act 2003, s 51, ACT Criminal Code, s 51.

[136] Defined in s 8(5): '"health and safety guidance" means any code, guidance, manual or similar publication that is concerned with health and safety matters and is made or issued (under a statutory provision or otherwise) by an authority responsible for the enforcement of any health and safety legislation'. See, generally, on Health and Safety legislation: www.hse.gov.uk/legislation/.

vague as a 'corporate culture',[137] is how the 'attitudes, etc' are proved. There is the potential for lengthy arguments and evidence comparing practices across the particular sector or industry. Imagine a prosecution of a rail company and the potential for the defence to adduce evidence of safety procedures and policies across the rail sector to demonstrate the quality of their own. No doubt the jury will have regard to the organization's overall objectives, published policy statements on safety, monitoring and compliance policies, attitudes to development of safety and to training and awareness, approaches to remedying previous health and safety infringements, etc.

There have been suggestions that English law could adopt a model of general corporate liability based on the 2007 Act approach.[138]

8.1.5.3 Reactive corporate fault

A yet more radical approach derives from the work of Australian academics Fisse and Braithwaite.[139] In short, they propose a model under which the company can become liable to court orders to investigate and remedy its conduct where there is an alleged criminal wrongdoing. Criminal liability would follow where the company subsequently failed to take adequate remedial measures.

8.1.5.4 Specific statutory offences

Another alternative is to create specific corporate forms of offences. An example is s 7 of the Bribery Act 2010. The s 7 offence provides:

(1) A relevant commercial organisation ('C') is guilty of an offence under this section if a person ('A') associated with C bribes another person intending—

(a) to obtain or retain business for C, or

(b) to obtain or retain an advantage in the conduct of business for C.

There is a due diligence defence in s 7(2) for C to prove that C had in place adequate procedures designed to prevent persons associated with C from undertaking such conduct.

The difficulties of the identification doctrine are avoided by specifically providing which individuals associated with a company will trigger liability for the company by their actions. In the case of s 7, it is a very wide range of individuals indeed. A person associated with a commercial organization is defined by s 8 as a person who performs services for or on behalf of the organization including employees, agents or subsidiaries. Employees are presumed to be performing services for their employer but otherwise the question is to be determined by reference to all the relevant circumstances. A person 'bribes' another for the purposes of this section if he commits an offence under ss 1 and 6 of the Act or aids and abets such an offence. It is irrelevant whether there has been a prosecution for it (s 7(3)), provided the prosecution show that the person would be guilty of the offence were that person prosecuted under this Act. There is no need for A to have a close connection to the UK as defined in s 12, provided C is a 'relevant commercial organisation'. 'Relevant commercial organisation' is defined (at s 7(5)) as: a body which is incorporated under the law of any part of the UK and which carries on business whether there or elsewhere; a partnership that is formed under the law of any

[137] Arguably it is no more difficult than proving a subjective state of mind such as recklessness of a human defendant. See Wells, *Corporations and Criminal Responsibility*, 155.

[138] See LCCP 195, Part 5 and Appendices B and C. Note s 21 of the Criminal Justice and Courts Act 2015, creating offences for corporate bodies or unincorporated associations based on breaches of duties owed to those whose care they manage where an individual carer neglects or ill-treats such a person. For discussion, see K Laird, 'Filling a Lacuna: The Care Worker and Care Provider Offences in the Criminal Justice and Courts Act 2015' (2016) 37 Stat LR 1.

[139] *Corporations, Crime and Accountability* (1993).

part of the UK and which carries on business there or elsewhere; or any other body corporate or partnership wherever incorporated or formed which carries on business in any part of the UK.

Other safeguards can be built into such offences. For example, s 7 is triable only on indictment (s 11(3)). No prosecution may be instituted in England and Wales except by or with the consent of the DPP or the Director of the Serious Fraud Office (s 10(1)). In the case of a partnership, proceedings must be brought in the name of the partnership (not in that of any of the partners) (s 15).[140]

Sections 45 and 46 of the Criminal Finances Act 2017 create two new corporate offences. Section 45 criminalizes corporates for failing to prevent the facilitation of domestic tax evasion, while s 46 criminalizes corporates for failing to prevent the facilitation of foreign tax evasion.[141] These offences are to a large extent modelled upon the offence found in s 7 of the Bribery Act 2010.[142] There is an important difference, however. Commission of the offence in s 7 of the Bribery Act 2010 is contingent upon the prosecution proving that the bribe was paid with the intention of obtaining or retaining business for the corporate. Insofar as the corporate is concerned, the s 7 offence is one of strict liability, but the prosecution must be able to prove the intention of the payer of the bribe. Neither of the new failure to prevent offences contained in the Criminal Finances Act require the prosecution to prove that the intention of the associated person in facilitating the tax evasion offence was to benefit the corporate. The corporate is liable for failing to prevent its associates committing crimes that potentially benefit someone else—not to prevent them committing crimes that benefit the corporate. This is significant, as the Law Commission, in drafting the Bribery Act, concluded that proof of fault would be a qualitative way of distinguishing the s 7 offence from a purely regulatory or administrative penalty.[143] The new offences lack this distinguishing feature.

These models of offence are different from the other approaches discussed earlier, since what is being criminalized is the organizational culture per se; it is only very indirectly if at all that the company is being held responsible for the wrongs done by its agents. Ashworth has convincingly argued that these offences represent a new generation of omissions-based liability that takes criminal responsibility to a new level. The question he poses is whether the wrong of failing to carry out the duty imposed by these new corporate offences is serious enough to justify criminalization or whether a regulatory response would be sufficient.[144]

A modified version of this model has been proposed by Mark Dsouza who suggests that the conduct and mental states of *any* employee acting in the course of their employment should be capable of being attributed to the company.[145] A person acts in the course of their employment when they act within their employer's area of real or ostensible authority. It has also been suggested that a causation-based approach would ensure that corporates are criminally liable for the unique, criminally proscribed harms that only they can cause.[146]

In 2017 the Ministry of Justice conducted a consultation exercise which sought views on whether the failure to prevent model ought to apply to other financial crimes, such as fraud and money laundering.[147] In November 2020, the Law Commission announced that the

---

[140] The maximum sentence is an unlimited fine. A fine imposed on a partnership is to be paid out of partnership assets (s 15(3)). See S Gentle [2011] Crim LR 101.

[141] For discussion, see K Laird, 'The Criminal Finances Act 2017—An Introduction' [2017] Crim LR 915.

[142] For discussion of this model, see A Ashworth, 'Positive Duties, Regulation and the Criminal Sanction' (2017) 133 LQR 606, 626–8.

[143] LC 313, *Reforming Bribery* (2008), para 6.100.

[144] A Ashworth, 'A New Generation of Omissions Offences?' [2018] Crim LR 354.

[145] M Dsouza, 'The Corporate Agent in Criminal Law—An Argument for Comprehensive Identification' (2020) 79 CLJ 91.

[146] R Lööf, 'Corporate Agency and White Collar Crime—An Experience-Led Case for Causation-Based Corporate Liability for Criminal Harms' [2020] Crim LR 275.

[147] Ministry of Justice, *Corporate Liability for Economic Crime: Call for Evidence* (2017) Cm 9370.

government had asked it to consider corporate criminal liability and make recommendations. Should the Bribery Act model of offence prove to be attractive, it will be necessary to consider whether the corporate's liability should be dependent upon whether the associated person, when he committed the substantive offence, intended to benefit the corporate.[148]

8.1.5.5 Extended vicarious liability

An alternative model would be to extend the approach to vicarious liability, as in some other jurisdictions such as some states in the United States, and introduce broader due diligence defences available to corporations.[149] The application of due diligence defences is considered in full in Ch 5. Again, this may not involve a drastic change from the present position. We turn now to consider the scope of vicarious liability.

8.2 Vicarious liability

8.2.1 Nature and scope of doctrine

The doctrine of 'vicarious liability'[150] is a mechanism by which the law attributes blame for the acts of another. Common examples include retail companies being responsible for the sale of items by managers and shop assistants in their stores, and of licensees being responsible for the acts of their employees. Unfortunately, English law's approach has the potential to operate very harshly. As the Law Commission commented, the doctrine can operate wholly unfairly and disproportionately by imposing liability on D for an offence committed by someone even though D had no reason to think that the delegated person would do as he did.[151] The doctrine ought therefore to be kept within strict limits; disappointingly, it remains of uncertain scope. Davis LJ observed in *Serious Fraud Office v Barclays Bank Plc*[152] that, 'the policy considerations which have driven the doctrine of vicarious liability in the law of tort simply do not apply in the same way in criminal law. This is in part because tort is focused on issues of *liability* (and the redress, ordinarily financial, involved). But, as Lord Diplock points out [in *Tesco v Nattrass*], the focus of the criminal law is different. For, other than in strict liability cases, the focus is on *culpability*'.[153]

8.2.1.1 Vicarious liability distinguished from personal duty

It is important to distinguish vicarious liability from liability for breach of a personal duty. Many statutes, particularly dealing with regulatory offences, create specific offences that can be committed by the specified person (eg the employer) in person. If the specified person is in breach of that duty, he commits the actus reus of the offence and, if it imposes strict liability, he is personally, not vicariously, guilty of the offence, though he may say with truth that he would not have been in breach but for the fault of his employees or agents. A good example is the Health and Safety at Work etc Act 1974. By s 3(1), the Act imposes on every employer a duty 'to conduct his undertaking in such a way as to ensure, so far as is reasonably practicable' that persons not in his employment are not exposed

---

[148] For discussion, see C Wells, 'Corporate Failure to Prevent Economic Crime—A Proposal' [2017] Crim LR 426.

[149] See GR Sullivan (1996) 55 CLJ 515.

[150] Williams, CLGP, Ch 7, and 'Mens Rea and Vicarious Responsibility' (1956) 9 CLP 57; P Glazebrook, 'Situational Liability' in *Reshaping the Criminal Law*, 108; PJ Pace, 'Delegation—A Doctrine in Search of a Definition' [1982] Crim LR 627; LH Leigh, *Strict and Vicarious Liability* (1982); F Sayre, 'Criminal Responsibility for the Acts of Another' (1930) 43 Harv LR 689; T Baty, *Vicarious Liability* (1916) especially Ch X. For proposals for the reform of the law, see Law Com WP No 43; LCCP 195.

[151] See LCCP 195, para 1.89.   [152] [2018] EWHC 3055 (QB).

[153] *Serious Fraud Office v Barclays Bank Plc* [2018] EWHC 3055 (QB), [67].

to risk. In *British Steel Plc*,[154] D's subcontractor, negligently conducting D's undertaking, caused V's death. D had not ensured so far as was, in the opinion of the court, reasonably practicable, that persons were not exposed to risk and D was therefore guilty. D was liable, not vicariously for the acts of the subcontractor which caused death, but for his own failure to ensure that there was no risk of such a thing happening. This was a case of personal liability being imposed by the statute.[155]

8.2.1.2 Strict liability and vicarious liability distinguished

It is also important to distinguish strict liability and vicarious liability;[156] they are by no means the same thing.[157] The point requires emphasis for there is an unhappy judicial tendency to confuse the two concepts. A statute may require mens rea and yet also impose vicarious responsibility under the delegation principle (discussed later). It has already been noted that supplying liquor to a constable on duty was an offence requiring mens rea,[158] yet a licensee may be vicariously liable for his agent/employee's act in so doing.[159] Conversely, it is clearly possible for a statute to create strict liability without imposing vicarious responsibility. Once a statute has been held to impose a duty with strict liability on a particular person, it is likely to be held that that person is liable for the acts of anyone through whom he performs that duty.[160] Where, however, the duty with strict liability is not imposed on particular persons but on the public generally, vicarious liability is inappropriate. For example, the offence of causing death by dangerous driving (in its previous form) was held to be an offence of strict liability, but it is surely inconceivable that vicarious liability would have been imposed.

8.2.1.3 Relationship with tortious doctrine

True vicarious liability is the general rule in the law of tort. An employer is held liable for all acts of his employee performed in the course of his employee's employment, or, as the courts now prefer to say, performed in close connection with it.[161] In the criminal law, an

---

[154] [1995] 1 WLR 1356. If work is part of D's undertaking—a question of fact—D is in breach of his duty if independent contractors whom he engages to perform it unreasonably expose others to risk: *Associated Octel Ltd* [1996] 4 All ER 846. See also *Environment Agency v Biffa Waste Ltd* [2006] EWHC 1102 (Admin). *Alphacell Ltd* (p 169) was, it is submitted, a case of personal liability and wrongly treated as a precedent for vicarious liability in *National Rivers Authority v Alfred McAlpine Homes (East) Ltd* [1994] 4 All ER 286, [1994] Crim LR 960 and commentary.

[155] See for an example: *Hatton Traffic Management Ltd* [2006] EWCA Crim 1156.

[156] The Court of Appeal in *St Regis Paper Co Ltd* [2011] EWCA Crim 2527 cited with approval the distinction drawn in the 12th edn of this work between questions of delegation and questions of strict liability.

[157] *Seaboard Offshore Ltd v Secretary of State for Transport* [1993] 1 WLR 1025, [1993] Crim LR 611; affd [1994] 2 All ER 99.

[158] *Sherras v De Rutzen* [1895] 1 QB 918.   [159] *Mullins v Collins* (1874) LR 9 QB 292.

[160] *Dicta* to the effect that an offence of strict liability necessarily imposes vicarious responsibility are not difficult to find: see eg *Barker v Levinson* [1950] 2 All ER 825 at 827; *James & Son Ltd v Smee* [1955] 1 QB 78 at 95 per Slade J; *Bradshaw v Ewart-James* [1983] 1 All ER 12 at 14.

[161] The doctrine has undergone a radical change in the law of tort, with a much wider scope of liability being imposed by the courts. Examples include *Dubai Aluminium v Salaam* [2003] 2 AC 366, where their lordships held that it is not a condition of vicarious liability that all the wrongful acts for which an employee was responsible had to have been committed in the course of employment, rather vicarious liability would not be imposed unless all the acts or omissions which were necessary to make him personally liable had taken place in the course of employment. See also *Lister v Hesley Hall Ltd* [2002] 1 AC 215; *Mattis v Pollock* [2003] EWCA Civ 887 (nightclub owner liable for bouncer stabbing V when club encouraged bouncer to be aggressive); *Various Claimants v Institute of the Brothers of the Christian Schools* [2012] UKSC 56 (a religious order was vicariously liable for the sexual abuse perpetrated by brother teachers at a residential school even though the order did not manage the school); and *Cox v Ministry of Justice* [2016] UKSC 10. See generally on tortious liability, Goudkamp and Nolan, *Winfield and Jolowicz on Tort* (20th edn, 2020) Ch 21; P Atiyah, *Vicarious Liability in the English Law of Torts* (1967) and C McIvor, 'The Use and Abuse of the Doctrine of Vicarious Liability' (2006) 35 CLWR 268; Lord Hope of Craighead, 'Tailoring the Law on Vicarious Liability' (2013) 129 LQR 514.

employer is generally not so liable. In one of the leading civil cases, *Lloyd v Grace, Smith & Co*,[162] a solicitor's managing clerk, without the knowledge of his employer, induced a widow to give him instructions to sell certain property, to hand over the title deeds and to sign two documents which were neither read over nor explained to her, but which she believed were necessary for the sale. The documents were, in fact, a conveyance to the clerk of the property, which he then dishonestly disposed of for his own benefit. It was held that, since the clerk was acting within the scope of his authority, his employer was liable. Today it is very likely that the clerk would be guilty of certain criminal offences; but it is perfectly clear that his employer could never have been made criminally liable for those acts even though the employer bore civil liability.

An employer is similarly liable in tort where the employee acting in the course of his employment commits a fraud involving a forgery,[163] and for acts which amount to fraud, assault and battery, manslaughter, and so on; but in none of these cases would the employer be *criminally* liable solely on the ground that his employee was acting in the course of his employment.

The doctrine of vicarious liability in tort developed in the early part of the eighteenth century, but there was to be no parallel development in the criminal law, as was made clear by the leading case of *Huggins*.[164] Huggins, the warden of the Fleet (equivalent to a prison governor), was charged with the murder of a prisoner whose death had been caused by the servant of Huggins' deputy. It was held that, though the servant was guilty, Huggins was not, since the acts were done without his knowledge. Raymond CJ said:[165]

It is a point not to be disputed, but that in criminal cases the principal is not answerable for the act of the deputy as he is in civil cases: they must each answer for their own acts, and stand or fall by their own behaviour. All the authors that treat of criminal proceedings proceed on the foundation of this distinction; that to affect the superior by the act of his deputy, there must be the command of the superior which is not found in this case.

This has been confirmed more recently in *R (Chief Constable of Northumbria) v Newcastle Magistrates' Court*,[166] where the court, referring to the 12th edition of this work, concluded that there is no doctrine of criminal vicarious liability at common law (except in relation to public nuisance, criminal libel (since abolished) and some forms of contempt of court).

8.2.2 Identifying criminal vicarious liability

An employer can be held liable for his employee's crimes, as a general rule, only where he is a participant in them within the rules governing secondary liability as discussed in Ch 6. Exceptions to the general rule have already been noted in public nuisance,[167] criminal libel (prior to its abolition—see Ch 30) and contempt of court, an employer has been held liable for his employee's acts although he, personally, played no part in the conduct and was unaware of it. These were the only exceptions at common law; but now, by statute, there are many such offences because Parliament is, of course, always at liberty to impose vicarious criminal liability.

---

[162] [1912] AC 716. As approved by the House of Lords in *Lister v Hesley Hall Ltd* [2001] UKHL 22.
[163] *Uxbridge Permanent Building Society v Pickard* [1939] 2 KB 248.   [164] (1730) 2 Stra 883.
[165] ibid, 885.
[166] [2010] EWHC 935 (Admin). The court offered an interesting analysis of the history of the principle.
[167] Although in *Rimmington* [2005] UKHL 63, [2006] Crim LR 153 and commentary, Lord Bingham commented that this is hard to reconcile with the modern approach to that subject in cases potentially involving the severest penalties, and may well be explained, as Mellor J did in *Stephens* (1866) LR 1 QB 702 at 708–9, [1861–73] All ER Rep Ext 2059 at 2060–1, by the civil colour of the proceedings, at [39].

As in the case of strict liability, in truth it appears that the imposition of vicarious liability is the work of the courts rather than of Parliament. Statutes do occasionally say, in terms, that one person is to be liable for another's crimes.[168] It is more common, however, for the courts to 'detect' such an intention in construing statutory offences. This judicial willingness to impose vicarious liability arises particularly in summary offences. The reason most commonly advanced by the judges for holding a person (usually an employer, but independent contractors may also be caught)[169] liable is that the statute would be 'rendered nugatory'[170]—and the will of Parliament thereby defeated—if he were not. It may seem rather odd for the courts to be willing to impose liability for the acts of another on grounds of expediency when the foundation of the criminal law is that a person should be liable only for his personal wrongdoing. This would be particularly unsatisfactory in the absence of clear evidence that the prosecution of an employer will render the legislation more effective by deterring that and other employers from similar breaches.

Atkin J in *Mousell Brothers Ltd v London and North-Western Railway Co*[171] provided guidance on the identification of statutory vicarious liability:

while *prima facie* a principal is not to be made criminally responsible for the acts of his servants, yet the legislature may prohibit an act or enforce a duty in such words as to make the prohibition or the duty absolute; in which case the principal is liable if the act is in fact done by his servants. To ascertain whether a particular Act of Parliament has that effect or not regard must be had to the object of the statute, the words used, the nature of the duty laid down, the person upon whom it is imposed, the person by whom it would in ordinary circumstances be performed, and the person upon whom the penalty is imposed.

The decision of the House of Lords in *Environment Agency v Empress Car Co (Abertillery) Ltd*[172] also has an impact in this area. As noted earlier, their lordships took an unorthodox approach to the issue of causation in the strict liability offences of 'causing' pollution under the Water Resources Act 1991. The House held that the conduct of a third party unknown to the defendants that released the pollutant from the defendant's storage tanks did not break the chain of causation. Hence, the defendants remained liable.[173]

8.2.3 The application of vicarious liability

Two quite distinct principles, differing somewhat in their effect, underlie the various decisions on vicarious liability. In the first place, a person may be held liable for the acts of another where he has delegated to that other the performance of certain duties cast on him by Act of Parliament. In the second place, an employer may be held liable because acts which are done physically by his employee may, in law, be the employer's acts. These two types of case require separate consideration.

---

[168] A striking example is the Road Traffic Offenders Act 1988, s 64(5), which provides that the owner of a vehicle (even if a corporation) shall be conclusively presumed to have been the driver at the time of the commission of certain offences and, 'accordingly, that acts or omissions of the driver of the vehicle at the time were his acts or omissions'.

[169] See eg *Quality Dairies (York) Ltd v Pedley* [1952] 1 KB 275.

[170] *Mullins v Collins* (1874) LR 9 QB 292 at 295 per Blackburn and Quain JJ; *Coppen v Moore (No 2)* [1898] 2 QB 306 at 314 per Lord Russell CJ; *Allen v Whitehead*, later.

[171] [1917] 2 KB 836 at 845.   [172] [1999] 2 AC 22.

[173] See *Milford Haven Port Authority* [2000] 2 Cr App R (S) 423. See also *Environment Agency v Biffa Waste Ltd* [2006] EWHC 1102 (Admin) which may appear to cast doubt on this, but is, it is submitted, a case turning on the facts of the subcontractual arrangement.

8.2.3.1 The delegation principle

A good illustration of the application of this principle[174] may be found in the case of *Allen v Whitehead*.[175] Section 44 of the Metropolitan Police Act 1839 provides an offence for a keeper of a refreshment house to 'knowingly permit or suffer prostitutes or persons of notoriously bad character to meet together and remain' there. D, the occupier of a cafe, although receiving the profits of the business, did not himself manage it, instead employing a manager. Having had a warning from the police, D instructed his manager that no prostitutes were to be allowed to congregate on the premises and had a notice to that effect displayed on the walls. He visited the premises once or twice a week and there was no evidence that any misconduct took place in his presence. Then, on eight consecutive days, a number of women, known to the manager to be prostitutes, met together and remained there between the hours of 8 pm and 4 am. It was held by the Divisional Court, reversing the Metropolitan Magistrate, that D's ignorance of those facts was no defence. The acts of the manager and his mens rea (knowing that the women present were prostitutes) were both to be imputed to his employer, not simply because he was an employee, but because the management of the house had been delegated to him.

So in *Linnett v Metropolitan Police Comr*[176] it was held, following *Allen v Whitehead*,[177] that one of two co-licensees was liable for the acts of the other in knowingly permitting disorderly conduct in the licensed premises, contrary to s 44 of the same Act, although the other was neither his servant nor his partner,[178] but simply his delegate in 'keeping' the premises.

The argument that vicarious responsibility is necessary if the statute is to be effective applies with special force to cases of this type. Where the statute is phrased in such a way that the offence can be committed only by the delegator, there would indeed be a real difficulty in making the statute effective without vicarious liability. For example, under s 44 of the Metropolitan Police Act 1839 (discussed earlier in this section), the offence may be committed only by a person 'who shall *have or keep* any house . . .' Presumably the mere manager in *Allen v Whitehead* was not such a person and if, therefore, the absentee 'keeper' were not liable for his manager's acts, the statute could be ignored with impunity. The position is the same in many of the offences under the Licensing Acts;[179] only the licensee can commit the offences. The difficulty has been well put by Lord Russell CJ:[180]

We may take as an illustration the case of a sporting publican who attends race-meetings all over the country, and leaves a manager in charge of his public-house; is it to be said that there is no remedy under this section[181] if drink is sold by the manager in charge to any number of drunken persons?

It is clear that there is no machinery by which the person actually selling can be convicted; a penalty can only be inflicted on the licensee.

---

[174] See Pace [1982] Crim LR 627.   [175] [1930] 1 KB 211.   [176] [1946] KB 290.   [177] See n 176.

[178] Both were, in fact, the employees of a limited company. The company was not charged, no doubt for the good reason that it was not the licensee.

[179] See generally S Mehigan, D Wilson, G Gouriet, J Phillips and J Saunders (eds), *Paterson's Licensing Acts* (2021).

[180] In *Commissioners of Police v Cartman* [1896] 1 QB 655 at 658. Yet when Parliament adds 'or his servant', the court holds that the delegation still applies to the licensee: *Howker v Robinson*, later. In *Boucher v DPP* (1996) 160 JP 650, it was held that where D is the licensee and owns a shop with P who is not a licensee, D cannot be vicariously liable for P's sales to a minor since P is not a servant but a co-owner.

[181] Licensing Act 1872, s 13. Cf *Cundy v Le Cocq* (1884) 13 QBD 207, which establishes that the offence is also one of strict liability.

Sub-delegation

It has been recognized that vicarious liability might be extended to cover the case where A delegates his responsibilities to B who sub-delegates them to C. Thus, if the licensee's delegate sub-delegates his responsibilities, the licensee is liable for the sub-delegate's acts,[182] but he is not liable for the acts of an inferior servant to whom control of the premises has not been delegated.[183]

What constitutes effective delegation?

There is some doubt as to the degree of delegation which is necessary to bring the principle into operation. In a leading case, *Vane v Yiannopoullos*, in the Divisional Court, whose view the House of Lords later affirmed,[184] Parker LCJ said that: 'It must be shown that the licensee is not managing the business himself but has delegated the management to someone else . . .'[185]

Lord Evershed[186] agreed with that and Lord Hodson said that the principle 'has never so far been extended so as to cover the case where the whole of the authority of the licensee has not been transferred to another'.[187] Lord Reid appears to have confined the principle to cases where the licensee is absent from the premises but leaves another in charge.[188] It was held that the principle was inapplicable in that case where the licensee was on the premises, but not on the same floor as a waitress whom he had instructed as to her rights to sell intoxicating liquor, at the time she made an illegal sale. However, in *Howker v Robinson*,[189] a licensee who was serving in one room of the pub (the public bar) was held liable for an illegal sale made by his barman in another room (the lounge). This does not seem to be a case where the whole authority of the licensee had been transferred or where he was not managing the business himself. The court regarded the question of whether there had been delegation as one of fact, which had been properly decided by the magistrates. *Winson*,[190] which the court followed, was entirely different, for there the licensee visited the premises only occasionally and had a manager who was in control.

In *Howker v Robinson*, the degree of delegation was no greater than is essential in any public house with more than one bar and it is submitted that not only does it go too far but it leaves the law in an uncertain state. It is apparently open to the magistrates to find as 'a fact' that there has or has not been delegation where the licensee is on the premises. The principle ought to be confined to the case where the licensee is not 'doing his job', but has handed it over to another. Where a licensee who is employed by a brewery is suspended, the brewery has the right, under an implied term in the contract of employment, to delegate the rights and duties of the licensee to another employee. Thus, sales of liquor on the licensed premises continue to be lawful and, presumably, the suspended licensee is liable for offences committed by the delegate.[191]

No delegation principle in strict liability offences?

According to Lord Parker, the delegation principle comes into play *only* in the case of offences requiring mens rea.[192] Where liability is strict, 'the person on whom liability is thrown is responsible whether he has delegated or whether he has acted through a servant'. According to this view, if D, the licensee, not having delegated his duties, is serving in the bar with E, the barmaid: (a) D will not be liable if E, without his knowledge, sells liquor to a

182   *Crabtree v Hole* (1879) 43 JP 799; *Sopp v Long* [1970] 1 QB 518.
183   *Allchorn v Hopkins* (1905) 69 JP 355.   184   [1965] AC 486.
185   [1964] 2 QB 739 at 745.   186   [1965] AC 486 at 505.   187   ibid, 510.
188   At 497; cf Pace [1982] Crim LR 627 at 629, 636.
189   [1973] QB 178, [1972] Crim LR 377. Contrast *McKenna v Harding* (1905) 69 JP 354.
190   [1969] 1 QB 371.   191   *DPP v Rogers* [1992] Crim LR 51.   192   *Winson* [1969] 1 QB 371 at 382.

constable on duty because that offence requires mens rea, but (b) D will be liable if E, without his knowledge, sells liquor to a drunken person because that offence does not require mens rea. If this is right, strict liability offences must be dealt with under the 'attributed act' principle (see the following section). The Court of Appeal stated, *obiter*, in *St Regis Paper Co Ltd* that in the context of the regulations under consideration in that case, the contrast between strict liability offences and those requiring mens rea was too striking to permit the application of the delegation principle.[193]

Legitimacy of the delegation principle

Some doubt was cast on the validity of the delegation principle by the House of Lords in *Vane v Yiannopoullos*.[194] Since there was no delegation in that case, their lordships' remarks were *obiter*. Lords Morris and Donovan could find no statutory authority for the doctrine and, though they did not find it necessary to pronounce on its validity, Lord Donovan thought that 'If a decision that "knowingly" means "knowingly" will make the provision difficult to enforce, the remedy lies with the legislature.' Lord Reid found the delegation principle hard to justify; but while it may have been unwarranted in the first instance, it was now too late to upset such a long-standing practice. Lord Evershed thought that a licensee may 'fairly and sensibly' be held liable where he has delegated his powers and Lord Hodson expressed no opinion. Subsequent cases[195] show that the doctrine continues unimpaired. Such a long-standing principle is perhaps unlikely now to be overruled by the Supreme Court. It should not, however, be readily extended.[196] In *Bradshaw v Ewart-James*,[197] the court declined to apply it to the case where the master of a ship delegated the performance of his statutory duty to his chief officer. That, however, was not a case of the full delegation which the doctrine seems to require, for the master remained on board and in command. As the master cannot personally direct the ship for 24 hours a day, some delegation is inevitable. In *St Regis Paper Co Ltd*, the Court of Appeal stated that the delegation principle is unlikely to be extended beyond its current boundaries.[198]

8.2.3.2 The 'attributed act' principle

This second vicarious liability principle occurs in cases of strict liability where the actus reus of the employee, etc is attributed to D. It arises in statutory offences involving acts of selling, possessing, using, etc.

Many of the reported cases are those in which 'selling' or 'supplying' is the central feature of the actus reus, under statutes like the Trade Descriptions Act 1968, the Food and Drugs Acts, etc. A 'sale' consists in the transfer of property in goods from A to B[199] and the seller, in law, is necessarily the person in whom the property is vested at the commencement of the transaction. It is not a great step and no surprise, therefore, for the court to say that the employer has committed the actus reus of 'selling' even though he was nowhere near when the incident took place. In *Coppen v Moore (No 2)*,[200] D owned six shops, in which he sold 'American hams'. He gave strict instructions that these hams were to be described as 'breakfast hams' and were not to be sold under any specific name of place of origin. In the absence

---

[193] [2011] EWCA Crim 2527.   [194] [1965] AC 486, [1965] Crim LR 401.

[195] *Ross v Moss* [1965] 2 QB 396; *Winson* [1969] 1 QB 371.

[196] cf *Howker v Robinson*, n 189. Yet Bristow J, while considering himself bound by the authorities to apply the delegation principle, hoped that it might be overturned by the House of Lords: [1972] 2 All ER 786 at 791.

[197] [1983] QB 671.

[198] [2011] EWCA Crim 2527, [28].

[199] This is so in the criminal as well as the civil law: *Watson v Coupland* [1945] 1 All ER 217.

[200] [1898] 2 QB 306. One partner may similarly be liable for the acts of another: *Davies v Harvey* (1874) LR 9 QB 433. Cf *Parsons v Barnes* [1973] Crim LR 537.

of D, and without the knowledge of the manager of the branch, one of the assistants sold a ham as a 'Scotch ham'. D was convicted[201] of selling goods 'to which any . . . false trade description is applied'. Lord Russell CJ said:[202]

It cannot be doubted that the appellant [the owner] sold the ham in question, although the transaction was carried out by his servants. In other words he was the seller, although not the actual salesman. It is clear also, as already stated, that the ham was sold with a 'false trade description' which was material. If so, there is evidence establishing a *prima facie* case of an offence against the Act having been *committed by the appellant*.

The court was clearly influenced by the fact that D (like many other employers) carried on his business in a number of branches and could not possibly be in direct control of each one so that, if actual knowledge of the particular transaction had to be proved, he could hardly ever be made liable. The court did not, however, apply the principle of delegation which is to be found in the licensing cases. By construing the Act in accordance with the principles of the civil law and so holding that D had himself committed an actus reus, the court introduced a more far-reaching principle. Comparison with *Allchorn v Hopkins*[203] shows that, under the delegation principle, D would not have been liable for the act of the assistant to whom control of the premises had not been delegated.[204] D is not liable under that principle unless the delegate is acting within the scope of the delegation. So, for example, D was not liable where an employee, who had no authority to sell anything, supplied his employer's whisky to a customer out of hours.[205]

A modern instance of the application of the attributed act principle is *Harrow London Borough Council v Shah and Shah*.[206] The Shahs, newsagents, were convicted of selling a national lottery ticket to a boy under 16, contrary to s 13(1)(c) of the National Lottery Act 1993, although they had taken all reasonable steps[207] to ensure that the regulations were complied with and, though one of them was on the premises, neither was present in the shop when the ticket was sold by their employee, H, who reasonably believed the boy was at least 16 years old.

The limits of the attribution principle

There are many cases not involving a sale where a similar principle has been invoked. Just as it is the employer who, in law, 'sells' goods with which his employee is actually dealing, so too is he 'in possession' of goods which are actually in his employee's hands[208] and so can be made liable for offences of 'being in possession' (of which there are many)[209] through his employees. A producer of plays was held under s 15 of the Theatres Act 1843 (now repealed),[210] to have 'presented' a play even though he was miles away when it was

---

201 Under the Merchandise Marks Act 1887, s 2(2).   202 [1898] 2 QB 306 at 313. Emphasis added.
203 See n 184.
204 It was within the scope of the employee's authority in *Coppen v Moore* (see earlier in this section) to sell hams.
205 *Adams v Camfoni* [1929] 1 KB 95.
206 [1999] 3 All ER 302, [2000] Crim LR 992. It is submitted that the court attributed excessive authority to *Moussell Bros Ltd v London and North-Western Rly Co Ltd* [1917] 2 KB 836, in holding that the offence imposed vicarious liability. The ruling of strict liability is also questionable, in the light both of the terms of the section and the subsequent decisions in *B (A Minor) v DPP* [2000] 2 AC 428, and *K* [2002] 1 AC 462, Ch 5. See [2000] Crim LR 694–6.
207 This is a common defence in such statutory offences. See, for a discussion in the context of vicarious liability: *R (Keam) v DEFRA* [2005] EWHC 1582 (Admin) (D's independent contractor allowing cow to go lame and not calling a vet—whether D taken all reasonable steps), and see Ch 5.
208 See n 227.   209 For examples, see p 166.   210 See Theatres Act 1968; see Ch 30.

performed, and when words were introduced into the performance, without his knowledge, which had not been allowed by the Lord Chamberlain.[211]

More controversially, it has been held that the owners of a van which was supplied by them to a bailiff of their farm, nevertheless commit the offence of 'keeping' a van which is not 'used solely for the conveyance of goods or burden in the course of trade' without a licence[212] if the bailiff uses it, without their knowledge or authority, to take his wife for a day out at Clacton.[213] An employer 'uses' his vehicle in contravention of the Motor Vehicles (Construction and Use) Regulations if his employee so uses it.[214] It is quite understandable that a court should hold that an employer 'presents' a play or 'keeps' a vehicle, for these verbs are apt to describe his function and inapt to describe that of his employees. It is less clear that this is so in the case of 'uses'.[215] This could very well refer to the employee's use.

Another case serves to illustrate the proper limits of the doctrine and the need for the statute to be considered in its context. In *A-G's Reference (No 2 of 2003)*,[216] D was held not to be vicariously liable for 'keeping' an embryo contrary to s 3(1)(b)[217] and s 41(2)(a) of the Human Fertilisation and Embryology Act 1990 ('keeping or using' an embryo, except in pursuance of a licence) where he was the consultant responsible for the supervision of two clinics licensed under the 1990 Act. The embryologist working within one of the clinics was convicted of offences, but D, the supervisor, was unaware of those activities and had not participated in them. In approving the trial judge's decision to acquit D, Judge LJ commented that the offence is committed by the person who contravenes s 3(1), and regarded it as difficult to see how the language could extend to create criminal liability for 'keeping' to D, who 'notwithstanding his statutory responsibilities, does not in fact keep the embryo at all'.[218]

Sales by a licensee

A new principle seemed to have emerged in *Goodfellow v Johnson*:[219] a licensee is liable for the act of another which can lawfully be performed only by virtue of the licence, even though the other is not his employee. A brewery employed D, a licensee, and P, a barmaid. The barmaid sold watered-down gin. The gin was at all times owned by the brewery. D, the licensee, who had no knowledge of the sale, was prosecuted.[220] *Coppen v Moore* (the hams case) did not apply since D (the licensee) was not the owner of the gin; the brewery was. The delegation principle did not apply because there was no delegation.

Some confusion arose as to the application of the case and the significance of the ownership of the property being sold.[221] It is important to note that the offence in question was not a licensing offence. Consider the position if the barmaid had sold adulterated lemonade (a sale for which no licence is required). It would be absurd to say that the brewery (and the barmaid) could be guilty of selling adulterated lemonade but not adulterated gin.

---

[211] *Grade v DPP* [1942] 2 All ER 118. The defendant had in fact been called up for service in the RAF. The result would have been different if D had been charged with 'causing' the play to be presented: *Lovelace v DPP* [1954] 1 WLR 1468.

[212] Contrary to the Revenue Act 1869, s 27 (repealed).   [213] *Strutt v Clift* [1911] 1 KB 1.

[214] *Green v Burnett* [1955] 1 QB 78; but not where a partner, or person authorized ad hoc, uses the vehicle, if there is also an offence of permitting: *Crawford v Haughton* [1973] QB 1; *Garrett v Hooper* [1973] Crim LR 61; *Cobb v Williams* [1973] Crim LR 243.

[215] See especially the disagreement in the Divisional Court in *Cambridgeshire CC v Associated Lead Mills Ltd* [2005] EWHC 1627 (Admin).

[216] [2004] EWCA Crim 785.   [217] Now s 3(1A)(a).   [218] At [20].

[219] [1966] 1 QB 83.   [220] Contrary to the Food and Drugs Act 1955.

[221] It was thought that this case meant that there could be no prosecution of, eg, a brewery whose defective beer was sold by a licensee. *Allied Domecq Leisure Ltd v Paul Graham Cooper* [1999] Crim LR 230 and commentary.

In *Nottingham City Council v Wolverhampton and Dudley Breweries Plc*,[222] clarification
was provided. It was acknowledged that the owner (brewery) could be convicted of an
offence of selling intoxicating liquor below the tolerance allowed in the Food Labelling
Regulations under the Food Safety Act 1990. Kennedy LJ accepted that in *Goodfellow*, Lord
Parker had misunderstood the provisions of the Food and Drugs Act 1955 by treating them
as absolute offences, and had misunderstood *Hotchin v Hindmarsh*. Kennedy LJ observed
that the owner (the brewery) through the barmaid could make an effective sale regardless
of the licensee (D) and that such a sale could involve the owner (the brewery) and not just
the licensee, D, in criminal liability.[223] Therefore, the responsibility of the licensee, D, under
licensing legislation does not relieve the owner (the brewery) of responsibility for conduct
relating to all other products.

8.2.4 Mode of participation of employer and employee

Where a statute creates an offence specifically for designated people (eg licensees) to do
the act in question, the principal offender is that designated person who is held vicariously
liable for the acts of his employee. He alone possesses the personal characteristic which is an
essential part of the actus reus and no one else is qualified to fill that role. The employee who
actually performs the act is plainly incapable of being a principal, since he is not a licensee,
etc, but he may be convicted as an accessory.[224] This seems strange since the employee is the
only participant in the crime who is present and doing anything.

The position is different where the actus reus of the offence can be committed by someone
who does not have to possess a personal characteristic, such as being a licensee. In such a case,
if the employee is capable of being a principal, then it seems that he may be held to be a joint
principal with his employer (the licensee). In crimes of 'selling' and being 'in possession', the
court allows the prosecution the best of both worlds by having regard to the legal act when
dealing with the employer and the physical act when dealing with the employee. So it is held
that the employee, as well as the employer, 'sells'[225] or is 'in possession';[226] and the employee
whose 'use' of a vehicle was held to be use by his employer was convicted in *Green v Burnett*
(see earlier) as a principal. It is submitted that when the employee is capable of being a principal it is logical to hold him liable as such (for he is the real offender) and not as an accessory.

Determining whether the employee is a principal or accessory, etc is of more than academic interest for two reasons. First, if the crime is one of strict liability, mens rea must
nevertheless be proved if he is to be convicted as an accessory but not if he is a principal.[227]
Secondly, where there is a statutory defence enabling someone held vicariously liable to
escape if he can bring the 'actual offender' before the court, it is difficult to suppose that the
production of an accessory (even though he is the real offender) will suffice. However, a joint
principal certainly will suffice in this scenario.[228]

8.2.5 No vicarious liability for abetting or attempting crimes

Abetting is a common law notion and therefore, as we have seen,[229] requires mens rea
even where the principal offence is one of strict liability. For the same reasons D cannot
be vicariously liable for E abetting an offence by P, even though the offence itself may be

222 [2003] EWHC 2847 (Admin).   223 At [18].
224 *Griffiths v Studebakers Ltd* [1924] 1 KB 102; *Ross v Moss* [1965] 2 QB 396.
225 *Hotchin v Hindmarsh* [1891] 2 QB 181. Cf *Goodfellow v Johnson* [1966] 1 QB 83, but note the *Nottingham*
case discussed in the previous section.
226 *Melias Ltd v Preston* [1957] 2 QB 380.   227 See p 214.
228 *Melias Ltd v Preston* [1957] 2 QB 380.   229 See Ch 6.

one imposing vicarious liability. In *Ferguson v Weaving*,[230] D, a licensee, was charged with abetting several of her customers in consuming liquor on the licensed premises outside the permitted hours.[231] It appeared that she had taken all proper means to ensure that drinking ceased when 'Time' was called. But the waiters in the concert room, contrary to their instructions, made no attempt to collect the customers' drinks and, while D was visiting the several other rooms in the premises, the offence was committed. It was assumed that control of the concert room had been delegated. The principal offence was committed by the customers (P). While accepting that the waiters (E) might have been guilty of abetting the customers who were the principal offenders, the court was emphatic that D could not be. Lord Goddard CJ said:[232]

She can aid and abet the customers if she knows that the customers are committing an offence, but we are not prepared to hold that their knowledge can be imputed to her so as to make her, not a principal offender, but an aider and abettor. So to hold would be to establish a new principle in criminal law and one for which there is no authority.

Had there been a substantive offence of *permitting* drinking on licensed premises after hours, it is fairly clear that the court could have held D guilty; for in that case the acts, and the mens rea, of the servant would have been attributed to her. Likewise, it has been said that there can be no vicarious liability for attempting to commit a crime, even though the crime attempted imposes vicarious liability.[233]

8.2.6 Reform of vicarious liability

Clause 29 of the Law Commission Draft Criminal Code would have imposed a welcome restriction on the application of vicarious liability to those circumstances in which Parliament expressly imposed such. Far greater clarity and certainty would have followed from the adoption of this restriction.

The Law Commission has provisionally proposed that a preferable method of imposing criminal liability in place of vicarious liability and delegation would be to create offences drafted in specific terms of 'failing to prevent someone to whom a duty of care has been delegated' from committing the offence.[234]

Further reading

J Gobert and M Punch, *Rethinking Corporate Crime*

A Norrie, *Crime, Reason and History: A Critical Introduction to Criminal Law*

C Wells, *Corporations and Criminal Responsibility*

---

[230] [1951] 1 KB 814. See also *Thomas v Lindop* [1950] 1 All ER 966; *John Henshall (Quarries) Ltd v Harvey* [1965] 2 QB 233. *Provincial Motor Club Co Ltd v Dunning* [1909] 2 KB 599 overlooks this principle and is a doubtful decision.
[231] Contrary to the Licensing Act 1921, s 4.   [232] [1951] 1 KB 814 at 821.
[233] *Gardner v Akeroyd* [1952] 2 QB 743.   [234] See LCCP 195.

9

Mental conditions, intoxication and mistake

9.1 Introduction

In this and the next chapter the most commonly occurring 'defences' are considered. There is no accepted hierarchy of defences in English law and none is adopted in this book.[1] It should also be noted that considerable disagreement persists over the precise theoretical lines between elements which ought properly to be regarded as part of the offence and those comprising defences.[2]

In this chapter, the pleas of insanity, intoxication and mistake are examined. It would be misleading to treat all of these as 'defences' in the true sense of the word since some involve a plea which simply puts the Crown to proof of the relevant issue. The 'defences' or 'pleas' of insanity, and intoxication, are based on a denial of sufficient capacity to deserve the imposition of a criminal sanction.[3] At the core of these topics—insanity, automatism, intoxication, mistake—is the basic principle of English criminal law that the defendant should be held liable only where he is of sufficient capacity to be blameworthy for his actions.[4] As Professor Hart famously explained, a person should only be blamed if he has the 'capacity and fair opportunity to change or adjust his behaviour to the law'.[5]

Chapter 10 deals with substantive defences in the true sense—where D has caused an actus reus with the appropriate mens rea but, despite both these elements of the offence being proved by the Crown, D is entitled to an acquittal owing to some justifying or excusing circumstance or condition. There are also special defences which apply to particular crimes (eg loss of self-control and diminished responsibility in murder). They are dealt with separately throughout the book where appropriate and their interrelationship with general defences is considered.

9.1.1 Defences and theories of justification and excuse

Historically, the common law distinguished between justification and excuse, at least in relation to homicide. Some homicides were justifiable and others were merely excusable. In both cases the accused who successfully raised the defence was acquitted of felony but, if the homicide was merely excusable, his goods were forfeited. In 1828, forfeiture was abolished and, ever since, there has been no difference, so far as the defendant is concerned, between the various general defences. If successfully raised, they result in a verdict of not guilty.

---

[1] See, however, the theoretical approach in PH Robinson, 'Criminal Law Defences: A Systematic Analysis' (1982) 82 Col LR 199; and for a ladder of defences see J Horder, *Excusing Crime* (2004) 103.

[2] See generally G Williams, 'Offences and Defences' (1982) 2 LS 233; K Campbell, 'Offence and Defence' in IH Dennis (ed), *Criminal Law and Criminal Justice* (1987). Tadros, *Criminal Responsibility* emphasizes the significance of the distinction. Defences, he argues, describe the conditions of criminal responsibility, but do 'not constitute essential features of D's conduct which express why he is deserving of conviction, where the defence is unavailable' (at 109). Thus, lack of consent is an element of the offence in rape.

[3] Loughnan seeks to move away from talking about defences and instead conceptualizes what are discussed in this chapter as doctrines. Her excellent account seeks to focus on the way mental condition doctrines relate to other aspects of the criminal law, rather than focusing on the moral evaluation that they might entail. See A Loughnan, *Manifest Madness: Mental Incapacity in Criminal Law* (2012). For a critique, see T Ward (2014) 77 MLR 527.

[4] Numerous theories abound as to whether criminal responsibility and defences are properly explained on the bases of D's capacity, choice or character. These philosophical arguments lie beyond the scope of this work. See, inter alia, Horder, *Excusing Crime* and Tadros, *Criminal Responsibility*, Ch 2.

[5] HLA Hart, *Punishment and Responsibility* (1968) 181. For discussion on the relationship of the insanity defence to questions of responsibility, see the Law Commission, *Criminal Liability: Insanity and Automatism, A Discussion Paper* (2013) (hereafter in this chapter LCDP), Appendix A. See also the supplementary material to the earlier Scoping Paper (2012) (hereafter in this chapter LCSP) available at https://consult.justice.gov.uk/law-commission/insanity-and-automatism/user_uploads/insanity_scoping_supplementary.pdf-1.

Insanity is distinct in this respect because it results in a 'special' verdict of not guilty by reason of insanity.

There has been a revival of academic interest in a distinction between justification and excuse.[6] On one simple version of the theory, an act is justified when society does not disapprove of it or where it is permitted.[7] An act is merely excused when society disapproves of it but thinks it is nevertheless not right to punish D. The distinction is often described in simple terms: whereas the justification speaks to the rightness of the act, the excuse relates to the circumstances of the individual actor.[8] Clearly, some such distinction exists in fact. There are examples which obviously fall into one category or the other. The nine-year-old child who deliberately kills his playmate is excused but no one would say his act of killing is justified. In contrast, nearly everyone would approve of the conduct of a man who in self-defence wounds an aggressor when that is the only way he can save the lives of his family.

However, these systems of classification into justifications and excuses suffer from a number of drawbacks. First, there is no agreement on the precise hierarchy,[9] nature or definition of either classification. Duff suggests that they have 'bred needless confusion'.[10] A number of sophisticated models of justification and excuse have been developed by legal philosophers.[11] Recent suggestions propose a fourfold system of classification with justifications,[12] warranted acts,[13] excuses[14] and exemptions.[15] Secondly, there is no consensus as to which classification

---

[6] G Fletcher, *Rethinking Criminal Law* (1978) Ch 10; S Yeo, *Compulsion in the Criminal Law* (1990); Smith, *Justification and Excuse*; G Williams, 'The Theory of Excuses' [1982] Crim LR 732; PH Robinson (1982) 82 Col LR 199; J Gardner, 'The Gist of Excuses' (1998) Buffalo Crim LR 575; Horder, *Excusing Crime*; Tadros, *Criminal Responsibility*; Duff, *Answering for Crime*, Ch 11; A Simester, 'On Justifications and Excuses' in L Zedner and JV Roberts (eds), *Principles and Values in Criminal Law and Criminal Justice* (2012); PH Robinson, 'Four Distinctions that Glanville Williams Did Not Make: The Practical Benefit of Examining the Interrelation Among Criminal Law Doctrine' in DJ Baker and J Horder (eds), *The Sanctity of Life and the Criminal Law: The Legacy of Glanville Williams* (2013).

[7] It is problematic to suggest that the question is whether society 'approves' of the conduct. A better basis for the classification is that it is 'permitted'. See generally the account in Duff, *Answering for Crime*, Ch 11. Cf P Westen (2008) 28 OJLS 563.

[8] For criticism, see J Gardner, 'Wrongs and Faults' in Simester, *Appraising Strict Liability*, 61–7.

[9] See DN Husak, 'On the Supposed Priority of Justification to Excuse' (2005) 24 L & Phil 557.

[10] *Answering for Crime*, 263.

[11] Debate continues as to whether D who relies on a justification should be seen as having done no wrong, or as having done wrong but being justified in doing it (see G Fletcher, 'The Nature of Justifications' in S Shute, S Gardner and J Horder (eds), *Action and Value in Criminal Law* (1993) 175). As for excuses, there is debate over whether D is excused because he has acted 'out of character' or because he lacked capacity (ie he has not lived up to the standards we can reasonably expect of someone in his circumstances). See generally J Gardner (1998) Buffalo Crim LR 575; V Tadros, 'The Characters of Excuses' (2001) 21 OJLS 495; and Horder, *Excusing Crime*, Ch 3.

[12] There are many theories of justification ranging from those based on whether the outcome of D's act was a good one; whether he acted for good reasons; etc. See Tadros, *Criminal Responsibility*, Ch 10; J Dressler, 'New Thoughts About the Concept of Justification in the Criminal Law' (1984) 32 UCLA L Rev 61; J Gardner (1998) Buffalo Crim LR 575.

[13] See Duff, *Answering for Crime*, 277 et seq. These arise where D had sufficient reason to believe he acted for a good reason.

[14] The theories of excuse are also numerous, with many accepting that there is no single definition. In short, it might be said that an excuse arises where D admits that his act was wrong, but claims not to deserve punishment because of the circumstances pertaining. See fully: Horder, *Excusing Crime*, especially Ch 6, Tadros, *Criminal Responsibility*, Ch 11; C Finkelstein, 'Excuses and Dispositions in Criminal Law' (2002) 6 Buffalo Crim LR 317. See for comparative review of approaches across Europe, J Blomsma, *Mens Rea and Defences in European Criminal Law* (2012) Chs VIII–X.

[15] Advocated by Horder, *Excusing Crime*, 103–6; Tadros, *Criminal Responsibility*, Chs 4, 10 and 11. D is exempted where his lack of capacity is a general continuing one whereas he will be excused if his lack of capacity relates to the particular incident alleged.

applies to which defence—for example, many see duress as excusatory but some treat it as justificatory. Thirdly, there seems to be little agreement as to what practical difference, if any, would result from classification of a particular defence into one category or another.

Few suggest that there is any difference so far as the acquittal of the person relying on the defence is concerned,[16] but it has been argued more widely that the distinction affects third parties in that (a) it is lawful to resist an aggressor whose aggression is merely excused but not one whose aggression is justified; and (b) there may be a conviction for aiding and abetting one who is merely excused[17] but not one who is justified. Some would also argue that particular judicial decisions on excuses are not to be regarded as being of any wider significance in precedent terms.[18] As Fletcher (whose work inspired the current interest) acknowledges,[19] Anglo-American criminal law has never expressly recognized these (as he thinks) fundamental distinctions.

Applying the version of the theory as expounded by Fletcher, D1 using force in arresting 'anyone who is in the act of committing an offence' would be justified but D2 arresting 'anyone whom he has reasonable grounds for suspecting to be [but who is not in fact] committing an offence' is merely excused. But both acts are equally sanctioned by English law—the Police and Criminal Evidence Act 1984, s 24A, provides that a person other than a constable may arrest without warrant anyone who is in the act of committing an indictable offence and anyone whom he reasonably suspects to be doing so.[20] The citizen incurs no criminal liability if he arrests in these circumstances. It is true, however, that the first 'arrestee' (of D1) would not be entitled to use force in self-defence (if the arrestor was using only reasonable force) whereas the second (of D2) might be.[21] The law does recognize that a person's act may be excused in the criminal law, while incurring civil liability. A person who makes an unreasonable mistake of fact which, if it were true, would amount to reasonable grounds for suspecting another to be in the act of committing an offence, has a defence to a criminal prosecution for false imprisonment or assault (because he lacks mens rea) but remains liable for the corresponding torts: the act done is not the act which the 1984 Act says he *may* do. Here the terminology of justification and excuse seems appropriate. The act is 'unlawful', but the actor is excused from criminal liability.

Any attempt to rely on the theories of justifications or excuses as the guiding principle by which to structure an analysis of defences would, in the present state of the law, be premature, and no such attempt is made in either this or the subsequent chapter.

9.1.2 Relationship between mental condition defences

Some of the pleas discussed in this chapter may overlap since they are concerned with D's denial that he was a responsible actor at the time of the commission of the offence. Their interrelationship may be usefully summarized at the outset.[22] In short, there are three categories.

(1) Situations where D suffers some malfunctioning of his body or mind owing to some disease or *internal* cause. These factors are treated in law as 'diseases of the mind' which render D liable to a special verdict of not guilty by reason of insanity. The category includes such unremarkable conditions as sleepwalking, epilepsy and diabetes. The label 'insanity' is profoundly misleading.

---

[16] cf Robinson (1982) 82 Col LR 199 considering special verdicts for those who are excused and also the distinctions he draws attention to in fn 6.

[17] As in *Bourne* (1952) 36 Cr App R 125 and *Cogan and Leak* [1976] QB 217. See p 234.

[18] Robinson, n 16.   [19] *Rethinking Criminal Law*, n 6.

[20] Subject to the conditions in s 24A(3). See *Blackstone's Criminal Practice* (2021) D1.29.   [21] See p 401.

[22] See LCDP, Ch 6 for a thorough analysis of the relationship between insanity, automatism and intoxication.

(2) Situations where, because of some *external* factor that has affected D's mind or body in such a way that he acts involuntarily, he is entitled to an acquittal. Examples include concussion, taking a *medically prescribed* drug or anaesthetic in accordance with instructions, and other 'external' factors. These may give rise to a defence of sane[23] automatism, but that defence is hedged with qualification and approached by the courts with considerable scepticism. A defence of sane automatism is available only where D suffers a complete loss of control over the functioning of his limbs. In addition, where the automatism is self-induced by taking alcohol or drugs, it may be a defence to crimes of specific intent (as explained later) but not generally to basic intent offences (explained later).

(3) Situations where the factors affecting D's capacity do not negate liability at all. Examples include the voluntary taking of drink or drugs (discussed at p 333), which will provide no excuse in crimes other than those of specific intent where D has become so intoxicated as to lack mens rea.

9.2 Insanity

Some form of defence *akin* to the current defence of insanity[24] is crucial to the criminal justice system.[25] It recognizes that the imposition of criminal punishment should be reserved for those who are rational and responsible beings.[26] There are two ways in which an accused person's mental condition or illness may be relevant in a criminal trial. First, the accused may claim that he lacked mental capacity at the time of the commission of the conduct alleged to constitute the criminal offence. Secondly, the accused may be claiming that at the time of trial he lacks mental capacity to be tried. It is convenient to deal with this second category here because of its very close relationship with the defence of insanity, although technically it is a matter not of substantive criminal law but of procedure.

9.2.1 Mental illness and trial
9.2.1.1 Mental condition rendering trial impracticable
In some cases, where D is held in custody awaiting trial, his mental condition will be so serious that he is transferred to hospital. If the Secretary of State is satisfied by reports from at least two medical practitioners that D is suffering from mental disorder,[27] he may order

---

23 Sometimes called non-insane automatism.

24 See generally the excellent, though now dated, discussion in RD Mackay, *Mental Condition Defences in Criminal Law* (1995). Proposals for the reform of the law are made in the Report of the Committee on Mentally Abnormal Offenders (The Butler Report, 1975) Cmnd 6244. See also the philosophical discussion in Tadros, *Criminal Responsibility*, Chs 11 and 12. For the Law Commission's review of this area and its provisional conclusions on reform, see LCDP. The present law is described in Ch 2. This paper was preceded by the LCSP in which the Commission sought evidence that the defences were causing problems in practice. See J Peay, 'Insanity and Automatism: Questions from and About the Law Commission's Scoping Paper' [2012] Crim LR 927. The supplementary materials to LCSP, Ch 2–4 set out the present law and problems in considerable detail.

25 Some have suggested that the defence could be abolished and the absence of mens rea would serve as a determinant of D's liability. See n 221 and C Slobogin, 'An End to Insanity: Recasting the Role of Mental Illness in Criminal Cases' (2000) 86 Virg LR 1199. See also LCDP, Ch 2 and references therein, and the supplementary material to LCSP, Appendix A.

26 See the valuable analysis of the relationship between the defences and responsibility in Appendix A of LCDP.

27 For definitions, see Mental Health Act 2007. The 2007 Act amends the Mental Health Act 1983, redefining 'mental disorder' as 'any disorder or disability of the mind'.

that D be detained in a hospital, if he is suffering from mental disorder of a nature or degree which makes it appropriate for him to be detained in a hospital for medical treatment; and he is in urgent need of such treatment; and appropriate medical treatment is available for him.[28] The defendant is normally brought to trial[29] when he is well enough. The basis for this practice is:

> that the issue of insanity should be determined by the jury whenever possible and the power should be exercised only when there is likely to be a scandal [ie serious concern about the propriety] if the prisoner is brought up for trial . . .[30]

Clearly, in order to maintain compatibility with Art 5(1) (deprivation of liberty only in accordance with law) and Art 6 (fair trial) of the ECHR, it is essential that this power to detain is exercised in accordance with law and sparingly.[31]

9.2.1.2 Unfitness to be tried

Introduction

It is an important principle that an accused should, wherever possible, have an opportunity to contest his guilt in a normal criminal trial.[32] Finding someone to be 'unfit' results in him being denied a full criminal trial and ought therefore to be an exceptional approach.[33]

Someone who is seriously mentally ill may nevertheless be 'fit to plead to the indictment and follow the proceedings at the trial and . . . if he is, he should ordinarily be allowed to do so, because it is in principle desirable that a person charged with a criminal offence should, whenever possible, be tried, so that the question whether he committed the crime may be determined by a jury.'[34]

At any trial in the Crown Court it might be alleged by the defence or the prosecution that D is 'unfit to plead' or 'unfit to stand trial'. If D is found by the judge to be unfit, the normal trial process is not applied to him. Instead, a jury determines the narrow question whether D did the act complained of (without considering his mens rea)—this is called a trial of the facts. At that hearing D might be acquitted (having been found not to have done the act) or

---

[28] Mental Health Act 1983, s 48 (as amended).

[29] See the Law Commission's description of the pathways through the criminal justice system for the mentally ill in Appendix A of supplementary material to LCSP. See also LC 364, *Unfitness to Plead* (2016) Ch 2.

[30] Report of the Royal Commission on Capital Punishment (1953) Cmd 8932. See eg *Ghanbary* [2006] EWCA Crim 2374.

[31] See P Bean, *Madness and Crime* (2008) Ch 3.

[32] *R (Hasani) v Blackfriars CC* [2005] EWHC 3016 (Admin). See the Law Commission's recommendation to allow for adjournment where there is a prospect of recovery so as to enable D to have a full trial: see LC 364, para 4.97.

[33] See LC 364, *Unfitness to Plead* (2016) especially Ch 2. On fitness to plead more generally, see RD Mackay and W Brookbanks (eds), *Fitness to Plead: International and Comparative Perspectives* (2018). For trends in the use of the plea, see RD Mackay and G Kearns, 'An Upturn in Unfitness to Plead?' [2000] Crim LR 532; RD Mackay, B Mitchell and L Howe, 'A Continued Upturn in Unfitness to Plead—More Disability in Relation to the Trial under the 1991 Act' [2007] Crim LR 530. Research appended to the LC Report reveals that the number of unfitness cases increased and has levelled off at around 100 per year. Legal guidance for the conduct of such cases is provided by the CPS: www.cps.gov.uk/legal-guidance/mental-health-suspects-and-defendants-mental-health-conditions-or-disorders.

[34] As expressed by witnesses before the Royal Commission on Capital Punishment, *Report* (1953) Cmd 8932, at 78. See generally LC 364, Ch 2, recommending greater availability of measures to assist defendants to participate in a full trial where possible. The judge must generally exercise this discretion to postpone where there is a reasonable chance that the prosecution case will be successfully challenged: *Webb* [1969] 2 QB 278. On the other hand, 'the case for the prosecution may appear so strong and the suggested condition of the prisoner so disabling that postponement of the trial of the issue would be wholly inexpedient': *Burles* [1970] 2 QB 191, per Parker LCJ.

be found to have done the act, and thereby be subjected to a range of disposal powers which are not 'sentences' since he has not been convicted.[35]

The issue of unfitness can be raised at any time. If raised at the start of the trial on arraignment, the Crown Court follows the procedure to determine D's fitness under ss 4 and 4A of the Criminal Procedure (Insanity) Act 1964.[36] The issue may also arise where D has been found unfit, he has been hospitalized and his condition has improved so that he is brought back to court to determine whether he remains unfit.[37] If, having decided D is unfit, D appears to have recovered before the court has begun to decide the trial of the facts alleged, the court should revisit the question of whether he is fit to be tried.

What constitutes unfitness?

At the first stage—inquiring whether D is unfit—the question is whether D has sufficient understanding to be tried. Astonishingly, the law is based on a test derived from a case decided in 1836 when any concern for and understanding of mental illness and the impact that might have on the ability of an individual to participate in the trial was limited.[38] The modern-day incarnation of the test was set out in the case of M.[39] The trial judge directed that the defendant had to have sufficient ability in relation to *all* of the following six things: (a) to understand the charges; (b) to understand the plea; (c) to challenge jurors; (d) to instruct counsel and his solicitor; (e) to understand the course of the trial; and (f) to give evidence if he chooses. If he is able to do all these things, he has *a right* to be tried, even if he is not capable of acting in his best interests.[40] The same principle must, theoretically, be applicable where the prosecution contend that D is fit to plead and he denies it; but it might be more leniently applied in such a case.

More recently the courts have sought to adopt more flexible and enlightened approaches.[41] The Law Commission Report recommends a shift in focus to whether a defendant can participate effectively given the particular allegations and likely nature of the trial, and the assistance that might be made available to him in the trial.[42] These imperatives were echoed by the Court of Appeal in *Marcantonio and Chitolie*:

In applying the *Pritchard* criteria the court is required to undertake an assessment of the defendant's capabilities *in the context of the particular proceedings*. An assessment of whether a defendant has the capacity to participate effectively in legal proceedings should require the court to have regard to what that legal process will involve and what demands it will make on the defendant. It should be addressed not in the abstract but in the context of the particular case. The degree of complexity of

---

[35] See LC 364, Ch 6. See *Wells et al* [2015] EWCA Crim 2, [2015] Crim LR 359; *Chinegwundoh* [2015] EWCA Crim 109.

[36] As substituted by the Criminal Procedure (Insanity and Unfitness to Plead) Act 1991 and amended by the Domestic Violence, Crime and Victims Act 2004, discussed by S White, 'The Criminal Procedure (Insanity and Unfitness to Plead) Act 1991' [1992] Crim LR 4; P Fennell, 'The Criminal Procedure (Insanity and Unfitness to Plead) Act 1991' (1992) 55 MLR 547. The 1964 Act replaced the Criminal Lunatics Act 1800. See LCCP 197, Part 2 for a history of the developments.

[37] Section 4A is mandatory and must be complied with in full in such cases: *Ferris* [2004] EWHC 1221 (Admin). See LC 364, Ch 5 and the discussion generally in *Sultan* [2014] EWCA Crim 2648. On the possibility for resumption see LC 364, Ch 9 recommending opportunities for defence and prosecution to apply for leave to resume a trial.

[38] *Pritchard* (1836) 7 C & P 303. See LC 364, Ch 3.

[39] [2003] EWCA Crim 3452.

[40] *Robertson* [1968] 1 WLR 1767. See also *R (Kenneally) v Snaresbrook Crown Court* [2002] QB 1169. For insights into how psychiatrists view these, see T Rogers et al, 'Fitness to Plead and Competence to Stand Trial' (2008) 19 J Forensic Psychiatry & Psychology 576.

[41] See also *Walls* [2011] EWCA Crim 443 suggesting use of special measures.   [42] See LC 364, Ch 3.

different legal proceedings may vary considerably. Thus the court should consider, for example, the nature and complexity of the issues arising in the particular proceedings, the likely duration of the proceedings and the number of parties. There can be no legitimate reason for depriving a defendant of the right to stand trial on the basis that he lacks capacity to participate in some theoretical proceedings when he does not lack capacity to participate in the proceedings which he faces. It is in the interests of all concerned that the criminal process should proceed in the normal way where this is possible without injustice to the defendant.[43]

It was held in *Podola*[44] that a person is fit to plead where an hysterical amnesia prevents him from remembering events during the whole of the period material to the question whether he committed the crime alleged, but whose mind is otherwise completely normal. The court was prepared to concede that a 'deaf mute'[45] is 'unfit' but declined:

to extend the meaning of the word to include persons who are mentally normal at the time of the hearing of the proceedings against them and are perfectly capable of instructing their solicitors as to what submission their counsel is to put forward with regard to the commission of the crime.[46]

But is a person suffering from hysterical amnesia capable in that sense? If the facts might justify a defence of accident or alibi but D is unable to remember them, the defence cannot be raised unless there are witnesses who come forward. On the other hand, it would be unsatisfactory if, for example, there could be no trial of a motorist who had suffered concussion in an accident, alleged to have been caused by his dangerous driving, and who could not remember what he did. It would be still less satisfactory in the case of one whose failure to recall the relevant events arose from voluntary drunkenness.[47]

The procedure for determining unfitness

The issue of unfitness may be raised by the judge on his own initiative or at the request of the prosecution or the defence. It is usually at the request of the defence at the start of the trial. Where neither party raises the issue, the judge should do so if he has doubts about the accused's fitness.[48] The Law Commission examined in detail the problems in practice with the need for expert evidence and the difficulties in identifying the likely unfitness of the accused.[49]

The issue of whether the accused is fit used to be tried by a jury.[50] Following s 22 of the Domestic Violence, Crime and Victims Act 2004, however, the issue is now to be determined

---

[43] [2016] EWCA Crim 14 at [7] per Lloyd Jones LJ. Cited with approval by Simon LJ in the subsequent case of *Ehi-Palmer* [2016] EWCA Crim 1844.

[44] [1960] 1 QB 325. The jury had found that Podola was not suffering from hysterical amnesia and the question before the Court of Criminal Appeal concerned the onus of proof of that issue; but the court held that this question could only arise if the alleged amnesia could in law bring Podola within the scope of s 2 of the Criminal Lunatics Act 1800. The court's decision on this point thus appears to be part of the *ratio decidendi* of the case.

[45] See also *Sharif* [2010] EWCA Crim 1709.

[46] [1960] 1 QB at 356. The word 'insane' was the one under consideration as that was the word used in the Criminal Lunatics Act 1800, and is not used in s 4 of the 1964 Act; but the law is unchanged. Cf CLRC, Third Report, *Criminal Procedure (Insanity)* (1963) Cmd 2149, at 7.

[47] *Broadhurst v R* [1964] AC 441 at 451. Butler (by majority) recommended the retention of the *Podola* rule.

[48] See LC 364, para 4.16. *MacCarthy* [1967] 1 QB 68, discussed by AR Poole, 'Standing Mute and Fitness to Plead' [1966] Crim LR 6. *Janaway* [2014] EWCA Crim 1073 demonstrates how difficult it can be to assess whether D is fit to stand trial if he refuses to cooperate. The Court of Appeal held that the trial judge's decision to continue the trial could not be criticized.

[49] See LC 364, Chs 3 and 4.

[50] Criminal Procedure (Insanity) Act 1964, s 4(5). See now *B* [2008] EWCA Crim 1997 on the position where D1 is unfit and D2 fit at the same trial. See also *MB* [2010] EWCA Crim 1684; on difficulties this creates see LCCP 197, para 7.27.

by a court without a jury. Such proceedings do not constitute 'criminal proceedings' since they cannot result in a conviction; the procedure is to ensure the protection of the defendant and the public. Accordingly, Art 6 of the ECHR does not apply.[51]

The defendant may not be found unfit to plead unless there is written or oral evidence to that effect by two or more registered medical practitioners, at least one of whom is approved by the Home Secretary as having special experience in the field of mental disorder.[52] This goes some way to ensuring that the criminal process is in step with medical practice.[53] The medical evidence is required to prove unfitness (not fitness).[54]

In *Lederman*,[55] the judge had rightly ruled that D was fit to stand trial where the medical evidence was divergent on that issue. D had attempted to commit suicide prior to his trial for causing death by dangerous driving. These suicidal intentions and mental fragility were not relevant to the *Pritchard* criteria for consideration of unfitness to plead.

When should the question of fitness to be tried be determined?

The general rule is that a defendant is presumed to be fit to be tried, and any challenge to fitness is to be determined as soon as it arises. If the accused is found by the judge to be fit and the trial proceeds, the case will be tried by a jury in the normal way.

If the defendant is found unfit, the trial of the facts occurs before a jury. The case against a person who is undoubtedly unfit to stand trial may be weak and capable of demolition by cross-examination of the prosecution witnesses by his lawyers. It would be wrong if he were to be found unfit and subjected to the disposals (including detention) which may follow from that finding without having an opportunity to test the prosecution's case. If the judge, having regard to the nature of D's supposed disability, thinks that it is expedient and in the interests of the accused to do so, he may postpone consideration of the question of fitness to be tried until any time up to the opening of the case for the defence.[56] This gives the defence the opportunity to test the prosecution's case in a normal trial. If at that point the judge takes the view that the prosecution case is insufficient to justify a conviction, the jury will be directed to acquit and the question of fitness to plead will not arise. If the judge finds that there is a case to answer, and that D is unfit, the trial of the facts will then be determined by the jury. The matter is regulated by statute.[57] In these exceptional cases, the issue is to be determined by the same jury by which the accused was originally tried.[58]

As the Court of Appeal emphasized in *Orr*,[59] s 4A is a:

mandatory statutory requirement which cannot be avoided by the court's general discretion to order proceedings otherwise however beneficial to the defendant they appear.[60]

---

[51] *H* [2003] UKHL 1 affirming *M, K and H* [2001] EWCA Crim 2024. On ECHR concerns with the operation of the procedure, see E Baker, 'Human Rights and McNaughten and the 1991 Act' [1994] Crim LR 84; Mackay, 'On Being Insane in Jersey Part Two' [2002] Crim LR 728, 'On Being Insane in Jersey Part Three—The Case of the *Attorney General v O'Driscoll*' [2004] Crim LR 219.

[52] The 1964 Act as amended, s 4(6). See also *Borkan* [2004] EWCA Crim 1642.

[53] But see LC 364, Ch 4 on the difficulties this can generate. It recognized that other health-care professionals or support workers are better qualified to give an assessment of the accused's ability to participate in his trial. See para 4.67.

[54] See *Ghulam* [2009] EWCA Crim 2285, [2010] Crim LR 796 and commentary.

[55] [2015] EWCA Crim 1308.   [56] See LC 364, para 4.97.

[57] Criminal Procedure (Insanity) Act 1964, as amended by the Criminal Procedure (Insanity and Unfitness to Plead) Act 1991 and the Domestic Violence, Crime and Victims Act 2004.

[58] Section 22 of the 2004 Act, amending the Criminal Procedure (Insanity) Act 1964, s 4(5) as substituted by the Criminal Procedure (Insanity and Unfitness to Plead) Act 1991, s 2.

[59] [2016] EWCA Crim 889. For comment, see A Owusu-Bempah and N Wortley, 'Unfit to Plead or Unfit to Testify?' (2016) 80 J Crim L 391.

[60] At [30] per Macur LJ.

Once it was determined that the defendant was no longer fit to fully participate, the procedure in s 4A(1) of the Criminal Procedure (Insanity) Act 1964 had to be followed.

The trial of the facts

Where D is found to be unfit, either on arraignment or at the end of the prosecution case,
the trial shall not proceed, or proceed further.[61] If the matter rested there, D might again
be subject to a loss of liberty on the grounds of his mental illness or condition even though
he has not been proved to have committed an offence. Even if the prosecution's evidence
has been heard and amounts to a case to answer, the defence may have an answer to it in
the shape of evidence—for example, of alibi. Section 4A (introduced by the 1991 Act, and
amended by the 2004 Act) therefore provides for a further hearing.[62]

At this hearing—the trial of the facts—the jury determines the question whether D 'did
the act or made the omission charged against him as the offence'.[63] The aim of such a hearing is to test the evidence rather than to hold D to account.[64] The judge should not direct the
jury as to what disposal powers might then be used against D if the jury were to find that
he did the act.[65]

In relation to this s 4A hearing, it was held in *Antoine*[66] that the words 'act' and 'omission'
mean the actus reus of the offence and that, accordingly, D could not rely on the defence
of diminished responsibility.[67] The decision creates problems by its presumption that all
offences divide neatly into elements only of actus reus and mens rea that can be readily
identified. On the *Antoine* approach, at a s 4A hearing, the defence can deny actus reus
elements but not mens rea elements.[68] The confusion is exemplified in the judgment itself.

---

[61] See generally LC 364, Ch 5. The judge in *O'Donnell* [1996] 1 Cr App R 286 went wrong at this point by
allowing the trial to proceed, by failing to appoint someone to put the case for the defence and by not directing
the trial jury that, now, the only question for them was whether D did the act. Conviction annulled and *venire
de novo* ordered. See also *Norman* [2008] EWCA Crim 1810—the duty on the court is to appoint the best person to represent D. Difficulties can arise where the accused refuses to be represented. As the Law Commission
notes in *Unfitness to Plead: Issues Paper* (2014) (para 2.82), questions arise as to the UK's obligations under
the UN Convention on the Rights of Persons with Disabilities to respect the rights, will and preferences of
disabled people.

[62] Controversy has arisen as to whether previous admissions made by D ought to be admissible in a trial of
the facts. In *B* [2012] EWCA Crim 1799, the Court of Appeal held that it was difficult to see how, if D was unfit
to plead, he was capable of understanding the right to caution, the caution itself and the significance of a police
interview. This issue was also considered in *Swinbourne* [2013] EWCA Crim 2329, although perhaps surprisingly, the Court declined to set aside the finding of fact in that case. In *B*, the court was critical of the fact that
it lacked the power to order a retrial in these circumstances and urged Parliament to address this lacuna. Such
sentiments echoed those in *McKenzie* [2011] EWCA Crim 1550 where it was recognized that there is no power
to order a retrial where the Court of Appeal quashes findings made under the Criminal Procedure (Insanity)
Act 1964, s 4A. See also *Roberts* [2019] EWCA Crim 1270.

[63] Problems arise where D has been found unfit to plead and his condition improves so that by the time of
the trial of the facts he is potentially fit to stand trial. See *Omara* [2004] EWCA Crim 431. See LC 364, Ch 5.

[64] The hearing is not a trial and D cannot be convicted: *Wells* [2015] EWCA Crim 2, [9].

[65] *Moore* [2009] EWCA Crim 1672.

[66] [2001] 1 AC 340, overruling *Egan* [1998] 1 Cr App R 121 which had 'held' that the words meant all the
ingredients of the offence as intended by the Butler Committee (1975, Cmnd 6244, para 10.24) on whose recommendations these provisions are based. RD Mackay and G Kearns, 'The Trial of the Facts and Unfitness to
Plead' [1997] Crim LR 644, however, demonstrated that this was not the meaning intended by ministers who
introduced the Bill in Parliament. The same words used in the Trial of Lunatics Act 1883, s 2, refer only to the
actus reus: *Felstead* [1914] AC 534. An application to Strasbourg was rejected as manifestly ill-founded: *Antoine
v UK* (App no 62960/00). For discussion see LC 364, Ch 5. The Law Commission recommends that the prosecution should have to establish all elements of the offence: para 5.85.

[67] That defence applies only when the actus reus (and, indeed, the mens rea) of murder has been established.

[68] See *Norman* [2008] EWCA Crim 1810 as a good illustration of the problems—D was charged with child
abduction and suffered from Huntingdon's Disease.

For example, Lord Hutton, with whom all their lordships agreed, said that the jury should take into account any objective evidence of mistake, accident or self-defence and should not find that D did the act unless it is sure that the prosecution has negatived the defence. But the 'defences' of mistake and accident are simply denials of mens rea, not of the actus reus, and self-defence has a vital mental element.[69] If this *dictum* is right, it is hard to see why any evidence, other than of a defect of reason from disease of the mind, suggesting the absence of mens rea,[70] should not be admissible, thus undermining the whole decision. Subsequently, it was held that D could not invoke the defence of provocation (as it then was).[71] That defence also applied only where all the elements of murder are proved so 'the act' of murder and of manslaughter by reason of provocation seem to be identical. Presumably the same approach would be taken to the new defence of loss of control. It appears that his lordship was anticipating that the s 4A inquiry is directed not merely to the actus reus, not to the full offence of actus reus and mens rea, but to an 'unlawful act'. The difficulty lies in what constitutes 'objective' evidence. In *Wells* (at [17]), it was held to include 'the background to the incident, the antecedents of the complainants and the circumstances of the [incident] as evidenced, for example by the injuries [and any] evidence of [a] co-defendant'.

It is possible to envisage some relatively straightforward cases where 'objective defences' ought to be capable of being pleaded. Difficult examples to test the precise limits of Lord Hutton's 'objective defences' might include a case in which the defence of sane automatism would have been advanced at trial. Consider, for example, a case where D has been hit on the head and in a state of concussion hit and killed V, and D has by trial become so traumatized by the event that he is unfit to be tried. At the trial of the facts under s 4A, is the automatism plea a denial of mens rea and forbidden? Or is it a denial of a 'voluntary act' and expressly recognized by Lord Hutton? Or is it in some third category of 'not unlawful act'? The Court of Appeal acknowledged the problem in *M*[72] where it was accepted that the actus reus/mens rea distinction was not one that could be rigidly adhered to in every case given the diverse nature of crimes. It also poses special problems in cases of secondary liability.

The practical difficulty posed by *Antoine* arose acutely in *B*, in which D was charged with voyeurism, contrary to s 67(1) of the Sexual Offences Act 2003.[73] The Court of Appeal accepted that the requirement in s 67(1) that D did an act 'for the purpose of sexual gratification' was pre-eminently an example of a mental element. It was therefore understandable why the judge had ruled that this element ought therefore to be excluded from the jury's consideration on a trial of the facts. However, the Court of Appeal disagreed with the judge's approach. In a voyeurism case, if that element was ignored all the Crown would have to prove was that D observed V doing a private act. Simply observing someone naked or in their underwear, even if done deliberately, is not a criminal offence. Having regard to the mischief at which the offence of voyeurism was designed to address, it was held that the link between deliberate observation and the purpose of sexual gratification of the observer is central to the offence. Relying upon Lord Hutton's phraseology in *Antoine*, it is that purpose which turns the deliberate observation of another doing an intimate act in private, into an

---

[69] This passage in the 13th edn was cited with approval by the Court of Appeal in *B* [2012] EWCA Crim 770.

[70] Clearly, the finding of an act or omission may include some elements of mens rea where they are a composite element of the actus reus: *R (Young) v Central Criminal Court* [2002] 2 Cr App R 12, [2002] Crim LR 588 and commentary. See the discussion in *Wells* [2015] EWCA Crim 2.

[71] *Grant (Heather)* [2002] QB 1030.

[72] [2003] EWCA Crim 357. See also *Wells* [2015] EWCA Crim 2. On the difficulties involved see RD Mackay and W Brookbanks, 'Protecting the Unfit to Plead' [2005] Juridical Review 173. See also the LCCP on provisional proposals to include all elements of the offence in the s 4A hearing as reformed.

[73] [2012] EWCA Crim 770. See p 855.

'injurious act'. The 'relevant act charged as the offence' was held to be the deliberate observation of another doing a private act where the observer *does so for the specific purpose of the observer obtaining sexual gratification*. Although this decision is an important one for the analysis and application of the principles espoused in *Antoine*, it only serves to highlight the problems.

Under the present law, the broader problem lies in defining with sufficient precision the level of inquiry that is appropriate at a trial of the facts under s 4A so as to: (a) avoid assessment of the accused's mental state at the time of the offence, because although he is the person best able to know that, by definition, he is now unfit to provide such evidence, or rebut allegations; and (b) prevent the hospitalization of those who would for reasons other than those of mental illness have secured a complete acquittal at a normal trial. The irony is that by seeking to protect defendants from (i) the rigours of a full trial which they would not be able to participate in effectively, and (ii) inquiry into their mental state at the time of the offence which it is supposed they are unable to defend at the trial of the facts, the system might place them in a worse position by subjecting them to a s 4A hearing.[74]

Where D has been found to be unfit and found at the s 4A hearing to have committed the actus reus, but his condition then improves and the question arises whether he is fit to be tried, the determination of his fitness and of whether he performed the actus reus must both be re-litigated. The prior determination of the actus reus being satisfied cannot be relied upon.[75]

Onus of proof

Podola's case decided, overruling earlier authorities, that where D raises the issue of fitness to plead the onus of proving that he is unfit is on him. By analogy to the rule prevailing when a defence of insanity is raised at the trial,[76] D is required to prove his case not beyond reasonable doubt but on a balance of probabilities. If the issue is raised by the prosecution and disputed by the defence then the burden is on the prosecution and the matter must be proved beyond reasonable doubt.[77] If the issue is raised by the judge and disputed by D, presumably the onus is again on the prosecution.[78]

The effect of *Podola*'s case is that a person may be convicted although a court was not satisfied that he was capable of making out a proper defence at his trial. Moreover, the reasoning of the court has been criticized on the ground, inter alia, that the prosecution, in bringing the charge at all, is implicitly alleging that D is fit to stand his trial; and that he, in denying that he is so fit, is merely denying that the prosecution have established all the elements in their case.

Disposal powers in relation to a person unfit to plead who 'did the act'

Until the reforms made by the 1991 Act took effect, the court was required to order that any person found unfit had to be admitted to the hospital specified by the Home Secretary where he might be detained without limitation of time, the power to discharge him being exercisable only with the Home Secretary's consent. Since the 1991 Act, a person who is found unfit but, following a s 4A hearing, not to have done the act or made the omission charged simply goes free. Where he is found to be unfit *and* to have done the act or made the omission, a

---

[74] This paragraph in the 13th edn was cited with approval by the Court of Appeal in *B* [2012] EWCA Crim 770. See LC 364, Ch 5.

[75] *Ferris* [2004] EWHC 1221 (Admin); cf *Omara*, n 63. See the Law Com Issues Paper, Ch 7.

[76] Per Edmund Davies J at first instance, [1960] 1 QB 325 at 329; *Robertson* [1968] 1 WLR 1767.

[77] *Antoine* [2001] AC 340, [2000] Crim LR 621. According to Podola's counsel, Mr FH Lawton, later Lawton LJ, it had been the normal practice in recent years for the prosecution to call the evidence.

[78] M Dean, 'Fitness to Plead' [1960] Crim LR 79 at 82.

wider range of disposals is now generally available, although these are frequently criticized as being inadequate.[79] Under s 24 of the 2004 Act inserting a new s 5 into the 1964 Act, in any case other than one of a fixed sentence, the court may make:[80]

(1) a hospital order (with or without a restriction order);[81]

(2) a supervision order; or

(3) an order for absolute discharge.

Magistrates' and youth courts

In magistrates' courts and youth courts[82] the procedure for dealing with defendants who may have mental illness or other difficulties preventing them participating in the trial effectively is quite different.[83] It is contained in s 37 of the Mental Health Act 1983.[84] In cases of alleged unfitness, *if* there exists medical evidence to justify making a hospital or guardianship order under s 37, the court has the power to make such an order. Ordinarily the court should first address whether the act alleged was done or the omission made by D. If it is not proved that D did the act or omission he will be acquitted. If the court finds that he did the act or omission it can make an order under s 37. However, if appropriate, where the court finds that D performed the act it can, instead of making an order under s 37, conduct a trial of the insanity plea.[85] At the conclusion of that trial the court's powers of disposal under s 37 remain available.

Reform

Numerous problems with the present law have been identified. It is based on an historic test and, as Toulson LJ stated in 2008, there is a 'mismatch between the legal test and the psychiatric understanding'.[86] The procedure has been cogently criticized for its focus on D's communicative ability and its failure to address the true problem—whether D is capable of providing a rational account of the incident to instruct his lawyer and of participating effectively in the trial process.[87] As the Law Commission's work has emphasized, the present test creates difficulties in practice. It fails to protect mentally ill defendants who, despite the unfitness procedure, are often tried in the normal way[88] although in some cases displaying

---

[79] See LC 364, Ch 6 on disposals including a revised supervision order: para 6.48. The Court of Appeal in *R* [2013] EWCA Crim 591 expressed uncertainty about whether an individual who has been found unfit to be tried and has 'done the act' has been acquitted. A finding that D did the acts was not a conviction because there had been no finding that D acted with mens rea. Similarly, a finding of unfitness and that D had done the act did not amount to an acquittal. There is thus no power to make a restraining order under s 5A of the Protection from Harassment Act, 1997: *Chinegwundo* [2014] EWCA Crim 2649, [2015] EWCA Crim 109.

[80] For discussion, see A Ashworth and L Zedner, *Preventive Justice* (2014) 209–14.

[81] See *Narey v Customs and Excise* [2005] EWHC 784 (Admin).

[82] *P v Barking Youth Court* [2002] EWHC 734 (Admin).

[83] The Law Commission Consultation Paper and Issues Paper examine the many defects in the procedure in the magistrates' and youth courts. LC 364 recommends the application of a statutory procedure in the magistrates' and youth courts for defendants who are unable to participate effectively in their trial: Ch 7.

[84] See A Samuels, 'Hospital Orders without Conviction' [1995] Crim LR 220. On the need to consider the suitability of such disposal, see *IA* [2005] EWCA Crim 2077. Note that the Mental Health Act 2007, Sch 1 amended s 37, so that the s 37 powers are available if D is suffering from any disorder or disability of the mind (the limitation to cases of mental illness or severe mental impairment is removed). See LCCP 197, Ch 8.

[85] *R (Singh) v Stratford MC* [2007] EWHC 1582 (Admin).

[86] *Murray* [2008] EWCA Crim 1792, [6].

[87] See also the psychiatrist's view—D Grubin, 'What Constitutes Unfitness to Plead' [1993] Crim LR 748, cf R A Duff, 'Fitness to Plead and Fair Trials' [1994] Crim LR 419.

[88] Examples include *Erskine* [2009] EWCA Crim 1425; *Moyle* [2008] EWCA Crim 3059.

bizarre behaviour.[89] It fails to protect enough defendants. Estimates are that 10 per cent of men in prison on remand display signs of psychosis, but only a very small number of unfitness pleas are made each year.[90] Moreover, the test is not always well suited to cases involving those with communication or learning difficulties rather than mental illness. The s 4A hearing is also defective since it fails to provide a fair opportunity for the accused to be acquitted.

The Law Commission recommendations seek to maximize the opportunity for the defendant to continue to participate in a full trial with assistance and support.[91] An adjournment would be available if D was likely to recover sufficiently for a full trial.[92] The defendant's ability to participate effectively would be tested against a modern statutory test drafted with the modern psychological and psychiatric understanding in mind.[93] The test is based on effective participation of the accused given the context of the trial.[94] There would be the opportunity for D to plead guilty if he wished and had the capacity to do so even if he lacked the capacity for a full trial.[95] The judge would have the power to divert an unfit defendant out of the criminal justice process where it was in the interests of justice.[96]

The Law Commission recommended amendment to the trial of the facts regime to require the prosecution to prove all elements of the offence.[97] The jury would be able to return three possible verdicts: an acquittal, that D did the acts complained of, or that D is not guilty by reason of insanity.[98] The disposals available to a judge would be hospital order, supervision or absolute discharge.[99] Resumption of the full trial would be possible where D has recovered and it was in the interests of justice subject to other safeguards where the Crown was seeking to resume the trial. The Commission also recommends the new scheme applies to trials in the magistrates' and youth courts.[100]

9.2.2 A plea of insanity

Whereas the plea of unfitness is concerned with the accused's mental state at the time of the trial, insanity is concerned with the accused's mental state at the time when he is alleged to have committed the crime.[101]

---

[89] See *Shulman* [2010] EWCA Crim 1034; *Grant* [2008] EWCA Crim 1870.

[90] See LCCP 197, para 2.61.

[91] See LC 364, Ch 2. For comment, see A Loughnan, 'Between Fairness and "Dangerousness": Reforming the Law on Unfitness to Plead' [2016] Crim LR 451 and H Howard, 'Lack of Capacity: Reforming the Law on Unfitness to Plead' (2016) 80 J Crim L 428. See generally M Bevan and D Ormerod, 'Reforming the Law of Unfitness to Plead in England and Wales: A Recent History' in RD Mackay and W Brookbanks (eds), *Fitness to Plead: International and Comparative Perspectives* (2018).

[92] LC 364, para 4.97

[93] Ch 3. Recommendations are made for more efficient use of a wider pool of relevant expertise.

[94] See para 3.136. See RD Mackay [2004] Crim LR 219. See also the Scottish Law Commission Report No 195 (2004) Ch 4 and cl 4. See LCCP 197, provisionally proposing a test of decisional competence, but awaiting a test being devised by psychiatrists. For critical comment see RD Mackay [2011] Crim LR 433.

[95] Para 3.156.   [96] Para 5.61.   [97] Para 5.85. See LCCP 197, Part 6.   [98] Para 5.132.

[99] Ch 6.   [100] See Ch 7.

[101] See generally Mackay, *Mental Condition Defences in Criminal Law*, Ch 2; A Loughnan, *Manifest Madness: Mental Incapacity in Criminal Law* (2012), and for a more philosophical account see Tadros, *Criminal Responsibility*, Ch 12. A comparative analysis of some European States is found in J Blosma, *Mens Rea and Defences in European Criminal Law* (2012) 483. For the Law Commission's review of this area, see the LCDP and the preceding LCSP, in particular, the supplementary materials available at https://consult.justice.gov.uk/law-commission/insanity-and-automatism/user_uploads/insanity_scoping_supplementary.pdf-1. The CPS provides guidance on prosecuting people with a mental disorder: www.cps.gov.uk/legal-guidance/mental-health-suspects-and-defendants-mental-health-conditions-or-disorders.

Although rarely raised in a magistrates' court, it applies in a summary trial as well as a trial on indictment.[102] The rules governing the plea of insanity derive from the common law, but in trials on indictment the procedure for dealing with the plea has been regulated by statute; the unamended common law operates in magistrates' courts.[103] Historically, a successful plea of insanity at a trial on indictment resulted in a mandatory order that D be admitted to a special hospital where he might be detained indefinitely. That was a significant deterrent to raising the plea. Since the 1991 Act,[104] a verdict of not guilty by reason of insanity means that the judge has more discretion in the disposal and can order hospitalization, a supervision order or an absolute discharge. Statistics suggest that this may be leading to more frequent reliance on the defence.[105]

9.2.2.1 Operation of the insanity defence

As a preliminary point it is worth emphasizing that legal and psychiatric understandings of 'insanity' are completely different.[106] Strangely, the fact that D suffers an extreme mental illness recognized by psychiatrists will not necessarily be sufficient to afford a defence in law. Conversely, the fact that D suffers an illness that no psychiatrist would normally regard as a form of 'insanity' (eg diabetes) may qualify him for the defence.[107] It seems astonishing that in the twenty-first century the law remains based not on any medical understanding of mental illness but on a distinct legal criterion of responsibility defined by the common law and set out in authoritative form in the 'M'Naghten Rules', formulated by judges as long ago as 1843.[108] Daniel M'Naghten, intending to murder Sir Robert Peel, killed Peel's secretary by mistake. His acquittal of murder[109] on the ground of insanity provoked controversy and was debated in the legislative chamber of the House of Lords, which sought the advice of the judges and submitted to them a number of questions.[110] The answers to those questions became the famous 'Rules'. Answers to hypothetical questions, even by all the judges, are not, strictly speaking, a source of law; but in *Sullivan*[111] it was accepted by the judicial committee of the House of Lords that the Rules have provided a comprehensive definition since 1843.[112] The M'Naghten Rules are binding law.

The importance of the Rules reduced greatly on the introduction of the defence of diminished responsibility and the abolition of the death penalty. Diminished responsibility is a (partial) defence only to murder. Insanity pleas remain rare, even on charges for murder (see Ch 13). Defendants seemingly prefer to risk conviction rather than incur the stigma

---

[102] See *R (Singh) v Stratford MC* [2007] EWHC 1582 (Admin).

[103] *Horseferry Road Magistrates' Court, ex p K* [1996] 2 Cr App R 574. See T Ward, 'Magistrates, Insanity and the Common Law' [1997] Crim LR 796.

[104] As amended by the Domestic Violence, Crime and Victims Act 2004.

[105] See RD Mackay, 'Ten More Years of the Insanity Defence' [2012] Crim LR 946, noting that there has been a gradual increase in the number of special verdicts returned but that it may now be plateauing and referring to Mackay's earlier empirical work; A Ashworth and L Zedner, *Preventive Justice* (2014) 209–14.

[106] For an analysis of the historical interaction between the two, see A Loughnan and T Ward, 'Emergent Authority and Expert Knowledge: Psychiatry and Criminal Responsibility in the UK' (2014) 37 Int'l J L & Psychiatry 25.

[107] See Ch 3 of the Law Commission supplementary materials to LCSP.

[108] (1843) 4 St Tr NS 847. For an engaging historical analysis of the case, see A Loughnan, 'M'Naghten's Case' in P Handler, H Mares and I Williams (eds), *Landmark Cases in Criminal Law* (2017).

[109] (1843) 10 Cl & Fin 200.

[110] On which judges signed the opinion see RD Mackay, 'The M'Naghten Rules—A Brief Historical Note' [2019] Crim LR 966.

[111] *Sullivan* [1983] 2 All ER 673 at 676.

[112] In *Johnson* [2007] EWCA Crim 1978 the Court of Appeal referred enigmatically to the fact that the Rules must, given their provenance, be treated with 'some caution'.

of a verdict of not guilty by reason of insanity. This remains true even though, since 1991, the disposal powers are not limited to automatic indefinite detention. But the stigma of the label 'insanity' remains: it is strikingly inappropriate when so much progress has been made regarding public attitudes to mental illness.

In some cases defendants will even prefer to plead guilty rather than risk a special verdict on grounds of insanity. The propriety of accepting a plea of guilty by a person who, on the evidence, is not guilty is open to question, but it has not been challenged in the Court of Appeal and the House of Lords left the matter open. It is unsatisfactory that the state of the law is such that people suffering from a mental condition feel compelled to plead guilty. One undesirable consequence is the disproportionately high number of inmates in prison with mental disorders, at least some of whom might satisfy a suitably reformed modern insanity defence.[113]

9.2.2.2 The test of insanity

Whatever the effect of the recent changes on procedure and disposal, the M'Naghten Rules remain of great importance symbolically and practically both because they provide the legal test of responsibility of the mentally abnormal and because they set a limit to the defences of automatism and, in theory, of diminished responsibility. The basic propositions of the law are to be found in the answers to Questions 2 and 3 of the M'Naghten Rules:[114]

the jurors ought to be told in all cases that every man is presumed to be sane, and to possess a sufficient degree of reason to be responsible for his crimes, until the contrary be proved to their satisfaction; and that to establish a defence on the ground of insanity, it must be clearly proved that, at the time of the committing of the act, the party accused was labouring under such a defect of reason, from disease of the mind, as not to know the nature and quality of the act he was doing, or, if he did know it, that he did not know he was doing what was wrong.

It will be seen that there are two lines of defence open to an accused person (often called the 'two limbs'):

(1) he must be found not guilty by reason of insanity if, because of a disease of the mind, he did not know the nature and quality of his act (effectively a denial of mens rea); or

(2) even if he did know the nature and quality of his act, he must be acquitted if, because of a disease of the mind, he did not know it was 'wrong'.

The Rules have been heavily criticized for being over-inclusive; 'disease of the mind' has been widely construed to include within the scope of insanity such commonplace illnesses as diabetes.[115] In addition, in some instances D qualifies for the defence even though he was responsible for his inability to appreciate the nature or wrongness of his actions. As Mackay has pointed out, some commentators have argued that the first limb is superfluous as anyone who did not know the nature and quality of the act must also not have known it was wrong.[116] Others, including Glanville Williams, argued that the second limb was superfluous since anyone who did not know the nature and quality of his act must also have lacked awareness that it was wrong.[117] The Rules are also criticized for focus on the cognitive state

---

[113] See in particular Lord Bradley's report, *People with Mental Health Problems or Learning Disabilities in the Criminal Justice System* (2009).

[114] 10 Cl & Fin at 210 per Lord Tindal CJ. R Moran, *Knowing Right From Wrong: The Insanity Defence of Daniel McNaghten* (1981).

[115] See LCSP, Chs 2–4 and LCDP, Ch 2.

[116] RD Mackay, '"Nature", "Quality" and *Mens Rea*—Some Observations on "Defect of Reason" and the First Limb of the *M'Naghten* Rules' [2020] Crim LR 588 arguing for a wider interpretation of limb 1.

[117] See RD Mackay, 'Righting the Wrong? Some Observations on the Second Limb of the M'Naghten Rules' [2009] Crim LR 80.

of D (has he appreciated the nature or wrongness) rather than on whether D had the *capacity* to be held responsible or to conform with criminal regulation.[118]

Disease of the mind

The two limbs of the Rule require separate consideration but the prior question, under either limb, is whether D was suffering from 'a defect of reason from a disease of the mind'. If D was unaware of the nature and quality of his act for some reason *other than* a defect of reason from a disease of the mind (eg mistake), he will usually be entitled to a straightforward acquittal on the ground that he lacked the necessary mens rea. Moreover, in such a case the onus of proof remains on the Crown, whereas it rests on D if he tenders evidence of a defect of reason arising from disease of the mind.[119] If D was unaware that his act was 'wrong' for some reason other than from a defect of reason from a disease of the mind, this will generally not amount to a defence at all. It is a cardinal principle that neither ignorance of the law[120] nor good motive will normally afford a defence.

The question whether D has raised the defence of insanity is one of law for the judge.[121] Whether D, or indeed his medical witnesses, would call the condition on which he relies 'insanity' is immaterial. The expert witnesses may testify as to the factual nature of the condition but it is for the judge to say whether that is evidence of 'a defect of reason, from disease of the mind', because, as will become apparent, these are legal, not medical, concepts. In the leading case of *Sullivan*,[122] the defence to a charge of assault occasioning actual bodily harm was that D attacked V while recovering from a minor epileptic seizure and did not know what he was doing. The House of Lords held that the judge had rightly ruled that this raised the defence of insanity. D had then changed his plea to guilty, notwithstanding that he was thereby pleading guilty to an offence for which he was manifestly not responsible. However, his conviction was upheld.

It seems that any disease which produces a malfunctioning of the mind is a disease of the mind.[123] Commonly the insanity plea will involve mental illness (schizophrenia being the most common basis)[124] but it is not restricted to diseases of the brain. Arteriosclerosis, a tumour on the brain, epilepsy, diabetes, sleepwalking, pre-menstrual syndrome and all physical diseases, may amount in law to a disease of the mind if they produce the relevant malfunction. The lack of correlation with medical definitions of mental illness renders this aspect of the test potentially incompatible with the ECHR (see later) where it results in D's loss of liberty or loss of private life.

Although the courts have adopted a very wide definition of disease of the mind, it is not without limit, as has been illustrated. In *Coley*,[125] D had probably suffered a psychotic

---

[118] See Tadros, *Criminal Responsibility*, Ch 12; A Brudner, *Punishment and Freedom: A Liberal Theory of Penal Justice* (2009). See also LCDP, Ch 2 and the supplementary materials to the LCSP available from the Law Commission website.

[119] The application of the burden of proof in these cases is critically explored by T Jones, 'Insanity, Automatism and the Burden of Proof on the Accused' (1995) 111 LQR 475; A Loughnan, 'Manifest Madness' (2007) 70 MLR 379, 398. It is surprising that there has not been a direct ECtHR challenge on this basis other than in 1990 in *H v UK* (App no 15023/89) in which the Commission dismissed the application. That decision has been very heavily criticized: see Jones, ibid. See also the discussion in LCDP, Ch 8 for a full discussion of the issues and a proposal to place the ultimate burden for the reformed defence on the Crown.

[120] cf the challenge by A Ashworth, 'Ignorance of the Law, and Duties to Avoid It' (2011) 74 MLR 1.

[121] See *Roach* [2001] EWCA Crim 2698.   [122] [1984] AC 156.

[123] *Kemp* [1957] 1 QB 399 at 406 per Devlin J, approved by Lord Denning in *Bratty*, n 135.

[124] See Mackay, Mitchell and Howe [2006] Crim LR 399.

[125] [2013] EWCA Crim 223. Also discussed in A Loughnan and N Wake, 'Of Blurred Boundaries and Prior Fault: Insanity, Automatism and Intoxication' in A Reed and M Bohlander (with N Wake and E Smith) (eds), *General Defences in Criminal Law—Domestic and Comparative Perspectives* (2014) 118–19 and 124.

episode following consumption of strong cannabis. D attacked his neighbour with a hunting knife (D had dressed in combat gear and wore a balaclava). It was suggested that he might have been acting out the role of a character in a computer game. He claimed to have 'blacked out'. The trial judge refused to leave the defence of insanity to the jury and that view was endorsed by the Court of Appeal. This was a case of voluntary intoxication and not a disease of the mind amounting to insanity. Hughes LJ said:

> The precise line between the law of voluntary intoxication and the law of insanity may . . . be difficult to identify in some borderline cases. But the present case falls comfortably on the side of the line covered by voluntary intoxication. . . . If the doctors were right about his state of mind, his mind was to an extent detached from reality by the direct and acute effects on it of the ingestion of cannabis. Every intoxicated person has his mind affected, and to an extent disordered, by the direct and acute effects of the ingestion of intoxicants; all intoxication operates through the brain. Not infrequently it would be perfectly legitimate to say of a very drunken man that his mind had become detached from reality by the intoxication . . . In order to engage the law of insanity, it is not enough that there is an effect on the mind, or, in the language of the *M'Naghten* rules, a 'defect of reason'. There must also be what the law classifies as a disease of the mind.[126]

In contrast, in *Harris*, conjoined with *Coley* on appeal, D was in the habit of binge drinking for several days at a time. Following a period of a week doing so, he took time to sober up before returning to work. After several days he then set fire to his home and was charged with aggravated arson. His defence was not one of intoxication—he was sober at the time of the fire-setting and his plea, if at all,[127] was one of insanity based on the disease of his mind caused by repeated chronic alcohol abuse. His past intoxication had produced a mental disorder—alcoholic psychosis amounting to a disease of the mind.

It is important to reiterate the distinction between pleas of insanity and pleas of sane automatism. A transitory malfunctioning of the mind is not a disease of the mind when it is caused by some external factor—a blow on the head causing concussion, the consumption of alcohol or drugs, or the administration of an anaesthetic. In such cases where there is a total loss of capacity sane automatism may be pleaded (discussed later in the chapter). Sane automatism imposes no burden of proof on D and, if successful, results in a complete acquittal. Insanity, including insane automatism, on the other hand, must be proved by D (on the balance of probabilities) and results in a special verdict of not guilty by reason of insanity. In terms of process and outcome, much turns on this distinction between internal and external causes of the malfunction of the mind, yet the basis for the distinction is unsatisfactory.[128]

In determining whether D suffers from a disease of the mind, it is clear that the law considers not only D's state of mind at the time the alleged offence was committed, but how it came about.[129] Devlin J thought that the object of the inclusion of the words 'disease of the mind' was to exclude 'defects of reason caused simply by brutish stupidity without rational power'; but it seems the words exclude more than that. In *Quick*,[130] D who had caused actual bodily harm called medical evidence to show that he was a diabetic and that he was suffering from a hypoglycaemic attack at the time of the alleged offence and was unaware of what he was doing. Bridge J ruled that he had thereby raised a defence of insanity, whereupon D

---

[126] At [18].

[127] Not on the facts as D clearly knew what he was doing and that it was wrong. Note also the discussion of *Taj*, below p 406.

[128] See LCDP, Ch 6.   [129] Contrary to the *dictum* of Devlin J in *Kemp* [1957] 1 QB 399 at 407.

[130] [1973] QB 910, [1973] Crim LR 434 and commentary; cf *Hennessy*. See p 324 and *Coley* [2013] EWCA Crim 223. See also LC 314, *Intoxication and Criminal Liability* (2009) para 2.88.

pleaded guilty. On appeal it was held that D's mental condition at the time of the offence was caused not by D's diabetes (an internal factor) but by his use of insulin prescribed by the doctor coupled with his failure to follow that prescription by eating after injecting insulin (an external factor). This use of the prescribed drug was an external factor and the plea of sane automatism should have been left to the jury. If D's mental condition had been caused by his diabetes the plea would have been insanity, being based on that internal factor of disease. The case illustrates the fine line between the two pleas although the consequence of pleading them successfully is markedly different.[131] The unsatisfactory nature of this distinction is further discussed in the next section.

Disease of the mind includes *physical* illnesses that manifest themselves by affecting reasoning. In *Kemp*,[132] D made an entirely motiveless and irrational attack on his wife with a hammer. He was charged with causing grievous bodily harm to her with intent. D suffered from arteriosclerosis which caused a congestion of blood in his brain, leading to a temporary lapse of consciousness during which he made the attack. It was conceded that D did not know the nature and quality of his act and that he suffered from a defect of reason but it was argued on his behalf that this arose, not from any mental disease, but from a purely physical one. It was argued that if a physical disease caused the brain cells to degenerate (as in time, it might), then it would be a disease of the mind; but until it did so, it was said, this temporary interference with the working of the brain was like a concussion or something of that sort and not a disease of the mind. Devlin J rejected this argument and held that D was suffering from a disease of the mind. He said:

The law is not concerned with the brain but with the mind, in the sense that 'mind' is ordinarily used, the mental faculties of reason, memory and understanding. If one reads for 'disease of the mind' 'disease of the brain,' it would follow that in many cases pleas of insanity would not be established because it could not be proved that the brain had been affected in any way, either by degeneration of the cells or in any other way. In my judgment the condition of the brain is irrelevant and so is the question of whether the condition of the mind is curable or incurable, transitory or permanent.

In the earlier case of *Charlson*,[133] where the evidence was that D was 'acting as an automaton without any real knowledge of that he was doing' as a result of a cerebral tumour, Barry J directed the jury to acquit if the defence might reasonably be true. Devlin J distinguished *Charlson* on the ground that there the doctors were agreed that D was not suffering from a mental disease.[134] As this is a question of law, the distinction seems unsound and in *Bratty*[135] Lord Denning approved *Kemp* and disagreed with *Charlson*. Lord Denning put forward his own view of a disease of the mind:

it seems to me that any mental disorder which has manifested itself in violence and is prone to recur is a disease of the mind. At any rate it is the sort of disease for which a person should be detained in hospital rather than be given an unqualified acquittal.

Quick casts some doubt on this *dictum*, and it is surely right to do so. The definition might fit a diabetic, but 'no mental hospital would admit a diabetic merely because he had a low blood sugar reaction', and it might be felt to be 'an affront to common sense' to regard such a person as insane. The court itself saw the weakness of the argument, agreeing with Devlin J

---

[131] See *Bingham* [1991] Crim LR 433.   [132] [1957] 1 QB 399 at 407.   [133] [1955] 1 WLR 317.
[134] A similar argument was rejected in *Sullivan* [1983] 2 All ER 673 at 677. The nomenclature adopted by the medical profession may change but the meaning of 'disease of the mind' in the M'Naghten Rules remains unchanged.
[135] *Bratty v A-G for Northern Ireland* [1963] AC 386 at 410–12.

that the disease might be 'curable or incurable . . . transitory or permanent'. Lord Denning's *dictum* has also been rightly criticized on the ground that it is tautologous and that a disease of the mind may manifest itself in wrongful acts other than violence, such as theft.[136] The test of disease of the mind is not one of whether D has a treatable condition.

'External' and 'internal' factors

The distinction between external causes, which may give rise to a defence of sane automatism, and internal factors which can only give rise to a defence of insanity, has been subjected to sustained and cogent criticism.[137] The supposed justification is that the internal factor will usually be a continuing condition which may cause a recurrence of the prohibited conduct, whereas the external factor—the blow on the head, the injection of drugs, the inhalation of toxic fumes,[138] etc—will usually have a transitory effect which will not recur. However, it is surely wrong to assume such a precise correlation between the source of the defect in D's 'mind' and likelihood of recurrence. The blow on the head may inflict permanent damage, which would be viewed thereafter as an internal factor giving rise to a defence of insanity. In cases of diabetes, it can hardly be suggested that there is a greater risk of recurrence from the diabetes itself causing a hyperglycaemic state (insanity) than from D forgetting to eat after taking insulin and going into a hypoglycaemic state (sane automatism). Distinguishing between external and internal causes is an unsatisfactory and deficient way of addressing the true mischief—the likelihood of danger posed by uncontrolled recurrence of the mental condition leading to a lack of capacity. The deficiency is exposed in Lord Lane's judgment in *Burgess*:

if there is a danger of recurrence that may be an added reason for categorising the condition as a disease of the mind. On the other hand, the absence of the danger of recurrence is not a reason for saying that it cannot be a disease of the mind.[139]

The passage serves to emphasize that the underlying bases for the courts' approach are pragmatism and policy rather than principle.

Range of conditions treated in law as 'a disease of the mind'

The concept of disease of the mind in the M'Naghten Rules extends to epileptics,[140] diabetics,[141] pre-menstrual syndrome sufferers,[142] sleepwalkers,[143] etc. It is astonishingly wide. Its application to sleepwalking has prompted interest[144] following first instance decisions

---

[136] N Walker, *Crime and Insanity in England* (1963) 117.

[137] See the dissent by Dickson J in *Rabey* (1981) 114 DLR (3d) 193; RD Mackay, 'Non-Organic Automatism' [1980] Crim LR 350; Williams, TBCL, 671. See LCSP, Chs 2–4 and LCDP, Chs 2 and 6.

[138] *Oakley* (1986) 24 CCC (3d) 351 at 362 per Martin JA.

[139] [1991] WLR 1206, 1212.

[140] *Sullivan* [1984] AC 156. RD Mackay and M Reuber, 'Epilepsy and the Defence of Insanity—Time for a Change' [2007] Crim LR 782.

[141] *Hennessy* [1989] 2 All ER 9; *Coley* [2013] EWCA Crim 223. See on diabetes and driving cases in particular, J Rumbold, 'Diabetes and Criminal Responsibility' (2010) 174 CLJW 21.

[142] *Smith* [1982] Crim LR 531 and see V St John, 'Premenstrual Syndrome in the Criminal Law' [1997] Auckland Uni LR 331; SM Edwards, 'Mad, Bad or Pre-Menstrual' (1988) 138 NLJ 456.

[143] *Burgess* [1991] 2 All ER 769. I Mackay, 'The Sleepwalker is Not Insane' (1992) 55 MLR 714. Cf the Canadian Supreme Court in *Parks* (1990) 95 DLR (4th) 27.

[144] See W Wilson et al, 'Violence, Sleepwalking and the Criminal Law' [2005] Crim LR 601 and 614; RD Mackay and B Mitchell, 'Sleepwalking, Automatism and Insanity' [2006] Crim LR 901 reviewing Canadian law which adopts a more holistic approach to the question rather than relying solely on the internal/external bifurcation. See also LCDP, p 110.

taking a generous approach and allowing a defence of sane automatism to be run.[145] Even if sleepwalking is classified as insanity, a more liberal approach is evident in some cases. For example, in one case D had killed V in the course of his sleepwalking/night terror, and pleaded insanity. The CPS discontinued the case since the result of an insanity verdict would have been hospitalization for D and that was not in the public interest.[146] Pressure has also been mounting for the reclassification of epilepsy to avoid the stigma of being labelled insane.[147]

Most if not all of the reported cases involve apparently purposive conduct. In *Bratty v A-G for Northern Ireland*,[148] D took off a girl's stocking and strangled her with it. There was medical evidence that he was suffering from psychomotor epilepsy which might have prevented him from knowing the nature and quality of his act. It was held to be evidence of insanity. This seems very far removed from a convulsive movement of the body of an epilepsy sufferer. It is a complex operation which has every appearance of being controlled by the brain. Whether or not D could have prevented himself from acting in this way, he appears to be a dangerous person and, in the absence of some other form of protection for the public, a simple verdict of acquittal seems inappropriate. Sullivan's conduct, like that of Kemp, Charlson, Quick and Rabey (see later) also seems to have been apparently purposive and, though he was less obviously a danger to the public than Bratty, his case may be indistinguishable in principle. Even the examples of epilepsy referred to in research into insanity suggest that commonly the actions are complex purposive ones. Of course, a convulsive movement of a person in an epileptic fit may result in injury to person or property but it would seem absurd either to convict the epileptic or hold him to be insane. If insanity is available as a defence for seemingly purposive action, it is not fanciful to suggest, bearing in mind the now increased flexibility of the courts' powers of disposal which will not result in automatic detention in hospital, that some unscrupulous pleas of insanity will be advanced, and the courts need to be alert to that fact.

It remains deeply unsatisfactory for this crucial 'disease of the mind' element to remain so ill-defined. First, a person with a mental condition of a non-severe nature and who poses no real future risk to society might end up labelled and treated as insane. Secondly, a challenge to the overbroad definition of disease of the mind may arise under the ECHR. Article 5(1)(e), in guaranteeing protection against arbitrary detention, allows for the detention of those suffering from mental illness where it is necessary for the protection of the public. The European Court of Human Rights has accepted that the State's power to detain in these circumstances is limited to cases where the mental illness is one recognized by objective medical expertise, and where the medical and legal definitions of mental illness have a close correlation.[149] If a defendant were ever to be detained as a result of a special verdict of insanity when the 'disease' he was suffering from was one which medical professionals would not normally classify as 'insanity', there might be an incompatibility. That may be unlikely as detention is regulated by the Mental Health Act. Although medical professionals are now

---

[145] See *Lowe* (2005) unreported, discussed in Wilson et al, n 144, and *Pooley* (2007) unreported, discussed in Mackay and Mitchell, n 144. See CPS guidance at www.cps.gov.uk/legal-guidance/mental-health-suspects-and-defendants-mental-health-conditions-or-disorders. See also I Ibrahim and P Fenwick, 'Sleep Related Automatism and the Law' (2008) 48 Med Sci Law 124.

[146] See http://news.bbc.co.uk/1/hi/wales/8370363.stm.

[147] See Mackay and Reuber [2007] Crim LR 782.   [148] [1963] AC 386.

[149] *Winterwerp v Netherlands* [1979] 2 EHRR 387, [1994] Crim LR 84; *Luberti v Italy* (1984) 6 EHRR 440; *Reid v UK* (2003) 37 EHRR 9. See P Sutherland and C Gearty, 'Insanity and the ECHR' [1992] Crim LR 418; Baker, n 51; Emmerson, Ashworth and Macdonald, HR&CJ, paras 18.23 et seq. The Law Commission examines the ECHR dimension to the defence in LCSP, Ch 5.

required to be involved in the trial of insanity,[150] it is debatable whether this ensures compatibility.[151] Medical professionals might well, in the course of providing expert evidence, be obliged to state that the disease is one that satisfies the legal test of insanity, but that is quite different from a medical professional recognizing the disease as a matter of psychiatry as one of mental illness.

Borderline cases: disease of mind (insanity) or external factor (sane automatism)?

Some of the most controversial problems on classification arise in relation to 'psychological blows'. Cases in other jurisdictions have addressed directly the question of whether a 'dissociative state' resulting from a 'psychological blow' amounts to insane or sane automatism. In the Canadian case of *Rabey*,[152] D, a student who had become infatuated by a girl, V, discovered that V did not regard him particularly highly and reacted to that news by hitting her on the head with a rock that he had taken from a geology laboratory. He was acquitted of causing bodily harm with intent on the ground of automatism. The trial judge accepted that D was in a dissociative state caused by the psychological blow of his rejection, which, it was held, was an external factor analogous to a blow to the skull where the skull is thin, causing concussion. The Ontario Court of Appeal allowed the prosecution's appeal and ordered a new trial. A further appeal to the Supreme Court of Canada was dismissed. That court approved the judgment of Martin J, who took the view that 'the ordinary stresses and disappointments of life which are the common lot of mankind do not constitute an external cause . . .'[153] The exceptional effect which this ordinary event had on D 'must be considered as having its source primarily in the [D's] psychological or emotional make-up'. Notwithstanding the powerful dissent by Dickson J, it is submitted that this is right and that in such a case if the evidence as to D's dissociative state is accepted at all,[154] it should be treated as evidence of insanity. Once the judge has so categorized the defence, D has the burden of proving on a balance of probabilities that he was in a dissociative state. If he and his medical witnesses are to be believed, he was not guilty, but he is a highly dangerous person.[155] Who is to say that the next ordinary stress of life will not lead him unconsciously to wield a deadly weapon? Policy clearly has a significant part to play here.

Martin J left open the question of the effect of an extraordinary event of such severity that it might reasonably be expected to cause a dissociative state in the average person. This would, it is submitted, be a case of sane automatism because D has done nothing to show that he is any more dangerous to others than anyone else; and he should be simply acquitted. It is, of course, difficult to identify what should constitute such a degree of extraordinariness. In *T*,[156] where the defendant had committed a robbery when suffering from

---

[150] By s 1 of the 1991 Act, a jury shall not return a special verdict of not guilty by reason of insanity (NGRI) except on the written or oral evidence of two or more registered medical practitioners of whom at least one is approved by the Home Secretary as having special experience in the field of mental disorder.

[151] In addition, Mackay, Mitchell and Howe [2006] Crim LR 399 identify cases in which NGRI verdicts have been returned without medical evidence.

[152] (1977) 37 CCC (2d) 461; affd [1980] SCR 513, 54 CCC (2d) 1. See also *Parnerkar* [1974] SCR 449, 10 CCC (2d) 253 and cases discussed by Mackay [1980] Crim LR 350.

[153] (1980) 54 CCC (2d) at 7.

[154] cf the scepticism of Williams about the acceptance of the evidence of 'over enthusiastic psychiatrists' in relation to the similar case of *Parnerkar* [1974] SCR 449, 10 CCC (2d) 253; Williams, TBCL (1st edn) 612–13. See LCDP, pp 107 et seq suggesting that the concern is really whether a person of reasonable fortitude might have withstood the trauma.

[155] In fact, D's expert witness said D had no predisposition to dissociate; but the court, while bound to take account of medical evidence, may also take account of the facts of the case and apply its common sense to all the evidence.

[156] [1990] Crim LR 256. And see *Huckerby* [2004] EWCA Crim 3251.

post-traumatic stress disorder as a result of having been recently raped, the trial judge ruled that the rape was to be treated as an external factor. It would be uncontroversial to regard the rape as an extraordinary event, but it is unclear which if any other traumatic events will suffice. Further judicial clarification of the scope of this exceptional category of sane automatism would be welcome.

In *Coley*, Hughes LJ remarked that the distinction between 'external factors inducing a condition of the mind and internal factors which can properly be described as a disease can give rise to apparently strange results at the margin'.[157] Despite the recognition that the distinction may be difficult to draw in some cases, it was ultimately confirmed that it is crucial given the different outcomes it dictates. The law is in urgent need of reform.

Defect of reason

For the insanity defence to apply, the disease of the mind must have given rise to a 'defect of reason'. It seems that D's powers of reasoning must be impaired and that D's mere failure to use powers of reasoning which he possesses does not bring him within the M'Naghten Rules. When D claimed that she had taken articles from a supermarket without paying for them because of absent-mindedness resulting from depression, it was held that even if she was suffering from a disease of the mind (which is arguable), she had not raised the defence of insanity but was simply denying that she had mens rea.[158] Tadros has suggested that this element of the defence warrants closer attention, since it could help to identify those who are morally responsible for failing to recognize either the nature and quality or wrongness of their act. This element should cause the courts to focus on whether there was a diminution of D's reasoning powers.

The nature and quality of his act: the 'first limb'

The phrase 'nature and quality of his act' refers to the physical nature and quality of the act and not to its moral or legal quality.[159] In modern terms, it means simply that D 'did not know what he was doing'.[160] It is of narrow application; illustrations given by leading writers are:

A kills B under an insane delusion that he is breaking a jar.[161]

and

the madman who cut a woman's throat under the idea that he was cutting a loaf of bread.[162]

Of course, a person who was under a delusion such as these, apart altogether from insanity, could never be convicted of murder, simply because he had no mens rea. The important practical difference, however, is that if the delusion arose from a disease of the mind, he will be liable to be indefinitely detained in a hospital,[163] whereas if it arose from some other

---

[157] [2013] EWCA Crim 223, [20].

[158] *Clarke* [1972] 1 All ER 219. For discussion see Tadros, *Criminal Responsibility*, 333.

[159] *Codère* (1916) 12 Cr App R 21; see *Johnson* [2007] EWCA Crim 1978. For cogent criticism see Mackay [2009] Crim LR 80 and '"Nature", "Quality" and *Mens Rea*—Some Observations on "Defect of Reason" and the First Limb of the *M'Naghten* Rules' [2020] Crim LR 588; cf J Child, H Crombag and GR Sullivan, 'Defending the Delusional, the Irrational, and the Dangerous' [2020] Crim LR 306.

[160] *Sullivan* [1983] 2 All ER 673 at 678.

[161] Stephen, *Digest* (8th edn) 6. On the difficulties in defining delusional, see also the discussion of *Taj* later, p 406.

[162] Kenny, *Outlines*, 76.

[163] The disposal powers for those found not guilty by reason of insanity in cases of murder are limited.

cause, he will go entirely free. A person whose acts are involuntary because he is unconscious does not 'know the nature and quality of his act'.[164]

Those who advocate abolition[165] of the defence of insanity suggest that the ability to plead
absence of mens rea can deal with those lacking mental responsibility. The approach has
been adopted in some US states, but has been criticized. The Law Commission rejected such
an approach after careful examination.[166] Such an approach distorts the mens rea test to
accommodate 'cases where the accused suffered from a mental disorder but could still form
a mental element for specific offences'.[167] Abolishing insanity and relying on the question
of mens rea also fails to accommodate the cases where D's mental illness led him to believe
that he had a defence, and those for whom mens rea is present because of the mental illness.

Insanity may be pleaded in respect of an offence irrespective of whether it is an offence of
mens rea. This was confirmed by the Divisional Court in *Loake v CPS*, which is discussed
later.[168]

Knowledge that the act is 'wrong': the 'second limb'

This second, alternative limb is not concerned with whether the accused is able to distinguish between right and wrong in general, but whether he was able to appreciate the wrongness of the particular act he was doing at the particular time alleged to constitute a crime. It
has always been clear that if D knew his act was contrary to law, he knew it was 'wrong' for
this purpose. Thus, in their first answer the judges in *M'Naghten*'s case said:[169]

notwithstanding the party accused did the act complained of with a view, under the influence of
insane delusion, of redressing or revenging some supposed grievance or injury, or of producing
some public benefit, he is nevertheless punishable, according to the nature of the crime committed, if he knew at the time of committing such crime that he was acting contrary to law; by which
expression we understand your lordships to mean the law of the land.

Even if D did not know his act was contrary to law, he was still liable if he knew that it was
wrong 'according to the ordinary standard adopted by reasonable men'.[170] The fact that
D thought his act was right was irrelevant if he knew that people generally considered it
wrong. This again seems to be supported by the M'Naghten Rules:[171]

If the question were to be put as to the knowledge of the accused solely and exclusively with reference to the law of the land, it might tend to confound the jury, by inducing them to believe that
an actual knowledge of the law of the land was essential to lead to a conviction: whereas the law is
administered upon the principle that everyone must be taken conclusively to know it, without proof
that he does know it. If the accused was conscious that the act was one which he ought not to do, and
if that act was at the same time contrary to the law of the land, he is punishable.

Modern cases, however, suggest that the courts are concerned only with D's knowledge of
legal, not moral, wrongness. In *Windle*,[172] D was unhappily married to a woman, V, who
was always speaking of committing suicide and who, according to medical evidence at
the trial, was certifiably insane. D killed V by the administration of 100 aspirins. He then
gave himself up to the police, saying, 'I suppose they will hang me for this'. A medical
witness for the defence said that D was suffering from a form of communicated insanity

---

[164] *Sullivan* [1983] 2 All ER 673 at 678.

[165] eg N Morris, 'The Criminal Responsibility of the Mentally Ill' (1982) 33 Syracuse LR 477.

[166] See LCDP, Ch 2 and Appendix A.   [167] Scottish Law Commission Report, para 2.16.

[168] [2017] EWHC 2855 (Admin).   [169] (1843) 10 Cl & Fin 200 at 209.

[170] *Codère* (1916) 12 Cr App R 21 at 27.   [171] (1843) 10 Cl & Fin 200 at 210.

[172] [1952] 2 QB 826. See J Manwaring, '*Windle* Revisited' [2018] Crim LR 987.

known as *folie à deux*. Rebutting medical evidence was called, but the doctors on both sides agreed that he knew he was doing an act which the law forbade. Devlin J thereupon withdrew the issue from the jury. That aspect of the case accords perfectly with the law as stated previously but, in the Court of Criminal Appeal, Lord Goddard CJ, in upholding the conviction, said:[173]

Courts of law can only distinguish between that which is in accordance with the law and that which is contrary to law. . . . The law cannot embark on the question and it would be an unfortunate thing if it were left to juries to consider whether some particular act was morally right or wrong. The test must be whether it is contrary to law. . . .

In the opinion of the court there is no doubt that in the M'Naghten Rules 'wrong' means contrary to law and not 'wrong' according to the opinion of one man or of a number of people on the question whether a particular act might or might not be justified.

Windle is in accordance with authority in rejecting the arguments of the defence that D should be acquitted if, knowing his act to be against the law, he also believed it to be morally right. In the Court of Appeal in *Johnson*,[174] it was confirmed that 'wrong' means only 'wrong' according to law. If D appreciates that his conduct is wrong according to law, he cannot rely on insanity. In practice it seems that juries commonly accept the defence in such cases.[175] There have been many calls for a wider reading of this limb.[176]

The High Court of Australia has refused to follow *Windle*. In *Stapleton v R*,[177] it made a detailed examination of the English law before and after *M'Naghten* and came to the conclusion that *Windle* was wrongly decided. The court's view was that if D believed his act to be right according to the ordinary standard of reasonable people, he was entitled to be acquitted even if he knew it to be legally wrong. This would extend the scope of the defence, not only beyond what was laid down in *Windle*, but beyond what the law was believed to be before that case. While such an extension of the law may be desirable, it is difficult to reconcile with the M'Naghten Rules and to justify on the authorities.[178] In *Johnson*, the court discussed *Stapleton* and rejected that approach.[179] It is not followed by the courts in England.[180] Should the defence be available where D kills a prostitute, knowing that to do so is murder, but believing that 'it is morally right to rid the streets of such women'?[181] The New Zealand Law Commission has questioned why this limb is needed or justified at all. It commented, in its 2010 report, 'it is still not clear why incapacity to reason *morally* is necessarily the right test for determining when it is not proper to hold the person responsible'.[182]

---

[173] ibid at 833, 834.

[174] [2007] EWCA Crim 1978. See RD Mackay [2009] Crim LR 79, for a valuable review.

[175] See Mackay and Kearns [1999] Crim LR 714 at 722.

[176] See recently, Child et al [2020] Crim LR 306.

[177] (1953) 86 CLR 358; see also *Weise* [1969] VR 953, especially at 960 et seq per Barry J. See also *Chaulk* [1990] 3 SCR 1303; *Oomen* [2004] 2 SCR 507. See generally for a comparative review S Yeo, 'The Insanity Defence in the Criminal Law of the Commonwealth Nations' [2008] Sing JLS 241.

[178] *Stapleton v R* is discussed in a note by N Morris, '"Wrong" in the M'Naghten Rules' (1953) 16 MLR 435, which is criticized by J Montrose, 'The M'Naghten Rules' (1954) 17 MLR 383.

[179] Referring with approval to this para in the 11th edn.

[180] See LCSP, paras 4.67–4.74. For criticism of *Stapleton* see also the New Zealand Law Commission in *Mental Impairment Decision-Making and the Insanity Defence*, R120 (2010) para 5.6.

[181] cf *Peter Sutcliffe* (1981) 30 Apr, CCC. See A Norrie, *Crime, Reason and History* (3rd edn, 2014) 267–8; cf Tadros, *Criminal Responsibility*, 326.

[182] *Mental Impairment Decision-Making and the Insanity Defence*, R120 (2010) para 5.8 (emphasis in original).

Insane delusions and insanity

Whereas the defence of insanity is excessively broad in defining diseases of the mind, it is unsatisfactorily narrow in respect of what constitutes a sufficient awareness of wrongdoing. The judges were asked in *M'Naghten*'s case:

If a person under an insane delusion as to existing facts commits an offence in consequence thereof, is he thereby excused?

They replied:[183]

the answer must, of course, depend on the nature of the delusion: but making the same assumption as we did before, namely, that he labours under such partial delusion only, and is not in other respects insane, we think he must be considered in the same situation as to responsibility as if the facts with respect to which the delusion exists were real. For example, if under the influence of his delusion he supposes another man to be in the act of attempting to take away his life, and he kills that man, as he supposes, in self-defence, he would be exempt from punishment. If his delusion was that the deceased had inflicted a serious injury to his character and fortune, and he killed him in revenge for such supposed injury, he would be liable to punishment.

This seems to add nothing to the earlier answers. The insane delusions that the judges had in mind seem to have been factual errors of the kind which prevent a person from knowing the nature and quality of his act or knowing it is wrong.[184] The example given seems to fall within those Rules.

Some caution is necessary with the proposition that the responsibility of the insane person 'must be considered in the same situation . . . as if the facts with respect to which the delusion exists were real'. It should always be remembered that there must be an actus reus, accompanied by the appropriate mens rea, for a conviction. Suppose that D strangles his wife's poodle under the insane delusion that it is her illegitimate child. If the supposed facts were real he would be guilty of murder—but that is plainly impossible as there is no actus reus.[185] In respect of the dog there is no crime because there was no mens rea (for a cruelty to animals or criminal damage offence). The Rule seems merely to emphasize that delusions which do not prevent D from having mens rea will afford no defence. As Lord Hewart CJ rather crudely put it, 'the mere fact that a man thinks he is John the Baptist does not entitle him to shoot his mother'. A case often discussed is that of a man who is under the insane delusion that he is obeying a divine command. Some US courts have held that such a belief affords a defence. Yet if the accused knows that his act is forbidden by law, it seems clear he is liable. Stephen certainly thought that this was so:

My own opinion is that if a special divine order were given to a man to commit murder, I should certainly hang him for it, unless I got a special divine order not to hang him.[186]

Irresistible impulse

It is recognized by psychiatrists that a person may know the nature and quality of an act, may even know that it is wrong and yet perform it under an impulse that is almost or quite uncontrollable. Such a person has no defence under the M'Naghten Rules. The matter was

---

[183] (1843) 10 Cl & Fin 200 at 211.

[184] For discussion of delusions that impact on beliefs about the existence of circumstances which would give rise to a defence (eg self defence) see Child et al [2020] Crim LR 306.

[185] Nor, notwithstanding *Shivpuri*, p 515 should an insane delusion entail liability for an attempt.

[186] II HCL, 160 fn 1. In some jurisdictions statutory reformulations have expanded the defence to accommodate decisions. See eg *Phillip v The Queen* [2007] UKPC 31.

considered in *Kopsch*:[187] D, according to his own admission, killed his uncle's wife. He said that he strangled her with his tie at her own request. (If this was an insane delusion, it would not, of course, afford a defence under the Rules stated earlier.) There was evidence that he had acted under the direction of his subconscious mind. Counsel argued that the judge should have directed the jury that a person under an impulse which he cannot control is not criminally responsible. This was described by Lord Hewart CJ as a 'fantastic theory . . . which if it were to become part of our criminal law, would be merely subversive'.[188]

The judges have steadily opposed acknowledging such a defence on the ground of the difficulty—or impossibility—of distinguishing between an impulse which proves irresist-ible because of insanity and one which is irresistible because of ordinary motives of greed, jealousy or revenge. The view has also been expressed that the harder an impulse is to resist, the greater is the need for a deterrent.[189]

English law does not recognize irresistible impulse even as a symptom from which a jury might deduce insanity within the meaning of the Rules.[190] If, however, medical evidence were tendered in a particular case that the uncontrollable impulse, to which the accused in that case had allegedly been subject, was a symptom that he did not know his act was wrong, it would be open to the jury to act on that evidence.[191] But it is not permissible for a judge to make use in one case of medical knowledge which he may have acquired from the evidence in another, in his direction to the jury.[192]

Although the M'Naghten Rules remain unaltered, a partial defence of irresistible impulse has now been admitted into the law of murder through the defence of diminished responsibility.[193]

9.2.2.3 Burden of proof

The M'Naghten Rules laid down that:

every man is presumed to be sane, and to possess a sufficient degree of reason to be responsible for his crimes, until the contrary be proved to [the jury's] satisfaction; and that to establish a defence on the ground of insanity, it must be clearly proved, etc.[194]

It seems from these words that the judges were intending to put the burden of proof squarely on the accused, and so it has always been subsequently assumed.[195] Insanity is stated to be the one exception at common law to the rule that it is the duty of the prosecution to prove the accused's guilt in all particulars.[196] He does not have to satisfy that heavy onus of proof beyond reasonable doubt which rests on the prosecution but is entitled to a verdict in his favour if he proves his case on a balance of probabilities, the standard which rests on the claimant in a civil action. If the jury think it is more likely than not that he is insane within the meaning of the Rules, then he is entitled to their verdict.

When, however, consideration is given to what has to be proved to establish insanity under the first limb of the Rules, there is an apparent conflict with the general rule requiring

---

187 (1927) 19 Cr App R 50. See also *True* (1922) 16 Cr App R 164; *Sodeman* [1936] 2 All ER 1138.

188 (1927) 19 Cr App R 50 at 51. See LCDP, paras 4.37 et seq.

189 As a Canadian judge, Riddell J, put it: 'If you cannot resist an impulse in any other way, we will hang a rope in front of your eyes, and perhaps that will help': *Creighton* (1909) 14 CCC 349.

190 *A-G for State of South Australia v Brown* [1960] AC 432.

191 ibid. See also *Sodeman* (1936) 55 CLR 192 at 203.   192 [1960] AC 432 at 449.   193 See Ch 13.

194 (1843) 10 Cl & Fin 200 at 210.

195 *Stokes* (1848) 3 Car & Kir 185; *Layton* (1849) 4 Cox CC 149; *Smith* (1910) 6 Cr App R 19; *Coelho* (1914) 10 Cr App R 210; *Bratty v A-G for Northern Ireland* [1963] AC 386.

196 *Woolmington v DPP* [1935] AC 462, per Viscount Sankey LC at 481.

the prosecution to prove mens rea.[197] This requires proof that the accused had the required mens rea with respect to all those consequences and circumstances of his conduct which constitute the actus reus of the crime with which he is charged (eg that the property he is damaging belongs to another). But, this is a requirement to prove that the accused *did* know the nature and quality of his act—at least in cases where the mens rea of the offence is intention or knowledge. The general rule, therefore, says that the prosecution must prove these facts; the special rule relating to insanity says that the defence must disprove them![198] Williams argued[199] that the only burden on the accused is the 'evidential' one of introducing sufficient evidence to raise a reasonable doubt in the jurors' minds; and that the burden of *proof* is on the prosecution.[200] This solution appears to be the best way of resolving the inconsistency.[201]

This problem does not arise when D's defence takes the form that he did not know that his act was wrong. Here he is setting up the existence of facts which are quite outside the prosecution's case and there is no inconsistency in putting the onus on him. It is very strange that the onus of proof should be on the Crown if the defence is based on the first limb of the Rules and on D if it should be on the second. Yet the authorities[202] seem clearly to establish that the onus in the case of the second limb is on the accused. It is not possible to argue that the courts really meant the evidential burden for they have said very clearly that the burden is one of proof 'on balance of probabilities', the same standard that the claimant in a civil action must satisfy. Whatever may be the position regarding the first limb of the defence then it seems clear that, under the second, the onus is on the accused.

The anomaly is emphasized by the decision of the House of Lords in *Bratty v A-G for Northern Ireland*[203] that, where the defence is sane automatism (ie arising otherwise than through a disease of the mind), the burden of proof is on the prosecution. It is difficult to see why a person whose alleged disability arises from a disease of the mind should be convicted whereas one whose alleged disability arises from some other cause, would, in exactly the same circumstances, be acquitted.[204]

9.2.2.4 The scope of the defence

Historically, Hale[205] thought insanity was a defence only to capital charges but that opinion is no longer tenable. In *Horseferry Road Magistrates' Court, ex p K*,[206] the court accepted the misleading proposition in *Archbold*,[207] relied on by the applicant, that the defence of insanity 'is based on the absence of *mens rea*'.[208] This may be true where D asserts that he did not know the nature and quality of his act, but it is not true where he asserts that he did not know the act was wrong.[209] Awareness of 'wrongness' is not an element in mens rea.

---

[197] For an explanation see *Foye* [2013] EWCA Crim 475 in which Lord Hughes stated at [35]: 'In the case of both insanity and diminished responsibility, the issue depends on the inner workings of the defendant's mind at the time of the offence. It would be a practical impossibility in many cases for the Crown to disprove (beyond reasonable doubt) an assertion that he was insane or suffering from diminished responsibility.' See also *Wilcocks* [2016] EWCA Crim 2043, [2017] Crim LR 706, Ch 13.

[198] See further Jones (1995) 111 LQR 475 for a compelling critique.   [199] CLGP, 165.

[200] See LCDP, Ch 8 for full discussion. In coroners' proceedings insanity has to be disproved to the criminal standard to sustain a verdict of unlawful killing—*R (O'Connor) v HM Coroner for Avon* [2009] EWHC 854 (Admin).

[201] cf, however, *Cottle* [1958] NZLR 999 at 1019 per North J.

[202] *Sodeman v R* [1936] 2 All ER 1138; *Carr-Briant* [1943] KB 607.   [203] [1963] AC 386.

[204] cf The Butler proposals on onus of proof.

[205] I PC, c 4, and Walker, *Crime and Insanity in England*, I, 80; S White (1984) 148 JPN 412 at 419.

[206] See n 103.   [207] 1996 edn, at 17.109.

[208] In *Foye* [2013] EWCA Crim 475, Lord Hughes expressed doubt as to whether insanity is essentially a denial of mens rea. At [31]. See now *Loake v CPS* [2017] EWHC 2855 (Admin).

[209] See also *Moore v The State* [2001] UKPC 4.

It seems that *Ex p K* misled the court in *DPP v H*[210] into holding that the defence does not apply to an offence of strict liability—in that case driving with excess alcohol.

In a welcome decision, *Loake v CPS*,[211] the Administrative Court, after a detailed examination of the law, held that the defence of insanity is not limited to denials of mens rea. L appealed against a decision of the Crown Court upholding her conviction in a magistrates' court for harassment contrary to s 2(1) of the Protection from Harassment Act 1997. L had been accused of sending a very large number of text messages to her husband, from whom she was separated. Before the magistrates and the Crown Court, she relied on the defence of insanity. However, the Crown Court ruled that the defence was not available for the offence of harassment since it was an offence of negligence in effect. The Administrative Court held that the M'Naghten Rules applied to the offence of harassment under s 2(1) of the 1997 Act just as they did to all other criminal offences. Accordingly, the defence of insanity was available to a defendant charged with harassment under s 2(1).[212] As the court noted, if the sole question on which criminal liability turned was whether a reasonable person in possession of the same information as the defendant would think his course of conduct amounted to harassment, that would lead to the conclusion that D would be guilty even if he did not know the nature and quality of his act, and thus was insane under the first limb of the M'Naghten Rules. That would produce startling results. The example given was a person suffering from severe dementia who repeatedly telephoned or texted the same individual, on each occasion believing he was doing so for the first time. Such an individual would not know the nature of his act in that he would not know of the sustained nature of the calls or texts. If the prosecution were right, such a person would be guilty because, viewed objectively, his conduct amounted to harassment. Furthermore, if the prosecution were right, the court observed that the defence of insanity would not apply to any offence with an objective form of mens rea. The court held that the decisions in *DPP v H* and *Ex p K* should not be followed. Both were founded on the inaccurate proposition that the defence of insanity is based on the absence of mens rea. The court confirmed that insanity in fact rests on a broader base than the mere absence of mens rea.[213] We examine the relationship between insanity and other mental condition defences later in this chapter and its relationship with other defences such as self-defence in Ch 10.[214]

9.2.2.5 The special verdict of insanity and the right of appeal

The Trial of Lunatics Act 1883 as amended provides that if it appears to the jury that the defendant 'did the act or made the omission charged but was insane as aforesaid at the time the jury shall return a special verdict that the accused is not guilty by reason of insanity'.[215] In *A-G's Reference (No 3 of 1998)*,[216] it was held that the words 'act' and 'omission' mean the actus reus of the offence.[217] The prosecution do not have to prove mens rea. To require them to do so would be inconsistent with the rule that the onus is on D to prove that he did not know the nature and quality of his act.

A right of appeal to the Court of Appeal and the Supreme Court is provided by s 12 of the Criminal Appeal Act 1968, subject to the same conditions as apply in criminal appeals generally.

---

210 [1997] 1 WLR 1406.   211 [2017] EWHC 2855 (Admin).   212 See [18], [61], [63].

213 At [54]. In doing so, the court agreed with the view expressed in successive editions of this work.

214 See p 406 and *Oye* [2013] EWCA Crim 1725 and *Taj* [2018] EWCA Crim 1743 in particular.

215 In *R* [2013] EWCA Crim 591, the Court of Appeal held that the special verdict constitutes a true acquittal, rather than something lying in between a conviction and an acquittal. This seems to have been assumed in the earlier case of *Smith* [2012] EWCA Crim 2566. Cf *Chinegwundoh* [2015] EWCA Crim 109.

216 [1999] 3 All ER 40.   217 As defined in the 8th edn of this book, at p 28. See p 27.

9.2.2.6 Function of the jury

It has been laid down for defences of both insanity and diminished responsibility that:[218]

it is for the jury and not for medical men [*sic*] of whatever eminence to determine the issue. Unless and until Parliament ordains that this question is to be determined by a panel of medical men [*sic*], it is to a jury, after a proper direction by a judge, that by the law of this country the decision is to be entrusted.

The law regarding insanity, however, is now modified by s 1 of the 1991 Act which provides that a jury shall not return a special verdict of not guilty by reason of insanity except on the written or oral evidence of two or more registered medical practitioners of whom at least one is approved by the Home Secretary as having special experience in the field of mental disorder.[219] The jury may still have to decide between conflicting medical evidence; but if the medical evidence is wholly in favour of a special verdict (or of diminished responsibility) and there is *nothing* in the facts or surrounding circumstances which could lead to a contrary conclusion, then a verdict of guilty (or guilty of murder as the case may be) will be upset.[220] If there are facts which, in the opinion of the court, justify the jury in coming to a conclusion different from that of the experts, their verdict will be upheld.

9.2.3 Proposals for reform of the insanity defence

Almost from the moment of their formulation the Rules have been subjected to vigorous criticism, primarily by doctors, but also by lawyers.[221] The Rules, being based on outdated psychiatric views, are too narrow, it is said, and exclude many persons who ought not to be held responsible. They are concerned only with defects of reason and take no account of emotional or volitional factors whereas modern medical science is unwilling to divide the mind into separate compartments and to consider the intellect apart from the emotions and the will.

There have been numerous attempts to reform the law including a 1923 review by Lord Atkin;[222] the 1953 Royal Commission on Capital Punishment;[223] and the 1978 Butler Committee review with a proposed verdict of 'not guilty on evidence of mental disorder'— 'a mental disorder verdict'. The Draft Criminal Code endorsed that approach[224] subject to including a presumption that the commission of the offence was attributable to the disorder but is rebuttable by proof beyond reasonable doubt. The Code would produce substantial improvements on the present position. It has been suggested, however, that it would still be incompatible with Art 5 of the ECHR.[225]

---

[218] *Matheson* (1958) 42 Cr App R 145; *Bailey* (1961) 66 Cr App R 31n *Sanders* (1991) 93 Cr App R 245,—all cases concerning diminished responsibility—but the same principle surely applies to insanity.

[219] On the true input of the jury in practice, see Mackay, Mitchell and Howe [2006] Crim LR 399.

[220] See *Golds* [2016] UKSC 61 considering *Brennan* [2014] EWCA Crim 2387. See Ch 13, p 586.

[221] S Dell, 'Wanted; An Insanity Defence that Can be Used' [1983] Crim LR 431. For a reappraisal of the defence seeking to explain its operation by reference to lay conceptions of abnormality, see A Loughnan, *Manifest Madness: Mental Incapacity in Criminal Law* (2012). See Mackay [2009] Crim LR 80, and calls for a more fundamental review made by M Hathaway, 'The Moral Significance of the Insanity Defence' (2009) 73 J Crim L 310.

[222] Cmd 2005.   [223] Cmd 8932.

[224] For an alternative approach to reform, see the recent Scottish reform: Criminal Justice and Licensing (Scotland) Act 2010, ss 168–71. For comment see: J Chalmers, 'Section 117 of the Criminal Justice and Licensing (Scotland) Bill: A Dangerous Loophole?' [2009] SCL 1240; E Shaw, 'Psychopaths and Criminal Responsibility' (2009) 13 Edin LR 497; G Maher, 'The New Mental Disorder Defences: Some Comments' [2013] SLT 1. The new Act implements recommendations contained in the Scottish Law Commission's Report No 195, *Insanity and Diminished Responsibility* (2004).

[225] See Horder, APOCL, 164.

9.2.3.1 The Law Commission's latest proposals

In 2012 the Law Commission published a Scoping Paper on Insanity and Automatism designed to elicit some evidence of the scale of the problem the defences pose in practice. The Scoping Paper was supplemented by material exploring the statistics around the use of the defences, the comparative approaches to mental disorder defences and a summary of the previous proposals. The responses to the Scoping Paper suggested that while the academic criticisms of the offence are justified, the defences caused few problems in practice. The Commission subsequently produced a Discussion Paper with provisional conclusions and proposals on reform of the insanity and automatism defences.

The principal proposal is that the common law insanity defence should be abolished and replaced with a new statutory defence where someone is not criminally responsible by reason of a qualifying recognized medical condition.[226] The party seeking to raise the defence would have to adduce expert evidence that at the time of the offence D wholly lacked one of the following capacities in relation to what they are charged with having done: (a) to make a judgement rationally; (b) to understand that they are doing something wrong; or (c) to control their actions. The lack of capacity would have to be due to a qualifying recognized medical condition. Not all recognized medical conditions would qualify for the defence and it would be a matter of law, not medicine, whether the condition qualified.[227] The Commission takes the view that as a matter of policy, not all medical conditions should qualify as 'recognized medical conditions', adopting the view of Hughes LJ that 'there will inevitably be considerations of legal policy which are irrelevant to the business of medical description, classification, and statistical analysis'.[228] Acute intoxication, for example, would not qualify, nor would anti-social personality disorders. The Commission sets out in detail how the new defence would operate with the rules on intoxication.[229]

The Commission proposes that there should be an elevated evidential burden on the accused—to call evidence from two experts—but that once that burden is satisfied, then it should fall to the Crown to disprove that defence.[230] The Commission proposes to retain the requirement for evidence from two experts, but proposes that only one of them need be a medical practitioner.[231]

The new defence would be available in relation to any kind of offence and would result in a new special verdict—'not criminally responsible by reason of a recognised medical condition'. Following this verdict, both the Crown Court and the magistrates' courts would be able to make a hospital order, a supervision order or an absolute discharge, and the Crown Court would be able to make a restriction order.[232] The Commission also recommends a new 'non-penal Youth Supervision Order' for under 18s following a special verdict.[233] Unlike the present law, under the proposals the jury verdict can be dispensed with if the accused is legally represented, no jury could reasonably reach any other verdict and the judge records the reasons for the verdict.[234]

Under the Commission's proposals, the breadth of the new recognized medical condition defence means that the defence of automatism becomes practically redundant. Physical and mental conditions can be dealt with under the new insanity defence. A new statutory defence of automatism (discussed later) would cover the situation where D had been unable

---

[226] Para 4.159.   [227] Para 4.161.   [228] See para 4.162 and *Dowds* [2012] EWCA Crim 281, [30].

[229] See Ch 7. For criticism, see A Loughnan and N Wake, 'Of Blurred Boundaries and Prior Fault: Insanity, Automatism and Intoxication' in A Reed and M Bohlander (with N Wake and E Smith) (eds), *General Defences in Criminal Law—Domestic and Comparative Perspectives* (2014). As the authors acknowledge, however, the Law Commission's terms of reference precluded it from reconsidering the law on intoxication.

[230] Para 4.164.   [231] Paras 4.165 and 7.53.   [232] Para 4.167.   [233] Para 4.168.

[234] Para 7.87.

to control his actions for reasons other than a recognized medical condition, for example in a reflex action case where D swerved to avoid a swarm of bees. The recognized medical condition defence and the automatism defence would be mutually exclusive. If successful, that plea would lead to an acquittal, as now. It is anticipated that very few such cases would come before the courts.[235]

The Commission also calls for a wider review of developmental immaturity as a defence. We consider that aspect of the Report in the next chapter.

9.3 Automatism

A claim by D that his consciousness was so impaired that he was acting in a state of physical involuntariness is a claim of automatism. Someone is an automaton or in a state of automatism where his conscious mind is dissociated from that part of the mind which controls action.[236] This concept—a denial of a voluntary act—has been discussed in Ch 2 in the context of the actus reus.[237]

9.3.1 Distinguishing types of automatism

The approach to automatism can be rather confusing. In reading what follows it is worth having in mind the two basic categories:

- automatism arising from an internal cause from a disease of the mind. This is a plea of insanity (insane automatism), D bears the burden of proof to show he did not know the nature and quality of his act;

- an external cause leading to total loss of control (sane automatism)—D is not guilty on any charge unless D was at fault in inducing that state of automatism.

A person who at the time he is alleged to have committed the offence was in a state of automatism (other than one induced by voluntary intoxication) cannot be guilty of it and the only question is whether he is to be found simply 'not guilty' or 'not guilty by reason of insanity'. The outcome (which is of great importance) depends on how the automatism arose. If it was caused by 'a disease of the mind', the proper verdict is not guilty by reason of insanity subject to the other elements of that defence being met. If it arose from any other cause, the verdict is simply not guilty. But as we have discussed earlier, whether a cause is a 'disease of the mind' is a question of law and that phrase has a wide meaning. Any 'internal factor', mental or physical, causing a malfunctioning of the mind is, in law, a disease of the mind.

Automatism caused by a cerebral tumour or arteriosclerosis, epilepsy or diabetes arises from a disease of the mind. These are all 'internal' to the accused. External factors include concussion, the administration of an anaesthetic or other drug, or hypnosis.[238] In a number

---

235 Para 5.123.   236 Wilson et al [2005] Crim LR 614, 615.

237 See the discussion in LCSP, Chs 2–4 and LCDP, Ch 5. See also the discussion in Scottish law as to whether the defence is one of a denial of mens rea or actus reus (PR Ferguson, 'The Limits of the Automatism Defence' (1991) 36 J Law Soc Scotland 446; I MacDougall 'Automatism—Negation of *Mens Rea*' (1992) 37 J Law Soc Scotland 57; JM Ross, 'A Long Motor Run on a Dark Night: Reconstructing *HMA v Ritchie*' [2010] Edin LR 193).

238 Lord Hughes in *Foye* [2013] EWCA Crim 475 observed that automatism may involve no abnormality of mind at all.

of cases, acts done while sleeping have been treated as sane automatism[239] but it has now been held[240] that they are the product of a disease of the mind and thus insanity.[241]

It will be recalled that the one exception at common law to the rule that the burden of proof is on the prosecution is the defence of insanity. If D claims that he was in a state of automatism because of an internal factor, he is raising the insanity defence and it will be for him to satisfy the jury on the balance of probabilities that this was so; but if he relies on an external factor and lays a proper foundation for the automatism defence, the onus is on the prosecution to satisfy the jury beyond reasonable doubt that it was not so.[242] If he alleges[243] that his condition was due to the administration of insulin (an external factor) inducing hypoglycaemia (too little blood sugar), he will be acquitted unless the prosecution can disprove his claim.[244] In contrast, if he alleges that it was due to diabetes (an internal factor) causing hyperglycaemia (excessive blood sugar), the onus will be on him to prove the defence on the balance of probabilities;[245] it must be supported by the evidence of two or more registered medical practitioners;[246] and, if he succeeds, he will be found not guilty by reason of insanity.[247]

A proper foundation for a defence of sane automatism (external cause) may be laid by introducing evidence from which it may reasonably be inferred that the act was involuntary. Whether such a foundation has been laid is a question of law. Lord Denning has said that D's own word will rarely be sufficient,[248] unless it is supported by medical evidence. The difficult questions that arise where there is evidence that the automatism was caused partly by a disease of the mind and partly by other factors are considered later.[249] This basic distinction between internal and external factors has recently been subdivided further by the Law Commission.

(1) Insane automatism arising from a 'disease of the mind' (eg epilepsy). If successful, this results in a special verdict of insanity. This is a plea of insanity and is discussed in full earlier. The other elements of the defence of insanity must also be present.[250]

(2) Automatism arising from an internal malfunctioning of the body which does not constitute a disease of the mind. This should give rise to a defence of sane, not insane,

---

239 *Boshears* (1961) The Times, 8 Feb; *Kemp* (1986) The Times, 3 May: D strangled his wife while experiencing a condition known as 'night terror'. Note that parasomnia caused by self-induced intoxication will not provide a defence of automatism.

240 *Burgess* [1991] 2 QB 92, and see news reports for 21 March 2005 of a killing when sleepwalking which led to an acquittal.

241 The Court of Appeal in *Coley* [2013] EWCA Crim 223 accepted that the distinction between external and internal factors can 'give rise to apparently strange results at the margin' but held that it was nevertheless binding upon the court.

242 See *Roach* [2001] EWCA Crim 2698, p 349.

243 In *De Boise* [2014] EWCA Crim 121, D claimed he was hypoglycaemic at the time he committed the relevant offences. The Court of Appeal rejected this argument on the basis that the expert instructed by D could only state that there was a possibility he was suffering from hypoglycaemia. Elias LJ affirmed that whilst the court does not look for certainty, there must be more than a mere possibility.

244 Assuming he has not acted recklessly as to becoming automaton by failing to follow his prescription, etc.

245 The Court of Appeal in *Coley* [2013] EWCA Crim 223 accepted that the distinction the law draws between these two scenarios is 'arguably unsatisfactory'.

246 Criminal Procedure (Insanity and Unfitness to Plead) Act 1991, p 349.

247 *Hennessy* [1989] 1 WLR 287 (this case was cited with approval by the Court of Appeal in *Coley* [2013] EWCA Crim 223); *Bingham* [1991] Crim LR 433. Cf *Pull* (1998) The Times, 20–1 Mar, discussed later. The distinction in terms of result highlights the unsatisfactorily incoherent nature of the law's categorization of automatism as sane or insane on the basis of its internal/external cause. See the cogent criticism of Wilson et al [2005] Crim LR 614.

248 In *Dervish* [1968] Crim LR 37, *Cook v Atchison* [1968] Crim LR 266 and *Stripp* (1978) 69 Cr App R 318, it was held that D's evidence that he had a 'blackout' was insufficient to raise the defence (see also *C* [2007] EWCA Crim 1862).

249 See p 349.   250 There must also be a 'disease of the mind', see *Sullivan* [1984] AC 156.

automatism. An example given by the Law Commission is of D, who is driving, who experiences a sudden cramp in his leg, causing him to press the accelerator and crash the car. This is not insane automatism because there is no impairment of D's mental functioning and therefore no disease of the mind in the sense adopted in *Sullivan*[251] which could found a defence of insane automatism. This should result in a complete acquittal unless D was at fault in inducing or failing to avoid the loss of control. There do not appear to be any reported cases of such automatism.[252]

(3) Automatism arising from voluntary taking of substances (eg the accused who, having taken insulin, suffers a hypoglycaemic episode). This results in a complete acquittal unless the accused was at fault in inducing or failing to avoid the loss of control (as discussed earlier). If D was at fault, either because he foresaw the likelihood of a loss of control and unreasonably failed to avert it or because he took a drug commonly known to create loss of control, he will be liable for any offences of basic intent charged.[253]

(4) Sane automatism arising from some external physical factor other than D taking substances. A classic example is the accused being stung by a wasp while driving.[254] If successful, this leads to a not guilty verdict for any offence charged.

We have examined the plea of insanity in full earlier and that discussion is relevant to insane automatism. That leaves us to consider the approach the law takes to sane automatism and self-induced automatism.

9.3.2 Sane automatism

It should be noted that where D makes a plea of sane automatism the defence will only succeed if his loss of control was complete; an impaired consciousness is not automatism.[255] This was reiterated by the Court of Appeal in *McGhee*, a case conjoined on appeal with *Coley* in which Hughes LJ stated that there must be a 'complete destruction of voluntary control'.[256] It is not sufficient that D is disinhibited. It was accepted that it is not necessary for D to be unconscious in the sense of being comatose. This is arguably an unduly strict approach.[257] In an indication of how strictly the courts regulate this defence, particularly in relation to diabetic drivers, the Court of Appeal has held, in an interlocutory prosecution appeal, that if D wants to advance a plea of sane automatism, he must provide evidence that:[258] he was totally unable to control his actions (driving) owing to an unforeseen hypoglycaemic attack; he could not reasonably have avoided the attack; and there were no

---

[251] [1984] AC 156.   [252] *Quick* [1973] QB 910, 922.

[253] Basic intent offences are discussed in detail at p 339. For present purposes, it can be equated with those offences for which the predominant mens rea is not intention, knowledge or dishonesty (this includes offences of recklessness, belief, negligence and strict liability).

[254] See Pearson J in *Hill v Baxter* [1958] 1 QB 277, 286; *Kay v Butterworth* (1945) 61 TLR 452, per Humphreys J. These examples are frequently used in the academic literature. See eg HLA Hart, *Punishment and Responsibility* (1968) 96.

[255] *A-G's Reference (No 2 of 1992)* [1994] QB 91. This is not always easy to establish, see *Nelson* [2004] EWCA Crim 333 (reliance on hearsay). The Draft Code would permit the defence in circumstances of impaired consciousness (cl 33).

[256] [2013] EWCA Crim 223, [22].   [257] See Mackay [2013] Crim LR 923.

[258] The mere possibility that D might have been experiencing a hypoglycaemic attack at the time he committed the actus reus of the offence will be insufficient, as the court confirmed in *De Boise* [2014] EWCA Crim 1121. See also J Rumbold and M Wasik, 'Diabetic Drivers, Hypoglycaemic Unawareness and Automatism' [2011] Crim LR 863.

advance warnings of its onset.[259] The narrow approach results in a further distinction from insanity: D may have some control over his actions and yet not know the nature and quality of his act or that it was wrong. He would qualify for insane automatism but not sane automatism subject to the other elements of the defences.

The plea of sane automatism can be made in relation to all offences (subject to what is said in the following section regarding self-induced automatism).

9.3.3 Self-induced sane automatism

Where D's state of automatism arises from his voluntary conduct (usually, ingesting substances), the following rules apply. The automatism plea is, of course, only available if D had a total loss of control.

(1) Where the automatism arises from D's taking a substance in bona fide compliance with his[260] medical prescription, the defence is a complete one to all crimes. For example, D has an adverse reaction to an anaesthetic and hits V. D will be acquitted on charges, whatever they may be, if he had totally lost control.

(2) Where the automatism arises *otherwise than* from D taking a substance in accordance with a medical prescription, if the crime with which D is charged is one of specific intent (discussed at p 333) the defence will result in acquittal. For example, D, a diabetic, takes insulin but ignores his prescription and takes too much, going into a coma. He punches V causing GBH. D will be acquitted on a s 18 charge.

(3) Where the automatism arises from D voluntarily taking a substance otherwise than in accordance with his medical prescription and the crime with which D is charged is one of basic intent (p 336), the automatism plea will fail if the substance ingested was one commonly known to create states of unpredictability or aggression (alcohol, alcohol combined with a drug that normally has soporific effects,[261] heroin, cannabis, cocaine, etc). Thus, D charged with reckless criminal damage will have no success with a defence based on his claim that he was 'completely out of it' and acting involuntarily when he swung his leg out and damaged V's property.

(4) Where the automatism arises from D's taking a substance otherwise than in accordance with his medical prescription and the crime with which D is charged is one of basic intent, and where the substance is not commonly known to create a state of unpredictability or aggression, the defence will result in an acquittal only if in taking the substance D was not subjectively reckless as to the effect it would have.[262] Thus, D who is charged with reckless criminal damage after taking a soporific drug will not succeed in his plea of automatism if he was aware when taking the drug that it posed the risk for him of a state of unpredictability of aggression.

Although the defence of automatism operates to deny the actus reus of the offence, in cases of self-induced automatism the approach is founded on the same policy concerns that underpin the rules relating to the plea of intoxication which, if accepted at all, operates as a denial of mens rea—there is no voluntary conduct element. The court in *Coley*, rejecting D's plea of sane automatism, referred to *Quick* and held that automatism is not available where

---

[259] C [2007] EWCA Crim 1862. See also *JG* [2006] EWCA Crim 1812.

[260] See the odd acceptance of the defence where D took his friend's 'pills' and mixed them with alcohol: *Buck* (2002), discussed by K Roberts (2002) 99 Law Soc Gaz 40.

[261] See *Coley* [2013] EWCA Crim 223.

[262] On the possible interpretations of the recklessness required, see LCDP, pp 127–31.

a defendant has induced an acute state of involuntary behaviour by his own prior fault. Hughes LJ commented:

> We do not, however, think it safe to say that in every case in which automatism is indeed a possible and legitimate conclusion, it should be removed from the jury if they have a decision to make about specific intent. That may particularly be so if the jury is invited to infer intent from the action, which may be a very short-lived action; if the action might indeed have been involuntary, such inference would not be safe and the jury ought in such a case to confront the issue of involuntary automatism before it goes on to intent.[263]

This is a recognition that, having ascertained that D had a total loss of control, it is important next to identify whether the external factor was involuntary or self-induced.

9.3.3.1 Reform of automatism

The Law Commission's provisional proposals for the reform of the automatism defence are to abolish the common law defence and replace it with a statutory defence available in respect of all offences. It would be available where D had a total loss of control other than one arising from a recognized medical condition. If D's loss of capacity to control his actions is due to something he culpably did or failed to do (as provided for by the common law), then the defence of automatism should not be available. The reformed automatism defence would not lead to a special verdict. If successful, this defence would result in a simple acquittal. It would be available in a much narrower set of circumstances than the present law.

9.4 Intoxication

It will come as no surprise to read that the law in this area is heavily policy-based. There is often little by way of principle underpinning the operation of the law. The relationship between intoxication and crime, particularly violent crime and public disorder, needs no elucidation here.[264] The following discussion analyses the three key distinctions drawn by the courts in their application of the plea of intoxication.[265]

(1) Is D's intoxication voluntary or involuntary?

(2) If voluntary, is the crime charged one of specific 'intent' or 'basic' intent?

(3) If basic intent, is the drug involved one of a dangerous nature (is it one known to create states of unpredictability or aggression)?

Before analysing these three issues, it is important to emphasize the general limits on the plea of intoxication. Intoxication is not, and never has been, a 'defence' in itself.[266] It is never a defence for D to say, however convincingly, that but for the drink he would not have behaved as he did.[267] Because alcohol and other drugs weaken the restraints and inhibitions which normally govern our conduct, a person may do things when drunk that he would

---

[263] At [25].   [264] See generally G Dingwall, *Alcohol and Crime* (2005); LC 314, para 1.1.

[265] The focus in this chapter is exclusively on D's intoxication. V's intoxication may affect the substantive law, eg in relation to sexual offences discussed at p 795. See LC 314, *Intoxication and Criminal Liability* (2009). The report provides a useful summary of the current law in Part 2. See for critical comment on the proposals, J Child, 'Drink, Drugs and Law Reform: A Review of Law Commission Report No 314' [2009] Crim LR 488.

[266] See the review by A Simester, 'Intoxication is Never a Defence' [2009] Crim LR 3; LC 314, para 1.15.

[267] *DPP v Beard* [1920] AC 479 at 502–4. This was emphasized in emphatic terms more recently in *Dowds* [2012] EWCA Crim 281.

never dream of doing when sober. This is echoed in the controversial judgment of the Court of Appeal in *Heard*[268] discussed in full later.

9.4.1 Intoxication as a denial of criminal responsibility

Before we examine the three key steps in detail, it is worth considering why intoxication might be relevant to criminal liability. Intoxication impairs a person's perception and judgement so that he may fail to be aware of facts, or to foresee results of his conduct, of which he would certainly have been aware, or have foreseen, if he had been sober.[269] So intoxication may be the reason why the defendant lacked the mens rea of the crime charged. When D relies on evidence of intoxication he does so for the purpose of disputing mens rea. This is its only relevance so far as liability to conviction (as opposed to sentence) is concerned.

It must always be borne in mind when considering intoxication that if D has the mens rea for the crime charged he is guilty. A drunken or drugged intent suffices for a crime of intention; a drunken or drugged awareness of a risk of the prohibited harm will suffice for a crime of recklessness. This is so even though drink or drugs impaired or negatived D's ability to judge between right and wrong or to resist temptation or provocation. It is so even though, in his drunken state, D found the impulse to act as he did irresistible. It is so if the state of intoxication was not self-induced by the accused—as where his drinks are laced. A drunken mens rea is still mens rea.

In many of the cases where intoxication is relevant, the plea, in substance, is one of mistake and the evidence of intoxication is circumstantial evidence that the mistake was made. Two examples quoted by Lord Denning[270] are: (a) where a nurse got so drunk at a christening that she put the baby on the fire in mistake for a log of wood;[271] and (b) where a drunken man thought his friend, lying in bed, was a theatrical dummy and stabbed him to death.[272] Lord Denning said there would be a defence to murder in each of these cases. These mistakes were highly unreasonable and, in the case of a sober person, it would be unlikely that a jury would believe that they might have been made. The relevance of the evidence of intoxication is simply that it makes these mistakes much more credible. Similarly, where D denies that he foresaw some obvious consequence of his action, his intoxicated state makes that more plausible. A denial which would be quite incredible in the case of a sober person may be readily accepted when there is evidence that D was intoxicated.

In *Beard*, it was said that intoxication was a 'defence' only if it rendered D *incapable* of forming the mens rea.[273] This goes too far. Proof of a lack of capacity to form mens rea is of course conclusive that mens rea was not present; but it is now established that it is not necessary to go so far. It is sufficient that D lacked mens rea on that occasion even though he was capable of forming the necessary intent. Equally, an intoxicated person may be capable, notwithstanding his intoxication, of forming the intent to kill and yet not do so. The nurse at the christening was capable of forming the intent to tend the fire, so she was probably capable of forming an intention to kill. The important thing is that she did not do so— and the intoxication was highly relevant to rebut the inference which might otherwise have arisen from her conduct. When, considering the three steps to be discussed, D's mens rea

---

268 [2007] EWCA Crim 125, [2007] Crim LR 654 and commentary.

269 For an analysis of how the modern approach to intoxication emerged at the end of the nineteenth century, see P Handler, 'Intoxication and Criminal Responsibility in England, 1819–1920' (2013) 33 OJLS 243.

270 In *A-G for Northern Ireland v Gallagher* [1963] AC 349 at 381m.

271 (1748) 18 *Gentleman's Magazine* 570; quoted in Kenny, *Outlines*, 29.

272 (1951) The Times, 13 Jan.

273 [1920] AC 479 at 501–2. For further discussion, see P Handler, '*DPP v Beard*' in P Handler, H Mares and I Williams (eds), *Landmark Cases in Criminal Law* (2017).

may be relevant, the correct question is, taking D's intoxicated state into account, did he in fact form the necessary mens rea?[274] The onus of proof—again contrary to certain *dicta* in *Beard*[275]—is clearly on the Crown to establish that, notwithstanding the alleged intoxication, D formed the mens rea.[276]

In *Sheehan*[277] the Court of Appeal stated:

in cases where drunkenness and its possible effect on the defendant's mens rea is in issue, we think that the proper direction to a jury is, first, to warn them that the mere fact that the defendant's mind was affected by drink so that he acted in a way in which he would not have done had he been sober does not assist him at all, provided that the necessary intention was there. A drunken intent is nevertheless an intent. Secondly, and subject to this, the jury should merely be instructed to have regard to all the evidence, including that relating to drink, to draw such inferences as they think proper from the evidence, and on that basis to ask themselves whether they feel sure that at the material time the defendant had the requisite intent.

The direction falls into two parts. The first is a warning to the jury that the mere fact that a defendant's mind was affected by drink does not assist him, provided the necessary intention was present, and that a drunken intent is still an intent. The second limb simply directs the jury to draw such inference as they think proper from the evidence. The reason why the court quashed the defendant's conviction in *Sheehan* was not because of the failure to give the suggested direction; it was because the judge misdirected the jury by telling them to consider whether the defendant was capable or incapable of forming the requisite intent. The true issue they had to consider was whether he did in fact form the requisite intent. The first limb of the test disabuses the jury of any misunderstanding they may have that drunkenness affords a defence. Failure to give such a direction may therefore be *favourable* to the defendant. The second limb of a *Sheehan* direction simply reminds the jury to consider all the evidence, including the defendant's intoxicated state, and to draw whatever inferences they think are proper about intent.

In the recent cases of *Mohamadi*[278] and *Campaneu*,[279] the Court of Appeal again emphasized that the correct question is about whether D formed the mens rea, not whether he was capable of doing so. A *Sheehan* direction is clearly required where there is sufficient evidence to suggest that the defendant was too drunk to know what he was doing and had not formed the necessary intent. In cases such as this, the jury should be reminded that they can only convict the defendant if they are sure that he formed the necessary intent, having regard to all the evidence, including the fact of his being intoxicated.

[274] *Pordage* [1975] Crim LR 575, following *dicta* in *Sheehan* [1975] 2 All ER 960, [1975] Crim LR 339 and commentary, *Cole* [1993] Crim LR 300. To the same effect are *Menniss* [1973] 2 NSWLR 113 and *Kamipeli* [1975] 2 NZLR 610. But cf *Groark* [1999] Crim LR 669.

[275] [1920] AC 479 at 502.

[276] *Sheehan*, n 274. *Bowden* [1993] Crim LR 379. When evidence emerges, whatever its source, of such intoxication as might have prevented D's forming a specific intent the judge must direct the jury on it: *Bennett* [1995] Crim LR 877. Cf *McKinley* [1994] Crim LR 944, where the point was left open. The absence of a *Sheehan* direction seems to be a fertile ground of appeal: see *Golding* [2004] EWCA Crim 858. See LC 314, paras 2.27–2.33. In *White* [2017] NICA 49, Morgan LCJ held that the absence of a *Sheehan* direction in that case did not render D's conviction unsafe. His lordship did emphasize, however, that 'where the evidence does raise an issue about the effect of alcohol on the specific intention necessary for a criminal offence there is an obligation on the court, whether or not the matter is raised by counsel, to ensure that the jury is properly directed in relation to it'. At [22].

[277] *Sheehan* [1975] 2 All ER 960, [1975] Crim LR 339.

[278] [2020] EWCA Crim 327 (16-year-old aiding and abetting rape being present—judge should have taken into account D's age when deciding whether to give *Sheehan* direction).

[279] [2020] EWCA Crim 362 (murder by stabbing pregnant girlfriend after taking cocaine).

In some cases, the courts have taken the unwelcome and, it is submitted, unduly restrictive approach to the question of when an intoxication plea gets off the ground. In *Soolkal and another v The State*,[280] *McKnight*[281] and *Porceddu*,[282] the courts have suggested that D is required to provide specific evidence to show that he was intoxicated and that he lacked mens rea. This burden is not satisfied by evidence that he had consumed so much drink/ drugs that he was intoxicated or by a loss of memory owing to intoxication. The courts are surely imposing too onerous a duty on D. If there is sufficient evidence as to consumption to make a lack of intent a realistic possibility, the direction should be given regardless of the nature of the defendant's defence.[283]

9.4.1.1 What amounts to intoxication?

The principles discussed in this chapter apply whether the intoxication is by alcohol, controlled drugs or other substances. In most cases, it is not in dispute that D was intoxicated, the dispute is as to the effect this had on his capacity. However, greater difficulties arise where D is not affected by the intoxicant at the time of the alleged offence but claims that the effects of earlier intoxication have affected his capacity to form an intent or see a risk, etc.

The orthodox approach to these cases has been to maintain a strict distinction between:

- cases in which D is intoxicated at the time of the offence—if the intoxicant is in his body and continuing to affect capacity: intoxication rules apply;
- cases in which D was previously intoxicated and, although now sober, is affected by the after-effects (eg a paranoid or psychotic state): rules on insanity apply since this is a claim that D is affected by an internal malfunctioning.[284]

The orthodox position was reiterated as recently as 2013 in *Harris*, conjoined on appeal with *Coley*.[285] The judge ruled that D's mental confusion at the time he started the fire (leading to his being charged with arson) was brought about by his previous binge drinking from which he had sobered up at the time of the act. The judge held that the rules on voluntary intoxication applied. The Court of Appeal rejected this argument, because it would represent a major expansion of the law if a mental disorder caused by D's prior fault were to be treated in the same way as drunkenness at the time of the offence.

This orthodox position was called into question by some broad *obiter dicta* in *Taj*.[286] D was convicted of attempted murder having attacked V with a tyre lever on a street in London. D claimed that he believed V to be a terrorist (V was a Muslim electrician, his broken-down car had electrical equipment in it), despite the police having attended the scene and left without concern about V's conduct. It was not in dispute that D had the ability to form an intent at the time of the alleged offence. The cause of his belief was a drug-induced/ drug-and-alcohol-induced paranoid state of mind. D admitted abusing drugs and alcohol from a very young age. He had recently been on a binge of drink and drugs but was sober at the time of the offence. D sought to rely upon self-defence on the basis that the defence is available even if the defendant is mistaken as to the circumstances as he genuinely believed them to be, whether or not the mistake was a reasonable one for him to have made.[287] D claimed that as there was no suggestion that he had alcohol or drugs present in his system at the time, he was not 'intoxicated' and so was not deprived of the defence.

A five-member Court of Appeal dismissed his appeal. Read strictly, the *ratio* of the case is simply that on these facts D was not able to rely on the plea of self-defence since his mistaken

---

280 [1999] 1 WLR 2011.   281 (2000) The Times, 5 May.   282 [2004] EWCA Crim 1043.
283 *Aidad* [2021] EWCA Crime 581.
284 For more sophisticated arguments dealing with whether the earlier voluntary intoxication causes insanity, see later, p 406.
285 [2013] EWCA Crim 223.   286 [2018] EWCA Crim 1743.   287 See later, p 406.

belief 'was attributable to intoxication' within the meaning of s 76(5) of the Criminal Justice and Immigration Act 2008.[288] More controversial are the *obiter* comments of the court about the relationship between intoxication and insanity. The court suggested that D is also unable to rely on self-defence where the mistake state of mind is:

immediately and proximately consequent upon earlier drink or drug-taking, so that even though the person concerned is not drunk or intoxicated at the time, the short-term effects can be shown to have triggered subsequent episodes of *e.g.* paranoia. This is consistent with common law principles. We repeat that this conclusion does not extend to long term mental illness precipitated (perhaps over a considerable period) by alcohol or drug misuse. In the circumstances, we agree with Judge Dodgson, that the phrase 'attributable to intoxication' *is not confined to cases in which alcohol or drugs are still present in a defendant's system. It is unnecessary for us to consider whether this analysis affects the decision in* Harris: it is sufficient to underline that the potential significance of voluntary intoxication in the two cases differs.[289]

If the principles governing intoxication are applicable in such cases, that would generate confusion and further incoherence with the rules on insanity. It is also possible to envisage disputes arising as to whether the ingestion of the intoxicant was sufficiently proximate to the offending. If D's mistaken belief in the need to use force was induced by a mental disorder that was triggered by drink or drug consumption, why should it matter whether it is proximate to the commission of the crime? Further clarification would be required as to what the court means by 'proximate ingestion' and how proximate the ingestion must be to the commission of the offence. Further, if the defendant suffers a psychotic episode triggered by drink or drugs, it is not clear why the court considers proximity to be relevant. The fault exhibited by the defendant is the same irrespective of proximity. The court's analysis also needs to be considered in the light of the recent judgments that have examined the relationship between diminished responsibility and intoxication.[290]

What is sorely needed is a judgment that considers the operation of the prior fault policy in a holistic fashion and analyses whether the distinctions that are presently drawn by the law are rational. It is possible to construct a statutory scheme that deals in a coherent way with intoxication, insanity and automatism and to make the application of those rules turn on whether D was at fault in his behaviour, the so-called 'prior fault approach'.[291] The Law Commission has proposed a workable scheme to that effect. But the present common law rules governing these three pleas should, it is respectfully submitted, respect the orthodox distinction above.[292]

9.4.1.2 Intoxicated mens rea

If D had the mens rea for the crime charged, it makes no difference whether his intoxication was voluntary or involuntary, nor whether the crime was one of specific or basic intent, nor whether the drug was of a dangerous or non-dangerous variety. In *Kingston*,[293] D may have given way to his paedophiliac inclinations only because E had surreptitiously laced his drink with intent that he should do so. D, however, knew what he was doing; he intended

---

[288] See p 403.   [289] At [60] (emphasis added).   [290] See p 574 and *Foy* [2020] EWCA Crim 270.

[291] It has been argued that the courts should reject *Taj* and interpret the insanity defence more permissively, taking account of circumstances and results when assessing D's understanding of his conduct, and taking account of belief in a defence when assessing D's knowledge of wrongfulness and when applying the delusional limb of the M'Naghten Rules. See Child et al [2020] Crim LR 306.

[292] We return later to examine the circumstances in which D's delusional beliefs as to circumstances which would deny him a defence are affected by the decision in *Taj*.

[293] [1994] 3 All ER 353. See J Horder, 'Pleading Involuntary Lack of Capacity' (1993) 52 CLJ 298; R Smith and L Clements, 'Involuntary Intoxication, The Threshold of Inhibition and the Instigation of Crime' (1995) 46 NILQ 210. See LC 314, para 2.75.

to commit a sexual assault on a 15-year-old boy. That was the mens rea of the offence. The judge had rightly directed the jury that a drugged intention is still an intention. The fact that, but for the secretly administered drug, he would not have formed the intent was a matter going only to mitigation of the sentence.[294]

9.4.2 Involuntary intoxication

Where, as a result of involuntary intoxication, D lacks the mens rea of the offence, it is submitted that he must be acquitted. This is so whether the crime charged is one of specific or basic intent. The offence has not been committed and there is absolutely no reason why the law should pretend that it has.[295] On a charge involving an offence of strict liability, the involuntary intoxication will not avail D if he claimed to lack mens rea as to that strict element since there is no mens rea for it to displace. In cases of alleged negligence, in principle, D ought only to be liable if the reasonable person would have acted in the same way had he suffered the effects of the involuntary intoxication.

In *Kingston*, Lord Mustill referred to a number of Scottish decisions to the effect that intoxication negates liability if it is 'based . . . on an inability to form *mens rea* as a result of some external factor which was outwith the accused's control and which he was not bound to foresee'. The *dicta* quoted all required an inability to form the intent. Inability is certainly a conclusive answer; but it is submitted that, whatever the position in Scotland, in England the ultimate question is whether D did form the mens rea and, if he did not—perhaps because he made a drunken mistake of fact—he must be acquitted, even though he was capable of forming the intent. This is the law in those cases where voluntary intoxication may be the basis of a defence to an offence of specific intent, and it ought to apply, *a fortiori*, to involuntary intoxication.

Involuntary intoxication is narrowly defined. If D knew he was drinking alcohol, he cannot claim that the resulting intoxication was involuntary merely because he underestimated the amount he was consuming[296] or the effect it would have on him. Intoxication is 'involuntary' if D was unaware that he was taking an intoxicant. So where D's lemonade is laced with vodka and he is unaware that he has consumed any alcohol, he can rely on evidence of his drunken condition.[297]

Similarly, perhaps, where D has taken drink under duress.[298] It also covers the special case where a person becomes intoxicated through taking drugs (presumably including alcohol) voluntarily in bona fide pursuance of medical treatment or prescription. This will rarely, if ever, be applicable to alcohol but it might apply where, for example, brandy is administered to D after an accident or shocking event.

---

[294] The case prompted interesting calls for a new defence applicable where D acted out of character. See GR Sullivan, 'Involuntary Intoxication and Beyond' [1994] Crim LR 272 and 'Making Excuses' in A Simester and ATH Smith (eds), *Harm and Culpability* (1996) 131; Tadros (2001) 21 OJLS 495; Tadros, *Criminal Responsibility*, Ch 11; and for a more recent review see C Crosby, 'Culpability, *Kingston* and the Law Commission' (2010) 74 J Crim L 434.

[295] See LC 314, para 1.22. See also the discussion in LC 314, Part 4.

[296] *Allen* [1988] Crim LR 698; cf the definition of voluntary intoxication proposed by the Butler Committee at para 18.56 and that in the Home Office Bill (see later) cl 19(3). LC 314, Part 3 proposes a non-exhaustive list of situations amounting to involuntary intoxication.

[297] See n 292. In *Majewski*, n 303, the Lord Chancellor pointed out that the drugs taken were not medically prescribed.

[298] cf *Kingston*, n 292. But what of the much more common case where D has voluntarily taken some drink and his companions surreptitiously add more? Probably, the jury should be told to convict only if satisfied that the drink voluntarily taken *contributed* to his lack of awareness. Cf LC 314, para 3.125.

As intoxication is nearly always voluntary, it is probably for D to raise the issue if he wishes to contend that it is involuntary. The onus of proof will then generally be on the Crown:[299] but s 6(5) of the Public Order Act 1986, for the purposes of offences under that Act, requires D to 'show' that his intoxication was not self-induced or caused by medical treatment. As the Divisional Court stated in *DPP v Smith*, under the 1986 Act: 'a drunken defendant is treated for the purposes of the issue of awareness as if he had been sober'.[300] This was presumably intended to put the onus of proof on D; but 'show', in contrast with 'prove' which is used in other sections of the Act, might be taken to impose no more than an evidential burden. This is more especially so given the impact of the HRA 1998, which gives force to Art 6(2) of the ECHR.[301]

9.4.3 Voluntary intoxication

9.4.3.1 Basic and specific intent crimes

D is entitled to an acquittal where his voluntary intoxication is such that he did not form the mens rea for the offence of specific intent.[302] It must be emphasized, once again, that this applies where there is a lack of mens rea, not merely a reduction of inhibition; a drunken intention is nevertheless an intention. The prosecution must prove mens rea.

In the case of a crime of basic intent, D may be convicted if he was voluntarily intoxicated at the time of committing the offence by a drug known to create unpredictability or aggression, though he did not have the mens rea required in all other circumstances for that offence and even though he was in a state of such intoxication to be effectively an automaton at the time of doing the act; if he would have had mens rea if sober.

The problem lies in identifying a way of distinguishing between crimes of basic and specific intent. Until very recently, it appeared to be settled that the distinction was between whether the predominant mens rea element of the crime was one of intention, knowledge or dishonesty which would lead to classification as a specific intent crime, or of something less (recklessness, negligence or strict liability) in which case the crime was one of basic intent. This was a largely pragmatic, but not unprincipled, method of classification. The decision of the Court of Appeal in *Heard*[303] casts doubt on this simple and established method of classification, although technically the comments of the court on the basic/specific distinction are *obiter*.

The rule in *Majewski*

In *DPP v Majewski*,[304] the House of Lords confirmed the rule, obscurely stated in *Beard*,[305] that evidence of self-induced intoxication negativing mens rea excuses a defendant on a charge of a crime requiring a specific intent but not to a charge of any other crime. In *Majewski*, D had assaulted a number of police officers when he was being restrained and arrested. He had taken a combination of drink and drugs and was very heavily intoxicated.

---

[299] *Stripp* (1978) 69 Cr App R 318 at 323; *Bailey* [1983] 2 All ER 503 at 507.

[300] [2017] EWHC 3193 (Admin) at [12] per Bean LJ.

[301] cf *Lambert* [2001] UKHL 37; *A-G's Reference (No 4 of 2002)* [2004] UKHL 40, p 20.

[302] See J Horder, 'The Classification of Crimes and the General Part' in Duff and Green, *Defining Crimes*. For extended analysis of the problems with the current law on voluntary intoxication, see R Williams, 'Voluntary Intoxication—A Lost Cause?' (2013) 129 LQR 264.

[303] [2007] EWCA Crim 125, [2007] Crim LR 654 and commentary. See LC 314, paras 2.2–2.28.

[304] [1977] AC 443, and commentary; G Williams, 'Intoxication and Specific Intent' (1976) 126 NLJ 658; AD Gold, 'An Untrimmed Beard' (1976) 19 Crim LQ 34; A Dashwood, 'Logic and the Lords in *Majewski*' [1977] Crim LR 532 and 591. Discussed in LC 314, paras 2.35–2.70.

[305] [1920] AC 479. Cf P Handler, 'Intoxication and Criminal Responsibility in England, 1819–1920' (2013) 33 OJLS 243.

He claimed that his self-induced intoxication had prevented him forming the mens rea, and that the evidence of the intoxication ought to be admissible to support that plea, relying on s 8 of the Criminal Justice Act 1967. He was convicted and this result was upheld by the House of Lords. He was charged with a crime of basic intent and it has long been recognized that voluntary intoxication was no defence to such a charge even if it did cause D to lack mens rea. Unfortunately, the House did not offer a unanimous basis for the distinction between crimes of specific intent and basic intent.

Rule of substantive law

On one interpretation, *Majewski* imposes a rule of substantive law that, where D relies on voluntary intoxication to a charge of a crime not requiring 'specific intent', the prosecution need not prove any intention or foresight, whatever the definition of the crime may say, nor indeed any voluntary act. D's prior fault in becoming voluntarily intoxicated supplies the mens rea. It follows that s 8 of the Criminal Justice Act 1967[306] has no application. There is, it appears, an implied qualification to every statute creating an offence and specifying a mens rea other than a specific intent. The mens rea must be proved—except, we must infer, where the accused was intoxicated through the voluntary taking of drink or drugs. It is assumed that D has the mens rea if he would have had it if sober. In *Richardson and Irwin*,[307] where DD dropped a fellow student from a balcony when drunk causing him grievous bodily harm, they were charged under s 20 of the 1861 Act. Their convictions were quashed by the Court of Appeal holding that the trial judge should have directed that the jury had to be sure that DD would have foreseen the risk of injury had they been sober.

On this first interpretation of *Majewski* it is fatal for a person charged with a crime not requiring specific intent, who claims that he did not have mens rea, to support his defence with evidence that he had taken drink and drugs. By so doing he dispenses the prosecution from the duty, which until that moment lay upon them, of proving beyond reasonable doubt that he had mens rea. Could the prosecution escape from this duty by leading evidence that D had taken drink so as to diminish his capacity to foresee the consequences of his acts? According to Lord Salmon[308] in *Majewski*, the question the House was deciding was whether the accused could rely *by way of defence* on the fact that he had voluntarily taken drink. But there are other *dicta* which suggest that D is held liable without the usual mens rea because he has taken the drink—the taking of the drink is the foundation of his liability[309]—a variety of mens rea—though not in the sense in which that term is used in this book. It is a form of 'prior fault', with D's liability for the crime based on his conduct at that time coupled with his fault in becoming intoxicated. If that is right, there is no reason why the prosecution should not set out to prove it, instead of seeking to prove mens rea in the sense of intention or recklessness.

In principled terms, this first interpretation of *Majewski* is problematical. It deems the defendant's negligence or recklessness in becoming voluntarily intoxicated—his 'prior fault'—to be sufficient mens rea for the crime.[310] This is despite the fact that there is no

---

[306] See p 135. See Simester, n 266, p 6.   [307] [1999] 1 Cr App R 192, see Simester, n 266.
[308] [1977] AC 443.
[309] 'His course of conduct in reducing himself by drugs and drink to that condition in my view supplies the evidence of *mens rea*, of guilty mind, certainly sufficient for crimes of basic intent': [1976] 2 All ER 142 at 150 per Lord Elwyn-Jones. 'There is no juristic reason why mental incapacity (short of M'Naghten insanity) brought about by self-induced intoxication to realize what one is doing or its probable consequences should not be such a state of mind stigmatized as wrongful by the criminal law; and there is every practical reason why it should be': at 153 per Lord Simon. For critical comment see LC 314, Part 2.
[310] For a theoretical analysis of the role played by prior fault, see A Loughnan and N Wake, 'Of Blurred Boundaries and Prior Fault: Insanity, Automatism and Intoxication' in A Reed and M Bohlander (with N Wake and E Smith) (eds), *General Defences in Criminal Law—Domestic and Comparative Perspectives* (2014) and J Child, 'Prior Fault: Blocking Defences or Constructing Crimes' in the same volume.

contemporaneity between the fault in becoming intoxicated and the commission of the actus reus of the crime. And, more importantly, that prior fault is deemed to be sufficient mens rea despite the fact that the degree of fault in becoming intoxicated (foresight or aware- ness of becoming intoxicated) bears no correlation to the mens rea that would normally be required—foresight or awareness of a risk of a prohibited harm specified in the offence. It is, with respect, not enough to say as Hughes LJ suggests in *Heard* (discussed later) that there is 'broadly equivalent culpability'.[311]

It seems that this rule applies whatever the degree of intoxication; if D claimed that it prevented him from foreseeing or knowing what he would have foreseen or known had he been sober he is guilty of the basic intent offence. It is true that Lord Elwyn-Jones at one point[312] posed the question before the House much more narrowly. His lordship spoke of a person who 'consciously and deliberately takes alcohol and drugs not on medical pre- scription, but in order to escape from reality, to go "on a trip," to become hallucinated . . .' Such a person is readily distinguishable from the ordinary 'social drinker' who becomes intoxicated in the course of a convivial evening. The former, intending to reduce himself to a state in which he will have no control over his actions, might well be said to be in some sense reckless as to what he will do while in that state. The same cannot be said of the latter. But the general tenor of the speeches, as well as earlier and subsequent cases, is against any such distinction.[313]

Professor Duff has suggested that we can make moral sense of *Majewski* if we accept that:

recklessness can be constituted either by awareness of a relevant risk [as elsewhere in criminal law] or by unawareness that results from voluntary intoxication: recklessness must be presumed given proof of such unawareness not because it can be inferred but because it is constituted by such.[314]

A rule of evidence?

An alternative view is that *Majewski* does not create a rule of substantive law, but one of evi- dence. On this second interpretation, once D has been shown to be voluntarily intoxicated in a basic intent crime, the evidence of intoxication is irrelevant to the question whether D held the mens rea, but the prosecution is still obliged to prove that D had the relevant mens rea. There is some authority that a jury must be directed to decide whether D was reckless, disregarding the evidence that he was intoxicated. In *Woods*,[315] D, charged with rape under the old sexual offences law, claimed that he was so drunk that he did not realize V was not consenting. He relied on s 1(2) of the Sexual Offences (Amendment) Act 1976[316] which required the jury to have regard to the presence or absence of reasonable grounds for a belief that the woman was consenting, 'in conjunction with any other relevant matters'. He said his intoxication was a relevant matter. The court said that self-induced intoxication is not 'a legally relevant matter' but 'the subsection directs the jury to look carefully at all the other relevant evidence before making up their minds on this issue'. The evidence of intoxication is undoubtedly logically relevant and may be the most cogent evidence. To ignore it in com- ing to a conclusion is to answer a hypothetical question. It is no longer, 'did he believe she was consenting?' and must become, 'would he have known she was consenting if he had not been drunk?' This is most obviously so in the case where D's intoxication has rendered him unconscious.

---

[311] For further analysis, see R Williams, 'Voluntary Intoxication—A Lost Cause?' (2013) 129 LQR 264, 268–9.

[312] [1977] AC 443 at 471.

[313] ACE Lynch, 'The Scope of Intoxication' [1982] Crim LR 139 makes a quite different distinction between 'complete intoxication' (to which *Majewski* would apply) and 'partial intoxication' (to which it would not); but there are many degrees of intoxication and the suggested distinction seems unworkable.

[314] *Answering for Crime*, 240–1.   [315] (1981) 74 Cr App R 312.

[316] Now repealed. See now Ch 17, p 824 and the discussion of the case of *Grewal* [2010] EWCA Crim 2448.

This second interpretation of *Majewski* as a rule of evidence also poses problems. Take *Lipman*, where D strangled V after taking LSD and believing that he was fighting off a serpent at the centre of the earth.[317] How can a judge seriously tell a jury to decide whether D *did* intend to do an unlawful and dangerous act to V—ignoring the undisputed evidence that he was unconscious at the time? Without this 'legally irrelevant' evidence, the *only* question the jury can sensibly answer is, 'would he have known that such an act was dangerous if he had not been intoxicated'? On facts like those in *Lipman*, there is only one possible answer. It is most regrettable that juries should be faced with questions which are, with all respect, nonsensical, even if their common sense will lead them to consider the only matter really in issue.

Distinguishing specific and basic intent crimes

In view of the rule in *Majewski*, the nature of 'specific intent' is a matter of great importance but a careful scrutiny of the authorities, particularly *Majewski* itself, fails to reveal any consistent principle by which specific and basic are to be distinguished.[318] A number of interpretations are possible. It is regrettable that the distinction is so obscure that the Law Commission recently felt unable confidently to state what the law was.[319]

Specific intent as 'ulterior intent'

One interpretation is that specific intent crimes are those in which there is an element of mens rea going beyond the immediate actus reus. There is, as it is often described, an 'ulterior intent'. For example, in the crime of indecent exposure it is necessary for D to have intentionally exposed his genitals with intent that someone will see them and be caused alarm or distress. There is a 'bolt on element of mens rea' (intent to cause alarm) beyond that relating to the immediate intentional conduct of exposing his genitals. The crime would therefore on this analysis be treated as one of specific intent. This approach derives some support from *Majewski* and from the decision in *Heard*. Lord Justice Hughes suggested, *obiter*, that if an offence requires 'proof of a state of mind addressing something beyond the prohibited act itself, namely its consequences', it is one of specific intent. The court 'regard[ed] this as the best explanation of the sometimes elusive distinction between specific and basic intent in the sense used in *Majewski*'.[320] It is submitted that it is an unsatisfactory basis for distinguishing between offences. The most compelling basis for rejecting this approach is that some crimes requiring no ulterior intent—conspicuously murder—have been consistently and unequivocally treated as crimes of 'specific intent' by all levels of court including the House of Lords. If the 'ulterior intent' approach is incapable of providing the correct classification for such an obvious example as murder, it cannot be worth serious consideration.[321] In addition, this approach produces some very odd results. For example, an offence can be one of specific intent even if it contains no element of intent at all—provided there is an ulterior mens rea: reckless criminal damage being reckless as to whether life is endangered

---

[317] [1970] 1 QB 152.

[318] cf S Gardner (1994) 14 OJLS 279 and J Horder, 'Intention in the Criminal Law—A Rejoinder' (1995) 58 MLR 678, who views the specific intent crimes as those in which the intent is integrally bound up with the nature and definition of the wrong involved. See the recommendation in LC 314. See also A Ward, 'Making Some Sense of Self-Induced Intoxication' (1986) 45 CLJ 247 and, for an historical account, A Loughnan, *Manifest Madness: Mental Incapacity in Criminal Law* (2012). Loughnan argues that the distinction between crimes of basic and specific intent has deep historical roots and is the reflection of a persistent lay understanding of the effects of alcohol. See LC 314, paras 2.29 et seq.

[319] See LC 229, para 3.27. In LC 314, Part 2, it was accepted again that the law was in a confused state.

[320] At [31].

[321] Indeed this was one of the principal bases on which *Majewski* was criticized. See Williams, TBCL, 429.

thereby would be a crime of specific *intention*. What of intentionally causing grievous bodily harm under s 18? On the simple form of the charge, there is no bolt on mens rea to be added. It looks then like a crime of basic intent, but every precedent confirms that it is one of specific intent.

Specific intent as 'purposive intent'

An alternative method of distinguishing between specific and basic intent is to ask whether the mens rea of the crime requires a direct or purposive intention (specific) or some other form of mens rea or strict liability (basic). This also derives some support from the speech of Lord Simon in *Majewski* who suggested that the distinguishing factor is that 'the *mens rea* in a crime of specific intent requires proof of a purposive element'. Lord Simon put it in this way:[322]

> The best description of 'specific intent' in this sense that I know is contained in the judgment of Fauteux J in *Reg v George* (1960) 128 Can CC 289, 301—'In considering the question of mens rea, a distinction is to be made between (i) intention as applied to acts considered in relation to their purposes and (ii) intention as applied to acts apart from their purposes. A general intent attending the commission of an act is, in some cases, the only intent required to constitute the crime while, in others, there must be, in addition to that general intent, a specific intent attending the purpose for the commission of the act.'

In *Heard*, Lord Justice Hughes also endorsed the distinction between basic and specific intent found in the speech of Lord Simon in *Majewski*,[323] and put it this way at [31]: 'crimes of specific intent are those where the offence requires proof of purpose or consequence, which are not confined to, but amongst which are included, those where the purpose goes beyond the *actus reus* (sometimes referred to as cases of "ulterior intent")'. It is submitted that it is also an unsatisfactory basis on which to distinguish crimes of specific and basic intent. The crime of murder, for example, has been consistently and unequivocally accepted by the Court of Appeal and House of Lords as a crime of specific intent, yet there need be no purposive element in the mens rea.[324]

Defining specific intent by reference to the predominant mens rea in the offence

A third approach to distinguishing between crimes of basic and specific intent is based on whether the crime in question is one for which the predominant mens rea is (a) intention, knowledge or dishonesty (specific) or (b) some lesser mens rea of recklessness negligence or strict liability (basic). In *Majewski*, Lord Elwyn-Jones LC suggested that the test is that crimes not requiring specific intent are crimes that may be committed recklessly.[325] In *Heard*, in an *obiter dictum*, the Court of Appeal rejected this simple practical approach.

The decision in *Heard*

The decision in *Heard* is a controversial one and a number of points are worth emphasizing. First, on its facts, it should never have given rise to problems. The accused had, while drunk, exposed his penis and rubbed it against the thigh of a police officer. D's plea was that he had no recollection of the incident. That is never a basis for a plea of intoxication and that should have been the end of the matter. However, D relied on his voluntary intoxication as negating his mens rea of an intention to touch for the purposes of s 3(1)(a) of the Sexual Offences Act 2003. The trial judge ruled that the intentional touching element of the offence required proof of a basic intent, and that it followed that voluntary intoxication was not a defence.

---

322 At 478H.   323 At 478B–479B.   324 See LC 314, paras 2.8 et seq.

325 Lord Edmund-Davies, a party to *Majewski*, was dismayed to think that, as a result of *Caldwell*, this opinion prevailed [1982] AC 341 at 361, [1981] 1 All ER 961 at 972.

Applying the predominant mens rea interpretation of *Majewski*, on a charge such as that under s 3 with the requirement of an 'intentional' touching, it was arguable at least that the crime was one of specific intent.[326] The court rejected that approach.

Secondly, we can assume that sexual offences under the 2003 Act in which the conduct is 'intended'[327] will be treated as basic intent crimes unless there is a clear ulterior purpose, as in indecent exposure, and offences in which D is acting 'for the purpose of obtaining sexual gratification'.[328] On policy grounds the court was clearly entitled to assume that Parliament had not intended to change the law, although it should be noted that under the pre-2003 law, the offence of indecent assault was not always a basic intent crime. The court could have adopted the predominant mens rea and created an exception for sex offences.

Thirdly, the court's radical reinterpretation of *Majewski* aligning specific intent with an ulterior or purposive mens rea produces difficulties, even within the scope of the s 3 offence. Someone like Lipman[329] who becomes so intoxicated that he thinks he is stroking an animal at the centre of the earth when in fact he is stroking a woman's breast will, on the court's approach, be guilty under s 3. But it is submitted that in such a case it would be difficult in any ordinary sense of the word to say that D 'intended' to touch V sexually as s 3 requires.

Fourthly, the court makes some very broad qualifications to the approach in s 3 (and other sexual offences and beyond, one assumes) in respect of accidents. Lord Justice Hughes stated that:

To flail about, stumble or barge around in an unco-ordinated manner which results in an unintended touching, objectively sexual, is not this offence. If to do so when sober is not this offence, then nor is it this offence to do so when intoxicated. It is also possible that such an action would not be judged by the jury to be objectively sexual, on the basis that it was clearly accidental, but whether that is so or not, we are satisfied that in such a case this offence is not committed. The intoxication, in such a situation, has not impacted on intention. Intention is simply not in question. What is in question is impairment of control of the limbs. . . . '[A] drunken intent is still an intent', the corollary [is] that 'a drunken accident is still an accident'.

In respect of someone who simply trips on the dance floor and grabs at the nearest thing to steady himself this makes perfect sense. But consider someone who,[330] fooling around when heavily intoxicated, pretends to strike the bottom of a woman who is bending and who misjudges the distance and strikes her bottom. He will be acquitted on the basis that his conduct is 'accidental'.[331] It is submitted that it would be a misuse of the word 'intention' to say that he had intended to touch her sexually. He intends to move his arm and intends to come close to touching her, but not to do so. It is also misleading to say it is accidental: D is reckless about that consequence, he has seen the risk and unjustifiably gone on to take it. There is a risk that the category of 'drunken accident' endorsed by *Heard* will be misunderstood and applied in cases of what are plainly recklessness.

Finally, there are several reasons why, it is submitted, the court's *obiter dicta* rejecting the predominant mens rea interpretation of *Majewski* in favour of a purposive approach should not be applied throughout the criminal law: it is more difficult to look for the 'bolt-on' element of additional mens rea in a crime in order to categorize it appropriately; the approach creates no fewer anomalies than the established interpretation of *Majewski*; and it creates confusion because specific intent might encompass crimes with no element of intent at all, such as reckless criminal damage being reckless as to whether life is endangered thereby.

---

[326] R Card, *Sexual Offences: The New Law* (2004) para 1.31; P Rook and R Ward, *Sexual Offences Law and Practice* (5th edn, 2016) paras 2.81–2.82.

[327] See *Grout* [2011] EWCA Crim 299.   [328] Section 12.   [329] *Lipman* (1969) 55 Cr App R 600.

[330] cf *Shimmen* (1987) 84 Cr App Rep 7.   [331] At [23].

9.4.3.2 A summary of the current law on basic and specific intent

Despite its obscure exposition in the House of Lords, and its unsatisfactory theoretical underpinnings, the *Majewski* approach had subsequently been knocked into pragmatic shape: the predominant mens rea approach was familiar and generally applied. Those virtues ought not to be undervalued. Despite *dicta* in *Heard*, it is submitted that any offence which may be committed recklessly ought to be held an offence of 'basic' and not 'specific' intent.

The safest approach seems to be that 'crime requiring specific intent' means a crime where evidence of voluntary intoxication negativing mens rea is an excuse. It may be easier to accept that the designation of crimes as requiring, or not requiring, specific intent is based not on principle but on policy. In order to know how a crime should be classified for this purpose, we can look only to the decisions of the courts. The following are crimes requiring specific intent: murder,[332] wounding or causing grievous bodily harm with intent,[333] theft,[334] robbery,[335] burglary with intent to steal,[336] handling stolen goods,[337] endeavouring to obtain money on a forged cheque,[338] causing criminal damage contrary to s 1(1) or (2) of the Criminal Damage Act 1971 where only intention to cause damage or, in the case of s 1(2), only intention to endanger life, is alleged,[339] an attempt to commit any offence requiring specific intent and post-*Jogee*, secondary participation in any offence.[340]

The following crimes do not require specific intent: manslaughter (apparently in all its forms),[341] rape,[342] sexual assault,[343] maliciously wounding or inflicting grievous bodily harm,[344] kidnapping and false imprisonment,[345] assault occasioning actual bodily harm,[346] assault on a constable in the execution of his duty,[347] common assault,[348] taking a conveyance without the consent of the owner,[349] criminal damage where intention or recklessness,

[332] *Beard*, n 267; *Gallagher* [1963] AC 349; *Sheehan* [1975] 1 WLR 739.
[333] *Bratty v A-G for Northern Ireland* [1963] AC 386, per Lord Denning; *Pordage* [1975] Crim LR 575; *Davies* [1991] Crim LR 469.
[334] *Ruse v Read* [1949] 1 KB 377, and *Majewski* at 152 per Lord Simon.   [335] As a corollary of theft.
[336] *Durante* [1972] 1 WLR 1612.   [337] ibid.   [338] *Majewski*, at 158 per Lord Salmon.
[339] *Caldwell* [1981] 1 All ER 961 at 964. The Court of Appeal in *Harris* [2013] EWCA Crim 223 declined to address the issue of whether causing criminal damage being reckless to whether life would be endangered is a crime of specific intent. Hughes LJ did, however, state that there was some force in the argument that voluntary intoxication ought not to be a 'defence' to crimes involving subjective recklessness.
[340] *Clarkson* [1971] 3 All ER 344 at 347. But cf comments in *Lynch v DPP for Northern Ireland* [1975] 1 All ER 913 at 942; see p 204.
[341] *Beard*, *Gallagher* and *Bratty v A-G Northern Ireland* [1961] 3 All ER at 533 per Lord Denning; *Lipman* [1970] 1 QB 152.
[342] *Grewal* [2010] EWCA Crim 2448; *Grout* [2011] EWCA Crim 299. *Majewski*, per Lords Simon and Russell and *Leary v R* (1977) 74 DLR (3d) 103, SCC, discussed 55 Can Bar Rev 691. But if this is right, and it seems almost certain that it is, *Cogan and Leak* (p 234) is wrongly decided; and *Morgan* (p 351) might have been decided simply on this ground. Cf *Fotheringham* (1988) 88 Cr App R 206, [1988] Crim LR 846 and commentary.
[343] *Heard* [2007] EWCA Crim 125.
[344] *Bratty* at 533 per Lord Denning; *Majewski*, per Lords Simon and Salmon.
[345] *Hutchins* [1988] Crim LR 379. Nor child abduction: *Hunter* [2015] All ER (D) 196 (Jan).
[346] *Bolton v Crawley* [1972] Crim LR 222; *Majewski*.   [347] *Majewski*.   [348] *A fortiori*.
[349] *MacPherson* [1973] RTR 157; *Gannon* (1987) 87 Cr App R 254. *Diggin* (1980) 72 Cr App R 204 is not, as it first appeared: [1980] Crim LR 656, an authority on intoxicated taking: [1981] Crim LR 563; but see S White, 'Taking the Joy Out of Joyriding' [1980] Crim LR 609.

or only recklessness, is alleged[350] and possibly an attempt to commit an offence where recklessness is a sufficient element in the mens rea,[351] as in attempted rape.[352]

It will be noted that for most specific intent offences there exists a basic intent offence that can be charged in the alternative (murder and manslaughter, ss 18 and 20 of the OAPA 1861, etc). The prosecution are usually therefore able to avoid an acquittal in cases of self-induced intoxication. Two problems arise in this regard, however. First, the jury will face confusing directions on charges such as ss 18 and 20 as to what use they may make of the evidence of intoxication. Secondly, there are some specific intent offences for which there is no basic intent equivalent: theft is an obvious example.

Specific and basic: a legitimate basis of distinction?

A classification of all crimes as offences of either specific or basic intent is oversimplified. The Court of Appeal in *Heard* even hints at rejecting the twofold classification by suggesting that it is not to be assumed that every offence is one of basic or specific intent.[353] It is submitted that this aspect of the Court of Appeal's decision should be taken as emphasizing that an offence is likely to have more than one element of mens rea. The question is what is the predominant mens rea.

Consider the offence under s 18 of the OAPA 1861 of unlawfully and maliciously wounding with intent to resist lawful apprehension. There is abundant authority to the effect that the words 'unlawfully and maliciously' when used in s 20 import only a basic intent; that is, *Cunningham* recklessness. Presumably they have the same effect in s 18. So as far as wounding goes, s 18 is an offence of basic intent. But the intent to resist lawful apprehension seems a clear case of specific intent. So it seems that a drunken person who intends to resist lawful arrest but, because of his drunkenness, does not foresee the risk of wounding, might be convicted, notwithstanding his lack of *Cunningham* recklessness. If, on the other hand, because of drunkenness, he does not realize that he is resisting lawful arrest, he must be acquitted.[354]

Intoxication and *Caldwell* recklessness

Where the offence is one of *Caldwell* recklessness, assuming that any such offences still exist, the impact of *Majewski* is reduced. Where, because he was intoxicated, D gave no thought to the existence of the risk, he was reckless and is liable to conviction without the invocation of the rule in *Majewski*.[355] This was the position in *Caldwell* itself. But *Majewski* may still have a significant sphere of operation.[356] D might say that he did consider whether there was a risk and decided there was none. He was then not *Caldwell*-reckless. But, if he would have appreciated the existence of the risk had he been sober, he will still be liable because of *Majewski*.

9.4.4 Dangerous or non-dangerous drugs in basic intent crime

In the case where D has become voluntarily intoxicated and the offence with which he is charged is one of basic intent, there remains one important issue to consider—whether the substance voluntarily ingested is 'dangerous'; that is, commonly known to create states of unpredictability or aggression.

---

[350] See Ch 27.   [351] Commentary on *Pullen* [1991] Crim LR 457 at 458.

[352] This possibility will depend upon whether the interpretation of attempts adopted in *Pace* [2014] EWCA Crim 186 prevails. The implication of the judgment is that, on a charge of attempted rape, the Crown would have to prove that D intended that V was not consenting. For discussion, see Ch 11.

[353] At [14]. But what is this other category that now exists? And what offences might fall into it? See the Law Commission's rejection in LC 314, Part 2.

[354] *Davies* [1991] Crim LR 469.   [355] This point was overlooked in *Cullen* [1993] Crim LR 936.

[356] This is overlooked by Lord Diplock at [1981] 1 All ER 968a.

The law in this area has developed principally in cases where D was intoxicated by alcohol. In *Lipman*,[357] it was held that the same principles apply to intoxication by other drugs but two later cases, *Bailey*[358] and *Hardie*,[359] suggest that drugs must be divided into two categories. Where it is common knowledge that a drug is liable to cause the taker to become aggressive or do dangerous or unpredictable things, that drug is to be classed alongside alcohol. Where there is no such common knowledge, as in the case of a merely soporific or sedative drug, different rules apply. There are obvious difficulties about classifying drugs in this way and it is surprising that it has not generated more case law.

In *Bailey*,[360] a diabetic failed to take sufficient food after insulin. He caused grievous bodily harm and his defence to charges under ss 18 and 20 of the OAPA was that, because of this failure, he was in a state of sane automatism. The recorder's direction to the jury that this was no defence was obviously wrong so far as s 18 was concerned for that is an offence of specific intent. The Court of Appeal held that it was also wrong for s 20 because 'self-induced automatism, other than that due to intoxication from alcohol or drugs, may provide a defence to crimes of basic intent'.[361] The court went on:

The question in each case will be whether the prosecution has proved the necessary element of recklessness. In cases of assault, if the accused knows that his actions or inaction are likely to make him aggressive, unpredictable or uncontrolled with the result that he may cause some injury to others and he persists in the action or takes no remedial action when he knows it is required, it will be open to the jury to find that he was reckless.

The automatism seems to have been treated as arising from the failure to take food, rather than from the taking of the insulin, but the court hinted at a distinction between two types of drug:

It is common knowledge that those who take alcohol to excess or certain sorts of drugs may become aggressive or do dangerous or unpredictable things. . . . But the same cannot be said, without more, of a man who fails to take food after an insulin injection.

In *Hardie*,[362] the court developed this further. D's defence to a charge of damaging property with intent to endanger the life of another or being reckless whether another's life be endangered, was that he had taken valium, a sedative drug, to calm his nerves and that this had resulted in intoxication precluding the mens rea for the offence. The judge, following *Majewski* and *Caldwell*, directed that this could be no defence. The Court of Appeal quashed the conviction. *Majewski* was not applicable because valium:

is wholly different in kind from drugs which are liable to cause unpredictability or aggressiveness. . . . [I]f the effect of a drug is merely soporific or sedative the taking of it, even in some excessive quantity, cannot in the ordinary way raise a conclusive presumption against the admission of proof of intoxication for the purpose of disproving *mens rea* in ordinary crimes, such as would be the case with alcoholic intoxication or incapacity or automatism resulting from the self-administration of dangerous drugs.[363]

This qualification to the normal rule for basic intent crimes applies where intoxication is self-induced otherwise than by alcohol or dangerous drugs. In these cases the test of liability

---

357 [1970] 1 QB 152; p 595.   358 [1983] 1 WLR 760.   359 [1985] 1 WLR 64.
360 [1983] 1 WLR 760.   361 See p 311.   362 [1985] 1 WLR 64.
363 This overlooks the fact that the *Majewski* principle is stated by the House of Lords to be a rule of substantive law and that the Criminal Justice Act 1967, s 8, precludes conclusive presumptions of intention or foresight. See p 134. For further discussion, see R Williams, 'Voluntary Intoxication—A Lost Cause?' (2013) 129 LQR 264, 266–9. The distinction is also unsatisfactory in pharmacological terms: M Weller and W Somers, 'Differences in the Medical and Legal Viewpoint Illustrated by *Hardie*' (1991) 31 Med Sci Law 152.

is stated to be one of recklessness: 'If [D] does appreciate the risk that [failure to take food/taking the non-dangerous drug] may lead to aggressive, unpredictable and uncontrollable conduct and he nevertheless deliberately runs the risk or otherwise disregards it, this will amount to recklessness.'[364]

It is clear that the recklessness which must be proved is:

(1) subjective—an actual awareness of the risk of becoming aggressive; but

(2) 'general'—not requiring foresight of the actus reus of any particular crime, such as is required in the case of a sober person charged with an offence of *Cunningham* recklessness. D will be liable for any crime of recklessness the actus reus of which he happens to commit under the influence of the self-induced intoxication. This flows from the rule in *Majewski*.[365]

Further:

(3) being aware that one may lose consciousness may be sufficient where a failure to exercise control may result in the actus reus of a crime, as in the case of careless or dangerous driving.

D's fault in voluntarily consuming the dangerous drugs with the awareness of their likely effect provides sufficient prior fault to warrant his conviction for basic intent crimes even though at the time of the commission of the offence D lacks the mens rea for that crime.

9.4.5 Intoxication and defences

9.4.5.1 Statutory defences prescribing a belief in circumstances

The *Majewski* rule has been held inapplicable where statute expressly provides that a particular belief shall be a defence to the charge. If D held that belief, he is not guilty, even though it arose from a drunken mistake that he would not have made when sober. In *Jaggard v Dickinson*,[366] D had a friend, H, who had invited her to treat his house as if it were her own. When drunk, D went to a house which she thought was H's but which in fact belonged to R, who barred her way. D gained entry by breaking windows and damaging the curtains. Charged with criminal damage, contrary to s 1(1) of the Criminal Damage Act 1971, she relied on s 5(2) of that Act[367] which provides that a person has a lawful excuse if D believed that the person entitled to consent to the damage would have done so had he known of the circumstances. D said that she believed that H would, in the circumstances, have consented to her damaging his property. Since s 1(1) creates an offence of basic intent, D could not have relied on her drunkenness to negative her recklessness as to whether she damaged the property of another. However, it was held, she could rely on her voluntary intoxication to explain what would otherwise have been inexplicable and give colour to her evidence about the state of her belief. The court thought that this was different from using drunkenness to rebut an inference of intention or recklessness. It seems, however, to be exactly the same thing.[368] Moreover, the court thought that s 5(2) of the 1971 Act provides that it is

364 *Bailey* [1983] 2 All ER 503 at 507.
365 Williams cogently argues that as a result of the current law intoxicated people can be convicted when they are inadvertent, provided they could have foreseen the risk when sober. By contrast, it is no longer permissible to convict sober people when they are inadvertent. See R Williams, 'Voluntary Intoxication—A Lost Cause?' (2013) 129 LQR 264, 270.
366 [1981] QB 527. Cf the unsatisfactory case of *Gannon* (1987) 87 Cr App R 254, criticized by G Williams, 'Two Nocturnal Blunders' (1990) 140 NLJ 1564.
367 See p 1107.   368 See p 1108.

immaterial whether a belief is justified or not if it is honestly held, and it was not open to the court to add the words 'and the honesty of the belief is not attributable only to self-induced intoxication'. Yet the courts have not hesitated to add similar words to qualify Parliament's express requirement of 'malice', or, *Cunningham* recklessness.

The result is anomalous. Where the defendant did not intend any damage to property but was reckless about damage he may be held liable because he was drunk; but where he did intend damage to property but thought the owner would consent he is not liable, however drunk he may have been. Suppose that D, because he is drunk, believes that certain property belonging to V is his own and damages it. His belief is not a matter of defence under s 5(2)[369] but negatives recklessness as to whether property *belonging to another* be damaged.[370] If D, being drunk, destroys X's property believing that it is the property of Y who would consent to his doing so, this is a defence; but if he destroys X's property believing that it is his own, it is not. The Law Commission recommendation to reverse the approach in *Jaggard*,[371] is a welcome one.

In the absence of parliamentary intervention, Elias LJ in *Magee v CPS*[372] stated that the principle enunciated in *Jaggard* ought to be construed narrowly. In *Magee*, D was found guilty of failing to stop after an accident, contrary to s 170(4) of the Road Traffic Act 1988. At the time the accident occurred, D was intoxicated and as a result of her intoxicated state the magistrates found that she had a genuine belief that there had been no accident. D was nevertheless convicted. Relying upon *Jaggard*, D argued that a mistaken view of the circumstances, even if induced by drink, could constitute a defence as long as the defendant genuinely did not believe an accident had occurred. Rejecting this proposition, Elias LJ held that the continuing validity of *Jaggard* is questionable, given subsequent developments in the case law.[373] His lordship further held that the onus was on D to negate the natural inference that once the accident had occurred she would have been aware of it. It was observed that there was no reason why the common law should be construed so as to allow D to pray in aid her own state of drunkenness as the reason for the mistake, and there was every reason of policy why it should not be extended in that way. This case demonstrates that even though the Law Commission's recommendations have not been acted upon, the courts will actively work to confine the scope of *Jaggard*, which, for the reasons already given, is welcome.

9.4.5.2 Self-defence

In relation to self-defence, the law has gone quite the other way from *Jaggard*. It is now settled that when D sets up self-defence, he is to be judged on the facts as he believed them to be, whether reasonably or not.[374] However, a mistake arising from voluntary intoxication cannot be relied upon, according to *O'Grady*[375] and *Hatton*, even on a charge of murder or other crime requiring specific intent. This has now been endorsed by Parliament in s 76(5) of the Criminal Justice and Immigration Act 2008.

In *O'Grady*, this conclusion was plainly *obiter* because the appellant had been acquitted of murder and was appealing only against his conviction for manslaughter; but in *O'Connor*,[376] the court, inexplicably, treated it as binding, while quashing the conviction of murder on another ground. This was followed in *Hatton*. H who had drunk more than 20 pints of beer

---

[369] *Smith (DR)* [1974] QB 354.   [370] ibid.   [371] LC 314, para 2.94.

[372] [2014] EWHC 4089 (Admin), [34].   [373] At [33]–[36].

[374] *Gladstone Williams* (1987) 78 Cr App R 276, p 354.

[375] [1987] QB 995 criticized by the Law Commission, LC 177, para 8.42, by H Milgate (1987) 46 CLJ 381 and JC Smith [1987] Crim LR 706. Relied upon in *Dowds* [2012] EWCA Crim 281 as an example of the 'general approach' that English law takes to intoxication.

[376] [1991] Crim LR 135; cf *Hatton* [2005] EWCA Crim 2951.

killed V with at least seven blows from a sledgehammer. H stated that he could not recall V's death but that he had a vague recollection that a stick fashioned in the shape of a samurai sword had been involved. H said that he believed that V had hit him with the stick and that he must have believed that V was attacking him. H wished to raise self-defence based on his own mistaken belief that he thought he was being attacked by an SAS officer (as V had earlier pretended to be) with a sword. The Court of Appeal, upholding his conviction, confirmed that the decision in *O'Grady* applied equally to cases of manslaughter and murder: a defendant seeking to rely on self-defence could not rely on a mistake induced by voluntary intoxication.[377] The case is controversial in extending the scope of *O'Grady* to murder, and in accepting unequivocally that the decisions in *O'Connor* and *O'Grady* were binding (but not, implicitly, feeling bound by *Gladstone Williams*). It is now beyond doubt by s 76(5).

As a matter of principle, this approach is flawed in a number of ways. First, it contradicts the approach taken in relation to mistakes in self-defence. If D has made a genuine but unreasonable mistake as to the need for force, he will be judged on the facts as he unreasonably believed them to be. If this is so when D is sober, logically it ought to be so when he is intoxicated since his intoxication explains the basis for the unreasonableness of his mistake. (The Law Commission rejects this argument in its report (at para 3.59).) Secondly, it is inconsistent with the application of the rules relating to specific and basic intent for offences. If D is charged with murder and pleads that he was so intoxicated that he did not form an intent, he is, if believed, entitled to an acquittal on that specific intent charge. In short, a killing in a state of voluntary intoxication is manslaughter. However, when D's intoxicated mistake to self-defence is pleaded it results in a murder conviction.

In cases of householder self-defence (see later, p 407), Sir Brian Leveson P questioned, *obiter*, whether the same approach to intoxication should apply.[378] His lordship said this because the common law (preserved by s 76 of the 2008 Act) requires an approach which it is at least arguable is unduly restrictive for householders. There is much to be said for the proposition that those who go about in public (or anywhere outside their own homes) must take responsibility for their level of intoxication: thus by s 76(5) of the 2008 Act, a defendant cannot rely on any mistaken belief attributable to intoxication that was voluntarily induced. Why that should be so in the defendant's own home in circumstances where he is not anticipating any interaction with someone D believes to be a trespasser is, perhaps, a more open question but that remains part of the test even in a householder case.

The law could have taken a different approach and said that D could be convicted of manslaughter by gross negligence if the jury judge his unreasonable mistake as to the need for force as a grossly negligent mistake (which a drunken mistake almost certainly is).[379] If self-defence is a defence to murder it does not necessarily follow that it needs to be a defence to manslaughter.

The Court of Appeal, in a purely policy-driven series of decisions, has created inconsistencies in an attempt to ensure that D cannot plead intoxicated self-defence: the basis for this seems to be a fear that jurors would acquit of all offences.[380] These decisions are difficult to defend. The court's attention does not appear to have been drawn to the recommendations of the Criminal Law Revision Committee, which complements those which the court

---

[377] See *Hatton* [2005] EWCA Crim 2951. Note also the Criminal Justice and Immigration Act 2008, s 76(5) which precludes D relying on a mistake in such circumstances which was attributable to him being voluntarily intoxicated. See also LC 314, paras 2.54–2.61.

[378] See *Collins* [2016] EWHC 33 (Admin), discussed in full in the next chapter.

[379] By Smith [1987] Crim LR 706. Cf the rejection arguments in LC 314, paras 3.59–3.64.

[380] See the critical comments by A Ashworth [2006] Crim LR 353; JR Spencer (2006) 65 CLJ 267; G Dingwall (2007) 70 MLR 127.

followed in *Gladstone Williams*.[381] The more logical view, it is submitted, is that a mistake arising from voluntary intoxication by alcohol or dangerous drugs ought to found a defence to crime requiring specific intent but not to one of basic intent if the prosecution prove that but for the intoxication the defendant would not have made the mistake.

9.4.5.3 Intoxication and partial defences to murder

The relevance of voluntary intoxication and alcohol dependence syndrome for the partial defences to murder (loss of control and diminished responsibility) is considered in Ch 13, p 566.

9.4.6 Intoxication induced with the intention of committing crime

We now turn to consider the rare situation where D, intending to commit a crime, takes drink or drugs in order to give himself 'Dutch courage' and then commits the crime, having, at the time of the act, induced a state of drunkenness as to negative a 'specific intent'. The problem was raised by *A-G for Northern Ireland v Gallagher*.[382] D, having decided to kill his wife, bought a knife and a bottle of whisky. He drank much of the whisky and then killed his wife with the knife. The defence was that he was either insane or so drunk that he did not form the necessary intent at the time he did the act. The Court of Criminal Appeal in Northern Ireland reversed his conviction for murder on the ground that the judge had misdirected the jury in telling them to apply the M'Naghten Rules to D's state of mind at the time before he took the alcohol and not at the time of committing the act. The majority of the House of Lords apparently did not dissent from the view of the Court of Criminal Appeal that such a direction would be 'at variance with the specific terms of the M'Naghten Rules which definitely fix the crucial time as the time of committing the act'.[383] They differed, however, in their interpretation of the summing up and held that it did direct the jury's attention to the time of committing the act. In that case, of course, it was not necessary to decide the problem because the jury, by their verdict, had found that D had mens rea and was not insane. Lord Denning, however, seems to have taken the view that the Court of Criminal Appeal's interpretation of the summing up was correct and that the direction, so interpreted, was right in law. He said:[384]

> My Lords, I think the law on this point should take a clear stand. If a man, whilst sane and sober, forms an intention to kill and makes preparation for it knowing it is a wrong thing to do, and then gets himself drunk so as to give himself Dutch courage to do the killing, and whilst drunk carries out his intention, he cannot rely on this self-induced drunkenness as a defence to a charge of murder, nor even as reducing it to manslaughter. He cannot say he got himself into such a stupid state that he was incapable of an intent to kill. So also, when he is a psychopath, he cannot by drinking rely on his self-induced defect of reason as a defence of insanity. The wickedness of his mind before he got drunk is enough to condemn him, coupled with the act which he intended to do and did do.

The difficulty about this is that an intention to do an act some time in the future is not mens rea.[385] The mens rea must generally coincide with the conduct which causes the actus reus. If D, being sober, resolves to murder his wife at midnight, drops off to sleep and, while still asleep, strangles her at midnight whilst still asleep, it is thought that he is not guilty of murder. The case of deliberately induced drunkenness, however, is probably different. The true analogy, it is thought, is the case where a man D uses an innocent agent as an instrument

381 See n 373.   382 [1963] AC 349.   383 See [1963] AC 349 at 376.
384 [1963] AC 349 at 382.   385 See p 128.

with which to commit crime. It has been seen[386] that if D induces X to kill, D is guilty of murder if X is an innocent agent. Arguably, the position is substantially the same where D induces in himself a state of irresponsibility with the intention that he will kill while in that state?[387] Should not the responsible D be liable for the foreseen and intended acts of the irresponsible D? Regarded in this way, a conviction would not be incompatible with the wording of the M'Naghten Rules. The result, certainly, seems to be one required by policy and it is thought the courts will achieve it if the problem should be squarely raised before them.

9.4.7 Reform of intoxication

England is becoming isolated in clinging to the *Majewski* principle.[388] Its abolition elsewhere does not seem to have led, as some anticipated, to increased crime or a collapse in respect for the law.[388] The Law Commission in a Consultation Paper published in 1993 reached a provisional conclusion that *Majewski* should be abolished.[390] The radical proposal was to introduce a new offence of criminal intoxication which would reflect more appropriately, in terms of label, the responsibility of the individual who commits a crime in a state of voluntary intoxication.[391] The consultation, however, persuaded the Commission to change its mind. In LC 229 it was recommended[392] that the rule be codified with minor amendment and attempted clarification, but in a draft Bill so complex that it is impossible to commend it.[393] That has not been taken forward. The Home Office then proposed a simplified model which it intended to enact in relation to offences against the person. That too has not been taken forward.[394]

The Law Commission's proposals in LC 314 would have provided a statutory framework, replacing the specific/basic intent distinction. The replacement for the 'specific intent' rule is to create a statutory list of 'integral fault elements' (intention, knowledge, belief, fraud and dishonesty), and if D is charged with an offence with such an 'integral fault element' D will only be liable if the prosecution proves he had the relevant fault element despite being voluntarily intoxicated (para 3.42). The general rule for all other offences (eg those requiring recklessness) is that if D was voluntarily intoxicated he will be treated 'as having been aware at the material time of anything which D would then have been aware of but for the intoxication' (para 3.35). This effectively replaces the basic intent rule. In relation to D's mistakes induced by voluntary intoxication, D's mistaken belief should be taken into account only if D would have held the same belief if D had not been intoxicated (para 3.53). If D's intoxication is involuntary (administered without consent or under duress or under proper medical instruction or without knowledge that it was an intoxicant) or 'almost entirely involuntary', that can be considered in all cases where D is charged with a crime of subjective fault (paras 3.105–3.126). Separate complex rules are proposed in relation to secondary and inchoate

---

[386] See p 188.   [387] See the discussion in Ch 2, p 71.

[388] For extended discussion of the options for reform, see R Williams, 'Voluntary Intoxication—A Lost Cause?' (2013) 129 LQR 264. She suggests a new offence of 'committing the *actus reus* of offence X while intoxicated'. For critique see J Child, 'Prior Fault: Blocking Defences or Constructing Crimes' in A Reed and M Bohlander (with N Wake and E Smith) (eds), *General Defences in Criminal Law—Domestic and Comparative Perspectives* (2014).

[389] G Orchard, 'Surviving without *Majewski*' [1993] Crim LR 426.   [390] LCCP 127 (1993).

[391] For a defence, see G Virgo, 'Reconciling Principle and Policy' [1993] Crim LR 415; for criticism, see S Gardner, 'The Importance of *Majewski*' (1994) 14 OJLS 279.

[392] LC 229 (1995). See J Horder, 'Sobering Up' (1995) 58 MLR 534; E Paton, 'Reformulating the Intoxication Rule' [1995] Crim LR 382.

[393] See S Gough, 'Intoxication and Criminal Liability' (1996) 112 LQR 335.

[394] See JC Smith, 'Offences Against the Person: The Home Office Consultation Paper' [1998] Crim LR 317.

liability (paras 3.85–3.104).[395] The then-government rejected the Law Commission's recommendations and stated that it would not be taking them forward.

The Code Team's report[396] to the Commission offered a simpler scheme. Other proposals for a *via media* have been made[397] but have not attracted support and are not pursued here.

The Law Commission's latest reform proposals for insanity and automatism do have one impact on intoxication. Under the Commission's proposed scheme, a defendant would be treated as pleading the new recognized medical condition defence if: he suffered from a recognized medical condition; took properly authorized medication for that condition and in accordance with the prescription (or in circumstances in which it was reasonable to take it); had no reason to believe he would suffer an adverse reaction; but suffered a total lack of a relevant capacity (see earlier).

9.5 Combined, consecutive and concurrent causes of loss of capacity

The internal and external factors which cause an individual defendant to lack capacity may operate consecutively or concurrently.[398] There is little authority on the complex questions which may arise and such as there is does not seem well thought out. From a theoretical perspective, Loughnan and Wake argue that co-morbidity poses two main issues.[399] The first relates to defendants who might have committed an offence whilst both mentally ill and intoxicated: D's mental illness might have been diagnosed prior to his committing the offence, or it may only have been stimulated by his intoxicated state. The second issue relates to defendants whose ingestion of an intoxicating substance has led them to develop some mental impairment. Their thesis is that the law currently places too much emphasis upon the cause of D's incapacity and does so in an inconsistent fashion. This part of the chapter will demonstrate that this issue poses practical problems in addition to theoretical ones. Some answers to the questions which may arise are suggested here.

9.5.1 Consecutive operation

9.5.1.1 Intoxication causes automatism

D, because he is drunk, sustains concussion and does the allegedly criminal act in a state of automatism resulting from the concussion. In *Stripp*,[400] the Court of Appeal thought, *obiter*, that D should be acquitted on the ground of automatism. That seems right—the intoxication is too remote from the act. The Law Commission concluded that the case suggests 'obiter, the possibility that where there is a course of automatism clearly separable in time or effect from the intoxication and supported by a foundation of evidence, then a defence of automatism may be available, but when the causal factors are less easily separable it would seem that the presence of the intoxication will on policy grounds adopted in *Majewski* exclude reliance on automatism'.[401] Distinguishing the degree of separateness of the factors will not always be easy.

---

[395] For critical comment see J Child, 'Drink, Drugs and Law Reform' [2009] Crim LR 488.

[396] LC 143 (1985) cl 26.   [397] See the 7th edn of this book, at p 230.

[398] For a discussion of the relationship between these defences see LCDP, Ch 6.

[399] A Loughnan and N Wake, 'Of Blurred Boundaries and Prior Fault: Insanity, Automatism and Intoxication' in A Reed and M Bohlander (with N Wake and E Smith) (eds), *General Defences in Criminal Law—Domestic and Comparative Perspectives* (2014).

[400] (1979) 69 Cr App R 318, 323. No foundation for automatism was laid.

[401] LCCP 127, para 2.33, Report (LC 143), para 6.44.LC 314, para 2.90.

9.5.1.2 Automatism causes intoxication

D having sustained concussion, drinks a bottle of vodka under the impression that it is water and does the allegedly criminal act, not knowing what he is doing because he is intoxicated. Since the intoxication is involuntary, both causes lead to an acquittal and D must be acquitted.

9.5.1.3 Intoxication causes insanity

Beard settles that insanity caused by drink operates in the same manner as insanity arising from any other cause. If excessive drinking causes actual insanity, such as delirium tremens, then the M'Naghten Rules will be applied in exactly the same way as where insanity arises from any other causes: 'drunkenness is one thing and the diseases to which drunkenness leads are different things; and if a man by drunkenness brings on a state of disease which causes such a degree of madness, even for a time, which would have relieved him from responsibility if it had been caused in any other way, then he would not be criminally responsible'.[402]

It has already been seen[403] that there are serious difficulties in defining a 'disease of the mind' and the distinction between temporary insanity induced by drink and simple drunkenness is far from clear-cut. The distinction becomes important in the case of a person who does not know that his act is wrong because of excessive drinking. If he is suffering from temporary insanity he is entitled to a verdict of not guilty on the ground of insanity; but if he is merely drunk he should be convicted.[404]

Note the conflict created by the *obiter dictum* discussed earlier in *Taj*. That *dictum* suggests that D who was suffering the effects of proximate intoxication is to be treated as relying on a plea of intoxication rather than one of insanity.[405]

9.5.1.4 Insanity causes intoxication or automatism

'Insanity' in the *M'Naghten* sense can strictly have no application here because it applies only in relation to a particular criminal act, whereas getting drunk or causing oneself concussion is probably not a criminal act at all and certainly not the criminal act with which we are concerned. However, D may not know the nature and quality of the act which causes the condition. The resulting intoxication is involuntary, so D should be acquitted. Insofar as automatism is caused by insanity, it is the result of an internal cause which looks as if the net result should be not guilty on the ground of insanity; but it would seem odd that, if D's insanity leads him to drink excessively, he should be acquitted absolutely whereas if it causes him to bang his head against a wall until he does not know what he is doing he should be subject to restraint. Policy may be best served by a verdict of not guilty on the ground of insanity in both cases.

9.5.1.5 Automatism causes insanity

Such cases will surely be rare, but, if one should arise, probably the answer should be as in the case where automatism and insanity are concurrent causes and for the same reason.[406]

---

[402] *Davis* (1881) 14 Cox CC 563 at 564 per Stephen J approved by the House of Lords in *DPP v Beard* [1920] AC 479 at 501. For discussion, see P Handler, 'Intoxication and Criminal Responsibility in England, 1819–1920' (2013) 33 OJLS 243. See also *Coley* [2013] EWCA Crim 223, [15].

[403] See p 308.

[404] 'In a case of simple drunkenness the judge should not introduce the question whether the prisoner knew he was doing wrong—for it is a dangerous and confusing question'—per Lord Birkenhead in *DPP v Beard* [1920] AC 479 at 506. Note that in the Scottish case of *Finegan v Heywood* 2000 JC 444, (2000) The Times, 10 May, a defence of sleepwalking triggered by intoxication was treated as not being one of 'automatism'.

[405] See p 406 and Child et al [2020] Crim LR 306.   [406] See p 349.

9.5.2 Concurrent operation

9.5.2.1 Intoxication and automatism

The circumstances of non-insane automatism being pleaded where D's level of intoxication renders him an automaton are discussed earlier (p 326).

9.5.2.2 Intoxication and insanity

D does not know what he is doing, partly because of a disease of the mind and partly because he is drunk. The choice is (or should be) between a verdict of not guilty on the ground of insanity and, in a crime not requiring specific intent, one of guilty. Two difficult cases cast doubt on this and illustrate the difficulty in dealing with combined causes in practice.

In *Burns*,[407] D was charged with indecent assault, a crime not requiring specific intent. He may not have been aware of what he was doing, partly because of brain damage and partly because of drink and drugs. It is unclear whether the drugs were prescribed to D.[408] The court accepted that if D did not know what he was doing, he was entitled to an absolute acquittal. If the only causes are alcohol and insanity it is difficult to see how this can be right, since neither of the concurrent causes entitled D to be absolutely acquitted. If the causes are alcohol, prescribed drugs and insanity the position is more complex. Since the crime is one of basic intent, it is arguable that the fact that D was taking non-dangerous drugs requires the prosecution to establish that D was not reckless in becoming aggressive and unpredictable.[409] Williams took the view that in such a case insanity was the correct verdict,[410] and analogy with *Beard* might suggest that this is the right verdict, but the House of Lords in *A-G for Northern Ireland v Gallagher*[411] thought otherwise, unless the alcohol caused some quite different type of disease, such as delirium tremens.[412]

9.5.2.3 Automatism and insanity

In *Roach*,[413] the Court of Appeal adopted a more pragmatic approach, focusing on which of the multiple concurrent causes of the lack of control was dominant. D was convicted of wounding with intent to cause grievous bodily harm having attacked V with a knife after a minor dispute. D claimed to have no knowledge or memory of the incident. D claimed that his voluntary intoxication by alcohol, coupled with his prescribed drugs might have had some causative effect on his latent mental illness being triggered leading to his lack of awareness. The expert evidence described a 'disease of the mind' and not surprisingly that was treated by the prosecution as the basis of a plea of insanity. Defence counsel argued that the 'disease of the mind' should lead to a defence of automatism, but the judge did not leave that defence to the jury.[414] The Court of Appeal allowed the appeal. It was accepted that automatism was sufficiently widely defined that if external factors were operative on an 'underlying condition which would not otherwise produce a state of automatism', then a defence of non-insane automatism ought to be left to the jury.[415] The court considered this to be a borderline case as identified in *Quick*, where the 'transitory effect caused by the

---

407 (1973) 58 Cr App R 364, [1975] Crim LR 155 and commentary.

408 In early editions of this work, it was suggested that the combination of the causes was intoxication and insanity alone. Mackay, *Mental Condition Defences*, at 158 criticizes that narrow view of the facts.

409 See Mackay, ibid, 159.   410 TBCL, 681.

411 [1963] AC 349, p 271 (effect of drink on a psychopath).

412 See p 574 for discussion of intoxication and the new diminished responsibility defence and *Dowds* [2012] EWCA Crim 281 in which the Court of Appeal held that acute intoxication is not a 'recognized medical condition' for the purposes of the defence.

413 [2001] EWCA Crim 2698.   414 At [17].   415 At [28].

application to the body of some external factor such as violence, drugs etc cannot fairly be said to be due to disease'. With respect, it is not clear that this is a faithful application of that principle. In *Quick*, the lack of control was due to hypoglycaemia, caused by taking insulin (an external event) on an underlying internal condition (diabetes). Is it true to say (as the Court of Appeal would) that the underlying condition in *Quick* would not otherwise have produced a state of automatism if the insulin had not been administered? Surely it would. D would have gone into a hyperglycaemic state if he had not taken the insulin. The state of automatism which would have resulted if the underlying condition had been left to its own devices would be hyperglycaemia, which is different from the state of automatism that resulted from the insulin—hypoglycaemia—but does that matter?

The court seems to accord precedence to the prescribed drugs rather than the internal cause and the voluntary intoxication. The lack of control seems to have been a combination of: (a) the 'psychogenic' personality (which would alone result in a special verdict); (b) prescribed drugs (which alone if taken as per the prescription would have resulted in acquittal); and (c) the voluntary intoxication (which on a specific intent charge such as this could have resulted in acquittal). It is submitted that the decision in *Roach* should be approached with considerable caution. It may be regarded as correctly decided on its facts since the judge gave confusing directions as to the relevant burdens of proof.[416]

9.6 Mistake

The rules relating to mistake are simply an application of the general principle that the prosecution must prove its case, including the mens rea or negligence which the definition of the crime requires and rebuttal of excuses raised. The so-called 'defence' is simply a denial that the prosecution has proved its case. Accordingly, only mistakes which relate to an issue which the prosecution have to prove will have any bearing on D's liability.

9.6.1 Mistakes as denials of mens rea

The 'landmark decision'[417] in *DPP v Morgan* endorsed by the House of Lords in *DPP v B*,[418] holds that D's mistake of fact will result in acquittal in all crimes of mens rea where it prevents D from possessing the relevant mens rea which the law requires for the crime with which he is charged. It is not a question of defence, but of denial of mens rea. As Lord Hailsham explains in *Morgan*:

Once one has accepted . . . that the prohibited act is [x], and that the guilty state of mind is an intention to commit [x], it seems to me to follow as a matter of inexorable logic that there is no room either for a defence of honest belief or mistake, or of a defence of honest and reasonable belief or mistake. Either the prosecution proves that the accused had the requisite intention, or it does not. In the former case it succeeds, and in the latter it fails.[419]

---

[416] The Law Commission considers the effect of its proposals on insanity and automatism on intoxication and successive and concurrent causes in LCDP, pp 145–8.

[417] [1976] AC 182. It has been described by Professor Farmer as a 'curious form of landmark case'. See L Farmer, '*DPP v Morgan*' in P Handler, H Mares and I Williams (eds), *Landmark Cases in Criminal Law* (2017).

[418] And subsequently by its ringing endorsement in *K* [2002] 1 AC 462 and *G* [2003] UKHL 50.

[419] At 214 per Lord Hailsham. For a powerful critique see J Horder, 'Cognition, Emotion and Criminal Culpability' (1990) 106 LQR 469.

Historically, mistake had been treated as a special defence and there were many *dicta* by eminent judges that *only* reasonable mistakes would excuse.[420] Lord Lane CJ[421] and the House of Lords,[422] in the light of *Morgan*, doubted these pronouncements and the House in *B v DPP*[423] made it very clear that they are wrong.

9.6.1.1 Evidence and proof

It should not be imagined that all D has to do is say 'I made a genuine mistake' to be acquitted. The reasonableness of his conduct will be important in evidential terms. Where the natural inference from D's conduct in the particular circumstances is that he intended or foresaw a particular result, the jury are very likely to convict him if he introduces no testimony that he did not in fact foresee; but the onus of proof remains throughout on the prosecution and, technically, D does not bear even an evidential burden.[424] Although D's belief need not be reasonable to excuse him, as a matter of practice, the more unreasonable it is, the less likely the jury is to accept that it was genuinely held.

9.6.1.2 Mistakes in crimes of subjective mens rea

Where the law requires intention, knowledge, belief or subjective recklessness with respect to some element in the actus reus, a mistake, whether reasonable or not, which precludes that state of mind will excuse D. The fact that a genuine though unreasonable mistake will negative D's mens rea or provide an excuse stems from the courts' endorsement of subjectivism in mens rea. Obviously, if a particular crime requires D's mens rea as to the proscribed conduct, circumstance or result to be based on his subjective intentions or beliefs, and because of a mistake of fact the intentions or beliefs D holds do not relate to the proscribed conduct, circumstance or result, D cannot be liable. Thus, where D genuinely though unreasonably believes that the thing he is shooting at is a scarecrow and not a human, he will lack the mens rea for murder—an intention to kill or do grievous bodily harm *to a person in being*.

Many commentators have suggested that the wholesale application of the subjectivist principles in the context of mistake is too simplistic an approach.[425] For example, in the context of sexual offences and consent, the ease with which D can ascertain the consent of his partner and the gravity of the harm done if the sexual act is non-consensual suggest that D's mistakes as to consent should be assessed objectively. This is in fact what Parliament has required in the Sexual Offences Act 2003. Beyond sexual cases, it can be argued that where D's mistake is unreasonable, in the sense that 'holding it or acting on it in a particular situation displays an unreasonable lack of the kind of respect and concern for others that the law demands' it should not lead to acquittal.[426] However, the present law generally adopts

[420] See, for historical accounts, E Keedy, 'Ignorance and Mistake in the Criminal Law' (1908) 22 Harv LR 75; Williams, CLGP, Ch 5; Hall, *General Principles*, Ch XI; G Williams, 'Homicide and the Supernatural' (1949) 65 LQR 491; C Howard, 'The Reasonableness of Mistake in the Criminal Law' (1961) 4 Univ QLJ 45.

[421] *Taaffe* [1983] 2 All ER 625, 628.

[422] *Westminster City Council v Croyalgrange Ltd* [1986] 2 All ER 353 at 399.

[423] See particularly Lord Nicholls at [2000] 1 All ER 836–9.

[424] G Williams, 'The Evidential Burden' (1977) 127 NLJ 156 at 158. But there is an evidential burden on D to get a particular mistake before the jury. 'Mistake is a defence in the sense that it is raised as an issue by the accused. The Crown is rarely possessed of knowledge of the subjective factors which may have caused an accused to entertain a belief in a fallacious set of facts': *Pappajohn v R* (1980) 52 CCC (2d) 481 at 494 per Dickson J. The judge does not have to direct the jury in every case of murder: 'You must be satisfied that D did not believe V was a turkey'; but he must give such a direction if D has testified that, when he fired, he thought V was a turkey.

[425] See Horder (1990) 106 LQR 469; Horder, APOCL, 239–42; R Tur, 'Subjectivism and Objectivism: Towards Synthesis' in S Shute, J Gardner and J Horder (eds), *Action and Value in Criminal Law* (1993) 213; P Alldridge, *Relocating Criminal Law* (2000) 88.

[426] Duff, *Answering for Crime*, 294.

the subjectivist stance as stated in *Morgan* and *DPP v B*. As Lord Nicholls observed in *B v DPP*, 'considered as a matter of principle, the honest belief approach must be preferable. By definition the mental element in crime is concerned with a subjective state of mind such as intent or belief.'[427] It is for Parliament to deviate from that in particular situations should it so choose.

9.6.1.3 Mistakes and crimes of negligence

Where the law requires mere negligence in respect of an element of the actus reus, then only a *reasonable* mistake can afford a defence; for an unreasonable mistake, by definition, is one which a reasonable person would not make and is, therefore, a negligent one.[428] In cases of gross negligence manslaughter, D's unreasonable mistake may excuse provided it is not regarded by the jury as a grossly unreasonable mistake. Parliament may, of course, specify in relation to any crime that only reasonable beliefs will excuse. An example of this is the Sexual Offences Act 2003 (see Ch 17).

9.6.1.4 Mistakes in crimes of strict liability

Where a crime is interpreted as imposing strict liability, then even a reasonable mistake as to that element of the actus reus for which liability is strict will not excuse. It is an oversimplification to say that mistakes are irrelevant in strict liability crimes since there are few such crimes in which every element of actus reus is regarded as strict.[429] Thus, in a sexual offence such as sexual assault on a child under 13 where liability as to the age of the victim is strict, D will still have to be proved to have *intentionally* touched V. Where he claims that because of a mistake he had not meant intentionally to touch a person, he will be denying mens rea, and an honest mistake will excuse. If he claims to have made a mistake about age, that is irrelevant because liability as to age is strict.

Bigamy: a special case?

On the explanation so far, the application of the principles of mistake would seem to be straightforward. However, there are skeletons lurking in the common law cupboard which suggest that in some cases D's mistake as to an element of actus reus must *always* be reasonable to provide an excuse. One particular problem relates to the cases on bigamy. In *Morgan*, the House of Lords showed no inclination to interfere with the line of authority[430] which asserted that D's mistaken belief in the death of his first spouse, or the dissolution or nullity of his first marriage, was a defence only where that mistake was reasonable. But in *B v DPP*, Lord Nicholls expressly disapproved of the requirement of reasonableness of belief in the leading bigamy case of *Tolson*.[431] It is submitted that a genuine though unreasonable belief ought now to be a sufficient excuse on a charge of bigamy.

In general terms the *Tolson* approach may be tolerable where we are concerned with so-called 'quasi-criminal', 'regulatory' or 'welfare' offences; but it should have no place in serious crimes—and, after *B v DPP*, *K* and *G* it seems less likely to do so, as discussed in Ch 5.

---

[427] For criticism see J Horder, 'How Culpability Can and Cannot be Denied in Under-Age Sex Crimes' [2001] Crim LR 15, arguing that D's mistake should be relevant if it relates to his 'guiding moral reason'.

[428] See Ch 4.

[429] See SP Green, 'Six Senses of Strict Liability' in Simester, *Appraising Strict Liability*, Ch 1.

[430] *Tolson* (1889) 23 QBD 168, CCR; *King* [1964] 1 QB 285; *Gould* [1968] 2 QB 65. As the opinions in *Morgan* relating to defences have been reconsidered so too may the opinions regarding bigamy, if the matter ever arises. The House also accepted the requirement of reasonable grounds for believing the use of force to be necessary in self-defence, but see *Beckford* and *Williams*.

[431] (1889) 23 QB 168.

9.6.1.5 Identifying the relevant mistake

What the discussion on bigamy exposes is the broader problem in many crimes of identifying which elements of actus reus require a corresponding mens rea requirement. In many serious offences there will usually be a strong if not complete correspondence; that is, that elements of the actus reus will each have corresponding elements of mens rea to be proved. For example, in *Westminster City Council v Croyalgrange Ltd*,[432] Robert Goff LJ referred to 'the ordinary principle that, where it is required that an offence should have been knowingly committed, the requisite knowledge must embrace all the elements of the offence'. On orthodox subjective principles intention, knowledge, belief or recklessness is required as to all the elements of the actus reus unless that is excluded expressly or by implication; and the more serious the crime, the more reluctant should the court be to find an implied exclusion.[433]

9.6.1.6 Summary

The most logical approach to mistakes is, it is submitted: (a) to identify the relevant mistake D claims to have made; (b) identify to which element of the actus reus of the offence it relates; (c) ascertain what mens rea, if any, attaches to that element of the actus reus in dispute; (d) apply the relevant rule as stated in the previous paragraphs: if the mens rea element is subjective D is entitled to acquittal on a genuine mistake; if it is objective/negligence, D's mistake must be a reasonable one to lead to acquittal; if liability on that element of actus reus is strict, D's mistake is irrelevant.

9.6.2 Mistakes and defences

The House of Lords in *Morgan* also left untouched the traditional requirement that mistakes as to the elements of defences had to be reasonable if they were to operate to excuse the accused. *Morgan*, although a case on the mens rea for rape and for that purpose no longer good law, was a landmark case in relation to mistake generally, for which it remains an authority for offences with subjective elements. In *Beckford v R*, the Privy Council recognized this:

Looking back, *Morgan* can now be seen as a landmark decision in the development of the common law, returning the law to the path upon which it might have developed but for the inability of an accused to give evidence on his own behalf.[434]

Beckford v R is itself of great importance in that it takes the principle of *Morgan* even further than the majority of the House were, at that time, prepared to go. In *Morgan*, the plea was a simple denial of the prosecution's case relating to the elements of the offence. By charging rape, the prosecution alleged that D had intercourse with a woman who did not consent and that he either knew that she did not consent or was reckless (at that time subjective recklessness was the prescribed mens rea for rape) whether she did so. D denied that he knew or was reckless, as alleged.

Where on the other hand D pleads a true defence, D admits the allegations made by the prosecution about actus reus and mens rea but asserts further facts which, in law, justify or excuse his action. Self-defence is an example. D admits that he intentionally killed or

---

[432] (1986) 83 Cr App R 155.

[433] There are, admittedly, many exceptions to this principle. LCCP 195, *Criminal Liability in Regulatory Contexts* (2010) also contains discussion of the significance of this principle and of the hierarchy of mens rea, see the discussion in Ch 5.

[434] [1987] 3 All ER 425 at 431.

wounded V but asserts that he did so because V was making a deadly attack on him and this was the only way he could save his own life. It may transpire that D was mistaken. V was not in fact making a deadly attack. The courts, until the 1980s, were consistent in asserting that the defence failed if there were no reasonable grounds for his belief. The majority of the House of Lords in *Morgan* did not intend to interfere with defences. They were concerned with a mistake as to an element of the offence. *Beckford* related to a mistake as to an element of a defence. The Privy Council rejected any distinction. The Board followed *Morgan* and approved the ruling of Lord Lane CJ in *Gladstone Williams*.[435] Discussing the offence of assault, he said:

The mental element necessary to constitute guilt is the intent to apply unlawful force to the victim. We do not believe that the mental element can be substantiated by simply showing an intent to apply force and no more.[436]

If D believed, reasonably or not, in the existence of facts which would justify the force used in self-defence, he did not intend to use *unlawful* force. *Beckford* clearly applies to all instances of private defence.[437] However, in duress, for example, the courts continue to state that D's belief in the alleged compelling facts must be based on reasonable grounds.[438] If, however, D is to be judged on the facts as he believed them to be when he sets up self-defence it is difficult to see why it is different in principle when he sets up duress. In both cases D is saying that, on the facts as he believed them to be, his act was not an offence. It is submitted that the principle of *Beckford* should be applicable to defences generally.

Since *Beckford*, *Albert v Lavin*[439] must be taken to be wrong in making a distinction in relation to assault between the definitional elements of an offence and the definitional elements of a defence. The same subjective test applies to both.

9.6.2.1 Summary

Whether the law recognizes the mistake made by D as to facts which if they existed would provide a valid defence, and whether in order to be recognized the mistake must be one of a reasonable or merely genuine nature, must be considered in the context of each defence (see the next chapter). Intoxicated mistake has been discussed previously (p 344).

The courts have adopted the subjective principle in some categories (eg self-defence),[440] but not others (eg duress).[441] Some commentators seek to distinguish the categories on the basis of whether the defence is one of a justificatory or excusatory kind, or whether the defence relates to a 'definitional element' of the offence. Since the law does not adopt such classifications, and they cannot be universally applied, it seems that these may confuse rather than illuminate matters.[442]

The correct approach to mistakes and defences is, it is submitted: (a) to identify the relevant mistake of fact the defendant claims to have made; (b) identify to which element of the defence it relates; (c) ascertain whether that element of the defence is one in which the courts have imposed an objective interpretation; (d) if the defence is one assessed objectively (eg the requirement of a reasonable belief in a threat of death or serious injury in duress) D will only be able to rely on the mistake if it is reasonable; if the element of the defence is

435 (1987) 78 Cr App R 276.
436 The HRA 1998, Art 2 (right to life), was thought by some to set a more demanding standard than 'honest belief', see Ch 10. See now *Duggan* [2014] EWHC 3343 (Admin) and *Da Silva* (2016) 63 EHRR 12.
437 See Ch 10.   438 *Hasan* [2005] UKHL 22, see Ch 10.   439 [1982] AC 546.
440 *Williams* [1987] 3 All ER 441.   441 *Graham* [1982] 1 All ER 801; *Hasan* [2005] UKHL 22.
442 See TBCL, 138; Tur, 'Subjectivism and Objectivism: Towards Synthesis' in Shute, Gardner and Horder (eds), *Action and Value in Criminal Law*, 213.

subjective (eg the requirement that D believes in the need for force in private defence) he will be entitled to rely on the mistaken belief as to the facts even if unreasonable.

9.6.3 Irrelevant mistakes

A mistake which does not preclude mens rea (or negligence where that is in issue) is irrelevant and no defence. Suppose D believes he is smuggling a crate of Irish whiskey. In fact the crate contains Scotch whisky. Duty is, of course, chargeable on both. D believes he is importing a dutiable item and he is importing a dutiable item. The actus reus is the same whether the crate contains Irish or Scotch. He *knows*, because his belief and the facts coincide in this respect, that he is evading the duty chargeable on the goods in the crate. If D had believed the crate to contain only some non-dutiable item, for example foreign currency (even if he had mistakenly believed it was dutiable), he would have lacked the mens rea for the offence.[443]

A much misunderstood case is that of *Taaffe*.[444] T imported 3.7 kilos of cannabis believing that he was importing large sums of money and that currency was subject to an import prohibition. The House of Lords upholding the decision of the Court of Appeal[445] concluded that an accused is to be judged upon the facts as he believed them to be. Taaffe held two mistaken states of mind. His mistake of fact was that he was importing currency when he was in fact importing cannabis. His mistake of law was that he thought currency was subject to a prohibition. T's belief as to the fact meant that he was not *knowingly* importing prohibited goods at all. If the jury accepted as genuine his mistaken belief as to the facts, there would be no knowing importation of prohibited goods. This is analogous to the example used earlier of D shooting the scarecrow. On that basis his mistaken belief negatived the mens rea. He could not be convicted of the substantive offence under s 170 of the Customs and Excise Management Act 1979.

T's mistaken belief as to the scope of criminal law is quite different. That belief could not, even if the jury accepted that he held it, have rendered him liable for importing the currency: there would be no criminal offence with which he could be charged either as a substantive offence under s 170 of the Customs and Excise Management Act 1979 or an attempt under s 1 of the Criminal Attempt Act 1981. The criminal law, even when inchoate forms of offending are involved, cannot extend that far: if D visits England and believes that adultery is an offence, he cannot be liable for any crime by committing adultery while here, nor for attempting to do so (see Ch 11).

The case of *Taaffe* provides for a defence only where D's belief is that he is importing goods of a particular description which, if it were true, would mean that as a matter of law he was not in fact importing goods which were subject to any prohibition. This should be contrasted with a second category of case of mistake: that in which D believes that he is importing or attempting to import prohibited goods, but in fact he is importing something not subject to a prohibition or restriction. This is illustrated by the decision in *Shivpuri* discussed at p 516. Shivpuri believed he was importing one type of prohibited goods when he was importing harmless material. The House of Lords concluded that there was no difficulty in convicting him of an attempt to import the prohibited goods. The case is, in one sense, the converse of *Taaffe*. Where D makes a mistake of fact that, if believed, would mean that he was not knowingly importing prohibited goods, he is to be acquitted: *Taaffe*. Where D

---

[443] See commentary on *Taaffe* [1983] Crim LR 536 at 537; affd [1984] AC 539. See *Forbes* [2001] UKHL 40 where D believed he was importing prohibited goods (adult pornography) and he was importing prohibited goods (child pornography). D evaded the prohibition on imports and intended to do so. See also *Matrix* [1997] 8 Arch News.

[444] [1984] AC 539.   [445] (1983) 77 Cr App R 82.

makes a mistake of fact that, if believed, would mean that he was importing goods subject to a prohibition, he can be convicted of an attempt to import those goods.

9.6.4 Mistakes of law

If D makes a mistake by thinking that some form of conduct is criminal when it is not, he cannot be guilty of an offence—there is no offence with which he can be charged, as in the example of the tourist who believes adultery is a crime in England.[446] These are exceptional and unlikely ever to come to light. It does not apply where D refuses, however honestly, to accept the judgment of a court,[447] just as it would be hopeless for him to argue that he did not accept the validity of an Act of Parliament.

Suppose that X obtains goods from V by fraud and gives them to D, who knows all the facts. We have already seen that it will not avail D to say he does not know handling stolen goods is a crime. Equally, it is thought it will not avail him to say that he did not know that it is against the criminal law to obtain goods by fraud and that goods so obtained are 'stolen' for this purpose. 'Stolen' is a concept of the criminal, not the civil, law and ignorance of it is no defence.

On the other hand, the 'leave' granted to a visitor to remain in the UK looks like a civil law concept, but the House of Lords has held that a mistake of law is no answer to a charge of knowingly remaining without leave.[448]

9.6.4.1 Mistake of criminal law

If D mistakenly believes that conduct which is a crime in England is not criminal he will, generally, have no defence.[449] This is because *usually* knowledge that the act is forbidden by law is no part of mens rea.[450] Where, for example, D, a visitor to England believes that his conduct is lawful because it does not constitute a crime in his homeland,[451] he will have no defence if that conduct is an offence in England. The harshness of the rule is tempered somewhat by the fact that most serious criminal offences are also well recognized as moral 'wrongs'. However, it is no defence even where the crime is not one commonly known to be criminal. Thus, ignorance of any of the thousands of regulatory offences is no defence. This position is ameliorated only slightly by s 3(2) of the Statutory Instruments Act 1946 providing a defence for D charged with an offence created by Statutory Instrument to prove that, at the time of the offence, the instrument had not been published nor reasonable steps taken to bring its contents to the notice of the public or the accused.[452] By analogy, where an offence in English law involves an issue of foreign law, it is arguable that D should only be liable if

---

[446] See DN Husak and A von Hirsch, 'Culpability in Mistake of Law' in Shute, Gardner and Horder (eds), *Action and Value in Criminal Law*.

[447] ibid.   [448] *Grant v Borg* [1982] 1 WLR 638.   [449] See p 478.

[450] cf the comments of Lord Woolf in the appeal in the Privy Council in the Pitcairn case discussed later in this section: *Christian v The Queen* [2006] UKPC 47. His lordship stated that '[A]s in this case the appellants suffered no prejudice in view of their state of knowledge an argument based on abuse of process would not be established. It may be the case that the argument under this head could be freestanding and not based on abuse of process. However if this be so the need for prejudice would still be a requirement. The great majority of criminal offences require mens rea. *If you do not know and are not put on notice that the conduct with which you are charged was criminal at the time you are alleged to have committed the offence, it can be the case that you do not have the necessary criminal intent*' (emphasis added). For discussion, see D Oliver (ed), *Justice, Legality and the Rule of Law: Lessons from the Pitcairn Prosecutions* (2009) in which it is argued that the Crown lacked jurisdiction to bring the prosecutions and that they amounted to an abuse of process.

[451] See *Esop* (1836) 7 C & P 456.

[452] cf A Ashworth, 'Excusable Mistake of Law' [1974] Crim LR 652 and p 478. See for a comparison with some other European States taking a less strict approach, J Blomsa, *Mens Rea and Defences in European Criminal Law* (2012) 466.

it is reasonable for him to discover that law.[453] Andrew Ashworth has advanced a powerful argument against the present position. He suggests that the rule is based on shaky foundations, examines many circumstances in which the rule gives rise to unfairness and identifies government obligations to provide clearer criminal law.[454]

The arguments that every citizen should have access to a clear statement of the law is a constitutional principle supported by Art 7 of the ECHR. As Lord Bingham observed in *Rimmington*,[455] 'Article 7 sustains [the] contention that a criminal offence must be clearly defined in law, and represents the operation of "the principle of legal certainty".'[456] The principle enables each community to regulate itself:

with reference to the norms prevailing in the society in which they live. That generally entails *that the law must be adequately accessible—an individual must have an indication of the legal rules applicable in a given case—and he must be able to foresee the consequences of his actions, in particular to be able to avoid incurring the sanction of the criminal law.*[457]

The ease with which a defendant could discover the law, and whether he might rely on a mistake as to the scope of the law where it was not readily discoverable, were in issue in the prosecution of a number of men in the Pitcairn Islands for sexual abuse of young women on the islands. In *Christian & others v The Queen (The Pitcairn Islands)*,[458] the defendants argued that the case should have been stayed as an abuse of process on the grounds, inter alia, that they did not know that English law applied and that they had no access on their remote Pacific island to English legal texts. Lord Woolf[459] accepted that:

it is a requirement of almost every modern system of criminal law, that persons who are intended to be bound by a criminal statute must first be given either actual or at least constructive notice of what the law requires. This is a requirement of the rule of law, which in relation to the criminal law reflects the need for legal certainty.

He had no difficulty with the principle of such an argument but found it had no application on the facts: it was clear that DD, although probably unaware of the terms of the Sexual Offences Act or even that there was legislation of that name or the sentences that could be imposed for those offences, were aware that their conduct was contrary to the criminal law. The moral wrong of rape and sexual abuse were so obvious that the claim of a lack of awareness of specific offences was irrelevant. Similarly, the Privy Council rejected the argument that the defendants could not have discovered the law had they tried[460] because the precise terms of the Sexual Offences Act had not been published on the island. This was because the fact that there were offences such as rape and possibly indecent assault was generally known because they had to be dealt with by the Pitcairn Supreme Court, requiring as they did greater punishment than was otherwise possible.

Interestingly, Lord Woolf acknowledged that:

The sheer volume of the law in England, much of which would be inapplicable . . ., creates real problems of access even to lawyers unless they are experts in the particular field of law in question. The criminal law can only operate . . . if the *onus is firmly placed on a person*, who is or ought to be

---

[453] See eg the argument in relation to sex tourism where D in England might mistakenly believe that to have sex with a 15-year-old in the host country is not criminal in that country. See Alldridge, *Relocating Criminal Law*, 149, discussing the Sexual Offences (Conspiracy and Incitement) Act 1996.

[454] See p 451.   [455] [2005] UKHL 63.

[456] See eg *Brumarescu v Romania* (2001) 33 EHRR 35 at para 61 and *Kokkinakis v Greece* (1993) 17 EHRR 397 at para 52.

[457] *SW v UK; CR v UK* (1995) 21 EHRR 363 (emphasis added).

[458] [2006] UKPC 47. See H Power, 'Pitcairn Island' [2007] Crim LR 609.   [459] At [40].

[460] cf Lord Hope at [83] who had he not concluded that they were aware of the wrongs which were criminal at common law, would have granted a stay.

on notice that conduct he is intending to embark on may contravene the criminal law, to take the action that is open to him to find out what are the provisions of that law.[461]

This places the emphasis on the duty of the citizen to ascertain the law rather than on the State to bring the law to every citizen's attention.[462]

9.6.4.2 Erroneous advice given to D

Where D has relied on erroneous advice provided by the relevant State authority he may in some circumstances be successful in an application to stay proceedings as an abuse of process.[463]

9.6.5 Mistake of fact or law?

Identifying whether a mistake allegedly made by D is one of criminal law or fact is not always easy. For example, if D mistakenly believes that the person grabbing hold of him is a thug about to rob him (it is in fact a police officer) and he resists, he has made a mistake of fact and cannot be guilty of assaulting with intent to resist arrest. Where, however, D is aware that the person who is grabbing him is a police officer, but mistakenly believes that the officer has no power of arrest on the facts as they exist, D has made a mistake of criminal law. But what of D who makes a mistake as to antecedent facts which, if they were as he believed them to be, would indeed preclude the officer's power of arrest?[464]

Where the mens rea involves some legal concept[465] or the absence of a claim of right then mistake may negative mens rea and be a defence.

An honest though unreasonable mistake as to the *civil* law may lead to acquittal where it prevents D from holding the mens rea of the criminal offence. For example, in *Smith (David)*,[466] D damaged property in his rented flat believing it was his own property—he made a mistake as to the ownership of the property. His conviction for criminal damage was quashed since D had no intent to damage property *belonging to another*. His mistake as to ownership prevented him having the relevant mens rea. As James LJ explained:

Applying the ordinary principles of *mens rea*, the intention and recklessness and the absence of lawful excuse required to constitute the offence have reference to property belonging to another. It follows that in our judgment no offence is committed under this section if a person destroys or causes damage to property belonging to another if he does so in the honest though mistaken belief that the property is his own, and provided that the belief is honestly held it is irrelevant to consider whether or not it is a justifiable belief.[467]

Further reading

J Horder, *Excusing Crime*

A Loughnan, *Manifest Madness: Mental Incapacity in Criminal Law*

A Simester and ATH Smith (eds), *Harm and Culpability*

V Tadros, *Criminal Responsibility*

461 At [44], emphasis added.
462 See for discussion of some European States' approaches, J Blomsa, *Mens Rea and Defences in European Criminal Law* (2012) 473.
463 See A Ashworth, 'Testing Fidelity to Legal Values' (2000) 63 MLR 633, 635–42 identifying the importance of Art 7 of the ECHR. One of the strongest examples is *Postermobile v LBC* (1997) 8 Dec, unreported, DC and the Editorial at [1998] Crim LR 435 (D receiving erroneous information from planning agency). See also G Williams, 'The Draft Code and Relevance of Official Statements' (1989) 9 LS 177. See for discussion of some European States' approaches, J Blomsa, *Mens Rea and Defences in European Criminal Law* (2012) 471.
464 See *Lee* [2001] Cr App R 293.   465 See 114.   466 [1974] QB 354.   467 ibid, 360.

10

General defences

This chapter deals with defences in the broader sense, not just those focused on the mental condition of the accused. In the cases in this chapter, D will usually have performed the actus reus with the appropriate mens rea, but despite both these elements of the offence being proved by the prosecution, the question arises whether D is entitled to an acquittal owing to some justifying, excusing or exempting circumstance or condition. There are special or partial defences which apply to particular crimes (eg loss of self-control and diminished responsibility in murder) which are dealt with separately although where appropriate their interrelationship is considered. Some reference back to the general discussion of defences at the beginning of Ch 9 may be necessary, particularly to the introductory comments on the theoretical underpinnings of defences and the theories of justifications and excuse.

10.1 Infancy

Infants or, in more modern terminology, children are persons under 18 years of age.[1] Although the civil law places restrictions on certain activities (eg writing a will) the criminal law imposes no such limitations on their ability to commit crimes, for, as Kenny put it, 'a child knows right from wrong long before he knows how to make a prudent speculation or a wise will'.[2] At common law the criminal law applied different rules to children in three categories, but under the present law only two categories remain.

10.1.1 Children under 10 years

At common law a child was entirely exempt from criminal responsibility until the day before his seventh birthday.[3] By statute, criminal responsibility now begins on the child's tenth birthday.[4] The common law rule was stated as a conclusive presumption that the child is *doli incapax,* and the statute uses the same language: 'It shall be conclusively presumed that no child under the age of ten years can be guilty of any offence.' Even though there may be the clearest evidence that the child caused an actus reus with mens rea, he cannot be convicted once it appears that he had not, at the time he did the act, attained the age of ten. This is not a mere procedural bar; no crime is committed by the child with the result that the one who instigated him to do the act is a principal and not a secondary party.[5] And where a husband and wife were charged with handling stolen goods in the form of a child's tricycle, knowing it to have been taken by their seven-year-old son, it was held that they must be acquitted on the ground that, since the child being only seven could not steal, the tricycle was not stolen.[6] Ten is a comparatively low age for the beginning of criminal responsibility, it is certainly much lower than many other European States; but, as the Ingleby Committee pointed out:[7]

In many countries the 'age of criminal responsibility' is used to signify the age at which a person becomes liable to the 'ordinary' or 'full' penalties of the law. In this sense, the age of criminal responsibility in England is difficult to state: it is certainly much higher than [ten].[8]

Numerous organizations including the UN Committee on the Rights of the Child (2002) and the European Committee on Social Rights (2005), have urged reform of English law. There is, of course, no international agreement on what the age should be.[9] As the Beijing Rules, adopted by the United Nations General Assembly in 1985 observe in their commentary on

---

[1] See H Keating, 'The Responsibility of Children in the Criminal Law' (2007) 19 CFLQ 183, and 'Reckless Children' [2007] Crim LR 546 and for an historical account see G Williams, 'The Criminal Responsibility of Children' [1954] Crim LR 493. Broader issues of youth justice are discussed in C Ball, 'Youth Justice: Half A Century of Responses to Youth Offending' [2004] Crim LR 167; J Fionda, *Devils and Angels: Youth, Policy and Crime* (2005); L Hoyano and C Keenan, *Child Abuse: Law and Policy* (2007).

[2] Kenny, *Outlines*, 80.

[3] A person attains a particular age at the commencement of the relevant anniversary of the date of his birth: Family Law Reform Act 1969, s 9(1).

[4] Children and Young Persons Act 1933, s 50, as amended by the Children and Young Persons Act 1963, s 16, which raised the age from eight. The Ingleby Committee had recommended that the age be raised to 12. Cmnd 1911 (1960). That is the age to be adopted in Scotland. The Welsh Justice Commission has recommended raising the age in Wales too. See J*ustice in Wales for the People of Wales (Cyfiawnder yng Nghymru dros Bobl Cymru)* (2019), see further C Hodgetts, 'An Evolution in Devolution? Welsh Criminal Justice and the Commission on Justice in Wales' [2021] Crim LR 34.

[5] See p 235.   [6] *Walters v Lunt* [1951] 2 All ER 645; and cf *Marsh v Loader* (1863) 14 CBNS 535.

[7] Cmnd 1191, at 30.   [8] The age then was eight. See n 4.

[9] See generally D Cipriani, *Children's Rights and the Minimum Age of Criminal Responsibility: A Global Perspective* (2009). The age in Scotland has now increased to 12—Criminal Justice and Licensing (Scotland) Act 2010, s 52.

the United Nations Standard Minimum Rules for the Administration of Juvenile Justice (Beijing Rules), Art 4(1):[10]

The minimum age of criminal responsibility differs widely owing to history and culture. The modern approach would be to consider whether a child can live up to the moral and psychological components of criminal responsibility; that is, whether a child, by virtue of her or his individual discernment and understanding, can be held responsible for essentially antisocial behaviour. If the age of criminal responsibility is fixed too low or if there is no lower age limit at all, the notion of criminal responsibility would become meaningless.

The law is out of step with psychological and neurological evidence[11] and is in urgent need of reform.

10.1.2 Children aged 10 and above

At common law, there was a *rebuttable* presumption that a child aged not less than ten but under 14 years ('a young person') was *doli incapax*: incapable of committing crime. The presumption was rebutted only if the prosecution proved beyond reasonable doubt, not only that the child caused an actus reus with mens rea, but also that he knew that the particular act was not merely naughty or mischievous, but 'seriously wrong'. If there was no evidence of such knowledge, other than that implicit in the act itself, the child had no case to answer. In *C v DPP*,[12] the Divisional Court held that this ancient rule of the common law was outdated and no longer law; but the House of Lords reversed this, ruling that it was not open to the courts so to hold. That decision was followed by a series of acquittals which caused disquiet.

In the Crime and Disorder Act 1998, Parliament responded by abolishing the rebuttable presumption.[13] This was intended to put children aged ten and above on an equal footing with adults, so far as liability (but not sentencing or mode of trial and procedure) is concerned. The Act is not well drafted. Section 34 of the Crime and Disorder Act 1998 provides:

The rebuttable presumption of criminal law that a child aged 10 or over is incapable of committing an offence is abolished.

Despite cogent arguments by Professor Walker that the section[14] left it open to a child under 14 to introduce evidence that he did not know that what he did was seriously wrong, the House of Lords finally decided the defence rather than the mere presumption had been abolished. In *T*,[15] the House of Lords concluded that there was no authority for the existence of the defence

---

[10] See further P Brown, 'Reviewing the Age of Criminal Responsibility' [2018] Crim LR 904 and the helpful discussion in Emmerson, Ashworth and Macdonald, HR&CJ, paras 11.01–11.05 concluding that it is 'difficult to see how the [current] age of criminal responsibility is in the child's best interests'. See also J Gillen, 'Age of Criminal Responsibility: The Frontier Between Crime and Justice' [2007] Int Fam LJ 7 and A Ashworth, 'Child Defendants and the Doctrines of the Criminal Law' in J Chalmers, L Farmer and F Leverick (eds), *Essays in Criminal Law in Honour of Sir Gerald Gordon* (2010).

[11] S-J Blakemore and S Choudhury, 'Development of the Adolescent Brain: Implications for Executive Function and Social Cognition' (2006) 47 J Child Psych & Psychol 296–312.

[12] [1996] AC 1. See the 8th edn of this book for detail, at p 195.

[13] Crime and Disorder Act 1998, s 34. See in particular: N Walker, 'The End of an Old Song' (1999) 149 NLJ 64; L Gelsthorpe and A Morris, 'Much Ado about Nothing—A Critical Comment on Key Provisions Relating to Children in the Crime and Disorder Act 1998' (1999) 11 CFLQ 209; J Fionda, 'New Labour, Old Hat: Youth Justice and the Crime and Disorder Act 1998' [1999] Crim LR 36; C Webb, 'Irrational Presumptions of Rationality and Comprehension' [1998] 3 Web JCLI.

[14] See Walker (1999) 149 NLJ 64. Cf the discussion by D Bailey, 'Interpreting Parliamentary Inaction' (2020) 79 CLJ 245 at 247.

[15] *T* [2009] UKHL 20. For critical comment see F Bennion, '*Mens Rea* and Defendants Below the Age of Discretion' [2009] Crim LR 757.

separate from the presumption and that Parliament's intention was clearly to abolish the con-cept of *doli incapax* as having any effect in law. There is no separate defence of *doli incapax* after s 34 of the Crime and Disorder Act 1998.[16] This is a disappointing though predictable outcome. The statute is clear that it is abolishing the presumption. The House of Lords' inter-pretation of the parliamentary debates is strained to achieve the pragmatic result desired.[17]

In the last twenty years, the law governing the procedure for trials of child defendants has developed[18] somewhat and this may assist some children. It has been recognized explicitly that a child defendant must be able to participate effectively in proceedings.[19] One of the criteria for determining whether a child has a sufficient understanding to be tried is whether he under-stands the seriousness of the consequences of his actions. In some cases, the child's lack of understanding of the wrongness of his conduct will be so great that it might preclude a trial.[20] In its Discussion Paper on insanity and automatism, the Law Commission observed that it is a matter of medical fact that children are neurologically immature as compared with adults.[21] Evidence suggests that developmental delay can be relevant to the question of capacity and criminal responsibility and that it impacts upon a number of specific competencies.[22]

The *presumption* of *doli incapax* still poses problems in prosecutions for historic sexual abuse where the conduct alleged to have been carried out by the defendant occurred when he was between the ages of 10 and 14.[23]

10.2 Duress

10.2.1 Duress by threats and circumstances

For centuries the law has recognized a defence of duress by threats.[24] The typical case is where D is told, 'Do this [an act which would be a crime if there were no defence of duress]—or you will be killed', and, fearing for his life, D does the required act. Relatively recently,

---

[16] T, aged 12 at the time of offending, pleaded guilty to 12 counts of causing or inciting a child under 13 to engage in sexual activity. Depending on the particular activity, this may be the sort of behaviour where a child might know that what he is doing is wrong or naughty, without seeing it as being seriously wrong resulting in his being on the sexual offender's 'register'.

[17] It has been argued that a new defence should be available for children up to the age of 14 that places emphasis on their relative lack of autonomy. See C Elliott, 'Criminal Responsibility and Children: A New Defence Required to Acknowledge the Absence of Capacity and Choice' (2011) 75 J Crim L 289.

[18] See references at n 1.   [19] *T & V v UK* (2000) 30 EHRR 121.

[20] Where there is evidence that D cannot understand, at the judge's discretion the process should switch to determining as a matter of fact whether the child performed the act alleged. There may be a sufficient delay between the act and the trial for D to have matured sufficiently to now understand the seriousness. See LCCP 197, *Unfitness to Plead* (2010); and LC 364, *Unfitness to Plead* (2016).

[21] Ch 9.

[22] P Kambam and C Thompson, 'The Development of Decision-Making Capacities in Children and Adolescents: Psychological and Neurological Perspectives and Their Implications for Juvenile Defendants' (2009) 27 Behavioral Sciences and the Law 173.

[23] *Andrew N* [2004] EWCA Crim 1236; *H* [2010] EWCA Crim 312; *PF* [2017] EWCA Crim 983 noting that independent evidence of naughtiness beyond the mere fact of the commission of the relevant acts was required.

[24] Although somewhat dated, there is a valuable discussion of the defences in LCCP 122, *Legislating the Criminal Code: Offences Against the Person and General Principles* (1992); LCCP 218, *Legislating the Criminal Code: Offences Against the Person and General Principles* (1993); LCCP 177, *A New Homicide Act for England?* (2005) Ch 7; LC 304, *Murder, Manslaughter and Infanticide* (2007) Ch 6. On the Commission's proposals, see A Ashworth, 'Principles, Pragmatism and the Law Commission Recommendations on Homicide Reform' [2007] Crim LR 333 at 340. The Law Reform Commission of Ireland has also produced a valuable analysis in its Consultation Paper, *Duress and Necessity* (2006): www.lawreform.ie; see also the review in the Victoria Law Reform Commission Report, *Defences to Homicide* (2006): www.lawreform.vic.gov.au.

the law has recognized another form of duress—duress of circumstances. Again, D does the act alleged to constitute the crime, feeling compelled to do so out of fear, but this time no human being is demanding that he do it.[25] D does it because he reasonably believes himself to be threatened with death or serious injury and that his only reasonable way of escaping the threat is to perform the conduct element of the offence. The defences are clearly closely related. For example, D is told he will be killed unless he acts as a getaway driver for a robbery. The compulsion on D to do the act is exactly the same whether the threat comes from someone demanding that he do it, or from an aggressor, or other circumstances. His moral culpability, or lack of it, seems exactly the same.[26] The discussion of the relationship of duress, duress of circumstances and necessity is postponed until each has been examined in detail (p 397).

The law relating to duress by threats is now well developed. Duress of circumstances is still relatively new, but it has developed by analogy to duress by threats so that there is a ready-made set of principles to govern it. By a strange coincidence, all the early cases on duress of circumstances concerned road traffic offences but there is no reason why it should be limited to such offences. *Pommell*,[27] *Safi*,[28] *Shayler*[29] and a host of other cases decide that it has the same range and is governed by the same principles as duress by threats. The result is that either form of duress is a general defence, except that neither applies to some forms of treason, or to murder or attempted murder, whether the defendant is a principal or a secondary party. There are only a few differences between the two defences in application.

10.2.1.1 Duress and voluntariness

It has often been said that the duress must be such that D's act is not 'voluntary'.[30] We are not, however, concerned here with the case where a person is compelled by physical force to go through the motions of an actus reus without any choice on his part. In such cases he will almost invariably[31] be guilty of no offence on the fundamental ground that he did no act.

If there be an actual forcing of a man, as if A by force takes the arm of B and the weapon in his hand and therewith stabs C whereof he dies, this is murder in A but B is not guilty.[32]

Nor are we concerned with the kind of involuntariness which arises from automatism where D is unable to control the movement of his body. When D pleads duress (or necessity) he admits that he was able to control his actions and chose to do the act with which he is charged, but denies responsibility for doing so.[33] He may say, 'I had no choice' but that is not strictly true.[34] The alternative to committing the crime may have been so exceedingly unattractive that no reasonable person would have chosen it; but there was a choice. It is clear that the courts recognize this because for some crimes, no matter how serious the threat D

---

[25] *Cole* [1994] Crim LR 582; *Ali* [1995] Crim LR 303.

[26] See the judicial affirmation that the defences are this closely linked: *Safi* [2003] EWCA Crim 1809; *Shayler* [2001] EWCA Crim 1977 but note p 397 later in this book.

[27] [1995] 2 Cr App R 607. The case was subsequently analysed as one of necessity rather than duress of circumstances because there is no immediate threat of death to D: see *Quayle* [2005] EWCA 1415.

[28] [2003] EWCA Crim 1809.   [29] [2001] EWCA Crim 1977.

[30] See M Wasik, 'Duress and Criminal Responsibility' [1977] Crim LR 453; A Norrie, *Crime, Reason and History* (3rd edn, 2014) 218–29; ATH Smith, 'On *Actus Reus* and *Mens Rea*' in *Reshaping the Criminal Law*, 104–6.

[31] cf *Larsonneur*, p 43.   [32] Hale, II PC, 534.

[33] In *Southward* [2012] EWCA Crim 2779 D sought to plead duress yet at the same time deny he had committed the offence. The trial judge refused to leave duress to the jury on the basis that it would be very confusing. The Court of Appeal rightly agreed with this assessment.

[34] *Hasan* [2005] UKHL 22 at [73] per Baroness Hale. See also Duff, *Answering for Crime*, 287.

faced, he cannot rely on duress. If D is threatened with harm or even death unless he kills V, he should, according to the English courts, withstand the pressure and suffer death himself. He will not have a defence to murder if he kills: his acts were voluntary.

In Canada, the Supreme Court (holding that necessity may be an excuse, but not a justification) described the act of a person under duress as '*morally* involuntary', the 'involuntariness' being 'measured on the basis of society's expectation of appropriate and normal resistance to pressure'.[35] This seems to mean only that even a person of goodwill and reasonable fortitude might have chosen to do the 'criminal' act. Duress in English law cannot be said to be a form of involuntariness. A person who kills when acting under duress cannot rely on that plea as a defence. If he succeeded only in wounding V he could rely on duress. Surely D's act is voluntary in both cases. It would be illogical to say his act was involuntary if he only succeeded in wounding V.[36] D intends to do the act which, but for the duress, would be a crime.

It has been recognized by the Court of Appeal and the House of Lords that the defence is not a denial of mens rea, but a true defence operating despite the existence of the actus reus and mens rea of the offence.[37]

In short, duress is a defence because 'threats of immediate death or serious personal violence so great as to overbear the ordinary powers of human resistance should be accepted as a justification for acts which would otherwise be criminal'.[38]

10.2.1.2 The onus of proof

The onus of disproving duress is on the prosecution.[39] If no facts from which duress might reasonably be inferred appear in the prosecution's case, then D has the 'evidential burden' of laying a foundation for the defence by introducing evidence of such facts.[40] There is considerable judicial scepticism regarding defences of duress and the defendant's burden to get the defence on its feet will not always be straightforward.[41] Indeed, it has been confirmed that the judge is only obliged to leave the issue to the jury if there is evidence of facts which if believed could cause a reasonable jury properly directed to accept the defence. In *Bianco*, Laws LJ stated that, 'if the case is one where no reasonable jury properly directed as to the law could fail to find the defence disproved, no legitimate purpose is served by leaving it to the jury.'[42] In *Batchelor*,[43] Elias LJ affirmed that there could be no purpose leaving a verdict to the jury that they, on considering the evidence, could not properly reach. His lordship stated that 'evidence' in this context means evidence that would, in principle, be sufficient to justify a jury concluding that the defence is established.[44] These sentiments were reaffirmed in unequivocal terms by the Court of Appeal in *Brandford*, although the court did state that

35 *Perka* (1984) 13 DLR (4th) 1.

36 *Howe* [1987] AC 417, per Lord Hailsham LC, citing Lords Kilbrandon and Edmund-Davies in *DPP for Northern Ireland v Lynch* [1975] AC 653 at 703 and 709–10.

37 *Fisher* [2004] EWCA Crim 1190; see also *Hasan* [2005] UKHL 22 at [18] per Lord Bingham.

38 *A-G v Whelan* [1934] IR 518, per Murnaghan J (Irish CCA). The judge probably did not have in mind any distinction between justification and excuse. If there is a material distinction, duress seems to be an excuse. Cf RA Duff, 'Rule Violations and Wrongdoing' in Shute and Simester, *Criminal Law Theory*, 63.

39 *Hasan* [2005] UKHL 22, [37]; *Gill* [1963] 1 WLR 841; *Giaquento* [2001] EWCA Crim 2696; *Bianco* [2001] EWCA Crim 2156, endorsed in *Bloomfield* [2007] EWCA Crim 1873 and *Brandford* [2016] EWCA Crim 1794.

40 Radically, the Law Commission recommended reversing the burden of proof on this defence, LC 218 (1993) para 33.16. It is doubtful whether this would be compatible with the ECHR (Art 6(2)). See the doubts expressed by Lord Bingham in *Hasan* at [20]. The Law Commission has subsequently recommended that the burden be reversed should the defence become available to a charge of murder: LC 304, Ch 6.

41 See *Hasan* at [20].   42 [2001] EWCA Crim 2516, [15].   43 [2013] EWCA Crim 2638.

44 The Court of Appeal recognized in *Hammond* [2013] EWCA Crim 2709 that there is a fine line between the judge making a ruling as to the law and coming to an impermissible resolution of a case on the facts. Moses LJ stated that this problem is especially acute when duress is pleaded but that it should not deter judges from taking a robust and reasoned approach where fanciful cases of duress are raised.

the power to withdraw the defence should be exercised with caution.[45] There is a particular judicial anxiety when the defence is raised late in the trial process.

The Law Commission's recommendation in relation to the availability of the duress defence in murder is to reverse the burden, so that the accused would be obliged to prove on the balance of probabilities that the elements of the defence were made out.[46] This is a controversial approach.[47] It is a clear compromise, with the Commission being keen to see the defence of duress available to murder (which at present it is not), but prepared to reverse the burden to deter spurious and unmeritorious defences being run. The Commission acknowledges the difficulty the prosecution may face in duress cases where D is often the sole source of evidence supporting the defence.[48]

10.2.1.3 The elements of the defence

Lord Bingham, in the leading modern authority from the House of Lords, *Hasan*, summarized the elements of the defence:[49]

(1) D reasonably believes there is a threat of death or serious injury;

(2) that threat must have been made to D or his immediate family or someone close to him or, someone for whom D would reasonably regard himself as responsible;

(3) D's perception of the threat and his conduct in response are to be assessed objectively— his belief that he is under such a threat must be reasonable and his decision to commit the crime in response must be reasonable;

(4) the conduct it is sought to excuse must have been directly caused by the threats D relies on;

(5) there must have been no evasive action D could reasonably take;

(6) D cannot rely on threats to which he has voluntarily laid himself open;

(7) the defence is unavailable to murder, attempted murder or treason.

(1) Threat of death or serious injury

The type of qualifying threat or danger

As a matter of policy the law places strict limits on the type of threat sufficient to trigger the defence. It is not simply a question of balancing in each case the gravity of the threat D faced against the gravity of the offence D committed in response. The threats must reach a threshold before the defence is triggered. That threshold is set at a deliberately high level. The only threat or danger which will found a defence in either type of duress is one of death or serious[50] personal injury.[51]

The House of Lords in *Hasan*, Lord Lane CJ in *Graham*[52] and Woolf LJ in *Conway*,[53] all required a threat of death or serious personal injury. This is in keeping with most modern codes in other jurisdictions.[54]

---

[45] [2016] EWCA Crim 1794.   [46] LC 304, para 6.115.

[47] For analysis of the potential ECHR implications, see LC 304, paras 6.116 et seq.

[48] cf LCCP 177, para 7.66 where it is suggested that the days when it was easy to raise and difficult to rebut are 'long gone'!

[49] *Hasan* [2005] UKHL 22, [21]. On the decision see, inter alia, D Ibbetson (2005) 64 CLJ 530; R Ryan and D Ryan (2005) 56 NILQ 421.

[50] In *Aikens* [2003] EWCA Crim 1573, it was doubted that a threat to punch V in the face would suffice.

[51] *Radford* [2004] EWCA Crim 2878. Cf the Criminal Damage Act 1971, s 5(2)(b).

[52] [1982] 1 WLR 294.   [53] [1989] QB 290.

[54] LC 218, para 29.1: 'the overwhelming tendency of the authorities as of modern codes, is to limit the defence to cases where death or serious injury is threatened . . . Consultation strongly supported that limitation on the defence of duress, which is imposed by clause 25(2)(a) of the Criminal Law Bill.'

The Court of Appeal confirmed in *Brandford* that mere pressure based on the exploitation of a relationship but without a relevant threat of death or really serious harm will not be sufficient to enable D to plead duress.[55] Pressure of this nature is not entirely irrelevant, however, as the court observed that it may operate in a cumulative manner alongside a threat of death or really serious harm.

It has been held that serious psychiatric injury can be grievous bodily harm for the purposes of the OAPA 1861 and it is probable that a threat to cause such injury could amount to duress.[56] A threat to make a person a nervous wreck could be just as terrifying as a threat to cause serious physical injury.

This threshold of serious injury in duress is narrowly construed by the courts.[57] In some circumstances the high threshold can lead to harsh results. For example, in *Joseph*, a case involving victims of human trafficking, the Court of Appeal rejected the argument that duress ought to be broadened to encompass a threat of false imprisonment.[58] As the defence in s 45 of the Modern Slavery Act 2015 (considered later) does not apply retrospectively, some victims of slavery and relevant exploitation will still have to rely upon the common law defence of duress. Unless there was a threat of death or really serious harm, such individuals will be unable to plead duress successfully.

What constitutes a threat of 'serious injury' for the defence has created difficulties. In *Brown*,[59] the court refused leave to appeal a conviction for possession of drugs when D, suffering from a degenerative disease, was cultivating cannabis for personal use to alleviate his pain. The court regarded the threat of 'injury' he faced as being only that additional pain he would suffer by having to rely on prescribed medication rather than the lower level of pain suffered with his condition if he used cannabis. The difference between the two levels of pain was not sufficient to constitute 'serious' injury.[60] In *Quayle*,[61] the Court of Appeal went further and rejected the pain experienced by a multiple sclerosis sufferer as sufficient to qualify as 'harm' as the defence of duress of circumstances requires.

While a threat of serious personal injury is the minimum which is acceptable to found the defence for offences to which it is available, a higher minimum may be required for crimes of great gravity. Historically, Hale required threats of death and so did the judges in *M'Growther*[62] and *Purdy*[63] but those were cases of treason. The Law Commission recommends that in a case of murder, duress will require proof that D was under a threat of death or 'life threatening injury'.[64]

The following *dictum* of Lords Wilberforce and Edmund-Davies no longer applies to killing but remains true for other acts:

the realistic view is that, the more dreadful the circumstances of the killing, the heavier the evidential burden of an accused advancing such a plea, and the stronger and more irresistible the duress needed before it could be regarded as affording any defence.[65]

---

[55] [2016] EWCA Crim 1794.   [56] *Baker and Wilkins* [1997] Crim LR 497.

[57] In *Hammond* [2013] EWCA Crim 2709, D's plea of duress to the charge of breaking prison based on D's fears of being touched sexually by another inmate was rejected. The sexual advances were 'miles away' from any threat to kill or cause really serious injury; the outcome could have been different had D feared he would be raped by the other inmate. The Court of Appeal did not cite the earlier case of *A (RJ)* [2012] EWCA Crim 434, in which Lord Judge CJ observed that although duress should not be confused with pressure, the requirement that there be a threat of death or serious injury would 'no doubt' be satisfied by a threat to rape, at [63].

[58] [2017] EWCA Crim 36. The court followed what had earlier been held in *van Dao* [2012] EWCA Crim 1717 in which Gross LJ stated that 'we would in this area place the requirements of practical policy ahead of those of strict logic'. At [44]–[49]. See the commentary at [2013] Crim LR 234.

[59] [2003] EWCA Crim 2637.   [60] A duress of circumstances case.

[61] [2005] EWCA Crim 1415, [2006] Crim LR 148 and commentary.   [62] (1746) Fost 13.

[63] (1946) 10 J Crim L 182.   [64] LC 304, para 6.75.   [65] *Abbott v R* [1976] 3 All ER at 152.

Threats of blackmail, no matter how effective, are not sufficient.[66] There is no modern[67] case in which a threat of injury to property has been admitted.[68] Some ancient cases do recognize that level of threat. In *M'Growther*,[69] it was held there was no defence where the Duke of Perth had threatened to burn the houses and drive off the cattle of any of his tenants who refused to follow him. But that was a case of treason and there is now clear authority that such a threat would not be enough even on some lesser charge.

If the wrong D would perpetrate by submitting to the threat (eg D being compelled to steal a chocolate bar) was clearly less than the wrong which would have been inflicted had he defied it (eg the threatening party burning down D's house), there are cogent reasons for allowing a defence; even if the threat was not of death or even grievous bodily harm. Williams argued strongly in favour of such a principle, which is closely analogous to that adopted in the American Model Penal Code in relation to necessity.[70] But there are problems with such an approach. It would in some cases still deny a defence to D even though the injury threatened was one which no ordinary person could be expected to endure. Secondly, there would be grave difficulty in balancing the two evils against one another when they are of a completely different character.[71] 'Proportionality' may be a prerequisite for necessity[72] but it seems inappropriate for duress. Duress requires a threat of death or serious injury.

From whom/what must the threat emanate

The threat must have some source extraneous to the defendant himself. In *Rodger and Rose*,[73] D who was serving a life sentence was informed that his tariff had been substantially increased. He broke out of prison and raised duress as a defence at his trial for prison-breaking. It was conceded for the purpose of the appeal that he broke out because he had become suicidal and would have committed suicide had he not done so. So there was a threat to his life, but since the threat did not come from an extraneous source, it was no defence. To allow it, said the court, 'could amount to a licence to commit crime dependent on the personal characteristics and vulnerability of the offender'. The Court of Appeal in *Quayle* relied upon this limitation to the defence to reject the defence of duress of circumstances where D cultivated cannabis for personal use to alleviate pain for his multiple sclerosis.[74]

No threat of death or GBH need exist in fact

There is no requirement for there to be a threat of death or serious injury in fact. It is sufficient that D reasonably believes that there is a threat of the relevant gravity. If the defence was only available where there was a threat in fact, D could not plead duress where threatened with an unloaded gun, nor where D escaped from prison erroneously believing it to be on fire. This would be unduly restrictive.

In *Safi and others*,[75] Afghan hijackers who had landed at Stansted airport claimed that their fear of persecution at the hands of the Taliban constituted a defence of duress of circumstances. The trial judge directed that the defence failed unless there was evidence that there was in fact, or might in fact have been, an imminent peril to the defendants or their families. S appealed on the basis that the defence should be available if he *reasonably* believed that if he had not acted in the way he had, he (and/or the family) would have been

---

[66] *Singh* [1973] 1 WLR 1600. [67] cf *Crutchley* (1831) 5 C & P 133.

[68] 'Well, the law must draw a line somewhere; and, as a result of experience and human valuation, the law draws it between threats to property and threats to the person', per Lord Simon [1975] AC 653.

[69] See n 62. [70] See p 397. [71] Law Com Working Paper No 55, paras 14–17.

[72] *Shayler* [2001] EWCA Crim 1977, see p 397. [73] [1998] 1 Cr App R 143.

[74] [2005] EWCA Crim 415. See M Watson, 'Cannabis and the Defence of Necessity' (1998) 148 NLJ 1260. See, for a philosophical consideration of such matters, SJ Morse, 'Diminished Capacity' in S Shute, S Gardner and J Horder (eds), *Action and Value in Criminal Law* (1993) 250–63.

[75] [2003] EWCA Crim 1809.

killed or seriously injured. The Court of Appeal allowed the appeal. Duress (or duress of circumstances) does not depend on there being an actual risk of death or serious injury to the accused; the defence can be made out if the accused was impelled to act as he did because, as a result of what he reasonably believed to be the situation, he had good cause to fear that otherwise death or serious injury would result.

In *Brandford*, the Court of Appeal confirmed that the threat does not have to be relayed directly to the defendant.[76] The fact that the threat was relayed to the defendant indirectly is not fatal to the defence being pleaded. The court held that the focus of the inquiry should be on immediacy, imminence and the possibility of taking evasion action. For this reason, the more indirectly the threat is relayed, then all other things being equal, the more the defendant will struggle to satisfy the elements of the defence. Therefore, although in theory a threat can be relayed indirectly, in practice it will make it very difficult for D to plead the defence successfully.

(2) Threats against whom?

Most of the cases naturally involve a threat or danger to the life or safety of D himself, but the defences are not limited to that situation. In *Hurley and Murray*,[77] the Supreme Court of Victoria held that threats to kill or seriously injure D's de facto wife amounted to duress. In *Wright*,[78] threats against D's boyfriend sufficed. In *Conway*,[79] the threat was to the passenger in D's car; and in *Martin*,[80] D's wife's threat to commit suicide if he did not drive while disqualified was held capable of founding a defence of duress of circumstances—though in fact it seems to have been one of duress by threats—'Drive or else . . .'[81] So threats against the life or safety of D's family certainly suffice. In *Shayler*,[82] the Lord Chief Justice, approving a statement of Rose LJ in *Hussain*, stated that:

the evil must be directed towards the defendant or a person or persons for whom he has responsibility or, we would add, persons for whom the situation makes him responsible; . . . [this extends], by way of example, [to] the situation where the threat is made to set off a bomb unless the defendant performs the unlawful act. The defendant may have not have had any previous connection with those who would be injured by the bomb but the threat itself creates the defendant's responsibility for those who will be at risk if he does not give way to the threat.

Lord Bingham in *Hasan* also suggested that the threat must be 'directed against the defendant or his immediate family or someone close to him or for whom he is responsible'. So, threats to D, his family and others to whom he owes a 'duty' will qualify, but arguably this is too narrow. If a bank robber threatens to shoot a customer in the bank unless D, the clerk, hands him the keys, D surely has a defence to a charge of assisting the robbery. The concept of those for whom D is 'responsible' is ill-defined, and ought to be given a liberal construction. It is submitted that the defence is so heavily qualified by the requirement of a threat of death or serious injury and the other objective elements, that there is little need to impose restrictions on the categories of individual to whom the threat must be made.

(3) Evaluating D's response to the threat

Several difficult issues arise in determining whether by committing the crime in response to the threats D's conduct should be excused. In particular, the courts have struggled with questions of whether it is sufficient that the individual defendant regarded it as a reasonable

---

[76] [2016] EWCA Crim 1794.   [77] [1967] VR 526.   [78] [2000] Crim LR 510.   [79] [1989] QB 290.
[80] [1989] 1 All ER 652. See also *Wright* [2000] Crim LR 510.
[81] See also *M* [2007] EWCA Crim 3228, where M sought to smuggle drugs into prison being threatened with violence by E, and hearing threats from Y in prison that if he did not get the drugs he would commit suicide.
[82] [2001] EWCA Crim 1977, [49]. This was accepted in *Hasan* [2005] UKHL 22, per Lord Bingham.

response to the threat he believed that he faced, or whether the defence is only available if the reasonable person would have responded in the same way if faced with the threat D genuinely believed he faced.

In *Howe*, the House of Lords held that the defence fails if:

the prosecution prove that a person of reasonable firmness sharing the characteristics of the defendant would not have given way to the threats as did the defendant.

The House held that the correct direction was that stated by Lane LCJ in *Graham*:[83]

(1) Was [D], or may he have been, impelled to act as he did because, as a result of what he reasonably believed [E] had said or done, he had good cause to fear that if he did not so act [E] would kill him or . . . cause him serious physical injury? (2) If so, have the prosecution made the jury sure that a sober person of reasonable firmness, sharing the characteristics of [D], would not have responded to whatever he reasonably believed [E] said or did by taking part in the [crime]?

The direction contains three objective elements:

(1) D must have *reasonably* believed in the circumstances of the threat;[84]

(2) D's belief must have amounted to *good cause* for his fear;

(3) D's response must be one which might have been expected of a *sober person of reasonable firmness*.

A fourth element is usually considered although not deriving from the *Graham* judgment:

(4) D must have had no *reasonable* opportunity to escape the threat.

Reasonable belief in circumstances of threat/good cause to fear

In imposing this objective regime on the defence, Lord Lane in *Graham* equated duress with self-defence which, it was then generally accepted, imposed an objective test. But less than two years later in *Gladstone Williams*,[85] Lord Lane, influenced by the judgment of Lawton LJ in *Kimber*,[86] held that an unreasonable belief, if honestly held, might found self-defence. Lawton LJ appreciated and applied the general effect of *DPP v Morgan*[87] which was not cited in *Graham*. Logically, if *Morgan* applies to self-defence, it ought equally to apply to duress.[88] It is arguable, however, that the defences are distinguishable since duress is generally regarded as excusatory and self-defence as justificatory in nature.[89] The decision in *Graham* may thus have been an unfortunate accident—but subsequently it has been approved by the House of Lords in *Howe* and more recently still the House of Lords in *Hasan* certainly did not seem to be inclined to depart from it.[90]

---

[83] (1982) 74 Cr App R 235 at 241. Cf *Lawrence* [1980] 1 NSWLR 122.

[84] The element of reasonableness was firmly endorsed in *Hasan* [2005] UKHL 22 at [23] per Lord Bingham. See also LC 304, para 6.77. In LCCP 177, para 7.46 fn 54 the Commission suggested that in an unpublished codification project, the reasonableness test would be endorsed, reversing an earlier Law Commission Report recommendation.

[85] See p 402.

[86] [1983] 3 All ER 316, (an honest belief that V was consenting was a defence to indecent (now sexual) assault).

[87] See p 350. See JC Smith, 'The Triumph of Inexorable Logic' in *Leading Cases of the Twentieth Century* (2000).

[88] In *Martin (DP)* [2000] 2 Cr App R 42 (discussed in [2000] 7 Arch News 6), Mantell LJ said at 49—apparently in error—that the subjective test in self-defence had been applied to duress in *Cairns* [1999] 2 Cr App R 137 where Mantell LJ also gave the judgment. See generally on the merits of the subjective and objective approaches, P Alldridge, 'Developing the Defence of Duress' [1986] Crim LR 433.

[89] See S Yeo, *Compulsion in the Criminal Law* (1990).

[90] Lord Bingham rejected comparison with other defences in *Hasan*. Cf LCCP 177, para 7.32. It is dangerous to place too much emphasis on comparisons with other defences when seeking to interpret the scope of duress. These common law defences evolved over centuries to meet the needs of individual cases and were not the product of a coherent structured scheme as one might expect from Parliament.

It is submitted that, in the first two respects, the direction in *Graham* lays down too strict a rule. D should surely be judged on the basis of what he honestly believed and what he genuinely feared.[91] If his genuine fear was such that the jury conclude that no person of reasonable firmness could have been expected to resist it, he should be excused. He may have been unduly credulous or stupid, but he is no more blameworthy than a person whose fear is based on reasonable grounds.[92] The Court of Appeal in *Martin (DP)*[93] held that D's characteristics—in that case, a schizoid affective disorder, making him more likely to regard things said as threatening and to believe that threats would be carried out—must be taken into account. This seems to be a substantial mitigation of the objective test. It is doubtful whether that decision can stand in the light of the emphasis on the objective nature of the defence in the House of Lords in *Hasan*.

As with mistake generally, lack of faith in the jury to detect the 'bogus defence' and the additional hardship for the prosecution probably lies at the root of the objective requirements. As with mistake generally, the more tenuous the grounds for his claim, the less likely is D to be believed.

The confusion and tension in this area is illustrated by the case of *Safi* (the Afghan hijack case discussed earlier). At the first trial the judge directed the jury that D's genuine belief in the threat of death was sufficient, on a retrial the second judge adopted an objective formulation. The Court of Appeal failed to clarify the position but seemed implicitly to be adopting an objective test.[94] In the case of *M*,[95] the Court of Appeal adopted an apparently subjective approach to the first question.

In two subsequent cases, the Court of Appeal again endorsed the objective approach in the first limb.[96] Further clarification from the House of Lords was not forthcoming in *Hasan*, but the tenor of the speech of Lord Bingham leaves little doubt that the *objective* formulation would be preferred. That would follow the decision in *Graham* which was approved in *Howe*.

The person of reasonable steadfastness

Since duress is (according to Lord Hailsham in *Howe* and Lord Bingham in *Hasan*) a concession to human frailty[97] and some people are frailer than others, it is arguable that the standard of fortitude required should also vary,[98] and that a subjective test should apply.[99] That is not the approach adopted in English law. *Graham* is consistent with a common

---

[91] See W Wilson, 'The Structure of Defences' [2005] Crim LR 108, 115–16. Courts occasionally lapse into such a formula, see *Mullally v DPP* [2006] EWHC 3448 (Admin).

[92] In *DPP v Rogers* [1998] Crim LR 202, Brooke LJ seems wrongly to have assumed that this is now the law, apparently anticipating a reform proposed by the Law Commission. Cf *Abdul-Hussain* [1999] Crim LR 570. If D reasonably believes there is a threat, it is immaterial that there is no threat in fact: *Cairns* [1999] 2 Cr App R 137. For a criticism of the Commission's 'slavish adherence to subjectivism', see J Horder, 'Occupying the Moral High Ground' [1994] Crim LR 334 at 341 and comments by JC Smith, 'Individual Incapacities and Criminal Liability' (1998) 6 Med L Rev 138 at 155–7.

[93] [2002] 2 Cr App R 42.   [94] At [25].

[95] [2003] EWCA Crim 1170. See also *Sewell* [2004] EWCA Crim 2322.

[96] *Blake* [2004] EWCA Crim 1238, [18]; *Bronson* [2004] EWCA Crim 903, [23].

[97] *Howe* [1987] 1 All ER 771 at 779–80; *Hasan* [2005] UKHL 22, [18].

[98] See KJM Smith, 'Duress and Steadfastness: In Pursuit of the Unintelligible' [1999] Crim LR 363. See also Tadros, *Criminal Responsibility*, Ch 13, on the need for defences including duress to take account of D's characteristics and RL Lippke, 'Chronic Temptation, Reasonable Firmness and the Criminal Law' (2014) 34 OJLS 75, for the argument that the law ought to make a concession for those who face chronic temptation to violate the law through no fault of their own.

[99] 'It is arguable that the standard should be purely subjective and that it is contrary to principle to require the fear to be a reasonable one': [1975] 1 All ER at 931 per Lord Simon. Cf Law Com Working Paper No 55, paras 11–13 and LC 83, paras 2.27–2.28; and *Hudson* [1965] 1 All ER 721 at 724.

approach of the law in deciding that the standard is an objective one. It is for the law to lay down standards of conduct. When attacked, D may use only a reasonable degree of force in self-defence. Under the loss of self-control defence, D must display a reasonable degree of tolerance and self-restraint. Similarly, *Graham* decides that a person under duress is required to display 'the steadfastness reasonably to be expected of the ordinary citizen in his situation'.[100] The court relied particularly on the analogy with the law of provocation as was then in force and the decision in *Camplin*.[101] That case suggests that account should be taken of not only the gravity of the threat to D but also the sex and age of D and such of D's characteristics[102] as would affect the gravity of the threat to him. The leading case on this issue in duress is *Bowen*.[103]

In *Bowen*, it was held that for a duress plea D's age[104] and sex may be relevant, depending on the circumstances, as may pregnancy[105] and serious physical disability. These might affect the gravity of the threat and D's ability to seek evasive action. In *Bowen*,[106] the court also accepted that a 'recognized mental illness or psychiatric condition, such as post-traumatic stress disorder leading to learned helplessness'[107] would be relevant. But, D's low IQ, short of mental impairment or mental illness, is not relevant: a person of low IQ may be expected to be as courageous and able to withstand threats as anyone else. That does not necessarily answer the argument—belatedly advanced on appeal—that D's ability to seek the protection of the police might have been impaired.

Cases of 'learned helplessness' are particularly difficult.[108] In *Emery*,[109] a case of cruelty to a child, it was said, *obiter*, that it would be right to admit 'an expert account of the causes of the condition of dependent helplessness, the circumstances in which it might arise and what level of abuse would be required to produce it'. 'A woman of reasonable firmness suffering from a condition of dependent helplessness' may seem a contradiction in terms; but the point appears to be that the alleged history of violence by D's partner, said to have produced that condition, was part of the duress.[110] That explanation did not seem attractive to the court in *Bowen*.

This matter is a question for the jury and expert evidence has been held inadmissible to show that D was 'emotionally unstable' or in 'a grossly elevated neurotic state',[111] or that he is unusually pliable or vulnerable to pressure.[112] The courts have also held inadmissible evidence of sexual abuse as a child, resulting in lack of firmness, not amounting to psychiatric disorder: *Hurst*.[113] In that case, Beldam LJ said, 'we find it hard to see how the person

---

[100] (1982) 74 Cr App R 235 at 241.   [101] [1978] AC 705, see p 564.

[102] Such as the schizoid affective disorder afflicting *Martin (DP)*, n 88.

[103] [1996] 2 Cr App R 157. In *Flatt* [1996] Crim LR 576, it was held that drug addiction was a self-induced condition, not a characteristic. For criticism of the approach in general for its failure to reflect psychiatric understanding, see A Buchanan and G Virgo, 'Duress and Mental Abnormality' [1999] Crim LR 517.

[104] cf *Ali* [1989] Crim LR 736.

[105] In *GAC* [2013] EWCA Crim 1472, Hallett LJ stated that: 'A threat of physical violence to a pregnant woman therefore might be more serious because of the risk to the unborn child' at [33].

[106] [1996] 2 Cr App R 157.   [107] This was held to be insufficient in *Moseley* [1999] 7 Arch News 2.

[108] For extensive analysis, see J Loveless, 'R v GAC: Battered Woman "Syndromization"' [2014] Crim LR 655.

[109] (1992) 14 Cr App R (S) 394. See also J Loveless, 'Domestic Violence, Coercion and Duress' [2010] Crim LR 93 analysing how the defence is formulated in such a way as to exclude battered women. The Court of Appeal took cognizance of the criticisms made in this article without expressing a view of them in *A (RJ)* [2012] EWCA Crim 434, [2013] Crim LR 240. In this case, D's conviction was upheld. She has since alleged a violation of Art 8 of the ECHR. See *RA v UK* [2014] ECHR 1288. In 2016, the European Court of Human Rights ruled that her case was inadmissible. See *RA v UK* (App no 75321/12), 2016.

[110] Arguably, in such a case D is still a person of reasonable firmness, just one with greater sensitivities.

[111] *Hegarty* [1994] Crim LR 353.   [112] *Horne* [1994] Crim LR 584: 'not a hero nor a coward'.

[113] [1995] 1 Cr App R 82 at 90.

of reasonable firmness can be invested with the characteristics of a personality which lacks reasonable firmness . . .' The Court of Appeal considered this issue directly in *GAC*.[114] D unsuccessfully relied upon learned helplessness to avoid a conviction for importing Class A drugs. The Court of Appeal, dismissing D's appeal, rejected her claim that she had exhibited battered women syndrome at the time she committed the offence or that the violence against her was of sufficient severity to make out the first element of duress. Hallett LJ held that a person who has suffered domestic abuse would not be able to plead duress unless they have been 'subjected to serious physical violence so bad' that they have lost their free will.

The application of this objective test is also difficult when D's condition is a 'recognized mental illness'. The acceptance of such an illness as a relevant characteristic for duress suggests that this element of the objective test has broken down and that we are moving closer to the test once proposed by the Law Commission: 'the threat is one which in all the circumstances (including any of [the defendant's] characteristics that affect its gravity) he cannot reasonably be expected to resist'.[115] Under the present law the court will be faced with drawing some fine distinctions between unusual vulnerability and recognized psychiatric conditions affecting the ability to withstand pressure.[116] This is demonstrated by *GAC*. The increasing shift towards subjectivity in this limb of the defence stands in contrast to the increased objectivity in the first limb. It highlights the incoherence of the defence as it has evolved at common law, underlining the need for a legislative response.

(4) The conduct it is sought to excuse must have been directly caused by the threats D relies on

Threats as a concurrent cause of the crime

It is said that D's will must have been 'overborne' by the threat.[117] Presumably this means only that he would not have committed the offence 'but for' the threat and that the threat was one which might cause a person of reasonable fortitude to do as he did. If the prosecution can prove that he would have done the same act even if the threat had not been made, it seems that the defence will fail.[118] But the threat need not be the only motive for D's action. In *Valderrama-Vega*,[119] D was under financial pressure and had been threatened with disclosure of his homosexual behaviour—neither matter being capable of amounting to duress—but it was wrong to direct the jury that the threats of death or serious injury also alleged to have been made must have been the sole reason for his committing the offence. If D would not have committed the offence but for the latter threats the defence was available even if he acted because of the cumulative effect of all the pressure on him. It is probably going too far to say that it is enough that the threats of death were 'the last straw' because the law will look for something more substantial than 'a straw' for an excuse; but threats

---

[114] [2013] EWCA Crim 1472. For extensive analysis, see J Loveless 'R v GAC: Battered Woman "Syndromization"' [2014] Crim LR 655.

[115] Draft Criminal Law Bill, cl 25, LC 218. The Commission's recommendation in relation to murder is that the jury should be permitted to take account of all the circumstances except D's capacity to withstand the duress.

[116] See *Antar* [2004] EWCA Crim 2708.

[117] cf the discussion of *Steane* [1947] KB 997. See also GR Rubin, 'New Light on *Steane's* Case' (2003) 24 *Legal History* 143. See eg the continued use of such statements which shed little light on the defence: *Rahman* [2010] EWCA Crim 235.

[118] In *DPP v Bell (Derek)* [1992] Crim LR 176, D, in terror of an aggressor, began to drive with excess alcohol. Although he admitted that, before the threat, he intended to drive, it was found as a fact (a finding with which the Divisional Court could not interfere) that he drove because of terror and so had a defence of duress of circumstances. But for the threat he might have changed his mind or been persuaded by his passengers not to drive.

[119] [1985] Crim LR 220 and commentary.

of death or serious bodily harm can never be trivial, so it is probably sufficient to tell the jury that D has the defence if he would not have acted but for the threats of violence. A jury direction that the defence was available only if D acted *solely* because of the relevant threats was upheld where it was suggested that he might also have been influenced by greed but the court thought it inadvisable to use the word 'solely' in a summing up.[120]

A nominated crime demanded?

In the paradigmatic case of duress by threats, the defendant will have been told 'perform this crime or else'. The question has arisen how specific the nomination of the crime must be for D to be able to rely on the threats.[121] In *Cole*,[122] D was convicted of robbing two building societies and pleaded duress on the basis that he had been threatened by money lenders to whom he was in debt. The Court of Appeal held that a plea of duress was not available as the money lenders had not stipulated that he commit robbery to meet their demands. This would place a very strict limitation on the defence. The Court of Appeal held, in addition, in *Cole* that there was not the degree of immediacy and directness required between the peril threatened and the offence charged. That is a better basis for the decision.

Subsequently, in *Ali*,[123] D, a heroin addict, was convicted of robbing a building society and D claimed that his supplier, X, who had a reputation for violence, had demanded repayment of the monies D owed him. Further, D claimed that X had provided D with a gun and told D to get the money by the following day from a bank or a building society. The Court of Appeal upheld his conviction but appeared to accept that a threat is capable of amounting to duress when D is charged with robbing a particular building society not specified by the person threatening him.

In a case of duress of circumstances there can be no nominated crime: D faced with an approaching tidal wave or tornado is not 'told' to 'steal that car to drive away', but he is entitled to the defence should he do so. It is submitted that the defence of duress by threats should be available even if the threatening party has not nominated the crime D commits.

(5) There is no 'reasonable' evasive action D can take

This element of the defence is more properly seen as part of a broader question which is whether the threat is still effective at the time D performs the conduct element of the offence. Historically it was recognized that:

> The only force that doth excuse, is a force upon the person, and present fear of death; and his force and fear must continue all the time the party remains with the rebels. It is incumbent on every man, who makes force his defence to show an actual force, and that he quitted the service as soon as he could.[124]

The Court of Appeal has reiterated the 'requirement that the accused must know or believe that the threat is one which will be carried out immediately or before the accused or the other person threatened, can obtain official protection'.[125] But in *Abdul-Hussain*,[126] where Iraqis hijacked an aircraft because they reasonably feared they would be killed if they were returned to Iraq, the court reinterpreted the requirement of immediacy, holding

---

[120] *Ortiz* (1986) 83 Cr App R 173.

[121] This issue was confronted directly by the Supreme Court of Canada in *Ryan* [2013] SCC 3. The court held that the defence is available only when D has been compelled to commit a specific offence under threats of death or bodily harm. See also *Khan* [2018] EWCA Crim 78.

[122] [1994] Crim LR 582. In *Hasan*, Lord Bingham approved the decision regarding the threat as lacking immediacy. See recently *Khan* [2018] EWCA Crim 78.

[123] [1995] 16 Cr App R (S) 692.

[124] *M'Growther* (1746) Fost 13 at 14 per Lee CJ.

[125] *Hurst* [1995] 1 Cr App R 82 at 93; *Flatt* [1996] Crim LR 576.   [126] [1999] Crim LR 570.

that the question was whether D's response to the 'imminent' threat was proportionate and reasonable.[127] This relaxation of the defence was controversial. In *Hasan*, Lord Bingham was at pains to reassert the primacy of the requirement of the 'immediacy of the threat' and D's inability to avoid it, which he described as the 'cardinal feature' of the defence.[128] His lordship was of the view that the defence would not be available if there was a delay of a day between D being threatened with being shot and his commission of the crime.[129] Surely this must depend on the circumstances, however. There may be instances where, despite the delay of a day, the defence ought to be available.

Duress where D has an opportunity to inform the police

If D is able reasonably to resort to the protection of the law, he must do so or the defence will be lost. In *Hasan*, Lord Bingham observed that it should be made clear to juries that unless D reasonably expects the threats to be carried out 'immediately or almost immediately' the defence may be lost because there may be little room for doubt that D could take evasive action. The question whether D had a reasonable opportunity to take evasive action ought *not* in Lord Bingham's view to be subsumed within the question whether D had a reasonable belief in the existence of the threat and whether a reasonable person in D's circumstances would have responded as D did.[130]

When the threat is withdrawn or becomes ineffective, D must desist from committing the crime as soon as he reasonably can. If, for example, having consumed excess alcohol, D is threatened and drives off in fear of his life, he commits a drink-driving offence only if the prosecution can prove that he continued to drive after the terror ceased.[131]

Where the threats operate, or D reasonably perceives them as operating on someone other than himself, the question whether the threat is still operative may be more difficult to determine. For example, in *Hurley*, D had ample opportunity to place himself under the protection of the police but the court held that the defence of duress might still be available because his de facto wife was held as a hostage by his oppressors. Though he himself was physically out of range, the threats against her were presently operative on his mind.

Hudson and Taylor[132] went further. Two young women, called as witnesses for the prosecution, gave false evidence because they had been threatened by a gang with serious physical injury if they told the truth, and they saw one of the gang in the public gallery of the court. The young women were charged with perjury. Duress was accepted as a defence even though they could have put themselves under the protection of the law by informing the court; and there were no threats to third parties. The court thought it immaterial that the threatened injury could not follow at once since (in its opinion) there was no opportunity for delaying tactics and they had to make up their minds whether to commit the offence while the threat was operating. The threat was no less compelling because it could not be carried out there if it could be carried out in the streets of Salford the same night. The case turns on the point

---

[127] See *Abdul-Hussain* [1999] Crim LR 570, where the court added 'if Anne Frank had stolen a car to escape from Amsterdam and been charged with theft, the tenets of English law would not, in our judgment, have denied her a defence of duress of circumstances, on the ground that she should have waited for the Gestapo's knock on the door'.

[128] At [25]–[26].

[129] The Supreme Court of Canada in *Ryan* [2013] SCC 3 affirmed that in Canadian law it must be demonstrated that any course of action other than inflicting the injury (or committing the crime) was 'demonstrably impossible' or that there was 'no other legal way out'.

[130] At [24].

[131] *DPP v Bell (Derek)*, n 118. See the reiteration of this in *Malcolm v DPP* [2007] EWHC 363 (Admin); *Mullaley* [2006] EWHC 3448 (Admin) and in *Brown v CPS* [2007] EWHC 3274 (Admin).

[132] [1971] 2 All ER 244; followed by *Lewis* (1992) 96 Cr App R 412 at 415. Described by Ryan and Ryan (2005) 56 NILQ 421, commenting on *Hasan* as a 'historical anomaly', at 427.

that police protection could not be effective. It was recognized to extend the possible ambit
of the defence widely for there would be few cases where the police can offer effective and
permanent protection against such threats.[133]

Subsequently, in *Hasan*, Lord Bingham regarded *Hudson and Taylor* as having had 'the
unfortunate effect of weakening the requirement that execution of a threat must be reasonably believed to be imminent and immediate'.[134] Such a strict standard may be supported
by the need to prevent the defence being misused and pleaded in spurious cases, but is it
right that a defendant who reasonably fears he will be shot tomorrow after perjuring himself today ought not to be allowed a defence of duress? His lordship seems to be focusing
the question on whether D could avoid compliance with the threat, which is in one sense
practically always possible. The real question is whether D could take action which would
negative the threat itself. If D genuinely, and perhaps reasonably, believes that the police
or others cannot protect him from the threat, should he be denied the defence?[135] What if
those under threat are held overseas beyond the protection of the British police? The Court
of Appeal in *Batchelor* went even further in expressing disapproval of *Hudson and Taylor*.[136]
Elias LJ, after citing Lord Bingham's reasoning in *Hasan*, stated that the Court of Appeal
in *Hudson* had allowed its sympathy for the defendants to distort legal principles.[137] Even
more recently, in *Brandford*,[138] one of the reasons for the Court of Appeal's rejection of the
defendant's reliance upon duress was the fact that the relevant threats lacked the immediacy
that would have precluded her from taking evasive action, such as by going to the police.

As a result of the recent case law, it is submitted that *Hudson and Taylor* should no longer
be followed. As noted earlier, however, the difficult question remains: should D be denied
the defence if he genuinely, and perhaps reasonably, believes the police cannot prevent the
threat being carried out?

As with the question whether the reasonable person would have withstood the pressure,
similar principles apply to the rule requiring D to escape from duress if possible. His defence
will fail if an ordinary person of his sex, age and other relevant characteristics would have
taken an opportunity to escape. Obviously, physical disabilities, for example that he had difficulties in walking, would be taken into account.[139] Following *Graham*, however, he must
presumably be taken to have been aware of opportunities of which he ought reasonably to
have been aware at the time the opportunity arose.[140] A better view, it is submitted, is that
if he was not in fact aware of the opportunity to escape, he should not be penalized for his

---

[133] See comment in [1971] Crim LR 359 and (by Goodhart) in 87 LQR 299 and 121 NLJ 909 and (by Zellick)
in 121 NLJ 845. In *K* (1983) 78 Cr App R 82, it was held that duress might be available as a defence to contempt
of court committed in the witness box by a prisoner who had been threatened with reprisals against himself
and his family, by the accused, a fellow prisoner. The Law Commission originally proposed: 'The threat must
be, or the defendant must believe that it is, one that will be carried out immediately, or before he (or the person
under threat) can obtain official protection: Criminal Law Bill, clause 25(2)(b). This provision, by allowing the
defence if the defendant believes that official protection will be ineffective, differs from previous treatments of
the point'—Report, para 29.2. In LC 304, the Law Commission now recommends an objective test.

[134] At [27]. Lord Bingham at one point suggests that the defence in *Hudson* should fail because there was no
question that DD had 'no opportunity to avoid'. That is surely too strict a view. The question is whether they
had a reasonable chance to avoid the threats. For examples of the strictness of *Hasan* being applied, see *N* [2007]
EWCA Crim 3479 and see *Hussain* [2008] EWCA Crim 1117 and *Khan* [2018] EWCA Crim 78.

[135] Consider the High Court of Australia case of *Taiapa* [2009] HCA 53 in which D was denied the opportunity to rely on the compulsion defence where, having been threatened at gun point that he, his pregnant
girlfriend and his mother would be shot unless he couriered drugs, D drove to collect the drugs and did not
report to the police. His asserted belief that the police would not protect him and his family was found not to
give rise to the defence.

[136] [2013] EWCA Crim 2638.   [137] At [15].   [138] [2016] EWCA Crim 1794.

[139] But the fact that he was voluntarily drunk or drugged might be considered irrelevant.

[140] *Aikens*, n 50.

stupidity or slow-wittedness. In view of recent judicial pronouncements in this area such an approach would probably be seen as too generous to the accused.

If the defence of duress is left to the jury and D seeks to explain his decision not to seek assistance from the authorities rather than commit the crime, it is not necessarily incumbent on the judge to spell out each of the risks to D if he had taken such a route.[141]

(6) D cannot rely on threats to which he has voluntarily laid himself open

A further important limitation on the defence is that the threat cannot be one that arises from D having voluntarily exposed himself to threats of violence. This has become an increasingly problematic area and the courts have sought to prevent the defence being too readily available to those involved in drug-related and terrorist crime, in particular where their involvement demonstrates a degree of prior culpability. The restriction is hedged in with qualifications. In *Hasan*,[142] the House of Lords expressed concern at the way in which the defence was being relied on more readily by defendants in more cases and that there was a danger that the restrictive elements of the offence were not being applied rigorously enough.[143]

Voluntary exposure to threats
D will be denied the defence if he voluntarily exposed himself to a risk of threats. An example is *Sharp*[144] where D, who was a party to a conspiracy to commit robberies, said that he wanted to withdraw when he saw his criminal colleagues equipped with guns, whereupon E threatened to blow his head off if he did not carry on with the plan. In the course of the robbery, E killed V. D's conviction for manslaughter was upheld after a jury had rejected his defence of duress. This had been the approach adopted in Northern Ireland in *Fitzpatrick* (duress no defence to a charge of robbery committed as a result of threats by the IRA because D had voluntarily joined that organization)[145] and the *dicta* of Lords Morris, Wilberforce and Simon in *Lynch*.[146] It would be different of course if D was compelled to join the violent organization by threats of death or serious bodily harm; then, in principle, he should not be deprived of the defence. Whether any lesser threat should suffice at this stage has not been decided. As Baroness Hale persuasively put the matter in *Hasan*, the question ought to be whether D by his joining exposed himself to the risk 'without reasonable excuse'.[147]

The types of organization
Most cases in this category involve D joining a criminal gang. In *Sharp*, the gang were armed robbers; in *Fitzpatrick*, a paramilitary organization. In *Lewis*,[148] the court construed this prior fault limitation on the defence strictly to be limited to associations such as 'a para-military or gangster-tyrant style of organization'. There are plenty of cases in which the defence has been denied where D has joined with others in a criminal enterprise which is not the equivalent of a terrorist organization. It is submitted that *Lewis* should be approached with caution. For example, in *Shepherd*[149] D voluntarily joined a gang of burglars but wanted to give up after his first outing and raised the defence of duress by the gang to a charge of a later burglary, it was held that it should have been left to the jury to decide whether he was taking a risk of being subjected to such a threat of violence when he joined the gang.

In *Ali*,[150] the Court of Appeal held that if D has joined with others whom he ought to have realized might subject him to threats of violence, he is denied the defence of duress. The

---

141 See *Aldridge* [2006] EWCA Crim 1970 where D had been threatened that his children would be beheaded with a samurai sword if he did not participate in a robbery.
142 [2005] UKHL 22, [2006] Crim LR 142 and commentary.
143 See especially Lord Bingham's speech at [22].
144 [1987] QB 853, [1987] Crim LR 566.   145 [1977] NI 20.   146 [1975] AC 653.   147 At [78].
148 (1993) 96 Cr App R 412; *Kleijn* [2001] All ER (D) 143 (May).   149 (1987) 86 Cr App R 47.
150 [2008] EWCA Crim 716.

defence is lost irrespective of whether he has joined an existing criminal gang. D was convicted of the robbery at knife point of a vehicle owner. His plea of duress had been rejected at trial on the basis that D had voluntarily joined with the alleged duressor, BH, a co-accused in the robbery. D knew that BH carried a knife and had been warned not to associate with BH. The trial judge directed the jury that duress does not apply if:

the defendant chooses voluntarily to associate with others where he ought to foresee that he might be subjected to compulsion by threats of violence . . . If you choose to join very bad company, such bad company that you can foresee that you are going to be liable to threats of some kind to do things, then you cannot complain and say I was forced to do them when you had voluntarily associated with those people.

The judge elaborated on what was meant by 'bad company' explaining that joining bad company:

doesn't just mean people who are going about doing bad things, it means people who you should have realised could would be likely to, or may, subject you to compulsion by threats of violence.

The Court of Appeal upheld the conviction. In *Hasan*,[151] Lord Bingham had answered the certified question by saying that:

the defence of duress is excluded when as a result of the accused's voluntary association *with others engaged in criminal activity* he foresaw or ought reasonably to have foreseen the risk of being subjected to any compulsion by threats of violence.[152]

The italicized words might suggest that the defence is only lost where D joins an existing criminal gang. *Ali* rejects any such limitation.

Active membership

It is too late if D attempts to withdraw from the organization when the particular enterprise which resulted in the charge is in contemplation. No defence of duress is available. But a person who joined a paramilitary organization in his youth can hardly be held to have forfeited his right to plead duress by that organization for life. If he has done all he can to sever his connection with it before the particular incident was in contemplation, should he not be able to rely on the defence?

The risk to which D was exposing himself by his association

In *Lewis*, D, who was serving a sentence for armed robbery, was savagely attacked in the prison yard by E, who was serving a sentence for the same robbery. D refused to testify against E because he was terrified of reprisals and was charged with contempt of court. It was held that duress ought to have been available as a defence to that charge. There was no evidence that D knew that he was exposing himself to the risk of this *sort of threat* when he participated in the armed robbery with E much earlier in time.

Initially the courts held that D would be denied the defence only where he voluntarily put himself in a position where he was aware of the risk of being subjected to pressure by way of violence *to commit offences of the type alleged* (*Baker and Ward*[153]). Subsequently a harsher view has been adopted. D will be denied the defence if he exposed himself to unlawful threats more generally: *Heath*,[154] *Harmer*.[155] Despite the cogent academic criticism of

---

151 [2005] UKHL 22, [39].   152 Emphasis added.   153 [1999] 2 Cr App R 355.
154 *Heath* [2000] Crim LR 109 (indebted drug user, aware that he might be subjected to threats, required to transport £300K of cannabis), distinguishing *Baker and Ward* (ibid) (inadequate direction).
155 [2001] EWCA Crim 2930.

this approach,[156] the House of Lords in *Hasan* confirmed this harsh view. Lord Bingham explained that:

The defendant is, *ex hypothesi*, a person who has voluntarily surrendered his will to the domination of another. Nothing should turn on foresight of the manner in which, in the event, the dominant party chooses to exploit the defendant's subservience. There need not be foresight of coercion to commit crimes, although it is not easy to envisage circumstances in which a party might be coerced to act lawfully.[157]

In *Ali*,[158] the court suggested a very harsh approach whereby D could not rely on the defence if he foresaw/ought to have foreseen that he was likely to be subjected to compulsion by threats. The court drew on the approval by Lord Bingham of the trial judge's direction in *Hasan*.[159] The approach in *Ali* and in *Hasan* is to deny the defence not only on the basis of D's association with a criminal gang, but on associating with anyone he ought to have foreseen *might* put him under compulsion by threats.

D's awareness of the risk to which he is exposing himself by his association

Hasan confirms that the duress defence is unavailable where the risk to which D exposes himself is pressure to commit any crime. A further question arises whether the defence can only be denied to D where he is proved to have been aware of that risk (subjectively), or whether it is sufficient that he ought to have been aware of that risk (objectively). As a matter of policy the House of Lords in *Hasan* suggests that the test is whether D ought to have known. Again, this restricts the availability of the defence.[160] In *Ali*, the Court of Appeal took the objective approach, holding that duress is not available if D *ought to have foreseen* that the others might threaten him.

The interpretation will operate very harshly for those involved in, inter alia, drug misuse. Many users of drugs will associate themselves with drug dealers and in many, if not most, cases the users ought to realize that the dealer might be likely to threaten them with violence. If the dealer does threaten the user with violence unless the user commits crimes (usually to pay the dealer), the user will be denied the defence of duress.[161] Baroness Hale's minority speech in *Hasan* adopts a more subjective approach, suggesting that the defence is denied only where D has himself foreseen a risk that he will be compelled by threats of violence to commit crime. It is submitted this is preferable approach, but it is not the law.

The policy of the law is clearly to discourage association with known criminals, and to be slow to excuse the criminal conduct of those who do so. If a person voluntarily becomes or remains associated with others engaged in criminal activity in a situation where he knows or ought reasonably to know that he may be the subject of compulsion by them or their associates, he cannot rely on the

---

[156] As JC Smith noted in commenting on *Heath* [2000] Crim LR 109, 'it is one thing to be aware that you are likely to be beaten up if you do not pay your debts, it is another that you may be aware that you may be required under threat of violence to commit other, though unspecified crimes, if you do not'.

[157] At [37]. Cf Baroness Hale's example of the battered woman compelled to perform lawful tasks of ironing, at [77].

[158] [2008] EWCA Crim 716.

[159] 'Did the defendant voluntarily put himself in the position, in which he knew he was likely to be subjected to threats? You look to judge that in all the circumstances . . . if someone voluntarily associates with the sort of people who he knows are likely to put pressure on him, then he cannot really complain, if he finds himself under pressure. If you are sure that he did voluntarily put himself in such a position, the defence fails and he was guilty. If you are not sure and you have not been sure about all of the other questions, then you would find him not guilty.' At [14].

[160] cf Baroness Hale commenting on the attractions of the subjectivist approach advanced by the Law Commission, at [75].

[161] cf *Heath* [2000] Crim LR 109. See also *Lal* [2009] EWCA Crim 2393 and *Mullally* [2012] EWCA Crim 687.

defence to excuse any act which he is thereafter compelled to do by them. It is not necessary in this case to decide whether or to what extent that principle applies if an undercover agent penetrates a criminal gang for *bona fide* law enforcement purposes and is compelled by the gang to commit criminal acts.[162]

(7) Offences to which duress/duress of circumstances available

Duress by threats has been accepted as a defence to manslaughter,[163] criminal damage,[164] arson,[165] theft,[166] handling,[167] perjury and contempt of court,[168] perverting the course of justice,[169] offences under the Official Secrets Acts[170] and drug offences.[171] The courts have also assumed that it would apply to buggery[172] (presumably therefore also to sex offences under the 2003 Act) and conspiracy[173] to defraud. It is available to strict liability crimes,[174] but, depending on the terms of the offence, not always to status crimes.[175]

Duress of circumstances has been held to be a defence to various road traffic offences, to hijacking, contrary to s 1(1) of the Aviation Security Act 1982[176] and to unlawful possession of a firearm. It now seems safe to say that either kind of duress may be a defence to any crime,[177] except some forms of treason, murder and attempted murder.[178]

Duress and treason

Although typically it is said that treason is a crime where duress is not a defence, it is quite clear that it may be a defence to at least some forms of treason.[179] As long ago as 1419 in *Oldcastle*'s case,[180] the accused, who were charged with treason in supplying victuals (food) to Sir John Oldcastle and his fellow rebels, were acquitted on the grounds that they acted through fear of death and desisted as soon as they could. The existence of the defence was admitted, *obiter*, by Lee CJ in *M'Growther*,[181] a trial for treason committed in the 1745 rebellion and by Lord Mansfield in *Stratton*:[182]

if a man is forced to commit acts of high treason, if it appears really force, and such as human nature could not be expected to resist and the jury are of that opinion, the man is not guilty of high treason.

Much more recently, in *Purdy*,[183] Oliver J directed a jury that fear of death would be a defence to a British prisoner of war who was charged with treason in having assisted with German

162 Lord Bingham at [38].   163 *Evans and Gardiner* [1976] VR 517 and *(No 2)* 523.

164 *Crutchley* (1831) 5 C & P 133.

165 *Shiartos* (Lawton J, 29 Sept 1961, CCA), unreported but referred to in *Gill*, n 166.

166 *Gill* [1963] 2 All ER 688.   167 *A-G v Whelan* [1934] IR 518.

168 *K* (1983) 78 Cr App R 82; *Lewis* (1992) 96 Cr App R 412.   169 *Hudson and Taylor* [1971] 2 QB 202.

170 *Shayler* [2001] EWCA Crim 1977.

171 *Valderrama-Vega* [1985] Crim LR 220; *Ortiz* (1986) 83 Cr App R 173.

172 *Bourne* (1952) 36 Cr App R 125.

173 *Verrier* [1965] Crim LR 732. In *Abdul-Hussain* [1999] Crim LR 570, the court doubted whether duress can be a defence to conspiracy; but if it is a defence to doing the act, it must surely be a defence to agreeing to do it.

174 *Eden DC v Braid* [1998] COD 259.

175 See *New Forest Local Education Authority v E* [2007] EWHC 2584 (Admin), n 177.

176 *Abdul-Hussain* [1999] Crim LR 570.

177 Its use in relation to a charge under s 444 of the Education Act 1996, where a parent was charged with failing to secure the attendance of a child was doubted: *New Forest Local Education Authority v E* [2007] EWHC 2584 (Admin).

178 It is not available to civil tax penalties: *Mu v Customs and Excise* [2001] VTD 17504.

179 [1975] 1 All ER at 920 per Lord Morris, at 940 per Lord Simon and at 944 per Lord Kilbrandon. In *Gotts* [1992] 2 WLR 284 at 300, Lord Lowry excepts 'most forms of treason'. This passage was cited by Lord Bingham in *Hasan*.

180 (1419) Hale, I PC, 50, East, I PC, 70.   181 (1746) Fost 13, 18 State Tr 391.

182 (1779) 21 State Tr 1045.   183 (1946) 10 J Crim L 182.

propaganda in the Second World War. Against this, Lord Goddard CJ said in *Steane*[184] that the defence did not apply to treason, but this remark appears to have been made *per incuriam*. Treason is an offence which may take many forms varying widely in seriousness and it would be wrong to suppose that threats, even of death, will necessarily be a defence to every act of treason. In *Oldcastle*'s case,[185] Hale emphasizes that the accuseds' act was *only* furnishing of victuals and he appears to question whether, if they had taken a more active part in the rebellion, they would have been excused. Stephen thought the defence only applied where the offender took a subordinate part.

Duress and murder

It was stated in the books from Hale onwards that duress could not be a defence to a charge of murder. As Blackstone put it, a man under duress 'ought rather to die himself than escape by the murder of an innocent'.[186] There was, however, no clear judicial authority in point and in 1969 in *Kray*[187] an inroad was made into the supposed rule when Widgery LJ said that a person charged as an accessory before the fact[188] to murder might rely on duress. In 1975, in *Lynch v DPP for Northern Ireland*,[189] the House of Lords, by a majority of three to two, held that a person charged with aiding and abetting murder[190] could have a defence of duress. The position of the actual killer was left open and in *Abbott*[191] in 1976, again by three to two, the Privy Council distinguished *Lynch* and held that the defence was not available to the principal offender, the actual killer. This was an illogical and unsatisfactory position because it is by no means always the case that the actual killer is the most dominant or culpable member of a number of accomplices, but under the law as it then stood he alone was excluded from the defence. The distinctions involved were technical and absurd.[192] Accordingly, when the matter came before the House of Lords in *Howe*,[193] there was a strong case for either going forward and allowing the defence to all alleged parties to murder, or backward, and allowing it to none. The House chose the latter course, overruling its own decision in *Lynch*. The speeches emphasize different aspects, but the following reasons for the decision appear among them.

(1) The ordinary person of reasonable fortitude, if asked to take an innocent life, might be expected to sacrifice his own.[194] Lord Hailsham would not 'regard a law as either "just;" or "humane" which withdraws the protection of the criminal law from the innocent victim and casts the cloak of its protection on the coward and the poltroon in the name[195] of a "concession to human frailty"'.

(2) One who takes the life of an innocent person cannot claim that he is choosing the lesser of two evils.[196]

---

[184] [1947] KB 997 at 1005.   [185] (1419) Hale, I PC, 50.   [186] Blackstone, *Commentaries*, iv, 30.

[187] [1970] 1 QB 125.

[188] A category of accessory that has become redundant since the abolition of felonies.

[189] [1975] AC 653.

[190] One who would have been a principal in the second degree under the law of felonies.

[191] [1977] AC 755.

[192] *Graham* [1982] 1 All ER 801 at 804 per Lane LCJ. See also IH Dennis, 'Duress, Murder and Criminal Responsibility' (1980) 106 LQR 208.

[193] [1987] AC 417, [1987] Crim LR 480 (sub nom *Burke*) and commentary. See also F Stark, '*R v Howe*' in P Handler, H Mares and I Williams (eds), *Landmark Cases in Criminal Law* (2017); H Milgate, 'Duress and the Criminal Law: Another About Turn by the House of Lords' (1988) 47 CLJ 61; L Walters, 'Murder under Duress and Judicial Decision Making in the House of Lords' (1988) 18 LS 61; Horder, *Excusing Crime*, 133–7.

[194] *Howe* [1987] 1 All ER 771 at 779–80.   [195] Referring to the 5th edn of this book, at p 215.

[196] Lord Hailsham, *Howe* (n 198) at 780. Art 2 of the ECHR will be engaged in cases of intentional killing.

(3) The Law Commission had recommended[197] ten years previously that duress should be a defence to the alleged principal offender, but Parliament had not acted on that recommendation.[198]

(4) Hard cases could be dealt with by not prosecuting—in some cases the person under duress might be expected to be the principal witness for the prosecution[199]—or by the action of the Parole Board in ordering the early release of a person who would have had a defence if duress had been an available defence.[200]

It is submitted that none of these reasons is at all convincing.

(a) If the defence were available, it would apply only when a jury thought a person of reasonable fortitude *would* have yielded to the threat. The criminal law should not require heroism, for, as Reed argues 'it is inapt to demand heroism as a pre-requisite for exculpation'.[201] Moreover, there are circumstances in which the good citizen of reasonable fortitude not only would, but probably should, yield to the threat because—

(b) to do so might clearly be to choose the lesser of two evils, as where the threat is to kill D and all his family if he does not do, or assist in, an act which he knows will cause grievous harm but not death (though, *ex hypothesi*, it has resulted in death and so constitutes murder).

(c) Parliament's failure to act on the Law Commission recommendation proves nothing. The government has not given Parliament the opportunity to consider the matter. By parity of reason, Parliament might be taken to have approved of *Lynch's* case, because there has been no move to overrule it.[202]

(d) Even if he were not prosecuted, the 'duressee' would be, in law, a murderer and, if he were called as a prosecution witness, the judge would, at the time of the decision in *Howe*, have been required to tell the jury that he was an accomplice in murder on whose evidence it would be dangerous to act in the absence of corroboration. A morally innocent person should not be left at the mercy of administrative discretion on a murder charge.

There is clearly a strong argument for reversing *Howe*.[203] Lord Bingham suggested that the logic of the argument is 'irresistible'.[204] The case of *Wilson*[205] illustrates the difficulties

---

[197] Lord Bridge, ibid at 784 and Lord Griffiths at 788.

[198] LC 83, *Report on Defences of General Application* (1977).　　[199] Lord Griffiths, *Howe* (n 198) at 790.

[200] Lord Griffiths, ibid at 791 and Lord Hailsham at 780–1. In non-murder cases the suggestion that the defence should be kept within strict limits and that no injustice will result because of the availability of sentencing discretion met with approval from Lord Bingham in *Hasan*, at [22], but cf Baroness Hale for convincing arguments against.

[201] A Reed, 'Duress and Normative Moral Excuse: Comparative Standardisations and the Ambit of Affirmative Defences' in A Reed and M Bohlander (with N Wake and E Smith) (eds), *General Defences in Criminal Law* (2014) 100.

[202] See generally D Bailey, 'Interpreting Parliamentary Inaction' (2020) 79 CLJ 245.

[203] On the need for reform see A Reed, 'The Need for a New Anglo American Approach to Duress' (1996) 61 J Crim L 209. See KJ Arenson, 'The Paradox of Disallowing Duress as a Defence to Murder' (2014) 78 J Crim L 65. Arenson argues that it is paradoxical that loss of control operates as a partial defence to murder but duress does not.

[204] *Hasan* at [21]. It is unlikely that the Supreme Court would change the position. Cf *Dunne v DPP* [2016] IESC 24 in which the Supreme Court in Ireland declined to do so. See also *R v Ryan* (2013) 290 CCC (3d) 477, Supreme Court of Canada declining to address this issue. In *Aravena* [2015] ONCA 250, the Ontario Court of Appeal held that duress is a defence to persons charged as parties to a murder. Although the constitutionality of the murder exemption as it applies to principals was not before the court, it stated that, 'subject to any argument the Crown might advance justifying the exception as it applies to perpetrators under s. 1 of the Charter, the exception must be found unconstitutional'.

[205] [2007] EWCA Crim 1251.

when duress cannot be a defence to a charge of murder, even if the person seeking to rely on that defence is a child and even if his alleged role in the murder was that of a secondary party acting out of fear of an adult perpetrator. The 13-year-old defendant was not able to plead duress, but argued instead that he had 'not known what he was doing in that his mind did not go with his actions'.[206] The Court of Appeal observed in *Wilson* that there 'might be grounds for criticising' a rule that denied a child any defence to a charge of murder on the grounds of adult or parental duress, but had no choice but to apply the law as it stood.[207]

The Law Commission in its *Murder, Manslaughter and Infanticide* Report recommended allowing the defence to the charge of murder, but controversially, recommended reversing the burden of proof.[208] The Commission[209] report addressed a range of options and concluded, rightly it is submitted, that if the jury find that D acted under duress within all the stringent requirements of the defence, he ought to be acquitted rather than guilty of manslaughter.[210]

Attempted murder and other related offences

In *Howe*, only Lord Griffiths[211] expressed a clear view that duress is not a defence to attempted murder and the House of Lords subsequently agreed with that view by a majority of three to two in *Gotts*.[212] This is logical, otherwise the effect would be that D's act would be excusable when done, and only become inexcusable if death resulted.

Logic would also require the exclusion of the defence on a charge under s 18 of the OAPA 1861 of causing grievous bodily harm with intent because here also, the offence becomes murder if death results from it. A distinction might be made between murder committed with intent to kill, where duress would not be a defence, and murder committed with intent to cause serious bodily harm, where it would. This would be reconcilable with the traditional statement of the law—a person 'ought rather to die himself than escape by the murder of an innocent'—which seems to postulate a decision to kill; but *Howe* seems too emphatic and uncompromising a decision to allow of any such refinement. *Gotts* indicates that the line is to be drawn below attempted murder, leaving the defence applicable to conspiracy to murder and assisting or encouraging murder. Indeed, in *Ness*[213] the judge ruled that duress is a defence to a charge of conspiracy to murder. Given that there exists no appellate decision directly on point, the judge chose to follow the 'closest authoritative statement' of Lord Lane in *Gotts* and endorsed the widely accepted view that duress is only excluded on a charge of murder, attempted murder and treason.

There is no point in raising the defence of duress to a murder charge; but suppose, as is frequently the case, that the evidence is such that the jury might properly acquit of murder and convict of manslaughter. If there is evidence that D may have been acting under duress[214] it is submitted that the judge should direct the jury that they must not convict of manslaughter either, unless they are sure that D was not acting under duress.

---

[206] His police interview did not support this defence, but suggested that he acted under duress from his father—the very defence he was precluded from running.

[207] See commentary by A Ashworth [2008] Crim LR 138.

[208] LC 304, para 6.116. See also LCCP 177 in which the Commission took a different view. Cf O Quick and C Wells, 'Getting Tough with Defences' [2006] Crim LR 514.

[209] LCCP 177, paras 7.18–7.19.   [210] LC 304, para 6.53.   [211] *Howe* (n 198) at 780 and 790.

[212] [1992] 2 AC 412. Lord Lowry, dissenting, thought it is 'the stark fact of death' which distinguishes murder from all other offences. See S Gardner, 'Duress in Attempted Murder' (1991) 107 LQR 389. The issues are discussed in LCCP 177, para 7.60.

[213] [2011] Crim LR 645 and commentary. See also *Moss v DPP* (2019) 9 May, unreported, Court of Appeal of the Bahamas.

[214] cf *Gilmour* [2000] 2 Cr App R 407 where D was roused from his bed and, unwillingly, drove the terrorist murderers to and from the scene of the crime.

10.2.2 Duress of circumstances

10.2.2.1 The emergence of the defence

The recognition of this defence occurred, more or less by accident, in *Willer*.[215] D was charged with reckless driving after he had driven very slowly on a pavement in order to escape from a gang of youths who were obviously intent on doing violence to him and his passengers. The trial judge declined to leave the defence of necessity to the jury. The Court of Appeal quashed D's conviction. They said that there was no need to decide on any defence of necessity that might have existed because 'the defence of duress[216] arose but was not pursued', as it ought to have been. It should have been left to the jury to say whether D drove 'under that form of compulsion, ie, under duress'. But this was not an instance of the previously recognized defence of duress by threats—the youths were not saying, 'Drive on the pavement—or else . . .' There is a closer analogy with self-defence.[217] But in substance the court was simply allowing the defence of necessity which it purported to dismiss as unnecessary to the decision. It should surely make no difference whether D drove on the pavement to escape from the youths, or a herd of charging bulls, a runaway lorry or a flood, if he did so in order to escape what he reasonably believed to be a threat of death or serious bodily harm.

Subsequent cases have not dismissed *Willer* as a case decided *per incuriam*. They have treated it as rightly decided but have recognized that it is not the long-established defence of duress but an extension of it—'duress of circumstances'—the relationship of which to necessity has not been settled (see later). In *Conway*,[218] another case of reckless driving, D's passenger, Tonna, had been the target of an attack on another vehicle a few weeks earlier when another man was shot and Tonna had a narrow escape. According to D, when two young men in civilian clothes came running towards D's parked car, Tonna shouted hysterically, 'Drive off'. D drove off because he feared a deadly attack on Tonna. Being pursued by the two men in an unmarked vehicle, he drove in a manner which the jury adjudged to be reckless. The two men were police officers who wished to interview Tonna. D's conviction was quashed because the defence of duress of circumstances had not been left to the jury.

Willer and *Conway* were followed in *Martin (Colin)*.[219] D, while disqualified, drove his stepson, who had overslept, to work. He said that he did so because his wife feared that the boy would lose his job if he were late and she threatened to commit suicide if D did not drive him. The wife had suicidal tendencies and a doctor stated that it was likely that she would have carried out her threat. The defence ought to have been left to the jury. According to the Court of Appeal, the defence:

can arise from other objective dangers threatening the accused or others . . . the defence is available only if, from an objective standpoint, the accused can be said to be acting reasonably and proportionately in order to avoid a threat of death or serious injury. . . . [The] jury should be directed to determine these two questions: First, was the accused, or may he have been impelled to act as he did as a result of what he reasonably believed to be the situation he had good cause to fear that otherwise death or serious physical injury would result; Second, if so, would a sober person of reasonable firmness, sharing the characteristics of the accused, have responded to that situation by acting as the accused acted?[220]

On the facts, the case seems to be strictly a case of duress by threats, where D is told, 'Commit the crime or else . . .' The defence, as with duress by threats, is available only so

[215] (1986) 83 Cr App R 225. On the emergence of the defence more generally see S Gardner, 'Necessity's Newest Invention' (1991) 11 OJLS 125.

[216] The 'very different' defence of duress according to the court in *Denton* (1987) 85 Cr App R 246 at 248.

[217] See p 398.   [218] [1989] QB 290.   [219] [1989] 1 All ER 652.   [220] At 653 per Simon Brown J.

long as the 'circumstances' continue to threaten. It may have been available (though the court did not decide the point) to a driver who drove off with excess alcohol in his blood to escape assailants; but it was not necessary for him to drive the two and a half miles to his home.[221] But where it was found that D, having consumed excess alcohol, drove off in fear of his life, he was guilty of an offence only if the prosecution could prove that he continued to drive after the terror ceased.[222] Similarly, in *Arnaot*,[223] where the court doubted there was any evidence that D was compelled by fear for her safety to drive dangerously following a road traffic incident.

In *S and L*,[224] S was charged with an offence of using unlicensed guards and sought to plead 'necessity' in that he had to deploy unlicensed guards in an emergency. The Court of Appeal referred to the trial judge's 'immaculate judgment' containing a clear and correct statement of the law of 'necessity'. For such a defence there had to be material on which a reasonable jury might conclude that:

(1) it had not been possible for S and L to obtain a licence before the threat to the premises became so acute as to compel them to deploy unlicensed guards. Although no specific threat must be identified as a matter of law, in the absence of such, it may be very difficult to identify material fit to go to a jury;[225]

(2) the deployment of the guards was directly caused by an immediate or imminent threat of death or serious injury;

(3) no other means could reasonably have been taken to avoid the risk. The judge found that the material relied on by the defence did not support the ingredients of the defence.

With respect, this sounds very much like a defence of duress of circumstances rather than one of necessity.

The Court of Appeal is clearly anxious to keep a tight degree of control over the defence of duress of circumstances (as with duress by threats).[226]

In *Quayle*,[227] the court heard a number of appeals and a related reference by the Attorney General. The issue in each case was whether the defence of necessity or 'necessity of circumstances' as it preferred to say, should be left to the jury in respect of offences of: possession, cultivation or production of cannabis where D genuinely and reasonably believed that such activities were necessary to avoid him suffering pain arising from a pre-existing medical condition or from conventional medicine to which he would otherwise resort to reduce the pain. Some of the appeals related to importation or possession with intent to supply cannabis for the purpose of alleviating pain suffered by others in similar circumstances. The defence argument was, in short, that the 'evil' of non-compliance with the Misuse of Drugs Act 1971 and the Customs and Excise Management Act 1979 was relatively minor compared with the risk of serious injury or pain to an individual defendant. It was argued that in any particular case it should be for the jury to weigh such potential ill-effects against the

---

[221] *DPP v Jones* [1990] RTR 34. Nor to drive 72 miles when intoxicated to escape a threat, *DPP v Tomkinson* [2001] EWHC Admin 182.

[222] *DPP v Bell (Derek)*, n 118. See also *CPS v Brown* [2007] EWHC 3274 (Admin).

[223] [2008] EWCA Crim 121.   [224] [2009] EWCA Crim 85.

[225] That is a rather ambiguous but potentially wide opportunity for a defence to be run.

[226] See eg statements in *Patel* [2010] EWCA Crim 976, [47]. Imminent danger that prevents a person from acting lawfully is a necessary ingredient of the defences; *Gregory* [2011] EWCA Crim 1712 in which Lord Judge CJ stated that 'The defence of duress of circumstances is of strictly limited ambit' at [12].

[227] [2005] EWCA Crim 1415; see further the commentary at [2006] Crim LR 148.

potential benefits to the particular defendant. This argument was supported by reference to the right to private life under Art 8 of the ECHR.

The prosecution argued, on policy grounds, that since Parliament had clearly and precisely regulated the medicinal use of drugs and had not provided for the use of cannabis, there were strong public policy grounds against allowing the defence of necessity. Alternatively, if the policy argument was rejected, the defence of necessity was not made out: an accused who was seeking to avoid his own pain was unable to show that there was an extraneous circumstance allegedly causing the commission of the offence. Similarly, in the case of those who were seeking to provide the means by which others could avoid pain, they could not reasonably be said to have a responsibility towards those for whose benefit they claimed to be acting. The Attorney General submitted further that the defence of necessity did not include the avoidance of serious pain, and should not be extended (in the present context at least) to do so.

The Court of Appeal held that there was no overarching principle applicable in all cases of 'necessity' to be derived from individual authorities. 'Necessity' should be developed on a case-by-case basis. The court made more general comments about the defence including that the defence required extraneous circumstances capable of objective scrutiny by judge and jury, capable of being checked and, where appropriate, met by other evidence. Otherwise abusive defences might arise.[228] It was emphasized also that there had to be an imminent danger of physical injury; otherwise, where pain was concerned (which required a large element of subjectivity in its assessment), there would be no clear, objective basis by reference to which to test or determine the defence. Perhaps predictably, the court rejected the Art 8 argument, concluding that Parliament had sanctioned interference with the private life of the sufferer in its legislative policy.

In *Altham*,[229] the Court of Appeal dismissed an appeal in similar circumstances where the drug user who was convicted of possession sought to rely on Art 3 of the ECHR to support his defence. The Court of Appeal concluded that the condition of the appellant was made no worse by the State and that there was no Art 3 claim.

In *Petgrave*,[230] the Court of Appeal held that a defendant who wishes to rely on the defence of duress of circumstances must advance the defence by evidence. In that case, D seriously injured a woman whilst driving on the pavement, and claimed to have been acting under duress of circumstances (having been threatened by two armed men). The issue had not been raised by the prosecution. The Court of Appeal held that the judge was right not to have acceded to a submission of no case to answer.

One further restriction which the Court of Appeal has sought to impose on the duress of circumstances defence is, it is submitted, unwarranted. In *Jones*,[231] involving intentional criminal damage to an air force base in an attempt to prevent the USAF and UK services continuing their bombardment of Iraq, the defendants sought to rely, inter alia, on defences of duress of circumstances to the charges. In particular, the defendants argued that the war on Iraq was illegal in international law and that their actions were therefore necessary to avert that crime being committed on civilians in Iraq. On an interlocutory appeal, the Court of Appeal held that the defence was not available, declaring that it is limited to a

---

[228] At [73].   [229] [2006] EWCA Crim 7, discussed with commentary by Ashworth [2006] Crim LR 633.
[230] [2018] EWCA Crim 1397.
[231] [2004] EWCA Crim 1981, [2005] Crim LR 122. Discussed in Norrie, *Crime, Reason and History*, 212 and S Gardner, 'Direct Action and the Defence of Necessity' [2005] Crim LR 371, although not on this point. For an analysis of the international law dimension to the case, see R Cryer, 'Aggression at the Court of Appeal' (2005) 10 J Conflict Law & Soc 209.

case of D being faced with a crime in national law. With respect, that cannot be right. The defence was available to *Martin* when his wife was threatening suicide (not a crime), moreover one can envisage many circumstances in which D, or those for whom he is responsible, face a threat of death or serious injury by non-criminal means (eg a rapidly engulfing forest fire leads D to steal a car to escape to safety). The House of Lords subsequently dealt with the appeal on the basis of the defence under s 3 of the Criminal Law Act 1967, and did not deal with the issues of duress of circumstances or necessity.[232]

10.3 Section 45 of the Modern Slavery Act 2015

Section 45[233] of and Sch 4 to the 2015 Act provide a statutory duress-like defence for a victim of slavery or trafficking who commits an offence.[234] In relation to a defendant (aged 18 or over) charged with an offence who has been 'compelled to do so' attributable to slavery or relevant exploitation, he has a defence if a reasonable person with relevant characteristics in the same position as the defendant would have no realistic alternative to committing the offence. Section 45 does not require the defendant to bear the legal or persuasive burden of proof of any element of the defence.[235]

There are other restrictions on the application of the defence. The offence alleged must be part of the slavery/trafficking itself or a direct consequence of the slavery/trafficking (subs (3)). It is not applicable to offences committed before the 2015 Act came into force. It will *not* apply to most serious sexual or violent offences. The defence differs from duress: it does not require a threat of death or really serious harm, but requires D to have been compelled to commit the criminal offence in question.[236] This compulsion must be attributable to slavery or relevant exploitation.[237] Compulsion is attributable to slavery or to relevant exploitation only if: it is, or is part of, conduct which constitutes an offence under s 1 of the Modern Slavery Act 2015 or conduct which constitutes relevant exploitation (s 45(3)(a)); or it is a direct consequence of a person being, or having been, a victim of slavery or a victim of relevant exploitation (s 45(3)(b)).

The relevant characteristics to be considered are age, sex, mental or physical illness and disability (subs (6)). The defence is not available in relation to Sch 4 offences.[238]

The Court of Appeal has stated that if there is evidence to suggest that a person charged with an offence may be a victim of modern slavery or trafficking, steps must be taken to

---

[232] [2006] UKHL 16, [2007] Crim LR 66.

[233] For detailed analysis, see K Laird, 'Evaluating the Relationship Between Section 45 of the Modern Slavery Act 2015 and the Defence of Duress: An Opportunity Missed?' [2016] Crim LR 395.

[234] A person is a victim of slavery/ trafficking if he is a victim of conduct which constitutes an offence under the Modern Slavery Act 2015, s 1, 2, or conduct which would have constituted an offence under s 1 or s 2 if s 1 had been in force when the conduct occurred: s 56(1), (2).

[235] *K(M); Gega* [2018] EWCA Crim 667.

[236] For an interesting analysis of how the concept of compulsion is relevant to English criminal law, see S Edwards, 'Coercion and Compulsion—Re-Imagining Crimes and Defences' [2016] Crim LR 876.

[237] If D is under 18, then by virtue of s 45(4)(b) it suffices if he commits the offence as a direct consequence of being, or having been, a victim of slavery or relevant exploitation.

[238] Sch 4 to the Modern Slavery Act 2015 lists a number of offences that have been excluded from the ambit of the new defences. Therefore, depending upon the offences they are alleged to have committed, some victims of slavery and trafficking will still have to rely upon the common law even after the implementation of s 45.

ascertain whether that is in fact the case. For example, in N[239] the Court of Appeal quashed the defendant's conviction, stating that had the proper inquiries been made, it was reasonable to conclude that a finding would have been made that the defendant was a victim of trafficking and that a defence under s 45 probably would have succeeded.

Section 46 provides for special measures (Youth Justice and Criminal Evidence Act 1999) to be available for witnesses in trials of slavery and trafficking offences.

10.4 Necessity

As with duress, we are again concerned with situations in which a person is faced with a choice between two unpleasant alternatives, one involving his committing a breach of the criminal law and the other some evil to himself or others. Unlike the defence of duress, the defence of necessity is more open-textured without prescribed thresholds. If the evil outweighs any evil involved in the breach of the letter of the law, it is arguable that the actor should have a defence of necessity. The courts have never recognized a defence in these broad terms and to what extent a defence of necessity prevails in English law is uncertain.[240] As early as 1552, Sergeant Pollard in an argument which apparently found favour with the judges of the Exchequer Chamber said that breaking the letter of laws might be justified 'where the words of them are broken to avoid greater inconveniences, or through necessity, or by compulsion . . .'[241] From an early period, other particular instances of necessity were recognized. It was justifiable (in the conditions of those days) to pull down a house to prevent a fire from spreading,[242] for a prisoner to leave a burning gaol contrary to the express words of a statute and for the crew of a ship or a passenger[243] to jettison the cargo in order to save the lives of the passengers. It was once held that prison officials may—indeed, must—forcibly feed prisoners if that was necessary to preserve their health and, *a fortiori*, their lives.[244] It was a defence to the offence of procuring an abortion to show that the act was done in good faith for the purpose only of preserving the life of the mother,[245] although at that time there was no provision for such a defence in any statute.[246]

Concerns about the ambiguity of the defence were expressed from the earliest times. Writing in the Victorian era, Stephen thought the law so vague that it was open to the judges to lay down any rule they thought expedient; and that the expediency of breaking the law in some cases might be so great that a defence should be allowed—but these cases could not be defined in advance.[247] In spite of these doubts, Glanville Williams in 1953 submitted 'with

---

[239] [2019] EWCA Crim 984.

[240] The Court of Appeal (Civ Div) has stated that there is no general defence of necessity. See *R (on the application of Nicklinson) v Ministry of Justice* [2013] EWCA Civ 961, [25]. This case examined whether necessity could be a defence to murder in the context of voluntary euthanasia and the court held that 'it is simply not appropriate for the court to fashion a defence of necessity in such a complex and controversial field; this is a matter for Parliament.' At [56].

[241] *Reniger v Forgossa* (1552) 1 Plowd 1 at 18.

[242] See now the Criminal Damage Act 1971, on which see Ch 27.

[243] *Mouse's Case* (1608) 12 Co Rep 63.

[244] *Leigh v Gladstone* (1909) 26 TLR 139 (Alverstone LCJ), not followed by Thorpe J in *Secretary of State for the Home Department v Robb* [1995] 1 All ER 677. The decision is heavily criticized—see G Zellick, 'The Forcible Feeding of Prisoners: An Examination of the Legality of Enforced Therapy' [1976] PL 153 at 159—and no longer applied in practice.

[245] *Bourne* [1939] 1 KB 687. Cf *Morgentaler* (1975) 20 CCC (2d) 449 (SCC), discussed by L Leigh, 'Necessity and the Case of Dr Morgentaler' [1978] Crim LR 151.

[246] See now Abortion Act 1967, on which see Ch 15 and *T v T* [1988] 1 All ER 613, Fam Div.

[247] II HCL, 108.

some assurance' that the defence of necessity is recognized by English law[248] and, particularly, by the criminal law,[249] arguing that the 'peculiarity of necessity as a doctrine of law is the difficulty or impossibility of formulating it with any approach to precision'.

Williams's confidence was entirely justified. In the late twentieth century, the defence had been recognized in the highest courts. Lord Goff has, on several occasions, recognized the existence of the defence and it was applied by the House of Lords in the *Bournewood Trust* case[250] to justify the detention of a person suffering from a mental disorder where there was no statutory authority on point.[251] It has been acknowledged in far more trivial cases: for example, where a police officer directed other persons to disobey traffic regulations as that was reasonably necessary for the protection of life and property.[252]

The precise scope and definition of the defence remain elusive. Indeed, there may be a greater degree of ambiguity arising from the case law development recognizing the emergence of duress of circumstances discussed earlier. In many cases, this is treated simply as an instance of necessity. On some occasions, the court has even merged the terms, as in *Quayle* where the reference is to 'necessity of circumstance'. The relationship of the defences is discussed later. Despite the explicit recognition of the defence the courts persistently adopt a restrictive approach to its application.[253] There is an underlying anxiety that the defence must be kept within strict limits to prevent defendants claiming generally that they thought their actions in breaking the law were reasonable and represented the lesser of two evils. This would be a Trojan horse for anarchy.[254] The speech of Lord Bingham in *Hasan* underlined these judicial anxieties with defences of circumstantial pressure. Norrie cogently explains why the courts have exhibited reluctance to incorporate necessity into English law in the following terms:

necessity operates to permit alternative political, ethical, economic and moral arguments to confront the formal logic of the law. Resting on a concept of moral involuntariness, it opens up the grounds upon which a defendant can say 'I could do no other'. For this reason, the law has fought shy of the defence, yet there remains at the same time a cogent reason for accepting it. It introduces broader ideas of justice, either in terms of social or environmental justice, or the requirements of a properly democratic polity. It requires the criminal law to be mindful of such ideas and the underlying social and political reasons which represent the only means of sustaining its legitimacy.[255]

10.4.1 Nature of threat

The traditional examples of necessity—escaping from the burning gaol, etc—do, like duress and duress of circumstances, involve danger to life. In relation to lesser threats, writers from Hale[256] onwards have denied that necessity can be defence to, for example, a charge of theft

---

[248] CLGP (1st edn) 216.   [249] ibid, 724 et seq.   [250] [1998] 3 All ER 289 at 297–8, 301–2.

[251] Note that the ECtHR in *HL v UK* (App no 45508/99) held that his being kept at Bournewood Hospital by doctors against the wishes of his carers under the common law of necessity amounted to a breach of Art 5(1) of the ECHR (deprivation of liberty) and of Art 5(4) (right to have lawfulness of detention reviewed by a court). Section 50 of the Mental Health Act 2007 amends the Mental Capacity Act 2005 so that it is unlawful to deprive a person of his liberty in a hospital or care home unless a standard or urgent authorization under Sch A1 to the 2005 Act is in force, or under an order of the Court of Protection. For discussion see LC 372, *Mental Capacity and Deprivation of Liberty* (2017).

[252] *Johnson v Phillips* [1976] 1 WLR 65. Cf *Wood v Richards* [1977] RTR 201.

[253] For criticism, see S Edwards, 'Good and Harm, Excuses and Justifications, and the Moral Narratives of Necessity' in A Reed and M Bohlander (with N Wake and E Smith) (eds), *General Defences in Criminal Law* (2014).

[254] cf Norrie, *Crime, Reason and History*, 207.   [255] ibid, 218.

[256] I PC, 54, and see Blackstone, *Commentaries*, iv, 31.

of food or clothing. In more modern times, Lord Denning has justified that limit on the ground that 'if hunger were once allowed to be an excuse for stealing, it would open a door through which all kinds of lawlessness and disorder would pass'.[257]

In that case, a civil action, it was held that homelessness did not justify even an orderly entry into empty houses owned by the local authority: 'If homelessness were once admitted as a defence to trespass, no one's house could be safe. Necessity would open a door which no man could shut.'[258] Probably, it is now the law that if the taking or the entry was necessary to prevent death or serious injury through starvation or cold there would be a defence of duress of circumstances; but if it were merely to prevent hunger, or the discomforts of cold or homelessness, there would be no defence.

There are some cases where what was in substance a defence of necessity was allowed without identifying a threat to life or serious injury. In *Gillick*'s case, one of the conditions stated of the lawfulness of the contraceptive advice or treatment given to a girl under 16 was that unless she receives it 'her physical or mental health or both are likely to suffer'.[259] In *F v West Berkshire Health Authority*,[260] it was held that it was lawful to carry out a sterilization operation on a woman who lacked the mental capacity to consent because otherwise there would be a grave risk of her becoming pregnant which would be disastrous from a psychiatric point of view.[261] Lord Goff founded his judgment on necessity. These cases would, however, involve at most a slight extension of duress of circumstances—comparable to MacNaghten J's interpretation of 'preserving the life of the mother' to include preserving her from becoming 'a physical or mental wreck' in *Bourne*,[262] a case which must now be regarded as one of duress of circumstances.

Lord Goff has also said, 'That there exists a defence of necessity at common law, which may in some circumstances be invoked to justify what would otherwise be a trespass to land, is not in doubt. But the scope of the defence is by no means clear.' He found it unnecessary to decide the important question raised in that case, whether the defence could justify forcible entry (which would otherwise be a crime) into the private premises of another in the bona fide, but mistaken, belief that there exists an emergency on the premises by reason of the presence there of a person who has suffered injury and who may require urgent attention.[263] In *Pipe v DPP*,[264] Owen J ruled that magistrates had been wrong to conclude that D could not plead necessity when he drove over the speed limit in order to get a young boy with a suspected fractured leg to hospital. Despite the fact that the boy's life was not in danger, he was in severe pain and the court ruled that necessity ought to have been considered. This case, again, could be seen as being a slight extension of duress of circumstances. Indeed, Owen J cited *Conway* in his judgment.

10.4.1.1 Statutory implication or exclusion of necessity defence

In England it has been argued that there is a principle of statutory interpretation:

that it requires clear and unambiguous language before the courts will hold that a statutory provision was intended to apply to cases in which more harm will, in all probability, be caused by complying with it than by contravening it.[265]

---

[257] *Southwark London Borough v Williams* [1971] 2 All ER 175 at 179.   [258] ibid.

[259] [1986] AC 112 at 174 per Lord Fraser.   [260] [1989] 2 All ER 545.

[261] See now the Mental Capacity Act 2005.   [262] [1939] 1 KB 687, see p 685.

[263] *Richards and Leeming* (on appeal from 81 Cr App R 125) (10 July 1986, unreported). The House agreed with Lord Goff's speech (thanks to Sir Anthony Hooper for this material). By s 17(5) of PACE 'all the rules of common law under which a constable has power to enter premises without a warrant are hereby abolished'. But does this abolish a justification which (if it exists at all) is available, not only to constables, but to persons generally?

[264] [2012] EWHC 1821 (Admin).

[265] P Glazebrook, 'The Necessity Plea in English Criminal Law' (1972A) 31 CLJ 87 at 93.

This principle, if it exists, seems to be little noticed in modern times. In *Buckoke v Greater London Council*,[266] Lord Denning MR said, *obiter*:

A driver of a fire engine with ladders approaches the traffic lights. He sees 200 yards down the road a blazing house with a man at an upstairs window in extreme peril. The road is clear in all directions. At that moment the lights turn red. Is the driver to wait for 60 seconds or more, for the lights to turn green? If the driver waits for that time, the man's life will be lost.

Lord Denning accepted the opinion of both counsel that the driver would (at that time) commit an offence against the Road Traffic Regulations if he crossed the red light. But the threat to the fictitious man at the upstairs window seems to be no less than the threat to Willer, to the passenger in Conway's car or to Martin. Lord Denning was stating the effect of the law as he then believed it to be; but he added that the hypothetical driver 'should not be prosecuted. He should be congratulated'—so Denning would welcome the defence of duress of circumstances. As Professor Packer says:

it seems foolish to make rules (or to fail to make exceptions to rules) that discourage people from behaving as we would like them to behave. To the extent that the threat of punishment has deterrent efficacy, rules such as these would condition people confronted with dilemmas to make the wrong choice, either through action or inaction. And the actual imposition of punishment would serve no useful purpose since we assume these people are not in need of either restraint or reform.[267]

The terms of a statute may, in effect, 'build in' a defence of necessity or, on the other hand, positively exclude one; and in either of these situations there is no room for the application of a general, common law defence. *Quayle*[268] is a good example of the courts rejecting a possible defence on the basis of the conflict it would create with a statutory scheme in which no such defence for possession or supply of drugs was included. A defence of duress by threats or of 'necessity by circumstances' might be available where the general scheme and policy of the legislation was not in question, but the use of cannabis on an individual basis conflicted with the purposes and effect of the legislation. Norrie makes the valuable point that in cases such as *Quayle* the main problem the courts face is in not being seen to sanction a systematic policy of self-help that would undermine the law.[269]

The Court of Appeal addressed this issue again in *S (C)*.[270] D and her husband were divorced and together had a daughter. When the husband applied for contact and residence orders, D alleged that he had sexually abused the daughter but a judge found that these allegations were unfounded. D continued to believe that her daughter was being sexually abused and took her out of the jurisdiction, without the consent of either the father or the court. D was then charged with child abduction. D sought to plead necessity but the judge, referring to *Quayle*, ruled that the defence was unavailable and she pleaded guilty. Sir John Thomas P, after referring to the Child Abduction Act 1984, concluded that given the legislative policy of the Act it was impossible to see how Parliament could have intended for necessity to operate when a parent removes a child who is subject to the court's protection from England and Wales.

These cases demonstrate that if D is charged with a statutory offence and seeks to plead necessity, the judge must determine whether the defence is implicitly excluded by the terms of the legislation. This will require the judge to examine the policy objectives underpinning the legislative scheme.

---

[266] [1971] 2 All ER 254 at 258. Statutory regulations now exempt the driver of the fire engine; but a contractor with a ladder on his lorry might find himself in the same position.

[267] H Packer, *The Limits of the Criminal Sanction* (1969) 114.   [268] [2005] EWCA Crim 1415.

[269] Norrie, *Crime, Reason and History*, 209–10.

[270] [2012] EWCA Crim 389, applied in *Ab* [2014] EWCA Crim 1642.

10.4.1.2 Necessity and responses to non-criminal threats

As noted earlier in the case of *Jones*, the Court of Appeal sought to limit the defence to cases where D faced a criminal threat (in fact it was stipulated that the crime must be one under national law not international law). It is submitted that no such restriction applies. D may rely on the defence where he is faced with naturally occurring disasters, accidents caused by human actors or criminal threats.

10.4.1.3 Necessity and negligence?

In *DPP v Harris*,[271] McCowan LJ was inclined to think that necessity can never be a defence to what would otherwise be the offence of driving without due care because the term 'due' in the section allows for consideration of all the circumstances that would be taken into account if the general defence applied. In *Backshall*,[272] the court preferred the opinion of Curtis J who thought it contrary to common sense to allow the defence in relation to the graver offence of reckless (now dangerous) driving and not to the lesser offence of careless driving; but the court recognized that it may make no difference. A person driving as a necessity, as required, is not failing to exercise 'due' care. The reasoning of McCowan LJ might be applicable to any crime where the prosecution must prove that an act was done unreasonably: if it was necessary so to act, it could hardly be unreasonable to do so. In *Harris*, the court was concerned with a statutory regulation which prescribes the circumstances in which a fire, police or ambulance vehicle may cross a red light; and as we have seen, such a specific provision may well be taken to exclude a defence of necessity when such a vehicle crosses in other circumstances. In *Harris*, all this was *obiter* because the court found that there was no necessity for D to drive as he did.

10.4.1.4 Necessity in strict liability and situational liability offences

In *Cichon v DPP*,[273] the court held that prohibition against allowing a pit bull terrier to be unmuzzled in a public place was 'absolute' and said that it followed that Parliament had excluded any defence of necessity; but if a general defence such as self-defence or duress—or necessity—is available even in offences requiring mens rea, it should *a fortiori* be available to an offence of strict liability. If the owner had removed the dog's muzzle on the orders of an animal rights fanatic armed with a sawn-off shotgun, he would surely have had a defence of duress. So too with necessity—though the fact that the dog in *Cichon* was afflicted with kennel cough might well be held insufficient to ground any such defence.

In *Santos v CPS*,[274] the CPS conceded that the magistrates were wrong to exclude the defence of necessity on the basis that D was charged with a strict liability offence. Foskett J held that there is clear authority that establishes that the defence of necessity is available for strict liability offences, citing *Martin* and *DPP v Mullally*.[275] This echoes what was said by Lord Judge in *Gregory*.[276] Lord Judge CJ stated that while duress of circumstances/necessity is of strictly limited ambit, it is possible to envisage circumstances in which, in the context of possession of a firearm, it might arise. His lordship gave the example of a bank robber who drops his gun, which is then seized by a member of the public who runs away with it to a safe place until the police arrive. Although Lord Judge did not state emphatically that the

---

[271] [1995] 1 Cr App R 170. Curtis J thought that if necessity (in effect, duress of circumstances) applied to reckless driving, it must apply to the lesser offence of careless driving. Cf *Symonds* [1998] Crim LR 280.

[272] [1999] 1 Cr App R 35 at 41.

[273] [1994] Crim LR 918.   [274] [2013] EWHC 550 (Admin).

[275] [2006] EWHC 3448 (Admin). It was accepted in this case that duress could be a defence to a charge of drink-driving, although there was no evidence that D in fact was acting under duress.

[276] [2011] EWCA Crim 1712.

defence would be applicable in such circumstances, he did observe that although prosecution would be unlikely that does not mean that the possible duress of circumstances/necessity defence would be bound to fail. It is submitted that despite the *obiter* nature of these observations, they have the benefit of according with common sense.

In *Hampshire County Council v E*,[277] the court held that the mother of a truanting child could not plead duress to a charge of 'being a parent of a child of compulsory school age' who was truanting.[278] The offence required no act by the mother, and thus the threats (from the child) could not affect her liability. Presumably no defence of necessity would be available to her either, which is a harsh result indeed, and seems wrong in principle.

10.4.1.5 Necessity and murder

One of the reasons given by the House of Lords in *Howe*[279] for refusing to allow a defence of duress to murder was that it had been decided in the famous case of *Dudley and Stephens*[280] that necessity was not a defence to murder. Whether that was the *ratio decidendi* of the case has been debated. One interpretation of the judgment is that the court found that no necessity existed[281] and the House of Lords later held that the case does decide that point. The facts are well known: three men and a boy of the crew of a yacht were shipwrecked. After 18 days in an open boat, having been without food and water for several days, the two accused suggested to the third man that they should kill and eat the boy. He declined but, two days later, Dudley killed the boy who was now very weak. The three men then fed on the boy's body and, four days later, they were rescued. The accused were indicted for murder. The jury, by a special verdict, found that the men would probably have died within the four days had they not fed on the boy's body, that the boy would probably have died before them and that, at the time of the killing, there was no appreciable chance of saving life, except by killing one for the others to eat. The accused were convicted of murder, but the sentence was commuted to six months' imprisonment.

In *Dudley and Stephens*,[282] Lord Coleridge CJ examined the pronouncements of writers of authority and found nothing in them to justify[283] the extension of a defence to such a case as this. Killing by the use of force necessary to preserve one's own life in self-defence was a well-recognized, but entirely different, case from the killing of an innocent person. Moreover, 'If . . . Lord Hale is clear—as he is—that extreme necessity of hunger does not justify larceny, what would he have said to the doctrine that it justified murder?'[284]

Apart from authority, the court clearly thought that the law ought not to afford a defence in such a case. They thought, first, that it would be too great a departure from morality;

---

[277] [2007] EWHC 2584 (Admin).   [278] Education Act 1996, s 444.

[279] [1987] AC 417 at 429, 453, n 193, see J Donoghue (2011) 74 MLR 216, 235 et seq.

[280] (1884) 14 QBD 273. On the instructions of Huddleston B the jury found the facts in a special verdict and the judge then adjourned the assizes to the Royal Courts of Justice where the case was argued before a court of five judges (Lord Coleridge CJ, Grove and Denman JJ, Pollock and Huddleston BB).

[281] Arguably this case is one of duress of circumstances as there is a threat of death or serious injury posed by the circumstances.

[282] On the case generally, see AWB Simpson, *Cannibalism and the Common Law* (1984).

[283] It has been argued that the problem with the judgment is that Lord Coleridge failed to draw a distinction between whether extreme circumstances can *justify* the taking of innocent life, and the separate question of whether such conduct, although unjustifiable, might nevertheless be *excusable*. See J Dressler, 'Reflections on *Dudley and Stephens* and Killing the Innocent: Taking the Wrong Conceptual Path' in D Baker and J Horder (eds), *The Sanctity of Life and the Criminal Law* (2013).

[284] (1884) 14 QBD at 283.

and, secondly, that the principle would be dangerous because of the difficulty of measuring necessity and of selecting the victim. The second reason is more convincing:

> Who is to be the judge of this sort of necessity? By what measure is the comparative value of lives to be measured? Is it to be strength or intellect, or what? It is plain that the principle leaves to him who is to profit by it to determine the necessity which will justify him in deliberately taking another's life to save his own.[285]

Williams finds as the 'one satisfying reason' in the judgment that it was no more necessary to kill the boy than one of the grown men and adds: 'To hinge guilt on this would indicate that lots should have been cast . . .'[286] If the boy had agreed to be bound by the casting of lots, he would have been consenting to die; and, arguably, consent in such a situation may be a defence. Captain Oates took his life when he left Scott and his companions; yet he was regarded not as a criminal but as a hero.[287] If the boy had not consented, the drawing of lots would be hardly more rational than trial by ordeal—yet more civilized than a free-for-all. In fact, the court disapproved, *obiter*, of a ruling in an American case, *United States v Holmes*,[288] that the drawing of lots in similar circumstances would legalize a killing. Holmes, a member of the crew of a wrecked ship, was cast adrift in an overcrowded boat. In order to prevent the boat sinking, the mate gave orders to throw the male passengers overboard and Holmes assisted in throwing over 16 men. No doubt, if his act was criminal at all, it was murder; but a grand jury refused to indict him for murder and so he was charged with manslaughter. The judge directed that the law was that passengers must be preferred to seamen; only enough seamen to navigate the boat ought to have been saved; and the passengers whom necessity requires to be cast over must be chosen by lot. As this had not been done (none of the officers or crew went down with the ship) the jury found him guilty.

Stephen thought the method of selection 'over refined'[289] and Lord Coleridge thought this 'somewhat strange ground . . . can hardly . . . be an authority satisfactory to a court in this country'.[290]

The English judges offered no alternative solution and, presumably, their view was that, in the absence of a self-sacrificing volunteer, it was the duty of all to die. This was also the view of the distinguished American judge, Cardozo J:

> Where two or more are overtaken by a common disaster, there is no right on the part of one to save the lives of some, by the killing of another. There is no rule of human jettison.[291]

The principle in *Dudley and Stephens* is distinguishable if there is no problem of selection.[292] D, a mountaineer who cuts the rope seconds before he would be dragged over a precipice by E, his falling companion, surely commits no offence. There is no question of choosing between D and E. E is going to die in a matter of seconds anyway. The question is whether he alone should die a few seconds earlier, or whether they should both die seconds later. At the inquest following the Zeebrugge ferry disaster a witness, an army corporal, gave evidence that he and numerous other passengers were trapped in the stricken ferry and in grave danger of drowning. A possible way of escape up a rope ladder was barred by a man, petrified by cold or fear, who could move neither up nor down. After fruitless attempts to persuade him to move, the corporal ordered those nearer to push him off the ladder. They

---

285 ibid, 287.   286 CLGP, 744.   287 Should it matter that Oates killed himself?
288 (1841) 26 Fed Cas 360.   289 II HCL, 108.   290 (1884) 14 QBD 273 at 285.
291 *Selected Writings*, 390.
292 On a more theoretical level, Dressler argues that Lord Coleridge CJ conflated justifiable with excusable conduct and that the circumstances the sailors found themselves in should have been seen as involving the latter. See n 283.

did so, he fell into the water and was not seen again. The trapped passengers were then able to climb up the ladder to safety. The coroner expressed the opinion that a reasonable act of self-preservation, or the preservation of others, is 'not necessarily murder'. So far as is known, no legal proceedings against the corporal were ever contemplated. Unlike the cabin boy, but like the falling mountaineer, the man frozen on the ladder was chosen by fate as the potential victim by his immobility there. He was preventing the passengers from going where they had a right and a most urgent need to go. He was, unwittingly, imperilling their lives.[293]

Similarly, the commander of an Australian naval ship 'took the decision to save the rest of his crew by sealing four sailors in the blazing engine room, consigning them to certain death, after rescuers were beaten back by the flames'.[294] It seems likely that the decision taken by the officer is that which any prudent officer of sound judgement would have taken. If so, it is inconceivable that he would ever be charged with, much less convicted of, murder. Surely the law should recognize this. In these examples the evil avoided outweighs that caused—one dies instead of two, or instead of many—not only is there extreme duress, but the conduct is justified. Indeed, the Australian officer would probably have been in breach of his duty if he had allowed his ship and most of her crew to be lost.

Re A: the conjoined twins

In the case of the conjoined twins,[295] the court held that, in the special circumstances of that case, it was lawful to kill the weaker twin, B, in order to save the life of the stronger, A. But this was not a simple choice between A and B, which the court would have been unwilling to make. The situation presented to the court was that if the operation was performed B would be killed but A would probably live—as indeed occurred—but, if the operation was not performed, both would die. Brooke LJ based his decision on necessity. The three requirements for the defence were stated to be:

(1) the act is needed to avoid inevitable and irreparable evil;

(2) no more should be done than is reasonably necessary for the purpose to be achieved; and

(3) the evil inflicted must not be disproportionate to the evil avoided.[296]

His lordship distinguished *Dudley and Stephens*. There was no problem of who was to be selected to be killed in this case. Like the man on the rope ladder in the Zeebrugge case and the falling mountaineer dragging his companion to his death, A was selected by the circumstances. Brooke LJ preferred necessity to private defence (discussed later) because here there was no 'unjust' aggression by A. But A was imperilling B's life and the private defence

---

[293] See further JC Smith, *Justification and Excuse*, Ch 3. And cf self-defence against a nine-year-old or insane person.

[294] (1998) The Times, 5 May.

[295] *Re A (Children)* [2000] 4 All ER 961, [2001] Crim LR 400 and commentary. See also J Rogers, 'Necessity, Private-Defence and the Killing of Mary' [2001] Crim LR 515. Cf the approach of the Canadian Supreme Court in *Latimer* [2001] 1 SCR 3, denying D a defence where he killed his severely disabled daughter. The court pronounced a defence based on three criteria: (a) imminent peril; (b) no reasonable legal alternative being available; (c) D's reaction being proportionate. See S Ost, 'Euthanasia and the Defence of Necessity' in C Erin and S Ost, *The Criminal Justice System and Health Care* (2007). For criticism of Ost, see F Stark, 'Necessity and *Nicklinson*' [2013] Crim LR 949.

[296] *Re A (Children)*, n 295, 1051. For discussion see W Wilson, 'How Criminal Defences Work' in A Reed and M Bohlander (with N Wake and E Smith) (eds), *General Defences in Criminal Law* (2014) 21. This passage in the 13th edn was cited with approval by Lord Dyson MR in *R (on the application of Nicklinson) v Ministry of Justice* [2013] EWCA Civ 466.

solution avoids the argument, valid or not, that necessity can never justify killing. Whatever its basis, the principle appears to be that it is lawful for D to kill A where, as D knows, A is doomed to imminent death but even the short continuation of his life will kill B as well. It remains important to appreciate the limited scope of this judgment. In rejecting the argument that this case is authority for the proposition that necessity is a defence to murder, the Court of Appeal has stated that, 'This case is too slender a thread on which to hang such a far-reaching development of the common law.'[297]

More analysis of the issue occurred in *R (on the application of Nicklinson) v Ministry of Justice*.[298] N sought to argue that voluntary euthanasia could be a defence to murder by relying upon the defence of necessity.[299] N relied upon *Re A* to demonstrate that the courts have evinced a willingness to extend the scope of the defence. Toulson LJ in the Divisional Court rejected the analogy with *Re A* and held that:

In a system governed by the rule of law, any such dispensing power requires great caution. It should not be used as a means of introducing major and controversial policy change. *In re A* was a case of highly exceptional facts, where an immediate decision was required.[300]

His lordship held that the common law develops incrementally, whilst major changes involving matters of controversial social policy are for Parliament: this issue falls into the latter category.[301] This passage also demonstrates that his lordship believes that *Re A* contains an element of immediacy that the facts of the instant case lacked. The same view was taken in the Court of Appeal. In the Supreme Court Lord Neuberger observed:[302]

As Lord Dyson MR and Elias LJ explained in para 25 of their judgment in the Court of Appeal, to extend the defence of necessity to a charge of assisted suicide would be a revolutionary step, which would be wholly inconsistent with both recent judicial dicta of high authority, and the legislature's intentions. As to judicial dicta, see *R v Howe* [1987] 1 AC 417, 429B–D and 453B–F, per Lord Hailsham and Lord Mackay respectively, *Airedale NHS Trust v Bland* [1993] AC 789, 892E–893A, per Lord Mustill, and *R v Inglis* [2011] 1 WLR 1110, para 37, per Lord Judge CJ. So far as legislative intention is concerned, in 1961, Parliament decided, through section 2(1), to create a statutory offence of assisting a suicide in a provision which admitted of no exceptions, and it confirmed that decision as recently as 2009 (when section 2(1) was repealed and re-enacted in more detailed terms) following a debate in which the possibility of relaxing the law on the topic was specifically debated.

Shooting down hijacked aircraft

Following the destruction of the World Trade Center in New York by hijacked aircraft, it now appears to be recognized that it would be lawful to shoot down a plane, killing all the innocent passengers and crew if this were the only way to prevent a much greater impending

---

[297] *Nicklinson* [2013] EWCA Civ 466, [63]. The Supreme Court also confirmed that *Re A* was an exceptional case.

[298] [2012] EWHC 2381 (Admin), [2013] EWCA Civ 466, [2014] UKSC 38.

[299] It has been argued that *Nicklinson* should not have been argued on the basis of necessity at all, but that consent would have made for a more viable argument, although one that would nevertheless have failed. See F Stark, 'Necessity and *Nicklinson*' [2013] Crim LR 949. Although not writing about *Nicklinson*, Professor Lewis has made the not dissimilar point that necessity is not a viable route towards the legalisation of euthanasia. See P Lewis, 'The Failure of the Defence of Necessity' in D Baker and J Horder (eds), *The Sanctity of Life and the Criminal Law* (2013).

[300] [2012] EWHC 2381 (Admin), [74].

[301] The Court of Appeal agreed with this analysis. See [2013] EWCA Civ 961. The Supreme Court ([2014] UKSC 38), in a complex judgment, also refused the relief sought. For discussion see J Rogers, 'Assisted Suicide Saga—The *Nicklinson* Episode' [2014] 7 Arch Rev 7.

[302] [2014] UKSC 38, [130].

disaster. This is doubted by Bohlander,[303] but without reference to the explicit statements in the Select Committee on Defence,[304] making it clear that government policy is to permit shooting down of civilian aircraft in such circumstances and that the basis for such action would be by application of a necessity principle:

In the last resort, it might be necessary to shoot down the civilian aircraft. MoD officials assured us . . . that they had properly examined the legal aspects of any such decision . . . we have satisfied ourselves with lawyers that there is a proper basis for doing this.

The MoD and Committee took the view that the test to be applied is that the act will be necessary and proportionate if:

(1) the act is needed to avoid inevitable and irreparable evil;

(2) no more should be done than is reasonably necessary for the purpose to be achieved; and

(3) the evil inflicted must not be disproportionate to the evil avoided.[305]

10.4.1.6 A doctor's defence of necessity

Without expressly acknowledging it, the courts appear to have recognized a special defence to murder by doctors.[306] Although a doctor knows that treatment will significantly accelerate the death of his patient—that is, kill him—he is not guilty of murder if his purpose is to give what, in the circumstances as he understands them, is proper treatment to relieve pain.[307] Even if this is right, there remains the possibility, where the doctor has made a grossly negligent assessment of the circumstances, of a conviction for manslaughter.

10.4.1.7 Necessity and a duty to act

Where D owes a duty of care to E it seems that necessity may impose on him a duty to act to the detriment of—even to kill—others. The Australian naval officer referred to earlier probably had a duty to kill the four sailors. While the doctors in the conjoined twins case remained in control, they apparently had a duty to kill the weaker twin. When the 'conflict of duties'[308] is resolved, D must fulfil the prevailing duty. If A, B and C are members of a mountaineering party and A sees that B is dragging C to the deaths of both, is he not bound to cut the rope, accelerating B's death but saving the life of C, if he can do so without risk? But what about a passer-by, D, who found himself in the same position as A? Presumably he would be justified in cutting the rope but probably not bound to do so.[309]

---

[303] 'In Extremis? Hijacked Airplanes, Collateral Damage and the Limits of Criminal Law' [2006] Crim LR 579. See for detailed analysis Norrie, *Crime, Reason and History*, 213–14 and T Hörnle, 'Hijacked Planes: May They Be Shot Down?' (2007) 10 New Crim LR 582.

[304] Sixth Report, *Defence and Security in the UK 2001–2002*, HC 518-I, para 8.   [305] ibid, para 9.

[306] See S Ost, 'Euthanasia and the Defence of Necessity' [2005] Crim LR 255, arguing that necessity would provide a better basis for a defence of euthanasia for doctors. For rejection of this argument, see P Lewis, 'The Failure of the Defence of Necessity' in D Baker and J Horder (eds), *The Sanctity of Life and the Criminal Law* (2013).

[307] Dr Moor's case, discussed by A Arlidge QC, 'The Trial of Dr David Moor' [2000] Crim LR 31 and a comment by JC Smith, 'A Comment on *Moor's Case*' [2000] Crim LR 41. See also A Ashworth, 'Criminal Liability in a Medical Context: The Treatment of Good Intentions' in A Simester and ATH Smith (eds), *Harm and Culpability* (1996).

[308] See the discussion of the judgment of Wilson J in *Perka v R* (1984) 13 DLR (4th) 1 at 36 by Ward LJ in *Re A (Children)* at [2000] 4 All ER 961 at 1015–16, by Brooke LJ at 1048–50 and by Walker LJ at 1065–6.

[309] On the 'duty' to assist in such cases, see Ch 2.

10.4.1.8 Necessity in other jurisdictions

In some other parts of the common law world a general defence of necessity is now recognized.[310]

In Australia the courts of Victoria recognized the existence of a general, if limited, defence in *Loughnan*[311] where D's defence to a charge of escaping from prison was that he feared he would otherwise be killed by other prisoners—but the defence was not made out on the facts. In *Perka*,[312] the Supreme Court of Canada held that necessity may be an 'excuse' but not a 'justification' (there seems to be no practical difference except that it perhaps made the court feel better) for an act which is 'inevitable, unavoidable and afford(s) no reasonable opportunity for an alternative course of action that does not involve a breach of the law'.

The American Model Penal Code, which has been adopted in many States of the United States, contains a general defence of necessity as follows:

Conduct which the actor believes to be necessary to avoid a harm or evil to him or to another is justifiable, provided that:

> (a) the harm or evil sought to be avoided by such conduct is greater than that sought to be prevented by the law defining the offence charged . . .[313]

No such general principle exists or is likely to be developed by English courts. Edmund Davies LJ clearly formulated the judicial attitude:

the law regards with the deepest suspicion any remedies of self-help, and permits these remedies to be resorted to only in very special circumstances. The reason for such circumspection is clear— necessity can very easily become simply a mask for anarchy.[314]

Until relatively recently, it seemed that, except in cases where necessity had already been recognized as a defence, the courts were likely to be satisfied by their power to grant an absolute discharge in hard cases.[315]

10.4.2 The relationship between duress, duress of circumstances and necessity

It seems now to be generally accepted that duress and duress of circumstances will be treated as identical by the courts as regards all elements other than the obvious one of the source of the threat.[316] This seems unobjectionable.

However, in *Shayler*,[317] it was stated that *Abdul-Hussain* 'reflects other decisions which have treated the defences of duress and necessity as being part of the same defence and the

---

[310] See for a review of the position in Oceanic countries, M Forsyth, 'The Divorce or the Marriage of Morality and Law?: The Defence of Necessity in Pacific Island Countries' (2010) 21 Crim Law Forum 121.

[311] [1981] VR 443.   [312] (1984) 13 DLR (4th) 1.

[313] §3.02. It is subject to qualifications not necessary to be noted here. See the fascinating discussions in L Alexander, 'Lesser Evils: A Closer Look at the Paradigmatic Justification' (2005) 24 L & Phil 611; M Berman, 'Lesser Evils: A Less Close Look' (2005) 24 L & Phil 681.

[314] *Southwark London Borough v Williams* [1971] 2 All ER 175 at 181.

[315] Glazebrook (1972A) 31 CLJ 87 at 118–19.

[316] See Wilson, *Central Issues*, Ch 10, pp 303 et seq; IH Dennis, 'On Necessity as a Defence to Crime: Possibilities, Problems and the Limits of Justifications and Excuses' (2009) 3 Crim L & Phil 29 examining the theoretical bases for the defence. See also P Westen and J Mangiafico, 'The Criminal Defense of Duress as Justification not Excuse and Why it Matters' (2003) 6 Buffalo Crim LR 833.

[317] [2001] EWCA Crim 1977.

extended form of the defence [ie duress of circumstances] as being different labels for essentially the same thing'.[318] But there are strong objections to this view.

(1) It is established that duress cannot be a defence to murder or attempted murder but, following *Re A* (the case of the conjoined twins) it is possible that necessity *may* be. This statement must be treated with due caution, however, given the Supreme Court's judgment in *Nicklinson*.[319]

(2) Imminent threats of death or grievous bodily harm are the only occasions for a defence of duress but not for necessity. It is surely a defence to a charge of battery that D was pushing a child to save him from some quite minor injury or even damage to his clothing. Suppose that in *Martin (Colin)* D's wife's threat had been not to kill herself but to leave D; and suppose further that the consequences of her doing so would have been disastrous for D and his family. Duress of circumstances is not open. Should it be a defence for D to demonstrate that the break-up of his marriage would be a social disaster beside which any effect of his driving a short distance while disqualified would pale into insignificance?

(3) Necessity is a defence only if the evil D seeks to avoid would be greater than that which he knows he is causing, whereas if D yields to torture which no ordinary person could be expected to resist, he should be excused however grave the consequences.

(4) Recent cases allowing evidence of the vulnerability to duress of the particular defendant have nothing to do with the proportionality of evils which is said to be required for necessity but are highly relevant to whether he should be excused for giving way to threats.

(5) Necessity may create a duty to act but mere duress can hardly do so.

(6) Duress is (generally accepted to be) an excuse, and necessity a justification.[320] It is quite inappropriate to talk of a surgeon's will being 'overborne' when he decides that it is necessary to carry out a sterilization or other operation, as in the *West Berkshire* case,[321] on a person who is unable to consent. The surgeon is making a reasoned and reasonable decision. Lord Brandon thought that not only would it be lawful, but that it would be the doctor's duty to operate. There is no question of excusing 'human frailty'. All this is true, *a fortiori*, of the decision of the court when it authorizes such an operation as in *Re A* (the conjoined twins).

It is disappointing that the appellate courts have been prepared to state that 'the distinction between duress of circumstances and necessity has, correctly, been by and large ignored or blurred by the courts'.[322] More recently, the Court of Appeal in *S*, taking cognizance of the criticisms made in this section in the 13th edition, ultimately held that, 'we can leave

---

[318] C Clarkson, 'Necessary Action: A New Defence' [2004] Crim LR 81, made a more radical suggestion that the defences of duress, necessity, duress of circumstances and self-defence should be collapsed into one defence of 'necessary action'. This would succeed in achieving its aim of avoiding the inconsistencies of the present law, but only by adopting a lowest common denominator for the defences which seems to be simply that the jury scrutinizes D's conduct to ascertain whether he faced a crisis and responded proportionately. It would be most unlikely to be adopted by the courts since they would be concerned that it opens the floodgates for spurious claims and perverse verdicts. For criticism see AP Simester, 'On Justifications and Excuses' in L Zedner and JV Roberts, *Principles and Values in Criminal Law and Criminal Justice* (2012).

[319] [2014] UKSC 38.

[320] See on this S Gardner, 'Direct Action and the Defence of Necessity' [2005] Crim LR 371.

[321] See p 389.

[322] *Shayler*, n 170, para 55; in *Hasan* [2005] UKHL 22, Lord Bingham seems to use the term necessity interchangeably with duress, eg at [22].

open the question as to whether there is a distinction between necessity and duress of circumstances'.[323]

10.5 Marital coercion

The defence of marital coercion was abolished by s 177 of the Anti-social Behaviour, Crime and Policing Act 2014.[324]

10.6 Superior orders

It is not a defence for D merely to claim that the act was done by him in obedience to the orders of a superior, whether military or civil.[325] Where a security officer caused an obstruction of the highway by checking all the vehicles entering his employer's premises, it was no defence that he was obeying his employer's instructions.[326] Both the House of Lords and the Privy Council have asserted, probably *obiter*, that there is no defence of superior orders in English law.[327] Both approved the statement of the High Court of Australia[328] that 'It is fundamental to our legal system that the executive has no power to authorize a breach of the law and that it is no excuse for an offender to say that he acted under the authority of a superior officer.'

The fact that D was acting under orders may, nevertheless, be very relevant. It may negative mens rea by, for example, showing that D was acting under a mistake of fact or that he had a claim of right[329] to do as he did, where that is a defence; or, where the charge is one of negligence,[330] it may show that he was acting reasonably.

10.7 Public and private defence

Force causing personal injury, damage to property or even death may be justified or excused because the force was reasonably used in the defence of certain public or private interests.[331] Public and private defence is therefore a general defence to any crime of which the use of force is an element or which is alleged to have been committed by the use of force.[332]

---

[323] [2012] EWCA Crim 389, [15].

[324] By virtue of s 177(3) the defence may still be pleaded in respect of an offence alleged to have been committed before the date when the provision came into force, 13 May 2014. For discussion of the defence, see the 13th edn, at p 375.

[325] See S Wallerstein, 'Why English Law Should Not Incorporate the Defence of Superior Orders' [2010] Crim LR 109 considering the influence of international law. See also P Rowe, 'The Criminal Liability of a British Soldier Merely for Participating in the Iraq War 2003' [2010] Crim LR 752 at 757.

[326] *Lewis v Dickson* [1976] RTR 431.

[327] *Clegg* [1995] 1 All ER 334 at 344, 428; *Yip Chiu-Cheung* [1994] 2 All ER 924 at 928. The implications of *Clegg* for firearms officers and servicemen are considered in S Skinner, 'Citizens in Uniform: Public Defence, Reasonableness and Human Rights' [2000] PL 266; J Rogers, 'Justifying the Use of Firearms by Policemen and Soldiers: A Response to the Home Office's Review of the Law on the Use of Lethal Force' (1998) 18 LS 486.

[328] *A v Hayden (No 2)* (1984) 156 CLR 532 at 540.   [329] *James* (1837) 8 C & P 131.

[330] *Trainer* (1864) 4 F & F 105.

[331] See, inter alia, Norrie, *Crime, Reason and History*, Ch 10; F Leverick, *Killing in Self-Defence* (2006); B Sangero, *Self Defence in Criminal Law* (2006).

[332] *Renouf* [1986] 2 All ER 449, (reckless driving). Force was not an element of the offence of reckless driving (now abolished) but the use of force was alleged to constitute the recklessness in that case. The Court of Appeal distinguished *Renouf* in *Bailey* [2013] EWCA Crim 378.

In *Riddell*, the Court of Appeal held that private defence is available as a defence to a charge of dangerous driving.[333] The court held that whilst being charged with this offence does not of itself convey that force has been used, the alleged facts relating to the driving charge may nevertheless be such that force has indeed been applied in response to threatened or actual force.[334] Private defence will therefore be available as a defence to some driving offences, dangerous driving and careless driving being the most obvious examples, but it will not be available to most other driving offences, since they necessarily do not involve the use of force.

The use of the word 'unlawfully' in a statutory definition of an offence is a reminder of the existence of the general defences but they apply whether or not the statute uses that word[335] unless expressly or impliedly excluded. It is clear that the burden of disproving claims of public or private defence rests on the prosecution.[336]

The law is to be found in a variety of sources. Defence of the person, whether oneself or another, is still regulated by the common law (a defence of private defence as it is called in this chapter) as 'clarified' in s 76 of the Criminal Justice and Immigration Act 2008; defence of property by the Criminal Damage Act 1971; and arrest and the prevention of crime by s 3 of the Criminal Law Act 1967 to be read in the light of s 76.

Because of its haphazard development, the law contains some inconsistencies and anomalies. In many cases the common law plea of private defence overlaps with the plea under s 3 of the Criminal Law Act 1967. It is important to bear in mind that s 3 is only available where D uses force *in the prevention of a crime*. Otherwise D must fall back on private defence at common law as now largely restated in s 76 of the Criminal Justice and Immigration Act 2008 (CJIA). Although the principles are very similar, technically they are different defences. One similarity that has been confirmed only relatively recently is that both defences can be pleaded by D who uses force on B in order to prevent C from committing a crime. In *Hichens*, Gross LJ stated that both defences, 'are capable of extending to the use of force against an innocent third party to prevent a crime being committed by someone else'.[337] His lordship did, however, recognize that circumstances giving rise to such a defence will be rare and placed a great deal of emphasis on the requirement of immediacy. This perhaps indicates that pleas of public or private defence in circumstances such as this will only be left to the jury in exceptional cases.

Section 76 provides in part:[338]

Reasonable force for purposes of self-defence etc.

(1) This section applies where in proceedings for an offence—

    (a) an issue arises as to whether a person charged with the offence ('D') is entitled to rely on a defence within subsection (2), and

    (b) the question arises whether the degree of force used by D against a person ('V') was reasonable in the circumstances.

(2) The defences are—

    (a) the common law defence of self-defence; and

    (aa) the common law defence of defence of property; and

    (b) the defences provided by section 3(1) of the Criminal Law Act 1967 . . .

---

[333] [2017] EWCA Crim 413.   [334] For criticism, see S Kyd [2017] Crim LR 637.

[335] *Renouf* (n 326); *Rothwell* [1993] Crim LR 626.

[336] The judge must give clear direction on the issue: *O'Brien* [2004] EWCA Crim 2900.

[337] [2011] EWCA Crim 1626, [30].

[338] Section 76 fails to clarify the law (cf s 76(9)), seeking merely to put some common law on a statutory footing.

(9) This section is intended to clarify the operation of the existing defences mentioned in subsection (2).

(10) In this section—

(a) 'legitimate purpose' means—

(i) the purpose of self-defence under the common law,

(ia) the purpose of defence of property under the common law; or

(ii) the prevention of crime or effecting or assisting in the lawful arrest of persons mentioned in the provisions referred to in subsection (2)(b);

(b) references to self-defence include acting in defence of another person; and

(c) references to the degree of force used are to the type and amount of force used.

In a case in which D is in a dwelling and uses violence on a trespasser (a householder case), different considerations apply.

10.7.1 General principle

The defences at common law and under s 3, as now both also regulated by s 76, can be conveniently described[339] in terms of trigger and response:

- the trigger being D's belief that the circumstances as he understands them render it reasonable or necessary for him to use force;[340] and

- the response being the use of a proportionate or reasonable amount of force to the threat that D believes he faces.[341]

The general principle is that the law allows such force to be used as is objectively reasonable in the circumstances as D genuinely believed them to be. The trigger is assessed subjectively (what did D genuinely believe);[342] the response objectively (would a reasonable person have used that much force in the circumstances as D believed them to be). For example, if D believed that he was being attacked with a deadly weapon and he used only such force as was reasonable to repel such an attack, he has a defence to any charge of an offence arising out of his use of that force. It is immaterial that he was mistaken. Indeed, it is immaterial that he was unreasonably mistaken. Section 76 of the 2008 Act confirms this established common law principle.

In terms of the force D uses in 'response' to the threat as he genuinely perceives it to be, the question, 'Was the force used reasonable in the circumstances as D supposed them

---

[339] Despite the simplicity with which private defence can be described, it is a difficult area of law and a careful direction to the jury will often be necessary. Indeed in *Hayes* [2011] EWCA Crim 2680, Moore-Bick LJ described this area of law as being 'notoriously difficult'.

[340] It is important not to lose sight of the fact that what D must have a genuine belief in is the necessity of using force. In *Yaman* [2012] EWCA Crim 1075 the judge directed the jury to evaluate whether D believed the men he attacked were burglars. It was rightly held that this was not what the jury ought to have been considering.

[341] See Wilson [2005] Crim LR 108 and W Wilson, 'How Criminal Defences Work' in A Reed and M Bohlander (with N Wake and E Smith) (eds), *General Defences in Criminal Law* (2014). Wilson argues that the requirement of proportionality in private defence is, in contrast to other defences, problematic on the basis that if the defence is constituted so as to vindicate the right to personal autonomy, it is unclear why D has to do anything other than that which is necessary to vindicate that right.

[342] This element of the defence has been criticized on the basis that it focuses too much on D's subjective belief. It has been suggested that the law should require an examination of why D was mistaken. See J Rogers, 'Culpability in Self-Defence and Crime Prevention' in GR Sullivan and IH Dennis, *Seeking Security: Pre-Empting the Commission of Criminal Harms* (2012).

to be?'[343] is a question to be answered by the jury or magistrates having regard to s 76. If D's use of force was reasonable given the threat he believed he faced, he is not liable for any harm that arises, even if the reasonable force he uses results in some greater harm which he had not foreseen. For example, D wrestles with V who is trying to steal D's wallet. V dies of a heart attack. If it was reasonable to use the amount of force to wrestle with V, D commits no offence even though it would not have been reasonable to kill V. In the important case of *Keane*[344] Hughes LJ summarized the law on these general principles set out in this paragraph. The judge need only leave private defence to the jury if there is prima facie evidence from which it could be inferred that the defence applies: *Mula*.[345]

10.7.1.1 D's belief in need for force—the trigger—is subjectively assessed

Section 76(3) of the CJIA 2008 provides:

> (3) The question whether the degree of force used by D was reasonable in the circumstances is to be decided *by reference* to the circumstances as D believed them to be, and subsections (4) to (8) also apply in connection with deciding that question.[346]

By s 76(4) of the 2008 Act:

If D claims to have held a particular belief as regards the existence of any circumstances—

> (a) the reasonableness or otherwise of that belief is relevant to the question whether D genuinely held it; but
>
> (b) if it is determined that D did genuinely hold it, D is entitled to rely on it for the purposes of subsection (3), whether or not—
>
> > (i) it was mistaken, or
> >
> > (ii) (if it was mistaken) the mistake was a reasonable one to have made.

Section 76(4) makes clear that the reasonableness of the force D uses is to be assessed on the facts and circumstances as D genuinely believed them to be, even if his belief as to the circumstances was mistaken and unreasonable.[347]

The common law authority for the proposition that D is to be judged on the facts as he believed them to be is *Gladstone Williams*,[348] repeatedly applied in the Court of Appeal[349] and by the Privy Council in *Beckford v R*. Williams was charged with an assault occasioning actual bodily harm to V. D's defence was that he was preventing V from committing an assault on X. But V may have been lawfully arresting X. The jury was directed that if V was acting lawfully, D had a defence only if he believed *on reasonable grounds* that V was

---

[343] But not in relation to s 5 of the Criminal Damage Act 1971, p 1107.

[344] [2010] EWCA Crim 2514. See also *Noye* [2011] EWCA Crim 650 at [9] and [55].

[345] [2013] EWCA Crim 1293. The Court of Appeal relied upon *DPP (Jamaica) v Bailey* [1995] 1 Cr App R 257, and *Bonnick* (1978) 66 Cr App R 266.

[346] Emphasis added.

[347] Subject to what is said later in relation to insane belief in the need for force. An unreasonable belief can be honestly held, but it is not a misdirection to omit this from jury directions: *Chuong* [2013] EWCA Crim 1716. On self-defence generally, see Leverick, *Killing in Self Defence*, Chs 5 and 9. On the admissibility of expert medical evidence to show why D may have been likely to perceive a threat, see *Ibrahim* [2014] EWCA Crim 121, [27] and *Press and Thompson* [2013] EWCA Crim 1849. See p 406.

[348] (1984) 78 Cr App R 276. But, where D is drunk, s 76(5), *Taj* [2018] EWCA Crim 1743. At common law see *O'Grady* [1987] QB 995 and *Hatton* [2005] EWCA Crim 2951, discussed at p 343. See also *Robinson* [2017] EWCA Crim 923 where D's evidence was that he panicked when he picked up a knife and stabbed V to death.

[349] *Jackson* [1985] RTR 257; *Asbury* [1986] Crim LR 258; *Fisher* [1987] Crim LR 334; *Beckford v R* [1988] AC 130. Failure to follow this closely will render the conviction unsafe, see *Duffy v Cleveland* [2007] EWHC 3169 (Admin).

acting unlawfully. It was held that this was a misdirection.[350] D had a defence if he honestly held the belief that there was a need to use force against V, whether his belief was reasonable or not.[351] The court referred to the recommendation of the Criminal Law Revision Committee (CLRC) that the common law of self-defence should be replaced by a statutory defence providing:

a person may use such force as is reasonable in the circumstances as he believes them to be in the defence of himself or any other person.[352]

The court declared that this proposition represented the common law, as stated in *Morgan*[353] and *Kimber*.[354]

If D is voluntarily intoxicated he cannot rely on any mistaken belief 'attributable' to that intoxication: s 76(5).[355] That section, a five-member Court of Appeal has recently stated, is:

broad enough to encompass both (a) a mistaken state of mind as a result of being drunk or intoxicated at the time and (b) a mistaken state of mind immediately and proximately consequent upon earlier drink or drug-taking, so that even though the person concerned is not drunk or intoxicated at the time, the short-term effects can be shown to have triggered subsequent episodes of *e.g.* paranoia. This is consistent with common law principles. We repeat that this conclusion does not extend to long term mental illness precipitated (perhaps over a considerable period) by alcohol or drug misuse. In the circumstances, we agree with Judge Dodgson, that the phrase 'attributable to intoxication' is not confined to cases in which alcohol or drugs are still present in a defendant's system.[356]

The court did not elaborate on what would be proximate in this context. The case involved a defendant who was sober at the time of his attack on V which led to charges of attempted murder. The defendant had, however, recently indulged in an excessive binge-drinking session. His mistaken and confused belief that V was a terrorist about to detonate a bomb arose because of his mental state following that period of intoxication. It is obvious on policy grounds why the court would be keen to preclude reliance on mistakes induced by such conduct. Read narrowly as a decision on the meaning of 'attributable to' in s 76(5), the decision is unassailable. However, as discussed in Ch 9, if the broader *obiter* statement is adopted, it does not sit easily with the broader approach to principles on intoxication.[357]

---

[350] It has been argued that this takes subjectivism too far for two reasons. First, that the more predisposed D is to assume unreasonably that he needs to use force, the more likely it is he will be acquitted, which puts the public at risk. Secondly, that permitting D to avoid liability altogether on the basis of an unreasonable belief could violate Art 2 and/or 3 of the ECHR. See C de Than and J Elvin, 'Mistaken Private Defence: The Case for Reform' in A Reed and M Bohlander (with N Wake and E Smith) (eds), *General Defences in Criminal Law* (2014) 135–6. Merely because the first limb of private defence is made out does not, however, mean that D will invariably be acquitted. On the ECHR point, see later.

[351] For further discussion, see Norrie, *Crime, Reason and History*, 287–91 and Horder, APOCL, 239–42.

[352] Fourteenth Report, para 72(a). The phrase 'may use' is inappropriate. The CLRC was concerned only with establishing a defence in criminal proceedings. The act should not be regarded as justified in the civil law; and, if the mistake was grossly negligent and caused death, it might be manslaughter.

[353] [1976] AC 182.

[354] [1983] 3 All ER 316, (D guilty of indecent assault only if he did not believe V was consenting and 'couldn't care less').

[355] See Ch 9, p 331. Cf *Goode* [2014] EWCA Crim 90, in which the Court of Appeal upheld the judge's direction to the jury that D was not entitled to rely upon a mistaken belief induced by the effects of alcohol. Section 76(5) was not cited by the Court of Appeal, it instead relied upon *Soames* [2001] EWCA Crim 2964.

[356] At [60].

[357] For critical comment, see J Child et al, 'Defending the Delusional, the Irrational, and the Dangerous' [2020] Crim LR 306.

10.7.1.2 Reasonableness of force—the response—is to be assessed objectively

The reasonableness of D's response and the amount of force used are to be assessed objectively on the facts as D believes them to be, by s 76(6) of the 2008 Act. Any possibility that D could have retreated is to be considered (so far as relevant) as a factor to be taken into account, rather than giving rise to a formal legal duty to retreat.[358]

The degree of force used by D is not to be regarded as having been reasonable in the circumstances as D believed them to be if it was disproportionate in those circumstances[359] (although in a householder case see the discussion later).

At common law, in *Shaw (Norman) v R*,[360] the Privy Council accepted the proposition that in determining whether D's response by using force is proportionate, D is to be judged on the circumstances *and danger* as he believed them to be. This is, it is submitted, a preferable approach. It was endorsed by the Court of Appeal in *Harvey*.[361]

D's belief that he is doing only what is reasonable may be evidence, but no more, that it *was* reasonable.[362] Lord Morris has said:[363]

If there has been an attack so that defence is reasonably necessary it will be recognized that a person defending himself cannot weigh to a nicety the exact measure of his necessary defensive action. If a jury thought that in a moment of unexpected anguish a person attacked had only done what he honestly and instinctively thought was necessary that would be most potent evidence that only reasonable defensive action had been taken. A jury will be told that the defence of self-defence, where the evidence makes its raising possible, will only fail if the prosecution show beyond doubt that what the accused did was not by way of self-defence.

This principle relates to self-defence but similar considerations apply to force used to prevent crime or to effect an arrest, etc.

10.7.1.3 Evidence of D's beliefs

There may be an issue as to what circumstances D genuinely believed to exist, especially where his claimed belief is, viewed objectively, an unreasonable one. In such a case, evidence of D's personal characteristics must, in principle, be admissible insofar as they bear upon his ability to be aware of, or to perceive, the circumstances.[364] Section 76(4)–(8) of the CJIA seeks to explain, based on the common law, what may be relevant to the question of D's beliefs. In particular, under s 76(7) in deciding whether D had a genuine belief in the need to use force:

the following considerations are to be taken into account (so far as relevant in the circumstances of the case)—

(a) that a person acting for a legitimate purpose may not be able to weigh to a nicety the exact measure of any necessary action; and

---

[358] By virtue of s 148 of the Legal Aid, Sentencing and Punishment of Offenders Act 2012, which inserted a new subs 76(6)(A).

[359] This was an issue in *Yaman* [2012] EWCA Crim 1075 in which the Court of Appeal identified a number of failings in the judge's summing up, but nevertheless upheld D's conviction. For commentary, see Ormerod [2012] Crim LR 896.

[360] [2002] 1 Cr App R 10.   [361] [2009] EWCA Crim 469.

[362] *Scarlett* [1993] 4 All ER 629 appeared to have significantly modified this rule but *Owino* [1996] 2 Cr App R 128 and *DPP v Armstrong-Braun* [1999] Crim LR 416, decide that *Scarlett* in no way qualifies the law as stated in *Gladstone Williams* (1984) 78 Cr App R 276.

[363] *Palmer v R* [1971] 1 All ER 1077 at 1078, applied in *Shannon* (1980) 71 Cr App R 192 and *Whyte* [1987] 3 All ER 416.

[364] Remorse is not necessarily evidence of D's reasonableness: *Dewar v DPP* [2010] EWHC 1050 (Admin).

(b) that evidence of a person's having only done what the person honestly and instinctively thought was necessary for a legitimate purpose constitutes strong evidence that only reasonable action was taken by that person for that purpose.

By s 76(8):

Subsection (7) is not to be read as preventing other matters from being taken into account where they are relevant to deciding the question mentioned in subsection (3).

At common law, *Martin (Anthony)*[365] held that evidence of D's *physical* characteristics may be admissible. Circumstances which would not be seen as threatening by a robust young man may appear so to a frail elderly woman. However, on policy grounds, the court held that psychiatric evidence that D would have perceived the supposed circumstances as being a greater threat than would a normal person is not admissible. The court rejected an analogy with provocation[366] where such evidence would have been admissible because provocation applied only to murder and was not a complete defence. Unfortunately, the court did not consider duress, where such evidence is admissible for a defence which applies to virtually all crimes except murder and is a complete defence. In the duress case of *Martin (DP)*,[367] psychiatric evidence was admitted that D was suffering from a schizoid affective disorder which made him more likely than a 'normal' person to regard things said as threatening, and to believe that threats would be carried out.

In *Oye*, the Court of Appeal considered the extent to which the plea of private defence could be founded on insane delusions.[368] D was charged with affray and inflicting GBH on a number of police officers. There was expert evidence that D was suffering from an insane delusion at the relevant time and believed that the police officers were evil spirits. At trial there was uncontradicted psychiatric evidence that supported the insanity plea. The judge allowed private defence and insanity to be left to the jury. The jury rejected both defences and D was convicted. On appeal the court held that although there is a subjective element to the question of whether the force used was reasonable in the circumstances as D believed them to be, the standard of reasonableness makes it overwhelmingly objective. Davis LJ stated that:

An insane person cannot set the standards of reasonableness as to the degree of force used by reference to his own insanity. In truth, it makes as little sense to talk of the reasonable lunatic as it did, in the context of cases on provocation, to talk of the reasonable glue-sniffer.[369]

Support for this conclusion was derived from *Martin (Anthony)* and *Canns*,[370] in which the Court of Appeal rejected the argument that the jury ought to have been directed to consider D's delusional state in private defence. In *Oye*, Davis LJ held that the enactment of s 76 did not undermine the validity of these authorities, given that the statute merely 'clarifies' the common law defence. His lordship held that the argument advanced on behalf of D would constitute a change in the law, rather than a clarification of it.[371] The Court of Appeal concluded that while D's physical condition may be taken into account in private defence, his psychiatric condition generally cannot. This outcome is unsurprising, as the argument that s 76 altered the common law in this respect was not one the Court of Appeal was ever likely to find convincing.

---

[365] [2001] EWCA Crim 2245, Child and Sullivan characterize this as a 'problematic authority'. See J Child and GR Sullivan, 'When Does the Insanity Defence Apply? Some Recent Cases' [2014] Crim LR 788.

[366] See p 568. [367] [2000] 2 Cr App R 42. [368] [2013] EWCA Crim 1725. [369] At [47].

[370] [2005] EWCA Crim 2264.

[371] Since the Crown accepted the psychiatric evidence, the Court of Appeal quashed D's conviction and substituted it for one of not guilty by reason of insanity.

The five-member Court of Appeal in *Taj*[372] also endorsed this reasoning. The court stated that in the case of Taj the judge could have withdrawn self-defence based upon the second limb of the defence, applying the judgment in *Oye*. Taj was seeking to rely on a mistaken belief in the need to use force. His paranoid and psychotic state had been induced by earlier binge drinking.

These decisions serve to highlight the difficult interaction between private defence and insanity. As the court observed in *Oye*, ensuring that mentally ill defendants receive the treatment they require complies with policy concerns about public safety.[373] This supports the idea that once D relies on insane beliefs he should be treated as though he is pleading insanity, which ought to 'trump'[374] private defence to preclude it from being left to the jury. To permit otherwise, it is argued, undermines the rationale for the existence of the insanity plea.[375] The counter-argument is that by withdrawing private defence D is denied an opportunity to advance a defence that might lead to a full acquittal;[376] by being forced to plead insanity D is at best going to receive the special verdict. The court in *Oye* did not state that private defence *must* be withdrawn when D relies on insane beliefs, but rather that in considering private defence the jury should ignore those beliefs when considering the second limb of the defence. But that approach also poses problems in practice for a judge trying to direct a jury coherently: when will it be appropriate to take into consideration D's psychiatric condition short of outright legal insanity if he pleads private defence?

If D uses force and relies on insane beliefs to explain why he did so but a reasonable person in his position would have had legitimate grounds to use the amount of force D actually used, why should D be precluded from pleading private defence and the possibility of securing a complete acquittal? It is different if a reasonable person would not have used any, or such, force in the circumstances but the reason D did so is because of his insanity. It is submitted that the Court of Appeal needs to provide clarity on exactly when insanity will 'trump' private defence.

Although the courts have generally demonstrated a reluctance to permit D's psychiatric condition to be considered as relevant to the belief he held, there are some cases in which it has been admitted. For example, in *Press* D pleaded private defence to the charge of causing GBH with intent and relied on psychiatric evidence that he suffered from PTSD to substantiate his claim that he had a mistaken belief in the need to use force.[377] D was convicted and appealed. One of the issues was the extent to which expert evidence was relevant to his plea of private defence. The court distinguished *Oye* on the basis that the expert evidence did not

---

[372] [2018] EWCA Crim 1743.

[373] It has been argued that the policy considerations the court relies upon can apply to any unreasonable mistake made by D and not just one induced by an insane delusion, at least where D's characteristics predispose him to make unreasonable mistakes about the circumstances. See C de Than and J Elvin, 'Mistaken Private Defence: The Case for Reform' in A Reed and M Bohlander (with N Wake and E Smith) (eds), *General Defences in Criminal Law* (2014) 135.

[374] cf RD Mackay [2014] Crim LR 544.

[375] J Child and GR Sullivan, 'When Does the Insanity Defence Apply? Some Recent Cases' [2014] Crim LR 788, arguing that the same approach ought to have been adopted in *B* [2013] EWCA Crim 3.

[376] In *Oye*, the Court of Appeal observed that the order in which the jury ought to be directed to consider the defences is important, but preferred not to express a view on the matter. At [58]–[59]. As the court pointed out, s 2(1) of the Trial of Lunatics Act 1883 precludes the judge from giving a judicial direction to the jury to find D insane.

[377] [2013] EWCA Crim 1849. See also *Ibrahim* [2014] EWCA Crim 121. Jackson LJ contrasted this case with *Oye*, which was characterized as one in which D suffered from a psychiatric condition that caused him to believe in a state of affairs which did not exist, whereas in the instant case it was D's contention that his ADHD caused him to return to the fray after having initially been struck by V.

suggest that D was acting under an insane delusion; rather, the evidence was that his PTSD could have caused D mistakenly to judge the need to use force and then exceed what was reasonable in the circumstances as he understood them to be.

Oye and *Press* demonstrate that there is no coherence of approach as to the extent to which the personal characteristics of the defendant are relevant when pleading private defence. This issue is not confined to private defence but has also arisen in the context of duress and loss of control. There may be good reasons for this lack of coherence if each of the defences has a separate theoretical foundation. The problem is that the courts continue to make occasional comparisons between each of the defences without exploring these theoretical distinctions. They also fail to explain why an approach that has been adopted in relation to one defence is not taken in relation to another.[378]

Within private defence, the balancing of the characteristics of the relevant individuals can give rise to difficult issues. What of the relatively slight woman who uses lethal force against a physically stronger male whom she believes is about to attack her?[379] The Law Commission in its 2004 consideration of the partial defence to murder recognized the difficulty that this posed in many trials and recommended a new Judicial Studies Board (now Judicial College) Direction:

It is insufficient to weigh the weapons used on each side; sometimes there is an imbalance in size and strength. You must also consider the relationship between the defendant and [the other party]. A defendant who has experienced previous violence in a relationship may have an elevated view of the danger that they are in. They may honestly sense they are in greater danger than might appear to someone who has not lived through their experiences. All these matters should be taken into account when considering the reasonableness of the force used.[380]

10.7.1.4 Householder cases

Section 43 of the Crime and Courts Act 2013 amends s 76 by inserting the following provisions.[381]

Use of force in self-defence at place of residence

(1) Section 76 of the Criminal Justice and Immigration Act 2008 (use of reasonable force for purposes of self-defence etc) is amended as follows.

(2) Before subsection (6) (force not regarded as reasonable if it was disproportionate) insert—

'(5A) In a householder case, the degree of force used by D is not to be regarded as having been reasonable in the circumstances as D believed them to be if it was grossly disproportionate in those circumstances.'

(3) In subsection (6) at the beginning insert 'In a case other than a householder case,'.

---

[378] The Court of Appeal recognized this issue in *Oye* and declined to draw comparisons between duress and loss of control. At [43].

[379] She might now rely on s 54 of the Coroners and Justice Act 2009 if she had lost self-control. If she had not lost self-control, she must rely on the defence of self-defence.

[380] LC 290, *Partial Defences to Murder* (2004) para 4.14 (adapted from suggested formulation by Justice For Women). Cf s 76(7). See Judicial College, *Crown Court Compendium* (2021).

[381] For the background to the enactment of the provision, see S Lipscombe, *Householders and the Criminal Law of Self-Defence* (2013). Available at http://researchbriefings.parliament.uk/ResearchBriefing/Summary/SN02959. See also Norrie, *Crime, Reason and History*, 285–6 and 300; C de Than and J Elvin, 'Mistaken Private Defence: The Case for Reform' in A Reed and M Bohlander (with N Wake and E Smith) (eds), *General Defences in Criminal Law* (2014) 138–41.

(4) After subsection (8) insert—

'(8A) For the purposes of this section 'a householder case' is a case where—

    (a) the defence concerned is the common law defence of self-defence,

    (b) the force concerned is force used by D while in or partly in a building, or part of a building, that is a dwelling or is forces accommodation (or is both),

    (c) D is not a trespasser at the time the force is used, and

    (d) at that time D believed V to be in, or entering, the building or part as a trespasser.'

For a number of years, there had been calls to reform the law to provide greater legal protection for householders who use force to defend themselves in their homes.[382] These calls went unanswered until 2010, when the Coalition Government committed to 'ensuring that people have the protection they need when they defend themselves against intruders'. The government achieved this commitment through the enactment of s 43 of the Crime and Courts Act 2013 which inserts a new s 76(5A) into the 2008 Act. The policy underlying this provision is controversial. For example, Norrie has questioned whether, if a different threshold is deemed appropriate in the context of householder cases, then perhaps there are other private defence situations where a context-specific standard could be justified.[383]

Section 76(5A) provides that in a 'householder case' the degree of force used by D is not to be regarded as reasonable in the circumstances as D believed them to be if it was grossly disproportionate in those circumstances. In non-householder cases it will be recalled that if D uses merely disproportionate force, then that is not to be regarded as reasonable.

On one interpretation, the impact of this change would be that in a householder case if D used grossly disproportionate force he was guilty and if not he was entitled to an acquittal. That is not the way the courts have construed the householder provision in the two leading cases, however.

In *R (on the application of Collins) v Secretary of State for Justice*, the Divisional Court rejected the argument that the statute dictates that the defendant is to be treated as having acted reasonably if the force he used was not grossly disproportionate.[384] Sir Brian Leveson P held that under s 76(5A) a householder who uses grossly disproportionate force will be guilty. Moreover, a householder can be regarded as having acted unreasonably where the degree of force used was merely disproportionate. If D has not acted grossly disproportionately the question will be whether his use of force was unreasonable. If it was, then D will be guilty.[385]

This aspect of the judgment in *Collins* has now been effectively superseded by *Ray*, in which a special Court of Appeal of five judges was convened.[386] Lord Thomas CJ, delivering the

---

[382] See S Miller, '"Grossly Disproportionate": Home Owners' Legal Licence to Kill' (2013) 77 J Crim L 299. A number of high-profile cases acted as a catalyst for reform, in particular the case of Munir and Tokeer Hussain. For criticism of some of the earlier private members' bills that had sought to amend the law, see S Skinner, 'Populist Politics and Shooting Burglars' [2005] Crim LR 275.

[383] Norrie, *Crime, Reason and History*, 285. See also L Bleasdale-Hill, 'Householders, Self-Defence and the Right to Life' [2015] Crim LR 407.

[384] [2016] EWHC 33 (Admin), [2016] Crim LR 438 and commentary.

[385] The Divisional Court's judgment generated a great deal of academic commentary. For example, see J Collins and A Ashworth, 'Householders, Self-Defence and the Right to Life' (2016) 132 LQR 377; M Dsouza, 'Understanding the "Householder Defence": Proportionality and Reasonableness in Defensive Force' (2016) 75 CLJ 192; JR Spencer, 'Using Force on Burglars' [2016] Arch Rev 6; MP Thomas, 'Defenceless Castles: The Use of Grossly Disproportionate Force by Householders in Light of *R (Collins) v Secretary of State for Justice*' (2016) 80 J Crim L 407.

[386] [2017] EWCA Crim 1391.

judgment of the court, endorsed the interpretation given to the legislation by Sir Brian Leveson P in *Collins*. His lordship agreed that if the degree of force used by the householder was grossly disproportionate then D will be liable. If it was not grossly disproportionate, then the question for the jury is whether that degree of force was reasonable, taking into account all the circumstances as D believed them to be. In a householder case, if the jury conclude that the degree of force used by D was not grossly disproportionate, it was held that their focus should be on whether that degree of force was reasonable. In assessing the reasonableness of the degree of force used by D, the Court of Appeal held that the judge should specify the kind of circumstances that are relevant to this inquiry. Examples given by the court include the shock of coming upon an intruder, the time of day, the presence of other help, the desire to protect the home and its occupants, the vulnerability of the occupants and the conduct of the intruder. The current state of the law is therefore as follows.

- In a householder case, D is liable if, in the circumstances as he believed them to be, the jury find he used grossly disproportionate force. He is also liable if the degree of force he used was disproportionate if and only if it was also unreasonable.

- In a non-householder case, D is liable if the amount of force used was in the jury's view unreasonable in the circumstances as he believed them to be.

The Court of Appeal's approach to proportionality and reasonableness

In *Keane*, the Court of Appeal had treated the concepts of reasonableness and proportionality as synonymous, in a non-householder case at least. In *Ray*, the court's approach creates a more complex picture. First, the court distinguishes between reasonableness and proportionality. The use of disproportionate force which is short of being grossly disproportionate is not, on the wording of the section, necessarily the use of reasonable force. Householder cases are, on a strict matter of statutory language, focused on proportionality. Non-householder cases are focused on the reasonableness of the force used by the defendant.

When it comes to the use of force which is disproportionate, the position is now as follows.

- In a householder case, the jury are entitled to form the view, taking into account all the circumstances, that the degree of force used was either reasonable or not reasonable. Therefore, the use of disproportionate force can be reasonable, but this will not necessarily be so in every case.

- In a non-householder case, the position is different as the degree of force cannot be regarded as reasonable if it was disproportionate.

As a result of *Ray*, the difference between the two types of case is that in non-householder cases the focus is exclusively on reasonableness. The householder cases can involve a distinction between what is disproportionate and what is unreasonable. That fine distinction cuts across the earlier decision in *Keane*.

The second problem with the decision in *Ray* is that having interpreted the provision to recognize the distinction between the tests based on reasonableness alone and those tests which are based on reasonableness and proportionality, the Court of Appeal stated that juries should not be presented with 'esoteric and conceptual distinctions' between what is disproportionate on the one hand and what is unreasonable on the other.

Thirdly, this distinction is difficult when set against the historical common law position which required consideration to be given to the role of necessity and proportionality in assessing the overall reasonableness of the defendant's use of force. The Court of Appeal in *Keane* held that the enactment of s 76 of the Criminal Justice and Immigration Act 2008 did not alter the common law position. This is exactly what the Court of Appeal appears to have done in *Ray*, however.

Fourthly, there is an impact on the likely ability of a jury to apply the test. The reason why the common law required consideration to be given to the necessity and proportionality of the defendant's use of force is that, without reference to these concepts, the jury has no criteria against which to assess the reasonableness of the force used by the defendant. That the force used by the defendant must be reasonable is required by the legislation, but the legislation does not state that reasonableness ought to be divorced from the concepts that have historically been relied upon to assist juries in their assessment of whether the force used was reasonable in the circumstances. To mitigate this difficulty, the court suggests that it is important for judges to give juries 'some colour to the issue of self defence which arises'. It is unclear, however, why the court considered it preferable to rely upon fact-specific examples rather than to continue to place reliance upon concepts that have broad application, and which can apply equally to non-householder cases as they can to householder cases.

Is this what Parliament intended?

A final potential problem is that this interpretation is, arguably, not what Parliament intended. In *Ray*, Lord Thomas CJ held that the court's 'narrow' construction of the legislation was in keeping with the aim the householder provision was intended to achieve, but as the parliamentary material cited by the court demonstrates, the government intended to amend the law to ensure it was 'on the side of people who defend themselves when confronted by an intruder in their home'. Given the court's conclusion that it is for the jury to assess whether the degree of force used was reasonable and that something less than grossly disproportionate force may be considered unreasonable, householders may be just as likely to be prosecuted now as they were before the enactment of s 76(5A). Parliament's intention has, on that view, been frustrated. Further evidence of the court's interpretation being contrary to that intended is derived from the MOJ circular that was cited by the court: 'if householders act honestly and instinctively to protect themselves or their loved ones from intruders using force that was reasonable in the circumstances as they saw them, they will not be guilty of an offence if the level of force turns out to have been disproportionate in those circumstances'. That statement of what was intended is not what *Ray* delivers. The Court of Appeal in *Ray* confirmed that the jury remain free to convict the householder on the basis that, despite the fact the degree of force he used was proportionate, it was nevertheless unreasonable in the circumstances as he believed them to be.

The fact that a five-member Court of Appeal presided over by the Lord Chief Justice was convened to consider the proper construction of s 76(5A) of the Criminal Justice and Immigration Act 2008 means that further challenge to the interpretation of the provision is now unlikely.

What is a householder case?

It is important to bear in mind that the different approach only applies in 'householder cases'. In s 76(5A), a 'householder case' is defined as one that has the following characteristics:

(1) the defence concerned is the common law of self-defence;

(2) the force concerned is force used by D while in or partly in a building, or part of a building, that is a dwelling or is forces accommodation (or is both);

(3) D is not a trespasser at the time the force is used; and

(4) at that time D believed V to be in,[387] or entering, the building as a trespasser.

---

[387] See *Cheeseman* [2019] EWCA Crim 149.

While the statute, in subsection (8F), clarifies that 'building' includes a vehicle or vessel,[388] it does not define what is meant by 'dwelling'. Historically, 'dwelling' could mean not only a person's home, but also the structures within the curtilage of a home, such as sheds, greenhouses, etc.[389] If D confronts V in his kitchen, that is clearly a householder case and the higher threshold applies. What if D confronts V attempting to steal the lawnmower from his shed? Further, what if D confronts V initially in the kitchen, but only uses force once both are struggling in the garden? The failure explicitly to define the scope of the provision is disappointing and could lead to difficulties in practice. It is submitted that 'dwelling' in this context ought to be narrowly defined and should not extend to buildings within the curtilage of a home. This has the benefit of ensuring a relative degree of certainty whilst also fulfilling the policy objective at which the legislation is aimed. It is questionable whether confronting an intruder in one's shed is as terrifying as confronting an intruder in one's living room. In the former case, D ought to be required to take greater care to ensure that he only uses force that is proportionate in the circumstances. The minister was explicit in debates on the clause in Parliament, after all, that s 76(5A) is not intended to be a vigilantes' charter.

Subsection (8B) makes clear that if a part of a building is where D dwells and it is internally accessible to another part that is a place of work for D or another person, then it is considered part of a dwelling. This is to deal with cases such as that of the pub landlord who lives above the pub and who confronts a trespasser behind the bar. This would constitute a householder case. It would not be a householder case if the pub were not connected to the landlord's accommodation by way of an internal means of access.

It is important to note that a householder case only arises when D is not a trespasser at the time when force is used. While this ought to be uncontroversial in most cases, it could require some consideration of the civil law. Crucially, the statute does not state that D must be the homeowner; he must simply not be a trespasser.[390] This would enable a guest of the homeowner to invoke s 76(5A) for example. Whether, for example, the boyfriend of the homeowner's daughter, who surreptitiously climbed through her window, is a trespasser, poses greater difficulty.[391] Subsection (8E) makes clear that a person is a trespasser if he derives title from a trespasser or has the permission of a trespasser. The squatter's guest, therefore, is no less a trespasser because he has an invitation. Again, this limitation is in keeping with the policy objective behind the enactment of the provision.

The final point to note is that at the time force is used D must have believed V to be in or entering the dwelling, or part of it, as a trespasser.

In *Cheeseman*, D attacked V, a fellow soldier. V who had been a guest in D's room in the army base was then locked out of the room and began damaging it. D regained entry and caused serious injury to V. D sought to rely on the householder defence. The Judge Advocate General ruled that the so-called 'householder defence' was only available in cases where the person who was injured was an intruder, as opposed to someone who had entered premises lawfully and then become an intruder. The Court Martial Appeal Court held that the language of the statute was clear—the question is whether, at the time of the incident, the defendant *believed* the other person to be in the dwelling as a trespasser. The defence is

---

[388] Ensuring that inhabitants of houseboats and caravans will also be able to invoke the provision.

[389] For discussion, see K Laird, 'Conceptualising the Interpretation of "Dwelling" in Section 9 of the Theft Act 1968' [2013] Crim LR 656. For further discussion, see p 1060.

[390] In *Day* [2015] EWCA Crim 1646, Laws LJ confirmed that self-defence is available not just to the property owner, but to anyone in lawful occupation of the dwelling who seeks to eject a trespasser. The court was not concerned with s 76, but the same principle applies.

[391] For discussion, see p 1048.

not directly concerned with the question whether someone was or was not a trespasser, but rather the defendant's belief as to V's status.

Two further questions arise in relation to this element of the householder provision. First, must D's belief be reasonable or does it suffice that it is genuinely held? Secondly, can D rely upon a belief induced by voluntary intoxication? Subsection (8D) provides that the provisions in subsections (4) and (5) also apply to subsection (8A)(d). The consequence of this is twofold: it suffices for D to have had a genuine belief that V was a trespasser;[392] and a belief induced by voluntary intoxication will not suffice. In relation to the latter, if D's mistake as to V's status as a trespasser is attributable to his voluntary consumption of alcohol, then he cannot rely upon the householder provision. This ensures there is consistency between householder cases and non-householder cases in relation to the nature of D's belief.[393] Interestingly, in *Collins*, Sir Brian Leveson P stated, *obiter*, that the common law requires an approach which it is at least arguable is unduly restrictive for householders. His lordship stated that whilst those who go about in public ought to be expected to take responsibility for their level of intoxication, whether the same ought to be expected of a defendant who is in his own home in circumstances where he is not anticipating any interaction with a trespasser is perhaps a more open question. It is submitted that there is much to be said for his lordship's characterization of the current state of the law and that this is something that merits Parliament's attention.[394]

10.7.1.5 The effect of the Human Rights Act 1998

There are arguments of some force[395] that the effect of Art 2 of the ECHR—the right to life—may be to invalidate the principle of *Gladstone Williams* and *Beckford* that a defendant is to be judged on the facts as he genuinely, though unreasonably, believed them to be. Article 2 provides:

(1) Everyone's right to life shall be protected by law. No one shall be deprived of his life intentionally save in the execution of a sentence of a court following his conviction of a crime for which this penalty is provided by law.

(2) Deprivation of life shall not be regarded as inflicted in contravention of this article when it results from the use of force which is no more than absolutely necessary:

(a) in defence of any person from unlawful violence;

(b) in order to effect a lawful arrest or to prevent the escape of a person lawfully detained;

(c) in action lawfully taken for the purpose of quelling a riot or insurrection.

It is argued by some eminent commentators, including in particular Ashworth and Leverick, that the present English law may be incompatible with this provision since a person's right to life is not sufficiently protected if he may be killed by force used without reasonable grounds.[396]

---

[392] That is also implicit in *Cheeseman*.

[393] The MOJ Circular reiterates that it suffices that D 'genuinely believed (rightly or wrongly)' that the person in respect of whom they used force is a trespasser, at para 16.

[394] [2016] EWHC 33 (Admin), [30].

[395] By A Ashworth, commenting on *Andronicou and Constantinou v Cyprus*, ECtHR, 9 Oct 1997 [1998] Crim LR 823. But see Buxton LJ, 'The Human Rights Act and the Substantive Criminal Law' [2000] Crim LR 331 at 336–7. See F Leverick, 'The Use of Force in Public or Private Defence and Article 2' [2002] Crim LR 347; JC Smith, 'The Use of Force in Public or Private Defence and Article 2' [2002] Crim LR 958; and F Leverick, 'The Use of Force in Public or Private Defence and Article 2: A Reply to Professor Sir John Smith' [2002] Crim LR 963. See also Leverick, n 331, Ch 10; Horder, APOCL, 142.

[396] See Leverick, previous note.

The arguments of incompatibility highlight a number of issues. First, the Article allows for life to be taken only where 'absolutely necessary'. A defendant in England could be acquitted even though his lethal attack turns out to have been completely unnecessary. Furthermore, the European Court has underlined the restrictive nature of the exceptional circumstances in which killing is permitted.[397] In *McCann v UK* and in *Andronicou*, the Court referred to the fact that the accused must have had 'good grounds' to use force. This looks like an objective test, which is not what English law requires: *Gladstone Williams* (and s 76) requires only a genuine belief in the need to use such force. Finally, it is noted that Art 2 restricts the circumstances in which a life may be taken to the purposes of quelling riots, etc or in defence of unlawful *violence*. In English law, it is possible for a defendant to be acquitted where he uses lethal force even in response to an attack merely on property.[398]

Despite these arguments of incompatibility, it was not clear that Art 2 or the ECtHR's jurisprudence (which is typically vague) *demanded* a change in the law to an objective test. The test of 'absolute necessity' applied in Strasbourg is not an inflexible one. In a recent assessment of the position, the Divisional Court in *R (Duggan) v HM Assistant Deputy Coroner*[399] recognized 'some ambiguity in the language used by the Strasbourg Court'. The court was not persuaded that an objective test of reasonableness was required to ensure that English law was compatible. The Court of Appeal subsequently agreed with this conclusion.[400]

Moreover, the ECtHR did not condemn English law when it had the opportunity to do so. The European Court's test was reiterated in *Bubbins v UK*[401] where the Court stated that D had an 'honest belief which was perceived for good reason to be valid at the time but which was mistaken'. There was no outright condemnation of the English test. In the most recent Strasbourg authority to consider this issue, the Grand Chamber held in *Da Silva v UK*[402] that it could not be said that the test applied in the law of England and Wales is significantly different from the standard applied by the Court in *McCann*. The Court concluded that the definition of self-defence in England and Wales did not fall short of the standard required by Art 2. As Emmerson, Ashworth and Macdonald[403] point out, the truth is that there is no case yet before the Strasbourg Court in which a use of lethal force in English law has been based on a wholly irrational mistake. If such a case arose, the Court would have to face the conflict between the Strasbourg jurisprudence and English law.

The English courts' approach to the ECHR question

In the English courts, it has been accepted that the current rules of English law on the use of potentially lethal force by the police are not incompatible with the ECHR as in *R (Bennett) v HM Coroner for Inner London*[404] and *R (Duggan) v North London Assistant Deputy Coroner*.[405] In both cases the principal issue was whether a killing committed by the police as a result of an honest but mistaken act of self-defence (not amounting to a crime, but possibly involving civil liability to pay compensation, etc) could be classed by a coroner's inquest as a 'lawful homicide'.

---

[397] See *Andronicou*, para 171; *Gul v Turkey* (2002) 34 EHRR 28, para 77; *McCann v UK* (1996) 21 EHRR 95. More recently, see *Ramsahai v Netherlands* (2006) 43 EHRR 39; *Huohuanainen v Finland* [2007] EHRLR 472.

[398] See the Joint Committee on Human Rights, *Fifteenth Legislative Report 2007–8* (2008), para 2.35.

[399] [2014] EWHC 3343 (Admin).

[400] *R (Duggan) v North London Assistant Deputy Coroner* [2017] EWCA Civ 142.

[401] [2005] 41 EHRR 24. See N Martin (2006) 69 MLR 242 for comment. Applied more recently in *Giuliani v Italy* (2012) 54 EHRR 10 and *Reynolds v UK* (2012) 55 EHRR 35.   [402] (2016) 63 EHRR 12.

[403] HR&CJ, para 18.33.   [404] [2006] EWHC 196 (Admin).   [405] [2017] EWCA Civ 142.

In the High Court in *Bennett* Collins J held, having regard to the case law, that:

the European Court of Human Rights has considered what English law requires for self defence, and has not suggested that there is any incompatibility with Article 2. In truth, if any officer reasonably decides that he must use lethal force, it will inevitably be because it is absolutely necessary to do so. To kill when it is not absolutely necessary to do so is surely to act unreasonably. Thus, the reasonableness test does not in truth differ from the Article 2 test as applied in *McCann*.

The Court of Appeal upheld that decision.[406]

Subsequently, in *Ashley and others v Chief Constable of Sussex Police*,[407] the House of Lords compared self-defence when used as a defence to a criminal charge and a defence in civil proceedings. In both criminal and civil proceedings, the conduct/degree of force in self-defence must objectively be reasonable but, in judging what was reasonable, the court must in either case have regard to all the circumstances, including the fact that the action may have been taken in the heat of the moment. However, there are differences: (a) in cases of mistaken self-defence an honest but unreasonable mistake may operate as a defence only in criminal proceedings. In civil proceedings, a mistaken view of the facts provides no defence in the absence of reasonable grounds for that mistake. (b) The burden of proof is different: in criminal proceedings, the burden of negativing self-defence is on the prosecution; but in civil proceedings the burden is on the defendant to establish that he acted in reasonable self-defence.[408]

Looking at the subject more broadly, one can argue that notwithstanding some unguarded language by the CLRC and the courts, English law does not say that D may take the life of another where there are no reasonable grounds for doing so. It says only that he is not guilty of a criminal offence, if he believes honestly though unreasonably that such ground exists. The killing is unlawful, but not criminal; D remains liable in tort. Parliament has now endorsed that principle in s 76. Where D's belief is unreasonable that will, of course, be a powerful reason for disbelieving his account and convicting him. But that is not all: the criminal law itself provides protection. If D's mistake is so unreasonable as to amount to gross negligence, D will be guilty of manslaughter.[409] That is, D will be guilty of criminal homicide if the jury think his conduct bad enough to amount to a crime—or, as is submitted later in the discussion in Ch 14, bad enough to deserve condemnation as manslaughter. The criminal law therefore does offer some protection. The fact that it is a conviction for manslaughter with a maximum life sentence cannot mean that the protection is inadequate.

Moreover, most force used in public or private defence is not intended to, and does not have, fatal results. Does the human rights argument require the *Beckford* principle to be outlawed *only* where it has fatal results? There would not seem to be any logic in that. The alternative is that it is invalidated entirely. It is submitted that this would be an undesirable and unnecessary conclusion and the English courts should not arrive at it unless compelled to do so. The present law, at least as regards protection against violence to the person, balances the need to protect life—and limb—against the ordinary rights of persons accused of crime.

In *R (Collins) v Secretary of State for Justice*, the focus of the judgment delivered by Sir Brian Leveson P was on whether the so-called 'householder provisions' were compatible

---

[406] [2007] EWCA Civ 617. The basis of appeal was principally that it had been a misdirection not to direct the jury to consider whether the officer's claim to have acted in self-defence was reasonable in the light of the requirement in the relevant ACPO manual to reassess at all times whether it was 'absolutely necessary' to shoot.

[407] [2008] UKHL 25; see the Court of Appeal's decision: [2006] EWCA Civ 1085.

[408] cf the decision at first instance [2005] EWHC 415 (QB).

[409] cf Leverick [2002] Crim LR 347 at 361. See Leverick, *Killing in Self Defence*, Ch 10. See on the need for careful direction, *Maddocks* [2006] EWCA Crim 3112. Use of lethal force is a last resort: *Noye* [2011] EWCA Crim 650.

with Art 2.[410] In assessing the compatibility of s 76(5A) with Art 2, the key question for the court was whether the criminal law of England and Wales effectively deters offences against the person in householder cases. His lordship held that although there may be cases when a jury consider the actions of a householder in self-defence to be more than what might be objectively described as the minimum proportionate response, this did not weaken the capacity of the criminal law to deter offences against the person in householder cases. The householder will only be able to plead self-defence if the degree of force he used was reasonable in the circumstances as he believed them to be. His lordship concluded that the criminal law provides reasonable safeguards against the commission of offences against the person in householder cases, which was sufficient to satisfy Art 2.

In addition to the right to life guaranteed in Art 2, the European Court has recognized that the rights in Arts 3 (freedom from torture and inhuman and degrading treatment) and 5 (right to liberty) are subject to an implied exception for injuries inflicted in self-defence.[411] D, who is protecting himself against an unlawful attack from V, will not infringe V's Art 5 rights by detaining him to prevent further attack.

10.7.2 Force used in the course of preventing crime or arresting offenders

The common law on this subject was both complex and uncertain;[412] but, by s 3 of the Criminal Law Act 1967:

(1) A person may use such force as is reasonable in the circumstances in the prevention of crime, or in effecting or assisting in the lawful arrest of offenders or suspected offenders or of persons unlawfully at large.

(2) Subsection (1) above shall replace the rules of the common law on the question when force used for a purpose mentioned in the subsection is justified by that purpose.[413]

Section 3 states a rule both of civil and criminal law. When the force is 'reasonable in the circumstances' it is justified in every sense. No civil action or criminal proceeding will lie against the person using it. The section says nothing specifically about any criminal liability of the user of the force. When that is in issue the ordinary principles of mens rea should apply. The use of force may be unjustified in the civil law because it is not in fact 'reasonable in the circumstances'; but D, while liable in tort, may nevertheless be excused from criminal liability if it was 'reasonable in the circumstances *as he believed them to be*'.[414] It has been held in a civil action in Northern Ireland[415] that, for the purpose of an identical provision, the objectives of the use of force are to be determined, not by the evidence of the user of the force, but by the court, applying an objective test. D, a soldier, said that his purpose in shooting was to arrest the occupants of a vehicle whom he believed on reasonable grounds to be determined terrorists who would probably continue to commit terrorist offences if they got away; but the court held that the use of force was not reasonable to make an arrest

---

[410] [2016] EWHC 33 (Admin). This aspect of the court's reasoning is discussed further in S Foster and G Leigh, 'Self-Defence and the Right to Life; the Use of Lethal or Potentially Lethal Force, UK Domestic Law, the Common Law and Article 2 ECHR' [2016] EHRLR 398.

[411] *Rivas v France* [2005] Crim LR 305; *RL v France* [2005] Crim LR 306.

[412] See the 1st edn of this book, at pp 230–8.   [413] See s 76 of the CJIA 2008, p 400.

[414] See *Duggan*, n 400. The court held that it would be inconsistent with the statutory regime governing inquests to say that a verdict of lawful killing was available only where the coroner's jury also concluded that there would be no civil liability.

[415] *Kelly v Ministry of Defence* [1989] NI 341. On whether the defence applies to British soldiers abroad, see Rowe, n 325.

but was justified because it was reasonable to prevent crime.[416] If this is right (and it is a per-suasive opinion) in a civil action, it is also right in criminal law. The only difference is that in the criminal case D need not have reasonable grounds for his honest belief in the circum-stances. The Court of Appeal confirmed in *Morris*[417] that it is a misdirection to direct the jury that D must have reasonable grounds for believing it is necessary to use force. So long as D has a genuine belief, this will suffice, even if it is a mistaken one. This case is welcome confirmation that the first limb of both private defence and the defence in s 3 embodies a subjective test.

10.7.2.1 Prevention of crime

Where D seeks to rely on the defence based on his belief that V was committing a crime, the question may well arise whether the offence was in fact occurring when D used force. In *Bowden*,[418] the issue was whether V had completed his appropriation of an article before D used violence to prevent what he understood to be a theft being perpetrated by V, but that is not a strong example. Similarly, in *Attwater*[419] D sought to rely on s 3 when he was charged with dangerous driving. He claimed that he drove in that manner (crashing with other vehicles) so that he could apprehend another driver X because X had been in an earlier incident and failed to stop. In short, D claimed to be apprehending X for his crime of failing to stop after a road traffic accident. On the facts, X's offence was probably already over.[420] More recently and to similar effect is *Williams*.[421] D had chased V who, having gate-crashed a house party, stabbed D in the arm and stolen D's necklace, fled the scene. D caught and fatally stabbed V. By the time D did so, 'he was not defending his property, nor was he pre-venting the commission of a robbery which had been completed sometime earlier. He was engaged in an act of retaliation or revenge . . .'[422]

In *R (DPP) v Stratford Magistrates' Court*, the Divisional Court emphasized that in order to plead the s 3 defence, there must be a link between the use of force and an imminently apprehended crime.[423] In that case, which involved protestors obstructing the passage of vehicles making their way to an exhibition centre, Simon LJ stated that there was a lack of clarity as to what crime was being committed and how force was preventing it. There was no evidence that the vehicles being obstructed were involved in anything other than lawful activity. As there was nothing to link the obstruction of the highway with an imminent or immediate crime, it was held that the defendants could not rely on the defence.

10.7.2.2 Arresting an offender

Where D seeks to rely on the defence to justify his use of force in arresting an offender, issues of civil powers of arrest may arise and the jury may well need further guidance on those pow-ers under s 24A of PACE, namely whether on the facts as D believed them to be: (a) an offence was being committed by V (s 24A(1)(a)); or (b) D had reasonable grounds to suspect that V was committing an offence (24A(1)(b)); or (c) D reasonably suspected V to have committed the offence (s 24A(2)(b)); and (d) he reasonably believed an arrest was necessary (s 24A(3)).[424]

---

[416] The ECtHR (App no 17579/90) observed that the 'prevention of crime' does not appear in the justifica-tions for taking life in Art 2 of the ECHR, but held that the shooting was justified to effect a lawful arrest. This decision is cogently criticized by JC Smith, 'The Right to Life and the Right to Kill in Law Enforcement' (1994) 144 NLJ 354.

[417] [2013] EWCA Crim 436, [2013] Crim LR 995.

[418] [2002] EWCA Crim 1279.   [419] [2010] EWCA Crim 2399.

[420] *Jackson* [1985] RTR 257. The court left open whether this was strictly speaking a matter that should have been left to the jury. The court had no doubt that a jury would have rejected the defence.

[421] [2020] EWCA Crim 193.   [422] At [19].   [423] [2017] EWHC 1794 (Admin), [42]–[44].

[424] See *Morris* [2013] EWCA Crim 436.

10.7.2.3 What is a crime for the purposes of s 3?

Section 3 operates only where D responds to prevent a 'crime'. In *Jones*,[425] the House of Lords concluded that the concept of 'crime' in this context can only have been intended to mean a crime recognized in English and Welsh law (ie not something which constitutes a crime only in international law).[426] The CLRC[427] explained the proposed s 3 in very broad terms:

the court, in considering what was reasonable force, would take into account all the circumstances, including in particular the nature and degree of force used, the seriousness of the evil to be prevented and the possibility of preventing it by other means; but there is no need to specify in the clause the criteria for deciding the question. Since the clause is framed in general terms, it is not limited to arrestable[428] or any other class of offences, though in the case of very trivial offences it would very likely be held that it would not be reasonable to use even the slightest force to prevent them.

Despite the breadth of this statement, the House of Lords' limitation in *Jones* seems warranted if the defence is to retain the degree of certainty desirable.

10.7.2.4 When is the use of force reasonable in s 3?

The CLRC,[429] in drafting the section, described it as set out in the last paragraph: 'reasonable force, would take into account all the circumstances, including in particular the nature and degree of force used, the seriousness of the evil to be prevented and the possibility of preventing it by other means'.[430]

It cannot be reasonable to cause harm unless (a) it was *necessary* to do so in order to prevent the crime or effect the arrest and (b) the 'evil' which would follow from failure to prevent the crime or effect the arrest is so great that a reasonable person might think himself justified in causing that harm to avert that 'evil'. It is likely, therefore, that even killing will be justifiable to prevent unlawful killing or grievous bodily harm, or to arrest a person where there is an imminent risk of his causing death or grievous bodily harm if left at liberty. The European Court has emphasized that the use of lethal force to stop a person suspected of a non-violent offence who does not pose an immediate risk of harm to anyone is contrary to Art 2.[431] The whole question is somewhat speculative. Is it reasonable to kill or cause serious bodily harm in order to prevent rape?[432] Or robbery, when the property involved is very valuable?[433] How much force may be used to prevent the destruction of a great work of art? The most extreme cases in which the police use lethal force are because they believed D to be a terrorist suicide bomber and in which any lesser force would have been futile.

It seems that the question, 'What amount of force is reasonable in the circumstances?' is always for the jury and never a point of law for the judge.[434] If the prosecution case does

---

[425] [2004] EWCA Crim 1981.
[426] See Lord Bingham at [31], Lord Hoffmann at [54] and Lord Mance at [105].
[427] Cmnd 2659, para 23.
[428] Since the Serious Organised Crime and Police Act 2005, all offences are potentially arrestable.
[429] Cmnd 2659, para 23.   [430] Note s 76, earlier.   [431] See *Nachova v Bulgaria* (2004) 39 EHRR 37.
[432] See Leverick, n 331, Ch 8.
[433] There are plenty of reported instances where the courts seem to have approved of the killing. See the more recent cases discussed by E Tennant (2003) 167 JP 804.
[434] *Reference under s 48A of the Criminal Appeal (Northern Ireland) Act 1968 (No 1 of 1975)* [1976] 2 All ER 937 at 947 per Lord Diplock.

not provide material to raise the issue, there is an evidential burden on the accused. If that burden is satisfied, that question for the jury is:

Are we satisfied that no reasonable person (a) with knowledge of such facts as were known to the accused[435] believed by him to exist (b) in the circumstances and time available to him for reflection (c) could be of the opinion that the prevention of the risk of harm to which others might be exposed if the suspect were allowed to escape, justified exposing the suspect to the risk of harm to him that might result from the kind of force that the accused contemplated using.[436]

At common law it was recognized that the standard of reasonableness should, as noted earlier, take account of the nature of the crisis in which the necessity to use force arises for, in circumstances of great stress, even the reasonable person cannot be expected to judge the minimum degree of force required to a nicety. This is now reflected in s 76(7) of the CJIA 2008. In holding quite considerable force to be justified to prevent an obstruction of the highway by a violent and abusive driver, Geoffrey Lane J said: 'In the circumstances one did not use jewellers' scales to measure reasonable force . . .'[437]

In *R (DPP) v Stratford Magistrates' Court*, the Divisional Court reiterated that citizens who apprehend a breach of the law are normally expected to call the police and not take the law into their own hands. Simon LJ emphasized that the use of force by individuals in the prevention of crime must be confined so as to avoid anarchy. His lordship stated that the use of force to prevent crime may be legitimate and enable D to plead the defence when individual action is necessary to prevent some imminent crime.[438]

10.7.2.5 Section 3 provides a defence only if force used

Section 3 excuses only the use of *force*. In *Blake v DPP*,[439] D, demonstrating against the Iraq war, wrote with a felt pen on a concrete pillar near the Houses of Parliament. He was charged with criminal damage and argued that his act was justified by, inter alia, s 3. The court held that his act was 'insufficient to amount to the use of force within the section'. This suggests that the defence might not have been ruled out on this ground (though it almost certainly would on other grounds) if D had used a hammer and chisel. It is odd that force should be excused when less serious acts might not be; but that is the effect of the section.[440]

The Court of Appeal considered this issue again in *Bailey*.[441] There was a collision between D's car and the car of a third party, C. C failed to stop and D sped after him, but struck V, who died. D sought to argue that he was using force to assist in the lawful arrest of C, who had committed the offence of failing to stop after an accident. The judge declined to leave the defence to the jury on the basis that D had not used force in attempting to stop C, indeed his evidence was that he had been a perfect gentleman throughout. Laws LJ stated: 'Giving chase in a motor car in order to ascertain the registration number of a car ahead cannot as a matter of language or good sense be regarded as a use of force.'[442] In addition, his lordship

---

435 Lord Diplock used the word 'reasonably' here and, in the light of his often stated opinion, it is likely that he would wish to continue to use it, were he still alive; but his remarks, in the light of *Gladstone Williams* and the cases following it, should be read as if 'reasonably' were omitted.

436 *Reference under s 48A of the Criminal Appeal (Northern Ireland) Act 1968 (No 1 of 1975)* [1976] 2 All ER 937 at 947 per Lord Diplock. The language is ill-suited to a jury direction.

437 *Reed v Wastie* [1972] Crim LR 221.   438 [2017] EWHC 1794 (Admin), [18].

439 [1993] Crim LR 586.

440 The illogicality of this restriction was noted by Brooke LJ in *Bayer v DPP* [2003] EWHC 2567 (Admin), calling for reform of the defences. See also *Riddell*, p 445.

441 [2013] EWCA Crim 378.

442 At [16]. His lordship distinguished *Renouf* on the basis that D in that case had forced another car off the road and rammed it to ensure that its occupants would still be there when the police arrived. That clearly did constitute the use of force.

observed that D was not attempting to assist the arrest of C, rather his aim was to get his insurance details. This would also have precluded him from relying upon s 3.

In *Jones*, the House of Lords expressed doubt as to whether s 3 ought to be relied on in cases of alleged damage to property. Section 5 of the Criminal Damage Act provides the appropriate defence. The House also doubted whether s 3 was intended to apply to peaceable protest activities such as those used by the defendants in that case—cutting wire and chaining themselves to armed service vehicles.

In *R (DPP) v Stratford Magistrates' Court*,[443] Simon LJ stated that the defence applies to the direct application of force, although the force does not necessarily have to be applied directly against a person. The example given by his lordship was a defendant who attached himself to a lorry which he believed to be carrying chemical weapons. By way of contrast, it was held that the defence would not be available to those who lie down in the road in front of lorries making their way to a place where crimes are believed to be taking place or who block access by chaining themselves to gates.

10.7.3 Force used in private defence

The Criminal Law Act 1967 made no reference to the right of private defence—the right to use force in defence of oneself or another against an unjustifiable attack.[444] Insofar as that position differed in effect from s 3 of the 1967 Act, the common law was probably modified by s 3. Private defence and the prevention of crime are sometimes indistinguishable. If D goes to the defence of E whom V is trying to murder, he is exercising the right of private defence but he is also seeking to prevent the commission of a crime. It would be absurd to ask D whether he was acting in defence of E or to prevent murder being committed and preposterous that the law should differ according to his answer. He was doing both.[445] The law cannot have two sets of criteria governing the same situation: s 3 of the Criminal Law Act is applicable. This is supported by the application of the same tests in s 76 of the 2008 Act to both the common law and s 3 defences.

The 1967 Act may be taken to have clarified the common law. Before the Criminal Law Act, the Court of Criminal Appeal equated the defence of others with the prevention of crime. In *Duffy*,[446] it was held that a woman would be justified in using reasonable force when it was necessary to do so in defence of her sister, not because they were sisters, but because 'there is a general liberty as between strangers to prevent a [crime]'. The principles applicable are the same whether the defence is put on grounds of self-defence or on grounds of prevention of crime. The degree of force permissible should not differ, for example, in the case of an employer defending his employee from the case of a brother defending his sister—or, indeed, that of a complete stranger coming to the defence of another under unlawful attack. As s 76(10)(b) of the 2008 Act makes clear, references to self-defence include acting in defence of another. The position is the same where D acts in defence of property, whether his own or that of another, which V seeks to steal, destroy or damage.

Where D is acting in defence of his own person it may be less obvious that he is also acting in the prevention of crime but this will usually be in fact the case. D's purpose is not the enforcement of the law but his own self-preservation; yet the degree of force which is permissible is the same.[447] An inquiry into D's motives is not practicable.[448]

---

[443] [2017] EWHC 1794 (Admin), [50].

[444] Thus where D knows that the actual or imminent danger he faces is not from an unlawful or criminal act he cannot rely on the defence: *Bayer v DPP* [2003] EWHC 2567 (Admin). See also *Cresswell v DPP* [2006] EWHC 3379 (Admin) where the defendants could not be acting to prevent a crime when DEFRA officials were within the law to take the badgers in dispute.

[445] See *Clegg* [1995] 1 All ER 334 at 343.   [446] [1967] 1 QB 63.

[447] *Devlin v Armstrong* [1971] NI 13 at 33; *McInnes* [1971] 3 All ER 295 at 302.   [448] See p 102.

As with s 3, the private law defence is limited to cases in which D responds to an unjusti-fied attack by using force. However, there is no requirement with the private law defence at common law that D is responding to a 'crime'. Therefore, where D believes that V's actions are unjustified because they are, for example, unlawful in international law, his use of force to prevent V's action may be justified.

10.7.4 Further elements of private and public defence

10.7.4.1 A duty to retreat?

There were formerly technical rules about the duty to retreat before using force, or at least fatal force. This is now simply a factor to be taken into account in deciding whether it was necessary to use force, and whether the force was reasonable.[449] The courts had developed the principle at common law (*Palmer v R*,[450] *Duffy v DPP*[451]) that it was a matter of evidence relevant to whether D was acting in self-defence but that there was no rule that a person had to retreat from threatened violence.[452] In *Jones*, the House of Lords emphasized the view that it is not for the citizen who apprehends a breach of the law to take matters into his own hands if there is an opportunity to summon official help.[453] Section 76(6)(A) now states explicitly that there is no duty to retreat. Rather, the possibility that D could have retreated is to be considered (so far as it is relevant) as a factor to be taken into account when considering whether the degree of force used by D was reasonable in the circumstances as he believed them to be. In *Ray*, discussed earlier, the Lord Chief Justice stated that if there is a threat of confrontation in the street, then the option to retreat may be important in determining whether the use of any force was reasonable. In the case of an intruder in the home, however, it was observed that the option of retreat is unlikely to arise in many cases and therefore the degree of force used, although otherwise appearing to be disproportion-ate, might nonetheless be assessed as reasonable.

10.7.4.2 Pre-emptive strikes

It has been accepted that a defendant need not wait for the attacker to strike the first blow before he defends himself. In *Devlin v Armstrong*,[454] following serious disturbances in Londonderry, D exhorted crowds of people who were stoning the police to build a bar-ricade and keep the police out and fight them with petrol bombs. D claimed that she had acted in this manner because she honestly believed that the police were about to behave unlawfully in assaulting people and damaging property in the area. The Northern Ireland Court of Appeal acknowledged that a 'plea of self-defence may afford a defence [where D used force] not merely to counter an actual attack, but to ward off or prevent an attack which he honestly anticipated. In that case, however, the anticipated attack must be immi-nent.'[455] In *Beckford*,[456] the Privy Council also acknowledged that circumstances may jus-tify a pre-emptive strike in self-defence. The availability of the defence in circumstances of pre-emptive strike has been narrowly construed by the courts. Where there is no evidence

---

[449] *McInnes*, n 447. But cf *Whyte* [1987] 3 All ER 416 at 419.

[450] [1971] AC 814. This passage then appearing in the 4th edn was approved by the Court of Appeal in *Bird* [1985] 2 All ER 513 at 516. Cf Horder, APOCL, 138 arguing that this should be seen as an exception to the gen-eral principle of a duty to avoid conflict.

[451] [2007] EWHC 3169 (Admin).   [452] See *M (ZM)* [2007] EWCA Crim 376.

[453] See Lord Mance at [78]–[81]. This point was also emphasized by Simon LJ in *R (DPP) v Stratford Magistrates' Court* [2017] EWHC 1794 (Admin). In *Thacker* [2021] EWCA Crim 97 the Court of Appeal held that this aspect of *Jones* was part of the ratio of the judgment and therefore binding.

[454] [1971] NI 13.   [455] At 33 per Lord MacDermott LCJ.

[456] [1987] 3 All ER 425, [1988] Crim LR 116.

to support a suggestion that D has acted in pre-emptive defence, no jury direction on the issue is needed.[457]

The requirement of imminence, strictly construed, prevents the widespread reliance on the defence where battered spouses kill their abusive partners. Commonly, the physical disparity between the parties means that the woman will seize her opportunity to kill the abuser when he is not poised about to strike her, but is instead in a position of vulnerability. This caused such individuals to rely on the partial defences of provocation and diminished responsibility.[458]

Under s 54 of the Coroners and Justice Act 2009, a defendant who kills with malice aforethought may rely on a defence of loss of control (LOSC) if he has lost his self-control and, inter alia, he fears serious violence from V towards himself or an identified person. The relationship between the LOSC defence and self-defence or defence of others under s 76 of the CJIA 2008 needs to be approached with caution. Self-defence is available on any charge; LOSC defence is available only on a charge of murder.[459] Self-defence results in an acquittal; LOSC in a verdict of manslaughter. With self-defence, D can only rely on a threat of (or believed threat of) *imminent* attack; with LOSC, D can rely on fear of future non-imminent attack. The defence of self-defence is available if D holds a genuine, though mistaken and unreasonable, belief of the threat to him of *any* violence. The LOSC defence is available if D genuinely, though mistakenly and unreasonably, believes himself to be at risk of *serious* violence.[460] Violence is undefined in the LOSC defence but includes sexual violence.[461] If the degree of force used by D in killing V is, viewed objectively, excessive, that will deprive D of the defence of self-defence,[462] but will not automatically deprive D of the LOSC defence.[463]

10.7.4.3 Defence against a provoked attack

In *Browne*,[464] Lowry LCJ in Northern Ireland said, with regard to self-defence, 'The need to act must not have been created by conduct of the accused in the immediate context of the incident which was likely or intended to give rise to that need.'

Self-defence is clearly not available where D deliberately provoked the attack with the intention of killing purportedly in self-defence.[465] Where D's act was merely 'likely' to give rise to the need, the proposition, with respect, is more questionable. If D did not foresee that his actions would lead to an attack on him, it is submitted that he should not be deprived of his usual right of self-defence. Even if he did foresee the attack, he may still be entitled to act in self-defence if he did not intend it. D intervenes to stop V from ill-treating V's wife.

[457] *Williams* [2005] EWCA Crim 669, cf *Carter* [2005] All ER (D) 372 (Apr); *Murphy* [2007] EWCA Crim 2810.

[458] See, generally, the discussion at p 551 and C Wells, 'Battered Woman Syndrome and Defences to Homicide: Where Now?' (1994) 14 LS 266; A McColgan, 'In Defence of Battered Women Who Kill' (1993) 13 OJLS 508; J Dressler, 'Battered Women Who Kill Their Sleeping Tormentors' in Shute and Simester, *Criminal Law Theory* arguing for a duress-type defence and J Horder, 'Killing the Passive Abuser: A Theoretical Defence' in ibid, 285.

[459] If there are multiple counts relating to different victims, care will be needed in directing the jury.

[460] See MOJ Circular 2010/13, para 25. Cf L Leigh, 'Two New Partial Defences to Murder' (2010) 53 Crim L & Justice Weekly 53 who states that the test is objective.

[461] MOJ CP 19/08, para 44.

[462] And therefore of a complete acquittal. See *Clegg* [1995]. See also Leverick, *Self Defence* (2007) 172 et seq.

[463] This analysis in the 13th edn was cited with approval by the Court of Appeal in *Dawes* [2013] EWCA Crim 322, [59].

[464] [1973] NI 96 at 107, discussed 24 NILQ 527. On 'prior fault' generally, see S Yeo, *Compulsion in the Criminal Law* (1990) Ch 5.

[465] cf *Mason* (1756) Fost 132. Under the Coroners and Justice Act 2009, the loss of self-control defence is not available in such circumstances. See Ch 13, p 553.

He knows that V may react violently. V makes a deadly attack on D. Surely D's right of self-defence is unimpaired. This suggestion was cited *obiter* with approval in *Balogun*.[466]

In *Rashford*,[467] the Court of Appeal made it clear that self-defence is available to the person who started the fight, if the person whom he attacks not only defends himself but goes over to the offensive. As a matter of principle, the defence ought to be available where D has prompted V's attack, and even where D has foreseen that V was likely to respond with violence, subject to the restriction that it should not be available where D deliberately provoked the attack with the intention of killing purportedly in self-defence. Considerable care will be necessary in directing the jury in such cases. In *Rashford*, Dyson LJ approved the Scottish decision in *Burns v HM Advocate*[468] as an important decision which should be more widely known. In that case,[469] it was said that the question:

depends upon whether the violence offered by the victim was so out of proportion to the accused's own actings as to give rise to the reasonable apprehension that he was in an immediate danger from which he had no other means of escape, and whether the violence which he then used was no more than was necessary to preserve his own life or protect himself from serious injury.

As the commentary in the *Criminal Law Review* points out, that test is inaccurate for English law as it suggests that the apprehension which D must have as to the threat of danger must be a reasonable one.[470]

The principles were reiterated in *Harvey*[471] in relation to self-defence relied on by an initial aggressor. The court followed *Rashford*. This is subject to a principle that D cannot rely on self-defence where he has set out to engineer an attack by V which will allow him, D, to respond with greater violence under the guise of self-defence. The difficulty of course lies in how to explain that to a jury. The court in *Harvey* emphasized that the direction on self-defence for initial aggressors is not always necessary simply because there is a dispute about 'who started it'. The Court of Appeal once again returned to this in *Keane*,[472] which provides a useful review, endorsing the guidance given in *Harvey* on the application of the defence where D provokes violence from another but on whom the tables are turned. Hughes LJ said:

It seems to us that that kind of homely expression, like 'the roles being reversed', can quite well encapsulate the question which may arise if an original aggressor claims the ability to rely on self-defence. We would commend it as suitable for a great many cases, subject only to this reminder.[473] ... We need to say as clearly as we may that it is not the law that if a defendant sets out to provoke another to punch him and succeeds, the defendant is then entitled to punch the other person ... The reason why it is not the law is that underlying the law of self-defence is the common-sense morality that what is not unlawful is force which is reasonably necessary ... Of course it might be different if the defendant set out to provoke a punch and the victim unexpectedly and disproportionately attacked him with a knife.

---

[466] [1999] 98/6762/X2.

[467] [2005] EWCA Crim 3377. Considered in *Marsh v DPP* [2015] EWHC 1022 (Admin).

[468] 1995 SLT 1090.   [469] At 1093H.

[470] cf *Williams (Gladstone)* [1987] 3 All ER 411; *Beckford v R* [1988] AC 130; Criminal Justice and Immigration Act 2008, s 76.

[471] [2009] EWCA Crim 469.   [472] [2010] EWCA Crim 2514.

[473] His lordship added that: 'Lord Hope's formulation of the rule [in *Burns*] makes it clear that it is not enough to bring self-defence into issue that a defendant who started the fight is at some point during the fight for the time being getting the worst of it, merely because the victim is defending himself reasonably. In that event there has been no disproportionate act by the victim of the kind that Lord Hope is contemplating. The victim has not been turned into the aggressor. The tables have not been turned in that particular sense. The roles have not been reversed' (at [18]).

10.7.4.4 Defence against lawful force

Lord Lowry CJ of Northern Ireland stated in *Browne*:[474]

Where a police officer is acting lawfully and using only such force as is reasonable in the circumstances in the prevention of crime or in effecting the lawful arrest of offenders or suspected offenders, self-defence against him is not an available defence.

Again, it may be respectfully suggested that this proposition is too wide. If D, an innocent person, is attacked by the police who mistakenly believe him to be a gunman and the police attack is such that it would be reasonable if D were the gunman, does the law really deny D the right to resist?[475] Again, if D reasonably supposes that the police are terrorists, he surely commits no crime by resisting, even if the police are in fact acting lawfully and reasonably. In *Oraki v DPP*,[476] D was convicted of obstructing an officer in the execution of his duty contrary to s 89(2) of Police Act 1996. D thought his mother was being assaulted by a police officer and intervened to prevent that from taking place. D was convicted on the basis that neither self-defence nor defence of another could be pleaded as defences to a charge of obstructing a police officer. Singh LJ stated that what was crucial was whether D genuinely believed he needed to use force to defend his mother from being assaulted. It was observed that the reasonableness of a mistaken belief on the part of a defendant is relevant to the question of whether it is a genuinely held belief but if it is a genuinely held belief, it does not matter that the belief is an unreasonable one. The Divisional Court held that the defence of self-defence or defence of another person is, as a matter of law, available in relation to the offence of obstructing a constable in the execution of his duty under s 89(2) of the Police Act 1996. It is submitted that the judgment in *Oraki* is correct as a matter of principle as it is faithful to the subjective nature of the first limb of the defences.[477] Although the judgment in *Browne* has not been overturned, it ought to be treated with considerable caution.

A person is not to be deprived of his right of self-defence because he has gone to a place where he might lawfully go, but where he knew he was likely to be attacked.

In a very limited number of cases, the attacker may not be committing a crime because, for example, he is a child under ten, insane, in a state of automatism or under a material mistake of fact. If D is unaware of the circumstances which exempt the attacker (eg the attacker's insanity), then s 3 of the Criminal Law Act will still, indirectly, afford D a defence to any criminal charge which may be brought, provided he is acting reasonably in the light of the circumstances as they appear, reasonably or not, to him; for he intends to use force in the prevention of crime, as that section allows, and therefore has no mens rea.

Where D does know of the circumstances which mean that the attack on him is not criminal, then s 3 is inapplicable, but it is submitted that the question should be decided on similar principles. A person should be allowed to use reasonable force in defending himself or another against an unjustifiable attack, even if the attacker is not criminally responsible.[478] Authority for this can now be found in the case of the conjoined twins, *Re A (Children)*.[479]

---

[474] [1973] NI 96 at 107.

[475] This passage in the 14th edn was cited with approval by the Divisional Court in *Oraki v DPP* [2018] EWHC 115 (Admin), [27]. *Mckoy* [2002] EWCA Crim 1628 suggests that D may resist unlawful restraint by a police officer. The judgment of Winn LJ in *Kenlin v Gardiner* [1967] 2 QB 510 is ambivalent. *Albert v Lavin* [1982] AC 546 (reversed by the House of Lords on another point) supports the view in the text. And see *Ansell v Swift* [1987] Crim LR 194 (Lewes Crown Court). Cf *Fennell* [1971] 1 QB 428,[1970] Crim LR 581 and commentary; p 739. These cases must now be read in the light of *Oraki*.

[476] [2018] EWHC 115 (Admin).

[477] In the subsequent case of *Wheeldon v CPS* [2018] EWHC 249 (Admin) the Divisional Court, relying upon *Oraki*, held that in principle there was no rule that the defence of self-defence was not available to a person who assaulted a police officer who was found to be acting in the execution of their duty contrary to s 89(1).

[478] *Bayer v DPP*, n 444.   [479] [2000] 4 All ER 961 (Civ Div) and commentary.

The court granted a declaration that it would be lawful to carry out an operation to separate the twins to enable A to live even though the operation would inevitably kill B. B's heart and lungs were too deficient to keep her alive. She lived only because A was able to circulate sufficient oxygenated blood for both. The evidence was that if the operation was not carried out both would die. The *ratio decidendi* of the three judges differed but it is submitted that Ward LJ rightly held that this was a case of self-defence. B was, of course, completely innocent but she was killing A. He equated the case with that of a six-year-old boy shooting all and sundry in a playground. It would be lawful to kill him if that was the only way to prevent the deaths of others. There is a great difference between the boy's active conduct and the pathetic inactivity of B; but neither is committing a crime. Whatever the position regarding necessity and duress, it has always been held that private defence may be an answer to a charge of murder.

10.7.4.5 D's reliance on unknown justifying circumstances

What of D who seeks to rely on facts that existed and would justify his use of force, but of which he was unaware at the time of acting?[480] The test proposed in the CLRC's Fourteenth Report and adopted as the law in *Gladstone Williams* and s 76 is stated exclusively in terms of D's belief. Its terms do not apply where D is unaware of existing circumstances which, if he knew of them, would justify his use of force. This line of reasoning accords with *Dadson*.[481] This is no accident. The Committee gave careful consideration to the matter and concluded that the *Dadson* principle was correct.[482]

Some academics take the view that where the circumstances justify his act, it is immaterial that D is not aware of them; where they can merely excuse his act, they do so only if he is aware of them.[483] Force used to make an arrest is said to be justified, not merely excused, so, it is argued, *Dadson* was a case of justification and is wrongly decided. Duress, which obviously requires awareness, is distinguishable because according to most commentators it merely excuses. But such an analysis based solely on justification and excuse is overly simplistic and does not provide a satisfactory explanation of *Dadson*. A boy who, knowing it is a wicked thing to do, deliberately kills his playmate has a defence if he was aged only nine at the time. Ten is the minimum age of criminal responsibility. He is excused, but no one would say he was 'justified' in killing his playmate because he was only nine. Is he to be liable for murder if he thought he was ten? Obviously not. He is excused by the fact, whether he knows of it or not. It is the policy of the law that a child under ten shall not be convicted of crime and the child's mistake cannot be allowed to defeat that policy.

Self-defence is, subject to s 76, still governed by the common law. Suppose that D shoots at V with intent to murder him and kills him. It turns out that D did so in the nick of time because, unknown to D, V was about to shoot D dead.[484] If D had only known he would certainly have had the defence of self-defence. Is D guilty of murder? According to orthodox justification/excuse theory, it depends on whether self-defence provides a justification or an

---

[480] See TM Funk, 'Justifying Justifications' (1999) 19 OJLS 630, arguing that *Dadson* represents a 'very principled, precedented, coherent and logically compelling decision'. See also PH Robinson, 'Competing Theories of Justification: Deeds v Reasons' in Shute and Simester, *Criminal Law Theory*, 45; R Christopher, 'Unknowing Justification and the Logical Necessity of the *Dadson* Principle in Self-Defence' (1995) 15 OJLS 229; J Gardner, *Offences and Defences*, Ch 5.

[481] (1850) 2 Den 35.   [482] The discussion is not included in the Fourteenth Report, paras 281–7.

[483] See in general GP Fletcher, *Rethinking Criminal Law* (1978); Smith, *Justification and Excuse*; ML Corrado (ed), *Justification and Excuse in the Criminal Law: A Collection of Essays* (1994); A Eser et al (eds), *Justification and Excuse: Comparative Perspectives* (1987). For monographs and essays providing sophisticated analyses of the theories, see especially R Schopp, *Justification Defences and Just Convictions* (1988) and Horder, *Excusing Crime*.

[484] This paradox of the unknowing justification is analysed by R Christopher (1995) 15 OJLS 229.

excuse for the use of force. Glanville Williams, who at one time thought self-defence merely an excuse, later concluded that it is a justification,[485] so he thought D would have a defence. But can it really be right that a person who has fired a gun at another with intent to murder should be beyond the reach of the law? One answer is that, though not guilty of murder, he is guilty of attempted murder under the Criminal Attempts Act 1981 (since, by that Act, he is to be treated for the purpose of an attempt charge as if the facts were as he believed them to be). But how can it be said that his act was both (a) justified and (b) attempted murder? What would a jury make of a direction to that effect? The better view is that the *Dadson* principle applies and that it is generally applicable to defences unless policy (as in the case of the nine-year-old, above) otherwise requires.

10.7.4.6 Defence of property

Where D is charged with criminal damage and his defence is that he was acting in defence of his own property—as where he kills V's dog which, he claims, was attacking his sheep, the matter is regulated by the Criminal Damage Act 1971, which is considered in Ch 27.[486] Where D is charged with an offence against the person, or any other offence, and his defence is that he was defending his property, he will generally be acting in the prevention of crime and, as in defence of the person, s 3 is likely to be held to provide the criterion. Following amendment to s 76 of the CJIA, it is clear that the provisions apply to '(ia) the purpose of defence of property under the common law'.

In *Faraj*,[487] the Court of Appeal considered the defence of protection of property where D had made a mistake in thinking that a gas repair man was a burglar and had threatened him with a knife. The court could see no reason why a householder should not be entitled to detain someone in his house whom he *genuinely* believed to be a burglar. 'The householder must honestly believe that he needs to detain the suspect and must do so in a way which is reasonable': *Gladstone Williams* applies to mistakes in relation to defence of property.

It can rarely, if ever, be reasonable to use deadly force merely for the protection of property.[488] Would it have been reasonable to kill even one of the Great Train Robbers to prevent them from getting away with their millions of pounds of loot, or to kill a man about to destroy a priceless painting (even assuming that no means short of killing could prevent the commission of the crime)? It will be recalled that Art 2 of the ECHR does not permit the use of lethal force otherwise than in preventing riot, etc, or unlawful 'violence'.

In the case of *Hussey*,[489] it was stated that it would be lawful for a person to kill one who would unlawfully dispossess him of his home. Even if this were the law at the time, it would seem difficult now to contend that such conduct would be reasonable; for legal redress would be available if the householder were wrongly evicted. Insofar as the householder was preventing crime, his conduct would be regulated by s 3 of the Criminal Law Act 1967 which replaces the rules of common law.

More recently, in *Burns*[490] the court emphasized the narrow scope of defences where D is protecting property. B was convicted of causing actual bodily harm to V, a prostitute whom B had picked up and driven to a secluded spot. Having decided not to have sex with V, and having paid her, B requested V to leave the car and when she refused, used force. The Court of Appeal upheld his conviction. B had not acted in self-defence nor in defence of anyone else; he had not been defending his property against threat or risk of damage; he was not acting for any purpose within s 3 of the Criminal Law Act 1967. The defence was one of

---

[485] Compare CLGP (1961) 25, (1982) 2 LS 233, 250.
[486] See D Lanham, 'Defence of Property in the Criminal Law' [1966] Crim LR 368.
[487] [2007] EWCA Crim 1033.   [488] See Leverick, *Killing in Self-Defence*, Ch 7.
[489] (1924) 18 Cr App R 160.   [490] [2010] EWCA Crim 1023.

'self-help'. That defence was always a last resort. It was a defence which the common law would be reluctant to extend. Lord Judge CJ added:

Recognising that to be lawful the use of force must always be reasonable in the circumstances, we accept that it might be open to the owner of a vehicle, in the last resort and when all reasonably practicable alternatives have failed, forcibly to remove an individual who has entered into his vehicle without permission and refuses to leave it. However, where that individual entered the car as a passenger, in effect at the invitation of the car owner, on the basis that they mutually understood that when their dealings were completed she would be driven back in the car from whence she had come, the use of force to remove her at the appellant's unilateral whim, was unlawful.

The court also doubted, as a matter of legal theory, whether the car owner's rights could be treated as analogous to those of a landowner to remove trespassers. However, caution is required since it does not seem the point was argued in full.

10.7.4.7 To what offences is public or private defence an answer?

These defences are most naturally relied on as answers to charges of homicide, assault, false imprisonment and other offences against the person. It is not clear to what extent public or private defence may be invoked as defences to other crimes.[491]

In *A-G's Reference (No 2 of 1983)*,[492] D made and retained in his shop petrol bombs at a time when extensive rioting was taking place in the area. He was acquitted of an offence under s 4(1) of the Explosive Substances Act 1883 of possessing an explosive substance in such circumstances as to give rise to a reasonable suspicion that he did not have it for a lawful object. It was a defence under the terms of the section for D to prove that he had it for a lawful object.[493] The Court of Appeal held that there was evidence on which a jury might have decided that the use of the petrol bombs would have been reasonable force in self-defence against an apprehended attack. If so, D had the bombs for 'a lawful object' and was not guilty of the offence charged. Yet it was assumed[494] that he was committing offences of manufacturing and storing explosives contrary to the Explosives Act 1875. The court agreed with the Court of Appeal in Northern Ireland in *Fegan*[495] that possession of a firearm for the purpose of protecting the possessor may be possession of a lawful object, even though the possession was unlawful being without a licence. The judgment is strangely ambivalent.

[D] is not confined for his remedy to calling in the police or boarding up his premises. He may still arm himself for his own protection, if the exigency arises, although in so doing he may commit other offences. That he may be guilty of other offences will avoid the risk of anarchy contemplated by the reference.

To say 'He may do it—but he will commit an offence if he does' seems inconsistent. There is, however, a clear statement that acts immediately preparatory to justifiable acts of self-defence are also justified. This must surely be right. If D becomes caught up in a shoot-out between police and dangerous criminals, picks up a handgun dropped by a wounded policeman and fires in order to defend his own and police lives, it would be astonishing if he

---

491 Clause 44 of the Draft Code ('Use of force in public or private defence') would not justify or excuse any criminal conduct not involving the use of force (except acts immediately preparatory to the use of such force); but the Code would leave it open to the courts to develop a wider defence at common law.
492 [1984] QB 456, [1984] 1 All ER 988, [1984] Crim LR 289 and commentary.
493 On which see *Copeland* [2020] UKSC 8; and *Flint and Holmes* [2020] EWCA Crim 1266.
494 *A-G's Reference (No 2 of 1983)* [1984] 1 All ER 988 at 992–3.
495 [1972] NI 80. Cf *Emmanuel* [1998] Crim LR 347.

had a defence to a charge of homicide but not to possessing a firearm.[496] Possibly, then, the passage earlier refers to preparatory, but not immediately preparatory, acts. This does not resolve the ambivalence. The law must say whether a person may, or may not, do such acts; and if it says they are crimes, he may not.

The matter must now be considered in the light of the defence of duress of circumstances.[497] A person may save himself from injury by an attacker by using force or by running away and *Willer* and *Conway*[498] are cases where this form of self-defence was an answer to a charge of reckless driving. In *Symonds*,[499] where a driver, charged under s 20 of the OAPA and with dangerous driving, raised self-defence, it was held that the same considerations applied to the driving charge as to the s 20 offence. Calling the defence to the driving charge 'duress of circumstances' may make no difference—but sometimes it may, because duress requires an objective test where the test for self-defence under s 76 is certainly subjective. As a matter of policy there is a great deal to be said for encouraging a threatened person to escape, even where that involves committing a minor offence, rather than using force against the aggressor.

A successful defendant will not care whether his defence is called 'duress of circumstances' or 'private defence'; but whether the defence succeeds may well depend on how it is categorized, because duress of circumstance is limited to threats to the person whereas self-defence extends to defence of property; and the former is governed by an objective test whereas a subjective test is applied to the latter. A disqualified driver who drove his Rolls-Royce to avoid its destruction by an aggressor could not plead duress (no threat of death or serious injury). Duress would not excuse possession of the handgun even if the possessor honestly believed that life was in danger, unless his belief was based on reasonable grounds (though D's self-defence would not be impaired). For the avoidance of such anomalies, acts immediately preparatory to public or private defence are better regarded as justified or excused by those defences.

The fears of the courts regarding a general defence of necessity[500] probably militate against a recognition that public and private defence may constitute a defence to crime generally; but, where contravention of *any* law is (a) necessary to enable the right of public or private defence to be exercised, and (b) reasonable in the circumstances, it ought to be excused. It is open to the courts to move in this direction.

The availability of private defence to a charge of dangerous driving was considered by the Court of Appeal in *Riddell*.[501] It was held that although the legal elements of that offence do not inherently involve the use of force, that does not preclude the availability of the defence where, on the particular facts of the case, use of responsive force was involved in the dangerous driving alleged. The court rejected the argument that a wholly uniform approach ought to apply that would preclude private defence from being pleaded by reference to the nature of the offence charged without reference to the underlying facts. It is submitted that there is much to commend the Court of Appeal's approach, as it ensures that focus is placed on the substance of what occurred, rather than on the offence D is alleged to have committed.

In *Oraki v DPP*[502] Singh LJ doubted whether it was right as a matter of principle that private or public defence is restricted to cases involving the use of force. The example his

---

[496] cf *Georgiades* (1989) 89 Cr App R 206; see also *Salih* [2007] EWCA Crim 2750; *McAuley* [2009] EWCA Crim 2130.

[497] See *Pommell*, p 363.

[498] See p 368. See DW Elliott, 'Necessity, Duress and Self-Defence' [1989] Crim LR 611.

[499] [1998] Crim LR 280.   [500] See p 387.   [501] [2017] EWCA Crim 413.

[502] [2018] EWHC 115 (Admin).

lordship gave of such a case was someone who blocks a police car by driving his own car in front of it, and in doing so enables a third party to escape. This person would commit the offence of obstructing a police officer and Singh LJ stated that the fact force was not used should not preclude someone from pleading the defence if he thought the police were in fact thugs chasing an innocent person. It is respectfully submitted that this *dictum* ought to be treated with caution, as the use of force is the hallmark of the defences discussed in this part of the chapter. Although there may appear to be an anomaly in that someone who does not use force will be unable to plead the defence, as Davis LJ stated in *Riddell*, 'self-defence ordinarily arises—putting it shortly—where a person uses force in order to meet actual or perceived force or threat of force'.[503] An individual who finds himself in the situation described by Singh LJ would be able to plead duress of circumstances, but not self-defence or defence of another.

10.7.4.8 Use of force excessive in the known circumstances

Generally, where D, being under no mistake of fact, uses force in public or private defence, he either has a complete defence or if he uses excessive force, no defence. In murder, if D used excessive force and lost his self-control he may (subject to the other elements of the defence being satisfied) be able to rely on the loss of self-control defence to reduce the offence to manslaughter. However, even in murder, if D has not lost his self-control, but has used excessive force, he will be guilty for the full offence of murder even if he genuinely (and reasonably) believed some force was necessary. This was affirmed by the House of Lords in *Clegg*.[504] D, a soldier on duty in Northern Ireland, fired four shots at a car (in fact stolen) which did not stop at the checkpoint he was guarding. The judge, sitting in a 'Diplock' court (without a jury), accepted that the first three shots had been fired in self-defence or defence of a colleague but that the fourth, which killed, was not, as the car had passed the soldiers and was already 50 feet down the road. D's conviction of murder was affirmed by the House of Lords, holding that it is established law that killing by excessive force in self-defence is murder and that if a change is to be made, it is for Parliament, not the courts, to make it. Where D has not lost control, but has used excessive force, there is no partial defence resulting in a manslaughter conviction, as with loss of control and diminished responsibility. The possibility was considered and rejected immediately after the *Clegg* decision.[505]

In *Palmer*,[506] the Privy Council explained why they saw no need for further refinement of the law in England:

If there has been an attack so that defence is reasonably necessary it will be recognized that a person defending himself cannot weigh to a nicety the exact measure of his necessary defensive action. If a jury thought that in a moment of unexpected anguish a person attacked had only done what he honestly and instinctively thought was necessary that would be most potent evidence that only reasonable defensive action had been taken. A jury will be told that a defence of self-defence, where the evidence makes it[s] raising possible, will only fail if the prosecution show beyond doubt that what the accused did was not by way of self-defence.[507]

---

[503] [2017] EWCA Crim 413, [41].

[504] [1995] 1 All ER 334, [1995] Crim LR 418 and commentary. See also M Kaye, 'Excessive Force in Self-Defence After *Clegg*' (1996) 61 J Crim L 448.

[505] See the *Inter-Departmental Review of the Law on Lethal Force in Self-Defence or the Prevention of Crime* (1996) paras 83–4.

[506] [1971] AC 814.

[507] On the importance of this direction and the potential for it to be underestimated, see LC 290, Part 4, paras 4.11–4.14.

The CLRC was persuaded that *Howe* was right in principle and recommended its adoption in relation to private defence of person and property and the prevention of crime.[508] It is submitted that the soundness of this recommendation is not impaired by *Clegg*.[509]

10.7.5 Reform of self-defence/private defence

The Law Commission's general proposals on defences are contained in Report No 218 which provides:

27(1) The use of force by a person for any of the following purposes, if only such as is reasonable in the circumstances as he believes them to be, does not constitute an offence—

(a) to protect himself or another from injury, assault or detention caused by a criminal act;

(b) to protect himself or (with the authority of that other) another from trespass to the person;

(c) to protect his property from appropriation, destruction or damage caused by a criminal act or from trespass or infringement;

(d) to protect property belonging to another from appropriation, destruction or damage caused by a criminal act or (with the authority of the other) from trespass or infringement; or

(e) to prevent crime or a breach of the peace.

(6) Where an act is lawful by reason only of a belief or suspicion which is mistaken, the defence provided by this section applies as in the case of an unlawful act, unless—

(a) D knows or believes that the force is used against a constable or a person assisting a constable, and

(b) the constable is acting in the execution of his duty.

10.8 Impossibility

Where the law imposes a duty to act, it has sometimes been held that it is a defence that, through no fault of his own, it was impossible for D to fulfil that duty.[510] The secretary of a limited company is not liable for failure to annex to an annual return a copy of a balance sheet laid before the company in a general meeting where there is no such balance sheet in existence: 'nobody ought to be prosecuted for that which it is impossible to do'.[511] A person is not liable for failure to leave a particular place if he is unaware of the order requiring him to do so.[512] In New Zealand, it has been held that a failure to leave the country after a revocation of a permit was not an offence if no airline would carry D because of the advanced state of her pregnancy.[513] Impossibility is a defence to a charge of failure to assist a constable to preserve the peace when called upon to do so.[514]

On the other hand, the failure of a driver to produce a test certificate is not excused by the fact that it is impossible for him to do so, the owner of the vehicle being unable or unwilling to produce it.[515]

---

[508] Fourteenth Report, para 228. Cf PF Smith, 'Excessive Defence—A Rejection of Australian Initiative' [1972] Crim LR 524.
[509] The Law Commission in cl 59 of the Draft Code have implemented the recommendation.
[510] CLGP, 746–8. See A Smart, 'Criminal Responsibility for Failing to do the Impossible' (1987) 103 LQR 532.
[511] *Stockdale v Coulson* [1974] 3 All ER 154 at 157 per Melford Stevenson J.
[512] *Lim Chin Aik v R* [1963] AC 160.   [513] *Finau v Department of Labour* [1984] 2 NZLR 396.
[514] *Brown* (1841) Car & M 314, per Alderson B.   [515] *Davey v Towle* [1973] RTR 328.

We find here the inconsistency which is so common in relation to strict liability. It cannot be asserted, therefore, that any *general* defence of impossibility is recognized at the present time. It has to be regarded as a question of the interpretation of the particular provision, with all the uncertainty that this entails.

When impossibility might be available as a defence, it will presumably fail if the impossibility has been brought about by D's own default.[516] The defence would also seem to be confined to cases where the law imposes a duty to act and not to cases of commission where the corresponding defence, if any, is necessity.[517]

Further reading

D Baker and J Horder (eds), *The Sanctity of Life and the Criminal Law: The Legacy of Glanville Williams*

ML Corrado (ed), *Justification and Excuse in the Criminal Law: A Collection of Essays*

F Leverick, *Killing in Self-Defence*

A Norrie, *Crime, Reason and History: A Critical Introduction to Criminal Law*

A Reed and M Bohlander (with N Wake and E Smith) (eds), *General Defences in Criminal Law: Domestic and Comparative Perspectives*

S Yeo, *Compulsion in the Criminal Law*

---

[516] But cf *Stockdale v Coulson*, n 511, and comment at [1974] Crim LR 375.

[517] See *Canestra* 1951 (2) SA 317 (AD) and EM Burchell and PMA Hunt, *South African Criminal Law and Procedure* (1970) 293–6.

11
Inchoate crime

11.1 Introduction

Attempts, conspiracies and assisting and encouraging under the Serious Crime Act 2007 are known collectively as 'inchoate offences'. 'Inchoate' means just begun, incipient; in an initial or early stage. Criminalizing inchoate offences raises particular difficulties because the conduct involved will often be far removed from the type of harm that would be needed to give rise to a charge under the relevant substantive offence.[1] For example, where A and B agree to burgle V's house, a conspiracy to burgle is complete even though they have never been near the house and have taken no further steps to commit that crime. It does not follow that inchoate offences will never involve a tangible harm—attempted murder can be charged just as appropriately where D shoots V who survives as where D is arrested before he has taken aim to shoot.

The actus reus of inchoate offences can extend to cover a wide range of behaviour, sometimes seemingly innocuous as, for example, with 'an agreement' in conspiracy, or mere words of encouragement in assisting and encouraging. However, there are sound reasons of policy and principle for punishing these types of wrongdoing, a central one being that the defendant has demonstrated by his actions his willingness that a substantive offence be committed.

There is nevertheless a clear risk of overcriminalization.[2] Since the actus reus is so broad, it is important that inchoates are kept within reasonable limits by requiring substantial mens rea elements. In inchoate crimes it is not uncommon to find that the mens rea requirements are for an intention or knowledge that the substantive offence will be committed. But this emphasis on mens rea does not mean that inchoates can be regarded as thought-crimes; there remains a requirement that the defendant's blameworthy state of mind manifests itself by some words or other conduct. In conspiracy, this is by agreement with others; in attempt by doing some act(s) beyond mere preparation towards the commission of the substantive crime, and in assisting and encouraging by doing acts capable of providing assistance and encouragement.

Inchoate offences always relate to a substantive offence.[3] So, there is no crime of attempt in the abstract, only crimes of, for example, attempted theft, attempted murder, etc. It should also be noted that liability for inchoate offences exists independently of accessorial liability. In the latter, the secondary party's liability derives from the commission of the full offence by the principal offender.[4] Inchoate offences are completed before the commission of any full offence. If D agrees with P to import drugs, that is a completed conspiracy even if neither party does any more. In contrast, D only becomes an accessory to the crime of importation if he aids, abets, counsels or procures P *and P does actually import drugs*.

Significant consequences flow from this distinction between secondary and inchoate liability. For example, there are defences of withdrawal for secondary parties who demonstrate a change of heart before the commission of the principal offence; inchoate liability, by contrast, is complete with the act of conspiracy or attempt or doing an act capable of assisting or encouraging, and any subsequent withdrawal goes only to mitigation in sentencing.[5] Arguably, inchoate offences better respect the principle of fair labelling, since the

---

[1] See generally LCCP 183, *Conspiracy and Attempt* (2007); and its report, LC 318, *Conspiracy and Attempts* (2009).

[2] See D Husak, *Overcriminalisation* (2008) 160 et seq. See on the importance of this, LCCP 195, para 4.61.

[3] For discussion of how the mens rea of the substantive offence ought to relate to the inchoate version of it, see J Child and A Hunt, 'Mens Rea and the General Inchoate Offences: Another New Culpability Framework' (2012) 63 NILQ 247.

[4] See C de Than and J Elvin, 'Towards a Rational Reconstruction of the Laws on Secondary Participation and Inchoate Offences' in A Reed and M Bohlander (eds), *Participation in Crime—Domestic and Comparative Perspectives* (2012).

[5] There have been suggestions that by analogy with counselling, such a defence should be available. For discussion see Wilson, *Central Issues*, 243–9.

description of D's conduct accurately reflects his personal behaviour; whereas in secondary liability the accessory's conduct may be fundamentally misdescribed because it is derivative on the conduct of the principal. For example, the getaway driver (accessory) in an armed robbery during which someone is intentionally killed is convicted, labelled and sentenced as a 'murderer'.[6]

A number of factors suggest that inchoate offences will become more commonplace in future, including, in particular, the shift from coercive to 'intelligence-led' policing where new powers and technological advances allow the police to gather evidence and intervene before substantive crimes are committed.[7] Aside from their prevalence, the study of inchoate offences is also of increased importance because of Parliament's willingness to enact new forms of substantive offence that take the form of inchoate offences.[8] Examples include the offence of sexual communication with a child,[9] offences of 'inciting' another to engage in sexual activity,[10] assisting or encouraging suicide,[11] expansive terrorist offences[12] and the wide-ranging offences under the Proceeds of Crime Act 2002.[13]

There are numerous such offences in the Terrorism Acts. They are often drafted in the style of an inchoate offence but they are in fact a substantive statutory offence. For example, s 57 of the Terrorism Act 2000 makes it an offence for a person to possess an article in circumstances which give rise to a reasonable suspicion that his possession is for a purpose connected with the commission, preparation or instigation of an act of terrorism. It is a defence for the defendant to prove that his possession of the article was not for one of these purposes. Examining that offence in *Rowe*,[14] the Lord Chief Justice noted that s 57 of the 2000 Act creates an inchoate offence in relation to terrorism. Comparing it to attempt, his lordship commented that:

Section 57, for good and obvious reason, makes criminal conduct that is merely preparatory to the commission of terrorist acts. While such conduct is highly culpable, it is not as culpable as attempting to commit, or actually committing, the terrorist acts in question. But the seriousness of the offence consists not merely in the culpability of the offender but the potential of his conduct to cause harm.[15]

The broad reach of inchoate liability was also expanded significantly when the government enacted a series of offences in Part 2 of the SCA 2007 to replace the common law offence of

---

[6] See Ch 6, and the discussion of the Law Commission's proposals in respect of secondary liability, LCCP 131 (1993), on which see JC Smith, 'Secondary Participation in Crime—Can We Do Without It?' (1994) 144 NLJ 679. See further LC 305.

[7] See GR Sullivan and IH Dennis (eds), *Seeking Security: Pre-Empting the Commission of Criminal Harms* (2012).

[8] LCCP 183, para 1.4. See eg s 45 of the Serious Crimes Act 2015 creating an offence of participating in the activities of an organized crime group.

[9] See s 15A of the Sexual Offences Act 2003, and Ch 17, p 846. On the prevalence of this, see A Gillespie, 'Child Protection on the Internet' (2002) 14 CFLQ 411 and 'Children, Chatrooms and the Law' [2001] Crim LR 435, and B Gallagher et al, 'International and Internet Child Sexual Abuse and Exploitation—Issues Emerging from Research' (2003) 15 CFLQ 353–70.

[10] Sexual Offences Act 2003, s 8, see p 836.   [11] See Ch 15.

[12] See eg Terrorism Act 2000, s 59; Anti-terrorism, Crime and Security Act 2001, s 50, discussed by C Walker, *The Anti-Terrorism Legislation* (3rd edn, 2014). The use of statutory inchoates is considered by the Law Commission: LCCP 183, Ch 15.

[13] See the discussion at Ch 33, and references therein.

[14] [2007] EWCA Crim 635.   [15] At [53].

incitement. Further expansion was also recommended when the Law Commission reviewed the offences of conspiracy and attempt relatively recently, and reference is made to the proposals throughout this chapter although the government has stated that it has no plans to enact any of the proposals at this time.[16]

11.2 Attempt

The common law of attempt[17] was repealed by the Criminal Attempts Act 1981 (in the rest of this part of the chapter referred to as 'the Act').[18] Section 1(1) creates a statutory offence:

If, with intent to commit an offence to which this section applies, a person does an act which is more than merely preparatory to the commission of the offence, he is guilty of attempting to commit the offence.

Liability turns on D doing more than merely preparatory acts with intent to commit an offence—in this chapter referred to as the 'substantive offence'. For example, for attempted theft, D must do acts more than merely preparatory to stealing. It is always essential to have in mind which substantive offence it is alleged D is intending to commit. Thereafter, it is a question of assessing D's conduct and mens rea.

11.2.1 Mens rea in attempts

In contrast to the usual approach to discussing crimes, mens rea is discussed before actus reus here because, as has often been remarked,[19] the mental element assumes paramount importance in attempts.[20] The actus reus may be a seemingly innocent and harmless act, as where D puts sugar in V's tea. If D intends to murder V and believes that the substance is a deadly poison when it is in fact sugar, he has committed attempted murder. The actus reus may be *any* act, provided it is done with intent to commit the offence and goes beyond mere preparation (see later). Although the terms of s 1 suggest that the mens rea requirement is straightforward—'with intent'—the position is more complex, and requires discussion of a number of elements of fault. It also requires consideration of the relevant mens rea in relation to the conduct of D, the circumstances of the substantive offence and the consequence elements of any such offence.

11.2.1.1 'Intentional' conduct

D must intend to perform the relevant *act* that goes beyond mere preparation towards the commission of the substantive offence. That is the conduct element of this offence. If D, carrying a knife, trips and accidentally stabs V, D does not intend to wound V. He is not guilty of attempting to murder him. The requirement of an intent to perform the conduct that is, as a matter of law, classified as going beyond mere preparation can only sensibly be understood to mean a 'purposive' or direct intent rather than an oblique intent.

---

16 As stated on the Law Commission website. Cf the MOJ, *Report on the Implementation of Law Commission Proposals* (2011).

17 See LCCP 183, Ch 13 for a review of the common law and see the 4th edn of this book, at pp 246–64. For a valuable theoretical examination of the offence, see RA Duff, *Criminal Attempts* (1996) and also G Yaffe, *Attempts* (2010) and G Yaffe, 'Criminal Attempts' (2014) 124 Yale LJ 92.

18 See generally IH Dennis, 'The Criminal Attempts Act 1981' [1982] Crim LR 5. See also P Glazebrook, 'Should We have a Law of Attempted Crime?' (1969) 85 LQR 28; Wilson, *Central Issues*, Ch 8.

19 See eg *Whybrow* (1951) 35 Cr App R 141.

20 See Duff, *Criminal Attempts*, Ch 1; Yaffe, *Attempts*, Ch 4; LC 318, Part 8. For comparisons with Dutch and German approaches, see J Keiler, *Actus Reus and Participation in European Criminal Law* (2013) 384 et seq.

11.2.1.2 Intention as to consequences

Where the substantive offence requires proof of a result or consequence, the offence of attempt will require proof of an intention as to that consequence. For example, wounding contrary to s 20 of the OAPA 1861 requires a result—wounding. For a charge of attempted s 20, D must intend that consequence. That is satisfied by proof of either direct or oblique intent.

This is straightforward enough where the mens rea of the substantive offence requires an intention as to the consequence: the mens rea is the same on the attempt. However, many substantive offences require proof of some mental element short of intention (eg recklessness) as to consequences. On a charge of attempt, an intention and nothing less must be proved as to any result element of the actus reus of the substantive crime.[21] So, for example, recklessness whether the relevant harm is caused is a sufficient mens rea for most non-fatal offences against the person, for criminal damage, and for many other offences, but it is not a sufficient mens rea on a charge of attempting to commit any of them.[22] So, in the example above, wounding contrary to s 20 of the OAPA requires a result—a break in the continuity of V's skin, but the mens rea is merely malice (which for these purposes is simply recklessness) as to some harm being caused. For a charge of attempted wounding, D must intend that V's skin is broken. Similarly, although an intention to cause grievous bodily harm is a sufficient mens rea for murder, that is plainly not an intention to commit murder and so is insufficient on a charge of attempted murder. Nothing less than an intention to kill will do on that charge.[23]

Purposive or oblique intention as to consequences?

As has been seen,[24] intention has a variable meaning in the criminal law so the question arises, what does 'intent to commit an offence' mean in s 1(1) of the Act? It was held in *Pearman*[25] that 'intent' in s 1 has the same meaning as in the common law of attempts, applying *Mohan*[26] where the court held that there must be proved:

a decision to bring about, in so far as it lies within the accused's power, the commission of the offence which it is alleged the accused attempted to commit, no matter whether the accused desired that consequence of his act or not.

The concluding words are difficult to reconcile with the main proposition, which certainly seems to embody the notion of 'trying' to cause, or striving for, a result.[27]

---

[21] On one interpretation of *A-G's Reference (No 3 of 1992)* [1994] 2 All ER 121 it may be sufficient that D has the mens rea (short of intention) sufficient for the full offence if he has completed that element in the course of his attempt. For discussion see LCCP 183, para 16.68. The final proposal in LC 318 was that the 1981 Act be amended to provide that, for the purposes of s 1(1), an intent to commit an offence includes a conditional intent to commit it: para 8.106.

[22] *Millard* and *Vernon* [1987] Crim LR 393. Cf D Stuart, '*Mens Rea*, Negligence and Attempts' [1968] Crim LR 647.

[23] cf *Whybrow*, *O'Toole* [1987] Crim LR 759. As the Court of Appeal accepted in *Morrison* [2003] All ER (D) 281 (May), an indictment containing a count of attempted murder includes, implicitly, an intention to cause grievous bodily harm with intent which can therefore be left as an alternative count. For comment on the need for proof in attempts of an intention as to the completed offence, see J Horder, 'Varieties of Intention, Criminal Attempts and Endangerment' (1994) 14 LS 335.

[24] See Ch 3, p 93.

[25] (1984) 80 Cr App R 259. For the common law position, see R Buxton, 'Inchoate Offences: Incitement and Attempt' [1973] Crim LR 656.

[26] [1976] QB 1. See K Arenson, 'The Pitfalls in the Law of Attempt' (2005) 69 J Crim L 146; LC 318, para 8.87.

[27] See the discussion in Duff, *Criminal Attempts* and Yaffe, *Attempts*.

In *Pearman*, the court thought that these words:

are probably designed to deal with a case where the accused has, as a primary purpose, some other object, for example, a man who plants a bomb in an aeroplane, which he knows is going to take off, it being his primary intention that he should claim the insurance on the aeroplane when the freight goes down into the sea. The jury would not be put off from saying that he intended to murder the crew simply by saying that he did not want or desire to kill the crew, but that was something that he inevitably intended to do.[28]

This is the meaning given to intention in criminal law generally after the series of cases culminating in *Woollin*.[29] Intention encompasses direct (purposive) intent and a jury may find intent from D's foresight of virtually certain consequences (oblique intent). This approach was applied to the offence of attempt by the Court of Appeal in *Walker*.[30] It seems, therefore, that the requirement of intention as to consequences can be satisfied by proof of oblique intention.

On the facts of *Walker*, the point may not have been in issue, since the jury had convicted on a direction that they must be satisfied that D was *trying* to kill. If he was trying to kill it was immaterial, as a matter of law, whether death was, or was known by D to be, virtually certain, highly probable or merely possible: a person may intend to kill even though the possibility of doing so is, and he knows it is, remote. Probability is no more than relevant evidence of the sufficient state of mind—it is easier to infer that D was trying to kill if he threw V from the window of the twentieth floor than if he threw him from the window of the ground floor. It was only if he was *not* trying to kill that the issue arose and in such cases *Woollin* requires foresight of virtual certainty; nothing less will do.[31] This issue of intention has been the subject of law reform proposals.[32]

11.2.1.3 Intention as to circumstances forming part of actus reus?

Where the substantive offence requires proof of intention or knowledge as to a circumstance, it is clear that nothing less will suffice for the attempt. So, for example, the substantive offence of handling stolen goods requires knowledge or belief as to the circumstance that the goods are stolen goods; D cannot be guilty of the offence of handling if he is merely reckless whether they are stolen. *A fortiori*, if D attempts to receive goods, being reckless whether they are stolen, he is not guilty of an attempt to handle stolen goods.

Where the fault element relating to circumstances forming part of the actus reus of the substantive offence is specified to include states of mind less than intention or knowledge, is it necessary always to prove intention as to that circumstance on a charge of attempt? For example, in the substantive crime of rape there is a circumstance element—that V is not consenting. The mens rea for that element of rape is that D did not reasonably believe in V's consent. For the offence of attempted rape, is it necessary to prove that D intended that V

---

28 (1984) 80 Cr App R 259 at 263.   29 [1999] 1 AC 82, p 102.

30 (1989) 90 Cr App R 226. In that case the court condoned the use by the judge of the phrase, 'very high degree of probability', but it is now clear that foresight of 'virtual certainty' is the minimum from which a jury may find intention.

31 For discussion of the philosophical dimensions of a distinction between trying to do something and trying to succeed, see J Hornby, 'On What's Intentionally Done' in S Shute, J Gardner and J Horder, *Action and Value in Criminal Law* (1993) 60; J Horder (1994) 14 LS 335: those who try without an intention to succeed are equivalent to those who recklessly endanger. See also Yaffe, *Attempts*, Ch 2.

32 The Law Commission in LC 318 recommended that an intent to commit an offence includes a conditional intent to commit it: paras 8.96–8.106. Cf the earlier proposals in LC 143; R Buxton, 'The Working Party on Inchoate Offences: Incitement and Attempt' [1973] Crim LR 656, 662; Draft Code, cl 49(2) and G Williams, 'Intents in the Alternative' (1991) 50 CLJ 120.

was not consenting or is it sufficient that he lacked a reasonable belief in her consent? Note that s 1 of the 1981 Act describes fault only in terms of 'intention'.

Stating the precise nature of the relevant mens rea for attempt is far from easy. This task is made more difficult by the existence of a number of Court of Appeal authorities that have reached different conclusions.

(1) In *Pace and Rogers*,[33] the Court of Appeal favoured a strict approach: even if reckless-ness or some lesser mens rea as to the circumstance element suffices for the substantive offence, for the attempt it is always necessary to prove intention as to circumstances.

(2) The Court of Appeal in *Khan*[34] approached the problem by accepting that unless the substantive offence requires mens rea of intention as to circumstances, then reckless-ness as to circumstances will suffice for the attempt. So if the substantive offence has a mens rea requirement of, for example, belief or suspicion or negligence as to circum-stances, proof of recklessness as to circumstances will suffice for a charge of attempt.

(3) In yet another case, *A-G's Reference (No 3 of 1992)*,[35] the Court of Appeal approached the problem by holding that the question is whether D has the mens rea of the sub-stantive offence sufficient to make up for the missing element of the actus reus of the substantive offence.

As there are Court of Appeal decisions adopting each view, it is necessary to examine them in further detail. A decision of the Supreme Court would be welcome to clarify the present state of the law.[36] This problem has become particularly acute since the Court of Appeal in *Pace* cast doubt on the validity of the approach in *Khan*—an approach that did not seem to have caused problems in over two decades.

(1) Nothing less than intention as to circumstances will suffice

Both 'direct' and 'oblique' intention can properly be used to describe mens rea in rela-tion to circumstances as well as consequences. D could be said to have a direct intention as to circumstances where the existence of the circumstance is part of the package of results he desires. For example, in criminal damage the circumstances include that the property belongs to another. D can hold an intention that the property he is going to destroy is that belonging to another.

In the context of circumstance elements of an offence, difficulties of distinguishing oblique intent from mere recklessness can be difficult. So, in *Pigg*,[37] before the Act, it was assumed without argument that a man might be guilty of attempted rape if he tried to have sex with a woman, intending to penetrate, but being reckless[38] whether she consented (ie being reckless as to the circumstance of her consent). Though the point was not spelled out in any case, it is submitted that this was right in principle.

The case which states that nothing less than intention will suffice is *Pace and Rogers*,[39] an appeal against conviction brought by two individuals who ran a scrap metal business. They had been approached by undercover police officers and offered metal which the officers hinted was stolen. The metal was not in fact stolen, but belonged to Thames Valley Police.

---

[33] [2014] EWCA Crim 186. Referred to subsequently in *Smith* [2014] EWCA Crim 1941 where D's conviction had to be quashed in the light of *Pace*. This also occurred in *Wheeler* [2014] EWCA Crim 2706.

[34] (1990) 91 Cr App R 29.   [35] (1993) 98 Cr App R 383.

[36] The Court of Appeal in *Pace and Rogers* did certify a question of law of general public importance. Leave was refused and there was no application made to the Supreme Court.

[37] (1982) 74 Cr App R 352, [1982] Crim LR 446 and commentary. See also S White, 'Three Points on *Pigg*' [1989] Crim LR 539, 541.

[38] That being the mens rea for rape in 1981 when the Criminal Attempts Act was passed.

[39] [2014] EWCA Crim 186.

If it had been stolen the defendants, by agreeing to buy it, would have committed the substantive offence under s 327 of the Proceeds of Crime Act 2002 (POCA) provided they had the relevant mens rea as to the circumstance element of that offence (that it was criminal property). The mens rea of the substantive offence requires proof that the defendants 'knew or suspected' the metal was stolen. Since the metal was not stolen, the defendants were charged with attempting to commit the offence in s 327.[40] The defendants were convicted and appealed.[41]

The question for the Court of Appeal was what mens rea was required for the charge of attempting the POCA offence? The court rejected the prosecution's argument that *Khan* was decisive. In departing from *Khan*, Davis LJ pointed out that the court in that case had made clear that it was not purporting to set out an approach that would apply to every offence. His lordship held that the starting point when considering the requisite mens rea for an attempt must be the text of s 1(1) of the 1981 Act. In a crucial passage, Davis LJ stated that:

Turning, then, to s 1(1) we consider that, as a matter of ordinary language and in accordance with principle, an 'intent to commit an offence' connotes an intent to commit all the elements of the offence. We can see no sufficient basis, whether linguistic or purposive, for construing it otherwise.

Applying this approach to the facts of the case, it was held that in order for DD to be guilty the Crown had to prove they intended for the property in question to be criminal property. As DD merely suspected the property to be criminal, the Court of Appeal quashed their convictions.

The decision in *Pace and Rogers* has been the subject of cogent criticism. Findlay Stark[42] makes the point that the court should have made reference to s 1(3)(b) of the 1981 Act. This provision requires the court to assume that facts the defendant believed to exist actually existed and in so doing provides the mens rea for impossible attempts. Therefore had it been proved that DD believed that the metal was stolen, then s 1(3)(b) mandates that the court proceed as though the property was in fact stolen. Stark makes the point that belief is a more culpable form of mens rea than suspicion so DD would have had 'the intent to commit an offence' had they believed that the metal was stolen. Given that it was only proved that DD suspected the metal to be stolen, Stark argues that the court was correct to quash their convictions but erred in casting doubt on the continued validity of *Khan*. Graham Virgo argues that the Court of Appeal has 'destabilised' the offence.[43] Like Stark he suggests that the court ought to have relied upon s 1(3), thus acquitting DD because there was no proof of belief whilst preserving the ambit of attempt. Virgo suggests that the decision should simply be ignored as *per incuriam*. Although the court referred to the relevant authorities, Virgo argues that they were misunderstood. Finally, Matthew Dyson suggests that although the court's interpretation of s 1(1) is plausible, for reasons of policy it should nevertheless not be followed.[44]

These criticisms are compelling.[45] It is submitted that the most significant problem with the approach adopted by the Court of Appeal in *Pace and Rogers* is that it may make it very

---

[40] A conviction for attempt to commit an offence might be proper, although the commission of that offence was impossible (eg D may be liable for attempting to handle stolen goods even though the goods are not in fact stolen, or for attempting to murder someone when the person is already dead). See p 516.

[41] The Criminal Attempts Act, s 1(3) requires us to treat D as if the facts were 'as he *believed* them to be' so the case should have been resolved on that basis without a need to engage with the controversy at all.

[42] F Stark, 'The *Mens Rea* of a Criminal Attempt' [2014] 3 Arch Rev 7.

[43] G Virgo, 'Criminal Attempts—The Law of Unintended Circumstances' (2014) 73 CLJ 244.

[44] M Dyson, 'Scrapping *Khan*?' [2014] Crim LR 445.

[45] Although see, for support of the decision, J Child and A Hunt, '*Pace and Rogers* and the *Mens Rea* of Criminal Attempt: *Khan* on the Scrapheap?' (2014) 78 J Crim L 220; P Mirfield, 'Intention and Criminal Attempts' [2015] Crim LR 140; AP Simester, 'The Mens Rea of Criminal Attempts' (2015) 131 LQR 169.

difficult to secure a conviction for attempting to commit a crime in circumstances where D, despite the fact he has not committed the substantive offence, has demonstrated a high degree of culpability. Take attempted rape for example. The defendant intends to penetrate V with his penis, irrespective of whether V consents or not. If there is no penile penetration, on the approach adopted in *Pace and Rogers*, D would only be guilty of attempted rape if the prosecution could prove not only that D intended to penetrate V with his penis, but also *intended* that V not consent to that penetration. This could be very difficult indeed, as it is more likely to have been the case that D did not care whether V consented, so was reckless as to the circumstance element of the offence. It is submitted that in a case such as this, where D has an intention to penetrate V with his penis irrespective of whether V consents or not, the fact that D was merely reckless as to whether V was consenting should not preclude him from being guilty of attempted rape. As Duff argues, D would be liable for the substantive offence if he succeeded in doing what he was trying to do with that level of mens rea as to circumstance, and it is logical therefore that he should be guilty of the attempt if he was unsuccessful in committing the substantive offence with the same mens rea.

Since the decision may well be subject to challenge, the alternative interpretations adopted by the Court of Appeal also merit consideration.

(2) A minimum of subjective recklessness as to circumstances is required for the attempt

In *Khan*,[46] the court, after considering conflicting opinions, held that for the purposes of the Criminal Attempts Act a man has an intention to commit rape if he intends penile penetration of a person, being reckless whether that person consents.[47] It is submitted that the approach in *Khan* is one that commends itself. The mens rea of the complete crime should be modified only insofar as it is necessary to accommodate the concept of attempt. Recklessness as to circumstances is a sufficient mens rea for the attempt unless the substantive crime requires proof of intent as to circumstances.

To take an example, if D, seeking to remove the satellite TV wiring from his rented accommodation sets out to damage the cable (intention as to a result), and at the time is reckless as to the ownership of the cable (a circumstance) because he is aware of the risk that it is the landlord's but is prepared to run that risk unjustifiably, he ought to be open to conviction for attempted criminal damage once he has gone beyond an act of mere preparation. The counter-argument to this—found persuasive by the court in *Pace and Rogers*—is that, as with all inchoate crimes, liability might arise where D has caused little if any tangible harm, and to avoid overbreadth, the law of attempts ought to require proof of a high level of culpability—in mens rea terms intention (perhaps even purposive intention) or knowledge.[48] This, however, ignores the fact that the law already compensates for the inchoate nature of the offence by always requiring proof of intention as to consequences. As Professor Sir John

---

46 (1990) 91 Cr App R 29. See further G Williams, 'The Problem of Reckless Attempts' [1983] Crim LR 365; R Buxton, 'Circumstances, Consequences and Attempted Rape' [1984] Crim LR 25; Duff (1991) 50 CLJ 100 and the response by Williams (1991) 50 CLJ 120. See LCCP 183, para 14.46; LC 318, para 8.129.

47 This was of course before the Sexual Offences Act 2003 redefined rape. Note the error in the Sexual Offences Act 2003, s 77: definitions and application of rebuttable and conclusive presumptions in ss 75 and 76 are, by s 77, applicable only in respect of the substantive offences, not inchoate versions. What then of D charged with attempted rape and rape, where the prosecution are unsure with what V was penetrated if anything, and D's plea is that V consented, whereas the complaint alleges that the penetration occurred while she was sleeping? See Ch 17.

48 See GR Sullivan, 'Intent, Subjective Recklessness and Culpability' (1992) 12 OJLS 381, 385 (relying on a concept of 'knowledge in the second degree') cf RA Duff, 'The Circumstances of an Attempt' (1991) 50 CLJ 100 at 100–1.

Smith pointed out in his seminal article,[49] the intuitive idea of an attempt means that D must have intended the consequences of his actions, but the same is not necessarily true of any circumstance elements of the substantive offence in question. It is submitted that the validity of this argument is not undermined when the circumstance element is at the core of the offence, such as lack of consent in rape. It could be argued, however, that there ought to be a higher mens rea attached to that element of the offence which is at its core.

Support for the *Khan* approach also derives from the most recent Law Commission recommendations on the subject. It was recommended that for substantive offences which have a circumstance requirement but no corresponding fault requirement (ie strict liability as to circumstances), or which have a corresponding fault requirement which is objective (eg negligence), it should be possible to convict D of attempting to commit the substantive offence only if D was subjectively reckless as to the circumstance at the relevant time.[50] In addition, it was recommended that where a substantive offence has fault requirements not involving mere negligence (or its equivalent)—that is, recklessness or knowledge—in relation to a fact or circumstance, it should be possible to convict D of attempting to commit the substantive offence if D possessed those fault requirements at the relevant time.[51]

Unfortunately, the courts have complicated the picture still further, not only in *Pace and Rogers*, as discussed earlier, but also in *A-G's Reference (No 3 of 1992)*.[52]

(3) Has D done his best to supply the missing element of the substantive offence?

Khan was extended in *A-G's Reference (No 3 of 1992)*[53] where the offence charged was attempted arson being reckless whether life be endangered, contrary to s 1(2) of the Criminal Damage Act 1971. DD had thrown petrol bombs at an occupied car and missed. The Court of Appeal stated a general principle:

a defendant, in order to be guilty of an attempt, must be in one of the states of mind required for the commission of the full offence, and did [*sic*] his best, so far as he could, to supply what was missing from the completion of the offence. It is the policy of the law that such people should be punished notwithstanding that in fact the intentions of such a defendant have not been fulfilled.[54]

Several comments must be made about this approach.[55] First, the decision goes beyond *Khan* by allowing a conviction for attempt where D's mens rea comprises only recklessness as to the existing *consequences* if there is an intention as to the missing *circumstances*. The full offence under s 1(2) of the Criminal Damage Act 1971 requires proof of a consequence: that property is damaged. There has never been a requirement in s 1(2) of an actual endangerment of any life. The required circumstance is that the property belonged to someone (not necessarily another). In addition, there was at the time of the decision a requirement

---

[49] JC Smith, 'Two Problems in Criminal Attempts' (1957) 70 Harv LR 422.

[50] LC 318, para 8.133.   [51] ibid, para 8.137.   [52] (1993) 98 Cr App R 383.

[53] ibid. For cogent criticism, see DW Elliott, 'Endangering Life by Destroying or Damaging Property' [1997] Crim LR 382, 393.

[54] See further on this approach J Stannard, 'Making Up for the Missing Element: A Sideways Look at Attempts' (1987) 7 LS 194.

[55] See RA Duff, 'Recklessness in Attempts (Again)' (1995) 15 OJLS 309 for an approach which seeks to explain the decision without distinctions between consequences and circumstances, focusing instead on the question whether D would have necessarily committed the full offence if he had carried out the actions. Mirfield argues that the decision no more accords with the language of s 1(1) than *Khan* but that the Supreme Court could find that it nevertheless has 'the valuable quality of being capable of practical application, obviating the need for strained judicial directions and jury headaches'. See P Mirfield, 'Intention and Criminal Attempts' [2015] Crim LR 140, 146.

that an ordinary prudent observer would have realized that life might be endangered by the damage.[56] Since the court in the *A-G's Reference* concluded that it was sufficient if D was (*Caldwell*) reckless as to that element of life endangerment, it would seem that recklessness as to consequences (where that is sufficient mens rea for the full offence) may also suffice for the mens rea of an attempt. This is, it is submitted, contrary to the clear wording of the Act which requires an intention as to *consequences.*

Secondly, the statement is overbroad.[57] Read literally, this approach would lead to the conviction for attempt of D who is merely reckless as to a consequence element of the offence provided he had an intention as to the relevant missing circumstance element(s). This is clearly not what the Act was intended to mean. Consider a tenant D, who is reckless as to whether his slapdash DIY will damage the TV cabling he is just about to try to remove (reckless as to consequence), but who intends/knows that it is property belonging to his landlord (intention as to circumstance). On any reading of s 1 he ought not to be guilty of attempt.

Thirdly, even if the case does not extend the law as regards the mens rea for consequences in attempt, it produces problems for the mens rea as to circumstances. On a broad interpretation, the case would introduce strict liability into the law of attempts. For example, if D tries to touch sexually a girl, V, whom he believes on reasonable grounds to be aged 16 but who is in fact only 12, he would on this approach be guilty of an attempt to commit the offence under s 7 of the Sexual Offences Act 2003. He has the state of mind required for the commission of the full offence (an intention to touch a person, who is in fact, whether he knows it or not, under the age of 13); and he has done his best 'to supply [in the language of the court] what was missing from the commission of the full offence'—sexual touching. There is a logical argument in favour of such an extension of inchoate liability;[58] but it goes beyond anything actually decided and beyond any recommendation of the Draft Code Team. It seems unlikely that the court in the *A-G's Reference* appreciated the point and the *dictum* should be regarded with caution.

Finally, at the time of the decision it was settled that *Caldwell* recklessness was sufficient for the full offence under the Criminal Damage Act and the court held that this was also the correct test on the attempt charge. Subjective recklessness (*Cunningham/G* recklessness) has long been thought to be an acceptable mens rea as to circumstances in attempt because it is a true state of mind. However, a person may be *Caldwell* reckless even if the possibility of the relevant risk (a bystander's perception of a danger to life) never enters his head. To hold that such an objective fault element is sufficient for attempt is, arguably, an unacceptable extension of liability for an inchoate offence.[59] The point does not appear to have been considered explicitly by the court. Given the overruling of *Caldwell* in *G*,[60] the issue assumes less significance in relation to criminal damage, but if it is interpreted more broadly so that recklessness, negligence or even strict liability as to a circumstance will suffice, it remains of fundamental importance.

---

[56] The latter requirement flowed from the application of the objective test in *Caldwell* as in *Sangha* (1988) 87 Cr App R 88. It is worth noting that since *Caldwell* has been overruled by *G*, it is arguable that the requirement relating to the perception of endangerment of life is not purely one of D's mens rea—that D intends or is subjectively reckless as to that danger—because recklessness requires also that the risk taking is unjustified, which implicitly requires that the risk is objectively present.

[57] See also for criticism: LCCP 183, paras 14.42 et seq.

[58] See JC Smith, 'Two Problems in Criminal Attempts' (1957) 70 Harv LR 422 at 433 and 'Two Problems in Criminal Attempts Re-Examined' [1962] Crim LR 135. See for further discussion RA Duff (1995) 15 OJLS 309, defending the more radical view.

[59] What of the person who does not give a thought to the relevant circumstance? He should be held sufficiently reckless if he was indifferent. Cf commentary on *Mousir* [1987] Crim LR 561 at 562.

[60] [2004] 1 AC 1034.

11.2.1.4 Conditional intention

The fact that D's intention is conditional upon some event or circumstance arising is no bar to conviction. D who picks up V's bag intending to steal anything worth keeping is guilty of theft. Great practical difficulty and much academic debate was caused by the decision of the Court of Appeal in *Husseyn*.[61] The defendants opened the door of a van in which there was a holdall containing valuable sub-aqua equipment. They were charged with attempted theft of the equipment. The judge directed the jury that they could convict if the defendants were about to look into the holdall and, if in the defendants' opinion its contents were valuable, to steal them. The Court of Appeal held that this was a misdirection: 'it cannot be said that one who has it in mind to steal only if what he finds is worth stealing has a present intention to steal'. This caused particular difficulties in the law of burglary because most persons charged with that crime intend to steal not some specific thing, but anything they find which they think is worth stealing.[62] The Court of Appeal[63] overcame this difficulty by holding that *Husseyn* applied only where, as in that case, the indictment named the specific thing which the defendant was alleged to have attempted to steal (the sub-aqua equipment). The Court of Appeal held that there would be no problem in convicting of an attempt if the indictment had charged an attempt to steal 'some or all of the contents' of the holdall—or car, handbag or house, as the case may be. This purely procedural device was rightly criticized. In *Husseyn*, for example, the only thing in the holdall was the sub-aqua equipment. If the defendant was guilty of attempting to steal 'some or all of the contents' he was obviously guilty of attempting to steal the sub-aqua equipment—there were no other contents—but if the indictment charged him with that he had to be acquitted!

Conditional intent under the 1981 Act

The Act does not expressly do anything about this absurd and unworthy distinction, and it remains part of the law.[64] The Act has, however, solved the problem because it is possible in such a case to charge D with attempting to steal something in the holdall even if it was empty. It is no bar to conviction under the Act if it is impossible for D to commit the substantive offence (because the holdall is empty). This reverses the common law position in *Haughton v Smith*.[65] In *Husseyn*, the jury must have found that D intended to steal anything in the holdall that he found to be of value. If he would have taken the sub-aqua equipment had he found it, he had certainly done an act that was more than merely preparatory to stealing it and he ought to be found guilty of attempting to do so. It might not, however, be possible for the jury to be satisfied that he would have taken that item. If he would not have taken it, it follows that he was looking for other things—we know not what and perhaps he did not know either—which were not there. He was attempting to steal all right, but his attempt was doomed to failure. This no longer matters since the Act reversed *Haughton v Smith*. He was no different in this respect from the person who attempts to steal from an empty pocket.

---

[61] (1978) 67 Cr App R 131n, [1978] Crim LR 219 and commentary; AR White, *Misleading Cases* (1991) 63. See also G Williams, 'The Three Rogues Charter' [1980] Crim LR 263. Described in LCCP 183 as 'wrong': para 16.74. See also LC 318, paras 8.96 et seq. See also J Child, 'Understanding Ulterior *Mens Rea*: Future Conduct Intention is Conditional Intention' (2017) 76 CLJ 311.

[62] Similarly, a person may be guilty of attempted burglary with intent to commit GBH if he attempts to enter, hoping to find someone inside whom he would wish to beat up. It is immaterial that there is no one in the house: *Toothill* [1998] Crim LR 876; LC 318, para 8.129.

[63] *A-G's References (Nos 1 and 2 of 1979)* [1980] QB 180; see also *Walkington* [1979] 2 All ER 716 and commentary. For discussion, see LCCP 183, para 5.11.

[64] *Smith* and *Smith* [1986] Crim LR 166.

[65] [1975] AC 476, p 517. Though there was an understandable inclination on the part of the Court of Appeal to carry on as if that case did not exist. See *Bayley and Easterbrook* [1980] Crim LR 503 and commentary.

A practical difficulty remains in how to form the indictment. The formula approved by the Court of Appeal, 'some or all of the contents', is unsatisfactory because the jury may not be satisfied that D intended to steal *any* of the actual contents and may indeed be satisfied that he did not intend to steal any of them. The indictment would be accurate, however, if it simply stated, 'attempted to steal from a holdall'. This represents the truth, whether there is anything there that he would have stolen or not. The failure to specify any subject matter is not an objection because there is in fact no subject matter to be specified. D must be dealt with on the basis that he intended to take anything he thought worth taking, whatever it might be. The problem is exactly the same in the empty pocket case.

In *Husseyn*, the court followed *Easom*[66] where D picked up a woman's handbag in a theatre, rummaged through the contents and put it back having taken nothing. The handbag was attached by a thread to a policewoman's wrist. D's conviction for stealing the handbag and the specified contents—tissues, cosmetics, etc—was quashed because there was no intention permanently to deprive the owner of these. Consequently, the court held, he was not guilty of attempting to steal the handbag or contents. Whether he was rightly acquitted of theft is debated[67] but, assuming he was, he was also innocent of attempting to steal the specific contents, but he was clearly guilty of an attempt to steal what was not there. Plainly, he was looking for money and therefore the handbag was, in effect, empty. The court posed a much-discussed example: 'If a dishonest postal sorter picks up a pile of letters intending to steal any which are registered, but, on finding that none of them are, replaces them, he has stolen nothing.' This is true; but he was then (before *Haughton v Smith*) and is now, guilty of attempting to steal registered letters.

Academic writing has produced a diverse range of classifications and terminology of conditional intentions but three broad categories are accepted: (a) 'non-comprehensive conditional intentions'—D intends to do 'x' if 'y';[68] (b) 'comprehensive conditional intentions'—D intends 'x' only if 'y'—D has a declared intentions as to his course of conduct in both eventualities: where y materializes and not; (c) unconditional intentions—D intends 'x' even if 'y'.[69] These have not been explicitly examined by the courts.

The Law Commission recommended that the 1981 Act be amended to provide that, for the purposes of s 1(1), an intent to commit an offence includes a conditional intent to commit it.[70]

The concept of conditional intent has gained prominence since the combined judgment of the Supreme Court/Privy Council in *Jogee; Ruddock*. This is discussed separately in Ch 6.

11.2.2 Actus reus in attempt

Although the mens rea of the offence is of primary importance, the actus reus of attempts remains significant.[71] It ensures that the offence does not extend to criminalizing thoughts, but rather applies only when D has exhibited some physical willingness to bring his criminal

---

[66] [1971] 2 QB 315.

[67] See Williams, TBCL, 651–3 and [1979] Crim LR 530; p 929.

[68] K Campbell, 'Conditional Intention' (1982) 2 LS 77 at 84–5.

[69] cf the view in LCCP 183, Part 5, see p 493.   [70] LC 318, para 8.106.

[71] See Duff, *Criminal Attempts*, Ch 2; Yaffe, *Attempts*, Ch 10; D Stuart, 'The *Actus Reus* in Attempts' [1970] Crim LR 505; W Wilson, 'Participating in Crime: Some Thoughts on the Retribution/Prevention Dichotomy' in A Reed and M Bohlander (eds), *Participation in Crime—Domestic and Comparative Perspectives* (2013). For comparisons with Dutch and German approaches see J Keiler, *Actus Reus and Participation in European Criminal Law* (2013) 359 et seq.

intentions to fruition. This, of course, begs the question how much of a physical manifestation of that intention it is necessary for D to perform in order for his conduct to be regarded
as an attempt to commit the crime.[72] The present law requires that D has done an act that is
more than merely preparatory to the commission of the substantive offence.

Whether an act is sufficient to satisfy this element of the offence of attempt is an extremely
controversial issue on many levels. First, on a practical level, the more broadly the law
extends the scope of attempt liability to include even the slightest conduct towards the commission of an offence, the greater the protection that can be afforded and the earlier the
police can intervene. The cost of that approach is in potentially overbroad criminalization
and oppressive and intrusive policing.[73]

Secondly, at a theoretical level, there is a division between the 'subjectivist' and 'objectivist' schools of thought. In short, it has been said that 'subjectivists require the relevant acts
to manifest an *intention* to commit the substantive offence whereas objectivists require the
relevant acts to manifest the *actual* attempt'.[74]

Thirdly, there is an even broader related question which is why the criminal law places as
much emphasis as it does on the *consequences* of the criminal actor's conduct. Why should
the outcome of the defendant's intentional conduct make so much difference to his criminal
liability? In the context of attempt, this raises the specific questions whether and why D
ought to be treated differently in terms of liability and punishment when he embarks on
carrying out his criminal intentions, but the proscribed harm does not occur.[75]

11.2.2.1 Common law

Before the 1981 Act, there was a sufficient actus reus for an attempt if D's steps towards the
commission of the offence were properly described as 'an attempt', in ordinary meaning.
At common law it was a matter of fact: was D's act sufficiently proximate to the substantive crime to be properly described as an attempt to commit it? This did not maximize
legal certainty nor clarity. Many steps may be taken towards the commission of a crime that
could not properly be described in this fashion. D, intending to commit murder, buys a gun
and performs target practice, studies the habits of V, reconnoitres a suitable place to lie in
ambush, puts on a disguise and sets out to take up his position. All are acts of preparation
but could scarcely be described as attempted murder. D takes up his position, loads the gun,
sees V approaching, raises the gun, takes aim, puts his finger on the trigger and squeezes
it, but the bullet, caught by a sudden gust of wind, misses V. D has now certainly committed attempted murder; but he might have desisted or been interrupted at any of the stages
described. At what point had D gone far enough to be guilty of an attempt?

In many cases, there would be a dispute about whether D's act was sufficiently proximate.
One situation where there was no dispute was where D had done the 'last act' that, as he knew,
was necessary to achieve the *consequence* alleged to be attempted: he was guilty of the attempt.[76]

---

[72] It has been argued that the case law suggests that there can only be an attempt when there has been a
'confrontation' with the victim (CMV Clarkson, 'Attempt: The Conduct Requirement' (2009) 29 OJLS 25) but
this is ultimately too simplistic an approach.

[73] For a discussion of an even broader approach in which attempt liability is founded not on D's physical
manifestation to commit crime but his disposition to do so, see PH Robinson, 'The Modern General Part: Three
Illusions' in Shute and Simester, *Criminal Law Theory*, 92–3.

[74] Wilson, *Central Issues*, 237. See also Yaffe, *Attempts*, Ch 1.

[75] See generally Duff, *Criminal Attempts*, Ch 12; Yaffe, *Attempts*, Ch 10; JC Smith, 'The Element of Chance in
the Criminal Law' [1963] Crim LR 63; and in particular the writings of Professor Ashworth: 'Belief, Intent and
Criminal Liability' in J Eekelaar and J Bell (eds), *Oxford Essays in Jurisprudence* (1987) and 'Criminal Attempts
and the Role of Resulting Harm under the Code and under the Common Law' (1988) 19 Rutgers LR 725.

[76] Even this, not very ambitious, rule was doubted by Lord Edmund-Davies in *Stonehouse* [1978] AC 55 at 86
but his lordship's doubts seem to relate to the last act of a secondary party which, admittedly, does not necessarily constitute an attempt. See [1977] Crim LR 547–9.

11.2.2.2 Common law and 1981 Act compared

The Law Commission, when proposing the 1981 Act, failed to identify a 'magic formula' to define precisely what constitutes an attempt. The proximity test (ie whether D's act is 'proximate' to the offence) was the only one broadly acceptable although it was imprecise. That was not the formula the Commission recommended. The Commission also rejected a test that limited attempts to the 'last act'.[77] The test proposed by the Law Commission was in substance adopted in the 1981 Act.[78]

The test in the 1981 Act—doing an act more than merely preparatory—was designed to focus not on when the commission of the offence begins, but on when mere preparation ends. The 1981 Act test is more suitable than the common law proximity test in one respect. The test of 'proximity' suggested that the attempter had to come 'pretty near'[79] to success; yet, where the attempt is to do the impossible (as where D attempts to murder using sugar that he believes to be poison), success is an infinity away. The 1981 Act test was not explicitly designed to change the scope of the offence. If any change has been made, it is to extend the scope of attempts because, if there is any 'middle ground' between mere preparation and a proximate act, an act in the middle ground now constitutes an attempt whereas formerly it did not do so.[80] It might be suggested, for example, that the assassin in the previous example was not proximate when he merely left home to the site of the intended assassination, but that conduct might now be regarded as being beyond mere preparation. However, it seems more likely that preparation and commission overlap than that there is any gap between them.[81]

11.2.2.3 Interpreting the 1981 Act test—'beyond mere preparation'

Every step towards the commission of an offence, except the last one, could properly be described as 'preparatory' to the commission of the offence.[82] When the assassin crooks his finger around the trigger that is an act preparatory to pulling it. If the section were to be interpreted in that narrow fashion, only the last act would amount to an attempt—a result which the Act was designed to avoid. The Act has not been read in that manner. An act can be more than merely preparatory and therefore sufficient to constitute an attempt without being the last act before the substantive offence is complete. D may be guilty of attempted murder where he has not yet fired the gun and D can be guilty of attempted rape though he has not physically attempted penile penetration.

The key word in interpreting the 1981 Act is 'merely'.[83] Not all preparatory acts are excluded, only those that are 'merely preparatory'. When does an act cease to be *merely*

---

[77] In particular, a test based on whether D had taken 'substantial steps'. Cf the American Model Penal Code, § 5.01(1)(c).

[78] See LC 102, paras 2.45–2.52. Criticized by G Williams, 'Wrong Turnings on the Law of Attempt' [1991] Crim LR 416.

[79] *Commonwealth v Kennedy*, 170 Mass 18 (1897) (OW Holmes J).

[80] See the discussion of reform throughout this chapter.

[81] The Law Commission suggested that the law must allow the flexibility judges need: LCCP 183, para 16.3.

[82] Arguments that the statute infringes Art 7 because of its ambiguity are rejected by Horder: J Horder, 'Criminal Attempt, the Rule of Law, and Accountability in Criminal Law' in L Zedner and JV Roberts (eds), *Principles and Values in Criminal Law and Criminal Justice* (2012).

[83] E Griew, *Current Law Statutes* (1981) says that, 'If "merely" adds anything at all, it is only emphasis'; but elsewhere in his note he recognizes that all acts but the last are in one sense preparatory and that the phrase, 'merely preparatory', indicates that 'there may, in any criminal transaction, be a point before which it is appropriate to describe the actor as not yet engaged in the commission of the offence but as *only* preparing to commit it' (emphasis added). 'Only' equals 'merely'. Griew seems to agree that not all preparatory acts are excluded, but only those that are 'only' or 'merely' preparatory. There is judicial support for the view that the word merely really matters. In *Tosti* [1997] Crim LR 746 the court held that D's acts were 'preparatory, but not merely so'.

preparatory? The answer, it seems, must be when D is engaged in the commission of the offence which he is attempting—as Rowlatt J put it many years ago, when D is 'on the job'.[84] The question whether D is in the 'executory stage' of committing the offence is another way of describing this.[85]

The first step for the court should be to determine precisely the nature of the substantive crime alleged to be attempted. That confirms the end stop and the court can then assess how preparatory D's acts are to that. The nature of the crime is also important since it has been recognized that where the substantive offence turns on the commission of a single act (eg killing or wounding) early acts are less likely to be regarded as beyond 'mere preparation' than where the crime in question is one continuing over time (eg fraud), where the 'moment of embarkation' may arise far earlier. This depends, of course, on the method by which the killing or the fraud is to be achieved.[86] Particular care is needed if the charge is one of an attempt to commit an offence which has, in its substantive form, an inchoate nature.[87]

Having identified the nature of the substantive crime and the nature of the conduct alleged to constitute acts beyond mere preparation, the court must determine whether the acts are indeed 'more than merely preparatory to the commission of the offence'. This is a question of fact. In a jury trial, it is of course for the judge to decide whether there is evidence sufficient in law to support such a finding and it is then for the jury to decide (a) what acts D did, and (b) whether they were more than merely preparatory.[88] If the judge decides there is not sufficient evidence, he directs a verdict of not guilty. Where he decides there is sufficient evidence, he must leave both questions of fact to the jury, even where the only possible answer in law is that D is guilty.[89] Where, for example, the evidence is that D has done the 'last act', the judge may not tell the jury that, if they find that D did that act, that *is* an attempt even though in law this is so. The judge may express a strong opinion, but he must not appear to take the question of fact out of the hands of the jury.[90]

The decision of the judge is not always easy. For example, in *K*[91] the defendant was convicted of attempting to cause a child to watch a sexual act. K spoke to some children playing near his office and asked children including a six-year-old if they wanted to look at pornography on K's laptop. There was no direct evidence that the laptop was in fact in K's nearby office. The judge explained to the jury that they had to be sure: that an invitation had been issued to the children, that the laptop had been in the office and that it had been used to show pornography. If they were sure of those facts then D's acts were more than merely preparatory. The Court of Appeal quashed the conviction. There was insufficient evidence

---

[84] *Osborn* (1919) 84 JP 63. Toulson LJ stated in *Moore v DPP* [2010] EWHC 1822 (Admin) that he found this phrase unhelpful, as it did not assist in determining when 'the job' begins. If it meant that D must have commenced the actus reus of the full offence, then his lordship doubted whether it was accurate.

[85] LCCP 183, para 14.5.   [86] *Qadir* [1997] 9 Arch News 1.

[87] See *Shergill* [2003] CLY 871 (Wolverhampton Crown Court) where the court rejected an indictment alleging an attempt to be knowingly concerned in the making of arrangements for facilitating entry of illegal entrants in to the UK (contrary to the Immigration Act 1971, s 25).

[88] See s 4(3) of the Act, which, in substance, codifies the common law as to the functions of judge and jury: *Stonehouse* [1978] AC 55. For a more recent affirmation of the correctness of this approach, see *Dyer* [2011] EWCA Crim 900. On the difficulty in application for jurors, see J Andrews, 'Uses and Misuses of the Jury' in *Reshaping the Criminal Law*, 55–6.

[89] *Wang* [2005] UKHL 9.

[90] *Griffin* [1993] Crim LR 515. If the judge does and the jury convict, the Court of Appeal used to have an easy route to upholding the conviction under the proviso to the Criminal Appeal Act 1968, s 2. Since the Criminal Appeal Act 1995, there is no proviso, and the court would have to quash the conviction if it was regarded as unsafe. LCCP 183 provisionally proposed removing this problem by leaving the judge to decide the issue of whether there has been an attempt: para 16.89. The proposal was dropped in LC 318.

[91] [2009] EWCA Crim 1931. The full offence is only committed if the child does watch.

in law to go before the jury and the directions given were inadequate. The mere invitation to the children and the presence of a laptop did not in law amount to an attempt to cause a child to watch sexual acts. There were acts that were merely preparatory and the judge should not have allowed the matter to go before the jury.[92] Contrast this with *R*[93] in which it was held that D's text message to a prostitute asking if she knew of any 12-year-olds available for sex was capable of constituting an attempt to arrange a sexual offence with a child (Sexual Offences Act, s 14).

It has been argued[94] that the judge and jury, in performing their respective functions, are not entitled to have regard to the word 'attempt'. The question to be determined is, in the words of s 4(3), simply whether D 'did an act falling within subsection (1) of [s 1]'; and that subsection does not use the word 'attempt'. While there is great force in this argument, it is submitted that it should not prevail. As observed earlier, all acts but the last one are preparatory. How then are we to determine whether an act is more than *merely* preparatory? To be more than merely preparatory, it must also be something else. What? Some other concept not mentioned in the section must be invoked to give it a sensible meaning. The answer seems to be that the act must be part of the commission of the intended offence, an act that is done by D 'on the job', that it is, in a word, an 'attempt'. The following section will outline the various judicial interpretations that have been given to the concept of an attempt over the years.

Judicial interpretations of the concept of attempt

A number of tests have been proposed at one time or another:

- whether D's act is the last act necessary; that is, for there to be a completed attempt, not the completed crime. It would be enough for attempted murder that D was about to pull the trigger; there is no need for the victim to have died, which is the last act of murder;
- whether D's act is proximate to the commission of the full offence;
- whether D's act was one of a series which would lead to the crime if uninterrupted;
- whether D's act was immediately connected with the substantive offence.

The narrowest interpretation[95] was that of Lord Diplock in *Stonehouse*[96] where, having cited the opinion in *Eagleton*[97] that only acts 'immediately connected' with the offence can be attempts, he continued: 'In other words the offender must have crossed the Rubicon and burnt his boats.' The 'Rubicon test' was initially accepted as representing the law under the 1981 Act[98] but was rejected in *Gullefer*.[99] In *Gullefer*, D, seeing that the dog he had backed in a greyhound race was losing, jumped onto the track to stop the race. He hoped that the stewards would declare 'no race' whereupon punters would be entitled to have their money back and he would recover his £18 stake. His conviction for attempting to steal the £18 was quashed. His act was held to be merely preparatory. It remained for him to go to the bookmaker and demand his money.

---

[92] The substantive offence involved is that contrary to s 12 of the Sexual Offences Act 2003 (for the purpose of obtaining sexual gratification, D intentionally causes a child to watch a third person engaging in an activity, or to look at an image of any person engaging in an activity), p 841.

[93] [2008] EWCA Crim 619. The full offence requires that there is an 'arrangement' not that a sex act occurs.

[94] Griew, *Current Law Statutes*.

[95] On which see Duff, *Criminal Attempts*, 390.

[96] [1978] AC 55 at 68. LCCP 183 suggests that Lord Diplock actually endorsed the proximity test despite his Rubicon comments.

[97] (1855) Dears CC 376, CCR at 515.   [98] *Widdowson* (1985) 82 Cr App R 314 at 318–19.

[99] [1990] 3 All ER 882, [1987] Crim LR 195 and commentary. Cf *Boyle* (1986) 84 Cr App R 270, [1987] Crim LR 111. Cf *Stevens v R* [1985] LRC (Crim) 17 (St Helena CA) discussed by L Blake (1986) 50 J Crim L 247.

In *Jones*,[100] applying *Gullefer*, the court upheld D's conviction of attempted murder where he got into V's car and pointed a loaded sawn-off shotgun at him, despite an argument by D that he had at least three acts to do: remove the safety catch, put his finger on the trigger and pull it. When he pointed the gun, there was evidence to leave to the jury. In the same vein is *Litholetovs*,[101] where D had done a sufficient act to be guilty of attempted arson by pouring petrol on V's door. It was unnecessary to prove that D had gone further by producing and operating the cigarette lighter he was carrying.

In *Gullefer*, Lord Lane CJ also referred to an alternative 'test' formulated by Stephen:[102] 'An attempt to commit a crime is an act done with intent to commit that crime and forming part of a series of acts which would constitute its actual commission, if it were not interrupted.' His lordship recognized the unhelpful nature of this test. It does not define where the 'series of acts' begins. Moreover, many acts that are obviously merely preparatory could be said to be part of such a series.[103] Lord Lane CJ said the 1981 Act requires a 'midway course' and that the attempt begins 'when the defendant embarks on the crime proper'. This seems the same as Rowlatt J's 'on the job' test.

Although it seemed that the court in *Gullefer* provided clear rejection of the narrow interpretation of the actus reus, there are numerous cases since in which an unduly narrow approach seems to have been taken. This is demonstrated most vividly in *Campbell*[104] where D was arrested by police when, armed with an imitation gun, he approached within a yard of the door of a post office with intent to commit a robbery therein. His conviction for attempted robbery was quashed: the court held there was no evidence on which a jury could 'properly and safely' find that his acts were more than merely preparatory. From the viewpoint of public safety, it is an unhappy decision. Though the police may lawfully arrest a person doing such preparatory acts because he is, or they have reasonable grounds for suspecting that he is, about to commit an offence,[105] they may feel obliged to wait until he has entered the post office and approached the counter before arresting him. The extra danger to post office staff, the public and the officers themselves is obvious.[106]

Geddes[107] is another example of an unsatisfactory narrow approach. D was found in the boys' toilet of a school, equipped in such a way as to suggest strongly that his purpose was kidnapping. His conviction for attempted false imprisonment was quashed. Even clear evidence of what D had in mind 'did not throw light on whether he had begun to carry out the commission of the offence'. Lord Bingham CJ distinguished between evidence that D was

[100] (1990) 91 Cr App R 351.   [101] [2002] EWCA Crim 1154.

[102] *Digest of Criminal Law* (5th edn, 1894) art 50.

[103] LCCP 183 considers this in examining the appropriate definition for the new offence of criminal attempt which is narrower than that at present.

[104] (1991) 93 Cr App R 350. But cf *Kelly* [1992] Crim LR 181.   [105] PACE, s 24(1), p 758.

[106] Campbell was convicted of the offence of carrying an imitation firearm and in similar cases it may be possible to convict of 'going equipped'; but the police may not know whether the suspect is armed or equipped and, whether they know or not, they will naturally wish to obtain a conviction for the more serious offence which they believe he intends to commit. For a philosophical discussion of the problem, see AP Simester, 'Prophylactic Crimes' in GR Sullivan and IH Dennis (eds), *Seeking Security: Pre-Empting the Commission of Criminal Harms* (2012), 72.

[107] [1996] Crim LR 894, per Bingham LCJ. The offence would now be one of trespass with intent to commit a sex offence contrary to the Sexual Offences Act 2003, s 63. For a discussion of whether the creation of substantive offences such as this one is justified, see W Wilson, 'Participating in Crime: Some Thoughts on the Retribution/Prevention Dichotomy' in A Reed and M Bohlander (eds), *Participation in Crime—Domestic and Comparative Perspectives* (2013). This case is not easy to reconcile with *Tosti* [1997] Crim LR 746 where DD were examining a door to decide how best to break in, it was held to fall on the other side of the line and to be sufficient evidence of attempted burglary. Clarkson argues that in the latter case, DD had confronted the 'victim' of the offence, ie the door, and that this explains the different outcomes, see CMV Clarkson, 'Attempt: The Conduct Requirement' (2009) 29 OJLS 25.

'trying to commit the offence . . . [and that] he had only got himself ready to put himself in a position or equipped himself to do so'. *Campbell* and *Geddes* served as a significant catalyst for the Law Commission's most recent recommendations for reform.[108]

The narrow approach in *Geddes* was echoed in the decision in *K*[109] discussed earlier relating to the pornography on the laptop. A similar approach was taken in *Mason v DPP*[110] holding that the act of opening a car door could not be characterized as more than merely preparatory to the act of driving the vehicle and, accordingly, D could not properly be convicted of an attempted drink-driving offence. In the Divisional Court, quashing the conviction, Nicol J said:[111]

In this case, the substantive offence, or the 'full offence', as it is referred to in the 1981 Act, is driving. In my view the appellant could not be said to have embarked on the 'crime proper' . . . until he did something which was part of the actual process of putting the car in motion. Turning on the engine would have been such a step, but starting to open the door of the car in my view was not capable of being so.[112]

It was thought that some pre-Act cases which were considered by judicial and academic critics to take too restrictive a view of attempts might be decided differently under the Act. Given the approach in *Geddes*, *K* and *Mason* this seems unlikely. One further example is *Robinson*.[113] D, a jeweller, having insured his stock against theft, concealed some of it on his premises, tied himself up with string and called for help. He told the police who came to his assistance that he had been knocked down and his safe robbed. The police were not satisfied with the story and discovered the property concealed on the premises. D confessed that he had hoped to get money from the insurers. His conviction for attempting to obtain by false pretences was quashed. If this case still represents the law, a judge, on these facts, should direct a jury to acquit of the attempt to commit that offence.[114] Notwithstanding the criticisms of the result, it is by no means clear that this conduct ought to be regarded as more than merely preparatory. The stage had been set; but the business of obtaining money from

[108] Is it an overreaction to just a couple of bad cases in which the defendants could have been convicted of other offences in any event? See LCCP 183, Part 12. The Commission accepted that it was unduly influenced by that case: LC 318, para 8.13. For suggestions of non-criminal responses to D who never gets beyond preparation, see D Ohana, 'Desert and Punishment for Acts Preparatory to the Commission of a Crime' (2007) 20 Canadian J L & Jurisprudence 113 and 'Responding to Acts Preparatory to the Commission of a Crime' (2006) 25 *Criminal Justice Ethics* 23. For a contrary view see L Alexander and K Kessler Ferzan, 'Risk and Inchoate Crimes: Retribution or Prevention' in GR Sullivan and IH Dennis (eds), *Seeking Security: Pre-Empting the Commission of Criminal Harms* (2012).

[109] [2009] EWCA Crim 1931.

[110] [2009] EWHC 2198 (Admin). See also *Ferriter* [2012] EWCA Crim 2211, where D struggled with V and put his hand in her trousers. Held to be an act beyond mere preparation, but no evidence it was to rape rather than assault sexually. See also *Beaney* [2010] EWCA Crim 2551, and *Bryan* [2015] EWCA Crim 433.

[111] At [19]–[20].

[112] As previously, the distinction between fact and law is important in s 4(3). Turning on the engine *may* be considered to be something more than mere preparation to drive, but whether it *does* in fact amount to an attempt remains a pure question of fact in each case. M might have committed the offence of 'being in charge of a motor vehicle on a road or other public place', when over the limit, contrary to s 5(1)(b), provided he was on a road or public place. In *Moore v DPP* [2010] EWHC 1822 (Admin), a court was fully entitled to find that D had attempted to drive on a public road where D started his car on private property (the inside perimeter fence of an atomic weapons establishment) and was stopped by an officer a few metres from the public road to which he was heading.

[113] [1915] 2 KB 342. Cf *Button* [1900] 2 QB 597.

[114] Interestingly it might be argued (as LCCP 183 assumes, para 13.15 fn 31) that D has attempted to defraud under the Fraud Act 2006 by making a false representation through conduct. But is it by the false representation of being tied up that he intends to gain? See p 972.

the insurance company was yet to begin. D was undoubtedly preparing to commit what today would be a crime of fraud, but his conduct thus far could only properly be described as mere preparation, which is insufficient to fall within the terms of the Act. *Widdowson*,[115] decided under the Act, was a rather similar case and the conviction was quashed.

The Law Commission suggested that the judicial interpretation of the test is so defective as to require at least rectification by specific guideline examples, and preferably full-blown statutory revision by the creation of new offences. Identifying the point at which D has moved from mere preparation into the territory of attempt is so difficult that the Law Commission initially proposed that the existing offence should be subdivided into: (a) an offence of criminal preparation, which is based on the conduct of D when performing acts which are more than merely preparatory to the commission of the substantive offence; and (b) an offence of attempt which will be narrower than the present law, requiring D to be performing the last acts needed to commit the intended offence. That was an odd solution which did not meet with support on consultation. The present problem is in identifying the boundary between mere preparation and attempt. The Commission proposed creating two boundaries between three categories: no liability, more than mere preparation and attempt. After consultation, the Commission rejected these initial proposals.

11.2.2.4 Attempt by omission

Section 1 of the 1981 Act is drafted in terms of an 'act' being more than merely preparatory. A crime of omission where the actus reus does not include any consequence resulting from the omission is, by its nature, incapable of being attempted.[116] This is not true of an offence including a consequence that may be committed by one having a duty to act. If the parents of a child deliberately withhold food from the child with the intent to kill it, they have set out to commit murder.[117] In fact, they are attempting to commit murder but, in the rare case where it cannot be proved that they did any act contributing to the death, it seems possible that, under the Criminal Attempts Act, they are not guilty of that offence.[118] They have done no 'act', as required by s 1(1). Though the government seems to have supposed that an attempt could be charged in such a case,[119] it would require bold judicial interpretation to read 'act' to include 'omission', although reference to the parliamentary debates would support liability for omissions in such a case.[120]

Cases will be rare where an intention to commit an offence by omission can be proved. In *Nevard*,[121] D seriously injured his wife by striking her with an axe and a knife. He then forced her to abandon her attempt to dial 999 to call for assistance. Despite D's efforts to prevent the emergency services attending, V was found with non-fatal injuries. D was charged with wounding with intent and with attempted murder. The judge directed the jury

---

[115] (1985) 82 Cr App R 314.

[116] For discussion of inchoate crimes as result or conduct crimes, see M Hirst, *Jurisdiction and the Ambit of the Criminal Law* (2003) 134 et seq.

[117] *Gibbins* and *Proctor* (1918) 13 Cr App R 134, p 49. Cf M Gunn and JC Smith, 'Arthur's Case and the Right to Life of a Down's Syndrome Child' [1985] Crim LR 705 at 706.

[118] They are, of course, guilty of the offence of wilful neglect of a young person under the Children and Young Persons Act 1933. See also the offences under the Domestic Violence, Crime and Victims Act 2004, s 5 (as amended by the Domestic Violence, Crime and Victims (Amendment) Act 2012), discussed in Ch 15.

[119] See IH Dennis, 'The Criminal Attempts Act 1981' [1982] Crim LR 5, 7. LCCP 183, paras 12.24, 16.83; LC 318, para 8.142.

[120] See also the discussion of the nurse who, intending to kill a terminally ill patient, omits to replace a life sustaining drip: P Palmer, 'Attempt by Act or Omission: Causation and the Problem of the Hypothetical Nurse' (1999) 63 J Crim L 158.

[121] [2006] EWCA Crim 2896.

to regard D's conduct in preventing the emergency services being contacted as an element of the overall evidence of D's intention to kill. The Court of Appeal upheld the conviction, but suggested that the judge should have made explicit to the jury that attempting to divert the emergency services could not in itself constitute attempted murder. But was not D's conduct in taking the return call and lying a sufficient 'act'? He took positive steps to prevent the emergency services responding to his wife's call. If V dies because D prevents the emergency services from reaching her, or from helping her if they do arrive (eg by keeping them away at gunpoint), that must make D a substantial cause of V's death, even if D was not the one who inflicted the original injuries. If D takes such positive measures to prevent the emergency services arriving, but despite his best efforts V lives, D must surely have attempted to cause V's death.

The Law Commission Report No 318 recommended that the 1981 Act be amended so that D may be convicted of attempted *murder* if (with the intent to kill V) D failed to discharge his legal duty to V (where that omission, unchecked, could have resulted in V's death).[122] The Commission's recommendation to extend liability in relation to murder only appears somewhat arbitrary.

11.2.3 Successful attempts

It has sometimes been argued that failure is essential to the very nature of an attempt so that D should not be convicted for attempting to commit a crime if he was successful in committing it.[123] Section 6(4) of that Act provided:

where a person is charged on indictment with attempting to commit an offence or with an assault or other act preliminary to an offence, but not with the completed offence, then (subject to the discretion of the court to discharge the jury with a view to the preferment of an indictment for the completed offence) he may be convicted of the offence charged notwithstanding that he is shown to be guilty of the completed offence.

This provision does not extend to summary trial. However, in *Webley v Buxton*,[124] it was held that an attempt to commit a misdemeanour did become subsumed within the completed offence at common law.

The 1981 Act makes no provision for this problem[125] so the matter is governed by the common law as stated in *Webley v Buxton*. As a matter of principle, this seems right. At a certain point in the transaction D is guilty of an attempt. The attempt may fail for many reasons, or it may succeed. There is no reason why, if it succeeds, it should cease to be the offence of attempt which, until that moment, it was. The greater includes the less. If D is convicted of attempted murder while his victim, V, is still alive and V then dies of injuries inflicted by D, D is now liable to be convicted of murder; but the conviction for attempt is not invalidated. It would, of course, be improper to convict D of both the attempt and the full offence at the same time. To that extent, the attempt is subsumed within the completed offence.

---

[122] Para 8.151.

[123] Hall, GPCL, 577: 'attempt implies failure . . .'; GP Fletcher, *Rethinking Criminal Law* (1978) 131. In *Commonwealth v Crow*, 303 Pa 91, 98 (1931), the court said 'A failure to consummate a crime is as much an essential element of an attempt as the intent and performance of an overt act towards its commission.' Cf the argument in L Alexander and K Kessler Ferzan with S Morse, *Crime and Culpability: A Theory of Criminal Law* (2009) 203.

[124] [1977] QB 481, overlooked in *Velasquez* [1996] 1 Cr App R 155, which is therefore wrong.

[125] LCCP 102, para 2.113.

11.2.4 Categories of offence which may be subject to an attempt

There are a number of limitations on the scope of the liability for attempt.

11.2.4.1 No liability for attempting summary only offences

At common law it was doubtful whether an attempt to commit an offence triable only summarily was a crime. Under the Act, it is clear that it is not, unless the provision creating the offence expressly provides that it shall be.[126]

Since 1981, the policy aimed at disposing of more cases in magistrates' courts has resulted in an increase in the number of offences that are triable only summarily, including common assault and battery. The effect was to abolish the former offence of attempted assault, which leaves an undesirable gap in the law.[127] It is submitted that there seems to be no good reason why it should not be an offence to attempt to commit a summary only offence and the policy should be reconsidered.[128]

11.2.4.2 Limits on liability for attempts of conspiracy and other secondary liability

Given that inchoate liability is, by definition, some distance removed from the full offence, there are obvious dangers in imposing double inchoate liability—prosecuting D for attempting to conspire with X to encourage Y to steal is preposterous. Limits on multiple inchoate liability need to be set. For attempts, the limits are set in the 1981 Act.

By s 1(4),[129] there can be no liability for attempting to commit crimes of conspiracy, whether common law or statutory,[130] nor offences of assisting an arrestable offender or compounding an arrestable offence contrary to ss 4(1) and 5(1) respectively of the Criminal Law Act 1967.[131] Liability for attempting these offences would be a considerable extension of the law, with the conduct involved being doubly remote from the substantive offence. Nevertheless, somewhat surprisingly, it is an offence under the Act[132] to attempt to commit an offence of assisting or encouraging under the SCA 2007.[133]

---

[126] The indictable offence of criminal damage is now triable only summarily if the damage is not more than £5,000: Magistrates' Courts Act 1980, s 22 and Sch 2. Only damage to the property itself is relevant, not any consequential damage: *R (on the application of Abbott) v Colchester Magistrates' Court* [2001] Crim LR 564, but it has been held that such 'low-value' criminal damage remains an indictable offence. *Bristol Magistrates' Court, ex p E* [1998] 3 All ER 798; *Fennell* [2000] 2 Cr App R 318. It is therefore still an offence to attempt to commit it, however low the value of the damage attempted.

[127] Although common law assault and battery are not indictable offences, they can be charged on indictment if the charge is part of a series of offences of the same or similar character as an indictable offence which is also charged. See s 40(1) of the Criminal Justice Act 1988. This provision was analysed in *Nelson* [2013] EWCA Crim 30, in which the Court of Appeal held that it did have the power to substitute D's conviction for attempted assault with one of attempted battery but declined to do so. The court's conclusion that attempted battery is an offence known to law is, with respect, in error. There must be an offence which is triable on indictment which battery is not, having regard to the definition of indictable offence under the Interpretation Act 1978.

[128] The Law Commission provisionally proposed to reverse the present rule: LCCP 183, para 6.67, cf LC 318, para 8.154.

[129] This result was achieved, rather curiously, by s 8 of the Computer Misuse Act 1990.

[130] See later. Cf the statements in *Harmer* [2005] EWCA Crim 1, [2005] Crim LR 482 and comment.

[131] See Ch 7. Reasons for excluding the offences under the Criminal Law Act 1967 are given in LCCP 102 at paras 2.124–2.126.

[132] As it was at common law, to attempt to commit the common law offence of incitement: *Dunnington* [1984] QB 472. For the common law, see JC Smith, 'Secondary Participation and Inchoate Offences' in *Crime, Proof and Punishment*, 21.

[133] It is possible for D to assist or encourage an attempt: SCA 2007, s 44.

The 1981 Act makes clear that it is not an offence to attempt to aid, abet, counsel, procure or suborn the commission of an offence: s 1(4)(b).[134] Of course, some substantive offences are drafted in terms of aiding and abetting, and in these cases an attempt to commit such an offence is an offence under the 1981 Act. Section 1(4)(b) does not apply because these are not instances of aiding, etc *an offence*. An 'attempt under a special statutory provision' (s 3(1) of the Act) is now governed by the same principles as attempts under the Act.[135]

11.2.4.3 Other exceptional cases where there is no liability for attempt

Apart from the statutory exceptions, there may be other crimes where an attempt charge cannot be pursued. In addition to those cases discussed earlier (summary only offences, conspiracy and aiding and abetting), modern-day offences where no attempt charge is possible include the following:

(1) Where any act done with the appropriate intent amounts to the complete crime. Such crimes are rare but one may be the form of treason known as compassing the Queen's death. The offence requires proof of an overt act but it seems that any act done with intent to kill the Queen would be enough.

(2) A crime defined as an omission[136] where the actus reus does not include any consequence of the omission, as in the case of some statutory offences of omission.

(3) It is difficult to conceive of an attempt where the actus reus is a state of affairs, such as 'being found' in particular circumstances.[137]

(4) It has been argued that there ought to be no liability for an offence that may be committed recklessly or negligently but not intentionally. The example most often used which comes readily to mind is involuntary manslaughter. The essence of this crime is that the killing is unintentional. An intentional killing (in the absence of diminished responsibility, the conditions for infanticide, loss of self-control[138] or a suicide pact) is necessarily murder. Section 1(1) of the 1981 Act requires an intention to commit the offence which D is charged with attempting and on this view an intent to commit involuntary manslaughter is not a concept known to law. What, however, of D who intends to commit a strict liability offence but is foiled in the process—why should he not be liable for attempting to commit that offence? If liability can arise for strict liability, why not for the offence of manslaughter?[139]

11.2.5 Jurisdictional issues

11.2.5.1 Attempt in England to commit an offence abroad

D may be prosecuted for attempt under the Act (as amended[140]) where D intends an offence to be committed outside England and Wales, provided that the more than merely preparatory act D performs is done in England or Wales and the result attempted would be both an

---

[134] For arguments as to whether the section is superfluous now that the SCA 2007, Part 2 is in force, see M Bohlander, 'The Conflict Between the Serious Crime Act and s 1(4)(b) of the Criminal Attempts Act 1981' [2010] Crim LR 483 and J Child who rejects the claim at [2010] Crim LR 924. There is considerable force in Bohlander's argument that the provision should have been repealed.

[135] The Law Commission's proposals in relation to double inchoate offences in LCCP 183, Ch 7 recommended that it should be an offence to attempt to conspire: para 7.57. This surely goes too far.

[136] Attempt by omission generally is considered at p 450.   [137] See p 43.

[138] For attempted infanticide, see *KA Smith* [1983] Crim LR 739 (Crown Court), p 663; and for attempt under provocation, *Bruzas* [1972] Crim LR 367 (Crown Court), and *Campbell* [1997] Crim LR 495 (Crown Court) (Sedley J) and commentary.

[139] cf Simester, Spencer, Stark, Sullivan and Virgo, CLT&D, 345.

[140] Subsection (1A), inserted by the Criminal Justice Act 1993, s 5(2).

indictable offence as defined by English law and an offence by the law of the other country.[141] If D, a British citizen, posts a letter bomb from England to V in France, intending to kill V in France, he is liable to conviction for attempted murder as soon as the letter is posted;[142] but, if he intends only to injure V, he is not guilty of an attempt to cause him grievous or actual bodily harm. This is because murder abroad by a British citizen is triable in England but lesser offences against the person are not. If D were a foreign citizen, then he could not be tried in England for attempted murder. This seems anomalous, particularly since two foreigners could, since 1977, be convicted of conspiring in England to commit murder abroad.[143]

The jurisdiction of the court has also been extended to certain cases where an act is done in England and Wales that would be an attempt under the Act, but for the fact that the offence, if completed, would not be triable in England and Wales.[144]

11.2.5.2 Attempt abroad to commit an offence in England

It was settled before the Act by the decision of the House of Lords in *DPP v Stonehouse*[145] that an act done abroad with intent thereby to cause the commission of an offence in England could be prosecuted here (even if done by an innocent agent[146]), at least if it had an effect in England. D, in Miami, falsely staged his death by drowning with the intent that his innocent wife in England should claim life assurance monies. He was guilty of attempting to enable his wife to obtain by deception. His acts abroad would have the 'effect' of communicating through the media to his wife and the insurance companies the false statement that he had died.[147] In *Somchai Liangsiriprasert v United States Government*,[148] the Privy Council, holding that a conspiracy abroad to commit an offence in England is indictable even though no overt act has been done within this jurisdiction, said, *obiter*, that the same rule applies to attempt. The Act has nothing to say on the question so it remains a matter of common law. This may be taken to have been settled by *Liangsiriprasert*.

11.2.5.3 Attempt abroad to commit an offence abroad

D, a British citizen, while in France, attempts to kill V in France or, knowing himself to be married, attempts to go through a ceremony of marriage there with X. If he succeeds he will be liable to conviction in England of murder and bigamy. Exceptionally, English law assumes jurisdiction over these crimes when committed abroad by a British citizen. Literally, then, the attempt is an offence under the Act. It has been argued that the presumption against the extraterritorial operation of the criminal law[149] requires the words 'does an act' to be construed as applicable only to acts done within the jurisdiction, or having, or being intended to have, some effect therein; but this argument has less weight after *Liangsiriprasert*. If the court has jurisdiction over the full offence when wholly committed abroad, why not over the attempt?

---

[141] See, generally, Hirst, *Jurisdiction and the Ambit of the Criminal Law*, Ch 4.

[142] See p 524.   [143] See p 480.

[144] This applies to an offence under s 3 of the Computer Misuse Act 1990: s 1(1A) and (1B) of the Act; and to a 'Group A offence' as defined in Part 1 of the Criminal Justice Act 1993: s 1A of the Act. This includes all the major offences under the Theft Act 1968, the Fraud Act 2006 and the Forgery and Counterfeiting Act 1981, and the common law offence of cheating the public revenue.

[145] [1978] AC 55.

[146] cf *Latif* [1996] 2 Cr App R 92, [1996] Crim LR 414 and commentary. But if D knows or believes E to have mens rea, he is guilty, not of an attempt, but under the offences in the SCA 2007, Part 2.

[147] Lord Keith insisted that an effect within the jurisdiction was essential but Lord Diplock thought otherwise. Why should the result have been different if D had been rescued from the sea and confessed before any report of his death appeared in England?

[148] (1991) 92 Cr App R 77 at 87–90.

[149] See Griew, *Current Law Statutes*, General Note.

11.2.6 Abandonment

Once D's steps towards the commission of an offence are sufficiently far advanced to amount to an attempt—they are beyond mere preparation—it can make no difference whether the failure to complete the crime is owing to a voluntary abandonment by D, the intervention of the police or any other reason.[150] In *Taylor*,[151] it was held that an attempt was committed where D approached a stack of corn with the intention of setting fire to it and lit a match for that purpose but abandoned his plan on noticing that he was being watched. Following the recommendation of the Law Commission,[152] the 1981 Act made no change to the common law in this respect. The principal argument in favour of an abandonment defence is that it might induce the attempter to desist—but this seems unlikely. The existence of such a defence would add to the problems of law enforcement authorities as defendants caught before the last act would no doubt claim that they were in the process of desisting and had no intention of going beyond the stage they had reached. In some jurisdictions, however, logic has given way to policy and a defence of free and voluntary desistance is allowed.[153]

11.3 Conspiracy

11.3.1 Introduction

A criminal conspiracy is, in simple terms, an agreement between two or more persons to commit a crime. The general statutory offence of conspiracy under the Criminal Law Act 1977 exists alongside some specific common law conspiracy offences that have been preserved.

Historically, at common law, conspiracy was defined as an agreement to do an unlawful act or a lawful act by unlawful means.[154] The word 'unlawful' was used in a broad sense to include crimes, even some torts, and some immoral acts. The offence therefore included agreements to perform not only any crime triable in England, even a crime triable only summarily, but also at least: (a) fraud; (b) the corruption of public morals; (c) the outraging of public decency; and (d) some torts. In this respect it went far beyond the other inchoate offences of incitement and attempt, where the result incited or attempted must be a crime. For many years until *DPP v Withers*,[155] in 1974 the crime of conspiracy was believed to be even wider, including any agreement to effect a public mischief.

---

[150] See M Wasik, 'Abandoning Criminal Intent' [1980] Crim LR 785; Duff, *Criminal Attempts*, 65–75; Yaffe *Attempts*, Ch 11. For comparisons with Dutch and German approaches, see J Keiler, *Actus Reus and Participation in European Criminal Law* (2013) 404 et seq.

[151] (1859) 1 F & F 511; see also *Lankford* [1959] Crim LR 209. It is doubtful whether Taylor's desistance was 'free and voluntary' in the sense that he was motivated by a desire to avoid detection.

[152] LC 102, paras 2.131–2.133.

[153] See D Stuart, 'The *Actus Reus* in Attempts' [1970] Crim LR at 519–21. See the Draft Scots Code which provides a defence where D 'voluntarily abandons his attempt as a result of repentance before all acts necessary for the commission of the offence were done', cl 18(2).

[154] By Lord Denman CJ in *Jones* (1832) 4 B & Ad 345, KB, at 349. But a few years later in *Peck* (1839) 9 Ad & El 686 at 690 he declared, 'I do not think the antithesis very correct.' For an historical account, see LCCP 183, Ch 3.

[155] [1975] AC 842. Conspiracy to commit the common law offence of public nuisance continues to be a potential source of expansion of the criminal law. See commentary on *Soul* (1980) 70 Cr App R 295. The House of Lords confirmed the ECHR compatibility of the offence of public nuisance: *Rimmington* [2005] UKHL 63.

It has long been the generally approved aim of the Law Commission that:

The crime of conspiracy should be limited to agreements to commit criminal offences: an agreement should not be criminal where that which it was agreed to be done would not amount to a criminal offence if committed by one person.[156]

The Criminal Law Act 1977 created a new offence of statutory conspiracy based on the policy that an agreement should not be criminal where that which it was agreed to be done would not amount to a criminal offence if committed by one person.[157] It is therefore an offence to agree with another that a crime (whether statutory or common law) will be committed.

However, the common law versions of conspiracy that are preserved alongside the 1977 Act are wider. Agreeing to engage in conduct which would not be criminal if performed by one actor alone may be criminal under those: conspiracy to defraud, conspiracy to corrupt public morals or to outrage public decency.[158] The retention of these common law conspiracies is controversial. The Law Commission has repeatedly proposed abolition,[159] but the government remains unwilling to run the risk by removing flexible common law offences that might prove necessary to deal with some unforeseen scenario that would fall outside the scope of statutory conspiracy.[160]

Despite amendment by the Criminal Attempts Act 1981 and the Criminal Justice Act 1987, the Criminal Law Act 1977, which is the principal topic under examination in this part of the chapter, remains an ill-drafted piece of legislation presenting numerous problems of interpretation. The arguments for reform to clarify the position seem compelling. In 2009, the Law Commission produced proposals in which recommendations for a wider, and yet more complex, form of conspiracy were advanced.[161]

11.3.2 Summary of present law

Whether a particular agreement between D1 and D2 is a statutory conspiracy under the Criminal Law Act or a conspiracy at common law, or both, the offence involves an agreement. That is not a mere mental operation, but must involve spoken or written words or other overt acts. If D1 repents and withdraws immediately after the agreement has been concluded, he is guilty[162] and his repentance is a matter of mitigation only.

---

[156] LC 76, *Conspiracy and Criminal Law Reform* (1976) para 1.113; see also Law Commission Working Paper No 50.

[157] LC 76, para 1.113; see also Law Commission Working Paper No 50.

[158] Cases since the 1977 Act (*May* (1989) 91 Cr App R 157; *Gibson* [1990] 2 QB 619; *Rowley* [1991] 4 All ER 649,) confirming that it is an offence for a person acting alone to do acts tending to corrupt public morals create a doubt whether there is any scope for the operation of common law conspiracy to do these things.

[159] As with the call for abolition of conspiracy to defraud in LC 276, *Fraud* (2002). See further Ormerod and Williams, *Smith's Law of Theft*, Ch 5.

[160] There is the irony—if it is so unforeseeable, prosecuting it is likely to run into difficulty under Art 7. See also *Norris v US* [2008] UKHL 16 holding that while price fixing in itself was not, prior to 2002, an offence under English law, when combined with other elements such as deliberate misrepresentation, it could lead to various offences such as fraud or conspiracy to defraud. See also *GG Plc* [2008] UKHL 17.

[161] See LCCP 183; LC 318.

[162] As in the *Bridgewater Case*, unreported, referred to by Lord Coleridge CJ in the *Mogul Steamship Case* (1888) 21 QBD 544 at 549.

11.3.2.1 Statutory conspiracy

It is an offence of conspiracy, triable only on indictment, to agree to commit any criminal offence, even an offence triable only summarily.[163] This is a 'statutory' conspiracy under the Criminal Law Act 1977. It is not limited to agreements to commit a statutory crime— agreements to commit the common law offence of murder are charged under this offence— rather, the term 'statutory conspiracy' is used to distinguish it from 'common law conspiracies'.

11.3.2.2 Common law conspiracies

It is an offence triable only on indictment to agree:

(1) to defraud, whether or not the fraud amounts to a crime or even a tort;[164]

(2) to do an act which tends to corrupt public morals or outrage public decency, whether or not that act amounts to a crime.

The 1977 Act has no part to play in the prosecution of such offences.

11.3.2.3 Relationship between common law and statutory conspiracies

Section 1(1) of the 1977 Act creates the offence of statutory conspiracy. It provides in effect that it is a conspiracy to agree to commit *any* offence. Section 5(2) and (3)[165] preserve common law conspiracies of conspiracy to defraud and conspiracies to corrupt public morals and outrage public decency. Statutory conspiracies and common law conspiracies to corrupt public morals or to outrage public decency remain mutually exclusive. Section 5 was amended to rectify an error in earlier drafting which rendered statutory and all common law conspiracies mutually exclusive.[166] But s 12 of the Criminal Justice Act 1987 provides that statutory conspiracy and conspiracy to defraud are not mutually exclusive. An agreement to commit a crime involving fraud or dishonesty is both a statutory conspiracy and a conspiracy to defraud. The prosecutor will frequently have a choice.[167] In *Dady*,[168] applying *Rimmington*,[169] it was held that where an agreement could be charged as a statutory conspiracy or as a conspiracy to defraud, it should ordinarily be charged as a statutory conspiracy unless there is good reason to charge conspiracy to defraud instead.

The broad and flexible nature of the conspiracy to defraud offence ensures its continued popularity with prosecutors. It is a 'not yet rusty and still trusty' weapon.[170]

---

[163] LCCP 183, para 6.58 on summary conspiracies. In LC 318 it was recommended to remove the present requirement for the DPP to give consent if proceedings to prosecute a conspiracy to commit a summary offence are to be initiated: para 4.35.

[164] See the House of Lords decision on the scope of the common law offence in *GG Plc* [2008] UKHL 17. See the extensive discussion in the Crown Court decision in *Evans and others* [2014] 1 WLR 2817 discussed by P Jarvis [2014] Crim LR 738.

[165] As amended by the Criminal Justice Act 1987.

[166] See *Ayres* [1984] AC 447. The House substantially modified the effect of *Ayres*, as generally understood, in the decision in *Cooke* [1986] AC 909.

[167] To be exercised in accordance with the Attorney General's guidance of 2007 issued to ensure appropriate use of conspiracy to defraud after the Fraud Act 2006 came into force and s 6 of the general guidance in the Code for Crown Prosecutors issued by the DPP under s 10(1) of the Prosecution of Offences Act 1985.

[168] [2013] EWHC 475 (QB).

[169] [2005] UKHL 63.

[170] Auld LJ in *Norris v US* [2007] EWHC 71 (Admin), [66]. But on the need to exercise care in charging the offence, note *Evans and others* [2014] 1 WLR 2817, Cardiff Crown Court, and the comment by P Jarvis [2014] Crim LR 738.

11.3.3 Statutory conspiracy

The offence of statutory conspiracy is defined by s 1(1) and s 1(2) of the Act.[171] Section 1(1) (as amended by s 5 of the Criminal Attempts Act 1981) provides:

Subject to the following provisions of this part of the Act, if a person agrees with any other person or persons that a course of conduct shall be pursued which, if the agreement is carried out in accordance with their intentions, either—

>   (a) will necessarily amount to or involve the commission of any offence or offences by one or more of the parties to the agreement, or

>   (b) would do so but for the existence of facts which render the commission of the offence or any of the offences impossible, he is guilty of conspiracy to commit the offence or offences in question.

Conspiracy is a crime where it is more difficult than usual to distinguish between actus reus and mens rea. The actus reus is said to be the agreement: but agreement is essentially a mental operation, though it must be manifested by or inferred from acts of some kind. 'In the case of conspiracy as opposed to the substantive offence, it is what was agreed to be done and not what was in fact done which is all important.'[172] The elements of the offence are best listed and examined separately rather than divided into sub-categories of mens rea and actus reus. They are:

(1) an agreement;

(2) that a course of conduct will be pursued;

(3) the course of conduct will necessarily amount to the commission of an offence if carried out in accordance with the defendants' intentions;

(4) the defendants had an intention to agree;

(5) the defendants had an intention that the agreement will be carried out;

(6) the defendants had an intention or knowledge as to any circumstances forming part of the substantive offence.

11.3.3.1 The agreement

Surprisingly, the courts have failed to define with precision what conduct suffices to constitute the completed agreement. It is not necessary to prove an agreement in the strict sense required by the law of contract,[173] but the parties must at least have reached a decision[174] that their unlawful object is to be carried out. Difficult questions may arise in cases where parties are at the stage of negotiating subject to final details being agreed, for example D1 agrees to sell D2 certain goods, known to both to be stolen, at 'a price to be agreed between

---

[171] For the background to Part I of the Criminal Law Act, see Law Commission Working Papers No 50, *Inchoate Offences* (1973); No 56, *Conspiracy to Defraud* (1974); No 57, *Conspiracies Relating to Morals and Decency* (1974); and No 63, *Conspiracies to Effect a Public Mischief and to Commit a Civil Wrong* (1975); and see LC 76, *Conspiracy and Criminal Law Reform* (1976). For the interpretation of the Act, see EJ Griew, 'Annotations on the Act' in *Current Law Statutes*; JC Smith, 'Conspiracy under the Criminal Law Act 1977 (1)' [1977] Crim LR 598 and 638; DW Elliott, '*Mens Rea* in Statutory Conspiracy' [1978] Crim LR 202; G Williams, 'The New Statutory Offence of Conspiracy' (1977) 127 NLJ 1164 and 1188; D Ormerod, 'Making Sense of Statutory Conspiracies' (2006) 59 CLP 185.

[172] *Bolton* (1991) 94 Cr App R 74 at 80 per Woolf LJ. See also the commentary at [1992] Crim LR 57.

[173] See G Orchard, 'Agreement in Criminal Conspiracy' [1974] Crim LR 297 at 335.

[174] cf Williams, CLGP, 212.

us'.[175] In *Walker*,[176] a conviction was quashed although it was 'perfectly clear' that D1 had discussed with D2 and D3 the proposition of stealing a payroll, because it was not proved that they had got beyond the stage of negotiation when D1 withdrew. Once the parties have agreed, the conspiracy is complete, even if they take no further action because, for example, they are arrested.

Conspiracy is a continuing offence.[177] The offence offers a significant attraction for prosecutors because of this opportunity to roll together a course of criminal conduct under one charge on the one indictment.[178]

The offence lies in agreeing with another that a crime will be committed. That is different from agreeing that D will commit the crime himself. D can be convicted of conspiracy even though he personally will not be participating in the commission of the substantive offence. The Law Commission's latest recommendation is that a conspiracy 'must involve an agreement by two or more persons *to engage in the conduct element of an offence* and (where relevant) to bring about any consequence element of the substantive offence'.[179] The recommendation would make a radical change to the law narrowing it considerably if each D must agree that he will engage in the conduct of the commission of the substantive offence. It is submitted that the recommendation should not be adopted. It ought to have reflected the present law—what is required is that D agrees and intends that the conduct of the substantive offence be performed by at least one party to the agreement.

Wheel and chain conspiracies

A conviction for conspiracy can arise without proof that the persons accused of conspiring together were in direct communication with one another. It may be that the conspiracy revolves around some third party, X, who is in touch with each of D1, D2 and D3, though they are not in touch with one another (a 'wheel conspiracy'). Provided that the result is that they have a common design—for example, to rob a particular bank—D1, D2 and D3 may properly be prosecuted for conspiring together though they have never been in touch with one another. The same is true of a chain conspiracy where D1 communicates with D2, D2 with D3, etc.[180] In either case it must be proved, of course, that each accused has agreed with another guilty person in relation to that single conspiracy.[181]

What has to be ascertained is always the same matter: is it true to say . . . that the acts of the accused were done in pursuance of a criminal purpose held in common between them?[182]

These propositions are well established,[183] but some of the older cases demonstrate some questionable application of the principles. In *Meyrick*,[184] D1 and D2, nightclub proprietors,

[175] *May and Butcher Ltd v R* [1934] 2 KB 17n.
[176] [1962] Crim LR 458; *Mulcahy v R* (1868) LR 3 HL 306 at 317. Careful jury direction is needed: *Webster* [2003] EWCA Crim 1946 (conspiracy to cheat the Revenue).
[177] *DPP v Doot* [1973] AC 807.
[178] See the comments of Lord Hope in *Saik* [2006] UKHL 18, [2006] Crim LR 998 and commentary.
[179] LC 318, recommendation 1, p 493. Surprisingly, this would enact the very error made by the House of Lords in *Anderson* [1986] AC 27.
[180] This passage in the 13th edn was cited with approval by the Court of Appeal in *Shillam* [2013] EWCA Crim 160.
[181] *Ardalan* [1972] 2 All ER 257 at 261.
[182] *Meyrick* (1929) 21 Cr App R 94 at 102 and *Griffiths* [1966] 1 QB 589, applied in *Chrastny* [1991] 1 WLR 1381; *Mintern* [2004] EWCA Crim 7; *Clark* [2012] EWCA Crim 1220; *Papachristos and Kerrison* [2014] EWCA Crim 1863; *Bhatti* [2015] EWCA Crim 1305.
[183] See eg *Cooper and Compton* [1947] 2 All ER 701; *Sweetland* (1957) 42 Cr App R 62. For a more recent analysis, see *Mehta* [2012] EWCA Crim 2824 and *Crocker* [2012] EWCA Crim 1762.
[184] See n 182.

each separately offered bribes to a police sergeant, E, to induce him to ignore breaches of the licensing laws in respect of their own premises. They were convicted of conspiring, inter alia, to contravene the licensing laws. The jury were directed that there must be a 'common design'. D1 and D2 were convicted, but it is difficult to see how the evidence justified this finding. The intent of each nightclub proprietor was simply to evade the licensing laws in respect of his own premises. There was no common design, merely parallel equivalent ones. *Meyrick* was distinguished in *Griffiths*[185] on the rather unconvincing ground that it related to a small geographical area (Soho), so the jury could come to the conclusion that 'the night-club proprietors in that district well knew what was happening generally in relation to the police'.[186] But this cannot be right. Even if D1 and D2 each knew that the other had made a similar agreement with E, it would seem that there were two separate and specific conspiracies, not one general one.

The challenge is often in distinguishing the existence of a common design as, for example, between D1, D2 and D3, rather than a series of parallel similar ones: D1 and D2, D1 and D3, etc. This is clear in the following example.

I employ an accountant to make out my tax return. He and his clerk are both present when I am about to sign the return. I notice an item in my expenses of £100 and say: 'I don't remember incurring this expense.' The clerk says: 'Well, actually I put it in. You didn't incur it, but I didn't think you would object to a few pounds being saved.' The accountant indicates his agreement to this attitude. After some hesitation I agree to let it stand. On those bare facts I cannot be charged with fifty others in a conspiracy to defraud [Inland Revenue] of £100,000 on the basis that this accountant and his clerk have persuaded 500 other clients to make false returns, some being false in one way, some in another, or even all in the same way. I have not knowingly attached myself to a general agreement to defraud.[187]

It is submitted that the position would be no different if the accountant had said: 'We do this for all our clients'; there would still have been a series of conspiracies, not one general conspiracy.[188] These difficulties in describing forms of conspiracy were addressed by the Court of Appeal in *Shillam*,[189] in which S and others were charged with conspiring with each other and with persons unknown, to supply cocaine. The evidence against them included text messages from people wanting to buy cocaine, quantities of the drug, quantities of cutting agent, etc. The prosecution case did not assert that S and R (one of the co-defendants) knew each other, but that both knew X (another co-defendant) and obtained drugs from him. The judge directed the jury that the critical question was: 'did the particular defendant whose case you are considering agree with at least one other person at some point during the period on the indictment that cocaine should be supplied to someone else?' The Court of Appeal quashed S's conviction. It was held that the jury may have been misled by the direction, as it allowed for the possibility that all three defendants could be convicted of separate conspiracies with different people. That was not what was charged. In quashing S's conviction, the court reiterated its earlier conclusion in *Mehta*:[190] conspiracy requires a single joint design between the conspirators within the terms of the indictment. It is always necessary that for two or more persons to be convicted of a single conspiracy each of them must be proved to have shared a common purpose or design. The court confirmed that although each conspirator need not necessarily know the identity or even the existence of all the other conspirators, there must be a shared criminal purpose or design in which all have joined, rather than merely similar or parallel ones. Toulson LJ emphasized that the prosecution should always think carefully

---

185 (1965) 49 Cr App R 279.   186 ibid, 291.

187 Paull J, ibid. Cf the argument of Maddocks in *Meyrick* (1929) 45 TLR 421 at 422.

188 The convictions in *Griffiths* were quashed as the evidence did not establish the single 'wheel conspiracy' alleged.

189 [2013] EWCA Crim 160.   190 [2012] EWCA Crim 2824.

before making use of the law of conspiracy, how to formulate the conspiracy charge or charges and whether charging a substantive offence or offences would be more appropriate.[191] The same points were reiterated more recently in *Johnson and others*.[192] Simon LJ observed that the need to show a common design and an awareness of the common design highlights the danger to the prosecution of charging a single conspiracy rather than what may be a series of substantive offences or different conspiracies, when the offending involves a group of people over a substantial period. Such offending may, on a proper analysis, be the result of a series of transactions or agreements, and a single conspiracy may be impossible to prove. Having the conspiracy correctly charged is, of course, also important when it comes to sentencing.[193]

Who can be a party to the agreement?
Corporations
A company may be convicted of an offence of conspiracy.[194] It must be proved that D conspired with another person but that other need not be identified.[195] If the managing director of a company resolves to perpetrate an illegality in the company's name, but communicates this to no other person, there is no conspiracy between him and the company[196] as was emphasized recently in *Alstom*.[197] In the civil law, as *Lee v Lee's Air Farming Ltd* demonstrates,[198] it is possible for there to be a conspiracy where the company is alleged to have conspired with only one human agent, who is the very person identified with that company. As others have argued,[199] there is no principled reason why the criminal law should deviate from the civil law in this regard.[200]

Statutory exceptions
In statutory conspiracies there are three cases in which the requirement of two parties is not satisfied. By s 2(2) of the Act, a person is not guilty of a statutory conspiracy:

if the only other person or persons with whom he agrees are (both initially and at all times during the currency of the agreement) persons of any one or more of the following descriptions, that is to say—

  (a) his spouse[201] or civil partner;

  (b) a person under the age of criminal responsibility; and

  (c) an intended victim of that offence or of each of those offences.

---

[191] For discussion of this issue, see P Jarvis and M Bisgrove, 'The Use and Abuse of Conspiracy' [2014] Crim LR 261. For an example of a case in which D's conviction was quashed because there was insufficient evidence that he was party to the same agreement as his alleged co-conspirators, see *Mehtab* [2015] EWCA Crim 1665. By way of contrast, D's conviction was upheld in *Dad* [2017] EWCA Crim 321, as Macur LJ held that the summing up alerted the jury to the requirement that they must be sure there was only one conspiracy.

[192] [2020] EWCA Crim 482 recognizing that the evidence may show the existence of a narrower conspiracy involving fewer people, in which case it is not intrinsically wrong for the jury to return guilty verdicts in relation to those people.

[193] *Griffin* [2018] EWCA Crim 2538.   [194] *ICR Haulage Ltd* [1944] KB 551.

[195] *Phillips* (1987) 86 Cr App R 18, discussed [1988] Crim LR at 338.

[196] To allow such an indictment would be to 'offend against the basic concept of a conspiracy, namely an agreement of two or more to do an unlawful act . . . it would be artificial to take the view that the company, although it is clearly a separate legal entity can be regarded here as a separate entity or a separate mind . . .', *McDonnell* [1966] 1 QB 233 (Nield J). Cf *ICR Haulage Ltd* [1944] KB 551. A conviction might ensue if D agrees with his company in his capacity as a person responsible for the acts of another corporation rather than as the person responsible for his company: see the Canadian cases cited in *McDonnell*. The validity of *McDonnell* was confirmed by the Court of Appeal in *A Ltd* [2016] EWCA Crim 1469.

[197] [2019] EWCA Crim 1318.   [198] [1961] AC 12.

[199] Simester, Spencer, Stark, Sullivan and Virgo, CLT&D, 335.

[200] For further discussion, see P Jarvis, 'Conspiring with Oneself' [2017] Arch Rev 7.

[201] The Court of Appeal in *Bala* [2016] EWCA Crim 560 held that the term 'spouse' means a husband or wife in a marriage recognized under English law. Therefore, if the defendants' marriage was void (eg being polygamous) under s 11 of the Matrimonial Causes Act 1973, they cannot rely upon s 2(2)(a) of the 1977 Act.

Spouses/civil partners   Paragraph (a) restates the rule of the common law[202] which adopted the fiction that husband and wife were one person with one will. The application of the rule to statutory conspiracies is based upon a social policy of preserving the stability of marriage.[203] The rule applies only where the parties are married at the time of the agreement. Marriage after the conspiracy or during its continuance is no defence.[204] A wife is guilty, though she agrees only with her husband, if she knows that there are other parties to the conspiracy.[205] There is no protection against prosecution should the couple be charged with the substantive offence having perpetrated the offence as they agreed. The protection extends only to conspiracies exclusive to the couple; if they agree with a third party the conspiracy can be prosecuted.[206] It is anomalous and anachronistic and the Law Commission has recommended abolition.[207] In declining to extend the exemption to unmarried couples in committed relationships, the Court of Appeal in *Suski* appears also to have taken the view that it is anachronistic.

Infants[208]   For the purposes of paragraph (b) a person is under the age of criminal responsibility 'so long as it is conclusively presumed by section 50 of the Children and Young Persons Act 1933,[209] that he cannot be guilty of any offence'[210]—that is, he is under the age of ten.

Victims   The Act does not define 'victim'. The Supreme Court in *Gnango*[211] suggested, *obiter*, that 'victim' in s 2 ought to be given a narrow meaning. Lord Phillips observed that if 'victim' were to be interpreted widely then it would produce the surprising result that an agreement by two persons that one will act as a suicide bomber would not attract criminal liability. The Supreme Court adopted the formulation of the victim rule advanced by Glanville Williams.[212] Williams thought that a person would be a victim where:

> the courts perceive the legislation is designed for the protection of a class of persons. Such people should not be convicted as accessories to an offence committed in respect of them when they cooperate in it. Nor should they be convicted as conspirators.[213]

It is unclear whether D and V who agree to engage in sadomasochistic activity together would commit a conspiracy to commit GBH or ABH at the time of the agreement,[214] although Lord Phillips in *Gnango* stated, *obiter*, that there would be no bar to convicting the 'victims' of the sadomasochistic acts of having aided and abetted offences against themselves.[215]

---

[202] See eg Hawkins, I PC, c 27, s 8 and *Mawji v R* [1957] AC 126.

[203] LCCP 76, paras 1.46–1.49. In *Suski* [2016] EWCA Crim 24, the Court of Appeal considered whether the exemption violates Arts 8 and 14 of the ECHR on the basis that it extends only to those couples who are married or in a civil partnership. The court rejected this argument and held that there was no reason to extend any further than statute required a rule of the common law which had come to be regarded as anomalous today.

[204] *Robinson's Case* (1746) 1 Leach 37.   [205] *Chrastny* [1991] 1 WLR 1381; *Lovick* [1993] Crim LR 890.

[206] *Chrastny*, ibid. See also *Singh* [2011] EWCA Crim 2992.   [207] See LC 318, para 5.16.

[208] The Law Commission recommended that the rule that an agreement involving a person of or over the age of criminal responsibility and a child under the age of criminal responsibility gives rise to no criminal liability for conspiracy should be retained. LC 318, para 5.45.

[209] See p 360.   [210] Section 2(3) of the Act.   [211] [2011] UKSC 59.

[212] Support for such an interpretation was derived from the SCA 2007, s 51, which explicitly refers to offences that exist wholly or in part for the protection of a particular category of persons. See p 503. It has been suggested that since s 2(1) of the Criminal Law Act 1977 does not use this terminology, it can plausibly be assumed that Parliament intended this section to be given a broad interpretation. See C de Than and J Elvin, 'Towards a Rational Reconstruction of the Law on Secondary Participation and Inchoate Offences: Conspiracy' in A Reed and M Bohlander (eds), *Participation in Crime—Domestic and Comparative Perspectives* (2013).

[213] G Williams, 'Victims and Other Exempt Parties in Crime' (1990) 10 LS 245.

[214] See *Brown* [1994] 1 AC 212, p 712.

[215] [2011] UKSC 59, [53]. For further discussion, see J Herring, 'Victims as Defendants: When Victims Participate in Crimes Against Themselves' in A Reed and M Bohlander (eds), *Participation in Crime—Domestic and Comparative Perspectives* (2013). This would be subject to proving the requisite mens rea of intention.

This is because GBH and ABH are not designed for the protection of a class of persons, but are offences of general application. By contrast, if a 14-year-old girl were to agree with her 16-year-old boyfriend that they will have sex, there would be no liability for conspiracy as the offences in ss 9 to 15 of the Sexual Offences Act 2003 are designed for the protection of a designated class, namely those under the age of 16. There appears to be no common law authority in point and the question seems unlikely to arise on a charge of conspiracy at common law since an agreement to defraud with the victim of the fraud is difficult to imagine. It remains to be seen whether the narrow interpretation the Supreme Court suggested in *Gnango* ought to be given to s 2 will prevail.

The Law Commission recommended reform of the rule.[216]

Solo conspirators

The 1977 Act does not deal with other cases where one of two parties to the agreement could not be liable to prosecution for the substantive offence, but it is clear that there may be a conspiracy although only one party is capable of committing the substantive offence as a principal. If, for example, the offence can be committed only by a licensee and A, who is a licensee, agrees with B, a customer who is incapable of committing the substantive offence as a principal (because B is not a licensee), that A will do so, there is a conspiracy to contravene the licensing legislation. The course of conduct will necessarily amount to the commission of the offence by one of the parties.[217]

In *Duguid*,[218] D agreed with E to remove a child of whom E was the mother from the possession of her lawful guardian. This would have been a crime by D under s 56 of the OAPA, but it was provided that a mother should not be liable to prosecution on account of taking her own child. It was held that E's 'immunity from prosecution for an act done by herself' was no bar to the conviction of D for conspiracy. The court did not find it necessary to decide whether E could have been convicted of the conspiracy.[219] This suggests that there may be a conspiracy with only one guilty party but the case is far from clear because the court may have accepted the argument of the prosecution that any bar to the prosecution of E was of a procedural nature. The better view is that there must be two conspirators.[220]

Mentally disordered conspirators

The Act does not deal with an agreement with a mentally disordered person so the common law, whatever it may be, applies to all conspiracies. In 1976 the Law Commission thought express provision unnecessary because 'a purported agreement with a person who is so mentally disordered as to be incapable of forming the intent necessary for the substantive offence will not be an agreement within clause 1(1) of the draft Bill [now, in substance, s 1(1) of the Act]'.[221] This seems to be right in the case of a mentally disordered person who does not know the nature and quality of the proposed act; but a person who, through mental disorder, does not know the proposed act is 'wrong' may be perfectly capable of forming the intent to commit it with full knowledge of the facts and circumstances.[222] In such a case it

---

[216] LC 318, para 5.35. The reform would result in the following: D1, aged 15, conspires with D2, 16, that P, 18, should have sex with D1. D1 has the defence, D2 does not.

[217] B will be liable as a secondary party if the offence is committed.

[218] (1906) 21 Cox CC 200. Cf *Sherry and El Yamani* [1993] Crim LR 537.

[219] The language used suggests that she might well have been guilty of conspiracy and of secondary participation in the ulterior offence if D had committed it, whether or not she could have been prosecuted. Section 56 has been repealed by the Child Abduction Act 1984, p 766 but the similar problems which could arise under that Act should be resolved in the same way.

[220] cf *Yip Chiu-Cheung*, p 91.   [221] LC 76, 22, n 156.

[222] cf *Matusevich v R* (1977) 51 ALJR 657 at 670 per Aickin J (High Ct of Aust).

is arguable that the party to the agreement who does not have a mental illness is guilty of a statutory conspiracy though the mentally ill person is not because it is sufficient that the carrying out of the agreement will amount to an offence by *one of the parties*.[223]

An agreement creating multiple conspiracies?

A single agreement between D1 and D2 may involve them in two or more conspiracies. There is nothing to prevent their being charged as such. Where D1 and D2 agreed to buy cannabis in Thailand and import it into the UK, a conviction in Thailand for conspiracy to possess cannabis for sale did not bar a prosecution in England for conspiracy to import the cannabis into England.[224] But where there is a general conspiracy to commit offences of a certain type, perhaps extending over a lengthy period, agreements to commit particular offences of that type may be treated simply as evidence of the general conspiracy.[225]

In *Ali*,[226] the Crown had originally alleged that D was party to a conspiracy to murder. At trial that count was amended so that it became more specific—to murder by detonating improvised explosive devices (IEDs) on transatlantic passenger aircraft. A second count alleging conspiracy to murder in general was added. The Court of Appeal accepted that on the unusual facts of the case, it was permissible for the Crown to charge two conspiracies though each involved an agreement to commit the same substantive offence of murder. A wider agreement or conspiracy would not preclude the existence of sub-agreements or sub-conspiracies to cause explosions in particular places. As a matter of law those sub-conspiracies or agreements could properly be charged as separate offences. However, it was essential that the conspiracies in the counts were different. Although the object was to commit the same underlying offence of murder, the court was satisfied that in this case they were distinct and different agreements as the first involved a more serious and sophisticated agreement to do so by detonating IEDs on aircraft.

Agreements to commit more than one offence

It has been held to be legitimate to charge a conspiracy alleging a single agreement embracing conduct involving several offences.[227] So, for example, D can be indicted for conspiracy to rob *and* murder as part of one agreement. Moreover, in some cases there is nothing to prevent charges being laid for conspiracy where D1 and D2 agree to commit offences 'X *or* Y' as one agreement.[228] The problem frequently arose in the context of money laundering conspiracies where until relatively recently there were two categories of substantive offence. Dealing with money from drug-related crime was one form of offence, and dealing with money from non-drug-related crime was another. If D1 and D2 agreed to deal with monies from X in the future, being unaware whether the money from X would be from drug crime or other crime, but knowing it will be one or the other, the agreement, if carried out, would necessarily lead to the commission of the offence contrary to the Drug Trafficking

---

223 Section 1(1).

224 *Lavercombe* [1988] Crim LR 435.

225 *Hammersley* (1958) 42 Cr App R 207, discussed in [1958] Crim LR 422–9 (acts alleged ranged over eight years and involved numerous illegal agreements with others, yet the Court of Criminal Appeal contrived to hold that only one conspiracy to obstruct the course of justice, evidenced by a large number of overt acts, was disclosed by the indictment). *Barratt and Sheehan* [1996] Crim LR 495 is a similar case. Cf *Edwards* [1991] Crim LR 45.

226 [2011] EWCA Crim 1260. Cf *Papachristos and Kerrison* [2014] EWCA Crim 1863, n 182.

227 *Roberts* [1998] 1 Cr App R 441; *Greenfield* [1973] 1 WLR 1151; *Taylor and others* [2001] EWCA Crim 1044.

228 *Hussain* [2002] EWCA Crim 6. Many of the cases on this involve the pre-POCA money laundering offences and are complicated by what are recognized in the wake of *Saik* [2006] UKHL 18 to be erroneous statements about the mens rea of conspiracy: *El-Kurd* [2001] Crim LR 234. The Law Commission discusses these in LC 318, Part 4.

Act 1994 and/or to the offence contrary to the Criminal Justice Act 1987. Such a count was not bad for duplicity; it alleged one agreement: *Suchedina*.[229] These cases on the procedure for indicting conspiracy effect significant extensions of an already broad offence.[230] It would be preferable for two counts to be included where that is possible.[231]

Timing of agreement

It is probably not essential that the agreement should have been made prior to the concerted action to bring about the criminal purpose. If, when D1 is taking steps towards the commission of a crime, D2 comes to his assistance and the two work in concert, they might thereby be held to have conspired;[232] but if D1 is unaware of, or rejects, D2's assistance, there is no conspiracy,[233] though D2 might be held to be an accessory of any offence or attempt consummated by D1.[234] Some of these principles derive from common law conspiracy cases, but it is submitted that they apply equally to statutory conspiracy.

Proof of the agreement

The question of what conduct amounts to a sufficient agreement to found a charge of conspiracy is complicated by a confusion between the substantive law and the law of evidence, as with several other questions in the criminal law. In most cases the agreement will probably be made in private. Direct evidence of it, even in an era of covert surveillance and telephone tapping, will rarely be available. Agreements are frequently proved by showing that the parties concerted in the pursuit of a common object in such a manner as to show that their actions must have been coordinated by arrangement beforehand.[235] The danger is that the importance attached to the acts done may obscure the fact that these acts do not in themselves constitute a conspiracy, but are only evidence of it. If the jury are left in reasonable doubt, when all the evidence is in, whether the two or more accused persons were acting in pursuance of an agreement, they should acquit, even though the evidence shows that they were simultaneously pursuing the same object.[236]

11.3.3.2 A 'course of conduct' which has been agreed

The words 'the agreement' mean the agreement that a 'course of conduct' shall be pursued. To consider D's liability for conspiracy, we therefore have to imagine that the course of conduct he intended was pursued and to ask, would it, when completed, have necessarily

---

[229] [2006] EWCA Crim 2543, and see LCCP 183, para 5.19 and Ch 4.

[230] Similarly where the parties agree to import 'prohibited drugs' which might be Class A or B or C—three separate offences: *Taylor (RJ)* [2002] Crim LR 203.

[231] See LC 318, Part 4, and para 4.25.

[232] *Leigh* (1775) 1 Car & Kir 28n; *Tibbits and Windust* [1902] 1 KB 77.

[233] *State v Tally*, 102 Ala 25 (1894); J Michael and H Wechsler, *Criminal Law and Its Administration: Cases, Statutes, and Commentaries* (1940) 699; *Hawkesley* [1959] Crim LR 211 (QB).

[234] *Rannath Mohan v R* [1967] 2 AC 187.

[235] *Cooper and Compton* [1947] 2 All ER 701; *Hammersley* (1958) 42 Cr App R 207. Lord Diplock thought that it is 'a legal fiction' (*DPP v Bhagwan* [1970] 3 All ER 97 at 104) and 'the height of sophistry' (*Knuller (Publishing, Printing and Promotions) Ltd v DPP* [1972] 2 All ER 898 at 921) that the offence lies not in the concerted action but in the inferred anterior agreement; but the law is clear that it is the agreement that is the offence. The concerted action is evidence of the crime, but not the crime itself. Cf JC Smith, 'Proving Conspiracy' [1996] Crim LR 386 and 'More on Proving Conspiracy' [1997] Crim LR 333.

[236] Where there are counts for both conspiracy and the substantive crime, and the only evidence of conspiracy is the collaboration of the parties in the completion of the substantive crime, the only logical verdicts are guilty of both conspiracy and the substantive crime or not guilty of both: *Cooper and Compton* [1947] 2 All ER 701, cf *Beach and Owens* [1957] Crim LR 687. See later on the use of substantive and conspiracy counts.

amounted to or involved the commission of any offence?[237] But the phrase 'course of conduct' is ambiguous. It might mean: (a) that the defendants have only to have agreed on the actual physical acts which they propose shall be done; or it might mean (b) that they must also have agreed on the consequences which they intend to follow from their conduct; and/or (c) on the relevant circumstances which they know, or believe, or intend, to exist.[238] The broader interpretation in (b) and (c) is, it is submitted, the correct interpretation. This deserves more detailed discussion.

The narrow view

At common law, in *DPP v Nock*,[239] the defendants agreed to extract cocaine from a particular substance by subjecting it to a certain process. The substance contained no cocaine. The House of Lords interpreted 'course of conduct' to mean proof only of the physical acts of applying a process to the chemicals. The 'course of conduct' was the conduct involved in applying the process to that substance. On the facts of that case there was no cocaine in the substance so producing a controlled drug was impossible; and the 'course of conduct' agreed to would not have resulted in the production of a controlled drug.[240] The law was changed by s 1(1)(b), added by the Criminal Attempts Act 1981, to ensure that in a case of statutory conspiracy the fact that the course of conduct relied on rendered the substantive offence impossible does not prevent a conviction for conspiracy. The section provides that if D1 and D2 agree that a course:

shall be pursued which, if the agreement is carried out in accordance with their intentions, either—

  (a) will necessarily amount to or involve the commission of any offence or offences by one or more of the parties to the agreement, or

  (b) would do so but for the existence of facts which render the commission of the offence or any of the offences impossible, they are guilty of conspiracy to commit the offence or offences in question.

On the facts in *Nock*, there could now be liability for the conspiracy even though the intended result was impossible. The subsection has nothing to say, however, about: (a) other consequences, which do not depend on the existence of facts believed to exist by the defendants; or (b) the existence of facts precluding the commission of the crime at the time it is to be carried out.

Consequences as part of the course of conduct

A wider interpretation of course of conduct is possible and, we suggest, preferable: course of conduct should be interpreted as including the conspirators' intended consequences. Suppose the defendants D1 and D2 agree to kill V by putting poison in his tea. This, surely, must be conspiracy to murder; but the act of putting poison in the tea will not necessarily result in murder. V may decide not to drink it. So, if the law adopts the *Nock* approach

237 cf *Barnard* (1979) 70 Cr App R 28, and commentary. *Bernard* was analysed extensively in *Mehta* [2012] EWCA Crim 2824, in which the Court of Appeal endorsed Professor Sir John Smith's criticisms of the decision. The impact of this is that on a charge of conspiracy, the greater includes the lesser such that, eg, if DD are charged with conspiracy to rob, the jury can find them guilty of conspiracy to commit theft. *Mehta* was subsequently considered and endorsed in *Shillam* [2013] EWCA Crim 160. For commentary, see A Shaw QC [2013] 5 Arch Rev 4.
238 See LC 318, Part 2 for discussion of what this should mean.
239 [1978] AC 979, [1978] Crim LR 483 and commentary. A case of common law conspiracy committed before, but decided after, the Act came into force.
240 They would now be guilty because of the addition of s 1(1)(b), discussed earlier, which was added by the Criminal Attempts Act 1981.

and treats the 'course of conduct' as merely putting poison in the tea, it is not conspiracy to murder—which is absurd.[241] Subsection (1)(b) has nothing to say on the matter because there is no question of impossibility. To avoid the absurdity, 'course of conduct' must be read to include the intended consequences—in this case, the death of V.[242]

Circumstances as part of the course of conduct

In determining whether conspiracy is committed, we have to look forward from the time of the agreement—will the agreed course of conduct necessarily amount to or involve the commission of an offence? But circumstances change and the commission of the offence may be perfectly possible at the time of the agreement and become impossible by the time it is to be performed. Where this may happen, how can we say that the pursuance of the course of conduct will *necessarily* amount to or involve the commission of an offence? Defendants agree to receive certain goods next Monday, which they know to be stolen; but, before next Monday, the goods may cease to be stolen goods by being restored to lawful custody. D1 and D2 may agree to marry next Tuesday, knowing that D1's wife is alive; but, before next Tuesday, she may die. These events may be unlikely, but they are possible, and therefore it cannot be said that the receipt of the goods or the going through with the marriage ceremony will *necessarily* amount to, or involve, the offences of handling stolen goods and bigamy respectively. If the contemplated receipt of the goods, or the marriage ceremony, is the 'course of conduct', the agreements do not amount to conspiracy to handle or commit bigamy.[243] Clearly, they ought to do so.

The obvious way out of this difficulty is to construe 'course of conduct' to include material circumstances *which the parties believe will (not may) exist*. There are two difficulties about this approach. First, under s 1(2) of the Act (discussed later) a person is not guilty of conspiracy unless he 'intends or knows' that circumstances necessary for the commission of the offence shall or will exist at the time when the conduct constituting the offence is to take place.[244] In the examples just given, D cannot 'know' that the circumstances will exist because, as we have seen, they may not do so. This was confirmed in *Saik*,[245] where the House of Lords held that it is not enough that D 'believes'[246] that the circumstances will exist; knowledge requires true belief. In the case of a conspiracy in relation to a future event this will not always be possible to prove. For example, if D1 and D2 are charged with conspiring to handle stolen goods, if they are to receive the goods at a future date, they cannot, at the time of the agreement, know that the goods will be stolen. That is a future circumstance. They may be guilty if they can be shown to have intended that the goods they will handle were to be stolen goods. It seems strange to say that D1 and D2 'intend' that they shall exist when the pair have, and know they have, no control over their existence.[247] The circumstance may, however, be held to be intended because it is part of an intended result.

---

[241] It would be conspiracy to attempt to commit murder, since putting poison in the tea necessarily amounts to an attempt. The Criminal Attempts Act 1981 does not rule out the possibility of such an offence, but it is a strange concept. An agreement to attempt to do something is, in practical terms, an agreement to do it. See LCCP 183, para 4.19. See LC 318, Part 3.

[242] This argument is discussed in full in Ormerod (2006) 59 CLP 185 and by Smith in [1977] Crim LR at 601–2. See also G Williams (1977) 127 NLJ 1164 at 1165 and see LCCP 183, para 4.19.

[243] They might be conspiracies to attempt. See LCCP 183, Part 7.   [244] See p 476.

[245] [2006] UKHL 18. The decision prompted the government to refer the subject to the Law Commission: LCCP 183, para 1.20. Since the decision and the Court of Appeal's clarification of the approach in *Suchedina*, n 229, it seems not to have given rise to problems in practice. See LC 318, Part 4.

[246] Lord Nicholls at [26]; Lord Hope at [78], cf Lord Brown at [119]; nor of suspicion: Lord Nicholls at [30].

[247] For a further discussion of 'intend or know', see Ormerod (2006) 59 CLP 185, and the 4th edn of this book at pp 220–2.

The second difficulty, which applies to both consequences and circumstances, arises following the amendment made by the Criminal Attempts Act 1981, which added s 1(1)(b). If 'course of conduct' includes the circumstances believed by the parties to exist, this provision is entirely unnecessary. It is necessary only if the narrow *Nock*[248] interpretation of 'course of conduct' is right. Arguably, by enacting s 1(1)(b) Parliament has accepted that interpretation, but taken the sting out of it so far as impossibility at the time of the agreement is concerned. The trouble with this approach is that it leaves other stings elsewhere. However, the argument that 'course of conduct' must include intended consequences and foreseen circumstances is so compelling that s 1(1)(b) might reasonably be regarded as an 'avoidance of doubt' provision, strictly unnecessary, but there for the guidance of the unwary. *Nock* is a discredited, though not overruled,[249] decision on the common law and should not be applied in interpreting the 1977 Act.

The Law Commission recommended that a conspirator must be shown to have intended that the conduct element of the offence, *and* (where relevant) the consequence element (or other consequences), should respectively be engaged in or brought about.[250]

Conditional agreements

The question of conditional agreements requires separate consideration, particularly in the light of s 1(1) of the Act.[251] The parties may agree on alternative courses of action depending on the existence of some fact to be ascertained or some event which may or may not happen.

It seems settled that there will be a conspiracy where the parties' objective is to commit a crime—but not if it proves too difficult or too dangerous—as where D1 and D2 agree that they will abandon their intention to commit burglary if they find the house surrounded by police. They agree to commit the burglary only if it is safe. If they go through with the agreed conduct *as intended* they must, of necessity, commit burglary. The fact that an agreement to commit a crime is subject to express or implied reservation does not necessarily preclude liability for conspiracy.[252]

There are far more difficult aspects to conditional intentions.[253] If one of the courses of action agreed upon involves the commission of a crime and the other does not, is this a conspiracy to commit the crime? Can it be said that, if the agreement is carried out in accordance with their intentions, the course of conduct pursued will *necessarily* amount to or involve the commission of an offence? Is not the agreement carried out in accordance with their intentions if, in the event, they take the non-criminal course? For example, D1 and D2 may agree that they will transfer money brought into their bureau de change even if it is criminal property. Is this an agreement to launder criminal property? What if, when it is delivered, the money is not from criminal activity and so is not criminal property after all? Can it be said that, if the agreement is carried out in accordance with their intentions, the course of conduct pursued will *necessarily* amount to or involve the commission of an offence?[254] This is a complex area and only an outline can be offered here by reference to scenarios involving the putative money launderers who agree to transfer monies brought into their bureau de change.[255]

---

[248] See p 514.   [249] See p 514.   [250] LC 318, para 2.56.

[251] See Campbell (1982) 2 LS 77. See LCCP 183, Part 5, taking a different view of these categories.

[252] *Mills* (1963) 47 Cr App R 49, and commentary. Cf *Hussein* [1978] Crim LR 219.

[253] For extensive analysis, see J Child, 'Understanding Ulterior *Mens Rea*: Future Conduct Intention is Conditional Intention' (2017) 76 CLJ 311.

[254] See further Ormerod (2006) 59 CLP 185; *Saik* [2006] UKHL 18; we are grateful to Tony Shaw QC for the very many valuable discussions on this topic and conspiracy in general.

[255] cf *Saik* [2006] UKHL 18. See LCCP 193 and LC 318, Part 2.

Agreements to do 'x' if 'y'

If D1 and D2 declare 'we will transfer the money if it is non-criminal property', there is no declared intention about what course of conduct they would adopt if the money is illicit. This is not, it is submitted, sufficient to constitute an agreement to launder money. D1 and D2 have, implicitly, seen the risk that the money will be illicit, but have not declared an intention to deal with criminal money. It cannot be said that D1 and D2 have agreed on a course of conduct that will *necessarily* involve them in the commission of an offence if carried out in accordance with their intentions. In fact, acting in accordance with their declared intentions, all we can assert is that they will *not* commit a money laundering offence.[256] The defendants' state of mind is declared only in relation to one possible eventuality.

Agreements to do 'x' only if 'y'

The money laundering duo might say: 'we will transfer the money *only if* the money is non-criminal property; if it is criminal we will not transfer it'.[257] There is no intention to pursue a course of conduct that will necessarily involve the commission of an offence: there can be no liability for conspiracy.[258] They differ significantly from the previous category because D1 and D2 have declared intentions as to their course of conduct in both eventualities: where y materializes and not.[259]

Agreements to do 'x' even if 'y'

Our money launderers D1 and D2 might acknowledge that 'the monies involved in the business might be criminal, and agree to pursue such conduct *even though* some of the monies we transfer will be criminal property'. Their agreement could be reconstructed as one which includes a confirmed intention: 'we intend to pursue a course of conduct (transferring money) which is not criminal and if certain circumstances transpire (the money is criminal property), we intend nevertheless to pursue a course of conduct (transferring money)'. The agreement will, if completed in accordance with one of their intentions, necessarily involve the commission of a crime. Campbell calls these unconditional intentions. They are generally regarded as a form of direct intention.[260]

In *Saik*, members of the House took different approaches to conditional agreements,[261] but the majority recognized that it had no part to play on the facts of that case as only suspicion and not intention was proved. Baroness Hale, dissenting, provided what is, it is submitted, a powerful example to support her conclusion that a conditional intention suffices for liability in a conspiracy. Where D1 and D2 consider having sex with a woman and agree that they will do so *even if* she turns out not to be consenting, they should be guilty of conspiracy since they have expressed an intent to rape.[262] The complex issue of conditional intentions may need to be addressed in further detail on a future occasion if it arises directly.[263]

---

[256] Kenneth Campbell in his useful analysis of the concepts describes these as 'non-comprehensive conditional intentions': Campbell (1982) 2 LS 77 at 84–5.

[257] The courts got muddled with this in the theft and burglary cases in the 1970s, in particular *Easom* [1971] 2 QB 315. See also L Koffman, 'Conditional Intention to Steal' [1980] Crim LR 463 and J Parry, 'Conditional Intents: A Dissent' [1981] Crim LR 6. See also the cogent criticism by Campbell (1982) 2 LS 77 at 78–80.

[258] Campbell calls these 'comprehensive conditional intentions', ibid.

[259] As Lynch observes ('Further Comment' [1978] Crim LR 205), conditional intentions provide that 'if A then B, if not A then C' (at 207).

[260] The Law Commission regards these as forms of recklessness not conditional intention. But that seems doubtful. In recklessness D has awareness of a risk. Here, D has beyond mere awareness of the risk, and demonstrated a commitment to perform the conduct even if the risk eventuates. See LC 318, Part 2.

[261] Lord Nicholls seems, strictly speaking, not to reject it outright, at [5]. Lord Brown finds it beguiling but reluctantly rejects it.

[262] At [99]. See the rejection of this in LC 318, Part 2, para 2.115.

[263] The Law Commission considers the matter in detail in LCCP 183, Part 5 and LC 318, Part 2. See also Appendix B.

Conditional agreements in the case law

The courts have been untroubled by these theoretical difficulties and have taken a broad-brush approach to conditional intention in a series of cases.

In *Reed*,[264] D1 and D2 were guilty of conspiring to aid and abet suicide (as the offence was then drafted) where they agreed that D1 would visit suicidal individuals and either discourage or actively help them, depending on his assessment of the appropriate course of action. D1 and D2 have agreed on a course of conduct which if carried out in accordance with their intentions will necessarily involve an offence. The court held that the following hypothetical case is distinguishable: D1 and D2 agree to drive from London to Edinburgh in a time which can be achieved without exceeding the speed limits, but only if the traffic which they encounter is exceptionally light. In this example, as in *Reed* itself, the parties have apparently agreed that, in a certain event, they will commit a crime. The difference appears to be that exceeding the speed limit is only incidental to the main object of the agreement—getting from London to Edinburgh in a certain time.

In *Jackson*,[265] D1 and D2 agreed with D3 that D3, if convicted of the burglary for which he was on trial, should be shot in the leg so that the court would sentence him more leniently. They were guilty of conspiring to pervert the course of justice. This was an agreement that D1 and D2 intended to shoot D3 if he was convicted. D1 and D2 agreed on a course of conduct which if carried out in accordance with their intentions will necessarily involve an offence.

In *O'Hadhmaill*,[266] it was held that an agreement by IRA members during the period of the IRA ceasefire to make bombs with a view to causing explosions, if, but only if, the ceasefire came to an end was a conspiracy to cause an explosion.[267]

11.3.3.3 The object of the conspiracy

An agreement to commit any offence is a conspiracy contrary to s 1 of the Act, triable on indictment.[268]

Summary offences

Proceedings for conspiracy to commit summary offences[269] may be instituted only with consent of the DPP.[270] The availability of trial on indictment for conspiracy to commit summary offences was introduced to meet the fear of[271] 'social danger involved in the deliberate planning of offences on a widespread scale'.

---

264 [1982] Crim LR 819. Cf *O'Hadhmaill* [1996] Crim LR 509.

265 [1985] Crim LR 442.   266 [1996] Crim LR 509. See LCCP 183, para 5.8.

267 Sullivan suggests that the decision is useful in 'refut[ing] any notion that, in legal discourse, one can never be found to have knowledge of facts relating to the future'. But, does this overlook the fact that the decision is more readily if not equally explicable on the basis of future intentions without detracting from the orthodox view that one cannot know the future? See also J Parry, 'Conditional Intents: A Dissent' [1981] Crim LR 6. Cf LCCP 183, para 5.5. Arguably the agreement was subject to further necessary agreement of the parties as to whether the ceasefire had ended, and was not a concluded intention on the unusual facts of this case. Cf LC 318, para 2.112.

268 There is one exception: Trade Union and Labour Relations (Consolidation) Act 1992, s 242. Section 3 of the Conspiracy and Protection of Property Act 1875 is repealed by 1977 Act: s 5(11). See JC Smith [1977] Crim LR 638.

269 But cf s 5(6) which limits this.

270 Section 4(1) or, where prosecution for the summary offence itself so requires, that of the A-G: s 4(2). The Law Commission recommends abolishing that requirement: LC 318, para 4.35.

271 LC 76, para 1.85. The Commission refers to *Blamires Transport Services Ltd* [1964] 1 QB 278, as a typical example of the sort of case they had in mind. The conspiracy to contravene certain provisions of the Road Traffic Acts extended over two years and included a large number of offences, all triable only summarily.

Conspiracies to commit inchoate offences

Although technically possible, conspiracies to commit other inchoate offences would be rare and in principle ought to be treated with caution since the remoteness from the substantive offence is so significant.[272] The matter is discussed in the Law Commission Report No 318.[273]

Conspiracies to aid and abet

The Criminal Attempts Act 1981[274] makes it clear that there can be no attempt to aid and abet an offence but it leaves open the question whether there can be a conspiracy to do so.[275] D1 and D2, knowing that E intends to commit a burglary, agree to leave a ladder in a place where it will assist him to do so. E is not a party to that agreement so is not a co-conspirator. If E uses the ladder and commits burglary, D1 and D2 will be guilty of aiding and abetting him to do so. Are they guilty of conspiracy to commit burglary? Conspiracy requires an agreement that will involve 'a course of conduct' amounting to or involving 'the commission of an offence'. If the course of conduct is placing the ladder, it seems clear that they are not guilty. Placing the ladder is not an attempt to aid and abet burglary, since the Criminal Attempts Act 1981[276] makes it clear that this is not an offence known to the law. However, it is argued earlier[277] that 'course of conduct' should be interpreted to include the consequences intended to follow from the conduct agreed upon, including the action of a person not a party to the agreement—for example, V, who takes up poisoned tea left by D and E and drinks it. So it might be argued, consistently with that, that the course of conduct ought to include E's use of the ladder in committing burglary. If that should be accepted, the next question would be whether the burglary is 'the commission of any offence by one or more of the parties to the agreement'. E is not a party to the agreement, so the question becomes, do the words 'commission of any offence' include participation in the offence as a secondary party? Since all the parties to a conspiracy to commit an offence will be guilty of that offence if it is committed, but s 1(1) contemplates that it may be *committed* by only one of them, it is clear that 'commission' means commission by a principal. It is submitted, therefore, that an agreement to aid and abet an offence is not a conspiracy under the Act.

The previous paragraphs were approved by the Court of Appeal in *Hollinshead*.[278] DD agreed to sell to X 'black boxes', devices for altering electricity meters to show that less electricity had been used than was the fact. They expected X to resell the devices to consumers of electricity for use in defrauding the electricity supplier. The House of Lords[279] did not find it necessary to decide whether there could be a conspiracy to aid and abet and Lord Roskill said that it should be treated as open for consideration *de novo* if the question arises again. But there was clearly an agreement to aid and abet the consumers to commit offences under what was then s 2 of the Theft Act 1978[280] against the electricity supplier. By upholding the conviction for conspiracy to defraud, the House implicitly[281] decided that an agreement to aid and abet the consumers to commit an offence against the suppliers was not a statutory conspiracy.[282] This, it is submitted, is the position under the Act. In *Kenning*,[283] Lord Phillips CJ confirmed this interpretation:

an agreement to aid and abet an offence is not in law capable of constituting a criminal conspiracy under section 1(1) of the 1977 Act.

---

[272] It is an offence to conspire to attempt and to conspire to commit an offence under SCA 2007, ss 44–6.

[273] Part 3.   [274] Section 1(4)(b).

[275] The question is discussed by JC Smith in *Crime, Proof and Punishment*, 21, 35–6 and 40–1. See also LC 318, Part 3.

[276] See p 452. See the possible offences under the SCA 2007, p 493.

[277] See p 466.   [278] [1985] 1 All ER 850 at 858.   [279] [1985] AC 975.

[280] The conduct in *Hollinshead* is now an offence under s 7 of the Fraud Act 2006.

[281] If that agreement were a statutory conspiracy, it could not under the then prevailing (though now repealed) rule in *Ayres*, n 166, be a conspiracy to defraud.

[282] See commentary on *Hollinshead* [1985] Crim LR 653 at 656.   [283] [2008] EWCA Crim 1534.

The Supreme Court of Hong Kong in *Po Koon-tai*[284] has held, however, that there may be a *common law* conspiracy to aid and abet an offence.

Care may be needed where the allegation is that D has conspired to commit an offence that, although appearing to be a form of secondary liability, is in fact a statutory offence in its own right giving rise to liability as a principal offender for those who commit it (assisted suicide was a good example). In *Dang*,[285] D and others were convicted on count 1 of a conspiracy, contrary to s 1(1) of the Criminal Law Act 1977, to be concerned in the production of cannabis by another in contravention of s 4(2)(b) of the Misuse of Drugs Act 1971. The Court of Appeal held that the convictions were safe. The offence charged as a conspiracy was the making of the agreement 'to *be concerned in*' the production of cannabis by others. There could be a lawful charge of conspiracy to commit the substantive offence of 'being concerned in' the unlawful production of cannabis, contrary to s 4(2)(b) of the 1971 Act. It was distinct from aiding and abetting production which could not found a conspiracy charge: *Kenning*.[286]

Conspiracy and voluntary manslaughter

What is the position where there is an agreement by D1 and D2 to kill where D2 would have a defence of diminished responsibility on a charge of murder? If the killing is to be done by D1 it will be murder and so the agreement is a conspiracy to murder. If it is to be done by D2, D1 will still be guilty of murder by virtue of s 2(4) of the Homicide Act 1957.[287] However if, as submitted earlier,[288] 'commission of any offence' means commission as principal this appears to be a conspiracy to commit manslaughter.

11.3.3.4 An intention to agree

Clearly, if D1 is unaware that his conduct is being construed by D2 as an assent or agreement to a criminal proposal he will have no liability for conspiracy since he will not be intending to form the necessary agreement. It might be argued that there are two elements to this part of the mens rea. First, it must be shown that D intended to perform the acts/speak the words that were capable of constituting an offer or acceptance of the agreement. This provides a very limited scope for denial of mens rea, but this might succeed where D is so intoxicated that he uses language or actions without being aware of their likely interpretation.[289] Secondly, the requirement of actus reus that there is an agreement suggests a corresponding mens rea requirement that D intentionally used conduct that he was aware might be understood to constitute an offer/acceptance in the non-contractual sense.[290]

11.3.3.5 Intention that the agreement will be carried out

Section 1 of the 1977 Act assumes the existence of an intention of the parties not merely to agree, but also to carry out their agreement. This is not surprising because the essence of conspiracy, like attempt, is the intent to cause the forbidden result. The Law Commission

---

284 [1980] HKLR 492.

285 [2014] EWCA Crim 348 in which the Court of Appeal, citing *Hollinshead* and *Kenning*, held that a mere agreement to sell equipment, one of the uses of which may be unlawful, cannot constitute a conspiracy. It has been cogently argued that there are differences between *Dang* and *Kenning* that the court ought to have considered in its analysis. See R Fortson [2014] Crim LR 675.

286 [2008] EWCA Crim 1534.   287 See Ch 12.   288 See n 286.

289 The Law Commission has recommended that it should be possible for a defendant to deny that he or she possessed the fault element for conspiracy because of intoxication, whether voluntary or involuntary, even when the fault element in question is recklessness (or its equivalent): LC 318, para 2.164. In other words, the proposed offence will be treated as a specific intent offence even though it would be one of recklessness.

290 cf *Prior* [2004] EWCA Crim 1147, [2004] Crim LR 849 and commentary discussing the mens rea for an 'offer' to supply drugs.

understood this well enough and their Report,[291] the draft Bill and the Bill which was introduced into Parliament, also expressly required proof of intention. Unwisely, this provision was deleted from the Bill because it was thought too complex; but, in agreeing to the amendment, the Lord Chancellor stated that the speeches in Parliament had conceded that 'the law should require full intention and knowledge before conspiracy can be established'.[292]

However, in *Anderson*,[293] Lord Bridge, in a speech with which all of the House agreed, said that it was sufficient that an alleged conspirator had agreed that the criminal course of conduct be pursued and that he would play his role, but that it was not necessary to prove in addition that he intended the crime to be committed.[294] Lord Bridge was concerned with cases like that of the owner of a car, D, who agrees with a gang to hire it to them for use in a robbery. D may be quite indifferent whether the robbery is committed or not. In that situation the gang members are certainly guilty of conspiracy for they do intend to carry out the robbery; and D is guilty of abetting the conspiracy by giving encouragement to its continuance. There was no need to dilute the requirement that the conspirators must intend the commission of a crime.[295]

In *Anderson*, D was convicted of conspiring with a number of others to enable one of them to escape from prison. D had agreed to supply diamond wire to cut bars. He had certainly intended to be a party to that agreement. But D said that he never intended the plan to be put into effect and believed that it could not possibly succeed. It was held that this was no defence. It was clear in that case that two or more of the alleged conspirators did intend to carry out the agreement, so D's conviction could have been upheld on the ground that he aided and abetted that conspiracy—which he undoubtedly did, encouraging the making or continuance of it by his offer to help.[296]

The decision that no intention need be proved on the part of one alleged principal offender in conspiracy would significantly alter the scope of the offence. If no intention needs to be proved on the part of conspirator A, then none needs to be proved on the part of another, B. But if A and B are the only parties, and neither has the intention that it should be carried out, how can there be a crime of conspiracy? A conspiracy which no one intends to carry out is an absurdity, if not an impossibility. Moreover, s 1(2)[297] of the Act requires the conspirators to have intention or knowledge as to facts or *circumstances* constituting an offence, and it would be very remarkable indeed if intention or knowledge were required for the circumstances of the principal offence and not for its *consequences*.

It is submitted that *Anderson* should not be followed in this respect. It has been overlooked or ignored more than once by the Court of Appeal.[298] In *Edwards*, where D had agreed to

[291] LC 76, *Report on Conspiracy and Criminal Law Reform* (1976) paras 1.25–1.41. For the common law, see *Mulcahy* (1868) LR 3 HL 306 at 317 per Willes J. *Yip Chiu-Cheung*, p 478, assumes that a person is guilty of conspiracy at common law only if he intends to carry out the agreement. See [1994] 2 All ER 924 at 928c per Lord Griffiths.

[292] HL, vol 379, col 55.

[293] [1986] AC 27, [1985] Crim LR 651, and commentary. See also PW Ferguson, 'Intention Agreement and Statutory Conspiracy' (1986) 102 LQR 26.

[294] It might be argued that D1 and D2 agreeing to the course of conduct is sufficient because if they intend that they can be inferred to intend its consequences—the offence. This is a very strained interpretation. *Anderson* is criticized in LCCP 183, paras 4.26–4.41. In LC 318 the Law Commission recommends that a conspirator must be shown to have intended that the conduct element of the offence, and (where relevant) the consequence element (or other consequences), should respectively be engaged in or brought about (para 2.56) See also LC 318, para 4.30.

[295] Sections 44–6 of the SCA 2007 will now extend to deal with such cases.

[296] See commentary on the decision of the Court of Appeal [1984] Crim LR 551, and, on conspiracy to aid and abet, p 471.

[297] See p 476.   [298] *Edwards* [1991] Crim LR 45; *Ashton* [1992] Crim LR 667; *Harvey* [1999] Crim LR 70.

supply amphetamine but there was a possibility that he intended to supply ephedrine, it was held that the judge had rightly directed the jury that they could convict of conspiracy to supply amphetamine only if D intended to supply amphetamine—that is, it was not sufficient that D agreed to supply amphetamine unless he intended to carry out the agreement.

Anderson was distinguished in *McPhillips*,[299] where the Court of Appeal of Northern Ireland, accepted the proposition in this book[300] that s 1(1) of the 1977 Act[301] assumes the existence of an intention of the parties to carry out the agreement. Lord Lowry CJ held that D, who had joined in a conspiracy to plant a bomb, timed to explode on the roof of a hall at 1 am when a disco would be at its height, was not a party to the conspiracy to murder of which his accomplices were guilty because, unknown to his accomplices, he intended to give a warning enabling the hall to be cleared. He did not intend that anyone should be killed. *Anderson* was distinguished relying on Lord Bridge's *dictum* that a 'perfectly respectable citizen' who joins in an agreement 'without the least intention of playing any part in the ostensibly agreed criminal objective but rather with the purpose of frustrating and exposing the objective of the other parties' is not guilty of conspiracy. The *dictum* may be correct[302] but hardly seems to fit *McPhillips*, whose convictions, arising out of the same facts, for conspiracy to cause explosions and offences under the Explosive Substances Act 1883, were upheld. He was rightly acquitted of conspiracy to murder as a principal offender simply because he lacked the required intention.

More debatable is the decision that he was not guilty as an abettor of the conspiracy to murder. He intentionally gave assistance or encouragement to what he knew to be a conspiracy to murder and that is normally sufficient for liability. This suggests that an intention to frustrate the object of the conspiracy is a special defence. There are clear public policy grounds for allowing such a defence, although any such withdrawal-type defence will need to be carefully prescribed in the context of inchoate liability.[303] Arguably, it should be limited to conduct of the conspirator who serves unequivocal notice of withdrawal on his co-conspirators and seeks to nullify the effects of any overt acts he has performed as part of the conspiracy.[304] It has been held that where D1 intends that the offence should be carried out, he is guilty of conspiracy although he had an ulterior motive to gather evidence of the criminal wrongdoing and expose it.[305] The Law Commission recommended that the defence of acting reasonably provided for by s 50 of the SCA 2007 should be applied to the offence of conspiracy.[306]

The 1977 Act does not deal specifically with the case where E purports to conspire with D but has no intention of going through with the plan. The question was formerly of no practical importance because D could be convicted of an attempt to conspire, but the 1977 Act provides that there is no such offence. The point has not arisen in England but in some jurisdictions it has been decided that there is no conspiracy.[307] It might be argued that,

---

[299] (1990) 6 BNIL.   [300] See the 6th edn of this book, at p 259.

[301] Art 9(1) of the Criminal Attempts and Conspiracy (Northern Ireland) Order 1983 is identical with s 1(1).

[302] *Edwards*, n 298. But cf *Yip Chiu-Cheung v R*, p 478, and *Somchai Liangsiriprasert v United States Government* (1990) 92 Cr App R 77 at 82 where the Privy Council left open the question whether law enforcement officers who entered into an agreement to import drugs into the United States with the object of trapping the dealers should be regarded as conspirators. For valuable discussion on the liability of state officials, see A Ashworth, 'Testing Fidelity to Legal Values: Official Involvement and Criminal Justice' in Shute and Simester, *Criminal Law Theory*, 299, 324–5.

[303] The Law Commission rejected a withdrawal defence in LC 318, paras 2.35–2.45.

[304] cf the earlier discussion in relation to secondary withdrawal, p 236.

[305] *Jones and Warburton* [2002] EWCA Crim 735.   [306] LC 318, Part 6.

[307] *Harris* [1927] NPD 347 (South Africa); *O'Brien* [1954] SCR 666 (Canada); *Delaney v State*, 164 Tenn 432 (1932) (Tennessee); *State v Otu* [1964] NNLR 113 (Nigeria). Cf *Thomson* (1965) 50 Cr App R 1. See GHL Fridman in (1956) 19 MLR 276.

looking at the facts objectively, there is such an agreement as (apart from the illegality) would be enforceable in the law of contract and that therefore there is an actus reus. D, who, with mens rea, has caused the actus reus should be guilty. An answer to this argument is that there is no actus reus unless E agrees in fact, that is, that an actual subjective agreement is required. If *Anderson*[308] is followed and E is held to be guilty of conspiracy notwithstanding his lack of intention, the problem disappears.

11.3.3.6 Intention to play some part in carrying out the agreement

According to Lord Bridge in *Anderson*,[309] the mens rea of conspiracy is established:

if, and only if, it is shown that the accused, when he entered into the agreement, intended to play some part in the agreed course of conduct in furtherance of the criminal purpose which the agreed course of conduct was intended to achieve.

No authority was cited for this novel *dictum* and the Court of Appeal has subsequently held that Lord Bridge is not to be taken as saying what he plainly did say (above); the court in *Siracusa* said that participation in conspiracy can be active or passive and D's intention to participate 'is established by his failure to stop the unlawful activity'.[310] D's liability is, however, complete when he joins the agreement, intending that it be carried out, and his failure to stop it is, at most, evidence of his agreement and intention. In truth, O'Connor LJ in *Siracusa* appears to have been using this as a mechanism to circumvent *Anderson*.

It is submitted that the correct statement of the law is that there is nothing in the section, nor in the common law, to require for every conspirator to have an intention to participate personally in the carrying out of the full offence.[311] All that need be contemplated is the commission of the offence 'by one or more of the parties to the agreement'. So an agreement between A and B that A will supply a controlled drug to B is a conspiracy between them to supply the drug.[312]

Unforeseen but inevitable consequences

It is submitted that, notwithstanding *Anderson*, the parties must intend that at least one of them will pursue the course of conduct agreed upon. If so, they must be proved to have intended the foreseen consequences.[313] Exceptionally, the agreed course of conduct may be such that it will necessarily cause a consequence not foreseen by the parties. For example, they agree to inflict a particular type of bodily harm, not appreciating that it will necessarily cause death. On a literal interpretation of the Act they are guilty of conspiracy to murder. In principle, that would be a wrong result, because killing is not intended and possibly not even foreseen as a possibility. It is thought that, as in interpreting other aspects of the offence, the answer lies in the construction of 'course of conduct'.[314] This should be read not only to include the consequences which are intended by the parties, but also to

---

[308] See p 473.

[309] [1986] AC 27 at 39. Strangely, the Law Commission recommendations (para 2.45) endorsed this.

[310] *Siracusa* (1989) 90 Cr App R 340; cf *Chambers* [2009] EWCA Crim 2742, following *Anderson*.

[311] In *King* [2012] EWCA Crim 805, Pitchford LJ noted the criticisms made in this section in the 12th edn but declined to enter into the debate about whether it is in fact necessary to prove an intention to play some part in the full offence being carried out.

[312] *Drew* [2000] 1 Cr App R 91. But an indictment alleging a conspiracy to supply 'another' will be taken to mean a conspiracy to supply someone other than the conspirators: cases cited in commentary at [1999] Crim LR 582.

[313] As noted earlier, Parliament deleted the provision in the Bill requiring an intention to cause any consequence which is an ingredient in the crime the parties are alleged to have conspired to commit.

[314] See p 465.

be limited to such consequences, whether they will in fact necessarily result or not. This is justifiable because it is the *agreed* course of conduct that we are concerned with; and the agreement does not include causing death.

If D1 and D2 agree to cause grievous bodily harm to V they are guilty of conspiring to commit an offence under s 18 of the OAPA but they are not guilty of conspiracy to murder although, if they carry out their intention and consequently V dies, they will be guilty of murder.[315] Similarly, an agreement to behave with gross negligence towards V is not a conspiracy to commit manslaughter, even though the parties will be guilty of manslaughter if they carry out the agreement and kill V.[316]

11.3.3.7 Intention or knowledge as to circumstances

Section 1(2) of the Act provides:

Where liability for any offence may be incurred without knowledge on the part of the person committing it of any particular fact or circumstance necessary for the commission of the offence, a person shall nevertheless not be guilty of conspiracy to commit that offence by virtue of subsection (1)above unless he and at least one other party to the agreement intend or know that the fact or circumstance shall or will exist at the time when the conduct constituting the offence is to take place.

The provision is intended to reflect the general principle that elements of mens rea in inchoate offences ought not to be diluted since that mens rea often forms the core of the wrongdoing in the absence of any tangible harm resulting from the actus reus. The aim of this section is to ensure that even if strict liability or recklessness as to circumstances are sufficient mens rea for the substantive crime, these are to have no place in conspiracy. Intention or knowledge as to *all* the circumstances of the actus reus is required *even* where the agreement is to commit a crime which in its substantive form may be committed recklessly, or is a crime of strict liability or one committed on the basis of D's suspicion or negligence.[317] Although the aim of s 1(2) is clear enough, a number of problems arise in its interpretation. These were addressed by the House of Lords in *Saik*.[318]

Scope of application

First, there is no express provision in s 1(1) requiring intention or knowledge as to circumstances. Section 1(2) is expressed to apply *only* to those conspiracies which involve an offence which in its substantive form has an element of strict liability as to a circumstance or requires only recklessness as to a circumstance. A strict interpretation would lead to the conclusion that the section does not apply where the conspiracy alleged is one involving a substantive crime in which there is a requirement of intention or knowledge (and not

---

[315] For an argument to the contrary, see 4th edn of this book, at pp 222–3 and [1977] Crim LR 638–9. Cf Williams (1977) 127 NLJ at 1169 and Williams, TBCL (1st edn, 1978) 357–9.

[316] A conspiracy to commit manslaughter seems a theoretical possibility in the case of a suicide pact or where the party to do the killing is suffering from diminished responsibility. See p 569.

[317] The Law Commission proposed to reverse this position. Two provisions are recommended. Where the agreement relates to a substantive offence for which fault as to circumstances is strict liability or negligence an alleged conspirator must be shown at the time of the agreement to have been merely reckless whether a circumstance element of a substantive offence (or other relevant circumstance) would be present at the relevant time (LC 318, para 2.137). Where the agreement relates to a substantive offence with fault requirements not involving mere negligence (or its equivalent), in relation to a fact or circumstance element, an alleged conspirator may be found guilty if shown to have possessed those fault requirements at the time of his or her agreement to commit the offence (para 2.146). The intention was to simplify the law.

[318] [2006] UKHL 18.

mere recklessness) as to a circumstance.[319] In *Saik*,[320] the House of Lords accepted that Parliament could not have intended a 'scandalous paradox'[321] whereby the requirement of mens rea should be greater on a charge of conspiring to commit an offence of strict liability or recklessness than on a charge of conspiring to commit an offence requiring knowledge.[322] Despite the unequivocal terms in which the House of Lords held that the mens rea as to circumstances must be knowledge and nothing less, recent cases demonstrate that errors are still made.[323]

What constitutes knowledge?

The knowledge required relates to the fact or circumstance which must be proved as part of the actus reus.[324] The full reading of s 1(2) might be, though it is unclear, that the parties are not liable for conspiracy to commit any crime where the actus reus includes proof of a circumstance which they do not know exists or intend will exist. In *Saik*, the House of Lords confirmed that within s 1(2) the requirement of 'knowledge' or 'intention' as to the fact or circumstances necessary for the commission of the substantive offence is not to be diluted. Knowledge is not satisfied by proof of 'belief'[325] nor of suspicion.[326] These states of mind will not suffice for the conspiracy even if they would for the substantive offence. In this respect, the offence of conspiracy is stricter than that of attempt where the courts have accepted that recklessness as to circumstances is a sufficient mens rea where that would suffice for the substantive crime attempted.[327]

What are the 'facts or circumstances' which must be known?

Suppose that D1 agrees to help D2 move out of his flat. D2 is unsure whether the cabling he has installed for his satellite TV belongs to him or to his landlord. D1 and D2 confer together and are uncertain, but agree, nevertheless, to remove it knowing their actions will result in damage in the process. They therefore have an intention to cause damage, and are reckless as to whether the property belongs to another. The substantive offence of criminal damage requires that D intends or is reckless as to the causing of damage (the result), *and* that D intends or is reckless as to whether the property belongs to another (circumstance).[328] If D1 and D2 went ahead, they would have sufficient mens rea to be convicted of the substantive offence. As for the conspiracy, in the *actual* circumstances that exist, the carrying out of the agreement 'will necessarily amount' to criminal damage; but on an orthodox reading of s 1(2), it is not a conspiracy to commit criminal damage. It would not be criminal damage in the circumstances which the parties *intend, or know, shall or will exist*. D1 and D2 are reckless as to the circumstance. Recklessness as to the circumstance of the actus reus (property belonging to another) is not a sufficient mens rea on a charge of conspiracy to commit a crime (criminal damage) even where it is a sufficient mens rea for the crime itself. If the Law Commission recommendations are accepted, the law will extend considerably. It is submitted that the law would be overbroad.

---

[319] Elliott [1978] Crim LR 204; LCCP 183, para 4.65.

[320] Lord Nicholls at [18].   [321] Elliott, n 319.

[322] Smith [1977] Crim LR 606; Williams (1977) 127 NLJ 1166. See LCCP 183, paras 4.45 et seq.

[323] See *Thomas* [2014] EWCA Crim 1958. See also the complexity involved when the substantive offences are technical ones such as immigration offences: *Ali* [2019] EWCA Crim 2448.

[324] See, generally, S Shute, 'Knowledge and Belief in the Criminal Law' (at 187) and GR Sullivan, 'Knowledge, Belief and Culpability' (at 215) in Shute and Simester, *Criminal Law Theory*, Chs 8 and 9 respectively.

[325] Lord Nicholls at [26], Lord Hope at [78]; cf Lord Brown at [119].

[326] Lord Nicholls at [30].   [327] *Khan* (1990) 91 Cr App R 29, p 437. LCCP 183, paras 4.145 et seq.

[328] *Smith (David Raymond)* [1974] QB 354. See p 1104.

For s 1(2) to apply there must be a fact or circumstance in the actus reus on which liability in the substantive offence is strict, based on negligence or for which D's recklessness suffices.[329] This has caused problems. For example, in a series of cases involving conspiracies to commit criminal damage being reckless as to whether life is endangered,[330] the Court of Appeal has held that it is sufficient to establish recklessness (rather than knowledge) on the part of the conspirators. These cases were based on the false assumption that the substantive offence requires proof of a fact that life is endangered. It does not: *Parker*.[331] Since life endangerment is not 'a circumstance' that needs to exist for the full offence, it is unnecessary in a conspiracy to prove that DD 'knew of' or intended it.[332]

This issue may arise following the decisions in *Ivey* and *Barton*. On a rather technical construction it is arguable that a 'fact' that makes the conduct criminal in dishonesty offences under the new test for dishonesty is that the conduct would be considered dishonest by ordinary decent people. Could it be argued, therefore, that for a statutory conspiracy to commit a dishonesty offence the defendant must now be proved to have known/intended that the agreed course of conduct would be considered dishonest by ordinary decent people?[333]

That is likely to be an unpalatable interpretation for the Court of Appeal. It would make such offences difficult to prove, would have the effect of reverting to the *Ghosh* test and would distinguish statutory conspiracy from conspiracy to defraud.[334]

Where only one party has mens rea

Section 1(2) makes it clear that, so far as the relevant circumstances are concerned, both parties to the agreement (or, where there are more than two parties, at least two of them) must have mens rea. If D1 and D2 agree to touch V sexually and D1 knows that she is only 15, there is no conspiracy if D2 reasonably believes that she is 16.

The Law Commission's rejected subsection from 1976 would have made similar provision for foresight of consequences, but there is no such provision in the Act. If, however, 'course of conduct' is construed, as suggested previously, to include intended consequences, and only intended consequences, the result is the same. As Lord Griffiths said in *Yip Chiu-Cheung*,[335] 'The crime of conspiracy requires an agreement between two or more persons to commit an unlawful act with the intention of carrying it out. It is the intention to carry out the crime that constitutes the mens rea of the offence.' If D1 intends death and D2 intends grievous bodily harm, this is a conspiracy to cause grievous bodily harm but not a conspiracy to murder.

Ignorance of criminal law no defence

There is no requirement that DD have knowledge of the relevant criminal law which renders their proposed conduct illegal.[336]

---

[329] This is discussed in full in Ormerod (2006) 59 CLP 185.
[330] *Mir* (1994) 22 Apr; *Browning* (1998) unreported; *Ryan* (1999) The Times, 13 Oct.
[331] [1993] Crim LR 856.
[332] See *Saik* [2006] UKHL 18, [2006] Crim LR 998. There are two arguments that these cases are not wrongly decided. First, they were all heard at a time when *Caldwell* recklessness was a sufficient mens rea for criminal damage. As such, although the offence did not require proof of a circumstance of a life being endangered, it did require proof of the reasonable person's awareness of a risk of life endangerment. That it is said could be a 'circumstance' in the substantive offence for which D must be held to have knowledge for the charge of conspiracy. Secondly, since *G* [2004] 1 AC 1034, [2004] Crim LR 369, the mens rea as to the endangerment of life is subjective. Arguably, however, there is still an 'objective circumstance' that must exist because even in a case of subjective recklessness, there must be proof that D 'unreasonably' took the risk he foresaw.
[333] This issue arose in *Nynyintono* [2020] EWCA Crim 454 but it was not considered in any great detail.
[334] Unless *Churchill v Walton* [1967] AC 224 applies.
[335] [1994] 2 All ER 924 at 928.
[336] *Churchill v Walton* [1967] 2 AC 224; *Broad* [1997] Crim LR 666.

11.3.4 Procedural issues relating to conspiracies

11.3.4.1 Conspiracy where the contemplated offence is committed

The courts discourage the charging of conspiracy where there is evidence of the complete crime.[337] However, one attraction of conspiracy charges is that evidence is admissible on a conspiracy charge which would not be admissible on a joint trial for the complete crime.[338] The real objections to conspiracy being charged reflect a concern expressed by Williams.[339] It is:

to the use of a conspiracy count to give a semblance of unity to a prosecution which, by combining a number of charges and several defendants, results in a complicated and protracted trial. The jury system is unworkable unless the prosecution is confined to a relatively simple issue which can be disposed of in a relatively short time.[340]

The length and complexity of trials for conspiracy raise doubts whether justice can be done.[341]

In *Dosanjh*,[342] the Court of Appeal held that it does not infringe the principle enunciated in *Rimmington* for the Crown to charge an individual with the statutory conspiracy to commit the common law offence of cheating the Revenue in circumstances where a substantive statutory offence was available.

Acquittal of the other alleged conspirators

Where D was alleged to have conspired with one other person, E, the acquittal of E, either before or after the trial of D, is no bar to, or ground for quashing, as the case may be, the conviction of D.[343] This is so whether tried separately or together:[344] see s 5(8) and (9) of the 1977 Act.

There may be evidence—usually a confession, but not necessarily so[345]—which is admissible against D but not against E, which shows that D conspired with E. In these circumstances, it is perfectly logical for the jury to be satisfied, as against D, that he conspired with E but not satisfied, as against E, that he conspired with D. It is only when the evidence against D and E is of equal weight, or nearly so, that the judge should direct the jury that they must either acquit both or convict both—being careful to add that, if they are unsure about the guilt of one, both must be acquitted.[346] The difficult question for the judge remains in

---

[337] Cockburn CJ, in *Boulton* (1871) 12 Cox CC 87 at 93. *West* [1948] 1 KB 709 at 720, and see *Gray and others* [1995] 2 Cr App R 100, sub nom *Liggins* [1995] Crim LR 45.

[338] For a discussion of the circumstances in which conspiracy should not be charged, see P Jarvis and M Bisgrove, 'The Use and Abuse of Conspiracy' [2014] Crim LR 261. In *Dady* [2013] EWHC 475 (QB), applying *Rimmington* [2005] UKHL 63, it was held that where an agreement could be charged as a statutory conspiracy or as a conspiracy to defraud it should ordinarily be charged as a statutory conspiracy unless there is good reason to charge conspiracy to defraud instead.

[339] CLGP, 684; and see *The Proof of Guilt* (3rd edn, 1963) Ch 9 and 'The Added Conspiracy Count' (1978) 128 NLJ 24.

[340] See also the speech of Lord Hope in *Saik* [2006] UKHL 18.

[341] eg the Jubilee Line Fraud. See S Lloyd Bostock, 'The Jubilee Line Jurors: Does their Experience Strengthen the Argument for Judge-Only Trial in Long and Complex Fraud Cases?' [2007] Crim LR 255.

[342] [2013] EWCA Crim 2366.

[343] *DPP v Shannon* [1975] AC 717. See eg *Zaman* [2010] EWCA Crim 209; *Thompson* [2018] EWCA Crim 2082. See also CW Coulter, 'The Unnecessary Rule of Consistency in Conspiracy Trials' (1986) 135 U Pa L Rev 223.

[344] ibid. D1 and D2 can be tried even if D3 has been acquitted earlier: *Austin* [2011] EWCA Crim 345.

[345] See *Testouri* [2003] EWCA Crim 3735.

[346] *Longman and Cribben* (1981) 72 Cr App R 121, [1981] Crim LR 38 and commentary. Cf the similar problem which arises with secondary parties, p 202 *Roberts* (1984) 78 Cr App R 41.

deciding whether there is a sufficient inequality between the weight of the cases against each conspirator. The required degree of difference has been explained as 'marked'[347] or 'substantial'.[348] Ultimately, the question would seem to be whether the difference is sufficient to displace a juror's reasonable doubt that they might otherwise have had. There is nothing to prevent the conviction of one conspirator at a retrial where his co-conspirator was acquitted at the original trial.[349]

11.3.4.2 Jurisdiction

The situation where there is an agreement in England to commit an offence abroad is now regulated by s 1A[350] of the Criminal Law Act 1977. The section applies where the pursuit of the agreed course of conduct would involve an act by one or more of the parties, or the happening of some event, in a place outside England and Wales which (a) would be an offence by the law of that place, and (b) would be an offence triable here but for the fact that it was committed abroad. Then, if, in England or Wales (a) a person became a party to the agreement, or (b) a party to the agreement did anything in relation to it before its formation, or did or omitted anything in pursuance of it, the agreement is indictable as a conspiracy, contrary to s 1(1) of the 1977 Act.[351] In the Crown Court the question is to be treated as one of law to be decided by the judge. This is a significant extension of the scope of the already broad-reaching offence of conspiracy.[352] It is indicative of Parliament's approach to extending the scope of the criminal law beyond the physical limits of the jurisdiction in general.[353]

The 1977 Act makes no express provision for agreements abroad to commit an offence in England. It has been clear since 1973[354] that, at common law, an agreement abroad to commit a crime in England is indictable here if an overt act is done in England in pursuance of the agreement. The Privy Council held in *Somchai Liangsiriprasert v United States Government*[355] that it is unnecessary to prove that any overt act was done in England. The only purpose of requiring an overt act could be to establish the link between the conspiracy and England or to show that the conspiracy was continuing and any other evidence that establishes this is just as good.

Agreements abroad to commit offences abroad deserve a brief mention. D1 and D2, British citizens in France, agree to kill V in France or to go through a ceremony of marriage there both knowing that D1 is married. The offences contemplated are triable in England even if committed in France so, literally, these are indictable conspiracies under the Act. It may

---

[347] *Longman* at n 346.   [348] *Roberts* at n 346.

[349] *James* [2002] EWCA Crim 1119; *Austin* [2011] EWCA Crim 345; *Thompson* [2018] EWCA Crim 2082.

[350] Inserted by the Criminal Justice (Terrorism and Conspiracy) Act 1998 and amended by the Coroners and Justice Act 2009, s 72. See also C Campbell, 'Two Steps Backwards: The Criminal Justice (Terrorism and Conspiracy) Act 1998' [1999] Crim LR 941; J Holroyd, 'The Reform of Jurisdiction over International Conspiracy' (2000) 64 J Crim L 323. See further LCCP 183, Part 11; LC 318, Part 7.

[351] There is, in effect, a presumption that the act or event is an offence by the foreign law unless the defence gives notice that, in their opinion, for which they must show grounds, it is not, and requires the prosecution to prove it: s 1A(8).

[352] Section 1A is not an offence in its own right: *Patel* [2009] EWCA Crim 67. In *Bina* [2014] EWCA Crim 1444. D argued that he ought to have been charged under s 1A, but the court rejected this argument on the basis that at all material times he was in the UK.

[353] See generally Hirst, *Jurisdiction and the Ambit of the Criminal Law*, 142–8 for critical analysis of the provisions.

[354] *DPP v Doot* [1973] AC 807.

[355] (1990) 92 Cr App R 77 (a case of extradition from Hong Kong to the United States, but applying the common law of England), followed in *Sansom* [1991] 2 All ER 145 where, however, one of the conspirators had acted in England in pursuance of the conspiracy. *Somchai* was applied in *Re Goatley* [2002] EWHC 1209 (Admin) to a case of cannabis importation. For discussion see LC 318, para 7.53.

be, however, that the presumption against the extraterritorial application of the criminal law will exclude agreements not made within the jurisdiction and not intended to have any effect therein, but this seems less likely after *Liangsiriprasert*.[356]

The Law Commission made proposals on jurisdiction which would, if enacted, bring the law for conspiracy broadly into line with that for assisting and encouraging under the SCA 2007, as discussed later.[357]

11.3.5 Common law conspiracies

All common law conspiracies require proof of an agreement as considered in relation to statutory conspiracies discussed earlier.

11.3.5.1 Conspiracy to defraud

This offence[358] is one of the most controversial in English criminal law, and there has been sustained pressure for its abolition.[359] It is excessively broad, vague and potentially criminalizes conduct by two or more that would not be criminal or even tortious when performed by an individual. It offends against the principles of legality, certainty and fair warning, and results in an offence which is commonly defined by reference only to the concept of dishonesty—a concept that is ill-suited to shoulder that responsibility[360] and arguable even more so in its new incarnation after *Ivey*[361] *and Barton*.[362] The Law Commission has commented that the offence is 'so wide that it offers little guidance on the difference between fraudulent and lawful conduct'.[363] Even the Home Office acknowledged that the offence was 'arguably unfairly uncertain and wide enough potentially to encompass sharp business practice'.[364] The Commission's conclusion was that the offence should be abolished with the implementation of the Fraud Act, but the government was insistent that conspiracy to defraud was to be retained as a safeguard against lacunae being revealed in the new scheme.[365]

Following the enactment of the Fraud Act 2006, a prosecutor should only select a charge of conspiracy to defraud having had regard to the Attorney General's guidelines. These provide that, in selecting charges in fraud cases, the prosecutor should first consider: whether the behaviour could be prosecuted under statute—whether under the Fraud Act 2006 or another Act or as a statutory conspiracy; and whether the available statutory charges

356 cf the corresponding problem in attempts, p 480.   357 See LC 318, Part 7.

358 See Smith, *Property Offences*, Ch 19; C Montgomery and D Ormerod (eds), *Fraud: Criminal Law and Procedure* (2008) Ch D7; Ormerod and Williams, *Smith's Law of Theft*. For an historical account see T Hadden, 'Conspiracy to Defraud' (1966) 24 CLJ 248. See also JC Smith, 'Fraud and the Criminal Law' in P Birks (ed), *Pressing Problems in the Law* (1995) vol 1, 49.

359 See for discussion Law Commission Working Papers No 56 (1974) and 104 (1988) and ATH Smith, 'Conspiracy to Defraud' [1988] Crim LR 508; LC 228, *Conspiracy to Defraud* (1994) and JC Smith, 'Conspiracy to Defraud: Some Comments on the Law Commission's Report' [1995] Crim LR 209. The Law Commission offered a defence of its approach: S Silber, 'The Law Commission, Conspiracy to Defraud and the Dishonesty Project' [1995] Crim LR 461, and see JC Smith, Letter [1995] Crim LR 519.

360 See the discussion below in Ch 18. As noted by the Law Commission in LCCP 155, *Legislating the Criminal Code: Fraud and Deception* (1999) in rejecting the idea of an offence based on an element of dishonesty because of anxiety that it would not be compatible with Art 7. See also D Ormerod, 'A Bit of a Con' [1999] Crim LR 789.

361 [2017] UKSC 67.   362 [2020] EWCA Crim 575.   363 LC 276, *Fraud* (2002) para 1.6.

364 See Home Office, *Fraud Law Reform: Consultation on Proposals for Legislation* (2004) para 6. For comment, see P Binning, 'When Dishonesty is Not Enough' (2004) 154 NLJ 1042 and the references cited in Ch 22.

365 See for detailed comment, Ormerod and Williams, *Smith's Law of Theft*, paras 5.65 et seq. HM Crown Prosecution Service Inspectorate, *Review of the Investigation and Criminal Proceedings relating to the Jubilee Line Case* (2006): para 11.88. The Ministry of Justice *Post-Legislative Assessment of the Fraud Act 2006* (2012) concluded that the common law offence of conspiracy to defraud works satisfactorily with the Fraud Act 2006.

adequately reflect the gravity of the offence. Statutory conspiracy to commit a substantive offence should be charged if the alleged agreement satisfies the definition in s 1 of the Criminal Law Act 1977,[366] provided that there is no wider dishonest objective that would be important to the presentation of the prosecution case in reflecting the gravity of the case.[367]

Scope of the offence

It was stated by the House of Lords in *Scott v Metropolitan Police Comr*[368] that:

it is clearly the law that an agreement by two or more by dishonesty to deprive a person of something which is his or to which he is or would be or might be entitled[369] and an agreement by two or more by dishonesty to injure some proprietary right of his, suffices to constitute the offence of conspiracy to defraud.[370]

In *Scott*, D agreed with the employees of cinema owners that in return for payment they would abstract films without the consent of their employers, or of the owners of the copyright, in order that D might make copies infringing the copyright, and distribute them for profit.

It was held that D was guilty of a conspiracy to defraud. It was held to be immaterial that no one was deceived; the offence is one of defrauding. Although the well-known definition of 'defraud' by Buckley J in *Re London and Globe Finance Corpn Ltd*[371] includes a reference to deceit ('to defraud is by deceit to induce a course of action'), there can be fraud without deceit. For example, larceny was an offence which had to be committed 'fraudulently', but deceit has never been a necessary ingredient of theft.

There are two versions of the offence of conspiracy to defraud. The most commonly encountered is that involving dishonest agreements relating to property.[372] In neither version of the offence is it necessary for the alleged co-conspirators to have met. The Court of Appeal in *Cook* stated that, 'It is not a requirement of a criminal conspiracy that the co-conspirators have met to devise their plan, or that any individual participant is aware of the identities of any of the others who are involved.'[373]

Defrauding by imperilling economic interests

In *Evans*,[374] Hickinbottom J, as he then was, preferred to describe the offence in terms of 'a proprietary right or interest of the victim [being] actually or potentially injured'[375] rather than by using the expression 'economic prejudice' which in his lordship's view 'has the potential for obfuscating the true requirement'.[376] It is respectfully submitted, however, that that may be an unduly narrow definition. The House of Lords in *Scott* held that it was sufficient that proprietary rights or interests were to be *affected* by D's dishonest agreement;

366 See *Dady* [2013] EWHC 475 (QB).
367 Available at www.gov.uk/guidance/use-of-the-common-law-offence-of-conspiracy-to-defraud--6.
368 [1975] AC 819.
369 In *Tarling v Government of the Republic of Singapore* (1980) 70 Cr App R 77 the House of Lords by a majority held that the intention of company directors to make and retain a secret profit for which they would have been accountable to the shareholders was not evidence of an intention to defraud. See, however, JC Smith, 'Theft, Conspiracy and Jurisdiction: *Tarling's Case*' [1979] Crim LR 220 at 225–6. In *Adams v R* [1995] 1 WLR 52, the court seems to have been of the view that, even if the agreement to make and retain the secret profit is not an offence, the agreement to take positive steps to conceal it is. See commentary [1995] Crim LR 561, 562.
370 At 1039 per Viscount Dilhorne.   371 [1903] 1 Ch 728 at 732, 733.
372 There is no need for any deprivation.   373 [2017] EWCA Crim 353, [11].
374 *Evans and others* [2014] 1 WLR 2817 (Cardiff Crown Court). After Hickinbottom J dismissed the charges against the defendants, the Serious Fraud Office sought a voluntary bill of indictment. Fulford LJ, sitting as a judge of the Queen's Bench Division, refused the SFO's application. See *SFO v Evans* [2014] EWHC 3803 (QB).
375 At [184].   376 At [169].

it did not hold that there had to be injury or potential injury to property. Moreover, the Law Commission in its Report No 276 catalogued those forms of conduct that are capable of being prosecuted only as conspiracy to defraud,[377] and these include examples in which there is no proprietary interest that is injured. Further, several cases demonstrate that the scope of the offence clearly includes cases where the agreement is to do an act that would not injure a property interest of the victim. In *Button*,[378] DD were convicted of conspiracy to use their employer's dyeing equipment, which they were not permitted to do, in order to make profits for themselves and so to defraud their employer of the profit. In using the dyes they no doubt stole them; but there was no theft of the profit DD made: the employer did not have a proprietary interest in the profit so that the appropriation of that did not constitute a substantive offence.[379] The great majority of agreements to defraud in this category will be agreements to commit offences under the Theft Act and/or the Fraud Act 2006 but clearly there are cases amounting to fraud within the definition. It is submitted that the above authorities demonstrate that conspiracy to defraud is broader than the judgment in *Evans* would suggest. Admittedly, in most cases there will be little difference in practice.

The offence as defined in *Scott* also applies to an agreement to deprive someone temporarily of their property. Parliament chose not to create a *general* offence of temporarily depriving another of his property in the Theft Act;[380] but it remains the case that an agreement so to do is clearly capable of amounting to conspiracy to defraud under *Scott*.[381] Likewise, it is a conspiracy to defraud where D1 and D2 dishonestly agree to shift D1's boundary fence so as to appropriate V's land—an act which is not theft.

It is clear that V is defrauded if he is induced to take an economic risk which he would not have taken but for a deception.[382] It is no answer that D believed that the speculation was a good one and that V had a good chance of making a profit. If V is induced to part with something of economic value, he is probably defrauded even if he does receive the promised return.[383]

In *Evans*, Hickinbottom J confirmed that it is not necessary under this head of conspiracy to defraud that anyone should be deceived, provided that there is a dishonest agreement that some proprietary right of the victim will or might be injured. His lordship also confirmed that in order for a dishonest agreement to amount to a conspiracy to defraud, either the object of the agreement had to be unlawful or, if the object was lawful, the means

---

[377] These included: deception which obtains a benefit which does not count as property, services or any of the other benefits defined in the Theft Acts; deception which causes a loss and obtains a directly corresponding gain, where the two are not the same property (other than a transfer of funds between bank accounts); deception which causes a loss and obtains a gain where the two are neither the same property nor directly correspondent; deception which does not obtain a gain, or cause a loss, but which prejudices another's financial interests; deception for a non-financial purpose; deception to gain a temporary benefit; deceptions which do not cause the obtaining of a benefit; conduct involving a view to gain or an intent to cause loss, but not deception; making a secret gain or causing a loss by abusing a position of trust or fiduciary duty; obtaining a service by giving false information to a machine; 'fixing' an event on which bets have been placed; dishonestly failing to fulfil a contractual obligation; and dishonestly infringing another's legal right. Most are now caught by the general fraud offence in the Fraud Act 2006, s 1.

[378] (1848) 11 QB 929.

[379] JC Smith, 'Embezzlement and the Disobedient Servant' (1956) 19 MLR 39. But see *A-G for Hong Kong v Reid* [1994] 1 AC 324 and p 998.

[380] The CLRC rejected such an offence: Eighth Report, para 29.

[381] The defendants intended to deprive the owners temporarily of the films but permanently of the profits the owners would otherwise have made; and the defrauding was the loss of the profits: [1974] 3 All ER 1032 at 1038.

[382] *Allsop* (1976) 64 Cr App R 29, [1976] Crim LR 738 and commentary; cf *Hamilton* (1845) 1 Cox CC 244; *Carpenter* (1911) 22 Cox CC 618.

[383] *Potger* (1970) 55 Cr App R 42.

of achieving that object had to be unlawful: it is not an offence of conspiracy to defraud to form a dishonest agreement to achieve a lawful object by lawful means.[384] The offence may be broader than this, however. Whilst not necessarily conclusive, there are a number of authorities that suggest conspiracy to defraud can encompass a dishonest agreement to achieve a lawful object by lawful means. For example, in *Cooke* Lord Bridge (repeating what he had earlier held in *Ayres*[385]) stated that:[386]

It is, I apprehend, precisely in order to maintain the criminality of certain forms of fraudulent conduct when agreed to be pursued by persons acting in concert which would not, of itself, be criminal conduct on the part of an individual acting alone that conspiracy to defraud at common law has been preserved.

Cooke was not cited in *Evans and others* and, although not conclusive, it is submitted that the judgment of the House of Lords does call into question what was held in *Evans* about the scope of conspiracy to defraud. Whilst it could be argued that as a matter of principle conspiracy to defraud ought to be confined to cases where there is an agreement to pursue an unlawful means or to attain an unlawful object (or both), there are, however, authorities that suggest the offence is in fact much broader than this.

The breadth and flexibility of the offence are both its vice and its virtue.

Agreement to deceive V to act contrary to public duty

The proposition in *Scott* is not an exclusive definition of conspiracy to defraud. A person is also defrauded if he is deceived into acting contrary to his public duty.[387]

In *Evans*, Hickinbottom J commented that for this form of the offence there is no need to establish any injury to the victim but 'there is a requirement for the victim to be deceived and, as a result of that deceit, act in a different way from that in which he would have acted if he had known the true position'.[388] His lordship stated that this form of the offence requires a causal nexus between the conspirators' agreement and the conduct of V.

It would therefore be a conspiracy to defraud if DD agree by deception to induce a public official to grant an export licence,[389] or to supply information[390] or to induce a professional body to accept an unqualified person as a member,[391] assuming, in each case, that it was the duty of the person so deceived not to do as asked in the actual circumstances of the case. If the public official is persuaded by means other than deception—for example, bribes or threats—to act contrary to his duty, he is obviously not defrauded and the agreement is not a conspiracy to defraud unless it can be said that those affected by the breach of duty have been defrauded—for example, those persons about whom the confidential information is disclosed or, more likely, perhaps, the official's superiors whose duty to keep the information secret has been vicariously violated. Many conspiracies to pervert the course of justice consist in agreements to deceive a public official so that he acts contrary to his duty and are conspiracies to defraud.

Some of their lordships in *Withers*[392] thought that this principle was strictly confined to public officials, and did not extend to the case, for example, of a bank manager deceived

---

384 At [160]. The Court of Appeal made the same point in *Barton* [2020] EWCA Crim 575, [122].
385 [1984] AC 447.
386 [1986] AC 909 at 919. We are grateful to Tony Shaw QC for discussions on this.
387 *Welham v DPP* [1961] AC 103. *Welham* was followed in *Terry* [1984] AC 374, (D, driving his own unlicensed vehicle, displayed on his dashboard an excise licence disc issued to another vehicle intending to cause police officers to act on the assumption that his vehicle was correctly licensed, had an intention to defraud, even though he intended to pay the licence fee).
388 At [48].   389 *Board of Trade v Owen* [1957] AC 602.
390 *DPP v Withers* [1975] AC 842.   391 *Bassey* (1931) 22 Cr App R 160.   392 [1975] AC 842.

into breaking his contractual duty.[393] However, in *Wai Yu-tsang v R*,[394] the Privy Council said that the cases concerned with public duties are not to be regarded as a special category but as examples of the general principle that conspiracy to defraud does not require an intention to cause economic loss. The Board, disapproving Lord Diplock's more restrictive statement in *Scott*,[395] preferred the broad propositions of Lord Denning—'If anyone may be prejudiced in any way by the fraud, that is enough'—and Lord Radcliffe, who agreed with Lord Denning and used similar language, in *Welham*.[396] This seems to open a very broad vista of potential criminal liability.

'Intention' to defraud

If a person is defrauded when he is 'prejudiced', conspirators clearly have a sufficient mens rea if it is their purpose to cause that prejudice by carrying out their agreement. There are *dicta* to the effect that such 'direct' intention in the form of a 'purpose' is required, but in *Wai Yu-tsang* the Privy Council thought this too restrictive and that it is enough that the parties have *agreed to cause* the prejudice. If they have agreed to cause it, that is, to defraud, they intend to defraud, and it is immaterial that defrauding is not their purpose.

The purpose of fraudsters is almost always to make a profit for themselves and not to cause loss to another. They act out of greed, not spite. Since they know that they can make a gain only by causing loss or prejudice, they intend to cause the loss or prejudice, even though they have no 'wish' to cause it and perhaps regret the 'necessity' of doing so in order to achieve their objective.

In the light of these principles, *A-G's Reference (No 1 of 1982)* (the 'whisky-label case')[397] is a doubtful decision. In that case the court suggested that the damage to the victim company by D's false labelling of whisky would have been merely 'a side effect or incidental consequence of the conspiracy and not its object'.[398] The defendants were charged with conspiracy to defraud X Co by causing loss by unlawful labelling, sale and supply of whisky, falsely purporting to be 'X label' products. The agreement was made in England but the whisky was to be sold in Lebanon. The *ratio decidendi* was that the trial judge had rightly held that he had no jurisdiction to try the indictment because the contemplated crime in Lebanon (obtaining by deception from the purchasers of the whisky) would not have been indictable in England. One reason for holding that there was no conspiracy to defraud X Co was that this was not the 'true object' of the agreement. This must now be considered in the light of the decision of the House of Lords in *Cooke*.[399] British Rail stewards boarded a train, equipped with their own food which they dishonestly sold to passengers, instead of that provided by their employers, intending to keep the proceeds of sale for themselves.[400] The House had no

[393] On the broad interpretation of public duty in the offence of misconduct in public office, see *A-G's Reference (No 3 of 2003)* [2004] EWCA Crim 868.
[394] [1991] 4 All ER 664 at 670.
[395] [1975] AC 819 at 840–1. But the court in *Wai* made no reference to *Withers* [1975] AC 842 decided by the same judicial committee at the same time as *Scott*, where Lords Simon and Kilbrandon agreed with Lord Diplock.
[396] [1961] AC 103 at 133 and 124 respectively.
[397] [1983] QB 751, [1983] Crim LR 534 and commentary.
[398] [1983] QB 751 at 757. But in *Governor of Pentonville Prison, ex p Osman* (1990) 90 Cr App R 281 at 298, it was held, distinguishing the whisky-label case, that a conspiracy to deprive V of dollars in the United States was only the means to effecting the 'true object' of the conspiracy which was the defrauding of V in Hong Kong. The distinction is not blindingly obvious.
[399] [1986] AC 909.
[400] They were probably guilty in law of going equipped to cheat the passengers and, when they sold food to them, of obtaining the price by deception. See p 1066.

difficulty in holding that they were guilty of conspiracy to defraud British Rail. It is true that the House was preoccupied with the problem of distinguishing *Ayres*, the 'whisky-label case' was not cited and it does not appear that it was argued that the loss to British Rail was 'a side effect or incidental consequence'. Nevertheless, it is clear that this was a case where the object of the conspirators was to make a profit out of the customers, not to defraud British Rail.

Of course, one must agree with Lord Lane CJ in the 'whisky-label case'[401] that 'it would be contrary to principle, as well as being impracticable for the courts, to attribute to defendants constructive intentions to defraud third parties based on what the defendants should have foreseen as probable or possible consequences'. Constructive intentions are unwelcome in criminal law; but presumably the House in *Cooke* thought that a jury could properly find that the defendants must have known that their conduct would, inevitably, cause loss to British Rail. If so, it was right to hold that they *intended*[402] to defraud British Rail and it should be immaterial that this was not their *purpose*.

The intention must always be proved.[403] The Privy Council in *Cassell v The Queen* emphasized that the mens rea for the offence is subjective.[404] Thus, the use abroad of a stolen chequebook and cheque card is capable of being fraud on a bank in England because the effect is to cause the bank in England to meet its legal or commercial obligation to honour the cheque; but, if D is charged with conspiracy to defraud the bank, the jury must be directed that he appreciated that his conduct would have this effect.[405] Subject to any jurisdictional problem, it is submitted that, on a proper direction, the whisky-label conspirators might properly have been convicted of conspiracy to defraud the X Co. They might have been more sophisticated in this respect than the stewards in *Cooke* and better able to appreciate the effect of their actions on third parties.

Prejudice includes putting at risk

If the conspirators know that the effect of carrying out the agreement will be, for example, to put V's property at risk, then they intend prejudice to V and, if they are dishonest, they are guilty of conspiracy to defraud him.[406] This is so notwithstanding that it turns out that V's property is unimpaired, or even that he makes a profit out of the transaction. A clear example would be where the conspirators agree to take V's money without his consent and then bet with it on a horse with odds at 20 to 1. They have agreed to defraud him and the conspiracy is not undone even if the horse wins and, as they intended throughout, they pay half the winnings into his bank account. This, it is submitted, is the best explanation of *Allsop*[407] in which D helped applicants for hire-purchase finance for cars to fill in forms using false information. D believed the finance company, V, would get its money; the applicant would get the car and the car dealer would get his sale. D also got his commission. The judgment is difficult because of its reliance on two *dicta* of Lord Diplock which were mutually inconsistent and have both since been disapproved; but the decision on the facts is readily explicable. D was a 'sub-broker' for a hire-purchase finance company, V. His function was to introduce prospective hire-purchasers who wished to acquire cars. In collusion with others, he filled in application forms with false statements about the value of the cars and the payment of deposits so as to cause V to accept applications for hire-purchase finance which, otherwise, it might have rejected. He expected and believed that the transactions he introduced would be duly completed, so that V would achieve its contemplated profit to the advantage of all

---

401 [1983] 2 All ER 721 at 724.   402 See p 95, Ch 3.

403 See eg *Sentamu* [2013] EWCA Crim 248. The court seemed to import the test for statutory conspiracy in *Saik* [2006] UKHL 18.

404 [2016] UKPC 19.   405 *McPherson and Watts* [1985] Crim LR 508.

406 See Ormerod and Williams, *Smith's Law of Theft*, para 5.28.   407 (1976) 64 Cr App R 29.

concerned, including D who got his commission. His defence was that he did not intend V to suffer any pecuniary loss or be prejudiced in any way. The court found that V was defrauded when it was induced to do the very acts which D intended it to do. V paid an excessive price for cars and advanced money to persons who were not as creditworthy as they were alleged to be. This not merely put it at risk of being defrauded, but actually defrauded it: 'Interests which are imperilled are less valuable in terms of money than those same interests when they are secure and protected.'[408] The result intended by D was, in law, the defrauding of V; and V was in law defrauded. It is wholly immaterial whether D would have regarded that result as 'fraud'. If he did not, he was making a mistake of criminal law.

According to this explanation, D intended to prejudice V. The facts admitted of no other interpretation. The judge in that case had directed the jury that they could convict if they were satisfied that D realized that his conduct was *likely to lead* to the detriment or prejudice of V. If this is taken literally, it is sufficient that D is reckless (in the *Cunningham/G* sense) whether prejudice—that is, defrauding—occurs. It is submitted that this would be going too far and take common law conspiracy out of line with statutory conspiracy. In *Wai Yu-tseng*, the Privy Council expressed a reluctance 'to allow this part of the law to become enmeshed in a distinction, sometimes artificially drawn between intention and recklessness'; but they then said, of *Allsop* and the instant case, that it is enough that:

the conspirators have dishonestly agreed to bring about a state of affairs which they realize will *or may* deceive the victim into so acting, or failing to act, that he will suffer economic loss or his economic interests will be put at risk.[409]

The use of the words, 'or may', admit recklessness as a sufficient mens rea—it is enough that the parties have taken a conscious risk of causing prejudice. This was probably not necessary to the decision since the trial judge had directed the jury that D was guilty if he knew what he had done 'would cause detriment or prejudice to another'.

Dishonesty in putting property at risk

The intention to defraud is readily discernible where there could be no question of D believing he has any right to do what he did. More difficult is the case where company directors take a risk with the company's property, perhaps hoping to make a large profit and so benefit the shareholders. If the risk taken was such that 'no director could have honestly believed . . . it was in the interest of that company that the risk should be taken',[410] then the company is defrauded. Whether a risk is unjustifiable is a question of judgement and a matter of degree. There is no clear dividing line between right and wrong, such as was crossed in *Allsop* when false statements were made, or in *Wai Yu-tseng* where the dishonouring of cheques was concealed in a bank account. Whether the risk is so grave that no director could believe it justified is equally a matter of judgement and degree. Conspiracy to defraud thus lacks the precision that we should normally look for in any offence, and certainly in one of this seriousness. The courts have made clear that care needs to be taken in drafting indictments to ensure that sufficient detail is provided,[411] *and* in particular making clear a distinction between the agreement alleged and the reasonable information given in respect of it.[412]

---

[408] ibid, at 32 per Shaw LJ.

[409] Emphasis in original. In *Bermingham* [2020] EWCA Crim 1662 the Court of Appeal held that a party to the agreement must intend that each of the relevant elements of the offence will be carried out.

[410] *Sinclair* (1968) 52 Cr App R 618.

[411] See eg *Landy* (1981) 72 Cr App R 237. See also more recently *Evans* [2014] 1 WLR 2817.

[412] *K* [2004] EWCA Crim 2685. It was noted, however, that it is only necessary to specify in detail in the indictment the agreement, and not how the participants intended individually to go about (or had gone about) defrauding V; and see *Giannakopoulos* [2005] EWCA Crim 247. See also *Fussell* [1997] Crim LR 812.

Dishonesty

Dishonesty is an essential constituent of the mens rea but historically there has been controversy about what 'dishonesty' means in this context. In *Landy*,[413] the court appeared to think that the ultimate test was whether the *defendant* thought his conduct dishonest. In *McIvor*,[414] the court reiterated this view, holding that the test in theft is different; but shortly afterwards in *Ghosh*[415] it was held that the same test should be applied in conspiracy to defraud as in theft. The *Ghosh* test applied until changed by the Supreme Court in *Ivey*. To preclude different tests for dishonesty applying to different offences, the test for dishonesty in this offence must follow that test: *Barton*[416] involving convictions for conspiracy to defraud.

It is at least arguable that the overwhelmingly objective nature of the *Ivey/Barton* test makes an already broad offence even broader. Even if D is genuinely unaware that no 'ordinary decent company director' would have taken the risk in question, he can still be dishonest applying *Ivey* and therefore guilty of the offence. It is disappointing that the desirability of this possibility was not addressed by the Supreme Court.

Fraud: by whom?

In statutory conspiracy it is expressly provided that the contemplated offence is to be committed 'by one or more of the parties to the agreement'.[417] In *Hollinshead*,[418] the Court of Appeal held that this was a restatement of the common law, so the same principle applied to conspiracy to defraud: the contemplated fraud must be one which is to be perpetrated by one of the parties to the agreement in the course of carrying it out. But complete execution of the agreement to sell the black boxes in that case would not defraud anyone. The parties contemplated that the fraud would be carried out by other persons, not yet ascertained, who would buy the boxes and use them to defraud the electricity suppliers. The court therefore quashed the convictions for conspiracy to defraud—but they were restored by the House of Lords. The House held that the 'purpose' of the defendants was to cause economic loss to the electricity suppliers. This is difficult to understand. Their purpose was to make a profit by selling the devices to the (as they thought) middleman. Presumably they did not care what happened to the boxes after they had sold them. If, post-sale, they had been accidentally destroyed in a fire, they would not consider that their enterprise had failed. On the contrary, they might have been pleased at the prospect of selling some more. The House seems to have been much influenced by the fact that the boxes were 'dishonest devices' with only one 'purpose', which was to cause loss. But 'purpose' is here used in the sense of 'function'. An inanimate thing cannot have a 'purpose' (any more than it can be 'dishonest') in the sense in which that word is used in the law of conspiracy. However that may be, *Hollinshead* seems to broaden the law of conspiracy to defraud to include the case where the defendants contemplate that the execution of their agreement will enable some third party to perpetrate a fraud.

Jurisdiction over conspiracy to defraud

An agreement in England or Wales to carry out a fraud abroad is not indictable at common law in England or Wales as a conspiracy to defraud.[419] This is now regulated by s 5(3) of the Criminal Justice Act 1993 which provides that, where the conspiracy would be triable in

413 [1981] 1 All ER 1172 at 1181.   414 [1982] 1 WLR 409.
415 [1982] QB 1053. See *Cox and Hodges* [1983] Crim LR 167 and commentary (fraudulent trading).
416 [2020] EWCA Crim 575.
417 Criminal Law Act 1977, s 1(1)(a), p 458.   418 [1985] 1 All ER 850 at 857, p 471.
419 See generally Hirst, *Jurisdiction and the Ambit of the Criminal Law*, 175–8.

England but for the fraud, which the parties had not envisaged intending to take place in England and Wales, a person may be guilty of conspiracy to defraud if:[420]

(a) a party to the agreement constituting the conspiracy, or a party's agent, did anything in England and Wales in relation to the agreement before its formation, or

(b) a party to it became a party in England and Wales (by joining it either in person or through an agent), or

(c) a party to it or a party's agent, did or omitted anything in England and Wales in pursuance of it.

ECHR

As has been noted, the offence is heavily dependent on the concept of dishonesty, and that test is one lacking in certainty.[421] Concerns were raised by Liberty and the Joint Parliamentary Committee on Human Rights as to whether the offence was compatible with Art 7 of the ECHR which prohibits criminal laws which lack sufficient certainty. The Law Commission acknowledged the force of the argument in its Report on *Fraud* by stating:

We continue to believe that a general dishonesty offence, by not requiring as an element some identifiable morally dubious conduct to which the test of dishonesty may be applied, would fail to provide any meaningful guidance on the scope of the criminal law and the conduct which may be lawfully pursued. We do not accept the argument that inherent uncertainty is satisfactorily cured by the promise of prosecutorial discretion.[422]

These views were echoed by the Joint Parliamentary Committee on Human Rights which, when scrutinizing the Fraud Bill, concluded:[423]

we remain concerned that the common law offence of conspiracy to defraud is a general dishonesty offence and as such is not compatible with the common law and ECHR requirements of legal certainty for the reasons given above.

A challenge seems most likely if the conspiracy to defraud offence is used in a case where it amounts to an allegation of an agreement to act dishonestly, even though that action would not constitute an agreement to perform a criminal offence.[424]

There is plenty of authority supporting the argument against such a broad common law offence being expanded.[425] Examples include confirmation from the House of Lords in *Jones*[426] that criminal law can only be extended by Parliament and that the English common law does not permit the creation of new offences nor the application of existing offences to activity previously regarded as outside the remit of the criminal law.[427] Similarly in *Goldstein and Rimmington*,[428] the House of Lords stated that:

Where Parliament has defined the ingredients of an offence, perhaps stipulating what shall and shall not be a defence, and has prescribed a mode of trial and a maximum penalty, it must ordinarily be proper that conduct falling within that definition should be prosecuted for the statutory offence and not for a common law offence which may or may not provide the same defences and for which the potential penalty is unlimited.[429]

---

[420] Hirst argues that s 5(3) should be charged separately from and in addition to conspiracy to defraud.
[421] See p 482.   [422] Para 5.28.   [423] Para 2.25.
[424] The challenge to the offence of cheating on this basis failed in *Pattni* [2001] Crim LR 570 (Southwark CC), and see more recently *Bermingham* [2020] EWCA Crim 1662.
[425] See in the case of the conspiracy to defraud offence, *Zemmel* (1985) 81 Cr App R 279.
[426] [2006] UKHL 16.   [427] At [28]–[29].   [428] [2005] UKHL 63.
[429] At [30]. See also the ECtHR decision in *Hashman and Harrup v UK* (2000) 30 EHRR 241. See *Dady*, n 366.

In the extradition case of *Norris v US*, the particular form of conduct that had not been pre-viously charged as a conspiracy to defraud involved the dishonest agreement between sup-pliers to fix prices or limit production. Such anti-competitive cartels are now proscribed by a series of specific offences introduced by the Enterprise Act 2002. The allegation in *Norris v US* and the related case of *GG* was that the conspirators routinely sold product to their cus-tomers under an agreement to avoid price competition. In effect, the allegation was that the conspirators 'defrauded their customers by requiring that they pay higher prices than they might otherwise have paid had there been no conspiracy'. The argument that this charge infringed Art 7 was rejected by the Administrative Court and the Court of Appeal.[430]

In the House of Lords[431] the House rejected the lower courts' approach, acknowledg-ing the 'consistent message . . . through cases decided from 1875 through to 1984 . . . that price-fixing was not of itself capable of constituting a crime . . . There was no reported case, indeed, it would appear, no unreported case, no textbook, no article which suggested oth-erwise.'[432] Their lordships, having regard to *Jones* and *Rimmington*, concluded that it would infringe the principle of legality to allow a first prosecution for conspiracy to defraud on the terms alleged.

Conspiracy to defraud and the Fraud Act 2006

In view of the breadth of offences created under the Fraud Act 2006, very little fraudulent conduct will now be chargeable *only* as conspiracy to defraud. The Home Office suggested that possibly the only instances of conspiracy to defraud not covered by the 2006 Act would be dishonestly failing to fulfil a contractual obligation;[433] deception for a non-financial pur-pose; 'fixing' an event on which bets have been placed; and dishonestly infringing another's legal right.[434] In respect of those situations, it is questionable whether they ought to be criminal at all: hence, the Law Commission's 2002 Report recommendation that conspiracy to defraud should be abolished.[435] Indeed, the Law Commission went so far as to describe the continued existence of the offence as 'indefensible'.[436] The Home Office had also stated:

if we achieve a proper and full definition of fraud there should be no need for a fall back offence of this kind.[437]

On public consultation by the Home Office, the majority were opposed to abolition of the offence.[438] The main arguments for retention of the offence of conspiracy to defraud despite the incredible breadth of the Fraud Act offences were that: abolition might leave an unfore-seen lacuna in the law;[439] retention would be necessary, even with the availability of the new fraud offences where, for example, a person allows his bank account to be used by a third party to transfer funds (typically from overseas) which form part of a conspiracy to defraud; retention was needed to deal with cases like *Hollinshead*;[440] most importantly, there are cases in which the use of the conspiracy to defraud charges, although not necessary, would render a prosecution far easier than if charges were brought under the 2006 Act.[441]

---

[430] The court was influenced by Sir Jeremy Lever QC and J Pike, 'Cartel Agreements, Criminal Conspiracy and the Statutory "Cartel Offence"' (2005) 26 ECLR 90.

[431] *Norris v US* [2008] UKHL 16; *GG Plc* [2008] UKHL 17.   [432] At [55].

[433] Now possibly an offence under s 3 of the Fraud Act 2006.

[434] Home Office, *Fraud Law Reform* (2004) para 38.

[435] See also LC 228, *Conspiracy to Defraud* (1994).   [436] LC 276, *Fraud* (2002) para 1.4.

[437] Home Office, *Fraud Law Reform* (2004) para 37.

[438] See Home Office, *Fraud Law Reform Responses to Consultation* (2004).   [439] See ibid, paras 39–45.

[440] This is misplaced. The conduct would be caught by s 7 of the Fraud Act 2006.

[441] Ormerod and Williams, *Smith's Law of Theft*, para 5.65.

As Jarvis makes clear in his discussion of *Evans*, 'It would be a mistake to assume that if the facts of a case reek of dishonesty but don't fit snugly into any of the statutory offences (such as the various fraud offences under the Fraud Act 2006) then conspiracy to defraud will catch them as a last resort.'[442]

11.3.5.2 Conspiracy to corrupt public morals

In *Shaw v DPP*,[443] the House of Lords (Lord Reid dissenting) held that a conspiracy to corrupt public morals is an offence. D published a booklet—the Ladies' Directory—which advertised the names and addresses of sex workers with, in some cases, photographs and, in others, particulars of sexual activities which they were willing to perform. He was convicted of inter alia conspiring to corrupt public morals and Obscene Publications Act offences. The House of Lords held that there was an offence of conspiring to commit a public mischief and that the corruption of public morals was a public mischief; but it did not reject the view of the Court of Criminal Appeal that to corrupt public morals is a substantive offence. Lord Simon in *DPP v Withers*[444] concluded that there were three possible *rationes decidendi*.

(1) There is a substantive offence of corrupting public morals, so an agreement to do so is a conspiracy.

(2) The corruption of public morals is a separate head of conspiracy.

(3) There is an offence of conspiracy to effect a public mischief and the corruption of public morals is a public mischief.

Lord Simon held that it was open to the House to reject *ratio* (3) and, indeed, the decision does so. Since Lord Tucker did not decide in *Shaw* that there is a substantive offence of corrupting public morals, it seems clear that the *ratio* must be taken to be (2).

It is therefore uncertain whether an agreement to corrupt public morals is a statutory conspiracy which should be charged under the 1977 Act; but judges of first instance may consider themselves bound by the decision of the Court of Criminal Appeal to hold that it is. *Shaw* was followed in *Knuller*[445] where, Lord Diplock dissenting, the House held that an agreement to publish advertisements to facilitate the commission of sexual acts between adult males in private was a conspiracy to corrupt public morals, although such conduct was by then not criminal.[446] Lord Reid maintained his view that *Shaw* was wrongly decided but held that it should nevertheless be followed in the interests of certainty in the law. Given the existence of the offence, he thought there was sufficient evidence of its commission on these facts.[447]

In *Shaw*, Lord Simonds used language which suggested that the House was asserting the right to expand the scope of the criminal law:[448]

In the sphere of criminal law I entertain no doubt that there remains in the courts of law a residual power to enforce the supreme and fundamental purpose of the law, to conserve not only the safety and order but also the moral welfare of the State, and that it is their duty to guard it against attacks which may be the more insidious because they are novel and unprepared for.

In *Knuller*, however, the House was emphatic that there is no residual power to create new offences; that is a task for Parliament. 'What the courts can and should do (as was truly

[442] P Jarvis, 'Conspiracy to Defraud: A Siren to Lure Unwary Prosecutors' [2014] Crim LR 738, 742.
[443] [1962] AC 220.   [444] [1974] 3 All ER 984 at 1003. See p 455.   [445] [1973] AC 435.
[446] See Ch 17.   [447] See [1972] 2 All ER 898 at 904.
[448] [1962] AC 220 at 267. For a judicial view to the contrary, see Stephen, III HCL, 359. See S Davies, *Annual Survey of English Law* (1932) 276–7. For criticism of *Shaw*, see D Seaborne Davies (1962) 6 J Society of Public Teachers of Law (NS) 104; A Goodhart (1961) 77 LQR 560; Williams (1961) 24 MLR 626; and [1961] Crim LR 470.

laid down in *Shaw*'s case) is to recognize the applicability of established offences to new circumstances to which they are relevant.'[449] This is no longer tenable. Moreover, a finding that conduct is liable to corrupt public morals was said to be one not lightly to be reached. It is not enough that it is liable to 'lead morally astray'. Lord Simon of Glaisdale went so far as to say that, 'The words "corrupt public morals" suggest conduct which a jury might find to be destructive of the very fabric of society.'[450]

There are very strong objections of principle to an offence based on such vague notions of morality. It is doubtful whether such an offence would withstand challenge under Art 7 of the ECHR for its uncertainty. If the allegations involve the publication of material it may also be that a defence under Art 10 arises.[451] In view of the range of specific statutory offences dealing with obscenity and indecent images, it is doubtful whether there is any need to retain the offence of conspiracy to corrupt public morals.[452] Unfortunately, the offence did not form part of the comprehensive review of sexual offences conducted in 2000.[453]

It is important to recall the House of Lords' confirmation in *Rimmington* that where Parliament has defined the ingredients of an offence, the statutory offence and not the common law offence should be relied on.[454]

11.3.5.3 Conspiracy to outrage public decency

A majority of the House in *Knuller* (Lords Reid and Diplock dissenting) held that there is a common law offence of outraging public decency[455] and, consequently, it is an offence to conspire to outrage public decency. But:

'outrage', like 'corrupt' is a very strong word. 'Outraging public decency' goes considerably beyond offending the susceptibilities of, or even shocking, reasonable people [T]he offence is concerned with recognized minimum standards of decency, which are likely to vary from time to time . . . [N]otwithstanding that 'public' in the offence is used in a locative sense, public decency must be viewed as a whole; and . . . the jury should be invited, where appropriate, to remember that they live in a plural society, with a tradition of tolerance towards minorities, and that this atmosphere of tolerance is itself part of public decency.[456]

This is a strict test. In *Choi*,[457] the defendant had secretly filmed women using a public lavatory in a supermarket. The court considered the meaning of the expression 'outraging public decency' and concluded that it involved activity which 'fills the onlooker with loathing or extreme distaste or causes them extreme annoyance'. Following the decisions of the Court of Appeal, including *Hamilton*,[458] recognizing the existence of a substantive offence of outraging public decency, it may well be prudent to charge the offence under s 1 of the 1977 Act. Statutory conspiracies and common law conspiracies to corrupt public morals or to outrage public decency remain mutually exclusive, under s 5(3) of the 1977 Act. The prosecutor cannot therefore hedge his bets.

---

[449] [1972] 2 All ER 898 at 932 per Lord Simon of Glaisdale. This seems impossible to square with *Rimmington*.

[450] cf Lord Devlin's views, p 10.   [451] This is discussed in Ch 30 on 'Publication offences'.

[452] A Hamilton, 'Live Streamed Sex Videos' (2003) 14(2) Computers and the Law 29, considers the possibility of prosecution for live video broadcasts on the internet.

[453] See especially *Setting the Boundaries* (2000), available at http://webarchive.nationalarchives.gov.uk/+/http://www.homeoffice.gov.uk/documents/vol1main.pdf?view=Binary and the discussion later in Ch 17.

[454] [2005] UKHL 63, [30].

[455] See Ch 30, following *Mayling* [1963] 2 QB 717.

[456] [1972] 2 All ER 898 at 936 per Lord Simon.   [457] [1999] 8 Arch News 3.

[458] [2007] EWCA Crim 2062, Ch 30. The Law Commission has proposed abolition of this common law conspiracy: LC 358, *Simplification of the Criminal Law: Public Nuisance and Outraging Public Decency* (2015).

11.3.6 Reform of conspiracy

Conspiracy is one of the most complex offences in English law. It is ill-defined and lacks even a clear rationale. Few would deny that reform is desirable. However, many of the complexities have developed as a result of a willingness of prosecutors to stretch the offence to breaking point, using it as a convenient 'device' for presenting a continuing course of conduct involving numerous defendants. Arguably, reform should look to deter prosecutors from stretching the boundaries of the offence, not encourage it. The Law Commission's recommendations in LC 318—particularly the dilution of mens rea—will extend the scope of the offence dramatically. Take D1 and D2 who own a bureau de change. If they intend that people transfer money in their business and foresee a risk that criminal property might be transferred by a third party through their business (this is surely inevitable in any such exchange) and agree nevertheless to continue to transfer any monies that do come into their business, it would appear that they would commit the offence of conspiring to launder money under the Commission's plan. Their foresight of a risk that some money will be the proceeds of crime, coupled with their willingness to take that risk, constitute a sufficient mens rea. That stands in stark contrast to the House of Lords' interpretation of the offence of conspiracy in *Saik* as requiring proof of intention or knowledge that criminal property will be transferred.

11.4 Encouragement and assistance under the Serious Crime Act 2007

11.4.1 Introduction

At common law it was an offence for D to incite another person, P, to do or cause to be done an act or acts which, if done by P, would involve the commission of the offence or offences by P.[459] It had to be shown that D intended or believed that P, if he acted as D encouraged him, would do so with the fault required for the offence or offences. The second element of mens rea required proof that D knew (or had deliberately closed his eyes) to any material circumstances which were necessary elements alongside the conduct and consequences (if any) of the offence he was inciting. For example, if D was inciting P to sexually assault V (a child under 13), D would have to have intended that P would sexually touch her (conduct) and D would have to have known that V would be under 13 (circumstance). D did not need to do any more than incite with that state of mind. D could be liable irrespective of whether P committed the offence.[460]

This was a simple offence that generated very few appeals. Unfortunately, it has been swept away with one of the most complex pieces of criminal legislation to have been drafted in recent times.[461]

---

[459] See, for detailed analysis, R Fortson, *Blackstone's Guide to the Serious Crime Act 2007* (2008) Ch 6; R Fortson, 'Inchoate Liability and the Part 2 Offences under the Serious Crime Act 2007' in A Reed and M Bohlander (eds), *Participation in Crime—Domestic and Comparative Perspectives* (2013). We are extremely grateful to Rudi Fortson QC for his valuable comments on a draft of this part of this chapter. We have drawn on the collaborative piece, D Ormerod and R Fortson, 'Serious Crime Act 2007: The Part 2 Offences' [2009] Crim LR 389.

[460] For a discussion of the offence see earlier editions of this work.

[461] For critical comment see Ormerod and Fortson [2009] Crim LR 389; JR Spencer and G Virgo, 'Encouraging and Assisting Crime' [2008] 9 Arch News 7. The complexity of the provisions has also been recognized by the House of Commons Justice Committee. The Committee expressed concern and recommended that the Ministry of Justice conduct a further post-legislative assessment of Part 2 and, in the interim, if the number of appeals increases to consider bringing forward legislative proposals for revising or even replacing Part 2 to meet the purpose of the legislation in a less tortuous fashion. The government disagreed and did not believe that further post-legislative scrutiny would serve any purpose.

Part 2 of the SCA 2007 has been in force since October 2008. It abolished the common law offence of incitement[462] replacing it with three new offences. They are based on the Law Commission's Report No 300[463] although the provisions as finally enacted differ from the Commission's recommendations. In summary, Part 2 of the SCA 2007 creates offences where:

- D does an act that is *capable* of encouraging or assisting another, P, *intending* to encourage or to assist P, to commit an offence (s 44);

- D does an act that is *capable* of encouraging or assisting P, *believing* that the offence by P will be committed and, D *believes* that his act will encourage or assist its commission (s 45);

- D does an act that is *capable* of encouraging or assisting the commission of one or more of a number of offence*s by P*, and he *believes* (a) that one or more of those offences will be committed (without having any belief as to which particular crime); and (b) that his act will encourage or assist the commission of one or more of them (s 46).

11.4.2 Background to the Act

It is doubtful whether these tortuously complex offences were necessary.[464] The law of incitement was well settled. Even if the breadth of the offences was necessary, the complex drafting style was not.

In Law Commission Report No 300, the Law Commission recommended two broad new offences. The first was relatively uncontroversial at least in terms of its breadth, if not its complexity: encouraging or assisting the commission of a criminal act *intending*[465] that the criminal act should be committed. This has been enacted in s 44 of the SCA 2007. The second proposal was for an offence with a wider mens rea for the assister or encourager: it would be sufficient if D *believed* that his encouragement or assistance would (not might) encourage or assist P in the commission of the criminal act, believing that P would (not might) commit it. Parliament produced a scheme of broader and more complex offences with wider mens rea.

In Part 4 of Report No 300, the Commission addressed the possible pros and cons of offences of assisting and encouraging. The pros included that such inchoate offences: (a) allow enforcement agencies to combat serious crime at an earlier stage; are based on strong utilitarian principles; (b) eliminate the element of risk inherent in making D's liability turn on whether P will act or not; (c) reflect D's culpability for the actions he has taken and contribute to a coherent scheme of offences; and (d) provide appropriate labels for the criminal conduct. Against the imposition of such inchoate liability are arguments that the offences: (a) are too broad and criminalize D's lawful conduct on the basis of his mens rea alone; (b) are too premature and may saddle D with liability unfairly; (c) create a disparity between the criminality of the assister who will be liable in every case and the principal who will only be liable if he performs the full offence; and (d) are likely to be in vague form

---

[462] Section 59. The many statutory offences of incitement have been retained and are set out in Sch 3. They include soliciting murder. See Ch 15. Statutory conspiracy under s 1 of the Criminal Law Act 1977, and criminal attempts under s 1 of the Criminal Attempts Act 1981, are unaffected. Similarly, liability as an accessory under s 8 of the Accessories and Abettors Act 1861 is not altered by the provisions. There will be a considerable degree of overlap.

[463] *Inchoate Liability for Assisting and Encouraging Crime* (2006). See also the HL Research Paper 07/52, and the Home Office Green Paper, *New Powers Against Organised and Financial Crime* (2006) Cm 6875 at 24 et seq.

[464] But see the statements in *New Powers Against Organised and Financial Crime* (2006) 25; and see GR Sullivan, 'Inchoate Liability for Assisting and Encouraging' [2005] Crim LR 1047.

[465] See LC 300, para 5.89.

with too great a degree of dependence on D's mens rea. The Law Commission rebutted the arguments against, being driven by the moral principle that D is culpable and deserving of punishment once he has performed his acts of assistance or encouragement irrespective of whether P performs the conduct of the substantive offence.[466]

The Law Commission's recommendations in LC 300 are only properly appreciated when read with LC 305 where the Law Commission provides a new range of offences to deal with all aspects of secondary liability.[467] If enacted, there would be eight separate offences to deal with assisting and encouraging.[468] Unless the recommendations in LC 305 are enacted, which is very unlikely, the law will be left in a rather imbalanced state. The inchoate offences in the 2007 Act were designed by the Law Commission to be of wide application, in part because the Commission proposed that the offences to replace secondary liability would be much narrower.

11.4.3 The scope and forms of liability

Four matters need to be understood from the outset.[469] First, the offences create inchoate liability. D (with the requisite fault) will be liable as soon as he has performed any act *capable*[470] of assisting or encouraging P irrespective of whether it has any effect on P, or whether P goes on to commit the offence, or even whether D had communicated with P.[471] As the Law Commission suggested:

If D sells P a weapon that D intends P will use to murder V, D has done everything that he or she intends to do. Nothing more turns on D's subsequent conduct whereas P has yet to take the step of attempting to commit the offence.[472]

Secondly, the offences apply also where D has done any act capable of assisting or encouraging P and it *has* assisted or encouraged. D will be liable in such circumstances even if P did not commit the anticipated offence. Again, D's liability is inchoate.[473]

Thirdly, the offences are also available against D even if P *has* committed the offence if D has done any acts capable of assisting or encouraging: s 49(1). This overlaps with D's secondary liability under the Accessories and Abettors Act 1861. This was a specific aim of the Law Commission. The result is to add to the breadth and confusion of the law. Under s 44, for example, D will be liable in relation to the criminal act that he *intended* (say, murder) rather than the actual offence committed by P (perhaps only wounding). In some cases the Crown would have the choice of charging D with aiding and abetting wounding or assisting and encouraging murder. There is a significant advantage in charging D with the offence under s 44 rather than as an accessory to P's act because it does not matter whether P has deliberately changed the manner of offence, or the identity of the victim.[474] Furthermore,

---

[466] ibid, para 4.18. See also the valuable discussion in RD Taylor, 'Procuring, Causation, Innocent Agency and the Law Commission' [2008] Crim LR 32; W Wilson, 'A Rational Scheme of Liability for Participating in Crime' [2008] Crim LR 3.

[467] See Wilson [2008] Crim LR 3 discussing the coherence that will be brought to bear when they are both enacted.

[468] See also the comments on LC 300 by GR Sullivan, 'Inchoate Liability for Assisting and Encouraging' [2005] Crim LR 1047.

[469] The discussion is based on s 44 because it is the simplest of the offences. The distinctions apply to the other sections.

[470] LC 300, para 5.22.   [471] *Ransford* (1874) 31 LT 488.   [472] LC 300, para 4.25.

[473] Where D does acts capable of encouraging P, his liability is in one sense wider than liability for conspiracy between D and P because P need not share his intention.

[474] See LC 300, para 5.5. This is different from the position where D is a secondary party, see Ch 6.

D could be liable under these provisions of the 2007 Act where P is incapable of committing the offence in relation to which D has done acts to assist or encourage.[475]

Fourthly, the offences are available not only against D, but also against P, the person D has assisted or encouraged. This may seem rather surprising, but is a logical application of the terms of the offences. Again, to take an example from the Law Commission's Report No 300,[476] P will be liable if:

P asks D to supply him or her with an article so that P can commit an offence, P is doing an act capable of encouraging D to do an act capable of assisting P to commit an offence. In other words, if D supplies the article to P, not only is D committing at least the [s 45] offence but, by encouraging D to commit the [s 45] offence, P is committing the [s 44] offence.[477]

The extent to which prosecutors will abandon reliance on other offences and rely on these offences to charge those whom we would currently regard as principals and secondary parties as well as inciters is open to debate. Graham Virgo makes the point that following the judgment in *Jogee* there is a growing disconnect between the breadth of inchoate liability and the court's more restrictive interpretation of accessorial liability. This disconnect is attributable to the fact that following *Jogee* the prosecution must be able to prove intention on the part of the accessory before he will be guilty as an accessory, whereas in the context of the 2007 Act recklessness may suffice as a substantive element. Virgo argues that this might lead prosecutors to prefer to charge D with the inchoate offence of assisting or encouraging despite the commission of the substantive offence.[478] The relationship between secondary liability and inchoate liability is discussed in more detail later.

11.4.3.1 Interpreting the 2007 Act

The offences are rendered complex because the sections (and the rest of that Part of the Act) include extended definitions of (a) what suffices as relevant conduct by D; and (b) the subdivision of the elements of the offence to be committed by P, into conduct, circumstances and consequences.[479] Unfortunately, several of the fundamental terms in the offences are left undefined, including core elements of the actus reus: 'encouraging' and 'assisting'.[480] The Law Commission Report No 300 will serve as an important interpretative document, but given the degree of difference between what was proposed and what was enacted, considerable caution is warranted. In addition, caution must be exercised in reading the statute itself since the true scope of the offences in ss 44 to 46 cannot be appreciated without reference to the ensuing 20 sections.

11.4.3.2 What must D's conduct have been capable of assisting or encouraging?

The Act describes D's conduct in terms of acts capable of encouraging or assisting the commission of '*an offence*'. Although at first sight the 2007 Act appears to require focus on whether D's act was capable of assisting or encouraging P's *crime*, in fact, the statute only requires proof that D's acts are capable of assisting or encouraging the *conduct element* of P's offence.[481] The Law

---

[475] LC 300, paras 4.22–4.26.   [476] Para 4.26.   [477] See also *Goldman* [2001] EWCA Crim 1684.

[478] G Virgo, 'The Relationship Between Inchoate Liability and Accessorial Liability after *Jogee*' [2016] 9 Arch Rev 6.

[479] For an alternative model by which inchoate offences may be analysed, see J Child and A Hunt, '*Mens Rea* and the General Inchoate Offences: Another New Culpability Framework' (2012) 63 NILQ 247. See also a reformulated version of this complex scheme in J Child, 'The Structure, Coherence and Limits of Inchoate Liability: The New Ulterior Intent' (2014) 34 LS 537.

[480] This has been a feature of legislation in which the draftsman introduces undue technicality in some aspects of the statute whilst failing to define the essentials. See the Sexual Offences Act 2003 and the Fraud Act 2006 for other examples.

[481] Section 47(2)–(4) explains what those expressions *really mean* (namely, the conduct element of the anticipated offence): s 47(2)—for s 44; s 47(3)—for s 45; s 47(4)—for s 46.

Commission proposal focused on whether D's *acts* were capable of assisting or encouraging P's 'criminal act', by which the Commission meant merely the conduct element of P's offence.[482] The Law Commission accepted that D ought not to be liable because he intends or believes that P should or will commit an 'act' that is criminal. The 'act' that is criminal in theft is the appropriation of property. It would be absurd if D could be criminally liable for doing nothing more than encouraging P to do that 'act' of mere appropriation by eg touching V's property.[483] The difference is significant because in some cases D's act of assistance or encouragement will be with intent towards a result which goes beyond the conduct element of P's offence.

11.4.4 Intentionally assisting or encouraging a crime: s 44

By s 44 of the SCA 2007:

(1) A person commits an offence if—

    (a) he does an act capable of encouraging or assisting the commission of an offence; and

    (b) he intends to encourage or assist its commission.

(2) But he is not to be taken to have intended to encourage or assist the commission of an offence merely because such encouragement or assistance was a foreseeable consequence of his act.[484]

This is the most straightforward of the offences. A simple example illustrates how the section is intended to operate: D commits the offence by supplying P with a gun, intending that P will use it in the murder of V. D is liable under s 44 (subject to mens rea) as soon as he has done the act of supply that is capable of encouraging or assisting P. D's liability is not affected by whether P commits the crime, as made clear in s 49. D is liable if P does nothing further because P gets cold feet, or has already died; or P attempts to commit the crime but fails because V is untraceable, or survives; or even where P does succeed and murders V. In all these cases D is liable for assisting or encouraging murder, and liable to be sentenced to life imprisonment.

Section 44 is triable in the same way as the 'anticipated offence' (ie the offence which D is intentionally assisting or encouraging P to commit but which P does not in fact need to commit[485] (in our example the murder)). Where the anticipated offence is murder, the maximum sentence on conviction under s 44 is life.[486] Where the anticipated offence is any offence other than murder, the maximum sentence is that available for the full anticipated offence if it had been committed.[487]

11.4.4.1 Actus reus

D's conduct must be 'capable' of 'assisting or encouraging' P. The focus is on D's conduct, not P's.[488] D's conduct can include a 'course of conduct'[489] as where D supplies a number of articles to P over time. This follows the Law Commission recommendation that D is liable

---

[482] See LC 300 Draft Bill, cl 17(2).

[483] LC 300, para 5.100. For telling criticism see Fortson, *Blackstone's Guide to the Serious Crime Act 2007*, 634.

[484] To be understood, this section must be read together with s 47(2), (5), (7), (8), and s 49(1) and (2).

[485] Section 55(1). Note that by 51A as introduced by the Coroners and Justice Act 2009, s 44 does not apply to an offence under s 2(1) of the Suicide Act 1961 (as now amended).

[486] Section 58(1).   [487] Section 58(2). See LC 300, paras 5.43 and 5.65.

[488] Note the trap for the unwary of confusing the use of the term 'act' in this part of the statute. 'Act' is used inconsistently and without clarification. Although from a reading of s 47, it might appear as if D's 'act' that is capable of giving assistance or encouragement might include 'a failure to act; the continuation of an act that has already begun; an attempt to do an act (except an act amounting to the commission of the offence of attempting to commit another offence)'. In fact the 'act' being discussed in that section is P's. Cf s 65(2)(b) where 'the act' refers to D. See further Fortson, *Blackstone's Guide to the Serious Crime Act 2007*, Ch 6.

[489] Section 67.

if he performs 'a number of acts, none of which would be regarded as having the capacity to encourage or assist the doing of a criminal act, if the cumulative effect of D's course of conduct would be regarded as having the capacity to encourage or assist'.[490]

There is no requirement that D's act does in fact encourage or assist P, or anyone. P might ignore D's assistance or encouragement, or find it of no encouragement or assistance at all. P need not be aware of D's acts which were intended to assist or encourage him.[491] This extends the scope of liability from that at common law for incitement where it was necessary that the incitement should have at least been communicated.[492]

The scope of the actus reus is extended in three ways by ss 65 and 66. First, s 65 provides that D's act is capable of encouraging or assisting the commission of an offence if D's conduct includes taking steps to reduce the possibility of criminal proceedings being brought in respect of that offence. D's assistance in providing a disguise for P who is about to commit a bank robbery is a simple example. An interesting question arises whether D's acts, which are capable of assisting or encouraging P, can include those relating to P's conduct *after* the entire actus reus of the substantive offence is committed by P. What of D who provides the getaway car which is available to P only *after* the robbery, or D providing false passports for P to flee the country after the robbery? Perhaps the Crown can meet such objections by arguing that the cases are the same: the provision of the disguise, getaway car, false passports, etc, 'encourage' P to commit the anticipated offence.

Secondly, by s 65(2)(b) D is liable if he fails to take reasonable steps to discharge a duty.[493] Whether there had been a failure to take reasonable steps to discharge a duty is a question of fact. To borrow the Law Commission's example, D would incur criminal liability in situations where he is a disgruntled security guard who fails to turn on a burglar alarm with the intention of assisting P to burgle the premises of D's employer.[494] Whether a duty existed is a matter of law, to be decided by the judge. Rudi Fortson makes the important point that s 65(2)(b) is restricted to cases in which D *deliberately* failed to take reasonable steps to discharge a duty 'but it does not apply where D failed to discharge a duty through inadvertence or forgetfulness'.[495]

The third extension of the actus reus is by s 66. If D arranges for P to do an act capable of encouraging or assisting X and P does that act, D is liable, being deemed also to have done it. This is not necessarily the same as encouraging/assisting D2 to encourage or assist P to commit an offence. The Law Commission provided an illustration:[496]

if D arranges for another person P to do something which has the capacity to encourage or assist another person to commit a criminal act, then D is also to be regarded as having done P's act. Thus, a person such as a gang leader can be held liable for the encouragement or assistance provided by a member of his gang in carrying out his instructions.

Encouraging

The 2007 Act offers no definition of this core term.[497] The Law Commission intended that 'encouraging' would have the same meaning as it had developed under the common law offence of incitement. It would include 'instigating', 'persuading', 'threatening' and

---

[490] LC 300, para A.101 fn 108.

[491] The Law Commission suggested that it is immaterial if no one was aware of D's words of encouragement: ibid, para 5.29.

[492] *Banks* (1873) 12 Cox CC 393; *Ransford* (1874) 31 LT 488.

[493] By s 65(3) a person is not to be regarded as doing an act that is capable of encouraging or assisting the commission of an offence merely because he fails to respond to a constable's request for assistance in preventing a breach of the peace. See Ch 7. LC 300, para 5.46.

[494] LC 300, para 5.62; LC 305, para 3.34.

[495] Fortson, *Blackstone's Guide to the Serious Crime Act 2007*, para 6.55.   [496] LC 300, para A.95.

[497] See Wilson [2008] Crim LR 3 at 12.

'coercing'.[498] In LC 300, the Commission proposed that the definition should also extend to conduct which 'emboldens a person who has already decided to commit an offence'. What of the provision of the getaway car in the earlier example?

There need not be actual (ie effective) encouragement: the 'act' need only be *capable of* encouraging or assisting another person to commit an offence.

Some guidance on the likely interpretation of the concept of encouragement might be drawn from the case law on incitement. In *Marlow*,[499] for example, D was convicted on the basis of 'encouraging' others by his publication of a book on cannabis cultivation.[500] Encouragement can be by hostile threats or pressure as well as by friendly persuasion.[501] It may be implied as well as express. It was held to be an incitement to advertise an article for sale, stating its potential to be used to do an act which is an offence. It was an act capable of encouraging P to commit that offence[502]—even when accompanied by a warning that the act is an offence. By contrast, it has been held that merely intending to manufacture and sell, wholesale, a device—which has no function other than one involving the commission of an offence—is not to incite the commission of that offence.[503] Arguably, there may be circumstances in which offering such devices for sale would be capable of constituting 'encouragement' for the purposes of Part 2 of the 2007 Act.

As stated above, there may be cases in which both D and P would be liable under Part 2 of the 2007 Act. Consider, for example, the facts in *Goldman*,[504] where it was held that D was liable where P published an advertisement inviting readers to buy indecent photographs of children. D replied to the advertisement offering to buy the photographs of children under 16. D was guilty of attempting[505] to incite P to distribute indecent photographs of children under 16,[506] contrary to s 1 of the Protection of Children Act 1978.[507] It is arguable (although the argument may be thought to be somewhat strained) that conduct such as subscribing to a website with indecent images of children may be caught by Part 2 of the 2007 Act,[508] particularly in the light of the decision in *O*.[509] In doing so D may be held to have encouraged P, the business offering

[498] LC 300, para 5.37. See further Wilson [2008] Crim LR 3.

[499] [1998] 1 Cr App R (S) 273. (A statutory offence of incitement, contrary to the Misuse of Drugs Act 1971, s 19.)

[500] Note the danger in using synonyms—see *Smith* [2004] EWCA Crim 2187, referring to the 10th edn of this book.

[501] It includes 'by threatening another person [P] or otherwise putting pressure on another person to commit the offence': s 65(1). *Race Relations Board v Applin* [1973] QB 815 at 827 per Lord Denning MR, followed in *Invicta Plastics Ltd v Clare* [1976] RTR 251.

[502] *Invicta Plastics Ltd*, ibid. (Indication that 'Radatex' may be used to detect police radar traps was incitement to an offence under s 1(1) of the Wireless Telegraphy Act 1949. Note that the licensing requirement was removed by SI 1989/123, and that no offence of 'obtaining information' is committed by the user of the apparatus: *Knightsbridge Crown Court, ex p Foot* [1999] RTR 21.) Cf the reports in The Times, 6 Aug 1998 that a student was convicted of 'inciting speeding offences' by the sale of a 'speed trap jammer'. In *Parr-Moore* [2002] EWCA Crim 1907, the court described D's publication of disclaimer on such a device serving only to illustrate their realization that the trade was illegal, at [3].

[503] *James and Ashford* (1985) 82 Cr App R 226 at 232, distinguishing *Invicta Plastics Ltd*, n 501. See also *Maxwell-King* [2001] 2 Cr App R (S) 28, 2 Jan: incitement to commit offence contrary to the Computer Misuse Act 1990, s 3, by supply of device to allow unauthorized access to satellite TV channels.

[504] [2001] EWCA Crim 1684.

[505] There is no explanation as to why the acts were not charged as incitement per se. They should have been. Cf *Jones* [2007] EWCA Crim 1118; see also [2007] Crim LR 979 and commentary.

[506] See now the Sexual Offences Act 2003, s 45.

[507] If P in this scenario is a State official, care must be taken to avoid a plea of 'entrapment', which, if successful, will lead to the proceedings being stayed as an abuse of process.

[508] *R (on the application of O) v Coventry Justices* [2004] EWHC 905 (Admin), [2004] Crim LR 948. The court in *O* did not discuss whether a corporation might be incited. The decision has been criticized in the Crim LR commentary but liability under the SCA 2007 may be less problematic given that words/acts of encouragement/ assistance need not be communicated to P.

[509] [2004] EWHC 905 (Admin).

for supply on the site, to continue doing so even though his communication had been with a wholly automated computer system. At common law there had to be contact with a person. Under s 44 it would seem that D is liable as soon as he sends his subscription details.

Assisting

This fundamental term is not defined. As noted, s 65 provides an extended definition to include D taking steps to reduce the prospect of criminal proceedings being brought[510] or by failing to take reasonable steps to discharge a duty.[511] Read literally, D should be liable if his act is capable of assisting (or encouraging) another person to *any* extent.[512] There is no requirement that D's conduct was, or could have been, a substantial contribution or assistance to P.[513]

Assisting or encouraging multiple offences

If D's act is capable of encouraging or assisting the commission of a number of offences, then by s 49(2), s 44 will apply separately in relation to each offence that he intends to encourage or assist to be committed. Presumably, therefore, each instance must be treated as a separate count in relation to each type or category of offence and not rolled up into one count. If D provides P with a gun which he intends P to use in threatening a number of debtors, D will be liable for each offence of robbery, blackmail, etc, which P commits provided that it was D's purpose to assist those offences.

11.4.4.2 Mens rea

The mens rea to be proved under s 44 is far from straightforward. D must: intend to perform the conduct which is capable of assisting or encouraging; intend to assist or encourage P; intend that P will perform the conduct element of the offence; intend believe or be reckless as to the consequences and circumstances required for P's offence; intend, believe or be reckless as to whether P will act with the mens rea required by the principal offence.

Intention to do acts capable of assisting or encouraging

There must be an intention to do the *act* which is capable of encouraging or assisting. In the earlier example, D must intend to do the act of supplying the gun which he intends P to use in the murder. This excludes liability where D has only been reckless or negligent about performing conduct which might assist P, as where D leaves his gun cupboard open and P helps himself.

Intention to assist or encourage

D must intend to encourage or assist the conduct element of P's offence.[514] Section 44(2) makes clear that this is not satisfied by proof that the encouragement was a foreseeable consequence of D's intentional acts.[515] This surely means (and s 44(2) should have said) D must have as his purpose to encourage or assist.[516] This element of the mens rea is in contrast with that in secondary liability where D's intention is satisfied by oblique intention.[517]

---

[510] Section 65(2)(a).   [511] Section 65(2)(b).   [512] LC 300, para 5.5.

[513] ibid, para 5.51. Cf the discussion by KJM Smith [1994] Crim LR 239, 246.

[514] ibid, para 5.89.

[515] Child (2012) 76 J Crim L 220, suggests that recklessness suffices. We disagree. The interpretation is not assisted by the unduly complex drafting of the Law Commission and the poor drafting of the Act. Section 44 requires an intention that the conduct element of the anticipated offence will be completed. One very clear indicator that intention is required under s 44 is that even in ss 45 and 46 there is a requirement that D believes that P will carry out the conduct element. It would be very odd indeed if the narrower offence in s 44 did not require that D intend the commission of the conduct element but instead had a lower level mens rea than the wider offences.

[516] See Sullivan [2005] Crim LR 1047.

[517] See p 93. See LC 305, paras 2.63–269; see generally *Jogee* [2016] UKSC 8.

D's mens rea as to P's mens rea

Where the anticipated crime (by P) is one of mens rea, then s 47(5)(a) states that it must be proved that:

(i) D believed that, were the act[518] to be done, it would be done with that fault;

(ii) D was reckless as to whether or not it would be done with that fault; or

(iii) D's state of mind was such that, were he to do it, it would be done with that fault.

As an example of how this will operate, consider D who encourages P to touch V sexually. D is liable under s 44 for encouraging the offence if he intentionally does acts capable of encouraging P to do so and (a) intends purposively to encourage *and* (b) intends or is (subjectively) reckless as to whether P would sexually touch V with intent (which is the relevant part of the mens rea required under s 3 of the Sexual Offences Act 2003).[519] Section 47(5)(a)(iii) deals with the cases where D would have mens rea if he committed the anticipated crime himself, even though he does not believe and is not reckless as to whether P would have such mens rea. For example, D encourages P to rape V. P has sex with V but lacks mens rea for rape. D is guilty of encouraging rape if D himself had the mens rea for rape even though he did not commit it and nor did P. Where this limb is relied on, D is presumed to be able to do the act in question; that is, there is no defence of impossibility for him (s 47(6)). So, in this example, D can be guilty for encouraging rape even if D is a woman.

D's mens rea as to consequences and circumstances of P's offence

D must also have mens rea as to any consequences and circumstances necessary for the commission of the anticipated offence. Therefore, by s 47(5)(b) it must be proved that:

(i) D believed [or (purposively[520]) intended[521]] that, were the act to be done, it would be done in those circumstances or with those consequences; or

(ii) D was reckless as to whether or not it would be done in those circumstances or with those consequences.

So, in the previous example of the sexual touching of a child, D must intend, or believe or be reckless as to whether, the child whom he has encouraged P to touch sexually would be under 13 when the act (by P) was done.

Similarly, this will apply where the anticipated crime is one of constructive liability. To take an example provided by the Home Office, D gives P a baseball bat and intends P to use it to inflict bodily harm on V. P, however, uses the bat to attack V and intentionally kills V. It would not be fair to hold D liable for encouraging and assisting murder, unless he also believes, or is reckless as to whether, V will be killed.[522]

Rudi Fortson demonstrates how technical this provision might be in practice, discussing the example[523] of D who hopes that P will cause grievous bodily harm to V and supplies P

---

[518] The act in question here is not D's, but P's. The Act uses the term 'act' inconsistently without clarifying whether the reference is to D or P. See Fortson, *Blackstone's Guide to the Serious Crime Act 2007*, para 6.47.

[519] Care will be needed here to distinguish between intending to encourage or assist—and the states of mind set out in s 47(5).

[520] Section 47(7)(b) provides that D is not to be taken to have intended that an act would be done in particular circumstances or with particular consequences merely because its being done in those circumstances or with those consequences was a foreseeable consequence of his act of encouragement or assistance. Once again, it seems that this should have said purpose.

[521] In this offence, by s 47(7)(a), the word belief is to be read as if it were a reference to intended or believed.

[522] Explanatory Notes, para 135.

[523] Based on the Law Com example LC 300—para 8.35.

with a baseball bat to do so, being unclear what P's exact intention might be. Assuming that P does not harm V, D cannot be liable for assisting or encouraging murder because although D would have acted with the fault for murder if he himself had committed the conduct element of that offence, s 47(5)(b)(i) is not satisfied 'because *D does not believe that V will be killed* (and it was not D's purpose that V should be killed)'.[524]

11.4.4.3 Defences and exemptions to s 44

The standard defences that are discussed in Chs 9 and 10 will apply. If when he hands P a weapon, D is an infant or insane or acting in self-defence, he will be entitled to an acquittal.[525] Four other issues relating to specific defences or exemptions need also to be considered. Two preliminary ones are: first, it is no defence that D is unaware that the conduct by P that D is intentionally encouraging or assisting would be a criminal offence.[526] Secondly, as noted, it is no defence for D to claim that no offence is actually committed by P: s 49(1). Two other more significant defences need to be discussed in detail.

Reasonable conduct

It is a defence for D to prove on the balance of probabilities that he acted reasonably. Section 50 provides:

(1) A person is not guilty of an offence under this Part if he proves—

    (a) that he knew[527] certain circumstances existed; and

    (b) that it was reasonable for him to act as he did in those circumstances.

(2) A person is not guilty of an offence under this Part if he proves—

    (a) that he believed certain circumstances to exist;

    (b) that his belief was reasonable; and

    (c) that it was reasonable for him to act as he did in the circumstances as he believed them to be.

(3) Factors to be considered in determining whether it was reasonable for a person to act as he did include—

    (a) the seriousness of the anticipated offence (or, in the case of an offence under section 46, the offences specified in the indictment);

    (b) any purpose for which he claims to have been acting;

    (c) any authority by which he claims to have been acting.

The defence is broader than that proposed in LC 300, where no such defence was recommended for intentional assisting or encouraging under s 44. Note that it is not enough that D thinks that his conduct is reasonable; it must be found to be reasonable by the jury. This objectively determined requirement provides a 'brake' on defences run under s 50 which the jury considers to be unmeritorious. No doubt challenges will be mounted to the ECHR compatibility of the imposition of the burden on D. Perhaps that burden will itself serve to prevent spurious claims being made.[528]

---

[524] Fortson, *Blackstone's Guide to the Serious Crime Act 2007*, para 6.113. D is, however, liable for intentionally encouraging or assisting the offence of causing grievous bodily harm with intent (OAPA 1861, s 18).

[525] But what if D gives P a bat anticipating that P would use it to unlawfully assault V? In the event, P uses the bat but, ironically, P acts in self-defence against V who got in his attack first and used excessive force! D has no defence since his liability is not dependent on P's.

[526] There is no reason for thinking that ignorance of the law would be a defence here.

[527] Note that it is not enough that D believed they existed.

[528] cf Fortson, *Blackstone's Guide to the Serious Crime Act 2007*, para 6.133.

Little guidance as to the precise scope and operation of the defence can be gleaned from the Law Commission Report. However, the Commission was of the view that it is unreasonable to perform acts of assistance with direct intent that the offence be committed. It is submitted that in such cases, the defence will rarely if ever succeed under s 44.[529]

Three specific examples of the defence in operation were offered by the Commission:[530]

> D, a motorist, changes motorway lanes to allow a following motorist (P) to overtake, even though D knows that P is speeding; D, a reclusive householder, bars his front door to a man trying to get into his house to escape from a prospective assailant (P); D, a member of a DIY shop's check-out staff, believes the man (P) purchasing spray paint will use it to cause criminal damage.

During parliamentary debates, Baroness Scotland of Asthal explained that the defence would be available to a civil servant whistleblower, but that the success of the defence turns on whether the jury accepts that argument.[531] It was recognized in Parliament, and by the Home Office and Law Commission, that 'unmeritorious defendants' will seek to rely on the defence. The breadth of the defence is also indicated, implicitly, by the government's decision that a separate defence of 'good purpose' is not necessary. The Law Commission had recommended such a defence for D whose acts capable of assistance or encouragement were reasonable and performed with the purpose of preventing or limiting harm.[532] Arguably, the defence would be open for undercover police officers and security service agents who may need to encourage criminal offences when undercover.

Defences for victim assisters

The *Tyrrell* principle is put in statutory form.[533] D will have a defence if he is a 'victim' of the offence that D intends to encourage P to commit—for example, where a 13-year-old, D, encourages her boyfriend, P, to have sex with her. The Supreme Court in *Gnango* characterized this section as being a 'limited exemption from criminal liability'.[534] Section 51 provides that a person does not commit an offence if:

(1) ...

　　(a) he falls within the protected category; and

　　(b) he is the person in respect of whom the protective offence was committed or would have been if it had been committed.

(2) Protective offence' means an offence that exists (wholly or in part) for the protection of a particular category of persons ('the protected category').

This works well enough where, for example, D (14) encourages P (35), to have sex with her, but the absence of further statutory definition leaves the scope of the defence unclear. For example, what of D aged 12 encouraging P aged 12? What of adult D encouraging adult P to engage in sadomasochism? What is a protected category?

11.4.4.4 Relationship with other forms of culpability

Relationship with liability as a principal

In some circumstances, D's liability under s 44 will be greater than that of the principal offender who carried out an offence as, for example, where D encourages P to murder and P merely wounds V. The Act also provides for an extended form of principal liability for

---

[529] See the discussion by Sullivan [2005] Crim LR 1047 as to whether the defence is truly one of justification which its name suggests or an excuse.

[530] LC 300, para A.63.　　　[531] Hansard, HL, 25 Apr 2007, col 744.　　　[532] See LC 300, para A.57.

[533] cf *Tyrrell* [1894] 1 QB 710.　　　[534] *Gnango* [2011] UKSC 59, [50].

D in cases where D has assisted or encouraged, and where the anticipated offence has been committed in full. In such a case, if it is unclear whether D merely assisted or encouraged or himself committed the full offence, by s 56 he may be convicted of the s 44 offence. As with accessorial liability, D may be convicted of an offence if the prosecution cannot prove whether he was a perpetrator, or an accessory, but it can be proved that he must have been one or the other.[535] Once again the breadth of the scheme is obvious.

Relationship with secondary liability

If P commits the anticipated offence D may also be liable as an accessory in the usual way. The elements of D's conduct as an accessory are considered in Ch 6. If D has performed acts *capable* of assisting or encouraging P's conduct, that will not necessarily mean that he will have done enough to render him liable as an accessory. P might never have heard D's words of encouragement, so D will not have aided in fact.[536] As for mens rea, if D has the mens rea for s 44, since the judgment in *Jogee* he will not necessarily have the mens rea to be liable as a secondary party. This is because recklessness no longer has any part to play in establishing liability as an accessory, but it can be a sufficient mens rea as to some elements in establishing liability under s 44. It has been argued that greater reliance may now be placed upon the offences in Part 2 of the Serious Crime Act in order to circumvent the strict mens rea requirements necessitated by the Supreme Court's judgment in *Jogee*.[537] Given the complexity of the offences contained in Part 2 and the difficulty in explaining them to a jury, it is submitted that secondary liability will continue to be a more attractive option for prosecutors, despite the more onerous mens rea requirements.

Relationship with conspiracy

D may be liable under s 44 in a wider range of circumstances than for conspiracy. Crucially, in a conspiracy DD must share a common purpose to commit the offence. Under s 44, D is liable irrespective of whether P has any intention to commit the anticipated offence.[538]

11.4.4.5 Double inchoate liability

Attempting or conspiring to commit: ss 44–46

Since D's acts need only be capable of assisting or encouraging, there would seem to be little practical scope for liability for D to be guilty of an attempt to commit a ss 44–46 offence. The possibility arises where, for example, D is about to post the letter to P containing details of how to break into V's safe. In addition, D may be liable for an attempt to commit a ss 44–46 offence where he mistakenly believes that the acts he will perform are capable of assisting or encouraging P's conduct element of his offence, but they are not, as a matter of fact, capable of doing so. The Act is ambiguous whether D can be liable for an attempt in either of these circumstances. As Fortson points out, it is not possible to impose liability on D for an attempt to assist or encourage by reference to s 47(8)(c) which deals with proving offences under s 44;[539] s 47(8)(c) 'must not be read as meaning that it is sufficient to found liability for an offence under ss 44–46 if D attempts to encourage or assist

---

[535] cf s 56(2). The purpose of s 56(2) is obscure.   [536] See Ch 6, p 195.

[537] G Virgo, 'The Relationship Between Inchoate Liability and Accessorial Liability after *Jogee*' [2016] 9 Arch Rev 6.

[538] See the discussion of *Anderson*, p 473.

[539] Section 47 focuses on P's acts, and includes expressly P attempting to do an act.

D2 to commit an offence'.[540] However, the fact that the *attempt* by D is not provided for in s 47(8) does not necessarily preclude the existence of that form of liability: D can attempt to commit as s 44–46 offence.

There seems to be nothing to prevent liability for conspiring to commit offences under ss 44 to 46: D1 agreeing with D2 that D1 will perform acts capable of assisting or encouraging P to commit an offence against V. Perhaps D1 and D2, serious drug villains, agree that D1 should supply a local criminal, P, with a weapon so that he will kill V, a competitor in the local drug market.[541] D can conspire to commit an offence under ss 44 to 46. Again, this is stretching liability so far that one begins to ask where criminal liability ends.

Assisting or encouraging attempts or conspiracies

The Law Commission[542] proposed that D should be liable for the inchoate offence of doing an act which is capable of encouraging or assisting P to *attempt* to commit an offence,[543] but *only if* it was his *direct intention* that P should do so.[544] Under s 44,[545] D can be convicted of an offence if he performs acts capable of assisting or encouraging P to *attempt* to commit an offence.[546] The Law Commission noted that, at common law, a charge of incitement to commit attempt is uncommon because D will nearly always be encouraging P to commit the full offence.[547]

As for assisting or encouraging conspiracy, under s 5(7) of the Criminal Law Act 1977 it was no offence to incite a conspiracy,[548] but the Law Commission has been recommending repeal of that provision since 1989.[549] In LC 300, the Commission recommended that D should be liable for acts capable of encouraging or assisting P to *conspire* to commit an offence, but only if it was D's *direct intention* that P should do so. D can be liable under s 44[550] where he does acts capable of assisting or encouraging P1 and P2 to *conspire* to commit an offence. Section 5(7) of the Criminal Law Act is repealed.[551]

Assisting or encouraging the act of assisting or encouraging

D can be liable for performing acts capable of encouraging or assisting P to encourage or assist P2. If D supplies a weapon to P knowing that the weapon will be passed to P2 to perpetrate a murder, D is liable under s 44. As the Law Commission explained:

If it is D's intention that P should encourage or assist X, his or her conduct should not be considered too remote from the principal offence merely because, were P to encourage or assist X, P would not intend X to commit the principal offence.[552]

---

[540] Fortson, *Blackstone's Guide to the Serious Crime Act 2007*, para 6.87.

[541] D1 and D2 might also separately (or jointly) be charged with a s 44 offence.

[542] LC 300, para 7.23.

[543] cf the original proposals in LCCP 131, *Assisting and Encouraging Crime* (1993) para 4.184 and see for discussion Fortson, *Blackstone's Guide to the Serious Crime Act 2007*, para 6.78.

[544] Note s 44(2).

[545] But not s 45 or 46 since Sch 3 to the Act removes attempt from the scope of their application.

[546] But not an act of assisting or encouraging an attempt to attempt: s 47(8)(c).

[547] LC 300, para 7.22.   [548] cf *Sirat* (1985) 83 Cr App R 41.

[549] See LC 177, *Criminal Law: A Criminal Code for England and Wales, Vol 2: Commentary on Draft Criminal Code Bill* (1989) para 13.15; and see LC 300, para 7.19.

[550] But not under s 45 or 46 as Sch 3 removes statutory conspiracy from the scope of their application. See later as to common law conspiracies.

[551] Para 54 of Part 2 of Sch 6 to the SCA 2007.   [552] LC 300, para 7.15.

11.4.5 Assisting or encouraging believing offence will be committed: s 45

By s 45 of the Act a person commits an offence if:

(a) he does an act capable of encouraging or assisting the commission of an offence; and

(b) he believes—

 (i) that the offence will be committed; and

 (ii) that his act will encourage or assist its commission.

A simple example of this section in operation is where D supplies a gun to P, *believing* that P will use it to commit a murder. Under the old law, D would not be liable for assisting or encouraging unless P committed the murder. D would not have been liable for conspiring with P unless there was a common agreement. Arguably, D could not have been charged with incitement unless there was encouragement rather than pure assistance. Under s 45, D can now be convicted of this new inchoate offence of assisting or encouraging the commission of a crime, even if P does not commit the crime (s 49(1)). The s 45 offence is triable in the same way as the 'anticipated offence' (ie the offence that P would commit if he did as D believed).[553] Where the anticipated offence is murder, the sentence on conviction under s 45 is life: s 58(1). Where the anticipated offence is any offence other than murder, the maximum sentence is that available for the full anticipated offence if it had been committed: s 58(2).

11.4.5.1 Actus reus

D's conduct needs only to be *capable* of assisting or encouraging. This will be satisfied by, for example, the provision of weapons, tools, advice, etc. There is no requirement that the conduct does in fact encourage or assist P or anyone. As under s 44, D fulfils the actus reus by a 'course of conduct'.[554] Similarly, conduct capable of assisting or encouraging includes threats or putting pressure on another person.[555] The extended definitions from s 65[556] (taking steps to reduce the possibility of criminal proceedings being brought, and failing to fulfil a duty) apply to s 45. Failing to assist a police officer preventing a breach of the peace does not amount to encouraging or assisting in the commission of an offence under s 45.[557] As with s 44, if D arranges for P to do an act capable of encouraging or assisting X, and P does that act, D is treated as also having done it: s 66.

11.4.5.2 Mens rea

This differs significantly from that under s 44. The mens rea turns on the requirement that D has a 'belief'. Belief is a state of awareness short of knowledge, but greater than mere suspicion.[558] Unlike s 44, D need not *intend* that the criminal act by P should be done. D must *believe* that P's criminal act *will* be done and that his (D's) act *will* encourage or assist the doing of the criminal act.[559] D must also believe or be reckless as to the circumstances and consequences of P's crime.

---

[553] Section 55(1).   [554] Section 67.   [555] Section 65(1).

[556] '(a) taking steps to reduce the possibility of criminal proceedings being brought in respect of that offence; (b) failing to take reasonable steps to discharge a duty.'

[557] Section 65(3).

[558] See Ch 26 on handling.

[559] Child takes issue with this proposition in J Child, 'Exploring the *Mens Rea* Requirements of the Serious Crime Act 2007: Assisting and Encouraging Offences' (2012) 76 J Crim L 220. For a response see R Fortson, 'Inchoate Liability and the Part 2 Offences under the Serious Crime Act 2007' in A Reed and M Bohlander (eds), *Participation in Crime—Domestic and Comparative Perspectives* (2013) 184–5 and 192–6.

Belief that conduct element of P's offence will be committed: s 45(b)(i)

It is sufficient that D believes that the conduct element of the anticipated offence *will* be committed.[560] Although in secondary liability the courts purport to apply a test of knowledge of what P might do, in practice they apply a much lower mens rea requirement satisfied by contemplation of the risk of a real possibility that P will commit it.[561]

Belief that acts will assist or encourage: s 45(b)(ii)

D must be proved to have intended or *believed* that his act (eg supplying the gun to P) *will* (not might) encourage or assist the P in his performance of the conduct element of the offence (eg murder).[562] For example, it is sufficient to prove that D believed that the act of supply would encourage or assist the doing of P's act in using the gun to kill V.[563] Under s 45, D must believe that an act will be done which 'would amount to the commission' of the anticipated offence.[564] In the example with the supply of the gun, D must believe that P will use the gun in the commission of a murder.

D's mens rea as to P's mens rea

Where the anticipated crime is one of mens rea, D must believe or be reckless as to whether P would perform the conduct element of the offence with the prescribed mens rea for that offence with which P would be charged.[565] For example, if D encourages P to touch V sexually, D is liable for encouraging the offence if he does acts capable of encouraging P and believes that they will encourage/assist and believes that P will sexually touch V with intent (which is a relevant aspect of the mens rea required under s 3 of the Sexual Offences Act 2003). As with s 44 discussed earlier, s 47(5)(a)(iii) deals with the cases where D would have mens rea if he committed the offence, even though he does not believe and is not reckless as to whether P would have it.

D's mens rea as to circumstances and consequences

D must also have mens rea as to the consequences and circumstances of the anticipated offence.[566] For example, in the previous illustration D must believe or be reckless as to whether the child whom he has encouraged P to touch sexually would be under 13 if the act (by P) was done. As a second example, in a case of encouraging P to use violence on V, D would only be liable for murder if D believed or was reckless as to that consequence, that is, that level of fatal violence.

11.4.5.3 Defences and exemptions to s 45

There is no requirement that any offence is actually committed by P: s 49(1). It is a defence for D to prove that he acted reasonably under s 50. D cannot be liable if he is a 'victim': s 51. These defences were considered previously when discussing s 44.

11.4.5.4 To which offences does s 45 apply?

Unlike s 44, there are several offences specifically listed by Parliament as not being capable of being assisted or encouraged under s 45. None of the listed statutory incitement offences in Sch 3 can be committed under s 45. D *cannot* be convicted under s 45 of encouraging or assisting a conspiracy to commit an offence, on mere belief that the offence (conspiracy) will

---

[560] Section 49(7).   [561] *Bryce* [2004] EWCA Crim 1231; cf *Webster* [2006] EWCA Crim 415.
[562] Section 45(b)(ii).   [563] Section 47(3)(b).   [564] Section 47(3)(a).
[565] Section 47(5).   [566] Section 47(5)(b).

be committed.[567] (He can be if he intends it: s 44.) Nor can D be liable under s 45 for doing an act that is capable of encouraging or assisting P to attempt to commit an offence, on a mere belief that the attempt will be committed.[568] (If he intends the attempt to be committed he is liable under s 44.) Nor can D be liable under s 45 for encouraging or assisting P to do an act which is capable of assisting X to commit a crime.[569] Under s 45 there is no double inchoate liability.

11.4.6 Encouraging or assisting one or more offences D believes will be committed: s 46

By s 46, D is guilty of this offence if:

(1) ...

    (a) he does an act capable of encouraging or assisting the commission of one or more of a number of offences; and

    (b) he believes—

        (i) that one or more of those offences will be committed (but has no belief as to which); and

        (ii) that his act will encourage or assist the commission of one or more of them.

(2) It is immaterial for the purposes of subsection (1)(b)(ii) whether the person has any belief as to which offence will be encouraged or assisted.

It is not necessary for the prosecution to specify in the indictment every offence that D potentially might have encouraged or assisted. Note that an offence charged under s 46 of the SCA 2007 is triable only on indictment: s 55(5).

This is the broadest, most complex and most controversial of the three offences.[570] It is introduced to deal with the problem encountered under secondary liability where D gives assistance and D is aware that P is likely to commit one of a number of offences, but is unsure which. For example, D drives P to a pub, being unsure whether D is going to commit robbery, murder, explosives offences or offences against the person, but knowing it will be one of them.[571] In secondary liability, the adequacy of D's mens rea has proved difficult to define with any precision. Section 46 creates an offence for D who does acts capable of encouraging more than one criminal act where D believes: that at least one of those acts *will* be done but without having any belief as to which it will be; and that his conduct *will* encourage or assist the doing of at least one of those acts. Note that this is markedly different from the form of secondary liability that may arise under *DPP v Maxwell*.[572] First, P need

---

[567] Sch 3, Part 2, para 32.   [568] ibid, para 33.

[569] Section 49(4). The Law Commission regarded this as an over-extension of criminal liability: LC 300, paras 7.12–7.13.

[570] Despite its breadth the Court of Appeal in *Sadique* [2011] EWCA Crim 2872, rejected the argument that it infringed Art 7 of the ECHR.

[571] As in *DPP for Northern Ireland v Maxwell* [1978] 1 WLR 1350, As the Law Commission puts it: 'D, a taxi driver, is asked by a group of armed men to drive to a public house in the East End of London. D believes that they *will* commit an offence of violence and, from their comments to each other, he concludes that the offence *might* be robbery or it *might* be causing grievous bodily harm with intent', LC 300, para A.52.

[572] Rudi Fortson also points out that it is inaccurate to argue that s 46 simply embodies the *Maxwell* principles. He makes the cogent point that the limits of liability under *Maxwell* are themselves ill-defined: [2014] Crim LR 61.

not perform any act or commit any offence; D's liability is inchoate, not dependent on P, and is complete as soon as D has performed his act. Secondly, D's mens rea under s 46 must be a belief that one of the crimes *will* be committed. Thirdly, it is unnecessary for the prosecution to specify every offence that D potentially might have encouraged or assisted but the indictment must specify all the offences which the prosecution allege D contemplated might be committed: s 46(3).[573]

As an example of its operation, D will be liable if:

(1) he supplies a weapon which is capable of encouraging or assisting the commission of one or more of a number of offences (eg one or more robberies or murders[574]); and

(2) D believes that his act of supplying the weapon to P *will* (not might) encourage or assist the commission of at least one of those offences; and

(3) although it cannot be proved that D had a belief or intent as to which *one* will be committed, it can be proved that D *believes* that one or more such offences *will* (not might) be committed;[575] and

(4) D believes or is reckless as to whether, when P is to perform the conduct element of the offence, P will do so with the mens rea required for that offence (or D's state of mind is such that were he to do it, it would be done with the fault required); and

(5) D believes or is reckless as to whether, were the conduct to be done by P, it would be done in those circumstances or with those consequences, if any, of which the offence requires proof.

It is as easy as that.

The maximum penalty for an offence under s 46 is life imprisonment if one of the anticipated offences is murder: s 58(5). If none of the anticipated offences is murder but one or more is an imprisonable offence, the maximum penalty is that for whichever offence has the highest or an unlimited fine.

11.4.6.1 Actus reus

D's conduct needs only to be *capable* of assisting or encouraging. There is no requirement that the conduct does in fact encourage or assist P or anyone. As under s 44, D's conduct can be a 'course of conduct'.[576] Similarly, conduct capable of assisting or encouraging includes threats or putting pressure on another person.[577] The extended definitions from s 65 apply[578] (taking steps to reduce the possibility of criminal proceedings being brought, and failing to fulfil a duty) but failing to assist a police officer preventing a breach of the peace does not amount to an offence.[579] Under s 66, if D arranges for P to do an act capable of encouraging or assisting X, and P does that act, D is treated as also having done it.

11.4.6.2 Mens rea

There are no fewer than five elements of mens rea to be proved (depending on the type of anticipated offence).

---

[573] Fortson, *Blackstone's Guide to the Serious Crime Act 2007*, para 6.71. This is subject to the caveat that the Court of Appeal initially took a different approach in *Sadique* [2011] EWCA Crim 2872, discussed later.

[574] Parliament may have had in mind different types/categories of offences rather than multiple offences of the same kind.

[575] Section 46(1)(b)(i).   [576] Section 67.   [577] Section 65(1).

[578] '(a) taking steps to reduce the possibility of criminal proceedings being brought in respect of that offence; (b) failing to take reasonable steps to discharge a duty.'

[579] Section 65(3).

D's belief that he will assist or encourage: s 46(b)(ii)

D must believe that his act *will* encourage or assist the conduct element of each offence. It is not necessary that the Crown establish a belief as to which offence will be committed.

D's belief as to offences: s 46(b)(i)

D must believe that one or more criminal acts *will* be committed. It is sufficient that D believes that the offence or one of the offences will be committed if certain conditions apply (s 49(7)). So, for example, if D encourages P to burgle the house and to use force to enter if necessary, D will be encouraging criminal damage and burglary.

D's belief as to one of a number of offences

If the allegation is that D believed one or more of a number of offences would be committed and that his act would encourage or assist the commission of one or more of them, by s 47(4), it is sufficient to prove that D believed:

(a) that one or more of a number of acts would be done which would amount to the commission of one or more of those offences; and

(b) that his act would encourage or assist the doing of one or more of those acts.

The aim of the provision is to allow for a conviction where, although it cannot be proved that D had a belief or intent as to which *criminal act* will be committed, it can be proved that D *believes* that one or more such acts *will* (not might) be committed, and subject to the further mens rea requirements of s 47(5). Note that the section refers to the 'act' of P. This suggests that if D does an act which might assist or encourage murder or arson, it is enough that he believes that at least one of the criminal *acts* (setting fire to a deserted building) would be done which *would* (not might) amount to the crime in question.[580]

In the first appeal in *Sadique*[581] (as an interlocutory appeal) the Court of Appeal held that since D must believe that an identified offence *will* be committed, each offence which his act is capable of assisting or encouraging (ie the reference offence) must be charged as a separate count on the indictment. Consider D who supplied P with a baseball bat and believed that P would use it, and that the offences P might use it to commit were assault or robbery or GBH or to kill, but D was not sure which. P was arrested before using the weapon. On the Court of Appeal's approach in this first *Sadique* appeal the Crown would have to have counts of assault, robbery, GBH and murder when charging D under s 46. If the jury returned a guilty verdict on one (or more of those), the judge would be able to sentence appropriately knowing the factual basis of the guilty verdict.[582]

This decision was welcomed by some commentators on the basis that it would make the task of the judge easier and fairer when sentencing defendants found guilty under s 46.[583] There were others, however, who took the view that the effect of the decision was to make the offence even more complex and effectively render it redundant.[584]

The Court of Appeal revisited the issue in a second appeal in the same case[585] (this time after conviction). In the second appeal, the Court of Appeal agreed with the criticism that

---

[580] See further Fortson, *Blackstone's Guide to the Serious Crime Act 2007*, para 6.71.

[581] [2011] EWCA Crim 2872.

[582] On the approach to sentencing defendants who have been convicted under s 46, see *McCaffery* [2014] EWCA Crim 2550 and *Hall* [2013] EWCA Crim 2499.

[583] Fortson [2012] Crim LR 449.

[584] G Virgo, 'Legislative Comment; Encouraging or Assisting More Than One Offence' [2012] 2 Arch Rev 6 and 'Making Sense of Section 46 of the Serious Crime Act 2007' [2013] 7 Arch Rev 4.

[585] *Sadique* [2013] EWCA Crim 1150

requiring the prosecution to specify each reference offence as a separate count on the indictment collapsed the distinction between ss 45 and 46. Lord Judge CJ held that if Parliament creates three distinct criminal offences (ss 44 to 46) it is not open to a court to set one or other of them aside. Although it did not explicitly say so, this later decision overturned the earlier one and so it is not necessary for the Crown to specify each reference offence as a separate count on the indictment.[586]

D's mens rea as to P's mens rea

Where the anticipated crime is one requiring mens rea, D must believe or be reckless as to whether P would act with the mens rea for one[587] (or more) of the anticipated offences with which he would be charged: s 47(5). For example, where D encourages P to commit sexual touching or rape on V, D is liable under the s 46 offence for encouraging if he does acts capable of encouraging P, and believes or is reckless (subjectively) as to whether P would commit either *one* of the offences with the mens rea for that offence. It is also sufficient under s 47(5)(a)(iii) that D's state of mind was such that, were he to do it, it would be done with that fault. This deals with the cases where D would have mens rea if he had committed the substantive offence personally, even though he does not believe and is not reckless as to whether P would have the mens rea.

D's mens rea as to circumstances and consequences of P's act

If the offence is one requiring proof of particular circumstances or consequences (or both), D must also have mens rea as to the consequences and circumstances of one of the[588] anticipated offences: s 47(5). D must either believe that, were the act to be done, it would be done in those circumstances or with those consequences; or be reckless as to whether or not it would be done in those circumstances or with those consequences. Using the sex offences example, D must believe or be reckless as to whether the person, V, whom he has encouraged P to touch sexually/rape would lack consent if P performed the relevant act (penetration or sexual touching). It is sufficient that D believes/is reckless as to the existence of the circumstances for *either* one offence.

11.4.6.3 Defences

There is no need for any of the anticipated offences to occur for D to be liable: s 47(4). It is sufficient to prove that D believed that one or more of a number of acts would be done which would amount to the commission of one or more of those offences; and that his act would encourage or assist the doing of one or more of those acts. There is no requirement that any offence is actually committed: s 49(1). It is a defence for D to prove that he acted reasonably under s 50. D cannot be liable if he is a 'victim': s 51.

11.4.6.4 Which offences are capable of being assisted or encouraged

In deciding under s 46 whether an act is capable of encouraging or assisting the commission of one or more of a number of offences, listed offences in Sch 3 are to be disregarded.[589] D *cannot* be convicted under s 46 of encouraging or assisting a conspiracy to

---

[586] The decision has been criticized. How is a judge to know how to sentence in the example posed? If P was going to commit murder the maximum sentence is life; if assault, six months. On the basis that an individual has a right under the ECHR to know the factual basis upon which he has been convicted and falls to be sentenced, and that s 46 as interpreted in *Sadique* [2013] EWCA Crim 1150 violates this principle, see Fortson [2014] Crim LR 61. Unsurprisingly, the decision was welcomed by Virgo. See [2013] 7 Arch Rev 4.

[587] See s 48(2).   [588] Section 48(2).

[589] Sch 3 offences are dozens of statutory forms of incitement including solicitation to murder.

commit an offence.[590] Nor can D be liable under s 46 for doing an act that is capable of encouraging or assisting P to attempt to commit an offence.[591] Nor can D be liable under s 46 for encouraging or assisting P to do act which is capable of assisting X to commit a crime.[592] Nor is there an offence of encouraging or assisting P to commit a statutory incitement of X.[593]

11.4.7 Procedure

Where a prosecuting authority has power to prosecute the substantive offence which D is alleged to have assisted or encouraged, it will also have power to initiate a prosecution for an offence of encouraging or assisting the commission of that substantive offence: s 54(2)(b).

Under s 55 if D is acquitted of an offence contrary to ss 44 to 46 of the Act, he may be found guilty of an 'alternative offence' as defined by s 57(4) and (9).

Where the substantive offence which D is alleged to have assisted or encouraged requires the consent of the Attorney General or the DPP before a prosecution can commence, that consent must be obtained before proceedings are initiated under Part 2 of the 2007 Act: s 54(2).

11.4.8 Jurisdiction

D may be liable in England and Wales no matter where he was at the time of the acts of encouragement or assistance provided he knows or believes that what he anticipates might take place wholly or partly in England and Wales: s 52(1). Where D does not know or believe that the acts of encouragement or assistance might take place in England and Wales he may only be guilty under s 45 if Sch 4 applies (as in relation to s 44). Paragraph 1 of Sch 4 provides jurisdiction where D does an act in England and Wales, capable of encouraging or assisting an offence, and knows or believes that what he anticipates might take place *outside England and Wales* but the full offence is one for which P could be tried in England and Wales if it were committed outside England and Wales, or relevant conditions exist that would make it so triable. D in England who sends a gun to P in Madrid to shoot V can be tried under s 44 because if P shot V the murder would be triable here.[594]

Schedule 4, para 2, provides jurisdiction where D does an act *in England and Wales*, capable of encouraging or assisting an offence, and knows or believes that what he anticipates might take place in a country *outside England and Wales* but what he anticipates is also an offence under the law in force in that country. Where D in England sends P in Paris a letter telling him to rape a child in France, D is guilty of the s 44 offence since rape of a child is an offence in French law.

Schedule 4, para 3, provides jurisdiction where D does an act *outside England and Wales*, capable of encouraging or assisting an offence, and knows or believes that what he anticipates might take place *outside England and Wales* but the offence is one for which it would be possible to prosecute the person who provides encouragement or assistance in England

---

[590] Sch 3, para 32.   [591] ibid, para 33.

[592] Section 49(4). The Law Commission regarded this as an over-extension of criminal liability: LC 300, paras 7.12–7.13.

[593] As noted earlier, if D arranges for P to do an act capable of encouraging or assisting and P does that act D is treated as also having done it: s 66.

[594] Without deciding the matter conclusively, the Court of Appeal (Civ Div) has stated that it is unnecessary for the English court to find that P has committed an offence triable in England and Wales. Rather, the question is whether any conduct which the UK national is assisting would be within the jurisdiction of the English court if P were a UK national. See *R (Khan) v Secretary of State for Foreign and Commonwealth Affairs* [2014] EWCA Civ 24, [15]–[16].

and Wales if he were to commit the offence as a principal in that place. D, a British citizen on holiday in Spain, sends to his friend P in France instructions on how to assassinate V in Paris. Since the murder could be tried in England, D would be liable for the s 44 offence.

Where the offence is one listed in Sch 4, the Attorney General's consent is required: s 53.

11.5 Inchoate crime and impossibility

The problem of impossibility is peculiar to the 'inchoate' offences that are the subject of this chapter.[595] If it is impossible to commit a crime, obviously no one can be convicted of committing it. It does not follow that no one can be convicted of attempting or conspiring or assisting/encouraging another to commit the crime. It is a fact that people sometimes do attempt, conspire and encourage others to do what is impossible. This happens only when D does not realize that what he has in view is impossible; that is, he is making a mistake of some kind, as for example when he tries to kill someone who (unknown to him) is already dead.

It is well established that in some circumstances a conviction for attempt, conspiracy or assisting/encouraging to commit an offence might be proper, although the commission of that offence was impossible. There has been great controversy about the circumstances in which impossibility will afford a defence and those in which it will not.

Several different categories of impossibility need to be considered in detail.

11.5.1 Impossibility and non-existent crimes

One category of case can be disposed of easily. That is where the crime is 'impossible' in the sense that the intended result is not a crime at all but D, because of his ignorance or mistake of criminal law, believes that it is. Here, the law is the same for all inchoate offences and it is clear that none of them is committed. Suppose that D comes from a country where adultery is a crime and he thinks that it is a crime in England. He may attempt the commission of adultery by chatting up his wife's friend. The 'offence' he has in mind is non-existent in England, its 'commission' is impossible and he is guilty of no offence.[596] The same is true for conspiracy and assisting/encouraging.

11.5.2 Impossibility in fact

In all the other cases to be considered below, we are discussing cases where there is a crime that exists and is capable of being committed and D has the mens rea of that ulterior offence—he intends that it shall be committed; but because of some *fact* as to which he is ignorant or mistaken, either:

(1) the result he intends cannot be achieved; or

(2) the result he intends, if achieved, will not be the crime that he believed would be committed.

Into category (1) fall cases where the means used are inadequate to achieve the intended result and where the subject matter or victim of the intended offence does not exist. Category

---

[595] See generally Duff, *Criminal Attempts*, Ch 3, and see S Christie, 'The Relevance of Harm as the Criterion for the Punishment of Impossible Attempts' (2009) 73 J Crim L 153.

[596] See the discussion in Ch 9, p 355, of the case of *Taaffe* [1983] 2 All ER 625, [1983] Crim LR 536 and commentary; *Taaffe* [1984] AC 539.

(2) comprises cases where some circumstance, which is an element of the intended crime, does not exist. D believes that he is committing a crime, because he is making a mistake, not of criminal law, but of fact. For example, D intends that he (or the person with whom he conspires[597]) shall have sexual intercourse with V, whom he believes to be 15. V is 16 and consequently the 'result' (intercourse with V) will not be the crime that D intended. At one time,[598] it was thought that the distinction between categories (1) and (2) was material but, as the law now stands, it makes no difference. The law now is that:

(1) common law conspiracies are governed by the common law;

(2) statutory conspiracy and attempt are governed by the Criminal Law Act 1977, s 1(1), as amended,[599] and the Criminal Attempts Act 1981, s 1(2) and (3), respectively. Assisting and encouraging are governed by the SCA 2007.

11.5.2.1 Impossibility in common law conspiracies

DPP v Nock[600] holds that impossibility *is* a general defence for common law conspiracies. It seems that the only exception is that D may be convicted where the impossibility results merely from the inadequacy of the means used, or to be used, to commit the offence.

So, for example, D will *not* be guilty of common law conspiracy where:

(1) the subject matter of the offence does not exist. D agrees with E to defraud V of her diamond ring. V had already sold it before D and E agreed.

On the other hand, D *may be* guilty of common law conspiracy to defraud where:

(2) he agrees with E to use a phishing scam on the internet to defraud investors, but the phishing software program will not operate on his computer.[601]

11.5.2.2 Statutory conspiracies and attempts

For statutory conspiracies the law is to be found in s 1(1) of the Criminal Law Act 1977[602] as amended by the Criminal Attempts Act 1981 and, for attempts, it is in s 1(2) and (3) of the Criminal Attempts Act 1981 which provides:

(2) A person may be guilty of attempting to commit an offence to which this section applies even though the facts are such that the commission of the offence is impossible.

(3) In any case where—

(a) apart from this subsection a person's intention would not be regarded as having amounted to an intent to commit an offence; but

(b) if the facts of the case had been as he believed them to be, his intention would be so regarded, then for the purposes of subsection (1) above he shall be regarded as having an intent to commit that offence.

Section 1(3) is strictly unnecessary but it was wise to include it as a matter of caution. It is unnecessary because under it no one will 'be regarded as having an intention to commit that offence' who does not in fact have that intent. It would be wholly wrong to impute a

---

[597] The 2007 Act makes no provision for impossibility under the new ss 44–6 offences. See later.

[598] See the first three editions of this book. See also RA Duff, 'Attempts and the Problem of the Missing Circumstance' (1991) 42 NILQ 87; and White, *Misleading Cases*.

[599] See p 458.   [600] [1978] AC 979, p 466.

[601] Where D agrees with E being unaware that E is a police officer, D's plea of impossibility will fail: *Gleeson* [2003] EWCA Crim 3357.

[602] See p 457.

non-existent intent to a defendant and the Act does not do so. In other words, the subsection does nothing—except forestall the following fallacious argument.

(1) D (believing them to be stolen) intends to handle certain goods.

(2) Those goods are not stolen.

(3) Therefore D does not intend to handle *stolen* goods.

Section 1(3) says he shall be regarded as having an intention to handle stolen goods. Of course, he has such an intention anyway. The fact that the goods are not stolen, being unknown to him, is wholly irrelevant in determining his intention.

The gist of the two provisions is that for both statutory conspiracy and attempt there must be an intention to commit the offence[603] contemplated. Once that intention is proved, it is immaterial that it is *in fact* impossible to commit the substantive offence if, in the case of conspiracy, there has been an agreement to commit it and in the case of an attempt, a more than merely preparatory step towards its commission. The provisions have no application to the cases considered previously where there is no crime to commit despite D's intention to do so (eg adultery in England).

As an example of the section in operation, if D tries to break into V's safe to steal a diamond but there is no diamond present, D is guilty of attempting to steal the diamond. Similarly, if D and E agree that they will use D's jemmy to break into V's safe and steal a diamond, but there is no diamond, D and E are guilty of conspiracy to steal the diamond.

The proper construction of the Criminal Attempts Act was controversial but it is now settled by the decision of the House of Lords in *Shivpuri*.[604] It seems reasonable to assume that the same interpretation will be put on the amended s 1(1) of the Criminal Law Act 1977 (statutory conspiracy), for that section was amended by s 5 of the Criminal Attempts Act 1981 to keep the law of attempt and conspiracy in line in this respect.

In the case of attempts, it must be proved that D had an intention to commit the crime in question. Once that is established, the only question is whether, with that intent, he has done an act which is 'more than merely preparatory' to the commission of the offence. Since, *ex hypothesi*, the offence is impossible, it is the offence envisaged by D to which the act in question must be more than merely preparatory. The effect is that the court must ask, 'would the act (eg breaking into the safe) have been more than merely preparatory to the commission of the offence (theft of the diamond) *if the facts had been as D believed them to be* (diamond within the safe)?'

In the case of conspiracy, it must be proved that D agreed with another or others that a course of conduct is to be pursued (breaking into the safe) which, in the circumstances believed by the parties to exist (diamond in the safe), will, in the event of their intention being achieved (theft of the diamond), amount to or involve the commission of the offence (theft).[605] It is then immaterial that the circumstances are in fact such that the offence is impossible, or that the results can never be achieved.

In the following examples, D *will be guilty* both of statutory conspiracy and attempt.

(1) D and E agree that they will administer a poison, which D has acquired, to V in order to kill him. D administers the poison. As a matter of fact, the poison is too weak ever to kill anyone. D and E are guilty of conspiracy, and D of an attempt to murder V.

(2) D and E agree that they will steal from V's safe. D attempts to break open the safe. It is empty. D and E are guilty of conspiracy, and D of an attempt to steal from the safe.

---

[603] For conspiracy, *pace* Lord Bridge in *Anderson*, p 473.   [604] [1987] AC 1.

[605] It has been argued earlier that this is the only sensible interpretation of the phrase 'course of conduct' and that the amendment by the 1981 Act was strictly unnecessary. The 1981 amendment may, however, be taken to reinforce this opinion, p 466.

(3) D and E agree that they will murder V. D shoots at V's heart but V is already dead. D and E are guilty of conspiracy to murder, and D of attempted murder.[606]

(4) D and E agree that they will receive from F certain goods which they believe to be stolen goods. D takes possession of the goods. The goods are not stolen goods. D and E are guilty of conspiracy, and D of an attempt to handle stolen goods.

(5) D and E agree that D will have consensual sexual intercourse with V, a girl whom they believe to be aged 15. D has sexual intercourse with her. In fact she is 16. D and E are guilty of conspiracy, and D of an attempt to engage in sexual activity with a child under the age of 16.

It is the cases exemplified by illustrations (4) and (5) which have been the subject of much controversy.[607] The reason is that, in these cases, if D succeeds in doing the precise thing that he set out to do, he will not commit a crime. D takes possession of the very goods he intended to take possession of—no other—and that is no offence, for the goods are not stolen goods. D has sexual intercourse with the girl he intends to have intercourse with. She is 16 and consents so there is nothing unlawful. How, then, can his taking steps towards the accomplishment of something that is no crime be a conspiracy or an attempt to commit it? Bramwell B ridiculed the idea in *Collins*[608] in 1864. He put the case of D who takes an umbrella from the stand near the door of his club, intending to steal it, but it turns out to be his own umbrella. Bramwell B thought it absurd that D should be convicted of attempting to steal it. Arguments of this kind prevailed in the House of Lords in *Anderton v Ryan*[609] but were then rejected in *Shivpuri*[610] barely a year later.

In *Anderton v Ryan*, D bought a video recorder for £110. Later she said to police, 'I may as well be honest, it was a stolen one I bought . . .' She was charged with handling and attempted handling. The prosecution, presumably believing that they were unable to prove that the video had in fact been stolen, offered no evidence on the first charge. The magistrates were not satisfied that the recorder had been stolen, though D believed it had. They dismissed the charge. The Divisional Court allowed the prosecution's appeal[611] but the House of Lords, Lord Edmund-Davies dissenting, restored the decision of the magistrates. Section 1(3) of the Criminal Attempts Act 1981, said Lord Roskill, 'does not compel the conclusion that an erroneous belief in the existence of facts which, if true, would have made his completed act a crime makes him guilty of an attempt to commit that crime'. Because the House thought the conclusion absurd, they were not going to reach it unless compelled to do so.

In *Shivpuri*, D was arrested by customs officials while in possession of a suitcase. He admitted that he knew it contained prohibited drugs. Analysis showed that the material in the suitcase was not a prohibited drug but a vegetable material akin to snuff. He was convicted of attempting to be knowingly concerned in dealing with a prohibited drug, contrary to s 1(1) of the Criminal Attempts Act 1981 and s 170(1)(b) of the Customs and Excise Management Act 1979. His appeal was dismissed by the Court of Appeal[612] and, overruling *Anderton v Ryan*, by the House of Lords. No distinction is to be drawn between 'objectively innocent' acts (taking one's own umbrella, receiving non-stolen goods, handling snuff) and 'guilty' acts, for the purposes of the law of attempts. The law is as stated previously.[613]

---

[606] See also the example of *Brown* [2004] EWCA Crim 744: D was rightly convicted of attempting to pervert the course of justice having put in train the machinery of public justice (by alleging he had been abused by V) which, if the matter were carried through in a way he wished or foresaw, would cause a risk to an innocent person (who was, unknown to D, already dead).

[607] The powerful article which influenced the decision in *Shivpuri* is G Williams, 'The Lords and Impossible Attempts' (1986) 45 CLJ 33.

[608] (1864) 9 Cox CC 497 at 498.   [609] [1985] AC 560.   [610] [1987] AC 1.

[611] [1985] 1 All ER 138.   [612] [1985] QB 1029.   [613] See p 514.

Since it must be proved that D intended to commit the crime in question, he is argued to be morally at least as bad as the person who actually commits the offence and, where the offence may be committed with some lesser degree of mens rea, perhaps he is worse. And in these impossibility cases D is as dangerous to whatever interest the particular law is designed to protect as the person who actually commits the offence. It is sometimes objected that he is punished solely for his thoughts but this is not true because it must be proved (in the case of an attempt) that he has taken such steps to put his intention into execution as would (if the facts were as he believed) be more than merely preparatory to the commission of the offence. In the case of conspiracy (not expressly considered in *Shivpuri* but presumably governed by the same principles), he must have agreed with another that the offence be committed—the usual actus reus of conspiracy.

It is also argued that the conclusion offends against the principle of legality (no one shall be convicted of doing something which has not been declared by the law to be an offence).[614] But the issue in these cases was the proper construction of the statute. If Parliament has said (and the House of Lords ultimately decided that it has) that it is to be an offence (attempt) to do any act which is more than merely preparatory with intent to commit an offence, the law may be criticized for being too wide-ranging; but the conviction of one who does any such act with that intent can no longer be criticized for breaching the principle of legality.

The breadth of the law is such that there may be cases where prosecution would be ill-advised. Bramwell B's man who took his own umbrella would no doubt be surprised to find himself charged with attempting to steal his own umbrella. D who has *succeeded* in having consensual sexual intercourse with V, a 16-year-old, might be astonished to find himself charged in consequence with *attempting* to commit a sexual offence against a person under 16. As such acts are objectively innocent, the offence is unlikely to come to light unless D advertises the fact that he acted with mens rea. There will be other cases, however, where a prosecution is in the public interest. The would-be drug smuggler, exemplified by *Shivpuri*, is an instance. It may well be that their lordships' change of mind was influenced by the fact that *Anderton v Ryan* would have required them to turn such dangerous persons loose on the public. Perhaps the most important case in practice is that of the person who receives goods wrongly believing them to be stolen. Mrs Ryan's was an unusual and trivial case. Typical of the case where a prosecution is likely to be brought is *Haughton v Smith* itself. A van, heavily laden with stolen meat products, was intercepted by the police. Having discovered that the intended recipient was D, the police allowed it to proceed on its way, but under the control of disguised policemen. D received the goods, believing them to be stolen. However, the meat ceased to be stolen goods when the police took control of it.[615] The House held that he was not guilty of attempted handling but now he could plainly be convicted. The public interest called for his conviction no less than if the police had never intercepted the goods.

Two doubtful cases
Mistakes of civil law
It has been noted that an intention to commit a non-existent crime (adultery) arising from a mistake as to the criminal law involves no liability.[616] A more difficult case is that where D has an intention to commit an offence that does exist because he is making a mistake of civil law. Believing that the law requires him to use money for a particular purpose, D

---

[614] B Hogan, 'The Principle of Legality' (1986) 136 NLJ 267. For comparative analysis of the problem of impossible attempts in England, the Netherlands and Germany, see J Keiler, *Actus Reus and Participation in European Criminal Law* (2013) 394–404.

[615] See p 1075.   [616] See p 355.

dishonestly uses the money for another purpose. If his belief was true, he would be guilty of theft. Actually the law allows him to do what he likes with the money and he commits no substantive offence.[617] He intends to steal and has done his best to do so. In principle, the case is difficult to distinguish from those where the intent to commit an offence is attributable to a mistake of fact; but the use of the word 'facts' in s 1(3)(b) is likely to exclude liability.

Reckless impossible attempts?

If we follow the decision in *Pace and Rogers*[618] the mens rea requirement for an attempt is intention as to *every element* of the substantive offence.

However, prior to that decision the leading authority was that of *Khan*[619] discussed earlier. That case recognized that for attempts recklessness as to circumstances will suffice, if that suffices for the substantive offence. That raised the spectre of the reckless/impossible attempt.[620] D burns V's rubbish on his bonfire, and V consents in fact to that act, but D is not sure whether V consented or not. Is D guilty of attempted criminal damage? In the context of subjective reckless rape, Glanville Williams thought a person who was not sure if V was consenting must be guilty of attempted rape even if V was consenting, but he thought that no prosecution should ensue. A possible answer is that s 1(3) of the Criminal Attempts Act requires us to treat D as if the facts were 'as he *believed* them to be' which removes the impossibility defence. This affords some ground for holding that even if *Khan* is followed (rather than *Pace*) the reckless/impossible attempt is still no offence. For the reasons given above, it is submitted that *Khan* adopts the correct interpretation of the mens rea for attempt.

11.5.2.3 Assisting and encouraging

The SCA 2007 makes no reference to the position regarding impossibility. The Law Commission believed that impossibility would be no defence under its scheme,[621] and that that is what the Act achieves by its silence.[622] If D encourages P or assists by providing him with the gun to kill V (who unknown to D is already dead), there are strong arguments for saying that D ought to be liable for assisting or encouraging murder. His conduct is no less blameworthy than those who attempt or conspire to murder in such circumstances. D has done an act capable of encouraging P to perform the conduct element of the offence of murder. The Act would seem to provide no defence of impossibility for D in such a case. The Commission provides the following example:

if D . . . provides P with a weapon believing that P will use it to attack V1 (intending to kill V1), D is guilty of assisting murder irrespective of whether P uses the weapon to attack anyone. Were P to attack and murder V2, instead of V1, D would be equally guilty of encouraging or assisting murder. If P attacked V2 because V1 was already dead at the time that D provided the weapon, D would still be guilty of encouraging or assisting murder. It may have been impossible for V1 to be murdered but, nonetheless, D had done an act capable of encouraging or assisting the conduct element of murder, namely an attack on any human being.[623]

This case would appear to be dealt with by the Act.

It is less clear that the silence of the Act deals with the case where D provides P with an article which he thinks is capable of assisting in the commission of a crime, but it is never going to be of assistance in committing any crime. Consider D who provides P with a plastic

---

[617] Commentary on *Huskinson* [1988] Crim LR 620 at 622.
[618] [2014] EWCA Crim 186, p 437.   [619] See p 437.   [620] G Williams [1983] Crim LR 365 at 375.
[621] LC 300, para 6.61.
[622] LC 318, para 5.42. The Law Commission conclusion appears in a footnote only.
[623] LC 300, para 6.63.

card which D believes is capable of assisting P to enter hotel bedrooms to steal therein. The card is not capable of opening any door. There is no magnetic strip and no data can be held on it. It would be arguable that because the card will not be 'capable of assisting or encouraging P' to commit the conduct element of the offence of burglary, impossibility is a defence. Consider D who sends P in prison a Monopoly 'get out of jail free' card. That act is clearly not capable of assisting or encouraging escape. What then of D who provides the would-be assassin with what he thinks are live bullets but are blanks? One answer is to charge D with attempting to assist or encourage in such situations.

11.5.3 The future of impossibility

In *Shivpuri*, Lord Hailsham, with whom Lord Elwyn-Jones and Lord MacKay concurred, offered reasons why *Anderton v Ryan* was distinguishable (even though they concurred in overruling it). That might suggest that *Shivpuri* was open to challenge. It is now surely too late to resurrect arguments which were in substance rejected in *Shivpuri*[624] and which have been settled for over 30 years.

Further reading

RA Duff, *Criminal Attempts*

DN Husak, *Overcriminalization: The Limits of the Criminal Law*

GR Sullivan and IH Dennis (eds), *Seeking Security: Pre-Empting the Commission of Criminal Harms*

G Yaffe, *Attempts: In the Philosophy of Action and the Criminal Law*

---

[624] See the analysis of Lord Hailsham's speech at [1986] Crim LR 539–41. For attempts to reconcile the two decisions, see RA Duff, 'Regarding Intention: The Criminal Attempts Act 1981 s 1(3)' (1990) XII(2) Liverpool L Rev 161, and Duff, *Criminal Attempts*, 378–84.

Part II
Particular Crimes

12
Murder

12.1 Definition

Although it is generally regarded as the most serious crime (apart perhaps from treason) the offence of murder has not been defined by statute. Indeed, the classic definition derives from a book from the seventeenth century. That definition, provided by Coke, is:

Murder is when a man of sound memory, and of the age of discretion, unlawfully killeth within any county of the realm any reasonable creature *in rerum natura* under the king's peace, with malice aforethought, either expressed by the party or implied by law, [so as the party wounded, or hurt, etc die of the wound or hurt, etc within a year and a day after the same].[1]

Over a decade ago, the Law Commission conducted a comprehensive review of the existing scope of the offence and concluded that the offence is a 'rickety structure set upon shaky foundations'.[2] The Commission made far-reaching recommendations for reform.[3] These are

---

[1] Co 3 Inst 47. As to the words in brackets, these are no longer part of the offence: see p 529.

[2] LCCP 177, *A New Homicide Act for England and Wales?* (2005) para 1.4. The history of the offence is summarized in LCCP 177 at paras 1.92–1.103.

[3] See LCCP 177 and LC 304, *Murder, Manslaughter and Infanticide* (2006). Both documents contain valuable analysis of the existing law meriting close attention. The chapters in A Reed and M Bohlander (eds), *Homicide in Criminal Law—A Research Companion* (2019) also contain valuable analysis of the current law.

discussed later in the chapter. The government initially indicated that it would consider legislative change,[4] but subsequently declined to take forward the recommendations.[5]

12.1.1 Who can commit murder?

'A man [*sic*] of sound memory and of the age of discretion' in Coke's definition means simply a person who is responsible according to the general principles which have been discussed in Ch 9. Such a person must be at least ten,[6] not insane within the M'Naghten Rules and, since 1957, not suffering from diminished responsibility.[7]

A corporation or other organization cannot be tried for murder because it cannot suffer the only penalty allowed by law, life imprisonment.[8]

12.1.2 Where murder can be committed

By s 9 of the OAPA 1861,[9] a murder (or manslaughter) committed by a British citizen[10] on land anywhere out of the UK may be tried in England or Northern Ireland as if it had been committed there.[11] Murder and manslaughter are among the exceptional cases where the English courts have jurisdiction over offences committed abroad.[12] Homicides on a British ship[13] or aircraft[14] are also triable here, whether committed by a British subject or not; those on a foreign ship (outside territorial waters[15]) may be triable if committed by a British citizen who 'does not belong' to that ship.[16] There are other statutory extensions under which murder may be tried in England and Wales irrespective of the killer's nationality.[17]

12.1.3 Who can be the victim?

Though it is only in relation to murder that a discussion arises as to who qualifies as a victim, it is clear that, in principle, the same rules must apply to assaults and offences against

---

[4] See the written Ministerial Statement of Maria Eagle, 12 Dec 2007.

[5] MOJ, *Report on the Implementation of Law Commission Proposals* (2011) para 54.

[6] See the discussion of the *doli incapax* defence, p 360.

[7] See s 2 of the Homicide Act 1957, as substituted by the Coroners and Justice Act 2009, see Ch 13.

[8] See p 631 for possible corporate liability for manslaughter.

[9] Which expands the territorial reach of common law murder and manslaughter: *Venclovas* [2013] EWCA Crim 2182, applying s 4 of the Suppression of Terrorism Act 1978. See commentary by Ormerod at [2014] Crim LR 684.

[10] Section 3 of the British Nationality Act 1948.

[11] See CLRC, *Offences Against the Person*, Working Paper No 67 (1976); Fourteenth Report (1980), 125. There is no provision enabling a murder committed in Scotland to be tried in England. See for discussion M Hirst, 'Murder in England or Murder in Scotland' (1995) 54 CLJ 488. Homicides committed abroad by non-British citizens may be tried here if the offences are under the War Crimes Act 1991, see *Sawoniuk* [2000] Cr App R 220. See also *Venclovas* [2013] EWCA Crim 2182—Lithuanian killing a Lithuanian in either Poland or England but unclear which.

[12] See generally on jurisdiction, M Hirst, *Jurisdiction and the Ambit of the Criminal Law* (2003) 226–32.

[13] As defined in the Merchant Shipping Act 1995, s 1. The jurisdiction applies not only when sailing on the high seas, but also when in the rivers of a foreign territory at a place below bridges, where the tide ebbs and flows and where great ships go: *Anderson* (1868) LR 1 CCR 161. See further the Merchant Shipping Act 1995, ss 281–2.

[14] Civil Aviation Act 1982, s 92. The Civil Aviation (Amendment) Act 1996, s 1(2), amending the 1982 Act, extends the jurisdiction to offences on foreign aircraft in specified circumstances. See also the Aviation Security Act 1982, s 6.

[15] Jurisdiction over offences within territorial waters is given by the Territorial Waters Jurisdiction Act 1878, s 2.

[16] Merchant Shipping Act 1995, ss 281–2.

[17] See especially the Suppression of Terrorism Act 1978, s 4 and *Venclovas* [2013] EWCA Crim 2182. In relation to British service personnel, see the Armed Forces Act 2006, s 42 and n 51.

the person generally.[18] Coke's expression 'reasonable creature in *Rerum natura*' means simply the 'person' who is the victim of an offence in the modern law of offences against the person—that is, any human being.[19] The problems are at what stage in the process of birth a foetus becomes a person; and at what stage in the process of death a person becomes a corpse. Article 2 of the ECHR provides a right to life, and this imposes on the State certain obligations to protect life, and investigate the taking of life, but the European Court of Human Rights has not directly addressed the issue of when life begins and ends.[20]

12.1.3.1 Child or foetus?

It is not murder to kill a foetus/child in the womb or in the process of leaving the womb. If the child is not capable of being born alive, destruction may be an offence under s 58 of the OAPA 1861.[21] A foetus of 24 weeks'[22] gestation is presumed capable of being born alive.[23] The prescription, supply, administration or use of the contraceptive pill, minipill and morning-after pill do not contravene s 58 of the OAPA.[24] Abortion in compliance with the 1967 Act does not contravene Art 2 of the ECHR.[25]

Where the child is capable of being born alive, it is an offence under the Infant Life (Preservation) Act 1929.[26] If the child has 'an existence independent of its mother' it is capable of being murdered. To have such an existence, the child must have been wholly expelled from its mother's body and be alive.[27] The cord and afterbirth need not have been expelled from the mother nor severed from the child.[28] The tests of independent existence which the courts have accepted are that the child should have an independent circulation, and that it should have breathed after birth. But there are difficulties with both these tests.

In *Brain*, Park J said:[29]

it is not essential that it should have breathed at the time it was killed; as many children are born alive and yet do not breathe for some time after their birth.

There is no simple and agreed way of determining precisely when foetal and maternal circulations become so dissociated that the child can live without the help of the mother. It should be noted that this dissociation may precede birth. There is therefore uncertainty about the precise moment at which the child comes under the protection of the law of murder, though the question does not seem to have troubled the English courts in recent years.

---

[18] In *Tait* [1990] 1 QB 290, the court held that the offence of threatening to kill under s 16 of the OAPA 1861 was not made out by threats to kill a foetus. Cited with approval in *CP (A Child) v First-tier Tribunal (Criminal Injuries Compensation)* [2014] EWCA Civ 1554.

[19] Draft Code, cl 53.

[20] See generally Emmerson, Ashworth and Macdonald, HR&CJ, paras 19.43–19.50. See also E Wicks, 'Terminating Life and Human Right: The Fetus and the Neonate' in C Erin and S Ost, *The Criminal Justice System and Health Care* (2007).

[21] See p 679.

[22] A woman would have exceeded her 24th week of pregnancy from midnight on the expiration of her 24th week: *R (on the application of British Pregnancy Advisory Service) v Secretary of State for Health and Social Care* [2019] EWHC 1397 (Admin).

[23] Human Fertilisation and Embryology Act 1990, s 37.

[24] *R (on the application of Smeaton) v Secretary of State for Health* [2002] All ER (D) 115 (Apr), [2002] Crim LR 664.

[25] *Paton v UK* [1981] 3 EHRR 408. At common law, it was a 'great misprision' (misdemeanour): Co 3 Inst 50. According to Hale, I PC, 433, 'a great crime'. Willes J said in 1866 (British Parliamentary Papers 21 at 274) that the crime was obsolete. (See MACL at 310.)

[26] See p 674. See generally DM Katkin and R Ogle, 'A Rationale for Infanticide Laws' [1993] Crim LR 903.

[27] See *Poulton* (1832) 5 C & P 329; *Enoch* (1850) 5 C & P 539.

[28] *Reeves* (1839) 9 C & P 25.

[29] (1834) 6 C & P 349 at 350. But see *C v S* and *Rance v Mid-Downs Health Authority*, p 674.

The last reported case that the Criminal Law Revision Committee could trace was in 1874.[30] The Committee recommended that the test should be that to be a victim for the purposes of murder the child should have been born and have an existence independent of its mother. With the rapid developments in medical science and its increasing ability to keep alive children born prematurely, the law should be careful to avoid any more rigid form of definition. As Brooke LJ observed, in holding that a conjoined twin with useless heart and lungs, dependent on her twin, was protected by the law of murder: 'Advances in medical treatment of deformed neonates suggest that the criminal law's protection should be as wide as possible, and a conclusion that a creature in being was not reasonable would be confined only to the most extreme cases of which this is not an example.'[31] In *Iby*,[32] the New South Wales Court of Appeal held that the decision of viability should be left largely to the jury. This is, with respect, not an approach that will promote certainty and consistency in the law. For this reason, it is hoped that it will not be adopted by the English courts.

The European Court of Human Rights has declined to decide directly whether the foetus is protected by the right to life in Art 2. In *Vo v France*,[33] a doctor caused fatal injury to a viable foetus after negligently mistaking the mother's identity for that of a similarly named patient. The French Criminal Court acquitted him on the basis that the foetus was not a human being for the purposes of the offence. On application to the ECtHR, the Court ruled that the issue was within the margin of appreciation for Member States to determine. The Court acknowledged that in:

the circumstances examined to date by the Convention institutions—that is, in the various laws on abortion—the unborn child is not regarded as a 'person' directly protected by Article 2 of the Convention and that if the unborn do have a 'right' to 'life', it is implicitly limited by the mother's rights and interests. The Convention institutions have not, however, ruled out the possibility that in certain circumstances safeguards may be extended to the unborn child . . .

The interpretation of Art 2 has involved the Court in balancing legal, medical, philosophical, ethical and religious issues. Since there is often no consensus at a national level, it is unsurprising that the Court has left States with considerable discretion in the matter—the issue of when the right to life begins comes within the margin of appreciation.[34]

12.1.3.2 Prenatal injury and postnatal death

Where D intentionally causes injury to, or attempts to kill, the foetus, but the child is born alive and dies of the injury sustained, D has caused the death of a person in being—the actus reus of murder.

Historically, the law took a strict stance. Coke[35] stated that such cases were murder. In *West*,[36] Maule J directed the jury that a woman was guilty of murder if, in attempting to

---

[30] *Handley* (1874) 13 Cox CC 79, followed by Wright J in *Pritchard* (1901) 17 TLR 310. Fourteenth Report, para 35.

[31] *Re A* [2001] 2 WLR 480, per Brooke LJ.   [32] [2005] NSWCCA 178, discussed at [2005] Crim LR 742.

[33] [2004] 2 FCR 577, on which see K O'Donovan, 'Taking a Neutral Stance on the Legal Protection of the Fetus' (2006) 14 Med L Rev 115 and Wicks, n 20. The Court of Appeal (Civ Div) in *CP (A Child) v First-tier Tribunal (Criminal Injuries Compensation)* [2014] EWCA Civ 1554 stated that 'it is clear from [*Vo*] that European learning on Article 2 cannot assist in determination of the matter before this court. This is an issue for individual states to determine and one which will be governed by domestic law.' At [55].

[34] In *X v Norway* (App no 867/60); *X v Austria* (1976) 7 DR 87; *X v UK* (1980) 1 DR 244, the Convention institutions declined to determine the issue of the time at which life begins.

[35] Co 3 Inst 50; Hawkins, I PC, c 31, s 16; East, I PC, 228; *contra* Hale, I PC, 433. See also *Kwok Chak Ming* (Hong Kong, 1963) discussed in [1963] Crim LR 748 and J Temkin, 'Pre-Natal Injury, Homicide and the Draft Criminal Code' (1986) 45 CLJ 414.

[36] (1848) 2 Cox CC 500.

procure an abortion, she caused the premature birth of her child who, consequently, died five hours later. The basis of that decision, however, appears to be that D caused the death by a felonious act, a type of 'constructive murder', which was abolished by the Homicide Act 1957.

The leading case in the modern law is *A-G's Reference (No 3 of 1994).*[37] D stabbed his girlfriend, V, who was 26 weeks pregnant with his child, X. V recovered but, because of the wound, X was born prematurely and, as a result of the premature birth, died after 120 days. The House of Lords accepted, *obiter*, as an established rule, that 'Violence towards a foetus which results in harm suffered after the baby has been born alive can give rise to criminal responsibility even if the harm would not have been criminal (apart from statute) if it had been suffered in utero.'

In practice, establishing mens rea in such a case is complex. An intention to cause death or injury to the foetus is not the mens rea of murder,[38] so that intent would not suffice for murder. If D intended the child to be born alive and then die or suffer serious injury, that would be murder. Alternatively, D might be liable for gross negligence manslaughter if there was an obvious and unjustifiable risk of, for example, premature birth and obvious and serious risk of early death.

In the *A-G Reference* case, the Court of Appeal had resolved the problem by holding that the foetus is an integral part of the mother, in the same way as her arm or leg. On that basis, an intention to kill or cause serious harm to the foetus would be an intention to cause such harm to the mother: that would be the mens rea of murder. But the House of Lords held that this approach was wrong. 'The mother and foetus were two distinct organisms living symbiotically, not a single organism with two aspects.'

Another proposed approach was by relying on the doctrine of transferred malice. D had intended GBH to the mother and that could be transferred to the child when born. The House rejected this approach too. That would involve extending the doctrine of transferred malice to what their lordships regarded as a double transfer of intent—from the mother to the foetus and from the foetus to the child. The House of Lords therefore held it was not murder. The House of Lords went on to hold that D was liable for manslaughter of the child by the unlawful and dangerous act of stabbing the mother. This is problematic for two reasons. First, it appears to be the application of transferred malice which the House had just rejected.[39] Secondly, D's act relied on for unlawful act manslaughter was not merely unlawful and dangerous—it was done with the mens rea of murder and, as it is acknowledged that it caused the death of the child, it is hard to see why it is not murder.

The decision of the House of Lords was considered in *CP (A Child) v First-tier Tribunal (Criminal Injuries Compensation).*[40] The claimant was a child who was born with foetal alcohol syndrome after her mother drank excessively during pregnancy. CP claimed criminal injuries from the Criminal Injuries Compensation Authority. Relying upon *A-G's Reference (No 3 of 1994)*, it was argued on behalf of CP that her mother had maliciously administered a noxious thing to her contrary to s 23 of the OAPA 1861 whilst she was in the womb. In rejecting this contention, both Treacy LJ and Lord Dyson MR held that 'it is well established that a foetus is not a "person;" rather it is a sui generis organism'[41] and that *A-G's Reference (No 3 of 1994)* did not undermine the validity of this proposition, but rather supported it.

---

[37] [1997] 3 All ER 936 at 942, reversing [1996] 1 Cr App R 351.

[38] cf Temkin (1986) 45 CLJ 414, and the Draft Code, cl 53.

[39] cf J Horder, 'Transferred Malice and the Remoteness of Unexpected Outcomes from Intentions' [2006] Crim LR 383. Note also *Grant* [2015] EWCA Crim 1815, above p 126.

[40] [2014] EWCA Civ 1554.   [41] At [39] and [62].

Historically, it was accepted, in *Senior*[42] that where D inflicted prenatal injury by gross negligence or with a mens rea sufficient only for manslaughter, and that conduct caused death to the child after it had been born, a conviction for manslaughter was appropriate. Logically, applying that reasoning, the mother should be guilty of manslaughter for gross prenatal *neglect* of the child leading to death after birth; but the courts have stopped short of this conclusion.[43] Neglect of the child by the mother after birth may give rise to liability; neglect before the birth does not. Note also that a woman is entitled to refuse medical treatment, even though she knows that the result may be the death of the foetus, or the child if it is born alive.[44]

12.1.3.3 Death

Similar problems could arise in determining the moment at which life ends, though surprisingly perhaps these do not seem to have troubled the courts very often.[45] Is V dead, and therefore incapable of being murdered, if his heart has stopped beating but a surgeon confidently expects to start it again, by an injection or mechanical means?[46] Is V dead if he is in a 'hopeless' condition and 'kept alive' only by an apparatus of some kind?[47] There is, at present, no certain answer to these questions.

The current medical view is that the test is one of brainstem death and that this can be diagnosed with certainty.[48] The law has not yet evolved a definition of its own and the CLRC declined to propose one[49] both because of the fluid state of medical science and the repercussions that such a definition might have on other branches of the law.[50]

12.1.3.4 Under the Queen's peace

Coke's requirement that to be murder the killing must be 'under the Queen's peace' recognizes that a British soldier killing an enemy in the heat of battle is not committing murder even though intending to kill. All persons appear to be 'under the Queen's peace'[51] for this purpose, even an alien enemy, 'unless . . . in the heat of war, and in the actual exercise thereof'.[52] In *Page*,[53] an argument that an Egyptian national who had been murdered in an

---

[42] (1832) 1 Mood CC 346.

[43] *Knights* (1860) 2 F & F 46; *Izod* (1904) 20 Cox CC 690 (Channell J); and see the discussion by Davies, MACL, 308–9.

[44] *St George's Healthcare NHS Trust v S* [1998] 3 All ER 673, 685–92 (Civ Div).

[45] See, however, *Re A (A Child)* [2015] EWHC 443 (Fam).

[46] G Williams, *Sanctity of Life and the Criminal Law* (1957) 18.

[47] J Herring, *Medical Law and Ethics* (8th edn, 2020) Ch 10 and references therein; IM Kennedy, 'Alive or Dead?' (1969) 22 CLP 102 and 'Switching Off Life Support Machines' [1977] Crim LR 443; B Hogan, 'A Note on Death' [1972] Crim LR 80; P Skegg, 'Irreversibly Comatose Individuals: Alive or Dead?' (1964) 33 CLJ 130; Broderick Committee, *Report of the Committee on Death Certification and Coroners* (1971) Cmnd 4810, paras 808–12; LC 230, *The Year and a Day Rule in Homicide* (1995); For more recent analysis, see J Munby, 'Medicine and the Law of Homicide: A Case for Reform?' (2012) 23 KLJ 207.

[48] *Re A* [1992] 3 Med LR 303; *British Medical Journal* and *The Lancet*, 21 Feb 1979. Cf *Malcherek* [1981] 1 WLR 690, p 78.

[49] Fourteenth Report, para 37.

[50] See also the discussion relating to the termination of patients' life-sustaining treatment, p 60.

[51] See M Hirst, 'Murder Under the Queen's Peace' [2008] Crim LR 541 arguing that the element ought now to focus on whether D is subject to the English law of homicide. On this see also ACE Lynch, 'British Subjects' Involvement in Foreign Military Clashes' [1978] Crim LR 257; P Rowe, 'The Criminal Liability of a British Soldier Merely for Participating in the Iraq War' [2010] Crim LR 752.

[52] Hale, I PC, 433. In *Adebelajo* [2014] EWCA Crim 2779, D was 'hopelessly misconceived' to think that because D thought *he* was at war with the UK his killing of a British soldier in London was not under the Queen's peace.

[53] [1954] 1 QB 170 (C-MAC). See further P Rowe, 'Murder and the Law of War' (1991) 42 NILQ 216.

Egyptian village by a British soldier serving there during the Suez crisis was not within the Queen's peace was rejected. Enemy soldiers who have been taken prisoner or have surrendered are protected by the law of murder.[54] In his analysis of the position of British service personnel in Iraq, Rowe concludes that the term is vague and, in particular, insufficiently precise to establish whether it applies to 'non-international armed conflict abroad to which the UK is a party'.[55] It is surprising that the argument did not arise in *Blackman*[56] where D killed an injured Afghan insurgent. D was ultimately successful in pleading diminished responsibility.

12.1.4 Death within a year and a day

The rule stated by Coke that the death must occur within a year and a day has been abolished by the Law Reform (Year and a Day Rule) Act 1996.[57] If an act can be shown to be the cause of death, it may now be murder, any other homicide offence or suicide, however much time has elapsed between the act and the death. The 1996 Act, however, requires the consent of the Attorney General to the prosecution of any person for murder, manslaughter, infanticide or any other offence of which one of the elements is causing a person's death, or assisting or encouraging suicide: (a) where the injury alleged to have caused the death was sustained more than three years before the death occurred; or (b) where the accused has previously been convicted of an offence committed in circumstances alleged to be connected with the death. The Attorney General's consent is therefore required if D has been convicted of wounding V, who has subsequently died of the wound within three years of D's causing it and it is proposed to prosecute D for murder or manslaughter.[58] It would seem that consent is also required if D has been convicted of, for example, a robbery, burglary or driving offence in the course of which V sustained an injury from which he subsequently died. This is not incompatible with the guarantee against double jeopardy in Art 4 of Protocol 7 to the ECHR.[59]

The year-and-a-day[60] rule continues to apply where any act or omission causing death was committed before 17 June 1996.

12.1.5 Unlawful

The requirement that the killing is unlawful is an important element of the offence. The most obvious example of its application is where the killing is in self-defence,[61] but the element applies more widely. For example, it was accepted by the Court of Appeal in *A-G's Reference (No 3 of 1994)*[62] that the doctor who performed a lawful abortion would not be liable for murder should the foetus be born alive and die from injuries sustained in the termination procedure. The doctor in such a case would have performed a lawful act under the Abortion Act 1967. Consent, which in many offences will render conduct lawful, has no part to play in the context of murder.

---

[54] Note also: a civilian of an enemy State in the custody of British forces is protected by Art 2 of the ECHR: *R (Al Skeini) v Secretary of State for Defence* [2007] UKHL 26; *Al-Skeini v UK* (2011) 53 EHRR 18.

[55] See n 50.   [56] [2017] EWCA Crim 190.

[57] For historical material on the rule, see D Yale, 'A Year and A Day in Homicide' (1989) 48 CLJ 202, and on the reform see LCCP 136, *The Year and a Day Rule in Homicide* (1994).

[58] By virtue of s 74(3) of PACE 1984, where D is convicted of, eg, causing grievous bodily harm with intent and V subsequently dies, his conviction for that offence is admissible at any later trial for murder of the same victim to prove the fact that D had caused V GBH with intent to do so: *Clift* [2012] EWCA Crim 2750.

[59] *Young* [2005] EWCA Crim 2963.   [60] For further details, see 7th edn of this book, at p 330.

[61] See generally F Leverick, *Killing in Self Defence* (2007).   [62] [1996] 2 All ER 10.

12.1.6 Causing death

It must be proved that D, by his own act or unlawful omission, caused death.[63] For this purpose, D, who, for example, procures E to murder D's wife, does not cause her death. D does not kill; E does. D is guilty of murder but as a secondary party. The principles of causation apply to 'result crimes' generally and are considered in detail in Ch 2. In fact, most of the leading cases concern causing death in homicide offences.

12.1.6.1 Accelerating death

What must be caused is some acceleration of death. Since everyone must die sooner or later it follows that every killing is merely an acceleration of death; and it makes no difference for this purpose that the victim is already suffering from a fatal disease or injury or is under sentence of death. Thus, in *Dyson*,[64] Lord Alverstone CJ said:[65]

The proper question [for] the jury was whether the prisoner accelerated the child's death by the injuries which he inflicted . . . For if he did, the fact that the child was already suffering from meningitis, from which it would in any event have died before long, would afford no answer to the charge of causing its death.

The administration of pain-saving drugs presents difficult problems. In *Adams*,[66] Devlin J directed the jury that there is no special defence justifying a doctor in giving drugs which would shorten life in the case of severe pain: 'If life were cut short by weeks or months it was just as much murder as if it were cut short by years.' He went on:

But that does not mean that a doctor aiding the sick or dying has to calculate in minutes or hours, or perhaps in days or weeks, the effect on a patient's life of the medicines which he administers. If the first purpose of medicine—the restoration of health—can no longer be achieved, there is still much for the doctor to do, and he is entitled to do all that is proper and necessary to relieve pain and suffering even if measures he takes may incidentally shorten life.

These passages are not easy to reconcile. If the doctor administers drugs with the sole object of relieving suffering of a dying person knowing that the drugs will certainly shorten life, then he intends to shorten life: he intends to kill. If, as Devlin J held, the doctor has a defence it cannot be because his act has not caused death nor because he did not intend so to do. It seems that the courts now do recognize a special defence for a doctor in these circumstances.[67] In *Airedale NHS Trust v Bland*,[68] Lord Goff referred, *obiter*, to:

---

[63] H Hart and T Honoré, *Causation in the Law*, especially Chs XII–XIV; G Williams, 'Causation in Homicide' [1957] Crim LR 429 and 510; F Camps and J Harvard, 'Causation in Homicide—A Medical View' [1957] Crim LR at 576. See also the discussion in Ch 2 and references therein.

[64] [1908] 2 KB 454.

[65] ibid, 457. And see Hale, I PC, 428; *Fletcher* (1841) Russell 417; *Martin* (1832) 5 C & P 128 at 130. See L Hoyano and C Keenan, *Child Abuse: Law and Policy* (2007) 135.

[66] [1957] Crim LR 365; S Bedford, *The Best We Can Do* (1958) 192; P Devlin, *Easing the Passing* (1985); Hart and Honoré, *Causation in the Law*, 344.

[67] cf *David Moor* (1999) Newcastle Crown Court (Hooper J) discussed by A Arlidge, 'The Trial of Dr David Moor' [2000] Crim LR 31 and JC Smith, 'A Comment on *Moor's Case*' [2000] Crim LR 41. See also J Goss, 'Postscript on the Trial of David Moor' [2000] Crim LR 568. The broader issues raised by assisted suicide and euthanasia lie beyond the scope of this work. See in particular R Dworkin, *Life's Dominion* (1993); J Herring, *Medical Law and Ethics* (8th edn, 2020) Ch 10; H Briggs, *Euthanasia, Death with Dignity and the Law* (2002); J Glover, *Causing Death and Saving Lives* (1977); S Ost, *An Analytical Study of the Legal, Moral and Ethical Aspects of the Living Phenomenon of Euthanasia* (2003); P Lewis, *Assisted Dying and Legal Change* (2007); M Wilks, 'Medical Treatment at the End of Life: A British Doctor's Perspective' in C Erin and S Ost, *The Criminal Justice System and Health Care* (2007).

[68] [1993] 1 All ER 821 at 868h–j. See also *R (Burke) v GMC* [2006] QB 273 and C Dupré, 'Human Dignity and the Withdrawal of Medical Treatment' (2006) 6 EHRLR 678.

the established rule that a doctor may, when caring for a patient who is, for example, dying of cancer, lawfully administer painkilling drugs, despite the fact that he knows that an incidental effect of that application will be to abbreviate the patient's life.

Lord Goff added:

Moreover, where the doctor's treatment of his patient is lawful, the patient's death will be regarded in law as exclusively caused by the injury or disease to which his condition is attributable.

But this approach involves a fiction and is therefore undesirable. It is not the doctor's *purpose* to kill but the brutal truth is that the doctor has foreseen death as virtually certain and he kills his patient. The ambiguity of the definition of intention in *Woollin*[69] allows the jury flexibility to conclude that the doctor is not a murderer: see Ch 3. If an unqualified and unauthorized person did the same act with the same knowledge he would presumably be guilty of murder. For the doctor, the killing is likely to be treated as unintentional or justified.[70] Despite the ambiguity of the position, the Supreme Court in *Nicklinson* acknowledged that, as Lord Sumption put it:[71]

Medical treatment intended to palliate pain and discomfort is not unlawful only because it has the incidental consequence, however foreseeable, of shortening the patient's life.[72]

However, it is not permissible, even for a doctor acting in good faith, *purposely to kill* in order to terminate pain. When painkilling drugs were no longer effective, Dr Cox,[73] in order to end the great suffering of his patient, administered a drug to stop her heart and end her suffering, not by the palliative effect of drugs but by death. He was held guilty of attempted murder (it was no longer possible to prove the actual cause of death). If he had administered a large dose of sedative causing her to lapse into a coma, he would probably have been on the right side of the law—even though that would have shortened life. In *R (Burke) v GMC*,[74] it was noted *obiter* that a doctor would have no defence to a charge of murder if he interrupted life-sustaining treatment in the face of the patient's express wish to be kept alive. Section 4 of the Mental Capacity Act 2005 deals with the circumstances in which treatment or its withdrawal is in the best interests of the patient. Section 4(5) stipulates that where the determination of what is in the best interests of the person relates to life-sustaining treatment, the person making the decision 'must not in considering whether the treatment is in the best interests of the person concerned, be motivated by a desire to bring about his death'.[75]

There is no defence of mercy killing in English law, no matter how tragic the circumstances. In *Inglis*,[76] D appealed against her conviction for the attempted murder and murder of her son, V, who had suffered catastrophic head injuries when aged 27. D tried to kill V by injecting him with heroin in his hospital bed. V was resuscitated but suffered substantial deterioration in his condition as a result. D was charged with attempted murder. While on bail D then injected V with a fatal dose of heroin. The court reviewed the current state of the law relating to 'mercy killing'. It was recognized that mercy killing is murder subject to

---

[69] [1999] AC 82.

[70] On the significance of offences and defences in murder, see Duff, *Answering for Crime*, 211–16.

[71] At [255].

[72] Citing *Airedale NHS Trust v Bland* [1993] AC 789, 867D (Lord Goff) and 892 (Lord Mustill); *R (Pretty) v DPP* [2002] 1 AC 800, 831H–832A (Lord Steyn).

[73] (1992) 12 BLMR 38.   [74] [2006] QB 273.

[75] The Law Commission declined to engage in reform of mercy killings and euthanasia, preferring to see that as part of a free-standing review: LC 304, para 1.6. No such review was undertaken.

[76] [2010] EWCA Crim 2637.

any partial defences that apply.[77] The law does not distinguish between murder committed for malevolent reasons and murder motivated by familial love. The defendant's subjective belief that he was acting out of mercy, however genuine, does not and cannot constitute any defence to the charge of murder.[78]

A nine-member Supreme Court reconsidered some of these issues in *R (Nicklinson) and another v Ministry of Justice and others*.[79] The claimants had each suffered catastrophic physical disabilities but their mental capacities were unimpaired. They wished to die but could not end their lives without third party assistance. The claimants sought declarations that, inter alia, the law of murder or of assisted suicide was incompatible with the right to respect for private life under Art 8 of the ECHR, insofar as it criminalized voluntary active euthanasia and/or assisted suicide. The case is discussed in more detail in Ch 15.

In the Supreme Court, Lord Neuberger confirmed that 'mercy killing involves the perpetrator intentionally killing another person, and therefore, even where that person wished to die, or the killing was purely out of compassion and love, the current state of the law is that the killing will amount to murder or (if one or more of the mitigating circumstances are present) manslaughter'.[80]

Lord Neuberger endorsed the fundamental difference between a positive action which caused death and an omission which resulted in a death and also between an act of administering the fatal drug to a person and setting up a machine so that the person can administer the drug to himself. The distinction is, in his lordship's view, founded on personal autonomy and morality:[81]

Where the act can be classified as an 'omission' (eg, to my mind somewhat uncomfortably in terms of common sense, switching off a life-supporting machine at least if done by an appropriately authorised person, as in *Bland*'s case and *In re B (Adult: Refusal of Medical Treatment)*), it seems to me that if the act which immediately causes the death is that of a third party that may be the wrong side of the line, whereas if the final act is that of the person himself, who carries it out pursuant to a voluntary, clear, settled and informed decision, that is the permissible side of the line. In the latter case, the person concerned has not been 'killed' by anyone, but has autonomously exercised his right to end his life.

12.1.7 The mens rea of murder
12.1.7.1 Malice aforethought

The mens rea of murder is traditionally called 'malice aforethought'.[82] This is a technical term and it has a technical meaning quite different from the ordinary popular meaning of the two words. The phrase, it has been truly said, 'is a mere arbitrary symbol . . . for the "malice" may have in it nothing really malicious; and need never be really "aforethought"'.[83]

---

[77] The Law Commission summary of the law on mercy killing in Ch 7 of LC 304, *Murder, Manslaughter and Infanticide* (2006) was endorsed as an accurate statement of the law.

[78] The latest statute to address the problem of mercy killing (Criminal Justice Act 2003, s 269 and Sch 21. Consolidated in the Sentencing Act 2020.), expressly includes as mitigation for the offence the offender's subjective belief that he was acting out of mercy. For discussion, see B Mitchell and JV Roberts, *Exploring the Mandatory Life Sentence for Murder* (2012) 19–20 and 46–7.

[79] [2014] UKSC 38. The case is discussed in more detail in Ch 15.

[80] At [17] per Lord Neuberger.   [81] At [94].

[82] See Lord Goff, 'The Mental Element in the Crime of Murder' (1988) 104 LQR 30 and G Williams, 'The *Mens Rea* for Murder: Leave it Alone' (1989) 105 LQR 387. For discussion of the comparative approaches to the fault element in murder, see S Yeo, *Fault in Homicide* (1997), and the extensive discussion in LCCP 177 and LC 304.

[83] Kenny, *Outlines* (15th edn, 1947) 153.

The House of Lords confirmed that the term means intention.[84] Thus, a parent who kills a suffering child out of motives of compassion is 'malicious' for this purpose; and there is sufficient 'aforethought' if an intention to kill is formed only a second before the fatal blow is struck. Neither ill-will nor premeditation[85] is necessary. The concept of premeditation is one which has been considered as an option for reform and wisely rejected. The fact that killing is premeditated is not necessarily an aggravating feature as, for example, where an abused spouse plans a killing of her abuser.[86]

The meaning of the term malice aforethought is critical since that is what determines whether an unlawful killing is murder or manslaughter. Murder is unlawful homicide with malice aforethought. Manslaughter is an unlawful homicide without malice aforethought.[87]

Malice aforethought is a concept of the common law with a long history but, since *Moloney*,[88] which held that malice aforethought means intention, it is no longer necessary to explore this. We can now state that the modern law defines malice aforethought as:

(1) an intention to kill any person or;

(2) an intention to cause grievous bodily harm to any person.

'Intention' has the meaning attributed to it in *Woollin*[89] as applied in *Matthews and Alleyne*.[90]

GBH: 'grievous bodily harm', at one time broadly interpreted to mean any harm sufficiently serious to interfere with health and comfort, must now be given its ordinary natural meaning. 'Grievous' means 'really serious'[91] and the word 'really' probably adds nothing but emphasis to the fact that the harm intended must be (actually or really) serious.[92] As Green LJ noted in *Sidhu*:[93]

Traditionally, judges use the expression 'really serious', and occasionally 'serious', to articulate the threshold. But when judges use such language they mean in effect 'an intention to cause serious harm or really serious harm sufficient to amount in law to murder'.

The Court of Appeal in *Bollom*[94] confirmed that the words are to be construed as ordinary English words and not assigned a specific legal definition.[95] The evaluation of whether the harm is sufficiently serious is based on the jury's assessment of the harm caused to the particular victim. The age and vulnerability of the victim will therefore be important. It is not a question of whether D thought that the harm he was causing was serious. This can present problems since it may, theoretically, give rise to murder by pinprick if D stabs with a needle V who is a

[84] *Moloney* [1985] AC 905.

[85] For a suggestion for reform on this basis, see B Mitchell, 'Thinking About Murder' (1992) 56 J Crim L 78. See also the support for such a view derived from Mitchell's research appended to LC 290, *Partial Defences to Murder* (2004). The Law Commission rejected redefinition in these terms in LC 304.

[86] See generally M Kremnitzer, 'On Premeditation' (1998) 1 Buffalo Crim LR 627. LCCP 177 rejected the approach on the basis of difficulties of proof. See also J Horder and D Hughes, 'Comparative Issues in the Law of Homicide' in J Horder (ed), *Homicide Law in Comparative Perspective* (2007).

[87] *Doherty* (1887) 16 Cox CC 306 at 307 per Stephen J.

[88] [1985] AC 905, p 100.   [89] [1999] AC 82.

[90] [2003] EWCA Crim 192, p 95. See also *Royle* [2013] EWCA Crim 1461 in which the judge adopted a less satisfactory definition although one more favourable to the defendant: 'You must be sure that he did not just realise that it could happen but acted on the basis that it would, or that he intended that it would.'

[91] *DPP v Smith* [1961] AC 290 at 334.

[92] *Saunders* [1985] Crim LR 230. It is for the judge to decide in each case whether it is necessary to direct the jury that the harm intended must be 'really serious'. Where the act was stabbing with a five-and-a-half inch knife blade, it was not necessary: *Janjua* [1999] 1 Cr App R 91.

[93] [2019] EWCA Crim 1034, [18].   [94] [2003] EWCA Crim 2846.

[95] cf other jurisdictions in which definitions based on lethality are used. See LCCP 177, paras 3.65 et seq.

haemophiliac, and the stabbing is judged to have been really serious bodily harm.[96] In its provisional proposals on homicide reform, the Law Commission defined the term as 'harm of such a nature as to endanger life or as to cause or be likely to cause permanent or long-term damage to a significant aspect of physical integrity or mental functioning',[97] The Commission's final recommendation was to retain the common law position, replacing the word injury for harm.

Although the expression GBH is ambiguous and forms a core element of the definition of such a serious offence carrying a unique sentence and stigma, it has been held, in Northern Ireland at least, to be compatible with the requirement in Art 7 of the ECHR of certainty.[98] There seems little doubt that this view would be followed by the courts in England.

Subjective test of mens rea: in 1960, in the notorious case of *DPP v Smith*, the House of Lords laid down a largely objective test of liability in murder—the test was 'not what the defendant contemplated, but what the ordinary reasonable man or woman would in all the circumstances of the case have contemplated as the natural and probable result'. That approach was modified by s 8 of the Criminal Justice Act 1967.[99] It can be consigned to history: in *Frankland and Moore v R*,[100] the Privy Council (comprising five judicial members of the House of Lords), acting on the *dicta* of Lord Diplock in *Hyam*,[101] Lord Bridge in *Moloney*[102] and Lord Scarman in *Hancock*,[103] held that *Smith* did not represent the common law of England.

12.1.7.2 Constructive malice

The common law of malice aforethought is now fully stated in the rule requiring an intention to cause death or grievous bodily harm. It is, however, still necessary to refer to s 1 of the Homicide Act 1957 which modified the common law.

(1) Where a person kills another in the course or furtherance of some other offence, the killing shall not amount to murder unless done with the same malice aforethought (express or implied) as is required for a killing to amount to murder when not done in the course or furtherance of another offence.

(2) For the purposes of the foregoing subsection, a killing done in the course or for the purpose of resisting an officer of justice, or of resisting or avoiding or preventing a lawful arrest, or of effecting or assisting an escape or rescue from legal custody, shall be treated as a killing in the course or furtherance of an offence.

The purpose of this section was, as the side-note in the statute indicates, to limit malice aforethought by the 'abolition of "constructive malice"'. 'Constructive malice' took two forms:

(a) it was murder to kill in the course or furtherance of a violent felony (or possibly any felony) so that an intention to commit the felony (eg rape or robbery) was a sufficient mens rea for murder where death resulted from such an intentional felony;[104]

(b) it was murder to kill while attempting to prevent lawful arrest or bring about escape from lawful arrest or custody, so that an intention to do these things was also malice aforethought where the act caused death.

---

[96] See LCCP 177, para 3.81. See also on the issues of this lack of definition: W Wilson, 'Murder and the Structure of Homicide' in B Mitchell and A Ashworth (eds), *Rethinking English Homicide Law* (2000).

[97] LCCP 177, para 3.159.   [98] *Anderson* [2003] NI 12.

[99] Section 8 applies not only to murder and its function is not to define what mens rea must be proved, but only *how* the mens rea required by the common law or other statutes is to be proved.

[100] [1987] AC 576.   [101] [1975] AC 55 at 94.

[102] [1985] AC 905 at 921 and 928.   [103] [1986] AC 455 at 473.

[104] This form of murder exists in some US states and in former British colonies, see eg *Griffith* [2004] UKPC 58 (Barbados) and *Foster* [2007] UKPC 20. See generally C Finkelstein, 'Merger and Felony Murder' in Duff and Green (eds), *Defining Crimes*.

Section 1(1) abolishes the first, and s 1(2) the second form of constructive malice. While eliminating constructive malice, the section leaves in existence 'express' and 'implied' malice. Although these terms have been used for centuries, their meaning is obscure and they certainly do not have any ordinary natural meaning.[105] At common law 'express malice' must now be taken to mean the intention to kill and 'implied malice' the intention to cause grievous bodily harm. Though the terms remain on the 'statute book', there is in practice no need to use them and the sooner they are repealed the better.

Constructive malice must be distinguished from constructive manslaughter, which is discussed in Ch 14 and remains very much a part of the common law.

It was at one time argued that s 1 also abolished intention to cause grievous bodily harm as a category sufficient for malice aforethought. That argument only worked if some other meaning was given to 'implied malice' since that concept is expressly preserved.[106] In *Cunningham*,[107] the House of Lords confirmed that intention to cause grievous bodily harm survived the Homicide Act as a category of mens rea.[108]

Both Lords Mustill and Steyn have criticized the rule that an intention to cause serious bodily harm is a sufficient mens rea for murder as a 'conspicuous anomaly' and an example of a 'constructive crime'.[109] Lord Steyn spoke of the result of the present definition being defendants 'classified as murderers who are not in truth murderers'.[110] The grievous bodily harm rule has been defended by some academic commentators, either as reflecting a general principle that the law imposes an obligation on an attacker to take the unforeseen consequences of his actions,[111] or as an appropriate response in cases of death caused by an 'attack'.[112]

The House of Lords had the opportunity in *Cunningham* to rid the law of the anomaly by requiring at least awareness of the risk of causing death. It declined. It seems unlikely that the Supreme Court will go to the lengths of overruling decisions in this area. The House of Lords endorsed the GBH rule as recently as *Rahman*.[113]

12.2 The sentence for murder

Until the Homicide Act 1957,[114] all persons convicted of murder were automatically sentenced to death. By s 5 of that Act certain types of murder were singled out and designated 'capital murder'. These continued to be punishable by death, while the

---

[105] See Lord Hailsham in *Cunningham* [1981] 2 All ER 863 at 867.

[106] The argument was that the only reason why intention to cause grievous bodily harm was malice aforethought before 1957 was that in 1803 Lord Ellenborough's Act created a felony of causing grievous bodily harm with intent to do so. If death resulted, that was murder because, and only because, the killing was in the course or furtherance of that felony. The argument was rejected in *Vickers* [1957] 2 QB 664 (a court of five judges). As the LCCP 177 discusses at para 1.119, the Lord Chief Justice in that case took a different approach to that which only a short time before he had assured Parliament he would take in such a case. Parliament had therefore enacted the 1957 Act on a misunderstanding as to the law. Lords Diplock and Kilbrandon accepted the argument in *Hyam* but the matter was left open because Lord Cross was not prepared to decide between the conflicting views.

[107] [1982] AC 566.

[108] It ante-dated Lord Ellenborough's Act as a form of malice aforethought, distinct from constructive malice.

[109] *A-G's Reference (No 3 of 1994)* [1998] 1 Cr App R 91, 93; *Powell and Daniels, English* [1998] 1 Cr App R 261 at 267–8, and *Woollin* [1999] 1 Cr App R 8 at 13.

[110] ibid. Cf Scots law and the requirement of wicked recklessness.

[111] J Horder, 'Two Histories and Four Hidden Principles of *Mens Rea*' (1997) 113 LQR 9.

[112] W Wilson, 'Murder and the Structure of Homicide' in Ashworth and Mitchell (eds), *Rethinking English Homicide Law*.

[113] *Rahman* [2008] UKHL 45. This aspect of the judgment has not been overruled by the Supreme Court's decision in *Jogee* [2016] UKSC 8.

[114] See M Wasik, 'Sentencing in Homicide' in Ashworth and Mitchell (eds), *Rethinking English Homicide Law*, 167.

remaining types of murder were punishable by imprisonment for life. In effect, there were two degrees of murder.

The distinction between the two degrees of murder proved to be unsatisfactory, and the death penalty for murder was suspended by the Murder (Abolition of Death Penalty) Act 1965.[115] All persons convicted of murder must now be sentenced to imprisonment for life. The mandatory sentence[116] was at that time unique in English law and the CLRC considered whether or not the judge should have discretion in sentencing as in all other crimes. It was deeply and almost evenly divided on the issue. Its Report[117] set out the arguments on both sides in some detail but made no recommendation.

Subsequently the matter was considered by a Select Committee of the House of Lords (the Nathan Committee) which recommended, with one dissent, that the mandatory sentence be abolished. The conclusion was that murder should be punishable with a maximum sentence of life but the judge should have the same discretion to impose lesser sentences as for other crimes.[118] The arguments in favour of this approach are overwhelming. Murders vary as greatly in their gravity, and murderers in their dangerousness, as for any other crime. The recommendation has not, however, found favour with the government, despite public opposition to the mandatory sentence,[119] and there seems to be no prospect of its implementation at the present time.

Prior to 2003, on sentencing a murderer, the judge would make a recommendation to the Home Secretary of the minimum period which should elapse before the prisoner was to be released on licence.[120] That power was successfully challenged as incompatible with Arts 5 and 6 of the ECHR since the minister was not an independent and impartial arbiter of the term of imprisonment.[121] (The mandatory sentence itself has been held not to be incompatible with Arts 3 and 5 of the ECHR.[122] Even a 'whole life tariff' is not incompatible with the ECHR.[123])

The Criminal Justice Act 2003 imposed a new regime for the sentencing and procedure for release of those sentenced to life imprisonment.[124] Under Sch 21 to the Sentencing Code (consolidating the Criminal Justice Act 2003) the judge must determine the length of the minimum term which will be served by the offender before he is eligible to be considered by the Parole Board for release on licence. The starting points for adult offenders are: (a) a whole-life term (ie where the offender will serve the rest of his life in prison)[125] in the most exceptional cases; (b) a 30-year minimum tariff for serious cases such as murders of police or prison officers, murders involving firearms, sexual or sadistic killings or killings aggravated by race, religion, sexual orientation, disability or transgender identity; (c) 25

---

[115] This, by virtue of affirmative resolutions of both Houses of Parliament on 16 and 18 Dec 1969, was to be permanently in force. See L Blom-Cooper, 'Life Until Death' [1999] Crim LR 899.

[116] For extensive discussion see B Mitchell and JV Roberts, *Exploring the Mandatory Life Sentence for Murder* (2012).

[117] Fourteenth Report, para 19.27.

[118] HL Paper 78-I (1989). See A Ashworth, 'Reform of the Law of Murder' [1990] Crim LR 75.

[119] See B Mitchell and J Roberts, *Public Opinion and Sentencing for Murder: An Empirical Investigation of Public Knowledge and Attitudes in England and Wales* (2010).

[120] See the review of the process since 1957—S Shute, 'Punishing Murderers: Release Procedures and the "Tariff"' [2004] Crim LR 873.

[121] *R v Home Secretary, ex p Anderson* [2002] UKHL 46; *Stafford v UK* (2002) 35 EHRR 121.

[122] *Pyrah* [2003] 1 AC 903.   [123] *Hutchinson v UK* (App no 57592/08) [2017] ECHR 65.

[124] See *Practice Direction (Criminal Proceedings)* [2013] EWCA Crim 1631; and Sentencing Act 2020, s 321 et seq. For academic comment, see N Padfield, 'Tariffs in Murder' [2002] Crim LR 192; J Saunders and J Roberts, 'Sentencing for murder: the adverse and unintended effects of Schedule 21 to the Criminal Justice Act 2003' [2020] Crim LR 900.

[125] The Grand Chamber of the ECtHR held in *Vinter v UK* [2014] Crim LR 81 that whole-life terms violated Art 3 of the ECHR. In *Hutchinson v UK* (App no 57592/08) [2017] ECHR 65, the Grand Chamber of the ECtHR departed from its earlier reasoning.

years for murders committed with a knife or other weapon taken to the crime; and (d) a 15-year minimum starting point for murders not falling within the two higher categories. Judges will have the opportunity to take into account aggravating and mitigating features: the starting points are just that.[126]

12.3 Proposals for reform of murder

Given the seriousness of the offence,[127] the sanctity of life, the unique stigma and the mandatory sentence, it is surprising that the offence remains so ill-defined in so many respects. Three main areas have been the subject of sustained criticism and focus for reform proposals.[128] First, there is the ambiguity over the definition of the concept of intention (as examined in Ch 3). This increases the opportunity for inconsistency in application and generates uncertainty in the law. Secondly, there is the grievous bodily harm rule—it is sufficient that D intends GBH. Murder is therefore a constructive crime, attracting all the criticisms normally levelled at such offences for a failure to respect principles of fair labelling and correspondence between actus reus and mens rea.[129] Thirdly, there is the sustained and cogent criticism of the mandatory sentence.[130] It is often assumed that the mandatory sentence is retained to reflect the will of the populus, but research does not always bear out such a conclusion.[131]

Although the government has been content to add, piecemeal, to the stock of homicide offences for over a century (see the infanticide offence, causing death by dangerous driving, the offence under s 5 of the Domestic Violence, Crime and Victims Act 2004, corporate manslaughter,[132] causing death by driving while uninsured, etc[133]), since 1957 it has avoided the reform of the most serious offence of them all—murder. Numerous reform proposals have been advanced, only a brief outline of which can be discussed here.[134]

---

[126] On public attitudes and expectations in sentencing of murder, see B Mitchell, in LCCP 177, Appendix A. Schedule 21 has affected other sentencing policy: D Jeremy [2010] Crim LR 593.

[127] See LCCP 177, Appendix G on the background information about murder.

[128] For a history of efforts to reform the law of homicide, see J Horder, *Homicide and the Politics of Law Reform* (2012) Ch 1.

[129] As regards labelling, Lord Steyn cited, n 110, that people are labelled murderers who are in truth not such. As for correspondence, the mens rea of intent to do GBH does not correspond with the actus reus—death. See, in particular, B Mitchell, 'In Defence of the Correspondence Principle' [1999] Crim LR 195; J Horder, 'A Critique of the Correspondence Principle in Criminal Law' [1995] Crim LR 759. See also N Lacey, 'Partial Defences to Homicide' in Ashworth and Mitchell, *Rethinking English Homicide Law*, Ch 5. Some might argue that there is no difficulty in holding D liable in a GBH case because his act of intentional GBH is an attack on V which shows sufficient culpability by its practical indifference for V's life. See Duff, *Answering for Crime*, 253–5.

[130] See generally B Mitchell, *Murder and Penal Policy* (1990).

[131] See the reports of Professor Mitchell's research as appended to LC 290, revealing that 62.9 per cent of the population surveyed thought that there ought *not* to be a mandatory sentence. Cf the findings in the LCCP 177, Appendix A.

[132] Corporate Manslaughter and Corporate Homicide Act 2007.

[133] See the Road Safety Act 2006.

[134] Horder is critical of the way in which legal experts have sought a privileged or elite position in the process of homicide law reform at the expense of the public at large. Horder's remedy for this is to conduct wider public consultation and require government periodically to consult on the substance of reforms made to what he terms 'violative crimes', such as homicide. See J Horder, 'Safe in Whose Hands? Judges, Experts, and Public Opinion in the Homicide Reform Process' in J Horder, *Homicide and the Politics of Law Reform* (2012). For a critique see A Cornford, 'The Architecture of Homicide' (2015) 34 OJLS 819, who is frustrated by Horder's failure to discuss explicitly why direct popular involvement in the reform process would be desirable.

12.3.1 Abolishing murder and manslaughter?

One unlikely way forward, which was rejected by the Law Commission in its 2006 Report, would be to replace murder and manslaughter with a single offence of unlawful killing in which the sentence is at the discretion of the trial judge (within guidelines). This view had some academic[135] and judicial support (from Lord Kilbrandon in *Hyam*) but was rejected by the CLRC.[136] Since this would remove the specific label of murder and the uniqueness that attaches to it, the option is unlikely ever to find much general support.[137] It is an unrealistic prospect in political terms,[138] but it has the merit of simplicity.

12.3.2 A victim-specific model?

A second model which has found little support would be to reform the law with a hierarchy of forms of homicide based on categories of victim. The most serious form of homicide would, under such a model, be applicable to those who kill children or the elderly or police officers, etc. This would, it is submitted, be an unsatisfactory reform. The sentencing regime under Sch 21 to the Sentencing Code already allows judges, and in some categories requires judges, to have particular regard to the characteristic of the victim.

12.3.3 Law Commission Consultation Paper No 177

The Law Commission in LCCP 177[139] provisionally proposed to create a new ladder of homicide offences in a hierarchical structure respecting the correspondence principle. This follows the model adopted in many other jurisdictions where the seriousness of the wrongdoing is reflected in a graduated scheme of offences.[140] The proposals were for a crime of first degree murder which would carry the mandatory life penalty. This would be restricted to cases of intentional killing. Second degree murder would be a wholly new form of offence and would be much broader with a discretionary life maximum penalty. Second degree murder would include killing where D did not intend to kill but did intend to do serious harm, and 'recklessly indifferent' killing, where D realized that his conduct involved an unjustified risk of killing, but pressed on with that conduct without caring whether or not death would result. Second degree murder would also encompass the partial defences to what would otherwise be 'first degree murder'. Below second degree murder would lie an offence of manslaughter capable of commission in one of two ways: by gross negligence; or through an intentional act intended to cause injury or involving recklessness as to causing injury. The maximum sentence for both would be a fixed term of years.

---

[135] See L Blom-Cooper and T Morris, *With Malice Aforethought: A Study of the Crime and Punishment for Homicide* (2004).

[136] In its Fourteenth Report on *Offences Against the Person* (1980). See R Buxton, 'The New Murder' [1980] Crim LR 521.

[137] For fascinating studies into the public perceptions of the scope of the offence, see B Mitchell, 'Public Perceptions of Homicide and Criminal Justice' (1998) 38 Brit J Crim 453 and 'Further Evidence of the Relationship Between Legal and Public Opinion on the Homicide Law' [2000] Crim LR 814.

[138] See J Horder and D Hughes, 'Comparative Issues in the Law of Homicide' in Horder (ed), *Homicide Law in Comparative Perspective*, 7. See also B Mitchell (2007) 71 J Crim L 318 recognizing that it would devalue the enormity of the worst cases.

[139] On the Commission's proposals see: W Wilson, 'The Structure of Criminal Homicide' [2006] Crim LR 471; A Norrie, 'Between Orthodox Subjectivism and Moral Contextualism: Intention and the Consultation Paper' [2006] Crim LR 486; C Wells and O Quick, 'Getting Tough with Defences' [2006] Crim LR 514; V Tadros, 'The Homicide Ladder' (2006) 69 MLR 601; J Rogers, 'The Law Commission's Proposed Restructuring of Homicide' (2006) 70 J Crim Law 223.

[140] See J Horder, 'The Changing Face of the Law of Homicide' in Horder (ed), *Homicide Law in Comparative Perspective*.

The Commission carried out extensive reviews of public perceptions of the offence of murder and the approach taken in other jurisdictions.[141]

12.3.4 Law Commission Report No 304

In its final recommendations in Report No 304,[142] the Law Commission made some significant changes. Most importantly, the Law Commission extended the proposed offence of first degree murder (which would still carry a mandatory life penalty). This offence would, under the final proposal, include both: (a) killing intentionally; and (b) killing where there was an intention to do serious injury, coupled with an awareness of a serious risk of causing death.

Second degree murder (which would carry a discretionary life maximum penalty) would include: (a) killing where D intended to do serious injury; (b) killing where D intended to cause some injury or a fear or risk of injury, and was aware of a serious risk of causing death; as well as (c) killing in which there is a partial defence (loss of self-control (gross provocation or fear of serious violence); diminished responsibility; participation in a suicide pact) to what would otherwise be first degree murder.

Manslaughter (also carrying a discretionary life maximum penalty) would include: (a) killing through gross negligence as to a risk of causing death; and (b) killing through a criminal act which is (i) intended to cause injury or (ii) where there was an awareness that the act involved a serious risk of causing injury.[143] These provisions relating to manslaughter are considered in Ch 14.

Special provision was also made for an offence of participating in a joint criminal venture in the course of which another participant commits first or second degree murder. This would be an offence of manslaughter where the circumstances are such that it should have been obvious that first or second degree murder might be committed by another participant.

The government has now decided it will not act upon these recommendations from the Law Commission.[144]

In 2016, the House of Commons Justice Committee held a single evidence-gathering session on the law of homicide. The session examined the effectiveness of the operation of the law of homicide and considered the proposals for reform discussed in this section. In his evidence, the then Minister of State for Courts and Justice, Sir Oliver Heald QC MP, stated that the government had no intention of reopening this area.[145]

Further reading

A Ashworth and B Mitchell (eds), *Rethinking English Homicide Law*

J Horder (ed), *Homicide Law in Comparative Perspective*

B Mitchell and JV Roberts, *Exploring the Mandatory Life Sentence for Murder*

---

[141] See also Horder, ibid.

[142] See A Ashworth, 'Principles, Pragmatism and the Law Commission's Recommendations on Homicide Law Reform' [2007] Crim LR 333; RD Taylor 'The Nature of "Partial Defences" and the Coherence of (Second Degree) Murder' [2007] Crim LR 345.

[143] See LC 304, para 1.67.

[144] See The Rt Hon Oliver Herald MP QC, 'Law of Homicide', MOJ, 24 Oct 2017, available at www.parliament.uk/business/committees/committees-a-z/commons-select/justice-committee/one-off-sessions/parliament-2015/law-of-homicide-16-17/.

[145] www.parliament.uk/business/committees/committees-a-z/commons-select/justice-committee/news-parliament-20151/law-of-homicide-evidence-16-17/.

13

Voluntary manslaughter

At common law, all unlawful homicides which are not murder are manslaughter. The offence has a broad scope, being limited by murder at one extreme and accidental killing at the other. There are an increasing number of statutory offences of unlawful killing including, for example, causing death by dangerous driving and corporate manslaughter.[1] Some of these statutory offences (notably corporate manslaughter) prohibit prosecution for manslaughter but in most cases manslaughter remains available as an alternative charge to the specific statutory offences.[2]

It is customary and useful to divide manslaughter into two main groups: 'voluntary' and 'involuntary' manslaughter. The distinction is based on D's intention at the time of the killing. Where there is no intention to kill or cause grievous bodily harm, the offence falls within the category of involuntary manslaughter. In contrast, voluntary manslaughter comprises cases where D had the intention to kill or do grievous bodily harm but some statutory defined mitigating circumstance—loss of self-control, diminished responsibility or killing in pursuance of a suicide pact—reduces what would be murder to the less serious grade of criminal homicide.[3] These partial defences to murder were originally introduced to avoid the death penalty. Today they subsist largely in order to avoid the mandatory life sentence for murder, but in an unsatisfactory state despite the main partial defences to murder—loss of control and diminished responsibility—being radically overhauled in the Coroners and Justice Act 2009.[4]

---

[1] These offences, their theoretical implications and the relationship with 'normal' manslaughter are considered in the valuable collection of essays edited by C Clarkson and S Cunningham (eds), *Criminal Liability for Non-Aggressive Death* (2008); see, in particular, A Ashworth, 'Manslaughter Generic or Nominate Offences' in that volume.

[2] See also V Tadros, 'The Limits of Manslaughter' in C Clarkson and S Cunningham (eds), *Criminal Liability for Non-Aggressive Death* (2008), who argues that the special offences discriminate and fail to optimize coherence in the law; see also Tadros, *Criminal Responsibility*, 348 et seq.

[3] *A-G of Ceylon v Perera* [1953] AC 200; *Lee Chun Chuen v R* [1963] AC 220; *Parker v R* [1964] AC 1369; *Smith (Clean) v R* [2002] 1 Cr App R 92; *contra, Holmes v DPP* [1946] AC 588 at 598 per Viscount Simon.

[4] For analysis of the defences of provocation and diminished responsibility under the law before the Coroners and Justice Act 2009, see the 12th edn of this book, Ch 15.

Three partial defences to murder exist:

(1) loss of control—where D kills with the mens rea for murder but at the time he had lost his self-control; one of the statutory qualifying triggers applied (governed by ss 54–6 of the Coroners and Justice Act 2009) and a person of D's age and sex with a normal degree of tolerance and self-restraint might have done as D did;

(2) diminished responsibility—where D kills with the mens rea for murder but he establishes on the balance of probabilities that he was suffering from diminished responsibility (under s 2 of the Homicide Act 1957);

(3) where D kills in pursuance of a suicide pact.[5] The problem of the suicide pact is examined in Ch 15 alongside the statutory crime of assisting or encouraging suicide.[6]

13.1 Loss of self-control

13.1.1 Background to the 2009 Act

The common law had recognized a partial defence of provocation for centuries.[7] That was modified by statute in s 3 of the Homicide Act 1957. The defence reduced murder to manslaughter.

The defence was extremely controversial.[8] Courts struggled with the application of the defence, in part because it was being used as a means of relieving the potential injustice of the mandatory life sentence for murder. There were disagreements as to the terms of the defence,[9] with numerous high-profile appeals including several to the House of Lords and Privy Council failing to adopt a consistent approach. For the appellate courts to fluctuate so often and so significantly on the interpretation of a defence in cases of such seriousness led to confusion and presented a disappointing spectacle.[10]

Even the theoretical foundation for the defence remained unclear: was the defence properly regarded as one of partial justification (D has gone beyond what would be an acceptable response to the provoking conduct, or that the deceased deserved it) or of partial excuse (D's loss of self-control was uncharacteristic, the bad character exhibited exceeds that to be expected in the circumstances)?[11] One of the most powerful influences for reform was the claim that the defence operated in a discriminatory fashion, which given its historical origins is hardly surprising.[12] Women who killed abusive partners were disadvantaged if they did not act in a state which could legally be described as one of 'sudden and temporary

---

5 See p 650. 6 See p 650.

7 *Duffy* [1949] 1 All ER 932n. On this case see S Edwards, 'Justice Devlin's Legacy' [2009] Crim LR 851. For a comprehensive review of the theoretical and historical context of the defence, see J Horder, *Provocation and Responsibility* (1992). See also JM Kaye, 'Early History of Murder and Manslaughter' (1967) 83 LQR 365.

8 There is a wealth of literature on the topic. LC 290, *Partial Defences to Murder* (2004) is a valuable starting point. The Law Commission documents leading to the new Act also include valuable discussion: see LCCP 177, *A New Homicide Act for England* (2005) and LC 304, *Murder, Manslaughter and Infanticide* (2006). Valuable articles and essays include the seminal piece by A Ashworth, 'The Doctrine of Provocation' (1976) 35 CLJ 292.

9 See LCCP 177, para 2.78.

10 This passage was cited with approval by Lord Judge CJ in *Clinton* [2012] EWCA Crim 2.

11 Horder, *Provocation and Responsibility*, Chs 6–9, in particular at 130–5. See further J Dressler, 'Provocation: Partial Justification or Partial Excuse' (1988) 51 MLR 467; F McAuley, 'Anticipating the Past: The Defences of Provocation in Irish Law' (1987) 50 MLR 133; V Tadros, 'The Characters of Excuses' (2001) 21 OJLS 495. See also the discussion in LC 290, paras 3.22 et seq and the Irish Law Reform Commission, LRC Consultation Paper No 27, *Homicide: The Plea of Provocation* (2003).

12 See Horder, *Provocation and Responsibility*.

loss of control'.[13] In addition, until relatively recently, the cumulative effect of years of abuse was not considered. Further, the mental characteristics arising from an abusive relationship (including what some recognize as battered woman syndrome)[14] could only be taken into account if that was relevant to the gravity of the provocation (ie the sting of the words or conduct that provoked D), but not to D's ability to exercise her self-control.[15] The abused woman is unlikely as a matter of fact to kill in self-defence (as that term is understood in law). Owing to relative limited physical strength, it is uncommon for women to respond lethally when facing an attack by an abusive male partner.[16] Women charged with murder were forced to rely on diminished responsibility, which aside from requiring expert evidence and imposing a burden of proof on the accused, stigmatized them as mentally abnormal.

A further general difficulty with the defence was its relationship with the partial defence of diminished responsibility. The elements were very different, with different burdens of proof, but they overlapped in many cases.

These serious problems with the provocation defence prompted reform. Law Commission papers examined numerous options for reform including whether it was even necessary or desirable to retain the defence if the mandatory sentence were to be abolished.[17] Fundamental questions included whether the purpose of the defence was to unshackle the judge from imposing the mandatory life sentence[18] or to label more distinctly those killers whose conduct might be regarded as morally different, despite their malice aforethought, owing to some mitigating feature of the killing. The unique stigmas and heightened emotions aroused by the stark fact of death generate strong views on these issues. Many other jurisdictions have faced similar difficulties where defence and reform proposals have been widely canvassed.[19]

13.1.2 Loss of self-control—the 2009 Act

By s 56 of the Coroners and Justice Act 2009 the common law defence of provocation is abolished and replaced by a new defence of loss of control (in this chapter 'LOSC'), contained in ss 54 and 55.[20] In *Clinton*, Lord Judge CJ emphasized that the old provocation

---

[13] S Edwards, *Sex and Gender in the Legal Process* (1996) Ch 6; O'Donovan (1991) 18 J Law & Soc 219; C Wells (1994) 14 LS 266; A McColgan, 'In Defence of Battered Women who Kill' (1993) 13 OJLS 508. For a valuable summary see LCCP 173, Ch 10.

[14] See L Walker, *Battered Women Syndrome* (1st edn, 1984; 3rd edn, 2008).

[15] See C Wells, 'Provocation: The Case for Abolition' in A Ashworth and B Mitchell (eds), *Rethinking English Homicide Law* (2000).

[16] On the availability of the defence, see A McColgan (1993) 13 OJLS 508; C Wells (1994) 14 LS 266; J Dressler, 'Battered Women Who Kill Their Sleeping Tormentors' and J Horder, 'Killing the Passive Abuser: A Theoretical Defence' both in Shute and Simester, *Criminal Law Theory*.

[17] See LC 290, Ch 2 and paras 3.35 et seq and the responses discussed to LCCP 173. Horder considers the arguments for abolition in *Provocation and Responsibility*, Ch 9.

[18] See C Wells, 'The Death Penalty for Provocation' [1978] Crim LR 662.

[19] For comparative material generally, see S Yeo, *Unrestrained Killings and the Law: Provocation and Excessive Self-Defence in India, England and Australia* (1998). See also eg the Victoria Law Reform Commission, 'Law Reform Defences to Murder' [2005] Crim LR 256 and for proposals in New South Wales, T Crofts and A Loughnan, 'Provocation, NSW Style: Reform of the Defence of Provocation in NSW' [2014] Crim LR 109.

[20] See A Norrie, *Crime, Reason and History* (3rd edn, 2014) Ch 11; A Reed and M Bohlander (eds), *Loss of Control and Diminished Responsibility: Domestic, Comparative and International Perspectives* (2011); C Withey, 'Loss of Control, Loss of Opportunity' [2011] Crim LR 263; R Fortson and AR Keene, *Current Law Statutes Annotation* (2010); J Glasson and J Knowles, *Blackstone's Guide to the Coroners and Justice Act 2009* (2010) Ch 8; S Edwards, 'Anger and Fear as Justifiable Preludes for Loss of Self-Control' (2010) 74 J Crim L 223.

defence is irrelevant in interpreting the 2009 Act and that 'The full ambit of the defence is encompassed within these statutory provisions.'[21] In relying on the Law Commission Report No 304[22] and earlier Law Commission Reports[23] and papers as sources of interpretation, care is needed since the enacted provisions differ in important respects from their proposals.[24]

Sections 54 and 55 replace the common law defence with a related but significantly different defence labelled 'loss of control'. This is designed to be a much narrower defence than at common law and under s 3 of the 1957 Act. Section 54 provides:

(1) Where a person ('D') kills or is a party to the killing of another ('V'), D is not to be convicted of murder if—

    (a) D's acts and omissions in doing or being a party to the killing resulted from D's loss of self-control,

    (b) the loss of self-control had a qualifying trigger, and

    (c) a person of D's sex and age, with a normal degree of tolerance and self restraint and in the circumstances of D, might have reacted in the same or in a similar way to D . . .

(7) A person who, but for this section, would be liable to be convicted of murder is liable instead to be convicted of manslaughter.

The LOSC defence is further defined in s 55. It comprises three main elements. In short, the requirements are:[25]

(1) a loss of self-control although not one that is necessarily sudden;

(2) D's loss of control must have been attributable to one or both of two specified 'qualifying triggers':

    (a) D's fear of serious violence from V against D or another identified person, and/or

    (b) things done or said (or both) which:

        (i) constitute circumstances of an extremely grave character, and

        (ii) cause D to have a justifiable sense of being seriously wronged;

(3) A person of D's sex and age, with a normal degree of tolerance and self-restraint and in the circumstances of D, might have reacted in the same or in a similar way to D.

---

[21] *Clinton* [2012] EWCA Crim 2, [2]. See also *Gurpinar* [2015] EWCA Crim 178: 'It should rarely be necessary to look at cases decided under the older law of provocation.' At [4] per Lord Thomas CJ.

[22] *Murder, Manslaughter and Infanticide* (2006).

[23] LC 290, *Partial Defences to Murder* (2004). See also LCCP 173 (2003) and LCCP 177, *A New Homicide Act for England and Wales?* (2005).

[24] The Law Commission proposal had no loss of control requirement nor did it exclude reliance on sexual infidelity as a sufficient trigger, see later for discussion. Lord Judge in *Clinton* stated, at [3], that the legislation does not sufficiently follow the recommendations of the Law Commission to allow the court to discern any link between the views and recommendations of the Law Commission and the legislation as enacted. See also *Gurpinar* [2015] EWCA Crim 178.

[25] As Lord Judge CJ emphasized in *Clinton*, each of these components is integral to the defence and if one is absent, then the defence fails. His lordship stated that the components ought to be analysed sequentially and separately, at [9]. See also *Gurpinar* [2015] EWCA Crim 178, per Lord Thomas CJ.

13.1.2.1 Commencement

Sections 54 to 56 were brought into force on 4 October 2010.[26] The LOSC defence will only apply if both D's act and V's death occurred after 4 October.[27]

13.1.2.2 The defence applies only to murder

The LOSC defence is available only to a charge of murder (and not attempted murder or any other charge) whether as a principal or secondary party.[28] The defence should, it is submitted, have no relevance to the determination of whether D committed the acts or omissions[29] causing death when he has been found unfit to plead under s 4A of the Criminal Procedure (Insanity) Act 1964.[30]

13.1.2.3 Withdrawing the defence from the jury

Under s 54(6), the LOSC defence must be left to the jury only if 'sufficient evidence is adduced to raise an issue with respect to the defence' and this is when 'evidence is adduced on which, in the opinion of the trial judge, a jury, properly directed, could reasonably conclude that the defence might apply'. This marks a significant change from the common law[31] and was one that the Court of Appeal was keen to assert in the early cases under the Act: *Clinton, Dawes, Gurpinar.*

The test to be applied by the trial judge under s 54(6) is to address each component of the defence separately and sequentially, ensuring that there is sufficient evidence to establish each one. In *Clinton,*[32] Lord Judge CJ observed that this exercise:

requires a common sense judgment based on an analysis of all the evidence. To the extent that the evidence may be in dispute, the judge has to recognise that the jury may accept the evidence which is most favourable to the defendant, and reject that which is most favourable to the prosecution, and so tailor the ruling accordingly. That is merely another way of saying that in discharging this responsibility the judge should not reject disputed evidence which the jury might choose to believe. Guiding himself or herself in this way, the more difficult question which follows is the judgment whether the circumstances were sufficiently grave and whether the defendant had a justifiable

---

[26] The Coroners and Justice Act 2009 (Commencement No 4, Transitional and Saving Provisions) Order 2010, SI 2010/816. The law of some Caribbean jurisdictions mirrors that of England prior to the enactment of the Coroners and Justice Act 2009, so the Privy Council may still have to consider provocation for some time to come.

[27] Para 7 of Sch 22 to the 2009 Act. Historical cases turning on the old law still arise: eg *Challen* [2019] EWCA Crim 916.

[28] Section 54(8): 'The fact that one party to a killing is by virtue of this section not liable to be convicted of murder does not affect the question whether the killing amounted to murder in the case of any other party to it.' This follows the position in relation to provocation: *Marks* [1998] Crim LR 676. Academics have suggested that provocation (and diminished responsibility) should be available to all offences—J Horder, *Excusing Crime* (2003) 143–6.

[29] It is possible to have an omission causing death and plead LOSC. Eg D is so angered by his wife's perpetual taunts that he loses control and leaves her to die when she has fallen and is critically injured despite having a duty to assist.

[30] That was the position with provocation: *Grant* [2001] EWCA Crim 2611.

[31] Under which if there was evidence of provocation and loss of self-control the provocation defence would be left to the jury even though that would undermine the defendant's plea of eg self-defence: *Bullard v R* [1957] AC 635; *Rolle v R* [1965] 3 All ER 582; *Lee Chun-Chuen v R* [1963] AC 220. Empirical work by B Mitchell ('Distinguishing Between Murder and Manslaughter in Practice' (2007) 71 J Crim L 318), reveals that 75 per cent of provocation pleas were accompanied by one or more other defence.

[32] This was reiterated in *Dawes* [2013] EWCA Crim 322, *Gurpinar* [2015] EWCA Crim 178 and *Martin* [2017] EWCA Crim 1359. This represents a change from the old law: see *Acott* [1997] 1 WLR 306, 312.

grievance because he had been seriously wronged. These are value judgments. They are left to the jury when the judge concludes that the evidential burden has been satisfied.[33]

In *Goodwin*,[34] the Court of Appeal reviewed the case law on this judicial gatekeeping function and summarized the current state of the law.

(1) The required opinion is to be formed as a common-sense judgement based on an analysis of all the evidence.

(2) If there is sufficient evidence to raise an issue with respect to the defence of loss of control, then it is to be left to the jury whether or not the issue had been expressly advanced as part of the defence case at trial.

(3) The appellate court will give due weight to the evaluation ('the opinion') of the trial judge, who will have had the considerable advantage of conducting the trial and hearing all the evidence and having the feel of the case. As has been said, the appellate court 'will not readily interfere with that judgment'.

(4) However, that evaluation is not to be equated with an exercise of discretion such that the appellant court is only concerned with whether the decision was within a reasonable range of responses on the part of the trial judge. Rather, the judge's evaluation has to be appraised as either being right or wrong: it is a 'yes' or 'no' matter.

(5) The 2009 Act is specific by s 54(5) and (6) that the evidence must be 'sufficient' to raise an issue. It is not enough if there is simply some evidence falling short of sufficient evidence.

(6) The existence of a qualifying trigger does not necessarily connote that there will have been a loss of control.

(7) For the purpose of forming his or her opinion, the trial judge, whilst of course entitled to assess the quality and weight of the evidence, ordinarily should not reject evidence which the jury could reasonably accept. It must be recognized that a jury may accept the evidence which is most favourable to a defendant.

(8) The statutory defence of loss of control is significantly differently from and more restrictive than the previous defence of provocation which it has entirely superseded.

(9) Perhaps in consequence of all the foregoing, 'a much more rigorous evaluation' on the part of the trial judge is called for than might have been the case under the previous law of provocation.

(10) The statutory components of the defence are to be appraised sequentially and separately.

(11) And not least, each case is to be assessed by reference to its own particular facts and circumstances.

In carrying out that assessment, the judge faces a difficult task. As Lord Judge CJ made clear in *Dawes*,[35] the use of the term 'opinion' in s 54(6) does not mean there is a discretion by which different judges may reasonably form different opinions on whether the partial defence ought to be left to the jury.[36] The temptation for the judge to leave the defence so as to avoid challenge on appeal has to be resisted: *Goodwin*. If there is not sufficient evidence of the defence, the jury deliberations should not be 'cluttered up' by such issues.[37]

---

[33] At [46].   [34] [2018] EWCA Crim 2287.   [35] [2013] EWCA Crim 322.

[36] This was reiterated in *Workman* [2014] EWCA Crim 575, in which the Court of Appeal emphasized that the judge is *required* to leave the partial defence to the jury if there is sufficient evidence to raise the issue. This is not a matter of discretion.

[37] *Skilton* [2014] EWCA Crim 154.

Although the test the judge has to apply has been articulated clearly—that of sufficient evidence of each limb of the defence—unless and until there is a clear definition of each substantive element, that remains a very difficult task. When asked to form an 'opinion' on whether there is sufficient evidence of loss of control, a judge might reasonably ask 'how is loss of control defined', but unfortunately the judge will receive no clear answer since the statute is silent and the Court of Appeal has yet to define the concept.[38] Similar problems are likely to arise with the third limb.

Lord Judge CJ in *Dawes* sought to emphasize that, provided there is sufficient evidence of each element of the defence the judge must leave the defence to the jury even if the defence has, for tactical reasons, decided not to plead LOSC.[39] Similarly, whether the prosecution has raised the question or not, at the end of the evidence the judge should examine it and decide whether sufficient evidence relating to all the ingredients of the defence has been raised. The Court of Appeal emphasized in *Jewell*[40] that judges need to be cautious. The judge should not reject evidence which the jury could reasonably accept and, of course, a jury may accept the evidence which is most favourable to a defendant. There will often be no other evidence to substantiate D's claim and the judge should not reject disputed evidence that the jury may well choose to believe. It is the judge's duty to consider whether, on the whole of the evidence, the defence arises.

Sufficient evidence of each of the elements of the defence may appear in the case presented by the Crown. If not, there is an evidential burden on D.[41] If no evidence is adduced by the Crown or D that D lost his self-control, then the judge will withdraw the defence.[42] Similarly if there is no sufficient evidence of the qualifying trigger.[43] Since the burden of proof is on the Crown, evidence which might leave a reasonable jury in reasonable doubt whether or not the element is satisfied is sufficient. There must be evidence of loss of self-control and of a qualifying trigger; mere speculation will not suffice.[44] The trial judge's task is not easy and assistance from the advocates must be provided.[45] As noted, the Court of Appeal will not lightly interfere with the trial judge's decision.[46]

13.1.2.4 No considered desire for revenge

The partial defence cannot apply where there is 'a considered desire for revenge' (s 54(4)) even if D lost control as a result of a qualifying trigger. This is a very important qualification and in many cases will be worth considering before any other element of the defence.[47] The restriction must also be seen in combination with the requirement in s 55(6)(a): even if D has lost his self-control, if that was caused by a thing which D incited to be done or said for the *purpose* of providing an excuse to use violence, the qualifying triggers are not available.

Prior to the 2009 Act, the requirement under the provocation defence of the 'sudden' loss of self-control was an (imperfect) mechanism for drawing the distinction between premeditated killings and those which occur in the heat of the moment.[48] The Law Commission

---

[38] Judges may identify evidence that seems consistent with loss of control, such as the frenzied nature of the killing, but that is not the test.

[39] For an example of a case in which the defence was left to the jury despite not being relied upon by the defence, see *Cox* [2014] EWCA Crim 804.

[40] [2014] EWCA Crim 414. See also *Gurpinar* [2015] EWCA Crim 178 per Lord Thomas CJ.

[41] It is submitted that as in provocation mixed statements could be relied on: *Jama* [2004] EWCA Crim 960. Care will need to be taken with reliance on D's lies: *Davies* [2004] EWCA Crim 1914 (under the old law).

[42] eg *Workman* [2014] EWCA Crim 575.   [43] cf *McDonald* [2016] EWCA Crim 1529.

[44] See in relation to provocation: *Miao* [2003] EWCA Crim 3486; *Van Dongen* [2005] EWCA Crim 1728.

[45] *Gurpinar* at [15] per Lord Thomas CJ.   [46] ibid.

[47] In *Davies-Jones* [2013] EWCA Crim 2809, the Court of Appeal observed that ascertaining the existence of a considered desire for revenge is a logical precursor to the consideration of loss of control.

[48] [1949] 1 All ER 932n.

recommended that the new partial defence should not require proof of loss of control, but also proposed an explicit safeguard against the defence being used for revenge killings.

As enacted, the provisions in the 2009 Act include a requirement for D to have lost self-control and for there to be no considered desire for revenge. The judge is required to identify whether there was a 'considered desire for revenge' bearing in mind that D must have lost control and satisfy a qualifying trigger. Aside from the theoretical incoherence which results from a requirement for a loss of self-control and a restriction on considered revenge killings, problems may arise in practice. An abused spouse who kills after years of torment might well have a desire for revenge and yet also be out of control at the time of killing.

The judge and jury face a difficult task. The word 'considered' which suggests that there is some element of premeditation, is likely to be significant, but is unfortunately undefined.[49] Lord Judge CJ suggested in *Clinton* that 'in reality, the greater the level of deliberation, the less likely it will be that the killing followed a true loss of self-control'.[50] Whilst this may be true, it is important not to conflate what ought to be two separate inquiries. It is possible for D to have lost his self-control *and* to act out of a considered desire for revenge. In such a case, D cannot plead the partial defence.

It is important to note also that under the 2009 Act there is no requirement for the loss of control to be 'sudden': s 54(2). The removal of that restriction means that in some cases it will be even harder for the court to determine whether the killing is one that is motivated by a considered desire for revenge or by other emotions. For example, to take cases from the old law, there was held to be sufficient evidence to go to the jury in *Thornton*[51] where a wife had previously declared an intention to kill her brutally abusive husband, and after a fresh provocation she went to the kitchen, took and sharpened a carving knife and returned to another room where she fatally stabbed him. Is that a 'considered desire for revenge'? Similarly, under the old law, in *Pearson*,[52] although DD had armed themselves in advance with the fatal weapon to attack their abusive father, and the killing was a joint enterprise, provocation was left. Is arming oneself evidence of a 'considered desire for revenge'? In *Baillie*,[53] where D, being greatly enraged, fetched a gun from an attic and drove his car to V's house (stopping for petrol on the way) before shooting him, provocation was also left to the jury. Would this be regarded as a 'considered desire for revenge'? In *Clinton*, the Court of Appeal approved the direction of the judge that a considered desire for revenge connoted a 'deliberate and considered decision . . . one that has been thought about'.[54]

If D acted in a considered desire for revenge the defence is denied whether or not the desire for revenge exists before any potential qualifying trigger—fear of serious violence or things said or done. It is enough that having been taunted or threatened with violence, D goes away for a period of time to brood and returns to kill V. It was suggested in Parliament that the courts should look to D's dominant motive at the time of the killing. That view was rejected by ministers[55] who stated a belief that:

the expression 'considered desire for revenge' achieves the right balance in ensuring that thought-out revenge killings are excluded without automatically barring every case where revenge may be part of a complex range of motivations.

---

[49] The language the Law Commission used to describe this element was adopted in the statute despite the Commission not having engaged in statutory drafting: LC 304, para 5.27. See also Horder, *Homicide and the Politics of Law Reform* (2012) 214 et seq.

[50] At [10].

[51] [1992] 1 All ER 306. The jury rejected the defence, presumably being satisfied that there was no 'sudden and temporary' loss of self-control.

[52] [1992] Crim LR 193. See on the old law, M Wasik, 'Cumulative Provocation and Domestic Killing' [1982] Crim LR 29.

[53] [1995] Crim LR 739.   [54] At [129]–[131].

[55] See https://publications.parliament.uk/pa/cm200809/cmpublic/coroners/memos/ucm2802.htm.

13.1.2.5 Loss of control

The requirement of a 'loss of control' lies at the heart of this partial defence but what it means is undefined—other than that we know it need not be a 'sudden' loss.[56] As observed in parliamentary debates, it could refer to the failure to exercise self-control or the inability to do so.[57] It is a subjective test. If D is of an unusually phlegmatic temperament and it appears that he did not lose his self-control, the fact that a reasonable person in like circumstances would have done so will not assist D in the least. It is submitted that the test may be best understood as founded on whether D has lost his ability to maintain his actions in accordance with considered judgement or whether he had lost normal powers of reasoning.[58] The threshold is a high one. As Lord Judge explained in *Dawes*: 'For the individual with normal capacity of self-restraint and tolerance, unless the circumstances are extremely grave, normal irritation, and even serious anger do not often cross the threshold into loss of control.'[59]

There must be a loss of control in fact. We have already noted the difficult task of the judge in forming an opinion on whether there is sufficient evidence of this undefined element. The judge, in deciding whether to leave the defence, and the jury in assessing the evidence if the defence is left, are entitled to take into account all the relevant circumstances. This will include the nature of the conduct which constitutes the qualifying trigger, and all the relevant conditions in which it took place, the sensitivity or otherwise of D,[60] and the time, if any, which elapsed between the qualifying trigger and the act which caused death. The length of time between the qualifying trigger and the killing will be important, but unlike under the provocation defence it is not critical that the time gap is short.[61]

D's failure to testify to his loss of self-control is not necessarily fatal to his case. In their evaluation of the defence as a whole, the jury should be directed to consider the loss of control element before examining the qualifying triggers.[62] However, if D's evidence is that he acted out of fear and panic, that may be indicative that he acted out of self-defence, but not from a loss of control.[63]

The requirement that there must be a loss of control is not satisfied by evidence that D acted 'instinctively', for example where a boxer punches V who had taunted him.[64] In one

---

[56] The Court of Appeal observed in *McGrory* [2013] EWCA Crim 2336 that: 'It is not a requirement of the law that this legal concept be explained to the jury in any precise defined form of words . . .' At [30] per Maddison J. See now the *Crown Court Compendium* (2021) Ch 19, section 2.

[57] See Hansard, HL, 7 July 2009, col 572.

[58] This definition proposed in the 13th edn was approved in *Jewell* [2014] EWCA Crim 414. In *Gurpinar* [2015] EWCA Crim 178, this test was challenged by the prosecution but the Court of Appeal found it unnecessary to resolve the issue. See the discussion on the old law in R Holton and S Shute, 'Self-Control in the Modern Provocation Defence' (2007) 27 OJLS 49.

[59] At [60]. At [47]. See also *Goodwin* [2018] EWCA Crim 2287 where the judge inferred from the 18 stab wounds that there was a frenzied attack. In *Islam* [2019] EWCA Crim 2419, the Court of Appeal made clear that the statutory requirement for 'sufficient' evidence to be adduced does not import a requirement that there be evidence of a frenzied attack. *Dawson* [2021] EWCA Crim 40 makes clear that evidence of frenzy does not necessarily provide sufficient evidence of loss of control.

[60] See under s 3, *Gregson* [2006] EWCA Crim 3364 (epileptic and mentally abnormal).

[61] See Hansard, HC Public Bills Committee, 3 Mar 2009, col 434. It has been argued with reference to social psychology that the partial defence is a mischaracterization, and a misleading approach to the psychological processes operating in emotionally motivated killings. Suggestions for its replacement with a reason-based defence are made by: S Sorial, 'Anger, Provocation and Loss of Self-Control: What Does "Losing It" Really Mean?' (2019) 13 Cr L & P 247.

[62] This was the case under s 3: *Brown* [1972] 2 All ER 1328 at 1333.

[63] *Islam* [2019] EWCA Crim 2419, [29].

[64] *Serrano* [2006] EWCA Crim 3182 decided under s 3. See also *Martin* [2017] EWCA Crim 1359, in which Davis LJ stated that 'a panicky or scared response to aggressive conduct of another person is not of itself necessarily indicative of the existence of an issue of loss of control'.

tragic case[65] under the old law in which D yielded to the entreaties of his incurably ill and suffering wife to put an end to her life, it was held that D had not lost his self-control. Indeed, the evidence was that he was so in control as to stop immediately when he thought, wrongly, that she had changed her mind. The case highlights the arbitrariness of a defence partially absolving those who kill in a state of anger or outrage, but not those who exercise mercy.[66]

The fact that the defence is available when the loss of self-control is not a 'sudden' one represents a significant change from the position at common law and under the 1957 Act. Under the old law the requirement of a 'sudden and temporary loss' of control had the potential to operate in a discriminatory way. It rendered the defence too readily available to those who are quick to temper (more commonly men), and less accommodating of those who endure the provoking circumstances before responding with lethal force (often women who kill abusive partners).[67] The requirement was tempered by cases such as *Thornton*[68] and *Ahluwalia*[69] to bring within the partial defence persons whose reaction to circumstances was delayed rather than instantaneous.[70]

Practically speaking, it may be harder to establish whether there was a loss of control if there is no suddenness element to it.[71] In *Dawes*, Lord Judge CJ gave the following guidance.

Provided there was a **loss of control**, it **does not matter** whether the loss was **sudden or not**. A reaction to circumstances of extreme gravity may be delayed. Different individuals in different situations do not react identically, nor respond immediately. Thus, for the purposes of the new defence, the **loss of control may follow** from the cumulative impact of earlier events. For the purposes of this first ingredient, the response to what used to be described as 'cumulative provocation' requires consideration in the same way as it does in relation to cases in which the loss of control is said to have arisen suddenly. Given the changed description of this defence, perhaps 'cumulative impact' is the better phrase to describe this particular feature of the first requirement.

Simply because D's response to the events was delayed does not necessarily mean there was no loss of control, but it will remain difficult to ascertain whether D in fact reached the point at which he lost self-control.[72]

---

[65] *Cocker* [1989] Crim LR 740, discussed by PR Taylor, 'Provocation and Mercy Killing' [1991] Crim LR 111.

[66] The focus of the defence on the element of anger and spontaneous loss of control as an excusing feature is critically examined by J Horder, 'Reshaping the Subjective Element in the Provocation Defence' (2005) 25 OJLS 123 who considers a defence akin to what is now s 55 of the 2009 Act.

[67] For a broader-ranging critique of the s 3 defence for its 'gendered and heterosexualist' nature and of measuring the reasonableness of killing across cultures, see H Power, 'Provocation and Culture' [2006] Crim LR 871. Other defences are also difficult to apply to these circumstances. See J Loveless, 'Domestic Violence, Coercion and Duress' [2010] Crim LR 93.

[68] [1992] 1 All ER 306. For a further appeal, see [1996] 2 Cr App R 108.

[69] [1992] 4 All ER 889. On which see D Nicolson and R Sanghvi, 'Battered Women and Provocation: The Implications of *R v Ahluwalia*' [1993] Crim LR 728.

[70] The issue has generated immense literature, see generally K O'Donovan, 'Defences for Battered Women Who Kill?' (1991) 18 J Law & Soc 219; C Wells, 'Battered Women Syndrome and Defences to Homicide: Where Now' (1994) 14 LS 266; and n 13.

[71] The test at common law (*Duffy* [1949] 1 All ER 932) suggested that the longer the period to cool off and calm down, the more likely the killing is a revenge killing. But this assumption was not borne out by psychological/physiological evidence: see P Brett, 'The Physiology of Provocation' [1970] Crim LR 634. The requirement of suddenness was criticized for restricting the defence and excluding cases of outraged retaliation: Horder, *Excusing Crime*, 69–71 et seq.

[72] In numerous reported cases the trial judge found that there was no evidence of a loss of control. See eg *Charles* [2013] EWCA Crim 1205 in which the court observed that the fact that there might have been a trigger for violence does not lead to the inference of a loss of control. In this case the trial judge observed that the deliberate nature of V's injuries was evidence that whoever had inflicted them was very much in control. In *Dawes*, D's own evidence was that he had acted out of shock rather than anger. See also *Barnsdale-Quean* [2014] EWCA Crim 1418; *Jewell* [2014] EWCA Crim 414; *Gurpinar* [2015] EWCA Crim 178; *Goodwin* [2018] EWCA Crim 2287 (Court of Appeal disagreeing with judge's assessment that there was evidence of loss of control); *Dawson* [2021] EWCA Crim 40 on frenzy.

The 'loss of self-control' element in s 54 raises several further issues. First, the loss of control must, presumably, still be temporary otherwise it would be a case of insanity.[73] Secondly, once D has raised evidence of it, the burden is on the prosecution to prove to the criminal standard that D had not lost self-control. It is important to note that the judge has greater control of this LOSC defence: as has already been explained, the judge should not leave the defence to the jury unless there is sufficient evidence on which a jury, properly directed, could conclude that the defence might apply.[74] Thirdly, a further element (considered later) of the LOSC defence is that D must be judged on the basis that he possesses a 'normal degree of tolerance and self restraint' (s 54(1)(c)). It would therefore seem relevant, when considering whether at the moment that V was killed D had lost his self-control, for the jury to consider the period available to D to reflect and to cool off.[75] The cooling-off period was construed generously to D in a number of cases under the old law.[76]

By including a requirement that D lost control for the defence to apply, it has been argued that the government has rendered the LOSC defence incoherent.[77] The loss of control requirement was not part of the Law Commission's scheme for the proposed defence.[78] The government added it to meet concerns that there was a risk of the partial defence being used inappropriately, for example where D killed in cold blood, or the killing was gang-feud related, or the killing was a so-called 'honour' killing,[79] and 'where a defendant has killed while basically in full possession of his or her senses, even if he or she is frightened, other than in a situation which is complete self-defence'.[80] The Law Commission's model was based on the qualifying triggers of fear and a sense of 'justified anger'.[81] To retain these qualifying limbs but to add a loss of control element renders the scheme unnecessarily complex and lacking logic; a person who has lost control cannot easily be described as acting in a state of 'justified' anger.[82]

Critics have also questioned the retention of the loss of control element given the government's expressed intention to amend the law to rectify imbalances that exist in the treatment of men and women. The Law Commission recognized that women's typical reactions might make it harder for them to demonstrate a loss of self-control, and hence rejected that element in its final proposal. By retaining a requirement of loss of control, the government may have reduced the availability of the defence for abused women. It may be difficult to describe as a 'loss of control' circumstances where a person executes a plan to protect herself—as with abused women who kill their abusers while they sleep.[83]

---

[73] The 'temporary' nature of the loss of self-control seems irrelevant, provided only that it extended to the fatal act. D should not be deprived of a defence because he continued to be berserk for days thereafter—but sudden losses of self-control are, in practice, temporary.

[74] Section 54(6). This follows a recommendation of LC 304, para 5.11(5); and see paras 5.25–5.32.

[75] cf *Jewell* [2014] EWCA Crim 414 in which there was a 12-hour cooling-off period. The judge withdrew the defence from the jury on the basis that there was no evidence (looking not just at the delay) from which it could reasonably be concluded that the defence might apply.

[76] *Pearson* [1992] Crim LR 193; *Ibrams* (1981) 74 Cr App R 154; *Baillie* [1991] Crim LR 383. In *Mann* [2011] EWCA Crim 3292, *Baillie* was regarded as a case decided upon its own special facts.

[77] See Norrie, n 20, 322–5; S Edwards, 'Anger and Fear as Justifiable Preludes for the Loss of Self-Control' (2010) 74 J Crim L 223 discussing potential difficulties for abused spouses.

[78] The Law Commission recommended abolishing the positive requirement that D lost his self-control on the grounds that the requirement was unnecessary and undesirable and see LC 304, para 5.19.

[79] Ministry of Justice Consultation Paper 19/08, *Murder, Manslaughter and Infanticide: Proposals for Reform of the Law* (CP 19/08).

[80] ibid, para 36.   [81] What Norrie describes as 'imperfect justifications' [2009] Crim LR 278.

[82] See the powerful critique by Norrie, n 20, 312–14.

[83] cf B Mitchell, 'Loss of Self-Control under the Coroners and Justice Act 2009: Oh No!' in A Reed and M Bohlander (eds), *Loss of Control and Diminished Responsibility* (2011). Mitchell would prefer there to be some form of mental or emotional disturbance at the core of the defence. See B Mitchell, 'Years of Provocation, Followed by a Loss of Control' in L Zedner and JV Roberts (eds), *Principles and Values in Criminal Law and Criminal Justice* (2012).

13.1.2.6 Qualifying triggers: s 55

Under the old law, there was no restriction on the words or conduct that were capable of founding the provocation defence, provided D lost his self-control. The provocation could arise from perfectly legal acts by V or others. As an extreme example, in *Doughty*[84] provocation should have been left to the jury as a defence to murder where there was evidence that the persistent crying of D's two-week-old baby had caused D to lose his self-control and kill it.

The LOSC defence, with the qualifying triggers as drafted in s 55, is designed to be narrower.[85] This was emphasized in *Dawes*, in which Lord Judge CJ noted that 'the circumstances in which the qualifying triggers will arise are much more limited than the equivalent provisions in the former provocation defence. The result is that some of the more absurd trivia which nevertheless required the judge to leave the provocation defence to the jury will no longer fall within the ambit of the qualifying triggers defined in the LOSC defence.'[86] Now, only qualifying triggers which cause the loss of self-control will be recognized. Section 55 provides:

> (2) A loss of self-control had a qualifying trigger if subsection (3), (4) or (5) applies.
>
> (3) This subsection applies if D's loss of self-control was attributable to D's fear of serious violence from V against D or another identified person.
>
> (4) This subsection applies if D's loss of self-control was attributable to a thing or things done or said (or both) which—
>
>   (a) constituted circumstances of an extremely grave character, and
>
>   (b) caused D to have a justifiable sense of being seriously wronged.
>
> (5) This subsection applies if D's loss of self-control was attributable to a combination of the matters mentioned in subsections (3) and (4).

Three preliminary points in relation to the qualifying triggers may be noted.[87] First, the statute requires that the loss of self-control is 'attributable to' a qualifying trigger and this raises the question whether that term should be construed as requiring something less than a formal causal link. Despite the ambiguity of the word 'attributable', it is submitted that the courts ought to treat this as a requirement of causation. Secondly, the presence or otherwise of a qualifying trigger is not determined by D and any assertions he might make in evidence. The Court of Appeal has confirmed that the existence of a qualifying trigger requires an *objective* assessment by the judge at the end of the evidence[88] and, if the defence is left, by the jury considering their verdict.[89] Thirdly, what would otherwise be sufficient for a qualifying trigger is to be disregarded if D brought that state of affairs upon himself by,

---

[84] (1986) 83 Cr App R 319. See J Horder, 'The Problem of Provocative Children' [1987] Crim LR 655.

[85] For an analysis of whether they restrict the scope of the defence too much, see RD Taylor, 'The Model of Tolerance and Self-Restraint' in A Reed and M Bohlander (eds), *Loss of Control and Diminished Responsibility* (2011). It has been argued that LOSC is not as restrictive as has been suggested and that it may be possible for the mercy killer to plead the partial defence. See B Livings, 'A New Partial Defence for the Mercy Killer: Revisiting Loss of Control' [2014] NILQ 187; with respect this seems unlikely.

[86] *Dawes*, [60]. Cited subsequently in *Charles* [2013] EWCA Crim 1205 and *Martin* [2017] EWCA Crim 1359.

[87] In *Clinton*, Lord Judge CJ made the additional point that, 'There is no point in pretending that the practical application of this provision will not create considerable difficulties', at [11].

[88] cf the exchange between the court and counsel in *McDonald* [2016] EWCA Crim 1529.

[89] *Dawes*, [61]; *Gurpinar* [2015] EWCA Crim 178.

for example, looking for a fight by inciting something to be said or done (s 55(6)(a) or (b)), as the case may be. The restriction in s 55(6) is:

(a) D's fear of serious violence is to be disregarded to the extent that it was caused by a thing which D incited to be done or said for the purpose of providing an excuse to use violence;

(b) a sense of being seriously wronged by a thing done or said is not justifiable if D incited the thing to be done or said for the purpose of providing an excuse to use violence.

Despite some clarification in *Dawes*, the law is not as clear as it could be.[90] Under the old law, the jury were told to take into account everything both done and said according to the effect which, in their opinion, it would have on a reasonable person, even where that which was done and said was a predictable result of D's own conduct. That was the decision in *Johnson*[91] (not following *dicta* of the Privy Council in *Edwards v R*)[92] where the Court of Appeal rejected the submission 'that the mere fact that a defendant caused a reaction in others, which in turn led him to lose his self-control, should result in the issue of provocation being outside a jury's consideration'.[93]

Read literally, however, the availability of the LOSC defence is wider. LOSC would only be removed from the jury if D's *purpose* was subsequently to use violence. D will not be able to rely on LOSC where D *deliberately* induces a state of affairs that will generate a qualifying trigger—D taunts V whom he wants to kill, to do an act so that D may kill him and rely on the defence and be convicted of manslaughter only. Such a situation may seem far-fetched.[94]

In *Dawes*, Lord Judge CJ held that the impact of *Johnson* has been diminished, but not wholly extinguished by the 2009 Act.[95] His lordship stated that 'the mere fact that in some general way the defendant was behaving badly and looking for and provoking trouble does not of itself lead to the disapplication of the qualifying triggers based on section 55(3)(4) and (5) unless his actions were *intended* to provide him with the excuse or opportunity to use violence.'[96] The focus of the inquiry under s 55(6)(a) and (b), it is submitted, should be narrow; namely whether D's *purpose* was to provide an excuse to use violence, not whether a violent reaction was the foreseeable consequence of what D was doing. As Lord Judge pointed out, consideration must also be given to whether D did in fact 'fear' serious violence if he was out to incite it and also whether he truly had a justified sense of being seriously wronged.

Fear of serious violence: s 55(3)

Section 55(3) provides:

This subsection applies if D's loss of self-control was attributable to D's fear of serious violence[97] from V against D or another identified person.

---

90 See *Dawes* [2013] EWCA Crim 322.

91 [1980] 1 WLR 740; was preferred to the *dicta* of the Privy Council in *Edwards* [1973] AC 648.

92 [1973] AC 648.   93 *Johnson*, 744.

94 Analogy should be drawn with the law on self-defence where D is the initial aggressor, see *Harvey* [2009] EWCA Crim 469; *Keane* [2010] EWCA Crim 2514, on which see Ch 10.

95 See commentary by Ashworth [2013] Crim LR 770.   96 *Dawes*, [58].

97 It has been argued that despite Lord Judge CJ stating in *Dawes* that each element of the qualifying triggers requires objective evaluation, whether D feared serious violence ought to be a subjective question, ie did D himself regard this violence as 'serious'. See T Storey, 'Loss of Control: The Qualifying Triggers, Self-Induced Loss of Control and "Cumulative Impact"' (2013) 77 J Crim L 189. Such an approach has the potential to render the partial defence extremely wide.

And by s 55(6):

In determining whether a loss of self-control had a qualifying trigger—

    (a) D's fear of serious violence is to be disregarded to the extent that it was caused by a thing which D incited to be done or said for the purpose of providing an excuse to use violence;

This qualifying trigger is the one which renders the LOSC defence quite distinct from the defence of provocation. It flows from a Law Commission recommendation.[98] It is designed primarily to accommodate within the partial defence regime those women who kill their violent and abusive partners.[99] The sudden and temporary requirement of the common law of provocation frequently proved a stumbling block for such women. The absence of a requirement of a 'sudden' loss of control and the breadth of this qualifying trigger will render the defence more widely available.[100] It clearly encompasses two quite distinct sets of circumstances: (a) where D kills in order to thwart an anticipated (albeit not imminent) attack; and (b) where D overreacts to what he perceived to be an imminent threat.[101] In the first category, the defence will be particularly useful for abused partners who kill. In that regard the reform is welcome. However, in relation to the second category, there is scope for the defence to be used in a very broad range of killings that were previously classed as murder and which attracted no defence. For example, D who stabs V in a fight in a pub might claim that he stabbed V having feared that V was going to stab him first. Even if D has used excessive force given the threat he thought he faced, and even if D has made an unreasonable mistake about the need for any force at all (so no self-defence plea is available), he will, if the jury believe his story may be true, be convicted of manslaughter. This is a significant change in the law.

    The defence is limited under this qualifying trigger to cases where D fears violence from V to himself or an identified other. That acts as a restriction, but it is unclear how narrowly it will be interpreted. What if D, who is in V's presence, hears V ordering X to commit an act of violence on D's fellow gang member who is miles away? D loses his self-control and kills V. Is this sufficient?

    The relationship between the LOSC defence and self-defence or defence of others under s 76 of the Criminal Justice and Immigration Act 2008 needs to be approached with care.[102] In *Martin*,[103] the Court of Appeal emphatically rejected the suggestion that where self-defence is raised in a murder case, then that will of itself also give rise to a potential defence of loss of control. It was held that not only was such a suggestion not the law but

---

[98] LC 304, para 5.55. Historically the common law defence of provocation *did* encompass reactions prompted by fear: LC 304, para 5.49.

[99] It has been argued that domestic violence is such a serious wrong that it would be relatively easy for women who lose control and kill their abusers to rely on the other qualifying trigger. See J Herring, 'The Serious Wrong of Domestic Abuse and the Loss of Control Defence' in A Reed and M Bohlander (eds), *Loss of Control and Diminished Responsibility* (2011).

[100] For an analysis of whether the provision will achieve this goal, see S Edwards, 'Loss of Self-Control: When His Anger is Worth More Than Her Fear' in A Reed and M Bohlander (eds), *Loss of Control and Diminished Responsibility* (2011).

[101] See MOJ CP 19/08, para 28.

[102] Lord Judge CJ cited this paragraph from the 13th edn with approval in *Dawes*, [59]. In *Skilton* [2014] EWCA Crim 154, Jackson LJ observed: 'There must be a clear distinction between the defence of self-defence, on the one hand, and the partial defence of loss of control on the other hand.' At [24]. The Court of Appeal held that the trial judge was correct not to leave loss of control to the jury, as D admitted in cross-examination that he was acting out of fear and was not out of control.

[103] [2017] EWCA Crim 1359. See also *Goodwin* [2018] EWCA Crim 2287 at [36] per Davis LJ: 'it is most emphatically by no means the case that a defence of self-defence in a homicide case necessarily of itself will carry with it a sufficient evidential basis in the alternative for a defence of loss of control. That most certainly is not the law.'

it was wholly contrary to the designedly limited nature of the defence as confirmed by the 2009 Act. It is important to note that the defences have the following distinguishing features.

Self-defence is available on any charge; LOSC is available only on a charge of murder.[104] Self-defence results in an acquittal; LOSC in a verdict of manslaughter. With LOSC, D can rely on fear of future non-imminent attack; with self-defence he can only rely on a threat (or believed threat) of imminent attack.[105] The defence of self-defence is available if D uses force in response to a perceived threat of *any* violence (including sexual violence[106]). The LOSC defence is available if D responds to a threat of *serious* violence.[107] Violence is undefined.[108] If the degree of force used by D in killing V is, viewed objectively, excessive,[109] that will deprive D of the defence of self-defence,[110] but will not automatically deprive D of the LOSC defence. Section 54(1)(c) (see later) requires a comparison of D's behaviour with that of a person of normal self-restraint. It has therefore been argued that if D uses excessive force in self-defence and kills, since a person of normal tolerance and self-restraint would, by defini-tion, not use excessive force, the defence ought not to be available. This view appears to be too strict. The requirement in s 54(1)(c) is to consider whether the person of normal self-restraint '*might* have reacted' as D did. Even people of normal self-restraint sometimes use excessive force and kill. It is submitted that it is not appropriate to read the LOSC defence as restricted in such a way.[111]

Particular problems may arise where on the facts there is evidence that might support self-defence or LOSC. If D has used excessive force, the complete defence of self-defence will fail, but D may still be able to rely on LOSC; the excessive amount of force being explicable by reference to the 'loss of self-control'. Directions to the jury will need to be approached with great care. A further problem is posed by s 54(5):

On a charge of murder, if sufficient evidence is adduced to raise an issue with respect to the defence under subsection (1), the jury must assume that the defence is satisfied unless the prosecution proves beyond reasonable doubt that it is not.

At first sight this seems to suggest that in a case where D pleads self-defence, the Crown will automatically be entitled to a manslaughter conviction in any case where D lost his self-control. However, when applied properly, this provision does not create the conflict it appears to. Section 54(5) requires only that sufficient evidence is adduced to raise an issue under s 54(1). Thereafter, the prosecution shoulders the legal burden of proving, to the crim-inal standard of proof, that the defence is not satisfied. Unless the prosecution discharges that burden, s 54(5) requires the jury to assume that the defence is satisfied.

(6) For the purposes of subsection (5), sufficient evidence is adduced to raise an issue with respect to the defence if evidence is adduced on which, in the opinion of the trial judge, a jury, prop-erly directed, could reasonably conclude that the defence might apply.

---

[104] If there are multiple counts relating to different victims, care will be needed in directing the jury.

[105] For discussion of how the two interact in the context of abused women, see N Wake, 'Battered Women, Startled Householders and Psychological Self-Defence: Anglo-Australian Perspectives' (2013) 77 J Crim L 433.

[106] MOJ CP 19/08, para 44.

[107] See MOJ Circular 2010/13, para 25. Cf L Leigh, 'Two New Partial Defences to Murder' (2010) 53 Crim L & Justice Weekly 53, who states that the test is objective.

[108] Fortson, n 20, argues that it includes psychological harm. It includes sexual harm: MOJ CP 19/08, para 27.

[109] By virtue of s 43 of the Crime and Courts Act 2013, if the case is a 'householder case' then if the degree of force was grossly disproportionate or unreasonable D will be denied the defence.

[110] And therefore of a complete acquittal. See *Clegg* [1995] and Ch 10. See also Leverick, *Self Defence* (2007) Ch 6.

[111] cf the suggestion by J Miles, 'The Coroners and Justice Act: Making a "Dog's Breakfast" of Homicide Reform' [2009] 6 Arch News 8. See on this Fortson, n 20.

It is essential in cases where D pleads self-defence and LOSC that the jury deal with self-defence before LOSC. If jurors address these matters in the wrong order, a manslaughter conviction becomes compulsory. This seems to be a case in which written directions instructing jurors of the steps to verdict would be valuable.[112] Lord Judge CJ in *Dawes* confirmed this view; the appropriate approach is to leave loss of control for the jury's consideration after it has rejected self-defence.[113]

Further problems may arise if D's fear of serious violence was based on an entirely mistaken interpretation of the facts by D.[114] Under the old law the authorities suggested that where D was provoked partly as the result of a mistake of fact, he was entitled to be treated as if the facts were as he mistakenly supposed them to be. This line of reasoning accords with the approach to other defences.[115] Given that the LOSC defence based on this first qualifying trigger is similar in many respects to self-defence, and a mistaken belief in the need for self-defence will not deprive a defendant of that defence, it is submitted that the defence should be available if D has a genuine mistaken belief in facts that would amount to a qualifying trigger of a fear of serious violence.

It is unclear whether a mistake induced by voluntary intoxication precludes reliance on the defence.[116] In self-defence, on policy grounds, mistakes due to intoxication are irrelevant, notwithstanding that murder is a crime of specific intent.[117] That would suggest that the defence of LOSC was not available. However, there are several arguments that could be marshalled in favour of adopting a more generous approach in LOSC. First, the policy-driven approach in relation to self-defence and intoxicated mistakes has been heavily and cogently criticized.[118] Secondly, this is a partial defence which leads to a manslaughter conviction—it is not the case that D will leave court with a complete acquittal if he is permitted to found his plea on an intoxicated mistaken view of the facts.[119] It is established that a drunken mistake may negative the mens rea of murder[120] and it is therefore consistent that such a mistake should be relevant in determining whether the killing should be reduced to manslaughter on the ground of LOSC. Thirdly, under the provocation defence an intoxicated mistake as to the facts did not preclude reliance on the defence. In *Brown*,[121] D, a soldier, wrongly, but apparently reasonably, supposed that V was a member of a gang who were attacking him and his comrade. He struck V with a sword and killed him. The judges were clearly of the opinion that this was only manslaughter. In the other cases the mistake arose from drunkenness. In *Letenock*,[122] the Court of Criminal Appeal substituted

---

[112] See generally the *Crown Court Compendium* (2021). [113] *Dawes*, [59].

[114] Edwards makes the important point that habituated gender thinking might impress upon what is considered sufficient to constitute both fear and serious violence. She states that women who are the victims of domestic violence can have a heightened awareness of their physical security. In cases in which D has killed in fear of an anticipated attack by V, if this is not made clear to juries then they might be inclined to think that D simply overreacted. See S Edwards, 'Loss of Self-Control: When His Anger is Worth More Than Her Fear' in A Reed and M Bohlander (eds), *Loss of Control and Diminished Responsibility* (2011).

[115] cf *Oye* [2013] EWCA Crim 1725 in which the Court of Appeal stated that it was best not to draw comparisons between loss of control and self-defence in relation to mistaken beliefs. With reference to the relationship between them, the Court of Appeal observed, *obiter*, that 'the highly complex provisions of ss 54–6 of the Coroners and Justice Act 2009 would seem to indicate no particular parliamentary intention that a corresponding approach is designed to be adopted'. At [43] per Davis LJ.

[116] See also the discussion of *Asmelash*, p 566 suggesting the Court of Appeal's reluctance to allow intoxication to be considered.

[117] *Hatton* [2006] 1 Cr App R 247. [118] See Ch 9, p 344.

[119] Although that is also true in relation to self-defence in murder because an unreasonable intoxicated mistake will lead to a conviction for manslaughter despite the courts' gloss on this in *O'Grady*. See p 344.

[120] See p 329. [121] (1776) 1 Leach 148. [122] (1917) 12 Cr App R 221.

a verdict of manslaughter in the case of a soldier who had stabbed another, where the 'only element of doubt in the case is whether or not there was anything which might have caused the applicant, *in his drunken condition*, to believe that he was going to be struck'.[123] Against this is, of course, the requirement that D has by definition lost his self-control.[124]

Things said or done; circumstances of an extremely grave character, etc: s 55(4)

This form of the defence bears greatest similarity to the old law of provocation. This version of the LOSC defence is available in s 55(4) if D's loss of self-control was:

attributable to a thing or things done or said (or both) which—

    (a) constituted circumstances of an extremely grave character, and

    (b) caused D to have a justifiable sense of being seriously wronged.

Section 55(6) further provides that:

In determining whether a loss of self-control had a qualifying trigger—

    (b) a sense of being seriously wronged by a thing done or said is not justifiable if D incited the thing to be done or said for the purpose of providing an excuse to use violence.

Under the provocation defence there was no requirement that the provoking acts or words were performed consciously, let alone with the deliberate intention to provoke.[125] The test under the LOSC defence is much stricter[126] although the statutory language is disappointingly vague. Even if a person with a normal degree of tolerance and self-restraint might have reacted in the circumstances as D did (see s 54(1)(c) and s 54(3)), this will not be enough unless those circumstances meet the thresholds as specified in s 55(4) of the 2009 Act. The Court of Appeal has confirmed that all the elements of s 55(4) require objective evaluation.[127]

Things done or said

As under the provocation defence, naturally occurring events (rather than something said or done) no matter how provocative, cannot be a sufficient basis for this qualifying trigger.[128] Loss of control by a farmer on his crops being destroyed by a flood, or his flocks by foot-and-mouth, or an author on his manuscript being destroyed by lightning, cannot constitute a qualifying trigger. An 'act of God' could hardly be regarded as 'something done' within s 55(4). There is no requirement that the things said or done be said or done by the victim (subject to the other elements of the defence). This follows the old law. For example,

---

   123 ibid, 224.

   124 This is one example of how the insertion of the loss of control element to the Law Commission's original proposal creates difficulties and illogicalities.

   125 This dilution of the concept of 'provocation' to mean merely words or conduct that *cause* the loss of control in the defendant has been heavily criticized by academics. See, in particular, T Macklem and J Gardner, 'Provocation and Pluralism' (2001) 64 MLR 815, and Tadros, *Criminal Responsibility*, 355–68. See LCCP 173, paras 4.8–4.11.

   126 The facts of *Zebedee* [2012] EWCA Crim 1428 illuminate how strict the qualifying triggers now are: D was convicted of the murder of his father. V was aged 94, suffered from senile dementia and was doubly incontinent. D claimed that he had lost his self-control after V soiled himself during the night, after which D cleaned him up, only for V to soil himself again 20 minutes later. The jury rejected his plea of loss of control. In the Court of Appeal, Spencer J observed that the jury must have concluded that whatever had triggered D's violence did not constitute circumstances of an extremely grave nature. A further example is *Dawson* [2021] EWCA Crim 40— no qualifying trigger where V had subjected D to years of harassment and been subjected to a restraining order. For an analysis of some of the cases that were successful under the old law, but which would now probably fail, see T Storey, 'Raising the Bar: Loss of Control and the Qualifying Triggers' (2013) 77 J Crim L 17.

   127 See *Clinton*, [12] and *Dawes*, [61].   128 *Acott* [1997] 2 Cr App R 94.

in *Davies*, D killed his wife, V having been provoked by X, her lover.[129] Bearing in mind that there is no restriction on the source of the words or conduct which cause D to lose control, it seems odd to distinguish cases where the trigger is words by a third party (defence available) and naturally occurring events (defence unavailable). If D may rely on the defence where the crops or the manuscript were destroyed by an unknown arsonist, why should it be different where no human agency was involved?

There must, as with the provocation defence, be some evidence of the qualifying trigger. In *Acott*,[130] the House of Lords held that for the defence of provocation it was not enough that D's loss of control may possibly have been the result of some unidentified words or actions by another. There must be 'some evidence of *what* was done or *what* was said to provoke the homicidal reaction'.[131] The trial judge is best placed to make this assessment.

There is no express provision in the 2009 Act to deal with the situation where D mistakenly believes that things were done or said. Several different situations may need to be distinguished. First, there is the position where D mistakenly believes that things were said or done when nothing was in fact said or done at all. In that case, it would be hard to see how the qualifying trigger is satisfied on a literal interpretation of the section. Secondly, there is the case in which words or acts occur, but D mistakes what was said or done. What of D who mishears V and thinks that V has issued a racist taunt when in fact V's words were completely innocuous? In that case, it could be argued that the defence ought to be available (subject to the other elements), even if D's mistake is an unreasonable one.[132] That raises the question of whether D can rely on this trigger for the LOSC defence if D acts on a mistaken belief induced by voluntary intoxication. Arguably, since the 'things done or said' must lead to a 'justifiable' sense of being seriously wronged, it will be appropriate to ignore intoxicated mistakes unless the mistake was one which D would have made had he been sober.

It is submitted that the defence will be available, as provocation was, if D sought to kill the person responsible for the acts or words but, by accident, missed him and killed an innocent person. The doctrine of transferred malice[133] should operate and D would be guilty of only manslaughter, as was held for provocation in *Gross*[134] where D, provoked by blows from her husband, shot at him, intending to kill him but missed and killed V.[135] If D knew it was virtually certain that she would hit V, she would have an independent mens rea with respect to V, probably sufficient to fix her with liability for murder[136] at common law; but now the acts or words of the third party would be a partial defence even for D's acts towards V.

---

[129] [1975] QB 691. Cf to the same effect by Lawton J in *Twine* [1967] Crim LR 710, where D's girlfriend's conduct caused D to lose his self-control and strike and kill the man she was with.

[130] [1997] 1 All ER 706. See also *Bharj* [2005] EWCA Crim 499 emphasizing that the jury would be looking at *all* the evidence.

[131] Emphasis in the original.

[132] Elvin questions whether an unreasonable belief could ever lead to a justifiable sense of being seriously wronged. See J Elvin, 'Killing in Response to "Circumstances of an Extremely Grave Character": Improving the Law on Homicide' in A Reed and M Bohlander (eds), *Loss of Control and Diminished Responsibility* (2011). Whether the two are in fact mutually exclusive is questionable.

[133] See p 125. For discussion, see M Bohlander, 'Transferred Malice and Transferred Defences' (2010) 13 New Crim LR 555.

[134] (1913) 23 Cox CC 455 (Darling J); and see *Porritt* [1961] 1 WLR 1372. Bohlander, n 133, doubts whether this case is one concerning the transfer of defences at all. Bohlander argues that in the same way that a temporary mental disease may exempt any and all actions D committed in that state from liability, so a temporary loss of control exempts any and all actions committed under its influence. We disagree. Given that the statute mandates that the defence is only available on a charge of murder, it is difficult to see how it exempts D from all liability. If D loses his self-control and causes criminal damage to his rival's car, he cannot plead loss of control.

[135] 23 Cox CC at 456.   [136] See p 93.

Historically, it used to be said that there was ~~no defence if acts or words were not done to the defendant;~~[137] but the 2009 Act as with the 1957 Act has ~~no~~ such ~~explicit requirement,~~[138] D can rely on the defence if V does acts to P that might cause D to lose his self-control and, in circumstances of extreme gravity, to kill V with intent and with a justifiable sense of being seriously wronged. For example, D might find V raping his child P.[139]

There is no statutory limitation to prevent a third party description or report being sufficient to satisfy the trigger, as where D loses his temper following X's report of V's admission that V had attacked D's child. That is, of course, subject to the other elements of the defence, and in particular it must be noted that the less plausible the account relayed to D, the less likely it will cause a loss of self-control and the less likely it will give rise to a justifiable sense of being seriously wronged.

There is nothing to prevent a lawful act by V being sufficient to constitute the trigger, although the fact that the acts or words were lawful will cast doubt on whether D had a justifiable sense of being seriously wronged (see later).[140] In particular, where the act is one which is not merely permitted, but which is positively praiseworthy, it is doubtful that a jury would find that it would cause D to lose his temper and to have a justifiable sense of being seriously wronged and that such action might have been performed by a person of normal tolerance and self-restraint in D's position.

Must constitute circumstances of an 'extremely grave character'

For the purposes of this second 'qualifying trigger' (s 55(4)), the threshold is that things said and done must constitute circumstances of an 'extremely grave character'. Presumably, grave means in all the circumstances. The intention is to restrict the scope of the defence from what was the position under the defence of provocation. The Law Commission offered the following guidance:

> The jury should be trusted to evaluate the relative grossness of provocation, in whatever form it comes, according to their own sense of justice in an individual case.[141]

It is disappointing that such a key term of the defence is left undefined. In *Hatter* (one of the cases conjoined with *Dawes*), it was observed that the **break-up** of a relationship, of itself, will **not normally constitute circumstances of an extremely grave nature** entitling the aggrieved party to feel a justifiable sense of being seriously wronged. Lord Judge CJ did state, however, that just as issues relating to sexual infidelity have to be examined in their overall circumstances, so the events surrounding the circumstances in the breakdown of a relationship will often but not always fall to be disqualified by s 55(6).[142]

'justifiable sense of being seriously wronged'

The defendant must have been caused by the things done or said to have a 'justifiable sense of being seriously wronged' (s 55(4)). This is much narrower than for provocation. It is intended to be an objective test.[143] It is, again, disappointing that the Act provides no further guidance on how the jury will approach this question. It was intended that it would

---

[137] But see *Fisher* (1837) 8 C & P 182 (Park J, *obiter*) (D discovering V raping D's son) and *Harrington* (1866) 10 Cox CC 370 (Cockburn CJ contemplating the possibility of a defence where D found his daughter being violently assaulted by her husband).

[138] cf J Elvin, 'Killing in Response to "Circumstances of an Extremely Grave Character": Improving the Law on Homicide' in A Reed and M Bohlander (eds), *Loss of Control and Diminished Responsibility* (2011).

[139] Examples under the 1957 Act included *Pearson* [1992] Crim LR 193.

[140] *Doughty* (1986) 83 Cr App R 319.   [141] LC 304, p 85 fn 31.

[142] *Dawes*, [65].

[143] Some commentators (eg Liberty) suggested that the provision was insufficiently clear and that it might be construed subjectively.

provide an opportunity to take into consideration cumulative abuse, which will be particularly important in domestic killings by abused women. At the same time, it was intended to exclude from the scope of the defence the cases of racist or 'honour' killings. For example, it is difficult to see how the defence could be left to the jury if D, a white supremacist, killed V, a black man, because V refused to give way to D on the staircase. No reasonable jury properly directed could conclude that D had a *justifiable* sense of being seriously wronged. The defence should be withdrawn from the jury. Similarly where D, a devout Muslim, kills his daughter because she has a sexual relationship before marriage, he cannot be said to have a justifiable sense of being seriously wronged.[144]

In many cases, of course, the judge will be obliged to leave the defence to the jury for their good sense. Note that the question for them is not whether D's act in *killing* was justifiable, but whether D had a justifiable sense of being seriously wronged. Again, it is presumably a question of whether the sense of serious wrong would be felt by someone in D's circumstances. In *Bowyer*, the other conjoined appeal in *Dawes*, D was a burglar who killed the householder from whose home he was intending to steal. Given the circumstances, the Court of Appeal held that it could hardly be said that V had given D any cause to feel justifiably wronged.[145] The same was true in *Meanza*.[146] In that case D's evidence was that he felt aggrieved at being asked to turn down the television in the secure unit in which he was being detained. He also felt aggrieved by the fact his meetings and encounters with his girlfriend had to take place on a supervised basis. The Court of Appeal held, rightly it is submitted, that D could have no justifiable grievance in relation to hospital and restriction orders that were lawfully imposed, nor in relation to the restrictions imposed upon his relationship with his girlfriend.

Sexual infidelity

Historically, one of the classic examples of extreme provocation recognized by the courts for centuries was where D killed having found his spouse in the act of adultery.[147] The government's intention was to prevent the LOSC defence from being run in such a case and to prevent obsessively jealous men using suspected infidelity on the part of the spouse or partner as a defence for killing.[148]

Under the LOSC defence, D's loss of control that is attributed to anything said or done which constitutes sexual infidelity is to be disregarded (s 55(6)(c)). This limitation did not form part of the Law Commission's original proposals and was introduced amid much controversy in Parliament. The restriction was met with anxiety by Lord Phillips, the former President of the Supreme Court, who admitted he was 'uneasy about a law which so

---

[144] cf *Mohammed* [2005] EWCA Crim 1880 where in cross-examination D claimed that 'it is part of our religion' to do as he did in killing his sexually active unmarried daughter. D's perception cannot be determinative of what is justifiable.

[145] *Dawes*, [66].   [146] [2017] EWCA Crim 445.

[147] Killing, in such a case, was 'of the lowest degree of [manslaughter]; and therefore . . . the court directed the burning in the hand to be gently inflicted, because there could not be a greater provocation': Blackstone, *Commentaries*, iv, 192. See also the case of *Manning* (1671) T Raym 212. For a contemporary case with exactly these facts, see *Christie* [2004] EWCA Crim 1338, D was convicted of murder. As an example of how significant this factor was, see *Evans* [2009] EWCA Crim 2243 where the Court of Appeal accepted that had E been aware of the infidelity of his wife he might have been able to plead provocation. For an analysis of the way sexual infidelity-related evidence has influenced perceptions of a homicide defendant's culpability, see J Horder and K Fitz-Gibbon, 'When Sexual Infidelity Triggers Murder: Examining the Impact of Homicide Law Reform on Judicial Attitudes in Sentencing' (2015) 74 CLJ 307.

[148] See Hansard, HC Public Bills Committee, 3 Mar 2009, col 439. For consideration of the more conceptual issues, see A Reed and N Wake, 'Sexual Infidelity Killings: Contemporary Standardisations and Comparative Stereotypes' in A Reed and M Bohlander (eds), *Loss of Control and Diminished Responsibility* (2011).

diminishes the significance of sexual infidelity as expressly to exclude it from even the possibility of amounting to provocation'.[149]

It is important to be clear about what s 55(6) forbids:

In determining whether a loss of self-control had a qualifying trigger . . .

(b) the fact that a thing done or said constituted sexual infidelity is to be disregarded.

The restriction on the defence presents difficulties of interpretation and application, and yet may well fail to defeat the intended mischief. The concern is that men are able to rely on loss of self-control defences when their anger and loss of control results from sexual jealousy. As Lord Judge CJ emphasized in *Clinton*, however, D remains at liberty to tell the jury the whole story about the relevant events, including the fact and impact of sexual infidelity.[150] The jury must still consider and ultimately evaluate this evidence.

Numerous problems of interpretation arise as recognized by the Court of Appeal in *Clinton*.[151] First, there is no definition of what 'sexual infidelity' means. Clearly, there can be infidelity outside marriage, but how 'solid' a relationship must there be before sexual acts with others outside that relationship constitute infidelity?[152] Lord Judge in *Clinton* accepted that 'infidelity' connotes a continuing relationship. His lordship accepted that the consequence of this is that a killing by a spouse or partner might fall outside the defence, but a killing by a jealous stalker would not.[153]

Secondly, the term 'sexual' infidelity can be read narrowly, so as to comprise only those incidents of, and conduct directly related to, sexual activity. Lord Judge accepted that a betrayal by one partner that involved telling the other about an illicit relationship was capable of falling within the prohibition.[154]

Thirdly, it seems that words might constitute sexual infidelity where, for example, D overhears his wife V saying 'I love you' to her lover, X.[155] But what of words spoken by V telling D that she loves X? Do her words 'I love someone else' constitute infidelity or are they a report of her infidelity? On a narrow view of the section, it can be argued that the words do not constitute sexual infidelity and they are not to be disregarded under s 55(6)(c).[156] In the debates in Parliament, in response to a question whether V bragging to D that he had been having an affair with D's wife would be sexual infidelity, the government spokesman said that the defence would turn on the facts, but that:

sexual infidelity in itself cannot and should not be an acceptable reason for a defence for murder.[157]

---

[149] The Times, 7 Nov 2008.   [150] At [28].

[151] Apart from the specific problems that arise from the drafting of this provision, it has been argued that exclusionary clauses in general give rise to difficulties when invoked in this context. See N Wake, 'Political Rhetoric or Principled Reform of Loss of Control? Anglo-Australian Perspectives on the Exclusionary Conduct Model' (2013) 77 J Crim L 512.

[152] The debates in Parliament do not reveal what types of relationship will qualify, but the references are usually to spouses, civil partners and in some instances to 'partners'.

[153] At [18].   [154] ibid.

[155] In *Clinton*, Lord Judge CJ stated that this may, or may not, provide evidence of *sexual* infidelity. In addition, his lordship observed that it may not *constitute* sexual infidelity. Whether it does so will depend upon the relationship between the parties, the person by whom and to whom it is spoken and the circumstances. His lordship stated that situations seemingly as simple as this one 'will give rise to manifold difficulties in the context of the prohibition on sexual infidelity as a qualifying trigger'. At [25]–[27].

[156] It was confirmed in *Clinton* that 'things said' includes admissions of sexual infidelity (even if untrue) as well as reports by others. Therefore it seems to be the case that if D is told by C that his wife, V, is having an affair, then that will be a 'thing said' for the purposes of the section.

[157] Hansard, HC, 9 Nov 2009, col 82 (Claire Ward) (emphasis added).

Fourthly, read literally s 55(6)(c) only forbids regard being had to the *fact* that the thing said or done constituted sexual infidelity when determining if there is a qualifying trigger sufficient for the defence to be left to the jury. The *effect on D* of the sexual infidelity is not to be disregarded, merely the words or acts that constituted it. This is disappointing legislative drafting.

Fifthly, provided there is some other thing besides the fact of sexual infidelity said or done which amounts to extreme circumstances which D claims caused him to lose his self-control and to have a justifiable sense of being seriously wronged, the trigger will be satisfied. It may be difficult to discern whether D's loss of self-control is attributable to things done or said by his sexual partner *other than* her act of infidelity. What related aspects can be taken into account in determining if the trigger is present? The MOJ[158] makes clear that:

it is only the fact of sexual infidelity that must be disregarded. The thing said or done can still potentially amount to a 'qualifying trigger' if (ignoring the sexual infidelity) it amounts to circumstances of an extremely grave character which caused the defendant to have a justifiable sense of being seriously wronged.[159]

Examples of the sorts of activity that might trigger the defence and would not be excluded by s 55(6)(c) include D who has found his wife in bed with her lover and killed the lover, saying in defence of the killing that it was not the act of sex that triggered the loss of self-control but the fact that the lover was D's best friend. Some such claims will be plausible. D will claim the thing that caused him to lose self-control in extremely grave circumstances having a justifiable sense of being seriously wronged was not the sex but, for example, 'the fact that V threatened to take the kids', or 'the fact that she taunted me about my erectile dysfunction' or 'the fact that she smashed up my prized possession as she was leaving', etc. In debates, the government spokesperson stated:

it is important to set out the position precisely and uncompromisingly—namely that sexual infidelity is not the kind of thing done that is ever *sufficient on its own* to found a successful plea of loss of control so as to reduce the verdict from murder to manslaughter.[160]

More extreme examples are easier to classify and were recognized in the debates: for example, where D comes home to find her husband, V, having sex with his young stepdaughter. In such a case, if D killed V, it would be open to D to argue that it was the fact of sexual abuse and not the sexual infidelity per se that formed the qualifying trigger. As has also been pointed out by others,[161] the combined impact of the statutory drafting and the judgment in *Clinton* is to undermine the practical impact of s 55(6)(c), given that it will be a rare case where sexual infidelity stands alone as a potential qualifying trigger.[162]

Finally, what is perhaps most surprising is that the drafting means that s 55(6)(c) only forbids regard to the sexual infidelity when considering whether there is a trigger, but not for the defence as a whole. As Lord Judge recognized in *Clinton*, sexual infidelity may be relevant to the third component of the defence: s 54(3) expressly excludes some of the

---

[158] MOJ Circular 2010/13.

[159] Para 30. This echoes statements in Parliament where the spokeswoman stated: 'If other factors come into play, the court will of course have an opportunity to consider them, but it will not be able to make the decision exclusively on the ground of sexual infidelity.' Hansard, HC, 9 Nov 2009, col 80 (Claire Ward).

[160] Hansard, HC, 9 Nov 2009, col 83 (Claire Ward) (emphasis added).

[161] N Wake, 'Loss of Control Beyond Sexual Infidelity' (2012) 76 J Crim L 193; A Clough, 'Sexual Infidelity: The Exclusion That Never Was?' (2012) 76 J Crim L 382; F Stark, 'Killing the Unfaithful' (2012) 71 CLJ 260.

[162] A point echoed by Norrie, n 20, 316.

defendant's circumstances from being considered and the fact that he has been 'sexually betrayed' is not one of them. Therefore:

sexual infidelity is not subject to a blanket exclusion when the loss of control defence is under consideration. Evidence of these matters may be deployed by the defendant and therefore the legislation proceeds on the basis that sexual infidelity is a permissible feature of the loss of control defence.[163]

Provided there is some other thing said or done which amounts to extreme circumstances which could have caused D to lose his self-control and to have a justifiable sense of being seriously wronged, the trigger will be satisfied. If the trigger is satisfied, s 54(1)(c) then requires the jury to consider whether:

> (c) a person of D's sex and age, with a normal degree of tolerance and self restraint and in the circumstances of D, might have reacted in the same or in a similar way to D.

And by s 54(3):

> (3) In subsection (1)(c) the reference to 'the circumstances of D' is a reference to all of D's circumstances other than those whose only relevance to D's conduct is that they bear on D's general capacity for tolerance or self-restraint.

The statute does not *at this final stage of the defence* preclude consideration of the fact of sexual infidelity. There are really two arguments to explain this apparent illogicality. First, it can be said that what is being considered in s 54(1)(c) is not the sexual infidelity but the effects of the sexual infidelity on D. A defendant in such cases might be exceptionally vulnerable in the sense of being more easily 'wounded' by such actions.[164] In psychiatric or psychological terms, the act causing the loss of control would be the *effects* of the unfaithfulness and the betrayal rather than the 'things said or done' which constitute sexual infidelity.[165] Section 54(1)(c) does not preclude reliance on such factors provided they are 'circumstances' and that they are relevant. They clearly are, and do not solely bear only on D's general capacity for tolerance and self-restraint. Secondly, it can be argued that the terms of s 54(1)(c) do not preclude reliance on the 'circumstance' of D discovering the sexual infidelity itself. This would allow the jury to have regard to the act/words in determining whether a person of D's age and sex, etc in his 'circumstances' (ie just discovering sexual infidelity) might have reacted as he did.[166]

On one view, these interpretations of s 54(1)(c) would seem to undermine the purpose of the provision in s 55. On another view, there is no conflict because there must be some trigger other than the mere fact of sexual infidelity for the defence to get to the jury, and what the government was seeking to prohibit was sexual infidelity as a sole basis for the trigger. It was acknowledged that:

If something else is relied on as the qualifying trigger, *any sexual infidelity that forms part of the background can be considered* but it cannot be the trigger. That is essentially what the legislation seeks to do—to stop the act of sexual infidelity being the trigger that enables people to say that these are extremely serious and grave circumstances.[167]

---

[163] At [37].

[164] See eg the acceptance that someone who was sexually abused is more likely to take offence at sexual advances than someone who was not: *Hill* [2008] EWCA Crim 76.

[165] But the government rejected an amendment that would have limited s 55(6)(c) to cases in which the motive for killing was punishment, sexual jealousy or sexual envy. Hansard, HC, 9 Nov 2009, col 84 (Claire Ward).

[166] The Court of Appeal in *Clinton* stated that this is the correct approach. Lord Judge observed that there will therefore be occasions when the jury will be both disregarding and considering the same evidence. His lordship characterized this as being 'counter intuitive', which is to put it mildly.

[167] Hansard, HC 9 Nov 2009, col 94 (Claire Ward) (emphasis added).

The Court of Appeal in *Clinton*, relying upon much of the analysis contained in this section in the 13th edition, was extremely critical of this component of the LOSC defence. Indeed, rather than stating that the court was interpreting the provision, Lord Judge CJ characterized the court's role as 'mak[ing] sense of it'. Lord Judge stated that the rationale behind the inclusion of the provision is to prohibit the 'misuse' of sexual infidelity as a potential qualifying trigger for loss of control in circumstances in which it was thought to have been misused in the former defence of provocation.

His lordship stated that to compartmentalize sexual infidelity and exclude it when it was integral to the facts as a whole would be difficult, unrealistic and could lead to injustice.[168] His lordship derived support for this conclusion from statements made by the minister that the government did not believe that sexual infidelity *by itself* ought to enable D to avoid liability for murder. This implies the government accepted that if there is evidence other than the sexual infidelity, then the partial defence should be left to the jury.

Despite the criticisms that have been made of *Clinton*,[169] it is submitted that the judgment is a sensible and pragmatic one that avoids the potential injustice alluded to by Lord Phillips. *Clinton* ensures that D will not be able to plead the partial defence if the only evidence is the sexual infidelity. Trial judges will have to make a judgement as to whether the sexual infidelity provides the context for the killing, in which case it may be considered, or whether it was the cause of it, in which case it is to be disregarded. As Ashworth pointed out, Lord Judge's interpretation of the language utilized in s 55(6)(c) is not the only plausible one.[170] As Ashworth also correctly observes, interpreting s 55(6)(c) in such a way that it only prohibits sexual infidelity from constituting the sole trigger conforms with ministerial statements about the government's legislative intention. For this reason, those who argue that Lord Judge has frustrated Parliament's intention seem somewhat misguided.

Combined qualifying triggers: s 55(5)
Section 55(5) provides:

This subsection applies if D's loss of self-control was attributable to a combination of the matters mentioned in subsections (3) and (4).

It is possible for D to rely on both qualifying triggers under s 55 in combination—that he killed having lost control because he was in fear of serious violence and that he also had a justifiable sense of being seriously wronged.[171] A striking example would be where D kills V whom he found raping his daughter at knifepoint. The two limbs might also be relied on by the woman who kills her abusive partner after years of torment when she lost control fearing another violent attack by him.

Where D relies on both limbs but there is insufficient evidence of each limb in isolation though in combination the evidence would satisfy s 54(5), it is submitted that the defence ought to be available. Lord Judge's *dicta* in *Clinton* support that approach.

13.1.2.7 Degree of tolerance and self-restraint: s 54(1)(c)
In addition to the loss of control and the qualifying trigger, the third element of the defence is an important limitation on its scope in the form of an objective requirement enacted in s 54(1)(c). The requirement is that 'a person of D's sex and age, with a normal degree of

---

[168] So long as sexual infidelity is 'integral to and forms an integral part of the context in which to make a just evaluation of whether a qualifying trigger properly falls within the ambit of subsections 55(3) and 55(4), the prohibition in section 55(6)(c) does not operate to exclude it'. At [39].

[169] See DJ Baker and LX Zhao, 'Contributory Qualifying and Non-Qualifying Triggers in the Loss of Control Defence: A Wrong Turn on Sexual Infidelity' (2012) 76 J Crim L 254.

[170] [2012] Crim LR 539.   [171] This was recognized in *Dawes*, [56].

tolerance and self-restraint and in the *circumstances* of D, *might* have reacted in the same or in a similar way to D'.[172] By s 54(3):

In subsection (1)(c) the reference to 'the circumstances of D' is a reference to all of D's circumstances other than those whose only relevance to D's conduct is that they bear on D's general capacity for tolerance or self-restraint.

In some respects the test is similar to the test under the 1957 Act which centred on whether a reasonable man might have done as D did. This element of the old test gave rise to confusion and numerous visits to the House of Lords.[173]

Under the old provocation defence the House of Lords and Privy Council had struggled to identify a clear position on which of the defendant's characteristics were to be considered when evaluating whether a reasonable person would have done as D did. In *Camplin*,[174] the House decided that the jury should be told that the reasonable man is a person having the power of self-control to be expected of an ordinary person of the sex and age of the accused, but in other respects sharing such of the accused's characteristics as they think would affect the gravity of the provocation to him; and that the question is not merely whether such a person would in like circumstances be provoked to lose his self-control but also whether he would react to the provocation as the accused did.[175] The distinction was central to subsequent decisions of the House of Lords: *Morhall*,[176] and Privy Council in *Luc Thiet Thuan v R*,[177] but the House shifted towards a much more subjective test in *Smith (Morgan)*.[178] Finally, in *A-G for Jersey v Holley*,[179] a specially convened nine-member Board of the Privy Council concluded that a distinction should be drawn between characteristics of the accused that were to be taken into account because they affected the gravity of the provocation, and those relating to the ability to exercise self-control which were not to be taken into account.[180] In *James and Karimi*,[181] the Court of Appeal took the radical and

---

172 Emphasis added.

173 *Camplin* [1978] AC 705; *Morgan Smith* [2001] AC 146: not followed in *A-G for Jersey v Holley* [2005] 2 AC 580.

174 [1978] AC 705.

175 This line of reasoning accords with the argument made earlier by Ashworth in a seminal article. The proper distinction is that individual peculiarities which bear on the gravity of the provocation should be taken into account, whereas individual peculiarities bearing on the accused's level of self-control should not: (1976) 35 CLJ 292. Cf the distinction made between provocativeness and provocability made in the commentary on *Morhall* [1995] Crim LR 890. For consideration of whether the questions can be kept separate, see A Norrie, 'From Criminal Law to Legal Theory: The Mysterious Case of the Reasonable Glue Sniffer' (2002) 65 MLR 538 at 547.

176 [1996] AC 90. A unanimous decision of the House which was virtually ignored in *Smith* [2001] AC 146.

177 [1996] 2 All ER 1033.

178 [2001] AC 146. For critical comment see, inter alia, T Macklem and J Gardner, 'Compassion without Respect: Nine Fallacies in *R v Smith*' [2001] Crim LR 623 and 'Provocation and Pluralism' (2001) 64 MLR 815. For a defence of the case see B Mitchell, RD Mackay and W Brookbanks, 'Pleading for Provoked Killers: In Defence of *Morgan Smith*' (2008) 124 LQR 675 arguing that the approach allowed for those who lacked capacity to control themselves to rely on the defence. *Rowland* [2003] EWCA Crim 3636, [41]. See Part 2 of LCCP 173, especially paras 21–2; LC 304, para 5.41.

179 [2005] UKPC 23. For commentary see Ashworth [2005] Crim LR 966; Virgo (2005) 64 CLJ 532. See also the discussion in LC 304, paras 5.34–5.39.

180 The minority disagreed. Lords Bingham and Hoffmann suggest that it is not rationally possible to consider the two in isolation. The majority regarded any difficulties of 'mental gymnastics' required of jurors in having regard to a defendant's 'characteristics' for one purpose of the law of provocation but not another as having been exaggerated. At [26]. Lord Carswell in dissent challenged that view, at [73].

181 [2006] EWCA Crim 14.

controversial step of endorsing the Privy Council decision in *Holley* over that of the House of Lords in *Smith*.[182]

The position under the LOSC defence

The requirement is that 'a person of D's sex and age, with a normal degree of tolerance and self-restraint and in the *circumstances* of D, *might* have reacted in the same or in a similar way to D'. It would therefore be wrong to assume that the combined effect of s 54(1)(c) and s 54(3) is to codify the decision of the majority of their lordships in *Holley*.[183] What constitutes a 'normal degree of tolerance and self-restraint' is a matter for the jury to determine according to their judgement and their collective experience of life. The reference to 'D's sex and age' is consistent with statements made in *Camplin*, and *Holley*, that the 'powers of self-control possessed by ordinary people vary according to their age and . . . their sex'.[184] Why sex was included at all[185] and why these are always relevant circumstances is not clear. Difficulties may arise for defendants of mental abnormality for their age since if read restrictively it is the age that is to be taken into account.[186]

However, in other respects the test is quite different.[187] First, the words that a person '*might*' have reacted in the same or similar way to D' creates a test that is more generous to D than the requirement in s 3 of the 1957 Act which was that 'the provocation is enough *to make* reasonable man do as he did'. There is no express restriction that D's acts must be proportionate to the threat/trigger he faced.[188] In *Clinton*, Lord Judge CJ explained the operation of this component of the defence in the following way:

> The defendant's reaction (that is what he actually did, rather than the fact that he lost his self-control) may therefore be understandable in the sense that another person in his situation and the circumstances in which he found himself, might have reacted in the same or in a similar way.[189]

Secondly, it is important to note that s 54(3) clarifies s 54(1)(c) so that the reference to 'the circumstances of D' includes '*all* of D's circumstances' except those which bear on D's 'general capacity for tolerance and self-restraint' (eg a propensity to violent outbursts). The words 'in the circumstances of D' may enable a jury to adopt a more generous approach when judging D's response than might have been possible under the old law. This opens up a broader range of subjective considerations than under the *Holley* test.[190] Judges will have to be vigilant to ensure that the broad nature of the test for including D's circumstances in considering how a person of his age, etc might have reacted does not lead to evidence of tenuous relevance being admitted and distracting the jury from the central inquiry.

---

[182] On the precedent issue, see J Elvin, 'The Doctrine of Precedent and the Provocation Defence' (2006) 69 MLR 819.

[183] See on *Holley* the comments of Lord Lloyd, Hansard, HL, 7 July 2009, col 572, and Lord Thomas, col 579.

[184] *Holley* [2005] UKPC 23, [13].

[185] For criticism, see N Cobb and A Gausden, 'Feminism, "Typical" Women and Losing Control' in A Reed and M Bohlander (eds), *Loss of Control and Diminished Responsibility* (2011). The authors question exactly how sex is relevant to capacity and argue that its inclusion could exacerbate the stereotyping and essentialism of women.

[186] cf Norrie, who makes the cogent point that what matters is not D's age, but rather his maturity. As he points out, 'age is no more than a rough and ready way of marking maturity'. See Norrie, n 20, 319–20.

[187] Norrie argues that the old law was 'under-demanding and over-enabling', but that the new law is 'narrow, harsh, and censorious'. He states that neither the new nor the old law fully captures the morally appropriate group. See Norrie, n 20, 308–12 and 316–19.

[188] cf *Van Dongen* [2005] EWCA Crim 1728 where the CA seemed to imply such despite the decision against in *Phillips v R* [2005] Crim LR 971.

[189] At [30].   [190] Indeed in *Clinton* it was held that sexual infidelity may be a circumstance. At [31].

A third distinguishing feature from the old law is that s 54(3) only appears to exclude a circumstance on which D seeks to rely if its *sole* relevance is to diminish D's self-restraint.[191] This could open up the opportunity for D to claim, for example, that his intake of alcohol or other intoxicants was a relevant circumstance and that the intoxication did not simply diminish his self-restraint, but also had some other relevance—for example, that it caused a relevant mistake. This may amount to no more than a plea of lack of intent on grounds of intoxication, but it will make directing the jury more complex. In *Asmelash*,[192] Lord Judge CJ held that there was nothing in the statutory language to indicate that Parliament had intended for the normal rules governing voluntary intoxication not to apply.[193] D's voluntarily intoxicated state is therefore not a matter to be taken into account by the jury when considering whether D exercised ordinary self-control. It was observed that if a sober individual in D's circumstances, with normal levels of tolerance and self-restraint, might have behaved in the same way as the defendant when confronted by the relevant qualifying trigger, then D would not be deprived of the loss of control defence just because he was intoxicated. It was held that the trial judge was correct to direct the jury that they had to be sure that a person of D's sex and age with a normal degree of tolerance and self-restraint in the same circumstances, but unaffected by alcohol, would not have reacted in the same or a similar way.

Equally, evidence that D was suffering from chronic alcoholism is *not* (unless the taunts related to D's alcoholism) a matter to be taken into account by the jury. If D had a severe problem with alcohol and was taunted about his addiction, then it was held that to the extent that it constituted a qualifying trigger, D's alcohol dependency would form part of the circumstances.

Although the facts of *Asmelash* did not present this possibility, an additional situation in which D's voluntary intoxication ought to be deemed a circumstance is if it causes him to make a relevant mistake. Suppose that D was so intoxicated that he mistook V's slap on the back as an attack rather than an exuberant act of friendship and consequently kills him. Although D's intoxication might bear on his general capacity for tolerance and self-restraint, in this situation it would not be its *sole* relevance and so falls within the 'gap'[194] left by the legislation.[195]

Section 54(3) excludes circumstances 'whose only relevance to D's conduct is that they bear on D's general capacity for tolerance or self restraint'. That restriction is similar to the

---

[191] It is important not to lose sight of the fact that a circumstance is excluded only if its *sole* relevance is that it bears on D's general capacity for tolerance and self-restraint.

[192] [2013] EWCA Crim 157.

[193] The Court of Appeal was heavily influenced by the earlier case of *Dowds*, see n 235, in which Hughes LJ held that voluntary intoxication could not constitute a recognized medical condition for the purposes of diminished responsibility. Lord Judge CJ held that the two partial defences ought to adopt the same approach to intoxication because 'in a fair proportion of cases both defences are canvassed before the jury, the potential for uncertainty and confusion which would follow the necessarily very different directions on the issue of intoxication, depending on which partial defence was under consideration, does not bear contemplation'. At [24]. However, since murder is a crime of specific intent and D will often seek to argue that his intoxication meant that he did not form the necessary mens rea, the jury will already have to approach the relevance of intoxication from more than one perspective.

[194] Ashworth [2013] Crim LR 599.

[195] Some commentators have expressed concern that this might lead to defendants making spurious claims with the aim of establishing that their intoxicated state had some other relevance. A Jackson and N Wortley, 'Loss of Control and the "Normal" Person: The Relevance of Self-Induced Intoxication' (2013) 77 J Crim L 292. No doubt, however, trial judges will be alive to this possibility and will scrutinize D's claim closely. Further, just because D's intoxicated state is permitted to be considered by the jury as a 'circumstance' in some situations, does not necessarily mean the partial defence will succeed.

old law in *excluding* certain features. However, there is now no positive requirement that D's individual circumstances have to affect the gravity of the triggering conduct in order for them to be *included* in the jury's assessment of what the person of D's age and sex might have done. So, where D has a learning disability and is provoked, his disability will be relevant even if the taunts relate to something completely different. Again, there is a need to be vigilant in avoiding evidence of marginal relevance from distracting the jury.

The question that arises is which, if any, of D's mental conditions are relevant. The answer, it is submitted, lies in the statutory formula. The evidence of D's mental illness would be a relevant circumstance so long as it had some relevance other than it bore on his general capacity for tolerance and self-restraint. One example already mentioned is that it induced D to make a relevant mistake.

A number of cases have considered this issue. In *McGrory*,[196] the Court of Appeal held that the judge was correct not to refer the jury to the evidence of the medical expert who testified that D's depression would have meant that he had a 'reduced ability to deal with taunting and to cope with those sorts of pressures compared to someone not suffering from depression'. Maddison J stated that this was not a relevant circumstance, as it was excluded by s 54(3). In *B*, Hughes LJ, as he then was, stated that: 's.54 of the Coroners and Justice Act 2009 . . . excludes from consideration those characteristics of the defendant which bear on his capacity for tolerance and self-restraint. Thus mental illness reducing that capacity would not be relevant to the partial defence of loss of control, but would be material if it amounted to insanity or (in the particular case of a murder charge alone) fulfilled the different criteria for the separate (also partial) defence of diminished responsibility.'[197]

In *Wilcocks*,[198] Holroyde J, as he then was, directed the jury that:

If and insofar as you conclude a personality disorder reduced his general capacity for tolerance and self-restraint, that would not be a relevant circumstance when you are considering the defence of loss of control. But it is important to emphasise that this exclusion only relates to any feature of a personality disorder which reduced his general capacity for tolerance and self-restraint. Let me give you an illustration. If you thought that [D] suffered from a personality disorder which made him unusually likely to become angry and aggressive at the slightest provocation, that would of course be relevant to diminished responsibility but it could not assist him in relation to loss of control. But if you thought that a personality disorder had caused him to attempt suicide, then you would be entitled to take into account as one of his circumstances the effect on him of being taunted that he should have killed himself.

The Court of Appeal endorsed this direction and it seems to reflect the statutory intent— that provided the mental condition is relevant to some aspect other than D's *general* capacity for tolerance and self-restraint, it should be considered by the jury in their deliberations on s 54(3). If, on the other hand, the mental condition's only relevance is that it bears on the defendant's general capacity for tolerance and self-restraint, then it should not be considered. For example, in *Meanza* it was conceded that D's paranoid schizophrenia and anti-social personality disorder could not be relevant circumstances within the meaning of s 54(1)(c).[199]

The leading case is now *Rejmanski*, in which the Court of Appeal accepted the analysis of the legislation advanced earlier.[200] The Court of Appeal held that the potential relevance of mental disorder to each of the elements of the LOSC defence is fact-specific: it depends on the nature of the defendant's disorder, the effect it has on the defendant, and the facts of the

---

[196] [2013] EWCA Crim 2336.   [197] [2013] EWCA Crim 3, [38].   [198] [2016] EWCA Crim 2043, [40].
[199] [2017] EWCA Crim 445.   [200] [2017] EWCA Crim 2061.

case. In relation to the final element of the partial defence, the court held that the wording of s 54(1)(c) makes clear that:

the defendant is to be judged against the standard of a person with a normal degree, and not an abnormal degree, of tolerance and self-restraint. If, and in so far as, a personality disorder reduced the defendant's general capacity for tolerance or self-restraint, that would not be a relevant consideration. Moreover, it would not be a relevant consideration even if the personality disorder was one of the 'circumstances' of the defendant because it was relevant to the gravity of the trigger. Expert evidence about the impact of the disorder would be irrelevant and inadmissible on the issue of whether it would have reduced the capacity for tolerance and self-restraint of the hypothetical 'person of D's sex and age, with a normal degree of tolerance and self-restraint'.[201]

If the mental disorder has some relevance to D's conduct other than its bearing on his general capacity for tolerance and self-restraint, it is not excluded by subs (3) and the jury will be entitled to take it into account as one of D's circumstances. The court emphasized, however, that it will be necessary to identify 'with some care' how the mental disorder is said to be relevant as one of D's circumstances.

Before permitting evidence of a mental disorder to be considered by the jury, trial judges must ensure that a sufficiently cogent case has been advanced that the disorder is relevant to something other than D's general capacity for tolerance or self-restraint. As the Court of Appeal observed, citing *Holley* and *Wilcocks*, in the majority of cases the disorder will be relevant to the gravity of the qualifying trigger. The example given by the court is a woman suffering from 'Battered Woman's Syndrome' or a personality disorder, who kills her abuser, and who may adduce evidence of her condition, on the basis that it may be relevant to both the loss of self-control and to the gravity of the provocation for her.[202] The court must not, however, be taken to have laid down a rule that this is the only relevance it can have. It is possible to envisage other ways in which the mental disorder may be relevant.

In a case in which the disorder is relevant to some factor other than the defendant's general capacity for tolerance and self restraint, the disorder must not be relied upon to undermine the principle that D's conduct is to be judged against 'normal' standards, rather than the abnormal standard of an individual defendant. The court in *Rejmanski* emphatically rejected the argument that if a disorder is relevant to the gravity of the qualifying trigger, and evidence of the disorder is admitted in relation to the gravity of the trigger, the jury would also be entitled to take it into account insofar as it bore on D's general capacity for tolerance and self-restraint. Whilst the disorder would be a relevant circumstance of the defendant, it would not be relevant to the question of the degree of tolerance and self-restraint which would be expected of the hypothetical person referred to in s 54(1)(c).

Given that loss of control and diminished responsibility may be pleaded together as alternatives, the court emphasized that the law does not ignore a mental disorder that, through no fault of the defendant, renders him unable to exercise the degree of self-control of a 'normal' person. In such a case, D could still plead diminished responsibility.

Rejmanski is a welcome judgment and ensures that D's reaction to the qualifying trigger is always assessed against the objective standard required by the legislation. It also confirms that the LOSC defence is more generous to defendants than provocation given that there is no positive requirement for D's circumstances to affect the gravity of the triggering conduct.

---

201 ibid, [25].

202 For an example of a case applying *Rejmanski*, see *Sargeant* [2019] EWCA Crim 1088 in which it was held that D's adjustment disorder with features of post-traumatic stress disorder, autistic spectrum disorder and mild intellectual disability were not relevant to the question of the degree of tolerance and self-restraint which would be exercised by the hypothetical normal person. They may have been relevant to the gravity of the qualifying trigger, however.

13.2 Diminished responsibility

Section 2 of the Homicide Act 1957 introduced a new defence to murder: 'diminished responsibility'.[203] The defence has been substituted with one of the same name contained in s 52 of the Coroners and Justice Act 2009. Diminished responsibility is not a general defence, but applies only to murder.[204] It is not available as a defence to attempted murder,[205] nor can it be raised on a finding of unfitness to plead.[206] If successful, the defence allows D to be found guilty only of manslaughter.[207]

By s 2(2) of the 1957 Act, the burden of proof is on D to prove the elements of the partial defence. It was held in *Foye*,[208] a case brought under the old law, that placing the burden upon D did not infringe the presumption of innocence enshrined in Art 6(2) of the ECHR. That was endorsed by the Court of Appeal in relation to the new law in *Wilcocks*.[209] Imposing a burden on D is said to be justified on the basis that: (a) diminished responsibility is an exceptional defence; (b) the defence depends upon the 'internal functioning of [D's] mental process'; (c) it would be impractical to require the Crown to disprove diminished responsibility whenever it was raised on the evidence. It has been held that, as in the case of insanity, the standard of proof required is not beyond reasonable doubt but on a balance of probabilities.[210]

13.2.1 The old law

Only the briefest outline of the old law is required. Under s 2 of the 1957 Act as enacted, the defence was available on a charge of murder where D could prove that 'he was suffering from such abnormality of mind (whether arising from a condition of arrested or retarded development of mind or any inherent causes or induced by disease or injury) as substantially impaired his mental responsibility for his acts and omissions in doing or being a party to the killing'.

---

[203] For historical and general accounts see Norrie, *Crime, Reason and History*, 248–56; RD Mackay, 'Diminished Responsibility and Mentally Disordered Killers' in Ashworth and Mitchell (eds), *Rethinking English Homicide Law* (2000); E Tennant, *The Future of the Diminished Responsibility Defence to Murder* (2001); S Dell, *Murder into Manslaughter: The Diminished Responsibility Defence in Practice* (1984).

[204] Given that LOSC and diminished responsibility will often be pleaded together (a fact noted by Lord Judge in *Dawes* (earlier)), Mitchell argues that the differences in the burdens and standards of proof of the respective partial defences could cause considerable difficulties for juries. See B Mitchell, 'Years of Provocation, Followed by a Loss of Control' in L Zedner and JV Roberts, *Principles and Values in Criminal Law and Criminal Justice* (2012). See also Norrie, n 203, 256–7.

[205] *Campbell* [1997] Crim LR 495, Sedley J. See also *Farrar* [1992] 1 VR 207.

[206] *Antoine* [2001] AC 340.

[207] The defence derives from the law of Scotland, where it was a judicial creation, originating in the decision of Lord Deas in *HM Advocate v Dingwall* (1867) 5 Irv 466. See TB Smith, 'Diminished Responsibility' [1957] Crim LR 354 and Lord Keith, 'Some Observations on Diminished Responsibility' [1959] Jur Rev 109. The Scottish version was redefined in the Criminal Procedure (Scotland) Act 1995, s 51B, inserted by s 168 of the Criminal Justice and Licensing (Scotland) Act 2010. The defence in Scotland now results in a conviction for 'culpable homicide on grounds of diminished responsibility'. The new statutory provisions implement recommendations made by the Scottish Law Commission in Report No 195, *Insanity and Diminished Responsibility* (2004); see for comment on those recommendations (2013) 77 J Crim L 512 and [2014] Crim LR 109.

[208] [2013] EWCA Crim 475. For compelling criticism, see Ashworth [2013] Crim LR 839.

[209] [2016] EWCA Crim 2043.

[210] *Dunbar* [1958] 1 QB 1. This rule is not affected by the HRA 1998: *Ali and Jordan* [2001] 1 All ER 1014. Where the medical evidence of diminished responsibility is based on certain facts, it is for the defence to prove those facts by admissible evidence: *Ahmed Din* (1962) 46 Cr App R 269; *Bradshaw* (1985) 82 Cr App R 79, [1985] Crim LR 733 and commentary.

The elements of the defence were therefore: (a) an abnormality of mind (b) which arose from one of the specified conditions (c) which substantially impaired (d) D's mental responsibility. None of the elements was defined with any precision and arguably the courts in collusion with psychiatrists were content to avoid definition so that the defence maintained its flexibility, thereby allowing for its application in deserving cases in which the mandatory sentence for murder would otherwise apply.[211]

There had been numerous calls for reform. The Law Commission Report No 290, *Partial Defences to Murder*, concluded that[212] there was 'overwhelming support' for reform. The old law was regarded by many as 'chaotic' and it was suggested that a rational sentencing exercise would be a better response for meeting the needs of mentally ill defendants. It was noted that the defence was 'grossly abused' and whether a defendant 'finds a psychiatrist who will be prepared to testify that, for example, depression was responsible for his behaviour is "a lottery"'. There was some pressure for abolition, particularly if the mandatory sentence was removed, but the Law Commission identified several arguments[213] for retention, including the need for 'fair and just labelling'.[214]

The Commission refined its original proposal from the Partial Defences Project.[215] The proposals were taken forward by the MOJ and the new defence as enacted in 2009 is very similar to those proposals (with the notable omission of a defence of developmental immaturity).

13.2.2 The reformed partial defence

Section 52 of the Coroners and Justice Act 2009 provides:[216]

(1) In section 2 of the Homicide Act 1957 (persons suffering from diminished responsibility), for subsection (1) substitute—

'(1) A person ('D') who kills or is a party to the killing of another is not to be convicted of murder if D was suffering from an abnormality of mental functioning which—

(a) arose from a recognised medical condition,

(b) substantially impaired D's ability to do one or more of the things mentioned in subsection (1A), and

(c) provides an explanation for D's acts and omissions in doing or being a party to the killing.

---

[211] LC 304, para 5.107.

[212] LC 290, para 5.10 and see Scottish Law Commission, Report No 195, *Insanity and Diminished Responsibility* (2004). See also J Horder, *Homicide and the Politics of Law Reform* (2012) 226.

[213] Justifications included the need for some defence other than insanity given the 'out-dated nature of the insanity defence' and its unsatisfactory scope and operation; the stigmatization of the label 'insanity'; the need to prevent jurors being faced with only the option of murder or acquittal lest they perversely acquit; allowing the central issue of culpability to be determined by a jury and not by the judge as part of the sentencing process; the need to ensure public confidence in sentencing which is more likely on a diminished verdict than on murder; the need for a jury to evaluate the expert evidence; the need to retain the defence for abused women 'driven to kill'; and the opportunity for the defence to provide a merciful but just disposition of mercy killing cases.

[214] LC 290, para 5.18.

[215] See V Tadros, 'The Limits of Manslaughter' in C Clarkson and S Cunningham (eds), *Criminal Liability for Non-Aggressive Death* (2008).

[216] See in particular Norrie, n 203, 251–4; A Reed and M Bohlander (eds), *Loss of Control and Diminished Responsibility—Domestic, Comparative and International Perspectives* (2011); L Kennefick, 'Introducing a New Diminished Responsibility Defence for England and Wales' (2011) 74 MLR 750; R Fortson and AR Keene, *Current Law Statutes Annotation* (2010); J Glasson and J Knowles, *Blackstone's Guide to the Coroners and Justice Act 2009* (2010) Ch 8; LH Leigh, 'Two New Partial Defences to Murder' (2010) Crim L & Justice Weekly 53; RD Mackay, 'The New Diminished Responsibility Plea' [2010] Crim LR 290.

(1A) Those things are—

    (a) to understand the nature of D's conduct;

    (b) to form a rational judgement;

    (c) to exercise self-control.

(1B) For the purposes of subsection (1)(c), an abnormality of mental functioning provides an explanation for D's conduct if it causes, or is a significant contributory factor in causing, D to carry out that conduct.'

Section 52 was brought into force on 4 October 2010.[217] Since the provision relates exclusively to a matter of substantive law, it will apply in relation to any murder which occurred on or after that date.[218]

Section 52 makes significant changes to the defence of diminished responsibility. The main aim is to modernize and clarify the defence. In particular, the aim is to redraft the provision with the needs and practices of medical experts in mind, and to clarify what is involved in the 'substantial impairment of the defendant's mental responsibility'. Strikingly, the word 'responsibility' no longer features in the terms of the defence at all.[219] The practical effects are, it would appear, to narrow the scope of the defence and to create the opportunity for experts to have even greater influence over the outcome.[220] Because the experts have a greater opportunity to provide a more definitive opinion on more of the elements of the offence, it remains unclear whether this will lead to a greater proportion of cases in which there will be accepted pleas. In 2017, Professors Mackay and Mitchell conducted a review into cases which have applied the partial defence in its current form. They compared CPS research into the new law (limited to only 90 cases) with the Law Commission's study of the old law.[221] Statistics reveal that the total number of successful diminished responsibility pleas under the old law was around 20 per year in the years immediately preceding amendment (down from around 70–85 per year in the 1980s).[222] The CPS study found a higher proportion of cases being dealt with as jury trials (43.3 per cent) than occurred in the earlier research (22.9 per cent) which indicates that more cases are being contested under the new law.[223]

13.2.2.1 The elements of the partial defence

The elements of the reformed partial defence are as follows.

    (1) An 'abnormality of mental functioning'. In itself this is not intended to be a change of substance, but rather one to adopt language preferred by psychiatrists.[224]

---

[217] The Coroners and Justice Act 2009 (Commencement No 4, Transitional and Saving Provisions) Order 2010, SI 2010/816.

[218] Para 7 of Sch 22 to the Coroners and Justice Act 2009.

[219] There has been a divergence of views expressed on whether this is desirable. Contrast L Kennefick, 'Introducing a New Diminished Responsibility Defence for England and Wales' (2011) 74 MLR 750 with R Fortson, 'The Modern Partial Defence of Diminished Responsibility' in A Reed and M Bohlander (eds), *Loss of Control and Diminished Responsibility* (2011).

[220] Jurors remain at liberty to disregard the expert evidence left to them and find D guilty of murder. *Golds* [2016] UKSC 61 provides a vivid example of this, as the jury rejected the unanimous evidence of the three experts, two for the defence and one for the Crown, who testified that the elements of the partial defence were present. See also *Brennan* [2014] EWCA Crim 2387.

[221] See RD Mackay and B Mitchell, 'The New Diminished Responsibility Plea in Operation: Some Initial Findings' [2017] Crim LR 18.

[222] See LC 290; LC 304, para 5.84.

[223] RD Mackay and B Mitchell, 'The New Diminished Responsibility Plea in Operation: Some Initial Findings' [2017] Crim LR 18 at 26.

[224] See LC 304, para 5.114. It received support in Parliament from Baroness Murphy (Visiting Professor of Psychiatry at Queen Mary, University of London): Hansard, HL, 30 June 2009, vol 712, col 177.

(2) The abnormality must arise 'from a recognised medical condition'. This is designed to be wider than the old list of bracketed causes in the original definition in s 2 of the 1957 Act. Again, it is designed to allow expert evidence to be received on a more meaningful basis.

(3) D's 'mental responsibility' must be substantially impaired. This means that his *ability* to do one or more of the things in s 2(1A), must be substantially impaired. The three things are:

(a) to understand the nature of D's conduct;

(b) to form a rational judgement;

(c) to exercise self-control.

This is a dramatic change from the old law. It is more specific and leaves less moral elbow room for the jury and is arguably harder for D to prove.

(4) The abnormality of mental functioning from a 'recognised medical condition' must be a cause or contributory cause of D's conduct in killing. There is some ambiguity as to whether the section requires a cause or merely an explanation.

Each element of the offence deserves more detailed consideration.

(1) 'an abnormality of mental functioning'

Under the old s 2 test (of 'abnormality of mind') the determination of 'abnormality' could be left entirely to the jury. In *Byrne*,[225] Lord Parker CJ stated that 'abnormality' of mind:

means a state of mind so different from that of ordinary human beings that the reasonable man would term it abnormal. It appears to us to be wide enough to cover the mind's activities in all its aspects, not only the perception of physical acts and matters and the ability to form a rational judgment whether an act is right or wrong, but also the ability to exercise will-power to control physical acts in accordance with that rational judgement.

That formula was appropriate when a jury was considering a concept as loose and general as the 'mind' and asking whether D's 'mind' deviated from the norm. But the expression 'abnormality of mind' has been superseded by the test of abnormality of 'mental functioning'. That test is, even if not a formal psychiatric test, one with a psychiatric flavour. The jury cannot have a sound grasp of that concept without expert evidence.[226] Nor, therefore, can the jury understand how far D's mental functioning deviates from the norm without expert evidence to assist them. As such, they cannot be left with as open a direction as in *Byrne*. Experts will express an opinion on whether there is an abnormal mental functioning. If there is uncontradicted expert evidence of the defence, the judge may withdraw murder from the jury, but should be cautious in doing so.[227] In such a case 'the judge needs to ensure that the Crown explains the basis on which it is inviting the jury to reject [the expert] evidence. He needs to ensure that the basis advanced is one which the jury can properly adopt.'[228] In *Blackman*,[229] the Lord Chief Justice emphasized that:

The fact that the prosecution calls no evidence to contradict a psychiatrist called by the defence is not in itself sufficient justification for doing so. In the light of the judgment in *Golds*, we see no

---

[225] [1960] 2 QB 396 at 403.

[226] This remains, however, a legal rather than a medical term. It has been argued that this fact demonstrates that the 'Law and psychiatry are based on opposing paradigms, they cannot work together'. See L Kennefick, 'Introducing a New Diminished Responsibility Defence for England and Wales' (2011) 74 MLR 750, 765. See also the discussion in Norrie, n 203, Ch 9.

[227] This is examined further at p 586.   [228] *Golds* [2016] UKSC 61 at [51] per Lord Hughes.

[229] [2017] EWCA Crim 190 (CMAC).

reason not to follow the broad approach of this court in *R v Khan (Dawood)* [2009] EWCA Crim 1569, [2010] 1 Cr App R 4, to which reference was made in *Brennan*, which we would express as follows: it will be a rare case where a judge will exercise the power to withdraw a charge of murder from the jury when the prosecution do not accept that the evidence gives rise to the defence of diminished responsibility.[230]

The reformed partial defence probably is stricter than the original s 2. Nevertheless, there is little doubt that on facts such as those in *Byrne*, the defence would still be available. Byrne strangled a young woman in a YWCA hostel and mutilated her corpse. Evidence was tendered that from an early age he had been subject to perverted violent desires; that the impulse or urge of those desires was stronger than the normal impulse or urge of sex, that he found it very difficult or, perhaps, impossible in some cases to resist putting the desire into practice and that the act of killing the girl was done under such an impulse or urge.[231] That would be an abnormality of mental functioning.

(2) 'a recognised medical condition'

The abnormality of mental functioning must arise 'from a recognised medical condition'. This new element to the test is designed to be wider than the list of sufficient causes in the original s 2 of the 1957 Act.[232] It is intended to produce clearer expert evidence from psychiatrists and psychologists and to allow sufficient flexibility for the new defence to develop in line with medical understanding and practice.[233] The immediate questions arising are: What kind(s) of medical condition? Recognized by whom?

'medical condition'

This new element of the definition will provide a clearer foundation for the defence. As the Royal College of Psychiatrists explained, it will:

encourage reference within expert evidence to diagnosis in terms of one or two of the accepted internationally classificatory systems of mental conditions (i.e. the World Health Organisation: International Classification of Diseases (ICD-10); and the American Psychiatric Association: Diagnostic and Statistical Manual of Mental Disorders (DSM-1V)) without explicitly writing those systems into the legislation.[234]

It must be noted that *any* medical condition *might* suffice subject to the restriction imposed in *Dowds*.[235] It will include physical conditions as well as psychological or psychiatric ones[236] and conditions such as diabetes or ADHD. Depressive illnesses resulting from

---

[230] At [43].

[231] The defence of irresistible impulse, which is not within the defence of insanity, is therefore included in the law (but only of murder) by way of diminished responsibility.

[232] The Law Commission originally wanted a wider formulation: that the source of the abnormality should be an 'underlying condition' (LCCP 177, para 10.21), which would not be limited to a mental condition existing independently of the external circumstances that gave rise to the commission of an offence. It would therefore have 'include[d] cases in which the origins of the condition itself lie in adverse circumstances with which the offender has had to cope': LCCP 177, para 6.54.

[233] See the MOJ CP 19/08.

[234] LC 304, para 5.114. See MOJ CP 19/08, fn 13.

[235] See p 575. In *Dowds* [2012] EWCA Crim 281, the Court of Appeal stated that just because a condition is transient or temporary does not preclude it from fulfilling this element of the partial defence. Hughes LJ suggested that concussion may be an example of such a condition, but did not resolve the matter conclusively, at [39].

[236] See the MOJ CP 19/08, para 49.

prolonged abuse will qualify,[237] and hence the defence remains available to battered women on those terms.[238]

Acute intoxication, that is, being drunk, does not constitute a recognized medical condition.[239] Alcoholic dependency will, however, qualify as a medical condition irrespective of whether it resulted in brain damage.[240] The Court of Appeal strongly doubted in *Lindo* whether a drug-induced psychosis standing alone would be sufficient to constitute a recognized medical condition. Hallett LJ stated that, 'public policy proceeds on the basis that an offender who voluntarily takes alcohol or drugs and behaves a way in which he would not have behaved when sober is not normally excused responsibility. People who take drugs run the risk of suffering side effects such as psychosis.'[241] Her ladyship held that it would be wrong to permit individuals such as the appellant to escape full responsibility for their actions simply on the basis that they took drugs at a time when they were at risk of developing a mental illness. As a result, if D voluntarily consumes drink or drugs which cause him immediately to suffer a psychosis, he will not be able to plead the partial defence. This interpretation was endorsed in *Foy*[242] where Davis LJ made crystal clear:

Where the killing occurs when the defendant is in a state of acute voluntary intoxication, even if that voluntary intoxication results in a psychotic episode, then there is no recognised medical condition available to found a defence of diminished responsibility: see *Dowds* [2012] EWCA Crim 281; *Lindo* [2016] EWCA Crim 1940. This is so whether the intoxicant is alcohol or drugs or a combination of each.

We discuss the further implications of this at p 583.

Although this element of the defence is much broader than the equivalent element under the 1957 Act, it should not create excessive breadth in the defence overall since the other elements are all, arguably, narrower.

During consultation on the reform proposals which led to the enactment of the reformed s 2, groups expressed concern that this element may in some circumstances be narrower than the old law because it will not apply to those who kill terminally ill relatives when the killer has 'acted rationally in response to persistent requests from a seriously ill loved-one'.[243]

---

[237] The Law Commission also took the view that most cases of 'mercy' killing, in which there was evidence of an abnormality of mental functioning resulting from depression arising from long-term care, would be covered by its proposed changes. See LC 304, paras 7.34–7.37. Mackay doubts whether the Law Commission's view was correct, on the basis that there may be no recognized medical condition from which D is suffering. See RD Mackay, 'The New Diminished Responsibility Plea: More than Mere Modernisation?' in A Reed and M Bohlander (eds), *Loss of Control and Diminished Responsibility*. See also M Gibson, 'Pragmatism Preserved? The Challenges of Accommodating Mercy Killers in the Reformed Diminished Responsibility Plea' (2017) 81 J Crim L 177. It has been argued that a specific provision ought to be enacted that provides a partial excusatory defence for those who kill out of compassion. See H Keating and J Bridgeman, 'Compassionate Killings: The Case for a Partial Defence' (2012) 75 MLR 697.

[238] Battered women's syndrome, having been included in 1992 in the standard British classification of mental diseases, is a relevant condition: *Hobson* [1998] 1 Cr App R 31.

[239] cf *Dowds* [2012] EWCA Crim 281.

[240] See *Kay and Joyce* [2017] EWCA Crim 647 and *Bunch* [2013] EWCA Crim 2489. Historically this was a confused area until the decision of the House of Lords in *Dietschman*. See *Tandy* [1989] 1 All ER 267. See since *Dietschman*: *Wood* [2008] EWCA Crim 1305; *Stewart* [2009] EWCA Crim 593; *Stewart (No 2)* [2010] EWCA Crim 2159; *Foy* [2020] EWCA Crim 270.

[241] [2016] EWCA Crim 1940, [42].

[242] [2020] EWCA Crim 270, [70].

[243] See the evidence of 'Dignity in Dying' to Joint Committee on Human Rights, Eighth Report, 2008–09, para 1.150; evidence 44–45. Cf *Cocker* [1989] Crim LR 740 who would not fit within this defence nor LOSC. It has been argued that loss of control will provide a more viable defence for mercy killers, see B Livings, 'A New Partial Defence for the Mercy Killer: Revisiting Loss of Control' [2014] NILQ 187.

However, it may be that some depressive illness would be likely to be diagnosed, as a 'medical condition'.[244]

'recognised'

The requirement that the medical condition is a 'recognised' one is also intended to prevent 'idiosyncratic diagnoses' being advanced as a basis for a plea of diminished responsibility.[245] However, during the debates in Committee in Parliament, the government recognized that it is important that the legislation must be sufficiently flexible to cater for emerging medical conditions. It expressed the view that it is open to the defence to call a 'recognized specialist who has had their work peer-reviewed, although it has *not quite got on the list* [ie in the psychiatric manuals DSM V or ICD-10] and that it would be for the jury to decide whether the evidence met the partial defence requirements'.[246] Care will be needed to ensure that 'quack' opinions are not received. The comment in Parliament might have been better expressed in terms of the recognized specialist being *not yet on the list*. This would reflect the desire to ensure flexibility for development.

Whether a condition in the manuals is 'recognised' is a matter of law. The Court of Appeal in *Dowds*[247] stated that it is necessary, but not always sufficient, that a condition is included in one of the diagnostic manuals. D sought to argue that voluntary acute intoxication (which is entirely different from alcohol dependency syndrome) was a recognized medical condition for the purposes of diminished responsibility.[248] Hughes LJ observed that the general principle that voluntary intoxication is no defence 'is well-entrenched and formed the unspoken backdrop for the new statutory formula'.[249] If Parliament had sought to alter this principle, then Hughes LJ stated that it would have made its intention to do so explicit.[250] It was observed that the diagnostic manuals are extremely broad and include many conditions of questionable legal impact. His lordship gave pyromania, unhappiness, suspiciousness and marked evasiveness, paedophilia, and intermittent explosive disorder as some vivid examples.

Whilst the Court of Appeal's judgment in *Dowds* is uncontroversial as it applies to voluntary intoxication, it leaves open the question as to how trial judges ought to determine whether a condition recognized by medical experts is a 'recognised medical condition' for the purposes of the partial defence. The problem arises due to the breadth of the term 'recognised medical condition'. Requiring trial judges to pick and choose which conditions are capable of founding the defence of diminished responsibility is inconsistent with the aim of reforming the law to ensure it conforms with modern psychiatric practice. Hughes LJ made explicit that the question of whether the classification system addresses the legal issue in a particular case 'will inevitably [involve] considerations of legal policy which are irrelevant

---

[244] See the evidence presented to the Public Bill Committee, 3 February 2009, written evidence (CJ/01); Joint Committee on Human Rights, *Eighth Report, 2008–09* (2009); para 1.151. For an engaging discussion of this issue, see M Gibson, 'Pragmatism Preserved? The Challenges of Accommodating Mercy Killers in the Reformed Diminished Responsibility Plea' (2017) 81 J Crim L 177.

[245] LC 304, para 5.114.   [246] Public Bill Committee Debates, 3 Mar 2009, col 414. Emphasis added.

[247] [2012] EWCA Crim 281, [2012] Crim LR 612.

[248] For discussion of how this issue is addressed in other common law jurisdictions, see N Wake, 'Recognising Acute Intoxication as Diminished Responsibility? A Comparative Analysis?' (2012) 76 J Crim L 71. For an early analysis, see M Gibson, 'Intoxicants and Diminished Responsibility: The Impact of the Coroners and Justice Act 2009' [2011] Crim LR 909.

[249] At [35].

[250] It has been suggested that one way of avoiding the issue that arose in *Dowds* would have been for Parliament to state explicitly that intoxication is incapable of forming the basis of the partial defence, as is the case in Scotland. See N Wake, 'Diminished Responsibility and Acute Intoxication: Raising the Bar?' (2012) 76 J Crim L 197.

to the business of medical description, classification, and statistical analysis'.[251] The Court of Appeal did not, however, elucidate what D will have to prove in addition to the fact that the condition is recognized by the medical profession in order to satisfy the first element of the defence. The list of conditions that are capable of constituting 'recognised medial conditions' will be determined on a case-by-case basis. The diagnostic manuals will be indicative and not determinative of the matter.

Developmental immaturity as a 'medical condition'?[252] The new diminished defence differs from the Law Commission's proposal principally because the new definition does not include, as a cause of impairment, 'developmental immaturity in a defendant under the age of 18', alongside abnormality of mental functioning arising from a mental condition. So, as it was put in debates:

An adult who acts like a 10-year-old gets that taken into account, but a 10-year-old who acts like a 10-year-old does not.[253]

The government rejected this proposal on the grounds that this was unnecessary and because the concept of a 'recognised medical condition' is designed to be wide enough to cover relevant conditions affecting those under 18 (eg learning disabilities and autistic spectrum disorders).[254]

There was widespread support for the Law Commission proposal.[255] Lord Phillips, the former President of the Supreme Court, is on record as regretting the omission of any reference to developmental immaturity, saying:

The Government has not accepted this argument for two reasons. The first is that they do not believe that the absence of such a provision is causing serious problems in practice. The second is, I quote: We think there is a risk that such a provision would open up the defence too widely and catch inappropriate cases.[256]

Since there is now no defence of *doli incapax*[257] the child who has killed has limited defence options. Arguably, there will be cases where a young defendant might be able to bring his developmental immaturity within the rubric of a 'recognised medical condition' for the purposes of the new defence. However, whatever the cause of the developmental immaturity, whether it is nature or nurture, unless it results in an *abnormal* mental functioning, D will not be able to meet the requirement under the new s 2(1)(a). The Law Commission was concerned that experts may find it impossible to distinguish between the impact of developmental immaturity on D's functioning and the impact of a mental abnormality on that functioning process. It concluded that it was 'wholly unrealistic and unfair' to expect medical experts to assess the impact of abnormal mental functioning whilst disregarding developmental immaturity.[258] The harshness of the inability to rely on developmental

---

[251] *Dowds*, [30].

[252] For further discussion, see R Fortson, 'The Modern Partial Defence of Diminished Responsibility' in A Reed and M Bohlander (eds), *Loss of Control and Diminished Responsibility* (2011), and A Ashworth *Positive Obligations in Criminal Law* (2013) 184.

[253] Public Bill Committee Debates, 3 Mar 2009, col 411.   [254] See CP 19/08, para 55.

[255] Supported by the Crown Court judges, the Criminal Bar Association, the Youth Justice Board, the Royal College of Psychiatrists, Dr Eileen Vizard, the NSPCC and a number of lawyers in Parliament.

[256] Lord Phillips' Essex University/Clifford Chance lecture on *Reforming the Law of Homicide*, delivered on 6 Nov 2008. What should matter, it is submitted, is whether there is disfunction of ability to exercise control and judgement, etc.

[257] *T* [2009] UKHL 20, Ch 10.   [258] LC 304, para 5.128.

immaturity to found a diminished responsibility plea might be felt most keenly in some cases of joint venture murder where a young vulnerable defendant has joined with an older gang, one of whose members kills V.

It must not be forgotten that the mere fact that D suffers from a particular medical condition is only one part of the defence; all the elements need to be established by D.[259]

(3) 'a substantial impairment of mental ability'

Under the old law, the matter that had to be substantially impaired was D's *mental responsibility* for acting as he did.[260] The test of *substantial* impairment of responsibility[261] was one of moral responsibility.[262] Under the new law, the matter that now has to be shown to be substantially impaired is D's *ability to do* any of the things mentioned in the new s 2(1A).

Under the old law the most authoritative case on the meaning of 'substantially' was *Lloyd*.[263] In that case counsel for D contended that 'substantially' can mean one of two things: that the impairment was real and not illusory, or that it was of a considerable amount. That decision was seen by some to be inconsistent with that of Lord Parker CJ in the earlier case of *Simcox*.[264] In *Ramchurn*,[265] Lord Judge CJ rejected the argument that the meaning of 'substantially' had been inconsistently applied under the 1957 Act. Lord Judge remarked that 'substantially' is an ordinary English word. The purpose of the term is to ensure that D does not escape liability for murder on account of any impairment of mental responsibility, no matter how trivial and insignificant, but also to ensure that D is not unduly burdened by having to prove that his mental responsibility was so grossly impaired as to be extinguished.

As a result of the partial defence being reformed, two questions fell for consideration. First, did the directions approved in *Lloyd* and *Simcox* really say the same thing and, secondly, did the 2009 reformulation of the partial defence alter the meaning to be attributed to the term 'substantial'?

The correct interpretation is now governed by the Supreme Court's decision in *Golds*.[266] The certified questions asked, first, whether the judge is required to direct the jury on the meaning of 'substantial', and secondly, whether it is 'to be defined as "something more than merely trivial," or alternatively in a way that connotes more than this, such as "something whilst short of total impairment is nevertheless significant and appreciable"?'[267]

The Supreme Court examined the history of the partial defence and the cases dealing with the concept of 'substantial' under the old law. The court concluded that the word 'substantially' had historically been held, in the diminished responsibility context, to mean 'having some substance' or 'important or weighty'. It was not synonymous with 'anything more than merely trivial'. The court held that that same interpretation applies to the defence under as it now stands in the Coroners and Justice Act 2009. In the absence of any indication

---

[259] Under the old law it was held that D's ADHD was not of itself enough to satisfy the defence: *Osborne* [2010] EWCA Crim 547 where D killed V in an unprovoked attack in anger and his illness was not a cause of the conduct.

[260] *Byrne*, n 225; *Simcox* [1964] Crim LR 402; *Lloyd* [1967] 1 QB 175. But cf R Sparks, 'Diminished Responsibility in Theory and Practice' (1964) 27 MLR 9, 16–19.

[261] *Campbell* (1986) 84 Cr App R 255 at 259.

[262] A person whose impulse is irresistible bears *no* moral responsibility for his act, for he has no choice; a person whose impulse is much more difficult to resist than that of an ordinary person bears a diminished degree of moral responsibility for his act.

[263] [1967] 1 QB 175.   [264] [1964] Crim LR 402.   [265] [2010] EWCA Crim 194, [15].

[266] [2016] UKSC 61.   [267] [2016] UKSC 61, [43].

to the contrary, Parliament was to be taken to have adopted the established sense in which the word 'substantially' had been used. The court observed that:

(1) Ordinarily in a murder trial where diminished responsibility is in issue the judge need not direct the jury beyond the terms of the statute and should not attempt to define the meaning of 'substantially'. Experience has shown that the issue of its correct interpretation is unlikely to arise in many cases. The jury should normally be given to understand that the expression is an ordinary English word, that it imports a question of degree, and that whether in the case before it the impairment can properly be described as substantial is for it to resolve.

(2) If, however, the jury has been introduced to the question of whether *any* impairment beyond the merely trivial will suffice, or if it has been introduced to the concept of a spectrum between the greater than trivial and the total, the judge should explain that whilst the impairment must indeed pass the merely trivial before it need be considered, it is not the law that *any* impairment beyond the trivial will suffice. The judge should likewise make this clear if a risk arises that the jury might misunderstand the import of the expression; whether this risk arises or not is a judgment to be arrived at by the trial judge who is charged with overseeing the dynamics of the trial. Diminished responsibility involves an impairment of one or more of the abilities listed in the statute to an extent which the jury judges to be substantial, and which it is satisfied significantly contributed to his committing the offence. Illustrative expressions of the sense of the word may be employed so long as the jury is given clearly to understand that no single synonym is to be substituted for the statutory word. . . .[268]

The Supreme Court's judgment was surprising given that Lord Judge CJ seemed to have adopted the more generous interpretation of 'substantial' in *Ramchurn*. It is submitted that there are a number of problems with the judgment in *Golds*. First, the Supreme Court's conclusion serves to narrow the defence, which has already been narrowed by its more medicalized recasting in 2009. Gibson cogently argues that the judgment, 'unduly compromises access to diminished responsibility'.[269] Limiting access to the partial defence could have harsh consequences. Professor Mackay gives the example of a post-natal mother who kills her 13-month-old child and who, because the child is older than 12 months, cannot rely upon the statutory defence of infanticide. She may also be unable to rely upon diminished responsibility because the psychiatrists and/or the jury consider the degree of impairment insufficient to reach the level now required by *Golds*.[270] Secondly, it is not clear that the decision is faithful to its own premise. The Supreme Court states that 'substantial' is an ordinary English word, with the consequence that the jury needs no assistance understanding its interpretation. However, if during the course of the trial someone has suggested otherwise, the jury are not simply to be told it is an ordinary English word but are to be given a further definition. If there is a technical definition that juries ought to adopt beyond the 'ordinary English one', why should every jury not hear it in all cases from the outset? Consequently, this may risk an inconsistent application of the law; some juries may receive an extended definition whereas others will not. Finally, the decision may generate more appeals. There is little to be lost in appealing a murder conviction in any event, but in the light of the vagueness of the basic instruction to the jury—to draw the line of 'substantially impaired' according to degree—future appeals on this point seem unavoidable.

---

[268] At [43].

[269] M Gibson, 'Diminished Responsibility in *Golds* and Beyond: Insights and Implications' [2017] Crim LR 543.

[270] RD Mackay, '*R v Golds*' [2017] 1 Arch Rev 4.

Despite its shortcoming, the courts have faithfully applied *Golds*. For example, in *Squelch*[271] three forensic psychiatrists agreed that S suffered from paranoid personality disorder (PPD), that he had an abnormality of mental functioning arising from that condition which had played some part in the killing. They disagreed, however, on whether the condition had substantially impaired S's ability to do one or more of the things listed in s 2 of the Homicide Act 1957. Two considered that it had, but the third concluded that the impairment was not substantial, only that it might be a partial cause for the incident. The judge directed the jury that:

'substantially' is an ordinary English word on which you will reach a conclusion in this case, based upon your own experience of ordinary life. It means less than total and more than trivial. Where you, the jury, draw the line is a matter for your collective judgment.

The Court of Appeal commended the judge's direction as concise and accurate.

Under the current formulation of the law, D has to show a substantial impairment of his ability to do one or more of these:

(1) to understand the nature of his own conduct;

(2) to form a rational judgement;

(3) to exercise self-control.[272]

Whether D has these abilities is a matter of psychiatry. The question is whether there is a 'substantial impairment' of one or more of these. It is submitted that it is a psychiatric question how far D's ability deviates from the normal level of ability to do those things. Giving the medical expert a greater role to play in this regard does not take the determination of the ultimate issue away from the jury, but merely ensures that they reach a verdict that is informed by medical expertise rather than intuition.[273]

If (1) and (2) are construed narrowly, they will be very similar to insanity and hence may be difficult for D to satisfy. If they are akin to insanity, in many cases D might well plead that complete defence rather than the partial defence of diminished responsibility.

To understand the nature of D's conduct

As commentators have observed, this is similar to the first limb of the insanity plea.[274] An example of how this element might be satisfied provided by the Law Commission[275] was of a ten-year-old boy with a recognized medical condition:[276]

who has been left to play very violent video games for hours on end for much of his life, loses his temper and kills another child when the child attempts to take a game from him. When interviewed, he shows no real understanding that, when a person is killed they cannot simply be later revived, as happens in the games he has been continually playing.

One aspect of this element of the defence is that the focus is exclusively on whether D has the ability to understand the nature of his own conduct; it does not encompass his ability to understand anyone else's. Will this accommodate D who believes that his victim is, for example, possessed? Does this apply to the person with a very distorted thinking process?

---

[271] [2017] EWCA Crim 204. For further discussion, see Gibson, n 269.

[272] See *Byrne* [1960] 2 QB 396; and *Khan* [2009] EWCA Crim 1569.

[273] See also the suggestion of LC 304, para 5.198 that it will be a question for the jury. See the most recent research by Mackay and Mitchell examining how often experts' reports deal with these matters, see n 221 and RD Mackay, 'The Impairment Factors in the New Diminished Responsibility Plea' [2018] Crim LR 462.

[274] See Mackay, n 216.   [275] LC 304, para 5.21.

[276] To reflect the provision as enacted we must amend the example so that he has an *abnormality* of mental functioning.

Baroness Murphy raised doubts about these in Parliament,[277] and such cases may be difficult to fit within limb (1).

Substantially impaired capacity to form a rational judgement
Examples from the Law Commission included:

(1) a woman who has been diagnosed as being in a state of learned helplessness consequent upon violent abuse suffered at her husband's hands comes to believe that only burning her husband to death will rid the world of his sins;

(2) a mentally subnormal boy believes that he must follow his older brother's instructions, even when they involve taking part in a killing. He says, 'I wouldn't dream of disobeying my brother and he would never tell me to do something if it was really wrong';

(3) a depressed man who has been caring for many years for a terminally ill spouse, kills her, at her request. He says that he had found it progressively more difficult to stop her repeated requests dominating his thoughts to the exclusion of all else, so that 'I felt I would never think straight again until I had given her what she wanted.'

In addition, Lord Judge CJ in *Clinton* observed that D's discovery that his partner has been sexually unfaithful may, and often will, be said to impair his ability to form a rational judgement (and/or exercise control).[278]

The case of *Conroy*[279] suggests that understanding the ability to form a rational judgement should not be 'over-refined'. The Court of Appeal held that the ability to form a rational judgement connotes not only rationality of outcome, but also rationality of thought process in achieving that outcome. All of a defendant's 'relevant circumstances preceding (and perhaps preceding over a very long period) the killing as well as any relevant circumstances following the killing',[280] can be taken into account. D submitted that the trial judge's summing up had significantly misdirected the jury because s 2 of the 1957 Act refers to the 'ability to form a rational judgment', requiring some rationality as to the final judgment, not the 'ability rationally to form a judgment'. The Court of Appeal dismissed the appeal and stated:

As it seems to us, while of course any jury will need in the light of the available psychiatric evidence to assess a defendant's thinking processes in the context of assessing his ability to form a rational judgment, it is likely to be over-refined to divorce that consideration relating to a defendant's thinking processes from the actual outcome. Indeed, in some cases it may actually be extremely difficult to separate out the thought processes on the one hand from the 'outcome' on the other hand. In some cases it may well be that the two may be entirely enmeshed. In our view, there is a potential danger in a direction such as this straying beyond what is actually stated in section 2 itself. The elements of section 2 should so far as possible not be glossed in a summing-up to the jury.[281]

The courts seem willing to take a wide interpretation of what constitutes a substantial impairment of the ability to form a rational judgement. In *Blackman*,[282] for example, the Court Martial Appeal Court (CMAC) found that, despite B's immediate recognition and admission that his actions in shooting a wounded Afghan insurgent constituted a breach of the Geneva Convention, his ability to form a rational judgement was substantially impaired.

---

277 Hansard, HL, 30 June 2009, vol 712, col 180.
278 At [33]. Note that the defence also requires proof of the recognized medical condition, etc.
279 [2017] EWCA Crim 81, [37].   280 ibid, [32].   281 At [37] per Davis LJ.
282 [2017] EWCA Crim 190 (CMAC).

The ability to exercise control

This might be construed very much more widely and render the defence available in a broader range of circumstances than under (1) and (2). As Rudi Fortson points out, it might be difficult to distinguish between cases of actual impairment of D's ability to exercise self-control from cases where D chose not to control his conduct.[283] It was acknowledged in *Blackman* that the defendant's ability to exercise self-control may be sufficiently impaired even where no loss of self-control is externally discernible. In that case, despite the deliberate nature of B's actions, the court still felt that he had exhibited a substantial loss of self-control.

(4) An explanation for (or cause of) the killing

The defence is narrowed by the further requirement that the abnormality of mental functioning, arising from a 'recognised medical condition' substantially impairing D's ability in a relevant manner must also 'explain' his acts in killing. By s 2(1B) 'an explanation' for D's conduct is provided 'if it causes, or is a significant contributory factor in causing, D to carry out that conduct'. Several problems arise. Section 2(1B) does not say that for the defence to succeed a sufficient explanation can *only* be provided if the abnormality of mental functioning is a 'cause'.[284] On this basis, a causal link is just one of the ways in which the killing might be explained. It has been suggested that the medical experts could agree that all the other elements of the defence are present, but then disagree about the presence of this one. Mackay argues that one way of circumventing this difficulty is for the courts to interpret this provision so that once all the other elements are established it is assumed that it is present also, unless there is evidence to the contrary.[285]

Although the wording of s 2(1B) might lend itself to the argument that the subsection provides merely one way in which the killing might be 'explained', the language of the parliamentary debates was clearly envisaging a causal link, although not necessarily 'but for' causation. In describing this element of the partial defence, the Supreme Court in *Golds* also used language that connoted the existence of some causal link. There may be cases where the abnormality provides an explanation sufficient to mitigate the conduct to manslaughter even if there is no causal link but it contributes in some way. In debates, the minister stated that:

> We do not believe that the partial defence should succeed where random coincidence has brought together the activity of the person and the recognised medical condition. . . . *[T]here must have been at least a significant contributory factor in causing the defendant to act as he did. We do not require the defence to prove that it was the only cause or the main cause or the most important factor, but there must be something that is more than a merely trivial factor.*[286]

Even if it is accepted that there must be some causal link, it is clear that the abnormality of mental functioning, etc need not be the sole cause of the killing. The Law Commission was clear that, for example, provocation might also be a relevant factor that caused D to kill. The government agreed with the Law Commission that it would be 'impracticable to require abnormality to be the sole explanation [for D's acts]' and that there must be 'some

---

[283] R Fortson, 'The Modern Partial Defence of Diminished Responsibility' in A Reed and M Bohlander (eds), *Loss of Control and Diminished Responsibility* (2011). As he also points out, given that the burden of proof is on the defendant, the problem weighs most heavily on his shoulders.

[284] See further *Blackstone's Criminal Practice* (2021) B1.

[285] See RD Mackay, 'The New Diminished Responsibility Plea: More than Mere Modernisation?' in A Reed and M Bohlander (eds), *Loss of Control and Diminished Responsibility*. See also RD Mackay [2021] Crim LR 442.

[286] Hansard, HC, 4 Mar 2009, col 416. Emphasis added.

connection between the condition and the killing in order for the partial defence to be justified'.[287]

Some commentators suggest[288] that s 2(1B) may be merely giving effect to the interpretation of the old s 2 in *Dietschmann*[289] and *Fenton*.[290] Under the old law, in *Dietschmann*[291] D killed the victim while D was heavily intoxicated. He was also suffering from a mental abnormality which all the medical witnesses described as an adjustment disorder arising from a 'depressed grief reaction' to the death of his aunt with whom he had a close physical and emotional relationship. In the House of Lords, Lord Hutton stressed that:[292] 'even if the defendant would not have killed if he had not taken drink, the causative effect of the drink does not necessarily prevent an abnormality of mind suffered by the defendant from substantially impairing his mental responsibility for his fatal acts'.[293] In other words, even if a factor (in that case, alcohol) other than the abnormality was the principal cause of the defendant killing V, the defence would be available. Adopting that approach to the section as amended in 2009, it would not matter that the abnormality of mental functioning from a recognized medical condition was not the principal cause of the killing.

Since the 2009 Act has been in force, the Court of Appeal has commented on this issue. In *Kay and Joyce*, the court stated that the killing must be caused by, or significantly caused by, the recognized medical condition. Therefore, an intoxicated defendant who would have killed even if he had not been suffering an abnormality will not be entitled to the defence.

Some commentators challenge the need for any causal element. Why should D have to prove a causal link given that the abnormality of mental functioning must be proved under s 2(1A) to have substantially impaired D's ability to understand his conduct or form a rational judgement or exercise control *in relation to the acts or omissions*, that is, killing?[294]

Intoxicated defendants

The issue of the extent to which there must be a causal link between the abnormal mental functioning and the killing is most likely to arise in cases where D kills when he suffers from an abnormality of mental functioning and at the time of the killing D had also taken alcohol or other intoxicants. The law on this issue has been helpfully summarised in *Foy*.[295]

As noted, in *Dietschmann* the House of Lords accepted that if a voluntarily intoxicated defendant kills, he is entitled to rely on diminished responsibility if the elements of the defence are made out even though he was intoxicated at the time of the killing. Subsequently in *Wood*[296] the Court of Appeal applied this reasoning to a case where D was suffering from alcohol dependency syndrome. D stated that giving in to his alcohol craving was not an involuntary act, and argued that an alcoholic not suffering from severe withdrawal symptoms who chose to accept a drink after he reached his normal quota was not drinking 'involuntarily'.[297] The Court of Appeal held that in the light of the decision in *Dietschmann* it was wrong to imply that unless the jury were of the opinion that every drink consumed by D was involuntary his alcohol dependency syndrome had to be disregarded. That was too strict an

---

[287] CP 19/08, para 51; and see Hansard, HC, 3 Mar 2009, col 414 (Maria Eagle).

[288] For discussion, see R Fortson, 'The Modern Partial Defence of Diminished Responsibility' in A Reed and M Bohlander (eds), *Loss of Control and Diminished Responsibility* (2011).   [289] [2003] 1 AC 1209.

[290] (1975) 61 Cr App R 26; *Gittins* [1984] QB 698.   [291] [2003] 1 AC 1209.

[292] Note that this case did not involve alcohol dependence syndrome.   [293] At [18].

[294] See Mackay [2010] Crim LR 299 and n 285.   [295] [2020] EWCA Crim 270, see at [70]–[76].

[296] [2008] EWCA Crim 1305. See also *Stewart* [2010] EWCA Crim 2159.

[297] The trial judge directed in accordance with *Tandy* [1989] 1 All ER 267 which drew distinctions between alcoholism that caused brain damage and otherwise. For critical comment see J Tolmie, 'Alcoholism and Criminal Liability' (2001) 64 MLR 688.

approach. The jury could have regard to D's alcoholism in considering the plea of diminished responsibility even if not every drink consumed that day by D was involuntary.[298]

The position under the new form of the defence was considered by the Court of Appeal in *Kay and Joyce*, in which the court confirmed that 'the law does not debar someone suffering from schizophrenia [the medical condition in this case] from relying on the partial defence of diminished responsibility where voluntary intoxication has triggered the psychotic state, but he must meet the criteria in section 2(1)'.[299] The court held that the authorities in *Dietschmann* and *Wood* apply with equal force to the amended version of diminished responsibility as they did under the former version. On the facts, there was no medical evidence available to K to show that his underlying illness was of such a degree that, independent of drug or alcohol abuse, it impaired his responsibility substantially. Therefore, once the jury rejected the defence's assertion that K was suffering from alcohol dependency syndrome, he no longer had a defence.

In *Foy*,[300] Davis LJ[301] again confirmed that under s 2 as amended by the 2009 Act, the abnormality of mental functioning did not need to be the sole cause of D's acts in killing: even if D would not have killed had he not taken alcohol, the causative effect of the drink does not necessarily prevent an abnormality of mind from substantially impairing the mental responsibility for the fatal acts.

Applying the policy behind *Dietschmann* and *Wood*, as endorsed with reference to the amended defence in *Kay and Joyce*,[302] and *Foy* the position is as follows:

(1) Where D has no medical condition other than acute intoxication, he cannot rely on the defence as there is no recognized medical condition: *Dowds*. If the voluntary intoxication (whether by alcohol and/or drugs) induces a psychotic episode, then there is no recognized medical condition: *Foy*.

(2) Where D suffers from a recognized medical condition other than alcohol dependency syndrome and is voluntarily intoxicated at the time of the killing,[303] the defence will succeed if D proves: that it is more probable than not that, ignoring his voluntary intoxication, that he suffered an abnormality of mental functioning arising from a 'recognised medical condition' so as to substantially impair his ability in a relevant way, and that abnormality of mental functioning was a cause, or a significant contributing factor, of the conduct by which D killed, even if D might not have killed had he been sober, provided the abnormality of mental functioning arising from the 'recognised medical condition' nevertheless 'explains' or 'causes' his conduct in killing.

(3) Where D suffers from a recognized medical condition in the form of alcohol dependency syndrome and is intoxicated at the time of the killing, the same approach should be taken. The jury should be entitled to have regard to the alcohol dependency syndrome and D's intoxication, leaving out of account, insofar as it is possible, his voluntary intoxication. D is entitled to the defence if he proves he suffered an abnormality of mental functioning arising from a 'recognised medical condition' so

---

[298] This approach was more confirmed as being the correct one in *Williams* [2013] EWCA Crim 2749, a reference by the CCRC under the old law.

[299] [2017] EWCA Crim 647, [16].   [300] [2010] EWCA Crim 270.

[301] His lordship also noted that the courts could have adopted a completely opposite but 'principled approach' to say that the defence is not available in such cases since the defendant voluntarily chose to take the intoxicant and must take the consequences. That would be consistent with the general principle of law, on policy grounds, that self-induced intoxication ordinarily is of itself no defence. At [73].

[302] [2017] EWCA Crim. See K Laird, '*R v Kay and Joyce*' [2017] Crim LR 881.

[303] But not suffering from acute intoxication which is not a recognized medical condition.

as to substantially impair his ability in a relevant way, and that abnormality of mental functioning explains or was a cause of the conduct by which D killed.[304]

(4) In categories (2) and (3), if an intoxicated defendant with a recognized medical condition would have killed even if he had not had an abnormality of mental functioning, the availability of the defence depends on whether s 2(1B) is interpreted as requiring proof of a causal link in every case. If a causal link is required, a voluntarily intoxicated defendant who would have killed even if he had not been suffering an abnormality will not be entitled to the defence. If, on the other hand, s 2(1B) is interpreted as meaning that the abnormality might explain the killing even if it did not cause it, the defence may be available. This is most likely to be relevant where the ability substantially impaired under s 2(1A) 'was D's ability to form a rational judgement rather than to exercise self-control'.[305]

The amendment to s 2 of the 1957 Act by the 2009 Act does not diminish the authority of cases such as *Byrne* and *Dix*,[306] confirming that medical evidence was a 'practical necessity' if the defence were to succeed.[307] This has been confirmed in *Bunch*[308] and by the Privy Council's opinion in the Jamaican case of *Brown*.[309]

Must D's medical condition cause the killing?

As to proof of a causal link generally, in many cases the causal link between the abnormality of mental functioning and D's act of killing, or being a party to the killing, may be self-evident. It is not going to be easy to prove that an intoxicated defendant with an abnormality of mind would have killed even if he had not had an abnormality of mental functioning.[310] Some commentators have questioned whether 'from a psychiatric perspective proving even a contributory causal link can be extremely difficult, if not impossible, to do in practice'.[311] Moreover, although the Royal College of Psychiatrists did not object to the requirement, it cautioned against 'creating a situation in which experts might be called on to "demonstrate" causation on a scientific basis, rather than indicating, from an assessment of the nature of the abnormality, what its likely impact would be on thinking, emotion, volition, and so forth'.[312]

The prior fault policy

The Court of Appeal's approach to intoxication and diminished responsibility is heavily influenced by the policy against allowing D to rely on his intoxicated state when it is self-induced. It is unclear, however, how fair that policy can be when it is taken in priority to the recognition of the medical condition.

The following situations may arise:

(1) D is acutely intoxicated and that is the sole claim of a recognized medical condition—no defence: *Dowds* adopting the prior fault policy.

(2) D suffers from a recognized medical condition and is intoxicated at the time of the killing—defence may be available: *Dietschmann, Kay, Foy* etc. D's recognized medical condition is not ousted by his also being voluntarily intoxicated.

---

[304] See especially *Stewart* [2009] EWCA Crim 593.
[305] See further *Blackstone's Criminal Practice* (2021) Part B1, 24.
[306] [1960] 2 QB 396 and (1982) 74 Cr App R 306 respectively.   [307] At [11].
[308] [2013] EWCA Crim 2498.   [309] [2016] UKPC 6.
[310] Even if D made an admission to that effect, how much reliance is to be placed on a confession made by someone who has an abnormality of mental functioning?
[311] J Miles, 'A Dog's Breakfast of Homicide Reform' [2009] 6 Arch News 8 and see the speech of Baroness Murphy, Hansard, HL, 30 June 2009, cols 177–80.   [312] LC 304, para 5.123.

(3) D's recognized medical condition was caused by his chronic substance misuse (eg he has developed alcohol dependency syndrome) and D was intoxicated at the time of the killing—defence may be available (this is merely an example of (2), but in the context of D's sustained 'fault' in his substance abuse bringing about the recognized medical condition).

(4) An underlying recognized medical condition suffered by D is triggered by his voluntary intoxication. For example, D has schizophrenia and is aware of that fact. He takes drugs voluntarily and triggers a schizophrenic episode. In such a case the defence is available, even if D was warned that taking drugs may trigger the schizophrenia: *Kay*.

(5) D's voluntary intoxication causes a drug induced psychosis (a recognised medical condition) where there was no pre-existing recognized medical condition—no defence: *Dowds, Lindo, Foy*.

It may seem odd that D can rely on the defence in (3) despite the fact that his sustained prior fault caused the recognized medical condition. It may also seem odd that D can rely on the defence in (4) where there is a considerable degree of prior fault in D triggering an existing recognized medical condition, but not in (5). Is the degree of prior fault in (5) that much greater than (4), or even (3)? It is submitted that these issues merit further consideration by the Court of Appeal.

13.2.2.2 The role of the expert and the jury

There is no statutory requirement of medical evidence, as there is with insanity, but surely the jury may not find that D is suffering from diminished responsibility unless there is medical evidence of a recognized medical condition and abnormality of mental functioning.[313] Indeed, in *Brennan*[314] Davis LJ stated that, 'most, if not all, of the aspects of the new provisions relate entirely to psychiatric matters. In our view it is both legitimate and helpful, given the structure of the new provisions, for an expert psychiatrist to include in his or her evidence a view on all four stages'. Under the old law, as with insanity,[315] whether the defence succeeded was a decision to be made by the jury, not the medical experts. They could reject unanimous medical evidence that D is suffering from diminished responsibility if there is nothing in the circumstances of the case to prevent them doing so.[316] The extent to which the jury remains free to do this will be considered later.

Under the old law, the 'abnormality of mind' element was a matter on which the psychiatric evidence was likely to be highly persuasive, but because the concept was a vague one, there was still an opportunity for the jury to apply its own understanding of the concept. Similarly, the crucial element of the old s 2 test involved moral rather than medical or legal evaluation: the 'substantial impairment' related not just to D's mental state, but to his 'responsibility'. In contrast, under the amended partial defence the expert may be offering opinions on: (a) whether there is an abnormality of mental functioning; (b) whether there is a recognized medical condition; (c) whether D had a substantial impairment of ability to understand/form a rational judgement/exercise control; and (d) whether it is a cause

---

[313] Medical evidence was required under the old law, indeed it was described as being a 'practical necessity' because the onus is placed on the defendant: *Byrne* [1960] 2 QB 396 at 402; *Dix* (1981) 74 Cr App R 306 at 311. The Court of Appeal in *Bunch* [2013] EWCA Crim 2498 confirmed the continued validity of *Byrne*. For further discussion, see T Storey, 'Diminished Responsibility: No Defence Without Evidence' (2014) 78 J Crim L 113.

[314] [2014] EWCA Crim 2387, [51].

[315] See p 308.

[316] eg *Salmon* [2005] EWCA Crim 70; *Eifinger* [2001] EWCA Crim 1855; cf the position if there was uncontradicted expert evidence and no other live issue: *Sanders* [1991] Crim LR 781. See generally LCCP 177, para 6.99.

or explanation for the killing. The Royal College of Psychiatrists expressed the view that medical experts ought not to be called upon to express an opinion on the 'ultimate issue'.[317] However, it is submitted that, in practice, it will often be difficult for an expert not to express an opinion from which it will be possible for the jury to draw a very clear inference as to the ultimate issue.

On one view, since the elements of the defence are now *all* capable of being subject to an opinion from an expert, there is much less, if anything, for the jury to consider, particularly if there was uncontradicted medical evidence for the defence. On the other hand, the courts may well continue to take the view that although the elements of the defence are now all capable of being subject to strong opinion evidence from an expert, the ultimate issue remains one for the jury. They must consider all the evidence, and the opinion of the expert is only that: an opinion. As was noted under the old law in *Walton v The Queen*:[318]

upon an issue of diminished responsibility the jury are entitled and indeed bound to consider not only the medical evidence but the evidence upon the whole facts and circumstances of the case.[319]

The Court of Appeal confronted this issue with reference to the amended partial defence in *Brennan*[320] and the Supreme Court considered it in *Golds*.

In *Brennan*, D was convicted of murder despite the fact that there was uncontradicted evidence from the experts that all the elements of the partial defence were satisfied. There was some evidence to suggest that V's murder was well planned. The defence expert, who was the only expert called, stated that such planning was not inconsistent with her finding that all the elements of the partial defence were satisfied, rather it was a facet of the mental condition from which D was suffering. Davis LJ characterized the case as one that brought to the fore two conflicting, but equally fundamental, principles. The first is that the ultimate issue on whether the partial defence is satisfied is a matter for the jury. The second is that the jury must base its verdict upon the evidence.[321] Davis LJ held that the experts can and should express a view on the ultimate issue. After reviewing the authorities analysed in this section, his lordship held that the judge ought to withdraw the murder charge from the jury if (a) the expert evidence is uncontested and (b) there is no other evidence which, looked at in the round, is at least capable of rebutting the defence.[322] In relation to this latter point, Davis LJ stated that even if there is some other evidence that might rebut the defence, there might be instances when that other evidence is too tenuous or, even if taken at its highest, is simply insufficient to permit a rational rejection of the partial defence.

In *Golds*,[323] the Supreme Court examined the reasoning in *Brennan*. The court commented, *obiter*, on the circumstances in which a judge should withdraw murder from the jury where there is uncontradicted medical evidence of diminished responsibility. The court made the preliminary observation that if a murder trial is contested, it is of considerable importance that the verdict be that of the jury. Therefore, despite the more medicalized nature of the amended partial defence, the Supreme Court affirmed in unequivocal terms that it is for the jury to determine whether all the elements are satisfied. The court also observed that the presence of a causal link between the mental abnormality and the killing and whether the impairment was substantial are elements of the partial defence that are essentially jury questions.

---

[317] Paras 5.118–5.120; and see *Khan* [2009] EWCA Crim 1569.   [318] [1978] AC 788.

[319] Lord Keith (at 793F), and see *Khan* [2009] EWCA Crim 1569, noting, in particular, the observations of the court at [18].

[320] [2014] EWCA Crim 2387.   [321] At [43]–[44].   [322] At [65]–[66].   [323] [2016] UKSC 61.

Lord Hughes offered the following, valuable guidance:

Where, however, in a diminished responsibility trial the medical evidence supports the plea and is uncontradicted, the judge needs to ensure that the Crown explains the basis on which it is inviting the jury to reject that evidence. He needs to ensure that the basis advanced is one which the jury can properly adopt. If the facts of the case give rise to it, he needs to warn the jury that brutal killings may be the product of disordered minds and that planning, whilst it may be relevant to self-control, may well be consistent with disordered thinking. While he needs to make it clear to the jury that, if there is a proper basis for rejecting the expert evidence, the decision is theirs—that trial is by jury and not by expert—it will also ordinarily be wise to advise the jury against attempting to make themselves amateur psychiatrists, and that if there is undisputed expert evidence the jury will probably wish to accept it, unless there is some identified reason for not doing so. To this extent, the approach of the court in *Brennan* is to be endorsed.[324]

The point was reiterated subsequently in *Blackman*, in which the Lord Chief Justice emphasized that the judge should exercise caution before accepting the applicability of the partial defence and removing the murder charge from the jury. It was held that the fact the prosecution call no evidence to contradict a psychiatrist called by the defence is not in itself sufficient justification for the judge to take that course of action. His lordship stated that, 'it will be a rare case where a judge will exercise the power to withdraw a charge of murder from the jury when the prosecution do not accept that the evidence gives rise to the defence of diminished responsibility'.[325] A more recent example of this principle in operation is *Hussain*,[326] in which the Court of Appeal held that the trial judge was right not to withdraw the murder charge from the jury despite the unanimous expert evidence. The court stated that the prosecution was entitled to invite the jury to reject the expert evidence on the basis that the defendant did not complain about symptoms said to indicate paranoid schizophrenia until he had been asked if he heard voices and he realized the extent of the evidence against him. Similarly, in *Sargeant*[327] the Court of Appeal accepted that the prosecution was able to advance a rational basis for contending that the defendant's ability to exercise self-control had not been substantially impaired, namely that it was a case of loss of temper in the context of a dispute about money rather than a loss of self-control. There was other evidence relied upon by the prosecution to show that the defendant was in control of herself and was looking for ways to avoid the consequences of what she had done.

13.2.2.3 Procedural relationship with insanity

One might assume that defendants charged with murder who have killed with malice aforethought would prefer a conviction for manslaughter on the ground of diminished responsibility to an acquittal by reason of insanity, and that would explain why reliance on the M'Naghten Rules has been greatly reduced since 1957 (see Ch 9). Where D, being charged with murder, raises the defence of diminished responsibility and the Crown have evidence that he is insane within the M'Naghten Rules, they may adduce or elicit evidence tending to show that this is so. This is now settled by s 6 of the Criminal Procedure (Insanity and Unfitness to Plead) Act 1964[328]—resolving a conflict in the cases. That Act also provides

---

[324] At [51]. In *Hussain* [2019] EWCA Crim 666, the Court of Appeal stated that in future it did not expect reliance to be placed on any judgment predating *Golds* on this issue.

[325] [2017] EWCA Crim 190 (CMAC), [43].   [326] [2019] EWCA Crim 666.

[327] [2019] EWCA Crim 1088.

[328] By s 52(2) of the 2009 Act, 'In section 6 of the Criminal Procedure (Insanity) Act 1964 (c. 84) (evidence by prosecution of insanity or diminished responsibility), in paragraph (b) for "mind" substitute "mental functioning".'

for the converse situation: where D sets up insanity, the prosecution may contend that he was suffering only from diminished responsibility.[329] The roles of the prosecution and defence may be strangely reversed, according to which of them are contending that D is insane. It seems clear in principle that the Crown must establish whichever contention it puts forward is beyond reasonable doubt.[330] It must follow that D rebuts the Crown's case if he can raise a doubt.[331] Where D relies on some other defence, such as loss of self-control, and evidence of diminished responsibility emerges, it seems that the most the judge should do is to draw the attention of D's counsel to it.[332] Diminished responsibility is an 'optional defence'. The defences of loss of self-control and diminished responsibility overlap in some respects,[333] and this can lead to a complex decision regarding trial tactics since the defences carry differing burdens. Similarly, a jury will have to be directed carefully on the respective burdens.

Where the defence rely on D's abnormal state of mind of whatever kind, it is open to the prosecution to allege, and to call evidence to prove, that the abnormality amounts to insanity or diminished responsibility and it is submitted this is so even where D is alleging that he was an automaton. This view is supported by the fact that the CLRC[334] was of the view that the prosecution could call evidence in cases such as *Kemp*.[335] The prosecution may not, however, lead evidence of D's insanity where the defence have not put the abnormality of D's mind in issue,[336] even though this course is desired by the defence.

Sentencing

The sentence available to the judge is discretionary with the maximum sentence being life imprisonment.[337] The available disposals on conviction are not something for the jury's consideration: *Edgington*.[338]

Further reading

A Ashworth and B Mitchell (eds), *Rethinking English Homicide Law*

C Clarkson and S Cunningham (eds), *Criminal Liability for Non-Aggressive Death*

J Horder, *Provocation and Responsibility*

A Reed and M Bohlander (eds), *Loss of Control and Diminished Responsibility: Domestic, Comparative and International Perspectives*

---

[329] It had been so held at common law by Elwes J in *Nott* (1958) 43 Cr App R 8.

[330] *Grant* [1960] Crim LR 424, per Paull J.

[331] In *Ranwell* (2019) 21 November, Exeter CC, May J ruled that s 6 does not affect the burden of proof.

[332] *Campbell* (1986) 84 Cr App R 255 at 259–60; *Kooken* (1981) 74 Cr App R 30.

[333] On the merits of such overlap and a potential merging of the defences under the old law before the 2009 Act, see Mackay and Mitchell [2003] Crim LR 745; Chalmers [2004] Crim LR 198; Gardner and Macklem [2004] Crim LR 213; Mackay and Mitchell [2004] Crim LR 219.

[334] (1963) Cmnd 2149, para 41.

[335] See p 310.

[336] *Dixon* [1961] 1 WLR 337, per Jones J.

[337] The Sentencing Council issued a definitive guideline in 2019. For discussion, see M Wasik, 'Reflections on the Manslaughter Sentencing Guidelines' [2019] Crim LR 315.

[338] [2013] EWCA Crim 2185.

14
Involuntary manslaughter

In the previous chapter we considered those categories of manslaughter in which the defendant has been proved to have killed with the mens rea for murder, but has a partial defence which results in a manslaughter verdict. In this chapter we consider the other forms of manslaughter—known collectively as involuntary manslaughter. This category of manslaughter includes varieties of homicide which are unlawful at common law but committed without the mens rea for murder. Given the breadth of cases that involuntary manslaughter must cover, it is not surprising that more than one form of the offence has evolved, and that the elements of each form of involuntary manslaughter are distinct, particularly as to the fault required. Equally, as the limits of the mens rea for murder are uncertain, it follows inevitably that there is a corresponding uncertainty at the boundary between murder and manslaughter. The difficulties do not end there, for there is another vague borderline between manslaughter and accidental death. Indeed, Lord Atkin observed:[1]

of all crimes manslaughter appears to afford most difficulties of definition, for it concerns homicide in so many and so varying conditions . . . the law . . . recognizes murder on the one hand based mainly, though not exclusively,[2] on an intention to kill, and manslaughter on the other hand, based mainly, though not exclusively,[3] on the absence of intent to kill, but with the presence of an element of 'unlawfulness' which is the elusive factor.

This ambiguity is unfortunate, since the offence is one of the most serious in the criminal calendar and carries a maximum life sentence. The upper and lower limits of the offence remain obscure, and there is little internal coherence between the forms of manslaughter currently recognized—other than the fact that D causes a death. Lumping together the many different types of behaviour that give rise to an unintentional unlawful killing under one label is unsatisfactory in principle, and can engender unmerited disparities in sentencing.[4] The Law Commission concluded that the offence of manslaughter was at risk of being devalued by being left as a 'residual, amorphous, "catch-all" homicide offence'.[5]

The forms of manslaughter overlap considerably. There are four broad categories of involuntary manslaughter:

(1) manslaughter by an unlawful and dangerous act;

(2) manslaughter by gross negligence;

(3) manslaughter by subjective recklessness;

(4) statutory corporate manslaughter.

The constituents of each of these categories require some degree of analysis.

14.1 Manslaughter by an unlawful and dangerous act

The modern form of this offence has evolved from a very harsh one dating to at least the seventeenth century.

By way of a brief overview of the history, the institutional writer Coke stated that an intention to commit *any* unlawful act was a sufficient mens rea for murder,[6] so that if D shot at V's hen with intent to kill it and accidentally killed V by the shot, this was murder, 'for the act was unlawful'. This savage doctrine was criticized by Holt CJ[7] and by the time Foster wrote his *Crown Law*,[8] it appears to have been modified by the proviso that to constitute murder the unlawful act which D intended to carry out had to be a felony (and not merely a misdemeanour or civil law wrong such as a tort). So, if D shot at the hen intending to steal it

---

[1] In *Andrews v DPP* [1937] AC 576 at 581.

[2] See p 535.   [3] See Ch 14.

[4] See M Wasik, 'Form and Function in the Law of Involuntary Manslaughter' [1994] Crim LR 883. But note that the Sentencing Council Definitive Guideline distinguishes them clearly.

[5] LC 304, para 2.9. To avoid drawing an arbitrary line between murder and manslaughter, the Commission recommended a middle tier of second degree murder. See Ch 12. For an argument that there ought to be aggravated murder and aggravated manslaughter to reflect different forms of killing, see C Elliot and C de Than (2009) 20 King's College Journal 69.

[6] Co 3 Inst 56. See Turner, MACL, 195 at 212 et seq for a discussion of the historical development.

[7] *Keate* (1697) Comb 406 at 409.   [8] *Discourses* (1762).

(a felony), the killing of V was murder even though D did not intend to kill any human. This doctrine of 'constructive murder' existed until the Homicide Act 1957. Alongside this doctrine of constructive murder, there existed a parallel doctrine of constructive manslaughter: any death caused while in the course of committing an unlawful act, other than a felony, was manslaughter. An act was unlawful for this purpose even if it was only a tort, so that the only mens rea which needed to be proved was an intention to commit the tort.

The present law is that D is guilty of unlawful act manslaughter (UAM) if he kills by an unlawful and dangerous act. The only mens rea required is an intention to do the unlawful act and any fault required to render it unlawful. It is irrelevant that D is unaware that it is unlawful or that it is dangerous.[9] It is enough that a reasonable and sober person would have been aware of the danger in the sense of a risk of some harm (not necessarily serious harm) to a person.[10] The offence is heavily and cogently criticized because of this constructive element by which D's liability for manslaughter turns on the consequence of death, which will often be unforeseen by D and indeed be regarded as a matter of 'bad luck' beyond his control.[11] The offender is labelled as a manslaughterer when he might only have foreseen, if at all, a risk of *some minor harm* being caused.[12]

It is a notoriously difficult crime to apply. A good starting point is to ask what offence D would have been charged with had no one died. That is the unlawful act on which the manslaughter may be constructed.

The crime comprises:[13]

(1) an unlawful act;

(2) intentionally performed;

(3) in circumstances rendering it dangerous;

(4) causing death.

As a simple example, consider D who throws a stone at V's greenhouse intending to break the window or being reckless as to the window being broken. V is kneeling close to the greenhouse tending his plants when the pane of glass shatters and a shard penetrates his eye and kills him. There is an unlawful act (criminal damage), the act (throwing the stone) is intentionally performed, given V's proximity to the greenhouse the reasonable and sober person would consider that there was a risk of some harm (not necessarily serious harm) to V by D's actions, and V's death is caused. D is guilty of manslaughter. The offence is commonly prosecuted where D has thrown a punch at V or scuffled with V in a drunken dispute.[14] If V falls as a result of the, perhaps minor, contact and on hitting his head V dies, D will be liable for manslaughter even though he intended or was reckless as to an assault. Several elements require further examination.

---

[9] *Newbury* [1977] AC 500; *Ball* [1989] Crim LR 730; *JF* [2015] EWCA Crim 351.

[10] *Watson* [1989] 2 All ER 865.

[11] See RA Duff, 'Whose Luck is it Anyway?' in C Clarkson and S Cunningham (eds), *Criminal Liability for Non-Aggressive Death* (2008). See generally on liability for consequences, A Ashworth, 'Taking the Consequences' in S Shute, J Gardner and J Horder (eds), *Action and Value in Criminal Law* (1993).

[12] On the issue generally, see G Williams, 'Convictions and Fair Labelling' (1983) 42 CLJ 85; B Mitchell, 'In Defence of a Principle of Correspondence' [1999] Crim LR 195; cf J Horder, 'A Critique of the Correspondence Principle in Criminal Law' [1995] Crim LR 759 and 'Questioning the Correspondence Principle: A Reply' [1999] Crim LR 206. See also the criticism in LC 304, paras 3.42 et seq.

[13] Per Lord Hope, *A-G's Reference (No 3 of 1994)* [1998] AC 830. Numerous cases have relied upon this formulation of the offence, for examples see *Webster v CPS* [2014] EWHC 2516 (Admin) and *Bristow* [2013] EWCA Crim 1540.

[14] For critical comment on the offence in such cases, see B Mitchell, 'More Thoughts about Unlawful and Dangerous Act Manslaughter and the One Punch Killer' [2009] Crim LR 502.

14.1.1 The unlawfulness

Issues requiring elaboration are whether the unlawful act must: (a) be criminal; (b) involve a completed crime; (c) be a crime of mens rea; (d) be one dependent on proof of an act, or whether an omission will suffice; (e) be a crime involving an offence against the person.

The current state of the law is that to be sufficient for unlawful act manslaughter, the unlawful act may be any criminal offence involving an act (but not an omission), with mens rea of more than mere negligence.

14.1.1.1 A crime

Historically, it was thought that even a tort which led to a death was sufficiently unlawful to trigger this offence. In *Fenton*,[15] D was liable for manslaughter when he threw stones down a mine and broke some scaffolding which caused a wagon to overturn with fatal results. D's act was a trespass and the only question was whether it caused V's death. Even in the nineteenth century the judges were sometimes troubled by the harshness of this approach. Some judges refused to apply it. For example, in *Franklin*,[16] D, walking on Brighton pier, took up 'a good sized box' from a refreshment stall and threw it into the sea where it struck a swimmer, V, and killed him. The prosecution argued that apart from any question of negligence, it was manslaughter if the commission of the tort of trespass against the stall-keeper had caused death. Field J, after consulting Mathew J who agreed, held that the case must go to the jury 'on the broad ground of negligence'. Expressing his 'great abhorrence of constructive crime', Field J asserted that 'The mere fact of a civil wrong committed by one person against another ought not to be used as an incident which is a necessary step to a criminal case.'

Under the present law, it is clear that D's 'act' must be a crime to found liability for manslaughter. In *Kennedy (No 2)*,[17] the House of Lords affirmed that to establish the crime of unlawful act manslaughter it must be shown: (a) that the defendant committed an unlawful act; (b) that such unlawful act *was a crime*; and (c) *that the defendant's unlawful act was a significant cause of the death of the deceased*. A good rule of thumb, as noted, is to identify the criminal charge that could be laid against D if no one had died as a result of his conduct.

In *Lamb*,[18] D pointed a loaded gun at his friend, V, in jest. He did not intend to injure or alarm V and V was not alarmed. There was therefore no assault. Because they did not understand how a revolver works, both thought there was no danger in pulling the trigger; but, when D did so, he shot V dead. D was not guilty of a criminal assault or battery because he did not foresee that V would be alarmed or injured. There was no mens rea for assault or battery. V did not fear violence so there was no assault. It was, therefore, a misdirection to tell the jury that this was 'an unlawful and dangerous act'.

This was confirmed by *Scarlett*.[19] D, a licensee, caused death by using excessive force while lawfully expelling a trespasser from his pub. His conviction for manslaughter was quashed because the judge had directed that D was guilty if he had committed a battery (used unnecessary and unreasonable force). What the judge should have said was that it was necessary to prove that the force used was excessive in the circumstances which D believed to exist[20]—that would be more than a mere tort of battery as D would, in such circumstances, have the mens rea of the *crime* of battery.

15 (1830) 1 Lew CC 179.   16 (1883) 15 Cox CC 163.   17 [2007] UKHL 38.
18 [1967] 2 QB 981. The case is a controversial one. Glanville Williams wrote that 'Lamb was a fool but there is no need to punish fools to that degree. There is no need to punish Lamb at all. He had killed his friend and that was punishment enough': 'Recklessness Redefined' (1981) 40 CLJ 252 at 281.
19 [1993] 4 All ER 629. The case must be read in the light of *Owino* [1995] Crim LR 743, p 404. See also *Jennings* [1990] Crim LR 588.
20 *Gladstone Williams* at 383.

In the unsatisfactory case of *DPP v Newbury*,[21] the House of Lords appeared to cast doubt on these cases. D threw a piece of paving stone from a bridge as a train approached. It killed the driver. The House of Lords failed to identify any crime rendering D's act unlawful. Throwing concrete in this way certainly looks like a criminal act, which explains why it was not argued to be lawful before the House.[22] The question for the House was whether D could properly be convicted of manslaughter if he did not foresee that his act might cause harm to another. As we have already outlined, UAM can be committed if D commits a crime by an intentional act provided also that a reasonable and sober person would see the risk of some harm to a person. The question is not whether D foresaw death or a risk of injury. It is whether he had mens rea for the offence that he would have been charged with if no one had died. In *Newbury*, D's act was not, on the facts, an assault or any of the usual offences against the person, all of which require mens rea. The only other likely crimes with which D could be charged were the offence of endangering passengers contrary to s 34 of the OAPA 1861 or an offence of criminal damage.[23] The House did not specify what offence was the base crime on which manslaughter was constructed.

The better view, it is submitted, is that as in *Lamb* and *Scarlett*, a criminal act must be identified and proved. *Kennedy (No 2)* supports this requirement.

The ambiguity of the concept of an 'unlawful' act has sometimes led the courts to gloss over the requirement for proof of a criminal offence. In *Cato*,[24] D caused V's death by injecting him with heroin with his consent. The court accepted that this was not an offence under the Misuse of Drugs Act and assumed for this purpose that it was not an offence under s 23 of the OAPA 1861.[25] However, the court said 'the unlawful act would be described as injecting the deceased with a mixture of heroin and water which at the time of the injection and for the purposes of the injection Cato had unlawfully taken into his possession'. The act was closely associated with other acts which are offences but it is submitted that neither this nor any moral condemnation attaching to that act should be enough to found liability for manslaughter.

14.1.1.2 The 'base' crime must be proved in full

The requirement of a criminal offence prompts a further question: whether it is necessary for the prosecution to establish all of the elements of the crime that would have been charged had no one died—that is, the 'base' crime on which the unlawful act manslaughter charge is constructed. In principled terms the element of 'unlawfulness' should require the prosecution to prove *all* the elements (mens rea and actus reus with no defence) of the base offence. Unfortunately, this apparently obvious interpretation of 'unlawful' has not been put completely beyond doubt by the case law.

It seems clear that the prosecution must prove the full mens rea of the base offence. In *Lamb*, the trial judge had directed the jury that it is an unlawful act 'whether or not it falls within any recognized category of crime'. The Court of Appeal found this to be a misdirection because '*mens rea* is now an essential element of the offence'.[26] L's conduct did not constitute an assault. First, because he lacked the mens rea: he had no intention to frighten, nor because of his lack of understanding of the operation of the firearm was he reckless as to causing apprehension in his victim. Secondly, there was no actus reus because his friend,

---

[21] [1977] AC 500.

[22] '. . . no question arose whether [Newbury's] actions were or were not unlawful': *Scarlett* [1993] 4 All ER at 635, per Beldam LJ.

[23] Using an offence against property seems as objectionable a basis for convicting of manslaughter as a tort (see later). There is no doubt criminal damage will suffice as the base offence: *JF* [2015] EWCA Crim 351.

[24] [1976] 1 All ER 260.

[25] See p 748. In fact D was convicted of the s 23 offence so the remarks discussed in the text may be *obiter*.

[26] At 986. See also *Reid* (1975) 62 Cr App R 109 (fright by threat to use firearm was sufficient).

believing that the whole thing was a joke, had no apprehension of immediate unlawful violence.[27] The court was categorical as to 'mens rea being now an essential element of the offence', and also accepted that counsel had put forward the correct view that for the 'act to be unlawful it must constitute at least what he then termed a technical assault'. Support also derives from *Arobieke*.[28] D pursued V onto railway lines 'looking for him'. V was killed. There was no evidence that D had actually threatened V, so no actus reus of assault could be established. The conviction for manslaughter was quashed.[29]

The courts all too often gloss over this aspect of the UAM offence, using language that implies that a mere voluntary act by D might suffice, as, for example, in *A-G's Reference (No 3 of 1994)*,[30] where Lord Hope referred to the requirement merely that D 'did what he did intentionally'.[31]

The proof of mens rea of the base offence is a necessary but not sufficient condition of unlawful act manslaughter. There must also be proof of actus reus. Where D, on facts similar to *Lamb*, thinks that the revolver is loaded and dangerous and he only intends to cause V to be frightened, but V does not apprehend violence because he does not believe the gun to be loaded, there is no complete assault. D has the mens rea, but the actus reus is not satisfied.[32] Again, it is submitted that a conviction for unlawful act manslaughter cannot be maintained.[33]

In addition to proving the mens rea and actus reus of the base offence, the prosecution must disprove any defences to the base offence raised by D.[34] If the defence itself is clearly defined, there is little difficulty in applying it in the unlawful act manslaughter context. Two particular problems fall for further discussion.

14.1.1.3 Problems of consent and unlawful act manslaughter

It is a matter of policy whether the law will recognize as valid the factual consent of an individual (ie an adult of full mental capacity), which leads to conduct where harm is intended or foreseen: *Brown*.[35] If D pleads that V consented to the base crime, that will be accepted where D's conduct falls within an established category for which V's consent is accepted in law; for example, boxing, surgery or horseplay. Since D commits no base crime as he has V's consent, there is no unlawful act manslaughter liability.[36] So, where D and V engage in a lawful boxing match and V is killed by D's blow within the rules of the sport, D is not criminally liable for V's death. In *A*,[37] D's post-exam celebrations included throwing V into

---

[27] *Bruce* (1847) Cox CC 262, Erle J supports this—on the facts, no assault as no apprehension by V or intent by D.

[28] [1988] Crim LR 314.

[29] Compare *Lewis* [2010] EWCA Crim 151 where D chased V and thereby assaulted him before V was knocked down.

[30] [1998] AC 245.   [31] At 274 per Lord Hope.

[32] It may be possible to charge a battery. There is no crime of attempted assault since it is a summary only offence. This point was not argued in *Lewis* [2010] EWCA Crim 151.

[33] If these 'fractions' of crimes are sufficient to form the basis for a UAM charge, that may tell us something about the underlying purpose of UAM. It would be clear that the punishment is based on the 'dangerousness' of the activity rather than on the technical 'unlawfulness'.

[34] *Jennings* [1990] Crim LR 588; *Scarlett* (1994) 98 Cr App R 290.

[35] [1994] AC 212; *A-G's Reference (No 6 of 1980)* [1981] QB 715.

[36] eg *Bruce* (1847) Cox CC 262 (no assault where D spun boy round in jest and killed V), and see Lord Mustill's speech in *Brown* [1994] AC 212 at 264. In *Morton* (2017) 14 July, Nottingham CC), D was charged with unlawful act manslaughter having caused V's death by strangulation in the course of what he argued was consensual sex. Carr J left the issue of consent to the jury on the basis that the relevant authorities do not impose a blanket prohibition on consent being relevant to D's liability in such circumstances.

[37] (2005) 69 J Crim L 394.

a river where he drowned. D claimed that he was entitled to a defence of belief in consent to the assault, his actions being mere horseplay. If he had consent to the assault there could be no manslaughter. The Court of Appeal confirmed that if D had caused V to fall in the river by a non-accidental act and D did not have a genuine belief in V's consent to the assault, D would be liable if all sober and reasonable people realized it was dangerous in the sense discussed later.

Where the consensual acts occur in the context of sexual activity, the law adopted the same position until the Domestic Abuse Act 2021. At common law, where D had not intended that a consensual assault would lead to any greater degree of harm than the mere assault or battery consented to by V, there was no base offence and therefore no manslaughter conviction: *Slingsby*.[38] Under s 71 of the Domestic Abuse Act 2021[39] where the 'violence' from D to V is in the context of sexual gratification, we must distinguish between cases on the basis of the level of harm that V consented to.

Where V consented to assault or battery and that is all the harm D intended to cause, but V died as a result (eg because V fell over hitting her head when D was assaulting her while engaging in role play), the 'defence' of consent applies, there is no crime of assault and no manslaughter liability for the death. The outcome in *Slingsby* would be the same.

Where the level of harm consented to between D and V in the context of sexual gratification is greater than assault and battery (s 47, 20 or 18 OAPA), then even if V has consented in fact, that factual consent will not be recognized in law. D will therefore commit an offence on V. If that offence leads to V's death, D can be liable for her manslaughter unless he intended to cause GBH in which case he would be liable for murder.

The Act creates an exception in relation to the transmission of sexually transmitted infections. If D had V's consent to the risk of acquiring an STI and V did contract such and died as a result, there would be no liability. D's act of infecting V with consent does not constitute a crime. There is, therefore, nothing on which to construct the manslaughter charge.[40]

14.1.1.4 Problems of intoxication and the unlawful act

Where the prosecution rely on an unlawful act which does not require a specific intent (eg a base crime that can be committed recklessly) and D was intoxicated at the time, it is immaterial that he lacked the mens rea of the crime in question and even that he was unconscious: *Lipman*.[41] In this memorable case D killed V by cramming a sheet into her mouth and striking her while he was on an LSD 'trip' and believed he was in the centre of the earth being attacked by serpents.[42] The unlawful act—the base crime—was the battery committed on V while D was unconscious. That battery required only the mens rea of recklessness, it was therefore a crime of basic intent, and D's self-induced intoxication provided no excuse. His prior fault satisfied that mens rea requirement.

---

[38] [1995] Crim LR 570 (D injuring V with a ring in course of consensual sexual touching, V dies of infection from wound).

[39] For the background to the changes, see the campaign group We Can't Consent To This at https://wecantconsenttothis.uk/ and the government policy paper at https://www.gov.uk/government/publications/domestic-abuse-bill-2020-factsheets/consent-to-serious-harm-for-sexual-gratification-not-a-defence.

[40] See p 718 and *Dica* and *Konzani*.

[41] [1970] 1 QB 152. The case was heavily criticized. See commentary by I Hooker [1969] Crim LR 547; G Orchard, 'Drunkenness, Drugs and Manslaughter' [1970] Crim LR 132; P Glazebrook, 'Constructive Manslaughter and the Threshold Tort' (1970) 28 CLJ 21; R Buxton, *Annual Survey of Commonwealth Law* (1970) 128 and 134. It was not followed in Australia: *Haywood* [1971] VR 755 (Crockett J) but was affirmed by the House of Lords in *Majewski* (at p 333). Cf the decision in *Heard* [2007] EWCA Crim 125.

[42] Though the jury convicted on the grounds that D was reckless or grossly negligent when, quite consciously, he took the drugs, the Court of Appeal upheld the conviction by applying the *Church* doctrine (p 600).

14.1.1.5 A crime of mens rea?

It is implicit in the decision in *Church*[43] that the base crime cannot be one where the fault is merely that D performed the act negligently. That case stipulates that for UAM the crime must involve an act which all sober and reasonable people would realize entailed the risk (ie an unjustifiable risk) of harm to others.[44] This is in accordance with the well-established rule that negligence sufficient to found liability in tort is not necessarily enough for criminal guilt and that death caused in the course of committing the tort of negligence is not necessarily manslaughter. Not only is it insufficient that D was negligent in civil law, it is insufficient for UAM if the unlawfulness of the criminal act arises *solely* from the negligent manner in which it is performed. Death caused by such an act will not necessarily be manslaughter. This follows from the decision of the House of Lords in *Andrews v DPP*.[45] In that case, at trial, Du Parcq J told the jury that if D killed V in the course of dangerous driving contrary to s 11 of the Road Traffic Act 1930, he was guilty of manslaughter. Lord Atkin (who clearly regarded dangerous driving in the 1930 Act as a crime of negligence)[46] said that, if the summing-up had rested there, there would have been misdirection:

There can be no doubt that this section covers driving with such a high degree of negligence as that, if death were caused, the offender would have committed manslaughter. But the converse is not true, and it is perfectly possible that a man may drive at a speed or in a manner dangerous to the public, and cause death, and yet not be guilty of manslaughter.[47]

Lord Atkin expressly distinguished[48] between acts which are unlawful because of the negligent manner in which they are performed and acts which are unlawful for some other reason:

There is an obvious difference in the law of manslaughter between doing an unlawful act and doing a lawful act with a degree of carelessness which the legislature makes criminal.

His lordship's next sentence implies that killing in the course of unlawful acts generally *was* manslaughter:

If it were otherwise a man who killed another while driving without due care and attention would *ex necessitate* commit manslaughter.

This passage has been severely criticized[49] and it is certainly unhappily phrased: 'doing a lawful act with a degree of carelessness which the legislature makes criminal' is a contradiction in terms, for the act so done is plainly not a lawful act. But the distinction evidently intended, *viz*, between acts which are unlawful because of negligent performance and acts which are unlawful for some other reason, is at least intelligible and, in view of the established distinction between civil and criminal negligence, a necessary limitation.

The natural reading of Lord Atkin's opinion is that the distinction is between acts which are unlawful because of negligent performance and acts which are unlawful for some other reason. An alternative (strained, but more attractive) reading is that only crimes of more

---

[43] [1996] 1 QB 59.

[44] The reference to 'an unlawful act' would be otiose if it did not mean unlawful in some other respect than negligence.

[45] [1937] AC 576.

[46] See Ch 32. The offence of dangerous driving was abolished by the Criminal Law Act 1977 but restored in a new form by the Road Traffic Act 1991, s 2.

[47] [1937] AC 576 at 584.   [48] ibid, 585.

[49] Turner, MACL, 238. Referred to by Devlin as 'the only obscure speech the great Lord Atkin ever made': 'Criminal Responsibility and Punishment: Function of Judge and Jury' [1954] Crim LR 661 at 672.

than mere negligence will suffice to ground an unlawful act manslaughter conviction. This is supported by the comments of Sachs LJ in *Lamb*: '*mens rea* being now an essential ingredient in manslaughter'.[50]

Despite the existence of authorities to the contrary, as a matter of principle it is submitted that the offence should be read restrictively and should be based on offences that require mens rea proper.[51] Gross negligence manslaughter is more than broad enough to deal with cases in which deaths are caused in other culpable circumstances.

A further issue which then arises is whether if it is insufficient to construct a manslaughter charge on a base crime of mere negligence, it is acceptable to construct such a charge on a base crime of strict liability. The issue has not been directly addressed by the appellate courts.[52]

This issue has been confronted at first instance. In the case of *Alliston*, D was charged with unlawful act manslaughter after V died as a result of his bicycle colliding with her as she was crossing the road.[53] The unlawful act relied upon by the prosecution was the offence of riding a bicycle on a public road without a front brake contrary to s 91 of the Road Traffic Offenders Act 1988 in conjunction with regs 6 and 7 of the Pedal Cycles (Construction and Use) Regulations 1983. HHJ Joseph QC accepted the prosecution's argument that there was nothing in the authorities to the effect that something more than a strict liability or 'regulatory offence' is necessary to establish the base offence of unlawful act manslaughter. She therefore concluded that there was no prohibition in law on a prosecution for unlawful act manslaughter being based upon the offence found in s 91 of the 1988 Act.[54]

In the earlier case of *Andrews*,[55] D gave V, with her consent, an injection of insulin in order to give her a 'rush'. V, who was also voluntarily intoxicated at the time, died as a result of the injection of insulin. D appealed against his conviction on the basis that the judge was wrong to rule that he would direct the jury that V's consent to the injection did not render D's act lawful. The Court of Appeal upheld the conviction, holding that ss 58(2)(b) and 67 of the Medicines Act 1968 made D's act unlawful because no consent could be pleaded to that offence. The fact that these offences are of strict liability was not challenged in the appeal.

14.1.1.6 Omissions as 'unlawful acts'

In *Lowe*,[56] the Court of Appeal held that D is not guilty of UAM simply on the ground that he has committed the offence under s 1(1) of the Children and Young Persons Act 1933 of neglecting his child so as to cause unnecessary suffering or injury to its health, and that neglect has caused death. The court disapproved *Senior*,[57] which, on similar facts, held that this was manslaughter. *Lowe* has now been overruled on its interpretation of the 1933 Act[58]

---

[50] [1967] 2 QB 981 at 988.

[51] It is for this reason that *Meeking* [2012] EWCA Crim 641 ought to be treated with considerable caution. In that case, the unlawful act relied upon was the offence of endangering road users, contrary to s 22A(1) of the Road Traffic Act 1988. As Ashworth points out, [2013] Crim LR 333, this is an offence of negligence and for that reason D should not have been prosecuted with UAM. As the Court of Appeal observes, D could have been charged with gross negligence manslaughter instead.

[52] For discussion, see Ormerod [2003] Crim LR 477; M Dyson, 'The Smallest Fault in Manslaughter' [2017] 6 Arch Rev 4. NB *Rebelo* [2019] EWCA Crim 633.

[53] See BBC News Online, 'Cyclist detained over pedestrian death', 18 Sept 2017 at www.bbc.co.uk/news/uk-england-41306738.

[54] *R v Alliston* (2017) 17 Sept, CCC.

[55] [2002] EWCA Crim 3021. See the commentary by Ormerod [2003] Crim LR 477.

[56] [1973] QB 702. See, generally, IH Dennis, 'Manslaughter by Omission' (1980) 33 CLP 255.

[57] [1899] 1 QB 283. On the difficulties of UAM in child abuse cases, see L Hoyano and C Keenan, *Child Abuse Law and Policy* (2007) 142.

[58] *Sheppard* [1981] AC 394 at 410 per Lord Edmund-Davies.

but on this point *Lowe* and not *Senior* represents the law. Death had certainly been caused by unlawful and dangerous conduct, but the court distinguished between omission and commission:

if I strike a child in a manner likely to cause harm it is right that if that child dies I may be charged with manslaughter. If, however, I omit to do something with the result that it suffers injury to its health which results in its death, we think that a charge of manslaughter should not be an inevitable consequence even if the omission is deliberate.

If the omission is no more than an act of negligence then it is right that the doctrine of the unlawful and dangerous act does not apply and D is not guilty of UAM (but may be of gross negligence manslaughter); but if the omission is truly *wilful*—a deliberate omission to summon medical aid, knowing it to be necessary—there seems to be no valid ground for the distinction.[59] Taylor makes a compelling case for a reinterpretation of the offence to include base offences perpetrated by omission.[60]

14.1.1.7 Other limitations of the category of unlawfulness

It has been questioned whether: (a) an inchoate offence might suffice for the base crime; and (b) whether the base crime must be one involving an offence to the person.

As for inchoate offences, attempted offences of violence would be the most obvious scenarios in which such an issue might arise. Consider D who intends to poison V and adds what he thinks to be poison to V's tea, but he has made a mistake and is simply adding a very concentrated sweetener. V is a diabetic and dies. There is probably no completed offence under s 23 of the OAPA 1861, but there is a possible attempted poisoning.[61] The issue does not appear to have arisen in any reported case. In *Willoughby*,[62] D had poured petrol around a building which he owned and which he planned to burn down and to claim the insurance money. D claimed that he was absent from the premises when a spark ignited the petrol and his associate who was assisting in spreading the petrol was killed. The conviction for manslaughter was upheld by the court, with the conclusion that the base offence was one of causing criminal damage to property being reckless as to whether life was endangered thereby, as the jury found. It is unclear if the question was raised whether D pouring petrol was a completed act of criminal damage, or one that was merely preparatory.[63]

There are plenty of decided cases confirming that the base crime need not be an offence against the person. Public order offences are capable of founding an unlawful act manslaughter charge. In *Carey*, the Court of Appeal held that there might be circumstances in which a verdict of UAM could properly be entered where the unlawful act was affray, although on the evidence that was not possible in that case.[64] On the facts the Court of Appeal quashed convictions where D1, D2 and D3 had committed an affray and D1 had hit V, a 15-year-old, apparently healthy, girl. V ran 109 metres away from DD. She died as a result of a heart condition which had not been diagnosed. The only sufficient dangerous act perpetrated on V had been the physical strike by D1. The other acts and threats used in the course of the affray were not dangerous in the relevant sense as against V. The judge should therefore have withdrawn the charge of manslaughter based on those acts. It would, it is

---

[59] See editorial comment in [1976] Crim LR 529, where Andrew Ashworth is heavily critical.

[60] RD Taylor, 'The Contours of Involuntary Manslaughter—A Place for Unlawful Act by Omission' [2019] Crim LR 3.

[61] Arguably D would not be liable not because of the unlawfulness element, but because there would be no objective risk of injury from the act.

[62] [2004] EWCA Crim 3365, [2004] Crim LR 389 and commentary.

[63] In such cases, a gross negligence charge might be difficult to substantiate.

[64] [2006] EWCA Crim 17, [2006] Crim LR 842 and commentary.

submitted, have been easier for the prosecution to argue that DD had assaulted V; that was an unlawful act, it was dangerous, and her death arose from V's foreseeable and reasonable flight and there was no break in the chain of causation since they must 'take their victim' as they find her.

Convictions have been upheld where D's unlawful act constituted criminal damage (eg *Goodfellow*)[65] and burglary (eg *Watson* (discussed later) and *Kennedy*).[66] In *JF*,[67] the arson committed in a derelict building in which homeless men were living was enough. In *Ball*[68] (discussed later), the court distinguished hypothetical examples posed by D's counsel on the ground that, unlike the case before the court, they were of acts 'not directed at V' (but with respect, that is irrelevant). The court therefore expressed no opinion on the example of D 'storing goods known to be stolen; if unknown to him the goods contain unstable explosive which explodes killing another, is that manslaughter?' The answer must surely be no, unless the sober and reasonable observer would have known of the danger. There is something to be said in favour of imposing some limitation to the offence. It does not seem appropriate that a person's guilt for homicide should depend on whether he was handling stolen goods or committing criminal damage or burglary. Cases of this sort would be better left to the next category of killing by gross negligence.[69]

14.1.1.8 No requirement that the unlawful act be 'directed at' the victim?

For a period in the 1990s the cases seemed to require that the unlawful act was directed at the victim. That was based on a statement in *Dalby*,[70] where Waller LJ said that, 'where the charge of manslaughter is based on an unlawful and dangerous act, it must be an act directed at the victim and likely to cause immediate injury however slight'. In *Goodfellow*,[71] D's argument that he was not guilty of manslaughter because his act was not directed against V was rejected. D, wanting to move from his local authority housing and seeing no prospect of exchanging it, set it on fire, attempting to make it appear that the cause was a petrol bomb. V died in the fire. The court said that in *Dalby*, Waller LJ was 'intending to say that there must be no fresh intervening cause between the act and the death'. It is true that that case could, and probably should,[72] have been decided on this ground, but it does not seem to have been the *ratio decidendi*.[73] It is also true that the act of burglary which causes the death of the obviously frail householder is not directed at him, but it is accepted in *Watson* that it may be manslaughter.[74] It now seems clear that there is no requirement that the unlawful act is directed at V.

---

[65] (1986) 83 Cr App R 23.

[66] (1993) 15 Cr App R (S) 141 (burglar dropped a match used to illuminate search of house).

[67] [2015] EWCA Crim 351.

[68] The point of law certified for the House of Lords postulated 'an act [not directed against V] which is the substantial cause of the death' and the court left open the question whether D was guilty of manslaughter by gross negligence which it could scarcely have done if it was deciding that D did not cause death.

[69] For a suggestion that the offence ought to be restricted to cases of 'attack' on another person, see C Clarkson, 'Context and Culpability in Involuntary Manslaughter: Principle or Instinct' in A Ashworth and B Mitchell (eds), *Rethinking English Homicide Law* (2000). The basis for this suggestion is that there is no wrong done by convicting D of a constructive crime of manslaughter because, by attacking V, D has shifted his moral stance vis-à-vis V. Since the concept of 'attack' has no foundation in English law, the proposal may generate uncertainty. As Ashworth and Mitchell observe, asking whether it is enough to say that choosing to engage in violence means you make your own luck begs the question (ibid, 13). See also J Gardner, *Offences and Defences* (2007) Ch 12.

[70] [1982] 1 All ER 916.

[71] (1986) 83 Cr App R 23. The conviction was upheld on the grounds of both unlawful act and reckless manslaughter.

[72] *Kennedy (No 1)* [1999] 1 Cr App R 54. In *Kennedy (No 2)* [2005] EWCA Crim 685, it was rightly accepted that there was no requirement that the act be 'aimed' at V.

[73] See n 69.   [74] [1989] Crim LR 730.

14.1.2 Dangerousness

The definitive statement of this element of the offence derives from *Church*. Edmund Davies J said:

For such a verdict inexorably to follow, the unlawful act must be such as all sober and reasonable people would inevitably recognize must[75] subject the other person to, at least, the risk of some harm resulting therefrom, albeit not serious harm.[76]

The test of dangerousness is objective. In *Newbury*, Lord Salmon stressed that 'the test is not did the accused recognize that it was dangerous but would all sober and reasonable people recognize its danger'.

The test describes the kind of act which gives rise to liability for manslaughter, not the intention or foresight, real or assumed, of the accused. Hence, the enactment of s 8 of the Criminal Justice Act 1967[77] had no effect on the law as stated in *Church*. The question is whether the sober and reasonable person would have appreciated that the act was dangerous in the light, not only of the circumstances actually known to the accused, but also of any additional circumstances of which that hypothetical person would have been aware.[78] There is, of course, a risk that in practice the fact that a death has occurred will be treated by the jury as conclusive evidence of the fact that the activity was dangerous. Judges' directions need to caution against such simplistic reasoning.[79]

If the victim has some peculiarity that is relevant if it would have been known to the sober and reasonable observer of the event, even if it was not known to the accused. This principle can be explained by comparing two cases. The burglary of a house in which V, a frail 87-year-old man resides, becomes a 'dangerous' act as soon as V's frailty and great age would be apparent to the reasonable observer. The unlawful act continues through the 'whole of the burglarious intrusion' so that if V dies of a heart attack caused by D's continuing in the burglary after it has become a dangerous, as well as unlawful, act, he will be guilty of manslaughter.[80] In contrast, where a petrol station attendant with a weak heart died in consequence of an attempted robbery where D was outside the station behind armour-plated glass, this was not manslaughter. The reasonable observer would not, at any point in the continuance of the robbery, have known of V's peculiar susceptibility—the act was not 'dangerous'.[81]

The objective nature of this limb was emphasized by the Lord Chief Justice in *JF*.[82] F, aged 14, and E, aged 16, were convicted of manslaughter. They had entered a derelict building and set alight a duvet on a pile of tyres before fleeing the building. They were unaware that

---

75 The degree of risk entailed is not further elaborated. See R Sparks, 'The Elusive Element of Unlawfulness' (1965) 28 MLR 601.

76 [1966] 1 QB 59 at 70. Cf R Buxton, 'By Any Unlawful Act' (1966) 82 LQR 174 suggesting that the law could return to a position whereby unlawful act manslaughter is restricted to cases where D intends to cause *serious* injury.

77 See p 134.

78 Confirmed as being the correct approach in *Bristow* [2013] EWCA Crim 1540.

79 Guidance is provided in the *Crown Court Compendium* (2021).

80 *Watson* [1989] 2 All ER 865. D's conviction was quashed because causation was not established. V's death may have been caused by the arrival of the emergency services. But did this predictable event break the chain of causation? Cf commentary [1989] Crim LR 734. If V has sustained a fatal shock before D has any opportunity to observe his frailty, D's liability seems to depend on whether his acts after he had that opportunity (now 'dangerous' acts) contributed to the death.

81 *Dawson* (1985) 81 Cr App R 150. Yet, before the Homicide Act 1957, this would have been murder (killing in the course or furtherance of a violent felony) and, according to one theory, Parliament's provision that it was not murder left it as manslaughter. See the 1st edn of this book, at pp 19–20. The theory has not taken root.

82 [2015] EWCA Crim 351.

anyone was in the building. In fact several homeless men lived in the building, and one of the men died. F had a low IQ (his understanding was comparable to a six-year-old child). At trial they were convicted of unlawful act manslaughter on the basis of the act of simple arson, which a reasonable person would have foreseen might have caused someone some harm, and which did in fact cause death. They were acquitted of the charge of aggravated arson which required proof that they had been reckless as to a life being endangered. The Court of Appeal upheld the convictions. The judge had directed the jury on the objective test as follows:

It is immaterial whether or not the defendant actually knew or actually realised that the act was dangerous in the sense I have defined it for you and whether or not he intended *any* harm to result therefrom. And the sober and reasonable man is endowed with the knowledge which the defendant possessed before and at the time of starting the fire.

The Court of Appeal rejected the argument that the objective test as to whether the act was a dangerous one was a test which should have been adapted to take into account the appellant's ages and, in the case of the appellant F, his mental capacity. The court held that it was for Parliament to act if there was a desire for a change in the law.

It is worth underlining three aspects of the *Church* doctrine. First, that there must be a 'likelihood' of harm. This suggests more than a mere possibility, but not perhaps that harm is more probable than not. Secondly, that the type of harm involved is only 'some' harm, not serious harm. This contrasts with the requirement in gross negligence manslaughter of a serious and obvious risk of death.[83] Thirdly, that there is no requirement that D himself foresees any risk of harm.[84] Historically, UAM was limited to cases in which the accused had at least foreseen injury of his victim resulting from his crime.[85] The *Fourth Report of HM Commissioners on Criminal Law*[86] described the offence in terms of 'death result[ing] from any unlawful act or omission done or omitted with intent to hurt the person'.[87] The decision in *Church* may have marked a significant deviation from the historical position. Buxton, writing extrajudicially, described it as a 'staggeringly severe ruling, and one which turns its back on the major part of the 19th century development of the law'.[88] There have been many suggestions to limit the offence to cases where D has committed an unlawful act likely to cause at least serious personal injury, and to restrict it further by a requirement that D intend or be reckless as to such.[89]

14.1.2.1 'Dangerousness' in crimes committed by multiple accused

An interesting issue arose in *Carey* (discussed earlier) as to whether, in considering the 'dangerousness of an act', it is permissible to aggregate the conduct of co-accused. It is submitted that, for the purposes of ascertaining whether there was a crime of a sufficiently dangerous nature to satisfy the *Church* test, there is no difficulty in aggregating the threats

---

[83] See *Kuddus* [2019] EWCA Crim 837, p 613.

[84] Reiterated by the Court of Appeal in *M (J)* [2012] EWCA Crim 2293, [20]. There is no requirement for D to foresee any harm let alone the type of harm V suffers.

[85] The case law bears examples, including *Sullivan* (1836) 7 C & P 641, where removing the trap-stick from a cart was sufficient to ground liability as D foresaw the risk of some harm arising.

[86] (1839); see Russell, 588.   [87] ibid, 589.   [88] See n 76.

[89] See also the Draft Scots Criminal Code, cl 38. A further attempt to narrow the offence was rejected by the Court of Appeal in *M (J)* [2012] EWCA Crim 2293. The Crown appealed against the judge's ruling that D could not be guilty unless 'the victim died as a result of the *sort of* physical harm that any reasonable and sober person would inevitably realise the unlawful act in question risked causing'. The Court of Appeal held that this placed 'a gloss on the ingredients of this offence which is not justified by the authorities and does not follow from the reasoning' (at [18]) and allowed the Crown's appeal. See Ashworth [2013] Crim LR 335.

of violence offered by, for example, D1, D2 and D3 where they acted together. If D1 is waving a machete around and D2 is shaking his fist at V, their affray comprises their combined conduct. Likewise, the dangerousness of the acts is properly assessed by looking at the combination of their conduct. Nor, it is submitted, is there a problem in aggregating the conduct of D1, D2 and D3 towards V1 and V2. Take a case where, in the course of a robbery, D1 issues serious threats against V1 and D2 issues threats to V2, and the obviously frail V2 dies from a heart attack induced by the shock. It is submitted that the actions of D1 and D2 could be aggregated in determining whether the conduct was sufficiently 'dangerous' in the sense required by *Church*.[90]

14.1.2.2 Fright, shock and harm as dangerous acts?

The courts have now acknowledged psychiatric injury to constitute actual bodily harm,[91] but it would be hard to prove that the risk of such harm would inevitably be recognized by all sober and reasonable people, especially as the law requires expert evidence to prove it. Fright and shock do not amount to 'actual bodily harm' but it does not necessarily follow that they are not 'harm' for the purposes of constructive manslaughter. In *Reid*,[92] Lawton LJ, upholding a conviction for manslaughter, said that 'the very least kind of harm is causing fright by threats'—in that case, by the use of firearms. But he was discussing the mental element of an accessory rather than the nature of the act, which is our present concern. The act was, in the opinion of the court, likely to cause death or serious injury and therefore was certainly 'dangerous'. In *Dawson*,[93] the court assumed without deciding that in the context of manslaughter 'harm' includes 'injury to the person through the operation of shock emanating from fright'. So it seems that it is not enough that the act is likely to frighten. It must be likely to cause such shock as to result in injury.[94]

Confusion was also caused by Lord Denning's *dictum* in the civil case of *Gray v Barr*,[95] which was criticized by Lord Salmon in *Newbury*.[96] Lord Denning said: 'the accused must do a dangerous act with the *intention* of frightening or harming someone or with *realisation* that it is likely to frighten or harm someone'. This is simply to require the mens rea of assault or battery. However, an act which is intended or known to be likely to frighten is not necessarily a 'dangerous' act; and whether it is dangerous is a question to be answered by an objective test. The *dictum* is correct if it is confined to the case where the unlawful act relied on is assault or battery.

In *Dhaliwal*,[97] D had struck his partner a minor blow and she had then committed suicide. This was against a history of domestic abuse amounting to psychological but not psychiatric injury by D. It was held that the infliction of mere psychological harm would not suffice to construct a manslaughter charge. The prosecution sought to rely for the relevant unlawful and dangerous act on D's conduct which caused psychological injury to V. The trial judge in his 'meticulous' judgment, and the Court of Appeal in turn, rejected this approach. It would have required an extension to the definition of grievous bodily harm. *Chan-Fook* and *Burstow* make it clear that psychiatric illness may amount to actual or indeed grievous

---

[90] Difficulties may arise in terms of different jurors concluding that the danger emanated from one defendant rather than the other. See the discussion in *Lewis* [2010] EWCA Crim 496.

[91] *Chan-Fook*, p 723.   [92] (1975) 62 Cr App R 109, 112.   [93] (1985) 81 Cr App R 150, 155.

[94] See M Stallworthy, 'Can Death by Shock be Manslaughter?' (1986) 136 NLJ 51; A Busuttil and A McCall Smith, 'Fright, Stress and Homicide' (1990) 54 J Crim L 257.

[95] [1971] 2 QB 554, 568. Lord Denning's emphasis.

[96] [1977] AC 500. Cf Blackstone, *Commentaries*, i, 109.

[97] [2006] EWCA Crim 1139.

bodily harm.[98] However, it is also clear that the Court of Appeal and House of Lords in those cases were not prepared to extend the definition of bodily harm to include emotional distress or any condition less than a 'recognisable psychiatric injury'. Attempts to dilute the definition further would exacerbate the already considerable problems of certainty in definition and proof.[99] However, in an *obiter dictum*, the Court of Appeal in *Dhaliwal*[100] left open the possibility that a manslaughter conviction might be available:

where a decision to commit suicide has been triggered by a physical assault which represents the culmination of a course of abusive conduct, it would be possible . . . to argue that the final assault played a significant part in causing the victim's death.[101]

14.1.3 Causing death

The principles of causation discussed in Ch 2 are applicable. The unlawful and dangerous act must cause death. Causation often gives rise to problems in UAM cases where there is frequently a factor other than D's unlawful dangerous act which plays a causal role in V's death. In the case of *Johnstone*,[102] for example, it could not be established that D's unlawful injury to V, fracturing his cheek and being abusive, had triggered the most direct cause of V's death which was a heart attack.[103]

14.1.3.1 Fright and flight cases

The question for the court is always: if there is a sufficient dangerous act, did *that* unlawful and dangerous act cause death? In some cases where D has performed a number of acts it depends which dangerous act is relied on. The tests to be applied are discussed in Ch 2. In short, the victim's conduct in trying to escape D will not break the chain of causation if it is 'reasonably foreseeable'.[104] Another variation which has developed is that V's conduct will break the chain if it is beyond a range of responses which might be regarded as reasonable, given the threat posed by D and V's circumstances.[105] In evaluating the reasonableness of the response the jury are to have regard to V's circumstances. In *Lewis*,[106] D was convicted of UAM having chased V into the road, where V was hit and killed by an oncoming car. The judge directed the jury to consider whether V running away from D was one of the responses which might have been expected from someone who found himself in V's situation. The Court of Appeal dismissed the appeal. In cases of death during flight from an unlawful act it had to be shown that there was cause and effect; that is, but for the unlawful act, flight and therefore death would not have taken place: *Williams*.[107] The court suggested that it would be appropriate to direct the jury to consider whether V's response was 'wholly disproportionate' or a 'daft response' to the nature of the threat posed by D.

---

[98] Expert evidence will be needed to prove the condition and that D caused it: *Morris* [1998] 1 Cr App R 386.

[99] Under the Offences Against the Person Bill (Home Office, *Reforming the Offences Against the Person Act 1861* (1998)) the definition of injury includes mental injury which encompasses any impairment of a person's mental health. See also LC 361, *Reform of Offences Against the Person* (2015) para 2.32.

[100] [2006] EWCA Crim 1139.

[101] See further, J Horder and L McGowan, 'Manslaughter by Causing Another's Suicide' [2006] Crim LR 1035, arguing that in an abusive relationship case V would not be a free actor, and that gross negligence manslaughter ought to be relied on.

[102] [2007] EWCA Crim 3133.

[103] See also *Warburton* [2006] EWCA Crim 627; *Fitzgerald* [2006] EWCA Crim 1655 (D, during a burglary, pushed 92-year-old V, injuring her, and she died later in hospital of pneumonia).

[104] *Roberts* (1971) Cr App R 95.   [105] *Williams* (1991) 95 Cr App R 1.

[106] [2010] EWCA Crim 151.   [107] (1991) 95 Cr App R 1.

14.1.3.2 Causation in drug supply cases

After a number of years in which the Court of Appeal created confusion in this area, the orthodox approach to causation was reasserted by the House of Lords in *Kennedy (No 2)*.[108] It was held that where D provides V with a syringe for immediate injection in the case of a fully informed and responsible adult V, it is 'never' appropriate to find D guilty of UAM. The criminal law generally assumes the existence of free will.[109] In its remarkably short unanimous judgment delivered by Lord Bingham, the House concluded that the Court of Appeal had been in error repeatedly in imposing liability in such cases.[110] There was no doubt that D committed an unlawful and criminal act by supplying the heroin to V. But that act of supplying, without more, could not harm V in any physical way, let alone cause his death. The crucial question was not whether D facilitated or contributed to administration of the noxious thing by supplying V but whether he went further and 'administered' it, that is, completed the offence under s 23 of the OAPA 1861. *Rogers*[111] was wrongly decided in concluding that where D assisted V by holding the tourniquet he had administered to V and could be liable for his death.[112]

14.1.3.3 Suicide

Homicide convictions have been upheld in a series of cases in which V has effectively committed suicide consequent upon being injured by D, but in each the decision was based on the fact that the injury inflicted by D was still an operating and substantial cause of the death, as, for example, in *Blaue*.[113] Similarly, in *Dear*,[114] the wounds inflicted by D were a continuing and substantial cause of death when V reopened them and bled to death. Similarly, in *People v Lewis*,[115] the conviction for murder was upheld where V had cut his throat to hasten his death when languishing from a gunshot wound inflicted by D, but again the decision was based on the gunshot wound being a substantial and operating cause.

Can D ever be liable for UAM where V has committed suicide and D's unlawful dangerous act is *not* at that moment of the suicide a continuing and operative cause of death? What if V jumps from a tower block fearing that D might be about to inflict an attack in physical terms? What of an abused spouse who takes her own life being in fear of D's continued psychological abuse?

If D has inflicted an injury, the question is whether that remains an operative cause of death. If V is seeking to escape the infliction (or further infliction) of injury by D the test to be applied is that from the flight cases discussed earlier: is V's act a proportionate one or a reasonably foreseeable one given the threat faced? That would cause the court to ask: can suicide ever be a reasonably foreseeable response to violence or further psychological harm? To adopt the language from *Williams* and *Lewis* discussed previously, that would mean asking: can suicide ever be within a range of reasonable responses to a threat of such harm? In *Dhaliwal*, the Court of Appeal gives *obiter* support to a suggestion that an unlawful and dangerous act (eg an assault) may be enough for a manslaughter conviction where

---

[108] *Kennedy (No 2)* [2007] UKHL 38; see generally W Wilson, 'Dealing With Drug Induced Homicide' in Clarkson and Cunningham, *Criminal Liability for Non-Aggressive Deaths*.

[109] At [14].   [110] [2007] UKHL 38. Cf *Keen* [2008] 1 Cr App R (S) 8.

[111] [2003] 1 WLR 1374.

[112] ibid, [31]. In *Burgess* [2008] EWCA Crim 516, the court considered convictions secured pre-*Kennedy (No 2)* where D had laid the tip of the needle against the vein for V. It was held that the fact that V depresses the plunger does not automatically entitle D to an acquittal. Cf the position in Scotland where *Kennedy (No 2)* was rejected: *MacAngus and Kane v HM Advocate* [2009] HCJAC 8.

[113] (1975) 61 Cr App R 271.   [114] [1996] Crim LR 595.   [115] 124 Cal 551 (1899).

the victim was of a 'fragile and vulnerable personality'.[116] There was no reference to any of the case law or issues in the discussion in this paragraph, and it is submitted that the Court of Appeal's *obiter dictum* ought to be treated with considerable caution.[117]

Where D's act *is* still a substantial and operative cause in the sense that the injury is persisting and V commits suicide to avoid further suffering, it is submitted that it is open to a jury to decide that V's act is a reasonably foreseeable and proportionate response (depending on the suffering) and hence not 'daft' and therefore not a break in the chain of causation.

In *Wallace*,[118] the Court of Appeal confirmed that the suicide of the victim will not necessarily break the chain of causation. In this case, V was left severely disfigured, permanently paralysed and in a state of unbearable physical and psychological suffering as a result of injuries inflicted by D. V travelled to Belgium, where euthanasia is lawful, and was euthanized by doctors in accordance with Belgian law. The Court of Appeal held that it was open to a jury to conclude that neither the acts of V in taking the decision to be euthanized nor the acts of the doctors in Belgium in carrying out his wishes broke the chain of causation. The judgment of the Court of Appeal confirms that, provided the jury concludes that the victim's act was a reasonably foreseeable response to the injuries inflicted by the defendant, there will be no break in the chain of causation between the defendant's unlawful act and the victim's death. This will remain the case even if the victim commits suicide.[119] The defendant can therefore be guilty not only of manslaughter, but also of murder if he possesses the requisite mens rea.

14.2 Gross negligence manslaughter

Although this form of manslaughter can be traced back to at least 1807[120] and remained well established in the twentieth century following *Bateman*,[121] its status was challenged when the law adopted objective recklessness in *Caldwell v MPC*.[122] In *Adomako*,[123] the House of Lords confirmed that gross negligence manslaughter (GNM) remained as a free-standing category and had not been subsumed within the category of objective reckless manslaughter. It requires proof that D was in breach of a duty of care under the ordinary principles of negligence; the negligence must have caused death; and it must, in the opinion of the jury, amount to *gross* negligence. The essential question is:

supremely a jury question ... having regard to the risk of death involved, [was] the conduct of the defendant ... so bad in all the circumstances as to amount in [the jury's judgement] to a criminal act or omission.[124]

---

[116] A Bill was introduced into Parliament to criminalize causing suicide, Hansard, HC Debates, 18 Dec 2006. It was not enacted.

[117] cf J Horder and L McGowan, 'Manslaughter by Causing Another's Suicide' [2006] Crim LR 1035.

[118] [2018] EWCA Crim 690.

[119] The position in relation to suicide is more straightforward than the facts of that case. In *Wallace* itself, the intervention was by a medical professional acting independently. In a case of suicide, the question is exclusively about whether V's acts have broken the chain of causation.

[120] *Williamson* (1807) 3 C & P 635.

[121] (1925) 19 Cr App R 8. The classic statement from Lord Hewart CJ appears at 11.

[122] [1982] AC 341.

[123] [1995] 1 AC 171. For comment, see JC Smith [1994] Crim LR 757; G Virgo (1995) 54 CLJ 14. It is unwise to refer to pre-*Adomako* cases: *Archbold* (2020) 19–125. See PA Ashall, 'Manslaughter: The Impact of *Caldwell*' [1984] Crim LR 467; A Briggs, 'In Defence of Manslaughter' [1983] Crim LR 764; G Syrota, '*Mens Rea* in Gross Negligence Manslaughter' [1983] Crim LR 776.

[124] At 187 per Lord Mackay.

The House reasserted the approach of Lord Hewart CJ in *Bateman*[125] that the crime turns on whether, in the opinion of the jury, the negligence of the accused went beyond a mere matter of compensation between subjects and showed such disregard for the life and safety of others as to amount to a crime against the State and conduct deserving of punishment.

The offence arises in a wide variety of contexts including deaths from medical treatment;[126] dangerous accommodation;[127] transportation accidents;[128] people-smuggling;[129] mis-handling firearms[130] and fireworks;[131] deaths in custody;[132] serving peanuts;[133] defective playground equipment;[134] neglect of children[135] or vulnerable adults;[136] deaths in the work-place;[137] neglect of drug addicts;[138] sadomasochistic sex;[139] and even rampaging bulls.[140]

In the recent years, there has been considerable refinement and development of the offence through a series of cases in the Court of Appeal, almost all of which were presided over by Sir Brian Leveson as President of the Queen's Bench Division. A full statement of the offence was provided by Sir Brian Leveson in *Rose*:[141]

The offence of gross negligence manslaughter requires breach of an existing duty of care which it is reasonably foreseeable gives rise to a serious and obvious risk of death and does, in fact, cause death in circumstances where, having regard to the risk of death, the conduct of the defendant was so bad in all the circumstances as to go beyond the requirement of compensation but to amount to a criminal act or omission.

---

[125] (1925) 19 Cr App R 8 at 11.

[126] *Adomako* [1995] 1 AC 171; *Misra* [2004] EWCA Crim 2375; *Sellu* [2016] EWCA Crim 1716; *Rudling* [2016] EWCA Crim 741; *Rose* [2017] EWCA Crim 1168; *Kovvali* [2013] EWCA Crim 1056 (plea: failure to diagnose obvious diabetes); *Garg* [2012] EWCA Crim 2520 (plea: failure to diagnose and forgery).

[127] *Singh* [1999] Crim LR 582 (carbon monoxide poisoning in accommodation); *Johnson* [2008] EWCA Crim 2976 (carbon monoxide from defective chimney repairs).

[128] *A-G's Reference (No 2 of 1999)* [2000] QB 796 (Southall rail crash); *Litchfield* [1998] Crim LR 508 (rigged schooner); *Devine* [1999] 2 Cr App R (S) 409 (drunk pedestrian stepping out killing motorcyclist).

[129] *Wacker* [2002] EWCA Crim 1944 (58 Chinese migrants suffocated in HGV).

[130] *S* [2015] EWCA Crim 558 (15-year-old shot girlfriend with gun he was minding).

[131] *Winter and Winter* [2010] EWCA Crim 1474 (storage of highly explosive unlicensed fireworks); *Pearson* [2019] EWCA Crim 455 (storage of fireworks).

[132] *Gray* [1988] QB 467; *R (W) v Deputy Coroner for Northamptonshire* [2007] EWHC 1649 (Admin).

[133] *Kuddus* [2019] EWCA Crim 837; *Zaman* [2017] EWCA Crim 1783. (Both takeaways supplying food with nuts to allergic customer.)

[134] *Thurston and Thurston* (2018) 9 May, unreported, Chelmsford CC; see also *York College* [2014] EWHC 122 (QB) (3-year-old hanged on slide at nursery).

[135] *Reeves* [2012] EWCA Crim 2613 (unattended infant drowned in bath); *C* [2011] EWCA Crim 3272 (failure to secure medical attention for child's burns).

[136] *Barrass* [2011] EWCA Crim 2629 (learning-disabled adult sister); *Brown (Toni)* [2010] EWCA Crim 2832 (allowed victim of stabbing to bleed to death in her home by refusing to call emergency services).

[137] *Winterton* [2018] EWCA Crim 2435 (excavation trench collapsing); *Crow* [2002] 2 Cr App R (S) 49 (JCB accident after inadequate training); *Mark* [2004] EWCA Crim 2490 (explosion of storage tank in cleaning); *Holthom* [2010] EWCA Crim 934 (excavated wall collapsed); *Babamiri* [2015] EWCA Crim 2152 (Health and Safety at Work etc Act 1974 guillotine tipped and trapped V); *Matthews* [2017] EWCA Crim 179 (construction site death); *McKenzie* [2017] NICA 29 (fall from roof during construction).

[138] *Khan and Khan* [1998] EWCA Crim 971 (drug supply to 15-year-old and abandonment when ill); *Evans* [2009] EWCA Crim 650 (drug supply to 16-year-old and failure to call emergency services when ill). Following *Kennedy (No 2)* [2008] 2 AC 169, D cannot be convicted of unlawful act manslaughter on the basis of the act of supply to V who self-administers the drugs.

[139] *Bowler* [2015] EWCA Crim 849 (bondage with cling film and PVC); *Pike* [1961] Crim LR 114 (sex with V rendered unconscious by consent); *Broadhurst* [2019] EWCA Crim 2026 (sadomasochistic beating, D left V severely injured and intoxicated).

[140] www.bbc.co.uk/news/uk-england-27311682.

[141] *Rose* [2017] EWCA Crim 1168 (optometrist failing statutory duty to inspect back of eye missing signs of V's fatal illness).

In the light of that decision, and the subsequent case of *Kuddus*,[142] there are six elements which the prosecution must prove in order for a person to be guilty of manslaughter by gross negligence:

(1) the defendant owed an existing duty of care to the victim;

(2) the defendant negligently breached that duty of care;

(3) there must be a serious and obvious risk of death. A recognizable risk of something serious is not the same as a recognizable risk of death. A mere possibility that an assessment might reveal something life-threatening is not the same as an obvious risk of death: an obvious risk is a present risk which is clear and unambiguous, not one which might become apparent on further investigation;[143]

(4) it was reasonably foreseeable that the breach of that duty gave rise to a serious and obvious risk of death. The question of whether there is a serious and obvious risk of death must exist at, and is to be assessed with respect to, knowledge at the time of the breach of duty;

(5) the breach of that duty caused the death of the victim;

(6) in the view of the jury, the circumstances of the breach were truly exceptionally bad and so reprehensible as to justify the conclusion that it amounted to gross negligence and required criminal sanction.

14.2.1 The House of Lords' decision in *Adomako*

In *Adomako*, D, an anaesthetist, failed to notice that the tube supplying oxygen to a patient had become detached. According to expert evidence, any competent anaesthetist would have recognized this immediately. The judge directed the jury that a high degree of negligence was required. The Court of Appeal upheld the conviction as this was the appropriate test to apply, and the House of Lords endorsed the gross negligence rather than recklessness test.

The House held that:[144]

(1) there is no separate offence of motor manslaughter. As Lord Atkin said in *Andrews*, 'The principle to be observed is that cases of manslaughter in driving motor cars are but instances of a general rule applicable to all charges of homicide by negligence';[145]

(2) there is no manslaughter by *objective* recklessness, in effect, though not formally, over-ruling *Seymour*. It would now be wrong to direct a jury on any charge of manslaughter in terms of *objective* recklessness (since the decision in *G* overruling *Caldwell*, it would be unthinkable to apply that test);[146]

(3) there is now a single, 'simple' test of gross negligence. D must have been in breach of a duty of care under the ordinary principles of negligence; the negligence must have caused death; and it must, in the opinion of the jury, amount to *gross* negligence. The question, 'supremely a jury question', is:

having regard to the risk of death involved, [was] the conduct of the defendant . . . so bad in all the circumstances as to amount in [the jury's judgement] to a criminal act or omission?

---

[142] [2019] EWCA Crim 837.   [143] *Rose* [2017] EWCA Crim 1168, [77].

[144] See commentary at [1994] Crim LR 757 and S Gardner, 'Manslaughter by Gross Negligence' (1995) 111 LQR 22. On the safety of convictions based on recklessness, see *Morgan* [2007] EWCA Crim 3313.

[145] See generally ID Brownlee and M Seneviratne, 'Killing with Cars After *Adomako*: Time for Some Alternatives' [1995] Crim LR 389. See also *Brown* [2005] UKPC 18.

[146] For a clear review of the development of fault in manslaughter from gross negligence, through forms of recklessness and back to gross negligence, see J Stannard, 'From *Andrews* to *Seymour* and Back Again' (1996) 47 NILQ 1.

Before examining the elements of the test in detail, it is necessary to point out that trials for gross negligence manslaughter often involve a great deal of expert evidence. Usually this evidence relates to whether D breached the duty of care he owed to V and whether the breach of duty was grossly negligent. The Court of Appeal emphasized in *Sellu* that despite the fact evidence of this nature will be crucial to the jury's assessment of whether D committed the offence, the experts cannot be permitted to undermine the role of the jury as the ultimate arbiter of guilt.[147]

14.2.2 A duty of care

The most obvious categories of duty in which liability might arise are those involving doctor and patient,[148] optometrist and patient,[149] transport carrier and passenger,[150] employer and employee,[151] parent and child,[152] landlord and tenant,[153] restaurateur and customer,[154] etc but the categories are limitless and involve duties arising in the course of hazardous activity (eg on the road,[155] smuggling illegal immigrants,[156] smuggling cocaine,[157] taking heroin,[158] storing fireworks,[159] minding a firearm[160]), or duties arising from relationships (eg failing to seek medical assistance for a spouse or someone to whose danger D has contributed).[161] It is impossible to catalogue all circumstances in which a duty will arise; rather, the approach

---

[147] *Sellu* [2016] EWCA Crim 1716, [142]. His lordship cited Lord Kerr's opinion for the Board in *Pora v The Queen* [2015] UKPC 9.

[148] See *Adomako* itself; *Misra* [2004] EWCA Crim 2375; RE Ferner, 'Medication Errors that Led to Manslaughter Charges' (2000) 321 BMJ 1212; RE Ferner and SE McDowell, 'Doctors Charged with Manslaughter in the Course of Medical Practice 1795–2005: A Literature Review' (2006) 99 J Royal Society of Medicine 309; O Quick, 'Prosecuting Gross Medical Negligence' (2006) 33 J Law Sco 421; M Childs, 'Medical Manslaughter and Corporate Liability' (1999) 19 LS 316. See also O Quick, 'Medical Killing: Need for a Special Offence' in Clarkson and Cunningham, *Criminal Liability for Non-Aggressive Death*, arguing that medical professionals do not deserve to be charged under the category of manslaughter based on gross negligence, but one based on recklessness. See his similar argument in 'Medical Manslaughter: The Rise and Replacement of a Contested Issue' in C Erin and S Ost (eds), *The Criminal Justice System and Health Care* (2007). See also in that volume the essay by M Brazier and N Allen 'Criminalising Medical Malpractice'. For a discussion of the issues that arise when sentencing doctors who are convicted of gross negligence manslaughter, see H Quirk, 'Sentencing White Coat Crime: The Need for Guidance in Medical Manslaughter Cases' [2013] Crim LR 871.

[149] *Rose* [2017] EWCA Crim 1168.

[150] See *Litchfield* [1998] Crim LR 507 (schooner); *Barker* [2003] 2 Cr App R (S) 22; *McGee* [2013] EWCA Crim 1012.

[151] *R v DPP, ex p Jones* [2000] IRLR 373; *Dean* [2002] EWCA Crim 2410; *Clothier* [2004] EWCA Crim 2629; *Crow* [2001] EWCA Crim 2968. For an analysis of the extent to which employers owe their employees a duty of care, see S Antrobus, 'The Criminal Liability of Directors for Health and Safety Breaches and Manslaughter' [2013] Crim LR 309.

[152] *Reeves* [2012] EWCA Crim 2613.   [153] *Harrison* [2011] EWCA Crim 3139.

[154] *Zaman* [2017] EWCA Crim 1783.

[155] Including a pedestrian killing a motorcyclist by being knocked down: *Devine* [1999] 2 Cr App R (S) 409.

[156] *Wacker* [2002] EWCA Crim 1944.

[157] See news reports for 14 Aug 2010 reporting conviction of Mr Newman. N had smuggled cocaine in concentrated form in a bottle of rum. V, who had been given the bottle, was unaware of the content, drank some and died.

[158] *Ruffell* [2003] Cr App R (S) 53; *Parfeni* [2003] EWCA Crim 159 (although this must surely have been a case of unlawful act manslaughter by D injecting V with heroin in order to steal from him).

[159] *Winter and Winter* [2010] EWCA Crim 1474.

[160] *S* [2015] EWCA Crim 558.

[161] *Hood* [2004] 1 Cr App R (S) 73. See also *Sogunro* [1997] 2 Cr App R (S) 89 (starving V believing her to be possessed) and see *Evans*, n 138. See also the sentencing case of *Barrass* [2011] EWCA Crim 2629 in which D pleaded guilty to the gross negligence manslaughter of his sister. It is unclear from the judgment whether the duty arose because of the familial relationship or because V was dependent upon D.

is to apply the 'ordinary principles of negligence' to determine whether the defendant owed a duty to the victim. So, for example, in *Yaqoob*,[162] D was a manager of a minicab firm and he had failed to inspect the tyres of a minibus involved in a fatal accident. It was held that it was *open to the jury* to find that there was a duty to inspect and maintain beyond that required for an MOT test, council inspections and other duties imposed by regulation. Moreover, the jury did not require expert evidence to assess that duty.[163]

In cases of positive acts, it is relatively easy to identify whether there was a duty based on whether the acts created a risk of death which was obvious to the ordinary prudent individual. In cases of omission, much greater care needs to be exercised as there will be situations in which a risk of death would be obvious, but where D has no duty—as with D witnessing a blind stranger walking towards a cliff. No doubt the courts will be prepared in many cases to recognize a duty arising from a combination of circumstances.[164] In *Willoughby*,[165] for example, D had, with V, spread petrol around D's property with the intention of burning it down to claim on the insurance. V died when the petrol ignited. The Court of Appeal concluded that D's ownership per se did not give rise to a duty, but because D engaged the deceased to participate in spreading petrol, and with a view to setting fire to D's premises for D's benefit, a duty existed.

The duty question in gross negligence should, according to Lord MacKay in *Adomako*, be founded on the 'ordinary principles of negligence'. However, this should not be regarded as incorporating all of the technicalities of the tort of negligence into the gross negligence offence. Thus, in *Wacker*[166] it was held that where D had smuggled 60 illegal immigrants into the UK and 58 had died of suffocation owing to his having shut the air vent in their container, he could not displace the duty by relying on the victims' being jointly engaged with him in a criminal enterprise—that is, a plea of *ex turpi causa*.[167]

The courts are clearly anxious to retain a degree of simplicity in this element of the offence which must be put before the jury. On some occasions the criminal courts seem readily to accept the existence of a civil law duty. In the case of *Winter and Winter*,[168] for example, MW and NW were convicted of manslaughter by gross negligence having stored fireworks of an extremely hazardous nature, in breach of their licence, in a container on a farm. A large explosion occurred, killing the fire service's civilian media awareness officer (V), who had been filming the fire for training purposes. V had ignored instructions to keep back from the container. The judge ruled that MW and NW owed a duty to take proper care in the storage and handling of explosives and that that duty was owed to all persons who were on the site or in the surrounding vicinity. The Court of Appeal held that it was reasonably foreseeable that civilian employees of the fire service might come on to and close to the site of a fire in order to film or photograph a fire.[169]

The courts have been willing to take an expansive interpretation of the scope of the duty where that appears appropriate on policy grounds. In *Evans*,[170] D was convicted of gross

---

[162] [2005] EWCA Crim 2169.   [163] *Oughton* [2010] EWCA Crim 1540.

[164] As in the cases of omission, especially in *Stone and Dobinson* [1977] QB 354 in which the duty arose from the cohabitation, blood relationship and voluntary assumption of responsibility.

[165] [2005] Crim LR 383.

[166] [2003] QB 1203, [2003] Crim LR 108 and commentary. Cf Scots law, *Transco plc v HM Advocate* 2004 SLT 41.

[167] cf the statutory recognition in relation to corporate manslaughter (see later).

[168] *Winter and Winter* [2010] EWCA Crim 1474.

[169] It was held that V's failure to comply with instructions might be relevant to the issue of causation and, in civil cases, to the issue of causation, *volenti* and contributory negligence. It was not arguable in the instant case that any failure to comply with instructions had the consequence that no duty of care was owed to V.

[170] [2009] EWCA Crim 650.

negligence manslaughter having supplied heroin to her half-sister V (a recovering addict). V self-administered the drug in the house with D and her mother (who was also convicted of manslaughter). D noticed that V looked as if she had overdosed, a condition D was familiar with. D, fearful of attracting the attention of the police, chose not to seek medical assistance and V died. The jury was directed that without D's involvement in the supply of heroin, there was no duty on D to act, even after she became aware of the serious adverse effect on V of the drug-taking. They were directed that if D *was* involved in supply, that fact, taken with the other undisputed facts, would and did give rise to a duty on D to act. On appeal, a five-member Court of Appeal held that having regard to the authorities on gross negligence manslaughter, it was an essential requirement of any potential basis for conviction that D was under a duty to act. The duty necessary to found gross negligence was plainly not confined to cases of a familial or professional relationship between the defendant and the deceased. For the purposes of gross negligence, a duty could arise if, inter alia, D had created *or contributed* to the creation of a state of affairs (V's danger) which D knew, or ought reasonably to have known, had become life-threatening. The duty on D was to act by taking reasonable steps to save the other's life by calling medical assistance.[171] This is a controversial decision.[172]

From where does the duty on D derive? A duty might be thought to arise at the time of and from the mere act of supply. That is not the law. Following the decision of the House of Lords in *Kennedy (No 2)*,[173] D cannot be convicted of unlawful act manslaughter on the basis of the act of supply to V who self-administers the drugs. D cannot be guilty of unlawful act manslaughter because if V is a free, informed, voluntary actor he breaks the chain of causation between D's unlawful act of supply and the resulting death.[174] If on such facts the prosecution was for gross negligence manslaughter, the same problem would arise: the mere act of supply will *not*, it is submitted, be sufficient to establish liability for manslaughter when V self-administers in a free, informed manner and dies. Although D might be said to owe a duty, have breached it and for there to have been a risk of death, the difficulty is that V's free, informed, voluntary act of self-administration breaks the chain of causation (as in cases of unlawful act manslaughter under *Kennedy (No 2)*).[175] Dealers who supply to their users, who are adults of full mental capacity, to self-inject are not liable for manslaughter—at least provided the dealer does not stay with the user and witness the user becoming ill.

The duty arises, the court held in *Evans*, at the point in time when D realized or ought to have realized that V was suffering life-threatening illness. The duty arises at that time because D created *or contributed to* the creation of the life-threatening situation. This conclusion was reached by an extended application of the decision in *Miller*. In that case D was liable for criminal damage when, having fallen asleep with a lit cigarette, he awoke, realized his accidental conduct had created a danger but did not take reasonable steps to prevent further harm arising.[176] In this case the defendants had deliberately supplied the drugs, but V had self-injected. How, applying *Miller* in this extended form, can D be said to be under

---

[171] Compare the recent decision of *Broughton* [2020] EWCA Crim 1093 on similar facts.

[172] There are other reported instances of drug suppliers being convicted on this basis. For an example, see *Phillips* [2013] EWCA Crim 358.

[173] [2008] 1 AC 269.

[174] There will be rare instances in which D is engaged in the act of injection to such an extent as to be liable for unlawful act manslaughter: *Burgess* [2008] EWCA Crim 516, p 76.

[175] In *Evans*, the Court of Appeal emphasized that 'The question in this appeal *is not whether the appellant may be guilty of manslaughter for having been concerned in the supply of the heroin which caused the deceased's death*' (emphasis added).

[176] Although Miller was charged with criminal damage which at that time was satisfied by proof of objective recklessness, the House of Lords held that his duty only arose on his subjective realization of the danger. Gross negligence manslaughter is also a crime based on objective fault, but in *Evans* the court holds that the duty arises when D realizes or *ought* to have realized the danger.

a duty of care given V's free, informed act to take the drugs? If D has not caused V's death when V self-injects (*Kennedy*), how can D have caused V to become ill when V has self-injected and therefore how can D owe a duty when V does become ill? The answer lies in the fact that the Court of Appeal used the broader expression 'created *or contributed*'.[177] A court may, it is submitted, conclude that a duty arises, applying that test, when D became aware (or ought to have become aware) of V's dangerous illness and either: (a) he was concerned in the supply to V; (b) D was in a pre-existing relationship with V (parent, carer, etc) which persists irrespective of V's self-administration (eg the husband of a woman who has self-injected and who realizes or ought to have realized that she is having breathing difficulty); (c) because D and V were engaged in a dangerous joint enterprise which went wrong;[178] or (d) where D has voluntarily assumed a duty to care for V who is in such a state[179] (eg where V becomes dependent on D's assistance as where D starts to care for V, who has overdosed at a party by moving him from one room to a more secluded space, but then abandons him, leaving V worse off as he is less likely to be seen and rescued by others).

The decision has been heavily criticized but, in policy terms, it might be asked when someone has died, what is wrong with looking to the conduct of those who contributed in some way to the danger *if they also* did not take reasonable steps to alleviate the danger when aware of it? To take an example unencumbered by the policy considerations of the drug supply cases, consider an electrician, D, who leaves half-completed wiring creating a risk of death and V makes an informed choice to use the electrical equipment, aware of its hazardous status. If V is in the process of being electrocuted and D realizes that, surely D has a duty to act responsibly to avoid a life-threatening situation to which he has contributed. Why should a failure at least to seek help on realizing V has been electrocuted not be considered manslaughter if the jury determines the breach sufficiently 'gross'?[180]

Historically the law was unclear whether the duty issue involved a pure question of law to be determined by the judge,[181] or whether the judge was to rule on whether there was evidence capable of establishing a duty, in which case that was to be left to be determined by the jury.[182] The matter has finally been resolved in *Evans*[183] in which the Court of Appeal held 'that whether a duty of care exists is a matter for the jury once the judge has decided that there is evidence capable of establishing a duty'. The court stated:[184]

In some cases, such as those arising from a doctor/patient relationship where the existence of the duty is not in dispute, the Judge may well direct the jury that a duty of care exists. Such a direction would be proper. But if, for example, the doctor were on holiday at the material time, and

---

[177] See for criticism, Glenys Williams [2009] Crim LR 631 and J Rogers [2009] 6 Arch News 6. The court's response might well be that V's free, deliberate, informed act might break the chain of causation if it was alleged that D's breach by supply per se caused V's death, but V's acts of supply do not become irrelevant when considering whether D *contributed* to the danger V now faces.

[178] See W Wilson, *Criminal Law: Doctrine and Theory* (3rd edn, 2008) 87.

[179] The court in *Evans* does not rule out this final possibility of duty in drug administration cases although it did not arise on the facts, at [36]. Arguably this is the basis for the decision in *Ruffell* [2003] 2 Cr App R (S) 53.

[180] An issue might arise as to whether D discharged the duty of care despite the fact that he failed to summon assistance. The facts of *Phillips* [2013] EWCA Crim 358 are instructive. D became aware that V was suffering from the effects of an overdose, but instead of summoning help, administered adrenaline. The Court of Appeal stated that 'the "gross negligence" alleged therefore was the appellant's failure to act once he knew that [V]'s life was in danger'. D did not fail to act, however. It is important not to lose sight of the fact that the jury must be sure that there was a breach of duty, taking into consideration any steps D took to mitigate the life-threatening situation.

[181] *Gurphal Singh* [1999] Crim LR 582.   [182] *Khan* [1998] Crim LR 830; *Sinclair* (1998) unreported.

[183] [2009] EWCA Crim 650. The court approved the commentary in *Willoughby* [2004] EWCA Crim 3365. On alternative interpretations that might have been drawn from tort law, see J Herring and E Palser, 'A Duty of Care in Gross Negligence Manslaughter' [2007] Crim LR 24.

[184] At [45].

the deceased asked a casual question over a drink, it may very well be that the question whether a doctor/patient relationship existed, and accordingly whether a duty of care arose, would be in dispute. In any cases where the issue is in dispute, and therefore in more complex cases, and assuming that the Judge has found that it would be open to the jury to find that there was a duty of care, or a duty to act, the jury should be directed that if facts A + B and/or C or D are established, then in law a duty will arise, but if facts X or Y or Z were present, the duty would be negatived. In this sense, of course, the jury is deciding whether the duty situation has been established. In our judgment this is the way in which *Willoughby* should be understood and, understood in this way, no potential problems arising from art.6 and art.7 of the ECHR are engaged.

14.2.3 Breach of duty

The breach can be by positive act or by omission.[185]

Whether there has been a breach of duty is quintessentially a question of fact for the jury. The test to be applied is an objective one, comparing the defendant's conduct with what could be expected of a reasonably competent and careful person in the defendant's position. 'The ordinary principles of the law of negligence apply to ascertain whether or not the defendant has been in breach of a duty of care towards the victim who has died.'[186] The duty may be set out in statute, arise under contract, by custom, etc. The standards to be expected of the person in complying with that duty could therefore derive from numerous sources. Expert evidence will be critical in establishing whether there has been a breach of the duty. Potential problems to be managed are: avoiding the expert evidence dominating the trial, becoming a distracting debate about industry practices and jurors' reliance on experts.

14.2.4 A serious and obvious risk of death

The proposition in *Adomako* refers to a risk of *death*, a point emphasized in *Gurphal Singh*.[187] The need for a risk of death to exist was not made as explicit as it might have been in *Adomako*.[188] A more explicit statement would have been welcome for at least two reasons. First, because there had been considerable debate about whether the offence extended to cases in which there was an objective risk of serious harm.[189] Secondly, because the element was often conflated with the question of whether death was reasonably foreseeable.

It is now clear that there must in all cases be proved to be a serious and obvious risk of death. This element is central to the offence because: 'There is no such thing as negligence in the abstract. Negligence is always in relation to a particular context.'[190] The question of whether the negligence was gross will have to be considered/assessed in the context of an existing risk of death that is both serious and obvious to someone in D's position possessed of the information available to him. It is necessary to avoid the jury reasoning, erroneously, that because there was a death, there must have been an obvious risk of death.

185 See, on omissions, *Watts* [1998] Crim LR 833; *Litchfield* [1998] Crim LR 507.
186 *Adomako* [1995] 1 AC 171 at 187B per Lord Mackay.
187 *Gurphal Singh* [1999] Crim LR 582. In *Brown* [2005] UKPC 18, the suggestion was of a 'high' risk of death. *Singh* was cited in *Webster v CPS* [2014] EWHC 2516 (Admin).
188 [1995] 1 AC 171, 187C–D. 'The jury will have to consider whether the extent to which the defendant's conduct departed from the proper standard of care incumbent upon him, involving as it must have done *a risk of death* to the patient, was such that it should be judged criminal.'
189 The debate has been a long-standing one. Going back 60 years, there were divergent views between eg Glanville Williams favouring the requirement for a risk of death (*Criminal Law the General Part* (1953) 111); and *Smith and Hogan* (1st edn, 1965) favouring 'death or really serious injury', p 228. Even *Bateman* (1925) can be read as requiring conscious disregard not negligence.
190 Williams, ibid, 93.

This element is also important as it takes some of the pressure off the causal element in the offence. To take an example, if D, a chef, grossly negligently cut V's finger and V contracted sepsis and died, D would not be liable as there was no serious and obvious risk of death (even though there would be no concern about causation as D must take his victim as found).

Confirmation that a risk of serious injury will not suffice was made in *Singh*:[191]

the circumstances must be such that a reasonably prudent person would have foreseen a serious and obvious risk not merely of injury, even serious injury, but of death.

The Court of Appeal echoed this requirement in *Misra*[192] and in *Rudling*:[193] at the time of the breach of duty, there must be a risk of death, not merely serious harm or illness; the risk must be serious; and the risk must be obvious. As a matter of policy, the CPS will not prosecute on evidence of anything less. If we are to have an offence of homicide by gross negligence at all, it seems right that it should be so limited.[194] The circumstances must be such that there is a serious risk, not merely of injury, even serious injury, but of death.

In *Kuddus*, the Court of Appeal confirmed explicitly that this element was distinct from the separate question of whether the serious and obvious risk of death was foreseeable. There must exist in fact a serious and obvious risk of death for it to be reasonably foreseeable:

the Defendant's breach of duty must give rise to (1) a risk of death, that was (2) obvious and (3) serious. These are objective facts, which are not dependent upon the state of mind or knowledge of the Defendant. If there is a real issue as to their existence, each must be proved by relevant and admissible evidence.[195]

In *Kuddus*, a 15-year-old girl died after suffering a severe allergic reaction to food ordered from the takeaway run by K. She had recorded her allergy (all be it ambiguously) on the online order form. The food delivered to her contained peanut proteins. V died in hospital two days later after suffering a severe allergic reaction. The judge directed the jury on reasonable foreseeability of the relevant risk, but rejected the submission that the jury should first be asked to consider whether there had been a serious and obvious risk of death to V specifically given that V's medical history was of only a mild allergy. The Court of Appeal held that in most cases there was no requirement to prove a serious and obvious risk of death for the specific victim. If that was an issue, the question was whether the breach had given rise to a serious and obvious risk of death to the class of persons to whom D owed a duty (of which V was one). If such a risk existed, it would not be a defence to say that V had been assessed as being at low risk of an allergic reaction or that she was only at risk of suffering injury rather than death. There was no separate and independent requirement that the prosecution had to prove the existence of a serious and obvious risk of death in respect of the particular victim:

The seriousness of the risk of death, as an objective fact, is itself a question of fact and is distinct from the question whether a reasonable person in the Defendant's position should have foreseen that the risk was serious (and obvious). As we have said, each of these objective facts is distinct from the question of foreseeability that was in issue in *Honey Rose* and *Zaman*: put simply, you cannot foresee something that does not exist.[196]

---

[191] [1999] Crim LR 582 (landlord and son failing to respond to tenant's concerns about fumes by installing working carbon monoxide detectors). See also *Yaqoob* [2005] EWCA Crim 2169 (duty to check roadworthiness of vehicle).

[192] [2004] EWCA Crim 2375, [51].   [193] *Rudling* [2016] EWCA Crim 741.

[194] cf the view of LH Leigh, 'Liability for Inadvertence: A Lordly Legacy?' (1995) 58 MLR 457, 459.

[195] [2019] EWCA Crim 837, [53].   [196] At [54].

There are further questions that may need to be resolved about this limb of the offence in an appropriate case, including how precisely defined the class must be and whether expert evidence is required to assist in defining the class. In some cases, expert evidence as to the risk of death will be very specific. For example, in *Sellu*,[197] where it was alleged that there were separate failings by the defendant's post-operative care of the victim which led to the death, the prosecution approached the medical evidence as to risks of death being evaluated in relation to each of the medical failings—the failure to give antibiotics (2 per cent), 9 per cent by the next morning, 15 per cent by later that second day and up to 99 per cent by the time of the operation. The prosecution put its case on any of the failings being sufficient in isolation or combination. That was to avoid the risk of a *Brown* direction being given. It is not clear that some of these incidents would satisfy the *Adomako* test in any event. There must be an 'a serious and obvious risk of death'. If the mortality risk was just 2 per cent, or even 9 per cent, it is far from clear that that constitutes a 'serious and obvious' risk of death. It might have been easier if the case had been focused on the cumulative effect of the failings.

A further issue, which was specifically left open in *Kuddus*, is whether a defendant's specific knowledge of the victim as distinct from the class of victim could affect this question. There is also the question of whether this element can be satisfied by a failure to put in place safe systems where that allegation is relied on as an alleged breach sufficient to ground liability.[198]

Whether the risk of death was obvious is a question of fact. The requirement is closely interwoven with other elements of the offence. The direction in *Singh*[199] should be followed: 'the circumstances must be such that a reasonably prudent person would have foreseen a serious and obvious risk not merely of injury, even serious injury, but of death'. In *Yaqoob* (discussed earlier), the Court of Appeal emphasized that a direction should expressly refer to the fact that it is the risk of death and not merely serious injury that is relevant. The seriousness of the risk speaks to the degree of risk—something much more than negligible. The word is there to qualify the risk, not the result: death is of itself always serious. It is difficult to be give any more guidance on what threshold it imposes. The obviousness suggests it must be 'immediately apparent', 'striking', 'glaring'.[200]

14.2.5 Reasonable foreseeability of the serious and obvious risk of death

The prosecution must prove that a reasonable person in D's position, possessed of the information available to D, would have foreseen a serious and obvious risk of death (nothing less). The leading authority is *Rose*.[201] Sir Brian Leveson P pointed out the crucial distinction:

a mere possibility that an assessment might reveal something life-threatening is not the same as an obvious risk of death. An obvious risk is a present risk which is clear and unambiguous, not one which might become apparent on further investigation.[202]

The question whether the serious and obvious risk of death was reasonably foreseeable is an objective question—not a question about whether D himself foresaw any such risk. In *S*,[203] S, aged 15, shot his girlfriend, aged 15, when a prohibited firearm (which he was minding)

---

[197] See n 197.

[198] See *Zaman* [2018] EWCA Crim 1783, where the facts alleged were: (a) failing to take reasonable steps to alert customers to the risk of the presence of peanuts; (b) failing to ensure that staff had been properly trained or instructed in food allergens; and (c) failing to provide a system to prevent cross-contamination.

[199] [1999] Crim LR 582.

[200] See also Law Comm Report No 237 (1996), para 5.27.

[201] At [77].   [202] See also *Rudling* [2016] EWCA Crim 741, [39]–[41].

[203] [2015] EWCA Crim 558.

went off at close range while he was showing it to her. There was no evidence that S had either known or believed the gun to be loaded. At trial, S claimed to have removed the magazine from the weapon and therefore believed that it was safe. Expert evidence was to the effect that an inexperienced 15-year-old may have reasonably believed it was safe (not being aware of the risk of a bullet still being in the chamber). The Court of Appeal rejected the argument that it was necessary to show that S knew, believed or personally foresaw the risk of death. Gross negligence manslaughter involves an objective test: whether a reasonable and prudent person of S's age and experience would have foreseen a serious risk of death and, if so, whether S's conduct fell so far below the standard of care required that it was grossly negligent such that it constituted a crime. Cranston J stated that:

In answering that objective question, it was open to the jury to conclude on the evidence before it that [S's] conduct fell below the standard of care in pointing a gun and pulling the trigger when just a short distance away from [V]. The judge distinguished ordinary negligence and said that whether this was gross negligence turned on the circumstances.[204]

A spate of cases involving medical error has led to a further refinement of the test. The focus of the Court of Appeal's attention has been on at what point the risk of death must be assessed as being obvious and in what context. The Court of Appeal has now decided that the risk must be obvious to the reasonable professional in D's shoes, who demonstrates the same level of negligence as D. In other words, the test is not whether the reasonable professional who had not been negligent would have appreciated the existence of a serious and obvious risk of death. The risk must be assessed with reference to D's negligent standard. The difference between these two approaches can be seen in the cases in which the applicable test has been forged.

In *Rudling*,[205] V, a 12-year-old boy, had died of Addison's disease (a very rare condition) after D, his GP, had failed to attend him. Addison's disease was not something any GP could be expected to recognize, but it was argued by the prosecution that the symptoms described to her by V's mother (including vomiting, soiling and black genitals) were so alarming that D ought to have visited him and had she done so she would then have seen that V needed immediate hospital admission. Had she arranged this, V would have been diagnosed and given life-saving treatment. The trial judge nevertheless accepted a submission of no case to answer and the Court of Appeal agreed with this. The thrust of the prosecution case was that a reasonably competent GP would have said to herself 'I cannot eliminate the possibility that this child may be suffering from a rare risk to life without the child being seen urgently', which equated to a serious and obvious risk of death. But according to the Court of Appeal:

At the time of the breach of duty, there must be a risk of death, not merely serious illness; the risk must be serious; and the risk must be obvious. A GP faced with an unusual presentation which is worrying and undiagnosed may need to ensure a face to face assessment urgently in order to investigate further. That may be in order to assess whether it is something serious . . . which may or may not be so serious as to be life-threatening. A recognisable risk of something serious is not the same as a recognisable risk of death.

What does not follow is that if a reasonably competent GP requires an urgent assessment of a worrying and undiagnosed condition, it is necessarily reasonably foreseeable that there is a risk of death. Still less does it demonstrate a serious risk of death, which is not to be equated with an 'inability to eliminate a possibility'. There may be numerous remote possibilities of very rare conditions which cannot be eliminated but which do not present a serious risk of death. Further,

---

204 At [20].   205 [2016] EWCA Crim 741.

and perhaps most importantly, a mere possibility that an assessment might reveal something life-threatening is not the same as an obvious risk of death. An obvious risk is a present risk which is clear and unambiguous, not one which might become apparent on further investigation.

These distinctions are not a matter of semantics but represent real differences in the practical assessments which fall to be made by doctors. . . .[206]

In *Rose*, the Court of Appeal addressed this issue more directly.[207] The court, drawing on *Rudling*, held that in assessing either the foreseeability of the risk of death or the grossness of the conduct in question, the jury were not entitled to take into account information which would, could or should have been available to the defendant had he not breached the duty in question: the test is objective and prospective.

Turning to the facts of *Rose*, D was a registered optometrist who conducted a routine eye test and examination on V. D failed to examine the internal structure of D's eyes, however, as she was required to do by statute. A few months after the eye examination, V died of acute hydrocephalus. Had D examined V's eyes in accordance with her statutory duty, she would have noticed the swelling of his optic nerve, the significance of which would have been clear. The experts agreed that a competent optometrist would have known the significance of that swelling and would immediately have referred the case on to others for urgent treatment. The judge rejected a submission of no case to answer, determining that D had failed to conduct a full examination of the internal structure of V's eyes, there was no good reason for that failure and thus she had breached her duty of care. He directed the jury to consider whether that risk would have been obvious to a reasonably competent optometrist with the knowledge that D would have had 'if she had not acted in breach of her duty to investigate the true position'. D appealed on the basis that the judge was incorrect to direct the jury that in evaluating whether the risk of death was reasonably foreseeable, they were entitled to consider the knowledge D would have had if she had conducted the eye examination in accordance with her statutory duty.

The Court of Appeal accepted D's submission. It was held that the objective nature of the test requires the notional exercise of putting a reasonably prudent professional in the shoes of the person whose conduct is under scrutiny and asking whether, at the moment of the breach of the duty relied on by the prosecution, that person ought reasonably to have foreseen a serious and obvious risk of death. On the facts of the case, the risk of death would only have been serious and obvious had D examined the internal structure of V's eyes. Sir Brian Leveson P concluded that there was no legitimate basis for altering what is a prospective test of foresight into one which judges with hindsight. D's conviction was therefore quashed. When directing the jury on whether it was reasonably foreseeable that D's breach of the duty gave rise to a serious and obvious risk of death, the reasonably prudent professional is to be endowed with the knowledge D had at the time of the breach of duty, not the knowledge D would or might have had if the breach had not occurred.

The court did add a caveat, however. It was held that the position might be different if V presented with symptoms which themselves either pointed to the risk of a potentially life threatening condition or provided a flag that alerted a competent optometrist to that risk. Sir Brian Leveson P stated that was not this case, however, given that D was conducting an entirely routine examination with no material pre-existing history.

The *Rose* test was repeated by the Court of Appeal in *Kuddus*.[208] In *Winterton*,[209] however, a construction site manager with overall responsibility for health and safety at the site

[206] At [39]–[41].   [207] *Rose* [2017] EWCA Crim 1168.

[208] The court was presided over by Sir Brian Leveson but also included Mr Justice Stuart-Smith, as he then was (the first instance judge in *Rose*).

[209] [2018] EWCA Crim 2435.

was convicted of gross negligence manslaughter, following a labourer's death after a trench collapsed that he was either standing in or at the edge of. The Court of Appeal accepted that D ought to have known (and arguably did know) that it was dangerously dug and 'the warning signs and serious and obvious risk of death were there' for all to see.[210]

The court rejected the argument that, as a result of *Rose*, the defendant could only be guilty if he actually saw the trench in an unsafe state with someone working inside. The court stated that the principle to be derived from *Rose* is that the question of available knowledge and risk is always to be judged objectively and prospectively as at the moment of breach, not but for the breach. The evidence in this case regarding the excavation of the trench clearly demonstrated the dangerous workmanship that posed a real and significant risk of death. It also stated that there was evidence that the defendant was aware of the dangerous state of the trench. Although there was a reference in *Winterton* to 'wilful blindness', it is submitted that the court was not using that term in the formal sense in which it is used to impute knowledge to a defendant. That is not a prerequisite for criminal liability for gross negligence manslaughter.

It is respectfully submitted that there are several problems with framing the test in the way *Rose* does.[211] First, it seems, in policy terms, to be counterintuitive since it appears to incentivize the person who owes the duty to do less—the less D engages, the less likely the reasonably competent person in his shoes would realize there was a risk of death. The optometrist who does not bother to examine the internal structure of the eye is less likely to be liable than one who does so badly. The counter-argument to this is that the test avoids the risk of medical and other professions being charged with gross negligence manslaughter by reason of negligent omissions to carry out routine eye, blood and other tests which in fact would have revealed fatal conditions notwithstanding that the circumstances were such that it was not reasonably foreseeable that failure to carry out such tests would carry a serious and obvious risk of death.[212] Stark argues that the approach is important in restricting the scope of gross negligence manslaughter to the worst cases of negligence causing death.[213]

Secondly, by endowing the reasonably competent professional with D's shortcomings, the Court of Appeal diminishes the objective nature of the test established in *Adomako*. The House of Lords in *Adomako* held that the standard against which D's conduct ought to be evaluated is that of a reasonably competent anaesthetist, optometrist, etc. If a reasonably competent optometrist would have performed a proper examination of the internal eye, why should D benefit from the fact that she failed to do so and therefore fell far below the standard expected of her? There is an important distinction between the facts of *Rose* and the facts of *Rudling* in this regard. In *Rose*, as D was an optometrist, any eye examination she conducted had to be in accordance with the Opticians Act 1989 and the Sight Test (Examination and Prescription) (No 2) Regulations 1989. These provisions specify that an optometrist, when conducting an eye examination, must perform an intra-ocular examination. There can be no doubt that the reasonably competent optometrist would have conducted V's eye examination in accordance with the duty imposed upon her by the applicable legislation. Had a proper intra-ocular examination been conducted, the reasonably prudent

---

[210] At [29].

[211] See further K Laird, '*R v Rose*' [2018] Crim LR 76 and 'The Evolution of Gross Negligence Manslaughter' [2018] 1 Arch Rev 6.

[212] This concern was expressed by the Court of Appeal in *Rose*, but whether a doctor's failure to diagnose a condition amounts to negligence depends upon a number of factors, including the symptoms presented, the diagnostic techniques available and the dangers associated with the alternative diagnoses. See M Jones, *Medical Negligence* (2017) 4–018.

[213] F Stark, 'In Praise of *Rose*' [2019] 8 Arch Rev 7.

optometrist would have noticed the swelling of V's optic nerve and would have referred him for urgent medical treatment. As has already been pointed out, on the court's interpretation of the test, had D conducted an intra-ocular examination but failed to appreciate the significance of the swelling of the optic nerve, she might have been guilty. By failing to conduct an intra-ocular examination, she was able to avoid liability altogether. The facts of *Rudling* are different, however. Owing to the equivocal nature of V's symptoms, there was disagreement as to whether a reasonably competent GP would have attended V having been told of the symptoms from which he was suffering. If a reasonably competent GP might not have attended V and therefore would also have failed to appreciate the seriousness of his condition, then D should not be penalized for also failing to do so. As the House of Lords confirmed in *Adomako*, D is not to be judged against the standard of more skilled professionals but by the standard of a reasonably competent professional. In *Rose*, had the Court of Appeal agreed with the trial judge's formulation of the relevant test, this would not necessarily lead to the adverse consequences for medical and other professionals described by the Court of Appeal and set out in the previous paragraph. Stark argues that the Court of Appeal's movement away from the House of Lords' focus on objective conduct is a virtue of the judgment in *Rose*.[214] He does so on the basis that it moves the law closer to analysing the defendant's actual beliefs, which is more relevant to assessing personal culpability regarding the risk of death than the failure to do as another person could have done.

A final difficulty is that the inquiry into whether the foresight of death was objectively identifiable will turn not just on the specific duty owed by D but by the critical context in which it arose. That will often be a less precise inquiry. Take a simple example of D the plumber who did not remove the front plate from a boiler to check its functioning. If the boiler subsequently explodes killing V, applying *Rose*, the question is whether the reasonable plumber in his shoes (not having taken off the front plate) would have realized there was a serious and obvious risk of death. That can only be determined by asking what the plumber was told to do when hired to examine the boiler. In a case where the plumber was called out because of a smell of gas, he may well be found liable; in a case where the call-out was to provide a routine service to the boiler, the jury may be less inclined to convict.

The problem is one which arises acutely in medical cases where the evidence of the 'context' will often be disputed and be based on what the deceased said. For example, in *Rudling*, the issue may turn on whether the mother described the boy's genitals as black (would have triggered a realization in a reasonable doctor of a risk of death) or discoloured (not immediately obvious that that suggests life-threatening illness).[215]

14.2.6 'Gross' negligence

The test is objective—the question is whether the risk would have been obvious to the reasonably prudent and skilful doctor, anaesthetist, electrician, motorist, restaurateur or person on the Clapham omnibus, as the circumstances require.

14.2.6.1 Relationship with recklessness

It is, at first sight, surprising that the gross negligence test should be more favourable to the defendant than a recklessness test—even *objective* recklessness.[216] The difference is that the recklessness test did not include the requirement that the jury must be satisfied that the defendant's conduct was bad enough to be a crime. A direction based on the test in

---

214 ibid.   215 See also *Bawa-Garba* [2016] EWCA Crim 1841.
216 See Leigh (1995) 58 MLR 457 and A Norrie, *Crime, Reason and History* (3rd edn, 2014) 66–9.

Lawrence terms deprived D of the chance of acquittal on that ground.[217] In *Prentice*, for example, there were many strongly mitigating factors in the doctors' conduct, which were irrelevant if the jury were concerned only with what was foreseeable, but highly relevant to question whether their behaviour was bad enough to deserve condemnation as manslaughter. Ever since *Bateman*, the courts have asserted that the test is whether the negligence goes beyond a mere matter of compensation and is bad enough to amount to a crime; but this is incomplete, if not plainly wrong. Careless driving amounts to a crime and deserves punishment but, manifestly, it does not on that ground alone amount to manslaughter, if it happens to cause death. Even dangerous driving causing death is not necessarily manslaughter. There are degrees of *criminal* negligence, and manslaughter requires a very high degree. Should not the jury be asked whether the negligence is bad enough to be condemned, not merely as a crime, but as the very grave crime of manslaughter?[218]

In *Misra*,[219] the defendants argued that gross negligence should be replaced with an offence of reckless manslaughter, relying on the fundamental rejection of objectivism in *G*, and the *dicta* in that case that all serious offences require proof of a blameworthy *state of mind*. The Court of Appeal concluded that such arguments had been duly considered and rejected in *Adomako*, and saw nothing in *G*[220] to cause them to regard *Adomako* as no longer binding.[221]

14.2.6.2 Relevance of D's state of mind

Since the test of gross negligence is purely objective, it might be thought that the state of mind of the particular accused is irrelevant to the inquiry. However, the courts have held that proof of the defendant's state of mind and in particular his foresight of the risk of harm or death is 'not a prerequisite to a conviction' whilst recognizing also that there may be cases in which the defendant's state of mind is 'relevant to the jury's consideration when assessing the grossness and criminality of his conduct'.[222] This approach has been endorsed on a number of occasions, and it has been recognized that it may operate in the accused's favour.[223]

In *A-G's Reference (No 2 of 1999)*,[224] Rose LJ stated:

Although there may be cases where the defendants state of mind is relevant to the jury's consideration when assessing the grossness and criminality of his conduct, evidence of his state of mind is not a prerequisite to a conviction for manslaughter by gross negligence. The *Adomako* test is objective, but a defendant is who is reckless may well be the more readily found to be grossly negligent to a criminal degree.

---

[217] Lord Mackay in *Adomako* did accept that 'it is perfectly open to the trial judge to use the word "reckless" in its ordinary meaning as part of his exposition of the law if he deems it appropriate in the circumstances of the particular case'. See the direction in *Winter and Winter* [2010] EWCA Crim 1474.

[218] cf *Litchfield* [1998] Crim LR 507 and commentary. Whether evidence was sufficient to satisfy a jury, and whether evidence of subjective recklessness is admissible on a charge of manslaughter by gross negligence, is considered in *DPP, ex p Jones* [2000] Crim LR 858 and commentary.

[219] [2004] EWCA Crim 2375. See O Quick, 'Medicine, Mistakes and Manslaughter: A Criminal Combination?' (2010) 69 CLJ 186 discussing a statistical breakdown of such prosecutions revealing low success rates and potential racial bias in prosecutions against doctors.

[220] [2004] 1 AC 1034.

[221] See also the same conclusion in *Mark* [2004] EWCA Crim 2490.

[222] *A-G's Reference (No 2 of 1999)* [2000] Crim LR 475 (Southall Rail crash case). Cf *S* [2015] EWCA Crim 558.

[223] *R v DPP, ex p Jones* [2000] IRLR 373; *R (Rowley) v DPP* [2003] EWHC 693 (Admin). Whether the two are consistent on this is debatable.

[224] (2000) 15 Feb, unreported.

In *R (Rowley) v DPP*,[225] Kennedy LJ stated:

Once it can be shown that there was ordinary common law negligence causative of death, and a serious risk of death, what remains to be established is criminality or badness. In considering whether there is criminality or badness, Lord Mackay [in *Adomako*] makes it clear that all the circumstances are to be taken into account.[226]

The Court of Appeal held in *Bannister*,[227] however, that taking into account the defendant's special skills in assessing liability in the context of s 2A(1) of the Road Traffic Act 1988 was inconsistent with the objective nature of the test.

14.2.6.3 Circularity of test

As Lord MacKay acknowledged, the test involves a degree of circularity. It may also be criticized, as was its predecessor, the '*Bateman* test', on the ground that it leaves a question of law to the jury. It has always been held that the negligence which suffices for civil liability is not necessarily enough for manslaughter, so someone has to decide whether the particular negligence is bad enough to amount to a crime, indeed this very grave crime. It is not necessary for the judge to refer to the distinction between civil and criminal liability, which might tend to confuse the jury.[228]

The jury appear to be left with the task of deciding the scope of the offence. The task is quite unlike that in, say, applying the definition of intention, which has been supplied by the judge. In such a case, the jury looks at the facts and applies the legal definition of intention as provided by the judge. In gross negligence, the jury has to determine whether on their view the conduct should be called grossly negligent, and if so that amounts to the crime. This seems objectionable in principle. In rejecting a challenge that the offence was insufficiently certain to be compatible with Art 7 of the ECHR, the Court of Appeal in *Misra* held that the jury's function in gross negligence cases is not to decide a point of law, but one of fact:

The decision whether the conduct was criminal is described [in *Adomako*] not as 'the' test, but as 'a' test as to how far the conduct in question must depart from accepted standards to be 'characterized as criminal'. On proper analysis, therefore, the jury is not deciding whether the particular defendant ought to be convicted on some unprincipled basis. The question for the jury is not whether the defendant's negligence was gross, and whether, *additionally*, it was a crime, but whether his behaviour was grossly negligent and *consequently* criminal. This is not a question of law, but one of fact, for decision in the individual case.[229]

With respect, it is doubtful whether this meets the criticisms that the test is circular, and that it requires the jury to determine the scope of the criminal law.

14.2.6.4 Guiding the jury

The Court of Appeal has recognized the need for the jury to receive greater assistance in determining whether a particular failing is 'grossly negligent'. The issue has arisen most acutely in cases of medical negligence.

In *Sellu*,[230] an experienced colorectal surgeon was convicted of gross negligence manslaughter for a series of errors in his treatment of the deceased who had undergone elective knee surgery. The post-operative treatment of a gastro-intestinal complication led

225 [2003] EWHC 693 (Admin) (carer left severely disabled man in bath unattended for five minutes).
226 At [34].   227 [2009] EWCA Crim 1571.
228 *Becker*, No 199905228/Y5, 19 June 2000, CA. For an argument that the circularity is not pernicious, see V Tadros, 'The Limits of Manslaughter' in Clarkson and Cunningham, *Criminal Liability for Non-Aggressive Death*.
229 At [62] (emphasis in original).   230 [2016] EWCA Crim 1716.

to V's death. The prosecution alleged that three specific breaches of S's duty of care to his patient had occurred: S failed to take urgent action when an x-ray showed that an intestinal perforation was likely; S failed to visit the deceased when learning of his condition despite the potential need to perform emergency surgery; S failed to operate within eight hours of CT scan results confirming the diagnosis and the need to operate to avoid fatal peritonitis. In summing up, the jury were directed that the issue to be assessed by them was as follows: first, did S behave negligently, in that no reasonable consultant colorectal surgeon in his position would have behaved as he did. Secondly, whether any gross negligence caused or significantly contributed to the deceased's death. Furthermore, and crucially, the trial judge's description of the required level of culpability referred only to whether S's conduct fell below the standard 'in a way that was gross or severe'.

The Court of Appeal held that the trial judge's approach to gross negligence, and in particular his direction to the jury, was inadequate. Following *Adomako*, *Bateman*, *Andrews* and *Misra* the direction ought to have made clear to the jury that the required conduct must have been 'truly exceptionally bad' and such a departure from the requisite standard that it consequently amounted to it being criminal. The conviction was therefore quashed. The Court of Appeal was also critical of the judge for not giving a route to verdict although he had given written directions. It was confirmed that, in complex cases, routes to verdict are now routinely expected.

The court gave further guidance to judges on how juries should be directed on this element of the offence. To repeat the word 'gross' is insufficient. The jury need to understand that they must be sure of a failure that was not just serious or very serious but 'truly exceptionally bad'.[231] Sir Brian Leveson P accepted that when directing the jury in cases of alleged gross negligence manslaughter, no formulation of the concept of gross negligence is mandatory, but, he added:

> What is mandatory is that the jury are assisted sufficiently to understand how to approach their task of identifying the line that separates even serious or very serious mistakes or lapses, from conduct which was 'truly exceptionally bad and was such a departure from that standard [of a reasonably competent doctor] that it consequently amounted to being criminal'.[232]

In the subsequent case of *Bawa-Garba*, the Court of Appeal emphasized once again that juries should be left in no doubt as to the truly exceptional degree of negligence which must be established if gross negligence is to be made out.[233] This emphasis on the high threshold for the very serious offence to be committed will have an impact on the likelihood of medical professionals being convicted (and prosecuted).

The court in *Sellu* also emphasized the importance of ensuring that the evidence elicited from the experts assists the jury in determining whether D's degree of negligence crossed the high threshold necessary for it to constitute gross negligence. Finally, the court reaffirmed that whether D's breach or omission was grossly negligent is ultimately a matter for the jury, not the experts. Trial judges must therefore take care to ensure that the jury's role is not usurped by the experts.

14.2.6.5 ECHR compatibility

The Court of Appeal in *Misra* concluded that gross negligence manslaughter was sufficiently clear and did not offend the requirement of legal certainty imposed by Art 7 or the common law. The court referred to the writings of Bacon and Blackstone to support its view that Art 7 merely

---

[231] At [152].

[232] ibid. Langley J's direction to the jury in *Misra* [2005] 1 Cr App R 21 was cited with approval.

[233] *Bawa-Garba* [2016] EWCA Crim 1841, [36].

confirmed the common law position on the principle of legal certainty. Thus, the court felt confident that the House of Lords, when framing the offence in *Adomako*, was not 'indifferent to or unaware of the need for the criminal law in particular to be predictable and certain'.[234] The court observed that Art 7 does not require absolute certainty but that offences are defined 'with sufficient precision to enable the citizen to regulate his conduct: he must be able—if need be with appropriate advice—to foresee to a degree that is reasonable in the circumstances, the consequences which any given action may entail'.[235] On the court's view, even applying the stricter interpretation of the test in *Hashman and Harrup v UK*,[236] the offence would be likely to satisfy Art 7, since gross negligence manslaughter depends on jury evaluation of conduct by reference to its consequences, and in gross negligence manslaughter the jury must be satisfied as to the 'risk of death' and of causation.

14.2.7 Causation

The breach of duty which posed a serious and obvious risk of death must be the cause of the death. Principles of causation in Ch 2 apply here. The prosecution is required to prove that D's breach of duty caused or made a significant contribution to the death.[237] The issue can be a difficult one in the context of medical negligence in particular. For example, in *Sellu*, Sir Brian Leveson P stated that what was crucial in that case was that the jury were sure D's failings were grossly negligent and went on to consider the question of causation, understanding that causation would not be established if that gross negligence occurred after the time that they could be sure V would have survived.[238] Similarly, in *Bawa-Garba*, the Court of Appeal held that the judge's direction to the jury that D could only be guilty if her acts or omissions made a significant contribution to D's dying as and when he did was unassailable.[239] Expert evidence will be necessary to help the jury assess whether D's gross negligence occurred at a time when V could still have survived.

The Court of Appeal returned to the issue of causation in the more recent case of *Broughton*.[240] The defendant had supplied his girlfriend with Class A drugs at a music festival. They left the main festival ground and went to nearby woodland. The victim experienced a bad reaction to the drugs and, after some time, the defendant asked someone to get medical assistance. However, he was mistaken as to the name of the forest they were in and the medical staff were wrongly directed. The prosecution's case was that, having supplied the victim with the drugs, the defendant was under a duty to secure timely medical assistance once he realized she was experiencing the adverse effects of taking the drugs such that her life was in danger. A medical expert gave evidence that had the victim received medical attention by a particular time in the evening, she would have stood a 90 per cent chance of survival. A submission of no case to answer was made on the basis that the medical evidence could not rule out the possibility that the victim would have died even if she had received medical attention. The trial judge rejected this submission and the defendant was convicted of gross negligence manslaughter. D appealed his conviction on the basis that the judge's direction needed to make clear to the jury that, in a case concerning negligent lack of medical attention, in order to establish that a breach of duty was a substantial and operative cause of death, the prosecution had to prove that the victim would have lived. The Court of

---

[234] At [34]; cf commentary on *Misra* [2005] Crim LR 234.
[235] *Sunday Times v UK* [1979] 2 EHRR 245.   [236] [2000] Crim LR 185.
[237] *Zaman* [2017] EWCA Crim 1783.   [238] [2016] EWCA Crim 1716, [127].
[239] [2016] EWCA Crim 1841, [33].   [240] [2020] EWCA Crim 1093.

Appeal agreed and quashed the defendant's conviction. The Court of Appeal articulated the applicable test in the following terms:

The prosecution must prove to the criminal standard that the gross negligence was at least a substantial contributory cause of death. That means that the prosecution must prove that the deceased would have lived in the sense that life would have been significantly prolonged. It is well established that being 'sure' is not the same as scientific certainty. See, for example, the discussion in *R v. Gian, Mohd-Yusoff* [2009] EWCA Crim 2553 at paragraphs 22 to 24. That case concerned a suggestion that there were theoretical or hypothetical possible causes of death which could not be excluded as a matter of theory but were entirely unrealistic. The jury must make judgements on 'realistic not fanciful possibilities'. To be sure that the gross negligence caused the death the prosecution must exclude realistic or plausible possibilities that the deceased would anyway have died.[241]

The court rejected the submission advanced on behalf of the prosecution that it would be sufficient for guilt for the defendant's omission to obtain timely medical attention to have made a material contribution to the victim's death. Practically speaking, this judgment will make it much more difficult to secure convictions for gross negligence manslaughter in cases involving the negligent lack of medical attention. In future, experts may be wary of stating definitively that the victim would have survived had they received medical attention in a timely fashion. The judgment may also have ramifications in other scenarios where gross negligence manslaughter is prosecuted, such as where a patient dies following treatment which is alleged to have been grossly negligent.

14.2.8 Challenges presented by the offence

The offence is one of the more difficult to apply in practice for a number of reasons. First, although expressed in simple terms in *Adomako*, the offence can prove complex in application. It involves questions of causation, omissions, duty, foreseeability, etc. all of which can generate difficulties. In particular, problems can arise in relation to liability for omissions.[242] Where D's positive acts cause death (eg negligent mistreatment), then it is sufficient to prove that D caused V's death. However, where it is alleged that D's omissions cause death (eg neglect of treatment), then the criminal law limitations on imposing liability for omissions will apply. Unless there is a pre-existing duty of care, a failure to act, even if it results in death, cannot amount to gross negligence manslaughter. It will be necessary to prove that D owed a duty of care—by reason of statute, contract, relationship, etc.[243] This has, on occasion, led the court to strive to find a duty from a combination of circumstances.[244] Difficult problems of causation can also arise not only where there are alleged intervening acts of the victim that may have broken the chain of causation (eg making informed voluntary choices to take substances supplied[245] or by neglect of an injury) but also where there are multiple concurrent causes of the death, including pre-existing conditions of the victim.[246] In some cases, depending on the way the prosecution puts the case, there is a need to consider a

---

[241] At [23].

[242] In criminal law there is a 'sharp distinction between acts and omissions': *Airedale NHS Trust v Bland* [1993] AC 789 at [10] per Lord Mustill.

[243] For critical discussion, see A Ashworth, 'Manslaughter by Omission and the Rule of Law' [2015] Crim LR 563.

[244] As in *Evans* [2009] EWCA Crim 650 (sister's duty to tend her comatose intoxicated sister to whom she supplied heroin).

[245] See eg *Evans*, ibid, where the court found it sufficient in that context that D had caused or contributed to V's death by her neglect of duty which arose when D was aware V, her sister had become ill from the drugs D supplied.

[246] See eg *Sellu* [2016] EWCA Crim 1716 (alleged neglect following surgery where V had co-morbidities).

'*Brown*'[247] direction. That will arise where the allegation is that there were multiple breaches of duty, each of which individually would suffice to amount to gross negligence.[248] The jury need to be agreed on the breach which satisfies all the elements to constitute the offence. Where there is a single breach of duty which is alleged to constitute gross negligence, no *Brown* direction is needed. Where there are multiple breaches which the prosecution allege cumulatively amount to gross negligence (but accept that none individually does so), there is no need for a *Brown* direction, but the jury must be sure that taken together the conduct amounts to gross negligence and they need to be sure that each alleged breach of duty is proven before they can convict.[249] The best approach is for the jury to work sequentially through the elements: they must decide what breach(es) of duty is/are proved, then proceed to deal with foreseeability and then causation and grossness on the breaches they have found proved. There is no doubt that multiple duties are conceptually more difficult to deal with, but the approach should be the same: decide on the duties; decide on which breaches, if any, occurred; did they give rise to serious risk of death, etc.

Secondly, the offence is an unusual one. There are few serious offences based on negligence in English law. It is also relatively rarely prosecuted.[250] As noted previously, it can arise in the most diverse range of circumstances. A lack of familiarity with the offence coupled with the complexities noted earlier may increase the difficulties faced by the trial judge. Assumptions that foundations of gross negligence manslaughter lie in the familiar law of 'negligence' will render it straightforward to apply may be misplaced. The criminal offence is quite distinct with different approaches to duty and the exclusions of duty. The pressure on the trial judge is enhanced by the fact that these are often high-profile cases with intense media interest. Some of that interest stems from the unusual factual circumstances which are newsworthy, for example with the Shoreham air crash,[251] or Hillsborough[252] or deaths of children.[253] There is also, understandably, pressure from the bereaved who expect someone to be held to account for the loss of a loved one.[254] There are other pressures involved in trying such cases given the heightened media interest. There is a risk of public misunderstanding of the nature of the offence and of the allegations. The need to ensure that there is a sound public understanding will be particularly important if there is a successful submission of no case.[255] It is not just the general public who seek clarity. The Williams Report (2018) into the prosecution of medical professionals for gross negligence manslaughter, noted:

A shared and accurate understanding of the law and how the threshold for gross negligence manslaughter is applied to healthcare professionals is the starting point for improving the consistency of investigations of suspected gross negligence manslaughter.[256]

---

[247] *Brown* (1984) 79 Cr App R 115.

[248] The argument was considered in *Sellu* [2016] EWCA Crim 1716 where the prosecution was advancing its case on the basis that the breaches of duty could be considered individually or accumulatively so that no *Brown* direction was necessary. The trial judge did not give a *Brown* direction and the Court of Appeal agreed at [128].

[249] See *Zaman* [2017] EWCA Crim 1783, [46]. The Court of Appeal regarded the conduct as a single breach.

[250] The Williams Review, *Gross Negligence Manslaughter in Healthcare: The Report of a Rapid Policy Review* (2018) at Annex A provides data from the CPS on the number of cases processed annually.

[251] www.bbc.co.uk/news/uk-england-47495885.

[252] www.bbc.co.uk/news/uk-england-merseyside-19710415.

[253] *Thurston and Thurston* (n 134). Similar incidents with exploding bouncy castles led to MPs calling for bans.

[254] eg the Shoreham Airshow disaster. The comments of Edis J commending the bereaved relatives' conduct after not guilty verdicts were widely publicized.

[255] *Rudling* [2016] EWCA Crim 741. This is also a concern in relation to challenges to coroners' decisions to leave unlawful killing to the jury: see eg *R (on the application of Secretary of State for Justice) v HM Deputy Coroner for the Eastern District of West Yorkshire* [2012] EWHC 1634 (Admin).

[256] Williams Review, n 250, para 7.1. The Report followed the conviction and striking off of Dr Bawa Garba, on which see earlier.

The infrequency and the diversity of the range of circumstances in which the offence is prosecuted make it more difficult to identify a sentence for gross negligence manslaughter that will be consistent with other cases.[257] This difficulty has been reduced by the Sentencing Council Definitive Guidelines.

Thirdly, expert evidence takes on a heightened significance. Gross negligence trials will commonly involve significant expert evidence and evidence of the guidance/protocols/systems to be followed within a profession or by those engaged in an activity.[258] Even in cases in which the duty is one that is obvious (eg parental duty to ensure treatment of child's injuries), expert evidence may well be vital in explaining the risks of death from delay and matters of causation.[259] There is no doubt that expert opinion evidence will assist the jury in determining whether D's degree of negligence crossed the high threshold necessary for it to constitute *gross negligence*. Such expert opinion evidence is clearly admissible, being outside the jury's common understanding and experience.[260] The experts may also testify as to the ultimate issues—was the degree of negligence in the case extremely bad and did it cause death?[261] However, careful handling will be necessary to: avoid the trial becoming dominated by the experts; avoid the trial being hijacked as an opportunity to challenge industry safeguards or as part of some broader campaign;[262] and guard against the jury's role as the ultimate decision-maker from being usurped by the experts. Although there is no prohibition on experts giving an opinion on the 'ultimate issue', guidance to the jury on their role in evaluating the expert evidence is likely to be essential.

The Court of Appeal in *Sellu* noted that in that case:

The jury was left on its own to trawl through the differing descriptions, which were adduced in evidence essentially by leading questions, essentially asking whether the behaviour under discussion was or was not gross negligence. In circumstances where those conclusions were not subject to any more detailed explanation and sat alongside a series of other descriptions which were also not expanded upon, the danger existed that the jury merely may have accepted without more that Mr Sellu had been grossly negligent on those occasions where he was stated to have been grossly negligent. Thus, notwithstanding the judge's direction, *the jury's role as the ultimate decision maker may have been supplanted.*[263]

The Williams Report raised serious misgivings about the approach of experts in the medical cases.[264]

Fourthly, the offence is ill-defined. The element of 'grossness' is not legally defined at all in the sense that it leaves to the jury the question of law: is D's conduct so bad that it

[257] See eg on the difficulties in medical cases before the Guideline, H Quirk, 'Sentencing White Coat Crime: The Need for Guidance in Medical Manslaughter Cases' [2013] Crim LR 871.

[258] An early example is *Rigmadon's case* (1833) 1 Lew 180 where experts testified as to the three methods of 'cask slinging' then in use in Liverpool.

[259] Another example is *R (Oliver) v DPP* [2016] EWHC 1771 (Admin): duty to protect those in custody is clear, but expert evidence on mortality rates and alcohol consumption, causation and delay in securing medical assistance.

[260] *Turner* [1975] QB 834.

[261] *Stockwell* (1993) 97 Cr App R 260. Oliver Quick's research found that medical experts too readily confused civil and criminal law and played too prominent a role in the trial: 'Expert Evidence and Medical Manslaughter' (2016) 38 J L & Soc 496. See also O Quick, 'Medicine, Mistakes and Manslaughter: A Criminal Combination?' (2010) 69 CLJ 186.

[262] As an example, see the challenges in *McKenzie* [2017] NICA 29 (conduct of construction worker in death at work).

[263] *Sellu* [2016] EWCA Crim 1716 at [142] per Sir Brian Leveson P (emphasis added).

[264] See the Williams Review, n 250, Ch 8.

deserves to be criminal.[265] As has already been examined, that test is widely acknowledged to be a circular one: the jury are told to find the grossness element as having been satisfied if they find the facts to be criminal in nature, and to find the facts criminal if they find them gross.[266] Although there is no empirical evidence that jurors struggle with the offence, it is a substantial burden to place on the jury who may well be dealing with complex expert evidence and will be conscious of the pressure from the bereaved relatives, and in a high-profile case generating media attention, for someone who has clearly been negligent to a degree which calls for them to be held to account. There is a real risk of *ex post facto* reasoning. The juror might reason: 'there was a death. It is clear D did something wrong . . . There must be gross negligence.' That has to be guarded against, particularly as it is clear (from recent cases especially) that the assessment of fault is one to be examined prospectively—was there a serious and obvious risk of death to someone in D's shoes at the time of the alleged wrongdoing. Despite what some (lawyers) may think, jurors are unlikely to be assisted by assurances that it is 'common sense' and 'just like negligence in civil law'. They are not (necessarily) civil lawyers and, in any event, the tort of negligence is far from straightforward! The advantages of written directions and routes to verdict are well established.[267] In this offence in particular there is a strong encouragement to provide them: *Sellu*.[268]

Fifthly, the offence is one that has generated such interest and controversy because it is heavily influenced by policy and always has been. The most obvious illustration of this arises in the context of medical negligence. Setting the boundaries of the offence too widely would have repercussions throughout that profession. The furore over the case of *Bawa-Garba*,[269] is a striking example of that. Hadiza Bawa-Garba, a junior doctor specializing in paediatrics, was convicted of gross negligence manslaughter in relation to a six-year-old patient. A medical practitioner's tribunal took into account multiple system failings at the hospital, and suspended her from the register for 12 months. The GMC appealed successfully to the High Court against the tribunal's ruling, and the court concluded that she should be struck off. After an outcry from the medical profession, an appeal was mounted (and crowdfunded) and the Court of Appeal (Civil Division) reversed that decision.[270] A later Medical Practitioners Tribunal Service hearing found that she should be permitted to practise again. (A finding of 'truly bad' conduct sufficient to lead to a conviction for gross negligence manslaughter was held not to be incompatible with future practice.) The Secretary of State for Health and Social Care established a government review on how the law of gross negligence manslaughter laws applies to medical professionals. The Williams Report[271] observed that:

recent cases have led to an increased sense of fear and trepidation, creating great unease within the healthcare professions. This has been compounded by a perceived arbitrariness and inconsistency in the investigation and subsequent prosecution of gross negligence manslaughter.[272]

---

[265] It is respectfully submitted that the denials of this by Judge LJ remain unconvincing: *Misra* [2004] EWCA Crim 2375. 'On proper analysis, therefore, the jury is not deciding whether the particular defendant ought to be convicted on some unprincipled basis. The question for the jury is not whether the defendant's negligence was gross, and whether, *additionally*, it was a crime, but whether his behaviour was grossly negligent and *consequently* criminal. This is not a question of law, but one of fact, for decision in the individual case.' At [62].

[266] Even Lord Mackay in *Adomako*: 'It is true that to a certain extent this involves an element of circularity, but in this branch of the law I do not believe that is fatal to its being correct as a test of how far conduct must depart from accepted standards to be characterised as criminal.' Lord Atkin before him also recognized the problem in *Andrews v DPP* [1937] AC 576.

[267] See the *Crown Court Compendium*, Ch 1.   [268] *Sellu* [2016] EWCA Crim 1716.

[269] [2016] EWCA Crim 1841.   [270] [2018] EWCA Civ 1879.

[271] Williams Review, n 250.   [272] At p 5.

Its recommendations included the need for:

An agreed and clear position on the law on gross negligence.

- Improving assurance and consistency in the use of experts in gross negligence manslaughter cases.
- Consolidating expertise of gross negligence manslaughter in healthcare settings in support of investigations.
- Improving the quality of local investigations.

The courts' have acknowledged the need to protect the medical profession for over 200 years. In *Williamson*,[273] Ellenborough CJ directed the jury:

if you find the prisoner guilty of manslaughter it will tend to encompass a most important and anxious profession with such dangers as would deter reflecting men from entering into it.

In *Crick*,[274] Pollock CB directed the jury:

if the prisoner had been a medical man, I should have recommended you to take the most favourable view of his conduct for it would be most fatal to the efficiency of the medical profession if no one could administer medicine without a halter around his neck.

The fact that so many of the elements of the offence are loosely defined allows the court to expand or contract the scope of the offence more freely than with many others. The lack of tight definitions across gross negligence manslaughter also increases the risk that prosecutors will push the boundary of the offence. The fact that a death has occurred and there is evidence of some fault, often by a professional, means there will often be significant pressure for charges to be pursued.

Sixthly, the offence has recently undergone considerable refinement. Over 30 cases are reported on Westlaw over the last decade. The evolving nature of the offence can make it less easy for a trial judge to determine its precise scope when applied in novel situations.

Seventhly, there are difficulties for the CPS in charging decisions. It has published guidance on its charging policy.[275] It faces a difficult task in making charging decisions.[276] It would be impossible to create exhaustive guidance given so many legal complexities, so much dependence at trial on expert evidence, ambiguities around the elements particularly that of grossness, the continually evolving nature of the offence, the limitless factual circumstances in which it can arise and a need to handle cases with a high degree of sensitivity.

It is not surprising that there have been several controversial judicial reviews of CPS decisions not to prosecute. Examples include: *R (Rowley) v DPP*,[277] *Lewin v CPS*,[278] *R (Oliver) v DPP*[279] and *R (Stephens) v DPP*.[280] Nor is it surprising that private prosecutions have been brought, including, most notably, in relation to Hillsborough in 2000.[281]

---

[273] (1807) 3 Car & P 635. See generally A Merry and A McCall Smith, *Errors, Medicine and the Law* (2001).

[274] (1859) 1 F & F 519, 520.

[275] For critical comment, see O Quick, 'Prosecuting "Gross" Medical Negligence: Manslaughter, Discretion and the Crown Prosecution Service' (2006) 33 J L & Soc 421.

[276] See eg the decision in relation to the Croydon tram crash at www.cps.gov.uk/cps/news/cps-statement-croydon-tram-crash-charging-decision.

[277] [2003] EWHC 693 (Admin) (carer left severely disabled man in bath for five mins unattended).

[278] [2002] EWHC 1049 (Admin) (D left V, heavily intoxicated, in a car on a hot Spanish day: held no duty).

[279] [2016] EWHC 1771 (Admin) (death in police custody).

[280] (2000) unreported, DC (collision of boats on St John's Ambulance training day).

[281] *Duckenfield*, www.theguardian.com/uk/2000/jul/27/davidward.helencarter.

Finally, in some cases there will be allegations of both unlawful act (constructive) manslaughter[282] and gross negligence manslaughter. They are not mutually exclusive.[283] There is potential overlap but only in limited circumstances. Particular care is needed as the manslaughter offences can include some traps for the unwary (eg unlawful act manslaughter cannot apply to omissions, gross negligence manslaughter can). The overlap is only where there is an unlawful act that can also be described as grossly negligent. An example might be possession of a loaded unlicensed firearm or a death in the course of poaching, or even in the context of a criminal venture to commit arson for fraud.[284]

14.3 Reckless manslaughter

Gross negligence is a sufficient, but not necessarily the only, fault for manslaughter. To some extent manslaughter by advertent recklessness—conscious risk-taking—still survives.[285] Where D kills by a reckless lawful act (therefore no UAM available) which he foresees might cause serious bodily harm (no gross negligence manslaughter available as no serious and obvious risk of death), this is reckless manslaughter.

Similarly, where D kills by a reckless omission (no UAM) which does not pose a serious and obvious risk of death (no gross negligence manslaughter), reckless manslaughter may apply if D foresaw a risk of serious injury to V. These used to be murder (*Hyam*) before the decision in *Moloney*,[286] so must still be manslaughter. Where death is so caused, the jury do not have to decide whether D's conduct is bad enough to amount to a crime. That question is appropriate only when we are concerned with degrees of negligence, there being no other way of determining the criminal degree. The jury are not asked this question in non-fatal offences against the person, which may be committed recklessly, so it would be quite inconsistent if it applied when death is caused. These cases are ones of reckless manslaughter even though that is not the articulated verdict.

The main concern with what is in practice the controversial form of manslaughter is to distinguish 'subjective recklessness' (manslaughter) from 'oblique intention' (murder).[287] The leading case is *Lidar*,[288] in which V died when run over by D's car to which he had been hanging on when pursuing D in the course of a fight. Although the trial judge directed that D's fault element would be satisfied by proof of recklessness (ie D's personal foresight) as to mere injury, the Court of Appeal held that this was not fatal to the safety of the conviction.

Subjective reckless manslaughter requires proof that D foresaw a risk that V would suffer serious injury (or death) and took the risk unjustifiably. In a sentencing appeal, the Court of Appeal recognized the existence of the offence. In *Hussain*,[289] D had killed a child, V, by driving with V trapped under the car. At trial, the prosecution expressly put its case on the

---

[282] Which requires an unlawful *act*; intentionally performed; in circumstances rendering it dangerous (in the sense that a reasonable and sober person possessed of information by presence at the scene would realize that it might cause some bodily harm to a person) causing death. See *Goodfellow* (1986) 83 Cr App R 23.

[283] *Willoughby* [2004] EWCA Crim 3465 (arson involving accelerant killing one participant in the venture).

[284] ibid.

[285] For an engaging analysis, see F Stark, 'Reckless Manslaughter' [2017] Crim LR 763 arguing that the offence does not exist but it ought to. We suggest that it is clear that it already does for the reasons explained in this section.

[286] See p 100.

[287] See p 93. See also J Horder, 'The Changing Face of the Law of Homicide' in J Horder (ed), *Homicide Law in Comparative Perspective* (2007) 26–33.

[288] [2000] 4 Arch News 3.   [289] [2012] EWCA Crim 188.

basis that D 'knew that it was a child who was under the car rather than some other object, that he foresaw the risk of serious injury or death by continuing to drive and yet chose to take that risk and death resulted'.

14.4 Reform

The reform debate[290] was rekindled by the Law Commission and MOJ agenda for reform of homicide which, although focusing principally on the appropriate scheme of murder and partial defences, has produced a coherent regime which integrates involuntary manslaughter offences.[291] The ladder structure of the Law Commission proposals allows for a clearer analysis of the relative degrees of culpability in the different forms of homicide.[292]

When considering the offences of manslaughter alongside that of murder and the proposed forms of murder, it is essential to bear in mind the numerous statutory offences of homicide—causing death by dangerous driving, causing death by careless driving, etc.[293]

14.4.1 Unlawful act manslaughter (UAM)

In view of the sustained principled criticism of the offence, it is no surprise that there have been calls for reform and indeed abolition. In the Law Commission's Consultation Paper No 135, *Involuntary Manslaughter*, it was observed that there was 'no prospect' of being able to devise any clear principled statement of the law based on concepts of unlawful act manslaughter.[294] In LCCP 135 the Law Commission provisionally proposed abolition of UAM without replacement.[295] By the time of the Report two years later, its opinion had changed. The Law Commission's final recommendation was that a person is guilty of careless killing (GCK) if he has intended to cause injury, or is aware of the risk of a new offence of injury and unreasonably takes the risk where the conduct causing or intended to cause the injury constitutes an offence. Keating[296] is critical of the failure to secure correspondence between the fault (foresight of injury) and the harm caused, regarding it as 'unfortunate' for the Law Commission to include a version of unlawful act manslaughter. The Home Office subsequently questioned whether some version of the constructive manslaughter offence ought to be retained.[297] It was unconvinced by the merits of the Law Commission proposal that it was wrong in principle to convict of an offence of death where the offender was aware only of a risk of injury. The example given by the Home Office is an extreme one of a person

---

[290] For a compelling review of the defects with the present law, see LC 237, *Involuntary Manslaughter* (1996) Part III. See also the Law Reform Commission of Ireland Report: *Homicide* (2008).

[291] See, generally, on the common law development of the homicide offences, J Horder, 'Homicide Reform and the Changing Character of Legal Thought' in Clarkson and Cunningham, *Criminal Liability for Non-Aggressive Death*.

[292] See, inter alia, Tadros, 'The Limits of Manslaughter' in Clarkson and Cunningham, *Criminal Liability for Non-Aggressive Death* suggesting that there needs to be a lower category of homicide offence for the least serious cases.

[293] See Ashworth, '"Manslaughter": Generic or Nominate Offences?' in Clarkson and Cunningham, *Criminal Liability for Non-Aggressive Death*, and S Yeo, 'Manslaughter versus Special Homicide Offences: An Australian Perspective' in the same volume.

[294] Para 5.4. On earlier reform proposals including those of the CLRC, Fourteenth Report, see S Prevezer, 'Criminal Homicides Other Than Murder' [1980] Crim LR 530.

[295] See Wasik [1994] Crim LR 883.

[296] See H Keating, 'The Restoration of a Serious Crime' [1996] Crim LR 535.

[297] Consultation Paper, *Reforming the Law of Involuntary Manslaughter* (2000) para 2.11.

causing a minor wound to the victim who is a haemophiliac.[298] The Home Office proposal would create liability where the accused intended some injury, in the course of the commission of a violent crime, and the death was not foreseen. As with the Law Commission proposal, there is no full correspondence between the fault (foresight of injury) and the harm (death) for which the defendant is punished. The Home Office offers no justification for basing liability on an accidental outcome rather than intention or foresight.

The Law Commission's latest recommendation is that the offence will be recast as killing another person:

(a) through the commission of a criminal act intended by the defendant to cause injury, or

(b) through the commission of a criminal act that the defendant was aware involved a serious risk of causing some injury ('criminal act manslaughter').[299]

14.4.2 Gross negligence manslaughter

In 1997, the Law Commission[300] proposed the reform, rather than abolition, of the gross negligence offence. The Law Commission's recommendations as part of the *Murder, Manslaughter and Infanticide* Report[301] are that gross negligence be recast as follows. A person is guilty of gross negligence manslaughter if:

(1) a person by his or her conduct causes the death of another;

(2) a risk that his or her conduct will cause death . . . would be obvious to a reasonable person in his or her position;

(3) he or she is capable of appreciating that risk at the material time; and

(4) . . . his or her conduct falls far below what can reasonably be expected of him or her in the circumstances . . .

As there seems to be an ever-greater culture of holding official error to account, particularly where it has led to serious harm, we might expect more challenges for deaths resulting from failings of public officials in particular. Consider, for example, cases such as *R (Secretary of State) v HM Coroner for East Yorks*[302] where V, a prisoner, committed suicide after D, a prison officer, spread false rumours that V was a sex offender. It was argued that this was gross negligence manslaughter. The court quashed the deputy coroner's decision to leave verdicts of unlawful killing to the jury on the basis of murder and gross negligence manslaughter. There appears also to be an ever-greater willingness to challenge deaths resulting from medical treatment. There has been a cultural shift—following national scandals involving the medical profession: Alder Hey, North Staffs, etc.

14.4.3 Reckless manslaughter

The Law Commission recommends abolition of this category of manslaughter. It is suggested that all cases will now be adequately catered for in either: (a) the new second degree murder offence where D realizes there is a serious risk of death from his conduct and intends to cause injury; or (b) the new version of gross negligence proposed earlier. What of D who

---

[298] This seemingly fanciful scenario has occurred: see *State v Frazier*, 98 SW 2d 707 (1936) (Mo).

[299] LC 304, para 2.163. In *JF* [2015] EWCA Crim 351, the Court of Appeal emphasized that it is for Parliament to change the law, not the courts.

[300] LC 237, *Legislating the Criminal Code: Involuntary Manslaughter* (1996). See also JR Spencer and M-A Brajeux, 'Criminal Liability for Negligence—A Lesson from Across the Channel' (2010) 59 ICLQ 1.

[301] LC 304, para 3.60.   [302] (2012) ACD 88.

has specialist knowledge of a risk of his lawful activity which is not known to the reasonable person and who foresees a risk of injury but not death by his conduct, but who kills V? D cannot be liable for gross negligence even though D's mental state can be considered by the jury in evaluating whether his conduct is grossly negligent, as there is no objective risk of death. Nor is D guilty of second degree murder unless he sees a risk of death.

14.5 The Corporate Manslaughter and Corporate Homicide Act 2007

14.5.1 Introduction

This long-awaited Act, which extends to the whole of the UK, received Royal Assent on 26 July 2007[303] and most of the Act was brought into force on 6 April 2008. Although the Act appears to create a broad-reaching offence in terms of bodies to which it will apply and the duties of care which will trigger liability, these are severely curtailed by the technical qualifications integral to the all important duty question and by the numerous and far-reaching exclusions designed to protect public bodies. The layers of technicality serve to restrict the scope of liability far more than would at first appear, and are also likely to lead to substantial practical difficulties in prosecution.[304] It has been argued that the Act has failed to live up to expectations.[305]

14.5.1.1 Background

Public disquiet with the lack of a specific offence for corporate killing increased with each successive failure to secure convictions for gross negligence manslaughter in any of the large-scale disasters such as the Southall, Paddington, Hatfield and Potter's Bar rail crashes, the Zeebrugge (*Herald of Free Enterprise*) and *Marchioness* shipping disasters and the Piper Alpha and King's Cross fires. With that list in mind, it seems startling that the Act was such a long time in coming. The immediate background to the Act is traceable to the Law Commission Report from 1996[306] recommending the creation of a new offence of 'corporate killing'.[307] A corporation would commit this offence if its 'management failure' were a cause

---

[303] On the Act, see generally D Ormerod and R Taylor, 'The Corporate Manslaughter and Corporate Homicide Act 2007' [2008] Crim LR 589. In this part of the chapter we have drawn heavily on that article. See also A Norrie, *Crime, Reason and History* (3rd edn, 2014) 124–8, who argues that the offence takes an 'uncomfortable' hybrid 'organizational–identitarian' approach; J Gobert, 'The Corporate Manslaughter and Corporate Homicide Act 2007' (2008) 71 MLR 413; J Horder, 'The Criminal Liability of Organisations for Manslaughter and Other Serious Offences' in S Hetherington (ed), *Halsbury's Laws of England Centenary Essays* (2007); M Hsiao, 'Abandonment of the Doctrine of Attribution in Favour of Gross Negligence Test in the Corporate Manslaughter and Corporate Homicide Act 2007' (2009) 30 Company Lawyer 110. Other background documents are on the Home Office website.

[304] It has been argued that the 2007 Act has failed to increase accountability, see S Field and L Jones, 'Five Years On: The Impact of the Corporate Manslaughter and Corporate Homicide Act 2007: Plus ça change?' (2013) 6 ICCLR 239. For an analysis of some of the criticisms that have been made of the legislation, see P Almond, *Corporate Manslaughter and Regulatory Reform* (2013). See also C Wells, 'Corporate Criminal Liability: A Ten Year Review' [2014] Crim LR 847.

[305] J Herbert, S Bittle and S Tombs, 'Obscuring Corporate Violence: Corporate Manslaughter in Action' (2019) 58 Howard J of Crim Justice 554.

[306] LC 237, *Legislating the Criminal Code: Involuntary Manslaughter* (1996).

[307] On which see H Keating, 'The Law Commission Report on Involuntary Manslaughter: (1) The Restoration of a Serious Crime' [1998] Crim LR 535; A McColgan, 'Heralding Corporate Liability' [1994] Crim LR 547. See also S Field and N Jorg, 'Corporate Liability and Manslaughter: Should We Be Going Dutch?' [1991] Crim LR 156.

of a person's death, and that failure fell far below what could reasonably be expected of the corporation in the circumstances. That proposal was, as Professor Wells noted, the start of the fundamental change in the UK to move the corporate manslaughter offence away from individual liability, bedevilled as it was by the identification doctrine discussed in Ch 8, towards liability based on 'management failure'.[308]

The Law Commission Report was followed by a Home Office Consultation Paper in which the government accepted the need for reform,[309] recognizing the need to restore public confidence that companies responsible for loss of life can properly be held accountable in law. The government stated its belief that 'the creation of a new offence of corporate killing would give useful emphasis to the seriousness of health and safety offences and would give force to the need to consider health and safety as a management issue'.[310] The government was prepared to go further than the Law Commission proposal by extending the offence to all 'undertakings' including unincorporated associations and other trades or businesses. Following a Report of the Home Affairs and Work and Pensions Committees in 2005,[311] the government produced another Bill[312] which, after much controversy in Parliament, became the present Act.

14.5.1.2 Problems with the old law

Aside from the symbolic benefits of a specifically labelled offence reflecting the particular wrongdoing involved in death caused by organizational mismanagement, three legal reasons for reform were apparent.

Identification doctrine

The identification principle was a major obstacle to securing a conviction under the common law offence of gross negligence manslaughter, particularly with a company of any size or with any complexity in its management structure. The doctrine is discussed in full in Ch 8. It required there to be an individual holding a sufficiently senior position in the company who could be identified with the company as its 'directing mind and will' and who individually fulfilled the elements of the gross negligence offence: fatality following a gross breach of a duty of care which posed a serious and obvious risk of death. The only successful prosecutions against corporate entities for gross negligence were in relation to small companies[313] where there was more likely to be a single person directly and immediately responsible for the death and who was senior enough to be regarded as the 'directing mind and will' of the company. There were few successful prosecutions for gross negligence manslaughter against corporations. Arguably, the 2007 Act retains this disproportionate effect

---

[308] C Wells, 'The Corporate Manslaughter Proposals: Pragmatism, Paradox or Peninsularity' [1996] Crim LR 545, 553. C Wells, 'Corporate Liability: A Ten Year Review' [2014] Crim LR 847 suggests that the Act provides 'an over-complex offence [with a] definition full of ambiguities and interpretive uncertainty'.

[309] *Reforming the Law on Involuntary Manslaughter: The Government's Proposals* (2000): www.corporateaccountability.org.uk/dl/manslaughter/reform/archive/homeofficedraft2000.pdf. See J Gobert, 'Corporate Killing at Home and Abroad: Reflections on the Government Proposals' (2002) 118 LQR 72; GR Sullivan, 'Corporate Killing—Some Government Proposals' [2001] Crim LR 31. For a different proposal based on causing death in the course of a specified 'scheduled' offence (eg one contrary to the Health and Safety at Work etc Act), see PR Glazebrook, 'A Better Way of Convicting Businesses of Avoidable Deaths and Injuries' (2002) 61 CLJ 405; see also C Clarkson, 'Corporate Manslaughter—Yet More Government Proposals' [2005] Crim LR 677.

[310] Para 3.1.9.   [311] HC 540 I-III.   [312] Cm 6755.

[313] See eg *Kite and OLL Ltd*, Winchester Crown Court, 8 Dec 1994 (1994) The Independent, 9 Dec; *R v Jackson Transport (Ossett) Ltd*, reported in Health and Safety at Work, Nov 1996, p 4; *R v Great Western Trains Company (GWT)* (1999) 30 June, CCC; *Roy Bowles Transport Ltd* (1999) The Times, 11 Dec.

on smaller companies since there is now a requirement that the senior manager(s) played a substantial part in the organizational failure leading to death. The smaller the company, the more likely the 'senior managers' will have had a hand in formulating and implementing the relevant policy on safety, etc; the breach of which led to the death.

Aggregation

Many critics of the identification doctrine questioned whether it must be proved that an *individual* controlling officer (whether identifiable or not) was guilty or whether it is permissible to 'aggregate' the conduct of a number of officers, none of whom would individually be guilty, so as to constitute, in sum, the elements of the offence.[314] In the context of gross negligence manslaughter, the argument was that *a company* owes a duty of care, and if its operation falls far below the standard required it is guilty of gross negligence. A series of minor failures by officers of the company might add up to a gross breach by *the company* of its duty of care. The argument was strengthened by the fact that such aggregation is permissible in tort[315] and the concept of negligence is the same in the criminal law, the difference being one of degree—criminal negligence must be 'gross'. This argument was, however, rejected by the Court of Appeal in *A-G's Reference (No 2 of 1999)*.[316] The prosecution arose from the Southall train crash in which seven passengers died. The trial judge ruled that the gross negligence manslaughter offence requires negligence to be proved under the identification doctrine. The Court of Appeal approved that ruling, holding that unless an identified individual's conduct, characterized as gross criminal negligence, could be attributed to the company, the company was not liable for manslaughter at common law.[317]

Killing of a human by a human

Historically, it was thought[318] that a corporation could not be convicted of an offence involving personal violence but, in *P&O European Ferries Ltd*,[319] Turner J held that an indictment for manslaughter would lie against the company in respect of the Zeebrugge disaster. The persuasive authority of this ruling is not impaired by the judge's subsequent decision that, on the evidence before him, the company had no case to answer. The requirement of an act or omission by a human being is not peculiar to manslaughter. All crimes involve acts or omissions, or the results of acts or omissions, by human beings. It is not manslaughter if a person is killed by an earthquake, or a thunderbolt, or a wild animal in the jungle.

---

[314] See RD Taylor, *Blackstone's Criminal Practice Bulletin* (Oct 2007).

[315] *WB Anderson & Sons Ltd v Rhodes (Liverpool) Ltd* [1967] 2 All ER 850, Cairns J, discussed by M Dean, 'Hedley Byrne and the Eager Business Man' (1968) 31 MLR 322.

[316] [2000] QB 796; considering *Great Western Trains Co* (1999) 3 June, CCC. It was also rejected in Scotland in *Transco v HM Advocate* 2004 SLT 41. See also *R (Bodycote) v HM Coroner for Hertfordshire* [2008] EWCA Crim 164.

[317] The court's conclusion that there can *in general* be no corporate liability in the absence of an identified human offender ignores the principle discussed earlier of corporate liability where a duty is specifically imposed on the corporation as a legal person: *Birmingham & Gloucester Railway* (1842) 3 QB 223.

[318] *Cory Bros Ltd* [1927] 1 KB 810 (Finlay J, holding that a corporation could not be indicted for manslaughter or an offence under the OAPA 1861, s 31), a ruling of which Stable J said in *ICR Haulage Ltd* [1944] KB 551, 'if the matter came before the court today, the result might well be different'.

[319] (1990) 93 Cr App R 72, [1991] Crim LR 695 and commentary. Streatfeild J ruled that an indictment for manslaughter would lie in *Northern Strip Mining Construction Co Ltd* ((1965) 1 Feb, unreported, Glamorgan Assizes) but the corporation was acquitted on the merits. Maurice J's decision in a civil action, *S and Y Investments (No 2) Pty Ltd v Commercial Co of Australia Ltd* (1986) 21 App R 204 at 217, required a ruling that a company was guilty of manslaughter. A company, OLL Ltd, was convicted of manslaughter at Winchester Crown Court, 8 Dec 1994, following a canoeing tragedy in Lyme Bay.

14.5.2 The 2007 Act

14.5.2.1 The offence

Section 1 of the 2007 Act provides:

> (1) An organisation to which this section applies is guilty of an offence if the way in which its activities are managed or organised—
>
> > (a) causes a person's death, and
>
> > (b) amounts to a gross breach of a relevant duty of care owed by the organisation to the deceased . . .
>
> (3) An organisation is guilty of an offence under this section only if the way in which its activities are managed or organised by its senior management is a substantial element in the breach referred to in subsection (1).

The offence follows many of the core aspects of gross negligence manslaughter. The crucial difference is that 'rather than being contingent on the guilt of one or more individuals, liability for the new offence depends on a finding of gross negligence in the way in which the activities of the organisation are run'.[320] The statutory offence, in a reversal of the common law, is focused on the aggregate responsibility of the senior managers. The Home Office Explanatory Notes describe this as the 'management failure', but that phrase is not found in the statute.[321]

The first successful prosecution was of a small firm (eight employees) for the death of a 27-year-old geologist who was buried under earth when a 3.5m trench collapsed on him when he was unsupervised.[322] The company's sole director was directly implicated in the acts.[323]

14.5.2.2 Relationship to other homicide offences

The Act abolishes gross negligence manslaughter as far as it applies to corporations and other bodies to which the 2007 Act applies (s 20).[324] The Act also provides that individuals cannot be liable as secondary parties to an offence of corporate manslaughter (s 18(1)). Individuals within companies can, of course, still be prosecuted for gross negligence manslaughter as principal offenders subject to what has been said previously.[325] This attempt

---

[320] Home Office Explanatory Notes, para 14.

[321] On the ambiguities of the term 'management' in the Act, see C Wells, 'Corporate Criminal Liability: A Ten Year Review' [2014] Crim LR 847, 854: 'the CMCH Act slips between two grammatical uses of the word management. "Management" can mean either "the action or manner of managing", or the "power of managing", or it could function as a collective noun for "a governing body".'

[322] *Cotswold Geotechnical Holdings Ltd* [2011] EWCA Crim 1337. See CPS blog relating to the Cotswold Geotechnical prosecution (http://blog.cps.gov.uk/2011/02/tuesday-15-february-afternoon-update.html).

[323] For a list of the prosecutions, see Wells [2014] Crim LR 847, 860.

[324] By s 27(4) 'any liability, investigation, legal proceeding or penalty for or in respect of an offence committed wholly or partly before the commencement of that section' remains, and by s 27(5) an offence is committed wholly or partly before the commencement if 'any of the conduct or events alleged to constitute the offence occurred before that commencement'. It is clear that there is no gap left in the law: gross negligence manslaughter remains available in all other relevant circumstances. In *Cornish; Maidstone and Tunbridge Wells NHS Trust* [2015] EWHC 2967 (QB), Coulson J rejected the submission that any prosecution for corporate manslaughter would have to be abandoned simply because it referred to an event that occurred before the commencement of the 2007 Act. Pre-commencement events could not *found* the charges, but it was held that evidence about them could be *relevant* to the charges that were brought under the 2007 Act.

[325] The Home Office Consultation Paper in 2000 had suggested that there should be responsibility for corporate manslaughter placed on individual directors in appropriate cases but this attracted strong opposition. For an analysis of the extent to which individual corporate officers can be liable for other homicide offences, see S Antrobus, 'The Criminal Liability of Directors for Health and Safety Breaches and Manslaughter' [2013] Crim LR 309. Wells [2014] Crim LR 847 is heavily critical of this aspect of the new offence.

at a strict division between organizational and individual fault may pose problems. If an individual defendant is charged alongside a company in the same proceedings, the jury will be faced with two different tests of manslaughter liability.

An organization can, although this is much less likely,[326] be convicted of unlawful act manslaughter in appropriate circumstances (eg where D is the manager of a company who encourages employee X to set fire to the company premises in an insurance scam which leads to the death of V on the premises). The corporation may also be liable as an accessory to the principal individual offender in other homicide offences, such as causing death by dangerous driving.[327]

In terms of Health and Safety Act offences,[328] an offending organization can be liable under the 2007 Act and under the relevant health and safety legislation (s 19(1)).[329] Additionally, nothing in the 2007 Act precludes prosecution of an organization which has already been convicted of corporate manslaughter for a health and safety offence (s 19(2)). The relationship between the health and safety legislation and the 2007 Act offence is an interesting one.[330] The government rejected a model of constructive manslaughter where a breach of health and safety legislation which led to death could found liability for corporate manslaughter. Liability under the Act is, instead, based on duties founded in the civil law of negligence. However, the breaches of health and safety legislation will not be irrelevant since the jury are directed that they must have regard to such breaches in establishing whether the organization has been grossly at fault (s 8).[331]

14.5.2.3 Which 'organizations' are caught?

Section 1(5) provides that the offence under this section is called: (a) 'corporate manslaughter', insofar as it is an offence under the law of England and Wales. This is rather misleading because it can also be committed by certain organizations other than corporations, for example an NHS Trust.[332] Section 1(2) defines the organizations to which the new offence applies, which includes, most obviously, corporations.[333] Section 1(2) also applies the offence to police forces, partnerships[334] (partnerships under the Limited Liability Partnerships Act 2000 are caught by the definition of corporation in any event), trade unions[335] and employers' associations,[336] if the organization concerned is an employer. Schedule 1 lists the government

---

[326] cf the argument advanced by C Wells, *Corporations and Criminal Liability* (2001) 120.

[327] See *JF Alford* [1997] 2 Cr App R 326.

[328] Defined in s 25 to mean 'any statutory provision dealing with health and safety matters, including in particular provision contained in the Health and Safety at Work etc Act 1974, and provisions dealing with health and safety matters contained in Part 3 of the Energy Act 2013'. See on corporate liability under the 1974 Act, *Chargot Ltd (trading as Contract Services) and others* [2008] UKHL 73.

[329] The overlap is considered by Wells [2014] Crim LR 847.

[330] cf Antrobus, n 325, and P Almond, *Corporate Manslaughter and Regulatory Reform* (2013). For criticism of the way the Act impacts on this relationship, see Wells [2014] Crim LR 847.

[331] See also FB Wright, 'Criminal Liability of Directors and Senior Managers for Deaths at Work' [2007] Crim LR 949.

[332] See *Cornish; Maidstone and Tunbridge Wells NHS Trust* [2015] EWHC 2967 (QB).

[333] By s 25, 'corporation' does not include a corporation sole but includes any body corporate wherever incorporated. This includes companies incorporated under companies legislation, as well as bodies incorporated under statute (as is the case with many non-departmental public bodies and other bodies in the public sector) or by Royal Charter.

[334] By s 25, 'partnership' means: '(a) a partnership within the Partnership Act 1890, or (b) a limited partnership registered under the Limited Partnerships Act 1907, or a firm or entity of a similar character formed under the law of a country or territory outside the United Kingdom.' See also *Stevenson & Sons*, p 275.

[335] By s 25, 'trade union' has the meaning given by s 1 of the Trade Union and Labour Relations (Consolidation) Act 1992.

[336] By s 25, 'employers' association' has the meaning given by s 122 of the Trade Union and Labour Relations (Consolidation) Act 1992.

departments to which the offence applies. There are over 40 such departments.[337] These include some in which it is not difficult to imagine how corporate manslaughter liability might arise because of the functions they perform, for example Department for Transport, HM Land Registry, Forestry Commission. With some it may seem a little less likely, for example Revenue and Customs, CPS, National Audit Office—but since liability can arise as a result of being an employer or occupier, it is not difficult so see how they might be liable for a death.[338]

In the course of debates in the House of Lords it was emphasized how important is the extension of the offence to public bodies:

> there is no reason why the death of an individual in one situation should be considered less of a death, or less deserving of justice, merely because that situation was presided over by government officials as opposed to privately employed foremen. Indeed, it is all the more of a tragedy and contravention of the natural principle of justice where the state itself acts with such gross negligence that the very lives of its own citizens are forfeit.[339]

Crown Immunity is removed by s 11. Section 11(2) provides that a Crown organization is to be treated as owing whatever duties of care it would owe if it were a corporation that was not a servant or agent of the Crown. However, as will be explained later there are a number of respects in which that liability is very heavily qualified in ss 3 to 7.

Partnerships are to be treated as owing whatever duties of care they would owe if they were a body corporate (s 14(2)).

14.5.3 Elements of the offence

In summary there must be:

- a relevant duty owed to the victim;
- the breach of the duty by the organization must be as a result of the way the activities are managed or organized;
- a substantial element of the breach of the duty must be due to the way the senior management managed or organized activities;
- the breach of the duty must be a gross one;
- V's death was caused by the breach of the duty.

14.5.3.1 A relevant duty

The definition of a 'relevant duty of care' is provided in s 2 of the Act:

(1) A 'relevant duty of care', in relation to an organisation, means any of the following duties owed by it under the law of negligence—

---

[337] Provision is made in s 16 for the circumstances in which relevant functions are transferred between one government department and another or between the other bodies listed in Sch 1, and for cases in which a relevant government agency is privatized.

[338] The list of organizations to which the offence applies can be further extended by secondary legislation, eg to further types of unincorporated association, subject to the affirmative resolution procedure (s 21). The list of government departments in Sch 1 may be changed by the negative resolution procedure (eg the name of a particular department) unless the change is to alter the range of activities or functions in relation to which the s 1 offence applies, in which case the affirmative resolution procedure applies. Since the Act was passed, the list in Sch 1 has been amended on a number of occasions.

[339] Hansard, HL, text for 15 Jan 2007, col GC 189 (Lord Hunt).

    (a) a duty owed to its employees or to other persons working for the organisation or performing services for it;

    (b) a duty owed as occupier of premises;

    (c) a duty owed in connection with—

        (i) the supply by the organisation of goods or services (whether for consideration or not),

        (ii) the carrying on by the organisation of any construction or maintenance operations,

        (iii) the carrying on by the organisation of any other activity on a commercial basis, or

        (iv) the use or keeping by the organisation of any plant, vehicle or other thing;

    (d) duty owed to a person who, by reason of being a person within subsection (2), is someone for whose safety the organisation is responsible [arising where V is in custody].

(2) Subsection (1) is subject to sections 3 to 7.

The duties reflect the duties of care arising at common law. The duty is that owed in the common law of negligence[340] or, where applicable, the statutory duty which has superseded the common law duty, for example the Occupiers' Liability Act 1957. It is made clear by s 2(4) that a duty owed under the law of negligence will apply if the common law duty of negligence has been superseded by statutory provision imposing strict liability. The Explanatory Notes give the example of the Carriage by Air Act 1961. The most important thing to remember is that the criminal offence does not impose new duties; it is based on the existing duties which are present in civil law—either by statute or common law. The requirement of proving a duty will add to the complexity of the prosecution.

The most frequently arising duties are likely to be from relationships as employers and occupiers, and duties arising from these activities are also of special significance when it comes to identifying the scope of the exemptions for certain types of organization/activity.[341]

It is easy to see how the categories might give rise to duties of care which, if breached, could lead to fatalities. Duties as employer would, for example, include duties to provide safe places of work. Note that the duty as an employer extends beyond the scope of employees as strictly defined and includes subcontractors, and volunteer workers, etc. Duties as occupiers of premises will render organizations liable if there are, for example, faulty electrical wiring, dangerous staircases, etc. 'Premises' includes land, buildings and moveable structures (s 25); a duty owed in connection with the supply by the organization of goods might arise from provision of foodstuffs; duties arising from the provision of services (whether for consideration or not), would include most obviously rail travel and other transport; duties from the carrying on by the organization of any construction or maintenance operations[342] would include building operations.[343] Duties arising from the carrying on by the organization of any other activity on a commercial basis was a category included in case activities such as

---

[340] Section 2(7) specifies, for the avoidance of doubt, that 'the law of negligence' includes, in relation to England and Wales, the Occupiers' Liability Act 1957, the Defective Premises Act 1972 and the Occupiers' Liability Act 1984.

[341] See p 641.

[342] Section 2(7) further defines 'construction or maintenance operations' to mean 'operations of any of the following descriptions—(a) construction, installation, alteration, extension, improvement, repair, maintenance, decoration, cleaning, demolition or dismantling of—(i) any building or structure, (ii) anything else that forms, or is to form, part of the land, or (iii) any plant, vehicle or other thing; (b) operations that form an integral part of, or are preparatory to, or are for rendering complete, any operations within paragraph (a).'

[343] This provision overlaps significantly with the previous category of supply of goods or services. It was included to avoid any lacunae where the construction operator was not acting 'commercially'—as might be argued with some public sector bodies.

farming or mining were not regarded as involving the provision of services, etc. Duties arising from the use or keeping by the organization of any plant, vehicle or 'other thing' could be extremely wide-ranging.

The most controversial category is that relating to duties arising from detention. Lord Ramsbotham, former Chief Inspector of Prisons, was successful in the House of Lords in amending the Bill to include what is now s 2(1)(d). There was considerable government opposition and the Bill almost lapsed. The final compromise position reached was that the commencement of this element required the further approval of Parliament. The most difficult issue, and one which engaged the House of Lords, was the question whether suicides in detention would give rise to liability where the relevant agency, for example the Prison Service, could or should have prevented it.[344]

Section 2(2) lists the various forms of custody or detention[345] which will trigger a duty:

(2) A person is within this subsection if—

  (a) he is detained at a custodial institution or in a custody area at a court or police station or customs premises;

  (aa) he is detained in service custody premises;

  (b) he is detained at a removal centre, a short-term holding facility or in pre-departure accommodation;

  (c) he is being transported in a vehicle, or being held in any premises, in pursuance of prison escort arrangements or immigration escort arrangements;

  (d) he is living in secure accommodation in which he has been placed;

  (e) he is a detained patient.

Deaths in custody give rise to problems because of the particular status of the victim; that by definition the activities will be occurring within 'premises'; and the fact that the organization providing the detention 'service' is one which will have to make public policy decisions as to allocation of resources, etc (and therefore in some cases the duty would be excluded under s 3).[346]

Even before s 2(1)(d) was introduced, the broad terms of s 2(1) could trigger liability for a death in custody in some circumstances. Subject to the exceptions in ss 3 to 7, there was possible liability under s 2(1)(b) if the organization's duty was as an occupier. As parliamentary debates accepted, if a brick fell off a wall because of poor maintenance and killed a prisoner that would trigger liability under the provisions already in force since the duty of care was the ordinary one owed by an occupier of premises.[347]

Duty issues under s 2

Given the potential breadth of the categories of duty and examination of the common law which might be necessary to determine whether a duty does exist, it is reassuring to see that the question whether a duty of care is owed is a question of law. It is for the judge to decide: s 2(5). Moreover, 'the judge must make any findings of fact necessary to decide that question'. This latter provision about the judge finding facts is highly unusual and should

---

[344] Under the new division of power, prisons come under the responsibility of the Ministry of Justice.

[345] The various categories are further defined in s 2(7). Section 23 provides a power to the Secretary of State to add to those categories listed in s 2(2), to whom a 'relevant duty of care' is owed by reason of s 2(1)(d).

[346] See p 641.

[347] See Taylor, n 314. See also S Griffin, 'Accountability for Deaths Attributable to the Gross Negligent Act or Omission of a Police Force: The Impact of the Corporate Manslaughter and Corporate Homicide Act 2007' (2010) 74 J Crim L 648.

be contrasted with the common law position on gross negligence manslaughter[348] where whether a duty of care exists is a matter for the jury once the judge has decided that there is evidence capable of establishing a duty.

Section 2(6) makes it clear that the duty of care will not be excluded by *ex turpi causa* and *volenti* doctrines.[349] This is potentially very important. The scope of liability at civil law is restricted in practice by the operation of these doctrines. However, the reason that they are excluded as defences or limits on criminal liability in this context is easy enough to deduce. The victim will in many cases not be properly described as taking a truly voluntary risk since he will be compelled to do so by the organization acting as his employer, etc.

14.5.3.2 The breach must be as a result of the way the activities are managed or organized

This second element of the offence is designed to ensure that the focus is on the so-called 'management failure'. This test is not linked to a particular level of management but considers how an activity was managed within the organization as a whole. It will now be possible to combine the shortcomings of a wide number of individuals within the organization to prove a failure of management *by the organization*. The language is designed to reflect the concentration on things done consistently with the organization's culture and policies more generally. It remains to be seen how easily this can be proved.

Senior management

The Act does, however, place a significant restriction on the organizational failure test. Under s 1(3), the offence is committed by an organization only if 'the way in which its activities are managed and organised by its senior management is a substantial element in the breach referred to in subsection (1)'.[350] Who are the senior managers? By s 1(4)(c): 'senior management', in relation to an organization, means the persons who play 'significant roles' in making:

decisions about how the whole or a substantial part of its activities are to be managed or organised, or the actual managing or organising of the whole or a substantial part of those activities.

This extends beyond the narrow category of senior individuals who would be caught at common law by the identification doctrine being the 'directing mind and will'.[351]

The senior managers' management and organization must be a 'substantial element' in the breach of duty leading to death. Two important consequences flow from this aspect of the offence. First, since the senior managers' involvement need only be a substantial element in the organization, etc, the involvement and conduct of others—'non-senior managers' who are involved in the management and organization of activities—is also relevant. Secondly, when assessing the management failure, the contribution of those individuals who are not senior management can be taken into account even if their involvement is 'substantial' provided it is not so great as to render the senior managers' involvement something less than substantial. There can be more than one substantial element. No doubt the courts will say that a 'substantial' involvement is something that the jury can evaluate as an ordinary English word.[352]

---

[348] *Evans* [2009] EWCA Crim 650.   [349] *Wacker* [2003] QB 1203.

[350] cf Norrie for the argument that this element of the offence demonstrates a problematic return to the identification approach. Norrie, *Crime, Reason and History*, 125.

[351] Is the test too restrictive? Will companies seek to avoid this by nominating people in less senior positions to take responsibility for all health and safety policies?

[352] In causation it is taken to mean more than trivial (p 79), in diminished responsibility it is taken to mean something more as in 'a substantial payment' (p 577).

14.5.3.3 A 'gross' breach of duty?

The requirement of a gross breach of duty is clearly designed to echo the gross negligence manslaughter offence at common law. Section 2(4)(b) provides a more detailed explanation of the concept—a breach of a duty of care by an organization is a 'gross' breach if the conduct alleged to amount to a breach of that duty *falls far below* what can reasonably be expected of the organization in the circumstances. The language chosen is similar to that proposed by the Law Commission as a suitable form of words to replace gross negligence. The test retains a degree of circularity, although not to the extent of that in the common law offence of gross negligence manslaughter.

The jury's duty in relation to determining the breach of duty is provided in s 8:

(1) This section applies where—

   (a) it is established that an organisation owed a relevant duty of care to a person, and

   (b) it falls to the jury to decide whether there was a gross breach of that duty.

(2) The jury must consider whether the evidence shows that the organisation failed to comply with any health and safety legislation[353] that relates to the alleged breach, and if so—

   (a) how serious that failure was;

   (b) how much of a risk of death it posed.

(3) The jury may also—

   (a) consider the extent to which the evidence shows that there were attitudes, policies, systems or accepted practices within the organisation that were likely to have encouraged any such failure as is mentioned in subsection (2), or to have produced tolerance of it;

   (b) have regard to any health and safety guidance that relates to the alleged breach.

(4) This section does not prevent the jury from having regard to any other matters they consider relevant.

This section deals with factors to be taken into account by the jury (the offence is only triable on indictment). Note that the jury 'must' consider these issues. Note also that the jury is obliged to consider whether the 'organization' complied, not just whether its senior management complied. This further supports the argument that the activities of non-senior managers are relevant in determining whether there has been a management failure. Section 8(3) emphasizes that the jury may have reference to general organizational and systems failures.[354] The inability to do so under the old law was a source of common complaint. How the 'attitudes, etc' are proved is problematic. There is the potential for lengthy arguments and evidence comparing practices across the particular sector or industry. Imagine a prosecution of a rail company and the potential for the company to adduce evidence of safety procedures and policies across the sector to demonstrate the quality of its own. No doubt the jury will have regard to the organization's overall objectives, published policy statements on safety, monitoring and compliance policies, attitudes to development of safety and to training and awareness, approaches to remedying previous health and safety infringements, etc.

---

353 Defined in s 8(5): '"health and safety guidance" means any code, guidance, manual or similar publication that is concerned with health and safety matters and is made or issued (under a statutory provision or otherwise) by an authority responsible for the enforcement of any health and safety legislation'.

354 This section has been influenced, as has much of this Act, by the Australian legislation and academic comment in Australia. See further B Fisse and J Braithwaite, *Corporations, Crime and Accountability* (1993).

14.5.3.4 Causing death

There must be a death of a person. Causation must be established in accordance with ortho-dox principles.[355] Difficulties may arise where the organization alleges that the individual employee has, with his free, voluntary, informed fatal act, broken the chain of causation.[356]

14.5.4 Excluded duties

The most important aspect of the legislation is not the scope of relevant duty and of poten-tial liability under s 1 and s 2, but rather what the government excluded from the scope of liability under ss 3 to 7. The excluded categories of duty are considerable. The different categories and sub-categories of duty also make the interpretation of whether a duty is owed rather more complex to unravel.

14.5.4.1 Public policy

The broadest exclusion is provided in s 3(1) and deals with decisions of public policy taken by public authorities.

Any duty of care owed by a public authority in respect of a decision as to matters of public policy (including in particular the allocation of public resources or the weighing of competing public interests) is not a 'relevant duty of care'.

This excludes liability where a death is due to a public authority's decision not to allocate appropriate resources to a particular service. The section is seeking to reflect the distinc-tion between 'operational' and 'public' policy matters in the law of tort.[357] The manner in which a public authority implements its duty in practice is justiciable in negligence, but the way it exercises its statutory discretion is not. In *X v Bedfordshire County Council*,[358] Lord Browne-Wilkinson said that, 'a common law duty of care in relation to the taking of decisions involving policy matters cannot exist'.[359] The courts have continually struggled with the dividing line and it has been recognized that the test is very difficult to apply.[360] It remains to be seen to what extent the criminal courts will be willing to engage in detailed evaluations of the common law on this issue.

As an example of the difficulty, if a relevant public authority decides not to deploy resources to buy a particular drug for patients suffering a particular illness, no duty arises. If, having made the decision to supply the drug, there is negligence in the way it is supplied/administered, etc, liability may arise. Interesting issues could arise in a trial in which the breach is of a duty owed by a private company and a public body where they have joint responsibility for managing an activity. The effect of the exemptions would be stark.

Section 3(2) provides a less extensive exclusion in relation to things done 'in the exercise of an exclusively public function':

(2) Any duty of care owed in respect of things done in the exercise of an exclusively public func-tion is not a 'relevant duty of care' unless it falls within section 2(1)(a), (b) or (d).

---

[355] See Ch 2.

[356] See *Kennedy (No 2)* [2007] UKHL 38. However, it is arguable that the decision in *Latif* [1996] 1 WLR 104 would apply because the employee and organization are acting in concert.

[357] See *Anns v Merton Borough Council* [1978] AC 728. See Horder, n 303, at 115.

[358] [1995] 2 AC 633.

[359] ibid, 738.

[360] See *Phelps v Hillingdon LBC* [2001] 2 AC 619, and also: *Gorringe v Calderdale Metropolitan Borough Council* [2004] UKHL 15; *Carty v Croydon London Borough Council* [2005] EWCA Civ 19; *Connor v Surrey County Council* [2010] EWCA Civ 286. See further, Horder, n 303.

(3) Any duty of care owed by a public authority in respect of inspections carried out in the exercise of a statutory function is not a 'relevant duty of care' unless it falls within section 2(1)(a) or (b).

(4) In this section—

'exclusively public function' means a function that falls within the prerogative of the Crown or is, by its nature, exercisable only with authority conferred—

(a) by the exercise of that prerogative, or

(b) by or under a statutory provision;

'statutory function' means a function conferred by or under a statutory provision.

The duty of care owed as employer or occupier or custodian under s 2(1)(a) or (b) or (d) still applies in these circumstances. This excludes only public functions involved in s 2(1)(c), notably the supply of goods or services and construction work, etc. The exemption was not supported by consultees in the government's consultation exercise.[361]

14.5.4.2 Military activities: s 4

Many of the activities performed by the armed forces[362] will be excluded by virtue of s 3(2) (above), but s 3(2) does not prevent liability arising as an employer or occupier. Section 4 goes further by providing a total exclusion for some activities. There is no relevant duty for:

operations, including peacekeeping operations and operations for dealing with terrorism, civil unrest or serious public disorder, in the course of which members of the armed forces come under attack or face the threat of attack or violent resistance.

Liability is also excluded for preparation and support of military operations of that description, or training of a hazardous nature, or training carried out in a hazardous way, which it is considered needs to be carried out, or carried out in that way, in order to improve or maintain the effectiveness of the armed forces with respect to such operations.[363]

The armed forces will owe a duty as an employer[364] or occupier other than in those circumstances.[365]

14.5.4.3 The police: s 5

The exemptions provided for police activities are also complex.[366] Two categories exist. Sections 5(1) and 5(2) create a total exemption—that is, no relevant duty arises for some types of policing activity—where, in short, there are operations in relation to terrorism or

---

[361] Home Office, *Summary of Responses to Corporate Manslaughter: The Government's Draft Bill for Reform* (Mar 2005) para 9.

[362] By s 12(1) 'the "armed forces" means any of the naval, military or air forces of the Crown raised under the law of the United Kingdom'.

[363] Will there be a problem in ECHR terms if the army cannot be prosecuted for killing? Arguably there will be no breach of Art 2 because an intentional killing can be prosecuted as murder on the part of the officer involved.

[364] By s 12(2), a person who is a member of the armed forces is to be treated as employed by the Ministry of Defence.

[365] There is no liability for special forces: 'Any duty of care owed by the Ministry of Defence in respect of activities carried on by members of the special forces is not a "relevant duty of care"' (s 4(3)). This is presumably necessary to allow for more extreme forms of training. By s 4(4), 'the "special forces" means those units of the armed forces the maintenance of whose capabilities is the responsibility of the Director of Special Forces or which are for the time being subject to the operational command of that Director'.

[366] See S Griffin, 'Accountability for Deaths Attributable to the Gross Negligent Act or Omission of a Police Force: The Impact of the Corporate Manslaughter and Corporate Homicide Act 2007' (2010) 74 J Crim L 648.

civil unrest. More fully, there is no duty on the organization where officers or employees[367] of the public authority[368] in question are engaged in operations for dealing with terrorism, civil unrest or serious disorder, which involve them coming under attack, or facing the threat of attack or violent resistance, or those involving the carrying on of policing or law enforcement activities (s 5(2)). Nor is there a duty when the police are preparing for those types of operations or training to enable them to carry out such operations.

In other circumstances, by s 5(3) a 'relevant duty of care' is owed where the organization is acting as employer, occupier or custodian (ie s 2(1)(a), (b) or (d)). This exemption will exclude circumstances where a member of the public has been killed in the pursuit of law enforcement activities. The Explanatory Notes suggest that this includes:

> decisions about and responses to emergency calls, the manner in which particular police operations are conducted, the way in which law enforcement and other coercive powers are exercised, measures taken to protect witnesses and the arrest and detention of suspects.

Professor Horder has suggested[369] that the extent of the exceptions in ss 4 and 5 is unwarranted and that the result may be to leave individuals at risk of liability when the agency is the one at fault. He suggests also that the exemption was unnecessary having regard to the need for the DPP's consent.[370] This is debatable. For Parliament to have fixed these activities as off-limits is one thing. To expect the DPP to have to make policy decisions such as the exemption of the police in a case of fatality is to subject him or her to media censure for whatever decision is made, and to diminish the level of certainty in the law.

14.5.4.4 Emergency services: s 6

In the law of tort, considerable difficulties have arisen in identifying the scope of the duty of care owed by the emergency and rescue services in the course of performing rescue activity. Section 6 puts beyond doubt that the corporate manslaughter offence does not apply generally to these agencies when responding to emergencies.[371] Approximate consistency with the civil law is secured by excluding liability arising from delay in response to an emergency, or the level of skill exercised in responding to the operation. The relevant emergency services protected by this exclusion are: the fire and rescue authorities and other emergency response organizations providing fire and rescue services; NHS bodies and ambulance services or blood/organ transport; the Coastguard and RNLI;[372] the armed forces (either responding to a military emergency such as a fire on a base or when assisting the civilian rescue services). By s 6(7), emergency circumstances are defined in terms of those that are life-threatening or which are causing, or threaten to cause, serious injury or illness or serious harm to the environment or buildings or other property.

The emergency services may still be liable for a death arising from their status as employer or occupier even where the death arises in the course of an emergency (s 6(5)). The exemption also does not apply to duties that do not relate to *the way in which* a body responds to an emergency, for example duties to maintain vehicles in a safe condition; these will be

---

[367] Section 13 provides that police officers are to be treated as the employees of the police force for which they work (and are therefore owed the employer's duty of care by the force). It also ensures that police forces are treated as occupiers of premises and that other conduct is attributable to them as if they were distinctly constituted bodies.

[368] This could include other authorities such as NCA or immigration officials: s 5(4).

[369] See n 303, at 119.

[370] See www.cps.gov.uk/legal-guidance/corporate-manslaughter. In reality, this consent can be granted by any prosecutor. It is not a significant safeguard.

[371] Emergency circumstances include circumstances that are believed to be emergency circumstances: s 6(8). This deals with the circumstances in which the response is to a hoax call.

[372] Those effecting sea rescue are also exempt in a very wide exclusionary provision.

capable of prosecution under the offence. There is no exemption from liability for medical treatment itself, or decisions about this (other than decisions that establish the priority for treating patients). Matters relating to the organization and management of medical services will therefore be within the ambit of the offence (s 6(4)).

14.5.4.5 Child protection and probation: s 7

Section 7 limits the duty of care that a local authority or other public authority owes in respect of the exercise of its functions under Parts IV and V of the Children Act 1989. In relation to the carrying on of those duties, a relevant duty arises for the purposes of s 1 only in relation to its activities as employer, occupier and duties relating to detention (s 2(1)(a), (b), (d)). There is no relevant duty, for example, if a child was not identified as being at risk and taken into care and was subsequently fatally injured. Similarly, any duty of care that a provider of probation services or other public authority owes in respect of the exercise by it of functions under Chapter 1 of Part 1 of the Criminal Justice and Court Services Act 2000 or the Offender Management Act 2007 is excluded. In relation to carrying out those duties, a relevant duty arises for the purposes of s 1 only in relation to its activities as employer, occupier and duties relating to detention (s 2(1)(a), (b), (d)).

14.5.5 Procedure

The offence of corporate manslaughter is triable only on indictment (s 1(6)), and a prosecution may not be instituted without the consent of the DPP (s 17(1)).[373] Proceedings against partnerships[374] for the offence are to be brought in the name of the partnership (and not in that of any of its members) (s 14(2)). Any fine imposed on a partnership is to be paid out of the funds of the partnership (s 14(3)). Further provision is made in s 15 for evidential and procedural mechanisms to apply to organizations which are not corporations. The section ensures that the relevant evidential and procedural provisions apply, in the same way as they apply to corporations, to all those government departments or other bodies listed in Sch 1, as well as to police forces and those unincorporated associations covered by the offence.

14.5.5.1 Jurisdiction

Section 28 deals with extent and territorial application. The Act extends to the whole of the UK. Section 1 applies if the harm resulting in death is sustained: in the UK; or within the seaward limits of the territorial sea adjacent to the UK; on a British registered ship, British-controlled aircraft; a British-controlled hovercraft; in, on or above, or within 500 metres of, an offshore installation in UK territorial waters or a designated area of the UK's continental shelf (s 28(3)).[375]

Section 28(4) provides that:

For the purposes of subsection (3)(b) to (d) harm sustained on a ship, aircraft or hovercraft includes harm sustained by a person who—

(a) is then no longer on board the ship, aircraft or hovercraft in consequence of the wrecking of it or of some other mishap affecting it or occurring on it, and

(b) sustains the harm in consequence of that event.

---

[373] cf L Jones and S Field, 'Corporate Criminal Liability for Manslaughter: The Evolving Approach of the Prosecuting Authorities and Courts in England and Wales' (2011) 32 JBL 80.

[374] Other than limited liability partnerships, which are corporate bodies and covered by the new offence as such.

[375] For difficulties in international waters, see the investigation into the death of a fisherman 15 miles off Cherbourg after a collision which resulted in no prosecution. See P Binning, 'Corporate Manslaughter on the High Seas' (2010) The Times, 28 Oct. Our thanks to Ms Chaynee Hodgetts for background information.

Section 1 will therefore still apply if the harm resulting in death is sustained as a result of an incident involving a British vessel, but the victim is not physically on board when he suffers that harm. It will not apply if the incident involves a non-British vessel in international waters.

14.5.5.2 Penalties

An organization guilty of corporate manslaughter is liable to an unlimited fine (s 1(6)).[376] Cotswold Geotechnical Holdings Ltd was fined £385,000. This fine was upheld despite the fact that it would lead the company into liquidation.[377] It was held that in some bad cases this may be an acceptable consequence. In addition, the court has power on the application of the prosecution to impose a remedial order against an organization convicted of corporate manslaughter requiring it to take specified steps to remedy: the breach; any matter appearing to have resulted from it and to have been a cause of the death; or any health and safety deficiency in the 'organisation's policies, systems or practices' appearing to be indicated by the breach (s 9(1) and (2)). This provision is also heavily influenced by Australian experience. Any such order must be on 'such terms (whether those proposed or others) as the court considers appropriate having regard to any representations made, and any evidence adduced, in relation to that matter by the prosecution or on behalf of the organisation' (s 9(2)).

Section 9(4) provides for the form of a remedial order. It must specify a period within which the remedial steps are to be taken and may require the organization to supply evidence of compliance. Periods specified may be extended or further extended by order of the court on an application made before the end of that period or extended period. An organization which fails to comply with a remedial order commits an offence triable only on indictment and punishable with an unlimited fine (s 9(5)). There appears to be nothing to prevent the conviction of a director as an accessory to this offence. In addition, the court has power to impose a 'publicity order' under s 10 'requiring the organisation to publicise in a specified manner' its conviction, specified particulars, the amount of any fine and the terms of any remedial order. Before imposing such an order, the court must ascertain the views of any relevant enforcement authority as it considers appropriate, and have regard to any representations made by the prosecution or the organization. The form of a remedial order must specify a period within which the publicity order must be complied with, and may require the organization to supply evidence of compliance. An organization which fails to comply with an order commits an offence triable only on indictment and punishable with an unlimited fine (s 10(4)). Section 10 was added to the Bill during its passage in the House of Lords. It is clearly predicated on the assumption (probably correct) that large organizations are more concerned about adverse publicity than a fine.

Further reading

P Almond, *Corporate Manslaughter and Regulatory Reform*

C Clarkson and S Cunningham (eds), *Criminal Liability for Non-Aggressive Death*

J Horder (ed), *Homicide Law in Comparative Perspective*

S Shute, J Gardner and J Horder (eds), *Action and Value in Criminal Law*

---

[376] The Sentencing Council has issued a definitive sentencing guideline which includes guidance on sentencing for corporate manslaughter and which is entitled *Health and Safety Offences, Corporate Manslaughter and Food Safety and Hygiene Offences: Definitive Guideline* (2015). For discussion of sentencing issues, see M Woodley, 'Bargaining Over Corporate Manslaughter—What Price a Life?' (2013) 77 J Crim L 33.

[377] [2011] EWCA Crim 1337.

15

Further homicide and related offences

15.1 Offences ancillary to murder

Murder remains a common law offence, but Parliament was not content to leave to the common law the punishment of acts preliminary to murder. The OAPA 1861 created offences of conspiracy, solicitation, attempt and threats to murder. The offences of attempt were particularly complicated[1] and were repealed by the Criminal Law Act 1967. Attempts to commit murder are now governed by the Criminal Attempts Act 1981.[2] The conspiracy provision was repealed by the Criminal Law Act 1977 and conspiracy to murder is governed by that Act. Those who assist or encourage murder might be convicted of offences under Part 2 of the Serious Crime Act 2007, as discussed in Ch 11, but there is also a specific offence of soliciting murder.

15.1.1 Solicitation

By s 4 of the OAPA 1861 (as amended by the Criminal Law Act 1977) it is an offence punishable with life imprisonment to 'solicit, encourage, persuade or endeavour to persuade or . . . propose to any person, to murder any other person'.

The offence is relied on commonly to deal with those who hire 'contract killers' (who turn out to be undercover police officers)[3] and has been used in more recent years to prosecute fundamentalist preachers who encourage their congregations to kill.[4] Sentences for the offence are high.[5]

15.1.1.1 A person

A child in the womb is not in law a 'person', so D encouraging X to kill the foetus while in the womb does not commit this offence.[6] But, in *Shephard*,[7] D's conviction was upheld when he wrote to a pregnant woman, 'When the kiddie is born you must lie on it . . . Don't let it live . . .' The decision seems reasonable on the facts—D *was* soliciting murder; that is, to kill the child once born—but the court based it on the strange ground that the offence only arose if the child was in fact born alive. This seems untenable.

15.1.1.2 Victim

The proposed victim need not be named. If the solicitation is to kill members of a group, it must be a sufficiently well-defined one. Where D was charged with the offence and the indictment alleged he had incited murder of 'sovereigns and rulers of Europe', Phillimore J thought 'rulers' a somewhat vague word, but there were some 18 or 20 sovereigns in Europe and that was a sufficiently well-defined class.[8] In *El-Faisal*,[9] the incitement was to kill all Jews, Christians, Americans, Hindus and non-believers, but it does not appear from the report to have been challenged as an insufficiently defined class.[10]

---

[1] See the 1st edition of this book, at pp 250–3.   [2] See Ch 11.

[3] See, as an example, *Singh Rai (Jagjit)* [2005] EWCA Crim 3126, [2006] 2 Cr App R (S) 13.

[4] See *El-Faisal* [2004] EWCA Crim 343 and *Abu Hamza* [2006] EWCA Crim 2918. The offence is considered, briefly, in LCCP 217, *Reform of Offences Against the Person: A Scoping Consultation Paper* (2014), and LC 361 *Reform of Offences Against the Person* (2015) Ch 8.

[5] See *Ahmad* [2012] EWCA Crim 959

[6] See *Re F (in utero)* [1988] Fam 122. Nor is it the offence of assisting or encouraging grievous bodily harm to the mother, since the foetus is not part of the mother; see p 527.

[7] [1919] 2 KB 125, CCA, a case found 'very hard to follow' in *Tait*, n 24.

[8] *Antonelli and Barberi* (1905) 70 JP 4.   [9] [2004] EWCA Crim 343.

[10] In *Rahman* [2008] EWCA Crim 2290, the offending words were made by D with a microphone referring to western forces in Iraq and Afghanistan. He said, among other things, 'We want to see them coming home in body bags. We want to see their blood running in the streets of Baghdad. We want to see their blood running in Fallujah. We want to see the Mujahideen shoot down their planes the way we shoot down the birds.' He then prayed to Allah, 'Don't leave any of them alive in Iraq. Don't leave any of them alive in Afghanistan.' D carried two different placards with slogans reading 'annihilate those who insult Islam' and 'behead those who insult Islam'.

There is no scope for an argument that the offence restricts the right to freedom of expression under Art 10 of the ECHR, since the limitation will, most obviously, be justified as necessary and proportionate for the protection of others.

15.1.1.3 Audience

The offence may be committed by the publication of an article in a newspaper and it is immaterial that the readers of the newspapers are not identified.[11] Logically, it must be capable of commission by email and by posts on the internet.[12] It seems, however, that the offence is not committed unless the mind of the person solicited, etc is reached: *Krause*.[13] In that case Lord Alverstone CJ applied this restricted reading even though the offence extends to an 'endeavour to persuade' which might be thought to cover an unsuccessful attempt to communicate. He held, however, that there was (what was then) a common law attempt to commit the statutory offence where it was not proved that the offending letters, though sent, had ever reached the addressee.[14] If it is proved that the letter or other publication did reach the addressee, it is not necessary to prove that his mind was in any way affected by it.[15]

15.1.1.4 'Solicitation'

A soliciting to kill, not merely to do serious harm, must be proved.[16] In deciding whether the words amount to a solicitation, etc, the jury will take account of: (a) the language used; (b) the occasion on which it was used; (c) the persons to whom the words were used; and (d) the circumstances surrounding their use. In *Diamond*,[17] Coleridge J left the jury to decide whether an article extolling the virtues of the assassins of tyrants was sufficient. The publication was just after an attempt on the life of the Viceroy of India, and the persons addressed were not 'a debating society of philosophers or divines' but 'anybody whom the paper would reach in this country or in Ireland'.

15.1.1.5 Offence solicited

It has been held to be sufficient that D incites P to act as an accessory to murder, as where D recruits P to act as the getaway driver in a murder.[18]

15.1.1.6 Mens rea

The section contains no explicit requirement that D intends or believes that his encouragement will be acted upon. It is likely that the offence follows the common law of incitement, as it existed before 2007.[19] It is submitted that the mens rea is that D intends or believes that the other person, if he acts as incited, shall or will do so with the fault required for the offence.

15.1.1.7 Jurisdiction

Section 4 is applicable where the person to be murdered is not a British subject or within this jurisdiction. The section also catches an alien who, within this jurisdiction, incites the commission of murder abroad, and who might otherwise be immune at common law under

---

[11] *Most* (1881) 7 QBD 244, CCR endorsed in *Jones* [2007] EWCA Crim 1118.

[12] See *Sheppard and Whittle* [2010] EWCA Crim 65, discussed in Ch 30 available free online. D could be tried in England because a substantial measure of his activities took place there.

[13] (1902) 66 JP 121. Contrast *Horton v Mead* [1913] 1 KB 154.

[14] See also *Banks* (1873) 12 Cox CC 393 at 399 per Quain J.

[15] *Diamond* (1920) 84 JP 211; *Most*, n 11; *Krause*, n 13.

[16] *Bainbridge* (1991) No 504/24/90, (1991) 93 Cr App R 32.   [17] See n 15.

[18] *Winter* [2007] EWCA Crim 3493.   [19] See the 11th edition of this work.

the rule in *Board of Trade v Owen*.[20] In *El-Faisal*,[21] the solicitation was sufficient where it was to murder all 'Hindus, Jews and non-believers [in Islam]' and it was contemplated that the killings incited might occur in any part of the world. In *Abu Hamza*,[22] the Court of Appeal, after an extensive survey of case law, held that s 4 makes the solicitation of murder an offence in England, even where the inciter is not British, the proposed killer is not British, the killing will be abroad and the proposed victim is not British. The act of incitement under s 4 may be an offence under English law, even if the act of murder, if carried out, would not be. Lord Phillips CJ observed that the motivation for the enactment of s 4 appeared to have been the activities of aliens in England in support of murders, or attempts to murder, committed by foreigners outside the jurisdiction. If so, it would have made no sense to have restricted the offence to situations where the murderers were to be British subjects. There was nothing in the wording that suggested that the conspirators, or the person incited, should be British subjects.

15.1.2 Threats to kill

Section 16 of the OAPA 1861 created an offence of making written threats to murder.[23] Schedule 12 to the Criminal Law Act 1977 replaced that provision with a new and broader s 16:

A person who without lawful excuse makes to another a threat, intending that that other would fear it would be carried out, to kill that other or a third person shall be guilty of an offence and liable on conviction on indictment to imprisonment for a term not exceeding ten years.

A foetus is not 'a third person' and so a threat to a mother to kill the foetus in her womb does not amount to this offence.[24] In *Tait*, the court thought that if the threat had been to kill the child after it was born it would still not be an offence—if that were an offence, they asked, why should it not be an offence to threaten a non-pregnant woman to kill any child she might have in the future? This, the court thought, 'seems to stretch the meaning of "any third person" altogether too far'. Perhaps so, but this was a threat to kill a particular person, already existing in embryo at least, which is altogether a different threat in terms of its impact on the mother—or anyone else. The decision in *Shephard*, discussed earlier,[25] suggests that this would have been the offence (if we ignore the strange and unsupportable *dictum*)—how could it be soliciting to kill a person and not threatening to kill a person? Moreover, it *is* a threat to kill a person, which the foetus will by then have become.

The threat may take any form[26] and may be implied as well as express.[27] There is no need for the words 'I will kill' to be explicitly used.[28] There is no need for the threat to be made to the person against whom the violence will be carried out.[29] The offence is made out if D

---

[20] [1957] AC 602, cf M Hirst, *Jurisdiction and the Ambit of the Criminal Law* (2003) 149, a view rejected by the CA in *Abu Hamza*, n 4.

[21] [2004] EWCA Crim 343.   [22] [2006] EWCA Crim 2918.

[23] See the 3rd edition of this book, at p 266.

[24] *Tait* [1990] 1 QB 290. Cited with approval by the Court of Appeal (Civ Div) in *CP (A Child) v Criminal Injuries Compensation Authority* [2014] EWCA Civ 1554. See also LCCP 217, *Reform of Offences Against the Person: A Scoping Consultation Paper* (2014) and LC 361, *Reform of Offences Against the Person* (2015) Ch 8.

[25] [1919] 2 KB 125, n 7.

[26] See n 28. See *Kennedy* [1999] 1 Cr App R 54.

[27] cf *Solanke* [1970] 1 WLR 1. See *Boucher* (1831) 4 Car & P 562. In *Dhir v Saddler* [2017] EWHC 3155 (QB) at [30], Nicklin J stated that 'I am quite satisfied that the words '*he threatened to slit my throat*' impute the commission of the offence of making a threat to kill under s.16.'

[28] As in *Robinson* [2009] EWCA Crim 375 where D had said to a police officer who asked if D was making a loose threat: 'I am making a semi automatic one and it is loaded.'

[29] See eg *Donovan* [2009] EWCA Crim 1258 (D informs prison officers he will kill V when he is released from present sentence).

makes a threat to A, intending that A would fear it would be carried out. It does not matter if the threat is to kill A or B.

In principle, it is thought that a threat should be 'made to another' only when communicated; but, since it has been held that a 'demand' is 'made' within s 21(1) of the Theft Act 1968 when and where a letter containing it is posted,[30] it is at least possible that the same might be decided in the case of a threat. The inclusion of the words 'to another' in this section makes no difference, since the demand under s 21 must impliedly be made to another. Threats to kill in England and Wales made by emails from abroad have been sufficient to constitute the offence.[31]

The offence is triable either way.[32] The statute makes a single threat to kill an offence and therefore where D has made repeated threats to kill over a period of time these ought not all to be charged in one count in the indictment.[33]

15.1.2.1 Lawful excuses

There would be a lawful excuse for making the threat if, in the circumstances known to D, the killing would be excusable if the threat were carried out, as where D makes the threat in self-defence.[34] A threat to kill may, however, be excusable where actual killing would not. To cause fear of death might be reasonable to prevent crime or arrest an offender, whereas actually to kill would be quite unreasonable.[35] In many cases it will be desirable to tell the jury this.[36] Where there is some evidence of a lawful excuse, the onus is on the Crown to prove its absence and the question is always one for the jury.[37]

15.2 Complicity in suicide and suicide pacts

15.2.1 Position at common law

Historically, it was a felony at common law for a sane person of the age of responsibility to kill himself either intentionally or in the course of trying to kill another.[38] Such a suicide was regarded as self-murder. Though the offender was, being dead, personally beyond the reach of the law, his guilt was not without important consequences at common law, since it resulted in the forfeiture to the Crown of his property.[39] The results were more important, however, where the attempt failed, for then:

(1) since the suicidal person had attempted to commit a felony he was guilty, under ordinary common law principles, of the misdemeanour of attempted suicide;

(2) if the suicidal person, in the course of trying to kill himself, killed another, he was guilty of murder under the doctrine of transferred malice.[40]

---

[30] *Treacy v DPP* [1971] AC 537; *Pogmore* [2017] EWCA Crim 925, see p 1037.

[31] *M* [2003] EWCA Crim 3067.   [32] Magistrates' Courts Act 1980, s 17 and Sch 1, para 5.

[33] See *Marchese* [2008] EWCA Crim 389 unless to do so is compatible with the Criminal Procedure Rules 2020, r 10.

[34] See p 399.

[35] The two preceding sentences were approved by the Court of Appeal in *Cousins* [1982] 2 All ER 115 at 117.

[36] *Cousins*, ibid.   [37] ibid.

[38] Hawkins, I PC, 77. For historical discussions on the implementation of the offences, see G Williams, *The Sanctity of Life and the Criminal Law* (1957) Ch 7; St John Stevas, *Life, Death and the Law* (1961) Ch 6; Second Report of the Criminal Law Revision Committee (1960) Cmnd 1187. See also on this historical position Toulson LJ in *Nicklinson* in the Divisional Court at [2012] EWHC 2381 (Admin) at [28] et seq.

[39] On the position now see *Re Ninian* [2019] EWHC 297 (Ch).

[40] *Hopwood* (1913) 8 Cr App R 143, CCA; *Spence* (1957) 41 Cr App R 80.

Though suicide was regarded as 'not a very serious crime',[41] an intention to commit it was the mens rea of murder. Moreover, someone who was an accessory to the suicide of another was guilty of murder as an accessory. It followed that the survivor of a suicide pact was also guilty of murder, for, even if he did not actually kill, he was an accessory to the other party's self-murder.

15.2.2 The Suicide Act 1961

Suicide ceased to be a crime by virtue of the Suicide Act 1961 which simply provides that: 'The rule of law whereby it is a crime for a person to commit suicide is hereby abrogated.'

There were very sound reasons for the abolition of the felony of suicide.[42] The 'felon' was dead and thus beyond the reach of punishment. The legal sanction was not an effective deterrent—there were some 5,000 suicides a year; and the effect was merely to add to the distress and pain of the bereaved relatives. The most important practical effect of the Act, however, was its repeal by implication of the crime of attempted suicide. If it was not a crime to commit suicide, it could not be a crime to attempt it. This also recognized the realities of the situation for it had been the practice for many years to institute proceedings only where it was necessary for the attempter's protection, for example because no relatives and friends were willing to give help. Thus, in 1959, of a total of 4,980 suicide attempts known to the police (and an estimated actual total of 25,000 concealed from the police) only 518 prosecutions were brought. The protection of the attempter may now be secured where necessary under the Mental Health Act 1983.

15.2.2.1 Complicity in another's suicide

In 1961, s 2 of the Suicide Act created a new offence for D to aid, abet, counsel or procure P in his suicide or attempt to commit suicide. The form of the offence was, in theoretical terms, an odd one. Since there was no principal offence committed by the suicidal person, so there was no crime for D to aid and abet. It had to be viewed as a specific statutory offence involving the use of the language of aiding and abetting even though there was no principal crime. Since the aiding, etc was the principal offence, it was possible to charge an attempt to aid, etc so that unsuccessful advice or encouragement was punishable.[43] That offence has now been replaced by one defined, more logically, in terms of doing acts capable of assisting or encouraging suicide.

From 1 February 2010, s 59 of the Coroners and Justice Act 2009 replaced s 2(1) of the Suicide Act with the following:

(1) A person ('D') commits an offence if—

    (a) D does an act capable of encouraging or assisting the suicide or attempted suicide of another person, and

    (b) D's act was intended to encourage or assist suicide or an attempt at suicide.

(1A) The person referred to in subsection (1)(a) need not be a specific person (or class of persons) known to, or identified by, D.

---

[41] *French* (1955) 39 Cr App R 192, per Lord Goddard CJ.

[42] In his judgment in *Nicklinson* [2014] UKSC 38, [212], Lord Sumption suggested the reason for decriminalization was not that suicide had become morally acceptable, but because it was recognized that imposing criminal sanctions was inhumane and ineffective.

[43] *McShane* (1978) 66 Cr App R 97, discussed by JC Smith in *Crime, Proof and Punishment*, 21 at 32–3. See more recently *Workman* [2006] EWCA Crim 2623 and *S* [2005] EWCA Crim 819.

(1B) D may commit an offence under this section whether or not a suicide, or an attempt at suicide, occurs.

(1C) An offence under this section is triable on indictment and a person convicted of such an offence is liable to imprisonment for a term not exceeding 14 years.

The changes are designed to clarify the law.[44] There is no intended extension of the law. The main change is to shift the basis of the offence from one of 'aiding and abetting' and 'attempting' to an inchoate form of the offence as defined in the modern terminology under Part 2 of the Serious Crime Act 2007 relating to the inchoate offence of intentionally[45] encouraging and assisting crime. Moving to an inchoate form of offence (subs (1B)) means that there is no need to prosecute under the Criminal Attempts Act 1981 for *attempt* to assist suicide where no one, as a result of the encouragement, actually commits or attempts to commit suicide. The *full* offence under s 2(1) is now committed by doing an act capable of encouraging or assisting suicide whether or not any suicide is committed or attempted. The only scope for the operation of the law of attempt is where D attempts to do, but does not succeed in doing, 'the act' he intended to do by way of encouragement—for example, posting the letter of encouragement to the suicidal person.

Subsection (1A) makes it clear that one can be liable for doing acts capable of encouraging or assisting persons unknown to commit suicide. Material on a website may be caught.[46] The Joint Parliamentary Committee on Human Rights expressed concern that the new offence might have a chilling effect on free speech.[47]

Section 59 of the 2009 Act[48] also inserts a new s 2A into the Suicide Act as follows:

2A Acts capable of encouraging or assisting

(1) If D arranges[49] for a person ('D2') to do an act that is capable of encouraging or assisting the suicide or attempted suicide of another person and D2 does that act, D is also to be treated for the purposes of this Act as having done it.

(2) Where the facts are such that an act is not capable of encouraging or assisting suicide or attempted suicide, for the purposes of this Act it is to be treated as so capable if the act would have been so capable had the facts been as D believed them to be at the time of the act or had subsequent events happened in the manner D believed they would happen (or both).

---

[44] The MOJ published a circular explaining the revised law on encouraging or assisting suicide, which came into effect on 1 Feb 2010, www.cps.gov.uk/legal-guidance/suicide-policy-prosecutors-respect-cases-encouraging-or-assisting-suicide.

[45] It is unclear whether the restricted interpretation of that term that applies to s 44 of the Serious Crime Act 2007 applies here. See Ch 11.

[46] The reform was prompted in part by concerns about internet sites offering encouragement. See *Safer Children in a Digital World: The Report of the Byron Review* (2008), www.iwf.org.uk/sites/default/files/inline-files/Safer%20Children%20in%20a%20Digital%20World%20report.pdf.

[47] It was suggested that the new offence might capture the publication of morbid poetry. The DPP in evidence to the Public Bill Committee gave assurance that this would not be caught because there would be no relevant intent.

[48] Section 61 of and Sch 12 to the 2009 Act regulate, in relation to encouraging and assisting suicide, the liability of (electronic) information society service providers within the EEA area, thereby making the s 2 offence consistent with the UK's obligations under the E-Commerce Directive (2000/31/EC). Paragraphs 1 and 2 of Sch 12 extend the liability of domestically based providers to acts done within the EEA. Paragraph 3 limits the circumstances in which proceedings for the s 2 offence may be brought in the UK against EEA-based (as opposed to domestically based) service providers. Schedule 12 also provides for some limited exceptions where the service provider in question acts as a 'mere conduit', or is providing 'caching' or 'hosting' services.

[49] This is problematical. D1 who merely encourages D2 to provide encouragement to P to kill himself does not seem to have 'arranged', unlike D1 who provides D2 with material to pass to P.

(3) A reference in this Act to a person ('P') doing an act that is capable of encouraging the suicide or attempted suicide of another person includes a reference to P doing so by threatening another person or otherwise putting pressure on another person to commit or attempt
suicide.

This new s 2A makes it clear: that the offence can be committed through an intermediary,[50]
that there is no defence of impossibility[51] and that encouragement by threats or other forms
of pressure is covered.[52] Section 2B clarifies that D's liability need not be based on an individual act but may be based on a course of conduct over a period of time. Again, none of this
is intended significantly to change the substance as opposed to the form of the previous law.
That is doubtful as, over a decade after they were enacted, the breadth of the assisting and
encouraging offences in the Serious Crime Act is yet to be fully tested.

During the passage of the Coroners and Justice Act 2009 Lord Falconer moved an
amendment in the House of Lords which would have created an exception to s 2 of the
1961 Act in the case of acts done for the purpose of enabling or assisting a person to travel
to a country in which assisted dying is lawful, subject to certain conditions. The amendment was defeated.

Prosecutorial policies

The operation of such an offence has given rise to considerable controversy because its scope
means that those who help other consenting adults to die fall within its terms.[53]

Challenges to the offence were raised on the basis that it might even criminalize the distribution of a booklet giving advice to any person who wishes to commit suicide on how to
do so efficiently and painlessly. It was held that this was not necessarily an offence under the
pre-2009 law. In *A-G v Able*,[54] Woolf J refused to grant a declaration that the distribution
was unlawful, holding that an offence would be committed only if the distributor intended
that the booklet would be used by someone contemplating suicide and that he would be (and
in fact was) assisted or encouraged to do so. This challenge was brought to the old s 2 offence
based on aiding and abetting and was in accordance with the ordinary principles of the law
of secondary participation.[55] The new offence requires only that the publisher intends to do
acts capable of assisting or encouraging and that his act was intended to encourage or assist
suicide or an attempt at suicide.

The crime covers a variety of situations varying in moral culpability from D who encourages V to commit suicide for the purpose of inheriting his property,[56] to that of D who
supplies a final fatal (over)dose to V of a prescribed drug to alleviate V's suffering when V is
anxious to accelerate the end,[57] or refastens the plastic bag over the head of his terminally ill

---

[50] eg D gives lethal pills to X to administer to V.

[51] eg D gives V harmless pills that D thinks are lethal.

[52] This could be very important with the types of bullying email and internet campaigns that lead to suicide.
See the Law Commission Report No 381, *Abusive and Offensive Online Communications: A Scoping Report*
(2018).

[53] See the references in n 68. The CPS reports that 'From 1 April 2009 up to 31 July 2020, there have been 162
cases referred to the CPS by the police that have been recorded as assisted suicide. Of these 162 cases, 107 were
not proceeded with by the CPS and 32 cases were withdrawn by the police.'

[54] [1984] QB 795, QBD. See Mental Capacity Act 2005, s 62 and Code, para 9.5. KJM Smith, 'Assisting
Suicide—The Attorney-General and the Voluntary Euthanasia Society' [1983] Crim LR 579. See Mental
Capacity Act 2005, s 62 and Code, para 9.5.

[55] See Ch 6.   [56] eg *Cumming* [2006] EWCA Crim 3223.

[57] The Court of Appeal in *Kennedy (No 2)* [2005] EWCA Crim 685, suggested that 'it would be an abuse to
prosecute someone assisting another to commit suicide for murder', at [32].

spouse as she desired.[58] The consent of the DPP is required in order to achieve consistency in prosecution practice.[59]

A series of important cases in the House of Lords and Supreme Court have grappled with the limits of assisted suicide offences in English law, the prosecution policies that apply and the ECHR dimension to criminalizing assisted suicide. As Toulson LJ explained in the Divisional Court in *Nicklinson* (discussed later): 'these are tragic cases. They present society with legal and ethical questions of the most difficult kind. They also involve constitutional questions'.[60]

R (on the application of Pretty) v DPP

In this landmark case it was held that the DPP had no power to give an undertaking that he would not prosecute the spouse, D, of a person, V, who suffered from an incurable disease which prevented her from committing suicide unaided. If D supplied V with the means of committing suicide when V requested it, D was liable to prosecution.[61] In *Pretty v UK*,[62] the European Court of Human Rights accepted that Art 2's protection provides a right to life, not a right to death. It was held that Arts 2, 3 and 9 were not engaged by the claim of a right to assisted death; Art 8 was engaged in such circumstances, but the UK's criminal prohibition on assisted suicide fell within Art 8(2).[63] The doctor who complies with the request of a competent adult who refuses life-sustaining/saving treatment does not assist his suicide.[64] As Lord Goff observed in *Bland*, the doctor who keeps a patient comfortable whilst he dies cannot be said to assist suicide: 'there is no question of the patient having committed suicide nor therefore of the doctor of having aided or abetted him in doing so. It is simply that the patient has, as he is entitled to, declined to consent to treatment which might or would have the effect of prolonging his life, and the doctor has, in accordance with

---

[58] See the prosecution of David March, discussed in S Burns, 'The Quality of Mercy' (2007) 157 NLJ 86.

[59] *R (on the application of Pretty) v DPP* [2002] 1 AC 800. See also on prosecution policy *Dunbar v Plant* [1997] 3 WLR 1261. According to the DPP's *Policy for Prosecutors in Respect of Cases of Encouraging or Assisting Suicide* (Feb 2010, updated Oct 2014), www.cps.gov.uk/publications/prosecution/assisted_suicide_policy.html, the DPP will only consent where the full code test is met (para 14), and these cases are dealt with by the Special Crime Division, the head of which reports directly to the DPP (paras 49, 50). Lord Hughes observed that: 'There is no reason to think that section 2(4) was inserted into the Suicide Act 1961 with any intention of doing more than keeping the prosecutions in reliable hands.' *Nicklinson*, [273].

[60] [2012] EWHC 2381 (Admin), [1].

[61] *R (Pretty) v DPP* [2002] 1 AC 800. The case decides that the ECHR does not oblige a State to legalize assisted suicide. For comment, see R Tur, 'Legislative Techniques and Human Rights—The Sad Case of Assisted Suicide' [2003] Crim LR 3. Cf D Calvert Smith and S O'Doherty, 'Legislative Technique and Human Rights—A Response' [2003] Crim LR 384.

[62] [2002] 35 EHRR 1.

[63] The House of Lords held that Art 8 was not engaged, since that Article was directed to the protection of personal autonomy whilst an individual was alive but did not confer a right to decide how or when to die: at [26] per Lord Bingham, at [61]–[62] per Lord Steyn and at [100]–[102] per Lord Hope. However, in *R (Purdy) v DPP* [2009] UKHL 45 (discussed later) the House of Lords departed from its decision in *Pretty* on this point and found Art 8(1) to be engaged: at [35]–[38] per Lord Hope, at [67]–[68] per Baroness Hall, at [83]–[84] per Lord Brown and at [95] per Lord Neuberger. For analysis, see M Freeman, 'Death, Dying and the Human Rights Act 1998' (1999) 52 CLP 218 and 'Denying Death its Dominion' (2002) 10 Med L Rev 245; B Hale, 'A Pretty Pass—When is there a Right to Die?' (2003) 32 Common Law World Rev 1; D Morris, 'Assisted Suicide under the European Convention on Human Rights: A Critique' [2003] EHRLR 65.

[64] *Re B (Refusal of treatment)* [2002] 2 All ER 449—also known as *Mrs B v NHS Trust*—in fact a hospital commits assault if they continue to treat her against her will and Butler-Sloss LJ awarded (albeit small) damages for assault.

his duty, complied with the patient's wishes.'[65] The Mental Capacity Act 2005 now provides for advance refusals of life-sustaining treatment.[66]

R (on the application of Purdy) v DPP

The second landmark challenge was to the sufficiency of the DPP's policy on prosecuting the offence.[67] P suffered from primary progressive multiple sclerosis for which there was no known cure. She would have liked to end her life when her continuing existence became unbearable, but at that stage in her disease she would be unable to travel to a country where assisted suicide was lawful without help. Her husband was willing to help her to travel. If P's husband helped her to travel outside the country, however, there was a substantial risk that he would be prosecuted. P challenged the lawfulness of the failure of the DPP to issue a crime-specific policy identifying the facts and circumstances that would be taken into account when deciding whether to prosecute an individual for assisting another to commit suicide. P sought information in order to make an informed decision about whether to ask for her husband's assistance in committing suicide.

In the House of Lords P argued that the offence of assisted suicide constituted an interference with her right to respect for her private life under Art 8(1) of the ECHR; and that the interference was not 'in accordance with the law' as required by Art 8(2), in the absence of an offence-specific policy. The House of Lords allowed her appeal holding that the right to respect for life contained in Art 8(1) was engaged. The ECtHR had determined that the very essence of the Convention was respect for human dignity and human freedom and it was under Art 8 that notions of the quality of life took on significance. Those notions covered the situation of people who were concerned that they should not be forced to linger on in old age or in states of advanced physical or mental decrepitude which conflicted with strongly held ideas of self and personal identity. For the purposes of Art 8(2), in order for s 2(4) of the 1961 Act to comply with the requirement that the law should be formulated with sufficient precision to enable the individual, if need be with advice, to regulate his conduct, the DPP had to create a code giving guidance on principles to be applied by Crown prosecutors in determining, in any case, whether proceedings for an offence under s 2(1) should be instituted. Such a code would be regarded for the purposes of Art 8(2) as forming part of the law in accordance with which an interference with the right of respect for private life might be held to be justified. In that way the requirements of accessibility and foreseeability would be satisfied.

The DPP was required to promulgate an offence-specific policy identifying the facts and circumstances which would be taken into account in deciding, in a case such as that which the claimant's case exemplified, whether or not to exercise the discretion to consent to a prosecution under s 2(4). The House did not prescribe what the guidance might say. The decision was controversial in constitutional terms, with the highest court of the land

---

[65] [1993] AC 789 at 864.

[66] See s 25(5) and (6). These provisions only apply to adults who have capacity: s 24(1). Note also: s 24 does not include the word 'care'. Para 9.28 of the Code of Practice issued pursuant to the Act states: 'An advance decision cannot refuse actions that are needed to keep a person comfortable (sometimes called basic or essential care). Examples include warmth, shelter, actions to keep a person clean and the offer of food and water by mouth'—see https://assets.publishing.service.gov.uk/government/uploads/system/uploads/attachment_data/file/921428/Mental-capacity-act-code-of-practice.pdf.

[67] *R (on the application of Purdy) v DPP* [2009] UKHL 45. But see also the judgment of Lord Hughes in *Nicklinson* at [275].

compelling the DPP to provide such guidance.[68] Interim guidance was published and, after consultation,[69] a final version was produced.[70]

The new prosecution policy does not 'decriminalize' the offence of encouraging or assisting suicide and does not give any express assurance that a person will be immune from prosecution if he does an act that encourages or assists another's suicide or attempted suicide. Sixteen factors that will be relevant and which will suggest that a prosecution is more likely to be required are listed. These include:

- the victim being under 18 years of age;
- the victim not having the capacity (as defined by the Mental Capacity Act 2005) to reach an informed decision to commit suicide;
- the victim not having reached a voluntary, clear, settled and informed decision to commit suicide;
- the victim not having clearly and unequivocally communicated his or her decision to commit suicide to the suspect;
- the victim not having sought the encouragement or assistance of the suspect personally or on his or her own initiative;
- the suspect not being wholly motivated by compassion, for example in that the suspect was motivated by the prospect that he or she or a person closely connected to him or her stood to gain in some way from the death of the victim;
- the suspect pressurizing the victim to commit suicide;
- the suspect not taking reasonable steps to ensure that any other person had not pressured the victim to commit suicide;
- the suspect having a history of violence or abuse against the victim;
- whether the victim could have herself performed the act that D did to assist V in her suicide;
- the suspect being unknown to the victim and encouraging or assisting the victim to commit or attempt to commit suicide by providing specific information via, for example, a website or publication;
- the suspect giving encouragement or assistance to more than one victim who were not known to each other;
- the suspect being paid by the victim or those close to the victim for his or her encouragement or assistance;

---

[68] See in particular on the decision, R Nobles and D Schiff, 'Disobedience to the Law—Debbie Purdy's case' (2010) 73 MLR 295; and K Greasley, '*R (Purdy) v DPP* and the Case for Wilful Blindness' (2010) 30 OJLS 301; J Rogers, 'Prosecutorial Policies, Prosecutorial Systems, and the Purdy Litigation' [2010] Crim LR 542; N Cartwright, '48 Years On: Is the Suicide Act Fit for Purpose?' (2009) 17 Med L Rev 467; A Mullock, 'Overlooking the Criminally Compassionate: What are the Implications of Prosecutorial Policy on Encouraging or Assisting Suicide?' (2010) 18 Med L Rev 442, P Lewis, 'Informal Legal Change on Assisted Suicide: The Policy for Prosecutors' (2011) 31 LS 119.

[69] See R Daw and A Solomon, 'Assisted Suicide and Identifying the Public Interest in the Decision to Prosecute' [2010] Crim LR 737 for an illuminating insight into how the policy was drawn up.

[70] See J Rogers, 'Prosecutorial Policies, Prosecutorial Systems, and the Purdy Litigation' [2010] Crim LR 542; A Mullock, 'Prosecutors Making (Bad) Law' (2009) 17 Med L Rev 290; R Heywood, 'Prosecutorial Guidelines on Assisted Suicide' (2010) 21 King's LJ 425. The DPP published the final policy on prosecuting cases of assisted suicide on 25 Feb 2010. A newer version of the policy with a short amendment was issued on 16 Oct 2014 following the Supreme Court's decision in *Nicklinson* (see n 59 and n 79).

- the suspect acting in his or her capacity as a medical doctor, nurse, other health-care professional, a professional carer (whether for payment or not) or as a person in authority, such as a prison officer, *and the victim was in his or her care*;[71]

- the suspect being aware that the victim intended to commit suicide in a public place where it was reasonable to think that members of the public may be present;

- the suspect acting in his or her capacity as a person involved in the management or as an employee (whether for payment or not) of an organization or group, a purpose of which is to provide a physical environment (whether for payment or not) in which to allow another to commit suicide.

A prosecution is less likely to be required if:

- the victim had reached a voluntary, clear, settled and informed decision to commit suicide;

- the suspect was wholly motivated by compassion;

- the actions of the suspect, although sufficient to come within the definition of the offence, were of only minor encouragement or assistance;

- the suspect had sought to dissuade the victim from taking the course of action which resulted in his or her suicide;

- the actions of the suspect may be characterized as reluctant encouragement or assistance in the face of a determined wish on the part of the victim to commit suicide;

- the suspect reported the victim's suicide to the police and fully assisted them in their inquiries into the circumstances of the suicide or the attempt and his or her part in providing encouragement or assistance.[72]

The first instance of the public interest factors of the policy being applied was consideration of whether to prosecute Caractacus Downes, son of Sir Edward and Lady Downes who committed suicide at the Dignitas clinic in Switzerland. Between 1998 and 2011, a total of 215 people from the UK used Dignitas and no one providing assistance in that connection has been prosecuted.[73] The first prosecution since the DPP's guidance was published was the case of *Howe*.[74]

R (on the application of Nicklinson) v DPP and R (on the application of AM) v DPP

The issue came to the fore once more in conjoined appeals heard before a nine-member Supreme Court.[75] The claimants—LM and N—suffered from degenerative medical conditions and expressed a strong, settled and reasoned wish to end their lives. Due to the

---

[71] This emphasis is in the guidance, as is this footnote: 'For the avoidance of doubt the words 'and the victim was in his or her care' qualify all of the preceding parts of this [bullet point]. This factor does not apply merely because someone was acting in a capacity described within it: it applies only where there was, in addition, a relationship of care between the suspect and the victims such that it will be necessary to consider whether the suspect may have exerted some influence on the victim.' The amendment is intended to clarify that the interpretation of the guidance given by Lord Judge CJ in *Nicklinson* [2013] EWCA Civ 961 is the correct one.

[72] For comment on the guidelines creating de facto defences, see the *Report of the Falconer Commission on Assisted Dying* (2012) 285–6. For careful analysis of the guidelines see the judgment of Lord Judge CJ in the Court of Appeal.

[73] *Nicklinson* at [48] per Lord Neuberger. On average 34 Britons die at Dignitas each year.

[74] [2014] EWCA Crim 114. The Court of Appeal gave guidance as to what the appropriate sentence is in cases such as this.

[75] [2014] UKSC 38.

debilitating nature of the claimants' medical conditions they would need assistance in order to carry out their wish to commit suicide. The Supreme Court held (by a majority),[76] that the offence in s 2 of the Suicide Act 1961 was within the margin of appreciation afforded to Convention States on the issue of whether to criminalize assisted suicide. The 1961 Act did not impose an impermissible 'blanket ban' which would take it outside the UK's margin of appreciation in this area.[77] The court recognized, by a majority,[78] that following the European Court's acceptance that it was for Convention States to decide whether their own law on assisted suicide infringed Art 8, the Supreme Court did have jurisdiction to the hold that s 2 infringed Art 8 and to consider a declaration of incompatibility. The court went on to hold by a majority (Baroness Hale and Lord Kerr dissenting) that it would not be appropriate for the Supreme Court to declare that s 2 of the 1961 Act was incompatible with the ECHR at least until such time as Parliament had considered specific legislation on assisted suicide.

The Supreme Court unanimously declined to order the DPP to amend the policy on prosecuting cases of alleged assisted suicide.[79] The policy was to provide transparency and consistency in the approach that would be taken. It was not for the court to dictate its contents.

As a result of the Supreme Court's judgment, the matter was very clearly one for Parliament to resolve, with the clear warning that if it did not do so, the Supreme Court may be forced to declare s 2 incompatible.

R (on the application of Conway) v Secretary of State for Justice

In a yet more recent case to consider this difficult issue, the claimant suffered from motor neurone disease.[80] C wished to have the option, when he had a prognosis of six months or less to live, of seeking assistance from a medical professional to end his life. The claimant argued that s 2 of the Suicide Act 1961 was incompatible with his rights under Art 8. He argued that alternative statutory regimes could be envisaged that sufficiently protected the weak and vulnerable but which did not impose a blanket prohibition on assisted suicide. The Administrative Court held that s 2 of the Suicide Act fell within Art 8(2). It was aimed at protecting the weak and vulnerable and was objectively justified under Art 8(2) on that basis. The court held that there was a rational connection between s 2 and the protection of the weak and vulnerable. The statute also reinforced a moral view regarding the sanctity of life and promoted relations of trust between doctors and patients. Finally, the court concluded that the prohibition on assisted suicide was necessary, as there was evidence to suggest that there was a real risk of vulnerable people seeking assistance to die were the prohibition on s 2 to be relaxed and that it struck a fair balance between the rights of people in the claimant's position and the wider community. The Court of Appeal upheld that decision.[81] The blanket ban on assisted suicide in s 2(1) of the Suicide Act 1961 was a necessary and proportionate interference with C's ECHR Art 8 rights.

---

[76] Upholding the decision of the Court of Appeal (Civ Div). Lady Hale and Lord Kerr held that the law was incompatible with Convention rights. The effect of the prohibition in s 2 was to create a law that was disproportionate in Art 8 terms since it applied to cases such as theirs. The two dissenting Justices would therefore have granted the declaration of incompatibility.

[77] Having regard to ECHR law, *Haas v Switzerland* (2011) 53 EHRR 33; *Koch v Germany* [2013] 1 FCR 595; and *Gross v Switzerland* [2013] 3 FCR 608.

[78] Lords Clarke, Sumption, Reed and Hughes dissenting.

[79] In doing so, the court reversed a majority decision of the Court of Appeal (Civ Div). The court did, however, indicate that the DPP should 'review' the policy to clarify certain inconsistencies—see [144] and [251]. In October 2014, the DPP issued amended guidance as discussed at n 59. See the challenge in *R (Kenward) v DPP* [2015] EWHC 3508 (Admin)

[80] [2017] EWHC 2447 (Admin).   [81] [2018] EWCA Civ 1431.

Jurisdictional issues

There was a dispute under the old law as to whether a prosecution could ensue if D assisted V's suicide abroad.[82] The issue gained a high profile with tragic cases such as that of Daniel James who travelled to the Dignitas clinic to commit suicide after having become paralysed.[83] Concern was raised that relatives would be prosecuted. Under s 2 as substituted in the 2009 Act, there seems no doubt that D will commit the offence if he performs acts in England and Wales that are capable of assisting V to commit or attempt suicide abroad.[84]

Transferred malice in suicides

Since suicide is not a crime, where D kills V in the course of trying to kill himself, there is now no room for the doctrine of transferred malice for there is no 'malice' to transfer. Where D kills V in the course of trying to kill himself, his liability depends on the general principles of murder and manslaughter. Thus, if the death of V was utterly unforeseeable, it would be accidental death; if there was gross negligence as to causing death or recklessness as to whether death or serious bodily harm was caused, it may be manslaughter; and if D foresaw death or serious bodily harm as virtually certain, it may be murder.[85]

Mercy killing

English law admits of no defence of mercy killing or euthanasia.[86] In *Inglis*,[87] where a mother killed her severely injured son in what she considered to be an act of mercy, she was prosecuted for murder. As the Lord Chief Justice emphasized, upholding her conviction:

the law does not recognise the concept implicit in the defence statement that [V] was 'already dead in all but a small physical degree'. The fact is that he was alive, a person in being. However brief the time left for him, that life could not lawfully be extinguished. Similarly, however disabled [V] might have been, a disabled life, even a life lived at the extremes of disability, is not one jot less precious than the life of an able-bodied person. [V]'s condition made him especially vulnerable, and for that among other reasons, whether or not he might have died within a few months anyway, his life was protected by the law, and no one, not even his mother, could lawfully step in and bring it to a premature conclusion. Until Parliament decides otherwise, the law recognises a distinction between

---

[82] M Hirst, 'Suicide in Switzerland: Complicity in England?' [2009] Crim LR 335 argued that if A helps or encourages B to travel from England to a jurisdiction (eg Switzerland) where assisted suicide is lawful in the knowledge that B will commit suicide there, A does not thereby commit any offence under the Suicide Act 1961, s 2(1). Lord Hope rejected this argument after careful consideration, referring to *Smith (Wallace Duncan) (No 4)* [2004] EWCA Crim 631.

[83] See http://news.bbc.co.uk/1/hi/england/hereford/worcs/7774802.stm.

[84] See M Hirst, 'Assisted Suicide after *Purdy*: The Unresolved Issue' [2009] Crim LR 870.

[85] See p 93.

[86] See Toulson LJ in the Divisional Court in *Nicklinson* citing the this passage in the 13th edn of this work (at p 589) with approval at [59]. On mercy killing in general, see: S McLean, *Assisted Dying: Reflections on the Need for Law Reform* (2007); R Huxtable, *Euthanasia, Ethics and the Law* (2007); M Otlowski, *Voluntary Euthanasia and the Common Law* (2000); H Biggs, *Euthanasia, Death with Dignity and the Law* (2001); J Keown, *Euthanasia, Ethics and Public Policy: An Argument against Legislation* (2002). See also more specifically in the criminal law context, S Ost, 'Euthanasia and the Defence of Necessity' [2005] Crim LR 355; M Wilks, 'Medical Treatment at the End of Life: A British Doctor's Perspective' in C Erin and S Ost, *The Criminal Justice System and Health Care* (2007); J Keown, 'Williams versus Kamisar on Euthanasia: A Classic Debate Revisited' in DJ Baker and J Horder, *The Sanctity of Life and the Criminal Law: The Legacy of Glanville Williams* (2013); P Lewis, 'The Failure of the Defence of Necessity as a Mechanism of Legal Change on Assisted Dying in the Common Law World' in Baker and Horder, ibid. For an analysis of the operation of diminished responsibility in the context of mercy killing, see M Gibson, 'Pragmatism Preserved? The Challenges of Accommodating Mercy Killers in the Reformed Diminished Responsibility Plea' (2017) 81 J Crim L 177.

[87] *Inglis* [2010] EWCA Crim 2637.

the withdrawal of treatment supporting life, which, subject to stringent conditions, may be lawful, and the active termination of life, which is unlawful.[88]

This position was confirmed by the Supreme Court in *Nicklinson*.[89]

There is no defence of mercy killing nor that the killing is in the best interests of the victim in some general sense, nor is there a defence of physician-assisted suicide.[90] Medical practitioners' obligations regarding the withdrawal of life-sustaining treatment are considered in Ch 2.[91] A competent but paralysed adult is entitled to refuse to continue medical treatment. This is not suicide and the health-care professionals are not assisting such.[92] There is no breach of Art 2 of the ECHR by the withdrawal of treatment in such cases.

The European Court in *Pretty v UK* declined to express a view on whether an assisted suicide provision would be compliant with Art 2. The Court concluded that the regulation of suicide was for the Member State's law, and that there was no State obligation to facilitate death. The ECtHR has held that there is no breach of Art 8 if a Member State does not facilitate assisted suicide: *Haas v Switzerland*.[93]

Reform

A Private Members' Bill for the Assisted Dying of the Terminally Ill, which would have enabled a competent adult who is suffering as a result of a terminal illness to receive medical assistance to die at his own request, and to make provision for a person suffering from a terminal illness to receive pain relief medication, was rejected in 2005.[94]

Several law reform agencies have reviewed the possibility of such a defence (or special offence) being available.[95] The Law Commission declined to engage fully with the issue in its Consultation Paper on Homicide[96] and accepted in its subsequent Report No 304 that the government ought to commission such a reform study. Public attitudes to mercy killing, as confirmed in Professor Mitchell's illuminating empirical research,[97] reveal that where there is clear evidence of the victim's wish to die, such cases are perceived as amongst the least serious homicide cases.[98] The Law Commission concluded:

There are three reasons why it is arguable that it would be more satisfactory if, in cases of rational 'mercy' killing, Parliament were to make 'mercy' killing a partial defence rather than purely a matter going to mitigation of the minimum term. First, for a genuine 'mercy' killer, a life long licence seems neither necessary nor appropriate. Secondly, if there is a dispute of fact as to D's motive for killing V, it might be thought better that the jury, rather than the trial judge, should decide the issue.

88 ibid, [38]–[39]. Cf *Webb* [2011] EWCA Crim 152.   89 See Lord Neuberger at [17].

90 E Jackson, 'Whose Death is it Anyway? Euthanasia and the Medical Profession' (2004) 57 CLP 415; cf the Netherlands on which see J Griffiths, 'Assisted Suicide in the Netherlands' (1995) 58 MLR 232; J Griffiths, H Weyers and M Adams, *Euthanasia and Law in Europe* (2009); J Keown, 'Euthanasia in the Netherlands' in J Keown (ed), *Euthanasia Examined* (1995) 261; P Lewis, *Assisted Dying and Legal Change* (2007).

91 See especially the decisions in *Nicklinson* and *R (Burke) v GMC* [2004] EWHC 1879 (Admin); overruled in the Court of Appeal [2006] QB 273; and see the ECHR application (App no 19807/06). For comment see J Coggan, 'Could the Right to Die with Dignity Represent a New Right to Die in English Law?' (2006) 14 Med L Rev 219, and generally on the ECHR position, Emmerson, Ashworth and Macdonald, HR&CJ, paras 18.48 et seq.

92 *B (Consent to Treatment)* [2002] 2 All ER 449.   93 App no 31322/07.

94 See S Evan and D Hewitt, 'A Question of Choice' (2006) 156 NLJ 44. See also the MOJ Consultation Paper 2009/06 which discusses these Bills.

95 See the CLRC, *Offences Against the Person*, Working Paper No 67 (1976) paras 79–87.

96 See Ch 8 of that Paper and the criticism levelled by J Rogers in 'The Law Commission's Proposed Restructuring of the Law of Homicide' (2006) 70 J Crim L 223 suggesting a distinction might be drawn in terms of availability of a defence to relatives as opposed to professional carers. The Law Commission rejected that argument—see LC 304, para 7.28.

97 Extracted in LCCP 177 and LC 304.   98 LC 304, para 7.17.

Thirdly, a partial defence would avoid the need for the practice, which concerns some of our consultees, of dressing up rational 'mercy' killing cases as ones of diminished responsibility by means of a sympathetic report from a pliant psychiatrist which the court and prosecution are content not to challenge.[99]

In *Inglis*,[100] the Lord Chief Justice referred to the Law Commission's 'careful analysis of this profoundly sensitive issue'.

The Law Commission provisionally proposed that a verdict of assisting suicide might be left as an alternative verdict on a charge of murder or manslaughter where D proves that he and V had intended to take part in a suicide pact.[101] That proposal was withdrawn in the final Report.[102] An attempt to reform the law was undertaken by Lord Falconer, whose Assisted Dying Bill had its first reading in the House of Lords in May 2014. The Bill reached Second Reading in July 2014. During a debate that lasted over nine hours, the Bill was debated in detail but no vote was held. In June 2015, Lord Falconer introduced an Assisted Dying Bill in materially similar terms to his earlier Bill. This time, however, the Bill was not given time for debate. In June 2016, Lord Hayward introduced a similar Bill, but Parliament was dissolved before it reached second reading. More recently, in January 2017, there was a brief debate following a question in the House of Lords about whether the government had any plans to legalize assisted dying for terminally ill adults with capacity, with appropriate safeguards.

15.2.3 Suicide pacts

A surviving party to a suicide pact who assists or encourages the other party to commit suicide is, of course, guilty of the assisting or encouraging offence discussed earlier.[103]

The survivor of such a pact may, however, have either himself killed the deceased or have procured a third party to do it. Such cases do not fall within the Suicide Act, but within s 4(1) of the Homicide Act 1957 which, as amended by the Suicide Act, provides:

It shall be manslaughter and shall not be murder for a person acting in pursuance of a suicide pact between him and another to kill the other[104] or be party to the other being killed by a third person.

'Suicide pact' is defined by s 4(3) of the Homicide Act as:

a common agreement between two or more persons having for its object the death of all of them, whether or not each is to take his own life, but nothing done by a person who enters into a suicide pact shall be treated as done by him in pursuance of the pact unless it is done while he has the settled intention of dying in pursuance of the pact.

The onus on a charge of murder of establishing the 'defence' of suicide pact is put by s 4(2) on the accused and the standard of proof required is the balance of probabilities. This is not incompatible with Art 6(2) of the ECHR.[105]

According to the Law Commission, writing in 2005, there are on average 10 to 15 successful suicide pacts per year.[106]

---

99 Para 7.48. 100 [2010] EWCA Crim 2637. 101 LCCP 177, para 8.95. 102 LC 304.

103 Until the enactment of the Suicide Act, this was manslaughter under the Homicide Act 1957, s 4. The public interest does not normally call for the prosecution of the survivor of a suicide pact: *Dunbar v Plant* [1997] 3 WLR 1261 at 1285 per Phillips LJ; followed in *Challen v Challen* [2020] EWHC 1330 (Ch).

104 If, otherwise than in pursuance of a suicide pact, D kills V at V's request, D is of course guilty of murder. Cf *Robinson*, p 218.

105 *A-G's Reference (No 1 of 2004)* [2004] EWCA Crim 1025, [130]–[132].

106 See LCCP 177, para 8.60.

The distinction between assisting or encouraging in suicide and manslaughter by suicide pact is not entirely satisfactory.[107] Manslaughter by suicide pact is punishable with life imprisonment and is evidently the more serious crime. However, since the person guilty of it always intends to die himself, it is difficult to see how it can compare in moral heinousness with the case of D who, for example, incites V to die in order that he may live and enjoy V's property.

The distinction between the two crimes may be very fine. If D and V agree to gas themselves with car exhaust fumes and D alone survives, it appears that he will be liable under the Homicide Act if he turned on the engine,[108] and possibly under the Suicide Act if V did. It may frequently be difficult to establish who did such an act and this is recognized by the provision in s 2(2) of the Suicide Act that, on the trial of an indictment for murder or manslaughter, the jury may find D guilty of assisting or encouraging in suicide if that is proved. If D is charged with murder and he establishes on a balance of probabilities that V committed suicide in pursuance of a suicide pact, he is entitled to be acquitted of murder and may presumably be convicted of assisting or encouraging in suicide since he has, in effect, admitted his guilt. If, however, D was charged with assisting or encouraging and it appeared that he had killed V, he would have to be acquitted. The Law Commission recently commented on the over- and under-inclusiveness of the offence.[109] It provides an undeserved defence to D who, as a leader of a cult, encourages followers to kill themselves but does not go through with the act himself. Yet it fails to deal with D's consensual killing of a terminally ill spouse, V, where D has secretly planned to kill himself once V is dead, but fails to achieve his own demise.[110]

15.2.3.1 Reform

There is considerable pressure for reform of the law. The Law Commission described the offence as having 'long outlived its usefulness' and having been flawed from the outset,[111] resting as it does on a promise from D to V that he will kill himself—a promise of no intrinsic moral value.[112] The Commission took the view that it presented no significant problem in practice.[113] However, although individuals prosecuted for manslaughter of their nearest and dearest may well receive low sentences, the pain and anguish of their bereavement is exacerbated by the criminal process.[114] Supporters of the law point to the significant protection it affords the vulnerable who face pressure to commit suicide when they perceive themselves to be a burden on carers. The defence is certainly more common among the elderly and, interestingly, empirical work reveals that the defence is more commonly relied on by men. One interpretation is that the defence is more readily relied on by dominant and controlling male partners.[115]

The Law Commission provisionally proposed the repeal of s 4, intending that all such cases would fall within its extended definition of diminished responsibility as cases where D suffered severe depression.[116] In its Report No 304, the Commission recognized that

---

[107] The Law Commission was not able to consider suicide in its review, LC 290, *Partial Defences to Murder* (2004). In its homicide review, LC 304, *Murder, Manslaughter and Infanticide* (2006) the Law Commission's recommendations for homicide provide only that the offence would be reclassified as second degree murder. The label seems unsuited to the actions of many of the cases to which it would apply.

[108] But if D pours out a glass of poison and V takes it, he may be liable under the Suicide Act 1961.

[109] LCCP 177, paras 8.21–8.25.

[110] See also the discussion of the differences in culpability between 'die together' cases and 'you then me' (homicide suicide) cases.

[111] LCCP 177, para 8.8.   [112] ibid, para 8.19.   [113] ibid, para 8.20.

[114] See *Blackburn* (2005) 14 Jan, unreported, CCC, suspended sentence for killing terminally ill wife in suicide pact, and see the news reports for 15 Jan 2005.

[115] See LCCP 177, paras 8.67–8.83.

[116] The research reveals that as many as 79 per cent of s 4 cases involve depressed individuals, para 8.63.

diminished responsibility would not deal with all depressed carer cases, nor with mercy killings. It was recommended that s 4 should not be repealed.[117] Some of the cases will fall within the new diminished responsibility defence (explained in Ch 13).

15.3 Infanticide

Section 1(1) of the Infanticide Act 1938 was amended in 2009.[118] From 4 October 2010 it now provides:

Where a woman by any wilful act or omission causes the death of her child being a child under the age of twelve months, but at the time of the act or omission the balance of her mind was disturbed by reason of her not having fully recovered from the effect of her giving birth to the child or by reason of the effect of lactation consequent upon the birth of the child, then if[119] the circumstances were such that but for this Act the offence would have amounted to murder or manslaughter, she shall be guilty of felony, to wit of infanticide, and may for such offence be dealt with and punished as if she had been guilty of the offence of manslaughter of the child.

The 1938 Act provision replaced a statute of 1922 which had confined the defence to killings by mothers of 'newly born' children. In one case, the Court of Criminal Appeal had held that to be inapplicable to a child of 35 days, so that the mother was convicted of murder.[120] The 1922 Act was itself the result of an agitation over very many years during which it was practically impossible to convict mothers of the murder of their young children because of the disapproval by public and professional opinion of a law which regarded such killings as ordinary murders. Where a conviction was obtained, the judge had to pronounce a sentence of death which everyone, except perhaps the offender, knew would not be carried out. A number of reasons were advanced why infanticide should be considered less reprehensible than other killings: (a) the injury done to the child was less, for it was incapable of the kind of suffering which might be undergone by the adult victim of a murder; (b) the loss of its family was less great; (c) the crime did not create the sense of insecurity in society which other murders caused; (d) generally, the heinousness of the crime was less, the motive very frequently being the concealment of the shame of the birth of an illegitimate child; and (e) where the killing is done by the mother, her responsibility may be reduced by the disturbance of her mind caused by the stress of the birth. It is, of course, the last of these considerations which is the governing one in the present legislation.[121] The killing of an infant by persons other than the mother, or by the mother if the balance of her mind is not disturbed, remains murder.

---

[117] See LC 304, Ch 7.

[118] See LCCP 177, Ch 8; LC 304, Ch 9. See also D Seaborne Davies, 'Child-Killing in English Law' (1937) 1 MLR 203; MACL, 301; G Williams, *The Sanctity of Life* (1957) 25–45; K O'Donovan, 'The Medicalisation of Infanticide' [1984] Crim LR 259; RD Mackay, 'The Consequences of Killing Very Young Children' [1993] Crim LR 21; A Wilczynski and A Morris, 'Parents who Kill their Children' [1993] Crim LR 31; D Maeir-Katkin and R Ogle, 'A Rationale for Infanticide Laws' [1993] Crim LR 903; M Jackson, 'Infanticide: Historical Perspectives' (1996) 146 NLJ 416; K Brennan, 'Beyond the Medical Model: A Rationale for Infanticide Legislation' (2007) 58 NILQ 505; A Loughnan, 'The "Strange" Case of the Infanticide Doctrine' (2012) 32 OJLS 685. The Court of Appeal called for its urgent reform: *Kai-Whitewind* [2005] EWCA Crim 1092, [2006] Crim LR 348.

[119] This replaced the words 'notwithstanding that'. In *Gore* [2007] EWCA Crim 2789, the Court of Appeal had construed that as meaning 'even if'. It is now clear it means merely 'if'.

[120] *O'Donoghue* (1927) 20 Cr App R 132.

[121] The validity of this psychiatric basis for the offence has been doubted, see N Walker, *Crime and Insanity in England* (1968) vol 1, 87–104, cf Maier-Katkin and Ogle [1993] Crim LR 903, 905–9.

This section is unusual in that it provides both a charge of infanticide and also a partial defence to murder: by s 1(2) as amended by the Coroners and Justice Act 2009, a woman indicted for the murder of her child under the age of 12 months may be acquitted of murder and convicted of infanticide if the conditions of s 1(1) are satisfied. The new subs (2) reads:

Where upon the trial of a woman for the murder of her child, being a child under the age of twelve months, the jury are of opinion that she by any wilful act or omission caused its death, but that at the time of the act or omission the balance of her mind was disturbed by reason of her not having fully recovered from the effect of giving birth to the child or by reason of the effect of lactation consequent upon the birth of the child, then the jury may, if the circumstances were such that but for the provisions of this Act they might have returned a verdict of murder or manslaughter, return in lieu thereof a verdict of infanticide.[122]

Where the charge is murder, an evidential burden on the issue of disturbance will fall on D; but the onus of *proof* remains with the Crown. Where the charge is infanticide, the onus of proving disturbance appears to be on the Crown; but this, of course, is unlikely to be contested.[123]

The 2009 Act amendment to the section came about following the case of *Gore*.[124] In that case, the Court of Appeal had construed the old s 1 as applying even if the mother was not charged with a homicide offence and held that it was available even if the mother lacked the mens rea for murder. The new section makes clear that infanticide as a defence and offence applies only in cases where the mother could otherwise have been convicted of murder *or manslaughter*.[125]

The CLRC thought that, because of the way in which the offence is drafted, it is not possible to charge a person with attempting to commit infanticide,[126] but McCowan J held that such an indictment will lie.[127]

It is worth emphasizing that there are several differences between the defence of diminished responsibility and infanticide. Infanticide requires that the balance of a woman's mind is disturbed at the time she kills her child, either by failure to make a full recovery from the effects of the birth or as a result of the effects of lactation; diminished responsibility requires proof of abnormality of mental functioning arising from a recognized medical condition that substantially impairs the defendant's ability to: (a) understand the nature of D's conduct; (b) form a rational judgement; (c) exercise self-control and that explains/causes her killing. Infanticide is both a partial defence to a charge of murder and an offence in its own right; diminished responsibility is only a partial defence. In infanticide, the burden of proof is on the prosecution; in diminished responsibility it is on the defendant on the balance of probabilities.[128]

In infanticide, unlike diminished responsibility, the defendant can rely on the plea if at the time of the killing the balance of her mind was disturbed either by birth or by the effects of lactation irrespective of whether that caused[129] her to kill the child. Infanticide

---

[122] Was it also necessary to insert 'or manslaughter' in the first line of s 1(2)? The effect of inserting it also into the opening words would be to make it clear that infanticide is an alternative verdict to a charge of manslaughter as well as to a charge of murder.

[123] See the numerous instances in LC 304, Appendix.   [124] [2007] EWCA Crim 2789.

[125] HC Research Paper 09/06, p 22. The government rejected the Law Commission recommendation for a trial judge to have power to order medical reports where any mother killed a child under the age of one and was convicted of murder.

[126] Fourteenth Report, para 113.   [127] *KA Smith* [1983] Crim LR 739 and commentary.

[128] The Court of Appeal in *Foye* [2013] EWCA Crim 475 stated that the reason why the burden of proof is on the defendant is because the defence is concerned with D's internal mental condition. The same conclusion was arrived at in relation to the amended version of the defence in *Wilcocks* [2016] EWCA Crim 2043.

[129] See the debate at p 582 on whether the new diminished plea requires a causal link.

is applicable only to biological mothers of the deceased and the deceased must have been under 12 months old at the time of death.[130]

The relationship between the offences gave rise to an interesting question of interpretation. In *Kai-Whitewind*, Lord CJ stated that the only circumstances relevant to the infanticide defence are whether the disturbance of the mother's mind must be due either to 'her not having fully recovered from the effect of giving birth' or to 'the effect of lactation consequent upon the birth of the child'.[131] However, in *Tunstill*[132] Treacy LJ held that this does not require the causes specified in the definition to be the *sole* cause of the balance of mind being disturbed. Treacy LJ stated:

as long as a failure to recover from the effects of birth is an operative or substantial cause of the disturbance of balance of mind that should be sufficient, even if there are other underlying mental problems (perhaps falling short of diminished responsibility) which are part of the overall picture.[133]

15.3.1 Reform

It is arguable that the principles on which the Infanticide Act was based may be no longer accepted and that mental illness is not now considered to be a significant cause of infanticide. In many cases, the relationship of incomplete recovery from the effects of childbirth or lactation to the child-killing is remote.[134] If the true trigger for the killing is a range of other social factors associated with caring for a young child, the offence/defence ought to apply to carers of either sex. The Court of Appeal has drawn attention to the unsatisfactory nature of the defence in this respect.[135] Moreover, when the Infanticide Act was passed, there was no defence of diminished responsibility to murder.[136]

The Butler Committee thought that diminished responsibility even under the pre-2009 Act law would probably cover all cases and recommended the abolition of the separate offence of infanticide.[137] The CLRC disagreed, at first on the ground that, so long as the prosecution are unable to charge manslaughter by reason of diminished responsibility, infanticide has the advantage that it avoids the necessity of charging the mother with murder;[138] and later on the ground that diminished responsibility might not cover all the circumstances[139] which in practice may be held to justify an infanticide verdict.[140]

---

[130] See *Gore*, n 124, [20].   [131] [2005] EWCA Crim 1092, [134].

[132] [2018] EWCA Crim 1696.   [133] At [31].

[134] Report of the Committee on Mentally Abnormal Offenders (The Butler Report (1975) Cmnd 6244, paras 19.23–19.24.

[135] See *Kai-Whitewind* [2005] EWCA Crim 1092.

[136] For comparison of the defence and offence, see Mackay [1993] Crim LR 21.

[137] ibid. For criticism, see Maier-Katkin and Ogle [1993] Crim LR 903. It has the advantage of applying to carers of either sex.

[138] CLRC, *Offences Against the Person*, Working Paper No 67 (1976) 26. The Committee tentatively suggested that a person apparently suffering from diminished responsibility should be indictable for manslaughter but later withdrew this proposal: CLRC/OAP/R, para 95.

[139] According to the Royal College of Psychiatrists, these circumstances include: (i) overwhelming stress from the social environment being highlighted by the birth of a baby, with the emphasis on the unsuitability of the accommodation etc; (ii) overwhelming stress from an additional member to a household struggling with poverty; (iii) psychological injury, and pressures and stress from a husband or other member of a family from the mother's incapacity to arrange the demands of the extra member of the family; (iv) failure of bonding between mother and child through illness or disability which impairs the development of the mother's capacity to care for the infant.

[140] Research reveals that half of women who plead or are convicted are not suffering any mental disorder. See Wilczynski and Morris [1993] Crim LR 31. See also the data in Appendix D of LC 304.

In order to bring the law into line with its practical operation, and because of the difficulty of establishing a direct connection between giving birth and the imbalance of the woman's mind, the CLRC recommended that the test should be whether the balance of her mind was disturbed by reason of the effect of giving birth to the child *or circumstances consequent upon that birth*.[141] A dissentient view was that the effect would be to make adverse social conditions a defence to child killing when it is not a defence to any other crime.[142] Because of the decision to recommend the broadening of the offence in this way (in law, if not in practice),[143] the CLRC abandoned its earlier tentative recommendation that the killing of older children of the family should be infanticide and not murder;[144] and recommended that the maximum penalty should be five years' imprisonment and not two, as they had previously been disposed to think.[145]

The Law Commission reviewed the scope of infanticide in LCCP 177 and LC 304. In LCCP 177,[146] its provisional proposals were to make minor amendment to the offence/defence so that it would apply where the deceased child was under two, and the reference to lactation in the defence would be removed since medical evidence did not support its retention. In LC 304, the Law Commission[147] considered extensive medical and psychiatric research,[148] along with the empirical survey[149] and recommended that no change be introduced to the offence/defence, save for a procedural amendment to allow an expedited appeal on medical evidence where a mother convicted of murdering her child under 12 months denied the killing. The 1938 Act was, somewhat disappointingly, described as a 'practicable legal solution'.[150]

15.4 The Domestic Violence, Crime and Victims Acts 2004 and 2012

Insurmountable problems arose in prosecutions for the non-accidental serious injury or death of a young child when the only individuals who had access to the child at the time of the incident (usually the two primary carers) denied responsibility.[151] Although clear that at least one of the carers was guilty of a serious crime, it was often impossible to prove beyond reasonable doubt that the ill-treatment was at the hand of one (or both) rather than the other. The death or injury may have occurred while one carer was absent. Further, it was also often impossible to prove whether the carer not directly responsible was guilty as an accomplice. Prior to the 2004 Act, if all that could be proved was that the offence was committed either by D1 or by D2, both had to be acquitted. Only if it could be proved that the one who did not commit the crime *must* have aided and abetted it could both be convicted.[152] This was as true where carers were charged with injury to their child as it was in the case of any other defendants. The only difference was that one carer may have a duty to intervene to prevent the ill-treatment of their child by the other when a stranger would

---

[141] Fourteenth Report, paras 103–6.   [142] See Annexes 7 and 8 to the Report.

[143] On the use of the offence in modern times see Mackay, n 118, and Wilczynski and Morris, n 118.

[144] Para 106.   [145] Para 108.   [146] Ch 7.   [147] Ch 6.

[148] Appendix E. Note also that the Royal College of Psychiatrists preferred a merger of the offence/defence with diminished responsibility: LC 304, para 8.35.

[149] Appendix D.   [150] Para 8.3.

[151] For further discussion, see SM Morrison, 'Should There Be a Domestic Violence Defence to the Offence of Familial Homicide?' [2013] Crim LR 826.

[152] See *Banfield* [2013] EWCA Crim 1394.

have no such duty. It was for the prosecution to prove that the carer who did not inflict the injuries must have aided and abetted the infliction by failure to fulfil that duty or otherwise.

In a series of cases, the Court of Appeal reluctantly accepted that trials in such circumstances would not normally proceed beyond a defence submission of no case to answer.[153] The result proved too much for some courts, and strained attempts to circumvent the problem were adopted. These were unsatisfactory.[154] The problem was a substantial one. Research revealed that in the UK no fewer than three children under the age of ten died or suffered serious injury each week, and only 27 per cent of cases led to a conviction.[155] The difficulties had exercised great academic minds, but no consensus was reached as to the optimal solution.[156] Was it better to create a new offence to catch A, who *ought to have been* aware of the wrongdoing of the other carer, B, who caused the injury? Alternatively (or additionally), was it appropriate to alter the procedure in such cases to upset the traditional burden of proof and presumption of innocence, or to admit pre-trial incriminating statements made by A against B, or to provide a statutory obligation to account for the death or injury?[157]

Following detailed consideration by the Law Commission, proposals for new offences and procedural changes were made, and provisions based on, though differing significantly from, those recommendations were implemented in s 5 of the Domestic Violence, Crime and Victims Act 2004.[158] To appreciate the full significance of the s 5 offence, it must be seen alongside s 6 of that Act,[159] which introduces controversial procedural changes whereby inferences can be drawn from a defendant's silence when charged with murder/manslaughter and the s 5 offence even where no case to answer would otherwise be established.

15.4.1 The Domestic Violence, Crime and Victims (Amendment) Act 2012

The Domestic Violence, Crime and Victims (Amendment) Act 2012 received Royal Assent on 8 March 2012. The Act extends the offence in s 5 of causing or allowing the death of a child or vulnerable adult.[160] As extended, the offence applies in relation to the death of *or serious physical harm* to a child or vulnerable adult. By a new subs (8), the maximum penalty in cases of serious injury is ten years' imprisonment. A new s 6A contains provisions relating to evidence and procedure.[161] Under the 2012 Act extension, the prosecution can

---

[153] *Russell and Russell* (1987) 85 Cr App R 388; *Lane and Lane* (1985) 82 Cr App R 5. For a valuable direction where one of two interrogating police officers has caused injury, see *Forman and Ford* [1988] Crim LR 677 (Judge Woods).

[154] *Gibson and Gibson* (1984) 80 Cr App R 24. See commentary [1984] Crim LR 615.

[155] See LC 282, *Children: Their Non-Accidental Death or Serious Injury (Criminal Trials)* (2003) Part II.

[156] See generally G Williams, 'Which of You Did It?' (1989) 52 MLR 179; E Griew, 'It Must Have Been One of Them' [1989] Crim LR 129.

[157] See LC 282 (2003) Part V.

[158] In particular, the Law Commission had proposed a new offence of aggravated child cruelty under s 1 of the Children and Young Person Act 1933, and had produced an offence which dealt with both serious injury and death in relation to children only. For comment on the Law Commission proposals, see P Glazebrook, 'Insufficient Child Protection' [2003] Crim LR 541, proposing an extremely wide offence which it is submitted would extend the ambit of the criminal law too far.

[159] See *Ikram* [2008] EWCA Crim 586 on difficulties that can arise as defendants shift their case in the course of the trial. Cf *Reid (Jason)* [2010] EWCA Crim 1478.

[160] In *McCarney* [2015] NICA 27, D was charged with 'causing the death of a child or vulnerable adult'. At the close of the prosecution case, D's application for the count to be quashed as not being an offence known to law was refused. The Northern Ireland Court of Appeal confirmed that s 5 creates a single offence of causing *or allowing* the death of a child or vulnerable adult.

[161] These provisions are controversial, but in *McCarney*, above, the Northern Ireland Court of Appeal held that the equivalent provisions in Northern Ireland were not incompatible with any of the rights guaranteed by Art 6. It can be assumed that the Court of Appeal in England and Wales would take the same approach.

allege in one count that D either caused serious physical injury (which does not include psychiatric injury) or allowed it to be caused. The extension was predictable: in 2003, the Law Commission recommended that the proposed offence extend to serious injury in relation to children, and the parliamentary debates on the 2004 Act acknowledged the possibility of extension if s 5 worked well.[162]

Parliamentary debates describe the evidence supporting such an extension. In 2010, six CPS areas identified 20 potential cases involving children and three involving vulnerable adults that could not be prosecuted under existing legislation, but which they believe could have been prosecuted under the proposed new offence.[163] The Metropolitan Police examined 179 cases between 2005 to 2008 in London, and suggested that of 69 cases where no prosecution took place, 39 would have been considered for prosecution under the extended s 5.[164]

15.4.2 The offence as extended

Section 5 provides the definition of the offence as amended:[165]

(1) A person ('D') is guilty of an offence if—

    (a) a child or vulnerable adult ('V') dies or suffers serious physical harm as a result of the unlawful act of a person who—

        (i) was a member of the same household as V, and

        (ii) had frequent contact with him,

    (b) D was such a person at the time of that act,

    (c) at that time there was a significant risk of serious physical harm being caused to V by the unlawful act of such a person, and

    (d) either D was the person whose act caused V's death or serious physical harm or—

        (i) D was, or ought to have been, aware of the risk mentioned in paragraph (c),

        (ii) D failed to take such steps as he could reasonably have been expected to take to protect V from the risk, and

        (iii) the act occurred in circumstances of the kind that D foresaw or ought to have foreseen.

(2) The prosecution does not have to prove whether it is the first alternative in subsection (1)(d) or the second (sub-paragraphs (i) to (iii)) that applies.

(3) If D was not the mother or father of V—

    (a) D may not be charged with an offence under this section if he was under the age of 16 at the time of the act that caused V's death or serious physical harm;

    (b) for the purposes of subsection (1)(d)(ii) D could not have been expected to take any such step as is referred to there before attaining that age.

(4) For the purposes of this section—

    (a) a person is to be regarded as a 'member' of a particular household, even if he does not live in that household, if he visits it so often and for such periods of time that it is reasonable to regard him as a member of it;

---

162 Hansard, HC, 27 Oct 2004, vol 425, col 1473.   163 Hansard, 21 Oct 2011, col 1181.
164 Public Bill Committee, 22 June 2011, col 7 (Sir Paul Beresford).
165 See L Hoyano and C Keenan, *Child Abuse: Law and Policy* (2007) 157–78; M Hayes, 'Criminal Trials Where the Child is the Victim: Extra Protection for Children or a Missed Opportunity' (2005) 17 CFLQ 307; C Colby, 'The Quest For Truth: Substantiating Allegations of Physical Abuse in Criminal Prosecutions and Care Proceedings' (2006) 20 I JLPF 317.

(b) where V lived in different households at different times, 'the same household as V' refers to the household in which V was living at the time of the act that caused V's death.

(5) For the purposes of this section an 'unlawful' act is one that—

  (a) constitutes an offence, or

  (b) would constitute an offence but for being the act of—

    (i) a person under the age of ten, or

    (ii) a person entitled to rely on a defence of insanity.

Paragraph (b) does not apply to an act of D.

The offence carries a maximum sentence of imprisonment for 14 years if death is caused and ten years if serious physical harm is caused.[166] The first reported cases under the provision were rather uncontroversial. In *Liu and Tan*,[167] there was physical abuse tantamount to torture of T's wife (a vulnerable adult) by T's mistress, L. T was aware of the gross mistreatment and was a participant. The provision has been used in high-profile cases such as the prosecutions relating to the death of 'Baby P'.[168]

Despite the attempts to define the key elements, many arbitrary distinctions persist and numerous issues will fall for judicial consideration.[169] In some respects the offence is unsatisfactorily wide; in particular, the Crown need not specify whether it is alleged that D killed/ seriously injured *or* failed to take reasonable steps to prevent the death/serious injury by the other member of the household.[170]

15.4.3 Who is protected?

The offence is limited to cases in which the victim is a child or vulnerable adult. A child is simply anyone under 16. The application of s 5 to vulnerable adults is less straightforward. The category under protection is less easily defined. 'Vulnerable adult' involves the more expansive definition in s 5(6):

a person aged 16 or over whose ability to protect himself from violence, abuse or neglect is significantly impaired through physical or mental disability or illness, through old age or otherwise.

This might have been intended primarily to protect the elderly cared for at home, but it may apply to domestic violence on much younger victims. In *Khan and others*,[171] S was convicted of murdering V, his wife aged 19 who was completely dependent on S and his extended family. S severely beat and inflicted serious injuries on V for weeks prior to killing her. S and others were convicted of allowing the death of a vulnerable adult, contrary to s 5(1). The Court of Appeal held that V was vulnerable at least from the time she suffered serious injuries in the weeks prior to the fatal attack. Adults, or near adults over the age of 16, are vulnerable if their ability to protect themselves from 'violence, abuse or neglect' is significantly impaired. The state of vulnerability need not be long-standing. The court was not prepared to exclude 'the possibility that an adult who is utterly dependent

---

[166] It has been argued that it is less than satisfactory that the jury cannot reflect the basis upon which they found the defendant guilty, given the maximum sentence available for the offences. See E Freer, '"Causing or Allowing the Death of a Child": Challenges to Working Out "Which of You Did It"?' [2016] Crim LR 618.

[167] [2006] EWCA Crim 3321.

[168] *Owen* [2009] EWCA Crim 2259.

[169] See also Home Office Circular 9/2005, *The Domestic Violence, Crime and Victims Act 2004*.

[170] Confusion can arise at trial as to which verdicts have been reached in relation to which defendants on which allegations: see *RN* [2020] EWCA Crim 1137 .

[171] [2009] EWCA Crim 2, [2009] Crim LR 348. See also *Watt and others* [2011] EWCA Crim 1325.

on others, even if physically young and apparently fit, may fall within the protective ambit of the Act'.[172] Moreover, the anticipation of a full recovery might not reduce the individual's temporary vulnerability.

The Court of Appeal in *Uddin* adopted an even broader interpretation than the one in *Khan*.[173] Hallett LJ rejected the argument that the term 'vulnerable adult' ought to be defined with reference to the words that precede it. Her ladyship held that the word 'otherwise' provided for an additional, third category or categories of potentially vulnerable adults who were not at the relevant time suffering from an illness, disability or old age. An adult may therefore fall within the ambit of the legislation by virtue of 'a cause (other than physical or mental disability or illness or old age) which has the effect on the victim of significantly impairing his ability to protect himself from violence, abuse or neglect'.[174] Her ladyship held that the cause of V's impaired ability to protect himself could be intrinsic or external and could be physical, psychological and/or arise from the victim's circumstances. Unlike Lord Judge CJ in *Khan*, however, Hallett LJ did not state that V had to be in a state of utter dependency. The example given was a victim of sexual or domestic abuse or modern slavery who might find himself in a vulnerable position, having suffered long-term physical and mental abuse leaving him scared, cowed and with a significantly impaired ability to protect himself.

Such a broad interpretation has the potential to create problems. It may make an already broad offence undesirably wide. The court's interpretation gives 'otherwise' within s 5(6) a meaning unconstrained by all of the words preceding it. As the statute introduces a positive duty to act, with a criminal sanction for failure to do so, a narrower approach to interpretation might have been expected. The s 5 offence applies to D2, who fails to protect a vulnerable person from death or serious injury, as well as to D1 who actually kills. Those who fail to protect are judged on a negligence-based standard—that they were or *ought to have been* aware of the significant risk to V. On a natural interpretation, there is no need for D2 to realize that V is a vulnerable adult: liability on that element of the offence is strict. If that is correct, D2's liability turns exclusively on the awareness/negligence as to V being at significant risk of serious injury from D1 and D2's failure to take reasonable steps to avoid that harm. If liability as to V's status is strict, and the definition of vulnerability is as ambiguous as it seems to be, the offence is remarkably wide. Since D2 need not (and arguably cannot) know whether V qualifies as a vulnerable adult, D2 is under a duty as soon as D2 ought to have realized that any member of the household is at significant risk from any other member of the household, whether V is a child or even a fit adult. If D2 ought to have been so aware, D2 will only be acquitted if either he took reasonable steps to avoid the harm or, *at trial* it is determined that V was not a vulnerable adult after all. However, it is implicit in the decision that the extent to which D2 did or did not know of V's vulnerability is highly material to what it was reasonable for D2 to be expected to do.[175]

15.4.4 What type of act or omission?

The actus reus of the offence is satisfied by either D's act or omission[176] which caused the death of the victim or caused V serious physical harm; or D's failure to take such steps as he could reasonably have been expected to take to protect V from the *significant*[177] risk of

---

[172] At [26].   [173] [2017] EWCA Crim 1072.   [174] At [37].

[175] Problems of proof might arise in the case of a person who is apparently fit: the physically fitter V is, the less likely that D2 will be aware that he is at significant risk of GBH from D1 (unless D1's treatment of V is extreme), particularly where D1's conduct takes the form of neglect rather than physical attack.

[176] Section 5(6) makes it clear that an act includes an omission.

[177] See *Mujuru* [2007] EWCA Crim 1249, [2008] Crim LR 54 and commentary.

serious physical harm by the unlawful act of a person living in the same household as V and having frequent contact with V. There is no requirement that the failure on D's part to protect V is a legal cause of death or serious physical harm.[178] The conduct which caused death or serious physical harm is not limited to that which would form specific crimes provided it was unlawful—offences of violence are the most obvious examples, and in relation to children under 16, but not vulnerable individuals, offences of child neglect. Section 5(6) confirms that 'serious' harm means harm that amounts to grievous bodily harm for the purposes of the OAPA 1861.

D1's conduct which results in V's death or causes V serious physical harm must occur in circumstances of 'the kind' which were/ought to have been foreseen by D2; there is no need for the conduct to be identical to that which D2 ought to have foreseen.[179] It is odd that the offence is restricted by this requirement. It means that D2 who foresees that D1 might use violence by punching V cannot be convicted if D1 kills or seriously injures V by poisoning.

The unlawful act by D1 of which D2 must be aware/ought to be aware can include a course of violent conduct as well as an *omission* to act. If D1 neglects a vulnerable member of the household to whom he owes a duty of care and is liable for gross negligence manslaughter, D2, a fellow member of the household, might then be liable under s 5 if he at least ought to have been aware of the risk of serious injury to V by D1's conduct. The fact that D1's act must be an 'unlawful' one (including an omission) does not mean that there must an unlawful 'act' as an element of the gross negligence manslaughter charge; rather, the gross negligence manslaughter qualifies because as a crime it is an unlawful act: s 5(5).

15.4.5 Household

The Act deliberately leaves undefined the concept of 'household'.[180] This is disappointing for an offence of this seriousness, even with the additional qualifying requirement that D has contact with the victim. Some categories of carer who have regular contact—for example, nannies—are seemingly not caught by the Act unless under s 5(4)(b). The focus of the offence is clearly on imposing burdens on household members to police the risk of harm.[181] In that respect it is illogical that the offence is not triggered where D is/ought to be aware of the risk posed by other carers in regular contact with the victim.

In *Khan*, it was held that membership of a household was a question of fact. There had to be 'frequent contact' between the household member and the eventual victim. The lack of certainty is unsatisfactory in an offence of this nature.[182]

15.4.6 What type of harm?

Serious harm is defined in the 2004 Act as 'harm that amounts to grievous bodily harm for the purposes of the Offences Against the Person Act 1861'.[183]

---

[178] D1's act in killing V will break the chain of causation. D2 will remain liable under this offence, not for an omission based on a duty (identified under the categories in Ch 2).

[179] See *Khan* at [39].

[180] Hansard, HL, 21 Jan 2004, col GC362: Baroness Scotland stated that it was a deliberate decision to leave the definition to courts.

[181] 'It is drafted with the idea that members of the household will know enough about the activities of the other members that they can be expected to be aware of the risk to the victim and take action. They are "complicit" in the offence, either directly or by proximity, through standing by during the preceding abuse or neglect and doing nothing. Therefore, in this context, if one were to ask, "Am I my brother's keeper?", the answer would be, "Yes".' Baroness Scotland, Hansard, 21 Jan 2004, col GC361.

[182] A point also made by A Ashworth, *Positive Obligations in Criminal Law* (2013) 99.

[183] Section 5(6).

15.4.7 What mens rea?

In terms of mens rea, it is effectively a crime of negligence since the fault on D's part if he is not the direct cause of the death or serious injury is a question of whether he *ought to have been* aware of the risk. The death or serious injury must have occurred *in the circumstances* that D ought to have foreseen. D who is aware that X has previously shaken his baby, V, violently might not be guilty if X caused V's death or serious injury by, for example, dipping its dummy in methadone to stop its incessant crying.[184]

In *Khan*, the court referred to the extension of the offence to 'those who chose to close their eyes to a risk of which they ought to have been aware, and which they ought to have foreseen'.[185] Technically, this confuses wilful blindness, where D has some awareness of the risk (at least suspicion), with negligence, where D need not have any awareness provided a reasonable person would. The test in s 5 is simply whether D *ought to have been* aware.

Another limitation on the scope of liability is that in s 5(1)(d)(ii): D's failure is to be assessed against the steps he could be reasonably expected to take. If D is a child or has a learning disability this will be relevant to determining what he could be expected to do. What of D2 who is petrified of D1? In addition, in assessing the reasonableness of the steps that ought to have been taken by D2, the question for the jury is, seemingly, whether the steps are reasonable for this particular defendant to take. Thus, juries might hesitate before convicting D2 who lives in an abusive and violent relationship with D1, and is aware that D1 batters their child as he does D2. In *Khan*, the Court of Appeal sought to allay fears[186] that the offence will be used inappropriately to victimize further those who, because they are themselves subjected to domestic abuse, have failed to take steps to protect a child or vulnerable adult from the risks posed by the abuser within the household. As the court observes, under s 5(1)(d)(ii) the protective steps which could have been expected of D2 depend on what reasonably could have been expected of *him* and the jury might therefore conclude that such a person's failure was reasonable in the circumstances.[187]

It should also be noted that the offence is qualified: the risk of which D2 ought to have been aware is a 'significant' one of 'serious injury'. The Law Commission had concluded that the level of risk to the child which must exist before a person is exposed to criminal liability ought to be 'relatively high'.[188] The Commission drew support for its proposal that the risk should be a 'real risk' more than 'a possibility', from the interpretation of the expression 'likely harm' in s 31 of the Children Act 1989 as construed in the House of Lords in *Re H and others*.[189] The Law Commission also accepted, however, that a test of 'serious likelihood' or 'serious risk' would set the standard too high and inhibit successful prosecution.[190] Parliament substituted the words 'significant risk' for the Law Commission's

---

[184] For an example of a s 5 case involving poisoning, see *V* [2010] EWCA Crim 721 where D drugged her children to make them sleep.

[185] At [32].

[186] Organizations such as Justice and Refuge cautioned during the Act's consultation process against the danger that the offence may be used to further victimize abused women by prosecuting them for allowing their abusive partners to kill the child: see eg Refuge, *Response to the Domestic Violence Crimes and Victims Bill 07/04*, a view echoed by J Herring, 'Familial Homicide, Failure to Protect and Domestic Violence: Who's the Victim' [2007] Crim LR 923. *Mujuru*, n 177, is one of the examples cited.

[187] The argument that there ought to be a specific domestic violence defence within the legislation is rejected by Morrison on the basis that it may exonerate culpable defendants and that the need for such a defence has not been established. Morrison states that the mens rea element of the offence is sufficient to ensure that the offence does not criminalize those who are themselves victims. See SM Morrison, 'Should There Be a Domestic Violence Defence to the Offence of Familial Homicide?' [2013] Crim LR 826.

[188] Para 6.21.   [189] [1996] AC 563 at 592 per Lord Nicholls.   [190] Para 6.23.

formula 'real risk'. Some commentators suggest that Parliament may, therefore, have intended to impose a higher threshold.[191] Comments made in the course of parliamentary debates also support that view. Baroness Scotland of Asthal stated that 'We should remember too that we are talking about "a significant risk of serious physical harm". *That is quite a high threshold. The signs of that risk would be very evident. In many cases, the risk of harm is all too evident from previous harm that a member of the household has inflicted on the child or on others.'[192]

One issue that was considered is whether it is appropriate for the judge to direct the jury to explain in a 'special verdict' the basis of their finding of guilt for an offence under s 5. In *Hopkinson*,[193] D was found guilty of causing or allowing the death of V. The jury also returned a 'special verdict' that D had caused the injuries from which V had died. The Court of Appeal observed that while it could not abolish the special verdict procedure, it had fallen into virtual desuetude. Lord Judge CJ held that directing the jury to return a special verdict in the context of s 5 was especially inappropriate given that the offence was created in order to address the difficulty of proving which of two was responsible when there are no other possible candidates. It is submitted that this is the appropriate conclusion.

15.5 Child destruction and abortion

It has already been observed that it is not murder to kill a child in the womb or while in the process of being born.[194] Nor is it, in itself, an offence against the person of the mother, since the foetus is not part of the mother.[195] Though the killing of the child in the womb after 'quickening'[196] was a misdemeanour at common law, the present law on the subject is statutory. There are two offences to consider:

- child destruction—s 1 of the Infant Life (Preservation) Act 1929 prohibits the killing of any child which is 'capable of being born alive'; and

- attempting to procure a miscarriage—s 58 of the OAPA 1861 (subject to the Abortion Act 1967)[197] prohibits attempts to procure miscarriage from any time after the conception of the child until its birth.

The two offences thus overlap. Procuring a miscarriage so as to kill a child capable of being born alive may amount to both offences. Killing a child in the process of being born is not procuring a miscarriage and can amount only to child destruction.

---

[191] R Ward and R Bird, *The Domestic Violence, Crime and Victims Act 2004: A Practitioner's Guide* (2005) para 3.24.

[192] Hansard, HL, 9 Mar 2004, col 1158 (emphasis added).

[193] [2013] EWCA Crim 795.

[194] See J Herring, *Medical Law and Ethics* (8th edn, 2020) Ch 7; B Bennett, *Abortion* (2004). See also the House of Commons Science and Technology Committee Report, *Scientific Developments Relating to the Abortion Act 1967* (2007) HC 1045-1. For historical accounts, see Williams, *Sanctity of Life*, 139–223 and 'The Legalization of Medical Abortion' (1964) The Eugenics Review; BM Dickens, *Abortion and the Law* (1966).

[195] *A-G's Reference (No 3 of 1994)*, p 527.

[196] 'Quickening' was an ambiguous term but was generally accepted to mean the time at which the mother felt the motion of the child. It was commonly treated as being around the 15th/16th week from conception.

[197] See p 680.

15.5.1 Child destruction

Section 1 of the Infant Life (Preservation) Act 1929 provides:[198]

(1) Subject as hereinafter in this subsection provided, any person who, with intent to destroy the life of a child capable of being born alive, by any wilful act causes a child to die before it has an existence independent of its mother, shall be guilty of an offence, to wit, of child destruction, and shall be liable on conviction thereof on indictment to imprisonment for life: Provided that no person shall be found guilty of an offence under this section unless it is proved that the act which caused the death of the child was not done in good faith for the purpose only of preserving the life of the mother.

(2) For the purposes of this Act, evidence that a woman had at any material time been pregnant for a period of twenty-eight weeks or more shall be prima facie proof that she was at that time pregnant of a child capable of being born alive.

While the actual physical condition in which a foetus would exist following birth is a matter for expert medical evidence, whether a foetus at that particular stage of its development can properly be described as 'a child capable of being born alive' is a question of law for the court. Differing interpretations have been proffered, including that the expression is limited to the child in the process of being born, that it extended to any viable foetus, and widest of all, that it extended to any foetus capable of being born alive, however short-lived its existence.[199]

In *C v S*,[200] the medical experts disagreed as to whether a foetus at the stage it will normally have reached by the 18th to the 21st week of pregnancy would be described as capable of being born alive. In the light of the evidence that it would never be capable of breathing, the court held it could not be capable of being born alive.[201] In *Rance v Mid-Downs Health Authority*,[202] a civil action, Brooke J thought the meaning of the phrase was clear and that a child is 'born alive' if 'after birth, it exists as a live child, that is to say breathing and living by reason of its breathing through its own lungs alone, without deriving any of its living or power of living by or through any connection with its mother'. It is not necessary that the child be capable of survival into old age or even for a period of days. Applying this test, Brooke J was satisfied to 'a very high standard of proof' that the particular child was capable of being born alive after 26 weeks of pregnancy and that therefore to kill him would have been the offence of child destruction. The Abortion Act 1967 uses the phrase 'protecting the life of the viable foetus' in respect of the provisions of the 1929 Act; but, rejecting the view that 'viable' has a different and more restrictive meaning, Brooke J held that it was merely used as convenient shorthand for 'capable of being born alive' and its use in 1967 had no effect on the meaning of the 1929 Act.[203]

198 See J Keown, 'The Scope of the Offence of Child Destruction' (1988) 104 LQR 120.

199 See J Keown for discussion of the merits of each interpretation. See also D Price, 'How Viable is the Present Scope of the Offence of Child Destruction' (1987) 16 Anglo Am LR 220. Cf *McDonald* (1999) NICC, 4 Mar (sufficient that foetus had a real chance of being born alive).

200 [1988] QB 135.

201 ibid, at 145–8 per Heilbron J. Cf G Wright, 'Capable of Being Born Alive?'(1981) 131 NLJ 188 and 'The Legality of Abortion by Prostaglandin' [1984] Crim LR 347; Tunkel [1985] Crim LR 133 and G Wright [1985] Crim LR 133.

202 [1991] 1 QB 587.

203 The 1990 amendments provide that no offence is committed under the 1929 Act provided that the pregnancy is terminated in accordance with provisions of the 1967 Act (see later).

The *Rance* test has the merit of being reasonably clear. However, it is not applicable to all situations. For example, in *Re A*, M never breathed on her own and yet, since she was clearly alive, was regarded as such by all involved and the point as to whether she was born alive was not taken with any seriousness.[204] The pressure on the law's ability to deal with these difficult issues will increase as medical advances allow, for example, for pre-birth treatment. It is now possible for a foetus to undergo surgery prior to birth, during the course of which it may be removed from the womb before being replaced in the mother. Is the child born? What if an individual was to burst in on the operating theatre and stab the foetus with murderous intent?

The Select Committee Report *Scientific Developments Relating to the Abortion Act 1967*[205] recognized the difficulty in defining the viability of a foetus or neonate. In relation to neonates, the Committee reported that 'it has been subject to a range of interpretations. At one extreme a baby could be defined as viable simply because it was born showing signs of life, for example, breathing or a heart beat . . . at the other extreme it could mean that a baby is capable of surviving through childhood with no or minimal disabilities.'[206] There is, as ever, a danger with loose language. In general, viability might mean the minimum age of gestation at which any neonate could survive, the minimum age at which this neonate could survive or the age at which the majority of neonates would survive.[207] The Committee heard evidence that viability means, in medical terms, capability of surviving into adulthood.[208]

In a controversial series of decisions, the European Court declined to decide whether the protection of Art 2 extends to the unborn child. It was acknowledged in *Vo v France*[209] that the Convention institutions have not 'ruled out the possibility that in certain circumstances safeguards may be extended to the unborn child'.[210] The Court noted that 'the unborn child is not regarded as a person directly protected by Article 2 of the Convention and that if the unborn do have a right to life it is implicitly limited by the mother's rights and interests'.[211] The decision has been cogently criticized.[212]

The jury may convict of child destruction on an indictment for murder, manslaughter, infanticide or an offence under s 58 of the OAPA 1861; and on an indictment for child destruction, they may convict of an offence under s 58.[213]

---

[204] See p 394. For a view that M was not 'born alive', see JK Mason, 'Conjoined Twins: A Diagnostic Conundrum' (2001) 5 ELR 226. On prenatal surgery, see Editorial, 'Progress in Understanding the Hemoglobin Switch' (2011) 365 N Engl J Med 852.

[205] (2007) HC 1045–1. See C Foster, 'Forty Years On' (2007) 157 NLJ 1517.

[206] Para 22.   [207] Para 23.   [208] Para 27.

[209] [2004] 2 FCR 577, ECtHR (Grand Chamber). See also *ABC v Ireland* [2010] ECHR 2032.

[210] Para 82.   [211] Para 80.

[212] See JK Mason, 'What's in a Name: The Vagaries of *Vo v France*' (2005) 17 CFLQ 97, calling for an offence of feticide which can be committed without an intent to kill—in cases of gross negligence. See also A Plomer, 'A Foetal Right to Life' [2005] EHRLR 311 criticizing the judgment and suggesting that cases of violence against the mother's life might be treated as beginning at the point of foetal viability. See also E Wicks, 'Terminating Life and Human Rights: The Fetus and the Neonate' in C Erin and S Ost, *The Criminal Justice System and Health Care* (2007) 201, discussing whether the right of the foetus might be subordinate to that of the mother, a violation of the foetus's right to life ought not to be justified on the basis of postnatal disability and suffering. For more recent analysis of the European Court's jurisprudence, see D Fenwick, '"Abortion Jurisprudence" at Strasbourg: Deferential, Avoidant and Normatively Neutral?' (2014) 34 LS 214.

[213] For an example of a conviction where D used violence against the pregnant woman with the intention of causing the death of the child, see *Virgo* (1988) 10 Cr App R (S) 427.

15.5.1.1 Interrelationship with the Abortion Act 1967

The Abortion Act 1967 legalizes abortion in certain circumstances and subject to certain formalities.[214] It originally provided that it should not affect the offence of child destruction but, as amended by the Human Fertilisation and Embryology Act 1990,[215] s 5(1) of the 1967 Act states that:

No offence under [the 1929 Act] shall be committed by a registered medical practitioner who terminates a pregnancy in accordance with the provisions of [the Abortion Act 1967].

The effect of this provision is that:

- if the doctor is complying with the terms of the 1967 Act, and causes the death of a child capable of being born alive, it is not an offence of child destruction under the 1929 Act;[216]
- if the death of such a child is caused by a doctor who is *not* complying with the provisions of the 1967 Act, or if the death is caused by any other person, then it is prima facie child destruction. There will, however, be a defence to a charge of child destruction under the 1929 Act if the act is done for the purpose only of preserving the life of the mother;
- but, even where the operation is to save the life of the mother, that will not amount to a defence to a charge under s 58 of the 1861 Act unless the *Bourne* defence of necessity has survived the 1967 Act—a matter of some doubt, considered below.[217]

On one reading, the defence to child destruction based on the words 'for the purpose only of preserving the life of the mother' was given a wide meaning by MacNaghten J in *Bourne*.[218] Strictly speaking, this was *obiter* so far as the Infant Life (Preservation) Act 1929 was concerned since the charge was brought under the OAPA 1861. However, MacNaghten J took the view that those words represented the common law and were implicit in the 1861 Act by virtue of the word 'unlawfully'. He said:

As I have said, I think those words ['for the purpose of preserving the life of the mother'] ought to be construed in a reasonable sense, and if the doctor is of opinion, on reasonable grounds and with adequate knowledge, that the probable consequence of the continuance of the pregnancy will be to make the woman a physical or mental wreck, the jury are quite entitled to take the view that the doctor who under these circumstances and in the honest belief, operates, is operating for the purpose of preserving the life of the mother.[219]

Looking to the language of the judgment as a whole, a narrower interpretation is also possible. Both before and after this passage the judge had stressed that the test was whether the operation was performed in good faith for the purpose of preserving the *life* of the mother. On that reading, the defence applied only where the doctor had formed a belief about the existence of circumstances that would have such an impact on the woman's health as to shorten life, because the judge had said 'life depends upon health and health may be so gravely impaired that death results'.[220]

---

[214] For analysis of whether the legal framework fulfils its intended aims, see S Sheldon, 'The Decriminalisation of Abortion: An Argument for Modernisation' (2016) 36 OJLS 334.

[215] On which see A Grubb, 'The New Law on Abortion: Clarification or Ambiguity' [1991] Crim LR 659. See also the Government's *Review of the Human Fertilisation and Embryology Act: Proposals for Revised Legislation (Including Establishment of the Regulatory Authority for Tissue and Embryos)* (Dec 2006) Cm 6989. See now the Human Fertilisation and Embryology Act 2008.

[216] M Bohlander, 'Of Shipwrecked Sailors, Unborn Children, Conjoined Twins and Hijacked Airplanes—Taking Human Life and the Defence of Necessity' (2006) 70 J Crim L 147 derives support from this for a defence of necessity applying to murder. That conclusion must be in considerable doubt following the decision in *Nicklinson* discussed earlier.

[217] See p 653.   [218] [1939] 1 KB 687.   [219] ibid, 694.   [220] ibid, 692.

Informed medical opinion construed the judgment in the wider sense[221] and this appears to have been vindicated. In *Bergmann and Ferguson*,[222] Morris J is reported to have said that the court will not look too narrowly into the question of danger to life where danger to health is anticipated. Then, in *Newton and Stungo*,[223] Ashworth J stated in his direction to the jury, 'Such use of an instrument is unlawful unless the use is made in good faith for the purposes of preserving the life *or health* of the woman', adding that this included mental as well as physical health. Newton was acquitted of manslaughter by criminal negligence, but convicted of manslaughter by unlawfully using an instrument and of the offence under s 58. He did not appeal (obviously the direction was favourable to him); but it is thought likely that Ashworth J's view would be accepted by the appellate courts.[224]

The defence as it has been applied by the courts is founded on the subjective belief of the actor; that is, the question is not whether the operation is in fact necessary to preserve the life of the mother but whether D *believes* it to be necessary.[225] In answering this question, the court will take account of the size of the fee, a large fee being evidence of bad faith;[226] and whether D followed accepted medical practice.[227] What is the position if the operation was in fact necessary, but was performed by D in bad faith, to oblige, as he thought, the mere convenience of the woman, and for a high fee? One view might be that there is no actus reus here,[228] but it is thought more likely that the defence will be limited to the case of a bona fide belief.[229] Thus, in *Newton*, it does not seem to have been decided that an operation was unnecessary; only that Newton did not bona fide believe it to be necessary.[230]

These cases all relate to s 58 of the 1861 Act, where they are probably no longer of relevance.[231] However, because they purport to be an interpretation of the proviso in the 1929 Act they cannot be ignored when construing the child destruction offence. On the other hand, it is quite possible that the court, when actually confronted with the interpretation of the proviso, might take a stricter and narrower view of what constitutes the preservation of the life of the mother.

15.5.2 Attempting to procure miscarriage

Historically, the common law misdemeanour of abortion applied only after the child had 'quickened' in the womb. To procure an abortion before this occurred was no crime. A statute of 1803[232] enacted that it should be a felony punishable by death to administer a poison with intent to procure the miscarriage of a woman quick[233] with child, and a felony punishable with imprisonment or transportation for 14 years to administer poison with a like intent to a woman who was not proved to be quick with child. The distinction between 'quick' and

[221] J Havard, 'Therapeutic Abortion' [1958] Crim LR 600 at 605.

[222] (1948) unreported; Williams, *Sanctity of Life*, 154; 1 BMJ 1008.

[223] [1958] Crim LR 469, fully considered by Havard [1958] Crim LR 600.

[224] See also *Paton v BPAS* [1979] QB 276: 'not only would it be a bold and brave judge . . . who would seek to interfere with the discretion of the doctors acting under the Abortion Act 1967, but I think he would really be a foolish judge who would try to do any such thing, unless, possibly, where there is clear bad faith and an obvious attempt to perpetrate a criminal offence', per Sir George Baker P.

[225] *Bergmann and Ferguson* cited in *The Sanctity of Life*, 165.

[226] A significant difference between the case of *Newton* and that of *Stungo* (who was acquitted) seems to have been that Stungo took a very small fee, Newton a high one.

[227] See Havard [1958] Crim LR at 607, 608.   [228] cf the discussion of *Dadson*, p 34.

[229] cf Williams, *The Sanctity of Life*, 166, who would agree with this conclusion on the ground that the crime is in the nature of an attempt. But it is just as much a substantive crime as burglary.

[230] But even if it was necessary to carry out the operation, it was probably not necessary to carry it out in the way it was done—in a consulting room, the patient being sent back to a hotel in a taxi afterwards.

[231] See later.   [232] 43 Geo 3, c 58 (Lord Ellenborough's Act 1803).

[233] See n 196; ie whether the mother felt the foetus.

'non-quick' women gave rise to complications and it disappeared in the re-enactment of the law by the Offences Against the Person Act 1837 which established the law substantially in its modern form. The current statute is the OAPA 1861, which provides by s 58:

Every woman being with child who, with intent to procure her own miscarriage, shall unlawfully administer to herself any poison or other noxious thing, or shall unlawfully use any instrument or other means whatsoever with the like intent, and whosoever, with intent to procure the miscarriage of any woman, whether she be or be not with child, shall unlawfully administer to her or cause to be taken by her any poison or other noxious thing, or shall unlawfully use any instrument or other means whatsoever with the like intent, shall be guilty of an offence, and being convicted thereof shall be liable . . . to imprisonment for life . . .

The extension of the law was of great practical importance, since most self-induced abortions occur before 'quickening'. Prescription, supply, administration or use of the contraceptive pill, mini-pill and morning-after pill does not contravene s 58 because the pill is not an abortifacient.[234] It has also been held that the fitting of an IUD was not an offence under s 58.[235]

The statute makes it clear beyond all doubt that the offence may be committed by the woman herself as well as by others, the only distinction being that if the woman herself is charged, it must be proved that she is in fact pregnant, whereas this is not necessary if the accused is someone other than the mother herself.[236] The Act is not confined to the use of a 'poison or other noxious thing' or 'any instrument'; the 'other means' include manual interference, even though no instrument is employed and the medical evidence is that the conduct could not, in the circumstances, cause a miscarriage.[237] The actus reus consists simply in the *administration* of the poison or other noxious thing or the *use* of the instrument or other means. The offence can be committed where the pregnant woman is not aware that the administration of the drug has been performed.[238] It is important to keep in mind that the actus reus does not require the actual procuring of a miscarriage, but rather an act done with the intention of procuring that result.

The Act distinguishes between 'poison' and 'noxious thing' and it has been held that in the case of something other than a 'recognized poison', the thing must be administered in such quantity as to be in fact harmful though not necessarily abortifacient.[239] A sleeping pill has been held not to be noxious;[240] and the administration in harmless quantities of oil of juniper was no actus reus;[241] but Denman J said that it would be otherwise if a thing, innocuous when administered in small quantities, were to be administered in such quantities as to be noxious.[242] Field and Stephen JJ thought that if the thing were a 'recognized poison' the offence might be committed even though the quantity given was so small as to be incapable of doing harm. The distinction is hardly a logical one for 'recognized poisons' may be beneficial when taken in small quantities and in such a case the thing taken is no more poisonous than the oil of juniper was noxious.

As noted, the section makes a distinction between the case where the woman administers, etc the thing to herself, in which case she must be proved to be pregnant, and the case where

---

[234] *R (on the application of Smeaton) v Secretary of State for Health* [2002] EWHC 610 (Admin), [2002] Crim LR 664. For critical comment on the decision, see J Keown, '"Morning After" Pills, "Miscarriage" and Muddle' (2005) 25 LS 296, and B Hewson, 'SPUC and the Morning-After Pill Saga' (2002) 152 NLJ 1004.

[235] *Dhingra* (1991) unreported but cited in E Jackson, *Medical Law: Text, Cases, and Materials* (5th edn, 2019).

[236] Section 2(3) of the Human Fertilisation and Embryology Act 1990 provides that 'for the purposes of the Act, a woman is not to be treated as carrying a child until the embryo has become implanted'.

[237] *Spicer* (1955) 39 Cr App R 189 (Dorset Assizes).

[238] See the case of *Magira* [2008] EWCA Crim 1939 where D secretly put into his wife's food abortifacient drugs that he had bought on the internet. D did not want a child.

[239] *Marlow* (1964) 49 Cr App R 49 (Brabin J); *Douglas* [1966] NZLR 45. Cf *Marcus* [1981] 2 All ER 833, p 750.

[240] *Weatherall* [1968] Crim LR 115 (Judge Brodrick).   [241] *Cramp* (1880) 5 QBD 307.

[242] Cf the interpretation of noxious substances under ss 23 and 24 of the OAPA, p 750.

it is administered to her by another, in which case she need not be. The importance of this distinction has been diminished by the decision in *Whitchurch*[243] that a woman who is not pregnant may be convicted of conspiring with another to procure her own abortion, and by the decision in *Sockett* that such a woman[244] may be convicted of aiding and abetting in the offence of the other, if it is complete. Thus, in effect, the woman will be excused on the ground that she is not pregnant only in cases where she is not acting in concert with another. One view is that this interpretation has wholly undermined the intention of Parliament.[245] But it has been argued elsewhere[246] that it would have been perfectly reasonable for Parliament to discriminate between the non-pregnant woman who calls in the back-street or professional abortionist and the non-pregnant woman who administers to herself an abortifacient in the solitude of her own bedroom.[247] The point is perhaps not of great practical importance as it appears that it is not the practice to prosecute the woman if she is not in fact pregnant.[248]

It is debatable whether s 1 of the Abortion Act (discussed later) allows for a defence only when a pregnancy is *successfully* terminated. There are cases where the abortion is unsuccessful.[249] In *RCN v DHSS*,[250] the House of Lords suggested that it would be 'absurd' and 'cannot have been the intention of Parliament' that anyone taking part in an unsuccessful termination would be unable to rely on defences in the Abortion Act so as to be guilty of an offence under the 1861 Act. Lord Edmund-Davies observed that 'Were it otherwise the unavoidable conclusion is that doctors and nurses could in such cases be convicted of what in essence would be the extraordinary crime of attempting to do a lawful act.'

15.5.3 Knowingly supplying or procuring poison, etc

Section 59 of the OAPA 1861 makes a substantive crime of certain preparatory acts, some of which might amount to counselling or abetting the offence under s 58. It provides:

Whosoever shall unlawfully supply or procure any poison or other noxious thing, or any instrument or thing whatsoever, knowing that the same is intended to be unlawfully used or employed with intent to procure the miscarriage of any woman, whether she be or be not with child, shall be guilty of a misdemeanour, and being convicted thereof shall be liable to imprisonment for any term not exceeding five years.

The word 'procure', on the first occasion on which it is used in the section, means 'get possession of something of which you have not got possession already'.[251] D's conviction was therefore quashed when there was no evidence as to how or when he had come into the possession of the instruments and the judge had misdirected the jury that the word was 'wide enough to include getting instruments or getting them together or preparing them for use'.[252]

This leaves a gap in the legislation. As prosecution counsel said:[253]

if a defendant went to a chemist and bought an instrument to abort A, he would have committed an offence, but if he then put the instrument away in a cupboard and later, for the purpose of aborting B, went to the cupboard and took the instrument he would not have committed an offence.

The meaning was further considered in the extraordinary case of *Ahmed*.[254] D was married to a woman who spoke no English who fell pregnant. D took her to an abortion clinic,

243 (1890) 24 QBD 420, CCR.   244 (1909) 1 Cr App R 101; p 242.
245 Williams, CLGP, 673.
246 B Hogan, 'Victims as Parties to Crime' [1962] Crim LR 683 at 690.
247 For an extraordinary case in which the woman committed the offence by aborting a foetus a few days before full term, see *Catt* [2013] EWCA Crim 1187.
248 Nor has it been for some time. Cf *The Sanctity of Life* at 146; *Peake* (1932) 97 JPN 353.
249 Or dealing with an attempt, where abortion is attempted but the woman turns out not to be pregnant.
250 [1981] AC 800.   251 *Mills* [1963] 1 QB 522, following *Scully* (1903) 23 NZLR 380.
252 ibid, 524.   253 ibid, 526.   254 [2010] EWCA Crim 1949.

telling her she was going for a minor operation for ovarian cysts. Staff at the clinic became concerned and provided an interpreter. No abortion occurred. D was convicted of an offence under s 59, but the conviction was quashed on appeal. One argument considered was that the surgical instruments which must have been available to carry out the intended abortion were procured by D, but the indictment referred only to medical or surgical procedures and not to instruments. The Court of Appeal noted that there was no evidence that any particular instruments had been selected for use at or brought to the place at which the operation would take place. 'Even if they had, we do not consider that the appellant could be said to have "procured" those instruments.' Referring to *Mills*, the court confirmed that the word 'procure' is not apt to describe a case in which the defendant brings about a situation in which a third person, here a nurse or doctor, will take possession of or use an instrument of some kind.

The meaning of 'thing' in s 59 was also considered in *Ahmed*.[255] The Court of Appeal held that D did not supply or procure any poison, any other noxious *thing* or any instrument. The Crown argued that a 'thing' was anticipated medical or surgical procedure. The Court of Appeal rejected that view—'the juxtaposition of the word "thing" with the word "instrument" which almost immediately precedes it, indicates that the "thing" must be some sort of article or object rather than something such as a medical procedure which has no physical existence'.[256]

The court drew support for this interpretation by comparing ss 59 and 58 of the 1861 Act. Section 58 extends to D who unlawfully uses 'any instrument or other means whatsoever'.

The words 'knowing that the same is intended to be unlawfully used' have been construed in an extraordinarily wide sense and one highly unfavourable to the accused. Their natural meaning is surely that some person other than the accused must intend to be the unlawful user and that the accused must know of that intention. But it has been held that it is enough if the accused *believes* that the poison, etc is to be so used, so that it is no defence for him to show that the person supplied did not intend to use it[257] or that the person supplied was a policeman who had obtained the thing by false representations about a purely fictitious woman.[258] This construction was defended by Erle CJ, the rest of the court concurring, on the extraordinary ground that, 'The defendant knew what his own intention was, and that was that the substance procured by him should be employed with intent to procure miscarriage.'[259] This attitude contrasts strikingly with the strict construction of the word 'procure'; and these two cases have been dissented from in Victoria,[260] though followed elsewhere in the Commonwealth.[261] In *Ahmed*, the court noted that a defendant such as Ahmed will not necessarily be liable since his lies might, the court thought, not have prevented the doctors concerned from forming the relevant medical opinions in the 1967 Act. D would not have been 'knowing' that the thing was 'intended to be *unlawfully* used or employed with intent to procure the miscarriage of any woman'.

15.5.4 The Abortion Act 1967

The law relating to abortion was modified in important respects by the Abortion Act 1967.[262] In the Act:

'the law relating to abortion' means ss 58 and 59 of the Offences Against the Person Act 1861, and any rule of law relating to the procurement of abortion.

---

[255] ibid.   [256] At [13] per Hughes LJ (emphasis added).
[257] *Hillman* (1863) 9 Cox CC 386.   [258] *Titley* (1880) 14 Cox CC 502 (Stephen J).
[259] (1863) 9 Cox CC 386 at 387.   [260] *Hyland* (1898) 24 VLR 101.
[261] *Scully* (1903) 23 NZLR 380; *Nosworthy* (1907) 26 NZLR 536; *Neil* [1909] St R Qd 225; *Freestone* [1913] TPD 758; *Irwin v R* (1968) 68 DLR (2d) 485.
[262] See J Hoggett, 'The Abortion Act 1967' [1968] Crim LR 247. On the changes introduced by the Act, see HLA Hart, 'Abortion Law Reform: The English Experience' (1972) 8 MULR 389; M Simms, 'Abortion Law Reform: Has the Controversy Changed' [1970] Crim LR 567, 573 and 'The Abortion Act: A Reply' [1971] Crim LR 86; JM Finnis, 'The Abortion Act: What Has Changed?' [1971] Crim LR 3; and generally S Sheldon, Beyond Control (1977) and K Greasley, 'Arguments about Abortion: Personhood, Morality, and Law' (2017).

Section 1 of the Act, as amended by s 37 of the Human Fertilisation and Embryology Act 1990, provides:[263]

(1) Subject to the provisions of this section, a person shall not be guilty of an offence under the law relating to abortion when a pregnancy is terminated by a registered medical practitioner if two[264] registered medical practitioners are of the opinion, formed in good faith—

   (a) that the pregnancy has not exceeded its twenty-fourth week and that the continuance of the pregnancy would involve risk, greater than if the pregnancy were terminated, of injury to the physical or mental health of the pregnant woman or any existing children of her family[265]; or

   (b) that the termination is necessary to prevent grave permanent injury to the physical or mental health of the pregnant woman; or

   (c) that the continuance of the pregnancy would involve risk to the life of the pregnant woman, greater than if the pregnancy were terminated; or

   (d) that there is a substantial risk that if the child were born it would suffer from such physical or mental abnormalities as to be seriously handicapped.[266]

(2) In determining whether the continuance of a pregnancy would involve such risk of injury to health as is mentioned in paragraph (a) or (b) of subsection (1) of this section, account may be taken of the pregnant woman's actual or reasonably foreseeable environment.

By s 1(3) and (3A), unless the abortion is carried out for the immediate saving of the life of the mother, the operation must be carried out in hospitals or other places as approved by the Secretary of State. In *BPAS v Secretary of State for Health*,[267] BPAS's claim to establish that it would be lawful to pilot and adopt a process of providing early medical abortion (EMA) whereby part of the treatment was administered at home was rejected by the Administrative Court.[268] 'Parliament has decided by section 1(3A) to give the Secretary of State the responsibility for approval of the types of medicine that can be used, the manner in which they can be used and the places where they can be used.'[269] Section 1(4) provides that the requirement for the opinion of two registered medical practitioners:

shall not apply to the termination of a pregnancy by a registered medical practitioner in a case where he is of the opinion, formed in good faith, that the termination is immediately necessary to save the life or to prevent grave permanent injury to the physical or mental health of the pregnant woman.

---

[263] See the valuable discussion of the amended Act by A Grubb, 'The New Law of Abortion: Clarification or Ambiguity?' [1991] Crim LR 659.

[264] The Select Committee Report, *Scientific Developments Relating to the Abortion Act 1967* (2007) HC 1045–1 discussed earlier, heard evidence that the practical reality of two doctors considering a case was a 'sham', para 86. See generally Ch 4 of that report. The Committee reported that it had not been presented with 'any good evidence' that in the first trimester of pregnancy the two signature rule safeguards the woman or the doctors or 'serves any useful purpose', at para 99.

[265] It has been argued that where an abortion is sought before a woman is 24 weeks pregnant, then in reality it is impossible to police the reasons why women seek an abortion and that a doctor would have a defence if an abortion was conducted on the grounds of gender: see K Swift and M Robson, 'Why Doctors Need Not Fear Prosecution for Gender-Related Abortions' (2012) 76 J Crim L 348. See also K Greasley, 'Is Sex-Selective Abortion Against the Law?' (2016) 36 OJLS 535. For factual reasons, in September 2013 the CPS declined to prosecute in two cases in which it was alleged that doctors had agreed to conduct abortions on the grounds that the women concerned did not want to give birth to girls. See http://blog.cps.gov.uk/2013/10/statement-from-director-of-public-prosecutions-on-abortion-related-cases.html. Section 84 of the Serious Crime Act 2015 requires the Secretary of State to examine this issue and publish a strategy. The response is available at www.gov.uk/government/publications/abortion-on-grounds-of-sex-of-the-foetus.

[266] See S McGuinness, 'Law, Reproduction, and Disability: Fatally "Handicapped"?' (2013) 21 Med L Rev 213 for critique of this exception.

[267] [2011] EWHC 235 (Admin).

[268] From 28 December 2018, women in England can take the second of the two abortion pills, misoprostol, at home.

[269] At [37].

In 2019, there were 207,384 abortions for women resident in England and Wales, the highest number since the Abortion Act was introduced. Of those, 82 per cent of abortions were performed at under ten weeks.[270] Where the pregnancy has not exceeded its 24th week,[271] the doctor must balance risks involved in an abortion against the risks to the woman or the existing child involved in the continuance of the pregnancy, and may perform the abortion only if it is his opinion that the latter are greater than the former. The Select Committee on Science and Technology reviewed the 24-week time limit to assess whether recent developments in medical science warranted a change in the law. The medical evidence suggested that around 89 per cent of foetuses born at 20 to 22 weeks are born dead.

Where the pregnancy has exceeded 24 weeks, the risks to the existing child(ren) are no longer a ground for abortion.[272] The Court of Appeal[273] has recently confirmed that in calculating the 24 weeks, time starts to run with the first day of the woman's last monthly period (LMP). That is 'day 0'. Adopting the standard approach adopted in many countries, the number of weeks and days used to date the pregnancy referred to the number of completed weeks and days, so that 23 weeks + 6 days would be considered the final day of the 24th week of pregnancy. At 24 weeks + 0 days, a woman entered the 25th week of pregnancy and it followed that she had exceeded her 24th week of pregnancy. Accepting that this was a medical construct, it was appropriate to adopt it to ensure a clear, consistent approach.

After 24 weeks, the abortion can be justified only on the grounds of risk of grave permanent injury to the woman or her death, or of the birth of a seriously handicapped child.[274] In *Jepson v Chief Constable of Mercia Police*,[275] D sought judicial review of the refusal to prosecute doctors who performed an abortion where the foetus had a cleft palate. The court concluded that the doctor had acted in good faith.[276]

Where the life of the woman is at risk, the doctor must engage in another balancing exercise and may terminate the pregnancy if he is of the opinion that this gives her a better chance of survival: 51/49 is enough. But where the risk is not to her life but of causing her 'grave permanent injury' the pregnancy may be terminated only if abortion is 'necessary' to prevent this. If the doctor is of the opinion that the woman will certainly suffer grave permanent injury if the pregnancy is not terminated, then termination is, undoubtedly, necessary.

---

[270] See https://assets.publishing.service.gov.uk/government/uploads/system/uploads/attachment_data/file/891405/abortion-statistics-commentary-2019.pdf.

[271] See the discussion by Grubb [1991] Crim LR 659. The Select Committee Report, *Scientific Developments Relating to the Abortion Act 1967* considered whether medical advances should lead to a period shorter than 24 weeks. The conclusion was that no evidence had been presented that 'survival rates below 24 weeks gestation time have significantly improved', Ch 2. See also Jackson, n 235.

[272] E Wicks, M Wyldes and M Kilby, 'Late Termination of Pregnancy for Foetal Abnormality: Medical and Legal Perspectives' (2004) 12 Med L Rev 285.

[273] *R (on the application of Christian Concern) v Secretary of State for Health and Social Care* [2020] EWCA Civ 1239.

[274] On this criterion, see the Select Committee Report, Ch 3, which is critical of the ambiguity of the wording and the difficulty in which this leaves doctors.

[275] [2003] EWHC 3318 (QB). A Grear, 'The Curate, a Cleft Palate and Ideological Closure in the Abortion Act 1967—Time to Reconsider the Relationship Between Doctors and the Abortion Decision' [2004] Web JCLI; R Scott, 'Interpreting the Disability Ground of the Abortion Act' (2005) 64 CLJ 388. See the interesting analysis by E Wicks, 'Terminating Life and Human Rights: The Fetus and the Neonate' in C Erin and S Ost, *The Criminal Justice System and Health Care* (2007), considering the difference in the degree of protection afforded to a foetus with severe disability and a newly born baby with such disability. See also S Smith, 'Dignity: The Difference Between Abortion and Neonaticide for Severe Disability' in the same volume.

[276] Jackson J did give leave, on the basis that the case raised an issue of public importance. West Mercia then reopened the case and the CPS decided not to prosecute, determining that the doctor had acted in good faith. See CPS press release: 16/3/2005. E Wicks, M Wyldes and M Kilby, 'Late Termination of Pregnancy for Reason of Fetal Abnormality: Medical and Legal Perspectives' (2004) 12 Med L Rev 285; S Sheldon and S Wilkinson, 'Termination of Pregnancy for Reason of Foetal Disability: Are there Grounds for a Special Exception in Law?' (2001) 9 Med L Rev 85.

It must be assumed, however, that Parliament, in distinguishing between grave permanent injury and death, intended that a higher degree of risk of grave permanent injury than of death is required to justify abortion. If so, termination is not 'necessary' simply because the doctor is of the opinion that grave permanent injury is more likely than not; that is, 51/49 is not enough. Whether necessity can be established somewhere between the balance of probabilities and virtual certainty is not clear. These balancing exercises do not pose problems under Art 2 of the ECHR. The European Court has recognized that 'if the unborn do have a "right to life" it is implicitly limited by the mother's rights and interests'.[277]

There is a similar problem of determining what is a 'substantial' risk of abnormality resulting in 'serious' handicap to the child—but these uncertainties have been with us since 1967 without troubling the courts (but note *Jepson* earlier in this section), however much they may have troubled the doctors. Clearly, something a good deal less than certainty may amount to a substantial risk and it is thought that most people would regard something well below a 50 per cent chance as substantial in this context.

Section 1(1)(a), on a literal reading, could justify the termination of most pregnancies in their early stages, since some risk is necessarily involved in childbearing whereas the risks involved in an abortion operation at this early stage are very slight.[278] The 1967 Act allowed the interests of the existing children of the woman's family to be taken into account for the first time. These expressions are not defined in the Act, but it has been argued[279] that 'family' means the sociological and not the legal unit, so as to include illegitimate children and perhaps children who have been accepted as members of the family. The view has been expressed[280] that a person over 21 could be a child of the family for this purpose if, for example, he were severely disabled.[281]

An incapacitated adult could be provided with an abortion if it was in her best interests.[282] The assessment would be in accordance with the Mental Capacity Act 2005.

15.5.4.1 Abortion and multiple pregnancies

Multiple pregnancies may be reduced by killing one or more of the foetuses. The Human Fertilisation and Embryology Act 1990 amended s 5(2) of the Abortion Act 1967 to deal with the matter as follows:

(2) For the purposes of the law relating to abortion, anything done with intent to procure a woman's miscarriage (or, in the case of a woman carrying more than one foetus, her miscarriage of any foetus) is unlawfully done unless authorised by section 1 of this Act and, in the case of a woman carrying more than one foetus, anything done with intent to procure her miscarriage of any foetus is authorised by that section if—

(a) the ground for termination of the pregnancy specified in subsection (1)(d) of that section applies in relation to any foetus and the thing is done for the purpose of procuring the miscarriage of that foetus, or

(b) any other grounds for termination of the pregnancy specified in that section applies.

[277] *Vo v France* [2004] 2 FCR 577, para 80. See G Puppinck, 'Abortion and the European Convention on Human Rights' (2013) 3 IJLS 142.

[278] '. . . it follows that a pregnancy may lawfully be terminated in order to secure a relatively small improvement in the woman's medical condition': *A Guide to the Abortion Act 1967*, at 11. The Act is not, however, interpreted in this way by the medical profession and administrators: Hart (1972) 8 MULR at 393–4. See also www.bma.org.uk/advice/employment/ethics/ethics-a-to-z/abortion.

[279] Hoggett [1968] Crim LR 247 at 249.   [280] ibid.

[281] Annual statistics break down the proportions of abortions carried out under each category: see Table A, https://assets.publishing.service.gov.uk/government/uploads/system/uploads/attachment_data/file/891405/abortion-statistics-commentary-2019.pdf.

[282] See eg *Re SG (Adult Mental Patient: Abortion)* [1991] 2 FLR 329; *Re B (Wardship: Abortion)* [1991] 2 FLR 426; *Re SS (An Adult: Medical Treatment)* [2002] 1 FLR 445—decided under common law pre-Mental Capacity Act 2005.

So, if one or more of several foetuses is identified as being substantially at risk of becoming a child suffering from such a mental or physical abnormality as would lead to its being seriously handicapped, that foetus, or those foetuses, may be aborted. Where no foetus is so identified, but the continuance of the multiple pregnancy would satisfy one of the other conditions in s 1, the doctor may reduce the number of foetuses in order to eliminate or reduce the risk. In this situation, the doctor must select which of a number of healthy foetuses is to die.[283]

15.5.4.2 Good faith of medical opinion

The Secretary of State for Health has exercised the powers under s 2 to require the opinion of medical practitioners to be certified in a particular form and notice of the termination of pregnancy and other information to be given. The question of the good faith of the doctors is essentially one for the jury. A verdict of guilty based on such bad faith where there is no evidence as to professional practice and medical probabilities is often likely to be regarded by the Court of Appeal as unsafe; but this depends on the nature of the other evidence.

An opinion may be absurd professionally and yet formed in good faith; conversely an opinion may be one which a doctor could have entertained and yet in the particular circumstances of a case may be found either to have been formed in bad faith or not to have been formed at all.[284]

If one or both of the doctors has expressed an opinion in bad faith but the operation is performed by a third, D, who is unaware of the bad faith, the conditions of the Act *authorizing the procurement of the miscarriage* are not satisfied but it is submitted that D has a defence. He lacks mens rea for, on the facts as he believes them to be, his act is a lawful one. The doctor in bad faith might, however, be convicted under Part 2 of the Serious Crime Act 2007 (see Ch 11) or the doctrine in *Cogan and Leak* or *Millward*.[285]

15.5.4.3 Termination 'by a registered medical practitioner'

The defences provided by the Act are available 'when a pregnancy is terminated by a registered medical practitioner'. When the conditions in the Act are satisfied and the pregnancy is terminated by the doctor, there is no actus reus. Those who assist him are therefore guilty of no offence. The Act obviously did not contemplate that every action in the steps leading to an abortion would be done personally by the doctor. If, however, the doctor were to delegate more and more of the process to others, there would come a point when it could no longer be said that the pregnancy had been terminated 'by a registered medical practitioner'—and at that point it would become unlawful. In *Royal College of Nursing of the United Kingdom v Department of Health and Social Security*,[286] the House of Lords by a majority of three to two, reversing a unanimous Court of Appeal judgment and restoring the judgment of Woolf J, held that a particular process for the extra-amniotic method of termination of pregnancies was lawful, notwithstanding the substantial part played by nurses in that process.[287] According to Lord Diplock, what the 1967 Act requires is that:

a registered medical practitioner . . . should accept responsibility for all stages of the treatment for the termination of the pregnancy. The particular method to be used should be decided by the doctor in charge of the treatment for the termination of the pregnancy; he should carry out any physical

---

[283] See Jackson, n 235. See also the Human Fertilisation and Embryology Act 2008.
[284] *Smith* [1974] 1 All ER 376 at 381.   [285] [1976] QB 217, see p 234.
[286] [1981] AC 800, n 250.
[287] See also the Select Committee Report, *Scientific Developments Relating to the Abortion Act 1967*, recognizing the ability of nursing staff to perform the modern abortion process, paras 103 et seq.

acts, forming part of the treatment, that in accordance with accepted medical practice are done only by qualified medical practitioners, and should give specific instructions as to the carrying out of such parts of the treatment as in accordance with accepted medical practice are carried out by nurses or other members of the hospital staff without medical qualifications. To each of them, the doctor, or his substitute, should be available to be consulted or called on for assistance from beginning to end of the treatment.

Thus, if the doctor were to direct the whole procedure by correspondence, over the telephone or by webcam, the operation would presumably be unlawful.

Treatment to terminate a pregnancy, which, if the treatment were successful, would be lawfully terminated, is lawful treatment,[288] notwithstanding (as apparently happens in 1 or 2 per cent of cases) an ultimate failure to terminate the pregnancy. If the conditions of the 1967 Act are otherwise fulfilled and known to be fulfilled, the steps taken to procure abortion are taken without mens rea—there is no intent *unlawfully* to administer anything or *unlawfully* to use any instrument. There is, moreover, no actus reus for the legalization of an abortion must include the steps which are taken towards it.

15.5.4.4 Necessity at common law

The provision in s 5(2) of the 1967 Act that, 'For the purposes of the law relating to abortion, anything done with intent to procure a woman's miscarriage . . . is unlawfully done unless authorised by section 1 of this Act . . .' appears to be intended entirely to supersede the law as stated in *Bourne*.[289]

Abortions, and the steps to procure them which are proscribed, are unlawful unless they can be justified by the Act. It is submitted, however, that this provision cannot have been intended entirely to eliminate the operation of general defences to crime. To take extreme examples, a child under the age of ten, or a person within the M'Naghten Rules, could surely not be convicted of committing or (slightly more likely) abetting an abortion. If this is conceded, then duress by threats ought equally to operate, so why not duress of circumstances or necessity? And so we are back to admitting *Bourne*'s case into the law. A possible interpretation of the Act would be to allow general defences other than necessity. Construing s 5(2) in the light of the previous law, a court might conclude that its obvious purpose was to overrule *Bourne*; and that it would be unreasonable to extend its operation beyond that.

A limited defence of necessity would seem desirable in principle. The defence would necessarily be limited in scope by the fact that, in the great majority of cases where it is necessary to procure an abortion, this is lawful by statute so that there is no room for the operation of any broader defence. Having regard to *Quayle*,[290] in which necessity defences were held to be ousted by the statutory scheme under the Misuse of Drugs Act, a similar argument could be advanced.[291] The Abortion Act is clearly intended to provide a scheme for the legalization of abortion—abortions outside the Act are unlawful and an offence. But suppose that a qualified doctor who is not a registered medical practitioner, and so does not come within the terms of s 1(4) discussed earlier, forms the opinion in good faith that immediate termination of a pregnancy is necessary in order to save the life of the mother

288 Per Lord Edmund-Davies, citing the 4th edition of this book, at p 346 [1981] 1 All ER 545 at 573.
289 See p 686. Cf the Canadian case of *Morgentaler* [1976] 1 SCR 616, 20 CCC (2d) 449 discussed by LH Leigh, 'Necessity and the Case of Dr Morgentaler' [1978] Crim LR 151 and *Davidson* [1969] VR 667 (Menhennit J).
290 [2005] EWCA Crim 1415.
291 Such an argument was also accepted in S (C) [2012] EWCA Crim 389. It was held that the existence of the statutory scheme in the Child Abduction Act 1984 precluded the possibility of there being any defence of necessity to a charge of child abduction.

who is in a remote place and beyond the help of any registered medical practitioner. Is it the law that he must let the woman die when he could save her by terminating the pregnancy?

In *Bourne*, MacNaghten J took the view that there was not only a right but a duty to perform the operation where a woman's life could be saved only by the doctor procuring an abortion:

if a case arose where the life of a woman could be saved by performing the operation and the doctor refused to perform it because of his religious opinions and the woman died, he would be in grave peril of being brought before this court on a charge of manslaughter by negligence. He would have no better defence than a person who, again from some religious reason, refused to call in a doctor to attend his sick child, where a doctor could have been called in and the life of the child could have been saved.[292]

Section 4 of the Abortion Act now provides:

(1) Subject to subsection (2) of this section, no person shall be under any duty, whether by contract or by any statutory or other legal requirement, to participate in any treatment authorised by this Act to which he has a conscientious objection:

Provided that in any legal proceedings the burden of proof of conscientious objection shall rest on the person claiming to rely on it.

(2) Nothing in subsection (1) of this section shall affect any duty to participate in treatment which is necessary to save the life or to prevent grave permanent injury to the physical or mental health of a pregnant woman.

The same people whose acts are rendered lawful by s 1 are given by s 4 the right in conscience to object to performing those same acts. The Supreme Court in *Greater Glasgow Health Board v Doogan* held that the term 'participate' ought to be given a narrow meaning synonymous with taking part in a 'hands-on' capacity and was not intended by Parliament to encompass hospital managers, caterers, cleaners, etc.[293] A person can only claim that right in respect of an act which would have amounted to an offence before the Abortion Act came into force. So, a secretary was not entitled, by s 4, to refuse to type a letter arranging an abortion rendered lawful by s 1. It was held that she would not, under the old law, have been guilty of the abortion as a secondary party; her intention would have been merely to carry out her contract of employment, not to counsel or procure.[294]

Section 4(2) does not create any duty, but it does appear to recognize at least the possibility of a duty at common law. The only authority for this appears to be *Bourne*. It will be noted that MacNaghten J dealt only with the case where the woman died, whereas the Act refers to grave permanent injury to physical or mental health. MacNaghten J appeared to regard the doctor's liability as one arising from gross negligence; and this, if a ground of liability at all, is indeed confined to cases where death is caused.[295] There is no general criminal liability for causing grievous bodily harm by gross negligence as distinct from recklessness.

If, however, the doctor is under a duty to act, and he knows all the circumstances giving rise to that duty and foresees the consequences of not fulfilling it, it would seem that he has the mens rea necessary to found a conviction for causing grievous bodily harm contrary to s 18 of the OAPA 1861.[296] The only doubtful link in this argument appears to be the existence of the duty; but the Act strengthens the case for its existence. Clearly, a doctor

---

[292] [1939] 1 KB 687 at 693.   [293] [2014] UKSC 68.
[294] *Salford Area Health Authority, ex p Janaway* [1989] AC 537, applied in *Greater Glasgow Health Board v Doogan* [2014] UKSC 68.
[295] See p 686.   [296] See p 729.

with conscientious objections[297] could fulfil his duty by referring the patient to another doctor who does not have such objections; and it is submitted that the doctor has a duty to do this where an abortion is necessary to save the woman from death or grave permanent injury. The question of a duty to participate in the operation can arise only where there is no effective substitute for the doctor concerned. Where the patient has conscientious objections there can be no duty to perform the operation since, clearly, it can only be lawfully performed with consent.

Abortion in compliance with the 1967 Act does not contravene Art 2 of the ECHR: *Paton v UK*.[298]

15.5.5 Concealment of birth

This offence when first created by statute in 1623[299] was limited to: (a) an illegitimate child who (b) was born alive and whose body was disposed of so as to conceal its death (c) by its mother. The current statute, s 60 of the OAPA 1861, is subject to none of these limitations; it applies to any child, legitimate or not and whether born alive or not, whose body is disposed of so as to conceal its birth, by anyone. The section provides:

If any woman shall be delivered of a child, every person who shall, by any secret disposition of the dead body of the said child, whether such child died before, at, or after its birth, endeavour to conceal the birth thereof, shall be guilty of [an offence triable either way], and being convicted thereof shall be liable, at the discretion of the court, to be imprisoned for any term not exceeding two years . . .

The expressed object of the original statute was to catch those women who would otherwise escape on a charge of murder because of the difficulty of proving that there had been a live birth.[300] Under a later Act,[301] which repealed the 1623 provision, a woman could only be convicted if she was acquitted on an indictment for murder. But the current offence is an independent substantive crime for which an indictment will lie irrespective of any other offences being alleged.[302]

The test of a 'secret disposition' seems to be whether there was a likelihood that the body would be found. Bovill CJ held therefore that there would be a secret disposition, 'if the body were placed in the middle of a moor in the winter, or on the top of a mountain, or in any other secluded place, where the body would not be likely to be found'.[303] If a body were thrown from a clifftop to the seashore, it might be a secret disposition if the place were secluded, but not if it were much frequented.[304] So, where the body was left in a closed but unlocked box in D's bedroom in such a way as to attract the attention of those who daily entered the room, it was held that there was no secret disposition.[305]

---

[297] See for arguments that the ECHR might impact on this claim, L Hammer, 'Abortion Objection in the UK within the Framework of the ECHR' [1999] EHRLR 564.

[298] [1980] 3 EHRR 408. Cf *Kelly v Kelly* 1997 SLT 896 and *Vo v France*, discussed earlier.

[299] 21 Jac 1, c 27.

[300] The original sentence was that the woman should suffer death as in the case of murder.

[301] 43 Geo 3, c 58.

[302] It was formerly the law that a person acquitted of murder, infanticide or child destruction might be convicted, on the same indictment, of concealment of birth; but this rule was abolished by the Criminal Law Act 1967, Sch 2. On its historical application, see MB Emmerichs, 'Trials of Women for Homicide in Nineteenth Century England' (1993) 5 *Women and Criminal Justice* 99.

[303] *Brown* (1870) LR 1 CCR 244. See *Hopkins* [2005] NICC 1 where the defendant initially secreted the body in the wardrobe and then sought to burn it in an open field.

[304] ibid.

[305] *George* (1868) 11 Cox CC 41. Cf *Sleep* (1864) 9 Cox CC 559; *Rosenberg* (1906) 70 JP 264.

D must be proved to have done some act[306] of disposition *after* the child has died. If the living body of the child is concealed and thereafter dies in the place of concealment, this offence is not committed,[307] though that is probably murder, manslaughter or infanticide.

According to Erle J in *Berriman*,[308] the child must have 'arrived at that stage of maturity at the time of birth that it might have been a living child'; so that the concealment of a foetus but a few months old would be no offence.[309]

15.5.6 Other offences

It is a common law misdemeanour to dispose of or destroy a dead body with intent to prevent an inquest from being held.[310] There is a common law offence of preventing the decent and lawful burial of a body. It is an offence under the Perjury Act 1911 wilfully to make a false statement relating to births or deaths, or the live birth of a child.[311] It is also a summary offence under s 36 of the Births and Deaths Registration Act 1953, to fail to give information concerning births and deaths when under a duty, as defined in the Act, to do so.

Further reading

D Baker and J Horder (eds), *The Sanctity of Life and the Criminal Law: The Legacy of Glanville Williams*

K Greasley, *Arguments about Abortion: Personhood, Morality, and Law*

J Griffiths, H Weyers and M Adams, *Euthanasia and Law in Europe*

G Williams, *The Sanctity of Life and the Criminal Law*

---

[306] *Derham* (1843) 1 Cox CC 56 (leaving body in privy where born not act of concealment).

[307] *Coxhead* (1845) 1 Car & Kir 623 (decided under 9 Geo 4, c 31, but the principle is the same); *May* (1867) 10 Cox CC 448.

[308] (1854) 6 Cox CC 388 at 390.

[309] *Colmer* (1864) 9 Cox CC 506 is to the contrary but is doubted by Russell, 611 fn 69.

[310] cf *Hunter* [1972] Crim LR 369. See M Hirst, 'Preventing the Lawful Burial of a Body' [1996] Crim LR 96. See also *R (Ghai) v Newcastle City Council* [2010] EWCA Civ 59, [2010] 3 WLR 737.

[311] Perjury Act 1911, s 4(1).

16

Non-fatal offences against the person

This chapter deals with offences against the 'person', and in relation to the offences under discussion that term means a human being. Associations, whether corporate or unincorporated, cannot be victims of these offences though these bodies might be guilty of committing some of the offences either as principal or as an accessory.[1] The meaning of 'person' as a victim has been discussed almost exclusively in relation to murder but it seems clear that the same principles must apply to non-fatal offences. The common law[2] position is usefully summarized in the Draft Criminal Code which provides[3] that victim 'means a person who has been born and has an existence independent of his mother and, unless the context otherwise requires, "death" and "personal harm" mean the death of, or personal harm to, such a person'.[4]

A foetus or a child in the process of being born could not, therefore, be the victim of an assault or any other offence against the person.[5] The attack might be an offence against the expectant mother where it affected her person, as distinct from the foetus which is not part of her. Statutory offences are probably to be construed in accordance with these common law principles.

---

[1] If a corporation may be guilty of manslaughter there is no logical reason why it should not be guilty of lesser offences against the person. See on corporate manslaughter, p 631. The 2007 Act deals only with corporate killings. In *R (on the application of Gladstone plc) v Manchester City Magistrates' Court* [2004] All ER (D) 296 (Nov), it was held that a private prosecution for assault may be brought by a registered company (the victim being the Chief Executive who was kneed in the groin at the AGM). The company's memorandum of association included power to lay an information in respect of the assault.

[2] cf *Tait*, p 649.   [3] Cl 53(1).   [4] For further reform, see p 732.

[5] In *A-G's Reference (No 3 of 1994)*, p 527, the Court of Appeal held that the foetus is part of the mother; but the House of Lords decided that it is not: [1997] 3 All ER 936, 943. 'The mother and the foetus were two distinct organisms living symbiotically, not a single organism with two aspects', per Lord Mustill.

16.1 Assault and battery

Assault and battery were two distinct crimes at common law and their separate existence (though now as statutory offences) is confirmed by s 39 of the Criminal Justice Act 1988:

Common assault and battery shall be summary offences and a person guilty of either of them shall be liable to an unlimited fine, to imprisonment for a term not exceeding six months, or to both.

Section 39 offers a valuable simplification of the law,[6] replacing the complex provisions in the OAPA 1861.

The courts continue to face technical challenges to the way that charges are described. It would be clearer for all concerned if the term assault was used only in relation to that offence and not as a compendious term to refer to both assault and battery.[7]

16.1.1 Definitions

An assault is any conduct by which D, intentionally or recklessly,[8] causes V to apprehend immediate and unlawful personal violence.[9] A battery is any conduct by which D, intentionally or recklessly, inflicts unlawful personal violence upon V.[10] But 'violence' here includes any unlawful touching[11] of another, however slight. As Blackstone explained:[12]

the law cannot draw the line between different degrees of violence, and therefore prohibits the first and lowest stage of it; every man's person being sacred, and no other having a right to meddle with it, in any the slightest manner.

This reflects the fact that the offences against the person protect the individual's personal autonomy by providing at least the opportunity for criminal punishment for the slightest unjustified infringement. This is supported by the protection offered by the ECHR, in Art 8 (respect for private life).[13] The other dimension to autonomy in this context—the purported freedom to do as you will with your body[14]—is less well respected in the current state of the law.[15]

---

[6] Common assault and battery were indictable offences at common law and under s 47, that element of s 47 was repealed by the 1988 Act, together with ss 42 and 43.

[7] See recently *R (Ward) v Black County Magistrates' Court* [2020] EWHC 680 (Admin): D charged with common assault, which was at trial amended to assault by beating. The Divisional Court accepted that a charge of 'common assault' incorporates the more specific 'battery' or 'assault by beating'. The word 'assault' was often used effectively as an abbreviation for 'assault and battery', and certainly was used to include 'battery' strictly so called.

[8] *Venna* [1976] QB 421 (a case of battery but the same principle surely applies to assault); *Savage* [1992] 1 AC 699, 740.

[9] In *Ireland* [1997] 4 All ER 225, 236, 239, the House of Lords applied this definition, originating in the 1st edn of this book, at p 262, adopted in *Fagan v Metropolitan Police Comr* [1968] 3 All ER 442 at 445 and approved in *Savage* [1992] AC 699, 740.

[10] *Rolfe* (1952) 36 Cr App R 4. Any amount of force will suffice, as emphasized in *Afolabi* [2017] EWHC 2960 (Admin).

[11] Note that the concept of touching may achieve a greater significance since it now forms the core of a number of offences under the Sexual Offences Act 2003. In *H* [2005] Crim LR 734, it was confirmed that touching of clothes would constitute the offence under s 3 of that Act. See Ch 17, p 818.

[12] *Commentaries*, iii, 120, cited by Goff LJ in *Collins v Wilcock* [1984] 3 All ER 374 at 378.

[13] For serious infringements, protection lies in Art 3—freedom from torture, inhuman and degrading treatment—and Art 5—freedom from unlawful deprivation of liberty. Art 4 protects against slavery. See the offence in the Modern Slavery Act 2015, s 1.

[14] On which see J Gardner, *Offences and Defences* (2007) 12.

[15] See the discussion of *Brown* later in this section.

In modern times, Lord Lane CJ described battery in expansive terms:

an intentional touching of another person without the consent of that person and without lawful excuse. It need not necessarily be hostile, or rude, or aggressive, as some of the cases seem to indicate.[16]

However, in *Brown*,[17] the majority of the House of Lords seem to have thought that hostility is an element in assault. But their lordships then interpreted 'hostile' in such a way as to deprive the word of all meaning. The case concerned sadomasochistic acts performed by a group of men on each other. All the acts were done for the mutual enjoyment of the participants, so they could not conceivably be assaults if hostility, in any ordinary meaning of the word, were required. The House of Lords suggested hostility was required but then upheld the convictions! Lord Jauncey said, 'If the appellants' activities in relation to the receivers [of the painful acts] were unlawful they were also hostile and a necessary ingredient of assault was present.' But the acts were only unlawful if they amounted to assaults. The reasoning appears to be circular. Notwithstanding the opinions of their lordships, it is submitted that the actual decision confirms the view that hostility is not an essential ingredient in the criminal offences of assault or battery. Some commentators suggest that there is value in requiring proof of hostility because otherwise an intentional touching which is nothing more than a faux pas, such as D's exuberant hug of a stranger at midnight on New Year's Eve, is potentially criminal.[18] It is submitted that such cases are not criminal because D will have a genuine belief in consent to that level of touching on that occasion. The concept of 'hostility' is unnecessary and ambiguous; it could cause undesirable complications in an offence which, because of the volume and summary nature of prosecutions, needs to be kept simple. The Court of Appeal has potentially added further confusion by conflating the issue of V's consent with whether D evinced hostility towards V. In *B*, Hughes LJ stated:[19]

The element of assault frequently and usefully described as hostility is a means of conveying to the jury that some non-hostile contact is an ordinary incident of life to which we all impliedly consent.

It is respectfully submitted that hostility is not an element of the offences and that the issue of consent ought not to be confused with it.

Assault and battery form the basis of many aggravated offences—for example, assaulting a police officer, assault with intent to resist arrest, etc.[20] It should be noted that assault and battery are also torts; and many, though not all, of the principles appear to be equally applicable in both branches of the law. Consequently, some of the cases cited here are civil actions.

The CPS Charging Standards now advise charging assault and battery where there is 'no injury or injuries which are not serious'. Previous versions of the guidance advised charging assault where: the injuries sustained amount to no more than: grazes; scratches; abrasions; minor bruising; swellings; reddening of the skin; superficial cuts; or a 'black eye'[21] and there are no aggravating features. The breadth of the offences results in wide prosecutorial discretion.

---

[16] *Faulkner v Talbot* [1981] 3 All ER 468 at 471, applied in *Thomas* (1985) 81 Cr App R 331 at 334; and see *Collins v Wilcock* [1984] 3 All ER 374 at 379; *Wilson v Pringle* [1987] QB 237, CA (Civ Div), criticized by Wood J in *T v T* [1988] 2 WLR 189 at 200, 203 (Fam Div); *Brown* [1992] 2 WLR 441 at 446.

[17] [1994] AC 212.   [18] Simester, Spencer, Stark, Sullivan and Virgo, CLT&D, 441.

[19] [2013] EWCA Crim 3.

[20] The Home Office identified over 70 such offences: *Violence. Reforming the Offences Against the Person Act 1861* (1998) para 3.5. See also LCCP 217, *Reform of Offences Against the Person: A Scoping Consultation Paper* (2014) Ch 2.

[21] See www.cps.gov.uk/legal-guidance/offences-against-person-incorporating-charging-standard#14382. See also C Clarkson, A Cretney, G Davis and J Shepherd, 'Assaults: The Relationship between Seriousness, Criminalisation and Punishment' [1994] Crim LR 4.

16.1.2 The relationship between assault and battery

Assault and battery are separate crimes, although as noted, they are not always recognized to be such.[22] The reason for the failure always to treat them as separate stems from the terminological problem: there is no acceptable verb corresponding to the noun, battery. As a result, 'assaulted' is almost invariably used to mean 'committed a battery against'. Sometimes, even statutes use the term 'assault' to mean 'assault or battery' but on other occasions both words are used.[23] It would be better if the terms 'assault' and 'battery' (rather than 'assault by beating') were consistently used.

Practical and procedural[24] problems flow from the loose use of the terms and the failure to treat assault and battery as separate offences. In *DPP v Little*,[25] a charge alleging that 'D . . . did unlawfully assault and batter J' was held to charge two offences and so to be 'bad for duplicity'.[26] More recently, in *R (on the application of Kracher) v Leicester Magistrates' Court* it was observed that:

> the offence of common assault can be committed in two ways which amount in law to different offences, namely assault by beating and an assault by putting another in fear of immediate silence [sic]. It is not possible to charge common assault in the alternative within the same charge.[27]

The failure properly to distinguish assault and battery also has repercussions for aggravated offences which depend on proof of an assault or battery. Consider the offence under s 47 of the OAPA 1861: 'Whosoever shall be convicted of an assault occasioning actual bodily harm shall be liable to [imprisonment for five years].' If D is charged under s 47 is it necessary for the Crown to spell out whether he assaulted or battered and occasioned ABH as a result or is it enough to use the term 'assault'? In *Savage*,[28] Lord Ackner's language when discussing s 47 suggests that that offence can be satisfied only if there is proof of an assault. But it would

---

[22] The CLRC Fourteenth Report, para 148, treated them as a single offence which may be committed in two ways and the Draft Code, cl 75, follows the CLRC's recommendation.

[23] There is a deplorable inconsistency in the statutory terminology. Even the Criminal Justice Act 1988, having made it crystal clear in s 39 that there are two offences, goes on in s 40(3)(a) to use 'common assault' in a context in which it can only sensibly mean—and has now been held to mean—'common assault or battery': *Lyndsey* [1995] 3 All ER 654. See also *R (Ward) v Black County Magistrates' Court* [2020] EWHC 680 (Admin) concluding that the word 'assault' was often used effectively as an abbreviation for 'assault and battery', that where a charge of simply 'common assault' was brought, it could usually be assumed that it was alleged that some degree of actual unlawful violence had been involved.

[24] The Domestic Violence, Crime and Victims Act 2004 remedied some procedural issues. Section 11 makes common assault an alternative verdict to more serious offences of assault, even if the count has not been preferred in the indictment. See *Nelson* [2013] EWCA Crim 30, [2013] Crim LR 689 for discussion although the decision is, it is submitted, in error. The court held that where a count for assault by beating is included in an indictment under the Criminal Justice Act 1988, s 40, then s 6(3A) does *not* enable a jury to return an alternative verdict of common assault on that count. The jury may return a verdict of assault on a charge of ABH. The court reasoned that if D threw a punch that missed, a verdict of 'attempted battery' may be returned on a charge of assault by beating. The Court of Appeal has overlooked the fact that attempted battery is not an offence known to law! The court's conclusion that common assault is not a permissible alternative on a charge of battery (because a battery can be inflicted on a victim who never saw the blow coming) is *per incuriam* because the case of *MPC v Wilson* [1984] AC 242, was not referred to.

[25] [1992] 1 All ER 299.

[26] ie that it makes more than one allegation in the same charge against the defendant. That is not generally permitted. Many earlier cases decided that a charge of assault and/or battery in a single information is duplicitous: *Jones v Sherwood* [1942] 1 KB 127 and *Mansfield Justices, ex p Sharkey* [1985] QB 613. But a blind eye appears to have been turned in *Notman* [1994] Crim LR 518.

[27] [2013] EWHC 4627 (Admin) at [11] per Saunders J. See Hickinbottom LJ's explanation of that case in *Black*, earlier.

[28] [1991] 4 All ER 698 at 711.

be incredible if D, who battered V without assaulting him (eg by hitting him on the back of the head so V did not apprehend the violence), was not guilty of an 'assault occasioning actual bodily harm'.

16.1.3 Common law or statutory offences?

On a literal reading, s 39 of the 1988 Act does not create any offence. It assumes the existence of offences of common assault and battery and merely prescribes the mode of trial and penalty. Laws LJ has asserted unequivocally that 'in truth, common assault by beating remains a common law offence'.[29] Nevertheless, in *DPP v Little*,[30] it was held that common assault and battery have been statutory offences since the enactment of s 47 of the OAPA 1861. The better view is that s 47 merely prescribed the penalty for the common law offences of common assault—as statutes do for other common law offences, for example murder, manslaughter and conspiracy to defraud.[31] Those offences all continue to exist at common law.

16.1.4 Actus reus of assault

The typical case of an assault as distinct from a battery is that where D, by some physical movement, causes V to apprehend that he is about to be struck. D runs towards or drives at V, or acts so as to appear to V to be on the point of striking, stabbing or shooting him. Assault was once regarded as 'attempted battery': D had embarked on an act which, if not stopped, would immediately result in an impact of some kind on V. Many 'attempted batteries' are assaults, but this is not necessarily so: D's acts may be unobserved by V, as where D approaches V from behind, or V is asleep, or insensible, or too young to appreciate what D appears likely to do. And there may be an assault where D has no intention to commit a battery but only to cause V to apprehend one.[32] The requirement is for apprehension, not fear.

16.1.4.1 Immediacy

What is required is that V is caused to apprehend immediate violence. The courts have tended to enlarge the scope of the offence by taking a generous, arguably too generous, view of 'immediacy' to include threats to V where the impending impact is remote. In part, this approach arose from the courts' desire to provide protection for those suffering harassment at a time before the Protection from Harassment Act 1997 was in force.[33]

In *Lewis*,[34] D was uttering threats to V from another room but was convicted of maliciously inflicting grievous bodily harm and therefore impliedly of an assault.[35] In *Logdon v DPP*,[36] D committed an assault by showing V a pistol in a drawer and declaring that he would hold her hostage. In *Ireland*,[37] the House of Lords held that words alone, or even silent telephone calls, are capable of amounting to an assault; but they found it unnecessary to decide whether they did so in that case. Words alone can cause someone to apprehend

---

[29] *Haystead v Chief Constable of Derbyshire* (2000) 164 JP 396, [2000] Crim LR 758. The defendant was in fact charged under s 39.

[30] See n 25.

[31] See [1991] Crim LR 900; *Blackstone* (2021) B2.1. The court in *Lyndsey*, n 23, noted the criticisms that have been made of *Little* but found it unnecessary to express any opinion.

[32] *Logdon v DPP* [1976] Crim LR 121.

[33] See C Wells, 'Stalking: The Criminal Law's Response' [1997] Crim LR 463.

[34] [1970] Crim LR 647.   [35] But see now *Wilson* [1984] AC 242, p 731.   [36] See earlier.

[37] See earlier. See G Virgo, 'Offences Against the Person—Do-It-Yourself Law Reform' (1997) 56 CLJ 251. J Horder, 'Reconsidering Psychic Assault' [1998] Crim LR 392, regards this dilution of the immediacy requirement as a welcome shift to an offence based on causing fear. On the merits of general threat offences, see P Alldridge, 'Threat Offences: A Case for Reform' [1994] Crim LR 176. See also LCCP 217, Ch 5.

immediate violence. If the caller said, 'There is bomb under your house which I am about to detonate', that would seem a clear case of assault. Lord Steyn said that the caller *may* be guilty of assault if he said, 'I will be at your door in a minute or two.' It seems to be a question of fact. Did the call in fact cause V to apprehend *immediate* unlawful violence? In *Constanza*,[38] V, who had for some time been harassed by D, received two letters from him eight days apart which she interpreted as clear threats. It was held that they amounted to an assault occasioning actual bodily harm. Was this two assaults or one continuing assault? It is easy to see that the letters might have caused V *immediate apprehension* of violence at some time in the future, but less easy to suppose that, as V read them, she apprehended *immediate violence.*

In *Smith v Chief Superintendent of Woking Police Station*,[39] D was convicted of assault by looking through the window of a bed-sitting room at V in her nightclothes with intent to frighten her. Kerr LJ limited his decision to a case where D 'is immediately adjacent, albeit on the other side of a window'. His lordship held that 'there can be no assault if it is obvious to V that D is unable to carry out his threat, as where D shakes his fist at V who is safely locked inside his car'. There may, of course, be an assault although D has no means of carrying out the threat.[40] The question is whether D intends or is reckless as to causing V to believe that he can and will carry it out immediately (mens rea) and whether V does so believe (actus reus). The question arises most obviously where D points an unloaded or imitation gun at V. If V knows the gun is unloaded or an imitation, there is no assault, because V could not apprehend being shot.[41] If V believes it is, or may be a real, loaded gun, there is an actus reus by D, for now V suffers the apprehension which is an essential element of assault.[42]

16.1.4.2 Assault by words alone

Ireland has now settled that an assault can be committed by words alone. This seems right— as a matter of fact, words, no less than a gesture, are capable of causing an apprehension of immediate violence.[43] It follows from *Constanza* that an assault by writing, email, tweet, text, etc is also possible.

Where D's actions would be an assault, but his words negate the effect of his actions, there is no offence.[44] If D's words are such that they amount to an implied threat or a conditional threat (eg 'as soon as we are alone I will hit you'), there may be an assault.[45]

It has generally been assumed that an act of some kind—even if it is only making a telephone call and remaining silent—is an essential ingredient of assault. One case[46] seems to support assault by omission but the court's actual decision was that D's conduct was a 'continuing act'. Where D inadvertently causes V to apprehend immediate violence (D is checking the sights on his gun when V walks into the room) and subsequently wilfully declines to withdraw the threat (by lowering the gun), his 'omission' might therefore constitute an assault.

---

[38] [1997] Crim LR 576. The court used ambiguous language, referring to the fact that she apprehended violence 'at some time not excluding the immediate future'. The House of Lords refused leave to appeal, but that does not imply approval of the decision.

[39] (1983) 76 Cr App R 234.   [40] *Pace*, Tindal CJ in *Stephens v Myers* (1830) 4 C & P 349.

[41] *Lamb*, p 597.   [42] *Logdon v DPP*, n 32.

[43] Previously the law was unclear although many authoritative writers asserted that words could not amount to an assault. See generally G Williams, 'Assault and Words' [1957] Crim LR 219.

[44] See *Tuberville v Savage* (1669) 1 Mood Rep 3—words 'if it were not assize time I would not take such language' negatived what would otherwise be an assault of D putting his hand on a sword in V's presence.

[45] See J Horder, 'Psychic Assault' [1998] Crim LR 392.

[46] *Fagan v Metropolitan Police Comr* [1969] 1 QB 439.

16.1.4.3 Attempt to assault

There can be no conviction for attempt to commit a common assault since common assault is a summary only offence.[47] There is no reason why there should not be attempt to commit a more serious offence of which assault forms an element; as where D points an unloaded gun at V, intending to frighten him in order to resist lawful arrest, but V, knowing the gun is unloaded, is unperturbed.[48]

16.1.5 Actus reus of battery

The actus reus consists in the infliction of unlawful personal violence by D upon V. V need not be aware of the touching as, for example, where he is asleep.[49] It used to be said that every battery involves an assault; but this is plainly not so, for in battery there need be no apprehension of the impending violence. A blow from behind is a battery even though V was unaware that it was coming.[50] It is generally said that D must have done some act and that it is not enough that he stood still and obstructed V's passage[51] like an inanimate object. But suppose D is sitting at the corner of a corridor with his legs stretched across it. He hears V running down the corridor and deliberately remains still with the intention that V, on turning the corner, shall fall over his legs. Why should this not be a battery? It would be if D had put out his legs with the intention of tripping up V. It would not be too difficult to conclude that D has a duty to V from the creation of the dangerous situation, applying the general principle recognized in *Miller*.[52] Further support for this proposition derives from *Santana-Bermudez*,[53] where D, an intravenous drug user, assured a police officer who was about to search him that he was carrying no 'sharps' and the officer stabbed her finger on a syringe in D's pocket. The court upheld the conviction, applying *Miller*:[54]

where someone (by act or word or a combination of the two) creates a danger and thereby exposes another to a reasonably foreseeable risk of injury which materializes, there is an evidential basis for the *actus reus* of an assault occasioning actual bodily harm. It remains necessary for the prosecution to prove an intention to assault or appropriate recklessness.[55]

By having the needles in his pocket and assuring the police officer about the contents of his pockets, D created a situation of danger. There may also be a battery where D inadvertently applies force to V and then wrongfully refuses to withdraw it. In *Fagan*,[56] where D accidentally drove his car on to a constable's foot and then intentionally left it there, the court held that there was a continuing act, not a mere omission.

There is certainly no battery where D has no control over the incident which causes the touching of V, as where D's horse unexpectedly runs away with him and into V;[57] but this might equally be explained because there is no mens rea. It might be otherwise if D foresaw, when he mounted the animal, that there was an unacceptable risk that this might happen.

---

[47] The point was not argued in *Lewis* [2010] EWCA Crim 151 (manslaughter where D chased V into the path of oncoming traffic).

[48] AF Noyes, 'Is Criminal Assault a Separate Substantive Crime or is it an Attempted Battery?' (1945) 33 Ky LJ 189; *State v Wilson*, 218 Ore 575, 346 P 2d 115 (1955). See also D White, 'Attempts: Initiatives in the Common Law Caribbean' [1980] Crim LR 780.

[49] See also *Thomas* (1985) 81 Cr App R 331.

[50] This passage in the 13th edn of this book was cited with approval by the Court of Appeal in *Nelson* [2013] EWCA Crim 30, [2013] Crim LR 689. The Court of Appeal held that the judge was wrong to leave a verdict of common assault to the jury as an alternative to battery. See n 24.

[51] *Innes v Wylie* (1844) 1 Car & Kir 257.   [52] [1983] AC 161.

[53] [2004] Crim LR 471, [2003] EWHC 2908 (Admin).   [54] [1983] AC 161.

[55] At [10].   [56] [1969] 1 QB 439.   [57] *Gibbons v Pepper* (1695) 2 Salk 637.

Although the courts have now interpreted 'bodily' harm to include psychiatric harm, and bodily harm may be inflicted without any impact on V's body by, for example, harassment over the phone, that certainly does not involve a battery.[58] Battery requires physical contact with V directly or indirectly.[59]

16.1.5.1 Battery with or via an instrument

Most batteries are *directly* inflicted, for example by D striking V with his fist or an instrument, or by a missile thrown by him, or by spitting upon V. But this is not essential: there can be an indirect battery. Where D punched W causing her to drop her baby, V, he was guilty of battery on V. It was found as a fact that D was reckless whether he injured V.[60]

Historically, in *Martin*,[61] Stephen and Wills JJ thought there would be a battery where D digs a pit for V to fall into or where he causes V to rush into an obstruction. In more modern times, the Divisional Court has recognized a battery by indirect means: in *DPP v K*,[62] D was convicted where he poured acid into a hand-drier in a toilet so that the next user sprayed himself with it.[63]

It is not a battery (nor an assault) for D to pull himself free from V who is detaining him, even though D uses force.[64]

It is submitted that it would undoubtedly be a battery to set a dog on another.[65] If D hit O's horse causing it to run down V, this would be battery by D.[66] No doubt the famous civil case of *Scott v Shepherd*[67] is equally applicable to the criminal law. D threw a squib (a firework) into a crowded area. First E and then F flung the squib away in order to save themselves from injury. It exploded and injured V. The acts of E and F were not 'fully voluntary' intervening acts which broke the chain of causation. This was battery by D.

If there is no violence at all, there is no battery; as where D puts harmful matter into a drink which is consumed by V.[68]

16.1.6 Mens rea of assault and battery

It is convenient to consider the mens rea of the two offences together. They are inextricably confused in some of the leading cases but need to be kept distinct if the separateness of the two offences is to be taken seriously. It was established by *Venna*[69] in 1975 that assault and battery may be committed recklessly as well as intentionally. *Venna* was a case of battery occasioning actual bodily harm but *dicta* concerning assault were relied on and it is safe to assume that the same principles apply to both offences.

---

[58] cf D Ormerod and M Gunn, 'In Defence of *Ireland*' [1996] 3 Web JCLI.

[59] The criminal law is not governed by the ancient forms of action at common law which would require directness.

[60] *Haystead v Chief Constable of Derbyshire* (2000) 164 JP 396, [2000] Crim LR 758 citing the 9th edn of this work. D could, alternatively, have been held guilty of an intentional assault by reason of transferred malice: p 125.

[61] (1881) 8 QBD 54.

[62] [1990] 1 All ER 331 overruled on other grounds by *Spratt* [1991] 2 All ER 210.

[63] It has been argued (M Hirst, 'Assault, Battery and Indirect Violence' [1999] Crim LR 557) that these authorities are inconsistent with the decision of the House of Lords in *MPC v Wilson* ([1984] AC 242, p 727 but all that case decided was that, though the word 'inflict' does not necessarily imply an assault, an allegation of inflicting harm may do so, and assault is therefore an 'included offence'. It does not follow that no indirect injury can ever be a battery.

[64] *Sheriff* [1969] Crim LR 260.

[65] *Murgatroyd v Chief Constable of West Yorkshire* [2000] All ER (D) 1742. But note the court's caution in *Dume* (1986) The Times, 16 Oct.

[66] *Gibbon v Pepper* (1695) 2 Salk 637 (*obiter*).   [67] (1773) 2 Wm Bl 892.

[68] *Hanson* (1849) 2 Car & Kir 912; but see fn 58.   [69] [1976] QB 421.

The mens rea of assault is an intention to cause V to apprehend immediate and unlawful violence, or recklessness whether such apprehension be caused.[70] Technically there is an argument that D should be shown to have intended or been reckless not only as to V's apprehension, but to have intended or been reckless that V's apprehension would be of *immediate* violence. It is unlikely the courts will adopt such a sophistication.

The mens rea of battery is an intention to apply force to the body of another or recklessness whether force be so applied.

16.1.6.1 Subjective recklessness

Venna approved the test of subjective, *Cunningham*-style recklessness. Despite some attempts to apply the *Caldwell* formulation of recklessness in *DPP v K*,[71] that decision was quickly overruled by the Court of Appeal in *Spratt*[72] which was followed by that court in *Parmenter*.[73] The House of Lords was not asked to decide the point but *dicta*[74] assume that *Cunningham* recklessness is required; and with the overruling of *Caldwell* in *G*, the point is now unarguable. The current law is that D must actually foresee the risk of causing apprehension of immediate violence (assault), or the application of it (battery), as the case may be, and go on unjustifiably to take that risk.[75]

16.1.6.2 Is the mens rea of assault and battery interchangeable?

Is it an offence to cause the actus reus of battery with the mens rea only of assault or the actus reus of assault with the mens rea only of battery? In principle, the answer is no.[76] D waves his fist, intending to alarm (assault) V but not to strike him and not foreseeing any risk of doing so; but V who does not see D, moves towards D, and is hit. D creeps up behind V, intending to hit him over the head without attracting his attention (battery), but V unexpectedly turns round and moves to avoid the blow. Taking the distinction between assault and battery seriously, in the former case D does not commit a battery but is attempting to commit an assault; and in the latter he does not commit an assault but is attempting to commit a battery; and these 'attempts' to commit summary offences are not offences. It remains to be seen whether the appellate courts will take the consequences of treating the offences as separate.

16.1.6.3 Assault and battery by an intoxicated person

Assault and battery are classified as offences of 'basic intent'[77] so it is no defence that D had no mens rea because of his voluntary intoxication. The reason appears to be that the offences may be committed by recklessness. If the prosecution specifically allege that D has *intentionally* assaulted or battered, it may be that they will be required to prove a 'specific

---

[70] cf *Savage* [1991] 4 All ER 698 at 711.   [71] [1990] 1 All ER 331.

[72] [1991] 2 All ER 210. In *Pinkney v DPP* [2017] EWHC 854 (Admin) despite the fact the district judge appeared to apply an objective test, D's conviction was upheld as Sir Wyn Williams reached the conclusion that on the facts D did commit an offence. With respect, the outcome of this case is surprising.

[73] [1992] 1 AC 699.

[74] 'Where the defendant neither intends nor adverts to the possibility that there will be any physical contact at all, then the offence under s 47 would not be made out. This is because there would have been *no assault*, let alone an assault occasioning actual bodily harm' ([1991] 4 All ER at 707): Lord Ackner of course means 'no battery'. Other *dicta* show that he recognized that an assault in the strict sense suffices for an offence under s 47 if it occasions actual bodily harm.

[75] Despite the ease with which the test can be stated, cases with questionable outcomes still occur. Cf *Katsonis v CPS* [2011] EWHC 1860 (Admin).

[76] See also LCCP 217, Chs 3 and 5.

[77] On the orthodox interpretation that basic intent offences are ones that can be committed without proof of intent; cf *Heard* [2007] EWCA Crim 125, p 337.

intent' and intoxication will be a defence.[78] Given the demonstrable link between alcohol and offences of violence, the courts might find this approach unpalatable.

16.2 Defences to assault and battery

16.2.1 Consent

It is clear that consent is an answer to a charge of common assault or battery (though not necessarily to the offence of assault occasioning actual bodily harm[79]). It remains unclear how consent negates liability for assault or battery. Is it because the *absence of consent* is an essential element in the offence, as in rape;[80] or is *consent* a defence to the charge? In *Brown*, Lord Jauncey, with whose reasoning Lord Lowry agreed, said that if it had been necessary to answer this question, which it was not, he would have held consent to be a defence. Lord Templeman also treated consent as a defence. Lord Mustill, on the other hand, regarded it as one factor negativing an actus reus; while Lord Slynn emphatically agreed with Glanville Williams that 'It is. . . inherent in the concept of assault and battery that the victim does not consent.'[81] The Law Commission regarded it as a defence.[82] However, Lord Woolf CJ stated that 'it is a requirement of *the offence* that the conduct itself should be unlawful'.[83]

This view—that it is an element of the offence—is, it is submitted, the better one. The importance of the question is demonstrated by the dissent of Lords Mustill and Slynn in *Brown*. The majority held that the sadomasochistic defendants were guilty of assaults occasioning actual bodily harm on, and unlawful wounding of, one another, notwithstanding the defendants' enthusiastic submission to, and the pleasure which they all derived from, the sadomasochistic 'assaults'. The question the majority asked themselves was 'Does the public interest require the invention of a new defence?' This is quite different from the question the minority were answering: 'Does the public interest require the offence to be construed to include sadomasochistic conduct?' It is not surprising that they led to different conclusions.[84]

While the distinction between offence and defence is fundamental in theory and in judicial law-making, in the practical functioning of the law in this area it is probably not very important.[85] It affects the evidential burden—if the absence of consent is an element of the

[78] cf *Caldwell* [1981] 1 All ER 961 at 964.

[79] There is a vast literature on this subject. Accessible discussions include LCCP 134, *Consent and Offences against the Person* (1994), on which see D Ormerod, 'Consent and Offences Against the Person: LCCP No 134' (1994) 57 MLR 928; and LCCP 139, *Consent in Criminal Law* (1995), on which see D Ormerod and M Gunn, 'Consent—A Second Bash' [1996] Crim LR 694; S Shute, 'Something Old, Something New, Something Borrowed—Three Aspects of the Consent Project' [1996] Crim LR 684. For a multifaceted analysis, see A Reed and M Bohlander (with N Wake and E Smith) (eds), *Consent: Domestic and Comparative Perspectives* (2017). For a review of the philosophical arguments, see P Roberts, 'The Philosophical Foundations of Consent in the Criminal Law' (1997) 17 OJLS 389. On consent more generally, see D Beyleveld and R Brownsword, *Consent in the Law* (2007).

[80] *Larter* [1995] Crim LR 75, see Ch 17, p 807, n 146.

[81] G Williams, 'Consent and Public Policy' [1962] Crim LR 74, 75.

[82] For criticism see S Shute [1996] Crim LR 684.

[83] *Barnes* [2005] EWCA Crim 3246, [16], [2005] Crim LR 381 and commentary.

[84] cf *Wilson*, p 715, where the court asked, 'Does public policy or the public interest demand that the appellant's activities [branding of wife's buttocks at her request] be visited by the sanctions of the criminal law?' and, unsurprisingly, answered, 'No.' By way of contrast, see *BM* [2018] EWCA Crim 560, which concerned body modification such as tongue splitting by a tattooist who had no medical qualification, discussed later, p 714.

[85] The Criminal Injuries Compensation Appeal Panel takes the view that the victim's consent is not determinative of whether an offence of violence has been committed: *R (E) v CICA* [2003] EWCA Civ 234.

offence, the prosecution must set out to prove it; if it is a defence, it is for the defendant to introduce evidence of it; but, in either case, the ultimate burden of proof is on the prosecution. In *Shabbir*,[86] S and others were acquitted by the magistrates of charges including assault. The charges arose from a prolonged violent attack in a city centre. The defendants raised the plea of consent, arguing that the Crown had the burden of proving an element of the offence—that V had not consented to being assaulted. The magistrates found that the Crown had failed to prove that matter and acquitted. The Divisional Court held that a lack of consent could be inferred from evidence (violent attack on strangers shown on CCTV) other than the direct evidence of the victim.

Whether or not consent is properly regarded as a defence or as an element of the offences of assault and battery (and therefore as an element of the aggravated assaults discussed later), it is valuable to consider its meaning here. In recent years the courts have been forced to deal with difficult issues including defining what constitutes effective 'consent' (ie whether frauds or pressure vitiate consent) and, if such factual consent is present, whether it ought to be recognized in law. In other words, in what circumstances it is appropriate for the State to apply the criminal sanction to punish conduct voluntarily engaged in by adults of full mental capacity. There are three distinct questions to address:

(1) Was there implied or express consent?

(2) Did the 'victim'[87] give effective consent to the act?

(3) Was the conduct performed in a context in which the law accepts that consent be validly given? [88]

16.2.1.1 Implied consent

Since the merest touching without consent is a battery, the needs of everyday life demand that there be an implied consent to that degree of contact which is necessary or customary in the ordinary course of daily life.

Generally speaking, consent is a 'defence' to battery; and most of the physical contacts of ordinary life are not criminal because they are impliedly consented to by all who move in society and so expose themselves to the risk of bodily contact. So no one can complain of the jostling which is inevitable from his presence in, for example, a supermarket, an underground station or a busy street; nor can a person who attends a party complain if his hand is seized in friendship, or even if his back is (within reason) slapped. Although such cases are regarded as examples of implied consent, it is more common nowadays to treat them as falling within a general exception embracing the limited physical contact which is generally to be expected and accepted in the ordinary conduct of daily life.[89]

---

[86] [2009] EWHC 2754 (Admin). Goldring LJ expressed astonishment and disappointment that such a 'wholly spurious' point would be taken on the facts of that case.

[87] The term 'victim' is adopted throughout this chapter, although it is acknowledged that if V has truly consented, it is illogical to view him as such.

[88] It has been argued that English law relies too much upon category-based decision-making and that a more suitable approach is the one propounded by the New Zealand Court of Appeal in *Lee* (2006) 22 CRNZ 568. This approach requires the court to engage with the facts of the individual case in a substantive fashion rather than simply basing its decision on the generic category of behaviour to which the facts belong. See J Tolmie, 'Consent to Harmful Assaults: The Case for Moving Away from Category Based Decision Making' [2012] Crim LR 656 and W Wilson, 'Consenting to Personal Injury' in A Reed and M Bohlander (with N Wake and E Smith) (eds), *Consent: Domestic and Comparative Perspectives* (2017).

[89] *Collins v Wilcock* [1984] 3 All ER 374 at 378 per Robert Goff LJ. In *F v West Berkshire Health Authority* [1989] 2 All ER 545 at 563 Lord Goff was more emphatic that the consent rationalization is 'artificial', pointing out that it is difficult to impute consent to those who through youth or mental disorder are unable to give it. See *Mepstead v DPP* [1996] Crim LR 111. In *Wainwright v Home Office* [2003] UKHL 53, Goff LJ was described as having 'redefined' the concept, at [9].

Touching a person for the purpose of engaging his attention has been held to be acceptable[90] but physical restraint is not. A police officer who catches hold of a person, not for the purpose of arresting him but in order to detain him for questioning, is acting unlawfully.[91] It is a technical assault for a police officer physically to detain a person without violence and without any intention to arrest him. Police officers can, however, make 'very brief' physical contact with members of the public in order to attract their attention.[92] So a constable who takes hold of the arm of a woman found soliciting in order to caution her was acting unlawfully. The fact that the practice of caution- ing sex workers is recognized by statute does not imply any power to stop and detain.[93] It may be difficult to determine whether a police officer is attempting to get someone's attention, or whether he has engaged in a form of unlawful restraint. This is essentially a question of fact and degree.

To 'detain' without any actual touching cannot be a battery. If the detention is effected by the threat of force, then it may be false imprisonment.[94] Article 5 of the ECHR has potential significance, but has been interpreted to protect against a 'deprivation of liberty not a minor restriction on freedom of movement'.[95]

In *H v CPS*,[96] the court rejected the submission that teachers in special needs schools must by their post 'impliedly consent' to the use of violence against them by pupils. The court accepted that the teachers were accepting a heightened risk of violence but that was not the same as saying that they implicitly consented to its infliction.

For this purpose, touching the 'person' of the victim includes the clothes he is wearing.[97] It is not necessary that V should be able to feel the impact through the clothes. In *Thomas*,[98] where D touched the bottom of V's skirt and rubbed it, the court said, *obiter*, that 'There could be no dispute that if you touch a person's clothes while he is wearing them that is equivalent to touching him.' Section 79 of the Sexual Offences Act 2003 defines touching for the purpose of that Act, as including touching with any part of the body, with anything else or *through anything*, and in *H*[99] the Court of Appeal confirmed that touching V's clothes sufficed.

In *Dica*,[100] the Court of Appeal confirmed that where V, who was unaware of D's HIV infected state, had consented to the act of unprotected sexual intercourse she could not be said to have *impliedly* consented to the risk of infection from that intercourse.

---

[90] *Wiffin v Kincard* (1807) 2 Bos & PNR 471; *Coward v Baddeley* (1859) 4 H & N 478. *Donnelly v Jackman* [1970] 1 WLR 562, where a police officer was held to be acting in the execution of his duty although he persisted in tapping V on the shoulder when V had made it clear that he had no intention of stopping to speak, is 'an extreme case': [1984] 3 All ER 374 at 379. See also *Walker v Commissioner of Police of the Metropolis* (2014) The Times, 16 July, CA (Civ Div) where the officer went beyond the permissible.

[91] *Kenlin v Gardiner* [1967] 2 QB 510. See *McKoy* [2002] EWCA Crim 1628. See for more recent examples *Iqbal* [2011] EWCA Crim 273; *Wood v DPP* [2008] EWHC 1056 (Admin); *Metcalf v CPS* [2015] EWHC 1091 (Admin), D may be guilty of obstructing a constable (making a lawful arrest, keeping the peace, etc) even if the officer, at some point, acts unlawfully (eg in pushing D out of the way). For discussion of whether the defences of private defence or defence of another can be pleaded in respect of these offences, see p 427, and the discussion in *Pegram v DPP* [2019] EWHC 2673 (Admin).

[92] *Pegram v DPP* [2019] EWHC 2673 (Admin).

[93] *Collins v Wilcock*, n 89; see eg *McMillan v CPS* [2008] EWHC 1457 (Admin) (touching when steadying a drunk person).

[94] See p 753.

[95] See discussion in Emmerson, Ashworth, and Macdonald, HR&CJ, paras 5.02 et seq; *Guzzardi v Italy* (1981) 3 EHRR 333, para 92. See the discussion of *Austin v MPC* [2009] UKHL 12, p 754. See also *R (AP) v Secretary of State for the Home Department* [2010] UKSC 24, in which it was held that when deciding if there is a deprivation of liberty within the meaning of Art 5 of the ECHR regard should be had to the subjective factors peculiar to the particular individual.

[96] [2010] All ER (D) 56 (Apr).   [97] *Day* (1845) 1 Cox CC 207. D slashed V's clothes with a knife.

[98] (1985) 81 Cr App R 331 at 334.   [99] [2005] EWCA Crim 732.

[100] [2004] EWCA Crim 1103, [2004] Crim LR 944 and commentary. The House of Lords refused leave to appeal— see House of Lords Session 2005–06, 15 Dec 2005. See for criticism of the case: M Weait, 'Criminal Law and the Transmission of HIV: *R v Dica*' (2005) 68 MLR 121; M Weait, '*Dica*: Knowledge, Consent and the Transmission of HIV' (2004) 154 NLJ 826; cf for a positive view of the case: JR Spencer, 'Retrial for Reckless Infection' (2004) 154 NLJ 762. See also M Davies, '*R v Dica*: Lessons in Practising Unsafe Sex' (2004) 68 J Crim L 498.

16.2.1.2 Effective consent

The principal problems to address in this context are:

- what mental capacity V must possess to be capable of issuing effective consent;
- what degree of prior knowledge of the acts V must have to be capable of giving a valid consent to them;
- what effect on V's apparent consent a fraud by D will have; and
- whether duress or pressure from D or another will vitiate consent by V.

We are not at this point examining D's belief in V's consent, but it must be borne in mind that D's belief that V is consenting to an act for which V's factual consent would be recognized in law[101] is a defence whether D's belief is based on reasonable grounds or not, provided D's belief is honestly held.[102]

Capacity

Those with a mental disorder or learning difficulty may lack sufficient capacity[103] to give consent,[104] as may someone who is temporarily incapacitated by intoxication or otherwise. Youth or immaturity is clearly also a potential impediment to the giving of effective consent.[105] In *Burrell v Harmer*,[106] where D tattooed boys aged 12 and 13, causing their arms to become inflamed and painful, the boys' apparent consent was held to be no defence to a charge of assault occasioning actual bodily harm. The court took the view that the boys were unable to understand the nature of the act. But in what sense did they not understand it? The case highlights the relative superficiality of the English criminal courts' approach to such fundamental questions underlying the issue of consent. In Wales, it is an offence to perform or make arrangements to perform an intimate piercing of a child under 18.[107]

The Mental Capacity Act 2005 provides a definition, at least for the purposes of that Act, of 'people who lack capacity'. The definition is as follows: 'a person lacks capacity in relation to a matter if at the material time he is unable to make a decision for himself in relation to the matter because of a temporary or permanent impairment of, or a disturbance in the functioning of, the mind or brain'. The section further provides that a lack of capacity cannot be established merely by reference to '(a) a person's age or appearance, or (b) a condition of his, or an aspect of his behaviour, which might lead others to make unjustified assumptions about his capacity'.

Even if the criminal courts do not adopt that definition directly in the context of offences against the person, they may be influenced in deciding whether a person lacks capacity by the 'principles' set out in s 1 of the Mental Capacity Act 2005 which include that a person: must be assumed to have capacity unless it is established to the contrary, and that a person is not to be treated as unable to make a decision merely because he makes an unwise decision.[108] The Act provides 'official recognition that capacity is not a blunt "all or nothing" condition, but is

---

[101] *Konzani* [2005] EWCA Crim 706.

[102] *Morgan* [1976] AC 182; p 350; *Albert v Lavin* [1981] 1 All ER 628.

[103] LCCP 139, Part V; LC 231, *Mental Capacity* (1995); see E Jackson, *Medical Law: Text, Cases, and Materials* (5th edn, 2019) Chs 4, 5 and 6.

[104] See *Re MB (An Adult) (Medical Treatment)* [1997] 2 FCR 541. Medical treatment in defiance of the (mentally normal) adult patient's wishes or in the case of a child in defiance of those of a parent will infringe Art 8: *Glass v UK* (App no 61827/00) 2000.

[105] See generally *Gillick v West Norfolk and Wisbech AHA* [1986] AC 112.

[106] [1967] Crim LR 169 and commentary thereon. It is now an offence to tattoo a person under the age of 18, except tattooing by a doctor for medical reasons: Tattooing of Minors Act 1969.

[107] Public Health (Wales) Act 2017, s 95. Intimate parts include the tongue.

[108] The Act is supplemented by a Code of Practice published in 2007. See also C [2009] UKHL 42, dealing with the offence in s 30 of the Sexual Offences Act 2003, discussed at p 794.

more complex, and is to be treated as being issue-specific. A person may not have sufficient capacity to be able to make complex, refined or major decisions but may still have the capacity to make simpler or less momentous ones, or to hold genuine views as to what he wants to be the outcome of more complex decisions or situations.'[109]

Informed consent

In principle, V cannot consent to some form of conduct without adequate knowledge of its nature, and the degree of knowledge required should depend on the degree of harm and risk of that harm to which V is exposing himself. In offences against the person, this issue seems to have received little attention until very recently. In sexual offences, it is implicit in the statutory formulation of the non-consensual offences that V must have capacity and have 'freely agreed', and that there must have been adequate information available to V to render his consent effective.[110] The issue overlaps with the next to be discussed—that of V's apparent consent in the face of deception by D. In sexual offences, the 2003 Act provides, inter alia, that it is conclusively presumed that there is no consent where D has deceived V as to the nature or purpose of D's act.[111] In non-sexual offences against the person, it remains unclear whether V can be said to have consented without having knowledge of the *purpose* of D's conduct even if V is aware of its *nature*. The issue has arisen in relation to cases in which D has infected V with HIV[112] in the course of sexual acts.[113]

In *Konzani*,[114] the Court of Appeal confirmed that if D engages in unprotected sexual intercourse with V, and D recklessly infects V with HIV, any defence of consent D seeks to advance will not be available unless V had made an informed consent to the risk of infection.[115] As the court explained:

If an individual who knows that he is suffering from the HIV virus conceals this stark fact from his sexual partner, the principle of V's personal autonomy is not enhanced if D is exculpated when he

[109] See *Re S and another (Protected Persons)* [2010] 1 WLR 1082, [53] concerning powers of attorney.

[110] See Ch 17.

[111] See s 76, p 809. As will be discussed later, deception is also relevant when considering the general definition of consent in s 74.

[112] See also *Golding* [2014] EWCA Crim 889 in which D pleaded guilty to transmitting genital herpes. See also LCCP 217, Ch 6.

[113] For detailed examination of the appropriate uses of the criminal law to tackle HIV transmission, see S Bronnit, 'Spreading Disease and the Criminal Law' [1994] Crim LR 21; D Ormerod and M Gunn, 'Criminal Liability for the Transmission of HIV' [1996] Web JCLI; D Ormerod, 'Criminalizing HIV Transmission—Still No Effective Solutions' (2001) 30 Common L World Rev 135; M Weait and Y Azad, 'The Criminalisation of HIV Transmission in England and Wales: Questions of Law and Policy' (2005) 10 HIV/AIDS Policy & Law Rev 1. See more generally, M Weait, *Intimacy and Responsibility: The Criminalisation of HIV Transmission* (2007). Cf S Matthiesson, 'Should the Law Deal with Reckless HIV Infection as a Criminal Offence or as a Matter of Public Health?' (2010) 21 KLJ 123 responding to Weait; R Bennett, 'Should We Criminalise HIV Transmission' in C Erin and S Ost (eds), *The Criminal Justice System and Health Care* (2007) 225; L Cherkassky, 'Being Informed: The Complexities of Knowledge, Deception and Consent when Transmitting HIV' (2010) 74 J Crim L 242; J Slater, 'HIV, Trust and the Criminal Law' (2011) 75 J Crim L 309; JG Francis and LP Francis, 'HIV Treatment as Prevention: Not an Argument for Continuing Criminalisation of HIV Transmission' (2013) 9 Int'l J Crim L in Context 520; the chapters in C Stanton and H Quirk (eds), *Criminalising Contagion: Legal and Ethical Challenges of Disease Transmission and the Criminal Law* (2016).

[114] [2005] EWCA Crim 706; M Weait, 'Knowledge, Autonomy and Consent: *R v Konzani*' [2005] Crim LR 763 arguing that the case extends the criminal law too far by criminalizing *reckless* non-disclosure of HIV-positive status. See more generally M Weait, *Intimacy and Responsibility: The Criminalisation of HIV Transmission* (2007) arguing that the act of recklessly exposing a sexual partner to the risk of HIV infection without her consent should be decriminalized and treated as a public health issue.

[115] For sentencing considerations in such cases, see *P (SJ)* [2006] EWCA Crim 2599—32 months on a plea. Darryl Rowe was sentenced to life imprisonment for intentionally transmitting HIV to a number of his sexual partners. See news reports for 18 April 2018.

recklessly transmits the HIV virus to V through consensual sexual intercourse. On any view, the concealment of this fact from her almost inevitably means that she is deceived. Her consent is not properly informed, and she cannot give an informed consent to something of which she is ignorant. Equally, her personal autonomy is not normally protected by allowing a defendant who knows that he is suffering from the HIV virus which he deliberately conceals, to assert an honest belief in his partner's informed consent to the risk of the transmission of the HIV virus. Silence in these circumstances not consistent with honesty, or with a genuine belief that there is an informed consent. Accordingly, in such circumstances the issue either of informed consent, or honest belief in it will only rarely arise: in reality, in most cases, the contention would be wholly artificial.[116]

Several aspects of the decision are of importance. First, to be effective, V's consent must be to the risk of HIV infection; V might well have consented to the act of sexual intercourse without consenting to the risk of HIV infection. Secondly, V cannot in law consent to intentional infection; V's consent is only effective if D is merely reckless as to transmission.[117] Thirdly, the decision appears to criminalize D who suspects that he is HIV-positive, without knowing that fact, if he then goes on to have unprotected intercourse with V without her consent as to the risk of infection.[118] This aspect of the decision has been heavily criticized for overcriminalizing.[119] Fourthly, the decision treats D's failure to disclose his HIV-positive status to V as sufficient to preclude informed consent by V. Several commentators have been critical of this aspect of the decision, arguing that V has some responsibility for taking precautions about her sexual safety, and that by assuming that by D's concealment V is not consenting, the law ignores that responsibility on V.[120] The question of whether D is liable where he has not informed V of his HIV status but, despite using a condom, he has infected V remains unresolved. D will surely argue that he was not reckless as to the risk of infection.[121]

It was accepted in *Konzani* that there may be circumstances in which V will have informed consent without express disclosure from D, as where the fact of D's HIV status becomes known in the course of medical treatment. That qualification to the general principle—that informed consent depends on D's honest disclosure—also poses problems. D will be able to plead that he did not know that V was not consenting to the risk, since he had a genuine belief that she knew of his HIV status although he had not disclosed the fact to her. In addition, D may be acquitted where V has in fact consented to the risk even if D did not know that she had consented because he was unaware of her having secured knowledge of his status from other sources. If absence of consent is an element of the actus reus, D cannot be guilty in such a case because the actus reus is not complete where V has, in fact, consented. If consent is a defence, D will have actus reus (infection) and mens rea (recklessness as to infection); but can he rely on the defence of consent based on the fact of V's awareness of his infected state of which D was ignorant at the time as it derived from other sources? Does the defence require proof that D was aware of the circumstances which would render his

---

[116] At [23].   [117] See later.

[118] Some argue that D has a 'right' not to know what his HIV status is and a right to act on that lack of knowledge: Tadros, *Criminal Responsibility*, 247.

[119] See S Ryan, 'Reckless Transmission of HIV: Knowledge and Culpability' [2006] Crim LR 981.

[120] See Weait (2005) 68 MLR at 128 and [2005] Crim LR 763. See also V Munro, 'On Responsible Relationships and Irresponsible Sex' (2007) 19 CFLQ 112.

[121] Some argue that consent may not be D's only way of avoiding liability in cases such as these and that there is ambiguity as to whether, in the absence of disclosure, D could avoid liability by using a condom and/or demonstrating that his viral load was very low, thereby diminishing the risk of transmission. It is argued that in these circumstances D is not being reckless and so lacks the requisite mens rea. See D Hughes, 'Condom Use, Viral Load and the Type of Sexual Activity as Defences to the Sexual Transmission of HIV' (2013) 77 J Crim L 136. See also LCCP 217, Ch 2.

conduct justified? Cooper and Reed[122] suggest that this resurrects the problems posed by *Dadson* (p 34). They point to the fact that D will be relying on a justifying circumstance (V's consent) of which D was unaware at the time of the act, and that this drives 'a coach and horses' through established doctrines of informed consent.

Parliamentary clarification of the issues would be welcome, but is unlikely given the controversial nature of such legislation in terms of broader public health policies and the desire to encourage responsible sexual behaviour.[123] The Law Commission has consulted on whether future reform of the offences against the person ought to include specific offences dealing with sexually transmitted infection.[124] In the subsequent Report, the Law Commission recommended that in any new statute governing offences against the person based upon the draft Home Office Bill, the offences of causing serious injury should be capable of including the intentional or (as the case may be) reckless transmission of disease. The Law Commission also recommended that if the government wished to consider the possibility of excluding criminal liability for the reckless transmission of disease, or of creating special offences for such transmission, this should follow a wider review.[125]

The approach in *Konzani*, in relation to the OAPA, by which V's informed consent rests on D providing information as to the relevant risk, does not sit easily with the courts' approach in sexual offences.[126] In relation to sexual offences, in *Monica*[127] the Lord Chief Justice stated that: 'deception which is closely connected with "the nature or purpose of the act", because it relates to sexual intercourse itself rather than the broad circumstances surrounding it is capable of negating a complainant's free exercise of choice'.

Consent procured by fraud

In offences against the person, D's fraud as to the conduct does not necessarily negative V's consent: it does so only if it deceives V as to D's identity or the nature of the act.[128] The common law approach to frauds vitiating consent remains unsatisfactorily complex and confused.

If V agrees to X touching her in a manner amounting to a mere battery, her consent is prima facie vitiated if D impersonates X and touches her. V's autonomy includes a right (generally) to choose *who* touches her. In *Richardson*,[129] D, a registered dental practitioner who was suspended from practice, carried out dentistry on patients who said they would not have consented had they known that D was suspended. D was convicted of assault occasioning actual bodily harm, the trial judge ruling that the mistake vitiated consent, being equivalent to a mistake of identity. The Court of Appeal disagreed since that would be to strain and distort the everyday meaning of 'identity'. The fraud was not as to who she was but whether she was licensed as a dentist.

---

[122] S Cooper and A Reed, 'Informed Consent and the Transmission of Sexual Disease: *Dadson* Revivified' (2007) 71 J Crim L 461.

[123] See J Rogers (2005) 64 CLJ 20, 22 pointing out that no government is likely to want to legislate.

[124] See LCCP 217, *Reform of Offences Against the Person: A Scoping Consultation Paper* (2014) Ch 6.

[125] See LC 361, *Reform of Offences Against the Person* (2015) Ch 6.

[126] See *Jheeta* [2007] EWCA Crim 1699, *Assange v Sweden* [2011] EWHC 2849 (Admin), *B* [2013] EWCA Crim 823; *R (Monica) v DPP* [2018] EWHC 3508 (Admin); *Lawrence* [2020] EWCA Crim 971; p 798. For discussion, see A Reed and E Smith, 'Caveat Amator—The Transmission of HIV and the Parameters of Consent and Bad Character Evidence' in A Reed and M Bohlander (with N Wake and E Smith) (eds), *Consent: Domestic and Comparative Perspectives* (2017) 125–30.

[127] At [72].   [128] See generally LCCP 139, Part VI.

[129] [1998] 2 Cr App R 200. *Richardson* now has to be read with *Tabassum* [2000] 2 Cr App R 328, p 811.

Richardson was distinguished, rightly it is submitted, in Melin.[130] D had administered Botox injections for cosmetic purposes to two women, both of whom suffered serious injury after their second injections. D was not medically qualified. Neither woman had met D before he administered the first injections. Both claimed that D told them, at different stages of the process, that he was medically qualified. Both said that they would not have allowed D to administer the injections had they known he was not medically qualified. The prosecution's case was that D had lied about his qualifications and that the women only consented in the belief that he was medically qualified. The Court of Appeal held that as a matter of common law, only deception as to identity or as to the nature of the act are capable of negating consent. The court accepted that it would be undesirable for all deceptions to negate consent, no matter how trivial. The court also accepted that there will be circumstances where a person's identity is inextricably linked to his professional status. Therefore, a person's being a doctor, where that is integral to his identity, could vitiate consent. *Richardson* was distinguished on the basis that the treatment in *Melin* was given by someone impersonating a doctor, whereas in *Richardson* the defendant was a qualified dentist but had been suspended.

It is submitted that there are some situations in which the status or attribute of the individual is inextricably bound up with his identity for the purposes of the specific activity he is performing. Indeed, it could be that the attribute is actually *more* important than the identity. For example, would a patient visiting a general practitioner and being told that a new doctor is taking the surgery be more concerned as to the 'status' of the person or his 'identity'? The same argument might apply to the attribute of being a police officer.[131]

The courts have had even greater difficulty dealing with the effect of frauds as to the nature of the act, and in particular in distinguishing frauds that relate to issues that affect the nature of the act and frauds that relate to a collateral issue. It would be undesirable for the law to treat all frauds as vitiating consent; otherwise the most trivial lies about the conduct could give rise to liability,[132] but this can give rise to difficult cases. In *Bolduc and Bird*, where D1, a doctor, by falsely pretending that D2 was a medical student, obtained V's consent to D2's presence at a necessary vaginal examination of V, it was held that there was no assault because the fraud was not as to the nature and quality of what was to be done.[133] Similarly, a woman was held to have consented to the nature of the act by agreeing to the introduction of an instrument into her vagina for diagnostic purposes when the operator was secretly acting only for sexual gratification.[134]

One of the leading cases in this area, and one which gave rise to considerable controversy, was *Clarence*.[135] D was charged with causing grievous bodily harm to his wife, V, when

---

[130] [2019] EWCA Crim 557.

[131] With powers to arrest, search, etc. See *Wellard* [1978] 1 WLR 921. It could be argued that there are circumstances in which the attribute or status of the actor is so crucial as to alter the *nature* of the act performed, as perhaps in a medical context. This would require the court to adopt a much wider reading of 'nature' than the orthodox interpretation which restricts the meaning to the mechanical acts, see eg *Williams* [1923] 1 KB 340. There is some Canadian authority supporting a wider test. See *Maurantonio* (1967) 65 DLR (2d) 674; *Harms* [1944] 2 DLR 61. See Ormerod, commentary at [1999] Crim LR 494.

[132] cf the quagmire the courts have found themselves in when interpreting the consent provisions of the SOA 2003, p 797. In appropriate cases, the law lowers the threshold of what constitutes a sufficient fraud or threat, as where the victim is mentally disordered—see Sexual Offences Act 2003, ss 30–44, p 848.

[133] *Bolduc and Bird* (1967) 63 DLR (2d) 82 (Sup Ct of Canada, Spence J dissenting), reversing British Columbia CA, 61 DLR (2d) 494; cf *Rosinski* (1824) 1 Mood CC 19.

[134] *Mobilio* [1991] 1 VR 339. See D Ormerod, 'A Victim's Mistaken Consent in Rape' (1992) 56 J Crim L 407.

[135] (1888) 22 QBD 23. For an interesting historical account of the case, see K Gleeson, 'The Problem of *Clarence*' (2005) 14 Nottingham LJ 1.

knowing that he was suffering from a sexually transmitted disease, he had unprotected sex with her and infected her. It was held that V had consented to intercourse with D and, although she would not have consented to the act of intercourse had she been aware of the disease from which D knew he was suffering, this was no assault. The court concluded that she had not been defrauded as to the *nature* of the act of intercourse (ie the physical mechanics of that act)[136] but merely as to the associated risk of disease. The flaw in this approach was in focusing on V's awareness of the nature of the act of intercourse. This was not a rape case where her understanding of the nature of sex might have been important. The court should have focused on the more important question: was V aware or was she deceived about the (risk of) harm which D was charged with causing—that of the infection. It was her awareness of the nature of *that* risk that ought to have been considered.

In the important case of *Dica*,[137] where D had infected two sexual partners with HIV, *Clarence* was regarded by the Court of Appeal as being no longer of useful application.[138] Where V, who was unaware of D's infected state, had consented to the act of unprotected sexual intercourse she could not be said to have impliedly consented to the risk of infection from that intercourse. In *Dica*, the court focused, appropriately it is submitted, on the question of whether D's fraud on V related to the infection—which represents the harm alleged—rather than the intercourse. The conclusion was that the victims had been defrauded as to the risk of infection and hence had not consented to bodily harm, but had not been defrauded as to the nature of the act of sexual intercourse and hence had not been raped.[139] The nature of intercourse is the same whether with an HIV-infected person or not. Where V has not consented to the risk of infection, D could be liable under s 20 of the OAPA 1861 if he was reckless as to whether he might infect V.[140] Subsequently, in *Konzani*[141] the court emphasized that 'there is a critical distinction between taking a risk of the various, potentially adverse and possibly problematic consequences of sexual intercourse and giving an informed consent to the risk of infection with a fatal disease'.[142] D will be liable if he fails to disclose or lies about his infection and is reckless whether he infects V.

Frauds as to the *nature* of the act (which, as *Dica* demonstrates, must be accurately categorized) are clearly sufficient to vitiate consent. Following *Tabassum*, it became unclear whether a fraud as to the 'quality' of the act (rather than its nature) would be sufficient to vitiate consent. In that case, D had persuaded three women to allow him to examine their breasts by falsely informing them that he was medically qualified and conducting research work for a cancer charity. D's conviction for indecent assault was upheld. The court accepted that the women had been aware of the nature of the act of touching their breasts, but defrauded as to the 'quality' of the act—they believed it to be for a medical purpose—and that vitiated their consent.[143] This was recognized to have profound repercussions. Where D

---

[136] cf *Williams* [1923] KB 340.

[137] [2004] EWCA Crim 1103, [2004] Crim LR 944 and commentary. See references in n 114.

[138] The various aspects of that decision had been eroded by the courts over recent years, with *R* [1992] 1 AC 599 dispensing with the marital rape exemption, and *Ireland and Burstow* [1998] AC 147 accepting that 'infliction' need not involve an assault or direct contact.

[139] The Court of Appeal allowed the appeal overturning the trial judge's ruling that the decision in *Brown* [1994] 1 AC 212 deprived V of the legal capacity to consent to such serious harm and that consent provided no defence. At his retrial Dica was convicted of inflicting grievous bodily harm contrary to s 20 and sentenced to four-and-a-half years' imprisonment. The House of Lords refused leave to appeal—see House of Lords Session 2005–06, 15 Dec 2005.

[140] If D intended to infect V he would be liable under s 18 irrespective of consent.

[141] [2005] EWCA Crim 706.   [142] At [22].

[143] There is no guidance in *Tabassum* on what might constitute the 'quality' of a particular act.

has sexual intercourse with V knowing (or possibly even being reckless as to whether) he is HIV-positive, D's fraud as to the infection could, on the *Tabassum* approach, be regarded as a fraud as to the 'quality' of the act. This could render V's consent to the intercourse invalid and D would be a rapist.[144]

The question of frauds as to purpose also arises. In B,[145] the Court of Appeal rejected the argument that D who has intercourse with V and conceals his HIV status is defrauding V as to the 'purpose' of the act of intercourse. Under the Sexual Offences Act 2003, it is conclusively presumed that V did not consent if D has defrauded V as to the nature *or a purpose* of his act. The court in B concluded that concealment of HIV will not be a fraud as to purpose in sex cases. It is submitted that at common law, in relation to offences against the person where the requirement is of a fraud or mistake as to the *nature* of the act and not merely its purpose, the court is now extremely unlikely to adopt a contrary view.

It is important to point out that the facts of B were framed as involving non-disclosure rather than fraud and the Court of Appeal treated the two as quite distinct. The outcome of the case could have been different had V specifically asked D about his HIV status and he lied to her about it. The distinction that was drawn in B, between non-disclosure and fraud, was rejected by the Court in *Lawrance*, and that removes a divergence of approach between non-fatal offences and sexual offences.[146]

In terms of failure to disclose: D will not be liable for an offence against the person, if he discloses his HIV status and obtains V's consent to the risk of transmission.[147] But, in the context of sexual offences if D says nothing about his status he will only be guilty of a non-consensual sexual offence if his HIV infected status is regarded as so closely connected to the nature or purpose of the act that the failure to reveal it means that V did not freely agree and D has no reasonable belief in consent.

In terms of lies: if V asks D about his HIV status and he lies, then he may be guilty of rape and, if V is infected, offences against the person. If V is not infected, then D may be guilty of rape but nothing else.

Duress

Duress may negative apparently valid consent. A threat to imprison V unless he submitted to a beating would probably invalidate V's consent to the beating. Possibly a threat to dismiss from employment[148] or to bring a prosecution[149] would have a similar effect. It is submitted that non-criminal threats and even threats of lawful action may also be sufficient. It is unclear whether, to negative consent, the threats must be such that they would have caused a person of reasonable firmness to succumb to the violence. An alternative view would be that consent should be invalid if D knew of the particular vulnerabilities of V which caused V to succumb although they might not have caused a reasonable person to do so. If the test is whether the threat would be sufficient to overcome the will of a reasonably steadfast person, the outcome must depend to some extent on the relationship between the gravity of the threat and the act to which V is asked to submit.

---

[144] Under the Sexual Offences Act 2003, s 76 a fraud as to the 'nature or purpose' (not quality) of the act is conclusively presumed to vitiate consent. Whether other frauds vitiate consent requires consideration to be given to the terms of the general definition of consent in s 74. See Ch 17 for discussion.

[145] [2006] EWCA Crim 2945. For criticism see L Leigh, 'Two Cases on Consent in Rape' [2007] 5 Arch News 6.

[146] For further discussion, see K Laird, 'Rapist or Rogue? Deception, Consent and the Sexual Offences Act 2003' [2014] Crim LR 491.

[147] Unless he takes steps to avoid transmission and therefore might lack mens rea—eg where he uses a condom.

[148] *McCoy* 1953 (2) SA 4 (AD) (threat to ground air hostess negativing her apparent consent to being caned).

[149] *State v Volschenk* 1968 (2) PH H283 (threat to prosecute held *not* to negative consent on rape charge).

Duress may be implied from the relationship between the parties—for example, where D is a teacher and V is a young pupil.[150] As in sexual offences,[151] submission is not consent. As noted, if D genuinely believes that V is consenting, even though she is in fact only submitting, D will lack mens rea.

16.2.1.3 Legal limits on the validity of consent

Having examined the circumstances in which V's apparent consent will be invalidated, we must turn to the yet more difficult question: if V has in fact given valid consent, is that consent recognized in law? Fundamental questions of morality are raised by the extent to which the State ought to use criminal sanctions to restrict an adult with full mental capacity in his consent to the infliction of harm on his person.[152] On a public policy basis, English law restricts the validity of consent by reference to the level of harm *and* the circumstances in which it is inflicted. Factual consent to mere assault or battery is valid in law. Factual consent to actual bodily harm or more serious levels of harm (wounding, serious harm, death) is not legally recognized unless the activity involved is one which the courts or Parliament have recognized to be in the public interest. Thus, as a matter of public policy, it is no defence to a charge of murder for D to say that V asked to be killed. On the other hand, V's consent to D's taking a high degree of risk of killing him is effective where it is justified by the purpose of the act, as it may be in the case of a surgical operation. Where the act has some social purpose, recognized by the law as valid, it is a question of balancing the degree of harm which will or may be caused against the value of that purpose.

Three issues require elucidation: (1) what level of harm is caused; (2) what level of harm is foreseen or intended; and (3) whether the activity in which the harm arises is one of the exceptional categories in which consent is recognized. Unfortunately, since this is an area in which the decisions of the appellate courts are based so heavily on public policy, it is not always easy to identify clear principles.

The level of harm

Consent to an assault or battery will always be valid consent, no matter what the circumstances (eg even if it is in a sadomasochist encounter) provided the consent is effective, as discussed earlier.

If D has caused actual bodily harm—injury of more than a merely transient or trifling nature—with intent to do so,[153] the factual consent of the victim will *not* be legally valid unless the conduct falls within one of the recognized exceptional categories discussed later. It is arguable that the law should recognize a person's consent as a valid defence to at least the level of harm of ABH. The Law Commission at one time proposed raising the level of harm to which a person is entitled to consent in general circumstances to harm falling below its proposed concept of 'serious disabling injury'.[154]

The role of intention and foresight of harms

Where D has intended or has been reckless as to the causing of actual bodily harm (or worse), liability arises even if V consents, subject to the exceptional categories examined later.

---

[150] *Nichol* (1807) Russ & Ry 130.

[151] See *Doyle* [2010] EWCA Crim 119, and *Ali* [2015] EWCA Crim 1279.

[152] See Williams [1962] Crim LR 74 and 154; LCCP 139, Part II, Appendix C; P Roberts (1997) 17 OJLS 389; J Feinberg, *The Moral Limits of the Criminal Law, Vol 1: Harm to Others* (1984).

[153] And probably also in cases where he does so recklessly. See the discussion of *Dica* earlier.

[154] See LCCP 139. For criticisms of the proposal and its incoherence with the offences against the person, see Ormerod and Gunn [1996] Crim LR 694. Many jurisdictions adopt a much higher threshold: see LCCP 139, Appendix B. See also LCCP 217, Ch 5 in which it is noted that creating a new offence of minor injury might allow for the threshold of harm to which consent is valid to rise to the proposed new form of ABH.

The law has struggled with cases where D has not caused that level of harm intentionally—where he intends or is reckless as to causing only assault or battery with consent, but the conduct leads to actual bodily harm. Some *obiter dicta* suggest that D is guilty if the harm was foreseen by D (if not intended), or even if it was objectively likely to occur. The problem flowed from an overbroad statement in the *A-G's Reference (No 6 of 1980)*[155] where two youths of 18 and 17 settled an argument by a fist fight and when one sustained a bleeding nose and bruises to his face, it was held that the other was guilty of assault occasioning actual bodily harm:

> it is not in the public interest that people should try to cause or *should cause* each other actual bodily harm for no good reason. Minor struggles are another matter. So, in our judgment, it is immaterial whether the act occurs in private or in public; it is an assault if actual bodily harm *is intended and/or caused*. This means that most fights will be unlawful regardless of consent.[156]

This passage was quoted with approval by all three of the majority in the leading case of *Brown* (discussed in the following section). It is submitted, however, that it goes too far. The difficulty is the words 'or should cause' and 'and/or'. These words imply that an offence is committed if D assaults or batters V with V's consent and D does not intend to cause bodily harm, but does so in fact. The passage suggests that D will be liable even if the bodily harm was not foreseen or even foreseeable. That seems a wholly unreasonable result. Subsequent case law is difficult to reconcile with the position, and it is submitted that the *dictum* no longer represents the law.

It is submitted that the following reflects the current state of the law.

(1) D intends to cause actual bodily harm and causes that level of harm (or worse) to V with consent (or belief in V's consent) to that level of harm. V's consent is invalid unless the harm occurs in the course of conduct within an exceptional category discussed later (pp 712 et seq). Unless it is an exceptional category case, D is liable for actual bodily harm (or whatever level of injury caused with appropriate mens rea). A good illustration would be one based on the case of *Donovan*[157] where D caned V, with her consent, for their mutual sexual enjoyment. If D had intended ABH, caused ABH and had V's consent to ABH, he would still be liable because the conduct is not in an exceptional category in which the courts accept that an individual can consent to that level of harm: D would be liable under s 47.

(2) D is reckless as to causing actual bodily harm and has V's consent (or belief in V's consent) to the risk of causing that level of injury which actually occurs. It is less clear whether V's consent is invalid in all cases irrespective of whether they fall within an exceptional category. *Dicta* in *Brown* and some decisions such as *Dica* suggest that the law treats V's factual consent as invalid only in respect of intentionally inflicted harms.

(3) D intends only to make physical contact with V at the level of battery with V's consent (or a belief in V's consent), but in fact D causes actual bodily harm not intending or being reckless as to that result. According to the *dictum* in *A-G's Reference* D is guilty, it being sufficient that actual bodily harm *is* caused.[158] This *dictum* has been rejected. The Court of Appeal in *Meachen*[159] concluded, correctly it is submitted, that where D

---

[155] [1981] QB 715.   [156] *A-G's Reference (No 6 of 1980)* [1981] 2 All ER 1057 at 1059 (emphasis added).
[157] [1934] 2 KB 498.
[158] D has committed the actus reus of actual bodily harm. He has the mens rea for actual bodily harm (it being the same as for assault/battery).
[159] [2006] EWCA Crim 2414.

intends[160] to cause the level of harm amounting only to battery and has V's consent to that level of harm, if D then causes actual bodily harm or worse, without being reckless in doing so or intending to do so, he is not guilty. There is no unlawful battery as the foundational element of the actual bodily harm.[161] The facts of *Meachen* illustrate how this operates. On D's account he intentionally digitally penetrated V's anus with her consent for their mutual sexual gratification. D had no intention to cause any injury, nor did he see the risk of doing so. V suffered serious anal injury and required a colostomy. D's conviction for inflicting grievous bodily harm contrary to s 20 (and indecent assault under the Sexual Offences Act 1956) was quashed because the trial judge had erroneously ruled that V's consent could not avail D in these circumstances.

(4) The *dictum* from the *A-G's Reference* was also rejected in *Slingsby*:[162] D and V engaged in 'vigorous' sexual activity, including D inserting his hand into V's vagina and rectum. This battery was activity to which V could lawfully, and did, consent. D was wearing a signet ring which caused internal injury to V resulting in infection which led to her death. D was charged with manslaughter by an unlawful and dangerous act. Judge J ruled that it would be contrary to principle to treat as criminal, activity which would not otherwise amount to an assault merely because an injury was caused. It is respectfully submitted that this is right.

(5) The decision in *Boyea*,[163] also needs to be re-evaluated in the light of the decision in *Meachen*. In *Boyea*, D's act of inserting his hand into V's vagina and twisting it caused actual bodily harm. It was held that there was an assault because the act was 'likely' to cause harm and D was guilty of an (indecent) assault even if he did not intend or foresee that harm was likely to be caused. This suggests that if, objectively, D's conduct is likely to lead to actual bodily harm there can be no defence of consent, even if D does not intend or foresee any harm over and above the battery to which he has consent. The Court of Appeal in *Meachen*, following *dicta* in *Dica*, concluded that *Boyea* is best treated as a decision in which V had not consented even to the assault/battery in the circumstances in which it was inflicted.

(6) D intends to cause actual bodily harm with V's consent (or belief in V's consent) but in fact causes only a battery. D ought not to be convicted of that offence. Consent is a valid defence to assault/battery; D has not caused actual bodily harm.[164] In *Barnes*,[165] Lord Woolf CJ asserted that 'When no bodily harm is caused, the consent of the victim to what happened is *always* a defence to a charge.'[166] It is submitted that this is the correct approach, even though D intended a level of harm to which consent would be no defence.[167]

(7) D is reckless as to causing actual bodily harm with V's consent (or belief in V's consent) as to that risk, but in fact causes only a battery. Arguably, since D has caused only a battery and has consent to that level of harm, he ought to be acquitted.

It need hardly be said, if this analysis is correct, that the law is in a dreadfully confused and unsatisfactory state.

---

[160] The court did not have to consider the case where D is reckless as to that harm; see [43].
[161] This passage in the 11th edn was referred to in *Meachen*, at [36].
[162] [1995] Crim LR 570.   [163] (1992) 156 JP 505, [1992] Crim LR 574.
[164] cf the view in *Donovan* [1934] 2 KB 498.   [165] [2005] Crim LR 381.
[166] Para 7 (emphasis added).
[167] Arguably D may be liable for attempted actual bodily harm provided he has the requisite mens rea.

Type of activity involved

The law recognizes the factual consent of V as valid consent to ABH or more serious harm only where the harm was caused in the course of certain categories of activity.

In *Brown*, a group of sadomasochistic men who had engaged in consensual beatings and genital torture that had not resulted in any participant receiving medical attention, were convicted of offences of assault occasioning actual bodily harm. The House of Lords, by a majority of three to two, upheld the convictions. In doing so, the House specified the categories of activity in which the law would recognize effective factual consent to injury as valid in law.[168]

Subsequently, in *Barnes*,[169] Lord Woolf candidly admitted that whether a particular activity is regarded as one to which consent may be valid is a matter of public policy. This 'renders it unnecessary to find a separate jurisprudential basis for the application of the defence in various different factual contexts in which an offence could be committed'. Perhaps even more candidly still, Lord Burnett CJ in *BM* stated that, 'the special categories hitherto identified in the cases do not lend themselves to a coherent statement of underlying principle. They are at best ad hoc, and reflect the values of society recognised from time to time by the judges.'[170] Such candour will do little to satisfy those advocating the need for a clear moral foundation to the law's approach, but is not a great surprise. This policy-based approach allows the courts to maintain the incoherent list of exceptions and to add or subtract from that list based on their perception of the social utility of particular conduct and the circumstances in which it occurs. Thus, the courts may continue to allow consensual buttock branding as akin to tattooing (*Wilson*)[171] but not nipple removal or tongue slicing (*BM*)[172] or sadomasochistic caning on the buttocks (*Brown*; *Donovan*). It has been argued that these cases demonstrate that criminality depends too much on an arbitrary assignment of the activity in question into one category or another and that this arbitrariness is compounded by the fact that the same activity could conceivably fall within two categories, one in which consent would provide a defence and another in which it would not.[173]

This categorization, on grounds of perceived public utility, of activities to which consent may and may not be validly given can be illustrated by comparing the case of a fist fight and a boxing match, both of which are intended or likely to cause actual bodily harm or worse. Boxing under the Queensberry Rules, or in the words of the Lord Chief Justice in *BM* 'when organised properly as a sport',[174] is lawful. A boxer, trying to knock out his opponent, certainly has an intention to cause harm, possibly even serious harm, which is a sufficient mens rea for murder, but no prosecutions have been brought against fighters operating under the professional rules and in *Brown* all of their lordships accepted that boxing is lawful. According to Lord Mustill, boxing is best regarded as a special case which, 'for the time being stands outside the ordinary law of violence because society chooses to tolerate it'.[175]

---

[168] On this, one of the most controversial decisions of the House of Lords in that period, see LCCP 139. D Kell, 'Social Disutility and Consent' (1994) 14 OJLS 121; M Giles, 'Consensual Harm and the Public Interest' (1994) 57 MLR 101; MJ Allen, 'Consent and Assault' (1994) 58 J Crim Law 183; N Bamforth, 'Sadomasochism and Consent' [1994] Crim LR 661; P Alldridge, *Relocating Criminal Law* (2000) 122 et seq. For an interesting analysis of the issues raised by the case that it is argued have been overlooked by many commentators, see J Herring, 'R v Brown' in P Handler, H Mares and I Williams (eds), *Landmark Cases in Criminal Law* (2017).

[169] [2005] Crim LR 381.   [170] [2018] EWCA Crim 560, [24].

[171] [1996] 2 Cr App R 241.   [172] [2018] EWCA Crim 560.

[173] J Tolmie, 'Consent to Harmful Assaults: The Case for Moving Away From Category Based Decision Making' [2012] Crim LR 656.

[174] [2018] EWCA Crim 560, [38].

[175] For a full discussion, see M Gunn and D Ormerod, 'The Legality of Boxing' (1995) 15 LS 181, and LCCP 139, XII. See also S Greenfield and G Osborn (eds), *Law and Sport in Contemporary Society* (2000); J Anderson, *The Legality of Boxing: A Punch Drunk Love?* (2007).

Where, however, two youths decide to settle an argument by a fight with fists[176] and one sustains a bleeding nose and bruises to his face, the other is guilty of assault occasioning actual bodily harm.

Exceptional categories in which consent to (intentionally inflicted)[177] harm has been recognized by the courts or Parliament to be valid include the following.

Sports

The law has long recognized the social utility of sport in enhancing the fitness of the population.[178] A number of principles seem to have developed. First, although by playing the sport V consents to whatever the rules permit, if the rules permit an unacceptably dangerous act, the law need not recognize the validity of V's factual consent. That is a matter of public policy. However, boxing continues to be lawful despite the life-threatening injury and participants' intention to cause grievous bodily harm. Secondly, where unlike boxing and martial arts, playing within the rules of the particular sport does not *necessarily* involve D causing actual bodily harm, but D intentionally inflicts actual bodily harm or worse, V's consent is irrelevant and D commits the offence: *Bradshaw*.[179] Thirdly, and most difficult in practical terms to apply, if in playing such a sport D was reckless only as to the causing of the injury, the question will be whether V impliedly consented to the risk of that level of injury in the context in which it was inflicted.

The question of whether the conduct was within the rules of the game is not the sole determinant of liability.[180] It would be too simplistic to suggest that V's consent is only valid for that which the rules of the game permit. V may well, as a matter of fact, impliedly consent to the *risk* of injury occurring in conduct outside the rules as in a late tackle in football, or an illegitimate bouncer in cricket.[181] It is therefore necessary to look to a broader range of factors. In *Barnes*, the Court of Appeal confirmed that it is appropriate to make an objective evaluation of these circumstances. The court adopted the approach in Canadian law[182] and advocated at one time by the Law Commission.[183] Relevant circumstances include the type of sport, the level at which it was being played, the nature of the act, the degree of force used, the extent of the risk of injury and D's state of mind. Prosecution is usually reserved for sufficiently grave conduct deserving to be regarded as criminal, having regard to the fact that most organized sports have their own disciplinary procedures and to the availability of civil remedies. What is accepted in one sport might not be covered by the implied consent

---

[176] A 'prize-fight' in public is unlawful at common law as a breach of the peace tending to public disorder. *Brown* [1993] 2 All ER 75 at 79, 86, 106, 119. Because the whole enterprise is unlawful, consent is not a defence even to a charge of common assault against the contestants: *Coney* (1882) 8 QBD 534.

[177] See earlier. Arguably the consent defence is only invalid where D has *intentionally* caused harm. See further *Dica* discussed earlier.

[178] See LCCP 139, Part XII and M Cutcheon, 'Sports, Violence and the Criminal Law' (1994) 45 NILQ 267. For an analysis that questions the objective approach to consent in sports, but denying the need for a uniform approach throughout the criminal law, see B Livings, 'A Different Ball Game' (2007) 71 J Crim L 534, disputing the arguments in C Elliott and C de Than, 'The Case for a Rational Reconstruction of Consent in Criminal Law' (2007) 70 MLR 225 who call for a unitary approach to consent throughout the criminal law. More recently, see M James, 'Consent—Revisiting the Exemption for Contact Sports' in A Reed and M Bohlander (with N Wake and E Smith) (eds), *Consent: Domestic and Comparative Perspectives* (2017).

[179] (1878) Cox CC 83.   [180] ibid.   [181] See *Moore* (1898) 14 TLR 229.

[182] See *Cicarelli* (1989) 54 CCC (3d) 121.

[183] LCCP 134. That approach was criticized by S Gardiner, 'The Law and the Sports Field' [1994] Crim LR 513, see also S Gardiner, 'Should More Matches End in Court' (2005) 155 NLJ 998 but received generally favourable responses: LCCP 139, paras 12.6–12.23. On *Barnes*, see also J Anderson, 'No Licence for Thuggery: Violence, Sport and the Criminal Law' [2008] Crim LR 751. See also B Livings [2018] Crim LR 430 on the CPS policy on prosecution in such cases.

in another. In highly competitive sports, conduct 'outside the rules' might be expected to occur in the heat of the moment, but even if such conduct justified not only being penalized but, for example, being sent off, it might not reach the threshold required for it to be criminal.

Horseplay

This exception is not confined to organized games. Consent by children to rough and undisciplined play may be a defence to a charge of inflicting grievous bodily harm if there is no intention to cause injury.[184] Equally, a genuine belief in consent, even an unreasonable belief, apparently leads to acquittal: *Jones*[185] where boys were injured by being tossed in the air by schoolmates. The decision recognizes that children have always indulged in rough and undisciplined play among themselves and probably always will; but the non-consenting child is rightly protected by the criminal law. The 'horseplay' exception seems to have been taken to extreme lengths in *Aitken*,[186] where the 'robust games' of Royal Air Force officers at a celebration in the mess included setting fire to one another's fire-resistant clothing. Two such incidents apparently caused no harm but on a third occasion V sustained severe burns. It was held that a ruling that it was not open to the court-martial to find that the 'activities' were lawful was wrong. If V consented to them, or if D believed, reasonably or not, that V consented to them, it was open to the trial court to find that there was no offence.

The courts have emphasized that horseplay can only be relied upon where V is consenting or D genuinely believes that to be the case. In the case of *A*,[187] D dropped V, a non-swimmer, off a bridge into a river where V drowned. V had been fighting for this not to happen and was clearly not consenting, nor was it credible that D believed he was. D's conviction for manslaughter was upheld.

Surgery

Consent to a surgical operation[188] for a purpose recognized as valid by the law is effective.[189] This includes gender reassignment surgery[190] and, presumably, cosmetic surgery and organ transplants. Where an adult of full mental capacity refuses consent to medical treatment, a failure to respect that decision will render the doctor liable for criminal offences, even in circumstances in which the treatment will be life-preserving.[191]

Body modification

Having one's hair cut is clearly lawful. Since cutting hair might amount to actual bodily harm, it is implicit that the law recognizes that consent to that activity will prevent liability: *DPP v Smith*.[192] Ritual[193] circumcision of males,[194] ear-piercing and tattooing of adults

---

[184] See LCCP 139.   [185] [1987] Crim LR 123.

[186] [1992] 1 WLR 1006, at 1011 (C-MAC).   [187] [2005] All ER 38 (D).

[188] See LCCP 139, Part VIII.

[189] Stephen, *Digest*, art 310. See P Skegg, 'Medical Procedures and the Crime of Battery' [1974] Crim LR 693 and (1973) 36 MLR 370. It was held in *BM* [2018] EWCA Crim 560 that there is a clear difference between surgery and body modification.

[190] *Corbett v Corbett* [1971] P 83 at 99.

[191] *St George's Healthcare NHS Trust v S* [1998] 3 All ER 673. See also the discussion previously of the Mental Capacity Act 2005.

[192] [2006] EWHC 94 (Admin).

[193] ie that performed otherwise than for medical reasons. See further LCCP 139. See *Brown* [1994] 1 AC 212 and *Re J* [2000] 1 FCR 307, CA (Civ). Professor Feldman advised the Law Commission that non-therapeutic circumcision might be in breach of Art 3 of the ECHR, para 3.25; see further H Gilbert, 'Time to Reconsider the Lawfulness of Ritual Male Circumcision' [2007] EHRLR 279; PW Edge, 'Male Circumcision after the Human Rights Act' (1998) 5 J Civil Liberties 320, see also L Vickers, 'Circumcision—The Unkindest Cut of All?' (2000) 150 NLJ 1694.

[194] See the Female Genital Mutilation Act 2003. Amendments made by the Serious Crime Act 2015, ss 70–5 extend the extraterritorial effect of the offence. By s 72, a new s 3A creates an offence of failing to protect a girl from the risk of genital mutilation (punishable on indictment with up to seven years' imprisonment).

are generally assumed to be lawful.[195] Presumably the same is true of some of the more exotic body-piercing of adults, although the Court of Appeal has held that unlicensed activities such as tongue splitting and ear removal cannot be consented to. In *BM*, Lord Burnett CJ appeared to go further and suggest that body modification was not an exceptional category:[196]

> we can see no good reason why body modification should be placed in a special category of exemption from the general rule that the consent of an individual to injury provides no defence to the person who inflicts that injury if the violence causes actual bodily harm or more serious injury. Even were the general rule to be revisited by Parliament or the Supreme Court and a different line drawn which allows consent to act as a defence to causing actual bodily harm and wounding, body modification causes really serious harm.

It is submitted that that statement is overbroad and should not be interpreted as casting doubt on the validity of consent in relation to hair cutting, body piercing, ritual male circumcision, etc (all of which are very different from the type of body modification being considered by the court in *BM*, which Lord Burnett CJ characterized as a series of *medical procedures* performed for no medical reason).

In *Wilson*,[197] D's branding of his initials on his wife's buttocks, at her request, in lieu of tattooing, was held to be equally lawful. The only distinction from *Donovan*[198] appears to be that Donovan's motive in caning V was sexual gratification whereas Wilson's was to bestow on his wife an adornment which she desired. Where the purpose of the act is one which the law condemns, consent may be no answer to the charge.[199] This is now the case with ear removal and tongue splitting, despite the fact that the customer may desire such extreme body modification.

Coke tells us that in 1604, 'a young strong and lustie rogue, to make himself impotent, thereby to have the more colour to begge or to be relieved without putting himself to any labour, caused his companion to strike off his left hand' and that both of them were convicted of mayhem.[200] Maiming, even with consent, was unlawful because it deprived the king of a fighting man. In early Victorian times when soldiers, as part of their training drill, had to bite cartridges, a soldier got a dentist to pull out his front teeth to avoid the drill. Stephen J thought that both were guilty of a crime.[201] Denning LJ followed these instances in discussing, *obiter*, the legality of a sterilization operation.[202] His opinion (that the operation is unlawful if done only to enable the man to have the pleasure of intercourse without the responsibility) is no longer tenable,[203] but it illustrates the continuing and changing influence of public policy.

---

[195] On consent in relation to medical treatment and body modification, see T Elliott, 'Body Dismorphic Disorder, Radical Surgery and the Limits of Consent' (2009) 17 Med L Rev 149. See also See LCCP 139, Part IX.

[196] *BM* [2018] EWCA Crim 560. On which see S Pegg, 'Not So Clear Cut: The Lawfulness of Body Modifications' [2019] Crim LR 579; R Clement, 'Consent to Body Modification in Criminal Law' (2018) 77 CLJ 451; R Williams, 'Body Modification and the Limits of Consent to Injury' (2019) 135 LQR 19. See also *Oversby* (1990) unreported, cited in LCCP 139, para 9.7.

[197] [1996] Crim LR 573.   [198] [1934] 2 KB 498.

[199] The court was also influenced by the fact that W was married to his victim, but this must be an irrelevance. If the criminal law governing consensual injury is applied differently to homosexuals and heterosexuals (or to men and women) or on the basis of marriage, this would almost certainly involve a violation of Arts 8 and 14 of the ECHR taken together.

[200] Co 1 Inst, 127a and b.   [201] *Digest* (3rd edn) 142.

[202] *Bravery v Bravery* [1954] 3 All ER 59 at 67, 68.

[203] The National Health Service (Family Planning) Amendment Act 1972 first authorized vasectomy services.

In circumstances where the body modification is for religious reasons, reliance on Art 9 of the ECHR guaranteeing respect for religious freedom would support the validity of consent. However, the courts have been unwilling to accommodate foreign cultural practices involving children, such as incision of cheeks.[204] In view of the recognition that ritual male circumcision practised by Jews and Muslims is lawful, the law's approach appears incoherent.

Sadomasochism

Sadomasochism beyond that amounting to mere assault or battery is not an activity that can be consented to.[205] There is, at common law, no defence of 'consent to rough sex' where the level of harm caused is ABH or more and D intended or foresaw that level of harm. This has been clear since at least the decision in *Brown*.

Public policy is clearly at the root of the decision in *Brown*. In the opinion of the majority, policy requires the conviction of men participating in consensual sadomasochistic encounters, resulting in actual bodily harm and wounding, to protect society against a cult of violence with the danger of the corruption and proselytization of young men and the potential for the infliction of serious injury: this notwithstanding that there was in fact no permanent injury, no infection and no evidence of medical attention being required.[206] The majority's reasoning that this was violence rather than sexual activity led to the conclusion that the activity should be unlawful.[207]

Public policy was invoked to justify conviction for a relatively slight degree of harm in *Donovan*.[208] D, for his sexual gratification, beat a 17-year-old girl with a cane in circumstances of indecency. He was convicted of both indecent assault and common assault. The judge failed to direct the jury that the onus of proving there was no consent was on the prosecution, but the Court of Criminal Appeal held that, if the blows were likely or intended to cause bodily harm, this omission was immaterial because D was guilty whether V consented or not.[209]

In *Brown*, the whole House agreed that consent is a complete defence to the two offences—common and indecent assault—with which Donovan was charged. The Court of Criminal Appeal's opinion (that he could have been convicted of these offences because he was guilty of assault occasioning actual bodily harm, an offence with which he was not charged), was unacceptable in *Brown* to both Lord Lowry[210] of the majority and Lord Mustill[211] of the minority. Subsequent cases nevertheless seem to treat the *dicta* in *Donovan* as correct, but

---

[204] *Adesanya* (1974) The Times, 16 July. See S Poulter, 'Foreign Customs and the English Criminal Law' (1975) 24 ICLQ 136.

[205] See LCCP 139, Part X.

[206] The majority cited no empirical evidence to substantiate their claim that those who engage in consensual sadomasochistic cruelty are prone to have their inhibitions loosened and escalate their conduct to more harmful acts of cruelty. See J Tolmie, 'Consent to Harmful Assaults: The Case for Moving Away From Category Based Decision Making' [2012] Crim LR 656.

[207] Peter Murphy argues that the real motivation for sadomasochistic acts is sexual gratification and therefore suggests it would be more appropriate to charge D with a sexual offence in such cases. See P Murphy, 'Flogging Live Complainants and Dead Horses: We May No Longer Need to Be in Bondage to *Brown*' [2011] Crim LR 758.

[208] [1934] 2 KB 498. See L Leigh, 'Sado-Masochism, Consent and the Reform of the Criminal Law' (1976) 39 MLR 130.

[209] The conviction was quashed because the question whether the blows were likely or intended to cause bodily harm was not put to the jury.

[210] 'If the jury, properly directed, had found that consent was not disproved, they must have acquitted the appellant of the only charges brought against him' [1993] 2 All ER 75 at 97.

[211] 'There is something amiss here' [1993] 2 All ER 75 at 112.

in the light of the decision in *Meachen* discussed earlier, it is submitted that if D intended to inflict only a battery, the consent he had to that level of harm should mean there is no criminal liability unless D intentionally or recklessly inflicted actual bodily harm.

In *Wilson* (wife's buttock branding),[212] the conduct was held to fall within an exceptional category on the basis that, unlike Donovan, Wilson was not seeking sexual gratification—his conduct was like that of a professional tattooist who embellishes (intimate) parts at the request of their owner.[213]

The decision in *Wilson* was distinguished, and *Brown* followed, in a further case of sado-masochism: *Emmett*.[214] D's conviction for recklessly occasioning actual bodily harm to V by, inter alia, setting fire to lighter fuel on her breasts with her consent, was upheld by the Court of Appeal. The court described the conduct as going 'beyond that which was established in *Wilson*'. But the charge was the same—assault occasioning actual bodily harm. Are the courts to start evaluating the validity of consent on the basis of some undeclared judicial barometer of the severity of harm? In *Meachen* and in *Dica*, *Emmett* appears to have been treated as a case of intentional infliction of actual bodily harm.

Rough sex

As noted, there is no defence of 'rough sex' to s 47, 20 or 18 OAPA at common law. Factual consent to causing that level of harm with intent is not a defence. Nevertheless, Parliament has chosen to attempt to reiterate that in statute.

Parliament has responded to concerns[215] about the use of the so-called 'rough sex defence' by introducing s 71 of the Domestic Abuse Act 2021. Section 71 seeks to address this by providing that:

71 Consent to serious harm for sexual gratification not a defence

(1) This section applies for the purposes of determining whether a person ('D') who inflicts serious harm on another person ('V') is guilty of a relevant offence.

(2) It is not a defence that V consented to the infliction of the serious harm for the purposes of obtaining sexual gratification (but see subsection (4)).

(3) In this section
—'relevant offence' means an offence under section 18, 20 or 47 of the Offences Against the Person Act 1861 ('the 1861 Act');
'serious harm' means—

(a) grievous bodily harm, within the meaning of section 18 of the1861 Act,

(b) wounding, within the meaning of that section, or

(c) actual bodily harm, within the meaning of section 47 of the 1861Act.

(4) Subsection (2) does not apply in the case of an offence under section 20 or 47 of the 1861 Act where—

(a) the serious harm consists of, or is a result of, the infection of V with a sexually transmitted infection in the course of sexual activity, and

(b) V consented to the sexual activity in the knowledge or belief that D had the sexually transmitted infection.

---

[212] [1996] Crim LR 573.

[213] In *Laskey* (a reference on the *Brown* case), the European Court distinguished *Wilson* because the injuries were not at all 'comparable in seriousness' with those in *Brown* even though they equally amounted to assault occasioning actual bodily harm

[214] (1999) The Times, 15 Oct.

[215] See the powerful campaign at https://wecantconsenttothis.uk/.

(5) For the purposes of this section it does not matter whether the harm was inflicted for the purposes of obtaining sexual gratification for D, V or some other person.

(6) Nothing in this section affects any enactment or rule of law relating to other circumstances in which a person's consent to the infliction of serious harm may, or may not, be a defence to a relevant offence.

The section appears to do no more than state the clear position at common law.

In truth, it seeks to address a different problem and it fails to do so. The problem that it really seeks to address is where D, charged with murder or manslaughter, claims that V's death was a result of rough sex (usually involving choking) in which D and V were consensually engaged. If the battery (the gripping of the neck) is consented to, then there is no unlawful act on which a manslaughter charge can be constructed: *Slingsby*.[216] Section 71 has no impact on such a case if D claims that he had consent to cause a battery and that he did not intend graver harm: see *Meachen*, *Slingsby*. Section 71 would serve to deny D a defence where he claims that V consented to more serious harms in the course of their sadomasochistic activity.

Religious flagellation

In *Brown*, Lord Mustill accepted this as a recognized, though rarely practised, exception. The protection of religious freedoms under Art 9 of the ECHR would support such a conclusion.[217]

The risk of sexually transmitted infection

The decision of the Court of Appeal in *Dica*[218] is that an adult is entitled to give valid consent to the risk of being infected with a potentially lethal sexually transmitted disease such as HIV.[219] The court distinguished between consensual acts of sexual intercourse where there might be a known risk to the health of one or other participants (consent valid) and those cases where participants were intent on spreading, or becoming infected with, disease (consent invalid). The court took the view that criminalization of consensual taking of risks would involve an 'impracticality of enforcement' and would undermine the general understanding of the community that sexual relationships were 'pre-eminently private'. Such arguments had not persuaded the House of Lords in *Brown*, albeit that case involved intentional harm. Many will find unconvincing the distinction in *Dica* between 'sexual' and 'violent' acts, with cases such as *Emmett* and *Boyea* treated as having 'sexual overtones' but being really concerned with 'violent crime'. These cases must all be read carefully in the light of *Meachen*. In *Konzani*,[220] the court confirmed that the consent will only be valid if V is informed of the risk of infection.

ECHR compatibility

The case of *Brown* was considered by the ECtHR in *Laskey v UK*,[221] with the Court unanimously holding that the prosecution, conviction and sentence did not contravene Art 8 of the ECHR.[222] It should be noted that the Court doubted whether the activities even fell

---

[216] Discussed in Ch 14, p 595.
[217] See LCCP 139, paras 10.2–10.7. However, note the conviction of Syed Mustafa Zaidi, a Shia Muslim, for child cruelty after he forced two boys (13 and 15) to whip themselves during a religious ritual using a handled implement with curved blades. See news reports for 28 Aug 2008.
[218] [2004] EWCA 1103, [2004] Crim LR 944 and commentary.
[219] For discussion of the potential criminalization of other types of infectious disease, see K Laird, 'Criminalising Contagion—Questioning the Paradigm' in H Quirk and C Stanton (eds), *Criminalising Contagion: Legal and Ethical Challenges of Disease Transmission and the Criminal Law* (2016).
[220] [2005] EWCA Crim 706.
[221] (1997) 24 EHRR 39; L Moran, 'Learning the Limits of Privacy' (1998) 61 MLR 77. See also *KA & AD v Belgium* (App no 42758/98) 2005.
[222] LCCP 139, Part III.

within the protection of Art 8. On the assumption that they did, the Court concluded that the prosecution was necessary and proportionate to the legitimate aim of the protection of health (and possibly also the protection of morals). The Court recognized that the margin of appreciation provided national courts the scope to prescribe the level of physical harm to which the law should permit an adult to consent.

16.2.2 Lawful chastisement

It was always the common law rule that punishment was unlawful:[223]

If it be administered for the gratification of passion or rage or if it be immoderate or excessive in its nature or degree, or if it be protracted beyond the child's powers of endurance or with an instrument unfitted for the purpose and calculated to produce danger to life and limb . . .[224]

In *A v UK*,[225] the rule of the common law entitling parents to inflict moderate and reasonable physical chastisement on their children was held to offend Art 3 of the ECHR, prohibiting torture and inhuman or degrading treatment or punishment. In that case, a jury had acquitted a man who had caned his nine-year-old stepson. It was accepted that the law then needed reform but there was considerable disagreement as what form reform should take. The English courts continued to acknowledge the parental right to chastise: *H*.[226] The judge had to give detailed directions to the jury to take account of the nature, context and duration of D's behaviour, the physical and mental effect on the child, the reasons for the punishment, and so on.

16.2.2.1 The Children Act 2004

Section 58 of the Children Act 2004 now provides:

(1) In relation to any offence specified in subsection (2), battery of a child cannot be justified on the ground that it constituted reasonable punishment.

(2) The offences referred to in subsection (1) are—

(a) an offence under section 18 or 20 of the Offences against the Person Act 1861 (wounding and causing grievous bodily harm);

(b) an offence under section 47 of that Act (assault occasioning actual bodily harm); an offence under section 1 of the Children and Young Persons Act 1933 (cruelty to persons under 16).

(3) Battery of a child causing actual bodily harm to the child cannot be justified in any civil proceedings on the ground that it constituted reasonable punishment.

(4) For the purposes of subsection (3) 'actual bodily harm' has the same meaning as it has for the purposes of section 47 of the Offences against the Person Act 1861.

---

[223] For a valuable discussion, see H Keating, 'Protecting or Punishing Children: Physical Punishment, Human Rights and English Law Reform' (2006) 26 LS 394.

[224] *Hopley* (1860) 2 F & F 202 at 206 per Cockburn CJ. Cf *Smith* [1985] Crim LR 42.

[225] [1998] TLR 578, (1999) 27 EHRR 611. See also *Costello-Roberts v UK* (1993) 19 EHRR 112 (seven-year-old slippered at public school); *Y v UK* (1992) 17 EHRR 238 (16-year-old caned at school). See generally B Phillips, 'The Case for Corporal Punishment in the UK—Beaten into Submission in Europe' (1994) 43 ICLQ 153.

[226] [2002] 1 Cr App R 59. J Rogers, 'A Criminal Lawyer's Response to Chastisement in the European Court' [2002] Crim LR 98; for trenchant criticism of the law, see C Barton, 'Hitting Your Children: Common Assault or Common Sense' [2008] Fam Law 65.

The effect is that reasonable and proportionate punishment amounting only to an assault or battery (that does not involve cruelty) is still protected by the defence of lawful chastisement. There is no longer a defence of lawful chastisement for punishment that involves a touching of the child and which constitutes the higher level of harm—actual bodily harm or cruelty.[227]

Given the ambiguity of the boundary between assault and actual bodily harm, neither parents nor children have gained a clear position of their rights. Reliance on Art 9 of the ECHR by parents claiming a right to inflict corporal punishment as an aspect of their religion will not preclude prosecution.[228]

In Wales, the Children (Abolition of Defence of Reasonable Chastisement) (Wales) Act 2020 will make the use of force against children as a form of chastisement unlawful from March 2022.[229]

The CPS reviewed a sample of cases where a child was assaulted by a parent or an adult acting *in loco parentis* after the coming into force of s 58 of the Children Act 2004. The report identified 12 cases where the reasonable chastisement defence was raised, which resulted in an acquittal or discontinuance. The report concluded that there is 'evidence to suggest that there have been cases where defendants charged with common assault have been acquitted or the case was discontinued, after running the reasonable chastisement defence. Of those cases, the file review suggests that it was possible that some defendants could have been charged differently.'[230]

16.2.2.2 Corporal punishment in schools

At common law, school teachers were in the same position as parents with regard to the conduct of the child at or on his way to or from school.[231] Now, by s 548 of the Education Act 1996, a 'member of staff' of a school has no right, by virtue of his position as such, to administer corporal punishment to a child.[232] 'Corporal punishment' does not include anything done for the purposes of averting an immediate danger of personal injury or damage to property (s 548(5)). Staff may use reasonable force to search a pupil for a prohibited item (ss 550ZA and 550ZB)[233] or to restrain pupils who are violent or disruptive (s 93 of the Education and Inspections Act 2006).

16.2.3 Necessity

As noted in Ch 10, necessity may negative what would otherwise be an assault, as where D pushes V out of the path of a vehicle which is about to run him down. The fire officer, the paramedic, the surgeon and nurse may all do things to a person rendered unconscious in

---

[227] A case may arise where, on the same facts, a charge under s 47 would be available but a prosecution for common assault would fail because of the defence.

[228] *R (on the application of Williamson) v Secretary of State for Education and Employment* [2002] EWCA Civ 1820. Confirmed in *R (Williamson) v Secretary of State for Education* [2005] UKHL 15. Baroness Hale's speech warrants close attention on these matters. See also *Seven Individuals v Sweden* (App no 8811/79) 29 DR 104, ECommHR. The ECHR issues are discussed in Emmerson, Ashworth and Macdonald, HR&CJ, paras 18–19. See also the conviction of Syed Mustafa Zaidi for child cruelty after he forced two boys (13 and 15) to whip themselves during a religious ritual. See news reports for 28 Aug 2008.

[229] Children (Abolition of Defence of Reasonable Chastisement) (Wales) Act 2020.

[230] *Reasonable Chastisement Research Report* (2007), http://dera.ioe.ac.uk/6886/10/chastisement.html.

[231] *Cleary v Booth* [1893] 1 QB 465; *Newport (Salop) Justices* [1929] 2 KB 416; *Mansell v Griffin* [1908] 1 KB 160.

[232] As substituted by the School Standards and Framework Act 1998.

[233] The powers in ss 550ZA and 550ZB apply only to schools in England. In Wales, members of staff may use reasonable force to search for weapons: s 550AA.

an accident, or by sudden illness, which would ordinarily be battery (or, in the case of the surgeon, wounding or grievous bodily harm) if done without consent; but they commit no offence if they are only doing what is necessary to save life or ensure improvement, or prevent deterioration, in health.[234]

Perhaps this is based on the presumption that V would consent if he knew of the circumstances, a principle which excuses conduct in other parts of the criminal law.[235] This is consistent with the view[236] that intervention cannot be justified if it is against V's known wishes.

So it seems that a passerby who prevents V, an adult of mental capacity, from committing suicide by dragging him from the parapet of a bridge is guilty of battery.[237]

16.2.4 Self-help

The circumstances in which a person may use reasonable force to protect himself or his property are dealt with in Ch 10. The Criminal Justice and Immigration Act 2008 regulates most such circumstances. *Burns*[238] dealt with a situation falling outside the scope of that Act. B was not in danger or protecting himself, others or his property. B was convicted of causing actual bodily harm to a sex worker V. B had picked her up, agreed a price for sex and driven her to a secluded place. He then changed his mind about the sex act and asked her to get out of his car. She refused to get out until he drove her back to where they had met. He forcibly removed her, causing minor injury. The Court of Appeal, having referred to authority from the seventeenth century, dismissed B's argument that he was entitled to use force as V became a trespasser on his property when he asked her to leave and she refused. B had not acted in self-defence nor in defence of anyone else; he had not been defending his property against threat or risk of damage; he was not acting for any purpose within s 3 of the Criminal Law Act 1967. The defence was one of 'self-help'. That defence was always a last resort. It was a defence which the common law would be reluctant to extend. Lord Judge CJ added:

Recognising that to be lawful the use of force must always be reasonable in the circumstances, we accept that it might be open to the owner of a vehicle, in the last resort and when all reasonably practicable alternatives have failed, forcibly to remove an individual who has entered into his vehicle without permission and refuses to leave it. However, where that individual entered the car as a passenger, in effect at the invitation of the car owner, on the basis that they mutually understood that when their dealings were completed she would be driven back in the car from whence she had come, the use of force to remove her at the appellant's unilateral whim, was unlawful.

16.3 Assault occasioning actual bodily harm

By s 47 of the OAPA 1861, 'whosoever shall be convicted on indictment of any assault occasioning actual bodily harm shall be liable to imprisonment for not more than five years'.

---

[234] *F v West Berkshire Health Authority* [1989] 2 All ER 545 at 564 at 566 per Lord Goff.

[235] eg the Theft Act 1968, ss 2(1)(b), 12(6), Criminal Damage Act 1971, s 5(2)(b).

[236] *F v West Berks*, n 235, at 566 per Lord Goff.

[237] cf Williams, TBCL, 616. Otherwise, perhaps, if V is in police custody: *Kirkham v Chief Constable of the Greater Manchester Police* [1990] 2 QB 283.

[238] [2010] EWCA Crim 1023.

16.3.1 Actus reus

16.3.1.1 Assault or battery

On its face, the section does not appear to create a separate offence but merely to provide a higher penalty for an assault at common law where actual bodily harm is occasioned, that is, caused. Historically, the offence was treated as a common law offence until the decision in *Courtie*,[239] and indeed for a period thereafter because it took some time for 'the penny to drop'. The current law is now clear that s 47 created a separate statutory offence[240] or, more accurately, two offences, assault occasioning actual bodily harm and battery occasioning actual bodily harm. Confusion on this still persists. For example, Lord Ackner in *Savage*[241] at one point describes the mens rea of the offence exclusively in terms of the battery and, at another, exclusively in terms of the assault. It is safe to assume that there are two offences and that their constituents, so far as the word 'assault' goes, are precisely the same as those of common assault and battery discussed previously. Most cases will involve battery, but not all. An assault occasioning actual bodily harm might be committed by words or gestures alone, without the need for any physical contact between the assailant and the body of the victim. D may cause V to apprehend immediate unlawful violence and V might injure himself in making reasonable escape attempts.

16.3.1.2 Occasioning

Once an assault or battery with appropriate mens rea is proved, it remains only to prove that it occasioned actual bodily harm. That is a question of causation[242] not requiring proof of any further mens rea or fault. This was established in *Roberts*,[243] where D in a moving car 'assaulted' V by trying to take off her coat (a battery), whereupon she jumped out and sustained injury. It was held that the only question was whether the 'assault' caused V's action—only if it was something that no reasonable person could be expected to foresee would the chain of causation be broken.[244] It is now firmly established that this is the law, after a remarkable series of cases had thrown the matter into doubt.[245] In *Savage* and *Parmenter*, the House of Lords held that the law was correctly stated in *Roberts*.[246]

The offence may be committed in circumstances of omission where D has created a dangerous situation, as in the case of *Santana-Bermudez v DPP*.[247]

16.3.1.3 Bodily harm

'Bodily harm', according to the House of Lords in *DPP v Smith*,[248] 'needs no explanation'. Since 'Grievous means no more and no less than really serious' it seems to follow that, under s 47, the harm need not be really serious. In *Miller*,[249] it was described as any hurt or injury calculated to interfere with the health or comfort of the victim. This is a very

---

[239] [1984] AC 463, [1984] 1 All ER 740, p 32.   [240] *Harrow Justices, ex p Osaseri* [1986] QB 589.

[241] [1991] 4 All ER 698 at 707 and 711.

[242] cf the view of J Gardner, 'Rationality and the Rule of Law in Offences Against the Person' (1994) 53 CLJ 502 at 509; J Gardner, *Offences and Defences: Selected Essays in the Philosophy of Criminal Law* (2007). See also J Stanton-Ife, 'Horrific Crimes' in RA Duff et al (eds), *Boundaries of the Criminal Law* (2010).

[243] (1971) 56 Cr App R 95.

[244] cf *Williams and Davies* (1991) 95 Cr App R 1.

[245] In *Spratt* [1991] 2 All ER 210, the court, very properly overruling *DPP v K* [1990] 1 All ER 331, held that only *Cunningham*, not *Caldwell*, recklessness would suffice to establish the assault but then went on, not referring to *Roberts*, to hold there must be recklessness as to the occasioning of actual bodily harm. *Savage* [1991] 2 All ER 220, decided on the same day, applied the law as stated in *Roberts* but without reference to that case. In *Parmenter* [1991] 2 All ER 225, the court, confronted with this conflict, preferred *Spratt*, again without reference to *Roberts*.

[246] [1992] 1 AC 699, reversing *Parmenter* (CA) and overruling *Spratt* on this point.

[247] [2003] Crim LR 471, discussed previously.

[248] [1961] AC 290 at 334.   [249] [1954] 2 QB 282.

low threshold for an offence carrying a five-year maximum sentence in the Crown Court. It includes a temporary loss of consciousness.[250] It would seem sufficient that the harm was more than merely transient and trifling.[251] It can include the cutting of a substantial amount of hair.[252] In *DPP v Smith*, the court held that having regard to the dictionary definitions, in ordinary language 'harm' was not limited to 'injury' and extended to 'hurt' or 'damage'. 'Bodily', whether used as an adjective or adverb, was 'concerned with the body'. It is settled law that evidence of external bodily injury, or a break in or bruise to the surface of the skin, is not required for there to be actual bodily harm. 'Bodily' encompasses all parts of the body including the victim's organs, his nervous system and his brain. Physical pain caused by the assault or battery is not a necessary ingredient of the offence, otherwise there could be no conviction where V was unconscious. Bodily harm can occur whether the tissue is alive beneath the surface of the skin or dead tissue above the surface of the skin; thus, hair is an attribute and part of the human body. There is no need for the harm to be permanent: a bruise suffices. The fact that hair will regrow is irrelevant; cutting hair is bodily harm.

It has been held that actual bodily harm is not limited to physical injury. It includes psychiatric injury. This represents a significant judicial extension of the offence. Neurotic disorders are included because they affect the central nervous system of the body, but emotions such as fear and anxiety ('brain functions') are not. While physical injury is within the ordinary experience of a jury, psychiatric injury is not; so, if the prosecution wish to rely on it, they must call expert evidence to prove that the alleged condition amounts to psychiatric injury.[253] Even where the victim can give evidence of physical and mental symptoms of psychiatric injury, expert evidence is necessary to prove causation.[254] The Court of Appeal has declined to extend the scope of the offence: psychological injury, not amounting to an identified or recognized psychological condition, cannot amount to 'bodily harm'.[255]

The CPS Charging Standard recommends s 47 be charged for injuries which are 'serious'. In determining 'seriousness', relevant factors may include the fact that there has been significant medical intervention, or that permanent effects have resulted. Examples may include injuries requiring a number of stitches (but not superficial steri-strips) or a hospital procedure under anaesthetic. Psychological harm which involves 'more than mere emotions such as fear, distress or panic' may suffice for this offence.[256]

16.3.2 Mens rea

The only mens rea that needs to be proved is the mens rea for the assault or battery. There is no mens rea requirement as to the bodily harm.

The absence of any requirement that D intends or foresees the additional harm for which he is punished over and above an assault or battery demonstrates the lack of correspondence of actus reus and mens rea in the offence and the conflict with the general principles of subjectivism.[257] This is a very clear example of a constructive crime.

---

[250] *T v DPP* [2003] Crim LR 622.   [251] ibid.

[252] *DPP v Smith* [2006] EWHC 94 (Admin). Presumably the same is true if D damages V's hair substantially by applying a permanent colouring.

[253] *Ireland* [1998] AC 147, [1997] 4 All ER 225 at 230–3, approving *Chan-Fook* [1994] 2 All ER 552. See also LCCP 217, Ch 5.

[254] *Morris* [1998] 1 Cr App R 386.   [255] *Dhaliwal* [2006] EWCA Crim 1139.

[256] (2005). See www.cps.gov.uk/legal-guidance/offences-against-person-incorporating-charging-standard#14382.

[257] Its constructive nature is defended on the basis that D has 'altered his normative position' towards V by choosing to assault V, and therefore must take the consequences of the further harm. See J Gardner (1994) 53 CLJ 502; J Horder, 'A Critique of the Correspondence Principle in Criminal Law' [1995] Crim LR 759. Cf B Mitchell, 'In Defence of a Principle of Correspondence' [1999] Crim LR 195. See on this the important article by A Ashworth, 'A Change of Normative Position: Determining the Contours of Culpability in Criminal Law' [2008] 11 New Crim LR 232. See also I Hare, 'A Compelling Case for the Code' (1993) 56 MLR 74.

16.4 Wounding and grievous bodily harm: OAPA 1861, s 20

Section 20 of the OAPA 1861 creates two forms of offence: wounding and inflicting grievous bodily harm. By s 20:

Whosoever shall unlawfully and maliciously wound or inflict any grievous bodily harm upon any other person, either with or without any weapon or instrument shall be guilty of [an offence triable either way] and being convicted thereof shall be liable to imprisonment for five years.

The two ways of committing the offence are: (a) malicious wounding, and (b) maliciously inflicting grievous bodily harm.

The element of unlawfulness should not be overlooked and should always be drawn to the jury's attention.[258]

16.4.1 Malicious wounding

16.4.1.1 To wound

In order to constitute a wound, the continuity of the whole skin must be broken.[259] Where a pellet fired by an air pistol hit V in the eye but caused only an internal rupturing of blood vessels and not a break in the skin, there was no wound.[260] It is not enough that the cuticle or outer skin be broken if the inner skin remains intact.[261] Where V was treated with such violence that his collarbone was broken, it was held that there was no wound if his skin was intact.[262] It was held to be a wound, however, where the lining membrane of the urethra was ruptured and bled. Evidence was given that that membrane is precisely the same in character as the membrane lining the cheek and the external and internal skin of the lip.[263] It is wrong to direct a jury that 'the surface of the skin' must be broken. On that direction a scratch would suffice which is clearly inadequate.[264]

Historically, under a predecessor offence to s 20[265] it was held that there was no wounding where V, in warding off D's attempt to cut his throat, struck his hands against a knife held by D and cut them;[266] nor where V was knocked down by D and wounded by falling on iron trams.[267] That old offence did not contain the words 'by any means whatsoever', and these cases would now surely be decided differently. Even under the earlier law, D was guilty where he struck V on the hat with a gun and the hard rim of the hat caused a wound.[268] It is unclear whether there can be a wounding by omission. It was formerly held that wounding must be the result of a battery but again, it is probably now sufficient that the wound be directly inflicted whether by a battery or not.[269] In *Marsh*,[270] D was convicted of wounding with intent to do grievous bodily harm after his Staffordshire terrier attacked V and D failed to call the dog off. The judge directed the jury that they could not convict D unless he had 'set his dog on' V. The Court of Appeal rejected the argument that there was no act sufficient

---

258 *Stokes* [2003] EWCA Crim 2977. In *Horwood* [2012] EWCA Crim 253, Hooper LJ stated, 'The word there [ie unlawful] means and relates to an absence of lawful justification such as self-defence or a similar kind of defence' at [7].

259 *Moriarty v Brooks* (1834) 6 C & P 684.   260 *C (A Minor) v Eisenhower* [1984] QB 331.

261 *M'Loughlin* (1838) 8 C & P 635.   262 *Wood* (1830) 1 Mood CC 278r.

263 *Waltham* (1849) 3 Cox CC 442. Contrast *Jones* (1849) 3 Cox CC 441.

264 *Morris* [2005] EWCA Crim 609.   265 7 Will 4 & 1 Vic, c 85, s 4.

266 *Beckett* (1836) 1 Mood & R 526 (Parke B); *Day* (1845) 1 Cox CC 207. Cf *Coleman* (1920) 84 JP 112.

267 *Spooner* (1853) 6 Cox CC 392.   268 *Sheard* (1837) 2 Mood CC 13.

269 *Wilson*, p 727. Cf *Taylor* (1869) LR 1 CCR 194; *Austin* (1973) 58 Cr App R 163.

270 [2012] EWCA Crim 1442.

to constitute the actus reus of wounding, which lends weight to the proposition that this is an offence that can be committed indirectly.

It may seem odd that the criminal law has a specific offence related to a type of injury. It is doubtful whether this specific form of injury (or indeed others in the OAPA such as throwing acid) warrants a separate offence in a modern code of offences. Some suggest that the specificity of label and the distinctions between the harms and the manner in which they are inflicted reflect important moral differences.[271]

16.4.1.2 Malice

The court in *Cunningham*[272] quoted with approval the definition of recklessness in Kenny's *Outlines of Criminal Law*: 'the accused has foreseen that the particular kind of harm might be done, and yet has gone on to take the risk of it'. According to that case, this definition applies whenever a statute defines a crime using the word 'malice'.

There is no doubt that malice in this context is a subjective test—*Caldwell* has no part to play, particularly since the decision of the House of Lords in *G*. It is submitted that the term 'malice' should be understood as meaning 'intentionally or recklessly' and 'reckless' should carry the definition used in *G*.[273] In *Brady*,[274] the Court of Appeal held that *G* does not require proof that D had foreseen 'an obvious and significant risk' in order to establish that he had acted recklessly. D was drunk when he climbed on railings at a nightclub and fell onto the dance floor below causing serious injuries to V. The court allowed the appeal, because the judge had failed to direct the jury as to recklessness in sufficiently clear and careful terms.

Although the definition of malice provided in *Cunningham* refers to D's foresight of a risk, there is no mention of the further element of the modern test of recklessness—that it is unjustifiable for D to take that risk known to him. There is no clear authority on whether malice includes that requirement under the 1861 Act. *Mowatt*[275] and *Savage*[276] involve discussion of intention or foresight, in accordance with *Cunningham*, but do not address the question whether it was justified to take the risk.[277] The court in *Brady*[278] did not specifically discuss the point, but the approach taken seemed consistent with that rule. It is submitted that the test of malice should incorporate the *G* definition of recklessness in its full measure: D acts with malice if he intends or foresees a risk and takes that risk unjustifiably.

D must intend or be reckless, but what is 'the particular kind of harm' that must be intended or foreseen? As a matter of general principle, the answer might be expected to be that it is necessary that D has mens rea as to all the elements of the actus reus—including the wounding or grievous bodily harm.[279] The law has developed differently. The law is that it is enough that D foresaw that *some* bodily harm, not necessarily amounting to grievous bodily harm or wounding, might occur.[280] Diplock LJ said in *Mowatt*:[281]

the word 'maliciously' does import upon the part of the person who unlawfully inflicts the wound or other grievous bodily harm an awareness that his act may have the consequence of causing some

---

[271] See the illuminating account by J Gardner (1994) 53 CLJ 502 and in J Gardner, *Offences and Defences* (2007) Ch 2.

[272] [1957] 2 QB 396. The case is discussed more fully at p 105.

[273] See [1992] 1 AC 699. *Savage and Parmenter* [1991] 4 All ER at 721, affirming *Mowatt* [1968] 1 QB 421.

[274] [2006] EWCA Crim 2413.   [275] [1968] 1 QB 421.   [276] [1992] 1 AC 699, 750.

[277] The leading speech in *Savage* describes the dissent in *Caldwell v Metropolitan Police Commissioner* [1982] AC 341, which does refer to justification, but the final conclusion was based on *Cunningham* and does not adopt the dissent in *Caldwell*.

[278] [2006] EWCA Crim 2413.   [279] cf p 724.   [280] See n 260.

[281] [1968] 1 QB 421 at 426. Reiterated post-*G* in *C* [2007] EWCA Crim 1068. See also *Dakou* [2002] EWCA Crim 3156, oversimplifying the issue of malice in s 18. Courts continue to make errors with this—see eg *DPP v W* [2006] EWHC 92 (Admin), where magistrates had acquitted on the basis that D had not foreseen the level of harm V suffered.

physical harm to some other person. That is what is meant by 'the particular kind of harm' in the citation from Professor Kenny.[282] It is quite unnecessary that the accused should have foreseen that his unlawful act might cause physical harm of the gravity described in [s 20], ie, a wound or serious physical injury. It is enough that he should have foreseen that some physical harm to some person, albeit of a minor character, might result.

It is sufficient to prove that D foresaw that *some* harm *might* result and took the risk unjustifiably. To tell the jury that it must be proved that D foresaw that it *would* result is too generous to the defendant.[283] It is not enough, however, whether the charge is one of wounding or inflicting grievous bodily harm[284] that D intended to frighten (unless he foresaw that the fright might result in psychiatric injury).

16.4.2 Maliciously inflicting grievous bodily harm

'Grievous bodily harm' was formerly interpreted to include any harm which seriously interferes with health or comfort;[285] but, in *Smith*,[286] the House of Lords said that the words should bear their ordinary and natural meaning.[287] It is not always necessary for the jury to be told to look for 'really' serious harm,[288] and it is not clear precisely what that word means when it is included.[289] The jury may take into consideration the totality of the injuries,[290] provided they have been inflicted in one attack or the relevant period specified accurately in the charge.[291] Although the determination of whether the injury constitutes grievous bodily harm is to be assessed objectively, and not merely on the basis of the victim's perception,[292] the characteristics of the victim may be taken into account—what is grievous bodily harm to a child might not be for an adult.[293] There is no need for the injury to be permanent or life-threatening.[294] Unconsciousness is capable of constituting grievous bodily harm.[295]

Grievous bodily harm may cover cases where there is no wounding as, for instance, the broken collarbone in *Wood*.[296] Conversely, there might be a technical 'wounding' which could not be said to amount to grievous bodily harm—as with an injection by a needle.[297]

---

[282] *Outlines*, 211. The citation is the passage approved by the Court of Criminal Appeal in *Cunningham* [1957] 2 QB 396; p 105.

[283] *Rushworth* (1992) 95 Cr App R 252 at 255, cited in *Pearson* [1994] Crim LR 534 which nevertheless left this point unresolved. Earlier *dicta* by Lords Diplock and Ackner are ambiguous.

[284] *Flack v Hunt* (1979) 70 Cr App R 51; *Sullivan* [1981] Crim LR 46.

[285] *Ashman* (1858) 1 F & F 88.

[286] [1961] AC 290; n 249; followed in *Metharam* [1961] 3 All ER 200.

[287] The Court of Appeal confirmed in *Golding* [2014] EWCA Crim 889 that the assessment of harm done in an individual case is a matter for the jury, applying contemporary social standards.

[288] *Janjua* [1999] 1 Cr App R 91. This was reiterated more recently in *Carey* [2013] EWCA Crim 482.

[289] In *Sidhu*, 'Traditionally, judges use the expression "really serious", and occasionally "serious", to articulate the threshold [for murder]. But when judges use such language they mean in effect "an intention to cause serious harm or really serious harm sufficient to amount in law to murder".' At [18] per Green LJ.

[290] *Grundy* [1977] Crim LR 543; *Birmingham* [2002] EWCA Crim 2608.

[291] See *Brown* [2005] EWCA Crim 359 (abuse of V over several days).

[292] *Brown* [1998] Crim LR 484.   [293] *Bollom* [2004] 2 Cr App R 50.   [294] ibid.

[295] *Hicks* [2007] EWCA Crim 1500—the issue being raised by the jury! See also *Foster* [2009] EWCA Crim 2214, [28] discussing the levels of unconsciousness and whether the 'Glasgow coma score' might assist in determining the severity of the unconsciousness in law.

[296] See n 265. *Lashley* [2017] EWCA Crim 260 provides a vivid example, in which V was on the ground when D reversed over him with his car.

[297] Although that is often charged under s 47. See eg *Gower* [2007] EWCA Crim 1655.

The absence of any clear definition of the term and the associated risk of inconsistent applications and a lack of predictability in verdicts is disappointing.[298]

It is settled that *serious* psychiatric injury amounts to grievous bodily harm.[299] This results in the possibility of convictions for inflicting grievous bodily harm by telephone—for example, a series of extreme threatening or obscene phone calls.[300] The actus reus may be readily established in such cases by proving that D inflicted the serious psychiatric injury. Proof of mens rea in such a case may be more difficult. The Court of Appeal in *Golding* reiterated that 'the ambit of bodily harm is restricted to recognisable psychiatric illness and does not cover psychological disturbance'.[301] The anguish V suffered as a result of learning that D had infected her with the genital herpes virus was therefore incapable of constituting grievous bodily harm.

Although the level of harm is ill-defined and rests on the jury's interpretation in each individual case, it has been held in Northern Ireland not to be contrary to Art 7 for want of certainty.[302]

16.4.2.1 Inflict

The current law is now settled—D can inflict injury without proof of an assault. The position had been unclear for over a century. In a series of cases[303] from 1861 until 1983, it was held or assumed that the words 'inflict' and 'wound' both imply an 'assault'. D could be convicted of an offence under s 20 only if it was proved that he wounded or caused grievous bodily harm by committing an assault. *Clarence*[304] held that D caused V harm by infecting her with gonorrhoea, but did not *inflict* it unless there was an assault. But a second line of cases[305] simply ignored the requirement of an assault and upheld convictions where D so frightened V that V jumped through a window,[306] or accidentally injured himself by putting his hand through a glass door under a 'well-grounded apprehension of violence'.[307] In *Martin*,[308] where, shortly before the end of a performance in a theatre, D put out the lights and placed an iron bar across the doorway, he was convicted of inflicting grievous bodily harm on those injured in the panic.

In 1983, the House of Lords in *Wilson*[309] resolved the matter by deciding, following the Australian case of *Salisbury*,[310] that 'inflict' does not, after all, imply an assault.[311] Arguably, the case decided no more than that; but Lord Roskill cited the opinion of the Australian court that 'inflict' has a narrower meaning than 'cause' (as used in s 18 discussed later) and requires 'force being violently applied to the body of the victim'. In *Burstow*,[312] the House

---

[298] In *Townsend* [2013] EWCA Crim 771, D was convicted of inflicting grievous bodily harm on the basis that he had fractured V's jawbone. It subsequently transpired, however, that V's jawbone was not in fact fractured and the Crown conceded that D's conviction therefore had to be quashed.

[299] *Ireland*, p 694.   [300] *Gelder* (1994) The Times, 25 May (news item).

[301] [2014] EWCA Crim 889 at [63] per Treacy LJ.   [302] See *Anderson* [2003] NICA 12.

[303] *Yeadon and Birch* (1861) 9 Cox CC 91; *Taylor* (1869) LR 1 CCR 194; *Clarence* (1888) 22 QBD 23; *Snewing* [1972] Crim LR 267; *Carpenter* (1979) 76 Cr App R 320n, cited [1983] 1 All ER 1004.

[304] (1888) 22 QBD 23.

[305] *Halliday* (1889) 61 LT 701; *Lewis* [1970] Crim LR 647; *Mackie* [1973] Crim LR 54; *Boswell* [1973] Crim LR 307; *Cartledge v Allen* [1973] Crim LR 530.

[306] *Halliday* (1889) 61 LT 701.   [307] *Cartledge v Allen* [1973] Crim LR 530.

[308] (1881) 8 QBD 54.   [309] [1984] AC 242 at 260.   [310] [1976] VR 452 at 461.

[311] The House nevertheless contrived to hold that a person charged under s 20 could be convicted on that indictment of a common assault by virtue of s 6(3) of the Criminal Law Act 1967—a much-criticized decision but approved by the House in *Savage* [1991] 4 All ER 698 at 711. See G Williams, 'Alternative Elements and Included Offences' (1984) 43 CLJ 290 and commentary at [1984] Crim LR 37.

[312] Heard and decided together with *Ireland* [1998] AC 147. Arguably the case is restricted to those cases involving the infliction of psychiatric injury. This would create an undesirable confusion in the law.

of Lords decided that 'inflict' does not bear this narrow meaning and that grievous bodily harm might be inflicted over the telephone or by other harassment, not involving the use of violence to the body or an assault. It remains necessary, as noted earlier, to prove that D foresaw that he might cause some harm, not necessarily serious psychiatric injury.

The distinction between 'cause' and 'inflict' seems then to have been substantially eliminated. The House thought that, while the words are not synonymous, there is 'no radical divergence' of meaning. Perhaps this is to be read to mean no 'material' difference.[313] If the courts were interpreting a modern statute, the use of different words in adjacent sections might compel the conclusion that different meanings were intended. No such inference can be drawn in the 1861 Act because that Act was never intended, and does not purport, to be a consistent whole.[314] *Clarence* can no longer be justified on the ground that there was no assault or violent application of force or that V consented.[315] It was not overruled but it appears to have been wrongly decided.[316] Following *Dica*, it now seems clear that as a matter of practice the terms can be treated as synonymous in almost every instance.[317]

In *Brady*, discussed earlier, the Court of Appeal questioned, *obiter*, whether it may be arguable that there was no actus reus, that is, no 'deliberate non-accidental conduct on the part of the accused that inflicted grievous bodily harm'. On D's account, he had deliberately perched precariously on a low railing above a crowded dance floor having consumed considerable quantities of alcohol and drugs. D argued that the act of falling was not deliberate and must, therefore, have been accidental; and that, since the actus reus of the offence contrary to s 20 required the inflicting of grievous bodily harm, the physical act of the falling that had caused the injury was not a direct assault. With respect, that argument is difficult to follow. There is no doubt that V suffered grievous bodily harm as she was rendered paraplegic. There is also no doubt that that injury was inflicted by D. The question is whether it was inflicted by D's blameworthy conduct. If the jury were satisfied that D realized that in perching as he did there was a risk of his falling and causing some injury to a person below, and that he went on unreasonably to take that risk, it is submitted that he would have committed the s 20 offence. Although the act of perching may look innocuous viewed in isolation, that is not the actus reus of the offence: the actus reus is D's whole conduct in perching *and* the resulting harm to the victim on the dance floor. The incident of D losing his balance and falling does not represent a break in the chain of causation; it is the very incident about which D was alleged to have been reckless/malicious. His reckless conduct in perching as he did caused the loss of balance which caused the fall and the resulting injury.[318]

---

[313] Lord Hope, however, said that 'inflict' implies that the consequence of the act is something that the victim is likely to find unpleasant or harmful whereas 'cause' may embrace pleasure as well as pain. But, if that is so, the sadomasochists in *Brown* [1994] 1 AC 212, discussed earlier, could not have been held to have been guilty of *inflicting* grievous bodily harm, contrary to s 20, because everyone was having a jolly good time. This would be surprising, as they were guilty of wounding, contrary to the same subsection on the ground that consent was no defence.

[314] CS Greaves, *The Criminal Law Consolidation and Amendment Acts* (2nd edn, 1862) 3–4, cited by Lord Steyn at 234.

[315] cf p 706.

[316] The draft Bill in the Home Office Consultation Paper of Feb 1998 expressly excludes from the proposed offences recklessly (but not intentionally) causing anything by disease. See now *Dica* [2004] EWCA Crim 1103. See also LCCP 217, Ch 6 and LC 361, Ch 4.

[317] The High Court of Australia in *Aubrey v The Queen* [2017] HCA 18 arrived at the same conclusion in respect of the equivalent legislation in New South Wales.

[318] Part of the problem in the court's analysis is that the events are all categorized as either deliberate or accidental. It is unclear what is meant by this, but it stems from the unsatisfactory way in which the case was presented.

16.4.2.2 Coexistence of s 20 and s 47

The coexistence of s 47 with that of maliciously inflicting grievous bodily harm contrary to s 20 of the same Act, also punishable with a maximum of five years' imprisonment, makes little sense.[319] The prosecutor's task is slightly easier under s 47 since it is not necessary to prove even the foresight of some bodily harm which is necessary under s 20. Proof of an assault or battery is required under s 47, but is not necessary under s 20; and s 20 no longer requires proof of a direct application of force. Section 20 is regarded in practice as the more serious offence. In *Parmenter*,[320] the Court of Appeal said that:

although the sentences imposed in practice for the worst s 47 offences will overlap those imposed at the lower end of s 20, nobody could doubt that the two offences are seen in quite different terms, whether by defendants and their advisers contemplating pleas of guilty, or by judges passing sentence under s 47 on defendants whose pleas of guilty have been accepted by the prosecution, or by subsequent sentencers casting an eye down lists of previous convictions.

16.5 Section 18 of the Offences Against the Person Act 1861

By s 18, as amended by the Criminal Law Act 1967:

Whosoever shall unlawfully and maliciously by any means whatsoever wound or cause any grievous bodily harm to any person with intent to do some grievous bodily harm to any person or with intent to resist or prevent the lawful apprehension or detainer of any person, shall be guilty of [an offence triable only on indictment], and being convicted thereof shall be liable to [imprisonment] for life.

The elements of the actus reus have been considered previously in relation to s 20. Note that under s 18 there is, technically, no need for the harm to be caused to another.

16.5.1 Mens rea

The mens rea of the offence differs slightly depending on which form of the offence is charged.

16.5.1.1 Intention

In every case the Crown must establish an ulterior intent which may be either intent to do grievous bodily harm or intent to resist or prevent the lawful apprehension or detainer of any person. Recklessness is not enough.[321] Where the allegation is of intentionally causing grievous bodily harm, it is sufficient that D intended to cause the harm he did, irrespective of whether *he personally* would regard that level of harm as really serious. As noted earlier in the context of s 20, proving an intention to cause psychiatric injury may be very difficult.

Intention has the same meaning as in the law of murder.[322] The prosecution must prove either: (a) that D acted in order to cause grievous bodily harm, or, if it was not his purpose, (b) that he knew that grievous bodily harm was a virtually certain consequence of his act. In case (b), the jury may then find that he had the requisite intent.[323] The jury need not be directed on this oblique intention definition except in rare cases.[324]

---

[319] cf the view of J Gardner (1994) 53 CLJ 502, and Ashworth, n 258.
[320] [1991] 2 All ER 225 at 233.
[321] *Re Knight's Appeal* (1968) FLR 81.   [322] *Bryson* [1985] Crim LR 669; cf *Belfon* [1976] 3 All ER 46.
[323] See p 93.   [324] See *Phillips* [2004] EWCA Crim 112.

If D intends to cause grievous bodily harm to X and, striking at X, he accidentally wounds another person, V, he may be indicted for wounding V with intent to cause grievous bodily harm to X.[325] If D intends to cause grievous bodily harm to X, and strikes the person he aims at, who is in fact V, he may be convicted of wounding V with intent to cause grievous bodily harm to V.[326] In addition, if D intends to kill X, for example by shooting him, but misses and instead causes really serious harm to V, D can be guilty of an offence contrary to s 18 for the harm caused to V. Additionally, the Court of Appeal in *Grant*[327] accepted the proposition that an intention to kill necessarily includes an intention to cause grievous bodily harm. The argument that the two are mutually exclusive or inconsistent was rejected.

Where the indictment specifies a particular form of the offence, the intent prescribed in that form of the offence must be proved; it is not enough to prove another variety of intent described in the section.[328] So D had to be acquitted where the charge was intent to do some grievous bodily harm and the jury found that the acts were done to resist and prevent D's apprehension *and for no other purpose*.[329] But if D intends to prevent his apprehension and, in order to do so, intends to cause grievous bodily harm, he may be convicted under an indictment charging only the latter intent. It is immaterial which is the principal and which the subordinate intent.[330]

The courts continue to create difficulties with the form of the mens rea. In *Taylor*,[331] the judge had directed that the jury on a s 18 charge must be sure that the prosecution had proved that D had intended to cause grievous bodily harm or to wound. This was a misdirection to the jury.

An intent to wound is insufficient. There must be an intent to cause really serious bodily injury.[332]

There was no evidence, upon which the jury could have relied, to show that D had intended really serious injury. The conviction was quashed and was replaced with a conviction for unlawful wounding. In *Purcell*,[333] the Court of Appeal suggested that at a trial of a person charged with causing grievous bodily harm the following direction should be given to the jury on the issue of intent:

You must feel sure that the defendant intended to cause serious bodily harm to the victim. You can only decide what his intention was by considering all the relevant circumstances and in particular what he did and what he said about it.

16.5.1.2 Malice

The meaning of malice has been considered earlier in relation to s 20.

Where, under s 18, the charge is of causing grievous bodily harm with intent to do grievous bodily harm, the word 'maliciously' obviously has no part to play. Any mens rea which

---

[325] *Monger* [1973] Crim LR 301, per Mocatta J holding that D could not be convicted where the indictment alleged intent to harm V. This is in accord with *Ryan* (1839) 2 Mood & R 213 and *Hewlett* (1858) 1 F & F 91 but contrary to *Hunt* (1825) 1 Mood CC 93 and *Jarvis, Langdon and Stear* (1837) 2 Mood & R 40. Cf the doctrine of transferred malice, p 125 and the comment on *Monger* in [1973] Crim LR 301.

[326] *Smith* (1855) Dears CC 559 at 560; *Stopford* (1870) 11 Cox CC 643.

[327] [2014] EWCA Crim 143. The court declined to consider the issue of whether D could be guilty of two or more attempted murders for a single act by which he intended to kill only one person. For criticism, see T Storey (2014) 78 J Crim L 214.

[328] There are numerous forms of the s 18 offence other than that commonly relied upon—grievous bodily harm with intent to do grievous bodily harm—wounding with intent to do grievous bodily harm; causing grievous bodily harm with intent to do grievous bodily harm; wounding with intent to resist or prevent apprehension or detention; causing grievous bodily harm with intent to resist or prevent apprehension or detention.

[329] *Duffin and Marshall* (1818) Russ & Ry 365; cf *Boyce* (1824) 1 Mood CC 29.

[330] *Gillow* (1825) 1 Mood CC 85.

[331] [2009] EWCA Crim 544. See also *Gregory* [2009] EWCA Crim 1374.

[332] ibid, [3].   [333] (1986) 83 Cr App R 45.

it might import is necessarily included within the ulterior intent. Even if 'wounding' is not foreseen, it is 'malicious'. The Court of Appeal has emphasized that generally judges ought not to give a direction on malice under s 18 in these cases.[334]

Where the charge is of malicious wounding or causing grievous bodily harm with intent to resist lawful apprehension, there is no difficulty in giving meaning to 'maliciously' and it is submitted that meaning should be given to that word.[335] A mere intent to resist lawful apprehension should not found liability for a charge of wounding or causing grievous bodily harm. It is submitted that the Court of Appeal went too far in *Mowatt*[336] in saying that 'In section 18 the word "maliciously" adds nothing.'

The indictment should spell out the alleged mens rea.[337] It is clear that there must be proof that D actually foresaw the specified result. Any doubt there may have been about this was dispelled by s 8 of the Criminal Justice Act 1967.[338] *Mowatt* was decided before the Act came into force, and certain observations in the case are therefore suspect.

If D has not admitted his malice, then it is submitted that it must be proved like every other element in the crime. The fact that the evidence appears to the judge to be overwhelming is not a good reason for not leaving it to the jury.

16.5.2 Alternative verdicts

A charge of 'causing' grievous bodily harm with intent contrary to s 18 has been held to include a charge of 'inflicting' grievous bodily harm contrary to s 20[339] which, in turn, includes a charge of assault occasioning actual bodily harm contrary to s 47.[340] The effect is that, on an indictment for the s 18 offence, the jury may find D guilty of an offence under s 20, or under s 47; and, on an indictment for the s 20 offence, of an offence under s 47. Whether to direct the jury that if they acquit of the offence charged they may convict of a lesser included offence is a matter for the discretion of the judge. Following *Coutts*,[341] if the possibility that D is guilty only of a lesser offence (s 20 or s 47) has been raised in the course of the evidence, the judge should leave the alternative offence to the jury, even in cases in which neither prosecution nor defence want the alternative offence to be left to the jury.[342] The Court of Appeal has reiterated the importance of this.[343]

---

[334] See *Brown* [2005] EWCA Crim 359, [17].

[335] *Morrison* (1989) 89 Cr App R 17. D was seized by a WPC as she was arresting him. D dived through a window pane and the WPC was dragged with him suffering serious facial injury. D clearly *intended* to resist arrest, the Court of Appeal held he must also be subjectively (*Cunningham*) reckless as to the grievous bodily harm.

[336] [1968] 1 QB 421. See R Buxton, 'Negligence and Constructive Crime' [1969] Crim LR 112. See also *Ward* (1872)LR 1 CCR 356.

[337] *Hodgson* [2008] EWCA Crim 895.   [338] See p 134.   [339] *Mandair* (1994) 99 Cr App R 250.

[340] *Wilson* [1984] AC 242.   [341] [2006] 1 WLR 2154.

[342] See *Ali* [2006] EWCA Crim 2906; cf *Foster* [2007] EWCA Crim 2869.

[343] *Foster* [2009] EWCA Crim 2214; *Green* [2009] EWCA Crim 2609; *Mathew* [2010] EWCA Crim 29; *Hodson* [2009] EWCA Crim 1590, [2010] Crim LR 249 and commentary. If s 20 is a realistically available verdict on the evidence, as an interpretation properly open to the jury, without trivializing the offending conduct, then the alternative should be left to the jury. The court emphasizes that it is particularly important that an alternative verdict was left to a jury where the offence charged required proof of a specific intent (s 18) and the alternative offence (s 20) did not. In *Caven* [2011] EWCA Crim 3239, the failure to leave the alternative offence resulted in D's conviction for an offence contrary to s 18 being quashed. In *Brown* [2014] All ER (D) 176 (Oct), D was charged with an offence of wounding with intent. Expert witnesses, however, agreed that no more than mild to moderate force would have been required to inflict the wound in question, which could easily have been sustained during a struggle, rather than as a result of a deliberate stabbing action. The jury should thus have been invited to consider the unlawful wounding option, but this was not done, so D's conviction for wounding with intent was quashed as unsafe and a conviction for the lesser offence was substituted.

In *Lahaye*,[344] the Court of Appeal's *per curiam* recommendation seems to have been that a s 20 offence ought to be included in the indictment from the outset in *any* s 18 case, and this goes beyond what was suggested by the House of Lords (Lords Mackay, Goff and Mustill) in *Mandair*,[345] namely that it may be desirable to include as an alternative where appropriate. Automatic inclusion of a s 20 count reduces the prosecution's freedom to select their indictment of choice, and increases the risk of compromise verdicts but it seems that such verdicts are already the practical reality. Beatson LJ's suggestion is, it is submitted, a sensible approach:

It is, on the authorities, the ultimate responsibility of the trial judge to leave an alternative verdict which is obviously raised by the evidence to the jury. While there is no universal rule about including a section 20 count in the indictment where there is an allegation of a section 18 offence, the decision of this court in *Lahaye* states that such a count should normally be included.[346]

Research has suggested that the moral distinction between the s 18 and s 20 offences has been eroded by the availability of the alternative verdicts and the frequency with which they are returned. In one study, albeit 20 years ago, only 23 per cent of those indicted for s 18 were convicted of that offence, whilst 53 per cent were convicted of s 20 and only one in ten of the contested s 18 trials led to an outright acquittal.[347]

16.6 Reform

The case for reform of these offences against the person (assault, battery, s 47, s 20, s 18) is compelling.[348] The Law Commission has commented that the law is 'defective on grounds both of effectiveness and of justice'.[349] In 2014 the Commission[350] published a scoping consultation paper in which it sought to assess the strength of the case for reform and in particular whether any future reform should be based on the draft Bill from the Home Office, *Consultation Paper on Violence*[351] in 1998. That Bill proposed a structured hierarchy of offences as follows:

1.—(1) A person is guilty of an offence if he intentionally causes serious injury to another.

(2) A person is guilty of an offence if he omits to do an act which he has a duty to do at common law, the omission results in serious injury to another, and he intends the omission to have that result . . .

(4) A person guilty of an offence under this section is liable on conviction on indictment to imprisonment for life.

[344] [2005] EWCA Crim 2847. See also *Hodson* [2010] Crim LR 248; *Brown* [2014] All ER (D) 176 (Oct).
[345] [1995] AC 208.
[346] *Vaughan* [2014] EWCA Crim 1456, [22].
[347] E Genders, 'Reform of the Offences Against the Person Act: Lessons from the Law in Action' [1999] Crim LR 689. See also LCCP 217, Ch 5.
[348] M Jefferson, 'Offences Against the Person: Into the 21st Century' (2012) 76 J Crim L 472; Genders [1999] Crim LR 689.
[349] LCCP 122, *Legislating the Criminal Code: Offences Against the Person and General Principles* (1992), on which see S Gardner, 'Reiterating the Criminal Code' (1992) 55 MLR 839; ATH Smith, 'Legislating the Criminal Code' [1992] Crim LR 396. See also LC 218, *Offences Against the Person and General Principles* (1993).
[350] LCCP 217.
[351] (1998) on which see JC Smith, 'Offences Against The Person: The Home Office Consultation Paper' [1998] Crim LR 317.

2.—(1) A person is guilty of an offence if he recklessly causes serious injury to another...

(3) A person guilty of an offence under this section is liable—

    (a) on conviction on indictment, to imprisonment for a term not exceeding 7 years;

    (b) on summary conviction, to imprisonment for a term not exceeding 6 months or a fine not exceeding the statutory maximum or both.

3.—(1) A person is guilty of an offence if he intentionally or recklessly causes injury to another ...

(3) A person guilty of an offence under this section is liable—

    (a) on conviction on indictment, to imprisonment for a term not exceeding 5 years;

    (b) on summary conviction, to imprisonment for a term not exceeding 6 months or a fine not exceeding the statutory maximum or both.

4.—(1) A person is guilty of an offence if—

    (a) he intentionally or recklessly applies force to or causes an impact on the body of another, or

    (b) he intentionally or recklessly causes the other to believe that any such force or impact is imminent.

(2) No such offence is committed if the force or impact, not being intended or likely to cause injury, is in the circumstances such as is generally acceptable in the ordinary conduct of daily life and the defendant does not know or believe that it is in fact unacceptable to the other person.

(3) A person guilty of an offence under this section is liable on summary conviction to imprisonment for a term not exceeding 6 months or [an unlimited fine] or both.

15.—(1) In this Act 'injury' means—

    (a) physical injury, or

    (b) mental injury.

(2) Physical injury does not include anything caused by disease but (subject to that) it includes pain, unconsciousness and any other impairment of a person's physical condition.

(3) Mental injury does not include anything caused by disease but (subject to that) it includes any impairment of a person's mental health.

[(4) In its application to section 1 this section applies without the exceptions relating to things caused by disease.] [The Law Commission recommended removing this clause.]

In 2015, the Law Commission published a scoping report, in which it recommended that future reform should be based upon the draft Home Office Bill.[352] The consequence of this is that the main injury offences would follow the correspondence principle, in which the harm required to be intended or foreseen matches the harm done. The Commission also recommended the creation of a new offence of 'aggravated assault', that would sit between the offence of intentionally or recklessly causing harm and the basic assault offences. It would be triable only in the magistrates' court.

---

[352] LC 361. For commentary, see S Demetriou, 'Not Giving Up the Fight: A Review of the Law Commission's Scoping Report on Non-Fatal Offences Against the Person' (2016) J Crim L 188; A Jackson and T Storey, 'Reforming Offences Against the Person: In Defence of "Moderate" Constructivism' (2015) 79 J Crim L 437; V Scully, 'Reforming Offences Against the Person—Seventh Time Lucky?' [2015] 10 Arch Rev 4.

16.7 Racially or religiously aggravated assaults

The Crime and Disorder Act 1998 created a new category of racially aggravated crimes, and the Anti-terrorism Crime and Security Act 2001 extended these to include religiously aggravated offences.[353] There has been a growing concern at the rise in violent hate crime.[354]

It is possible for a judge when sentencing to take into account hostility on grounds of race, religion, sexual orientation, gender identity or disability.[355] Some questioned, therefore, whether it was necessary to create offences applicable where certain categories of base offence (including many offences of violence) are committed with racial or religious hostility.

In a clear statement the House of Lords unequivocally supported such offences. Baroness Hale opined that they properly reflect the 'qualitatively distinct order of gravity' involved when racial hostility is demonstrated.[356] In addition, establishing separate offences rather than leaving matters of racial aggravation purely for sentencing means that *the jury* must be satisfied of that distinctive stigmatizing aspect of the alleged wrongdoing.

16.7.1 The offences

Section 28(1) of the Crime and Disorder Act provides two forms which the racial and religious aggravation can take. The difference between the two is extremely important but unfortunately appears to be frequently overlooked.[357]

Offences involving a demonstration of hostility. Section 28(1)(a) applies where at the time of[358] committing the relevant offence (assault, s 47, s 20, public order offences, harassment, etc) or immediately[359] before or after doing so, the offender demonstrates towards the victim[360] of the offence racial or religious hostility based on the victim's membership of a racial or religious group. The question is whether, *objectively*, D's words or conduct demonstrate hostility based on race or religion. D's motivation is not relevant.

Offences motivated by hostility. Section 28(1)(b) applies where the relevant offence is motivated wholly or partly by hostility towards members of a racial or religious group based on their membership of that group. This is a *subjective* question. D's motivation for the use of the words or conduct is crucial in determining whether it was racially or religiously hostile.

---

[353] See generally M Malik, 'Racist Crime: Racially Aggravated Offences in the Crime and Disorder Act 1998' (1999) 62 MLR 409; M Idriss, 'Religion and the Anti-Terrorism, Crime and Security Act 2001' [2002] Crim LR 890; A Tomkins, 'Legislating Against Terror: The Anti-terrorism, Crime and Security Act 2001' [2002] PL 205; PW Edge, 'Extending Hate Crime to Religion' (2003) 10 J Civ Lib 5; E Burney, 'Using the Law of Racially Aggravated Offences' [2003] Crim LR 28; and LCCP 213, *Hate Crime: The Case for Extending the Existing Offences* (2013) and LC 348, *Hate Crime: Should the Current Offences be Extended* (2014). For a theoretical discussion, see J Waldron, *The Harm in Hate Speech* (2012).

[354] See generally J Perry, *Facing all the Facts: Connecting on Hate Crime Data in England & Wales* (2020).

[355] It has been held that where D pleads to a non-aggravated form of the offence and no evidence is offered on the racially aggravated form of the offence, the judge cannot then sentence on the basis that the offence was racially aggravated: *McGillivray* [2005] Crim LR 484. See LC 348, paras 2.65 et seq.

[356] See note I Hare, 'Legislating Against Hate—The Legal Response to Bias Crimes' (1997) 17 OJLS 415 at 416–17.

[357] See *Jones v Bedford and Mid Bedfordshire Magistrates' Court* [2010] EWHC 523 (Admin). See LC 348, Ch 2.

[358] Where D uttered racist words and then attacked V several minutes later, the Court of Appeal regarded the incident as properly viewed as one in which D's racial hostility was present throughout: *Babbs* [2007] EWCA Crim 2737.

[359] This qualifies both acts before and after—a 20-minute delay after the act before D made the racist remark demonstrating hostility was too long: *Parry v DPP* [2004] EWHC 3112 (Admin).

[360] Who need not be present: *Parry v DPP* [2004] EWHC 3112 (Admin). In *Valentine* [2017] EWCA Crim 207, the Court of Appeal held that the trial judge had erred in presenting 'X' to the jury as the victim in his summing-up, as it was another person who had presented evidence of distress. The charge had therefore lacked accuracy.

There are numerous offences (some public order offences, harassment, criminal damage, etc) that can be aggravated in either of these ways (by demonstrations of hostility or motivated by hostility) but for the purposes of this part of this chapter, the relevant offences are contained in s 29. A person commits an offence under s 29 if he commits:

(1) an offence under s 20[361] of the OAPA 1861 (malicious wounding or grievous bodily harm); or

(2) an offence under s 47 of that Act (p 721); or

(3) a common assault;

which is 'racially aggravated' for the purposes of s 29.

Offences (1) and (2) are punishable on indictment with seven years' imprisonment (compared with five years for the basic, non-aggravated offence) and offence (3) with two years, the basic offence being triable only summarily.

16.7.2 Definitions

'Race' is widely defined to include colour, nationality (including citizenship) or ethnic or national origins.[362] The courts have taken an extremely wide and non-technical view of what constitutes a 'race' and racial group. It has been confirmed that the terms will be satisfied by non-inclusive expressions if, for example, D demonstrates hostility to V by calling him 'non-white' or 'foreign'.[363] 'Religious group' means a group of persons defined by reference to religious belief or lack of religious belief.[364] The Act gives no further guidance. Given the broad interpretation in Art 9 of the ECHR, it would seem likely that the domestic courts will interpret the offence as affording protection to a religion as widely understood.[365] By analogy with the interpretation of race, non-inclusive terms will suffice, for example 'unbeliever' or 'gentile'.[366]

Racial or religious hostility can be demonstrated by D towards someone of his own racial or religious group.[367] Note also that there is no need for D's presumption about V's race or religion to be accurate: as where D calls V a 'Paki' when V is from India. In Rogers,[368] the House of Lords confirmed that though D must have formed the view about V's racial group, the words used by D and which are alleged to demonstrate racial hostility need not refer expressly to that group to which V belongs. A racially aggravated assault might also be committed by one white person on another.[369] It is submitted that this is a perfectly appropriate interpretation of the Act. There is no need for the aggravating words to be repeated, or for the intended target to hear them or be present.[370]

[361] There is clearly no need for aggravation for s 18 which carries the maximum life sentence.
[362] 'African' does not denote an ethnic, but does denote a racial, group: White [2001] Crim LR 576, but see commentary on difficulties this creates. Applying the House of Lords' approach in Rogers, both terms are capable of being construed as demonstrations of hostility based on the victim's membership of a racial group. For further analysis see MA Walters, 'Conceptualizing "Hostility" for Hate Crime Law: Minding "the Minutiae" when Interpreting Section 28(1)(a) of the Crime and Disorder Act 1998' (2014) 34 OJLS 47.
[363] Rogers [2007] UKHL 8. See also DPP v M [2004] EWHC 1453 (Admin); A-G's Reference (No 4 of 2004) [2005] EWCA Crim 889; H [2010] EWCA Crim 1931 (question for jury whether D's repeated references to V as a 'monkey' or 'black monkey' constituted a demonstration of hostility based wholly or partly on race or whether it was mere vulgar abuse unconnected with hostility based on race).
[364] In Hewlett [2016] EWCA Crim 673, the Court of Appeal held that Romany gypsies were capable of being recognized as a racial group. D's reference to his neighbour as a 'pikey' was capable of being seen as a pejorative reference to Romany gypsies, which meant that he had committed the offence.
[365] See Pendragon v UK (1999) 27 EHRR CD 179.　　[366] DPP v M [2004] EWHC 1453 (Admin).
[367] White [2001] Crim LR 576.　　[368] [2007] UKHL 8.
[369] DPP v Pal [2000] Crim LR 756 per Simon Brown LJ. Cf Johnson v DPP [2008] EWHC 509 (Admin).
[370] Dykes v DPP [2008] EWHC 2775 (Admin).

16.7.2.1 Assault and contemporaneous demonstration of hostility: s 28(1)(a)

The courts have made clear that the offence under s 28(1)(a) is not limited to cases in which D is motivated solely or even mainly by racial malevolence. It is designed to extend to cases which may have a racially neutral gravamen but in the course of which there is, *objectively viewed*, hostility demonstrated towards the victim based on V's race (or presumed membership of that race).[371] So, for example, the offence applies where other bases for hostility exist—because V has, for example, taken D's car parking space, etc. In relation to s 28(1)(a), it has been held that no subjective intent needs to be proved. It is not a question of D intending to express hostility; the test is objective and the prosecution merely has to show the hostile behaviour.[372] As a matter of statutory interpretation, the key term in the section is that the hostility is '*based on*' V's race. By contrast, under s 28(1)(b) the motivation behind the behaviour has to be proved—that is a requirement expressed in the section.[373]

The parliamentary debates show that this broad interpretation of s 28(1)(a) was intended, since it was felt that proving a sole racial motive for the offence would be too difficult a task for the prosecution.[374] In consequence, s 28(1)(a) is extremely broad. Lord Monson in the debates on the Bill described the section as Orwellian in that it seeks to police people's emotions.[375] At present, only insults relating to religion and race are criminalized in this way.[376] This highlights the arbitrariness of the legislation. In terms of broader social objectives of the legislation, the section may be regarded as a success if it deters individuals from using racist language in any context. Whether this will be the effect or whether those convicted will bear such resentment at the stigma as to become hardened in their racist attitudes is debatable.[377]

16.7.2.2 Racially/religiously motivated assaults: s 28(1)(b)

The s 28(1)(b) offence is much narrower and less controversial, being focused on the defendant's state of mind and one of his *motivations* for the crime being one of racial or religious hostility, although not necessarily against the victim in person. It provides an interesting example of an offence in which the motivations rather than intentions of the defendant become crucial in substantive criminal law, and not merely as a matter of evidence.

There must be evidence of racial or religious motivation for the offence. In *DPP v Howard*,[378] D chanted 'I'd rather be a Paki than a cop' at his neighbours who were white police officers. Charges were based on s 28(1)(b). The magistrates concluded that there was insufficient

---

[371] *Woods* [2002] EWHC 85 (Admin) at [11] per Maurice Kay J. See also *DPP v Green* [2004] All ER (D) 70 (May); *DPP v MacFarlane* [2002] All ER (D) 78 (Mar); *DPP v M* [2004] EWHC 1453 (Admin).

[372] See *Jones v Bedford and Mid Bedfordshire Magistrates' Court* [2010] EWHC 523 (Admin), the magistrates erred in applying the reasoning from s 28(1)(b) when dealing with a case that was charged under s 28(1)(a).

[373] See *Jones v Bedford and Mid Bedfordshire Magistrates' Court* [2010] EWHC 523 (Admin). Section 28(3) provides that it is irrelevant whether in a s 28(1)(a) case D's hostility is 'also' based to any extent on another factor besides his racism. Read literally, this suggests that the section does include an examination of whether D had some racialist intent in his hostility. On that interpretation, if D's hostility was exclusively based on non-racialist grounds, he would not be within the s 28(1)(a) offence. The decision in *Jones* precludes that argument.

[374] In *Pal* [2000] Crim LR 756, the Divisional Court accepted that the racial statement 'whiteman's arse licker' was not in itself sufficient to prove hostility based on racial grounds. Simon Brown LJ stated that he did 'not regard the fact that D would not have used such a term but for V's race as a *sine qua non* of the racial hostility'. His lordship did note that the use of racially abusive insults will 'ordinarily no doubt be found sufficient'. *Pal* has since been described as turning on its own facts. In *Rogers*, Baroness Hale suggests at [15] that the case might also have been disposed of by arguing that the racial hostility was based on the caretaker's association with whites. With respect, that argument was addressed by the Divisional Court at [12] and it is not clear that that alternative approach meets the problem—the argument could still be made that the basis for hostility was the ejection and V's conduct, not his race or affinity with members of other races.

[375] HL, 12 Feb 1998, col 1266.   [376] But see the sweeping reform proposals discussed later.

[377] See generally E Burney and G Rose, *Racially Aggravated Offences: How is the Law Working?* (2002) HORS 244.

[378] [2008] EWHC 608 (Admin).

evidence on which they could be satisfied that the racially aggravated public order offence had been made out. They found that the evidence showed that D's hostility was motivated *only* by his intense dislike of the neighbours and not even as a result of his intense dislike of the police. There was, they concluded, insufficient evidence to establish (even in part) that the reason why those words were shouted was hostility towards Pakistani people. The Divisional Court dismissed the prosecution appeal, concluding that the magistrates were entitled to come to the conclusion they did: there was an abundance of evidence that the *sole* motivation for D's chanting was his hostility toward the officers personally. Moses LJ suggested that:

> prosecutors should be careful not to deploy [s 28(1)(b)] where offensive words have been used, but in themselves have not in any way been the motivation for the particular offence with which a defendant is charged. It diminishes the gravity of this offence to use it in circumstances where it is unnecessary to do so and where plainly it cannot be proved.[379]

It is a question of fact whether the motivation is found to be exclusively for non-racist reasons. Thus, in contrast to *Howard*, in *Kendall v DPP*[380] the magistrates were entitled to find that displaying posters of black men convicted of manslaughter with the title 'Illegal Immigrant Murder Scum' was evidence of motive even though D claimed that his purpose was to drum up support for the BNP.

Reform

The Law Commission has previously recommended that the offences could be extended to deal with hostility towards people on grounds of disability, sexual orientation and transgender identity. Definitions of those characteristics were based on the definitions in s 146 of the Criminal Justice Act 2003 (Sentencing Act 2020, s 66).

More recently, the Law Commission has published a consultation paper[381] with wide-ranging questions about extending the scope of the offences to include migration and asylum status and/or language within the definition of race and to extend the aggravated offences to include sexual orientation; transgender,[382] non-binary and intersex identity and disability. The Commission seeks views on extending the aggravated offences to include age, subcultures, sex workers, homelessness, philosophical beliefs and gender or sex. In addition, the Commission proposes reforming the current test of hostility or motivation to one of motivation by 'hostility or prejudice' towards the protected characteristic. The offences that can be aggravated would include GBH contrary to s 18 of the OAPA 1861; and arson with intent or reckless as to whether life is endangered contrary to s 1(2) and (3) of the Criminal Damage Act 1971 (notwithstanding that the maximum penalty for the offence without aggravation is already life imprisonment). The Commission seeks views on whether property or fraud offences ought to be capable of being aggravated.

16.8 Aggravated assaults

Assault forms the basis for a number of more serious offences based on attacks on specified classes of people or in particular circumstances—we can call these aggravated assaults. Three introductory points should be noted about this. First, a person cannot be convicted

---

[379] At [12]. Cf *Johnson v DPP* [2008] EWHC 509 (Admin).

[380] [2008] EWHC 1848 (Admin).

[381] LCCP 250, *Hate Crime Laws* (2020).

[382] It is proposed that the definition of 'transgender' be revised to include people who are or are presumed to be transgender, people who are or are presumed to be non-binary, people who cross-dress (or are presumed to cross-dress) and people who are or are presumed to be intersex.

of an aggravated assault unless he is guilty of assault. Subject to what was said earlier relating to consents and assault, if D has a defence to the charge of assault, he is not guilty of the aggravated assault. This proposition is not always understood. For example, in *Blackburn v Bowering*,[383] D was convicted of assaulting an officer of the court in the execution of his duty.[384] His defence was that he did not believe V was a bailiff—he thought he was using reasonable force against a trespasser. D's mistake was as to the legal status of the victim. The trial judge ruled correctly that liability as to that element of the offence was strict,[385] but he held that D's mistaken belief was no defence, remarking on the 'extraordinary situation' if that could have been a defence to common assault. D's conviction was quashed. If D was not guilty of assault because he lacked mens rea owing to a mistake, he could not be guilty of the aggravated form of the offence of assault on an officer of the court. Liability is strict as regards the status of the person assaulted, but there must still be an assault.[386] If the assault had been proved—for example, if D had used force which was excessive even against a trespasser—it would have been no defence that he believed (even on reasonable grounds) that V was not an officer but a thug.

Secondly, this range of aggravated offences do not form a coherent scheme, let alone a nicely structured ladder of offences. Rather they form a motley collection which has evolved over time. Many of the offences are found within the OAPA 1861. Some of these were, no doubt, intended to deal with matters causing public concern at the time, and appear rather curious today. Thus, obstructing or assaulting a clergyman in the discharge of his duties in a place of worship or burial place, or who is on his way to or from such duties, is an offence triable either way, punishable on indictment with two years' imprisonment under s 36![387] Assaulting a magistrate or other person in the exercise of his duty concerning the preservation of a vessel in distress or a wreck is an offence punishable on indictment with seven years' imprisonment under s 37. Such provisions are rarely invoked in the modern day and need not be considered further, save to note that for some, the explicit labelling and differentiation between the offences by reference to the manner and circumstances in which they were caused reflects important moral distinctions that ought to be retained and replicated in a modern criminal code.[388]

Thirdly, these aggravated offences, including those considered in this chapter, represent some of the starkest examples of constructive crimes—those which do not respect the correspondence principle—that is, D may be convicted of an offence requiring proof of actus reus elements A *and* B even though he has mens rea relating only to element A.[389]

---

[383] [1994] 3 All ER 380, CA (Civ Div). The appeal came to the Civil Division because the offence was in the nature of a contempt of court. Referred to by Lord Nicholls in *B v DPP* [2000] 2 AC 428 at 463: 'The Crown advanced no suggestion to your Lordships that any of these recent cases was wrongly decided. This is not surprising, because the reasoning in these cases is compelling.' See also its endorsement in *Oraki v DPP* [2018] EWHC 115 (Admin).

[384] Contrary to the County Courts Act 1984, s 14(1)(b). See LCCP 217, paras 2.139 et seq; LC 361, Ch 5.

[385] Following *Forbes and Webb* (1865) 10 Cox CC 362 (assaulting constable). In this regard s 14 was rightly treated as akin to s 51 of the Police Act 1964 which has now replaced by s 89 of the Police Act 1996, p 739.

[386] See p 743. This offence is an example of 'constructive crime' because the mens rea of a lesser offence, common assault, must be proved.

[387] There was one reported instance of this offence in 2001, and one in 2002: HC Written Answer, 21 Nov 2005 (Hazel Blears). The number of prosecutions is miniscule: see the Law Commission Scoping Paper, para 2.148 and Ch 5.123.

[388] See J Horder, 'Rethinking Non-Fatal Offences Against the Person' (1994) 14 OJLS 335 arguing that the offences serve valuable labelling functions and J Gardner (1994) 53 CLJ 502 arguing that they are valuable in terms of clarity. See LCCP 217, Ch 3; LC 361, Ch 5.

[389] Horder [1995] Crim LR 759; cf Mitchell [1999] Crim LR 195, and see references in n 258.

16.8.1 Assault with intent to resist arrest

By s 38 of the OAPA 1861:

Whosoever shall assault any person with intent to resist or prevent the lawful apprehension or detainer of himself or of any other person for any offence is guilty of an offence triable either way and punishable with two years' imprisonment.

It may be assumed that the section creates two offences, assault with intent and battery with intent. For each version, D must be shown to have committed all the elements of the assault/battery *and* that he intended to resist, etc. Thus, threatening the arrester (V) with a weapon to make him let go of the arrestee would be the assault, poking him with it would be battery. Dragging the arrestee from V's grasp, being reckless whether this causes V to fall to the ground, will be a reckless battery with intent to resist arrest if V does fall. D has an intention to prevent 'apprehension' when he tries to prevent the arrest taking place, and an intention to prevent the 'detainer' when he tries to bring the arrest to an end. The section applies only where the arrest is 'for any offence'; so it does not apply to an arrest in civil process or for a breach of the peace not amounting to crime. It is immaterial whether the arrest is by a police officer or a citizen; but D's claim that he did not know the arrester was a plain-clothes officer may be crucial where his defence is that he believed he was being attacked by thugs.[390]

The intent must be to resist 'lawful' arrest.[391] It is important to distinguish between D's mistakes of fact and law. If D knows of the factual circumstances which make the arrest lawful, he probably has a sufficient intent even though he believes, on the circumstances known to him, the arrest to be unlawful: for example, having read in an out-of-date law book that conspiracy is not an arrestable offence, he resists arrest for conspiracy. The law of arrest is treated as part of the criminal law for this purpose[392] and his mistake or ignorance of criminal law is no defence.[393] D's honest and, indeed, true belief that he is not, in fact, guilty of any offence is not per se a defence: the arrest may be lawful because the arrester has reasonable grounds for suspicion. But, if D makes a mistake of fact he should be judged on the circumstances as he believed them to be—in accordance with general principle. If D believes the arrester has no reasonable grounds to suspect that D is guilty, and D believes that the arrester knows he has no such grounds,—matters of fact—D should be acquitted if he resists. Whatever the true facts, D does not *intend* to resist *lawful* arrest. It may be that the principle of *Fennell*[394] leaves D liable for common assault or battery but it would be wrong in principle to convict him of the aggravated offence when mens rea with respect to the aggravating factor is not proved.

16.8.2 Assault on, resistance to, or obstruction of constables

By s 89 of the Police Act 1996:

(1) Any person who assaults a constable in the execution of his duty, or a person assisting a constable in the execution of his duty, shall be guilty of an offence and liable on summary

---

[390] *Brightling* [1991] Crim LR 364; *Blackburn v Bowering*, p 738.

[391] *Lee* [2001] 1 Cr App R 293 and see commentary at [2001] Crim LR 991. 'Whether or not an offence has actually been committed or is believed by the defendant not to have been committed is irrelevant', per Rose LJ.

[392] cf cl 25(2)(b) of the Code Team's Draft Code (LC 143), a provision not included in the Law Commission's draft (LC 177).

[393] Talfourd J put his decision on this ground in *Bentley* (1850) 4 Cox CC 406. See more recently *Hewitt v DPP* [2002] EWHC 2801 (Admin).

[394] [1971] 1 QB 428. Cf *Ball* (1989) 90 Cr App R 378. See the quashing of the conviction in *McKoy* [2002] EWCA Crim 1628.

conviction to [an unlimited] fine or to imprisonment for a term not exceeding six months or to both.

(2) Any person who resists or wilfully obstructs a constable in the execution of his duty, or a person assisting a constable in the execution of his duty, shall be guilty of an offence and liable on summary conviction to imprisonment for a term not exceeding one month or to a fine not exceeding level 3 on the standard scale, or to both.[395]

Though the section is headed 'Assaults on Constables', it contains three crimes, only one of which necessarily amounts to an assault. Resistance to a constable may occur without an assault, as where D has been arrested by V and D tears himself from V's grasp and escapes.[396] Obstruction, as explained later, includes many situations which do not amount to an assault. On the other hand, both resistance and obstruction clearly may include assaults. The nature of assault and resistance requires no further consideration but obstruction presents problems and is examined in some detail later.

Common to all three crimes is the requirement that the constable[397] is acting in the course of his duty. But the mens rea of assault and resistance, on the one hand, and obstruction on the other require separate consideration.

There is now also the scope to deal with those who use or threaten violence against a police officer under the Assaults on Emergency Workers (Offences) Act 2018. Section 1 of that Act makes provision for increased sentencing powers for offences of common assault and battery (as considered earlier) committed against an emergency worker acting in the exercise of functions as such a worker. Since the sentencing powers available under that Act are greater than under s 89, the CPS policy is to use the 2018 Act where both offences apply to the facts. The offence may apply more widely than s 89 since it is not restricted to V 'executing his duty'.

16.8.2.1 A constable acting in the execution of his duty

Identifying whether a police officer is acting in the course of his duty is a question that can give rise to difficult problems.[398] There are numerous examples of an officer's action falling on the wrong side of the line, taking him outside his duty such that when the constable is assaulted this offence is not committed.[399] Police officers have no power to detain a person (in ways that go beyond levels of conduct that would be acceptable from any ordinary member of the public).[400] If an officer does so, even briefly, without intending to exercise the power of arrest, the detention is a false arrest and amounts to false imprisonment. A constable who restrained D under the mistaken belief that D had been lawfully arrested by another officer was held not to be acting in the execution of his duty.[401]

Caution is required when interpreting the word duty. There are many things which a constable on duty may do (eg rescuing a stranded cat or helping to deliver a baby)[402] which he is probably not under any 'duty' in the strict sense to do; that is, he would commit no

---

[395] See LCCP 217, paras 2.139 and 2.145 on the volume of offending.

[396] *Sheriff* [1969] Crim LR 260.

[397] ie a person holding the *office*, not the rank of constable. A prison officer acting as such is a constable for this purpose: Prison Act 1952, s 8 see also the extended power in s 8A (but immigration detention centre officials are not constables—*Yarl's Wood Immigration v Bedfordshire Police Authority* [2008] EWHC 2207 (Admin)). It is also an offence to assault a member of other police-related agencies such as the NCA.

[398] It is for the prosecution to prove: *R (Ahmad) v Bradford MC* [2008] EWHC 2934 (Admin).

[399] For a recent example, see *Ahmed v CPS* [2017] EWHC 1272 (Admin), in which the injunction and power of arrest had erroneously cited repealed statutory provisions.

[400] *Pegram v DPP* [2019] EWHC 2673 (Admin).   [401] *Kerr v DPP* [1995] Crim LR 394.

[402] Or assisting a landlord to expel drunk and disorderly people under the Licensing Act 2003, s 143(4) (see *Semple v DPP* [2009] EWHC 3241 (Admin)).

crime or tort or even breach of police regulations by not doing it. In *Coffin v Smith*,[403] the Divisional Court held that a constable could be in the execution of his duty for the purposes of this section even if he was doing something that he was not obliged to do. Officers, who had been summoned to a club to ensure that certain people left, were assaulted. It was held that the officers were there in fulfilment of their duty to keep the peace and were plainly acting in the execution of their duty. But duty surely cannot be equated with being 'on duty'.

A constable may be acting in the execution of his duty by being present, and by intervening when a breach of the peace occurs or is imminent, but acting outside his duty if he takes it upon himself to expel a trespasser.[404] In a leading case, *Waterfield*,[405] the Court of Criminal Appeal provided welcome clarification:

it would be difficult, and in the present case it is unnecessary, to reduce within specific limits the general terms in which the duties of police constables have been expressed. In most cases it is probably more convenient to consider what the police constable was actually doing and in particular whether such conduct was *prima facie* an unlawful interference with a person's liberty or property. If so, it is then relevant to consider whether (a) such conduct falls within the general scope of any duty imposed by statute or recognized at common law and (b) whether such conduct, albeit within the general scope of such a duty, involved an unjustifiable use of powers associated with the duty.

If the police officer's conduct falls within the general scope of the 'duty' to prevent crime and to bring offenders to justice, then it would seem to be within the protection of the statute, if it was lawful. The officer may ask questions of individuals whom he suspects to be involved in offending.[406]

If, in the course of carrying out his duty to prevent crime and to bring offenders to justice, the officer exceeds his powers, then he is no longer acting in the execution of his duty for this purpose.[407] Query whether he is performing a function for the purposes of the 2018 Act.

Where the charge against D is that he assaulted or obstructed etc a police officer, V, in the execution of his duty and the assault etc occurred in the course of V performing an arrest for a criminal offence, the fact that the offence for which the officer was effecting an arrest is subsequently not prosecuted to conviction does not mean that V was not acting in the execution of his duty.[408] However, where the constable has not arrested D and uses violence on D, D's resistance will not be an offence even if the constable would have been empowered to arrest D in the first place.[409]

Where D is arrested or detained by an officer unlawfully, for example where the officer has not used words of arrest or told D the grounds of arrest, the officer is not acting in the execution of his duty.[410] In such a case, D cannot be liable for resisting other officers in the execution of their duty when they are merely assisting the unlawful arrest.[411] A constable

---

[403] (1980) 71 Cr App R 221. Cf the approval of Sedley LJ in *Porter v MPC* (1999) 20 Nov, unreported, CA (Civ).

[404] In *Chief Constable of Devon and Cornwall, ex p Central Electricity Generating Board* [1982] QB 458. On the police powers to prevent breach of the peace, see also P Thornton et al, *The Law of Public Order and Protest* (2010) paras 6.125 et seq.

[405] [1964] 1 QB 164 at 170.

[406] *Sekfali v DPP* [2006] EWHC 894 (Admin); cf *D v DPP* [2010] EWHC 3400 (Admin) dealing with powers of a PCSO.

[407] *Ludlow v Burgess* [1971] Crim LR 238; *Pedro v Diss* (1981) 72 Cr App R 193.

[408] *Burrell v DPP* [2005] EWHC 786 (Admin).   [409] *Wood v DPP* [2008] EWHC 1056 (Admin).

[410] cf *Saliu v DPP* [2005] EWHC 2689 (Admin), D assaulted PC who had yet to arrest. See also *Sobczak v DPP* [2012] EWHC 1319 (Admin), in which the officer failed to follow s 2 of PACE by not informing D of his name, police station, the object of the search and the grounds for making it. The police officer was, however, attempting to remove B's leg from the jaws of a police dog. For that reason it was held that the police officer was acting in the exercise of his duty and D's conviction was therefore upheld.

[411] *Cumberbatch v CPS* [2009] EWHC 3353 (Admin).

who is not acting in the execution of his duty because he is a trespasser begins to act in the execution of his duty as soon as circumstances justifying his presence arise—as where he reasonably apprehends a breach of the peace. He does not have to leave the premises and re-enter.[412] Even if an officer is not acting in the execution of his duty, for example where he is trespassing, the conduct of the defendant might nevertheless constitute a simple assault.[413]

Importantly, the Divisional Court in *Oraki v DPP*[414] confirmed that the defences of self-defence and defence of another person are, as a matter of law, available in relation to the offence of obstructing a constable in the execution of his duty contrary to s 89(2) of the 1996 Act.

16.8.2.2 Trivial touchings by officers

A police officer investigating crime is entitled to speak to any person from whom he thinks useful information can be obtained, even though that person declares that he is unwilling to reply,[415] but the officer has no power to detain for questioning so the use of reasonable force to escape from such detention is not an assault;[416] (it may be obstructing[417]) and the use of excessive force, while it may be a common assault (or wounding, etc) would not be an offence under s 89.

Where the question is whether something is trivial or *de minimis*, it is perhaps to be expected that assessments will differ. In *C v DPP*,[418] the officer's taking hold of a 14-year-old girl's arm to escort her home when she was reported missing by her parents was not in the exercise of his duty and hence her boyfriend was not guilty of assaulting the officer in the execution of his duty. As Kerr J explained recently:

when not making an arrest, a police officer has no more right than an ordinary citizen to make physical contact with another person; but a police officer has his rights as a citizen like any other. In applying the test of 'generally acceptable standards of conduct', whether by a police officer or any other citizen, account is taken of the context. In the case of a police officer that includes the duty to investigate crime.[419]

Officer preventing breach of peace

Probably the most important application of s 89 is in the context of the constable's duty to prevent breaches of the peace which he reasonably apprehends.[420] That power is one which must be scrutinized with the utmost care since it allows an officer (and indeed a civilian) to restrain or arrest D where D has not committed, and is perhaps not even about to commit, a crime. The House of Lords confirmed that a power to arrest or take less intrusive action arises where: (a) a breach of the peace has been committed; or (b) a breach has occurred and a further breach is threatened; or (c) the officer reasonably believes that a breach will be committed imminently. If an officer reasonably believes one of the above three circum-stances pertains, he is under a duty to take such steps, whether by arrest or otherwise,[421] as he reasonably thinks are necessary.[422] Where a reasonable apprehension of an imminent

---

[412] *Lamb* [1990] Crim LR 58.   [413] See eg *Syed v DPP* [2010] EWHC 81 (Admin).

[414] [2018] EWHC 115 (Admin). See also *Wheeldon v CPS* [2018] EWHC 249 (Admin). For further discussion, see p 742. See also E Cape [2018] Crim LR 388.

[415] Code of Practice A, code issued under the Police and Criminal Evidence Act (1984); *Weight v Long* [1986] Crim LR 746. See also *Sekfali*, p 745.

[416] *Kenlin v Gardner* [1967] 2 QB 510; *Ludlow v Burgess* [1971] Crim LR 238; *Lemsatef* [1977] 1 WLR 812. Cf *Daniel v Morrison* (1980) 70 Cr App R 142.

[417] See *Sekfali*, p 745.   [418] [2003] All ER (D) 37 (Nov).

[419] *Pegram v DPP* [2019] EWHC 2673 (Admin), [22].   [420] *Duncan v Jones* [1936] 1 KB 218.

[421] *King v Hodges* [1974] Crim LR 424; *Blench v DPP* [2004] All ER (D) 86 (Nov). The requirement for an 'imminent' breach of the peace was interpreted very widely in *Wragg v DPP* [2005] EWHC 1389 (Admin).

[422] *Piddington v Bates* [1960] 3 All ER 660.

breach of the peace exists, the preventive action taken must be reasonable and proportionate; and there is no power to take action short of an arrest when a breach of the peace is not so imminent as would be necessary to justify arrest.[423]

The most difficult cases are likely to be those in which the police seek to intervene to prevent conduct which is not objectively violent nor provocative to others but which may amount to a breach of the peace. In *Laporte*, Lord Rodger observed that:

Sometimes lawful and proper conduct by A may be liable to result in a violent reaction from B, even though it is not directed against B. If B's resort to violence can be regarded as the natural consequence of A's conduct, and there is no other way of preserving the peace, a police officer may order A to desist from his conduct, even though it is lawful. If A refuses he may be arrested for obstructing a police officer in the execution of his duty.[424]

Even where no breach of the peace is anticipated, a constable may be under some other duty to give instructions to members of the public—for example, to remove an obstruction from the highway[425]—and a deliberate refusal to obey such an instruction may amount to an obstruction of the police.

A constable who makes a lawful arrest is acting in the execution of his duty even though the arrest subsequently becomes unlawful when he fails to communicate the ground to the arrestee.[426]

16.8.2.3 Mens rea in cases of assault and resistance

The only mens rea required in the case of an allegation of assaulting a constable is the mens rea for assault or battery. In a case of resisting, the mens rea is an intention to resist. A reckless battery might be inflicted by hitting or flailing arms or legs around at arresting officers or even by biting, as where D uses his teeth to try to snatch something from the hand of the officer restraining him, being aware that he might make contact with the officer's hand in the process.[427]

There is no requirement to prove that D knew that the person he was assaulting was a police officer, still less that D knew that V was on duty. Liability in relation to the status of the arrester and whether the constable was in the execution of his duty is strict. Although the original authority for this was a ruling by a recorder in a direction to a jury in *Forbes and Webb*,[428] this has now been repeatedly accepted.[429] It is submitted that a better view[430] is that D should only be liable if he was at least reckless as to whether V was a police officer in the execution of his duty when he committed the assault.[431] Such a view avoids any difficulty arising from the fact that s 36[432] of the 1861 Act used the words 'to the knowledge of

---

[423] *R (Laporte) v Chief Constable of Gloucestershire* [2007] 2 WLR 46.

[424] At [78]. See *R (Moos) v MPC* [2012] EWCA Civ 12.

[425] It is in the course of a constable's duty to require pickets to move where they would otherwise obstruct lawful passage on the highway by others; *Kavanagh v Hiscock* [1974] QB 600, applying *Broome v DPP* [1974] AC 587. See also *Austin v MPC*, text accompanying n 532.

[426] *DPP v Hawkins* [1988] 3 All ER 673.   [427] *DPP v D* [2005] EWHC 967 (Admin).

[428] (1865) 10 Cox CC 362, applying s 38 of the OAPA 1861.

[429] In *Prince* (1875) LR 2 CCR 154 (six judges accepted it as correct); *Maxwell* (1909) 73 JP 176, (1909) 2 Cr App R 26; *Mark* [1961] Crim LR 173 (Judge Maxwell Turner). See also *Blackburn v Bowering*, p 738. See F Fairweather and S Levy, 'Assaults on the Police: A Case of Mistaken Identity' [1994] Crim LR 817.

[430] See the dissenting judges in *Reynhoudt* (1962) 36 ALJR 26.

[431] This was the view of the majority of the court in *Galvin (No 2)* [1961] VR 740, overruling *Galvin (No 1)* [1961] VR 733. Barry J thought actual knowledge necessary. Scholl J adhered to his view in *Galvin (No 1)* that the offence was one of strict liability. See also *McLeod* (1954) 111 CCC 106.

[432] See p 738.

the offender', whereas no such words were used in s 38 or its successors. Nevertheless, the present English law is that laid down in *Forbes*. This is implicit in *McBride v Turnock*,[433] where D struck at O, who was not a constable, and hit V, who was. Although he had no intention of assaulting V, the Divisional Court held that he was guilty of assaulting a constable in the execution of his duty. The mens rea for this crime being only that of a common assault/battery, D's 'malice' was transferable.[434] No better illustration could be given of the unsatisfactory nature of strict liability in this context. Following the landmark decisions of the House of Lords in *DPP v B*[435] and *R v K*,[436] it is arguable that this approach deserves reconsideration.[437]

If D is unaware (whether reasonably or not) that V is a constable and believes in the existence of circumstances of justification or excuse for his use of force, he should be acquitted:[438] he will not intend or be reckless as to an *unlawful* assault. If, however, D knows that V is a constable, it seems that a mistaken belief—even an honest and reasonable belief—that the constable is acting outside the course of his duty will not always be a defence. In *Fennell*,[439] the court assumed that a father might lawfully use reasonable force to free his son from unlawful arrest by the police; but he acted at his peril and, if the arrest proved to be lawful, he was guilty.

16.8.2.4 Wilful obstruction

The meaning of obstruction

There must be obstruction in fact. If D does an act with intent to obstruct but which fails to do so he commits no offence—and it cannot be an attempt.[440] A wide interpretation of 'obstruction' has been accepted in England.[441] It is not necessary that there should be any interference with the officer himself by physical force or threats. The focus is on whether D has made it more difficult for the officer to carry out his duty.

Where the police tell an offender to desist from an offence, his deliberate refusal may amount to an obstruction, as where D is obstructing the highway and refuses to obey the instructions of a constable to move.[442] It is not necessary that the constable should anticipate a breach of the peace. But a constable has no power to arrest D for obstructing him, unless the obstruction was such that it actually caused, or was likely to cause, a breach of the peace.[443]

Equally, to give a warning to a person who *has* committed a crime so as to enable him to escape detection by police is enough. Thus, in *Betts v Stevens*,[444] D committed the offence by warning drivers who were exceeding the speed limit that there was a police trap ahead. *Hinchliffe v Sheldon*[445] might be thought to go further than *Betts v Stevens* in that it was only *suspected*, and not proved, that an offence was being committed; but there the warning was tantamount to a physical obstruction.[446] D, a publican's son, shouted a warning to his

---

[433] [1964] Crim LR 456. This was also assumed to be the law in *Blackburn v Bowering*, p 738.

[434] See p 125.   [435] [2000] 2 AC 428, see Ch 5.   [436] *K* [2002] 1 AC 462, see Ch 5.

[437] See also the criticism in LCCP 217, paras 5.123 et seq.

[438] *Gladstone Williams* (1984) 78 Cr App R 276, p 354. *Mark*, n 430, requiring reasonable grounds for the belief, can no longer be regarded as good law.

[439] [1971] 1 QB 428, [1970] Crim LR 581 and commentary; and cf *Ball* (1989) 90 Cr App R 378, [1989] Crim LR 579 and commentary.

[440] Because it is triable only summarily. Cf *Bennett v Bale* [1986] Crim LR 404 and commentary.

[441] See for an historical account, J Coutts, 'Obstructing the Police' (1956) 19 MLR 411.

[442] *Tynan v Balmer* [1967] 1 QB 91; *Donaldson v Police* [1968] NZLR 32.

[443] *Wershof v Metropolitan Police Comr* [1978] 3 All ER 540 (May J); *Gelberg v Miller* [1961] 1 WLR 153; *Riley v DPP* [1990] Crim LR 422.

[444] [1910] 1 KB 1.   [445] [1955] 3 All ER 406.   [446] See Coutts (1956) 19 MLR 411.

parents that the police were outside the public house. It was 11.17 pm and the lights were on in the bar, so presumably the police suspected that liquor was being consumed after hours. There was a delay of eight minutes before the police were admitted and no offence was detected. The police had a right to enter under statute[447] whether an offence was being committed or not; an entry under this statutory right was in execution of their duty; and their *entry* was obstructed. Lord Goddard CJ defined 'obstructing' as 'Making it more difficult for the police to carry out their duties.'[448] This is far wider than was necessary for the decision.

Where defendants warn individuals who *are about to commit* offences, the courts have had difficulties. In *Green v Moore*,[449] the distinction was drawn between advising a person to *suspend* his criminal activity, so that he will not be found out by the police (warning motorists so they do not speed until past the speed trap), which is an offence; and advising him to give it up altogether (ie never speed again)—in which case he will not be found out by the police—which is not an offence.[450]

Presumably it must be proved that some named officer was obstructed;[451] it would hardly be enough that D warned E in general terms that if he did not stop committing an offence he would be found out.

Obstructing by not assisting

Lord Goddard CJ's *dictum* defining 'obstructing' as 'Making it more difficult for the police to carry out their duties'[452] goes too far in some senses. Surely a solicitor who advises his client to say nothing cannot be guilty of an offence, though he undoubtedly makes things more difficult for the police; and why should a solicitor be in a different situation from anyone else? The fact that the refusal is expressed in abusive and obscene terms should, in principle, make no difference.[453] If D's language amounts to some other offence, such as that under s 4 of the Public Order Act 1986,[454] he should be charged with that.

It has been held that refusal to answer a constable's question, though it undoubtedly makes it more difficult for the police to carry out their duties, does not amount to wilful obstruction: *Rice v Connolly*.[455] However, where there is more than a mere refusal the offence may be committed. In *Sekfali v DPP*,[456] police officers approached the defendants who had been acting suspiciously. The officers identified themselves as such whereupon the defendants all ran off. They were convicted of wilfully obstructing police officers in the execution of their duty. The Divisional Court held that the police officers were entitled in the execution of their duty to approach the men and ask questions. The court confirmed that a citizen has no legal duty to assist the police, whilst noting that most people would accept that they have a moral and social duty to do so. The court then went on:

section 89(2) makes it an offence to willfully [*sic*] obstruct a police officer in the execution of his duty. The appellants would have been entitled to remain silent and not answer any questions put to them. They could have refused, if they had not been arrested, to accompany the police to any particular place to which they might have been requested by the police to go. They could have said that

---

[447] See now Licensing Act 2003, s 180(1).   [448] [1955] 3 All ER 406 at 408.

[449] [1982] QB 1044. Cf *Moore v Green* [1983] 1 All ER 663. Explaining *Bastable v Little* [1907] 1 KB 59. See also *DPP v Glendinning* [2005] EWHC 2333 (Admin), holding that warning motorists of a speed trap was not necessarily sufficient to amount to the offence of obstructing a police officer in the execution of his duty unless the drivers being warned were speeding or were likely to be speeding. How fine a line is that? How will anyone know if they are likely to be?

[450] What then of the maps and apps published of all speed camera sites, or the devices which warn motorists as they approach a speed trap?

[451] *Syce v Harrison* [1981] Crim LR 110n.   [452] [1955] 3 All ER 406 at 408.

[453] See Marshall J in *Rice v Connolly* [1966] 2 QB 414 at 420.   [454] See Ch 31.

[455] [1966] 2 QB 414.   [456] [2006] EWHC 894 (Admin).

they had no intention of answering questions and they could, no doubt, have said that as a result they were intent on going on their way and have done so without giving rise to a case which would entitle the court to conclude that in departing they were intending to impede the police officers and obstruct the police officers in the execution of their duty. Had they responded in that way, then it would have been for the police to have decided whether to arrest them; but they ran off, as the magistrates found to avoid apprehension. That being a wilful act, taken so as to obstruct the police, was an act capable of constituting an offence contrary to section 89(2).

Telling the police a false story is also quite different from merely remaining silent and is clearly an obstruction.[457] Refusing to reveal the whereabouts of a prohibited drug is not an obstruction; but burying it to hide it from an officer searching for it might be, when the officer's task is made more difficult.[458] These difficulties would not arise if the Act had been held to be limited to physical interference.

Lawful acts as obstruction?

It is not necessary that the act relied on as an obstruction should be unlawful independently of its operation as an obstruction of the police.[459] The conferment of powers and imposition of duties on the police may, impliedly, impose duties on others not to impede the exercise by the police of these powers and duties: the right of a constable to enter licensed premises where he believes an offence might be committed imposes an obligation on the licensee and others to let him in;[460] the right to conduct a lawful search of premises;[461] the right of a constable to require a driver in certain circumstances to provide a specimen of breath[462] implies a duty on the motorist (though he has not been arrested) to remain 'there or nearby' until the constable has had a reasonable opportunity to carry out the test.[463] If, when D is found to have consumed an excess of alcohol, it is the duty of a constable to remove D's car from the highway, there is an implied duty on D to hand over the keys of the car.[464]

Whether a duty thus to cooperate with the police is to be implied depends on whether this is a compelling inference from the nature of the police duty or right. To some extent it is a question of policy—so, the courts have held there is no duty to answer police questions but there is a duty not to give misleading answers.[465] Whether D's conduct is an act rather than an omission is only one factor in determining whether there is an obstruction. Omissions may amount to obstruction even when the omission is not an offence independently of s 89.[466] There is a separate common law offence of refusing to aid a constable who is attempting to prevent or to quell a breach of the peace and who calls for assistance.[467]

Mens rea for obstruction

Unlike 'assault' and 'resist', if D is charged with 'obstruction', it must be proved that that was 'wilful'. D must intend to behave in such a way as to make it more difficult for the police to carry out their duties. His conduct need be neither hostile to, nor aimed at, the police, as some cases have suggested.[468] So, in *Lewis v Cox*[469] where D persisted in opening the door of a van in which X, who had been arrested, was about to be driven away, D's purpose was

---

[457] *Rice v Connolly*, n 454.   [458] See note on *Syce v Harrison* [1981] Crim LR 110.

[459] *Dibble v Ingleton* [1972] 1 QB 480. See G Williams, 'Criminal Law—The Duty Not To Obstruct Your Own Conviction' (1972) 30 CLJ 193.

[460] Licensing Act 2003, s 180.   [461] *Sykes v CPS (Manchester)* [2013] EWHC 3600 (Admin).

[462] Road Traffic Act 1988, s 7.   [463] *DPP v Carey* [1970] AC 1072 at 1097.

[464] *Stunt v Bolton* [1972] RTR 435.   [465] *Rice v Connolly*, n 454.

[466] eg *Stunt v Bolton*, n 465. Cf *Dibble v Ingleton*, n 460.

[467] *Waugh* (1976) The Times, 1 Oct 1976.

[468] *Willmott v Atack* [1977] QB 498; *Hills v Ellis* [1983] QB 680.   [469] [1985] QB 509.

not to obstruct the police but to find out where X was being taken, but, since he must have known that he was preventing the police officer from driving off, the justices were bound to find that he intended to make it more difficult for them to carry out their duty.[470]

In *Rice v Connolly*,[471] it was said that 'wilfully' means not only 'intentionally' but also 'without lawful excuse'. This is difficult to follow. 'Wilfully' must surely refer to the state of mind of the defendant. But whether he has a lawful excuse for what he does generally depends on D's conduct and the circumstances in which he acts.[472] In that case, D would have been no more 'wilful' if he had told a false story. The difference seems to lie in the conduct which the court considers to be permissible. 'Wilfully' may of course import the absence of any *belief* on D's part of circumstances of lawful excuse. If the story told by D were in fact false, but D believed it to be true, the constable might be obstructed, but he would not be 'wilfully' obstructed.

As to mistakes about the status of the officer, in cases of obstruction, liability is not strict. Since the decision in *Gladstone Williams*,[473] it is sufficient that the mistaken belief was genuinely held even if it was unreasonable.

Note also the summary offence of obstructing without reasonable excuse an emergency worker—fire and rescue personnel, paramedics, lifeboat crew, etc—under the Emergency Workers (Obstruction) Act 2006. By s 1(3), a person is responding to emergency circumstances if the person: (a) is going anywhere for the purpose of dealing with emergency circumstances occurring there; or (b) is dealing with emergency circumstances or preparing to do so. Emergency is defined in s 1(4).[474]

16.9 Ill-treatment or neglect

Section 44 of the Mental Capacity Act 2005, which has been in force since 1 April 2007, creates the offences of ill-treatment and wilful neglect.[475] On summary conviction, D is liable to imprisonment for a term not exceeding 12 months or a fine not exceeding the statutory maximum, or both. On conviction on indictment, D may be imprisoned for a term not exceeding five years or a fine or both. As is evident, the offence can be committed if D either ill-treats P or wilfully neglects P.[476] In *Turbill*,[477] the Court of Appeal held that 'wilful' denotes a subjective state of mind, but it is not equivalent to subjective recklessness. It is respectfully submitted that 'wilful' is now generally accepted to mean intention or subjective recklessness.[478]

The offences in s 44 is only made out if D has care of a person[479] who lacks, or whom D reasonably believes lacks, capacity.[480] It is important to point out that lack of capacity is defined by reference to ss 2 and 3 of the 2005 Act. These provide a complex series of tests

---

[470] cf the discussion of intention, p 93.   [471] See p 745.
[472] See comment at [1966] Crim LR 390.   [473] (1987) 78 Cr App R 276, p 353.
[474] The offence can include eg making hoax calls: *McMenemy* [2009] EWCA Crim 42.
[475] See A Brammer, 'Carers and the Mental Capacity Act 2005: Angels Permitted, Devils Prosecuted?' [2014] Crim LR 589 evaluating whether the offence adds to the pre-existing legal framework.
[476] It was confirmed in *Nursing* [2012] EWCA Crim 2521 that the section creates two separate offences.
[477] [2013] EWCA Crim 1422.
[478] See the further discussion at Ch 3 and the case comment at [2014] Crim LR 388.
[479] The offence also applies where D is the donee of a lasting power of attorney, or an enduring power of attorney for V or is a deputy appointed by the court for V. It is not necessary for an enduring power of attorney to have been registered in accordance with the Act. The wording of s 44(1)(b) imposes no such requirement: *Kurtz* [2018] EWCA Crim 2743.
[480] *Kurtz* [2018] EWCA Crim 2743.

that purport to define the circumstances in which an individual is to be treated as if he is unable to make decisions for himself.[481] The Lord Chief Justice, in *Nursing*,[482] held that s 44 does not create an absolute offence and that 'actions or omissions, or a combination of both, which reflect or are believed to reflect the protected autonomy of the individual needing care do not constitute wilful neglect'.[483]

Section 44 offences can be committed without proof of any requirement that D's conduct was performed 'in a manner likely to cause unnecessary suffering or injury to health'. As was made clear in *Patel*,[484] it is no defence that V, a patient who was wrongly denied CPR when she stopped breathing, would have died even if that treatment had been provided.

Section 20 of the Criminal Justice and Courts Act 2015 creates a new offence for care workers who ill-treat or wilfully neglect those in their care. By s 21, corporate or unincorporated care providers may be liable for negligence or neglect in the way their activities are organized which amounts to a gross breach of a duty of care owed to the individual receiving care.[485]

16.10 Administering poison

Sections 23 and 24 of the OAPA 1861 create offences, punishable with ten and five years' imprisonment respectively, with a similar actus reus. The offences apply to conduct in England and Wales.[486]

16.10.1 Section 23

The section (as amended) provides:

Whosoever shall unlawfully and maliciously administer to or cause to be administered to or taken by any other person any poison or other destructive or noxious thing, so as thereby to endanger the life of such person, or so as thereby to inflict upon such person any grievous bodily harm, shall be guilty of [an offence] and being convicted thereof shall be liable . . . to [imprisonment] for any term not exceeding ten years . . .

By s 25, a person charged under s 23 may be convicted of an offence under s 24.[487]

16.10.1.1 Actus reus

Administer, cause to be administered, cause to be taken

Lord Bingham described s 23 as providing three distinct offences: (a) administering a noxious thing to any other person; (b) causing a noxious thing to be administered to any other person; and (c) causing a noxious thing to be taken by any other person. His lordship explained:

Offence (1) is committed where D administers the noxious thing directly to V, as by injecting V with the noxious thing, holding a glass containing the noxious thing to V's lips, spraying V with acid

---

[481] See *A* [2014] EWCA Crim 299.   [482] [2012] EWCA Crim 2521.
[483] ibid, [18].   [484] [2013] EWCA Crim 965.
[485] For detailed discussion of these offences, see K Laird, 'Filling a Lacuna: The Care Worker and Care Provider Offences in the Criminal Justice and Courts Act 2015' (2016) 36 Stat LR 1.
[486] The court would not therefore issue a summons against Tony Blair for authorizing the use of depleted uranium bullets in Iraq: *R (on the application of Defending Christian Arabs) v Guildford Magistrates' Court* [2020] EWHC 1850 (Admin).
[487] See generally LCCP 217, paras 2.189 et seq and LC 361, Ch 7.

or corrosive substances, or (as in *R v Gillard*[488]) spraying the noxious thing in V's face. Offence (2) is typically committed where D does not directly administer the noxious thing to V but causes an innocent third party TP to administer it to V. If D, knowing a syringe to be filled with poison instructs TP to inject V, TP believing the syringe to contain a legitimate therapeutic substance, D would commit this offence. Offence (3) covers the situation where the noxious thing is not administered to V but taken by him, provided D causes the noxious thing to be taken by V and V does not make a voluntary and informed decision to take it. If D puts a noxious thing in food which V is about to eat and V, ignorant of the presence of the noxious thing, eats it, D commits offence (3).[489]

The words 'administer' and 'take' are to be construed by the court and not left as a question of fact to the jury.[490] The words are disjunctive. 'Takes' assumes some 'ingestion' by the victim. It seems that the thing is not 'administered' until it is taken into the body.[491] To leave the poison, intending it to be taken by an unwitting victim, may be an attempt to administer it.[492] There is no requirement that the 'administration' under s 23 involves surreptitious conduct.[493]

In *Kennedy*,[494] D handed to V a syringe containing heroin with which V injected himself and, in consequence, died. At his trial he was convicted of manslaughter. The Court of Appeal said, *obiter*, that it could see no reason why D should not have been convicted of an offence under s 23. There is a very good reason, simply that D did not administer the thing to V or cause V to take it. V, a person of full age and capacity, not labouring under any mistake, administered it to himself. Such an act breaks the chain of causation. After seemingly returning to orthodoxy in *Dias*, the Court of Appeal again returned to this revolutionary approach to causation in *Rogers*,[495] and *Finlay*.[496] In *Kennedy (No 2)*,[497] the House of Lords finally laid this heresy to rest. Where D hands V a syringe with which V injects himself, there is no administering by D. Nor is it possible to say that D is jointly responsible or jointly engaged in administering the heroin.[498]

In *Kennedy (No 2)*, the House of Lords also rejected the approach of the Court of Appeal in *Finlay* which had adopted the *Empress Car* approach to causation. Since V has voluntarily taken the decision to inject himself, his free, informed act breaks the chain of causation. It is different if D secretly puts the noxious thing into V's drink and V consumes it. V's consumption is then not a fully voluntary act—he believes he is drinking nothing but, say, coffee and has no intention to take the noxious thing. D has then 'administered' it to him or caused him to take it.[499]

---

[488] *Gillard* (1988) 87 Cr App R 189. See also *Cronin-Simpson* [2000] 1 Cr App R (S) 54, D surreptitiously pouring petrol into neighbour's house through loft pipe; *Potter* [2005] EWCA Crim 3050—splashing petrol on V and threatening to ignite (surely better charged as a threat to kill?).

[489] *Kennedy (No 2)* [2007] UKHL 38, [9]–[10].

[490] *Gillard* (1988) 87 Cr App R 189 at 194.

[491] *Cadman* (1825) Carrington's Supplement 237. The report to the contrary in Ryan and Moody 114 is said to be inaccurate: *Harley* (1830) 4 C & P 369, per Parke J: and 6 Cox CC 16 n (c). But see *Walford* (1899) 34 L Jo 116, per Wills J.

[492] Prior to the Criminal Attempts Act, a judge could tell a jury it was an attempt, as Wightman J did in *Dale* (1852) 6 Cox CC 14.

[493] It has been prosecuted where eg D doused people with petrol and threatened to ignite it: *Potter* [2005] EWCA Crim 3050.

[494] [1999] Crim LR 65. Cf *Khan* [1998] Crim LR 830.   [495] [2003] Crim LR 555.

[496] [2003] EWCA Crim 3868.   [497] [2005] EWCA Crim 685.

[498] See Ch 2 for detailed comment. But see *Burgess* [2008] EWCA Crim 516.

[499] *Harley* (1830) 4 C & P 369; *Dale* (1852) 6 Cox CC 14. D would have been more appropriately charged with 'causing . . . to be taken'. And see *Field* [2021] EWCA Crim 380.

Noxious

Some substances are noxious per se, as, for example, with radioactive isotope polonium-210 used to murder Russian dissident, Alexander Litvinenko. In *Marcus*,[500] a case under s 24, 'noxious' was broadly interpreted. A substance which may be harmless if taken in small quantities is noxious if administered in sufficient quantity to injure, aggrieve or annoy.[501] The meaning is taken to be coloured by the purpose which D may have in view. It is not necessary that the substance should be injurious to bodily health: '"noxious" mean[s] something different in quality from and of less importance than poison or other destructive things'. The court quoted the *Shorter Oxford Dictionary* meaning, 'injurious, hurtful, harmful, unwholesome', and suggested that the insertion of the celebrated snail allegedly in the ginger beer bottle in *Donoghue v Stevenson*[502] would create a noxious substance. It was held that the insertion of sedative and sleeping tablets into a bottle of milk was an attempt to commit an offence under s 24. While the tablets would cause no more than sedation or possibly sleep, they might be a danger to a person doing such normal but potentially hazardous acts as driving or crossing the street.[503]

That approach was endorsed in *Veysey*[504] where D, a serving prisoner, threw urine and faeces at a prison officer and was convicted under s 24. D's submission that a substance cannot be a noxious thing unless it has the capacity to cause some impairment or harm to a person's faculties or functioning, whether because of its intrinsic quality or because of the quantity in which it was administered, was rejected. The Court of Appeal held that where a substance is administered in a manner and a quantity which is in fact harmful, and the requisite intent is proved, then the offence will be made out even though the same substance in a lesser quantity, or administered in a different manner, may not have been harmful. Where an issue arises as to whether a substance is a noxious thing for the purpose of the 1861 Act, it will be for the judge to rule as a matter of law whether the substance concerned, in the quantity and manner in which it is shown by the evidence to have been administered, could properly be found by the jury to be injurious, hurtful, harmful or unwholesome. If it can be properly so regarded, it will be a matter for the jury whether they are satisfied that it was a noxious thing within that definition.

The earlier decision of the Court of Appeal in *Cato*[505] (a case under s 23) is wrong in saying that a thing could not be noxious merely because it was harmful if taken in large quantities.[506] The actual decision, however, that heroin is a noxious thing even where it is administered to a person with a high tolerance to whom it is unlikely to do any particular harm, is right. Heroin is noxious because 'it is liable to cause injury in common use'.[507] It was no answer that V was experienced in taking heroin and had a high tolerance. Ecstasy has been held to be a noxious substance for these purposes.[508] It has been argued that HIV could be regarded as a noxious substance capable of being administered in the course of sexual activity.[509] Charges under s 20 (discussed earlier) are more likely.

[500] [1981] 1 WLR 774.
[501] Following *Hannah* (1877) 13 Cox CC 547 and *Cramp* (1880) 5 QBD 307. Cf *Marlow* (1964) 49 Cr App R 49 (Brabin J).
[502] [1932] AC 562.
[503] See also *T* [2006] EWCA Crim 2557, where D (46) plied V (14) with alcohol and amphetamines.
[504] [2019] EWCA Crim 1332.   [505] [1976] 1 WLR 110; cf *Dalby* [1982] 1 WLR 425.
[506] 'It is not in doubt that heroin is a noxious thing, and the contrary was not contended': *Kennedy (No 2)* [2007] UKHL 38 at [10] per Lord Bingham.
[507] [1976] 1 All ER at 268. See also *MK* [2008] 2 Cr App R (S) 437 (administering methadone to child).
[508] See *Gantz* [2004] EWCA Crim 2862.
[509] See Ormerod and Gunn [1996] 1 Web JCLI; Bronnit [1994] Crim LR 21.

Whether consenting to the administration of a noxious substance that might cause grievous bodily harm or endanger life is valid consent in law must be subject to the policy on consent adopted in *Brown*.[510] The courts have repeatedly asserted that factual consent will not necessarily provide a legal defence to a charge under s 23.[511] However, it must be the case that V can consent in some contexts to the administration of a noxious substance, even one that is potentially fatal. Otherwise, V could not consent to anaesthetic for surgery. The validity of consent will, it seems, turn on public policy factors, so that while informed adult consent in a medical context or in horseplay may be legally recognized, in other contexts it will not be. In *Dica*, it was accepted that V could validly consent to the risk of infection by HIV. The court acknowledged that in some instances a person would be willing to take that risk, for example to conceive or to respect a religious prohibition on contraception. The court held that V could not consent to an intentional infection.

Section 23 was considered by the Court of Appeal (Civil Division) in *CP (A Child) v Firsttier Tribunal (Criminal Injuries Compensation)*.[512] The claimant was a child who was born with foetal alcohol syndrome after her mother drank excessively during pregnancy. CP claimed compensation from the Criminal Injuries Compensation Authority. It was argued on behalf of CP that her mother had maliciously administered a noxious thing to her contrary to s 23 of the OAPA 1861 whilst she was in the womb. In rejecting this contention, both Treacy LJ and Lord Dyson MR held that 'it is well established that a foetus is not a "person"; rather it is a *sui generis* organism'.[513] A foetus was not 'any other person' for the purposes of s 23, and as the harm had been inflicted on the child while she was in the womb, the child was not entitled to criminal injuries compensation.[514]

'Thereby'

The use of the term 'thereby' in s 23 could represent a significant restriction on the offence if it is interpreted in as narrow a fashion as that term has been understood in relation to the life-endangering offences under the Criminal Damage Act 1971. If the life endangerment arises from consequences other than the noxious substance itself, it is arguable that the offence is not committed. For example, if D laces V's coffee and V then drives to work, if V's life is endangered by the manner of his driving which was affected by the noxious substance which induced drowsiness,[515] but not by the noxious substance administered, it is arguable that life is not endangered 'thereby'.

16.10.1.2 Mens rea

Under s 23, the only mens rea required is intention or recklessness as to the administration of a noxious thing. The use in the section of the word 'maliciously' makes this clear as held in the leading case of *Cunningham*.[516] Whereas in s 24 the offence uses the expression 'with intent to', in s 23 the expression is simply 'so as thereby to'. This suggests that in s 23 no additional mens rea is required as to the element of endangering life or inflicting grievous bodily harm. That was the interpretation adopted in *Cato*. The requirement of 'malice'

---

[510] [1994] AC 212.
[511] *Cato; McShane* (1977) 66 Cr App R 97. Cf the CLRC Fourteenth Report, para 190.
[512] [2014] EWCA Civ 1554.   [513] At [39] and [62].
[514] *A-G's Reference (No 3 of 1994)* in relation to homicide does not undermine that conclusion.
[515] cf *Steer* [1988] AC 111.
[516] [1957] 2 QB 396: D tore the gas meter from the wall of an unoccupied house to steal money from it. The gas seeped into the neighbouring houses and was inhaled by V, whose life was endangered. D's conviction under s 23 was quashed because the judge directed the jury only that 'malicious' meant 'wicked'. See now Criminal Damage Act 1971, s 1(2), see Ch 29.

was satisfied by the deliberate injection of heroin into V's body. No mens rea was required as to the danger to life or the infliction of grievous bodily harm. In *Cunningham*, the Court of Criminal Appeal thought the jury should have been told that D must have foreseen that the gas he caused to be administered to V by breaking the gas pipe might cause injury to someone. The court did not say D must have foreseen that life would be endangered. This is an extraordinary result, in that a less culpable state of mind is required for the more serious offence (s 23) than the less serious (s 24).

16.10.2 Section 24

The section as amended provides:

Whosoever shall unlawfully and maliciously administer to or cause to be administered to or taken by any other person any poison or other destructive or noxious thing, with intent to injure, aggrieve, or annoy such person, shall be guilty of [an offence], and being . . . convicted thereof shall be liable to [imprisonment for a term not exceeding 5 years] . . .

By s 25, a person charged under s 24 may not be convicted of an offence under s 23.[517]

16.10.2.1 Actus reus

The elements of administration, etc have been considered earlier in relation to s 23. Section 24 might be seen as an inchoate offence, with the focus on the conduct whereas s 23 is a result-oriented crime.[518]

It is arguable that V ought to be able to provide valid consent to the administration of a substance under s 24. However, the level of harm likely is that of injury, which seems to be on a par with the threshold at which consent is generally treated as invalid in *Brown*.[519] The public policy exceptions as in *Brown* will apply.

16.10.2.2 Mens rea

This offence requires an ulterior intent: 'with intent to injure, aggrieve, or annoy such person'.

When a drug is given to V with intent to keep him awake it seems that whether this amounts to an intention to injure depends on whether D has a malevolent or a benevolent purpose. If D, a paedophile, gives the drug to V, a child, with the motive of ingratiating himself with V or rendering him susceptible to sexual offences, he has an intention to injure: *Hill*.[520] It would probably be otherwise if D's intention was to enable V to stay awake to enjoy the fireworks or greet his father on return from work. The administration of a drug to the pilot of an aircraft to keep him awake is probably not an offence. The administration of the same drug for the purpose of carrying out a prolonged interrogation may be.[521] This casts doubt on *Weatherall*.[522] D put a sleeping tablet in V's tea to enable him to search her handbag for letters proving that she was committing adultery. It was held that there was insufficient evidence of intent to injure, aggrieve or annoy: but there was surely evidence of a 'malevolent' purpose, as there would be if D gave V a sleeping tablet with intent to

---

517 cf *Stokes* (1925) 19 Cr App R 71.

518 See A Ashworth, 'Defining Criminal Offences without Harm' in *Criminal Law Essays*, 13.

519 cf the remarks in sentencing in *Sky* [2000] 2 Cr App R (S) 260, [6].

520 (1986) 83 Cr App Rep 386. The offence under s 61 of the Sexual Offences Act 2003 will apply, see p 851.

521 Examples taken from *Hill*, ibid.

522 [1968] Crim LR 115 (Judge Broderick). See also *A-G's Reference (No 71 of 2012)* [2012] EWCA Crim 3071 where D laced his colleagues' coffee with amphetamine and reported them to a supervisor for drug taking.

rape her. The test of malevolence is presumably objective. The paedophile's belief that the drugged child will enjoy and profit from the sexual experience is never going to be regarded as capable of being a 'benevolent' purpose. The question of intention comes perilously close to being one of motive, and at least on orthodox approaches to mens rea, this is irrelevant.

16.10.3 Other poisoning offences

16.10.3.1 Administering substances in relation to sexual offences

The Sexual Offences Act 2003 introduced s 61—intentional administration of a substance/causing it to be taken by V without consent with intent to stupefy/overpower to enable any person to engage in sex with V. See Ch 17, p 851.

16.10.3.2 Terrorist related poisonings

Section 38 of the Public Order Act 1986 creates what is in effect an offence of food terrorism applicable where, for example, D puts poisons or harmful objects in food products in supermarkets.[523] Sections 113 and 114 of the Anti-terrorism, Crime and Security Act 2001 create very broad offences of using or threatening to use a noxious substance or thing to cause harm and intimidate.[524]

16.11 False imprisonment

False imprisonment, like assault and battery, is both a crime at common law and a tort.[525] The civil remedy is commonly invoked and most of the reported cases on this subject are civil actions, but it features as a count in many indictments. As will appear, there are some important distinctions between the crime and the tort.

False imprisonment is committed where D unlawfully and intentionally or recklessly restrains V's freedom of movement from a particular place without lawful justification. 'Imprisonment' is probably a wider term than, and includes, 'arrest'.[526]

16.11.1 Article 5: deprivations of liberty and arrest

Article 5 of the ECHR provides a guarantee against arbitrary deprivation of liberty, but that has been interpreted more narrowly than the concept of 'restricting movement' which lies at the heart of false imprisonment. 'Article 5 is concerned with the *deprivation* of liberty and not with mere *restrictions* on freedom of movement.'[527] The distinction is not always easy to identify since the difference is 'merely one of degrees or intensity, and not one of nature or substance'.[528] In *Gillan v MPC*,[529] the House of Lords held that a brief stop (20 mins) could

---

[523] See *Cruikshank* [2001] EWCA Crim 98.

[524] For discussion, see C Walker, *Blackstone's Guide to the Anti-Terrorism Legislation* (3rd edn, 2014) 215–16.

[525] See J Goudkamp and D Nolan, *Winfield and Jolowicz on Tort* (20th edn, 2020) Ch 4. See also the discussion in LC 355, *Simplification of Criminal Law: Kidnapping and Related Offences* (2014).

[526] *Rahman* (1985) 81 Cr App R 349 at 353. *Brown* [1977] Crim LR 291 and commentary thereon and articles by D Telling, 'Arrest and Detention—The Conceptual Maze' [1978] Crim LR 320 and K Lidstone, 'A Maze in Law!' [1978] Crim LR 332. Care must be taken with the articles' references to powers of arrest as these have changed significantly. See LC 355, Ch 2.

[527] *Engel v Netherlands* (1976) 1 EHRR 647, para 58; *Guzzardi v Italy* (1980) 3 EHRR 333, para 92; *Raimondo v Italy* (1994) 18 EHRR 237, para 39; *HM v Switzerland* (App no 39187/98), 26 Feb 2002. See generally Emmerson, Ashworth and Macdonald, HR&CJ, Ch 5.

[528] *Guzzardi v Italy* (1980) 3 EHRR 333, para 92; *Ashingdane v UK* (1985) 7 EHRR 528, para 41; *Engel v Netherlands* (1976) 1 EHRR 647, paras 58–9. See also *Blume v Spain* (2000) 30 EHRR 632.

[529] [2006] UKHL 12; see [2006] Crim LR 751 and commentary.

not be regarded as a 'deprivation of liberty' within the meaning of Art 5; those subjected to a stop and search were merely 'detained in the sense of kept from proceeding or kept waiting'. The ECtHR disagreed, unanimously finding a violation of Art 8, that the use of coercive powers to require an individual to submit to a detailed search of his person, his clothing and his personal belongings amounted to a clear interference with the right to respect for private life: *Gillan and Quinton v UK*.[530] The Strasbourg Court expressly disagreed with the assessment of the House of Lords that the safeguards provided by the English legislation provided adequate protection against arbitrary interference.[531] In *Austin v MPC*,[532] the House of Lords concluded that the police detention of several thousand people on Oxford Street did not amount to a deprivation of liberty within the meaning of Art 5.[533] The Grand Chamber of the Strasbourg Court agreed and held that there was no violation of Art 5, basing its decision upon the exceptional facts of the case.[534] The Court reiterated that determining whether there has been a deprivation of liberty as that term is utilized in Art 5 as opposed to a mere restriction on liberty is one of degree or intensity as opposed to nature or substance. Extraordinarily, the Grand Chamber reached its conclusion without referring to the earlier judgment in *Gillan and Quinton*. Given that the applicants in *Austin* were detained for hours as opposed to the 20-minute police stop in *Gillan and Quinton*, the two cases are hard to reconcile.[535]

16.11.2 Actus reus

16.11.2.1 'Imprisonment'

For the purposes of the offence of false imprisonment, the 'imprisonment' may consist in confining V in a prison,[536] a house,[537] even V's own house,[538] a mine[539] or a vehicle;[540] or simply in detaining V in a public street[541] or any other place.

---

[530] (2010) 50 EHRR 45. See also *R (AP) v Secretary of State for the Home Department* [2010] UKSC 24, in which it was held that when deciding if there is a deprivation of liberty within the meaning of Art 5 of the ECHR regard should be had to the subjective factors peculiar to the particular individual.

[531] The authorization power under the Terrorism Act 2000, s 44 required only that it be expedient to make the authorization, not that it be necessary or proportionate. See Ashworth, commentary [2010] Crim LR 415. See now: the Protection of Freedoms Act 2012 dealing with the maximum length of detention without trial in terrorism cases, and stop and search under the Terrorism Act 2000. On which see E Cape, 'The Counter-Terrorism Provisions of the Protection of Freedoms Act 2012: Preventing Misuse or a Case of Smoke and Mirrors?' [2013] Crim LR 385.

[532] [2009] UKHL 5.   [533] See Ashworth, commentary [2010] Crim LR 415.

[534] (2012) 55 EHRR 14.   [535] See Ashworth's criticisms at [2012] Crim LR 545.

[536] *Cobbett v Grey* (1849) 4 Exch 729; *R v Governor of Brockhill Prison, ex p Evans (No 2)* [2001] 2 AC 19. On the difference between positive acts of imprisonment and omissions, see *Iqbal v Prison Officers Association* [2009] EWCA Civ 1312.

[537] *Warner v Riddiford* (1858) 4 CBNS 180.

[538] See eg *Cooksey* [2019] EWCA Crim 1410 where false imprisonment occurred within the context of coercive and controlling behaviour in a domestic setting. False imprisonment in V's own home has been recognized to suffice for the offence for centuries: *Termes de la Ley*, approved by Warrington and Atkin LJJ (1920) 122 LT at 51 and 53. See also *Secretary of State for the Home Department v JJ* [2007] UKHL 45 considering the power to make control orders: s 1(2) of the Prevention of Terrorism Act 2005. See also *Secretary of State for the Home Department v E* [2007] UKHL 47; *Secretary of State for the Home Department v MB; Secretary of State v AF* [2007] UKHL 46.

[539] *Herd v Weardale Steel, Coal and Coke Co Ltd* [1915] AC 67.

[540] By driving at such a speed that V dare not alight: *McDaniel v State*, 15 Tex Crim 115 (1942); *Burton v Davies* [1953] QSR 26. See also *Bowell* [2003] EWCA Crim 3896, single count of false imprisonment split where D detained V in the car, and detained her again when she escaped and injured herself.

[541] Blackstone, *Commentaries*, iii, 127; *Ludlow v Burgess* [1971] Crim LR 238; *Austin v MPC*, discussed earlier.

A false imprisonment may arise for a short duration. The restraint need be only momentary, so that the offence would be complete if D tapped V on the shoulder and said, 'You are my prisoner.'[542] It is not necessary that the victim be physically detained; there may be an arrest by words alone, but only if V submits. If V is not physically detained and does not realize he is under constraint, he is not imprisoned.[543] If V agrees to go to a police station voluntarily, he has not been arrested even if the constable would have arrested him if V had refused to go.[544] If it is then made clear to V that he will not be allowed to leave until he provides a laboratory specimen, it has been suggested that, though he has never been 'arrested', he is 'under arrest'.[545] If this distinction is valid it would seem to be enough for false imprisonment that V is 'under arrest'.

It is enough that D orders V to accompany him to another place, and V goes because he feels constrained to do so. V is not imprisoned if, on hearing D use words of arrest, he runs away or makes his escape by a trick.[546] An invitation by D to V to accompany him cannot be an imprisonment if it is made clear to V that he is entitled to refuse to go. Thus, Lord Lyndhurst CB thought there was no imprisonment where D asked a policeman to take V into custody, and the policeman objected, but said that if D and V 'would be so good as to go with him', he would take the advice of his superior.[547] The distinction between a command, amounting to an imprisonment, and a request not doing so, is a difficult one.[548] Probably Alderson B went too far in *Peters v Stanway*[549] in holding that V was imprisoned if she went to the police station with a constable voluntarily but nevertheless in consequence of a charge against her.

Though some of the older authorities[550] speak of false imprisonment as a species of assault, it is quite clear that no assault need be proved.[551] In *Linsberg*,[552] the Common Sergeant held that V, a doctor, was falsely imprisoned where D locked the door to prevent him leaving a woman in childbirth. A battery is not necessarily an imprisonment. In *Bird v Jones*,[553] V was involved in 'a struggle during which no momentary detention of his person took place'.

There is little authority on the question of how large the area of confinement may be. It is not an imprisonment wrongfully to prevent V from going in a particular direction, if he is free to go in other directions. This was decided in *Bird v Jones*,[554] where Coleridge J said: 'A prison may have its boundary large or narrow, visible and tangible, or, though real, still in the conception only;[555] it may itself be moveable or fixed: but a boundary it must have . . .' It would be otherwise if V could move off in other directions only by taking an unreasonable risk. It could hardly be said that a man locked in a second-floor room was not imprisoned because he could have climbed down the drainpipe. It has been suggested that it would be tortious to confine V to a large country estate or the Isle of Man;[556] but it could hardly be

---

[542] *Simpson v Hill* (1795) 1 Esp 431, per Eyre CJ; *Sandon v Jervis* (1859) EB & E 942, 'a mere touch constitutes an arrest, though the party be not actually taken', per Crowder J.

[543] *Alderson v Booth* [1969] 2 QB 216, [1969] 2 All ER 271.

[544] *Campbell v Tormey* [1969] 1 WLR 189. See Emmerson, Ashworth and Macdonald, HR&CJ, para 5.03.

[545] ibid, per Ashworth J.   [546] *Russen v Lucas* (1824) 1 C & P 153.

[547] *Cant v Parsons* (1834) 6 C & P 504.

[548] G Williams, 'Police Interrogation Privileges and Limitations under Foreign Law: England' in CR Sowle (ed), *Police Power and Individual Freedom: The Quest for Balance* (1962) at 43.

[549] (1835) 6 C & P 737, followed in *Conn v David Spencer Ltd* [1930] 1 DLR 805.

[550] eg Hawkins, I PC, c 60, s 7; *Pocock v Moore* (1825) Ry & M 321.

[551] *Grainger v Hill* (1838) 4 Bing NC 212; *Warner v Riddiford* (1858) 4 CBNS 180.

[552] (1905) 69 JP 107.   [553] See later.   [554] (1845) 7 QB 742 (Denman CJ dissenting).

[555] eg V is forbidden to move more than ten yards from the village pump.

[556] (1845) 7 QB 742. But 'Napoleon was certainly imprisoned on St Helena': *Winfield and Jolowicz on Torts* (20th edn, 2020) 71. In *Re Mwenya* [1960] 1 QB 241 a writ of *habeas corpus* was sought for V who was confined to an area of some 1,500 square miles but he was released before it became necessary to decide whether he was imprisoned for the purpose of *habeas corpus*.

false imprisonment to prevent V from leaving Great Britain, still less to prevent him from entering. However, a person who has actually landed and is not allowed to leave an airport building is imprisoned.[557] Is V also imprisoned, then, if he is not allowed to leave the ship which has docked in a British port?

Merely deciding to restrain a person if he attempts to leave does not amount to imprisonment.[558] But if steps are in fact taken to prevent his leaving, as by placing a policeman at the door, he is imprisoned although he is not aware of it: *Meering v Grahame-White Aviation Co Ltd*[559] where Atkin LJ said:

> It appears to me that a person could be imprisoned without his knowing it. I think a person can be imprisoned while he is asleep, while he is in a state of drunkenness, while he is unconscious, and while he is a lunatic . . . though the imprisonment began and ceased while he was in that state.

A contrary decision[560] was not cited and *Meering* has been heavily criticized,[561] although cited with approval by the House of Lords in *Murray v Minister of Defence*;[562] the arguments advanced against awarding damages in this situation are, however, not applicable to the crime. D's conduct may not be damaging to V if V knows nothing about it, but it is not necessarily any less blameworthy for, in most cases, the fact that V remains in ignorance must be a matter of mere chance.

Like other crimes, false imprisonment can be committed through an innocent agent.[563] So D is responsible for the actus reus if, at his direction or request, a policeman takes V into custody,[564] or he signs the charge-sheet when the police have said they will not take the responsibility of detaining V unless he does.[565] However, if D merely gives information to a constable, which causes him to make an arrest, that is not a false imprisonment in tort by D, if D is acting in a bona fide way.[566] A fortiori, it should not be *criminal*, because D will also lack mens rea. But this raises the question whether D will be guilty if he deliberately supplies false information to a constable who, acting on his own authority but relying exclusively on D's information, arrests V.[567] D has surely caused the actus reus with mens rea. Note that

---

[557] *Kuchenmeister v Home Office* [1958] 1 QB 496.

[558] *Bournewood Community and Mental Health NHS Trust, ex p L* [1998] 3 All ER 289 at 298; but Lord Steyn, dissenting, more realistically thought (at 306): 'The suggestion that L was free to go is a fairy tale.' Note the European Court's finding of a breach of Art 5 in *HL v UK* (App no 45508/99), and see the Mental Health Act 2007, ss 4 and 5. See also the discussion of *Cheshire West and Chester Council v P* [2014] UKSC 19 that 'deprivation of liberty' in the context of the living arrangements of a mentally incapacitated person was to be given the same meaning in domestic law as in Art 5 of the ECHR.

[559] (1919) 122 LT 44, Duke LJ dissenting, where two policemen were stationed outside the door of a room to prevent V leaving. He was as effectively imprisoned as if the door had been locked. *Meering* was approved in *Murray v Ministry of Defence* [1988] 2 All ER 521 at 529.

[560] *Herring v Boyle* (1834) 1 Cr M & R 377 (Court of Exchequer).

[561] G Williams in *Police Power and Individual Freedom* (1962) 45–6; C Witting, *Street on Torts* (14th edn, 2015) Ch 9.

[562] [1998] 1 WLR 692.

[563] There is no vicarious liability for false imprisonment (nor generally in criminal law for common law offences: *R (Chief Constable of Northumbria) v Newcastle Magistrates' Court* [2010] EWHC 935 (Admin)).

[564] *Gosden v Elphick and Bennett* (1849) 4 Exch 445. Note also the tort of procuring an arrest, see *Martin v Watson* [1996] 1 AC 74.

[565] *Austin v Dowling* (1870) LR 5 CP 534. It is otherwise if D signs the charge-sheet as a matter of form, when the police are detaining V on their own responsibility: *Grinham v Willey* (1859) 4 H & N 496.

[566] *Gosden v Elphick and Bennett*, n 565; *Grinham v Willey*, n 566; 'We ought to take care that people are not put in peril for making complaint when a crime has been committed', per Pollock CB. Cf *O'Hara v Chief Constable of RUC* [1997] AC 286.

[567] See *Hough v Chief Constable of Staffordshire* [2001] EWCA Civ 39.

where D is initially liable for false imprisonment, his liability ceases on the intervention of some judicial act[568] authorizing the detention or on any other event, breaking the chain of causation.[569] So, in the case of the false information leading to arrest, D may be liable for the act of the constable but not the judicial act of the magistrate.[570]

Whatever the position in the law of tort,[571] it should be immaterial in the criminal law that the imprisonment was not 'directly' caused by D; and it ought to be sufficient that D caused it with mens rea—as by digging a pit into which V falls and is trapped.[572]

Another issue in the law of tort is whether, in view of the requirement of a trespass, it is possible to falsely imprison by mere omission. In *Herd v Weardale Steel, Coal and Coke Co Ltd*,[573] V voluntarily descended into D's mine and, in breach of contract, stopped work and asked to be brought to the surface before the end of the shift. D's refusal to accede to this request was not a false imprisonment: he was under no duty to provide facilities for V to leave in breach of contract. Clearly, the result would be different if D were to take positive steps to prevent V from leaving in breach of contract,[574] as by locking him in a factory. Buckley and Hamilton LJJ[575] thought that mere omission could not have been false imprisonment, even if it occurred when the shift was over. V's only civil remedy would have been in contract; but the House of Lords expressed no opinion on this point.

In *Mee v Cruickshank*,[576] Wills J held that a prison governor was under a duty to take steps to ensure that his officers did not detain a prisoner who had been acquitted. In that case there were acts of imprisonment by the prison officers but they were not the servants of D, the governor, and it seems to have been D's omission which rendered him liable in tort. As the House of Lords accepted in *Ex p Evans*, the failure to release a prisoner on the due date gives rise to an action in false imprisonment, even if the failure was in good faith. And it ought to make no difference that D's duty to release V arises out of a contract:

If a man gets into an express train and the doors are locked pending its arrival at its destination, he is not entitled, merely because the train has been stopped by signal, to call for the doors to be opened to let him out.[577]

But if he is kept locked in for a day at his destination this surely ought to be false imprisonment. And even if there is no remedy in tort this is no reason why the omission should not be held to be criminal. The CLRC was of the opinion that the crime of false imprisonment is, and ought to be, capable of commission by omission.[578]

---

[568] *Lock v Ashton* (1848) 12 QB 871. Cf *Marrinan v Vibart* [1963] 1 QB 528.

[569] *Harnett v Bond* [1925] AC 669. D's report caused V to be taken to an asylum; D was not liable for the imprisonment after the doctor at the asylum had examined V and decided to detain him. Cf *Pike v Waldrum* [1952] 1 Lloyd's Rep 431.

[570] See *Austin v Dowling* (1870) LR 5 C & P 534 at 540.

[571] R Clayton and H Tomlinson, *Civil Actions against the Police* (3rd edn, 2005) para 4–046. See also *Ahmed v Shafique* [2009] EWHC 618 (QB).

[572] cf *Clarence* (1888) 22 QBD 23 at 36 per Wills J.   [573] [1915] AC 67.

[574] Unless, perhaps, the contract was that V should be entitled to leave only on the fulfilment of some reasonable condition: *Robinson v Balmain New Ferry Co Ltd* [1910] AC 295. *Sed quaere* whether one is entitled to restrain another from leaving even if it is a breach of contract for him to do so. The contract can hardly be specifically enforceable.

[575] [1913] 3 KB at 787 and 793.   [576] (1902) 20 Cox CC 210.

[577] *Herd v Weardale Steel, Coal and Coke Co Ltd* [1915] AC 67 at 71 per Lord Haldane. See M Amos, 'A Note on Contractual Restraint of Liberty' (1928) 44 LQR 464; KF Tan, 'A Misconceived Issue in the Tort of False Imprisonment' (1981) 44 MLR 166.

[578] Fourteenth Report, paras 253, 254.

16.11.2.2 Unlawful restraint

The imprisonment must be 'false'; that is, unlawful. A convicted person sentenced to imprisonment may be lawfully confined in any prison and, as against prison officers so confining him in good faith, he has no 'residual liberty'. If he is subjected to intolerable conditions he may have other remedies[579] but he cannot sue (or, it may be assumed, prosecute) the officers for false imprisonment.[580] It might, however, be false imprisonment for a fellow prisoner, or an officer acting in bad faith outside the scope of his duty, to lock him in a confined space, such as a hut, within the prison. In *Iqbal v Prison Officers Association*,[581] the failure to allow I, a serving prisoner, out of his cell on the day of unlawful strike action by prison officers, did not give rise to a claim for false imprisonment against the officers.

A parent may lawfully exercise restraint over a child, so long as he remains within the bounds of reasonable parental discipline and does not act in contravention of a court order,[582] or s 58 of the Children Act 2004. Where a girl of 14 or 15 was fostered out by her father with the consent and assistance of the local authority and he abducted her against her will and with intent to take her to her country of origin, it was for the jury to say whether they were satisfied that this was outside the bounds of legitimate parental discipline and correction.[583] A defendant charged with false imprisonment may rely on other justifications, such as the prevention of crime.[584]

The question of false imprisonment most commonly arises in connection with the exercise of powers of arrest. If such powers are exceeded, there is a false imprisonment. The principal powers are as follows.

Arrest by a constable under a valid warrant

Where a warrant is issued but the justice lacks jurisdiction to issue the warrant, the constable who arrests under the warrant is statutorily protected[585] from any 'action' if he acts in obedience to it. As the term 'action' is inappropriate to a criminal proceeding, a constable could not rely on the Act as a defence to criminal prosecution; but he would probably have a good defence on the ground of lack of mens rea.[586] An arrest under warrant for a civil matter is unlawful if the arresting officer does not have the warrant in his possession.[587]

Arrest without warrant under PACE

The powers of police constables and others to arrest are governed by PACE. See ss 24 and 24A and the common law powers preserved under PACE.

---

[579] See *Krgozlu v MPC* [2006] EWCA Civ 1691.

[580] *Hague v Deputy Governor of Parkhurst Prison* [1991] 3 All ER 733. What if the conditions are so intolerable as to found a defence of necessity to a charge of escape (see Ch 10)? Is it false imprisonment to prevent such a prisoner from leaving the prison?

[581] [2009] EWCA Civ 1312.   [582] *Rahman* (1985) 81 Cr App R 349. Cf *D* [1984] AC 778.

[583] *Rahman*, ibid. In fact, D pleaded guilty, and his appeal was dismissed. Note s 121 of the Anti-social Behaviour, Crime and Policing Act 2014 which makes it an offence to use violence, threats or any other form of coercion for the purpose of causing another person to enter into marriage and the Forced Marriage (Civil Protection) Act 2007, which creates forced marriage protection orders.

[584] D acting to prevent theft relied on s 3 of the Criminal Law Act 1967: *Bowden* [2002] EWCA Civ 1279. See also *Morris* [2013] EWCA Crim 436, p 416; *Faraj* [2007] EWCA Crim 1033 (see Ch 10, p 425).

[585] The Constables Protection Act 1750, s 6. See *O'Connor v Isaacs* [1956] 2 QB 288.

[586] See later.

[587] *De Costa Small v Kirkpatrick* (1978) 68 Cr App R 186, [1979] Crim LR 41.

Arrest for breach of the peace

The House of Lords held in *R (Laporte) v Chief Constable of Gloucestershire*[588] that an arrest for an anticipated breach of the peace can only be legitimate where there is a reasonable apprehension[589] of an *imminent* breach of the peace.[590] Moreover, in the absence of such an apprehension, there is no power to take preventive action falling short of arrest.

In *Austin v MPC*,[591] the House of Lords held that there was no false imprisonment when, in order to maintain order and public safety and to prevent the commission of offences, the police held several thousand people in a cordon on Oxford Street in London. Some of those people were not demonstrators. The containment of the individuals amounted to imprisonment, but it was not false imprisonment because the police were acting lawfully. The police action was found to be necessary in order to avoid an imminent breach of the peace (and the causing of serious injury) by some members of the crowd. The circumstances in which the police can detain V in order to avoid danger because of an imminent breach of the peace by X were said to be very strictly limited to extreme and exceptional circumstances. There is a breach of the peace whenever harm is actually done or is likely to be done to a person, or in his presence to his property, or a person is in fear of being so harmed through an assault, an affray, a riot or other disturbance.[592] Public alarm, excitement or disturbance is not of itself a breach of the peace, unless it arises from actual or threatened violence.

16.11.3 Mens rea

Since the great majority of the reported cases are civil actions,[593] there is little authority on the nature of the mens rea required for false imprisonment but, in *Rahman*,[594] the court stated that 'false imprisonment consists in the unlawful and intentional or reckless restraint of a victim's freedom of movement from a particular place'. This was confirmed by *Hutchins*[595] which held that the offence is one of 'basic intent' so that a belief caused by self-induced intoxication that the victim is consenting is no defence. The courts did not specify what kind of recklessness they had in mind; but a common law offence would naturally require *Cunningham* recklessness. This may be taken to be established now that it is settled that assault requires *Cunningham* recklessness.[596] Assault and false imprisonment are both common law offences and are so closely related that it is inconceivable that they should be governed by different principles of mens rea.

16.11.4 Reform

The Law Commission recommends the replacement of the common law offence of false imprisonment with a statutory offence entitled 'unlawful detention' but which in other

---

[588] [2007] 2 WLR 46.

[589] The Court of Appeal has confirmed that on appeal it is not for the court to form its own assessment of whether a breach of the peace was imminent, rather it must evaluate the reasonableness of the apprehension of the police. See *R (Moos) v Commissioner of Police of the Metropolis* [2012] EWCA Civ 12.

[590] This principle was affirmed in *R (Wright) v Commissioner of Police for the Metropolis* [2013] EWHC 2739 (QB) and *R (Hicks) v Commissioner of Police of the Metropolis* [2014] EWCA Civ 3.

[591] [2009] UKHL 5. The Grand Chamber of the Strasbourg Court dismissed the claimants' application. See (2012) 55 EHRR 14.

[592] *Howell* (1981) 73 Cr App R 31 at 37. Lord Denning has said that even the lawful use of force is a breach of the peace: *Chief Constable of Devon and Cornwall, ex p Central Electricity Generating Board* [1981] 3 All ER 826 at 832; but this can hardly subject the person using such force to arrest.

[593] Reckless indifference suffices for the tort: *Muuse v Secretary of State for the Home Department* [2010] EWCA Civ 453.

[594] (1985) 81 Cr App R 349 at 353, n 583.   [595] [1988] Crim LR 379.   [596] See p 105.

respects retains the elements of the current law.[597] The offence would be indictable only and carry a maximum life sentence.[598]

16.12 Kidnapping

Kidnapping has long been regarded as an aggravated form of false imprisonment[599] so the rules of lawful excuse are, no doubt, the same. Both are common law offences, punishable with imprisonment or fine at the discretion of the court. It is generally regarded as important to have a separate offence of kidnap to reflect the distinctive wrongdoing involved in the taking or carrying away which distinguishes kidnap from false imprisonment.[600]

In *D*,[601] the House of Lords gave what purported to be an authoritative account of the law of kidnapping:

First, the nature of the offence is an attack on, and infringement of, the personal liberty of an individual. Second, the offence contains four ingredients as follows: (1) the taking or carrying away of one person by another, (2) by force or by fraud, (3) without the consent of the person so taken or carried away and (4) without lawful excuse. Third, until the comparatively recent abolition by statute of the division of criminal offences into the two categories of felonies and misdemeanours (see s1 of the Criminal Law Act 1967), the offence of kidnapping was categorised by the common law as a misdemeanour only. Fourth, despite that, kidnapping was always regarded, by reason of its nature, as a grave and (to use the language of an earlier age) heinous offence. Fifth, in earlier days the offence contained a further ingredient, namely that the taking or carrying away should be from a place within the jurisdiction to another place outside it; this further ingredient has, however, long been obsolete and forms no necessary part of the offence today. Sixth, the offence was in former days described not merely as taking or carrying away a person but further or alternatively as secreting him; this element of secretion has, however, also become obsolete, so that, although it may be present in a particular case, it adds nothing to the basic ingredient of taking or carrying away.

In defining the offence in that way, Lord Brandon's attempts to consolidate earlier interpretations resulted in a considerable degree of overlap and this prompted the Law Commission to recommend a simplification of the offence in a statutory form.

Following decisions in which the Court of Appeal has struggled to identify whether the core of the offence lies in the wrong of taking and carrying away by fraud or force or the harm in terms of deprivation of liberty, the law is in a state of some confusion.[602]

---

[597] See LC 355, para 4.238.   [598] See *Trifonova (Rossitza)* [2017] EWCA Crim 240.

[599] East, I PC, 429. On the history, see D Napier, 'Detention Offences at Common Law' in *Reshaping the Criminal Law*, 198. More recently, in *Vu* [2012] 2 SCR 411, the Supreme Court of Canada analysed the common law origins of the offence.

[600] See the analysis in LC 355, paras 4.66 et seq in which the Law Commission identifies the additional mischiefs in kidnap over and above those, or at least different to those, in false imprisonment, including the additional danger in which V is placed by being made to travel with D, the greater anxiety that would cause V and the enhanced wrong on D's part by demonstrating such control over V's autonomy by compelling V to remain in his continued presence. These aggravated harms and wrongs are most obvious when D uses force or threats to cause V to move with him.

[601] [1984] AC 778, [1984] Crim LR 558. Kidnapping had not previously been satisfactorily defined: see Napier, n 600. The Law Commission Draft Criminal Code, cl 81, proposed radical amendment to the offence by restricting it to cases of carrying away for ulterior purposes—to commit a serious offence.

[602] For further analysis, see LCCP 200, *Simplification of the Criminal Law: Kidnapping* (2011). See also J Herring, 'What's Wrong with Kidnapping?' [2012] Crim LR 343; LC 355, para 2.10.

In *Cort*,[603] D had on a number of occasions stopped his car at bus stops, falsely stating to women in the queue that the bus they awaited had broken down and offered them a lift. On two occasions women got into the car. One changed her mind and asked to be let out of the car and D complied; the other was taken to her destination without being assaulted by D in any way. D was convicted of two counts of kidnapping. The Court of Appeal upheld the conviction, finding that D had defrauded VV as to the nature of the act. In this case it was held that the complainants did not consent to the events; they only consented to a ride in the car, but the ride in the car was a 'different thing' from that with which D was charged. That decision is no longer to be followed in the light of the decision in *Hendy-Freegard*.[604] H was convicted of two offences of kidnapping and a number of offences of dishonesty. H had 'an astonishing capacity to deceive', and managed to persuade three victims that he was an MI5 agent who had been investigating an IRA cell at their college. He persuaded them to leave the college and travel around the country, with periods of settlement, for a period of up to ten years. During that period, he financially exploited them. H's conviction for kidnapping was quashed as the Court of Appeal, rightly it is submitted, concluded that because H did not accompany the victims this meant that there was no kidnap. In the course of the judgment, the Lord Chief Justice emphasized that the prosecution had to establish that the victim was deprived of his or her liberty.

Confusion remains as to the relationship between the elements of: (a) the deprivation of liberty; (b) the absence of consent; (c) being taken or carried away; (d) the use of force or fraud; and (e) the absence of a lawful excuse. In particular, it is difficult to determine whether the force or fraud must be the means of carrying away (as Lord Brandon's speech and *Cort* suggest) or the reason for the lack of consent. A further question is whether the consent must be: (a) to the taking or carrying away; (b) the deprivation of liberty; (c) both; or (d) being taken by force or fraud.[605]

It is submitted that there must be an act of force or fraud which results in V being taken or carried away and that by that act of taking or carrying away without consent, V must be deprived of liberty without lawful excuse.

16.12.1 Deprivation of liberty

The definition offered in *D* fails to clarify whether the offence requires proof of a deprivation of liberty. Prior to *D*, commentators had expressly defined the offence in terms of a deprivation of liberty and carrying away from the place where the victim wanted to be.[606] It is difficult to see how there could be a kidnap if V was not deprived of his liberty. It is submitted that following the decision in *Hendy-Freegard*, this is now reconfirmed as a core element of the offence. Whether someone is deprived of his liberty is to be determined in the same way as for the offence of false imprisonment. A deprivation of liberty is a necessary but not a sufficient basis of liability for kidnap.

It seems clear that if V has consented to the deprivation of liberty there can be no kidnapping. If V consents, for example, to being locked up (either as part of a prank or a role play in sadomasochism, etc) there is no offence of false imprisonment or of kidnap. There is consent to the deprivation of liberty.

Applying orthodox principles discussed earlier in this chapter, if D has deprived V of her liberty by deceiving her as to the nature of the act or as to his identity, there will be no

---

[603] [2003] EWCA Crim 2149.   [604] [2007] EWCA Crim 1236.

[605] These criticisms were cited with approval by the Lord Chief Justice in *Kayani* [2011] EWCA Crim 2871.

[606] See the 5th edn of this book, at p 388; *Archbold* (40th edn, 1979) para 2796.

valid consent. The usual difficulties will arise as to whether the fraud was as to the nature or identity. The case of *Wellard*[607] might be best interpreted as involving a fraud as to identity. In *Wellard*, D was held to have 'taken' V when by impersonating a police officer he tricked V into his car in order to submit to a 'drugs search'. That case also suggests that there is a sufficient deprivation of liberty if V does not believe that she can move. This will usually arise because of D's deception.[608]

16.12.2 Taking and carrying away

There is no doubt that this is also an important element of the offence. The requirements of carrying away and the use of force or fraud seem to be the principal factors distinguishing kidnapping from false imprisonment.[609] It seems that every kidnapping is also a false imprisonment but a detention without any taking away or force or fraud (eg D merely turns the key intentionally locking V in the room) is only the latter offence. Where D has taken or carried V away by force or fraud, he may be convicted of both offences.[610] The crime is complete when V is deprived of her liberty and carried away from the place where she wished to be.[611]

The courts have failed to define what the term 'taking or carrying away' means. Lord Brandon used the terms as alternatives, which suggests that there is some difference between them. Carried implies some movement, and as we know from *Hendy-Freegard*, D must accompany V. If 'takes' implies a different action, it could mean 'seizes', but if that means no more than a stationary capture of V by D, that would be difficult to reconcile with the requirement in *Hendy-Freegard*. It is submitted that the word 'takes' here should not be construed so as to extend the offence of kidnap to include stationary detention that would amount to no more than false imprisonment.

The courts have failed to spell out the relationship between the element of taking or carrying away and the deprivation of liberty.[612] It is submitted that the most logical interpretation of the offence may be that the act of taking or carrying away must be the *cause of* the deprivation of liberty. The decision in *Hendy-Freegard* supports this interpretation by concluding that there is no kidnap where V is taken or carried away by force or fraud (as in *Cort*) unless V is also deprived of her liberty. In *Cort*, for example, it would now seem to be accepted that the passengers accepting the lifts were defrauded as to being carried away, but not deprived of their liberty since they would be free to leave at any time they wished—as demonstrated by the fact that D did let one of the women out of the car immediately when she so requested. *D* could be interpreted more narrowly, to require deprivation of liberty in the course of taking or carrying away.

In *Hendy-Freegard*, Lord Phillips CJ stated that:

We cannot see that there was justification for extending the offence of kidnapping to cover the situation in which the driver of the car has no intention of detaining his passenger against her will nor of doing other than taking her to the destination to which she wishes to go, simply because in some such circumstances the driver may have an objectionable ulterior motive. The consequence of the

607 [1978] 3 All ER 161.   608 See LC 355, para 4.190.
609 See also the Canadian Supreme Court's analysis of the English common law in *Vu* [2012] 2 SCR 411. It was observed that, 'it is the element of movement that differentiated kidnapping from the lesser included offence of false imprisonment and made kidnapping an aggravated form of false imprisonment. The underlying concern was that by carrying the victim away, the kidnappers would be taking him or her beyond the protection of the country's laws.' At [31].
610 *Brown* [1985] Crim LR 398 (five years' imprisonment concurrent on both counts upheld).
611 *Wellard* [1978] 1 WLR 921.   612 See LC 355, paras 2.4 and 4.197.

decision in *Cort* would seem to be that the mini-cab driver, who obtains a fare by falsely pretending to be an authorised taxi, will be guilty of kidnapping.[613]

It is clear, following *Hendy-Freegard*, that D must accompany V at the time that V is alleged to be taken or carried away. The Crown's expansive interpretation argued for in *Hendy-Freegard* would have rendered guilty the practical joker who telephoned V and induced him to attend a hospital and remain there on the pretext that his wife had been in an accident. That would clearly go too far.[614]

Interpreting *D* in the light of subsequent cases, the taking and carrying away must be by force or fraud (see the following section). It is not enough, then, that D asks V to accompany him and practises no fraud and offers no menace or threat to V, even if V is then deprived of liberty at their destination. As noted previously, it is submitted that to constitute kidnapping, the taking or carrying away must also be such as will deprive V of her liberty at that time. On a narrow interpretation of *D*, it is not sufficient that D persuades V by some fraud to accompany him to a place where he proposes to deprive her of her liberty if, during the period of her transmission to that place, D is prepared to release her at any time she requests. That would seem to follow from the decision in *Hendy-Freegard* interpreting *Cort*.[615]

In *D*, Lord Brandon states, explicitly, that the taking or carrying away must be by force or fraud *and without consent*. If a deprivation of liberty is also an essential element of the offence, and a lack of consent is an integral part of that element of the offence, the question arises: what part does consent have to play in taking and carrying away? If V is not consenting to the deprivation of her liberty, D ought to be guilty of kidnap irrespective of whether the force or fraud used to take or carry V away was sufficient to vitiate V's consent *to that act* of being carried or taken away.[616]

16.12.2.1 'Force or fraud'

The formulation in *D* creates problems. It is necessary to prove a taking or carrying away by force or fraud and absence of consent (whether that absence of consent was because of the force or fraud or not). If D's force or fraud taking V away also causes V's lack of consent, then no problem arises. If D's force or fraud that causes V to be taken or carried away is not of such gravity that it vitiates consent (eg a deception about a peripheral matter), it must be shown that V did not consent for some other reason. More problematic still is a case where D uses force or fraud and V is not consenting for a reason unconnected to force or fraud (eg a general lack of capacity). There would, on a literal reading of *D*, be no offence unless the taking was shown to be 'by' force or fraud.

Force or fraud and consent

For the reasons discussed in the previous paragraph, it is submitted that if the force or fraud vitiates the consent to the taking or carrying away and that taking or carrying away causes V to be deprived of her liberty without consent, the offence will be committed.

---

[613] At [55]. The Lord Chief Justice referred to the criticisms of *Cort* made in the 11th edn. *Cort* was also doubted by the Court of Appeal in *Nnamdi* [2005] EWCA Crim 74.

[614] The difficulty is to identify any serious offence in such cases. If D phones V and tells her falsely that D holds X hostage and that he will kill X unless V goes to a particular venue and remains there, what crime has been committed? There is no threat to X, nor to V. Is it a threat to kill? See p 649.

[615] In *Archer* [2011] EWCA Crim 2252, the Court of Appeal upheld D's conviction for kidnapping when he forced D, by threatening her with serious assault, to drive V and two others to a particular location. D did not take control of the car, it was driven by V. As Ashworth notes, this amounts to a 'carrying away' if not literally a 'taking' but nevertheless falls within the mischief at which the offence is aimed. Problematically, the Court of Appeal came to this conclusion with little citation of authority.

[616] That may be an assault.

Force

Clearly, where D forces V by violence or threats[617] of violence to be taken or carried away that should be sufficient to satisfy this element of the offence. It may be that lesser threats or trivial force ought to be sufficient for kidnapping. The Court of Appeal has suggested that the element of force sufficient to vitiate consent may be established by no more than submission.[618] Presumably the same is true of force sufficient to lead to taking away. The force used must be sufficient to cause V to be taken or carried away. In addition, if it is alleged that the taking or carrying away is by force, that taking or carrying away (and hence the force used to achieve it) must be sufficient to deprive V of her liberty without her consent. The relationship between deprivation of liberty and being taken away once again arises.

Fraud

What types of fraud will suffice? The answer is, it is submitted, contained within the previous analysis. The fraud used must be sufficient to cause V to be taken or carried away. Any fraud (not just those as to identity and nature) may suffice to cause V to be carried away. There is also a question of whether V is consenting to being taken and carried away. The absence of consent may arise from D's fraud or from some other basis (eg lack of capacity). It is possible to envisage a case in which D uses fraud on V to cause her to be carried away, but in which V is not actually deprived of her liberty by that act of taking away. This would seem to follow from *Hendy-Freegard*'s interpretation of *Cort*.

Adopting general principles to frauds vitiating consent, any fraud as to the identity of the actor should suffice. In this context, it is submitted that there is a stronger claim than in most circumstances for a fraud as to certain attributes of the actor and not just his correct name or identity being sufficient.[619] Thus, as in *Wellard*,[620] the impersonation of a police officer should suffice to negative the consent of the person. Other examples might include impersonation of State officials, paramedics, etc.

In addition to frauds as to identity, it is recognized that frauds as to the *nature* of the act will vitiate consent. This is where the most significant difficulties arise, as illustrated by the cases on sexual offences discussed in Ch 17. There is also the question of whether a fraud as to the 'purpose' of the taking will suffice to vitiate consent. Consider D who falsely tells V that her husband is injured and he drives her home (because he enjoys her company). Or consider D, who tells his 17-year-old daughter that they are to travel abroad to visit an ailing relative when his true motive is for her to take part in an arranged marriage.[621] The destination, manner of transport, etc are identical so the nature of the carrying away is not affected by the fraud. But note the decision in *Nnamdi*,[622] in which on the facts the court did not find it necessary to determine, on a charge of conspiracy to kidnap, whether telling V that she should meet D to join his modelling agency would be a sufficient fraud.

Force or fraud sufficient to vitiate consent to deprivation of liberty

On this literal approach to D, the elements of force or fraud represent routes through which the prosecution might establish the absence of consent to the fundamental question whether V was consenting to the deprivation of liberty arising from the taking or carrying away. It

---

[617] The Court of Appeal accepted in *Archer*, n 616, that the reference to force in D extends to a threat of force and is not limited to the actual infliction of force. As noted earlier, there was little analysis of previous authorities.

[618] See *Greenhalgh* [2001] EWCA Crim 1367.

[619] See *Melin* [2019] EWCA Crim 557, n 131.   [620] [1978] 3 All ER 161.

[621] NB: s 121 of the Anti-social Behaviour, Crime and Policing Act 2014. Under s 121(3) it is an offence to practise deception with intent to lure the victim into a forced marriage abroad.

[622] [2005] EWCA Crim 74.

is an interpretation which resonates with Lord Brandon's emphasis in *D* that, 'the nature of the offence is an attack on, and infringement of, the personal liberty of an individual'.

16.12.2.2 Without lawful excuse

What amounts to a lawful excuse is left completely at large; and whether a taking by a parent amounts to kidnapping is likely to be resolved in the same way whether the court proceeds by the route of deciding (as the majority in *Reid*[623] would), whether there is a lawful excuse or by deciding (as Lord Bridge would) whether the offence extends to those further circumstances. If a 12-year-old child refuses to return home from a visit to his grandmother's and his father forcibly carries him off, he surely commits no offence. The majority would say, presumably, because the father has a lawful excuse and Lord Bridge, because kidnapping does not extend to those circumstances. The result is the same. The question must be whether the parent has gone beyond what is reasonable in the exercise of parental authority.

Where V is not D's child and D is not acting in pursuance of any statutory authority or power of arrest, 'lawful excuse' is likely to be narrowly confined. In *Henman*,[624] D was guilty of attempted kidnapping when he tried to take by force an acquaintance whom he believed to be in moral and spiritual danger from a religious sect to which she belonged. There was no lawful excuse because there was no 'necessity recognized by the law as such' for D's conduct.

16.12.2.3 Who may be kidnapped?

It was held in *Reid*[625] that a husband may be convicted of kidnapping his wife and in *D* that a father may be guilty of kidnapping his child. It was recognized that, until modern times, it may be that an indictment of a father for kidnapping his child would have failed because of the paramount stature of his position in the family; but common law principles adapt and develop in the light of radically changed social conventions and conditions. Lord Bridge held that parental kidnapping includes the case (as in *D*) where the parent acts in contravention of the order of a competent court, leaving open the question whether a parent might be convicted in any other circumstances; but the majority preferred to hold simply that the parent is guilty where he acts 'without lawful excuse'.[626]

In cases of fraud, the offence might be regarded as seriously deficient in protecting children. V must be deprived of her liberty without consent, and it will be possible to say that in the case of a young child[627] who lacks the understanding or intelligence to give consent, the absence of consent is a necessary inference. However, the present definition requires there to be a carrying or taking away *by* force or fraud. In the case of a young child, D may not need to use force or fraud (unless those words are very broadly construed) to succeed in taking V away, as where a toddler is persuaded by true statements ('I'll buy you sweets') to accompany D. Arguably, such cases need not be kidnapping since they constitute false imprisonment which is equally punishable so, though it looks a little odd if a baby cannot be kidnapped,[628] but there is no lacuna in the law.

---

[623] [1973] QB 299.   [624] [1987] Crim LR 333.   [625] [1973] QB 299.

[626] In *Kayani* [2011] EWCA Crim 2871, Lord Judge CJ observed that simply because a child has been taken by a parent, it no longer necessarily follows that for policy reasons a charge of kidnapping must always be deemed inappropriate. The court invited the Law Commission to address the question whether cases in which children are removed from one parent by the other should be treated as kidnapping offences. See now LC 355, Ch 5.

[627] In the case of an older child, it is a question of fact for the jury whether (a) the child has sufficient understanding and, if so, (b) it in fact consented. Lord Brandon thought that a jury would usually find that a child under 14 lacked sufficient understanding to give consent; but this surely underestimates the capacity of the modern child. Reliance might be placed on the Mental Capacity Act 2005, discussed earlier. Cf *Cooper* [2009] UKHL 42 on the capacity concept in consent in sex cases.

[628] See G Williams, 'Can Babies be Kidnapped?' [1989] Crim LR 473. See the comments of Munby LJ in *Re HM* [2010] EWHC 870 (Fam) calling for law reform in this area.

16.12.2.4 Reform

The Law Commission has recommended that the common law offence be abolished and a simple statutory offence of kidnapping be created. The offence would be committed where D: (a) without lawful authority or reasonable excuse; (b) intentionally uses force or threats of force; (c) in order to take V or otherwise cause V to move with him. The offence would be indictable only and carry a maximum life sentence.[629]

16.13 Other abduction offences

16.13.1 Abduction of children

The Child Abduction Act 1984, as amended including by the Children Act 1989, creates two offences of abduction of a child under the age of 16. The offences encompass a broad spectrum of criminal behaviour, as Lord Judge CJ recognized in *Kayani*.[630]

16.13.1.1 Abduction by parents/guardians

The first offence, under s 1, arises where a child is taken or sent out[631] of the UK 'without the appropriate consent'.

Takes or sends

There is a clear lacuna since as the Divisional Court held in *Nicolaou* that the expression 'takes or send out of the United Kingdom' relates to the removal of the child from the jurisdiction, not to the position once the child has left the country. The issue is whether the appropriate consent existed at the time the child left the jurisdiction. The court rejected the submission that the phrase connotes a continuing activity. The Law Commission has recommended that the lacuna be closed and that the offence apply to detaining[632] as well as taking and sending.

Connection with the child

The offence may be committed as a principal[633] only by a person 'connected with' the child. A person 'connected with' a child is: (a) the child's parent; (b) in the case of a child whose parents were not married or civil partners at the time of the birth, a man in respect of whom there are reasonable grounds for believing him to be the father; (c) a guardian; (d) a special

---

[629] LC 355, para 4.231.

[630] [2011] EWCA Crim 2871. His lordship stated that: 'Child abduction, like every other offence, can take many forms. It may include the abduction of a child for a few days, or even a week or two, followed by the child's return, effectively undamaged, and, more important, although the parent from whom the separation was effected has suffered distress and anxiety in the meantime, with the loving relationship between parent and child quite unharmed. At the other extreme there are offences of forced marriage which ultimately culminate in what in reality is rape, or cases like the present, where the child is deliberately taken abroad and separated from one of its parents for many years, and the ordinary loving relationship which each should enjoy with the other is irremediably severed.' At [2]. *Kayani* [2012] 2 Cr App R (S) 38 and *SB* [2012] 2 Cr App R (S) 408 and 'a number of other decisions of this court' were considered in *RH* [2016] EWCA Crim 1754.

[631] In *R (Nicolaou) v Redbridge Magistrates' Court* [2012] EWHC 1647 (Admin). Given the fact that the purpose of the offence is the protection of children, such a narrow interpretation of s 1 is somewhat surprising. For further criticism, see N MacEwan [2013] Crim LR 54.

[632] See LC 355, Ch 5.

[633] A person who is not 'connected with' the child may be convicted as a secondary party or conspirator: *Sherry and El Yamani* [1993] Crim LR 537.

guardian;[634] (e) a person in whose favour 'a residence order'[635] is in force with respect to the child; or (f) a person having custody.

The 'appropriate consent' is the consent of each of the child's mother, the child's father if he has 'parental responsibility'[636] for him, any guardian, any special guardian, any person named in a child arrangements order as a person with whom the child is to live and any person having custody of him; or the leave of the court under the Children Act 1989 or, in the case of any person having custody, the leave of the court which awarded custody.

A person does not commit an offence under this section by taking or sending a child out of the UK without obtaining the appropriate consent if he is a person named in a child arrangements order as a person with whom the child is to live and he takes or sends the child out of the UK for a period of less than one month; or he is a special guardian of the child and he takes or sends the child out of the UK for a period of less than three months unless, in either case, this is a breach of an order under Part II of the Children Act 1989.

The Act provides defences for which D bears an evidential burden and the prosecution the burden of proof where:

(1) D believes that he has the appropriate consent or that he would have it if the person or persons whose consent is required were aware of all the relevant circumstances; or

(2) he has taken all reasonable steps to communicate with those persons but has been unsuccessful; or

(3) the other person has unreasonably refused to consent.

The Court of Appeal held in *S(C)*[637] that necessity cannot be pleaded as a defence to a charge under s 1. The court reasoned that it would be inimical to the aims of the legislation for individuals to avoid liability by pleading such a defence. Whether this is true of other common law defences remains to be seen, but it is submitted that the court's reasoning applies with equal force to duress of circumstances. It may therefore be the case that the only defences that can be pleaded to a charge of child abduction are those that exist within the legislative scheme.

16.13.1.2 Abduction otherwise than by parents/guardians

The second offence, which arises under s 2, requires an intentional or reckless taking or detention of a child under the age of 16.[638] It cannot be committed by the following:

(1) where the father and mother of the child in question were married to or civil partners of each other at the time of his birth, the child's father and mother;

(2) where the father and mother of the child in question were not married to or civil partners of each other at the time of his birth, the child's mother; and

(3) any other person who is a guardian of the child, or he is a special guardian of the child or he is a person named in a child arrangements order as a person with whom the child is to live or he has custody of the child.

The offence arises where any other person takes or detains the child without lawful authority or reasonable excuse:

(i) so as to remove him from the lawful control of any person having lawful control of him; or

(ii) so as to keep him out of the lawful control of any person entitled to lawful control of him.

---

[634] As inserted by the Adoption Act 2002.   [635] As defined in the Children Act 1989, s 8(1).

[636] As defined in ibid, s 3.   [637] [2012] EWCA Crim 389.

[638] D will not be guilty if he had a genuine belief that V was over the age of 16: s 2(3)(b). The court emphasized in *Heys and Murtagh* [2011] EWCA Crim 2112 that the belief need not be reasonable.

There are therefore four ways in which the offences can be committed.

'Detaining' is defined in s 3 to include causing the child to be detained or inducing the child to remain with the accused or another person. 'Taking' is defined in s 3 so as to include causing or inducing the child to accompany the accused or any other person or causing the child to be taken. 'Remove' does not require any 'geographical' removal—it is not the removal of the child but removal of control of the child which is material. 'Lawful control' is not defined in the Act and the courts have declined to define it. The concept varies according to the person said to have control—for example, parent, schoolteacher or nanny. A relevant question is whether the child was deflected by D from doing that to which his lawful controller had consented into some other activity. Has D substituted his authority or will for that of the lawful controller? There was evidence on which a jury could find that D had taken control where he persuaded a 14-year-old boy on his way home from school to go to D's flat,[639] and where he persuaded children to go with him to look for a bicycle which he said had been stolen.[640]

It is immaterial that the child consented to the lawful removal from the lawful control.[641] In the case of X,[642] D was convicted of abducting a child, V, contrary to s 2(1)(b). D, a woman, was a drug addict and sex worker and had befriended V aged 13. V was dressed in a manner suggesting she was soliciting.[643] V persistently ran away from home. V was found in the company of D in the red light district. V said in her evidence that she had no intention of returning to her mother whether she was with D or not. On those facts, it was debatable whether the conduct of D was any cause at all of V's absence, but the Court of Appeal held that the issue was rightly left to the jury.[644]

The words 'so as to' are ambiguous. Two conflicting decisions added to the confusion. In Mousir,[645] the Court of Appeal held that the words import an element of actus reus (that D's conduct had the objective consequence of removing the child from lawful control) but not mens rea (that D intended to remove lawful control). That has been confirmed to be the correct interpretation despite contrary comments in the extradition case of Re Owens.[646] The Divisional Court in Foster[647] favoured the conclusion in Mousir as did the Court of Appeal in Pringle.[648]

In Mousir, the court held that D's conduct had to bring about a sufficient degree of interference with the lawful control of the child,[649] but that the concept of control did not require an assessment of the individual child's maturity. The conclusion that the words import such an element of actus reus seems, with respect, to be correct in principle. The natural meaning of the term 'so as to' is 'with the effect of' removing the child from lawful control. It introduces a causal element additional to the actus reus of 'taking' or 'detaining'.[650]

---

[639] Mousir [1987] Crim LR 561.

[640] Leather (1993) 98 Cr App R 179. See also Norman [2008] EWCA Crim 1810 (D unfit to plead on facts).

[641] A [2001] Cr App R 418.   [642] [2010] EWCA Crim 2367.

[643] The judge's direction on recklessness was appealed but, although unnecessary on the facts, was held not to be in error following, as it did, Foster v DPP [2005] 1 WLR 1400 discussed later.

[644] See also A [2000] 2 All ER 177.   [645] [1987] Crim LR 561.   [646] [2000] 1 Cr App R 195.

[647] [2004] EWHC 2955 (Admin). Cf Wakeman [2011] EWCA Crim 1649. See also Hunter [2015] All ER (D) 196 (Jan): the crime is one of basic intent. The judge had correctly explained that the prosecution had to prove their allegation that the defendant had deliberately encouraged the complainant to get into his car, following which she had been raped by his co-defendants.

[648] [2019] EWCA Crim 1722.

[649] Where, as in that case, the charge is one of attempt, the issue is whether the acts are more than merely preparatory to that effect.

[650] It is possible that D might remove or detain a child without lawful excuse but without causing him to be removed from lawful custody where D also removed or detained the lawful custodian.

The Divisional Court considered the scope of the offence in *Shepherd v CPS*.[651] The appellant had been served with a Child Abduction Warning Notice informing him that a mother had not given him permission to communicate with her daughter or allow her daughter to enter or stay in his home or be in his company. The daughter, who was 14 years old at the time, went to D's house and asked if she could come to roll up a cigarette. D allowed her in and he was charged with detaining a child without lawful authority. It was submitted on behalf of D that the child had voluntarily entered his home and that he had therefore done nothing to cause her to be detained so as to be out of her mother's lawful control. The Divisional Court, in dismissing his appeal, held that the wishes of the child were irrelevant to whether D had committed the offence. There was an inducement by D's positive act of allowing the child to remain. Furthermore, D's action in allowing the child to enter and remain in his house was sufficient to constitute the keeping of a child who was under the control of her mother.

The mens rea of the offence is as summarized in *Foster*[652] and endorsed by the Court of Appeal in *Pringle*.

the *mens rea* of the offence of abduction under section 2 is an intentional or reckless taking or detention of a child under the age of sixteen, the effect or objective consequence of which is to remove or to keep that child within the meaning of section 2(1)(a) or (b). [It is not] necessary to require an intention to remove the child from the lawful custody of another, or to keep the child against the entitlement of the grandmother, to arrive at the same result had a prosecution proceeded. The offence is not committed if the defendant has lawful authority or a reasonable excuse for taking or detaining the child.

Note that Art 8 of the ECHR—the right to respect for private life—may impose positive obligations on the State to respect family life. This may include an obligation on the State to provide safeguards against abduction.[653]

16.14 Harassment

16.14.1 Background

Prior to 1997, the criminal law struggled to provide protection for those who suffered at the hands of so-called 'stalkers'.[654] It was difficult for the law to tackle an activity which was in part an infringement of privacy,[655] in part an offence against the person, with some forms of the conduct also having a public order dimension. The use of tortious remedies to tackle behaviour which amounted to stalking was severely curtailed by the decision of the House of Lords in *Hunter v Canary Wharf*[656] when it was held that only those who had a right to exclusive possession of the land could sue in nuisance. Recourse was had to the criminal law and prosecutors relied on offences of public nuisance, specific offences relating to malicious communications or telecommunications where possible, or public order offences and

---

[651] [2017] EWHC 2566 (Admin).　　[652] [2004] EWHC 2955 (Admin).

[653] *Iglesias Gil and AIU v Spain* (App no 56673/00) 2003; *Maire v Portugal* (App no 48206/99) 2003; *D (A Child) (Abduction: Rights of Custody)* [2006] UKHL 51. See also *Ljungkvist v Sweden* [2014] ACD 173(60).

[654] See R Babcock, 'The Psychology of Stalking' in P Infield and G Platford, *The Law of Harassment and Stalking* (2000); N Addison and T Lawson-Cruttenden, *Harassment Law and Practice* (1998). The offence is further amended by the Serious Organised Crime and Police Act 2005, s 125.

[655] See Alldridge, *Relocating Criminal Law*, Ch 4.

[656] [1997] 2 All ER 426. See also *Wong v Parkside Health NHS Trust* [2003] 3 All ER 932.

offences against the person. These efforts to combat what was perceived as a growing social menace were assisted by the courts' acceptance that psychiatric injury was a sufficient basis for a finding of actual or grievous bodily harm[657] and by the House of Lords' acceptance that assault could be committed by words alone or even by a silent telephone call.[658] These extended interpretations were not always well received[659] but led to convictions.

Parliament nevertheless felt that a specific offence was needed and, following consultation[660] and an unseemly rush through Parliament, the Protection from Harassment Act 1997 was enacted.[661] The drafter faced a formidable difficulty in defining 'stalking' without overcriminalizing. The conduct complained of as harassing behaviour may include acts of apparent kindness, such as repeated sending of flowers or seemingly innocuous conduct, such as walking by the victim's house. As the minister stated:

> Stalkers do not stick to activities on a list. Stalkers and other weirdos [sic] who pursue women, [sic] cause racial harassment and annoy their neighbours have a wide range of activity which it is impossible to define.[662]

As Wells observes, the Act follows a pattern all too common in recent years of 'addressing a narrowly conceived social harm with a widely drawn provision, often supplementing and overlapping with existing offences'.[663] The flexibility allows for the offence to be used in respect of stalking, persistent protestors, bullying,[664] etc.

In *Smith*,[665] the Court of Appeal defined 'harassment' as follows: 'Essentially, it involves persistent conduct of a seriously oppressive nature, either physically or mentally, targeted at an individual and resulting in fear or distress.' The definition was considered more recently in *N*.[666] At trial the judge defined harassment by reference to s 7(2), but equated harassment with alarm or distress, rather than directing the jury that harassment *includes* alarm or distress. The Court of Appeal held that this was a misdirection. The danger of equating harassment with alarm or distress, according to the court, is that not all conduct, even though it may be unattractive, unreasonable and does in fact cause alarm or distress, will be sufficient to justify the sanction of the criminal law. The judge's direction to the jury failed to include a reference for the need to be sure that D's conduct was oppressive. The court held that the requirement of oppression serves as a yardstick that helps the law to draw a sensible line between, 'the give and take of daily life and conduct which justifies the sanctions of the criminal law'.[667] The definition provided by s 7 is clearly inclusive and not exhaustive. 'Harassment' is generally understood to involve improper oppressive and

---

[657] *Chan Fook* [1994] 2 All ER 552; *Burstow* [1998] AC 147.

[658] *Ireland* [1998] AC 147.   [659] C Wells, 'Stalking the Criminal Law Response' [1997] Crim LR 463.

[660] See Home Office, *Stalking: The Solutions* (1996).

[661] See the analysis by E Finch, *The Criminalisation of Stalking* (2001); MJ Allen, 'Look Who's Stalking' [1996] Web JCLI. For a comparative review of stalking laws, see B Clarke and L Meintjes-Van der Valt (1998) 115 South African LJ 729.

[662] D MacLean, Home Office Minister, HC, 17 Dec 1996, col 827.

[663] C Wells [1997] Crim LR 463 at 464.

[664] See A Gillespie, 'Cyber-Bullying and Harassment of Teenagers: The Legal Response' [2006] J Social Welfare & Fam Law 123; N Geach, 'Regulating Harassment: Is the Law Fit for the Social Networking Age?' (2009) 73 J Crim L 241. The House of Lords in *Majrowski v Guy's and St Thomas' Hospital* [2006] UKHL 34, [2007] 1 AC 224, held that the Act applies in the workplace and that employers may be vicariously liable for failing to take appropriate preventative action to prevent employees being bullied. Note also the powers inserted by the Domestic Violence, Crime and Victims Act 2004, in respect of restraining orders in domestic violence cases.

[665] [2012] EWCA Crim 2566, [24].   [666] [2016] EWCA Crim 92.

[667] At [32]. In the subsequent case of *Tan* [2017] EWCA Crim 493, D's conviction was upheld on the basis that despite the fact the judge did not use the word 'oppression', his direction nevertheless accurately conveyed to the jury the threshold that must be crossed before an offence is committed.

unreasonable conduct that is targeted at an individual and calculated to produce the consequences described in s 7. By s 1(3) of the Act, reasonable and/or lawful courses of conduct may be excluded.

The CPS has issued guidance on prosecuting harassment.[668] The CPS introduces the guidance by stating:

This legal guidance addresses behaviour which is repeated and unwanted by the victim and which causes the victim to have a negative reaction in terms of alarm or distress. Cases involving stalking and harassment can be difficult to prosecute, and because of their nature are likely to require sensitive handling, especially with regard to victim care. The provision of accurate and up-to-date information to the victim throughout the life of the case, together with quality support, and careful consideration of any special measures requirements are essential factors for the CPS to consider.

16.14.2 Harassment defined

1.—(1) A person must not pursue a course of conduct—

(a) which amounts to harassment of another, and

(b) which he knows or ought to know amounts to harassment of the other.

(1A) A person must not pursue a course of conduct—

(a) which involves harassment of two or more persons, and

(b) which he knows or ought to know involves harassment of those persons, and

(c) by which he intends to persuade any person (whether or not one of those mentioned above)—

(i) not to do something that he is entitled or required to do, or

(ii) to do something that he is not under any obligation to do.

2.—(1) A person who pursues a course of conduct in breach of section 1(1) or (1A) is guilty of an offence.[669]

16.14.2.1 Course of conduct

The offences under the Act are dependent on proof of a course of conduct, which is merely an element of each offence and not a crime in itself.

By s 7:

(1) A 'course of conduct' must involve—

(a) in the case of conduct in relation to a single person (see section 1(1)), conduct on at least two occasions in relation to that person, or

(b) in the case of conduct in relation to two or more persons (see section 1(1A)), conduct on at least one occasion in relation to each of those persons.

(3A) A person's conduct on any occasion shall be taken, if aided, abetted, counselled or procured by another—

(a) to be conduct on that occasion of the other (as well as conduct of the person whose conduct it is); and

(b) to be conduct in relation to which the other's knowledge and purpose, and what he ought to have known, are the same as they were in relation to what was contemplated or reasonably foreseeable at the time of the aiding, abetting, counselling or procuring.

---

[668] See www.cps.gov.uk/legal-guidance/stalking-and-harassment.

[669] Section 1A was added by the Serious Organised Crime and Police Act 2005, s 125.

The course of conduct is at the core of both crimes (and the tort). The provision is far from clear, with little further elaboration other than that words are sufficient (s 7(4)). One of the major problems under the Act has been in determining when two incidents are sufficiently closely associated to constitute a course of conduct. Although seeking to identify the idea of 'persistence' that lies at the heart of stalking, Parliament refrained from attempting further to define the proscribed behaviour. In debates on the Bill, Michael Howard, then Home Secretary, referred to the lack of definition, but regarded harassment as a concept 'interpreted regularly by the courts since 1986'.[670] It is extremely wide in scope and applies to protest and neighbourhood disputes[671] as well as what might more usually be regarded as stalking.

It has been accepted that D's conduct can amount to a course of conduct even where that involves some action by V. In *James v CPS*,[672] D was receiving care from a social services team in his area. D repeatedly phoned the services team to complain about his care. The team manager, V, returned D's calls as she was duty-bound to do and D was abusive to her. That pattern of behaviour was repeated. The Divisional Court held that the fact that V returned the calls was irrelevant. As Elias LJ observed:

If I am continually abusive to someone who comes within my vicinity, that may still be capable of constituting a course of conduct, even if the victim chooses to come within my vicinity. The fact that he or she chooses to do so might arguably be relevant to the question of whether there is harassment, but not to the question of whether there is a course of conduct.[673]

As the court observed in *Curtis*,[674] s 7 of the Act does not provide an exhaustive definition of harassment. There will be conduct which might alarm or distress someone without being harassing.[675] The use of information in the public domain is capable of constituting harassment. Use of private email might, therefore, amount to conduct that is beyond what is unattractive and unreasonable and amount to harassment.[676]

One act or two?

Is there a 'course of conduct' when an individual engages in one continuous activity—for example, sitting outside V's house for a whole day? In *Hills*,[677] it was stressed that it is not just enough to count the incidents, nor to direct the jury in such terms.[678] In *Kelly v DPP*,[679] D, who had just been released on licence after conviction for harassing V, made three abusive and threatening phone calls to a mobile phone belonging to V between 2.57 am and 3.02 am. V did not answer any of the calls at the time and they were recorded on her voicemail. V subsequently listened to the messages one after the other, without pause. It was held that the closeness of time within which the calls were made was only *a* factor to be taken into account when determining whether there had been repetitious behaviour for the purposes of proving the commission of an offence of harassment. The case raises questions about

---

[670] HC, 17 Dec 1996, vol 287, col 784.

[671] Inciting a dog to bark is sufficient to form part of a course of conduct: *Tafurelli v DPP* [2004] EWHC 2791 (Admin).

[672] [2009] EWHC 2925 (Admin).   [673] At [12].   [674] [2010] EWCA Crim 123.

[675] In that case repeated incidents of domestic violence.

[676] *Hilson v CPS* [2019] EWHC 1111 (Admin). Other conduct included emailing the victim's private email address, commenting in court on details of the judge's private life and sending the judge a birthday card to her home address stating 'Keep up the good work stealing for profit. Don't drink too much raspberry gin and stagger back to Sarf, London.'

[677] [2001] Crim LR 318. See also *Sahin* [2009] EWCA Crim 2616.

[678] *Patel* [2005] Crim LR 649, [2004] EWCA Crim 3284.

[679] [2003] Crim LR 43.

where the courts will draw the line. Consider D who phones V, V answers the call and immediately she identifies D and terminates the call. D calls back immediately. V sees that D's number appears on the 'caller ID' facility. Is this a course of conduct? In *Loake v CPS*, D was convicted of harassment after sending her husband, from whom she was separated, a very large number of text messages over a period of time.[680]

In *Hills*, Latham LJ stated that repetition was a significant factor in determining whether there is a course of conduct, but there is no requirement that acts be similar or repeated. Any combination of bouquets of flowers, menacing calls or letters, loitering outside the victim's home, etc will suffice. As was suggested in *Lau*,[681] the question of whether there is a course of conduct should be determined by whether there is a sufficient nexus between the two acts, taking account of all of the circumstances. The courts have acknowledged that the question is a difficult one.[682] In *DPP v Hardy*,[683] the court accepted that 95 phone calls made over a 90-minute period were capable of constituting harassment, especially since they included threats to continue that behaviour all night.[684]

One actor or two?

Section 7(3A)[685] ensures that where D performs a harassing act towards V aided by B, and subsequently D alone commits a further act of harassment towards V, the two acts may be regarded as a course of conduct. This extension of the scope of a 'course of conduct' was enacted to deal with protestors. A campaign of collective harassment by two or more people can amount to a 'course of conduct'. The knowledge and purpose of the aider, abetter, counsellor or procurer is judged at the time that the conduct was planned and not when it is carried out. The provision seeks to pre-empt a defence by D that, when he counselled B to commit a second act towards V, D was unaware that his first act towards V had caused distress. Since it is enough that D ought to have known that the act would cause distress at the time that the subsequent act was commissioned, he will be liable.

The offence can be committed by D communicating with X which causes harassment to V.[686]

One victim or two?

The course of conduct under s 1(1) must relate to 'another'. In *DPP v Williams*,[687] D had put his hand through a bathroom window startling the occupant V1 who was showering. She then informed V2, her flatmate, who was scared by the event as reported to her. Two days later D peered through the bedroom window, this time frightening V2 directly. The magistrates convicted, holding that 'another' could be read as 'others'. The Divisional Court decided the case on the basis that V2 had been distressed on both occasions and therefore the offence was made out. The interpretation was rightly criticized for extending the offence considerably and for giving rise to practical problems.[688] In *Caurti v DPP*,[689] it was held that

---

[680] [2017] EWHC 2855 (Admin).   [681] [2000] Crim LR 580 and commentary.

[682] See *Buckley* [2008] EWHC 136 (Admin) graveside altercation and spitting at V in cemetery car park.

[683] [2008] All ER (D) 315 (Oct).

[684] D had called an employment agency to request information about why he had been rejected for a job, so his calls had been legitimate to begin with, but they had clearly escalated into conduct that was capable of constituting harassment.

[685] As inserted by the Criminal Justice and Police Act 2001.

[686] *C v CPS* [2008] EWHC 148 (Admin).

[687] *DPP v Williams* (DC, 27 July 1998, Rose LJ and Bell J).

[688] A charge under the 1997 Act, s 1(1), might be bad for duplicity where it names two complainants when they are members of a 'close knit identifiable group': *Mills v DPP* (1998) 17 Dec, DC.

[689] [2002] Crim LR 131 and commentary.

in relation to the more serious s 4 offence (causing fear of violence, see later) the course of conduct must have its impact on *one* complainant, even where it is aimed at another.

Under s 1(1A), it is clear that the harassment can be to two or more persons, provided the additional element of intention in s 1(1A)(c) can be established. The provision will prove useful in criminalizing, for example, the conduct of protestors who target people connected with animal breeding and vivisection organizations.[690] Section 1(1A) will catch threats and intimidation intended to force an individual or individuals to stop trading.

The complainant must be an individual and not a corporate body:[691] s 7(5) of the Act provides that references to a 'person' are references to 'a person who is an individual'. But a company can commit the offence.[692]

No need for temporal proximity or similarity

Is there a course of conduct where different acts are separated by a considerable period of time? For example, are two acts separated by one year, say, two birthday cards, a 'course of conduct'? In *Lau v DPP*,[693] two incidents four months apart were held to be capable of amounting to a course of conduct. The court observed that 'one can conceive of circumstances where incidents, as far apart as a year, could constitute a course of conduct'. The example given was of racial harassment outside a synagogue on the Day of Atonement. In *Baron v CPS*,[694] it was accepted that the less proximate in time and the more limited in number the incidents, the less likely that there was a course of conduct. In *Pratt v DPP*,[695] D threw water over his estranged wife and three months later chased her through the matrimonial home swearing and questioning her constantly. The magistrates found these actions to be a course of conduct and the Divisional Court did not find this to be an irrational decision. However, it was noted that prosecuting authorities should be cautious in bringing charges for the offence of harassment in circumstances where only a small number of incidents had occurred. The prosecution should ensure not merely that two or more incidents had occurred, but that such repetitious behaviour had caused harassment to the other person.[696] Examples of prosecution agencies overusing harassment charges persist. In *Curtis*,[697] D had in the course of a relationship with V, a fellow police officer, engaged in conduct including minor assaults on V and pulling the handbrake of a car V was driving, causing it to skid. This was charged as harassment. The court quashed the conviction. The court defined harassment as 'tormenting a person by subjecting them to constant interference or intimidation'. The conduct had to be oppressive, unreasonable and unacceptable to a degree that would sustain criminal liability. Although D's conduct had been deplorable and the incidents had been far from trivial, it could not be concluded that, in the course of a volatile relationship where there had been aggression on both sides, the six incidents over a nine-month period amounted to a course of conduct amounting to harassment within the meaning of the Act. Reference was made to *Majrowski* (see earlier)[698] where it was emphasized that:

Courts are well able to recognise the boundary between conduct which is unattractive, even unreasonable, and conduct which is oppressive and unacceptable. To cross the boundary from the

---

[690] See the Home Office document: *Animal Welfare: Human Rights—Protecting People from Animal Rights Extremists* (2004). See the Serious Organised Crime and Police Act 2005, s 145.

[691] *DPP v Dziurzynski* (2002) 166 JP 545; cf *Daiichi UK Ltd and others v Huntingdon Animal Cruelty and others* [2003] EWHC 2337 (QB): person does not include a limited company as a victim.

[692] See *Kosar v Bank of Scotland* [2011] EWHC 1050 (Admin).

[693] [2000] Crim LR, [2000] 1 FLR 799.   [694] (2000) 13 June, unreported.

[695] [2001] EWHC 483 (Admin).

[696] Note that the CPS acknowledges that the Act is 'widely drafted, and could incorporate many minor forms of behaviour'. Reference should be had to Home Office Circular 34/1997, making it clear that the Act is not intended to supplant existing powers to deal with incidents that do not reach the threshold of harassment.

[697] [2010] EWCA Crim 123.   [698] [2007] 1 AC 224 at [30] per Lord Nicholls.

regrettable to the unacceptable the gravity of the misconduct must be of an order which would sustain criminal liability under section 2.

Baroness Hale observed[699] that the definition had been deliberately left wide open and it had been left to the wisdom of the courts to distinguish between the ordinary banter and badinage of life and genuinely offensive and unacceptable behaviour. It cannot be a requirement that each of the acts alleged to constitute part of the course of conduct is itself criminal.[700]

It is submitted that the events making up the 'course of conduct' under the Act require a nexus, as is implicit within the expression, which suggests a 'series' of events with some connection. The main connecting factor will be that the acts are aimed at a particular victim, but that will not of itself be sufficient, in the same way that two visits to the hospital by the same patient would not necessarily be described as a course of treatment. There must be something more connecting them—in the case of the treatment, one would expect it to be for the same ailment. The mere fact that D made two harassing calls to the same victim a year apart will not necessarily constitute a course of conduct. If the calls were made on a particular anniversary, there would be a greater nexus and the course of conduct would be more likely to be established. The question must turn on all the circumstances of the case.

When does the course of conduct begin?

In many instances, D will be involved in what might be considered to be, initially at least, neutral conduct towards V. Does his course of conduct only begin when he is aware of the distress he is causing V, or when it causes V harassment or when the reasonable person would see it as harassing? In *King v DPP*,[701] the alleged harassment was by offering the victim a plant, writing letters to her, rummaging in her rubbish, stealing her discarded underwear from refuse bags and filming her secretly. The Divisional Court held that 'repeated offers of unwelcome gifts or the repeated sending of letters could well amount to harassment, nevertheless, the *single* offer of a gift of modest value *and* the sending of one innocuous letter in the circumstances of this case cannot amount to harassment within the meaning of the 1997 Act. Nor could the letter and the gift be treated as the first stage or the first two stages of a course of conduct amounting to harassment . . .' The magistrates were wrong to treat these incidents as forming part of a course of conduct. The decision is difficult to square with the terms of the section. There is no limitation as to the types of conduct amounting to harassment in the statute.

A victim may be held to be aware of a course of conduct through indirect knowledge, as where V is told that D has been calling her, provided there is evidence on the basis of which the court can properly conclude that D was pursuing a course of conduct with the necessary mens rea.[702]

Mens rea as to the course of conduct

There is no requirement that the harasser intended or directed his conduct to harass V, it is sufficient that 'a reasonable person in possession of the same information would think the course of conduct amounted to harassment of another'.[703] The leading case is that of *Colohan*[704] where it was held that the test is entirely objective.[705] In that case it was held that D's schizophrenia could not be taken into consideration in evaluating whether the reasonable person would have realized that the conduct was harassing. On the facts, it was unclear

[699] ibid, [66].   [700] See *R (Jones) v Bedfordshire MC* [2010] EWHC 523 (Admin), [27].

[701] (2000) 20 June, DC.   [702] *Kellett v DPP* [2001] EWHC 107 (Admin).

[703] Section 1(2).   [704] [2001] EWCA Crim 1251, [2001] Crim LR 845 and commentary. See Ch 4.

[705] Affirmed more recently by the Divisional Court in *R (Aylesbury Crown Court) v CPS* [2013] EWHC 3228 (Admin). Note that in *Loake v CPS* [2017] EWHC 2855 (Admin) the Divisional Court confirmed that insanity is available as a defence to harassment. See p 320.

whether D was denying that he knew what he was doing in writing the allegedly harassing letters, or denying that he knew that the letters constituted a course of harassing conduct, or was claiming simply that the harassment was reasonable. Given the clear policy behind the legislation, it is not surprising that the court rejected the defence claims. The prosecution of mentally disordered individuals under this offence not only ensures the protection for victims of stalking, but also increases the chances of the offender receiving psychiatric assessment and treatment.

To be liable under s 1(1A), D must also intend to persuade the person(s) to refrain from something that they are entitled or to do something they are not; for example, for an animal breeding unit to stop trading with a vivisection lab.

In possession of the same information

Section 1(2) is unusual in requiring that the person whose course of conduct is in question *ought to know* that it amounts to harassment of another if a reasonable person 'in possession of the same information' would do so. The section is designed to endow the reasonable person with knowledge of circumstances that would render otherwise seemingly innocuous conduct harassing (eg when D knows that previous advances towards V have been rejected and continues to send gifts). In such cases D's inculpatory state of mind is taken into account. Should the reasonable person also be possessed with knowledge about D's exculpatory states of mind in order to assess whether the conduct is harassment? This is not the same as asking whether a reasonable person with the characteristics of D would regard it as harassment, particularly where the characteristic inhibits cognition of the wrongdoing. In *Colohan*, the strong policy grounds of protection on which the Act is founded justified the court's rejection of any attempt to diminish the purely objective stance. In *Pelham*,[706] D was charged under the racially aggravated form of the offence and denied that she had the mens rea on the basis that she was of low IQ and lacked an understanding of the racial nature of her comments. The court refused to allow expert evidence as to this aspect of the mens rea, in line with the general rule against expert evidence being permitted on mens rea issues.

Defences justifying the course of conduct

Section 1(3) provides:

> (3) Subsection (1) or (1A) does not apply to a course of conduct if the person who pursued it shows—
>
>   (a) that it was pursued for the purpose of preventing or detecting crime;
>
>   (b) that it was pursued under any enactment or rule of law or to comply with any condition or requirement imposed by any person under any enactment, or
>
>   (c) that in the particular circumstances the pursuit of the course of conduct was reasonable.

Paragraph (a) seems clear, although debate might arise over whether it is restricted to State officials engaged in criminal investigations or whether investigative journalists might also be able to rely on this defence.[707] It might apply to the busybody Neighbourhood Watch coordinator, although the courts have suggested that s 1(3)(a) was framed with law enforcement

---

706 [2007] EWCA Crim 1321.

707 Note also s 12 providing that the Secretary of State may issue certificates that render conduct of specified individuals conclusively reasonable (eg security service operatives). Note *Trimingham v Associated Newspapers Ltd* [2012] EWHC 1296 (QB), where Tugendhat J referred to *Thomas v News Group Newspapers Ltd* [2001] EWCA Civ 1233 to hold that journalism amounting to a course of conduct is reasonable under s 1(3)(c) unless, in the particular circumstances of the case, the course of conduct is so unreasonable that under Art 10 of the ECHR it is necessary proportionately to prohibit or sanction it under Art 10(2) including the protection of the rights of others.

agencies and not private individuals in mind. If a private individual relies on s 1(3)(a) he must show some rational basis for his conduct, judged on an objective basis.[708]

The Supreme Court considered what the appropriate standard ought to be in *Hayes v Willoughby*,[709] a civil case. Lord Sumption, who delivered the judgment of the majority, held that the word 'purpose' connotes a subjective state of mind.[710] Section 1(3)(a) does not, therefore, embody a wholly objective test. His lordship further stated, however, that Parliament could not have intended for there to be no limits placed on the pursuit of the course of conduct, no matter how irrational D's state of mind. It was held that the necessary control mechanism is found in the concept of rationality. His lordship distinguished rationality from reasonableness, which was characterized as an 'external, objective standard applied to the outcome of a person's thoughts or intentions'. Rationality, on the other hand:

applies a minimum objective standard to the relevant person's mental processes. It imports a requirement of good faith, a requirement that there should be some logical connection between the evidence and the ostensible reasons for the decision, and (which will usually amount to the same thing) an absence of arbitrariness, of capriciousness or of reasoning so outrageous in its defiance of logic as to be perverse.[711]

In future, therefore, before an alleged harasser can be said to have had the purpose of preventing or detecting crime, he must have sufficiently applied his mind to the matter. He must have thought rationally about the material suggesting the possibility of criminality and formed the view that the conduct said to constitute harassment was appropriate for the purpose of preventing or detecting it. Lord Sumption stated explicitly that the court should not test D's conclusions against the standard of what a reasonable person in D's circumstances would have concluded. Lord Reed dissented on the basis that Parliament did not specify that D's pursuit of the course of conduct had to be rational; the statute should not be construed as extending beyond the limits which Parliament itself made clear in its enactment; and that criminal liability should not turn on the subtle distinction between what is unreasonable and what is irrational. It is submitted that there is considerable force in Lord Reed's three points. The most pertinent one is, however, his lordship's third point. Formulating a new test of rationality adds an additional layer of uncertainty. It is submitted that not only might judges find it difficult to direct juries on how they ought to approach the test of rationality, judges themselves might have difficulty in delineating between the various states of mind now demanded by the Supreme Court's judgment when determining whether the defence ought to be left. A better approach, it is submitted, would be the one suggested by Lord Reed, namely a wholly subjective test. This would not necessarily lead to specious defences being pleaded successfully, as the jury or magistrates could still conclude that D did not have as his purpose the prevention or detection of crime.

Paragraph (b) is uncontroversial. It protects the right of free speech and expression. In a civil case which was one of the first cases under the Act, Eady J commented that the Act was not intended to be used to stifle discussion of public interest on public demonstrations.[712]

---

[708] *Howlett v Holding* (2006) The Times, 8 Feb, QBD (D conducted a campaign against the V, a local councillor, by flying banners from his aircraft referring to her in derogatory and abusive terms).

[709] [2013] UKSC 17.

[710] The Supreme Court did not reach a conclusion on whether preventing or detecting crime must be the sole purpose, or whether the dominant purpose will suffice. His lordship did intimate, however, that he favoured the latter formulation. The Commercial Court in the subsequent case of *Starbev GP Ltd v Interbrew Central European Holdings* [2014] EWHC 1311 (Comm) stated that the relevant purpose is the dominant one.

[711] At [14].

[712] *Huntingdon Life Sciences v Curtin* (1997) The Times, 11 Dec, [1998] Env LR D9. See also *Bayer Crop Science Ltd* [2009] WL 4872821.

More difficult is the defence under para (c), particularly in cases where D claims that his action was part of a campaign of legitimate protest. In *Baron v DPP*,[713] the court emphasized that:

a line must be drawn between legitimate expression of disgust at the way a public agency has behaved and conduct amounting to harassment. The right to free speech requires a broad degree of tolerance in relation to communications. It is a legitimate exercise of that right to say things which are unpleasant or possibly hurtful to the recipient.

The defence under s 1(3)(c) does not involve the question whether the reasonable person regards the course of conduct as harassment, but whether it *is* reasonable harassment.[714]

It seems to arise only where it is accepted that the course of conduct is harassing. Furthermore, the question is whether the conduct was, as a whole, 'reasonable' which suggests a purely objective assessment. In some cases involving protest campaigns the courts may face difficult issues of evaluating the reasonableness of a form of protest. These may involve arguments based on rights of freedom of expression under Art 10 of the ECHR.[715]

The burden is on the defendant to prove, on the balance of probabilities,[716] that the conduct is reasonable. It has been held that pursuit of conduct in breach of an injunction will preclude a defence under s 1(3)(c).[717]

16.14.2.2 The s 2 offence

2.—(1) A person who pursues a course of conduct in breach of section 1(1) or (1A) is guilty of an offence.

(2) A person guilty of an offence under this section is liable on summary conviction to imprisonment for a term not exceeding six months, or [an unlimited] fine, or both.

The offence is based on the course of conduct and it has been held that prosecutions are not therefore time-barred if at least one of the incidents forming part of the course of conduct occurs within the six-month limitation period for the laying of informations in the magistrates' court.[718]

The s 2 offence requires two or more acts by D constituting a course of conduct. There need be only one result from their cumulative effect—the harassment of the victim. Section 7(2) provides that 'harassing a person' includes 'alarming the person or causing the person distress' and this has been treated as a non-exhaustive definition.[719] There is no requirement that any violence is threatened (or feared) for the offence under s 2. The section criminalizes conduct such as that in *Chambers and Edwards v DPP*[720] where protestors persistently but non-violently blocked the surveyor's theodolite beam, since the Divisional Court held that such conduct would amount to harassment for the purposes of the Public Order Act 1986. In many cases the section has been used successfully in respect of 'classic' stalking behaviour.[721]

---

[713] (2000) 13 June, unreported.

[714] Nothing that involves cultural or racial differences should be taken into account, unless it is relevant and supported by proper evidence: *C v CPS* [2008] EWHC 148 (Admin).

[715] See *Debnath* [2006] 2 Cr App R (S) 25, where a restraining order against D prohibiting any publication against V whether true or not was upheld.

[716] See p 23, on the appropriateness of the burden under the HRA 1998 and Art 6(2).

[717] *DPP v Mosely* (1999) The Times, 23 June.

[718] *DPP v Baker* [2004] EWHC 2782 (Admin).   [719] *DPP v Ramsdale* (2001) The Independent, 19 Mar.

[720] [1995] Crim LR 896.

[721] For critical comment on the scope of the offence, see E Finch, 'Stalking the Perfect Stalking Law: An Evaluation of the Efficacy of the Protection from Harassment Act 1997' [2002] Crim LR 702. See also J Harris, Home Office Research Study No 203, *An Evaluation of the Use and Effectiveness of the Protection from Harassment Act 1997* (2000).

16.14.2.3 Causing a fear of violence: s 4

Section 4 provides:

(1) A person whose course of conduct causes another to fear, on at least two occasions, that violence will be used against him is guilty of an offence if he knows or ought to know that his course of conduct will cause the other so to fear on each of those occasions.

(2) For the purposes of this section, the person whose course of conduct is in question ought to know that it will cause another to fear that violence will be used against him on any occasion if a reasonable person in possession of the same information would think the course of conduct would cause the other so to fear on that occasion.

(3) It is a defence for a person charged with an offence under this section to show that—

(a) his course of conduct was pursued for the purpose of preventing or detecting crime,

(b) his course of conduct was pursued under any enactment or rule of law or to comply with any condition or requirement imposed by any person under any enactment, or

(c) the pursuit of his course of conduct was reasonable for the protection of himself or another or for the protection of his or another's property.

Section 4 is triable either way, carrying a maximum sentence on indictment of ten[722] years' imprisonment, or a fine or both. This is a high maximum sentence for a negligence-based offence. A judge who rules that there is no case to answer on a charge under s 4 may allow the jury to consider an alternative verdict under s 2.[723]

The essential difference between this offence and that in s 2 (and the tort in s 3) is that the victim must be caused to fear on at least two occasions, that violence will be used 'against him'. The other important difference is that the only defence available to this charge is that the harasser proves that his conduct was for the purpose of preventing or detecting crime, was lawfully authorized or was reasonable for the protection of *himself or another or of property*.[724]

Section 4 has been criticized as being too narrow because of this requirement.[725] Whereas s 2 explicitly requires, inter alia: (a) a course of conduct (b) which must amount to harassment of another, s 4 requires that the victim is caused, by the course of conduct, to fear violence on at least two occasions. In *Curtis*, the court concluded that the s 4 offence requires proof also that the course of conduct has to amount to harassment.[726] Section 4 does not expressly require that the course of conduct which causes the victim to fear violence constitutes harassment. Section 4 contains the stricter limitation that the course of conduct has to cause fear (it being insufficient even to frighten the victim as to what might happen (*Henley*)). Arguably, s 4 represents a distinct offence focused not on harassment but on the graver wrong of creating fear of violence. However, the court's preferred interpretation is one which construes s 4 in the broader context of the Act and sits more comfortably with the fact that s 2 is an included alternative offence.[727] Interpreting s 4 so as not to require the

---

[722] See s 175 of the Policing and Crime Act 2017 (in force from 3 Apr 2017).

[723] *Livesey* [2006] EWCA Crim 3344.

[724] A failure to direct on these defences may well render a conviction unsafe—*Wilkes* [2004] EWCA Crim 3136.

[725] See Finch [2002] Crim LR 702, n 722, suggesting a new offence of intentional harassment to bridge the gap between the narrow s 4 and the wide and overused s 2.

[726] *Curtis* was followed in the subsequent case of *Widdows* [2011] EWCA Crim 1500. Although these authorities ultimately bound it as a matter of precedent, the Court of Appeal in *Haque* [2011] EWCA Crim 1871 stated that it applied them 'reluctantly'. The court took cognizance of the scepticism expressed in the commentary at [2011] Crim LR 959.

[727] Furthermore, it is consistent with the approach that seems to have been taken in previous authorities holding that the victim has been put in 'fear of violence *by harassment*', such as *Patel* [2004] EWCA Crim 3284 (emphasis added).

course of conduct to constitute 'harassment' would only be of practical significance if there are circumstances in which two or more incidents with a sufficient nexus caused a fear of violence without also being harassing. That would seem unlikely.

Section 4 has no requirement of immediacy as in assault. In *Qosja*,[728] Carr J stated that:

In our judgment, a plain and natural reading of the wording of section 4A(1)(b)(i) of the Protection from Harassment Act 1997 reveals that the section is wide enough to look to incidents of violence in the future and not only to incidents giving rise to a fear of violence arising directly out of the incident in question. Nor is there any requirement for the fear to be of violence on a particular date or time in the future, or at a particular place or in a particular manner, or for there to be a specific threat of violence. There can be a fear of violence sufficient for the statute where that fear of violence is of violence on a separate and later occasion. The position can be tested simply by reference to the example of somebody saying 'I'll come back and get you'. On [counsel for D's] interpretation that would be insufficient fear to fall within the scope of the section; that is not a position that we consider to be correct.[729]

It is submitted that this interpretation of the offence is in keeping with the broad approach intended by Parliament and that it ought to apply equally to the offence in s 4(1). In the subsequent case of *Pendlebury v CPS*,[730] the court emphasized that the point being made in the passage quoted from *Qosja* is that the fear of violence must be real and not remote, or hypothetical.

The prosecution does not have to prove that the fear will be fulfilled. Fear that something 'will take place' is a belief, not a proof that the thing feared will in fact arise. Moreover, the distinction between a fear that something 'will' happen, and a fear that something 'might' happen is not necessarily easy to formulate. The two words are descriptors of the degree of fear: in a sense no fear can be other than a fear that something 'might' happen, until it actually does so.[731]

Unlike s 8 of the Public Order Act 1986, no definition of violence is provided in the 1997 Act. In *Henley*,[732] H's harassment of the complainant and her family included threats to kill. He was charged under s 4. The trial judge failed properly to direct the jury, wrongly suggesting that to 'seriously frighten her' would suffice and failed to clarify that the person must *himself* fear violence, not violence towards others. It was emphasized that a direction on the mens rea under s 4(2) should be routinely given. It is 'good practice' for the judge to direct the jury to consider whether the incidents about which they were sure were so connected in type and in context as to justify the conclusion that they could amount to a course of conduct.[733]

A fear of violence may be inferred from threats and behaviour other than explicit threats of violence issued to the victim in person (eg threats to his dog), but the victim must fear that violence will be used against himself.[734] Threats to burn down the family house will suffice.[735]

16.14.2.4 Racially and religiously aggravated harassment

The Crime and Disorder Act 1998, as amended by the Anti-terrorism, Crime and Security Act 2001, provides racially and religiously aggravated offences of harassment and putting people in fear of violence.

---

[728] [2016] EWCA Crim 1543.   [729] At [31].   [730] [2018] EWCA Crim 3567.
[731] At [20] per Irwin LJ.   [732] [2000] Crim LR 582. See also *Curtis* [2010] EWCA Crim 123.
[733] *Sahin* [2009] EWCA Crim 2616.
[734] *R v DPP* [2001] Crim LR 396; *Henley* [2000] Crim LR 582; *Caurti v DPP* [2002] Crim LR 131 and commentaries.
[735] *R (A) v DPP* [2005] ACD 61.

Section 32:

(1) A person is guilty of an offence under this section if he commits—

   (a) an offence under s 2 of the Protection from Harassment Act 1997 (offence of harassment); or

   (b) an offence under s 4 of that Act (putting people in fear of violence), which is [racially or religiously aggravated] for the purposes of this section.

An aggravated offence under s 32(1)(a) is triable either way and punishable on indictment with a maximum sentence of two years' imprisonment. An offence under s 32(1)(b) is triable either way and carries a maximum 14 years' imprisonment on conviction on indictment. The nature of racial and religious aggravation is discussed earlier.[736]

16.14.2.5 Harassment in the home

Section 126 of the Serious Organised Crime and Police Act 2005 introduced a new offence into s 42A of the Criminal Justice and Police Act 2001. This offence is triable summarily only[737] and carries a maximum sentence of six months' imprisonment or a fine not exceeding level 4 on the standard scale, or both. 'Dwelling' has the same meaning as in s 8 of the Public Order Act (see Ch 31).[738]

Regard should also be had to s 1(3)–(3A) of the Protection from Eviction Act 1977. In short, it is an offence to do acts likely to interfere with the peace or comfort of the residential occupier or members of his household, or persistently withdraw or withhold services reasonably required for residential occupation with intent to cause the residential occupier either: (a) to give up the occupation or (b) to refrain from exercising any right or pursuing any remedy in respect of the premises.

16.14.2.6 Stalking

In February 2012 the report of the Independent Parliamentary Inquiry into Stalking Law Reform was published.[739] The report concluded that the current legislative regime was inadequate and in need of reform. Sections 111 and 112 of the Protection of Freedoms Act 2012 amend the 1997 Act with the effect that stalking is, for the first time in England and Wales, a criminal offence in its own right. These provisions have been in force since November 2012 and amend ss 2 and 4 of the 1997 Act in the following ways: s 2A(1) contains the offence of stalking; s 4A(1)(b)(i) creates the offences of 'stalking causing fear of violence'; and s 4A(1)(b)(ii) creates the offence of 'stalking causing serious alarm or distress'. As was stated earlier, conduct constituting 'stalking' as that term is commonly understood already falls within the terms of the 1997 Act.[740] What these news provisions do, therefore, is to label explicitly conduct of this nature as 'stalking', rather than harassment. Section 2A(2) provides:[741]

(2) For the purposes of subsection (1)(b) (and section 4A(1)(a)) a person's course of conduct amounts to stalking of another person if—

   (a) it amounts to harassment of that person,

   (b) the acts or omissions involved are ones associated with stalking, and

---

[736] Note also the Law Commission proposals to extend the aggravated offences to protect a broader range of characteristics. See text at n 382.

[737] Section 42A(4).　　[738] Section 42A(7).

[739] The Justice Unions' Parliamentary Group, 'Independent Parliamentary Inquiry into Stalking Law Reform: Main Findings and Recommendations' (2012).

[740] For an analysis of whether the new provisions will deal with the phenomenon of 'cyberstalking', see N MacEwan, 'The New Stalking Offences in English Law: Will They Provide Effective Protection From Cyberstalking?' [2012] Crim LR 767.

[741] By virtue of s 2(A)(4) this is a summary only offence.

(c) the person whose course of conduct it is knows or ought to know that the course of conduct amounts to harassment of the other person.

The legislation provides some guidance as to what is meant by the requirement that D's 'acts or omissions . . . are ones associated with stalking'. The legislation does not, however, provide a definition of stalking. Section 2A(3) gives the following examples:

(a) following a person,

(b) contacting, or attempting to contact, a person by any means,

(c) publishing any statement or other material—

   (i) relating or purporting to relate to a person, or

   (ii) purporting to originate from a person,

(d) monitoring the use by a person of the internet, email or any other form of electronic communication,

(e) loitering in any place (whether public or private),

(f) interfering with any property in the possession of a person,

(g) watching or spying on a person.

D cannot be guilty unless his conduct first constitutes harassment. It is important that this element of the offence is considered separately from whether D's acts or omissions are ones associated with stalking. The list of examples provided in the legislation is not exhaustive and it is possible for an act or omission not included on the list to constitute an act or omission associated with stalking.

Section 4A(1)(b)(i) and (ii) creates the aggravated offences of 'stalking causing fear of violence' and 'stalking causing serious alarm or distress which has a substantial adverse impact on day-to-day activities'.[742] These are either way offences. Section 4A provides:

4A Stalking involving fear of violence or serious alarm or distress

(1) A person ('A') whose course of conduct—

   (a) amounts to stalking, and

   (b) either—

      (i) causes another ('B') to fear, on at least two occasions, that violence will be used against B, or

      (ii) causes B serious alarm or distress which has a substantial adverse effect on B's usual day-to-day activities, is guilty of an offence if A knows or ought to know that A's course of conduct will cause B so to fear on each of those occasions or (as the case may be) will cause such alarm or distress.

(2) For the purposes of this section A ought to know that A's course of conduct will cause B to fear that violence will be used against B on any occasion if a reasonable person in possession of the same information would think the course of conduct would cause B so to fear on that occasion.

(3) For the purposes of this section A ought to know that A's course of conduct will cause B serious alarm or distress which has a substantial adverse effect on B's usual day-to-day activities if a reasonable person in possession of the same information would think the course of conduct would cause B such alarm or distress.

---

[742] By virtue of s 4(A)(5)(a) a person convicted is liable on conviction on indictment to imprisonment for a term not exceeding ten years, or a fine, or both. On summary conviction, the maximum term of imprisonment is six months or a fine not exceeding the statutory maximum.

(4) It is a defence for A to show that—

    (a) A's course of conduct was pursued for the purpose of preventing or detecting crime,

    (b) A's course of conduct was pursued under any enactment or rule of law or to comply with any condition or requirement imposed by any person under any enactment, or

    (c) the pursuit of A's course of conduct was reasonable for the protection of A or another or for the protection of A's or another's property.

This offence is similar to the one in s 4. There are, however, a number of important differences. First, D's course of conduct must amount to stalking. Secondly, in addition to D causing another, V, to fear on at least two occasions that violence will be used against her, D can also be guilty if he 'causes another serious alarm or distress which has a substantial adverse effect on her usual day-to-day activities'.[743] None of these terms are defined.[744] It submitted that this is a subjective question, so irrespective of whether V's 'usual day-to-day activities' are idiosyncratic, if they are substantially adversely affected then that will suffice. Section 4A(3) makes clear that D commits the offence if a reasonable person with the same information as D would think the course of conduct would have a substantial adverse impact on V's day-to-day activities. Therefore D cannot escape liability by claiming that he did not realize that his conduct would have this effect; the test is an objective one. It is also clear that the legislation imposes a threshold, as D will not be guilty unless he causes V *serious* alarm or distress that has a *substantial* adverse effect on her usual day-to-day activities. If tried on indictment, the maximum sentence for this offence is ten years' imprisonment and/or a fine.[745] If tried summarily, the maximum sentence is six months' imprisonment and/or a fine.

16.15 Domestic abuse

The offences of assault, battery and those under ss 47, 20 and 18 of the OAPA apply as equally in the context of a cohabiting relationship as elsewhere. Other offences in the OAPA may also have particular relevance in that context (including the offence of choking under s 21 as well as the poisoning offences under ss 23 and 24). There are numerous procedural problems in prosecuting those offences effectively in a domestic abuse context—not least the pressures on the complainant not to report and the pressures to pursue the prosecution.[746] The low rates of prosecution for such offences had broader impacts on likely reporting and on

---

[743] Home Office Circular 018/2012 states that the offence 'is designed to recognize the serious impact that stalking may have on victims, even where an explicit fear of violence is not created by each incident of stalking behaviour'. Available at www.gov.uk/government/publications/a-change-to-the-protection-from-harassment-act-1997-introduction-of-two-new-specific-offences-of-stalking.

[744] This is recognized in the circular. The Home Office does, however, give some examples of what it considers will constitute 'substantial adverse effect': the victim changing their routes to work, work patterns or employment; the victim arranging for friends or family to pick up children from school (to avoid contact with the stalker); the victim putting in place additional security measures in their home; the victim moving home; physical or mental ill-health; the victim's deterioration in performance at work due to stress; the victim stopping/or changing the way they socialize.

[745] The maximum sentence was increased from five years by s 175(1)(b) of the Policing and Crime Act 2017. For an extreme case see *McNeill* [2019] EWCA Crim 1566.

[746] See M Madden Dempsey, *Prosecuting Domestic Violence: A Philosophical Analysis* (2009); L Ellison, 'Prosecuting Domestic Violence Without Victim Participation' (2002) 65 MLR 834.

victims' confidence in the criminal justice system. The offences under the Protection from Harassment Act also have an important role to play, and they capture an important aspect of the wrongdoing—that it involves a course of conduct against the victim.

It has long been recognized that these offences do not provide an adequate response to domestic abuse.[747] In particular, the harms and wrongs involved in that behaviour were not accurately reflected in the range of mainstream criminal offences.[748] As a result, a more targeted criminal offence has been created which seeks to criminalize the different, often more subtle, forms of abuse within intimate partner relationships. These include non-violent conduct which impacts on a person's day-to-day life choices within the relationship. Not only is there an advantage in terms of fair labelling, but also in raising public awareness. Section 76 of the Serious Crime Act 2015 provides:

(1) A person (D) commits an offence if—

(a) D repeatedly or continuously engages in behaviour towards another person (V) that is controlling or coercive,

(b) at the time of the behaviour, D and V are personally connected,

(c) the behaviour has a serious effect on V, and

(d) D knows or ought to know that the behaviour will have a serious effect on V.

The maximum penalty for an offence, is five years' imprisonment and/or a fine on indictment and six months and/or an unlimited fine summarily (ss 76(11) and 86(14)).[749]

Several distinctive features of the offence are worth noting. It is not gender-specific.[750] The offence only applies within particular relationships that are further defined in s 76. For these purposes, D and V are 'personally connected' if: D is in an intimate personal relationship with V (s 76(2)(a)); or D and V live together[751] and they are members of the same family (s 76(2)(b)(i)); or they have previously been in an intimate personal relationship with each other (s 76(2)(b)(ii)). The distinctive harm that is described by the offence is that it has a 'serious effect' on V which is defined to include, on at least two occasions, of violence and/or serious alarm or distress which has a substantially adverse effect on V's day-to-day activities. There is no need for proof of any assault or the threat or infliction of any physical harm or violence. The offence is targeting the 'psychological abuse' and 'mental cruelty' that is at the heart of the abusive intimate relationship. In terms of mens rea, the offences extends to D who knows (or *objectively* should know) that his conduct is having a serious impact on

[747] See generally M Burton, *Legal Responses to Domestic Violence* (2009); N Groves and T Thomas, *Domestic Violence and Criminal Justice* (2014); E Stark, *Coercive Control: How Men Entrap Women in Personal Life* (2009); V Tadros, 'The Distinctiveness of Domestic Abuse: A Freedom Based Account' (2004–5) 65 La L Rev 989; S Edward, 'Coercion and Compulsion—Re-Imagining Crimes and Defences' [2016] Crim LR 876 (considering the overlap with modern slavery).

[748] V Bettinson and C Bishop, 'Is the Creation of a Discrete Offence of Coercive Control Necessary to Combat Domestic Violence?' (2015) 66 NILQ 177; Home Office, *Strengthening the Law on Domestic Abuse Consultation—Summary of Responses* (Dec 2014).

[749] See generally *Katira* [2020] EWCA Crim 89.

[750] L Martin, 'Debates of Difference: Male Victims of Domestic Violence and Abuse' in V Bettinson and S Hilder (eds), *Domestic Violence: Interdisciplinary Perspectives on Protection, Prevention and Intervention* (2016) 181–201.

[751] For these purposes D and V are members of the same family if: they are or have been married to each other (s 76(6)(a)); they are or have been civil partners of each other (s 76(6)(b)); they are relatives (s 76(6)(c)); they have agreed to marry one another (whether or not the agreement has been terminated) (s 76(6)(d)); they have entered into a civil partnership agreement (whether or not the agreement has been terminated) (s 76(6)(e)); they are both parents of the same child (s 76(6)(f)); they have or have had parental responsibility for the same child (s 76(6)(g)).

V's ability to live her life. A specific, and highly controversial, defence is also introduced by s 76(8) where D believed she was acting in V's best interests and her behaviour was reasonable.

The offence has already been subjected to some telling criticism in terms of its drafting[752] and application.[753] Further legislative developments are inevitable, including that the new protection order will only be applicable to those aged 18 or over but, where it is applicable, it will empower the police to exclude D from certain properties, from contacting V, and so on.

Postscript

The government supported amendment to the Domestic Abuse Act 2021 inserts a new offence of strangulation or suffocation into the Serious Crime Act 2015. Strangulation is typically a gendered form of violence that can cause primal fear, serious physical harm and psychological harm.[754]

The offence requires that a person (A) intentionally strangles another person (B), or does any other act to B that affects B's ability to breathe and constitutes battery of B. Consent to the strangulation is a defence unless B suffered serious harm (grievous bodily harm, wounding, or actual bodily harm) and A intended to cause B serious harm or was reckless as to causing such harm to B. There is no definition of the concept of strangulation. The breadth of the battery form of the offence is so wide that the lack of definition will be unproblematic unless there are cases of strangulation that merit prosecution but do not affect B's breathing. The section does not make clear whether, in relation to the battery form of the offence, A also needs to know or believe that their battery will affect B's ability to breathe. There will be work for the Courts to do in interpretation. There is also a need for a sentencing guideline, enhanced police and judicial training and for greater public awareness of the serious harms involved.[755] Section 73 of the 2021 Act gives extraterritorial application to ss 47, 20, 18, 23 and 24 of the OAPA where the offence is committed in a country or territory outside the UK by a UK national or by a person ordinarily resident in England and Wales, but only where the conduct in question is also an offence of some description under local law.

Further reading

J Anderson, *The Legality of Boxing: A Punch Drunk Love?*

J Gardner, *Offences and Defences: Selected Essays in the Philosophy of Criminal Law*

A Reed and M Bohlander (with N Wake and E Smith) (eds), *Consent: Domestic and Comparative Perspectives*

C Stanton and H Quirk (eds), *Criminalising Contagion: Legal and Ethical Challenges of Disease Transmission and the Criminal Law*

M Weait, *Intimacy and Responsibility: The Criminalisation of HIV Transmission*

---

[752] V Bettinson, 'Criminalising Coercive Control in Domestic Violence Cases: Should Scotland Follow the Path of England and Wales?' [2016] Crim LR 165; P McGorrery, 'Criminalising "The Worst" Part: Operationalising the Offence of Coercive Control in England and Wales' [2019] Crim LR 957. See also J Youngs, 'Domestic Violence and the Criminal Law: Reconceptualising Reform' (2015) 79 JCL 55 preferring a model based on D's motivations rather than the effect on V.

[753] C Bishop and V Bettinson, 'Evidencing Domestic Violence, Including Behaviour That Falls Under the New Offence of "Controlling or Coercive Behaviour"' [2018] E & P 3.

[754] On the gender and context specific nature of strangulation see Susan Edwards, 'The strangulation of female partners' [2015] Crim LR, 12, 949'.

[755] See generally R Kelly and D Ormerod [2021] Crim LR (Issue 7).

17

Sexual offences

17.1 Introduction

The Sexual Offences Act 2003 (SOA 2003)[1] came into force on 1 May 2004.[2] The Act represents the most comprehensive and radical overhaul of the law relating to sexual offences ever undertaken in England and Wales. Previously, most of the relevant law was contained in the Sexual Offences Act 1956, but that was itself merely a consolidation of various statutes dating back to the late nineteenth century, and the 1956 Act had been amended incrementally to tackle numerous specific problems.[3] The 2003 Act redefines many of the offences found in the old legislation, but introduces scores of new ones. It is not, however, a complete codification of sexual offences; some regulation remains elsewhere—for example, that relating to prostitution[4] and indecent images.[5] Parliament continues to add new sexual offences and to amend those in the 2003 Act.[6]

It is worth pointing out that the 2003 Act was result of a fundamental review: the Home Office Review of sex offences, *Setting the Boundaries: Reforming the Law on Sex Offences*[7] *and the Review*

---

[1] See generally on the Act: P Rook and R Ward, *Sexual Offences: Law and Practice* (5th edn, 2016); K Stevenson, A Davies and M Gunn, *Blackstone's Guide to the Sexual Offences Act 2003* (2004); R Card, M Hirst and A Gillespie, *Sexual Offences* (2008). See generally SP Green, *Criminalizing Sex: A Unified Liberal Theory* (2020).

[2] Where the prosecution has not demonstrated whether the events constituting the charge occurred before or after this date, it was held that the prosecution cannot continue: *Newbon* [2005] Crim LR 738 (HHJ Glenn); *C* [2005] EWCA Crim 3533. The government responded by introducing s 55 of the Violent Crime Reduction Act 2006. In short, s 55 applies if the offence now charged is an offence under the SOA 2003 and the conduct alleged amounts to an offence under one of the repealed offences listed in subs (2), and the *only thing* preventing D being found guilty is that it cannot be proved beyond reasonable doubt whether the conduct took place before or after the commencement of the SOA 2003. If so, where the maximum penalty of imprisonment available was lower under the old law that will be conclusively presumed to apply. If the penalties are the same, then it shall be conclusively presumed that the conduct took place after the commencement of the SOA 2003. The section presents difficulties: how can it be known that the 'only thing' preventing the accused being guilty is that the date has not been proved? Many other issues will determine guilt. It is also potentially unfair: why should it not be that the version of the offence (not penalty) which is more favourable to the defendant is adopted? In *C* [2009] EWCA Crim 52 it was held that for s 55 'to have been relied upon each offence should have been charged in the alternative under the new regime and the old'. This is still not always understood by prosecutors. See also *F* [2008] EWCA Crim 994.

[3] For the previous law see the 10th edn of this book, Ch 16.

[4] The Home Office consultation process on prostitution: *Paying the Price* (2004) (see on this B Brooks Gordon, 'Clients and Commercial Sex' [2005] Crim LR 425; M Madden Dempsey, 'Rethinking Wolfenden' [2005] Crim LR 444) led to the new offences in the Policing and Crime Act 2009: s 14 created a new offence of paying for sexual services of a prostitute who is subject to exploitation; s 16 amends the Street Offences Act 1959, s 1. A new offence of soliciting was created by s 19 of the 2009 Act, which inserted s 51A into the SOA 2003; this offence effectively replaces the offences under the Sexual Offences Act 1985. See TK Paz and N Levenkron (2009) 29 LS 438.

[5] See the Protection of Children Act 1978, s 1; and s 160 of the Criminal Justice Act 1988 as amended by the Criminal Justice and Immigration Act 2008. See generally A Gillespie, *Child Pornography: Law and Policy* (2011); S Ost, *Child Pornography and Sexual Grooming: Legal and Societal Responses* (2009); M Taylor and E Quayle, *Child Pornography: An Internet Crime* (2003).

[6] See eg the possession of extreme image offences discussed in Ch 30 and the amendments in the Violent Crime Reduction Act 2006, the Criminal Justice and Immigration Act 2008, the Coroners and Justice Act 2009 and the Policing and Crime Act 2009, and the Serious Crime Act 2005.

[7] (2000). See N Lacey, 'Beset by Boundaries' [2001] Crim LR 3; J Temkin, *Rape and the Legal Process* (2nd edn, 2002), 60–7.

of Part 1 of the Sex Offenders Act 1997.[8] Following consultation, these led to a Government White Paper, *Protecting the Public: Strengthening Protection Against Sex Offenders and Reforming the Law on Sexual Offences.*[9] The laudable aims of these reviews cannot be criticized. Unfortunately, whilst trying to achieve some of those aims, such as a measure of gender neutrality[10] and modernization of the language, the Act creates numerous difficulties, many of a significant and substantial nature.

17.2 Recurring fundamental concepts in the 2003 Act

17.2.1 Consent

At the core of some of the most serious offences in the 2003 Act is the element of consent.[11] It has long been recognized that determining the consent of the complainant is not restricted to ascertaining whether there has been the use or threat of force,[12] nor whether the sexual acts were against his or her will.[13] However, beyond these negative observations the law has struggled to define, in positive terms, the scope of consent.[14] It is important to remember that the absence of consent is an element of the actus reus, not an element of a defence. As Duff points out,[15] the description of the conduct must be descriptive of the proscribed wrong, and if consent was part of the defence, sexual intercourse would have to be the wrong.[16]

Defining consent was acknowledged to be one of the major difficulties under the 1956 Act,[17] where the leading authority of *Olugboja*[18] simply left the question to the jury to apply their common sense, giving consent its 'ordinary meaning'. This approach prompted stringent academic criticism: Glanville Williams regarded it as 'one more manifestation of the deplorable tendency of the criminal courts to leave important questions of legal policy to the jury'.[19]

---

[8] (2001). Described by Lord Ackner in the Debates as a 'pamphlet': HL, 13 Feb 2003, col 846.

[9] (2002) Cm 5668.

[10] cf the Gender Recognition Act 2004 relating to gender-specific offences. On the importance of gender neutrality, see P Rumney and M Morgan-Taylor, 'Recognising the Male Victim: Gender Neutrality and the Law of Rape' (1997) 26 Anglo-American LR 198.

[11] For discussion of a multitude of issues surrounding consent, see A Reed and M Bohlander (eds), *Consent—Domestic and Comparative Perspectives* (2017).

[12] Until relatively recently judges continued erroneously to direct juries that the use of force by the defendant and resistance by the complainant were essential ingredients of the offence of rape. See *Howard* [1965] 3 All ER 684.

[13] *Camplin* (1846) 1 Cox CC 220: Tindal CJ and Parke B were of the view that rape was ravishing a woman 'where she did not consent' and not ravishing her 'against her will'.

[14] See generally the discussion in the Law Commission Policy Paper appended to *Setting the Boundaries*. For more philosophical analysis, see eg H Hurd, 'The Moral Magic of Consent' (1996) 2 Legal Theory 168; J McGregor, 'Why When She Says No She Doesn't Mean Maybe and Doesn't Mean Yes' (1996) 2 Legal Theory 175.

[15] See Duff, *Answering for Crime*, 208–11.

[16] For an argument that it is prima facie wrong to penetrate a vagina or anus see M Madden Dempsey and J Herring, 'Why Sexual Penetration Requires Justification' (2007) 27 OJLS 467. See also J Wall, 'Sexual Offences and General Reasons Not to Have Sex' (2015) 35 OJLS 777; J Gardner, 'The Opposite of Rape' (2018) 38 OJLS 48; J Conaghan, 'The Essence of Rape' (2019) 39 OJLS 151.

[17] For a review of circumstances in which consent was held to be absent under the old law, see *Setting the Boundaries*, para 2.2.2.

[18] [1981] 3 All ER 443.

[19] Williams, TBCL, 551. Although see S Gardner, 'Appreciating *Olugboja*' (1996) 16 LS 275 for a defence of this approach emphasizing that it focused correctly on the issue of the victim's autonomy. See also G Dingwall, 'Addressing the Boundaries of Consent in Rape' (2002) 13 KCLJ 31.

Remedying this shortcoming was one of the most important objectives of the law reform. *Setting the Boundaries* emphasized the need for clarity in 'the most private and difficult area of sexual relationships . . . so that the boundaries of what is acceptable, and of criminally culpable behaviour, are all well understood'.[20] It was stressed that this is particularly important because in sexual activity consent often involves 'verbal and non-verbal messages [which] can be mistaken and where assumptions about what is and is not appropriate can lead to significant misunderstanding'.[21] Given such determination to clarify the law of consent, echoed as forcefully as it was by ministerial statements,[22] the provisions in the 2003 Act are rather disappointing. Although there is greater clarity than under *Olugboja*, the jury is still left with considerable discretion since the statutory definitions are not as clear or as comprehensive as they could be. In particular, it is doubtful whether the Act succeeds in providing any solution to some of the more frequently encountered difficulties such as the complainant who was, at the time of the sexual act, voluntarily and heavily intoxicated[23] or who succumbed to threats or pressure short of violence, or to deceptions.[24]

17.2.1.1 'Definition' of consent

Three sections in the Act seek to clarify what is meant by consent. Under s 76, where the defendant, A,[25] intentionally deceives the complainant, B, as to the nature or purpose of the act or his identity, it is conclusively presumed that there is a lack of consent and that A has no reasonable belief in consent. Under s 75, six specified circumstances give rise to a rebuttable presumption that there was no consent and that A did not have a reasonable belief in B's consent. Finally, s 74 provides a general definition of consent which may be relevant in combination with ss 75 and 76 in appropriate cases, and independently governs all other situations. It is unclear whether the three-tiered approach to consent reflects a hierarchy of circumstances in which consent is absent.[26]

These 'deeply ambiguous'[27] definitions apply throughout Part I of the Act (in particular for the non-consensual offences of rape, assault by penetration, sexual assault and causing a person to engage in sexual activity without consent). One very significant failure of the drafting of the Act was not to extend ss 75 and 76 beyond the substantive offences, to inchoate forms of those offences.[28]

In *H*,[29] the Court of Appeal rightly emphasized that it is not necessary in every case for the judge to direct on all aspects of the law of consent when they do not arise on the facts.

---

[20] Home Office Consultation Paper, *Setting the Boundaries: Reforming the Law on Sexual Offences* (2000) paras 2.7.2 and 2.10.1.

[21] ibid. See on this DN Husak, *The Philosophy of Criminal Law: Selected Essays* (2010) Ch 9. See also P Rumney, 'The Review of Sex Offences and Rape Law Reform: Another False Dawn' (2001) 64 MLR 890 emphasizing that consent should involve a dialogue between the parties.

[22] See Lord Falconer speaking of the need for 'crystal clarity', HL Deb, 13 Feb 2003, col 772. See also *Protecting the Public*, para 30.

[23] See *Bree* [2007] EWCA Crim 804 and discussion at p 795.

[24] See eg *Jheeta* [2007] EWCA Crim 1699 and the many other cases discussed at p 798.

[25] Throughout this chapter 'A' will be used to denote the principal defendant and 'B' the complainant reflecting the distinctive drafting style in the 2003 Act.

[26] See the influential article by J Temkin and A Ashworth, 'Rape, Sexual Assaults and the Problems of Consent' [2004] Crim LR 328. See also J Miles [2008] 10 Arch News 5, suggesting that s 74 should be construed subject to s 76. This seems to be a strained reading of the sections and, as will be discussed, it is not one the courts have found favourable. For analysis, see K Laird, 'Rapist or Rogue? Deception, Consent and the Sexual Offences Act 2003' [2014] Crim LR 492; M Gibson, 'Deceptive Sexual Relations: A Theory of Criminal Liability' (2020) 40 OJLS 82.

[27] See Tadros (2006) 26 OJLS 521.

[28] See HHJ Rodwell, 'Problems with the Sexual Offences Act 2003' [2005] Crim LR 290.

[29] [2006] EWCA Crim 853. See also *Taran* [2006] EWCA Crim 1498, where B was raped at gunpoint and there was no need to explain to the jury the intricacies of ss 75 and 76, discussed later.

There will, however, be cases of greater difficulty in which a careful direction will be needed. As the analysis that follows will demonstrate, one of the most intractable difficulties is the approach the judge ought to take when it is alleged that A has deceived 'B, in circumstances in which the deception does not fall within s 76.

Section 74

Section 74 provides that 'a person consents if he agrees by choice, and has the freedom and capacity to make that choice'. In *R (on the application of 'Monica') v DPP*, the Lord Chief Justice stated that in enacting the Sexual Offences Act 2003 and placing the offence of rape on a statutory footing for the first time, there was no reason to suppose that Parliament had intended any change to the understanding of consent that had developed under the common law.[30] The Lord Chief Justice returned to this issue in *Lawrance*, in which he stated that there was 'no sign that Parliament intended a sea change in the meaning of consent when it legislated in 2003'.[31]

This definition, based on 'free agreement', is intended to emphasize that the absence of the complainant's protest, resistance or injury does not necessarily signify his consent. Although the Act is silent as to the precise moment at which B's consent or agreement must be present, it is clear that the relevant time is that of the alleged sexual wrongdoing. This may present problems where, for example, B has indicated to A his willingness to engage in sexual activity later that evening, but then becomes so heavily intoxicated that at the time of the sexual act B is incapable of making any coherent decision.[32] *A fortiori* where B initially indicates his disinclination to engage in sexual activity but later does so when voluntarily intoxicated.

'Freedom', it is submitted, is too loose a word to use in defining this crucial element of such serious offences. Freedom is a term which is heavily context-dependent and always implies 'freedom from' something.[33] The jury will have to address the existence and weight of this 'other' pressure from which B might have been acting freely. It may therefore be desirable for the jury to address the question of freedom by reference to proportionality. The greater the 'pressure' facing B, the less 'freedom' she has to make her choice to engage in sexual activity. This may involve the jury in a difficult assessment of a wide range of factors when the degree of freedom is inhibited by, for example, A's threat to terminate B's employment unless she has sex. This may lead to further difficulties such as the source of the pressures, particularly where the defendant is not directly responsible for bringing them to bear. Beyond freedom from physical pressure, it is unclear what degree of freedom is envisaged to validate consent. In particular, issues may arise as to B's economic freedom, as where B, an underprivileged employee of a wealthy businessman, agrees to his sexual advances to retain her position. Other examples might involve B's religious freedom as where a dependent young member of a strict religion agrees to sexual activity with an elder whom in all other respects she has been taught never to question.[34] The answer to 'what level of pressure negates freedom' will depend on a whole range of factors and will be decided on a case-by-case basis. It is helpful to consider some of the cases to identify examples of how the Court of Appeal views the position.

---

[30] [2018] EWHC 3508 (Admin), [29].   [31] [2020] EWCA Crim 971, [42].

[32] See also the Law Commission's Policy Paper appended to *Setting the Boundaries*, para 4.54. See generally Temkin, *Rape and the Legal Process*, 90–116 and the excellent analysis in P Jarvis, 'The Timing of Consent' [2019] Crim LR 394.

[33] As Temkin and Ashworth point out, n 26, freedom is only used to rule out the suggestion of some or all of its antitheses; see p 336 of Temkin and Ashworth, citing JL Austin, 'A Plea for Excuses' in H Morris (ed), *Freedom and Responsibility* (1961) 8.

[34] Difficulties also arise because A will claim that he had a reasonable belief in B's consent.

In the case of *Kirk*,[35] it was accepted by the Court of Appeal that the homeless teenage complainant, B, who had been sexually abused for years by A, had not consented to sex with A where she had done so to gain £3.25 from him in order to buy food. It cannot be said that B has truly 'agreed by choice' if she has been groomed or frightened into submission by A. A further instructive case on this issue is *C*,[36] where the question was whether A had sexually abused B between the ages of 5 and 15 and then raped her after she was 16. Once the jury found that A had sexually abused B when she was under 16, it was open to them to conclude that her consent to the sexual acts that occurred after she turned 16 was indeed apparent and not real. This was the effect of the dominance and control that A had exerted over B from a young age. *C* illustrates that the impression of consent can be negated by A's dominance and control over B.

This question of interpreting freedom also raises the difficult relationship between 'consent' and 'submission', which continues to feature in the courts' analysis. Under the 1956 Act, in *Olugboja*[37] the court placed considerable emphasis on the difference between consent and submission, but never fully identified what the distinction was. For example, B may reluctantly submit to sexual intercourse only because her fiancé threatens that he will break off their engagement if she does not. Such a case is very far removed from rape but it seems to be one of submission. At the other extreme, B may submit because A is holding a knife to her throat. This is plainly rape; there is no consent.[38] In both cases B yields because a threat is made; it is not easy to see how the term 'submission' helps to distinguish them. The confusion in addressing these terms was in part a result of the *dictum* of Coleridge J in *Day*:[39] 'every consent involves a submission; but it by no means follows that a mere submission involves consent'. It is submitted that this is wrong. B who joyously embraces her reluctant lover, A, undoubtedly consents to the acts that follow but it would seem inappropriate, to put it mildly, to say that B 'submits' to the sexual activity that she clearly wants. On the other hand, B who 'gives in' to threats from her fiancé does in fact agree, although not freely. Whether any useful distinction can be drawn in this context between threats ('do this or I will sack you') and promises ('do this and I will give you a pay rise') is debatable.

The language of submission and consent was used in *Kirk* (earlier in this section), and the Court of Appeal addressed this issue directly in *Doyle*[40] where A had used violence against his ex-partner (holding her head under water and tying her up) before demanding sex. B refused, protesting until he had penetrated her; she then ceased to resist, explaining at trial that she 'just let him get on with it'. A's conviction for rape was upheld.[41] There was no consent. The court acknowledged that there would be circumstances where a jury would require assistance with the distinction between (a) reluctant but free exercise of choice, especially in a long-term loving relationship, and (b) unwilling submission due to fear of worse consequences, but the instant case did not call for such assistance.[42]

---

[35] [2008] EWCA Crim 434 (under the old law).   [36] [2012] EWCA Crim 2034.

[37] (1981) 73 Cr App R 344.

[38] This may now give rise to a presumption of non-consent under s 75(2)(a).

[39] (1841) 9 C & P 722 at 724.   [40] [2010] EWCA Crim 119.

[41] The judge directed that 'submission to do something which she did not want to happen does not amount to consent. In deciding if [B] consented or whether she merely submitted to something which she did not want, you should apply your combined good sense, your experience, and your knowledge of human behaviour and modern behaviour to all the relevant facts, including, obviously, their relationship and what you have heard about that. The law does not require a complainant to have resisted physically, and nor is it necessary to show that a woman's submission was induced by force or fear, although obviously, in this case, as you know, the prosecution evidence is that [B] did say no, and physically resisted until the defendant penetrated her.'

[42] In cases where a direction on submission is needed, the old JSB Direction 53 offers an illustration taken from Pill J's ruling in *Zafar*: 'V may not particularly want sexual intercourse on a particular occasion, but because it is her husband or her partner who is asking for it, she will consent to sexual intercourse. The fact that such consent is given reluctantly or out of a sense of duty to her partner it is still consent.' See now the *Crown Court Compendium* (2021).

In *Robinson*,[43] Elias LJ reaffirmed that the division between consent and submission is a matter for the jury, applying its common sense, experience and knowledge of human behaviour. In reaching this conclusion his lordship cited *Olugboja* with approval. *Olugboja* was also cited with approval in the more recent case of *Ali*,[44] in which the prosecution alleged that the defendants groomed young girls from troubled backgrounds. The prosecution contended that, as a result of such grooming, the girls become sexually compliant and that any apparent consent on their part was not genuine. Upholding the defendants' convictions, Fulford LJ stated that, 'one of the consequences when vulnerable people are groomed for sexual exploitation is that compliance can mask the lack of true consent on the part of the victim'.[45] It was observed that individuals in circumstances such as these may have been manipulated to the extent that they are unaware of, or confused about, the distinction between acquiescence and genuine agreement. His lordship held that evidence of exploitation is a factor the jury can take into account when deciding whether or not there was genuine consent. The continued reliance on the approach in *Olugboja* is somewhat problematic, however, given that s 74 was enacted with the express intention[46] that consent would not simply be a matter for the jury's common sense.

The distinction the law has traditionally drawn between consent and submission seems to have been called into question in *Watson*.[47] In this case, Burnett LJ, as he then was, stated, *obiter*, that 'it is possible for a person to submit to a demand which he or she feels unable to resist, but without lacking the capacity or freedom to make a choice'.[48] His lordship characterized this as being an example of 'reluctant consent'. If an individual truly feels unable to resist a demand for sex, then it is difficult to see how he or she has the freedom to make a choice. Surely this is an example of submission rather than consent? To the extent that it calls into question the existence of a distinction between consent and submission, the *dictum* in *Watson* is contrary to the weight of Court of Appeal authority. Indeed, in *Ali* the distinction between consent and submission was described as being 'critical'.

Section 74 also lists 'choice' as a factor in determining consent. Choice presupposes that B has options from which to choose and that, in turn, surely presupposes B is possessed of adequate information about each to make an 'informed' choice between them.[49] In *R (on the application of F) v DPP*,[50] Lord Judge CJ held that 'choice' is crucial to the issue of consent. His lordship stated that the evidence relating to choice and freedom to make a choice ought to be approached in a 'broad commonsense way'. Again, s 74 fails to offer any guidance as to the necessary degree of information about the activity (eg penetration) that B is to engage in and this will be a particularly difficult issue in cases in which it is alleged that B's consent has been procured by deception. One of the most controversial areas in which this issue arises is in cases where A is HIV-positive and has not informed B of that fact. The Court of Appeal has confirmed that a complainant's consent to the risk of contracting HIV has to be an informed consent.[51] However, it is important to reiterate[52] that the current position in English law is that if A who is HIV-positive fails to inform B of that fact before having unprotected intercourse, A will not commit rape. The appropriate charge is under the OAPA 1861. Indeed, it has been held that A's failure to disclose his HIV status did not

---

43 [2011] EWCA Crim 916.   44 [2015] EWCA Crim 1279.   45 At [57].

46 *Setting the Boundaries: Reforming the Law on Sexual Offences, Vol I*, para 2.10.2.

47 [2015] EWCA Crim 559.   48 At [34].

49 Tadros argues that there is a paradox in the present law in that it is possible for B to agree by choice while lacking freedom or capacity: if one lacks capacity and freedom one cannot agree by choice at all: (2006) 26 OJLS 521.

50 [2013] EWHC 945 (Admin).   51 *Konzani* [2005] EWCA Crim 706.

52 See the full discussion in Ch 16.

affect the issue of consent in rape where there were no allegations that A had deceived B. In *B*,[53] it was held that the evidence of A's HIV status should have been excluded: the fact that a defendant may not have disclosed his HIV status is not relevant to the issue of consent under s 74.

A different approach may be adopted by the court where B asks A whether he is HIV-positive and A lies. In *McNally*,[54] the Court of Appeal distinguished *B* on the basis that it was a case concerning non-disclosure. Leveson LJ stated that non-disclosure should not be equated with active deception. His lordship held that it was possible for the latter to vitiate consent within the meaning of s 74.[55] However, subsequently, in *Lawrance*, that distinction between positive lies and failures to disclose has been rejected by the Court of Appeal.

The element of 'capacity' is similarly not further defined. It is clearly 'integral to the concept of choice'.[56] In this context it is clearly intended to mean mental capacity. It is submitted that the crucial issue should be whether B has the capacity to choose to perform the specified act with A on the occasion in question.[57] The test is not one focusing on B's status—that is, whether B has a particular mental disability or not. The question is focused on B's capacity to make the decision about engaging in this sexual act with this person. Determining B's capacity is necessarily a contextually sensitive issue. The Court of Appeal has stated that the process is, 'largely visceral rather than cerebral, and owes more to instinct and emotion rather than to analysis'.[58]

The leading authority on the concept of capacity to consent under the 2003 Act is *Cooper* in which the House of Lords considered that term in the context of the offence under s 30: sexual activity with a person with a mental disorder impeding choice.[59] Some aspects of the decision inform a general understanding of consent. B was a 28-year-old woman with a history of serious mental disorders manifesting themselves in episodes of impulsive and aggressive behaviour, delusions, hallucinations, depression or manic episodes. She developed irrational concerns for her safety. A befriended her, gave her crack cocaine and made her perform oral sex on him and a co-defendant. B said that she had performed the acts out of fear of violence. A argued that B's capacity was only impaired and that she did not lack capacity to choose in the sense of lacking sufficient understanding of the nature of the act or its consequences. In short, A argued that B knew what oral sex was and that was sufficient for her to have capacity to consent. The judge directed the jury that if B had an irrational

---

[53] [2006] EWCA Crim 2945.   [54] [2013] EWCA Crim 1051.

[55] The distinction between active deception and non-disclosure is one that Sharpe characterizes as 'morally problematic'. See A Sharpe, 'Criminalising Sexual Intimacy: Transgender Defendants and the Legal Construction of Non-Consent' [2014] Crim LR 207 and more recently A Sharpe, 'Expanding Liability for Sexual Fraud Through the Concept of "Active Deception": A Flawed Approach' (2016) 80 J Crim L 28. For further discussion of the deception/disclosure bifurcation, see A Reed and E Smith, 'Caveat Amator—Transmission of HIV and the Parameters of Consent and Bad Character Evidence' in A Reed and M Bohlander (eds), *Consent—Domestic and Comparative Perspectives* (2017). See also S Ryan, '"Active Deception" v Non-Disclosure: HIV Transmission, Non-Fatal Offences and Criminal Responsibility' [2019] Crim LR 4.

[56] *Bree* [2007] EWCA Crim 804 at [23] per Sir Igor Judge P.

[57] C Elliott and C de Than, 'The Case for a Rational Reconstruction of Consent in Criminal Law' (2007) 70 MLR 225 argue that the test of capacity should focus on whether B was capable of understanding at the material time the nature and reasonable foreseeable consequences of the act and able to communicate her consent effectively, at 242.

[58] *A* [2014] EWCA Crim 299, [28]. Citing with approval *Re M* [2014] EWCA Civ 37.

[59] Technically these comments might be seen as *obiter* on the scope of capacity in s 74 since the appeal dealt with the meaning of the words 'unable to communicate' a choice in s 30(2). By s 30(2), a person is unable to refuse if—(a) he lacks the capacity to choose whether to agree to the touching (whether because he lacks sufficient understanding of the nature or reasonably foreseeable consequences of what is being done, or for any other reason), or (b) he is unable to communicate such a choice to the alleged offender.

fear or confusion of mind arising from her mental disorder she may lack capacity to choose whether to agree to sexual touching. The Court of Appeal[60] took a much narrower view of capacity and held that an irrational fear that prevents the exercise of choice cannot be equated with a lack of capacity to choose. The House of Lords unanimously held that this approach was wrong. In a welcome judgment delivered by Baroness Hale,[61] it was stressed that the law on capacity recognizes that to be able to make a decision:

(1) a person must be able to understand the information relevant to making it, and

(2) must be able to weigh that information in the balance to arrive at a choice.[62]

A mentally disordered person might appreciate the sexual nature of the act but not be able to weigh the information in the balance so as to be able to arrive at a choice. The capacity to choose under the 2003 Act is situation- and person-specific. 'One does not consent to sex in general. One consents to this act of sex with this person at this time and in this place.'[63] These general sentiments in relation to capacity are important in construing s 74.

In short, at present there appear to be the following categories relevant to whether V is lacking capacity in relation to sexual conduct under the 2003 Act:

- B lacks mental capacity to make the choice—no consent;
- B lacks ability to refuse because of mental disorder—unable to refuse; if the inability also amounts to inability to choose B also gives no consent;
- B lacks ability to refuse for reasons unrelated to mental disorder—if inability amounts to inability to choose (eg being heavily intoxicated) also gives no consent;
- B has mental capacity to choose, but *mentally* (not physically)[64] incapable of communicating choice to this defendant—unable to refuse; arguably[65] also lacking consent.

The Court of Appeal has confirmed that where capacity to consent is at issue in criminal proceedings, the burden of proving incapacity falls upon the party asserting it.[66] This will, inevitably, be the prosecution. The prosecution must discharge this burden to the criminal standard; they must make the jury sure that B did not have the capacity to consent. If the jury cannot be sure, then Macur LJ stated that they must assume that B did have the capacity to consent. Her ladyship then went on to state that:

The issue for them then will be an examination of all the facts and circumstances to determine whether or not the complainant consented to the act or acts in question and whether the alleged assailant knew they did not consent or did not believe that they did so or were unreasonable in their belief that there was consent.[67]

---

[60] [2008] EWCA Crim 1155. For critical comment see T Elliott [2008] 6 Arch News 5. The Court of Appeal relied heavily on Munby J in *X City Council v MB* [2006] EWHC 168 (Fam).

[61] The central issue was the scope of s 30. The issue of capacity under that section is made clear by the Act. As the House concluded under s 30(2)(a), a person is unable to refuse if she lacks the capacity to choose to agree to the touching whether because she lacks sufficient understanding of the nature or reasonably foreseeable consequences of what is being done 'or for any other reason'.

[62] [2009] UKHL 42, [24].

[63] At [27] per Baroness Hale. Such an approach is in keeping with the concept of autonomy in matters of private life guaranteed by Art 8 of the ECHR.

[64] B lacks physical ability to communicate consent to this defendant—presumptively no consent (s 75).

[65] Stevenson et al, n 1, regard these as all non-consensual cases.

[66] *A* [2014] EWCA Crim 299.   [67] At [29].

If capacity is in issue, then it may be necessary to call an expert to provide evidence that would not otherwise be within the common experience of the jury. Her ladyship emphasized, however, that the expert evidence must only deal with the matter in issue, namely capacity. In the instant case, the expert strayed beyond her remit and gave her own interpretation of the facts as to whether B was consenting or not.

Intoxicated consent

A engages in sexual activity with B who is intoxicated.[68] How intoxicated must B be to lack capacity for the purposes of the 2003 Act? This has provoked controversy and a number of high-profile appeals. In the 2002 White Paper, *Protecting the Public*, the Home Secretary, when stating the government's intention to create a set of evidential presumptions, indicated that these would not cover voluntary intoxication leading to incapacity falling short of sleep or a lack of consciousness:

I have rejected the suggestion that someone who is inebriated could claim they were unable to give consent—as opposed to someone who is unconscious for whatever reason, including because of alcohol—on the ground that we do not want mischievous accusations.

In *Dougal*,[69] the trial judge directed the jury to enter a 'not guilty' verdict when the prosecutor informed the judge that he did not propose to proceed further because the prosecution were unable to prove that the complainant had not given consent because of her level of intoxication.[70] The decision to drop the case was controversial since all that B had said was that she 'could not remember'. Following the furore over that case the government raised the issue in a Consultation Paper, *Convicting Rapists and Protecting Victims*,[71] asking 'Does the law on capacity need to be changed. Should there be a statutory definition of capacity?' Subsequently, the Court of Appeal has sought to pre-empt the need for further legislative intervention by encouraging trial judges to leave the issue to the common sense of the jury where there is evidence that B might not have been consenting owing to intoxication.[72] That is likely to lead to inconsistency of decisions, but is a pragmatic response to a seemingly intractable problem.

In *Bree*,[73] A aged 25, and B, aged 19, had both voluntarily consumed a large amount of alcohol and it was accepted by both parties that sexual intercourse had taken place. A was charged with rape on the basis that B had effectively been unconscious throughout most of the sexual activity. B gave evidence that she was not unconscious. It was a fundamental part of A's case that B had been conscious throughout and had in fact consented. A claimed that

---

[68] If B is involuntarily intoxicated by A's conduct, s 75(2)(f) might be applicable: presumption of no consent. Note also the offence under s 61, p 851.

[69] (2005) 1 Nov, unreported, Swansea CC.

[70] This CPS decision was criticized in *Bree* [2007] EWCA Crim 804.   [71] (2006).

[72] On jury attitudes to intoxicated rape complainants, see also E Finch and V Munro, 'Breaking Boundaries; Sexual Consent in the Jury Room' (2006) 26 LS 303.

[73] [2007] EWCA Crim 804. See for critical comment on the case, P Rumney and R Fenton, 'Intoxicated Consent in Rape: *Bree* and Juror Decision-Making' (2008) 71 MLR 279 calling for better guidance and S Wallerstein, 'A Drunken Consent is Still a Consent—Or Is It?' (2009) 73 J Crim L 318 arguing that the law does not go far enough and that a drunken consent is not consent. See also G Firth, 'Not an Invitation to Rape: The Sexual Offences Act 2003, Consent and the Case of the "Drunken" Victim' (2011) 62 NILQ 99. For more recent discussion, see C de Than and J Elvin, 'Capacity and Consent' in A Reed and M Bohlander (eds), *Consent—Domestic and Comparative Perspectives* (2017).

B's intoxication did not mean that she had lacked the capacity to consent, indeed, she had removed her own pyjamas and responded to questions such as whether she had a condom. A was convicted, but the Court of Appeal allowed the appeal. In cases of rape arising after voluntary[74] consumption of alcohol, the question was whether the evidence proved that A had had sexual intercourse with B without her consent. On the proper construction of s 74, where B had voluntarily consumed alcohol but remained *capable* of *choosing* whether or not to have intercourse, and in her drunken state agreed to do so, that would not be rape.[75] However, if, through drink or some other reason, B had temporarily lost her capacity to choose whether to have intercourse on the relevant occasion, she was not consenting and, subject to questions about A's mens rea, if intercourse took place, that would be rape.[76] The question is not whether the alcohol had made either or both less inhibited than they would have been if sober, nor whether either or both might afterwards have regretted what had happened and indeed wished that it had not.[77] The court remarked pithily that the 'capacity to consent can evaporate well before unconsciousness occurs'.[78] The court also emphasized that the jury should in such cases be given assistance with the meaning of 'capacity'. The court has made clear in *Kamki* that judges need to consider the following issues in drafting suitable directions for the jury:[79]

a. A person consents if he or she agrees by choice and has the freedom and capacity to make that choice,

b. When a person is unconscious, there is no such freedom or capacity to choose,

c. Where a person has not reached a state of unconsciousness and experiences some degree of consciousness, further considerations must be applied,

d. A person can still have the capacity to make a choice and have sex even when they have had a lot to drink (thereby consenting to the act),

e. Alcohol can make people less inhibited than when they are sober and everybody has the choice whether or not to have sex,

f. If through drink a [person] has temporarily lost the capacity to choose to have sexual intercourse, she would not be consenting,

g. Before a complete loss of consciousness arises, a state of incapacity to consent can nevertheless be reached. Consideration has to be given to the degree of consciousness or otherwise in order to determine the issue of capacity,

h. . . . the jury would have to consider the evidence of B to determine what her state of consciousness or unconsciousness was and to determine what effect this would have on her capacity to consent,

i. If it is determined that the complainant did have the capacity to make a choice, it would then have to be considered whether she did or may have consented to sexual intercourse.

---

[74] See D Warburton (2007) 71 J Crim L 394 on whether the decision is restricted to cases of voluntary intoxication.

[75] In *Kamki* [2013] EWCA Crim 2335, the Court of Appeal held that as long as the relevant issues are explained to the jury, it is unnecessary for the judge to use the precise phrase 'a drunken consent remains a consent'. For further discussion, see D Warburton, 'Intoxication and Consent in Sexual Offences' (2014) 78 J Crim L 207.

[76] At [34] per Sir Igor Judge P. See also the valuable commentary by Ashworth [2007] Crim LR 903.

[77] Moreover, it was not a question of whether either or both might have a very poor recollection of precisely what had happened. That might be relevant to the reliability of their evidence.

[78] At [32]. The language echoes that of the law on intoxicated defendants, but the analogy is flawed: see Wallerstein, n 74.

[79] [2013] EWCA Crim 2335, [18]. See also *Evans* [2012] EWCA Crim 2559.

In *Hysa*,[80] the defence argued that, first, the fact that the intoxicated 16-year-old complainant rejected the advances of two men accompanying A meant that she clearly had capacity to consent. The Crown's case was that she could not remember whether or not she had consented: the Crown simply could not exclude the possibility that the complainant had said 'yes'. The Court of Appeal, in an interlocutory appeal by the Crown, concluded that the judge erred in withdrawing the case from the jury. The pre-2003 Act case of *Malone*[81] was referred to as authority for the proposition that:

there is no requirement that the absence of consent has to be demonstrated or that it has to be communicated to the defendant for the *actus reus* of rape to exist. . . . It is not the law that the prosecution in order to obtain a conviction for rape have to show that the complainant was either incapable of saying no or putting up some physical resistance, or did say no or put up some physical resistance.

The court was critical of the defence submissions which were 'based to a large extent on the premise that because the complainant cannot remember if she consented or not, that is fatal to the prosecution'. That was, in the court's words 'expressly disavowed' in *Bree*.[82]

In *Seedy Tambedou*,[83] B stated that she would not have consented to having sex with A, but because of her intoxicated condition on the night in question, she was unable to say categorically that she did not consent. The judge rejected A's submission of no case and he was convicted. The Court of Appeal dismissed A's appeal. It was held that the jury had been entitled to consider the issue of the absence of consent and to distinguish it from absence of memory. B's evidence that she could not remember was insufficient for the judge to remove the case from the jury.

There have been repeated calls for reform, including the proposal by Wallerstein arguing that drunken consent is not consent.[84] Wallerstein proposes a two-step test: (a) was B drunk so as to make her incapable of giving a valid consent; and, if so, (b) was there pre-intoxication consent? If the answer to (b) is yes, there is consent. If not, there is no consent. The courts have yet to tackle this problem case of B who agrees when sober to have sex with A, and whether her consent given when sober is lost when she is heavily intoxicated.[85]

Consent induced by deception

One issue that generated controversy when the 2003 Act was enacted centred on the nature of the relationship between ss 74 and 76, specifically whether deception perpetrated to induce consent is capable of falling within the scope of s 74.[86] The applicability of s 76 is limited to

---

[80] [2007] EWCA Crim 2056. *Bree* was distinguished in *Wright* [2007] All ER (D) 267 (Nov) where B had been so heavily intoxicated as to be unconscious.

[81] [1998] 2 Cr App R 447.

[82] Hallett LJ emphasized that it would be a rare case indeed where it would be appropriate for a judge to stop a case in which, on one view, a 16-year-old girl, alone at night and vulnerable through drink, is picked up by a stranger who has sex with her within minutes of meeting her and she says repeatedly she would not have consented to sex in these circumstances. At the recommended trial the jury took just 40 minutes to convict.

[83] [2014] EWCA Crim 954.   [84] Wallerstein, n 74.

[85] See *Ashlee* (2006) 212 CCC (3d) 477 where the Alberta Court of Appeal held that consent becomes vitiated on unconsciousness. See also *JA and the AG of Canada* [2011] 2 SCR 440. See also Jarvis, n 32.

[86] For further background, see K Laird, 'Rapist or Rogue? Deception, Consent and the Sexual Offences Act 2003' [2014] Crim LR 492. For discussion of the how the internet has facilitated this form of deception, see A Gillespie, 'The Electronic Spanish Prisoner: Romance Frauds on the Internet' (2017) 81 J Crim L 217.

those categories of deception listed within it, whilst s 74 makes no mention of deception. Commentators took divergent views on whether s 76 was intended to be exhaustive,[87] but the courts have now settled the matter conclusively. In *Assange v Sweden*,[88] Sir John Thomas P stated that, 's 76 deals simply with a conclusive presumption in the very limited circumstances to which it applies. If the conduct of the defendant is not within s 76, that does not preclude reliance on s 74.' This outcome was reached as a matter of statutory construction, as his lordship stated that, 'It would, in our view, have been extraordinary if Parliament had legislated in terms that, if conduct that was not deceptive could be taken into account for the purposes of s 74, conduct that was deceptive could not be.' The language of the provision aside, his lordship's reluctance to rely upon s 76 is understandable, given the draconian nature of conclusive presumptions.[89]

Although it is clear that s 76 is not exhaustive of the circumstances in which deceptions may vitiate apparent consent, s 74 has a role to play. The appellate courts have now addressed this issue, in various guises, on numerous occasions cases under the 2003 Act. But the circumstances in which deceptions under s 74 will vitiate apparent consent are unclear. Despite the government's explicit intention in enacting the 2003 Act that 'It is vital that the law is as clear as possible about what consent means',[90] the courts have failed to deliver. Only relatively recently did the courts articulate an overriding principle to be applied in these cases. In *Monica*, the Lord Chief Justice stated that:

deception which is closely connected with 'the nature or purpose of the act', because it relates to sexual intercourse itself rather than the broad circumstances surrounding it is capable of negating a complainant's free exercise of choice for the purposes of section 74 of the 2003 Act.[91]

The application of that principle has already been demonstrated to create difficulties in practice, as shown by the case of *Lawrance*. It is worth cataloguing some of the judicial pronouncements on consent in cases of deception. These include:[92]

- *B*[93]—the defendant's failure to disclose his HIV-positive status did not negate consent to sexual intercourse and ejaculation;
- *Jheeta*[94]—A deceiving B that a police officer was encouraging her to perform sexual acts with her partner was not a deception as to the nature or purpose of the act under s 76 but was capable of negating consent applying s 74;
- *Bingham*[95]—deceptions as to identities assumed by A to cause his girlfriend to perform sexual acts online were not deceptions as to the purpose of the acts under s 76, but were capable of negating consent under s 74;

---

[87] Temkin and Ashworth took the view that s 76 was not exhaustive, [2004] Crim LR 328, while Miles opined that it was, [2008] 10 Arch News 5.

[88] [2011] EWHC 2849 (Admin).

[89] Rogers argues that this decision is wrong because the purpose of the non-consensual offences is to protect a person's sexual autonomy, not their health or desire not to have a child. He states that it is a mistake to conflate concerns about sexual health/pregnancy with sexual autonomy. Sexual autonomy means one's willingness to be used to provide sexual stimulation and, it is argued, given the presence of that willingness here, there was no violation of sexual autonomy and it ought to follow no liability either. See J Rogers, 'The Effect of "Deception" in the Sexual Offences Act 2003' [2013] 4 Arch Rev 7.

[90] Home Office White Paper, *Protecting the Public* (2002) Cm 5668, para 28.   [91] At [72].

[92] See also *Matt* [2015] EWCA Crim 162. What these cases highlight is the unpredictable range of behaviours and the lengths to which some will go to defraud other (even existing partners) to engage in sexual acts.

[93] *B* [2006] EWCA Crim 2945; [2007] 1 WLR 1567.   [94] [2007] EWCA Crim 1699.

[95] [2013] EWCA Crim 823.

- *Devenauld*[96]—deception as to A's true purpose for encouraging B to masturbate online was a deception as to the purpose of the act and fell within s 76;

- *McNally*[97]—A's deception as to their biological sex negated B's apparent consent to digital penetration by A (the court noted *obiter* that deceptions as to wealth or employment would 'obviously' not be sufficient to vitiate consent);

- *R (F) v DPP*[98]—A's deception about whether he would withdraw before ejaculating in B's vagina was capable of negating her consent to sexual intercourse;

- *Assange*[99]—A's deception about using a condom during sex was capable of negating B's apparent consent;

- *Monica*[100]—A's deception about environmental beliefs and his employment as an undercover police officer was not sufficient to vitiate consent to sexual intercourse;

- *Lawrance*[101]—A's deception about having had a vasectomy was not capable of vitiating consent.

The courts' failure to adopt a consistent application of an overriding principle can be illustrated by reference to four of these cases.

In *R (on the application of F) v DPP*, A knew that B's consent to sex was contingent upon his either wearing a condom or withdrawing before ejaculation. A intentionally ejaculated inside B, who sought judicial review of the CPS's decision not to prosecute him for rape. In allowing the claim, Lord Judge CJ placed significant reliance upon the terms of s 74 and in particular the concepts of freedom and choice. His lordship held that evidence relating to choice and freedom ought to be approached in a 'broad, commonsense way'. The evidence demonstrated that A deemed B subservient to his control and that what he did was his method of asserting that control. Importantly, Lord Judge stated that B was deprived of choice relating to the crucial feature on which her original consent to sex was based and for that reason her consent was negated. Therefore the circumstances of the case fell within the statutory definition of rape.

In *McNally*,[102] A was biologically female but identified as male. A joined a social networking site and listed her status as male. A began a relationship with B and the evidence demonstrated that B was unaware of the fact A was in fact biologically female. A penetrated B's vagina on a number of occasions. B's mother began to have suspicions about A's gender and confronted her. Once it emerged that she was biologically female, A was charged with six counts of assault by penetration, contrary to s 2(1) of the 2003 Act. A pleaded guilty, but sought to vacate her plea on the basis that she had received inaccurate legal advice as to the interpretation of the relevant provisions of the 2003 Act. In dismissing A's appeal, Leveson LJ conceptualized the case as one concerning active deception rather than a failure to disclose.[103] As has already been discussed, it was held that only the former that can come within

---

[96] [2008] EWCA Crim 527.   [97] [2013] EWCA Crim 1051.
[98] [2013] EWHC 945 (Admin).
[99] *Assange v Swedish Prosecution Authority* [2011] EWHC 2849 (Admin).
[100] *R ('Monica') v DPP* [2018] EWHC 3508 (Admin).
[101] [2020] EWCA Crim 971.   [102] [2013] EWCA Crim 1051.
[103] Sharpe vigorously contests the conclusion that the case concerned active deception, on the basis that transgender people are not engaging in a form of pretence. See A Sharpe, 'Criminalising Sexual Intimacy: Transgender Defendants and the Legal Construction of Non-Consent' [2014] Crim LR 207; A Sharpe, 'Expanding Liability for Sexual Fraud Through the Concept of "Active Deception": A Flawed Approach' (2016) 80 J Crim L 28.

the scope of s 74. His lordship placed reliance upon *Assange* and *F* as authorities that substantiated the proposition that s 76 is not exhaustive. Importantly, his lordship observed that:

In reality, some deceptions (such as, for example, in relation to wealth) will obviously not be sufficient to vitiate consent. In our judgment, Lord Judge CJ's observation that 'the evidence relating to "choice" and the "freedom" to make any particular choice must be approached in a broad commonsense way' identifies the route through the dilemma.

It was accepted that, in a physical sense, the acts of assault by penetration of the vagina are the same whether perpetrated by a male or a female, but that the sexual nature of the act is different where the complainant is deliberately deceived into believing that the person performing those acts is male. This led Leveson LJ to the conclusion that A's deception had deprived B of the freedom to choose to have sexual encounters with a boy, in addition to her freedom to choose whether to have sex with a girl.[104] Had she known the truth, B may have consented to being penetrated by A, but the latter's deception deprived her of that choice.

McNally appeared to confirm that only active deception (and not failure to disclose) falls within the scope of s 74, although the distinction between these two might be difficult to draw.[105] This must now be doubted given that the Lord Chief Justice in *Lawrance* declared that 'it makes no difference to the issue of consent whether, as in this case, there was an express deception or, as in the case of *B*, a failure to disclose'.[106] This statement is surprising given that this distinction appears to have been crucial in both *McNally* and *B*. However, the Lord Chief Justice's clarification is welcome given that what should really matter is the exercise of choice, which presupposes sufficient information to make an informed choice. *Lawrance* aligns sexual offences with non-fatal offences against the person, as it has long been accepted that non-disclosure is sufficient to negate consent under the latter.[107]

In *McNally*, Leveson LJ suggested that deception as to wealth would obviously be insufficient to vitiate consent. What, however, in s 74 precludes deception as to wealth from potentially vitiating consent? In *F*, upon which Leveson LJ placed reliance, it will be recalled that Lord Judge CJ held that B was deprived of choice relating to the crucial feature on which her original consent to sex was based. If B's original consent to sex was based upon A's wealth, when it transpires that A is in fact not wealthy, does this not suffice to vitiate B's consent? Of course, a jury might be sceptical about whether B in fact based her consent on A's wealth, but suppose there are other features which B says influenced her that juries might find more important than wealth, such as religion.

The next controversy for the courts to grapple with was whether there ought to be a limit placed on those features capable of vitiating consent[108] or whether this is something that is

---

[104] Sharpe, n 103, states that this argument casts doubt on the authenticity of the gender identities of transgender people.

[105] Rogers states that it is unclear whether reliance was in fact placed upon s 74 as opposed to s 76. With respect, given Leveson LJ's invocation of *Assange* and *F*, it seems clear beyond doubt that the outcome was dictated by the terms of s 74. See J Rogers, 'Further Developments Under the Sexual Offences Act' [2013] 7 Arch Rev 7.

[106] [2020] EWCA Crim 971, [41].   [107] See *Konzani* [2005] EWCA Crim 706.

[108] See A Sharpe, 'Criminalising Sexual Intimacy: Transgender Defendants and the Legal Construction of Non-Consent' [2014] Crim LR 207 for the argument that there are policy reasons for why every material fact ought not to be capable of vitiating consent. The example given is the anti-Semite who does not want to have sex with people who are Jewish. Sharpe asks whether that person ought to be able to give effect to their prejudice by invoking the criminal law. The arguments are also made that the right to sexual autonomy is not an unlimited right and that prosecution produces inconsistency.

best left for juries to determine, applying the broad common-sense approach advocated by Lord Judge.[109] That opportunity arose in *R (on the application of 'Monica') v DPP*.[110]

The claimant applied for judicial review of the DPP's decision not to prosecute a former police officer for offences of rape, procurement of sexual intercourse and misconduct in public office. When the claimant entered into the sexual relationship with the former police officer, he was portraying himself as a member of the same environmental protest group of which she was a member. The decision was taken not to prosecute the former police officer with any offences. In rejecting the submissions made on behalf of the claimant, the court stated that there was no defined list of circumstances which, for the purposes of s 74, were capable of vitiating consent. The common law position before the 1956 Act was that only fraud as to the nature of the sexual act and as to the identity of the perpetrator were capable of vitiating consent. Analysing the position under the 2003 Act, the court held that deception which was closely connected with 'the nature of purpose of the act', because it related to sexual intercourse itself rather than the broad circumstances surrounding it, was capable of negating a complainant's free exercise of choice for the purposes of s 74. The court stated that the claimant's case was founded on the proposition that various *dicta* in the case law should be extrapolated to establish a new understanding of consent for the purposes of rape and sexual offences. The court concluded that this would be a leap for Parliament to take, rather than the courts.

In concluding that the CPS's decision not to prosecute the interested party was lawful, the court made significant observations about the scope of s 74. The court rejected the claimant's submission that there are no longer any constraints as to the categories of deception which are capable of vitiating consent under s 74. The court conducted an extensive analysis of the relevant case law. It concluded that the law had long accepted that deceptions which were not closely connected to the performance of the sexual act (or intrinsically so fundamental, owing to that connection, that they can be treated as cases of impersonation), were capable of vitiating consent. To put the point another way, unless the deception falls within one of these categories, then it will not be capable of vitiating consent.

The most recent pronouncement from the Court of Appeal demonstrates how difficult the application of the principle pronounced in *Monica* can be in practice.

In *Lawrance*,[111] having met on a dating website, A assured B in the course of a sexually explicit text message exchange, that he had had a vasectomy. On B's account, A repeated that assertion to her shortly before they twice had unprotected intercourse. A admitted the following day that he was fertile (B became pregnant and had a termination). On appeal, A's convictions on two counts of rape were quashed. Distinguishing *Assange* and *R (F) v DPP*, and applying *Monica*, the Court of Appeal held that A's lie about fertility was not sufficiently closely connected to the performance of sexual intercourse to negate consent under s 74.

The Lord Chief Justice concluded:

In our opinion, a lie about fertility is different from a lie about whether a condom is being worn during sex, different from engaging in intercourse not intending to withdraw having promised to do so and different from engaging in sexual activity having misrepresented one's gender.

Unlike the woman in *Assange*, or in *R (F)*, the complainant agreed to sexual intercourse with the appellant without imposing any physical restrictions. She agreed both to penetration of her

---

[109] Whether this is best left to juries is questionable. Spencer has made the valid point that the practical distinction between deceptions that vitiate consent and those that do not is 'murky and uncertain', in JR Spencer, 'Sex by Deception' [2013] 9 Arch Rev 6.

[110] [2018] EWHC 3469. See on the earlier challenge in *AJA v Commissioner of Police for the Metropolis* [2013] EWCA Civ 1342; C McCartney and N Wortley, 'Raped by the State' (2014) 78 J Crim L 1.

[111] [2020] EWCA Crim 971.

vagina and to ejaculation without the protection of a condom. In so doing she was deceived about the nature or quality of the ejaculate and therefore of the risks and possible consequences of unprotected intercourse. The deception was one which related not to the physical performance of the sexual act but to risks or consequences associated with it.[112]

Can the Court of Appeal maintain a clear distinction between: unprotected intercourse with a deception as to withdrawal resulting in D ejaculating in V (F—rape); unprotected intercourse with a deception as to use of a condom resulting in D ejaculating into V (*Assange*—rape); and unprotected intercourse with deception that the ejaculate will not contain sperm because of a vasectomy (*Lawrance*—not rape)? In each case, there is an active deception by the defendant as to a factor known by the defendant to be a condition precedent of the complainant's consent. The decision has broader consequences than exposing apparent inconsistencies in the jurisprudence. In practical terms, it does not render any easier the prosecutor's task in determining which deceptions reported by complainants constitute rape. Nor, in policy terms, is the message one that maximizes the protection of sexual autonomy. Applying the reasoning in the above paragraph, a complainant's autonomy is afforded less protection in law where she is deceived about her partner's need to use a condom (leading her to impose no 'physical restrictions') than about whether he was actually wearing a condom.

   Is it time for the Supreme Court to step up and resolve the problems? What options would be open to that court? Could it reject the idea that lines are to be drawn, accepting instead that a deception or failure to inform on any factor is capable of negating consent? Admittedly, that leaves the mens rea of these offences to do all the work. To adopt this approach, the court would first have to conclude that s 74 does not, as has been held by the Lord Chief Justice, merely codify the common law. Would the Supreme Court, instead, prefer to refine the Court of Appeal's model by identifying a principled way of distinguishing factors about which deceit is capable of negating apparent consent? Any such test has to be capable of consistent application by prosecutors and courts alike and has to reflect attitudes to sexual conduct and the protection of autonomy. Alternatively, might the court attempt to create a list of decisive factors (eg as to risks of STI and pregnancy) about which deceit will negate consent? Would that inevitably lead to yet more line drawing and frustrate Parliament's clear choice to adopt an open-textured test of consent as provided in s 74 in contrast to one that is overly prescriptive?

   The Court of Appeal in *Lawrance* concluded by stating that 'these issues require debate as matters of social and public policy'.[113] The court is clearly right to acknowledge the breadth and sensitivity of the policy questions at stake, but if Parliament is to legislate there are some difficult issues to tackle. Should any fraud as to any matter be capable of nullifying apparent consent? If so, what label is it appropriate to apply to such conduct? Some commentators have argued for a resurrection of the offence from the Sexual Offences Act 1956 of procuring sex by false pretences. Section 3 of the 1956 Act made it an offence to procure sexual intercourse by false representations and had it been re-enacted would have given prosecutors the option of charging A with an offence other than rape in cases involving deception. Both the Law Commission and the Sexual Offences Review recommended that this offence be re-enacted in a more modernized form, but the government failed to implement that proposal. The 2003 Act therefore repealed, but did not replace, this offence. As we noted immediately after the Act,[114] this was an obvious lacuna. It has since been characterized by Spencer as 'glaring and obvious';[115] and may have led to the difficulties examined in this

---

[112] At [36]–[37].   [113] At [42].   [114] See the 11th edn of this book, Ch 18.

[115] JR Spencer, 'Three New Cases on Consent' (2007) 66 CLJ 490.

section. However, re-enacting this offence could create the perception of two-tier protection for autonomy and produce practical problems of charging for the CPS. Furthermore, re-enactment of the offence would not necessarily address the fundamental issue, which is whether legally speaking any deception ought to be capable of vitiating consent.

The one clear benefit of the Court of Appeal's approach is that it clarifies that deceptions as to the circumstances surrounding sexual intercourse, such as wealth, will not be capable of vitiating consent. Whether they should be now appears to be a matter for Parliament to determine.

Section 75: evidential presumptions

If A is proved to have performed the relevant act[116] for the offence in question (eg penile penetration for rape), and it is proved that any of the circumstances listed in s 75(2) exists and A knows[117] it exists, B is taken not to have consented and A not to have a reasonable belief in B's consent unless sufficient evidence is adduced to raise the issue.

The circumstances in s 75(2) are:

(a) any person was, at the time of the relevant act or immediately before it began, using violence against the complainant or causing the complainant to fear that immediate violence would be used against him;

(b) any person was, at the time of the relevant act or immediately before it began, causing the complainant to fear that violence was being used, or that immediate violence would be used, against another person;

(c) the complainant was, and the defendant was not, unlawfully detained at the time of the relevant act;

(d) the complainant was asleep or otherwise unconscious at the time of the relevant act;

(e) because of the complainant's physical disability, the complainant would not have been able at the time of the relevant act to communicate to the defendant whether the complainant consented;

(f) any person had administered to or caused to be taken by the complainant, without the complainant's consent, a substance which, having regard to when it was administered or taken, was capable of causing or enabling the complainant to be stupefied or overpowered at the time of the relevant act.

Although A has to know that '*those* circumstances existed',[118] the requirement is in fact only that his knowledge of any *one* circumstance is proved.[119] The Act is silent on whether this must be proof by the prosecution.[120] There is no requirement that the existence of the circumstances listed in (a) to (f) *caused* B's lack of consent.[121] The absence of consent is simply presumed. Controversially, s 75 relates to both the issue of consent and the issue of A's belief in consent. Section 75 creates a rather odd set of presumptions since A can raise evidence sufficient to rebut the presumption without challenging the actual circumstance on which the presumption arises. So, for example, where the prosecution allege that B was asleep, A might raise evidence which will rebut the effect of the Crown's evidence without denying

---

[116] See s 77.

[117] Knowledge means 'true belief' as we have been reminded by the House of Lords in a different context: *Saik* [2006] UKHL 18.

[118] Section 75(1)(c).   [119] Section 75(1)(b).

[120] What if D2 seeks to prove the existence of the circumstance in the course of showing that he lacked knowledge of it but D1 did not?

[121] cf the proposals in *Setting the Boundaries*, para 2.10.9.

the fact that B was asleep. A can claim that he believed, reasonably, that despite being asleep B was consenting (based on their previous sexual practices).[122] A is obliged not to rebut the *fact* giving rise to the presumption, but the *legal consequences* of that presumption.

If the prosecution prove the three elements—the relevant act, A's knowledge and the circumstance giving rise to the presumption—A is obliged to raise sufficient evidence to rebut the issue. This can be done by calling evidence, testifying or by cross-examination of a Crown witness.[123] The obligation on A is *to satisfy the judge*, from the evidence, that there is a real issue about consent that is worth putting to the jury. If there is such evidence, it will be for the jury to determine whether they accept it. This means that the section is more likely to withstand ECHR challenge[124] than the original version in the Bill which incorporated reverse burdens for A's belief in consent.[125] Creating such presumptions has an important symbolic value,[126] and was widely welcomed in principle.[127] The Canadian courts have interpreted similar provisions as requiring that any claims by the defence have an 'air of reality'.[128]

In the leading English case of *Cicarelli*,[129] A met B at a party and touched her sexually when he found her unconscious at the end of the night. A was charged with sexual assault and sought to argue that despite B's unconsciousness he had a reasonable belief in consent on the basis of a single sexual advance he alleged she had made at the beginning of that evening. The trial judge ruled that there was insufficient evidence to rebut the presumption and directed the jury accordingly. The Court of Appeal agreed and held that, in order to rebut the presumption once it has arisen, A must adduce some evidence that is more than merely speculative or fanciful. The Lord Chief Justice emphasized that the issue of A's reasonable belief will only be considered by the jury *provided that* there is evidence which is sufficient to raise that issue. This language requires the judge to evaluate carefully the relevant evidence. It was concluded that the judge in this case had engaged in such an exercise and that her conclusion was justified. Given the factually sensitive nature of evaluating whether A has adduced sufficient evidence to cross the threshold imposed by s 75, it is unsurprising that the Court of Appeal was reluctant to interfere with the trial judge's ruling. Although it has been confirmed that A must adduce evidence that is more than merely speculative, it is submitted that it should not render it necessary for the defence to produce corroborative independent evidence, in the formal sense, to rebut the presumption.[130]

A jury should not ordinarily be directed as to s 75 at all unless the trial judge decides that there has been no evidence capable of rebutting s 75.[131] If there is evidence that is

---

[122] Note, however, that in *P* [2009] EWCA Crim 1110, Hughes LJ stated that 'We have no doubt that . . . there is no real prospect of a jury considering that a belief in consent might be reasonably based on the proposition that because a defendant has had sexual intercourse on a number of previous occasions with a comatose or unconscious or asleep complainant, who after discovery of those occasions has not overtly objected, that this gives rise to an advance consent which the defendant could reasonably rely upon in the future to indulge in like sexual activity whenever she was in a similar condition.' At [29].

[123] Note that an earlier version of the Bill specifically stated that cross-examination of the complainant would not be sufficient to raise the issue as to V's consent unless the equivalent of an admission of consent.

[124] cf the views expressed in Stevenson et al, *Blackstone's Guide to the Sexual Offences Act 2003* (2004) para 2.4.3.

[125] HL, 2 June 2003, cols 1062–3 (Lord Thomas of Gresford).

[126] See HC Standing Committee B, 15 Oct 2002, col 26 (Beverley Hughes).

[127] See Home Affairs Committee, Fifth Report 2002–03, HC 639.

[128] A striking example cited by P Rook and R Ward, *Sexual Offences: Law and Practice* (5th edn, 2016), is of *Filice* (1999) Carswell Ont 1262 where evidence that B had (as was her custom) taken out her false teeth before sex was sufficient to give the claim an air of reality. See further *Pappajohn* [1980] 2 SCR 120 discussed by Lord Steyn in *R v A (No 2)* [2002] 1 AC 67. For discussion on this, see Temkin, *Rape and the Legal Process*, 132.

[129] [2011] EWCA Crim 2665.   [130] *Osolin* [1993] 4 SCR 595; *Park* [1995] 2 SCR 836.

[131] The use of s 75 is often misunderstood—see eg *Tamanda K* [2013] EWCA Crim 560.

capable of establishing consent (including A's testimony to that effect), s 75 ceases to have any application and the jury have no need to hear of s 75. In *White*,[132] A sent B a photo of him digitally penetrating her vagina. They had been in a sexual relationship. A claimed he took the image with her consent. B claimed he must have taken it while she slept. The Court of Appeal quashed the conviction where the judge had directed on s 75 in a confusing manner.[133] Under s 75, A is to be taken not to have reasonably believed that B consented *unless* sufficient evidence is adduced to raise an issue as to whether A reasonably believed it. The Court of Appeal stated:

> There must be some foundation in the evidence and it must not be merely speculative or fanciful for there to be sufficient evidence. However, *it is vital to understand that if the trial judge decides (presumably at the close of the evidence) that there is sufficient evidence to raise an issue as to whether the complainant consented and/or the accused reasonably believed that the complainant was consenting, then the judge will put the issues to the jury in accordance with the key sections (ie 74 and 1(2)), and the section 75 route is barred.* In the relatively rare cases where the judge decides that there is not sufficient evidence on one or both of the issues, a section 75 direction must be given on that issue.[134]

If the judge has ruled that s 75 has no part to play, the jury should then be directed to deal with the issue of consent under the general guidance in s 74. If sufficient evidence of consent has *not* been raised and there is no other defence available to A, the jury will be bound to find A guilty. Judges must avoid directing the jury to convict.[135]

In view of the complexity of the s 75 provision, it is perhaps no surprise that there are few reported instances in which it has been relied on.[136] Section 75 will clearly have an impact on the process of the trial. In practical terms it will render it more likely that A will testify.[137] In addition, it will have a significant impact on the way that sexual offences are investigated and on the manner of police interviews. If the complainant alleges that one of the s 75(2) circumstances was present, the suspect will be under considerable pressure to offer an explanation in interview and advance his defence at an earlier stage.

Aside from these general concerns about creating presumptions, the individual circumstances listed in s 75(2) also pose problems.

Threats of violence

The use/threats of immediate violence need not emanate from A before they are treated, presumptively, as vitiating B's consent. This is a welcome extension of the law. Section 75(2)(a) will operate in circumstances such as those in *Dagnall*,[138] where A had grabbed B and dragged her off the road telling her that he would rape her. Under threat, B told A that he could 'do what he liked as long as he did not harm her'. A was apprehended before

---

[132] [2010] EWCA Crim 1929.

[133] The court approved the recommendation in *Blackstone's Criminal Practice*. See now *Blackstone's Criminal Practice* (2021) B3.

[134] Emphasis added.   [135] *Mba* [2012] EWCA Crim 2773.

[136] There are occasional examples. In addition to the cases already discussed, see eg *Zhang* [2007] EWCA Crim 2018 in which the Court of Appeal rejected the submission that the trial judge's summing up had inadvertently elevated the rebuttable presumptions in s 75 to conclusive ones.

[137] See Explanatory Notes Sexual Offences Act 2003, Ch 42, which makes it clear that evidence given by the defendant himself may constitute 'sufficient evidence'. This must be read in the light of subsequent case law confirming that a mere assertion from the defendant that is unsubstantiated by evidence is insufficient. There is a threshold the defendant's evidence must cross before the jury will be permitted to consider the reasonableness of his belief. See *Cicarelli*, n 129.

[138] [2003] EWCA Crim 2441.

penetrating B and convicted under the 1956 Act of attempted rape.[139] The fact that B had explicitly assented to sexual acts did not in these circumstances mean that she was consenting. However, there are difficulties with s 75(2)(a). It is unclear why the requirement is one of 'immediate' violence. Arguably, it should be sufficient that A threatens B that he will 'make her suffer one day' unless she has sex with him at once. It may be that the concept of 'immediacy' is interpreted expansively by the courts.[140] Of course, even without the presumption, in a case of threats of a non-immediate nature B's consent might still be absent when applying the general test of free agreement under s 74.

Although it might appear sensible for a threat of violence to give rise to a conclusive presumption of non-consent, it is clear that in some circumstances even the most explicit threats of violence to B might not vitiate consent as, for example, where A and B are sado-masochists.[141] The rebuttability of the presumption provides for this scenario.

'Violence' is not defined. It is clear from the parliamentary debates that it was intended to be limited only to violence to the person, but that does not appear on the face of the statute. Where A threatens to damage B's property unless she engages in sexual activity, s 75 does not apply and the jury are left to determine the question of B's consent by reference to the criteria in s 74.

It is disappointing that the 2003 Act provided no replacement for the offence under s 2 of the 1956 Act, despite contrary recommendations in *Setting the Boundaries*. Section 2 provided an offence of procuring sexual intercourse by threats. A broader gender-neutral version of causing sexual activity by threats would have provided a useful backstop offence for cases in which the threats fall short of violence so that the jury were not sure there was a lack of consent, but considered the conduct criminally blameworthy. For example, in *Olugboja*[142] reference was made to an unreported case in which Winn J held that a constable had no case to answer where he induced B to consent to sexual intercourse by threatening to report her for an offence; whereas in *Wellard*,[143] A was said to have a previous conviction for rape (for which he was sentenced to six years' imprisonment) by masquerading as a security officer and inducing a girl to consent by threatening to report to her parents and the police that she had been seen having intercourse in a public place. Other examples are easy to envisage: A threatens that if B does not consent he will: (a) tell the police of a theft she has committed; (b) tell her relatives/employer of her previous misconduct; (c) dismiss her from her present employment; (d) not give her a rise in salary; (e) never take her to the cinema again.[144] Clearly, a line must be drawn somewhere, but the boundary of consent in such cases is difficult to draw and the Act ought to have provided more guidance in s 74.

Section 75(2)(b) also relates to threats of violence, applying where B is caused to fear that violence was being used, or that immediate violence would be used, against another person. This is an extremely broad presumption, but it has been welcomed as 'clarifying the common law regarding the fear of violence to third parties'.[145] There is no requirement that A is

---

[139] See also *Low* [1997] Crim LR 692 where B performed oral sex on A after persuading him not to rape her vaginally as she was pregnant. Note that there is a potential problem with applying the s 75 presumption to attempts. See HHJ Rodwell QC [2005] Crim LR 290.

[140] See the interpretation of 'immediate' in assault, p 694. The court did not tackle the issue in the case of *C* [2007] EWCA Crim 378 where the threats were to mother and child. Counsel had wrongly advised as to whether s 75 could apply to allow the Crown to rely on earlier threats which lacked immediacy.

[141] See N Bamforth, 'Sado-Masochism and Consent' [1994] Crim LR 661.   [142] [1982] QB 320 at 347–8.

[143] (1978) 67 Cr App R 364 at 368. See p 762. The court made no comment on the propriety or otherwise of the conviction.

[144] Note that in the case of mentally disordered complainants, ss 34–7 provide offences based on 'inducement, threat or deception' where the degree of threat is not limited—it could include a threat to break friends with the complainant.

[145] Temkin and Ashworth [2004] Crim LR 328.

in any way involved in the causing of the complainant's fear. So, in theory, A who is aware that B, an immigrant, has heard on the TV of ongoing violent atrocities against the population of her homeland, who then performs a relevant sexual act with B is presumed to have done so without consent. Although this may seem like a fanciful example which is unlikely to present problems in practice, because of the ease with which the presumption could be rebutted, it demonstrates the unsatisfactory nature of the overbroad drafting.

Unlawful detention

Section 75(2)(c) seems to be an uncontroversial provision. Where, for example, B has been kidnapped, and A is aware of B's detained status, it is legitimate to presume that B is not consenting to sexual activity. This arises where, for example, A kidnaps his former lover and sexually assaults her.[146] Although there are instances of hostages forming a sexual bond with their kidnappers, it is unlikely that A will be able easily to rebut this presumption.

Unconsciousness

The presumption in s 75(2)(d) requires proof that A knows that B is unconscious.[147] At common law, it was held that unconsciousness (including lack of consciousness through sleep) was sufficient to vitiate consent.[148] There are numerous cases of sexual activity when the complainant was asleep resulting in a conviction.[149] Indeed, this seems to be more commonplace than many might imagine.[150] Arguably, the *presumption* in s 75(2)(d) provides less protection than had been afforded at common law where consent was conclusively rebutted. It is arguable therefore that this circumstance of 'unconsciousness' ought to give rise to a *conclusive* presumption of non-consent by B.[151] However, if B is unconscious and A is aware of that fact, there may be circumstances in which A will be readily capable of rebutting a presumption of non-consent. For example, A, who performs a relevant sexual act (note that the presumption applies to offences of touching and not just penetrative acts) on his sleeping partner as a gesture of intimacy to wake her, ought not to be conclusively presumed guilty.

There is no stipulation as to the cause of the lack of consciousness; it could arise from self-induced intoxication. At common law, if a complainant, through alcohol or drugs, was not capable of exercising a judgement on consent, she was not consenting.[152] Such circumstances now only give rise to *a presumption* of a lack of consent. It is clear that the Sexual Offences Review envisaged that consent would be lacking in such a case.[153]

Inability to communicate owing to physical disability

At common law, and under the 1956 Act, there was no requirement that the absence of consent has to be demonstrated or communicated to A.[154] As a matter of logic it is unclear why the physical inability to *communicate* should be seen as presumptive of a lack of consent. The statutory formula seems to presuppose that B has the capacity to make the choice of free agreement, but merely lacks the physical ability to communicate to this defendant. The Act makes specific provision for those with mental disorders who are unable to communicate (ss 30–44).[155]

---

[146] eg *David T* [2005] EWCA Crim 2668.

[147] cf the view expressed in Stevenson et al, *Blackstone's Guide to the Sexual Offences Act 2003*, para 2.4.1.3.

[148] See *Larter and Castleton* [1995] Crim LR 75; *Howard* [1966] 1 WLR 13.

[149] See *Johnston* [2003] All ER (D) 266 (Jun).

[150] See eg *Garvey* [2004] EWCA Crim 2672; *Blacklock* [2006] EWCA Crim 1740; *Ekatette* [2008] EWCA Crim 3137 where X filmed A having sex with unconscious B.

[151] See eg Temkin and Ashworth [2004] Crim LR 328.

[152] *Malone* [1998] 2 Cr App R 454. See *Bree* [2007] EWCA Crim 804 and the discussion earlier. See also *Zhang* [2007] EWCA Crim 2018.

[153] See *Setting The Boundaries*, 18, paras 2.10.7 et seq.   [154] *Malone* [1998] 2 Cr App R 447.

[155] See *Cooper* [2009] UKHL 42. In particular note Lord Rodger at [30] distinguishing physical inability to communicate and other bases.

It is notable that the presumption only applies if B's physical disability inhibits his communication with *this* defendant. This may be significant if B has a particular speech or sign pattern that can be understood by some individuals.

Causing to be taken by the complainant, without consent, a substance capable of causing or enabling the complainant to be stupefied or overpowered at the time of the relevant act

This provision was introduced late in the Bill's progress as a response to the growing concern over 'drug-assisted rape'.[156] The Act seeks to combat this problem by the presumption in this section and the introduction of the new offence in s 61.[157] The presumption of non-consent applies to both sexes and to sexual acts other than intercourse.

Although targeted at drugs which induce states of incapacity such as Rohypnol and GHB (gamma hydroxyl butyrate acid), there is no statutory limitation on the type of substance which will trigger the presumption. Alcohol is certainly capable of satisfying the definition,[158] so A who surreptitiously laces B's soft drink with spirits will be caught. Similarly, there is no limitation on the manner of the administration. Unless it is established that A knew or believed that the substance was capable of rendering B stupefied or overpowered, the presumption will not apply. This will depend on the type of drug involved. The section does not apply to the 'seductive blandishments to have "just one more drink"'.[159]

The presumption will also apply where A 'caused [the substance] to be taken by the complainant'; this includes A deceiving B into self-administration of the substance as where the substance is mixed with an innocuous one (laced drinks). If B's consumption is purely voluntary and fully informed the presumption does not apply.[160]

The section makes clear that it is irrelevant who administers or causes B to take the substance, provided that one is administered and that B is therefore presumed not to consent. The presumption would apply where X administers in the company of A who performs a sexual act on B.

In those cases in which the presumption applies, A can argue that although he administered the drug being aware of its effects, B nevertheless consented to the sexual acts that finally ensued. If, for example, B indicated at the beginning of the date that she would not have sex with A, and A surreptitiously laces B's drink with potent alcohol, it may be that B later willingly engages in sexual activity with him (not being unconscious nor stupefied); her inhibitions having been lowered.

Section 75(2)(f) will increase the pressure on A to testify and strengthen the hand of the police in interview since they can inquire why A thought that B was consenting given the circumstance of his administering the substance. It will also render prosecution far easier in some circumstances.

Section 76: conclusive presumptions

If it is proved that A performed the relevant act[161] and any one of the circumstances specified in s 76(2) existed, it is to be *conclusively presumed* that the complainant did not consent to the relevant act, and that A did not believe that the complainant consented. There is an important labelling issue here: if A engages in these forms of conduct (deceiving the complainant) and commits the relevant act, he is conclusively proved to be a sexual offender; this is not merely a matter of evidence.[162] It is questionable whether, since these are conclusive

156 For comprehensive analysis, see E Finch and V Munro, 'Intoxicated Consent and the Boundaries of Drug Assisted Rape' [2003] Crim LR 773 and 'The Sexual Offences Act 2003: Intoxicated Consent and Drug Assisted Rape Revisited' [2004] Crim LR 789.
157 See p 851.　　158 See HC Standing Committee B, 14 Oct 2002, col 54 (Beverley Hughes).
159 *Bree* at [24] per Sir Igor Judge P.
160 See eg *Abbess* [2004] EWCA Crim 1813 where no trace of GHB was found.
161 Section 77.　　162 See Tadros (2006) 26 OJLS 515.

presumptions, they are intended by Parliament to represent the worst forms of non-consent. It seems doubtful that they outrank the sexual offence in the course of a violent attack, but some would argue that the element of deception renders the position more serious because of the potential guilt felt by the complainant in being tricked.[163]

The circumstances giving rise to a conclusive presumption are:

(1) the defendant intentionally deceived the complainant as to the *nature or purpose* of the relevant act;

(2) the defendant intentionally induced the complainant to consent to the relevant act by *impersonating a person known personally* to the complainant.

It is sufficient that any *one* of the deceptions is proved. In both instances, the section goes further than the common law. The provisions are open to challenge on the basis that it is unclear why these are conclusive of anything beyond A's absence of a belief in consent.[164] These are also arguably objectionably wide as *conclusive* presumptions especially since they apply in relation to offences other than one of penetration, for example, touching.

There are many well-established difficulties in drawing a line between the kinds of fraud which ought to be treated as a matter of conclusive presumption that B is not consenting. Should they be based on frauds which would render a contract invalid, should they relate only to the nature or purpose or identity, etc? Suggestions have been made to move towards a more coherent approach to the issue in offences against the person and in sexual offences.[165]

Nature or purpose

At common law, a fraud as to the nature of the act vitiated consent.[166] Thus, there was no consent where B was unaware that she was submitting to sexual intercourse because, for example, she had been persuaded by A that he was performing a surgical operation as in *Flattery*.[167] She was deceived as to the very nature of the act, believing it was surgery rather than sexual intercourse. Similarly, in *Williams*,[168] A persuaded his voice pupil that he was opening an air passage to improve her singing voice when he was having sex with her.[169] In that case, B was unaware of sexual matters and was held not to have consented. When analysing what 'nature' means in this context it is important to note that in each of these cases, B was deceived as to the physical mechanics of what A was about to do to her. She had no idea of what sexual intercourse involved. Neither was a case in which B understood the mechanics of sex, that is, penile penetration of the vagina, but did not understand its significance because she believed it was also a cure for fits/for a singing

---

[163] Similar arguments led the Sexual Offences Review to conclude that stranger rape was not worse per se than acquaintance rape where the complainant may feel an element of self-blame in misjudging her attacker. Temkin and Ashworth [2004] Crim LR 328, 337, cf the debate on theft regarding the relative seriousness of being deceived into acting as opposed to actions being performed against the will. See also C Gallavin, 'Fraud Vitiating Consent to Sexual Activity: Further Confusion in the Making' (2008) 23 NZLR 87.

[164] cf Stevenson et al, *Blackstone's Guide to the Sexual Offences Act 2003* who regard this as unarguable, para 242.

[165] See eg R Williams, 'Deception, Mistake and the Vitiation of the Victim's Consent' (2008) 124 LQR 132; M Gibson, 'Deceptive Sexual Relations: A Theory of Criminal Liability' (2020) 40 OJLS 82.

[166] See *Flattery* (1877) 2 QBD 410. For discussion, see R Williams, '*R v Flattery*' in P Handler, H Mares and I Williams (eds), *Landmark Cases in Criminal Law* (2017). See also *Williams* [1923] 1 KB 340.

[167] (1877) 2 QBD 410.

[168] [1923] 1 KB 340. G Williams, TBCL, 561–2 thinks *Williams* 'clearly wrong' because it was not proved that B did not know the facts of life and may merely have been persuaded that sexual intercourse improves breathing. If that were all, it was not rape; but Hewart LCJ said that the girl never consented to sexual intercourse but only a necessary operation.

[169] Did she understand the mechanics of the act but misunderstand whether the act would improve her voice or simply misunderstand what he was about to do to her, having no idea about what sexual intercourse entailed?

exercise. If that had been the case one might argue that B was deceived as to the purpose of the act (understanding it was sex but deceived also into thinking the act will also cure fits/improve vocal range).

Under the 2003 Act, where B has been defrauded as to the nature *or* purpose of the acts A performs, s 76 creates a conclusive presumption that B is not consenting.[170]

It is important to note that s 76 applies only in cases of *intentional* deceptions by A. Where A has not intentionally deceived B, s 76 has no application—as where B has unilaterally formed a false understanding as to the nature, purpose or identity.[171] In such cases, B's mistake, even if A is aware of it but has not intentionally caused it, will be relevant to the consideration under s 74 of whether B is consenting. It will be likely that B is not consenting within s 74 if the mistake is as to any of these matters listed in s 76.

Nature Three further problems have arisen under s 76. First, there is the question of what the 'nature' of sexual intercourse means. Can the 'nature of the act' be read widely so as to render A guilty of rape under s 76 for deceiving B as to whether he will use a condom in penetrative sex? There is an argument that unprotected intercourse is different in *nature* from protected intercourse so that s 76 is engaged and A is conclusively presumed guilty of rape in such a case. Such a wide reading would not have been likely under the old law, but some argued that it should be under the new. In *Assange v Sweden*,[172] the Divisional Court acknowledged this argument, citing the 12th edition of this work. Sir John Thomas P ultimately held, however, that the materiality of wearing a condom to the presence of consent is one that ought to be considered under s 74. His lordship stated that s 76 ought to be given a narrow interpretation, given that it contains conclusive presumptions.

Restricting the applicability of s 76 to near vanishing point has been a trend of the case law examining this issue.[173] This trend is also evident from *McNally* (discussed earlier) in which it was held that A deceived B as to her gender. Again, the court concluded that s 76 was inapplicable[174]—the deception was not as to the nature of the act—but consent was vitiated under s 74. Leveson LJ stated that while in a physical sense the act of sexual penetration is the same irrespective of whether it is done by someone who is male or female, the sexual nature of the act will differ.[175] The outcome in these cases is attributable to the judiciary's aversion to conclusive presumptions that mandate guilt. This is understandable given the seriousness of the offences under consideration. It is submitted

---

[170] Read literally there is no need to establish that there was no consent. It is sufficient that A has deceived B about the nature/purpose of the act. This is another example of the poor drafting in the 2003 Act.

[171] This seems to be underplayed in the radical proposals offered by J Herring, 'Mistaken Consent' [2005] Crim LR 511. Cf M Bohlander, 'Mistaken Consent to Sex, Political Correctness and Correct Policy' (2008) 71 J Crim L 412. Bohlander suggests that Herring's approach demeans rape. It has been argued that criminalizing sex by deception has difficult implications. See J Rubenfeld, 'The Riddle of Rape-by-Deception and the Myth of Sexual Autonomy' (2013) 122 Yale LJ 1372. For Herring's response, see J Herring, 'Rape and the Definition of Consent' (2014) 26 NLSI Rev 62.

[172] [2011] EWHC 2849 (Admin).

[173] The same approach was adopted in *R (on the application of F) v DPP* [2013] EWHC 945 (Admin).

[174] Rogers questions whether the court did place reliance upon s 74 as opposed to s 76. J Rogers, 'Further Developments Under the Sexual Offences Act' [2013] 7 Arch Rev 7. With respect, the court's reliance upon s 74 seems beyond doubt.

[175] It has been argued that gender history should not be deemed capable of vitiating consent on the basis that it casts doubt upon the authenticity of the gender identities of transgender people. See A Sharpe, 'Criminalising Sexual Intimacy: Transgender Defendants and the Legal Construction of Non-Consent' [2014] Crim LR 207; A Sharpe, 'Expanding Liability for Sexual Fraud Through the Concept of "Active Deception": A Flawed Approach' (2016) 80 J Crim L 28. Once it was held that deception is capable of coming within s 74, there is nothing in the language of that section to constrain what forms of deception are capable of vitiating consent.

that the appropriate course, therefore, is to err on the side of caution and rely upon s 74, rather than attempt to invoke s 76 in circumstances where it might not be applicable. The approach in *Lawrance*[176] appears to bring s 74 closer to s 76 in terms of the *types* of deception which are capable of vitiating consent. Section 74, despite its broad terms, in effect only encompasses those types of deception which are explicitly enumerated within s 76 or those closely connected to such deceptions.

Quality Secondly, there is a question as to how s 76 deals with frauds as to 'quality' rather than the nature of the act. Under the old law, it was unclear whether a deception as to 'quality' as opposed to the 'nature' of the act would be sufficient to vitiate consent. In *Tabassum*,[177] A, who was not medically qualified, persuaded women to allow him to measure their breasts by representing (perhaps truthfully) that he was doing so for the purpose of a breast cancer database he was preparing for doctors. His convictions for indecent assault were upheld, although the women were fully aware of the nature of the acts to be done because (a) they would not have consented to these acts if they had not believed that he had medical qualifications and (b) the defendant knew that this was so. Following *Tabassum*, it seemed that although the complainant was aware of the nature of the act, her consent may be negatived if she was mistaken as to its *quality*. This appeared to be a new distinction for which there was no prior authority.[178] The concept of a deception as to 'quality' has not been explicitly included in the Act, but the inclusion of *'purpose'* in s 76(2)(a) confirms that the legislation is designed to extend the protection of the law. In any event, evidence of A's deception as to the quality of the act should be available to the jury in determining whether consent was present under s 74.

Purpose Thirdly, there is the question of how widely the concept of 'purpose' should be construed under the Act. Deceptions as to the 'purpose' of the act are most likely to arise in relation to sexual touching and non-penile penetration, although it is possible that a deception as to the purpose of the act of intercourse will arise.[179] The presumptions apply in respect of male and female complainants. They would operate, for example, in cases such as *Green*,[180] where a doctor had conducted bogus medical examinations of young men, including wiring them to monitors while they masturbated, allegedly so that he could assess their potential to become impotent.[181] The men understood the nature of the acts they were performing but were deceived as to the purpose for doing so. The issue is not one of A's motive, nor what the complainants thought, but whether the act (masturbation) was being performed for a different purpose than that which A alleged. The purpose of the act of masturbation was different in *Green* since it was not for a medical reason, it was for sexual gratification. *Green* is a relatively easy case.

A slightly more difficult example is *Piper*,[182] where A's touching of B when measuring her for a bikini was a sexual assault given that he had invited B on the basis that he was running a modelling agency. A pleaded guilty. He had sexually touched the women wearing their bikinis. The purpose which A alleged was that this was for the purpose of assessing her modelling statistics, etc. The true purpose was for his sexual gratification.

The question then arises whether s 76 permits a wider approach so as conclusively to presume guilt in cases such as *Linekar*.[183] In that case, A procured a prostitute to have

[176] [2020] EWCA Crim 971.   [177] [2000] 2 Cr App R 328.
[178] *Setting the Boundaries* gave the example of a false representation of a medical examination, para 2.10.9 at 19.
[179] eg where A claims it is to procreate but really it is for his gratification.
[180] [2002] EWCA Crim 1501.
[181] This passage was cited with approval in *Jheeta* [2007] 2 Cr App R 34.
[182] [2007] EWCA Crim 2151.
[183] [1995] 2 Cr App R 49. See A Reed, 'Analysis of Fraud Vitiating Consent in Rape Cases' (1995) 59 J Crim L 310.

intercourse with him by promising to pay her £25. He never intended to pay. It was held under the 1956 Act that this was not rape. The deception did not go to the 'nature' of the act, since the prostitute knew the nature of the conduct of intercourse. Under the 2003 Act, it might be argued that the deception as to payment alters the *'purpose'* of the act for the prostitute. On this interpretation, A would as a result of a conclusive presumption, be classified as a rapist.

The Court of Appeal in *Jheeta*[184] has taken a clear line against overextending the scope of s 76. In this bizarre case, A's deception to B was that she must have intercourse with him to avoid being fined by the police and to avoid his committing suicide. That did not engage s 76. B knew what the act of intercourse entailed and agreed. It will no doubt be suggested by some that the Court of Appeal is taking too narrow a view of 'purpose', restricting it to almost the same meaning as 'nature'. In *Jheeta*, the complainant was not deceived as to the nature of the mechanics of intercourse (ie vaginal penetration with a penis). Nor, it is submitted, was she deceived as to the purpose. She understood it to be for sexual gratification which is what it was for. It is submitted that this is the correct approach to limiting the draconian conclusive presumption provision in s 76. The question of A's deceptions can be left to the jury in their consideration of consent under s 74.

A more difficult case is *Devonald*.[185] B was a 16-year-old boy who had been in a relationship with A's daughter. The relationship had broken down and, believing B to have treated his daughter badly, A sought to teach B a lesson by deliberately embarrassing him. A set up a fake email account pretending to be a young woman. A then corresponded with B and persuaded B to masturbate in front of a webcam. A was convicted, having changed his plea to guilty following a ruling by the judge, of an offence of causing a person to engage in sexual activity without consent. The trial judge ruled that s 76(2)(a) applied. The Court of Appeal dismissed an application for leave to appeal, holding that it was open to the jury to conclude that B had been deceived as to the purpose of the act. Was B deceived as to A's purpose? It was 'difficult to see how the jury could have concluded otherwise than that B had been deceived into believing that he was indulging in sexual acts with, and for the sexual gratification of, a young woman with whom he was having an online relationship'. B's act was undoubtedly sexual, A's purpose in causing B to engage in it was not to secure sexual gratification. A's purpose was to cause B to engage in a sexual act. It is submitted that the decision is out of step with that in *Jheeta*.[186]

There are dangers in taking a wider reading of 'purpose'. If 'purpose' is read widely, many bigamists and adulterers would become rapists *on the basis of a conclusive presumption*. The Court of Appeal took cognizance of this danger in *Bingham*.[187] The facts of this case were

184 [2007] EWCA Crim 1699. The pressure to treat such conduct as rape is increased because the Act fails to include any provision analogous to s 3 of the 1956 Act, criminalizing procuring sexual intercourse by false pretences (short of those which would vitiate consent, namely deception as to the nature of the act and the identity of A). John Spencer (2007) 66 CLJ 490 has suggested that the framers of the 2003 Act assumed that instances of behaviour that would have constituted an offence under s 3 of the 1956 Act would fall within s 4 of the 2003 Act, ie causing another to engage in sexual activity without consent. A similar view was expressed in *Dica* in which Judge LJ stated that s 4 re-enacts the s 3 offence, 'in slightly different terms', at [36]. It is submitted, however, that it is far from obvious that this is what was intended. Eg the separate deception offence that the Sexual Offences Review recommended was confined to cases where A obtained consent to *sexual penetration* by deception, whereas the offence in s 4 applies to causing any sexual activity without consent. In addition, it makes no reference to deception. For further discussion, see K Laird, 'Rapist or Rogue? Deception, Consent and the Sexual Offences Act 2003' [2014] Crim LR 492.

185 [2008] EWCA Crim 527; see also the comment by J Rogers (2008) 72 J Crim L 268.

186 Was there a deception as to the identity of a person known to B if that person (Cassie on the internet) did not really exist? See B Fitzpatrick (2008) 72 J Crim L 11 discussing this in the context of *Jheeta*.

187 [2013] EWCA Crim 823.

similar to those in *Jheeta* and just as bizarre. A met B through a social networking site using a false name and purporting to be someone by the name of G. B sent A topless photographs of herself at A's request. A then threatened to publish the topless photographs online if B did not engage in further sexual acts over a webcam. B capitulated. A then contacted B purporting to be someone else, C. B performed further sexual acts over a webcam, in response to more threats by A to publish the photographs. A's scheme was uncovered and he was charged with seven counts of causing a person to engage in sexual activity without consent, contrary to s 4(1) of the 2003 Act. The prosecution sought to rely upon s 76 on the basis that A had deceived B as to the purpose of the act, drawing an analogy with *Devonald*. Counsel for A, relying upon *Jheeta*, argued that s 76 was inapplicable. The judge ruled in favour of the prosecution. Delivering the judgment of the Court of Appeal, Hallett LJ noted how, in the 13th edition of this work, it was argued that there was an inconsistency between *Jheeta* and *Devonald*. Her ladyship pointed out that the 2003 Act does not provide a definition of 'purpose' and that the courts have therefore been left to define it. It was noted that this is a far from straightforward task, given that it may be difficult to ascertain what the purpose of a sexual act was and that a sexual act may have had more than one purpose. Further, her ladyship pointed out that s 76 does not specify whose purpose matters and that sexual partners may have different purposes when engaging in sex. For these reasons, it was held that there exists a danger that purpose will be defined too widely and that a wide definition would bring within the remit of s 76 situations never contemplated by Parliament.

Given that s 76 embodies a conclusive presumption that effectively removes from the defendant his only line of defence to a serious criminal charge, it was held that the normal rules of statutory construction dictated that it ought to be construed strictly. Hallett LJ held that, to the extent that there does exist a conflict between *Jheeta* and *Devonald*, the former ought to be followed. In *Bingham*, B had never been asked what her purpose was or what her understanding of A's purpose of the sexual acts was. B could have been in no doubt from what A coerced her into doing that the motive was at least in part sexual gratification. For this reason it was observed that, on one view, there was no deceit as to purpose. Nevertheless, the Court of Appeal accepted the submission of counsel for A that if s 76 is relied upon the judge ought to direct the jury's attention specifically to the evidence that is relevant to deception as to the purpose of the relevant act.[188] Given the accumulation of these factors, A's conviction was quashed and a retrial was ordered.

This decision, it is submitted, is a welcome one. As has already been observed, conclusive presumptions such as those contained in s 76 are draconian. Narrowing the applicability of s 76 will ensure that cases in which A is deprived of a defence due to a conclusive presumption will be rare. This is welcome considering the gravity of the offences to which s 76 applies. Further, there is no injustice done to complainants, given that the issue of whether there was consent can still be evaluated with reference to the general definition of consent in s 74. As Hallett LJ pointed out, the prosecution in *Bingham* needed to look no further than s 74. Given A's persistent threats to post the topless pictures of B online, it could be argued that she lacked the freedom to choose whether to engage in sexual activity over the webcam.

While s 76(2)(a) has not been rendered wholly obsolete, it remains uncertain when it would be appropriate for the prosecution to rely upon it. Some fundamental ambiguities persist, for example whether there must be deception as to the dominant purpose or whether deception as to one purpose suffices. If B thinks the purpose is solely sexual gratification, whereas A's purpose is sexual gratification and humiliation, would this be sufficient to fall within

---

[188] The difficult question left by the sections on consent and s 77 on what is a relevant act is 'has A deceived B as to the nature or purpose of A intentionally causing B to engage in sexual activity?'; another illustration of the unduly complex drafting.

s 76(2)(a)? This issue remains unresolved despite *Bingham*, as Hallett LJ did not provide a definition of purpose beyond stating that the term ought to be construed narrowly. It would be wise, therefore, to err on the side of caution and rely upon s 74. Section 74 is available in all cases, given that it has been confirmed that deceptions perpetrated to induce consent to sex are capable of vitiating consent under the general definition of consent. Of course, the important difference is that under s 74 A can argue that he had a reasonable belief that B was consenting, despite the fact that he deceived her. It will be for the prosecution to prove that A lacked a reasonable belief in consent, although a jury might be inclined to conclude that because A believed he had to deceive B in order to obtain her consent to sex, *a fortiori*, he lacked a reasonable belief in consent.

Perhaps the principal circumstances in which s 76(2)(a) will be engaged will be where A tells B that the purpose of the relevant act is medical, when in fact it is solely for A's sexual gratification. There are other circumstances in which s 76(2)(a) may be successfully relied upon, however. Once such case is *M*.[189] A told B that he was making a pornographic film and that any sexual activity would be simulated. This was not the case, however, and sexual activity in fact took place. The prosecution successfully argued that s 76(2)(a) applied on the basis that A had deceived B as to the sexual purpose of the activity that was due to take place. A therefore pleaded guilty. The Court of Appeal rejected A's application to vacate his guilty plea. Irwin J, as he then was, stated: 'The ostensible purpose of the activity, on the facts as presented by the Crown and accepted by the defence, was not sexual pleasure but simulated sexual pleasure for commercial reasons.' This form of deception was sufficient for the conclusive presumption to apply.

Some commentators have argued for an extremely broad reading of s 76. Writing before the case law limiting the applicability of s 76, Herring went so far as to suggest that where B has *made a mistake* about a matter relating to the sexual conduct with A, including a mistake about A's state of mind, which, had she known the truth, she would not have agreed to, there is no consent and if A knows or *ought to have known*[190] that B was mistaken and would not have consented had she known the truth, he is guilty. This is concerning in its ramifications: where B discovers that she made a mistake about A's marital status, wealth, sexual prowess or love for her, A becomes a rapist. The results are unrealistic in practical application.[191] The breadth of the proposal is striking since it includes a unilateral mistake by B as to a state of mind held by A. Of course, such a radical approach could not be brought within s 76 since it is based on B's mistakes when the 2003 Act is founded on A's deceptions.[192]

Alex Sharpe has three objections to Herring's approach, specifically in how it applies to transgender people: (a) it is potentially discriminatory; (b) the right to sexual autonomy does

---

[189] [2015] EWCA Crim 162.

[190] J Herring, 'Mistaken Sex' [2005] Crim LR 511. As Hyman Gross makes clear in his powerful response ('Rape, Moralism and Human Rights' [2007] Crim LR 220) why should A be liable on that basis for a mistake he has not induced?

[191] Herring himself now appears to take a contrary view—that sex is unlike the activities to which contractual rules can apply in criminal law (n 171). Cf Peter Alldridge's proposal that consent should be vitiated if without mistake, consent would not have been given and the person to whom it was given knew: 'Sex Lies and the Criminal Law' (1993) 44 NILQ 250. It has been argued that the standard of consent that applies in contractual cases may be inappropriate in the context of the criminal law: J Stannard, 'The Emotional Dynamics of Consent' (2015) 79 J Crim L 422.

[192] With mistakes unilaterally formed by B, it is doubtful whether in such circumstances there is any legal obligation on A to disabuse B of his misconception, although if A admits to being aware of B's confusion, this may assist the prosecution in proving his mens rea—that he did not reasonably believe in B's consent to that sexual act. Cf Miles [2008] 10 Arch News 5, arguing that if B makes a mistake of a type governed by s 76 there is no consent and that if B makes a mistake other than one of the type within s 76 there is consent even if A induced the mistake. This seems to reduce the operation of s 74 too much. See Rook and Ward, *Sexual Offences: Law and Practice*, para 1.207.

not necessarily trump the right to privacy; and (c) there are compelling public policy concerns in allowing an individual's prejudices against certain people to form the basis of criminal liability.[193] In relation to the final point, Herring has argued that individuals should not fall outside the law's protection simply because others do not agree with the reasons behind their sexual decisions.[194]

In practice, s 76 might have little scope for application with penile penetration. It is difficult to conceive of many cases in twenty-first-century England where an adult is deceived as to the *nature* of penile penetration, or indeed its primary purpose.[195] With other sexual conduct, there is a much stronger argument for relying on s 76—A may tell B he is digitally penetrating her for a medical purpose. She is not defrauded as to the 'nature' of the action (ie a finger entering her vagina), but is as to purpose. She thinks it is for a medical purpose and it is actually for a sexual one. Arguably, this should trigger a conclusive presumption of lack of consent.

Difficulties may arise in all cases of deceptions where A acts with more than one purpose. As has already been mentioned, it is possible for A to have multiple purposes, only some of which are legitimate and about which the accused has been honest with B. What for example, of A, a doctor performing a *necessary* intimate medical examination of B, with the additional aim of allowing his friend, X, to watch for his sexual gratification?[196] It is submitted that on these facts there is a deception as to the 'purpose' and, even after *B*, A would be guilty.

Section 76(2)(b): identity fraud?

By s 142(3) of the Criminal Justice and Public Order Act 1994, it was rape for a man to induce a woman to have intercourse with him by impersonating her husband. At common law, this was extended to include impersonation of long-term heterosexual partnerships.[197] Section 76(2)(b) extends the law beyond any particular category or duration of relationship; it also extends beyond the offence of rape to other acts of penetration and sexual activity. This is a welcome extension.

The conclusive presumption in s 76(2)(b) is more limited than that in para (a) since it is not sufficient for A to have lied about his identity, or even to have lied successfully and deceived B, it must be *by that* impersonation that B is induced to consent. The prosecution must prove this causal link.

The section poses other difficulties in interpretation, particularly regarding the limitation expressed in the formula 'known personally to' the accused. This is clearly intended to prevent the presumption arising when A claims to be a celebrity with whom B has no personal acquaintance, but for whom B may be expected to hold an attraction. Are all people B has ever met 'known personally to' him? Is it only those with whom B has had some greater degree of intimacy? Can a person be known personally to B by email correspondence? Consider the couple who arrange to meet after internet dating. X gets cold feet and decides he cannot face meeting B. A, his friend, steps in. Is there a conclusive presumption that B was not consenting to any sexual acts which follow?

Disappointingly, despite Law Commission recommendations to the contrary,[198] the Act does not deal expressly with the problem of deception as to the defendant's attributes (eg A claiming

---

[193] A Sharpe, 'Criminalising Sexual Intimacy: Transgender Defendants and the Legal Construction of Non-Consent' [2014] Crim LR 207.

[194] J Herring, 'Rape and the Definition of Consent' (2014) 26 NLSI Rev 62.

[195] Unless a much broader view of purpose is adopted so that, eg, sex for procreation is treated as purposively different from that for recreation.

[196] cf *Bolduc and Bird* (1967) 63 DLR (2d) 82.   [197] *Elbekkay* [1995] Crim LR 163.

[198] The Law Commission Report *Consent in Sex Offences* submitted to the Home Office, *Sex Offences Review* (2000) para 5.25. The Commission concluded 'that it should be open to a jury to decide that, for the purposes of a particular act, the "identity" of the actor included the possession of a professional qualification or other authority to do the act in question, and that if the defendant had no such authority then he or she did without consent'.

to have a medical qualification, be a police officer, etc) or other personal authority to perform the act.[199] In *Richardson*[200] (D practised as a dentist although suspended), the court rejected the argument that the concept of the identity of a person extended to cover the qualifications or attributes of the practitioner on the basis that the patients only consented to treatment by a qualified dentist and not a suspended one. The court felt that this would be straining and distorting the definition of identity. However, that case was distinguished in *Melin*,[201] where the court recognized that in some instances the attribute of the individual was integral to their identity (in that case, D's claim to be medically qualified caused V to allow D to inject Botox).[202]

17.2.2 Sexual: s 78

Most offences in the Act involve proof of 'sexual' activity of one kind or another. The concept of 'sexual' is therefore of great significance, and the Act seeks to define it in a fashion similar to that propounded in the House of Lords in the pre-Act case of *Court*:[203]

[P]enetration, touching or any other activity is sexual if a reasonable person would consider that—

(a) whatever its circumstances or any person's purpose in relation to it, it is because of its nature sexual, or

(b) because of its nature it may be sexual and because of its circumstances or the purpose of any person in relation to it (or both) it is sexual.

The first limb requires consideration only of the nature of the act divorced from its circumstances. Where the nature of the activity is unambiguously sexual[204] (eg penile penetration, oral sex, etc) the activity *is* sexual irrespective of the defendant's purpose. Even this limb may be difficult to apply.[205]

The second limb deals with cases where the nature of an activity is ambiguous. Such actions are only 'sexual' if the circumstances or the defendant's purpose render them such. The leading case is that of *H*[206] in the Court of Appeal. B was walking across some fields, when A said to her 'Do you fancy a shag?' She ignored that remark and continued walking. A then grabbed her tracksuit bottoms by the fabric, attempted to pull her towards him and, without succeeding, attempted to place his hand over her mouth. She broke free and escaped. A was convicted of sexual assault, contrary to s 3. It had been submitted that nothing had occurred which a reasonable person might regard as being 'sexual' within the meaning of s 78. According to the Court of Appeal in *H*, the approach should be as follows:

1. If the conduct is unambiguously sexual in the eyes of reasonable people, s 78(a) applies and the conduct is sexual irrespective of what A claims.

2. If the conduct is not unambiguously sexual in the eyes of reasonable people, the jury must ask themselves

---

[199] See *Richardson* [1999] Crim LR 62.   [200] [1998] 2 Cr App R 200.

[201] [2019] EWCA Crim 557.   [202] See p 706.

[203] [1989] AC 28. See on this G Williams, 'The Meaning of Indecency' (1990) 12 LS 20; GR Sullivan, 'The Need for A Crime of Sexual Assault' [1989] Crim LR 331.

[204] The unambiguous nature of the indecency is relevant to whether a proved assault is indecent. It is not relevant to the question whether there is an assault in the first place. *Tabassum* [2000] 2 Cr App R 328, n 178, is surely wrong in this respect.

[205] What of A who pulls B's head towards his naked penis. It looks unambiguously sexual, but what if A claims he is confirming to B, his partner, that he has not recently had sex. We are grateful to Sally O'Neill QC for the example.

[206] [2005] EWCA Crim 732. See also A Gillespie, 'Indecent Images, Grooming and the Law' [2006] Crim LR 412.

(i) whether they as 12 reasonable people considered that the conduct in the particular circumstances before them because of its nature might be sexual and[207]

(ii) whether they, as reasonable people considered that in view of the circumstances or the purpose of the person in relation to the conduct or both it was in fact sexual.

The court's approach to s 78 has the effect of extending the potential scope of the offences dependent on proof of 'sexual' conduct well beyond the former offences in which the requirement was of indecency. In more general terms, the fact that jurors remain sole arbiters of what is 'sexual' is not conducive to the development of a consistent jurisprudence on a fundamental statutory term. Can a jury really be expected to keep the two questions under s 78(b) separate? Taking a shoe fetishist touching B's foot as an example, is there not a danger that the jury will, in answering (i), conclude that the conduct is capable of being sexual by referring, illegitimately, to A's secret motive, particularly when viewed against the backdrop of B having complained?

Few problems arise in relation to s 78(a) in practice where A's conduct is inherently sexual (eg oral sex). The difficulty with s 78(a) is that it might be regarded as overly strict. For example, on facts such as those in *Court*,[208] A, an assistant in a shop, pulled a girl aged 12 who was in the shop across his knee and spanked her on her clothed bottom. When asked why he did it, he said 'buttock fetish'. The House held (Lord Goff dissenting) that because the act was ambiguous, it was necessary to prove an indecent intention. Under the 2003 Act, on facts such as those in *Court*, if A had pulled down B's shorts, the case may well fall immediately into s 78(a), with the nature of the act rendering it unambiguously sexual. What, however, if in pulling down B's shorts, A had a merely (admittedly bizarre) disciplinary motive? Arguably there should be an opportunity for A's explanation, but that only arises if the case is decided under s 78(b).[209] Conversely, there may be some acts of an unambiguously sexual nature where A's purpose is to perpetrate an act of violence not sex, but A's purpose is irrelevant.

The more significant aspect of the section is s 78(b). Examples of the operation of s 78(b) might include where A induces B to remove clothing, or an intimate examination involving digital penetration of the vagina or anus. If performed by a doctor for a medical purpose, and in appropriate medical circumstances, these would be non-sexual; A's purpose may make them sexual. As interpreted in *H*, s 78(b) catches a wide range of conduct as sexual. It is submitted that practically any seemingly innocuous conduct *may* be capable of being regarded by a reasonable person as being sexual. Fetishism knows no bounds.[210] The s 78(b) test could give rise to difficulties in practice. Take the case of *Pratt*[211] as an example: A made two young boys strip and point a torch at each other's genitals while he watched. A claimed that he was looking for cannabis. Under s 78, if the jury believed A's explanation for his actions it will be treated as a non-sexual purpose, and provided they do not conclude that the act is sexual per se (category (a)) A will be acquitted.

---

[207] In relation to this first question, evidence as to the circumstances before or after the conduct was irrelevant.

[208] [1989] AC 28.

[209] A similar argument is developed by I Bantekas, 'Can Touching Always be Sexual When There is No Sexual Intent?' (2008) 72 J Crim L 251.

[210] For criticism of this interpretation see Gallavin, n 163.

[211] [1984] Crim LR 51. Note that he is not guilty of sexual assault since he does not touch the boys; the charge would be under s 4. See *Thompson (Andrew)* [2014] EWCA Crim 836 where A's drying off naked boys after swimming was ambiguous.

Section 78 also creates difficulties with odd sexual fetishes. In *George*,[212] A attempted to remove a girl's shoe from her foot because this gave him sexual gratification. Streatfeild J, rejecting an argument that A's indecent motive made this an indecent assault, held that there were no circumstances of indecency. This decision was not followed under the 2003 Act in *H*. Stroking a woman's shod foot is not unambiguously sexual (leaving aside the extreme cases): s 78(a) does not apply. However, assuming a reasonable person would consider that stroking a woman's foot '*may be*' sexual, A's purpose would render it such: s 78(b). The less overtly sexual the fetish, the less likely the reasonable jury might regard it as being sexual and the less likely it will be caught by the section.

The significant shift from the 1956 Act offences based on 'indecent' conduct to the 2003 Act focus on 'sexual' conduct fails to address other difficulties. For example, in the case of *CW*[213] it was questioned whether A's touching of a 13-year-old's 'belly bar piercing' was 'indecent' under the 1956 Act. It is no clearer whether this is sexual under the 2003 Act than whether it was indecent under the old law. More commonly occurring questions might be whether a kiss is inherently sexual and if not then its categorization would depend on the circumstances and purpose of the kisser (thus, not where a hairy old aunt issues a slobbering greeting to a reluctant nephew). Distinguishing on the basis of whether the kissing involved is 'deep'[214] or otherwise is not an accurate basis of distinction. In *Davies*,[215] a 22-year-old woman kissing an 11-year-old girl on the mouth with an open mouth was sufficient for the s 7 offence—sexual touching of a child under 13.

Does an act that is seemingly sexual lose that quality if it is performed exclusively for reasons of violence in A's mind? In *AJ*,[216] A was convicted of sexual touching of B (his 19-year-old stepdaughter) whom he had tied up (wrists and feet) and pinned down while he told her she needed to 'do more' around the house, that being part of an ongoing argument between them. B claimed that she thought that he was going to rape her. Her tracksuit bottoms 'fell down' in the course of the struggle with him. He did not touch her genitals.[217] In *Deal*,[218] A was convicted of two counts of sexual touching, one being for the act of standing behind a female police officer and rubbing her arms with his hands, whilst making comments to her which she was unable to hear. It might even be argued in an extreme case that an act of penetration is not sexual: in *Hill*,[219] A had, in the course of a violent argument with his partner, 'forcefully inserted his finger in her vagina' as the Court of Appeal described it: 'without her consent and . . . as some form of aggressive humiliation rather than a sexual act'.[220] A nevertheless pleaded guilty to a 'sexual' penetration.

17.2.3 Touching: s 79(8)

Under the 1956 Act, the offences other than those of intercourse centred predominantly on acts involving 'assault' as explained in the Court of Appeal in *Court*:[221]

The offence . . . included both a battery, or touching, and psychic assault without touching. If there was touching, it was not necessary to prove that the victim was aware of the assault or of the circumstances of indecency. If there was no touching, then to constitute an indecent assault the victim must be shown to have been aware of the assault and of the circumstances of indecency.

---

[212] [1956] Crim LR 52. Such cases are not uncommon: see *Price* [2004] 1 Cr App R 12, [2003] EWCA Crim 2405, where A stroked B's leg and boot and admitted it was because he had a shoe fetish.

[213] *CW* [2004] EWCA Crim 340.

[214] See Williams (1990) 10 LS 29 (presumably his definition turns on whether tongues are involved).

[215] [2005] EWCA Crim 3690.   [216] [2006] EWCA Crim 2956.

[217] Evidence was admitted that D had spent the previous hour viewing online pornography.

[218] [2006] EWCA Crim 684.   [219] [2006] EWCA Crim 2575.   [220] ibid, [4].

[221] [1987] 1 All ER 120 at 122.

The 2003 Act creates offences based on 'touching' which includes touching:

(1) with any part of the body;[222]

(2) with anything else;

(3) through anything,[223]

and in particular includes touching amounting to penetration.

As elsewhere in the Act, there is no further definition of any of the terms, and this may lead to a regrettable inconsistency in the application of the law.

The leading case is *H* (see earlier) where the question was whether A's touching of B's tracksuit bottoms alone constituted a 'touching' of another person within the meaning of s 79(8). Although s 79(8) offers an extended and non-exhaustive interpretation of that term, including 'touching through anything', some commentators had suggested that the Act required physical contact with B's *body*.[224] The Court of Appeal held that where a person was wearing clothing, touching of that clothing constituted touching for the purposes of the Act. It was unnecessary for there to be some form of pressure brought against the body of the individual who was alleged to have been assaulted for touching to occur for the purposes of s 3.[225] This is consistent with the decisions in relation to battery generally. For example, in *Thomas*,[226] A had touched the bottom of B's skirt and the court said *obiter* that 'There could be no dispute that if you touch a person's clothes while he is wearing them that is equivalent to touching him.' There are numerous instances of convictions for sexual assault through clothing under the Act. For example, in *Swinscoe*,[227] A approached an eight-year-old and asked to see her knickers before touching her through her underwear (s 7).

The shift from 'assault' under the 1956 Act to 'touching' under the 2003 Act is significant. Although assault did not require any element of hostility,[228] 'touching' might appear to be broader than even a non-hostile assault. It is submitted that as with the old law, there is no room for any '*de minimis*' exception.[229] In other circumstances it seems that the law has been narrowed. Thus, sexual words do not constitute a touching but might well have been assaults. Similarly, where A walks towards B with his penis exposed,[230] this could have been an assault: the old law did not require any apprehension of indecent touching.[231] Note that it is enough that A makes contact and the act is sexual; B need not be aware that there is a touching or, presumably, that the act is sexual.[232] So, in *Farrar*,[233] A committed the offence

---

[222] Note that under s 79(3) surgically reconstructed body parts are included as parts of the 'body' with which touching can occur.

[223] This covers D who engages in frottaging (rubbing his genitals against a fellow passenger on public transport): see eg *Tanylidiz* [1998] Crim LR 228.

[224] Card suggested that 'lightly touching an outer garment so thick that no physical contact is made with B's body would not suffice'. R Card, *Sexual Offences: The New Law* (2003), para 2.32.

[225] Interestingly, A's counsel's argument had been that A had pulled the shorts away from B not touching her at all. Our thanks to Ian West for this point.

[226] (1985) 81 Cr App R 331 at 334.   [227] [2006] EWCA Crim 2412.

[228] Although cf the House of Lords in *Brown* [1994] 1 AC 212 and p 692. More recently, in *B* [2013] EWCA Crim 3, Hughes LJ stated that: 'The element of assault frequently and usefully described as hostility is a means of conveying to the jury that some non-hostile contact is an ordinary incident of life to which we all impliedly consent', at [44].

[229] *Ananthanarayanan* (1994) 98 Cr App R 1 at 5 per Laws J. See *Mills* [2003] EWCA Crim 3723, two-second touching of barmaid's breasts by customer.

[230] *Rolfe* (1952) 36 Cr App R 4.

[231] *Sargeant* (1996) 161 JP 127, [1997] Crim LR 50, where the assault was a threat with a knife and the circumstance of indecency was A's demand that B masturbate into a condom in a public place.

[232] *Bounekhla* [2006] EWCA Crim 1217 (A secretly ejaculating over B while dancing closely with her in a nightclub).

[233] [2006] EWCA Crim 3261.

by blindfolding a child, B, and masturbating on him. There is still the question whether it is sufficient that A ejaculates on B without touching B in the process.[234] Surely this is sufficient.

It is unclear whether there can be a touching by omission. What, for example, of cases such as *Speck*,[235] where A's failure to remove B's hand, which she had voluntarily placed on his penis, caused it to become erect? Does this constitute a touching? There is a touching between A and B, but it is more difficult to describe A as touching B. Is it a sexual touching if the sexual element derives from B and not A? It is submitted that it is capable of being sexual.[236]

17.3 Non-consensual offences

17.3.1 Rape

Rape was an offence at common law. Although placed on a statutory basis in s 1 of the Sexual Offences Act 1956, there was no statutory definition of the offence, and this position continued until the Sexual Offences (Amendment) Act 1976[237] introduced a partial definition of the mens rea requirement and the Criminal Justice and Public Order Act 1994 extended the offence to include anal rape. There had been sustained calls for reform of the offence, particularly the mental element and the opportunity for an acquittal on the basis of a mere honest belief in the complainant's consent since the controversial decision in *Morgan*.[238] The need for this issue to be addressed and for clearer definition of this the most serious sexual offence were significant catalysts for reform, as was the low conviction rate for rape: by 1999, only one in 13 alleged rapes led to conviction.[239]

The 2003 reform prompted several radical suggestions for rape to be subdivided into different categories of offence. One suggestion was to distinguish between cases on the basis of whether there was a previous relationship between the accused and complainant (acquaintance rape) and the more stereotypical but far less common stranger rape. This was rejected. There is no doubt that rape by an acquaintance, including as it does an abuse of trust, can be as traumatic as stranger rape. The Court of Appeal has accepted that, in sentencing terms, there is in general no difference between a stranger rape and an acquaintance rape.[240] The 2003 Act also rejected the possibility of structuring different offences of rape based on the extent of mental fault.[241]

---

[234] The Scottish legislation specifically provides that such conduct is an offence: s 3(2)(d) of the Sexual Offences (Scotland) Act 2009.

[235] [1977] Crim LR 689. See also *B* [2004] EWCA Crim 319 where A had allowed B to touch his genitals and where B had placed A's hand on her genitals.

[236] cf the s 4 case of *Aveya* [2009] EWCA Crim 2640 where A forced B's hand onto A's penis and moved it.

[237] The Sexual Offences Act 1956, s 1(1), simply provided 'It is a felony for a man to rape a woman', whilst s 1(2) provided 'A man who induces a married woman to have sexual intercourse with him by impersonating her husband commits rape.'

[238] [1976] AC 182; see p 350. For discussion, see L Farmer, '*DPP v Morgan*' in P Handler, H Mares and I Williams (eds), *Landmark Cases in Criminal Law* (2017).

[239] Home Office, *Rape and Sexual Assault of Women, Findings from the BCS* (2002).

[240] See also the Sentencing Advisory Panel's advice to the Court of Appeal, Foreword by the Chairman, 1 May 2002, paras 32–5. On the court's controversial qualification of this, see P Rumney, 'Progress at a Price: The Construction of Non-Stranger Rape in the *Millbery* Sentencing Guidelines' (2003) 66 MLR 870.

[241] See Temkin, *Rape and the Legal Process*, Ch 3, H Power, 'Towards a Redefinition of the *Mens Rea* of Rape' (2003) 23 OJLS 379, a view also considered by the Heilbron Committee, *Report of the Advisory Group on the Law of Rape* (1975) paras 79–80. For a proposal to subdivide the offence into categories based on the reason for the absence of consent (eg intoxicated, under threat of violence, etc) see Tadros (2006) 26 OJLS 515.

Despite the rejection of these more radical proposals, the new rape offence represents a significant change from the 1956 Act. It provides:

(1) A person (A) commits an offence if—

    (a) he intentionally penetrates the vagina, anus or mouth of another person (B) with his penis,

    (b) B does not consent to the penetration, and

    (c) A does not reasonably believe B consents.

(2) Whether a belief is reasonable is to be determined having regard to all the circumstances, including any steps A has taken to ascertain whether B consents.

Rape is triable only on indictment (except for certain cases where there is provision for trial in the Youth Court).[242] The maximum penalty is life imprisonment.[243]

17.3.1.1 Actus reus
Penile

The Sexual Offences Review team wanted the offence of rape to reflect the general public's understanding of the term, and concluded that although it would perpetuate gender inequality, penile penetration should nevertheless remain an essential element of the offence. The Review considered that penile penetration was a distinctive act, carrying as it can risks of pregnancy and disease transmission, and that it should, therefore, be treated separately from other penetrative assaults. This strong commitment to the principle of fair labelling is especially important in sexual offences where the stigma of conviction is most acute. If jurors are to apply the offences appropriately it is also important that the offences reflect society's general understanding of the wrongdoing involved. By restricting rape to penile penetration,[244] s 1 reflects this principle.

Because the offence requires penetration by a penis, rape remains one of the few offences capable of being committed only by a male (as a principal offender).[245] However, in a welcome extension of the offence, a post-operative transsexual can commit rape with her reconstructed penis[246] (hence, presumably, the drafting in terms of 'a person' rather than 'a man').[247] A female can aid and abet the offence[248] as where she encourages or assists a male, A, to penetrate B without B's consent. It may be possible for the female aider and abettor to be convicted even though A is acquitted of rape on the basis of his lack of mens rea.[249] In such circumstances, a female can also be charged with an offence under s 4—causing a person to engage in sexual activity (see later).

The conclusive presumption that boys under 14 were incapable of sexual intercourse was abolished by s 1 of the Sexual Offences Act 1993 for acts done after 20 September 1993. It has been held that a boy under ten years old cannot commit an offence and so cannot be procured to commit rape,[250] but this reasoning seems flawed.[251]

---

[242] Magistrates' Courts Act 1980, s 24, as amended, and Sch 9, para 64.   [243] SOA 2003, s 1(4).

[244] *Setting the Boundaries*, Ch 2, para 2.8.4.

[245] The Sexual Offences Act 1993 removed the common law presumption that boys under the age of 14 are incapable of intercourse. In a prosecution for historic offences pre-20 March 1993, a defendant cannot be guilty of charges involving acts of sexual intercourse perpetrated when he was aged under 14. See *W* [2003] 10 Arch News 2, *PF* [2017] EWCA Crim 983 and D Ormerod, 'A Presumption of Intercourse' [2003] 1 Arch News 2. For a more theoretical debate see N McKeever, 'Can a Woman Rape a Man and Why Does it Matter?' (2019) 13 Crim L & P 599.

[246] Under s 79(3).   [247] Section 79(3). See *Setting the Boundaries* recommendation at para 2.8.4.

[248] *Ram* (1893) 17 Cox CC 609; *Lord Baltimore's case* (1768) 1 Black, W 648.

[249] *Cogan and Leak* [1975] 2 All ER 1059.   [250] *DPP v K and C* [1997] 1 Cr App R 36 at 42.

[251] See commentary in [1997] Crim LR 121, and see n 245. See also *C* [2005] EWCA Crim 2817.

Penetration

Penetration is not defined in the Act, although s 79(2) provides that it is a continuing act, thus putting on a statutory footing the decisions of the Privy Council in *Kaitamaki*[252] and the Court of Appeal in *Cooper and Schaub*.[253] Penetration continues until withdrawal,[254] and A can be convicted of rape where, having initially penetrated B with consent, B subsequently withdraws that consent and A, being aware of that retraction of consent, does not remove his penis.[255] Presumably, A will not commit the offence until he either knows or could reasonably be expected to know that consent had been withdrawn.

The Act does not provide any clarification of the degree of penetration necessary. Presumably the common law rule applies so that the slightest degree of penetration will suffice. In relation to vaginal rape, this will include any penetration of the vulva,[256] and thus, the common law rule that it is not necessary to show that the hymen was ruptured remains.[257] In *F*,[258] 'vagina' was held to be used in the general sense of the female genitals, not in its strict anatomical sense.[259] There is no express provision making clear that rape is complete upon penetration without ejaculation,[260] but this must surely still represent the law. The fact that the Act creates numerous other offences of non-penile penetration supports this view.

If the prosecution fail to establish that there was penetration by a penis, a verdict of attempted rape may be returned if A's conduct amounted to more than mere preparation to penile penetration.

Of the vagina, anus or mouth

'Vagina' is to be interpreted as including the vulva.[261] Section 79 of the Act provides further relevant definition, including welcome confirmation that penetration of a surgically reconstructed vagina suffices.[262] At common law, rape protected only against penetration of the vagina, indeed historically it was an offence protecting virginity.[263] Section 142 of the Criminal Justice and Public Order Act 1994 introduced the offence of anal rape. The 2003 Act extends the offence of rape yet further by including non-consensual penile penetration of the mouth. The Sexual Offences Review acknowledged that non-consensual oral sex is as 'abhorrent, demeaning and traumatising' as vaginal and anal penetration by the penis.[264] There is no doubt that this form of conduct deserves appropriate condemnation by the law in terms of labelling and sentence, but some argued that it would have been more appropriately dealt with as non-consensual penetration under s 2 (which also carries a life sentence). There may, of course, be greater forensic difficulties in establishing oral sex as opposed to

---

[252] [1985] AC 147.   [253] [1994] Crim LR 531.

[254] For criticism of *Kaitamaki* see the 10th edn of this book, where it was emphasized that the offence requires penetration without consent as an essential part of the actus reus of rape and this act of penetration must be accompanied by the mens rea.

[255] See *Leaver* [2006] EWCA Crim 2988 and under the previous law also *Tarmohammed* [1997] Crim LR 458; *Greaves* [1999] 1 Cr App R (S) 319.

[256] Section 79(3).

[257] *Hughes* (1841) 9 C & P 752; *Lines* (1844) 1 C & K 393; *Allen (Henry)* (1839) 9 C & P 31; *M'Rue* (1838) 8 C & P 641.

[258] [2002] EWCA Crim 2936.   [259] cf *Holland* (1993) 117 ALR 193, High Ct of Aust.

[260] cf s 44 of the Sexual Offences Act 1956.   [261] Section 79(9).

[262] Section 79(3). This puts on a statutory footing the ruling in *Matthews*, Oct 1996, unreported. See also M Hicks and G Branston, 'Transexual Rape—A Loophole Closed?' [1997] Crim LR 526.

[263] Temkin, *Rape and the Legal Process*, 57.

[264] *Setting the Boundaries*, para 2.8.5. See the government response to the *Home Affairs Committee Fifth Report*.

vaginal or anal penetration, although that in itself should not militate against it being classified as rape.[265] The Court of Appeal has confirmed that sentencing should not distinguish between the orifice(s) penetrated.[266]

Without consent

The critical element of rape remains the absence of consent. Without that, penile penetration is not merely not criminal, it is an explicit expression of intimacy. The Act's approach to consent is discussed earlier.

17.3.1.2 Mens rea
Intentional penetration

The requirement that the defendant *intentionally* penetrate the relevant orifice should not give rise to difficulty in practice. One circumstance in which A might realistically claim that penile penetration was 'accidental' might include those where A intended to penetrate B's vagina with her consent, but accidentally penetrated her anus, for which act he knew he did not have consent, or to which he could not reasonably believe that he had consent (whether from previous knowledge or from B's expression of non-consent once A penetrated her anally).[267] It has been held that to charge A with rape where the allegation is that he penetrated either B's vagina or her anus is not to allege two offences.[268] Nevertheless, if A has a reasonable belief in consent to vaginal sex and unintentionally penetrates B's anus, it is submitted that he has not raped B.

Despite this element of the offence being expressed in terms of intention, it would seem, following *Heard*,[269] that a mistake of this nature induced by voluntary intoxication cannot be relied upon.[270] The offence is one of basic intent.

Mens rea as to consent

One of the most dramatic changes under the 2003 Act was to redefine the mens rea for rape. Under s 1(1) of the Act, the prosecution have to prove that A intentionally penetrated the vagina, anus or mouth of B, and that A did not have a *reasonable* belief that B was consenting. It is important to understand the development of the move to a more objective mens rea.[271]

In 1975 the House of Lords in *Morgan* held that rape was not proved if the man may have honestly believed that the woman was consenting, even if that belief was unreasonable. Lord Hailsham held that the mens rea required an 'intention of having intercourse, willy-nilly, not caring whether the victim consents or not'.[272] Another way of putting this was to ask, 'Was A's attitude one of "I could not care less whether B is consenting or not, I am going to have intercourse with her regardless"?'[273] Thus, the mens rea under the old law required proof that A intentionally had sexual intercourse with B: (a) knowing that B did not consent or (b) being aware that there was a possibility that B did not consent.

---

[265] In its Definitive Guideline, the Sentencing Council does not draw distinctions based upon the orifice penetrated, p 10.

[266] *Ismail* [2005] EWCA Crim 397.

[267] See *Gabbai* [2019] EWCA Crim 2287. See also *Pigg* [1983] 1 WLR 56 and discussion by S White, 'Three Points on *Pigg*' [1989] Crim LR 539.

[268] *K* [2008] EWCA Crim 1923.   [269] [2007] EWCA Crim 125.

[270] cf *Woods* (1981) 74 Cr App R 132. See now *Grewal* [2010] EWCA Crim 2448.

[271] See the recent discussion of reform in Ireland: Y Daly, 'Knowledge or Belief Concerning Consent in Rape Law: Recommendations for Change in Ireland' [2020] Crim LR 478.

[272] [1976] AC 182 at 215. See also the *Heilbron Report of the Advisory Group on the Law of Rape* (1975) Cmnd 6352, para 77.

[273] *Taylor* (1984) 80 Cr App R 327; *Haughian* (1985) 80 Cr App R 334.

Following widespread public concern with this approach, the Heilbron Committee[274] reviewed the position and, while endorsing *Morgan*, recommended some statutory clarification. The Sexual Offences (Amendment) Act 1976 provided that the jury was to consider the presence or absence of reasonable grounds for such a belief as relevant matters, in considering whether A believed he had consent. This was largely a public relations provision explaining the jury's role in evaluating a defendant's mistaken beliefs of facts; it did not enact any rule peculiar to rape.

There was little empirical evidence that *Morgan* defences were successfully run, so jurors were presumably not readily believing defendants' spurious claims. Even if generally unsuccessful, the plea was easy to run and difficult to disprove, and sent an undesirable message to society—that it is acceptable to take unreasonable risks as to your partner's consent to sexual conduct.[275] Unsurprisingly, many submissions to the Sexual Offences Review were highly critical of the approach. *Setting the Boundaries* regarded this 'defence' as in direct conflict with the ordinary perceptions of contemporary society. A more objective approach to the issue of mens rea as to consent was desirable, or even necessary, but further difficulty lay in determining the appropriate degree of objectivity.

One key issue of the reform agenda became whether the mens rea (for rape in particular) ought to be rendered wholly objective (would a reasonable person have realized that B was not consenting?). Although the general trend of English criminal law had been increasingly favouring subjective approaches to mens rea—even in serious sexual offences[276]—there are powerful arguments against adopting a purely subjective approach in this context. When the conduct in question is of a sexual nature, the ease with which the defendant can ascertain the consent of his partner, coupled with the catastrophic consequences for the complainant if the defendant acts without consent, militate strongly against the purely subjective approach. The generosity the law extends to accepting a defendant's genuine but unreasonable mistakes in, for example, matters of self-defence need not be replicated in sexual cases because the conduct in question calls for a qualitatively different degree of vigilance on his part.[277]

The government took a strong stance on this aspect of the reform.[278] In early versions of the Sexual Offences Bill, it was proposed that the defendant would bear a *legal* burden (on the balance of probabilities) to show that he did believe that the complainant consented. This may well have been in breach of Art 6(2) of the ECHR. The final version as enacted is less objective, and although to be welcomed for extending the mens rea, the Act is not as clear as it might be, and may still leave the opportunity for *Morgan*-type pleas to be run (although they will be even less likely to succeed).

The mens rea in rape and the other non-consensual offences (ss 1–4) comprises two elements:

(1) A does not reasonably believe B consents.

(2) Whether a belief is reasonable is to be determined having regard to all the circumstances, including any steps A has taken to ascertain whether B consents.

274 (1975) Cmnd 6352. See [1976] Crim LR 97.
275 See the Law Commission's Policy Paper in *Setting the Boundaries* (2000) vol 2.
276 See *K* [2001] UKHL 41; *DPP v B* [2000] 2 WLR 452.
277 This passage was cited with approval by the Court of Appeal in *B* [2013] EWCA Crim 3. See generally on this issue J Horder, 'Cognition, Emotion and Criminal Culpability' (1990) 106 LQR 469, 477; T Pickard, 'Culpable Mistakes' (1980) 30 U Toronto LJ 75; C Wells, 'Swatting the Subjectivist Bug' [1982] Crim LR 209. There have been suggestions for strict liability rape offences. For discussion see K Huigens, 'Is Strict Liability Rape Defensible' in Duff and Green, *Defining Crimes*, 196 discussing a hypothetical case where B was under the self-imposed mistaken belief that A was a serial rapist, so she acquiesced in all A did. A was unaware and thought B was consenting.
278 See HL, 31 Mar 2003, col 1089 (Lord Falconer).

The provisions do not render the test *wholly* objective.[279] The defendant's personal characteristics and beliefs remain important, but both the concluded belief as to consent and the manner by which A reached it are to be assessed by reference to some objective criteria.

A does 'not reasonably believe'

This encompasses cases in which: (a) A's purpose is to act without B's consent; (b) A is aware that B might not be consenting; (c) A has no belief whether B is consenting or not; (d) A holds a belief that B is consenting but that is an unreasonable belief. What is not made completely clear is whether in (d) the question is as to (i) A's purely subjective belief about consent measured against a standard of reasonableness applied by the jury or magistrate, or (ii) A's assessment that his own belief as to consent was reasonable. It is submitted that the correct interpretation is that in (i).[280] The dilution of the purely objective test originally proposed to accommodate those with limited capacity has not been that substantial. A, with a learning disability,[281] who believes B is consenting will have the mens rea if the reasonable juror concludes that the belief was an unreasonable one, irrespective of the fact that the basis for belief is understandable, given A's limited capacity.

In *B*,[282] the Court of Appeal stated unequivocally that a belief in consent induced by psychotic illness or personality disorder could not be reasonable. Hughes LJ observed that a delusional belief in consent would, by definition, be irrational and thus unreasonable.[283] In this case A was suffering from paranoid schizophrenia and had sex with B, who did not consent. It was held that the trial judge was correct to direct the jury to ignore A's condition when evaluating whether his belief in consent was reasonable. It would only be relevant if A sought to plead insanity. A caveat was, however, added to this general proposition. Hughes LJ stated that it did not follow that there will never be a case in which the personality or abilities of A might be relevant to whether his belief in consent was reasonable. His lordship gave the example of a situation in which the reasonableness of a belief in consent depends upon A's ability to read subtle social signals. In these circumstances it was held that A's impaired ability would be relevant to the reasonableness of his belief. His lordship stated that a situation such as this one could be distinguished from the facts of the instant case, because such a belief in consent might not be irrational and might not be unreasonable, despite the fact that it is a belief that would not be held by most members of society. It is submitted that while the decision is in keeping with Parliament's intention to make the mens rea for the non-consensual sexual offence more objective, difficulties might arise in future. A's mental condition must only be left out of the equation when the belief it leads him to form can be classified as being wholly irrational. If it is not wholly irrational, then it may be taken into consideration when determining whether A's belief in consent was reasonable. There is scope for the exercise of a great deal of judicial discretion in determining what types of mental condition will fall into this latter category.[284] The further issue, it is submitted, is that judges may be reluctant to make the initial determination that A's belief was irrational, since that would seem to lead inexorably to a conviction, unless A seeks to plead insanity.[285]

---

[279] See Ch 4 for discussion of negligence.

[280] HC, col 639 refers ambiguously to the 'focus on the defendant's belief', at para 23.

[281] Under the old law, A's Asperger's was relevant: see *Tipu Sultan* [2008] EWCA Crim 6.

[282] [2013] EWCA Crim 3.

[283] Although it did not reach a conclusion on the matter, this issue was alluded to by the Court of Appeal in the earlier case of *MM* [2011] EWCA Crim 1291.

[284] In *MM* [2011] EWCA Crim 1291, the expert concluded that A's bipolar state caused him to misinterpret ambiguous messages that he received from B and her family, eg that he was described as being her boyfriend. Whether this evidence would be left to the jury after *B* is questionable.

[285] It has been suggested that if A has a delusional belief that B is consenting, he should be denied any access to the statutory claim of reasonable belief and be instructed that he is raising a defence of insanity. See J Child and GR Sullivan, 'When Does the Insanity Defence Apply? Some Recent Cases' [2014] Crim LR 788.

If this is an accurate assessment of the situation, then the scope of the *dicta* in *B* will be greatly diminished, but this remains to be seen.

Reasonable having regard to all the circumstances including the steps taken

The reasonableness test does not oblige the defendant to have taken any specific steps to ascertain consent; the government was keen to emphasize that there would be no need to have 'blank consent forms by the bedside'. However, where steps have been taken they must be taken into account by the jury in deciding whether the defendant's claimed belief in consent was reasonable.[286] Also, importantly, the issue of the reasonableness of belief will now be worth pursuing in police interviews with the suspect. The objective test has an impact on the evidential provisions regarding cross-examination of sexual complainants.[287]

Ministerial statements[288] suggested that the expression 'all the circumstances' in s 1(2) will allow juries, when determining the reasonableness of the belief, to take account of any *relevant* characteristics of the defendant. Ministers rejected the idea that the very narrow interpretation of similar provisions in New Zealand might be followed, creating a purely objective test.[289] It is clear, then, that the defendant's age; general sexual experience; sexual experience with this complainant;[290] learning disability; and any other factor that could have affected his ability to understand the nature and consequences of his actions, and particularly the ability to appreciate the risk of non-consent, may be relevant depending on the circumstance of the particular case. What weight will attach to these characteristics will be a matter for judicial direction.

Several difficulties flow from the breadth of this provision. First, there is the question as to which characteristics of the defendant might be *excluded* from the jury's deliberation. On the basis of the long-established position that rape is a crime of basic intent, the jury should not take into account the defendant's self-induced intoxication by drink or drugs.[291] What of other characteristics, such as those which are inherently unreasonable in the context of sexual conduct? For example, what of A who claims that women who invite him for coffee are automatically agreeing to sex? Or that dressing in a short skirt is an invitation to be touched in a sexual manner?[292] Ministers reassured Parliament that the jury would not be asked to take into account such characteristics.[293] The crucial question for the courts is in defining the limits on which less strikingly unreasonable characteristics are legally relevant. This created difficulty elsewhere in the law, particularly with provocation.[294] Careful judicial direction is critical. Once again, it is disappointing that such an important issue is not resolved by clearer policy and drafting in the Act.

Secondly, and related to this point, the statute does not expressly preclude the most objectionable of the *Morgan*-type pleas from being advanced. A could claim that he had taken

---

[286] HC, 3rd reading, 17 June 2003, col 669.

[287] See *Bahadour* [2005] EWCA Crim 396 and J McEwan, 'I Thought She Consented' [2006] Crim LR 961.

[288] HC, 2 June 2003, col 1073 (Lord Falconer of Thoroton); HC, 17 June 2003, col 674 (Baroness Scotland of Asthal).

[289] HC, 17 June 2003, col 674 (Baroness Scotland of Asthal).   [290] *McAllister* [1997] Crim LR 233.

[291] *Grewal* [2010] EWCA Crim 2448; *Heard* [2007] EWCA Crim 125; *Fotheringham* (1988) 88 Cr App R 206.

[292] The disturbing report of Amnesty International revealed that one-third of the UK population believe that women who had flirted were wholly or partially responsible for a sexual assault on them. See the Home Office Report, *Convicting Rapists and Protecting Victims* (2006). Cf H Reece, 'Rape Myths: Is Elite Opinion Right and Popular Opinion Wrong?' (2013) 33 OJLS 445.

[293] Lord Falconer of Thoroton stated: 'Introducing a requirement that all of the personal characteristics of the defendant should be taken into account would mean that the jury would be asked to take into account characteristics that should not absolve him from his guilt: for example, the fact that he has a quick temper or that the sight of a girl in a mini-skirt will always turn him on and make him unable to resist her. That cannot be the intention.' HL, 17 June 2003.

[294] Especially in relation to provocation. Guidance may be derived from the Court of Appeal's approach in self-defence cases where D has a belief formed owing to a psychiatric condition: *Canns* [2010] EWCA Crim 2264; *Press and Thompson* [2013] EWCA Crim 1849.

reasonable steps to ascertain the consent of the complainant by asking her friends, or by seeking the confirmation of her husband (as in *Morgan*). Could A also claim that it was reasonable for him to ignore B's explicit 'no' since he believes that all women sometimes say 'no' and mean 'yes'?[295] Such pleas are never likely to be considered to be 'reasonable' by any right-thinking jury. Nevertheless, the 2003 Act provisions allow for the plea to be run adding to the distress of the complainant. It should be noted that *Setting the Boundaries* recommended a significantly wider list of circumstances presumptively vitiating consent including where a person has agreement given for them by a third party.[296] This was rejected because of concerns that a person with a learning disability, A, might be easily deceived by X and have sex with B believing her to be consenting on the basis of X's false statement.[297]

As the Court of Appeal noted in *Taran (Farid)*:[298]

A direction upon absence of reasonable belief clearly falls to be given when, but only when, there is material on which a jury might come to the conclusion that (a) the complainant did not in fact consent, but (b) the defendant thought that she was consenting. Such a direction does not fall to be given unless there is such material. It is, of course, the fact, as all trial judges know well, that a direction of this kind, as of many other kinds, may have to be given even when it is not the case of either the Crown or the defendant that it arises . . . Reasonable belief in consent on an indictment for rape can certainly be [an] example, but only where there is material on which a jury may think that there might have been a misunderstanding, that is to say that the complainant did not in fact consent but that the defendant may have thought that she did.[299]

Mistakes as to the identity of B

What is the liability of A who claims that he thought on reasonable grounds that X would be consenting to the sexual act which he then mistakenly performed on B? Can A claim he has a reasonable belief in consent? In *Whitta*,[300] A had agreed with X that they would have sex later after the party they were both attending. Both A and X were adults but drunk. A, having removed his glasses, later entered a bedroom and digitally penetrated B, the sleeping 51-year-old mother of the party host. B was also very drunk. A desisted as soon as he realized his mistake. The trial judge ruled that mistake as to the identity in this context was irrelevant—liability was strict. The judge's approach draws support from the peculiar drafting of the sections with their reference to A and B. The Court of Appeal disagreed with this analysis of the sections. The effect of the judge's ruling was that it is not a defence to a charge if the defendant has made a mistake, however reasonable, as to the identity of the person to whom the sexual activity is directed. That is not the law. It would mean that A who kissed his wife's identical twin sister would be liable for sexual assault irrespective of the reasonableness of his mistaken belief that he was kissing his wife. It is submitted that the correct question is whether A's belief was a reasonable one.

17.3.2 Assault by penetration: s 2

A person, A, commits an offence if he intentionally penetrates the vagina or anus of another person (B), sexually, with a part of his body or anything else, where B does not consent to the penetration, and A does not reasonably believe that B consents. This offence introduced in

---

[295] See also Husak, n 21, Ch 9. Note, however, that in *P* [2009] EWCA Crim 1100 the court observed that 'Any counsel accordingly advising a defendant facing a charge of rape, whose instructions are that he had a genuine belief in consent, will have to advise him as to the likelihood of a jury nonetheless concluding that in the circumstances the belief was unreasonable.'

[296] *Setting the Boundaries*, 20, para 2.10.9.   [297] See Temkin and Ashworth [2004] Crim LR 328, 339.

[298] [2006] EWCA Crim 1498.   [299] At [12]. See also *Saad* [2009] EWCA Crim 2781.

[300] [2006] EWCA Crim 2626.

the 2003 Act carries a maximum life sentence. It is designed to reflect the seriousness of non-consensual penetration with objects other than the penis. Acts of penetration with bottles, knives, fingers, etc are caught by s 2. Such acts would have been charged as indecent assault under the old law, and thus lacked a sufficiently accurate or stigmatizing label and sentencing power.[301] The Court of Appeal has made clear that long sentences may be appropriate for some acts of digital penetration.[302] The offence has proved useful where B cannot recall, could not tell or lacks the capacity to tell whether the penetration was by a penis or other object.[303]

17.3.2.1 Actus reus

Penetration is discussed earlier. Unlike rape, the penetration need not be by a penis; where it is, the charge ought to be under s 1. Where there is doubt as to with what the complainant was penetrated the charge should be under s 2. The offence can be committed by a person of either sex on a person of either sex. The act of penetration is regarded as continuing until withdrawal. Since the degree of penetration need only be slight, and 'vagina' includes 'vulva',[304] oral sex is caught by s 2. An allegation that A penetrated B's vagina or anus is not an allegation of two offences.[305] The requirement that the penetration is 'sexual' (as discussed earlier) excludes from the scope of the offence medical examinations, intimate body searches, etc. If the prosecution cannot establish the 'sexual' element, there is no actus reus, and the offence is not committed even if the complainant is not consenting to the penetration. Such acts should be charged as offences against the person.

The absence of consent is an element of the actus reus and if B has consented to the acts of penetration with any form of object, provided A's intention is only to perform acts amounting to a battery, his penetration of B will not render him liable for an offence of violence if injury is in fact caused. Where the act of penetration is intended or likely to cause actual bodily harm or worse and is performed for a sexual purpose, A may be liable for an offence against the person, even if B consents.[306]

17.3.2.2 Mens rea

The penetration must be intentional; there is no crime of reckless sexual penetration.[307] However, following *Heard*,[308] the voluntarily intoxicated defendant cannot rely on his intoxicated state to support his claim that his penetration of V with an object/part of his body was not intentional. Such circumstances are, however, unlikely to be commonplace. The mens rea regarding consent is determined in accordance with the principles discussed at p 823. Sections 75 and 76 relating to presumptions on consent apply.

It is now clear, following the approach in section 3 below, that there is no element of mens rea as to the 'sexual' nature of the penetration: *AG's Ref (No 1 of 2020)*.[309] As a matter of principle, it would be desirable for each element of the actus reus to have a corresponding element of mens rea. In the absence of any requirement to prove that A realised or intended

---

[301] A maximum ten years.   [302] *Corran* [2005] EWCA Crim 192.

[303] See eg *Minshull* [2004] EWCA 2673 (B severely disabled); and *Lyddaman* [2006] EWCA Crim 383.

[304] Section 79.

[305] *P* [2010] EWCA Crim 164, following *K* [2008] EWCA Crim 1923 in relation to rape.

[306] See *Meachen* [2006] EWCA Crim 2414, discussed at p 710. Cf P Murphy, 'Flogging Live Complainants and Dead Horses: We May No Longer Need to be in Bondage to *Brown*' [2011] Crim LR 758.

[307] See *Phillips* [2008] EWCA Crim 2830 where A claimed to have digitally penetrated B while he, A, was asleep.

[308] [2007] EWCA Crim 125.

[309] [2020] EWCA Crim 1665.

the conduct was sexual there is no opportunity for A to claim, for example, that his penetration of B's vagina with an object such as a bottle was motivated solely by a desire to cause injury, being performed with a violent and not a sexual intent. It was always doubtful that such a plea would be successful, and A would, in any event, have thereby admitted an offence against the person.[310] There are bizarre instances of penetrative conduct that would appear to be motivated by such non-sexual motives.[311] It may be that penetrative acts would be dealt with, additionally, as offences against the person where performed as acts of torture.[312]

17.3.3 Sexual assault: s 3

Under the law prior to the 2003 Act there were separate offences of 'indecent assault', protecting males and females.[313] For the want of anything more specific, these offences dealt with all non-consensual conduct: non-penile penetrations of the vagina and anus, oral sex; the merest touching in an indecent manner; and even technical assaults (where A caused B to apprehend immediate unlawful force on her body) in circumstances of indecency. The label on conviction did not differentiate between the vastly different forms of conduct and their disparate gravity.[314] Many of the activities dealt with previously as indecent assaults would now be rape (oral sex) or s 2 (most commonly digital penetration of the vagina).

The 2003 Act introduces a much wider offence with greater ambiguity stemming from the broad definition of the central elements of 'sexual' and 'touching'.

A commits an offence if he intentionally touches another person (B), sexually, and B does not consent to the touching, and A does not reasonably believe that B consents. The maximum sentence of imprisonment is ten years on indictment; and six months summarily.

17.3.3.1 Actus reus

The elements of 'sexual' and 'touching' have been discussed previously. In combination, the terms render the offence very broad indeed. There is no element of hostility required; a kiss could be sufficient provided it is regarded as sexual, as could A stroking B's clothing without her awareness. Although described as 'sexual assault' there is no need for a technical assault or battery; a touching is what is needed. As such, conduct that constitutes a psychic assault will not satisfy the actus reus.[315] If the touching is in non-sexual circumstances there is no sexual offence—for example, where a police officer pats down a suspect, or a rugby player grabs the testicles of an opponent in the scrum. If the complainant is not consenting to such touching the conduct should be charged, if at all, as an offence against the person.

The sexual touching must be proved to be without consent. The presumptions in ss 75 and 76 (discussed earlier) apply. Given the breadth of the activity covered, there is a potential for problems with the conclusive presumptions. What, for example, of Dr A who tells B, accurately, that a breast examination is necessary, but who also nurses a secret sexual purpose in performing it? Is there a deception as to 'purpose'?[316]

---

[310] See *Hill* [2006] EWCA Crim 2575—penetration with fingers in forceful manner. OAPA 1861, s 18.

[311] In *C* [2001] 1 Cr App R (S) 533, D paid a prostitute to fellate him and surreptitiously inserted live maggots into her vagina while she did so.

[312] In *Aydin v Turkey* (1997) 25 EHRR 251 it was recognized that rape by a State official could constitute torture.

[313] Sections 14 and 15 of the Act.

[314] Temkin (2000) 150 NLJ 1169, 1170 described them as 'mindless' (meaning that they did not describe the essence of the wrongdoing, particularly in serious cases).

[315] cf *Rolfe* (1952) Cr App R 4, n 231.   [316] See p 814.

17.3.3.2 Mens rea

The touching must be intentional. Applying the established interpretation of *Majewski*, on a charge such as that under s 3 with the requirement of an 'intentional' touching, it was at least arguable that the crime is one of specific intent.[317] However, following the decision in *Heard*, the offence should be treated as one of basic intent: it is no excuse for A to rely on his voluntary intoxication as an excuse that he did not intend to touch the complainant in a sexual manner. As noted,[318] on its facts, *Heard* should never have given rise to problems. A had, while drunk, exposed his penis and rubbed it against the thigh of a police officer, B. A's plea was that he had no recollection of the incident. That is never a basis for a plea of intoxication and that should have been the end of the matter. However, A relied on his voluntary intoxication as negating his mens rea of an intention to touch for the purposes of s 3(1)(a). The trial judge ruled that the intentional touching element of the offence required proof of a basic intent, and that it followed that voluntary intoxication was not a defence. The Court of Appeal concluded that A could not rely on that voluntary intoxication to negative mens rea. The full implications are considered in Ch 9. On policy grounds, the court was clearly entitled to assume that Parliament had not intended to change the law (although it should be noted that under the pre-2003 law, the offence of indecent assault was not always a basic intent crime).

A claim that a touching was not intended to be 'sexual', but rather was an act of pure violence could in some circumstances have seemed a more plausible plea, certainly more so than in circumstances of penetration under s 2 discussed previously. However, it is now clear that there is no mens rea required as to the sexual nature of the touching: *AG's Ref (No 1 of 2020)*.[319]

17.3.4 Intentionally causing someone to engage in sexual activity: s 4

A commits an offence if he intentionally causes another person (B) to engage in an activity, the activity is sexual, B does not consent to engaging in the activity and A does not reasonably believe that B consents.

This was an entirely new and potentially very useful offence, which has as one of its purposes criminalizing the actions of women who compel or procure men to penetrate them. Under the old law this conduct would have been prosecuted as indecent assault only. Examples of other types of conduct caught by this offence would include requiring a person to masturbate him/herself[320] or to masturbate another person.[321] It is an extremely broad offence and could also include A who, for example, causes B to act as a sex worker.

Aggravated versions of the offence (which attract a maximum of life imprisonment rather than the standard maximum ten years on indictment/six months summarily) are created by subs (4). These involve penetration of B's anus or vagina; penetration of B's mouth with a person's penis; penetration of a person's anus or vagina by B with his body or otherwise; or penetration of a person's mouth with B's penis. Applying *Courtie*,[322] there are separate offences created and this must be reflected in the indictment.

---

[317] R Card, *Sexual Offences: The New Law* (2003) para 1.31; Rook and Ward, *Sexual Offences: Law and Practice*, para 2.82.

[318] [2007] EWCA Crim 125. See p 337.

[319] [2020] EWCA Crim 1665.

[320] As in *Sargeant* [1997] Crim LR 50; see *Devonald* [2008] EWCA Crim 527, p 812.

[321] See *Basherdost* [2009] EWCA Crim 2883 where A forced B and C to engage in sex together while he filmed them.

[322] [1984] AC 463.

17.3.4.1 Actus reus

The offence can be committed by words alone, and there is no explicit requirement that A is present when B engages in the activity nor that A participate in the activity. It is commonly prosecuted where A causes B to perform sex acts on camera.[323] The offence could also involve a third party, who might also be a victim if neither the third party nor B consents.[324] However, this is not a preliminary offence: the sexual activity must take place for A to be guilty. Although A must 'cause' the action, following orthodox principles of causation[325] it appears to be sufficient for A to be 'a' cause of the sexual activity without being the 'sole' cause. It is doubtful that an omission to prevent sexual activity occurring is a sufficient actus reus.[326]

The presumptions regarding consent in ss 75 and 76 (discussed earlier) apply.

17.3.4.2 Mens rea

As with rape, discussed previously, the reasonableness of belief is determined by reference to 'all the circumstances' including 'any steps A has taken to ascertain B's consent'.

There is a requirement of 'intention', which in this context would apparently include oblique intention—foresight by A that B's engaging in the sexual activity is a virtually certain consequence of A's action, even though it might not be his 'direct intention'.[327]

Despite the requirement of intention to cause B to engage in the activity, following *Heard*, s 4 creates a basic intent offence. A who in a voluntarily intoxicated state jokingly encourages B to strip might claim that there was no such intent, but drunken intent is still intent.

17.4 Offences against children under 13 (ss 5–8)

The offences in ss 5 to 8[328] are very similar to those in ss 1 to 4, except that they relate only to offences against children under 13, and there is no requirement to prove the absence of consent.

- Section 5 criminalizes penile penetration of the vagina, anus or mouth of a child under 13.
- Section 6 criminalizes sexual penetration of the vagina or anus of a child under 13.
- Section 7 criminalizes sexual touching of a child under 13.
- Section 8 criminalizes causing or inciting a child under 13 to engage in sexual conduct.

Under the old law a child under 16 could not consent to indecent assault, but could consent to sexual intercourse.[329] Determining whether a child consented to sexual intercourse involved an assessment of her understanding of the activity.[330] Consent is no longer an issue.

---

[323] eg *A* [2006] EWCA Crim 2103; *Hinton-Smith* [2005] EWCA Crim 2575. Note the new offence introduced by s 67 of the Serious Crime Act 2015 where the sexual communication is to someone under 16.

[324] As in *Basherdost* [2008] EWCA Crim 2883.   [325] Discussed in Ch 2.

[326] See *Clarkson and Carroll* [1971] 3 All ER 344. Card, *Sexual Offences*, n 318.   [327] See Ch 3, p 45.

[328] See generally F Bennion, 'Criminalizing Children under the Sexual Offences Bill' (2003) 167 JP 784; JR Spencer, 'Child and Family Offences' [2004] Crim LR 347; L Hoyano and C Keenan, *Child Abuse: Law and Policy* (2007) 192–215 dealing with comparative materials. For sentencing guidance, see *Corran* [2005] EWCA Crim 192. See also L James, 'Children Who Commit Sex Offences' (2007) Howard Jnl 493. The Criminal Justice and Immigration Act 2008 extends the territorial reach of a number of offences under the Act in relation to children: s 72 of the SOA 2003 as substituted by s 72 of the 2008 Act.

[329] It was arguable that since all acts of intercourse must include an indecent assault, the law was irremediably incoherent.

[330] *Howard* [1966] 1 WLR 13.

This shift proved to be very controversial as the legislation progressed through Parliament. The commendable underlying policy of the offences is to protect the child from the 'predatory' older offender, and to guard against exploitation of young people, but the breadth of the offences raises a number of problems.

First, the legislation makes no attempt to distinguish between exploitative sexual activity against a child under 13 (whether by an older individual or not) and that of fully informed consensual sexual experimentation between children under that age.

Secondly, denying the relevance of the factual consent of the under-13-year-old clashes with the law's willingness to accept their capacity to consent to, for example, invasive medical procedures. The Home Secretary stated in a press release on the Act receiving Royal Assent that there would be no prosecution for sexual activity between children under the age of 16 where the activity is genuinely consensual. This rather begs the question why the Act is not drafted so as to include a requirement of an absence of consent.[331]

Thirdly, this gave rise to challenges under the ECHR. In the controversial case of G,[332] the defendant who was aged 15, pleaded guilty to rape of a child under 13 (s 5). G's basis of plea was that V consented and that he reasonably believed her to be older than 13, because she had so informed him. One ground of appeal was that the offence was incompatible with Art 8 since G claimed he should have been charged under ss 9 and 13 (sexual activity with a child under 16), if at all. The charge and conviction under s 5 (sex with child under 13) breached his right to respect for private life by labelling him publicly as a child rapist, subjecting him to a maximum penalty of life imprisonment and attracting sexual offender notification requirements.[333] Compliance with the proportionality requirement in Art 8 would, he argued, mean that no prosecution should ensue;[334] or prosecution should be under ss 9 and 13, with its lower maximum penalty of five years and limited notification requirements. The House of Lords (Lords Hope and Carswell dissenting) held that s 5 was compatible with Art 8. Convicting G of rape contrary to s 5 even in circumstances where the agreed basis of plea established that his offence fell properly within the ambit of s 13 did not infringe Art 8. The issue drew some striking comments from the Law Lords.[335] Baroness Hale doubted whether Art 8 was engaged at all but, if it was, held that there was no breach.[336] Similarly, Lord Mance accepted that Art 8 might be engaged, but that prosecution was justified to protect children. In the minority, Lord Hope concluded that the prosecution ought not to have pursued a s 5 conviction once G's basis of plea was accepted. His lordship did not go as far as to say that it was disproportionate to use s 5 even in cases where children had mutually agreed to have sex. Lord Carswell agreed, deprecating the 'crude generalisation' involved in using the term 'statutory rape'.[337] In G v UK,[338] the ECtHR accepted that Art 8 was engaged by G's conviction. Despite the fact the court accepted that the Member States' margin of appreciation is narrow where intimate aspects of private life are concerned, G's application

---

[331] See the Home Office, *The Sexual Offences Act 2003: A Stocktake of the Effectiveness of the Act since its Implementation* (2006) 9.

[332] [2008] UKHL 37, [2008] Crim LR 818 with a valuable commentary by Andrew Ashworth.

[333] See now the decision of the Supreme Court in *R (F) v Secretary of State for the Home Department* [2010] UKSC 17.

[334] The government had given an assurance that consensual sexual activity between minors would not inevitably be prosecuted, but relied on prosecutorial discretion to achieve the correct balance, and this was not a satisfactory protection for rights. Cf the position in Ireland: *CC v Ireland* [2006] IESC 33 (Irish Supreme Court) and C O'Sullivan, 'Protecting Young People from Themselves' (2009) Dublin Uni LJ 386.

[335] Lord Hoffmann opined that 'This case is another example of the regrettable tendency to try to convert the whole system of criminal justice into questions of human rights', at [10]. Lord Hoffmann went as far as to suggest that Convention rights have nothing to do with prosecutorial policy. This was denied by Lord Hope at [34]. See the discussion by R Buxton, 'Private Life and the English Judges' (2009) 29 OJLS 413.

[336] At [54].   [337] At [60].   [338] (2011) 53 EHRR SE25.

was declared inadmissible on the basis that Art 8(2) was satisfied, given the powerful countervailing interests in protecting young people from premature sexual activity, exploitation and abuse.[339]

There is no additional restraint on prosecution such as a requirement for the DPP's prior consent. In R,[340] the Administrative Court doubted whether criminal prosecution was always appropriate where the conduct is less serious conduct between children; that case concerned two children with learning disabilities with A touching B's breast over her clothes. In R (S) v DPP,[341] the prosecutor did abandon the s 5 charge against a boy of 15 in favour of proceeding under s 13 when it appeared that the conduct had been consensual. Challenges to such decisions to prosecute will be rare: R (Tolhurst) v CPS.[342]

The final general point to note is that the breadth of the new offences means that in cases of consensual sexual activity between 12-year-olds they will both commit an offence—for example, as penetrator (s 5) and penetrated (s 9). In this context, the drafting undermines the principle in Tyrrell[343] whereby a child 'victim' could not be convicted as a participant in the offence. The gloss that the Supreme Court placed on the Tyrrell principle in Gnango[344] adds an extra layer of difficulty. The Supreme Court held that the 'victim rule' is only applicable when the offence in question is one that is intended to protect an identified class. This suggests that in the case of consensual sexual activity between 12-year-olds, neither ought to be prosecuted, given that they are both within the class that the offences are intended to protect, namely children. It remains to be seen how the Supreme Court's reformulation of the principle in Tyrrell will impact upon these offences. As noted, challenges under Art 8 of the ECHR were mounted by consenting 15-year-olds.[345]

The degree of overlap of ss 9 to 10 and s 13 (dealing with children under 16) with ss 5 to 8 is notable. For example, a person guilty of s 5 could be guilty of s 9 or s 13 also ('touching' including penetration). The sections have considerable sentencing discrepancy—s 5 carries a maximum of life, s 9 (over 18s) a maximum 14 years, s 13 (under 18s) a maximum five years on indictment/six months if summary.

In relation to an adult defendant committing offences under ss 5 to 8, the CPS guidance[346] is that 'a prosecution will usually take place unless there are public interest factors tending against prosecution which clearly outweigh those tending in favour'. In relation to child defendants, the CPS emphasizes that the 'overriding public concern is to protect children. It was not Parliament's intention to punish children unnecessarily or for the criminal law to intervene where it is wholly inappropriate.'[347] Prosecutors are to have regard to various factors including the age and understanding of the offender, the complainant's willingness to enter into the sexual activity, the parties' emotional and physical development and

---

[339] As Ashworth points out in his commentary, what both the ECtHR and the House of Lords failed to discuss was the impact of this conviction on someone who was himself a child. Ashworth states that the real issue is whether a decision to prosecute a *child* for an offence under s 5 is necessary in a democratic society, given the availability of the lesser alternative in s 9. See [2012] Crim LR 47.

[340] [2007] EWHC 1842 (Admin).   [341] [2006] EWHC 2231 (Admin).

[342] [2008] EWHC 2976 (Admin).

[343] [1894] 1 QB 710. For a catalogue of the circumstances in which the Act ignores the Tyrrell principle, see M Bohlander, 'The Sexual Offences Act 2003 and the Tyrrell Principle Criminalising Victims' [2005] Crim LR 703.

[344] [2011] UKSC 59.

[345] See G [2008] UKHL 37; G v UK (2011) 53 EHRR SE25, n 338. Cf the view in E v DPP [2005] EWHC 147 (Admin), in which it was held that Art 8 was not infringed by s 6 of the 2003 Act.

[346] See www.cps.gov.uk/legal-guidance/rape-and-sexual-offences-overview-and-index-2020-updated-guidance.

[347] The Guidance emphasizes the need to gather as much information as possible from sources, such as the police, and any professionals assisting those agencies about the defendant's home circumstances and the circumstances surrounding the alleged offence, as well as any information known about the complainant.

the nature of the acts. This may include whether the offender has been subjected to any exploitation, coercion, threat, deception, grooming or manipulation by another which has led him or her to commit the offence. The relative ages of the parties are also important.[348]

It is recognized that 'it is not in the public interest to prosecute children who are of the same or similar age and understanding that engage in sexual activity, where the activity is truly consensual for both parties and there are no aggravating features, such as coercion or corruption'. The abolition of the *doli incapax* defence renders the position more strict for young children.[349]

17.4.1 Rape of a child under 13: s 5

There had been much discussion of the merits of a 'statutory rape' offence, commonly found in the United States, and s 5 introduces one: a person commits an offence if he intentionally penetrates the vagina, anus or mouth of another person with his penis, and the other person is under 13.

As noted earlier, the Sexual Offences Review was anxious for the offence of rape to continue to reflect everyday conceptions of that term, hence the requirement of penile penetration. In this instance, the unique stigma of 'rape' has been applied to conduct which seems to be lacking the most important aspect of the everyday conception of the offence—an absence of consent. The maximum sentence is one of life imprisonment. Given that it is rape, it will be more difficult for the CPS to declare that it is not in the public interest to prosecute, particularly in the face of pressure from the complainant's parents.[350]

17.4.1.1 Actus reus

Each element of the actus reus—penetration, with a penis, of the vagina, anus or mouth—has already been discussed in the section on rape. The additional element of the actus reus is that B is aged under 13. Given the significance of B's age, it is crucial that this element is proved strictly via the usual mechanisms. The defendant may be of any age, although criminal liability as an offender arises at the age of ten.[351] It has already been noted that this is a very broad offence: B, aged 12, who willingly performs oral sex on her 12-year-old boyfriend thereby renders him a rapist (and she arguably commits offences under ss 7 and 9). The absence of any requirement of consent means that it is less likely that a complainant will face the ordeal of giving evidence.

17.4.1.2 Mens rea

Penetration must be intentional, as discussed earlier. There is no opportunity for a plea of consent, and thus no plea of mistaken belief as to consent, however reasonable.[352] Similarly, there is no scope for a plea of mistake, however reasonable, as to the age of the complainant.

---

[348] In *G* [2008] UKHL 37, Lord Hope concludes that 'The context suggests however that a child under 18 ought not to be prosecuted under section 5 for performing a sexual act with a child under 13 of the kind to which that section applies unless the circumstances are such as to indicate that it plainly was an offence of such gravity that prosecution under section 13 would not be appropriate. It suggests that a child under 18 (and more especially a child as young as 15) should not be prosecuted under section 5 (rape of a child under 13) if the complainer says that he or she consented to sexual intercourse.' At [23]. (See also Baroness Hale at [48].)

[349] See *JTB* [2009] UKHL 20, and see Ch 10. The defence remains important in some historic cases: *PF* [2017] EWCA Crim 983.

[350] See HC Standing Committee B, 11 Sept 2003, col 107 (Mr Malins). In *G* [2008] UKHL 37, Lord Hope noted that 'The creation of an offence of this kind, carrying the stigma and maximum sentence of life as it does, applicable as it is to child defendants places a "heavy responsibility" on the prosecuting authorities, where both parties are of a similar young age, to distinguish the consensual experimentation from the exploitative', at [14].

[351] See Ch 10 on defences.   [352] See the discussion in Ch 5.

In G,[353] G, who was aged 15, pleaded guilty to rape of a child under 13, where B consented and he reasonably believed her to be older than 13, because she had so informed him. The House of Lords confirmed that s 5 creates an offence of strict liability; belief in consent or the age of the victim is irrelevant.[354] The presumption of mens rea is negatived by necessary implication, arising from the contrast of the express references to reasonable belief that a child was over 16, in other sections—s 9 of the 2003 Act—and the absence of any such reference in relation to children under 13. This was Parliament's 'deliberate choice'.[355] The consequence is, as Lord Hoffmann put it:

The policy of the legislation is to protect children. If you have sex with someone who is on any view a child or young person, you take your chance on exactly how old they are.[356]

The House of Lords also confirmed that s 5 as a strict liability offence is compatible with Art 6.[357] G sought to argue before the ECtHR that his conviction infringed Art 6. The complaint was, however, declared inadmissible. It was held that Parliament's decision not to make available a defence based on reasonable belief that the complainant was aged 13 or over did not give rise to an issue under Art 6(1) or (2).[358]

17.4.1.3 Defences for secondary liability

Concern was expressed in Parliament as to the potential for such broad offences to criminalize the actions of teachers and health-care workers who advise young people about sex education and safe sexual practices in general. For example, there was concern that the doctor who provided contraceptives to the 12-year-old girl to protect her in her consensual sexual acts with her partner would be aiding and abetting her 'rape'. To meet this difficulty, s 73 of the Act provides that there is no liability for aiding and abetting or counselling if the purpose of the actor is to protect the child from sexually transmitted diseases or pregnancy or to protect physical safety or promote emotional well-being, unless the actor's purpose is to gain sexual gratification or to cause or encourage the relevant sexual act.

17.4.2 Assault of a child under 13 by penetration: s 6

It is an offence for a person intentionally to penetrate the vagina or anus of a person under 13 with a part of the body or anything else where that penetration is sexual.

This is identical to that in s 2, except that there is no requirement that the complainant is not consenting. Again, there is no scope for a plea of mistaken belief in consent or mistaken reasonable beliefs as to the age of the victim. This is a very broad offence which criminalizes consensual sexual (eg digital) penetration between 12-year-olds. As with the offence under s 5, there is no liability for aiding and abetting or counselling if the purpose of the assistance is to protect the child unless the actor's purpose is to gain sexual gratification or to cause or encourage the relevant sexual act.[359] Section 6 is triable on indictment only and carries a maximum sentence of life imprisonment.

17.4.3 Sexual assault of a child: s 7

It is an offence intentionally to touch a person under 13, where that touching is sexual. This offence is identical to that in s 3 (discussed earlier), except that there is no requirement that the complainant is not consenting. There is no scope for a plea of mistaken belief in consent

---

[353] [2008] UKHL 37.

[354] The Supreme Court in *Brown* [2013] UKSC 43 held that the same analysis applied to the equivalent offences in Northern Ireland.

[355] Lord Hope at [21].   [356] At [3]. (See also Baroness Hale at [45]–[48].)

[357] Art 6 is concerned with procedural protection not the substantive law. (See Lord Hope at [27].) See Ch 5.

[358] (2011) 53 EHRR SE25, [2012] Crim LR 47.   [359] Section 73.

or mistaken reasonable belief as to the age of the victim. This is an excessively broad offence which criminalizes consensual kissing between 12-year-olds.[360] It also applies, of course, where the adult offender preys on children.[361] The defence applicable to abetting or counselling applies as under ss 5 and 6.[362]

17.4.4 Causing or inciting a child under 13 to engage in sexual activity: s 8

It is an offence intentionally to cause a person under 13 to engage in an activity, which is sexual. It is also an offence intentionally[363] to incite a person under 13 to engage in a sexual activity. These are broader than the offence under s 4 discussed earlier. Separate offences carrying a maximum of life imprisonment (rather than the standard 14 years on indictment/six months summarily) are created under s 4(4) if the activity involves causing or inciting:

(a) penetration of B's anus or vagina;

(b) penetration of B's mouth with a person's penis;

(c) penetration of a person's anus or vagina by B; or

(d) penetration of a person's mouth with B's penis.

17.4.4.1 Actus reus

The offence can be committed by *causing* B to engage in sexual activity, in which case it is identical to that under s 4 except that there is no requirement that B is not consenting. A, who persuades his 12-year-old girlfriend to touch herself sexually, commits the actus reus of this offence.

In addition, there is an offence of 'incitement' of B. It is submitted that the word incitement should carry its technical legal meaning.[364] The inclusion of a specific offence of incitement enables a prosecution where the child incited would not herself commit an offence (and would not be liable under a common law charge of incitement). This offence is much broader and does not require that any sexual activity occurs. It covers the case where A, the friend of B, aged 12, encourages B to have oral sex with B's boyfriend C. The Court of Appeal has taken a very wide interpretation of s 8 and of the concept of incitement in this context. In *Walker*,[365] the Court of Appeal rightly held that s 8 created two offences:[366] (a) intentionally causing and (b) intentionally inciting a child under 13 to engage in sexual activity. The allegation was centred on the concept of incitement and the court held that it was not a necessary ingredient for incitement of sexual activity that A had intended that sexual activity would take place. So, when A said over the phone to a child he was watching in a nearby public telephone booth, 'show us your fanny' there was no need for proof that he ever intended her to do anything sexual. But how can there ever be an incitement without intention from A that the act by B will occur? The Court of Appeal would no doubt defend the interpretation on the basis that the wrong targeted by the offence is making that kind of sexual suggestion to a child irrespective of whether there is any intent or likelihood of it influencing

---

[360] Section 7 is triable either way. The maximum sentence is 14 years on indictment; six months summarily.
[361] See for an unusual example *PE* [2007] EWCA Crim 231 where A, a scout leader, tied up young boys—clothed—and video-recorded the incidents. A derived sexual gratification from the acts.
[362] Section 73.   [363] See also *Rae* [2013] EWCA Crim 2056.
[364] See Ch 11.   [365] [2006] EWCA Crim 1907.   [366] See *Grout* [2011] EWCA Crim 299.

the child. The new offence of sending sexual messages to children, in s 67 of the Serious Crime Act 2015, will meet that mischief more directly.

The Court of Appeal took an equally broad interpretation of the s 8 offence in *Jones*. The defendant wrote graffiti on train and station toilets seeking girls aged eight to 13 for sex in return for payment. He gave a mobile telephone number for them to contact. Following a complaint by a journalist, the police began an undercover operation using an officer pretending to be aged 12. The defendant was charged with attempting to incite her to sexual activity.

At trial the defendant alleged that the charge disclosed no offence known to law, because the defendant did not intend to incite any actual person under the age of 13 (the officer being older) and therefore could not have had the requisite intent. He was convicted. The Court of Appeal held that s 8 of the 2003 Act did not require incitement of an identified or identifiable child.[367] The criminality at which the offence was directed was the incitement. It mattered not that this was directed at a particular child, a very large group of children or whether they could be identified or not. There was no significance in the use of the term 'another' in s 8 as opposed to 'any other'; they meant the same. Therefore, the offence could have been charged without identifying a particular person, and it could not be said that the police created the offence. A who leaves messages on a children's website[368] or scribbled on the walls of a children's play area inciting sex commits the s 8 offence. Whilst this may seem like a desirable result in terms of protection of under-13s, it presents problems. If it is unnecessary for A to be targeting the message at a particular individual, whenever A sends a message *capable* of being read by under-13s, the charges can now be brought under s 8. In other words, unless A targets a child over 13, he will always be at risk of prosecution for the more serious s 8 offence. What of A who leaves a message on a blog: 'sex is great: I recommend trying it with your first girlfriend/boyfriend'? This might have been intended only for consumption by older children, but, assuming it amounts to a sufficient encouragement to constitute incitement, it is now caught by s 8. Following G, liability is strict. The charge under s 10 discussed later allows A an excuse if he has a reasonable belief that the person is 16 or over (unless V is under 13). In cases of untargeted messages such as the blog example earlier, A will be denied the opportunity to rely on that excuse because he cannot know the age of those who might read his message.

The offence is used where A incites B to have sex with him.[369] Unlike ss 5 to 7, there is no defence for 'abetting or counselling' to protect the child.[370] Thus, teacher A, approached by B, 12, who asks whether she should engage in full sex with her boyfriend X as he would like, commits the offence if A incites her by suggesting that since she and X are only 12 they should stick to other intimate activities short of sex (even perhaps just kissing). The offence applies where A causes or incites sexual activity abroad (see p 858).[371]

---

[367] The defendant's acts were more than merely preparatory and done with the intention of committing the offence. The fact that commission of the actual offence was on the true facts impossible because the police substituted an adult for a child did not mean that there was a defence in law to the charge. That is uncontroversial.

[368] ie many of the offences are by text or social media, see *Butcher* [2009] EWCA Crim 1458.

[369] eg *A* [2006] EWCA Crim 2103; *Hinton-Smith* [2005] EWCA Crim 2575, or even to cause B to show him her bra strap: *Grout* [2011] EWCA Crim 299.

[370] Section 73.

[371] See eg *Charnley* [2010] All ER (D) 127 (Jun). A had used the internet to procure and watch the rape of children in the Philippines.

17.5 Sexual offences against children aged 13 to 15

The legal age of consent remains at 16.[372] Under the pre 2003 law the protection afforded to children under 16 years included specific offences which had been incrementally amended and lacked coherence.

The 2003 Act created a series of specific offences targeting a wider range of sexual activity with children under 16. These reflect the Act's stated policy of protecting children from sexual exploitation. There is no time limit on prosecution as there was under some of the 1956 Act offences, which reflects the growing awareness of frequent delays in disclosing childhood sexual abuse.[373]

Widespread public concern that the Act criminalized consensual sexual activity between children produced ministerial assurances that the use of these offences in prosecuting children will be limited:

> The creation of such broad ranging offences raises a number of difficulties. There are no convictions at present [for kissing]. The guidelines [for the CPS] will be strong and I do not think that there will be prosecutions in the future for less serious consensual activity between children.[374]

Parliament expressly rejected the approach in other jurisdictions whereby liability for consensual sexual activity with those under 16 would be criminal only where one of the parties was older than the other by a specified amount—for example, two years as in Canada.[375] One of the principal reasons for rejection was the recognition that many offences against children are committed by children.[376]

17.5.1 Sexual activity with a child: s 9

It is an offence intentionally to touch a person, B, where that touching is sexual and either:

(1) B is under 16 and A does not reasonably believe that B is 16 or over; or

(2) B is under 13.

The offence under s 9 can be committed by a person aged 18 or over.[377] The maximum sentence is 14 years' imprisonment. Sexual touching in these circumstances committed by offenders below 18 is criminalized in identical terms by s 13.[378]

A separate offence[379] is created by subs (2) where the touching involves (a) penetration of B's anus or vagina, (b) penetration of B's mouth with a person's penis, (c) penetration of a person's anus or vagina by B, or (d) penetration of a person's mouth with B's penis. This offence carries a maximum penalty of 14 years' imprisonment and is triable on indictment only.

---

[372] *Setting the Boundaries*, recommended that age of consent remain at 16—para 3.5.7 (recommendation no 17); the age of consent is lower in most other European countries—para 3.9.9. For discussion of the age of consent and its purpose, see A Gillespie and S Ost, 'The "Higher" Age of Consent and the Concept of Sexual Exploitation' in A Reed and M Bohlander (eds), *Consent—Domestic and Comparative Perspectives* (2017). Somewhat anomalously, although an individual is legally capable of consenting to sex once they reach the age of 16, they cannot consent to being photographed naked. By virtue of s 1 of the Protection of Children Act 1978, it is an offence to make an indecent photograph of someone under the age of 18. See *M* [2011] EWCA Crim 2752, [2012] Crim LR 789.

[373] See the problems created by *J* [2004] UKHL 42; *Cottrell* [2007] EWCA Crim 2016; and *K* [2009] EWCA Crim 2117.

[374] See HC, 3 Nov 2003, col 622 (Paul Goggins).   [375] Criminal Code 1985, s 150.1.

[376] E Lovell, *Children and Young People who Display Sexually Harmful Behaviour* (2002) NSPCC.

[377] On the difficulties in charging when it is unclear whether B is under 13 and therefore whether the offence should be charged under s 9 or eg s 8, see *Rae* [2013] EWCA Crim 2056.

[378] The sentence is six months' imprisonment summarily, five years on indictment: s 13.

[379] See earlier in chapter.

17.5.1.1 Actus reus

The elements of 'touching' and 'sexual' are discussed earlier in the chapter. There is no requirement that B is not consenting. A, 18, kissing/touching his consenting 15-year-old girlfriend is guilty if his conduct is 'sexual touching' which is to be decided by the jury. Passionate embracing and kissing suffices.[380] The offence can, of course, be committed by women on young boys.[381]

17.5.1.2 Mens rea

The touching must be intentional as discussed previously in relation to s 3. If B is under 13 there is no other element of mens rea. A's pleas of honest (and reasonable) belief in consent or age are irrelevant. Liability is strict.[382] If B is under the age of 16, but over the age of 13, A must also be proved not to have had a reasonable belief that B was aged over 16.[383] Belief in consent remains irrelevant in such a case.

17.5.1.3 Defences

As with ss 5 to 7, the defence under s 73 applies to aiding and abetting or counselling for the child's protection. A marriage defence was deleted in the final stages of the Bill.

17.5.2 Causing or inciting a child to engage in sexual activity: s 10

It is an offence intentionally to cause and an offence intentionally to incite a person under 16, B, to engage in a sexual activity, if either B is under 16 and A does not reasonably believe that B is 16 or over, or B is under 13.[384]

A separate offence is created by s 10(2) for penetrative touching (as in s 9 discussed earlier). That offence carries a maximum penalty of 14 years and is triable on indictment only. These offences can be committed by a person under the age of 18, in which case the sentence is one of six months summarily, five years on indictment: s 13. These are extremely broad offences, technically capable of criminalizing much schoolyard banter. Section 10 is commonly used to prosecute the sender of explicit text messages by mobile phone.[385] It has also proved useful as an offence supporting that of 'grooming' under s 15.[386]

17.5.2.1 Actus reus

There are two offences: an act 'causing' B to engage, and any conduct 'inciting' B to engage in the activity. The relevant elements are discussed earlier in relation to s 8. The offences are very broad. A, 18, who begs his 15-year-old girlfriend to strip for him, commits an offence whether she declines or willingly assents. Examples of inciting sexual activity might

---

[380] *Lister* [2005] EWCA Crim 1903.

[381] See *Angela C* [2006] EWCA Crim 1781 (43-year-old having sex with 14-year-old boyfriend of her daughter) in which numerous cases of this nature are reviewed.

[382] This represents a direct reversal of the House of Lords' decisions in *DPP v B* [2000] AC 428 and *K* [2002] 1 AC 462.

[383] This is a more generous defence than the 'young man's defence' under the 1956 Act which was limited to cases where D faced his first charge of this nature and was under 24. See *Kirk and Russell* [2002] EWCA Crim 1580.

[384] See the unusual case of *B (Piara)* [2010] EWCA Crim 315 where a Bangladeshi-born mother who spoke no English arranged a 'marriage' by custom (but not recognized in law) between her 15-year-old daughter and a man in his late 30s who abused her sexually. The mother claimed not to know about the age of consent in England.

[385] See eg *Howell* [2007] EWCA Crim 1863. See eg *Morell* [2012] EWCA Crim 1410; *Brocklebank* [2013] EWCA Crim 1813. See now s 67 of the Serious Crime Act 2015.

[386] See A Gillespie, 'Indecent Images, Grooming and the Law' [2006] Crim LR 412.

include the conduct in *DPP v B* where the defendant invited the girl to give him 'a shiner' (perform oral sex on him). It includes A causing/inciting B to engage in sexual activity with a third party. Following the decision in *Walker*,[387] incitement is construed so broadly as to include circumstances in which A has no intention that the act will be carried out. Following *Jones*, where A has not targeted a specific child or age range, it will always be possible to prosecute him for the more serious offence under s 8.

The breadth of the actus reus in terms of causing or inciting leaves no room for the application of the defence under s 73.

17.5.2.2 Mens rea

A must 'intend' to cause or incite. It is submitted that in this context intention extends to oblique intention. There is no scope for a plea of consent. If B is under 13 there is no other element of mens rea. A's pleas of honest (and reasonable) belief in consent or age are irrelevant. Liability is strict. If B is aged between 13 and 15, A must also be proved not to have had a reasonable belief that B was aged over 16. Belief in consent remains irrelevant in such a case.

17.5.3 Engaging in sexual activity in the presence of a child: s 11

It is an offence intentionally to engage in sexual activity, when a person under 16, B, is present or is in a place from which A can be observed, where for the purpose of obtaining sexual gratification A engages in it knowing or believing that B is aware, or intending that B should be aware, that he is engaging in it, and either B is under 16 and A does not reasonably believe that B is 16 or over, or B is under 13.[388]

This was another entirely novel offence introduced in 2003. It covers much of the activity that might previously have been charged as gross indecency. It is triable either way. The maximum sentence is ten years' imprisonment on indictment/six months summarily. The offence can also be committed by a person under 18, for which the sentence is one of six months summarily, five years on indictment: s 13.

17.5.3.1 Actus reus

A must engage in a sexual[389] activity. B's position is far from clear. There is no requirement that B is actually witnessing the act, merely that B is present or in a position from which A can be observed. Since observation includes viewing directly or viewing an image,[390] the offence can be committed via a webcam.[391] To that extent, it is unclear what degree of physical proximity B must have to A. There is also no guidance as to whether the observation has to be in real time. There is no requirement that B is aware of the sexual activity, but B must actually be under 16; an undercover officer witnessing the event will not suffice. B's consent to being present or witnessing the events is irrelevant.

The offence is directed primarily at the defendant who masturbates in front of a child but it has the potential to criminalize a much wider range of conduct. Sexual thrill seekers ('doggers' as they are called) who have sex in public places might commit the offence by having sex in a park visible from a nearby children's play area.[392]

---

[387] See n 364.
[388] See eg *Chevron* [2005] All ER (D) 91 (Feb), masturbating in sight of 12-year-old on beach.
[389] As defined in s 78 and discussed at p 816.   [390] Section 79(4) and (5).
[391] See eg *W* [2013] EWCA Crim 1475.
[392] See *Vaiculevicius (Andrius)* [2013] EWCA Crim 185 where D was convicted of outraging public decency for sex in a park in the presence of children. See also the case of *WT* [2005] EWCA Crim 2448. Husband and wife convicted of taking photos of 14-year-old daughter naked and of having their nine-year-old daughter photograph them in acts of intercourse and in posed lewd positions.

17.5.3.2 Mens rea

There are four elements of mens rea: (a) A must intentionally engage in the sexual activity; (b) A must have as his 'purpose' (which is presumably narrower than his intention and is restricted to 'direct' intention)[393] to derive sexual[394] gratification from B's presence. It remains unclear whether A's *sole* purpose must be to derive sexual pleasure from B's watching. A and C will not commit the offence if their child, B, walks in on their sexual activity in the parental bedroom; (c) A must 'know or believe' that B is aware or 'intend' that B should be aware of the activity; (d) in the case of B being between 13 and 16, A must be shown not to have had a reasonable belief that B is 16 or over. In *B and L*,[395] the issue for the Court of Appeal was whether the person engaging in sexual activity had the necessary purpose of obtaining sexual gratification by simply engaging in sexual activity in the knowledge or belief that a child was present or observing and aware of the activity, or whether the sexual gratification had to be obtained *from* the knowledge or belief that the sexual activity was being carried out in the presence of, or under the observation of, a child. The court held that the prosecution must prove a link between 'for the purpose of obtaining sexual gratification' and the presence or observation of a child. It was therefore insufficient for the prosecution to prove that a child just happened to be present when sexual activity was taking place. The court concluded that the offence has the following elements: (a) A intentionally engages in an activity that is sexual; (b) in the presence or under the observation of a child (B); (c) A does so for the purpose of A's obtaining (some) sexual gratification from B's presence or observation; (d) A knew or believed that B was aware of the activity or intended that B should be aware of the activity; and (e) B was under 16 and A did not reasonably believe that B was 16 or over or B was under 13.

The gravamen of the offence is not that a child happens to be within sight of the defendants' sexual activity. The offence is much narrower than that. The prosecution must be able to prove that the defendants, in having sex in the presence of or under the observation of a child, had as their purpose sexual gratification.

17.5.4 Causing a child to watch a sexual act: s 12

It is an offence intentionally to cause another person under 16, B, to watch a third person engaging in an activity, or to look at an image of any person engaging in a sexual activity, where A acts for the purpose of obtaining sexual gratification, and is aware that B is under 16 and does not reasonably believe that B is 16 or over, or B is under 13.

This offence was included to supplement that in relation to grooming discussed later. Research suggests that paedophiles often diminish the sexual inhibitions of children by exposing them to explicit pornography to facilitate subsequent sexual acts. The offence under s 12 is wider than that under s 11 because the activity/image B is watching is not restricted to one involving A. It is a very wide offence: A aged 18 who shows his willing 15-year-old girlfriend a pornographic film for their mutual sexual enjoyment commits the offence. The obvious cases of application will be where an adult gets a child to watch sexual DVDs, etc. It applies to causing a child to read explicit text messages or other social media.[396]

The offence is triable either way and carries a maximum ten-year sentence on indictment. By s 13 it can be committed by a child under the age of 18, in which case the maximum sentence is five years' imprisonment.

---

[393] And renders the offence one of specific intent following *Heard* [2007] EWCA Crim 125.
[394] Section 78 (see earlier).   [395] [2018] EWCA Crim 1439.
[396] *L* [2006] EWCA Crim 2225 where images of the offender masturbating were sent by phone to B.

17.5.4.1 Actus reus

A must cause B to watch the activity/image. Ordinary principles of causation apply here as elsewhere. Omitting to prevent B from watching the activity/image will not ground liability, as where a parent A turns a blind eye to B watching a pornographic film. In such a case, A would also lack the mens rea of acting for the purpose of sexual gratification. 'Image' is widely defined to include moving or still images however produced and 3D images.[397] The broadest definition possible was created to include, for example, cartoons and 'etchings' as well as video and computer-generated pseudo-images. The image must be sexual as defined in s 78. B must watch the activity or image. This involves using the visual sense. It must be proved that B was under 16; again, an undercover officer being caused to watch an act will not suffice.

In *Abdullahi*,[398] the Court of Appeal held that the act must be done 'for the purpose of obtaining sexual gratification'—but the gratification need not be contemporaneous; so A is guilty if his act is done in order to 'groom' a child with a view to sexual activity later. A caused the 13-year-old complainant, whom he plied with drink and drugs, to watch a pornographic film depicting heterosexual and homosexual sexual activity. Subsequently, in his room, A touched B's penis. A was charged with offences under ss 12 and 14. It was sufficient that A showed the images for the purpose of obtaining sexual gratification, either by enjoying seeing the complainant looking at the images or with a view to engaging in sexual activity with B later.

17.5.4.2 Mens rea

The elements of mens rea are that A must (a) intend to cause B to watch, and (b) act for the 'purpose' of sexual gratification. As in s 11, 'purpose' is to be narrowly construed. If A has a dual purpose, for example to explain sexual matters to B, but also to derive some sexual gratification from the activity, it is submitted that A commits the offence. Although there is no explicit element of mens rea in relation to the 'sexual' nature of the activity in s 12(1)(b), the courts might imply a requirement of knowledge. This could create problems. Since what is 'sexual' is to be defined retrospectively by the jury, A might claim that he did not realize it was sexual when he caused B to watch the image. In particular, this argument might be advanced when the images are regarded as 'art'.

17.5.5 Arranging or facilitating commission of a child sex offence: s 14

It is an offence for A intentionally to arrange or facilitate something that A intends to do, intends another person to do or believes that another person will do, in any part of the world, and doing it will involve the commission of an offence under any of ss 9 to 13 (discussed earlier).

This is a controversial 'sweeper' provision. It is a form of inchoate offence and can be committed in a number of ways. Its breadth in the original Bill caused consternation among youth and health-care workers (and teenage magazine advice columnists) anxious that by giving legitimate advice to teenagers about safe sexual practices they would expose themselves to prosecution. As a result, the offence is markedly narrower than its original draft.

---

[397] Section 79(4).   [398] [2006] EWCA Crim 2060.

17.5.5.1 Actus reus

The element of 'arranging' is not defined. The Home Office provides as an example the case where A approaches an escort agency and requests a 15-year-old girl for sex.[399] In R,[400] A asked an adult sex worker whether she knew of any young girls, aged 12 or 13, who were sex workers. She said that she did not. A then sent text messages to her asking whether she had 'got the 12-year-old sorted yet?' The sex worker reported the matter to the police and A was prosecuted under s 14. The trial judge ruled that there was no conduct amounting to that offence or an attempt to commit it. The Crown appealed. The Court of Appeal reversed the trial judge's decision. The court held that s 14 does not require any 'agreement'.[401] A asked the sex worker to arrange things for him, but she did not do so and therefore A could not be said to have done more than attempt to commit the s 14 offence. On the facts there was a possible attempt. Whether A's acts went beyond mere preparation for the purposes of an attempt would be a question of fact for the jury. Moses LJ suggested that:

> The section does not require an agreement or arrangement. It does not require the consent or acquiescence of anyone else. An arrangement may be made without the agreement or acquiescence of anyone else. A defendant may take steps by way of a plan with the criminal objective identified in the section without involving anyone else and the mere fact that no-one else is involved would not necessarily mean that no arrangement was made. In those circumstances, we reject the submission . . . that, absent any agreement, formal or informal, there can be no arrangement.

Section 14 was acknowledged to be wider than attempt because it does not require proof of any act that is 'more than merely preparatory' to one of the relevant child sex offences. The section 'does not limit the stage at which criminal liability is imposed to what would hitherto be regarded as an attempt; in other words, to a proximate stage before the commission of the full offence. The section widens liability to steps taken with the requisite criminal intent by way of preparation.'

The case went back for trial and A was convicted. He appealed successfully on the basis that the judge had this time directed in such a way that the jury were bound to convict.[402] On a retrial he was convicted and appealed, again seeking to distinguish the two earlier appeal decisions, in his own case. In this third appeal the Court of Appeal held that the agreement was not necessary for the offence of arrangement to be concluded.[403]

The offence is extremely broad. A, 18, who agrees with his willing 15-year-old girlfriend to meet later for sex commits the offence. It is particularly wide since it governs arranging or facilitating acts anywhere in the world; it seems that A who arranges to marry B, 14, in her native country in which the age of consent is 14 commits the offence.

'Facilitating' is not defined. It is intended to cover the case where A lets his room to C so that C can have sex with B aged 15. This is also an overbroad offence. It applies also to suppliers of pornography which might be used in ss 11 and 12 offences. A, the father of a 15-year-old girl who would rather she had sex with her boyfriend at home than elsewhere, appears to facilitate that action (although he may have a defence under s 14(3)(b) discussed later).

17.5.5.2 Mens rea

A must intend the activity. In this context it would seem that oblique intention would be sufficient. However, the offence is limited in the sense that A must intend that an offence under ss 9 to 13 *will* be committed.

---

[399] See eg *Jordan* [2006] EWCA Crim 3311 where A asked a sex worker to get him an under-age girl. See also *R* (2008) 16 Jan, unreported, CA (Crim Div).

[400] [2008] EWCA Crim 619.

[401] Since A's request had not been acted on by the sex worker it seems difficult to regard his conduct as amounting to 'arranging or facilitating' any ulterior offence.

[402] [2008] EWCA Crim 2912.   [403] [2009] EWCA Crim 1472. See A Gillespie (2009) 73 J Crim L 378.

17.5.5.3 The exceptions

In view of the overbroad terms of the offence, the statutory exceptions provided in s 14 are extremely important. These provide:

(2) A person does not commit an offence under this section if—

(a) he arranges or facilitates something that he believes another person will do, but that he does not intend to do or intend another person to do, and

(b) any offence within subsection (1)(b) would be an offence against a child for whose protection he acts.

(3) For the purposes of subsection (2), a person acts for the protection of a child if he acts for the purpose of—

(a) protecting the child from sexually transmitted infection,

(b) protecting the physical safety of the child,

(c) preventing the child from becoming pregnant, or

(d) promoting the child's emotional well-being by the giving of advice, and not for the purpose of obtaining sexual gratification or for the purpose of causing or encouraging the activity constituting the offence within subsection (1)(b) or the child's participation in it.

These are designed to safeguard the health-care worker who provides condoms and sex education and the teacher who advises children under 16 on sexual matters. Although well intentioned, major ambiguities remain, in particular in defining 'emotional well-being' in s 14(3)(d). The courts are left to flesh out these issues.

17.5.6 Meeting a child following sexual grooming, etc: s 15

Paedophiles and others intent on sexually exploiting children and young people often use the internet, in particular 'chat rooms', to contact and 'groom' children before meeting them with a view to committing sexual acts. This is acknowledged as a widespread problem.[404] Under the pre-2003 law, the principal offences available were those of attempt which required the investigating authorities to wait until confident that the offender had gone beyond acts of mere preparation to the substantive sexual offence.[405] This was unsatisfactory since it exposed the child to a risk of harm. In response, the government created the much publicized 'grooming' offence. The seriousness with which this risk is considered by the government is evidenced by the maximum sentence of ten years' imprisonment on indictment/six months summarily. The definition as amended[406] is:

15.—(1) A person aged 18 or over (A) commits an offence if—

(a) A has met or communicated with another person (B) on one or more occasions and subsequently—

(i) A intentionally meets B,

(ii) A travels with the intention of meeting B in any part of the world or arranges to meet B in any part of the world, or

(iii) B travels with the intention of meeting A in any part of the world,

---

[404] On the scale of this type of activity, see A Gillespie, 'Child Protection on the Internet—Challenges for Criminal Law' (2002) 14 CFLQ 411. The offence was amended by the Criminal Justice and Immigration Act 2008, s 73.

[405] For a comprehensive analysis of the old law and its failings, see A Gillespie, 'Children, Chatrooms and the Law' [2001] Crim LR 435.

[406] By the Criminal Justice and Immigration Act 2008, s 73 and Sch 15 and by the Criminal Justice and Courts Act 2015, s 36.

(b) A intends to do anything to or in respect of B, during or after the meeting mentioned in paragraph (a)(i) to (iii) and in any part of the world, which if done will involve the commission by A of a relevant offence,

(c) B is under 16, and

(d) A does not reasonably believe that B is 16 or over.

The offence can be committed by an adult where a child under 16 travels to meet the adult or the adult agrees to meet the child in any part of the world, following at least one communication and the adult intends to commit a relevant sexual offence during or after the meeting.

In one of the first reported cases under the provision, *Mansfield*,[407] Sir Douglas Brown explained the paternalist nature of the provision: 'The law is there to protect young girls against their own immature sexual experimentation and to punish much older men who take advantage of them.'[408] The offence also protects boys of course.[409]

17.5.6.1 Actus reus

There must be at least one communication. There is no restriction on the manner of communication. There is no requirement that the messages are sexual in nature.[410] The offence is headed 'meeting a child *following* sexual grooming etc' but that is rather misleading. The phrase 'sexual grooming' does not appear in the section.[411] The aim of the section is to penalize those who use relationships to break down a child's inhibitions before arranging a meeting with a view to sexual offending. The initial communication(s) need therefore not be sexual. They may well be seemingly innocuous precisely in order to win the child's confidence. An offence is committed whether or not a meeting actually takes place. It is enough that having communicated with B before, A travels with the intention of meeting B or arranges to meet B or B travels with the intention of meeting A. What is crucial is proving A's intention to engage in a child sex offence on B during or after the meeting.

It is not enough that, during the course of a meeting, started without any such intention, A then decides to take advantage of the situation and commit an offence: the crime then will be the commission of or the attempt to commit that offence. The offence contained within s 15 is not engaged.[412]

Moreover, there is no clear limit on the period of time between the previous meeting/communication and the planned meeting. This raises the problem at what point must A believe B to be over 16—in the course of communication or at the time of the proposed meeting? What if B turns 16 in the interim?

Despite its laudable aims, anxieties must be raised by the breadth of the offence. A, 18, writes love letters to B, 15, arranging to meet at the local club. A might commit the offence depending on his mens rea.[413]

Arguably, however, the offence is too narrow. An elderly man, A, who is a paedophile, posts internet messages to B, believing her to be 15. She is X, an undercover woman police officer aged over 16. No substantive offence is committed. A might be liable for an attempt.

---

[407] [2005] EWCA Crim 927.   [408] Endorsed in *Mohammed* [2006] EWCA Crim 1107.

[409] See eg *A-G's Reference (No 91 of 2007)* unreported.

[410] *Gaviria* [2010] EWCA Crim 1693, citing this para in the 13th edn with approval.

[411] See Rook and Ward, *Sexual Offences Law and Practice*, para 4.211, noting that the government resisted amendments to the Bill to restrict the offence in that way.

[412] *Gaviria* [2010] EWCA Crim 1683 at [17] per Leveson LJ.

[413] ie if he hopes that the evening may involve sexual conduct with B, he commits the offence when he travels to the club.

17.5.6.2 Mens rea

There is a requirement of intention. It is submitted that given the lack of any requirement for manifest wrongdoing in communicating and setting out to meet B, this element should be very strictly construed by the courts. In lobbying Parliament during the passage of the Bill, the offence was likened to a 'thought-crime' because of the absence of any tangible harm.[414]

17.5.7 Sexual communication with a child: s 15A

Section 67 of the Serious Crime Act 2015 inserts a new s 15A into the SOA 2003. This new offence, entitled 'sexual communication with a child', is committed where A, aged 18 or over, intentionally communicates with a person, B, who is aged under 16, for the purposes of sexual gratification when the communication is sexual or is intended to encourage the recipient to make a communication that is sexual and the offender does not reasonably believe that B is 16 or over.[415] In respect of the s 15 offence, even if A were discovered to have been communicating sexually with a person under the age of 16, he would not commit an offence until he and B actually met or at least arranged to meet. This new offence closes what was perceived by many to be a lacuna. The offence is triable either way. On summary conviction, the maximum sentence is 12 months' imprisonment and/or a fine. On conviction on indictment, the maximum sentence is two years' imprisonment and/or a fine.

17.6 Offences of abuse of trust

The Sexual Offences (Amendment) Act 2000[416] created new offences of abuse of a position of trust.[417] The 2003 Act replaced them with four offences where A (aged over 18) in a position of trust to B (under 18): sexually touches B (s 16);[418] causes or incites B to engage in sexual activity (s 17);[419] engages in sexual activity in B's presence for the purpose of sexual gratification (s 18); or causes B to watch a sexual image or activity for the purpose of obtaining sexual gratification.

The most notable feature of the offences is that they criminalize consensual conduct with those under 18. Although 16- to 18-year-olds may consent to sexual activity in other circumstances, they cannot do so with those who regularly 'look after' them.[420] This reflects the Act's theme of preventing exploitation. The category of those in positions of trust is widely defined and includes, for example, pupils and students, but is not all-embracing; there is no specific inclusion of categories such as clergy and non-professional carers such as scout leaders. Individuals in these positions may fall within the terms of the offences depending on the circumstances of their responsibility for B.[421]

---

[414] See Liberty and Criminal Bar Association responses to the government's White Paper, *Protecting the Public*.

[415] For further discussion, see K Laird, 'Parts 5 and 6 of the Serious Crime Act 2015—More than Mere Miscellany' [2015] Crim LR 789.

[416] See Burnside [2001] Crim LR 425.   [417] See the 10th edn of this book, at p 478.

[418] eg a teacher's kiss to a 6th former at the leavers' ball: *Lamb* [2007] EWCA Crim 1766; *Wootton* [2005] EWCA Crim 2137, teacher engaged in sex with 15- and 16-year-olds; *Wilson* [2007] EWCA Crim 2762.

[419] See eg *Vallente* [2011] EWCA Crim 294.

[420] As defined in ss 21 and 22. The requirement of regularity may be unduly restrictive. Does it catch the supply teacher? See also the amendment by the Social Services and Well-being (Wales) Act 2014 (Consequential Amendments) Regulations 2016/413 in relation to care homes.

[421] It has been argued that a better approach would be to focus on whether the actual relationship between A and B is exploitative. See A Gillespie and S Ost, 'The "Higher" Age of Consent and the Concept of Sexual Exploitation' in A Reed and M Bohlander (eds), *Consent—Domestic and Comparative Perspectives* (2017).

The offences place a burden on A, where his position of trust arises in an institutional setting, to present evidence that he did not know nor could he reasonably be expected to know that he was in a position of trust towards B. This may well be a difficult plea to raise unless A and B are in a large institution.

No offence is committed where A has a reasonable belief that B is aged over 18 (unless B is under 13). There is a defence for A to prove that he was lawfully married[422] to B (aged 16 or over) or that immediately before the position of trust arose there existed a lawful sexual relationship between them. This covers cases where, for example, A and B had a sexual relationship before A became a teacher at B's school.

17.7 Family offences

The 2003 Act creates two sets of offences to deal with offences within the family. In relation to children, ss 25 and 26 criminalize the same forms of activity as ss 9 and 12 (see earlier): sexual touching and causing a child to engage in sexual activity. These are welcome extensions, protecting vulnerable individuals against acts other than sexual intercourse. Sections 25 and 26 differ from ss 9 and 12 in two important respects: B must be under 18 and A must be a family member. Family membership is defined in very broad terms in the Act (and has been further extended by the Criminal Justice and Immigration Act 2008, Sch 15), extending well beyond blood relationships to reflect the diverse structures of modern families. It protects, for example, the stepchild,[423] foster child[424] and adopted child.[425] Family members include adoptive relationships,[426] wider family members who live, or have lived, in the same household as the child or who are, or have been, regularly involved in caring for, training or supervising or being in sole charge of the child[427] and others who are living in the same household as the child and who hold a position of trust or authority in relation to the child at the time of the alleged offence.[428] The breadth of the extended family[429] caught by the Act reflects the shift in emphasis in the legislation from a blood relationship-based offence of heterosexual intercourse (incest)[430] to one based on gender-neutral exploitation of sexual vulnerability in the home environment.

There are defences in s 28 where A is lawfully married to B[431] at the time of engaging in the sexual activity, and under s 29 where A proves that a lawful sexual relationship existed between A and B immediately before the familial relationship arose.[432]

---

[422] 'Person who is married' includes a person who is married to a person of the same sex: see Marriage (Same Sex Couples) Act 2013, Sch 3, para 1(1)(c), (2), (3).

[423] See eg *R (Danny)* [2005] EWCA Crim 1296 where A asked his 12-year-old stepdaughter to allow him to perform oral sex on her; *DA* [2012] EWCA Crim 1825 where A engaged in a sexual relationship with his 16-year-old stepdaughter that resulted in her giving birth to his child.

[424] *Thomas (Robert)* [2005] EWCA Crim 2343.

[425] Section 27 of the 2003 Act, as amended by the Criminal Justice and Immigration Act 2008, Sch 15, para 3.

[426] Parents, current or former foster parents, grandparents, brothers, sisters, half-brothers, half-sisters, aunts and uncles.

[427] Step-parents, cousins, stepbrothers and stepsisters, current or former foster siblings.

[428] This offence will not be committed if A has a lawful sexual relationship with the child after the familial relationship has ceased, even where the child is under 18.

[429] This is so wide that it has been argued that sports coaches will be caught: C Brackenridge and Y Williams, 'Incest in the "Family" of Sport' (2004) 154 NLJ 179. See the Safeguarding Vulnerable Groups Act 2006.

[430] Founded historically in part at least on eugenics arguments: V Bailey and S Blackburn, 'The Punishment of Incest Act 1908: A Case Study in Law Creation' [1979] Crim LR 708; S Wolfram, 'Eugenics and the Punishment of Incest Act 1908' [1983] Crim LR 308; J Temkin, 'Do We Need a Crime of Incest?' (1988) 44 CLP 185; HH Peter Bowsher, 'Incest—Should Incest Between Consenting Adults be a Crime?' [2015] Crim LR 208.

[431] Note the amended definition in the Civil Partnerships Act 2004.

[432] eg two 16-year-olds are in a sexual relationship and the girl's father and boy's mother subsequently marry. As amended by the Criminal Justice and Immigration Act 2008, Sch 15, para 4.

The 2003 Act also creates controversial sexual offences involving consenting adult relatives. Section 64 makes it an offence for A aged 16 or over to intentionally penetrate sexually
(anally, vaginally or orally) a relative B who is aged 18 or over if he knows or could reasonably have been expected to know that B is his relative. The converse offence is provided for
in s 65: A aged 16 or over commits an offence by consenting to being penetrated sexually
by a relative B aged 18 or over if he knows or could reasonably have been expected to know
that B is his relative. The concept of a 'relative' is broadly defined.[433] Where the prosecution
establish that A is related to B, A will be taken to have known or to have reasonably been
expected to know that they were related in that way unless A raises sufficient evidence as to
whether he knew or could reasonably have been expected to know. These are broad, gender-
neutral offences. They have been heavily criticized.[434] Both offences are triable summarily
or on indictment and have a maximum penalty of two years' imprisonment. Together, ss 64
and 65 make both parties to sexual activity guilty, so who is the law trying to protect? Will
this be found to be compatible with Art 8 of the ECHR for consenting adults? In *Stubing v
Germany*,[435] the ECtHR accepted that a legal ban on sexual intercourse with the applicant's
willing sister was an interference with his right to respect for his private life. The court went
on to find, however, that the ban fell within Art 8(2) as being necessary in a democratic society. The State's decision to criminalize sexual intercourse between even consenting adult
relatives was held to fall within the margin of appreciation.[436]

17.8 Offences involving mental disorder

The Act provides three specific groups of offences to protect those with a mental disorder.[437]
In each category the types of behaviour criminalized are roughly the same as those in relation to children. In short, the activities prohibited are:

- sexual touching of B;
- causing or inciting sexual activity by B;
- engaging in sexual activity in B's presence;
- causing B to watch sexual activity.

---

[433] Parent, grandparent, child, grandchild, brother, sister, half-brother, half-sister; and blood relationships of uncle, aunt, nephew or niece. Criminal Justice and Immigration Act 2008, Sch 15 provides
that adopted child/parent relationships are caught where A is over 18. The Human Fertilisation and
Embryology (Parental Orders) Regulations 2010, SI 2010/985, amended the Sexual Offences Act, ss 64 and
65, so that references to an adoptive relationship include references to the comparable relationship under
a parental order.

[434] See Bowsher [2015] Crim LR 208. JR Spencer, 'Child and Family Offences' [2004] Crim LR 347, doubts
that they could ever be properly used. But what of the situation where eg X aged 17 penetrates his 19-year-old
sister, Y, having secured her agreement with a threat which is not sufficient to vitiate consent under s 74? This
constitutes an offence under s 64, but not any other serious offence, and it may well be proper to prosecute it.
X commits the s 64 offence (X being over 16 and Y being over 18), but not the child offences (Y is over 16), nor
the family offences (Y being over 18).

[435] [2013] 1 FCR 107.

[436] For criticism, see JR Spencer, 'Incest and Article 8 of the European Convention on Human Rights' (2013)
72 CLJ 5.

[437] For criticism see J Stanton-Ife, 'Mental Disorder and Sexual Consent' in DJ Baker and J Horder, *The
Sanctity of Life and the Criminal Law* (2013). Stanton-Ife examines four legal tests for attempting to set the
threshold at which a severely mentally disordered person can give valid consent to sexual activity and concludes that the test utilized in the 2003 Act focuses too much upon B's cognitive state, which may lead to a result
that is not in her best interests. See also *IM v LM* [2014] EWCA Civ 37.

In the offences dealing with children, the Act has decreed that it is sufficient to prove that one of these activities is intentionally performed; liability as to the factor of vulnerability—that is, age—is strict. Applying strict liability would be too harsh in the present context[438] since there may not necessarily be physical signs that the adult complainant is a vulnerable person. Thus, only when these activities arise in an exploitative context are they criminalized. The three prohibited contexts for such activity are:

- ss 30 to 33 where B is mentally disordered and *'unable to refuse'*;[439]
- ss 34 to 37 where B is mentally disordered and the activity is caused by *'threats or deception or inducement'* which need not vitiate consent under s 74;
- ss 38 to 41 where B is mentally disordered and A is *'in a relationship as a carer'*.[440]

There are numerous welcome improvements in the 2003 Act scheme. Creating specific offences produces much fairer labelling—defendants are convicted of offences that better describe their actions. The language has been modernized, and gender specificity has been removed. This is not mere political correctness: for example, one result is that mentally disordered men are protected against heterosexual abuse. The offensive terminology of the 1956 Act was replaced by the appropriate (but technical) language of the Mental Health Acts. The Mental Health Act 2007 adopts broader definitions and produces yet wider offences. 'Mental disorder' under the 2007 Act means any disability or disorder of the mind and includes conditions such as autism and bipolar disorder.

As elsewhere in the Act, there is tremendous prolixity. Many of the definitions are complex and their interrelationship with other provisions in the Act exacerbates this problem. For example, the relationship between the s 30 offence of sexual touching with a person with mental disorder impeding the ability to refuse and the general offence of non-consensual sexual touching in s 3 is confusing.[441] Thus, s 30(2) provides:

B is unable to refuse if:

(a) he lacks the capacity to choose whether to agree to the [activity] (whether because he lacks sufficient understanding of the nature or reasonably foreseeable consequences of what is being done, or for any other reason), or

(b) he is unable to communicate such a choice to A.

The definition of 'inability to refuse' includes cases where B lacks capacity: in such cases there is clearly no consent. Inability to refuse includes, in the alternative, an inability to communicate a choice to this defendant. The House of Lords in C[442] confirmed that s 30(2)(b)

---

[438] *Setting the Boundaries*, para 4.6.4.

[439] In *Hulme v DPP* [2006] EWHC 1347 (Admin), the Divisional Court considered the offence under s 30, concluding that on the facts a magistrates' court was entitled to reach the decision that a woman suffering from a mental disorder was unable to refuse to be touched sexually. The defendant, a 73-year-old, had touched the complainant, a cerebral palsy sufferer with a low mental age. B was unable to refuse because she did not know what to say or how to say it. She was physically capable of speaking, but was too confused and scared to do so. This was held to be an inability to refuse. The conviction was upheld despite the magistrates having been incorrectly advised as to the interpretation of s 30.

[440] This is broadly construed as where B was suffering from postnatal depression and was in a vulnerable state when her social worker had sexual intercourse with her: *Bradford* [2006] EWCA Crim 2495.

[441] This issue was alluded to in *A* [2014] EWCA Crim 299. The Court of Appeal was extremely critical of the decision to charge A with rape and sexual assault instead of one of the offences found in s 30. Macur LJ stated that: 'it behoves us to say that "charging" decisions in relation to the prosecution of offences concerning complainants where there is or may be an issue of capacity to consent, would benefit from a measured consideration of the full array of offences created by section 30, and following, of the 2003 Act and which incorporate the full range of criminal sexual activity', at [32].

[442] *C* [2009] UKHL 42.

did not require that a complainant was physically unable to communicate by reason of her mental disorder. There is considerable overlap with the offences under ss 1 to 4.

It is arguable that too much discretion lies in the hands of the CPS which faces an especially difficult task in deciding whether to prosecute in cases where, for example, A and B are both mentally disordered, or where a carer claims that the actions were performed for the appropriate sex education of an individual with learning disability. In many instances it will still be necessary to determine the capacity of the complainant and this will involve her giving evidence—albeit under the Youth Justice and Criminal Evidence Act 1999 special measures regime.

Symbolically it was very important for the Act to criminalize exploitative behaviour, but the message is confused when it overcriminalizes and potentially inhibits the appropriate sexual behaviour of those with a learning disability.[443]

Note that the offences involving mental incapacity do not have to be charged where the complainant has such a disability. It is possible to rely on the straightforward non-consensual offences of rape, penetration, etc.[444]

17.9 Other sexual offences

17.9.1 Prostitution and pornography

The Act provides specific protection against the sexual exploitation of children in a number of contexts. Section 47 provides an offence of paying (as widely defined) for the sexual services of a child[445] and s 48 provides wider supporting offences of causing or inciting child sexual exploitation or pornography, being designed to catch those who recruit vulnerable children into such activities.

Further broadly defined offences provide protection against child sexual exploitation[446] and arranging or facilitating the sexual exploitation of a child.[447]

Provisions to deal with adult sexual exploitation were strengthened with a range of offences introduced to deal with causing or inciting[448] or controlling prostitution for gain.[449] The rise in trafficking for prostitution was combated by offences of trafficking into, within and outwith the UK, but these have been repealed and replaced with the relevant offences found in the Modern Slavery Act 2015.

17.9.2 Indecent photographs of children

There are offences of taking, making, permitting to take, distributing, showing, possessing with intent to distribute and advertising indecent photographs or pseudo-photographs of children under 18.[450] There is a defence if the child is aged 16 or over and A proves that he

---

[443] The Parliamentary Joint Committee on Human Rights, *Scrutiny of Bills: Further Progress Report. Twelfth Report of Session 2002–03* (2003) HL 199, HC 765, concluded that the provisions were probably compatible with ECHR obligations under Art 8.

[444] See eg *Wragg* [2006] EWCA Crim 2022 (A touched B, who was a cerebral palsy sufferer, in a community home). Note the comments by Macur LJ in *A*, however.

[445] See *Y* [2014] EWCA Crim 413.

[446] Section 49. The Serious Crime Act 2015, s 68 renamed these offences 'sexual exploitation' instead of 'child prostitution and pornography'.

[447] Section 50.   [448] Section 52.   [449] Section 53.

[450] On the prevalence of this activity, see B Gallagher, K Christmann, C Fraser and B Hodgson, 'International and Internet Child Sexual Abuse and Exploitation—Issues Emerging from Research' (2003) 15 CFLQ 353.

and the child were married or living together as partners in an enduring family relationship, that the child consented to the image being taken and that the image shows no one other than B (and A).[451] This is an area of considerable controversy.

The strictness of the offences has given rise to concern in some cases, particularly as regards the definition of creation, which can occur by the act of downloading an image to view it on the screen of a computer and then immediately deleting it without consciously saving it.[452] Because of the strictness of liability in relation to age, other difficulties arise where A downloads images of teenagers claiming that he was led by the website to believe the models to be older. There are also broader concerns about freedom of expression.[453] Existing offences were extended by s 69 of the Criminal Justice and Immigration Act 2008: these are considered briefly in Ch 30, free online.

17.9.3 Preliminary offences

17.9.3.1 Administering drugs

The Act introduces three important new preliminary sex offences. Section 61 introduces an offence of intentional administration of a substance/causing it to be taken by B without consent with intent to stupefy/overpower to enable any person to engage in a sexual activity that involves B.[454] This is a further response to the problem of drug-assisted rape (see also s 75(2)(f) discussed earlier).[455] The offence is much wider than that in s 4 of the 1956 Act, being gender-neutral and relating to all sexual activity rather than just sexual intercourse. The offence covers A spiking B's drinks[456] as well as administering drugs such as GHB and Rohypnol. It does not extend to A encouraging B to get drunk so that A could more readily persuade B to have sex.

Section 61 applies where A himself administers the substance to B, and where A causes the substance to be taken by B, by for example persuading C to administer it to B. There is no requirement that the intended sexual activity involve A. It is a preliminary offence in the sense that there is no requirement that B actually is involved in any sexual activity. It is unclear whether those who manufacture or supply the drugs will be liable as aiders and abettors, or under the SCA 2007, or for offences under s 61.

17.9.3.2 Committing an offence with intent to commit a sexual offence

Section 62 introduces an offence of 'committing an offence with intent to commit a sexual offence'. The offence was designed primarily to tackle cases where A kidnaps B so that he can rape her or assaults B to subdue her.[457] The offence as drafted is much wider: there is no requirement that the preliminary offence is directed at B, the person against whom the

---

[451] On the complex and unsatisfactory nature of the offences, see A Gillespie, 'The Sexual Offences Act 2003: (3) Tinkering With 'Child Pornography' [2004] Crim LR 361.

[452] See *Okoro (No 3)* [2019] 1 Cr App R 2 (15) and Ch 30.

[453] See I Cram, 'Criminalising Child Pornography—A Canadian Study in Freedom of Expression and Charter-Led Judicial Review of Legislative Policy Making' (2002) 66 J Crim L 359 on the decision of the Canadian Supreme Court in *Sharpe* [2001] 1 SCR 45.

[454] See *Wright* [2006] EWCA Crim 2672; *Spall* [2008] 1 Cr App R (S) 250.

[455] cf the offences of poisoning under ss 23 and 24 of the OAPA 1861. See also *Coomber* [2005] EWCA Crim 1113 (scout leader drugging boys to abuse them when asleep). On the prevalence of intoxicated complainants, see M Horvath and J Brown, 'The Role of Drugs and Alcohol in Rape' (2006) 46 Med Sci Law 219 concluding that the complainant's state of intoxication is more significant than the defendant's.

[456] As in the case of *W* [2014] EWCA Crim 2232 where B suffered a seizure as a result of being drugged by A.

[457] See the first sentencing case on the offence: *Wisniewshi* [2004] EWCA Crim 3361. See also *Vageesan S* [2008] EWCA Crim 346 (assault prior to rape) and *Fairweather* [2011] EWCA Crim 1783.

substantive sexual offence is committed.[458] A, 18, speeding in his car to B, 15, to have consensual sex with her commits the offence. Stalking under the Protection from Harassment Act 1997 will suffice as the preliminary crime.[459] It will also apply in the more commonplace cases such as those of a physical assault by A in preparation for a sexual assault or rape.[460]

At common law it was uncertain whether the offence of assault with intent to rape exists. There is no doubt that an indictment for assault with intent to rape would lie at common law but it is not certain whether it was a specific offence or an example of a wider common law offence of assault with intent to commit a felony. If the latter, it ceased to exist with the abolition of felonies by the Criminal Law Act 1967 and the repeal of the words in s 38 of the OAPA 1861 which provided that assault with intent to commit a felony was punishable with two years' imprisonment. The better view is that there was no general offence of assault with intent to commit a felony at common law, and that assault with intent to rape was, and is, a specific offence which was not abolished by the 1861 Act or by the repeal of the general statutory offence. Most significantly, it was treated by the draftsman of the 1861 legislation, CS Greaves, as continuing to exist after the 1861 Act.[461] Most cases of assault with intent to rape will amount to attempted rape under the Criminal Attempts Act 1981 but there will be instances where the assault is a 'merely preparatory' act.[462] In such cases the most obvious charge is that under s 62.

17.9.3.3 Trespass with intent to commit a sexual offence

The third preliminary offence is that under s 63: 'trespass with intent to commit a sexual offence'. This is committed where A intends to commit a sexual offence whilst he is on any premises as a trespasser, either knowing or being reckless[463] as to whether he is trespassing. A person is a trespasser if he is on any premises without the owner's or occupier's consent, or other lawful excuse. This replaces the offence under s 9 of the Theft Act 1968, in relation to burglary with intent to rape. It is clearly wider since it involves any trespass and includes sexual offences beyond rape.[464] It is not necessary for the Crown to specify which sexual offence the trespasser was intent on committing. In *Pacurar*[465] the Court of Appeal held that it was sufficient for the prosecution to allege in the particulars of offence that P was going to commit one of a specified number of offences against specific individuals at an identified time and place.

17.9.4 Miscellaneous sexual offences

17.9.4.1 Exposure

Section 66 creates an offence if A intentionally exposes his or her genitals with the intention that another person will see them and be caused alarm or distress. This extends the previous law to include female exposure, although that is a particularly rare phenomenon. It is not necessary that anyone should have seen the genitals or have been caused alarm or distress.

---

[458] *Little* [2012] EWCA Crim 3099.

[459] Where the preparatory offence is kidnapping or false imprisonment, the offence is triable on indictment only, and has a maximum penalty of life imprisonment. In all other cases, the offence is triable summarily or on indictment and has a maximum penalty of ten years on indictment.

[460] See *Seevaratnarajah* [2008] EWCA Crim 346.

[461] CS Greaves (ed), *Russell on Crime* (4th edn, 1865) 927.   [462] See Ch 9.

[463] This is one of the few offences in the 2003 Act that includes a reckless mens rea element.

[464] See eg *H* [2007] EWCA Crim 2622. The offence is triable summarily or on indictment and has a maximum penalty of ten years. See Ch 25.

[465] [2016] EWCA Crim 569.

In addition to the commonplace incidents of flashing, and more serious examples,[466] the offence has been used to tackle the more unusual exposers: see the case of *Bullen*,[467] where A went to a women's dress shop and exposed himself when trying on clothes.[468] There was much controversy over the offence when originally introduced since it was feared that it would criminalize naturism.[469] As finally enacted, the offence would not apply to a naturist unless his exposure is with intention to cause alarm or distress. Similarly, it is unlikely that 'streakers' at sports events will be prosecuted. In many such cases A intends to distress by the disruption to play not by the exposure of genitals.[470] There is an overlap between the statutory offence and the common law offence of outraging public decency.[471] For further analysis of the latter see Ch 30.

17.9.4.2 Voyeurism

Section 67 creates an offence where A, for the purposes of sexual gratification,[472] observes another person doing a 'private act' in the knowledge[473] that the other person does not consent to being observed for that purpose. The Court of Appeal in *B*[474] stated that the social mischief that the new offence of voyeurism was created to tackle is 'the anti-social nature of deliberate observation by a person of another doing intimate acts in private, where the purpose of the observation is to obtain sexual gratification for the observer and, secondly, the fact that this activity has been linked to more serious offending behaviour by the observer'. The offence extends beyond simple peeping Toms looking through keyholes.[475] Subsection (2) creates an offence of A 'operating equipment' with the intention of enabling another person, C, for their sexual gratification, to observe B doing a 'private act' in the knowledge that B has not consented to this being done for another person's sexual gratification. This provision was enacted in response to the numerous instances reported in the news of people setting up illicit cameras. In *Vigon v DPP*,[476] surreptitious viewing of customers changing into swimwear in a market stall cubicle was held capable of being 'insulting behaviour' for the purposes of s 5 of the Public Order Act 1986.[477] The common law offence of outraging public decency was also prayed in aid when a defendant secretly filmed women urinating in a supermarket toilet. 'Disgusting conduct' was held to be that which fills an onlooker with loathing or extreme distaste or causes the onlooker extreme annoyance: *Choi*.[478] That offence is

---

[466] eg *Nicholson* [2014] EWCA Crim 2710 (D on suicide watch in prison summoning women officers to watch him masturbate).

[467] [2006] EWCA Crim 1801.

[468] See also *Whitton* [2006] EWCA Crim 3229 (A masturbating and exposing himself to child pedestrians as he drove).

[469] See eg *Lindsky* [2009] All ER (D) 263 (Nov) where A was convicted having been naked in his own garden.

[470] The offence is triable summarily or on indictment with a maximum penalty of two years' imprisonment.

[471] In *Hardy* [2013] EWCA Crim 2125, the Court of Appeal observed that, since there exist no sentencing guidelines for the offence of outraging public decency, the guidelines applicable to s 66 could be relied upon instead.

[472] In *B* [2012] EWCA Crim 770, it was held that the use in s 67(1)(b) of the terms 'his' and 'he' indicates that the purpose of the deliberate observation by A must be his own 'sexual gratification' and not someone else's.

[473] In *B*, this was interpreted as importing the requirement to prove *actual* knowledge that the other person does not consent to being deliberately observed for the specific purpose of A obtaining sexual gratification from that observation.

[474] [2012] EWCA Crim 770, [63].

[475] Or placing mirrors under changing room cubicles: *Sayed* [2009] EWCA Crim 1922.

[476] [1998] Crim LR 289.

[477] It was then sufficient that the defendant was aware that his conduct may be insulting, so there was no need to prove that he intended to insult the customer—it is no defence that he concealed the camera.

[478] [1999] 8 Arch News 3.

considered in Ch 30, and it has been put to recent use in relation to conduct including 'up skirting' (filming illicitly up women's skirts).[479] (See s 67A below.)

The Law Commission in its report *Public Nuisance and Outraging Public Decency* (2015) recognized the continued value of that common law offence in relation to upskirting. It recommended creating a statutory form of the outraging public decency offence.[480]

Section 67(3) makes it an offence for a person A to record B doing a 'private act' with the intention that A or a third person will, for the purposes of sexual gratification, look at the recorded image, when it is known that B does not consent to being recorded for that purpose.[481] Finally, s 67(4) creates an offence for a person to install equipment, or to construct or adapt a structure,[482] with the intention of enabling himself, or another person, to commit an offence under s 67(1).[483]

For each of these offences a 'private act' is defined in s 68 as 'an act done in a place and in circumstances where the person would reasonably expect privacy and either the person's genitals, buttocks or female[484] breasts are exposed or covered only by underwear,[485] or the person is using a lavatory or the person is doing a sexual act that is not of a kind ordinarily done in public'. There is much scope for judicial interpretation.[486]

The leading case is *Bassett*.[487] A was convicted of voyeurism. He used a video camera hidden in a bag in men's changing rooms at a public swimming pool, to film B, a man, who was in the shower in his trunks. The showers were open to the general view of the changing room. A had 'observed' B for the purpose of obtaining sexual gratification, and B did not consent to that. The judge ruled that B was in a place in circumstances which would reasonably be expected to provide privacy. The Court of Appeal disagreed and allowed the appeal. The case is important in emphasizing the centrality of the privacy expectation element of the offence. A will escape liability even if he observes B in a state of nakedness, derives sexual gratification from doing so and lacks B's consent to being observed for the purpose of sexual gratification *unless* it is also proved that there is a reasonable expectation of privacy. The reason that no offence was committed in *Bassett* is that although it is possible to have a reasonable expectation of privacy without being wholly enclosed, there was no reasonable expectation of privacy in the circumstances. Hughes LJ remarked that it was 'normally inevitable' that users must expect to be observed unclothed by other users of public swimming pools and changing facilities in sports and leisure complexes. It is to be left to the jury to determine if there is reasonable expectation of privacy. In determining whether there is a reasonable expectation of privacy in the circumstances, the court suggests that there A's purpose may be relevant but it is 'the nature of the observation rather than the purpose of the observer which may be relevant to the expectation of privacy'.[488] Presumably, then, a

---

[479] See A Gillespie, '"Up-Skirts" and "Down-Blouses": Voyeurism and the Law' [2008] Crim LR 370 on whether a voyeurism-based offence such as that in New Zealand should be adopted here.

[480] LC 358, paras 3.178–3.181.

[481] See the case of *Sippings* [2008] EWCA Crim 46 where A had video-recorded from his kitchen window B, his neighbour's teenage daughter, undressing in her bedroom when she left the curtains open.

[482] 'Structure' includes 'a tent, vehicle or vessel or other temporary or movable structure'.

[483] The offence is triable summarily or on indictment with a maximum penalty of two years' imprisonment.

[484] See *Bassett* [2008] EWCA Crim 1174.

[485] See the Northern Ireland case of *PSNI v MacRitchie* [2008] NICA 26 holding that a bikini was not underwear when worn by B in a changing cubicle at the local swimming pool. A had sought to video her changing in her own cubicle while he remained in his.

[486] See the sentencing cases of *Henderson* [2006] EWCA Crim 198 (filming in public toilets); *Turner* [2006] EWCA Crim 63 (sports centre manager filming changing rooms); *IP* [2004] EWCA Crim 2646 (filming 24-year-old stepdaughter in shower); *McCann* [2006] EWCA Crim 1078 (surveillance camera hidden in neighbour's bathroom).

[487] [2008] EWCA Crim 1174.   [488] At [11].

casual glance at B naked in the communal shower from which A derives a sexual thrill is not enough, but determined ogling might be, *a fortiori* if A starts filming. In the subsequent case of *B*,[489] the Court of Appeal held that the use of the verb 'observes' connotes a deliberate decision on the part of A to look at someone doing a 'private act'. Aikens LJ stated, *obiter*, that this excludes both the careless and the reckless perception. It was also held that the question of whether A's purpose is sexual gratification entails an evaluation of his thought process; it is thus a subjective question. Whether A actually obtains sexual gratification is largely irrelevant, although it was observed that proof that he had would be evidence of the purpose of deliberate observation.

It is worth noting the position in relation to consent in such cases. It will not excuse A that B impliedly consented to being viewed in a state of nakedness in a place in which privacy would be expected if B has not consented to being observed *for the purposes of sexual gratification*.[490]

In *Richards*,[491] A had sex with two sex workers (separately). He filmed the two complainants without their consent. One said that she enjoyed being filmed but charged extra for that service and did not consent to being filmed by A. The other said she had not consented and would not have consented because of concerns she had about images being put online. A claimed he had paid a higher price for filming the sexual encounters. A argued that for the purposes of s 67(3), an offender could never be a participant in an act that was being recorded and it was therefore not a private act. The prosecution argued that the absence of consent for the filming by the two complainants created a reasonable expectation of privacy. Whether there was, in fact, a reasonable expectation of privacy was intended by Parliament to be considered by a jury and it is a matter of fact and degree depending on the kind of observation that occurred. For example, where a doctor examines a patient's genitalia or breasts for medical examination, the expectation is that they will be viewed once. If the doctor covertly filmed the examination it would be open to a jury to conclude that there was a reasonable expectation of privacy against the secret filming for the purposes of the doctor's subsequent sexual gratification. The Court of Appeal concluded that where there is deliberate and covert filming of consensual intercourse, it is necessary to consider whether the recording met the specific circumstances of s 67(3). Following *Bassett*, there was a private act at which they were the only people who witnessed what occurred. There was a case for a jury to consider that there would have been an expectation that there would have been no publicity or display of that private act, nor any secret observation or recording. D's presence in the bedroom would not lessen the expectation of privacy; that expectation being that what occurred would not be available for later viewing, even if only by D. The court accepted that it may be an unexpected decision; that one can be guilty of voyeurism in respect of an act in which one participates. But the court emphasized that it is clear that the behaviour under consideration was of the type that s 67(3) was created to tackle.

Section 67A: upskirting

The s 67 offence of voyeurism was inadequate to deal with 'upskirting': someone operating film-recording equipment beneath the victim's clothing, with the intention of viewing the victim's genitals or buttocks—whether exposed or covered with underwear—for the

---

[489] [2012] EWCA Crim 770.

[490] See *Sippings* [2008] EWCA Crim 46 in which A pleaded guilty to observing from his kitchen window V (aged 14–19) over a five-year period when she was undressing in her bedroom in a neighbouring house with the lights on and the curtains open. Is there a reasonable expectation of privacy in a room with the lights on and curtains open?

[491] [2020] EWCA Crim 95.

purpose of obtaining sexual gratification or humiliating, distressing or alarming the victim. Where the conduct of taking an intimate recording occurs in an ordinary public context, such as where a person is riding on public transport, the 'private act' element of the voyeurism offence under s 67 of the Sexual Offences Act 2003 cannot be established. Further, as Gillespie notes, where a photograph is taken up a person's skirt in a public place such as a shopping centre, the person is not engaged in a 'private act' because they are not exposing their genitals or buttocks (with underwear or otherwise) in that place; they are covered by clothing. There is also a difficulty in using s 67 because the fault element of sexual gratification may also not be satisfied, where such images are taken and disseminated to humiliate, or to be humorous, for example.[492]

The Voyeurism (Offences) Act 2019[493] creates a new offence—s 67A of the Sexual Offences Act 2003. It applies where D, for the purpose of either obtaining sexual gratification or humiliating, alarming or distressing another person (V), and without that person's consent: (a) operates equipment beneath V's clothing with the intention of enabling himself or another person (X) to observe V's genitals, buttocks or underwear; or (b) he records an image beneath the clothing of V of V's genitals, buttocks or underwear with the intention that D or another person (X) will look at the image.

D is liable on conviction on indictment to imprisonment for a term not exceeding two years, or on summary conviction to imprisonment for a term not exceeding six months, to a fine not exceeding the statutory maximum, or to both.

17.9.4.3 Bestiality

Section 69 creates an offence for A intentionally to penetrate the vagina[494] or anus of a living animal with his penis where he knows or is reckless as to whether that is what he is penetrating.[495] It also creates an offence for A intentionally to cause or allow her vagina or his or her anus to be penetrated by the penis of a living animal where he or she knows or is reckless as to whether it is the penis of a live animal that is penetrating him/her. Note also the offences of extreme pornography discussed in Ch 30.

17.9.4.4 Necrophilia

Section 70 makes it an offence for A intentionally to penetrate sexually[496] any part of the body of a dead person B with A's penis, any other body part or any other object, knowing or being reckless as to whether A is penetrating any part of a dead body.[497] A commits no offence if B dies during intercourse unless A realizes and continues to penetrate B.[498] The penetration must be sexual but it remains unclear whether A must have any mens rea in relation to that element of the actus reus. As a matter of principle, that would be desirable.

---

[492] A Gillespie, '"Up-Skirts" and "Down-Blouses": Voyeurism and the Law' [2008] Crim LR 370.

[493] By the Voyeurism (Offences) Act 2019, s 1(2).

[494] The reference to vagina or anus in this context is further explained at s 79(9) and (10). References to 'vagina' include vulva and in relation to an animal, references to the vagina or anus include references to any similar part.

[495] For criticisms of the offence, see I Jones, 'A Beastly Provision: Why the Offence of "Intercourse With an Animal" Must be Butchered' (2011) 75 J Crim L 75. NB *Boyd* [2013] EWCA Crim 2384 in which D had trained his dog to have sex with humans.

[496] Hence pathology staff will not commit the offence by penetrating the corpse with a finger or instrument for medical purposes. Following the *AG's Ref (No 1 of 2020)* [2020] EWCA Crim 1665, presumably there is no mens rea requirement as to the sexual nature of the penetration.

[497] The offence is triable summarily or on indictment and has a maximum penalty of two years. It could be charged in some extreme cases: eg Mark Dixie who claimed to have performed sex with the corpse of, but not to have killed, his victim: http://news.bbc.co.uk/1/hi/england/london/7254628.stm. He was convicted of murder.

[498] The offence is triable summarily or on indictment and has a maximum penalty of two years' imprisonment.

17.9.4.5 Sexual activity in a public lavatory

Section 71 creates an offence for A to engage in sexual activity[499] in a public lavatory.[500] There is no requirement that any person is alarmed or distressed by the activity. This is the only offence in the Act which is triable summarily only.[501] Section 320 of the Criminal Justice Act 2003 made the common law offence of 'outraging public decency' triable summarily as well as on indictment. The offence under s 71 is wider since there is no need for the act to have shocked, disgusted or revolted a member of the public.

17.10 Overarching problems with the 2003 Act

17.10.1 Undue complexity

In terms of technicality and complexity there are several problems with the Act.[502] First, it takes 80 sections to set out the many new offences, and these often contain numerous sub-categories of offence. For example, many involve aggravated versions for penetrative acts, and since these are indictable only and carry a different sentence, following *Courtie*[503] each represents a separate offence. Although it might be argued that it is better to have too many offences than too few in an area dealing with serious matters such as these, it is questionable whether tighter drafting and structure could have achieved adequate protection. This is not just a criticism levelled at the length of the Act; practical problems arise when there are too many charging options.[504] It produces confusion and inhibits optimal development of case law, with no guarantee that similar conduct will be treated consistently by the CPS and by courts. Recognizing the extent of the options available to prosecutors, the CPS guidelines[505] state that:

When choosing which offences to charge, prosecutors should choose the most appropriate offence to fit the circumstances of the case, taking account of the courts' sentencing powers. Counts on the indictment *must*:

- Reflect the seriousness and extent of the offending supported by the evidence;
- Give the court adequate powers to sentence and impose appropriate post-conviction orders; and,
- Enable the case to be presented in a clear and simple way.

. . .

Section 25 (familial child sex offence) where the complainant is 13 or over should be charged rather than section 9 (Sexual Activity with a Child), as long as all the elements can be proved. Adopting this approach makes clear the context in which an offence is committed.

---

[499] An activity is sexual if a reasonable person would, in all the circumstances, but regardless of any person's purpose, consider it to be sexual.

[500] 'Public lavatory' is defined as a lavatory to which the public or a section of the public has or is permitted to have access, whether on payment or otherwise. See C Ashford, 'Sexuality, Public Space and the Criminal Law: The Cottaging Phenomenon' (2007) 71 J Crim L 506.

[501] It carries a maximum penalty of six months' imprisonment or a fine.

[502] See JR Spencer, 'The Drafting of Criminal Legislation: Need It Be So Impenetrable?' (2008) 67 CLJ 585.

[503] [1984] AC 463.

[504] See *Grout* [2011] EWCA Crim 299. In some instances, it would appear that the objective in including a new crime is to trigger the availability of possible sexual offender orders under Part 2 of the Act.

[505] See CPS guidance at www.cps.gov.uk/legal-guidance/rape-and-sexual-offences-overview-and-index-2020-updated-guidance.

Parliament's decision to create so many offences is especially ironic given that the Sexual Offences Review was described as seeking to 'focus the law more sharply' and 'to abolish the unnecessary and useless offences which have accumulated over the years'.[506]

Secondly, the complexity is also exacerbated by the obsession with detail and with describing the manner in which the offence is committed rather than with the harm caused: whilst this shows commendable respect for the principles of fair labelling and maximum certainty, it creates confusion and density[507] in the legislation which renders it less accessible than it ought to be.[508] An example of this detail can be seen in s 67 (voyeurism): A, for the purpose of obtaining sexual gratification, observes or records or enables another to observe (with equipment or otherwise) B doing a 'private act' knowing B does not consent to observation for that purpose. By s 68 'private acts' are those 'in a private structure in which one would expect privacy and B's genitals, buttocks or [female] breasts are exposed or covered only with underwear, or B is using the lavatory, or B is doing a sexual act not of a kind ordinarily done in public'! This obsession with exhaustive definition is sadly lacking in some of the key definitions of fundamental issues such as 'consent'.

Finally, the number of offences and the minute definition of many elements produce some glaring examples of incoherence. One of the most striking is that although a person can engage in sexual activity at 16, it is still illegal to have a sexual relationship with his carer until over 18, or to engage in sexual conduct with certain members of the extended family even though he could marry them. Similarly, whilst it is legal for A to have intercourse with B aged 16, consensually taking or possessing her nude photo will not be legal unless A is married to her, or living with her in an enduring family relationship.

17.10.2 Overcriminalization?

In addition to the volume and complexity of the offences, there are many examples of the Act providing what are arguably overbroad offences. One obvious example is s 62: 'committing an offence with intent to commit a sexual offence'. This contains no limitation to the types of offence and no requirement that the preliminary offence is directed at the person who will be the victim of the sex offence.[509] The offence has been used diversely to prosecute acts such as committing criminal damage with intent to commit a sexual offence where A wrote graffiti on trains inciting underage girls to text him for sex.[510] Ironically, despite the detail and number of other offences in the Act, this section has proved important in making up for the shortfalls in drafting elsewhere.[511]

A further argument that the Act overcriminalizes can be based on the jurisdictional reach of the offences. As amended by the Criminal Justice and Immigration Act 2008, many of the offences (including ss 1–4, 5–8, 10–19, 25, 26, 30–41) can be prosecuted in England and Wales even if performed abroad if the victim was under 18 and the offender is a UK national or UK resident.[512] In the case of a UK national, it is no defence that the conduct was not criminal in the country in which it took place.

[506] Temkin (2000) 150 NLJ 1169.
[507] See the definition of foster siblings at s 27 for an example, p 848.
[508] Other memorable examples include the degree of detail in defining offences such as intercourse with an animal, where the Act goes so far as to extend the definition to the 'vagina or anus' to include references 'to any similar part' in animals—eg those functionally equivalent body parts in amphibians and crustaceans.
[509] A, 18, criminally damaging the condom machine to gain condoms to have consensual sex with B, 15, commits the offence.
[510] *Jones* [2007] EWCA Crim 1118, p 837.
[511] See the importance of this as noted by Woolf LCJ in *H*, p 816 and its use for kidnap cases, eg *Royle* [2005] EWCA Crim 279 (D kidnapped V at roadside and forced her to undress, she then escaped).
[512] Section 72 as amended by the Criminal Justice and Immigration Act 2008.

A further controversial aspect of the Act is the heavy reliance on strict liability in many contexts—most notably the offences committed against children under 13. There is, of course, a clear and legitimate objective in providing protection against sexual exploitation of young people. However, the criminal law should be reserved for the clearest cases of wrongdoing. The offences in relation to children impose strict liability as to age and can be committed irrespective of the age of the offender, his reasonable belief in the age of the victim or whether the acts were in a consensual or exploitative environment. Lord Millett's observations in the House of Lords only two years previously in *K* went unheeded: 'the age of consent has long ceased to reflect ordinary life, and in this respect Parliament has singularly failed to discharge its responsibility for keeping the criminal law in touch with the needs of society'.[513]

Some of the offences introduced demonstrate the clashes of principle which arise when criminal law seeks to regulate activities such as sexual behaviour. Examples include the difficulty in providing adequate protection for children and those with learning or mental disability without denying them an opportunity to express their sexual behaviour in non-exploitative relationships. The government claimed that it was not seeking to prosecute consensual conduct between youths that was not previously prosecuted. Given that the 2003 Act criminalizes a broader range of consensual sexual activities (eg watching sexual activity), this is doubtful. Moreover, even if the new offences were no broader and not prosecuted more frequently, this is not an adequate justification for creation of offences criminalizing consensual sexual activity (short of penetration) between minors and carrying a maximum of 14 years. The Act is supposed to modernize the law and to reflect the sexual mores of the twenty-first century. Implementing broad offences in the context of sexual conduct also poses a danger of sending conflicting messages to young members of society. In general, the Act sought to encourage and re-educate people about the significance of respecting the autonomy of individuals by obtaining their consent.[514] But with children under 16 that message may be undermined by a starker one—even if you do act responsibly and seek and gain consent in your sexual experimentation you will still commit a serious offence.

Parliament received repeated ministerial assurances that the volume, strictness and breadth of the offences would not lead to overcriminalization in practice because the CPS would exercise their discretion not to prosecute.[515] Aside from the fact that the Act leaves some very hard decisions to be made, in terms of principle, it is undesirable that such significant issues are a matter of discretion, not law. As the Joint Parliamentary Committee on Human Rights observed in the Twelfth Report.

Creating catch all offences and then relying on the prosecutor's discretion to sort things out satisfactorily undermines [the rule of law]. It leaves prosecutors to do the job that Parliament should be doing, and gives them discretion to prosecute (or not to prosecute) people who ought never to have been within the scope of criminal liability in the first place.[516]

---

[513] [2001] UKHL 41, [44]. On the House of Lords' approach to strict liability and age in sexual offences, see J Horder, 'How Culpability Can and Can't be Denied in Under Age Sex Crimes' [2001] Crim LR 15. See also A Ashworth, *Positive Obligations in Criminal Law* (2013) 120–2.

[514] On the criminal law's role in facilitating conditions in which autonomy can be promoted, see N Lacey, *Unspeakable Subjects* (1998) 151. Rubenfeld argues that rape should not be conceptualized as a violation of sexual autonomy and in fact it is a 'red herring'. He argues that a better approach is to compare rape to slavery and torture, which are violations of an individual's fundamental right to self-possession. See J Rubenfeld, 'The Riddle of Rape-by-Deception and the Myth of Sexual Autonomy' (2013) 122 Yale LJ 1372. For a defence of autonomy, see J Herring, 'Rape and the Definition of Consent' (2014) 26 NLSI Rev 62.

[515] The CPS policy is available from www.cps.gov.uk/legal-guidance/rape-and-sexual-offences-overview-and-index-2020-updated-guidance.

[516] Para 2.11.

Another unfortunate feature of the Act is that it perpetuates the growing trend of creating 'quasi-crimes'—civil orders that are backed by a criminal sanction for breach. These have become a common feature—Criminal Behaviour Orders, Football Banning Orders, exclusion orders, etc—and they pose many problems.[517] The 2003 Act introduced new orders including FTOs (Foreign Travel Orders), SHPOs (Sexual Harm Prevention Orders, as they are now) and RSHOs (Risk of Sexual Harm Orders).[518]

17.10.3 ECHR issues

In ECHR terms, the Act is only a partial success. Although succeeding in removing several incompatible offences (gross indecency, buggery, etc), it creates new problems of ECHR incompatibility. One of the most obvious and heavily criticized examples is the criminalization of sexual conduct between consenting children, particularly those aged 13 to 16.[519] The Parliamentary Joint Committee on Human Rights[520] suggested that some sections of the Act were overbroad in criminalizing all sexual touching between children. The decision of the House of Lords in G is disappointing.

Further reading

RA Duff and S Green, *Defining Crimes: Essays on the Special Part of the Criminal Law*

SP Green, *Criminalizing Sex: A Unified Liberal Theory*

J Temkin, *Rape and the Legal Process*

---

[517] See generally A Ashworth, 'Social Control and Anti-Social Behaviour: The Subversion of Human Rights?' (2004) 120 LQR 263.

[518] See S Shute, 'New Civil Preventative Orders: Sexual Offences Prevention Orders; Foreign Travel Orders; Risk of Sexual Harm Orders' [2004] Crim LR 417. In relation to England and Wales, the Anti-social Behaviour, Crime and Policing Act 2014, s 113 and Sch 5 abolished these orders and replaced them with 'Sexual Harm Prevention Orders' and 'Sexual Risk Orders' from 8 Mar 2015.

[519] See G discussed earlier. *Laskey v UK* (1997) 24 EHRR 39; *Sutherland v UK* (1997) 24 EHRR CD22; note also the Northern Irish case of S [2006] NICA 34 in which the Court of Criminal Appeal concluded that A lacked status as a victim and inclined to the view that the offence was justifiable to protect young girls from themselves.

[520] *Twelfth Report*, 2002–3, *Scrutiny of Bills: Further Progress Report*, 2003 (HL 119; HC 765).

18

Theft

18.1 Interpreting the Theft Acts

The law governing dishonesty-related offences is to be found in the Theft Acts 1968 and 1978, the Theft (Amendment) Act 1996 and the Fraud Act 2006.[1] These Acts are not a restatement of the common law and its numerous statutory additions. They provide a code of the most important offences of dishonest dealing with the protection of property (with the notable exception of the common law offence of conspiracy to defraud). They are based on a fundamental reconsideration of the principles by the Criminal Law Revision Committee (CLRC)[2] and the Law Commission.[3]

The law of theft is concerned with infringements against the proprietary interests of others but the law of property is not explained in any detailed fashion in the Theft Acts. It is a matter of civil law. The Theft Acts assume the existence of the civil law on personal and real property. The criminal courts, including the appellate courts, have sometimes shown impatience with arguments based on 'the finer distinctions in civil law',[4] but many of the fundamental issues of criminal liability turn on these civil law concepts. For example, whether property 'belongs to another' for the purposes of theft 'is a question to which

---

[1] See Ormerod and Williams, *Smith's Law of Theft*; Griew, *Theft*; Smith, *Property Offences*; for a more theoretical analysis, see Green, *13 Ways*.

[2] Eighth Report, para 7. And see Thirteenth Report (1977) Cmnd 6733.

[3] See especially LC 276, *Fraud* (2002).

[4] *Baxter* [1971] 2 All ER 359 at 363; *Morris* [1984] AC 320.

the criminal law offers no answer and which can only be answered by reference to civil law principles'.[5] Equally, the Acts provide no definition of what constitutes 'a proprietary right or interest' for the purposes of s 5 of the 1968 Act. Theft offences sometimes necessarily involve consideration of 'the finer distinctions in civil law'.[6] It follows, of course, that changes in the civil law may affect the scope of the criminal law.[7] The Acts, by protecting property rights per se, also serve to protect the vitally important mechanisms for creating and exchanging property rights.[8]

Unfortunately, the interpretation of the Theft Acts has produced a great deal of complex case law. In interpreting the Acts, the courts have usually aimed to give words and expressions their ordinary meaning so as to avoid undue technicality and subtlety. This is a sensible approach, but it has led to the practice of leaving the interpretation of 'ordinary' words and expressions to the jury.[9] The interpretation, even of ordinary words, must sometimes be a matter for the court to maintain respect for the rule of law and to ensure certainty, consistency and clarity in the definition and interpretation of the law. To leave interpretation in the hands of the juries (or more frequently the magistrates) is to risk their taking different views on indistinguishable facts. Even such ordinary words in the Theft Act as 'dishonesty', 'force', 'building', etc may involve definitional problems on which a jury may require guidance if like is to be treated as like. This poses potential problems of compatibility with Art 7 of the ECHR which protects against retrospective criminalization, and includes a requirement that crimes are defined with sufficient certainty and predictability.

One final aspect of the interpretation of the Theft Acts should also be emphasized from the outset. The appellate courts have demonstrated a distinct willingness to uphold the convictions of those found to have been dishonest even though there are fundamental errors with the conviction in other respects.[10] This has not generated the level of clarity and certainty of principle in the law that is desirable. In addition, such an approach places a degree of emphasis on the concept of dishonesty, which as we shall see, it is ill-suited to bear.[11] The Supreme Court has recently adopted a new approach to the interpretation of the concept of dishonesty which the Court of Appeal has now wholeheartedly endorsed.[12] We consider that significant change in detail later, along with the impact it will have in practice.

The offence of theft is an extremely broad one as will soon be appreciated. In an empirical study Green and Kugler questioned the merits of having such a broad single offence which fails to distinguish the different harms and wrongs involved in various activities which all result in the same outcome—D acquiring V's property.[13] In Green's recent work, he uses this empirical data to argue that the law of theft took a wrong turn with the enactment of the

---

[5] *Dobson v General Accident Fire and Life Assurance Corpn plc* [1989] 3 All ER 927 at 937 per Bingham LJ.

[6] See *Shadrokh-Cigari* [1988] Crim LR 465, p 899; *Wheeler* (1990) 92 Cr App R 279, p 879. See also JC Smith, 'Civil Law Concepts in the Criminal Law' (1972) 31 CLJ 197; GR Williams, 'Theft, Consent and Illegality' [1977] Crim LR 127 and 205; G Treitel, 'Contract and Crime' in *Crime, Proof and Punishment*, 81.

[7] See discussion of *Floyd v DPP*, p 895.

[8] See A Simester and GR Sullivan, 'On the Nature and Rationale of Property Offences' in Duff and Green, *Defining Crimes*, 173–83.

[9] See G Williams, 'Law and Fact' [1976] Crim LR 472; DW Elliott, 'Law and Fact in Theft Act Cases' [1976] Crim LR 707. See also *Brutus v Cozens* [1973] AC 854, cf *Chandler v DPP* [1964] AC 763, and DW Elliott, '*Brutus v Cozens*, Decline and Fall' [1989] Crim LR 323.

[10] See eg Lord Steyn in *Hinks*, at 844, discussed at p 873.

[11] See further Ormerod and Williams, *Smith's Law of Theft*, Ch 1.

[12] See *Barton and Booth* [2020] EWCA Crim 575 discussed at p 910.

[13] The study involved students ranking relative blameworthiness of D acquiring V's bike by theft, robbery, embezzlement, fraud, burglary, blackmail, etc. See SP Green and M Kugler, 'Community Perceptions of Theft Seriousness: A Challenge to Model Penal Code and English Theft Act Consolidation' (2010) 7 J Empirical Legal Studies 511.

1968 Act. Green's thesis is that abolishing the array of common law offences and replacing them with a single offence of theft fails to capture the gradations of moral culpability inherent in different kinds of conduct.[14]

18.2 The offence of theft

By s 1(1) of the Theft Act 1968:

A person is guilty of theft if he dishonestly appropriates property belonging to another with the intention of permanently depriving the other of it; and 'thief' and 'steal' shall be construed accordingly.

The maximum sentence is now seven years (s 7) on indictment.[15] The Sentencing Council has produced (revised) guidance.

The vast majority of thefts can be prosecuted without further difficulty by applying the straightforward meaning of the terms in the section. This is worth emphasizing before turning to detailed consideration of the elements of the offence.

18.3 Actus reus

The actus reus of theft consists: (a) in the appropriation of (b) property (c) belonging to another.

18.3.1 Appropriation

By s 3 of the Theft Act 1968:

(1) Any assumption by a person of the rights of an owner amounts to an appropriation, and this includes, where he has come by the property (innocently or not) without stealing it, any later assumption of a right to it by keeping or dealing with it as owner.

(2) Where property, or a right or interest in property is or purports to be transferred for value to a person acting in good faith, no later assumption by him of rights which he believed himself to be acquiring shall, by reason of any defect in the transferor's title, amount to theft of the property.

The CLRC did not provide a full definition of 'appropriation'[16] because it rather optimistically[17] assumed that people would realize that it was simply a different label for what they

---

[14] Green, *13 Ways*, Ch 1.

[15] Criminal Justice Act 1991, s 26. Originally it was ten years, but few people ever received sentences over seven years, although there were even some theft sentences as high as the maximum. We are grateful to Simon Price for pointing this out. Section 22A of the Magistrates' Courts Act 1980, added by the Anti-social Behaviour, Crime and Policing Act 2014, s 176, as amended by the Criminal Justice and Courts Act 2015, s 52 provides that low-value shoplifting (goods not in excess of £200 in value) will be triable only summarily unless the defendant is 18 or over and elects trial in the Crown Court. For discussion of this provision which has generated much confusion, see *Maxwell* [2017] EWCA Crim 1233; *Harvey* [2020] EWCA Crim 354. Under the Penalties for Disorderly Behaviour (Amount of Penalty) Order 2002, SI 2002/1837 (as amended), a fixed penalty may be awarded.

[16] For early comment on this element, see L Koffman, 'The Nature of Appropriation' [1982] Crim LR 331; D Stuart, 'Reform of the Law of Theft' (1967) 30 MLR 609.

[17] 'Conversion' is a complex tort and not even all tort lawyers have a full understanding of the concept. See A Dugdale, M Jones and M Simpson (eds), *Clerk and Lindsell on Torts* (23rd edn, 2020) Ch 17.

saw as the 'familiar concept of [the tort of] conversion . . .'[18] Appropriation was preferred because it aptly describes the kind of conduct in question and was felt broad enough to describe various types of conduct that had been separate offences under the previous law.[19]

Three basic problems in interpreting 'appropriation' have arisen, each having a significant impact on the scope of the offence:

(1) Is there an appropriation if D assumes only *a right* of the owner, not *all* the rights of that owner?

(2) Can D 'assume' rights when the alleged assumption is an act done with the consent of the owner?

(3) Can there be an appropriation when the effect is that the entire proprietary interest in the thing then belongs indefeasibly to the alleged thief?

Controversially, all three questions were answered in the affirmative by the House of Lords: the first two in *Gomez*,[20] and the third in *Hinks*.[21]

18.3.1.1 Assumption of 'a' right: *Morris*

Section 3 requires an assumption of 'the rights of an owner' which seems prima facie to mean all the rights, not one, or some, of the rights of the owner in question. But in *Morris* Lord Roskill nevertheless held that it is an appropriation if D assumes a single right. But surely, if D assumes *a right to* the thing, he treats it as *his*, something in which he owns *all* the rights. It is hard to see how a reference to 'rights' can point to a conclusion that the assumption of 'a right' is sufficient, but that is now the law.

Many think Lord Roskill's conclusion was obviously wrong,[22] but it formed an element in the *ratio decidendi* of *Morris*. It was endorsed by the House of Lords in *Gomez*. We must take it that the law is settled: any assumption of *any of* the rights of an owner amounts to an appropriation. This extends the scope of the offence so that D's acts, which might naturally be regarded as mere preparation or attempts because they involve the assumption of a single right, constitute the actus reus of the full offence.

Morris was concerned with a formerly common scenario where D switches the labels on two articles displayed on the shelves of a supermarket with the intention of buying the more expensive article for the price of the less expensive one. The right to label the goods is a right of the owner, so the label-switching amounted to an appropriation and theft. D, of course, intended to deceive the cashier and to obtain the goods by deception.[23] On the interpretation in *Morris*, D has appropriated the goods as soon as he switches the label even if D abandons the venture and leaves the goods with the switched labels safely on the shelf. It is important to remember that on these facts, to be guilty of theft D must be shown to have mens rea—the intention permanently to deprive and dishonesty; there would not necessarily be a completed theft where D moves articles in a supermarket as a prank or protest.

---

[18] Eighth Report, para 34.   [19] Larceny, embezzlement, conversion.

[20] [1993] AC 442, [1993] Crim LR 304 and commentary. On which see also M Davies, 'Consent after the House of Lords: Taking and Leading Astray the House of Lords' (1993) 13 LS 308; S Cooper and M Allen, 'Appropriation After *Gomez*' (1993) 57 J Crim L 186.

[21] [2000] 4 All ER 833. On which see especially: JC Smith [2001] Crim LR 162; ATH Smith, 'Theft or Sharp Practice: Who Cares Now?' (2001) 60 CLJ 21; J Beatson and A Simester, 'Stealing One's Own Property' (1999) 115 LQR 372; S Shute, 'Appropriation and the Law of Theft' [2002] Crim LR 445.

[22] See E Melissaris, 'The Concept of Appropriation and the Offence of Theft' (2007) 70 MLR 581 for support of the decision.

[23] At that time probably an offence under s 15 of the 1968 Act, and now an offence of making a false representation under ss 1 and 2 of the Fraud Act 2006

18.3.1.2 Appropriation with consent: *Gomez*

Section 3 is not drafted in terms of requiring a 'misappropriation'. In *Morris*, Lord Roskill, for a unanimous House, said, 'In the context of s 3(1), the concept of appropriation involves not an act expressly or impliedly authorized by the owner but an act by way of adverse interference with or usurpation of those rights.'[24] This, however, was *obiter*, because the label-switching was plainly unauthorized by the shop and there was no need to say anything about authorized acts. In *Gomez*, the House held that the Lord Roskill's *dictum* was wrong: the current law is that there can be an appropriation even if D acts with V's consent in relation to the property.

This is an issue that had been considered in several cases before *Gomez*. The House of Lords first considered the point in *Lawrence*,[25] in which D, a taxi driver, was convicted of stealing from V, an Italian who spoke little English. V showed D a note bearing an address and tendered £1 to be taken there. The authorized fare was about 50p but D indicated that £1 was not enough and took from V's still open wallet a £1 note and a £5 note. V permitted him to do so. D was convicted of theft. On appeal D argued that he took the money with V's consent. This was rejected. One of the questions certified for the House was whether the offence of theft was to be construed as if it contained the words 'without the consent of the owner'. The answer was, rightly, an emphatic 'no'. [26] The definition of theft was based on certain offences in the Larceny Act 1916 which had been replaced by the Theft Act.[27] Those offences did not include the phrase, 'without the consent of the owner' and it had never been suggested that someone acting with consent could be guilty of those offences. The CLRC intended no change in the law in that respect when it drafted the Theft Act. *Gomez* follows *Lawrence*.

The matter arose once more in the civil case of *Dobson v General Accident Fire and Life Assurance Corpn plc*,[28] which applied *Lawrence*. In *Dobson*, the plaintiff had been deceived by a rogue, R, into accepting a worthless cheque when selling his expensive watch and ring. Dobson brought an action in civil law to recover from his insurers the value of the watch and ring. The policy covered only loss by theft. It was not enough for Dobson to prove (this being a civil case) that his property had been obtained by deception (as it undoubtedly had). The insurers argued that there was no theft.[29] Parker LJ held that the making of the contract over the phone days before the delivery constituted the act of appropriation—it was an assumption of ownership by R.[30] There was an appropriation even if Dobson had consented to R's conduct.

Gomez, the assistant manager of a shop, persuaded the manager to sell goods to the value of £17,000 to his accomplice, X, and to accept payment by two cheques. The cheques, as Gomez and X knew, were stolen and worthless. They should have been charged with obtaining the goods by deception, contrary to s 15 of the 1968 Act;[31] but, for some reason, they were

---

[24] [1983] 3 All ER at 292. See LH Leigh, 'Some Remarks on Appropriation in the Law of Theft after *Morris*' (1985) 48 MLR 167.

[25] [1972] AC 626. For defence of *Lawrence* on pragmatic grounds, see P Glazebrook, 'Thief or Swindler: Who Cares?' (1991) 50 CLJ 389.

[26] For a contrary view see N Tamblyn, 'Reforming Theft: Taking Without Consent' [2020] Crim LR 594.

[27] The offences of fraudulent conversion and larceny by a bailee. On the value of these distinct offences, see A Steele, 'Taking Possession: The Defining Element of Theft?' (2008) 32 Melbourne University L Rev 1030.

[28] [1990] 1 QB 274.

[29] Ownership passed when a contract of sale was made over the phone two days before delivery so that R, when he collected the goods, was taking delivery of his own property.

[30] On the insurance implications of the definition of theft generally, see M Wasik, 'Definitions of Crimes in Insurance Contracts' [1986] J Bus Law 45.

[31] It would now be a straightforward case under s 2 of the Fraud Act 2006.

charged with theft.[32] The Court of Appeal, following *Morris*, quashed their convictions. The House of Lords in *Gomez*, relying heavily on the judgment of Parker LJ in *Dobson*, restored the convictions holding that, on the issue of the effect of consent, *Lawrence* and *Morris* were irreconcilable. The proposition in *Lawrence* was *ratio decidendi*, that in *Morris* an *obiter dictum*: *Lawrence* prevailed.

18.3.1.3 Theft where consent is given without deception by D

The point of law of general importance certified for the decision of the House in *Gomez* was whether there is an appropriation where 'consent has been obtained by a false representation', as occurred in that case. It was not necessary for the House to go beyond that and consider cases in which no deception was involved.[33] Nevertheless, the House chose to confirm explicitly that there could be an appropriation even where D has practised no deception on V. This was illustrated by their example of a label-switcher in the supermarket. Their lordships were in no doubt that D, in that scenario, appropriates property when he touches the article on the shelf, although he has, as yet, practised no deception.[34]

The conclusion in *Gomez* that an appropriation can occur with the owner's consent, irrespective of that consent being induced by deception, is further illustrated by the overruling of *Fritschy*.[35] The owner of some Krugerrands (a South African gold coin with a portrait of President Kruger on the obverse) instructed Fritschy to take them to Switzerland, F did so and then took them for himself as he planned all along. The Court of Appeal held that since everything F did in England was with the consent of the owner, F committed no appropriation and therefore no theft within the jurisdiction. The House of Lords in *Gomez* held that that was wrong. Fritschy committed theft the moment he first got his hands on the property in England with intent to steal it, although there was no finding of any deception.

Gomez also overruled *Skipp*.[36] There D, 'posing as a genuine haulage contractor' (presumably that was itself an operative deception), collected three loads from different places in London with instructions to deliver them in Leicester. D deviated from the route to Leicester and transferred the goods to an accomplice, as he had planned all along. The Court of Appeal in *Skipp* held that though D may have had mens rea—a dishonest intention permanently to deprive at the time he received each of the three loads—he had done nothing inconsistent with the rights of the owners until he diverted the goods from their proper destination. According to the court in *Skipp*, that was the point at which D stole. Since *Gomez* it is now clear that he committed three thefts, one each time he collected a load.[37]

[32] For consideration of when ownership passed, see R Heaton, 'Deceiving without Thieving' [2001] Crim LR 712.
[33] There was powerful, though, it is submitted, mistaken, academic support suggesting that there can be an appropriation where the consent was by a false representation. See G Williams, 'Theft and Voidable Title' [1981] Crim LR 666, and see the reply by JC Smith at [1981] Crim LR 677. See also a letter by GV Hart [1982] Crim LR 391.
[34] Arguably he commits the general fraud offence contrary to s 1(2)(a) and s 2 of the Fraud Act 2006 in relation to *both* items as soon as he switches the labels. There is a false representation as to the more expensive item and by that representation D intends to cause loss to the shopkeeper. The cheaper item is now falsely represented to have a higher price. If D's intent is that X will pay that amount for it he intends to cause loss to X; if it is his intent that no one will, but it remains at its inflated price, he commits fraud against the shopkeeper because he intends the keeper to be exposed to the risk of loss on the sale of that item.
[35] [1985] Crim LR 745. A charge of obtaining property by deception was withdrawn from the jury.
[36] [1975] Crim LR 114.
[37] Each theft being also an offence of obtaining property by deception which existed at that time.

18.3.1.4 Appropriation of indefeasible title to property: *Hinks*

It was argued that despite the incredible breadth of the concept of appropriation as interpreted in *Gomez*, there remained one necessary limitation to that concept. In all the decided cases, any proprietary right acquired by D's appropriation was voidable:[38] the owner was entitled to rescind the transaction and get his property back. Following *Gomez* these appropriations could nevertheless constitute theft. In contrast, where D gets an absolute, indefeasible right to the property, he has the right to retain the property. It was thought by some to be unacceptable—impossible applying orthodox civil law rules relating to personal property—for a criminal court to hold that a transaction which resulted in D obtaining such a right amounted to a theft of the property by him. If D has a right to retain the property, or even to recover it from the alleged victim, it could hardly be held to be theft for him to take and keep it.[39] This argument underestimated the determination of some judges including, as it happened, a majority of a particular committee of the House of Lords, to uphold convictions of those found by a jury to be dishonest.

In each of a series of three cases, D received a substantial gift from V, a person of a vulnerable mental state, over whom D had acquired some influence. Importantly, in each case V was of sufficient mental capacity in law to make a gift of property.[40] On those facts in civil law, in each case there was a valid gift to D.[41] The Court of Appeal Criminal Division adopted different approaches in the three cases but in the last of the three, *Hinks*,[42] the Court of Appeal held that it was immaterial whether there was a valid gift. That court held that the only question was whether D, the recipient of the gift, was dishonest—and the jury had found that she was. The House of Lords, Lords Hutton and Hobhouse dissenting, upheld the conviction.

The conduct of the accused in all these cases was despicable.[43] They were, as the jury must have found in each case, dishonestly taking an unfair advantage of a person with failing mental powers. If the donors were mentally incapable of making a valid gift owing to their diminished mental capacity, the cases were unanswerable. But the prosecutions were not made on the basis that the victims lacked mental capacity to make decisions to give their property away. We must assume they were capable and had done so. It should be reiterated at this point that the offence of theft was drafted with the purpose of protecting property rights, not protecting against exploitation per se.[44] Farmer has suggested that the aims of property offences have not shifted. Rather than protecting property rights 'as defined in the

---

[38] Where one party to a transaction is acting under a fundamental mistake the transaction is void and no property passes. Where, in contrast, the party is acting under a non-fundamental mistake, the transaction is voidable and property does pass.

[39] If it were theft by D, the civil law would be assisting D to enjoy, or to recover, the fruits of his crime by providing protection through the law relating to conversion!

[40] The gift might, in civil law, have been voidable because of the exercise of undue influence by D, but the juries were not asked to consider that question, so we must take it that it was not.

[41] For the argument that it is difficult to determine with certainty whether the civil law would in fact provide a remedy in circumstances such as these, see SP Green, 'Theft and Conversion—Tangibly Different?' (2012) 128 LQR 564.

[42] [1998] Crim LR 904. The court derived 'some comfort' from Simon Gardner's article, 'Property and Theft' [1998] Crim LR 35.

[43] All would now likely be guilty of the offence of fraud under s 4 of the Fraud Act 2006.

[44] cf AL Bogg and J Stanton-Ife, 'Protecting the Vulnerable: Legality, Harm and Theft' (2003) 23 LS 402. See also S Shute, 'Appropriation and the Law of Theft' [2002] Crim LR 445. Green also defends the decisions of the House of Lords in *Lawrence*, *Gomez* and *Hinks*. Green relies extensively upon Peter Westen's work on consent to argue that the victims in these three cases did not truly consent to the taking of their property. He uses the cases to illuminate the role that lack of consent plays in defining the moral content of theft crimes. See Green, *13 Ways*, 105–8.

civil law', the key concern is now to protect 'the interests of the vulnerable against conduct which poses a threat to the security of property and the securing of confidence in institutions such as the market in which property is transferred'.[45] With the advent of the fraud offence of abusing a position of financial trust,[46] which is explicitly designed to criminalize exploitative dishonest conduct, there is a yet stronger argument that the courts should reconsider the actus reus of theft to return it to acceptable limits based on the protection of property rights.[47]

The result of the decision of the House of Lords in *Hinks* is that the recipient of a valid gift may now be guilty of stealing it—provided that a jury is satisfied that his mind was dishonest in the sense to be considered later. As Professor Smith commented, 'At its outer reaches theft becomes something akin to "thought crime".'[48] Aside from creating an astonishingly broad offence of theft, this creates numerous problems.

First, although there is a theft there are sometimes no stolen goods because the donor never has any right to restitution:[49] the property belongs absolutely to D forever.

Secondly, there is the problem of the relationship between civil and criminal law.[50] There are principled arguments for the criminal law not extending beyond the civil law, in particular in the area of theft where the criminal law is necessarily developed on the foundations of civil law concepts of property, ownership, etc. The majority of the House in *Hinks* acknowledged, with surprising equanimity, that their decision creates a conflict between the civil and the criminal law.[51] D who has V's consent to appropriate the property will commit no civil law wrong and, indeed, will be able to rely on the civil law to enforce the transfer of property, but will be exposed to prosecution for theft. In *Hinks*, Lord Steyn states, however, that 'it would be wrong to assume on a priori grounds that the criminal law rather than the civil law is defective' in creating this conflict. If we were constructing a new code of civil and criminal law, it would certainly be open to the legislator to prefer a principle of the criminal law to one of the civil law, but that is not the position. The Theft Acts assume the existence of the civil law of property rights and the criminal courts are, or should be, bound to take it as they find it.

The implications of the decision are significant. Suppose that D is selling a painting of Salisbury Cathedral. V becomes very excited on seeing the painting and, thinking he is about to get a bargain, offers D £100,000 for it. D realizes that V thinks the painting is by Constable, but D knows that it was painted by his sister and is worth no more than £100. He accepts V's offer. D has made an enforceable contract and he is entitled to recover and to

---

[45] L Farmer, *Making the Modern Criminal Law: Civil Order and Criminalization* (2016) 223.

[46] See p 997.

[47] It has been argued that it is wrong to assume that a general fraud offence is fit for the purpose of penalizing exploitation. See J Collins, 'Exploitation of Persons and the Limits of the Criminal Law' [2017] Crim LR 169.

[48] 'Theft or Sharp Practice Who Cares Now?'(2001) 60 CLJ 21, 22. For a view that even after *Hinks* the argument is still open that a valid gift cannot be dishonest, see *Arlidge and Parry on Fraud* (6th edn, 2020) paras 2.035 and 2.049.

[49] See s 24(3) of the Theft Act 1968, p 1075. Assuming a valid gift, the goods were never out of lawful custody or possession and the donor never had a right to restitution. Hinks was ordered to pay £19,000 compensation to Dolphin. Compensation for what? For keeping a gift which she was entitled to keep? The jury's verdict did not decide that she did not have an *indefeasible* title to the property. Was the judge entitled to decide that her title was defeasible?—for misrepresentation, undue influence, or what? Could Hinks have an argument that the order was contrary to her right to peaceful enjoyment of her possessions under Art 1, Protocol 1 to the ECHR?

[50] See on this more generally: Smith (1972B) 31 CLJ 197; Williams [1977] Crim LR 127 and 205; ATH Smith, 'Gifts and the Law of Theft' (1999) 58 CLJ 10.

[51] Contrast with the argument in *Ivey*, p 914, that the criminal law test of dishonesty must change to avoid conflict with the civil law definition of that concept.

retain the money.[52] To take another scenario, consider a buyer, D2, who knew that a picture was in fact by Constable and bought it for a very small sum from a seller, V2, who, as D2 was aware, did not know its provenance. A jury might well regard the conduct in these examples as dishonest—and, of course, V would not have consented in either case, had he known the true facts. The effect of *Hinks* is that if the jury is satisfied that these defendants were dishonest, they are guilty of stealing the property—property to which they are absolutely entitled in civil law.

A third problem with the decision in *Hinks* is with the requirement that at the time of appropriation there must be property belonging to another. In the trilogy of cases *Mazo*, *Hopkins and Kendrick* and *Hinks*, the property belonged to the donor, V, until the instant when the dishonest act of receiving the gift (appropriation) was done. D's acquisition of the entire proprietary interest and the appropriation were simultaneous. If, however, D acquires the entire interest first and then, after an interval, does the act alleged to be an appropriation, it seems he cannot, even after *Hinks*, be guilty: he has not then appropriated property belonging to another—it is already his.[53] For example, consider a case where V, infatuated by a wealthy man, D, sends a valuable gift to D's house where it arrives while D is absent abroad. When D comes home, he treats it as his own—which it is. However dishonest a jury might think his conduct at that point in time, this cannot be theft. The property is already D's.

18.3.1.5 The consequences of the House of Lords' interpretation of appropriation

In the trilogy of cases—*Morris*, *Gomez* and *Hinks*—the House has adopted an interpretation of appropriation at odds with that intended and with very significant ramifications.[54]

Overextending the scope of the offence

The effect of the overbroad reading of the element of appropriation is to render the offence of theft an extraordinarily wide one, embracing conduct which would more naturally be regarded as merely preparatory acts, not even amounting to an attempt to steal. Where V is the absolute owner of property, the general principle in civil law is that only he has any right to do anything to or with it. Anyone else who does anything to or with it is therefore exercising a right of the owner. If V has consented to or authorized the exercise of that right by D we would not, it is submitted, ordinarily describe that exercise as an 'assumption' or 'appropriation'; but, since it has been decided that consent and authority are immaterial, it is both. And since the assumption of any one of the owner's rights in the property is an appropriation of the property itself, this amounts to theft if done dishonestly and with an intention permanently to deprive.

---

[52] cf *Smith v Hughes* (1871) LR 6 QB 597 (sale of oats enforceable by seller although he knew that the buyer thought they were old oats, new oats being useless to him, and that the oats were in fact new). Another example may be the case where a finder has in law a better right to the thing found than the landowner: p 891. However dishonest the finder may be, he should not be guilty of theft by appropriating that which the law says he may appropriate.

[53] See Lord Hobhouse at [2000] 4 All ER 855f–g.

[54] E Meliassaris, 'The Concept of Appropriation and the Offence of Theft' (2007) 70 MLR 581 has suggested that appropriation should be understood as occurring only when D develops a 'proprietary subjectivity' for the property, ie thinks of the property as his own. This might produce results which are as unpalatable as under the present law. Eg in *Fritschy*, as with other bailments, appropriation may be at the time of taking physical control of the goods even if within the terms of the bailment. The donee of a gift could, on this test, be held to have appropriated it, as in *Hinks*. See also on the interpretation of appropriation, N Weinrich, 'German Cures For English Ailments? Appropriation Versus Taking Away—Significance and Consequences of Conceptual Differences Between the English and the German Law of Theft' (2005) 69 J Crim L 427.

Theft might now be defined as follows:

Anyone doing anything whatever to property belonging to another, with or without his consent, appropriates it; and, if he does so dishonestly and with intent by that, or any subsequent act, permanently to deprive, he commits theft.

Prosecutors may, as a result of the broad interpretation, find it easier to secure convictions for theft in most cases, but problems may arise in identifying the precise time and place of the act which constitutes the appropriation. Astonishing though it may sound, despite the incredible breadth of the offence as currently interpreted, prosecutors may well be advised to prefer the offence of fraud in many cases since that is even wider and requires no proof of loss, gain, appropriation or intention permanently to deprive.[55] It is obvious that the combination of the interpretation of theft and the offences of fraud provide English criminal law with some of the most wide-reaching dishonesty offences imaginable.

Overemphasis on mens rea

By reducing the actus reus almost to vanishing point, theft becomes (too) dependent on mens rea, placing additional emphasis on dishonesty. It loses what Fletcher would describe as its 'manifest criminality'.[56] It should be noted that a minority of academics welcomed this shift. For example, Gardner regarded the decision in *Gomez* as 'unimpeachable' in following the decision in *Lawrence*, and 'desirable from first principles . . . [since] the quality of the dishonest conduct is not necessarily altered by the victim's consent'.[57]

The overlap with obtaining property by deception under s 15

The effect of *Gomez* was that virtually[58] all offences of obtaining property by deception contrary to s 15 were also theft (except obtaining land, which, the Act provides, cannot be stolen). The creation of this degree of overlap made life much easier for prosecutors, but was not what the Act's drafters intended,[59] which was to maintain a difference between offences of obtaining ownership by deception and theft.[60]

The distinction between obtaining *possession* of property and obtaining outright *ownership* had troubled the courts for years. The old law had separate offences: one to deal with cases where D by deception caused V to transfer possession (larceny by trick) and one where D by deception caused V to transfer ownership (obtaining by false

---

[55] See Ch 22.

[56] G Fletcher, *Rethinking Criminal Law* (1978) 82. See M Giles and S Uglow, 'Appropriation and Manifest Criminality in Theft' (1992) 56 J Crim L 179 and see Steele (2008) 32 Melbourne University L Rev 1030.

[57] S Gardner, 'Appropriation in Theft: The Last Word' (1993) 109 LQR 194. See also P Glazebrook, 'Revising the Theft Acts' (1993) 52 CLJ 191 pointing out that D's moral blameworthiness is as great in these cases where V consents.

[58] R Heaton, 'Deceiving without Thieving' [2001] Crim LR 712, describes cases where the obtaining of goods may still not amount to theft, including eg goods delivered under a mail order contract.

[59] Strikingly, in *Briggs* [2004] 1 Cr App R 34, the Court of Appeal resisted a wide reading of appropriation, by relying on an argument that to do otherwise would mean that there was too great an overlap between theft and deception. This is precisely the reasoning that had on three occasions failed to persuade the House of Lords against creating an almost total overlap between the offences. For an illustration of how the overlap caused courts to be too lax in their scrutiny of the allegations, see *Clarke v CPS* [2007] EWHC 2228 (Admin).

[60] This is quite distinct from the expressly intended overlap between, eg, theft and robbery, where all robberies must contain a theft. This point undermines the argument in S Gardner, 'Appropriation in Theft: The Last Word' (1993) 109 LQR 194.

pretences).[61] The two offences were complex in application but generally thought to be mutually exclusive.[62]

The CLRC, when drafting the Theft Act, decided to create an offence of obtaining property by deception (s 15) to cover all cases of conduct that would have been larceny by a trick or obtaining by false pretences. So, under the Theft Act as enacted, the prosecutor could not go wrong if he charged s 15 whenever D had obtained any interest in property—whether possession or ownership—by any kind of trick or false pretence. Some cases in which D obtained possession of the property with consent but had not obtained ownership would be theft, as well as obtaining by deception, but the intention was that if a deception was involved, s 15 should be charged.[63]

Unfortunately, some prosecutors and judges failed to recognize the distinction in the 1968 Act. Lawrence, the dishonest taxi driver, should have been charged with obtaining by deception[64] but the argument was not properly presented to the House of Lords in that case.[65] Gomez should also have been charged with obtaining by deception. In *Gomez*, the appellant invited the House to look at the Report of the CLRC to discover the way the 1968 Act was intended to operate. The majority declined as it would 'serve no useful purpose' to do so. Lord Lowry, dissenting, demonstrated convincingly that reference to the Report would have shown that there was no intention for theft to include cases where D obtained ownership with V's consent. The law should have been as stated in the *dictum* in *Morris*, not the decision in *Lawrence* (on this point); and Gomez was wrongly convicted of theft. Some may think that there would have been 'a useful purpose' in looking at the CLRC Report.

In terms of labelling, 'theft' and 'deception' reflect separate moral wrongs.[66] The judicial blurring of such distinctions undermines the coherence of the Act's scheme of offences.

Creating confusion in the lower courts

The initial reaction of the Court of Appeal to *Gomez* seemed to have been one of incredulity. In *Gallasso*,[67] an appeal heard on the very day that judgment was given in *Gomez*, the court said that although a taking with consent may be an appropriation, 'there must still be a taking' (in that case the theft was by a nurse caring for a vulnerable person). That would have imposed drastic limitations on theft, but it is an untenable opinion. There is no requirement for 'appropriation' to include a physical taking. *Gallasso* appears indistinguishable from *Fritschy* and must be taken as wrongly decided.

---

[61] See G Ferris, 'The Origins of Larceny by Trick and Constructive Possession' [1998] Crim LR 17. On the moral differences between the types of dishonest conduct and public perceptions of such, see SP Green and M Kugler, 'Community Perceptions of Theft Seriousness: A Challenge to Model Penal Code and English Theft Act Consolidation' (2010) 7 J Empirical Legal Studies 511.

[62] On the moral differences between the types of dishonest conduct and public perceptions of such, see Green and Kugler (2010) 7 J Empirical Legal Studies 511.

[63] cf Smith, *Property Offences*, para 5.17. See the confusion where both theft and deception were available: *Clarke v CPS* [2007] EWHC 2228 (Admin). The repeal of the deception offences means that the overlap will now be with the Fraud Act 2006.

[64] He obtained ownership of the excessive fare by deception, since V permitted him to take the money only because D had told him, falsely, that £1 was not enough.

[65] For an opinion as to the questions which the House ought to have been asked, see [1971] Crim LR 53, 54.

[66] See in particular S Shute and J Horder, 'Thieving and Deceiving: What is the Difference' (1993) 56 MLR 548, 'the thief makes war on a social practice from the outside, the deceiver is the traitor within'; C Clarkson, 'Theft and Fair Labelling' (1993) 56 MLR 554. See, for a more pragmatic view, Glazebrook (1991) 50 CLJ 389 and (1993) 52 CLJ 191. Shute and Horder suggest that the true distinction lies in the voluntariness of the transfer. This test, it is submitted, carries its own substantial difficulties, some of which are addressed by Clarkson.

[67] [1993] Crim LR 459. See also [1993] Crim LR at 307. Griew, *Theft*, para 2.89 thought the 'strange judgment' may 'defy rationalisation'; and Smith, *Property Offences*, para 5.56, concludes that it is 'simply wrong'.

The Court of Appeal's apparent disbelief at the breadth of the offence of theft in the wake of *Gomez* and *Hinks* continues to manifest itself. In *Ashcroft*,[68] D, a haulier, was alleged to have conspired to steal items from sealed containers in transit. The court regarded as 'some way removed from reality' D's argument that the theft occurred when D originally took possession of the goods in his lorries (in Scotland). Having referred to *Atakpu* (discussed later), the court commented that in this case 'there never was in any ordinary sense of the word an "appropriation" of the stolen goods until the conspirators removed them from the containers . . .'[69] True enough, but since *Gomez*, the word appropriation does not bear the 'ordinary' meaning that its drafters had intended.[70] It is difficult to distinguish the case from *Skipp* or *Fritschy*, neither of which was cited by the court.

The greater importance of timing

In some cases there will be a greater significance on the precise time at which the appropriation occurs. Consider *Dip Kaur v Chief Constable for Hampshire*.[71] While in a shop D found a pair of shoes one of which was labelled £6.99 and the other £4.99. These were in a rack of shoes which she knew to be properly priced £6.99 a pair. She took the pair to the cashier, and, as she hoped, the cashier saw the lower and not the higher price. She paid £4.99 and left the shop with the shoes. Her conviction for theft was quashed on the ground that the cashier had authority to accept D's offer to buy at the lower price and the ownership passed to D. It now seems clear, in the light of *Gomez*, that D was guilty of theft as soon as she did anything with the shoes with a dishonest intent—probably when she picked them up and noticed the price discrepancy and decided to act on it, certainly not later than when she tendered them to the cashier.

Jurisdictional matters

The significance of the timing of the appropriation can be important if there is a cross-jurisdictional aspect to the crime. The House of Lords' decision in *Gomez* was therefore applied, with great reluctance, by the Court of Appeal in *Atakpu*.[72] D and E hired cars in Germany and Belgium and drove them to England intending to sell them to bona fide purchasers. They were detained in Dover and charged with conspiracy to steal. The trial judge, applying the Court of Appeal's decision in *Gomez*, held that there was no theft outside the jurisdiction (ie England and Wales) because everything that was done there (Germany and Belgium) was done with the consent of the owner. The judge went on to hold that theft would have been committed in England when D and E retained the cars after the expiration of the hire period with the dishonest intention of permanently depriving the owners.[73] However, by the time *Atakpu* reached the Court of Appeal, the House of Lords had allowed the appeal in *Gomez*. The Court of Appeal felt bound to conclude that theft was committed outside the jurisdiction when the cars were obtained irrespective of the consent of the owner which D and E had induced by their deception. The court concluded that while theft may continue as long as the thief is 'on the job', and that this is a question for a jury, no jury could reasonably decide that these thefts were continuing days after D and E had first obtained the cars. Theft is a finite act and this theft ended outside the jurisdiction of the English courts.

---

68 [2003] EWCA Crim 2365.   69 At [45].

70 For an early discussion of the two senses of the word 'appropriation', see A Halpin, 'The Appropriate Appropriation' [1991] Crim LR 426 and A Halpin, *Definition in the Criminal Law* (2004) 166–81.

71 [1981] 2 All ER 430. D was probably guilty of obtaining by deception by representing that the authorized price was £4.99 when she knew it was £6.99.

72 [1994] QB 69.

73 This was *Fritschy* in reverse. D and E were guilty of conspiracy to steal in England.

There was a conspiracy (now under s 1 and s 1A of the Criminal Law Act 1977[74]) in England to steal in Germany and Belgium, but not to steal *in England*.[75]

Conflict with the civil law

Glanville Williams argued that no act should amount to theft unless it is contrary to the civil law. Nearly all thefts do amount to the civil wrongs of trespass, conversion or breach of trust but it does not follow that civil unlawfulness is a necessary constituent of the offence.[76] The definition of theft does not use the word 'unlawfully' nor does it say '*mis*appropriate'.[77]

The courts are extremely reluctant to admit consideration of civil law into criminal cases, even where it is inevitable, and these arguments have not been judicially accepted.[78] After *Gomez* and *Hinks*,[79] the arguments appear untenable. The removal of goods from the shelves of a supermarket is not a civil wrong merely because the act is done with a secret dishonest intent, but it is now theft. Fritschy committed no civil wrong by carrying out his employer's instructions to take the Krugerrands to Switzerland, but since *Gomez* we know he was a thief.

In *Hinks*, the House of Lords recognized that the decision led to a conflict, but took comfort from Gardner's argument that the criminal law can 'float free' of the civil law in this context. It is submitted that this ignores the underlying purpose of the offence of theft and others in the Theft Acts being designed to protect property—a civil law concept.[80] Shute suggests an alternative argument; dishonest conduct such as that in *Hinks* might not constitute a civil law wrong, it 'may nonetheless have a *tendency* to undermine property rights either directly by attacking the interests that they protect, or indirectly by weakening an established system of property rights and so threatening the public good that the system represents'.[81] It is submitted that such vague concepts of harm do not form a sufficiently clear or solid foundation for an offence that is serious, commonplace and for which a clear rationale—protecting property rights—has existed since its inception. The consequence of accepting the arguments supporting the *Hinks* proposition is, of course, that the offence becomes almost entirely dependent on the concept of dishonesty. It becomes an offence protecting against exploitation not property rights.[82]

---

[74] See p 480. See further M Hirst, *Jurisdiction and the Ambit of the Criminal Law* (2003) para 2.26.

[75] See G Sullivan and C Warbrick, 'Territoriality, Theft and *Atakpu*' [1994] Crim LR 650 at 659 for an argument that the court was misled by the phrase 'theft abroad is not triable in England' and that so-called 'theft abroad' is not theft under English law; D and E had come by the cars without stealing them so their later assumption of a right to the cars in England would have amounted to an appropriation; the cars were to be stolen in English law for the first time when appropriated in England. For a counter-argument see the 12th edn of this book.

[76] '. . . the aims and purposes of the civil law are not co-extensive with the criminal', Smith, *Property Offences*, para 5.06; but see also paras 5.11–5.52.

[77] Although this is regarded as 'the very essence of the offence' by Simester and Sullivan in Duff and Green, *Defining Crimes*, 173.

[78] A partner has been held guilty of theft of the partnership property, even though his act did not amount to the tort of conversion. The court did not think it necessary to look for any other civil wrong—in fact, the act must have been a breach of contract: *Bonner* [1970] 2 All ER 97n.

[79] See Lord Hobhouse at [2000] 4 All ER 865b.

[80] See also J Beatson and A Simester, 'Stealing One's Own Property' (1999) 115 LQR 372. It is a decision described by Simester and Sullivan in Duff and Green, *Defining Crimes* as 'subversive', at 179.

[81] Shute [2002] Crim LR 445, 455.

[82] Simester and Sullivan in Duff and Green, *Defining Crimes*, 180. See also SP Green, *Lying, Cheating and Stealing: A Moral Theory of White Collar Crime* (2006) Ch 6: recognizing that to steal is to violate 'in some fundamental way, another's rights of ownership [or possession]', at 89–90. For a more substantive (and compelling) account of the wrongfulness of theft, see Green, *13 Ways*, 91–131. At the risk of oversimplifying Green's sophisticated argument, it is that theft has both a primary wrong and a secondary wrong. The primary wrong is the wrong that is the consequence of depriving someone of his property rights. The secondary wrong is the means by which that deprivation is effected. Green argues that it is this secondary wrong that has been blunted by the abolition of the various common law offences and their replacement with a monolithic offence of theft.

18.3.1.6 Theft without loss

The offence of theft does not require proof of loss. This is illustrated by *Chan Man-sin v A-G of Hong Kong*.[83] A company accountant drew a forged cheque on the company's bank account. He was guilty of stealing the company's credit balance, or its contractual right to overdraw from the bank (which is property in the form of a 'thing in action'). This was theft even though applying settled banking law, the company, on discovering the unauthorized debit, was entitled to have it reversed and would lose nothing. In law, D's actions were wholly ineffective, the company was never a penny the worse off; but it was held that there was an appropriation—because D assumed the rights of an owner over the credit balance—and an intent permanently to deprive—because he intended to treat the thing as his own to dispose of regardless of the company's rights.[84]

The Privy Council has subsequently endorsed the broad effect of *Hinks*, rejecting an argument that there is a requirement to prove loss to V[85] in *Wheatley v Commissioner of Police of the British Virgin Islands*.[86] As Lord Bingham observed:

it is certainly true that in most cases of theft there will be an original owner of money or goods who will be poorer because of the defendant's conduct. But in one of the two cases in *Morris* the defendant was arrested before paying the reduced price for the goods, so that the supermarket suffered no loss, and, in *R (A) v Snaresbrook Crown Court*,[87] it was accepted that the alleged theft was carried out for a purpose which could financially benefit the company.[88]

18.3.1.7 Appropriation by 'keeping' and 'dealing'

Section 3 provides that there can be an appropriation not only by assuming the right of an owner as discussed so far in this chapter, but also by keeping or dealing with property as owner. It is difficult to conceive of D being held to be 'dealing' with the property where he has done nothing at all in relation to the goods, even though he has made up his mind to steal them.[89] Arguably, however, 'keeping' is somewhat broader.

Suppose that D, having borrowed V's bike for a week, resolves at the end of the week to keep it. It would clearly be an appropriation, at the end of the week, to refuse to return it on demand,[90] or to deny V access to it or for D to claim it as his own. Such conduct shows that he is keeping it as owner. It would also constitute appropriation if D were to use the bike after the end of the week because that use would be an assumption of one of the owner's rights. But what if D, on the expiry of the loan, merely leaves the bike where it is in his garage, hoping that V will forget about it, and intending to keep it? Literally, the case falls within s 3 since D is 'keeping . . . it as owner' and there is no justification for giving the words other than their plain meaning. Of course, it would be very difficult to prove D's mens rea in the form of the intention permanently to deprive, but he satisfies the appropriation requirement of keeping as owner. Proof would be even more difficult in the case of some forms of property. As the court has underlined in *Gresham*,[91] '"keeping" as owner in relation to a bank account may be difficult to prove in a case where [D] does no more than refrain from bringing the mistake to the attention of the bank'.[92] Some positive act such as making out a cheque, or authorizing a payment, on the account may be necessary.

83 [1988] 1 All ER 1.   84 Presumably the same principle applies to tangible property.
85 [2006] UKPC 24.   86 ibid.   87 [2001] All ER (D) 123, [25].   88 At [11].
89 But see *A-G's Reference (No 1 of 1983)* [1985] QB 182.
90 cf *Wakeman* (1912) 8 Cr App R 18.   91 [2003] EWCA Crim 2070.
92 Approving the statements in *Ngan* [1998] 1 Cr App R 331 at 336, *Gresham*, [22].

18.3.1.8 Appropriation: requirement of a positive act towards the property by D?

Theft requires proof of an 'act' by D towards the property that belongs to another, subject to what was said in the previous section about 'keeping' and 'dealing'. As appropriation is defined in terms of an 'assumption' of the right(s) of another that seems to require conduct on D's part demonstrating such an assumption. What of cases in which D induces V to hand over property to him? Can there be an appropriation before the point in time at which D first has physical contact with, possession or control of the property?

In *Hilton*,[93] where D, who had direct control of a bank account belonging to a charity, gave instructions for the transfer of the charity's funds to settle his personal debts, it was held that he stole the property[94] belonging to the charity. *Hilton* might be regarded as a straightforward case since D always had control of the bank account and instructed his agent (the bank) to act in relation to the property. D acted in relation to the property.

The courts treat differently cases where D, by deception, induces, V, the owner and controller of the bank account, to transfer funds from it. Although in such a case V's property[95] has gone, D did not 'appropriate' it.[96] The Court of Appeal affirmed this distinction in *Briggs*[97] where D had, by deception, induced her elderly relatives to transfer to her proceeds of their house sale. The Court of Appeal quashed a conviction for theft.[98] The court held that the word 'appropriation' connoted a physical act rather than a more remote action triggering the payment that gave rise to the charge.[99] The court relied heavily on Sir John Smith QC's commentary on *Caresena*:

It is true that D procures the whole course of events resulting in V's account being debited; but the telegraphic transfer is initiated by V and his voluntary intervening acts break the chain of causation. It is the same as if V is induced by deception to take money out of his safe to pay to D. D does not at that moment 'appropriate' it—V is not acting as his agent. D commits theft only if and when the money is put into his hands.

This approach remains correct after *Gomez* and *Hinks*, as recognized in *Darroux*.[100] The court quashed a care home manager's conviction for theft where it was alleged that she had been falsely and dishonestly inflating overtime on her time sheets (which she signed off). Whereas the defendants in *Kohn* and *Hilton* had assumed rights of an owner in procuring payments to themselves out of accounts over which they had control, in this case the defendant was not, by submitting her timesheets, assuming any rights of an owner with regard to the bank account. The forms the defendant completed conferred no rights upon her with regard to the bank account. The defendant had no contact with the bank and no control over the bank account, so her conduct was too far removed to be an act of appropriation.

Despite these authorities endorsing the distinction, it is submitted that *Gomez* and *Hinks* make it very much harder to draw any clear distinction between: (a) D's direct acts towards

---

93 [1997] 2 Cr App R 445, [1997] Crim LR 761 and commentary.
94 A thing in action representing the charity's right to payment of that sum from its bank.
95 The thing in action in the form of his credit balance, or part of it.
96 *Caresana* [1996] Crim LR 667; *Naviede* [1997] Crim LR 662. See also JC Smith [1996] 9 Arch News 4.
97 [2004] EWCA Crim 3662, [2004] Crim LR 455.
98 There was some confusion as to what D was alleged to have stolen. It appears to be the credit balance representing the proceeds of the sale.
99 Despite the court's approving reference to the *Oxford English Dictionary* definition of appropriation involving a 'taking', it is submitted that a physical 'taking' or 'touching' is only a sufficient but not a necessary element of the offence, otherwise there would be no protection for intangible property.
100 [2018] EWCA Crim 1009.

V's property, with V's fraudulently obtained consent (appropriation); and (b) D's acts causing V to transfer his property with V's fraudulently obtained consent (no appropriation
until D acquires it). The distinction seems to be that V's act of transfer in (b) breaks the
chain of causation.[101] In *Darroux*, Davis LJ made two observations:

(1) While the above cited statement in *Naviede*, as restated in *Briggs*, may in general terms frequently represent the correct position, as will be gathered we do not think that such statement
should be taken as an inflexible statement of principle of invariable application. As we see it, there
may be cases where a deceptive representation inducing an account holder to make payment out of
his bank account could constitute an appropriation (within the meaning of the 1968 Act). It would
depend on the circumstances.

(2) It has been suggested, most notably by Professor Sir John Smith, that cases where a cheque
is dishonestly obtained and presented are different from cases where payment out of an account is
procured in circumstances where the bank uses electronic or automated means. In common with
the court in *Hilton*, we have some difficulty with that. It is at all events hard to see how or why (as is
suggested) the latter scenario may give rise to a break in the chain of causation but the former not.
That said, as will also be gathered, we do not regard the causative impact of a deception as of itself
determinative of whether there has been an appropriation by a defendant with regard to a bank
account in any particular case.[102]

D can, of course, be liable for theft if he induces another party to conduct a transfer on his
behalf. If D uses an innocent agent, E, to effect the transfer of V's property, or to extinguish
it, there would be no difficulty in establishing a theft charge at the moment that E assumes
any right in relation to V's property.[103] Similarly, where D deceives V as to the nature and
quality of the act of transfer (as where V is naive or vulnerable) that would suffice. The fact
that V has the authority to act in this way by transferring the property and to consent is,
according to *Gomez* and *Hinks*, irrelevant. By setting in motion the transaction D could,
in that circumstance, be regarded as having started the continuing act of appropriation.[104]

18.3.1.9 Offers to sell as an act of appropriation?

Before 1968, D could be liable for larceny by offering to sell property belonging to another.
Under the 1968 Act, on a charge of theft, the question would now be whether he appropriated the property offered for sale. It has been argued that a purported sale of V's property
by D might not be an assumption of a right of another.[105] The better view is that although D
may lawfully *contract* to sell V's property to X at some future date (D hoping that he will be
able to buy it from V in order to sell it to X in the meantime),[106] a purported present sale to
a bona fide purchaser seems to be an appropriation. The property D offered for sale nearly
always continues to belong to the original owner, so theft generally has no effect on the owners' rights, as such.

   Even in the light of *Gomez*, the earlier case of *Pitham* remains difficult to justify. D, knowing that V was in prison, took Pitham to V's house and offered to sell V's property to Pitham.

---

[101]   cf R Heaton, 'Cheques and Balances' [2005] Crim LR 747.

[102]   At [64].

[103]   This might be thought to be the answer to a case like *Darroux*—the better answer is to charge fraud under
the Fraud Act 2006.

[104]   We are grateful to Tony Shaw QC for discussion. Cf *Arlidge and Parry on Fraud*, para 9.107.

[105]   Smith, *Property Offences*, 'whereas the owner has a right against others that they shall not deliver his
property to third persons (because that involves a tortious interference) he has no general right that they shall
not contract to sell it, or purport to pass ownership in it', at para 5.49.

[106]   cf Sale of Goods Act 1979, s 5.

It was held that the offer amounted to a completed theft of V's property.[107] Pitham, the buyer, knew that D had no authority to sell V's property and D knew that Pitham knew that. D did not purport to be the owner or have the owner's authority to sell the property. It was not really an offer to sell at all, but a proposal for a joint theft of the property.[108]

18.3.1.10 Continuing appropriation

An offence that is complete at a particular moment may nevertheless continue being committed for some time thereafter.[109] It is often important to know how long a particular theft continued. A person may be guilty of a theft by aiding and abetting it while it is being committed by another, but he cannot aid and abet once the theft is over. A person may be guilty of robbery if he uses force while theft is being committed but not by using force when the theft is at an end. A person may be guilty of the offence of handling stolen goods only if he does a proscribed act 'otherwise than in the course of the stealing'. A person may use reasonable force in preventing a crime, in this case theft, while it is being committed.[110]

Theft may certainly be committed in an instant, so that D could be convicted of the offence even if he was immediately arrested. It does not follow that the offence is over in an instant, though that seems to have been the opinion of the court in *Pitham*.[111] In *Atakpu*,[112] after a careful review of the pre-*Gomez* authorities, Ward J summarized the law as follows:[113]

(1) theft can occur in an instant by a single appropriation but it can also involve a course of dealing with property lasting longer and involving several appropriations before the transaction is complete; (2) theft is a finite act—it has a beginning and it has an end; (3) at what point the transaction is complete is a matter for the jury to decide upon the facts of each case; (4) though there may be several appropriations in the course of a single theft or several appropriations of different goods each constituting a separate theft as in *R v Skipp*, no case suggests that there can be successive thefts of the same property . . .

The court thought that, on a strict construction, *Gomez* left 'little room for a continuous course of action'. The court did not welcome that consequence of the *Gomez* decision and preferred the view that appropriation continues so long as the thief can sensibly be regarded as in the act of stealing, or in more understandable words, so long as he is 'on the job'.[114] In *Atakpu*, it was not necessary for the court to decide the matter because no jury could have reasonably concluded that the theft of the cars in Frankfurt or Brussels in that case was continuing when the cars were brought, days later, into England. It is thought that this is the better view and that to treat appropriation simply as an instantaneous act would be inconsistent with the provisions of the Act relating to robbery and handling, which presuppose that there can be a course of stealing.

---

[107] This was significant because it meant that when the goods were delivered to Pitham he received them 'otherwise than in the course of the stealing' and was therefore guilty of handling stolen goods: see Ch 26.

[108] The jury acquitted Pitham of theft although 'The evidence that they had bought property knowing that it was stolen, arose from the fact that they said they had bought considerably under price', (1976) 65 Cr App R 45 at 47. How can a buyer knowing that the seller by selling the property is stealing it, not be guilty of theft? See also Williams, TBCL, 764; Ormerod and Williams, *Smith's Law of Theft*, para 2.103.

[109] G Williams, 'Appropriation: A Single or Continuous Act' [1978] Crim LR 69.

[110] See *Bowden* [2002] EWCA Crim 1279, where D claimed a defence under s 3 of the Criminal Law Act 1967 when detaining youths whom he believed to have stolen car keys. The Court of Appeal held that the judge was right to leave to the jury the issue of whether the youths' crime of theft of the keys was still continuing at the time of D's actions. See also *Morris* [2013] EWCA Crim 436.

[111] See n 107.   [112] See p 872.   [113] [1993] 4 All ER 215 at 223.

[114] As it was put in the 7th edn of this book, at p 513.

18.3.1.11 Appropriation: when and where?

Where the thief and the property are in different places does the theft take place where and when D acts, or where and when his act affects the property? The problem usually arises in relation to the theft of things in action—intangible property—but it is equally possible with tangible property. D, in England, may dishonestly assume V's rights of ownership over goods in a warehouse in Scotland by selling, or purporting to sell, them to E.[115] The cases have not all taken a consistent approach to the problem. In *Tomsett*,[116] the Court of Appeal accepted without argument that the theft occurred at the location of the property in question. Similarly, in *Kohn*,[117] Lane LJ said, *obiter*, that where D had drawn cheques to himself on V's bank account, the theft did not take place until the account was debited. In extradition cases, the courts took different views. In *Ex p Osman*,[118] Osman, in Hong Kong, sent a telex assuming the rights of the owner of a bank account in New York. It was held that this could be theft in Hong Kong. In *Ex p Levin*,[119] the court held that a computer operator in Russia committed theft in the United States by operating on magnetic discs on a computer server in the United States.

In *Ngan*,[120] a large sum intended for V had been mistakenly paid into D's bank account in England. By virtue of s 5(4) of the 1968 Act (discussed later) this property was to be regarded as belonging to V. D dishonestly signed blank cheques on the account and sent them to her sister in Scotland who presented them there for payment. The court, equating the presentation of the cheque with the sending of the telex in *Osman*, held that the theft took place in Scotland. The act of presenting the cheque was the point of appropriation. The signing and issuing of the cheques were preparatory acts to the theft, but the appropriation occurred before the account was debited.

These problems are less likely to arise since the bringing into force of Part 1 of the Criminal Justice Act 1993 and s 1A of the Criminal Law Act 1977, but they are still significant and require resolution. In the light of the broad notion of appropriation followed since *Gomez*, it may be that the theft is committed where and when D does some act which only the owner could properly do; but that it continues to the time when and place where it affects the property.

18.3.1.12 The exception in favour of bona fide purchasers: s 3(2)

The definition of appropriation in s 3 includes an important exception:

Where property or a right or interest in property is or purports to be transferred for value to a person acting in good faith, no later assumption by him of rights which he believed himself to be acquiring shall, by reason of any defect in the transferor's title, amount to theft.

The CLRC explained this exception as follows:[121]

A person may buy something in good faith, but may find out afterwards that the seller had no title to it, perhaps because the seller or somebody else stole it. If the buyer nevertheless keeps the thing or otherwise deals with it as owner, he could . . . be guilty of theft. It is arguable that this would be

---

[115] See Ormerod and Williams, *Smith's Law of Theft*, para 2.108.

[116] [1985] Crim LR 369. D, a telex operator, had transferred funds from V bank to an account in Geneva. The theft occurred in Geneva. His conviction for conspiracy was quashed. This would not be so today. See Criminal Law Act 1977, s 1A.

[117] (1979) 69 Cr App R 395, p 880.

[118] *Governor of Pentonville Prison, ex p Osman* [1989] 3 All ER 701. This issue was not discussed in the House of Lords: [1997] AC 741. The Divisional Court comprised of Lloyd LJ and French J, both members of the court in *Tomsett*.

[119] *Governor of Brixton Prison, ex p Levin* [1997] QB 65.

[120] [1998] 1 Cr App R 331. The availability of theft charges was accepted in *Ali* [2009] EWCA Crim 1131.

[121] Eighth Report, para 37. But this exception may now be neutralized by the money laundering legislation, Ch 33.

right; but on the whole it seems to us that, whatever view is taken of the buyer's moral duty, the law would be too strict if it made him guilty of theft.

The exception operates in favour only of a person acquiring his interest (eg by buying the property from D or by acquiring other rights over it) in good faith and for value—a 'BFP'. The 'BFP' who discovers that the property is stolen is not guilty of handling if he disposes of it to an innocent person.[122] But the property in the hands of the 'BFP' continues to belong to the owner from whom it was stolen. If the 'BFP' sells it and represents himself as having title to the property, he may be guilty of fraud.[123]

18.3.2 Property

Those types of property which may be stolen are defined in s 4 of the Theft Act 1968.[124] The broad effect of the section is that all property may be stolen subject to certain exceptions in relation to land, things growing wild and wild creatures. It is important to reiterate that the offence of theft is founded on orthodox civil law concepts of property.[125]

Legal conceptions of property are constantly evolving to reflect developments in society, and in recent years the particular concern has been for the law to reflect the rapid developments in information technology and the way in which data is stored and accessed. There have been calls to expand the definition of property to provide protection in this area.[126] More radically, there is pressure for the law to recognize a diverse range of rights and interests as species of property (eg environmental rights and welfare rights).[127] Irrespective of the validity of this re-conceptualization of property, it is submitted that the law of theft is certainly not the most appropriate mechanism for securing protection of these rights under the criminal law. Empirical research has also called into question whether thefts of different forms of property, even when equal in value, ought to be treated alike. Green and Kugler distinguish between 'thefts' of items of equal monetary value but different physical and legal form.[128] In the empirical work, those surveyed consistently ranked the theft of tangible goods as more blameworthy than the theft of intangibles, and the theft of intangible goods as more blameworthy than the theft of services.

Under the 1968 Act, the definition of property is extremely broad, and coupled with the breadth of the definition of appropriation this renders the actus reus minimal. The structure of the Act avoids defining offences by distinctions based on the type of property involved, and focuses instead on the manner of the harm being caused. Section 4(1) provides the general definition:

'Property' includes money and all other property, real or personal, including things in action and other intangible property.

---

[122] See p 1087.

[123] See *Wheeler* (1990) 92 Cr App R 279. D did not obtain by deception in selling stolen goods to V but only because the sale, though not the delivery, took place before D became aware that they were stolen.

[124] For a sophisticated theoretical analysis about what types of property ought to be capable of being stolen, see Green, *13 Ways*, Ch 4. To help to determine what ought to count as property for the purposes of the law of theft (as opposed to the civil law), Green relies upon the economic concepts of commodifiability, rivalrousness, excludability and zero-sumness.

[125] It has been argued that the criminal law takes a more robust definitional and practical approach to the interference with intangible items of property, such as choses in action, than the civil law. See SP Green, 'Theft and Conversion—Tangibly Different?' (2012) 128 LQR 564.

[126] See eg J Lipton, 'A Revised Property Concept for the New Millennium' (1999) 7 Int'l J L & IT 171.

[127] See N Lacey, C Wells and O Quick, *Reconstructing Criminal Law* (4th edn, 2010) 399.

[128] These were: tangible good (a book in their example); an intangible good (a computer file downloaded from a website); a supply of a service which was not limited (attendance at a full lecture) and a service the supply of which was limited (attendance at a lecture in which the hall was half empty). See Green and Kugler (2010) 7 J Empirical Legal Studies 511. For further analysis, see Green, *13 Ways*, Ch 4.

The definition is wide enough to include property which is unlawful or illegal or prohibited. D can therefore be guilty of stealing from V the drugs V unlawfully possesses.[129] There are specified exceptions relating to land, animals and plants to be discussed later.

18.3.2.1 Things in action

The one limitation on the generality of the definition of property, apart from the specified exceptions, is that the property must be capable of appropriation. Intangible property may be appropriated by any assumption of any of the rights of an owner over it.[130] This is best illustrated by reference to one of the most commonplace forms of intangible property—bank accounts.

Where a bank account is in credit, the relationship between banker and customer is that of a debtor and creditor. In law, the customer, V, does not have 'money in the bank';[131] there is no specific pile of money that is designated as his. The property that he has is a 'thing in action', a right to payment by the bank of the sum of money it owes him.[132] Thus, if D dishonestly causes a bank to debit V's account, D does not appropriate V's money, he appropriates a thing in action belonging to V (V's right to payment of that sum from the bank) and may be guilty of theft of that property.[133] D has reduced or, if he has reduced the credit to zero, extinguished V's right to that payment from the bank. Where V has an overdraft with the bank, V has a right to payment from the bank of the sum up to the limit of that agreed overdraft, and that is property—a thing in action—that D may steal by dishonestly causing the bank to debit V's account. The operation of this aspect of the law of theft is illustrated by *Kohn*.[134] D, an accountant employed by a company to write cheques to pay the company's debts, wrote cheques on the company's account to pay his own debts and was held guilty of theft of the thing in action.

Care must always be taken to ascertain the state of V's account at the time of the alleged theft by D. If V is overdrawn and has no overdraft facility, D's drawing of a cheque on V's account cannot amount to theft because there is no property to steal—V has no contractual right to any payment from the bank. D's action might amount to attempted theft, like an attempt to steal from an empty pocket.

In terms of conduct by D in relation to bank accounts over which he has control, care must also be taken. In *Hilton*,[135] discussed earlier, where D, who had direct control of a bank account belonging to a charity, gave instructions for the transfer of the charity's funds to settle his personal debts, it was held that he stole the thing in action belonging to the charity. On the other hand, D does not steal from his *own* bank where he uses his banker's card to make a purchase, knowing that his own account is overdrawn and that his authority to use the card has terminated.[136] The bank is obliged to meet the cheque and its own funds will

---

[129] See *Smith* [2011] EWCA Crim 66, citing Ormerod and Williams, *Smith's Law of Theft*, 80, with approval.

[130] See *Storrow and Poole* [1983] Crim LR 332.

[131] 'Although we talk about people having money in the bank, the only person who has money in the bank is the banker', *Davenport* [1954] 1 All ER 602 at 603 per Goddard LCJ.

[132] As Sarah Green points out, although the Act distinguishes between things in action and money, there is a diminishing difference between the two in practical terms. See SP Green, 'Theft and Conversion—Tangibly Different?' (2012) 128 LQR 564.

[133] *Chan Man-sin v A-G for Hong Kong* [1988] 1 All ER 1, p 874; *Ex p Osman* [1989] 3 All ER 701; *Williams* [2001] 1 Cr App R 362.

[134] [1997] 2 Cr App R 445, [1997] Crim LR 761 and commentary. As discussed in *Darroux* at p 875, it may be different where D, by deception, induces V, the owner and controller of the bank account, to transfer funds from it. V's credit balance, or part of it, has gone, but arguably D did not 'appropriate' it until he took control/possession: *Caresana* [1996] Crim LR 667; *Naviede* [1997] Crim LR 662; *Briggs* [2004] Crim LR 455.

[135] *Navvabi* [1986] 1 WLR 1311.

[136] (1979) 69 Cr App R 395. See further EJ Griew, 'Stealing and Obtaining Bank Credits' [1986] Crim LR 356.

be thereby diminished. D has caused the bank to become indebted but he has not assumed a right over any specific property of the bank. If D withdraws money from an ATM at his bank in excess of his overdraft and without authorization, he may commit theft of the cash.[137]

Stealing or obtaining cheques

Where a cheque (ie the piece of paper from a chequebook) is alleged to have been stolen, a different problem arises.[138] A cheque is a piece of paper which, if given for consideration, creates a thing in action—it gives the person in whose favour it is made out a right to sue the person who made out the cheque for the sum stated. So, where V writes a cheque payable to D, as well as obtaining the piece of paper into his physical possession, D also obtains a thing in action—a right to sue V's bank for the sum specified on the cheque. However, it is crucial to note that the particular thing in action obtained by D is *not* an item of property that previously belonged to V; the thing in action D obtains is D's right to sue V's bank. This is a new item of property, distinct from that which V owned before he wrote the cheque to D; the previous item of property was *V's* right to sue his bank. In *Preddy*,[139] the House accepted this to be the correct state of the law. *Preddy* confirms that the thing in action D obtains belonged from the instant of its creation to him. It never belonged, or could belong, to V. A chose in action is, remember, a right to sue someone, and D could not sue himself!

Where D dishonestly induces V to write out a cheque in D's favour and D attempts to cash the cheque, he would at that point commit fraud contrary to s 1 of the Fraud Act 2006. If D presents the cheque for the credit of his own account, he is at that point guilty of theft of a different thing in action which does belong to V, namely V's credit balance (or right to overdraw if such a facility exists) at his bank.[140] On presenting the cheque,[141] D has assumed V's right to destroy that part of V's property.[142]

D also acquires the cheque itself, the physical thing in the form of the piece of paper. *Preddy* did not decide whether D might be guilty of obtaining this item of property. Lord Goff noted that it does belong to V but said that D would not be guilty because he had no intention permanently to deprive—he knew that the cheque form (ie the piece of paper) would, after presentation, be returned to V via his bank (or at least be available for V's collection).[143] It is submitted that this was *obiter* (as well as wrong) but the Court of Appeal in *Graham*[144] treated it as *ratio* and in *Clark*[145] held that it was bound by that decision. So, under the current law a cheque form (piece of paper) cannot be stolen if D intends to present it for payment. A cheque is still a piece of paper and can be stolen if D intends merely to retain the piece of paper. For example, D might steal from V a cheque which V has never cashed because it was signed by someone famous and V had retained it as a souvenir.[146]

---

[137] See *Poland v Ulatowski* [2010] EWCA Crim 2673 (Admin); *Chodorek v Poland* [2017] EWHC 995 (Admin); *Adamczewski v District Court in Jelenia Gora Poland* [2014] EWHC 2958 (Admin) (at [11] et seq).

[138] See JC Smith, 'Obtaining Cheques by Deception or Theft' [1997] Crim LR 396, 'Stealing Tickets' [1998] Crim LR 723 and commentaries on *Horsman* [1998] Crim LR 128 and *Aston* [1998] Crim LR 498; see also *Arlidge and Parry on Fraud*, paras 9.20–9.21.

[139] [1996] AC 815.   [140] *Burke* [2000] Crim LR 413, and *Williams (Roy)* [2001] 1 Cr App R 362.

[141] *Ngan* [1998] 1 Cr App R 331.

[142] Prior to the Fraud Act coming into force (15 Jan 2007) D committed no offence of obtaining property by deception because D's increased credit balance (a thing in action belonging to D—his right to sue his bank) was never 'property belonging to another', *Burke* [2000] Crim LR 413, applying *Preddy*. See also *White* [2014] EWCA Crim 714.

[143] This assumes the cheques (as pieces of paper) will all be retained for V; modern banking practice is not to do so. D may intend to return the piece of paper, but not the valuable security: see later. That may make an allegation of theft of the valuable security an attractive one.

[144] [1997] 1 Cr App R 302.   [145] 2001] EWCA Crim 884.

[146] See *Roach* [2011] EWCA Crim 918 (blank cheque D never going to present).

So far the discussion has concluded that D does not obtain a thing in action from V (the thing in action D acquires has never belonged to V), and D does not steal the cheque form (ie the paper). There is an argument that D could also be convicted of theft of the cheque not as a piece of paper, but as a 'valuable security'. A cheque is recognized as a 'valuable security' by s 20 of the 1968 Act. This is a highly technical area of law explored elsewhere[147] but it is easy enough to understand that a cheque is special—not just any piece of paper which will cause, say, a bank clerk to hand over £1,000; but a cheque will do that. Of course the cheque *is* (a) a piece of paper which (b) *creates* a thing in action but it is also (c) a valuable security. A valuable security is an item of property that may be stolen; and that means, not the theft of the thing in action, nor a mere piece of paper, but the instrument, the physical thing with certain writing on it.[148] The Supreme Court of Victoria in *Parsons*[149] accepted this argument. The English Court of Appeal found it 'highly persuasive' but, unlike the Victorian court, was unable to follow it. The question of D's liability for theft may still be open to argument.[150] D will, of course, be liable under the Fraud Act if he makes any false representation relating to the account, the cheque form or his right to use them, provided he also has the relevant mens rea.

A final point to note is that a cheque creates a thing in action *only if it is given for valuable consideration*.[151] If D induces V to make him a gift of a cheque for £50, that cheque does not create a thing in action—but it is still a cheque and, it is submitted, a valuable security. Unless V stops it, the cheque will enable D to deprive V of £50. When D gets his hands on it, he has a valuable, tangible, thing in his possession. It is submitted that such a cheque is a valuable security capable of being stolen.

18.3.2.2 Other intangible property

The reach of the law of theft is extended yet further by s 4(1) beyond things in action to include 'other intangible property'.[152] An illustration is provided by *A-G of Hong Kong v Chan Nai-Keung*.[153] The export of textiles from Hong Kong was prohibited except under licence, and exports were regulated by a quota system. An exporter who, in a given year, could not meet his quotas could sell his surplus export quotas to an exporter who could meet them, and there was a flourishing market in these quotas. D, a director of the 'A' exporting company, without the authorization of the A company, sold surplus

---

[147] 'A cheque is not a piece of paper and no more . . . It is a piece of paper with certain special characteristics', *Kohn* (1979) 69 Cr App R 395 at 409 per Lord Lane CJ.

[148] *Arnold* [1997] 4 All ER 1. D was convicted of stealing a valuable security, a bill of exchange, signed by V, creating a thing in action which V could never own but was nevertheless property belonging to him. But cf *Horsman*, n 138.

[149] [1998] 2 VR 478; affd 73 ALJR 27, High Ct of Aust.

[150] A point of law of general importance was certified; the House refused leave on the ground that the offence of obtaining a money transfer by deception and other offences are adequate. That is not correct. In *Marshall*, considered at p 891, it was argued that if a cheque cannot be stolen from the person who made out the cheque on his account, a ticket cannot be stolen from the company issuing it. The court dismissed this argument as impossible, but it is submitted that it is right. The cheque and the ticket are both papers which create and embody a thing in action against the issuer. In neither case can the thing in action be stolen or obtained from the person issuing it—it cannot belong to him—but that is no reason why the paper, which does belong to him and which is a valuable thing, cannot be stolen from him. For an argument against this approach relying on the valuable security, see *Arlidge and Parry on Fraud*, paras 9.154–9.156.

[151] ie any consideration sufficient to support a simple contract or an antecedent debt or liability: Bills of Exchange Act 1882, s 27(1).

[152] For extensive theoretical analysis, see Green, *13 Ways*, 234–69. Green distinguishes between intangibles and semi-intangibles, analysing each separately. An example of the latter would be wi-fi.

[153] [1987] 1 WLR 1339. The law of theft in Hong Kong was identical in this respect to the law of England.

quotas at a gross undervalue to the 'B' exporting company in which D had an interest as a director. It was held that the quotas, though they were not things in action, were nevertheless 'other intangible property'—the quotas were things of value which could be bought and sold and by knowingly selling them at an undervalue. D had appropriated them.[154]

The definition of property is so broad that it is easier to focus on the things that do not constitute property for the purposes of the Act. Some of these limitations on what constitutes property are contained in the Act (land, wild animals, electricity) and some are the result of case law—for example, confidential information. Each merits consideration.

18.3.2.3 Limitations on the theft of land

It would have been technically possible to make land generally stealable (eg where D moves his boundary fence a few inches into V's garden), since rights over land are just as capable of appropriation as rights in goods. But the decision not to do so was made for reasons of policy. In drafting the Theft Act, the CLRC considered that there were numerous reasons[155] for not treating this as theft, including: that appropriating land by encroachment was rare and could be dealt with adequately by civil remedies;[156] and it might create conflict with the civil law (D could get good title by occupation for 12 years and it would be odd if he remained even theoretically guilty of theft for ever afterwards). Section 4(2) therefore limits the scope of theft of land, and provides:

A person cannot steal land, or things forming part of land and severed from it by him or by his directions, except in the following cases, that is to say—

(a) when he is a trustee or personal representative, or is authorised by power of attorney, or as liquidator of a company, or otherwise, to sell or dispose of land belonging to another, and he appropriates the land or anything forming part of it by dealing with it in breach of the confidence reposed in him; or

(b) when he is not in possession of the land and appropriates anything forming part of the land by severing it or causing it to be severed, or after it has been severed; or

(c) when, being in possession of the land under a tenancy, he appropriates the whole or part of any fixture or structure let to be used with the land.[157]

(1) *Appropriation by trustees etc.*[158] Exceptionally, land, or things forming part of the land, are capable of being stolen by trustees, etc. A trustee may appropriate land held in trust by an unauthorized disposition. Of course, an unauthorized dealing is not, of itself, theft since the other elements of the offence must be present. If, for example, a trustee is authorized to sell the land only to A and he sells it to B because B is offering a much better price, the unauthorized sale by the trustee might not be dishonest.

---

[154] *Pilgram v Rice-Smith* [1977] 2 All ER 658; *Bhachu* (1976) 65 Cr App R 261.

[155] Eighth Report, paras 40–4. Cf Smith, *Property Offences*, paras 3.32–3.33, 3.38.

[156] But the Committee observed (ibid, para 42) that moving boundaries was a 'real problem, especially in crowded housing estates'. Rarity did not prevent the CLRC creating the offence under s 11 (Ch 20) which seems to owe its origin to *three* known instances of its occurrence.

[157] For the purposes of this subsection 'land' does not include incorporeal hereditaments (eg easements); 'tenancy' means a tenancy for years or any less period and includes an agreement for such a tenancy, but a person who after the end of a tenancy remains in possession as statutory tenant or otherwise is to be treated as having possession under the tenancy; and 'let' shall be construed accordingly.

[158] See R Brazier, 'Criminal Trustees?' (1975) 39 Conv (NS) 29. Such individuals would be liable for fraud under s 4 of the Fraud Act 2006.

Cases under this provision are rare and care must be taken in interpreting and applying the provision. For example, in *Gimbert*,[159] V was a woman with an IQ of 57. She signed forms transferring her house to a cousin for £1 and the property was then transferred to a third party for £53,000. In this way, the property belonging to V was transferred away for effectively no consideration paid to, or received by, her. The prosecution's case was that D1, her cousin, had taken dishonest advantage of his status in exercising enduring powers of attorney for her. D claimed that since the enduring power was in fact invalid in this case, he was being charged with theft of land when he was not an attorney and therefore not within s 4(2). The Court of Appeal quashed his conviction. There was no justification for writing 'is (or purportedly is) authorised' or 'is (or believes himself to be) authorised' into the s 4(2) exception. The power of attorney was null, the exception could not apply and the land in question could not therefore be the subject of theft. Since s 4(2) states that a person cannot steal land, unless the case falls within one of the three exceptions contained in s 4(2)(a)–(c) of the 1968 Act, the court's conclusion is clearly right. A simple solution would be to charge defendants with an offence under the Fraud Act 2006, either fraud by false representation or fraud by failure to disclose.

(2) *Appropriation by persons not in possession.* It is not theft for D to appropriate land without severing it, as where he moves his boundary fence so as to incorporate a strip of V's land into his own.[160] However, a person not in possession can steal anything forming part of the land by severing it or by appropriating it after it has been severed. So, if D helps himself to the topsoil in V's garden, or to a gate, or to rose bushes or even to growing grass, it may be theft.[161] In each case the appropriation is complete upon severance,[162] but where the thing is already severed, as where the gate is lying in V's yard for repair, the appropriation would be complete, at the latest, when D takes control of it.

(3) *Appropriation of fixtures by tenants.* A tenant cannot steal the land which he possesses by virtue of the tenancy, nor of things forming part of the land. If D, a tenant, removes topsoil from the premises, say to sell it to a neighbour, he is appropriating property of another (the landlord) but he is not guilty of theft. A tenant may be guilty of theft, however, where he appropriates (and here severance is not required) any fixture or structure let to be used with the land. A fixture here means something annexed to land for use or ornament, such as a washbasin, cupboards or a fireplace, and a structure seems to mean some structure of a moveable or temporary character, such as a garden shed or a greenhouse. A house would not be a structure in this sense.

(4) *Appropriation by persons not in possession.* In contrast if D, who is living with the tenant, removes the topsoil to sell it D would be guilty of theft because he is not 'in possession' of the land although he happens to live there.

To determine potential liability for theft, it may, therefore, be important to determine whether a particular article forms part of the land. Generally, appropriation will involve severance, so non-possessors will be caught by s 4(2)(b) while tenants are caught by s 4(2)(c). But if a licensee in possession appropriates a structure, it is vital to know whether it forms

---

[159] [2018] EWCA Crim 2190.

[160] The arguments for and against making land the subject of theft are summarized in the Eighth Report, 21–2.

[161] By human hand or by grazing cattle: *McGill v Shepherd*, unreported; M Williams and C Weinberg, *The Australian Law of Theft* (3rd edn, 1986) 116. In 1972, a man was prosecuted at Leeds Crown Court for stealing Cleckheaton railway station by dismantling and removing it. He was acquitted on the merits, the jury accepting that on this bold enterprise he was acting under a claim of right. But railway stations are stealable by severance.

[162] Note that if D is caught in the act of severing he is guilty only of an attempt. By attempting to sever D is, of course, assuming the rights of an owner and in other circumstances (p 864) this alone constitutes a complete appropriation. But in this case the effect of the subsection is to insist upon severance to complete the theft.

part of the land. This is a question of land law and the answer depends on the degree of annexation and the object of annexation.[163]

18.3.2.4 Limitations on the theft of things growing wild

There is a long-standing cultural tradition in Britain of picking fruits from the land for consumption.[164] Section 4(3) of the Act provides some limited protection from theft charges in such circumstances:

A person who picks mushrooms growing wild on any land, or who picks flowers, fruit or foliage from a plant growing wild on any land, does not (although not in possession of the land) steal what he picks, unless he does it for reward or for sale or other commercial purpose.

For the purposes of this subsection, 'mushroom' includes any fungus and 'plant' includes any shrub or tree.[165]

In some ways it might be thought that s 4(3) is rather unnecessary. It exempts from liability for theft someone who picks wild mushrooms, or one who picks flowers, fruit or foliage '*from a plant*' (thus a person who takes the whole plant may be convicted of theft)[166] growing wild on land unless done for sale or other commercial purpose. Picking holly branches around about Christmas time for the purpose of sale may amount to theft, as may picking elderberries for making wine if the purpose is to sell the wine. The whole matter might have been left to the common sense of the prosecutor who would hardly institute proceedings where the appropriation was trivial. However, the CLRC thought that, 'a provision could reasonably be criticized which made it even technically theft in all cases to pick wild flowers against the will of the landowner'.[167]

In some instances liability might also arise under the Criminal Damage Act 1971.

18.3.2.5 Limitations on the theft of wild creatures

Section 4(4) of the Act provides:

Wild creatures, tamed or untamed, shall be regarded as property; but a person cannot steal a wild creature not tamed nor ordinarily kept in captivity, or the carcase of any such creature, unless either it has been reduced into possession by or on behalf of another person and possession of it has not since been lost or abandoned, or another person is in course of reducing it into possession.

It is possible, therefore, to steal wild creatures where these have been tamed or are ordinarily kept in captivity. A tiger may be stolen from a zoo, and if it has escaped it may be stolen while at large because it is 'ordinarily' kept in captivity.

Wild animals while at large are not owned by anyone, nor does a landowner have a proprietary interest in such animals even where they constitute game. The landowner has, however, the right to take wild animals, and once a wild animal is caught or killed it immediately becomes the property of the landowner where this takes place. The taker (ie the

---

[163] See *Elitestone Ltd v Morris* [1997] 1 WLR 687. The chattel must be actually fixed to the land, not for its more convenient use as a chattel, but for the more convenient use of the land. Compare *Elitestone v Morris* [1997] 1 WLR 687—timber bungalow on concrete stand on land only removable by destroying part of land, held to be part of land; cf *Chelsea Yacht and Boat Club v Pope* [2001] 2 All ER 409—houseboat secured to riverbed pontoon and river walls by mooring ropes is not part of land. For more recent analysis, see *Tristmire Ltd v Mew and others* [2011] EWCA Civ 912.

[164] See M Welstead, 'Season of Mists and Mellow Fruitfulness' (1995) 150 NLJ 1499.

[165] For discussion of the legal protection of trees, see *Palm Developments Ltd v Secretary of State for Communities and Local Govt* [2009] EWHC 220 (Admin).

[166] This raises interesting possibilities in the case of GM protestors who remove seedlings.

[167] Eighth Report, para 47. The Wildlife and Countryside Act 1981 makes it an offence to kill, possess or sell certain creatures; and to pick, uproot or destroy certain wild plants.

killer, trapper, etc) would be guilty of theft were it not for the protection afforded by s 4(4). He is guilty instead of a minor offence of poaching.

The CLRC recommended[168] that poaching should be theft when done 'for reward or for sale or other commercial purpose'. Parliament rejected that proposal. Poaching is unlawful but it was felt that it would be going too far, even in such cases, to turn this traditional country pastime into theft.

Wild animals may be stolen when they are in the process of being reduced into possession by or on behalf of another. A lazy poacher who picks up the pheasants shot from the skies by V is a thief, as is a gamekeeper who keeps for himself a pheasant which he shot for his employer. And if V, having shot a pheasant, cannot find it in the brush and gives up the search, a subsequent appropriation by D makes him a thief from the landowner.[169]

In *Cresswell v DPP*,[170] the Divisional Court considered whether badgers which had been enticed into traps set by officials from DEFRA had become 'property' for the purposes of the Criminal Damage Act 1971 (identically worded in this respect to the Theft Act). The defendants who had destroyed the traps sought to argue that the badgers were property and they had a defence to destruction of the traps on the basis that they were protecting property—the badgers. Keene LJ, rejecting the argument, stated that 'merely to entice a wild animal, whether it be a badger or a game bird or a deer, to a particular spot from time to time by providing food there, even with the objective ultimately of killing it in due course, does not form part of the course normally of reducing it into possession. If the creature were thereby to become the property, say, of the landowner providing the food, it would mean that it could not then be lawfully shot by the adjoining landowner on or over whose land it passed.'[171] Walker J was more hesitant, declining to express a concluded view on what constitutes property.[172]

18.3.2.6 Electricity

On the face of it all property is capable of appropriation, but there were formerly doubts whether electricity was capable of appropriation.[173] The dishonest use, wasting or diverting of electricity was a separate offence under the Larceny Acts and the position was preserved by s 13 of the Theft Act. The CLRC observed that, 'This has to be a separate offence because owing to its nature electricity is excluded from the definition of stealing in . . . [s] 1(1) of the [Act].'[174] The Committee's view was endorsed in *Low v Blease*[175] where it was held that, electricity not being property capable of appropriation, D could not be convicted of burglary in entering premises and making a telephone call from them.[176] Heat is a thing of value, as anyone paying the heating bill well knows, but it seems that it would not be theft to assume

---

[168] Eighth Report, para 52.   [169] As to abandonment, see p 904.

[170] [2006] EWHC 3379 (Admin).   [171] At [11].

[172] His lordship examined, at [38], whether an animal is to be regarded as wild or domestic.

[173] Ofgem conducted a review into electricity 'theft', which it was estimated costs the industry approximately £250m annually. The review concluded that electricity providers were not doing enough to detect this behaviour and that consumers were bearing the cost. To ameliorate the problem, Ofgem proposed changes to the regulatory framework governing the provision of electricity. No changes to the criminal law were recommended. The material produced by Ofgem refers to electricity theft, but electricity cannot in fact be stolen. See www.ofgem.gov.uk/electricity/retail-market/market-review-and-reform/electricity-theft.

[174] Eighth Report, para 85. See further Griew, *Theft*, paras 2.162–2.165; Williams, TBCL, 736–7; Ormerod and Williams, *Smith's Law of Theft*, Ch 11.

[175] [1975] Crim LR 513. Cf *Flack v Baldry* [1988] 1 WLR 214, treating electricity as a 'noxious thing' for the purposes of Firearms Act 1968, s 5(1)(b).

[176] See *P* (2000) 11 Aug, CA, No 0003586 Y5, where D entered his neighbour's property as a trespasser and made phone calls to premium-rate sex chatlines.

the right to heat belonging to V, by diverting V's hot water so as to warm D's premises.[177] The heat is energy (as is electricity) but is not property.

Section 13 of the Theft Act 1968 provides:[178]

A person who dishonestly uses without due authority, or dishonestly causes to be wasted or diverted, any electricity shall on conviction on indictment be liable to imprisonment for a term not exceeding five years.

This provision will ordinarily be applied to the case where D dishonestly[179] uses some device to bypass an electricity meter, but beyond that it is capable of some curious applications.[180] It has recently been used to prosecute commuters who charge their mobile phones on the London Underground. Applied strictly there might be an offence under this section where D borrows an electrically driven vehicle such as an environmentally friendly car, golf buggy or disabled person's scooter, though there would be no theft of the vehicle, nor an offence of taking a conveyance under s 12.[181] But proceedings under s 13 in such a case are perhaps very unlikely. There might be some reluctance to prosecute when the substance of what D does is not criminal, even though there is technically some incidental offence.[182]

In terms of actus reus, it is enough under s 13 that D causes electricity to be wasted or diverted; he need not be shown to have made any use of the electricity for himself. An employee who, out of spite for his employer, puts on all the lighting and heating appliances in the office would commit the offence; but a fellow employee, or even a stranger, who, knowing what D has done, chooses to stay in the office to enjoy the warmth, would not: 'use' implies some consumption of electricity which would not occur but for the accused's acts.[183] The offence extends only to the abstraction of electricity, whether from the mains or a battery source. Gas and water, if dishonestly appropriated, can form the subject of a theft charge. Despite the upsurge in using more environmentally friendly energy sources (solar and wind, etc) the s 13 offence only protects against the dishonest abstraction of these forms of power once converted.[184]

The mens rea of s 13 is dishonesty. The partial definition of dishonesty in s 2 (see later) does not apply; the test of dishonesty does.[185] Although it has been held in cases of electricity meter tampering that the defendant must be shown to have an intention not to pay, this is too generous to the defence; it is one factor to be considered in the overall question of dishonesty.[186] There is a potential problem with mens rea: D may plausibly claim that he did not

<hr/>

[177] *Clinton v Cahill* [1998] NI 200. Nor is it theft of the hot water, unless all, or substantially all, of the heat is exhausted, so as to deprive the water of its 'virtue'.

[178] For recent use of the offence, see *Handford* [2016] EWCA Crim 1838.

[179] See *Boggeln v Williams* [1978] 2 All ER 1061, p 912. Care must be taken when the offence alleged is against a number of occupants of a property in which the meter has been bypassed—*Hoar and Hoar* [1992] Crim LR 606; *Collins and Fox v Chief Constable of Merseyside* [1988] Crim LR 247.

[180] cf Ormerod and Williams, *Smith's Law of Theft*, para 2.176. It has been prosecuted where, eg, D has wired his house to run appliances from the nearby council street lamp.

[181] See Ch 20.

[182] Prosecutions have been brought for stealing the petrol consumed where D has borrowed a motor vehicle, but this was never regarded as satisfactory, and the offence of taking motor vehicles was introduced. Cf *Low v Blease*, n 175, where it was apparently assumed that a dishonest user of a telephone may commit the offence under s 13. See also *R v Sui-Tak-Chee* (1984) unreported, in which abstracting electricity valued at one-eighth of a Hong Kong cent by using a computer without authorization led to a conviction; referred to in S Fafinski, 'Access Denied' (2006) 70 J Crim L 424.

[183] This sentence was approved in *McReadie and Tume* (1992) 96 Cr App R 143.

[184] There are strong policy arguments for saying that if D prevents V's solar panels from working by blocking the sun over his property or deprives V's turbines of wind, V's remedy should be through the civil law, and not the criminal law.

[185] *Melwani* [1989] Crim LR 565, applying *Ghosh* [1982] QB 1053, but now the appropriate test would be that in *Ivey* [2017] UKSC 67, [74]; and *Barton* [2020] EWCA Crim 575, [84] and [108].

[186] See *Collins and Fox v Chief Constable of Merseyside* [1988] Crim LR 247; Griew, *Theft*, para 2.164.

consider the fact that he was causing the electricity to be used, and thus lacks the necessary mens rea, as, for example, where D makes unauthorized use of a telephone. It was perhaps for these reasons that the law was amended by the Theft Act 1968[187] to create the specific offence of dishonestly using a communication system with intent to avoid payment.[188] This provides an appropriately labelled charge and avoids the prosecution appearing strained.

18.3.2.7 Confidential information

It has been held[189] that confidential information, though it has a value and can be sold, is not property within s 4(1). Accordingly, an undergraduate was not guilty of theft where he unlawfully acquired an examination paper and returned that original piece of paper after he had read its contents.[190] The 'theft' of information is a serious problem, particularly in the form of industrial espionage, for which the civil law arguably provides inadequate remedies. However, as Griew observes,[191] the Theft Act is not the appropriate instrument to deal with this specialized kind of mischief. Examining the issue from a more theoretical perspective, Green argues that while it would be conceptually possible for intangibles such as confidential information to fall within the scope of the law of theft, caution ought to be exercised. Green makes the point that not every appropriation of information ought to be capable of constituting theft, especially if it does not deprive its owner of substantial use of it. The practical consequence of this, Green argues, is that prosecutors and juries might find it difficult to identify when a given instance of appropriation of information ought to constitute theft.[192] The Law Commission has reviewed the possibility of introducing a specific offence of the misuse of trade secrets,[193] and in view of the significance and prevalence of the problem, legislation would seem desirable. The Law Commission's proposal was to criminalize non-consensual use or disclosure of another's trade secrets.

18.3.2.8 Services

Services do not constitute property, so it is not theft for D dishonestly to walk off without paying for his haircut.[194] Specific offences were originally included in the Theft Act 1978

---

[187] Sch 2, Part 1, para 8, see now Communications Act 2003, s 125: dishonestly obtaining an electronic communications service with intent to avoid payment of a charge applicable to that service. In *Mariusz Mikolajczak v District Court in Kalisz, Poland* [2013] EWHC 432 (Admin), Keith J suggested, *obiter*, that this might be the appropriate offence to charge when an individual obtains mobile phone credit by charging the cost to another user. But this does not cover 999 calls since no payment is involved; it is, however, an offence under s 5(2) of the Criminal Law Act 1967 to cause any wasteful employment of the police.

[188] Punishable, on summary conviction, by six months' imprisonment and/or a fine not exceeding the statutory maximum; and, on indictment, by two years' imprisonment. As to the intent, cf *Corbyn v Saunders* [1978] Crim LR 169.

[189] *Oxford v Moss* (1978) 68 Cr App R 183, [1979] Crim LR 119 and commentary.

[190] But see commentary at [1979] Crim LR 119.

[191] Griew, *Theft*, para 2.25. See further R Hammond, 'Theft of Information' (1984) 100 LQR 252; JT Cross, 'Protecting Confidential Information under the Criminal Law of Theft and Fraud' (1991) 11 OJLS 264; AL Christie, 'Should the Law of Theft Extend to Information?' (2005) 69 J Crim L 349; A Coleman, *Intellectual Property Law* (1994). See also L Weinreib, 'Information and Property' (1988) 38 UTLJ 117, and the Canadian Supreme Court in *Stewart* (1988) 50 DLR 1. See also the excellent article by A Taylor and M O'Floinn, [2021] Crim LR 163 considering whether crypto currencies can be stolen.

[192] Green, *13 Ways*, Ch 4.

[193] See LCCP 150, *Legislating the Criminal Code: Misuses of Trade Secrets* (1997), and the reviews by J Hull, 'Stealing Secrets: A Review of the Law Commission Consultation Paper' [1998] Crim LR 246; A Trenton and C Steele, 'Trade Secrets: The Need for Criminal Liability' (1998) 20 EIPR 188. For a recent review of the criminal law's general protection for intellectual property, see C Davies, 'Protection of Intellectual Property—A Myth?' (2004) 68 J Crim L 398.

[194] Green argues that a distinction ought to be made between public and private services. This distinction has consequences for whether the service in question ought to be capable of being stolen. See Green, *13 Ways*, 230–4.

to deal with this problem, and now the Fraud Act 2006 provides an offence of dishonestly obtaining services which was described by the Law Commission when drafting it as 'akin to theft'.[195]

18.3.3 Belonging to another

The third element of the actus reus of theft is that the property which D appropriates must belong to another.

18.3.3.1 The general rule

Section 5(1) of the Theft Act 1968 provides:

Property shall be regarded as belonging to any person having possession or control of it, or having in it any proprietary right or interest (not being an equitable interest arising only from an agreement to transfer or grant an interest).

The onus is on the prosecution to prove that the property in question belonged to someone.[196] Frequently this is self-evident and not disputed at trial, but not always.

In the ordinary case, property is stolen from someone who both owns and possesses it, by someone who has no interest in the property whatever, as where V's wallet is stolen by a stranger, D. Section 5(1) covers this case, of course, but it goes much further. Two partners both own the whole of the partnership property; but if one of them dishonestly makes off with it to the exclusion of the other, he steals it from the other.[197] As a further example of the breadth of s 5(1), suppose that V lends a book to X and that X is showing the book to Z when D snatches the book from Z's hands and makes off with it. Here D has stolen the book from Z (who has control of it), and X (who has possession of it), and V (who also has a proprietary interest—ownership—in it).

Moreover, under s 5(1) D can still be guilty of stealing an item of property if he has an interest (ie possession or control) in that property, provided someone else, V, also has a proprietary interest in it at the same time and it is D's intention dishonestly to deprive V permanently of his interest. So, in the above illustration, if Z were dishonestly to appropriate the book he would steal it from both V and X,[198] and if X were dishonestly to appropriate the book he would steal it from V. Even an owner may steal his own property. So, if A owns a book, and lends it to B, while the book is in B's possession it belongs to B for the purposes of s 5(1). When A appropriates it, there is 'another' who has a proprietary interest: B. It is important to note that s 5 does not place any limitations on the class of persons who may steal. It is possible for a person to steal property even where he has a better proprietary claim than the victim. So D can be liable for theft of his book on loan to V even though D is the owner and V has mere possession of it.

Of course, it will be rare for D's appropriation of his own property to amount not just to an appropriation but to a complete theft because D will be unlikely to possess mens rea: he

---

[195] See p 1004.

[196] The person to whom the property belongs will usually be known and identified in the charges, but if the owner is unknown D may be charged with stealing the property of a person unknown provided that this does not result in D being unable to ascertain the nature of the case he has to meet. Cf *Gregory* [1972] 2 All ER 861 at 866, (handling property of person unknown).

[197] *Bonner* [1970] 1 WLR 838.

[198] cf *Thompson* (1862) Le & Ca 225. D made off with a sovereign [coin] which V handed him to buy a ticket for her because she was unable to make her way through the crowd before a ticket office. This would be theft by D. Cf *Rose v Matt* [1951] 1 KB 810.

may easily be able to plead a claim of right,[199] or be unlikely to be found dishonest generally. But consider *Turner (No 2)*.[200] D had left his car with V for repair, promising to pay for the repairs when he returned to collect the car the following day. D, however, returned a few hours later and surreptitiously took back his car using the spare keys. Although D claimed that he was entitled to do as he did, it was clear from the circumstances that he was acting dishonestly, and his conviction for stealing the car from V was affirmed. At first sight this seems obviously right because D was out to cheat V of his right to retain the property until the debt for the service work was satisfied (technically known as his 'lien'). V had a proprietary right or interest in the property and, even as against the owner, D, the car could be properly regarded as belonging to V so long as he had his lien. Unfortunately, the trial judge told the jury to disregard the question of the lien. Thus, the case is authority for a much broader proposition: that D may steal his own property from V who is D's 'bailee at will' (ie where D is entitled to terminate the bailment *at any time*). It is obvious that so long as V remains in possession of D's property he has a 'proprietary right or interest' as against third parties. Should X have come along and taken Turner's car while it was in V's possession, there would be no difficulty in saying X stole it from V. But it seems odd to regard V as having a 'proprietary interest' as against D (ignoring the lien), when D could take back his property as he is entitled to do.

Turner is difficult to justify.[201] A better decision is that of Judge da Cunha in *Meredith*.[202] D surreptitiously removed his car from a police pound where it had been lawfully placed by the police for causing an obstruction. It was held that D could not be convicted of stealing the car. The police were lawfully in possession of it so that a third party could have stolen it from them. But, they had no right to retain it from D: they had a right to enforce the statutory charge for its removal from the compound, but not to retain it from him. It is useful to compare the position of the police and the repairer in *Turner (No 2)*. There are differences,[203] but, if the police were not liable in *Meredith*, Turner should not have been liable (ignoring the repairer's lien as the courts in that case did).

18.3.3.2 Possession or control

Possession and control may overlap, and it is not important to pursue any possible distinction between them because property is treated as belonging to V if he has *either* possession or control. It is the limits of these concepts which are important, not the difference between them.

Possession requires both an intention to possess and some degree of control in fact. If V and D both see a wallet on the pavement, both may have the same intent to possess it, but until one of them seizes it neither has possession. Once V seizes it he has both possession and control. If he hands it to D just to show D what he has got, it would normally be said that V retains possession while D has control.

Possession and control are not, however, always as clear-cut as in this illustration where V's intent existed in respect of a specific article (wallet) and he reduced it into his actual control—he had it in his hands. But it is not necessary to have, or ever to have had, control of a thing in this sense in order to have possession. A drinks vending-machine supplier may

---

[199] See p 968.   [200] [1971] 2 All ER 441.

[201] Insofar as *Turner* decided that V's possession need not be lawful, it is obviously right and was approved on this point in *Kelly* [1998] 3 All ER 741 at 750. It may be theft to take the stolen property from a thief; the law protects his possession. But the point in *Turner* is that D (in the absence of a lien) had every right to take his own property back. If the owner takes his property from a thief who is unlawfully detaining it, does he steal it if he mistakenly thinks it is someone else's property?

[202] [1973] Crim LR 253.

[203] The police were not bailees of the car (they came into possession by a statutory power to take the car).

have possession of the coins inserted in the machine without knowing at any given moment how many coins, if any, are in the machine.[204] Similarly, a householder normally has possession of the whole contents of his house even though he cannot itemize all his goods.

It is not, then, essential that V's intent to possess should exist in respect of a specific thing: it may be enough for V's intent to exist in respect of all the goods situated about his premises. In *Woodman*,[205] V owned some disused business premises. V sold all the scrap metal on the premises to X; X removed most of it but left some as being too inaccessible to be worth the expense of removal. D then entered the premises to take some of this scrap and was held to have been rightly convicted of theft from V. V continued to control the site and by erecting fences and posting notices V showed that he intended to exclude others; that was enough to give V control of the scrap which he did not wish to remove.

This principle was exemplified in the cases involving the theft of golf balls from lakes and water features on courses with a view to the balls being resold (reportedly producing a £15,000 to £30,000 annual turnover). In *Rostron*,[206] the Court of Appeal confirmed that the issue was whether there was evidence that golf balls hit into a lake were property belonging to another—the club owning the course.[207] It remains necessary for the prosecution to prove that the golf ball retrievers were acting dishonestly in order to sustain a theft conviction, and that may be no easy task. Possibly a finder who was not trespassing—a visitor playing a round of golf or a person crossing the course under a public right of way—would have a better right than the club to the ball. If so (and it is a question of civil law turning on whether they had exercised control over the course to assert title to the property on it), it is submitted that he could not be guilty of theft.

Dependence on civil law

In some instances the question of who has a proprietary interest will turn on technical issues of civil law. In *Marshall*,[208] D obtained part-used Underground tickets and travel cards from members of the public passing through railway barriers and resold them to other potential customers, so depriving London Underground Ltd (LUL) of the revenue it would have gained from the potential customers. D was convicted of theft of the part-used tickets from LUL. The court assumed that those tickets, though in the possession of the passengers, continued to belong to LUL because there was a contract term to that effect on the reverse of each ticket.[209] If reasonable efforts had been made by LUL to bring that term to the passenger's notice, the passenger was merely in possession of a ticket belonging to LUL. It could be stolen from him and from LUL.[210] If sufficient notice of the term was not given to the

---

[204] cf *Martin v Marsh* [1955] Crim LR 781 (electricity meters). But see [1956] Crim LR 74.

[205] [1974] QB 754. See also *Hibbert v McKiernan* [1948] 2 KB 142 (theft of golf balls 'lost' on club premises) criticized by R Hickey (2006) 26 LS 584 for its 'cavalier' reasoning, at 600; *Williams v Phillips* (1957) 41 Cr App R 5 (theft of refuse from dustbins).

[206] [2003] EWCA Crim 2206.

[207] See L Toczek, 'Never Plead Guilty!' (2002) 146 SJ 455. See also the detailed analysis by Hickey, n 205, considering whether it would matter if the balls were in the ground (in a water feature or embedded, etc) or on the ground, and suggesting that the criminal courts ought to follow the civil law where the property is found on the land—asking whether the landowner had evidenced an intention to control the land and anything on it. Where the item is found in the land, title should be with the landowner.

[208] [1998] 2 Cr App R 282, discussed by JC Smith, 'Stealing Tickets' [1998] Crim LR 723. For consideration of the case and offences that may have been committed, see also K Reid and J MacLeod, 'Ticket Touts or Theft of Tickets and Related Offences' (1999) 63 J Crim L 593.

[209] Even if such a term existed, it is for the jury to determine whether LUL had taken reasonable steps to bring that condition to the notice of the 'buyer'—as the passenger probably thought himself to be: see the contract case of *Parker v South Eastern Rly Co* (1877) 2 CPD 416.

[210] He was a buyer of the right to travel on the railway, a thing in action.

passenger, the ticket belonged only to the passenger who had originally purchased it, LUL had no proprietary interest in it and D could not properly be convicted of stealing from LUL. The availability of the theft charge turns on the application of the law of contract. (See also later p 893 in relation to equitable interests.)

18.3.3.3 Proprietary interests and treasure trove

At common law, the rules of treasure trove governed whether the Crown owned articles of gold or silver whose original owner or successors in title could not be found.[211] The Treasure Act 1996 abolished the law relating to 'treasure trove', replacing it by a wide concept of 'treasure' including, as well as any object which would previously have been treasure trove, other specified objects at least 300, or in some cases 200, years old.[212]

18.3.3.4 Any proprietary right or interest

Property is also to be regarded as belonging to any person having in it 'any proprietary right or interest'. Obviously, then, property may be stolen from the owner although at the time of the appropriation the owner is not in possession or control, as where V lends his library book to X and D steals the book from X. Furthermore, property may be stolen from the owner even though he may never have been in possession or control. If X sells goods to V (ownership passing to V) but X remains in possession of them until V has collected them, if D dishonestly appropriates them, he steals from both X and V.[213] Moreover, on those facts if X, after he has sold the goods to V, dishonestly appropriates them (eg by selling them to Y) X steals the property from V even though X was still in possession of the property; X has usurped V's proprietary right in the property. Similarly, if V dishonestly removed from X's premises the property he has bought (with intent to avoid paying for the property), then V steals from X because he usurps X's remaining interest in the property.[214]

D may appropriate property which belongs to V in any of the senses described in s 5(1). It does not matter that V's interest is precarious or that it may be short-lived. For example, flowers left on a grave remain the property of the leaver.[215] Nor does it matter that someone exists who has a better right to the property than V: a thief may steal from a thief.[216] This is a well-established principle. It does not matter that it is impossible for the victim (the original thief) to assert his title in a civil court: public policy which prevents the wrongdoer from enforcing a property right should have no application to criminal proceedings brought in the name of the Crown. The criminal law is concerned with keeping the Queen's peace, not vindicating individual property rights.[217]

18.3.3.5 Equitable interests

The term 'any proprietary right or interest' in s 5 extends to both legal and equitable proprietary interests. Where property is subject to a trust it belongs to both the trustee (legal interest) and beneficiary (equitable interest) and it may be stolen from either. The question

---

[211] See *Hancock* (1989) 90 Cr App R 422 and the discussion in earlier editions of this work.

[212] See generally EM Paintin, 'The Criminal Offence under the Treasure Act' (2001) Art Antiquities & Law 101 and J Marston and L Ross, 'Treasure and Portable Antiquities in the 1990s still Chained to the Ghosts of the Past: The Treasure Act 1996' [1997] Conv 273, criticizing the Act for offering only piecemeal protection.

[213] Frequently the thief will have no idea of the identity of the owner, or owners, of the property; it suffices that he knows the property belongs to *another*.

[214] cf *Rose v Matt* [1951] 1 KB 810 (D pawned a clock and dishonestly retook it from pawnbroker).

[215] According to *Bustler v State*, 184 SE 2d 24 (1944). Cf *Edwards and Stacey* (1877) 13 Cox CC 384.

[216] cf *Clarke*, referred to at [1956] Crim LR 369–70; *Meech* [1974] QB 549; and see *Rose* [2008] EWCA Crim 239.

[217] *Smith* [2011] EWCA Crim 66, citing this work and Ormerod and Williams, *Smith's Law of Theft* on the point.

whether V has an equitable interest in property alleged to have been stolen from him may involve difficult issues of civil law as, for example, in *Clowes (No 2)*,[218] where the criminal court had to consider various Chancery decisions and to rely on the principles of equity relating to tracing into mixed funds to determine whether there was property belonging to another. The criminal law becomes dependent on the civil law here, and if the scope of the civil law's definition of who has a 'proprietary interest' changes, that affects the scope of the criminal law. See the discussion of s 5(4) later.[219]

Under s 5(1) property is not to be regarded as belonging to a person who has an equitable interest arising *only* from an agreement to transfer or grant an interest. A specifically enforceable contract to sell property may give the intending buyer an equitable interest in the property[220] and the provision makes it clear that the seller cannot commit theft by reselling the property to another, however dishonest this may be thought to be.

18.3.3.6 Trust property

Section 5(2) of the Theft Act 1968 provides:

Where property is subject to a trust, the persons to whom it belongs shall be regarded as including any person having a right to enforce the trust, and an intention to defeat the trust shall be regarded accordingly as an intention to deprive of the property any person having that right.

In the ordinary case, appropriation of trust property[221] by a trustee is covered not only by this subsection but also by s 5(1) because the beneficiary ordinarily has a proprietary interest and accordingly the trust property belongs to another—the beneficiary—within s 5(1). In *Sanders*,[222] D, the executor of a will, appropriated £100,000 of the legacy. He admitted doing so and admitted that he did so dishonestly. He argued that this was not theft since subsequently it had come to light that there was a second will naming him as the beneficiary. The Court of Appeal upheld his conviction. Once probate had been granted a trust was established, and if D had discovered that he was the beneficiary under a second will he ought to have sought an amendment of probate. As the court noted, in some cases there would be a ground for arguing that D was not dishonest in such action.

In some exceptional circumstances there will be no ascertained beneficiary. This occurs in the case of 'purpose' trusts, whether charitable[223] or private,[224] where the object is to effect some purpose rather than to benefit ascertainable individuals. To meet such cases s 5(2) goes further than s 5(1) by providing that the property is to be treated as belonging to anyone who has a right to enforce the trust.[225] As far as charitable trusts are concerned, the trustees are the legal owners of the charity's funds but, if they misappropriate the money, they steal not from the donors to that charity, but from the Attorney General who has the right to enforce the trust.[226]

---

[218] [1994] 2 All ER 316. See also MC Davies, 'After *R v Clowes No 2*: An Act of Theft Empowered—A Jury Impoverished' (1997) 61 J Crim L 99 commenting that with a trial based on complex legal issues the effect is to reduce the issues that fall to be determined by the jury, potentially displacing the importance of, eg, s 2(1)(a) of Theft Act 1968.

[219] See p 898.   [220] See Ormerod and Williams, *Smith's Law of Theft*, para 2.196.

[221] Brazier (1975) 39 Conv (NS) 29.   [222] [2003] EWCA Crim 3079.

[223] eg where money is given to D in trust for the improvement of schools in a particular locality.

[224] eg where money is given to D in trust for the maintenance of a tomb, or for the upkeep of animals.

[225] In these examples this would be, respectively, the A-G and the person entitled to the residue of the estate.

[226] *Dyke and Munro* [2002] 1 Cr App R 404.

18.3.3.7 Property received for a particular purpose

Section 5(3) of the 1968 Act provides that:

When a person receives property from or on account of another, and is under an obligation to the other to retain and deal with that property or its proceeds in a particular way, the property or proceeds shall be regarded (as against him) as belonging to the other.

If there is no legal obligation on D to retain and deal with the property in a particular way, it is his to do as he likes with, and it cannot be theft for him to do what he is entitled to do. But where there is such an obligation, it seems right that the property should be capable of being stolen by D. A straightforward example would be where D agrees to do certain work for V and V makes an advance payment of £100. D's failure to do the work or return the £100 will be a breach of contract but no criminal offence.[227] But if V had given D the money *for a specified purpose*, such as to buy materials for the job, that would create the obligation on D to retain and deal, so that D's dishonest disposal of the money for some other purpose would be theft under s 5(3).

Breadth of application

Section 5(3) covers a very wide range of cases. Every bailment seems to be included. So does every trust. Section 5(1) is so wide that in many cases it is unnecessary to rely on s 5(3). So where D has received property from or on account of V in the circumstances described in the subsection, V will usually have a legal or equitable interest in the property or proceeds.[228]

If D dishonestly appropriates the property, he will be stealing it from V who has retained a proprietary right or interest. The case is covered by s 5(1) and so s 5(3) is, strictly speaking, unnecessary, but it is useful because it allows the prosecution to make out their case more easily, without the need to resort to the technical question whether V retains an interest.

'From or on account of another'

The section applies only where the property is 'received from or on account of another'. This creates a difficulty where the property is credited to D's account by a bank transfer.[229] *Preddy* decides that since the credit is new property, a thing in action which belongs to D and has never belonged to anyone else, D could not be guilty of obtaining property *belonging to another* by deception. The property has only ever been D's. On one interpretation, D has not 'received' the property from another or on account of another. The property of the other, V, was the thing in action—V's right to sue his bank—and that was extinguished when D's new item of property was created. On that interpretation, s 5(3) does not apply and D can be guilty of theft only if the person whose bank account has been debited retains an equitable interest in the new property owned by D. An alternative interpretation is to suggest that D has received the thing in action that never previously existed and never belonged to anyone other than him. On that interpretation, s 5(3) would apply. The issue may be academic since D may be guilty of a Fraud Act offence in such cases.

---

[227] Of course, if D never intended to do the work, he would be guilty of fraud under s 2 of the 2006 Act and, since *Gomez*, of theft of it. But if he was acting honestly at the time he received the money, once he had received it he was the absolute owner of it and there was nothing belonging to another for him to steal.

[228] cf *Klineberg and Marsden* [1999] Crim LR 419. *Klineberg* was straightforward, since the money was paid to D on the understanding that it would be 'safeguarded by trusteeship'.

[229] Though it is commonly called a bank transfer, in law it is not a 'transfer' at all.

'Obligation'

It is settled that an 'obligation' to retain and deal with property in a certain way in s 5(3) (and (4) to be discussed later) means a legal, not a merely moral or social, obligation. That much is straightforward; determining whether there is such an obligation is far less so. Where the relevant transaction which allegedly creates the obligation is wholly in writing, it is for the judge to decide as a matter of law whether it does create the legal obligation and to direct the jury accordingly.[230] Where the obligation is alleged to have been created wholly or partly by word of mouth, or by conduct, the judge should direct the jury that if they find the necessary facts (which he must refer them to specifically) proved, there *is* an obligation—not that it is 'open to them' to find that there is an obligation.[231] Aside from the correct procedure for determining whether a legal obligation existed, the substance of that question will often involve complex issues of civil law.[232]

Obligation owed to V

It is plain that the obligation must be owed by D to V. It is not enough that D is under an obligation to a third party to deal with the property for the benefit of V. The case of *Floyd v DPP*[233] is difficult to square with this principle. D collected money in weekly premiums from colleagues who had ordered goods from a Christmas hamper company—V Ltd. She failed to pay the money to V Ltd and her conviction for stealing it from V Ltd was upheld in reliance on s 5(3). The court said it was unnecessary to show that V Ltd had any legal or equitable interest in the money. D may have had a contract with her colleagues (V was not privy to that) but now, under the Contracts (Rights of Third Parties) Act 1999,[234] D's contract with colleagues may 'purport to confer a benefit' on V, resulting in D having an obligation to V: s 5(3) then applies.

Examples of s 5(3) in operation

If D is under no legal obligation to retain and deal with property which has been delivered to him, he can lawfully do what he likes with it and it is incapable of being stolen, as are its proceeds. This is ordinarily the position where money is lent. It is not always easy to determine whether D was under an obligation to retain and deal or at liberty to dispose of the property entirely as he wished. It is, to underline the point, a question of civil law.

Advance payments

As noted earlier, this includes if V has given D money *for a specified purpose*, as an advance such as to buy materials for the job. That would create the obligation on D to retain and deal, so that D's dishonest disposal of the money for some other purpose would be theft.

Deposits

If V were to pay a deposit to D, a trader, for goods to be supplied D's liability under s 5(3) will depend on whether D is under an obligation to deal with that deposit in a particular way. The difficulties in application are well illustrated by *Hall*.[235] D, a partner in a firm of travel agents, had received money from V and others as deposits for flights to the United States. The flights never materialized and the deposits, which had been paid into the firm's general

---

[230] *Clowes (No 2)* [1994] 2 All ER 316, holding that a brochure inviting the payment of money for investment in gilts was a contractual document creating a trust.

[231] *Dubar* [1995] 1 All ER 781, following *Mainwaring* (1981) 74 Cr App R 99 and disapproving *dicta* in *Hall* [1972] 2 All ER 1009 at 1012 and *Hayes* (1976) 64 Cr App R 82 at 85 and 87.

[232] See eg *Breaks and Huggan* [1998] Crim LR 349 (contractual obligations of insurance brokers placing insurance with Lloyds).

[233] [2000] Crim LR 411.   [234] Applying to contracts made on or after 11 May 2000.

[235] [1972] 2 All ER 1009, and see *Hayes* (1976) 64 Cr App R 82.

trading account, were never returned to V and other customers. The Court of Appeal had no difficulty in accepting the jury's verdict that D had acted dishonestly in spending this money, but quashed D's conviction for theft on the ground that D had *not* received the money under an obligation to deal with it *in a particular way*. The court reached this conclusion with obvious reluctance (as ever when there has been a finding of dishonesty).[236]

The case shows that if D owes money to V and he dishonestly disposes of his assets so that when the time comes for payment to V he has no funds from which to meet his debts, he will not be under an obligation for the purposes of s 5(3). Moreover, it makes no difference, as far as the law of theft is concerned, that D has acted in this way in order to defeat his creditors. A liability to pay V is accordingly not enough under s 5(3) unless D is obliged to keep in existence a fund representing that property.

This issue was also considered in *Foster*[237] in which D collected sums of money from work colleagues for the purpose of pooling them to place large bets on sporting events. D pooled those funds with others, not subject to any such restriction, and drew on the global fund for his own purposes. D was convicted of theft on the basis that he dishonestly appropriated over £1.4m of the investors' property for his own purpose and benefit. D appealed and argued that s 5(3) did not apply to the sum he had appropriated for his own benefit.

Citing *Hall*, the Court of Appeal stated that the crucial issue was whether the property was given to D in circumstances where he had to retain or deal with it or its proceeds in a particular way. It was held that this was a matter for the jury and that the judge had been right to leave it to them to evaluate whether there was such a legal obligation. The problem, however, was that on the facts of the case there were around 8,500 individuals who had invested in D's scheme and it was impossible to say which investors had imposed which obligations on the monies. All of the monies had been placed into a mixed fund, which made the task even more difficult. D's conviction was quashed on the basis that it was impossible to tell whether the monies he had used for his own purposes were subject to an obligation that they be used for a particular purpose.

Foster makes clear that even if D is under an obligation to deal with some of the funds in a particular way, within the meaning of s 5(3), if these are pooled with funds that are not subject to the obligation or there is doubt about whether there is such an obligation, then D cannot be guilty if it is funds from this mixed pool it is alleged that he has used for his own purpose. Of course, if D has separated the funds such that it is possible to determine whether he has only used those funds subject to the obligation for his own purposes, the position will be different. As the Court of Appeal observes, however, this is an unlikely scenario and indeed D now has an incentive to pool the funds.

Breaches of contract

Section 5(3) may apply to cases of mere breach of contract not covered by s 5(1). For example, D who buys a non-transferable ticket may become the owner of the ticket, but be under a contractual obligation to 'retain and deal with it in a particular manner' in the sense of 'not dealing' with it.[238] In the case of a rail ticket, such as that in *Marshall*, his ownership of the ticket involved his contractual obligation not to assign it to another. But note that the property must be 'received'. Where D enters into a contract to deal with his own property in his own possession the subsection does not apply.[239]

---

[236] [1972] 2 All ER 1009 at 1011. See *Re Kumar* [2000] Crim LR 504, where there was such an obligation.

[237] [2011] EWCA Crim 1192.

[238] cf Smith [1998] Crim LR 723 at 726. It is pointed out that this is not theft of the thing in action, but whether it is theft of the thing in possession (the ticket) is not considered.

[239] It may, however, create an equitable interest. Cf commentary on *Arnold* [1997] Crim LR at 834. The case involved an odd application of s 5(3).

Charity sponsorship

A common situation in which s 5(3) is used is where D receives property from V for onward transmission to, or for the benefit of, E. The required obligation may be imposed on D either by D's relationship with V, or his relationship with E, or both. After a strange decision in *Lewis v Lethbridge*,[240] the court in *Wain*[241] rightly held that where D obtained sponsorships in favour of a charity (E) and received money from sponsors (V), D is under an obligation and guilty of theft if he disposes of the property dishonestly.

Obligations imposed by statute

It is possible for the obligation to be imposed on D by statute. No doubt when the State pays housing benefit to D to enable D to pay his rent, the expectation is that D will use that money to pay his landlord, but it was held in *Huskinson*[242] that D was not guilty of theft where he spent some of the money received as housing benefit on himself. There was nothing in the relevant legislation suggesting that D was bound to pay *that* money or its proceeds to the landlord. D could have met his legal obligation to pay the rent from any source, such as an unexpected win on the lottery, and spent the benefit as he chose.

Obligations and agency

An obligation to deal with property in a specified way may be imposed on D in civil law through the acts of his agents. However, if D is unaware of the facts giving rise to that obligation, the prosecution cannot rely on s 5(3).[243] Moreover, if D knew the facts but owing to his mistake of civil law believed that there was no obligation and that the money was his to do as he liked with, he would not be dishonest and should be acquitted on that ground.

If D receives a bribe in contravention of his duty to his principal, V, the principal may recover the amount of the bribe in a civil action; and D can steal the amount of the bribe. This is a complex question of civil law that has only relatively recently been resolved. In *FHR European Ventures LLP v Cedar Capital Partners LLC*,[244] the Supreme Court addressed the conflict between earlier cases.[245] It was held that V *does* have a proprietary interest in the money. This decision substantially enlarges the scope of the criminal law[246] and for that reason it is important that criminal practitioners and those who administer the criminal law recognize its impact.

For s 5(3) to apply, it is not necessary that the fiduciary duty arises out of the transaction between D and the person delivering the property to him; it is enough that D's fiduciary duty arises out of a relationship with a person other than the person delivering the property.

---

[240] [1987] Crim LR 59. D not guilty for spending £54 charity money he raised.

[241] [1995] 2 Cr App R 660, following *Davidge v Bunnett* [1984] Crim LR 297, where, by agreement between flatmates to share the costs of gas, etc, D received money from the others for the gas bill and spent it on Christmas presents. Domestic arrangements are commonly not intended to give rise to legal relationships but here the parties were not members of the same family and presumably intended their agreement to be legally binding. Equally doubtful is the case where a woman was held guilty of stealing money entrusted to her by her cohabitee to buy food, etc for their household: *Cullen*, No 968/C74 of 1974, unreported.

[242] [1988] Crim LR 620.   [243] *Wills* (1990) 92 Cr App R 297.

[244] [2014] UKSC 45. For critical comment, see W Gummow, 'Bribes and Constructive Trusts' (2015) 131 LQR 21.

[245] *Lister & Co v Stubbs* (1890) 45 Ch D 1 (holding V has no proprietary interest); *A-G for Hong Kong v Reid* [1994] 1 AC 324 (holding that a bribe should be treated as being held on constructive trust for V from the moment it is received). See also *Cullum* (1873) LR 2 CCR 28; CLRC, Eighth Report, para 38; Williams, TBCL, 756; ATH Smith, 'Constructive Trusts in the Law of Theft' [1977] Crim LR 395; JC Smith (1956) 19 MLR 39, 46. It has been said that in none of the cases in which a fiduciary has been held liable to account for profits did the question arise whether the defendant was a trustee as opposed to being merely accountable: J Glister and J Lee, *Hanbury and Martin, Modern Equity* (21st edn, 2018).

[246] See JC Smith, 'Contracts—Mistake, Frustration and Implied Terms' (1994) 110 LQR 400.

18.3.3.8 Property got by mistake

Section 5(4) of the Theft Act provides:

Where a person gets property by another's mistake, and is under an obligation to make restoration (in whole or in part) of the property or its proceeds or of the value thereof, then to the extent of that obligation the property or proceeds shall be regarded (as against him) as belonging to the person entitled to restoration, and an intention not to make restoration shall be regarded accordingly as an intention to deprive that person of the property or proceeds.

This provision was enacted to deal with the problem encountered in the case of *Moynes v Cooper*.[247] D was given an advance on his pay by his employer, V. Later that week, unaware that an advance had been made, V's wages' staff paid D the full weekly wage. D dishonestly kept all of the money. The difficulty in treating this as theft by D is that in law the whole of the full weekly wage belonged to D. Under the pre-Theft Act law D was acquitted. The payroll staff made a mistake of course, but that mistake was not such as would prevent ownership of all the money passing to D. This type of case is now covered by s 5(4): D steals the excess payment if he dishonestly appropriates it. Although D becomes the owner of the full weekly wage he is under a legal obligation, at the very least, to repay the value of the excess payment.

Section 5(4) was applied in these circumstances in *A-G's Reference (No 1 of 1983)*.[248] D's salary was paid into her bank account by direct debit and on one occasion her employers mistakenly overpaid her by £74.74. Section 5(4) was held to apply. The 'money in the bank' was entirely hers to do with as she liked, but she was under an obligation to repay an equivalent sum (the value) to her employers. On these facts, subject to proof of dishonesty, her failure to do so meant she was guilty of theft.

The law is clear as to V's position in circumstances of making a mistaken payment: if, owing to a mistake of fact, V believes that he is legally obliged to make a payment and he does so, he is entitled in civil law to recover the equivalent of the sum he mistakenly paid.[249] It is less clear what D's civil law position is where he has received a payment made in error. The issue whether D was under a legal obligation to repay the value was resolved in the *A-G's Reference (No 1)* without difficulty, but it will be appreciated that it will not always be so straightforward.

The law of unjust enrichment[250] is one of complexity and subtlety which has developed considerably in recent years in *Kleinwort Benson Ltd v Lincoln City Council*,[251] and *Westdeutsche Landesbank v Islington LBC*.[252] D's liability for theft may turn upon a consideration of fine points of civil law remote from the central question of D's dishonesty. There was no evidence in the *A-G's Reference (No 1)* that D had spent the money that was overpaid or that she had done any act in relation to it. To meet a possible argument that in doing nothing D cannot intend permanently to deprive the owner, s 5(4) further provides that an intention not to make restoration shall be regarded as an intention permanently to deprive.[253]

A further difficulty with cases such as this follows from the decision in *Preddy* and the need to identify which item of property is in issue. In *Gresham* (discussed later), D's mother

---

[247] [1956] 1 QB 439. See also the discussion in W Swadling, 'Rescission, Property and the Common Law' (2005) 121 LQR 123 at 135.

[248] [1985] QB 182.

[249] *Norwich Union Fire Insurance Society Ltd v William H Price Ltd* [1934] AC 455.

[250] See R Goff and G Jones, *The Law of Unjust Enrichment* (9th edn, 2016).

[251] [1999] 2 AC 349, followed in a number of other decisions, including *Deutsche Morgan Grenfell v IRC* [2006] UKHL 49.

[252] [1996] AC 669.   [253] 'Keeping' is a sufficient appropriation. See p 874.

had been in receipt of pension payments from her former employer which were made by automatic transfers to her bank account. D failed to inform her former employer (the Department of Education) and the bank of his mother's death. The payments continued to be credited for ten years after her death and D having had the power of attorney to act for her when she was alive, continued to use this power to cash cheques drawn on her account. The cheques drawn by D reduced the credit balance in his mother's account. D was convicted of theft and obtaining a money transfer by deception (contrary to the offence then in force under s 15A of the 1968 Act). The credit balance that D diminished by drawing cheques was not an item of property that belonged to the Department of Education within the terms of s 5(1). The prosecution relied instead on the fact that the payments had been by mistake and that s 5(4) applied. The court upheld convictions for theft on this basis, rejecting an argument that s 5(4) has no application where D has induced V's mistake by deception as 'eccentric'.

Is s 5(4) superfluous?

The foregoing discussion of s 5(4) assumes, as seemingly did the CLRC, that the entire proprietary interest in the money mistakenly paid passes to D, who is no more than a debtor. That is the position *at law*. Section 5(4) was felt to be necessary to vest a fictitious interest in V who had paid money by mistake. However, some cases have now held that as a matter of equity, where V pays money by mistake to D, V retains an equitable interest. If that is right, V has a proprietary right or interest under s 5(1) in such cases and there would be no need for s 5(4).

In *Chase Manhattan Bank NA v Israel–British Bank (London) Ltd*,[254] the X bank by mistake paid $2m.[255] Goulding J held that V who pays money (or, presumably, delivers any property) to D under a mistake of fact retains an equitable interest[256] in the money and the conscience of D is subject to a fiduciary duty to respect V's proprietary right.[257] The reasoning underpinning this decision was disapproved by Lord Browne-Wilkinson in *Westdeutsche Landesbank v Islington LBC*[258] but his lordship commented *obiter* that stolen monies should be treated as being held on constructive trust by the thief, and therefore would be traceable by the original owner of those monies. Having regard to the decision in *Kleinwort*,[259] it now seems that a mistake of fact or law may ground a claim in unjust enrichment, and so an obligation to make restitution may arise where the mistake caused the payment to be made (or other benefit to be transferred). Adopting that approach, in *Moynes v Cooper*, V retained an equitable interest in the money overpaid and D, on these facts, could now be convicted of theft even if s 5(4) had not been enacted.

The *Chase Manhattan* principle was relied on by the Court of Appeal (Criminal Division) in *Shadrokh-Cigari*.[260] The O bank had, in error, credited a child's account at the V bank

---

[254] [1981] Ch 105—doubted, but not so as to affect its application in criminal cases, by Lord Browne-Wilkinson in *Westdeutsche Landesbank Girozentrale v Islington LBC* [1996] AC 669 at 715. *Westdeutsche* has been followed in *Bank of America v Arnell* [1999] Lloyd's Rep 399; *Clark v Cutland* [2003] EWCA Civ 810. For a helpful discussion see G Virgo, *Principles of the Law of Restitution* (3rd edn, 2015) 598–602.

[255] The payment was from the X bank to the Y bank for the account of the Z bank which subsequently went into liquidation. The X bank was, of course, entitled to a dividend in the liquidation but it sought to recover the whole of its loss.

[256] Section 5(1) extends to equitable interests, see p 889.

[257] Accordingly, the X bank was entitled to the restoration of the whole of the money mistakenly paid and was not relegated to claiming a dividend in the liquidation.

[258] [1996] AC 669.   [259] See p 898.

[260] [1988] Crim LR 465. See further G MacCormack, 'Mistaken Payments and Proprietary Claims' [1996] Conv 86.

with £286,000 instead of £286! D, the child's guardian, got the child to sign authority for the V bank to issue banker's drafts, and when D was arrested only £21,000 of the £286,000 remained in the account. Upholding D's conviction for theft from the V bank, the court said that the drafts belonged to the bank and although legal ownership passed to D by delivery, the bank retained an equitable interest in them by virtue of the *Chase Manhattan* principle and D had appropriated property belonging to another (V) within the broad terms of s 5(1). It was accordingly not necessary to rely on s 5(4) though that subsection provided an alternative route to conviction.[261]

Subsequent decisions have applied *Shadrokh-Cigari* without hesitation. In *Webster*,[262] the Court Martial Appeal Court upheld D's conviction for theft of a medal which he had sold on eBay. The medal was sent in error to Captain X (it was an unsolicited duplicate). X gave it to D, his administrative officer, to deal with. There was some confusion as to what the procedure was for the issue and return of medals, but the court had no doubt that medals are akin to gifts from the sovereign, and that in this case there had been a fundamental error by the Ministry of Defence in supplying a duplicate. The Crown retained an interest in that medal, it was property belonging to another as against D.[263]

Identifying the property got by mistake

Section 5(4), or the *Chase Manhattan* principle, applies though only part of the property is got by mistake. In *Moynes v Cooper*,[264] D appropriated only the amount by which he was overpaid. In such a case it would be impossible to identify the coins which represented the overpayment but the prosecution are not required to do so because the relevant property is sufficiently identified if it is proved to be part of an identifiable whole. This principle was applied in *Davis*.[265] By a computer error, D was sent two cheques a month in respect of housing benefit when he was entitled to only one. It was held that where D had cashed these cheques he could be convicted of stealing the proceeds (the cash) of one of the cheques and it was not necessary for the prosecution to establish which proceeds he had stolen and which he had not.[266]

Requirement of legal obligation

It will be evident from the previous discussion that 'obligation' in s 5(4) can only refer to a legal obligation imposed by the civil law. This is confirmed by *Gilks*,[267] though the case has its complications. V, a bookmaker, mistakenly believing that D had backed a winning horse, overpaid D on the bets he had placed and D, aware of the error, dishonestly decided not to return the overpayment. Since V had made no mistake either as to the amount or the recipient, ownership of the money passed to D. The court was clear that s 5(4) was inapplicable. As this was a betting transaction, as a matter of civil law, as the law then stood V had no right of restitution in respect of the overpayment, so D could be under no legal obligation to make restoration. But the court went on, relying upon an antique and questionable authority under the law of larceny,[268] to uphold D's conviction on the

---

[261] See also the statements in *Gresham* [2003] EWCA Crim 2070.   [262] [2006] EWCA Crim 2894.

[263] Was this not obvious? Was there not also X's proprietary interest? He had not authorized the sale, and after *Gomez* that would not matter in any event. See also the comments of the Administrative Court in *Re Holmes* [2004] EWHC 2020 (Admin) expressing the provisional view that the property which D had fraudulently transferred by automated process from a German to a Dutch bank was subject to a constructive trust. Cf *Ngan* [1998] 1 Cr App R 331 in which s 5(4) was not discussed.

[264] See p 898.   [265] (1988) 88 Cr App R 347.

[266] On the civil law position for tracing into mixed funds, see *Westdeutsche Landesbank v Islington LBC* [1996] AC 669.

[267] [1972] 1 WLR 1341.   [268] *Middleton* (1873) LR 2 CCR 38.

ground that since V would not have made the overpayment but for his mistake, ownership in the money did not pass to D. This is at odds with the civil law and the decision needs to be reconsidered. It is a further example of the courts striving to uphold the convictions of those found to be dishonest, at the expense of clarity and principle in the definition of the Theft Act offences. After *Westdeutsche Landesbank v Islington LBC* (discussed earlier), it is clear under civil law that if D was aware that a part of the money had been mistakenly overpaid to him, then D would be required to hold that overpayment on constructive trust for the payer, V.

18.3.3.9 Property of corporations

A corporation such as a limited company is, in law, a person distinct from its members. It can own property and be the victim of theft and other offences under the Theft Acts. A member of the corporation can be guilty of stealing the property of the corporation—it is property belonging to another: the company. If a director, D, of a limited company misappropriates the company's property the injury is suffered by the company's shareholders (or, if it is insolvent, its creditors); but the property D has appropriated does not belong to the directors and D is guilty of theft, not from them, but from the company.[269] This is straightforward where D is misappropriating the property because he is acting without authority. The matter is more difficult if the alleged theft from the company is, say, an act authorized by the board of directors at a properly constituted meeting. Although it exists as a separate legal person, a company can act only through its human controlling officers and, in some contexts at least, they are identified with the company—their acts are the company's acts.[270] If company directors resolve to use the company's assets for their personal advantage instead of for the company's proper purposes, and if this act is the company's act (ie the company authorizes it (albeit by the directors' decision)), it might be thought difficult to characterize it as theft; no one can steal from himself. It is different if the act is *ultra vires* the company because then it is not the company's act at all; but the courts seem to have regarded the question of *ultra vires* as irrelevant.

The problem is most acute where the directors, say, D and E, are also the sole shareholders. If D and E, as the controlling mind of the company, C, agree that C shall pay them money for their personal use, have they stolen the money from C? Historically, judicial opinion was divided about this situation. One view was that this was theft from the company.[271] The other was that an act done with the authority of the company cannot in general amount to an appropriation.[272] Since *Gomez* it is clear that this is wrong. The current law is clear: a dishonest appropriation is theft, even if the owner consents. In *Gomez*, Lord Browne-Wilkinson (with whom three judges, including Lord Lowry who dissented on the main issue, agreed) said that their lordships' decision rendered 'the whole question of consent by the company irrelevant'.

D and E in the example above might object, saying they were not merely acting with the consent of the company: they *were* the company. If I give away all my property with the intention of defrauding my creditors, it is impossible to hold that I have committed theft because I have not appropriated something belonging to another. However, Lord Browne-Wilkinson also said that even if consent was relevant to appropriation, there would still be a theft.[273]

---

[269] *R (on the application of A) v Snaresbrook Crown Court* (2001) 165 JPN 495.   [270] See Ch 8.

[271] *A-G's Reference (No 2 of 1982)* [1984] QB 624; *Phillipou* (1989) 89 Cr App R 290.

[272] *McHugh and Tringham* (1988) 88 Cr App R 385, 393. See also *Roffel* [1985] VR 511, discussed by JC Smith (1985) 9 Crim LJ 320.

[273] [1993] 1 All ER 1 at 40.

Where a company is accused of a crime the acts and intentions of those who are the directing minds and will of the company are to be attributed to the company. That is not the law where the charge is that those who are the directing minds and will have themselves committed a crime against the company.

It must now be conceded, following *Gomez*, that in these cases D appropriates property belonging to another, but there is still difficulty in seeing how it can be a *dishonest* appropriation.[274] The act is not dishonest vis-à-vis the shareholders because they are the appropriators and therefore it is unreal to say that it is dishonest with respect to the company, which exists for the benefit of the shareholders. It may well be dishonest with respect to the company's creditors, but the property does not belong to them.[275] The illogicality of the position is demonstrated further when comparison is made with the position of partnership property. If D and E were not the directors of a company but the sole members of a partnership, they could not be guilty of theft of the partnership's assets, even if they disposed of them in riotous living with intent to defeat their creditors.[276] There does not seem to be any difference in substance.

18.3.3.10 Ownerless property

A person cannot be guilty of stealing property that is not owned by another at the time of the appropriation. If there is no person to whom the property belongs in any of the senses set out in s 5, that property cannot be stolen. Property that is capable of belonging to another may be ownerless because it has never been made the subject of ownership. D can commit no offence where, for example, he takes a swarm of bees not presently owned by another.

18.3.3.11 Property it is unlawful to possess

There is nothing to stop a theft charge where the property in question was held by V, someone who had no lawful right to it. A thief can steal from a thief. Equally, it does not matter whether the property is of a type that V was not lawfully permitted to possess. In *Smith*,[277] D was convicted of robbery having appropriated V's heroin by force. Initially D and others were charged with robbery of cash (£50) but the indictment was amended to charge robbery of drugs to the value of £50. D argued that the controlled drugs did not amount to property within the meaning of the Theft Act 1968. In particular that they could not be guilty of theft (and hence of robbery) if the article that had been taken was unlawfully in the possession of V. Moreover, it was argued that there could be no appropriation of the rights of the owner where the owner had no rights of possession because possession was prohibited by law. The Court of Appeal rejected these arguments. On settled law, the sole question was whether the owner had possession or control of the property. There was no ground whatever for qualifying the words 'possession or control', in any way. It was sufficient that the person from whom the property was taken, or to use the words of the Act, appropriated, was at the time in fact in possession or control of the property. The criminal law is concerned with keeping the Queen's peace, not with protecting private property rights.[278]

---

[274] DW Elliott, 'Directors' Thefts and Dishonesty' [1991] Crim LR 732; Griew, *Theft*, paras 2.86–2.87.

[275] GR Sullivan, Letters to the Editor [1991] Crim LR 929 argues that the interests of the creditors of an insolvent or doubtfully solvent company are the interests of the company, and as such D and E are rightly guilty of theft in such circumstances. But it is not clear that this is an established principle or that it is the foundation of the cases holding that the sole director may steal the company's property.

[276] Note the offence of fraudulent trading by a sole trader under s 9 of the Fraud Act 2006.

[277] [2011] EWCA Crim 66.

[278] If the argument of S in this case was accepted, it would, nevertheless, be an offence to steal drugs from the exhibit room in court or from a police officer.

18.3.3.12 Corpses and living body tissue

Historically, at common law, the rule was that there is no property in a corpse or part of a corpse.[279] Executors or administrators or others with a legal duty to inter a body have a right to custody and possession of it until it is buried; but it seems the corpse is incapable of being stolen from them. In *Doodeward v Spence*,[280] the High Court of New South Wales (having examined the English authorities) held that a proprietary interest could be acquired by one who expended work and skill on the corpse with a view to its preservation on scientific or other grounds. This decision was applied in *Kelly*,[281] where parts of bodies preserved as anatomical specimens and taken from the Royal College of Surgeons were held to have been stolen.

In *Yearworth v North Bristol NHS Trust*,[282] the Court of Appeal (Civil Division) has moved away from this principle that recognized property rights in body tissue only on the basis of expended skill. The claimants who were undergoing cancer treatment had stored their sperm with the defendant hospital for potential future use; they sought damages when the hospital failed to store the sperm properly. One issue at trial was whether each man's sperm was 'property' belonging to him. It was removed from his body but unlike most other removed tissue was capable of performing the same function it had when in the body. The Court of Appeal, accepting that the men had ownership of the tissue for the purposes of the claim, acknowledged that developments in medical science require a re-analysis of the common law's treatment of ownership of body products.[283] The Lord Chief Justice accepted that the storage of sperm in liquid nitrogen represented 'an application to the sperm of work and skill', but regarded *Doodeward* as illogical:

we are not content to see the common law in this area founded upon the principle in *Doodeward*, which was devised as an exception to a principle, itself of exceptional character, relating to the ownership of a human corpse.[284]

The Human Tissue Act 2004[285] provides a framework for issues of donation, storage and use of body parts, organs and tissue. The Act is a response to the concerns raised by events at Alder Hey Children's Hospital and the Bristol Royal Infirmary.[286] Many difficult issues relating to proprietary interests in body parts arise in other areas of the law and these may have an impact on future interpretations of s 5. For example, in *L v Human Fertilisation and Embryology Authority*[287] it was doubted whether there was anyone who had authority to remove or authorize removal of gametes from a deceased person without effective advance consent.

[279] See ATH Smith, 'Stealing the Body and its Parts' [1976] Crim LR 622 and *Property Offences*, paras 3.03–3.06; P Skegg, 'Criminal Liability for the Unauthorized Use of Corpses for Medical Education and Research' (1992) 32 Med Sci L 51; M Pawlowski, 'Dead Bodies as Property' (1996) 146 NLJ 1828; A Maclean, 'Resurrection of the Body Snatchers' (2000) 150 NLJ 174.

[280] (1908) 95 R (NSW) 107.

[281] [1998] 3 All ER 741. Cf *Dobson v North Tyneside Health Authority* [1996] 4 All ER 474, CA (Civ Div).

[282] [2009] EWCA Civ 37. See M Quigley (2009) 17 Med L Rev 457; C Hawes, 'Property Interests in Body Parts: *Yearworth v North Bristol NHS Trust*' (2010) 73 MLR 130; M Quigley, 'Property in Human Biomaterials—Separating Persons and Things?' (2012) 32 OJLS 659; S Douglas and I Goold, 'Property in Human Biomaterials: A New Methodology' (2016) 75 CLJ 478, who argue that the Court of Appeal sidestepped the established rules of acquisition of property rights.

[283] See the discussion at [31]–[45].   [284] At [45].

[285] The Human Tissue Act 2004 provides safeguards and penalties in relation to improper retention of tissue and organs without consent. See also J Herring, *Medical Law and Ethics* (8th edn, 2020) Ch 9.

[286] See Department of Health guidelines: *The Removal, Retention and Use of Human Organs and Tissue from Post-Mortem Examination* (2001).

[287] [2008] EWHC 2149 (Fam).

18.3.3.13 Property of the deceased

In *Sullivan and Ballion*,[288] the defendants had appropriated the £50,000 they found on their friend who had died of natural causes in their company the night before. The deceased was a drug dealer and the money represented his takings. They were charged with theft of the money. Dismissing the charges, the trial judge ruled that the property did not 'belong to another' when it was taken.[289] As pointed out in the commentary to the case, the property must have belonged to someone other than the thieves (who had no rights to it). Since there may be a conviction of theft of property of a person unknown, it follows that it is enough to show that the property must have belonged to someone and that the defendants knew it belonged to someone other than themselves. The money did not belong to those who had purchased drugs from the deceased (in this case a group known as 'The Firm') because, as the judge held, they had parted with their entire proprietary interest in the money; but the proprietary interest can hardly have vanished into thin air—it passed to the deceased or, if he was acting as an agent, his principal. At the time of the alleged theft, the money must have belonged either to the deceased's principal, if any, or to those entitled under his (or their) will or intestacy; or, if they did not exist, to the Crown as *bona vacantia* (ownerless property, which by law passes to the Crown).[290] There remains the difficulty in establishing the defendants' mens rea. If the defendants supposed, or may have supposed, that the property belonged to no one and could be taken by the first person to come across it, then they are not guilty. But if they knew it must belong to someone other than themselves, it is immaterial that they did not know who that person was.

18.3.3.14 Abandonment

Property which has at one time been owned may become ownerless by abandonment.[291] But abandonment is not something to be lightly inferred: property is abandoned only when the owner is indifferent to any future appropriation of the property by others. It is not enough that V had no further use for the goods. A farmer who buries diseased animals has no further use for them but he would clearly intend that others should not make use of them and retains ownership of the carcasses.[292] It is legitimate for magistrates to conclude that a person who leaves bags of goods outside a charity shop has not abandoned the items.[293] When D takes the bags he can be convicted of theft—subject to his mens rea. The person leaving the bags does so with the intention of making a legitimate donation and has attempted to effect

---

[288] [2002] Crim LR 758.

[289] Hale, I PC, 514: 'If A dies intestate, and the goods of the intestate are stolen before administration committed, it is felony, and the goods shall be supposed to be *bona episcopi* de D. ordinary of the diocese, and if he made B his executor the goods shall be supposed bona B tho he hath not proved the will, and they need not show specifically their title as ordinary or executor because it is of their own possession, in which case a general indictment as well as a general action of trespass lies without naming themselves as executor or ordinary, and so for an administrator.' See also East, II PC, 652 and *Russell on Crime* (2nd edn, 1843) ii, 99 stating the law in similar terms.

[290] A suggested direction for such cases is supplied in the commentary, n 288.

[291] On abandonment, see AH Hudson, 'Is Divesting Abandonment Possible at Common Law' (1984) 100 LQR 110 and 'Abandonment' in N Palmer and E McKendrick (eds), *Interests in Property* (1993). See also the interesting article discussing the civil and criminal law approaches to abandonment: R Hickey, 'Stealing Abandoned Goods: Possessory Title in Proceedings for Theft' (2006) 26 LS 584. On the potential for theft charges against 'freegans'—those who take food from supermarket refuse areas when it has been discarded because it has passed its sell by date—see the detailed analysis by S Thomas, 'Do Freegans Commit Theft' (2010) 30 LS 98. The argument advanced in that article that the goods are not abandoned may not be likely to persuade the courts, but the argument based on mens rea is, it is submitted, a stronger one.

[292] cf *Edwards and Stacey* (1877) 36 LT 30.

[293] *R (Ricketts) v Basildon Magistrates' Court* [2010] EWHC 2358 (Admin).

delivery.[294] Whether the charity shop had either kept and resold those items or disposed of them, they still would have come within its possession and control but the shop did not have possession or control when D appropriated. Importantly, then, a householder who puts rubbish in his dustbin has no further use for the rubbish, but he puts it there to be collected by the authorized refuse collectors and not as an invitation to all-comers to help themselves.[295]

In *Toleikis*[296] D was convicted of handling stolen goods when he was found in possession of several bags of clothes that had been intended for charity. Householders left the clothes in clearly marked bags outside their homes for the charity to collect, but they instead ended up in D's van. One of the issues on appeal was whether the clothes constituted property belonging to another. Sir John Thomas P held that the correct approach was that the clothes did belong to the charity in question on the application of the law of gift. Even though the bags of clothes had not yet been collected by the charity, the President held that a gift could be completed by delivery. Given that this was the case, the bags of clothes constituted property belonging to another. It is submitted that *Toleikis* simply applies the principle that was confirmed earlier by the Divisional Court in *Ricketts*. The homeowners left the bags of clothes outside their homes with the intention of conferring the proprietary interest in them to the charity. Given this intention, the clothes were not abandoned and could therefore be stolen.

A shipowner who runs aground and whose cargo is cast onto the land has not lost his proprietary interest in the cargo.[297] Nor is property abandoned because the owner has lost it and has given up the search.[298] A husband may have lost his wedding ring and long since given up the search but will not have abandoned it.

18.4 Mens rea

Theft requires an intention to appropriate property belonging to another,[299] and that the appropriation be dishonest. As the Law Commission stated in its Consultation Paper No 155, 'in theft . . . dishonesty is now the principal determinant of criminality'.[300]

18.4.1 View to gain immaterial

Section 1(2) of the 1968 Act provides, 'It is immaterial whether the appropriation is made with a view to gain, or is made for the thief's own benefit.'

---

[294] That gift would be complete when the shop took possession of the items. Until then, the donor has not relinquished ownership. D faced a second count of theft of bags left by the charity shop in its dustbin. The property was deemed to belong to the shop at the time of appropriation by D. See also *Rostron* [2003] EWCA Crim 2206. At trial, it would of course be important to deal fully with D's belief that he was not acting dishonestly, under s 2 of the Act and under *Ivey* [2017] UKSC 67 and *Barton* [2020] EWCA Crim 575, and that he lacked an intent to deprive.

[295] cf *Williams v Phillips* (1957) 121 JP 163. The availability of theft charges in such circumstances is important in dealing with those who rummage through the refuse of celebrities for information to sell to tabloid newspapers, and those who appropriate confidential industrial or financial information from refuse. There is a specific offence under s 60 of the Environmental Protection Act 1990 of interfering with waste receptacles.

[296] [2013] EWCA Crim 600.

[297] R Glover, 'Can Dishonesty be Salvaged? Theft and the Grounding of the *MSC Napoli*' (2010) 74 J Crim L 53; J Lowther, R Glover and M Williams, 'Salvage, Pollution or Looting? The Stranding of the *Napoli*'s Cargo' (2009) 15 J Int'l Maritime Law 65.

[298] *Hibbert v McKiernan* [1948] 1 All ER 860, discussed in (1972B) 31 CLJ at 213–15 (lost golf balls not abandoned), and see the references in n 291.

[299] *Ingram* [1975] Crim LR 457 (absent-minded taking a defence to charge of shoplifting). *Small* [1987] Crim LR 777 (D who believes, reasonably or not, that property has been abandoned, does not intend to appropriate property belonging to another (or, *ex hypothesi*, permanently to deprive)).

[300] Para 3.2.

This section is designed to defeat arguments such as that which might be made by D, a shop worker who charged a friend, E, for only some of the goods in E's trolley. The fact that the gain was for E does not prevent D stealing from the shop owner. Similarly, the section renders prosecution easier in cases of D causing only loss to V, without a corresponding gain to himself. Thus, if D takes V's letters and puts them down a lavatory or throws V's iPad off a cliff, he is guilty of theft notwithstanding the fact that he intends only to cause loss to V and not gain for himself or anyone else. It might be thought that these instances could safely and more appropriately have been left to other branches of the criminal law—criminal damage to property, for instance. But there are cases where there is no such damage or destruction of the property which would be sufficient to found a charge under another Act. For example, D takes V's diamond and flings it into a deep pond. The diamond lies unharmed in the pond and a prosecution for criminal damage would fail. It seems clearly right that D should be guilty of theft.[301] As Lord Bingham observed, 'In providing that an appropriation may be dishonest even where there is a willingness to pay, [the section] shows that the prospect of loss is not determinative of dishonesty.'[302]

18.4.2 Dishonesty

The concept of dishonesty in theft needs to be approached in two stages:

(1) By understanding the statutory situations in which it is made clear that certain conduct is not to be regarded as dishonest. These exclusions from dishonesty are not found in all dishonesty offences—they apply to theft.

(2) By understanding the common law definition of dishonesty. This has changed significantly following the Supreme Court's decision in *Ivey*[303] as now wholeheartedly endorsed in *Barton* by a five-member Court of Appeal.[304]

There is now no doubt that the test adopted by the Supreme Court in *Ivey* should apply to all offences in which the term dishonesty is used. The same principle applies throughout the Theft Acts, the Fraud Act 2006 and the common law of conspiracy to defraud as well as other statutory offences,[305] such as fraudulent trading under the Companies Act 2006. There is one test of dishonesty in English criminal law and *Ivey/Barton* define the test.

This approach to defining dishonesty raises interesting questions about the role that the element has to play in the offence of theft generally. Dishonesty operates both as a peg on which to hang claims of an exculpatory nature—that is, as equivalent to an element of unlawfulness or lack of blameworthiness—and also as a positive element of mens rea. Professor Horder describes dishonesty as a concealed excuse, 'taking the form of a morally open textured mental element'.[306] This overlap between 'dishonesty' as a state of mind (requiring a factual inquiry from the jury) and as a concept describing the wrong done (requiring a moral

---

[301] An alternative solution would be to consider creating an offence of unlawfully depriving the owner of the use of his property.

[302] *Wheatley and Penn v Commissioner of Police of the British Virgin Islands* [2006] UKPC 24.

[303] [2017] UKSC 67. For comment, see D Ormerod and K Laird, '*Ivey v Genting* Casinos—Much Ado About Nothing?' (2019) 9 Supreme Court Yearbook 1; K Laird, '*Ivey v Genting Casinos (UK) Ltd (t/a Crockfords)*' [2017] Lloyd's Law Reports: Financial Crime 576; [2018] Crim LR 395; M Dyson and P Jarvis, 'Poison *Ivey* or Herbal Tea Leaf?' (2018) 134 LQR 198.

[304] [2020] EWCA Crim 575. See D Ormerod and K Laird, 'The Future of Dishonesty—Some Practical Considerations' [2020] 6 Arch Rev 8.

[305] eg benefit fraud offences under the Social Security Acts: *Department for Work and Pensions v Costello* [2006] EWHC 1156 (Admin).

[306] J Horder, *Excusing Crime* (2004) 49. See A Steel, 'The Harms and Wrongs of Stealing: The Harm Principle and Dishonesty in Theft' (2008) 31 UNSWLJ 712.

evaluation by the jury) is perpetuated by the case law. A further complexity with the element of dishonesty (beyond the law of theft per se) has been described by the Law Commission:

> In some crimes, such as conspiracy to defraud, the other elements of the offence are not prima facie unlawful, so dishonesty renders criminal otherwise lawful conduct. However, in deception offences the other elements of the offence, if proved, would normally be unlawful in themselves. If someone has practised a deception in order to gain a benefit their conduct is prima facie wrongful. Therefore dishonesty can be raised to rebut the inference that conduct was in fact wrongful . . . The former type of crime [can be described] as having a positive requirement of dishonesty, and the latter as having a negative requirement.[307]

It is regrettable that there is no statutory definition of dishonesty, particularly since the common law definition which supplements s 2 is so vague, and as noted earlier, dishonesty has assumed an elevated importance following the excessively broad interpretations of the actus reus elements of the offence.[308]

18.4.2.1 Statutory circumstances which are *not* dishonest

The CLRC thought that 'dishonesty' could probably be left undefined and it did not define it but merely sought to clarify its meaning in certain respects.[309] By s 2 of the Act:

(1) A person's appropriation of property belonging to another is not to be regarded as dishonest—

    (a) if he appropriates the property in the belief that he has in law the right to deprive the other of it, on behalf of himself or of a third person; or

    (b) if he appropriates the property in the belief that he would have the other's consent if the other knew of the appropriation and the circumstances of it; or

    (c) (except where the property came to him as trustee or personal representative) if he appropriates the property in the belief that the person to whom the property belongs cannot be discovered by taking reasonable steps.

(2) A person's appropriation of property belonging to another may be dishonest notwithstanding that he is willing to pay for the property.[310]

It will be noticed that this section specifies three situations in which an appropriation of property belonging to another is *not* to be regarded as dishonest, and one in which it may be. By this negative approach, the section assists somewhat in defining the meaning of dishonesty, but the section does not specify any state of mind that *must* be regarded as dishonest.

Belief in the right to deprive

D is not dishonest if he believes, whether reasonably or not,[311] that he has the legal right[312] to do the act which is alleged to constitute an appropriation of the property of another. The prosecution must disprove any belief in such a right that D claims to have held.[313] The Act

---

[307] LC 276, *Fraud* (2002) para 5.12. For criticism of this as unhelpful, see P Kiernan and G Scanlon, 'Fraud and the Law Commission: The Future of Dishonesty' (2003) 24 Comp Law 4.

[308] cf the Law Commission's subsequent view that no definition is possible: LC 276, Part V.

[309] See also Smith, *Property Offences*, Ch 7; *Arlidge and Parry on Fraud*, Ch 2; LC 276, Part V.

[310] Care must be taken when considering the concept of dishonesty since s 2 is not applicable to all of the offences under the Theft Acts.

[311] See *Terry* [2001] EWCA Crim 2979.

[312] It is irrelevant that no such right exists in law. A *dictum* to the contrary in *Gott v Measures* [1948] 1 KB 234, is irreconcilable with the decision in *Bernhard* [1938] 2 KB 264. The belief need not relate to a 'property' right: *Wood* [1999] Crim LR 564 and commentary.

[313] There must be some evidence of the belief in a claim of right to be left to the jury before the judge is obliged to leave it: *Hall* [2008] EWCA Crim 2086.

refers specifically to a belief in a right *in law* as inconsistent with dishonesty. This does not *necessarily* mean that a belief in a merely moral right will be insufficient to negative dishonesty.[314] The common law position was that taking another's property was not justifiable, even where it is necessary to avoid starvation, and that suggests that even the strongest moral claim to deprive another is not enough to rebut dishonesty. However, under the 1968 Act it is now a jury question. There is nothing in the Act to say that a belief in a moral right does not rebut dishonesty, and a jury would be likely to find that a truly starving person was not dishonest.

D's belief in the legal right of another, X, will also negative D's dishonesty. Thus, in *Close*,[315] an employee, who took his employer's property without consent because he was owed money by the employer, was apparently held not to be dishonest by a jury. Where D specifically pleads a belief in a claim of right, the jury ought, it is submitted, to be directed in relation to s 2 and not left to deal with the issue under the general test of dishonesty (discussed later).[316] In *Barton*, one of the claims made by the defendant was that he believed that the property in question was freely given to him by people of full capacity. The Court of Appeal did not regard the judge's failure to provide a direction tailored to s 2(1)(a) as problematic: it was 'not required'.[317]

Belief that the owner would consent

It is sufficient that D holds a mistaken though genuine belief that the person to whom the property belonged would have consented had he known of the circumstances. Thus, D will not be dishonest where he helps himself to his flatmate's milk from the fridge if he holds a belief that this would be consented to. Numerous appropriations of this nature occur every day and a specific provision dealing with the matter precludes capricious prosecutions. Following *Hinks*, the issue of mistaken beliefs will be of particular importance in cases in which D claims that he was acting with the owner's consent.[318]

Belief that the person to whom the property belongs cannot be discovered by taking reasonable steps

Though the Act makes no reference to 'finding', this provision is obviously intended to preserve the substance of the common law rule relating to finding. The finder who appropriates property commits the actus reus of theft (assuming that the property does belong to another and has not been abandoned) but is not dishonest unless he believes the owner *can* be discovered by taking reasonable steps. There is no requirement that D's belief about the traceability of the owner is reasonable; merely that his belief about the steps necessary to trace the owner is reasonable. This will depend on the nature of the property in question.[319]

If D's initial appropriation of lost property is innocent (either because he does not believe that the owner can be discovered by taking reasonable steps or because he intends to return the thing to the owner when he takes it), a dishonest later assumption of a right to it by

---

[314] A belief in a moral right was not a defence to larceny: *Harris v Harrison* [1963] Crim LR 497. Cf Williams, CLGP, 322.

[315] [1977] Crim LR 107.

[316] See *Rostron* [2003] EWCA Crim 2206, where D believed that he had a legal right to collect 'lost' golf balls. Cf *Smith (Paul Adrian)* [1997] 7 Arch News 4. On charges to which s 2 does not apply the test enunciated in *Ivey/Barton* must perform the function.

[317] At [129].

[318] See p 866. See especially Lord Hutton's dissent focusing on dishonesty and the question of whether D can be convicted if he has a claim of right—consent, but not if he has a mere belief in a claim of right—under s 2(1)(a). See the discussion in relation to freegans taking from supermarket rubbish bins: Thomas, n 291.

[319] See eg the implausible defence in *Sylvester* (1985) CO/559/84 where D alleged that the car he was stripping of parts in a car park was abandoned and therefore s 2(1)(c) applied.

keeping or dealing with it as owner will be theft by virtue of s 3(1).[320] While this provision was intended primarily for the case of finding, it is not confined to that case and there are other instances where it would apply. Suppose that V arranges with D that D shall store V's furniture in D's house without payment. V leaves the town and D loses touch with him. Some years later D, needing the space in his house and being unable to locate V, sells the furniture.[321] This is undoubtedly an appropriation of the property of another and D is liable to V in conversion; but he appears to be saved from any possibility of conviction of theft by s 2(1)(c). Though the purchase money probably belongs to V, D's immunity under the Act for lack of dishonesty must extend to the proceeds of sale.

Where property has come to D as a trustee or personal representative and he appropriates it, he may be dishonest even though he believes that the person to whom the property belongs cannot be discovered by taking reasonable steps. This seems to provide a particularly strict approach.

Dishonest appropriation, notwithstanding payment

Section 2(2) is intended to deal with the kind of situation where D takes bottles of milk from V's doorstep but leaves in its place the full price. Certainly D has no claim of right and he intends to deprive V permanently of his property. Doubts had, however, arisen as to whether this was dishonest. This subsection resolves them. The mere fact of payment does not negative dishonesty but the jury are entitled to take into account all the circumstances and these may be such that even an intention to pay for property, let alone actual payment, may negative dishonesty. The fact of payment, or intention to pay, may be cogent evidence where D's defence is that he believed V would have consented, as where D takes milk bottles from V's unattended delivery van and leaves the price, claiming that he assumed that V would have been very happy to sell him the milk had he been there, but that he had not time to wait for V to return. If D is believed—and the fact of repayment would be persuasive evidence—it would seem that he has no dishonest intent. The section is important in emphasizing that D's willingness to pay the market value for appropriated property will not necessarily negate dishonesty, otherwise there would be no theft where D takes V's original work of art that he has long coveted, leaving its listed valuation price.

18.4.3 Dishonesty as an element of the offence

18.4.3.1 A summary of the current law

After initial confusion and inconsistency, the definition of dishonesty became settled following the case of *Ghosh*.[322] Despite considerable academic criticism of that test,[323] it was rarely challenged on appeal and had attracted little adverse comment in practice for 35 years. In 2017, the Supreme Court, in a civil case, *Ivey v Genting Casinos (UK) Ltd (t/a Crockfords Club)*, overruled the decision in *Ghosh*.[324]

The current test for dishonesty in all criminal offences which require proof of such an element is therefore:

When dishonesty is in question the fact-finding tribunal must first ascertain (subjectively) the actual state of the individual's knowledge or belief as to the facts. The reasonableness or otherwise of his belief is a matter of evidence (often in practice determinative) going to whether he held the

---

[320] See p 874.   [321] cf *Sachs v Miklos* [1948] 2 KB 23; *Munro v Wilmott* [1949] 1 KB 295.
[322] [1982] QB 1053.   [323] Examined later.
[324] [2017] UKSC 67. In truth the outcome was not surprising as the Court of Appeal seemed to have been keen to overturn *Ghosh* for some time. See *Starglade* [2010] EWCA Civ 1314 and *Cornelius* [2012] EWCA Crim 500.

belief, but it is not an additional requirement that this belief must be reasonable; the question is whether it is genuinely held. When once his actual state of mind as to knowledge or belief as to facts is established, the question whether his conduct was honest or dishonest is to be determined by the fact-finder by applying the (objective) standards of ordinary decent people. There is no requirement that the defendant must appreciate that what he has done is, by those standards, dishonest.[325]

The Supreme Court redefined the test in *obiter dicta* in a civil case and there were some questions raised about whether it would be adopted by the Court of Appeal (Criminal Division). Following the decision in *Barton*, in which a specially convened five-member Court of Appeal[326] endorsed the test in *Ivey*, it is now clear that *Ghosh* is not to be followed. The law is as stated in *Ivey*. The Court of Appeal in *Barton* summarized the new two-limb test as follows:

> (a) what was the defendant's actual state of knowledge or belief as to the facts; and
>
> (b) was his conduct dishonest by the standards of ordinary decent people.[327]

We consider the implications of this new test later. Before doing so, it is important to understand: (a) the evolution of the *Ghosh* test; (b) the criticisms that led to it being rejected in *Ivey* in such a significant fashion (why, as Jackson LJ put it, the 'tectonic plates' on the subject moved[328]); (c) the decision in *Ivey*; and (d) the explanation and endorsement of *Ivey* in *Barton*.

18.4.3.2 The evolution of the *Ghosh* test
The CLRC drafting of the Theft Act

In the legislation before the Theft Act, the term used was 'fraudulently'. Under the Larceny Act, it was probably for the judge to say whether D's state of mind was to be characterized in law as 'fraudulent' subject to the jury finding given facts.[329] When drafting the 1968 Act, the CLRC seems to have overlooked the limited role that word had in the Larceny Act.[330] In its Eighth Report[331] and in drafting the 1968 Act, the CLRC used 'dishonestly' rather than 'fraudulently', not because the meaning was any different but because it thought it to be more easily understood:

> 'Dishonestly' seems to us a better word than 'fraudulently'. The question 'Was this "dishonest"?' is easier for a jury to answer than the question 'Was this "fraudulent"?' 'Dishonesty' is something which laymen can easily recognize when they see it, whereas 'fraud' may seem to involve technicalities which have to be explained by a lawyer.

This passage suggests that it is for jurors to decide whether 'this' (D's conduct) is dishonest. Of course, it is for jurors to decide all questions of fact, including the state of mind of the

---

[325] At [74].

[326] Which included the Lord Chief Justice, the President of the Queen's Bench Division and the Vice President of the Court of Appeal (Crim Div).

[327] [2020] EWCA Crim 575, [84].   [328] *SRA v Wingate* [2018] EWCA Civ 366, [90].

[329] *Williams* [1953] 1 QB 660; *Cockburn* [1968] 1 All ER 466.

[330] Commentators on the Larceny Act 1916 disagreed as to the function, if any, of the word 'fraudulently' (which was the precursor to 'dishonesty'). JWC Turner (writing as editor of *Russell on Crime* (12th edn, 1964) 996), concluded that the word added nothing to 'without a claim of right' (now found in s 2(1)(a)). Others thought it had the limited function of exculpating the taker who believed the owner would have consented if it had been possible to ask him—a case now expressly covered by s 2(1)(b) of the 1968 Act: see Wing-Commander Lowe, 'The Fraudulent Intent in Larceny' [1956] Crim LR 78. Others that it exculpated the taker of money or other 'fungibles' (substitutable property) who intended to, and had no doubt that he could, return, not the identical thing, but an equivalent (a case which is not expressly provided for in the 1968 Act): JC Smith, 'The Fraudulent Intent in Larceny: Another View' [1956] Crim LR 238. See also the analysis by A Steel, 'The Meanings of Dishonesty in Theft' (2009) 38 Common L World Rev 103.

[331] Para 39. On the CLRC intentions, see also DW Elliott, 'Dishonesty in Theft: A Dispensable Concept' [1982] Crim LR 395 at 405.

defendant—what was his intention and belief, including his belief as to his legal rights. But, that was not how fraudulently was interpreted. The CLRC unwittingly made a significant change to the law. This was one factor which led Lord Hughes in *Ivey*, see later, to adopt a new interpretation of the test for dishonesty.

Possible approaches to interpretation

There are, in simple, terms three ways in which the courts could have construed the concept of dishonesty under the 1968 Act.

(1) As a subjective test—did D believe his conduct was dishonest? The danger of such a test is obvious—the more warped the moral standards of D, the more likely he will escape liability since he will not believe his conduct to be dishonest.

(2) As a predominantly objective test—was D's conduct dishonest by the standards of reasonable and honest people? This was the test first adopted in a case called *Feely*, rejected in *Ghosh*, but reaffirmed as correct by the Supreme Court in *Ivey*, albeit with a subjective dimension.

(3) As a hybrid test involving objective and subjective elements. This was the approach settled in *Ghosh* which reigned for 35 years until being overturned in *Ivey*.

A subjective approach. Perhaps not surprisingly, the courts rarely applied a purely subjective test based on whether D thought what he did was dishonest. A rare instance was *Gilks*,[332] where D kept the overpayment made by a bookmaker, the judge invited the jury to 'try and place yourselves in [D's] position at that time and answer the question whether in your view he thought he was acting dishonestly'. The Court of Appeal thought this was a proper and sufficient direction, agreeing apparently that if D may have held the belief he claimed, the prosecution had not established dishonesty. This applied not the standards of ordinary decent people, but the defendant's own standards, however deplorable they might be. The present law certainly, and we suggest correctly, rejects the idea of a purely subjective test.

An objective approach. Possibly influenced by the approach in the CLRC Report, the Court of Appeal in *Feely*[333] held that it is for the jury in each case to decide not only what the defendant's state of mind was but also, subject to s 2, whether that state of mind is to be categorized as dishonest.

Jurors, when deciding whether an appropriation was dishonest can be reasonably expected to, and should, apply the current standards of ordinary decent people. In their own lives they have to decide what is and what is not dishonest. We can see no reason why, when in a jury box, they should require the help of a judge to tell them what amounts to dishonesty.

Only a moment's comparison with the approach to other mens rea requirements is needed to illustrate how much of a departure from the pre-1968 Act law and from orthodoxy this is. For example, in a case involving recklessness, the judge defines that concept and directs the jury to determine whether, on the facts as they find them to be, D's state of mind is within that legal definition. The jury are not invited to decide for themselves what recklessness means. *Feely*,[334] when read properly, required: (a) determination of the conduct/facts; and (b) an objective assessment of the conduct/facts (having regard to *D's state of mind* about them, albeit this latter aspect was not made explicit[335]) applying the standards of ordinary decent people. It is an objective test with a subjective dimension.

---

[332] See p 900; [1972] 3 All ER 280 at 283. On the very early cases, see DW Elliott, 'Dishonesty Under the Theft Act' [1972] Crim LR 625.
[333] [1973] QB 530, [1973] Crim LR 193 and commentary.   [334] *Feely* [1973] QB 530 at 541.
[335] See Griew, *Theft*, paras 2-132 et seq.

The court in *Feely* was heavily influenced by the opinion of the House of Lords in *Brutus v Cozens*[336] that the meaning of an ordinary word of the English language is not a question of law for the judge but one of fact for the jury. 'Dishonestly' is such a word and so it should be for the jury to attribute to it such meaning as they thought proper. *Feely* did at least provide a standard—that of 'ordinary decent people', as understood by the jury—against which the defendant's intentions and beliefs were to be tested.

A hybrid approach: Ghosh. Concerns about the bluntness of a purely objective or purely subjective test led the court in *Ghosh*[337] to adopt a hybrid test:

(1) Was what was done dishonest according to the ordinary standards of reasonable and honest people? If no, D is not guilty. If yes:

(2) Did the defendant realize that reasonable and honest people regard what he did as dishonest?[338] If yes, he is guilty; if no, he is not.

If there was any evidence to suggest that D's attitude was, 'Whatever others may think, I did not consider this dishonest', the direction had to be given. Where there was no such evidence, it was probably unnecessary. Where this direction was necessary, the exact form of words had to be used.

This got away from the extreme and unacceptable subjectivism of *Gilks*. It addressed the concern expressed in *Boggeln v Williams* that D's state of mind was relevant to the test. In that case, the court expressly rejected an argument that D's belief as to his own honesty was irrelevant and held that, on the contrary, it was crucial. D, whose electricity had been cut off, reconnected the supply through the meter. He knew that the electricity company did not consent to his doing so, but he notified them and believed, not unreasonably, that he would be able to pay at the due time. It was held that the question was whether he believed that what he did was honest.

Following *Ghosh*, D was not to be judged exclusively by his own standards of honesty. *Ghosh* attempted a compromise between a predominantly objective *Feely*-type test which some regarded as too harsh, and a purely subjective test such as that in *Gilks* which would create a thief's charter. Properly understood, *Ghosh* required: (a) determination of the conduct/facts; (b) objective assessment (standards of reasonable honest people) of whether the conduct was dishonest; and (c) D's state of mind as to (a) and (b), ie the conduct and what reasonable honest people would think of it.

Ghosh generated considerable academic criticism.[339] The principal concern, and the one which led to *Ghosh* being overruled, was that in seeking to achieve a compromise between objective and subjective elements, *Ghosh* introduced unnecessary confusion in the form of the second limb. Why should the jury inquire into whether D believed that his conduct was dishonest by the standards of honest and reasonable people? Campbell[340] cogently argued

---

[336] [1973] AC 854.   [337] [1982] QB 1053.

[338] The Court of Appeal held in *Chitate* [2014] EWCA Crim 1744 that the judge did not misdirect the jury by deviating slightly from this formulation.

[339] EJ Griew, 'Dishonesty—The Objections to *Feely* and *Ghosh*' [1985] Crim LR 341; M Wasik, '*Mens Rea*, Motive and the Problem of Dishonesty in the Law of Theft' [1979] Crim LR 543; Elliott [1982] Crim LR 395 at 398. Elliott's solution is to dispense with the word 'dishonestly' altogether but to add a new s 3(2): 'No appropriation of property belonging to another which is not detrimental to the interests of the other in a significant practical way shall amount to theft of the property.' In *Cornelius* [2012] EWCA Crim 500, a five-member court was convened as it was initially thought that the case gave rise to an issue about the validity of the *Ghosh* test. The issue did not, however, arise.

[340] K Campbell, 'The Test of Dishonesty in *Ghosh*' (1994) 43 CLJ 349, where Campbell suggests that if the aim is to provide this hybrid test it should be: whether a reasonable jury, applying ordinary standards of honesty, is prepared to excuse D's failure to recognize that his own behaviour would be regarded as dishonest by the standards of ordinary people.

that this additional limb is superfluous if under the first limb the jury is properly directed to take account of all the circumstances. Taking the oft-quoted example of D who fails to pay a travel fare because he is new to the country and is accustomed to free public transport at home, it should not be necessary to rely on the second limb to conclude that D is not dishonest. A properly directed jury would so conclude under the first limb. As Lord Hughes noted in *Ivey*:

> In order to decide whether this visitor was dishonest by the standards of ordinary people, it would be necessary to establish his own actual state of knowledge of how public transport works. Because he genuinely believes that public transport is free, there is nothing objectively dishonest about his not paying on the bus.[341]

18.4.3.3 The problems with *Ghosh*

In *Ivey*, Lord Hughes identified the following problems with the *Ghosh* direction, and particularly the second limb. It is respectfully submitted that some of the arguments are not as convincing as they might at first appear:

(1) the more warped the defendant's standards of honesty, the less likely was a conviction—that is not a strictly accurate representation of the *Ghosh* test. The *Ghosh* test required an analysis of what D thought the reasonable person would think was dishonest; an entirely warped belief would not suffice unless (the jury believed) it prevented D from appreciating that the jury would realize his conduct was dishonest;

(2) the rule was not necessary to preserve the principle that dishonesty had to depend on the defendant's actual state of mind—Lord Hughes convincingly demonstrates this is the case by suggesting that the defendant's state of mind should be considered as part of limb (1) under the reformulated test;

(3) it set a test which jurors often found puzzling—in arriving at this conclusion, his lordship relied on his own vast experience and the anecdotal evidence of many judges, but no empirical evidence was adduced to substantiate it;

(4) it had led to a divergence between the test for dishonesty in criminal and civil cases—this is clearly the case, but in other areas of theft the appellate courts have been happy for the criminal law to 'float free' of the civil law.[342] In addition, the civil law and the criminal law have different purposes, which means that it was not necessarily unprincipled for the test for dishonesty to be framed in different terms depending upon the context in which it was being invoked;

(5) it represented a significant departure from the pre-1968 Act law, when there was no indication that such a change had been intended; and it had not been compelled by earlier authority—this is accurate, but it is at least arguable that the force of this criticism had diminished 50 years after the enactment of the Theft Act and 35 years after the Court of Appeal set the law on a steady course in *Ghosh*.

As a result of these factors, as is discussed in detail later, the Supreme Court in *Ivey* held that the second stage should not represent the law and directions based on it should no longer be given.

Three other criticisms of the *Ghosh* test are worth noting. First, it had been recognized from the outset that the attempted compromise in *Ghosh* was argued to fail in its intended

---

341 [2017] UKSC 67, [60]. See D Ormerod and K Laird, '*Ivey v Genting* Casinos—Much Ado About Nothing?' (2019) 9 Supreme Court Yearbook 1.

342 See the discussion of *Hinks* earlier.

purpose—to prevent the 'Robin Hood defence'. It was not clear that *Ghosh* did prevent it because the defendant would have to be acquitted 'if the jury thought *either* (a) that what Robin Hood did (rob the rich to feed the poor) was not dishonest *or* (b) that Robin Hood thought the reasonable and honest man would not consider what he did as dishonest'.[343] Take the more modern example of a peace protestor who takes from an army depot armaments destined for a war zone because he thinks they are being used against civilians. He would certainly not regard his own conduct as dishonest and so would escape under the rule as stated in *Gilks*. He might have been acquitted under *Ghosh*.[344] A jury of pacifists would be likely to agree with him; and it might be difficult to satisfy any jury that the defendant did not believe that all right-thinking people would agree with him. Peace protestors probably do so believe. But this surely *should* be theft. One who deliberately deprives another of his property should not be able to escape liability because of his disapproval, however profound and morally justified, of the lawful use to which that property was being put by its owner. In deciding whether a certain state of mind should be regarded as dishonest, it is not irrelevant to consider how the matter will be regarded by the ordinary decent citizen who is the victim of the offence. The owners of the armaments will certainly consider that their property has been stolen, even though they are fully aware of the state of mind of the takers. The law fails in one of its purposes if it does not afford protection to a person against what he quite reasonably regards as a straightforward case of theft. *Ivey* ensures that this is more likely to be regarded as theft.

Furthermore, the test impacted adversely on criminal procedure. As has already been explained, perhaps the most trenchant critic of the *Ghosh* test was Professor Griew,[345] who catalogued its numerous deficiencies. Griew suggested that the test confused the state of mind with the concept of dishonesty;[346] led to more trials as defendants have little to lose by pleading not guilty and hoping that the dishonesty element is not made out; and led to longer trials as the dishonesty issue is a 'live' one in all cases.

18.4.3.4 *Ivey v Genting Casinos (UK) Ltd (t/a Crockfords)*

The test adopted in the Supreme Court is as follows:

(1) What was D's knowledge or belief as to the facts (a subjective test; the reasonableness of the belief is a matter of evidence of the belief being genuinely held)?

(2) In the light of the conclusion in relation to question (1), was D's conduct honest or dishonest applying the (objective) standards of ordinary decent people?

Ivey: the facts

The claimant, a professional gambler, used a technique called 'edge sorting' to give himself a competitive advantage when playing a card game called Punto Banco. By noting minute physical differences on the reverse of the cards, the claimant was able to increase his odds

---

[343] Such examples contradict the view of some commentators that apart from 'morons and lunatics' the only people likely to rely on a claim that they did not realize that ordinary honest people would regard their conduct as dishonest are business people who assert that their activities are the norm in that context, *Arlidge and Parry on Fraud* (2nd edn, 1996) para 1.027. This phrase is not found in the most recent edition.

[344] This is an instance in which it appears motive, which is generally regarded as irrelevant to mens rea in practice, assumes an importance. The defendant's character may also take on an elevated significance: *Bailey* [2004] EWCA Crim 2530.

[345] Author of *The Theft Acts 1968 and 1978* (7th edn, 1995) and 'Objections to *Feely* and *Ghosh*' [1985] Crim LR 341.

[346] See also K Campbell, 'The Test of Dishonesty in *Ghosh*' (1994) 43 CLJ 349 at 354 criticizing *Ghosh* for confusing the state of mind and the defendant's standards of honesty.

of winning. To do so, however, he needed to ensure that the deck of cards was not changed. The claimant pretended to be superstitious, and persuaded the croupier to use the same pack of cards and to turn 'lucky' cards around, enabling him to predict which cards would emerge from the shoe. By virtue of this technique, the gambler was able to increase his odds of winning and ultimately won £7.7m. The casino discovered that the claimant used 'edge sorting' to win and refused to pay him his winnings. As a matter of fact, the trial judge found that although the gambler was genuinely convinced that what he had done was not cheating, he had in fact and law cheated, thus breaching the implied term against cheating in his contract with the casino. The claimant argued that the test of what was cheating was the same for the implied contractual term as for the criminal offence of cheating at gambling, contained in s 42 of the Gambling Act 2005. Furthermore, it was argued that cheating necessarily involved dishonesty, which had not been demonstrated in his case, meaning that the claimant was entitled to recover his winnings.

Ivey: the decision

In a unanimous judgment delivered by Lord Hughes, it was held that s 42 leaves open the question of what is and what is not cheating. Although it was sensible to interpret the concept of cheating contained in s 42 in the light of the meaning given to cheating over many years, his lordship held that it made no sense to interpret cheating by reference to dishonesty, an expression introduced into the criminal law for different purposes in 1968. 'Cheating', in the context of games and gambling, carried its own inherent stamp of wrongfulness. Although 'honest cheating' was an improbable concept, it was held that it did not follow that all cheating ordinarily attracted the description 'dishonest' or that anything was added to the legal concept of cheating by an additional legal concept of dishonesty. Lord Hughes held that, as an element of a criminal charge, dishonesty was not a defined concept. His lordship stated that it is not a matter of law but a jury question of fact and standards. Except to the limited extent that s 2 of the 1968 Act required otherwise, judges must not attempt to define it. Likewise, whether conduct amounted to cheating, given the nature of the game, is a jury question. The addition of the legal element of dishonesty would unnecessarily complicate the question. The judge's conclusion that the gambler's actions amounted to cheating was unassailable. The key factor in this determination was the fact that the claimant had contrived a situation that enabled him to know whether the next card was of a high or low value. He had therefore taken positive steps to fix the deck. In a game which depended on the random delivery of unknown cards, it was held that such conduct was inevitably cheating.

The crucial aspect of the Supreme Court's judgment for present purposes is its restatement of the test for dishonesty. The court held that, when dishonesty is an issue, the fact-finding tribunal first has to ascertain, subjectively, the actual state of the individual's knowledge or belief as to the facts. The reasonableness of that belief is a matter of evidence going to whether the defendant held the belief, but it is not an additional requirement that the belief had to be reasonable; the question is whether it was genuinely held. When the defendant's state of mind has been established, the question of whether his conduct was honest or dishonest is to be determined by applying the objective standards of ordinary decent people. There is no requirement that the defendant must appreciate that the conduct was dishonest by those standards.

18.4.3.5 *Barton—Ivey* rooted in the criminal law

Despite the *obiter* nature of the Supreme Court's analysis of the test for dishonesty in the criminal law, it was almost immediately clear that the judgment in *Ivey* would be treated as authoritative. Within a matter of weeks in *Patterson*, Sir Brian Leveson P stated that, 'Given the terms of the unanimous observations of the Supreme Court expressed by Lord Hughes, who does not shy from asserting that *Ghosh* does not correctly represent the law, it is difficult to imagine the Court of Appeal preferring *Ghosh* to *Ivey* in the future.'[347] The Court of Appeal's approving reference in *Pabon*,[348] and the explicit advice to judges in the *Crown Court Compendium* to follow *Ivey*, meant that the outcome in *Barton* was no surprise.

Barton—The facts

The first defendant ran a nursing home. Over many years, he targeted, befriended and 'groomed' wealthy and vulnerable (and childless) elderly residents of the home in order to profit from them. A number of these residents made him the residuary beneficiary of their wills, usually within a short time of arriving at the home. They also allowed him to assume control of their finances, by making him next of kin or granting him power of attorney, or by making him executor of their estates. The defendant obtained over £4m from the residents. The second defendant was responsible for managing the domestic affairs at the home and was described as being the first defendant's 'eyes and ears'. After a lengthy trial, the judge directed the jury in accordance with *Ivey*, rather than *Ghosh*. The defendants were convicted and appealed on the basis that he was wrong to do so.

Barton—The decision

In dismissing the argument that the Supreme Court's rejection of *Ghosh* was not binding, the Lord Chief Justice stated that 'where the Supreme Court itself directs that an otherwise binding decision of the Court of Appeal should no longer be followed and proposes an alternative test that it says must be adopted, the Court of Appeal is bound to follow what amounts to a direction from the Supreme Court even though it is strictly *obiter*'. [349]

The Court of Appeal remarked that it was not following *Ivey* reluctantly, given the compelling nature of Lord Hughes's reasoning. The court endorsed the Crown's argument that the test for dishonesty remains a test of the defendant's state of mind—his or her knowledge or belief—to which the standards of ordinary decent people are applied.

The test was that articulated by the Supreme Court: (a) what was the defendant's actual state of knowledge or belief as to the facts; and (b) was his conduct dishonest by the standards of ordinary decent people?

Barton as a refinement of *Ivey*?

Following the decision of the Supreme Court, it was clear that the substance of the change from *Ghosh* was that the defendant's belief that reasonable people would not consider his conduct dishonest was no longer determinative of dishonesty. What was less clear was the way in which the two limbs of the new test for dishonesty were to be interpreted and applied.

It is clear that the new first limb is designed to address the well-worn example of the foreign tourist who does not realize that people must pay to use public transport in the UK.[350] Whereas previously the second limb of *Ghosh* would come to the 'rescue'[351] to ensure acquittal, now it is intended for the first limb to fulfil this purpose. What *Ivey* did not make clear was the scope of the jury's inquiry: what facts or beliefs which the defendant might have held are the jury to take into consideration? Did the Supreme Court in *Ivey*, by

---

[347] *DPP v Patterson* [2017] EWHC 2820, [16]. See also *Pabon* [2018] EWCA Crim 420 and *Wingate v SRA* [2018] EWCA Civ 366.

[348] *Pabon* [2018] EWCA Crim 420.

[349] On this controversial interpretation of the *stare decisis* principle, see GR Sullivan and AP Simester, 'Judging Dishonesty' (2020) 136 LQR 523.

[350] As Campbell pointed out decades ago, if *Feely* [1973] QB 530 was applied properly *Ghosh* did not need to deal with this by creating the second limb. See K Campbell, 'The Test of Dishonesty in *Ghosh*' (1994) 43 CLJ 349.

[351] Williams, TBCL, 728.

removing the second limb of *Ghosh* but retaining subjectivity in this first limb, mean to (a) render totally irrelevant D's belief as to the perceptions of others about the honesty of the conduct? Or (b) remove the binding nature of that belief—if D did not believe others would consider his conduct dishonest, he would be entitled to an acquittal under *Ghosh*?

The court in *Barton* provided the answer: the reference in *Ivey* to the 'actual state of mind as to knowledge of belief as to the facts' was to *all* the circumstances known to the accused and not limited to consideration of past facts. Lord Burnett CJ explained that:

> [a]ll matters that lead an accused to act as he or she did will form part of the subjective mental state, thereby forming a part of the fact-finding exercise before applying the objective standard. That will include consideration, where relevant, of the experience and intelligence of an accused.[352]

It is submitted that this test requires the jury, in the first limb, to have regard not only to D's state of mind as to the facts, but also as to his beliefs about whether the conduct would be seen as dishonest (that would be a matter which may 'lead' him to act as he did). Part of the difficulty in understanding what the Supreme Court intended is attributable to the fact that there is some ambiguity over whether the civil test Lord Hughes adopted in *Ivey* contains a subjective element.[353]

The Supreme Court in *Ivey* had also failed to expand on the relationship between the subjective and objective limbs of the reformulated test for dishonesty. Unfortunately, the Court of Appeal in *Barton* did not offer any explicit guidance on this.[354] Having regard to the way that the first limb is expressed (see at [84], cited earlier and *Ivey* at [60]), it cannot, we suggest, have been intended for the two limbs of *Ghosh* simply to be inverted. That would require the jury to ask what the defendant thought others would think was dishonest and then apply an objective assessment of dishonesty *constrained by* what the defendant thought others would consider was dishonest.[355] Accepting that approach to be untenable, what is the correct interpretation?

Under the first limb, the jury is required to assess the defendant's conduct *and* state of mind broadly including D's beliefs about all the circumstances. We suggest that defendants are entitled to adduce evidence of their perceptions of the honesty of their conduct. When the jury is using that information in applying the second (objective) limb, the jury must surely have regard to that evidence but, crucially, they should not treat what the defendant believed about others' perceptions of honesty as determinative.

The relationship between the limbs and the way the jury is to be directed has real practical significance in some cases. In *Hayes*,[356] for example, D was accused of conspiring dishonestly to manipulate the LIBOR lending rate. He argued that his behaviour was not dishonest by the standards of those working in that market. It was submitted on his behalf that the objective aspect of the dishonesty direction (then under *Ghosh*) must sometimes be modified so as to invite the jury to consider not just the standards of honest and reasonable people generally, but the standards set by the particular market or business in which the defendant is operating. The trial judge rejected that submission and the Court of Appeal upheld the conviction. The Court of Appeal in *Hayes* confirmed, however, that evidence of the kind D wanted to adduce was relevant to the second, subjective limb of the *Ghosh* test. *Ivey* has abolished that subjective limb of the *Ghosh* test. We suggest that D's beliefs are now relevant to the first limb of the *Ivey/Barton* test. In cases like *Hayes*, a defendant should be entitled to adduce evidence

---

[352] *R v Barton; R v Booth* [2020] EWCA Crim 575, [108] (emphasis added).

[353] For discussion, see G Virgo, 'The Role of Fault in the Law of Restitution' in A Burrows and A Roger (eds), *Mapping the Law: Essays in Honour of Peter Birks* (2006).

[354] The analogy is not perfect: in self-defence, the jury assesses D's subjective perception of one issue (the need to use force) and then applies an objective assessment of a different issue (the amount of force used).

[355] That would be closer to the self-defence test.

[356] [2015] EWCA Crim 1944.

about industry practices but the jury is no longer *bound* to acquit if the defendant held a belief that ordinary decent people would not regard his conduct as dishonest.

Where necessary, juries should be directed to approach the issue of dishonesty as follows.

(1) What were the facts or circumstances at the time D did what he is alleged to have done by the prosecution?

(2) What was D's knowledge or belief as to those facts or circumstances? You are entitled to consider D's explanation for his conduct, his experience and his intelligence.

(3) Having regard to the facts *and* D's state of mind about them, was his conduct dishonest according to the standards of ordinary decent people?

(4) D's belief about the honesty of his conduct, or what others think of his conduct, is not conclusive. The standard of honesty in law is that of ordinary decent people, which is a matter for you and not the defendant.

A critique of the law as stated in *Ivey/Barton*

There is no question that the change is a significant one. In some respects, it has less impact than some other recent decisions of the Supreme Court. By contrast to the change in *Jogee*, for example, it does not generate any risk of appeals out of time since the previous test in *Ghosh* was more generous to defendants.[357] It is submitted that there are nevertheless numerous unresolved problems.

(1) The manner by which the change was effected

Ivey is a civil case and did not concern the concept of dishonesty in the criminal law at all. It is less than ideal that a change to the criminal test for dishonesty occurred in the context of a purely civil case. None of the arguments which might have been advanced for retaining *Ghosh* were placed before the court.[358] The Supreme Court's casting aside of the *Ghosh* test of dishonesty without detailed argument left many issues unresolved. The judgment in *Barton* is of enormous significance for the law of precedent and all offences of dishonesty, but the law remains far from satisfactory. *Barton* only begins to provide the answers. Given the prominence of the role of dishonesty in so many very wide-reaching offences, further clarification is desperately needed.

(2) Dishonesty remains undefined

Adopting an objective test of this nature presents some difficulties. One major difficulty about this view is that juries—and magistrates—are likely to give different answers to the second limb of the test (objective limb) on facts which are indistinguishable. This creates very obvious injustices that risk bringing the criminal law into disrepute.

(3) The significance of the dishonesty concept in the criminal law

In terms of principle, the criticisms levelled at the failure to provide a clear definition of dishonesty are rendered all the more cogent for several reasons. First, the test applies in a great volume of cases in English courts—all those involving an element of dishonesty, which includes all Theft Act, Fraud Act and common law conspiracy to defraud cases, and many other offences under specific legislation (although it seems that dishonesty had not created enormous problems in practice).[359] Secondly, broad interpretations of the elements of actus reus have left dishonesty as the principal determinant of criminality in theft. As

---

[357] This was a point made by Gross LJ in *Pabon* [2018] EWCA Crim 420.

[358] For comment see Sullivan and Simester, n 82.

[359] See eg Magistrates' Association response to LCCP 155, reported in LC 276, para 5.14. And see the Commission's conclusion at para 5.18.

the Law Commission commented, 'where the conduct elements of an offence are morally neutral [as, for example, appropriation may be], the element of dishonesty has to do more than simply exclude specific types of conduct which, though *prima facie* wrongful, do not deserve to be criminal'.[360]

(4) Article 7

The change in law brought about by *Ivey* and *Barton* raises ever greater potential for challenges to the law under Art 7 of the ECHR[361] on the basis of lack of certainty. In relation to the offence of theft, the elements of actus reus—that there must be an appropriation of property belonging to another—are likely to be held to be sufficient, even after the extensive interpretation in *Gomez* and *Hinks*, to ensure that the offence of theft is not incompatible with Art 7. It is not yet an offence based solely on the concept of dishonesty (despite the best efforts of the House of Lords in *Morris*, *Gomez* and *Hinks*). It had been held at first instance that dishonesty under *Ghosh* was not itself incompatible with Art 7.[362] Given that the test for dishonesty under *Ivey/Barton* is now more objective, an individual could be convicted even though he may genuinely have held a belief that no ordinary decent people would consider his conduct to be dishonest. Even if he sought legal advice, in marginal cases it would be impossible to advise such an individual with certainty on whether a jury would consider his conduct to be dishonest. The Court of Appeal has so far resisted challenges to *Ivey/Barton* on this basis.[363]

This issue is perhaps more acute when it comes to the other offences for which dishonesty is the mens rea, such as fraud and conspiracy to defraud. As other chapters discuss, the actus reus of these offences is extremely broad indeed and the conduct involved often lawful but for dishonesty. To mitigate the potential harshness of the *Ivey* test as it applies to those offences, it will be important to direct the jury to pay close attention to limb (1), which requires them to ascertain the facts or circumstances as the defendant believed them to be, as explained in *Barton*.

(5) The assumptions made about jurors' approaches to dishonesty

One of the most detailed doctrinal studies of the concept of dishonesty was that by Professor Griew. Many of the criticisms he made of *Ghosh* remain pertinent in relation to the test pronounced in *Ivey* since they are effectively criticisms of the failure to provide a definition in law of the concept of dishonesty. The objective question (the first limb of *Ghosh* and the second limb of *Ivey*): assumes a community norm within the jury in that they must agree on the ordinary standards of honesty; assumes that jurors are honest, or at least that they can apply ordinary standards of honesty even if they do not adhere to them in their personal lives; and is unsuitable in specialized cases such as complex commercial frauds where the 'ordinary' person is unlikely to understand the honesty or otherwise of the activities;[364]

---

[360] LCCP 155, para 5.6.

[361] Art 7 guarantees not only against retrospective criminalization in strict terms, but also that 'legal provisions which interfere with individual rights must be adequately accessible, and formulated with sufficient precision to enable the citizen to regulate his conduct', *G v Federal Republic of Germany* (1989) 60 DR 252 at 262. So vague are the elements of dishonesty under *Ghosh* that LCCP 155 provisionally took the view that a Home Secretary could not safely be advised to make a statement of compatibility in relation to a Bill creating a general dishonesty offence. Subsequently, the Law Commission reversed its opinion in LC 276, *Fraud* (2002).

[362] *Pattni* [2001] Crim LR 570.   [363] See *Bermingham* [2020] EWCA Crim 1662.

[364] On the suitability of dishonesty in these cases, see also DW Elliott, 'Directors' Thefts and Dishonesty' [1991] Crim LR 732 arguing that insufficient attention has been paid to the issue of dishonesty in cases of sole traders committing theft from the company. See *Hayes* [2015] EWCA Crim 1944.

and leaves a question of law to the jury[365] which may lead to inconsistent decisions with the potential for different juries to reach different verdicts on identical facts, thus presenting acute problems in respect of Art 7 of the ECHR.

The *Ivey/Barton* approach endorses the CLRC's view of dishonesty relying on the common sense of members of society and a consensus about the appropriate benchmarks for protecting private property. As Norrie[366] points out, however, this view of private property might not be an accurate reflection of current values, particularly in relation to specific types of misappropriation—for example, petty pilfering from the workplace and omissions from tax returns. A national survey in 2007 found that more than 33 per cent of people admitted that they had paid in cash to a cleaner, plumber or other tradesman to avoid paying tax, 20 per cent had taken something from work; just under one-third, if handed too much change in a shop or business transaction, would just keep it, and one in ten avoids paying their television licence. About 6 per cent of people have 'padded out' an insurance claim[367] and one in four people admit not paying for at least one item when they use a self service checkout in a shop, leading to a loss to retailers of £3.2 billion per year.[368] Of course, it might well be that people do not generally assume their own moral standards when sitting as jurors.

(6) In what circumstances and how is the jury to be directed?

The Court of Appeal has frequently stressed that it is not necessary for the jury to be given a direction in every case.[369] It is unnecessary where D's claim is a lack of dishonesty owing to forgetfulness.[370] Nor is it necessary where, for example, D, a shop worker, simply denies taking the property and does not claim, for instance, that he borrowed it from the till.[371] Under *Ghosh*, it was accepted that a direction would be necessary where D's claim was that the ordinary person would not regard the conduct as dishonest,[372] but it was only in such cases that the direction should be given.[373]

Should juries now be directed on how to approach dishonesty in every case? This is a very real problem because the *Ivey/Barton* test may not reflect the ordinary understanding of the word dishonesty. It requires the jury to consider the facts or circumstances known to the defendant, including why he behaved as he did. We suggest that there will be many cases where, if no explanation or direction on dishonesty is provided, there would be a risk that jurors would simply apply an objective assessment without having proper regard to the defendant's knowledge or belief as to the facts. The safest course may be for at least the two-limb *Barton* direction[374] to be given in every case.

---

[365] For an argument in support of leaving such issues to the jury, see R Tur, 'Dishonesty and the Jury Question' in A Phillips Griffiths (ed), *Philosophy and Practice* (1985). The Law Commission provisionally concluded that 'the circumstances in which such conduct may be found to be non-dishonest cannot be circumscribed by legal definition. Where dishonesty is a positive element, it *must* be open to the fact-finders to find that particular conduct is not dishonest, even if the legislation does not say so.' LCCP 155, *Legislating the Criminal Code: Fraud and Deception* (1999) para 5.6.

[366] At 42. See also N Lacey, C Wells and O Quick, *Reconstructing Criminal Law* (4th edn, 2010) 399.

[367] See The Times, 24 June 2007; S Karstedt and S Farrall, *Law Abiding Majority? The Everyday Crimes of the Middle Classes* (2007). The report found that 61 per cent of 1,807 people in England and Wales aged between 25 and 65 had committed at least one of a number of offences against business, government or their employers.

[368] 'Self-scan shoplifters stealing £3bn a year', The Times, 27 Dec 2017.

[369] See in particular *Roberts* (1985) 84 Cr App R 177; *Price* [1990] Crim LR 200. Cf A Halpin, 'The Test for Dishonesty' [1996] Crim LR 283 at 291.

[370] *Atkinson* [2004] Crim LR 226.   [371] *Cobb* [2005] EWCA Crim 1549.

[372] *Wood* [2002] EWCA Crim 832, where D claimed that his trespassing into empty premises, to remove the entire stock of curtain fabric, was not dishonest since he believed it to be abandoned.

[373] See *Jouman* [2012] EWCA Crim 1850, in which the Court of Appeal reaffirmed that unless the question of the subjective element was properly raised, it was not necessary for the trial judge to give a full *Ghosh* direction. See also *Roberts* (1987) 84 Cr App R 117.

[374] At [84].

Finch's recent mock jury research however leads her to conclude that 'giving the jury no direction on dishonesty confuses them less and creates less conflict than giving them a test, irrespective of its wording and whether it is objective or subjective in nature.'[375]

(7) An expanded direction in specialist cases?

As noted, the Court of Appeal had a rare opportunity to consider the objective limb of dishonesty in *Hayes*[376] (as part of the *Ghosh* test). The Court of Appeal refused to allow evidence of industry practices to dilute the objective limb of the *Ghosh* test. Lord Thomas CJ stated:

> Not only is there is no authority for the proposition that objective standards of honesty are to be set by a market, but such a principle would gravely affect the proper conduct of business. The history of the markets have shown that, from time to time, markets adopt patterns of behaviour which are dishonest by the standards of honest and reasonable people; in such cases, the market has simply abandoned ordinary standards of honesty. Each of the members of this court has seen such cases and the damage caused when a market determines its own standards of honesty in this way. Therefore to depart from the view that standards of honesty are determined by the standards of ordinary reasonable and honest people is not only unsupported by authority, but would undermine the maintenance of ordinary standards of honesty and integrity that are essential to the conduct of business and markets.[377]

Some argued that the decision in *Hayes* had unwittingly changed the test in *Ghosh* by limiting the factors the jury can take into consideration when assessing whether D's conduct was dishonest.[378] It has been clear for decades that the objective limb of the test (as the first limb under *Ghosh* and now the second limb under *Ivey/Barton*) should not be altered to accommodate the particular context or market in which the alleged acts occurred. In *Robertson*,[379] for example, it was wrong to amend the objective test by reference to 'reasonable and honest people *engaged in business*'.[380] There is no separate first limb test for commercial fraud or market standards or market ethos, standard practice in an industry or any common understanding amongst employees. That would dilute the test since within certain sectors practices can develop that would be regarded as dishonest by all reasonable people even though they are adopted within the sector.

The Court of Appeal in *Hayes* confirmed that evidence of the kind D wanted to adduce was relevant to the second, subjective limb of the *Ghosh* test. Although *Ivey/Barton* has abolished that subjective limb of the *Ghosh* test, such evidence is, we submit, relevant to the first limb of the *Ivey* test, which requires the tribunal of fact to determine the actual state of the individual's knowledge or belief as to the facts.

In cases like *Hayes*, a defendant should be entitled to adduce evidence about industry practices (as they were entitled to do under the subjective limb of the *Ghosh* test), but the jury is no longer *bound* to acquit if the defendant held a belief that ordinary decent people would not regard his conduct as dishonest.

(8) The impact of Ivey/Barton on corporate liability

As we have seen in Ch 8, a company can only commit a crime if a corporate officer who is sufficiently senior to constitute its directing mind and will (DMW) has the necessary *mens rea*.[381] In *SFO v Barclays Plc*,[382] Davis LJ confirmed that since liability for an offence under the Fraud Act 2006 requires a 'dishonest state of mind' a company could only be liable if a DMW behaved dishonestly. Following *Ivey* and *Barton*, fraud turns more on the presence of a dishonest course of conduct than a dishonest state of mind. Whether this makes it easier to prosecute corporates remains to be seen, but that may prove to be the case.

---

375 E Finch, 'The Elephant in the Jury Room' [2021] Crim LR (issue 7).
376 [2015] EWCA Crim 1944.   377 At [32].
378 N Dent and A Kervick, '*Ghosh*: A Change in Direction?' [2016] Crim LR 553.
379 [2006] EWCA Crim 1289.   380 See also *Lockwood* [1986] Crim LR 244.
381 For discussion, see the 15th edn of this book, at Ch 8.
382 *SFO v Barclays Plc* [2018] EWHC 3055 (QB), [129] and [131].

(9) Secondary liability for dishonesty offences

To be guilty as an accessory, a defendant must have knowledge or belief about any 'facts' necessary to make the principal's conduct in question criminal.[383] Similarly, for a statutory conspiracy the defendant must intend or know the facts necessary for the commission of the offence.[384] Following *Ivey* and *Barton*, on a rather technical construction it is arguable that a 'fact' that makes the conduct criminal in dishonesty offences is that the principal's conduct would be considered dishonest by ordinary decent people. Could it be argued, therefore, that to be an accessory or a statutory conspirator the defendant must now be proved to have known/intended/believed that the principal's conduct would be considered dishonest by ordinary decent people?[385]

That is likely to be an unpalatable interpretation for the Court of Appeal. It would make such offences difficult to prove, would distinguish statutory conspiracy from conspiracy to defraud[386] and would mean that *Ghosh* was effectively retained in such cases, resulting in different tests for different offences,[387] thereby defeating Lord Hughes's aim of maximizing consistency of approach. Moreover, on an examination of the elements discussed, it seems to be an oversimplification to say that the objective assessment of conduct is what renders it dishonest. Properly read, *Barton* requires an objective assessment of the conduct *and* the defendant's state of mind about it.

(10) Dishonesty test in non-theft cases

Note that in cases of theft, s 2 of the Act stipulates that D is not dishonest if he has a (subjective) belief in a right in law to act as he did. In other offences for which dishonesty is the gravamen of the wrongdoing, s 2 does not apply. Where there is an overlap, the selection of charge by the CPS can mean entirely different approaches are adopted in relation to the same legal concept: dishonesty.

18.4.3.6 Reform of dishonesty

The Law Commission commented that it found the criticisms of *Ghosh* 'compelling'.[388] In the light of the volume and strength of such criticisms, it was not surprising, therefore, that numerous reform proposals have been advanced. Professor Elliott went so far as to suggest the removal of the element of dishonesty from the definition of theft. His proposal was to leave s 2 to deal with the bulk of cases and to add a further exculpatory element to the definition of the offence for conduct 'not detrimental to the interests of the owner in a significant practical way'.[389] It is unclear that such a proposal would offer any greater degree of certainty and promote any greater degree of consistency than the present law. There have been many other proposals, each with their strengths and defects.[390]

---

[383] See p 212.   [384] p 476.

[385] This issue arose in *Nyonyintono* [2020] EWCA Crim 454 but it was not considered in any great detail.

[386] Unless *Churchill v Walton* [1967] AC 224 applies.

[387] Almost reminiscent of the position in *McIvor* (1982) 1 All ER 49, the court in *Ghosh* sought to resolve.

[388] LCCP 155, para 5.32.

[389] See DW Elliott [1982] Crim LR 395. See also DW Elliott [1991] Crim LR 732. Cf G Williams, 'Innocuously Dipping into Trust Funds' (1983) 5 LS 183. This solution would require legislation and that seems very unlikely. Why should the taking of £20 from Bill Gates' wallet not amount to theft?

[390] See, inter alia, Glazebrook (1993) 52 CLJ 191 who provides a list of excepted circumstances that are not dishonest. This approach is developed by A Halpin, 'The Test for Dishonesty' [1996] Crim LR 283 at 294—'1. The treatment by a person of the property of another is to be regarded as dishonest where it is done without a belief that the other would consent to that treatment if he knew of all the circumstances, unless the person believes that the law permits that treatment of the property. 2. The treatment by a person of the property of another is not to be regarded as dishonest if done (otherwise than by a trustee or personal representative) in the belief that the person to whom the property belongs is unlikely to be discovered by taking reasonable steps.' See further, A Halpin, *Definition in the Criminal Law* (2004) 162–6, and Green, *13 Ways*, Ch 5. Green does not suggest a model theft statute, but instead drafts a list of principles that he says ought to inform future efforts to reform the law of theft.

One attractive solution would be a provision that a person appropriating property belonging to another *is* to be regarded as dishonest unless one of the three existing exemptions (in s 2) apply or, fourthly:

he intends to replace the property with an equivalent and believes that no detriment whatever will be caused to the owner by the appropriation.

This would excuse the employee who 'borrows' £5 from the till when closing the shop on Saturday afternoon, having no doubt that he will be able to replace it when he opens up on Monday morning, only to be robbed and rendered penniless on his way home from the pub on Saturday night.[391] His actions would be unlawful (in civil law) although not dishonest. It probably would not save the postmaster who 'borrows' from the post office till to keep his ailing grocery business going, in the hope that business will improve.

This test might, however, be thought too severe, leaving no escape route for hard cases such as the parents taking food for their starving children. But perhaps the concept of dishonesty is not the right vehicle for such cases. Suppose that the person breaks a window to get at the food and is charged with criminal damage. The definition of criminal damage does not require dishonesty. It would not make much sense to acquit the parent of theft and convict instead of criminal damage. They should stand or fall together. The parent might claim he had a 'lawful excuse' for the doing the damage—that is, the general defences of necessity or duress of circumstances—and this is the right approach for theft. If dishonesty were defined appropriately as a state of mind, exculpatory claims would be dealt with under the general defences which are applicable equally to theft and criminal damage. It is important, of course, to distinguish elements of unlawfulness and dishonesty. D may be acting unlawfully (and be aware that he is), and yet not be aware that he is acting dishonestly.

18.4.4 Intention permanently to deprive

The Theft Act preserves the rule of the common law and of the Larceny Act 1916 that appropriating the property of another with the intention of depriving him only temporarily of it is not stealing. There is no general offence in English law of stealing the use or enjoyment of a chattel or other property. The taking of motor vehicles and of articles from public places are exceptions, considered later. Apart from those cases, the 1968 Act left the law substantially unchanged; so that, if D takes V's iPad without authority and uses it for an afternoon, a week or a month, he commits no offence under the 1968 Act if he has an intention to return the iPad at the end of this period.[392] This is a mens rea requirement. It is not a question of whether V was in fact deprived permanently of the property; what matters is D's intention.

18.4.4.1 Deprivation of persons with limited interests

As we have seen, theft may be committed against a person having possession or control of property or having any proprietary right or interest in it. The element of permanence relates to the intended deprivation of V, not to the proposed benefit to D. Where V has an interest less than full ownership, it appears that an intention by D to deprive him of the whole of that interest, whatever it might be, is sufficient.[393] Thus, if as D knows, V has hired a car from X for a month, and D takes it, intending to return it to X after the month has expired, this appears to be theft from V, who is permanently deprived of his whole interest

---

[391] This proposal goes back substantially to the explanation offered many years ago for the meaning of 'fraudulently' in the Larceny Act 1916 and to that made by JC Smith in the first two editions of *Law of Theft*.
[392] *Neal v Gribble* [1978] RTR 409 (taking of a horse), p 950.
[393] cf Smith, *Property Offences*, para 6.05.

in the property, but it is not theft from X. The question is one of intention; so, if in the above example, D, when he took the car, believed V to be the owner, he would apparently not commit theft from V (because he intended to return it) even though V was, in fact, deprived of his whole interest.

18.4.4.2 Section 6 and the common law

It is valuable to consider the scope of the old law, first to understand what problems the 1968 Act was seeking to address and, secondly, because the courts continue to make reference back to the common law position when interpreting the scope of s 6.

Under the law before the 1968 Act the phrase 'intention permanently to deprive' was held to include the cases where:

(1) D took V's property with intention that V should have it back only by paying for it— for example, he took V's property so that, pretending that it was his own, he could sell it to V[394] ('ransom' cases).

(2) D took V's property intending to return it to V only when he had completely changed its substance—for example, D, being employed by V to melt down iron, took an axle belonging to V and melted it down in order to increase his output and consequently his earnings;[395] or D wrongfully fed V's oats to V's own horses;[396] or took V's horse intending to kill it and to return the carcass.[397]

(3) D took V's property and pawned it, intending to redeem and restore it to V one day but with no reasonable prospects of being able to do so.[398]

The draft Bill proposed by the CLRC contained no definition or elaboration of the phrase 'intention of permanently depriving'. The Committee assumed that the old law would be applied without any difficulty under that expression. The government had other ideas and introduced a clause which, after much amendment, became s 6.[399]

Section 6(1) provides:

A person appropriating property belonging to another without meaning the other permanently to lose the thing itself is nevertheless to be regarded as having the intention of permanently depriving the other of it if his intention is to treat the thing as his own to dispose of regardless of the other's rights, and a borrowing or lending of it may amount to so treating it if, but only if, the borrowing or lending is for a period and in circumstances making it equivalent to an outright taking or disposal.

As Spencer has written,[400] and the Court of Appeal was inclined to agree,[401] s 6 'sprouts obscurities at every phrase'.

On one view s 6 was intended to cover the cases that had been included under the old law and no more. In *Lloyd*,[402] the Court of Appeal approved academic opinions that s 6 only need be referred to in exceptional cases and then the question for the jury should not be 'worded in terms of the generalities' of the section but be related to the particular facts. The court cited the opinion of Edmund Davies LJ,[403] that 'Section 6 . . . gives illustrations, as it

---

[394] *Hall* (1849) 1 Den 381. See also *Raphael* [2008] EWCA Crim 1014 (discussed later).

[395] *Richards* (1844) 1 Car & Kir 532.　　　[396] *Morfit* (1816) Russ & Ry 307.

[397] cf *Cabbage* (1815) Russ & Ry 292.

[398] *Phetheon* (1840) 9 C & P 552; *Medland* (1851) 5 Cox CC 292. Cf *Trebilcock* (1858) Dears & B 453 and *Wynn* (1887) 16 Cox CC 231, which are inconclusive on the point.

[399] See JR Spencer, 'The Metamorphosis of Section 6 of the Theft Act' [1977] Crim LR 653. See more recently A Steele, 'Permanent Borrowing and Lending: A New View of Section 6 Theft Act 1968' (2008) 17 Nottingham LJ 3.

[400] Spencer [1977] Crim LR 653.　　　[401] *Lloyd* [1985] QB 829 at 834.　　　[402] [1985] QB 829.

[403] *Warner* (1970) 55 Cr App R 93 at 97.

were, of what can amount to the dishonest intention demanded by s 1(1). But it is a misconception to interpret it as watering down s 1', and concluded, 'we would try to interpret the section in such a way as to ensure that nothing is construed as an intention permanently to deprive which would not prior to the 1968 Act have been so construed'.

However, before and since *Lloyd*, courts have given the words of the section their wider ordinary meaning; *Downes*,[404] *Chan Man-sin*,[405] *Re Osman*,[406] *Bagshaw*.[407]

The current judicial opinion seems to be that s 6 is to be given its wider ordinary meaning (whatever that may be) and is not necessarily restricted to the scope of the common law meaning of the concept. The court in *Raphael*[408] expressly doubted whether the statutory framework created by the Act should always be restrictively interpreted by reference to the previous law. This was reiterated in more explicit terms by the Court of Appeal in *Vinall*.[409] Pitchford LJ stated that there was nothing in s 6(1) or (2) that indicated the governing and general words in subs (1) were intended to be limited to specific common law exceptions. Section 6 certainly has to be applied to situations which did not arise at common law, like the theft or obtaining of a thing in action.[410] Subject to that, it is submitted that in view of the acknowledged obscurity of s 6, the better opinion is that it should, in general, be treated as a narrow restatement of the common law.[411]

18.4.4.3 Disposal of the property as one's own

Adopting the broader meaning of s 6, as the courts have done, presents some difficulties. It is submitted that an intention merely to use the thing as one's own is not enough, and that 'dispose of' is used in the sense given by the *Shorter Oxford Dictionary*: 'To deal with definitely; to get rid of; to get done with, finish. To make over by way of sale or bargain, sell.'[412] In *DPP v Lavender*,[413] however, the Divisional Court seems to have held D's intention to *treat* the thing as his own, regardless of the owner's rights, as crucial and to have minimized the importance of 'to dispose of'. D, a council tenant, without authority removed two doors from another property belonging to the council to replace doors in the council property he occupied. Did he not, in fact, treat the doors as the property of the council, like the rest of the premises he occupied? If an office worker surreptitiously swaps his keyboard for the similar model operated by a colleague (because he believes it works better), does he steal the keyboard from his employer? He may well steal it from his colleague whom he does intend to deprive permanently of his limited interest.

It is submitted that, on a similar basis, there is no reason why there should not be a conviction for theft (rather than having to rely on s 11) in a case like that of the taker of the Goya from the National Gallery: 'I will return the picture when £X is paid to charity.' Substantially, the taker is offering to sell the thing back and his case is, in principle, the same as those contemplated by s 6(1). Nor should it make any difference that the price demanded is something other than money. 'I will return the picture when E (who is imprisoned) is given a free pardon'—this should be sufficient evidence of an intention permanently to deprive. The general principle might be that it is sufficient that there is an intention that V shall not have the property back unless some consideration is supplied by him or another; or, more generally still, unless some condition is satisfied.

404 (1983) 77 Cr App R 260, [1983] Crim LR 819 and commentary.
405 [1988] 1 All ER 1.   406 [1988] Crim LR 611.   407 [1988] Crim LR 321.
408 [2008] EWCA Crim 1014.   409 [2011] EWCA Crim 6252.
410 Since the thing in action is often extinguished and replaced by another (eg V's bank credit being extinguished and D's being created), there can only be permanent deprivation of that item of property belonging to V. The question is of D's mens rea as to that deprivation.
411 cf Griew, *Theft*, para 2.103.   412 This passage was cited in *Cahill* [1993] Crim LR 141.
413 [1994] Crim LR 297.

The Court of Appeal commented that it was hard to find a better example of an intention on the part of the thief to 'treat the thing as his own to dispose of regardless of the other's rights'[414] than on the facts of *Raphael*.[415] D had stolen V's car using violence and then contacted V offering to sell the car back to him.

18.4.4.4 Borrowing or lending

Where money or anything which is consumed by use—like petrol—is 'borrowed', the dishonest 'borrower' has an intention permanently to deprive even though he intends to replace the money or the article with another which is just as good. He intends to deprive the owner of the specific thing he has appropriated.[416] In the case of a true borrowing it appears that there can be no theft, however dishonest the borrower may be, because, by definition, he does intend to return the specific thing taken. Yet by s 6(1), if the borrowing 'is for a period and in circumstances making it equivalent to an outright taking . . .' the borrower may be regarded as having the intention of depriving the owner permanently. This is a rather puzzling provision, because it would seem, prima facie, that borrowing cannot be an 'outright taking'. Clearly, however, this part of the subsection is intended to do something and, therefore, certain borrowings are to be treated as the equivalent of outright takings. Once this is accepted, it is not difficult to identify the kind of borrowings which are intended to be covered: they are those where the taker intends not to return the thing until the virtue is gone out of it: D takes V's non-rechargeable battery, intending to return it to V when it is exhausted; or V's season ticket, intending to return it to V when the season is over. Similar in principle are those cases where D intends to return the thing only when it is completely changed in substance.[417]

Where property belonging to another has been entirely deprived of an essential characteristic, which has been described as its 'virtue', the matter seems reasonably clear as, for example, with a person stealing a ticket which will be returned only after it has been used. What if the virtue has not been entirely eliminated—but very nearly? D takes V's season ticket for Arsenal's matches intending to return it to him in time for the last match of the season. Is this an 'outright taking' so as to amount to theft of the ticket? If it is, is it theft if D intends to return the ticket in time for two matches?—or three, four, five or six—where should the line be drawn? The difficulty of drawing a line suggests that it should not be theft of the ticket unless D intends to keep it until it has lost *all* (or, at least, substantially all) of its virtue.[418] (The difficulty might satisfactorily be overcome in this particular case by holding that the right to see each match is a separate thing in action, of which V is permanently deprived once that match is over.) This means, of course, that if D takes V's car and keeps it for ten years, he will not be guilty of theft if, when, as he intended all along, he returns it to V, it is still a roadworthy vehicle, though the proportion of its original value which it retains is very small. If it can no longer be described as a car, but is scrap metal, then, if D intended to return it in this state, he has stolen it.[419]

The provision regarding lending appears to contemplate the situation where D is in possession or control of the property and he lends it to another, X. If D knows that the effect is that V, the owner, will never get the property back again, he clearly has an intention permanently to deprive V. Similarly, if D knows that when V gets the property back again the virtue will have gone out of it, this is equivalent to an outright disposal. The examples of the non-rechargeable battery, season ticket, etc are applicable here, though they seem less likely to arise in the context of lending than of borrowing.

---

[414] At [47].   [415] [2008] EWCA Crim 1014.   [416] *Velumyl* [1989] Crim LR 299.

[417] See cases cited earlier. *Dicta* in *Bagshaw* [1988] Crim LR 321 concerning the 'virtue' test seem inappropriate to the facts of that case.

[418] cf *Chan Wai Lam v R* [1981] Crim LR 497.

[419] cf *DPP v J* [2002] EWHC 291 (Admin), holding that the magistrates were wrong to accept a submission of no case where D had taken V's headphones, snapped them and returned them.

18.4.4.5 Parting with property under a condition as to its return

Section 6(2) provides:

Without prejudice to the generality of subsection (1) above, where a person, having possession or control (lawfully or not) of property belonging to another, parts with the property under a condition as to its return which he *may not* be able to perform, this (if done for purposes of his own and without the other's authority) amounts to treating the property as his own to dispose of regardless of the other's rights.

This is clearly intended to deal with the kind of case which gave difficulty under the old law, where D, being in possession or control of V's goods, pawns them. If D has no intention of ever redeeming the goods, he would now clearly be guilty of theft, apart from s 6(2). But what if D does intend to redeem? The answer now is that if he knows that he may not be able to do so, he is guilty of theft. The subsection does not seem to allow any distinction to be drawn between the case where D knows that the chances of his being able to redeem are slight and the case where he believes the chances are high; in either case, the condition is one which he knows he may not be able to perform.

The question under the Theft Act is a purely subjective one: D must *intend* to dispose of the property regardless of the other's rights, and s 6(2) merely describes what he must intend.[420] If then D is in fact *convinced*, however unreasonably, that he will be able to redeem the property, he does not come within the terms of s 6(2) because he intends *to dispose of it under a condition which he will be able to perform*.[421]

This is not necessarily conclusive, however, for s 6(2) is without prejudice to the generality of s 6(1); and it might reasonably be argued that even the person who is convinced, when pawning the goods, of his power to redeem them intends to treat the goods as his own to dispose of, regardless of the other's rights. This would be equally true if the person pawning the goods in fact had power to redeem; and, since pawning is not 'lending', there is no need to prove that it was equivalent to an outright disposal.[422]

On the whole it would seem that the better approach is to hold that D who is sure of his ability to redeem does not have an intention permanently to deprive. Such a person, in some circumstances, may well be found by the jury not to be dishonest. For example, D, a tenant for a year of a furnished house, being temporarily short of money, pawns the landlord's clock, knowing that he will certainly be able to redeem it and intends to do so before the year expires. A prosecution for theft of the clock could fail on the grounds that he has no intent permanently to deprive. In contrast, if D does not know that he will be able to redeem the clock, then the situation will be different. In the extradition case of *Balint v Municipal Court in Prague, Czech Republic*, Jackson LJ reiterated that, 'The fact that a defendant hopes that he may one day be in a position to repay the money taken is not a defence to theft.'[423]

---

[420] Historically, the common law cases suggested that it was theft, notwithstanding an intention to redeem the goods, if the person pawning them had no reasonable prospects of being able to redeem them: *Phetheon* (1840) 9 C & P 552; *Medland* (1851) 5 Cox CC 292; *Trebilcock* (1858) Dears & B 453; and *Wynn* (1887) 16 Cox CC 231 are inconclusive.

[421] cf A Steele (2008) 17 Nottingham LJ 3 in a comprehensive review of the case law suggests that an intention permanently to deprive is established: 1. Automatically if D pawns V's property subject to a condition that D cannot control. There is no need to prove any intent in such cases; 2. If D's borrowing V's property is objectively equivalent to an outright taking but where D intends that it will be returned; 3. Where D lends V's property to X and D does not intend that V's property will be returned to him; 4. In all other cases the subjective intention of D must be proved.

[422] The difficulty about this interpretation is that it makes it very difficult to see why s 6(2) is there at all; if D's disposition of property under a condition which he is able to perform is theft under subs (1), why refer specifically to the case of a condition which he may not be able to perform?

[423] [2011] EWHC 498 (Admin), [45].

18.4.4.6 Abandonment of property

Where the property is abandoned, s 6(2) does not apply because D does not part with the property under a condition. D might, however, be regarded as having an intention to treat the thing as his own to dispose of regardless of the other's rights. If D borrows the thing and then leaves it where he knows the owner or someone on his behalf will certainly find it, he clearly does not have an intention permanently to deprive. But if he abandons the thing in circumstances such that he knows that it is quite uncertain whether the owner will ever get it back, then it would not be unreasonable to hold that he has an intention to treat the thing as his own to dispose of regardless of the other's rights.

Care must be taken with arguments that property has been abandoned and that D has therefore demonstrated an intent to deprive permanently. In *Mitchell*,[424] D was charged with robbery having been one of four men who had seized V's vehicle having crashed their own vehicle in a police chase. They abandoned V's car and took another one which they subsequently abandoned and burnt out.[425] The trial judge ruled that there was sufficient evidence from the taking of the first car and abandoning capable of amounting to an intention to dispose of property regardless of owner's rights pursuant to s 6(1) of the Act. The Court of Appeal allowed the appeal confirming that s 6(1) was not intended to dilute the definition of theft in s 1(1). None of the earlier authorities extended the scope of s 6 to a case, even of violent taking of a car for its brief use before abandoning it where it could easily be discovered.

By analogy to the pawning case discussed earlier, it would seem that it should be immaterial whether D believes that the chances of V's getting the property back are large or small; it is sufficient that he intends to risk the loss of V's property. In *Fernandes*,[426] Auld LJ concluded that 'section 6 may apply to a person in possession or control of another's property who dishonestly and for his own purpose deals with that property in such a manner that he knows he is risking its loss'.[427] The Court of Appeal cited this passage with approval in *Vinall*.[428] Pitchford LJ stated that what s 6(1) requires is a state of mind in D which Parliament regards as the equivalent of an intention permanently to deprive, namely an 'intention to treat the thing as one's own to dispose of regardless of the other's rights'. His lordship went on to observe that:

The subsection does not require that the thing has been disposed of, nor does it require that the defendant intends to dispose of the thing in any particular way. No doubt evidence of a particular disposal or a particular intention to dispose of the thing will constitute evidence of the defendant's state of mind but it is, in our view, for the jury to decide upon the circumstances proved whether the defendant harboured the statutory intention.

His lordship accepted that if the prosecution cannot establish an intention permanently to deprive at the moment of the taking, it may nevertheless establish that D later exercised such a dominion over the property that it can be inferred that at the time of the taking he intended to treat the property as his own to dispose of regardless of the owner's rights. A subsequent disposal of property may therefore be *evidence* either of an intention at the time of the taking or evidence at the time of the disposal. When the allegation is one of theft, this later appropriation will suffice.

In *Vinall*, the Court of Appeal held that it was open to the judge to invite the jury to consider whether D's later abandonment of V's bicycle was evidence from which it could be inferred that, at the time of the taking, he intended to treat it as his own to dispose of

---

424 [2008] EWCA Crim 850.

425 It was conceded by the prosecution that the second vehicle had not been stolen.

426 [1996] 1 Cr App R 175. Cf *Mitchell* [2008] EWCA Crim 850 in which D was not guilty of robbery where he had taken a car by force and abandoned it. Relying upon *Fernandes*, it was emphasized in *Balint v Municipal Court in Prague, Czech Republic* [2011] EWHC 498 (Admin).

427 At [188].   428 [2011] EWCA Crim 6252

regardless of V's rights. If, however, D is charged with robbery, then this later appropriation will be insufficient because there will be no coincidence of theft and force.[429]

18.4.4.7 Other things to be returned—but for a price

A problem arises with the theft of a railway ticket or any other ticket which entitles the holder to services or goods when he returns it.[430] If D takes the ticket from another passenger, V, there is no difficulty. D intends to deprive V permanently not only of the piece of paper but also of the thing in action (V's contractual right to travel) which it represents. But if D takes the ticket from the rail company intending to use it, he may well intend to give it up at the end of the journey.[431] The rail company own the piece of paper but they cannot own the contractual right to travel. As with a cheque,[432] it may be said that D intends to return a different thing, a cancelled ticket with a hole punched in it; it has lost its virtue.

An alternative explanation is that D intends that the rail company shall have the ticket only by paying for it—through the provision of a ride on their train. That should be enough. This explanation has the advantage that it extends to things which are intended to be returned (but only for value) in an unchanged form. For example, D takes tokens from a coffee shop intending to return them in exchange for his espresso; or gaming chips from the proprietor of a gaming club, intending to return them in exchange for the right to play.[433] In all these cases there is probably a conditional intention permanently to deprive in the literal sense. The ticket, tokens and chips will probably not be returned at all if the taker realizes that he is not going to receive the value they represent.

18.4.4.8 Conditional intention to deprive

Consider a case where D takes V's bag, intending to take anything of value which he finds in it. Is such a 'conditional' intention sufficient? In *Easom*,[434] the Court of Appeal held, controversially, that 'a conditional appropriation will not do'. A difficulty with this proposition is that all intention is conditional, even though the condition is unexpressed and not present to the mind of the person at that time. In that case, D picked up a woman's handbag in a cinema, rummaged through the contents and put it back having taken nothing. The handbag was attached by a thread to a policewoman's wrist. D's conviction for stealing the handbag and the specified contents—tissues, cosmetics, etc—was quashed because D never had any intention of permanently depriving V of any of those things. It followed that he was not guilty of attempting to steal any of them. No doubt he intended to steal things which were not there—presumably money—and might have been convicted of attempting to steal on a suitably worded indictment.[435] D had no intention permanently to deprive and, consequently, he was not guilty of attempting to steal the handbag, or the specified contents either.

In *Husseyn*,[436] DD opened the door of a van in which there was a holdall containing valuable sub-aqua equipment. They were charged with attempted theft of the equipment. The judge directed the jury that they could convict if DD were about to look into the holdall and, if its contents were valuable, to steal it. The Court of Appeal, following *Easom*, held that this was a misdirection: 'it cannot be said that one who has it in mind to steal only if what he

---

429 See Ch 19.   430 cf *Marshall* [1998] 2 Cr App R 282, p 891.

431 At the time the Act was drafted, everyone knew that all tickets had to be given to the collector at the end of the journey but now some stations are open and some have barriers. If I travel to an open station, I expect (and intend) to retain my ticket; but if I am travelling to a closed station I expect (and intend) to give it up.

432 See p 881.

433 cf correspondence in [1976] Crim LR 329 and commentary on *Pick* [1982] Crim LR 238 which should have been read in the light of the Gaming Act 1968, s 16 which was overlooked.

434 [1971] 2 QB 315 at 319.   435 Discussed later.

436 (1977) 67 Cr App R 131n, [1978] Crim LR 219 and commentary; discussed at [1978] Crim LR 444 and 644.

finds is worth stealing has a present intention to steal'. In *Re A-G's References (Nos 1 and 2 of 1979)*,[437] the Court of Appeal held that these words were applicable only to an indictment which alleged an intention to steal a specific object, such as sub-aqua equipment. If the indictment had charged an attempt to steal 'some or all of the contents of the holdall' or, in *Easom*, of the handbag, there would be no problem. Yet, in *Husseyn* the sub-aqua equipment *was* the contents of the holdall—there were no other contents; so, according to the court, D was not guilty of attempting to steal the equipment if it was described as such, but he was guilty if it was described as the 'contents of the holdall'. At that time it was clear law that there could be no conviction for attempting to steal a thing that was not there—it was the sub-aqua equipment or nothing. Since the Criminal Attempts Act 1981,[438] this is no longer so. A person looking for money in an empty handbag might now be convicted of attempting to steal money.

The real problem in cases of this kind is the form of the charges. The formula approved in the *A-G's References* is not satisfactory because, in these cases, the defendant did not intend (or it was not proved that he intended) to steal any of the contents. But he undoubtedly intended to steal something—something which was *not* 'all or any of the contents'.[439] The charge would be accurate if it alleged simply that D attempted to steal from the handbag, or holdall.[440] This is so whether or not there is anything there that D would have stolen. D's intention to steal anything he finds which he thinks worth stealing is a present intention to steal, at least so far as the law of attempts is concerned. The failure to specify any subject matter cannot be an objection since the Criminal Attempts Act 1981.[441]

It is submitted that the better view is that an assumption of ownership, which is conditional because there is an intention to deprive only in a certain event, is theft. For example, D takes V's ring intending to keep it if the stone is a diamond, but otherwise to return it. He takes it to a jeweller who says the stone is paste. D returns the ring to V. It is submitted that he committed theft when he took the ring. The fact that he returned it is relevant only to mitigation in sentence. A similar problem may arise where D takes the property of V, say a ring, intending to claim a reward from V for finding it. If he intends to return the ring in any event and hopes to receive the reward, he is not guilty of stealing the ring though he is of fraud and of an attempt to steal the reward. But if he intends to retain the ring unless he receives the reward, he seems to be in substantially the same situation as the taker who sells the property back to the owner. It might be said, however, that in this example, the taker is not treating the property as his own. There are two possible answers to this: the assertion of a better right to possession might be regarded as treating the property as one's own; or, s 6 not providing an exclusive definition, this might be regarded as an analogous case falling within the general principle.

18.5 Corporations and their officers

As far as offences under the Theft Acts generally are concerned, the liability of corporations for them falls to be determined in accordance with the general principles applicable to the liability of corporations for crime.[442] Where a corporation commits a crime it must be the

---

[437] [1980] QB 180, [1979] Crim LR 585 and commentary.

[438] See p 434.   [439] cf *Bayley and Easterbrook* [1980] Crim LR 503 and commentary.

[440] cf *Smith and Smith* [1986] Crim LR 166 and commentary.

[441] As with the law of burglary, this is an instance in which it appears motive, which is generally regarded as irrelevant in mens rea in practice, assumes an importance, p 103. It may be different where the charge is theft. A lorry driver was held (in a civil action) not guilty of theft of the goods loaded on his lorry when he drove off intending to steal the load 'if and when the circumstances were favourable': *Grundy (Teddington) Ltd v Fulton* [1983] 1 Lloyd's Rep 16; but he had assumed a right of the owner (cf *Gomez*) and the only question is whether the conditional intention was enough.

[442] See Ch 8.

case that the crime has been committed by a person, or persons, in control of the corporation's affairs.[443] Such persons are, of course, liable in accordance with the ordinary principles governing liability for crime.

18.6 Reform

Over the last century the central focus of acquisitive crimes has shifted from protecting the possession of tangible goods against transportation to the protection of ownership of property (as broadly construed) against misuse. Those interests being protected, and which form essential elements of the actus reus—property and ownership—have expanded. The constant concept has been that of mens rea—fraud or dishonesty. So it seems that it will be in the future. It may be that the actus reus of the offences will disappear almost to vanishing point as the interests the law seeks to protect become more diffuse, diverse and indefinable.

There is also a growing pressure to use the criminal law to protect other 'interests' from misuse—trade secrets and crypto currencies being strong examples. The law may need to be more forward-thinking by protecting 'rights' and 'interests' such as the 'use' and 'value' derived from 'having access' to facilities. As these interests are harder to define, the mental element of dishonesty offences will become ever more important.

Although the Theft Acts have generated some complex and controversial case law, one view is that there is not very much wrong with them if properly handled.[444] An alternative view is that the Acts are now in need of some radical reappraisal since they represent a pragmatic but unprincipled patchwork of overlapping and technical offences. Tamblyn has recently suggested that radical reform by the judiciary could be achieved to recast the offence under s 1 of the Theft Act as one of intentionally or recklessly taking or keeping another's property without consent.[445]

Further reading

SP Green, *13 Ways to Steal a Bicycle: Theft Law in the Information Age*

E Griew, *The Theft Acts 1968 and 1978*

D Ormerod and D Williams, *Smith's Law of Theft*

---

[443] A corporation may, of course, be vicariously liable for crimes even though the crime is not committed by a person in control of its affairs: see p 281. But vicarious liability would not apply in connection with offences under the Theft Act 1968.

[444] See JC Smith, 'The Sad Fate of the Theft Act 1968' in W Swadling and G Jones (eds), *The Search for Principle, Essays in Honour of Lord Goff of Chieveley* (1999) 97. See also JC Smith, 'Conspiracy to Defraud: Some Comments on the Law Commission's Report' [1995] Crim LR 210 (a view shared by the Model Criminal Code Committee of the Attorney-General's Department, Australia, Final Report (1995) Chs 3, 6) and JC Smith, 'Reforming the Theft Acts' (1996) 28 Bracton LJ 27. See also DW Elliott, 'Dialogues on the Theft Act' in Glazebrook, *Reshaping the Criminal Law*, 287.

[445] See N Tamblyn, 'Reforming Theft: Taking Without Consent' [2020] Crim LR 597.

19
Robbery

19.1 Robbery under the Theft Act 1968

Robbery was a common law offence, and was put on a statutory footing in s 8 of the 1968 Act:

(1) A person is guilty of robbery if he steals, and immediately before or at the time of doing so, and in order to do so, he uses force on any person or puts or seeks to put any person in fear of being then and there subjected to force.

(2) A person guilty of robbery, or of an assault with intent to rob, shall on conviction on indictment be liable to imprisonment for life.

Robbery[1] is an extremely serious offence, carrying a maximum life sentence, and attracting substantial sentences in practice.[2] It is triable only on indictment.

The offence is very broad, applying to thefts in many circumstances ranging from the work of sophisticated gangs[3] and armed bank robbers, to extreme forms of playground bullying.[4] There have been cogent calls for reform to subdivide the offence into categories based on the gravity of the threat or use of violence involved.[5] This would provide offences which would have more appropriate labelling and sentencing.

Since the offence necessarily includes theft,[6] and will usually also involve an offence against the person,[7] it might be thought that a separate offence of robbery is otiose and that the combination of the two charges would cater adequately in terms of labelling and

---

[1] See generally Ormerod and Williams, *Smith's Law of Theft*, Ch 7; J Andrews, 'Robbery' [1966] Crim LR 524; Griew, *Theft*, Ch 3; Smith, *Property Offences*, Ch 14.

[2] The Definitive Guideline was published by the Sentencing Council on 28 Jan 2016 and came into effect on 1 Apr 2016. Available at www.sentencingcouncil.org.uk/publications/item/robbery-definitive-guideline-2/.

[3] See M Gill, *Commercial Robbery* (2000).

[4] See *FA and others* [2003] 2 Cr App R (S) 84.

[5] See A Ashworth, 'Robbery Reassessed' [2002] Crim LR 851. See also Green, *13 Ways*. Green notes that under the US Model Penal Code only those thefts involving the infliction or threat of immediate 'serious bodily injury' are treated as robbery.

[6] *Guy* (1990) 93 Cr App R 108.

[7] Robbery is not an offence of violence per se: *Baker* [2000] Crim LR 700.

sentencing powers. Despite the overlap, it is submitted that a specifically labelled offence of robbery is desirable, not least because in cases of a theft with a threat of violence, unless the threat is to kill, the only offence against the person likely to have been committed will be that of assault.[8] In short, with robbery the whole is greater than the sum of the parts.

19.1.1 Requirement of theft

As defined, robbery is essentially an aggravated form of theft; and if there is no theft, or attempted theft, there can be no robbery or attempted robbery. All of the elements of theft must be proved. So it would not be robbery where D by force takes a bag from V in the belief that he has the legal right to it (no dishonesty under the Theft Act 1968, s 2);[9] or where D is merely begging for money;[10] or where D by force takes a car from V not intending to deprive V permanently of it. In the first case D may be guilty of an assault,[11] and in the last of both an assault and an offence under s 12 of the Theft Act (taking a motor vehicle without authority), but in neither case is he guilty of robbery.

The requirement of an intention permanently to deprive has generated considerable case law. In *Raphael*,[12] R had been convicted of conspiracy to rob V by forcibly taking his car and then offering V the opportunity to buy it back. The Court of Appeal referred to s 6 (see the previous chapter) and concluded that this was clearly capable of amounting to robbery. In contrast, in *Mitchell*[13] DD took V's car as a getaway car and abandoned it later with no attempt to conceal it: no intention permanently to deprive was found and, hence, no theft and therefore no robbery. The same result occurred in *Vinall*[14] and *Zerei*.[15] In these latter two cases, the Court of Appeal accepted that D's later abandonment of the property was evidence from which the jury could infer an intention permanently to deprive. It was critical that the jury were directed that D could only be guilty of robbery if they were sure there was an intention permanently to deprive at the moment the property was appropriated by force. In both cases, the Court of Appeal reiterated the need for the judge to draw a distinction between the requirement for there to be an appropriation and the requirement for the defendant to have an intention permanently to deprive. If the two issues are conflated, this may be fatal to the safety of any ensuing conviction. Robbery does not require D to keep the property, rather only that he has the intention permanently to deprive V at the time of the appropriation, as where D takes V's headphones by force, snaps and returns them in 'useless' form.[16]

Problems can arise in relation to indirect threats. In *Waters*,[17] D had been with a group in a park and they had approached V. A mobile phone was taken from V, and D had said to V that the phone would be returned if another named man, X, could be persuaded to come and talk to them. The judge directed the jury that, if D had made it clear that the phone would be returned if he was able to talk to X, it would still constitute the 'intention to permanently deprive' element of the offence of theft. The Court of Appeal allowed the appeal.

---

8 Ashworth [2002] Crim LR 851 at 863.

9 cf *Skivington* [1968] 1 QB 166; *Robinson* [1977] Crim LR 173; *Forrester* [1992] Crim LR 793; *Hall* [2008] EWCA Crim 2086—some evidence of the belief in right to the property is needed before the judge must leave it to the jury.

10 cf *Codsi* [2009] EWCA Crim 1618.

11 D's claim that he believes himself to be entitled to the property appropriated does not of itself legitimate his use of force. The fact that V unlawfully possesses the property does not preclude a robbery conviction if D takes it by force: *Smith* [2011] EWCA Crim 66.

12 [2008] EWCA Crim 1014, [2008] Crim LR 995 and commentary.   13 [2008] EWCA Crim 850.

14 [2011] EWCA Crim 6252.   15 [2012] EWCA Crim 1114.

16 Magistrates wrong to accept submission of no case: *DPP v J* [2002] EWHC 291 (Admin).

17 [2015] EWCA Crim 402.

The jury might have been left with the erroneous impression that even if X could be found in the near future and it was likely that the phone would be soon returned, nonetheless there had been an intention to permanently deprive in respect of the phone. That was not a correct conclusion. The court did not refer to the 'ransom' cases. As the Court of Appeal made clear in *Lloyd*,[18] it is theft and therefore can be robbery if:

a defendant takes things and then offers them back to the owner for the owner to buy if he wishes. If the taker intends to return them to the owner only upon such payment, then, on the wording of section 6(1) that is deemed to amount to the necessary intention permanently to deprive . . .[19]

It makes no difference if the ransom demand is for action rather than money. In short, the jury needed to be sure that D intended to 'treat the thing as his own to dispose of regardless of the other's rights'.

The offence of robbery is complete when the theft is complete, that is when the appropriation is complete. Following recent interpretations of that concept,[20] a robbery can now be completed much earlier than at common law, and than the drafters of the Theft Act intended. So, in *Corcoran v Anderton*,[21] where D and E sought to take V's handbag by force, it was held that the theft was complete when D snatched the handbag from V's grasp, though it then fell from D's hands and the defendants made off without it. It is now arguable that the theft in such a case is complete when D first touches the handbag, for by that conduct he is assuming a right of an owner.

For robbery, the appropriation element of theft will normally be by D 'taking' V's property since it is difficult to imagine realistic situations in which robbery might arise by appropriation without taking.[22] One possibility is where D has borrowed V's property and refuses to return property to V, and backs this refusal with a threat of force. Taking a different scenario, it is unclear whether D can be said to have completed the robbery where he issues a threat to V and demands that V hand over his property and V is in the process of doing so, but D has not yet touched it.[23] A safer course is to charge an attempted robbery in such circumstances.[24]

19.1.2 Use or threat of force

Any use or threat of 'force' against the person suffices. 'Force' is wider than the concept of 'violence' used at common law, and might be regarded as a more neutral word. The courts have not defined it, and treat it as an ordinary English word, which should be left to the jury to determine.[25] It is submitted that no jury could reasonably find that the slight physical contact that might be involved where D picks V's pocket would amount to a use of force.[26] However, very little may be required to turn a case of theft into one of robbery; to push or

---

[18] [1985] QB 829.   [19] At 836.

[20] Discussed in Ch 18. The significance of when robbery ends can be important in sentence in a murder case where D is alleged to have killed for gain: see Sch 21, para 5 of the Criminal Justice Act 2003 and *Cullen* [2007] 2 Cr App R (S) 394.

[21] (1980) 71 Cr App R 104.   [22] See Andrews [1966] Crim LR 524, for possible instances.

[23] cf *Briggs* [2004] Crim LR 495. Cf *Farrell* (1787) 1 Leach 332. D apprehended before V handed over the property.

[24] For an example of a case in which such an approach was upheld by the Court of Appeal, see *Dyer* [2011] EWCA Crim 900.

[25] *Dawson and James* (1976) 64 Cr App R 170.

[26] See eg *Monaghan and Monaghan* [2000] 1 Cr App R (S) 6 where 'jostling' to pick V's pockets was charged as theft.

nudge the victim so as to cause him to lose his balance is capable of being a use of force.[27] If D causes a substance to come into contact with V, in an effort to incapacitate V in order to facilitate theft, then it is submitted that D would be guilty of robbery.

The offence can be committed in one of three ways.

(1) Where D uses force. This poses few problems. It is no defence that V was unaware that D was using force, as where D strikes V from behind rendering V unconscious so that D can steal from him.

(2) Where D 'puts' any person in 'fear' of being then and there subjected to force. Here, the language of the section does leave some ambiguity. Is it a requirement of robbery that (a) V is put in 'fear' or (b) is it sufficient that he apprehends[28] that force may be used if he resists? The Divisional Court confirmed in *R v DPP*[29] that robbery does not require proof that V was actually put in fear. It is submitted that this must be correct, otherwise the commission of the offence would turn on the courage of the victim. That case does not, however, answer the question whether it is necessary for the victim to apprehend that force will be used.[30] In this form of the offence, it would seem to be a necessary element. Support for that proposition is derived from *Grant v CPS*,[31] although the court in *R v DPP* cast doubt on that case.

(3) Where the allegation is that D *seeks* to put V in fear of force. Here, there is no need for V to be in fear, nor it seems to apprehend force; the offence turns solely on D's intention. It is important to emphasize that it is sufficient that D's intent is to produce a state of mind where V *apprehends* force; it is not necessary for D to intend that V will be afraid. Hence, D cannot plead that he thought V was macho enough not to be afraid of the threats. *Tennant* makes clear that D may threaten a use of force and satisfy the requirement of the offence of robbery although V is not made to apprehend the immediate infliction of force on him which is necessary to constitute an assault.[32]

A threat of force may be implied as well as express. Where D threatens V with force unless V complies with D's demands and at a later stage D takes property from an unprotesting V, D may be convicted of robbery if he intends, and V understands, the threat to continue even though D's original threats were not made for the purpose of taking V's property.[33] This might be a common occurrence where D threatens V who subsequently escorts D to V's bank ATM and withdraws cash to hand over to D.

[27] *Dawson and James*, n 25. See Williams, TBCL, 825, suggesting a distinction based on 'gentle force' used to take by stealth as opposed to force used to overcome resistance. See also Griew, *Theft*, para 3.05; Smith, *Property Offences*, para 14.10.

[28] Clearly a different state of mind from fear as is obvious from the law in relation to assault, see p 691.

[29] [2007] EWHC 739 (Admin).

[30] In *B (JJ)* [2012] EWCA Crim 1440, the Court of Appeal observed that robbery could be committed without any force actually being used on V. It was held that the consequence of this is that if there is only a charge of robbery on the indictment and the jury were to find D not guilty of that charge, then the only possible alternative verdict made possible by the introduction of s 6(3A) of the Criminal Law Act 1967 is one of common assault. This observation, however, is overbroad and surely depends upon the facts of the case. The jury might not be sure that D used force in order to steal and therefore find him not guilty of robbery, but nevertheless be sure that there was an unlawful touching and find him guilty of battery or a more serious non-fatal offence against the person, depending upon the circumstances. The Court of Appeal confirmed in *Ali* [2016] EWCA Crim 375 that the offence of ABH is not a statutory alternative to the offence of robbery. The ABH could be seen as being separate to and independent from the robbery.

[31] *Grant v CPS* (2000) 10 Mar, unreported, QBD.   [32] *Tennant* [1976] Crim LR 133, CC.

[33] *Donaghy and Marshall* [1981] Crim LR 644 (Judge Chavasse).

19.1.2.1 Force to the person

Historically, prior to the Theft Act, robbery was thought of as stealing accomplished by force against the person, the force being used to overpower V's resistance and not merely to seize the property.[34] The CLRC in drafting the 1968 Act had the same distinction in mind, stating it would 'not regard mere snatching of property, such as a handbag, from an unresisting owner as using force for the purpose of the definition'.[35] The requirement that the force be administered directly to a person and not the property being stolen was meant to be retained by the words in s 8: '. . . if he steals . . . and in order to do so, he uses force *on any person* or seeks to put *any person* in fear of being then and there subjected to force'. But, in *Clouden*,[36] the distinction was rejected and D's conviction for robbery was upheld where he wrenched a shopping basket from V's hand and ran off with it. In the view of the court, the old distinction could not stand with the words of s 8, and it was open to a jury to find on such facts that force had been used on V with intent to steal. *A fortiori*, it will be robbery where, for example, a struggle, even a fleeting one, takes place for possession of a handbag[37] or where an earring is snatched tearing the lobe of the ear.[38] The decision in *Clouden* is an interesting illustration of the ambiguity over the true foundation of robbery: it is a hybrid offence protecting property and personal safety, and the courts refuse to narrow it down by defining its concepts in an unduly technical fashion.

The Administrative Court examined the meaning of 'force' in *P v DPP*[39] in which D snatched a cigarette from the hand of V. D was convicted in the Youth Court of robbery and appealed by way of a case stated. The issue for the court was whether the snatching of a cigarette, in the absence of any physical contact between D and V, was sufficient to constitute 'force'. Mitting J observed that under the Larceny Act 1916, which used the term 'violence', the answer would be in the negative. His lordship cited with approval a passage from *Smith's Law of Theft*[40] and concluded that the snatching of a cigarette in these circumstances was insufficient to constitute 'force' within the meaning of s 8. Although 'force' has a broader meaning than 'violence', it was held that the facts of this case were analogous to cases of pickpocketing in which there is no physical contact between D and V. As this case involved no physical contact whatsoever, D's conviction was quashed. It was observed that the appropriate charge on these facts was theft of the cigarette.[41] His lordship did, however, accept that force could be applied indirectly, for example when D wrenches a shopping bag from V. Mitting J stated that the snatching of the cigarette could not constitute force because it could not have caused any pain to D. We suggest that *dictum* be treated with caution. As has already been pointed out, s 8 does not require pain to be caused to V; it simply requires the use of force on any person. For example, if D wrenches a prosthetic leg from V, this, it is submitted, would be sufficient to constitute 'force' even if V was not caused any pain.

---

[34] *Gnosil* (1824) 1 C & P 304; *Harman's Case* (1620) 2 Roll Rep 154.   [35] Eighth Report, para 65.

[36] [1987] Crim LR 56. Griew believes the case to be wrongly decided: para 3.05. See also eg *Symons* [2009] EWCA Crim 83 where D pulled at V's bag. In *Yohannes* [2011] EWCA Crim 1362, the Court of Appeal noted Professor Smith's criticisms of *Clouden* but did not express any concluded view of them. In that case D was convicted of robbery but acquitted of being in possession of an imitation firearm with intent to commit an indictable offence. The prosecution's case was that an imitation firearm was brandished in front of V and then a box containing a valuable watch was snatched from him. The Court of Appeal accepted D's contention that the verdicts were inconsistent and substituted his conviction for robbery with one for theft.

[37] *Corcoran v Anderton* (1980) 71 Cr App R 104.

[38] cf *Lapier* (1784) 1 Leach 320. This passage was cited with approval by the Court of Appeal in *Martin* [2021] EWCA Crim 223.

[39] [2012] EWHC 1657 (Admin).   [40] Ormerod and Williams, *Smith's Law of Theft*, para 7.08.

[41] It has been cogently argued that charging relatively trivial cases such as this as robbery undermines the distinctive harmfulness of the offence which justifies it being an offence triable only on indictment. See Horder, APOCL, 408.

19.1.2.2 In order to steal

If D assaults V and, having incapacitated him without any intention of stealing from him, opportunistically takes V's wallet, there is no robbery. D commits offences against the person and theft.[42]

19.1.3 On *any* person

In most cases of robbery, D will use or threaten force against the person in possession of the property. But the offence is not so limited. Provided the force is used or threatened *in order* to steal, it will be robbery.

If, for example, the only force used at the time of the [Great Train Robbery] in 1963 had been on a signalman [rather than the train driver or guard], this would under the [Act] have been sufficient.[43]

It does not matter that the person against whom the force is used or threatened has no interest whatever in the property; it would be robbery to overpower a security guard in his office at X Co, because his office overlooks a factory Y Co across the road from which the thieves wish to steal, and they fear that he will notice them and raise the alarm.

It does not amount to robbery where D threatens to use force on X (who has no knowledge of the threat) in order to overcome V's reluctance to part with his money. Take the case of D a bank robber. If D hands V, a bank clerk, a note which reads 'I have a gun pointed at a customer',[44] V who is safely behind the armour-plated glass is not apprehending force to himself (not robbery). The customer, X, is unaware of what D has in mind and has written on the note. X is not apprehending violence. However, if D reads the note aloud, that is sufficient for robbery if the customer, X, then apprehends violence. There is no glaring failing in the law in these situations since all cases of this type could be treated as blackmail under s 21 of the Act.

19.1.4 Immediately before or at the time of stealing

Strictly interpreted, this expression might suggest that force used only a second after the theft is technically complete would not suffice for robbery, a view which may be said to receive further support from the requirement that the force be used 'in order to steal'. The argument was advanced in *Hale*.[45] D and E entered V's house and while D was upstairs stealing a jewellery box, E was downstairs tying up V. Their convictions for robbery were upheld although the appropriation of the jewellery box might have been completed before the force was used. The court regarded appropriation as a 'continuing act' and it was open to the jury on these facts to conclude that it continued while V was tied up. The matter needs to be looked at in a commonsense way; while the force must be used at the time of the theft and *in order to steal*,[46] the theft needs to be looked at in its entirety.

There is, arguably, an ever-greater need for the courts to adopt a pragmatic approach to this issue following the extension of the concept of appropriation in *Hinks*. Technically, where D first touches V's property he has appropriated it, but it would render the offence of robbery useless if the theft was deemed complete at that time and D applied force a second later. For example, where D has already gained access to V's car, and locked himself in, and

---

[42] *Harris* (1998) The Times, 4 Mar; *James* [1997] Crim LR 598.

[43] Eighth Report, para 65. Cf *Smith v Desmond and Hall* [1965] AC 960.

[44] *Taylor* [1996] 10 Arch News 2. Cf *Reane* (1794) 2 Leach 616.

[45] (1978) 68 Cr App R 415. Confirmed post-*Gomez* in *Lockley* [1995] Crim LR 656. Cf *Gregory* (1981) 74 Cr App R 154. Cf *Atakpu*, p 872.

[46] Failure to direct the jury on this point renders the conviction unsafe: *West* (1999) 14 Sept, unreported, CA.

V is only threatened by D's driving at him to escape, the theft might be said to be continuing and a robbery committed.[47] But a line has to be drawn somewhere. If, having taken the car from V without using or threatening force, D is subsequently stopped by a police officer in the street and knocks him down in order to avoid arrest, this would not amount to robbery. Force used to retain possession of property not obtained by force would not ordinarily be thought of as robbery.[48] Even on a broad view, the use of force is neither at the time of, nor in order to commit, the theft.[49] There may be merit in extending the offence by legislation to include force or the threat of force 'immediately after' a theft.[50] This would resonate with the existing underlying approach which is that robbery protects against the use of force in the acquisition of property.

'Immediately before' must add something to 'at the time of' the theft. The interpretation taken in some Australian decisions—that it means 'no intervening space or lapse of time or event of any significance'[51]—may be too restrictive. Clearly, if a gang overpower V, the security guard at the main gate of a depot, this would be a use of force immediately before the theft, although some minutes must elapse before the gang reaches the part of the depot where the safe is housed.[52] And it can make no difference that V is not present at the depot at all; it would be robbery where some members of the gang detain V by force at his home while the other gang members open the safe in the depot miles away. It does not seem to be possible to put any specific temporal limit on 'immediately'. All the circumstances have to be considered including the time when, and the place where, the force was used or threatened in relation to the theft. Force converts theft into robbery only when its use or threat is in a real sense directly part of the theft and is used in order to accomplish the theft.

It is not enough that D gets V to part with property by threatening to use force on a separate and/or future occasion. This may well amount to blackmail but the fact that V is intimidated or frightened is not in itself enough for robbery unless he is put in fear of being 'then and there' subject to force. But suppose a gang, by threats of force, persuade V, the depot security guard, to stay away from work the following evening, and on that evening they steal from the depot uninterrupted. At the time of the theft the threat of force still operates on V's mind; he stays at home because he is afraid of what will happen if he goes to work. But this does not seem to amount to robbery. At the time of the theft V is not put in fear of being 'then and there' subjected to force. In *Khan*,[53] V, at D's request, withdrew cash from his bank to hand over to D. V stated that he was in fear that D would be attacked by X, a violent man to whom D claimed to be in debt, and that he feared that if X beat up D, D would then come and beat up him, V. The Court of Appeal quashed D's robbery conviction: there was no evidence that V feared that he would be subjected *then and there* to force.

19.1.5 Mens rea

Obviously, robbery requires at least an intention to steal, which in this context will usually be a purposive, direct intent.[54] But it seems to require more than this. What of the mens rea requirement in relation to the use or threat of force? It could be argued that liability in respect of the force is strict, and that if D intends to steal it will be robbery if in fact there is some use of force, or if in fact he puts someone in fear, whether he intends to do so or not.

---

[47] *Hayward v Norwich Union Insurance Ltd* [2000] Lloyd's Rep IR 382. Whether the offence is one of theft or robbery may be of special significance for V's insurance claim: see generally M Wasik, 'Definitions of Crime in Insurance Contracts' [1986] JBL 45.

[48] *Harman's Case* (1620) 2 Roll Rep 154 (subject to the point at n 22 above).

[49] cf Eighth Report, para 65.   [50] Griew, *Theft*, para 3.08.   [51] *Stanischewski* [2001] NTSC 86.

[52] It would surely be open to the jury so to find. Cf *Hale* (1978) 68 Cr App R 415.

[53] [2001] EWCA Crim 923.   [54] See p 93.

But in principle this would not be a desirable interpretation. It seems clear that D must use or threaten force *in order* to steal, and a merely accidental use of force would not be done in order to steal.[55] Moreover, it should be proved that D intended to use the force in relation to a person, and not merely to property.[56]

It is enough that D seeks to put another in fear of being subjected to force. Fear here means to apprehend, and it would be no less a robbery because V was not afraid. Even if V does not apprehend that he will be subjected to force (because, perhaps, plain-clothes police are present and D has walked into a trap), it will be robbery if D intended to make him fear. But it would not be enough that V is in fact put in fear unless D intended to put V in fear. A timorous witness to a smash-and-grab raid might well fear that the thieves will turn on him, but if the thieves do not intend to put him in fear of being there and then subjected to force, the offence cannot amount to robbery.

Further reading

SP Green, *13 Ways to Steal a Bicycle: Theft Law in the Information Age*
E Griew, *The Theft Acts 1968 and 1978*

---

[55] cf *Edwards* (1843) 1 Cox CC 32.
[56] Intention here might include oblique intention, p 93.

20

Offences of temporary deprivation

In general it is not theft dishonestly to use the property of another unless there is an intention to deprive the other permanently of the property.[1] There may be a case for creating a general offence, which need not necessarily be termed theft, of dishonest use or unauthorized use of another's property.[2] Arguably, the case for such an offence is growing stronger as so much property derives its particular value to a person from its availability for *immediate* use.

At the time of drafting the Theft Act 1968, the CLRC decided against any such offence and its view, though subject to vigorous assault in Parliament, was accepted. The Committee concluded that there was no evidence of a need for such a considerable extension of the criminal law was not called for at that time.[3] But Parliament accepted that there are particular cases in which temporary deprivation of property is considered to be sufficiently serious to justify criminalization. The taking of vehicles (which was first made an offence by s 28 of the Road Traffic Act 1930) is one obvious instance; and the taking of vessels (which was made an offence by s 1 of the Vessels Protection Act 1967)[4] is another. These offences are now dealt with in s 12 of the Theft Act 1968 that extends the offence to a much wider range of 'conveyances' as the Act calls them.

In addition, the Theft Act 1968 added a further and entirely new offence of temporary deprivation; that of removing articles from places open to the public. Before the Act there had been a number of notorious 'borrowings' of famous works of art from galleries

---

[1] See generally Ormerod and Williams, *Smith's Law of Theft*, Ch 10; Griew, *Theft*, Ch 5; Smith, *Property Offences*, Ch 8.

[2] See especially G Williams, 'Temporary Appropriation Should Be Theft' [1981] Crim LR 129.

[3] Eighth Report, para 56.   [4] As repealed by the Theft Act 1968.

and exhibitions. For example, someone removed Goya's portrait of the Duke of Wellington from the National Gallery. The CLRC thought that the problem was 'serious enough to justify the creation of a special offence'.[5]

20.1 Removal of articles from places open to the public

Section 11 of the Theft Act 1968 provides:

(1) Subject to subsections (2) and (3) below, where the public have access to a building in order to view the building or part of it, or a collection or part of a collection housed in it, any person who without lawful authority removes from the building or its grounds the whole or part of any article displayed or kept for display to the public in the building or that part of it or in its grounds shall be guilty of an offence. For this purpose 'collection' includes a collection got together for a temporary purpose, but references in this section to a collection do not apply to a collection made or exhibited for the purpose of effecting sales or other commercial dealings.

(2) It is immaterial for purposes of subsection (1) above, that the public's access to a building is limited to a particular period or particular occasion; but where anything removed from a building or its grounds is there otherwise than as forming part of, or being on loan for exhibition with, a collection intended for permanent exhibition to the public, the person removing it does not thereby commit an offence under this section unless he removes it on a day when the public have access to the building as mentioned in subsection (1) above.

(3) A person does not commit an offence under this section if he believes that he has lawful authority for the removal of the thing in question or that he would have it if the person entitled to give it knew of the removal and the circumstances of it.

(4) A person guilty of an offence under this section shall, on conviction on indictment, be liable to imprisonment for a term not exceeding five years.

It is questionable why special protection should be provided for the temporary deprivation of this category of items in such specific circumstances when the temporary removal of non-exhibited property of individuals or companies will commonly be a cause of much greater concern and pose the risk of much greater financial hardship to the victim.

20.1.1 Actus reus

On the face of it the offence under s 11 is one of considerable complexity. The draftsman's intention was to deal with the specific mischief discussed, and care has been taken to confine the operation of the section to that mischief. Numerous points arise for consideration.

20.1.1.1 Public access to a building

For the offence to apply, the public must have access to the building, not merely its grounds. Access must be *public* access; access limited for a particular section of the public will not

---

[5] CLRC, para 57(ii). See the allegations against D Cartrain who visited Damian Hirst's installation *Pharmacy* at Tate Britain and removed a few of the rare 'Faber Castell dated 1990 Mongol 482 Series' pencils. Cartrain then produced a 'wanted' poster: 'For the safe return of Damien Hirst's pencils I would like my artworks back that DACS and Hirst took off me in November. It's not a large demand . . . Hirst has until the end of this month to resolve this or on 31 of July the pencils will be sharpened. He has been warned.' The pencils were worth £500,000. See news reports for 4 Sept 2009.

suffice.[6] It does not matter that members of the public are required to pay for the privilege of access, nor whether the purpose of imposing the charge is merely to cover expenses or to make a profit.[7] But the access must be to a building or part thereof. So if D removes a statuette displayed in the open in a local authority park this behaviour would not be within the section.[8] If, however, the park consists of a building and its grounds, and the public have access to the building in order to view, D's removal of the statuette would be within this section.

Normally, no doubt, D will have entered the building in consequence of the owner's invitation[9] to the public to view. But as long as the public have access to view, D may commit the offence although he entered as a trespasser or although he is the owner's guest and is temporarily residing in the building.

20.1.1.2 In order to view

For the offence to apply, the access to the building must be *in order* to view the building (or part of the building) or a collection (or part of a collection) housed in it. It has been held that the question whether access is 'in order to view' is to be determined by reference to the occupiers' intention in allowing access.[10] The public might have access to a building (eg a shopping precinct or arcade) where collections are from time to time exhibited in the lanes connecting the shops; but in such circumstances access exists in order to shop and access to view the collection is only incidental to that shopping purpose. If, however, the collection is housed in a cordoned off part of the precinct and access is given to that part specifically so that the collection may be viewed, it would be within the protection of s 11.

20.1.1.3 Articles displayed or kept for display

The offence prohibits the removal of *any* articles displayed or kept for display, and is not confined to works of art. The coronation stone (something which the CLRC expressly considered)[11] is clearly for this purpose an article displayed to the public though it is not a work of art. The criterion is only whether the article, which may be priceless in either sense of the term, is displayed or kept for display to the public.

'Display' here is presumably used in the sense of 'exhibit' and not merely in the sense of able to be seen; the article must be displayed or exhibited *to the public*.[12] Consequently, the removal of a fire extinguisher from a building housing exhibits would not be within the section even though it can be seen by members of the public, but it would be within the section if the fire extinguisher was itself exhibited, perhaps as an example of an early type of extinguisher, or as an example of unique design, or even nowadays if it was acclaimed as a work of modern 'art'.

It is enough that the article, though not displayed, is 'kept' for display, as where a painting is kept in the gallery's storeroom.[13]

20.1.1.4 Removal

To complete the actus reus of the offence the article must be removed from the building *or* from its grounds. Thus, removal from the building to the grounds or vice versa will suffice. The removal, as s 11(2) makes clear, need not be during the times at which the public have

---

[6] But the exclusion of a particular class, eg the exclusion of children from an exhibition considered unsuitable for them, would not prevent access being public access.   [7] But see p 943.
[8] cf the discussion in relation to burglary, Ch 25.
[9] *Barr* [1978] Crim LR 244 (Deputy Judge Lowry) and commentary.   [10] ibid.
[11] Eighth Report. Cf *Barr* [1978] Crim LR 244.   [12] So linked in *Barr*.
[13] cf *Durkin* [1973] QB 786.

access. If the collection is permanently[14] exhibited (which would be the case, eg, with public galleries and museums) removal at any time, even during a holiday when the building is closed to the public, may amount to an offence. But if the exhibition is temporary only, the removal must take place on a day when the public have access to the building in order to view. This serves to illustrate how unduly complex the provision is as a result of its being tailored to meet such a particular mischief. It underlines the fact that the offence is driven in part by a desire to criminalize the abuse of trust of those given access to public exhibitions.[15]

20.1.1.5 Commercial exhibitions

This limitation on the scope of the offence creates considerable ambiguity. As has been seen,[16] s 11 applies notwithstanding that the owner charges the public for admission. It applies even though he admits the public only to make profit. But the section does not apply where the owner admits the public only to view a collection,[17] if the collection is 'made or exhibited for the purpose of effecting sales or other commercial dealings'.

If it is such an exhibition, s 11 has no application whether entry is free or not. It seems odd that the law draws this distinction. The reason for this restriction upon the offence was to avoid creating an unduly wide offence, involving a very substantial exception to the general principle that temporary deprivation should not be criminal.[18] It would have meant, for example, that a removal from the premises of an ordinary commercial bookseller would have been an offence even where D has no intent permanently to deprive. In addition, since the section protects things at risk because they are on display to the public, it is thought to be reasonable for that risk to be borne by the commercial exhibitor.

As it stands, only where the collection is made or exhibited for *the purpose*[19] of sale or other commercial dealings does this exclusion from liability apply. If, then, a commercial bookseller, for the purpose of encouraging local art, arranges exhibitions in a room of his bookshop to which the public are admitted, D's removal of the paintings, or of any other article displayed or kept for display in his premises, would fall within the section whether or not it was available for sale.

20.1.2 Mens rea

D must intend to remove the article from the building *or* its grounds. Dishonesty is not required but D would not be guilty of an offence if he removed an article in the belief (and clearly the test of D's belief is here subjective) that he had lawful authority or that the person entitled to give consent would have done so. Strictly interpreted, it would be an offence for D to remove a statuette from the house to the garden because he thinks the setting better, provided D does not believe the person entitled to give consent would have done so.

---

[14] In this context 'permanently' means for an indefinite period: *Durkin* [1973] QB 786.

[15] See Griew, *Theft*, para 5.08.

[16] See p 941.

[17] Note that if the owner admits the public to view the building as well as the collection, D may commit the offence by removing anything displayed (including articles forming part of the collection) although the collection is exhibited for commercial purposes. Cf Ormerod and Williams, *Smith's Law of Theft*, Ch 10.

[18] The clause as originally drafted would have excluded not only the case where the public were invited to view the contents for a commercial object, but also where the public were invited to view the building for a commercial object. The latter limitation was removed; cf n 17.

[19] Presumably it is the dominant one that matters.

20.2 Taking conveyances

Because of the ease of tracing intact vehicles via their identification numbers, it is often difficult to establish that D intended permanently to deprive V of his vehicle when taking it.[20] Theft is therefore not an appropriate charge. An example is *Mitchell*,[21] in which D took V's car from her with violence in the course of his attempt to evade capture by the police who were pursuing him. He abandoned the car, intact with hazard lights flashing. There was no theft and no robbery.[22] Since such conduct is not theft, a specific offence criminalizing temporary deprivation of conveyances is necessary.[23] Section 12 of the Theft Act 1968 (as amended) now provides:

(1) Subject to subsections (5) and (6) below, a person shall be guilty of an offence if, without having the consent of the owner or other lawful authority, he takes any conveyance for his own or another's use or, knowing that any conveyance has been taken without such authority, drives it or allows himself to be carried in or on it.

(2) A person guilty of an offence under subsection (1) above shall . . . [be liable on summary conviction to [an unlimited fine], to imprisonment for a term not exceeding six months, or to both].

(3) [Repealed]

(4) If on the trial of an indictment for theft the jury are not satisfied that the accused committed theft, but it is proved that the accused committed an offence under subsection (1) above, the jury may find him guilty of the offence under subsection (1) [and if he is found guilty of it, he shall be liable as he would have been liable under subsection (2) above on summary conviction].

[Subs 4A–C deal with procedural issues for commencement of prosecution]

(5) Subsection (1) above shall not apply in relation to pedal cycles; but, subject to subsection (6) below, a person who, without having the consent of the owner or other lawful authority, takes a pedal cycle for his own or another's use, or rides a pedal cycle knowing it to have been taken without such authority, shall on summary conviction be liable to a fine not exceeding [level 3 on the standard scale].

(6) A person does not commit an offence under this section by anything done in the belief that he has lawful authority to do it or that he would have the owner's consent if the owner knew of his doing it and the circumstances of it.

---

[20] See S White, 'Taking the Joy Out of Joy-Riding' [1980] Crim LR 609; Ormerod and Williams, *Smith's Law of Theft*, Ch 10; Griew, *Theft*, Ch 6; Smith, *Property Offences*, Ch 9. For a practical analysis, see K McCormac (ed), *Wilkinson's Road Traffic Offences* (29th edn, 2019) Ch 15; and for a more broad-ranging socio-legal review of car crime, see C Corbett, *Car Crime* (2003). The CPS has issued guidance on the offence—see www.cps.gov.uk/legal-guidance/theft-act-offences.

[21] [2008] EWCA Crim 850.

[22] cf *Raphael* [2008] EWCA Crim 1014, discussed at p 925, where D took V's car and attempted to sell it back to him. This was theft as D had an intention permanently to deprive V within the extended meaning of s 6 of the Act. In *Vinall* [2011] EWCA Crim 6252, discussed at p 928, D's conviction for robbery was quashed as the judge failed to direct the jury that in order to convict they had to be sure at the time D appropriated V's bicycle, he intended permanently to deprive him of it. The Court of Appeal held that the judge was correct to state that D's later abandonment of the bicycle was evidence from which the jury could infer an intention permanently to deprive, but when the charge is robbery the jury must be directed in unambiguous terms that if the intention only formed at the time of the abandonment D is not guilty. See also *Zerei* [2012] EWCA Crim 1114. This serves to emphasize the importance of charging the appropriate offence.

[23] Technically, charges of theft of the fuel might succeed.

(7) For purposes of this section—

    (a) 'conveyance' means any conveyance constructed or adapted for the carriage of a person or persons whether by land, water or air, except that it does not include a conveyance constructed or adapted for use only under the control of a person not carried in or on it, and 'drive' shall be construed accordingly; and

    (b) 'owner', in relation to a conveyance which is the subject of a hiring agreement or hire-purchase agreement, means the person in possession of the conveyance under that agreement.

By s 37(1) of the Criminal Justice Act 1988, the offence is now triable only summarily.[24] When a jury acquits of theft of a conveyance it may convict of an offence under s 12, in which case the offender is punishable as he would have been on summary conviction.[25] Proceedings under s 12 cannot be commenced after the end of a period of three years from the date on which the offence was committed, and six months after the date on which sufficient evidence to justify the proceedings comes to the knowledge of the prosecutor.[26]

20.2.1 Taking for own or another's use

20.2.1.1 Taking

The offence is committed where D 'takes any conveyance for his own or another's use'. D 'takes' when he (a) assumes possession or control *and* (b) moves the conveyance, or causes it to be moved. Where possession is assumed, abandoned and resumed there is a second taking.[27] It is not enough that D uses the conveyance for some purpose (say to sleep or shelter in it) since he must also take it. The offence can be completed only by some movement, however slight, of the conveyance.[28] The taking must be intentional.[29] In the case of a motor vehicle, the taking will be most frequently accomplished by driving but the taking may be accomplished in some other way, as by pushing or towing or even by removing the conveyance on a transporter. In *Pearce*,[30] D's conviction was upheld when he took an inflatable dinghy and drove off with it on his trailer; the court rejecting an argument that the offence could be committed only where D took the conveyance by moving it in its own medium (ie in this case by sailing it as a boat). The court also held that there was no need for D to have been conveyed *on* the boat.

Although the offence is commonly regarded as one relating to temporary deprivation of use, the requirement of a physical taking demonstrates that the offence does not protect against deprivation generally. Thus, where D intentionally hides V's car keys, depriving V of the use of the vehicle, he does not commit the offence under s 12.[31]

---

[24] Punishable by an unlimited fine, or by six months' imprisonment, or by both. Although triable summarily only, a count under s 12 may be included in an indictment under s 40 of the Criminal Justice Act 1988.

[25] For the position in the magistrates' court, see *R (H) v Liverpool City Youth Court* [2001] Crim LR 487. On the substitution of charges under s 12 when the original allegation is attempted theft, see *DPP v Hammerton* [2009] EWHC 921 (Admin).

[26] Theft Act 1968, s 12(4A), inserted by the Vehicles (Crime) Act 2001, s 37(1).

[27] *DPP v Spriggs* [1994] RTR 1.

[28] *Bogacki* [1973] QB 832. Cf *Miller* [1976] Crim LR 147 (boarding boat anticipating journey but no movement in fact), and *Diggin* (1980) 72 Cr App R 204. Because the offence is now summary only, no attempt charge is available, but the Criminal Attempts Act 1981, s 9, creates a specific offence of interference with a motor vehicle with the intention that an offence under s 12(1) shall be committed.

[29] The offence was not committed where D accidentally put his foot on the accelerator in an automatic car: *Blayney v Knight* [1975] Crim LR 237.

[30] [1973] Crim LR 321.

[31] The actus reus of theft does not, of course, require a physical moving of the vehicle. See also the discussion in relation to criminal damage at p 1098.

20.2.1.2 For his own or another's use

The essence of the offence was thought by the CLRC to be 'stealing a ride'.[32] Strictly, however, D may steal a ride without committing this offence. A hitch-hiker who jumps on to the back of a passing lorry literally steals a ride but does not commit the offence since in no sense has he *taken* the vehicle for his own or another's use. So, too, if D releases the handbrake of a car so that it runs down an incline (without his being on board), or releases a boat from its moorings so that it is carried away by the tide; such conduct would not fall within the section.[33] In neither case is the conveyance taken by D for his own or another's use.

Considering these last two examples, the Court of Appeal in *Bow*[34] expressed the firm view that the reason why D was not guilty of an offence was that although the conveyance had been moved, it would not have been 'used' as a conveyance. In other words, the court thought 'use' means, and means only, use as a conveyance. No doubt in the vast majority of cases D's purpose in taking the conveyance is to transport himself from one place to another, but it is not entirely clear that the offence is, or ought to be, confined to takings with that purpose. It is not clear from the facts of *Pearce* why D took the dinghy but in *Marchant and McCallister*[35] the Court of Appeal assumed that the conviction was based on D's intended use of the dinghy as a conveyance and confirmed that taking a conveyance with intent to use it on some future occasion as a conveyance sufficed.[36] *Bow* suggests, and *Marchant* appears clearly to confirm, that if D in *Pearce* had some use other than as a conveyance in mind (eg to use the dinghy as a paddling pool for his children) he could not be convicted under s 12. *Stokes*[37] is to the same effect. There it was held that D did not commit the offence where he pushed V's car around the corner to make V think it had been stolen.[38]

The courts have interpreted s 12(1) as though the words 'as a conveyance' had been inserted after 'use'. But on the face of the provision 'use' is capable of extending to uses other than use as a conveyance.[39] It should be recalled that this provision was inserted to deal with the problem of temporary deprivations. The mischief aimed at is surely that the use of the conveyance is denied to V and it should not be significant to what use D puts it when he takes it.

Even if use is restricted so that the offence applies only where D's uses it as a conveyance, any such use suffices for the offence. It is enough that D releases a boat from its moorings so that he can be carried downstream in it. So, in *Bow*,[40] where D released the handbrake of V's car and coasted some 200 yards down a narrow road in order to enable him to remove his own obstructed car, it was conceded that no distinction could be drawn between driving the motor and allowing it to freewheel. In that case it was argued that D had not used the car as a conveyance, merely to move it as an obstruction. The court accepted that to push an obstructing vehicle a yard or two to get it out of the way would not involve the use of the vehicle as a conveyance,[41] but once it was proved that the vehicle was necessarily used as a conveyance, the taker cannot claim it was not intended for that use. In that case D did not use V's car in order to convey himself from one end of the lane to the other. It so happened

---

[32] Eighth Report, para 84.

[33] Even though the owner temporarily loses the use of his car or boat and is equally inconvenienced.

[34] (1977) 64 Cr App R 54, [1977] Crim LR 176 and commentary.

[35] (1985) 80 Cr App R 361.

[36] Equally a conditional intent (eg an intent to use should it prove suitable) will suffice.

[37] [1983] RTR 59.

[38] The outcome of the case may have been different had D got into the car and steered it round the corner.

[39] See White [1980] Crim LR 609 at 611.

[40] (1977) 64 Cr App R 54.

[41] In such circumstances D might in any case have lawful authority for the removal, see p 949.

that to remove it as an obstruction required its removal not for two yards but for 200. It is not easy to see why the distance involved should make all that difference if all D is doing is to remove a conveyance as an obstruction.[42]

20.2.1.3 Taking by unauthorized use

The discussion so far has assumed that D is not in possession or control of the conveyance but it may happen that D already has lawful possession or control of the conveyance and the question arises whether D can be said to 'take' it by using it in an unauthorized way. Suppose, for example, that D, authorized to use V's van in the course of V's business, uses the van to take his family to the seaside. It seems clear that under this section he may commit the offence for he now 'takes [the van] for his own . . . use'. D does not have the consent of V for the taking for his, D's, own use. This was the view taken by the Court of Appeal in *McGill*,[43] a case decided under s 217 of the Road Traffic Act 1960. D, given permission to use V's car to drive E to the railway station and on condition that he returned it immediately, subsequently drove it elsewhere and did not return it for some days. D's conviction for taking the car without the consent of the owner, in relation to his use after the trip to the station, was upheld. The same result must follow under s 12 of the Theft Act even though there is no requirement for driving away and where the emphasis is squarely placed on taking 'for his own or another's use'. So, in *McKnight v Davies*,[44] the conviction of a lorry driver was upheld when instead of returning the lorry to the depot at the end of the working day he used it for his own purposes and did not return it until the early hours of the following morning. It would seem that an unauthorized use in terms of either the destination involved or time of taking[45] or duration will constitute the offence. Equally, it has been held that the offence is committed where D allows some third party to drive the vehicle, being aware that the owner would not have consented to that person driving.[46]

McGill, *McKnight v Davies* and *McMinn* were cases where the use by D was plainly outside the scope of the terms of the authorisation so there was no difficulty in finding that D took it for his own use. It is thought, however, that not every deviation by D would constitute a taking for his own use. For the offence to be committed there must be a use that is sufficiently at variance with the terms of the contract to demonstrate that D has replaced use on behalf of another by use on his own behalf.[47] Note that there is an exception in the case of a hirer under a hire-purchase agreement. His unauthorized use cannot amount to an offence because by s 12(7) he is treated as owner for the purposes of the section.

20.2.1.4 Without owner's consent or lawful authority

The ordinary run of cases where D takes V's vehicle without reference to V presents no problem. It follows from the discussion in the previous paragraph that where D has obtained V's permission to use the vehicle for a particular purpose and for a given time, D may be

---

[42] In *Bow*, D was probably engaged in a poaching expedition and V's car had been deliberately placed to block D's route of exit. But if D finds a vehicle blocking the highway he is presumably entitled to remove it whether he is on his way to or from a crime. The CPS legal guidance simply states that it is 'not appropriate' to charge a defendant with a s 12 offence 'when a vehicle has been moved only a short distance because it was causing an obstruction'. Neither 'moved' nor 'short distance' are defined. See www.cps.gov.uk/legal-guidance/theft-act-offences.

[43] [1970] RTR 209.   [44] [1974] RTR 4.   [45] *Wibberley* [1966] 2 QB 214.

[46] *McMinn v McMinn* [2006] 3 All ER 87 at 93, applying *McKnight*.

[47] 'Not every brief, unauthorised diversion from his proper route by an employee in the course of his working day will necessarily involve a "taking" of the vehicle for his own use', *McKnight v Davies* [1974] RTR 4 at 8 per Lord Widgery CJ. See also *Wibberley* [1966] 2 QB 214; *Phipps* and *McGill* [1970] RTR 209. In determining whether an employee has taken his employer's vehicle, it would seem proper to consider whether for civil purposes D is acting in the course of his employment.

convicted of the offence if he uses it beyond that time for a different purpose: *McGill*.[48] There is no difficulty in such a case in saying that D has taken the vehicle for his own use, and that particular use is clearly one to which V has not consented.

20.2.1.5 Consent by fraud

McGill is a clear case. Suppose, however, that D made some false representation to induce V to allow him to take the car. The falsity might relate to: (a) some attribute of D (eg his being licensed to drive); (b) some fundamental issue such as D's identity; or (c) D's purpose in taking the vehicle.[49]

Taking the first of these issues, what if D had falsely represented that he was licensed to drive in order to borrow V's car for the trip to the station? There is perhaps no compelling reason why D should not be guilty of the offence since he knows perfectly well that V has 'consented' only because he has been misled. But on a strict interpretation of the section all that is required is that V should have consented to D taking the car for the trip to the station (the taking for D's own use) and to this V may be said to have consented even though he would never have consented had he known that D was unlicensed. The point arose in *Whittaker v Campbell*.[50] D and E required a vehicle to transport goods but D was not licensed to drive and E had only a provisional licence. Somehow they came into possession of T's driving licence and D, representing himself as T, hired a vehicle from V. Their convictions for taking a vehicle without consent were quashed. The court thought that while there might be a taking without consent where the owner is by force compelled to part with possession,[51] where he is induced to do so by fraud it could not be said 'in commonsense terms' that he had not consented to the taking. Distinguishing between agreements induced by force and fraud in this manner is at odds with the general approach of the criminal law and undermines the principle that consent necessarily involves an agreement made freely, and which is based on adequate, accurate information. On the other hand, the broad common-sense approach to consent is less problematic in this context given the mischief at which the section is aimed.

The court in *Whitaker v Campbell* also considered the second issue—whether the offence would be committed where the fraud is such as to induce what in contract law amounts to a 'fundamental mistake'. The court thought that it would not make sense, having regard to the mischief at which the offence was aimed, to have D's liability turn upon whether the transaction was voidable for fraud or void for mistake. That distinction is one that presents complexity in civil law. Moreover, it does not sit easily with the criminal law's approach to the concept of consent. Suppose that D telephones V and impersonates V's brother, thereby inducing V to agree the loan of his car to his brother and to leave the keys in an accessible spot while V is out of town. If D then avails himself of this trick to take possession of the car while V is away, it would be an astonishing conclusion to say that V had consented to D taking his car. It is submitted that the issue of consent by fraud under s 12 deserves reconsideration by the courts.[52]

As for the third problem of falsity, in *Whittaker v Campbell* there was no suggestion of any misrepresentation as to the use to which D and E proposed to put the vehicle and their

---

[48] [1970] RTR 209, n 43.

[49] The CPS legal guidance implies that *any* case in which the taking was obtained by fraud would not be appropriate for a charge under s 12—see www.cps.gov.uk/legal-guidance/theft-act-offences.

[50] [1984] QB 318.   [51] See *Hogdan* [1962] Crim LR 563.

[52] cf Smith, *Property Offences*, paras 9–23.

actual use was within the terms of the hire.[53] Suppose, however, that D obtains possession of the conveyance by describing to V a use that he knows V will consent to while secretly proposing to use the vehicle for a use to which he knows V would not consent. D might, for example, secure V's consent to the use of his vehicle for the transportation of goods from Leeds to London knowing that V would not consent had he known that the goods were stolen. The case is essentially indistinguishable from *Whittaker v Campbell*. V has consented to the use of his vehicle for that journey though he would not have agreed to incur criminal liability as a handler of stolen goods.

Suppose, though, that D's *purpose* is not to drive to London and back but to take the vehicle on a fortnight's holiday to the south of France. The point arose in *Peart*.[54] D persuaded V to lend him a van by pretending that he needed it for an urgent appointment in Alnwick and that he would return it by 7.30 pm. In fact, D wanted the van for a journey to Burnley where he was found with the van by the police at 9 pm, and he knew all along that V would not have consented to this use. It was held, quashing D's conviction, that V's consent was not vitiated by the deception since V had merely been deceived as to *the purpose* for which the van was to be used. Reliance was placed on this decision by the court in *Whittaker v Campbell*.

But there are difficulties with *Peart*. By reason of the direction given to the jury by the trial judge, the Court of Appeal had to consider the position at the time when the van was borrowed in the afternoon:

> There was no issue left to [the jury] whether, in this particular case, there could have been a fresh taking . . . at some time after it was originally taken away at 2.30 pm. The consent which has to be considered is thus a consent at the time of taking possession of the van with licence to drive and use it.[55]

It seems, then, that even if he did not commit an offence at the time of the taking he would, like the defendants in *McGill* and *McKnight v Davies*,[56] have done so as soon as he departed from the Alnwick road and set course for Burnley.

There is, however, a difference. In *McGill* and *McKnight v Davies*, there was no evidence that the defendants had the unauthorized use in mind when they obtained possession. In *Peart*, in contrast, that could be proved—D frankly admitted it—and it is submitted this case also ought to be reconsidered. Given the use for a journey to which V had consented, D *took* it for a journey for which no consent was given. As a practical matter of evidence, it will often be necessary to prove a departure from the stated use in order to prove that D intended to use the vehicle in other than the authorized way, but this cannot affect the substantive criminal law.

20.2.1.6 Lawful authority

D commits no offence where he takes a vehicle, even without the consent of the owner, when acting under 'other lawful authority'. This is appropriate to cover the growing number of cases where local authorities or the police are authorized under various statutory powers to

---

[53] In *Singh v Rathour (Northern Star Insurance Co Ltd, third party)* [1988] 2 All ER 16, a civil case where the issue was whether D was insured under his policy which covered him when driving any vehicle 'provided he had the consent of the owner', it was held that D did not have the consent of the owner where he was aware that the consent given did not extend to the use to which he put the vehicle. See J Birds, 'Consent of the Owner under a Motor Policy' [1998] JBL 421.

[54] [1970] 2 QB 672.

[55] [1970] 2 All ER 823 at 824. It seems surprising that the proviso which was then available to the Court of Appeal was not applied.

[56] See p 947.

remove vehicles. No doubt D would be acting lawfully in moving V's vehicle a few yards so that he can obtain access to the highway for his own vehicle, even though he may know that V does not consent to the removal.[57]

It may fairly be assumed that general defences such as self-defence and duress are available on charges for this offence.

20.2.1.7 Conveyance

Section 12(7) provides:

For purposes of this section—

> (a) 'conveyance' means any conveyance constructed or adapted for the carriage of a person or persons whether by land, water or air, except that it does not include a conveyance constructed or adapted for use only under the control of a person not carried in or on it, and 'drive' shall be construed accordingly.

'Conveyance' has been interpreted to mean a mechanical contrivance of some kind. While it includes conveyances such as cars and motorcycles, it does not include horses;[58] horses are clearly not constructed, though they may be suitable for the carriage of persons, and the argument that they might be 'adapted' by the use of halter and bridle was rejected. Because the essence of the offence was thought to be stealing a ride,[59] conveyance is defined, in effect, to exclude conveyances that are not meant for riding.[60] Thus, though it would be an offence to take an aircraft, hovercraft or railway engine, it is not an offence within this section to take, for example, a lawnmower which, though power-driven, is operated by a person who is not carried in or on it.[61]

20.2.2 Mens rea

The taking must be intentional. It is not enough that the vehicle is accidentally moved.[62]

Section 12(6) provides that a person does not commit an offence by anything done in the belief that he has lawful authority to do it or that the owner would have consented. The test of belief appears to be subjective. If D honestly believes that V has consented to his use of V's car, it is not relevant to inquire whether V did in fact consent or whether V would have consented had he known of the circumstances—for example, that D was uninsured,[63] or even that D was unlicensed to drive. If D takes a vehicle 'without having the consent of the owner' and does not believe that the owner would have consented had he known of the taking, he may be convicted though the owner subsequently says that he would have consented;[64] the offence is constituted not by taking a conveyance without the owner's consent, but in taking it without *having* the consent of the owner.

---

[57] But see *Bow* (1977) 64 Cr App R 54, n 34.

[58] *Neal v Gribble* (1978) 68 Cr App R 9.

[59] cf Eighth Report, para 84. Earlier (para 82) the Committee seemed to have viewed the mischief of the offence as the danger, loss and inconvenience which often result from it. See HL, 12 Mar 1968, vol 290, col 141 (Lord Stonham).

[60] But on this see Ch 32.

[61] Recently, concern has arisen over electric mobility scooters and whether these can be 'stolen' or taken without the owner's consent. Insurance companies have been more concerned about the theft of the very expensive batteries on which they run.

[62] *Blayney v Knight* (1974) 60 Cr App R 269.   [63] *Clotworthy* [1981] RTR 477.

[64] *Ambler* [1979] RTR 217

If D takes a conveyance not caring whether the owner would or would not have consented, it would seem that he may be convicted. For in such a case he does not *believe* that the owner would have consented.[65]

Taking a conveyance has been held to be a crime of basic intent so that evidence of intoxication is not relevant as tending to show that D lacked mens rea.[66] Arguably, where D's belief as to the consent of the owner is based on a mistake induced by voluntary intoxication he can rely on that mistake.[67]

20.2.3 Driving or being carried

Section 12 creates a second version of the offence to deal with the person who allows himself to be carried or who himself drives a vehicle which has already been taken, but who might not be caught by ordinary principles of accessorial liability since he might not have been a party to the taking acting with the necessary intent.

If, when D allows himself to be carried, he is aiding and abetting the taking of the conveyance by E, he may be convicted of the primary offence as a secondary party. But if the 'taking' has come to an end, the primary offence has ceased and it is no longer possible to aid and abet it. In such a case, the second version of the offence is applicable being based on D 'allowing' himself to be carried. 'Allow' is probably a word of wider ambit than 'aid, abet, counsel or procure'. If D allows himself to be driven by a person who, as he knows, would drive the car whether D was there or not, it will not necessarily be proved that he assisted or encouraged, or intended to assist or encourage, the driver.[68]

Where E takes a conveyance without consent or other lawful authority, it is an offence for D, knowing the conveyance has been so taken, to drive it or allow himself to be carried in or on it. A hitch-hiker would therefore not be guilty of an offence where, unknown to him, the driver is using his employer's van, contrary to the employer's instructions, to go to Blackpool for the day. If the driver tells the hitch-hiker that he is using the van in that unauthorized way then the hitch-hiker will be liable if he allows himself to be carried further.[69]

20.2.3.1 Carried

D's mere presence in or on the conveyance, knowing that it has been taken without consent or authority, does not suffice unless he allows himself to be 'carried' in or on it and this requires some movement of the conveyance.[70]

20.2.3.2 Driving

In *DPP v Alderton*,[71] merely sitting in the car with the engine on, gear engaged and the wheels spinning was held to be 'driving'. In *Planton v DPP*,[72] D stopped his vehicle on a causeway, awaiting an opportunity to cross at low tide. D claimed he was not 'driving' for the purposes of a drink-driving offence since his vehicle was not moving. The Divisional

---

[65] cf the discussion of recklessness, Ch 3.

[66] *MacPherson* [1973] RTR 157; *Gannon* (1988) 87 Cr App R 254. G Williams is heavily critical of *Gannon*, 'Two Nocturnal Blunders' (1990) 140 NLJ 1564. For a contrary view, see White [1980] Crim LR 609.

[67] By analogy with the decision in *Jaggard v Dickinson* [1981] QB 527, decided under s 5(2) of the Criminal Damage Act 1971 which uses similar terms. See Griew, *Theft*, para 6.20.

[68] cf Ch 6.

[69] *Boldizsar v Knight* [1980] Crim LR 653. For more detailed analysis, see Ormerod and Williams, *Smith's Law of Theft*, paras 8–13. There are problems of proof where the prosecution seek to rely on D informing E that the vehicle has been taken: *Francis* [1982] Crim LR 694.

[70] *Miller* [1976] Crim LR 147; *Diggin* (1980) 72 Cr App R 204.   [71] [2004] RTR 367.

[72] [2001] EWHC 450 (Admin).

Court held that he was driving: a driver who had stopped at traffic lights was in a similar position but was still driving. It seems to be a question of fact and degree whether a cessation of movement has been so long that it could not reasonably be said that a person was still driving.

20.2.3.3 Mens rea

It must be proved that D *knew* the conveyance had been taken without authority when he drove it or allowed himself to be carried in or on it as the case may be. The vehicle must actually have been taken; one cannot know a thing to be so unless it is so.[73] 'Wilful blindness' may be enough, as in the case of other statutes.[74] Such a state of mind is dangerously close to that of belief that the conveyance had been so taken.[75] D would be wilfully blind where he thinks it quite possible that E might have taken the vehicle without authority but makes no inquiries to ascertain whether this is so or not. It could happen that E believes he has authority to take the conveyance but D knows that E has not. In such a case D would be guilty of an offence since he knows it was taken without authority. And no doubt D knows the conveyance has been taken without authority, and may be convicted under this provision,[76] though he knows that E has in fact stolen the conveyance.[77]

20.2.4 Pedal cycles

Section 12(5) creates an offence of taking pedal cycles,[78] which has broadly similar elements to the offence under s 12(1). A small difference is that the offence under s 12(5) is not committed by one who allows himself to be carried on the cycle knowing that it has been taken without authority. The offence is summary only.[79]

20.3 Aggravated vehicle-taking

The so-called 'joyrider' (or 'twocker') under s 12 is liable to relatively limited punishments. He is additionally liable for any offence involved in taking the vehicle (most obviously criminal damage caused in gaining access to the conveyance and in interfering with the locks and the electrical ignition systems in order to get it started) and the driver, whether or not he is the original taker, is liable for any offence committed whilst driving the vehicle (eg driving whilst uninsured, careless driving, dangerous driving). And, of course, a person who allows himself to be carried in or on a conveyance may be liable as a secondary party to these further offences under the principles which govern aiding and abetting or under the version of the s 12 offence discussed earlier.[80]

It might be thought therefore that s 12 was entirely adequate to deal with the taker, those who subsequently drive the taken conveyance and those who allow themselves to be carried in or on it. In the normal case, the unlimited fine and/or six months' imprisonment would seem adequate. In the abnormal case where the driver drives dangerously, or kills whilst

---

[73] See the discussion of the House of Lords of the concept of knowledge in *Saik* [2006] UKHL 18.
[74] Edwards, *Mens Rea*, 202–5; Williams, CLGP, 159.
[75] See s 22(1).
[76] cf *Tolley v Giddings* [1964] 2 QB 354.
[77] Where E's conviction is proved by certificate under s 74 of PACE, and D was in the vehicle at the time of the taking to which E's conviction relates, that is prima facie evidence of E's guilt, but it must also be shown that D *knew* it was taken: *DPP v Parker* [2006] EWHC 1270 (Admin).
[78] It is a moot point whether this extends to electronically powered cycles or stand-on scooters.
[79] Thus there can be no attempt charge.   [80] See Ch 6.

driving dangerously or carelessly, additional charges can be added for that and again the punishment (imprisonment in this case) would seem to be adequate. But in the early 1990s the taking of motor vehicles increased to an extent that it was described as epidemic. As the activity increased, so did the risks. Youngsters (usually male) used the vehicles they had taken to demonstrate their driving 'skills' or become involved in high-speed chases when pursued by the police.[81] The hazards of either are obvious. Even in the face of this 'epidemic', it might be argued that s 12 and the range of driving offences and ordinary criminal charges for damage and injury inflicted were adequate in the sense that the activity would always be capable of being punished and the penalties provided seemed appropriate.[82]

There was an additional problem. In many cases, the taking is performed by a group, and the vehicle is damaged or injury inflicted but it is difficult to prove whether it was D or E or F who damaged the vehicle or caused the injury. One or more of them is able to claim that the damage was done before he joined the criminal venture. And where, as not infrequently happens, the vehicle is found burned out, all three would say that this must have been done by someone else after they had abandoned the vehicle.

It was to deal with all of these problems, and what was seen as a rapidly growing social menace, that s 12A of the Theft Act 1968 was inserted by the Aggravated Vehicle-Taking Act 1992.[83] It provides:

(1) Subject to subsection (3) below, a person is guilty of aggravated taking of a vehicle if—

    (a) he commits an offence under section 12 (1) above (in this section referred to as a 'basic offence') in relation to a mechanically propelled vehicle; and

    (b) it is proved that, at any time after the vehicle was unlawfully taken (whether by him or another) and before it was recovered, the vehicle was driven, or injury or damage was caused, in one or more of the circumstances set out in paragraphs (a) to (d) of subsection (2) below.

(2) The circumstances referred to in subsection (1)(b) above are—

    (a) that the vehicle was driven dangerously[84] on a road or other public place;

    (b) that, owing to the driving of the vehicle, an accident occurred by which injury was caused to any person;

    (c) that, owing to the driving of the vehicle, an accident occurred by which damage was caused to any property, other than the vehicle;

    (d) that damage was caused to the vehicle.

(3) A person is not guilty of an offence under this section if he proves that, as regards any such proven driving, injury or damage as is referred to in subsection (1)(b) above, either—

    (a) the driving, accident or damage referred to in subsection (2) above occurred before he committed the basic offence; or

    (b) he was neither in nor on nor in the immediate vicinity of the vehicle when that driving, accident or damage occurred.

---

[81] See B Rix, D Walker and R Brown, *A Study of Deaths and Serious Injuries Resulting from Police Vehicle Accidents* (1997) HORS, noting that 27 per cent of those in police vehicle accidents were in stolen cars at the time.

[82] It is not suggested that the answer or solution lies in the penalty, merely that the penalty is adequate in relation to the crime. The answer lies in foolproof (or is it expert-proof?) immobilizing devices.

[83] See JN Spencer, 'The Aggravated Vehicle Taking Act 1992' [1992] Crim LR 69.

[84] In *Tame* [2012] EWCA Crim 573, D appealed his conviction for aggravated vehicle-taking on the ground that the judge ought to have directed the jury as to what was meant by 'dangerously'. The Court of Appeal accepted that a direction ought to have been given, but held that the omission did not render the conviction unsafe, as there was no factual dispute about the nature of D's driving.

(4) A person guilty of an offence under this section shall be liable on conviction on indictment to imprisonment for a term not exceeding two years or, if it is proved that, in circumstances falling within subsection (2)(b) above, the accident caused the death of the person concerned, fourteen years.[85]

(5) If a person who is charged with an offence under this section is found not guilty of that offence but it is proved that he committed a basic offence, he may be convicted of the basic offence.

Since there is a different maximum sentence for those cases in which death results, there are technically two offences created by the section.[86]

The prosecution must first prove that D has committed the basic offence under s 12(1) of the 1968 Act as described earlier in relation to a mechanically propelled vehicle—the offence does not apply to conveyances generally.

Secondly, the prosecution must prove that at any time after the vehicle was unlawfully taken (proof of the identity of the taker is not required) and before it was recovered (ie restored to the owner or other lawful custody: s 12A(8)), the vehicle was driven or injury or damage was caused in one or more of the circumstances specified in s 12A(2). Initially, the provision was interpreted as requiring no proof of fault on the part of D, or D and others involved in the enterprise—liability was strict if injury to the person or damage to property was owing to the driving,[87] or if damage was caused to the vehicle taken, whether by driving or not.[88] On that interpretation, D's driving might be impeccable, but he would not escape liability if the injury, damage or death arose.[89] Moreover, each of the participants in the enterprise commits the offence though they were not driving the vehicle. In *Taylor*,[90] a seven-member Supreme Court rejected that strict liability interpretation. D was charged with s 12A (having taken a work vehicle without consent) and with causing the death of a scooter rider while driving uninsured contrary to s 3ZB of the Road Traffic Act 1988. D was later found to have been over the drink-drive limit and uninsured at the time of the accident. At trial the Crown accepted that D's driving did not involve any fault. In light of the decision of the Supreme Court in *Hughes*,[91] the judge held that fault had to be proved in relation to the accident on the aggravated vehicle-taking count. The Crown appealed relying on *Marsh*.[92] The Supreme Court, following *Hughes*, held that no offence contrary to s 12A(1) and (2)(b) of the 1968 Act is committed when, following the basic offence and before recovery of the vehicle, the defendant drove the vehicle and, without fault in the manner of his driving, the vehicle was involved in an accident which caused injury to a person. D was not criminally responsible for the death where his own driving had been completely faultless. The approach to causation adopted in *Hughes* in the context of the offence of 'causing the death of another person by driving a motor vehicle on a road' (Road Traffic

---

85 Criminal Justice Act 2003, s 285(1).

86 They should therefore be charged separately: *Courtie* [1984] AC 463; *Sherwood* [1995] RTR 60.

87 The Court of Appeal in *Marsh* [1997] 1 Cr App R 67 held that the words 'owing to the driving of the vehicle' were plain and simple and no gloss ought to be provided by referring the jury to the manner of the driving. See [1997] Crim LR 205 and comment. If D has used the car as a weapon, he will still be caught by the section: 'accident' includes deliberate causing of injury: *B* [2005] 1 Cr App R 140.

88 *Dawes v DPP* [1995] 1 Cr App R 65 at 72, 73.

89 See eg *Clifford* [2007] EWCA Crim 2442.

90 [2016] UKSC 5. See K Laird, 'The Decline of Criminal Law Causation Without Limits' (2016) 132 LQR 566.

91 [2013] UKSC 56. See Ch 32.   92 [1997] 1 Cr App R 67.

Act 1988, s 3ZB) applied equally to the offence of aggravated vehicle-taking s 12A. D would be liable if there was:

at least some act or omission in the control of the car which involved some element of fault, whether amounting to careless/inconsiderate driving or not, and which contributed in some more than minimal way to the death.[93]

The offence is unusually broad in the way it approaches liability of those involved in the joint venture. So if D and E commit the basic offence (s 12), each of them is liable if either one of them causes injury or damage when driving the vehicle. More remarkably, if during the enterprise D chooses to damage the vehicle by slashing the seats, E commits the offence under s 12A though he does not assist or encourage D in slashing the seats or even if E tries to dissuade D from so doing.[94] This highlights the draconian nature of the provision. Even if E is no longer in the vehicle—he may, for example, be walking away from it when D decides to set fire to it[95]—E is liable provided he is still 'in the immediate vicinity' of the vehicle. The offence creates guilt by association, but also guilt by approximation.

Section 12A(3) deals with the problem of proof identified above. The prosecution may prove, or D may admit, that D committed the basic offence but D may claim that he had left the enterprise before the injury or damage was done or that he joined the enterprise after the injury or damage had been done. In such circumstances, it is for D to prove on the balance of probability that the dangerous driving or the accident or the damage took place before he committed the basic offence; or that, having committed the basic offence, he was no longer in, nor on, nor in the immediate vicinity of the vehicle when one of those events took place.

The activity known as 'carjacking'—where D causes V to stop his car and D then forcibly ejects V from the car and drives V's vehicle away—is more appropriately prosecuted by offences of theft, robbery, offences against the person, etc. In particular, in cases where V is caused to stop by D's minor collision with V's vehicle, aggravated vehicle-taking will not be a suitable charge because the damage will have occurred prior to the taking.

It is unclear whether an attempt to commit aggravated vehicle-taking is an offence. The s 12A offence requires proof of the basic offence under s 12 which is triable summarily only (and therefore cannot be the subject of an attempt charge), but the s 12A offence itself is triable either way. It is submitted that in an appropriate case a charge of attempt would be available, as where D is apprehended trying to break into a high-powered vehicle and admits that his intention was to take it for an evening's 'racing' against his friend's car.

---

[93] At [32] per Lord Sumption.

[94] 'A passenger may be liable even though the passenger has protested at the driving which has caused damage to the vehicle': *Dawes v DPP* [1995] 1 Cr App R 65 at 72 per Kennedy LJ. See also *Wiggins* [2001] RTR 37 on the sentencing implications in such cases.

[95] Or allow it to roll downhill causing damage to property. See *DPP v Hughes* [2010] EWHC 515 (Admin).

21

Making off without payment

21.1 Making off under the Theft Act 1978

By s 3[1] of the Theft Act 1978 as amended:

(1) Subject to subsection (3) below, a person who, knowing that payment on the spot for any goods supplied or service done is required or expected from him, dishonestly makes off without having paid as required or expected and with intent to avoid payment of the amount due shall be guilty of an offence.

(2) For purposes of this section 'payment on the spot' includes payment at the time of collecting goods on which work has been done or in respect of which service has been provided.

(3) Subsection (1) above shall not apply where the supply of the goods or the doing of the service is contrary to law, or where the service done is such that payment is not legally enforceable.[2]

By s 4 the offence, which is triable either way, is punishable on summary conviction by imprisonment and/or an unlimited fine, and on indictment by imprisonment for a term not exceeding two years and/or a fine.

This offence aims to deal in a simple and straightforward way with a person who having consumed a meal in a restaurant, or filled the tank of the car with fuel, or reached their destination in a taxi, leaves without paying. Although factually simple, difficulties arise in prosecuting such cases as theft.[3] There are no such difficulties under s 3. Under s 3, there is no requirement that D's conduct amounts to theft or fraud or that he has practised any deception at all. There is no requirement to prove that D was dishonest when he ordered the meal or began to fill his car; it is sufficient if the dishonesty occurs at the point of making off.

The offence may have been rendered redundant in many situations by the Fraud Act 2006. Before that Act, the old deception offences applied and D could only be liable for one of those if his deception occurred *before* the relevant property passed to him (or the service was provided etc depending on which type of deception offence was charged). In contrast, under s 2 of the Fraud Act 2006, D may be liable even if he dishonestly makes a false representation

---

[1] See generally Ormerod and Williams, *Smith's Law of Theft*, Ch 6; Griew, *Theft*, Ch 13; Smith, *Property Offences*, Ch 20; JR Spencer, 'The Theft Act 1978' [1979] Crim LR 24, 35; G Syrota, 'Annotations to Theft Act 1978' in *Current Law Statutes* 1978 and 'The Theft Act 1978' (1979) 42 MLR 301, 304.

[2] Section 3(4) was repealed by the Serious Organised Crime and Police Act 2005, Sch 17, Part 2, para 1.

[3] See eg *DPP v Ray* [1974] AC 370, p 982; *Edwards v Ddin* [1976] 1 WLR 942.

after the entire proprietary interest has passed to him, provided that there is an intention to make a gain or cause a loss thereby. It follows that if, after D has transferred fuel to the tank in his vehicle and the entire proprietary interest in the fuel has passed to him, he then falsely represents to V (the cashier) that it will be paid for by D's firm, D commits fraud under s 2.[4] A prosecution under s 3 of the 1978 Act may nevertheless be preferable because it describes precisely what D did, and it does not involve proof of a false representation. Moreover, in some cases s 3 of the 1978 Act will be the necessary charge because the fraud offence is limited to cases of intending to gain or cause loss in terms of *property*.[5]

The s 3 offence creates an exception to the general principle that it is not an offence dishonestly to avoid the payment of a debt.[6] This might be thought to pose a potential problem of overcriminalizing[7] and has predictably generated academic interest. Green suggests that there are two ways of reconciling the making off offence with the general principle that it is not an offence to avoid payment of a debt. The first is to presume that D never intended to pay for the goods or services in question. The second approach is the one adopted in *DPP v Ray*,[8] namely that D *at some point* formed the intention never to pay for the goods or services. Green rejects these two theories as being artificial and suggests that the individual who falsely represents that he intends to pay is treated less harshly than he ought to be (had he been charged with fraud), while the individual who only formed the intention never to pay at some later point is treated more harshly than he deserves. It is the difficulty of recognizing into which category a given case falls that explains the existence of the offence, which he argues represents a compromise.

In practical terms, the offence creates a desirable exception to the general principle. A dishonest debtor who can be traced can be coerced into payment via civil remedies without resort to criminal sanctions. In contrast, where someone makes off from the point of payment the person becomes difficult, if not impossible, to trace. Enforcement can usually only occur on the spot.[9]

21.1.1 Actus reus

21.1.1.1 Makes off

The term 'makes off' might be thought to have a pejorative connotation implying some requirement of stealth in the manner of the making off. Certainly, the offence extends to such cases (the diner who waits until the manager leaves the room or exits via the cloakroom window) but it cannot be confined to such cases. A diner who brazenly walks out of the restaurant after finishing his pudding is properly said to make off though his act is done openly and without stealth; so, too, a heavyweight boxer whose departure cannot be prevented by a timorous restaurant owner.[10]

'Makes off' appears to mean simply that D leaves one place (the place where the payment is required) for another place. The offence does not necessarily require that D should have

---

[4] cf under the old law *Collis-Smith* [1971] Crim LR 716, CA.   [5] See p 970.

[6] See further GH Treitel, 'Contract and Crime' in *Crime, Proof and Punishment*, 89.

[7] See Green, *13 Ways*, 89–90. One could also plausibly argue that the offence is not a compromise but simply reflects the fact that English law does not recognize the moral distinction between D who never intended to pay and D who only formed the intention later on.

[8] [1974] AC 370.

[9] Hence originally by s 3(4) a power of arrest was conferred which was necessary since the offence carries only a maximum two-year sentence and was not, before the Serious Organised Crime and Police Act 2005, automatically arrestable.

[10] See F Bennion, 'Letter to the Editor' [1980] Crim LR 670.

'made off' from V's premises. The spot from which D makes off is simply the place where payment is required[11] and this may be a food stall or an ice-cream van on the highway. In the case of a taxi ride, it will be the agreed destination.[12] If D has not left the first place he has not made off, but if he is in the process of leaving there may be an attempt.[13] Presumably, this element of the actus reus continues for such time as D can be said to be in the process of 'making off'.[14]

If D leaves with V's consent it may be more difficult to say that D has made off. Suppose that D, having determined never to pay, gives his correct name and address to V and is allowed to go. It would be a strained reading of the section to say that D had made off; D has left without paying but the offence requires something more than that. A more difficult case is that where E, who also intends never to pay, gives a false name and address to V and is allowed to go. The two cases differ in that D can be traced and coerced into payment under the civil law while E cannot be traced at all. Spencer[15] argues that the difference between these cases is material. The mischief aimed at by this section, he argues, is the customer who cannot be traced.[16]

There is force in Spencer's argument that the applicability of the offence turns on the traceability of the defendant, but is not easy to square with the language of s 3. It can lead to some illogical results. For example, assume that F is V's best customer of many years' standing. One day F determines not to pay and decamps from the premises via the toilet window. All the elements of the offence appear to be present unless it is to be said that F did not make off. It may puzzle us all to wonder why F should have thought that he could get away with his conduct but he seems clearly to have made off even though he is clearly traceable by the owner and he knows that at the time of leaving. A customer using a wheelchair would surely make off if he decamps without paying though he does not at all fancy his chances of outpacing the restaurateur.[17] If the untraceability of D was the touchstone of the offence, it is arguable that the offence would then fail to protect the proprietor (eg the restaurant owner) who knows who D is, but is unlikely to pursue D's small debt via the civil courts.[18] The CLRC[19] certainly regarded the purpose of the offence as to protect legitimate business.

Section 3 does not, on a natural interpretation, mean that D does not make off if he gives a correct identification but that E does make off if he gives a false one. Suppose in the latter case that V orders a taxi for E and bids him a cheery farewell from the hotel lobby. Can it really be said that E has made off?[20]

---

[11] Payment may be legitimately required at more than one spot: *Moberly v Allsop* [1992] 156 JP 514. See also *Aziz* [1993] Crim LR 708.

[12] Although not necessarily at the moment the taxi arrives at its destination. If V, the taxi driver, permits D to leave the taxi with the purpose of getting money to pay the fare, the time at which payment is expected will be deferred. See *Morris* [2013] EWCA Crim, [2013]. The *ex turpi causa* doctrine prevents D from recovering damages where the cab driver injures him in attempts to prevent the making off: *Beaumont v Ferrer* [2016] EWCA Civ 768 (those engaged in the commission of a crime should not be able to recover for the consequences of their criminal conduct).

[13] *Brooks and Brooks* (1982) 76 Cr App R 66; making off, said the court, 'may be an exercise accompanied by the sound of trumpets or a silent stealing away after the folding of tents'.

[14] This was important for determining the lawfulness of arrests: *Drameh* [1983] Crim LR 322.

[15] [1983] Crim LR 573.

[16] He supported this argument by the fact that, as originally enacted, V had a power of arrest; it would be highly undesirable if V could arrest a customer of whose identity he is aware, that power being required for the unidentifiable defendant.

[17] For further views on this difficult aspect of the offence, see Williams, TBCL, 878; F Bennion, Letter, 'The Drafting of Section 3 of the Theft Act 1978' [1980] Crim LR 670 and Letters [1983] Crim LR 205, 574; Griew, *Theft*, paras 13–16.

[18] See Griew, paras 13–16.   [19] Thirteenth Report (1977) Cmnd 6733, para 19.

[20] cf *Hammond* [1982] Crim LR 611, n 32.

If, however, V permits D to leave the spot where payment is required for a purely tempo-rary purpose (eg to answer a telephone call or to collect his wallet from his overcoat which he has deposited in the cloakroom) expecting him to return to settle up, it is submitted that D commits the offence if he then decamps. In such cases V has not consented to D leaving without paying; quite the contrary, in the latter example he has consented to D taking steps to facilitate payment. So where V, a taxi driver, permits D to leave so that D, as he claims, may go into his house to get the fare it would appear that D, if he then runs off, has made off within the meaning of this section.[21]

21.1.1.2 Goods supplied or service done

The offence requires that the goods[22] be *supplied* or that a service be *done*. Most obviously, goods are supplied where V delivers them to D but the offence cannot be limited only to cases of delivery by V. Petrol is clearly supplied to D at a self-service filling station though D supplies himself and, similarly, goods taken by D from the shelves in a supermarket are supplied.[23] 'Supplied' in this context suggests goods proffered by V and accordingly taken by D. Hence, it would not be an offence under this section, though it may be theft, for D to take goods in a shop which is not self-service; such goods are not proffered until tendered by V or his assistant. It is submitted that goods may be supplied for the purpose of s 3 even though D has a dishonest intent from the outset and therefore steals the goods. It can hardly have been intended that theft and making off should be mutually exclusive since the effect of that would create difficulties for prosecutors.

Where 'service' is concerned, the service must be 'done'. An obvious example of a service done is the provision of hotel accommodation, or a meal in a restaurant, but it will also apply to the collection of goods, such as clothes, shoes or cars, on which work (repair, etc) has been done. A service may be done (as goods may be supplied) though nothing is physically done by V other than proffering the service of which D takes advantage, as where D is permitted to park his car on V's parking lot.

There is no definition of 'service' in s 3. 'Service' is not the same as the extended meaning of 'services' which was contained in s 1 of the 1978 Act.[24]

21.1.1.3 Unenforceable debts

The offence under s 3, unlike the repealed offence under s 1 of the 1978 Act, cannot be com-mitted where the supply of the goods or the doing of the service is contrary to law; or where the service done is such that payment is not legally enforceable.[25] Thus, it is no offence for D to make off from a brothel without paying.

Whether a supply of goods or services is contrary to law or whether payment for a service is not legally enforceable involves a consideration of the general law of contract and can-not be detailed here.[26] But the distinction that s 3 makes may be illustrated by reference

---

[21] This approach was approved in *Morris* [2013] EWCA Crim 436. The court may have gone further by stat-ing that D simply failing to return is sufficient.

[22] As defined in s 34 of the 1968 Act, applicable to the 1978 Act by s 5(2).

[23] *Contra* ATH Smith, 'Shoplifting and the Theft Acts' [1981] Crim LR 586. Cf Griew, *Theft*, para 13.07; Ormerod and Williams, *Smith's Law of Theft*, para 6.12.

[24] See on that *Sofroniou* [2003] EWCA Crim 3681, and p 773 in the 11th edn of this work. Section 1 was repealed by the Fraud Act 2006.

[25] The reason for the distinction is that while the aim of s 1 was to punish fraud, the aim of s 3 is to protect legitimate business.

[26] For a general review of the relationship and consideration of s 3, see Treitel, 'Contract and Crime' in *Crime, Proof and Punishment*, 81.

to transactions entered into by a minor.[27] As a matter of civil law, the supply of unnecessary services to a minor will not create a legally enforceable contract. It is a question of law whether the items are necessary. To be necessary they must be of a nature suitable to the child's condition in life and actually required by him at the time and he must not already be otherwise sufficiently provided with them.[28] So, if a landlord of a pub supplies beer to a minor, the transaction is contrary to law and the minor commits no offence in making off without payment. If the minor has a service provided to him which is not a 'necessary' one (say, flying lessons) he commits no offence in making off since payment for that service is not legally enforceable. If the minor is supplied with non-necessary *goods* (say, 11 fancy waistcoats) and makes off he commits the offence; while payment for the waistcoats is not legally enforceable, the supply of these *goods* is not contrary to law.

The courts do not seem to have been troubled by defence claims that although performance of the contract was not contrary to law, some collateral aspect of V's conduct in the supply of the goods or services was contrary to law and therefore unprotected by s 3. It was anticipated by some that this would give rise to problems in cases such as D's failure to pay the unlicensed taxi driver.[29]

21.1.1.4 Without having paid as required or expected

It is implicit in the section that V requires or expects payment on the spot and that the payment is due in fact and law. If a taxi driver, in the course of a journey, commits a breach of contract entitling his passenger to rescind the contract, the passenger does not commit an offence by making off.[30] Where the money is due, does a person who gives a worthless cheque in 'payment' of the debt commit the offence? The offence would be under s 2 of the Fraud Act 2006 as D makes a false representation that the cheque will be honoured.[31] In the one reported case (although only at first instance)[32] in which the matter has arisen the judge ruled that the s 3 offence was not committed because a worthless cheque was not the same as counterfeit money, and that D was not making off because he departed with V's consent. The true answer may well be that D is guilty because he has not paid 'as required or expected'. V requires and expects payment in legal tender or by a good cheque. Payment by a worthless cheque does not satisfy this requirement or expectation any more than would payment in counterfeit money. In the rare cases in which payment by cheque nowadays occurs, it will inevitably be backed by a cheque guarantee card, and depending on the conditions of its issue, D may have paid as required or expected although his authority to use the card has been withdrawn or even if it has been stolen.[33] The same is true of payment by credit card.[34] V has been paid if the bank or card issuer is bound to honour the cheque or card, and that is a question of civil law. The offence is not committed if the supplier consents to D's leaving without payment, even if the consent was obtained

---

[27] cf P Rowlands, 'Minors: Can They Make Off Without Payment' (1981) 145 JP 410: cf Smith, *Property Offences*, para 20.69.

[28] *Bainbridge v Pickering* (1779) 2 Wm Bl 1325.   [29] See Griew, *Theft*, para 13.10.

[30] *Troughton v Metropolitan Police* [1987] Crim LR 138.

[31] See G Syrota, 'Are Cheque Frauds Covered by Section 3 of the Theft Act 1978?' [1980] Crim LR 413.

[32] *Hammond* [1982] Crim LR 611 (Judge Morrison).

[33] cf *First Sport Ltd v Barclays Bank plc* [1993] 3 All ER 789.

[34] cf *Re Charge Card Services Ltd* [1988] 3 All ER 702.

by fraud, as where D deceives V into accepting postponement of payment.[35] Payment in such a case is not required or expected at *that* time. This may be an offence under s 2 of the Fraud Act 2006.

21.1.2 Mens rea

The offence requires that D should make off: (a) dishonestly; (b) knowing that payment on the spot is required or expected from him; and (c) with intent to avoid payment.

21.1.2.1 Dishonesty

Reference may be made to the general discussion of dishonesty and the application of the *Ivey/Barton* test.[36] It does not matter at what stage D decides to act dishonestly as long as he is dishonest when he makes off. Dishonesty is a question for the jury. If D genuinely believed that no payment was due at that time or that none was due owing to the poor standard or deficient goods, following *Ivey*[37] and *Barton*.[38] it would be for the jury to determine whether D was dishonest in refusing to pay for goods or a service. D's perception of how reasonable people would view his conduct is no longer fundamental since the rejection of the *Ghosh* test.

21.1.2.2 Knowing that payment on the spot is required or expected of him

The offence is concerned only with cases where payment on the spot is required. Such transactions are difficult to define in abstract terms. They are usually easy enough to identify[39] by reference to normal trading practices, although these may in particular instances be modified by the course of dealing between the parties.[40] If D believes that the transaction is on credit terms, he cannot be convicted of this offence for he does not *know* the transaction to be an on-the-spot transaction. Where D believes that payment is to be made by another (eg where he believes that E will pay for the meal) he does not commit the offence because he does not know that payment is to be required of him.[41] Presumably D would not be liable if, having drunk too much alcohol with his meal, he staggers out of the restaurant without paying and is so intoxicated that he does not know what he is doing.

21.1.2.3 Intention to avoid payment

Section 3 does not explicitly require an intention to make permanent default, and commentators tended to favour the view that a dishonest intention temporarily to avoid payment would suffice. However, *Allen*[42] holds that the offence requires an intention to make permanent default. D had left an hotel without settling his bill and the trial judge directed the jury that all that was required was an intention to make default at the time payment was

---

[35] *Vincent* [2001] EWCA Crim 295. See also *Evans v Lane* (1984) CO/137/84, CA.

[36] See p 914.   [37] [2017] UKSC 67, [74]. For discussion, see p 918.   [38] [2020] EWCA Crim 575.

[39] Section 3(2) provides that it includes 'payment at the time of collecting goods on which work has been done or in respect of which service has been provided'. But this seems to have been added from an abundance of caution and adds nothing.

[40] It cannot be enough that V requires a payment to be made on the spot, eg seeing D who owes him £10 lent a month ago, V demands payment on the spot. The reference is to those transactions where payment *customarily* follows immediately upon the provision of the goods or service.

[41] *Brooks and Brooks* (1982) 76 Cr App R 66.   [42] [1985] AC 1029.

required. The Court of Appeal held, however, that an intention to make permanent default was required because s 3 required both (a) a making off without paying on the spot; and (b) an intention to avoid payment. In view of the requirement in (a), (b) made sense only if permanent default was intended. The House of Lords endorsed this view and drew further support for it by reference to the fact that the CLRC had intended permanent default to be necessary.[43]

The Home Office rejected a reform proposal suggested by garage owners[44] which would have extended the offence to include cases where D acts with intent to defer payment.

Further reading

SP Green, *13 Ways to Steal a Bicycle: Theft Law in the Information Age*

---

[43] Thirteenth Report (1977) Cmnd 6733, para 18.

[44] Home Office, *Fraud Law Reform: Consultation on Proposals for Legislation* (2004) para 45. Complaining of individuals who, having filled their cars with fuel, claimed to have left their wallets at home and promised to pay at a later date. That may be an offence under s 2 of the Fraud Act 2006.

22

The Fraud Act 2006

22.1 Background

22.1.1 Common law and legislation before the Fraud Act 2006

Fraudulent conduct has long been dealt with at common law by the offence of conspiracy to defraud. The Theft Act 1968 included deception offences,[1] each requiring that D's conduct: (a) constituted a representation; (b) that the representation caused V to form a false belief; (c) that belief (caused by the representation) led V to behave in a prescribed way (transfer property, a valuable security, etc); and (d) that as a result of the behaviour D (or another) gained. Those result crimes caused problems. The requirement for an operative deception meant that the offences were restricted in application. If V knew that D's statement was false,[2] or if V would have acted in the same way even if he had known it,[3] or if V did not rely on the false statement but arrived at the same erroneous conclusion from his own observation or some other source,[4] or, of course, if V did not read or hear the false statement made by D, no deception offence was committed. Numerous technical issues arose[5] including such fundamental matters as: whether a representation could be made impliedly,[6] whether V's indifference as to the truth of a representation precluded a finding of an operative deception[7] and whether there could be a deception of a machine.[8] The courts were forced to adopt broad interpretations and the concept of deception was, arguably, being misconstrued.

It was thought that to offer adequate protection from the growing problem of fraud, a more structured and coherent package of offences was necessary to keep pace with technology and modern methods of property transfer.[9] The solution to these problems was to repeal the deception offences and replace them with a 'general fraud offence'.

22.1.2 Evolution of the Fraud Act 2006

The Law Commission produced a Consultation Paper No 155, *Legislating the Criminal Code: Fraud and Deception* (1999)[10] rejecting the idea of a general fraud offence because it would be too wide. This hesitant, unambitious approach was heavily criticized.[11]

In the light of consultation responses, the Law Commission changed its opinion and in its Law Commission Report No 276, *Fraud* (2002)[12] made recommendations for a fraud offence. The government responded with the Home Office Consultation Paper, *Fraud Law*

---

[1] The offences were: obtaining property: 1968, s 15; obtaining a money transfer: 1968, s 15A; obtaining a pecuniary advantage: 1968, s 16; procuring the execution of a valuable security: 1968, s 20(2); obtaining services: 1978, s 1; securing the remission of a liability: 1978, s 2(1)(a); inducing a creditor to wait for or to forgo payment: 1978, s 2(1)(b); obtaining an exemption from or abatement of liability: 1978, s 2(1)(c). See generally C Montgomery and D Ormerod, *Montgomery and Ormerod Fraud: Criminal Law and Procedure* (2008).

[2] *Ady* (1835) 7 C & P 140; *Mills* (1857) Dears & B 205; *Hensler* (1870) 11 Cox CC 570; *Light* (1915) 11 Cr App R 111.

[3] *Edwards* [1978] Crim LR 49, and commentary at 50.   [4] *Roebuck* (1856) Dears & B 24.

[5] For a detailed account see JC Smith, *The Law of Theft* (8th edn, 1997) Ch 4; and Ch 19 of the 11th edn of this book.

[6] *Ray* [1974] AC 370.   [7] *Charles* [1977] AC 177; *Lambie* [1982] AC 449.

[8] A more robust stand on this has now been adopted: there cannot be deception of machines for the purposes of dishonesty offences. See *Chodoreck v Poland* [2017] EWHC 995 (Admin) and *Poland v Ulatowski* [2010] EWHC 2673 (Admin), [32].

[9] LC 276, *Fraud* (2002).

[10] See www.lawcom.gov.uk/app/uploads/2015/03/cp155_Legislating_the_Criminal_Code_Fraud_and_Deception_Consultation.pdf.

[11] See D Ormerod, 'A Bit of a Con' [1999] Crim LR 789.

[12] See www.lawcom.gov.uk/app/uploads/2015/03/lc276_Fraud.pdf. Described by Dominic Grieve MP as a 'model of its kind': Hansard, HC, 12 June 2006, col 546.

Reform (2004) which developed the Law Commission's proposals.[13] The Bill was, in general, very warmly received in Parliament where the law lords approved of practically all of its terms (except the retention of the offence of conspiracy to defraud).[14] The Bill was passed almost unchallenged. The Act received Royal Assent on 8 November 2006.

22.1.3 The merits of a general fraud offence

The merits of general fraud offences have been debated for decades.[15] Such an offence was considered by the CLRC when preparing the Theft Act 1968[16] but ultimately rejected. Several eminent commentators doubted whether a general fraud offence could ever be drafted which does not extend potential criminal liability too far.[17] There were, however, numerous strong supporters of such reform.[18] Most supporters argued for a model requiring not only that the prosecution prove that the defendant behaved dishonestly and with intent to gain/cause loss but also that there were economic interests actually imperilled by that conduct. The Fraud Act adopts a wider model with no requirement to prove that the conduct imperilled economic interests or caused the victim to believe the representations.

22.2 The general fraud offence

The principal offence is the general fraud offence created by s 1 in the following terms:

(1) A person is guilty of fraud if he is in breach of any of the sections listed in subsection (2) (which provide for different ways of committing the offence).

(2) The sections are—

    (a) section 2 (fraud by false representation),

    (b) section 3 (fraud by failing to disclose information), and

    (c) section 4 (fraud by abuse of position).

Interestingly, there has been no attempt to provide a clear definition of what constitutes fraud.[19] The offence of fraud can be committed in one of three ways as described by ss 2 to 4. Each is based on dishonest conduct against property interests, and carries a maximum

---

[13] See http://webarchive.nationalarchives.gov.uk/+/http://www.homeoffice.gov.uk/documents/cons-fraud-law-reform/. The proposals were endorsed after further consultation in 2004 in which additional proposals were suggested. The government drew support for introducing broader, less technical offences from the deficiencies in the old law and from the need to combat the rising volume of fraud. See HC Research Paper 06/31, at 3. See also press reports of 7 Mar 2007.

[14] See eg Hansard, HL, 22 June 2005, col 1661.

[15] The merits were discussed in Law Com WP 104, *Conspiracy to Defraud* (1987), and in LCCP 155, Parts 4 and 5. The model offered was an offence for 'Any person who dishonestly causes another to suffer [financial] prejudice, or who dishonestly makes a gain for himself or another', para 5.2.

[16] Eighth Report, paras 97–100. Cl 12(3) of the CLRC Draft Bill of 1966: 'A person who dishonestly, with a view to gain for himself or another, by any deception induces a person to do or refrain from doing any act shall on conviction on indictment be liable to imprisonment for a term not exceeding two years.'

[17] JC Smith, 'Fraud and The Criminal Law' in P Birks (ed), *Criminal Justice and Human Rights—Pressing Problems in the Law* (1995) vol 1, 49. Similar sentiments were expressed by another great theft scholar: Griew, *Theft*, 141. See also the conclusions in Law Com WP 56, *Criminal Law: Conspiracy to Defraud* (1974) paras 65, 81–2.

[18] See GR Sullivan, 'Fraud and Efficacy in the Criminal Law: A Proposal for a Wide Residual Offence' [1985] Crim LR 616 and 'Framing an Acceptable General Offence of Fraud' (1989) 53 J Crim L 92.

[19] Cf N Yeo, 'Bull's Eye' (2007) 157 NLJ 212 at 213, suggesting that in practical terms the government has succeeded in defining fraud.

ten-year sentence on indictment.[20] They are incredibly wide offences deliberately drafted to avoid technicality. The offence of fraud can be charged in one of three forms: s 1(2)(a) (fraud by false representation under s 2); s 1(2)(b) (fraud by failure to disclose under s 3); s 1(2)(c) (fraud by abuse of position under s 4). The particularity and complexity of this scheme was unnecessary. Sections 2 to 4 could have been free-standing offences in their own right.

22.2.1 General matters of interpretation

The 2006 Act[21] is a short statute designed to be unburdened by the technicality which bedevilled the old law. The Act is not a codifying Act. The Law Commission Bill attached to the *Fraud* Report No 276 serves as a useful interpretative tool,[22] especially given the government's refusal to define many core elements of the offence in an attempt to ensure the broadest interpretation.[23]

As noted, the offences are extremely broadly drafted. To date, sensible prosecution decisions have avoided the most extreme possible uses of the legislation, identified throughout this chapter. Reflecting on the Fraud Act a decade after it came into force, Virgo argues that:

Legal analysis needs to strike a balance between principle and pragmatism. The Fraud Act on its face might be criticised for infringing fundamental criminal justice principles, by virtue of its breadth and uncertainty, but if the legislation enables appropriate responses to be reached, assisted by judicial interpretation where appropriate, it can be defended. This is the case with the Fraud Act 2006. Initial concerns about the ambit and interpretation of the legislation have largely proved unfounded. It remains a model of criminal legislation which remains fit for purpose.[24]

It remains disappointing that Parliament created such wide and ill-defined offences, leaving to prosecutorial discretion the fair and efficient administration and application of the offences. There is no guarantee that all prosecution agencies will adopt (equally) rigorous prosecution policies, nor that each agency will apply such policies with internal consistency.[25] Even if the prosecution agencies do all manage to achieve a sensible, measured, consistent approach to the Act, that does not prevent inappropriate exploitation of the breadth of the offences by private prosecutors.

The offences, especially s 2, overlap with theft, but fraud requires no element of appropriation, no loss, no gain, no intention permanently to deprive and carries a higher sentence. The CPS reminds prosecutors of the benefits of a charge under the 2006 Act.[26]

---

[20] See Sentencing Council, *Fraud, Bribery and Money Laundering Offences: Definitive Guideline* (2014) (with application to all individual offenders and organizations sentenced on or after 1 Oct 2014).

[21] In force from 15 Jan 2007: Fraud Act 2006 (Commencement) Order 2006, SI 2006/3200; Fraud Act 2006, Sch 2, paras 2 and 3. See *Goldsmith* [2009] EWCA Crim 1840.

[22] In addition to the Law Commission Consultation Paper and Report, valuable insights may be gleaned from Home Office, *Fraud Reform: Government Response to Consultations* (2004) and the House of Commons Research Paper 06/31, *The Fraud Bill [HL]* (2006).

[23] See eg the lack of definition of the term 'abuse' in s 4 noted in *Pennock and Pennock* [2014] EWCA Crim 598. In general, the government was reluctant to provide rigorous analysis of any terms.

[24] G Virgo, 'The Fraud Act 2006—Ten Years On' [2017] 10 Arch Rev 6.

[25] The larger scale frauds which come under scrutiny from the most senior lawyers are those to which more detailed attention is likely to be paid, and ironically it may be those to which the Act's provisions are applied most cautiously.

[26] The credit/debit status of any bank accounts is irrelevant to the Fraud Act offences. All that is in issue is D's right to use the account; it is not necessary to prove or demonstrate any consequences of fraud (though they will clearly be material to sentence, compensation and confiscation). '*Preddy*'-type difficulties will not arise (where the property obtained had not belonged to another); Fraud Act offences do not require an intent permanently to deprive; a charge should describe what actually happened and reflect the true criminality; and the indictment should be as simple as reasonably possible. See www.cps.gov.uk/legal-guidance/fraud-act-2006.

22.2.2 Jurisdiction

The courts continue to have jurisdiction when property is fraudulently gained/lost in England or Wales, even though the conduct causing this result has taken place in another country (or countries as where D in the United States makes false representations to V in Canada causing V's London bank account to be debited). The Criminal Justice Act 1993 provides that if any act or omission, proof of which is required for conviction of a relevant crime (a 'relevant event'), takes place here it will be capable of prosecution in England and Wales. Schedule 1 to the 2006 Act amends the 1993 Act to extend the meaning of 'relevant event' to include:

(a) if the fraud involved an intention to make a gain and the gain occurred, *that occurrence*;

(b) if the fraud involved an intention to cause a loss or to expose another to a risk of loss and the loss occurred, *that occurrence*.[27]

Where, however, D performs one of the elements of the fraud offence abroad (eg making the false representation under s 2, or abusing the financial position under s 4), but intends to make a gain which will occur in England and Wales or cause a loss in this jurisdiction, the 1993 Act (as amended by the 2006 Act) will not apply unless *there is an actual gain or loss within England and Wales*. The Act could have extended the meaning of 'relevant event' to include the making of the false representation, etc with intent rather than the result (given that these are now conduct crimes), but oddly did not do so. [28]

22.2.3 Common elements of the fraud offence

22.2.3.1 Dishonesty

The principal element of mens rea for the offence of fraud in each of its three forms is that of dishonesty. The Law Commission and the Home Office intended that the *Ghosh* definition should apply, and this was confirmed repeatedly[29] in the parliamentary debates. That test, and the changes introduced by the Supreme Court's judgment in *Ivey v Genting Casinos UK Ltd (t/a Crockfords Club)*,[30] and *Barton*[31] are examined in detail in Ch 18.

No statutory definition for dishonesty was adopted in relation to this offence. Parliament presumed that the *Ghosh* test would apply. The test for dishonesty in this offence is now that articulated in *Ivey*.[32]

The court in *Barton* succinctly stated the test for dishonesty as follows:

(1) what was the defendant's actual state of knowledge or belief as to the facts; and

(2) was his conduct dishonest by the standards of ordinary decent people.[33]

Several further points are worth noting.

First, it is, we suggest, unthinkable that the courts will entertain a challenge to the application of *Ivey* in the context of fraud on the basis that it was not the test anticipated by Parliament. Had Parliament wanted to impose a specific dishonesty test it could have done so. Had it wanted to put *Ghosh* on a statutory footing it could have done so. Instead, it

---

[27] Para 25(3) (emphasis added).

[28] See *Blackstone's Criminal Practice* (2021) B5.3, noting the difficulty with the lack of transitional provisions in respect of jurisdiction.

[29] See Hansard, HL Debates, 19 July 2005, col 1424 (Attorney General); House of Commons Research Paper 31/06, at 14; Standing Committee B, 20 June 2006, col 8 (Solicitor General).

[30] [2017] UKSC 67.   [31] [2020] EWCA Crim 575.   [32] At [74].

[33] [2020] EWCA Crim 575, [84] (emphasis added).

intended for the common law test to apply and in doing so must be taken implicitly to have accepted that the common law is subject to change.

Secondly, reliance on dishonesty as the key element of mens rea and as ill-defined as it is, with its inherent unpredictability, increases the chances that more cases will go to trial as defendants have little to lose by 'trying their luck' with a jury. This remains the case even after the reformulation of the test for dishonesty in *Ivey/Barton*. In terms of principle, the lack of certainty in the substantive law and inefficiency in the criminal justice system render this undesirable.

Thirdly, care will be needed in applying the beguilingly simple test in *Barton* in cases of complex fraud where D claims that he had a genuine (and perhaps reasonable) belief that his conduct was honest by, for example, reference to professional standards. Clearly, *Ghosh* precluded liability where D had no realization that reasonable and honest people would see the conduct as dishonest. What is the position under *Ivey/Barton*? There was some ambiguity about the extent to which the Supreme Court in *Ivey*, by removing the second limb of *Ghosh* but retaining subjectivity in this first limb of the test, mean to (a) render totally irrelevant D's belief as to the perceptions of others about the honesty of the conduct or (b) remove the binding nature of that belief—if D did not believe others would see it as dishonest, he would be entitled to an acquittal under *Ghosh*. That ambiguity has been resolved by the decision in *Barton*. Lord Burnett provided the answer: the reference in *Ivey* to the 'actual state of mind as to knowledge of belief as to the facts' was to *all* the circumstances known to the accused and not limited to consideration of past facts. Lord Burnett CJ explained that:

> [a]ll matters that lead an accused to act as he or she did will form part of the subjective mental state, thereby forming a part of the fact-finding exercise before applying the objective standard. That will include consideration, where relevant, of the experience and intelligence of an accused.[34]

We suggest, therefore, that in a prosecution for fraud that requires the jury to have regard not only to D's state of mind as to the facts but also as to his beliefs about whether the conduct would be seen as dishonest (that would be a matter which may 'lead' him to act as he did), a defendant should be entitled to adduce evidence about industry practices (as they were entitled to do under the subjective limb of the *Ghosh* test). But the jury is no longer *bound* to acquit if the defendant held a belief that ordinary decent people would not regard his conduct as dishonest. In an appropriate case, it may therefore be necessary for an expanded definition to be provided to the jury. We discuss this issue in more detail in Ch 18.

Claim of right

There is no equivalent to s 2 of the Theft Act 1968, so D's claims to be acting under a claim of right are no guarantee of acquittal. Dishonesty under the Act is based solely on the common law test as articulated in *Ivey/Barton*.[35] The Supreme Court confirmed in *Ivey* that the tribunal of fact must first ascertain (subjectively) the actual state of the defendant's knowledge or belief as to the facts before considering whether he was dishonest according to the standards of ordinary decent people. It is submitted therefore that if D has a claim of right to the property he should not ordinarily be at risk of criminal liability.[36] It is unlikely in practice that any defendant would be found to be dishonest in such circumstances, although that cannot be guaranteed.

---

[34] ibid, [108].

[35] *Ivey v Genting Casinos (UK) Ltd (t/a Crockfords Club)* [2017] UKSC 67, [74]. For extensive discussion, see p 906.

[36] cf the Law Commission recommending that a claim of right ought not be a defence in all cases, LC 276, para 7.66, which was a reversal of its position in LCCP 155.

Equally, it is submitted that there should be no criminal liability for D who genuinely believes that he has a claim of right to the property which he seeks to gain, or indeed where D genuinely believes that he has a claim of right to cause V to lose that property. It is unlikely, though not impossible, that in practice such conduct would be found to be dishonest applying the test enunciated in *Ivey/Barton*. A jury might well think D is dishonest where he made a deliberately false representation even where D did so to get something to which he thought he was entitled. The fact that D can now be guilty even though he was genuinely unaware that his conduct would be considered dishonest by the standards of ordinary decent people makes the absence of an equivalent to s 2 of the Theft Act 1968 more keenly felt.

To avoid increasing the scope of fraud, which is a consequence that the Supreme Court presumably did not intend in *Ivey* or it would have made that explicit, in cases where D genuinely believes he has a claim of right, it will be crucial for the trial judge to direct the jury to consider the facts and circumstances as D believed them to be, before directing the jury to consider whether D's conduct was objectively dishonest.

It is submitted that a mistake of civil law giving rise to a belief in a claim of right ought therefore to avoid liability.[37] One argument in support of such an interpretation is the desire to maintain coherence between the offence of theft and that of fraud. If D believes the property to be his, whether through a mistake of fact or a mistake of law, he has a defence if the charge is brought as theft. There are good reasons to suggest that he should have the same defence if the charge is brought under s 1 of the 2006 Act. If the judge has to direct the jury expressly on the theft charge that claim of right is a defence (and it is submitted that he should), then it is desirable that he should also have to do so on the fraud charge, instead of leaving the jury to deduce this from the general dishonesty direction.

Counter-arguments can be advanced. One is that theft and fraud are quite separate offences with distinct moral wrongs: theft is designed to protect property rights and associated rights of transfer of property, etc; fraud is to protect against dishonest exploitation of others. We refute that. The House of Lords' broad interpretation of theft in *Hinks* and *Gomez* (p 866) undermines such a distinction. A more telling counter-argument is that the offence under the 2006 Act is focused on the dishonesty of means: it is an offence of dishonestly making a false representation rather than making a false representation with intent to dishonestly make a gain.

The absence of an automatic and complete defence of a claim of right may lead to liability where, for example, D makes a false statement in a company prospectus and includes a disclaimer that, for instance, 'no investment should be made on the basis of the information in this document alone'. A jury may well find such conduct dishonest when viewed in the round.

Irrespective of the argument about an explicit direction echoing that in s 2 of the 1968 Act, in the event of a prosecution for an alleged fraud where D has a claim of right or a belief in a claim of right, it is important that the jury is directed that dishonesty is a separate element of the offence. D may deliberately make a false representation, yet not act dishonestly in doing so.[38] The jury should always be directed that they must be satisfied that the conduct alleged under ss 2 to 4 as appropriate was done dishonestly.

---

[37] The CPS has issued guidance to prosecutors stating that: 'The criminal law is not a suitable vehicle to regulate such disputes [that is, arguments over ownership of property]. Before a criminal charge can proceed the ownership of any property must be absolutely clear. If that ownership is in real dispute the criminal law should not be invoked until ownership has been established in the civil courts.' See www.cps.gov.uk/legal-guidance/fraud-act-2006.

[38] See *Wright* [1960] Crim LR 366; *Griffiths* [1966] 1 QB 589; *Talbot* [1995] Crim LR 396.

Article 7

The shift in emphasis brought about by *Ivey* and *Barton* increases the likelihood of a challenge under Art 7 of the ECHR.[39] A defendant might claim that (even with legal advice), he could not have anticipated that a jury would consider his conduct to be dishonest.

The Parliamentary Joint Committee on Human Rights, in its Fourteenth Report[40] scrutinizing the Fraud Bill, concluded that the new offence is compatible with Art 7 of the ECHR and common law requirements of certainty:

the new general offence of fraud *is not* a general dishonesty offence. Rather, it embeds as an element in the definition of the offence some identifiable morally dubious conduct to which the test of dishonesty may be applied, as the Law Commission correctly observed is required by the principle of legal certainty. We are therefore satisfied that, as defined in the Bill, the new general offence of fraud satisfies the common law and ECHR requirement that criminal offences be defined with sufficient clarity and precision to enable the public to predict with sufficient certainty whether or not they will be liable.[41]

The Committee did, however, confirm that:

a general dishonesty offence would be incompatible with the common law principle of legality. In our view it would also be in breach of the requirement of legal certainty in Articles 5 and 7 ECHR for the same reasons.[42]

Even in the *Ghosh* era, the validity of this argument was questionable.[43] It is not strikingly obvious that in all cases there will have been 'morally dubious' conduct over and above dishonesty. In the s 2 offence, the additional morally dubious conduct seems to be little more than making a false representation—that is, lying, which might also be fairly described in many contexts at least as 'being dishonest': the 'additional' element which the Committee regards as preventing the offence being one solely of dishonesty! It is true that there is also the element of an intent to gain or cause loss, but that is extremely wide and can be morally neutral in some cases, particularly perhaps where D intends only to get that to which he is entitled (which is nevertheless an intent to gain[44]).

At its widest, D could be liable under s 2 for dishonestly making a statement which he knew might be misleading with intent to gain his own property temporarily. Since dishonesty now has a more objective definition under *Ivey/Barton*, it is submitted that the risk of there being an infringement of Art 7 is theoretically much greater than under *Ghosh*, although the courts have continued to resist Art 7 challenges as in *Bermingham*.[45]

22.2.3.2 With intent to gain or cause loss or to expose to a risk of loss

A second common element in each of the ways fraud can be committed is the element under s 5 defining the meaning of 'gain' and 'loss' for the purposes of ss 2 to 4.

(1) The references to gain and loss in sections 2 to 4 are to be read in accordance with this section.

(2) 'Gain' and 'loss'—

    (a) extend only to gain or loss in money or other property;

    (b) include any such gain or loss whether temporary or permanent;

---

[39] See generally D Ormerod and K Laird, '*Ivey v Genting Casinos*—Much Ado About Nothing?' (2019) 9 Supreme Court Yearbook 1, available at https://ukscy.org.uk/doi/10.19152/ukscy.762.

[40] (2006).

[41] Para 2.14 (emphasis added). See also the AG's statements in debate: Hansard, 19 July 2005, col 1424.

[42] Fourteenth Report, para 2.12.   [43] See earlier.   [44] See p 1025.

[45] [2021] EWCA Crim 1662. D Ormerod and K Laird, '*Ivey v Genting Casinos*—Much Ado About Nothing?' (2019) 9 Supreme Court Yearbook 1, available at https://ukscy.org.uk/doi/10.19152/ukscy.762.

and 'property' means any property whether real or personal (including things in action and other intangible property).

(3) 'Gain' includes a gain by keeping what one has, as well as a gain by getting what one does not have.

(4) 'Loss' includes a loss by not getting what one might get, as well as a loss by parting with what one has.

The definitions are essentially the same as those in s 34(2)(a) of the Theft Act 1968.[46] Under these definitions, 'gain' and 'loss' are limited to gain and loss in money or other property. 'Property' is defined as in s 4(1) of the Theft Act 1968[47] and covers all forms of property; to ensure coherence with the Theft Act.[48] None of the special exceptions in s 4 of the 1968 Act apply: there can be fraud with intent to gain/cause loss of land, wild animals and flora, but they cannot be stolen.

Loss or gain

In most cases 'an intention to gain' and an 'intention to cause loss' will go hand in hand; V's loss will be D's gain. The phrase, 'intent to cause loss' is not, however, superfluous. There may be circumstances in which D intends to cause a loss to V without any corresponding gain to D, for example where D lies to V to pay X. Problems arose in some cases under the old law because the deception might cause a gain which did not correspond to a loss.[49] If the prosecution specify one particular intent (say intent to gain) then they must prove that intent, and evidence of the alternative intent (to cause loss) is not sufficient.[50]

The consequence of making the intentions alternative[51] sufficient bases for liability is that the general fraud offence is even broader than may appear. For example, D who starts a false rumour that V is going out of business, commits the s 2 form of the offence if he does so with intent to lead customers away from V, intending by those actions that V will lose or be exposed to a risk of loss and is regarded as dishonest in doing so.[52] There is no requirement that D seeks to gain by these actions. It is debatable whether such conduct ought properly to be described as a criminal fraud.

Intention

Intention should bear its ordinary meaning, and should extend as elsewhere in the criminal law to include the foresight of a virtually certain consequence.[53] This may be significant in extending the scope of the offences.[54]

22.2.3.3 Remoteness

Although the fraud offence is not a result-based crime, the element of intent to gain/cause loss does involve a causal link that must be established. Under s 2, for example, it is '*by the*' false representation that D must intend to make the gain or cause the loss. This prompts the

---

[46] cf in particular their use in relation to false accounting, the Theft Act 1968, s 17, p 1018. They are also used in the Trade Marks Act 1994.

[47] See Ch 17, p 880.   [48] See Standing Committee B, 20 June 2006, col 32 (Solicitor General).

[49] The *Guinness* case was one famous example of this. See *Saunders* [1996] Cr App R 463, and more generally, N Kochan and H Pym, *The Guinness Affair* (1987).

[50] *Bush* [2019] EWCA Crim 29, [134].

[51] C Withey, 'The Fraud Act 2006' (2007) 71 J Crim L 220 suggests that both an intent to gain and an intent to cause loss must be proved, but this is difficult to square with the words of the section.

[52] See LC 276, para 4.13.

[53] See Hansard, HL, 19 July 2005, col 1414 (Attorney General). Cf the definition advanced by the House of Lords in the context of murder in *Woollin* [1998] AC 82.

[54] See the explanation of the concept in Ch 3.

question: how remote can D's intentions be? Suppose that D makes false representations to induce V, a wealthy banker, to marry him. Is D guilty of the s 2 offence if one intention is to enrich himself? Presumably such matters will be left to the jury to determine.[55] The importance of this element of the offence has already been emphasized by the Court of Appeal. In *Gilbert*,[56] G, S and H were charged with various offences including fraud contrary to s 2 for dishonestly making false representations in support of an application to open a bank account. H dishonestly informed the bank that savings and assets were also going to be used along with the loan to fund property developments. Subsequently, they defaulted on payments to a supplier and were charged with a fraud based on the false representation made to the bank to open the account. The recorder directed the jury that they could convict if the intent was to make the gain *either* by the false representations to the bank in opening the account or by their subsequent property business.

The Court of Appeal quashed G's conviction, with Roderick Evans J stating that:

> The jury must, therefore, be sure that the defendant intended to make a gain or cause loss or exposure to loss by making the false representation and it is a matter for the jury on the facts of each case whether the causative link between the intention and the making of the false representation, required by the section, is established.[57]

Despite the fact that there might have been a false representation to the bank, there was no evidence that it was *by that falsity* that G intended to gain or cause a loss.[58]

There are other circumstances where this issue could arise.[59] One obvious example is where D makes a number of representations in relation to a sale: for example, that a car is a genuine VW, that it has a specific mileage and that it has had one careful owner. Can D argue that the final representation, though false, is not one by which he intended to make a gain? This may well become subsumed within his plea of a lack of dishonesty, but it is a distinct element of the offence and deserves to be drawn to the jury's attention. The jury will properly have regard to all the circumstances. The fact that the representation relates to a peripheral matter will not *entitle* the defendant to an acquittal.[60] What is in issue is solely a matter of D's intent. It seems then to be a question of fact and degree in every case whether what was said was intended to be a misrepresentation by which the gain or loss would be made.

The jury would have to be sure under, for example, s 2 that: (a) D made a representation that was untrue or misleading, and in relation to *that* representation;[61] (b) D knew it was or might have been false; and (c) that D made the representation dishonestly; and (d) that D, by making *that* representation, intended to make a gain/cause loss, etc.

The problem may be dealt with more easily where D has made two or more false representations. In such a case, the prosecution may incorporate all the representations in one count indicting the conduct as, for example, 'falsely representing the details of the car for sale' and

---

[55] The Court of Appeal seems reluctant to impose clear rules of remoteness in criminal law contexts. See eg *Kennedy (No 2)* [2005] EWCA Crim 785, cf the decision of the House of Lords [2008] UKHL 37. In *Idress* [2011] EWHC 624 (Admin), a conviction under s 2 was upheld where D had persuaded X to sit his driving test for him representing himself to be D. Presumably the property D was to gain was the driving licence.

[56] [2012] EWCA Crim 2392.   [57] At [29].

[58] The false representation was to secure the opening of an account which might not constitute 'property' for the purposes of s 1 depending on the terms of the account.

[59] See the correspondence between Ormerod and Gardner [2007] Crim LR 661.

[60] A proposal that the misrepresentation must be a 'material' one was expressly rejected by the Attorney General during the debates: Hansard, HL, 19 July 2005, cols 1419–20. See also *Lancaster* [2010] EWCA Crim 370 on the element of materiality not needing to be causal in false accounting—p 1022.

[61] Each representation if there are many charged.

rely on the two statements (original form of vehicle and previous ownership) as evidence of the dishonest intent to gain. Prosecutors will wrap up a number of representations in one count. In a long-running investment fraud this matter might be critical and inhibit the defendant's case, especially if he wants to deny causal intent. It risks a '*Brown* problem':[62] six jurors might think that D is guilty because of representation A and six because of representation B.

Things are yet more straightforward where D uses a false representation in order to secure a contract, and intends to fulfil the terms of the contract and give value for money. To be liable in such a case, the prosecution have to show that D acted in order to, or foresaw that it was virtually certain that his conduct in making the false representation would lead him to, gain. There are numerous instances of convictions under the Act for D making a false representation as to his eligibility to work in the UK, securing employment and working to be paid[63] or even making false representations as to having a clean driving licence which was a prerequisite for the job.[64]

Claims of entitlement to the gain

A defendant who intends to recover what he believes he is entitled to still has the intention to gain (and/or to cause loss). Should it be fraud for A to lie to B to get back money owed to him? Authority on the construction of the same expression in false accounting[65] suggests that liability will arise. The Court of Appeal has held that the element of intent to gain is satisfied by proof of an intention to 'acquire' even that property to which D is entitled. *A fortiori*, there will be a relevant intention where D genuinely though mistakenly believes that he is entitled to the gain (or to cause the loss). Such cases will be rare. Greater emphasis will therefore be placed on the dishonesty element. As discussed previously, if D believes he has a right to the gain or loss he seeks then it will be for the jury to determine whether he is dishonest applying the test in *Ivey/Barton* and bearing in mind that the dishonesty related to the making of the false representation (in s 2) and not the gain or loss.

Arguably, the definition in s 5 is too wide since it criminalizes the situation where D intends V not to get something which V might have gained, even though V was not entitled to it. For example, under s 2, if V asks D for a loan and D denies it him by saying falsely (dishonestly?) that he has no money to spare, D has made a false representation with intent to cause V not to gain that which he might[66] have obtained.[67] V has at most suffered a loss of a chance. D might avoid liability by arguing that a simple refusal, however malicious or dishonest, is not a 'representation' but an explanation for the refusal. Even if it is a representation, D might claim that the words were not intended to cause loss or damage but designed solely to ease the loss and damage caused by the refusal. D's additional, or alternative, excuse is that he is probably not going to be regarded as dishonest in those circumstances.[68]

Criminal liability seems broad, including as it does making a misleading statement with intent to cause someone to be exposed to the risk of temporarily not being able to get that which he might otherwise have got. How will the prosecution prove the intention to cause loss by not getting what one might get? Is it enough in practice that D believes that there was a chance that V would make a gain?

---

62 See *Brown* (1984) 79 Cr App R 115.
63 See *Dziruni* [2008] EWCA Crim 667; *Haboub* [2007] EWCA Crim 3327.
64 *Asif* [2008] EWCA Crim 3348.
65 *A-G's Reference (No 1 of 2001)* [2002] Crim LR 844.
66 The offence would have been much tighter with a requirement that D intended that loss/gain *would* occur.
67 See GR Sullivan, 'Fraud and Efficiency in the Criminal Law' [1985] Crim LR 616.
68 See Standing Committee B, 20 June 2006, cols 33–5.

Exposure to temporary loss

Unlike theft, there is no requirement that D acts with intent to deprive V *permanently* of any property. It would seem to be sufficient under s 2, for example, that D makes a false representation to V with intent to cause V to lend D property[69] which D intends to return in an unaltered form. The offence comes close to criminalizing dishonest deprivation of the value of an item's usefulness. This strains the property-based foundation of the offence. It supports the argument that the offence is one centred on the wrong of lying.[70]

Intention to expose another to a risk of loss

It is sufficient that D intends that V will be exposed to the risk of loss; there is no need for the prosecution to prove that D had a more specific intention that V will actually lose. D who makes a dishonest false representation on his health insurance form will be liable (under s 2). He intends the insurance company to be exposed to a risk of loss, even though he desperately hopes that he will remain healthy and the insurance company will not incur actual loss. He also intends to deny them the higher premium to which they are entitled.

D, who makes a false statement in a job reference for V, will be liable if he intends that V will thereby not be promoted and attain the higher salary appropriate to that post.

22.3 Section 2: fraud by false representation

The offence created by s 1(2)(a) of the Act is incredibly broad. This offence is described in s 2, which provides:

(1) A person is in breach of this section if he—

    (a) dishonestly makes a false representation, and

    (b) intends, by making the representation—

        (i) to make a gain for himself or another, or

        (ii) to cause loss to another or to expose another to a risk of loss.

(2) A representation is false if—

    (a) it is untrue or misleading, and

    (b) the person making it knows that it is, or might be, untrue or misleading.

(3) 'Representation' means any representation as to fact or law, including a representation as to the state of mind of—

    (a) the person making the representation, or

    (b) any other person.

(4) A representation may be express or implied.

(5) For the purposes of this section a representation may be regarded as made if it (or anything implying it) is submitted in any form to any system or device designed to receive, convey or respond to communications (with or without human intervention).

Section 1 provides that the maximum sentence on indictment is ten years' imprisonment.

The actus reus requires proof that D: made a representation, which is untrue or misleading, and the mens rea requires proof that D knew the representation was, or knew that it

---

[69] Even that to which D is already entitled. Cf *Zemmel* [1985] Crim LR 213, and the Law Commission Working Paper No 104, *Conspiracy to Defraud* (1988) para 4.4 rejecting this as a sufficient basis for criminal liability.

[70] See D Ormerod, 'Criminalising Lying' [2007] Crim LR 193; cf J Horder (2011) 127 LQR 37.

might be, false, and he acted dishonestly in making that representation, and with intent to gain or cause loss or expose to a risk of loss. In its judgment in *Varley*, the Court of Appeal cited this paragraph with approval and held that it represented the proper construction of the 2006 Act.[71] Gross LJ stated that the actus reus of the offence is the making of an objectively untrue or misleading representation. The mens rea is made up of the requisite knowledge, dishonesty and intention. His lordship stated that the actus reus is therefore contained in s 2(2)(a), with the mens rea found in s 2(2)(b), s 2(1)(a) and s 2(1)(b). This led the court to conclude that the offence is one that can be committed through an innocent agent.

22.3.1 Conduct-based offence

Crucial to an understanding of the operation and scope of the offence is an appreciation of the conduct-based nature of liability[72] and why that model was adopted to meet the problems under the 1968 Act and 1978 Act deception offences. Under the old law,[73] it had to be proved that D's conduct actually deceived V and caused V to do whatever act was appropriate to the offence charged. Under s 2, there is no need to prove: a result of any kind; that the alleged victim or indeed any person believed any representation; that any person acted on a representation; or that D succeeded in making a gain or causing a loss by the representation.

This shift from a result-based to conduct-based offence has numerous other practical implications. The principal aim is to make the offence easier to prove,[74] and there is little doubt that in most cases this objective will be achieved. The effect is that D may be liable for the false representations even where they had no bearing on V.[75]

Classic problems which recurred under the old law are greatly diminished, if not eradicated. For example, in *Laverty*,[76] a case under s 15 of the 1968 Act, D changed the number plates and chassis identification plate of a car and sold it to V. It was held that by his conduct D represented that the car was the original car to which these numbers had been assigned; but D's conviction for obtaining the price of the car by deception from V was quashed on the ground that it was not proved that the deception operated on V's mind. There was no direct evidence to that effect—V said he bought the car because he thought D was the owner—and it was not a necessary inference.[77] Under s 2 of the 2006 Act, the offence is committed as soon as D dishonestly changes the number plate or at the latest offers it for sale with intent to gain.

---

[71] [2019] EWCA Crim 1074, [106] and [108].

[72] It has been argued that the new fraud offence is a substantive offence drafted in the inchoate mode defined in such a way as to penalize conduct before it reaches the stage of causing harm. See A Ashworth and L Zedner, *Preventive Justice* (2014) 97–8. Horder suggests that the inchoate mode is common among acquisitive offences. See J Horder, 'Harmless Wrongdoing and the Anticipatory Perspective on Criminalisation' in GR Sullivan and IH Dennis (eds), *Seeking Security: Pre-Empting the Commission of Criminal Harms* (2012).

[73] Even under the pre-1968 law, it was necessary to show that the false pretences *caused* the loss. Cf S Farrell, N Yeo and G Ladenbury who suggest that the 2006 Act is a return to the pre-1968 position—*Blackstone's Guide to the Fraud Act 2006* (2007) para 1.09.

[74] This passage in the 15th edn of this work was cited by approval by the Court of Appeal in *Varley* [2019] EWCA Crim 1074, [104].

[75] This passage in the 14th edn of this work was cited with approval by Gross LJ in *Proctor v The Chief Constable of Cleveland Police* [2017] EWCA Civ 1531, [41].

[76] [1970] 3 All ER 432. Cf *Talbot* [1995] Crim LR 396.

[77] The court did not substitute a conviction for an attempt, possibly because there was also insufficient evidence that D intended to deceive V into buying the car by this representation. The purpose of changing the plates may well have been not to deceive the buyer but to deceive the police, the true owner and anyone else who might identify the vehicle. It would have been better to allege that D had made a representation by conduct that he had a right to sell the car.

22.3.1.1 Time of commission of the offence

One of the most important consequences of the shift to a conduct-based offence is that the s 2 crime is complete before the point in time at which any person acts in response to the false representation (as would have been required for a deception offence). A s 2 offence may also be completed later in time. For example, under the s 2 offence D can be liable if he makes a false representation after the entire proprietary interest has passed to him. If, after D, a motorist, fills his tank so that the entire proprietary interest in the fuel has passed to him, he falsely represents to V, the garage cashier, that it will be paid for by D's employer, he commits the offence irrespective of the fact that the property in the petrol has passed.[78] He intends by the dishonest false representation about payment to cause loss to the garage.

22.3.1.2 A victimless crime?

No specific victim(s) need to be identified, because no loss needs to have been incurred and no person needs to have believed or acted on D's representation.[79] The fact that D must have acted with the intention to gain or cause loss[80] means, however, that the offence will remain focused on the potential effect a false representation might have had on the economic interests of others.

Although under s 2 there is clearly no need to call a victim since there need be no result, in most instances, prosecutors may still prefer to call a victim or intended victim who can give unequivocal evidence of the representation being made and the surrounding circumstances which will support the allegations that it was made dishonestly, with knowledge as to its falsity and with intent to gain or cause loss. It is possible to invite the jury to infer that the false representation was made without calling evidence of that fact from a victim.[81]

22.3.2 Actus reus

22.3.2.1 'Makes a representation'

Whether a representation is made is a question of fact for the jury.

By whom representation may be made

The offence can be committed by any 'person' who makes a false representation. Clearly, this can include a corporation as where a false representation is contained in a corporation's prospectus for potential investors.[82]

---

[78] cf under the old law *Collis-Smith* [1971] Crim LR 716. He may also be guilty of making off without payment. See Ch 21.

[79] On this concept, see H Packer, *The Limits of the Criminal Sanction* (1968) 151–2. Packer suggests that victimless crimes pose a peculiar problem for criminal justice because the State is more likely to resort to the use of covert surveillance. Unlike the paradigm examples offered by Packer, fraud is not a 'victimless crime'. Rather, by bringing forward in time the completion of the actus reus of the offence (ie completion being as soon as the relevant representation is made, the offence is committed without the requirement that anyone actually believes it, let alone acts on it), Parliament has therefore *created* a victimless crime that is quite unlike the traditional understanding of 'fraud'.

[80] See p 970.

[81] See eg *Greig* [2010] EWCA Crim 1183 in which the reason for the payments by the vulnerable V to the 'cowboy' builders were plain enough for the conviction to be safe.

[82] Such representations were already criminalized by the Financial Services and Markets Act 2000, s 397. Within that section a distinction was made between recklessly and knowingly making a false statement. See *Bailey* [2005] EWCA Crim 3487. Section 397 has been repealed and replaced by the Financial Services Act 2012, s 89, in similar terms.

D will be liable for his personal representations. He might also be liable for representations of third parties which he can be said unambiguously to have adopted as, for example, where a manager adopts statements made by his predecessor.[83]

It is important also to recall the significance of the fact that it is sufficient under s 2 that D intends *either* to gain *or* to cause loss. If D offers a credit card for payment for goods in a shop, he makes a representation to the shopkeeper that payment will be made and that he has the authority to use the card.[84] If the latter representation is false but D knows that the shop will be paid by the credit card company, D still commits the offence. He is making a false representation to the retailer with intent to cause loss/expose to a risk of loss the credit card company (if they pay) or the retailer (if the credit card company will not pay because, for example, the card is outside the expiry date and the shop ought to have refused it).[85] However, only one offence is created despite the different elements of intent to gain, intent to cause loss and intent to expose to a risk of loss.

When is a representation made?

Potential difficulties with this element of timing may arise. It could be argued that the representation is made either: (a) as soon as D articulates it; (b) only if it is also addressed to something; or (c) only when it is actually perceived as such by a person, that is, when it is communicated. If D stands alone in the middle of an empty market and shouts 'Guaranteed solid gold watch for sale', if the watch is not solid gold and D knows that it is not, he is making a false statement, but is it a representation? Under the old law, where D had to cause V to believe the representation, the issue did not arise because there had to be a completed communication between D and V.

It is significant that the Act uses the term 'representation' rather than 'communication'.[86] The latter term would ordinarily imply that there was a recipient of the statement which D made, even if that recipient ignored the statement completely. However, even that restrictive interpretation of the concept of communication cannot be asserted beyond doubt. In *DPP v Collins*,[87] the House of Lords held that the offence of making a grossly offensive communication[88] could be committed even if no person was in receipt of the communication. It is submitted that under s 2 of the Fraud Act 2006 there need not be a completed communication in the sense that a person must read or hear or see D's statement in order for it to constitute a representation. A representation would seem to be 'made' as soon as articulated, but in accordance with the ordinary use of the word, a representation must be made 'to' someone or something. A representation could include a statement being made to the whole world.[89] If this interpretation is correct, it will typically render the full offence complete far earlier in time than would have been possible with deception offences.

---

[83] This passage in the 15th edn of this work was cited by approval by the Court of Appeal in *Varley* [2019] EWCA Crim 1074, [64].

[84] See p 985. For a case in which D was convicted based upon similar facts, see *Ahmed* [2016] EWCA Crim 104.

[85] See further p 985.

[86] cf C Withey, 'The Fraud Act 2006' (2007) 71 J Crim L 220, suggesting that the offence is not committed unless a communication is completed. This is difficult to square with the statutory wording and intent.

[87] [2006] UKHL 40.   [88] Communications Act 2003, s 127.

[89] See *Silverlock* [1894] 2 QB 766 (fraudulent advert in newspaper).

Representations to machines

One of the catalysts for enacting the Fraud Act was the concern that the law was failing to keep pace with technology. The prevailing opinion under the old law, from the cases[90] and academics,[91] was that it is not possible in law to deceive a machine. The problem of how to criminalize the 'deception' of a machine became an acute one as businesses relied increasingly on automated facilities to pay by credit card via automated telephone systems and the internet.[92] Such activity is, of course, not restricted to the consumer context.[93] Sections 1(2) and 11 of the 2006 Act deal with the problem.

To ensure that such conduct is within the scope of s 2, the government introduced an amendment to cl 2 to include *any* statements made to machines and computers as where D types in his PIN on a chip and PIN device.[94] Section 2(5) now provides:

> For the purposes of this section a representation may be regarded as made if it (or anything implying it) is submitted in any form to any system or device designed to receive, convey or respond to communications (with or without human intervention).

Section 2(5) is not without its difficulties. Aside from the complexity of the drafting, difficulties also stem from the breadth of the subsection. The terms used in s 2(5) were obviously intended to provide the broadest scope of liability, but they are not unambiguous. For example, is a document 'submitted' when the defendant saves the typing to his hard drive on the computer, or is it only 'submitted' when he sends it via email? There is a clear argument for suggesting that the document is submitted as soon as D saves it. However, if that is the case, how is it any different from D who writes his false representation on a piece of paper and locks it in his safe? That does not seem like a representation, but it is difficult to distinguish it from the case of saving data to a hard drive. Arguably, the individual who has submitted it to his computer is in a position in which he may more readily communicate it, but that mere possibility does not adequately justify any difference in criminality. The legislature might have intended to criminalize the conduct only when the representation was submitted to the ISP or system designed to act on it, but the subsection is not so narrowly drafted.

The criminal courts may follow the much narrower approach adopted in e-commerce. In business-to-business contracts it seems to be accepted that all contractually relevant communications only have operative effect when they are received.[95] In other contexts, it has been argued that the normal 'postal rule' of contract applies in relation to email contact so that the time of acceptance is the time when the electronic message was received by the ISP's network, and the place of acceptance is therefore that 'node' of the network which received the message. The courts have permitted contracting parties to stipulate in advance

---

[90] 'To deceive is . . . to induce a man to believe that a thing is true which is false, and which the person practising the deceit knows or believes to be false': *Re London and Globe Finance Corpn Ltd* [1903] 1 Ch 728 at 732. *Davies v Flackett* [1974] RTR 8. Deceit can be practised only on a human mind: (1972) Law Soc Gaz 576 and Law Com WP No 56 (1974) 51. Some devices used to operate machines are now 'instruments' for the purposes of the law of forgery. See also I Walden, *Computer Crimes and Digital Investigations* (2016) paras 3.89–3.92. See, however, the first instance civil decision of HHJ Seymour QC concluding that an action for deceit can be founded on lies told to a machine: *Renault UK v Fleetpro Technical Service* [2007] EWHC 2541 (QB).

[91] Griew, *Theft*, paras 8–12; see also Williams, TBCL, 794 and Smith, *Property Offences*, para 11.02. *Arlidge and Parry on Fraud*, para 4.072.

[92] Following implementation of the Fraud Act 2006, offences involving theft from an automatic machine using a plastic card are now regarded, and recorded, as false representation (cheque, plastic card and online banks).

[93] See eg the automated banking practices in issue in *Holmes* [2004] EWHC 2020 (Admin), [2005] Crim LR 229 and commentary. See also the Administrative Court in *Mikolajczak v Poland* [2013] EWHC 432 (Admin) citing the 11th edn of this work.

[94] Hansard, HL, 14 Mar 2006, col 1108 (AG).   [95] C Reed, *Computer Law* (2012).

where and when the relevant communications will have legal effect.[96] The implications are important. Consider D who types his false statements into a document on his computer and proposes to send that document to V later via email. If by saving it he has 'submitted' it in a form to a device designed to receive, etc he commits the offence at that point, even though it has not yet been released from D's control. For example, suppose D intends to circulate his investment brochure full of false statements by email at 8 am the following day, and he puts his false prospectus in a 'draft mail to be sent' folder.[97]

Section 2(5) clearly extends the meaning of representation in cases involving 'submission to any system or device designed to receive, convey or respond to communications (with or without human intervention)', but what of those in which there is no 'submission' to such a system or device?[98] Is the concept of representation to be given an equally broad interpretation? What of the case in which D simply writes his representation on a piece of paper. Has he at that time made a representation? It is submitted that s 2(5) must be regarded as informing the general interpretation of the word representation. There is no need for completed communication to V. It suggests, implicitly, that there is no requirement that a representation should be addressed to anyone specifically, or to a human being, provided of course that it is addressed to someone or something.

There will be few instances where this element of s 2 will give rise to problems in practice. There is no doubt that if D makes a statement otherwise than to a system or device as defined in s 2(5), and it cannot be proved that it was represented to someone or something, D may nevertheless be liable for an attempted offence under s 1(2)(a) and s 2.

Attempted representation?

Since the s 2 form of the fraud offence can be committed as soon as D has dishonestly made a false representation, there is only limited scope for a charge of attempt. Possible examples include where D, having prepared documents containing false statements, is apprehended en route to post those to V. It may be that liability for the full offence arises even earlier if D decides to make his representations via a 'system' as defined in s 2(5) discussed above.

The most important circumstances in which an attempt will be charged may well be those in which D has unwittingly made a true statement. An historical example illustrates the problem well. In *Deller*,[99] D induced V to purchase his car by representing, inter alia, that it was free from encumbrances, that is, that D had ownership and was free to sell it. In fact, D had previously executed a document that purported to mortgage the car to a finance company and, no doubt, he thought he was telling a lie. He was charged with obtaining by false pretences.[100] However, the document by which the transaction had been effected was probably void in law for the technical reason that it was as an unregistered bill of sale. If the document was void the car *was* free from encumbrances: 'quite accidentally and, strange as it may sound, dishonestly, the appellant had told the truth'.[101] D's conviction was, therefore, quashed by the Court of Criminal Appeal, for, though D had mens rea, no actus reus had been established. Under the 2006 Act, D could be convicted of an attempted fraud as soon as he made the true representation with intent.

---

[96] ibid.

[97] In such a case, could D also argue that he was not intending by *that representation* as made to his own computer to make a gain or cause loss. This is unlikely to succeed as a plea: D does intend to gain by *that* representation eventually—when it is sent

[98] Neither term is further defined. Presumably the government was anxious not to use terminology which might become outdated or too difficult to define as, eg, with 'computer'.

[99] (1952) 36 Cr App R 184. Cf *Brien* (1903) 3 SRNSW 410; *Dyson* [1908] 2 KB 454.

[100] Under the Larceny Act 1916, s 32. The same principles are applicable.

[101] (1952) 36 Cr App R 184 at 191.

The Court of Appeal agreed with this interpretation in *Cornelius*.[102] D was convicted of a number of counts of fraud and money laundering. It transpired, however, that the very technical representations he made were in fact true. The Court of Appeal quashed his convictions and confirmed that he could be guilty of attempting the offences.

Where the representation occurs

The actus reus requires that a representation is made, and hence the offence should be regarded as occurring in the place in which D acts in making that representation. The discussion earlier is pertinent. A representation may be articulated and received at different locations and even in different jurisdictions.

Representations by words, conduct or other means

The most obvious forms of the offence will involve D's physical action in the form of oral or written representations. D satisfies the 'making' element of the offence as much by saying to a customer: 'this is a genuine Chippendale chair I have for sale' as by describing the chair in those terms in his catalogue. The offence will catch false representations on mortgage application forms, or loan application forms,[103] or as to the need for building work to be performed on an elderly person's home;[104] or by falsifying documents relating to a will[105] or by use of false identity documents to secure work.[106] In *Formhals*, for example, D was convicted of falsely representing that various items of memorabilia were signed by Winston Churchill, when in fact the signatures were forged by D.[107] The s 2 form of the offence is also designed to tackle 'phishing' on the internet. D who posts on the internet a website purporting to be that of a bank or financial institution, encouraging account holders to reveal their passwords and confidential information, will commit the offence. It does not matter that the website is ignored by everyone; a false representation has been made.

Forms of physical conduct other than speech or writing will suffice as where D nods assent in response to the question 'Is this a genuine Chippendale chair?' Conduct was capable of providing a relevant representation for the deception offences, and some of the old authorities remain valuable. In *Barnard*,[108] D went into an Oxford shop wearing a fellow-commoner's cap and gown. He induced the shopkeeper to sell him goods on credit by an express representation that he was a student; but Bolland B said, *obiter*, that he would have been guilty even if he had said nothing: he was making an implied representation that he was a student. In an Australian case,[109] the wearing of a badge was held to be a 'false pretence' when it indicated that the wearer was entitled to take bets on a racecourse. This would seem to constitute a 'representation'. Similarly, wearing a false press badge to gain entry to a sporting event or a members' tie in order to gain entry to the enclosure at Lords may constitute representations. There will remain some forms of conduct which give rise to doubt—is it enough that D represents that he is authorized to be 'present' in a virtual place, by having logged on illicitly to a website or secure terminal? The representation is not, of course, the entire offence—there must be dishonesty and an intention to gain or cause loss in terms of property for a completed offence.

In early versions of the Bill the definition of 'representation' expressly referred to the fact that it could be by 'words or conduct' but that term is omitted from the section as enacted. Almost all representations will be by words or conduct, but Parliament's deletion

102 [2012] EWCA Crim 500.
103 See cases under the Act including: *Viera* [2009] EWCA Crim 528; *Cleps* [2009] EWCA Crim 894.
104 See eg *Cowan* [2007] EWCA Crim 3402; *Hamilton* [2008] EWCA Crim 2518.
105 *Hursthouse* [2011] EWCA Crim 3064.
106 See eg *Kapitene* [2010] EWCA Crim 2061; *Haboub* [2007] EWCA Crim 3320.
107 [2013] EWCA Crim 2624.   108 (1837) 7 C & P 784.   109 *Robinson* (1884) 10 VLR 131.

of that expression raises the question whether the offence might also be committed by silent inaction.

Representation by omission/continuing representations

A simple example of a representation by omission is provided by the CPS: where D omits 'to mention previous convictions or County Court Judgments on an application form'.[110] It seems clear that D would be falsely representing himself as being of 'good character or financial probity'. This could, of course, be seen as a case of positive action—completing a form with false information.[111]

The interrelationship between ss 2 and 3 is important in considering representations by omission. Section 3 is considered in full later, but in short it criminalizes failing to disclose information. However, s 3 is limited to cases in which D is under a 'legal duty' to disclose information; a broad reading of s 2 would not be so limited. Several scenarios deserve to be considered in more detail. An important distinction always to bear in mind is that if D made a representation as to a future event (eg a future payment) and he never intended to keep the promise he made, that will be a false representation under s 2.[112] In contrast, if D breaks his promise but at the time he made that promise there was no false representation as to his state of mind (ie at the time he made it he intended to pay), he will not commit a section 2 offence.

The first scenario to examine is where D has not actively misrepresented any fact or opinion to V, but realizes that V is acting under a misconception as to the matters D has expressed. D may be liable under s 3 only *if* he is under a legal duty to correct V's error. In considering D's potential liability under s 2, it is important that the criminal law reflects the civil law's *caveat emptor* principle. We suggest that liability for the failure to remedy V's misunderstanding of non-false statements ought to be restricted to that which may arise under s 3 where D has a legal duty to disclose.[113] Support for this approach derives from the Attorney General in early parliamentary debates on the Bill, when the Attorney General accepted that there are occasions when:

something that most of us naturally might think of as a non-disclosure is transformed by a fiction of the law into an implicit misrepresentation. But it is a fiction; it is not how people think about it. People will frequently say, 'I was not misled because I understand that he was implicitly making this representation to me. He just did not disclose something; he was dishonest in not disclosing it; and the purpose of that was to make a gain or to do something else'. One can think of many other examples where that would be the true basis on which a charge would be laid.[114]

Under the old deception offences, in *Firth*,[115] a consultant was held to have deceived a hospital by failing to inform the hospital that certain patients were private patients. D knew that the effect would be that the patients would be treated on the NHS and not have to pay. The court apparently regarded this omission, which constituted a breach of D's contractual duty, as 'conduct' for the purposes of determining whether there was a deception.[116] Under the 2006 Act this would be an offence under s 3 as he had a legal duty to inform the employer.[117] We suggest that to maximize clarity and certainty such cases should be prosecuted under s 3 and ought not to be within the scope of s 2.

---

[110] See www.cps.gov.uk/legal-guidance/fraud-act-2006.   [111] See eg *D* [2012] EWCA Crim 2181.

[112] See eg *Shabbir* [2012] EWCA Crim 1482.

[113] See eg H Beale, *Chitty on Contracts* (33rd edn, 2020) Ch 6.

[114] Hansard, HL, 19 July 2005, cols 1411–12.

[115] (1989) 91 Cr App R 217, [1990] Crim LR 326 and commentary. Cf *Shama* [1990] 1 WLR 661.

[116] And s 4 (if there was an expectation that D would not act contrary to the financial interests of the hospital).

[117] *Smith v Hughes* (1871) LR 6 QB 597.

A second scenario is where D makes a representation to V which is not false within the meaning in s 2 but subsequently, to D's knowledge but not V's, circumstances change in a way that materially affects the accuracy of D's original representation. Where D is under a legal duty to disclose the change in circumstances to V (eg in a contract of insurance) he will be liable under s 3, but the question remains whether in those cases in which D is not under a legal duty, he ought to be liable under s 2. Once D is aware of the change of circumstances, might D be said to be impliedly making a fresh, and now false, representation? Can D's conduct be seen as amounting to a continuing representation that is false?

Under the old law, in *DPP v Ray*,[118] it was established that D who enters a restaurant and orders a meal impliedly represents that he intends to pay for the meal before leaving,[119] and probably also represents, in the absence of an agreement for credit, that he has the money to pay.[120] In that case, D's implied representation was true when made and continued to be true until the end of the meal, but when D changed his mind and decided to leave without paying it became false. Under the 1968 Act, it was essential to prove that V acted on the false representation and that the result of V acting was that D obtained the property or the service as the case may be.[121] It was held that the waiter acted on the false statement by leaving the room thereby allowing D an opportunity to leave, when he would not have done so had he known the truth, that D intended to leave without paying. Importantly for present purposes, Lord Pearson referred to there being a continuing representation: 'By 'continuing representation' I mean in this case not a continuing effect of an initial representation, but a representation which is being made by conduct at every moment throughout that course of conduct . . .'

Under the 2006 Act, the Administrative Court considered this issue with reference to s 2 in *Government of the United Arab Emirates v Allen*.[122] A obtained a loan from a bank in Abu Dhabi in order to buy a property. A agreed to repay the loan in monthly instalments that were to be taken from her account with the bank. A provided the bank with a post-dated check that they could cash in order to recoup the amount if she defaulted on the loan. (This was standard banking practice in the UAE.) Some months later A defaulted but when the bank presented the cheque there were, unsurprisingly, insufficient funds in her account to honour it. This constituted a criminal offence in the UAE and the issue for the Administrative Court was whether it would also constitute an offence in England and Wales so that A could be extradited. Counsel for the UAE sought to argue that this would be a fraud under s 2 as there was a continuing representation made by A that there were sufficient funds in her account to honour the cheque. Toulson LJ rejected the analogy with *Ray*. A gave no undertaking to the bank that she would inform it of any changes in her financial circumstances after it had advanced the loan monies and there was no basis for construing an implied representation to this effect into the loan agreement. His lordship went on to observe that: 'Implied representations are legal constructs intended to give effect to that which honest parties involved in a transaction would reasonably read into the conduct of the other.' Although there might be cases in which there is a duty to inform the representee if there is a change of circumstances, such as in the course of contractual negotiations, this was not one of them.[123]

---

[118] [1974] AC 370; *Nordeng* (1975) 62 Cr App R 123 at 129.

[119] *DPP v Ray* [1974] AC 370 at 379, 382, 385, 388, 391.   [120] ibid, 379, 382.

[121] It was accepted that if D had decided only once the waiter left the room that he would not pay and then made off while the waiter was out of the room, he would not have committed the offence. On the facts, D's continued presence was essential to the prosecution's case.

[122] [2012] EWHC 1712 (Admin).

[123] In *Government of the United Arab Emirates v Amir* [2012] EWHC 1711 (Admin), a case that was heard with *Allen*, the Administrative Court allowed the appeal against the District Judge's dismissal of an extradition request. It was held that there was a prima facie case of fraud against D. The different outcome between the two cases was due to differences in their facts. This demonstrates that in some circumstances there can be a continuing representation sufficient to found liability.

A third scenario to consider when interpreting the interrelationship between s 2 and s 3 is that where D makes a false representation but at the time he makes it he believes it to be true. If D discovers that the statement is false and thereafter does not seek to rectify any misunderstanding, might he be liable?[124] The resolution of this issue is not self-evident because of the manner in which s 2 is drafted. At the time of making the representation, D makes a statement which is inaccurate (untrue or misleading), but it is not false under s 2 unless at that time D also knows that it is or might be false. The falsity of the statement is dependent on proof of an element of mens rea. If D believes he is making a true statement then, for the purposes of s 2, there is no false statement actually made. To avoid this problem, the courts would have to interpret the concept of representation as being a continuing one. For the reasons expressed by Toulson LJ above, they may be reluctant to do so.

As a matter of general principle, it is submitted that considerable caution should be exercised in interpreting s 2 to prevent undesirable extension of the criminal law where D is neither responsible nor at fault in causing V to interpret the representation in an erroneous manner nor under a legal duty to disclose the fact of V's error. The criminal law ought to take its lead from the civil law. The maxim *caveat emptor* ought to operate to restrict the scope of liability. In commercial transactions, D, though under a duty to do nothing to confirm any misunderstanding by V, has no duty to correct it even though he is fully aware of it. '[T]he passive acquiescence of the seller in the self-deception of the buyer does not entitle the buyer to avoid the contract.'[125] This ought not to amount to a s 2 offence and the Administrative Court seems to have accepted that it does not in *Allen*. It is possible for there to be liability in such circumstances if there is a continuing representation. Whether this is so depends upon the terms of the agreement between the two parties and the Administrative Court in *Allen* demonstrated a marked reluctance lightly to infer such a representation.[126] The CPS has issued important guidance on the public interest test in prosecuting frauds which states that:

The borderline between criminal and civil liability is likely to be an issue in alleged Fraud Act offences particularly those under Section 1. Prosecutors should bear in mind that the principle of *caveat emptor* applies and should consider whether civil proceedings or the regulatory regime that applies to advertising and other commercial activities might be more appropriate. Not every advertising puff should lead to a criminal conviction but it is also the case that fraudsters prey on the vulnerable. Prosecutors should guard against the criminal law being used as a debt collection agency or to protect the commercial interests of companies and organisations. However, prosecutors should also remain alert to the fact that such organisations can become the focus of serious and organised criminal offending. The criminal law should not be used to protect private confidences.[127]

---

[124] cf *Rai* [2000] 1 Cr App R 242 under the old law where D failed to inform the local authority that his mother had died and allowed them to continue their installation of disability aids to her house to which he was not entitled. See a similar scenario in *Ali* [2006] All ER (D) 270 (May), where D was not in receipt of student support when applying for local authority benefit, but when he received student support he failed to disclose this change in circumstances to the local authority. The prosecution was under s 111A of the Social Security Administration Act 1992. See also *R (Pearson) v Greenwich MC* [2008] EWHC 300 (Admin). For an example of the nuances in its interpretation, see *Croydon LBC v Shanahan* [2010] EWCA Crim 98. See further *Arlidge and Parry on Fraud*, paras 4.053–4.054. For a prosecution under s 3 there must be an identified legal duty on D: *D* [2019] EWCA Crim 209 (local authority council tax payments).

[125] *Smith v Hughes* (1871) LR 6 QB 597.

[126] A different conclusion was reached in *Government of the United Arab Emirates v Amir* [2012] EWHC 1711 (Admin) due to differences in the facts and the terms of the agreement between the parties.

[127] See www.cps.gov.uk/legal-guidance/fraud-act-2006.

A representation may be express or implied: s 2(4)

Section 2(4) was included late in the passage of the Bill through the House of Lords[128] for the avoidance of doubt. Express representations will rarely give rise to difficulty, at least where they relate to facts (as opposed to states of mind). Greater difficulty is likely to arise in interpreting 'implied' representations, judging by experiences with the old law. A person who registers as a guest in a hotel represents that he intends to pay the bill at the end of his stay.[129] A wine waiter employed at a hotel impliedly represents that the wine he offers is his employer's, not his own.[130] A car dealer who states that the mileage shown on the odometer of a second-hand car 'may not be correct' represents that he does not know it to be incorrect.[131] A bookmaker, it is submitted, represents, when he takes a bet, that he intends to pay if the horse backed wins.[132] A person who takes a taxi represents that he intends to pay, and has the means of paying, at the end of the ride.[133]

Representations and cheques

When D offers a stolen cheque in payment for goods he is clearly making a false representation since he has no authority to write the cheque in the first place. Where D offers a cheque on his own account in payment for goods he may also be committing a s 2 offence, but that will depend on identifying the false representation. He makes three implied representations: (a) that he has an account on which the cheque is drawn; (b) that he has authority to draw on the bank for that amount; and (c) that the state of facts existing at the time he offers the cheque is that in the ordinary course of events payment will be made when it is presented by the recipient for payment.

This was the accepted orthodoxy from cases as early as *Hazelton*,[134] where Pollock B stated that the representation is that 'the existing state of facts is such that in the ordinary course the cheque will be met'. In *Gilmartin*, the Court of Appeal thought that 'this terse but neat epitome of the representation . . . should properly be regarded as an authoritative statement of the law'.[135]

Where D postdates a cheque, his liability will depend on his state of mind at the time of offering the cheque. Toulson LJ in *Government of the United Arab Emirates v Allen*, stated:

To summarise, it is easy to see that a person who obtains goods or services by giving a cheque in payment which he knows that he is not going to be in a position to meet, but who does not disclose that fact to the supplier, carries out a form of deception. . . .

As a matter of common law, a representation must be capable of being expressed as a statement of the past or present. A statement which amounts only to a statement as to the future may have effect as a contractual promise, but it will not come within the legal classification of a representation. A promise may carry with it an implied statement as to the promissor's present intention and circumstances, but that is a representation of present fact.[136]

If D genuinely believes, at the time he writes the cheque, that there will be funds in the account when it is presented for payment, he is not making a false representation at the time he offers the cheque. If D's state of mind at the time he offers the cheque is such that he has no belief that the cheque will be paid, he is making a false representation. As the

---

[128] Hansard, HL, 14 Mar 2006, col 1107.   [129] *Harris* (1975) 62 Cr App R 28.

[130] *Doukas* [1978] 1 All ER 1061. The decision is to be preferred to *Rashid* [1977] 2 All ER 237.

[131] *King* [1979] Crim LR 122.   [132] cf *Buckmaster* (1887) 20 QBD 182.

[133] cf *Waterfall* [1970] 1 QB 148.

[134] (1874) LR 2 CCR 134, the source of the proposition in Kenny, *Outlines*, 359, adopted in *Page* [1971] 2 QB 330 at 333.

[135] (1983) 76 Cr App R 238 at 244.   [136] At [39] and [41].

Administrative Court made clear, when an individual presents a post-dated cheque as security for a loan, there is no general obligation to inform the lender if the balance in his account has dwindled such that the cheque may not be honoured. Of course, if there is a term in the loan agreement that requires disclosure of any change in circumstances, then D may be liable under s 3. Close attention needs to be paid to the terms of the agreement to ascertain whether D is liable.

Credit cards and debit cards

When a person presents his credit or debit card he makes a representation (a) that he has the authority to use that card, and (b) that payment will be made. Under the old law problems arose because the representation had to cause the obtaining. That difficulty is removed because under the 2006 Act the requirement is only that the representation that is made is false and D intends to gain/cause loss *by* that false representation. There are, however, two problems which do need to be considered.

The first relates to whether there is a false statement about authority to use the card and payment being made. As a matter of banking law, the issuing of debit cards includes an undertaking by the bank that, if the conditions on the card are satisfied, the payment will be honoured. The position with credit cards is similar.[137] The bank issuing the card enters into contracts with the trader, agreeing to pay the trader the sum shown on a voucher signed by the customer/confirmed by chip and PIN when making a purchase, provided that the conditions on the credit or debit card are satisfied. Conditions on both types of card may be satisfied although the holder is exceeding his authority. The trader accepting either type of card will usually accept the card simply because the conditions on the card are satisfied. He will not know whether the customer is exceeding his authority and using the card in breach of contract with the bank. He will get his money in any event. This is neither immoral nor unreasonable. The whole object of these cards is to avoid the trader concerning himself with the relationship between the cardholder and his bank. The trader is perfectly entitled to take advantage of the facility which the banks offer to him.

If D is unaware of the banking practice whereby the trader is guaranteed to receive payment, he will unwittingly be making a true statement that payment will be made. Since he intends to make a false representation, he would theoretically also be liable for an attempt. However, resort to such technicalities is unnecessary. The fact that D makes a true representation that payment will be made is not the end of the matter because in many of these cases D will be making a separate, false representation. When D presents the card knowing he is lacking authority to do so—for example, because it is not his own card, etc—he makes a false representation subject to the specific contractual terms on which the card was issued. If that representation is made (even impliedly), the element of the offence is satisfied. D will be aware that he is making that representation and that it is false.[138]

The second problem is the requirement that it must be *by the* false representation that D intends to gain/cause loss or expose another to a risk of loss. If D has made a false representation

137 In the case of credit cards, the contract between the bank and the trader precedes the purchase by the customer, whereas in the case of the debit card the contract is made when the trader accepts the customer's cheque, relying on the card which is produced. See W Blair, G Walker, J Chuah and L Oyesanya, *Encyclopedia of Banking Law* (2020) D23; *First Sport Ltd v Barclays Bank plc* [1993] 1 WLR 1229, CA (Civ Div), holding, Kennedy LJ dissenting, that the bank was bound even though the cheque was a forgery. Lord Roskill's opinion in *Lambie* (all their lordships concurring) that the customer was making a contract as agent for the credit card company is powerfully criticized by F Bennion, 'Credit or Theft: The *Lambie* Cases' (1981) 131 NLJ 431.

138 cf the decisions of the Administrative Court in *Poland v Ulatowski* [2010] EWHC 2673 (Admin) and *Chodorek v Poland* [2017] EWHC 995 (Admin).

as to his authority to use the card, it seems clear that he has *by* that false representation intended to expose another (the credit card company and/or the trader) to a risk of loss. Arguably, by that false representation D also intends to gain by keeping that which he has (s 5(3)). Subject to dishonesty, all the other elements also appear to be satisfied:[139] it is no excuse that D also intends the trader to receive payment (ie not to make a loss). But, perhaps the trader does not care whether D has authority (because) the trader will receive his payment as explained earlier. Can D claim therefore that it was not *by* his false representation to the trader that he intended to make a gain/cause a loss? Although this is a plea that D can raise, alongside one of a lack of dishonesty in such circumstances, it is submitted that it will be unlikely to succeed. The trader's apparent disinterest in D's representations is in fact more apparent than real.[140] If D uses X's card because D knows X's PIN, D dishonestly makes a false representation as to authority to use the card. X might be recompensed by his bank for any loss and the trader might (probably will) be paid by the bank, but the bank will lose out. In that sense, it does appear that neither X nor the shopkeeper particularly 'care' if the card is misused—neither will lose out, but there is an argument which suggests that beneath that superficiality they do 'care'. If X or the trader became aware that D was misusing the card, and chose to endorse that misuse, then he would become party to the fraud against the bank. X and the trader 'care'—not because they may suffer financial loss, but because they might otherwise become accessories to a criminal offence and, on becoming accessories, they would lose their right to recompense.

Some commentators argue that there is not a false representation in such circumstances.[141] It is submitted that this interpretation places too much emphasis on the likely significance of the representation to V. That issue is no longer of relevance under the 2006 Act because the question is not whether V might be deceived or believe a matter, it is whether it is a representation to the trader that is false. If D has no authority to use the card, the trader would not accept his card because otherwise the trader would be an accomplice to D's fraud on the bank.

Representations as to 'fact'

Representations as to present facts will present little difficulty for the courts. If D asserts that he is selling a solid gold watch and it is, to his knowledge, made of brass, he commits the offence. Greater difficulty arises if his statements included making a representation as to future facts.[142] As noted previously, statements that are not representations of D's present state of mind or the present state of facts are merely promises as to the future and do not amount to representations in law. In *Government of the United Arab Emirates v Allen*,[143] the Administrative Court held that a statement that amounts *only* to a statement as to the future may have effect as a contractual promise, but will not fall within the definition of 'representation' in s 2(3).

Representations as to 'law'

Section 2(3) expressly provides that 'any representation' as to law will suffice. Representations of law ought to be caught as, for example, where D and V are reading a legal document and

---

[139] Arguably the trader will also be exposed to the risk of loss.

[140] For consideration of the bank's obligation where it is suspected that there was no genuine transaction with an unauthorized card, see *Do-buy 925 Ltd v National Westminster Bank plc* [2010] EWHC 2862 (QB).

[141] The argument is that there can only be a representation as to authority by D if he thinks that it will matter to V, and since the trader, V, will not care whether D is authorized, there is no false representation. *Arlidge and Parry on Fraud*, paras 4.068–4.070.

[142] Section 2(3) defines a representation as meaning '*any* representation as to fact . . .', but the term 'any' relates to the type of representation, not the type of fact; it is designed to encourage the most expansive reading of 'representation'.

[143] [2012] EWHC 1712 (Admin).

D deliberately misrepresents its legal effect. This would seem to be false representation of law since the construction of documents is a question of law. If D does so with the intent to gain or cause loss, for example by inducing V to pay money for the release of his rights, this would seem to amount to fraud contrary to s 2. Greater difficulty will arise where the state of the law contained in the representation is uncertain. For a representation to be 'false' within s 2, not only must it be untrue or misleading in fact but D must know it is or might be untrue or misleading. Where there is some ambiguity as to the state of the law, D will only be making a false representation where it is untrue or misleading *and* he does not believe it to be true. The following proposition formulated by Street for the law of the tort of deceit is probably equally true of the concept of representation in this context:

If the representations refer to legal principles, as distinct from the facts on which those principles operate, and the parties are on an equal footing, those representations are expressions of belief only and of the same effect as expressions of opinion between parties on an equal footing. In other cases where the defendant professes legal knowledge beyond that of the claimant . . ., the potential arise for an action in deceit. However, liability is likely to arise in clear cases of misrepresentation of the law only, given the often contentious nature of legal rules.[144]

Representations as to 'states of mind'

Section 2(3) provides that a representation as to a state of mind of any person will suffice. A representation as to a present intention of either D or some other person will therefore be sufficient. Representations as to present intentions may be expressed or implied.

If D states that his intention is that he will pay V tomorrow, he is making a representation as to his present state of mind. The prosecution must, of course, go further and prove that the representation as to D's state of mind was false; that is, it must be proved that at the time of making the representation as to the present state of mind, D knew that it was false. If D, at the time of making the representation, intended to carry out his promise but later changed his mind he is guilty of a breach of contract. He is also guilty under s 3 of the 2006 Act if he is under a legal duty to disclose that information (ie the change of intention).

Representations as to the present intentions of a person other than D seem to be rare. Examples would include where an agent obtains property for his principal by representing that the principal intends to render services or supply goods, well knowing that the principal has no such intention, or where an estate agent says that a particular building society is willing to advance half the purchase price of a house, knowing that this is not so. Where the representation is as to the state of mind of another, it may be more common for the prosecution to allege, in proving falsity, that D knew not that it was untrue but that it *might* be untrue or misleading.

Statements of opinion

Difficulties have arisen in determining whether a statement of opinion is sufficient to constitute a representation. D who says 'this is a Swiss-made watch' is making a representation of fact. But what of D who says 'the quality of the mechanism in this watch is as good as a Swiss made one': is this a representation of fact? Is it a representation as to D's state of mind—also capable of being treated as a representation of fact under s 2?

In the old case of *Bryan*,[145] D obtained money from V by representing that certain spoons were of the best quality. These statements were false to D's knowledge.[146] Nevertheless, ten out of 12 judges[147] held that his conviction must be quashed on the ground that this was

---

[144] C Witting, *Street on Torts* (15th edn, 2018) 343.   [145] (1857) Dears & B 265.
[146] D's counsel said: 'I cannot contend that the prisoner did not tell a wilful lie . . .'
[147] Willes J *dissentiente* and Bramwell B *dubitante*.

mere exaggerated praise by a seller of his goods to which the statute was not intended to apply. It is submitted that the case went too far.[148] D's statement that the spoons had as much silver in them as a famous brand was a statement of fact.[149]

Difficulties will no doubt arise in distinguishing representations of fact from opinion, particularly when it comes to exaggeration as to value or excessive quotation. It has been held[150] that it is a misrepresentation of fact for DD to state 'that they [had] effected necessary repairs to a roof [which repairs were specified] that they had done the work in a proper and workmanlike manner and that [a specified sum] was a fair and reasonable sum to charge for the work involved'. The evidence showed that nothing needed to be done to the roof, what had been done served no useful purpose and it could have been done for £5, whereas £35 was charged. It might be argued that representations as to quotations for goods or services could be interpreted as including an implied representation of fact that the price quoted is one reflecting only a fair profit margin. But even this strained reading will not assist in all cases. What of the vendor's description of his tenant as 'a most desirable tenant' when the rent was in arrears and, in the past, had only been paid under pressure? This was held by the Court of Appeal to be a sufficient misrepresentation to found an action in deceit.[151]

Deliberate misstatements of opinion will be likely to be generally condemned as dishonest, no less dishonest, indeed, than misstatements of other facts—for whether an opinion is held or not is a fact. The question now ought to be not 'Is it a matter of opinion?' but, 'If it is a matter of opinion, was it D's real opinion?' If the opinion is not honestly held there is a misrepresentation of fact, for D's present state of mind is a question of fact.

22.3.2.2 'False' representation

Whether a representation is false usually depends on the meaning intended or understood by the parties and that too is a question for the jury, even where the statement is made in a document. Where the issue is as to the legal effect of a document, it is for the judge to decide.[152] For example, where the enforceability of a contract is in issue, it is for the trial judge to decide that matter of law.[153]

Section 2(2)(a) provides that a representation may be false by either being 'untrue' or 'misleading'. It is necessary for the prosecution to establish as a matter of actus reus that the representation is false or misleading aside from any issue about D's knowledge as to its truth or otherwise. However, the states of mind of the parties are likely to be important. Indeed, rather oddly the Act provides that a statement is only false if D knows it is or knows it might be false. The definition of falsity turns not solely on the objectively discernible fact of its lack of accuracy, but on D's subjective awareness of that fact or its possibility.

Untrue

The word is an ordinary English word and no doubt the courts will suggest that juries should be directed to approach it as such. The only potential difficulties in application relate to

---

[148] It may be a significant fact that at the time *Bryan* was decided, it was not possible for the prisoner to give evidence in his own defence. In *Ragg* (1860) Bell CC 208 at 219, Erle CJ, referring to *Bryan*, said, 'if such statements are indictable a purchaser who wishes to get out of a bad bargain made by his own negligence, might have recourse to an indictment, on the trial of which the vendor's statement on oath would be excluded, instead of being obliged to bring an action where each party would be heard on equal terms'.

[149] *Ardley* (1871) LR 1 CCR 301.

[150] *Jeff and Bassett* (1966) 51 Cr App R 28. Cf *Hawkins v Smith* [1978] Crim LR 578 ('Showroom condition throughout' a false trade description of a car which has interior and mechanical defects).

[151] *Smith v Land and House Property Corpn* (1884) 28 Ch D 7.

[152] *Adams* [1994] RTR 220, [1993] Crim LR 525 and commentary. Cf *Deller*, p 979.

[153] *Whatcott* [2019] EWCA Crim 188 (enforceability of late payment and cancellation fees relating to the supply of domestic energy performance certificates for judge to decide).

those representations made by D which are not *wholly* untrue. It should be noted that there is no requirement that the falsity relates to a material particular. Where D's representation contains one falsity, even if it relates to a peripheral matter in his dealings with V, he may be convicted subject to the jury concluding that the use of that falsity was dishonest, and that it is *by that falsity*[154] that he intended to gain or cause loss. This may give rise to difficulties in a range of circumstances from the street trader who exaggerates his wares to the investment fraudster who falsely embellishes certain aspects of the deal.

Where the requirement to prove that D's statement was untrue involves the prosecution proving a negative and D knows the affirmative facts that will establish the truth of the statement, there may be an onus on him to introduce some evidence of the affirmative fact. For example in *Mandry and Wooster*,[155] street traders selling scent for 25p, said, 'You can go down the road and buy it for 2 guineas in the big stores.' The police checked the price at certain stores but it was admitted in cross-examination that they had not been to Selfridges. It was held that it was not improper for the judge to point out that it was impossible for the police to go to every shop in London and that 'if the defence knew of their own knowledge of anywhere it could be bought at that price . . . they were perfectly entitled to call evidence'. Even though no evidence was called to show that the perfume was on sale at Selfridges or anywhere else, the convictions were upheld.

D may often be able to argue that it was not *by* the particular falsity alleged that he intended to make the gain/cause the loss. This issue is discussed earlier.[156] Simply because D's representation relates to a peripheral matter will not *entitle* the defendant to an acquittal. It will be a question of fact and degree in every case whether what was said was intended to be a misrepresentation by which the gain or loss would be made. Ironically, the jury may be more likely to acquit a person whose lie is a whopper of such proportions that the jury accept that, although knowingly false, no one could have intended that it would be believed. In general, the defence are going to be faced with the difficult obstacle which is the juror's natural inclination to ask—'if D did not intend that his representation would lead to the gain or loss why did he make it?'

Or misleading

The inclusion of this alternative suggests that the draftsman intended that it constitute a distinct route to establishing falsity. The Home Office has suggested a very wide interpretation of the term 'misleading' proposing that it means 'less than wholly true and capable of an interpretation to the detriment of the victim'.[157] Being 'untrue' and being 'misleading' are, it is submitted, distinct.[158] An untrue statement is one which is literally false. A statement can be misleading even though it is literally true. Common examples are where D fails to provide a comprehensive answer to a question. For example, V asks D a car salesman 'Have you had many faults reported with this model?' and D replies, 'Only one this year'. That may be a literally true statement, but is highly misleading if there were 200 faults reported the previous year.[159] To display a cheap fake with a collection of originals by a well-known artist may amount to a misleading representation that the fake is by the famous artist.

---

[154] See p 972 and *Gilbert* [2012] EWCA Crim 2392.

[155] [1973] 3 All ER 996; cf *Silverman* (1987) 86 Cr App R 213.

[156] At p 972.   [157] Para 19.

[158] Although Arlidge and Parry dispute this. See *Arlidge and Parry on Fraud*, para 4.089.

[159] There is little problem in practice in saying that the misrepresentation is by something not literally true but meant to be misunderstood: *Moens v Heyworth* (1842) 10 M & W 147. There are academic debates as to which conduct is more blameworthy and whether the victim of one or the other suffers greater harm. One view is that the victim who is misled feels more aggrieved since he has played a part in his own loss by inferring facts which D did not expressly represent. See generally Green, *Lying, Cheating and Stealing*.

There are, arguably, important moral distinctions between the conduct of someone who lies outright and someone who is merely economical with the truth, allowing the hearer to infer facts for which he must take some responsibility—*caveat auditor!*[160] These distinctions find no place in the 2006 Act.

Whether a representation is misleading can be a matter of degree. Is a 'trade puff' misleading? The main riposte by a street trader to an allegation that he made a false representation may be that there was no dishonesty. The second argument that he may rely on is that he did not intend by his exaggerated banter to cause anyone to believe him and that he did not therefore intend *by* that admittedly false representation to gain or cause loss. Such arguments may sometimes be difficult to sustain in a court remote in time and atmosphere from the theatre of a street market.[161]

Proof of falsity

Proving whether a representation is untrue will be far easier when it relates to a fact (or law) that exists at the time of the making of the representation[162] than when it relates to the state of mind of an individual. If the representation is untrue, there is no explicit defence that the representation was made for good reason or with lawful excuse, as where D said he made the false representation in order to recover property belonging (he believed) to him. In such a case, the defendant must rely on the claim of a lack of dishonesty,[163] and, as noted, the Act does not provide a special defence of belief in claim of right.

22.3.3 Mens rea

22.3.3.1 'Knowing that the representation is' or 'knowing that it might be' false

Knowledge is a strict form of mens rea; much stricter than 'belief', 'suspicion', 'having reasonable grounds to suspect' and even 'recklessness'.[164] In this offence, knowledge is in a diluted form—the prosecution need only prove knowledge that the representation either: (a) is untrue; or (b) is misleading; or (c) might be untrue; or (d) might be misleading. The Court of Appeal confirmed in *Augunas*[165] that it is insufficient that the reasonable person might have known that the representation is or might be false. What matters is the defendant's knowledge: this is a subjective test.

In the context of representations as to existing facts, the proof of knowledge will be least difficult to establish. It will require proof, often by inference, that D possessed knowledge of the existence of the falsity of the representation. More difficult will be cases where the falsity relates to the representation which is about D's present state of mind. Even with the opportunity for the prosecution to succeed on proof of knowledge that D knew that the representation might be misleading, difficulties may arise.

---

[160] See Green, *Lying, Cheating and Stealing*, 78.

[161] See earlier and the correspondence between Ormerod and Gardner [2007] Crim LR 661.

[162] The A-G accepted that it is implicit in the drafting of s 2 that 'the only time at which one can make a judgment about whether the defendant thinks his representation is, or might be, untrue, is when he makes the representation. So if he believes it to be true at the time he makes it, he cannot have been dishonest', Hansard, HL, 19 July 2005, col 1420.

[163] See p 968.

[164] See the House of Lords discussion of the definition of knowledge in the context of conspiracy: *Saik* [2006] UKHL 18.

[165] [2013] EWCA Crim 2046.

It is sufficient that D is shown to have known that his representation *might be* false. Is the offence rendered too wide by this alternative mens rea? D tells a customer that he has a Renoir for sale. D knows that there is a risk, as with all art, that the painting might be a fake. Does D know that the statement *might be* misleading? He will only be guilty if he made a false statement and he was dishonest. Many competent art dealers will acknowledge that there is always a risk that a painting might be a forgery. In short, a dealer who believes that his attribution in respect of this painting is true, acts honestly. He has an honest belief based upon provenance, history, his own expertise, reliance on the expertise of others or a combination of any of these factors. The dealer who actually thinks it might be untrue, acts, it is submitted, dishonestly. If the painting in question turns out to be a forgery, a representation has been made. The element of dishonesty once again serves as the principal determinant of guilt.[166] Interestingly, in debates in Parliament the Attorney General had no difficulty with this example,[167] saying that it would be for a jury to decide if the art dealer was dishonest and thus guilty of fraud.

If an art dealer said, 'This is a painting by Renoir', knowing that that statement can have a huge impact on the value of the painting—but not knowing whether it is true and thinking that it might be untrue—it would be for a jury to decide whether he was dishonest. If he was dishonest, I see no difficulty in saying that he is guilty of fraud in those circumstances.[168]

Is this an oversimplification? Is the Attorney General treating as sufficient D's *thinking* that a statement might be untrue or misleading?[169] But did the art dealer know it might be misleading? He might argue that acceptance or knowledge that a thing might be untrue is different from thinking that it in fact is or might in fact be untrue. In the former case, the dealer, while accepting that nothing can be certain in the art market, believes that his attribution is true, and therefore acts honestly. The issue is properly regarded as one of dishonesty and not knowledge. It is easy to see that a person who has bought an item which has been wrongly attributed by an auction house might use the criminal law in s 2 to support his civil claim for misrepresentation.

It seems inevitable then that in practice this mens rea element will blur unsatisfactorily into the element of dishonesty.

Wilful blindness

The breadth of this fault element may extend even further if the courts interpret knowledge as including 'shutting one's eyes to an obvious means of knowledge' or 'deliberately refraining from making inquiries the results of which the person does not care to have'.[170] The Court of Appeal in *Augunas* stated, *obiter*, that 'if an accused person wilfully shuts his eyes to the obvious doubts as to the genuineness of the misrepresentation that he is making, then he knows that it might be untrue or misleading and he would be guilty of the offence'.[171] The concept is discussed further in Ch 3, but it suffices to say that this aspect of the decision in *Augunas* has the potential to expand significantly the scope of the offence.[172]

---

[166] Hansard, HL, 19 July 2005, col 1416 (Lord Kingsland).

[167] Nor did the Home Office in its *Response to Consultations*, observing that if it caused sellers to be more careful that was a desirable result: para 18.

[168] Hansard, HL, 19 July 2005, col 1417. The Home Office thought likewise in its *Response to Consultations*, para 17.

[169] cf the old law in which reckless deceptions sufficed: Theft Act 1968, s 15(4).

[170] *Roper v Taylor's Garage* [1951] 2 TLR 284, per Devlin J.

[171] [2013] EWCA Crim 2046, [9].

[172] See also *Manifest Shipping Co Ltd v Uni-Polaris Shipping Co Ltd and others* [2003] 1 AC 469.

Not negligence

What must certainly be guarded against is any slippage into regarding as a sufficient mens rea test negligence or constructive knowledge. The courts have rejected the idea that constructive knowledge is sufficient in the context of deception offences[173] and this state of negligence should have no part under the Fraud Act.[174] The government rejected as too wide mens rea alternatives which were proposed on consultation, including a test based on whether D had 'no reasonable grounds for believing' the representation to be true, and that he 'ought to have known' it to be false.

Knowledge and mistake of law

Where the alleged false representation is one relating to law, and D denies that he has knowledge as to the relevant law, if that is a denial of criminal law there is no excuse, but if D is denying a knowledge of civil law that may be a sufficient excuse.

22.3.3.2 Dishonesty

The test for dishonesty applies, as noted previously. This is potentially problematical in the s 2 form of the offence since the criminality turns almost exclusively on dishonesty, and the definition of that term is left to the jury to determine on a case-by-case basis. In addition, as noted, there is since *Ivey* and *Barton* no guarantee of acquittal where D has a claim of right or belief in a claim of right to the property he intends to gain by his false representation.

22.3.3.3 With intent to gain or cause loss

This element is discussed at p 970.

22.4 Section 3: fraud by failing to disclose information

Section 3 provides the second form of the general fraud offence introduced by s 1. It is far less heavily used. Section 3 provides:

A person is in breach of this section if he—

(a) dishonestly fails to disclose information to another person, which he is under a legal duty to disclose, and

(b) intends, by failing to disclose the information—

(i) to make a gain for himself or another, or

(ii) to cause loss to another or to expose another to a risk of loss.

22.4.1 General

The elements of this version of the fraud offence are, as with s 2, easy enough to describe. None of the elements is, however, defined in detail in the section. The actus reus comprises: failing to disclose information to a person; being under a *legal* duty to disclose. The mens rea comprises acting dishonestly, with an intention to make a gain/cause loss/expose to loss.

---

[173] *Flintshire CC v Reynolds* [2006] EWHC 195 (Admin).
[174] See *Augunas* [2013] EWCA Crim 2046, [9].

The important overriding principle of interpretation is that criminal liability under s 3 should not be imposed where the civil law imposes no duty on D. As has been emphasized throughout, it is desirable for the criminal law to respect the civil law foundations on which the offences are created.[175] This interpretation derives explicit support from the comments of the Attorney General in the course of parliamentary debates where he stated that 'the Government believe that it would be undesirable to create disparity between the criminal and the civil law; it should not be criminal to withhold information which you are entitled to withhold under civil law'.[176]

This overriding interpretative principle is also underlined by the fact that the offence is much narrower than original formulations proposed by the Law Commission. These included breaches of 'moral duties' or duties arising from an expectation in the mind of the person with whom D is dealing.[177] The Home Office expressly rejected these proposals as creating offences which would be too ambiguous and which would trespass on the *caveat emptor* principle.[178]

22.4.2 Relationship with s 2

This form of offence is much narrower than that under s 2, but their relationship warrants close attention.[179] Arguably, many cases in which there is a legal duty to disclose information might be regarded as involving an implied false representation within s 2.[180] As a matter of principle, it is preferable for the charges to be brought under s 3. The various scenarios were discussed earlier, p 981. This ensures an accuracy of labelling in the offence and conviction, and in practical terms it will be easier for juries to understand the wrongdoing in terms of failing to disclose.

A good example of the application of s 3 is the case of *Forrest and others*.[181] Four individuals were charged with several counts of fraud. One of the counts alleged that DD had dishonestly made a false representation on a mortgage application form. Another count alleged that DD had failed to disclose to the mortgage company what they were under a legal duty to disclose, namely that the funds for the deposit were coming not from their savings but from their limited company. DD accepted that there was a legal duty to provide the information sought by the mortgage application form truthfully, but argued that there was otherwise no legal duty to make disclosure of matters relating to the circumstances of the application. The judge acceded to this submission and the prosecution appealed. The Court of Appeal held that the failure to disclose the true source of the deposit in the mortgage application form was insufficient to fall within the scope of s 3 and that the trial judge had been correct in ruling as he did. Despite the fact they had made a false representation, DD had discharged the duty the application form imposed on them. Pitchford LJ observed that the prosecution's case was fatally undermined by its failure to assert that the representation in the mortgage application form was false. This case illustrates the importance for the prosecution to choose carefully between ss 2 and 3 and serves to reinforce the point that not every false representation can give rise to possible liability for failing to disclose.

---

175 See Sullivan [1985] Crim LR 617.   176 Hansard, HL, 19 July 2005, col 1426.

177 Home Office *Fraud Law Reform* (2004) paras 18–22.

178 See Home Office, *Fraud Reform: Government Response to Consultations* (2004) paras 21–5.

179 See p 981. See also Hansard, HL, 19 July 2005, col 1411.

180 Provided the failure to disclose when under such a duty can be seen as synonymous with a false representation by omission.

181 [2014] EWCA Crim 308.

22.4.3 Actus reus

22.4.3.1 A person

There is nothing to prevent a corporation being liable for a failure to disclose information under s 3 when the obligation is imposed by law on the corporate entity.[182]

22.4.3.2 Legal duty to disclose

For the purposes of determining when and where the offence occurs, it appears to be committed at the point at which the failure to disclose under the duty arises. D's duty must, it is submitted, be one arising under English law. It may arguably extend to some international law obligations to the extent that these are incorporated within domestic law.

Types of duty

The core element of the s 3 form of the fraud offence is the concept of 'legal duty'.[183] Unfortunately, this critical concept is not defined in the Act, nor even in the Home Office Explanatory Notes. It is necessary to turn to the Law Commission's Report for further guidance on which forms of legal duty were envisaged as being caught by the section. The Law Commission's Report *Fraud*,[184] stated that:

Such a duty may derive from statute (such as the provisions governing company prospectuses), from the fact that the transaction in question is one of the utmost good faith (such as a contract of insurance), from the express or implied terms of a contract, from the custom of a particular trade or market, or from the existence of a fiduciary relationship between the parties (such as that of agent and principal).

For this purpose there is a legal duty to disclose information not only if D's failure to disclose it gives V a cause of action for damages, but also if the law gives V a right to set aside any change in his legal position to which he may consent as a result of the non-disclosure.[185]

That opens an extremely broad vista of criminal liability. Some of the examples offered are already criminalized (eg the failure to disclose information in a company prospectus is criminalized by the Financial Services Act 2012).[186] Other categories will also be straightforward as, for example, with insurance contracts where a person fails to disclose that he has a medical condition when taking out life insurance; or with job applications where there is a failure to reveal criminal convictions.[187] There may be duties that arise in equity, contract and even in tort. In *Razoq*,[188] for example, D was a doctor who worked for the NHS. In addition, D also worked privately for a locum agency. When he joined the locum agency,

---

[182] For the liability of corporate officers, see s 12 of the 2006 Act.

[183] The requirement of a legal duty was endorsed by the 'Rose Committee' of senior judges: Hansard, HL, 12 June 2006, col 536.

[184] Paras 7.28 and 7.29.

[185] eg where a person in a fiduciary position has a duty to disclose material information when contracting with a beneficiary: a failure to make such disclosure will entitle the beneficiary to rescind the contract and to reclaim any property transferred under it. This section might be applicable in acrimonious divorce settlements where D withholds disclosure of his true assets. See D Salter, 'It's Criminal Not to Disclose' (2007) 37 Fam L 432.

[186] One example is that in the case of *Butt* [2005] EWCA Crim 1163, where D's duty arose from his role as an 'introducer' for the company making the representations about high-yield investment.

[187] See *Daley* [2010] EWCA Crim 2193. See also *Mashta* [2010] EWCA Crim 2595. In *D* [2012] EWCA Crim 2181, D was convicted of fraud by false representation for falsely asserting that she had no criminal convictions.

[188] [2012] EWCA Crim 674.

D signed a form stating that if he was subject to any disciplinary proceedings he had to inform the locum agency. D failed to inform the locum agency that there were disciplinary proceedings pending against him. In these circumstances, the Court of Appeal had no difficulty in finding that D was under a legal duty to disclose the fact that he was subject to disciplinary proceedings. Given that the terms of the contract signed by D were express, it was a question of fact for the jury whether D had received them and was aware of their content.

Some categories will, however, be less straightforward, particularly when this involves the criminal court in an assessment of complex matters of civil law.[189] Difficult matters of proof will arise where the question is whether a duty arises in the trade or custom or was agreed to orally, etc. What is essential is that no matter how strongly one might assume there is a legal duty in a particular context, the specific legal source of that duty must be identified and confirmed to apply. In D,[190] for example, D ceased paying her council tax having told the local authority, falsely, that she had moved and was renting the property to another party. She was not liable under s 3 because the prosecution could find no statutory duty on D to inform the council that she remained living in the property.

Since liability only arises on proof of a 'legal' duty, the question must, it is submitted, be one of law for the judge,[191] with the jury being directed to conclude that if they find certain facts, as identified by the judge, proved, they can conclude that in law there is a duty to disclose information.[192] Several Lords expressed doubts in Parliament as to whether judges would struggle in explaining this issue to the jury.[193] The element was, however, endorsed by the 'Rose Committee'—a committee of the Senior Judiciary.[194] The Home Office rather optimistically regarded this as a 'relatively uncomplicated' requirement.[195]

The criminal courts have demonstrated a marked reluctance to become embroiled in civil law issues in their interpretation of the Theft Acts[196] despite the fact that those offences, being specifically designed to protect property and property rights, necessarily rely upon the civil law's understanding of those concepts. Under s 3, the criminal courts are statutorily obliged to have regard to the civil law.

Scope of duty

The difficulties in applying the civil law are exacerbated because the civil law will be essential not only in identifying the relevant circumstances in which a duty arises, but also in cases where D has revealed some information in assessing whether it was a sufficient disclosure to satisfy the duty imposed upon him. Clearly, where the Prosecution can show that D has failed completely to comply with his civil duty, he will be liable. Beyond that, where

---

[189] A number of cases involve some alleged failure of disclosure in the context of mortgage applications. The Court of Appeal seems to have taken a minimalist approach to whether there is a legal duty in these circumstances, in that it is reluctant to infer a duty to disclose beyond what is required by the terms of the mortgage application. Eg in *White* [2014] EWCA Crim 714, D was under no legal duty to disclose that he was unemployed when applying for a mortgage. Nevertheless, D did make a false representation and could have been guilty of fraud on that basis. This highlights the delicate relationship between ss 2 and 3.

[190] [2019] EWCA Crim 209.

[191] Consistent also with the decision in *Whatcott* [2019] EWCA Crim 188 on s 2.

[192] cf the A-G's view that this was a question of fact: Hansard, HL, 19 July 2005, col 1428. In *Razoq* [2012] EWCA Crim 674, the Court of Appeal also asserted that this was a question of fact. In that case, however, the issue was straightforward given that the terms of D's contract stated expressly that he was under a duty to disclose any disciplinary proceedings against him.

[193] Hansard, HL, 19 July 2005, col 1427 (Lord Lyell of Markyate).

[194] Hansard, HL, 12 June 2006, col 536.   [195] Home Office Responses (2004) para 21.

[196] See especially *Morris* [1984] AC 320 at 324.

D claims that he has fulfilled the duty of disclosure it will be a matter of degree. The case of *Forrest* is a good example of this, as the Court of Appeal accepted that DD had fulfilled the legal duty imposed on them by the terms of the mortgage application. It was held that there was nothing extraneous to the application that imposed a more onerous duty of disclosure. As such, the judge was correct to accede to a submission of no case to answer. It is important to point out that such issues go not only to the question of the duty and its scope, but also relate to D's dishonesty.

Awareness of a duty?

It is unclear whether liability is strict as to the existence of a duty. If it is, D's denial of awareness will be subsumed within the general plea of a lack of dishonesty—once again, that is the element of the offence which is the principal determinant of liability. The court in *Razoq* seemed to require D to know of the duty. It is interesting to note that the Law Commission in its original proposals suggested that liability as to the existence of the duty ought not to be strict. However, that recommendation was made in the context of a range of much broader proposals. Once the government restricted its scope to cases of breach of a legal duty, it is arguable that imposing strict liability as to the existence of such duties is less problematical. Arguably, D ought to be aware of his duties in civil law. The counter-argument is that his mistake as to the civil law ought not to give rise to criminal liability.

Despite the landmark decisions of the House of Lords in *DPP v B*[197] and *K*,[198] holding that there is a constitutional principle of a presumption of mens rea in English criminal law, the courts are often willing to find that the presumption is rebutted by necessary implication.

Information

The duty must be one which is to disclose 'information'. That concept is not defined. It is submitted that the word is an ordinary English word and that few difficulties in interpretation should arise. It will take its meaning in part from the circumstances and terms of the duty in question.

To whom duty must be owed?

The section does not limit liability to those cases in which D is under a duty to disclose to V and fails to disclose to V. For example, D might be a company director and in breaching his duties to the company he might intend to expose to a risk of loss V, an investor. Again, the scope of criminal liability is determined by the particular civil law obligation imposed.

22.4.3.3 Failing to disclose

As noted, the question of whether there has been a sufficient degree of failure in disclosure may give rise to problems. The opportunity for the defence to claim that there has been adequate disclosure may well be exploited.[199] If D has fulfilled his civil law duty in terms of the type/quantity of disclosure there should be no criminal liability. This may involve the courts in some complex issues of civil law. Particularly difficult examples might include those in which the allegation of a failure to comply with a duty arises from the trade or custom. Such duties are less likely to be clearly prescribed and must take their form, to some extent, from the circumstances in which they arise and from the parties' expectations. Expert evidence may play an important role.

---

[197] [2000] 2 AC 428.   [198] [2002] 1 AC 462.
[199] See the argument in *Ali* [2006] All ER (D) 207 (May) where D had failed to disclose a change in benefit entitlement.

22.4.4 Mens rea

22.4.4.1 Dishonesty

As discussed previously, the *Ivey/Barton* test for dishonesty will apply. The element of dishonesty will be especially important in cases where D claims that he was not aware of his duty and/or that he believed that he had satisfied that duty.[200]

22.4.4.2 With intent to gain or cause loss or expose to risk of loss

This element of the mens rea is discussed earlier. There is no requirement that the intention is to cause a loss by which D gains. Nor need there be any intention for the loss to be caused to the person to whom the duty is owed.

22.5 Section 4: fraud by abuse of position

The third form of the general fraud offence is perhaps the most controversial and is provided for in s 4. Section 4 provides:

(1) A person is in breach of this section if he—

    (a) occupies a position in which he is expected to safeguard, or not to act against, the financial interests of another person,

    (b) dishonestly abuses that position, and

    (c) intends, by means of the abuse of that position—

        (i) to make a gain for himself or another, or

        (ii) to cause loss to another or to expose another to a risk of loss.

(2) A person may be regarded as having abused his position even though his conduct consisted of an omission rather than an act.

22.5.1 Interpretation

As with ss 2 and 3, the terms of the offence are easy to describe. The actus reus comprises abusing a position of financial trust and the mens rea comprises acting dishonestly and intending by the abuse to make a gain/cause loss. Once again, it is disappointing that none of the terms of this form of the offence are defined in the Act. The provision met with some opposition in Parliament, being described as 'woolly',[201] and as a 'catch all provision that will be a nightmare of judicial interpretation . . . and help bring the law into disrepute'.[202]

22.5.2 Actus reus

22.5.2.1 A 'position'

Critical to understanding this offence is the concept of 'position'. Unfortunately, despite repeated requests for clarification in the course of parliamentary debates, the government refused to define with any particularity what this element of the fraud means. The most

---

[200] The Court of Appeal emphasized in *Razoq* [2012] EWCA Crim 674 that the judge did not need to give a *Ghosh* direction in every case. The court stated that the judge was correct in not giving a *Ghosh* direction, as to do so would have 'muddied the waters', as cited with approval in *Jackson-Mason* [2014] EWCA Crim 1993. This principle will be as equally applicable to the test enunciated by the Supreme Court in *Ivey* and the Court of Appeal in *Barton*.

[201] Hansard, HC, 12 June 2006, col 549. [202] Standing Committee B, 20 June 2006, col 25.

obvious interpretation of this element would be to treat it as synonymous with a requirement that D owed a 'fiduciary duty' to the other. That would have involved the criminal courts in yet more close analysis of complex civil law questions, but it would have secured certainty and ensured coherence between the civil and criminal law. Unfortunately, the government rejected this logical interpretation, being persuaded by arguments that the definition of 'fiduciary duty' would be unduly technical and would restrict the scope of the offence.[203] It preferred to allow s 4 to extend the criminal law into ambiguous territory, although, interestingly, few if any of the examples provided by government spokesmen or in government documents go beyond circumstances in which D does in fact owe a fiduciary duty.

The Home Office Explanatory Notes[204] provide little assistance, simply referring the reader back to the Law Commission explanation in its Report No 276. The Law Commission explained the meaning of 'position' at para 7.38:

> The necessary relationship will be present between trustee and beneficiary, director and company, professional person and client, agent and principal, employee and employer, or between partners. It may arise otherwise, for example within a family, or in the context of voluntary work, or in any context where the parties are not at arm's length. In nearly all cases where it arises, it will be recognised by the civil law as importing fiduciary duties, and any relationship that is so recognised will suffice. We see no reason, however, why the existence of such duties should be essential. This does not of course mean that it would be entirely a matter for the fact-finders whether the necessary relationship exists. The question whether the particular facts alleged can properly be described as giving rise to that relationship will be an issue capable of being ruled upon by the judge and, if the case goes to the jury, of being the subject of directions.[205]

This offers a very broad and ill-defined scope of liability. The Home Office gave examples of relevant 'positions' as including those where D is given access to V's premises, equipment, records or customers.[206] It also provided other obvious examples, including that of a software company employee who abused his employment position to clone software products with the intention of selling them, and employees in care homes who were entrusted to look after the financial affairs of the elderly or disabled person and drew money for their own purposes.[207] These give no meaningful guidance on any limits of this serious offence.[208] The only other advice was that the offence applies wherever V has 'voluntarily' put D in such a position.[209] It would apply to cases of insider dealing and to cases where auditors have acted dishonestly in not safeguarding investors, etc.[210]

Section 4 was considered in *Valujevs*.[211] V and others were charged with fraud by abuse of position. They were gangmasters and had made unwarranted deductions from their workers' earnings, had grossly inflated the rents workers owed to them, withheld work until a worker accrued debts to them, etc. At the close of the prosecution's case the defence successfully made a submission of no case to answer. The judge ruled that since the gangmasters

---

[203] See ibid, cols 24–7 (Solicitor General).   [204] Para 20.

[205] Referred to in debates by the AG (Hansard, HL, 19 July 2005, col 1431) and the Solicitor General (Hansard, HC, 12 June 2006, col 558).

[206] Para 23.

[207] This would also be theft: *Hopkins and Kendrick* [1997] 2 Cr App R 524; *Hinks* [2001] 1 Cr App R 18.

[208] Section 4 will overlap with theft in some cases, eg *Chan Man-sin v A-G for Hong Kong* [1988] 1 All ER 1; cf *A-G for Hong Kong v Reid* [1994] AC 314. See on insider dealing generally, S Clarke, *Insider Dealing: Law and Practice* (2nd edn, 2019).

[209] LC 276, para 7.37, repeated in the Home Office Consultation Paper (2004) para 23.

[210] See as an example of civil law duty, *Manutzfarg v Freightliner* [2007] EWCA Civ 910.

[211] [2014] EWCA Crim 2888. For further discussion, see J Collins, 'Fraud by Abuse of Position and Unlicensed Gangmasters' (2016) 79 MLR 354.

were providing work and accommodation on the 'open market', they could not be in a position where they were 'expected to safeguard, or not to act against, the financial interests of another' as required by s 4. The prosecution appealed against this ruling.

The Court of Appeal allowed the appeal. The court had regard to the regulations governing the role of gangmasters and concluded that s 4 of the 2006 Act was broad enough to apply in these circumstances because the gangmasters had in this case gone beyond merely supplying workers and had taken responsibility for collecting and distributing the workers' wages. The judge was therefore wrong to hold that as a matter of law a gangmaster was not in a position where he was 'expected to safeguard, or not to act against, the financial interests of another'. More generally, it was noted that s 4 is not restricted to cases in which the fraudster owes a fiduciary duty to the victim. Fulford LJ stated that the question of whether the position held by the defendant is one which qualifies for the purpose of the offence in s 4 is an objective one that is not determined by the perception of the defendant or the victim as to the nature of D's position.[212]

The court made clear that no crime under s 4 is committed by a person who charges excessive rent. Although accepting the breadth of s 4, the court concurred with the trial judge that s 4 should not apply:

in 'the general commercial area where individuals and businesses compete in markets of one kind or another, including labour markets, and are entitled to and expected to look after their own interests'. We repeat, the critical factor in this case is that there is evidence that the defendants arguably assumed control of, and responsibility for, collecting the wages of the workers, or they controlled the wages at the moment that they were paid over, and the fact that they were acting as gangmasters merely provided the vital context relied on by the prosecution in which that role was assumed.[213]

As noted, the government was unwilling to accept that the scope of liability for s 4 should be restricted to circumstances of fiduciary duties, arguing that the definition of fiduciary duty was too narrow and too complex. The Solicitor General referred to the definition of that concept provided by Millet LJ in *Bristol & West Building Society v Mothew*,[214] but misinterpreted his lordship's definition to conclude that a fiduciary duty would restrict the offence unnecessarily because it would require proof that the person under the fiduciary duty has a single loyalty.[215]

Cases of fiduciary duty

In the more obvious situations in which s 4 might be relied on, the existence of the duty will present no problem: D's civil law duties will saddle him with liability. Even in these cases, there may be practical problems with the criminal courts identifying with precision the duty, and its terms. This may pose further questions as to the respective functions of judge and jury. If the scope of liability under s 4 had been restricted to cases of fiduciary duty, there would have been a strong argument for saying that the judge must determine whether D's 'position' is within s 4 and to direct the jury as to what evidence of that they must find in order to convict. However, since a fiduciary duty will be a *sufficient* but not a *necessary* basis for liability, it is more questionable who has responsibility for determining D's status. The Law Commission clearly thought that whether the particular facts alleged can properly be described as giving rise to that relationship will be 'an issue capable of being ruled upon by the judge and, if the case goes to the jury, of being the subject of directions'.[216]

---

[212] At [41] per Fulford LJ.   [213] At [44] per Fulford LJ.
[214] [1998] Ch 1. J Glister and J Lee, *Hanbury and Martin on Modern Equity* (21st edn, 2018) Ch 22.
[215] HC Standing Committee B, 20 June 2006, col 27.   [216] LC 276, para 7.38.

One area of fiduciary duty in which the s 4 offence will be useful is that relating to secret profits. Historically, the common law had become extremely confused on this issue. In *Tarling*,[217] the House of Lords held that the company directors' failure to disclose a secret profit made in breach of a fiduciary duty, even if it was dishonest, did not constitute a conspiracy to defraud. In *Adams*,[218] the Privy Council held that the company director had been correctly convicted when making a secret profit. Adams seems to have gone further than Tarling by actively concealing the profits. The position was inconsistent and incoherent. Under the 2006 Act, s 4 is wide enough to tackle both situations: it catches secret profiteers from the waiter who sells his bottle of wine passing it off as one from the restaurant,[219] to the director who makes personal millions by trading company stock in breach of his fiduciary duty.

Whether there was a breach of fiduciary duty was considered by the Court of Appeal in *Pennock*.[220] V was elderly and suffering from the early signs of Alzheimer's. He sold his house and moved in with the defendants, one of whom was his great-niece. The proceeds from the sale were placed into a joint account to which the defendants and V were signatories. DD removed £100,000 from the account and used it to buy a bungalow. DD were named as holders of the legal title to the property, but there was nothing to indicate that V held an equitable interest in it. Therefore, V's financial contribution to the purchase price was in no way recognized. Subsequently, DD transferred legal title to their daughter. The Court of Appeal quashed DD's convictions for fraud by abuse of position based on DD having abused their position by transferring ownership of the bungalow to their daughter without recognizing or protecting V's interest. The Court of Appeal accepted that although DD held the legal title to the bungalow, V would have had an equitable interest in it, given that he contributed to the purchase price. It was held that if DD made the transfer in such a way that V's equitable interest was not protected, they were in breach of their fiduciary duty towards him. If they did this dishonestly and with a view to gain, this was sufficient to constitute an offence under s 4. Notwithstanding this conclusion, the Court of Appeal went on to observe that V's equitable interest in the property remained intact despite the transfer of legal title to DD's daughter. This was because she was not a bona fide purchaser for value; she had not given any value for the transfer. Since this fact was not brought to the jury's attention, the conviction was unsafe: the jury may have wrongly assumed that the transfer of legal title destroyed V's equitable interest in the bungalow. The case highlights how important the civil law is to any consideration of s 4. It was the failure to recognize important features of the transaction, which have their origin in the law of equity, that led to DD's convictions being quashed, something that the Court of Appeal 'regretted'.

In cases involving a breach of a fiduciary duty, there may well be an overlap with s 3 where the fiduciary fails to disclose information, and/or under s 2 when there is a false representation. Note, however, that liability is potentially wider under s 4 because there is no need for the prosecution to prove any positive act on D's part; an omission will do.

Liability in the absence of a fiduciary duty

The s 4 offence has the potential to criminalize acts or omissions by someone who is not under a formal legal duty of a fiduciary nature. The organization Justice criticized the offence on these grounds when it was first proposed, suggesting that it 'compromised legal certainty'.[221] The Law Commission's examples, noted earlier, which list the family and other voluntary arrangements as being caught, highlight the potential reach of s 4. Will

---

[217] (1980) 70 Cr App R 77. The application of the offence in this context is discussed in the Home Office, *Fraud Law Reform: Response to Consultations*, Annex B, para 14.

[218] [1995] 1 WLR 52.   [219] *Doukas* [1978] 1 All ER 1071.   [220] [2014] EWCA Crim 598.

[221] Briefing Document for House of Lords (2006) para 8.

the breadth of the offence open up the possibility of civil actions becoming the subject of prosecution?[222] Concerns were expressed in Parliament that the offence would, for example, catch D who breaches a confidentiality agreement with his employer.[223]

Employee A of X Ltd will be caught by passing up an opportunity to seal a lucrative contract so that his friend B, working for Y Ltd, can take advantage.[224] D who is employed to secure three tenders for a lucrative contract and chooses instead to obtain one which turns out to be a disastrous selection may be caught. Section 4 seems to apply whether D is motivated by malice or laziness. Beyond that, the scope of the offence is astonishingly wide. Its ambit lies in the hands of those defining the qualifying 'position'. To take an extreme example, what of an employee who persistently arrives late for work? He occupies a position in which he is expected not to act against the financial interests of the employer. Arguably, he abuses that position intending thereby to make a gain. Subject to a finding of dishonesty, he may be guilty.

The offence is so wide that it also has the potential to apply to financial misgovernance by public officials. Many public officials are in a position in which they are expected to safeguard or not to act against the financial interests of another person (ie the public or the prosecution). There may be overlap with a number of the offences contained in the Bribery Act 2010[225] and misconduct in public office.[226]

Unless kept within sensible limits, the offence has the potential to elevate all sorts of trivial contractual and familial disputes into criminal matters. The government suggested that 'something more than a breakdown of relationships' would be needed to trigger s 4, but did not elaborate on this.[227] For the reasons expressed previously, it is doubtful whether that ill-defined element can shoulder such a burden in an offence carrying a maximum of ten years' imprisonment.

The CPS has listed examples of circumstances in which s 4 should be charged to guide prosecutors. These demonstrate the reach of the offence. There have been few reported cases under s 4. In *Marshall*, the offence was used to prosecute a care home worker who was misusing residents' bank accounts.[228] In *Gale*,[229] G had abused his position as a shipping handler when he certified cargo as 'approved' for shipment to the United States when he was in fact unaware of its contents (a prohibited substance). The offence is used across a range of activities from sophisticated frauds involving kick-back payments *(Knowles)*[230] to cases in which a person retains payments that he is obliged to distribute to others *(Waqanika)*.[231]

---

[222] This will be a significant stick with which employers can beat employees: Standing Committee B, 20 June 2006, col 15 (Mr Geoffrey Cox QC, MP).

[223] Standing Committee B, 20 June 2006, col 15.

[224] The CPS has issued guidance on public policy interests of prosecuting fraud and has stated that 'The criminal law should not be used to protect private confidences'—see www.cps.gov.uk/legal-guidance/fraud-act-2006.

[225] See eg *Ross River v Cambridge FC* [2007] EWHC 2115 (Ch), where the fraudulent representations involved bribery of a member of the defendant's board.

[226] See C Nicholls et al, *Corruption and Misuse of Public Office* (3rd edn, 2017) Ch 5. In *Akpom* [2013] EWCA Crim 2662, D was convicted of misconduct in a public office and fraud after it was discovered that he was issuing birth certificates for children who had never been born in order to facilitate benefit fraud. Dismissing his appeal against conviction, the Court of Appeal held that it was not inappropriate for the CPS to charge D with both a common law offence and a statutory one. The Court of Appeal accepted that it is good practice to observe the primacy of statutory offences over common law offences, but that it was appropriate to deviate from that principle in this case given the consequences of the offences for the public. D was in this case not charged with an offence contrary to s 4, but rather s 7.

[227] See Home Office, *Fraud Law Reform: Response to Consultations* (2004) para 27.

[228] [2009] EWCA Crim 2076.   [229] [2008] EWCA Crim 1344.

[230] [2013] EWCA Crim 646.   [231] [2014] EWCA Crim 902.

22.5.2.2 'Occupies'

The section applies only in relation to the positions D 'occupies'. It is clear that the 'abuse' with intent to gain or cause loss must arise while D is in occupation of that position in order for s 4 to apply. Where D has, whilst in a position of trust, obtained financial information, and then after leaving his position uses that information with intent to gain or cause loss, has the s 4 offence been committed? Arguably, the answer will turn on whether D intends *at the time of the obtaining* to use the information to gain or cause loss. If he obtains the information with that intention, he is abusing the position he then occupies. More difficult will be the case where D obtains such information while occupying a relevant 'position', and at the time of obtaining he has no intention by that obtaining to gain or cause loss then or in the future. Perhaps he has an intention to keep the information as a safeguard against any future allegation that he was involved in a dubious aspect of a particular deal that was being undertaken in the organization within which he occupied the position.[232] Subsequently, having left that position, D realizes that there is the potential to use the information to make a gain or cause a loss and he decides to do so. He is not at that time abusing a position which he 'occupies'. Such a person commits the offence under s 6 of the Act: possession of an article for use in fraud (see later) if he intends it to be used in fraud—which is, of course, much narrower than intending to use it for gain or to cause loss or expose to a risk of loss.

According to the Solicitor General in the course of debates in the Standing Committee:

A person can occupy a position where they owe a duty that goes beyond the performance of a job. A contract that is entered into that obliges a person to have duties of confidentiality, perhaps, can go well beyond the time when that employment ceases. The duty may, however, still arise. The person entered into the duty at the beginning of the employment and it exists indefinitely. Therefore a person may still occupy a position in which there is a legitimate expectation. That may well, by virtue of a contract and the agreement that the employee entered into voluntarily, go beyond redundancy or the point when he leaves the post.[233]

22.5.2.3 Expectation

The scope of the concept of 'position' which D must occupy is to some extent dependent on the definition of the term 'position in which he is expected to safeguard'.[234] The critical question, and one which Parliament spectacularly left unanswered, is: whose expectation counts?[235] If it is the potential victim's this could be a very wide scope of liability subject to D denying liability by way of a lack of dishonesty. If it is a test based on what D thinks his financial duties are, it might be very limited and difficult to prove. In *Valujevs* (p 999) the court held that this issue is to be determined objectively, based on the position of the reasonable person rather than that of the victim or of the defendant.

22.5.2.4 Financial interests

The term is not defined. There is little doubt that the courts will be encouraged to adopt a very wide reading. There is no restriction that the financial interests be regarded as long-term ones.

---

[232] Is that an abuse? It is doubtful that a jury would regard it as such where the defendant is protecting himself against allegations that he was involved in criminal conduct by the organization; that does not sound like abuse, even though it is contrary to the interests of that organization.

[233] Standing Committee B, 20 June 2006, col 23.

[234] If the conduct is perpetrated by a public official, there may be an offence of misconduct in public office.

[235] See the discussion in the Commons Standing Committee where it was proposed that the word 'expected' be replaced by a requirement that D had a 'fiduciary duty': HC, Standing Committee B, 20 June 2006, col 11; rejected by the Solicitor General at col 20.

22.5.2.5 Abuse

The term 'abuse' is not defined. The Home Office makes clear in the Explanatory Notes that it is deliberately left undefined as the term is intended to cover a wide range of conduct. Coupled with the breadth of the concept of 'positions' of responsibility this makes the offence extremely wide. If positions of financial responsibility were restricted to legal/fiduciary duty cases the issue of abuse would be resolved by asking simply whether the defendant had breached the legal/fiduciary duty he owed.

The word 'abuse' may well fall to be interpreted as an ordinary English word which, although straightforward, will do nothing to promote certainty and consistency in an offence of such seriousness. If guidance is needed, the dictionary definitions suggest that it involves acting 'wrongly' or 'improperly' or treating in a harmful or injurious way. The Court of Appeal in *Pennock* (discussed earlier) stated that 'uses incorrectly' or 'puts to improper use' were appropriate working meanings.[236]

Although not an element of the offence, jurors might be unwilling to conclude that there has been abuse unless some loss is in fact caused (or some gain accrued) or at least that someone is exposed to the risk of loss. The abuse is of the 'position', but it may be that D holds a position of financial responsibility towards B (eg the company), but acts with intent to cause loss to C (an investor) by the abuse of his position vis-à-vis B.

The original proposal contained a requirement of secrecy in D's actions of abuse,[237] but the Home Office removed this element, despite its widespread approval on the grounds that it was difficult to define and created unnecessary complication.[238]

22.5.2.6 Act or omission

Section 4(2) makes clear that the offence can be committed by omission as well as by positive action. An obvious example is where D, an employee, fails to perform his duty under the contract of employment so that a rival company wins the tender at the expense of D's employer.

22.5.3 Mens rea

There is no explicit mens rea requirement as to any awareness of the defendant as to the existence of the expectation that he must safeguard the financial interests of another. It would appear that liability is strict. D's lack of awareness that he is in such a position must be subsumed in a plea of lack of dishonesty.

22.5.3.1 Dishonesty

The elements have been discussed previously. As noted, there is a very heavy burden placed on dishonesty. It is interesting to consider the ECHR compatibility of this form of the fraud offence. In cases in which there is no legal or fiduciary duty on D, it is difficult to see what additional element of conduct which is morally dubious prevents the offence being one based solely on dishonesty. As the Parliamentary Joint Committee on Human Rights recognized, such an offence would be likely to infringe Art 7.[239]

---

[236] [2014] EWCA Crim 598.

[237] Indeed, the CPS said: 'In the absence of an element of secrecy, it is accepted that the new offence would probably be too wide.' However, the deletion of this requirement was supported by Lord Lloyd, Hansard, HL, 22 June 2005, col 1665.

[238] See Home Office, *Fraud Law Reform: Response to Consultations* (2004) para 28.

[239] See p 970.

22.5.3.2 Intent to gain/cause loss

One particular aspect of this element to note in the context of s 4 is that the definition of gain and loss includes intangible property which may well have a significant role to play in the context of abuse of a financial position.

22.6 Section 11: obtaining services dishonestly

Section 11 replaces the offence of obtaining services by deception in s 1 of the Theft Act 1978.[240] As noted earlier, it was increasingly apparent that the Theft Acts failed to protect against the obtaining of services via wholly automated processes. The Law Commission's proposal as endorsed by the Home Office was to remove the troublesome element of deception from the offence and to place the emphasis on dishonesty.

The section provides:

(1) A person is guilty of an offence under this section if he obtains services for himself or another—

   (a) by a dishonest act, and

   (b) in breach of subsection (2).

(2) A person obtains services in breach of this subsection if—

   (a) they are made available on the basis that payment has been, is being or will be made for or in respect of them,

   (b) he obtains them without any payment having been made for or in respect of them or without payment having been made in full, and

   (c) when he obtains them, he knows—

      (i) that they are being made available on the basis described in paragraph (a), or

      (ii) that they might be, but intends that payment will not be made, or will not be made in full.

The offence carries a maximum six months' imprisonment and a fine in the magistrates' court and five years and a fine in the Crown Court.

22.6.1 Interpretation

This is a result crime, and is quite distinct from the three forms of fraud offence provided for in ss 1 to 4.[241] There must be an actual obtaining of a service. The actus reus comprises: (a) an act resulting in the obtaining; (b) of services; (c) for which payment is or will become due; and (d) a failure to pay in whole or in part. The mens rea comprises (a) dishonesty; (b) knowing that the services are to be paid for or knowing that they might have to be paid for; (c) with intent to avoid payment in whole or in part.

According to the Law Commission in its Report No 276, 'This offence would be more analogous to theft than to deception, because it could be committed by "helping oneself" to the service rather than dishonestly inducing another person to provide it.'[242]

---

[240] See generally the Home Office, *Fraud Law Reform* (2004) paras 32–5; the Home Office, *Fraud Law Reform: Response to Consultations* (2004) para 35; the Home Office Explanatory Notes, paras 34–6; the House of Commons Research Paper 31/06, at 17.

[241] cf Arlidge and Parry who suggest that 'A person who lies to obtain a service is guilty of the same offence as a person who lies to obtain property', para 9.003.

[242] LC 276, para 8.8.

22.6.2 Actus reus

22.6.2.1 An act

Unusually, the offence is restricted to conduct in the form of a positive act. It is made explicit that it is not possible to commit the offence by omission. If an unsolicited service is offered, perhaps in the mistaken belief that a customer has paid for it, no dishonest 'act' has taken place. A rather unrealistic example provided in Parliament was of D, who sits on a boat and does not alight when he hears an announcement that anyone who has not paid for the next trip should alight. It was suggested that he commits no offence under this section.[243] This restriction may be rather illusory in its practical impact. In this example, there is no doubt that D commits a fraud offence under s 2 by making an implied representation by conduct that he will pay for the trip. He does so with intent to cause loss in terms of property within s 5 to the travel company and/or to gain by keeping that which he has (s 5(3)). In addition, it is difficult to see why D is not obtaining a service in the form of the return trip by his positive act of sitting on the boat to take the return trip.

22.6.2.2 Obtaining

As noted, this is a result crime. D's dishonest act must be a cause of the obtaining of a service. The obtaining may be for D or another.

22.6.2.3 Service

Service is not further defined. But the offence is restricted in that it only applies to services for which payment is required. This follows the old offence under s 1 of the 1978 Act which did not apply to gratuitous services. Some of the situations in which D obtains a service for free by making a false representation will be caught by s 2 (discussed earlier). Note that ss 1 to 4 apply only in relation to *property* (see s 5) whereas s 11 applies in relation to dishonest obtaining of *services*. As under the old law, an application for a bank account or credit card will only be caught by this offence if the service is to be paid for: *Sofroniou*.[244] What is not made clear is whether the offence extends to services which are not legally enforceable. Can the offence occur, for example, in respect of prostitution or corrupt services?[245]

The offence obviously extends well beyond the electronic 'deception'-type case. It covers, for example, the case where D climbs over a wall and watches a football match without paying the entrance fee (such a person is not deceiving the provider of the service directly, but is obtaining a service which is provided on the basis that people will pay for it). But not to cases where D watches the game from the window of a property adjoining the ground.[246] It has been held that the section does not apply to the individual who tops up his mobile telephone with credit by charging the cost to other mobile telephone users: D is obtaining credit not services.[247]

As the Home Office explains, it also covers the situation where a person attaches a decoder to his television to enable viewing access to cable/satellite television channels for which he has no intention of paying.[248] It was suggested that it would also catch illegally downloading music where the provision of the music constituted a service.[249]

---

[243] The government also emphasized the need to avoid criminalizing those who received unsolicited services from unscrupulous companies: Standing Committee B, 20 June 2006, col 54.

[244] [2003] EWCA Crim 3681.   [245] *Linekar* [1995] QB 250.

[246] Standing Committee B, 20 June 2006, col 52.

[247] *Mikolajczak v Poland* [2013] EWHC 432 (Admin). The court did observe that D could perhaps have been guilty of dishonestly obtaining electronic communication services, contrary to s 125 of the Communications Act 2003.

[248] See Home Office Explanatory Notes, para 36.   [249] ibid.

22.6.2.4 Without payment

One problem with the s 11 offence which does not seem to have been foreseen was that it may be inapplicable in the commonplace situation where D obtains the relevant service by using a credit card or debit card. Even though the use of the card is unauthorized, the payment will be made by the bank/issuing company provided that the PIN is correct and the security number accurate, etc. The offence will not apply in such circumstances because the requirement as expressed in the section is not that D himself does not pay, but that payment has not been made at all, or in part. The fact that D is unaware of the banking practice and believes that no payment will be made, cannot make him liable under s 11 if payment has in fact been made. He may, of course, be liable for an attempt.

In many cases where D obtains a service by use of a credit card in such circumstances he will also obtain some element of property (eg the ticket for the travel or for entry to the theatre, etc) and will therefore commit an offence under s 2 of the Act because his false representation (that he is authorized to use the card), coupled with a dishonest intention to cause either loss to the credit card company and/or expose to a risk of loss the service provider, suffice for that offence. He might also be regarded as making a false representation with intention to gain by keeping what he has—that is, the money he would otherwise have had to spend. Alternatively, s 6 of the 2006 Act might be used with charges of possession of the article with intent to commit fraud.

22.6.3 Mens rea

22.6.3.1 Dishonesty

Dishonesty has been discussed previously. This is the principal mens rea element of the s 11 offence. The test applied is that expressed in *Ivey/Barton*.

22.6.3.2 Knowing that payment is required/might be required

The additional requirement that D knows that the services are to be paid for or knows that they might have to be paid for imposes a relatively strict test. Arguably, the offence is too wide in including cases where D knows only that payment *might* have to be made. This form of the mens rea was included to deal with electronic purchasing over the internet and cases where D might have alleged that he was unsure what the obligations to pay were.[250] Perhaps the statute is right to extend the offence this far: if D knows that payment might be due the onus is on him to make inquiries before he engages the services, and not to act dishonestly.

Other difficulties might arise where there is uncertainty over whether the knowledge is that payment will be due immediately or at some later date.

22.6.3.3 Intention that payment avoided

This requirement that D acts with intent to avoid payment in whole or in part marks a departure from the old offence under s 1 of the 1978 Act and narrows the scope of the crime.

Intends that 'payment will not be made'

As noted, there is no liability under s 11 for D who obtains a service by use of a credit card, where payment is made by the card-issuing company, although D was unaware of that fact and intended that no payment would be made.

If D intends that payment will be made, whether by himself or by the card company, he will also be acquitted. The Law Commission was keen to emphasize the limits of the s 11

---

[250] Home Office, *Fraud Law Reform* (2004) para 35.

offence in this regard and provided an example that DD, parents of D, who lie about their religion in order to get D into a private school where they will be charged and pay the full fees, commit no offence under s 11.[251]

22.7 Section 6: possession of articles for fraud

The scope of the criminal law's proscription of acts merely preparatory to the commission of acquisitive crime is extended dramatically by s 6 which provides:

(1) A person is guilty of an offence if he has in his possession or under his control any article for use in the course of or in connection with any fraud.

The offence carries a maximum six-month sentence in the magistrates' court and a maximum five years in the Crown Court.

This is a disturbingly wide offence which the courts have narrowed only slightly in scope. The Law Commission in its 2002 Report, *Fraud*, had proposed simply to replace that form of s 25 of the Theft Act offence of 'going equipped'[252] which covered going equipped with implements for 'deception'[253] with one covering going equipped for 'fraud'.[254] The going equipped offence is limited in two significant ways: (a) the offence cannot be committed by possession of the materials at the defendant's abode, thereby respecting the unique privacy rights attaching to that space; and (b) the s 25 offence is designed to deal with the defendant who has set out to commit the specified wrong—albeit this might be mere preparation and hence not an attempt, nevertheless it does require evidence that D has a degree of proximity to the offence although the defendant need not be on his way to commit a crime at that moment and need not have identified a target.

The Home Office in its consultation exercise in 2004 proposed much wider reform, noting in particular the need to deal with the use of home computers for fraud.[255] The Home Office went on to explain its desire for an offence of mere possession of, for example, computer software for use in 'the course of or in connection with' a fraud.[256] One particular concern was the widespread use of software to read credit cards, and the impact this has on the volume of fraud and, more generally, the public's fear of fraud and of 'identity theft'.[257]

The government's argument is not as compelling as it might at first seem. There is now the extremely wide offence in s 1 of the 2006 Act with which to prosecute frauds. The fraudster who works from home is caught by that provision just as easily as anyone else. There is also the scope for charging inchoate offences such as conspiracy to commit a s 1 offence.[258] Similarly, the fraudster who has *attempted* to commit frauds from his home will be caught. Section 6 extends to those who have not yet even attempted to commit fraud. Section 6 may turn out to be a powerful weapon in prosecuting the peripheral players in major frauds.

[251] There has been considerable controversy over whether s 1 applies in relation to parents making false representations in order to enhance their chances of securing places in schools which the parents would like their children to attend. See C Monaghan, 'Fraudsters? Putting Parents in the Dock' (2010) 174 CJLW 581; C Monaghan, 'School Application Forms and the Criminal Law' [2015] Crim LR 270. It is difficult to identify what property D intends to gain. See also the Report to the Secretary of State for Children Schools and Families on Fraudulent or Misleading Applications for Admission to Schools (2009), see also http://news.bbc.co.uk/1/hi/8334503.stm and www.telegraph.co.uk/education/6486725/Warning-over-school-admissions-theft.html.
[252] See Ch 25.   [253] Confusingly termed 'cheat' in s 25 of the 1968 Act.
[254] See Law Commission, Fraud (2002), Draft Bill.
[255] Para 39.   [256] Para 41.
[257] The Home Office explained that the target included articles which are specifically 'made or adapted' for committing frauds at para 42.
[258] See eg *Pakiyanthur* [2010] EWCA Crim 2312.

If the key players are prosecuted under ss 2 to 4 or for conspiracy to defraud, there will be many who have assisted in some way who could be more easily prosecuted under s 6 than for assisting or encouraging or conspiring.

22.7.1 Actus reus

22.7.1.1 An article

The concept of article has been given a wide reading under the s 25 offence,[259] but the 2006 Act provides a yet broader definition of the term in s 8.

> (1) For the purposes of—
>
>> (a) sections 6 and 7, and
>>
>> (b) the provisions listed in subsection (2),[260] so far as they relate to articles for use in the course of or in connection with fraud, 'article' *includes* any program or data held in electronic form.[261]

The Home Office Explanatory Notes state that:

> Examples of cases where electronic programs or data could be used in fraud are: a computer program can generate credit card numbers; computer templates can be used for producing blank utility bills; computer files can contain lists of other peoples' credit card details or draft letters in connection with 'advance fee' frauds.[262]

There is no requirement that the program or data is designed exclusively for fraud. Any word-processing or spreadsheet program is capable of being used to produce false invoices or false utility bills. Any email software is capable of sending false representations and thus for committing frauds under s 2, and so on. It is difficult to see any restriction on the concept of article which might limit the offence. A printer and computer, an iPhone,[263] a memory stick,[264] paper[265] or even a humble pen are articles and capable of being used in the course of or in connection with fraud and are capable of being possessed.

22.7.1.2 A person

The offence is designed primarily to tackle the *individual* but would seem also on the application of general principles of interpretation to apply to corporate defendants. The company director who is aware of the DVD-copying machine or the software for producing false bills, etc, which is loaded onto the company's computers may render the company liable.

---

[259] See Home Office, para 50.

[260] Offences of having in possession and powers under PACE, etc.

[261] Emphasis added. See on the wide interpretation of the concept of article in the Terrorism Act 2000, s 57, to include electronic data, the case of *M* [2007] EWCA Crim 218; cf *Rowe* [2007] EWCA Crim 635; *Zafar* [2008] EWCA Crim 184 as approved in this respect in *G* [2010] 1 AC 43.

[262] Para 28.

[263] See eg *Nimley* [2010] EWCA Crim 2752—recording films in cinema to upload to website.

[264] Used for downloading data from ATM machines in *Ciorba* [2009] EWCA Crim 1800.

[265] As in *Kazi* [2010] EWCA Crim 2026 where D was going to pass the paper off as bundles of used banknotes that had been blacked out by the Bank of England. The victim would be told that these could be washed clean with a special chemical sold to them for a high price. This is commonly known as a 'wash wash' or 'black money' fraud. The victim is persuaded to buy the paper by the fraudster demonstrating the process on a real note on which an easily removable dye has been added. See also the cases on 'Lebanese loop' frauds by which the rogues trap cards in ATMs and retrieve them for illegitimate use: *Munteanu* [2012] EWCA Crim 2231; *Giomaga* [2012] EWCA Crim 2679.

22.7.1.3 Has in his possession

The concept of possession has given rise to problems for the courts, particularly in relation to drugs offences.[266] Any article in the possession of the person whether at home, in public or at work is capable of satisfying this element of the offence. Whereas the concept of possession has created few problems with the going equipped offence, it might be suggested that this is in part at least because the offence only applies where D is not at his abode. That restriction makes it more likely that the articles will be on D's person or in very close proximity to him for the offence to be triggered. With the offence under s 6, there is no such restriction. A person might be said to have in his possession many thousands of articles around his home and workplace.

Personal possession?

One ambiguity within the provision is whether it is possible for D to be in possession through an agent or intermediary. Does D have in his possession the software held on his teenage son's computer? Does the employer possess all the software loaded onto each of his employees' computers? Such cases might be thought to be cases of 'control' by D, if within the offence at all. In *Montague*,[267] the Court of Appeal considered what 'possession' means in this context. The Court of Appeal adopted the approach that was taken towards the Misuse of Drugs Act 1971 in *Searle*.[268] It was held that an individual can be in possession of an article and therefore guilty as a principal offender if he can draw upon an article from a common pool. In that case D was in joint possession of various articles—false identity documents—and his conviction was therefore upheld.[269]

The question nevertheless arises: what limits on liability are there? Does D possess an article in the form of data if it is stored only on a server outside the jurisdiction and accessible via the internet? If so, does D possess all that software or data on the internet to which he has instant access? Surely not. What about the case where D takes an annual subscription to an electronic product, which can be used in fraud, stored on a server outside the jurisdiction, which by virtue of his subscription he can access from the UK? Might he have possession of an article, through the internet, for use in connection with fraud?

Knowing possession?

As it must now be shown that D intended that the article be used in the course of fraud,[270] this will obviously impose a natural limitation on the scope of the offence as a whole, although it will do nothing to restrict the scope of the concept of possession. On one view there should also be an element that D knew he was in possession of the article. But D who intends that the article will be used for fraud is almost inevitably likely to 'know' that it is in his possession, other than in exceptional cases.[271]

---

[266] See generally R Fortson, *Misuse of Drugs: Offences, Confiscation and Money Laundering* (6th edn, 2012).

[267] [2013] EWCA Crim 1781.   [268] [1971] Crim LR 592.

[269] In the earlier case of *Tarley* [2012] EWCA Crim 464, the trial judge similarly placed reliance on the Misuse of Drugs Act 1971 and observed that 'possession' as it is used in the context of the Fraud Act suggests a wider meaning than the concept of absolute possession adopted in the Proceeds of Crime Act 2002. While the Court of Appeal did not explicitly endorse this reasoning, it did agree with the judge that D was in joint possession and therefore upheld his conviction.

[270] See *Sakalauskas*, n 290.

[271] What of D who is party to a gang of would-be fraudsters and is aware of a device that the gang possesses which could be used for fraud, and he intends that it should be used for their proposed fraud, but is unaware that it has been left in his garage by the gang?

The CPS suggests in its guidance that it is 'probable' the courts are likely to draw on the case law on possession of drugs.[272] In that context, the courts have held that D must 'know' that he is in possession of something which is, in fact, a controlled drug.[273]

If it must be proved that D 'knew' that he possessed the article that is alleged to be for use in fraud, particular difficulties may arise in the case of electronic data. Even in cases of tangible articles problems may arise: what of D who claims that he was unaware of the credit card cloning machine being stored in his son's bedroom or his office storeroom? In the drugs context, in *Lewis*[274] it was held that the judge had not misdirected the jury by telling them that the tenant of a house might be found to be in possession of articles (drugs) found on the premises although he did not know they were there, provided he had had an opportunity to find out that they were. But this seems to go too far.[275] It is submitted that D does not possess 'articles' for use in fraud if the prosecution can only establish that he had an opportunity to discover that they were on his property.

Knowledge of the fraudulent 'nature' of the article

If the courts do incorporate an element of mens rea requiring proof that D must know he has the thing which he is alleged to possess, the question arises whether there is a further element which must be established—that D must know or comprehend the *nature* of the article?[276] What if D knows of the existence of the software that he possesses, but not its function? On one view, he is still in possession, a position akin to the container cases in drugs law. It is submitted that this should not pose any great problems. As there is a requirement that D intends that the article be used for fraud, it will be very rare for D to be able to raise a plausible plea of this type. Where the prosecution establishes D's intention as to fraudulent use, it will be possible but unlikely that he did not also know of the nature of the article. In contrast, if D lacks *any* understanding as to the nature of the article and its use, he must also lack an intention that it be used for fraud.

Possession of electronic data

Where the article comprises electronic data on a computer, being perhaps one of many thousands on D's office machine, proving possession may be more difficult. The prosecution's task will be even harder if the courts interpret the provision as requiring proof that D 'knew' he had possession of the article. What of a case where D claims to have deleted the relevant data or software and therefore not to have it in his possession even though an IT expert could recover the material from D's computer? This argument as a basis for denial of possession was accepted in the case of *Porter*[277] in the context of possession of indecent images of children. The Court of Appeal held that 'if a person cannot retrieve or gain access to an image, in our view he no longer has custody or control of it. He has put it beyond his reach just as does a person who destroys or otherwise gets rid of a hard copy photograph.'[278] It is questionable whether that is a faithful analogy. It is not as if D has burnt the hard copy photograph; rather, he has put the hard copy in a safe and thrown away the key. Someone

[272] See www.cps.gov.uk/legal-guidance/fraud-act-2006.

[273] *Warner v Metropolitan Police Comr* [1969] 2 AC 256; *Boyesen* [1982] AC 768; *McNamara* (1988) 87 Cr App R 246; *Lambert* [2002] 2 AC 545. Cf in relation to firearms *Zahid* [2010] EWCA Crim 2158.

[274] (1987) 87 Cr App R 270, [1988] Crim LR 517 and commentary.

[275] 'First of all man does not have possession of something which has been put into his pocket or into his house without his knowledge': *McNamara* (1988) 87 Cr App R 246 at 248.

[276] *Boyesen* [1982] AC 768. (It is immaterial how minute the quantity provided only that it amounts to something and D knows he has it.)

[277] cf *Porter* [2006] EWCA Crim 560, [2006] Crim LR 748. See also *Leonard* [2012] EWCA Crim 277.

[278] At [21].

with the relevant skills can allow him to access it. Similarly, someone who has deleted the data from his computer could still be said to be in control of it in the sense that he possesses the machine on which it is stored and controls access to it, even if that access must be by another (more skilled) person. It is arguable that the charge should be focused on controlling such an article in these circumstances. Again, the fact of deletion proves that D possessed the article pre-deletion and if it can be shown that he had the relevant intent at that stage he is guilty.

22.7.1.4 'Control'

Use of the words possession *or* control must suggest that Parliament intended them to be capable of applying differently. Possession is intended to mean merely having custody of the article and the word 'or' does not extend the meaning of possession, but signifies that 'under his control' is a discrete, alternative version of the offence. The CPS guidance suggests that the phrase is intended to suggest something 'looser' than the concept of absolute possession.[279]

How far does the concept of control extend in this context? Does D control all material that is present on any of D's premises, or in his car, etc? To what extent can D be said to be in control of an article which he cannot access instantly? In some instances D will have possession where the article is in a pool for use by all his associates.[280] In some offences based on having control of an article, the scope of the control is defined by the nature of the article or the illegal uses to which it is to be put. Given the breadth of the definition of article, there is no such implicit restriction in this offence. The courts might follow the interpretation in relation to electronic articles at least, in the offences under the Regulation of Investigatory Powers Act 2000,[281] in which the Court of Appeal held that a person has a right to control where he has the ability to authorize and forbid access.[282]

There is no obvious way in which 'control' will be limited by the courts to incorporate some requirement of D's physical proximity to or ease of access to the article. In the absence of any such limitation, the question arises whether any geographical limit can be placed on the concept in this context. Does D control the articles in his safety deposit box or locked in his safe many miles away? If so, does it matter that the articles are in D's safe in Liechtenstein rather than in London? It does not seem to be an abuse of language to say that someone sitting at a computer terminal in London can be in control of data on a server in the United States which he intends to be used to send false representations to the UK with intent to cause loss to the recipients here. In *Ex p Levin*,[283] an extradition case, the court thought that the fact that a computer operator was physically in Russia was of far less significance than the fact that he was looking at, and operating, on magnetic disks in the United States: he had committed theft in the United States and could be extradited to that country. That again prompts the question—can D be in control of data that are instantly accessible to him because they are posted on the internet? It is submitted that this would be going too far. The courts may be able to avoid such a broad reading by concluding that material/data, etc stored on a site to which D does not have the ability to regulate access is not within his control. If D controls the website, he can regulate access to the data and can be said to be in control of them.

---

[279] See www.cps.gov.uk/legal-guidance/fraud-act-2006.   [280] See *Montague*, n 267.

[281] Section 1(6) of that Act provided: 'The circumstances in which a person makes an interception of a communication in the course of its transmission by means of a private telecommunication system are such that his conduct is excluded from criminal liability under subsection (2) if—(a) he is a person with a *right to control* the operation or the use of the system; or (b) he has the express or implied consent of such a person to make the interception' (emphasis added).

[282] *Stanford* [2006] EWCA Crim 258.   [283] *Governor of Brixton Prison, ex p Levin* [1997] QB 65.

Knowing control?

As with the element of possession, there is a question mark over whether the prosecution must show that D knows he is in control of the article. As it must be proved that D intended the article be used for fraud, there is arguably no need to include a further element of mens rea that D knew he was in control of the article. D who intends that the article will be used for fraud is almost inevitably likely to know that it is under his control.

22.7.1.5 'For use in the course of or in connection with'

This form of words is identical to that in going equipped. The offences of fraud are so wide that the items which might be used 'in connection with' such activities are endless. It is not necessarily a defence that D did not intend to use the article while in the physical commission of the contemplated crime. If, for example, he intended to use it only in the course of covering his tracks after the commission of the offence, this is sufficient because it is use 'in connection with' the offence.[284] Similarly, if he intended to use the article while doing preparatory acts, the offence would be committed.

22.7.1.6 'Any fraud'

This clearly extends to the offence under s 1 of the 2006 Act. Presumably it also extends to ss 9 and 11. Is it limited to frauds under the Act? Is conspiracy to defraud caught as well? The Act provides no guidance on whether 'fraud' is to be construed as meaning a general fraud offence under s 1 or some wider collection of offences.[285] It is submitted that the offence does not extend to articles for use in connection with all dishonest offences. Some support for this is derived from the refusal of the Home Office in its responses to consultation to extend the proposal to include possession of articles for use in theft.[286]

22.7.2 Mens rea

The section makes no reference to mens rea.[287] The Home Office Explanatory Notes suggest that 'A general intention to commit fraud will suffice.'[288] The courts have thankfully adopted that interpretation to avoid innocent people being at risk of prosecution for the possession of innocuous articles.[289]

In *Sakalauskas*,[290] the Court of Appeal adopted the interpretation in *Ellames*[291] where in construing the going equipped offence the court said that:

> An intention to use must necessarily relate to use in the future. . . . It seems to us impossible to interpret section 25(1) as if it read 'has with him any article for use or *which has been used* in the course of or in connection with any burglary, theft or cheat' . . . In our view, to establish an offence under section 25(1) the prosecution must prove that the defendant was in possession of the article, and intended the article to be used in the course of or in connection with some future burglary, theft or cheat. But it is not necessary to prove that he intended it to be used in the course of or in connection

---

[284] This interpretation was endorsed in *Smith* [2020] EWCA Crim 38.

[285] eg what of the offences involving copyright infringement under the Copyright, Designs and Patents Act 1988 where D records films at the cinema on his iPhone and uploads them to a website for general viewing: see eg *Nimley* [2010] EWCA Crim 2752.

[286] Para 49.

[287] For criticism, see Justice, *Briefing for the Fraud Bill, House of Lords Committee* (2006) paras 18–21; and debates in Parliament: Hansard, HL Committee, 19 July 2005, col 1451; Hansard, HL, Standing Committee B, 20 June 2006, cols 38–42; D Ormerod, 'The Fraud Act 2006—Criminalising Lying' [2007] Crim LR 193.

[288] At [25].

[289] In its original proposal, the Home Office had implicitly envisaged a strict liability offence of pure possession, see para 43 of the consultation document.

[290] [2013] EWCA Crim 2278.   [291] [1974] 3 All ER 130.

with any *specific* burglary, theft or cheat; it is enough to prove a general intention to use it for *some* burglary, theft or cheat; we think that this view is supported by the use of the word 'any' in section 25(1). Nor, in our view, is it necessary to prove that the defendant intended to use it himself; it will be enough to prove that he had it with him with the intention that it should be used by someone else.[292]

In *Sakalauskas*, Mitting J stated that this passage applied with equal force to s 6 of the Fraud Act 2006. His lordship observed that if a different interpretation were to be adopted then it would be easy to see how an innocent person who knew that an article had been used by somebody else for the purpose of fraud would commit an offence under s 6 if he knowingly had it in his possession. That outcome cannot have been the intention of Parliament.

22.7.3 Defences

Note that there is no defence of lawful excuse or lawful authority. The Home Office in its responses to consultation regarded this as unnecessary given the mens rea requirement—which is unfortunately not spelt out on the face of the statute. The investigative agency, which possesses such materials as a part of an undercover operation, etc, will be protected by the lack of mens rea and/or by the absence of any public interest in prosecution.[293] The Home Office explanation for the absence of such a defence was that the 'dishonesty test' would protect those in undercover operations.[294] This seems to demonstrate a fundamental misunderstanding of s 6, which contains no dishonesty element!

22.7.4 Inchoate liability

The s 6 offence is capable of extending even further when inchoate versions are considered—for example, D who seeks to purchase a device for use in fraud from a police officer in a sting operation attempts to possess.[295] However, it is submitted that it is not necessary to fall back on the use of an attempt charge where there is a potential impossibility problem.[296] The full offence may well be committed. For example, D is proved to be in possession of an article which he thinks will be able to clone credit cards, but which is in fact a useless piece of software which will be incapable of doing so. He is in possession of an article and he intends that the article will be used for fraud. He commits the full offence, even though it would be impossible for the article to be used to commit fraud.

22.8 Section 7: making or supplying articles for use in frauds

22.8.1 Section 7 of the Fraud Act 2006

Section 7 provides for a further broad offence:

> (1) A person is guilty of an offence if he makes, adapts, supplies, or offers to supply any article—
>
> > (a) knowing that it is designed or adapted for use in the course of or in connection with fraud, or
> >
> > (b) intending it to be used to commit, or assist in the commission of, fraud.

[292] ibid at 136 per Browne J, citing the 3rd edn of this book (1973) at pp 484, 485.
[293] Paras 47–8.
[294] Home Office, *Fraud Law Reform: Response to Consultations* (2004) para 48.
[295] See also the liability for conspiracy in *Pakiyanthur* [2010] EWCA Crim 2312.
[296] See p 516.

In the magistrates' court the maximum penalty is six months' imprisonment and a fine and in the Crown Court the maximum is ten years' imprisonment and a fine.

22.8.1.1 The forms of the offence

There are several distinct versions of the offence contained in s 7. There are obviously differences between making, adapting, supplying and offering to supply. There are also important differences between s 7(1)(a) which requires that the article *is*[297] for use in connection with fraud and s 7(1)(b) where there is no requirement that the article is so designed, etc provided D intends it to be used. Section 7(1)(b) is in that respect much wider, and that difference may be important particularly where the charges allege supply/offer to supply.[298] In a different respect, s 7(1)(b) seems narrower than s 7(1)(a), being restricted to articles for use in the commission of fraud, whereas s 7(1)(a) is wider—encompassing use in connection with fraud. Whether the courts will be willing to draw such a distinction remains to be seen.

22.8.1.2 Scope of offence

This is far from being the straightforward offence that the government proposed. The Home Office had suggested that the offence would extend only to cases where the article was 'specifically designed to commit fraud or where the manufacturer knows the article is to be used to commit frauds'.[299] Clearly, the offence extends much wider than this. The only example of its operation provided in the Explanatory Notes to the Act is that where 'a person makes devices which when attached to electricity meters cause the meter to malfunction. The actual amount of electricity used is concealed from the provider, who thus makes a loss.'[300] Such conduct was capable of being prosecuted as conspiracy to defraud where there was more than one actor involved in the agreement, as in *Hollinshead*,[301] discussed in Ch 13.

Section 7 has the potential to apply to a much wider range of circumstances. It will catch the software manufacturer who produces programs that are designed solely for criminal purposes—those that clone credit card data, etc. In that respect, it is a welcome addition to the prosecution's armoury.

There seems to be no doubt that the section could apply to the corporate defendant. The companies producing blank cards for use in credit card cloning, or designing software for the production of phishing sites, etc may all be caught.

22.8.1.3 Actus reus
Any article

The definition of article has been considered previously. By virtue of s 8, it includes electronic data. The scope of the actus reus is extremely broad. An allegation based on articles 'designed or adapted for' use in fraud will be relatively narrow but will still encompass, for example, computer software for credit card cloning, etc.[302] In comparison, if the allegation is that the article is 'intended for use in' fraud and it was made or supplied or offered for supply, the offence extends much wider and could include articles such as mobile phones.[303] It seems clear that the offence is committed irrespective of whether the article is capable of being used by itself or in combination with other articles.[304]

---

[297] Otherwise there could be no knowledge that it is for such use: *Montila* [2004] UKHL 50 and *Saik* [2006] UKHL 18.

[298] If the allegation is that D made or adapted the article, it is likely to be caught by s 7(1)(a) in any event.

[299] Response to Consultations (2005) para 52.   [300] Para 27.

[301] [1985] 1 All ER 850 at 858 and commentary at [1985] Crim LR 653 at 656.

[302] See eg *Yew* [2013] EWCA Crim 809 where D was running a counterfeit bank payment card factory.

[303] See eg *Nimley* [2010] EWCA Crim 2752 where D pleaded guilty to offences under ss 6 and 7 for filming screenings in a cinema on his iPhone and uploading them to a share site on the internet.

[304] cf Misuse of Drugs Act 1971, s 9A, inserted by Drugs Trafficking Offences Act 1986, s 34(1).

As noted earlier, where the charge is laid under s 7(1)(a), it is necessary that the prosecution establishes that the article *is* designed or adapted for use in fraud. The article must be such in order for D to know that it is such.

'Makes'

This is an ordinary English word, and in this context is used in the sense of 'manufactures'. It seems not to give rise to difficulties in practice. Where D has made the article, it will be most likely that he also knows that it is designed for or adapted for use in fraud and the charge will be under s 7(1)(a). It is possible, however, that D has made some article which is not designed or adapted for fraud, but which he nevertheless intends to use for that purpose. This would fall under s 7(1)(b) and could extend as widely as, for example, the making of special paper which D intends to use to print false cheque forms.

Where the allegation involves electronic data, the courts might draw upon the interpretation of the word 'makes' from the offences dealing with indecent images of children. In that context, it has been held that D makes an image when he downloads it to his computer cache from the internet.[305] If such an interpretation is adopted under s 7, it will broaden the offence considerably. The individual who downloads software, even if he does not then adapt it or alter it or use it, may be liable if the prosecution can establish either: (a) that it was designed or adapted for use in fraud (s 7(1)), for example credit card cloning software; or (b) even if it is entirely innocuous software such as a spreadsheet program, that D intended to use it for the commission of fraud (s 7(1)(b)).

'Adapts'

Adapts is a term which may have been chosen with the application of this offence to electronic data in mind. To describe the action of creating software or other electronic data as 'making' an article would be an unnatural use of that word (unless the courts adopt the interpretation in the previous paragraph in which case downloading constitutes making). Moreover, it will often be the case that D has not created the software from scratch but has changed a form of software which has pre-existing legitimate uses and has 'adapted' it for fraudulent use. There is no requirement that the article which D adapts must have been in his possession, ownership or control.

'Supplies'

This is a term which, like possession, has created difficulties for the courts in a number of contexts. However, given that in this context we are dealing with the supply of articles for illegal purposes, it is unlikely that the courts will take a restrictive or unduly technical approach to the term.

The word 'supply', in its ordinary natural meaning,[306] conveys the idea of furnishing or providing to another something which is wanted or required in order to meet the wants or requirements of that other. It suggests more than the mere transfer of physical control of some chattel or object from one person to another.

There is no restriction that the supply has to be for money or money's worth or that it is restricted to commercial supply.[307] D handing over a blank credit card to his friend for free is as guilty as the commercial provider of software programs for, for example, decoding satellite TV boxes.

Where D is alleged to have supplied an article, the prosecutor will have to exercise considerable care over the description of the charge. If D has supplied the article and knows that

---

[305] *Atkins v DPP* [2000] 1 WLR 1427.

[306] As the House of Lords adopted in relation to supply of drugs—*Maginnis* [1987] AC 303.

[307] cf s 1(4) of the Video Recordings Act 1984 now re-enacted as the Video Recordings Act 2010 where an extended definition makes this clear.

it is designed or adapted for use in fraud, the correct charge is under s 7(1)(a). That charge will only be available where the article supplied is actually designed or adapted for use in fraud. Where the articles are not designed or adapted for fraud, the charges will have to be brought under s 7(1)(b).[308]

'Offers to supply'

This expression is also one with which the courts will be familiar from s 4(1)(b) and s 4(3)(a) of the Misuse of Drugs Act 1971. It seems likely that the courts will follow the interpretation developed under that Act, and an offer will therefore be capable of being made by words or conduct. Whether the words or conduct amount to an 'offer' will be a question of fact. Further, it will not be necessary for D making the offer to have in his possession or control the article he is offering to supply. The manufacturer, or someone acting as his agent, who has yet to make the articles in question may be liable for offering to supply them.[309] Whether D intends to perform the act of supplying what he is offering will be irrelevant; the offence is complete as soon as an offer to supply is made.[310] Perhaps most importantly, as an overriding principle of interpretation, the courts have held that this is not an area in which it will be helpful to refer to principles of contract law in determining whether there is an offer.

Where the article is one designed or adapted for use in fraud and D knows that his offer to supply it will be caught under s 7(1)(a), there is no need to show that D is aware/intends that the recipient intends to use it for fraud.[311] Where D merely has an intention that the articles he offers to supply will be used in the commission of fraud, he commits the s 7(1)(b) form of the offence, irrespective of whether the articles are in fact designed or adapted for fraud. Again, there is no need for the prosecution to prove that D has any intent or knowledge of the offeree's mens rea. In this respect, the offence is stricter than assisting and encouraging where D's liability turns in part on his mens rea as to the incitee's likely criminality.

In the course of or connection with any fraud

This expression suggests a very broad scope of application. It would seem to include articles not only for use in performance of the actual elements of the fraud offence, but also articles for use in preparation and/or concealment of the offence.

To commit or assist in the commission of

In contrast to the expression 'in the course of or connection with', this expression seems to be more restricted. A reasonable argument can be advanced that the expression denotes the elements of the fraud offence, and does not extend to the acts preparatory or ancillary to that offence whether before or after its commission.

For use in 'any fraud'

As with the s 6 offence, it is unclear whether the offence can be committed where the 'fraud' offence is one which is proscribed by common law (conspiracy to defraud) or by legislation other than the Fraud Act 2006. Are articles for use in a conspiracy to defraud caught? The Home Office's use of the example based on *Hollinshead* suggests that the s 7 offence does apply to conspiracy to defraud. Whether the s 7 offence extends further and applies, for

---

[308] Or as charges of attempt under the Criminal Attempts Act 1981.
[309] *Mitchell* [1992] Crim LR 723; *Haggard v Mason* [1976] 1 WLR 187.
[310] *Gill* (1993) 97 Cr App R 215.
[311] cf eg the offence under s 126(2) of the Communications Act 2003 in which it is an offence to possess or supply apparatus knowing or believing that the intentions of the person to whom it is supplied are dishonestly to obtain, etc communication services. See, similarly, the requirement of mens rea in s 2(3)(b) of the Mobile Telephones (Re-programming) Act 2002.

example, to supply of articles for use in the commission of other dishonesty offences generally and in specific fraud-based offences such as those under the Taxes Management Act and the Value Added Taxes Act remains to be seen.

22.8.1.4 Mens rea
Section 7(1)(a)
'Knowing' that it is designed or adapted for such use
This is a relatively strict mens rea requirement. Knowledge involves a state of mind of true belief as the House of Lords acknowledged in *Montila*.[312] It is difficult to see how the doctrine of wilful blindness has any application in the context of design, although it is possible in the context of adaptation.

The prosecution must establish that the article which D has made, adapted, supplied or offered to supply is designed or adapted for use in the course of or in connection with fraud. In addition, the prosecution must prove that D knew that the article was designed or adapted for such use. There is no requirement that D intends or believes or knows that the person to whom the article is supplied or offered will commit any fraud offence. The CPS suggests, with some optimism, that the 'use to which the article can be put is likely to provide sufficient evidence of the defendant's state of mind'.[313]

Section 7(1)(b)
Intending it to be used to commit or assist in committing
The s 7(1)(b) form of the offence applies where D makes, adapts, supplies or offers to supply any article, whether it is designed or adapted for use in fraud or not, with the intention that the article will be used in the commission of fraud or to assist in the commission of fraud. Intention here will presumably include not only direct intention in the sense of purpose, but also an oblique intention where D sees the use of the article for fraud as virtually certain.

It is submitted that it is not necessary that D intends that the person to whom he supplies or offers to supply the article will act with mens rea.

Further reading

J Fisher, J Bewsey, A Herd and A Milne, *Arlidge and Parry on Fraud*
C Montgomery and D Ormerod, *Montgomery and Ormerod Fraud: Criminal Law and Procedure*

[312] [2004] UKHL 50.
[313] See www.cps.gov.uk/legal-guidance/fraud-act-2006.

23

Other offences involving fraud

23.1 False accounting

Section 17 of the Theft Act 1968 provides:

(1) Where a person dishonestly, with a view to gain for himself or another or with intent to cause loss to another,—

(a) destroys, defaces, conceals or falsifies any account or any record or document made or required for any accounting purpose; or

(b) in furnishing information for any purpose produces or makes use of any account, or any such record or document as aforesaid, which to his knowledge is or may be misleading, false or deceptive in a material particular;

he shall, on conviction on indictment, be liable to imprisonment for a term not exceeding seven years.

It has been suggested that the section creates six forms of the offence, although the courts acknowledge that 'false accounting' is the appropriate way to refer to the offence however committed.[1] False accounting can be a useful charge to reflect accurately the scale of dishonest wrongdoing without the need to deal with the complex issues of when and where property transferred or was acquired (whether as bank credits or otherwise). False accounting is also often the most suitable charge where the conduct did not involve a scheme which was fraudulent from the outset but became so when, for example, a legitimate business got into financial difficulties. The offence overlaps with others, especially forgery and fraud. The offence under s 17 is wider than forgery; not every false statement renders the document a forgery.[2] False accounting is narrower than the general Fraud Act offence because it is

---

[1] *Bow Street Magistrates, ex p Hill* (1999) 29 Nov, unreported, DC.
[2] See Ch 29 and *Dodge* [1972] 1 QB 416.

restricted to falsity, etc in relation to accounts. The Fraud Act applies under s 2 to any false representation and under ss 3 and 4 where D is under a legal duty to reveal information or where he is in a position in which he is expected to safeguard V's financial interests as, for example, where he is the auditor or accountant.

23.1.1 Section 17(1)(a)

23.1.1.1 Actus reus

The offence may be committed by any person who falsifies, etc any document 'made or required' for an accounting purpose. It is not necessary to prove that anyone accepted or acted on the falsified document; this is a conduct offence, not an offence of deception requiring a result caused by D's conduct. The falsification, etc is a sufficient manifestation of criminal intent to warrant criminalization irrespective of whether it causes loss or results in gain.

The account or record

'Account' is an ordinary English word. 'Any account or any record' encompasses a set of written financial accounts but is interpreted widely to include a mechanical or electronic or digital accounting device such as a computer or a taximeter. It has even been held to include[3] a turnstile which records the number of paying customers[4] as the admission of two people through one movement of the turnstile amounts to falsification by the omission of a material particular. A completely false set of accounts is also 'an account' for the purposes of the section.[5]

'Made or required for'

It is enough that the document was either made or required for an accounting purpose.[6] This restriction means that s 17 does not apply to all documents or records.

Unfortunately, the courts have failed to adopt a consistent approach to identifying whether particular documents were made or required for accounting purposes. Two issues arise: (a) whether a document is made or required for an accounting purpose; and (b) on what evidence the jury is to be satisfied of that fact.

In relation to the first issue, neither 'made for' or 'required for' is to be read restrictively. Each term should be given its ordinary meaning having regard to the context[7] and potential purpose for which the document was required. They should not be treated as technical terms of 'forensic accounting'.[8] It has been persuasively suggested that 'made for' refers to the purposes of the maker of the document and 'required for' to the purposes of the recipient.[9] A set of financial accounts is prima facie made for an accounting purpose. Any other record or document is 'made for' an accounting purpose where that is its primary purpose. It has also been held that it is enough that *one of the purposes* of the document or record is for an accounting purpose.[10] This is a controversial extension of the offence.[11]

In relation to the second issue, the question of what evidence is needed for the jury to be satisfied of the accounting purpose, the courts have distinguished between two categories of case. First, those types of documents which a jury, with such experience and knowledge

---

[3] cf *Solomons* [1909] 2 KB 980.   [4] *Edwards v Toombs* [1983] Crim LR 43.

[5] *Scot-Simonds* [1994] Crim LR 933.

[6] *Baxter v Governor of HM Prison Brixton* [2002] EWHC 300 (Admin).

[7] See *Neil* [2008] EWCA Crim 476.   [8] ibid at [22] per Auld LJ.

[9] Some support for this view is implicit in Auld LJ's judgment in *Baxter*.

[10] *A-G's Reference (No 1 of 1980)* [1981] 1 WLR 34, (personal loan proposal forms addressed to finance company).

[11] See *Arlidge and Parry on Fraud*, Ch 12.

of the world as jurors may be expected to have, could by examining the document, be satisfied that it was required for an accounting purpose. Secondly, those from which no such inference could safely be drawn. In this second category, the prosecution must adduce evidence of the purpose of the document. The court or jury may infer from the circumstances that the document is so required[12] but only if sufficient evidence exists for this conclusion to be drawn. One of the difficulties with the offence is that jurors cannot be assumed to know about accounting practices,[13] and the types of document that might be required for accounting purposes are extremely wide-ranging.

In *O and H*[14] (a prosecution appeal against a terminatory ruling), the court sought to clarify the position of the evidence that may be required, at least in relation to the commonly occurring problem of false information on a commercial mortgage or loan application form. The Court of Appeal held that an application made by a person for a mortgage was a document required for an accounting purpose because, if successful, it would lead to the lender providing funds and thus the opening of a mortgage account in favour of D in the books of the lender. That account would inevitably include the name and address of D as set out on the form and any bank details supplied by D. It would be inevitable (so the jury could find) that the account formed part of the accounting records of the lender. No direct evidence was required to prove that. A jury was entitled to conclude that an application for a mortgage or a loan made to a commercial institution was a document required for an accounting purpose.

The court conducted a comprehensive review of all the earlier authorities. It was accepted that not all of the decisions were reconcilable. In some earlier authorities, the court had taken a wide view of the likely uses the recipient would make of such documents. For example, a 'Report on Title' was required by a building society for an accounting purpose,[15] namely to decide whether to grant a mortgage advance. Similarly, in *Osinuga v DPP*[16] a form claiming entitlement to housing benefit was held to be a 'document made or required for' an accounting purpose. In *Manning*,[17] it was held that it would be open to a jury to conclude that an insurer's cover note was 'required' in the terms of this section simply by looking at the document because it set out what the client owed—but it was a borderline case. On other occasions the court had taken a narrower view. For example, in *Okanta*[18] the court was not satisfied that a falsified letter which induced a mortgage advance was required for an accounting purpose. Similarly, in *Sundhers* the court had held that claim forms for an insurance company had not been demonstrated to be required for an accounting purpose.[19] The cases adopting this narrower view would be decided differently applying *O* because the focus would be on whether the forms would have led to the opening of an account or the making of an account transfer. This is, with respect, one of the difficulties with the decision in *O*. Although it makes the prosecution's obligation on proof clear, caution must be exercised in applying the decision. The court is not saying, it is submitted, that an accounting purpose in s 17 can *only* arise where an account will be created or transfers into or from

---

12 *Osinuga v DPP* [1998] Crim LR 216; *Baxter*, n 6.   13 *Sundhers* [1998] Crim LR 497.

14 [2010] EWCA Crim 2233, [2011] Crim LR 401 and commentary.

15 *Cummings-John* [1997] Crim LR 660.

16 [1998] Crim LR 216. Cf at first instance HH Judge Jackson in *S* [1997] 4 Arch News 1, which must be regarded as wrongly decided. Note: the offence under s 111A of the Social Security Administration Act 1992 was amended by the Social Security Fraud Act 2001, s 16, but only in respect of the offence(s) of failing to notify the authorities of a change of circumstances relating to benefits. The specific offence relating to producing a document which is false in a material particular with a view to gaining social security benefits (s 111A(1)(b)) is still in force.

17 [1998] 2 Cr App R 461.   18 [1997] Crim LR 451. Distinguished in *Doncaster* [2008] EWCA Crim 5.

19 *Sundhers* [1998] Crim LR 497.

an account will be caused. That would render the offence far too narrow and would be irreconcilable with many earlier decisions. What the court is saying, it is submitted, is that because in cases of commercial mortgage or loan applications an account will be created, the application document is necessarily one that is required for an accounting purpose. *Mallett* is clear that it is the *document* that must be made or required for an accounting purpose. A further reason for caution when applying this reasoning is that the focus on the fact that the application document leads to an account being created must not be allowed to cloud the very clear law holding that there is no requirement under s 17 to prove that D's false statement, etc caused any result. False accounting is a conduct offence.

Given the inconsistent authorities on this element of the offence, prosecutors may well prefer, where possible, to rely on the general fraud offence under s 1 of the 2006 Act in which no such restriction as to the document applies.[20]

Particular difficulty arises where the document is one that is not a set of formal accounts and is being sent to a private individual rather than a lending company or equivalent. For example, in alleged high-yield investment frauds and pyramid frauds, application forms sent to a potential investor which include false statements as to the rate of return on investments may constitute documents made or required for any accounting purpose since they would be retained by the investor: 'it was the sort of document he would put in a wall safe not a waste paper basket'.[21]

'Any accounting purpose'

The section further extends its reach to any document, so long as it is made or required for *any* accounting purpose, though the document itself is not in the nature of an account and though the falsification does not relate to figures. So, if in a hire-purchase proposal form D enters false particulars relating to a company director, the case falls within the plain words of s 17(1)(a).[22]

Destruction, defacement, etc

For the s 17 offence, some account or record must be destroyed, defaced, concealed or falsified by D or as a result of information provided by D. It is not enough that D is cheating V, for example by selling his own property as V's, if that transaction is not recorded in any account.[23]

The courts do not seem to have provided any detailed consideration of the terms 'destruction', 'defacement' or 'concealment'. Destruction and defacement should present few, if any, problems. Some cases of defacement might also constitute forgery under the Forgery and Counterfeiting Act 1981. 'Concealment' raises the interesting question of whether it is necessary for D to be hiding some record, etc being aware that he is under a duty to disclose it, or whether it is sufficient simply that D conceals it. Arguably, concealment requires some 'act' and cannot be committed by a mere omission. The issue will commonly be rolled up with that of dishonesty since knowing concealment commonly implies a lack of honesty. Secrecy and dishonesty are, however, not coextensive, nor are transparency and honesty.

---

[20] The likelihood that the Fraud Act would be relied on was noted by the Court of Appeal in *O*.

[21] *Baxter v Governor of HM Prison Brixton* [2002] EWHC 300 (Admin).

[22] *A-G's Reference (No 1 of 2001)* [2002] EWCA Crim 1768. The charge is available in relation to alleged fraud of parliamentary expenses and is not ousted by art 9 of the Bill of Rights 1688: *Chaytor* [2010] UKSC 52. For discussion, see J Saunders, 'Parliamentary Privilege and the Criminal Law' [2017] Crim LR 521.

[23] *Cooke* [1986] AC 909.

Falsification

The more important issues arise in relation to falsification. Under s 17(1)(a) the offence is committed by falsification of the account, etc whereas under s 17(1)(b) it is committed by *use* of a falsified account, etc. Section 17(2) provides an extended though non-exhaustive definition of falsity:

> For the purposes of this section a person who makes or concurs in making in an account or other document an entry which is or may be misleading, false or deceptive in a material particular, or who omits or concurs in omitting a material particular from an account or other document, is to be treated as falsifying the account or document.

The extended meaning attaches only to documents and accounts, not records. Falsification may be by omission, as where D omits to include information relating to his true income on an application form for housing benefit.[24] The case law has extended the scope of the actus reus far beyond that simple proposition. In *Shama*,[25] D, an international telephone operator, was required for each call to fill in a 'charge ticket' which was then used for an accounting purpose. He connected certain favoured subscribers without filling in a charge ticket, so they were not charged. The prosecution were unable to produce any falsified document. Upholding D's conviction, the court said that 'failure to complete a charge ticket by omitting material particulars from a document required for an accounting purpose' constituted the offence. But how can the omission to make a document at all be the omission of material particulars from it? The omission of material particulars seems necessarily to imply the existence of a document from which those particulars are omitted.[26]

The offence applies irrespective of whether D is under a formal duty to account, but if D is acting under such a duty that will prescribe the scope of his obligation to include material in the documents.[27]

Material particular

Where the allegation is of falsification, that must relate to a material particular.[28] This aspect of the offence has also been interpreted broadly. Information is 'material' if it is something that matters to V in making up his mind about action to be taken on the document.[29] It need not be material to the accounting purpose directly. In *Mallett*, the Court of Appeal approved the trial judge's description of a material particular as 'an important matter; a thing that mattered'. It was not specified to whom it must be shown to have been important. The particulars may be material precisely for the purpose of auditing and detecting fraud. Thus, omitting the name of an account holder to whom bank payments were to be made is a material particular since the name would have revealed instantly that the payment was unauthorized.[30] The particular can be material for the purposes of the section even if it would not have been the direct cause of the gain being made or the loss caused. That

---

[24] See *Lancaster* [2010] EWCA Crim 370, [2010] Crim LR 776 and commentary.

[25] [1990] 2 All ER 602.

[26] Presumably, D, at the end of his shift returned a bundle of charge tickets to his employers. Effectively it was his work record for the shift and was required for an accounting purpose. The 'record' might be regarded as a single document though it records each transaction on a separate page; on this view the document would be false by omitting to record some of the transactions. The best course now might be to charge under s 2 of the Fraud Act 2006: when the operator handed in the forms there was presumably an implied, if not an express, representation that there was a form for each call, it must still be shown that D intended to gain/cause loss.

[27] *Keatley* [1980] Crim LR 505 (Judge Mendl).

[28] If it is of destruction, etc, it is the whole document or record or, presumably, a relevant part.

[29] *Mallett* [1978] 1 WLR 820.

[30] *Taylor* [2003] EWCA Crim 1509, D dishonestly authorizing £73,000 payments from his employer to his parents.

applies whether the allegation is one of positive falsification or omission. For example, if D, when completing an application form for a mortgage, omits to mention that he is married, although that information had it been revealed would have been unlikely to have led to the mortgage being refused, it can be regarded as a material particular for the purposes of s 17.[31]

In cases of omission, it will only be possible to evaluate the materiality of the omitted particular in the context of the account as a whole. Whether the omission was significant would depend on the nature of the document and the context. The test is objective, although it is doubtful whether it would be helpful to use that language when directing a jury on the matter. Evidence may be admissible to explain significance. There is no hard-and-fast rule that any omission to supply information required by an application form must *necessarily* amount to the omission of a material particular.

There does not appear to be a clear mens rea requirement as to materiality: it is not clear that D must know or believe that the 'particular' he has omitted (or falsified) is or may be material.

23.1.1.2 Mens rea

The mens rea of the s 17(1)(a) offence requires that D:

(1) intentionally destroys, defaces, conceals or falsifies the document; and

(2) does so dishonestly; and

(3) acts with a view to gain for himself or another, or with intent to cause loss to another.

Given the breadth of the actus reus (in the previous section) it is desirable in principle for specificity and clarity in each element of mens rea. However, the courts have relied heavily on the dishonesty as the gravamen, avoiding unduly technical separation of the issues of knowledge and falsity.[32]

Intentionally making the statement in the account or record

Proving this element of the mens rea may be difficult if D is completing large numbers of similar records containing routine information. In *Atkinson*,[33] a pharmacist completed forms to secure repayment of prescription costs. She admitted to filling in the forms while watching TV and playing with her children. Some forms were false in a material particular. The trial judge directed the jury to concentrate on her dishonesty, commenting that it was sufficient if the jury were sure that she knew it was *likely* that some of the forms were false in a material particular. The Court of Appeal regarded this as a dilution of the element of intention, coming close to mere recklessness. There must be a view to gain or intent to cause loss (see later), which would not be satisfied by proof that D saw the falsity of a statement as 'likely'.[34] There is a distinct requirement that D 'deliberately and intentionally' makes the statement in the account or document. It is important to keep this element separate from the question of intention to gain since there are cases in which D will act with knowledge of

---

[31] See *Lancaster* [2010] EWCA Crim 370. Toulson LJ did express doubt whether all incomplete or incorrect answers would be material (eg ethnic monitoring in government forms, or profiling questions in commercial forms).

[32] In *Atkinson* [2003] EWCA Crim 3031 the court's suggestion that 'only lawyers would think of breaking [the mens rea] into component parts' is, with respect, an odd one. Is this not one element of the art of statutory construction one would expect of lawyers?

[33] [2004] Crim LR 226.

[34] It is acceptable to say that D intends result A (causing loss/making gain) if he does an act B (making false statement) which is likely to bring about the result A, provided D also has an intention to perform act B.

falsity but with no ulterior intent to gain or cause loss.[35] This is an important element of the offence because the exercise of completing standard records and accounts is such that there is often great potential for recklessness or negligence in the recording of data. Such failings should not give rise to liability under this offence.

Knowledge as to falsity

Since s 17(2) extends the offence to cover cases in which the statement 'is or may be' misleading, false or deceptive, it is arguable that D is guilty if he intentionally makes statements in the account or record, knowing that they *may be false* and acts with a view to gain or intent to cause loss. The learned authors of *Arlidge and Parry*[36] suggest that it can hardly be intended that the subsection should apply where it is uncertain whether the proposition in question is true or false. The conclusion is that the expression 'or may be' must relate *only* to the s 17(1)(b) offence which includes the terms 'deception' and 'misleading'.[37] In *Bush*,[38] which involved a prosecution arising out of a £250m discrepancy in Tesco's financial accounting, it was alleged that D and others had improperly recognized and adopted certain commercial income figures to provide a false account of the company's true earnings. The prosecution conceded that they must prove that each defendant knew that income was being improperly *and* unlawfully recognized. On the facts, the prosecution could not establish that the income was being improperly accounted.[39] It was not sufficient to prove merely that the defendants were aware of the unusual and complex accounting practice that turned out to be unlawful; it was necessary to prove that they were aware of the unlawfulness of the practice.

'Dishonesty'

The term should be interpreted, as far as possible, consistently with its application in other sections of the 1968 Act. No statutory definition for dishonesty was adopted in relation to this offence. The test to be applied is that from *Ivey v Genting Casinos UK Ltd (t/a Crockfords Club)*,[40] and *Barton*[41] which is examined in detail in Ch 18. The shift to a more objective focus in the application of the dishonesty test may well have an impact in false accounting cases. As noted, the activity of recording transactions can be monotonous and errors can readily occur, even in situations where large sums are at stake. Whereas under *Ghosh* D could never be liable unless he realized that ordinary decent people would regard his conduct as dishonest, that safeguard has gone. A serious accounting error involving a large sum of money may well be regarded by some jurors as dishonest applying an objective standard.

Section 2 of the Theft Act does not apply. It is unclear whether the concept of a claim of right has any relevance here, as it does in s 1.[42] Does s 17 apply to D who falsifies accounts to get property to which he believes he has a claim of right? One argument is that this should not excuse false accounting: the legitimacy of the end, or the belief in the legitimacy of the end, should not justify an illegality in the means of securing that end. D should not falsify documents. A further argument is that the essence of this offence is to recognize the

---

[35] See further Ormerod and Williams, *Smith's Law of Theft*, Ch 4 and cases cited therein.
[36] *Arlidge and Parry on Fraud*, para 12.022.
[37] See ibid, para 12.022. Would this have been a better charge for *Atkinson*, n 32.
[38] [2019] EWCA Crim 29.
[39] As the Court of Appeal observed, 'It can be done lawfully and properly (for example where the activity linked to the income is brought forward), it can be done lawfully but be unwise commercially; or it may be done unlawfully or via the use of false accounting', at [123].
[40] [2017] UKSC 67.   [41] [2020] EWCA Crim 575.
[42] *Wood* [1999] Crim LR 564. Williams, TBCL, 890.

separate obligation of honesty in the creation of documents that will serve as a *means* by which D can acquire property. If D has a genuine belief in the claim of right to the money to which he acts with a view to gain, there is no reason why he should use false means (evidencing his dishonesty) to acquire that money.

In *A-G's Reference (No 1 of 2001)*,[43] X had been charged with an offence in the United States, which attracted high-profile media coverage. A fund was established with payments from well-wishers. An appeal committee placed donations received in the fund account, irrespective of whether the donors expressly stated whether the payment was for X and her parents (G and S) or for the fund. G and S submitted false invoices in respect of expenses incurred in attending their daughter's trial. That was alleged to amount to false accounting. The judge accepted the submission that because some of the money transferred to the fund was money originally donated to G and S to use as they chose, the prosecution could not prove that the amount of money obtained on the false invoice was not the money of G and S. No claim of a belief in a claim of legal entitlement was made. It is easy to see how even though G and S had a 'view to gain' in the sense of acquiring the property, a jury might have found, applying the *Ghosh* test, that they were not dishonest in submitting the false invoices if they believed they had a legal right to acquire the property. Applying *Ivey* and *Barton*, there is a greater likelihood that such conduct would be regarded as dishonest.

In *Gohill v DPP*,[44] D1 and D2 were charged with offences of theft and false accounting arising from their management of a plant hire shop. They had accepted 'tips' for allowing others to use the plant for a short time without payment. On these occasions, D1 and D2 recorded each such short use as if the plant had not been hired at all. They claimed that these actions were not dishonest but were promoting customer relations. The justices acquitted, not being satisfied beyond a reasonable doubt that the defendants' actions had been dishonest by the ordinary standards of reasonable and honest people. The prosecution's appeal was allowed, Leveson LJ concluding that it was impossible to find that it was not dishonest by the ordinary standards of reasonable and honest people to falsify a record in this way, particularly since company policy, of which the defendants had been aware, did not permit an alteration of those records. The same would be true applying *Ivey* and *Barton*. The decision rests on what was the first limb of *Ghosh*—the objective test—which is preserved and prioritized by *Ivey* and *Barton*.

Gain and loss

'Gain' and 'loss' are defined in s 34(2)(a) which is discussed elsewhere.[45] There might be a view to gain or an intention to cause loss in falsifying the account although the gain or loss has already taken place.

It is sufficient that D intends to gain or to cause loss, but where the prosecution allege specifically that D intended to gain, that must be proved.[46]

'Gain' includes a gain by keeping what one has. This has created some difficulties in interpretation. D commits an offence under s 17 where, having already appropriated property of V, he destroys, defaces, conceals or falsifies an account so that he will not be found out, or to put off the evil day when he will be called to account. An intent to gain or cause loss on a temporary basis may therefore suffice: *Eden*.[47] There is one decision that seems to contradict that interpretation. In *Golechha*,[48] it was held that D's falsifications by which he intended

---

[43] [2002] Crim LR 844.   [44] [2007] EWHC 239 (Admin).
[45] See p 1043. Cf *Lee Cheung Wing v R*, n 55.
[46] In *Bush* [2019] EWCA Crim 29, the judge rightly acceded to a submission of no case where there was no evidence of intent to gain even though there was some evidence of intent to cause loss.
[47] [1971] Crim LR 416.   [48] [1989] 3 All ER 908 (sub nom *Choraria and Golechha*).

to postpone V enforcing a debt was not an act with intent to gain. It is submitted that in such circumstances D's act involves both an intent to gain and cause loss. It is not easy to reconcile this decision with *Eden*. Putting off the evil day when D will have to repay his debt would seem clearly to constitute a 'gain' to D. *Golechha* has been described as a case turning very much on its own facts[49] and it has been held, for example, that a 'deed of postponement', postponing the priority of a registered charge in favour of another obligation, does 'cause loss'.[50]

Where D falsifies accounts to exaggerate the profit which his department is making in order to induce his employer to continue his employment, it seems he has both a view to gain (he does this to keep his job and his salary) and an intent to cause loss (insofar as it causes him to continue to operate an uneconomic department).[51] It may be that there is no appropriation, or intended appropriation, of any money or goods belonging to the employer and therefore no theft; but, clearly, D is acting dishonestly. In *Masterson*,[52] D's falsification of invoices in an attempt to 'improve relations with his co-directors' who were unhappy with the acquisitions he had recently made was not sufficient to constitute the necessary view to 'gain'. D knew that there was no question of losing his position and could not therefore be said even to be falsifying them with a view to retaining that 'which he had'.

'With a view to gain' was construed, in a different context, in *Dooley*[53] as requiring more than foresight or awareness of a likelihood of the prohibited consequence. It is sufficient that the consequence (in this case 'gain') was 'one of' the reasons for D acting in that fashion.

It has been held that there can be a view to gain even if D has a (belief in a) claim of right to that which he is acquiring. In *A-G's Reference (No 1 of 2001)*,[54] discussed in the previous section, G and S accepted that there was evidence that their expenses invoice was false, but argued that some of the money the committee had transferred to the trust was in fact money originally donated to G and S to use as they chose. On this basis, they argued that the prosecution could not prove that the amount G and S sought to obtain via the false invoice was not theirs. They argued that they had not 'gained' anything within the meaning of s 34(2)(a) because the trustees had incorporated into the trust some money which in fact belonged to G and S. The judge accepted that submission and ruled that G and S should be acquitted. The Court of Appeal held that this was wrong. Where D has provided false information with a view to obtaining money or other property it is not necessary for the prosecution to prove that D had no legal entitlement to the money or other property in question.

In *Lee Cheung Wing*,[55] D was an employee of a company offering facilities for dealing in futures. Employees were not allowed to use these facilities. D, in breach of his employment contract, opened an account in the name of a friend, X. The transactions D conducted were profitable and D signed withdrawal slips in X's name. The question was whether the slips were made 'with a view to gain'. D said he was withdrawing money to which he was entitled. Since a person has a view to gain even if he is entitled to the property demanded,[56] Lee's conviction might perhaps have been upheld on that ground. The Privy Council, however, concluded that D was not entitled to the money because he would have been bound to account to his employer for a profit made by improper use of his position as an employee.[57] The Board added that, in any event, action by D to recover the profits would probably have been met by a plea of *ex turpi causa non oritur actio*.[58] *Lee Cheung Wing*[59] is not a sufficiently

---

[49] *Masterson* (1996) 30 Apr, unreported, CA.   [50] *Cummings (John)* [1997] Crim LR 660.
[51] cf *Wines* [1953] 2 All ER 1497.   [52] (1996) CA 94/2221/X5.   [53] [2005] EWCA Crim 3093.
[54] [2002] EWCA Crim 1768.   [55] (1991) 94 Cr App R 355.
[56] *A-G's Reference (No 1 of 2001)* [2002] EWCA Crim 1768.
[57] *Reading v A-G* [1951] AC 507 at 516, 517.
[58] That the party will be unable to enforce an action if it arises in connection with his own illegal act.
[59] (1991) 94 Cr App R 355.

clear and weighty authority to cast doubt on the reasoning in the *A-G's Reference* because in *Lee Cheung Wing* it was not actually necessary to decide whether D would have been guilty had he been entitled to keep the money.

As for the intention to cause loss, it is unclear whether the intent must be direct or whether an oblique intention (where D sees a loss as virtually certain barring some unforeseen intervention) will suffice. The motives for intending to cause the loss are irrelevant. Thus, in *Leedham*,[60] D, a policeman, so disliked the government ban on handguns (imposed after the Dunblane shootings) that he completed compensation forms falsely and dishonestly to cause loss to the Home Office by allowing claims for ineligible items owned by others.

Strict liability as to accounting purpose

The actus reus requires proof that the document is made or required for an accounting purpose. As a matter of principle, this ought to involve proof of corresponding mens rea. It has been held,[61] however, that there is no requirement to prove D's intent or awareness of the purpose for which the document is required. A person may be guilty of false accounting although he has no idea, perhaps reasonably so, that this is what he is doing—as, for example, where the document is one which subsequently requires expert evidence to show that it is required for an accounting purpose. This imposition of strict liability as to an essential element of a serious offence seems objectionable.

Awareness of materiality?

Where the allegation is one of falsifying the document, etc a further element of actus reus is involved—the falsity must relate to a material particular. There has been no detailed judicial scrutiny of whether D must know or be aware of the materiality of the particular. In *Bowie and McVicar*,[62] HH Judge Atherton ruled that it was necessary for the prosecution to establish that additional element of mens rea.[63]

Historically, this issue would often have been subsumed within the question of dishonesty. Under *Ghosh*, D would claim that he had no realization that ordinary people would regard his conduct as dishonest. That is no longer a determinative feature of whether D is in law dishonest. If, for example, D makes an application for insurance and in doing so he makes a false statement—perhaps out of embarrassment—as to his marital status, he knows that what he has written is false, but is arguably unaware of the materiality of that status in affecting the insurance rate he will be offered. The lack of awareness or recklessness as to the materiality should be capable of being addressed within the broader questions of whether D is dishonest and is acting with a view to gain.

In practice, it is difficult to envisage circumstances in which D will be able to plead simultaneously that he accepts that he was dishonest, but that he lacked mens rea as to the materiality and should therefore be acquitted.[64] All such cases can, it is submitted, be prosecuted under s 1(2)(a) and s 2 of the Fraud Act 2006, where it is sufficient that D has made a false representation with intent to gain/cause loss irrespective of the materiality of the falsity.

---

[60] No 200200135/Y3.   [61] *Graham* [1997] 1 Cr App R 302 at 314.

[62] (2003) 19 Feb, Manchester CC.

[63] The charges arose from the sale of the defendants' portfolio of properties, which had been let to various tenants. The details of the properties were, in some cases, inaccurate in recording that the rents were paid from housing benefit rather than privately by the tenants. These were false statements, and arguably material since they would affect the security of future payments. The defendants denied that they had acted 'intentionally' or 'recklessly' either as to the falsehood or the materiality of that falsehood, but were convicted.

[64] cf Smith, *Property Offences*, para 24.07a.

23.1.2 Section 17(1)(b)

23.1.2.1 Actus reus

The offence under s 17(1)(b) involves 'using' rather than destroying, falsifying, etc the account. This is an extremely broad offence since it applies where D uses the document, etc for *any* purpose. A document may be misleading or false within the subsection by its failure to include material particulars, even though it is accurate in the sense that each statement which is contained is true.[65] It is notable that the prosecution need to show only that information in the account may be (not is) misleading or deceptive. Difficulties may arise in establishing the misleading, false or deceptive particular, and expert accounting evidence may be necessary. The elements relating to accounts and records or documents made or required for any accounting purpose are interpreted as in relation to s 17(1)(a), as are the requirements relating to falsity.

23.1.2.2 Mens rea

The mens rea for the s 17(1)(b) offence comprises: (a) intentionally using a document; (b) knowing it is or may be false; (c) dishonestly; and (d) with a view to gain for himself or another, or with intent to cause loss to another. It is important to note that the mens rea differs here in one important respect from the elements as discussed in relation to s 17(1)(a). D may commit the offence in furnishing information not only where he knows that the material particular is false, but also where he knows that the document *may* be false or misleading in a material particular; evidently wilful blindness suffices.

23.2 Corporations and their officers

As far as offences under the Theft Acts generally are concerned, the liability of corporations for them falls to be determined in accordance with the general principles applicable to the liability of corporations for crime.[66] Where a corporation commits a crime it must be the case that the crime has been committed by a person, or persons, in control of the corporation's affairs.[67] Such persons are, of course, liable in accordance with the ordinary principles governing liability for crime. Section 18 contains a special provision relating to false accounting. The section provides:

(1) Where an offence committed by a body corporate under section 17 of this Act is proved to have been committed with the consent or connivance of any director, manager, secretary or other similar officer[68] of the body corporate, or any person who was purporting to act in any such capacity, he as well as the body corporate shall be guilty of that offence, and shall be liable to be proceeded against and punished accordingly.

(2) Where the affairs of a body corporate are managed by its members, this section shall apply in relation to the acts and defaults of a member in connection with his functions of management as if he were a director of the body corporate.

---

[65] See *Kylsant* [1932] 1 KB 442.   [66] See Ch 8.

[67] A corporation may, of course, be vicariously liable for crimes even though the crime is not committed by a person in control of its affairs: see p 281. But vicarious liability would not apply in connection with offences under the Theft Act 1968.

[68] See *Boal* [1992] 3 All ER 177, limiting this to those in positions of real power.

This provision was explained by the Criminal Law Revision Committee as follows:[69]

The [section] follows a form of provision commonly included in statutes,[70] where an offence is of a kind to be committed by bodies corporate and where it is desired to put the management[71] under a positive obligation to prevent irregularities, if aware of them. Passive acquiescence does not, under the general law, make a person liable as a party to the offence, but there are clearly cases (of which we think this is one) where the director's responsibilities for his company require him to intervene to prevent fraud and where consent or connivance amount to guilt.

The Committee was suggesting that, without such a provision, in some circumstances the director might not be liable under the general principles governing liability for crime. The circumstances in which the director does not incur liability as a joint perpetrator or acces-sory will be relatively few. Suppose, for example, that D, a director, learns that E, a fellow director, proposes to falsify accounts but D does nothing about it. The effect of s 18 appears to be that D incurs criminal liability in respect of the false accounting because the offence has been committed with his consent. There would be no need to show that D communicated to E his approval of the falsification. Possibly, however, D would be liable under general principles for he has a clear duty to control the actions of E in this situation and his deliberate failure to perform his duty, coupled with his guilty knowledge, may make him an accessory.[72]

There are many provisions based on s 18 applying to very different areas of criminal law.[73] The Court of Appeal[74] has considered a similar provision and, it is submitted correctly, con-firmed that these provisions do not create discrete offences for the director, but rather they make the director liable as a secondary party to the company's principal offence.

23.3 False statements by company directors

Section 19 of the Act provides:

(1) Where an officer of a body corporate or unincorporated association (or person purport-ing to act as such), with intent to deceive members or creditors of the body corporate or association about its affairs, publishes or concurs in publishing a written statement or account which to his knowledge is or may be misleading, false or deceptive in a material particular, he shall on conviction on indictment be liable to imprisonment for a term not exceeding seven years.

(2) For purposes of this section a person who has entered into a security for the benefit of a body corporate or association is to be treated as a creditor of it.

(3) Where the affairs of a body corporate or association are managed by its members, this section shall apply to any statement which a member publishes or concurs in publishing in connection with his functions of management as if he were an officer of the body corporate or association.

The offence is designed to deal with cases where directors publish false prospectuses to members. It is one of a range of legislative provisions seeking to protect investors.[75]

---

[69] Eighth Report, para 104.   [70] See further p 271.

[71] Note that s 18 imposes criminal liability only on the management; this may include (s 18(2)) any member who is in fact in control even though he may not formally hold a managerial post.

[72] See p 198; *Tamm* [1973] Crim LR 115.

[73] These include s 12 of the Fraud Act 2006; s 18(1) of the Terrorism Act 2006; s 18(1) of the Safeguarding Vulnerable Groups Act 2006 and s 14 of the Bribery Act 2010.

[74] *Wilson* [2013] EWCA Crim 1780, p 272.

[75] See generally *Arlidge and Parry on Fraud*, paras 12.030–12.034; M Gale, 'Fraud and the Sale of Shares' (2001) 22 Company Lawyer 98. Investor protection has taken on a greater significance as increasing numbers of the general public have personal investment portfolios.

In two senses the offence is a narrow one. First, it may be committed only by an officer[76] of a body corporate or unincorporated association. 'Officer' in relation to a body corporate includes a director, manager or secretary.[77] Secondly, it may be committed only where the intention is to deceive[78] members or creditors of the corporation or association, and not the public at large, about its affairs. This is much narrower than the scope of liability under s 2 of the Fraud Act 2006 which is not restricted to company officers nor does it require an intent to deceive.

In another sense, the offence is a wide one for it extends to the publication of any *written* statement of account that *may be* misleading in a material particular. Recklessness suffices. It is not necessary to show that there is any view to gain or intention to cause loss in publishing the statement or account, though no doubt either or both will often be present. There is no requirement that D acted dishonestly, although it has been suggested that there is no practical difference between defining the mens rea as an intent to deceive or dishonesty.[79] The prosecution will depend in many cases on the expert accountancy evidence as to whether the accounts were misleading. The offence might be committed where an officer, in order to inspire confidence in the company, falsely publishes that a well-known person has been appointed to the board. It might also include a false statement, 'made in order to appeal to persons interested in a particular area, that a company had arranged to build a factory in that area'.[80]

In view of the breadth of the general fraud offence under the Fraud Act 2006, it is surprising that s 19 was not considered for repeal in the Fraud Act 2006.

Note also the specific offence to protect investors, found in s 89 of the Financial Services Act 2012.[81] This section creates an offence when D does one of the following: (a) makes a statement which he knows to be false or misleading in a material respect; (b) makes a statement which is false or misleading in a material respect, being reckless as to whether it is; or (c) dishonestly conceals any material facts whether in connection with a statement made by D or otherwise. D must make the statement or conceal facts with the intention of inducing, or being reckless as to whether making it will induce, another person (whether or not the statement is made to that person) to (a) enter into or offer to enter into a relevant agreement or (b) to exercise, or refrain for exercising, any rights conferred by a relevant investment. In addition to s 89, Part 7 of the Act creates two other offences of giving misleading impressions and making misleading statements, etc in relation to benchmarks.

23.4 Suppression of documents

By s 20 of the Theft Act 1968:

(1) A person who dishonestly, with a view to gain for himself or another or with intent to cause loss to another, destroys, defaces or conceals any valuable security, any will or other testamentary document or any original document of or belonging to, or filed or deposited in, any court of justice or any government department shall on conviction on indictment be liable to imprisonment for a term not exceeding seven years.[82]

---

[76] The officers of a body corporate are frequently defined in the articles or by-laws of a corporation. See Companies Act 2006, Part 3, Ch 2. An auditor may be an officer: *Shacter* [1960] 2 QB 252.

[77] Companies Act 2006, s 1173(1).   [78] As to intent to deceive, see *Welham v DPP* [1961] AC 103.

[79] See *Shuck* [1992] Crim LR 209.   [80] Eighth Report, para 105.

[81] See V Callaghan and Z Ullah, 'The LIBOR Scandal—The UK's Legislative Response' (2013) 28 J Int'l Business & Law 160. The offence has been amended by, inter alia, SI 2016/1680.

[82] Section 20(2) of the Theft Act 1968 created a very important offence of 'procuring the execution of a valuable security'. This was repealed by the Fraud Act 2006.

This provision is not likely to be of great practical importance; it was included because:

It seemed to us that it might provide the only way of dealing with a person who, for example, suppressed a public document as a first step towards committing a fraud but did not get so far as attempting to commit the fraud. In accordance with the scheme of the [Act] the offence is limited to something done dishonestly and with a view to gain or with intent to cause loss to another.[83]

Section 20(3) provides that:

For purposes of this section . . .[84] 'valuable security' means any document creating, transferring, surrendering or releasing any right to in or over property, or authorising the payment of money or delivery of any property, or evidencing the creation, transfer, surrender or release of any such right, or the payment of money or delivery of any property or the satisfaction of any obligation.

The wide definition of valuable security renders this offence available in a diverse range of circumstances and it is rather surprising that it is not often prosecuted.[85] Presumably, the evidential difficulties in establishing the destruction, etc of the document lie behind this.[86] Note also that the Proceeds of Crime Act 2002 creates offences including that under s 327: concealing, disguising, converting or transferring criminal property or removing it from the jurisdiction.[87] In addition there are offences of making false statements in statutory documents.[88]

23.5 Cheating the public revenue

Historically, cheating was a misdemeanour at common law and was developed most vigorously during the eighteenth century. The authorities suggest an incredibly broad definition. Hawkins[89] defined cheating as 'deceitful practices, in defrauding or endeavouring to defraud another of his own right by means of some artful device, contrary to the plain rules of common honesty'.

The common law offence of cheating still retains significant importance because, though s 32(1) of the Theft Act abolished cheating (along with common law offences against property), it did so only 'except as regards offences relating to the public revenue'.[90] The punishment is imprisonment and/or a fine without limit.

As a practical matter, the offence of cheating has been used, on any scale at all, only in connection with frauds against the public revenue. Given the available sentence and the breadth of the offence, it is not surprising that it is popular with prosecutors and is frequently prosecuted in preference to specific offences under the Theft Acts, Taxes Management Act and VAT Act.

---

83 Eighth Report, para 106.   84 Words repealed by the Fraud Act 2006.
85 See, in the extradition context, *Cholewinski v Poland* [2013] EWHC 3648 (Admin), where Bean J reviewed the authorities. CHAPS orders, cheques, bills of exchange and other negotiable instruments are 'valuable securities', but insurance policies are not.
86 Smith states that criminal damage will 'almost certainly' be committed by a person who falls within the terms of the offence. See Smith, *Property Offences*, 780. This would not, however, be true if D merely concealed the relevant document. For further discussion, see J Jaconelli, 'Wills as Public Documents—Privacy and Property Rights' (2012) 71 CLJ 147 at 154–7.
87 See Ch 33.   88 Perjury Act 1911, s 5.   89 I PC, 318.
90 D Ormerod, 'Cheating the Public Revenue' [1998] Crim LR 627 and 'Summary Evasion of Income Tax' [2002] Crim LR 3.

In *Hudson*,[91] the Court of Criminal Appeal upheld D's conviction on a charge of making false statements to the prejudice of the Crown and the public revenue with intent to defraud where it appeared that D had falsely stated to the Inland Revenue the profits of his business. It was argued that the indictment disclosed no offence known to the law, but the court, relying on *dicta* of Lord Mansfield CJ in *Bembridge*,[92] and statements by Hawkins[93] and East,[94] held that it was an offence for a private individual, as well as a public officer, to defraud the Crown and public. The argument that there was no such offence was raised again in *Mulligan*[95] and was just as forthrightly rejected by the Court of Appeal.

The CLRC was minded to abolish the offence, and its retention was the result of special pleading by the revenue authorities who wished to retain it for serious revenue frauds where penalties under other provisions were seen by them as inadequate. Perhaps, too, the Revenue was attracted by the expansive terminology of Hawkins's definition. In all events, the Revenue's fondest hopes for the offence of cheating must have been realized by the decision in *Mavji*.[96] D had dishonestly evaded value added tax to the tune of over £1m. Charged, as he might have been, under what was then s 38(1) of the Finance Act 1972 with the fraudulent evasion of tax, he would have been liable to a maximum of two years' imprisonment and/or a fine of £1,000 or three times the tax, whichever was the greater. Convicted, as he was, of cheating he was sentenced to six years' imprisonment and made criminally bankrupt in the sum of £690,000. The Court of Appeal, affirming D's conviction and sentence, rejected counsel's submission that cheating required a positive act such as a deception, and not merely an omission to make a VAT return. The court held that D was under a duty to make such a return and his failure to do so with intent to cheat the Revenue of money to which it was entitled constituted the offence.[97] This conclusion was, with respect, a novel extension of the offence. *Hudson*,[98] which was treated in *Mavji* as the leading case, appears to assume that cheating requires the use of a false representation or false device. Even the expansive language of Hawkins is conditioned by the requirement 'by means of some artful device'. What artful device was employed by D in *Mavji*?

Mavji was considered in *Dosanjh*,[99] in which D and a number of others were convicted of conspiring to cheat the Revenue after setting up a complex scheme involving the non-payment of VAT. It was estimated that the total loss to the Revenue caused by the scheme was £39m. D was sentenced to 15 years' imprisonment and appealed against his sentence on the basis that it was contrary to the principle declared by the House of Lords in *Rimmington*.[100] Counsel for D contended that it was contrary to the intention of Parliament for the courts to permit prosecutors to avoid the constraints, such as maximum sentence, which Parliament had imposed upon one of the statutory offences he could have been charged with, for example fraud, by charging him with a common law offence. It was conceded on behalf of D that the decision in *Mavji* was inconsistent with this line of reasoning, but it was argued that that decision was no longer valid in light of the House of Lords' comments in *Rimmington*. In rejecting this argument, the Court of Appeal held that by not abolishing the common law offence of cheating the Revenue, despite the proliferation of statutory offences that could be charged in the alternative, it could be inferred that Parliament had made a conscious

---

91 [1956] 2 QB 252, discussed by 'Watchful' [1956] BTR 119.   92 (1783) 22 State Tr 1 at 156.

93 I PC, 322.   94 II PC, 821.   95 [1990] Crim LR 427.

96 [1987] 1 WLR 1388. *Mavji* was followed in *Redford* (1988) 89 Cr App R 1. The proposition in *Mavji* that the statutory offences coexist with the common law offence of cheating the public revenue was confirmed by the House of Lords in *Revenue & Customs Commissioners v Total Network SL* [2008] UKHL 19, [136].

97 Cheating is a 'conduct offence' and it is not necessary to prove that D caused any loss: *Hunt* [1995] 16 Cr App R (S) 87.

98 See earlier.   99 [2013] EWCA Crim 2366.   100 [2005] UKHL 63. See p 489.

decision to retain the offence for those exceptional revenue frauds where none of the statutory offences would accurately reflect D's criminality. Lord Bingham's judgment in *Rimmington* was distinguished on the basis that his lordship had accepted that his general approach would not apply when there was 'good reason' to deviate from it. This was a case in which there was such a 'good reason' for charging the common law offence, despite the existence of a statutory offence with which D could have been charged.

The actus reus of the offence has become so wide that the definition is almost best stated in negative terms. There need not be a dishonest act; an omission will suffice.[101] The act or omission must be intended to prejudice HMRC[102] or the Department for Work and Pensions. The offence cannot be committed in respect of a local authority[103] nor, it is submitted, against the EU.[104] There is no requirement of an operative deception[105] nor of a need to prove actual loss to the Revenue,[106] or to any other. It is not necessary to prove that the accused's conduct resulted in any gain to himself[107] nor for the defendant to be a government official.[108] The types of behaviour caught include: failing to account for VAT,[109] withholding PAYE and National Insurance,[110] failing to register for VAT[111] or simply failing to disclose income.[112] It is a particularly useful offence in cases of carousel frauds where there is no duty to pay VAT arising. It is unclear precisely when the offence commences. Is D cheating the Revenue when he has determined not to declare his profits but has yet to make a false declaration in his tax return?[113] Does it matter whether he has done some act—such as keeping a false set of books?[114]

It is difficult to see how the offence could be stated in more expansive terms. The offence is, of course, even broader when charged as a statutory conspiracy to cheat, as it often is. The breadth of the offence means that often the only live issue at trial will be dishonesty.

The jury's difficulty in applying the dishonesty test in commercial settings has been considered in Ch 18. In relation to carefully planned tax schemes, the problems appear obvious: it seems ludicrous to ask jurors to apply the test of whether a reasonable and honest person would see it as dishonest when they (probably) have little or no understanding of the very

---

101 *Steed* [2011] EWCA Crim 75 was an appeal against a confiscation order made following a plea of guilty to cheating the public revenue by failing to submit accounts for tax. At [11], Moses LJ restated the basic principle that the offence can be committed by omission. 'Cheating consists of any form of fraudulent conduct, whether by making positive false representations, as in *Hudson*, or by concealing or omitting to disclose liability or income with the result that money is diverted from the Revenue and the Revenue is deprived of money to which it is entitled.'

102 *Blake* (1844) 6 QB 126; *Tonner* [1985] 1 WLR 344.   103 *Lush v Coles* [1967] 1 WLR 685.

104 On fraud in the EU, see L Kuhl, 'The Criminal Law Protection of the Communities' Financial Interests Against Fraud' [1998] Crim LR 259 and 323, especially at 264–6 and 330.

105 *Mavji* [1987] 1 WLR 1388.

106 *Hunt* [1994] STC 819 at 827 per Stuart-Smith LJ. Hence its use in VAT carousel frauds. See also *Matthews* [2008] EWCA Crim 423.

107 *Hunt* [1994] STC 819.   108 *Mulligan* [1990] STC 220.   109 *Ryan* [1994] STC 446.

110 *Less* (1993) The Times, 30 Mar.   111 *Redford* [1988] STC 845.

112 *Anderson* (1992) 13 Cr App R (S) 564.

113 This may be important in determining whether the property in the form of the tax not yet paid is already criminal property for the purposes of the Proceeds of Crime Act 2002, s 340. In *Williams* [2013] EWCA Crim 1262, the Court of Appeal held that the effect of ss 327 and 340(6) of the Proceeds of Crime Act 2002 is that D who cheats the Revenue by failing to pay the tax due is taken to have obtained a benefit which is the same as the amount of tax unpaid. In cases where D misrepresents the turnover, the benefit is the tax due on the undeclared income. Importantly, Elias LJ held that the criminal property as defined by s 340 is the entirety of the undeclared turnover and not merely the tax due. The reason for so holding is that the benefit is represented in part by that sum.

114 cf *Doncaster* [2008] EWCA Crim 5; *IK* [2007] EWCA Crim 491, [2007] Crim LR 645 and commentary.

complex civil law tax position or commercial background.[115] Some have suggested it is tantamount to retrospective criminalization and may well offend the protection in Art 7 of the ECHR.[116] That argument gains force under the more objective test in *Ivey* and *Barton*, but has been rejected in general terms by the Court of Appeal in *Bermingham*.[117]

Care needs to be taken in charging the offence when the wrongdoing alleged spans a period of time and involves numerous transactions.[118]

Notwithstanding the criticism of the cheating offence, the government introduced a statutory version of the offence which is triable either way. Section 144 of the Finance Act 2000 criminalized 'being knowingly concerned in the evasion of income tax'.[119] The offence is now found in s 106A of the Taxes Management Act 1970, which was inserted into the 1970 Act by the Taxation (International and Other Provisions) Act 2010. The offence requires proof of knowledge; recklessness will not suffice.[120] This is an ill-defined and extremely broad offence, but for numerous reasons has proved less successful than the Revenue anticipated.

Further reading

ATH Smith, *Property Offences: The Protection of Property Through the Criminal Law*

---

[115] eg the difficulty in cases where D is alleged to have created sham transactions and avoided tax: *Kumar* [2005] EWCA Crim 1979.

[116] cf *Pattni* [2000] Crim LR 570 at first instance. See LCCP 155, *Legislating the Criminal Code: Fraud and Deception* (1999) para 3.23.

[117] [2020] EWCA Crim 1662.

[118] See *Lunn* [2017] EWCA Crim 34.

[119] See D Ormerod, 'Summary Evasion of Income Tax' [2002] Crim LR 3. Section 144 was repealed on 1 Apr 2010 by the Taxation (International and Other Provisions) Act 2010, Sch 10, Part 12, para 1.

[120] *Godir* [2018] EWCA Crim 2294.

24

Blackmail and related offences

24.1 Blackmail

Historically, the word 'blackmail' was used to describe the tribute paid to Scottish chieftains by landowners in the border counties in order to secure immunity from raids on their lands.[1] In the early stages of its development the crime of blackmail seems to have been coextensive with robbery and attempted robbery,[2] but over the years the definition has been extended to embrace more subtle methods of extortion. The law is now set out in s 21 of the Theft Act 1968:[3]

(1) A person is guilty of blackmail if, with a view to gain for himself or another or with intent to cause loss to another, he makes any unwarranted demand with menaces; and for this purpose a demand with menaces is unwarranted unless the person making it does so in the belief—

(a) that he has reasonable grounds for making the demand; and

(b) that the use of the menaces is a proper means of reinforcing the demand.

(2) The nature of the act or omission demanded is immaterial, and it is also immaterial whether the menaces do or do not relate to action to be taken by the person making the demand.

(3) A person guilty of blackmail shall on conviction on indictment be liable to imprisonment for a term not exceeding fourteen years.

---

[1] Ormerod and Williams, *Smith's Law of Theft*, Ch 12; Griew, *Theft*, Ch 14; CLRC, Eighth Report, paras 108–25.

[2] W Winder, 'The Development of Blackmail' (1941) 5 MLR 21; G Williams, 'Blackmail' [1954] Crim LR 7; J Lindgren, 'The Theory, History, and Practice of the Bribery-Extortion Distinction' (1993) 141(5) U Pa L Rev 1695; M Hepworth, 'The British Conception of Blackmail' (1975) 3 Int'l J of Criminology and Penology 1.

[3] B MacKenna, 'Blackmail' [1966] Crim LR 467; B Hogan, 'Blackmail' [1966] Crim LR 474; CR Williams, 'Demanding with Menaces: A Survey of the Australian Law of Blackmail' (1975) 10 Melb LR 118, especially at 136–44.

When unravelled, this rather complicated provision comprises an actus reus of a demand with menaces, and mens rea requirements of an intention to make the demand with menaces, with a view to gain or intention to cause loss, in the absence of a belief that there are reasonable grounds for making the demand and an absence of belief that the menacing is a proper means of enforcing the demand. The offence is complete upon the demand being made, irrespective of whether any property is transferred.

Blackmail is triable only on indictment. There are relatively few reported appellate court decisions on the substance of the offence; those that are reported relate mostly to sentencing, and it should be noted in that regard that the offence is one of the most serious in the criminal calendar attracting long-term imprisonment.[4] Mobile telecommunications, advances in information technology, the internet and social media have created new opportunities for blackmail.[5]

Although the offence appears in the Theft Act 1968, and its requirement of an act with a view to loss or gain demonstrates that it serves to protect property, in many cases blackmail is more appropriately viewed as an offence against privacy.[6] Correctly identifying the harm or interest being protected by the offence has generated a wealth of academic literature.[7] It has been suggested that the wrong of blackmail is done even if the demand is nothing to do with payment[8] but that seems to be over-inclusive: the offence as defined in English law is restricted to cases in which the demand is for property.

24.1.1 The demand

A demand may take any form, and may be implicit as well as explicit. It extends well beyond the obvious '£1,000 or I will publish the photographs exposing your adultery'. The demand could be oral, in writing, by gestures or by D's demeanour provided that, objectively viewed, it is a demand. The essence of this offence is that D's communication conveys the message to V that a menace will materialize unless V complies with the demand. D may be guilty of blackmail where, for example, he apprehends V in the act of stealing and, without any formal demand, makes it clear to V that if he pays D money he will hear no more of the matter.[9]

---

[4] On sentencing, see eg *Roberts* [2019] EWCA Crim 1931.

[5] See the case of *Breakwell* [2009] EWCA Crim 2298, where D sent digitally altered images of Vs' faces on nude bodies with demands that they send him real photos of them nude on threat of him publishing the fakes online. See also the increasingly common practice of hackers threatening to corrupt or to disable a company's website unless payment is made. See M Griffiths, 'Internet Corporate Blackmail: A Growing Problem' (2004) 168 JP 632. See also S Morris, *The Future of Netcrime* (2004) HORS 62/04, at 15. Greater difficulties of proof might arise in electronic cases: *Robinson* [2006] Crim LR 427. Blackmailers also plant viruses on people's computers and identify embarrassing material which they use to make demands: the CPS discuss such a case— *Ringland* (2006) 9 Nov, CCC.

[6] See P Alldridge, 'Attempted Murder of the Soul: Blackmail, Privacy and Secrets' (1993) 13 OJLS 368 and *Relocating Criminal Law* (2000) Ch 4. See also the suggestion that blackmail is a 'serious offence against the person, even where the threat is one of exposure rather than violence': A Simester and GR Sullivan, 'The Nature and Rationale of Property Offences' in Duff and Green, *Defining Crimes*, 188. For a sociological view of the activity, see M Hepworth, *Blackmail, Publicity and Secrecy in Everyday Life* (1975); for an historical account of its expansion in the last century, see A McLaren, *Sexual Blackmail* (2002).

[7] See, inter alia, 'Blackmail—A Symposium' (1993) 141 U Pa L Rev and L Katz, *Ill-Gotten Gains: Evasion, Blackmail, Fraud, and Kindred Puzzles of the Law* (1996). For English material, see W Block, 'The Logic of the Argument of Legalising Blackmail' [2001] Bracton LJ 61; W Block and R McGee, 'Blackmail as a Victimless Crime' [1999] Bracton LJ 24.

[8] See Simester and Sullivan in Duff and Green, *Defining Crimes*, 188.

[9] cf *Collister and Warhurst* (1955) 39 Cr App R 100: 'the demeanour of the accused' was sufficient. See also *Lambert* [2009] EWCA Crim 2860.

D's humblest form of request may be a demand.[10] But, whether express or implied, there must actually be a demand. If, having caught V in the act of stealing, D receives and accepts an unsolicited offer to buy his silence, D would not be guilty of blackmail (but might commit the offence of withholding for gain information relating to an offence, see p 253).

A demand may be made through an intermediary.[11] It may be complete though it has not been communicated to V because, say, V is deaf. A demand by letter is made where and when it is posted.[12] This issue has now been addressed with reference to communications by email. The Court of Appeal in *Pogmore*[13] considered whether the English courts had jurisdiction to try D for blackmail where the communication, containing an unwarranted demand with menaces, was sent from abroad to V, who was in this country. Simon LJ held that so far as blackmail is concerned, the communication of a demand was sufficient to give the court jurisdiction if it was sent either (a) from a place in England and Wales to a place elsewhere, or (b) from a place elsewhere to a place in England and Wales.

In these cases, D has done the final act necessary to communicate the demand. The offence is complete irrespective of V's compliance with the demand. It has been argued that the wide interpretation of 'demand' means that there is little or no room for a crime of attempted blackmail,[14] although there are hypothetical scenarios of D being intercepted on his way to the post, or where the email is not sent, etc. Treating the full offence as committed before the demand has been communicated emphasizes that the gravamen of the offence is the making of unwarranted demands per se.

Normally D will demand money or other property but s 21(2) provides that 'the nature of the act or omission demanded is immaterial'. At first sight, this seems to undermine the foundation of the offence being one of protecting *property*. However, it does not go that far because the offence can be committed only if D also has a view to gain or an intention to cause loss in money or other property.[15] The purpose of s 21(2) seems to have been to forestall a possible argument that D cannot be guilty unless his demand is for some specific item of property.[16] If D demands with menaces that he be given paid employment or demands that V sign a promissory note provided by D,[17] he may be guilty of blackmail if he acts with a view to gain. Demands for sexual intercourse or other acts of a sexual nature are not within the scope of the offence and are dealt with under the Sexual Offences Act 2003.[18]

---

[10] cf *Robinson* (1796) East, II PC, 1110, where the words 'Remember, Sir, I am now only making an appeal to your benevolence' were held in the circumstances capable of importing a demand. In *Miah* [2003] 1 Cr App R (S) 379, D sent videos of child pornography to Vs with a return address and when they returned them D contacted Vs informing them that their fingerprints were on the videos and 'urging' them or 'inviting' them to call a telephone number. D pleaded guilty and no issue arose as to whether these 'invitations' to call the number were a 'demand'.

[11] *Thumber* (1999) No 199900691, 29 Nov, CA.

[12] *Treacy v DPP* [1971] AC 537. See PJ Pace, 'Demanding with Menaces' (1971) 121 NLJ 242.

[13] [2017] EWCA Crim 925.

[14] See *Moran* (1952) 36 Cr App R 10 at 12; cf JL Edwards, 'Criminal Attempts' (1952) 15 MLR 345.

[15] Theft Act 1968, s 34; and see p 1043.   [16] cf Eighth Report, Annex 2.

[17] cf *Phipoe* (1795) 2 Leach 673, where Mrs Phipoe, armed with a carving knife, 'in the French language threatened, amidst the most opprobrious expressions, to take away [V's] life' unless he signed a promissory note on paper and with materials provided by her.

[18] See Ch 17. Note that the offence of procuring a woman to have sexual intercourse by threats contrary to s 2 of the Sexual Offences Act 1956 has not been replicated in the 2003 Act. There are reported convictions for blackmail in these circumstances (eg *Downer* (2000) 17 Oct, CA), but these must be erroneous.

24.1.2 Menaces

The word 'menace' is an ordinary English word which in most cases will be understood by a jury without the need for elaboration.[19] On one view, it might suggest only threats of violence to persons or property, but under the former law[20] 'menace' was given a much wider meaning. The CLRC intended to retain this extended meaning in its suggestions for reform. The Committee was well aware of the meaning 'menace' had acquired and deliberately chose to use this word when they might have chosen another.[21] It extends to threats to damage property and to make damaging allegations whether truthful or not. In *Thorne v Motor Trade Association*,[22] Lord Wright said[23] that a menace was a threat of 'any action detrimental to or unpleasant to the person addressed'. This is a very wide definition.[24] The CLRC chose 'menaces' in preference to 'threats' because, 'notwithstanding the wide meaning given to "menaces" in *Thorne's* case … we regard that word as stronger than "threats", and the consequent slight restriction on the scope of the offence seems to us right'. In view of Lord Wright's definition of menaces, it might be thought that any theoretical distinction between menaces and threats is wholly illusory in practice,[25] but it does perhaps serve to emphasize that there is a limit below which conduct will not be regarded as a menace.

Three situations need to be distinguished:

(1) Where D has made a demand with a 'menace' that would cause a person of ordinary firmness to succumb, V's subsequent refusal to accede to the demand cannot relieve D of liability. There can be a menace even if V is not intimidated. Thus, D may be guilty of blackmail where he threatens to assault V unless V pays him money, even though V is in no way frightened and squares up to D with the result that D runs away.[26]

(2) The law will not treat as a menace words or conduct which would not intimidate or influence *anyone* to respond to the demand. So, in *Harry*,[27] where the organizers of a student charity 'Rag' event had written to shopkeepers offering them immunity from any 'inconvenience' resulting from Rag activities in return for donations, the trial judge ruled that there was not sufficient evidence of a menace. Some shopkeepers had complained of the veiled threat in the letter but this menace was not, to use the words of Sellers LJ in *Clear*,[28] 'of such a nature and extent that the mind of an ordinary person of normal stability and courage might be influenced or made apprehensive so as to accede unwillingly to the demand'.

(3) D's conduct may, however, amount to a menace even though a person of ordinary firmness would not accede to the demand where, *to D's knowledge*, the particular victim, owing to such factors as infirmity, youth, timidity or even plain cowardice, will accede to the demand.[29] Indeed, the blackmailer will often select his victim precisely because he is aware of the victim's vulnerability.[30] If D intends that his menace should

---

[19] *Lawrence and Pomroy* (1971) 57 Cr App R 64.
[20] Although not called blackmail, see ss 29–31 of the Larceny Act 1916.
[21] Eighth Report, para 123.   [22] [1937] AC 797.   [23] ibid, 817.
[24] For an argument that the offence ought to be limited to threats to do unlawful acts, see Green, *Lying, Cheating and Stealing*, Ch 17. See also Green, *13 Ways*, 120–2. For an argument that the definition is so wide that drug dealers might be guilty of blackmailing addicted customers by 'selling protection from withdrawal symptoms', see P Alldridge, *Relocating Criminal Law*, 205–6.
[25] See n 22 and L Katz, *Ill-Gotten Gains: Evasion, Blackmail, Fraud, and Kindred Puzzles of the Law* (1996) 157.
[26] cf *Moran* [1952] 1 All ER 803n. See also *Garwood* [1987] 1 WLR 319 and *Southward* [2012] EWCA Crim 2779.
[27] [1974] Crim LR 32 (Judge Petre).   [28] [1968] 1 All ER 74 at 80.
[29] ibid; *Garwood* [1987] 1 WLR 319.   [30] cf *Tomlinson* [1895] 1 QB 706.

operate on the mind of V and knows of circumstances that will make V unwillingly accede to the demand, D may properly be convicted of blackmail. Since the offence is completed irrespective of the demand being successfully communicated to V, it is somewhat illogical for this aspect of the offence to be interpreted by reference to the victim's susceptibilities.[31]

The case of *Lambert*[32] emphasized that blackmail is committed if D threatens V that something will happen to V even if D could not carry out that threat. D in that case claimed to have X held hostage when he did not. D demanded money from V on threat of injuring X. It was not within D's power to carry out the threat to injure X there and then. At trial D argued that s 21 is limited to situations where the person making the demand is proposing to carry out the menace or had it in his power to do so. That would certainly be the typical circumstances of many blackmail charges. The trial judge and Court of Appeal rejected the argument, referring to s 21(2) which states that it is 'immaterial whether the menaces relate to action to be taken by the person making the demand'. That provision was expressly inserted to confirm that there is no need for the demander to be the one who will carry out the menace.[33] However, it seems that s 21 does not quite meet Lambert's argument head-on. His argument was that the person issuing the menaces must be capable of controlling the carrying out of the threat, even if it is be performed by another. Read literally there is nothing in the statute to justify such a restriction as a matter of law. Of course, the fact that the party making the demand might not be in a position to carry out the action he threatens is something which might affect whether his conduct constitutes a menace in the particular case. A chain letter in which D asserts that some unpleasantness will befall X unless V pays Y may therefore satisfy the offence subject to the sufficiency of the menace. Nor is there any restriction that the menace will involve actions directly against the person to whom the menace/demand is issued. Such a limitation would render the offence very narrow indeed: it would be an offence to demand property backed by a threat to harm V, but where the threat is to harm V's child. That cannot be right.[34]

24.1.3 Unwarranted demand

Not every demand accompanied by a menace will amount to blackmail. Clearly, it ought not to be blackmail to demand payment of a debt from V and threaten civil proceedings in the event of his failure to comply. There is a menace (a threat of action detrimental to or unpleasant to the person addressed) but it is in the circumstances a perfectly lawful demand accompanied by a justifiable threat. At the other extreme, a demand by D for property to which he is not legally entitled accompanied by a threat to kill V would be an obvious instance of blackmail.

24.1.3.1 The paradox of blackmail

Between these two extremes in the previous paragraph, less clear-cut cases emerge: D may threaten to expose V's immoral relationship with D unless V pays money which he had promised D;[35] D may threaten to publicize V as a defaulter unless he pays a gaming debt;[36] D may threaten to publish memoirs which expose V's discreditable conduct unless

---

[31] See Smith, *Property Offences*, 15–18.   [32] [2009] EWCA Crim 2860.
[33] Eighth Report, Annex 2, 131.
[34] See *Ceesay* [2013] 1 Cr App R (S) 529 (101), where D faked his own kidnap and sent demands to his pregnant partner.
[35] cf *Bernhard* [1938] 2 KB 264.   [36] cf *Norreys v Zeffert* [1939] 2 All ER 187.

V 'buys' them from D.[37] It is arguable whether the conduct in these cases *ought* to be blackmail. Indeed, there is an apparent paradox in that while it is lawful for D to make a demand for payment of a debt owed by V, and it is lawful for D to expose or threaten to expose V's immorality, it is blackmail to perform the two in combination.[38] This paradox has given rise to an extensive academic literature, and a diverse range of theories has been employed in an attempt to justify criminalizing that paradox and indeed the inclusion of the offence of blackmail in a coherent and principled code of criminal law.[39] These theories include: analyses of the offence in terms of its economic efficiency;[40] claims that blackmail is outlawed as a means of prohibiting private law enforcement,[41] and the growth of an industry trading on confidential material which generates fear and inhibits everyday life;[42] and assertions that the offence prevents D being unjustly enriched through the use of another's interests (V's confidential information and/or the public's 'right to know' about that information).[43] Some of the most cogent theoretical explanations for the offence are focused on the coercion and exploitation it involves, even in the paradox cases.[44] Far from seeing the paradox as creating an anomaly, some eminent American academics have treated blackmail as a paradigmatic crime with its core involving D placing V in a subordinate position.[45] There are those who argue that the optimal method of solving the paradox of blackmail is to align the law with the layperson's view of what ought to constitute blackmail.[46]

Given the accumulation of academic commentary, perhaps the following assessment is the most accurate: 'Only one proposition is common to all modern academic writing on blackmail, and that is the proposition that all accounts other than that proposed by the instant author have failed to persuade.'[47]

---

[37] cf the case discussed in Lord Denning's Report (1963) Cmnd 2152, paras 31–6.

[38] Even more odd, perhaps, is the acceptance that even if a person is committing blackmail this does not of itself mean that that person has no right to freedom of expression. Lord Atkin pointed out in *Thorne* that the blackmailer may even be under a duty to disclose the information. Cf *AMH v HXW* [2010] EWHC 2457 (QB) in which Tugendhat J stated that the fact D is a blackmailer 'is a factor in deciding whether that person has any Art 10 rights …', at [38].

[39] For an interesting review of many of the theories, see J Isenbergh, 'Blackmail from A to C' (1993) 141 U Pa L Rev 1905. There are those who argue that the paradox of blackmail has been overstated: see P Westen, 'Why the Paradox of Blackmail Is So Hard To Resolve' (2012) 9 Ohio State J Crim L 585. Westen argues that the paradox only arises in a narrow range of factual scenarios.

[40] See further DH Ginsburg and P Shechtman, 'Blackmail: An Economic Analysis of the Law' (1993) 141 U Pa L Rev 1849; R Posner, 'Blackmail, Privacy and Freedom of Contract' (1993) 141 U Pa L Rev 1817.

[41] JG Brown, 'Blackmail as Private Justice' (1993) 141 U Pa L Rev 1935.

[42] R Epstein, 'Blackmail Inc' (1983) 50 U Chi LR 553.

[43] See further J Lindgren, 'Unravelling the Paradox of Blackmail' (1984) 84 Col L Rev 670.

[44] See further S Altmann, 'A Patchwork Theory of Blackmail' (1993) 141 U Pa L Rev 1639; G Lamond, 'Coercion, Threats and the Puzzle of Blackmail' in A Simester and ATH Smith (eds), *Harm and Culpability* (1996). More recently, see S Galoob, 'Coercion, Fraud, and What is Wrong with Blackmail' (2016) 22 Legal Theory 22.

[45] See G Fletcher, 'Blackmail: The Paradigmatic Crime' (1993) 141 U Pa L Rev 1617 and L Katz, 'Blackmail and Other Forms of Arm-Twisting' (1993) 141 U Pa L Rev 1567. The offence continues to excite public and academic interest. See eg SE Sachs, 'Saving Toby: Extortion, Blackmail and the Right to Destroy' (2006) 24 Yale Law & Policy Rev 251 discussing the case of a website where the owner of a rabbit (which was pictured) demanded money from readers to spare it from being killed and eaten.

[46] PH Robinson, MT Cahill and DM Bartels, 'Competing Theories of Blackmail: An Empirical Research Critique of Criminal Law Theory' (2010) 89 Texas L Rev 291. For criticism, see SP Green, 'Taking It to the Streets' (2010) Texas L Rev 61.

[47] DA Dripps, 'The Priority of Politics and Procedure over Perfectionism in Penal Law, or, Blackmail in Perspective' (2009) 3 Crim L & Phil 247, 248.

24.1.3.2 Subjective approach

The Theft Act's pragmatic solution to defining the type of demand that will be *un*warranted is provided in s 21. It renders the element something akin to a mens rea element. D's demand will be unwarranted unless made in the belief (a) that there are reasonable grounds for making it, *and* (b) that the use of the menaces is a proper means of enforcing the demand. The test is subjective: did D believe in the reasonableness of the grounds for making the demand and the propriety of using a menace to enforce the demand? D's belief in the reasonableness of the demand may derive from the fact that V owes him money, or from D's presumption that he has a legal claim against V, or from some other source.[48] D's belief that the use of menaces is a proper way of enforcing that demand may stem from such factors as his upbringing, and his relationship and past dealings with V.[49]

Suppose that V promises that he will pay D £100 for the sexual favours which he has received from her; V fails to keep his promise whereupon D threatens to expose the relationship to V's regular sexual partner unless V pays.[50] D's liability would turn upon whether she believed that she had reasonable grounds for demanding the £100, *and* that her threat to expose V was a proper way of enforcing the demand. All the circumstances have to be taken into account insofar as they are relevant as tending to show or negative the authenticity of D's beliefs. D might have believed (wrongly) that she was legally entitled to the £100 (reasonable grounds) and that it was lawful for her to threaten to expose V to get it (proper means of enforcement). Alternatively, D might have believed that she was morally entitled to enforce payment in this way; this would be enough provided she believed in fact that this was reasonable and proper. One person (eg a lawyer) might feel that she was morally entitled to something and yet recognize that her moral claim would not afford her reasonable grounds for making the demand. Another person might genuinely think that her moral right affords her reasonable grounds. In practice, D may not think precisely in terms of the legality or morality of her conduct, but more in terms of whether or not it is, in a broad way, reasonable.

In *Harvey, Ulyett and Plummer*,[51] D and his associates paid V £20,000 for what V claimed was a consignment of cannabis but which turned out to be 'a load of rubbish'. Incensed by this swindle, the defendants kidnapped V's wife and child and made threats of serious bodily harm to them and to V unless the money was returned. No doubt a lawyer (or even a reasonably well-informed layman) would have appreciated that in these circumstances the money was not recoverable since it was paid in pursuance of an illegal contract. Such a person might have difficulty in forming a belief that there were reasonable grounds for the demand. But in *Harvey* the particular defendants felt that they had been swindled ('ripped off to the tune of £20,000' as the trial judge put it) and it was for the jury to determine whether as a matter of fact they believed that their demand was reasonable.[52]

---

[48] cf *Kewell* [2000] 2 Cr App R (S) 38, where V owed a debt to D but there was little difficulty in establishing that D knew it was improper to threaten to reveal embarrassing but consensually taken photos of V from their period of cohabitation. See now the so-called 'revenge porn' offence in the Criminal Justice and Courts Act 2015, s 33. See also *Walker* [2010] EWCA Crim 2184 where D threatened that unless paid he would kill V's dog which he had found.

[49] Several cases of car clamping have given rise to blackmail charges, see eg *Williams* [2012] EWCA Crim 1483. Note the offence in the Protection of Freedoms Act 2012, s 54.

[50] cf *Bernhard* [1938] 2 KB 264.   [51] (1981) 72 Cr App R 139.

[52] See also *Lambert* [2009] EWCA Crim 2860 where D's argument that the threat to injure was to recover a debt was also rejected.

It has been argued[53] that this goes too far: that it is not right that D's own moral standards should determine the rightness or wrongness of his conduct.[54] The criticism is that the mens rea turns not merely on D's subjective beliefs about the circumstances in which he is acting (as in offences where the mens rea is recklessness, etc), but also on D's beliefs about appropriate moral standards. There are a number of responses to this. First, as a practical matter most people do act according to generally accepted legal and moral standards, and the cases must be rare where D can *genuinely* rely on his own moral standards where these are seriously at odds with accepted norms. Secondly, it is important to note that it is not enough that D feels that his conduct is justified or that it is in some way right for him; 'proper' in this context involves a consideration of what D believes would be generally thought of as proper. While the test of D's belief is subjective, that belief refers to an external standard—that of propriety; D cannot, therefore, take refuge in his own standards when he knows that these are not thought proper by members of society in general.[55] In this respect, the test reflects that found in the now discredited *Ghosh*[56] formula of dishonesty. Thirdly, there is a further limitation on the opportunity for D to claim that his own standards apply in evaluating what is a proper means of enforcing a demand. It has been held that if D knows that he is threatening to commit a crime, he cannot maintain that he believes such a threat to be proper.[57] This is a questionable limitation. The focus must surely remain on the question of D's belief as to the propriety of his use of menaces. The fact that D is aware that his menace would be a crime may be strong evidence that he did not believe it to be a proper means of enforcing the demand, but it is not conclusive.

One consequence of this subjective approach is that D may, in theory, be guilty of blackmail where he believes that he has no reasonable grounds for his demand or that the use of the menaces is improper, even though, viewed objectively, his demand is perfectly reasonable and his threat perfectly proper. Concentrating to this extent on D's state of mind as the criterion of criminality represents something of an innovation in English criminal law, but cases where the matter arises must inevitably be rare.[58]

This element of the offence can also generate problems in evidential terms. In *Ashiq*,[59] the Court of Appeal confirmed that following *Harvey*[60] D had to raise the issue of his belief, and that once it was raised it was for the prosecution to disprove it before the jury could be sure the demand was unwarranted. It was only necessary to give the jury a direction on this matter if there was a live issue raised before them in evidence as to whether the defendant did believe that he had reasonable grounds for making the demand and did believe that the use of menaces was the proper means for reinforcing it.

---

[53] By Sir Brian MacKenna, 'Blackmail' [1966] Crim LR 467 at 469.

[54] See *Lambert* [1972] Crim LR 422 (Newcastle Crown Court), where Judge John Arnold appears to have accepted that the effect of the section is that the law should give 'efficacy to the defendant's moral judgments whatever they may be'.

[55] cf Griew, *Theft*, para 14.30. In *Harrison* [2001] EWCA Crim 1314, where D had been demanding money to which he believed himself to be entitled as compensation for being sacked by V, the judge directed the jury that '"proper" was a word of wide meaning—wider than lawful, but no act which was not believed to be lawful could be believed to be proper within the subsection. The test is not what the defendant regarded as justified but what he believed to be proper ...' The Court of Appeal commented that the directions contain a rogue sentence 'proper in that sense ... meant a suitable and apt way, not threats of unlawful or criminal actions'.

[56] [1982] QB 1053, p 910, prior to the decision of the Supreme Court in *Ivey v Genting Casinos UK Ltd (t/a Crockfords Club)* [2017] UKSC 67 to overrule the second limb of that test. See p 908.

[57] *Harvey, Ulyett and Plummer* (1980) 72 Cr App R 139.

[58] This subjectivism goes even further than that which prevails in the law of attempts. In the context of legally impossible attempts, just because D believes he is doing something that constitutes an offence, D cannot be guilty if no such offence exists as a matter of law. See *Taaffe*, p 151.

[59] [2015] EWCA Crim 1617.   [60] See n 51.

It should be noted that s 21(2) provides that it is immaterial whether or not the menaces relate to action to be taken by the person making the demand. Consequently, it may amount to blackmail if D makes a demand of V and threatens that E will assault V if he does not comply. The provision was included to prevent any possible argument on this matter.[61]

24.1.4 View to gain or intent to cause loss

It has been noted earlier[62] that the requirement of a view to gain or intent to cause loss operates as a limiting factor on the offence of blackmail. It anchors it, albeit rather precariously, in the scheme of offences protecting property interests.[63] A threat by D to prosecute V for a theft she has committed unless she has sexual intercourse with D would not amount to blackmail under s 21(1) of the Act, though it might constitute some other offence.[64] The Theft Act 1968 is concerned with invasions of economic interests, and gain and loss are defined accordingly in s 34(2)(a):

'gain' and 'loss' are to be construed as extending only to gain or loss in money or other property, but as extending to any such gain or loss whether temporary or permanent; and—

(i) 'gain' includes a gain by keeping what one has, as well as a gain by getting what one has not; and

(ii) 'loss' includes a loss by not getting what one might get, as well as a loss by parting with what one has.

In the ordinary case of blackmail, D will have both a view to gain (for himself) and an intention to cause loss (to V), but either suffices. D may commit the offence where he intends to cause loss to V without making a gain for himself, as where he demands by threats that Z destroy property belonging to V. In such a case, D clearly intends to cause loss to 'another' even though the person threatened is not the person to whom the loss is caused. Conversely, D may act with a view to gain although there is no intention to cause loss. D might demand that V appoint him as a paid director in V's company: here D has a view to gain for himself but it may well be that, far from intending to cause V loss, he intends to bring him increased profits.

Most often D's view to gain will be obvious: a blackmailer's prime objective is normally to get money or other property from V, intending to deprive V permanently of property. Section 34(2)(a) makes it clear, however, that there is no need for the intended gain or loss to be permanent. D might be guilty of blackmail, for example, where by menaces he demands that V make a loan of property. This, again, reflects the fact that the gravamen of the offence is that an unwarranted demand has been made. But will any view to gain—no matter how remote—suffice?[65] Clearly, there may be a view to gain although the gain is not to materialize for a period of time, or even though the gain may never materialize. D might, by threats, cause his sister to destroy their grandmother's will on the assumption that this shall be to D's financial advantage; it can make no difference that granny is on her death bed or is in the best of health, or that she has made another will revoking the one destroyed.[66] The essence of blackmail is the demand with menaces and the offence is complete whether D succeeds in making a gain thereafter or not.[67] The interpretation of the concept of 'view to gain' has not

---

[61] Eighth Report, Annex 2. See also *Lambert*, n 52.   [62] At p 1036.

[63] There is a view to gain where D at gunpoint demands that a doctor give him an injection of morphine (morphine is property) to relieve pain: *Bevans* (1987) 87 Cr App R 64. It is not uncommon for blackmail charges to be laid where one drug gang has demanded drugs from another, backed by threats of violence, eg *Hart* and *Bullen* [1999] 2 Cr App R (S) 233.

[64] See Ch 17.   [65] See Ormerod and Williams, *Smith's Law of Theft*, paras 12.20–12.21.

[66] See *Custance* [2007] EWCA Crim 520.   [67] cf *Moran* [1952] 1 All ER 803n.

been fully explored in the case law under s 21, although the courts have acknowledged that the expression does not connote motive.[68] The academic approach has been to interpret the expression as simply a form of intention.[69] What is important is that D should have the view to gain in his mind at the time of making the demand; the fact that it has crossed his mind at some stage that there may be a gain involved might not be enough. While it is probably not necessary to show that D's *primary* purpose in making the demand was to make a gain for himself or another, it must be one of his objectives.[70] Equally, where it has to be shown that D *intended* to cause loss to another, the mere foresight that another might suffer some likelihood of loss would be insufficient. Arguably, it should be sufficient that D demands something and in doing so realizes that it is virtually certain to result in his causing loss to V. In *Dooley*,[71] the Court of Appeal expressly left open that question.[72]

Subparagraphs (i) and (ii) of s 34(2)(a) were introduced to meet a possible argument that D would not be acting with a view to gain, or with intent to cause loss, where the gain or loss had already taken place. An example might be where D owes V £10 and demands by threats that V forgo his claim to the debt; it is quite clear[73] that D would be acting with a view to gain.

A further difficulty under this section is whether D can be said to have a view to gain or intent to cause loss where he acts under a supposed legal claim of right to the property demanded (the paradox position earlier). Suppose that D, who is owed £100 by V, threatens to expose to V's employers the fact that V is a paedophile unless V pays the debt. D can satisfy the requirement that he believes he has reasonable grounds for making the demand, but it can be assumed (almost invariably) that D does not believe that the use of the menace is a proper means of reinforcing the demand. It was clearly intended by the CLRC that D might be guilty of blackmail if he failed to meet *either* of the criteria in paras (a) and (b) of s 21(1), irrespective of whether or not D acted under a legal claim of right to the property demanded:

The essential feature of the offence will be that the accused demands something with menaces when he knows either that he has no right to make the demand or that the use of the menaces is improper. This, we believe, will limit the offence to what would ordinarily be thought should be included in blackmail. The true blackmailer will know that he has no reasonable grounds for demanding money as the price of keeping his victim's secret: *the person with a genuine claim will be guilty unless he believes that it is proper to use the menaces to enforce his claim*.[74]

The offence of blackmail is, however, governed in all cases by the requirement of D having a view to gain or intent to cause loss. It might be argued[75] that where D demands property to which he is *legally* entitled (or believes himself to be legally entitled), he has no view to make a gain for himself or to cause loss to another: ie that he makes no gain in getting what he is legally entitled to, and V sustains no loss in paying his lawful debts. In other statutory contexts, gain is sometimes treated as economic gain or profit. However, it has also been held to mean 'acquisition' and this is not necessarily to be equated with the narrower concept of 'profit'.[76]

---

[68] *J Lyons and Sons v Wilkins* [1899] 1 Ch 255 at 269–70 per Chitty LJ, considering the offence under s 7 of the Conspiracy and Protection of Property Act 1875. See also *Bevans* (1988) 87 Cr App R 64: D's unwarranted demand with menaces for painkillers was sufficient for blackmail as he did so with a view to gain even though his motive was to alleviate pain.

[69] See eg Williams, TBCL, 830.

[70] This sentence in the 11th edn was approved by the Court of Appeal in *Dooley* [2005] EWCA Crim 3093, [14].

[71] [2005] EWCA Crim 3093.

[72] See further the commentary at [2006] Crim LR 544. In that case, it was held that D possesses child pornography 'with a view to' it being shown to others if he intends to do so; and it is not enough that he knew that others could access it from his computer if he did not actually 'want' this.

[73] Or is it? See *Golechha* [1989] 3 All ER 908, p 1025.   [74] Eighth Report, para 121 (emphasis added).

[75] B Hogan, 'Blackmail' [1966] Crim LR 474, 476. Cf Ormerod and Williams, *Smith's Law of Theft*, para 12.28. Cf Griew, *Theft*, paras 14.25–14.28.

[76] cf Ormerod and Williams, *Smith's Law of Theft*, para 12.28; and authorities there cited.

To construe it as meaning acquisition would certainly be consistent with the CLRC's intentions.[77] In *Lawrence and Pomroy*,[78] where D and E were convicted of blackmail in making threats to recover a debt, it appears to have been assumed by the Court of Appeal, though the point was not directly argued,[79] that D and E had a view to gain. This accords with s 21(2) which emphasizes that the 'nature of the act or omission demanded is immaterial'. A literal interpretation should mean that a demand for a debt legally owed will suffice for the offence.[80]

By the same token, D intends V to lose a particular item even if D is prepared to replace it with one of identical value.[81]

24.2 Unlawful harassment of debtors

Section 40 of the Administration of Justice Act 1970 which creates an offence of unlawful harassment of debtors is worth noting. The offence was created to curb the growing practice of enforcing the payment of debts in a fashion that is unreasonable, unfair or improper; such as where a creditor calls at the debtor's house to make a demand and is accompanied by large, fierce and hungry-looking Rottweilers. The offence is wider than blackmail in that it may cover conduct that the creditor believes to be proper as a means of enforcing the debt.

24.3 Other offences based on threats

There are numerous other offences based on threats, including: threats to kill,[82] assaults,[83] robbery,[84] threats to damage property,[85] threats of food terrorism,[86] threats of violence for the purpose of securing entry to premises,[87] sending malicious communications[88] and demanding payment for unsolicited goods with threats.[89] There is disappointingly little coherence in English law's approach to threat offences.[90] The Law Commission has recommended the creation of an offence of threat to rape.[91]

Further reading

E Griew, *The Theft Acts 1968 and 1978*

L Katz, *Ill-Gotten Gains: Evasion, Blackmail, Fraud, and Kindred Puzzles of the Law*

---

[77] As expressed in the passage cited at n 73. But the Committee also characterized blackmail as an offence of dishonesty (cf paras 118 and 122) and one who demands that to which he believes he is legally entitled is not acting dishonestly: cf *Skivington* [1968] 1 QB 166 and *Robinson* [1977] Crim LR 173, p 933.

[78] (1971) 57 Cr App R 64.

[79] The point was argued in *Parkes* [1973] Crim LR 358 (Judge Dean), where it was ruled that a person demanding money undoubtedly owed to him did have a view to gain and approved in *A-G's Reference (No 1 of 2001)* [2002] EWCA Crim 1768.

[80] Considered in *A-G's Reference (No 1 of 2001)* [2002] EWCA Crim 1768, in the context of false accounting. Cf *Houston* [2011] EWCA Crim 3030 in which the Court of Appeal observed that 'blackmail in order to collect a debt is always a serious matter', at [14].

[81] See Ormerod and Williams, *Smith's Law of Theft*, para 12.31.

[82] OAPA 1861, s 16.   [83] Criminal Justice Act 1988, s 39.   [84] Theft Act 1968, s 8.

[85] Criminal Damage Act 1971, s 2.   [86] Public Order Act 1986, s 38.

[87] Criminal Law Act 1977, s 6(1).

[88] Malicious Communications Act 1988, s 1, as extended by the Criminal Justice and Police Act 2001, s 43.

[89] Unsolicited Goods and Services Act 1971, s 2(2).

[90] This passage in the 13th edn was cited with approval by Lord Judge CJ in *Chambers v DPP* [2012] EWHC 2157 (Admin), [27]. See further on this point, P Alldridge, 'Threats Offences: A Case for Reform' [1994] Crim LR 176.

[91] See LC 361 (2015).

25

Burglary and related offences

Burglary is an offence under the Theft Act 1968 and is much broader than the common (mis)understanding of a 'breaking and entering' in order to steal.

25.1 Burglary

Section 9 of the Theft Act 1968 provides:[1]

(1) A person[2] is guilty of burglary if—

    (a) he enters any building or part of a building as a trespasser and with intent to commit any such offence as is mentioned in subsection (2) below; or

    (b) having entered any building or part of a building as a trespasser he steals or attempts to steal anything in the building or that part of it or inflicts or attempts to inflict on any person therein any grievous bodily harm.

---

[1] For further analysis see Ormerod and Williams, *Smith's Law of Theft*, Ch 8; Griew, *Theft*, Ch 4; Smith, *Property Offences*, Ch 28.

[2] In *Deutsche Genossenschaftsbank v Burnhope* [1996] 1 Lloyd's Rep 113, 123, the majority of the House of Lords found on the facts of that case that the company in question had not committed a burglary. However, Lord Steyn, dissenting, had no doubt that a company could commit burglary where, eg, a company chairman dishonestly instructs an innocent employee to enter V's warehouse and remove valuables.

(2) The offences referred to in subsection (1)(a) above are offences of stealing anything in the building or part of a building in question, of inflicting on any person therein any grievous bodily harm . . .[3] therein, and of doing unlawful damage to the building or anything therein.

(3) A person guilty of burglary shall on conviction on indictment be liable to imprisonment for a term not exceeding—

    (a) where the offence was committed in respect of a building or part of a building which is a dwelling, fourteen years;

    (b) in any other case, ten years.[4]

(4) References in subsections (1) and (2) above to a building, and the reference in subsection (3) above to a building which is a dwelling, shall apply also to an inhabited vehicle or vessel, and shall apply to any such vehicle or vessel at times when the person having a habitation in it is not there as well as at times when he is.[5]

Section 9(1)(a) describes three separate ways the offence can be committed (entering with intent to steal, commit grievous bodily harm or unlawful damage), each of which can be committed by entry into either a dwelling (a 'domestic burglary')[6] or other building. Because there are separate sentencing provisions depending on whether the building in question is a dwelling, s 9(1)(a) effectively creates six separate offences. Each of these offences is committed once D has entered as a trespasser with the necessary intent,[7] irrespective of whether or not he succeeds in the intended theft, grievous bodily harm, etc.[8]

Section 9(1)(b) creates four separate forms of burglary (attempting to steal, stealing, attempting to inflict grievous bodily harm and inflicting grievous bodily harm). Again, each of these forms can be committed as either a domestic burglary or otherwise, with separate sentencing regimes applying for domestic burglaries.

A person charged with an offence under s 9(1)(b) may be convicted of an offence under s 9(1)(a) because (however contrary to the facts it may seem) the allegation of an offence under s 9(1)(b) is held to include an allegation of an offence under s 9(1)(a).[9]

The law seems to be unduly technical, and is very different from the layman's conception of burglary. More importantly, the offence definition does not reveal the principal harms and wrongs against which it offers protection—possibilities are the invasion of private space, the risk of violent confrontation or aggravated forms of theft.[10] There are powerful arguments that the offence encompasses so many qualitatively different types of wrongdoing under

---

[3] The offence of entering a building with intent to commit rape was repealed by the SOA 2003, Sch 7, para 1. Section 63 of that Act creates a much broader offence: see p 1064.

[4] For current sentencing practice, see Sentencing Council, *Burglary Offences: Definitive Guideline* (2011). Sentencing for burglary is controversial, arousing strong public emotion, common misunderstanding and a high volume of appeals; see M Davies, 'Filling in the Gaps' [2003] Crim LR 243.

[5] Section 9(3) and (4) as substituted by the Criminal Justice Act 1991, amended by the Powers of Criminal Courts (Sentencing) Act 2000 (PCC(S)A 2000), s 111 see now the Sentencing Act 2020, s 314.

[6] Under s 314 Sentencing Act 2020. Burglary comprising the commission of, or an intention to commit, an offence triable only on indictment and burglary in a dwelling where any person in the dwelling was subjected to violence or the threat of violence are triable on indictment only: Magistrates' Courts Act 1980, Sch 1, para 28; *McGrath* [2003] EWCA Crim 2062.

[7] *Watson* [1989] Crim LR 733; *Toothill* [1998] Crim LR 876.

[8] D can, if successful, still be charged under s 9(1)(a): *Taylor* [1979] Crim LR 649.

[9] *Whiting* (1987) 85 Cr App R 78, applying *Wilson and Jenkins* [1984] AC 242. *Whiting* is criticized at [1987] Crim LR 473. See also the CLRC Eighth Report, para 76 and *Chevannes* [2009] EWCA Crim 2725, n 111.

[10] See Horder, APOCL, 411.

one label that it deserves reformulation.[11] It is qualitatively different from a mere attempt to commit theft or damage or cause injury.[12]

25.1.1 Actus reus

25.1.1.1 Enters

At common law, it was sufficient that any part of the body, however small, was inserted into the building or structure. Where D pushed in a windowpane and the forepart of his finger was observed inside the building that was enough.[13] The 1968 Act gives no express guidance on this issue and Parliament seems to have assumed that the common law rules would apply.[14] In the famous case of *Collins*,[15] D, naked but for his socks, had climbed up a ladder to a bedroom window with intent to rape the woman inside the bedroom. The woman, believing him to be her boyfriend and seeing him on the windowsill silhouetted with an erect penis invited him in. It was not clear whether he was on the sill outside the window or on the inner sill at the moment when she made her invitation and he ceased to be a trespasser. Generations of law students have pondered whether any part of D might have been inside the building at that point in time. Edmund Davies LJ in *Collins* held that to constitute burglary there must be 'an effective and substantial entry' as a trespasser. Later cases, however, do not support this interpretation. In *Brown*,[16] there was a sufficient entry where D's feet were on the ground outside a shop and the top half of his body was inside the broken shop window, as if he was rummaging for goods. The court said that the word 'substantial' did not materially assist but the entry must be 'effective' and here it was: D was presumably in a position to steal. In *Ryan*,[17] D became trapped by the neck with only his head and right arm inside the window, but the court rejected the argument that because D could not have stolen anything this was not capable of constituting an entry. But strictly, *Ryan* decided only that there was evidence on which a jury could find that D had entered.

It is submitted that it cannot be required that D must have got so far into the building as to be able to accomplish his unlawful purpose. D who intends to inflict grievous bodily harm is guilty of burglary when he enters through the ground-floor window even though V is on the fourth floor. The act of entry need not, therefore, be either an 'effective' or a 'substantial' entry. It is unsatisfactory that such a crucial actus reus element of a serious offence should be left for a jury to determine; the best course would be to accept the continued existence of the common law rule: any entry no matter how slight should suffice.

At common law, if D inserted an instrument into the building for the purpose of committing the ulterior offence (theft, etc), there was an entry even though no part of the body was introduced into the building. It was enough that hooks were inserted into the premises to drag out the carpets (theft), or that the barrel of a gun was introduced with a view to shooting someone inside (GBH). However, the insertion of an instrument merely for the purpose of gaining entry and not for the purpose of committing the ulterior offence was *not* an entry if no part of the body entered.[18] If D bored a hole in a door with a drill for

---

[11] B Mitchell, 'Multiple Wrongdoing and Offence Structure' (2001) 64 MLR 393.

[12] GR Sullivan and AP Simester, 'On the Nature and Rationale of Property Offences' in Duff and Green, *Defining Crimes*, 168 at 192; Duff, *Answering for Crime*, 127–8. See also G Yaffe, *Attempts* (2010) Ch 12; J Gardner, *Offences and Defences* (2010); Green, *13 Ways*.

[13] *Davis* (1823) Russ & Ry 499.   [14] HL Deb, 11 Mar 1968, vol 290, cols 85–6.

[15] [1973] QB 100 at 106. This was at a time when burglary included trespassing with intent to rape.

[16] [1985] Crim LR 212.   [17] [1996] Crim LR 320, (1996) 160 JP 610.

[18] eg *Horncastle* [2006] EWCA Crim 1736 (pole through letterbox to hook door keys from shelf).

the purpose of gaining entry, the emergence of the point of the drill bit on the inside of the door was not an entry. Under the 1968 Act, even if the courts are willing to follow the common law in holding that the intrusion of any part of the body is an entry, they may be more reluctant to preserve these technical rules regarding instruments. The rules do seem to produce outlandish results—there would be an entry if a stick of dynamite is thrown into the building, or if a bullet is fired from outside the building into it, or if a bomb is sent by post (assuming that such acts are not done merely to gain access to the building). The 1968 Act was said to be written in 'simple language as used and understood by ordinary literate men and women', but these examples are not what an ordinary person would describe as an 'entry'. Perhaps D must at least be present at the scene, or 'on the job'. Arguably, a distinction should be drawn between cases where D causes an instrument to enter V's building (eg by throwing it), and those where the instrument entering V's building represents an extension of D's body (as where he uses a telescopic pole).[19] These issues do not seem to have given rise to practical difficulty under the Act, perhaps due to the sensible use of more suitable charges such as theft or GBH or attempting such.

If it is conceded that inserting an inanimate instrument is not an entry, are we to distinguish between inanimate and animate instruments? Suppose that instead of an instrument, D sends in a monkey. Is that an entry? At common law, burglary could be committed by an innocent agent as, for example, if D sent a child under the age of ten into the building to steal.[20]

25.1.1.2 As a trespasser

In all cases of burglary it must be shown that D entered the building as a trespasser.[21] Trespass is a legal concept and it is necessary to look to the law of tort to understand its meaning.[22] It would appear that as a matter of civil law any intentional, reckless or (possibly) negligent entry into a building is a trespass if the building is in fact in the possession of another who does not consent to the entry. In burglary there must be a trespass in fact and the prosecution must show that D knew or was reckless as to whether or not he was a trespasser. Trespass can be proved without evidence from the occupier in person.[23]

What if D's entry is involuntary? So if, having been dragged against his will into V's house and left there by drunken companions, he steals V's vase and leaves, this is not burglary at the time of the entry. That offence is committed not at that point, but when the ulterior crime is committed; at that time D knew that he had entered as a trespasser.[24]

In tort, a mistake as to the building being entered is no defence: if D on a very dark night entered his neighbour's house by mistake he would be regarded as having intentionally entered and trespassed. It would be a tortious trespass even if D's mistake was a reasonable one, and even more so if it were negligent as, for example, if D made the mistake because he was drunk. In criminal law, for D to be guilty of burglary it is necessary to show he was a

---

[19] cf Griew, *Theft*, para 4.21. The offence has been used successfully where, eg, D has used a mechanical digger to steal a cash dispenser by ripping it from the wall of a bank: *Richardson and Brown* [1998] 2 Cr App R (S) 87; cf *Sang* [2003] EWCA Crim 2411 (going equipped for burglary with fishing rod bound with Sellotape to extract car keys through letterboxes).

[20] Hale, I PC, 555.

[21] In *McEneff* [2014] EWCA Crim 1633, the Crown conceded that the judge had misdirected the jury by seeming to introduce into the law of burglary the concept of trespass *ab initio*. This concept has no place here. If D enters a building otherwise than as a trespasser, he is not guilty of burglary.

[22] See J Goudkamp and D Nolan, *Winfield and Jolowicz on Tort* (20th edn, 2020) Ch 14.

[23] *Maccuish* [1999] 6 Arch News 2.

[24] The common law doctrine of trespass *ab initio* was held not to apply to burglary under the Theft Act: *Collins* [1973] QB 100 at 107. See JC Smith, *The Law of Theft* (2nd edn, 1972) paras 377–8 and (4th edn, 1979) paras 338–9.

trespasser (as defined in the civil law) but that is not sufficient: the criminal law also requires mens rea. If D is charged under s 9(1)(a), it need not be proved that D knew that as a matter of *law* that he was a trespasser. It must, however, be proved that, when he entered, he knew *the facts* which caused him to be a trespasser, or at least that he was reckless as to whether or not those facts existed.[25] A merely negligent entry, as where D enters another's house honestly but unreasonably believing it to be his own, is not enough to constitute burglary. D would also lack the mens rea for burglary if he believed he had a right to enter. Imagine that D, being separated from his wife, wrongly supposes that he has a right to enter the matrimonial home of which she is the owner-occupier and D enters with intent to inflict grievous bodily harm upon her. Even if he is a trespasser in law, D is not a burglar.[26]

Problems can arise when D has been invited to enter for a particular purpose or by a person in the household who is not the owner. In *Collins*,[27] D was invited in to have sex by the daughter of the householder. It was held that, whatever the position in the law of tort, the daughter's invitation, even without the knowledge or consent of the occupier (parent), meant that D was not a trespasser for the purpose of burglary.

Where the invitation to enter is issued by a member of the household, it is submitted that the crucial question will often be that of D's mens rea: did D know, or was he reckless as to whether or not, the invitation from that person was issued without the relevant authority? If in *Collins* she had invited her lover, D, into her parent's house to steal her parent's property that ought to be burglary if D realized that she had no right to invite him in for this purpose. This issue highlights the problem that burglary protects against a number of harms—the trespass, and the ulterior harms—and the interests being protected may be those of different individuals.[28]

In *Jones and Smith*,[29] the occupier's son, D, had a general permission to enter his father's house. He entered the house with E for the purpose of stealing. This constituted burglary. D had knowingly exceeded the permission granted to him by his father. It is perhaps noteworthy that this was a case 'where [D and E] took elaborate precautions, going there at dead of night'; and that, even if D's entry was covered by his father's general permission, this would scarcely extend to the entry of his accomplice. If E's entry was unlawful, D abetted it. Glanville Williams[30] argued that *Jones and Smith* is wrongly decided, being inconsistent with *Collins*,[31] because Collins exceeded permission since he entered intending to rape *if necessary*; that is, if the woman in the bedroom had not consented. But as the girl saw him to be 'a naked male with an erect penis' it seems that she invited him in expressly for the purpose of sexual intercourse, that he knew he was so invited and that any intention to rape must have lapsed by the time of the trespass when he entered the building.

Mistake as to identity, where identity is material, generally vitiates consent. So where V's invitation to enter is based on a mistake as to the identity of D who is being invited in, there will be a trespass if D knew the mistake was being made. If Collins had known of the woman's mistake as to his identity he would have intentionally entered as a trespasser.

---

[25] *Collins* [1973] QB 100 at 104–5. 'Reckless' is used in the subjective sense: *Cunningham* [1957] 2 QB 396 and *G* [2003] UKHL 50. See p 104. D need not know the civil law of trespass. The jury may need an express direction on recklessness: *Phillips* [2012] EWCA Crim 2149.

[26] There are of course other offences, particularly those of violence, with which he could be charged.

[27] [1973] QB 100 at 107. Cf *Robson v Hallett* [1967] 2 QB 939 (invitation by occupier's son effective until withdrawn by occupier).

[28] Burglary does not require that the ulterior offence should concern the occupier. If D and E enter V's house without V's consent, technically it would amount to burglary were D to steal E's wallet or inflict on E grievous bodily harm.

[29] [1976] 3 All ER 54.   [30] TBCL, 846–50.

[31] cf Mason J in *Barker v R* (1983) 7 ALJR 426 at 429: 'The foundation for [Williams'] conclusion is too frail.'

Where D gains entry by deception he enters as a trespasser.[32] For example, D is a trespasser if he gains admission to V's house by falsely pretending that he has been sent by the utility company to check the meter. The courts have taken a broad reading of trespass and this has serious consequences for the offence of burglary.

A person with limited authority to enter for a particular purpose enters as a trespasser, though he practises no deception, if he has an unlawful purpose outside the scope of that limited authority. Thus, in *Taylor v Jackson*,[33] D, who had express permission to go on V's land and hunt for rabbits, went there instead to hunt for hares. The Divisional Court held that this was evidence of trespass in pursuit of game, contrary to s 30 of the Game Act 1831. In *Hillen and Pettigrew v ICI (Alkali) Ltd*,[34] members of a stevedore's gang who had permission to enter a barge for the limited purpose of unloading it were held to be trespassers when they placed kegs on the hatch covers, knowing that this was a wrong and dangerous thing to do.[35] Lord Atkin stated:

As Scrutton LJ has pointedly said: 'When you invite a person into your house to use the staircase you do not invite him to slide down the banisters.'[36] So far as he sets foot on so much of the premises as lie outside the invitation or uses them for purposes which are alien to the invitation he is not an invitee but a trespasser. . . .

In *Farrington v Thomson and Bridgland*,[37] an Australian court held that a police officer was a trespasser when he entered a hotel for the purpose of committing a tort. The implied invitation to the public to enter the hotel did not extend to persons entering for the purpose of committing torts or crimes. In *Barker v R*,[38] V asked his neighbour, D, to keep an eye on his house while he was away on holiday. Having been told the whereabouts of a concealed key in case he needed to enter, D entered the house in order to steal. The High Court of Australia held that D had committed burglary: 'If a person enters for a purpose outside the scope of his authority then he stands in no better position than a person who enters with no authority at all.'[39] One decision goes against this view. In *Byrne v Kinematograph Renters Society Ltd*,[40] Harman J held that it was not trespass to gain entry to a cinema by buying tickets with the purpose, not of seeing the film, but of counting the patrons. This decision is against the weight of authority and, it is submitted, should not be followed.

It seems, therefore, that a person who enters a shop for the *sole* purpose of shoplifting is a burglar, though two of the majority in *Barker* thought otherwise. In their view, where the permission to enter is not limited by reference to purpose, a person with permission to enter is not a trespasser merely because he enters with a secret unlawful intent. It was argued that the shopkeeper's invitation to the public is not limited by reference to a specific purpose: 'the mere presence of the prospective customer upon the premises is itself likely to be an object of the invitation and a person will be within the invitation if he enters for no particular

---

[32] There is no need to distinguish between entry under a licence that is void and one that is merely voidable; entry under either is a trespass.

[33] (1898) 78 LT 555.   [34] [1936] AC 65.

[35] They were not therefore entitled to damages for injury when the covers collapsed.

[36] *The Carlgarth* [1927] P 93 at 110.

[37] [1959] VR 286 (Smith J). See also *Gross v Wright* [1923] 2 DLR 171.

[38] (1983) 7 ALJR 426 (Murphy J dissenting).   [39] At 429 per Mason J.

[40] [1958] 2 All ER 579 at 593; distinguished in *Jones*, p 1050, and by Mason J in *Barker v R* (1983) 7 ALJR 426 at 429 on the ground that 'the invitation by the lessee of the cinema to the public to enter the cinema was in very general terms and could on no view be said to be limited in the way in which was contended'. See more recently also *Taylor* [2004] VSCA 189 and *Lambourn* [2007] VSCA 187.

purpose at all'.[41] It is doubtful, however, if the shopkeeper's invitation can be said to extend to those who enter for the *sole* purpose of shoplifting. It is only in the exceptional case that it will be possible to prove this particular intent at the time of entry—as where there is evidence of a previous conspiracy, or system, or preparatory acts such as the wearing of a jacket with special pockets. Such an entry may be no more than a merely preparatory act to stealing (and so not amount to attempted theft); but it ought to be possible, where there is clear evidence, to secure a conviction for burglary. Few would object to the conviction of burglary of bank robbers who enter the bank flourishing firearms, for they are clearly outside the invitation extended by the bank to the public. A person who enters a shop for the sole purpose of murdering the manager is surely a trespasser; the case of the intending thief is no different in principle.

This extension of the law beyond what was intended by the CLRC[42] is significant in terms of the number of people potentially at risk of prosecution for burglary. This wider interpretation echoes the view expressed by Fletcher that the emphasis in burglary has shifted from an act of manifest illegality—'breaking' and entering—to an illicit entry where the principal element of blameworthiness lies in the criminal intent.[43] The cumulative effect of the extension in *Jones and Smith* with that of the major House of Lords decisions in theft cases must also be considered.[44] Consider D, an antiques dealer who calls on vulnerable older people with the intention of tricking them into selling him their priceless heirlooms for a gross undervalue. This is clearly fraud, but following *Hinks* seemingly also theft with the result that D could be guilty of burglary.

The decision in *Jones and Smith* does, however, have the advantage of emphasizing the importance of mens rea and reducing the reliance within the criminal law on the intricacies of the civil law of trespass.[45] It has been suggested that to keep the *Jones and Smith* extension within desirable limits, a distinction might be drawn between buildings that are open to the public and others that are not,[46] but such a distinction might create an unnecessary layer of technicality. Buildings are increasingly commonly quasi-public[47] (consider, eg, large shopping centres) and this distinction might cast further doubts on the ability of the tort of trespass to provide a sufficiently clear foundation for the offence in this context.

25.1.1.3 The victim of the burglary

Trespass is an interference with possession. Burglary is therefore committed against the person in possession of the building entered. Thus, where the premises are rented, burglary is committed against the tenant and not against the landlord. The landlord could commit burglary of the premises, the tenant could not.[48] Historically, it was held that where an employee occupies premises belonging to his employer (eg a caretaker living on site), the employer is not a trespasser if he enters the premises.[49] In such a case it is, of

[41] Brennan and Deane JJ (1983) 7 ALJR at 436. See also Williams, TBCL, 'a person who has a licence in fact to enter does not become a trespasser by reason of his criminal intent', at 846, see further 846–9; PJ Pace, 'Burglarious Trespass' [1985] Crim LR 716; ATH Smith, 'Shoplifting and the Theft Acts' [1981] Crim LR 586. A burglarious shoplifter should be sentenced in accordance with shoplifting guidelines rather than burglary guidelines: *Creed* [2005] EWCA Crim 215.

[42] See Eighth Report, para 35.   [43] See G Fletcher, *Rethinking Criminal Law* (1977) 128.

[44] See p 864.   [45] Horder, APOCL, 412.

[46] Smith, *Property Offences*, paras 28–14, referring to the American Model Penal Code, § 221.1.

[47] See K Gray and S Gray, 'Civil Rights, Civil Wrongs and Quasi-Public Space' [1999] 1 EHRLR 46, discussed in the breach of the peace case, *Porter v MPC* (1999) 20 Oct, unreported, CA (Civ Div).

[48] In contrast, a guest in a hotel will not ordinarily have sufficient possession of his room in law to enable him to sue in trespass. A burglary of a hotel room will be against the hotelier. Sentencing in such cases is as if the burglary was a domestic one: *Cook* [2007] EWCA Crim 7 and see *Chipunza* [2021] EWCA Crim 597.

[49] *Mayhew v Suttle* (1854) 4 E & B 347; *White v Bayley* (1861) 10 CBNS 227.

course, necessary to look at the precise terms of the arrangement between the parties. If the employee has been given exclusive possession, he would be the victim of a trespass. In cases where the employee is not the victim of a trespass by his employer, that does not mean that the employee cannot be the victim of trespass by a third party.[50] The position of a lodger also depends on the precise terms of his contract. If he has exclusive possession so that he can refuse entry to the landlord, then he may maintain trespass. Many lodgers, however, do not have such possession and in such cases an unauthorized entry by a third party is a trespass against the landlord.

It seems to follow that burglary is not committed where an hotelier enters the room of a guest, even though the entry is with intent to steal and is without the guest's consent. Depending on the terms of the contract, the same may be true in the case of an employer entering premises occupied by his employee for the purposes of his employment or a landlord entering the rooms of his lodger. There is no glaring deficiency in the law since charges of attempted or actual theft will lie in either case.

It is possible to charge burglary even though the indictment does not allege that the building was the property of anyone.[51] There must be a trespass, so evidence must be offered that someone other than the accused was in possession.

25.1.1.4 Any building or part of a building

The meaning of 'building' has frequently been considered by the courts in interpreting numerous statutes.[52] The meaning of the term varies according to context,[53] and many things have been held to be buildings for other purposes. According to Lord Esher MR, its 'ordinary and usual meaning is, a block of brick or stone work, covered in by a roof'.[54] It seems clear, however, that for the purposes of the offence of burglary, it is not necessary that the structure be of brick or stone to be a building. All dwellings are protected, regardless of their material of construction, and the Act expressly includes 'an inhabited vehicle or vessel'.

To constitute a building, the structure must have some degree of permanence.[55] Moveable structures which are intended for use as offices, workshops and stores ('portakabins') may fairly be regarded as buildings though their intended use on a given site is only temporary. It has been generally assumed that a tent cannot be a building,[56] notwithstanding that it is occupied on a particular site indefinitely. A structure may be a building even though its construction is flimsy.

The structure does not need to be one occupied by people. Farm outbuildings (eg stables, barns or silos) used to house animals or products are buildings for the purposes of burglary,

[50] Though in *White v Bayley*, ibid, Byles J thought, *obiter*, that an action could not have been maintained by the servant against a stranger (10 CBNS at 235).

[51] cf the Larceny Act 1916 which required that the breaking and entering be of the dwelling-house *of another*. See JN Adams, 'Trespass under the Theft and Firearms Act' (1969) 119 NLJ 655.

[52] An early example is *Manning and Rogers* (1871) LR 1 CCR 338.

[53] See the explicit statement to this effect from Lord Neuberger MR in *R (Ghai) v Newcastle City Council* [2010] EWCA Civ 59, [22].

[54] *Moir v Williams* [1892] 1 QB 264. Cf Byles J in *Stevens v Gourley* (1859) 7 CBNS 99 at 112: 'a structure of considerable size and intended to be permanent or at least to endure for a considerable time'. This statement was put into context in the *Ghai* case where it was suggested that 'building in normal parlance is naturally used to describe a significantly wider range of structures than would be included in Lord Esher's inclusion of brick or stonework covered by a roof', at [24].

[55] There is authority that a structure is capable of being a 'building' notwithstanding that it is 'implanted within another building': *Royal Exchange Theatre Trust v The Commissioners* [1978] VATTR 139.

[56] See CLRC, Eighth Report, para 78. This is certainly questionable in the case of, eg, a substantial marquee housing many facilities. Cf *Storn* (1865) 5 SCR (NSW) 26.

as are factory buildings and stores. The detached garage, shed or greenhouse in the grounds of a dwelling are similarly protected.

Potential problems also arise regarding at which point in the process of erection a structure becomes a building. In *Manning and Rogers*,[57] Lush J said: 'it is sufficient that it should be a connected and entire structure. I do not think four walls erected a foot high would be a building.' In that case all the walls were built and the roof was on, so it was obvious that the structure was a building. It is possible that a structure with a roof and no walls, such as a bandstand, is a building. So too, a structure which is intended to have a roof—a house where the walls are complete but not yet roofed or a house which has lost its roof in a hurricane. It has been held in a different context that 'a mere structure or superstructure composed of a steel and concrete frame [as yet] having no roof' could constitute a building.[58]

Lines must be drawn and it will not always be easy to do so.[59] The courts would probably hold, following *Brutus v Cozens*,[60] that 'building' is an ordinary word the meaning of which is 'a matter of fact and degree' to be determined by the trier of fact. The judge must at least rule whether or not there is evidence on which a reasonable jury could find the structure to be a building. As with the concept of entry, it is unfortunate that one of the essential elements of the offence is left to be determined by the trier of fact.

The extent of a 'building'

Historically, under the very complex pre-1968 law, the entry had to be into a particular dwelling-house, office, shop, garage, etc. A single structure might contain many dwelling-houses (eg a block of flats) or many offices, shops or garages. If D entered through the window of Flat 1 with intent to pass through it, to go to the communal staircase and steal in Flat 45, the breaking and entering of Flat 1 was neither burglary nor housebreaking because D did not intend to commit a crime therein.[61]

Under the Theft Act, everything depends on the extent of a 'building'.[62] In its ordinary natural meaning, this term could certainly include a block of flats. Adopting that meaning, D's entry through the window of Flat 1 as a trespasser with intent to pass through, go to the communal stairs and steal in Flat 45 is an entry of a building as a trespasser with intent to steal therein—it is burglary. The effect is to criminalize as burglary what was previously, at most, an attempt, and probably only an act of preparation. There are good reasons why the law should be extended in this way: it enables the police to intervene at the earliest possible

---

[57] (1871) LR 1 CCR 338.

[58] *Ealing London Borough Council, ex p Zainuddain* [1994] 2 PLR 1 at 4 per Tucker LJ.

[59] Contrast *B and S v Leathley* [1979] Crim LR 314 (Carlisle CC) and *Norfolk Constabulary v Seekings and Gould* [1986] Crim LR 167 (Norfolk CC). In the former, it was held that a freezer container detached from its chassis, resting on railway sleepers and used to store frozen food, was a building; in the latter it was held that two similar containers, still on their wheeled chassis, remained vehicles though they were, as in the first case, being used by a supermarket to provide temporary storage space. Cf *King* [1978] 19 SASR 118 (walk-in freezer could be a building).

[60] [1973] AC 854.

[61] cf *Wrigley* [1957] Crim LR 57. It was probably not even an attempt, not being sufficiently proximate to the intended crime.

[62] In *Hedley v Webb* [1901] 2 Ch 126, Cozens-Hardy J held that two semi-detached houses were a single building for the purpose of determining whether there was a sewer within the meaning of the Public Health Act 1875, s 4. In *Birch v Wigan Corpn* [1953] 1 QB 136, the Court of Appeal (Denning LJ dissenting) held that one house in a terrace of six was a 'house' within the meaning of s 11(1) and (4) of the Housing Act 1936 and not 'part of a building' within s 12 of that Act. Since the sections were mutually exclusive, the house could not be both a 'house' and 'part of a building' for the purpose of the Act; otherwise Denning LJ would have been disposed to say that the house was both. Romer LJ also thought that 'for some purposes and in other contexts two "houses" may constitute one building'. Cf Ormerod and Williams, *Smith's Law of Theft*, paras 8.31–8.36.

moment to prevent such offences, and forestalls the unmeritorious plea by D: 'I had no intention to steal in the flat—I was only using it as a passage to steal in another flat which I never reached'. It is submitted, therefore, that the word 'building' should be given its natural meaning.

Part of a building

It is sufficient if the trespass takes place in part of a building. So, for example, one lodger may commit burglary by entering the room of another lodger within the same house, or by entering the part of the house occupied by the landlord. Similarly, a guest in a hotel may commit burglary by entering the room of another guest. A customer in a shop who goes behind the counter and takes money from the till would be guilty of burglary. He enters that part of the building as a trespasser, even though he entered the shop (the building) with the shopkeeper's permission. The permission did not extend to his going behind the counter.[63]

What is 'a part' of the building may be a difficult and important question. Take a case put by the CLRC:[64] D enters a shop lawfully[65] but conceals himself on the premises until closing time and then emerges with intent to steal. When concealing himself D may or may not have entered a part of the building to which customers are not permitted to go. Even if he did commit a trespass at this stage because the area was off limits to customers, D may not have done so with intent to commit an offence in that part of the building. For example, D hides in the cleaning cupboard of a supermarket, intending to emerge and steal goods. The cupboard is not an area that customers are permitted to enter. D's entry of that room, even during opening hours, is a trespass. It is a trespass committed with intent to steal, but is not burglary, for D has no intent to steal in the part of the building (cupboard) that he has entered as a trespasser. When he emerges from the cupboard after the shop has closed, he is a trespasser. He is just as much a trespasser as if he had been told in express terms to leave the shop, for he knows perfectly well that his permission to remain on the premises terminated when the shop closed.[66] He has, then, entered a part of the building—the main floor of the shop—with intent to steal. Suppose, however, having entered lawfully, D merely remained concealed until after closing time behind a stack of boxes in the main hall of the supermarket. This was not a trespass because he had a right to be there. When he emerged and proceeded to steal, still in the main hall of the supermarket, was he entering another part of the building? It is submitted that every step he took was 'as a trespasser', but it is difficult to see that he entered any part of the building as a trespasser; the whole transaction took place in a single part of the building which he had lawfully entered.[67] It is illogical to treat these two cases differently.

The word 'part' has no precise meaning in relation to buildings. Its significance for the purpose of the section is that a person may lawfully enter one part of a building, yet be a trespasser on setting foot in another. This was the view taken in *Walkington*.[68] D, having entered a department store, went into an area bounded by a moveable three-sided counter where he opened a cash till. It was held that there was evidence on which the jury could find that the counter area was a 'part' of the building from which the public were excluded and

---

[63] *Walkington* [1979] 1 WLR 1169.　　[64] Eighth Report, para 75.

[65] ie without intent to steal; p 1058.

[66] The CLRC thought: 'The case is not important, because the offender is likely to go into a part of the building where he has no right to be, and this will be a trespassory entry into that part.' But he has no right to be in any part of the building after closing time and the only question, it is submitted, is whether he went into *another* part.

[67] cf *Laing* [1995] Crim LR 395.　　[68] [1979] 1 WLR 1169.

that if D knew that, he entered it as a trespasser. For the purposes of burglary, it seems that buildings fall into two parts: those parts where D is entitled to be, and those where he is not.

If D is lawfully in Flat 1 and, without leaving the building, he enters Flat 2 as a trespasser with intent to pass through it into Flat 3 and steal therein, his entry into Flat 2 does not constitute burglary if each flat is regarded as a separate part. He has not entered *Flat 2* with intent to steal *therein*. Yet, as we have seen, if he had entered Flat 2 from outside the building as a trespasser, there would have been no problem; he would have entered the *building* as a trespasser with intent to steal *therein*.[69] Perhaps it may fairly be said, however, that the building is in two parts: one part comprising the flat, where D is lawfully present, and the other part comprising *all* the remaining flats, where D may not lawfully go. On this view, D would commit burglary by entering that part (ie the remainder of the building) as a trespasser with the appropriate intent.

Inhabited vehicle or vessel

Whilst all 'buildings' are protected by the law of burglary, vehicles and vessels are protected only where they are 'inhabited'.[70] The obvious cases which are brought within the protection of burglary by this provision are a caravan or houseboat which is someone's home. There seems to be no reason whatever why a home should lack the ordinary protection of the law because it is mobile.[71] The limits of the extended definition should be noted. 'Inhabited' implies not that there is someone present inside the vehicle at the moment of the entry as a trespasser, but that someone lives there. My sports car is not an inhabited vehicle because I happen to be sitting in it when D enters against my will. The caravan or houseboat that is a person's home is expressly protected, whether or not the occupier is there at the time of the burglary.

Owners of camper vans might use them for the ordinary purposes of a car during most of the year but live in them while on holiday. While the vehicle is being lived in, it is undoubtedly an inhabited vehicle.[72] When being used for the ordinary purposes of a car it is submitted that it is not. The exact moment at which the camper van becomes an inhabited vehicle may be difficult to ascertain.[73]

Applying ordinary principles of construction of criminal offences, to be guilty of burglary D must know of the facts which would make him, in law, a trespasser in a building. Just as *Collins*[74] shows that D must know (or be reckless as to) the facts which render him a trespasser, so too D should not be convicted of burglary unless he knew of the facts which make the thing entered 'a building' in law. Suppose D enters a camper van parked by the side of the road. If he knew that V was living in the vehicle, there is no problem. But what if he did not know? It would seem that he must be acquitted of burglary unless it can be shown that he was at least reckless as to whether anyone was living there or not; this involves showing that the possibility was present in his mind.

'Dwelling'

Since the Criminal Justice Act 1991, it has become crucial to identify whether the building entered is a dwelling, rendering the offence a 'domestic burglary' for sentencing purposes. This issue is discussed later.

---

[69] cf S White, 'Lurkers, Draggers and Kidnappers' (1986) 150 JP 37 at 56.

[70] Section 9(3).

[71] Arguably, on this rationale, the offence should also extend to protect tent dwellers.

[72] *Quaere* whether the unoccupied boat or caravan, which is visited and lived in only during holidays is protected. See Smith, *Property Offences*, paras 28–39 (no); Williams, TBCL, 841 (yes); Griew, *Theft*, paras 4–27 (no).

[73] Ormerod and Williams, *Smith's Law of Theft*, paras 8.43–8.46. Cf *Bundy* [1977] 1 WLR 914, p 1068.

[74] [1973] QB 100, p 1048.

25.1.2 Mens rea

25.1.2.1 Intention to enter as a trespasser

As discussed, burglary requires proof that D knew (or was reckless as to) the facts that, in law, make his entry trespassory: *Collins*.[75] It would follow that if D sets up an honest belief in a right to enter, it would be for the Crown to prove that D's belief was not held.

25.1.2.2 The ulterior offence

It must be proved that D *either*:

(1) entered with intent[76] to commit one of the following offences:

    (a) stealing,

    (b) inflicting grievous bodily harm,

    (c) unlawful damage to the building or anything therein;[77] or

(2) entered and committed *or* attempted to commit one of the following offences:

    (a) stealing,

    (b) inflicting grievous bodily harm.

Where the charge is one of entering with intent, it must be proved that at the time of entry D held an intention to cause the harm in question. In many such cases, D's intent may be conditional at the time of entry, in the sense that he intends to steal if there is anything worth stealing, or intends to cause grievous bodily harm if V, his enemy, happens to be in the building. D may be guilty even if there is nothing in the building worth stealing or V is out of town.[78] If D intends to steal a specific item only (should it be present), it seems that the s 9(1)(a) offence is not committed.[79]

Intention as to the ulterior offence must be proved; it is not sufficient that D is shown to have been reckless at the time of entry as to whether or not the ulterior offence would be committed.[80] Although intention in this context will usually be direct or purposive, it is possible that D will have an oblique intention: as where he intends to remove from V's premises an item of property that is D's, but foresees that in doing so he is virtually certain to cause criminal damage to V's property.

The offences in s 9(1)(a) may be accurately described as inchoate versions of the three ulterior offences (theft, GBH and criminal damage). Since the trespassory intrusion represents a free-standing harm to V's interests, it is generally accepted that it is appropriate in principle to criminalize these actions by a specific offence—burglary.

It might be questioned why the offence of burglary is limited to the ulterior intent to commit such a limited number of specified offences, and to the commission of an even smaller number. There have been suggestions to criminalize trespass with intent to commit any indictable offence; that would create considerable overlap with offences of inchoate liability, and would not appear to be necessary.[81]

---

[75] ibid.

[76] The crime is one of specific intent: *Durante* [1972] 1 WLR 1612, p 339.

[77] The further alternative of rape was repealed by the SOA 2003. See later.

[78] *A-G's References (Nos 1 and 2 of 1979)* [1980] QB 180. See the discussion at p 442. This interpretation of intention illustrates the flexibility of that concept: A Ashworth, 'The Elasticity of Mens Rea' in *Crime, Proof and Punishment*, 45, 49.

[79] Ormerod and Williams, *Smith's Law of Theft*, para 8.51.

[80] *A v DPP* [2003] All ER (D) 393 (Jun).

[81] See LCCP 183, *Conspiracy and Attempts* (2007) para 16.61.

Stealing

This clearly means theft, contrary to s 1 of the Theft Act 1968.[82] Following *Gomez* this has an especially broad meaning.[83]

Grievous bodily harm

The intention to inflict grievous bodily harm in s 9(1)(a) must be an intention to commit an offence, that is, to inflict that harm unlawfully. The offence in question would be causing grievous bodily harm with intent to do so, contrary to s 18 of the OAPA 1861. It is arguable that s 23 of that Act may also be a qualifying offence since it involves administering or causing to be administered poisons or noxious substances so as thereby to endanger life *or inflict grievous bodily harm.*

If there is no evidence that D had, at the time of entry, intent to do GBH, the charge under s 9(1)(a) should not be left to the jury, even if the occupiers have been assaulted.[84]

Section 9(1)(b) does not use the word 'offence', but simply requires that D inflicts or attempts to inflict on any person in the building any grievous bodily harm. The omission of the word 'offence' is in fact a legislative accident,[85] but in *Jenkins*[86] the Court of Appeal held that the infliction need not amount to an offence of any kind. The court gave this example:

An intruder gains access to the house without breaking in (where there is an open window for instance).[87] He is on the premises as a trespasser and his intrusion is observed by someone in the house of whom he may not even be aware, and as a result that person suffers a severe shock, with a resulting stroke ... Should such an event fall outside the provisions of s 9 when causing some damage to property falls fairly within it?

The court posed this question plainly expecting the answer, 'no'. It is submitted that the right answer is an emphatic 'yes'. Otherwise, a person may become guilty of burglary in consequence of a wholly unforeseen and unforeseeable event. The analogy with damage to property is misplaced: causing damage to property does not fall within the provisions of s 9(1)(b). There must be an actual intention to cause damage at the time of the trespassory entry to constitute the offence under s 9(1)(a). This requires a mens rea which is wholly absent in the example put by the court. The House of Lords allowed the appeal in *Jenkins*[88] but on a different point and no allusion was made to the interpretation by the Court of Appeal of s 9(1)(b). The case, therefore, stands as an authority—but, it is submitted, a bad one. When para (b) is read in the context of s 9(1) and (2), it is reasonably clear that the infliction of bodily harm required must be an offence—in effect, under s 18, or possibly s 23, of the OAPA 1861.

What if D enters with intent to murder? It would be very strange if an entry with intent to inflict grievous bodily harm amounted to burglary, and an entry with intent to murder did not. It is submitted that the greater includes the lesser and that an intention to kill is enough.

---

82 Electricity is not property for the purposes of theft and cannot therefore found a burglary charge, as where D enters property and makes a telephone call: *Low v Blease* [1975] Crim LR 513.

83 *Dobson v General Accident Fire and Life Assurance Corpn plc* [1990] 1 QB 274, p 865.

84 *O'Neill, McMullen and Kelly* (1986) The Times, 17 Oct.

85 See JC Smith, 'Burglary under the Theft Bill' [1968] Crim LR 367 and commentary on *Jenkins* [1983] 1 All ER 1000, [1983] Crim LR 386.

86 [1983] 1 All ER 1000 at 1002. Cf *Watson* (1989) 89 Cr App R 211 (death caused after entry is caused in the course of committing an offence under s 9(1)(a)).

87 It is not clear why the court thought this was relevant.

88 [1983] 3 All ER 448, [1984] Crim LR 36 and commentary.

Unlawful damage to the building or anything therein

The damage intended must be such that to cause it would amount to an offence. It might be any of the offences of causing damage created by the Criminal Damage Act 1971. In the case of every one of the offences which is likely to be invoked under this provision, the elements of the actus reus must be committed intentionally or recklessly.

The location of the object of the ulterior crime

Is it necessary that the object of the ulterior crime be in the building before the trespassory entry? In other words, is it burglary if D drags V into a barn with intent to rob, or inflict grievous bodily harm on him?[89] Similarly, what of D who enters with the aim of removing a piece of property to damage it outside? Must it be proved only that the property was in the building or part thereof, or that the damage would occur in the building or part thereof? The words of the section do not supply a clear answer, but the purpose of the offence—the protection of persons and things in a building—suggests that the crime does not extend to these cases.

25.2 Burglary in respect of a dwelling

Since the Criminal Justice Act 1991, burglary in respect of a dwelling is a separate offence[90]— a new aggravated form of burglary. In *Miller*,[91] the Court of Appeal recognized that where it is alleged that a burglary has been committed in relation to a dwelling, it is necessary to specify as much in the particulars of the offence.[92] Arguably, this represents a return to the origins of the offence being a crime against 'habitation',[93] and has significance in labelling the conduct appropriately. The only constituent of the offence that requires consideration is 'dwelling', but it must be looked at in respect of both actus reus and mens rea.

25.2.1 Actus reus

'Dwelling' is not defined but it is submitted that it ought to mean substantially the same as 'dwelling-house' in the former offence of burglary at common law and under the Larceny Acts.[94] 'House' would be too narrow a definition and the word 'dwelling' better describes many forms of accommodation that should be protected. Unfortunately, the term 'dwelling' has been subject to differing interpretations in the context of dwelling burglary. For example, it has sometimes been interpreted to include those buildings that are within the

---

[89] See S White, 'Lurkers, Draggers and Kidnappers' (1986) 150 JP 37 at 56.

[90] See p 1056. See *Courtie*, p 32. For a more extended discussion see K Laird, 'Conceptualising the Interpretation of "Dwelling" in Section 9 of the Theft Act 1968' [2013] Crim LR 656.

[91] [2010] EWCA Crim 809.

[92] In *Love* [2013] EWCA Crim 257, the Court of Appeal upheld the judge's decision to allow an application by the prosecution to amend the indictment by substituting 'dwelling' for 'building'. It was held that the power to amend the indictment existed notwithstanding that the defendants had already entered pleas of guilty to the original indictment.

[93] Blackstone, *Commentaries*, iv, 220.

[94] See the 1st edn of this book (1965) 399; *Russell on Crime* (12th edn, 1964) 826. Cf Public Order Act 1986, s 8: '"dwelling" means any structure or part of a structure occupied as a person's home or as other living accommodation (whether the occupation is separate or shared with others) but does not include any part not so occupied, and for this purpose "structure" includes a tent, caravan, vehicle, vessel or other temporary or movable structure'. Cf Terrorism Act 2000, s 121: '"dwelling" means a building or part of a building used as a dwelling, and a vehicle which is habitually stationary and which is used as a dwelling . . .'

boundary of a person's home but which are not physically attached to it, such as a shed.[95] In other instances, this interpretation has been rejected in favour of a narrower one.[96] Such inconsistency is unwelcome given the frequency with which burglary is charged and the fact that it attracts a higher sentence than non-dwelling burglary. A more satisfactory interpretation would be to accept that a person dwells in that building where he sleeps rather than where he spends his waking hours where those places are different, and that the definition does not extend to those buildings within the boundary of the premises that encompass the home, but are not physically attached to it. A building, such as a block of flats, may contain many dwellings. Entering the 'public' parts of the block may be burglary but perhaps not burglary in 'a dwelling'. In *Le Vine v DPP*,[97] the laundry room within the sheltered housing block was not a dwelling for the purposes of the Public Order Act 1986.

Premises that qualify as a dwelling will not cease to be such because of the temporary absence of the inhabitants, provided that at least one of them intends to return. A person may have more than one dwelling, as where he has a flat in London and a house in the country, sleeping sometimes in one and sometimes in the other. The camper van considered previously will probably be a dwelling while the owners are living in it, but will cease to be a dwelling when they stop doing so.[98] The Court of Appeal in *Flack*[99] declined to give guidance as to how 'dwelling' ought to be interpreted, as it was held to be largely a question of fact. See also recently the discussion of hotel rooms as dwellings: *Chipunza*.[99a]

The Divisional Court affirmed the validity of this approach in *Hudson v CPS*.[100] The defendant was convicted of committing dwelling burglary after he burgled a house that was uninhabited but was ready for new tenants to move in, although none had yet been identified. The defendant appealed by way of case stated. The Crown argued that as a matter of ordinary language, the word 'dwelling' is capable of including not only a building dwelt in, but also a building designed to be dwelt in, although at the relevant time it might have been vacant or not ready for occupation. Delivering the judgment of the Divisional Court, Gross LJ stated that 'dwelling' is an ordinary English word and that its meaning is a question of fact for the jury, magistrates or District Judge. His lordship held that a building that would otherwise be a dwelling if it were lived in does not cease to be a dwelling the moment it becomes unoccupied. Where a dwelling has become unoccupied, it is a question of fact and degree—not law—as to whether it is no longer a dwelling.[101] It was held that the more habitable a building as a matter of fact, then the more, other things being equal, it is likely to be a 'dwelling' for the purposes of s 9(3)(a) of the Act. The Divisional Court's conclusion was heavily influenced by the desire to avoid fine distinctions and the introduction into standard burglary cases of disputes about the tenancy status of the property in question. The court was also keen to ensure the law deters the burglary of both residential and apparently residential buildings.

It is respectfully submitted that there is a tension between the court's conclusion that apparently residential properties can constitute dwellings for the purposes of s 9(3)(a) and the justification for treating dwelling burglary as a more serious offence than non-dwelling

---

[95] *Alexander* [2008] EWCA Crim 2834.   [96] *Miles* [2003] EWCA Crim 2892.

[97] [2010] EWHC 1128 (Admin).

[98] In *Coleman* [2013] EWCA Crim 544 the Court of Appeal, in interpreting s 111(5) of the PCC(S)A 2000 which defines a 'domestic burglary' as one committed 'in respect of a building or part of a building which is a dwelling', held that it encompassed a houseboat.

[99] [2013] EWCA Crim 115.   [99a] 2021 EWCA Crim 597.   [100] [2017] EWHC 841 (Admin).

[101] The court distinguished the earlier case of *Sticklen* [2013] EWCA Crim 615, in which the Court of Appeal held that the burglary of an unoccupied house was not a dwelling burglary and so D ought to have been sentenced on the basis that he had committed simple burglary.

burglary. If there is no one residing[102] in the building who can feel a sense of 'violation and insecurity'[103] by its being burgled, then why should the defendant be subject to a harsher penalty than if he had burgled a commercial building? The court was confident that its conclusion would not lead to unfairness on the basis that the fact the property was temporarily vacant can be reflected in arguments as to mitigation. However, if it is the defendant's third dwelling burglary, then the court must sentence him to a minimum sentence of three years' imprisonment. It would have been preferable for the court to have laid down a bright-line rule to the effect that non-inhabited buildings cannot be dwellings for the purposes of the offence. This would have the benefit of not only ensuring greater consistency, but would also be in keeping with the justification for treating dwelling burglary as a more serious offence than non-dwelling burglary.[104]

25.2.2 Mens rea

As 'dwelling' is an aggravating element in the offence warranting a higher maximum sentence of imprisonment, it should, in principle, import a requirement of mens rea. A person who commits burglary in a dwelling should be convicted only of simple burglary unless he had awareness that it was a dwelling. Given the potentially counterintuitive interpretation of 'dwelling' endorsed in *Hudson v CPS*, proving such awareness could be made more difficult. In principle and by analogy to the construction of 'as a trespasser' in *Collins*,[105] recklessness should be enough. If D entered being aware that someone might be living there, and someone was, he should be guilty of burglary in respect of a dwelling.

25.3 Aggravated burglary

By s 10 of the Theft Act 1968:

(1) A person is guilty of aggravated burglary if he commits any burglary and at the time has with him any firearm or imitation firearm, any weapon of offence, or any explosive; and for this purpose—

    (a) 'firearm' includes an airgun or air pistol, and 'imitation firearm' means anything which has the appearance of being a firearm, whether capable of being discharged or not; and

    (b) 'weapon of offence' means any article made or adapted for use for causing injury to or incapacitating a person, or intended by the person having it with him for such use; and

    (c) 'explosive' means any article manufactured for the purpose of producing a practical effect by explosion, or intended by the person having it with him for that purpose.

(2) A person guilty of aggravated burglary shall on conviction on indictment be liable to imprisonment for life.

The reason given by the CLRC for the creation of this additional offence is that 'burglary when in possession of the articles mentioned . . . is so serious that it should in our opinion be punishable with imprisonment for life. The offence is comparable with robbery (which will

---

[102] There is no need for the building to be resided in on a permanent basis. As has already been pointed out, a person may have more than one dwelling.

[103] *Brewster* [1998] 1 Cr App R (S) 181 at 185.

[104] In the subsequent case of *Distill* [2017] EWHC 2244 (Admin), the Divisional Court held that the definition of 'dwelling' in s 8 of the Public Order Act 1986 did not include a private garden.

[105] At p 1048.

be so punishable). It must be extremely frightening to those in the building, and it might well lead to loss of life.'[106] The offence can be committed in dwellings or other buildings.

25.3.1 The articles of aggravation

'Firearm' is not defined in the Act, except to the extent that it includes an airgun or air pistol. The term is given a very wide meaning by the Firearms Act 1968,[107] but since that statutory definition has not been incorporated in the Theft Act it is submitted that the word should not be given a meaning any wider than that which it naturally bears; and that the term 'imitation firearm' be similarly limited.[108]

The definition of 'weapon of offence' is marginally wider than that of 'offensive weapon' in s 1(4) of the Prevention of Crime Act 1953.[109] It includes: (a) articles made for causing injury to a person; (b) articles adapted for causing injury to a person; (c) articles which D has with him for that purpose; (d) any article made for incapacitating a person; (e) any article adapted for incapacitating a person; and (f) any article which D has with him for that purpose. Articles *made* for incapacitating a person might include a pair of handcuffs; articles *adapted* for incapacitating might include a pair of socks made into a gag; articles *intended* for incapacitating a person might include sleeping pills to put in the security guard's tea, a rope to tie him up, a sack to put over his head, pepper to throw in his face, and so on.

The definition of 'explosive' closely follows that which was used in s 3(1) of the Explosives Act 1875 which, after enumerating various explosives, adds: 'and every other substance, whether similar to those above mentioned or not, used or manufactured with a view to produce a practical effect by explosion or by a pyrotechnic effect . . .'

It will be observed that the definition in the Theft Act is narrower. The Explosives Act, if read literally, is wide enough to include a box of matches—these produce a 'pyrotechnic effect'—but it seems clear that a box of matches would not be an 'explosive' under the Theft Act. The main difficulty about the definition (this is unlikely to be important in practice) lies in determining the meaning of 'practical effect'. Perhaps it serves to exclude fireworks which, so it has been said in connection with another Act, are 'things that are made for amusement'.[110]

25.3.2 'At the time' of commission of burglary

It must be proved that D had the article of aggravation with him *at the time* of committing the burglary. Where the charge is one of entry with intent (s 9(1)(a)) this is clearly at the time of entry. Where the charge is one of committing a specified offence, having entered (s 9(1)(b)), it is at the time of commission of the specified offence. Care must be taken to identity precisely whether the charge is under s 9(1)(a) or (b) and what articles were present at the time of entry and afterwards[111] and under whose control.[112]

---

[106] Eighth Report, para 80.

[107] See s 57 and *Bewley* [2012] EWCA Crim 1457 and note s 125 of the Policing and Crime Act 2017. Note that the possession of a firearm with intent to commit an indictable offence (including burglary) is an offence carrying a maximum life imprisonment: Firearms Act 1968, s 18.

[108] The term has been widely construed under the Firearms Act 1968, but a jury cannot conclude that D pointing a finger inside his coat at V is sufficient: *Bentham* [2005] UKHL 18.

[109] See Ch 34. Note that defences of lawful authority or reasonable excuse available under the 1953 Act do not apply here.

[110] *Bliss v Lilley* (1862) 32 LJMC 3, per Cockburn CJ and Blackburn J, but Wightman J thought that a fog-signal was a 'firework'. Cf *Bouch* [1982] 3 All ER 918; *Howard* [1993] Crim LR 213. See also the definition in s 1(1) of the Fireworks Act 2003.

[111] *Chevannes* [2009] EWCA Crim 2725.   [112] See *Downer* [2009] EWCA Crim 1361.

Burglary is not aggravated merely because a weapon is used against the occupier outside the building or is held by an accomplice in a getaway car.[113] Nor is it enough to prove an armed entry by D as a trespasser unless that entry is accompanied by one of the specified intents (theft, GBH, criminal damage). If D, having no such intent at the time of entry, discards his weapon and thereafter commits one of the specified offences, he is not guilty of aggravated burglary[114] though he would be so guilty if he rearmed himself for this purpose.[115] It is debatable whether or not D who arms himself only to escape, having already completed the burglary (eg by stealing), is guilty of the aggravated offence.[116] By analogy with the court's approach in *Watson*,[117] and the courts' willingness to treat Theft Act offences as continuing,[118] it is likely that the offence would be held to have been committed.

25.3.3 'Has with him'

The expression 'has with him' appears in the Prevention of Crime Act 1953 and reference should be made to the discussion of that Act,[119] particularly as regards the controversial issue of D claiming to have forgotten that he has with him the forbidden article.[120] The Court of Appeal has reiterated that what matters for the purpose of s 10 is whether the weapon was within D's control so that it could be taken up and used if necessary (not whether he was holding it).[121] In *Henderson*,[122] which was a case concerning s 139(1) of the Criminal Justice Act 1988, the Court of Appeal held that the following are relevant considerations when determining whether a person has a weapon 'with him': possession of a weapon by D is a wider concept than D having it 'with him'; D having a weapon 'with him' is a wider concept than D carrying it; the 'propinquity' between D and the weapon; whether the weapon is immediately available to D; the accessibility of the weapon; the context of any criminal enterprise embarked upon; the purposes of the applicable statute. In this case, the weapon in question was found by police in a bag in the boot of D's car. The court quashed D's conviction on the basis that there was no close geographical, temporal or purposive link between the knife, which was in a public place, and D who was in a private flat. Furthermore, the court did not consider that it could be said that the knife was immediately available or readily accessible to D. The outcome of this case is unsurprising, given that the recorder seems to have conflated the concepts of 'possession' and 'having with one'. The case is a useful reminder that the two concepts are distinct.

When the prosecution have proved that the article was made or adapted for causing injury or incapacitating, they need not prove that D intended to use the weapon in the course of the burglary. Where the article was not made or adapted for causing injury or incapacitating, but the prosecution prove D had it with him for such use, it is not necessary to show that he intended so to use it *in the course of the burglary*. D's conviction was accordingly upheld in *Stones*,[123] where at the time of the burglary he had with him an ordinary kitchen knife that, he claimed, he was carrying to use in self-defence in case he was attacked by a gang. The court held that the mischief at which the section is aimed is that if a burglar has a weapon

---

[113] *Klass* [1998] 1 Cr App R 453; followed in *Wiggins* [2012] EWCA Crim 885.

[114] *Francis* [1982] Crim LR 363.   [115] *O'Leary* (1986) 82 Cr App R 34.

[116] See Smith, *Property Offences*, para 28.61.   [117] *Watson* (1989) 89 Cr App R 211.

[118] *Atakpu* (1994) 98 Cr App R 254.

[119] See Ch 34. See also *Pawlicki and Swindell* (1992) 95 Cr App R 246, ('have with him' under Firearms Act 1968, s 18(1)), and *North* [2001] EWCA Crim 544. In respect of the Firearms Act offence, it has been held that the question of 'propinquity' is to be approached in a commonsense way. A person could not, therefore, be said to 'have with him' a firearm stored two or three miles away: *Bradish* (2004) 148 SJ 474.

[120] See especially *Jolie*, Ch 34.   [121] See *Chevannes*, n 111.   [122] [2016] EWCA Crim 965.

[123] [1989] 1 WLR 156. See NJ Reville, 'Mischief of Aggravated Burglary' (1989) 139 NLJ 835.

which he intends to use to injure some person unconnected with the premises burgled, he might nevertheless be tempted so to use it if challenged during the course of the burglary. Clearly, a conditional intent to use a weapon suffices for the offence.

Under the Prevention of Crime Act 1953, it has been decided that a person carrying an inoffensive article for an innocent purpose does not become guilty of having an offensive weapon with him merely because he uses that article for an offensive purpose. The 1953 Act is directed against the *carrying* of articles intended to be used as weapons, not against the *use* of an article as a weapon. It was to be expected that the same construction would be put upon the similar words of s 10 of the Theft Act but, in *Kelly*,[124] it was held that D, who had used a screwdriver to gain entry to premises, became guilty of aggravated burglary when he used it to prod V in the stomach. The court purported to apply the ordinary meaning of the words of the subsection, but they seem indistinguishable in this respect from the words of the Prevention of Crime Act (and the same considerations of policy seem applicable to the two provisions). *Kelly* seems a dubious decision.

It has also been held under the 1953 Act that no offence is committed where a person arms himself with a weapon for instant attack on his victim;[125] if *Kelly* is right, it seems that such a decision can hardly apply to s 10. So, if D, being interrupted in the course of stealing after a trespassory entry, picks up a paperweight (or any object) and throws it with intent to cause injury, he will thereby become guilty of aggravated burglary. He could be adequately dealt with by a charge of simple burglary and a second count charging whatever offence against the person he has committed; it is submitted that this is the proper course. On the other hand, if D picks up a stone outside the building to use as a weapon should he be disturbed after entry, the subsequent burglary would properly be held to be aggravated: D has armed himself before an occasion to use violence has arisen; and the stone is a weapon of offence.[126] In *O'Leary*,[127] D, having entered V's house as a trespasser, took up a kitchen knife and proceeded upstairs where by use of the knife he forced V to hand over property. It was held that he was rightly convicted of aggravated burglary. Burglary is committed under s 9(1)(b) at the time when the ulterior offence is committed; before its commission, D had armed himself for use in connection with it.

25.4 Trespass with intent to commit a sexual offence

Section 63 of the Sexual Offences Act 2003 introduced a new offence to replace burglary with intent to rape.[128]

   (1) A person commits an offence if—

      (a) he is a trespasser on any premises,

      (b) he intends to commit a relevant sexual offence on the premises, and

      (c) he knows that, or is reckless as to whether, he is a trespasser.

---

[124] (1993) 97 Cr App R 245, [1993] Crim LR 763 and commentary. See *Eletu* [2018] EWCA Crim 599 for more recent discussion and vivid illustration of the issues that can arise in directing juries.

[125] *Ohlson v Hylton* [1975] 2 All ER 490; *Giles* [1976] Crim LR 253; *Bates v Bulman* (1979) 68 Cr App R 21; *Byrne* [2004] Crim LR 582; *Szewczyk* [2019] EWCA Crim 1811.

[126] See *Reid* [2017] EWCA Crim 2571 as an example of the need to deal carefully with this where there are accessories not entering the property.

[127] (1986) 82 Cr App R 341.

[128] See generally P Rook and R Ward, *Rook and Ward on Sexual Offences: Law and Practice* (6th edn, 2021) paras 14.51 et seq.

(2) In this section—

'premises' includes a structure or part of a structure;

'relevant sexual offence' [is all those in that Part of the Act];

'structure' includes a tent, vehicle or vessel or other temporary or movable structure.

The offence, carrying a maximum sentence of ten years on indictment, is significantly wider in a number of respects than the old law where it was burglary to enter a building as a trespasser with intent to rape. Under s 63 any trespass is sufficient and there is no need to prove a trespassory *entry*. The trespass may arise as a result of D exceeding permission for the purposes for which entry was granted; or exceeding permission in terms of the areas or parts of premises entered. Secondly, the trespass relates to 'premises', which is wider than the concept of a building or part of a building. It is a term used in many statutes, including criminal ones, and is usually widely construed.[129] Technically, it could extend to all areas of land which could be the subject of a lease and will include open spaces (fields and parks). Thirdly, the concept of 'structure' is given a wide definition and will, unlike in burglary, include a car or other vehicle.[130] Fourthly, as with s 9(1)(a) of the Theft Act there is no need for the ulterior (sexual) offence to occur. Indeed, there is no need for any intended victim to be on the premises. Finally, the list of ulterior offences to which this section applies is much wider than under the old law which applied only to rape; it extends to all those in Part 1 of the 2003 Act.[131] By s 72 of the 2003 Act the offence is committed if D, who is a British national, does an act abroad against an under-18-year-old which would, if committed in the UK, constitute an offence under s 63.

The mens rea of the offence requires proof that D intended to perform the relevant sexual offence, and knowledge or subjective recklessness as to the facts that render him a trespasser.

In *Pacurar*,[132] the Court of Appeal observed that there will be many cases where the evidence points to a specific sexual offence D intended and the prosecution will be in a position to make clear what is alleged, by identifying the sexual offence in the particulars of the offence. The court also noted that there will be other cases where the prosecution allege it is obvious from all the circumstances that D intended to commit *a* sexual offence, but it is impossible to specify which one and upon whom. The court had no doubt that Parliament intended s 63 to cover both situations. Therefore, there is no need for the prosecution to specify any particular sexual offence it is alleged the defendant intended to commit, nor for the trial judge to direct the jury that they had to agree on the sexual offence intended. It suffices for the jury to be directed that they have to agree that D intended to commit *a* sexual offence contained in Part 1 of the 2003 Act.

---

[129] eg in the Criminal Law Act 1977, s 12(1)(a): 'premises' means any building, any part of a building under separate occupation, any land ancillary to a building, the site comprising any building or buildings together with any land ancillary thereto.

[130] 'Structure' is a term used in numerous statutes, but its interpretation is heavily dependent on context. One example is the Criminal Justice and Police Act 2001, where s 66 provides (as amended) '"premises" includes any vehicle, stall or moveable structure (including an offshore installation [or other marine installation]) and any other place whatever, whether or not occupied as land'. Section 48 of the RIPA 2000 similarly provides that 'premises' includes any vehicle or moveable structure and any other place whatever, whether or not occupied as land. This suggests that 'structure' is wider than 'building'. For proposals to extend the law, see LCCP 183, *Conspiracy and Attempts* (2007) para 16.61(3).

[131] See eg *Fulton* [2006] EWCA Crim 960 (D had forced his way into the house of a 60-year-old woman and forced her to watch him masturbate). See also *C* [2006] EWCA Crim 1024 and *Ralston* [2005] EWCA Crim 3279 (sexual touching); and *H* [2007] EWCA Crim 2622.

[132] [2016] EWCA Crim 569.

25.5 Going equipped

Many of the offences in the Theft Acts (and Fraud Act) have been criticized for their considerable breadth, particularly in view of the generally wide interpretations adopted by the courts. It is possible for D to be convicted of theft from the moment that he touches an item or acts in a way that assumes any single right of an owner, provided he has the proscribed state of mind.[133] Similarly, it is possible for D to be convicted of burglary where he has only got as far as entering as a trespasser with a proscribed intent.[134] With charges also available for attempted theft where D has gone beyond any act of mere preparation, the reach of the criminal law in this area is vast. The offence under s 25 (like those under ss 6 and 7 of the Fraud Act) goes further still, criminalizing conduct of a more preliminary nature than even attempt.

By s 25(1) and (2) of the Theft Act 1968:

(1) A person shall be guilty of an offence if, when not at his place of abode, he has with him any article for use in the course of or in connection with any burglary or theft.[135]

(2) A person guilty of an offence under this section shall on conviction on indictment be liable to imprisonment for a term not exceeding three years.[136]

This useful inchoate offence is expressed to be directed against acts preparatory to: (a) burglary contrary to s 9; (b) theft contrary to s 1;[137] (c) taking and driving away a conveyance, contrary to s 12.[138]

25.5.1 Actus reus

The cross-heading in the statute, 'Possession of house-breaking implements, etc', and the side-note, 'Going equipped for stealing, etc', indicate that the offence[139] is aimed primarily at someone setting out on an expedition equipped with a jemmy, skeleton keys and such like. However, in *Re McAngus*,[140] an extradition case, it was held that there was evidence of the offence when undercover agents said that D had agreed to sell them counterfeit clothing and had shown them shirts, wrongly bearing an American brand name, in a bonded warehouse.

D was certainly 'equipped' for criminal deception and, when visiting the warehouse, was not at his place of abode. If he had been hawking the shirts from door to door it would have been a straightforward case, but D did not 'go' anywhere with the articles. The side-note is not part of the section but might now be considered as a legitimate aid to statutory construction;[141] it might be taken to show that 'going' is the essence of the offence.[142] Presumably, it would have made no difference if the shirts had been kept in D's own warehouse (which does not seem substantially different from keeping them at home).

---

[133] See the discussion of *Gomez* [1993] AC 442 and *Hinks* [2001] 2 AC 241, p 867.

[134] See s 9(1)(a), p 1048.

[135] The form of the offence in terms of going equipped to cheat was abolished by the Fraud Act 2006.

[136] See generally JK Bentil (1979) 143 JP 47; Williams, TBCL, 853–7; Griew, *Theft*, Ch 16; Smith, *Property Offences*, para 31.1.

[137] References to deception under s 15 of the Act were repealed by the Fraud Act 2006.

[138] By s 25(5), 'theft' in this section includes an offence under s 12(1).

[139] Like its predecessor, s 28 of the Larceny Act 1916.

[140] [1994] Crim LR 602, and commentary.

[141] *M* [2004] UKHL 50; cf R Munday, 'Bad Character Rules and Riddles: "Explanatory Notes" and True Meanings of s 103(1) of the Criminal Justice Act 2003' [2005] Crim LR 337.

[142] As the long title showed that 'carrying' was the essence of the offence under the Prevention of Crime Act 1953, Ch 34.

D must have with him 'any article'; the article need not be made or adapted for use in committing one of the specified offences. It is sufficient that D intended to use it in the course of, or in connection with, one of the specified offences. The article may therefore be as innocuous as a tin of treacle (intended for use in removing a pane of glass), a diving suit (to allow D to steal balls from a lake on a golf course),[143] a pair of gloves (to be worn to avoid leaving fingerprints) or a charity collecting tin (which D is not authorized to use).[144] It was implicit in numerous decisions that the offence of going equipped to cheat caught such conduct as possession of a sliced loaf and a bag of tomatoes[145] or bottles of wine[146] which D intended to pass off as the property of his employer and sell to customers.[147]

D can hardly be committing an offence by wearing his shoes or any other item of everyday clothing, yet it was argued above that possession of gloves for the avoidance of leaving fingerprints would amount to this offence.[148] This suggests that one way of restricting the scope of the offence is to limit it to articles D would not be carrying with him 'but for' the contemplated offence. So there might be a difference between a pair of latex gloves and a pair of woollen gloves that D was wearing to keep his hands warm on a freezing night, even though he did intend to keep them on so as to avoid leaving fingerprints. The latter pair of gloves is hardly distinguishable, for this purpose, from D's overcoat, which seems to fall into the same category as his shoes. Arguably, this 'but for' analysis is too simplistic. What of D who picks up his gloves with a view to avoiding leaving fingerprints at a burglary that he is about to commit, but on opening his front door sees that it is snowing and would ordinarily have picked up his gloves on seeing snow outside? There is no difference between wearing the woolly gloves, for a dual purpose, and wearing latex gloves, for a sole purpose. In both cases, D wears the gloves in order to avoid detection.

The offence is extremely wide, and in some instances the actus reus might be regarded as negligible. The emphasis is on the proof of mens rea; for that reason, care must be taken to avoid overly broad application.

The expression 'has with him'[149] is the same as that found in s 10(1)(b) of the Act as discussed earlier. Questions as to D's knowledge of the nature of the thing can hardly arise here, since it must be proved that he intended to use it in the course of, or (more broadly) in connection with, one of the specified offences. If a number of defendants are charged jointly with going equipped it must be proved that all the members of the enterprise knew of the existence of the articles and had the common purpose to use those articles in the specified offence.[150]

No doubt D has an article with him if it is in his immediate possession or control; he will be guilty if the article is only a short distance away and he can take it up as he needs it, as where a ladder has been left in a garden by an accomplice and D enters the garden intending to use the ladder to make an entry to the house. If the article is found in D's car some distance from the scene of the crime this will be evidence that D was in possession of the article when driving the car. The tenor of decisions on the interpretation of 'has with him' indicates that mere momentary possession will not suffice,[151] as where D is apprehended on picking up a stone which he intends to use to break a window in order to commit burglary. But, in *Minor v DPP*,[152] it seems to have been decided that D may be convicted of going equipped (in this case,

---

[143] *Rostron* [2003] EWCA Crim 2206.   [144] *Armson* [2005] EWCA Crim 2528.

[145] *Rashid* (1977) 64 Cr App R 201; cf *Cooke* [1986] AC 909, applied in relation to s 25 in *Whiteside* [1989] Crim LR 436.

[146] *Doukas* [1978] 1 WLR 372.

[147] This series of cases place unwarranted emphasis on the question of whether the intended victim would be deceived, when the true issue is, it is submitted, whether D intends to obtain property by deception. See Ormerod and Williams, *Smith's Law of Theft*, para 3.96; Griew, *Theft*, paras 16.11–16.13.

[148] cf *Ellames* [1974] 3 All ER 130; p 1068, where gloves were included in the charge.

[149] See Ch 34.   [150] *Reader, Connor and Hart* (1998) 7 Apr, CA.   [151] See Ch 34.

[152] (1987) 152 JP 30.

to steal petrol from cars) though he did not take the equipment (petrol cans and a hose) with him but somehow came across it while he was removing the cap from the petrol tank of a car. It appears to have been regarded as enough that the theft 'was to be posterior to the acquisition of the articles'. On this view, the burglar who picks up a nearby stone to break a window to gain entry would commit the offence of going equipped; it is respectfully submitted that 'has with him' requires more than that the acquisition of the article should precede the theft.

'Place of abode' is a term that suggests a place, that is a site, where D lives.[153] Clearly, this offence is not committed when D has articles for housebreaking, etc, in his own home,[154] but place of abode is apt to cover the whole of the premises where D lives so that D does not commit the offence by having the articles in his garage or even in his car while that is on his premises. Once D steps into the street with the articles, or drives off with them in his car, the offence may be committed. The ambit of the exemption is presumably based on a respect for D's privacy. Though a car or a caravan may constitute a place of abode while stationary at some site, they can never constitute a *place* of abode while D is in transit; if he then has the articles with him, he may commit the offence.[155]

25.5.2 Mens rea

The mens rea for the offence would appear to consist in D's:

(1) knowledge that he possesses the article; and

(2) intention to use the article in the course of or in connection with any of the specified crimes.

It was held in *Ellames*[156] that the 'intent to use' must necessarily relate to use in the future so that D was not guilty of this offence where the evidence showed only that he was in possession of certain articles (masks, guns, gloves, etc) after a robbery and was trying to get rid of them. Given an intent to use the article in the future, the expression 'in the course of or in connection with' any burglary, theft is wide enough to cover not only articles intended for use in the perpetration of the crime, but also articles intended for use before or after its commission.[157]A car intended for use to make an escape after the commission of a robbery falls within the offence. But the article must be intended for some direct use in connection with the crime; it has been held that D's possession of a stolen driving licence so that he could obtain a job which would give him an opportunity to steal is not within the offence.[158]

In *Ellames*,[159] it was said that D could commit the offence where he possessed the articles for future use by another, so that D would have been guilty in that case had he been hiding away the guns, etc, for their future use by others. The court also thought that it was not necessary to show that D intended the article to be used in connection with a particular theft; the section requires only intended use in connection with *any* burglary or theft. No doubt a conditional intent (eg possessing a jemmy to use if necessary) suffices, but D must have made up his mind, even if only contingently, to use the article. If D had not so determined he does not commit the offence.[160] Section 25(3)[161] provides:

---

[153] *Bundy* [1977] 2 All ER 382; *Kelt* [1977] 3 All ER 1099, [1977] Crim LR 556 and commentary.
[154] It may be an offence under the Fraud Act 2006, s 6.   [155] *Bundy* [1977] 2 All ER 382.
[156] [1974] 3 All ER 130.
[157] In the context of the similar offence of possession of articles for fraud, the Court of Appeal has confirmed that possession of articles to cover up a fraud will be caught: *Smith* [2020] EWCA Crim 38.
[158] *Mansfield* [1975] Crim LR 101.   [159] [1974] 1 WLR 1391.
[160] So in *Hargreaves* [1985] Crim LR 243, the jury were misdirected when told they could convict if satisfied that D might have used the article.
[161] As amended by the Fraud Act 2006, Sch 1, para 8.

Where a person is charged with an offence under this section, proof that he had with him any article made or adapted for use in committing a burglary or theft . . . shall be evidence that he had it with him for such use.

This is probably no more than enactment of the general rules regarding proof of intent.[162] It puts upon D an evidential burden. If he offers no explanation then the jury may be told that there is evidence upon which they may find that he had the necessary intent, but they must be satisfied so they are sure that he in fact had that intent.[163] If D does offer an explanation then the jury should be told to acquit if they think it may reasonably be true, and to convict only if satisfied so that they are sure that the explanation is untrue. The provision does not reverse the burden of proof and poses no difficulty under Art 6(2) of the ECHR.[164]

Where the article in question is not made or adapted for use in any specified offence, mere proof of possession without more will not amount to prima facie evidence—that is, the case will have to be withdrawn from the jury.[165] It is a question of law for the judge at what point proof of other incriminating circumstances amounts to a case fit for submission to the jury.

The Fraud Act 2006 introduced offences of possession of articles for use in fraud (s 6) and making, adapting, supplying or offering to supply articles for fraud (s 7).[166] The Law Commission made provisional proposals for a wider general offence of possession of an article away from one's home with intent to use it in a specified offence.[167]

25.6 Other trespass offences

English law criminalizes numerous other types of trespass.[168] These include trespassing on various types of property (railways,[169] aerodromes,[170] etc) and areas protected for their significance in national security.[171] In addition, there are offences of trespass with weapons.[172] Further, there are old offences of being found in specified places for unlawful purposes, for example 'being found in or upon any dwelling house, warehouse, coach house, stable or outhouse, or in any enclosed yard garden or area for any unlawful purpose'.[173]

Further reading

E Griew, *The Theft Acts 1968 and 1978*

ATH Smith, *Property Offences: The Protection of Property Through the Criminal Law*

---

[162] cf Criminal Justice Act 1967, s 8; p 95.

[163] cf the case where the alleged receiver is proved to have been in possession of recently stolen property and offers no explanation: *Abramovitch* (1914) 11 Cr App R 45.

[164] *Whiteside* [1989] Crim LR 436.

[165] cf *Harrison* [1970] Crim LR 415.   [166] See p 1013.

[167] See LCCP 183, *Conspiracy and Attempts* (2007) para 16.61(4). These were not taken forward by government.

[168] See generally P Thornton et al, *The Law of Public Order and Protest* (2010) Ch 5.

[169] British Transport Commission Act 1949, s 55. CPS Legal Guidance on Transport Offences sets out the offences dealing with railway trespass and includes s 55. The others are s 16 of the Railway Regulation Act 1840 and s 23 of the Regulation of the Railways Act 1868: www.cps.gov.uk/legal-guidance/transport-offences.

[170] Civil Aviation Act 1982, s 39.

[171] Official Secrets Act 1911. The Act does not use the word 'trespass' but s 1(1) makes it an offence to approach, inspect or pass over, or be in the neighbourhood of, or *enter* any 'prohibited place' (defined in s 3).

[172] Criminal Law Act 1977, s 8.

[173] Vagrancy Act 1824, s 4 and see *L v CPS* [2008] 1 Cr App R 8 and *Akhurst v DPP* [2009] EWHC 806 (Admin).

26

Handling and related offences

26.1 Handling stolen goods

By s 22 of the Theft Act 1968:[1]

(1) A person handles stolen goods if (otherwise than in the course of the stealing) knowing or believing them to be stolen goods he dishonestly receives the goods, or dishonestly undertakes or assists in their retention, removal, disposal or realisation by or for the benefit of another person, or if he arranges to do so.

(2) A person guilty of handling stolen goods shall on conviction on indictment be liable to imprisonment for a term not exceeding fourteen years.

English law has, since the nineteenth century, provided a specific offence of handling, treating this conduct as an independent crime rather than one of being a secondary party to theft.[2] The diversity of the activities it is sought to criminalize results in a broad and complex offence—Glanville Williams memorably described s 22 as a 'draftsman's omelette'.[3]

Note that the maximum sentence is twice that available for theft, reflecting Parliament's desire to deter the professional 'fence' so that the market for stolen goods will diminish and the incidence of theft will decrease.[4] The particular moral wrong involved lies in dealing in stolen goods—with the idea being that stolen goods 'are a form of contraband, like

---

[1] See generally Ormerod and Williams, *Smith's Law of Theft*, Ch 13; Griew, *Theft*, Ch 15; Smith, *Property Offences*, Ch 30; CLRC, Eighth Report (1966) paras 127–32. The law is cogently criticized by DW Elliott, 'Theft and Related Problems—England, Australia and the USA Compared' (1977) 26 ICLQ 110, 135–44.

[2] J Hall, *Theft, Law and Society* (2nd edn, 1952) 55–8; cf Hale, I PC, 618. G Fletcher, *Rethinking Criminal Law* (1978) 645–6, regards this as an illustration of the gradual replacement of the offence of being an accessory after the fact.

[3] Williams, TBCL, 858.

[4] *Shelton* (1986) 83 Cr App R 379; *Tokeley-Parry* [1999] Crim LR 578 (deterring removal of antiquities from Egypt). See also M Sutton, K Johnston and H Lockwood, *Handling Stolen Goods and Theft: A Market Reduction Approach* (1998); M Sutton, 'Supply by Theft: Does the Market for Second-Hand Goods Play a Role in Keeping Crime Figures High?' (1995) 35 Brit J Crim 400; JL Schneider, 'Stolen Goods Markets' (2005) 45 Brit J Crim 129.

drugs or counterfeit currency, which law-abiding persons should not, knowingly, acquire'.[5] It has been argued that the offence is aimed at two distinct yet complementary aspects of the handler's conduct.[6] Green terms these backward-looking and forward-looking. The former focuses upon the fact that the handler perpetuates the wrongful interference with the victim's property rights, while the latter's focus is upon the handler's encouragement of the commission of future thefts. It is argued that the law as it is currently formulated focuses only upon the backward-looking basis, as the handler can be guilty in the absence of evidence that the thief will commit theft again. Green's thesis is that to perpetuate an owner's loss of property is less culpable than to cause that loss in the first place, so the handler ought to be punished *less* severely than the thief. Given that in English law the sentence for handling is twice that for theft, Green argues that handling is overcriminalized.

In practical terms, the substantial differences between the sentencing of large-scale professional handlers and, for example, those receiving low-value stolen goods for personal use[7] prompts suggestions that the offence ought to be subdivided to reflect more accurately the criminality involved.[8]

There are similar offences contained in other statutes. For example, s 17(1) of the Cultural Property (Armed Conflicts) Act 2017 adds an offence of dealing in 'unlawfully exported cultural property' (as defined in s 16 of that Act), knowing or having reason to suspect that it has been unlawfully exported. It does not extend to property imported into the UK before commencement.

26.1.1 Actus reus

The actus reus is drafted in extremely broad terms, creating an offence that can be committed in many different ways.[9] It is obvious from s 22 that there is no requirement that the handler ever comes into physical possession of the stolen goods, and that the concept of stolen goods itself carries an extended meaning.

The questions that require detailed consideration are: what are 'goods', when are they 'stolen' and what is 'handling'?

26.1.1.1 Stolen goods

By s 34(2)(b), '"goods", except in so far as the context otherwise requires, includes money and every other description of property except land, and includes things severed from the land by stealing'. This definition differs from that of 'property' for the purposes of theft. Clearly, it is such a wide definition that problems will rarely arise other than in relation to land and choses in action which we discuss in more detail.

Land

Since land generally is excluded from theft by s 4(2), the effect is that, subject to the small exceptions discussed below, property which can be stolen can be the subject of a handling charge.

---

[5] A Simester and GR Sullivan, 'The Nature and Rationale of Property Offences' in Duff and Green, *Defining Crimes*, 190. It is this same philosophy that lies behind the far-reaching and draconian offences in the Proceeds of Crime Act 2002, criminalizing dealing not just with stolen goods but the proceeds of criminal activity.

[6] Green, *13 Ways*, 180–94.

[7] Low monetary value goods received for a handler's own use will attract a modest fine or conditional discharge. For analysis of the activities of the professional handler, see CB Klockars, *The Professional Fence* (1975).

[8] See DA Thomas, 'Form and Function in Criminal Law' in Glazebrook, *Reshaping the Criminal Law*, 23–4.

[9] *Nicklin* [1977] 1 WLR 403.

A 'thing', attached to or forming part of the land, can be stolen (s 4(2)(b)[10]) and can therefore always be the subject of handling since the stealing necessarily involves severance of the thing in question. Under s 4(2)(c), on the other hand, a fixture or structure can be stolen whether severed from the land or not. Only if it is severed can it be the subject of handling. So, if E, an outgoing tenant, dishonestly sells to D, the incoming tenant, a fixture which actually belongs to V, the landlord, D cannot be guilty of handling if the fixture is not severed.[11] If after D's tenancy the incoming tenant is F who knows all of the facts about how D came to have the fixture, F is not guilty of handling even though F has knowingly taken possession of a stolen fixture.

Land which is stolen contrary to s 4(2)(a) (by trustees or personal representatives) will rarely be capable of being handled since the kind of conduct contemplated by s 4(2)(a) will not normally involve severance.

Land may be the subject of both fraud and blackmail, both of which create 'stolen' goods for the purposes of handling.[12] Again, severance of the land may or may not take place and handling is possible only if it does so.

Things in action

Things in action (an item of property comprising a right to sue another) are expressly mentioned in s 4(1) of the 1968 Act as capable of being the subject of theft but are not mentioned in s 34(2)(b). They must, however, be included in the all-encompassing words 'every other description of property except land' within that section. Things in action may then constitute stolen goods, but a further question is whether they can be handled. Some forms of the actus reus in s 22—for example, 'realisation' and 'disposal'—would, on a natural interpretation, extend to D's dealings with things in action. This is uncontroversial. Whether things in action can be the subject of a charge of 'receiving' is less clear. Prior to the Theft Act, the law referred to taking control of a physical thing and would not be apt to apply to things in action. But there would seem to be no good reason for fettering the interpretation of s 22 in this way. If 'receiving' is given its ordinary meaning there is no reason why D cannot receive a thing in action. So, if D opens a bank account into which he pays stolen money and subsequently assigns the balance in that bank account to E, on a natural use of the language E 'receives' that balance.[13] The Court of Appeal took this broad view in *A-G's Reference (No 4 of 1979)*[14] concluding:

it is clear that a balance in a bank account, being a debt, is itself a thing in action which falls within the definition of goods and may therefore be goods which directly or indirectly represent stolen goods for the purposes of s 24(2)(a).

In *Forsyth*,[15] the court had no doubt that there could be an offence of handling of a thing in action. It is submitted that this view makes good sense.

[10] See p 884.   [11] This is true whether or not his act is in the course of stealing.
[12] See p 1073.
[13] This forestalls any argument that because only some forms of the conduct (realization, disposal, etc) specified in s 22 (but not receiving) are applicable to things in action, they can never be handled.
[14] [1981] 1 All ER 1193 at 1198, [1981] Crim LR 51 and commentary. But see *Preddy* [1996] AC 815 and discussion at p 894. If part of the balance in the thief's account is transferred to the credit of the receiver's, it cannot 'represent the goods originally stolen with s 24(2)(a)' because, following *Preddy*, a new thing in action is created which belongs to the receiver and has never been in the hands of a thief or handler and so is not stolen. Section 24A must be relied on in such cases.
[15] [1997] 2 Cr App R 299, p 1078. The conviction was quashed on other grounds.

Meaning of 'stolen'

By s 24(4):

For purposes of the provisions of this Act relating to goods which have been stolen (including sub-sections (1) to (3) above) goods obtained in England or Wales or elsewhere either by blackmail or [, subject to subsection (5) below by fraud (within the meaning of the Fraud Act 2006)][16] shall be regarded as stolen; and 'steal', 'theft' and 'thief' shall be construed accordingly.[17]

By s 24A(8):

References to stolen goods include money which is withdrawn from an account to which a wrongful credit[18] has been made, but only to the extent that the money derives from the credit.

And by s 24(1):

The provisions of this Act relating to goods which have been stolen shall apply whether the stealing occurred in England or Wales or elsewhere, and whether it occurred before or after the commencement of this Act, provided that the stealing (if not an offence under this Act) amounted to an offence where and at the time when the goods were stolen; and references to stolen goods shall be construed accordingly.

The effect of these provisions is that goods are 'stolen' for the purposes of the Act if they:

(1) have been stolen contrary to s 1;[19]

(2) have been obtained by blackmail contrary to s 21;

(3) have been obtained by fraud contrary to s 1 of the Fraud Act 2006;

(4) consist of money dishonestly withdrawn from a wrongful bank credit; or

(5) have been the subject of an act done in a foreign country which was:

(a) a crime by the law of that country, and which

(b) had it been done in England, would have been theft, blackmail or fraud contrary to s 1 or s 21 of the Theft Act 1968 or s 1 of the Fraud Act 2006.[20] The jurisdictional scope means that if T steals property in, for example, Greece by performing an act that is theft under Greek law and would be theft if performed in England, and D, in England, handles that property with mens rea, D can be convicted of handling under s 22.[21]

If the information or indictment specifies that the goods were stolen from a specific entity (person or corporation), the prosecution are obliged to prove that issue, if the ownership by the entity is integral to the case.[22]

---

[16] Words substituted by the Fraud Act 2006, Sch 1, para 6, in force from 15 Jan 2007.

[17] By s 24(5): 'Subsection (1) above applies in relation to goods obtained by fraud as if—(a) the reference to the commencement of this Act were a reference to the commencement of the Fraud Act 2006, and (b) the reference to an offence under this Act were a reference to an offence under section 1 of that Act.'

[18] See s 24A (dishonestly retaining a wrongful credit), p 1092.

[19] This will include goods obtained by offences of robbery and burglary which involve theft. See eg *Pitham and Hehl* (1976) 65 Cr App R 45.

[20] Handling is a Group A offence for the purposes of the Criminal Justice Act 1993. See generally M Hirst, *Jurisdiction and the Ambit of the Criminal Law* (2003) 180 et seq.

[21] The question whether D commits theft in England if he performs acts in, eg, Greece amounting to theft under Greek law and transports the goods to England, is considered at p 872; *Atakpu* [1994] QB 69; and GR Sullivan and C Warbrick, 'Territoriality, Theft and *Atakpu*' [1994] Crim LR 650. D who commits theft abroad and returns to England with the criminal property might commit a money laundering offence contrary to s 329 of the Proceeds of Crime Act 2002, see Ch 33.

[22] *Iqbal v DPP* (2004) All ER (D) 314 (Oct).

The 'thief' must be guilty

Though s 22 does not say so expressly, the goods must have been stolen in fact.[23] To take a simple example, magistrates had erred when they concluded that a credit card was stolen when it was found in D's house three weeks after its owner had realized it was missing. D could, as he had claimed, have found it in the street but forgotten to hand it in to the police. There was insufficient evidence that the card had been stolen at the time it came into D's possession.[24]

It is not sufficient for the prosecution to prove that D believed the goods to be 'stolen' if they were not. If, because of a mistake of fact (or of civil law) D wrongly believed the goods to be stolen, he might be guilty of theft or an attempt to handle under the Criminal Attempts Act 1981. If D says he knew the goods were stolen because T told him so, this is evidence of D's mens rea but it is not evidence that the goods were stolen in fact.[25] D's admission is based on hearsay[26] and is of no more value than the hearsay itself. It is a misdirection to tell the jury that they are entitled to take such an admission into account, except as evidence of mens rea.[27] In contrast, D's admission of facts that he himself perceived (by, eg, seeing T steal the goods) is evidence of those facts from which a jury could infer that the goods were stolen. In a more likely scenario, D's admission that he bought goods in a pub at a ridiculously low price *is* prima facie evidence that those goods were stolen; similarly, where a television is bought in a betting shop or where a publican buys cases of whisky from an HGV driver.[28] The conduct of a person, T, who offers a bag of jewellery to a stranger, D, for £2,000 and then accepts £100 for it, suggests strongly, as a matter of common sense, that the jewellery is stolen.[29]

If the alleged thief, T, is not guilty, the handler, D, cannot be convicted for there are no stolen goods for him to handle. So, for example, if the alleged thief turns out to have been under the age of ten at the time of the alleged theft, then the goods appropriated cannot be stolen goods and there can be no conviction for handling them.[30] If D believed the 'thief' was ten or above, he might be convicted of an attempt to handle.[31] Whatever his belief as to the 'thief's' age, the more appropriate charge would be theft of the goods. In considering the liability of the handler and the question of whether there has been a theft, the courts have not drawn any distinctions between types of defences or cases in which the alleged thief is acquitted on the basis of a justification—for example, necessity—or an excuse—for example, duress.

If the appropriator of the goods is guilty of theft (or the fraudster or blackmailer guilty of those offences), it is submitted that the goods acquired may be the subject of handling although the appropriator is immune from prosecution by reason, for example, of diplomatic immunity.[32]

---

[23] *Haughton v Smith* [1973] 3 All ER 1109 at 1112, 1119 and 1124.

[24] *Defazio v DPP* [2007] All ER (D) 262 (Jul).

[25] *Porter* [1976] Crim LR 58; *Marshall* [1977] Crim LR 106; *Lang v Evans (Inspector of Police)* [1977] Crim LR 286; *Hack* [1978] Crim LR 359; *Overington* [1978] Crim LR 692.

[26] An out-of-court assertion relied on for the truth of its content; see now the impenetrable Criminal Justice Act 2003, s 115. See *Riat* [2012] EWCA Crim 1509. Under the Criminal Justice Act 2003, such conduct will only be hearsay if (one of) T's purpose(s) was to cause D to believe that fact or to act upon the truth of the statement that the goods were stolen.

[27] *Hulbert* (1979) 69 Cr App R 243.

[28] An example put by Lawton LJ in *McDonald* (1980) 70 Cr App R 288. See also *Barnes* [1991] Crim LR 132.

[29] *Korniak* (1983) 76 Cr App R 145.

[30] *Walters v Lunt* [1951] 2 All ER 645 therefore remains good law.

[31] See *Toye* [1984] Crim LR 555.

[32] cf *Dickinson v Del Solar* [1930] 1 KB 376; *AB* [1941] 1 KB 454; *Madan* (1961) 45 Cr App R 80.

It must be proved, as against an alleged handler, that another person was guilty of steal-ing the goods. If the thief, T, and handler, D, are tried together, the verdict acquitting T is not necessarily inconsistent with one convicting D; evidence admissible against D may have been inadmissible against T. In separate trials, the fact that T has been acquitted of stealing the goods is no bar to the prosecution of the handler and is, indeed, inadmissible in evi-dence. But the fact that T has been convicted of stealing the goods is admissible at D's trial for handling and, when it is admitted, T must be taken to have committed the theft unless the contrary is proved.[33] Under this evidential provision, if D claims that T did not steal the goods—ie that T was wrongly convicted—it is for D to prove it on a balance of probabilities.

26.1.1.2 When goods cease to be stolen

It is obvious that goods that have once been stolen cannot continue to be regarded as 'stolen' so long as they continue to exist thereafter. A line must be drawn somewhere, and the Act draws it in the same place as the common law did. By s 24(3) of the Act:

But no goods shall be regarded as having continued to be stolen goods after they have been restored to the person from whom they were stolen or to other lawful possession or custody, or after that person and any other person claiming through him have otherwise ceased as regards those goods to have any right to restitution in respect of the theft.

Consider a case where T steals goods, but the stolen goods are taken back by the owner or someone acting on his behalf, or by the police,[34] but then in a police sting operation returned to the thief so that he may hand them over to D. That person, D, will not be guilty of handling because the goods he receives are no longer stolen goods.[35] A charge of attempted handling is available, and it may also be theft. D might also be convicted of handling if his acts of 'arranging' occurred after the theft but before the goods had been 'restored'.

Difficult questions arise over whether goods have in fact been 'restored to the person from whom they were stolen or to other lawful possession or custody'. It cannot be enough to constitute restoration that V (the owner or his agent) knows that T has stolen the goods and follows T to his destination so that the handler can be caught red-handed;[36] nor that V marks the goods after the theft so that they can be identified in the hands of the handler.[37] A more difficult case in this context is *King*.[38] A parcel containing a stolen fur coat was handed by T, the thief, to a policeman who was in the act of examining the parcel when the telephone rang. The caller was D, the proposed receiver. The policeman stopped his examination, and D was told to come along as arranged. He did so, and received the coat. It was held that D was guilty of receiving stolen goods because the coat had not been reduced into the possession of the police—though it was admitted that in a few minutes it would have been, had the telephone not rung. The case has, however, been criticized. It is easy to accept that if the police are examining a parcel to see whether it contains stolen goods, they do not take possession of the contents until they decide that this is what they are looking for.[39] In *King*, however, T had admitted to the policeman the theft of the coat and produced

---

[33] See s 74 of PACE 1984, *O'Connor* (1986) 85 Cr App R 298 at 302, and R Munday, *Cross and Tapper on Evidence* (13th edn, 2018) 117.

[34] *A-G's Reference (No 1 of 1974)* [1974] QB 744.

[35] cf *Dolan* (1855) Dears CC 436; *Schmidt* (1866) LR 1 CCR 15; *Villensky* [1892] 2 QB 597.

[36] In *Haughton v Smith* [1975] AC 476, the police accompanied the driver of a van containing stolen goods to its destination to trap the handler. Lords Hailsham and Dilhorne questioned whether the prosecution was right to concede that the goods had been 'restored' to lawful custody.

[37] *Greater London Metropolitan Police Comr v Streeter* (1980) 71 Cr App R 113.

[38] [1938] 2 All ER 662.   [39] cf *Warner v Metropolitan Police Comr* [1969] 2 AC 256.

the parcel. One might have expected, therefore, that the policeman had made up his mind to take charge of it before the telephone rang. The court presumably made the decision on the assumption that the police officer had not done so. On that assumption the decision would now be the same under the Theft Act.[40]

This view is supported by the decision in *A-G's Reference (No 1 of 1974)*[41] that whether the police officer has taken possession depends primarily on his intentions. In that case an officer, correctly suspecting that goods in the back of a car were stolen, immobilized the car and kept watch until T returned to it. He questioned T and in view of T's unsatisfactory response arrested him. It was held that the jury ought to have been directed to consider whether the officer had decided, before T's appearance, to take possession of the goods or whether he was of an entirely open mind, intending to decide after he had questioned T. Possession[42] requires both an intention to possess and some act of possession. To immobilize a car does not necessarily involve an intention to possess the car or its contents but, along with other circumstances, it may be evidence of such an intention. The approach adopted by the courts is hardly conducive to certainty and consistency in the law in deciding whether goods cease to be stolen.

It is clear that the goods cease to be stolen in the case where the police take control acting without the authority of the owner, for they are clearly in 'other lawful possession or custody of the goods'. Indeed, it would seem to be enough that the goods fall into the possession of *any* person provided that person intends to restore them to the person from whom they were stolen.

Section 24(3) also provides that the goods lose their character of being 'stolen goods' if the person from whom they were stolen has ceased to have any *right to restitution* in respect of them. Whether a 'right to restitution' exists is a complex question of civil law. A person whose goods have been wrongfully converted (under the Torts (Interference with Goods) Act 1977) does not have a *right* to have those goods restored to him. He has a right to damages to compensate him for the conversion, but it is in the discretion of the court whether to order the goods to be delivered to him.[43] Section 24(3) is not intended to be limited to only those cases in which a court would exercise its discretion to order the goods to be returned to V. In the criminal proceedings, it would be impossible to identify such cases and it is submitted that the subsection is applicable to all cases in which V *could* succeed in a civil action based on his proprietary interest in the thing, whether in conversion or for the protection of an equitable interest.[44]

As drafted, the provision seems to have been intended to bear a still wider meaning. The CLRC explained it as follows:[45]

if the person who owned the goods when they were stolen no longer has any title to them, there will be no reason why the goods should continue to have the taint of being stolen goods. For example, the offence of handling stolen goods will . . . apply also to goods obtained by criminal deception

---

[40] In *A-G's Reference (No 1 of 1974)* [1974] 2 All ER 899 at 904, Lord Widgery CJ said that *King* 'might be thought to be a rather bold decision'.

[41] ibid.

[42] For the purposes of s 24(3), possession *or control* suffices. Arguably in both the above cases the police officer had at least control of the goods but control, like possession, must involve an intention to take charge.

[43] Torts (Interference with Goods) Act 1977, s 3. See generally J Goudkamp and D Nolan, *Winfield and Jolowicz on Tort* (20th edn, 2020).

[44] In view of the recent expansion of the opportunities to claim for restitution or unjust enrichment, this might be enlarged, particularly in cases where there has been a transfer of property under a mistake. See Ch 18, p 898.

[45] Eighth Report, para 139.

under [s 15[46]]. If the owner of the goods who has been deceived chooses on discovering the deception to ratify his disposal of the goods he will cease to have any title to them.

It is clear that 'title' is here used in a broad sense to include a right to rescind. The Committee clearly had in mind a case where property passes from V to D at the moment when the goods are obtained by fraud. In such a case, V, strictly, has no 'title' and his right to recover the goods (or much more likely, their value) will only arise on his rescinding the contract.[47] Such a potential right is, it is submitted, clearly a 'right to restitution' within the Act.

26.1.1.3 Goods representing those originally stolen may be stolen goods
By s 24(2) of the Act:

For the purposes of those provisions references to stolen goods shall include, in addition to the goods originally stolen and parts of them (whether in their original state or not),—

(a) any other goods which directly or indirectly represent or have at any time represented the stolen goods in the hands of the thief as being the proceeds of any disposal or realisation of the whole or part of the goods stolen or of goods so representing the stolen goods; and

(b) any other goods which directly or indirectly represent or have at any time represented the stolen goods in the hands of a handler of the stolen goods or any part of them as being the proceeds of any disposal or realisation of the whole or part of the stolen goods handled by him or of goods so representing them.

The CLRC[48] accepted that this provision:

may seem technical; but the effect will be that the goods which the accused is charged with handling must, at the time of the handling or at some previous time, (i) have been in the hands of the thief or of a handler, and (ii) have represented the original stolen goods in the sense of being the proceeds, direct or indirect, of a sale or other realisation of the original goods.

The effect is best explained by an example. Suppose D steals an Audi car from V and subsequently that car passes, by way of sale, exchange or otherwise, through the hands of E, F and G. The Audi remains stolen until such time as it ceases to be stolen by virtue of s 24(3) (ie until the Audi is restored to the owner or other lawful custody or until the owner ceases to have a right to restitution in respect of it). It follows that until such time any person acquiring the Audi may be convicted of handling it, if he acquires it knowing or believing it to be stolen. It is not necessary for every person in the chain to have been a handler for the Audi to remain stolen. So, where F acquires the stolen car but F did not know or believe it to be stolen, F is not a handler. F acquired it innocently. But, if G acquires it from F and G knows or believes it to be stolen, G is a handler even though F was not.

The position with regard to the *proceeds* of stolen goods rather than the goods themselves is different. Assume that D steals the Audi from V and D then swaps the stolen Audi with E for a BMW. The BMW is now notionally stolen for the purposes of the offence because it directly represents the proceeds of the stolen Audi *in the hands of the thief*, D. Assume that E was aware that the Audi was stolen. E is a handler. If E exchanges the Audi with F for a Citroën. The Citroën is now notionally stolen because it represents the proceeds of the stolen Audi *in the hands of the handler*, E. Assume, then, that D sells the BMW to H who buys in good faith for £5,000. The BMW now ceases to be stolen goods as V has no right to restitution and (unlike with actual stolen goods in the example of the Audi with G and F above) once *notionally* stolen goods cease to be stolen goods; they cannot revert to being notionally stolen because they are subsequently acquired by someone who is aware of their provenance.

---

[46] Now repealed.   [47] cf Ch 22, p 994.   [48] Eighth Report, 66.

The £5,000 now in D's hands, however, *is* notionally stolen because it indirectly represents the proceeds of the stolen Audi *in the hands of the thief* (as D was the original thief). A recipient of all or part of that £5,000 would, if aware of its provenance, be guilty of handling. The position may be a little more complex where D banks the £5,000. If the £5,000 represents all that D has in the account, money which D draws from the account is stolen goods and a receiver of it, having the requisite knowledge, would be guilty of handling. Where, however, D has other innocently acquired money in his account, say a further £5,000, it may be difficult to prove that a cheque made out by D for £2,000 that is cashed by E represents the proceeds of the stolen £5,000. It is not enough to establish that the recipient believed that the cheque for £2,000 represented proceeds of the stolen £5,000—that it represented his share of the ill-gotten £5,000.[49] This will establish the recipient's mens rea, which would be enough to convict him of an attempt but, to establish the full offence, it must additionally be proved that D intended the £2,000 to represent the proceeds of the stolen money.

In the difficult case of *Forsyth*,[50] T stole funds in a company's bank account and transferred them to a series of other banks in which T had accounts. It was held that 'in the hands of' means 'in the possession or control of' and therefore that the new credit balances remained under T's control. This renders the handling offence even wider. The balances were new property, distinct from that stolen,[51] but they 'represented' that stolen money and, 'being in the hands of' the thief, were accordingly stolen goods. More difficult to follow is the court's assumption that the actual banknotes withdrawn, on T's instructions, by D from one of the accounts were also stolen, so that D was guilty of handling them when she took physical possession of them. The notes belonged exclusively to the bank and had never been in the hands of a thief or handler until D received them and therefore could not have been stolen goods under s 24(2). If A pays stolen money into a bank account and, in payment of a debt he owes to B, gives B a cheque drawn on that account, B, if he cashes the cheque, does not receive stolen money. The actual cash in the form of pound coins in the hands of the bank is not stolen goods. B is not the thief, nor is he receiving stolen goods. He is not guilty of handling. Nor is it permissible to argue that B is a handler and therefore that the goods are stolen because they are in his hands. That is a circular argument.

In that example, however, B is acting on his own behalf. In *Forsyth*, D was acting as an agent for T, the original thief. For the reason given above, D (it is submitted) was not *receiving* stolen goods. But because D, unlike B in the example, was acting as agent for the thief, the cash, though physically in D's hands, was in law 'in the hands of' T—that is, it 'indirectly represented the stolen goods in the hands of the thief' (s 24(2)(a))—and was therefore stolen goods. D was not a receiver of stolen goods—the cash became stolen only when she received it. She then had stolen goods in her hands. That is not an offence; but she then went on to assist in the retention, etc, of the stolen goods for the benefit of T; and that is the offence of handling.

26.1.1.4 Forms of handling

Section 22 of the 1968 Act creates a broad offence[52] capable of being committed in any one of several (as many as 18) ways. These are:

(1) *Receiving* the goods.

(2) *Undertaking* the retention, removal, disposal or realization of the goods by or for the benefit of another person.

---

[49] *A-G's Reference (No 4 of 1979)* [1981] 1 WLR 667.

[50] [1997] 2 Cr App R 299, [1997] Crim LR 589 and additional commentary.

[51] *Preddy* [1996] AC 815.

[52] Under the old law in s 33(1) of the Larceny Act 1916, the only way of committing the offence was by 'receiving' the stolen goods.

(3) *Assisting* in the retention, removal, disposal or realization of the goods by or for the benefit of another person.

(4) *Arranging* to do (1), (2), (3).

Although in the leading case of *Bloxham*[53] Lord Bridge said, 'It is, I think, well settled that this subsection creates two distinct offences but no more than two', this must be wrong. It is generally accepted that s 22 creates only one offence[54] which may be committed in a variety of ways. What was well settled before *Bloxham* (and remains so) was that where the evidence justified it, the proper practice was to have one charge for receiving (or perhaps arranging to receive) and a second charge for all the other forms of handling.[55] In law, however, the subsection creates only one offence.[56]

If D is charged specifically with receiving only, he may not be convicted on that indictment of some other form of handling;[57] and vice versa. Since receiving is 'a single finite act', each receipt of stolen goods is a separate offence. Therefore, a single count for receiving a whole quantity of goods found in D's possession may be defective because it alleges more than one offence in the single charge (it is 'bad for duplicity') if the receipt of various portions of that whole took place on more than one occasion.[58]

Receiving

All forms of handling other than receiving or arranging to receive are subject to the qualification that it must be proved that D was acting 'for the benefit of another person'. If, as will frequently be the case, there is no evidence of this then it must be proved that D received or arranged to receive the goods and evidence of no other form of handling will suffice.[59]

So, to establish receiving, it must be proved that either:

(1) D took possession or joined with others to share possession (whether actual or constructive), intending to possess the goods; or

(2) D took control of the stolen property or joined with others to share control of it with intent to do so.

'Receiving' the thief by welcoming him as a person who has the goods in his possession does not necessarily amount to receiving the goods. If the thief, T, retains exclusive control, there is no receiving by D.[60] There may, however, be a joint possession by the thief and receiver, so it is unnecessary to prove that the thief ever parted with possession—it is sufficient that he shared it with the alleged receiver.

The question is what joint possession means in these circumstances. In *Smith*,[61] it was held that a jury had been correctly directed that they could convict D of handling if they believed that the stolen watch was in the custody of the thief, that D was aware of that and

---

[53] [1983] 1 AC 109 on which see L Blake, 'The Erstwhile Innocent Purchaser of Stolen Goods' (1982) 46 J Crim L 220.

[54] *Griffiths v Freeman* [1970] 1 All ER 1117.

[55] *Willis and Syme* [1972] 3 All ER 797; *Deakin* [1972] 3 All ER 803.

[56] Thus in *Nicklin* [1977] 2 All ER 444, it was held that an indictment alleging unparticularized handling was not bad for duplicity as it charges only one offence. Particulars should be given so as to enable the accused to understand the ingredients of the charge he has to meet: *Sloggett* [1972] 1 QB 430. The maximum number of counts for a single instance of handling in the ordinary case is two: *Ikpong* [1972] Crim LR 432.

[57] *Nicklin*, n 56.

[58] *Smythe* (1980) 72 Cr App Rep 8. But note the flexibility offered by r 10(2) of the Criminal Procedure Rules 2020.

[59] The Theft Act does not further define receiving and it must be assumed that old authorities all remain valid.

[60] *Wiley* (1850) 2 Den 37.   [61] (1855) Dears CC 494. See also *Gleed* (1916) 12 Cr App R 32.

that D had absolute control over the thief to the extent that if D demanded it, the thief would hand it to him. Lord Campbell CJ said that if the thief had been employed by D to commit theft, so that the watch was in D's control, D was guilty of receiving. This situation is slightly odd because usually handling occurs because a previous theft has been committed. In this situation, however, there has been no *previous* theft so D may become a handler by some act done only *after* the theft. It is, of course, important to identify the point at which D receives the stolen goods since it is at that point that he must have the relevant mens rea.[62] D would be guilty of theft and receiving but, since virtually all handling is now theft, it is the general rule that the two offences are committed simultaneously.[63]

As is clear from *Smith*, it is not necessary to prove personal physical possession or control by D. It is enough if the goods are received by his agent with D's authority.[64] There are few other limits on what constitutes receiving: D might receive them for a merely temporary purpose such as concealment from the police;[65] and it is unnecessary that the receiver should receive any profit or advantage from the possession of the goods.[66] However, it is not enough that D took possession by 'finding' goods that were stolen; there must be a receipt *from* another.[67] If D took possession of goods from the thief without his consent, this appears to be capable of being both theft and handling, since it is clear that the two offences can be committed by one and the same act.[68]

In all cases of receiving, it continues to be essential for the judge to give a careful direction as to possession or control.[69] If the only evidence against D is that he ran away on being found by the police in a house where stolen property had been left, there would appear to be no case to leave to a jury. Likewise, where the evidence is consistent with the view that D went to premises where stolen goods were stored with the intention of assuming possession but had not actually done so,[70] or where the only evidence of receiving, for example, a stolen car is that D's fingerprint was found on the rear-view mirror.[71] The mere fact that the stolen goods were found on D's premises is not sufficient evidence to establish receiving. It must be shown that the goods had come either by invitation or arrangement with him or that he had exercised some control over them.[72] It has even been held that D is not necessarily in possession of a stolen safe simply because he assists others in trying to open it.[73]

Arranging to receive

Where it is impossible to prove an actual receipt by D, the evidence may nevertheless show that D has arranged to receive the goods. Where D has merely made preparations to receive and has not yet reached the stage of attempting to do so, the preparations may constitute a sufficient arrangement. The difficulties in a case like *King*[74] (the fur coat case discussed earlier) will be overcome if it appears that the arrangement to receive was concluded before there was a possibility of the goods ceasing to be stolen. Presumably it is enough if the

---

[62] *Brook* [1993] Crim LR 455.   [63] *Sainthouse* [1980] Crim LR 506.

[64] *Miller* (1854) 6 Cox CC 353. In several areas of law (eg drugs offences and fraud offences) the courts have been prepared to accept that D is in possession of an article if he can draw upon it from a common pool of articles shared with his associates. See *Montague* [2013] EWCA Crim 1781, [2014] Crim LR 327 and commentary.

[65] *Richardson* (1834) 6 C & P 335.   [66] *Davis* (1833) 6 C & P 177.

[67] *Haider* (1985) unreported, discussed in Griew, *Theft*, para 13.

[68] This was formerly only larceny (from the thief) and not receiving: *Wade* (1844) 1 Car & Kir 739.

[69] *Frost and Hale* (1964) 48 Cr App R 284.

[70] *Freedman* (1930) 22 Cr App R 133. But this might be sufficient evidence of an arrangement to receive.

[71] *Court* (1960) 44 Cr App R 242.

[72] *Cavendish* [1961] 2 All ER 856; *Lloyd* [1992] Crim LR 361.

[73] *Tomblin* [1964] Crim LR 780.

[74] See p 1075. And similarly the difficulties of *Haughton v Smith* [1975] AC 476, n 36.

proposed receipt is by an agent of D. The arrangement must be made after the theft, since D must know or believe the goods to be stolen when he makes the arrangement.[75]

It is difficult to envisage an arrangement that does not involve an agreement with another, although there is no such express requirement in the Act. Such an agreement will therefore almost always amount to a conspiracy to receive so the breadth of the crime created by this provision is less concerning than might appear. Clearly, an arrangement made by D with an innocent person is enough (provided D has the relevant mens rea), as is an arrangement that does not involve another party at all, if that can be envisaged.

This form of the offence is complete as soon as the proposed receipt is arranged. It is immaterial (except as to sentence) that D repents or does nothing in pursuance of the arrangement. In this respect, it is clear that the substantive offence of arranging to receive has developed as a form of inchoate offence, rather than a form of secondary participation.

Undertaking and assisting

Handling under the 1968 Act extends to acts of 'undertaking and assisting' in the retention, removal, disposal or realization of stolen goods. Before 1968, such conduct was not criminal at all, not even by way of an attempt. Section 22 created far-reaching and overlapping forms of the offence. 'Undertaking' presumably covers the case where D sets out to retain, etc the stolen goods, on his own initiative. It appears more apt to describe the activity of the seller of stolen goods rather than that of the buyer. 'Assisting' seems more apt to cover the case where D joins the thief or another handler in doing so.[76]

Retention

In *Pitchley*,[77] the court suggested that retention means 'keep possession of, not lose, continue to have'. It is a continuing activity. The obvious cases of retaining will be where D stores stolen goods for the thief. An example of assisting in retention would be where D's ten-year-old son, T, brings home a cycle which he has stolen: D assists in its retention if: (a) he agrees that T may keep the cycle in the house; or (b) he tells the police there is no cycle in the house; or (c) he gives T a tin of paint so that he may disguise it.

Merely to *use* goods knowing them to be stolen does not in itself amount to assisting in their retention. D did not commit the offence by using a stolen heater and battery charger in his father's garage,[78] nor by erecting stolen scaffolding in the course of a building operation.[79] Nothing was done with the purpose, or with the effect, of assisting in retention.

It must be proved that D assisted in retention by concealing the goods or making them more difficult to identify or some other such conduct. It has been held that it is sufficient that D's passive conduct may constitute such assistance.[80] But, according to *Kanwar*,[81] 'something must be done by the offender, and done intentionally and dishonestly, for the purpose of enabling the goods to be retained'. In that case, it was sufficient that D told lies to protect her husband who had dishonestly brought the stolen goods into the house. She knew that, if the deception succeeded, the effect would be that her husband would be enabled to retain the goods.

Disposal

This would most obviously cover cases of D destroying the stolen goods, or using stolen money to pay for goods or services.[82] It extends beyond that to cases where D negotiates with E to sell him goods which D knows to have been stolen by T. Although D is never in

---

[75] *Park* (1987) 87 Cr App R 164.   [76] But cf *Deakin* [1972] 3 All ER 803.

[77] (1972) 57 Cr App R 30.   [78] *Sanders* (1982) 75 Cr App R 84.

[79] *Thornhill* (unreported; discussed in *Sanders* (1982) 75 Cr App R 84).

[80] *Burroughes* (2000) 29 Nov, unreported.   [81] [1982] 2 All ER 528.

[82] cf Williams, TBCL, 867, interpreting disposal as being limited to alienation.

possession or control of the goods,[83] he would appear to have undertaken or assisted in the disposal of stolen goods.

A person does not 'assist' in the disposal of stolen property merely by accepting any benefit deriving from that disposition. There must be proof that D gave help or encouragement; an omission to act will not generally ground liability. In *Coleman*,[84] D knew that his wife was using stolen money to pay solicitors' fees relating to the purchase of a flat in the couple's joint names. That did not in itself amount to assisting though it was evidence from which a jury might infer that he had assisted by telling his wife to use the stolen money or agreeing that she should do so.

Removal

This would occur where, for example, D assists T to lift from a van a barrel of gin which he knows to have been stolen by T or another. Even if D never has possession or control,[85] he has assisted or undertaken the removal of the stolen goods. D who lights the way for T to carry stolen goods from a house to a barn so that he may negotiate for the purchase of them,[86] has assisted in the removal of the goods and even if that were the full extent of his intended dealing with the goods he would still be liable to conviction (though his sentence might be lighter).

Realization

According to the House of Lords in *Bloxham*, this means 'exchanging goods for money or other property'. This form of the offence overlaps with disposal.

Assistance

The undertaking or assisting must relate to the retention, etc of the goods. The assistance can be by words or conduct. It was said in *Kanwar* that, 'The requisite assistance need not be successful in its object'. But is it true to say that one who attempts to assist and fails nevertheless 'assists'? This seems to involve reading the section as if it read, 'does an act with the purpose of assisting'. The would-be assister who fails to assist in any way would surely be more properly convicted of an attempt.

In all cases of undertaking it is necessary for the prosecution to prove that D was acting by or for the benefit of another, and in cases of 'assisting in' D must be assisting another.

Arranging to undertake or assist

The extension of the law to undertaking and assisting is far-reaching, but the 1968 Act goes further still. The mere arrangement to do any of the acts amounting to undertaking or assisting amounts to the complete offence of handling. The goods must, of course, be stolen by the time of such an arrangement. It is, presumably, enough that D agreed to negotiate the sale of the stolen goods, for example to lift down the barrel of stolen gin or to do any act for the purpose of enabling T to retain, remove or dispose of the stolen goods.

26.1.1.5 Handling by omission

'Receiving', 'undertaking' and 'arranging' all suggest that some positive conduct is required, though as little as a nod or a wink might suffice in particular circumstances. 'Assisting', however, may be constituted by inactivity provided it is in circumstances where that inactivity does in fact provide assistance.[87] Take a simple case. D, a wife, could hardly be liable

---

[83] cf *Watson* [1916] 2 KB 385.   [84] [1986] Crim LR 56.
[85] *Gleed* (1916) 12 Cr App R 32; *Hobson v Impett* (1957) 41 Cr App R 138.   [86] *Wiley* (1850) 2 Den 37.
[87] See n 80.

as a handler because T, her husband, each dawn returns to *his* house with the fruits of the night's burglaries. As has been shown earlier, D would not become a handler even if she used the goods, provided such use did not involve assistance in their retention, etc.

Knowledge of the whereabouts of stolen goods cannot suffice to make D a handler; nor does D become a handler simply by refusing to answer police questions as to the whereabouts of the goods[88] since there is no obligation to help the police with their inquiries.[89] So, in *Brown*,[90] where T secreted stolen goods in D's flat and told D he had done so, it was a misdirection to tell the jury that assisting in the retention of the goods could be inferred from D's refusal to reveal the presence of the stolen goods when questioned about them by the police. The conviction in *Brown* was, however, upheld by applying the proviso then available to the Court of Appeal. D had tacitly, if not expressly, permitted T to hide the goods on his premises and had thereby assisted in their retention. This is not to say that knowledge of the presence of stolen goods on his premises always renders the occupier a handler. Obviously, D does not assist in the retention of stolen goods where D knows that T is wearing a stolen coat and invites T into his premises, even if D puts it in the cloakroom for the duration of T's stay. But if D's premises are used, as they were used in *Brown*, to house the goods and D allows them to remain there he can properly be said to be assisting in their retention just as plainly as if he had initially given permission. What is important here is that D has control of premises and has chosen to allow their use for the storage of stolen goods.

Contrast the case of *Kousar*[91] decided under the Trade Marks Act 1994 in which K's conviction for unauthorized use of a trade mark was quashed. K's home was searched after her husband's market stall was found to be selling counterfeit goods. Counterfeit goods were in the loft and in a van parked outside. The van was not the family transport and K did not use it. K was prosecuted on the basis that she was in *possession, control or custody* of the goods as a principal offender, not as an aider and abettor of her husband. The Court of Appeal held that in terms of possession, proof of K's knowledge or acquiescence of the presence of the goods was not enough. There was no evidence that K was in possession of the goods in the loft, and *a fortiori*, she did not have possession of the goods in the van outside. As far as control was concerned, *actual* control of the goods was needed. It was not enough that she had the ability to control the storage of the goods.

Pitchley[92] is similar to *Brown*. T, D's son, gave D stolen money telling him that he had won it gambling and D paid it into his bank account. Two days later D became aware that the money was stolen but he did nothing about it until questioned by the police four days later. D's conviction for handling by assisting in the retention of the stolen money[93] was upheld because he had continued to retain possession after he became aware that the money was stolen. D had assumed control of the money and had, with guilty knowledge, retained control for the benefit of T. But the stolen money had in fact ceased to exist and it appears that the thing in action which replaced it was not 'stolen' because D was neither a thief nor a handler at the time of the 'realisation'.[94] It is thus very doubtful whether Pitchley was rightly convicted. A better charge would have been theft. The thing in action, being the proceeds of the stolen money, probably continued to belong to V; and D, by keeping it as owner, appropriated it: s 3(2).

---

[88] Though D may become a handler (assist in the retention of the goods) if lies are told to put the police off the scent: *Kanwar* [1982] 1 WLR 845, n 81.

[89] See p 257. Although cf *Sekfali v DPP* [2006] EWHC 894 (Admin).

[90] [1970] 1 QB 105.   [91] [2009] EWCA Crim 139.

[92] (1972) 57 Cr App R 30. Cf *Tamm* [1973] Crim LR 115.

[93] The decision overlooks the fact that when D acquired his knowledge there was no longer any 'stolen' money to handle (see Ormerod and Williams, *Smith's Law of Theft*, para 13.70 fn 3) but this does not affect the point at issue.

[94] See Griew, *Theft*, paras 15–23 fn 62; Williams, TBCL, 873.

26.1.1.6 Otherwise than in the course of the stealing

The offence is committed only if the conduct that amounts to handling occurs otherwise than in the course of the original stealing; that is, causing the goods to be stolen goods in the first place before the alleged handling arose.[95] (Almost every handling is also a second theft—the handler dishonestly appropriates property belonging to another with the intention permanently to deprive the other of it—but that is not significant for this issue.)

If D was a party to the original theft, his participation in that theft cannot also render him liable for the offence of handling stolen goods. This limitation is necessary to keep handling within proper bounds. Without it, virtually every instance of theft by two or more persons would also be handling by one or the other or, more likely, both of them. This restriction assists in separating these two distinct forms of conduct that carry vastly different sentences and particular labels to which different stigmas attach.

The courts have emphasized that charging and jury directions should be kept simple where these issues arise.[96] It is often a sensible course for alternative counts of theft and handling to be left to the jury.[97]

The duration of the course of stealing

Identifying when the stealing stops and the handling begins is important. The duration of 'the course of the stealing' depends on the extent to which appropriation is a continuing act.[98] The issue has become even more complex following *Gomez*, and the extension of the concept of appropriation, rendering what were previously mere preparatory acts to completed thefts. As noted, one case involving handling, *Pitham and Hehl*,[99] suggested that appropriation is an instantaneous act, concluded at the moment the goods are stolen. If this were right, the words 'in the course of the stealing' would be rendered nugatory. It is submitted that, in the light of *Hale*[100] and *Atakpu*,[101] cases concerned with robbery and theft respectively, *Pitham* must be wrongly decided in this respect.

Atakpu adopts the transaction test—was D still 'on the job'? Although providing a pragmatic guideline, this does not, of course, solve all the problems. A thief is likely to be held to be on the job while he is in a building that he has entered for the purpose of stealing and from which he intends to remove the stolen goods. But is he still in the course of theft as he walks down the garden path with the goods? As he drives home? As he shows them to his wife at home? Griew[102] suggests that the scope of theft is determined by looking at 'the total process of the effective appropriation, including the getaway', but it is doubtful that this is any improvement on the test of the thief being 'on the job'.

It does not necessarily follow that the theft is still in the course of being committed because the stolen property has not yet been removed from the premises on which it was stolen. If D and T agree to steal from their employer V and in pursuance of the plan D steals goods which he places in T's locker so that T may remove them from the premises, T is a thief and not a handler even though some time elapses between D's appropriation of the goods and T's removal of them. It is one enterprise for the theft of V's goods. If, however,

---

[95] See generally ATH Smith, 'Theft and/or Handling' [1977] Crim LR 517 and *Property Offences*, paras 30.71–30.82.

[96] See *Bosson* [1999] Crim LR 596.

[97] The Court of Appeal confirmed in *Read* [2014] EWCA Crim 687 that it is also permissible to leave alternate counts of robbery and handling to the jury.

[98] See p 877. See also G Williams, 'Appropriation: A Single or Continuous Act?' [1978] Crim LR 69.

[99] (1976) 65 Cr App R 45, p 894.

[100] (1978) 68 Cr App R 415, p 937. The offence of robbery under s 8 requires theft 'at the time of' whereas s 22 focuses on 'the course of'.

[101] [1994] QB 69, p 877.   [102] Paras 15–46.

D steals V's goods and secretes them on the premises, a *subsequent* arrangement with T for T to remove them from the premises constitutes T being a handler. T is not a party to the original theft.

In the very old case of *Atwell and O'Donnell*,[103] D1 and D2, bent on stealing some of their employer's property, moved it nearer the warehouse door during the course of the morning. Later that day, E1 and E2 arranged to buy the goods from them and all returned later that evening to take away the goods from the warehouse. It was held that E1 and E2 were thieves and not receivers; the theft was a continuing transaction as to those (E1 and E2) who joined the plot before the goods were finally removed from the warehouse. Arguably, if these facts were to recur under the 1968 Act, E1 and E2 would be handlers and not thieves. The theft (the appropriation) may have been complete before E1 and E2 became aware of it.

Proof of handling or theft

It has been held that in an ordinary case, the words, 'otherwise than in the course of the stealing', have little importance and the jury should not even be told about them. But where the evidence is such that a reasonable jury might think it reasonably possible that the alleged handler was a participant in the theft, they should surely be told that, if this was so, the law says that he is not guilty of handling.

There have been some odd applications of this principle in various cases. In *Cash*,[104] it was held that the words 'otherwise than in the course of stealing' do not constitute an element in the offence that has to be proved in order to establish a prima facie case of handling. In *Cash*, stolen goods were found in D's possession on 25 February. The property was stolen (by a burglar) not later than 16 February. It was held that it was not open to the jury to infer that D was the burglar rather than a receiver. Perhaps the evidence was insufficient to satisfy the jury beyond reasonable doubt that D was the burglar but might they not, given the opportunity, have thought that it was reasonably possible, if not probable, that he *was* the burglar? Is it unheard of for burglars to retain possession of the stolen property for nine days? In *Greaves*,[105] it was held that the judge had properly left it open to the jury to convict of burglary where the time lapse was 17 days. In *Wells*,[106] *Cash* was described as a decision which makes 'entirely good sense'[107] and held to apply in any case in which there is no evidence to be left to the jury suggesting that D was a burglar/thief.

There are at least four possible incriminating explanations for D's recent possession in these types of case: (a) that he is the thief; (b) that he took part in the theft and received the goods in the course of it; (c) that he was implicated in the theft and only received his proceeds later; (d) that he was not involved in the theft and received the stolen goods at a later date.[108] If all that can be proved by the prosecution beyond a reasonable doubt is that D was in possession with a dishonest state of mind, how can handling be satisfactorily established?

---

[103] cf *Atwell and O'Donnell* (1801) East, II PC, 768.

[104] [1985] QB 801, [1985] Crim LR 311 and commentary.

[105] (1987) The Times, 11 July. *Cash* was also distinguished in *Bruce* [1988] VR 579. Failure to add alternative theft counts can be fatal to the indictment: *Suter* [1997] CLY 1339 (Judge Bull, Guildford CC).

[106] [2004] EWCA Crim 79.

[107] Para 1. On inferences from possession, see *M v DPP* [2009] EWHC 525 (Admin) (inference) from M's claim to have bought a mobile phone from X very cheaply without packaging or charger, but with a SIM card. On the difficulty of proving continuity of the evidence—ie that the goods allegedly stolen are those allegedly handled, etc, see *Lamb v DPP* [2009] EWHC 238 (Admin).

[108] See M Hirst, 'Guilty but of What' (2000) 4 E & P 31.

26.1.1.7 For the benefit of another person

Each of the nouns 'retention', 'removal', 'disposal' and 'realization' is governed by the words 'by or for the benefit of another person'.[109] It must therefore be proved that:

(1) D undertook or arranged the retention, removal, disposal or realization *for the benefit of another person*; or

(2) D assisted or arranged the retention, removal, disposal or realization *by another person*.[110]

Every thief either retains, removes, disposes of or realizes the stolen goods, so this requirement of conduct being 'for the benefit of another' prevents all thieves from also being handlers. The italicized words are an essential part of the offence and the indictment must allege that the handling was 'by or for the benefit of another person'.[111] The thief may himself be guilty of handling (by undertaking) if he himself retains, removes, etc the goods for the benefit of another person. It would seem to be immaterial that the other person is guilty of no offence and even unaware of what is going on.

However, an important limitation was imposed in *Bloxham*.[112] It was held that when deciding whether the handling was by or for the benefit of another person, a purchaser of stolen goods is not 'another person' within the section. So, where D sells stolen goods to E, D's act is not for the benefit of the buyer, E; it is for D's own benefit. Sellers usually sell for their own benefit, not the benefit of the purchaser; that much is uncontroversial. However, in the opinion of Lord Bridge even if the sale could be described as for the purchaser's benefit, it would not be within the ambit of the section. This gives a special, though obscure, meaning to the term 'another person'. Griew lucidly summarizes the interpretation—something will be for the benefit of another when it is 'an act done on behalf of another person; it is an act that the other might do himself'.[113]

In *Bloxham*, D, acting in good faith, purchased a stolen car for £1,300. Eleven months later, suspecting that it was stolen, he sold it for £200 to a person unknown who was prepared to buy it without official documents. D was charged with handling by undertaking or assisting in the realization of the car for the benefit of the buyer. A submission of no case to answer was rejected, whereupon he pleaded guilty. His conviction was upheld by the Court of Appeal who thought that the buyer's use of the car, for which he had paid less than its true value, was a benefit to him. Maybe it was; but it seems a travesty to say that the sale was for his benefit. The House of Lords quashed the conviction, holding that the buyer was not 'another person'. In fact, of course, he was 'another person'; but the sale was certainly not effected 'on his behalf'.

Bloxham was distinguished in *Tokeley-Parry*[114] where D was charged with undertaking or assisting in removal by E, whom he had procured to smuggle stolen antiquities from Egypt. An argument that D and E were one person was firmly rejected. E was 'another person' in fact and in law. Further, *Roberts*[115] decides that if A and B are jointly charged in one count with an act of handling 'by or for the benefit of another', the other must be some

---

[109] *Sloggett* [1971] 3 All ER 264 at 267.

[110] cf L Blake, 'The Innocent Purchaser and Section 22 of the Theft Act' [1972] Crim LR 494, arguing that there is no need that the third party benefits if he retains, removes, realizes or disposes.

[111] *Sloggett* [1972] 1 QB 430.   [112] See n 53.

[113] Paras 15–22. See also Spencer's suggestion 'the requirement that the act be "for the benefit of another" serves no intelligible purpose unless it limits the offence to those who act on another's behalf': 'The Mishandling of Handling' [1981] Crim LR 682 at 685, commenting on the Court of Appeal decision in *Bloxham*.

[114] [1999] Crim LR 578. It is questionable how this was for the benefit of anyone other than D.

[115] No 93/0075/Z2, 9 July 1993, unreported, see [1996] Crim LR 495 and see *Gingell* [2000] 1 Cr App R 88.

person other than A or B. This seems logical if, indeed, only one act, jointly done by A and B, is alleged.[116] A might, however, arrange the disposition of the goods *by* B; and B might undertake the disposition *for the benefit of* A. In that case, both have committed an offence under s 22 and there is no need to show that any third person was involved.

Conspiracy to handle

Notwithstanding *Roberts*, an agreement by A and B that B would, for example, dispose of the goods for the benefit of A is a conspiracy to handle. A and B have agreed that B will commit the offence of handling, and that is enough. If B does dispose of the goods as agreed, he commits the offence under s 22; and obviously A has counselled or procured him to do so. They are both guilty of the same offence. There seems to be every reason, *pace* the court in *Roberts*, why A and B should be jointly charged with committing it.[117]

26.1.1.8 Innocent receipt and subsequent retention with mens rea

If D receives the stolen goods innocently (ie either believing them not to be stolen or knowing them to be stolen but intending to return them to the true owner), he commits no offence.[118] Suppose he subsequently discovers the goods to be stolen or decides not to return them to the true owner or disposes of them. He has dishonestly undertaken the retention of, or has disposed of, stolen goods knowing them to be stolen. Whether he is guilty of an offence depends on a number of factors.

(1) Where D does not get ownership of the goods (the normal situation where goods are the product of theft):

  (a) D gives value for the goods.

    (i) D retains or disposes of the goods for his own benefit. This is not theft because of s 3(2);[119] nor is it handling by undertaking, assisting or arranging since it is not for the benefit of another.[120] D might be guilty of handling by aiding and abetting the receiving by the person to whom he disposes of the goods, if that person has mens rea.

    (ii) D retains or disposes of the goods for the benefit of another. This is not theft (s 3(2)) but is handling.

  (b) D does not give value.

    (i) D retains or disposes of the goods for his own benefit. This is theft but not handling unless it amounts to aiding and abetting receipt by another.

    (ii) D retains or disposes of the goods for the benefit of another. This is theft and handling.

(2) Where D gets ownership of the goods:

  (a) D gives value for the goods.

    Retention or disposal of the goods cannot be theft since V has no property in the goods. It is not handling since V has lost his right to restitution,[121] his right to rescind being destroyed on the goods coming into the hands of D who was a bona fide purchaser for value.

  (b) D does not give value.

---

[116] Why this should only apply if they are jointly charged is less logical, see R Harrison, 'Handling Stolen Goods for the Benefit of Another' (2000) 64 J Crim L 156.

[117] See *Slater and Suddens* [1996] Crim LR 300.

[118] *Alt* [1972] Crim LR 552.   [119] See p 878.   [120] *Bloxham* [1983] 1 AC 109.   [121] See p 1077.

Again this cannot be theft, since V has no property in the goods, but it may be handling since V's right to rescind and secure restitution of his property is not extinguished by the goods coming into the hands of one who does not give value. It will be handling if this is so *and* D either aids and abets a guilty receipt by another or disposes of the goods for the benefit of another.

26.1.1.9 Handling by the thief

Any thief may be convicted of handling goods stolen by him by receiving them—if the evidence warrants this conclusion.[122] In the majority of cases the thief can only be guilty of handling by receiving where he is assisting or encouraging the receipt by another because he is already in possession or control and therefore cannot receive as the principal offender. In some circumstances, however, a thief might be convicted of handling the stolen goods by receiving them as the principal offender. For example, D steals goods and, in the course of the theft, delivers them to E. Two days later E returns the goods to D.

26.1.2 Mens rea of handling

D's mens rea as described later must coincide in time with the conduct constituting the actus reus. In the case of receiving, this is when D first receives the goods or makes the arrangement to receive.[123] In the case of other forms of handling, which may be continuing in nature, it is sufficient that the mens rea exists at some point in that continuum, for example where D has taken possession innocently but has subsequently become aware of the provenance of the goods and then acts for the benefit of another.[124]

26.1.2.1 Knowledge or belief

It must be proved that the goods were stolen and that D handled them 'knowing or believing them to be stolen goods'.[125] It is vital that the belief or knowledge is D's, not merely that of the reasonable person, since this is a subjective mens rea requirement.[126]

The CLRC apparently intended to include the concept of 'wilful blindness', which is often held by the courts to be included in the word 'knowing':[127]

It is a serious defect of the [pre-1968] law that actual knowledge that the property was stolen must be proved. Often the prosecution cannot prove this. In many cases indeed guilty knowledge does not exist, although the circumstances of the transaction are such that the receiver ought to be guilty of an offence. The man who buys goods at a ridiculously low price from an unknown seller whom he meets in a public house may not *know* that the goods were stolen, and he may take the precaution of asking no questions. Yet it may be clear on the evidence that he believes that the goods were stolen. In such cases the prosecution may fail (rightly, as the law now stands) for want of proof of guilty knowledge.[128]

If this was the Committee's intention, it has not been achieved. Liability based on wilful blindness involves D having a strong suspicion that something is so (in this case goods are

---

[122] *Dolan* (1975) 62 Cr App R 36; *Stapylton v O'Callaghan* [1973] 2 All ER 782. See ATH Smith [1977] Crim LR 517.

[123] *Alt* (1972) 56 Cr App R 45.   [124] See V Tunkel (1983) 133 NLJ 844.

[125] See in particular E Griew, 'Consistency, Communication and Codification—Reflections on Two *Mens Rea* Words' in Glazebrook, *Reshaping the Criminal Law*, 57; S Shute, 'Knowledge and Belief in the Criminal Law' in Shute and Simester, *Criminal Law Theory*, 171; GR Sullivan, 'Knowledge, Belief and Culpability' in ibid, 207; AR White, *Misleading Cases* (1991) 133; Tadros, *Criminal Responsibility*, Ch 9 and *The Ends of Harm* (2011) 144.

[126] *Bellenie* [1980] Crim LR 43; *Brook* [1993] Crim LR 455.   [127] See p 116.

[128] Eighth Report, 64. Cf *Woods* [1969] 1 QB 447. See also G Williams, 'Handling, Theft and the Purchaser Who Takes a Chance' [1985] Crim LR 432.

stolen) and consciously decides not to take steps that he could take to confirm or deny that fact. But the courts have repeatedly said that, for the purposes of s 22, suspicion, however strong, is not to be equated with belief that the goods are stolen.[129] It is a misdirection to tell the jury that it is enough that D, 'suspecting that the goods were stolen deliberately shut his eyes to the consequences'.[130]

Proof of either knowledge or belief will suffice. What, if anything, does 'believing' add to 'knowing'? According to *Hall*:[131]

A man may be said to know that goods are stolen when he is told by someone with first-hand knowledge (someone such as the thief or the burglar) that such is the case. Belief, of course, is something short of knowledge. It may be said to be the state of mind of a person who says to himself: 'I cannot say I know for certain that these goods are stolen but there can be no other reasonable conclusion in the light of all the circumstances, in the light of all that I have heard and seen.'

This seems to be merely a distinction between two *sources* of D's state of mind. But s 22 suggests a distinction between two states of mind that might be held, not two modes of arriving at the same state of mind. The case suggests that if D had direct evidence, he knows; if he has mere circumstantial evidence, he believes; but it would surely be more accurate to describe knowledge in terms of the accuracy of the belief, not the directness of the evidence leading to the belief. As Shute has suggested, the distinctions between the concepts are twofold: knowledge constitutes a true belief, and belief includes acceptance of the proposition in question whereas knowledge does not.[132] In *Forsyth*,[133] the court said that the judgment in *Hall* is 'potentially confusing'.[134] In *Moys*,[135] the court suggested simply that the question whether D knew or believed that the goods were stolen is a subjective one and that suspicion, even coupled with the fact that D shut his eyes to the circumstances, is not enough.

In practical terms, D may be left in varying degrees of certainty as to the provenance of the goods whether or not he has been told by the thief or deduced the fact from his own observation. What matters is that D is caused to be certain that the goods are stolen; there is no significance for these purposes in the source of information. Although what seems to be implied in *Hall* is that the person with direct information is certain and the person with circumstantial evidence is nearly certain, it would be dangerous in such terms to direct a jury because 'near certainty' is strong suspicion and that is not enough. It is unclear whether it is sufficient that D considers the likelihood that the goods are stolen to be 'virtually certain'; presumably not. It is clearly not enough for D to believe that the goods are 'probably' stolen.[136]

In general, it seems that a judge cannot go wrong by simply directing the jury in accordance with the words of the section and offering no elaboration or explanation of

---

[129] *Forsyth* [1997] Crim LR 581; *Grainge* [1974] 1 All ER 928; *Saik* [2006] UKHL 18. Cf *Woods* [1969] 1 QB 447; *Ismail* [1977] Crim LR 557 and commentary. Cf Griew, *Theft*, paras 15.30–15.33; Spencer [1985] Crim LR 101. See S Shute, 'Knowledge and Belief in the Criminal Law' in Shute and Simester, *Criminal Law Theory*.

[130] *Griffiths* (1974) 60 Cr App R 14. *Atwal v Massey* [1971] 3 All ER 881, is definitely misleading on this point and seems to have misled the judge in *Pethick* [1980] Crim LR 242, where it was said that suspicion, 'however strong', does not amount to knowledge.

[131] (1985) 81 Cr App R 260 at 264.   [132] At n 129.

[133] See n 129. A *Hall* direction is not necessary in every case—*Toor* (1987) 85 Cr App R 116.

[134] It is the second part of *Hall* that presents a problem: *Adinga* [2003] EWCA Crim 3201.

[135] (1984) 79 Cr App R 72.

[136] *Reader* (1977) 66 Cr App R 33 at 36. For consideration of whether this ought to be a sufficient mens rea, see JR Spencer, 'Handling, Theft and the Mala Fide Purchaser' [1985] Crim LR 92 at 95–6; Williams [1985] Crim LR 432 at 435; JR Spencer, 'Handling and Taking Risks: A Reply to Professor Williams' [1985] Crim LR 440.

'believing'.[137] Of course, it may be that the jury will then apply the word as if it included wilful blindness, but no one will ever know. This is another example of the appellate refusal to interpret elements of crimes definitively, which is unsatisfactory but which remains uncorrected because the cloak of jury secrecy avoids the true shortcomings of the interpretation being exposed.

Some have called for a further extension of the offence to include reckless handling.[138] There are, of course, competing policy arguments: on the one hand, there is the need to avoid stifling trade of honest dealers and, on the other, the recognition that in most cases dishonest defendants could escape liability by not confirming mere suspicions.[139] If there were a high incidence of low-value handling by individuals (dealing through eBay and car boot sales, etc) such arguments might have greater force. The argument would become greater still if different offences distinguished professional fences from individuals trading in low-value items.

Knowledge or belief of what?

It is sufficient that D knows or believes that the goods, whatever they are, are stolen. His knowledge or belief need not extend to the identity of the thief, or the owner,[140] or the nature of the stolen goods.[141] If D knows he is in possession of a box containing stolen goods, it is no defence that he does not know what the contents are and is shocked to discover that the box contains guns; nor would it be a defence that he believed the box contained stolen watches. Equally, it is enough for D to know or believe that the goods are stolen in the extended meaning that term has under s 24. So, it does not matter that D believed the goods to be the product of blackmail when they were in fact the product of a theft. In line with general principle, it is not necessary for D to know the criminal law: it is sufficient that D has knowledge or belief as to the facts and circumstances that render it criminal.

26.1.2.2 Dishonesty

'Dishonestly'[142] shares the same meaning as elsewhere in the Theft Acts. That now means the *Ivey/Barton* test discussed earlier.[143]

(1) What was the defendant's actual state of knowledge or belief as to the facts; and

(2) was his conduct dishonest by the standards of ordinary decent people?

D may receive goods knowing or believing them to be stolen and yet not be guilty if, for example, he intends to return them to the true owner or turn them in to the police.[144] Section 2 of the Act does not apply, so D's claim of a belief in right is not necessarily going to negate dishonesty. The question will be a matter for the jury and they are unlikely to regard such conduct as honest where D knows or believes the goods to be stolen, except where they believe that D's claim that he intends to return the goods to the owner was or may be true.

---

[137] *Reader* (1977) 66 Cr App R 33; *Harris* (1986) 84 Cr App R 75; *Toor* (1986) 85 Cr App R 116.

[138] See J Spencer [1985] Crim LR 92.

[139] Some argue that there would be a significant setback to economic efficiency if there was an obligation to investigate whether suspicious-looking goods were stolen. See Tadros, *The Ends of Harm*, 144.

[140] *Fuschillo* [1940] 2 All ER 489; but it may be necessary to name the owner where the property is of a common and indistinctive type: *Gregory* [1972] 2 All ER 861. See *Webster* [2002] EWCA Crim 1346.

[141] *McCullum* (1973) 57 Cr App R 645.

[142] cf *Ivey v Genting Casinos UK Ltd (t/a Crockfords Club)* [2017] UKSC 67; p 909.

[143] *Barton* [2020] EWCA Crim 575, [84].   [144] cf *Matthews* [1950] 1 All ER 137.

26.1.2.3 Proof of mens rea

The general principles of evidence in criminal cases apply to the proof of offences of theft and handling as they apply to other crimes. This is not the place to examine those rules in full.

The 'doctrine' of recent possession

Where D is found in possession of, or dealing with, property which has recently been stolen, a jury may properly infer that he is guilty of an offence if he offers no explanation or if they are satisfied beyond reasonable doubt that any explanation he has offered is untrue. They are not bound so to infer and must not do so unless they are sure that D was in fact guilty of the particular offence. The onus of proof remains on the Crown throughout. Whether D offers an explanation or not, the jury must not convict unless they are sure that he committed the offence in question.[145]

These principles are frequently misleadingly referred to as 'the doctrine of recent possession'. The 'doctrine' is nothing more than the application of the ordinary principles of circumstantial evidence to this commonly recurring situation.

The difficulty which arises is that a jury may be quite certain that D was either the thief or a receiver but not satisfied beyond reasonable doubt that he was one rather than the other. A solution which has been adopted in some jurisdictions, following *Langmead*,[146] is to direct the jury that if they are satisfied beyond reasonable doubt that D was *either* the thief *or* a receiver, they may convict of the offence which they think more probable—that is, it is enough that they are satisfied on a balance of probabilities that D was the thief, or that he was the receiver. As the jury is unlikely to find that the evidence is exactly evenly balanced, this is a practical solution, and one that should be Art 6(2) compliant.[147] It was, however, rejected by the Privy Council in *A-G of Hong Kong v Yip Kai-foon*.[148] D was charged with robbery and with handling the goods that were stolen. The Privy Council held that the jury had been rightly directed to consider the robbery charge first. Once they had decided that they were not sure that D was guilty of robbery, he was to be presumed to be innocent of the theft of the goods and it followed that any handling that occurred took place 'otherwise than in the course of the stealing' so there was no need for more than a passing reference to those words. This is a novel use of the presumption of innocence *against* a defendant. Because the jury are not satisfied beyond reasonable doubt that D was guilty of theft it is apparently to be conclusively presumed that he was not guilty of that offence. If the jury are satisfied that he was guilty of one offence or the other, it follows inevitably that he was guilty of handling. But this is arbitrary. The outcome depends on which offence the jury consider first, and it becomes critical for the jury to be directed carefully as to the order in which they approach the verdicts.[149] A more fundamental objection is that the approach treats the acquittal as proof of guilt and may offend Art 6(2) of the ECHR.[150]

Because of the difficulty of proving guilty knowledge, the Theft Act provides for the admission of certain evidence on a receiving charge that would not (at least at the time of enactment) be admissible in criminal cases generally. By s 27(3):

Where a person is being proceeded against for handling stolen goods (but not for any offence other than handling stolen goods),[151] then at any stage of the proceedings, if evidence has been given

---

[145] *Abramovitch* (1914) 11 Cr App R 45; *Aves* (1950) 34 Cr App R 159; *Hepworth* [1955] 2 QB 600.

[146] (1864) Le & Ca 427.

[147] If the approach was applied more widely it would pose problems particularly where more than two alternatives are left, leading to possible conviction of an offence of which the jury are not even sure D is probably guilty. See further M Hirst, *Jurisdiction and the Ambit of Criminal Law* (2003).

[148] [1988] AC 642, followed in *Foreman* [1991] Crim LR 702; but see commentary at 704.

[149] *Fernandez* [1997] 1 Cr App R 123.   [150] See Hirst (2000) 4 E & P 31.

[151] cf *Anderson* [1978] Crim LR 223 (Judge Stroyan).

of his having or arranging to have in his possession the goods the subject of the charge, or of his undertaking or assisting in, or arranging to undertake or assist in, their retention, removal, disposal or realisation, the following evidence shall be admissible for the purpose of proving that he knew or believed the goods to be stolen goods:

(a) evidence that he has had in his possession, or has undertaken or assisted in the retention, removal, disposal or realisation of, stolen goods from any theft taking place not earlier than twelve months before the offence charged;[152] and

(b) (provided that seven days' notice in writing has been given to him of the intention to prove the conviction) evidence that he has within the five years preceding the date of the offence charged been convicted of theft or of handling stolen goods.[153]

The Law Commission called for the abolition of the provisions.[154] The provisions are now merely supplementary to the wide-reaching statutory rules permitting admissibility of previous misconduct[155] under s 101 of the Criminal Justice Act 2003.[156]

26.2 Dishonestly retaining a wrongful credit

Section 24A of the Theft Act 1968 (inserted by s 2 of the Theft (Amendment) Act 1996) provides:

(1) A person is guilty of an offence if—

(a) a wrongful credit has been made to an account kept by him or in respect of which he has any right or interest,

(b) he knows or believes that the credit is wrongful; and

(c) he dishonestly fails to take such steps as are reasonable in the circumstances to secure that the credit is cancelled.

(2) References to a credit are to a credit of an amount of money.[157]

The offence is punishable on indictment with imprisonment for ten years.

The effect is that D1, a thief or fraudster, who has credited to his account[158] a wrongful credit commits an offence if he does not take steps within a reasonable time to divest himself of his ill-gotten gains. The provision is not, of course, aimed at him but at D2, where D1 has procured the crediting, not of his own, but of D2's account. If this was done with D2's connivance, D2 would be guilty as a secondary party to D1's original offence which generated the proceeds which were credited to D1's account. There would be no need to invoke s 24A.

---

[152] There is no requirement for D to have been convicted on this earlier occasion. As to what detail may be admitted, see *Bradley* (1979) 70 Cr App R 200, [1980] Crim LR 173 and commentary.

[153] These provisions have attracted both judicial and academic criticism: see *Hacker* [1995] 1 Cr App R 332, overruling *Fowler* (1987) 86 Cr App R 219; R Munday, 'Handling the Evidential Exception' [1988] Crim LR 345. See Ormerod and Williams, *Smith's Law of Theft*, paras 13.102–13.120 for more detailed treatment.

[154] See LC 273, *Evidence of Bad Character in Criminal Proceedings* (2001) Cm 5257, paras 4.13–14.23, 11.53–11.55. On such prejudice generally, see S Lloyd-Bostock, 'The Effects on Juries of Hearing About the Defendant's Previous Criminal Record: A Simulation Study' [2000] Crim LR 734.

[155] See ss 98–112 of the Criminal Justice Act 2003.

[156] Or in some odd cases at common law if s 98(a) applies. R Munday, *Cross and Tapper on Evidence* (13th edn, 2018) Ch VIII; *Blackstone's Criminal Practice* (2021) F12.39.

[157] As amended by the Fraud Act 2006, Sch 1, para 7.

[158] By Sch 1, para 7 to the Fraud Act 2006: '(9) "Account" means an account kept with—(a) a bank; (b) a person carrying on a business which falls within subsection (10) below; or (c) an issuer of electronic money (as defined for the purposes of Part 2 of the Financial Services and Markets Act 2000).'

Suppose, however, that the credit was made without D2's connivance. One day D2 finds that an unexpected credit has been made to his account by D1. As soon as he knows or believes that the credit has been made in such circumstances as to amount to an offence, he comes under a duty to divest himself of this unforeseen windfall. If he fails to do so within a reasonable time he commits the offence. It is an offence of omission,[159] rather like theft where s 5(4) applies. Whereas, however, s 5(4) requires D to intend to 'make restoration' of the property, s 24A(1)(c) merely requires him to cancel the credit.

D does not do this merely by withdrawing the money to spend. In *Lee*,[160] L relied on a passage in previous editions of this work to the effect that if D withdraws the money to spend for his own benefit, he cancels the credit and might escape liability under s 24A—'if the draftsmen meant "make restoration" he should have said so—but, by section 24A(8), the money withdrawn is stolen goods so he will be guilty of receiving stolen goods'. The Court of Appeal rejected this submission noting that if it were correct it would lead to a 'surprising conclusion, since it is clear from the terms of the section itself that the offence consists in retaining the credit rather than taking reasonable steps to cancel it'. The conclusion was that 'the word "cancelled" as used in section 24A(1)(c) means cancelling the original credit so as to achieve the same effect as if it had not been made in the first place. In many cases that will be achieved by a corresponding debit reversing the original entry in the account'.[161]

The section extends to other conduct which was not an offence even before the decision of the House of Lords in *Preddy*. Section 24A(2A)[162] provides:

(2A) A credit to an account is wrongful to the extent that it derives from

    (a) theft;

    (b) blackmail;

    (c) fraud (contrary to section 1 of the Fraud Act 2006); or

    (d) stolen goods.

So D2 may be guilty of the offence if:

    (1) D1 steals money and pays it into D2's account;

    (2) D1 obtains money by blackmail and pays that money into D2's account;

    (3) D1 obtains money by fraud and pays that into D2's account;

    (4) D1 receives stolen money and pays it into D2's account.

In each of these cases the credit in D2's account is a new item of property—a thing in action belonging to D2—which has never been 'in the hands' of a thief or handler and so is not 'stolen goods' within s 24(2). D2 is not guilty of handling by retaining it. Now, however, he commits an offence under s 24A(1) if he dishonestly fails to cancel 'the wrongful credit' within a reasonable time. Cancelling, according to *Lee*, means cancelling it as if it had never been made and not simply withdrawing that amount. In any event, s 24A(8) provides that any money which is withdrawn from a wrongful credit will be stolen goods and subject to the general law of handling so D2 may commit an offence under s 22. An incidental effect is that the thief, blackmailer or handler who pays the proceeds of his offence into his own account commits another offence when he fails to take reasonable steps to cancel the credit. This is so because the Law Commission thought: 'It would be

---

[159] The argument of the Law Commission that this is necessary is found in LC 243, *Offences of Dishonesty: Money Transfers* (1996) 39.

[160] [2006] EWCA Crim 156.   [161] At [22].   [162] As inserted by the Fraud Act 2006.

difficult, if not impossible, to devise a simple way of excluding the case where A dishonestly secures a credit to his own account, while including the case where A dishonestly secures a credit to B's.'[163]

Section 24A(5) provides that it is immaterial whether an account is overdrawn before or after a credit is made. So if D2's account is overdrawn to the tune of £100 when a wrongful credit of £50 arrives, he is under a duty, somehow, to get his overdraft restored to its former level. There is no provision corresponding to s 24(3).[164] Nor is there any exemption for the bona fide purchaser such as is to be found in s 3(2).[165] Suppose that D sells his car in good faith to A who pays him with stolen money. After learning that the money was stolen, D spends it. He did not commit any offence before the enactment of s 24A. He still commits no offence if A paid him in cash and he spends the cash. But if D paid the cash into his own bank account, or if he was paid by a cheque which he has paid into that account, he has received a wrongful credit and it appears that he will (subject to proof of dishonesty) commit an offence under s 24A when he spends the money, because he has failed to take reasonable steps to disgorge.

That would create not only an unsatisfactory anomaly but also a conflict with the civil law.[166] The money, whether in cash or in the bank, is surely his to dispose of as he chooses. How then can he be guilty of a crime by doing so? It may be that a court will think it necessary to read into s 24A(1)(c) some such qualification as 'except where no person has any right to restitution of the credit', on the ground that Parliament could not have intended to change, or create a conflict with, such a fundamental rule of the civil law. This would introduce a limitation to the same effect as that relating to stolen goods generally in s 24(4).

26.3 Advertising for the return of stolen goods

The existence of this offence might come as a surprise given the number of such advertisements that are commonly seen.[167] By s 23 of the Theft Act 1968 it is an offence publicly to advertise for the return of stolen goods indicating that no questions will be asked about how the person returning the goods came by them. An offence of this type has existed since 1828[168] and it was retained, after some hesitation, in the Theft Act because it was thought that advertisements of this kind might encourage dishonesty.[169] Though such advertisements may encourage dishonesty in other people, dishonesty is not required of the perpetrator. It operates harshly in preventing the advertiser offering to pay the (innocent) bona fide purchaser of the advertiser's stolen goods.

Indeed, the offence has been held to be one of strict liability so that the advertising manager of a newspaper in which such an advertisement appeared committed the offence,

---

[163] LC 243, paras 6.16–6.17. The Commission comforted itself with the consideration that there was already an enormous degree of overlap in the existing offences under the Theft Acts.

[164] Stolen goods cease to be 'stolen' when they are restored to lawful custody or when the owner and any others claiming through him have ceased to have any right to restitution of the goods, p 1075.

[165] See p 878.

[166] A transferee of stolen currency for value and without notice gets a good title: *Miller v Race* (1758) 1 Burr 452.

[167] See JC Smith, 'Rewards for the Return of Lost or Stolen Property' in N Palmer (ed), *The Recovery of Stolen Art* (1998).

[168] See *Hall* (1985) 81 Cr App R 260, [1985] Crim LR 377 on its history. See also Smith, *Property Offences*, Ch 31B.

[169] Eighth Report, para 144.

though he was unaware that it had appeared in the paper.[170] In the light of the House of Lords' reiteration of the presumption of mens rea a court may be persuaded that strict liability is inappropriate.[171] However, when analysing the offence, Goff LJ in *Denham* regarded the section as creating a 'quasi criminal' offence, and that is a factor pointing towards strict liability.

Further reading

S Green, *13 Ways to Steal a Bicycle: Theft Law in the Information Age*

M Sutton, K Johnston and H Lockwood, *Handling Stolen Goods and Theft: A Market Reduction Approach*

---

[170] *Withers* [1975] Crim LR 647; *Denham v Scott* (1983) 77 Cr App R 210.
[171] See *DPP v B* [2000] 2 AC 428; *K* [2002] 1 AC 462. See p 154.

27

Offences of damage to property

The principal offences of damage to property are governed by the Criminal Damage Act 1971 which replaced the complicated provisions of the Malicious Damage Act 1861. Like the Theft Act, the Criminal Damage Act is a code, and it must be approached and interpreted in the same fashion.[1] The Criminal Damage Act is largely the product of a Law Commission Report, and reference to that helps in understanding the underlying policies and in elucidating the provisions of the Act.[2]

---

[1] See p 861.

[2] See LC 29, *Criminal Law: Report on Offences of Damage to Property* (1970). See also Law Com Working Paper No 23, *Malicious Damage* (1969) and generally DW Elliott, 'Criminal Damage' [1988] Crim LR 403.

The Law Commission sought to align the law governing damage to property with that governing appropriating property as found in the Theft Act 1968. Complete parity for theft and criminal damage is neither practicable nor desirable, but it is important that there should be no conflict of principle if the whole range of criminal offences is to be consistent and harmonious. Differences are obvious: while land cannot in general be stolen, there is no reason why criminal damage to land should go unpunished. On the other hand, it is clearly desirable that if it is not generally an offence to pick another's wild mushrooms, it should not be an offence to destroy or damage them and the Criminal Damage Act makes that clear.

27.1 Destroying or damaging property of another

By s 1(1) of the Criminal Damage Act 1971:

A person who without lawful excuse destroys or damages any property belonging to another intending to destroy or damage any such property or being reckless as to whether any such property would be destroyed or damaged shall be guilty of an offence.

And by s 4 the offence is punishable by imprisonment for ten years on indictment.[3]

27.1.1 Destroy or damage

The expression 'destroy or damage' was commonly used in the Malicious Damage Act 1861 and decisions on the meaning of these words under that Act, though no longer binding, retain a persuasive value.

'What constitutes criminal damage is a matter of fact and degree and it is for the [jury or magistrates], applying their common sense, to decide whether what occurred was damage or not'.[4] In *Samuels v Stubbs*,[5] Walters J said:

It seems to me that it is difficult to lay down any very general and, at the same time, precise and absolute rule as to what constitutes 'damage'. One must be guided in a great degree by the circumstances of each case, the nature of the article and the mode in which it is affected or treated . . . It is my view, however, that the word . . . is sufficiently wide in its meaning to embrace injury, mischief or harm done to property, and that in order to constitute 'damage' it is unnecessary to establish such definite or actual damage as renders the property useless, or prevents it from serving its normal function . . .

Under the usual principles, a court or jury must not be allowed to find that the result constitutes damage when no reasonable tribunal could so find. A magistrates' court may be corrected, as a magistrate was in *Samuels v Stubbs*,[6] if it finds that the result was not damage when, in law, it was. The lack of firm definition does nothing to promote consistency in the law.

What is contemplated by 'destroy or damage' is actual destruction or damage; that is, some *physical* alteration, harm, impairment or deterioration. This will usually be capable

---

[3] Although originally the same as theft, this is now more severe than theft (maximum seven years). Penalty notices are often imposed: criminal damage contrary to s 1(1) attracts a fixed penalty—the Penalties for Disorderly Behaviour (Amount of Penalty) Order 2002, SI 2002/1837 (as amended).

[4] *Roe v Kingerlee* [1986] Crim LR 735.

[5] [1972] 4 SASR 200 at 203. Following this, in *Previsic* [2008] VSCA 112 Ashley JA stated that absence of cost of repair is a circumstance that a jury might take into account in deciding whether it was satisfied to the criminal standard that the accused had damaged property.

[6] [1972] 4 SASR 200 at 201.

of being perceived by human senses,[7] but it is the property that must be tangible for the purposes of this offence, not the damage.[8] The damage can be caused by act or omission.[9] It is not enough to show that what has been done amounts to a civil wrong as, for example, a trespass to land or goods for neither requires proof of actual damage. So, in *Eley v Lytle*[10] D was not guilty when, during a game of football, he ran over V's land and committed trespass without actual damage. The same result would follow under the 1971 Act. Actual damage, however, need only be slight. It has been held that grass can be damaged by trampling it down,[11] and is easily and rapidly damaged by football, cricket or even bowls.[12]

The overarching question in determining whether there is damage is to ask whether there has been physical alteration of the property. Several problems arise in practice.

First, a machine or other property comprising many separate parts may be damaged by the removal of one or more parts even if those part(s) remain physically intact. The property (machine) has been damaged as there has been a physical alteration of it as a whole. The courts often examine such cases by reference to whether the usefulness of the property has been impaired.

Applying this approach, there is damage to property where one part is removed intact and unaltered in state, but its removal renders the whole machine inoperable. A car is damaged just as much by uncoupling the brake cable as by cutting it with a pair of pliers. So a machine may be damaged by removing some integral part,[13] or tampering with some part so that it will not work although no part is removed or broken.[14] In this sense, a thing may be damaged in the sense of being physically impaired though nothing is actually broken or deformed. Though a machine or a structure may be damaged by the removal of a part or by dismantling, it does not necessarily follow that *the parts* are damaged by the removal or dismantling; if the parts are undamaged, D can be charged only with damaging the whole machine.[15] Care must be taken in drafting the charge accurately.

The challenge in applying the true test of whether there is a change to the physical integrity of the property—not whether there is impaired functionality—is illustrated by *Lloyd v DPP*.[16] It was argued that clamping a car was, by itself, damage to the car, but the court rejected that and the decision was followed in *Drake v DPP*[17] where it was held that clamping involved no intrusion into the physical integrity of the vehicle. The clamp renders the vehicle useless for its purpose for the time being, just as the removal of an essential working part does, but it does not harm any integral part. In *Lloyd*, a large yellow sticker was also

---

[7] But no doubt a non-rechargeable battery is damaged by exhausting the charge. The damage cannot be perceived by the eye but it has been rendered useless. Similarly, with the erasure of recordings from audio, video and storage media: it was held that a card containing a computer program is damaged by erasure of the program: *Cox v Riley* (1986) 83 Cr App R 54. But as to the modification of computers and computer material, see now the Computer Misuse Act 1990, Ch 28, and s 10(5) of the Act (as inserted) discussed later. On these cases see also I Walden, *Computer Crimes and Digital Investigations* (2nd edn, 2016).

[8] See p 44.   [9] *Miller* [1983] 2 AC 161, p 54.   [10] (1885) 50 JP 308.

[11] *Gayford v Chouler* [1898] 1 QB 316.   [12] cf *Laws v Eltringham* (1881) 8 QBD 283, n 40.

[13] cf *Tacey* (1821) Russ & Ry 452. Charges of criminal damage were brought against the person who sabotaged floodlights at a premiership football game intending to fix bets: The Times, 13 Feb 1999.

[14] cf *Fisher* (1865) LR 1 CCR 7 and see *Getty v Antrim County Council* [1950] NI 114 (dismantling).

[15] *Woolcock* [1977] Crim LR 104 and 161; *Morphitis v Salmon* [1990] Crim LR 48.

[16] [1992] 1 All ER 982.

[17] [1994] RTR 411. Cf the position in Scotland discussed by A Phillips, 'Criminal and Civil Aspects of Wheel Clamping on Private Property' (1993) 38 J of the Law Soc of Scotland 187. Section 54 of the Protection of Freedoms Act 2012 makes it an offence to immobilize a vehicle on private land without lawful authority with a view to preventing its removal by the owner. Before Parliament the minister stated that the rationale for the offence was to abolish the 'menace of intimidation and extortion' that is associated with private clampers. Hansard, HC, 1 Mar 2011, vol 524, col 209.

affixed firmly to the windscreen, rendering it impossible to drive the car until considerable effort had been put into removing it. Brian Hogan contended strenuously, and reasonably, that this must be criminal damage. But applying the court's test, it did not intrude into the 'integrity' of the vehicle any more than the clamp. Affixing with glue can hardly be more intrusive than affixing with steel bolts.

Other cases that may appear inconsistent if viewed by reference to the question of 'impaired usefulness' are clearer when understood to be decided on the basis of whether there is an alteration to the physical state of the property.[18] For example, the courts have accepted that damage was caused to a blanket and police cell where D stuffed the blanket in the toilet in his cell and repeatedly flushed the toilet causing flooding. The water was clean and the floor was waterproof, but the suggestion that this was not damage was 'incomprehensible'. The floor and blanket were rendered temporarily unusable[19] and implicitly the court is acknowledging that the blanket, at least, was physically altered by being soaked with water from a toilet bowl.

Care must be taken to avoid an overly broad approach of an offence of 'damage' to criminalize impairment of 'usefulness'. Consider a case where an owner is deprived of access to a house or car by the theft or borrowing of keys to the front door or ignition keys. It would not be a natural use of language to describe these actions as damaging the house or car (even though the owner may be put to expense before he can put the house or car to their intended uses).[20] The crucial point is that the physical integrity of the house or car is unaltered.

The Australian High Court recently held that simply impairing the functionality of property does not amount to damage.[21] The majority held that there must be some physical contact or connection with the property which caused a physical alteration to it. The minority held that mere physical interference would suffice. The distinction is a useful one which may be attractive to the English courts.

In some cases, the courts have found it useful, in deciding the critical question whether there has been physical alteration, to ask whether there is a reduction in value of the property. Again, care is needed. In holding that there was damage to land by depositing rubble on the land that reduced it in value, the better view is that the court was implicitly recognizing that the land had been physically altered.[22] A car is damaged if the paintwork is scratched and food is damaged by spoiling, as is milk when diluted with water.[23] In each of those cases there is a physical interference. Smith[24] argues that focusing on the impact of D's conduct on the value of V's property is an erroneous approach under the 1971 Act since it could lead to prosecution for criminal damage in wholly unsuitable circumstances.[25] This serves to remind us, again, that the offence requires that property must be physically altered.

In some cases where the physical alteration to property is of a trivial kind, the courts have been influenced in deciding whether there is damage by considering whether expense will

---

[18] See K Grevling, 'Damaging Property' [2020] Crim LR 497.   [19] *Fiak* [2005] EWCA Crim 2381.

[20] *Henderson and Battley* (1984) unreported, CA, but extensively cited in *Cox v Riley* (1986) 83 Cr App R 54.

[21] *Grajewski* [2019] HCA 8.

[22] cf *Foster* (1852) 6 Cox CC 25. Cf *King v Lees* (1948) 65 TLR 21(passenger urinating in taxi held to have caused injury for purposes of London Hackney Carriage Act 1831, s 41).

[23] cf *Roper v Knott* [1898] 1 QB 868.   [24] Smith, *Property Offences*, para 27.16.

[25] The example given is that of the taking of the examination paper in *Oxford v Moss* (1978) 68 Cr App R 183, but the offence would surely not be made out in that case because the harm done (whether damage or not) is to the interest in confidentiality which does not constitute property for criminal damage (nor for theft).

be incurred by the owner in repair.[26] This is perhaps best seen as merely *evidence* of whether there is physical alteration.

In *Samuels v Stubbs*,[27] D had jumped on a policeman's hat resulting in 'temporary functional derangement'. This was held to constitute damage though there was no evidence that the cap might not have been restored to its original state without any real cost or trouble to the owner.[28] By contrast, in *Hardman v Chief Constable of Avon and Somerset Constabulary*,[29] it was held that pavement drawings in water-soluble paint constituted damage to the pavement where the local authority incurred expense in removing them with high-pressure water jets. This seems entirely right, because the property was altered, albeit temporarily. No one would maintain that property which has been daubed by slogans or drawings was not damaged simply because the rain would eventually remove all trace of them[30] or because the householder could remove them more quickly with soap and water. *Samuels v Stubbs* is, perhaps, a less clear case. If an article is accidentally trodden upon (and for the purpose of determining whether there has been damage it can make no difference that it is intentionally trodden upon) and the owner finds that it takes a matter of moments to press it back into shape, surely he would say that no damage had been done? In *A (A Juvenile) v R*,[31] it was held that spitting on a policeman's raincoat did not damage the raincoat where the spittle could be removed by a wipe with a damp cloth. No doubt it would have been otherwise had the raincoat material been capable of being stained by the spittle.[32]

In deciding whether there is damage to property, the defendant's opinion that what he did was not damage is irrelevant if damage is caused in law and fact. V's wall is damaged by D's graffiti irrespective of whether D regards it as an improvement.[33]

Interestingly, the Police and Justice Act 2006 inserted a new s 10(5) which provides that for the purposes of the Criminal Damage Act 'a modification of the contents of a computer shall not be regarded as damaging any computer or computer storage medium unless its effect on that computer or computer storage medium impairs its physical condition'.[34]

'Destroy' clearly goes beyond damage and does not contemplate half measures. The word is a useful addition. It more accurately describes certain forms of conduct; for example: to 'destroy' structures by pulling them down or demolishing them, or to destroy crops or other growing things by laying them to waste, or to break machines, or to kill animals.[35]

---

[26] The problem arises disproportionately frequently with criminal damage because the activities of protestors commonly involve a symbolic act of relatively minor damage—daubing slogans, decapitating statutes of former prime ministers, snipping perimeter fencing of air force bases, etc. See also *Grajewski* [2019] HCA 8.

[27] [1972] 4 SASR 200 at 203.

[28] The test was not one endorsed in *Grajewski*, at [46]: 'Whatever its origin, the concept of "temporary functional derangement" is not a useful criterion for the determination of criminal damage to property. It is an effect or product of damage.'

[29] [1986] Crim LR 330 (Judge Llewellyn Jones and Justices).

[30] For a call for criminal damage prosecutions of dog owners who allow their dogs to foul pavements, see P Alldridge, 'Incontinent Dogs and the Law' (1990) 140 NLJ 1067.

[31] [1978] Crim LR 689 (Judge Streeter and Justices).

[32] But would it not be reasonable for the policeman to insist that even rain-proofed material should be dry cleaned after it had been spat upon?

[33] Nor is D's motive (eg painting fig leaves over parts he considers indecent) relevant. Cf *Fancy* [1980] Crim LR 171 (whiting out National Front slogans). This passage in the 13th edn was cited with approval by the Administrative Court in *Seray-Wurie v DPP* [2012] EWHC 208 (Admin). See also M Watson, 'Graffiti—Popular Art, Anti-Social Behaviour or Criminal Damage' (2004) 168 JP 668 and see the valuable discussion in I Edwards, 'Banksy's Graffiti: A Not So Simple Case' (2009) 73 J Crim L 345, considering whether there is damage, whether D needs to be aware it is damage and whether there is a lawful excuse.

[34] Police and Justice Act 2006, Sch 14, para 2.

[35] cf *Barnet London Borough Council v Eastern Electricity Board* [1973] 2 All ER 319.

27.1.2 Property

Section 10(1) of the Criminal Damage Act provides:

In this Act 'property' means property of a tangible nature, whether real or personal, including money and—

(a) including wild creatures which have been tamed or are ordinarily kept in captivity, and any other wild creatures or their carcasses if, but only if, they have been reduced into possession which has not been lost or abandoned or are in the course of being reduced into possession; but

(b) not including mushrooms growing wild on any land or flowers, fruit or foliage of a plant growing wild on any land.

For the purposes of this subsection 'mushroom' includes any fungus and 'plant' includes any shrub or tree.

The clarifications in para (a) and the exceptions in para (b) are, of course, to keep the law of damage to property closely in line with the law of theft,[36] but there are three significant differences.

First, land, which in general cannot be stolen, may be the subject of criminal damage. The policies against applying theft to appropriating land[37] do not apply when the conduct is damaging land. While D cannot steal his neighbour's beautifully tended lawn by annexing it,[38] he may commit criminal damage by turning it over to grow vegetables.

Secondly, while it is now possible to steal intangible property, it is not possible to commit criminal damage to it. 'Offences of criminal damage to property', said the Law Commission, 'in the context of the present law connote physical damage in their commission, and for that reason we have not included intangible things in the class of property, damage to which should constitute an offence'.[39] Consequently, such intangible property as easements and profits, patents and copyrights, are excluded for the purposes of criminal damage.[40]

Thirdly, whereas it is theft to pick wild mushrooms, fruit and foliage, etc for commercial purposes, this would not result in a criminal damage charge irrespective of whether the picker had commercial motives.[41] It is important to note that the limitation extends only to fruit or foliage of plants growing on the land. The land itself may be damaged by, for example, environmental protest against GM crops.[42]

Turning to animals, in *Cresswell v DPP*,[43] the Divisional Court considered whether badgers which had been enticed into traps set by officials from DEFRA had become 'property' for the purposes of s 10. The defendants sought to argue that the badgers were no longer wild, but property under s 10 and that the defendants had a defence to destroying the traps because they were protecting other property—the badgers. Keene LJ, rejecting the argument, stated that 'merely to entice a wild animal, whether it be a badger or a game bird or a deer, to a particular spot from time to time by providing food there, even with the objective ultimately of killing it in due course, does not form part of the normal course of reducing it into possession. If the creature were thereby to become the property, say, of the landowner

---

[36] But note that the destruction of, or damage to, wild animals and plants may be an offence under other legislation; see eg the Wildlife and Countryside Act 1981 and the Protection of Badgers Act 1992. For an analysis of the 1992 Act, see *Foster v CPS* [2013] EWHC 3885 (Admin).

[37] See p 883.   [38] He might steal from the land by removing the turf.   [39] LC 29, para 34.

[40] cf *Laws v Eltringham* (1881) 8 QBD 283. D and others had been charged with damaging Newcastle Town Moor by playing bowls upon it. It was held that the property could not be laid in the freeman who had merely the (incorporeal) right of herbage; the property ought to have been laid in Newcastle Corporation as the freeholder.

[41] On the relationship of the provisions with the Wildlife and Countryside Act 1981, see M Welstead, 'Seasons of Mists and Mellow Fruitfulness' (1995) 145 NLJ 1499.

[42] See M Stallworthy, 'Damage to Crops' (2000) 150 NLJ 728 at 801.   [43] [2006] EWHC 3379 (Admin).

providing the food, it would mean that it could not then be lawfully shot by the adjoining landowner on or over whose land it passed.'[44] Walker J was more hesitant, declining to express a concluded view on what constitutes property.[45]

A person does not constitute property for the purposes of this offence.[46]

27.1.3 Belonging to another

The offence under s 1(1) may be committed only where D destroys or damages property 'belonging to another'. Here, again, the policy of the law of criminal damage, which must be to protect interests in addition to ownership, is very much the same as that for the law of theft. Section 10 of the Criminal Damage Act therefore provides:[47]

> (2) Property shall be treated for the purposes of this Act as belonging to any person—
>
> > (a) having the custody or control of it;
> >
> > (b) having in it any proprietary right or interest (not being an equitable interest arising only from an agreement to transfer or grant an interest); or
> >
> > (c) having a charge on it.
>
> (3) Where property is subject to a trust, the person to whom it belongs shall be so treated as including any person having a right to enforce the trust.
>
> (4) Property of a corporation sole shall be so treated as belonging to the corporation notwithstanding a vacancy in the corporation.

It is, then, enough that V has some proprietary interest in the property which D damages, and it does not have to be shown that V is the owner of the property. D may, for example, damage property which V has borrowed or rented. Further, D may commit an offence where the property belongs to him provided that V *also* has a proprietary interest in the property. So, where D owns a car and loans it to V, but then D damages the car during the loan period, he damages property 'belonging to another'. In such cases, it may be difficult to prove that D acted with mens rea or without lawful excuse,[48] but, given that, D may commit criminal damage though he both owns and has custody and control of the property. Just as a co-owner of property may steal it by appropriating the other's share,[49] a co-owner may commit criminal damage by destroying or damaging the property.

V must have some *proprietary* right or interest in the property.[50] Where property is insured the insurer acquires an interest in the property, but the interest is not a proprietary one.[51] If D destroys his own property which he has insured with V, he does not destroy property belonging to another even though he may have destroyed it with a view to making a dishonest claim against V.[52] In *Appleyard*,[53] where D, the managing director of a company, set fire to the company's premises, it was argued that he could not be convicted of arson since he was 'in effect' the owner of the premises. D's conviction for arson was nevertheless upheld apparently on the basis that he was not the owner of the premises and knew he was not.

---

[44] At [11].   [45] His lordship did express some more general views on the concept of wild animals, at [38].

[46] *Baker* [1997] Crim LR 497.

[47] See for comparison s 5 of the Theft Act 1968, p 889.   [48] See p 1104.

[49] *Bonner* [1970] 1 WLR 838, p 889.   [50] See p 1103.

[51] An insurer has an interest in the safety of the insured property but, without more, this does not constitute a proprietary interest. Cf *Lucena v Craufurd* (1806) 2 Bos & PNR 269 at 302 per Lawrence J.

[52] cf *Denton* [1981] 1 WLR 1446, n 94. Such offences were included in the Malicious Damage Act 1861, ss 3 and 59.

[53] (1985) 81 Cr App R 319.

Property is also to be treated as belonging to a person who has a 'charge' on it. At least that is what the Law Commission intended by its conclusion that this was an interest worthy of protection.[54] The expression does not expressly appear in s 5 of the Theft Act 1968 and is probably unnecessary in either Act, since a charge is almost certainly a 'proprietary interest'.

It will be noted that the definition of property belonging to another in s 10 of the Criminal Damage Act contains no provision equivalent to s 5(4) of the Theft Act—property got by another's mistake. This distinction can be of no practical importance: if someone obtains property by another's mistake he may be tempted to keep it but will be unlikely to decide to damage it. There do not seem to have been difficulties over allegations of damaging abandoned property.[55] In *Cresswell*, it was accepted that there may well be some items of property which do not belong to another (eg because they are abandoned) and some which are not capable of so belonging (eg with wild animals in a state of being reduced into possession).[56]

Where D is the owner of property in which no other person has *any* proprietary right or interest, his destroying or damaging it cannot amount to an offence under s 1(1).[57] Nor generally is it an offence to damage one's own property apart from the special case dealt with in s 1(2).[58] It is not an offence for D to destroy a work of art which he owns or to lay waste to his plentiful stocks of food at a time of acute shortage. Such acts may be properly described as wanton but they are not criminal because there is no compelling policy reason for making them criminal. But where such a reason does exist, and cruelty to animals one owns provides an illustration, particular offences can be created which deal with harm by an owner to his own property.[59]

27.1.4 Mens rea

Section 1(1) requires that the destruction or damaging of the property should be intentional or reckless, and without lawful excuse.

27.1.4.1 Intention and recklessness

The mens rea requirement in the Malicious Damage Act offences was intention or malice.[60] The Law Commission expressly stated its intention that the offences under the Criminal Damage Act 1971 should require the same mens rea. The only difference was to be a change of language from malice to 'recklessness', reflecting the Commission's aim for greater simplicity and clarity. The term 'maliciously'[61] was avoided because:

It is evident from such cases as *Cunningham*[62] and *Mowatt*[63] that the word can give rise to difficulties of interpretation. Furthermore, the word 'maliciously' conveys the impression that some ill-will is required against the person whose property is damaged.[64]

The Law Commission recommended proof that D's conduct was intended by D to cause the damage in question or was foreseen by D as creating a risk of causing that damage which risk he then went on unjustifiably to take. In other words, recklessness was to be interpreted in its subjective sense.

---

[54] LC 29, para 39.　　[55] cf theft of 'abandoned' property: p 904.　　[56] Walker J at [41].
[57] If, in a case like *Hinks*, p 867, the donee is given a chattel, he may steal it, but he can then damage or destroy it with impunity. Where the donee's title is voidable, it may be arguable that it is different.
[58] See p 1117.　　[59] Examples would include protection of listed buildings.
[60] cf the general discussion of intention and recklessness, Ch 3.
[61] 'Maliciously' was the expression most commonly used in the Malicious Damage Act 1861 to describe mens rea.
[62] [1957] 2 QB 396, p 105.　　[63] [1968] 1 QB 421, p 725.　　[64] LC 29, para 44.

27.1.4.2 Mens rea as to circumstances and consequences

There must be mens rea proved as to the damage (consequences) and that the property damaged belongs to another (circumstances). It is not enough that D intends to do the act which causes the damage unless he intends to cause the damage itself; proof that D intended to throw a stone is not proof that he intended to break a window.[65] Nor is it enough that D intends or is reckless as to damaging property if he does not intend or is not reckless as to the damage being to property *of another*. Since D commits no offence under s 1(1) of the Act in damaging or destroying his own property, it follows in principle that he ought not to be guilty where he destroys V's property under the mistaken impression that it is his own. Whether D's mistake is one of fact or law, he commits no crime for he lacks mens rea, and this view was firmly endorsed by the Court of Appeal in *Smith*.[66] At the end of his tenancy of a flat, D had caused £130 worth of damage in removing wiring which he had himself installed and boarded over. As a matter of property law, the landlord became the owner of the wiring and boarding as fixtures, and the trial judge directed the jury that D could have no lawful excuse since he had in law no right to do as he did. D's appeal against conviction was allowed. James LJ said on behalf of the court:[67]

Applying the ordinary principles of *mens rea*, the intention and recklessness and the absence of lawful excuse required to constitute the offence have reference to property belonging to another. It follows that in our judgment no offence is committed under this section if a person destroys or causes damage to property belonging to another if he does so in the honest though mistaken belief that the property is his own, and provided that the belief is honestly held it is irrelevant to consider whether or not it is a justifiable belief.

The mistake in *Smith* was a mistake as to the civil law; D knew all the facts and drew the wrong conclusion of law from them. The result is the same as far as criminal liability is concerned whether the mistake is one of fact or law as long as the mistake negatives mens rea.[68] As such, D commits no offence in pulling down a house if he honestly believes the house is his whether his mistake is one of fact or civil law and however egregious his error may have been.[69] It makes no difference that D's conduct might be described as wanton (as where he destroys a work of art) or that his purpose is a crime of fraud (eg to defraud insurers). If D does not intend to destroy or damage property of *another*, nothing can render him liable to a charge under s 1(1). In *Appleyard*,[70] discussed earlier, if D had believed that he owned the company's premises then he could not have been convicted of this offence whatever his motive (to defraud insurers or creditors, to inflict loss on the shareholders) may have been.

27.1.4.3 Mens rea as to consequences (damage)

The Act extends liability not merely to damage which is caused intentionally but also damage which is caused recklessly. The Law Commission recommended subjective recklessness as to consequences as noted earlier.[71] As Lord Edmund-Davies pointed out,[72] that was surely in the draftsman's mind when he drafted the Criminal Damage Act. This was not the view taken in *Caldwell*,[73] where the criminal law was plunged into unnecessary confusion and

---

[65] cf *Pembliton* (1874) LR 2 CCR 119.

[66] [1974] QB 354. See also *Seray-Wurie v DPP* [2012] EWHC 208 (Admin).

[67] [1974] 1 All ER 632 at 636.   [68] See generally p 351.   [69] cf *Langford* (1842) Car & M 602.

[70] (1985) 81 Cr App R 319.

[71] 'A person is reckless if, (a) knowing that there is a risk that an event may result from his conduct or that circumstances may exist, he takes that risk, and (b) it is unreasonable for him to take it, having regard to the degree and nature of the risk he knows to be present': Working Paper No 31, *The Mental Element in Crime* (1970). See also LC 89, *Criminal Law: Report on the Mental Element in Crime* (1978).

[72] *Caldwell* [1982] AC 341.   [73] [1982] AC 341.

complexity,[74] and the breadth of the offence posed risks of serious unfairness.[75] Fortunately, the House of Lords subsequently acknowledged that the decision of the majority in *Caldwell* constituted a misinterpretation of the 1971 Act, and for that reason and for sound reasons of policy and principle as discussed in Ch 3, in *G*[76] the orthodox subjective interpretation of recklessness which the Law Commission intended has been re-established. *Caldwell* is overruled.

In *G*,[77] the two defendants aged 11 and 12, when on a camping expedition, entered the yard of a shop and set fire to bundles of newspapers leaving some lit newspaper under a large plastic wheelie bin. The newspapers set fire to the wheelie bin and the fire spread causing £1m worth of damage. The boys had expected the fires to extinguish themselves on the concrete floor; neither had appreciated that there was any risk of the fire spreading in the way that it did.[78] They were convicted of arson contrary to ss 1(1) and 1(3) of the Criminal Damage Act applying the *Caldwell* formula of recklessness, although the jury acknowledged some difficulty in applying fairly an objective standard to children whose capacity to see risk was limited by their immaturity.[79] In overruling *Caldwell*, Lord Bingham observed that:

section 1 as enacted followed, subject to an immaterial addition, the draft proposed by the Law Commission. It cannot be supposed that by 'reckless' Parliament meant anything different from the Law Commission. The Law Commission's meaning was made plain both in its Report (Law Com No 29) and in Working Paper No 23 which preceded it. These materials (not, it would seem, placed before the House in *R v Caldwell*) reveal a very plain intention to replace the old-fashioned and misleading expression 'maliciously' by the more familiar expression 'reckless' but to give the latter expression the meaning which *R v Cunningham* . . . and Professor Kenny had given to the former. In treating this authority as irrelevant to the construction of 'reckless' the majority fell into understandable but clearly demonstrable error. No relevant change in the mens rea necessary for proof of the offence was intended, and in holding otherwise the majority misconstrued section 1 of the Act.[80]

As Lord Bingham made clear, the definition of recklessness to be applied in criminal damage is now that found in cl 18(c) of the Draft Criminal Code:

A person acts recklessly within the meaning of section 1 of the Criminal Damage Act 1971 with respect to—

(i) a circumstance when he is aware of a risk that it exists or will exist;

(ii) a result when he is aware of a risk that it will occur; and it is, in the circumstances known to him, unreasonable to take the risk.

The courts have applied the new test unhesitatingly.[81]

The doctrine of transferred malice[82] applies to the offence, so that if D intends, or is reckless as to, damage to property of A, he may be liable where he in fact causes damage, neither intentionally nor recklessly, to property of B.

---

[74] See *G* [2004] AC 1034 at [57] per Lord Steyn.

[75] See at [33] per Lord Bingham in *G*: 'It is neither moral nor just to convict a defendant (least of all a child) on the strength of what someone else would have apprehended if the defendant himself had no such apprehension. Nor, the defendant having been convicted is the problem cured by imposition of a nominal penalty.'

[76] [2004] AC 1034.   [77] ibid.

[78] Lord Bingham noted that they would have had little defence to a charge in relation to the wheelie bin, at [33].

[79] See the interesting analysis of H Keating, 'Reckless Children' [2007] Crim LR 546 on whether the children were likely to have foreseen damage and public attitudes to punishing such acts by children.

[80] *G* at [29]. See also Lord Steyn at [45] and Lord Rodger at [64].

[81] See p 112.   [82] See p 125.

The intention or the recklessness need not be related to the particular property damaged, provided that it is related to another's property. If, for example, D throws a stone at a passing car intending to damage it, but misses and breaks a shop window, he will have the necessary intention in respect of the damage to the window as he intended to damage the property of another. But if in a fit of anger he throws a stone at his own car he will not have the requisite intention if it misses and damages V's. In this case the question of whether he has committed an offence will depend upon whether in throwing the stone at his own car he was reckless as to whether any property belonging to another would be destroyed or damaged.[83]

D would not commit an offence of criminal damage where he throws a stone at V but misses him and breaks a window, unless of course D was subjectively reckless as to the risk of breaking the window.[84]

Arson, as we will see later, is a separate offence carrying a higher punishment than damage caused by other means and its mens rea requires not merely the intentional or reckless damaging of property but the intentional or reckless damaging of property *by fire*. Williams rightly suggests[85] that transferred malice would not apply where D, intent on damaging property other than by fire, accidentally starts a fire in circumstances where he had no foresight of a risk of fire.

Obviously, mens rea cannot be supplied by an afterthought. If D inadvertently breaks V's window he cannot become liable when, having learned that V is his sworn enemy or a hated tax inspector, he rejoices in the harm caused. On the other hand, if D inadvertently sets fire to V's property and subsequently becomes aware[86] that he has done so, he may be criminally liable if, intending or being reckless that *further* damage ensue to V's property, he lets the fire take its course when it lies within his power to prevent or minimize that further damage.[87]

Judges may have to provide careful directions on the issues of intention and recklessness if both are alleged.[88]

27.1.5 Lawful excuse

The Law Commission took the view that in most cases:

there is a clear distinction between the mental element and the element of unlawfulness, and in the absence of one or other element no offence will be committed, notwithstanding that damage may have been done to another's property. For example, a police officer who, in order to execute a warrant of arrest, has to force open a door of a house is acting with lawful excuse although he intends to damage the door or the lock. On the other hand a person playing tennis on a properly fenced court who inadvertently hits a ball on to a greenhouse roof, breaking a pane of glass, acts without lawful excuse, but will escape liability because he has not the requisite intention.[89]

This distinction drawn by the Law Commission between the 'mental element' and the element of 'unlawfulness' may be a distinction of convenience but it is also a distinction generally adopted in this book. It is thought convenient to consider separately, as far as the

---

[83] LC 29, para 45.   [84] cf *Pembliton* (1874) LR 2 CCR 119.

[85] (1983) 42 CLJ 85 at 86. Cf A Ashworth, 'Transferred Malice and Punishment for Unforeseen Consequences' in Glazebrook, *Reshaping the Criminal Law*, 77, 92. The issue is discussed in detail in J Horder, 'A Critique of the Correspondence Principle in Criminal Law' [1995] Crim LR 759 at 769–70. Horder argues that what really matters is 'the representative label: is it right to label D as an arsonist if he did not intend to start a fire . . .' Cf B Mitchell, 'In Defence of a Principle of Correspondence' [1999] Crim LR 195.

[86] It is not enough that D ought to have been aware, or was not aware because he gave no thought to it: *Miller* [1983] 2 AC 161.

[87] *Miller*, ibid. See p 53.   [88] *Mason* [2005] All ER (D) 04 (Feb).   [89] LC 29, para 49.

situation permits, the issue of intention or recklessness as to the damaging of the property and the various grounds of exculpation or justification that may exist for damage deliberately done.

Section 5 of the Act provides a partial definition of 'lawful excuse'. The section in part provides:

(2) A person charged with an offence to which this section applies[90] shall, whether or not he would be treated for the purposes of this Act as having a lawful excuse apart from this subsection, be treated for those purposes as having a lawful excuse—

(a) if at the time of the act or acts alleged to constitute the offence he believed that the person or persons whom he believed to be entitled to consent to the destruction of or damage to the property in question had so consented, or would have consented to it if he or they had known of the destruction or damage and its circumstances; or

(b) if he destroyed or damaged or threatened to destroy or damage the property in question . . . in order to protect property belonging to himself or another or a right or interest in property which was or which he believed to be vested in himself or another, and at the time of the act or acts alleged to constitute the offence he believed—

(i) that the property, right or interest was in immediate need of protection; and

(ii) that the means of protection adopted or proposed to be adopted were or would be reasonable having regard to all the circumstances.

(3) For the purpose of this section it is immaterial whether a belief is justified or not if it is honestly held.

(4) For the purposes of subsection (2) above a right or interest in property includes any right or privilege in or over land, whether created by grant, licence or otherwise.

The Court of Appeal confirmed in *Cairns*[91] that the offence is not one of destroying or damaging property without the consent of the owner. It is incumbent upon the prosecution to prove that D had no lawful excuse for what he did only if D can adduce sufficient evidence to raise this issue.

27.1.5.1 Belief in consent

D's belief is judged by the single criterion that it be honestly held; a point which, if it is not clear enough from the wording of s 5(2)(a), is put beyond doubt by s 5(3). Section 5(2)(a) closely follows the pattern of s 2(1)(b) of the Theft Act 1968,[92] and it is right that it should.[93]

The provision covers a number of mistaken beliefs. First, and most obviously, this provision covers the case where D believes that the owner *has consented* to the destruction or damage. So, in *Denton*,[94] it was held that D was not guilty of arson in setting fire to his employer's mill when D believed that his employer had encouraged him to do so (even though this was in order to make a fraudulent claim against the insurers). Secondly, the provision covers the case where D believes the owner *would have consented* as, for

---

90 The section applies to an offence under s 1(1); as to other offences, see later.
91 [2013] EWCA Crim 172.   92 See p 908.
93 Note that the question of dishonesty is now governed by a largely objective test otherwise than under s 2 of the Theft Act. In some cases, D may be able to rely on a lack of dishonesty to deny a charge of eg burglary, but not be able to rely on s 5 of the 1971 Act since there is no evidence that the property D claimed to be defending was in fact in need of protection: *Scott* [2017] EWCA Crim 1000.
94 [1981] 1 WLR 1446.

example, where D comes across an injured animal and, believing that the owner *would have consented* had he been able to contact him, D kills the animal to put it out of its misery.[95] Thirdly, the provision covers the case where D rightly believes that X is a person *entitled to consent* to the destruction or damage and wrongly believes that he *has consented*. Thus, for example, an employee destroying or damaging property belonging to the firm would commit no offence where he believed that some person in authority (say, a foreman) was entitled to consent, and had consented.[96] Fourthly, the provision applies where D honestly but wrongly believes that X is the person *entitled to consent* and also wrongly believes that X *would have consented* to the damage if asked. Mistakes as to the identity of the person entitled to consent, the status of the person, the presence of consent and the likelihood of conditional consent are therefore all accommodated in this extremely wide defence.

One controversial example of the breadth of the defence is that in *Jaggard v Dickinson*[97] where D had permission to treat the house of a friend, X, as her own. One night when D was heavily intoxicated she took a taxi to the street where X lived. D then attempted to enter what she mistakenly believed to be X's house, smashing a window in the process. The magistrates had rejected the s 5(2)(a) defence since D's belief in consent was brought about by self-induced intoxication. The Divisional Court quashed the conviction because of the explicitly subjective focus of s 5(3): 'a belief can be just as much honestly held if it is induced by intoxication, as if it stems from stupidity, forgetfulness or inattention'.[98] Williams exposes the breadth of the decision by posing the case of D, intoxicated by LSD, who believes that the owner of a Rolls Royce has instructed him to roll it over a cliff.

Based on subjective beliefs though the defence is, it seems that a belief that God is entitled to, and does, consent to the damage is no answer.[99]

27.1.5.2 Defence of property

D has a lawful excuse within s 5(2)(b) if:

(1) he destroyed or damaged the property in question in order to protect property which he *believed* to be vested in himself or another.[100] Some decisions have interpreted this as importing an objective element into the defence. It is submitted that this element ought, on a natural interpretation of the language, to be construed entirely subjectively;

---

[95] There is also a specific defence under the Wild Mammals (Protection) Act 1996, to the offence under that Act of inflicting unnecessary suffering on a wild animal, where D attempts to kill a wild mammal as an act of mercy if D shows that the mammal had been so seriously disabled otherwise than by his unlawful act that there was no reasonable chance of its recovering (s 2). Note also the Animal Welfare Act 2006, ss 4–8 (as amended), which create offences of harm to protected animals. For analysis of these provisions, see *R (Gray) v Crown Court at Aylesbury* [2013] EWHC 500 (Admin).

[96] cf *James* (1837) 8 C & P 131.

[97] [1981] 3 All ER 716. Note that in *Magee v CPS* [2014] EWHC 4089 (Admin), the Divisional Court went as far as to say 'there is considerable doubt whether *Jaggard* is still good law in the light of such cases as *O'Connor* [1991] CLR 135 and *R v Hatton* [2005] EWCA Crim 2951 . . ., in any event I am satisfied that *Jaggard* could, and should, be narrowly rather than widely construed. *Jaggard* turned on the construction of the specific defence in section 5 of the 1971 Act', at [32]–[34] per Elias LJ.

[98] At 532 per Mustill J. See G Williams, 'Two Nocturnal Blunders' (1990) 140 NLJ 1564.

[99] *Blake v DPP* [1993] Crim LR 586, p 418 and commentary suggesting difficulties also because God is not a 'person'.

[100] In *Cresswell* [2006] EWHC 3379 (Admin), the argument that these words were superfluous was rejected. They may be necessary to deal with abandoned property.

(2) he *believed* the property to be in immediate need of protection. The courts have construed this as a hybrid test by importing an objective element—ie does D have a *reasonable* belief;

(3) he *believed* that the means of protection adopted were reasonable having regard to all the circumstances. This is interpreted as an entirely subjective question.[101]

Origin and type of threat

A person is entitled to take measures to protect his own property, real or personal, from harm caused by, or by the use of, property belonging to another. The origin of the threat to D's property might be animate (eg trespassing cattle) or inanimate (eg a caravan). If, for example, a dog is attacking sheep it may be shot if D believes that he needs to do so in order to protect the sheep.[102] A right of way over land belonging to another, being a 'right or privilege in or over land', is 'property' and may be defended, in appropriate circumstances, by the demolition of a wall obstructing it.[103] The owner clearly has this right where the risk to his property exists in fact, but the Act goes further in providing defences.

In *Jones*,[104] the Court of Appeal concluded that there is no requirement that the threat to the item of property D believed to be in need of protection is a threat of *unlawful* damage. It is clear that s 5 does not, on its face, restrict the scope of the defence to the prevention of unlawful damage. In *Cresswell* (the badger case), however, the Divisional Court suggested that the s 5(2) defence was not available to D who argued that he had believed the badgers to be in immediate need of protection from DEFRA. It is not the purpose of the section to prevent an owner destroying or damaging his property.[105] In *Creswell*, on D's argument that he believed the badgers to be owned by DEFRA, there would be no unlawful act perpetrated against the badgers by DEFRA (if they were the owners) if they killed them. Keene LJ suggested that if there was an unlawful act another defence would arise.[106]

Threat to 'property'

The property which D believes he is acting in order to protect must exist.[107] It is, of course, for the prosecution to disprove D's claim as long as D meets the evidential burden by laying a foundation for his claim to lawful excuse. The obligation is interpreted strictly: it is not for

---

[101] cf the Northern Irish case of *McCann* in which the Court of Appeal summarized the position as follows: 'there are three elements to the defence . . . firstly, that the defendant acted in order to protect property; secondly that he honestly believed that that property was in immediate need of protection; and, thirdly, that he honestly believed that his actions were reasonable having regard to all the circumstances. It is clear that the second and third elements of the defence involve the application of a subjective test, ie did the defendant honestly believe that the conditions therein arose in the particular case. Different considerations arise in relation to the first element of the defence, however.' That interpretation was also the one of the Divisional Court in *DPP v Unsworth* [2010] EWHC 3037 (Admin).

[102] Where there is no such justification, injuring the animal may constitute an offence under the Animal Welfare Act 2006, s 4 (as amended). Cf *Isted v CPS* (1997) 162 JP 513, decided under the old law.

[103] *Chamberlain v Lindon* [1998] 2 All ER 538. It was accepted in *Unsworth* [2010] EWHC 3037 (Admin), without any consideration being given to the question, that the right to light is 'property' and that the applicant's property was therefore being threatened by her neighbour's 12ft-high conifer trees. As the Law Commission notes, however, the right to light is different from other rights over land. See LCCP 210, *Rights to Light* (2013) and LC 356, *Rights to Light* (2014).

[104] [2005] QB 259.   [105] At [16] per Keene LJ.

[106] If D peers through my window and sees me about to destroy my original Picasso in my living room, can he rely on s 5(2)(b) as a defence to breaking down my door? I would be committing no crime, but should D have a defence?

[107] Per Keene LJ in *Cresswell*, n 100, at [10].

the judge to raise the defence and it has even been suggested that D must raise the defence by testifying.[108]

'In order to'

This aspect of the s 5(2)(b) provision has caused most difficulty. In a series of cases, the courts have said that the words 'in order to protect property' have an objective meaning. The insistence that the test is objective is difficult to reconcile with the wording of the statute which suggests a purely subjective test.

In *Hunt*,[109] D, who assisted his wife in her job as warden of a block of old people's flats, set fire to some bedding. He said he did so in order to demonstrate that the fire alarm was not working and so to protect the flats from immediate danger by getting it put right. The court concluded that while this act was done in order to draw attention to the defective state of the fire alarm, it was not done in order to protect property. Roskill LJ was clear that the question whether or not a particular act of destruction or damage or threat of destruction or damage was done or made 'in order to' protect property belonging to another must be an objective test.

In *Ashford and Smith*[110] and *Hill and Hall*,[111] the defendants were convicted of possessing articles with intent to damage property, namely the perimeter fences surrounding military bases. They each claimed to have a lawful excuse because the military bases, being an obvious target for enemy attack, constituted an immediate danger to property in the neighbourhood, and they acted in order to have the bases, and with them, the danger, removed. In both cases, the court said that the defence had rightly been withdrawn from the jury: *objectively*, the defendants did not act in order to protect property.[112]

In *Johnson v DPP*,[113] D, a squatter, damaged the door frame of a house in order to replace the locks with one of his own. He said that he did so in order to protect his property which he believed to be in immediate need of protection. The court purporting to apply an objective test (but in fact, it seems, simply disbelieving D) said that his purpose was not to protect property but to enable him to use the door; and, in applying a subjective test, that he did not believe his property was in immediate need of protection and that the means of protection were reasonable. It should be noted that a person may act with more than one purpose, and it is sufficient that one of those purposes was to protect property.[114]

As the court in *Hill and Hall* accepts, there are two distinct matters to be addressed. The first matter to be decided is D's actual state of mind. If D is asked, 'Why did you do this act?' and answers 'In order to protect the flats from fire', or 'To save the houses from damage by enemy attack' or 'To protect my property from thieves', he may be disbelieved but, if his answer is or may be true, if this was, or may have been, his reason for acting, it is impossible to say, rationally, that he did not act 'in order to' protect property. A purpose can exist only in the mind; it need not have an objective existence. If A sticks pins into a wax model of Buckingham Palace in order to destroy it, all reasonable people will agree that

---

[108] And not through defence statements or counsel: *Jones* [2003] EWCA Crim 894 at [14] per Buxton LJ.

[109] (1977) 66 Cr App R 105. Cf *Phillips v Pringle* [1973] 1 NSWLR 275, (action pursuant to a UN resolution against racialism not a lawful excuse for damaging goalposts).

[110] [1988] Crim LR 682.   [111] (1988) 89 Cr App R 74.

[112] In *Hill and Hall*, it was added that there was no evidence on which it could be found that D believed the property was in immediate need of protection.

[113] [1994] Crim LR 673. See also *Scott* [2016] EWCA Crim 1000.

[114] In *Chamberlain v Lindon* [1998] 1 WLR 1252, n 103, it was held that it was immaterial that D may have had a second purpose of avoiding civil litigation. This attitude has not been reflected in other cases, including *Mitchell* [2004] Crim LR 139 where the court rejected the common law defence of recaption where D had removed wheel clamps. Self-help is a last resort, but see *Unsworth v DPP* [2010] EWHC 3037 (Admin).

the act does not imperil the Palace. 'Objectively' the act is quite harmless; but no amount of objectivity can alter the fact that A acts 'in order to' destroy property if that is why he is acting. Similarly, if he acts in order to *protect* property. This issue should be assessed on D's subjective belief.

It may be that all three cases above can be justified without the need to interpret 'in order to' as having an objective meaning. The more acceptable basis for the decisions is that in each case the need, even as asserted by the defendants, was not an *immediate* need.[115]

'In immediate need of protection'

The courts' importation of an objective element into this question of D's alleged belief that the property was 'in immediate need of protection' is also difficult to reconcile with the statutory language but is, in policy terms, easier to justify.

Under s 5(2)(b)(i) and (ii) it is irrelevant that the belief was wholly unreasonable if it was, or may have been, actually held. Unreasonableness is only evidence which assists the trier of fact in determining the ultimate question: whether the belief was honestly held or not. But, once D's belief is ascertained, however unreasonable the existence of the belief, the question whether it is a belief of the kind specified in the section is an objective question—a question of law or, perhaps, mixed fact and law. Whether the need for protection, as seen by D, is an 'immediate' need is a question for the court or jury. For example, if Johnson had said that he believed his goods would be in need of protection when he moved them into the premises in a week's time, the court may believe him but not accept that this belief is a belief in an 'immediate' need for protection.

The courts have followed the approach in *Hill and Hall* to deny the defence where protestors had caused criminal damage as a symbolic gesture of protest where there was no 'direct and proximate' threat to their property.[116] In *Jones*, D was convicted of causing £65,000-worth of damage to council premises in a protest over planning permission. Buxton LJ[117] accepted that the objective evaluation of beliefs in the defence was no different from the court deciding whether a defendant's claim that his intent was to break the victim's nose amounted in law to grievous bodily harm.[118] The absence of any 'immediate' need for protection has also been used by the courts to prevent defendants relying on s 5(2)(b) when they have damaged wheel clamps attached to their vehicles.[119]

Belief in the reasonableness of the action

Once again the subjective terms of s 5(2)(b) need to be emphasized. There is no requirement that D's belief be reasonable, still less that D's conduct must meet some objective standard of reasonableness. The section does require that D must believe that it was reasonable for him to do as he did. In theory, D might justify destroying an oil refinery because he believes it is polluting the air and damaging his geraniums. However, a jury is unlikely to believe he did think, or could possibly have thought, that this was reasonable.[120] This example was discussed in *DPP v Unsworth*[121] where the court quashed D's conviction for criminal damage

---

[115] In *Chamberlain v Lindon*, n 103, it was held that D, within the meaning of the Act, believed the right of way was in immediate need of protection because the wall across it was an existing obstruction and delay would be evidence of acquiescence in it.

[116] *Jones* [2003] EWCA Crim 894.   [117] Citing this part of the 10th edn of this book with approval.

[118] *Jones* [2003] EWCA Crim 894, [19]. Whether the harm amounts to GBH is not for D to dictate.

[119] See *Lloyd v DPP* [1992] 1 All ER 982; *Mitchell* [2004] Crim LR 139.

[120] *Hunt* might be different. There was some evidence that efforts had been made to get the council to repair the fire alarm but these had proved unavailing. D may thus have reached the end of his tether and his claim that he believed the action reasonable might carry some credibility.

[121] [2010] EWHC 3037 (Admin).

to her neighbour's trees which D claimed to have cut down to protect the right to light that D believed she had. The defence had been misapplied at trial. Munby LJ pointed out that:

The protection, the safeguard, against such extravagant attempts to rely upon the defence is of course, . . . that a jury is unlikely in the circumstances postulated to believe that the defendant did think or could possibly have thought that what he was doing was reasonable.[122]

The problem is that in practice, because of the theoretical availability of such a defence, protestors are able to advance the plea at trial, and maintain maximum publicity for their cause throughout the trial.

Relationship with other defences

Section 5(2)(b) is in line with general principles of defences insofar as it relates to beliefs in facts or circumstances. However, it goes well beyond the norm by providing that D's *belief* that the means employed *were reasonable* will excuse him. This must be contrasted with the position in self-defence/prevention of crime where D may use such force as *is found by a jury to be reasonable* in the circumstances which D believed to exist.[123] In self-defence, D's belief in the trigger for the defence is assessed on a subjective basis but the response to it is assessed objectively. The disparity between the 1971 Act and the common law was acknowledged in *DPP v Bayer*,[124] where Brooke LJ noted that the degree of incoherence provided a further illustration of the urgent need for codification.

The breadth of the defence in s 5(2) may be thought to carry subjectivity to excessive lengths. It departs from the general principle of criminal law that standards are set by the law, in practice by the jury or magistrates, not by every person for himself. The effect may be that D's right under s 5 to use force to defend his dog, which is property, may be more fully protected by the law than his right relying on private defence to use force to defend his child, who is not property.[125]

Prophylactic measures in defence of property

D may not destroy or damage property of another merely because he honestly believes that harm may occur to D's property at some time in the future. On the other hand, it is not unlawful for D to take defensive measures in relation to his own property. It is an offence under s 31 of the OAPA 1861 to set traps so as to endanger life,[126] and it is an offence under s 1(2) of the Criminal Damage Act 1971 to destroy or damage property intending or being reckless as to the endangerment of life,[127] but it is not otherwise an offence merely to take defensive measures (to set broken glass on walls, erect spiked fences, etc) for the purpose of discouraging or preventing incursions by persons on their property.[128] In such cases, the question of criminal liability can arise only where some harm is caused to the person or property of another.

So far as harm to another's property is concerned, D will ordinarily have taken his defensive or protective measures at some stage before his property was in 'immediate need of

122 At [42].
123 See p 404. Note that an apparent attempt in *Scarlett* [1993] 4 All ER 629 to introduce a similar subjective standard into the law of self-defence and prevention of crime has been resoundingly rejected. See now the Criminal Justice and Immigration Act 2008, s 76.
124 [2004] 1 Cr App R 38. Some of the broader statements in *Bayer* regarding defences were doubted in *Cresswell*, n 100.
125 Section 5(2)(b) does not apply to damage to property in order to protect a person: *Baker and Wilkins* [1997] Crim LR 497.
126 See *Cockburn* [2008] EWCA Crim 316.   127 See p 1117.
128 cf potential civil liability under the Occupiers' Liability Act 1984, on which see J Goudkamp and D Nolan, *Winfield and Jolowicz on Tort* (20th edn, 2020) Ch 9.

protection', and when the harm occurs D may be absent and unaware of it. It is submitted that where what D has done is a normal method of protecting property, say a barbed wire fence erected by D, a farmer, he would not be liable though a trespasser tears his best suit in climbing through the fence, notwithstanding that D himself could not have justified ripping open the trespasser's suit as a use of reasonable force to eject him.[129] But where D adopts unusual defensive measures, say traps calculated to maim animals, it would normally not be difficult to show that he did not honestly believe this was a reasonable way to protect his property. In determining whether D thought the protective measure was reasonable, regard would be had to D's knowledge of the risk of accidental as opposed to deliberate trespass, of the risk to children not capable of looking properly to their own protection, of the propensities of the particular dog and other similar factors.

There are related offences relating to animals—the Guard Dogs Act[130] criminalizes the person who leaves an unchained dog loose on his premises overnight. Such a person could be liable under the Criminal Damage Act if property is damaged by the dog attacking a trespasser unless he believed that the keeping of an uncontrolled guard dog was reasonable having regard to all the circumstances.[131]

Another common case calling for the protection of property is where a dog is worrying livestock. In such a case, s 5(2)(b) will ordinarily provide a lawful excuse for the killing of the dog. The civil law provides further protection.[132] The law in such circumstances is further complicated by the availability of charges under the Animal Welfare Act 2006, but no offence is committed if an animal is destroyed in an appropriate and humane manner.[133]

Protecting interests that D believes he has

In most cases no doubt D will be the owner of the property which he seeks to protect, but even if D is not the owner he will not incur criminal liability if he honestly believes himself to be the owner and the other circumstances set out in the section exist.

The scope of the defence under s 5(2)(b) is again rather surprising. By s 5(4), property is expressly defined to include any right or privilege in or over land. Consequently, D commits no crime where, honestly but mistakenly believing he has a right of way across V's land, he tears down a hut erected by V which, as D thinks, obstructs his imagined right of way. Moreover, D is in the same position where he believes that he has a right or interest in property which he protects, but that imagined right is not a right or interest which is recognized by law. D has a defence in such a case because by s 5(3) it is immaterial whether a belief is justified or not so long as it is honestly held. Suppose, for example, that D has a right to kill and take game on O's land, and D kills V's dog which he sees chasing and destroying game.

---

[129] Note the specific powers to remove trespassers under the Criminal Justice and Public Order Act 1994, s 69.

[130] The Guard Dogs Act 1975 makes it a summary offence, punishable by a fine, to use or permit the use of a guard dog (ie a dog kept for the purpose of protecting persons or property or a person guarding the same) unless a person capable of controlling the dog, the handler, is present and controlling it, except where the dog is secured and not at liberty to go about the premises: see ss 1, 5 and *Hobson v Gledhill* [1978] 1 WLR 215. The Act shall not be construed as conferring any civil right of action, or as derogating from any remedy (whether civil or criminal) in proceedings instituted otherwise than by virtue of the Act: s 5(2).

[131] In *Cummings v Granger*, the Court of Appeal held that keeping an uncontrolled guard dog was not, in the circumstances of that case, unreasonable; and conduct is not necessarily unreasonable even though it involves a breach of the criminal law. Cf *Buckoke v Greater London Council* [1971] 1 Ch 655, p 390.

[132] Under the Animals Act 1971, s 9, D has a defence to a civil claim for killing V's dog in this situation provided that D is a person entitled to act for the protection of the livestock and that he gives notice within 48 hours to the officer in charge of a police station of the killing or injury. That is true even if the dog *has been* worrying livestock—so there is no current threat to D's sheep: s 9(3)(b). It is submitted that in these circumstances D would commit no criminal offence. See the discussion of *Workman v Cowper* [1961] 1 All ER 683.

[133] Section 4(4).

In such a case, D has in law no right or interest in property to protect; until D himself reduces the game into his possession (ie shoots it) he has no proprietary interest in it whatever.[134] But if D believes he has a right or interest in the game, he would incur no criminal liability in killing V's dog provided the other circumstances required for the defence exist.[135] In such a case as this, D's belief that he has a right in property to protect is understandable, but even if D's belief is absurd it suffices to provide him with the defence if honestly held.

Protecting interests of others

The position is essentially the same where D claims to act to protect the property of another. An employee who caused damage to V's property in defending property belonging to his employer would commit no offence given his belief that the measures were reasonable and were immediately needed. But there need be no nexus whatever between the person intervening to protect the property and the owner of it. An officious bystander who chooses to intervene to protect the property of another will be free from criminal liability if he acts honestly on the same terms.

D must have at least a belief that there is some *property interest* that he is protecting. Thus, the defence was correctly held to be unavailable where D decapitated a statue of Baroness Thatcher. He explained his motive as being that he held her responsible for developments in world politics with which he disagreed and that he genuinely feared for the future of his son growing up in this world.[136] D had no belief that he was protecting property.

27.1.5.3 Cases not falling within the Act

By its terms, s 5(2) recognizes that there may be other circumstances which would constitute lawful excuse on a charge of criminal damage, and s 5(5) further provides:

This section shall not be construed as casting any doubt on any defence recognized by law as a defence to criminal charges.

It is clear that certain general defences (eg insanity and duress) are available on a charge of criminal damage and these are discussed elsewhere in this book.[137] But some particular matters call for further discussion here.

Self-defence, necessity and duress of circumstance

So far as necessity is concerned, the law relating to defence of property is a particular, and well-defined, instance where necessity is recognized as a defence. Are there cases in which it is permissible to destroy or damage property on the grounds of necessity in circumstances which, because there is no defence of property or belief in such a defence on the facts, would not amount to a defence under s 5 of the 1971 Act? As a starting point, it must be obvious

---

[134] A point echoed in *Cresswell* at [41].

[135] On the facts of *Gott v Measures* [1948] 1 KB 234, D would now be acquitted.

[136] *Kelleher* [2003] EWCA Crim 2486. Bizarrely, at his first trial the prosecution conceded the defence of 'lawful excuse' under s 5(2)(b) was available to D. As an indication of the difficulty if these defences are allowed to go to the jury in cases of protest, it should be noted that in that first trial the jury failed to reach a verdict. The Court of Appeal has confirmed that *Kelleher* is one of those exceptional cases in which the judge was correct to rule that the explanation advanced by D was incapable in law of amounting to a lawful excuse. The fact that a defence might be considered by the judge to be hopeless on its merits is not, however, a sufficient reason for it to be withdrawn from the jury. Withdrawing a defence from being considered by the jury is only appropriate if it would be contrary to the 'essential nature and purpose of the offence' for D to advance it successfully. See *Asmeron* [2013] EWCA Crim 435.

[137] Chs 9 and 10. As to intoxication, see pp 342 et seq.

that just as harm to the person may be justified on the grounds of self-defence of the person, so too the destruction of or damage to property may be justified in defence of the person.[138]

Where D damages property because he faces (or believes he faces) an attack involving the commission of a crime recognized by English law,[139] as will be commonly the case, the situation would be covered by s 3 of the Criminal Law Act 1967.[140] That section provides D with a defence if he uses such force as is reasonable in the circumstances in the prevention of crime. For example, if V sets his dog to attack D, and D kills the dog, D would not commit an offence of criminal damage if using reasonable force to defend himself. Section 3 in the 1967 Act is narrower than the defence under s 5 of the 1971 Act because s 3 has been interpreted to include an objective requirement of reasonableness.[141] D could not rely upon this section where the force used is unreasonable even though D himself honestly believed it was reasonable. Thus, there appears to be the odd situation that if D is defending his property it is enough (under s 5) that he *honestly* believed that the force used was reasonable, but if he is defending his person his honest belief will not save him unless the force used was in fact reasonable in the circumstances.[142]

It may also be noted that s 5(2)(b) of the Criminal Damage Act provides a wider defence in connection with offences of damage to property than is afforded by the common law defence of duress of circumstances. Duress of circumstances is available only where D faces (or reasonably believes he faces) a threat of death or serious bodily harm.[143] But s 5(2)(b) does not require any such threshold. Where it applies it permits a purely utilitarian calculation. Suppose there is a flood affecting the properties of X and Y and the fire service is called. Their assessment is that while X's house is not in danger there will be serious damage to Y's house by flooding unless X's fence is knocked down to allow the floodwaters to recede. A few pounds worth of damage needs to be done to the fence in order to prevent damage of several thousand pounds to the house. The firemen ask X for permission to knock down the fence, which he refuses, but the firemen nonetheless knock down the fence.[144] The firemen would have a lawful excuse to a charge of criminal damage if damaging the fence is reasonable in the circumstances. But if, additionally, the firemen have to restrain X because he resists their efforts to knock down the fence they would not be able to avail themselves of the common law defence of duress of circumstances since there is no threat of any harm to the person, let alone death or serious injury. They could rely only on the uncertain common law defence of necessity. If their action were regarded as not merely excused but justified, it may be that X would have no right to use force to defend his property.

Claim of right

It is clear that D cannot commit an offence under s 1(1) of the Act by destroying or damaging property which is, or which he believes to be, his own. The position would appear to be the same where D, though he does not believe he is the owner of the property which he destroys or damages, nevertheless acts under a claim of legal right.

Two historical examples support that interpretation. In *Twose*,[145] a case decided under the Malicious Damage Act, where it appeared that persons living near a common had

---

[138] So if D lawfully repelling an attack by E causes E to fall through F's window, D cannot be convicted of criminal damage to F's window: *Sears v Broome* [1986] Crim LR 461.

[139] *Jones* [2006] UKHL 16. For more recent discussion, see *R (Al Rabbat) v Westminster Magistrates' Court* [2017] EWHC 1969 (Admin).

[140] See p 419.   [141] See p 1112.

[142] Perhaps, then, if D kills V's dog that has been set upon him, D should say that he feared for the safety of his trousers rather than his ankles! Section 5 would then be available as a defence.

[143] See p 383.   [144] The illustration is based on fact except that X readily gave his permission.

[145] (1879) 14 Cox CC 327.

occasionally burnt the furze in order to improve the growth of grass, it was accepted that D's belief in a right to burn the furze would be a good defence though there was no such right. Here D's belief was at least understandable, but in *Day*,[146] again under the old law, it was held that D was not guilty of an offence in maiming sheep belonging to V which he had distrained,[147] where he did so in the honest belief that he was entitled to do so upon V's refusal to pay compensation for damage done by the sheep. It would seem clear that cases such as these would be decided in the same way under the Criminal Damage Act where the clear emphasis is upon honest belief in right without any objective qualification.

In similar vein, it is thought that a person who destroys or damages property found by him in circumstances where he believes the owner cannot be traced by taking reasonable steps can no more be convicted of criminal damage than he can be of theft by appropriating the property.

Protest defences

While the foregoing discussion deals with the more obvious categories of lawful excuse for damage to property, there are certainly other cases. Moreover 'lawful excuse', like 'lawful authority or reasonable excuse',[148] may have an inbuilt elasticity which enables courts to stretch it to cover new situations so that it is never possible to close the categories that might constitute lawful excuse.

Criminal damage is commonly committed in the course of political protest, as in the cases of *Hill and Hall*, *Jones* and *Kelleher*. The courts have also dealt with two different claims of defence to charges under the Act. First, although accepting that an act of criminal damage (eg the snipping of wire fence at a nuclear weapons base) could be regarded as an act of expression for the purposes of Art 10 of the ECHR,[149] the courts have held that the criminalization of such activity is a proportionate response to the legitimate aims within Art 10(2).[150]

Secondly, the courts have rejected attempts to argue that the commission of criminal damage is lawfully excused when done in response to actions of the State which D believes to be contrary to international law.[151] In *Pritchard and others*,[152] the conduct involved possession of articles to cause damage on an RAF base. The defendants pleaded that the action was necessary and lawful to attempt to prevent what they believed was the UK's unlawful act of war against Iraq. At first instance, Grigson J held that the non-justiciability of the legality of the war did not preclude reliance on s 5 defences. On an interlocutory appeal, the Court of Appeal held that the s 5 defence would be available to D irrespective of the determination as to the legality of the war. D is entitled to defend his property against threats of a non-criminal and even of a lawful nature. The only objective element in the defence in s 5(2)(b) of the Criminal Damage Act 1971 was whether it could be said that, on the facts as the defendant believed them to be, the criminal damage alleged could amount to something done to protect another's property; subject to that, the court and the jury were concerned simply with the question of a defendant's honestly held beliefs. The judge was therefore right to rule that no issue arose in relation to this defence which involved consideration of the legality of the war in Iraq. The House of Lords in the conjoined appeals of *Jones and Ayliffe*,[153] subsequently dealt with the appeals in these and related cases on the basis of pleas

---

146 (1844) 8 JP 186.   147 Taken out of V's possession pending compensation.
148 See p 1106.   149 See *Steel v UK* (1999) 28 EHRR 603.
150 *Hutchinson v Newbury Magistrates' Court* (2000) The Independent, 20 Nov.
151 Early cases on this included *Hutchinson v Newbury Magistrates' Court* (2000) The Independent, 20 Nov; *Pritchard and others* [2004] EWCA Crim 1981.
152 [2004] EWCA Crim 1981.   153 [2006] UKHL 16.

of necessity and self-defence (rather than under s 5) concluding that a belief in a need to protect property from action which D believes constitutes a crime in international law could not found a defence in English law.[154]

27.2 Destroying or damaging property with intent to endanger life

Section 1(2) of the Criminal Damage Act 1971 provides:

A person who without lawful excuse destroys or damages any property, whether belonging to himself or another—

    (a) intending to destroy or damage any property or being reckless as to whether any property would be destroyed or damaged; and

    (b) intending by the destruction or damage to endanger the life of another or being reckless as to whether the life of another would be thereby endangered;

shall be guilty of an offence.[155]

By s 4, the offence is punishable by imprisonment for life. The section creates aggravated offences of criminal damage and arson.[156]

This subsection incorporates what is essentially an offence against the person into the Criminal Damage Act. The Law Commission was aware of this and expected that the matter would be reviewed when offences against the person were reformed.[157] That has not occurred.

The actus reus is the destruction of or damage to property. The destruction or damage which occurs in fact may be quite different from that envisaged by D. Where there is such a difference, it is the destruction or damage which D intended, or as to which he was reckless, to which we must look in order to determine whether *by that damage* he intended to endanger, or was reckless whether he endangered, the life of another.[158] Thus, if D aimed to throw his petrol bomb through the window of an occupied house, but the bomb hits the outer wall causing only trivial damage to the target, it is D's intended damage to the interior which is relevant. The question is as to D's state of mind when he did the act and we cannot, at that point, know for certain what, if any, destruction or damage will be caused. The offence is not committed unless D's act caused some destruction or damage—there must be an actus reus—but whether the terms of s 1(2)(b) are satisfied has been predetermined. The nature of the destruction or damage actually caused may be very good evidence of what D intended, or of his recklessness, but that is all.

The actus reus does not require that any life is in fact endangered. Thus, in *Parker*,[159] D was convicted under s 1(2) of criminal damage, being reckless as to the endangerment

---

[154] On the Court of Appeal's decision, see R Cryer, 'War and Armed Conflict: Aggression at the Court of Appeal' (2005) 10 J of Conflict and Security Law 209.

[155] See DW Elliott, 'Endangering Life by Destroying or Damaging Property' [1997] Crim LR 382.

[156] The trial of a person accused of arson being reckless as to whether life would be endangered must be heard by a full-time judge: *Jones (Stephen)* (1999) The Times, 20 May, CA.

[157] LC 29, para 27.

[158] *Dudley* [1989] Crim LR 57 and commentary as cited with approval by the Court of Appeal in *Webster and Warwick*. The requirement is to be at least reckless as to the endangerment of the life of another. Suicide attempts with explosions and fire, etc may suffice if D is reckless as to nearby residents, etc.

[159] [1993] Crim LR 856.

of his neighbours' lives when he started a fire in his semi-detached house. The fact that the neighbours were absent and therefore never at risk did not preclude conviction.

The life that D must intend or be reckless about endangering by the damage he intends or is reckless about causing must be the life of another.[160] So, D's conviction was quashed where, in order to commit suicide following the break-up of his marriage, he set fire to his own car when he was in it or close to it, but parked 7–8 metres away from his wife's house. There was no evidence of an intent to endanger any life but his own by the damage that he intended to his own car in that location.[161]

The most controversial aspect of the offence is that it requires 'a dismal distinction'.[162] In *Steer*,[163] it was held that the offence requires intention or recklessness as to the endangering of life *by the damaging or destruction of property*, not merely by D's act. D fired rifle shots at the windows of a house occupied by V, against whom he had a grudge. The House of Lords held that the charge under s 1(2) was misconceived. Danger to life was caused by the bullets, not by any damage to the windows or property in the bedroom. The question, as we have seen, is not whether or how life was endangered in fact, but what D intended, or as to what result he was reckless.[164] While there was certainly cogent evidence that D was reckless as to danger to life from the bullets, he did not commit the offence unless he foresaw danger to life from, say, flying broken glass and there was no evidence of that. The contrary interpretation would also produce potential anomalies. Lord Bridge gave an example of A and B firing bullets into the air, being reckless whether life was endangered. It would be absurd if A alone was liable because only his bullet damaged property.

In *Webster*, D pushed a heavy stone from a bridge onto a passenger train passing below. Only a corner of the stone penetrated the roof but the passengers were showered with glass-fibre and other material. The judge failed to direct the jury that D was guilty only if his mens rea was as to the endangerment of life from the damage to the carriage, not merely from the stone, so the conviction had to be quashed. In *Warwick*,[165] D drove a stolen car from which E threw bricks at a pursuing police car, smashing a window and showering officers with glass. It was held that there was evidence from which a jury could infer recklessness whether the police driver might lose control through being so showered, thus endangering life. Recklessness whether he might lose control through being hit by the brick would not be enough. The distinction applied in each of these cases is indeed 'dismal' but inevitable on the proper construction of the Act.

The fact that the damage may be to D's own property adds to the anomalous nature of the offence.[166] Suppose that D, the owner of a house, removing unwanted electrical equipment belonging to him, cuts a cable also belonging to him and exposes the live wire in such a way that he foresees a risk to the life of another. The actus reus is the 'damage' to the cable. It is no answer that the cable belongs to D and that he is entitled to cut the cable if he wants to. It seems extraordinary that this should be an offence of damage to property, but that seems to be the implication of *Merrick*.[167] O, a householder, employed D to remove old television cable.

---

[160] *Thakar* [2010] EWCA Crim 2136.

[161] T was drunk and it would have been open to T to argue that his consumption of a bottle and a half of vodka prevented him forming mens rea: reckless aggravated criminal damage being a specific intent offence according to *Heard* [2008] QB 43. See Ch 9.

[162] *Webster* and *Warwick* [1995] 2 All ER 168 at 173.   [163] [1988] AC 111.

[164] *Dudley* [1989] Crim LR 57.

[165] [1995] 1 Cr App R 492. Similar incidents are not uncommon—see eg *Ratcliffe* [2008] EWCA Crim 471.

[166] There have been a number of cases in which D has set fire to his own property intent on committing suicide, and has been reckless as to the endangerment of neighbours' lives: eg *Brewis* [2004] EWCA Crim 1919. Cf *Harris* [2013] EWCA Crim 223 and Ch 9, p 330.

[167] [1996] 1 Cr App R 130.

D did so, leaving the live cable exposed for six minutes. His conviction was upheld. It would appear that the result would have been the same if O had done the act himself instead of through an agent. It would be understandable if the offence were simply the endangering of life; but the gravamen of the conduct in a case like *Merrick* has nothing to do with damage to property. Why should it be different if the danger arose not from cutting old cable but from the installation of new? The implications of the result are 'absurd and alarming'.[168]

The offence has features both of an offence against property and an offence against the person. In some circumstances (as where D severs the brake cable of V's car intending V to drive to his death), the offence will overlap with the offence of attempted murder, but it is wider than attempted murder in two respects. One is that it does not require the intent to kill which is necessary on a charge of attempted murder:[169] intention or recklessness as to the endangering of life will suffice. On facts such as those occurring in *Cunningham*,[170] for example, it could be that when D severed the gas pipe he did not intend to asphyxiate V but was reckless whether her life would be endangered; he would not be guilty of attempted murder but he would be guilty of the s 1(2) offence under the Criminal Damage Act.[171] The other is that the offence under s 1(2) may be committed where the acts done by D are too remote to constitute an attempt[172] to murder. If, for example, D were to sever the brake cable of O's car intending thereafter to induce V to drive the car to his death, D's act of damaging the car might be too preparatory to support a charge of attempting to murder V but it would support a charge under the 1971 Act.

Certain general features of the offence under s 1(2) (eg destruction or damage, property, intention and recklessness) are the same as for the offence under s 1(1) which has already been discussed. The following additional matters need to be discussed in relation to the offence under s 1(2).

27.2.1 Intention and recklessness

Intention and recklessness in relation to destroying or damaging property have been discussed previously.[173] That discussion applies to intention and recklessness in relation to endangering the life of another,[174] and reference may also be made to the general discussion of intention and recklessness elsewhere in this book.[175] It need not be shown that life was in fact endangered by the damage nor that the damage in fact done created any risk to life so long as D, by damaging the property, intended or was reckless as to the endangering of life.[176] Where D starts a fire in an unoccupied building with no one present, he might be reckless whether he endangers the lives of firemen, if he foresees a risk of a life being endangered by the damage.

Recklessness, following *G*, is subjective. In *Cooper*,[177] the Court of Appeal suggested that the risk be one that was 'obvious and significant' to D. Thus, where D has realized that there is a risk but has dismissed it as negligible, it could not be said that he was taking an obvious and significant risk. This is an unusual interpretation of the subjective form of recklessness.

---

[168] Elliott [1997] Crim LR 382 at 389. Note that the mens rea at that time was *Caldwell* recklessness.

[169] See p 434.   [170] [1957] 2 QB 396, p 105.

[171] And also, of course, of the offence under s 23 of the OAPA 1861. It might be noted in passing that the toxic elements are now removed from gas used for domestic purposes and natural gas does not contain them; hence domestic gas can cause death only by asphyxiation, and even this risk is almost nil. But there remains a very high risk of explosion which is a serious danger to life.

[172] See p 445.   [173] At p 1103.   [174] *Hardie* [1985] 1 WLR 64.   [175] See Ch 3.

[176] *Sangha* [1988] 2 All ER 385; *Dudley* [1989] Crim LR 57. The definition of recklessness applied was that under *Caldwell*.

[177] [2004] EWCA Crim 1382.

It is submitted that the correct test is whether D has foreseen *a* risk of life being endangered by the damage that he intends or about which he is reckless and that he takes *that* risk unjustifiably. In *Castle*,[178] D had burgled an empty office and started a fire. That spread to the unoccupied residential flats above. D pleaded guilty to burglary but denied reckless endangerment as he claimed to have been unaware that there were residential flats above the office. The Court of Appeal confirmed that the question should have been whether D had acted recklessly with respect to: a circumstance when he was aware of a risk that had or would have existed; or a result when he was aware of a risk that it would occur, and it was in the circumstances known *to him*, unreasonable to take the risk.

Following the Court of Appeal's decision in *Heard*,[179] the element of intention or recklessness as to endangering life is an ulterior mens rea which means that it is not a basic intent but is a specific intent crime. Voluntary intoxication is available as a plea by D where his intoxication was such that he did not appreciate the risk of endangering life.

There must be a causal connection between the destroying or damaging of the property and the intended or reckless endangerment of life. If, to extend an example used earlier, D were to damage the lock in the process of entering V's garage in order to sever the brake cable of V's car, there would be no offence under s 1(2). D intends to damage the lock and he further intends to endanger V's life, but he does not intend '*by the destruction or damage to endanger the life of*' V. It is only when D damages the brake cable that he would commit the offence under s 1(2). So in *Steer*,[180] discussed earlier, it was held that the offence was not committed where D fired off some shots at the bedroom window where V and his wife were standing. While D must have foreseen that the shooting would cause damage by smashing the bedroom window and also endanger the lives of V and his wife, D would not have foreseen that their lives would be endangered *by the damage to the window*, because it was not by that damage that they were, or were likely to be, endangered. In *Wenton*,[181] D smashed a window in V's house in which V was present with children. D then threw through the window a petrol can and a burning piece of paper. The paper did not ignite the petrol canister. No fire ensued. He was convicted of an offence under s 1(2) of the 1971 Act, namely reckless aggravated criminal damage. D appealed arguing that the damage that he caused and about which he was reckless was the broken window; there was no life endangered by that nor did he intend or was he reckless whether life would be endangered by that damage to the window. The Court of Appeal accepted this ground of appeal and quashed the conviction.[182]

On the other hand, it may be that if, having destroyed or damaged property belonging to V (eg having set fire to V's premises), D subsequently realizes that V's life is in danger, D would commit the offence under s 1(2), if, provided it lies within D's power to prevent or minimize the further harm, he then omits to do so, intending that or being reckless whether, V's life should be endangered.[183]

In *A-G's Reference (No 3 of 1992)*,[184] it was said that the property which D intends to damage need not be the same as the property which endangers life, instancing the case of a man who cuts the rope (the first property) of a crane, causing its load to crush the roof of a car

---

[178] [2004] All ER (D) 289 (Oct).   [179] [2007] EWCA Crim 125, [2007] Crim LR 654 and commentary.
[180] [1988] AC 111.   [181] [2010] EWCA Crim 2361.
[182] Is it impossible to argue that: (a) the canister and petrol were property; (b) D intended to damage that property by fire; (c) he did cause some damage to that property; (d) he intended by the damage to the canister and the petrol that a life would be endangered? Equally can it be argued: (a) the canister and petrol were property; (b) D was reckless whether the petrol and canister would be damaged; (c) he damaged the property; and (d) he was reckless whether a life would be endangered by the damage about which he was reckless? Or was it an attempt?
[183] *Miller* [1983] 1 All ER 978, p 53.
[184] (1993) 98 Cr App R 383. The case was primarily concerned with the law of attempt, p 440.

(the second property) which kills the driver. But this seems to make far too heavy weather of the problem. Cutting the rope damages the crane, of which the rope is part, and the question then is whether D foresaw that the damaged crane might endanger life. It makes no difference whether the danger arises from the falling object or the car roof—it is caused by the damage to the crane.

27.2.2 Lawful excuse

Since the gist of the offence under s 1(2) lies in intending or being reckless as to the endangering of life *by* destroying or damaging property, it is understandable that D may commit the offence whether he destroys or damages the property of another or himself. The risk is just the same whether D severs the brake cable on V's car, or severs the brake cable on his own car before lending it to V to drive.

It is equally understandable that the partial definition of lawful excuse in s 5(2) should not be applicable here, and s 5 does not apply to offences under s 1(2). It ought not to be a defence to an offence of this nature that, say, D, with the assent of E, severed the brake cable on E's car before lending it to V to drive. Equally, D ought to have no lawful excuse in damaging property, although done for the purpose of protecting other property, where in so doing he knowingly creates a risk to life.

Clearly, then, Parliament's intention in enacting the offence under s 1(2) was that certain matters (eg destruction by D of his own property, destruction with owner's consent, destruction in defence of property) which constitute lawful excuse where D is charged with an offence under s 1(1) do not constitute lawful excuse where D is charged under s 1(2). This does not mean that there can never be a lawful excuse where D is charged under s 1(2), because s 1(2) expressly states that the offence may be committed only by one 'who *without lawful excuse* destroys or damages any property'. It follows that there may be circumstances, presumably of an exceptional character, where D would have lawful excuse for destroying or damaging property even though he does it realizing that he may endanger life. An exceptional case of this character would be where D damages property in self-defence; when it is legitimate for D to kill in order to prevent himself being killed, D would not commit an offence under s 1(2) because he happened to use, and damage, property belonging to another in killing his attacker.[185] Similarly, the police might have lawful excuse for damaging property where this was done to prevent the commission of a serious crime against the person, even though what was done might endanger the life of the criminal. And if necessity is a defence where D chooses to put one life at risk in order to save many others,[186] it would extend to damaging property to do so.

27.2.3 Endangerment offences

The problems of the s 1(2) offence stem in part from the confusion between its objective in penalizing endangerment, and the requirement for that endangerment to be founded on damage to property.[187] This has called some to question why English law does not adopt a general offence of life endangerment, and this is certainly an issue which deserves further

---

[185] cf *Sears v Broome* [1986] Crim LR 461.   [186] See p 387.

[187] Despite its name, it is debatable whether it is properly regarded as an endangerment offence in every case in which it can apply. See further RA Duff, 'Criminalising Endangerment' in Duff and Green, *Defining Crimes*. Duff distinguishes between crimes of attack where the intention is to harm some value of interest (and which be unconsummated as in an attempt) and endangerment offences proper which arise where D creates a significant risk that another will suffer harm. See also RA Duff, 'Criminalising Endangerment' (2005) 65 La L Rev 941.

consideration by the Law Commission.[188] To date, English law has created endangerment offences only in relation to specific activities, for example causing explosions[189] or specific circumstances such as behaviour on an aircraft.[190] There is no general property endangerment offence.[191]

27.3 Arson

There is a separate offence of arson—that is, of destroying or damaging property by fire[192]—in the Act despite the Law Commission's view that this was unnecessary.[193] Parliament preferred a specific offence.[194]

Section 1(3) of the Act provides:

An offence committed under this section by destroying or damaging property by fire shall be charged as arson.

And by s 4 it is punishable by imprisonment for life. Arguably, the retention of a separate offence was desirable to provide a more appropriate label and reflect public anxiety about the offence. Arson remains disturbingly prevalent, particularly in certain types of property such as schools.

The provision is a mandatory one—'*shall* be charged as arson'. Where D destroys or damages property by fire the proper course would appear to be to charge him with an offence under s 1(3).[195] Where there is also an allegation of endangerment, there should be separate counts of arson with intent to endanger life and of arson being reckless that life is endangered.[196]

The general features of arson are the same as for the offences under s 1(1) and s 1(2) except that the destruction or damage is to be by fire. For the offence to be complete some property must be destroyed or damaged by fire. The damage may, of course, be quite insignificant (eg it would be enough that wood is charred)[197] but there must be some damage *by* fire; it

---

[188] This was an issue considered by the Law Commission in its most recent work on reforming offences against the person. See LCCP 217, *Reform of Offences Against the Person: A Scoping Consultation Paper* (2014) and LC 361, *Reform of Offences Against the Person* (2015). See generally KJM Smith, 'Liability for Endangerment: English Ad Hoc Pragmatism and American Innovation' [1983] Crim LR 127; D Lanham, 'Danger Down Under' [1999] Crim LR 960. The dangers are that such offences overcriminalize and render the law too vague. See generally DN Husak, *Overcriminalization: The Limits of the Criminal Law* (2008) 162–3.

[189] Explosive Substances Act 1883, s 2.

[190] Aviation Security Act 1982, ss 2–3. See *R (Hilali) v Governor of Whitemoor Prison* [2008] 1 AC 805.

[191] cf the Scottish Draft Criminal Code, cl 82 which provides for causing a risk of unlawful damage to property.

[192] LC 29, paras 28–33.

[193] The Commission proposed that such conduct would be punishable on indictment by imprisonment for life. This seemed a sensible way to meet the case and avoided complication of the substantive law.

[194] See HC, 19 May 1971, vol 817, cols 1433 et seq. The reasons given for singling out damage by fire would be equally applicable to singling out damage by explosives; that 'arson' is such a splendidly evocative term cannot have been unimportant in securing its retention.

[195] *Booth* [1999] Crim LR 144. *Booth* was distinguished in *Drayton* [2005] EWCA Crim 2013. D was charged under s 1(1) and (3) of the 1971 Act, but the word 'arson' did not appear in the information. The Court of Appeal held that the charge was in that context in the magistrates' court a valid charge. The use of the word 'arson' was described as desirable. The information alleged 'damage by fire' and that was synonymous with arson. It complied with the requirements of the Criminal Procedure Rules 2005, r 7.2 (now reproduced in the Criminal Procedure Rules 2020).

[196] In sentencing, the court has the more specific verdict of the jury: *Hoof* (1980) 72 Cr App R 126. But cf *Flitter* [2001] Crim LR 328.

[197] cf *Parker* (1839) 9 C & P 45. No visible flame is necessary: *Stallion* (1833) 1 Mood CC 398.

would not be enough that property is merely blackened by smoke though there might well be an attempt in such a case. D must intend, or be reckless as to, destruction or damage *by fire*. Consider a case where D, aided by E, throws a bottle which, unknown to E, D filled with petrol in order to set fire to V's house. D may be convicted of arson but E may not.[198] E, however, may be convicted of simple criminal damage in respect of any damage caused by the throwing of the bottle.

27.4 Racially or religiously aggravated criminal damage

Section 30 of the Crime and Disorder Act 1998 (as amended)[199] provides:

(1) A person is guilty of an offence under this section if he commits an offence under section 1(1) of the Criminal Damage Act 1971 (destroying or damaging property belonging to another) which is racially or religiously aggravated for the purposes of this section.

Definitions of 'racially aggravated' and 'religiously aggravated' and a discussion of the racial and religious aggravation offences in general are set out in Ch 16. The offence is punishable on summary conviction by imprisonment for six months or a fine not exceeding the statutory maximum or both, and, on conviction on indictment, by imprisonment for 14 years or a fine or both. The racial or religious hostility must be roughly contemporaneous with the damage being caused.[200]

27.5 Threats to destroy or damage property

Section 2 of the Criminal Damage Act 1971 provides:

A person who without lawful excuse makes to another a threat, intending that that other would fear it would be carried out—

(a) to destroy or damage any property belonging to that other or a third person;[201] or

(b) to destroy or damage his own property in a way which he knows is likely to endanger the life of that other or a third person;

shall be guilty of an offence.

The offence is punishable by a maximum ten years' imprisonment: s 4(2).

27.5.1 The conduct threatened

In order to constitute an offence under this section the conduct threatened must be conduct that would be an offence under s 1. D would commit the offence where, without lawful excuse, he threatened to destroy or damage the property of another (whether property of

[198] *Cooper (G) and Cooper (Y)* [1991] Crim LR 524.
[199] By the Anti-terrorism, Crime and Security Act 2001, s 39(5)(b) and (6)(b).
[200] *Parry v DPP* [2004] EWHC 3112 (Admin) (20-minute delay between throwing nail varnish on V's door and calling him an Irish so-and-so). See also *Babbs* [2007] All ER (D) 383 (Oct), where D's hostility although not contemporaneous, was evinced over a continuing period. See LC 348, *Hate Crime: Should the Current Offences be Extended?* (2014), and *Hate Crime Laws* (2020) LCCP 250.
[201] The Court of Appeal has confirmed that the offence in s 2(1)(a) is an offence solely concerned with damage to property and does not involve an assault on, or injury, or threat to, a third party within the meaning of s 80(2A)(b) of PACE 1984. For this reason, if the threat is directed at D's spouse or civil partner he is not a compellable witness. This is not so if D is charged with an offence contrary to s 2(1)(b). See *A (B)* [2012] EWCA Crim 1529.

the person threatened or of a third party), or where he threatened to destroy or damage his own property in a way which he knows is likely to endanger the life of another (whether the life of a person threatened or the life of a third party).

If D is charged under s 2(a), 'lawful excuse' has the meaning ascribed to it by s 5 so that D would not commit an offence where, for example, he threatens to shoot V's dog should he find it attacking his sheep.[202] But by s 5(1) the partial definition of lawful excuse in the section does not apply to an offence 'involving a threat by the person charged to destroy or damage property in a way which he knows is likely to endanger the life of another . . .' This does not mean that there cannot be a lawful excuse for an offence under s 2(b), merely that the partial definition of lawful excuse in s 5 cannot apply.[203] Where D threatens to destroy property of another with intent to endanger life he would have to be charged under s 2(a), and cannot be charged under s 2(b). Curiously, it would seem that if in such a case D is charged under s 2(a) there would be a lawful excuse if it appeared that he believed the owner would have consented to the threatened destruction or damage (s 5(2)(a)), but if he is charged under s 2(b) it would not be a lawful excuse that he was threatening to destroy his own property. But the distinction can be of small practical importance: if D threatens to destroy V's property in order to endanger the life of X then it would be difficult to show that D honestly believed that V would have consented to the threatened destruction 'had [V] known of the destruction or damage *and its circumstances*', that is, the endangerment of X's life.[204]

27.5.2 The threat

The threat may take any form. The Law Commission said:

There seems to be no good ground for limiting threats to written threats, for a telephonic threat, particularly if repeated, can cause more alarm in the recipient than any written threat. If the law is to be extended to cover telephonic threats, then logically there is no reason why it should not be extended to all threats, however made. The only limitation that needs to be imposed is that the threats should be intended to create a fear that what is threatened will be carried out.[205]

This last limitation needs to be imposed because the gist of the offence is the threat and, given that D intends that V should believe that the threat will be carried out, there ought to be no requirement that D himself should have intended to carry his threat into effect.

In *Cakmak*,[206] the accused had threatened to set fire to herself as a protest when on the London Eye. The charges were laid under s 2(a), even though the threat was to set fire to herself. The Court of Appeal held that despite this the jury were entitled to find a threat of damage to property of another, because there was an implied threat to damage such property. Whether there is an implied threat is an objective question: would a reasonable person in the particular circumstances regard the words used as a threat to damage the London Eye?

If D intends that V would fear the threat would be carried out, D commits the offence only if, judged objectively, the nature of the threat would have caused V to believe that the threat would be carried out. The actual thoughts and fears of the person threatened are irrelevant according to the court in *Cakmak*. It would seem that the threat need not be a threat to do the damage immediately, but immediacy may be a relevant factor, along with other circumstances, in determining whether there is something that can be called a threat.

27.5.3 Mens rea

In *Cakmak*, the court held that whether an offence under s 2(a) or (b) is charged, the jury must be satisfied that D made a threat to another with the intention (recklessness not being a sufficient mens rea) that the other would fear that it would be carried out. In *Ankerson*,[207] D went to social services offices and, according to the officials there, threatened to burn down the family home irrespective of who was in it before committing suicide. D denied threatening anything more than suicide: he claimed not to have threatened to burn the house down and he did not intend that the officials should fear that such a threat would be carried out. It was clear that under s 2 there must be (a) words or actions which objectively speaking constitute a threat; (b) the threat must be one which, again objectively considered, amounts to a threat to damage any property though it is not relevant that the particular listener perceived it to be a threat if objectively it would not have been so construed; (c) D must intend that the person hearing the threat would fear that the threat would be carried out.

The Court of Appeal held that the judge had not directed adequately on the third limb. Although in some parts of the summing up the judge repeated the statutory formula that D must have intended that the social worker would fear that the threat *would* be carried out, in other places he said the test was whether D intended her to fear that he *might* carry out the threat. Nevertheless, the conviction was safe. In this case:

there is no material difference between a defendant who intends that the listener should fear that the threat will be carried out and one who intends that the listener should fear that it might be carried out. It seems to us that the critical word is 'fear'. To fear that something will happen is not to be equated with a belief that it will happen. It is to be anxious about the possibility it will happen. That anxiety or fear arises where there is a risk that it might happen. So in our view it is enough if the intention is to create in the mind an objective listener the genuine fear that the threat might be carried out. The listener can have that fear even where he or she is not certain that the threat will be carried out. It is in circumstances where the threat is understood to be serious that the authorities will likely be alerted with all the adverse consequences flowing from that. It will not be enough if the risk, objectively viewed, is merely fanciful because then there would not be a real and genuine fear that the threat would be carried out.

As the court recognized, the purpose of the offence is to ensure that the defendant does not make threats that he may or may not intend to carry out but that he intends V to worry just might be carried out. Some of the language of the decision may go too far, however, in suggesting that fear that it 'might' happen is sufficient; the Act requires fear that it will.

Section 2(a) deals exclusively with the property of a person other than the defendant. It is only in relation to s 2(b) that the prosecution must prove that D knew that the damage or destruction threatened was likely, if carried out, to endanger the life of a person other than the defendant.

27.6 Possession offences

By s 3 of the Act:

A person who has anything in his custody or under his control intending without lawful excuse to use it or cause or permit another to use it—

(a) to destroy or damage any property belonging to some other person; or

(b) to destroy or damage his own or the user's property in a way which he knows is likely to endanger the life of some other person;

shall be guilty of an offence.

---

[207] [2015] EWCA Crim 432.

The offence is punishable by imprisonment for a maximum ten years: s 4(2).

In line with the offence of threatening under s 2, the possession of the thing must be for the purpose of committing an offence under s 1 of the Act. There is, of course, no need for the commission of an offence of destruction or damage, but there must be an intention to use the thing, or allow another to use it, for the purpose of committing what would be an offence under s 1.[208] Accordingly, the same provisions apply in relation to lawful excuse as apply to charges under s 2.[209]

27.6.1 Custody or control

Although it is convenient to talk of this offence as one of possession, the section speaks only of custody or control which the Law Commission preferred so as to avoid the complexities often associated with the word possession.[210] It may well have been a wise decision to avoid the term 'possession', but what really helps to simplify the situation is the clear requirement for mens rea.

As the Law Commission observed:

Problems which may arise where a substance, such as a stick of gelignite, is slipped into a person's pocket without his knowledge will be wholly academic, because if that person has no knowledge of its presence he cannot have an intention to use it or permit or cause another to use it. If he has no intention to use it or permit or cause it to be used, he does not commit an offence . . .[211]

But there must be custody or control; a mere intention to use something to commit an offence of criminal damage will not suffice. D may be about to pick up stones from the road to throw through a shop window, but since at this stage he does not have custody or control of the stones he commits no offence under this provision. D need not, of course, be the owner of the thing in order to have custody or control of it, but he must have the charge of it. Where D is charged with permitting E to use the thing, D must be in a position where, as against E, he might properly have prevented E from using it.

27.6.2 The things used

There is no limitation on the things which may be possessed with intent to commit criminal damage—'anything' may do for the purpose.

The essential feature of the proposed offence is to be found not so much in the nature of the thing—for almost any everyday article, from a box of matches to a hammer or nail, can be used to destroy or damage property—as in the intention with which it is held.[212]

By way of example, in *Akhtar* the Court of Appeal held that a petrol bomb is an offensive weapon per se, it being impossible to see an innocent purpose to which a petrol bomb could be put.[213] Clearly, the nature of the thing may have significance in proving that D possessed the thing with intent to commit criminal damage (the possession of a box of matches may be one thing and the possession of a ton of dynamite quite another) but given that the intent can be proved, the nature of the thing is immaterial.

---

[208] *Fancy* [1980] Crim LR 171. For reform proposals, see LCCP 183, *Conspiracy and Attempts* (2007) para 16.61.
[209] See p 1124.   [210] LC 29, para 59.   [211] ibid.
[212] ibid, para 60.   [213] [2015] EWCA Crim 176.

27.6.3 Mens rea

The offence may be committed only where D intends to use, or cause or permit another to use, the thing to destroy or damage property. It is not enough that D realizes that the thing may be so used: he must intend or permit such use. But it is not necessary that D should intend an immediate use of the thing. The offence is aimed at proscribing what is essentially a preparatory act and it is therefore enough that D possesses the thing with the necessary intent even though he contemplates its actual use of the thing at some time in the future. It would also seem to be clear that a conditional intent (an intention to use the thing to cause damage should it prove necessary) will suffice.[214]

27.7 Kindred offences

In keeping with the aim of codification,[215] the Criminal Damage Act 1971 contains, as near as may be, the whole of the law relating to damage to property. The Act abolished the common law offence of arson, repealed most of the provisions of the Malicious Damage Act 1861 and repealed the Dockyards Protection Act 1772 and a large number of statutory provisions containing miscellaneous offences of damage to property.

But the Criminal Damage Act leaves untouched the Explosive Substances Act 1883.[216] The Law Commission had at first planned to repeal s 2 (causing an explosion likely to endanger life or to cause serious injury to property) and s 3 (possessing explosives with intent to endanger life or cause serious injury to property, and doing an act to cause an explosion likely to endanger life or cause serious injury to property) since these might easily have been brought within the scheme of the Criminal Damage Act. But in the end the Law Commission did not do this because it was felt that the Explosive Substances Act belonged to the area of public order offences, and its replacement should be considered in the context of a review of offences relating to public order. This means that on given facts there may be an offence both under the Criminal Damage Act and the Explosive Substances Act, and it should be noted that there are differences in relation to the mens rea that has to be established.

The Criminal Damage Act did not repeal the following provisions of the Malicious Damage Act 1861: s 35 (placing wood etc on rail lines or obstructing signals with intent to obstruct or overturn any engine);[217] s 36 (obstructing railway engines);[218] and the retention of these offences made necessary the further retention of general provisions of the Malicious Damage Act relating to malice (s 58) and jurisdiction (s 72). It will be seen that none of these offences would necessarily (or even ordinarily) involve damage to property, though the ultimate aim may be to cause damage to property. Frequently such acts might amount to an attempt to commit criminal damage, but insofar as the acts might be merely preparatory these provisions render the preparatory acts criminal. These offences have

---

[214] *Buckingham* (1976) 63 Cr App R 159; cf *Bentham* [1973] QB 357.   [215] See Ch 1.

[216] Proceedings for a crime under this Act shall not be instituted except by or with the consent of the A-G: Explosive Substances Act 1883, s 7(1).

[217] See *Buxton* [2010] EWCA Crim 2923 for a rare application of s 35.

[218] See *Mirahessari* [2016] EWCA Crim 1733 and *Bard* [2014] EWCA Crim 463 for applications of s 36.

been used to prosecute environmental protestors who obstruct freight trains carrying coal to power stations.

Nor does the Act repeal offences of damage arising under other legislation where the liability for the damage may be grounded in negligence or where there is strict liability for the damage. In particular cases, there may be thought valid policy reasons for imposing criminal liability for damage to property caused negligently, or even for imposing strict liability for offences of damage to property.[219] These offences are perhaps best considered in relation to a review of criminal liability for negligence and a review of strict liability.

Further reading

ATH Smith, *Property Offences: The Protection of Property Through the Criminal Law*

---

[219] eg s 85(1) of the Postal Services Act 2000 creates an offence of sending by post a postal packet which encloses any creature, article or thing of any kind which is likely to injure other postal packets in the course of their transmission by post or any person engaged in the business of a postal operator.

28

Computer misuse

The impact of computer technology on society has been profound.[1] From simple beginnings in arithmetical calculations, it has spawned immense data retrieval systems; systems controlling traffic by land, sea and air; systems indispensable to the functioning of industry, health care, education, banking and commerce. All this is to the common good or nearly all to the common good because, inevitably, some will use the technology for anti-social purposes. These may range from simple 'snooping', as where the hacker gains access to computer systems just for the fun of it (perhaps to demonstrate his computing ability), or for industrial or State espionage, or to perpetrate frauds, or disrupt systems with viruses, worms or Trojan horses[2] with serious commercial and possibly life-threatening consequences.

The law before the Computer Misuse Act 1990 could deal with some of these problems.[3] Appropriating property belonging to another is just as much theft[4] when it is done by picking a pocket as by causing a computer to debit one account and to credit another. Should someone cause death or injury not with a blunt instrument but by interfering with a traffic control system, he would be equally liable to conviction for a homicide offence or an offence against the person. But there were gaps in the protection offered by the criminal law. The 1990 Act seeks to address these and is based on a Law Commission Report from 1989. This free online chapter analyses the following offences:

(1) Section 1—unauthorized access to computer material.

(2) Section 2—unauthorized access with intent to commit or facilitate further offences.

(3) Section 3—unauthorized acts with intent to impair or recklessness as to impairment of a computer.

(4) Section 3ZA—impairing a computer such as to cause serious damage.

(5) Section 3A—making, supplying or obtaining articles for use in offences under s 1 or s 3: s 3ZA.

A FULL DISCUSSION IS CONTAINED IN THE CHAPTER, AVAILABLE **FREE** ONLINE—www.oup.com/he/SHO-textbook16e

---

[1] See E Brynjolfsson and A Mcafee, *The Second Machine Age: Work, Progress, and Prosperity in a Time of Brilliant Technologies* (2014); I Walden, *Computer Crimes and Digital Investigations* (2nd edn, 2016) Ch 3.D; I Lloyd, *Information Technology Law* (8th edn, 2017) 189–254; J Hörnle, *Internet Jurisdiction: Law and Practice* (2021). For more historical accounts, see M Wasik, *Crime and the Computer* (1991) and 'The Computer Misuse Act 1990' [1990] Crim LR 767; Smith, *Property Offences*, Ch 11; N MacEwan, 'The Computer Misuse Act 1990: Lessons from its Past and Predictions for its Future' [2008] Crim LR 955.

[2] For a comparative analysis of legal regulation of viruses, see M Klang, 'A Critical Look at the Regulation of Computer Viruses' (2003) 11 Int'l J L & IT 162.

[3] See C Tapper, 'Computer Crime: Scotch Mist?' [1987] Crim LR 4.

[4] cf the problem of deceiving a machine, discussed at p 978.

29
Forgery

Forgery and counterfeiting are now regulated by the Forgery and Counterfeiting Act 1981.[1] This Act is largely based upon the recommendations of the Law Commission.[2]

Forgery overlaps with many other offences. It is usually done as a preparatory step to the commission of some other crime, most often a crime involving fraud. Despite the many available dishonesty offences, forgery is retained as a separate offence because it has long been regarded as a serious offence, and the conduct is regarded as distinctive enough to warrant a particular label within the criminal law.

The offences of forgery may be paraphrased as follows:

(1) making a false instrument (s 1);

(2) copying a false instrument (s 2);

(3) using a false instrument (s 3);

(4) using a copy of a false instrument (s 4);

(5) having custody or control of specified kinds of false instrument (s 5(1)); and

(6) making or having custody or control of machines, paper, etc for making false instruments of that kind (s 5(3)).

All of the forgery offences require proof that D intended to induce somebody to accept a false instrument as genuine, which as a result causes V to do or not to do some act to his own or any other person's prejudice. Forgery does not require proof of dishonesty.[3]

Forgery is triable either way.[4] The maximum sentence is ten years' imprisonment on indictment, six months' imprisonment or a fine not exceeding the statutory maximum or both summarily.

A FULL DISCUSSION IS CONTAINED IN THE CHAPTER, AVAILABLE **FREE** ONLINE—www.oup.com/he/SHO-textbook16e

---

[1] Smith, *Property Offences*, Ch 23, *Arlidge and Parry on Fraud* (5th edn, 2016) Ch 11.

[2] LC 55, *Report on Forgery and Counterfeit Currency* (1973). See also Law Com Working Paper No 26, *Forgery* (1970). The history is considered by JWC Turner, 'Documents in the Law of Forgery' (1946) 32 Virg LR 939.

[3] *Campbell* (1984) 80 Cr App R 47; *Winston* [1999] 1 Cr App R 337.

[4] Forgery and Counterfeiting Act 1981, s 6.

30

Obscene communication and publication offences

The criminal law has used a range of offences to deal with obscene communications conveyed through various media. Such criminal regulation clearly engages important issues relating to freedom of expression and the appropriate limits on restricting communication.

The Obscene Publications Act 1959 deals with publishing 'obscene' articles. The Act has distinctive features which render it worthy of study by law students. It contains presumptions, reverse burdens and, unusually, a defence that publication was justified as being in the public good. Challenging questions have been raised about its application in a modern digital world in which images are shared instantaneously across continents.

More modern statutes have criminalized various other types of publication. For example, the Communications Act 2003 makes it an offence to send, by means of a public electronic communications network, a message or other matter that is grossly offensive or of an indecent, obscene or menacing character. Section 63 of the Criminal Justice and Immigration Act 2008 (as amended in 2015) criminalizes the possession of extreme pornographic images. These offences have also raised interesting questions of definition, jurisdiction and as to their application to social media. We examine these offences in the chapter which is free online.

The Protection of Children Act 1978 and the Criminal Justice Act 1988 create offences to deal specifically with the making and possession of indecent images of children (we do not examine those offences in detail in this chapter).

A FULL DISCUSSION IS CONTAINED IN THE CHAPTER, AVAILABLE **FREE** ONLINE—www.oup.com/he/SHO-textbook16e

31

Offences against public order

Public order offences are commonly prosecuted. Many of the prosecutions are, simply, forms of violence or threatening behaviour against individuals. However, some cases will involve human rights arguments (Arts 10 and 11 of the ECHR) or take on a constitutional dimension about the legitimate limits that the State can place on protest and collective disobedience.

The offences are largely found in the Public Order Act 1986 which replaced the ancient common law offences.[1] The offences examined in the online chapter are, in descending order of gravity:

(1) riot (s 1);

(2) violent disorder (s 2);

(3) affray (s 3);

(4) threatening, abusive or insulting conduct intended, or likely, to provoke violence or cause fear of violence (s 4);

(5) threatening, abusive or insulting conduct intentionally causing harassment, alarm or distress (s 4A); and

(6) threatening or abusive conduct likely to cause harassment, alarm or distress (s 5).

The less serious offences (4–6 above) have become heavily used. Note that some 1986 Act offences can be committed in 'private' although they remain 'public order' offences. As the courts have repeatedly emphasized, it is important to keep sight of the public order foundations of these offences and not treat them as merely additional offences against the person. With the lower level offences under ss 4, 4A and 5, one might question whether they are protecting against a general endangering of public safety and security.

A FULL DISCUSSION IS CONTAINED IN THE CHAPTER, AVAILABLE **FREE** ONLINE—www.oup.com/he/SHO-textbook16e

---

[1] For the law before the 1986 Act, see the 5th edn of this book, Ch 20; for the background to the 1986 Act, see the Home Office, *Review of the Public Order Act and Related Legislation* (1980) Cmnd 7891 and Law Com Working Paper No 82, *Offences Against Public Order* (1982) and LC 123, *Offences Relating to Public Disorder* (1983).

32
Selected road traffic offences

Road traffic legislation is voluminous, technical and complex and it is neither possible nor appropriate in a work of this kind to deal in a comprehensive way with the plethora of offences created. Nevertheless, there are some road traffic offences that illustrate important principles of criminal law in operation. For example, there are many of the offences that involve strict liability, the road traffic offences which relate to causing death generate interesting issues involving causation, and careless and dangerous driving are rare examples of English law providing endangerment offences.

This chapter is available free online. Our aim is not to offer comprehensive coverage, but to focus attention on the following, most serious, offences which offer insights into general principles of criminal law:

(1) causing death by dangerous driving (s 1 of the Road Traffic Act 1988);

(2) dangerous driving (s 2 of the Road Traffic Act 1988);

(3) careless driving (s 3 of the Road Traffic Act 1988); and

(4) some of the related offences contained in the Road Traffic Acts, such as causing death by careless or inconsiderate driving when under the influence of drink or drugs.

The additions to the legislative scheme in the Road Safety Act 2006 (as subsequently amended in 2015) included some controversial offences in which it was sought to impose liability for a death arising while unlawfully on the roads irrespective of whether the death was due to some defect in the manner of the driving. These provoked considerable concern and led to a powerful Supreme Court decision in *Hughes* (2013). These offences are also considered in this chapter.

THE CHAPTER IS AVAILABLE **FREE** ONLINE—www.oup.com/he/SHO-textbook16e

33
Money laundering

The Proceeds of Crime Act 2002 creates a number of offences which target those who assist in the disposal of criminal proceeds. There are a raft of measures providing for confiscation, asset recovery, civil recovery, restraint proceedings and prevention orders. In some respects, the offences of money laundering share a similar rationale to handling: to target the individuals who render criminal activity profitable rather than those committing the substantive crime itself. However, the money laundering offences are concerned not just with stolen goods but with criminal proceeds more generally. The legislation has been driven by international treaty obligations, and these are relied upon by the courts as an aid to interpretation. This chapter, which is available free online, offers only an overview of the three principal money laundering offences to serve as a contrast to the offence of handling. These offences are:

(1) Section 327—concealing, disguising, converting, transferring or removing criminal property.

(2) Section 328—entering into or becoming concerned in an arrangement which D knows or suspects facilitates (by whatever means) the acquisition, retention, use or control of criminal property by or on behalf of another person.

(3) Section 329—acquiring, using or possessing criminal property.

THE CHAPTER IS AVAILABLE **FREE** ONLINE—www.oup.com/he/SHO-textbook16e

34
Offensive weapons

Legislation regulating the possession and use of firearms and offensive weapons is of major importance in the prevention of offences against the person. In earlier editions of this book[1] an account was given of the principal offences under the Firearms Act 1968 and other legislation. Consideration is given in this chapter, which is available free online, to important offences of general interest relating to offensive weapons and bladed articles:

(1) The Prevention of Crime Act 1953;

(2) The Criminal Justice Act 1988;

(3) The Offensive Weapons Act 2019.

THE CHAPTER IS AVAILABLE **FREE** ONLINE—www.oup.com/he/SHO-textbook16e

---

[1] See the 6th edn of this book, at pp 416–22.

Bibliography

A comprehensive bibliography, including all references used throughout the book, is now available free online. Readers can quickly and easily locate specific references by using the online, alphabetized bibliography, or alternatively can download and print the entire listing free.

In addition to this, all references are available in the footnotes throughout the text. www.oup.com/he/SHO-textbook16e.

Bibliography

The following list contains all the references from the book. You can also view the list in printable ⬇ PDF format.

A - B - C - D - E - F - G - H - I - J - K - L - M - N - O - P - Q - R - S - T - U - V - W - X - Y - Z

Abbott, C, *Enforcing Pollution Control Regulation* (2009).

Abortion Law Reform Association, *A Guide to the Abortion Act 1967* (1971).

Adam, S, N Cosette- Basecqz and M Nihoul (eds), *Corporate Criminal Liability in Europe* (2008).

Adams, JN, 'Trespass under the Theft and Firearms Act' (1969) 119 NLJ 655.

Addison, N, *Religious Discrimination and Hatred Law* (2007).

Addison, N and T Lawson-Cruttenden, *Harassment Law and Practice* (1998).

Akdeniz, Y, 'Section 3 of the Computer Misuse Act 1990 – An Antidote for Computer Viruses' [1996] 3 Web Jnl CLI.

Akdeniz, Y, 'Cybercrime', in *E-Commerce Law & Regulation Encyclopaedia* (2003).

Alexander, L, 'Criminal Liability for Omissions: An Inventory of Issues' in S Shute and A Simester (eds), *Criminal Law Theory: Doctrines of the General Part* (2002).

Alexander, L, 'Lesser Evils: A Closer Look at the Paradigmatic Justification' (2005) 24 Law and Phil 611.

Alexander, L, K Ferzan and S Morse, *Crime and Culpability* (2009).

Index